THE YEAR'S WORK 2007

KU-305-822

The Year's Work in
English Studies
Volume 88

Covering work published in 2007

Edited by
WILLIAM BAKER
and
KENNETH WOMACK
with associate editors

THERESA SAXON
KIRSTIE BLAIR
KIM WORTHINGTON
OLGA FISCHER
JAMES DECKER
MATTHEW STEGGLE
MARY SWAN
CHRISTOPH LINDNER

Published for
THE ENGLISH ASSOCIATION
by

OXFORD JOURNALS
OXFORD UNIVERSITY PRESS

DBS Library
13/14 Aungier Street
Dublin 2
Phone: 01-4177572

LIBRARY COPY
DO NOT REMOVE

OXFORD

UNIVERSITY PRESS

Great Clarendon Street, Oxford ox2 6DP, UK

Oxford University Press is a department of the University of Oxford.
It furthers the University's objective of excellence in research, scholarship,
and education by publishing worldwide in
Oxford New York
Athens Auckland Bangkok Bogotá Buenos Aires Cape Town
Chennai Dar es Salaam Delhi Florence Hong Kong Istanbul Karachi
Kolkata Kuala Lumpur Madrid Melbourne Mexico City Mumbai Nairobi
Paris São Paulo Shanghai Taipei Tokyo Toronto Warsaw

Oxford is a registered trade mark of Oxford University Press
in the UK and in certain other countries

©The English Association 2009

The moral rights of the author have been asserted
Database right Oxford University Press (maker)
First published 2008

All rights reserved. No part of this publication may be reproduced,
stored in a retrieval system, or transmitted, in any form or by any means,
without the prior permission in writing of Oxford University Press,
or as expressly permitted by law, or under terms agreed with the appropriate
reprographics rights organization. Enquiries concerning reproduction
outside the scope of the above should be sent to the Rights Department,
Oxford University Press, at the address above

You must not circulate this publication in any other binding or cover
and you must impose this same condition on any acquirer

British Library Cataloguing in Publication Data
Data available
ISSN 0084-4144
ISBN 9780199583232
1 3 5 7 9 10 8 6 4 2
Typeset by Cepha Imaging Pvt. Ltd., Bangalore, India
Printed in Great Britain on acid-free paper by the MPG Books Group,
Bodmin and King's Lynn

DUBLIN BUSINESS SCHOOL
LIBRARY
RECEIVED

1 DEC 2009

The English Association

The object of The English Association is to promote the knowledge and appreciation of English language and its literatures.

The Association pursues these aims by creating opportunities of co-operation among all those interested in English; by furthering the recognition of English as essential in education; by discussing methods of English teaching; by holding lectures, conferences, and other meetings; by publishing several journals, books, and leaflets; and by forming local branches overseas and at home. English Association Fellowships recognize distinction and achievement in the field of English worldwide.

Publications

The Year's Work in English Studies. An annual narrative bibliography which aims to cover all work of quality in English studies published in a given year. Published by Oxford University Press.

The Year's Work in Critical and Cultural Theory. An annual narrative bibliography which aims to provide comprehensive cover of all work of quality in critical and cultural theory published in a given year. Published by Oxford University Press.

Essays and Studies. A well-established series of annual themed volumes edited each year by a distinguished academic.

English. This internationally-known journal of the Association is aimed at teachers of English in universities and colleges, with articles on all aspects of literature and critical theory, an extensive reviews section and original poetry. Four issues per year. Published by Oxford University Press.

Use of English. The longest-standing journal for English teachers in schools and colleges. Three issues per year.

English 4–11. Designed and developed by primary English specialists to give practical help to primary and middle school teachers. Three issues per year.

English Association Studies. A new monograph series published in association with Boydell & Brewer.

Issues in English. Occasional pamphlet series.

Membership

Membership information can be found at http://www.le.ac.uk/engassoc or please write to The English Association, University of Leicester, University Road, Leicester LE1 7RH, UK or email: engassoc@le.ac.uk.

The Year's Work
in English Studies

Subscriptions for Volume 88

Institutional (combined rate to both *The Year's Work in English Studies* and *The Year's Work in Critical and Cultural Theory*) print and online: £281.00/$492.00/ €422.00. *Institutional* (*The Year's Work in English Studies* only) print and online: £189.00/$350.00/€284.00.

Please note: £/€ rates apply in Europe, US$ elsewhere. All prices include postage, and for subscribers outside the UK delivery is by Standard Air. There may be other subscription rates available. For a complete listing, please visit www.ywes.oxford journals.org/subinfo.

Online Access

For details please email Oxford University Press Journals Customer Services on: jnls.cust.serv@oxfordjournals.co.uk.

Order Information

Full prepayment, in the correct currency, is required for all orders. Orders are regarded as firm and payments are not refundable. Subscriptions are accepted and entered on a complete volume basis. Claims cannot be considered more than FOUR months after publication or date of order, whichever is later. All subscriptions in Canada are subject to GST. Subscriptions in the EU may be subject to European VAT. If registered, please supply details to avoid unnecessary charges. For subscriptions that include online versions, a proportion of the subscription price may be subject to UK VAT.

Methods of payment. (i) Cheque (payable to Oxford University Press, Cashiers Office, Great Clarendon Street, Oxford OX2 6DP, UK) in GB£ Sterling (drawn on a UK bank), US$ Dollars (drawn on a US bank), or EU€ Euros. (ii) Bank transfer to Barclays Bank Plc, Oxford Group Office, Oxford (bank sort code 20-65-18) (UK), overseas only Swift code BARC GB 22 (GB£ Sterling to account no. 70299332, IBAN GB89BARC20651870299332; US$ Dollars to account no. 66014600, IBAN GB27BARC20651866014600; EU€ Euros to account no. 78923655, IBAN GB16BARC20651878923655). (iii) Credit card (Mastercard, Visa, Switch or American Express).

Back Issues

The current plus two back volumes are available from Oxford University Press. Previous volumes can be obtained from the Periodicals Service Company, 11 Main Street, Germantown, NY 12526, USA. Email: psc@periodicals.com; tel: +1 (518) 537 4700; fax: +1 (518) 537 5899.

Further information. Journals Customer Service Department, Oxford University Press, Great Clarendon Street, Oxford OX2 6DP, UK. Email: jnls.cust.serv@oxfordjournals. org; tel (and answerphone outside normal working hours): +44 (0) 1865 353907; fax: +44 (0) 1865 353485. *In the US, please contact:* Journals Customer Service Department, Oxford University Press, 2001 Evans Road, Cary, NC 27513, USA. Email: jnlorders@oxfordjournals.org; tel (and answerphone outside normal working hours): 800 852 7323 (toll-free in USA/Canada); fax: 919 677 1714. *In Japan, please contact:* Journals Customer Services, Oxford Journals, Oxford University Press, Tokyo, 4-5-10-8F Shiba, Minato-ku, Tokyo 108-8386, Japan. Email: custserv.jp@ oxfordjournals.org; Tel: +81 3 5444 5858; Fax: +81 3 3454 2929.

The Year's Work in English Studies (ISSN 0084 4144) is published annually by Oxford University Press, Oxford, UK. Annual subscription price is £281.00/$492.00/ €422.00. *The Year's Work in English Studies* is distributed by Mercury International, 365 Blair Road, Avenel, NJ 07001, USA. Periodicals postage paid at Rahway, NJ and at additional entry points.

US Postmaster: send address changes to *The Year's Work in English Studies*, c/o Mercury International, 365 Blair Road, Avenel, NJ 07001, USA.

The Table of Contents email alerting service allows anyone who registers their email address to be notified via email when new content goes online. Details are available at http://ywes.oxfordjournals.org/cgi/alerts/etoc.

Permissions

For permissions requests, please visit www.oxfordjournals.org/permissions.

Advertising

Inquiries about advertising should be sent to Oxford Journals Advertising, Oxford University Press, Great Clarendon Street, Oxford, OX2 6DP, UK. Email: jnlsadvertising@oxfordjournals.org; tel: +44 (0) 1865 354767; fax: +44 (0) 1865 353774.

Disclaimer

Statements of fact and opinion in the articles in *The Year's Work in English Studies* are those of the respective authors and contributors and not of the English Association or Oxford University Press. Neither Oxford University Press nor the English Association make any representation, express or implied, in respect of the accuracy of the material in this journal and cannot accept any legal responsibility or liability for any errors or omissions that may be made. The reader should make his/her own evaluation as to the appropriateness or otherwise of any experimental technique described.

© The English Association 2009. All rights reserved; no part of this publication may be reproduced, stored in a retrieval system, or transmitted in any form of by any means, electronic, mechanical, photocopying, recording, or otherwise without the prior written permission of the Publishers, or a licence permitting restricted copying issued in the UK by the Copyright Licensing Agency Ltd, 90 Tottenham Court Road, London W1P 9HE, or in the USA by the Copyright Clearance Center, 222 Rosewood Drive, Danvers, Massachusetts 01923, USA.

DUBLIN BUSINES▸ ▸CHOOL
LIBRAF▸
RECEIVE▸

1 0 DEC ▸▸▸9

Contents

CONTENTS

Abbreviations

1. Journals, Series and Reference Works

1650–1850	*1650–1850 Ideas, Aesthetics, and Inquiries in the Early Modern Era*
A&D	*Art and Design*
A&E	*Anglistik und Englishunterricht*
AAA	*Arbeiten aus Anglistik und Amerikanistik*
AAAJ	*Accounting, Auditing and Accountability Journal*
AAR	*African American Review*
ABäG	*Amsterdamer Beiträge zur Älteren Germanistik*
ABC	*American Book Collector*
ABELL	*Annual Bibliography of English Language and Literature*
ABM	*Antiquarian Book Monthly Review*
ABQ	*American Baptist Quarterly*
ABR	*American Benedictine Review* (now *RBR*)
ABSt	*A/B: Auto/Biography Studies*
AC	*Archeologia Classica*
Academy Forum	*Academy Forum*
AcadSF	*Academia Scientiarum Fennica*
ACar	*Analecta Cartusiana*
ACF	*Annuli, Facolta di Lingue e Litterature Straniere di Ca'Foscari*
ACH	*Australian Cultural History*
ACLALSB	*ACLALS Bulletin*
ACM	*Aligarh Critical Miscellany*
ACR	*Australasian Catholic Record*
ACS	*Australian-Canadian Studies: A Journal for the Humanities and Social Sciences*
Acta	*Acta* (Binghamton, NY)
AdI	*Annali d'Italianistica*
ADS	*Australasian Drama Studies*
AEB	*Analytical and Enumerative Bibliography*
Æstel	*Æstel*
AF	*Anglistische Forschungen*
AfricanA	*African Affairs*
AfrSR	*African Studies Review*
AfT	*African Theatre*
AgeJ	*Age of Johnson: A Scholarly Annual*
Agenda	*Agenda*
Agni	*Agni Review*
AGP	*Archiv für Geschichte der Philosophie*
AH	*Art History*
AHR	*American Historical Review*
AHS	*Australian Historical Studies*
AI	*American Imago*

AICRJ	American Indian Culture and Research Journal
AILA	Association Internationale de Linguistique Appliqué
AIQ	American Indian Quarterly
AJ	Art Journal
AJGLL	American Journal of Germanic Linguistics and Literatures
AJIS	Australian Journal of Irish Studies
AJL	Australian Journal of Linguistics
AJP	American Journal of Psychoanalysis
AJPH	Australian Journal of Politics and History
AJS	American Journal of Semiotics
AKML	Abhandlungen zur Kunst-, Musik- and Literaturwis-senschaft
AL	American Literature
ALA	African Literature Association Annuals
ALASH	Acta Linguistica Academiae Scientiarum Hungaricae
Albion	Albion
AlexS	Alexander Shakespeare
ALH	Acta Linguistica Hafniensia; International Journal of Linguistics
Alif	Journal of Comparative Poetics (Cairo, Egypt)
ALitASH	Acta Literaria Academiae Scientiarum Hungaricae
Allegorica	Allegorica
ALN	American Literary Nationalism Newsletter
ALR	American Literary Realism, 1870–1910
ALS	Australian Literary Studies
ALT	African Literature Today
Alternatives	Alternatives
AmasJ	Amerasian Journal
AmDram	American Drama
Americana	Americana
AmerP	American Poetry
AmerS	American Studies
AmLH	American Literary History
AmLS	American Literary Scholarship: An Annual
AMon	Atlantic Monthly
AmPer	American Periodicals
AmRev	Americas Review: A Review of Hispanic Literature and Art of the USA
Amst	Amerikastudien/American Studies
AN	Acta Neophilologica
Anaïs	Anaïs
AnBol	Analecta Bollandiana
ANF	Arkiv för Nordisk Filologi
Angelaki	Angelaki
Anglia	Anglia: Zeitschrift für Englische Philologie
Anglistica	Anglistica
Anglistik	Anglistik: Mitteilungen des Verbandes Deutscher Anglisten
AnH	Analecta Husserliana
AnL	Anthropological Linguistics
AnM	Annuale Mediaevale
Ann	Annales: Économies, Sociétés, Civilisations
ANQ	ANQ: A Quarterly Journal of Short Articles, Notes and Reviews (formerly American Notes and Queries)
AntColl	Antique Collector
Anthurium	Anthurium: A Caribbean Studies Journal

Antig R	*Antigonish Review*
Antipodes	*Antipodes: A North American Journal of Australian Literature*
ANStu	*Anglo-Norman Studies*
ANZSC	*Australian and New Zealand Studies in Canada*
ANZTR	*Australian and New Zealand Theatre Record*
APBR	*Atlantic Provinces Book Review*
APL	*Antwerp Papers in Linguistics*
AppLing	*Applied Linguistics*
APR	*American Poetry Review*
AQ	*American Quarterly*
Aquarius	*Aquarius*
AR	*Antioch Review*
ArAA	*Arbeiten aus Anglistik und Amerikanistik*
ARAL	*Annual Review of Applied Linguistics*
Arcadia	*Arcadia*
Archiv	*Archiv für das Stadium der Neueren Sprachen und Literaturen*
ARCS	*American Review of Canadian Studies*
ArdenS	*Arden Shakespeare*
ArielE	*Ariel: A Review of International English Literature*
Arion	*Arion: A Journal of the Humanities and the Classics*
ArkQ	*Arkansas Quarterly: A Journal of Criticism*
ArkR	*Arkansas Review: A Journal of Criticism*
ArQ	*Arizona Quarterly*
ARS	*Augustan Reprint Society*
ARSR	*Australian Religion Studies Review*
ArtB	*Art Bulletin*
Arth	*Arthuriana*
ArthI	*Arthurian Interpretations*
ArthL	*Arthurian Literature*
Arv	*Arv: Nordic Yearbook of Folklore*
AS	*American Speech*
ASch	*American Scholar*
ASE	*Anglo-Saxon England*
ASInt	*American Studies International*
ASoc	*Arts in Society*
Aspects	*Aspects: Journal of the Language Society* (University of Essex)
AspectsAF	*Aspects of Australian Fiction*
ASPR	*Anglo-Saxon Poetic Records*
ASSAH	*Anglo-Saxon Studies in Archaeology and History*
Assaph	*Assaph: Studies in the Arts (Theatre Studies)*
Assays	*Assays: Critical Approaches to Medieval and Renaissance Texts*
ASUI	*Analele Stiintifice ale Universitatii 'Al.I. Cuza' din Iasi (Serie Noua), e. Lingvistica*
Atlantis	*Atlantis: A Journal of the Spanish Association for Anglo-American Studies*
ATQ	*American Transcendental Quarterly: A Journal of New England Writers*
ATR	*Anglican Theological Review*
AuBR	*Australian Book Review*
AuFolk	*Australian Folklore*
AuFS	*Australian Feminist Studies*
AuHR	*Australian Humanities Review*

AuJL	*Australian Journal of Linguistics*
AUMLA	*Journal of the Australasian Universities Language and Literature Association*
Aurealis	*Australian Fantasy and Science Fiction Magazine*
AuS	*Australian Studies*
AuSA	*Australian Studies* (Australia)
AusCan	*Australian-Canadian Studies*
AusPl	*Australian Playwrights*
AusRB	*Australians' Review of Books*
AustrianS	*Austrian Studies*
AuVSJ	*Australasian Victorian Studies Journal*
AuWBR	*Australian Women's Book Review*
AvC	*Avalon to Camelot*
AY	*Arthurian Yearbook*
BakhtinN	*Bakhtin Newsletter*
BALF	*Black American Literature Forum*
BAReview	*British Academy Review*
BARS Bulletin	*British Association for Romantic Studies Bulletin & Review*
BAS	*British and American Studies*
BASAM	*BASA Magazine*
BathH	*Bath History*
BaylorJ	*Baylor Journal of Theatre and Performance*
BayreuthAS	*Bayreuth African Studies*
BB	*Bulletin of Bibliography*
BBCS	*Bulletin of the Board of Celtic Studies*
BBCSh	*BBC Shakespeare*
BBN	*British Book News*
BBSIA	*Bulletin Bibliographique de la Société Internationale Arthurienne*
BC	*Book Collector*
BCan	*Books in Canada*
BCMA	*Bulletin of Cleveland Museum of Art*
BCS	*B.C. Studies*
BDEC	*Bulletin of the Department of English* (Calcutta)
BDP	*Beiträge zur Deutschen Philologie*
Belfagor	*Belfagor: Rassegna di Varia Umanità*
Bell	*Belgian Essays on Language and Literature*
BEPIF	*Bulletin des Itudes Portugaises et Brésiliennes*
BFLS	*Bulletin de la Faculté des Lettres de Strasbourg*
BGDSL	*Beiträge zur Geschichte der Deutschen Sprache and Literatur*
BHI	*British Humanities Index*
BHL	*Bibliotheca Hagiographica Latina Antiquae et Mediae Aetatis*
BHM	*Bulletin of the History of Medicine*
BHR	*Bibliothèque d'Humanisme et Renaissance*
BHS	*Bulletin of Hispanic Studies*
BI	*Books at Iowa*
Biblionews	*Biblionews and Australian Notes and Queries: A Journal for Book Collectors*
Bibliotheck	*Bibliotheck: A Scottish Journal of Bibliography and Allied Topics*
Biography	*Biography: An Interdisciplinary Quarterly*
BioL	*Biolinguistics*
BIS	*Browning Institute Studies: An Annual of Victorian Literary and Cultural History*
BJA	*British Journal of Aesthetics*

BJCS	British Journal of Canadian Studies
BJDC	British Journal of Disorders of Communication
BJECS	British Journal for Eighteenth-Century Studies
BJHP	British Journal for the History of Philosophy
BJHS	British Journal for the History of Science
BJJ	Ben Jonson Journal
BJL	Belgian Journal of Linguistics
BJPS	British Journal for the Philosophy of Science
BJRL	Bulletin of the John Rylands (University Library of Manchester)
BJS	British Journal of Sociology
Blake	Blake: An Illustrated Quarterly
BLE	Bulletin de Littérature Ecclésiastique
BLJ	British Library Journal
	Borrowers and Lenders: The Journal of Shakespeare and Appropriation
BLR	Bodleian Library Record
BMC	Book and Magazine Collector
BMJ	British Medical Journal
BN	Beiträge zur Namenforschung
BNB	British National Bibliography
BoH	Book History
Bookbird	Bookbird
Borderlines	Borderlines
Boundary	Boundary 2: A Journal of Postmodern Literature and Culture
BP	Banasthali Patrika
BPMA	Bulletin of Philadelphia Museum of Art
BPN	Barbara Pym Newsletter
BQ	Baptist Quarterly
BRASE	Basic Readings in Anglo-Saxon England
BRH	Bulletin of Research in the Humanities
Brick	Brick: A Journal of Reviews
BRMMLA	Bulletin of the Rocky Mountain Modern Language Association
BRONZS	British Review of New Zealand Studies
BS	Bronte Studies
BSANZB	Bibliographical Society of Australia and New Zealand Bulletin
BSE	Brno Studies in English
BSEAA	Bulletin de la Société d'Études Anglo-Américaines des XVIIe et XVIIIe Siècles
BSJ	Baker Street Journal: An Irregular Quarterly of Sherlockiana
BSLP	Bulletin de la Société de Linguistique de Paris
BSNotes	Browning Society Notes
BSRS	Bulletin of the Society for Renaissance Studies
BSSA	Bulletin de la Société de Stylistique Anglaise
BST	Brontë Society Transactions
BSUF	Ball State University Forum
BTHGNewsl	Book Trade History Group Newsletter
BTLV	Bijdragen tot de Taal-, Land- en Volkenhunde
Bul	Bulletin (Australia)
Bullán	Bullán
BunyanS	Bunyan Studies
BuR	Bucknell Review
BurlM	Burlington Magazine
BurnsC	Burns Chronicle

BWPLL	Belfast Working Papers in Language and Linguistics
BWVACET	Bulletin of the West Virginia Association of College English Teachers
ByronJ	Byron Journal
CABS	Contemporary Authors Bibliographical Series
CahiersE	Cahiers Élisabéthains
CAIEF	Cahiers de l'Association Internationale des Études Françaises
Caliban	Caliban (Toulouse, France)
Callaloo	Callaloo
CalR	Calcutta Review
CamObsc	Camera Obscura: A Journal of Feminism and Film Theory
CamR	Cambridge Review
CanD	Canadian Drama/L'Art Dramatique Canadienne
C&L	Christianity and Literature
C&Lang	Communication and Languages
C&M	Classica et Medievalia
CanL	Canadian Literature
CAnn	Carlyle Annual
CanPo	Canadian Poetry
CapR	Capilano Review
CARA	Centre Aixois de Recherches Anglaises
Carib	Carib
Caribana	Caribana
CaribW	Caribbean Writer
CarR	Caribbean Review
Carrell	Carrell: Journal of the Friends of the University of Miami Library
CASE	Cambridge Studies in Anglo-Saxon England
CathHR	Catholic Historical Review
CatR	Catalan Review
CaudaP	Cauda Pavonis
CBAA	Current Bibliography on African Affairs
CBEL	Cambridge Bibliography of English Literature
CCL	Canadian Children's Literature
CCor	Cardiff Corvey: Reading the Romantic Text
CCRev	Comparative Civilizations Review
CCS	Comparative Critical Studies
CCrit	Comparative Criticism: An Annual Journal
CCTES	Conference of College Teachers of English Studies
CCV	Centro de Cultura Valenciana
CDALB	Concise Dictionary of American Literary Biography
CDCP	Comparative Drama Conference Papers
CDIL	Cahiers de l'Institut de Linguistique de Louvain
CdL	Cahiers de Lexicologie
CE	College English
CEA	CEA Critic
CEAfr	Cahiers d'Études Africaines
CE&S	Commonwealth Essays and Studies
CentR	Centennial Review
Cervantes	Cervantes
CF	Crime Factory
CFM	Canadian Fiction Magazine
CFS	Cahiers Ferdinand de Saussure: Revue de Linguistique Générale

CH	*Computers and the Humanities*
Chapman	*Chapman*
Chasqui	*Chasqui*
ChauR	*Chaucer Review*
ChauS	*Chaucer Studion*
ChauY	*Chaucer Yearbook*
ChE	*Changing English*
ChH	*Church History*
ChildL	*Children's Literature: Journal of Children's Literature Studies*
ChiR	*Chicago Review*
ChLB	*Charles Lamb Bulletin*
CHLSSF	*Commentationes Humanarum Litterarum Societatis Scientiarum Fennicae*
CHR	*Camden History Review*
CHum	*Computers and the Humanities*
CI	*Critical Idiom*
CILT	*Amsterdam Studies in the Theory and History of the Language Sciences IV: Current Issues in Linguistic Theory*
Cinéaste	*Cinéaste*
CinJ	*Cinema Journal*
CIQ	*Colby Quarterly*
CISh	*Contemporary Interpretations of Shakespeare*
Cithara	*Cithara: Essays in the Judaeo Christian Tradition*
CJ	*Classical Journal*
CJE	*Cambridge Journal of Education*
CJH	*Canadian Journal of History*
CJIS	*Canadian Journal of Irish Studies*
CJL	*Canadian Journal of Linguistics*
CJR	*Christian–Jewish Relations*
CK	*Common Knowledge*
CL	*Comparative Literature* (Eugene, OR)
CLAJ	*CLA Journal*
CLAQ	*Children's Literature Association Quarterly*
ClarkN	*Clark Newsletter: Bulletin of the UCLA Center for Seventeenth- and Eighteenth-Century Studies*
ClassW	*Classical World*
CLC	*Columbia Library Columns*
CLE	*Children's Literature in Education*
CLet	*Confronto Letterario*
CLIN	*Cuadernos de Literatura*
ClioI	*Clio: A Journal of Literature, History and the Philosophy of History*
CLQ	*Colby Library Quarterly*
CLS	*Comparative Literature Studies*
Clues	*Clues: A Journal of Detection*
CMCS	*Cambridge Medieval Celtic Studies*
CML	*Classical and Modern Literature*
CN	*Chaucer Newsletter*
CNIE	*Commonwealth Novel in English*
CogLing	*Cognitive Linguistics*
Cognition	*Cognition*
ColB	*Coleridge Bulletin*
ColF	*Columbia Forum*

Collections	*Collections*
CollG	*Colloquia Germanica*
CollL	*College Literature*
Com	*Commonwealth*
Comitatus	*Comitatus: A Journal of Medieval and Renaissance Studies*
Commentary	*Commentary*
Comparatist	*Comparatist: Journal of the Southern Comparative Literature Association*
CompD	*Comparative Drama*
CompLing	*Contemporary Linguistics*
ConcordSaunterer	*Concord Saunterer: Annual Journal of the Thoreau Society*
Configurations	*Official Journal of the Society for Literature, Science and the Arts*
ConfLett	*Confronto Letterario*
ConL	*Contemporary Literature*
Connotations	*Connotations*
ConnR	*Connecticut Review*
Conradian	*Conradian*
Conradiana	*Conradiana: A Journal of Joseph Conrad Studies*
ContempR	*Contemporary Review*
ConTR	*Contemporary Theatre Review*
Coppertales	*Coppertales: A Journal of Rural Arts*
Cosmos	*Cosmos*
Costume	*Journal of the Costume Society*
CP	*Concerning Poetry*
CQ	*Cambridge Quarterly*
CR	*Critical Review*
CRCL	*Canadian Review of Comparative Literature*
CRev	*Chesterton Review*
CRevAS	*Canadian Review of American Studies*
Crit	*Critique: Studies in Modern Fiction*
CritI	*Critical Inquiry*
Criticism	*Criticism: A Quarterly for Literature and the Arts*
Critique	*Critique* (Paris)
CritQ	*Critical Quarterly*
CritT	*Critical Texts: A Review of Theory and Criticism*
CrM	*Critical Mass*
CRNLE	*CRNLE Reviews Journal*
Crossings	*Crossings*
CRUX	*CRUX: A Journal on the Teaching of English*
CS	*Critical Survey*
CSASE	*Cambridge Studies in Anglo-Saxon England*
CSCC	*Case Studies in Contemporary Criticism*
CSELT	*Cambridge Studies in Eighteenth-Century Literature and Thought*
CSLBull	*Bulletin of the New York C.S. Lewis Society*
CSLL	*Cardozo Studies in Law and Literature*
	Critical Studies in Media Communication
CSML	*Cambridge Studies in Medieval Literature*
CSNCLC	*Cambridge Studies in Nineteenth-Century Literature and Culture*
CSPC	*Cambridge Studies in Paleography and Codicology*
CSR	*Cambridge Studies in Romanticism*
CSRev	*Christian Scholar's Review*

CStA	*Carlyle Studies Annual* (previously CAnn)
CTC	
CTR	*Canadian Theatre Review*
Cuadernos	*Cuadernos de Literatura Infantil y Juvenil*
CulC	*Cultural Critique*
CulS	*Cultural Studies*
CulSR	*Cultural Studies Review*
CUNY	*CUNY English Forum*
Current Writing	*Current Writing: Text and Reception in Southern Africa*
CV2	*Contemporary Verse 2*
CVE	*Cahiers Victoriens et Edouardiens*
CW	*Current Writing: Text and Perception in Southern Africa*
CWAAS	*Transactions of the Cumberland and Westmorland Antiquarian and Archaeological Society*
CWS	*Canadian Woman Studies*
Cycnos	
DA	*Dictionary of Americanisms*
DAE	*Dictionary of American English*
DAEM	*Deutsches Archiv für Erforschung des Mittelalters*
DAI	*Dissertation Abstracts International*
DAL	*Descriptive and Applied Linguistics*
D&CN&Q	*Devon and Cornwall Notes and Queries*
D&S	*Discourse and Society*
Daphnis	*Daphnis: Zeitschrift für Mittlere Deutsche Literatur*
DC	*Dickens Companions*
DerbyM	*Derbyshire Miscellany*
Descant	*Descant*
DFS	*Dalhousie French Studies*
DHLR	*D.H. Lawrence Review*
DHS	*Dix-huitième Siècle*
Diac	*Diacritics*
Diachronica	*Diachronica*
Dialogue	*Dialogue: Canadian Philosophical Review*
Dickensian	*Dickensian*
DicS	*Dickinson Studies*
Dictionaries	*Dictionaries: Journal of the Dictionary Society of North America*
Dionysos	*Dionysos*
Discourse	*Discourse*
DisS	*Discourse Studies*
DLB	*Dictionary of Literary Biography*
DLN	*Doris Lessing Newsletter*
DM	*Dublin Magazine*
DMT	*Durham Medieval Texts*
DNB	*Dictionary of National Biography*
DOE	*Dictionary of Old English*
Dolphin	*Dolphin: Publications of the English Department* (University of Aarhus)
DOST	*Dictionary of the Older Scottish Tongue*
DownR	*Downside Review*
DPr	*Discourse Processes*
DQ	*Denver Quarterly*
DQR	*Dutch Quarterly Review of Anglo-American Letters*
DQu	*Dickens Quarterly*

DR	*Dalhousie Review*
Drama	*Drama: The Quarterly Theatre Review*
DrS	*Dreiser Studies*
DS	*Deep South*
DSA	*Dickens Studies Annual*
DSNA	*DSNA Newsletter*
DU	*Der Deutschunterricht: Beiträge zu Seiner Praxis und Wissenschaftlichen Grundlegung*
DUJ	*Durham University Journal*
DVLG	*Deutsche Viertejahrsschrift für Literaturwissenschaft und Geistesgeschichte*
DWPELL	*Dutch Working Papers in English Language and Linguistics*
EA	*Études Anglaises*
EAL	*Early American Literature*
E&D	*Enlightenment and Dissent*
E&S	*Essays and Studies*
E&Soc	*Economy and Society*
EarT	*Early Theatre*
EAS	*Early American Studies*
ESt	*Englisch Amerikanische Studien*
EBST	*Edinburgh Bibliographical Society Transactions*
EC	*Études Celtiques*
ECan	*Études Canadiennes/Canadian Studies*
ECCB	*Eighteenth Century: A Current Bibliography*
ECent	*Eighteenth Century: Theory and Interpretation*
ECF	*Eighteenth-Century Fiction*
ECI	*Eighteenth-Century Ireland*
ECIntell	*East-Central Intelligencer*
ECLife	*Eighteenth-Century Life*
ECN	*Eighteenth-Century Novel*
ECon	*L'Époque Conradienne*
ECr	*L'Esprit Créateur*
ECS	*Eighteenth-Century Studies*
ECSTC	*Eighteenth-Century Short Title Catalogue*
ECW	*Essays on Canadian Writing*
ECWomen	*Eighteenth-Century Women: Studies in their Lives, Work, and Culture*
EDAMN	*EDAM Newsletter*
EDAMR	*Early Drama, Art, and Music Review*
EDH	*Essays by Divers Hands*
EdL	*Études de Lettres*
EdN	*Editors' Notes: Bulletin of the Conference of Editors of Learned Journals*
EDSL	*Encyclopedic Dictionary of the Sciences of Language*
EEMF	*Early English Manuscripts in Facsimile*
EF	*Études Francaises*
EHR	*English Historical Review*
EI	*Études Irlandaises* (Lille)
EIC	*Essays in Criticism*
EinA	*English in Africa*
EiP	*Essays in Poetics*
EIRC	*Explorations in Renaissance Culture*
Éire	*Éire-Ireland*

EiTET	*Essays in Theatre/Études Théâtrales*
EIUC	
EJ	*English Journal*
EJES	*European Journal of English Studies*
EL	*Études lawrenciennes*
ELangT	*ELT Journal: An International Journal for Teachers of English to Speakers of Other Languages*
ELet	*Esperienze Letterarie: Rivista Trimestrale di Critica e Cultura*
ELH	*English Literary History*
ELing	*English Linguistics*
ELL	*English Language and Linguistics*
ELN	*English Language Notes*
ELR	*English Literary Renaissance*
ELS	*English Literary Studies*
ELT	*English Literature in Transition*
ELWIU	*Essays in Literature* (Western Illinois University)
EM	*English Miscellany*
Embl	*Emblematica: An Interdisciplinary Journal of English Studies*
EMD	*European Medieval Drama*
EME	*Early Modern Europe*
EMedE	*Early Medieval Europe* (online)
EMLS	*Early Modern Literary Studies* (online)
EMMS	*Early Modern Manuscript Studies*
EMS	*English Manuscript Studies, 1100–1700*
EMu	*Early Music*
EMW	*Early Modern Englishwomen*
Encult	*Enculturation: Cultural Theories and Rhetorics*
Encyclia	*Encyclia*
English	*English: The Journal of the English Association*
EnT	*English Today: The International Review of the English Language*
EONR	*Eugene O'Neill Review*
EPD	*English Pronouncing Dictionary*
ER	*English Review*
ERLM	*Europe-Revue Littéraire Mensuelle*
ERR	*European Romantic Review*
ES	*English Studies*
ESA	*English Studies in Africa*
ESC	*English Studies in Canada*
ESQ	*ESQ: A Journal of the American Renaissance*
ESRS	*Emporia State Research Studies*
EssaysMedSt	*Essays in Medieval Studies*
EST	*Eureka Street*
Estudios Ingleses	*Estudios Ingleses de la Universidad Complutense*
ET	*Elizabethan Theatre*
Etropic	*Etropic*
EurekaStudies	*Eureka Studies*
EuroS	*European Studies: A Journal of European Culture, History and Politics*
EWhR	*Edith Wharton Review*
EWIP	*Edinburgh University, Department of Linguistics, Work in Progress*
EWN	*Evelyn Waugh Newsletter*

EWPAL	Edinburgh Working Papers in Applied Linguistics
EWW	English World-Wide
Excavatio	Excavatio
Exemplaria	Exemplaria
Exit	
Expl	Explicator
Extrapolation	Extrapolation: A Journal Science Fiction and Fantasy
FC	Feminist Collections: A Quarterly of Women's Studies Resources
FCEMN	Mystics Quarterly (formerly Fourteenth-Century English Mystics Newsletter)
FCS	Fifteenth-Century Studies
FDT	Fountainwell Drama Texts
FemR	Feminist Review
FemSEL	Feminist Studies in English Literature
FFW	Food and Foodways
FH	Die Neue Gesellschaft/Frankfurter Hefte
Fiction International	Fiction International
FilmJ	Film Journal
FilmQ	Film Quarterly
FilmS	Film Studies
Fiveb	Fivebells
FiveP	Five Points: A Journal of Literature and Art (Atlanta, GA)
FJS	Fu Jen Studies: Literature and Linguistics (Taipei)
FLH	Folia Linguistica Historica
Florilegium	Florilegium: Carleton University Annual Papers on Classical Antiquity and the Middle Ages
FLS	Foreign Literature Studies (Central China Normal University, Wuhan, People's Republic of China)
FMLS	Forum for Modern Language Studies
FNS	Frank Norris Studies
Folklore	Folklore
FoLi	Folia Linguistica
Forum	Forum
FranS	Franciscan Studies
FreeA	Free Associations
FrontenacR	Revue Frontenac
Frontiers	Frontiers: A Journal of Women's Studies
FS	French Studies
FSt	Feminist Studies
FT	Fashion Theory
FuL	Functions of Language
Futures	Futures
GAG	Göppinger Arbeiten zur Germanistik
GaR	Georgia Review
GBB	George Borrow Bulletin
GBK	Gengo Bunka Kenkyu: Studies in Language and Culture
GEGHLS	George Eliot–George Henry Lewes Studies
GeM	Genealogists Magazine
Genders	Genders
Genre	Genre
GER	George Eliot Review
Gestus	Gestus: A Quarterly Journal of Brechtian Studies
Gettysburg Review	Gettysburg Review

GG@G	Generative Grammar in Geneva (online)
GHJ	George Herbert Journal
GissingJ	Gissing Journal
GJ	Gutenberg-Jahrbuch
GL	General Linguistics
GL&L	German Life and Letters
GlasR	Glasgow Review
Glossa	Glossa: An International Journal of Linguistics
GLQ	A Journal of Lesbian and Gay Studies (Duke University)
GLS	Grazer Linguistische Studien
GPQ	Great Plains Quarterly
GR	Germanic Review
Gramma	Gramma: Journal of Theory and Criticism
Gramma/TTT	Tijdschrift voor Taalwetenschap
GrandS	Grand Street
Granta	Granta
Greyfriar	Greyfriar Siena Studies in Literature
GRM	Germanisch-Romanische Monatsschrift
Grove	The Grove: Working Papers on English Studies
GSE	Gothenberg Studies in English
GSJ	Gaskell Society Journal
GSN	Gaskell Society Newsletter
GURT	Georgetown University Round Table on Language and Linguistics
HamS	Hamlet Studies
H&T	History and Theory
HardyR	Hardy Review
Harvard Law Review	Harvard Law Review
HatcherR	Hatcher Review
HBS	Henry Bradshaw Society
HC	Hollins Critic
HCM	Hitting Critical Mass: A Journal of Asian American Cultural Criticism
HE	History of Education
HEAT	HEAT
Hecate	Hecate: An Interdisciplinary Journal of Women's Liberation
HEdQ	History of Education Quarterly
HEI	History of European Ideas
HeineJ	Heine Jahrbuch
HEL	Histoire Épistémologie Language
Helios	Helios
HEng	History of the English Language
Hermathena	Hermathena: A Trinity College Dublin Review
HeroicA	Heroic Age: A Journal of Early Medieval Northwestern Europe
HeyJ	Heythrop Journal
HFR	Hayden Ferry Review
HistJ	Historical Journal
History	History: The Journal of the Historical Association
HistR	Historical Research
HJEAS	Hungarian Journal of English and American Studies
HJR	Henry James Review (Baton Rouge, LA)
HL	Historiographia Linguistica
HLB	Harvard Library Bulletin

HLQ	Huntingdon Library Quarterly
HLSL	(online)
HNCIS	Harvester New Critical Introductions to Shakespeare
HNR	Harvester New Readings
HOPE	History of Political Economy
HPT	History of Political Thought
HQ	Hopkins Quarterly
HR	Harvard Review
HRB	Hopkins Research Bulletin
HSci	History of Science
HSE	Hungarian Studies in English
HSELL	Hiroshima Studies in English Language and Literature
HSJ	Housman Society Journal
HSL	University of Hartford Studies in Literature
HSN	Hawthorne Society Newsletter
HSSh	Hunganan Studies in Shakespeare
HSSN	Henry Sweet Society Newsletter
HT	History Today
HTR	Harvard Theological Review
HudR	Hudson Review
HumeS	Hume Studies
HumLov	Humanistica Lovaniensia: Journal of Neo-Latin Studies
Humor	Humor: International Journal of Humor Research
HUSL	Hebrew University Studies in Literature and the Arts
HWJ	History Workshop
HWS	History Workshop Series
Hypatia	Hypatia
IAL	Issues in Applied Linguistics
IAN	Izvestiia Akademii Nauk SSSR (Moscow)
I&C	Ideology and Consciousness
I&P	Ideas and Production
ICAME	International Computer Archive of Modern and Medieval English
ICS	Illinois Classical Studies
IEEETrans	IEEE Transactions on Professional Communications
IF	Indogermanische Forschungen
IFR	International Fiction Review
IGK	Irland: Gesellschaft and Kultur
IJAES	International Journal of Arabic-English Studies
IJAL	International Journal of Applied Linguistics
IJB	International Journal of Bilingualism
IJBEB	International Journal of Bilingual Education & Bilingualism
IJCL	International Journal of Corpus Linguistics
IJCT	International Journal of the Classical Tradition
IJECS	Indian Journal for Eighteenth-Century Studies
IJES	Indian Journal of English Studies
IJL	International Journal of Lexicography
IJPR	International Journal for Philosophy of Religion
IJSL	International Journal of the Sociology of Language
IJSS	Indian Journal of Shakespeare Studies
IJWS	International Journal of Women's Studies
ILR	Indian Literary Review
ILS	Irish Literary Supplement
Imaginaires	Imaginaires

Imago	*Imago: New Writing*
IMB	*International Medieval Bibliography*
Imprimatur	*Imprimatur*
Indexer	*Indexer*
IndH	*Indian Horizons*
IndL	*Indian Literature*
InG	*In Geardagum: Essays on Old and Middle English Language and Literature*
Inklings	*Inklings: Jahrbuch für Literatur and Ästhetik*
Ioc	*Index to Censorship*
Inquiry	*Inquiry: An Interdisciplinary Journal of Philosophy*
Interactions	*Interactions: Aegean Journal of English and American Studies*
InteractionsAJ	*Interactions: Aegean Journal of English and American Studies/ Ege Ingiliz ve Amerikan Incelemeleri Dergisi*
Interlink	*Interlink*
Interpretation	*Interpretation*
Intertexts	*Intertexts*
Interventions	*Interventions: The International Journal of Postcolonial Studies*
IowaR	*Iowa Review*
IRAL	*IRAL: International Review of Applied Linguistics in Language Teaching*
Iris	*Iris: A Journal of Theory on Image and Sound*
IS	*Italian Studies*
ISh	*Independent Shavian*
ISJR	*Iowa State Journal of Research*
Island	*Island Magazine*
Islands	*Islands*
Isle	*Interdisciplinary Studies in Literature and Environment*
ISR	*Irish Studies Review*
IUR	*Irish University Review: A Journal of Irish Studies*
JAAC	*Journal of Aesthetics and Art Criticism*
JAAR	*Journal of the American Academy of Religion*
Jacket	*Jacket*
JADT	*Journal of American Drama and Theatre*
JAF	*Journal of American Folklore*
JafM	*Journal of African Marxists*
JAIS	*Journal of Anglo-Italian Studies*
JAL	*Journal of Australian Literature*
JamC	*Journal of American Culture*
JAmH	*Journal of American History*
JAmS	*Journal of American Studies*
JAP	*Journal of Analytical Psychology*
JAPC	*Journal of Asian Pacific Communication*
JArabL	*Journal of Arabic Literature*
JAS	*Journal of Australian Studies*
JASAL	*Journal of the Association for the Study of Australian Literature*
JAStT	*Journal of American Studies of Turkey*
JBeckS	*Journal of Beckett Studies*
JBS	*Journal of British Studies*
JBSSJ	*Journal of the Blake Society at St James*
JCAKSU	*Journal of the College of Arts* (King Saud University)
JCanL	*Journal of Canadian Literature*
JCC	*Journal of Canadian Culture*

JCERL	*Journal of Classic and English Renaissance Literature*
JCF	*Journal of Canadian Fiction*
JCGL	*Journal of Comparative Germanic Linguistics*
JChL	*Journal of Child Language*
JChLS	*Journal of Children's Literature Studies*
JCL	*Journal of Commonwealth Literature*
JCP	*Journal of Canadian Poetry*
JCPCS	*Journal of Commonwealth and Postcolonial Studies*
JCSJ	*John Clare Society Journal*
JCSR	*Journal of Canadian Studies/Revue d'Études Canadiennes*
JCSt	*Journal of Caribbean Studies*
JDECU	*Journal of the Department of English* (Calcutta University)
JDHLS	*Journal of D.H. Lawrence Studies* (formerly *The Journal of the D.H. Lawrence Society*)
JDJ	*John Dunne Journal*
JDN	*James Dickey Newsletter*
JDTC	*Journal of Dramatic Theory and Criticism*
JEBS	*Journal of the Early Book Society*
JEDRBU	*Journal of the English Department* (Rabindra Bharati University)
JEGP	*Journal of English and Germanic Philology*
JEH	*Journal of Ecclesiastical History*
JELL	*Journal of English Language and Literature*
JEMCS	*Journal of Early Modern Cultural Studies*
JEn	*Journal of English* (Sana'a University)
JEngL	*Journal of English Linguistics*
JENS	*Journal of the Eighteen Nineties Society*
JEP	*Journal of Evolutionary Psychology*
JEPNS	*Journal of the English Place-Name Society*
JES	*Journal of European Studies*
JETS	*Journal of the Evangelical Theological Society*
JFR	*Journal of Folklore Research*
JGE	*Journal of General Education*
JGenS	*Journal of Gender Studies*
JGH	*Journal of Garden History*
JGL	*Journal of Germanic Linguistics*
JGN	*John Gower Newsletter*
JH	*Journal of Homosexuality*
JHI	*Journal of the History of Ideas*
JHLP	*Journal of Historical Linguistics and Philology*
JHP	*Journal of the History of Philosophy*
JHPrag	*Journal of Historical Pragmatics*
JHSex	*Journal of the History of Sexuality*
JHu	*Journal of Humanities*
JHuP	*Journal of Humanistic Psychology*
JIEP	*Journal of Indo-European Perspectives*
JIES	*Journal of Indo-European Studies*
JIL	*Journal of Irish Literature*
JIPA	*Journal of the International Phonetic Association*
JIWE	*Journal of Indian Writing in English*
JJ	*Jamaica Journal*
JJA	*James Joyce Annual*
JJB	*James Joyce Broadsheet*

JJLS	*James Joyce Literary Supplement*
JJQ	*James Joyce Quarterly*
JKS	*Journal of Kentucky Studies*
JL	*Journal of Linguistics*
JLH	*Journal of Library History, Philosophy and Comparative Librarianship*
JLLI	*Journal of Logic, Language and Information*
JLP	*Journal of Linguistics and Politics* ·
JLS	*Journal of Literary Semanitcs*
JLSP	*Journal of Language and Social Psychology*
JLVSG	*Journal of the Longborough Victorian Studies Group*
JmedL	
JMemL	*Journal of Memory and Language*
JMEMS	*Journal of Medieval and Early Modem Studies*
JMGS	*Journal of Modern Greek Studies*
JMH	*Journal of Medieval History*
JMJS	*Journal of Modern Jewish Studies*
JML	*Journal of Modern Literature*
JMMD	*Journal of Multilingual and Multicultural Development*
JMMLA	*Journal of the Midwest Modern Language Association*
JModH	*Journal of Modern History*
JMRS	*Journal of Medieval and Renaissance Studies*
JMS	*Journal of Men's Studies*
JNLH	*Journal of Narrative and Life History*
JNPH	*Journal of Newspaper and Periodical History*
JNT	*Journal of Narrative Theory* (formerly *Technique*)
JNZL	*Journal of New Zealand Literature*
Jouvert	*Jouvert: A Journal of Postcolonial Studies*
JoyceSA	*Joyce Studies Annual*
JP	*Journal of Philosophy*
JPC	*Journal of Popular Culture*
JPCL	*Journal of Pidgin and Creole Languages*
JPhon	*Journal of Phonetics*
JPJ	*Journal of Psychology and Judaism*
JPolR	*Journal of Politeness Research: Language, Behavior, and Culture*
JPrag	*Journal of Pragmatics*
JPRAS	*Journal of Pre-Raphaelite and Aesthetic Studies*
JPsyR	*Journal of Psycholinguistic Research*
Jpub	
JPW	*Journal of Postcolonial Writing*
JQ	*Journalism Quarterly*
JR	*Journal of Religion*
JRAHS	*Journal of the Royal Australian Historical Society*
JRH	*Journal of Religious History*
JRMA	*Journal of the Royal Musical Association*
JRMMRA	*Journal of the Rocky Mountain Medieval and Renaissance Association*
JRSA	*Journal of the Royal Society of Arts*
JRT	*Journal of Religion and Theatre*
JRUL	*Journal of the Rutgers University Libraries*
JSA	*Journal of the Society of Archivists*
JSaga	*Journal of the Faculty of Liberal Arts and Science* (Saga University)

JSAS	Journal of Southern African Studies
JScholP	Journal of Scholarly Publishing
JSem	Journal of Semantics
JSoc	Journal of Sociolinguistics
JSP	Journal of Scottish Philosophy
JSPNS	
JSSE	Journal of the Short Story in English
JSTWS	Journal of the Sylvia Townsend Warner Society
JTheoS	Journal of Theological Studies
JVC	Journal of Victorian Culture
JWCI	Journal of the Warburg and Courtauld Institutes
JWH	Journal of Women's History
JWIL	Journal of West Indian Literature
JWMS	Journal of the William Morris Society
JWSL	Journal of Women's Studies in Literature
KanE	Kansas English
KanQ	Kansas Quarterly
KB	Kavya Bharati
KCLMS	King's College London Medieval Series
KCS	Kobe College Studies (Japan)
KDNews	Kernerman Dictionary News
KJ	Kipling Journal
KN	Kwartalnik Neoflologiczny (Warsaw)
KompH	Komparatistische Hefte
Kotare	Kotare: New Zealand Notes and Queries
KPR	Kentucky Philological Review
KR	Kenyon Review
KSJ	Keats-Shelley Journal
KSMB	
KSR	Keats-Shelley Review
Kuka	Kuka: Journal of Creative and Critical Writing (Zaria, Nigeria)
Kunapipi	Kunapipi
KWS	Key-Word Studies in Chaucer
L&A	Literature and Aesthetics
L&B	Literature and Belief
L&C	Language and Communication
L&E	Linguistics and Education: An International Research Journal
Landfall	Landfall: A New Zealand Quarterly
L&H	Literature and History
L&L	Language and Literature
L&LC	Literary and Linguistic Computing
L&M	Literature and Medicine
L&P	Literature and Psychology
L&S	Language and Speech
L&T	Literature and Theology: An Interdisciplinary Journal of Theory and Criticism
L&U	Lion and the Unicorn: A Critical Journal of Children's Literature
Lang&S	Language and Style
LangF	Language Forum
LangQ	USF Language Quarterly
LangR	Language Research
LangS	Language Sciences

Language	*Language* (Linguistic Society of America)
LanM	*Les Langues Modernes*
LATR	*Latin American Theatre Review*
LaTrobe	*La Trobe Journal*
LawL	*Law and Literature*
LawLi	*Law and the Literary Imagination*
LB	*Leuvense Bijdragen*
LBR	*Luso-Brazilian Review*
LCrit	*Literary Criterion* (Mysore, India)
LCUT	*Library Chronicle* (University of Texas at Austin)
LDOCE	*Longman Dictionary of Contemporary English*
LeedsSE	*Leeds Studies in English*
LeF	*Linguistica e Filologia*
Legacy	*Legacy: A Journal of Nineteenth-Century American Women Writers*
Lemuria	*Lemuria: A Half-Yearly Research Journal of Indo-Australian Studies*
L'EpC	*L'Epoque Conradienne*
LeS	*Lingua e Stile*
Lexicographica	*Lexicographica: International Annual for Lexicography*
Lexicography	*Lexicography*
LFQ	*Literature/Film Quarterly*
LH	*Library History*
LHY	*Literary Half-Yearly*
LI	*Studies in the Literary Imagination*
Library	*Library*
LibrQ	*Library Quarterly*
LIN	*Linguistics in the Netherlands*
LingA	*Linguistic Analysis*
Ling&P	*Linguistics and Philosophy*
Ling&Philol	*Linguistics and Philology*
LingB	*Linguistische Berichte*
LingI	*Linguistic Inquiry*
LingInv	*Linvisticæ Investigationes*
LingP	*Linguistica Pragensia*
LingRev	*Linguistic Review*
Lingua	*Lingua: International Review of General Linguistics*
Linguistics	*Linguistics*
Linguistique	*La Linguistique*
LiNQ	*Literature in Northern Queensland*
LiRevALSC	*Literary Imagination: The Review of the Association of Literary Scholars and Critics*
LIT	*LIT: Literature, Interpretation, Theory*
LitComp	*Literature Compass*
LiteratureC	*Literature Compass*
LitH	*Literary Horizons*
LitI	*Literary Imagination: The Review of the Association of Literary Scholars and Critics*
LitR	*Literary Review: An International Journal of Contemporary Writing*
LittPrag	*Litteraria Pragensia: Studies in Literature and Culture*
LJCS	*London Journal of Canadian Studies*
LJGG	*Literaturwissenschaftliches Jahrbuch im Aufrage der Görres-Gesellschaft*

LJHum	*Lamar Journal of the Humanities*
LMag	*London Magazine*
LockeN	*Locke Newsletter*
LocusF	*Locus Focus*
Logos	*Logos: A Journal of Catholic Thought and Culture*
LongR	*Long Room: Bulletin of the Friends of the Library* (Trinity College, Dublin)
Lore&L	*Lore and Language*
LP	*Lingua Posnaniensis*
LPLD	*Liverpool Papers in Language and Discourse*
LPLP	*Language Problems and Language Planning*
LR	*Les Lettres Romanes*
LRB	*London Review of Books*
LSE	*Lund Studies in English*
LSLD	*Liverpool Studies in Language and Discourse*
LSoc	*Language in Society*
LSp	*Language and Speech*
LST	*Longman Study Texts*
LTM	*Leeds Texts and Monographs*
LTP	*LTP: Journal of Literature Teaching Politics*
LTR	*London Theatre Record*
LuK	*Literatur und Kritik*
LVC	*Language Variation and Change*
LW	*Life Writing*
LWU	*Literatur in Wissenschaft und Unterricht*
M&Lang	*Mind and Language*
MÆ	*Medium Ævum*
MAEL	*Macmillan Anthologies of English Literature*
MaComere	*MaComère*
Magistra	*Magistra: A Women's Spirituality in History*
MagL	*Magazine Littéraire*
Mana	*Mana*
MAS	*Modern Asian Studies*
M&H	*Medievalia et Humanistica*
M&L	*Music and Letters*
M&N	*Man and Nature/L'Homme et la Nature: Proceedings of the Canadian Society for Eighteenth-Century Studies*
M&T	
Manuscripta	*Manuscripta*
MAR	*Mid-American Review*
Margin	*Margin*
MarkhamR	*Markham Review*
Matatu	*Matatu*
Matrix	*Matrix*
MBL	*Modern British Literature*
MC&S	*Media, Culture and Society*
MCI	*Modern Critical Interpretations*
MCJNews	*Milton Centre of Japan News*
McNR	*McNeese Review*
MCRel	*Mythes, Croyances et Religions dans le Monde Anglo-Saxon*
MCV	*Modern Critical Views*
MD	*Modern Drama*
ME	*Medieval Encounters*

Meanjin	*Meanjin*
MED	*Middle English Dictionary*
MedFor	*Medieval Forum* (online)
MedHis	*Media History*
Mediaevalia	*Mediaevalia: A Journal of Mediaeval Studies*
MedPers	*Medieval Perspectives*
MELUS	*MELUS: The Journal of the Society of Multi-Ethnic Literature of the United States*
Meridian	*Meridian*
MES	*Medieval and Early Modern English Studies*
MESN	*Mediaeval English Studies Newsletter*
MET	*Middle English Texts*
Met&Sym	
METh	*Medieval English Theatre*
MFF	*Medieval Feminist Forum* (formerly *Medieval Feminist Newsletter*)
MFN	*Medieval Feminist Newsletter* (now *Medieval Feminist Forum*)
MFS	*Modern Fiction Studies*
MH	*Malahat Review*
MHL	*Macmillan History of Literature*
MHLS	*Mid-Hudson Language Studies*
MichA	*Michigan Academician*
MiltonQ	*Milton Quarterly*
MiltonS	*Milton Studies*
MinnR	*Minnesota Review*
MissQ	*Mississippi Quarterly*
MissR	*Missouri Review*
Mittelalter	*Das Mittelalter: Perspektiven Mediavistischer Forschung*
MJLF	*Midwestern Journal of Language and Folklore*
ML	*Music and Letters*
MLAIB	*Modern Language Association International Bibliography*
MLing	*Modelès Linguistiques*
MLJ	*Modern Language Journal*
MLN	*Modern Language Notes*
MLQ	*Modern Language Quarterly*
MLR	*Modern Language Review*
MLRev	*Malcolm Lowry Review*
MLS	*Modern Language Studies*
M/M	*Modernism/Modernity*
MMD	*Macmillan Modern Dramatists*
MMG	*Macmillan Master Guides*
MMisc	*Midwestern Miscellany*
MOCS	*Magazine of Cultural Studies*
ModA	*Modern Age: A Quarterly Review*
ModET	*Modern English Teacher*
ModM	*Modern Masters*
ModSp	*Moderne Sprachen*
Mo/Mo	*Modernism/Modernity*
Monist	*Monist*
MonSP	*Monash Swift Papers*
Month	*Month: A Review of Christian Thought and World Affairs*
MOR	*Mount Olive Review*
Moreana	*Moreana: Bulletin Thomas More* (Angers, France)

Mosaic	*Mosaic: A Journal for the Interdisciplinary Study of Literature*
MoyA	*Moyen Age*
MP	*Modern Philology*
MPHJ	*Middlesex Polytechnic History Journal*
MPR	*Mervyn Peake Review*
MQ	*Midwest Quarterly*
MQR	*Michigan Quarterly Review*
MR	*Massachusetts Review*
MRDE	*Medieval and Renaissance Drama in England*
MRTS	*Medieval and Renaissance Texts and Studies*
MS	*Mediaeval Studies*
MSC	*Malone Society Collections*
MSE	*Massachusetts Studies in English*
MSEx	*Melville Society Extracts*
MSh	*Macmillan Shakespeare*
MSNH	*Mémoires de la Société Néophilologique de Helsinki*
MSpr	*Moderna Språk*
MSR	*Malone Society Reprints*
MSSN	*Medieval Sermon Studies Newsletter*
MT	*Musical Times*
MTJ	*Mark Twain Journal*
Multilingua	*Multilingua: Journal of Cross-Cultural and Interlanguage Communication*
MusR	*Music Review*
MW	*Muslim World* (Hartford, CT)
MWQ	*Mid-West Quarterly*
MysticsQ	*Mystics Quarterly*
Mythlore	*Mythlore: A Journal of J.R.R. Tolkein, C.S. Lewis, Charles Williams, and the Genres of Myth and Fantasy Studies*
NA	*Nuova Antologia*
Names	*Names: Journal of the American Name Society*
NAmR	*North American Review*
N&F	*Notes & Furphies*
N&Q	*Notes and Queries*
Narrative	*Narrative*
Navasilu	*Navasilu*
NB	*Namn och Bygd*
NCaS	*New Cambridge Shakespeare*
NCBEL	*New Cambridge Bibliography of English Literature*
NCC	*Nineteenth-Century Contexts*
NCE	*Norton Critical Editions*
NCFS	*Nineteenth-Century French Studies*
NCI	*New Critical Idiom*
NCLE	*Nineteenth-Century Literature in English*
NConL	*Notes on Contemporary Literature*
NCP	*Nineteenth-Century Prose*
NCS	*New Clarendon Shakespeare*
NCSR	*New Chaucer Society Readings*
NCSTC	*Nineteenth-Century Short Title Catalogue*
NCStud	*Nineteenth-Century Studies*
NCT	*Nineteenth-Century Theatre*
NDQ	*North Dakota Quarterly*
NegroD	*Negro Digest*

NELS	*North Eastern Linguistic Society*
Neoh	*Neohelicon*
Neophil	*Neophilologus*
NEQ	*New England Quarterly*
NERMS	*New England Review*
NewA	*New African*
NewBR	*New Beacon Review*
NewC	*New Criterion*
New Casebooks	*New Casebooks: Contemporary Critical Essays*
NewComp	*New Comparison: A Journal of Comparative and General Literary Studies*
NewF	*New Formations*
NewHR	*New Historical Review*
NewR	*New Republic*
NewSt	*Newfoundland Studies*
NewV	*New Voices*
NF	*Neiophilologica Fennica*
NfN	*News from Nowhere*
NFS	*Nottingham French Studies*
NGC	*New German Critique*
NGS	*New German Studies*
NH	*Northern History*
NHR	*Nathaniel Hawthorne Review*
NIS	*Nordic Irish Studies*
NJES	*Nordic Journal of English Studies*
NJL	*Nordic Journal of Linguistics*
NL	*Nouvelles Littéraires*
NLAN	*National Library of Australia News*
NL&LT	*Natural Language and Linguistic Theory*
NLH	*New Literary History: A Journal of Theory and Interpretation*
NLitsR	*New Literatures Review*
NLR	*New Left Review*
NLS	*Natural Language Semantics*
NLWJ	*National Library of Wales Journal*
NM	*Neuphilologische Mitteilungen*
NMAL	*NMAL: Notes on Modern American Literature*
NMer	*New Mermaids*
NMIL	*Notes on Modern Irish Literature*
NML	*New Medieval Literatures*
NMS	*Nottingham Medieval Studies*
NMW	*Notes on Mississippi Writers*
NN	*Nordiska Namenstudier*
NNER	*Northern New England Review*
Nomina	*Nomina: A Journal of Name Studies Relating to Great Britain and Ireland*
NoP	*Northern Perspective*
NOR	*New Orleans Review*
NorfolkA	*Norfolk Archaeology*
NortonCE	*Norton Critical Edition*
Novel	*Novel: A Forum on Fiction*
Novitas-ROYAL	*Research on Youth and Language*
NOWELE	*North-Western European Language Evolution*
NPS	*New Penguin Shakespeare*

DUBLIN BUSINESS SCHOOL LIBRARY

NR	Nassau Review
NRF	La Nouvelle Revue Française
NRRS	Notes and Records of the Royal Society of London
NS	Die neuren Sprachen
NSS	New Swan Shakespeare
NTQ	New Theatre Quarterly
NVSAWC	Newsletter of the Victorian Studies Association of Western Canada
NwJ	Northward Journal
NWR	Northwest Review
NWRev	New Welsh Review
NYH	New York History
NYLF	New York Literary Forum
NYRB	New York Review of Books
NYT	New York Times
NYTBR	New York Times Book Review
NZB	New Zealand Books
NZJAS	New Zealand Journal of Asian Studies
NZListener	New Zealand Listener
NZW	NZWords
OA	Oxford Authors
OB	Ord och Bild
Obsidian	Obsidian II: Black Literature in Review
OBSP	Oxford Bibliographical Society Publications
OED	Oxford English Dictionary
OEDNews	Oxford English Dictionary News
OENews	Old English Newsletter
OELH	Oxford English Literary History
OET	Oxford English Texts
OH	Over Here: An American Studies Journal
OHEL	Oxford History of English Literature
OhR	Ohio Review
OL	
OLR	Oxford Literary Review
OnCan	Onomastica Canadiana
OPBS	Occasional Papers of the Bibliographical Society
OpenGL	Open Guides to Literature
OpL	Open Letter
OPL	Oxford Poetry Library
OPLiLL	Occasional Papers in Linguistics and Language Learning
OPSL	Occasional Papers in Systemic Linguistics
OralT	Oral Tradition
Orbis	Orbis
OrbisLit	Orbis Litterarum
OS	Oxford Shakespeare
OSS	Oxford Shakespeare Studies
OT	Oral Tradition
Outrider	Outrider: A Publication of the Wyoming State Library
Overland	Overland
PA	Présence Africaine
PAAS	Proceedings of the American Antiquarian Society
PacStud	Pacific Studies
Paideuma	Paideuma: A Journal Devoted to Ezra Pound Scholarship

PAJ	*Performing Art Journal*
P&C	*Pragmatics and Cognition*
P&CT	*Psychoanalysis and Contemporary Thought*
P&L	*Philosophy and Literature*
P&P	*Past and Present*
P&R	*Philosophy and Rhetoric*
P&SC	*Philosophy and Social Criticism*
P&MS	
PAns	*Partial Answers*
PAPA	*Publications of the Arkansas Philological Association*
Papers	*Papers: Explorations into Children's Literature*
PAPS	*Proceedings of the American Philosophical Society*
PAR	*Performing Arts Resources*
Parabola	*Parabola: The Magazine of Myth and Tradition*
Paragraph	*Paragraph: The Journal of the Modern Critical Theory Group*
Parergon	*Parergon: Bulletin of the Australian and New Zealand Association for Medieval and Renaissance Studies*
ParisR	*Paris Review*
Parnassus	*Parnassus: Poetry in Review*
PastM	*Past Masters*
PaterN	*Pater Newsletter*
PAus	*Poetry Australia*
PBA	*Proceedings of the British Academy*
PBerLS	*Proceedings of the Berkeley Linguistics Society*
PBSA	*Papers of the Bibliographical Society of America*
PBSC	*Papers of the Biographical Society of Canada*
PCL	*Perspectives on Contemporary Literature*
PCLAC	*Proceedings of the California Linguistics Association Conference*
PCLS	*Proceedings of the Comparative Literature Symposium* (Lubbock, TX)
PCP	*Pacific Coast Philology*
PCRev	*Popular Culture Review*
PCS	*Penguin Critical Studies*
PEAN	*Proceedings of the English Association North*
PE&W	*Philosophy East and West: A Quarterly of Asian and Comparative Thought*
PELL	*Papers on English Language and Literature* (Japan)
Pequod	*Pequod: A Journal of Contemporary Literature and Literary Criticism*
Performance	*Performance*
PerfR	*Performance Review*
Peritia	*Peritia: Journal of the Medieval Academy of Ireland*
Perspicuitas	*Perspicuitas: Internet-Periodicum für Mediävistische Sprach-, Literature- und Kulturwissenschaft*
Persuasions	*Persuasions: Journal of the Jane Austen Society of North America*
Philament	*Philament: Online Journal of the Arts and Culture Phonology*
Philosophy	*Philosophy*
PhilRev	*Philosophical Review: A Quarterly Journal*
PhiN	*Philologie im Netz*
PHist	*Printing History*
Phonetica	*Phonetica: International Journal of Speech Science*

PHOS	*Publishing History Occasional Series*
PhRA	*Philosophical Research Archives*
PhT	*Philosophy Today*
PiL	*Papers in Linguistics*
PIMA	*Proceedings of the Illinois Medieval Association*
PinterR	*Pinter Review*
PJCL	*Prairie Journal of Canadian Literature*
PLL	*Papers on Language and Literature*
PLPLS	*Proceedings of the Leeds Philosophical and Literary Society, Literary and Historical Section*
PM	*Penguin Masterstudies*
PMHB	*Pennsylvania Magazine of History and Biography*
PMLA	*Publications of the Modern Language Association of America*
PMPA	*Proceedings of the Missouri Philological Association*
PNotes	*Pynchon Notes*
PNR	*Poetry and Nation Review*
PoeS	*Poe Studies*
Poetica	*Poetica: Zeitschrift fur Sprach- und Literaturwissenschaft* (Amsterdam)
PoeticaJ	*Poetica: An International Journal of Linguistic-Literary Studies* (Tokyo)
Poetics	*Poetics: International Review for the Theory of Literature*
Poétique	*Poétique: Revue de Théorie et d'Analyse Littéraires*
Poetry	*Poetry* (Chicago)
PoetryCR	*Poetry Canada Review*
PoetryR	*Poetry Review*
PoetryW	*Poetry Wales*
POMPA	*Publications of the Mississippi Philological Association*
PostS	*Past Script: Essays in Film and the Humanities*
PoT	*Poetics Today*
PP	*Penguin Passnotes*
PP	*Philologica Pragensia*
PPA	*Philosophical Perspectives Annual*
PPMRC	*Proceedings of the International Patristic, Mediaeval and Renaissance Conference*
PPR	*Philosophy and Phenomenological Research*
PQ	*Philological Quarterly*
PQM	*Pacific Quarterly* (Moana)
PR	*Partisan Review*
Pragmatics	*Pragmatics: Quarterly Publication of the International Pragmatics Association*
PrairieF	*Prairie Fire*
Praxis	*Praxis: A Journal of Cultural Criticism*
PRep	
Prépub	*(Pré)publications*
PRev	*Powys Review*
PRIA	*Proceedings of the Royal Irish Academy*
PRIAA	*Publications of the Research Institute of the Abo Akademi Foundation*
PRMCLS	*Papers from the Regional Meetings of the Chicago Linguistics Society*
Prospects	*Prospects: An Annual Journal of American Cultural Studies*

Prospero	Prospero: Journal of New Thinking in Philosophy for Education
Proteus	Proteus: A Journal of Ideas
Proverbium	Proverbium
PrS	Prairie Schooner
PSt	Prose Studies
PsyArt	Psychological Study of the Arts (hyperlink journal)
PsychR	Psychological Reports
PTBI	Publications of the Sir Thomas Browne Institute
PubH	Publishing History
PULC	Princeton University Library Chronicle
PURBA	Panjab University Research Bulletin (Arts)
PVR	Platte Valley Review
PWC	Pickering's Women's Classics
PY	Phonology Yearbook
QDLLSM	Quaderni del Dipartimento e Lingue e Letterature Straniere Moderne
QE	Quarterly Essay
QI	Quaderni d'Italianistica
QJS	Quarterly Journal of Speech
QLing	Quantitative Linguistics
QQ	Queen's Quarterly
QR	Queensland Review
QRFV	Quarterly Review of Film and Video
Quadrant	Quadrant (Sydney)
Quarendo	Quarendo
Quarry	Quarry
QWERTY	QWERTY: Arts, Littératures, et Civilisations du Monde Anglophone
RadP	Radical Philosophy
RAL	Research in African Literatures
RALS	Resources for American Literary Study
Ramus	Ramus: Critical Studies in Greek and Roman Literature
R&C	Race and Class
R&L	Religion and Literature
Raritan	Raritan: A Quarterly Review
Rask	Rask: International tidsskrift for sprong og kommunikation
RB	Revue Bénédictine
RBPH	Revue Belge de Philologie et d'Histoire
RBR	Rare Book Review (formerly ABR)
RCEI	Revista Canaria de Estudios Ingleses
RCF	Review of Contemporary Fiction
RCPS	Romantic Circles Praxis Series (online)
RDN	Renaissance Drama Newsletter
RE	Revue d'Esthétique
Reader	Reader: Essays in Reader-Oriented Theory, Criticism, and Pedagogy
ReAL	Re: Artes Liberales
REALB	REAL: The Yearbook of Research in English and American Literature (Berlin)
ReAr	Religion and the Arts
RecBucks	Records of Buckinghamshire

RecL	*Recovery Literature*
RECTR	*Restoration and Eighteenth-Century Theatre Research*
RedL	*Red Letters: A Journal of Cultural Politics*
REED	*Records of Early English Drama*
REEDN	*Records of Early English Drama Newsletter*
ReFr	*Revue Française*
Reinardus	*Reinardus*
REL	*Review of English Literature* (Kyoto)
RELC	*RELC Journal: A Journal of Language Teaching and Research in Southeast Asia*
Ren&R	*Renaissance and Reformation*
Renascence	*Renascence: Essays on Values in Literature*
RenD	*Renaissance Drama*
Renfor	*Renaissance Forum* (online)
RenP	*Renaissance Papers*
RenQ	*Renaissance Quarterly*
Rep	*Representations*
RePublica	*RePublica*
RES	*Review of English Studies*
Restoration	*Restoration: Studies in English Literary Culture, 1660–1700*
Rev	*Review* (Blacksburg, VA)
RevAli	*Revista Alicantina de Estudios Ingleses*
Revels	*Revels Plays*
RevelsCL	*Revels Plays Companion Library*
RevelsSE	*Revels Student Editions*
RevR	*Revolution and Romanticism, 1789–1834*
RFEA	*Revue Française d'Études Américaines*
RFR	*Robert Frost Review*
RG	*Revue Générale*
RH	*Recusant History*
Rhetorica	*Rhetorica: A Journal of the History of Rhetoric*
Rhetorik	*Rhetorik: Ein Internationales Jahrbuch*
RhetR	*Rhetoric Review*
RHist	*Rural History*
RHL	*Revue d'Histoire Littéraire de la France*
RHT	*Revue d'Histoire du Théâtre*
RIB	*Revista Interamericana de Bibliografía: Inter-American Reviews of Bibliography*
Ricardian	*Ricardian: Journal of the Richard III Society*
RL	*Rereading Literature*
RLAn	*Romance Languages Annual*
RLC	*Revue de Littérature Comparée*
RL&C	*Research on Language and Computation*
RLing	*Rivista di Linguistica*
RLit	*Russian Literature*
RLM	*La Revue des Lettres Modernes: Histoire des Idées des Littératures*
RLMC	*Rivista di Letteratura Moderne e Comparate*
RLT	*Russian Literature Triquarterly*
RM	*Rethinking Marxism*
RMR	*Rocky Mountain Review of Language and Literature*
RM	*Renaissance and Modern Studies*
RMSt	*Reading Medieval Studies*

ROA	*Rutgers Optimality Archive*
Romania	*Romania*
Romanticism	*Romanticism*
RomN	*Romance Notes*
RomQ	*Romance Quarterly*
ROMRD	
RomS	*Romance Studies*
RomText	*Romantic Textualities: Literature and Print Culture, 1780–1840 (formerly Cardiff Corvey)*
RoN	*Romanticism on the Net*
ROO	*Room of One's Own: A Feminist Journal of Literature and Criticism*
RORD	*Research Opportunities in Renaissance Drama*
RPT	*Russian Poetics in Translation*
RQ	*Riverside Quarterly*
RR	*Romanic Review*
RRDS	*Regents Renaissance Drama Series*
RRestDS	*Regents Restoration Drama Series*
RS	*Renaissance Studies*
RSQ	*Rhetoric Society Quarterly*
RSV	*Rivista di Study Vittoriani*
RUO	*Revue de l'Université d'Ottawa*
RUSEng	*Rajasthan University Studies in English*
RuskN	*Ruskin Newsletter*
RUUL	*Reports from the Uppsala University Department of Linguistics*
R/WT	*Readerly/Writerly Texts*
SAC	*Studies in the Age of Chaucer*
SAD	*Studies in American Drama, 1945–Present*
SAF	*Studies in American Fiction*
Saga-Book	*Saga-Book (Viking Society for Northern Research)*
Sagetrieb	*Sagatrieb: A Journal Devoted to Poets in the Pound–H.D.–Williams Tradition*
SAIL	*Studies in American Indian Literatures: The Journal of the Association for the Study of American Indian Literatures*
SAJL	*Studies in American Jewish Literature*
SAJMRS	*South African Journal of Medieval and Renaissance Studies*
Sal	*Salmagundi: A Quarterly of the Humanities and Social Sciences*
SALALS	*Southern African Linguistics and Applied language Studies*
SALCT	*SALCT: Studies in Australian Literature, Culture and Thought*
S&S	*Sight and Sound*
SAntS	*Studia Anthroponymica Scandinavica*
Salt	*Salt: An International Journal of Poetry and Poetics*
SAP	*Studia Anglica Posnaniensia*
SAQ	*South Atlantic Quarterly*
SAR	*Studies in the American Renaissance*
SARB	*South African Review of Books*
SARev	*South Asian Review*
Sargasso	*Sargasso*
SASLC	*Studies in Anglo-Saxon Literature and Culture*
SatR	*Saturday Review*
SB	*Studies in Bibliography*
SBHC	*Studies in Browning and his Circle*
SC	*Seventeenth Century*

Scan	*Scandinavica: An International Journal of Scandinavian Studies*
ScanS	*Scandinavian Studies*
SCel	*Studia Celtica*
SCER	*Society for Critical Exchange Report*
Schuylkill	*Schuylkill: A Creative and Critical Review* (Temple University)
Scintilla	*Scintilla: Annual Journal of Vaughan Studies and New Poetry*
SCJ	*Sixteenth Century Journal*
SCL	*Studies in Canadian Literature*
ScLJ	*Scottish Literary Journal: A Review of Studies in Scottish Language and Literature*
ScLJ(S)	*Scottish Literary Journal Supplement*
SCLOP	*Society for Caribbean Linguistics Occasional Papers*
SCN	*Seventeenth-Century News*
ScotL	*Scottish Language*
ScottN	*Scott Newsletter*
SCR	*South Carolina Review*
Screen	*Screen* (London)
SCRev	*South Central Review*
Scriblerian	*Scriblerian and the Kit Cats: A Newsjournal Devoted to Pope, Swift, and their Circle*
Scripsi	*Scripsi*
Scriptorium	*Scriptorium: International Review of Manuscript Studies*
ScTh	*Scottish Journal of Theology*
SD	*Social Dynamics*
SDR	*South Dakota Review*
SECC	*Studies in Eighteenth-Century Culture*
SECOLR	*SECOL Review: Southeastern Conference on Linguistics*
SED	*Survey of English Dialects*
SEDERI	*Journal of the Spanish Society for Renaissance Studies (Sociedad Española de Estudios Renacentistas Ingleses)*
SEEJ	*Slavic and East European Journal*
SEL	*Studies in English Literature, 1500–1900* (Rice University)
SELing	*Studies in English Linguistics* (Tokyo)
SELit	*Studies in English Literature* (Tokyo)
SELL	*Studies in English Language and Literature*
Sem	*Semiotica: Journal of the International Association for Semiotic Studies*
Semiosis	*Semiosis: Internationale Zeitschrift für Semiotik und Ästhetik*
SER	*Studien zur Englischen Romantik*
Seven	*Seven: An Anglo-American Literary Review*
SF&R	*Scholars' Facsimiles and Reprints*
SFic	*Science Fiction: A Review of Speculative Literature*
SFNL	*Shakespeare on Film Newsletter*
SFQ	*Southern Folklore Quarterly*
SFR	*Stanford French Review*
SFS	*Science-Fiction Studies*
SH	*Studia Hibernica* (Dublin)
Shakespeare	
ShakB	*Shakespeare Bulletin*
ShakS	*Shakespeare Studies* (New York)
Shandean	*Shandean*
Sh&Sch	*Shakespeare and Schools*
ShawR	*Shaw: The Annual of Bernard Shaw Studies*

Shenandoah	*Shenandoah*
SherHR	*Sherlock Holmes Review*
ShIntY	*Shakespeare International Yearbook*
Shiron	*Shiron*
ShJE	*Shakespeare Jahrbuch* (Weimar)
ShJW	*Deutsche Shakespeare-Gesellschaft West Jahrbuch* (Bochum)
ShLR	*Shoin Literary Review*
ShN	*Shakespeare Newsletter*
ShortS	
SHPBBS	*Studies in the History of Philosophy of Biological and Biomedical Sciences*
SHPS	*Studies in the History and Philosophy of Science*
SHR	*Southern Humanities Review*
ShS	*Shakespeare Survey*
ShSA	*Shakespeare in Southern Africa*
ShStud	*Shakespeare Studies* (Tokyo)
SHW	*Studies in Hogg and his World*
ShY	*Shakespeare Yearbook*
SiAF	*Studies in American Fiction*
SIcon	*Studies in Iconography*
SidJ	*Sidney Journal*
SidN	*Sidney Newsletter and Journal*
Signs	*Signs: Journal of Women in Culture and Society*
SiHoLS	*Studies in the History of the Language Sciences*
SIL	*Studies in Literature*
SiMed	*Studies in Medievalism*
SIM	*Studies in Music*
SiP	*Shakespeare in Performance*
SIP	*Studies in Philology*
SiPr	*Shakespeare in Production*
SiR	*Studies in Romanticism*
SJC	
SJS	*San José Studies*
SL	*Studia Linguistica*
SLang	*Studies in Language*
SLCS	*Studies in Language Companion Series*
SLI	*Studies in the Literary Imagination*
SLJ	*Southern Literary Journal*
SLRev	*Stanford Literature Review*
SLSc	*Studies in the Linguistic Sciences*
SMART	*Studies in Medieval and Renaissance Teaching*
SMC	*Studies in Medieval Culture*
SMed	*Studi Medievali*
SMELL	*Studies in Medieval English Language and Literature*
SMLit	*Studies in Mystical Literature* (Taiwan)
SMRH	*Studies in Medieval and Renaissance History*
SMRT	*Studies in Medieval and Renaissance Teaching*
SMS	*Studier i Modern Språkvetenskap*
SMy	*Studia Mystica*
SN	*Studia Neophilologica*
SNNTS	*Studies in the Novel* (North Texas State University)
SO	*Shakespeare Originals*
SOA	*Sydsvenska Ortnamnssällskapets Årsskrift*

SoAR	*South Atlantic Review*
SoC	*Senses of Cinema* (online)
Sociocrit	*Sociocriticism*
Socioling	*Sociolinguistica*
SocN	*Sociolinguistics*
SocSem	*Social Semiotics*
SocT	*Social Text*
SohoB	*Soho Bibliographies*
SoQ	*Southern Quarterly*
SoR	*Southern Review* (Baton Rouge, LA)
SoRA	*Southern Review* (Adelaide)
SoSt	*Southern Studies: An Interdisciplinary Journal of the South*
Soundings	*Soundings: An Interdisciplinary Journal*
Southerly	*Southerly: A Review of Australian Literature*
SovL	*Soviet Literature*
SP	*Studies in Philology*
SPAN	*SPAN: Newsletter of the South Pacific Association for Commonwealth Literature and Language Studies*
SPAS	*Studies in Puritan American Spirituality*
SPC	*Studies in Popular Culture*
Spectrum	*Spectrum*
Speculum	*Speculum: A Journal of Medieval Studies*
SPELL	*Swiss Papers in English Language and Literature*
Sphinx	*Sphinx: A Magazine of Literature and Society*
Spiritus	*Spiritus: A Journal of Christian Spirituality*
SpM	*Spicilegio Moderno*
SpNL	*Spenser Newsletter*
Sport	*Sport*
Sprachwiss	*Sprachwissenschalt*
SpringE	*Spring: The Journal of the e.e. cummings Society*
SPub	*Studies in Publishing*
SPWVSRA	*Selected Papers from the West Virginia Shakespeare and Renaissance Association*
SQ	*Shakespeare Quarterly*
SR	*Sewanee Review*
SRen	*Studies in the Renaissance*
SRSR	*Status Report on Speech Research* (Haskins Laboratories)
SSEL	*Stockholm Studies in English*
SSELER	*Salzburg Studies in English Literature: Elizabethan and Renaissance*
SSELJDS	*Salzburg Studies in English Literature: Jacobean Drama Studies*
SSELPDPT	*Salzburg Studies in English Literature: Poetic Drama and Poetic Theory*
SSELRR	*Salzburg Studies in English Literature: Romantic Reassessment*
SSEng	*Sydney Studies in English*
SSF	*Studies in Short Fiction*
SSILA Newsletter	*Newsletter of the Society for the Study of the Indigenous Languages of the Americas*
SSL	*Studies in Scottish Literature*
SSLA	*Studies in Second Language Acquisition*
SPap	*Sydney Papers*
SSR	*Scottish Studies Review*
SSt	*Spenser Studies*

SStud	Swift Studies: The Annual of the Ehrenpreis Center
Staffrider	Staffrider
StaffordS	Staffordshire Studies
STAH	Strange Things Are Happening
StCH	Studies in Church History
STGM	Studien und Texte zur Geistegeschichte des Mittelalters
StHR	Stanford Historical Review
StHum	Studies in the Humanities
StIn	Studi Inglesi
StLF	Studi di Letteratura Francese
STP	Studies in Theatre and Performance
StQ	Steinbeck Quarterly
StrR	Structuralist Review
StTCL	Studies in Twentieth-Century Literature
StTW	Studies in Travel Writing
StudiesAmNaturalism	
StudWF	Studies in Weird Fiction
STUF	Sprachtypologie und Universalienforschung
Style	Style (De Kalb, IL)
SUAS	Stratford-upon-Avon Studies
SubStance	SubStance: A Review of Theory and Literary Criticism
SUS	Susquehanna University Studies
SussexAC	Sussex Archaeological Collections
SussexP&P	Sussex Past & Present
SVEC	Studies on Voltaire and the Eighteenth Century
SWPLL	Sheffield Working Papers in Language and Linguistics
SWR	Southwest Review
SwR	Swansea Review: A Journal of Criticism
Sycamore	Sycamore
Symbolism	Symbolism: An International Journal of Critical Aesthetics
TA	Theatre Annual
Tabu	Bulletin voor Taalwetenschap, Groningen
Takahe	Takahe
Talisman	Talisman
TC	Textual Cultures: Texts, Contexts, Interpretation
T&C	Text and Context
T&L	Translation and Literature
T&P	Text and Performance
T&S	Theology and Sexuality
TAPS	Transactions of the American Philosophical Society
TCBS	Transactions of the Cambridge Bibliographical Society
TCE	Texas College English
TCL	Twentieth-Century Literature
TCS	Theory, Culture and Society: Explorations in Critical Social Science
TCWAAS	Transactions of the Cumberland and Westmorland Antiquarian and Archaeological Society
TD	Themes in Drama
TDR	Drama Review
TEAMS	Consortium for the Teaching of the Middle Ages
TEAS	Twayne's English Authors Series
Telos	Telos: A Quarterly Journal of Post-Critical Thought
TennEJ	Tennessee English Journal

TennQ	*Tennessee Quarterly*
TennSL	*Tennessee Studies in Literature*
TeReo	*Te Reo: Journal of the Linguistic Society of New Zealand*
TSLL	*Texas Studies in Language and Literature*
Text	*Text: Transactions of the Society for Textual Scholarship*
Textus	
TH	*Texas Humanist*
THA	*Thomas Hardy Annual*
Thalia	*Thalia: Studies in Literary Humor*
ThC	*Theatre Crafts*
Theater	*Theater*
TheatreS	*Theatre Studies*
Theoria	*Theoria: A Journal of Studies in the Arts, Humanities and Social Sciences* (Natal)
THES	*Times Higher Education Supplement*
Thesis	*Thesis Eleven*
THIC	*Theatre History in Canada*
THJ	*Thomas Hardy Journal*
ThN	*Thackeray Newsletter*
ThoreauQ	*Thoreau Quarterly: A Journal of Literary and Philosophical Studies*
Thought	*Thought: A Review of Culture and Ideas*
Thph	*Theatrephile*
ThreR	*Threepenny Review*
ThS	*Theatre Survey: The American Journal of Theatre History*
THSJ	*Thomas Hardy Society Journal*
THSLC	*Transactions of the Historic Society of Lancashire and Cheshire*
THStud	*Theatre History Studies*
ThTop	*Theatre Topics*
THY	*Thomas Hardy Yearbook*
TiLSM	*Trends in Linguistics: Studies and Monographs*
Tip	*Theory in Practice*
Tirra Lirra	*Tirra Lirra: The Quarterly Magazine for the Yarra Valley*
TJ	*Theatre Journal*
TJS	*Transactions* (Johnson Society)
TJAAWP	*Text: Journal of the Australian Association of Writing Programs*
TkR	*Tamkang Review*
TL	*Theoretical Linguistics*
TLJ	*The Linguistics Journal*
TLR	*Linguistic Review*
TLS	*Times Literary Supplement*
TMLT	*Toronto Medieval Latin Texts*
TN	*Theatre Notebook*
TNWSECS	*Transactions of the North West Society for Eighteenth Century Studies*
TP	*Terzo Programma*
TPLL	*Tilbury Papers in Language and Literature*
TPQ	*Text and Performance Quarterly*
TPr	*Textual Practice*
TPS	*Transactions of the Philological Society*
TR	*Theatre Record*
Traditio	*Traditio: Studies in Ancient and Medieval History, Thought, and Religion*

Transition	*Transition*
TRB	*Tennyson Research Bulletin*
TRHS	*Transactions of the Royal Historical Society*
TRI	*Theatre Research International*
TriQ	*TriQuarterly*
Trivium	*Trivium*
Tropismes	*Tropismes*
TSAR	*Toronto South Asian Review*
TSB	*Thoreau Society Bulletin*
TSLang	*Typological Studies in Language*
TSLL	*Texas Studies in Literature and Language*
TSWL	*Tulsa Studies in Women's Literature*
TTR	*Trinidad and Tobago Review*
TUSAS	*Twayne's United States Authors Series*
TWAS	*Twayne's World Authors Series*
TWBR	*Third World Book Review*
TWQ	*Third World Quarterly*
TWR	*Thomas Wolfe Review*
Txt	*Text: An Interdisciplinary Annual of Textual Studies*
TYDS	*Transactions of the Yorkshire Dialect Society*
Typophiles	*Typophiles* (New York)
UCrow	*Upstart Crow*
UCTSE	*University of Cape Town Studies in English*
UCWPL	*UCL Working Papers in Linguistics*
UDR	*University of Drayton Review*
UE	*Use of English*
UEAPL	*UEA Papers in Linguistics*
UES	*Unisa English Studies*
Ufahamu	*Ufahamu*
ULR	*University of Leeds Review*
UMSE	*University of Mississippi Studies in English*
Untold	*Untold*
UOQ	*University of Ottawa Quarterly*
URM	*Ultimate Reality and Meaning: Interdisciplinary Studies in the Philosophy of Understanding*
USSE	*University of Saga Studies in English*
UtopST	*Utopian Studies*
UTQ	*University of Toronto Quarterly*
UWR	*University of Windsor Review*
VCT	*Les Voies de la Création Théâtrale*
VEAW	*Varieties of English around the World*
Verbatim	*Verbatim: The Language Quarterly*
VIA	*VIA: The Journal of the Graduate School of Fine Arts* (University of Pennsylvania)
Viator	*Viator: Medieval and Renaissance Studies*
Views	*Viennese English Working Papers*
VIJ	*Victorians Institute Journal*
VLC	*Victorian Literature and Culture*
VN	*Victorian Newsletter*
Voices	*Voices*
VP	*Victorian Poetry*
VPR	*Victorian Periodicals Review*
VQR	*Virginia Quarterly Review*

VR	*Victorian Review*
VS	*Victorian Studies*
VSB	*Victorian Studies Bulletin*
VWM	*Virginia Woolf Miscellany*
WAJ	*Women's Art Journal*
WAL	*Western American Literature*
W&I	*Word and Image*
W&L	*Women and Literature*
W&Lang	*Women and Language*
Wasafiri	*Wasafiri*
WascanaR	*Wascana Review*
WBEP	*Wiener Beiträge zur Englischen Philologie*
WC	*World's Classics*
WC	*Wordsworth Circle*
WCR	*West Coast Review*
WCSJ	*Wilkie Collins Society Journal*
WCWR	*William Carlos Williams Review*
Wellsian	*Wellsian: The Journal of the H.G. Wells Society*
WEn	*World Englishes*
Westerly	*Westerly: A Quarterly Review*
WestHR	*West Hills Review: A Walt Whitman Journal*
WF	*Western Folklore*
WHASN	*W.H. Auden Society Newsletter*
WHR	*Western Humanities Review*
WI	*Word and Image*
WLA	*Wyndham Lewis Annual*
WL&A	*War Literature, and the Arts: An International Journal of the Humanities*
WLT	*World Literature Today*
WLWE	*World Literature Written in English*
WMQ	*William and Mary Quarterly*
WoHR	*Women's History Review*
WolfenbütteleB	*Wolfenbüttele Beiträge: Aus den Schätzen der Herzog August Bibliothek*
Women	*Women: A Cultural Review*
WomGY	*Women in German Yearbook*
WomHR	*Women's History Review*
WorcesterR	*Worcester Review*
WORD	*WORD: Journal of the International Linguistic Association*
WQ	*Wilson Quarterly*
WRB	*Women's Review of Books*
WS	*Women's Studies: An Interdisciplinary Journal*
WSIF	*Women's Studies: International Forum*
WSJour	*Wallace Stevens Journal*
WSR	*Wicazo Sa Review*
WstA	*Woolf Studies Annual*
WTJ	*Westminster Theological Journal*
WTW	*Writers and their Work*
WVUPP	*West Virginia University Philological Papers*
WW	*Women's Writing*
WWR	*Walt Whitman Quarterly Review*
XUS	*Xavier Review*
YCC	*Yearbook of Comparative Criticism*

YeA	*Yeats Annual*
YER	*Yeats Eliot Review*
YES	*Yearbook of English Studies*
YEuS	*Yearbook of European Studies/Annuaire d'Études Européennes*
YFS	*Yale French Studies*
Yiddish	*Yiddish*
YJC	*Yale Journal of Criticism: Interpretation in the Humanities*
YLS	*Yearbook of Langland Studies*
YM	*Yearbook of Morphology*
YNS	*York Note Series*
YPL	*York Papers in Linguistics*
YR	*Yale Review*
YREAL	*The Yearbook of Research in English and American Literature*
YULG	*Yale University Library Gazette*
YWES	*Year's Work in English Studies*
ZAA	*Zeitschrift für Anglistik and Amerikanistik*
ZCP	*Zeitschrift für celtische Philologie*
ZDA	*Zeitschrift für deutsches Altertum und deutsche Literatur*
ZDL	*Zeitschrift für Dialektologie und Linguistik*
ZGKS	*Zeitschrfit für Gesellschaft für Kanada-Studien*
ZGL	*Zeitschrift für germanistische Linguistik*
ZPSK	*Zeitschrift für Phonetik Sprachwissenshaft und Kommunikationsforschung*
ZSpr	*Zeitschrift für Sprachwissenshaft*
ZVS	*Zeitschrift für vergleichende Sprachforschung*

Volume numbers are supplied in the text, as are individual issue numbers for journals that are not continuously paginated through the year.

2. Publishers

AAAH	Acta Academiae Åboensis Humaniora, Åbo, Finland
AAH	Australian Academy of Humanities
A&B	Allison & Busby, London
A&R	Angus & Robertson, North Ryde, New South Wales
A&U	Allen & Unwin (now Unwin Hyman)
A&UA	Allen & Unwin, North Sydney, New South Wales
A&W	Almqvist & Wiksell International, Stockholm
AarhusUP	Aarhus UP, Aarhus, Denmark
ABC	ABC Enterprises
ABC CLIO	ABC CLIO Reference Books, Santa Barbara, CA
Abbeville	Abbeville Press, New York
ABDO	Association Bourguignonne de Dialectologie et d'Onomastique, Dijon
AberdeenUP	Aberdeen UP, Aberdeen
Abhinav	Abhinav Publications, New Delhi
Abingdon	Abingdon Press, Nashville, TN
ABL	Armstrong Browning Library, Waco, TX
Ablex	Ablex Publishing, Norwood, NJ
Åbo	Åbo Akademi, Åbo, Finland
Abrams	Harry N. Abrams, New York
Academia	Academia Press, Melbourne
Academic	Academic Press, London and Orlando, FL

Academy	Academy Press, Dublin
AcademyC	Academy Chicago Publishers, Chicago
AcademyE	Academy Editions, London
Acadiensis	Acadiensis Press, Fredericton, New Brunswick, Canada
ACarS	Association for Caribbean Studies, Coral Gables, FL
ACC	Antique Collectors' Club, Woodbridge, Suffolk
ACCO	ACCO, Leuven, Belgium
ACLALS	Association for Commonwealth Literature and Language Studies, Canberra
ACMRS	Arizona Center for Medieval and Renaissance Studies
ACP	Another Chicago Press, Chicago
ACS	Association for Canadian Studies, Ottawa
Adam Hart	Adam Hart Publishers, London
Adam Matthew	Adam Matthew, Suffolk
Addison-Wesley	Addison-Wesley, Wokingham, Berkshire
ADFA	Australian Defence Force Academy, Department of English
Adosa	Adosa, Clermont-Ferrand, France
AEMS	American Early Medieval Studies
AF	Akademisk Forlag, Copenhagen
Affiliated	Affiliated East–West Press, New Delhi
AFP	Associated Faculty Press, New York
Africana	Africana Publications, New York
A–H	Amold-Heinemann, New Delhi
Ahriman	Ahriman-Verlag, Freiburg im Breisgau, Germany
AIAS	Australian Institute of Aboriginal Studies, Canberra
Ajanta	Ajanta Publications, Delhi
AK	Akadémiai Kiadó, Budapest
ALA	ALA Editions, Chicago
Al&Ba	Allen & Bacon, Boston, MA
Albatross	Albatross Books, Sutherland, New South Wales
Albion	Albion, Appalachian State University, Boone, NC
Alderman	Alderman Press, London
Aldwych	Aldwych Press
AligarhMU	Aligarh Muslim University, Uttar Pradesh, India
Alioth	Alioth Press, Beaverton, OR
Allen	W.H. Allen, London
Allied Publishers	Allied Indian Publishers, Lahore and New Delhi
Almond	Almond Press, Sheffield
AM	Aubier Montaigne, Paris
AMAES	Association des Médiévistes Angliciste de l'Enseignement Supérieur, Paris
Amate	Amate Press, Oxford
AmberL	Amber Lane, Oxford
Amistad	Amistad Press, New York
AMP	Aurora Metro Press, London
AMS	AMS Press, New York
AMU	Adam Mickiewicz University, Posnan
Anansi	Anansi Press, Toronto
Anderson-Lovelace	Anderson-Lovelace, Los Altos Hills, CA
Anma Libri	Anma Libri, Saratoga, CA
Antipodes	Antipodes Press, Plimmerton, New Zealand
Anvil	Anvil Press Poetry, London
APA	APA, Maarssen, Netherlands

APH	Associated Publishing House, New Delhi
API	API Network, Perth, Australia
APL	American Poetry and Literature Press, Philadelphia
APP	Australian Professional Publications, Mosman, New South Wales
Applause	Applause Theatre Book Publishers
Appletree	Appletree Press, Belfast
APS	American Philosophical Society, Philadelphia
Aquarian	Aquarian Press, Wellingborough, Northants
ArborH	Arbor House Publishing, New York
Arcade	Arcade Publishing, New York
Archon	Archon Books, Hamden, CT
ArchP	Architectural Press Books, Guildford, Surrey
Ardis	Ardis Publishers, Ann Arbor, MI
Ariel	Ariel Press, London
Aristotle	Aristotle University, Thessaloniki
Ark	Ark Paperbacks, London
Arkona	Arkona Forlaget, Aarhus, Denmark
Arlington	Arlington Books, London
Arnold	Edward Arnold, London
ArnoldEJ	E.J. Arnold & Son, Leeds
ARP	Australian Reference Publications, N. Balwyn, Victoria
Arrow	Arrow Books, London
Arsenal	Arsenal Pulp Press
Artmoves	Artmoves, Parkdale, Victoria
ASAL	Association for the Study of Australian Literature
ASB	Anglo-Saxon Books, Middlesex
ASchP	Australian Scholarly Publishing, Melbourne
ASECS	American Society for Eighteenth-Century Studies, c/o Ohio State University, Columbus
Ashfield	Ashfield Press, London
Ashgate	Ashgate, Brookfield, VT
Ashton	Ashton Scholastic
Aslib	Aslib, London
ASLS	Association for Scottish Literary Studies, Aberdeen
ASP	Australian Scholarly Publishing
AStP	Aboriginal Studies Press, Canberra
ASU	Arizona State University, Tempe
Atheneum	Atheneum Publishers, New York
Athlone	Athlone Press, London
Atlantic	Atlantic Publishers, Darya Ganj, New Delhi
Atlas	Atlas Press, London
Attic	Attic Press, Dublin
AuBC	Australian Book Collector
AucklandUP	Auckland UP, Auckland
AUG	Acta Universitatis Gothoburgensis, Sweden
AUP	Associated University Presses, London and Toronto
AUPG	Academic & University Publishers, London
Aurum	Aurum Press, London
Auslib	Auslib Press, Adelaide
AUU	Acta Universitatis Umensis, Umeå, Sweden
AUUp	Acta Universitatis Upsaliensis, Uppsala
Avebury	Avebury Publishing, Aldershot, Hampshire

Avero	Avero Publications, Newcastle upon Tyne
A-V Verlag	A-V Verlag, Franz Fischer, Augsburg, Germany
AWP	Africa World Press, Trenton, NJ
Axelrod	Axelrod Publishing, Tampa Bay, FL
BA	British Academy, London
BAAS	British Association for American Studies, c/o University of Keele
Bagel	August Bagel Verlag, Dusseldorf
Bahri	Bahri Publications, New Delhi
Bamberger	Bamberger Books, Flint, MI
B&B	Boydell & Brewer, Woodbridge, Suffolk
B&J	Barrie & Jenkins, London
B&N	Barnes & Noble, Totowa, NJ
B&O	Burns & Oates, Tunbridge Wells, Kent
B&S	Michael Benskin and M.L. Samuels, Middle English Dialect Project, University of Edinburgh
BAR	British Archaelogical Reports, Oxford
Barn Owl	Barn Owl Books, Taunton, Somerset
Barnes	A.S. Barnes, San Diego, CA
Barr Smith	Barr Smith Press, Barr Smith Library, University of Adelaide
Bath UP	Bath UP, Bath
Batsford	B.T. Batsford, London
Bayreuth	Bayreuth African Studies, University of Bayreuth, Germany
BBC	BBC Publications, London
BClarkL	Bruccoli Clark Layman Inc./Manly Inc.
BCP	Bristol Classical Press, Bristol
Beacon	Beacon Press, Boston, MA
Beck	C.H. Beck'sche Verlagsbuchandlung, Munich
Becket	Becket Publications, London
Belin	Éditions Belin, Paris
Belknap	Belknap Press, Cambridge, MA
Belles Lettres	Société d'Édition les Belles Lettres, Paris
Bellew	Bellew Publishing, London
Bellflower	Belflower Press, Case University, Cleveland, OH
Benjamins	John Benjamins, Amsterdam
BenjaminsNA	John Benjamins North America, Philadelphia
BennC	Bennington College, Bennington, VT
Berg	Berg Publishers, Oxford
BFI	British Film Institute, London
BGUP	Bowling Green University Popular Press, Bowling Green, OH
BibS	Bibliographical Society, London
BilinguaGA	Bilingua GA Editions
Bilingual	Bilingual Press, Arizona State University, Tempe
Bingley	Clive Bingley, London
Binnacle	Binnacle Press, London
Biografia	Biografia Publishers, London
Birkbeck	Birkbeck College, University of London
Bishopsgate	Bishopsgate Press, Tonbridge, Kent
BL	British Library, London
Black	Adam & Charles Black, London
Black Cat	Black Cat Press, Blackrock, Eire
Blackie	Blackie & Son, Glasgow
Black Moss	Black Moss, Windsor, Ontario

Blackstaff	Blackstaff Press, Belfast
Black Swan	Black Swan, Curtin, UT
Blackwell	Basil Blackwell, Oxford
BlackwellR	Blackwell Reference, Oxford
Blackwood	Blackwood, Pillans & Wilson, Edinburgh
Bl&Br	Blond & Briggs, London
Blandford	Blandford Press, London
Blaue Eule	Verlag die Blaue Eule, Essen
Bloodaxe	Bloodaxe Books, Newcastle upon Tyne
Bloomsbury	Bloomsbury Publishing, London
Blubber Head	Blubber Head Press, Hobart
BM	Bobbs-Merrill, New York
BMP	British Museum Publications, London
Bodleian	Bodleian Library, Oxford
Bodley	Bodley Head, London
Bogle	Bogle L'Ouverture Publications, London
BoiseSUP	Boise State UP, Boise, Idaho
Book Enclave	Book Enclave, Shanti Nagar, Jaipur, India
Book Guild	Book Guild, Lewes, E. Sussex
BookplateS	Bookplate Society, Edgbaston, Birmingham
Booksplus	Booksplus Nigeria Limited, Lagos, Nigeria
Boombana	Boombana Press, Brisbane, Queensland
Borealis	Borealis Press, Ottawa
Borgo	Borgo Press, San Bernardino, CA
BostonAL	Boston Athenaeum Library, Boxton, MA
Bouma	Bouma's Boekhuis, Groningen, Netherlands
Bowker	R.R. Bowker, New Providence, NJ
Boyars	Marion Boyars, London and Boston, MA
Boydell	Boydell Press, Woodbridge, Suffolk
Boyes	Megan Boyes, Allestree, Derbyshire
Br&S	Brandl & Schlesinger
Bran's Head	Bran's Head Books, Frome, Somerset
Braumüller	Wilhelm Braumüller, Vienna
Breakwater	Breakwater Books, St John's, Newfoundland
Brentham	Brentham Press, St Albans, Hertfordshire
Brepols	Brepols, Turnhout, Belgium
Brewer	D.S. Brewer, Woodbridge, Suffolk
Brewin	Brewin Books, Studley, Warwicks
Bridge	Bridge Publishing, S. Plainfield, NJ
Brill	E.J. Brill, Leiden
BrillA	Brill Academic Publishers
Brilliance	Brilliance Books, London
Broadview	Broadview, London, Ontario and Lewiston, NY
Brookside	Brookside Press, London
Browne	Sinclair Browne, London
Brownstone	Brownstone Books, Madison, IN
BrownUP	Brown UP, Providence, RI
Brynmill	Brynmill Press, Harleston, Norfolk
BSA	Bibliographical Society of America
BSB	Black Swan Books, Redding Ridge, CT
BSP	Black Sparrow Press, Santa Barbara, CA
BSU	Ball State University, Muncie, IN
BuckUP	Bucknell UP, Lewisburg, PA

Bulzoni	Bulzoni Editore, Rome
BUP	Birmingham University Press
Burnett	Burnett Books, London
Buske	Helmut Buske, Hamburg
Butterfly	Butterfly Books, San Antonio, TX
BWilliamsNZ	Bridget Williams Books, Wellington, New Zealand
CA	Creative Arts Book, Berkeley, CA
CAAS	Connecticut Academy of Arts and Sciences, New Haven
CAB International	Centre for Agriculture and Biosciences International, Wallingford, Oxfordshire
Cadmus	Cadmus Editions, Tiburon, CA
Cairns	Francis Cairns, University of Leeds
Calaloux	Calaloux Publications, Ithaca, NY
Calder	John Calder, London
CALLS	Centre for Australian Language and Literature Studies, English Department, University of New England, New South Wales
CambridgeSP	Cambridge Scholars Publishing, Newcastle upon Tyne, United Kingdom
Camden	Camden Press, London
CamdenH	Camden House (an imprint of Boydell and Brewer), Rochester, NY
C&G	Carroll & Graf, New York
C&W	Chatto & Windus, London
Canongate	Canongate Publishing, Edinburgh
Canterbury	Canterbury Press, Norwich
Cape	Jonathan Cape, London
Capra	Capra Press, Santa Barbara, CA
Carcanet	Carcanet New Press, Manchester, Lancashire
Cardinal	Cardinal, London
CaribB	Caribbean Books, Parkersburg, IA
CarletonUP	Carleton UP, Ottawa
Carucci	Carucci, Rome
Cascadilla	Cascadilla Press, Somerville, MA
Cass	Frank Cass, London
Cassell	Cassell, London
Cavaliere Azzurro	Cavaliere Azzurro, Bologna
Cave	Godfrey Cave Associates, London
CBA	Council for British Archaeology, London
CBS	Cambridge Bibliographical Society, Cambridge
CCEUCan	Centre for Continuing Education, University of Canterbury, Christchurch, New Zealand
CCP	Canadian Children's Press, Guelph, Ontario
CCS	Centre for Canadian Studies, Mount Allison University, Sackville, NB
CDSH	Centre de Documentation Sciences Humaines, Paris
CENS	Centre for English Name Studies, University of Nottingham
Century	Century Publishing, London
Ceolfrith	Ceolfrith Press, Sunderland, Tyne and Wear
CESR	Société des Amis du Centre d'Études Supérieures de la Renaissance, Tours
CETEDOC	Library of Christian Latin Texts
CFA	Canadian Federation for the Humanities, Ottawa

CG	Common Ground
CH	Croom Helm, London
C–H	Chadwyck–Healey, Cambridge
Chambers	W. & R. Chambers, Edinburgh
Champaign	Champaign Public Library and Information Center, Champaign, IL
Champion	Librairie Honoré Champion, Paris
Chand	S. Chand, Madras
Chaucer	Chaucer Press
ChelseaH	Chelsea House Publishers, New York, New Haven, and Philadelphia
ChLitAssoc	Children's Literature Association
Christendom	Christendom Publications, Front Royal, VA
Chronicle	Chronicle Books, London
Chrysalis	Chrysalis Press
ChuoUL	Chuo University Library, Tokyo
Churchman	Churchman Publishing, Worthing, W. Sussex
Cistercian	Cistercian Publications, Kalamazoo, MI
CL	City Lights Books, San Francisco
CLA	Canadian Library Association, Ottawa
Clarendon	Clarendon Press, Oxford
Claridge	Claridge, St Albans, Hertfordshire
Clarion	Clarion State College, Clarion, PA
Clark	T. & T. Clark, Edinburgh
Clarke	James Clarke, Cambridge
Classical	Classical Publishing, New Delhi
CLCS	Centre for Language and Communication Studies, Trinity College, Dublin
ClogherHS	Clogher Historical Society, Monaghan, Eire
CLUEB	Cooperativa Libraria Universitaria Editrice, Bologna
Clunie	Clunie Press, Pitlochry, Tayside
CMAP	Caxton's Modern Arts Press, Dallas, TX
CMERS	Center for Medieval and Early Renaissance Studies, Binghamton, NY
CML	William Andrews Clark Memorial Library, Los Angeles
CMST	Centre for Medieval Studies, University of Toronto
Coach House	Coach House Press, Toronto
Colleagues	Colleagues Press, East Lansing, MI
Collector	Collector, London
College-Hill	College-Hill Press, San Diego, CA
Collins	William Collins, London
CollinsA	William Collins (Australia), Sydney
Collins & Brown	Collins & Brown, London
ColUP	Columbia UP, New York
Comedia	Comedia Publishing, London
Comet	Comet Books, London
Compton	Compton Press, Tisbury, Wiltshire
Constable	Constable, London
Contemporary	Contemporary Books, Chicago
Continuum	Continuum Publishing, New York
Copp	Copp Clark Pitman, Mississuaga, Ontario
Corgi	Corgi Books, London
CorkUP	Cork UP, Eire

Cormorant	Cormorant Press, Victoria, BC
Cornford	Cornford Press, Launceston, Tasmania
CornUP	Cornell UP, Ithaca, NY
Cornwallis	Cornwallis Press, Hastings, E. Sussex
Coronado	Coronado Press, Lawrence, KS
Cosmo	Cosmo Publications, New Delhi
Coteau	Coteau Books, Regina, Saskatchewan
Cowley	Cowley Publications, Cambridge, MA
Cowper	Cowper House, Pacific Grove, CA
CPP	Canadian Poetry Press, London, Ontario
CQUP	Central Queensland UP, Rockhampton
Crabtree	Crabtree Press, Sussex
Craftsman House	Craftsman House, Netherlands
Craig Pottoon	Craig Pottoon Publishing, New Zealand
Crawford	Crawford House Publishing, Hindmarsh, SA
Creag Darach	Creag Durach Publications, Stirling
CreativeB	Creative Books, New Delhi
Cresset	Cresset Library, London
CRNLE	Centre for Research in the New Literatures in English, Adelaide
Crossing	Crossing Press, Freedom, CA
Crossroad	Crossroad Publishing, New York
Crown	Crown Publishers, New York
Crowood	Crowood Press, Marlborough, Wiltshire
CSAL	Centre for Studies in Australian Literature, University of Western Australia, Nedlands
CSLI	Center for the Study of Language and Information, Stanford University
CSP	Canadian Scholars' Press, Toronto
CSU	Cleveland State University, Cleveland, OH
CTHS	Éditions du Comité des Travaux Historiques et Scientifiques, Paris
CUAP	Catholic University of America Press, Washington, DC
Cuff	Harry Cuff Publications, St John's, Newfoundland
CULouvain	Catholic University of Louvain, Belgium
CULublin	Catholic University of Lublin, Poland
CUP	Cambridge UP, Cambridge, New York, and Melbourne
Currency	Currency Press, Paddington, New South Wales
Currey	James Currey, London
Cushing	Cushing Memorial Library & Archives
CV	Cherry Valley Edition, Rochester, NY
CVK	Cornelson-Velhagen & Klasing, Berlin
CWU	Carl Winter Universitätsverlag, Heidelberg
Da Capo	Da Capo Press, New York
Dacorum	Dacorum College, Hemel Hempstead, Hertfordshire
Daisy	Daisy Books, Peterborough, Northampton
Dalkey	Dalkey Archive Press, Elmwood Park, IL
D&C	David & Charles, Newton Abbot, Devon
D&H	Duncker & Humblot, Berlin
D&M	Douglas & McIntyre, Vancouver, BC
D&S	Duffy and Snellgrove, Polts Point, New South Wales
Dangaroo	Dangaroo Press, Mundelstrup, Denmark

DavidB	David Brown Books
Dawson	Dawson Publishing, Folkestone, Kent
DawsonsPM	Dawsons Pall Mall
DBAP	Daphne Brasell Associates Press
DBP	Drama Book Publishers, New York
Deakin UP	Deakin UP, Geelong, Victoria
De Boeck	De Boeck-Wesmael, Brussels
Dee	Ivan R. Dee Publishers, Chicago, IL
De Graaf	De Graaf, Nierwkoup, Netherlands
Denoël	Denoël S.A.R.L., Paris
Dent	J.M. Dent, London
DentA	Dent, Ferntree Gully, Victoria
Depanee	Depanee Printers and Publishers, Nugegoda, Sri Lanka
Deutsch	André Deutsch, London
Didier	Éditions Didier, Paris
Diesterweg	Verlag Moritz Diesterweg, Frankfurt am Main
Dim Gray Bar Press	Dim Gray Bar Press
Doaba	Doaba House, Delhi
Dobby	Eric Dobby Publishing, St Albans
Dobson	Dobson Books, Durham
Dolmen	Dolmen Press, Portlaoise, Eire
Donald	John Donald, Edinburgh
Donker	Adriaan Donker, Johannesburg
Dorset	Dorset Publishing
Doubleday	Doubleday, London and New York
Dove	Dove, Sydney
Dovecote	Dovecote Press, Wimborne, Dorset
Dovehouse	Dovehouse Editions, Canada
Dover	Dover Publications, New York
Drew	Richard Drew, Edinburgh
Droste	Droste Verlag, Düsseldorf
Droz	Librairie Droz SA, Geneva
DublinUP	Dublin UP, Dublin
Duckworth	Gerald Duckworth, London
Duculot	J. Duculot, Gembloux, Belgium
DukeUP	Duke UP, Durham, NC
Dundurn	Dundurn Press, Toronto and London, Ontario
Duquesne	Duquesne UP, Pittsburgh
Dutton	E.P. Dutton, New York
DWT	Dr Williams's Trust, London
EA	English Association, London
EAS	English Association Sydney Incorporated
Eason	Eason & Son, Dublin
East Bay	East Bay Books, Berkeley, CA
Ebony	Ebony Books, Melbourne
Ecco	Ecco Press, New York
ECNRS	Éditions du Centre National de la Recherche Scientifique, Paris
ECW	ECW Press, Downsview, Ontario
Eden	Eden Press, Montreal and St Albans, VT
EdinUP	Edinburgh UP, Edinburgh
Edizioni	Edizioni del Grifo
Educare	Educare, Burnwood, Victoria

EEM	East European Monographs, Boulder, CO
Eerdmans	William Eerdmans, Grand Rapids, MI
EETS	Early English Text Society, c/o Exeter College, Oxford
1890sS	Eighteen-Nineties Society, Oxford
Eihosha	Eihosha, Tokyo
Elephas	Elephas Books, Kewdale, Australia
Elibank	Elibank Press, Wellington, New Zealand
Elm Tree	Elm Tree Books, London
ELS	English Literary Studies
Ember	Ember Press, Brixham, South Devon
EMSH	Editions de la Maison des Sciences de l'Homme, Paris
Enitharmon	Enitharmon Press, London
Enzyklopädie	Enzyklopädie, Leipzig
EONF	Eugene O'Neill Foundation, Danville, CA
EPNS	English Place-Name Society, Beeston, Nottingham
Epworth	Epworth Press, Manchester
Eriksson	Paul Eriksson, Middlebury, VT
Erlbaum	Erlbaum Associates, NJ
Erskine	Erskine Press, Harleston, Norfolk
EscutchP	Escutcheon Press
ESI	Edizioni Scientifiche Italiane, Naples
ESL	Edizioni di Storia e Letteratura, Rome
EUFS	Editions Universitaires Fribourg Suisse
EUL	Edinburgh University Library, Edinburgh
Europa	Europa Publishers, London
Evans	M. Evans, New York
Exact Change	Exact Change, Boston
Exeter UP	Exeter UP, Devon
Exile	Exile Editions, Toronto, Ontario
Eyre	Eyre Methuen, London
FAB	Free Association Books, London
Faber	Faber & Faber, London
FAC	Federation d'Activites Culturelles, Paris
FACP	Fremantle Arts Centre Press, Fremantle, WA
Falcon Books	Falcon Books, Eastbourne
FALS	Foundation for Australian Literary Studies, James Cook University of North Queensland, Townsville
F&F	Fels & Firn Press, San Anselmo, CA
F&S	Feffer & Simons, Amsterdam
Farrand	Farrand Press, London
Fay	Barbara Fay, Stuttgart
F–B	Ford–Brown, Houston, TX
FCP	Four Courts Press, Dublin
FDUP	Fairleigh Dickinson UP, Madison, NJ
FE	Fourth Estate, London
Feminist	Feminist Press, New York
FictionColl	Fiction Collective, Brooklyn College, Brooklyn, NY
Field Day	Field Day, Derry
Fifth House	Fifth House Publications, Saskatoon, Saskatchewan
FILEF	FILEF Italo–Australian Publications, Leichhardt, New South Wales
Fine	Donald Fine, New York
Fink	Fink Verlag, Munich

Five Leaves	Five Leaves Publications, Nottingham
Flamingo	Flamingo Publishing, Newark, NJ
Flammarion	Flammarion, Paris
FlindersU	Flinders University of South Australia, Bedford Park
Floris	Floris Books, Edinburgh
FlorSU	Florida State University, Tallahassee, FL
FOF	Facts on File, New York
Folger	Folger Shakespeare Library, Washington, DC
Folio	Folio Press, London
Fontana	Fontana Press, London
Footprint	Footprint Press, Colchester, Essex
FordUP	Fordham UP, New York
Foris	Foris Publications, Dordrecht
Forsten	Egbert Forsten Publishing, Groningen, Netherlands
Fortress	Fortress Press, Philadelphia
Francke	Francke Verlag, Berne
Franklin	Burt Franklin, New York
FreeP	Free Press, New York
FreeUP	Free UP, Amsterdam
Freundlich	Freundlich Books, New York
Frommann-Holzboog	Frommann-Holzboog, Stuttgart
FS&G	Farrar, Straus & Giroux
FSP	Five Seasons Press, Madley, Hereford
FW	Fragments West/Valentine Press, Long Beach, CA
FWA	Fiji Writers' Association, Suva
FWP	Falling Wall Press, Bristol
Gale	Gale Research, Detroit, MI
Galilée	Galilée, Paris
Gallimard	Gallimard, Paris
G&G	Grevatt & Grevatt, Newcastle upon Tyne
G&M	Gill & Macmillan, Dublin
Garland	Garland Publishing, New York
Gasson	Roy Gasson Associates, Wimbourne, Dorset
Gateway	Gateway Editions, Washington, DC
GE	Greenwich Exchange, UK
GIA	GIA Publications, USA
Girasole	Edizioni del Girasole, Ravenna
GL	Goose Lane Editions, Fredericton, NB
GlasgowDL	Glasgow District Libraries, Glasgow
Gleerup	Gleerupska, Lund
Gliddon	Gliddon Books Publishers, Norwich
Gloger	Gloger Family Books, Portland, OR
GMP	GMP Publishing, London
GMSmith	Gibbs M. Smith, Layton, UT
Golden Dog	Golden Dog, Ottawa
Gollancz	Victor Gollancz, London
Gomer	Gomer Press, Llandysul, Dyfed
GothU	Gothenburg University, Gothenburg
Gower	Gower Publishing, Aldershot, Hants
GRAAT	Groupe de Recherches Anglo-Américaines de Tours
Grafton	Grafton Books, London
GranB	Granary Books, New York
Granta	Granta Publications, London

Granville	Granville Publishing, London
Grasset	Grasset & Fasquelle, Paris
Grassroots	Grassroots, London
Graywolf	Graywolf Press, St Paul, MI
Greenhalgh	M.J. Greenhalgh, London
Greenhill	Greenhill Books, London
Greenwood	Greenwood Press, Westport, CT
Gregg	Gregg Publishing, Surrey
Greville	Greville Press, Warwick
Greymitre	Greymitre Books, London
GroC	Grolier Club, New York
Groos	Julius Groos Verlag, Heidelberg
Grove	Grove Press, New York
GRP	Greenfield Review Press, New York
Grüner	B.R. Grüner, Amsterdam
Gruyter	Walter de Gruyter, Berlin
Guernica	Guernica Editions, Montreal, Canada
Guilford	Guilford, New York
Gulmohar	Gulmohar Press, Islamabad, Pakistan
Haggerston	Haggerston Press, London
HakluytS	Hakluyt Society, c/o British Library, London
Hale	Robert Hale, London
Hall	G.K. Hall, Boston, MA
Halstead	Halstead Press, Rushcutters Bay, New South Wales
HalsteadP	Halstead Press, c/o J. Wiley & Sons, Chichester, W. Sussex
Hambledon	Hambledon Press, London
H&I	Hale & Iremonger, Sydney
H&L	Hambledon and London
H&M	Holmes & Meier, London and New York
H&S	Hodder & Stoughton, London
H&SNZ	Hodder & Stoughton, Auckland
H&W	Hill & Wang, New York
Hansib	Hansib Publishing, London
Harbour	Harbour Publishing, Madeira Park, BC
Harman	Harman Publishing House, New Delhi
Harper	Harper & Row, New York
Harrap	Harrap, Edinburgh
HarrV	Harrassowitz Verlag, Wiesbaden
HarvardUP	Harvard UP, Cambridge, MA
Harwood	Harwood Academic Publishers, Langhorne, PA
Hatje	Verlag Gerd Hatje, Germany
HBJ	Harcourt Brace Jovanovich, New York and London
HC	HarperCollins, London
HCAus	HarperCollins Australia, Pymble, New South Wales
Headline	Headline Book Publishing, London
Heath	D.C. Heath, Lexington, MS
HebrewUMP	Hebrew University Magnes Press
Heinemann	William Heinemann, London
HeinemannA	William Heinemann, St Kilda, Victoria
HeinemannC	Heinemann Educational Books, Kingston, Jamaica
HeinemannNg	Heinemann Educational Books, Nigeria
HeinemannNZ	Heinemann Publishers, Auckland (now Heinemann Reed)
HeinemannR	Heinemann Reed, Auckland

Helm	Christopher Helm, London
HelmI	Helm Information
Herbert	Herbert Press, London
Hermitage	Hermitage Antiquarian Bookshop, Denver, CO
Hern	Nick Hem Books, London
Hertfordshire	Hertfordshire Publications
Heyday	Heyday Books, Berkeley, CA
HH	Hamish Hamilton, London
Hilger	Adam Hilger, Bristol
HM	Harvey Miller, London
HMSO	HMSO, London
Hodder, Moa, Beckett	Hodder, Moa, Beckett, Milford, Auckland, New Zealand
Hodge	A. Hodge, Penzance, Cornwall
Hogarth	Hogarth Press, London
HongKongUP	Hong Kong UP, Hong Kong
Horsdal & Schubart	Horsdal & Schubart, Victoria, BC
Horwood	Ellis Horwood, Hemel Hempstead, Hertfordshire
HoughtonM	Houghton Mifflin, Boston, MA
Howard	Howard UP, Washington, DC
HREOC	Human Rights and Equal Opportunity Commission, Commonweath of Australia, Canberra
HRW	Holt, Reinhart & Winston, New York
Hudson	Hudson Hills Press, New York
Hueber	Max Hueber, Ismaning, Germany
HUL	Hutchinson University Library, London
HullUP	Hull UP, University of Hull
Humanities	Humanities Press, Atlantic Highlands, NJ
Huntington	Huntington Library, San Marino, CA
Hurst	C. Hurst, Covent Garden, London
Hutchinson	Hutchinson Books, London
HW	Harvester Wheatsheaf, Hemel Hempstead, Hertfordshire
HWWilson	H.W. Wilson, New York
Hyland House	Hyland House Publishing, Victoria
HyphenP	Hyphen Press, London
IAAS	Indian Institute of Aveanced Studies, Lahore and New Delhi
Ian Henry	Ian Henry Publications, Homchurch, Essex
IAP	Irish Academic Press, Dublin
Ibadan	Ibadan University Press
IBK	Innsbrucker Beiträge zur Kulturwissenschaft, University of Innsbruck
ICA	Institute of Contemporary Arts, London
IHA	International Hopkins Association, Waterloo, Ontario
IJamaica	Institute of Jamaica Publications, Kingston
Imago	Imago Imprint, New York
Imperial WarMuseum	Imperial War Museum Publications, London
IndUP	Indiana UP, Bloomington, IN
Inkblot	Inkblot Publications, Berkeley, CA
IntUP	International Universities Press, New York
Inventions	Inventions Press, London
IonaC	Iona College, New Rochelle, NY

IowaSUP	Iowa State UP, Ames, IA
IOWP	Isle of Wight County Press, Newport, Isle of Wight
IP	In Parenthesis, London
Ipswich	Ipswich Press, Ipswich, MA
IrishAP	Irish Academic Press, Dublin
ISI	ISI Press, Philadelphia
Italica	Italica Press, New York
IULC	Indiana University Linguistics Club, Bloomington, IN
IUP	Indiana University of Pennsylvania Press, Indiana, PA
Ivon	Ivon Publishing House, Bombay
Jacaranda	Jacaranda Wiley, Milton, Queensland
JadavpurU	Jadavpur University, Calcutta
James CookU	James Cook University of North Queensland, Townsville
Jarrow	Parish of Jarrow, Tyne and Wear
Jesperson	Jesperson Press, St John's, Newfoundland
JHall	James Hall, Leamington Spa, Warwickshire
JHUP	Johns Hopkins UP, Baltimore, MD
JIWE	JIWE Publications, University of Gulbarga, India
JLRC	Jack London Research Center, Glen Ellen, CA
J-NP	Joe-Noye Press
Jonas	Jonas Verlag, Marburg, Germany
Joseph	Michael Joseph, London
Journeyman	Journeyman Press, London
JPGM	J. Paul Getty Museum
JT	James Thin, Edinburgh
Junction	Junction Books, London
Junius-Vaughan	Junius-Vaughan Press, Fairview, NJ
Jupiter	Jupiter Press, Lake Bluff, IL
JyväskyläU	Jyväskylä University, Jyväskylä, Finland
Kaibunsha	Kaibunsha, Tokyo
K&N	Königshausen & Neumann, Würzburg, Germany
K&W	Kaye & Ward, London
Kangaroo	Kangaroo Press, Simon & Schuster (Australia), Roseville, New South Wales
Kansai	Kansai University of Foreign Studies, Osaka
Kardo	Kardo, Coatbridge, Scotland
Kardoorair	Kardoorair Press, Adelaide
Karia	Karia Press, London
Karnak	Karnak House, London
Karoma	Karoma Publishers, Ann Arbor, MI
Katha	Katha, New Delhi
KC	Kyle Cathie, London
KCL	King's College London
KeeleUP	Keele University Press
Kegan Paul	Kegan Paul International, London
Kenkyu	Kenkyu-Sha, Tokyo
Kennikat	Kennikat Press, Port Washington, NY
Kensal	Kensal Press, Oxford
KentSUP	Kent State University Press, Kent, OH
KenyaLB	Kenya Literature Bureau, Nairobi
Kerosina	Kerosina Publications, Worcester Park, Surrey
Kerr	Charles H. Kerr, Chicago
Kestrel	Viking Kestrel, London

K/H	Kendall/Hunt Publishing, Dubuque, IA
Kingsley	J. Kingsley Publishers, London
Kingston	Kingston Publishers, Kingston, Jamaica
Kinseido	Kinseido, Tokyo
KITLV	KITLV Press, Leiden
Klostermann	Vittorio Klostermann, Frankfurt am Main
Kluwer	Kluwer Academic Publications, Dordrecht
Knopf	Alfred A. Knopf, New York
Knowledge	Knowledge Industry Publications, White Plains, NY
Kraft	Kraft Books, Ibadan
Kraus	Kraus International Publications, White Plains, NY
KSUP	Kent State UP, Kent OH
LA	Library Association, London
LACUS	Linguistic Association of Canada and the United States, Chapel Hill, NC
Lake View	Lake View Press, Chicago
LAm	Library of America, New York
Lancelot	Lancelot Press, Hantsport, NS
Landesman	Jay Landesman, London
L&W	Lawrence & Wishart, London
Lane	Allen Lane, London
Lang	Peter D. Lang, Frankfurt am Main and Berne
Latimer	Latimer Trust
LehighUP	Lehigh University Press, Bethlehem, PA
LeicAE	University of Leicester, Department of Adult Education
LeicsCC	Leicestershire County Council, Libraries and Information Service, Leicester
LeicUP	Leicester UP, Leicester
LeidenUP	Leiden UP, Leiden
Leopard's Head	Leopard's Head Press, Oxford
Letao	Letao Press, Albury, New South Wales
LeuvenUP	Leuven UP, Leuven, Belgium
Lexik	Lexik House, Cold Spring, NY
Lexington	Lexington Publishers
LF	LiberFörlag, Stockholm
LH	Lund Humphries Publishers, London
Liberty	Liberty Classics, Indianapolis, IN
Libris	Libris, London
LibrU	Libraries Unlimited, Englewood, CO
Liguori	Liguori, Naples
Limelight	Limelight Editions, New York
Lime Tree	Lime Tree Press, Octopus Publishing, London
LincolnUP	Lincoln University Press, Nebraska
LINCOM	LINCOM Europa, Munich, Germany
LIT	Lit Verlag
LITIR	LITIR Database, University of Alberta
LittleH	Little Hills Press, Burwood, New South Wales
Liveright	Liveright Publishing, New York
LiverUP	Liverpool UP, Liverpool
Livre de Poche	Le Livre de Poche, Paris
Llanerch	Llanerch Enterprises, Lampeter, Dyfed
Locust Hill	Locust Hill Press, West Cornwall, CT
Loewenthal	Loewenthal Press, New York

Longman	Pearson Longman Wesley, Harlow, Essex
LongmanC	Longman Caribbean, Harlow, Essex
LongmanF	Longman, France
LongmanNZ	Longman, Auckland
Longspoon	Longspoon Press, University of Alberta, Edmonton
Lovell	David Lovell Publishing, Brunswick, Australia
Lowell	Lowell Press, Kansas City, MS
Lowry	Lowry Publishers, Johannesburg
LSUP	Louisiana State UP, Baton Rouge, LA
L3	L3: Liege Language and Literature, University of Liege, Belgium
LundU	Lund University, Lund, Sweden
LUP	Loyola UP, Chicago
Lutterworth	Lutterworth Press, Cambridge
Lymes	Lymes Press, Newcastle, Staffordshire
Lythrum	Lythrum Press, Adelaide
MAA	Medieval Academy of America, Cambridge, MA
Macleay	Macleay Press, Paddington, New South Wales
Macmillan	Macmillan Publishers, London
MacmillanC	Macmillan Caribbean
Madison	Madison Books, Lanham, MD
Madurai	Madurai University, Madurai, India
Maecenas	Maecenas Press, Iowa City, Iowa
Magabala	Magabala Books, Broome, WA
Magnes	Magnes Press, The Hebrew University, Jerusalem
Mainstream	Mainstream Publishing, Edinburgh
Maisonneuve	Maisonneuve Press, Washington, DC
Malone	Malone Society, c/o King's College, London
Mambo	Mambo Press, Gweru, Zimbabwe
ManCASS	Manchester Centre for Anglo-Saxon Studies, University of Manchester
M&E	Macdonald & Evans, Estover, Plymouth, Devon
M&S	McClelland & Stewart, Toronto
Maney	W.S. Maney & Sons, Leeds
Mango	Mango Publishing, London, United Kingdom
Manohar	Manohar Publishers, Darya Gan, New Delhi
Mansell	Mansell Publishing, London
Manufacture	La Manufacture, Lyons
ManUP	Manchester UP, Manchester
Mardaga	Mardaga
Mariner	Mariner Books, Boston, MA
MarquetteUP	Marquette UP, Milwaukee, WI
Marvell	Marvell Press, Calstock, Cornwall
MB	Mitchell Beazley, London
McDougall, Littel	McDougall, Littel, Evanston, IL
McFarland	McFarland, Jefferson, NC
McG-QUP	McGill-Queen's UP, Montreal
McGraw-Hill	McGraw-Hill, New York
McIndoe	John McIndoe, Dunedin, New Zealand
McPheeG	McPhee Gribble Publishers, Fitzroy, Victoria
McPherson	McPherson, Kingston, NY
MCSU	Maria Curie Skłodowska University
ME	M. Evans, New York

Meany	P.D. Meany Publishing, Port Credit, Ontario
Meckler	Meckler Publishing, Westport, CT
MelbourneUP	Melbourne UP, Carlton South, Victoria
Mellen	Edwin Mellen Press, Lewiston, NY
MellenR	Mellen Research UP
Menzies	Menzies Centre for Australian Studies
MercerUP	Mercer UP, Macon, GA
Mercury	Mercury Press, Stratford, Ontario
Merlin	Merlin Press, London
Methuen	Methuen, London
MethuenA	Methuen Australia, North Ryde, New South Wales
MethuenC	Methuen, Toronto
Metro	Metro Publishing, Auckland
Metzler	Metzler, Stuttgart
MGruyter	Mouton de Gruyter, Berlin, New York, and Amsterdam
MH	Michael Haag, London
MHRA	Modern Humanities Research Association, London
MHS	Missouri Historical Society, St Louis, MO
MI	Microforms International, Pergamon Press, Oxford
Micah	Micah Publications, Marblehead, MA
MichSUP	Michigan State UP, East Lansing, MI
MidNAG	Mid-Northumberland Arts Group, Ashington, Northumbria
Miegunyah	Miegunyah Press, Carlton, Victoria, Australia
Mieyungah	Mieyungah Press, Melbourne University Press, Carlton South, Victoria
Milestone	Milestone Publications, Horndean, Hampshire
Millennium	Millennium Books, E.J. Dwyer, Newtown, Australia
Millstream	Millstream Books, Bath
Milner	Milner, London
Minuit	Éditions de Minuit, Paris
MIP	Medieval Institute Publications, Western Michigan University, Kalamazoo
MITP	Massachusetts Institute of Technology Press, Cambridge, MA
MLA	Modern Language Association of America, New York
MIM	Multilingual Matters, Clevedon, Avon
MLP	Manchester Literary and Philosophical Society, Manchester
MnaN	Mkuki na Nyota Publishers, Dar es Salaam, Tanzania
Modern Library	Modern Library (Random House), New York
Monarch	Monarch Publications, Sussex
Moonraker	Moonraker Press, Bradford-on-Avon, Wiltshire
Moorland	Moorland Publishing, Ashbourne, Derby
Moreana	Moreana, Angers, France
MorganSU	Morgan State University, Baltimore, MD
Morrow	William Morrow, New York
Mosaic	Mosaic Press, Oakville, Ontario
Motilal	Motilal Books, Oxford
Motley	Motley Press, Romsey, Hampshire
Mouton	Mouton Publishers, New York and Paris
Mowbray	A.R. Mowbray, Oxford
MR	Martin Robertson, Oxford
MRS	Medieval and Renaissance Society, North Texas State University, Denton

MRTS	MRTS, Binghamton, NY
MSUP	Memphis State UP, Memphis, TN
MtAllisonU	Mount Allison University, Sackville, NB
MTP	Museum Tusculanum Press, University of Copenhagen
Mulini	Mulini Press, ACT
Muller	Frederick Muller, London
MULP	McMaster University Library Press
Murray	John Murray, London
Mursia	Ugo Mursia, Milan
NAL	New American Library, New York
Narr	Gunter Narr Verlag, Tübingen
Nathan	Fernand Nathan, Paris
NBB	New Beacon Books, London
NBCAus	National Book Council of Australia, Melbourne
NCP	New Century Press, Durham
ND	New Directions, New York
NDT	Nottingham Drama Texts, c/o University of Nottingham
NEL	New English Library, London
NELM	National English Literary Museum, Grahamstown, S. Africa
Nelson	Nelson Publishers, Melbourne
NelsonT	Thomas Nelson, London
New Endeavour	New Endeavour Press
NeWest	NeWest Press, Edmonton, Alberta
New Horn	New Horn Press, Ibadan, Nigeria
New Island	New Island Press
NewIssuesP	New Issues Press, Western Michigan University
NH	New Horizon Press, Far Hills, NJ
N-H	Nelson-Hall, Chicago
NHPC	North Holland Publishing, Amsterdam and New York
NicV	Nicolaische Verlagsbuchhandlung, Berlin
NIE	La Nuova Italia Editrice, Florence
Niemeyer	Max Niemeyer, Tübingen, Germany
Nightwood	Nightwood Editions, Toronto
NIUP	Northern Illinois UP, De Kalb, IL
NUSam	National University of Samoa
NLA	National Library of Australia
NLB	New Left Books, London
NLC	National Library of Canada, Ottawa
NLP	New London Press, Dallas, TX
NLS	National Library of Scotland, Edinburgh
NLW	National Library of Wales, Aberystwyth, Dyfed
Nodus	Nodus Publikationen, Münster
Northcote	Northcote House Publishers, Plymouth
NortheastemU	Northeastern University, Boston, MA
NorthwesternUP	Norhwestem UP, Evanston, IL
Norton	W.W. Norton, New York and London
NorUP	Norwegian University Press, Oslo
Novus	Novus Press, Oslo
NPF	National Poetry Foundation, Orono, ME
NPG	National Portrait Gallery, London
NPP	North Point Press, Berkeley, CA
NSP	New Statesman Publishing, New Delhi
NSU Press	Northern States Universities Press

NSWUP	New South Wales UP, Kensington, New South Wales
NT	National Textbook, Lincolnwood, IL
NUC	Nipissing University College, North Bay, Ontario
NUP	National University Publications, Millwood, NY
NUSam	National University of Samoa
NUU	New University of Ulster, Coleraine
NWAP	North Waterloo Academic Press, Waterloo, Ontario
NWP	New World Perspectives, Montreal
NYPL	New York Public Library, New York
NYUP	New York UP, New York
OakK	Oak Knoll Press, New Castle, DE
O&B	Oliver & Boyd, Harlow, Essex
Oasis	Oasis Books, London
OBAC	Organization of Black American Culture, Chicago
OberlinCP	Oberlin College Press, Oberlin, OH
Oberon	Oberon Books, London
O'Brien	O'Brien Press, Dublin
OBS	Oxford Bibliographical Society, Bodleian Library, Oxford
Octopus	Octopus Books, London
OdenseUP	Odense UP, Odense
OE	Officina Edizioni, Rome
OEColl	Old English Colloquium, Berkeley, CA
Offord	John Offord Publications, Eastbourne, E. Sussex
OhioUP	Ohio UP, Athens, OH
Oldcastle	Oldcastle Books, Harpenden, Hertfordshire
Olms	Georg Ohms, Hildesheim, Germany
Olschki	Leo S. Olschki, Florence
O'Mara	Michael O'Mara Books, London
Omnigraphics	Omnigraphics, Detroit, MI
Open Books	Open Books Publishing, Wells, Somerset
Open Court	Open Court Publishing, USA
OpenUP	Open UP, Buckingham and Philadelphia
OPP	Oxford Polytechnic Press, Oxford
Orbis	Orbis Books, London
OregonSUP	Oregon State UP, Corvallis, OR
Oriel	Oriel Press, Stocksfield, Northumberland
Orient Longman	Orient Longman, India
OrientUP	Oriental UP, London
OriginalNZ	Original Books, Wellington, New Zealand
ORP	Ontario Review Press, Princeton, NJ, United States
Ortnamnsarkivet	Ortnamnsarkivet i Uppsala, Sweden
Orwell	Orwell Press, Southwold, Suffolk
Oryx	Oryx Press, Phoenix, AR
OSUP	Ohio State UP, Columbus, OH
OTP	Oak Tree Press, London
OUCA	Oxford University Committee for Archaeology, Oxford
OUP	Oxford UP, Oxford
OUPAm	Oxford UP, New York
OUPAus	Oxford UP, Melbourne
OUPC	Oxford UP, Toronto
OUPI	Oxford UP, New Delhi
OUPNZ	Oxford UP, Auckland
OUPSA	Oxford UP Southern Africa, Cape Town

Outlet	Outlet Book, New York
Overlook	Overlook Press, New York
Owen	Peter Owen, London
Owl	Owl
Pace UP	Pace University Press, New York
Pacifica	Press Pacifica, Kailua, Hawaii
Paget	Paget Press, Santa Barbara, CA
PAJ	PAJ Publications, New York
Paladin	Paladin Books, London
Palgrave	Palgrave, NY
Pan	Pan Books, London
PanAmU	Pan American University, Edinburgh, TX
P&C	Pickering & Chatto, London
Pandanus	Pandanus Press, Canberra, Australia
Pandion	Pandion Press, Capitola, CA
Pandora	Pandora Press, London
Pan Macmillan	Pan Macmillan Australia, South Yarra, Victoria
Pantheon	Pantheon Books, New York
ParagonH	Paragon House Publishers, New York
Parnassus	Parnassus Imprints, Hyannis, MA
Parousia	Parousia Publications, London
Paternoster	Paternoster Press, Carlisle, Cumbria
Patten	Patten Press, Penzance
Paulist	Paulist Press, Ramsey, NJ
Paupers	Paupers' Press, Nottingham
Pavilion	Pavilion Books, London
PBFA	Provincial Booksellers' Fairs Association, Cambridge
Peachtree	Peachtree Publishers, Atlanta, GA
Pearson	David Pearson, Huntingdon, Cambridge
Peepal Tree	Peepal Tree Books, Leeds
Peeters	Peeters Publishers and Booksellers, Leuven, Belgium
Pelham	Pelham Books, London
Pembridge	Pembridge Press, London
Pemmican	Pemmican Publications, Winnipeg, Canada
PencraftI	Pencraft International, Ashok Vihar II, Delhi
Penguin	Penguin Books, Harmondsworth, Middlesex
PenguinA	Penguin Books, Ringwood, Victoria
PenguinNZ	Penguin Books, Auckland
Penkevill	Penkevill Publishing, Greenwood, FL
Pentland	Pentland Press, Ely, Cambridge
Penumbra	Penumbra Press, Moonbeam, Ontario
People's	People's Publications, London
Pergamon	Pergamon Press, Oxford
Permanent	Permanent Press, Sag Harbor, NY
Permanent Black	Permanent Black, Delhi, India
Perpetua	Perpetua Press, Oxford
Petton	Petton Books, Oxford
Pevensey	Pevensey Press, Newton Abbot, Devon
PH	Prentice-Hall, Englewood Cliffs, NJ
Phaidon	Phaidon Press, London
PHI	Prentice-Hall International, Hemel Hempstead, Hertfordshire
PhilL	Philosophical Library, New York
Phillimore	Phillimore, Chichester

Phoenix	Phoenix
Piatkus	Piatkus Books, London
Pickwick	Pickwick Publications, Allison Park, PA
Pilgrim	Pilgrim Books, Norman, OK
PIMS	Pontifical Institute of Mediaeval Studies, Toronto
Pinter	Frances Pinter Publishers, London
Plains	Plains Books, Carlisle
Plenum	Plenum Publishing, London and New York
Plexus	Plexus Publishing, London
Pliegos	Editorial Pliegos, Madrid
Ploughshares	Ploughshares Books, Watertown, MA
Pluto	Pluto Press, London
PML	Pierpont Morgan Library, New York
Polity	Polity Press, Cambridge
Polygon	Polygon, Edinburgh
Polymath	Polymath Press, Tasmania, Australia
Poolbeg	Poolbeg Press, Swords, Dublin
Porcepic	Press Porcepic, Victoria, BC
Porcupine	Porcupine's Quill, Canada
PortN	Port Nicholson Press, Wellington, NZ
Potter	Clarkson N. Potter, New York
Power	Power Publications, University of Sydney
PPUBarcelona	Promociones y Publicaciones Universitarias, Barcelona
Praeger	Praeger, New York
Prakash	Prakash Books, India
Prestel	Prestel Verlag, Germany
PrestigeB	Prestige Books, New Delhi
Primavera	Edizioni Primavera, Gunti Publishing, Florence, Italy
Primrose	Primrose Press, Alhambra, CA
PrincetonUL	Princeton University Library, Princeton, NJ
PrincetonUP	Princeton UP, Princeton, NJ
Printwell	Printwell Publishers, Jaipur, India
Prism	Prism Press, Bridport, Dorset
PRO	Public Record Office, London
Profile	Profile Books, Ascot, Berks
ProgP	Progressive Publishers, Calcutta
PSUP	Pennsylvania State UP, University Park, PA
Pucker	Puckerbrush Press, Orono, ME
PUF	Presses Universitaires de France, Paris
PUPV	Publications de l'université Paul-Valéry, Montpellier 3
PurdueUP	Purdue UP, Lafayette, IN
Pushcart	Pushcart Press, Wainscott, NY
Pustet	Friedrich Pustet, Regensburg
Putnam	Putnam Publishing, New York
PWP	Poetry Wales Press, Ogmore by Sea, mid-Glamorgan
QED	QED Press, Ann Arbor, MI
Quarry	Quarry Press, Kingston, Ontario
Quartet	Quartet Books, London
Quaternary	The Quaternary Institute
QUT	Queensland University of Technology
RA	Royal Academy of Arts, London
Rainforest	Rainforest Publishing, Faxground, New South Wales
Rampant Lions	Rampant Lions Press, Cambridge

R&B	Rosenklide & Bagger, Copenhagen
R&L	Rowman & Littlefield, Totowa, NJ
Randle	Ian Randle, Kingston, Jamaica
RandomH	Random House, London and New York
RandomHAus	Random House Australia, Victoria
RandomHNZ	Random House New Zealand Limited, Auckland, New Zealand
Ravan	Ravan Press, Johannesburg
Ravette	Ravette, London
Ravi Dayal	Ravi Dayal Publishers, New Delhi, India
Rawat	Rawat Publishing, Jaipur and New Delhi
Reaktion	Reaktion Books, London
Rebel	Rebel Press, London
Red Kite	Red Kite Press, Guelph, Ontario
Red Rooster	Red Rooster Press, Hotham Hill, Victoria
Red Sea	Red Sea Press, NJ
Reed	Reed Books, Port Melbourne
Reference	Reference Press, Toronto
Regents	Regents Press of Kansas, Lawrence, KS
Reichenberger	Roswitha Reichenberger, Kessel, Germany
Reinhardt	Max Reinhardt, London
Remak	Remak, Alblasserdam, Netherlands
RenI	Renaissance Institute, Sophia University, Tokyo
Research	Research Publications, Reading
RETS	Renaissance English Text Society, Chicago
RH	Ramsay Head Press, Edinburgh
RHS	Royal Historical Society, London
RIA	Royal Irish Academy, Dublin
RiceUP	Rice UP, Houston, TX
Richarz	Hans Richarz, St Augustin, Germany
RICL	Research Institute for Comparative Literature, University of Alberta
Rivers Oram	Rivers Oram Press, London
Rizzoli	Rizzoli International Publications, New York
RobartsCCS	Robarts Centre for Canadian Studies, York University, North York, Ontario
Robinson	Robinson Publishing, London
Robson	Robson Books, London
Rodopi	Rodopi, Amsterdam
Roebuck	Stuart Roebuck, Suffolk
RoehamptonI	Roehampton Institute London
Routledge	Routledge, London and New York
Royce	Robert Royce, London
RS	Royal Society, London
RSC	Royal Shakespeare Company, London
RSL	Royal Society of Literature, London
RSVP	Research Society for Victorian Periodicals, University of Leicester
RT	RT Publications, London
Running	Running Press, Philadelphia
Russell	Michael Russell, Norwich
RutgersUP	Rutgers UP, New Brunswick, NJ
Ryan	Ryan Publishing, London

SA	Sahitya Akademi, New Delhi
Sage	Sage Publications, London
SAI	Sociological Abstracts, San Diego, CA
Salamander	Salamander Books, London
Salem	Salem Press, Englewood Cliffs, NJ
S&A	Shukayr and Akasheh, Amman, Jordon
S&D	Stein & Day, Briarcliff Manor, NJ
S&J	Sidgwick & Jackson, London
S&M	Sun & Moon Press, Los Angeles
S&P	Simon & Piere, Toronto
S&S	Simon & Schuster, New York and London
S&W	Secker & Warburg, London
Sangam	Sangam Books, London
Sangsters	Sangsters Book Stores, Kingston, Jamaica
SAP	Scottish Academic Press, Edinburgh
Saros	Saros International Publishers
Sarup	Sarup, New Delhi
SASSC	Sydney Association for Studies in Society and Culture, University of Sydney, New South Wales
Saur	Bowker-Saur, Sevenoaks, Kent
Savacou	Savacou Publications, Kingston, Jamaica
S-B	Schwann-Bagel, Düsseldorf
ScanUP	Scandinavian University Presses, Oslo
Scarecrow	Scarecrow Press, Metuchen, NJ
Schäuble	Schäuble Verlag, Rheinfelden, Germany
Schmidt	Erich Schmidt Verlag, Berlin
Schneider	Lambert Schneider, Heidelberg
Schocken	Schocken Books, New York
Scholarly	Scholarly Press, St Clair Shores, MI
ScholarsG	Scholars Press, GA
Schöningh	Ferdinand Schöningh, Paderbom, Germany
Schwinn	Michael Schwinn, Neustadt, Germany
SCJP	Sixteenth-Century Journal Publications
Scolar	Scolar Press, Aldershot, Hampshire
SCP	Second Chance Press, Sag Harbor, NY
Scribe	Scribe Publishing, Colchester
Scribner	Charles Scribner, New York
SDSU	Department of English, South Dakota State University
Seafarer	Seafarer Books, London
Seaver	Seaver Books, New York
Segue	Segue, New York
Semiotext(e)	Semiotext(e), Columbia University, New York
SePA	Self-Publishing Association
Seren Books	Seren Books, Bridgend, mid-Glamorgan
Serpent's Tail	Serpent's Tail Publishing, London
Sessions	William Sessions, York
Seuil	Éditions du Seuil, Paris
7:84 Pubns	7:84 Publications, Glasgow
Severn	Severn House, Wallington, Surrey
SF&R	Scholars' Facsimiles and Reprints, Delmar, NY
SH	Somerset House, Teaneck, NJ
Shalabh	Shalabh Book House, Meerut, India
ShAP	Sheffield Academic Press

Shaun Tyas	Paul Watkins Publishing, Donington, Lincolnshire
Shearsman	Shearsman Books, Exeter
Shearwater	Shearwater Press, Lenah Valley, Tasmania
Sheba	Sheba Feminist Publishers, London
Sheed&Ward	Sheed & Ward, London
Sheldon	Sheldon Press, London
SHESL	Société d'Histoire et d'Épistemologie des Sciences du Langage, Paris
Shinozaki	Shinozaki Shorin, Tokyo
Shinshindo	Shinshindo Publishing, Tokyo
Shire	Shire Publications, Princes Risborough, Buckinghamshire
Shoal Bay Press	Shoal Bay Press, New Zealand
Shoe String	Shoe String Press, Hamden, CT
SHP	Shakespeare Head Press
SIAS	Scandinavian Institute of African Studies, Uppsala
SIL	Summer Institute of Linguistics, Academic Publications, Dallas, TX
SIUP	Southern Illinois University Press
Simon King	Simon King Press, Milnthorpe, Cumbria
Sinclair-Stevenson	Sinclair-Stevenson, London
SingaporeUP	Singapore UP, Singapore
SIUP	Southern Illinois UP, Carbondale, IL
SJSU	San Jose State University, San Jose, CA
Skilton	Charles Skilton, London
Skoob	Skoob Books, London
Slatkine	Éditions Slatkine, Paris
Slavica	Slavica Publishers, Columbus, OH
Sleepy Hollow	Sleepy Hollow Press, Tarrytown, NY
SLG	SLG Press, Oxford
Smith Settle	Smith Settle, W. Yorkshire
SMUP	Southern Methodist UP, Dallas, TX
Smythe	Colin Smythe, Gerrards Cross, Buckinghamshire
SNH	Société Néophilologique de Helsinki
SNLS	Society for New Language Study, Denver, CO
SOA	Society of Authors, London
Soho	Soho Book, London
SohoP	Soho Press, New York
Solaris	Solaris Press, Rochester, MI
SonoNis	Sono Nis Press, Victoria, BC
Sorbonne	Publications de la Sorbonne, Paris
SorbonneN	Publications du Conseil Scientifique de la Sorbonne Nouvelle, Paris
Souvenir	Souvenir Press, London
SPA	SPA Books
SPACLALS	South Pacific Association for Commonwealth Literature and Language Studies, Wollongong, New South Wales
Spaniel	Spaniel Books, Paddington, New South Wales
SPCK	SPCK, London
Spectrum	Spectrum Books, Ibadan, Nigeria
Split Pea	Split Pea Press, Edinburgh
Spokesman	Spokesman Books, Nottingham
Spoon River	Spoon River Poetry Press, Granite Falls, MN

SRC	Steinbeck Research Center, San Jose State University, San Jose, CA
SRI	Steinbeck Research Institute, Ball State University, Muncie, IN
SriA	Sri Aurobindo, Pondicherry, India
Sri Satguru	Sri Satguru Publications, Delhi
SSA	John Steinbeck Society of America, Muncie, IN
SSAB	Sprakförlaget Skriptor AB, Stockholm
SSNS	Scottish Society for Northern Studies, Edinburgh
StanfordUP	Stanford UP, Stanford, CA
Staple	Staple, Matlock, Derbyshire
Starmont	Starmont House, Mercer Island, WA
Starrhill	Starrhill Press, Washington, DC
Station Hill	Station Hill, Barrytown, NY
Stauffenburg	Stauffenburg Verlag, Tübingen, Germany
StDL	St Deiniol's Library, Hawarden, Clwyd
Steel Rail	Steel Rail Publishing, Ottawa
Steiner	Franz Steiner, Wiesbaden, Germany
Sterling	Sterling Publishing, New York
SterlingND	Sterling Publishers, New Delhi
Stichting	Stichtig Neerlandistiek, Amsterdam
St James	St James Press, Andover, Hampshire
St Martin's	St Martin's Press, New York
StMut	State Mutual Book and Periodical Source, New York
Stockwell	Arthur H. Stockwell, Ilfracombe, Devon
Stoddart	Stoddart Publishing, Don Mills, Ontario
StPB	St Paul's Bibliographies, Winchester, Hampshire
STR	Society for Theatre Research, London
Strauch	R.O.U. Strauch, Ludwigsburg
Streamline	Streamline Creative, Auckland, New Zealand
Stree	Stree/Bhatkal, Kolkata, India
Studio	Studio Editions, London
Stump Cross	Stump Cross Books, Stump Cross, Essex
Sud	Sud, Marseilles
Suhrkamp	Suhrkamp Verlag, Frankfurt am Main
Summa	Summa Publications, Birmingham, AL
SUNYP	State University of New York Press, Albany, NY
SUP	Sydney University Press
Surtees	R.S. Surtees Society, Frome, Somerset
SusquehannaUP	Susquehanna UP, Selinsgrove, PA
SussexAP	Sussex Academic Press
SussexUP	Sussex UP, University of Sussex, Brighton
Sutton	Alan Sutton, Stroud, Gloucester
SVP	Sister Vision Press, Toronto
S–W	Shepheard–Walwyn Publishing, London
Swallow	Swallow Press, Athens, OH
SWG	Saskatchewan Writers Guild, Regina
Sybylla	Sybylla Feminist Press
SydneyUP	Sydney UP, Sydney
SyracuseUP	Syracuse UP, Syracuse, NY
Tabb	Tabb House, Padstow, Cornwall
Taishukan	Taishukan Publishing, Tokyo

Talonbooks	Talonbooks, Vancouver
TamilU	Tamil University, Thanjavur, India
T&F	Taylor & Francis Books
T&H	Thames & Hudson, London
Tantivy	Tantivy Press, London
Tarcher	Jeremy P. Tarcher, Los Angeles
Tartarus	Tartarus Press
Tate	Tate Gallery Publications, London
Tavistock	Tavistock Publications, London
Taylor	Taylor Publishing, Bellingham, WA
TaylorCo	Taylor Publishing, Dallas, TX
TCG	Theatre Communications Group, New York
TCP	Three Continents Press, Washington, DC
TCUP	Texas Christian UP, Fort Worth, TX
TEC	Third Eye Centre, Glasgow
Tecumseh	Tecumseh Press, Ottawa
Telos	Telos Press, St Louis, MO
TempleUP	Temple UP, Philadelphia
TennS	Tennyson Society, Lincoln
TexA&MUP	Texas A&MUP, College Station, TX
Text	Text Publishing, Melbourne
TextileB	Textile Bridge Press, Clarence Center, NY
TexTULib	Friends of the University Library, Texas Tech University, Lubbock
The Smith	The Smith, New York
Thimble	Thimble Press, Stroud, Gloucester
Thoemmes	Thoemmes Press, Bristol
Thornes	Stanley Thornes, Cheltenham
Thorpe	D.W. Thorpe, Australia
Thorsons	Thorsons Publishers, London
Times	Times of Gloucester Press, Gloucester, Ontario
TMP	Thunder's Mouth Press, New York
Tombouctou	Tombouctou Books, Bolinas, CA
Totem	Totem Books, Don Mills, Ontario
Toucan	Toucan Press, St Peter Port, Guernsey
Touzot	Jean Touzot, Paris
TPF	Trianon Press Facsimiles, London
Tragara	Tragara Press, Edinburgh
Transaction	Transaction Publishers, New Brunswick, NJ
Transcendental	Transcendental Books, Hartford, CT
Transworld	Transworld, London
TrinityUP	Trinity UP, San Antonio, TX
Tsar	Tsar Publications, Canada
TTUP	Texas Technical University Press, Lubbock
Tuckwell	Tuckwell Press, East Linton
Tuduv	Tuduv, Munich
TulaneUP	Tulane UP, New Orleans, LA
TurkuU	Turku University, Turku, Finland
Turnstone	Turnstone Press, Winnipeg, Manitoba
Turtle Island	Turtle Island Foundation, Berkeley, CA
Twayne	Twayne Publishing, Boston, MA
UAB	University of Aston, Birmingham
UAdelaide	University of Adelaide, Australia

UAlaP	University of Alabama Press, Tuscaloosa
UAlbertaP	University of Alberta Press, Edmonton
UAntwerp	University of Antwerp
UArizP	University of Arizona Press, Tucson
UArkP	University of Arkansas Press, Fayetteville
UAthens	University of Athens, Greece
UBarcelona	University of Barcelona, Spain
UBCP	University of British Columbia Press, Vancouver
UBergen	University of Bergen, Norway
UBrno	J.E. Purkyne University of Brno, Czechoslovakia
UBrussels	University of Brussels
UCalgaryP	University of Calgary Press, Canada
UCalP	University of California Press, Berkeley
UCAP	University of Central Arkansas Press, Conway
UCapeT	University of Cape Town Press
UChicP	University of Chicago Press
UCDubP	University College Dublin Press
UCL	University College London Press
UCopenP	University of Copenhagen Press, Denmark
UDelP	University of Delaware Press, Newark
UDijon	University of Dijon
UDur	University of Durham, Durham, UK
UEA	University of East Anglia, Norwich
UErlangen-N	University of Erlangen-Nuremberg, Germany
UEssex	University of Essex, Colchester
UExe	University of Exeter, Devon
UFlorence	University of Florence, Italy
UFlorP	University of Florida Press
UFR	Université François Rabelais, Tours
UGal	University College, Galway
UGeoP	University of Georgia Press, Athens
UGhent	University of Ghent
UGlasP	University of Glasgow Press
UHawaiiP	University of Hawaii Press, Honolulu
UHertP	University of Hertfordshire Press
UHuelva	Universidad de Huelva Publicaciones
UIfeP	University of Ife Press, Ile-Ife, Nigeria
UIllp	University of Illinois Press, Champaign
UInnsbruck	University of Innsbruck
UIowaP	University of Iowa Press, Iowa City
UKanP	University of Kansas Press, Lawrence, KS
UKL	University of Kentucky Libraries, Lexington
ULavalP	Les Presses de l'Université Laval, Quebec
ULiège	University of Liège, Belgium
ULilleP	Presses Universitaires de Lille, France
ULondon	University of London
Ulster	University of Ulster, Coleraine
U/M	Underwood/Miller, Los Angeles
UMalta	University of Malta, Msida
UManitobaP	University of Manitoba Press, Winnipeg
UMassP	University of Massachusetts Press, Amherst
Umeå	Umeå Universitetsbibliotek, Umeå
UMichP	University of Michigan Press, Ann Arbor

UMinnP	University of Minnesota Press, Minneapolis
UMirail-ToulouseP	University of Mirail-Toulouse Press, France
UMIRes	UMI Research Press, Ann Arbor, MI
UMissP	University of Missouri Press, Columbia
UMontP	Montpellier University Press
UMP	University of Mississippi Press, Lafayette
UMysore	University of Mysore, India
UNancyP	Presses Universitaires de Nancy, France
UNCP	University of North Carolina Press, Chapel Hill, NC
Undena	Undena Publications, Malibu, CA
UNDP	University of Notre Dame Press, Notre Dame, IN
UNebP	University of Nebraska Press, Lincoln
UNevP	University of Nevada Press, Reno
UNewE	University of New England, Armidale, New South Wales
UnEWE, CALLS	University of New England, Centre for Australian Language and Literature Studies
Ungar	Frederick Ungar, New York
Unicopli	Edizioni Unicopli, Milan
Unity	Unity Press, Hull
UnityP	Unity Press Woollahra
Universa	Uilgeverij Universa, Wetteren, Belgium
UNMP	University of New Mexico Press, Albuquerque
UNorthTP	University of North Texas Press
UNott	University of Nottingham
UNSW	University of New South Wales
Unwin	Unwin Paperbacks, London
Unwin Hyman	Unwin Hyman, London
UOklaP	University of Oklahoma Press, Norman
UOslo	University of Oslo
UOtagoP	University of Otago Press, Dunedin, New Zealand
UOttawaP	University of Ottawa Press
UPA	UP of America, Lanham, MD
UParis	University of Paris
UPColorado	UP of Colorado, Niwot, CO
UPennP	University of Pennsylvania Press, Philadelphia
UPittP	University of Pittsburgh Press, Pittsburgh
UPKen	University Press of Kentucky, Lexington
UPMissip	UP of Mississippi, Jackson
UPN	Université de Paris Nord, Paris
UPNE	UP of New England, Hanover, NH
Uppsala	Uppsala University, Uppsala
UProvence	University of Provence, Aix-en-Provence
UPSouth	University Press of the South, NO
UPValéry	University Paul Valéry, Montpellier
UPVirginia	UP of Virginia, Charlottesville
UQDE	University of Queensland, Department of English
UQP	University of Queensland Press, St Lucia
URouen	University of Rouen, Mont St Aignan
URP	University of Rochester Press
USalz	Institut für Anglistik and Amerikanstik, University of Salzburg
USantiago	University of Santiago, Spain
USCP	University of South Carolina Press, Columbia

USFlorP	University of South Florida Press, Florida
USheff	University of Sheffield
Usher	La Casa Usher, Florence
USPacific	University of the South Pacific, Institute of Pacific Studies, Suva, Fiji
USQ, DHSS	University of Southern Queensland, Department of Humanities and Social Sciences
USydP	University of Sydney Press
USzeged	University of Szeged, Hungary
UtahSUP	Utah State UP, Logan
UTampereP	University of Tampere Press, Knoxville
UTas	University of Tasmania, Hobart
UTennP	University of Tennessee Press, Knoxville
UTexP	University of Texas Press, Austin
UTorP	University of Toronto Press, Toronto
UTours	Université de Tours
UVerm	University of Vermont, Burlington
UVict	University of Victoria, Victoria, BC
UWalesP	University of Wales Press, Cardiff
UWAP	University of Western Australia Press, Nedlands
UWarwick	University of Warwick, Coventry
UWashP	University of Washington Press, Seattle
UWaterlooP	University of Waterloo Press, Waterloo, Ontario
UWI	University of the West Indies, St Augustine, Trinidad
UWIndiesP	University of West Indies Press, Mona, Jamaica
UWiscM	University of Wisconsin, Milwaukee
UWiscP	University of Wisconsin Press, Madison
UWoll	University of Wollongong
UYork	University of York, York
Valentine	Valentine Publishing and Drama, Rhinebeck, NY
V&A	Victoria and Albert Museum, London
VanderbiltUP	Vanderbilt UP, Nashville, TE
V&R	Vandenhoeck & Ruprecht, Göttingen, Germany
Van Gorcum	Van Gorcum, Assen, Netherlands
Vantage	Vantage Press, New York
Variorum	Variorum, Ashgate Publishing, Hampshire
Vehicule	Vehicule Press, Montreal
Vendome	Vendome Press, New York
Verdant	Verdant Publications, Chichester
Verso	Verso Editions, London
VictUP	Victoria UP, Victoria University of Wellington, New Zealand
Vieweg	Vieweg Braunschweig, Wiesbaden
Vikas	Vikas Publishing House, New Delhi
Viking	Viking Press, New York
VikingNZ	Viking, Auckland
Virago	Virago Press, London
Vision	Vision Press, London
VLB	VLB Éditeur, Montreal
VP	Vulgar Press, Carlton North, Australia
VR	Variorum Reprints, London
Vrin	J. Vrin, Paris
VUP	Victoria University Press, Wellington, New Zealand
VUUP	Vrije Universiteit UP, Amsterdam

Wakefield	Wakefield Press
W&B	Whiting & Birch, London
W&N	Weidenfeld & Nicolson, London
Water Row	Water Row Press, Sudbury, MA
Watkins	Paul Watkins, Stanford, Lincsolnshire
WB	Wissenschaftliche Buchgesellschaft, Darmstadt
W/B	Woomer/Brotherson, Revere, PA
Weaver	Weaver Press
Webb&Bower	Webb & Bower, Exeter
Wedgestone	Wedgestone Press, Winfield, KS
Wedgetail	Wedgetail Press, Earlwood, New South Wales
WesleyanUP	Wesleyan UP, Middletown, CT
West	West Publishing, St Paul, MN
WHA	William Heinemann Australia, Port Melbourne, Victoria
Wheatsheaf	Wheatsheaf Books, Brighton
Whiteknights	Whiteknights Press, University of Reading, Berkshire
White Lion	White Lion Books, Cambridge
Whitston	Whitston Publishing, Troy, NY
Whittington	Whittington Press, Herefordshire
WHP	Warren House Press, Sale, Cheshire
Wiener	Wiener Publishing, New York
Wildwood	Wildwood House, Aldershot, Hampshire
Wiley	John Wiley, Chichester, New York and Brisbane
Wilson	Philip Wilson, London
Winter	Carl Winter Universitätsverlag, Heidelberg, Germany
Winthrop	Winthrop Publishers, Cambridge, MA
WIU	Western Illinois University, Macomb, IL
WL	Ward Lock, London
WLUP	Wilfrid Laurier UP, Waterloo, Ontario
WMP	World Microfilms Publications, London
WMU	Western Michigan University, Kalamazoo, MI
Woeli	Woeli Publishing Services
Wolfhound	Wolfhound Press, Dublin
Wombat	Wombat Press, Wolfville, NS
Wo-No	Wolters-Noordhoff, Groningen, Netherlands
Woodstock	Woodstock Books, Oxford
Woolf	Cecil Woolf, London
Words	Words, Framfield, E. Sussex
WP	Women's Press, London
WPC	Women's Press of Canada, Toronto
WSUP	Wayne State UP, Detroit, MI
WUS	Wydawnictwo Uniwersytetu Slaskiego
WVT	Wissenschaftlicher Verlag Trier
WVUP	West Virginia UP, Morgantown
W-W	Williams-Wallace, Toronto
WWU	Western Washington University, Bellingham
Xanadu	Xanadu Publications, London
XLibris	XLibris Corporation
YaleUL	Yale University Library Publications, New Haven, CT
YaleUP	Yale UP, New Haven, CO and London
Yamaguchi	Yamaguchi Shoten, Kyoto
YorkP	York Press, Fredericton, NB
Younsmere	Younsmere Press, Brighton

Zed	Zed Books, London
Zell	Hans Zell, East Grinstead, W. Sussex
Zena	Zena Publications, Penrhyndeudraeth, Gwynedd
Zephyr	Zephyr Press, Somerville, MA
Zomba	Zomba Books, London
Zwemmer	A. Zwemmer, London

3. Acronyms

AAVE	African-American Vernacular English
AmE	American English
AusE	Australian English
BrE	British English
DP	Determiner Phrase
ECP	Empty Category Principle
EFL	English as a Foreign Language
EIL	English as an International Language
ELF	English as a Lingua Franca
ELT	English Language Teaching
eModE	early Modern English
ENL	English as a Native Language
EPNS	English Place-Name Society
ESL	English as a Second Language
ESP	English for Special Purposes
HPSG	Head-driven Phrase Structure Grammar
LF	Logical Form
LFG	Lexical Functional Grammar
ME	Middle English
MED	*Middle English Dictionary*
NZE	New Zealand English
ODan	Old Danish
OE	Old English
OED	*Oxford English Dictionary*
OF	Old French
ON	Old Norse
OT	Optimality Theory
PDE	Present-Day English
PF	Phonological Form
PP	Prepositional Phrase
SABE	South African Black English
SAE	South African English
SingE	Singapore English
TESOL	Teaching English to Speakers of other Languages
TMA	Tense, Mood and Aspect
UG	Universal Grammar

Preface

The Year's Work in English Studies is a narrative bibliography that records and evaluates scholarly writing on English language and on literatures written in English. It is published by Oxford University Press on behalf of the English Association.

The Editors and the English Association are pleased to announce that this year's Beatrice White Prize has been awarded to Pamela M. King for *The York Mystery Cycle and the Worship of the City* (D.S. Brewer; ISBN 1 8438 4098 7).

The authors of *YWES* attempt to cover all significant contributions to English studies. Writers of articles can assist this process by sending offprints to the journal, and editors of journals that are not readily available in the UK are urged to join the many who send us complete sets of current and back issues. These materials should be addressed to The Editors, *YWES*, The English Association, The University of Leicester, University Road, Leicester LEI 7RH, UK.

Our coverage of articles and books is greatly assisted by the Modern Language Association of America, who annually supply proofs of their *International Bibliography* in advance of the publication of each year's coverage.

The views expressed in *YWES* are those of its individual contributors and are not necessarily shared by the Editors, Associate Editors, the English Association, or Oxford University Press.

We would like to acknowledge a special debt of gratitude to Joy Davies and Eva Gooding for their efforts on behalf of this volume. We are especially grateful to Amy Mallory-Kani for her superlative work on behalf of this issue. We also with to thank Jacki Mowery and Judy Paul at Penn State Altoona and Jayne Crosby at Northern Illinois University for their kindness, professionalism, and unwavering support.

The Editors

I

English Language

VERENA HASER, ANITA AUER, JEROEN VAN DE WEIJER,
MARION ELENBAAS, WIM VAN DER WURFF, BEÁTA
GYURIS, JULIE COLEMAN, EDWARD CALLARY,
LIESELOTTE ANDERWALD, ANDREA SAND, CAMILLA
VASQUEZ AND DAN MCINTYRE

This chapter has twelve sections: 1. General; 2. History of English Linguistics; 3. Phonetics and Phonology; 4. Morphology; 5. Syntax; 6. Semantics; 7. Lexicography, Lexicology and Lexical Semantics; 8. Onomastics; 9. Dialectology and Sociolinguistics; 10. New Englishes and Creolistics; 11. Pragmatics and Discourse Analysis; 12. Stylistics. Section 1 is by Verena Haser; section 2 is by Anita Auer; section 3 is by Jeroen van de Weijer; sections 4 and 5 are by Marion Elenbaas and Wim van der Wurff; section 6 is by Beáta Gyuris; section 7 is by Julie Coleman; section 8 is by Edward Callary; section 9 is by Lieselotte Anderwald; section 10 is by Andrea Sand; section 11 is by Camilla Vasquez; section 12 is by Dan McIntyre.

1. General

Several books on linguistic evolution have been published in 2007. *The Genesis of Grammar: A Reconstruction* by Bernd Heine and Tania Kuteva is perhaps most fascinating for the authors' well-argued hypotheses concerning the shape of early hominid grammar. Yet the book offers much more than informed speculations on the organization of early linguistic systems. Heine and Kuteva's work is a lucid and extremely well-structured account of language evolution addressing a very wide range of topics. Though not designed as such, it would also make an excellent textbook. The authors' overarching goal is to solve some long-standing puzzles concerning linguistic evolution, utilizing insights from grammaticalization theory as their methodological tool. The book is divided into five parts. The introductory chapter gives an overview of previous studies in the field and introduces central research questions. Chapter 2 aims at reconstructing the emergence of functional categories, taking as its foil key findings on common paths of grammaticalization. Chapters 3 and 4 explore animal cognition and pidgins in the context of language evolution, while the following two chapters offer a sketch of the paths which may have led to the emergence of morphosyntax and recursivitiy. Finally, the concluding sections answer a number of questions raised in the first part of the book, often going beyond the confines of the grammaticalization research that has dominated the exposition in earlier chapters. Issues tackled in these sections include the evolutionary sequence in which syntax and lexicon emerged, the function of early language (cognition vs. communication), and the question whether language evolved gradually or in an abrupt switch.

In another book devoted to linguistic evolution, David Armstrong and Sherman Wilcox make a case for *The Gestural Origin of Language*. In recent years, several theorists have been occupied with a possible historical trajectory from gesture to language. What most distinguishes the present authors' work from that of their predecessors is its firm grounding in cognitive linguistic ideas. Armstrong and Wilcox cite compelling evidence from, *inter alia*, research on sign languages in support of their conjectures. Their model presents language as emerging from visual gestures via processes of ritualization. Given that understanding gestures amounts to understanding iconic signs, it is the ability to use and understand icons—rather than symbols in the generativist sense—which the authors identify as the pivotal feature of human language. As demonstrated by Armstrong and Wilcox, the study of sign languages holds out considerable promise for models of language evolution that attempt to trace language to gestures. The question to what extent the non-conventional sign languages used by some deaf children ('homesigns') offer insights into the genesis of language is further explored in a paper by Rudolf Botha, 'On Homesign Systems as a Potential Window on Language Evolution' (*L&C* 27:i[2007] 41–53). Like Armstrong and Wilcox's work on *The Gestural Origin of Language*, this paper is likely to provide new impetus for research on the study of sign language in the context of evolutionary linguistics.

Jean-Louis Dessalles's *Why we Talk: The Evolutionary Origins of Language* addresses a wide range of pertinent topics. Of particular interest is the author's account of why language evolved in the first place. His principal hypothesis is that language is the result of an accidental change in the social organization of early hominids. In order to survive, our ancestors were forced to find a comparatively large group of allies. Language emerged as a means of 'showing off' one's value to the group by demonstrating one's ability to notice relevant phenomena in the environment. This line of argument has some intriguing implications which are bound to arouse controversy: if it weren't for a rather fortuitous development in hominid societies, language might not have developed at all, or it might have developed in a completely different way. Dessalles's hypotheses concerning the 'political' origins of language form the concluding chapter of a book which is full of illuminating, even if sometimes debatable, observations on the nature of language. The first part of the book ('The Place of Language in Human Evolutionary History') features an insightful comparison of human and animal language and elaborates on the familiar conception of language as a 'code'. As will be seen below, this idea has been challenged by some proponents of the embodied cognition hypothesis.

The second part covers issues relating to 'The Functional Anatomy of Speech', including the question that takes centre stage in Armstrong and Wilcox's book: did language evolve from manual gestures? Dessalles's answer, incidentally, is negative. The third part ('The Ethology of Language') reflects on two modes of communication, the informative and the argumentative. The author relates the informative mode to the 'language' used by our hominid forebears, and the argumentative mode to the type of languages used today, sketching likely reasons for the emergence of these two modes. The final section draws together several strands of argument encountered in the preceding pages, reconstructing the genesis of language as a three-stage process.

The above-mentioned books on linguistic evolution, notably Armstrong and Wilcox's *Gestural Origin of Language*, sound a recurrent theme in several publications that have appeared in 2007: the rejection of the idea of language as a symbol-manipulating system along the lines of classical cognitive science. Indeed, advances in connectionist modelling and the concurrent decline of symbol-processing artificial intelligence have heralded a sea-change in the way many scientists now view human thought. Cognition is situated (embodied), or so the proponents of the 'new' paradigm argue; the notorious brains in vats are incapable of thinking, disconnected as they are from an environment. Brain processes do not operate on physical symbols in the way suggested by the mind-as-computer metaphor. Following the 'distributed cognition' view, cognition and language should be construed in terms of reciprocal relations between brain, bodies, and reality—rather than in terms of localized phenomena (i.e. information-processing performed by individual cognitive systems). As outlined by Stephen Cowley in his editorial introduction (*LangS* 29:v[2007] 575–83), the contributions to a special issue of *Language Sciences* put flesh on these ideas and map out their implications for the nature of language and thought. Thus, in 'Good Prospects: Ecological and Social Perspectives on Conforming, Creating, and Caring in Conversation' (*LangS* 29[2007] 584–604), Bert Hodges observes that the essence of language acquisition cannot be captured either in terms of 'rule-governed creativity' or of 'social conformity'. The author associates these two positions with the work of scholars such as Noam Chomsky and Michael Tomasello respectively, urging us to adopt an alternative view according to which language is a 'values-realizing activity'. His article draws on ecological accounts of mind and language as well as influential studies investigating the impact of majority opinions on human decision-making. Per Linell in 'Dialogicality in Languages, Minds and Brains: Is There a Convergence between Dialogism and Neuro-Biology?' (*LangS* 29[2007] 605–20) espouses an approach to cognition that casts doubt on the notion of mind as essentially a means of representing the outer world. According to Linell, the foremost function of the human mind is to enable individuals to interact with the world and with other individuals. The framework of dialogism investigates this type of physical and social embodiment (situatedness). Linnell's article sketches the ways in which dialogism and modern neuroscience have arrived at similar insights into language and cognition. Richard Menary reflects on 'Writing as Thinking' (*LangS* 29[2007] 621–32), exploring the impact of writing on human cognitive capacities. Angelo Cangelosi, 'Adaptive Agent Modeling of Distributed Language: Investigations on the Effects of Cultural Variation and Internal Action Representations' (*LangS* 29[2007] 633–49), puts forward a computational model of language which aims at integrating internal and external factors in language development. Alexander Kravchenko's contribution reflects on 'Essential Properties of Language, or, Why Language Is Not a Code' (*LangS* 29[2007] 650–71). The author advocates a 'bio-cognitive' framework, which he argues is better suited than traditional paradigms to reveal the true nature of language 'as a biologically based, cognitively motivated, circularly organized semiotic activity in a consensual domain of interactions aimed at adapting to . . . the environment' (p. 650). As already indicated in the title, Kravchenko jettisons the idea of language as a code, offering cogent observations on the notions of representation, sign, interpretation and related concepts central to human cognition. Like Kravchenko, Philip Carr reconsiders long-standing views of language as a digital code. His paper on 'Internalism, Externalism and Coding' (*LangS* 29[2007] 672–89) attempts to undermine the idea that languages constitute codes in the first place. In a similar vein, the question raised in the title of Nigel Love's contribution, 'Are Languages Digital Codes?' (*LangS* 29[2007] 690–709), receives a negative answer from the author, who argues (on different grounds than Kravchenko) that languages should not be conceived of as codes. Finally, Don Ross in '*H. Sapiens* as Ecologically Special: What Does Language Contribute?' (*LangS* 29[2007] 710–31) identifies the high degree of sociality—behavioural co-ordination—as the distinguishing feature of human beings. The author hypothesizes that it is language which crucially facilitates co-ordination of behaviour among members of the human species.

Proceeding from a broadly 'bio-cognitive' approach to language and thought, many contributions to this special issue of *Language Sciences* challenge tenets that form the bedrock of the Chomskyan programme. Generative linguists in turn have launched a new journal, *Biolinguistics*, in 2007, which champions a radically different perspective on the biological foundations of language. The first editorial by Cedric Boeckx and Kleanthes Grohmann (*BioL* 1[2007] 1–8) sketches 'The Biolinguistics Manifesto'. Issues that will take centre stage in the journal include such key concerns of generative linguistics as the nature and acquisition of language, its evolution and especially its biological underpinnings. This first issue contains four articles, including a paper by Noam Chomsky himself, 'Of Minds and Language' (*BioL* 1[2007] 9–27), who glances back at the development of the biolinguistic enterprise. Frédéric Mailhot and Charles Reiss are concerned with 'Computing Long-Distance Dependencies in Vowel Harmony' (*BioL* 1[2007] 28–48), setting forth a procedural, as opposed to constraint-based, model of vowel harmony. Rosalind Thornton and Graciela Tesan shed light on language acquisition from a generativist perspective, reflecting on 'Categorical Acquisition: Parameter Setting in Universal Grammar' (*BioL* 1[2007] 49–98). The authors specifically assess the relative merits of different models of parameter-setting on the basis of their own longitudinal study of linguistic development in four children. Finally, Juan Uriagereka aims at 'Clarifying the Notion "Parameter"' (*BioL* 1[2007] 99–113), introducing a distinction between three different types of variation which are of fundamental importance to the language faculty. The final section of the paper reconsiders the relation between the minimalist programme and optimality theory.

Cognitive linguistics is one of the most popular approaches to have emerged in recent decades. *The Oxford Handbook of Cognitive Linguistics*, edited by Dirk Geeraerts and Hubert Cuyckens, is a treasure trove of information on all aspects of the cognitivist framework. The contributors to the volume include two of the founding fathers of the cognitivist framework (Leonard Talmy, Ronald Langacker), and many other scholars who are closely associated with cognitive linguistics or related approaches, such as the editors themselves, as well as Joan Bybee, William Croft, René Dirven, Gilles Fauconnier, Raymond Gibbs, Joseph Grady, Richard Hudson, Klaus-Uwe Panther, Linda Thornburg, John Taylor, Mark Turner, Chris Sinha, Michael Tomasello and Jordan Zlatev, to name but a few.

The book contains forty-nine papers, including a succinct introduction by the editors that maps out crucial ideas associated with the cognitivist enterprise and sketches future developments in the field. The book is organized into six parts. Part I ('Basic Concepts') features sixteen papers which explore key concepts such as, *inter alia*, embodiment, construal, entrenchment, metaphor, image schemata and spatial semantics. The second part ('Models of Grammar') contains three contributions from major proponents of cognitive approaches to grammar: Ronald Langacker (cognitive grammar), William Croft (construction grammar), and Richard Hudson (word grammar). Part III aims at 'Situating Cognitive Linguistics', containing pertinent articles on the relation between cognitive and functional linguistics (Jan Nuyts), and between cognitive linguistics and autonomous linguistics (John Taylor) respectively. A paper by Brigitte Nerlich and David Clarke situates the cognitivist enterprise within a broader historical perspective.

While parts I to III offer more general accounts of key issues and concepts in cognitive linguistics, the final three parts contain papers that flesh out the theoretical model. Part IV ('Linguistic Structure and Language Use') contains thirteen intriguing case studies, too numerous to list in detail, which deal with various aspects of linguistic structure, from phonology to discourse structure. 'Linguistic Variation and Change' is the overarching theme of part V, which contains papers on diachronic linguistics (Joan Bybee), lexical change (Stefan Grondelaers, Dirk Speelman and Dirk Geeraerts), linguistic relativity (Eric Pederson), and signed languages (Sherman Wilcox). The contribution by Johan van der Auwera and Jan Nuyts considers the relation between the cognitive approach and typology, while Gary Palmer is concerned with the relation between cognitive linguistics and anthropological linguistics. Part V also contains a paper on language acquisition from a cognitive linguistic perspective (Michael Tomasello). The final part opens up 'Applied and Interdisciplinary Perspectives' and consists of seven important contributions on topics such as 'Cognitive Linguistics and Cultural Studies' (René Dirven, Hans-Georg Wolf and Frank Polzenhagen), 'Cognitive Poetics' (Margaret Freeman) and 'Cognitive Linguistics, Psychology, and Cognitive Science' (Chris Sinha).

Vyvyan Evans's relatively slim *Glossary of Cognitive Linguistics* is an excellent companion to the hefty volume edited by Geeraerts and Cuyckens. Evans's much-needed work provides accessible and succinct definitions of key terms used in cognitive semantics and cognitive accounts of grammar. The glossary is complemented by helpful suggestions for further reading. The book is highly recommendable, especially in conjunction with the textbook by Vyvyan Evans and Melanie Green, *Cognitive Linguistics: An Introduction* [2006], since the entries selected for the glossary are for the most part terms that feature in the textbook.

Criticism of work in the otherwise rather disparate disciplines of generative grammar and cognitive linguistics is often based on a common complaint—a perceived lack of empirical support for theories which ostensibly rely on 'mere' intuition. Two books published this year are among the publications which go some way towards rectifying this problem. The first is *Methods in Cognitive Linguistics*, edited by Monica Gonzalez-Marquez, Irene Mittelberg, Seana Coulson and Michael Spivey, which surveys various empirical methods that can profitably be employed in cognitive linguistic research. The book has four parts. The first part focuses on fundamental methodological questions, including the most basic one raised by Raymond Gibbs: 'Why Cognitive Linguists Should Care More about Empirical Methods'. The second part discusses and illustrates the use of corpora in cognitive linguistic research, while part III is concerned with 'Sign Language and Gesture'. The final two chapters review psycholinguistic and neurolinguistic methods respectively. The papers are written by experts in the field such as Dirk Geeraerts, Raymond Gibbs, Rachel Giora and Eve Sweetser.

The second book takes a different approach. Attempts at adjudicating between different generative models of grammar occasionally draw on data from child language acquisition. William Snyder's *Child Language: The Parametric Approach* investigates child language with a view to its relevance for grammatical theory. The framework adopted is emphatically formalist in nature. This is reflected in the absence of any discussion of functionalist approaches to language acquisition along the lines of Michael Tomasello's *Constructing a Language: A Usage-Based Theory of Language Acquisition* [2003]. Similarly, functionalist accounts of cross-linguistic variation—another prominent topic in the book—do not play a role in Snyder's argument. The term 'contemporary syntactic theory' seems to be construed as a synonym for 'formalist syntactic theory'. Thus the chapter which 'surveys the ideas on cross-linguistic variation that are prominent in contemporary syntactic theory' (p. 4) does not contain references to functionalist approaches to syntax, notably William Croft's *Radical Construction Grammar: Syntactic Theory in Typological Perspective* [2001]. The latter book would have deserved mention in this context on various grounds. For one thing, Croft's book presents a substantial contribution to syntactic theory from a distinctly cross-linguistic perspective. For another, Croft's approach has been a source of inspiration for (functionalist) models of language acquisition. At least the existence of these functionalist models might have been acknowledged in a work such as Snyder's, the more so since it is targeted at a wider readership. Despite these provisos, Snyder's book is an invaluable companion for scholars concerned with the parametric approach to child language. The term 'parametric' in this context covers 'any kind of abstract grammatical knowledge, regardless of how it is implemented' (p. 1), including not only parameters in the narrow sense, but also concepts such as constraint rankings. The first two chapters afford brief and, even for relative novices, highly readable entries into 'contemporary syntactic theory' (principles-and-parameters framework; minimalist program) and phonological theory (from the perspective of optimality theory and government phonology), with particular emphasis on the acquisitional predictions that can be derived from the respective accounts. The chapters that follow contain a wealth of practical suggestions for scholars intending to conduct research on child language, including sections on diary studies and on how to run computerized searches with the help of the CHILDES corpus. Chapters 5 ('Statistical Methods for Longitudinal Studies') and 6 ('Experimental and Statistical Methods for Cross-Sectional Studies') deal with statistical and experimental methods. Chapter 7 presents a number of studies which illustrate the methods discussed in the previous parts of the book. A major finding of this line of research is that child language contains surprisingly few syntactic mistakes of commission. As discussed in chapter 8, the insight that child language is grammatically conservative is likely to have considerable impact on formalist views of explanatory adequacy and the language faculty in general.

The Oxford Handbook of Linguistic Interfaces, edited by Gillian Ramchand and Charles Reiss, is a collection of articles designed to address what generativists view as the 'crucial issue facing generative linguistics—the internal structure of the language faculty' (p. 2). The volume explores linguistic interfaces in the sense of boundaries and relations between the various hypothesized domains or 'modules' of grammar. The book is divided into four parts. Part I ('Sound') contains five contributions. The first two chapters by James Scobbie and Charles Reiss offer interestingly divergent accounts of the phonetics–phonology interface. The former throws doubt on the notion of a strict demarcation between phonetics and phonology, while the latter supports a very clear-cut distinction between the two. Mark Hale and Madelyn Kissock's article is also concerned with the phonetics–phonology interface, shedding light on problems faced by most accounts of language acquisition in OT. The final two papers in this section deal with the morphology–phonology and phonology–syntax interfaces. C. Orhan Orgun and Andrew Dolbey's paper expounds the morphology–phonology interface from the perspective of Sign-Based Morphology and OT, solving some knotty issues regarding the phonology–morphology interface in Turkic and Bantu languages. Gorka Elordieta reviews different models of the phonology–syntax interface that have been proposed in the past two decades, and discusses data from Basque which challenge these models.

The second part of the book offers fresh perspectives on the syntactic module and its interfaces: are the syntactic and morphological modules guided by the same rules or should we assume a strict separation of syntax and morphology? Is it necessary to posit the lexicon as a separate module (involving distinct primitives and rules)? As in the previous sections, the chapters complement each other very well, some of them offering relatively subtle differences in perspective (for example Peter Ackema and Ad Neeleman vs. Edwin Williams, where both papers support a distinction between the morphological and syntactic modules), others presenting sharply contrasting views (for example Thomas Stewart and Gregory Stump vs. Marit Julien, the former two authors positing a word-based interface that mediates between morphology and syntax, the latter viewing words as epiphenomena of other processes). Apart from the previously mentioned authors, the second section also contains contributions by Sara Thomas Rosen, Peter Svenonius, David Embick and Rolf Noyer. Rosen's paper reconsiders phenomena which have formerly been assigned to the semantic module. Specifically, she focuses on argument licensing and argument placement, suggesting that these processes are syntactic in nature, and elaborates on cross-linguistic differences with regard to the functional projections employed in argument licensing. Svenonius examines the link between 'dominant' (in the sense of Joseph Greenberg) word-order patterns and basic morphological patterns. According to Svenonius, the word-order patterns observed across languages can be accounted for in terms of movement. Finally, Embick and Noyer elaborate on the Distributed Morphology model of the interface between morphology and syntax, which denies the existence of a separate lexical module.

Part III ('Meaning') features four papers, which *inter alia* address the interfaces between syntax and semantics/pragmatics and between semantics and pragmatics. James Higginbotham's contribution is concerned with compositionality. Daniel Büring expounds the interfaces between information structure (which he views as part of syntactic representation) and meaning, as well as between information structure and prosody. Christopher Potts's paper amounts to little short of a 'resuscitation' of conventional implicatures, which have long been considered of marginal interest to linguistic pragmatics. His account casts new light on the syntax–semantics and semantics–pragmatics interfaces. The focus of David Beaver and Henk Zeevat's account is on the semantics–pragmatics interface, more specifically on semantic/pragmatic accommodation, the process of recovering missing presuppositions in order to make sense of an utterance.

The final part ('Architecture') provides a more global perspective, discussing in general terms various models of grammar in generativist and related research. Cedric Boeckx and Juan Uriagereka survey the development of generativist linguistics from the early days to the present, making a case for the supremacy of the minimalist program over previous models. Mark Steedman sketches a non-derivational model of grammar, viz. Combinatory Categorial Grammar, which he argues compares favourably with the minimalist model. He suggests that integrating a number of features of Categorial Grammar, notably the rejection of traditional surface constituents, will lead to highly desirable modifications of the minimalist architecture. Finally, Jonas Kuhn takes a look at the concept of interfaces (construed in a broad sense) in constraint-based theories of grammar, focusing on Lexical-Functional Grammar and Head-Driven Phrase Structure Grammar.

Modularity in the sense of separation between linguistic and other cognitive processes is also the principal issue addressed in *Automaticity and Control in Language Processing*, edited by Antje Meyer, Linda Wheeldon and Andrea

Krott. Three questions take centre stage in many papers. Is the modularity thesis in line with recent findings from psycho- and neurolinguistic studies? Was Jerry Fodor correct in assuming that the central linguistic processes work in separation from other cognitive processes? Are central linguistic processes really for the most part automatic? The book comprises eleven contributions which invariably present cutting-edge research in language processing. All contributors are leading scholars in the fields of psycho- or neurolinguistics, including Simon Garrod and Martin Pickering ('Automaticity of Language Production in Monologue and Dialogue'), Victor Ferreira ('How Are Speakers' Linguistic Choices Affected by Ambiguity?'), and Peter Hagoort ('The Memory, Unification, and Control (MUC) Model of Language').

Hard on the heels of Matthew Traxler and Morton Ann Gernsbacher's voluminous *Handbook of Psycholinguistics*, published in its second edition in 2006, comes the first edition of a similar and hardly less comprehensive reference work for psycholinguists: *The Oxford Handbook of Psycholinguistics*, edited by Gareth Gaskell. The two books complement each other very well, inevitable overlaps in issues notwithstanding. Even in the case of syntactic parsing, a topic which in both volumes is presented by the same authors (Roger van Gompel and Martin Pickering), each individual paper is not rendered superfluous by the existence of the other. The new *Oxford Handbook* consists of six sections, all of which present state-of-the art overviews of the respective topics: 'Word Recognition' (section I), 'The Mental Lexicon' (section II), 'Comprehension and Discourse' (section III), 'Language Production' (section IV), 'Language Development' (section V) and 'Wider Perspectives' (section VI). The authors of the forty-nine contributions are leading scholars in the field: James McQueen, William Marslen-Wilson, Roger van Gompel, Martin Pickering and Michael Tanenhaus, to name but a few. Despite their relative brevity, all the papers offer a wealth of information on key areas of debate, which will be most welcome to researchers in the field but possibly at times overpowering to novices.

Readers searching for a more elementary introduction to psycho- and neurolinguistics need look no further than John Ingram's *Neurolinguistics: An Introduction to Spoken Language Processing and its Disorders*. This textbook is a stand-alone introduction to research on the relation between language and the brain, focusing on language comprehension and linguistic impairments. The first part outlines fundamental concepts, including Chomskyan and Fodorian modularity, and provides a sketch of the neuro-anatomy of speech. Part II surveys crucial findings on speech perception and impairments of auditory processing. The third part is devoted to semantics and morphology, including the mental lexicon and word structure (chapter 9), semantic networks (chapter 10), and lexical semantic disorders (chapter 11). The final sections deal with sentence comprehension and discourse respectively. Ingram presents the central areas of debate with great clarity. The only niggling point is that very occasionally a more extensive discussion might have been desirable. Cases in point are Ingram's outline of Edward Gibson's theory of syntactic complexity—which the author concedes is somewhat simplified—and the sections on Herbert Paul Grice and Relevance Theory. Overall, however, the book is essential reading for students of neuro- and psycholinguistics.

Advances in neurophysiological techniques have yielded insights into the dynamics of language processing that are beyond the reach of purely behavioural methods. In testing factors such as reaction time, behavioural techniques tend to measure the product of the various processes involved in speaking, listening, or writing, rather than the processes themselves. By contrast, methods for recording electrical activity in the brain while subjects are presented with certain stimuli (event-related potentials or ERPs) afford a window into the very processes at work in language comprehension. Readers who wish to familiarize themselves with this area of cognitive science (and especially with studies implementing ERPs) may turn to the collection of articles in *Brain Research in Language*, edited by Zvia Breznitz. The title is slightly misleading since, according to the introduction, the volume is devoted specifically to cognitive processes involved in reading. Even so, some chapters are of more general interest. For example, a paper by Marta Kutas and Katherina Delong describes various types of research implementing ERPs and illustrates the relevance of this technique to the study of language in general. Specialists on metaphorical language will turn to the contribution by Abraham Goldstein, Yossi Arzouan and Miriam Faust, whose research lends support to the idea that the comprehension of literal and metaphorical language is based on the same mechanisms.

Much of the literature on linguistic philosophy is notoriously elusive. Alexander Miller's *Philosophy of Language* enables readers to get a grip on the agendas of major thinkers in the field. The second edition, published in 2007, features a number of improvements on the original text. Most importantly, the author presents more up-to-date coverage of the controversy inspired by Saul Kripke's take on the later Wittgenstein. Throughout the book Miller's exposition combines accessibility with depth of analysis. Another asset of the book lies in its remarkable breadth of coverage, which extends beyond the founding fathers of modern linguistic philosophy (Frege, Wittgenstein, Bertrand Russell, Willard van Orman Quine) to discussions of more recent work by Simon Blackburn, Crispin Wright, Colin McGinn and others, whose arguments cast new light on the classical texts. The book has nine chapters devoted to the most important topics in linguistic philosophy: sense, reference, and definitive descriptions (chapters 1 and 2), logical positivism (chapter 3), scepticism about sense (chapters 4 and 5), proposals for 'saving' the notion of sense (chapter 6), Herbert Paul Grice's and John Searle's account of meaning (chapter 7), and Donald Davidson's approach to meaning and truth-conditions (chapter 8). In the concluding chapter the author takes a broader look at the relation between language and reality, elucidating the controversy between realism and anti-realism (Michael Dummett, Crispin Wright) and Putnam's externalism.

We will conclude our review with a couple of books that are geared specifically to the needs of interested laypersons and newcomers to the field of linguistics. Two general linguistic reference works have been published in a second edition in 2007. The first is Peter Matthews's *Concise Oxford Dictionary of Linguistics*, which has been updated especially with regard to sociolinguistic terminology. For reasons specified in the introduction, the dictionary does not cover all fields that are commonly held to be part of linguistics. For example, no entries are provided for applied and computational linguistics. Despite a number of inevitable omissions, the dictionary features no fewer than 3,000 entries that are generally in line with the book's title in being concise and very well written.

Larry Trask's popular *Language and Linguistics: The Key Concepts*, edited by Peter Stockwell, contains far fewer entries (approximately 300) than the *Oxford Dictionary*, offering in compensation more extensive coverage of basic concepts. The entries relate to the core linguistic disciplines (phonetics, phonology, syntax, semantics) as well as to sociolinguistics, discourse analysis, psycholinguistics and cognitive linguistics. As is pointed out by Stockwell, the second edition has been considerably expanded. Particularly helpful are suggestions for further reading, though in a few cases a greater number of works, or more recent publications, might have been added.

Ingo Plag, Marie Braun, Sabine Lappe and Mareile Schramm offer a comparatively brief *Introduction to English Linguistics*, which familiarizes students with the core areas of research—phonetics, phonology, morphology, syntax, semantics and pragmatics. The book also provides very short introductions to work in historical linguistics, sociolinguistics and psycholinguistics. Full of pertinent examples and lucidly written, the chapters offer stimulating reading for the linguistic novice. Due to limitations of space the authors use Standard BrE and RP as their points of reference. Differences between varieties of English are not covered in detail. A number of exercises (both basic and advanced) allow students to put their newly acquired knowledge to the test. Along with a number of other introductions that have appeared in recent years, such as Bernd Kortmann's *English Linguistics—Essentials* [2005] and Ralph Fasold and Jeffrey Connor-Linton's *An Introduction to Language and Linguistics* [2006], this book can be strongly recommended to all undergraduate students.

Another introduction to crucial linguistic concepts comes in the guise of Keith Denning, Brett Kessler, and William Leben's second edition of *English Vocabulary Elements*, which straddles the areas of applied and theoretical linguistics. The aims of the book are twofold: first and foremost, it is designed to 'expand vocabulary skills by teaching the basic units of learned, specialized and scientific English vocabulary' (p. v). In doing so it also provides a succinct introduction to phonetics, morphology, semantic change, the history of English and other Indo-European languages, and to some extent even sociolinguistics.

The Stuff of Thought: Language as a Window into Human Nature by Steven Pinker is a 'popular science' publication similar in style to the author's previous works addressed to a wider audience. The common thread that runs through all the chapters is the idea that language—the meaning and use of words and constructions—reveals crucial insights about the workings of the human mind, specifically about the categories constituting a hypothesized language of thought. Pinker broaches a wide range of issues which are at the heart of current linguistic theory: construction grammar (argument structure alternations), the language of thought-debate, radical pragmatics, conceptual metaphor, linguistic determinism, and non-literal language. The author displays an uncanny facility for explaining complex issues in a few paragraphs—the sections dealing with the theory of names as rigid designators are an object lesson in this respect. Nevertheless, some background in (psycho)linguistics or philosophy of language will enhance one's enjoyment of the book, and might at the same time arouse critical objections in cases where one might have expected a more extensive or balanced coverage. For example, in his discussion of spatial semantics, Pinker asserts that 'when the mind conceptualizes an entity in a location or in motion, it tends to ignore the internal geometry of the object and treat it as a dimensionless point or featureless blob' (p. 48). Examples from English are designed to illustrate Pinker's point (which can ultimately be traced to the work of Leonard Talmy). However, some languages do focus on the internal geometry of the figure to be localized: see Stephen Levinson's 'Relativity in Spatial Conception and Description' (in John Gumperz and Stephen Levinson, eds., *Rethinking Linguistic Relativity* [1996]). As a result, Pinker's extrapolation of facts about the human mind from linguistic data may be somewhat rash in this case. In general, however, the book makes for highly stimulating and occasionally provocative reading.

2. History of English Linguistics

The year 2007 saw the publication of the proceedings of the second Late Modern English conference (Pérez-Guerra, González-Alvarez, Bueno-Alonso and Rama-Martínez, eds., *'Of Varying Language and Opposing Creed': New Insights into Late Modern English*), which took place at the University of Vigo in 2004. A couple of papers contained in this volume contribute to our understanding of the history of English linguistics. For instance, Joan C. Beal's '"To Explain the Present": Nineteenth-Century Evidence for "Recent" Changes in English Pronunciation' sheds light on selected consonantal variants associated with 'Estuary English', namely happY-tensing, th-fronting, glottalization, and labiodental /r/, whose diffusion has been argued to have taken place in recent years. Based on a range of sources from the eighteenth and nineteenth centuries such as pronouncing dictionaries and usage manuals, as well as literary representations of dialects, the author shows convincingly that, for instance, the variant happY-tensing was recorded in Newcastle as found in Thomas Spence's *Grand Repository of the English Language* [1775] and has therefore already been part of polite Newcastle speech in the eighteenth century. If the diffusion had started out in the south, this particular variant had certainly reached the north of England a lot earlier than has hitherto been assumed. In her conclusion, Beal states that conclusions drawn from apparent-time evidence 'might become monolithic and model-driven' and should therefore be anchored 'in real time that can be provided by historical data' (p. 44). The contribution by González-Díaz, entitled '*Worser* and *Lesser* in Modern English', focuses on 'social development of the double suppletive forms *worser* and *lesser*' (p. 238) during the period 1500–1900 and the role that standardization and prescriptivism might have played in the development of these forms. The investigation is based on a usage corpus, which largely consists of genres that captured oral language of the time, and a precept corpus, which comprises metalinguistic comments that contemporary grammarians made on double forms. In order to put the development of *lesser* and *worser* into context, González-Díaz first describes the development of double periphrastic comparatives in ModE. The data and the comparison of the usage and precept corpora reveal that double periphrastic comparative forms were still accepted in educated environments at the end of the sixteenth century. However, from then onwards 'a qualitative shift in the social consideration of these double forms' (p. 249) started taking place, which resulted in a process of stigmatization of the form during the seventeenth century. As regards the development of *worser*, the author shows that the social downgrading of the form started at a later date than that of the remaining double periphrastic forms. *Lesser*, on the other hand, appears to have become established as part of StE during the time of Charles Dickens. Even though *lesser* was largely stigmatized in eighteenth-century grammars, a shift in attitude towards the form can be observed in the second half of the nineteenth century—as also reflected by actual usage of the form. As concerns the influence of grammarians' comments on the development of double periphrastic comparatives and in particular *lesser* and *worser*, González-Díaz warns 'against invoking too readily the influence of prescriptive grammars on actual usage' (p. 273).

The year 2007 saw the publication of some more papers that were concerned with language standardization and prescriptivism. For instance, Sylvia Adamson's 'Prescribed Reading: Pronouns and Gender in the Eighteenth Century' (*HLSL* 7[2007] online) aims at measuring to what extent prescriptive rules had an effect on a speech community by focusing on the interpretative habits, i.e. readings and misreading, of members of that community. After commenting on pronouns and gender in PDE as well as pronoun variability in EModE, with a specific focus on interrogatives *who/what*, relativizers *who/which*, anaphoric pronouns (*he/she/it*), and the emergence of the neuter possessive *its*, the author takes a close look at the codification of gender in eighteenth-century grammar and interpretations, i.e. eighteenth-century readings. Adamson notes that during the seventeenth century the English pronominal system was acquired 'by intuition or imitation' while it was 'reinforced, or modified, by precept' during the eighteenth century. It was an eighteenth-century innovation to give the pronoun a substitutive function of a noun, i.e. also to make a 'link between gender in the language system and sex in the world'. Two grammarians who were influential in propagating the close link between nature and language were James Harris and Robert Lowth. A binary opposition between 'persons' and 'things' was established which associated things with inanimacy and personhood with animacy, the latter of which included the attribute of rationality. The more categorical the rules on pronoun usage became, which led to the suppression of variable practices, the more did the reading community start to misinterpret earlier readings. For instance, in 1672 Dryden considered Jonson's *heaven...his* instead of *heaven...its* as a grammatical error and did not recognize the former version as obsolete usage. In this article Adamson convincingly shows that misreading can give us an insight into 'internalised grammars of successive interpretive communities and so provide crucial aids to our understanding of the historical changes through which languages pass'. In 'Marginalia as Evidence. The Unidentified Hands in Lowth's *Short Introduction to English Grammar* (1762)' (*HL* 34[2007] 1–18), Karlijn Navest closely investigates the annotations found in the two Winchester College copies of Lowth's grammar in order to verify whether, as earlier claimed by R.C. Alston, one of these copies was owned by Lowth and the other copy was used as the basis for the second edition [1763] of his grammar. A careful investigation of Lowth's autograph letters and a comparison to the annotations reveals that they were made by a different hand. Moreover, as the annotations found in one of the copies do not concur with the additions made in the 1763 grammar edition, it is unlikely that this copy served as the basis for the latter edition. By investigating the hands of the in-letters received by Robert Lowth, Navest is able to show that the owner of the latter Winchester copy was most likely William Warburton (1698–1779) and thus a contemporary and acquaintance of Robert Lowth. Another study concerned with the grammarian Robert Lowth by Anita Auer and Ingrid Tieken-Boon van Ostade, 'Robert Lowth and the Use of the Inflectional Subjunctive in Eighteenth-Century English', appeared in a Festschrift for Herbert Schendl edited by Ute Smit, Stefan Dollinger, Julia Hüttner, Ursula Lutzky and Gunther Kaltenböck, *Tracing English through Time: Explorations in Language Variation* (pp. 1–18). It takes a close look at Lowth's account of the mood in different editions of his grammar and then compares his precepts to the actual use of the subjunctive in his letters. The grammar analysis of the authors reveals that Lowth did not prescribe the use of the inflectional subjunctive and that he only gave his opinion on the correct use of the past subjunctive. Only around the time when his grammar was published did Lowth use the inflectional past subjunctive form in the 'correct' context in his correspondence. After a short period of time his use of the form declined, which suggests that the grammarian did not strictly follow his own suggestions on 'correct' language use.

Lowth also features in the article 'The Syntactic Status of English Punctuation' (*ES* 88[2007] 195–216) by Karsten Schou. Most notably, this article focuses on the historical development of English punctuation theory. Nowadays it is largely believed that punctuation is a grammatical marking that is 'only sporadically related to speech and intonation' (p. 195) while throughout history punctuation was often considered to be a prosodic phenomenon that related writing to speech. By analysing grammatical accounts of punctuation from the seventeenth century onwards, Schou observed that punctuation theory became increasingly associated with syntax. For instance, during the late eighteenth century, when grammatical descriptions of English became independent of Latin, distinctions between punctuation marks were explained and defined both in terms of rhetoric and syntax. From 1800 onwards the rhetorical aspect of punctuation theory gradually started declining.

The end of the eighteenth century is the main period of investigation in Jane Hodson's monograph *Language and Revolution in Burke, Wollstonecraft, Paine and Godwin*, which closely investigates political language use in Britain at the time of the French Revolution. Hodson analyses texts written by prominent people who did not only contribute to the public debate on the

French Revolution but who were also concerned with the style of political language. By discussing reflections on grammar, logic and stylistics in the late eighteenth century as well as examining reviews on the selected texts, the author shows how salient the politico-linguistic debate was at the time. Her analyses of literary devices such as rhetorical questions and figurative language in selected texts throws a critical light on the authors' self-perceptions as well as contemporary criticism. Hodson is successful in demonstrating that it is too simplistic to view 'the French Revolution debate as a straightforward conflict between radical and conservative', which led to a linguistic revolution; instead, she argues that we can observe 'a series of skirmishes, in which writers on all sides attempt to lend authority to their writings by justifying their stylistic choices in terms of contemporary ideas about language' (p. 184).

Prescription versus description is the topic of Charlotte Brewer's article 'Pronouncing the "P": Prescription or Description in 19th- and 20th-Century English Dictionaries?' (*HL* 34[2007] 257–80). This article investigates how the pronunciation of Greek-derived words that begin with a p-, in particular the ps-words, are represented in English dictionaries from the nineteenth and twentieth centuries. While more than a dozen dictionaries published during the nineteenth century suggested that the [p] should be dropped, a change in viewpoint can be observed in the first two decades of the twentieth century. Most notably, the chief editor of the *OED*, J.A.H. Murray (1837–1915) disapproved of dropping the [p] and recommended that the reader should change his or her habits. Even though the *OED* claims to describe actual language usage, the prescriptive attitudes of editors could slip into the dictionary by way 'of supposedly objective definitions or labels or etymologies' (pp. 266–7). Brewer also investigates whether Murray's p- precept was adopted by actual language users as well as succeeding dictionaries. She successfully demonstrates that during most of the twentieth century the initial [p] was primarily silent. Moreover, the dictionaries reveal great inconsistency of record regarding the pronunciation of [p], which, according to Brewer, suggests that its existence was mainly 'a dictionary chimera rather than...a true reflection of the way English speakers have pronounced these words' (p. 274). Michael K.C. MacMahon in his article 'The Work of Richard John Lloyd (1846–1906) and "The crude system of doctrine which passes at present under the name of phonetics"' (*HL* 34[2007] 281–331) takes a close look at the phonetic works of Richard John Lloyd (1846–1906), who was well known as a Liverpool businessman but also had a strong interest in phonetics, English language and literature, sociology, philosophy, mathematics and physics. The main focus of his work in phonetics was vowel acoustics and sound transitions. MacMahon points out that even though Lloyd has been grouped with the 'minor phoneticians' so far and his work might not have had a great influence on others, 'the quality of his work, the extent of it, and the manner in which he went about it, signal a need to reappraise his position in the community of late 19th-century British phoneticians' (p. 321). In fact, Lloyd's work is comparable to that of articulatory and experimental phonetics in the twentieth century.

Another worthwhile article published in 2007, written by Julie Coleman, focuses on 'Howard N. Rose's *Thesaurus of Slang* (1934): Its Purpose, Structure, Contents, Reliability, and Sources' (*HL* 34[2007] 351–61). While contemporary reviewers of the thesaurus 'found it wanting in various respects' (p. 351), Coleman concludes that this criticism largely had to do with the misleading title of the work, *Thesaurus of Slang*, as it was not a thesaurus and not all of the words listed can be categorized as slang. Interestingly, Maurice Weseen's *Dictionary of American Slang*, which was published in the same year, received far more favourable reviews, which was mainly because of its size rather than its quality. This suggests that Rose's thesaurus was criticized by reviewers most likely for its title and the small size.

In 'On the History of English Teaching Grammars' (in Schmitter, ed., *Sprachtheorien der Neuzeit III/2: Sprachbeschreibung und Sprachunterricht*, pp. 500–25). Emma Vorlat provides an overview of available teaching grammars for native speakers published from the sixteenth to the nineteenth centuries. She focuses in particular on the overall structure of the grammars, the grammatical categories of the grammars and the influence of the Latin paradigm and/or universal grammar, and the pedagogy of the grammars. This paper serves as a suitable introduction to beginners in the field of English grammar writing. In the article 'Innovation and Continuity in English Learners' Dictionaries: The Single-Clause *When*-Definition' (*IJL* 20[2007] 393–9) Noel E. Osselton demonstrates that the use of single-clause *when*-definitions for nouns, e.g. 'Destruction: when something is destroyed' (p. 393), which has hitherto been considered a recent innovation in English learners' dictionaries, can already be found in a seventeenth-century English dictionary by Elisha Coles, who 'proclaims himself to be 'School-Master and Teacher of the Tongue of Foreigners' (p. 394). It is noteworthy that Coles did not restrict the single-clause *when*-definitions to nouns but that he also used the pattern for verbs and adjectives. Osselton points out that the evolution of defining techniques has largely been neglected, and that even though they are working in widely different periods, 'dictionary compilers may quite independently arrive at similar solutions to similar problems' (p. 398). Another interesting article published in 2007 is 'The Architecture of Joseph Wright's *English Dialect Dictionary*: Preparing the Computerised Version' (*IJL* 20[2007] 355–68) by Manfred Markus and Reinhard Heuberger. This paper is concerned with the tasks, problems and difficulties the project faces during the digitization of the *English Dialect Dictionary*, in particular regarding the challenges of the entry structure. An analysis of the dictionary identified eight recurrent fields within the entries, namely (1) headwords (2) parts of speech (3) labels (4) counties, regions, nations (5) phonetic transcription (6) definitions or meaning(s) (7) citations, and (8). A detailed investigation revealed that Wright did not use any of the eight parameters with total consistency. For instance, many variant forms of headwords are not found in the headword list but mentioned in the field of labels of entries. Moreover, compounds and derivations were not given headword status by Wright. The project aims to compensate for these shortcomings in the structure of the dictionary in the digitized version in order to provide a user-friendly electronic version for the international research community (see also section 7 below).

3. Phonetics and Phonology

/H/-dropping in different varieties of English is a phonological phenomenon that inspires interest up to the present day. Both the exact environment in which it is obligatory or optional (cf. *vehicle* without /h/ and *vehicular* with /h/) and the sociolinguistic status of this rule are topics of debate. It is interesting to note, for instance, that /h/-dropping in the weak form of articles (*him, her*) is perfectly acceptable, while /h/-dropping in content words (*horse, harm*) is frowned upon in most varieties. A situation like this with extensive geographical and social variation suggests that /h/-dropping is an old rule— one which has been present in the language for a long time. In her article 'Were they 'Dropping their Aitches'? A Quantitative Study of H-Loss in Middle English' (*ELL* 11[2007] 51–80), Paola Crisma presents extensive quantitative evidence that it is possible to distinguish different Middle English varieties on the basis of the treatment of word-initial /h/. The data presented suggest that /h/ loss was never generalized, i.e. that variation has persisted through many centuries.

Philip Carr and Patrick Honeybone have put together a special double issue on English phonology and linguistic theory (*LangS* 29:ii–iii[2007]). It is wonderful to note that many topics in the field continue to yield new and surprising viewpoints. In their introductory article the guest editors point out the various ways in which English phonology has contributed to phonological theory over the years, for instance with respect to the tense-lax distinction in vowels, the organization of the grammar and the place of the phonological component(s), and the treatment of lenition. Let us briefly discuss some articles in this volume. Lenition is also the main topic in Csaba Csides's study 'A Strict CV Approach to Consonant Lenition: Bidirectional Government in English Phonology' (*LangS* 29[2007] 177–202), where the author examines flapping in AmE from a Government-Phonology perspective. Here the interesting viewpoint is defended that a distinction needs to be made between governing relations established in the lexicon and those established post-lexically to account for the environments in which there is no lenition. The same framework is adopted in 'Branching Onsets and Syncope in English' (*LangS* 29[2007] 408–25) by Peter Szigetvari, to analyse the status of clusters like *pl-* in *police* where schwa in the initial syllable has been deleted: does this cluster have the same status as *pl-* in *please*?

The phenomenon of intrusive /r/ in BrE has often attracted attention in these pages. One question is whether this is an arbitrary, quirky historical accident or whether /r/ in environments like *Shah* /r/ *of Persia* can be motivated on independent phonetic or phonological grounds. In 'Intrusive [r] and Optimal Epenthetic Consonants' (*LangS* 29[2007] 451–76), Christian Uffmann takes the (minority) position that intrusive /r/ is a phonologically natural phenomenon. This bold stand is based on the idea that other 'default' consonants like glottal stops and semivowels like /j, w/ are not permitted in the intrusive-r environment. This sounds like grist to the mill of OT, and indeed this framework is adopted for this purpose. However, the same framework is attacked in another contribution to the same volume, that by April McMahon, 'Who's Afraid of the Vowel Shift Rule?' (*LangS* 29[2007] 341–59), where, on the basis of the Great Vowel Shift and its contemporary successor rules, she argues that it is perfectly acceptable to adopt OT for some, but not all, phenomena that phonologists wish to describe. OT would be more suited to prosodic phenomena—for the analysis of which it has, of course, traditionally been most often employed—while segmental phenomena are better captured by traditional segmental rules.

A number of articles deal with voicing. Gregory K. Iverson and Sang-Cheol Ahn discuss 'English Voicing in Dimensional Theory' (*LangS* 29[2007] 247–69). The authors analyse two apparently disparate phenomena in English phonology as structurally related: the lexically specific voicing of fricatives in plural nouns like *wives* or *thieves* and the prosodically governed 'flapping' of medial /t/ (and /d/) in North American varieties (cf. also Csides's article, mentioned above). A non-formalist account is presented in David Eddington, 'Flaps and Other Variants of /t/ in American English: Allophonic Distribution without Constraints, Rules, or Abstractions' (*CogLing* 18[2007] 23–46). Wouter Jansen presents a more laboratory-phonology oriented article in his 'Phonological "Voicing", Phonetic Voicing, and Assimilation in English' (*LangS* 29[2007] 270–93), which investigates regressive voicing assimilation by means of a quantitative acoustic study of British English obstruent clusters, and finds that these effects are best treated in terms of co-articulation.

Finally, a number of contributions in this special issue deal with English stress, as of course in this area there have been major contributions to phonological theory. Luigi Burzio, 'Phonology and Phonetics of English Stress and Vowel Reduction' (*LangS* 29[2007] 154–76), examines the relation between vowel reduction under lack of stress and the identifiability of the place of articulation of consonants following such vowels (which is of course reduced as a result of vowel reduction), paying special attention to the status of coronals. Jean-Michel Fournier, in 'From a Latin Syllable-Driven Stress System to a Romance versus Germanic Morphology-Driven Dynamics: In Honour of Lionel Guierre' (*LangS* 29[2007] 218–36), sets out to disprove the idea that the English stress system is, to a great degree, still modelled on classical Latin metrical rules. Sanford Schane, 'Understanding English Word Accentuation' (*LangS* 29[2007] 372–84), also argues against the 'received' treatment of English stress, and presents a set of metrical rules to derive stress in underived words on a par with morphologically complex words, making use of unary, binary and ternary feet. Finally, Ives Trevian, in 'Stress-Neutral Endings in Contemporary British English: An Updated Overview' (*LangS* 29[2007] 426–50), draws attention to variation in words with certain suffixes such as *-ed*, *-ing*, *-ly*, *-atory* or *-able*, on the basis of original database research by Lionel Guierre, to whom this special issue is dedicated, and a comparison with contemporary sources.

On the borderline between phonology and syntax is the article by Colleen M. Fitzgerald, 'An Optimality Treatment of Syntactic Inversions in English Verse' (*LangS* 29[2007] 203–17), which looks at syntactic inversions, i.e. disruption to the syntax so as to better satisfy the metrical constraints in verse. Such inversions are best modelled by interleaving syntactic and metrical constraints in OT. A purely phonetic study on vowel reduction is Edward Flemming and Stephanie Johnson's 'Rosa's Roses: Reduced Vowels in American English' (*JIPA* 37[2007] 83–96), which investigates whether and how the two reduced vowels in *Rosa* and *roses* are different: it is found that the first vowel is indeed schwa-like, while the second is barred-i-like.

In these pages we have paid attention before to measuring the difference between dialects: is there an objective way to say two dialects A and B are *more different* than two other dialects C and D, or is there an objective way of saying that a dialect C is *more closely related* to A than to B, etc.? Two articles contribute to this debate. The first is by April McMahon, Paul Heggarty, Robert McMahon and Warren Maguire, 'The Sound Patterns of Englishes: Representing Phonetic Similarity' (*ELL* 11[2007] 113–42), who illustrate a method for measuring phonetic similarity in a sample of cognate words for a number of (mainly British) varieties of English, and show how these results can be displayed in network diagrams. Robert G. Shackleton, Jr, in 'Phonetic Variation in the Traditional English Dialects: A Computational Analysis' (*JEngL* 35[2007] 30–102), deals with exactly the same topic. A future topic of discussion might be whether 'mixed' dialects can also be represented in terms of 'mixed' grammars, for example in terms of OT grammars.

A number of articles deal with the specific characteristics of dialects in Britain and across the globe. For England, clear ('palatalized') and dark ('velarized') liquids in Leeds and Newcastle take pride of place in Paul Carter and John Local's 'F2 Variation in Newcastle and Leeds English Liquid Systems' (*JIPA* 37[2007] 183–99), where the authors describe the effects of laterals on vowels, distinguishing between different positions and the effect on stressed and unstressed vowels. This article may contribute to ongoing debate in the area of r- (and l-) loss and the effect of these changes on the vocalic system, which is also the topic of Wyn Johnson and David Britain's 'L-Vocalisation as a Natural Phenomenon: Explorations in Sociophonology' (*LangS* 29[2007] 294–315), which deals specifically with the Fenland area. The authors pay specific attention to the relation between /l/-allophony, i.e. the alternation between clear and dark /l/ according to position, and the degree to which final /l/ is being lost. Relatedly, Derek Britton, 'A History of Hyper-Rhoticity in English' (*ELL* 11[2007] 525–36), investigates the history of what is usually referred to as 'hyper-rhoticity', i.e. the appearance, in rhotic accents, of epenthetic, non-etymological rhyme-/r/, usually taking the form of /r/-colouring in modern accents (for example *clorth* for *cloth*, reported for Bristol English), and finds evidence for this already in EModE stages. This may have repercussions for our understanding for the reverse process, loss of postvocalic /r/.

The phonetics of Liverpool English, which is, as is well known, influenced to some extent by Irish English settlers, forms the subject matter of a short contribution by Kevin Watson ('Liverpool English', *JIPA* 37[2007] 351–60). The pronunciation of Scottish English in the Shetland and Orkney islands was discussed last year. A contribution by Peter Sundkvist, 'The Pronunciation of Scottish Standard English in Lerwick, Shetland' (*EWW* 28[2007] 1–21), now adds to this.

The study of intonational variation is a topic of increasing attention. Alan Cruttenden, 'Intonational Diglossia: A Case Study of Glasgow' (*JIPA* 37[2007] 257–74), describes the intonational patterns in two different styles (conversation and reading) in one Glaswegian speaker. It is shown that these styles are entirely distinct, and it is interesting to observe that the more formal of these styles is more akin to intonation in RP than the more informal one. Of course more investigation in this area is called for.

Perhaps the only dialect of English which is not typically regional is RP. Anne H. Fabricius, 'Variation and Change in the TRAP and STRUT Vowels of RP: A Real Time Comparison of Five Acoustic Data Sets' (*JIPA* 37[2007] 293–320), examines evidence for change in real time within the short vowel subsystem of the RP accent of English over the course of the twentieth century. Not only are the individual changes in these vowel realizations uncovered, but the relation between the two changes is also captured, providing a welcome systemic perspective on the study of vowel shift phenomena.

Variation in AmE at large is dealt with in Ewa Jacewicz, Robert A. Fox and Joseph Salmons, 'Vowel Duration in Three American English Dialects' (*AS* 82[2007] 367–85), where the duration of the vowels in words like *hid, head, had, hayed* and *hide* is compared for the Inland North, Midlands, and South of the United States. Reverting to the theme of measuring and modelling dialectal variation mentioned above, it should be observed that the Midlands not only take up a geographically intermediate position but also behave phonetically so. Specific dialect studies deal with Charleston, South Carolina (Maciej Baranowski's 'Phonological Variation and Change in the Dialect of Charleston, South Carolina', supplement 92.1 to *AS* 82[2007]), the Bonin Islands (Daniel Long's 'English on the Bonin (Ogasawara) Islands', supplement 92.2 to *AS* 82[2007]), Atlanta, Georgia (Phil Harrison's 'The Lost Consonants of Atlanta' *LangS* 29[2007] 237–46), Kentucky (Terry Lynn Irons's 'On the Status of Low Back Vowels in Kentucky English: More Evidence of Merger', *LVC* 19[2007] 137–80) and Vermont (Julie Roberts's 'Vermont Lowering? Raising Some Questions about /ai/ and /au/ South of the Canadian Border', *LVC* 19[2007] 181–97).

A follow-up on Labov's classic study on Martha's Vineyard deserves special mention: in 'Forty Years of Language Change on Martha's Vineyard' (*Language* 83[2007] 615–27), Jennifer Pope, Miriam Meyerhoff and D. Robert Ladd investigate the present-day linguistic situation on Martha's Vineyard and comment on the usefulness and validity of the apparent-time method in sociolinguistics.

Three articles deal with varieties of English in Africa. 'Global and Local Durational Properties in Three Varieties of South African English' by Andries W. Coetzee and Daan P. Wissing (*TLR* 24[2007] 263–89), discusses phrasal lengthening in the light of the distinction between stress-timed and syllable-timed languages. Yves Talla Sando Ouafeu presents 'Intonational Marking of New and Given Information in Cameroon English' (*EWW* 28[2007] 187–99), showing that speakers of this variety mark new information in the discourse somewhat differently from speakers of other varieties, namely by varying intensity and duration, rather than pitch. Finally, Augustin Simo Bobda ('Some Segmental Rules of Nigerian English Phonology', *EWW* 28[2007] 279–310) outlines differences in rules and rule ordering, compared to common English phonological rules.

Across the waves, NZE continues to be thoroughly investigated by an active group of researchers. Its general phonetics is illustrated in *JIPA* by Laurie Bauer, Paul Warren, Dianne Bardsley, Marianna Kennedy and George Major ('New Zealand English', *JIPA* 37[2007] 97–102). In addition, there are specific studies on Niuean English, spoken on the island of Niue, by Donna Starks, Jane Christie and Laura Thompson in 'Niuean English: Initial Insights into an Emerging Variety' (*EWW* 28[2007] 133–46), and on the realization of the vowels in the lexical sets FLEECE and DRESS by Margaret Maclagan and Jennifer Hay ('Getting Fed Up with our Feet: Contrast Maintenance and the New Zealand English "Short" Front Vowel Shift', *LVC* 19[2007] 1–25), where the authors find a merger of these vowels in certain subsets of these groups of words, in particular before voiceless codas.

Finally, one article on loanwords from English should be mentioned. This is Michael Kenstowicz's 'Salience and Similarity in Loanword Adaptation: A Case Study from Fijian' (*LangS* 29[2007] 316–40), in the special issue of *LangS* mentioned above, where different theories of loanword adaptation are put to the test on the basis of data from Fijian: what exactly is the role of the native language phonology, and what changes are due to general phonetic tendencies? These issues are important but not always easy to tease apart. Also relevant in this respect is the study of interference in general. Two important studies deal with interaction of languages spoken in the Far East. These are Barış Kabak and William J. Idsardi's paper 'Perceptual Distortions in the Adaptation of English Consonant Clusters: Syllable Structure or Consonantal Contact Constraints?' (*LSp* 50[2007] 23–52), where the authors present a meticulous account of the role of phonotactic restrictions in Korean in the perception of English consonantal sequences. Finally, Lei Sun and Vincent J. van Heuven, in 'Perceptual Assimilation of English Vowels by Chinese Listeners: Can Native-Language Interference be Predicted?' (*LIN* 24[2007] 150–61), investigate to what extent the errors made by Chinese learners of English at different levels can be predicted on the basis of a contrastive analysis of native and target language.

4. Morphology

We have enjoyed reading the *Handbook of English Linguistics*, edited by Bas Aarts and April McMahon. Its thirty-two chapters include a wealth of information, pitched—we feel—at exactly the right level: there is no great amount of technical machinery originating in this or that theoretical framework but there is accessible in-depth analysis of a wide variety of topics. It contains four chapters that deal with morphological issues; other ones will be discussed in the next section. Ricardo Bermúdez-Otero and April McMahon write about 'English Phonology and Morphology', (pp. 382–410) aiming—and, we would say, admirably succeeding—to 'sift through the intricate debate...that surrounds English morphophonology and to identify key concepts and issues that deserve our continued attention, regardless of major shifts in the theoretical landscape' (p. 383). Illustrating various theoretical approaches to the facts, they discuss several alternations (including vowel shortening and Northern Irish dentalization) and use these to probe deeper into the interaction between phonology and morphology, focusing in particular on phenomena invoking the need for domains, cycles and levels. James Blevins addresses 'English Inflection and Derivation' (pp. 507–36), engaging in detailed consideration of the (few) inflections of the language and then at greater speed going over a number of derivational issues, such as category-preserving and changing processes, productivity and analogy. The issue of 'Productivity' is addressed at greater length by Ingo Plag (pp. 537–56), who surveys qualitative and quantitative approaches to it, sketches the questions it raises for the mental lexicon and then considers restrictions on productivity.

All of the above matters are also addressed in the textbook by Francis Katamba and John Stonham, *Morphology*, a second edition of the book that Katamba authored alone in 1993 (see *YWES* 74[1996] 20). The overall structure of the first edition has been retained, as has its generative slant, but there has been some updating and thankfully also a weeding out of the many typos that marred the earlier work. After an introduction to word structure, there are chapters on types of morphemes, productivity, lexical morphology, templatic morphology, prosodic morphology, OT in morphology (this is new), inflection, mapping of grammatical functions and the interface between lexicon, morphology and syntax. Data and examples, also in the in-text and end-of-chapter exercises, come from a wide range of languages, and the authors do not hesitate to go into considerable technical detail. All of this means that this is clearly a work for more advanced students—but a very rewarding work.

Heidi Harley's *English Words: A Linguistic Introduction* gives a very accessible introduction to the analysis of lexical items from various perspectives. It has chapters on the phonology of words, lexical semantics, acquisition, the historical forces that have helped shape the English lexicon and—most relevantly here—three chapters concerned with morphological analysis. One is all about the creation of new words, through processes like back formation, clipping, initializing, affixation, compounding and blending. Another chapter considers more closely the processes and results of derivation and a third one elaborates on this by introducing notions such as root irregularity, suffixal restrictions, suppletion, productivity and blocking. Many examples are given of each notion and process, and there are practically oriented study problems at the end of the chapter. As we can attest, this book works well in classes for beginners in the topic.

On specific inflectional matters, comparatives and superlatives have attracted attention in three articles. There is Claudia Claridge's 'The Superlative in Spoken English' (in Facchinetti, ed., *Corpus Linguistics 25 Years On*, pp. 121–48), based on a 4 million-word spoken subpart of the BNC. She examines not only that staple of superlative analysis, the alternation between inflected and periphrastic forms, but also considers the spread of adjective types, superlative syntax and semantics, finding that—in speech—superlatives commonly express intensifying and absolute meanings, rather than factual comparison. Britta Mondorf looks at comparatives, noting several 'Recalcitrant Problems of Comparative Alternation and New Insights Emerging from Internet Data' (in Hundt, Nesselhauf and Biewer, eds.,

Corpus Linguistics and the Web, (pp. 211–32), a timely collection of papers of which we review several more below). Mondorf uses a combination of corpus and web data to investigate the relation between comparative form and concrete vs. abstract meaning of the head noun; the occurrence of forms like *they became friendlier and more friendly* in earlier English; and the choice between comparative compounds like *more broad-based* vs. *broader-based* (shown to depend on the degree of entrenchment of the ADJ + N base). In a more theoretical mode, David Embick's 'Blocking Effects and Analytic/ Synthetic Alternations' (*NL&LT* 25[2007] 1–37) argues that the inflected forms are formed post-syntactically by affixation under adjacency, adopting the theory of Distributed Morphology.

We have not seen much on verbal inflection. Lieselotte Anderwald's '*He rung the bell* and *She drunk ale*: Non-Standard Past Tense Forms in Traditional British Dialects and on the Internet' (in Hundt, Nesselhauf and Biewer, eds., pp. 271–85) shows that forms like *I/you/(s)he/we/they sung/rung/ begun* are plentiful not only in UK dialectal speech but also within the '.uk' domain of the web. This is brought out well by Google, but the WebCorp results are somewhat disappointing. Adrian Pablé and Radoslaw Dylewski trace the development of 'Invariant BE in New England Folk Speech: Colonial and Postcolonial Evidence (*AS* 82[2007] 151–84]. Using a range of sources, they argue that the plural use of finite *be* was a feature brought from Britain but singular use developed in New England itself in the late seventeenth century. The various linguistic constraints are investigated, including *be*'s preference for clause-final position, as in ' "Men is different," said Sally Jinks. "Yes, they be." '

Derivational matters are put in a historical context in D. Gary Miller's *Latin Suffixal Derivatives in English and their Indo-European Ancestry*. After an introduction explaining relevant concepts and terminology, it contains lists of Latin verbal suffixes that have been borrowed into English, with information being given about their form(s) and meaning(s) in Latin, followed by a set of English words in which they occur, the Latin forms and meaning of these words and their reconstructed proto-Indo-European sources. This book is therefore similar to an etymological dictionary, except that the information is ordered by affix rather than lexical item. The affixes are grouped according to the bases they take and the resulting word class and much fuller information is given about the etymology of the affixes than is normally the case. Correspondingly, there is very little about the intermediate stage that many of the relevant words went through, i.e. (Old) French. But even without this the amount of detail is staggering. Indexes for Indo-European roots, English and Latin words allow the reader to find the desired information easily.

A general introduction to 'Compounds and Minor Word-Formation Types' by Laurie Bauer (in Aarts and McMahon, eds., pp. 483–506) first discusses the main types of compounds, their phonology, grammatical structure and semantics, and then goes on to deal with minor word formation types such as clipping, 'alphabetization' (initialisms and acronyms) and blends. Bauer also devotes some attention to the process of word manufacturing, i.e. the conscious and planned creation of new words (though this remains an under-studied topic). Anette Rosenbach considers the alternation between genitive constructions (e.g. *driver's licence*) and compounds (*driver licence*) in 'Exploring Constructions on the Web: A Case Study' (in Hundt, Nesselhauf and Biewer, eds., pp. 167–90). She notes the unreliability of Google results (which silently include tokens with a genitive when the compound type is searched for) and then investigates data from WebCorp, which show that animacy of the possessor promotes use of the genitive, especially in US English. Don Chapman and Ryan Christensen, 'Noun–Adjective Compounds as a Poetic Type in Old English' (*ES* 88[2007] 447–64), argue that the characteristics of OE noun–adjective compounds (e.g. *hilde-hwate* 'battle-brave') make them more poetic than other compounds.

Adverbs with the suffix *-wise* are the subject of Hans Lindquist's article 'Viewpoint *-wise*: The Spread and Development of a New Type of Adverb in American and British English' (*JEngL* 35[2007] 132–56). Lindquist shows that viewpoint adverbs in *-wise*, which originated in AmE, are increasing in both AmE and BrE due to functional and social factors, are more frequent in BrE, and are twice as frequent in spoken than in written corpora.

5. Syntax

(a) Modern English

Do your students know the difference between realism and mentalism? Or how the status of binarity differs in morphology, syntax and phonology? Or what the general methods of linguistic data collection are? And can they use slashes, curly brackets, pointed brackets, phis and thetas accurately? Do they know how to pronounce C.S. Pierce? (and whether C.S. is a man or a woman?). Can they make glosses? If not, tell them to consult Laurie Bauer's *The Linguistics Student's Handbook*. This delightful book is aimed at students that need guidance on the host of puzzling things that they are expected to understand, some of them sometimes taught (but not therefore automatically assimilated) and others never explicitly discussed. The books has six parts: 'Fundamentals' (these are matters that are essential but not always included in linguistics syllabuses), 'Notation and Terminology' (including lists of ambiguous and synonymous terminology), 'Reading Linguistics' (covering the IPA, accents and diacritics, names and subjects of journals, statistics and online resources), 'Writing and Presenting' (with notes on essay-writing, glossing, spelling), 'Referencing' (the great divider of the neophytes and the cognoscenti) and a 'Language File' (giving basic information and references for some 280 languages).

There are also some straightforward textbooks this year. Deborah Cameron has written the concise and accessible *The Teacher's Guide to Grammar*. After introducing the topic of grammar (chapter 1), it pays attention to identifying word classes (chapter 2), the structure of words (chapter 3), the structure of sentences (chapter 4), the structure of noun phrases (chapter 5), verb forms and their meanings (chapter 6), organizing information by joining clauses (chapter 7), dialectal variation (chapter 8), register variation (chapter 9) and cross-linguistic and L1/L2 variation (chapter 10). All chapters present practical pointers on how to approach the issues at hand in the classroom and on how to approach and comment on pupils' writing.

A third edition has appeared of Michael Swan's well-known *Practical English Usage* (the blurb mentions 'over one and a half million copies sold worldwide'). The book remains an excellent source of information about the practicalities of English grammar, (some) vocabulary and usage-based issues. The alphabetically arranged entries tell intermediate and advanced learners about *it's* vs. *its*, StE vs. dialects, participle clauses, the uses of *rather*, final < e >, tense simplification in subordinate clauses and some 600 other matters. The explanations and advice provided are eminently sensible and illustrated with many example sentences. Alongside these, plenty of negative input is also provided, with the indispensable font effect of 'strikethrough' being used to good purpose in visualizing for learners what kinds of forms or constructions they should not ('NOT') ~~to~~ use.

Another, more specialized, textbook is Mick Randall's *Memory, Psychology and Second Language Learning*, which is intended for those teaching or studying second-language (L2) learning. It draws on insights from cognitive linguistics and psychology concerning the way in which second languages are processed and learned. In addition, it discusses the methods that are used to teach English (and other languages) as a second language. The book is divided into two sections, the first of which provides a survey of contributions from linguistics and psychology to our understanding of language processing and learning. The second section is a workbook section, which contains exercises that complement the chapters in the first section. After the introduction, chapter 1 discusses what the fields of linguistics and psychology can tell us about L2 learning, reviewing various models of processing and considering evidence from brain imaging. Chapter 2 adopts the information-processing approach in explaining how spoken language is comprehended and looks at implications for the L2 learner. Chapter 3 is concerned with processes underlying word recognition, considering the linguistic features that are relevant to word recognition (such as phonological representation and semantics). Chapter 4 examines the way in which stored knowledge of the world is used in the interpretation of language messages. It is shown that language recognition procedures are less automatic for L2 learners than for native speakers of a language, due to an increased cognitive load. Chapter 5 focuses on the way in which lexical items of L1 and L2 are stored and retrieved. Chapter 6 describes 'the process by which basic learning of language takes place in Working Memory' (p. 145) and shows that this process is governed by a monitoring supervisory attentional system (SAS). It is this SAS that the L2 learner has to train in order to achieve automatic language processing. Chapter 7 assesses the methodologies of L2 teaching in terms of cognitive processing, focusing on current communicative approaches to L2 learning. The first section is concluded by an endnote in which Randall briefly considers how the working memory model adopted in the book deals with a number of issues in language learning, such as automaticity. The exercises in the workbook section allow the reader to put theory into practice.

Günter Radden and René Dirven have written the textbook *Cognitive English Grammar*. It has four parts: part I introduces the reader to the cognitive framework, part II concentrates on the expression of conceptual entities as nouns and noun phrases, part III deals with the grammatical expression of temporal information (aspect, tense and modality) and part IV looks at the way in which the conceptual structure of situations is represented in terms of sentence structure. The book is well-presented throughout and provides study questions as well as suggestions for further reading at the end of each chapter.

A textbook for an introduction to formal syntax is Liliane Haegeman's *Thinking Syntactically: A Guide to Argumentation and Analysis*. Meant for complete beginners, it deals with all the necessary topics in a clear and systematic fashion, bringing the student to a level where they could go on to tackle more advanced textbooks on generative syntax. The book contains chapters on the nature of studying language scientifically, on the basic structure of the clause, on lexical and functional projections, on multiple subject positions and on the pre-IP field and what happens there (i.e. wh-movement and lots of other interesting stuff). Two distinguishing features of the work are the consistent focus on argument rather than outcome and the inclusion of many exercises that ask the student to consider a range of facts and phenomena. Example sentences mainly come from English, but there is a fair sprinkling of other Germanic languages as well.

Many of the chapters in Aarts and McMahon, eds., *Handbook of English Linguistics*, are also eminently suitable for teaching purposes. For syntax, it contains sensible and instructive discussion of the foundational topics of 'English Word Classes and Phrases' by Bas Aarts and Liliane Haegeman (pp. 117–45), 'Verbs and their Satellites' by D.J. Allerton (pp. 146–79), 'Clause Types' by Peter Collins (pp. 180–97) and 'Coordination and Subordination' by Rodney Huddleston and Geoffrey K. Pullum (pp. 198–219). There is nothing wrong with a syntactic education based on these, we would say. It could be complemented by further study of verb-related categories through 'Tense in English' by Laura Michaelis (pp. 220–43), 'Aspect and Aspectuality' by Robert Binnick (pp. 244–68) and 'Mood and Modality in English' by Ilse Depraetere and Susan Reed (pp. 269–90). Discourse-related factors impinging on syntax are dealt with in Betty Birner and Gregory Ward's 'Information Structure' (pp. 291–317) and the boundary between lexis and syntax is explored from a construction grammar perspective in 'English Construction' by Adele Goldberg and Devin Casenhiser (pp. 343–55).

The same volume could also be used to increase students' awareness of issues of data and theory in the study of English linguistics. Kersti Börjars presents an introduction to 'Description and Theory' (pp. 9–32), sketching the basics of what it means to describe a language, the complications that arise when theory is brought in and the main features of three theoretical models, minimalism, lexical-functional grammar and OT. A good follow-up is the chapter by Charles F. Meyer and Gerald Nelson on 'Data Collection' (pp. 93–113), which discusses and compares the methods of introspection, experiment and corpus-building. Andrew Linn's 'English Grammar Writing' (pp. 72–92) presents an engaging historical overview of descriptive English grammars, from William Bullokar in 1586 via the Great Tradition created by Dutch twentieth-century grammarians to the Quirkian approach and other recent work. Also in Aarts and McMahon, eds., there are two chapters focusing on the properties of spoken English. Jim Miller's 'Spoken and Written English' (pp. 670–91) uses established findings about written English to explore in what ways speech is different (situational, morphological and especially syntactic), while Paola Quaglio and Douglas Biber analyse 'The Grammar of Conversation' (pp. 692–793). Drawing on the *Longman Grammar of Spoken and Written English* (*YWES* 80[2001] 20), they provide a list of grammatical features studied in earlier work on speech grammar and then relate these to the situational characteristics of conversation. Straddling the borderline between syntax and discourse is the slippery field of 'English Usage: Prescription and Description', explored by Pam Peters (pp. 759–80). She clarifies some of the central questions raised by usage guides, reviews studies of eighteenth- to twentieth-century examples and investigates the actual impact that prescriptive work has had on English usage.

While on this topic, we should also—even if somewhat belatedly—mention Pam Peters's own usage guide: *The Cambridge Guide to English Usage*. This is an A–Z of issues in grammar, spelling, text type conventions and other matters which is linguistically well-informed, corpus-based and inclusive of all the major varieties of English worldwide. The tone is welcoming, the advice is sensible and the coverage is comprehensive, with entries ranging from punctuation through grammatical conundrums to usage in modern electronic media. If students are made to look up specific items in this work, they are bound to read a lot more and in the process learn a great deal about the proper way to think about usage-related questions.

The volume *Language in the British Isles*, edited by David Britain, presents a comprehensive overview of the languages and dialects spoken and signed in the British Isles, and follows up on Peter Trudgill's *Language in the British Isles* [1984]. It contains much that is not syntactic but we mention here James Milroy's chapter on the history of English, which highlights the key phonological, syntactic, morphological and vocabulary (including semantic) changes that have taken place in the history of English, and the chapter by David Britain that 'reviews the literature on grammatical variation in the non-standard dialects of England since the mid-1980s' (p. 75). Chapters 5–10 are devoted to several regional varieties of English: chapter 5 (Paul A. Johnston, Jr) looks at Scottish English and Scots, chapter 6 (Kevin McCafferty) deals with Northern Irish English, chapter 7 (Raymond Hickey) examines Southern British English, chapter 8 (Robert Penhallurick) is concerned with English in Wales, chapter 9 (Andrew Hamer) looks at English on the Isle of Man (Manx) and chapter 10 (Heinrich Ramisch) looks at English in the Channel Islands. All of these include some syntactic information as well (for more information, see section 9).

More on English dialect syntax can be found in the special issue 'English Dialect Syntax' (*ELL* 11:ii[2007]), edited by David Adger and Graeme Trousdale (see also section 9). In the introductory article 'Variation in English Syntax: Theoretical Implications' (*ELL* 11[2007] 261–78), David Adger and Graeme Trousdale discuss the relationship between research on syntactic variation in the dialects of English and theoretical research into the structure of language. Alison Henry and Siobhan Cottell, 'A New Approach to Transitive Expletives: Evidence from Belfast English' (*ELL* 11[2007] 279–99), explain the presence of transitive expletives in Belfast English (e.g. *There have lots of people eaten their lunch already*) versus their absence in StE through an analysis in which the expletive is merged in SpecTP (its associate is merged in SpecvP) in Belfast English and in SpecvP in StE. Next, Joan Bresnan, Ashwini Deo and Devyani Sharma, in 'Typology in Variation: A Probabilistic Approach to *Be* and *N't* in the *Survey of English Dialects*' (*ELL* 11[2007] 301–46), present a Stochastic Optimality Theory (SOT) analysis of individual and dialectal variation in subject agreement and synthetic negation (*n't*) for the verb *be* and suggest that individual grammars are 'sensitively tuned to frequencies in the linguistic environment, leading to isolated loci of variability in the grammar' (p. 301). Emily M. Bender's article, 'Socially Meaningful Syntactic Variation in Sign-Based Grammar' (*ELL* 11[2007] 347–81), explores how sociolinguistic variation can be dealt with in models of syntactic competence, proposing an HSPG performance-plausible sign-based grammar, based on a case study of AAVE variable copula absence. Another more theoretical article is Richard A. Hudson's 'English Dialect Syntax in Word Grammar' (*ELL* 11[2007] 383–405). Hudson argues that the cognitive-linguistic theory Word Grammar can adequately handle the inherent variability found in English dialects, illustrating this on the basis of the *was/were* alternation in Buckie. The last article in the *ELL* special issue, 'A Construction Grammar Account of Possessive Constructions in Lancashire Dialect: Some Advantages and Challenges' (*ELL* 11[2007] 407–24), by Willem Hollmann and Anna Siewierska, looks at the Lancashire dialect. It is shown that reduction of 1SG possessives in possessive-noun constructions (e.g. *me brother*) in the Lancashire dialect patterns according to the (in)alienability hierarchy, which has previously been argued not to play a role in English. Widening the scene to the entire globe, a survey of 'Syntactic Variation in English: A Global Perspective' is provided by Bernd Kortmann (in Aarts and McMahon, eds., pp. 603–24). It offers an inventory of variation in world Englishes associated with the NP, the VP, negation, agreement and subordination, complemented with reflection on the proper interpretation and implication of the facts.

An introduction to 'English Corpus Linguistics' is given by Tony McEnery and Costas Gabrielatos (in Aarts and McMahon, eds., pp. 33–71). They discuss the fundamentals of the enterprise, debates about concrete practices, the implications of corpus findings for our conception of the language, their importance for reference works and for teaching and their use in the study of changes in English. Many actual corpora are mentioned, and there is a useful list of further reading.

There is a lot more on corpus linguistics this year, much of it in volumes in the thriving series Language and Computers from Rodopi. Several papers on general trends and developments appear in Facchinetti, ed., *Corpus Linguistics 25 Years On*. One of the pioneers in the field, Jan Svartvik, surveys 'Corpus Linguistics 25 + Years On' (pp. 11–26), offering personal memories of his earliest and later contributions to the field and sketching the various ways in which it has evolved over the twenty-five years since the first ICAME conference. In the same volume, Antoinette Renouf considers 'Corpus

Development 25 Years On: From Super-Corpus to Cyber-Corpus' (pp. 27–49), singling out for special attention the Birmingham Corpus, the 'dynamic' corpus and the 'Web-as-corpus' and commenting on various practical and theoretical issues that led to their development. Also in this volume, Stig Johansson advocates 'Seeing through Multilingual Corpora' (pp. 51–71). He shows how the use of corpora made up of parallel texts (i.e. in original and translated versions) offers opportunities for contrastive analysis, demonstrating how this can be done for the English nouns *person* and *thing* in English-Swedish and Norwegian corpora. 'Corpora and Spoken Discourse' by Anne Wichmann (pp. 73–86) highlights several problems posed by speech (including prosodic) analysis of corpus materials, arguing strongly in favour of keeping accessible the original sound files. Mark Davies reports on a project enabling 'Semantically-Based Queries with a Joint *BNC/WordNet* Database' (pp. 149–67), so that researchers can search for, say, the frequency across text types of synonyms or hyponyms of specific words; those interested can try it out on http://view.byu.edu (a site that we can recommend for the easy searches that it allows of a growing range of corpora of different types). Ron Cowan and Michael Leeser reflect on 'The Structure of Corpora in SLA Research' (pp. 289–303), considering how greater use of larger L2 corpora would allow insight into the nature of L2 grammars, the U-shaped development that learners sometimes go through and the influence of the L1 in SLA.

An entire volume on *Corpora in the Foreign Language Classroom* has been edited by Encarnación Hidalgo, Luis Quereda and Juan Santana. It contains twenty papers on a wide variety of topics, ranging from the general benefits of corpora use in the classroom through the implications for teaching of the analysis of tourism texts to the (in)transitivity of mental verbs in English and Spanish. The papers are grouped under three headings: general, theoretical issues in corpus design and exploitation, and practical classroom applications. What comes out clearly in many papers is the role of corpora in raising learner awareness, the positive effects of exposure to 'raw' data and the greater accuracy that corpus use brings to the learning and teaching of a host of lexical, grammatical and pragmatic features—features of English, we should add, because this volume is entirely focused on English-language classrooms.

But, as editors Andrew Wilson, Dawn Archer and Paul Rayson say in the first sentence of their preface to *Corpus Linguistics around the World*: 'The scope of corpus-based research is becoming ever wider.' Their volume has chapters on corpus work in Basque, Danish, Maltese, French, Slovene, Spanish, German, Polish, Russian, Dutch, Brazilian Portuguese and Chinese. On English, there are Khurshid Ahmad, David Cheng, Tugba Taskaya, Saif Ahmad, Lee Gillam, Pensiri Manomaisupat, Hayssam Traboulsi and Andrew Hippisley, who gauge 'The Mood of the (Financial) Markets: In a Corpus of Words and Pictures' (pp. 17–32). They analyse the text and figures in a corpus of financial reporting, with a view to extracting the sentiments expressed. In the somewhat misleadingly titled 'Analysing a Semantic Corpus Study across English Dialects: Searching for Paradigmatic Parallels' (pp. 121–40), Sarah Lee and Debra Ziegeler investigate the use of *get*-causatives of the type *we got him to redo it* in SingE, BrE and NZE. No real differences emerge, but it appears to be the case that SingE is sometimes using paradigmatically parallel *ask* in the same function. Judy Noguchi, Thomas Orr and Yukio Tono 'Us[e] a Dedicated Corpus to Identify Features of Professional English Usage: What Do "We" Do in Science Journal Articles?' (pp. 155–66), analysing the way the word *we* is used in a corpus of science texts, with respect to the types of verbs it combines with and their tense-aspect properties.

Efforts by linguists to harness the power of the World-Wide Web continue this year. Hundt, Nesselhauf and Biewer, eds., *Corpus Linguistics on the Web*, contains several important contributions on the general issues that arise in this attempt. The first article, 'Using Web Data for Linguistic Purposes' by Anke Lüdeling, Stefan Evert and Marco Baroni (pp. 7–24) is a helpful guide through the problems (instability, duplication of pages, the need to rely on commercial search machines, etc.) and possibilities (the availability of huge amounts of data, the creation of corpora drawn from the web, pre- and post-processing of web data, etc.) of this field. Some of these issues are also discussed in William H. Fletcher's 'Concordancing the Web: Promise and Problems, Tools and Techniques' (pp. 25–46), but with a somewhat stronger emphasis on practical solutions. One of these is the author's own KWiCFinder, a search engine which produces concordances for key search terms in context. Antoinette Renouf, Andrew Kehoe and Jayeeta Banerjee describe 'WebCorp: An Integrated System for Web Text Search' (pp. 47–67) that has been developed at the University of Central England. After explaining what WebCorp can currently do for you (it interfaces with commercial search engines but, like KWiCFinder, it yields concordance lines for search terms), the authors analyse the various problems faced by it and sketch an ambitious programme meant to result in WebCorp doing much more for you. A specific set of data available on the web, transcripts of CNN programmes, is explored by Sebastian Hoffmann in 'From Web Page to Mega-Corpus: The CNN Transcripts' (pp. 69–86). He explains how he created a corpus of this material and provides a sample investigation focusing on intensifier *so*. A different type of material on the web is explored in Claudia Claridge's 'Constructing a Corpus from the Web: Message Boards' (pp. 87–108). She describes the techniques she used and then carries out a small study of the corpus, focusing on the lexical and grammatical expressions of emotion and attitude in this text type. Also concerned with text types on the web are Douglas Biber and Jerry Kurjian in 'Towards a Taxonomy of Web Registers and Text Types: A Multi-Dimensional Analysis' (pp. 109–31). They show that the two domains of Home and Science recognized on Google are not internally homogeneous; instead they propose to classify web texts on the basis of Biberian multi-dimensional analysis, and demonstrate how this would work. A more reflective chapter is Geoffrey Leech's 'New Resources, or Just Better Old Ones? The Holy Grail of Representativeness' (pp. 133–50). It contains thoughts on the construction of corpora, old and new, and the precise meaning (or lack thereof) of claims about 'balance', 'comparability' and 'representativeness'. Graeme Kennedy also expresses some reservations about the current drive to go online, pointing out that there is 'An Under-Exploited Resource' and suggesting ways of 'Using the BNC for Exploring the Nature of Language Learning' (pp. 151–66). He considers data from collocations (such as *lose* + direct object and *find* + direct object, which are shown to have very different profiles) and discusses the relevance of frequent expressions for language learning. Of course, we may also expect that in some cases web data and corpus data will simply show the same patterns. This is what was found by Günter Rohdenburg in 'Determinants of Grammatical Variation in English and the Formation/Confirmation of Linguistic Hypotheses by Means of Internet Data' (pp. 191–210). Inspecting several constructions known to be undergoing change (e.g. *much fewer* vs. *many fewer*, *have difficulty* (*in*) V-*ing*, *it depends* (*on*) + wh-clause, *advise* + *to*-infinitive vs. *advise* + V-*ing*), he finds that in each case Google data and traditional corpus data point in the same direction and thus allow him to test his explanations for the changes.

Further contributions to (or based on) corpus work are found in Eileen Fitzpatrick, ed., *Corpus Linguistics Beyond the Word: Corpus Research from Phrase to Discourse*. It has chapters on a wide range of topics, including the technicalities of corpus annotation (also for discourse/pragmatic categories), and the use of corpora in the development of machine translation, in semantic analysis, in the register analysis of Spanish, in the study of the Albanian personal pronouns and in various forms of teaching (with one paper even describing the teaching of German grammar through a corpus made up of the Grimm fairy-tales). Of more direct relevance to English syntax is Angus B. Grieve-Smith's contribution, 'The Envelope of Variation in Multidimensional Register and Genre Analyses' (pp. 1–20). The author points out that some of the factors in Biber's multidimensional framework can be interpreted as being grammatical in nature, rather than text-typical. The remedy he proposes is to consider the frequency of linguistic features relative to the number of sites where they could have been used, rather than per number of words.

On the more theoretical side of the linguistic spectrum, Richard Hudson contributes *Language Networks: The New Word Grammar*, in which he sets out a comprehensive theory of linguistic analysis. The guiding idea is that language is a local network (of symbols), which is organized along the same lines as other areas of cognition. In the introduction, Hudson describes the fundamental properties and relations of linguistic networks (such as the 'isa' relation, default inheritance and spreading activation), and in the subsequent chapters he shows how this model can be applied to the areas of morphology, syntax, semantics and sociolinguistics. Crucially, phenomena in all these areas are shown to be analysable using the same type of network and network relations. Many facts from English are addressed (including—in a separate chapter—the properties of gerunds, which are taken to be both nouns and verbs at the same time) but cross-linguistic data are also analysed. Altogether, this book is a carefully argued plea for a non-generative, non-modular, non-derivational linguistics. There is also some work to report on the generative front. Nirmalangshu Mukherji, Bibudhendra Narayan Patnaik and Rama Kant Agnihotri have edited *Noam Chomsky: The Architecture of Language* [2000, but not seen by us until the paperback edition of 2006]. It gives the text of a lecture delivered by Chomsky in Delhi in 1996, followed by an edited transcript of the following discussion session, complemented by Chomsky's later written reactions to the questions that were handed in in writing. The volume gives an excellent sense of the excitement that the lecture engendered, the overall motivation of the generative enterprise and the state of Chomskyan thinking at that point in time (with minimalism truly being programmatic). The editors provide a helpful introduction and notes.

Movement and Silence is a collection of twelve of Richard Kayne's papers written (and previously published) in the 2000s. The two major themes of the collection are that comparative work sheds abundant light on syntactic structure and that this light often reveals the presence of antisymmetric effects. Numerous cases of movement (all leftward, and often of the remnant type) and empty categories (nominal and adjectival) are explored from this perspective. The empirical data from English that are addressed include focus *too*-constructions, the words *here* and *there* (analysed as demonstrative elements, associated with an empty PLACE noun, also in combinations like *thereof*), causatives such as *He made Paul do the work* (argued to have a causee introduced by a silent preposition), antecedent–pronoun relations as in *John thinks he's smart* (derived through movement of *John* from the DP [*John he*]), eliminating the need for binding condition C), the quantified expressions like *lots of money* (argued to involve movement of *lots* to the specifier of *of*), other quantifiers (which can come in unpronounced guise too), sentences like *He was seven* and *It is seven* (which have silent YEAR and HOUR), the puzzling *?the people who John think should be invited* (analysed as having a silent auxiliary in front of *think*) and heavy NP shift (derived, antisymmetrically, through merging the determiner at the VP level).

Two other big names in syntax, Peter Culicover and Ray Jackendoff, have written *Simpler Syntax*, which in many ways is the complete antithesis of Kayne's approach. Their model is constraint-based rather than derivational. It features multiple branching and hence quite flat phrase structures, no projections of functional categories, no movement and only minimal use of Kaynian silences, i.e. non-overt elements. After setting out the details of the model (which has several similarities with Head-Driven Phrase Structure Grammar and Lexical-Functional Grammar), the authors apply and refine it in analyses of phenomena including non-sentential utterances, sluicing, gapping, VP ellipsis, wh-constructions, aspects of binding theory and control and 'subordinating' *and* (as in *One more word and I am leaving*). The history of the generative enterprise is also briefly reviewed (in terms of principles and mechanisms proposed and accepted, with an emphasis on the resulting complexity of the complete edifice). The final chapter provides some reflections on future directions, as well as a syntactic-semantic analysis of the word *interesting*, as found in the alleged minimalist reaction to Simpler Syntactic ideas: 'If this approach is right, then syntax isn't very interesting' (p. 540).

The minimalist program itself is explained in two books. Cedric Boeckx does so in the lucid *Linguistic Minimalism: Origins, Concepts, Methods, and Aims*. This is not for devotees of technicalities but for those interested in the place of minimalist thinking within the larger philosophical-scientific enterprise. It sketches the roots of minimalism in early Chomskyan thought, the principles currently guiding its development, the implications of the program and several examples of minimalism in action (engaging with phenomena like control, multiple wh-fronting, successive cyclicity, sluicing and parasitic gaps). Much further technical detail can be found in Željko

Boškovic and Howard Lasnik, eds., *Minimalist Syntax: The Essential Readings*. This is meant as a textbook for a graduate syntax class (indeed, the material was so used by the two authors). It contains excerpts, ranging from a single paragraph to more than twenty pages, of works from the 1990s and 2000s that have helped shape the minimalist program. After an introduction by the editors highlighting the main features of minimalism, there are sections on the basic design of language (levels of representation and interfaces), on the push to eliminate the notion of government (with repercussions for the understanding of case, PRO and locality), on minimalist structure-building (using bare phrase structure, merge-over-move and the cycle), verbal morphology, antisymmetry and c-command, copy theory, existentials and the syntax–semantics interface. The authors whose work is excerpted include Noam Chomsky, the two editors, Samuel Epstein, Norbert Hornstein, Chris Collins, Norvin Richards, Cedric Boeckx, Richard Kayne and Danny Fox. None of these, of course, is known to shun complications, and the result of packing them all together like this is indeed a very dense book, understanding of which will only be possible with expert assistance from a teacher.

Gisbert Fanselow, Caroline Féry, Ralf Vogel and Matthias Schlesewsky have edited the volume *Gradience in Grammar: Generative Perspectives*. In their introduction (pp. 1–21) the editors provide a sketch of what gradience involves (basically, the existence of non-discrete effects in language) and then discuss the ways this is visible in the formal properties of linguistic elements, phonology as well as syntax. The following chapters deal in further depth with the nature of gradience, its role in phonology and syntax and the specific case of gradience in wh-constructions. In the syntactic contributions, it is mainly graded judgements that are addressed. Eric Reuland's 'Gradedness: Interpretive Dependencies and Beyond' (pp. 45–69) argues, using facts of binding and coreference from English and Dutch, that gradedness in sentence judgements does not mean that any drastic changes to the generative model are needed: some gradedness comes from outside the linguistic system and some may simply follow from the number of violations that a particular sentence incurs in various parts of the derivation. Leonie Cornips considers 'Intermediate Syntactic Variants in a Dialect: Standard Speech Repertoire and Relative Acceptability' (pp. 85–105) and describes the way intermediate speakers may show gradience in judging sentences due to uncertainty about their own dialect. Antonella Sorace, in 'Gradedness and Optionality in Mature and Developing Grammars' (pp. 106–23), argues that gradedness can come either from optionality or from structures operating at the interface of syntax and discourse, where more complex computation is required than for non-interface structures. John Hawkins, not entirely surprisingly, interprets 'Gradience as Relative Efficiency in the Processing of Syntax and Semantics' (pp. 207–26); drawing on facts of word order inside the VP in English and Japanese, he suggests that selection preferences in this area are due to the principle of Minimize Domains, which basically promotes quick processing. Frank Keller does things differently in 'Linear Optimality Theory as a Model of Gradience in Grammar' (pp. 270–87), attributing graded acceptability judgements directly to properties of the grammar, specifically to differences in numerical weight

among constraints in Optimality Theory. Ralf Vogel's 'Degraded Acceptability
and Markedness in Syntax, and the Stochastic Interpretation of Optimality
Theory' (pp. 246–69) argues that graded judgements are due to grammatical
factors (the interaction of various principles and mechanisms, to be precise)
but that no numerical information needs to be imported into the grammar. In
'What's What' (pp. 317–35), Nomi Erteschik-Shir addresses the difference
between *What did John say that he'd seen t* vs. **What did John lisp that he'd seen
t*. She attributes it to a difference in focusing: if the matrix verb is focused
(likely in the case of *lisp* but less so for *say*), the subordinate clause is not
focused; extraction from a non-focused constituent is impossible. Other
gradience effects come from processing difficulty. Finally, in 'Prosodic
Influence on Syntactic Judgements' (pp. 336–58), Yoshihisa Kitagawa and
Janet Dean Fodor present some intriguing findings from a grammaticality
judgement experiment comparing written and spoken stimuli. It turned out
that grammatical sentences requiring a non-default prosody were more often
rejected when read than when heard. The authors propose that in reading too,
a prosody is mentally constructed for sentences—failure to construct the
appropriate non-default prosody results in erroneous rejection of the sentence.

In her article 'The Syntax of English Comitative Constructions'
(*FoL* 41[2007] 135–69), Niina Ning Zhang shows that the syntactic structure
of English comitative constructions (e.g. *John is friends with Bill*) can best be
analysed as a complex DP containing the two DPs (in base-generated position)
and is headed by *with* (carrying the features [D, Plural, Case assigning]):
[[$_{DP1}$ *John*] *with* [$_{DP2}$ *Bill*]]. She further shows that two types of comitative
constructions, symmetrical and asymmetrical, can be distinguished and
proposes a syntactic analysis of these two types.

More theoretical insights about DPs are offered by Arthur Stepanov,
'Morphological Case and the Inverse Case Filter' (*LingB* 211[2007] 255–76),
who argues in favour of eliminating the Inverse Case Filter ('Every potential
Case licensor must license Case on some DP', p. 263) from the syntax and
considering it as part of the morphological component ('Every morphological
case licensor must license case on some DP, at the level of Morphology
(between syntax and PF)', p. 264).

John Payne, Rodney Huddleston and Geoffrey K. Pullum, 'Fusion of
Functions: The Syntax of *Once, Twice* and *Thrice*' (*JL* 43[2007] 565–603),
propose a new analysis of the English expressions *once, twice* and *thrice*, in
which they are treated as NPs consisting of 'a determinative base (numerical
on·, twi·, thri·) and a noun base *·ce* (meaning 'time')' (p. 588), which are fused
through 'fusion of functions' (FF), as proposed in the Cambridge Grammar
of the English Language (CGEL) framework.

Various types of nonsententials come under scrutiny in Catherine Fortin's
article 'Some (Not All) Nonsententials are Only a Phase' (*Lingua* 117[2007]
67–94), in which she proposes a minimalist analysis in which nonsententials
are phases. Ana Carrera Hernández 'Gapping as a Syntactic Dependency'
(*Lingua* 117[2007] 2106–33) proposes an analysis of gapping in which it is a
syntactic dependency 'between the projection of a null [+V,-N] head and
its antecedent' (p. 2130). The syntactic operation of rightward movement
is the topic of Joseph Sabbagh's article 'Ordering and Linearizing

Rightward Movement' (*NL&LT* 25[2007] 349–401). Sabbagh argues that rightward movement in general is a case of unbounded movement and that apparent bounded instances can be explained by assuming that rightward movement is constrained with respect to ordering and linearization.

We now turn to studies dealing with specific syntactic elements, first of all the NP. Possessive NPs remain the topic of much linguistic debate. Lars Hinrichs and Benedikt Szmrecsanyi, 'Recent Changes in the Function and Frequency of Standard English Genitive Constructions: A Multivariate Analysis of Tagged Corpora' (*ELL* 11[2007] 437–74), add to this debate by investigating 'the ongoing shift away from the *of-* and toward the *s*-genitive' (p. 440) on the basis of a multivariate analysis of data from the Brown, Frown, LOB and FLOB corpora. Also writing on possessive NPs, Anette Rosenbach, 'Emerging Variation: Determiner Genitives and Noun Modifiers in English' (*ELL* 11[2007] 143–89), argues that a semantic shift in ModE created contexts compatible with both determiner genitives and noun modifiers, explaining why variation between these two arose. Another article focusing on possessive NPs is Peter Willemse's 'Indefinite Possessive NPs and the Distinction between Determining and Nondetermining Genitives in English' (*ELL* 11[2007] 537–68). This article presents a descriptive account of English indefinite possessive NPs (e.g. *a friend's house*), arguing that determining genitives can be clearly distinguished from nondetermining (classifying) genitives.

Several articles were published that deal with other elements inside the NP. The already highly grammaticalized expressions *kind/sort/type of* are investigated by Liesbeth De Smedt, Lieselotte Brems and Kristin Davidse in 'NP-Internal Functions and Extended Use of the "Type" Nouns *Kind, Sort* and *Type*: Towards a Comprehensive, Corpus-Based Description' (in Facchinetti, ed., pp. 225–55). After surveying earlier work, they provide a classification of the many uses of these words (ranging from head use, as in *five types of animals*, to semi-suffix use, as in *an iMac sorta phone* and even quotative, as in *these little kids kinda 'Señorita Flynn?'*) and then present corpus data showing that NP-related uses predominate in newspaper language while adverbial and discourse marker uses are most frequent in teenage speech. Lieselotte Brems, 'The Grammaticalization of Small Size Nouns: Reconsidering Frequency and Analogy' (*JEngL* 35[2007] 293–324), argues that the grammaticalization of infrequent small size nouns, such as *a jot of*, is brought about not just by analogy with frequent counterparts such as *a bit of*, but rather by analogy with various quantifier expressions, which serve as distant models. More quantifiers are found in Richard S. Kayne's '*Several, Few* and *Many*' (*Lingua* 117[2007] 832–58), which argues that these words should be analysed as modifiers of the unpronounced counterpart of the noun *number* (NUMBER). Floating quantifiers are the topic of Mana Kobuchi-Philip's article 'Floating Numerals and Floating Quantifiers' (*Lingua* 117[2007] 814–31). She proposes an analysis in which quantification in the case of floating quantifiers takes place in the verbal domain, whereas quantification in the case of non-floating quantifiers takes place in the nominal domain.

Subject-verb inversion after sentence-initial *thus* is studied by Solveig Granath in 'Size Matters—or *Thus can meaningful structures be revealed in large corpora*' (in Facchinetti, ed., pp. 169–85). Using a 250 million-word PDE corpus, the author demonstrates that the choice of (non-)inversion depends on the precise semantics of *thus* in the sentence in question. A wider variety of inversion-inducing elements is included in Rolf Kreyer's 'Inversion in Modern Written English: Syntactic Complexity, Information Status and the Creative Writer' (in Facchinetti, ed., pp. 187–203). He finds—not unexpectedly—that the first element is usually discourse-old and short while the subject is discourse-new and heavy. But he finds further effects: inversion, he argues, is also a device for writers to creatively achieve 'observer effects' and iconically mirror the order of natural processes.

Verbs and their forms continue to receive a great deal of attention. Christoph Rühlemann's article, 'Lexical Grammar: The GET-Passive as a Case in Point' (*ICAME* 31[2007] 111–28), presents the results of a study on various characteristics of the GET-passive, using the BNC, and proposes that the GET-passive should not be regarded simply as a grammatical structure, but as a construction on the grammar-lexis cline. Another study of passive verbs is Nicholas Smith and Paul Rayson's 'Recent Change and Variation in the British English Use of the Progressive Passive' (*ICAME* 31[2007] 129–60), in which they investigate the recent development of the progressive passive (e.g. *the TV is being repaired*), which is shown to continue to expand in BrE. The progressive in general is the topic of Seung-Ah Lee's article '*Ing* Forms and the Progressive Puzzle: A Construction-Based Approach to English Progressives' (*JL* 43[2007] 153–95), in which Lee argues that progressivity is a constructional property rather than a lexical property. Colette Moore, 'The Spread of Grammaticalized Forms: The Case of *Be + Supposed to*' (*JEngL* 35[2007] 117–31), investigates the diffusion of the grammaticalized semi-modal *be supposed to* on the basis of corpus data, concluding that frequency and genre can create pragmatic conditions that help spread the construction.

The volume *Imperative Clauses in Generative Grammar: Studies in Honour of Frits Beukema*, edited by Wim van der Wurff, contains ten articles, each of which examines aspects of the structure of imperative clauses from a generative perspective. Most articles explore imperative clauses in languages other than English: Dutch, German (Old) Scandinavian, Spanish and South Slavic. Two articles focus specifically on English imperative clauses. Eric Potsdam's 'Analysing Word Order in the English Imperative' (pp. 251–72) looks at the structure of inverted English imperatives such as '*Don't you leave!*' (p. 251) and proposes an analysis in which the subject in these inverted imperatives occupies SpecIP and the auxiliary occupies the C position, after head-movement from the I position. Inverted interrogatives are thus treated on a par with polar interrogatives such as *Did Mary leave?*, which is supported by the identical scope facts of the two sentence types. The analysis proposed by Potsdam explicitly argues against an analysis of inverted imperatives in which the subject occupies a position lower than SpecIP and in which the auxiliary stays put in the I position. This type of analysis is defended by Laura Rupp, in her article ' "Inverted" Imperatives' (pp. 297–323). Rupp argues that the subject in English inverted imperatives occupies SpecFP (having moved there from SpecVP), FP being a functional projection between V and I. Rupp shows that Potsdam's CP analysis makes the wrong predictions regarding scope ambiguity, and disagrees with Potsdam that the CP analysis is more advantageous than the SpecFP analysis when it comes to the similarities in scope between inverted imperatives and polar interrogatives. In non-inverted imperatives such as '*Everybody DO give it a try!*' (p. 314), Rupp assumes the subject has moved from SpecFP (originating in SpecVP) to SpecIP, supporting this with the observation that 'flexibility in the distribution of subjects would appear to be a more general feature of imperatives across Germanic languages' (p. 314).

On the topic of tense, there is Tim Stowell's 'The Syntactic Expression of Tense' (*Lingua* 117[2007] 437–63), which appeared in a special issue 'Approaches to Tense and Tense Construal' (*Lingua* 117:iii[2007]). Stowell shows that general principles of syntactic theory can capture many aspects of the syntax and semantics of tense, if the semantic features of tense are syntactically decomposed. Taking a descriptive angle, Ylva Berglund and Christopher Williams report on 'The Semantic Properties of *Going To*: Distribution Patterns in Four Subcorpora of the British National Corpus' (in Facchinetti, ed., pp. 107–20). They find several patterns in the use of this future marker, with respect to form (*going to, gonna*), meaning (intention, prediction), type of following lexical verb, subject person/number and text type. Further description of tense and aspect usage is found in Marianne Hundt and Carolin Biewer's 'The Dynamics of Inner and Outer Circle Varieties in the South Pacific and East Asia' (in Hundt, Nesselhauf and Biewer, eds., pp. 249–69). They compare the use of the past tense and the perfect in BrE, AmE, AusE, NZE, SingE, Fiji and Philippine English online newspapers with the aim of identifying possible shifts in influence of inner on outer circle varieties. The results are not conclusive—the complexity of the conditioning factors makes comparison difficult.

There is a collection of papers on *Finiteness: Theoretical and Empirical Foundations*, edited by Irina Nikolaeva. After an introduction by the editor (pp. 1–19) sketching the problems for the simple idea that finiteness inheres in verbs, the chapters are arranged in four sections. The first is on formal theories, and has David Adger exploring 'Three Domains of Finiteness: A Minimalist Perspective' (pp. 23–58), in which the properties of the functional head Fin are investigated; and Peter Sells considering 'Finiteness in Non-Transformational Syntactic Frameworks' (pp. 59–88), specifically Head-Driven Phrase Structure Grammar and Lexical-Functional Grammar, where a distinction is proposed between finiteness as a property of clauses and its morphological expression in a word, with the two normally but not always going together. The second section is on functional and typological theories, with Sonia Cristofaro's 'Deconstructing Categories: Finiteness in a Functional-Typological Perspective' (pp. 91–114), which looks at the cross-linguistic correlations between TMA-agreement marked verbs and phenomena such as nominal marking of verbs, the presence of overt complements and the marking of subjects as possessors; Walter Bisang on 'Categories that Make Finiteness: Discreteness from a Functional Perspective and Some of its Repercussions' (pp. 115–37), proposing that finiteness resides in categories obligatorily expressed in main clauses but not subordinate clauses; and the editor studying 'Constructional Economy and Nonfinite Independent Clauses' (pp. 138–80), focusing on the way certain independent clauses—such as the imperative—show reduced finiteness, in ways explored in detail. The third section is on individual languages (Nakh-Daghestanian, Russian and Turkish), and the fourth section deals with diachrony and acquisition, with Adam Ledgeway looking at 'Diachrony and Finiteness' in Italian dialects (pp. 335–65); Nicholas Evans at 'Insubordination and its Uses' (pp. 366–431), providing data on the cross-linguistic properties of subordinate clauses used as main clauses; and Petra Gretsch and Clive Perdue focusing on 'Finiteness in First and Second Language Acquisition' (pp. 424–84).

Marianne Hundt's *English Mediopassive Constructions: A Cognitive, Corpus-Based Study of their Origin, Spread, and Current Status* is a detailed study of sentences of the type *The two ends anchor securely into the ground*, aka middles. It has chapters on the basic properties of the mediopassive, the earlier literature on them (generative and cognitive), its proper theoretical analysis (with Hundt favouring a prototype perspective, incorporating Randolph Quirk's idea of serial relationship), their usage and frequency in PDE and their historical development. Among the conclusions is the finding that, in spite of claims in the literature, mediopassives occur often without an adverbial, that they are largely restricted to the simple present and past tense and that they are especially common in advertising language. With respect to their history, Hundt is able to show that it is not likely they developed from passivals (as in *Coffee is serving*) or from reflexive constructions. It appears more likely that they developed from ergatives, i.e. clauses like *the door opened/closed*, which became more common in the EModE period. She relates both changes to a typological change that affected English around this time, whereby subjects came to have a wider range of semantic roles than just the agentive one predominant in early English.

Verb complementation can always count on receiving a good deal of attention. Kate Kearns, 'Epistemic Verbs and Zero Complementizer' (*ELL* 11[2007] 475–505), argues that a zero complementizer following epistemic verbs such as *think* correlates with a shift in informational prominence, the subordinate clause becoming more prominent than the main clause. In 'Native and Nonnative Use of Multi-Word vs. One-Word Verbs' (*IRAL* 45[2007] 119–39), Anna Siyanova and Norbert Schmitt discuss the results of a questionnaire-directed study on the use of multi-word versus one-word verbs by natives and advanced non-natives, which showed that advanced learners of English are less inclined to use multi-word verbs than native speakers of English. Hiromi Onozuka, 'Remarks on Causative Verbs and Object Deletion in English' (*LangS* 29[2007] 538–53), argues that object deletion is not a good diagnostic tool for distinguishing causative verbs from non-causative verbs. Alan Clinton Bale, 'Quantifiers and Verb Phrases: An Exploration of Propositional Complexity' (*NL&LT* 25[2007] 447–83), draws conclusions about the semantic interpretation of non-stative, transitive verbs, on the one hand, and intransitive and stative, transitive verbs on the other hand on the basis of facts about syntactic complexity involving the adverb *again*. Focusing on the complements of the verb *try*, Charlotte Hommerberg and Gunnel Tottie, '*Try to or Try and?* Verb Complementation in British and American English' (*ICAME* 31[2007] 45–64), report on differences between *try*-complementation in BrE and AmE, raising questions regarding usage and why it diverged. Looking at complement-taking verbs in general, Kasper Boye and Peter Harder, 'Complement-Taking Predicates: Usage and Linguistic Structure' (*SLang* 31[2007] 569–606), explore the structure and usage of complement-taking predicates, showing how these two aspects can be integrated in a functional linguistic approach. Contrastive differences in complementation form the topic of 'Transitive Verb Plus Reflexive Pronoun/ Personal Pronoun Patterns in English and Japanese: Using a Japanese-English Parallel Corpus' by Makoto Shimizu and Masaki Murata (in Facchinetti, ed., pp. 333–46). Their data show up all kinds of differences between the two languages; a general point that emerges is that the choice between, say, *he blamed himself* and *he blamed them* should not be considered as being based on independent selection of each individual word—rather, it is necessary to recognize the existence of phrases as independent units of meaning.

Turning now to adjuncts and that ilk, we begin with Dagmar Haumann's *Adverb Licensing and Clause Structure in English*. This extensive monograph presents an in-depth study of a range of English adverbs focusing on the relation between their distribution and their interpretation in terms of clause structure. Chapter 1 provides the necessary background to studying the syntax and semantics of adverbs. Chapter 2 contributes to the debate of whether syntax determines semantics or vice versa by discussing the (functional) specifier analysis and the opposing adjunction-based semantic scope analysis. Haumann concludes that the empirical arguments against the specifier analysis are not compelling and adopts this analysis throughout the rest of the book. Chapter 3 takes a closer look at the structural position of adverbs within the lexical VP (e.g. manner adverbs such as *carefully*). Haumann assumes a split VP structure, containing several agreement projections as well as a VP and various other functional projections. In this domain, adverbs are merged in the specifier of a functional projection part of the split VP and are licensed in a specifier–head relation with a functional head. Chapter 4 provides a specifier analysis of English adverbs within the inflectional layer (e.g. subject-related adverbs such as *cleverly*). Adverbs occurring within the inflectional domain are assumed to occupy the specifier of a designated functional projection and are licensed in a specifier–head relation with the functional head. Chapter 5 considers adverbs that occur within the complementizer domain (including speaker-oriented adverbs such as *honestly*). In Haumann's analysis, such adverbs are not raised to designated functional projections within the complementizer domain, but are merged as specifiers of these projections. Chapter 6 provides an overall conclusion to the book, summarizing the most important aspects of the analysis, which contains a very elaborate inventory of functional projections.

A study of the adverb *absolutely* can be found in Hongyin Tao's 'A Corpus-Based Investigation of *Absolutely* and Related Phenomena in Spoken American English' (*JEngL* 35[2007] 5–29). Tao examines the discourse properties of the free-standing adverb *absolutely* (i.e. modifier without a head) in spoken AmE, treating it as an instance of grammar emerging out of discourse (Emergent Grammar). Geoffrey Pullum and Kyle Rawlins, 'Argument or No Argument?' (*Ling&P* 30[2007] 277–87), argue that *X or no X* adjuncts in English (where X is a nominal) do not provide any convincing arguments for the (non-)context-freeness of English.

Michael Stubbs, in 'An Example of Frequent English Phraseology: Distributions, Structures and Functions' (in Fachinetti, ed., pp. 89–105), investigates PPs of the type *at the end of the* and *as a result of the*, which are among the most frequent five-word frames in English. Using a BNC-based phraseology database, he explores their semantics and pragmatics and discusses the processes of grammaticalization which, due to their high frequency, they are prone to. Gossé Bouma, Petra Hendriks and Jack Hoeksema, 'Focus Particles Inside Prepositional Phrases: A Comparison of Dutch, English, and German' (*JCGL* 10[2007] 1–24), present the results of a corpus investigation into the possibility of focus particles (e.g. *only, even*) occurring inside PPs in Dutch, English and German, showing that, although this is most readily allowed in English, it is also an option in Dutch and German. David Minugh has studied 'The Filling in the Sandwich: Internal Modifications of Idioms (in Facchinetti, ed., pp. 205–24), looking at the frequency and types of idiom modifiers aimed at anchoring the idiom in surrounding discourse, as in 'They sought to restore some political coals to Newcastle'. Contrary to what earlier commentators had suggested, this usage is found to be fairly rare in actual texts, at around 3 per cent of all idioms examined.

Sentential complements of verbs are the topic of Peter Öhl's article 'Unselected Embedded Interrogatives in German and English: S-Selection as Dependency Formation' (*LingB* 212[2007] 403–38). Öhl discusses the selectional properties involved in German and English Unselected Embedded Questions (UEQs) and proposes an analysis in which the licensing of UEQs is explained through the presence of a polarity sensitive head π on factive epistemic predicates. Juhani Rudanko's article 'Text Type and Current Grammatical Change in British and American English: A Case Study with Evidence from the Bank of English Corpus' (*ES* 88[2007] 465–83) explores changes in the sentential complements (notably *to*-infinitive and *to ing*-complements) of the adjective *accustomed* in eighteenth-, nineteenth-, and early twentieth-century BE as well as in current BrE and AmE.

The well-known optionality between an overt and covert relativizer in English relative clauses is analysed by Barbara A. Fox and Sandra A. Thompson in 'Relative Clauses in English Conversation: Relativizers, Frequency, and the Notion of Construction' (*SLang* 31[2007] 293–326). They show that the choice between overt relativizer and Ø-relativizer in English relative clauses is regulated by a set of pragmatic-prosodic factors. Focusing on non-restrictive relative clauses, Doug Arnold's article 'Non-Restrictive Relative Clauses are not Orphans' (*JL* 43[2007] 271–309) counters the 'radical orphanage' approach to non-restrictive relative clauses (in which they are outside the syntactic representation of the clause that contains them) with a 'syntactically integrated' approach. In this approach, non-restrictive relative clauses are syntactically like restrictive relative clauses, but differ from these semantically and pragmatically.

Exceptions to the well-known claim that adjuncts are islands for extraction are discussed in Robert Truswell, 'Extraction from Adjuncts and the Structure of Events' (*Lingua* 117[2007] 1355–77). Truswell provides a semantically based analysis of extraction from adjunct secondary predicates, showing that this is permitted 'if the event denoted by the secondary predicate is identified with an event position in the matrix predicate' (p. 1359). Liliane Haegeman, 'Operator Movement and Topicalisation in Adverbial Clauses' (*FoL* 41[2007] 279–325), looks at the impossibility of argument fronting in English adverbial clauses. This is explained through the adoption of a generative syntactic analysis in which adverbial clauses are derived by movement of an operator to their left periphery, which results in intervention effects in English, but not in Romance languages, which allow Clitic Left Dislocation patterns.

Robert Fiengo has been *Asking Questions: Using Meaningful Structures to Imply Ignorance*. As he points out, there is a large literature on the syntax of questions and a reasonable amount of work on the questioning speech-act. What Fiengo does in this book is argue that the pragmatics of questions is more varied than has so far been realized (with questions needing to be viewed in relation to assertions) and that the analysis of this pragmatics needs to be carried out in conjunction with (but separately from) analysis of question syntax. Fiengo interprets questions as expressing a lack and discusses in detail the factors that will lead people with a lack to choose a particular question type. He then uses the results to reflect on the nature of speech acts, drawing on Austin's categorization of assertive speech-acts and suggesting that they are all matched by questioning speech-acts.

(b) Early Syntax

We start with an important general work, *Diachronic Syntax* by Ian Roberts. This is a generous textbook, with its 500 pages taking the reader on an extended tour leading from the basics of historical syntax to a wide variety of topics in current research. Many examples from a range of different languages are given, there are plenty of tree structures and other diagrams, detailed guides to further reading and a glossary of technical terms. The theoretical approach taken is 'an informal version of minimalism' (p. 7), but good use is also made of tools and concepts of the pre-minimalist era which have so far not received a minimalist reworking. The five chapters cover the topics of historical syntax in the principles-and-parameters model (presenting the well-known parameters associated with null subjects, V-to-I/V-to-T, negative concord, overt vs. covert wh-movement, and head-complement order, and showing how these can change historically), types of syntactic change (such as re-analysis, grammaticalization, changes in argument structure), the relation between acquisition and change (with a strong case made for a role being played in change by factors of markedness), the diffusion of syntactic change (including the topics of optionality, the constant rate effect, grammar competition, drift, cascading parameter changes and syntactic reconstruction) and a final chapter on language contact and the changes this can trigger (as evidenced in the phenomena of borrowing, substrata and creoles). Although the book clearly demands diligence and application from the student and ample guidance from the teacher, phenomena and interpretations are set out with maximum clarity and we think this will be a successful course text at advanced undergraduate or postgraduate level.

After it, students would do well to read another important general work published this year, Olga Fischer's *Morphosyntactic Change: Functional and Formal Perspectives*. This offers ample discussion of the following question: in explaining change, should we focus on formal aspects (as Roberts and others do) or is it best addressed through study of functional factors (as is done in many grammaticalization studies and in functionally inspired historical work)? Adherents of the two perspectives usually take their own approach to be self-evidently superior, but Fischer makes a strong case for the need to combine the two, not only in principle but also in concrete practice. In making this case, she provides an illuminating review of representative work from the two sides, carefully distinguishing what is helpful from what is not, and showing how a combined approach makes greatest sense of the data. Among the changes analysed in detail—mostly from English—are the developments in the English modal auxiliaries, various instances of alleged clause union (shown to be rather doubtful in most cases) and changes leading to subjectification (a type of change different from grammaticalization). Fischer's own model of change accords a crucial place to the concept of analogy, not only as a source of new forms and functions but also as an important mechanism of language acquisition.

There are two textbooks on the history of English to report this year, continuing on from the four that we reviewed last year (see *YWES* 87[2008] 62–4). Laurel J. Brinton and Leslie K. Arnovick's *The English Language: A Linguistic History* provides twelve substantial chapters covering general issues, the sound and writing systems, language change, the IE and Germanic background and then two chapters apiece for OE, ME and EModE, with a concluding chapter on ModE (where the focus is on North America). The text is highly accessible throughout and includes numerous clearly presented and explained tables, examples, in-text exercises (with a Key at the back) and weblinks. A good amount of linguistic detail is covered and, where appropriate, attention is also paid to the social background. A third edition has appeared of Dennis Freeborn's *From Old English to Standard English: A Course Book in Language Variation across Time*. Like the earlier editions, this work is quite philological in orientation, with detailed attention being paid to matters of spelling and palaeography, contemporary evidence for changes, historical dialect differences and manuscript comparison (the book abounds with facsimiles). This of course means that students require hands-on supervision from a tutor. If this is provided, they will end up with a vast amount of knowledge of the philology of English. The chapters are arranged in chronological order, with a preponderance towards the earlier periods, and there is a companion website which contains recordings of historical texts from the book, a Word Book and Text Commentary Book.

An introduction to OE for students with no prior linguistic knowledge is given in Carole Hough and John Corbett's *Beginning Old English*. The authors have managed to keep a clear distance from the traditional approach, with its focus on decontextualized forms and paradigms. Instead, they discuss the ways in which OE is still alive today (in translations of its literature, in the *Lord of the Rings* and of course in the modern language), give detailed and concrete advice about how to learn OE words, present paradigms (not too many) in the context of discussions about how language is used to express particular meanings, and introduce points of grammar through initial short OE texts, preceded by some explanation of the context, a few comprehension questions and a number of vocabulary items. The book starts with a chapter on the history and literature of the period and has a separate chapter on translations of *Beowulf*. The last hundred pages are taken up by four OE texts (*Cynewulf and Cyneheard*, the *Battle of Maldon*, the *Dream of the Rood* and a passage from *Beowulf*), each divided up into smaller chunks with comprehension questions, vocabulary and comment. As this brief summary makes clear, OE is here presented as a language used for communication, and we think this will be a successful textbook for undergraduate modules.

Adrian Beard has written *Language Change*, published in Routledge's Intertext series. Meant for British A-level students, it presents materials showing change in (mostly) twentieth-century and contemporary English. There are abundant (short) authentic texts, many of them part of exercises. Some technical terminology is introduced and there is a strong emphasis on the role of discourse factors (in the widest sense of the word) in promoting or constraining change—this includes matters relating to visual representation, from pictorial to orthographic.

At a more scholarly level, Christian Mair and Geoffrey Leech investigate 'Current Changes in English Syntax' (in Aarts and McMahon, eds., pp. 318–42). After reviewing the few earlier studies of twentieth-century syntactic change, they discuss several cases, including the increasing prominence of the progressive and of non-finite verbal forms, the decline of some of the modals (*may, must, shall, ought to*), the lesser frequency of the *be*-passive and wh-relatives and the growth of premodified NPs. Data come from the Brown/Frown and LOB/FLOB corpora. The next step is of course to go online, and that is what Christian Mair has done in 'Change and Variation in Present-Day English: Integrating the Analysis of Closed Corpora and Web-Based Monitoring' (in Hundt, Nesselhauf and Biewer, eds., pp. 233–47). Looking at quite simple Google data for *different from/than/to*, the passive progressive and *save* NP (*from*) V-*ing*, he finds that they show the kind of patterning that is expected on the basis of work on traditional corpora and that—interpreted with due caution—they are valid sources of insight and hypotheses.

Various elements inside NPs have received historical attention. Yumi Yokota, 'Disambiguation of Definite Article *þo* and Demonstrative *þo* in Middle English Texts from the West Riding of Yorkshire' (*N&Q* 54[2007] 236–9), shows that the definite article *þo* 'the' and demonstrative *þo* 'those' in texts from the West Riding of Yorkshire were functionally disambiguated. Florian Haas, 'The Development of English *Each Other*: Grammaticalization, Lexicalization, or Both?' (*ELL* 11[2007] 31–50), shows on the basis of a corpus study that the historical development of the English reciprocal marker *each other* involved both grammaticalization (in the form of syntactic context expansion) and lexicalization (in the form of univerbation and fossilization). Elizabeth Closs Traugott's 'The Concepts of Constructional Mismatch and Type-Shifting from the Perspective of Grammaticalization' (*CogLing* 18[2007] 523–57) addresses the possible factors in the diachronic development of partitive constructions into degree modifier constructions from the point of view of grammaticalization.

Nadja Nesselhauf has studied the development of the future time markers *will*, *shall* and *'ll* in nineteenth-century English and reports the results in 'Diachronic Analysis with the Internet? *Will* and *Shall* in ARCHER and in a Corpus of E-Texts from the Web' (in Hundt, Nesselhauf and Biewer, eds., pp. 287–305). The two corpora show rather different frequency patterns, which Nesselhauf attributes to their non-comparability in terms of text types and also to the influence of individual preference and style. The same author's article, 'The Spread of the Progressive and its "Future" Use' (*ELL* 11[2007] 191–207), shows that the spread of the progressive with future time reference (e.g. *He's leaving for London tomorrow*) has contributed to the general spread of the progressive construction, although the factors involved in the increase of the 'future' progressive do not always coincide with the factors involved in the general increase of the progressive construction. Michiko Ogura, 'Old English *Agan to* Reconsidered' (*N&Q* 54[2007] 216–18), shows that the modal auxiliary *ought to* became established as a result of semantic expansion (possession to obligation) combined with a syntactic reanalysis (*again* + *to*-infinitive to *agan to* + infinitive) in the OE period.

Prepositional complement constructions are the focus of Günter Rohdenburg's article 'Functional Constraints in Syntactic Change: The Rise and Fall of Prepositional Constructions in Early and Late Modern English' (*ES* 88[2007] 217–33). Rohdenburg explores the implications of the *horror aequi* principle and of the Complexity Principle for syntactic change in these constructions. Meiko Matsumoto, 'The Verbs *Have* and *Take* in Composite Predicates and Phrasal Verbs' (*SN* 79[2007] 159–70), looks at the development of the state versus event contrast in composite predicates and phrasal verbs with the verbs *have* and *take*.

Focusing on the position of adverbs is Eric Haeberli and Richard Ingham's 'The Position of Negation and Adverbs in Early Middle English' (*Lingua* 117[2007] 1–25). Haeberli and Ingham identify similarities and differences in the distribution of the negator *not* and adverbs in early ME, arguing that *not* already occupies SpecNegP in early ME. John R. Rickford, Thomas Wasow, Arnold Zwicky and Isabelle Buchstaller contribute 'Intensive and Quotative ALL: Something Old, Something New' (*AS* 82[2007] 3–31). They trace the history of both uses in detail, comparing them with competing variants and showing that intensifying *all* is old, but has recently gained in strength and scope, while quotative *all* arose in the early 1980s in California teenage speech, then gained in popularity but is now receding fast. Their detailed analysis shows that these two areas of lexico-grammar have been subject to considerable amounts of flux and variation over time (involving both the inventory of items and their constraints); see also section 9.

Next, we turn to studies on clauses (and the elements that connect them) in Early English. Ursula Lenker and Anneli Meurman-Solin have edited

Connectives in the History of English, which presents a collection of papers on various aspects of some individual clausal connectives in the history of English, based on corpus investigations. The introduction by the editors (pp. 1–10) is followed by María José López-Couso's article on the history of *lest* (pp. 11–29). The author shows that adverbial connectives can belong to more than one category. In her article on infinitival *to* (pp. 31–60), Bettelou Los argues that the *to*-infinitive represents a sententialized *to*-PP already in OE. Matti Rissanen's article (pp. 61–75) provides an account of the history of *op* and its replacement by *till*. Laurel Brinton (pp. 77–96) discusses the relatively recent rise of the conjunctive use of {*any, each, every*} *time*, suggesting that this use is the result of a grammaticalization process. Rafał Molencki (pp. 97–113) examines the evolution of *since* in ME, arguing that it involves grammaticalization. The same is argued for by Elina Sorva in her article on the history of the concessive connective *albeit* (pp. 115–143), in which she also shows that it was syntactically polyfunctional. Ana I. González-Cruz studies the semasiological development of *while*-constructions (pp. 145–166), showing that subjectification as well as positional specialization is involved. Carsten Breul (pp. 167–192) argues that the semantic development of clausal connectives involves an increase in relevance, which comprises (but does not reduce to) informativeness. Ursula Lenker's article (pp. 193–227) explores the historical development of causal connectives in English. Claudia Claridge presents (pp. 229–254) the results of a corpus study on the functions of conditional *if*-clauses in the history of English. Anneli Meurman-Solin (pp. 255–287) presents the findings of a corpus study of original manuscripts, i.e. without editorial modernization of sentence structure, on relatives used as sentential connectives. The final article in the volume is by Thomas Kohnen (pp. 289–308), who suggests a 'connective profile' as a tool for analysing clause-level connectives, especially their distribution and frequency across texts and text types.

Hendrik de Smet's '*For . . . To*-Infinitives as Verbal Complements in Late Modern and Present-Day English: Between Motivation and Change' (*ES* 88[2007] 67–94) shows that the diachronic development of *for . . . to*-infinitives in Late ModE and PDE involves 'diffusion', i.e. 'spreading to an ever widening set of complement-taking verbs' (p. 69), and argues that mechanisms of change make use of the motivating principles behind *for . . . to*-infinitives, extending these principles to other domains. Øystein Heggelund, 'Old English Subordinate Clauses and the Shift to Verb-Medial Order in English' (*ES* 88[2007] 351–61), presents the results of a pilot study on word order in OE subordinate clauses, showing that SVX is the most common order in this environment, that the information value of subjects is generally lower in subordinate clauses than in main clauses, and suggesting that verb-medial order might first have been established in subordinate clauses. Tomoyuki Tanaka, 'The Rise of Lexical Subjects in English Infinitives' (*JCGL* 10[2007] 25 – 67), presents a minimalist account of the historical changes in the distribution of lexical subjects in English infinitival clauses, paying special attention to the role of the infinitival morpheme and to changes in the infinitival marker *to*.

A different type of clause is the focus of Javier Calle-Martín and Antonio Miranda-Carcía's 'On the Use of *Ond*-Clauses in the Old English Gospels' (*SN* 79[2007] 119–32), in which the results of a corpus study on the syntax of *ond*-clauses in the West Saxon gospels are presented, showing that *ond*-clauses mostly have V2 rather than VF order (although there exists variation between the different gospels in this regard) and that *ond*-clauses and subordinate clauses with subjects have the same word order (SVX being the most frequent order). On relative clauses there is Christine Johansson's 'The Use of Relativizers across Speaker Roles and Gender: Explorations in 19th-Century Trials, Drama and Letters' (in Fitzpatrick, ed., pp. 257–77). While it might be expected on the basis of EModE and PDE that less formal texts or passages by more vernacular speakers would have a high incidence of *that* in the nineteenth century as well, this is not confirmed by the data, which instead show high levels of WH use throughout, with *that* being prominent only in certain linguistic contexts (such as clefts and following indefinite pronouns) and in women's letters of the beginning of the century.

Writing on inversion in Late ME, Anthony Warner's 'Parameters of Variation Between Verb–Subject and Subject–Verb Order in Late Middle English' (*ELL* 11[2007] 81–111), shows that, in fourteenth- and fifteenth-century prose, syntactic considerations as well as considerations of weight 'are likely to play a considerable role in the patterning of inversions and late subjects' (p. 107), suggesting that inversion involves an interaction between syntax and pragmatics. Finally, Elizabeth Closs Traugott, 'Old English Left-Dislocations: Their Structure and Information Status' (*FoL* 41[2007] 405–41), examines the structural and discourse-functional properties of subject and object left-dislocations in OE, showing that OE left-dislocations are 'considerably less constrained than Present Day English left-dislocations are said to be' (p. 436).

6. Semantics

One of the highlights of 2007 is *Questions in Dynamic Semantics*, edited by Maria Aloni, Alastair Butler and Paul Dekker, a fine collection of recent work on the formal study of questions from the perspective of an 'Amsterdam-style' approach to semantics/pragmatics that originated in Jeroen Groenendijk and Martin Stokhof's dissertation *Studies on the Semantics of Questions and the Pragmatics of Answers* [1984]. The general features of this approach, the relevant notions and the most influential theories (with particular reference to Groenendijk and Stokhof's work, but also to its contenders), as well as the 'burning issues' in contemporary research, are carefully outlined in the editors' introduction, as are the major claims made in the contributions, and the reasons why they are relevant for each other. Three out of the four main sections of the book start with a classical paper (or a revised version of one) that in the 1990s revolutionized thinking about particular phenomena, followed by two other papers written for this volume that develop the theme raised in the first paper. Part I, 'Update Semantics', opens with Jeroen Groenendijk's seminal 1999 paper 'The Logic of Interrogation' (pp. 43–62), which explores the possibility of basing logic on co-operative information exchange instead of valid reasoning (given that 'cooperative information exchange seems a more prevailing linguistic activity' (p. 43) than reasoning), and thereby creates an integrated theory of semantics and pragmatics. The two other papers here,

'Axiomatizing Groenendijk's Logic of Interrogation' (pp. 63–82), by Balder ten Cate and Chung-chieh Shan, and 'Optimal Inquisitive Discourse' (pp. 83–101), by Paul Dekker, illustrate the directions one can go in from here, the former providing a sound and complete axiomatization of Groenendijk's logic, and the latter investigating the formal properties of optimal discourses. Part II, on 'Topic and Focus', starts with Gerhard Jäger's 'Only Updates: On the Dynamics of the Focus Particle *Only*' (pp. 105–22), where a particular context dependency related to *only* was first described, namely the one enabling the interpretation of *Only Socrates is wise* to vary depending on whether the sentence is uttered as an answer to *Who is wise?* or to *Which Athenian is wise?* The paper introduces a dynamic logic that handles the observed context dependencies. 'The Dynamics of Topic and Focus' (pp. 123–45), by Maria Aloni, David Beaver, Brady Clark and Robert van Rooij, and 'Nobody (Anything) Else' (pp.147–58), by Paul Dekker, present proposals that render the effects of domain restriction in more sophisticated ways, in view of a number of problems that Jäger's original proposal ran into. The third part, on 'Implicatures and Exhaustiveness', features Henk Zeevat's paper, 'Exhaustivity, Questions, and Plurals in Update Semantics' (pp. 161–92), which provides a semantic analysis for exhaustification effects, by proposing an exhaustification operator in update semantics which is capable of explaining such effects not only with respect to the interpretation of questions and answers, but also with respect to that of focus, quantifiers, or scalar implicatures. In the face of some of the problems presented by Zeevat's semantic approach to exhaustification, Robert van Rooij and Katrin Schulz, in '*Only: Meaning and Implicatures*' (pp.193–223), and Benjamin Spector, in 'Scalar Implicatures: Exhaustivity and Gricean Reasoning' (pp. 225–49), propose to handle the same effects in terms of pragmatics. The papers in the last section, 'Intonation and Syntax', are concerned with how intonational and syntactic information contributes to the interpretation of questions, and includes 'Nuclear Accent, Focus, and Bidirectional OT' (pp. 253–68), by Maria Aloni, Alastair Butler and Darrin Hindsill, 'Counting (on) Usage Information: WH Questions at the Syntax-Semantics Interface' (pp. 269–93), by Alastair Butler, and 'Nuclear Rises in Update Semantics' (pp. 295–313), by Marie Šafářová.

Another volume on the meaning of questions but written from the perspective of a language philosopher, is *Asking Questions*, by Robert Fiengo. It defends a complex approach to the meaning of sentences that are used to ask questions, which equally takes their form and the uses they are put to into account, and which is concerned with the types of questions that can be asked, and with the factors determining how a speaker decides on a particular occasion which type to use. The author argues that a fundamental distinction exists among questioning speech-acts, which divides them into 'open questions' and 'confirmation questions', cross-cutting the sentence-type differences between *yes-no*-questions and *wh*-questions. Whereas open questions have so far enjoyed a lot of attention from linguists, confirmation questions, such as *You are talking to who?* or *It's raining?* (the first signalling that I cannot complete what I set out to say, and the second that I do not have enough confidence to assert that it is raining) have mostly been neglected in previous investigations. Fiengo argues that all question types used in questioning speech-acts share the feature of incompleteness; with open questions this happens on the formal side, whereas for confirmation questions incompleteness resides in the requisite beliefs of the speaker, since she presents herself, according to Fiengo, as lacking the beliefs necessary for performing the corresponding assertion. Regarding open *wh*-questions, the author puts forward an explanation for the differences between the interpretation of questions containing expressions of the type 'which N' vs. 'what N', proposes an account for the differences in the syntactic distribution of *which* versus other *wh*-expressions, particularly *who* and *what*, and presents a typology of questioning speech-acts corresponding to J.L. Austin's [1953] typology of assertive acts, by which he also aims to account for the choice of *wh*-expressions in expressing particular meanings.

The fact that 'there have been only very few studies devoted to the task of illuminating the relationship between truth and illocutionary force' (p. 1) was the main motivation for Dirk Greimann and Geo Siegwart to edit *Truth and Speech Acts*, a collection of seventeen solicited foundational papers on the relationship between the descriptive and the interpersonal dimensions of language. Among contributors are the eminent philosophers of language William Alston and John Searle, the former putting forward his commitment-based perspective on illocutionary acts, the latter reflecting among other things on the function of expressions like *true* and *false* 'to assess success in the word-to-world direction of fit' (p. 36) arising with assertive acts. Among the papers most closely related to the analysis of natural language semantics, Wolfram Hinzen's contribution, 'Truth, Assertion, and the Sentence' (pp. 130–56), stands out in its provocative defence of the primacy of form over function. Elaborating on ideas by Andrew Carstairs-McCarthy [1999], Hinzen speculates on the viability of 'Nominalized English', an artificial language lacking the distinction between noun phrases and sentences. Headlinesque expressions like 'Victory for Bush' are used as tools for eliminating the reference/truth distinction and for dissociating assertive potential from 'sentences', the aim being to argue that the co-incidence of (declarative) sentence, truth, and assertion may have been an evolutionary accident. In their 'Truth as a Normative Modality of Cognitive Acts' (pp. 280–306), Gila Sher and Cory Wright take a glance at linguistic theories of modal expressions in trying to assess the relation between alethic terms like *it is true* and epistemic modalities like (subjective) necessity and possibility. They argue against reductionist approaches such as that of Frank Palmer [1990]. The characterization of interpersonal or expressive meaning is also the topic of Christopher Potts's target article in *Theoretical Linguistics*, 'The Expressive Dimension' (*TL* 33[2007] 165–98), which proposes a formal theory of expressives like *damn* and *bastard*, viewed as acting on and actively changing the expressive setting of the context of interpretation determined by a class of expressive indices, and which is followed by commentaries by Pranav Anand, Bart Geurts, Timothy Jay and Kristin Janschewitz, Peter Lasersohn, Uli Sauerland, Philippe Schlenker and Malte Zimmermann.

The contributions to the collection *Presupposition and Implicature in Compositional Semantics*, edited by Uli Sauerland and Penka Stateva, are also concerned with the semantics–pragmatics interface. A number of them look at particular phenomena, with the aim of investigating whether they should be analysed with the help of the tools of truth-conditional semantics or in terms of presuppositions or implicatures. These include Orin Percus's study 'A Pragmatic Constraint on Adverbial Quantification' (pp. 178–213), concerned with the interpretation of sentences containing individual-level predicates and temporal quantifiers, as in *The student who finished first was always Swedish*, as well as Regine Eckardt's ('Licensing *or*', pp. 34–70) and Danny Fox's ('Free Choice and the Theory of Scalar Implicatures', pp. 71–120) papers on the so-called free-choice effect with disjunction (illustrated by the equivalence between *Some linguists were having coffee or tea* and *Some linguists were having coffee and some linguists were having tea*). Two contributions study the interaction between implicatures and truth conditions. Manfred Krifka, 'Negated Antonyms: Creating and Filling the Gap' (pp. 163–77), offers a pragmatic solution for the non-equivalence of examples like *John is happy* vs. *John is not unhappy*, whereas Benjamin Spector ('Aspects of the Pragmatics of Plural Morphology: On Higher-Order Implicatures', pp. 243–81) gives an account of cases where plural NPs do not require plural reference (as in *The homework does not contain difficult problems*, which is identical in meaning to *The homework does not contain any difficult problem*) in terms of higher-order implicatures. The remaining three papers are concerned with the interaction between presuppositions and truth conditions. Sigrid Beck ('Quantifier Dependent Readings of Anaphoric Presuppositions', pp. 12–33) proposes a way to account for the presuppositions introduced by the adverb *again* by claiming that it is determined by an anaphoric element present in the syntax that can be free, bound, or internally complex like all natural language variables. Gerhard Jäger ('Partial Variables and Specificity', pp. 121–62) puts forward a new semantic analysis for specific indefinites which assumes that they introduce free variables into the logical representation, where the descriptive content of the indefinite is interpreted as a precondition for the corresponding variable to denote, and implements this idea formally in an extension of classical predicate logic with partial variables. Philippe Schlenker ('Transparency: An Incremental Theory of Presupposition Projection', pp. 214–42) argues against considering the notion of presuppositions as basic and aims to derive it from general pragmatic principles, including the principle 'Be Articulate' proposed by him, which puts a constraint on the use of lexical items that express more than one separate truth-conditional contribution simultaneously.

The volume *The Grammar–Pragmatics Interface*, edited by Nancy Hedberg and Ron Zacharski, is a collection of essays written in honour of Jeanette K. Gundel on the three main topics that have been at the centre of Professor Gundel's attention throughout her work and to which she has made significant contributions. The first part, 'Pragmatics and Syntax', contains papers investigating the grammar–pragmatics interface at the sentential level, inspired by Gundel's work on the information-structural properties of various topic- and focus-marking constructions, including *it*-clefts and *wh*-clefts, also from a contrastive perspective. Laura Michaelis and Hartwell Francis, 'Lexical Subjects and the Conflation Strategy' (pp. 19–48), investigate the properties of topical subjects in a corpus of spoken English, showing that pronominal subject NPs far outnumber lexical NPs, which they attribute to the satisfaction of Knud Lambrechts's [1994] Principle of Separation of Reference and Role (which, however, can be violated for reasons of speaker economy). Nancy Hedberg and Lorna Fadden, 'It-Clefts, Wh-Clefts and Reverse Wh-Clefts in English' (pp. 49–76), investigate the information structure of the three constructions in the title, arguing that they are similar from the point of view of 'referential givenness'—since the cleft clause is presupposed in all of them and thus must be at least uniquely identifiable (making them analogous to definite descriptions)—but differ with respect to their 'relational information structure': whereas the cleft clause in wh-clefts always presents the topic of the sentence and the cleft constituent the focus, no similar regularity is to be observed with respect to the other two construction types. Gregory Ward, Jeffrey P. Kaplan and Betty J. Birner, in 'Sistemic Would, Open Propositions, and Truncated Clefts' (pp. 77–90), compare sentences with epistemic would—where the subject NP is anaphoric to the variable in a salient open proposition in the context, as in That would be me—to truncated clefts like That would be me that you are talking about, addressing the question whether the former could be analysed in terms of the latter. The second part of the book addresses the interface at the level of the NP, inspired by Gundel's work on reference, and by Gundel, Hedberg and Zacharsi's 1993 study on the six cognitive statuses of referring expressions. Kaja Borthen's 'The Correspondence between Cognitive Status and the Form of Kind-Referring NPs' (pp. 143–69), applies the results of the latter work to the analysis of generic nominals, while Michael Hegarthy, in 'Context Dependence and Semantic Types in the Interpretation of Clausal Arguments' (pp. 171–88), addresses questions related to the accessibility of clausal denotations to reference with different pronominal forms, in addition to discussing under what circumstances clauses can have properties, situations, facts and events as denotations. Francis Cornish, in 'Implicit Internal Arguments, Event Structure, Predication and Anaphoric Reference' (pp. 189–216), discusses the conditions under which internal arguments of transitive or ditransitive predicates may remain implicit and the interpretations available for these arguments, while Thorstein Fretheim's 'Switch-Polarity Anaphora in English and Norwegian' (pp. 217–43) presents a contrastive study of the uses of English otherwise—a discourse connective with an anaphoric function—and the switch-polarity anaphor else, compared to Norwegian ellers, which is often used as the translation correspondent of the latter two, based on data from a bidirectional translation corpus. The studies in the third part of the book relate the results of the two main directions of Gundel's work to pragmatics in the wider sense, namely, to the study of social variables.

The contributions to the volume Interfaces and Interface Conditions, edited by Andreas Späth, are concerned with problems of differentiating between linguistic and extralinguistic (conceptual) knowledge, i.e. with the structure of the interfaces that make it possible to transform the former into the latter (particularly the two systems of performance: the system of articulation and perception, and the conceptual-intentional system), as well as the interfaces between the various levels of the linguistic system.

Several publications have addressed various recent challenges to the principle of semantic compositionality. This was also the topic of a special issue of the journal Research on Language and Computation, edited by Frank Richter and

Manfred Sailer (*RLandC* 5:iv[2007]). In 'Against Opacity' (*RLandC* 5[2007] 435–55) Marcus Egg looks at cases with no direct one-to-one mapping between (surface) syntactic and semantic structure (that is, where the meaning of a complex constituent depends on the inner structures of its parts), and proposes interface rules that derive underspecified representations for them, based on a surface-oriented syntactic analysis. In 'Compositionality: The Very Idea' (*RLandC* 5[2007] 287–308), Marcus Kracht claims that many recent and contemporary syntactic and semantic theories confuse syntactic and semantic structures, and that the principle of compositionality can serve, if properly understood, as a tool to gain insight into sentential structure. In a different paper, 'The Emergence of Syntactic Structure' (*Ling&P* 30[2007] 47–95), the same author proposes a definition of meaning devoid of the latter pitfalls that 'bans all mentioning of syntactic structure' (p. 47), and relocates many phenomena often thought to belong to syntax (like Θ-roles or linking) within semantics. The collection *Direct Compositionality*, edited by Chris Barker and Pauline Jacobson, takes a new look at the hypothesis of direct compositionality, which can be formulated in its simplest form as saying that 'The syntax and the semantics work together in tandem' (p. 1); in other words, that for every syntactic operation there must be a corresponding semantic one. Whereas direct compositionality was associated with the dominant trend in the formal semantics of the 1970s and 1980s, it has now been mostly replaced by the view prevalent in generative grammar, according to which semantic interpretation only takes place after syntax has created complete abstract representations at the level of Logical Form. One group of papers in the collection concentrates on some general issues concerning the concept of direct compositionality, its consequences, and the organization of the grammar it assumes. This includes 'Compositionality as an Empirical Problem' (pp. 23–101), by David Dowty; 'Direct Compositionality on Demand' (pp. 102–31), by Chris Barker, studying the status of Type-Logical Grammar with respect to compositionality; 'Linguistic Side Effects' (pp. 132–63), by Chung-chieh Shan, which devises a metalanguage to handle cases of apparent non-compositionality in natural languages based on the treatment of analogous phenomena in programming languages; and 'Type-Shifting with Semantic Features: A Unified Perspective' (pp. 164–87), by Yoad Winter, which argues that type-shifting operations are triggered by two kinds of type-mismatch. A second group of papers concentrates on empirical phenomena that appear to challenge direct compositionality, and have therefore played a great role in previous discussions about this. This section includes 'Direct Compositionality and Variable-Free Semantics: The Case of "Principle B" Effects' (pp. 191–236), by Pauline Jacobson, which argues that binding theory, in particular Principle B effects, should not be viewed (contrary to appearances) as stating constraints on non (strictly) local chunks of representations (that are incompatible with the idea of reasonably strong versions of direct compositionality). Next there are 'The Non-Concealed Nature of Free Relatives: Implications for Connectivity in Specificational Sentences' (pp. 237–63), by Ivano Caponigro and Daphna Heller, and 'Connectivity in a Unified Analysis of Specificational Subjects and Concealed Questions' (pp. 264–305), by Maribel Romero, both of which are concerned with the question whether direct compositionality is compatible with the connectivity effects in specificational copular sentences (illustrated by the fact that in *What John is is proud of himself* the reflexive is licensed in spite of it not being c-commanded by a local binder), but proposing opposite answers. Further papers in this section include 'Degree Quantifiers, Position of Merger Effects with their Restrictors, and Conservativity' (pp. 306–35), by Rajesh Bhatt and Roumyana Pancheva, which discusses several empirical challenges to direct compositionality, as well as to other analyses of the relevant data, and 'Two Reconstruction Effects' (pp. 336–59), by Yael Sharvit, which analyses the problems that a direct compositional theory versus a (non-directly compositional) reconstruction theory faces in accounting for superlative constructions such as *The longest book John said Tolstoy had written was Anna Karenina* on the reading that the book in question was merely said by John to have been written by Tolstoy (and may have in fact been written by someone else). Two more papers in the collection are concerned with the possibility of working out directly compositional analyses for domains to which such accounts have never been applied before, namely, 'Online Update: Temporal, Modal and *De Se* Anaphora in Polysynthetic Discourse' (pp. 363–404), by Maria Bittner, and 'The Dimensions of Quotation' (pp. 405–31), by Christopher Potts.

The contributions to the volume *Computing Meaning*, edited by Harry Bunt and Reinhard Muskens, discuss data, methods and problems concerning the computation of meaning in natural language. One group of papers is concerned with new or not satisfactorily analysed data pertaining to various types of ambiguity in natural languages providing suggestions for formalizing them in a manner intelligible for computational applications. Among those focusing on English, the following deserve particular attention. Massimo Poesio, Uwe Reyle and Rosemary Stevenson, in 'Justified Sloppiness in Anaphoric Reference' (pp. 11–31), identify two cases on the basis of a corpus study and psychological experiments, where apparently ambiguous anaphoric expressions do not seem to result in communication problems. 'Interpreting Concession Statements in Light of Information Structure' (pp. 145–72), by Ivana Kruijff-Korbayová and Bonnie L. Webber, studies the role the information structure of utterances plays in the interpretation of discourse connectives, particularly the connectives signalling concession, distinguishing between two senses of the latter. In 'Meaning, Intonation and Negation' (pp. 195–212), Marc Swerts and Emiel Krahmer report on the results of perception and production experiments concerning the different roles intonation can play in the interpretation of negation phrases, resulting in descriptive and metalinguistic readings. They argue for an OT approach to model the observed interactions between semantics and pragmatics. The other papers are concerned, on the one hand, with proposing underspecified semantic representations (which seem to be the most efficient way to model the ambiguity and incompleteness of the meaning of natural-language utterances) or with comparing existing representations or representation strategies for well-known language data, such as the interpretation of anaphors, ellipsis, intonation, tense, the relative scope of quantifiers and the contribution of context to meaning and, on the other hand, with investigating the problems that annotating corpora with semantic information run into. Also concentrating on the consequences of underspecification but from a different perspective are the papers collected in *Aspects of Meaning Construction*, edited by Günther Radden, Klaus-Michael Köpcke, Thomas Berg and Peter Siemund. The individual contributions, using the methodology of cognitive linguistics, examine three of the general principles underlying meaning construction (that is, the process enabling linguistic units having an underspecified meaning to 'evoke a whole scenario' (p. 9)), namely, metonymy, metaphor and conceptual blending, by means of data pertaining to the meaning of lexical items, phrases, discourse-connectives and speech-act types. According to the editors' introduction, underspecification occurs in language when linguistic units verbalize meanings implicitly or indirectly, when the meaning of a linguistic unit is indeterminate (or vague) and when linguistic units are incompatible, which forces the interlocutors to reconcile the meaning conflict between them.

We can also report on two semantics textbooks of very high quality. *An Introduction to English Semantics and Pragmatics*, by Patrick Griffiths, which appeared in 2006, is a concise but well-proportioned textbook, presenting exactly the amount of material that can be covered in the first one-semester course in semantics/pragmatics at BA level. The nine chapters of the book provide a discussion of the most basic concepts in semantics and pragmatics from the perspective of English, making constant reference to the most up-to-date research findings in the field, without showing commitment to any particular theoretical framework. The topics include the subject matter of semantics and pragmatics; definitions of types of meaning and explanations of some key concepts in semantic investigations such as compositionality and entailment; the characteristics of adjective meanings, with the help of which the various meaning relationships of similarity and oppositeness are introduced; basic issues in the semantics of nouns; the meanings of verbs, with particular reference to causative constructions and the Vendlerian system of predicate classes; issues in the interpretation of figurative uses of language; tense and aspect (this is the only case where the restriction to English data, where some aspectual distinctions are grammaticalized but others are not, leads to an incomplete presentation of the relevant phenomena); modality, scope and quantification; classic issues in pragmatics, such as conversational implicatures, presuppositions and speech acts; and, finally, basic concepts of information structuring, such as the interpretation of (in)definite NPs, clefts and passives, and (English-style) phonologically marked focus. The usefulness of the distinctions introduced is illustrated by the discussion of actually occurring examples. Each chapter is complemented by a list of further reading, and a set of exercises, for which solutions are also provided.

Semantics: A Coursebook, by James R. Hurford, Brendan Heasley, and Michael B. Smith (which is the second edition of an 1983 work by the first two authors, updated and supplemented by the third author), distinguishes itself from the range of semantics textbooks in its workbook format, with exercises forming an integral part of the presentation of the material, intended both to prepare readers for the information that follows and to check whether they have understood it. The fact that the solutions to these unit-internal exercises are also available, and that each unit closes with a summary of the main points that readers are expected to understand, makes the work an ideal companion for individual study for more advanced students as well. The six parts of the book cover the topics normally dealt with in introductory courses, such as the basic ideas in semantics (its subject matter, the distinction between sentences, utterances and propositions, and between reference and sense), issues in investigating reference (referring expressions, predicates, the universe of discourse, deixis and definiteness, extensions and prototypes), issues in investigating sense (sense properties and stereotypes, identity and similarity vs. oppositeness and dissimilarity of sense, ambiguity), logic (the subject matter of logic, ways of representing simple propositions, and various connectives), word meaning (dictionary definitions, meaning postulates, properties of predicates, derivation and participant roles), and interpersonal and non-literal meaning (speech-acts, perlocutions and illocutions, felicity conditions, direct and indirect illocutions, propositions and illocutions, conversational implicature, and idioms, metaphor and metonymy). Although I find this work one of the best among introductory textbooks not necessarily committed to the formal semantic paradigm, instructors and students with a more formal background might find the employment of an idiosyncratic quasi-logical language instead of the standard logical languages more disturbing than helpful.

Turning now to the study of 'classical' topics within semantics, *Recent Advances in the Syntax and Semantics of Tense, Aspect and Modality*, edited by Louis de Saussure, Jacques Moeschler, and Genoveva Puskás, contains a selection of the written versions of the papers presented at the sixth Chronos colloquium in Geneva. From the point of view of the semantics of English, the most noteworthy contributions to the volume include Sheila Glasbey's 'Aspectual Composition in Idioms' (pp. 71–87), who claims that the fact that the (Vendlerian) aspectual class membership might differ for literal and idiomatic interpretations of the same phrase or sentence does not mean that the latter cannot be derived compositionally. Arie Molendijk's 'The Passé Simple/Imparfait of French vs. the Simple Past/Past Progressive of English' (pp. 109–21) offers a contrastive analysis of the two tense forms in the two languages, concentrating on the temporal relationships that can be established by these tense forms in narrative discourse. Björn Rothstein, in 'A Modified *Extended Now* for the Present Perfect' (pp. 89–107) takes a new look at the present perfect puzzle (illustrated by *Sigurd has come yesterday) and its kin (involving the (in)compatibility of various temporal adverbials with perfect tenses) in English, German and Swedish, and argues for a combined syntactic-semantic account. Tim Stowell, 'Sequence of Perfect' (pp. 123–46), proposes a solution why the infinitival perfect (HAVE + -en) may function like the finite preterit *past*, claiming that it is a PAST polarity item, serving as the head of a time-denoting expression, rather than as a true past-shifting tense. Pranav Anand and Valentine Hacquard, in 'When the Present Is All in the Past', propose a novel ingenious answer to why a present tense embedded under a past tense need not always refer to the utterance time in English, as in *Caesar declared that he would execute any senator who stirs up rebellious sentiment in the Roman Empire*.

In a special issue of *Lingua* on syntactic and semantic approaches to tense and tense construal, Toshiyuki Ogihara's 'Tense and Aspect in Truth-Conditional Semantics' (*Lingua* 117[2007] 392–418) provides an informed overview of the basic data and key formal semantic analyses of various tense and aspect constructions in English, which can be highly recommended as a first reading even for those unfamiliar with the results of the field. In the same issue, Carlota S. Smith argues, in 'Tense and Temporal Interpretation' (*Lingua* 117[2007] 419–36), that the time talked about in a sentence does not only depend on tense or temporal adverbials, but also on context and on the Discourse Mode (Narrative, Report, Description, Information and Argument) of the text where the sentence appears, and analyses the combined contribution of these within a DRT-based framework. In 'A Cross-Linguistic Discourse Analysis of the Perfect' (*JPrag* 39[2007] 2273–2307), Henriëtte de Swart establishes that the perfect constructions in English, French, Dutch and German have similar aspectual properties, and are all Reichenbachian perfects, but differ in additional constraints imposed upon the possible relations between the event time E and other times/events in the sentence or the surrounding discourse. Ana Arregui, 'When Aspect Matters: The Case of *Would*-Conditionals' (*NLS* 15[2007] 221–64), offers a unified semantics for *would*-conditionals with simple morphology in the antecedent, as in *If your plants died next week, I would be very upset*, vs. those with perfect morphology in the antecedent, as in *If your plants had died next week, I would have been very upset*, which accounts for their interpretational differences, while Nicholas Asher and Eric McCready, '*Were, Would, Might*, and a Compositional Account of Counterfactuals' (*JSem* 24[2007] 93–129), propose a new dynamic account of epistemic modal operators, and complement it with an analysis of conditionals and irrealis moods to result in a fully compositional semantics of indicative and counterfactual conditionals. Maria Aloni, 'Free Choice, Modals, and Imperatives' (*NLS* 15[2007] 65–94), accounts for the differences between imperatives and possibility and necessity statements with respect to the licensing of free choice *any* and *or* (illustrated, on the one hand, by the contrast between *Vincent may be anywhere*, and *To continue push any key* vs. *Vincent must be anywhere*, and, on the other hand, by the fact that whereas the sentence *Vincent may be in Paris or in London* entails *Vincent may be in Paris and Vincent may be in London*, the corresponding entailment does not hold for necessity statements with *must*). Paul Portner, 'Imperatives and Modals' (*NLS* 15[2007] 351–83), argues that imperatives, interpretable with many subvarieties of directive force, contribute to a component of the discourse context called the 'addressee's To-Do List', which serves as a contextual resource for the interpretation of non-dynamic root modals in their deontic, bouletic and teleological readings. Benjamin Russell's 'Imperatives in Conditional Conjunction' (*NLS* 15[2007] 131–66) provides a compositional semantic analysis of the English conditional conjunction with imperative first conjuncts as in *Everyone drink another can of beer and we'll set a record*, combining semantic theories of imperatives, the future tense, modal subordination and speech-act conjunction. In 'Quantifiers and Verb Phrases: An Exploration of Propositional Complexity' (*NLLT* 25[2007] 447–83), Alan Clinton Bale argues that VPs containing intransitive and stative, transitive verbs are propositionally complex (containing more than one proposition), but those containing non-stative, transitive verbs are propositionally simple.

We turn now to the semantics of nominal expressions. In 'At least et al.: The Semantics of Scalar Modifiers' (*Language* 83[2007] 533–59), Bart Geurts and

Rick Nouwen challenge the accepted view that the meaning of comparative scalar modifiers like *more than* is analogous to superlative ones like *at least*, and propose that the latter have a modal interpretation. In 'Bare Nominals and Reference to Capacities' (*NL&LT* 25[2007] 195–222), Henriëtte de Swart, Yoad Winter and Joost Zwarts look at bare nominals in Germanic and Romance languages, and argue that in the syntactic configurations where they are allowed to occur, bare nominals refer to 'capacities', which are analysed as entities of type *e*, sortally distinct from regular individuals as well as kinds. 'Article Choice in Plural Generics' (*Lingua* 117[2007] 1657–76), by Donka F. Farkas and Henriëtte de Swart, shows that the contrast between two kinds of language that differ in using bare versus definite plurals in the expression on kind reference and in generic generalization, can be captured in terms of two OT syntactic constraints, while 'Exceptions to Generics: Where Vagueness, Context Dependence and Modality Interact', by Yael Greenberg (*JSem* 24[2007] 131–67), discusses the exceptions-tolerance property of generic sentences with indefinite singular and bare plural subjects. In 'The Gifted Mathematician that You Claim to Be: Equational Intensional "Reconstruction" Relatives' (*Ling&P* 30[2007] 445–85), Alexander Grosu and Manfred Krifka provide a semantic interpretation for relative constructions like the one in the title that considers surface representation to be the input to semantic representation. In 'Parasitic Scope' (*Ling&P* 30[2007] 407–44), Chris Barker makes a proposal for a compositional semantic account of the meaning of *same*, treating it as a scope-taking adjective, both in terms of quantifier-raising at LF and in a continuation-based Type-Logical Grammar in the style of Michael Moortgat [1997]. In a special issue of *RLandC* (5:i[2007]) on 'Semantic approaches to binding', Edward L. Keenan, in 'On the Denotations of Anaphors' (*RLandC* 5[2007] 5–17) works out direct interpretations for anaphors such as *himself, herself, everyone but himself, no student but himself, both himself and the teacher*, etc., in the framework of generalized quantifier theory, and proposes a syntax-independent definition of 'anaphor'.

Turning to the interpretation of discourse anaphora, the collection *Anaphors in Text: Cognitive, Formal, and Applied Approaches to Anaphoric Reference*, edited by Monika Schwarz-Friesel, Manfred Consten and Mareile Knees, is devoted to the discussion of the representation and interpretation of definite descriptions used as anaphors in text and discourse from cognitive, text- and discourse-linguistic, syntactic, semantic and computational-linguistic perspectives, and the results of neurolinguistic investigations on the reception of anaphoric reference, in a variety of languages. 'Accessibility and Definite Noun Phrases', by Klaus von Heusinger, studies the interaction of definite NPs and the accessibility structure, a network of semantically related sets of ranked discourse items associated with the predicates that have introduced them, and argues that not only does the accessibility structure determine the definiteness status of referring expressions, but definite NPs also change this accessibility due to their descriptive content. Discourse interpretation is the topic of the papers in *Connectivity in Grammar and Discourse*, edited by Jochen Rehbein, Christiane Hohenstein and Lukas Pietsch, which investigates the linguistic devices that interconnect units of text and discourse, ranging from subordinating connectives through 'serialization' by means of converbs, to co-ordinative devices that not only link phrases and clauses but also complete utterances, sentences, or parts of text or discourse to each other in a variety of languages, from descriptive and theoretical perspectives, as well as from the perspectives of languages, language change and language acquisition.

Parentheticals, edited by Nicole Dehé and Yordanka Kavalova, is a remarkable collection of papers devoted to the syntactic, semantic-pragmatic or prosodic properties of particular subtypes of parentheticals in a variety of languages which have traditionally been considered peripheral and therefore neglected in linguistic research. In their very instructive introduction, the editors outline some of the main challenges for the study of parentheticals, which include, first, the controversy between their forming a linear constituent of the sentence and their showing signs of structural independence, 'interrupt[ing] the prosodic flow of the utterance' (cf. Dwight Bolinger [1989]), thus not contributing to truth-conditional meaning but typically functioning as modifiers, additions to or comments on the current talk, and, second, the variation among expressions traditionally considered to be parentheticals in length/complexity, category and function, ranging from one-word expressions like *what*, *say*, *like*, sentence adverbials, comment clauses (*I think*, *you know*), reporting verbs, nominal appositions, to non-restrictive relative clauses, question tags and whole clauses (with or without a connector, elliptical or non-elliptical). The introduction also outlines the major views about the syntactic relation between the host structure and the interpolated parenthetical structure, which most of the contributions in the volume are concerned with, as well as issues concerning the semantic/pragmatic relations between parentheticals and their hosts.

The Grammar of Names, by John M. Anderson, aims to propose a grammar for proper names (that describes their syntax as well as their lexical subclasses) following the tradition of notional grammar dominant in linguistics until the twentieth century, whose basic assumption is that the syntactic categories have a notional basis. This means, according to the author, that the defining distributional properties of a syntactic category are those that characterize prototypical members of the category semantically. This seems to carry a touch of circularity since it presupposes that there should be some independent criteria other than syntactic ones for determining what elements constitute a category (otherwise there would be no way of knowing among what elements to search for central ones). In spite of the reservations of the linguist trained in contemporary linguistic theory about the idea of a notional grammar, the monograph, with its detailed discussion of cross-linguistic empirical data about proper names as well as overviews of the history of their investigation within onomastics, philosophy and linguistics, provides highly recommendable reading for anyone interested in the study of proper names.

The volume *The Categorization of Spatial Entities in Language and Cognition*, edited by Michel Aurnague, Maya Hickmann and Laure Vieu, collects contributions concerned with the categorization of spatial entities from the perspective of descriptive linguistics (studying the distinctions made by various languages among spatial entities, with the aim of specifying underlying concepts and distinctions), psycholinguistic studies (examining the relation between linguistic and cognitive categories) and formal semantics and formal ontology (concerned with the characterization of the categories of spatial entities that play a role in language and cognition in logical formalisms). Among the papers in the last category, Achille C. Varzi's 'From Language to Ontology: Beware of the Traps' (pp. 269–84) calls attention to some phenomena that call into question the possibility of basing ontological analysis on the results of linguistic analysis. Philippe Muller, 'The Temporal Essence of Spatial Objects' (pp. 285–306), argues for a 'four-dimensionalist' or spatio-temporal ontological theory to formally define some differences between categories of concrete objects referred to in natural language, namely those concerned with mass terms and count nouns, singular and plural, and object and event reference. Nicholas Asher, in 'Objects, Locations and Complex Types' (pp. 337–61), proposes a rich system of lexical types in which locations and physical objects are distinct types of things, and a logic that accounts for the data where terms can denote both kinds of things at the same time. *Space, Time, and the Use of Language: An Investigation of Relationships*, by Thora Tenbrink, re-examines the popular view that temporal terms are closely related to and conceptually (and historically) based on spatial terms (expressed by Martin Haspelmath [1997], among others), and concludes, on the basis of studying various synchronic(!) corpora for German and English that there is no dependency relationship between the two kinds of expression, and that their shared features are due to the shared features of the underlying conceptual domains of space and time, and to various discourse processes.

Renewed interest in the linguistic applications of game theory, a mathematical framework originally developed for the analysis of economic behaviour, is manifested in *Game Theory and Linguistic Meaning*, edited by Ahti-Veikko Pietarinen. Fifteen papers provide an interesting interdisciplinary perspective on broad issues such as the origins of communication, social conventions and semantics and ontology, as well as on narrowly focused problems in the area of quantifier scope and anaphora resolution. Well represented are the two major schools of game-theoretical approaches to meaning. Evolutionary Game Theory, inspired by the biologist Maynard-Smith's work on population dynamics, privileges the interactional, 'pragmatic', dimensions of meaning and applies concepts like co-operation, stability, resource allocation and signalling strategy. Game-Theoretic Semantics, developed by the philosopher and logician Jaakko Hintikka, concentrates on dialogic aspects of providing truth conditions for logical forms of sentences. The editor's introduction 'An Invitation to Language and Games' (pp. 1–15), helpfully unravels these different strands and points out related ideas in the philosophical works of Charles Sanders Peirce and Ludwig Wittgenstein. In the chapter 'Game Dynamics Connects Semantics and Pragmatics' (pp. 103–17), Gerhard Jäger uses the evolutionary approach in order to provide an analysis of scalar implicatures arising from existential quantifiers like *some* (implicating *not all*). Ahti-Veikko Pietarinen devotes his 'Semantic Games and Generalised Quantifiers' (pp. 183–206) to extending Hintikka's classical approach to the full set of quantificational expressions available in natural language. Robin Clark argues for a synthesis of approaches in 'Games, Quantifiers and Pronouns' (pp. 207–27). Accordingly, sentence-internal interpretation is done

Hintikka-style, while aspects of evolutionary approaches play a role in cross-sentential processes like anaphora resolution. Still on the applications of game theory in natural language semantics, Robin Clark and Prashant Parikh, 'Game Theory and Discourse Anaphora' (*JLLI* 16[2007] 265–82), develop a theory of discourse anaphora (the relationship between a pronoun and an antecedent earlier in the discourse) where the strategic inferences involved in finding the referent of the anaphor are modelled by means of games of partial information.

This year we have seen a particularly high number of publications addressing topics of interest for natural language semanticists from the perspective of philosophy.

As is well known, the attractive view that the meaning of proper names reduces to their referent is seriously challenged by pairs of identity statements like *Cicero is Cicero* and *Cicero is Tully*. Although both names refer to the same famous Roman orator, the second statement is perceived to be informative while the former statement is not. Kit Fine, in his monograph *Semantic Relationism*, addresses this challenge by assuming that semantic values can be or can fail to be 'co-ordinated'. If they can, this preserves the information that they have been 'represented-as-same' already on the syntactic level by the use of identical expressions. Lack of co-ordination, for example when two semantic values are the same 'by co-incidence', is responsible for informativity effects. Fine goes on to apply this method to the analysis of beliefs regarding identity statements and the treatment of variables in predicate logic. In the course of the discussion, brief but helpful descriptions of rival views, such as those of David Kaplan and Saul Kripke, are provided. In *Simple Sentences, Substitution, and Intuitions*, Jennifer Saul reconsiders the puzzle of why co-referential names fail to be freely substitutable in simple sentences such as *Clark Kent went into the phone booth and Superman came out* vs. *Superman went into the phone booth and Clark Kent came out*, making these construction types analogous to 'opacity-producing' constructions where substitution failure is known to occur, as in *Lois believes that Superman flies* vs. *Lois believes that Clark Kent flies*. In the course of reviewing all standard accounts of substitution failure, the author shows that there is no semantic theory that yields truth conditions that could accord with the latter intuitions, no way to explain away the intuitions, and no way to attribute the intuitions to implicated, asserted, implicited or expressed propositions with truth-conditions matching the intuitions, or to the presence of any other such intuition-matching propositions available to conversational participants in all cases. She also explores the possibility that the intuitions are to be explained with reference to the states of mind of those having the intuitions, rather than of the conversational participants. Saul then proposes that the relevant intuitions about substitutability are due to the fact that information associated with one name is stored separately from information associated with the other name, and these two kinds of information are not always integrated reliably and immediately, which is also supported by psychological experiments confirming the tendency to segregate information known to be about a single individual, and by theoretical assumptions about the differences between the mental representations speakers hold when encountering the phone-booth examples described above.

In *Language Turned on Itself: The Semantics and Pragmatics of Metalinguistic Discourse*, Herman Cappelen and Ernie Lepore propose a new, 'minimal' theory of quotation, after delineating the problems they find with all main previous semantic approaches to the phenomenon, including theories that treat quotations as names, demonstratives or quantifiers (in particular, as definite descriptions), as well as those pragmatic ones according to which quotations lack a semantic function altogether. The predictions of these previous theories are checked against the twelve basic properties of quotation that have been identified in the literature, which are carefully delineated in the first part of the book, making it an excellent first read for those (students) new to the topic.

In the monograph *Minimal Semantics* (which appeared as a hardback in 2004 and as a paperback in 2006), Emma Borg argues that the only tasks an adequate theory of linguistic meaning is supposed to perform are to reveal, on the one hand, how the meanings of complex expressions are determined given the meaning of their component expressions and the latter's mode of composition, and, on the other hand, what relations hold between those complex expressions (like the inferential relations between sentences); it should not, however, be expected to answer metaphysical or epistemic questions, and it should not be tied too strictly to communicative concerns. The author claims that traditional formal theories of semantics satisfy exactly the latter requirements, and therefore the criticism against such approaches by particular use-oriented semantic theories, referred to as 'dual pragmatic' theories by the author (representatives of which would be Dan Sperber and Deirdre Wilson's relevance theory, Recanati's contextualism and Kamp's dynamic representation theory), which argue that pragmatic processes do not only have a role in the post-semantic domain to determine the implicatures of an utterance but also enter into the calculation of truth-conditional or propositional content, is unwarranted. Borg finds formal semantic theories preferable also because she considers them compatible with Jerry Fodor's important modularity account of human cognitive architecture. In the selected essays constituting the volume *Language in Context*, Jason Stanley takes up a position contrary to Borg's. In Stanley's theory an utterance acquires the truth-conditions it intuitively possesses in the following manner. Each term in a sentence uttered has a content that is determined by its context-independent meaning together with extra-linguistic context, although the function of the context cannot be to expand the content of a term relative to that context. As a last step, these contents are put together into truth-conditions by composition rules determined by the syntactic configuration of the sentence, which are not sensitive to context (although ambiguity between different composition rules is possible).

The aim of *An Essay on Names and Truth*, by Wolfram Hinzen, is to argue for an internalist conception of language use, according to which it is the result of causes due to the internal organization of the organism, and not the result of the organism's encounters with the environment. He argues, in particular, that meaning begins not from relations of reference between word and things, but from the concepts that we as human beings possess. Therefore, truth and reference, which correspond to the meanings of particular kinds of expressions in natural language, and as such, are central to most formal theories of semantics, are specific and contingent forms of intentionality, and have a crucial structural basis in the specific format of language.

The range of topics addressed in various journal publications includes focus interpretation. In 'Focus Interpretation in Thetic Statements: Alternative Semantics and Optimality Theory Pragmatics' (*JLLI* 16[2007] 15–33), Kjell Johan Sæbø argues for a theory that explains the choice between one broad focus vs. two narrow foci in English thetic sentences (as in *[Champagne had been offered]$_F$* vs. *[Champagne]$_F$* *[had been declined]$_F$*) by combining the results of Alternative Semantics with OT. In 'On the Meaning of Some Focus-Sensitive Particles' (*NLS* 15[2007] 1–34), Michaela Ippolito proposes that the meaning differences between the aspectual, marginality and concessive uses of the grading particles *still* and *already* correlate with the type of the object denoted by the phrase in the scope of the particle. 'When Semantics Meets Phonetics: Acoustical Studies of Second-Occurrence Focus' (*Language* 83[2007] 245–76), by David Beaver, Brady Zack Clark, Edward Flemming, T. Florian Jaeger and Maria Wolters, is the first study presenting the details of systematic production and perception experiments investigating the prosodic properties of second-occurrence (SO) focus (the semantic focus of a focus-sensitive operator, like *only*, which, however, is a repeat of an earlier focused occurrence), showing that SO foci occurring after a nuclear accent are prosodically marked, generally by longer duration and greater energy, and optionally by pitch rise. A variety of topics in semantics, including focus interpretation are also discussed in the contributions to *Coreference, Modality, and Focus*, edited by Luis Eguren and Olga Fernández Soriano from a generative perspective, on the basis of data from a variety of languages.

Finally, we call attention to some more articles on less frequently discussed topics. 'On the Role of Semantics in a Theory of Adverb Syntax' (*Lingua* 117[2007] 1008–33), by Thomas Ernst, uses two kinds of evidence to argue that adverbs are adjoined and licensed largely by semantically based principles, instead of syntactic ones, proposed, for example, by Guglielmo Cinque [1999], according to which adverbs are licensed in specifier positions by empty functional heads. Tamina Stephenson, 'Judge Dependence, Epistemic Modals, and Predicates of Personal Taste' (*Ling&P* 30[2007] 487–525) analyses the interpretation of epistemic modals in Peter Lasersohn's [2005] framework of judge dependency, which was proposed to handle the interpretation of predicates of personal taste, and discusses modifications of the latter system that are necessitated by the transfer to the new domain. In 'Talking about Taste: Disagreement, Implicit Arguments, and Relative Truth' (*Ling&P* 30[2007] 691–706), however, Isidora Stojanovic argues that a contextualist account like Lasersohn's, modelling the judge parameter as an implicit argument to the taste predicate, and a relativist account modelling it as a parameter of the circumstances of evaluation are semantically equivalent.

7. Lexicography, Lexicology and Lexical Semantics

This section begins with a discussion of publications in the field of lexicology, with general discussions preceding the historical. These are followed by books and articles on lexical semantics and metaphor. Publications on dictionary research are discussed as follows: historical dictionary research, the *OED*, other modern dictionaries for native speakers, and bilingual and learners' dictionaries.

M.A.K. Halliday and Colin Yallop's *Lexicology: A Short Introduction* was reissued this year. It remains a useful and clearly written introduction to the field for beginners, but it would have been helpful to update the last chapter 'The Future of Lexicology', which refers to the availability of the *OED* on CD-ROM and provides only a brief overview of the use of corpora by lexicologists. Lexicological studies concentrating on particular historical periods include Richard Coates's 'Goldhwite: An Unrecognized Middle English Bird-Name?' (*TPS* 105[2007] 188–91), which finds place-name evidence to support the possibility that this term was used as a bird name before its first record in Ray's *Collection of English Words* [1674]. Coates also argues, in 'Fockynggroue in Bristol' (*N&Q* 54[2007] 373–6), that this fourteenth-century place-name pre-dates the first *OED* citation, from 1568, for the verbal noun *fucking*. In 'Colours of the Landscape: Old English Colour Terms in Place-Names' (in Biggam and Kay, eds., *Progress in Colour Studies*, vol. 1: *Language and Culture*, pp. 181–98), Carole Hough provides place-name evidence for colour terms in Old English. In 'Middle English **Wrestman*' (*N&Q* 54[2007] 22–3), Hough posits an otherwise undocumented word meaning 'ploughman', and in 'Old English *Weargbeorg*' (*N&Q* 54[2007] 364–5) suggests that 'wolf hill' is a better analysis than 'gallows hill'. C.P. Biggam's 'Political Upheaval and a Disturbance in the Colour Vocabulary of Early English' (in Biggam and Kay, eds., pp. 159–79) asks why the native colour term *hæwan* was replaced by the French borrowing *blue* when all other basic colour terms remained stable. R. Carter Hailey's 'To "Finde wordes newe": Chaucer, Lexical Growth, and *MED* First Citations' (in Considine and Iamartino, eds., *Words and Dictionaries from the British Isles in Historical Perspective*, pp. 14–24) argues that Chaucer had 'a large and demonstrable effect in the expansion of the English lexicon' (p. 21). William Sayers argues, in 'Lubber, Landlubber' (*N&Q* 54[2007] 376–9), that *landlubber* originated among non-mariners as a term for rustics unskilled in the ways of city life. In '"Lightography" in a Letter by Thomas Hood' (*N&Q* 54[2007] 140–1), Rodney Stenning Edgecombe finds that an apparent nonce word of 1839 has been reinvented in contemporary English. In 'Idioms in Journalese: A Synchronic and Diachronic Study of Food and Drink Idioms in 200 Years of *The Times*' (in Considine and Iamartino, eds., pp. 178–91), Laura Pinnavaia finds that idioms reoccur in related articles through their links with particular themes.

Mark Kaunisto's *Variation and Change in the Lexicon. A Corpus-based Analysis of Adjectives in English Ending in -ic and -ical* demonstrates the value of corpora in lexicological research. Kaunisto finds that where competing forms are not differentiated semantically, there is a tendency for one of the two to be ousted. Earlier scholars have differed over whether the -*ic* or -*ical* form has a greater tendency to survive, and some have argued that there are no discernible trends. Kaunisto finds that these studies have tended to rely on intuition and contemporary evidence, and thus cannot offer reliable comment on historical developments. Kaunisto's own study considers the productivity of -*ic* and -*ical* in different periods, and finds that -*ical* forms were overtaken by coinages with -*ic* in the first half of the eighteenth century. A parallel chapter considers obsolescence of one of the forms in each pair, finding that from a total of twenty-eight pairs, the -*ic* form dominates over or completely supplants its longer equivalent in twenty cases. He also examines the use of six surviving semantically differentiated adjective pairs in detail: *classic/classical, comic/comical, economic/economical, electric/electrical, historic/historical* and *magic/magical,* and finds that the differences in use are often rather subtle. Minor pairs (*diabolic/diabolical, fantastic/fantastical, optic/optical,* and *politic/ political*) are considered in less depth. Kaunisto concludes that -*ic* forms are now preferred for new coinages, but that -*ical* was preferred in the sixteenth century. He argues that adjectives formed from proper nouns are the most likely to use -*ic* forms (e.g. *Byronic*), and that pre-nineteenth-century adjectives relating to the sciences are most likely to use -*ical* forms (e.g. *chemical*), though -*ic* forms predominate from the nineteenth century onwards (e.g. *linguistic*). Kaunisto predicts that the shorter forms will continue to dominate, particularly where semantic differences between paired terms are slight. Although modestly written, this volume provides a model for future lexicological studies.

Publications concentrating on contemporary English include Tony Devarson's consideration of some terms and usages peculiar to NZE in 'Kiwi Lollies: Sweet As' (*NZWords* 11[2007] 3–5). Desmond Hurley's 'Premier Words' (*NZWords* 11[2007] 7–8) discusses terms derived from the names of New Zealand prime ministers. The volume edited by Mina Gorji, *Rude Britannia,* explores the idea that Britain is now less civilized than in the past. The introduction looks particularly at the history of the censorship of tabooed terms in Britain, and considers the perceived relationship between obscenity and low social status. Most of the contributions are not linguistic in focus— their subjects range from McGill's smutty postcards to *Viz* magazine to page three girls in *The Sun*—but a few chapters on dictionaries are considered below. Two more general chapters include Tom Paulin's 'Rude Words', which documents non-standard words and phrases used in Belfast in the middle of the twentieth century, and Tony Crowley's exploration of the rules governing football chants in 'Boundaries of Football Rudeness'. Crowley finds that although obscenity is commonplace, racist chants are now rare. John Humphrys's *Beyond Words: How Language Reveals the Way We Live Now* is an account of the broadcaster's linguistic likes and dislikes. His particular bugbears are imprecision and, though he denies it, change. Humphrys does provide some interesting observations about current trends in, for example, capitalization in advertising. He offers a useful perspective on the current use of words and phrases like *respect, trust,* and *work–life balance.* Susie Dent's *The Language Report. English on the Move 2000–2007* is a similarly popular account, but one that takes a largely celebratory stance on neologisms.

Dent also provides a summary of contentious but ephemeral utterances that hit the headlines, which will be especially useful in years to come. Although there are comments on developments in grammar and pronuniciation, Dent concentrates largely on lexis, and considers the influence of catchphrases, business English, the internet and newspaper headlines. She presents a glossary of possible stayers, which include *go-bag* 'a bag for use in an emergency evacuation', *meh* 'whatever', and *urbeach* 'an urban beach'. Georgeta Ciobanu looks at the influence of English on other European languages in 'Dictionary Symbols Used to Mark Changes of Languages in Contact' (in Sica, ed., *Open Problems in Linguistics and Lexicography*, pp. 163–77), considering particularly the treatment of various types of loans in two major projects: *The English Elements in European Languages*, directed by Rudolf Filipović, and *English in Europe*, directed by Manfred Görlach.

In *Main Trends in Historical Semantics*, Marcin Grygiel and Grzegorz A. Kleparski provide an overview of developments in semantics. Most of the examples are from English, and the volume includes numerous diagrams produced by various theorists, some of which are helpful in understanding the theoretical approaches underlying them. The authors argue that cognitive theories have returned semantics to a central place in grammar, but the volume concentrates largely on pre-cognitive approaches. Following the introductory chapter, they consider causes of semantic change, the types and mechanisms involved, and they end by discussing the search for 'Rules of Semantic Change'. Although hardly cutting-edge, this volume provides a useful and accessible introduction to the history of semantics.

Zoltán Kövecses's *Metaphor in Culture: Universality and Variation* was first published in 2005, but came out as a paperback in 2007. It aims to provide a more comprehensive and sophisticated version of the current cognitive linguistic view of metaphor, which does not account for all the data available. Kövecses argues that the theory ought to explain universality and its absence, as well as variation, though he concedes that cognitive linguists cannot offer proof, only hypotheses: proof depends on cognitive psychologists, and he makes good use of the data that they provide. Examination of conceptual metaphors involving the emotions, event structure, time and the inner life provide evidence for universality or near-universality in general terms, but cross-cultural and intra-cultural variations in their application undermine any attempt to generalize. Chapter 5 is an interesting discussion of differences in metaphor use within societies: by men and women, or by different ethnic, regional, or religious groups. Kövecses analyses metaphors into eleven components, including 'source domain', 'target domain', 'experiential basis' and so on. Part III uses this categorization to explore variation between metaphors. LIFE IS A JOURNEY, for example, is mapped differently in biblical usage and in contemporary Western culture, where the biblical metaphor is based on a moral journey with a single goal and a single route to it. An analysis of TIME IS MONEY in English and Hungarian reveals different emphases in a metaphor that is allegedly cross-cultural. Kövecses usefully emphasizes the importance of creativity, whose application and value varies between cultures. This is an interesting, wide-ranging and thought-provoking account that will undoubtedly provide new direction to its field.

L. David Ritchie's *Context and Connection in Metaphor* builds on the work of previous theorists with an emphasis on the communicative function of metaphors as well as the cognitive processes involved. Ritchie also provides a valuable summary of work in the field to date, considering conceptual metaphor theory, conceptual blending, relevance theory, context-based cognition and context-limited simulation. From this discussion arises 'Context-Limited Simulators Theory', which argues that associations and interpretations that are not relevant to the context are suppressed rather than activated and then discounted. Various fields of meaning will be associated with a particular conceptual field and, Ritchie argues, it is more useful to identify these fields of meaning than to look for single root metaphors. For example, *she attacked my argument* could be understood as arising from ARGUMENT IS WAR, but it may also be interpreted with reference to a variety of sporting activities. The underlying conceptual field *CONTENTIOUS ACTIVITIES* accounts for these multiple interpretations. Having posited this theory, Ritchie applies it to the problems posed by earlier theorists, with convincing results. The discussion also incorporates the notion that metaphorical language is often playful. Context-limited simulation accounts for the operation of some types of humour and also offers the possibility of understanding metaphors in their social contexts. Using metaphor to understand cognitive processes can only ever offer theories, however; only cognitive neuroscience can provide definitive results.

This was also a good year for historical dictionary research. Fredric Dolezal's 'Writing the History of English Lexicography: Is There a History of English Lexicography after Starnes and Noyes?' (in Considine and Iamartino, eds., pp. 1–13) contends that, although dictionary research has developed and diverged since the publication of that seminal work, scholars still rely on its outdated overview. Gabriele Stein offers a contribution to the work of updating the overview in 'The Emergence of Lexicology in Renaissance English Dictionaries' (in Considine and Iamartino, eds., pp. 25–38), in which she asks how the compilers of early English dictionaries conceptualized their task. R.W. McConchie's paper 'The Real Richard Howlet' (in Considine and Iamartino, eds., pp. 39–49) provides an account of the evidence available for the life of this little-known lexicographer. Paola Tornaghi considers the importance of a manuscript glossary in the early history of Old English lexicography in ' "Certaine things to be considered & corrected in Will": Dugdales Saxon-Lexicon' (in Considine and Iamartino, eds., pp. 50–80). Elisabetta Lonati presents an account of an early medical dictionary in 'Blancardus' *Lexicon Medicum* in Harris's *Lexicon Technicum*: A Lexicographic and Lexicological Study' (in Considine and Iamartino, eds., pp. 91–108). In 'Alphabet Fatigue and Compiling Consistency in Early English Dictionaries' (in Considine and Iamartino, eds., pp. 81–90), N.E. Osselton discusses how and why early dictionaries are more thorough in their treatment of the first part of the alphabet. In 'Letters, Sounds and Things. Orthography, Phonetics and Metaphysics in Wilkins's *Essay* (1668)' (*HL* 34[2007] 213–56), Michael M. Isermann argues that Wilkins represented contemporary developments with some sophistication at a turning point in Western thought.

Kusujiro Miyoshi's *Johnson's and Webster's Verbal Examples: With Special Reference to Exemplifying Usage in Dictionary Entries* compares Johnson's and Webster's practice with reference to their views of the English language and their own historical contexts. Miyoshi charts changes in the lexicographers' standpoints as they gained in experience. Johnson began work on his dictionary determined to fix the language but came to recognize that, though desirable, this was not possible. Webster moved from prescriptivism to descriptivism through the course of his dictionary. Miyoshi follows earlier students of Johnson in selecting the letter L for analysis from both dictionaries. There is a particular emphasis on the lexicographers' use of biblical citations, and the analysis demonstrates, for example, that although both provide numerous biblical citations, Webster preferred to use them to illustrate contemporary usage. Johnson had a tendency to use invented examples for prepositional adverbs and modal auxiliaries, while Webster used them throughout his dictionary. Webster also made substantial use of Johnson's citations, but often interpreted them afresh. Miyoshi also finds that Webster was more skilful in his treatment of compound words and that he provided more information about usage. Tables showing the frequency of use of different sources for citations in various types of entry are fascinating, but it would have been useful to subject these figures to statistical analysis to determine probability.

In ' "The Bad Habit": *Hobson-Jobson*, British Indian Glossaries, and Intimations of Mortality' (*Henry Sweet Society Bulletin* 46–7[2006] 7–22), Javed Majeed compares Yule and Burnell's dictionary with other nineteenth-century colonial glossaries, and finds that *Hobson-Jobson* is distinctive in its opposition to the use of terms and phrases from Indian languages by speakers of English. Manfred Markus and Reinhard Heuberger discuss 'The Architecture of Joseph Wright's *English Dialect Dictionary*: Preparing the Computerized Version' (*IJL* 20[2007] 355–68). They break Wright's entries into eight fields of information, including 'headwords', 'labels' and 'definitions or meaning(s)', but find that these fields are not used consistently with regard to either content or order. Julie Coleman's 'Expediency and Experience: John S. Farmer and William E. Henley's *Slang and its Analogues*' (in Considine and Iamartino, eds., pp. 136–65) explores the effects of changing methodology through the course of a multi-volume slang dictionary. In 'Howard N. Rose's *Thesaurus of Slang* (1934): Its Purpose, Structure, Contents, Reliability, and Sources' (*HL* 34[2007] 351–61), Coleman describes an early attempt to provide broad coverage of different varieties of American slang. She finds that it is not a thesaurus and that its contents are by no means all slang. In 'Poubellication: In the Lexical Dunny with the Furphy King from Down Under' (in Gorji, ed., pp. 35–55), Valentine Cunningham ambles through Partridge's publications in search of obscenity.

Charlotte Brewer's *Treasure-House of the Language. The Living OED* is a detailed and fascinating account of events following the publication of the last instalment of *OED1* in 1928. The volume takes a people-centred approach to the *OED*, in that it is concerned with questions such as pension arrangements for long-serving lexicographers, the treatment of female staff and relationships between the editors. Many useful insights into these matters are provided by reference to correspondence in the dictionary's archives. However, Brewer also offers a critical account of the contents of *OED1* and its supplements and provides a brief introduction to *OED-online*. Chapters exploring the public reception of the dictionary are particularly interesting, and Brewer successfully demolishes the myth that *OED* lexicography ceased between the first and second supplements. Word-collectors continued to send slips to the *OED*, and James M. Wyllie was tasked with the job of sorting and supplementing these so that modern material was available to the editors of other Oxford dictionaries. As Wyllie's mental health declined, his relationships within the Press became increasingly difficult, and he was dismissed in 1954. By this time it was clear that the *OED* was in need of revision, or at least supplementation, and Raymond C. Goffin had begun work on this project. Robert Burchfield was appointed editor in 1956, and Brewer's narrative of his early days in the office offer an interesting counterpoint to some of his own later accounts. This volume is an invaluable contribution to the continuing scrutiny of the history and methodology of the *OED*.

Brewer also considers the vexed question of 'Reporting Eighteenth-Century Vocabulary in the *OED*' (in Considine and Iamartino, eds., pp. 109–35), and suggests that *OED3* could do more to fill the gaps of the first edition. Peter Gilliver's 'The Great *Un-* Crisis: An Unknown Episode in the History of the *OED*' (in Considine and Iamartino, eds., pp. 166–77) explores the pressure on Craigie to reduce his treatment of this uniquely productive prefix. In ' "Decent Reticence": Coarseness, Contraception, and the First Edition of the *OED*' (*Dictionaries* 28[2007] 1–22), Lynda Mugglestone finds that considerations of propriety extended further in *OED1* than the omission of a few high-profile tabooed terms. Not only are sexual and contraceptive senses treated briefly or omitted altogether, but terms relating to female emancipation are also, apparently, unsuitable for inclusion. Mugglestone's ' "The Indefinable Something". Representing Rudeness in the English Dictionary' (in Gorji, ed., pp. 23–34) examines the *OED* treatment of, for example, *cock*, *twat*, *trousers* and *anus* for signs of prudity. Sarah Ogilvie considers dictionary content and contributors in 'New Zealand and the *OED*' (*NZWords* 11[2007] 6–7). In 'Pronouncing the "P": Prescription or Description in 19th- and 20th-Century English Dictionaries' (*HL* 34[2007] 257–80), Charlotte Brewer investigates the representation in dictionaries of Greek-derived words with a silent initial *p*, such as *pneumatic, psalm* and *ptarmigan*. She finds that many dictionaries followed Murray's recommendation in the *OED* that the *p* should be pronounced, but argues that his recommendation was based on personal preference rather than contemporary usage.

Alex Games's *Balderdash and Piffle* is a popular look at the development of English. It arises from the BBC television series, *Balderdash and Piffle*, which asked viewers to help locate ante-datings and origins for terms in (or not yet in) the *OED*. The book consists of thematic chapters dealing with terms for insanity, clothes, criminality and sex; chapters on insults and euphemisms; and chapters on words and phrases, including or apparently including names. Perhaps the oddest chapter looks at compounds and phrases of *dog*. The 'Endword' describes the words whose *OED* entries were altered as a result of the *Balderdash and Piffle* Wordhunt: *balti, Beeb, boffin, bog-standard, bomber jacket, bonk, chattering classes, cocktail, codswallop, cool, full monty, mackem, made-up, management-speak, (gas) mark, minger, moony, mullered, mushy peas, ninety-nine, nip and tuck, nit comb, nit nurse, nutmeg, pass the parcel, phwoar, ploughman's lunch, pop one's clogs, on the pull, ska, smart casual, snazzy, something for the weekend* and *back to square one.* What is perhaps most interesting for dictionary researchers is the range of sources now accepted by the *OED*: from various special interest magazines and television scripts to school exercise books, diaries and autograph books.

'Working Knowledge' (*Dictionaries* 28[2007] 131–62) is a discussion of neologism and its treatment by contemporary dictionaries. Contributors on English neologisms include David K. Barnhart, Orin Hargraves, Ian Brookes, John Simpson, Allan Metcalf and Victoria Neufeldt. They explore particularly the possibilities and problems posed by the availabilty of the huge, democratic, unedited (and often uneducated) corpus that is the internet. The inclusion of topical neologisms undoubtedly helps to sell dictionaries, but they can be a distraction from the task of updating the definitions of more commonly used terms. In 'Considered and Regarded: Indicators of Belief and Doubt in Dictionary Definitions' (*Dictionaries* 28[2007] 48–67), Joseph Pickett analyses techniques for expressing faith and uncertainty in a variety of modern dictionaries of AmE, using definitions for terms including *tooth fairy, reincarnation, Aryan, Brownie point* and *bitch* to explore how attitudinal indicators subtly change the meaning of definitions for problematic terms. Pamela Faber, Pilar León Araúz, Juan Antonio Prieto Velasco and Arianne Reimerink consider the interplay between linguistic and graphical descriptions of specialized contexts in 'Linking Images and Words: The Description of Specialized Concepts' (*IJL* 20[2007] 39–65). They find that current dictionary illustrations do not always mesh with the content or focus of written definitions. Muffy E.A. Siegel's 'What Do You Do with a Dictionary? A Study of Undergraduate Dictionary Use' (*Dictionaries* 28[2007] 23–47) finds that undergraduate first-language users want their dictionaries to be more accessible, particularly by including pictures and listing the most frequent senses first, but also to contain detailed information about etymology and pronunciation.

Heming Yong and Jing Peng's *Bilingual Lexicography from a Communicative Perspective* presents a triangular communicative model of lexicography which encompasses three interdependent standpoints: those of the compiler, user and context. Their evidence is largely drawn from the Chinese–English bilingual tradition, but their conclusions may be more widely applicable. Their discussion of the problem of alphabetizing idioms, for example, offers a useful structural categorization of idioms, and their account of illustrative examples wrestles with the question of whether invented examples are acceptable or not. They also offer a detailed account of dictionary macrostructure, and find that front matter is more predictable than back matter in monolingual and bilingual learners' dictionaries. They conclude with twelve separate recommendations, often differentiating between what is required in dictionaries for encoding and in those for decoding. These range from 'lexicographers should have a clear idea of what purpose their work is intended for' (p. 196) to the recommendation that etymological information should be provided only sparingly 'with emphasis laid on culturally-loaded and morphologically difficult words' (p. 214).

Reinhard Hartmann's *Interlingual Lexicography. Selected Essays on Translation Equivalence, Contrastive Linguistics and the Bilingual Dictionary* consists of twenty-four of his own essays, all previously published elsewhere from 1969 to 2005. One essay originally published in German is translated here into English, perhaps in recognition of the compartmentalizing tendency that he notes in lexicographic research: papers considering dictionaries in a particular language or group of languages will often only be read by researchers interested in those languages. Hartmann defines 'interlingual', in this context, as referring to dictionaries providing information about more than one language. It can be used to emphasize the contrast with monolingual dictionaries or to group together bilingual and multilingual dictionaries. There is no conclusion to draw together the findings of the various papers, but the introduction does offer an overview of their perspectives and purpose. Hartmann offers six perspectives on interlingual dictionaries: dictionary history, dictionary criticism, dictionary typology, dictionary structure, dictionary use and computational lexicography, and follows these with a list of ten research priorities. In this volume, Hartmann's papers are grouped into sections on translation equivalence, contrastive linguistics, interlingual dictionaries and dictionary research. They are edited to avoid repetition and to achieve uniformity of presentation; a single bibliography is provided, and some cross-references are inserted, but the papers are not otherwise altered or updated. For libraries and scholars interested in this area of dictionary research, the republication of these essays will undoubtedly save time spent in the frustrating task of tracking them down in their original contexts. Hartmann returned to the task of listing priorities for dictionary-making and dictionary research in 'Desiderata in Lexicography: Looking Back at Some Problems and Forward to Solutions' (in Sica, ed., pp. 155–61).

Wolfgang Teubert's edited collection, *Text Corpora and Multilingual Lexicography*, represents the results of an EU-funded project called Trans-European Language Resources Infrastructure (TELRI). TELRI took a different approach than earlier machine-translation projects, in that it did not begin from a multilingual conceptual ontology. Instead it took a 'bottom-up approach' (p. viii), and started by looking at translation equivalence in parallel corpora comparing, for instance, translations of Plato's *Republic* in various different languages. Many of the papers included deal with the generation of machine-usable lexicons rather than people-friendly dictionaries, but several will be of interest to lexicologists, lexicographers and dictionary researchers.

Primož Jakopin's 'Distance between Languages as Measured by the Minimal-Entropy Model' (in Teubert, ed., pp. 39–47) offers a technique for calculating relationships between languages. Mihail Mihailov and Hannu Tommola's paper 'Compiling Parallel Text Corpora. Towards Automation of Routine Procedures' (in Teubert, ed., pp. 59–67) describes an automated use of collocation to select translation equivalents. Hana Skoumalová presents the use of 'Bridge Dictionaries as Bridges Between Languages' (in Teubert, ed., pp. 83–91), by which partially translated learners' dictionaries can be used as the basis for new bilingual or multilingual dictionaries. Teubert's own paper, 'Corpus Linguistics and Lexicography' (in Teubert, ed., pp. 109–33), explores the place of corpus linguistics as a sub-branch of linguistics.

Herbert C. Purnell introduces and describes a bilingual dictionary of a language used in northern Laos and Thailand in 'Reference Works in Progress: Excerpts from *An Iu Mien-English Dictionary with Cultural Notes*' (*Dictionaries* 28[2007] 69–130). After twenty years' work, the project is nearing completion. Wang Fu Fang and Lu Gu Sun (referred to as Gusun throughout the article) discuss 'Inheritance Plus Innovation: On the Revision of the *English–Chinese Dictionary*' (*IJL* 20[2007] 1–38). They consider particularly the task of determining which new words should be included and how the evidence should be collected. Villy Tsakona's 'Bilingualisation in Practice: Terminological Issues in Bilingualising a Specialised Glossary' (*IJL* 20[2007] 119–45) offers a theoretical discussion emerging from the production of a glossary in Greek of English sociolinguistic terminology, emphasizing the importance of using corpora to determine the frequency and usage of terms in the target language. Wen Xiu Yang writes 'On Pragmatic Information in Learners' Dictionaries, with Particular Reference to *LDOCE₄*' (*IJL* 20[2007] 147–73), and identifies strengths and weaknesses in the fourth edition of the *Longman Dictionary of Contemporary English*'s provision of pragmatic information. N.E. Osselton's 'Innovation and Continuity in English Learners' Dictionaries: The Single-Clause *When*-definition' (*IJL* 20[2007] 393–9) finds that Elisha Coles used definitions of the type: '**Obtuse angle**, when two lines include more than a square' as early as 1676.

8. Onomastics

Onomastics books published in 2007 were rare, but three are particularly noteworthy, two on place-names and a very welcome treatment of the theory of names from a linguistic and pragmatic perspective.

The first of the two place-name volumes is Keith Baca's *Native American Place Names in Mississippi*, a welcome addition to a long-neglected aspect of American place-naming, one which for too many years has been dismissed as 'insignificant' or patronized as 'merely descriptive'. Keith Baca, a career archaeologist with the Mississippi Department of Archives and History, has selected just under 600 names, overwhelmingly from Choctaw or Chickasaw, closely related Muskogean languages and the main indigenous languages of Mississippi. Many of these are based upon a small number of Choctaw words (usually with close cognates in Chickasaw), such as *Bogue* (< *bok*) 'stream', *chitto* 'big', *oka* 'water', and *homa* 'red', which provide the roots for such names as *Bogue Chitto* 'big creek', *Okahatta* 'white water', and *Tallahoma* 'red rock'. The entries include the name, location of the community or natural feature, the current local pronunciation and discussion of previously suggested etymologies and derivations (with references), followed by criticisms and Baca's own interpretations where earlier suggestions are non-existent or shown to be false. Baca's primary purpose is to determine the actual (or at least most probable) etymology for each name. To this end he holds previous suggestions to the light of Choctaw and Chickasaw vocabularies, rejecting many proposals, and in more than a hundred instances where no previous etymologies have been offered or are obviously erroneous he has provided his own, exposing many myths, legends and folk tales surrounding the names in the process. This is a valuable contribution to the growing body of literature showing the considerable impact of native names on the American landscape.

The Place-Names of County Durham by the late Victor Watts—whose monumental *Cambridge Dictionary of English Place-Names* was reviewed in this section one year ago—and edited by Paul Cavill, is volume LXXXIII in the Survey of English Place-Names series. This particular issue is the first of several projected volumes dealing with the names of County Durham which draws upon the materials collected by Victor Watts from his home county over a thirty-year period. His lamentable passing in late 2002 left the final editing to Paul Cavill, who is to be commended for seeing this book through the publication process in so exemplary a manner. The present volume deals with only a part of County Durham. The organization proceeds from Stockton Ward itself to the twenty-two parishes contained within that ward to the townships within each parish. The names of not only communities but also those of ways, roads, buildings and fields are included as well. A welcome feature is the outstanding twenty-six-page appendix of the elements of place-names and field-names which appear among the names of Stockton Ward. This volume is an exceptional example of place-name research, a model for future scholars.

Willy Van Langendonck's *Theory and Typology of Proper Names* is the first comprehensive study of proper names in a quarter-century since John Algeo's *On Defining the Proper Name*, which was published in 1973. Van Langendonck is to be commended for bringing a considerable body of interdisciplinary material to bear on the issue of proper names. This is in essence a linguistic analysis of names, but it also includes evidence from philosophical, psycholinguistic, dialinguistic and neurolinguistic perspectives, which Van Langendonck uses to delineate the semantic and grammatical status of names and the boundaries between names and other nouns and noun-like objects. In the process he provides a typology of proper names based upon their grammatical, semantic and pragmatic properties. Especially impressive is Van Langendonck's use of neurolinguistic studies as major contributors to onomastic theory, especially those of Carlo Semenza and Marina Zettin, which allow him to conclude that proper names do not have lexical meaning in the same way that common nouns do and that the function of proper names is essentially referential. Van Langendonck defines a proper name as 'a noun that denotes a unique entity at the level of established linguistic convention to make it psychosocially salient within a given basic level category. The meaning of the name, if any, does not (or not any longer) determine its denotations. An important reflex of this pragmatic-semantic characterization of names is their ability to appear in such close appositional constructions as *the poet Burns, Fido, the dog, the River Thames*, or *the City of London*' (p. 116). Note that psycho-social saliency is a pragmatic function, the meaning is a semantic function, and these combined create the syntactic function of a proper name. There is a great deal more of both theoretical and practical interest in this book; hypotheses which will keep onomastic researchers busy for years to come. For instance, Van Langendonck claims that proper names are 'the prototypical nominal category' (p. 119), that names 'like personal pronouns . . . are inherently referential and definite' and that they are 'singular, countable, nonrecursive and show third person on the lexical level' (p. 182). Van Langendonck distinguishes four classes of names, ranging from personal and place-names (the prototypical category) through brand names and autonyms to appellatives. This is an important book and it is best to approach it directly. A review by Frank Nuessel appeared in *Lingua* (118[2008] 1233–8).

Before proceeding with summaries of some of the onomastic articles which were published in 2007, I would like to bring to readers' attention three collections of essays, all of which make strides towards both defining the discipline and extending its boundaries. The long-delayed 2004 issue of *Onoma* (number 39) is devoted to teaching about names, a welcome issue on a long-ignored subject but one which is being given greater and greater attention. In fact the three most recent triennial meetings of the International Congress of Onomastic Sciences (ICOS) included sessions on the teaching of names. The selections in this issue of *Onoma* are highly varied; most are concerned with the teaching of names in particular institutions or particular countries: in Finland, in Italy, in Croatia, in Germany, in Norway; others deal with including onomastic units in courses devised primarily for other purposes, such as geography, anthropology, or the history of a particular language; still others survey the state of teaching onomastics in a particular location. The languages in which the contributions are written are likewise variable; here I will summarize only those written in English and concerned with onomastics in primarily English-speaking countries.

In 'Teaching Names: A Personal Account' (*Onoma* 39[2004] 19–28), W.F.H. Nicolaisen recounts his more than half-century of teaching and research and how he has given scores of talks on onomastics and conducted courses (both credit and non-credit) at the university level in the US and in Scotland. Nicolaisen provides a discussion of the differences between lexical and onomastic items, the lexicon and the onomasticon, sets out the goals for a course in onomastics and concludes with a useful appendix of a course outline for names in north-east Scotland. The appendix contains information useful to anyone contemplating a course on names or even giving an informal lecture on the subject. Grant Smith, in 'Teaching Onomastics in the United States' (*Onoma* 39[2004] 45–60), surveys the history of teaching names in colleges and universities in the US, focusing on the classes taught by himself, William G. Loy at the University of Oregon and Thomas J. Gasque at the University of South Dakota. Smith laments that onomastics courses are now generally absent from the curricula of American colleges and universities, citing among other reasons the fact that since individual departments want to hold onto their own students for purposes of generating enrolment 'place name courses seem to suffer from what seems to be their greatest strength, their interdisciplinarity' (p. 49). And I agree wholeheartedly with Smith's claim that unfortunately there are no courses currently taught in which the primary content is names. Smith proceeds to describe a Shakespeare seminar which he devoted primarily to names, in particular 'to use the analysis of names as a way of understanding language and literature in general and of appreciating Shakespeare more profoundly' (p. 51). Several appendices describing the class and its goals are included. Finally, an article relevant to anyone contemplating a course on onomastics is Naftali Kadmon's very informative 'Teaching Toponymy at University Level' (*Onoma* 39[2004] 275–87), a particularly useful aspect of which is the appendix where Kadmon lists several dozen topics included in the course he teaches, ranging from grammatical aspects of toponyms, to transliterating names, to political and cultural aspects of names, to present names authorities and names standardization.

Names (55:iii[2007]), was a special issue devoted to 'Women in Onomastics', edited by Dorothy Dodge Robbins and Christine De Vinne. The issue contains four essays on aspects of women's names in the larger onomastic world. Beth DiNatale Johnson and Christine De Vinne (*Names* 55[2007] 199–228) consider the names of women's colleges in the US; Laurie K. Scheuble and David R. Johnson report on 'Social and Cognitive Factors in Women's Marital Name Choice' (*Names* 55[2007] 229–51), finding that women who make non-conventional name choices upon marriage (i.e. retaining their own surname or hyphenating their surname with that of their new husband) tend to marry later, live in larger communities, and are better educated than those who assume their husband's surname; Eileen Quinlan writes on 'Ritual Circles to Home in Louise Erdrich's Character Names' (*Names* 55[2007] 253–75) and Lynn Westney, in 'From Courtesans to Queens: Recipes Named for Women' (*Names* 55[2007] 277–86), considers some of the many recipes which have been named after women, from omelette Agnès Sorel to Melba toast to cantaloupe Lillian Russell.

Names (55:iv[2007]) was a Festschrift in honour of Edwin D. Lawson, a tribute to Lawson for his nearly fifty years of social science research in onomastics, for his promotion of name study, for his encouragement of onomasts around the world, and for his work on behalf of the American Name Society, which he served as president in 1995 and 1996. The Festschrift contains twenty-one essays, obviously far too many to summarize here. Some titles, however, can be mentioned both to convey the flavour of the contributions and to appeal to readers with particular onomastic interests: 'Naming the Goodyear Blimp' (*Names* 55[2007] 326–34) 'Compass Points in English Surnames' (*Names* 55[2007] 343–8), 'Names, Registration Plates, and Identity' (*Names* 55[2007] 354–62), 'Two Worldviews Regarding Chinese American Names' (*Names* 55[2007] 363–71), and 'War Names in the Zimbabwean Liberation War' (*Names* 55[2007] 427–36). In addition there are essays on the translation of proper names, the use of nicknames by politicians and the influence of popular culture on given names.

I have grouped the following onomastic articles into traditional categories: those dealing with the theory and practice of onomastics, those concerned primarily with geographical names, those emphasizing personal names and finally those best called socio-onomastic.

D.K. Tucker has been a primary contributor to the methodology of onomastic research for the past decade. His article in *Nomina* (30[2007] 5–22) continues his search for revealing ways to graphically present the distribution of name types and tokens from very large databases. Here he expands on an occupied frequency technique where a graph can be plotted from a desktop program such as Excel. These plots, which look like saggital sections of ships (Tucker once called them 'Viking longboats') show that surname distributions, regardless of country of origin, follow Zipf's law, a power law relationship of the form X times Y equals a constant.

The retrieval of names, especially those with more than a few variants, has long been an issue in onomastics. In recent times the search for a mechanism to retrieve similar names dates from at least 1918 when Richard Russell developed the well-known Soundex system, which attempted to retrieve name clusters that sounded similar, regardless of the different ways they might be spelled. This became an important issue in the US in the 1930s with the establishment of the social security system. An article by Ronald J. Leach (*Names* 54[2006] 321–30) reports an attempt to improve on both the Soundex and Daitch–Mokotoff retrieval systems by including essentially etymological information. The example used here is the habitational name Shirecliff, which has some fifty known variants. Adding the habitational field raised the success rate from 86 per cent for the two most common encodings in Soundex to 88 per cent, and from 86 per cent in Daitch–Mokotoff to 92 per cent. But as Leach cautions: 'At present, the state of name matching leaves quite a bit to be desired' (p. 328).

In 2007 Marc Picard (*OnCan* 89[2007] 27–51) continued his investigations, which have shown the great value of internet resources in replacing otherwise 'unidentified' or 'uncertain' origins of surnames with solid etymologies. Here, Picard removes more than 150 surnames from these categories and, conversely, shows that an additional sixty or so which were claimed to be from a given language in the *Dictionary of American Family Names* are in fact from other sources.

Newsletters are usually the repositories of chatty news items concerning an organization's business affairs, activities of its members, announcements of forthcoming meetings and the like. Rarely are they the home of serious, extended scholarly research. *The Newsletter of the Society for the Study of the Indigenous Languages of the Americas* (at least the January 2007 issue) is a welcome exception since it offers etymologies and derivations for three Native American names, two of which were previously problematic. David Costa, perhaps the world's leading authority on the now extinct Miami-Illinois language, reconsiders the origin and significance of the name Illinois, which has been taken to mean 'tribe of superior people' and tacitly accepted as the name by which the Illinois referred to themselves. Costa (*SSILA Newsletter* 25[Jan. 2007] 9–12) makes the case that the self-designation of the Illinois was Inoca, a name of unknown origin and meaning. The name from which Illinois is derived apparently originated in Miami-Illinois, was taken into Ojibwa and subsequently into French. Rather than meaning 'superior people', Illinois more likely means 'I speak in the regular way.' Michael McCafferty (*SSILA Newsletter* 25[Jan. 20072007] 13–14) takes on the origin and meaning of Peoria, a name for which at least seven meanings have been proposed. McCafferty suggests a derivation from Proto-Algonquian through Miami-Illinois and the meaning 'to dream with the help of a manitou'.

The *Journal of the English Place-Name Society* contains its usual mix of articles, shorter items and reviews. Keith Briggs (*JEPNS* 39[2007] 7–44) takes on the task of explaining the motivation for the one hundred plus place-names in Europe meaning 'seven springs' or 'seven streams' (the appended gazetteer lists sixty-six in Britain, including 'seven wells'). Briggs suggests that in pre-Christian folklore the 'seven springs' were likely considered sacred. When the church was unsuccessful in suppressing superstitions it in effect took them over and turned them to its own advantage, redefining them as the seven types of wisdom which flowed from Christ and which neutralized the seven deadly sins. Sound changes in English caused the etymologies to become obscure and the meanings to become opaque.

Richard Coates, of the University of the West of England in Bristol, is one of the pre-eminent and highly prolific contemporary onomasts. In 2007 he produced a number of articles of significance. In 'Shoreditch and Car Dyke: Two Allusions to Romano-British Built Features in Later Names Containing OE dīc, With Reflections on Variable Place-Name Structure' (*Nomina* 30[2007] 23–33), Coates suggests an origin for 'shore' which is much older than previously thought and which derives from Brittonic **Skor* meaning 'fort' or 'rampart'. As to 'Car Dyke', after considering previous work and especially looking at earlier spellings, Coates proposes that the first element is not from a Scandinavian personal name as had been suggested but is rather 'an Old English rendering of Primitive Welsh . . . *kair, "civitas, city" ' (p. 28). The same formative is found in Carlisle, Cardew, Cardinham and Carburton. A significant feature of this article is Coates's reference to the Onymic Default Principle, which, as far as I can determine, was coined and first introduced to onomastics by him at the 21st International Congress of Onomastic Sciences, held at Uppsala, Sweden, in 2002. As conceived by Coates, the Onymic Default Principle is a kind of folk etymology which holds that the interpretation of any string of opaque linguistic units will default to a proper name (real or imagined), especially where personal names are 'found' within otherwise opaque place-names. Examples given by Coates include 'Ludgate', associated with the legendary King Lud, 'Edinburgh' for King Edwin of Northumbria, and 'Shoreditch' for Jane Shore, the mistress of King Edward IV.

Coates (*JEPNS* 39[2007] 59–72) looks into the etymology of 'Domball', which he calls 'a not previously noted place-name element' (p. 59). After considering a number of possibilities and after providing copious historical and geographical relevancies, he suggests (tentatively) an origin which includes 'a lost regional lexical word meaning "pasture subject to (occasional) tidal flooding" ', which itself may have its roots 'in a local Scandinavian expression **dunnu-ból*, "mallard's, duck's lair or bed" ' (p. 66). Coates contributed several additional articles to *JEPNS*, a substantial one of some seventy pages, which deals with a number of minor names, each in its own section, the concerns of which can be gathered by considering the title: 'Azure Mouse, Bloater Hill, Goose Puddings, and One Land Called Cow: Continuity and Conundrums in Lincolnshire' (*JEPNS* 39[2007] 73–143). A useful part of this article is the appended list of name formatives which appear in the text. These include

'Cloot', 'Tid', 'Willow' and the ever-popular 'Tom Turd', the generic name given to gatherers of night soil.

In 'Bordastubble, a Standing Stone in Unst, Shetland, and Some Implications for English Toponymy' (*JSPNS* 1[2007] 137–9) Coates shows how a single, isolated name can shed light not only on other names but on cultural aspects of locales as well. He suggests that 'Bordastubble' is from an ON descriptive for 'battle axe pillar/post', which leads him to conjecture that there was in former times a similar standing stone in at least five English places with variant names, including 'Barnstable' in Devon and probably 'Bastow Hill' as well. This is onomastic detective work at its finest and Coates demonstrates a remarkable range and depth of knowledge of not only British history but of related cultures and languages in this article and in many others. And, speaking of onomastic detective work, Coates likely has antedated by more than a century the first attestation of one of the most often denounced but most frequently used and certainly one of the most discussed words in English (remarkable for the fact that it has been both supported and condemned without using the word itself) by elucidating the history of the no longer existing field name which will immediately be obvious to all speakers of English, 'Fockynggroue', in his article 'Fockynggroue in Bristol' (*N&Q* 54[2007] 373–6).

Jay H. Bernstein, in a creative article titled simply 'New York Placenames in Film Titles' (*Names* 55[2007] 139–66), shows how a simple list (in this case the titles of the nearly 400 films made between 1914 and 2006 with titles referring to New York, its boroughs, neighbourhoods, streets, or locations) can be used to provide insights into the 'psychological map' (in this instance a conflicted one) of a culture. 'New York', 'Manhattan', 'Broadway' and 'Times Square' have been used by movie-makers since the beginning of the medium to evoke the collective imaginary of glitz, glamour and grandeur, the über-sophistication of the big city, while at the same time using such names as 'Harlem', 'The Bowery' and 'Hell's Kitchen' to elicit images of the squalor, hopelessness and despair of the tenements and the ethnic neighbourhoods.

In a study related to one reported here last year showing that baseball players with nicknames tended to live about two years longer than those without nicknames, Ernest Abel and Michael L. Kruger (*PandMS* 104[2007] 179–82) looked at baseball players whose initials spelled out 'positive' words (e.g. ACE, LAF, WOW) compared to those whose initials spelled out 'negative' words (e.g. DED, MAD, SOB), and found that players with positive initials lived an astounding average of thirteen years longer than those with negative or neutral initials. The authors attribute this effect to the likelihood that having positive initials is part of the 'implicit self-esteem people associate with their names' (p. 181). Abel and Kruger are certainly among the more creative name scholars. In an article dealing with the phonetics of pet names (*Names* 55[2007] 53–64) they look at naming practices of dogs and cats in terms of their phonetic properties as related to human names and as given in two countries: the US and Australia. Hypothesizing that sex stereotyping of pets would take the same forms it does with humans, they found in general that 'people applied the same gender-related naming practices for pets that they used for both male and female children' (p. 53). In particular both the final letter and the final phoneme differentiated female pets from male pets just as they do for male and female human names. Somewhat surprisingly, cats (which are generally thought of as female) were not as a group characterized by a 'female' final letter or phoneme. In another article dealing with the naming of pets, Abel (*Names* 55[2007] 349–53) found that dogs (and to a slightly lesser extent cats) were given human names more often than other species of pets. Nearly 50 per cent of dogs were given human names. Abel concludes that 'pets kept in cages [birds, hamsters, rabbits] are less likely to be given human names than are pets allowed to roam freely within the home [dogs, cats]' (p. 349).

In a creative use of a newly available database Iman Makeba Laversuch (*Names* 54[2006] 331–62) investigated the personal names of fugitive slaves, classifying them into plant and animal names (most of which, such as 'Monkey' and 'Buckwheat', were derogatory); place-names such as 'Bristol', 'London' and 'Shrewsbury'; biblical names such as 'Esther' and 'Matthew'; classical names such as 'Cato' and 'Hector'; names from the British royal house such as 'Charles' and 'Henry'; traditional African names, especially day names such as 'Quashee' and 'Kofi'; and surnames, often of their owners. This is an interesting descriptive article but one which wanders too far into speculation, as when the author attempts to impute the heroic classical characteristics of, say, 'Julius' or 'Pompey' to escaped slaves, or, when this model does not fit, to simply brush it off with a too nimble 'sometimes [the exact] opposite was the case' (p. 347). An important finding is that apparently the names of female fugitives were —as is the case with contemporary names— considerably more diverse than male names: just under 40 per cent of male name tokens came from only fifteen name types.

Frank Exner, Little Bear, discusses personal names of North American Indians in their historical and contemporary forms in 'North American Indians: Personal Names with Semantic Meaning' (*Names* 55[2007] 3–16), emphasizing the problems different name forms can create cross-culturally. Currently, Native American names are of three forms: traditional (e.g. 'Little Bear'), European (e.g. 'Frank Exner'), and mixed (e.g. 'Frank Exner, Little Bear'). Native American names differ from European names in that one name may be followed by an entirely different name at another time, and names may be concurrent, so one individual may have multiple names at any given time, and the social situation will dictate which is the appropriate name and conversely, the particular name used often elicits a specific response. As Exner, Little Bear, notes, in a Native American setting, if Severt Young Bear is asked to perform at a gathering there is no pressure on him to comply, but if he is asked as Hehaka Luzahan ('Swift Elk') then it is difficult for him to refuse.

Onomastica Canadiana publishes twice a year and carries articles in French as well as English; thus on average about half of the articles which appear in *OnCan* are appropriate for this volume. In ' "Ils appellent le soleil Iesus": Linguistic Interaction among Montagnais, Basques, and Jesuits in New France' (*OnCan* 89[2007] 53–61), William Sayers takes what appears to be a simple and straightforward folk etymology and turns it into a revealing account of pidginization among social and linguistic groups in seventeenth-century Canada. A Jesuit report that local Montagnais called the sun 'Jesus' led to Sayers's conclusion that the source was *eguzki*, a Basque word for 'sun' which had become part of the trade jargon developed between the Montagnais and Basque whalers. The expected /eguski/ was rendered by the Montagnais (or more likely hopefully heard by French priests) as /dzezykri/.

Herbert Barry III (University of Pittsburgh, emeritus) continued his research into the psychological implications of names in literature, especially authorial 'self-naming', in which authors name characters, if not directly for themselves, with their own name. In 'Characters Named Charles or Charley in Novels by Charles Dickens' (*PRep* 101[2007] 497–500) Barry notes that in his fourteen completed novels Dickens created twelve fictional characters named Charles or Charley. In the early novels (*Pickwick Papers, Oliver Twist* and *Nicholas Nickleby*) these namesakes tend to be characterized by humour and spirit, but they become less so in the later novels (*Dombey and Son, David Copperfield, Bleak House*), and especially in *Tale of Two Cities* and *Our Mutual Friend*, written towards the end of his career and after Dickens's estrangement from his wife.

For nearly three decades Donna Lillian has been tracking the use of 'Ms' as a courtesy title for women in general corresponding to 'Mr' as a courtesy title for men. Using fifteen scenarios involving hypothetical women with imputed attributes and soliciting responses electronically, she found that, since 1995, although use of 'Ms' had increased from slightly more than half of all responses to nearly three-quarters in the intervening decade, the usage had become stereotyped and 'used in a manner that is almost the complete opposite of its intended usage' (in Reich, Sullivan,. Lommel and Griffen, eds., *LACUS Forum 33: Variation*, pp. 211–18) and had been 'turned into a tool for more precisely identifying a woman's marital status' (p. 211). 'Specifically, a woman is more likely to be addressed with *Ms.* if she is divorced, separated, or widowed, if she is a lesbian, or if she is single and past the age of about 25' (p. 217).

A reasonably new aspect of onomastics and one which will likely gain in application and significance is associated with the discipline of forensic linguistics, which offers linguistic expertise at various points in the judicial process. Although the testimony offered by linguists is currently confined largely to North America, its use appears to be spreading, especially in Europe. There is now an International Association of Forensic Linguists, which publishes *The International Journal of Speech, Language and the Law*. Much expert testimony concerns names, in particular trade names and other registerable marks. One of the leading forensic linguists who has written extensively on names and the law is Ronald Butters. Butters, in 'Changing Linguistic Issues in US Trademark Litigation' (in Turrell, Spassova and Cicres, eds., *Second European IAFL Conference on Forensic Linguistic / Language and the Law*, pp. 29–42) gives a good overview of the kinds of contributions forensic linguists (onomasts in particular) can make to the legal process, as well as pointing out some of what he refers to as the changes and challenges in US trademark litigation. Butters presents a scale of trademark strength, which ranges from the weakest (true generics; in other words, common nouns) to descriptives (nouns which have taken on secondary meanings) to suggestives (nouns with positive connotations) to the strongest (arbitrary and fanciful names manufactured for the purpose of providing a trademarkable name). Butters illustrates extensively from cases on which he has provided expert opinion, especially the case questioning the genericness of the name 'kettle chips'.

9. Dialectology and Sociolinguistics

This year's review starts with textbooks. Nikolas Coupland has written what is probably the first textbook on *Style: Language Variation and Identity*, and at the same time the first book-length introduction to postmodern concepts of the term. Coupland gives an excellent overview of the concept of style through time, from variationist sociolinguistics (William Labov's idea that *style* is 'attention to speech') via Howard Giles's and Allan Bell's idea of style as 'audience design' to the late modern idea that speakers actively employ style to stylize themselves through discourse, and indeed that all speech is performance. The individual chapters deal with 'Style and Meaning in Sociolinguistic Structure' (especially with the meaning potential of standard vs. non-standard speech), 'Style for Audiences' (note Giles's idea of style above), 'Sociolinguistic Resources for Styling' (relating the discussion to Pierre Bourdieu's concept of *habitus*, which we will meet again below), 'Styling Social Identities' (discussing 'acts of identity', 'gender' as well as 'crossing' on the way), 'High Performance and Identity Stylisation', where 'high performance' is meant to indicate public performances with a heightened (more intense) character. The crucial point is, of course, that every performance has some elements of 'high performance'. Stylization can also be thought of as 'pastiche', or recycling, of (perhaps stereotyped) features of variants for a variety of reasons, from identity construction to parody and meta-parody. Throughout, the book is thoughtful as well as thought-provoking, full of text extracts and Coupland's own in-depth analyses, while Coupland's thesis that 'style is performance' is explored throughout the text. As the author himself notes, the book moves away 'from one every particular, consolidated, disciplined and productive perspective [on style, viz. the variationist one] to a much more open, critical but speculative perspective' (p. 177). A highly enjoyable and informative must-read for advanced students and researchers alike.

But before you think that postmodernism has finally arrived in linguistics, well, at least in sociolinguistics, it has to be said that the bulk of publications, perhaps with the exception of publications on gender (see below) are still written from a very traditional, highly objectivist perspective. A good example for this set of mind is the collection of introductory essays in the *Routledge Companion to Sociolinguistics* edited by Carmen Llamas, Louise Mullany and Peter Stockwell. Extremely short (eight- to twelve-page) articles provide introductions to variationist methods and analysis techniques, the traditional extralinguistic variables (class, gender, age, ethnicity, speech community), what the editors call 'socio-psychological factors' (style, identity, mobility, accommodation, attitudes, politeness and power), 'socio-political factors' (standard language, mass media, multilingualism, education, language planning), and language change (curiously encompassing mainly creole studies, but also an article on language death). The list of contributors reads like a who's who in sociolinguistics, from Peter Auer to Walt Wolfram. Nevertheless, this is mainly a repetition of articles we have read in almost identical form many times before; the entries are too short to be really useful as introductions, but too long to function as lexicon entries, and the collection is too old-fashioned to be really fascinating.

On the subject of applied linguistics, Carolyn Temple Adger, Walt Wolfram and Donna Christian have written an updated second edition of *Dialects in Schools and Communities*, geared towards non-specialists (for example teachers or speech therapists), therefore paying particular attention to the fact that variation is inherent in language and systematic. They discuss lay perceptions of dialect and language variation before introducing more sociolinguistic ways of investigating and thinking about language variation. They also look at the role language plays in social interaction, and how dialect and cultural differences can lead to misunderstandings in the classroom. In addition, they deal with more narrowly relevant topics such as how to test language skills in the light of language differences, a discussion of the influence (and perhaps the value) of the vernacular in writing and in teaching reading skills, and the drawing up of a programme of dialect awareness for students. Throughout, this book is superbly informed, yet at the same time accessible to readers with no previous knowledge of sociolinguistics. It tries to dispel a range of popular myths about language that are not only ill informed from the point of view of sociolinguistics, but have very real repercussions on (dialect-speaking) students' lives. Not surprisingly, the keyword of this book is 'fairness', and we can only hope that as many teachers and other non-specialists as possible will make use of this resource, now up-to-date.

Robert Bayley and Ceil Lucas have edited the in-depth *Sociolinguistic Variation: Theories, Methods, and Applications*, a volume dedicated to Walt Wolfram and obviously very much inspired by his work. Contributions are divided into the three parts of the subtitle, 'Theories' (eight chapters), 'Methods' (three chapters) and, indeed, 'Applications' (six chapters). The first part is the most interesting, since it provides a forum for the discussion of such important topics as the treatment of variation in phonological theories (Greg Guy), a discussion of syntactic variation (Lisa Green), inherent variability (Ralph Fasold and Dennis Preston), historical variationist studies (Kirk Hazen, but also Michael Montgomery), variation in second-language acquisition (Robert Bayley), and variation in sign language (Ceil Lucas)—topics often neglected in more standard sociolinguistic compendiums. Part II, the shortest, on methods in sociolinguistics, only features a chapter on sociolinguistic fieldwork (Natalie Schilling-Estes), one on quantitative analysis (Sali Tagliamonte) and one on 'Sociophonetics' (Erik Thomas)—surely not doing justice to the wide field of sociolinguistics as such, and not even to variationist sociolinguistics. Where are more modern ethnographic approaches, where is James and Lesley Milroy's network approach, where is the Community of Practice? The third part is a hotchpotch of topics not always discussed in other collections, from the more predictable relation to education (Carolyn Temple Adger and Donna Christian, and Angela and John Rickford), or to language acquisition (Ida Stockman), up to topics not usually found in sociolinguistics books, viz. 'Sociolinguistic Variation and the Law' (Ron Butters), an interesting introduction to forensic linguistics, or 'Attitudes towards Variation and Ear-Witness Testimony' (John Baugh), where 'linguistic profiling' is introduced, defined (and condemned). Finally, completing this collection, Roger Shuy writes a very personal and memorable afterword on Walt Wolfram. A very interesting collection, useful as introductory or supplementary texts, that should sit on every self-respecting sociolinguist's desk (then again, if you know Walt Wolfram, you probably contributed to this volume yourself), and which will be useful in advanced and graduate classes too.

Ethnography (and in particular linguistic ethnography (LE)), though perhaps missing from Bayley and Lucas, eds., is the subject of a special issue of the *Journal of Sociolinguistics* (11:v[2007]), edited by Karin Tusting and Janet Maybin. Particularly relevant to English sociolinguistics is Ben Rampton's contribution in which he traces 'Neo-Hymesian Linguistic Ethnography in the United Kingdom' (*JSoc* 11[2007] 584–607) through persons, career paths and institutions, pointing out that LE in Britain has been the domain of sociolinguists, rather than anthropologists, and that as an interdisciplinary region it 'sits comfortably in the much broader shift from mono- to inter-disciplinarity in British higher education' (p. 584). Alison Sealey puts 'Linguistic Ethnography in Realist Perspective' (*JSoc* 11[2007] 641–60), exploring answers that LE can provide to the basic sociolinguistic question of 'which people use which kinds of language in what circumstances and with what outcome(s)?' (p. 641). Sealey argues that LE, especially linked theoretically to social (or sociological) realism, can provide better answers than other approaches, in particular when it comes to taking into account speakers' agency and the fact that social categories are mediated through discourse. It is especially this link to social realism that Sealey advocates and hopes to promote.

Moving to more general discussions of sociolinguistics and dialectology, the treatment of non-standard data in more abstract linguistic theories also plays a large role this year. Helmut Weiss calls for co-operation between theoretical (read: generative) linguistics and sociolinguistics in his paper 'A Question of Relevance: Some Remarks on Standard Languages' (in Penke and Rosenbach, eds., *What Counts as Evidence in Linguistics: The Case of Innateness*, pp. 181–208). Weiss makes the interesting point that English, like German, has a standard language heavily influenced by prescriptivism, and is therefore at least to some degree 'unnatural', while the data from dialects would present theoretical linguistics with more natural input. Graeme Trousdale and David Adger have edited a special issue of *English Language and Linguistics* (11:ii[2007]) on English dialect syntax, or perhaps more precisely, the treatment of variation in various syntactic frameworks (or syntactic theories). As the editors, they correctly point out that non-standard data have so far not really played a prominent role in theory-building, be it in the generative camp or elsewhere. (David Adger and Graeme Trousdale, 'Variation in English Syntax: Theoretical Implications', *ELL* 11[2007] 261–78). What is more, 'syntactic variation in English dialects has been a thorny issue for dialectologists, sociolinguists, and theoretical linguists alike' (p. 266), so that this topic has really been doubly (or trebly?) neglected, if you will—an oversight that this special issue sets out to remedy. Contributions range from Word Grammar to stochastic OT to Principles and Parameters, and the phenomena under discussion span an equally wide range from copula deletion to possessive constructions. Individual contributions are discussed in the regional subsections below. Perhaps even more abstract is William A. Kretzschmar Jr's contribution on 'What's in the Name "Linguistics" for Variationists' (*JEngL* 35[2007] 263–77), geared especially towards the American linguistics scene which is dominated by structuralists or generativists, and as this subsection has repeatedly pointed out, generative grammar and linguistic variation are difficult to reconcile if you take variation seriously. Kretzschmar's advice in this difficult situation is that (theoretical) linguists need to 'accept the idea that there are many different valid ways to study human language' (p. 276).

After this more general overview, we now move to an overview of publications dealing with Great Britain. The collection of essays in David Britain, ed., *Language in the British Isles*, is in a way a new edition of Peter Trudgill's first edition from 1984, taking over the basic division of chapters into English, Celtic and 'Other Languages'. It is *not* just a new edition in that all the chapters are brand new, and especially the chapters on English (which, just, make up the bulk of this volume) deal with new subdivisions that would have been inconceivable twenty-five years ago (or so). In part, the chapters read like a miniature version of the 2004 *Handbook of the Varieties of English*, edited by Bernd Kortmann and Edgar Schneider (*YWES* 85[2006]), but going beyond mere regional varieties. Thus, James Milroy deals with 'The History of English', Paul Kerswill discusses differences between 'Standard and Non-Standard English', Paul Foulkes and Gerard Docherty present 'Phonological Variation in England', David Britain gives an overview of the relatively new field of studies on 'Grammatical Variation in England' in a chapter that stands out by virtue of its depth and width of coverage, Paul A. Johnston Jr writes on 'Scottish English and Scots', Kevin McCafferty summarizes research on 'Northern Irish English', Raymond Hickey does the same for 'Southern Irish English', and Robert Penhallurick describes 'English in Wales'. The rough regional divisions inside England (English in the north, Midlands, south-west, south-east, East Anglia) of the *Handbook* are not mirrored here in separate sections, for this the general phonological/morphological overview chapters have to suffice. Interesting for comparative reasons might be the chapters on the Celtic languages (there are chapters on Gaelic, Irish and Welsh, as well as an overview of the 'History of the Celtic Languages in the British Isles'), and of course the third ('Other') part, which ranges from Caribbean creoles, Indic languages and Chinese to Channel Island French or Angloromani, and this reviewer at least would be hard pushed to name another publication with as wide a range of languages discussed. The fourth part, 'Applied Sociolinguistic Issues', deals with languages in the classroom from two perspectives: internal variation (a chapter by Ann Williams) and speakers of languages other than English (Ben Rampton, Roxy Harris and Constant Leung). In sum, this is an up-to-date (or at least it was, some four years ago) summary of much dialectological and sociolinguistic work done on language in the British Isles. Seeing the dynamics of this field, we look forward to a new edition in just a few years' time. The more specifically regional contributions are also discussed below in the regional sections of this chapter.

Also overview-like in character are contributions to *A History of the English Language*, edited by the late Richard Hogg and David Denison, from last year (unaccountably overlooked by this reviewer then, our apologies). Hogg and Denison stress that the whole volume takes variation as a central theme, and this is perhaps clearest in Hogg's own chapter on 'English in Britain' (pp. 352–83), a thirty-page introduction to questions and methods of historical as well as present-day dialectology, and in Edward Finegan's mirror-chapter on 'English in North America' (pp. 384–419) (see below). Hogg's tour through the (dialectal nature of) the English language from Old English until today stresses that even in the age of mass media and high mobility, dialects are not just disappearing (although for rural dialects this is probably the case), but that there are also many innovative features in urban dialects, which, as he writes, have often been ignored for ideological reasons. Hogg also effortlessly moves from a discussion of historical to traditional dialectology and includes results from more modern variationist sociolinguistics.

Also taking a wide regional sweep of the country, and linking empirical variationist evidence with theoretical arguments, Joan Bresnan, Ashwini Deo and Devyani Sharma draw up a 'Typology in Variation: A Probabilistic Approach to *Be* and *N't* in the *Survey of English Dialects*' (*ELL* 11[2007] 301–46). The authors, with an interesting methodological twist, extract individual answers from the *SED* and model the ensuing variation in stochastic OT. General observations are that person distinctions of the singular tend to be levelled in the plural; person distinctions in positive contexts are levelled under negation to prevent 'overloading of a single lexical form with multiple semantic features such as negation, person, and number' (p. 305). Where systems are variable, 'variation is idiosyncratic and inherent in individual grammars' (p. 340), which can be reduced to two invariant systems; interestingly (almost) always consisting of a vernacular system and the standard English system. In other words, variation is played out between the 'social prestige of the standard variety and [the] geographical continuity of vernacular varieties' (p. 331), suggesting that 'standard grammar is perturbing the vernacular grammar but not necessarily replacing it' (p. 312).

Also on the basis of the *SED*, Robert G. Shackleton Jr analyses 'Phonetic Variation in the Traditional English Dialects: A Computational Analysis' (*JEngL* 35[2007] 30–102) in what would probably win the prize for longest article this year. Based on the *SED* and the derived *Structural Atlas of the English Dialects* (Peter M. Anderson [1987]), this dialectometrical analysis uses clustering, phylogenetic methods, regression analysis, barrier analysis and principal component methods to measure the distance between traditional dialects of England and identify the features that distinguish the dialect regions. Shackleton finds that 'phonetic variation in the dialects is simply not very systematic, but instead tends to involve largely uncorrelated variations' (p. 42), and that 'the [phonetic] distance measures are fairly closely correlated with geographic distance' (p. 47). Interestingly, the General American 'control' speaker is most similar to south-western dialects, in fact Somerset. Shackleton also identifies seven major dialect regions of England: the far north, the upper north and the lower north, the central Midlands, the upper south-west, the lower south-west, and the south-east (including East Anglia), rather similar to Peter Trudgill's traditional dialect areas but notably different from many other approaches based on the same material.

Perceptual dialectology, more precisely over 5,000(!) informants' reactions to English accents, are reported by Nikolas Coupland and Hywel Bishop in 'Ideologised Values for British Accents' (*JSoc* 11[2007] 74–93), confirming that standard accents are linked to higher prestige and attractiveness, and urban accents (Birmingham, Liverpool, Glasgow) are systematically downgraded. What is new is that younger informants rate StE less highly, and that females in general produce more favourable evaluations.

In our regional overview, we will begin by looking at studies on Irish English. As noted above, Ireland features twice in Britain's *Language in the British Isles*. Kevin McCafferty distinguishes three varieties of 'Northern Irish English' on phonological grounds (pp. 122–34), namely Ulster Scots (which has the Scottish Vowel Length Rule), Mid Ulster (a transitional zone with 'phonemic vowel length...but Northern Irish vowel quality', p. 125), and South Ulster English. Grammatical features mentioned (but not necessarily distinctive of the three varieties) are the *after*-perfect, habitual *be, do be* or *bes*, modal *be to* (rarely noted elsewhere), subordinating *and*, the Northern Subject Rule, punctual *whenever*, *for-to* infinitives, and (the much more widespread) zero relatives, especially in existentials (again as in many other dialects). For 'Southern Irish English' (pp. 135–51), Raymond Hickey pays considerable attention to a periodization of Irish English, noting that language acquisition (of English) was largely unguided and took place over several centuries. Hickey distinguishes several dialect areas in Ireland, based on their settlement history (twelfth-century settlement in Dublin vs. seventeenth-century planta-tions in Ulster vs. Irish Gaelic-speaking population on the west coast), and relates this to the dialect features present, also pointing out which features Irish dialects have in common (the *after*-perfect, habitual *be*, negative concord or *it*-clefting). Hickey also discusses the research traditions (the substratists vs. the retentionists) and draws up a consensus table of putative origins of individual features.

In even more detail, Hickey presents a book-length introduction to *Irish English: History and Present-Day Forms*, pointing out that 'the political division of Ireland has a linguistic equivalent' (p. 2), although dialect differences of course go beyond the 'basic split' between Northern Ireland and the Republic. Hickey looks at the two settlement periods in two separate chapters, the twelfth-century settlement in the south, and the sixteenth-century settlement ('plantation') of Ulster, then discusses the 'Emergence of Irish English' as a contact phenomenon with all its consequences, mainly concentrating on the grammar (such as the *after*- perfect, the habitual, subordinating *and*, or cleft structures). Hickey also discusses the pronunciation of 'Present-Day Irish English', and here contrasts the rather conservative rural areas with the urban areas of Belfast, Derry, Coleraine and Dublin, a rare case of integration of these divergent systems (and studies) that is highly welcome. Especially the new developments in Dublin English rely on studies Hickey has reported on before (e.g. *YWES* 80[1999]). Hickey also reports on 'the pragmatics of Irish English', again a sub-field that is not usually integrated into more mainstream dialectological work. The final chapter, 'Transportation Overseas', is a useful outlook pointing out where in the world Irish settlers have influenced the local vernaculars (almost everywhere, according to Hickey, from Britain to, of course, the United States and Canada, but also Australia and New Zealand). The appendices contain outlines of the history, text extracts from the highly conservative language enclaves of Forth and Bargy, and a host of useful maps. In sum, this is probably the most comprehensive book on the subject yet, taking account of most previous work, and as such an ideal start for getting acquainted with the fine details of Irish English.

Alison Henry and Siobhan Cottell present 'A New Approach to Transitive Expletives: Evidence from Belfast English' (*ELL* 11[2007] 279–99), the phenomenon under investigation being transitive constructions with *there*, as in *There've lots of people passed the test*. Although this construction resembles similar constructions in other languages, for example Icelandic, it seems to have none of the features associated with it in earlier generative analyses. Transitive expletives seem to be an innovation of Belfast English, and the authors link it to the extensive use of subject contact clauses, to which they bear a superficial resemblance (cf. *There's somebody bought the book*). Especially with contracted auxiliaries, a reanalysis from *there is* to *there has* is possible, and bingo, there's your transitive expletive.

John Wilson and Karyn Stapleton deal with a possibly more serious topic in 'The Discourse of Resistance: Social Change and Policing in Northern Ireland' (*LSoc* 36[2007] 393–425), where they investigate the discourse of nationalist Catholic women in Belfast through which they pragmatically 'block off institutional... forms of interpretation, and then reinterpret... all messages within an alternate social world' (p. 395). 'Pragmatic blocking' is used as a term for the process of challenging (explicit or implicit) assumptions in prior talk, and offering an account for that challenge. In this way, an anti-police *habitus* (in Bourdieu's sense) is passed on to each new generation, where the women deny that the (formerly mainly Protestant, Unionist) police force, long seen as the enemy, has changed at all, despite political changes from above. Perhaps rather rarely for linguistic analysis, this one also has serious real-world implications, for policing policy in Northern Ireland.

Moving across the Irish Sea we turn to English in Scotland. Paul A. Johnston Jr's 'Scottish English and Scots' (in Britain, ed., pp. 105–21), not surprisingly, seeing the title, proposes a cline from Scottish Standard English (SSE) to the Scots end of a continuum, which, over the last centuries, has evolved (or devolved?) from a written standard language to a 'localised vernacular, complete with working-class associations and the stigmatisation that goes with them' (p. 106). As Johnston points out, SSE 'also forms the basis of Highland and Hebridean English', where Gaelic was traditionally spoken and broad Scots therefore never had a chance of disseminating. The complementary area, if this makes sense, is discussed more fully in Robert McColl Millar's small monograph *Northern and Insular Scots*. 'Northern' Scots here refers to the varieties spoken in pockets rather than contiguous areas of northern Scotland where Gaelic was not spoken, encompassing in particular the areas around Aberdeen (also sometimes called the *Doric*, cf. Derrick McClure in *YWES* 83[2002]), Inverness and Caithness, which is the furthest north-west corner of (mainland) Scotland including the towns of Wick, Thurso and (famously) John O'Groats. As McColl Millar notes, 'all of these dialects are bounded on a least one side by the sea, and on another by areas where the local population spoke Gaelic until recently' (p. 3). Insular Scots is more easily delimited, being spoken on Orkney and the Shetland Islands. Memorable not just for its title photograph, which exhorts 'Dunna Chuck Bruck' (for non-Scotticists, 'Don't throw away litter'—obviously part of the 'Keep Shetland Tidy' campaign), McColl Millar discusses in exhaustive detail the phonetics and phonology (mostly of vowels), morphosyntax (where differences are mostly of degree, rather than absolute) and lexis (based on 'anecdotal, personal and indicative' instances, p. 79) of these non-Lowlands and non-Highlands varieties, noting that these regions are relic areas whose distinctive history can also be traced in the Gaelic and Scandinavian influences on the language. The book also contains two chapters that are more appendix-like, one a 'Survey of Previous Works and Annotated Bibliography', possibly a great help for further research, the other a collection of representative texts from Shetland, Orkney, Caithness, the Black Isle (the peninsula north of Inverness) and some more general 'northern' dialect areas.

Also, with respect to a rather marginal area (even by Scottish standards), Peter Sundkvist discusses 'The Pronunciation of Scottish Standard English in Lerwick, Shetland' (*EWW* 28[2007] 1–21), finding that speakers are bi-dialectal and using SSE increasingly. The most striking phonetic feature is the effect of a voiced consonant on a preceding short vowel, which is raised, fronted, or diphthongized (in words like *bin*, *don* or *badge*), a 'highly salient localized process referred to as "vowel mutation" or "vowel softening"' (p. 18), which contributes to the distinctiveness of this dialect.

Richard Hudson integrates an analysis of inherent variability (exemplified by taking Jennifer Smith's data on *was*/*were* variation in Buckie, northern Scotland) with his theory of Word Grammar in 'English Dialect Syntax in Word Grammar' (*ELL* 11[2007] 383–405), coming to the conclusion that 'a model of I-language should be able to include very specific linguistic categories such as "the *was* of *we was*" and to link these linguistic categories to particular kinds of speakers defined in terms of whatever social categories are available in the speaker's social cognition ("I-society")' (p. 400), accounting for example for the fact that, in Buckie, middle-aged women prefer *we were*, whereas young men tend to say *we was*. In this way, Hudson claims, his framework of Word Grammar can model acts of identity. The acquisition of variable forms in Buckie by small children is the subject of Jennifer Smith, Mercedes Durham and Liane Fortune in '"Mam, my trousers is fa'in doon!": Community, Caregiver, and Child in the Acquisition of Variation in a

Scottish Dialect' (*LVC* 19[2007] 63–99). The authors find that in the two variables under investigation (the *house* diphthong, which is sometimes a monophthong /uː/ *hoose*, and variable -*s* in third-person-plural environment, following the Northern Subject Rule), the social and linguistic constraints (of the variable) evident in the speech of the mothers are matched by the speech of their small children, suggesting that 'input from the primary caregiver is crucial' (p. 63).

Moving to the west coast, Jane Stuart-Smith, Claire Timmins and Fiona Tweedie are '"Talking Jockney"? Variation and Change in Glaswegian Accent' (*JSoc* 11[2007] 221–60), where their analysis of eight consonant features (TH, alveolar taps for TH, L-vocalization, T-glottaling, apico-alveolar /s/, /x/, /hw/ and postvocalic /r/) in thirty-two speakers shows that middle-class speakers (i.e. those speakers with weaker social network ties, higher mobility and more contact with English English speakers) are maintaining traditional Scottish variants (e.g. /x/, /hw/ and postvocalic /r/), whereas more working-class speakers start to use non-local features like the notorious TH-fronting (*bruvver*) and have reduced rhoticity, perhaps contrary to what one would expect. The authors propose that 'local context is the key to these findings', namely that middle-class speakers actively reject working-class innovations, and that 'working-class speakers try to be as anti-middle-class, and anti-establishment as possible' (p. 251), especially the adolescents, for fear of sounding 'posh'. The local history of Glasgow city repeatedly destroying working-class living areas and disrupting neighbourhoods may also have a role to play.

Moving south, but staying with the 'Celtic fringes' just briefly, 'English in Wales' is discussed by Robert Penhallurick (in Britain, ed., pp. 152–70). Penhallurick takes great care to chart the Welsh phonetic system by going through Wells's set of lexemes one by one, noting Welsh influence where plausible, but he also devotes some space to morphology and syntax, where he discusses features such as predicate fronting (*a weed it is*), periphrastic verbs and a wider range of uses of the progressive to indicate habitual action.

The north of Britain features in a number of publications this year. Christoph Schubert provides a general overview of 'Dialect and Regional Identity in Northern England' (in Ehland, ed., *Thinking Northern: Textures of Identity in the North of England*, an interdisciplinary collection of essays, pp. 73–90). The author draws attention to pervasive stereotypes that are exploited in the media—from Joseph, the epitome of a Yorkshire dialect speaker in *Wuthering Heights* in the nineteenth century, to more recent British films such as *Brassed Off* or *Michael Eliot*, where the regional variety is on a par with terraced houses and the cloudy sky, constituting the 'resilient Northerner, hard-working and humorous, blunt speaking and straight-forward' (p. 86). Going into some more grammatical detail, Willem Hollmann and Anna Siwierska give 'A Construction Grammar Account of Possessive Constructions in Lancashire Dialect: Some Advantages and Challenges' (*ELL* 11[2007] 404–24). They find that the construction patterns according to alienability (or not) of the possessum (*my football shoes* vs. *me brother*), which may be caused by underlying frequency effects. The north-east is the topic in Carmen Llamas's account of '"A Place Between Places": Language and Identity in a Border Town' (*LSoc* 36[2007] 579–604), the town in question being Middlesbrough, whose political affiliation has changed four times over the last thirty years. Llamas investigates glottalization of the voiceless stops /p, t, k/, a stereotypical feature of Newcastle and Tyneside English (to the north of Middlesbrough) but not of Yorkshire English (to the south of Middlesbrough) and shows that 'shifting...from an orientation towards Yorkshire to one toward the North East' (p. 599) correlates with a higher use of glottalized /p/, which may, however, index a more specifically Middlesbrough identity for speakers today.

Moving across the ocean to North America, let us begin by looking at studies dealing with Canada. *Language Issues in Canada: Multidisciplinary Perspectives*, edited by Martin Howard, curiously mainly deals with French, although Howard admits that 'English has dominant status' (p. 1). Three chapters may be of interest to English sociolinguistics, namely the overview by Howard himself on 'Language in Canada' (pp. 1–23), a brief overview of language policy issues in this multilingual state, 'Legislating for Language: The Canadian Experience of Language Policy and Linguistic Duality' by Maeve Conrick (pp. 24–39), and an article by Shana Poplack, James A. Walker and Rebecca Malcolmson, 'An English "Like No Other"?: Language Contact and Change in Quebec' (pp. 156–85), where the English are in the (unusual) position of being in the minority. Poplack et al. investigate spontaneous speech of speakers of Quebec city, Montreal and the anglophone-controlled Oshawa and find that unselfconscious borrowings from French are surprisingly rare. Instead, anglophone speakers use French lexemes rhetorically or metalinguistically. In this situation, structural repercussions on Quebecois English are highly unlikely. One persistent feature of Quebec English is investigated further by James A. Walker in '"There's bears back there": Plural Existentials and Vernacular Universals in (Quebec) English' (*EWW* 28[2007] 147–66), indeed one of the prime candidates for a general feature of non-standard English attested in practically all varieties. Walker's study supports the impression that *there's* has lexicalized and is therefore as good as invariant, whereas singular agreement patterns differently, which would also argue for not considering *there is/there's* in future studies on variable agreement. Quebec is also featured in the special May issue of the *International Journal of the Sociology of Language* (185[2007]), on 'Official Language Minorities in Canada'. John A. Dickinson provides a historical overview of the Anglophone community in 'The English-Speaking Minority of Quebec: A Historical Perspective' (*IJSL* 185[2007] 11–24), claiming that, at least before 1977, the anglophones' minority status in the province was offset by its political and economic clout' (p. 12). A detailed demographic investigation shows, however, that in terms of percentage, the anglophone population already 'peaked in the 1860s and has declined ever since' (p. 13), while the old 'consociational arrangement' whereby elites negotiated compromises for their part of the population came to an end with the rise of the nationalist movement. This was marked especially by the 1973 Bill making French the (only) official language in Quebec, which has led to an exodus of anglophones from the province ever since. Continuing this investigation, Jack Jedwab proposes 'Following the

Leaders: Reconciling Identity and Governance in Quebec's Anglophone Population' (*IJSL* 185[2007] 71–87), looking at recent debates on 'how and by whom political advocacy and representation are conducted' (p. 71) for the anglophone minority. Although institutional representation is very good, the anglophones nevertheless lack a strong sense of group consciousness, and may even lack any meaningful self-definition. Patricia Lamarre discusses 'Anglo-Quebec Today: Looking at Community and Schooling Issues' (*IJSL* 185[2007] 109–32), claiming that young speakers in Montreal today are not only bilingual, they are bicultural, shown (*pace* Poplack et al.) by extensive code-switching, 'blurring... individual and collective identity' (p. 110) (which might of course constitute the new identity of Montrealers, or Quebecois), in stark contrast to the situation, say, a generation ago. In fact, the English-sector school system is a stronghold of bilingual programmes.

Moving to the rest of Canada, Sali Tagliamonte and Alexandra D'Arcy put 'The Modals of Obligation/Necessity in Canadian Perspective' (*EWW* 28[2007] 47–87). They show that, in Toronto, 'the system of obligation/necessity... has undergone nearly complete specialization to *have to*' (p. 47), and in this respect CanE 'seems to be at the forefront of change' (p. 47) compared with other (British and) North American varieties. Deontic *must*, on the other hand, is noticeably less frequent than in other varieties of English, and has 'all but run its course' (p. 68). Our overview of articles dealing with Canada is completed by looking at Susanne Wagner, who asks: 'Unstressed Periphrastic *do* — from Southwest England to Newfoundland?' (*EWW* 28[2007] 249–78) (incidentally, the answer is 'No'). Periphrastic *do* is a dialect feature of the English south-west, and (with slightly different semantics) of Irish English, the two main founder populations of Newfoundland, but is noticeably absent from that dialect. Wagner argues that settlers at most brought a variable system with them, which competed with habitual -*s* and a more standard system and which in this situation was not adopted.

Studies on 'English in North America' are summarized by Edward Finegan (in Hogg and Denison, eds., pp., 384–413), concentrating mainly on lexis and onomastics, but some syntactic patterns (always in contrast to BrE) are noted as well. Phonological patterns and dialect areas follow Labov's *Atlas of North American English* (*ANAE*). Social variation is rather inelegantly dealt with in a page and a half, ethnic varieties are given a little more space, but two pages of running text obviously cannot do the complex structure of AAVE justice, so that this overview chapter might really only be helpful for someone with no previous knowledge whatsoever. Adding much more linguistic detail, Ewa Jacewicz, Joseph Salmons and Robert A. Fox compare 'Vowel Duration in Three American Dialects'' (*AS* 82[2007] 367–85), i.e. in Wisconsin (for the Inland North), Ohio (for the Midland) and North Carolina (for the South), an area of phonetics that is not much studied in sociolinguistics and dialectology. This is rather surprising, since the authors find robust systematic differences in the vowels in *hid, head, had, hayed* and *hide*. In all cases, the vowels had 'the longest durations in the South and the shortest in the Inland North, with the Midlands in an intermediate but distinct position' (p. 367), opening up an interesting new area of comparative dialectology.

More specifically regional, Julie Roberts discusses 'Vermont Lowering? Raising Some Questions about /ai/ and /au/ South of the Canadian Border' (*LVC* 19[2007] 181–97). She finds fronting for /au/, and raising, as well as possibly backing, for /ai/ for the older speakers, whereas the younger speakers 'show a more typical Canadian raising pattern' (p. 194). An old classic is revived this year by Jennifer Pope, Miriam Meyerhoff and D. Robert Ladd, who trace 'Forty Years of Language Change on Martha's Vineyard' (*Language* 83[2007] 615–27) by replicating as closely as possible Labov's seminal study from the early 1960s. In this way, Labov's apparent-time design is complemented by a real-time comparison, validating his original approach, *pace* Renée Blake and Meredith Josey [2002] (cf. *YWES* 83[2002]). The authors find that the iconic (icons not in the Peircean sense, but as 'icons' (stereotypes) of the dialect area) diphthongs (ay) and (aw) are still centralized most by islanders with positive attitudes towards island life, in particular the fishermen, but that this change seems to have accelerated, especially for (aw) (not studied by Blake and Josey). As the authors note, 'the antipathy toward the summer people that Labov documented was still very much present in 2002' (p. 621), not least because of the high cost of living on the island due to the super-rich tourists (see also section 3 above).

William Labov himself distinguishes 'Transmission and Diffusion' (*Language* 83[2007] 344–87) in a family-tree model. Based on his data from the *ANAE*, Labov argues that the transmission of linguistic change *within* a speech community is characterized by faithful reproduction, and extension, of a pattern (as children incrementally advance the change in the same direction, increasing the distance between branches on the family tree), whereas the diffusion *across* communities (promoted by adult learning) may show weakening of the pattern and loss of structural features (across branches on the family tree, decreasing their distance). Labov illustrates these assumptions with data on short-*a* tensing (diffused from New York to four other communities) and on the Northern Cities Shift (diffused from Chicago to St Louis). Labov admits, however, that this model only works for relatively abstract chain shifts, which may be more typical of America than, say, of Europe.

Adrian Pablè and Radosław Dyłewski investigate 'Invariant *Be* in New England Folk Speech: Colonial and Postcolonial Evidence' (*AS* 82[2007] 151–84), which, they argue (rather controversially), is a genuine New England innovation, at least in its use as the singular indicative (*What be I doing here?*). The authors trace this form to the seventeenth century, arguing that the settlers brought with them invariant *be* used in the plural only, and that the expansion into the singular happened in both British and American varieties independently of each other. Perhaps one should say it *was* a genuine American innovation, since it seems to have disappeared in the 1940s or 1950s and hasn't been revived to date.

Moving south a little, Terry Lynn Irons reports 'On the Status of Low Back Vowels in Kentucky English: More Evidence of Merger' (*LVC* 19[2007] 137–80) in this important transitional area between Midland and Southern dialects. In the Midland region, the *cot–caught* merger is expanding, whereas in the South the vowels are still distinct. Evidence of the low back merger that

Irons finds in rural areas might be an indication that this is an independent development resulting from 'back upglide loss' (p. 138), which in turn might be linked to a 'negative social evaluation and rejection of this feature as a stigmatized marker of local identity' (p. 167). Not far from Kentucky, Brian José discusses whether there may be 'Appalachian English in Southern Indiana? The Evidence from Verbal -*s*' (*LVC* 19[2007] 249–80). Appalachian English is characterized by a distinctive (non-)concord pattern similar to the Northern Subject Rule (see above), as well as a range of other morphosyntactic similarities. José argues for what he calls a 'family resemblance account' (p. 254) between the two dialects since they have similar historical connections to Scots-Irish immigrants and a very similar mix of morphosyntactic features that is very unlikely to result from coincidence.

Moving west, the perceptual dialectology of California is the topic of Mary Bucholtz, Nancy Bermudez, Victor Fung, Lisa Edwards and Rosalva Vargas, winning the prize for greatest number of co-authors this year, in 'Hella Nor Cal or Totally So Cal?' (*JEngL* 35[2007] 325–52), based on map-labelling tasks inside California. The most salient boundary is between northern California and the south, linked to the salience (not necessarily the actual usage) of English vs. Spanish. Interestingly, the north is associated with unmarked or 'normal' speech, although it is simultaneously associated with ruralness (although not by the same informants). The lexical marker commented on most is *hella* from the title (*nor* stands for *North* and *Cal* for *California*, by the way ...), probably a lexicalization of *a hell of*, which can be used as a quantifier (*There were hella people there*) or as an intensifier (*He runs hella fast*).

The topic of age and ageism is taken up by Gerline Mautner, who undertakes 'Mining Large Corpora for Social Information: The Case of *Elderly*' (*LSoc* 36[2007] 51–72), obviously a contested term. Mautner shows that *elderly* is mainly found in discourses of 'disability, illness, care, and vulnerability to crime' (p. 63), which leads her to conclude that the ageist *elderly*, rather than designating chronological age, really indicates a social stereotype.

Jenny Cheshire investigates 'Discourse Variation, Grammaticalisation and Stuff Like That' (*JSoc* 11[2007] 155–93) in the speech of adolescents in three English towns, and finds that 'general extenders' like *and stuff* in the title or *and things* are rather middle-class, whereas working-class speakers prefer *and that* or *and everything*. As Cheshire points out, 'the multifunctionality of the general extenders caused problems for a rigorous analysis of their pragmatic functions' (p. 155), which are precisely multifunctional and often simultaneously so; this of course throws up important questions of how to conduct quantitative analyses of discourse forms like these at all.

An all-time favourite of this section, quotatives, is discussed again this year by John R. Rickford, Thomas Wasow, Arnold Zwicky and Isabelle Buchstaller in 'Intensive and Quotative *All*: Something Old, Something New' (*AS* 82[2007] 3–31). On the basis of a variety of data (sociolinguistic interviews, but also data from the internet), the authors find that intensifier *all* (as in *my Mom is all mad at me*) is not a new phenomenon (indeed, there are even attestations from OE), but has expanded its syntactic scope, such that it can now be used with verbs (*I all screamed when we hit the skunk*)—note that the example comes from the original. In fact, intensifier *all* is the fourth most frequent intensifier after *really*, *so* and *very*. Quotative *all* (or, more precisely, *BE all*), on the other hand, is new and probably originated in California in the 1980s, but has already peaked, as studies also from recent years have shown in detail. The most popular quotative of the day is now *BE like*, and, interestingly, the two can be used together, as in *he's all like 'I have to wear socks on my ears'* (cf. *YWES* of the last few years). Alexandra D'Arcy looks at the rival discourse marker and quotative (and its responsibility for ruining the English language . . .) in '*Like* and Language Ideology: Disentangling Fact and Fiction" (*AS* 82[2007] 386–419). As she puts it, the 'enduring belief that young people are ruining the language and that, as a consequence, the language is degenerating' (p. 386) is often linked to the perceived over-use of, precisely, *like*. This use is criticized as being, like, meaningless, promoted by women, an Americanism, and introduced by the Valley girls. Based (not only) on data from Toronto, D'Arcy bravely argues against these myths. There are four functionally different variants of *like* (the quotative, the approximative use, the discourse marker and the discourse particle), only some of which are favoured by women, and the discourse marker can be traced back at least to the nineteenth century. In other words, perhaps with the exception of the quotative use, the vernacular functions of *like* are 'complex and historically long-standing features of English dialects' (p. 412). However, it is highly improbable that with the publication in a scholarly journal this repudiation of popular misconceptions will have much effect on laypeople's ideas. (Then again, this may be a good thing, since several female linguists trying to repel widespread language myths have recently been receiving death threats—so good luck to you, Alex!).

Sali A. Tagliamonte and Alexandra D'Arcy deal with *be like* at the community level in 'Frequency and Variation in the Community Grammar: Tracking a New Change through the Generations' (*LVC* 19[2007] 199–217), testing whether we are dealing with age-grading, a generational or indeed a communal change in Toronto English. The authors find that indeed, '*be like* overshadows all other forms among speakers under age 30', whereas for the older speaker, *say* dominates. This 'dramatic division' or even 'catastrophic shift' in the population is linked to the different function of *be like*, which seems to have started out as a marker of quoted thought, a niche that already existed before *be like* entered the system.

A slightly larger range of quotatives is investigated by Federica Barbieri, in particular their use by 'Older Men and Younger Women: A Corpus-Based Study of Quotative Use in American English' (*EWW* 28[2007] 23–45). Her examination of the role gender and age play in the use of *be like*, *go*, *be all* and *say* shows that, perhaps not surprisingly, 'the quotative *be like* is the favored choice for young women in their late teens and early to mid-20s' (p. 26), whereas for men it is the 'older' men (in their late twenties and thirties) who favour *be like* and *go*. Barbieri proposes some kind of convergence since it is a truth universally acknowledged that 'men in their late 20s to early 30s . . . generally aspire to, and thus socialize with slightly younger women'

(p. 42), suggesting that these dating practices are reflected in the use of quotatives.

The field of gender studies boasts many publications again this year, from the more traditional variationist sociolinguistic ones to new methodologies, one of them Judith Baxter's monograph *Positioning Gender in Discourse: A Feminist Methodology* (originally from 2003, now reprinted in paperback). Baxter here tries to establish feminist post-structuralist discourse analysis (FPDA) in the field of gender studies, stressing the constructivist notion that 'relationships . . . are always discursively produced, negotiated and contested *through* language' (p. 91) and paying attention to several 'polyphonic voices' rather than just the one 'authorial voice'. Baxter employs FPDA in two case studies on power, one on classroom interaction between students, and one on a management team study. Her accessible book shows the ethnographic approach 'in action' and makes clear what is meant by investigating gender polarization, or the 'culturally accreted discourse of gender differentiation' (p. 183), precisely *in* discourse.

Liz Morrish and Helen Sauntson provide us with *New Perspectives on Language and Sexual Identity*, a monograph on the discourse of lesbian women, in some ways a counterpart to Paul Baker [2005] (cf. *YWES* 86[2005]). Morrish and Sauntson analyse narratives of 'coming out', the discourse of 'shame, risk and concealment', and a corpus of lesbian erotica, where differences from gay men's erotica are particularly revealing. They also analyse the construction of the stereotypes 'butch' and 'femme' in a number of films, finding that these stereotypes in turn draw on linguistic gender stereotypes of 'male' vs. 'female'. Finally, the authors investigate 'How the British Broadsheet Press Learned Gay Slang', here, however, focusing on two male politicians (Michael Portillo and Peter Mandelson), rather than on lesbians (it is not quite clear what motivated this choice; perhaps there are no high-profile lesbians in British politics?). Anyway, the authors show convincingly how 'camp codes of homosexuality have been used to taunt unpopular politicians, with the presumed intent of trivializing their work and undermining their credibility' (p. 166)—subtle enough not to call libel lawyers on the plan but transparent enough for readers to guess at the message.

Kathryn Campbell-Kibler adds an interesting study on the perception of the variable (*–ing*) in 'Accent (ing), and the Social Logic of Listener Perceptions' (*AS* 82[2007] 32–64). In a matched guise experiment, she finds that the non-standard alveolar variant (*-in*) is perceived as being more Southern (US), less educated, more rural and more masculine, confirming older studies, but adds the interesting detail that the standard, velar nasal or variant (*-ing*) is perceived as more educated, more urban, and less masculine; instead, it is perceived as 'metrosexual', or even decidedly gay—a finding with its link of non-standard speech and (heterosexual) masculinity that would go a long way towards explaining the covert prestige of non-standard varieties.

Continuing his studies from last year (see *YWES* 87[2008]), Erez Levon puts 'Sexuality in Context: Variation and the Sociolinguistic Perception of Identity' (*LSoc* 36[2007] 533–54), examining the identification of gayness in male speakers through the auditory perception of pitch range and sibilant duration (corresponding to the popular perceptions of 'gay' high voices and a 'gay men's lisp'). Levon again uses the mechanically manipulated gay men's speech, but also uses a heterosexual control whose pitch range was widened. Levon finds that shortening the sibilants and decreasing the pitch range (in conjunction) increases the perception of a speaker as 'masculine', and that pitch range 'is acting as indexical of sexuality for the listener population' (p. 546). Manipulating the 'straight' speaker did not result in any different perception, however. Indexicality is clearly a more complex, contingent phenomenon. Also on the subject of sounding gay, Robert J. Podesva discusses 'Phonation Type as a Stylistic Variable: The Use of Falsetto in Constructing a Persona' (*JSoc* 11[2007] 478–504), the persona being a gay 'diva', which is indexed, together with other linguistic and non-linguistic resources, by the use of a falsetto voice (technically: rapid vocal fold vibrations that raise the fundamental frequency f0 to between 240 and 634 Hz, contrasting with the usual 100 Hz for men and 200 Hz for women)—'a socially marked behaviour [which is] at odds with more culturally normative pitch practices for men, and may be involved in the performance of stereotypical gay identity' (p. 480). The subject under investigation uses falsetto significantly more frequently at a barbeque with his friends than when talking on the phone or to a patient. Part of the 'gay diva' stereotype is 'sounding flamboyant', a style that a falsetto voice with its connotations of 'performing expressiveness' (p. 482) seems particularly apt to underline, since both expressiveness and falsetto constitute 'non-normative behaviour' (p. 496) for men.

Moving to ethnic varieties, but also related to the recurrent theme of stereotypes, Jacquelyn Rahman discusses 'An *Ay* for an *Ah*: Language of Survival in African American Narrative Comedy' (*AS* 82[2007] 65–96), stereotypical rendering of AAVE (by AAVE comedians for a primarily AAVE audience) here relying to a large degree on the monophthongal variant (ah) in words like *time*, while the diphthong (ay) is linked stereotypically to white, middle-class speech. Rahman argues that vernacular AAE constituted in this way 'indexes a self-empowering ideology that is prevalent in the narratives and that serves as a source of strength for African Americans in the face of perceived racism' (p. 66). Elaine M. Stotko and Margaret Troyer have discovered 'A New Gender-Neutral Pronoun in Baltimore, Maryland: A Preliminary Study' (*AS* 82[2007] 262–79), the new pronoun being *yo* as in *yo handing out the papers (he/she...)* in the language of (mostly black) schoolchildren. On the basis of elicitation data from more than 200 middle-school students, Stotko and Troyer distinguish third-person *yo* from second-person uses (*yo mamma*), to which it seems unrelated, and from focusing *yo*, as in *yo, get away from my locker*, which they present very tentatively as a possible source. *Yo* is used when the referent is known, so the original motivation cannot therefore have been unknown gender. But before you try this out yourself, a note of warning: it is apparently disrespectful to refer to a teacher as *yo*.

Tracy Weldon contributes a missing detail to the debate of the origins of AAVE with her analysis of 'Gullah Negation: A Variable Analysis' (*AS* 82[2007] 341–66). Based on data from very rural, older, Southern speakers of Gullah with little formal education, Weldon suggests that the variation between *ain't* and *didn't* in past-tense contexts at least allows for the possibility that Gullah and AAE are related.

An old favourite of AAVE studies, copula deletion (or copula absence) is the topic of Emily M. Bender in her discussion of 'Socially Meaningful Syntactic Variation in Sign-Based Grammar' (*ELL* 11[2007] 347–81), i.e. in HSPG. Bender makes the interesting point that 'syntactic constraints and social meaning are intertwined' (p. 347) and investigates what the 'identity turn' (the third wave in Eckert's conceptualization of sociolinguistics) means for syntactic theory; more precisely, how can we model the fact that social meaning is attached to linguistic features smaller than whole varieties which speakers are free to choose from to constitute their identity? Bender argues that, in order to model this behaviour, syntactic theory has to include 'social meaning, prefabricated "chunks" of linguistic structure, and some reflection of probabilistic (or frequentistic) aspects' (p. 359) as parts of grammar.

Other ethnic groups that play a role this year are Mexican Americans; here Petra Scott Shenk proposes '"I'm Mexican, remember?"': Constructing Ethnic Identities via Authenticating Discourse' (*JSoc* 11[2007] 194–220). Authenticating discourse, Shenk writes, is 'part of an ongoing ordinary interactional routine through which speakers take overt authentication stances' (p. 195). The initial sentence of her title illustrates nicely how ethnicity is continually constructed and co-constructed in and through discourse and 'subject to shared ideological interpretation' (p. 197). The Mexican American (college student) speakers under investigation here take three constructs as central: presumed purity of bloodline, purity of nationality and fluency in Spanish, also indicating the important role language and language choice have in identity construction. In fact, Shenk points out that 'a speaker's ability to produce well-formed Spanish utterances is tantamount to her/his ability to maintain an ethnic identity as Mexican' (p. 201). This concludes our review of publications dealing with dialectology and sociolinguistics this year.

10. New Englishes and Creolistics

The most important publication on English as a world language is undoubtedly Edgar W. Schneider's *Postcolonial English: Varieties Around the World*, which is based on his article in *Language* 79[2003] (cf. *YWES* 84[2005] 88–9) and elaborates the model of the development of the New Englishes presented there. In his introduction, Schneider discusses the development of English as a world language, pointing out that despite the individual social and historical circumstances the processes of linguistic nativization are similar for each variety of English outside the British Isles. In the second chapter, he charts the development of linguistic research into English as a world language, presenting various models of accounting for the different varieties. Schneider prefers the term 'Post-colonial Englishes' over more common labels such as 'New Englishes' (p. 4). In the third chapter, Schneider presents his model for the development of Post-colonial Englishes. He distinguishes between the English-speaking settlers or colonialists as the

'STL [i.e. 'settlers'] strand' of the development and the InDiGenous
population as the 'IDG strand', whose group identities and attitudes towards
and uses of English are of importance in the course of the evolution of a new
variety. According to Schneider, the Post-colonial Englishes develop in
five phases, which will be summarized briefly. In Phase 1, 'Foundation',
English-speaking settlers arrive in the area. The IDG and the STL group are
characterized by a relationship of otherness, but within the STL group, dialect
levelling or koinéization occurs, evening out differences between the different
varieties spoken by the settlers. Phase 2, 'Exonormative Stabilization', involves
political stabilization, usually in the form of an official colony during which
the STL group begins to develop a 'British-cum-local' (p. 37) identity which
also leads to changes in the English spoken by them, mainly in the form of
borrowed words. As more members of the IDG acquire English, 'Structural
Nativization', the hallmark feature of Phase 3, is also under way. This phase is
also characterized by political semi-autonomy with regard to the colonial
mother country, for example as members of the Commonwealth. In Phase 4,
political independence has been gained and 'Endonormative Stabilization' sets
in, as the STL and the IDG strands begin to view themselves as members of
the newborn nation. This leads to the acceptance and codification of local
norms. In Phase 5, finally, the focus shifts from a larger national identity to
smaller group identities, whether regional or social, leading to linguistic
'Differentiation'. Schneider also presents variations of this basic pattern,
before he proceeds to discuss the linguistic aspects of nativization in greater
detail in chapter 4. Chapter 5 is devoted to a total of sixteen case studies,
from Fiji, Australia and New Zealand, via Asian varieties, such as SingE and
IndE, to African varieties, such as SAE or NigE, to Caribbean varieties from
Barbados and Jamaica to Canada. Chapter 6 presents a test case from
hindsight, namely the case of AmE, which Schneider argues is exemplary for
the developmental cycle outlined in chapter 3. The conclusions include
a summary of the main facts, as well as a number of points related to the
applicability of the model, which is designed to account for pidgin and creole
varieties as well as for standard or standardizing varieties. Schneider's model,
drawing on earlier work by Salikoko Mufwene, as well as Sarah Thomason
and Terence Kaufman, is without doubt a very important step towards
a unified but yet comparative approach to accounting for the emergence of
the New Englishes. While not every linguist may agree with Schneider's
analysis (cf. the review of Mukherjee's article on IndE below), it is without
doubt a book which will generate a lively discussion in the field and certainly
inspire more research.

Another monograph on English as a world language with a completely
different angle is Alastair Pennycook's *Global Englishes and Transcultural
Flows*, in which the author examines the effects of the global spread of hip-hop
music and culture on linguistic usage. After three introductory chapters on the
issue of English as a global language, a wide range of theories of transgression,
and questions of performativity, Pennycook gives a large number of examples
of how rap and hip-hop have led to new forms of localization while at the same
time providing global identification. The linguistic result of this twofold aim is
often mixed codes or new vernacular forms of English which borrow from

the originally African-American hip-hop as well as from local indigenous languages. The examples include rap lyrics from Japan, Malaysia, Senegal or Australia, which Pennycook ties in with a discussion of research on hip-hop culture in Asia, Africa, Europe and the Pacific. Pennycook stresses the transgressive potential of hip-hop language or 'raplish' (p. 4) and therefore does not consider these uses of English as instances of cultural imperialism along the lines of Robert Phillipson and others. Pennycook's arguments are supported by Jamie Shinhee Lee's article '*I'm the illest fucka*: An Analysis of African American English in South Korean Hip Hop' (*EnT* 23:ii[2007] 54–60), which illustrates the processes of linguistic borrowing from AAVE but at the same time localization by creating new lexical items from English and Korean morphological material.

A number of shorter publications also deal with English as a world language. Barbara A. Fennel's contribution on 'Colonial and Postcolonial Varieties' (in Llamas, Mullany and Stockwell, eds., pp. 192–8) offers a very concise overview of relevant issues and concepts. Joseph A. Foley offers 'English as a Global Language: My Two Satangs' Worth' (*RELC* 38[2007] 7–17), addressing issues of standards and norms and the native-speaker teacher of English and questions of linguistic ownership. Similarly, Keith Davidson discusses 'The Nature and Significance of English as a Global Language' (*EnT* 23:i[2007] 48–9), coming to the conclusion that native speakers need to adjust their ways of speaking in a global context in order to communicate successfully.

A number of articles specifically address English as a lingua franca (ELF). Martin Dewey's article 'English as a Lingua Franca and Globalization: An Interconnected Perspective' (*IJAL* 17[2007] 332–54) provides a comprehensive overview of current ELF research and proposes a transformationalist approach in dealing with ELF as its realizations are necessarily dynamic rather than static. Luke Prodromou asks 'Is ELF a Variety of English?' (*EnT* 23:ii[2007] 47–53), and comes to the conclusion that despite various claims made by ELF researchers, there is no empirical proof of a homogenous variety of ELF. Similarly, Sandra Mollin wonders 'New Variety or Learner English? Criteria for Variety Status and the Case of Euro-English' (*EWW* 28[2007] 167–85), and argues quite convincingly that there is no empirical evidence for a variety of English which could be called 'Euro-English'. Nevertheless, Nicos Sifakis calls for 'The Education of Teachers of English as a Lingua Franca: A Transformative Perspective' (*IJAL* 17[2007] 354–75), claiming that teacher education for TESOL should be informed by the ELF context and include native-speaker and non-native-speaker interaction. An empirical analysis of ELF communication is provided by Anne Kari Bjørge's study of 'Power Distance in English Lingua Franca Email Communication' (*IJAL* 17[2007] 60–80), which is based on a corpus of e-mails written by international students in Norway to two professors. Bjørge's analysis of the greetings and complimentary close formulae reveals that not only the medium of communication and the students' L1 influence the linguistic choices made in the English-language e-mails, but also the politeness conventions of their home culture.

Two publications compare data from a wider range of Englishes and are therefore included in this introductory section. Christian Mair looks at 'Varieties of English around the World: Collocational and Cultural Profiles' (in Skandera, ed., *Phraseology and Culture in English*, pp. 437–68), establishing typical collocational patterns in L1 and L2 varieties of English from Great Britain, Canada, Australia, New Zealand, India, Singapore, the Philippines, Jamaica, Kenya and Tanzania on the basis of the web, the *BNC* and the International Corpus of English (ICE). The study shows that while huge amounts of data are necessary to arrive at any conclusions, the study of collocational or phraseological patterns is very promising also with regard to identifying varieties of English. Ulrike Gut compares 'First Language Influence and Final Consonant Clusters in the New Englishes of Singapore and Nigeria' (*WEn* 26[2007] 346–59), showing that despite similarities between the L1s of the speakers analysed, there is actually a high degree of variation in the realizations of final consonant clusters by educated Singaporean and Nigerian speakers of English. Gut attributes these differences to the different status of English in the two countries under analysis and differences in norm orientation which have led to a higher degree of nativization in the case of Singapore.

As in past years, we will begin the survey of the individual varieties with those from the southern hemisphere. A special issue of *JAPC* (17[2007]), edited by Yinxia Zhu and Herbert Hildebrandt, on the topic of *Culture, Contexts, and Communication in Multicultural Australia and New Zealand: An Introduction* contains a number of contributions dealing with AusE and NZE which will be reviewed individually below. Two publications compare AusE and NZE. Deanna Wong and Pam Peters provide 'A Study of Backchannels in Regional Varieties of English, Using Corpus Mark-Up as the Means of Identification' (*IJCL* 122[2007] 479–509) on the basis of the telephone conversations in the Australian and New Zealand subcorpora of *ICE*. Comparing their findings to earlier research based on AmE they come to the conclusion that speakers of NZE and AusE use a similar repertoire of backchannels, but the AusE speakers showed more repetition while the NZE speakers employed a greater variety of forms. In comparison to previous research on AmE, the Southern Hemisphere varieties are significantly different from AmE, which indicates a great potential for the analysis of regional variation elsewhere. Gina Poncini is 'Exploring the Image of New World Wine Producers: Website Texts for Wineries in Australia and New Zealand' (*JAPC* 17[2007] 105–25) on the basis of the evaluative linguistic devices used and the strategies for building up shared knowledge.

AusE has received most scholarly attention this year. Peter Collins provides a comprehensive description of the semantics of '*Can/Could* and *May/Might* in British, American and Australian English: A Corpus-Based Account' (*WEn* 26[2007] 474–91) on the basis of ICE-GB, ICE-AUS and a specially compiled corpus of AmE, showing that there are significant regional differences in the usage of these modals. Peter Collins also looks at 'Modality across World Englishes: The Modals and Semi-Modals of Prediction and Volition' (in Butler, Downing and Lavid, eds., *Functional Perspectives on Grammar and Discourse*, pp. 447–68), comparing the functions of *will*, *shall*, *be going to*, *gonna, want to, wanna* and *be about to* on the basis of the same AusE, BrE and AmE corpora. Bert Peeters discusses 'Australian Perceptions of the Weekend: Evidence from Collocations and Elsewhere' (in Skandera, ed., pp. 79–107), defining 'weekend' as a cultural key term in Australian English based on expressions such as 'the land of the long weekend' or 'Mondayitis'. Pam Peters looks at 'Similes and other Evaluative Idioms in Australian English' (in Skandera, ed., pp. 235–55) in the Australian Corpus of English, ICE-AUS and the web. Peters shows the productivity of many expressions and patterns, e.g. *as* ADJ *as a bandicoot*, whether they are based on an older British expression or local inventions. Thérèse Lalor and Johanna Rendle-Short report on '"That's so gay": A Contemporary Use of *Gay* in Australian English' (*AuJL* 27[2007] 147–73), which is especially common among younger speakers with a negative meaning of 'boring' or 'stupid' and found most frequently in constructions with BE and an inanimate subject. Johanna Rendle-Short also discusses '"Catherine, you're wasting your time": Address Terms within the Australian Political Interview' (*JPrag* 39[2007] 1503–25) during the time leading up to the federal election in 2004. Using CA methodology, Rendle-Short shows distinct differences in the address strategies of journalists and politicians, in the choice of address terms as well as in the sequential positioning of the address.

Gerhard Leitner examines 'Australia's "Asia Competence" and the Uneasy Balance between Asian Languages and English' (*JAPC* 17[2007] 29–60) in the light of Australian language policy since the 1980s. Verna Robertson Rieschield looks at 'Influences of Language Proficiency, Bilingual Socialization, and Urban Youth Identities on Producing Different Arabic-English Voices in Australia' (*Novitas* 1[2007] 34–52) on the basis of interview data and matched-guise experiments. She comes to the conclusion that there is no uniform Arabic-AusE ethnolect, but rather a range of different varieties, depending on the speaker's individual background. In addition to that, younger speakers also make use of the mixed code Arabizi or the urban variety Lebspeak, which combines Arabic-heritage-AusE, global hip-hop language and Arabic loanwords, to express group identity and solidarity.

Three publications deal with Australian Aboriginal English. Ian G. Malcolm and Ellen Grote provide a brief survey of the features of 'Aboriginal English: Restructured Variety for Cultural Maintenance' (in Leitner and Malcolm, eds., *The Habitat of Australia's Aboriginal Languages: Past, Present and Future*, pp. 153–79), including information on linguistic processes involved in its development, its functions and uses and information on regional, social and stylistic variation. Diana Eades explores the uses of 'Aboriginal English in the Criminal Justice System' (in Leitner and Malcolm, eds., pp. 299–326) on the basis of court transcripts of a number of cases in which the Aboriginal English spoken by the defendants led to misunderstandings in the courtroom or in which linguistic evidence was used to identify fabricated confessions. Eades concludes that all legal professionals in Australia should be educated with regard to the specific features of Aboriginal English in order to avoid fatal miscommunication. Ian G. Malcolm and Farzad Sharifian discuss 'Multiword Units in Aboriginal English: Australian Cultural Expression in an Adopted Language' (in Skandera, ed., pp. 375–98) on the basis of a large corpus of interview and free speech data. The analysis shows that Aboriginal English contains a wide range of multi-word units which differ from General AusE due to different discourse strategies and encoding conventions.

Moving on to New Zealand, Martin East, Nick Shackleford and Gail Spence look at ways of 'Promoting a Multilingual Future for Aotearoa/New Zealand: Initiatives for Change from 1989 to 2003' (*JAPC* 17[2007] 11–28), examining the language policy of the New Zealand government during this period with regard to its effectiveness. Laurie Bauer, Paul Warren, Dianne Beardsley, Marianna Kennedy and George Major provide a very concise overview of educated Pakeha NZE pronunciation in 'Illustrations of the IPA: New Zealand English' (*JIPA* 37[2007] 97–102). Margaret Maclagan and Jennifer Hay focus on 'Getting *Fed* Up With Our *Feet*: Contrast Maintenance and the New Zealand English "Short Front Vowel Shift"' (*LVC* 19[2007] 1–25), showing that for some younger speakers of NZE, the DRESS vowel completely overlaps the space of the FLEECE vowel which has led to a subsequent diphthongization of the latter in order to maintain the phonemic distinction. John Macalister discusses '*Weka* or *Woodhen*? Nativisation through Lexical Choices in New Zealand English' (*WEn* 26[2007] 492–506) on the basis of a diachronic analysis of twelve Maori-English synonym pairs to determine which factors lead to the use of a Maori loanword when an English equivalent exists.

David Cooke, T. Pascal Brown and Yunxia Zhu look 'Beyond Language: Workplace Communication and the L2 Worker' (*JAPC* 17[2007] 83–103) on the basis of data from three New Zealand worksites, showing that small talk is used in the exercise of power and that L2 workers have to struggle considerably in participating in verbal exchanges. The authors thus formulate implications for language teaching and the need for consciousness-raising measures at workplaces with L2 speakers of English. Angela Chan examines 'Same Context, Different Strategies: A Company Director's Discourse in Business Meetings' (*JAPC* 17[2007] 61–81) on the basis of audio and video recordings of a New Zealand IT company director in business meetings, identifying the discourse strategies employed in dealing with his subordinates.

Moving on to further southern hemisphere varieties, Marianne Hundt and Carolin Biewer report on 'The Dynamics of Inner and Outer Circle Varieties in the South Pacific and East Asia' (in Hundt, Nesselhauf and Biewer, eds., pp. 249–69) on the basis of a newspaper corpus downloaded from the web which includes AusE, NZE, AmE and BrE as inner-circle varieties and Singapore E, Philippine E and Fiji E as outer-circle varieties. The analysis of the occurrences of present perfect and past tense forms showed that some of the outer-circle varieties pattern with BrE while others have developed their own norms. It remains to be seen if NZE or AusE are sources of exonormative orientation in the southern hemisphere. Donna Starks, Jane Christie and Laura Thompson discuss 'Niuean English: Initial Insights into an Emerging Variety' (*EWW* 28[2007] 133–46) as spoken by Niueans in New Zealand with regard to its phonological and suprasegmental features. Their research is another step in the analysis of the Pasifika Englishes spoken in New Zealand. Finally, Daniel Schreier examines 'Greetings as Acts of Identity in Tristan da

Cunha English: From Individual to Social Significance?' (in Skandera, ed., pp. 353–74), looking at the social functions of the Tristanian greeting formula *How you is?*. Finally, a special volume supplement of *American Speech* (*AS* 91:i[2007]) deals with the Bonin Islands, where a variety of English has been spoken since the late nineteenth century. While most of the contributions are concerned with Japanese and various indigenous languages, a number of articles in this volume also deal with the development of English on the Bonin Islands, for example Peter Trudgill's 'Late-Nineteenth-Century Bonin English' (*AS* supplement 91[2007] 99–120). As very little research has been done on Bonin Islands English so far, this collection is a very valuable contribution to the field.

With regard to English in Asia, we welcome the publication of the five volumes on *Asian Englishes*, edited by Kingsley Bolton and Braj B. Kachru. With this collection, many key publications on Asian Englishes, dating back into the nineteenth century, have been made available to the interested linguist. Volume 1 is concerned with *South Asian English, 1837–1938*, including seminal text such as Henry Yule's 'Hobson-Jobsonia' (originally published in the *Asiatic Quarterly Review* in 1886). Volume 2 is dedicated to the phenomenon of *Baboo English, 1890–1891*, collections of letters and petitions written by Westerners, for example the journalist Arnold Wright, mocking the elaborate English style of Indian writers. These have strongly influenced stereotypes of IndE until the present day. Volume 3 presents *Features of Indian English, 1907–1954*, namely George Clifford Whitworth's book *Indian English: An Examination of the Errors of Idiom Made by Indians in Writing English* [1907], which has been reprinted many times and was used in Indian schools until very recently, and *G. Subba Rao*'s study of *Indian Words in English: A Study in Indo-British Cultural and Linguistic Relations* [1954], which shows the development of Indian loanwords in English. Volume 4 is dedicated to *Debating English in India, 1968–1976* and contains Amritlal B. Shah's book *The Great Debate: Language Controversy and University Education* [1968] and Klayan K. Chatterjee's work *English Education in India: Issues and Opinions* [1976], both illustrating the post-independence language controversy about the role of English and Hindi in India. Volume 5, finally, presents *East Asian Varieties of 'Pidgin English' 1836–1960*, including various accounts of Canton and Chinese Pidgin English from the nineteenth century, as well as Yokohama Pidgin and Korean and Japanese Bamboo English, which refer to the English spoken by American GIs who were stationed in Japan or Korea and which led to a kind of Pidgin English in interaction with the local population. While the collection is very much focused on Indian English, it nevertheless provides very important early writing on Asian Englishes which is often difficult to obtain today. It thus gives research on Asian, and especially IndE, more historical perspective. Another collection concerned with Asian Englishes focuses on the present-day situation and the more recent past. Amy B.M. Tsui and James W. Tollefson are the editors of *Language Policy, Culture and Identity in Asian Contexts*, which covers a wide range of Asian countries, from South Korea to Cambodia. The contributions of interest to the linguist working on the New Englishes will therefore be reviewed below in the sections concerned with the individual countries.

Most scholarly attention has been devoted to the study of English in Hong Kong and China this year. Loretta Fung and Ronald Carter provide interesting insights into 'Cantonese E-Discourse: A New Hybrid Variety of English' (*Multilingua* 26[2007] 35–66) based on Hong Kong university students' communication via the web-based message service ICQ. The corpus reveals code-switching between Cantonese and English, but also loan translations and borrowings as well as prosodic effects realized by spelling and punctuation changes. Amy B.M. Tsui examines 'Language Policy and the Construction of Identity: The Case of Hong Kong' (in Tsui and Tollefson, eds., pp. 121–41), tracing the development of national identity and language policy from the colonial into the postcolonial period. It becomes quite clear that today English and Cantonese are an integral part of Hong Kong's identity. Empirical support of Tsui's conclusions is provided by Mee Ling Lai's contribution on 'Exploring Language Stereotypes in Post-Colonial Hong Kong through the Matched-Guise Test' (*JAPC* 17[2007] 225–44) with regard to English, Cantonese and Putonghua. The results from testing more than a thousand secondary students showed that English rates highest with regard to power and Cantonese received highest marks for solidarity, whereas Putonghua rated lowest in both dimensions. With regard to the teaching of English in Hong Kong, Cheung Yin Ling and George Braine studied 'The Attitudes of University Students towards Non-Native Speakers English Teachers in Hong Kong' (*RELC* 38[2007] 257–77), revealing that the attitudes of third-year students were more favourable towards non-native teachers than those of first-year students. This is explained by their ability to judge the advantages and disadvantages of non-native-speaker English teachers in terms of teaching effectiveness and strategies. Along similar lines, Andy Kirkpatrick is concerned with 'Setting Attainable and Appropriate English Language Targets in Multilingual Settings: A Case for Hong Kong' (*IJAL* 17[2007] 376–91), criticizing the native-speaker model used in Hong Kong's language policy and promoting an ELF approach in language teaching in multilingual countries like Hong Kong. This is echoed in David C.S. Li's article on 'Researching and Teaching China and Hong Kong English' (*EnT* 23:iii and iv[2007] 11–17), who also advocates a focus on ELF and World Englishes in lieu of the current (American) native-speaker models in the teaching of English in those two countries.

Bertha Du-Babcock looks at 'Language-Based Communication Zones and Professional Genre Competence in Business and Organizational Communication: A Cross-Cultural Case Approach' (*JAPC* 17[2007] 149–71) on the basis of data from the US, Taiwan, Hong Kong and mainland China. Sylvia Xiaohua Chen and Michael Harris Bond work on 'Explaining Language Priming Effects: Further Evidence for Ethnic Affirmation among Chinese-English Bilinguals' (*JLS* 26[2007] 398–406) within a framework of accommodation theory. In a survey of over 450 university students from China and Hong Kong, who were fluent in Chinese and English, they found that the Chinese students identified more with Western and Chinese cultures, while the Hong Kong students scored lower on both, probably due to a stronger identification with local Hong Kong culture.

Moving on to Singapore, Lionel Wee looks at 'Singapore English *X-self* and *Ownself*' (*WEn* 26[2007] 360–72), discussing the semantic and functional differences between these reflexive forms in Colloquial SingE. Lisa Lim reports on 'Mergers and Acquisitions: On the Ages and Origins of Singapore English Particles' (*WEn* 26[2007] 446–73), tracing the development of the discourse particles *lah, ah, what, lor, hor, leh, meh* and *ma* and identifying their most likely substrates on the basis of sociolinguistic profiles for various phases in Singapore's history. While *lah* and *ah* are found to have originated in Hokkien or Bazaar Malay, Lim attributes the other particles to borrowing from Cantonese while maintaining their original tonal structure. Rani Rubdy examines 'Singlish in the School: An Impediment or a Resource?' (*JMMD* 28[2007] 308–24) on the basis of two surveys in Singapore primary schools, and comes to the conclusion that despite the government's campaign against the use of the local vernacular variety it could even be instrumentalized as a pedagogical resource in the education system. Viniti Vaish discusses 'Bilingualism without Diglossia: The Indian Community in Singapore' (*IJBEB* 10[2007] 171–87) based on findings from the Sociolinguistic Survey of Singapore conducted in 2006. The survey covers language use in various public and private domains, and while the trend of language shift from Tamil to English among the Indian community in Singapore is indeed confirmed, there are also tendencies of language maintenance, often more situation- than domain-dependent. Wendy D. Bokhorst-Heng, Lubna Alsagoff, Sandra McKay and Rani Rubdy also look at the linguistic behaviour of another ethnic group in Singapore, namely 'English Language Ownership among Singaporean Malays: Going Beyond the NS/NNS Dichotomy' (*WEn* 26[2007] 424–45). The researchers recorded eight Malay informants of varying age and social class while they completed a questionnaire of acceptability judgements to gain insights into their English-language norms. They found a strong adherence to exonormative standards, but also a growing sense of linguistic ownership especially among the younger informants. These findings are also mirrored in Phyllis Ghim-Lian Chew's study 'Remaking Singapore: Language, Culture, and Identity in a Globalized World' (in Tsui and Tollefson, eds., pp. 73–93), which is based on a survey of language attitudes among Singaporeans during the government's Speak Good English Movement campaign. Chew found that Singlish is especially mentioned with regard to a Singaporean identity, while English is viewed as a useful and non-threatening global language.

Joanne Rajadurai offers 'Sociolinguistic Perspectives on Variation in Non-Native Varieties of English: The Case of Malaysian English' (*Multilingua* 26[2007] 409–26) on the basis of recorded speech from various domains and follow-up interviews. Rajadurai is able to show how skilfully speakers use educated and colloquial Malaysian English according to the demands of the context. Maya Khemlani David and Subramaniam Govindasamy discuss 'The Construction of National Identity and Globalization in Multilingual Malaysia' (in Tsui and Tollefson, eds., pp. 55–72). After providing a brief survey of Malaysia's sociolinguistic background and development, the authors examine current Malaysian English textbooks with regard to their success in representing the official policy of national integration. Mukul Saxena reports on 'Multilingual and Multicultural Identities in Brunei Darussalam' (in Tsui and Tollefson, eds., pp. 143–62), which involve an intricate balance of local Malay, English and various other indigenous languages and cultures in a concept of governance that consists of Muslim, Hindu and Western values and ideologies.

Two articles deal with the specific linguistic requirements of outsourced call centres in Asia. Eric Friginal studies 'Outsourced Call Centers and English in the Philippines' (*WEn* 26[2007] 331–45) by analysing the English communication and Transaction monitoring scores of seventy-four Filipino customer-service representatives over a period of seven months. The study showed the importance of job-related language training, but also of task-specific skills, such as intercultural pragmatics. Claire Cowie examines 'The Accents of Outsourcing: The Meanings of "Neutral" in the Indian Call Centre Industry' (*WEn* 26[2007] 316–30) on the basis of an ethnographic analysis of a call-centre training institute in Bangalore, South India. Cowie concludes that the growing acceptability of an educated Indian accent, the traditional use of the British model in the education system and the customer demand for American accents come into conflict in call-centre language training resulting in mixed messages for the trainees.

Moving on to South Asia, Joybrato Mukherjee discusses 'Steady States in the Evolution of New Englishes: Present-Day Indian English as an Equilibrium' (*JEL* 35[2007] 157–87), taking Edgar Schneider's dynamic model reviewed above as a departing point for a closer look at IndE. Unlike Schneider (cf. pp. 161–73), Mukherjee claims that IndE has progressed to the stage of endonormative stabilization while retaining some features from the stage of nativization. While Schneider's model entails that eventually all New Englishes progress to stage 5 (development of dialects), Mukherjee puts forward arguments in favour of a steady-state situation, in which conservative and progressive forces hold each other in check. He views IndE thus as a semi-autonomous variety, which includes the common core of international English, structures taken over from indigenous languages but also developing its own norms with regard to English. Joybrato Mukherjee and Sebastian Hoffmann examine 'Ditransitive Verbs in Indian English and British English: A Corpus-Linguistic Study' (*AAA* 32[2007] 5–24), looking at the complementational profiles of ditransitive verbs in IndE and BrE on the basis of various synchronic and diachronic corpora. They find that there are significant differences between the two varieties and that the new patterns in IndE are not retentions of earlier BrE norms but rather innovations by means of extensions of an existing paradigm. Claudia Lange has worked on 'Focus Marking in Indian English' (*EWW* 28[2007] 89–118), analysing the functions of the forms *only* and *itself* in ICE-India. Lange is able to show that the forms have acquired additional presentative functions in IndE and have developed a distributional pattern according to text type. Kanthimathi Krishnasamy presents a case of code-mixing in southern India, namely 'English in Tamil: The Language of Advertising' (*EnT* 23:iii–iv[2007] 40–9), giving many examples of the linguistic creativity, for example wordplay, of advertisers in combining Tamil and English to make their ads work for a bilingual audience.

R.K. Agnihotri discusses 'Identity and Multilinguality: The Case of India' (in Tsui and Tollefson, eds., pp. 185–204), tracing the history of language policy in India, with a special focus on the language debate after independence and the status and functions of English in present-day India. Other South Indian states in which English plays an important role in terms of language policy are also represented in the same volume. Selma K. Sonntag presents 'Change and Permanence in Language Politics in Nepal' (in Tsui and Tollefson, eds., pp. 205–17), pointing out that, unlike in the past, the current political developments are not conducive to the learning and teaching of English. Tariq Rahman looks at 'The Role of English in Pakistan with Special Reference to Tolerance and Militancy' (in Tsui and Tollefson, eds., pp. 219–39), providing data on the sociolinguistic profile, current language policy and current uses of English in education, the media, and government and administration. Tania Hossain and James W. Tollefson report on 'Language Policy in Bangladesh' since independence (in Tsui and Tollefson, eds., pp. 241–57), especially with regard to the education system and the rivalry with Bengali. Sebastian M. Rasinger has tackled *Bengali-English in East London: A Study in Urban Multilingualism*, more precisely, whether the English spoken by first-generation immigrants from Bangladesh, whose L1 is Sylheti, in the Tower Hamlets community represents an identifiable variety of English. Rasinger's study is based on the qualitative analysis of sociolinguistic interview data as well as on the quantitative analysis of questionnaire data. He comes to the conclusion that the first-generation immigrants do not speak a focused variety of English, but rather a very variable kind of Sylheti–English interlanguage. However, he has found evidence that second-generation younger speakers have indeed developed their own variety, sometimes dubbed *Benglish*. To conclude this section on Asian English, I would like to refer to Priyanvada Abeywickrama's article 'Do We Codeswitch or Codemix in Sri Lanka?' (*JMD* 2[2007] 63–77), in which it is argued that in conversations code-switching between Sinhala and English gives way to a mixed code.

With regard to English in Africa, there is a wide range of publications on a larger number of varieties than usual. Augustin Simo Bobda offers a comparative analysis of 'Patterns of Segment Sequence Simplification in Some African Englishes' (*WEn* 26[2007] 411–23), examining a large number of varieties mainly on the basis of previous research and identifying similar patterns, for example in the monophthongization of diphthongs or in consonant cluster reduction.

West Africa is a major focus in the study of African Englishes this year. Rotimi Taiwo, Akin Odebunmi and Akin Adetunji have edited a volume on *Perspectives on Media Discourse*, which mainly contains contributions on pragmatic aspects of Nigerian media discourse. Rotimi Taiwo looks at 'Language, Ideology and Power Relations in Nigerian Newspaper Headlines' (pp. 40–60), using CDA (Critical Discourse Analysis) methodology in the analysis of a corpus of headlines collected from six Nigerian newspapers. Olatunde Ayodabo reports on 'Pragmatic Functions of Newspaper Cover Lead News Headlines in Nigeria' (pp. 114–39) on the basis of a different corpus of headlines from six Nigerian newspapers, with a view to their adherence to the Co-operative Principle and the speech-act type employed.

Akin Odebunmi discusses 'Explicatures and Implicatures in Magazine Editorials: The Case of Nigerian *TELL*' (pp. 84–99), looking at the Generic Structure Potential in the editorials of sixty editions of *Tell* magazine. Moses Alo examines 'Representation of People in the News in the Nigerian Print Media' (pp. 100–13) on the basis of the linguistic strategies in naming and referring to people in NPs in a corpus compiled from five Nigerian newspapers. Akin Adetunji provides an analysis of 'Meaning Death Mediation: A Pragmatic Study of Obituaries in Nigerian Newspapers' (pp. 198–221) on the basis of obituaries sampled from Nigeria's major newspapers. Innocent Chiluwa discusses 'Discourse Features of the Language of Nigerian News Magazines' (pp. 222–49), analysing lexical usage, graphological elements and strategies of cohesion in a corpus compiled from three widely read news magazines, *Tell*, *The News* and *Newswatch*. Godwin Eliarekhian Oboh provides 'Tidbits on News and Editorial Writing in Nigerian Weekly Magazines' (pp. 280–95), showing that the editorials analysed are not so much opinion pieces but rather summaries of the news reported elsewhere. Oni Olawale and Oluseye Abiodun B. report on 'The Mass Media and Public Opinion: A Content Analysis of Newspaper Coverage of Alamieyeseigha's Bail Jump Saga' (pp. 296–325) in three major Nigerian newspapers in order to assess the role of public opinion in Nigerian news reporting. Kate Azuka Omenugha remarks on 'Playing Unfair: The Synergy of Culture and Sexism in Nigerian News Discourse' (pp. 156–81) on the basis of data collected from four Nigerian newspapers, showing which images of women are presented there. Mafhouz Adedimeji provides 'A Speech Acts Analysis of Cigarette Advertising in the Nigerian Media' (pp. 267–79) taken from nine advertising billboards in south-western Nigeria. Finally, S.A. Aladeyomi discusses 'Errors of Segmental Phonemes in the Spoken English of Nigerian Television Newscasters' (pp. 182–97) on the basis of recordings of sixty television newscasters from state and federal television stations, including speakers of all major and a number of minority languages. Aladeyomi uses error analysis to discuss various features, such as consonant and vowel substitutions, and concludes by recommending pronunciation training for newscasters.

Efurosibina Adegbija provides a comprehensive account of 'Language Policy and Planning in Nigeria' (in Kaplan and Baldauf, eds., *Language Planning and Policy in Africa*, vol. 2: *Algeria, Côte d'Ivoire, Nigeria and Tunisia*, pp. 190–255), discussing the language profile of Nigeria and questions of language spread through education and the media, as well as language policy since the colonial period. Adegbija specifically discusses the role of English and Nigerian Pidgin, predicting that without political measures to ensure the maintenance of the indigenous languages, the shift towards English and Nigerian Pidgin will continue because of their economic value and the prestige of English, especially in urban areas. Augustin Simo Bobda presents a detailed study of 'Some Segmental Rules of Nigerian English Phonology' (*EWW* 28[2007] 279–310), which consists mainly of the reanalysis of previous research. His focus is on the identification of phonological rules and their sequencing in contrast to RP. Grace Ebunlola Adamo discusses 'Nigerian English: Is It—Can It Be—Part of a Quest for Cultural Expression and

Identity?' (*EnT* 23:i[2007] 42–7), coming to the conclusion that despite considerable nativization English is not a language suited to be Nigeria's national language as it lacks the facilities for cultural self-expression. Bolanle Akeredolu Ale reports on 'Good English for What? Learners' Motivation as a Factor in Declining Learners' Performance in English Language Acquisition and Use in Nigerian Schools' (*ChE* 14[2007] 231–45), arguing that the growing acceptance of a local variety of English is reflected in the results of nationwide school examinations in English.

Jean-Paul Kouega has compiled *A Dictionary of Cameroon English Usage*, which does not only contain dictionary entries of current Cameroon English usage, but also some background information on the geographical and linguistic situation in Cameroon, a brief survey of CamE features, as well as a short chapter on the sources of the dictionary. In the appendix there is a list of proverbs and sayings, a list of common names and a bibliography containing recent literary works by Cameroonian writers. Despite the very short introductory chapters, the dictionary will be very useful for interested linguists as it provides the most comprehensive collection of CamE lexical items, including a large number of abbreviations for state agencies and institutions. Yves Talla Sando Ouafeu looks at 'Intonational Marking of New and Given Information in Cameroon English' (*EWW* 28[2007] 187–99) on the basis of interview and reading passage data. The author is able to show that, in contrast to some other New Englishes, there is an intonational distinction between given and new information in CamE, but new information is not highlighted by using a higher pitch but rather by increasing intensity and duration. Daniel Nkemleke wonders ' "You will come when?": The Pragmatics of Certain Questions in Cameroon English' (*TLJ* 2[2007] 128–42). Using rather unusual terminology, Nkemleke analyses 160 tokens of questions with the *wh*-word *in situ* from conversational data, coming to the conclusion that this question type is used in informal situations and is modelled on the interrogative patterns of various Bantu languages spoken in Cameroon. He is not aware of the fact that this pattern is common in many varieties of English. Hans-Georg Wolf and Frank Polzenhagen discuss 'Fixed Expressions as Manifestations of Cultural Conceptionalizations: Examples from African Varieties of English' (in Skandera, ed., pp. 399–435) on the basis of the Cameroon English Corpus and a thematic database from unidentified African sources on the web. Their analysis is based on conceptual metaphors in the Lakoffian tradition and Anna Wierzbicka's cultural key words, and it reveals differences from the BrE and AmE corpora which are corroborated by a questionnaire survey. The same data are also used in Frank Polzenhagen and Hans-Georg Wolf's study of 'Culture-Specific Conceptualisations of Corruption in African English: Linguistic Analyses and Pragmatic Applications' (in Sharifan and Palmer, eds., *Applied Cultural Linguistics: Implications for Second Language Learning and Intercultural Communication*, pp. 125–68). Anne Schröder looks at 'Camfranglais—A Language with Several (Sur)Faces and Important Sociolinguistic Functions' (in Bartels and Wiemann, eds., *Global Fragments: (Dis)Orientation in the New World Order*, pp. 281–98), showing that this mixed code spoken by younger urban francophone Cameroonians has two major varieties, one based on French syntax, the other on the syntax of Cameroonian Pidgin English.

Three articles deal with SAE phonetics and phonology. Ian Bekker and Georgina Eley provide 'An Acoustic Analysis of White South African English (WSAE) Monophthongs' (*SALALS* 25[2007] 107–14), more precisely of the speech of ten younger speakers of the prestige variety spoken in the northern suburbs of Johannesburg. The analysis reveals that this variety is indeed characterized by a number of distinct vowel qualities. Andries W. Coetzee and Daan P. Wissing compare 'Global and Local Durational Properties in Three Varieties of South African English' (*LingRev* 24[2007] 263–89), namely WSAE, Afrikaans English and Tswana English. While the last of these reveals a more syllable-timed pattern, the two former varieties are stress-timed just like RP and other L1 varieties of English. Philippa Louw and Febe De Wet investigate 'The Perception and Identification of Accent in Spoken Black South African English' (*SALALS* 25[2007] 91–105), addressing the question whether Nguni and Sotho L1 speakers can determine each other's L1 via their accent when speaking English. The analysis reveals that the correlation between L1 and pronunciation is not straightforward enough for a reliable recognition.

Rajend Mesthrie discusses 'Dialect Representation versus Linguistic Stereotypes in Literature: Three Examples from Indian South African English' (in Bartels and Wiemann, eds., pp. 261–80). After briefly outlining key features of the Indian South African speech community, Mesthrie tests samples from a satirical radio show and two literary texts as to how realistically they depict the variety under analysis, showing that the authors of the texts skilfully exploit stereotypical features for a comic or satirical effect rather than aiming at dialect realism. Nkonko M. Kamwangamalu reports on 'One Language, Multi-Layered Identities: English in a Society in Transition: South Africa' (*WEn* 26[2007] 263–75), using the concepts of Acts of Identity and John Gumperz's [1982] notion of *we*-code and *they*-code. He comes to the conclusion that as English takes on the role of a *we*-code for black South Africans, indigenous languages are endangered by language shift. Similarly, Bongi Bangeni and Rochelle Kapp investigate 'Shifting Language Attitudes in a Linguistically Diverse Learning Environment in South Africa' (*JMMD* 28[2007] 253–69), tracing how black students develop a dual affiliation towards English during their undergraduate studies at a formerly 'white' university, even if they had negatively associated English with 'whiteness' before. Similarly, Joel M. Magogwe's article 'An Investigation into Attitudes and Motivation of Botswana Secondary School Students towards English, Setswana and Indigenous Languages' (*EWW* 28[2007] 311–28) reveals that despite students' loyalty to Setswana, the official language, English is preferred as medium of instruction.

Sinfree Makoni, Janina Brutt-Griffler and Pedzisai Mashiri explore 'The Use of "Indigenous" and Urban Vernaculars in Zimbabwe' (*LSoc* 36[2007] 25–49), i.e. those mixed codes that combine morphological material from various indigenous languages and English, such as the Harare urban vernaculars, which fulfil a number of functions in multilingual societies. Along similar lines, Christina Higgins examines 'Shifting Tactics of Intersubjectivity to Align Indexicalities: A Case of Joking Around in Swahinglish'

(*LSoc* 36[2007] 1–24), a mixed code of Swahili and English used in urban Tanzania by a group of journalists in a jocular conversation, which is analysed according to ethnographic principles. Based on the same data, Christina Higgins also writes on 'Constructing Membership in the In-Group: Affiliation and Resistance among Urban Tanzanians' (*Pragmatics* 17[2007] 49–70), showing how the outsider in the group is ethnified by the others but resists this process of ethnification and thus manages to be reintegrated.

Moving on to the Caribbean, there is one article which covers both standard Jamaican English and JC. Alicia Beckford Wassink, Richard A. Wright and Amber D. Franklin discuss 'Intraspeaker Variability in Vowel Production: An Investigation of Motherese, Hyperspeech, and Lombard Speech in Jamaican Speakers' (*JPhon* 35[2007] 363–79) pointing out differences between Jamaican English and Jamaican Creole speakers with regard to five acoustic parameters in the various speech modes analysed, as well as within the speech of individuals, which are attributed to style-shifting between Creole and English.

A number of publications deal with creole languages in general or provide a comparative analysis. We welcome the long-overdue publication of *Comparative Creole Syntax: Parallel Outlines of 18 Creole Grammars*, edited by John Holm and Peter L. Patrick. The volume contains contributions on creoles with a large number of European and non-European lexifiers, which are all ordered in the same way for easier reference and comparison. After a brief introduction of the variety, they deal with the unmarked verb, the anterior marker, the progressive marker, habitual aspect, completive aspect, irrealis, complementizers, dependent clauses, negation, passive constructions, verbal functions of adjectives, the copula, serial verbs, the NP, possession, personal pronouns, co-ordinating conjunctions, prepositions and word order. The chapters dealing with English-lexifier creoles are 'Jamaican Patwa' (by Peter L. Patrick), 'Krio (Creole English) or Sierra Leonian' (by Sorie M. Yillah and Chris Corcoran), 'Ndyuka' (by Mary Huttar) and 'Tok Pisin (Pidgin/Creole English)' (by Nicholas Faraclas). This volume is highly interesting for all creolists as it combines relevant morphosyntactic information on a broad scope of creoles in an easily accessible format and with—at least largely—comparable terminology. Summary tables at the end of each section make typological comparison even easier, but it must be pointed out that these tables necessarily represent simplifications.

The editors of *Deconstructing Creole*, Umberto Ansaldo, Stephen Matthews and Lisa Lim, set out to critically examine some widespread beliefs about creoles, such as their grammatical simplicity, their exceptional diachrony or their inadvertent decreolization, as Umberto Ansaldo and Stephen Matthews explain in the introduction to the volume, 'Deconstructing Creole: The Rationale' (pp. 1–18). I will concentrate on those contributions which deal with creoles in general or specific English-lexifier creoles. Joseph T. Farquharson offers insights on 'Typology and Grammar: Creole Morphology Revisited' (pp. 21–37), providing counter-evidence to the claim that creoles do not possess morphology. Enoch O. Aboh and Umberto Ansaldo use Salikoko Mufwene's concept of the feature pool to account for 'The Role of Typology in Language Creation' (pp. 39–66), based on the development of Sranan and Sri Lanka Malay. David Gil assesses 'Creoles, Complexity and Associational Semantics' (pp. 67–108) on the basis of experimental data from speakers of Sranan, Bislama and Papiamentu as well as various African, Asian European and Semitic languages. He finds that the creoles under analysis do not exhibit the simplest semantic associations, which would be counter-evidence to John McWhorter's claim that creoles are the simplest languages due to their relative youth. Jeff Siegel discusses the importance of 'Sociohistorical Contexts: Transmission and Transfer' (pp. 167–201) in creole genesis, pointing out the crucial role of SLA in this process. Nicholas Faraclas, Don E. Walicek, Mervyn Alleyne, Wilfredo Geigel and Luis Ortiz examine 'The Complexity that Really Matters: The Role of the Political Economy in Creole Genesis' (pp. 227–64), developing a matrix of creolization in the Caribbean based on the economies, political systems and prevalent ideologies of the territories involved. These factors had a considerable influence on the actual linguistic outcome of the creolization process because they determine interaction types and attitudes.

Salikoko S. Mufwene provides a very concise overview of 'Creoles and Pidgens' discussing their features and development (in Llamas, Mullany and Stockwell, eds., pp. 175–84). Marlyse Baptista discusses 'Properties of Noun Phrases in Creole Languages: A Synthetic Comparative Exposition' (in Baptista and Guéron, eds., *Noun Phrases in Creole Languages: A Multi-Faceted Approach*, pp. 461–70), summarizing the findings from a larger number of contributions on creoles with various European lexifiers, pointing out the importance of the concept of 'specificity' in the creole NP. As in the past, there is a lot of interest in issues of creole genesis. Jeff Siegel provides 'Recent Evidence against the Language Bioprogram Hypothesis: The Pivotal Case of Hawai'i Creole' (*SLang* 31[2007] 51–88), critically examining Bickerton's work and pointing out features of Hawai'i Creole, which are not in line with Bickerton's claims, which were based on his analysis of this particular variety. Anna L. Moro's article 'An Exploration of Colour Terms in English-Lexifier Atlantic Creoles' (*Lingua* 117[2007] 1448–61) provides evidence for substrate influence and universal tendencies in the development of the colour termin-ology of creoles such as Jamaican Creole, Bahamian Creole, or Cameroon Creole. Darlene LaCharité proposes an important role for 'Multilingualism in Creole Genesis' (*JPCL* 22[2007] 159–64) based on widespread bi- and multilingualism in Africa and its role in the adaption of loanwords.

A special issue of the *Journal of Pidgin and Creole Languages* (22:i[2007]) is devoted to the question of 'Substrate Influence in Creole Formation', as the editors, Bettina Migge and Norval Smith, explain in their introduction (*JPCL* 22[2007] 1–15). The contributions concentrate on the Suriname creoles because they are widely considered as very conservative creoles, on which a lot of research is being done. Richard Price offers 'Some Anthropological Musings on Creolization' (*JPCL* 22[2007] 17–36), tracing the spread of the concept of creolization into the fields of anthropology and history, especially in the study of slavery in the Americas. James Essegbey and Felix K. Ameka compare the semantics of '"Cut" and "Break" in Gbe and Sranan' (*JPCL* 22[2007] 37–55), pointing out that the semantics of the verbs in Sranan are closer to their Dutch and English etyma, but their syntax is strongly influenced by the Eastern Gbe varieties. This is a counter-argument against the relexification hypothesis. George L. Huttar, James Essegbey and Felix K. Ameka also study 'Gbe and other West African Sources of Suriname Creole Semantic Structures: Implications for Creole Genesis' (*JPCL* 22[2007] 57–72) in a large-scale project on the semantics structures of Ndyuka by comparing a large set of lexemes with corresponding lexemes in various Gbe languages, other Kwa languages, such as Akan or Ga and non-Kwa Niger–Congo languages. The data analysis revealed that some features are widespread enough to be considered areal features, but others can be traced to specific languages, which played an important role in various periods of creole development. Donald Winford and Bettina Migge report on 'Substrate Influence on the Emergence of the TMA Systems of the Surinamese Creoles' (*JPCL* 22[2007] 73–99), assessing the role of various Gbe languages in the development of the TMA system of the Suriname creoles, based on contemporary data from a variety of languages and historical data from Sranan. Their analysis reveals enough similarities to posit substrate influence in the formation of the TMA systems, but a number of differences also point towards the influence of other European languages and mechanisms of language change. Norval Smith and Vinije Haabo examine 'The Saramaccan Implosives: Tools for Linguistic Archaeology?' (*JPCL* 22[2007] 101–22), using the presence or absence of implosive voiced stops as a means to identify different historical strata in the Saramaccan lexicon. They also argue that Fon must have contained implosive stops in the seventeenth century which were subsequently lost. All the articles in this special issue reveal that, while substrate influence is more or less undisputed today in creole genesis, its exact nature is very complex and often difficult to assess for lack of data.

Moving on to research on the Surinamese and other Atlantic creoles, Adrienne Bruyn discusses 'Bare Nouns and Articles in Sranan' (in Baptista and Guéron, eds., pp. 339–81), showing that the uses of bare nouns and NPs with articles and demonstratives in Sranan differ both from constructions in English and in the Gbe substrate languages. Bettina Migge looks at 'Code-Switching and Social Identities in the Eastern Maroon Community of Suriname and French Guiana' (*JSoc* 11[2007] 53–73) within the framework of Carol Myers-Scotton's Markedness Model. She finds that code-switching between various creole varieties fulfils similar functions in creating interactional meaning as have been shown for bilingual speech communities. Miriam Meyerhoff and James A. Walker discuss 'The Persistence of Variation in Individual Grammar: Copula Absence in Urban Sojourners and their Stay-at-Home Peers, Bequia (St Vincent and the Grenadines)' (*JSoc* 11[2007] 346–66), showing that Bequians who have spent considerable time abroad may sound very different from those who have not left the island, but an analysis of their grammatical system reveals only very superficial restructuring. The constraints governing copula absence remain the same and only the overall frequency of the feature is reduced in the speech of the returnees. Janina Fenigsen traces a development 'From Apartheid to Incorporation: The Emergence and Transformations of Modern Language Community in Barbados, West Indies' (*Pragmatics* 17[2007] 231–61), evaluating the sociolinguistic stratification of Bajan and Barbadian English with a view to colonial and later postcolonial, national ideologies. Aonghas St Hilaire reports on 'National Development and the Language Planning Challenge in St Lucia,

West Indies' (*JMMD* 28[2007] 519–36) during the colonial period and thereafter, especially with regard to the relationship of the French-lexifier Kweyol and English.

Stephanie Hackert and Magnus Huber examine 'Gullah in the Diaspora: Historical and Linguistic Evidence from the Bahamas' (*Diachronica* 24[2007] 279–325), providing convincing evidence for a close relationship between Bahamian Creole and English and Gullah, which runs counter to previous claims which regarded Bahamian Creole English as a diaspora variety of AAVE. John Victor Singler also looks at the relationship of Atlantic creoles and AAVE, comparing the situation in 'Samaná and Sinoe' in two of his columns, 'Part I: Stalking the Vernacular' (*JPCL* 22[2007] 123–48) and 'Part II: Provenance' (*JPCL* 22[2007] 309–46). The Settler English spoken by descendants of ex-slaves in Sinoe County, Liberia, and the English spoken by African-Americans on the Samaná peninsula in the Dominican Republic are compared and a number of differences are identified, the possible causes of which are discussed in the second part, namely the differences between free and emancipated slaves, whose provenance from the north or south of the US must have played an important role in the linguistic development.

Michele M. Stewart reports on 'Aspects of the Syntax and Semantics of Bare Nouns in Jamaican Creole' (in Baptista and Guéron, eds., pp. 383–99), reanalysing *dem*, which has been considered a plural marker, as a marker of inclusiveness. She also identifies definite and indefinite senses in NPs lacking overt modification, which leads her to reject the term 'bare NP' in these cases. Dagmar Deuber and Lars Hinrichs examine the 'Dynamics of Orthographic Standardization in Jamaican Creole and Nigerian Pidgin' (*WEn* 26[2007] 22–47), pointing out that due to the increased presence of these predominantly oral varieties in computer-mediated communication, a process of grassroots spelling standardization is taking place, which mainly relies on English orthography but also shows deviations for phonological reasons. Lothar Peter and Hans-Georg Wolf provide 'A Comparison of the Varieties of West African Pidgin English' (*WEn* 26[2007] 3–21), that is WAPE as spoken in Nigeria, Ghana and Cameroon, based on their own research and previous research. Their survey includes phonological, morphosyntactic and a smaller number of lexical features.

Finally in this section on English-lexifier creoles, Pacific creoles will be considered. Toshiaki Furukawa studies 'No Flips in the Pool: Discursive Practice in Hawai'i Creole' (*Pragmatics* 17[2007] 371–85) on the basis of data obtained from a local comedy show in which Hawai'ians of Filipino origin ('Flips') are constructed as the social Other by means of code-switching between Hawai'i Creole and English. Peter Mühlhäusler discusses 'The Pitkern-Norf'k Language and Education' (*EWW* 28[2007] 215–47), pointing out that the language policy in favour of English, among other factors, has led to a considerable decline of Norf'k on Norfolk Island. John Harris reports on 'Linguistic Responses to Contact: Pidgins and Creoles' (in Leitner and Malcolm, eds., pp. 131–51) in Australia, such as Macassan Pidgin, which was spoken in the nineteenth and early twentieth centuries by Aborigines and white settlers in north Australia, or Northern Territory Kriol, a creole language still spoken mainly by Aborigines in the Northern Territory. The article provides a good survey of pidgins and creoles spoken in Australia and their socio-historical background.

11. Pragmatics and Discourse Analysis

As Emmanuel Schegloff explains in the introduction, his *Sequence Organization in Interaction: A Primer in Conversation Analysis*, volume 1 is the first of what is to be a three-volume introductory series on conversation analysis. This first volume is concerned with sequence organization. Schegloff describes sequences as stretches of talk, larger than a turn, that somehow 'hang together'. How these sequences are organized into larger units of spoken interaction is the focus of the volume. Each chapter centres on conversation analysis (CA) topics such as adjacency pairs, pre-expansions, insert expansions, post-expansions, and preference/dispreference. Although Schegloff's prose is characteristically dense, the use of technical terminology specific to CA is aided by numerous examples and excerpts from transcripts which helpfully illustrate the phenomena under discussion. A further excellent feature is that the book provides a URL for a companion website which features audio and video files of the transcript excerpts reproduced in the book. The book's status as a primer, or basic introduction, to the subject of sequence organization is somewhat questionable—a point which Schegloff himself addresses in his introduction. Furthermore, Schegloff's recommendation in the book's conclusion that the reader re-read the entire text immediately after the initial reading is certainly well taken: it contains a wealth of information to process. Consequently, there is no doubt that Schegloff's first volume in this series will serve as an excellent resource for slightly more advanced students of talk and social interaction, and will quickly become a classic and authoritative work on the basics of CA.

Elizabeth Holt and Rebecca Clift's volume, *Reporting Talk: Reported Speech in Interaction* brings together ten chapters by different authors, each of whom examines different aspects of reported speech and related phenomena. Topics explored include the use of reported speech in witness testimony in the courtroom (Renata Galatolo's chapter 'Active Voicing in Court') to the sequential organization in the talk of mediums, who claim the ability to communicate with the spirit world (Robin Wooffitt's 'The Dead in the Service of the Living'). The majority of the contributions adopt a CA approach, concentrating on the details of talk, specifically on the 'design and placement of reported speech—and thought—in sequences of conversation' (p. 2). This CA approach is enhanced by contributors such as Charles Goodwin, whose close analysis of excerpts of interaction in 'Interactive Footing' include attention to speakers' gazes, gestures and body placement as an integral part of the analysis of talk, and Elizabeth Couper-Kuhlen, whose own analysis of reported speech and thought in non-narrative contexts ('Assessing and Accounting') is enriched by acoustic analysis of selected excerpts. It is encouraging to see that not only Couper-Kuhlen's chapter, but also chapters such as those by Markku Haakana ('Reported Thought in Complaint Stories') and by John Rae and Joanne Kerby ('Designing Contexts for Reporting

Tactical Talk') include increasing attention to reported thought; in other words, there is growing awareness of quoted material that does not necessarily represent only speech. This volume is a welcome contribution for scholars interested in reporting discourse.

Stancetaking in Discourse, edited by Robert Englebretson, offers a number of interesting papers addressing the topic of stance from various perspectives. The collection is prefaced by the editor's introduction, which discusses the heterogeneity of approaches and perspectives found in current research on stance. Englebretson begins with a metalinguistic analysis of 'stance', a corpus-based exploration of how the term is used in everyday speech and writing. This is followed by a more traditional literature review, in which he explains the relationship of subjectivity, evaluation, and interaction to stance. The introductory chapter concludes with an overview of the remainder of the volume. Although the individual contributors emphasize different aspects of stance, a theme that clearly underlies all of the papers in the volume is a stress on the situated, pragmatic and interactional nature of stance. A chapter by John W. Du Bois presents his framework (employing a heuristic of 'stance triangle') for analysing stance, which highlights the intersubjective, sequential, and context-bound nature of stance-taking. Du Bois's framework is not only elegant but also useful, as is illustrated by a number of chapters by other authors who adopt it in their own analyses. For example, Elise Karkkainen draws on Du Bois's framework in her analysis of the discourse marker *I guess*, which—as she illustrates—functions more as a marker of evidentiality than of epistemicity. Similarly, Pentti Haddington combines Du Bois's framework with the methods of CA in an analysis of alignment in news interviews. Other chapters of interest in this volume include Susan Hunston's, in which she combines quantitative and qualitative approaches to the analysis of corpora, and illustrates how stance is constructed at the level of phraseology, rather than at the level of lexis. Also of note is Barbara Johnstone's chapter, in which she demonstrates how stance emerges as speakers in a sociolinguistic interview both discuss—and perform—a regional dialect.

Person Reference in Interaction: Linguistics, Cultural, and Social Perspectives, a volume edited by N.J. Enfield and Tanya Stivers, offers a cross-linguistic examination of person reference (mostly initial third-person reference), in order to understand marked versus unmarked usage in everyday conversation. The volume begins with a clear and focused introduction by Stivers, Enfield and Steven Levinson, which defines what is encompassed by the term 'person reference', provides some background on how the topic has been approached by the disciplines of cognitive science, philosophy, anthropology and linguistics, and discusses similarities as well as differences in person reference across languages. This introductory chapter is followed by a brief chapter by Harvey Sacks and Emmanuel Schegloff, originally written in 1973, which includes a number of assumptions about reference that are taken up by some of the other authors included in this volume: assumptions such as the preference for minimization (i.e. reference is preferably done with a single form) and a preference for using 'recognitionals' (for example, in English, the use of first names). Stivers's chapter identifies four specific types of 'alternative recognitionals' (i.e. pragmatically marked types of person-reference) and illustrates how their use works to manage relationships between speaker, addressee and referent. Drawing on an earlier unpublished paper from 1979, Schegloff's 'Conveying Who You Are: The Presentation of Self, Strictly Speaking' examines a set of phone-call openings to determine how it is that speakers do self-reference. Recipient design as well as a preference for minimization are the fundamental concepts that Schegloff uses to understand the patterns he finds in his data. John Heritage's chapter 'Intersubjectivity and Progressivity in Person (and Place) Reference' illustrates how, in conversation, the recognition of a reference to a person or place is assumed by a speaker unless a recipient indicates otherwise. He also shows how, in talk-in-interaction, the preference for progressivity (i.e. moving the talk along) appears to be stronger than that for intersubjectivity, or securing common ground. Finally, a number of other chapters which explore referring practices in specific languages (e.g. Lao, Korean, Yucatec Maya, Tzeltal) offer fascinating reading as well.

Ian Hutchby's *The Discourse of Child Counselling* offers a concise and tightly focused CA study of one particular type of institutional discourse. In this work, Hutchby examines talk produced by counsellors and children whose parents are going through separation. The book opens with a discussion of different sociological approaches to the study of children's social competence. This is followed by a chapter which outlines the methodological approach that Hutchby adopts (i.e. CA, specifically CA in institutional settings). The next four chapters constitute the analysis provided by the book. Chapter 3 examines the ways in which participants orient to being audio-recorded in the setting; chapter 4 explores how the perspective-display series (PDS) is used by counsellors to topicalize 'difficult issues' in these interactions; chapter 5 focuses on the ways in which counsellors do 'active listening'; and chapter 6 looks at the resources children use to resist responding to counsellors' questions. The concluding chapter offers a compact summary of the main points of the analysis, and presents some implications for counselling practitioners. With its clear analysis and straightforward prose, Hutchby's discussion of features of this type of institutional discourse is accessible even for readers with little background knowledge of these types of interactions.

Another work that looks at various types of institutional discourse is *Discursive Research in Practice: New Approaches to Psychology and Interaction*, edited by Alexa Hepburn and Sally Wiggins. The editors' introductory chapter offers a clear and helpful discussion of the various points of theoretical and methodological convergence and divergence between CA and discursive psychology (DP), as well as an overview of the remainder of the volume. The volume consists of three parts. The first section includes chapters that all illustrate how discursive psychology differs from other psychological approaches, in that it represents 'an action-orientated approach to what have traditionally been characterized as inner states' (p. 17), such as emotions, for example. Derek Edwards's chapter is a nice illustration of such an approach: in it, he examines how subjectivity is constructed and managed in talk. The second part of the book includes DP analyses of various institutional interactions, focusing especially on 'how clients and professionals display their concerns and orientations in the unfolding features of interaction' (p. 25), in environments as diverse as gender-identity clinics, sex-offender group meetings, and family medical practice settings. The last part, 'Youth in Institutions', centres specifically on examinations of child–adult interactions, such as Wiggins and Hepburn's own chapter, which examines child and adult discussions of 'troubled' eating. This volume represents a contribution to the growing literature on institutional discourse from a DP perspective.

Political Discourse in the Media: Cross-Cultural Perspectives, edited by Anita Fetzer and Gerda Eva Lauerbach, is a collection of studies that take a comparative/contrastive approach to the analysis of political discourse on television. Genres analysed include political interviews, political debates and political speeches. The editors' introduction provides an overview of relevant theoretical issues (i.e. the notion of 'culture' as it applies to studies of international media in an era of globalization), in addition to an overview of the volume. The volume is organized into three sections. The first section includes chapters which take a form-to-function approach to analysis. For example, in a chapter by Anne-Marie Simon-Vandenbergen, Peter R.R. White and Karin Aijmer, the authors examine the marker of expectation 'of course' (and its equivalents in Flemish and Swedish) and its functions in radio/television interviews and debates. Another chapter in this section examines the metaphors used in televised election coverage in Britain, the US and Germany. The second section concentrates on various discursive practices in political interviews, and includes chapters on topics such as represented discourse in interview answers from French and British political interviews (Marjut Johansson), and patterns of challenge and support in Arabic and Hebrew television news interviews (Elda Weitzman, Irit Levi and Isaac Schneebaum). The volume's third and final section takes a macro-perspective in the examination of larger media events, and includes chapters which address, for example, multimodality in televised Christmas messages delivered by different European heads of state (Christoph Sauer), and cross-cultural analyses of election night coverage in three countries (Gerda Eva Lauerbach).

The papers in *Healthcare Interpreting*, edited by Franz Pöchhacker and Miriam Shlesinger, were originally published as a special issue of the journal *Interpreting* in 2005. In addition to legal settings and educational contexts (i.e. interpreting for the deaf), health care represents another institutional domain which has seen a dramatic rise in interpreting, or 'mediated communication'. Nevertheless, in their introduction the editors point out that in spite of increased attention to communication in medical fields over the last fifteen years or so, health-care interpreting remains a relatively under-explored field of enquiry. Following the editors' introduction, which contextualizes the collection of papers within the literature on medical interpreting more broadly, the volume consists of five papers and three book reviews. All five papers in the volume represent discourse analyses of interpreter-mediated interaction. Topics range from the interpreter's role in interaction in pediatrics, to the use of reported speech by interpreters in psychotherapeutic encounters. Because this volume represents one of the first collections of research focusing exclusively on interpreting in health care, it is clear that much more work remains to be done in this area.

The collection of essays in *Narrative: State of the Art Narrative* edited by Michael Bamberg, was originally published as a special issue of the journal *Narrative Inquiry* (16:i[2006]), for which Bamberg also serves as editor. In his introduction to this most recent volume (a slightly expanded version of his introduction to the original special issue), Bamberg explains that the recent profusion in theorizing on narrative from various disciplinary perspectives has resulted in a field of narrative of studies which is 'not necessarily coherent or homogenous' (p. 2). The volume's chapters—which certainly do attest to this diversity of perspectives—were kept deliberately short in order to include as wide a variety of approaches to narrative as possible. Following Bamberg's brief introduction, the volume consists of twenty-five essays, with an average length of ten pages per essay. Contributions in the volume focus on the following questions posed by the editor: 'What was it that made the original turn to narrative so successful? What has been accomplished over the last 40 years of narrative inquiry? What are the future directions for narrative inquiry?' (p. 4). While the volume's authors represent a wide spectrum of disciplines, from internal medicine to philosophy, approximately half of the contributors represent some domain of psychology (clinical, personality, social, discursive, counselling, etc.). Discourse analysts whose work is represented in this volume include Jan Blommaert, and Derek Edwards and Elizabeth Stokoe. In 'Applied Ethnopoetics', Blommaert offers a more critical perspective to narrative analysis. Blommaert argues that an ethno-poetic approach to narrative analysis can be an especially useful tool for understanding stories told in interactions where 'different systems of meaning-making' converge. Blommaert illustrates this approach with data from cross-cultural bureaucratic encounters: stories told by African asylum-seekers to Belgian immigration officials. Discursive psychologists Stokoe and Edwards examine how speakers formulate and orient to the telling of a narrative in naturally occurring talk-in-interaction in their chapter, 'Story Formulations in Talk-in-Interaction'. Finally, the central chapters by applied linguist Alexandra Georgakopoulou ('Thinking Big with Small Stories in Narrative and Identity Analysis'), narrative psychologist Mark Freeman ('Life "on Holiday"? In Defense of Big Stories'), and narrative psychologist/editor Bamberg ('Stories: Big or Small—Why Do We Care?') provide some of the richest and most interesting discussion of the critical issues in narrative studies these days.

Selves and Identities in Narrative and Discourse, edited by Michael Bamberg, Anna De Fina and Deborah Schiffrin, is a collection of various studies of narrative, the focus of which is on narrative as the site for construction of identity; or, more specifically, the theme that underlies chapters in the volume is that of the generative, dynamic and emergent nature of identity as it takes shape in narratives. (Georgakopoulou—see below—describes this approach to the analysis of identity in narrative as a 'microgenetic' one.) Different methodological approaches are represented in this collection. For example, it includes chapters by scholars approaching narrative analysis from socio-linguistic traditions, such as variationism (for example Catherine Evans Davies's 'Language and Identity in Discourse in the American South: Sociolinguistic Repertoire as Expressive Resource in the Presentation of

Self') and ethnography of communication (for example Amanda Minks on Miskitu children's narratives of spirit encounters, and Cecilia Castillo Ayometzi on Mexican immigrants' narratives of religious conversion). Other contributors offer analyses that are more informed by ethno-methodological approaches to the study of talk in interaction, such as MCA, or membership categorization analysis (such as Eleni Petraki, Carolyn Baker and Michael Emmison's analysis of how mothers and daughters project their identities in stories they tell, in their chapter, ' "Moral Versions" of Motherhood and Daughterhood in Greek-Australian Family Narratives'). Overall, the volume contains a number of interesting papers, with a wide variety of narrators (and thus, identities) represented.

One of the most exciting publications on narrative this year is Alexandra Georgakopoulou's monograph, *Small Stories, Interaction and Identities*. Her primary objective in this work is 'to put small stories firmly on the map of narrative analysis, as a timely and needed antidote to the longstanding tradition of "big stories" ' (p. 147). In addition to arguing for the validity and importance of studying 'small stories'—which she defines as 'fleeting moments of narrative orientation to the world' (p. vii)—Georgakopoulou also engages with a number of other theoretical and methodological issues in narrative analysis. For example, challenging the dominant Labovian model, she offers a well-articulated reconceptualization of narrative structure. She also demonstrates how some of the tools of CA (for example, sequentiality and Membership Category Analysis) can be usefully and appropriately applied to narrative analytic studies focusing on identity. Because Georgakopoulou uses ethnographic data to illustrate her points, it is not surprising to find that she aptly draws on linguistic anthropological notions such as a 'practice-based view of language', 'indexicality' and 'recontextualization' in her work. The book has five chapters: the first introduces central concepts associated with narrative; the second defines, explains and exemplifies different types of small stories; and the third focuses on issues of structure in small stories. Whereas the first three chapters are more theoretical, chapters 4 and 5—with their focus on identity and positioning, respectively—offer more fine-grained analyses. Throughout the book, Georgakopoulou's prose is clear and convincing. There is no doubt that *Small Stories, Interaction and Identities* will quickly become essential reading for any scholars who work with narrative.

Another work which explores the relationship between language and identity is Nikolas Coupland's *Style: Language Variation and Identity*. Although the book is framed in sociolinguistic terms, the topics that Coupland explores in it also very much represent areas of interest to many discourse analysts. The focus of the book is on linguistic 'style' and speaker identity. The introduction presents a brief overview of the different ways that 'style' has been addressed in sociolinguistic research over the past decades. Chapter 2 discusses more traditional variationist approaches to the topic by focusing on style, stratification and standards. Chapter 3 explores the topics of accommodation and audience design. The following three chapters discuss 'styling' and 'performance' of identities and the ways that these concepts have been applied in more recent sociolinguistic/discourse analytic work (for example, work by Ben Rampton). The concluding chapter ties together a number of themes explored throughout the book, discusses the role of new media in shaping language and identity, and situates them in late modernity. One of the highlights of Coupland's book is the numerous examples and illustrations he offers of each phenomenon discussed—many from his own work, and many from the work of other researchers. Another highlight of the book is the way in which Coupland weaves in relevant social theory to the topics being discussed. *Style* demonstrates that there are often no clear boundaries between discourse analysis, sociolinguistics and linguistic anthropology.

Functional Perspectives on Grammar and Discourse, edited by Christopher S. Butler, Raquel Hidalgo Downing and Julia Lavid, brings together a diverse collection of topics. Following three more general opening papers (including one by Talmy Givón on 'Grammar as an Adaptive Evolutionary Product') the remainder of this Festschrift is conceptually organized around the three Hallidayan metafunctions of language: experiential, textual and interpersonal. Included among the first group are chapters such as J. Lachlan Mackenzie's, which examines 'Double-Possessive Nominalizations in English'. Chapters in the textual portion of the volume focus on different aspects of discourse structure: for example, Bruce Fraser's study, which examines the functions of 'The English Contrastive Discourse Marker *instead*'. Finally, the third section, which is concerned with the interpersonal functions of language, includes chapters such as Gordon Tucker's on apologies ('"Sorry to muddy the waters": Accounting for Speech Act Formulae and Formulaic Variation in a Systemic Functional Model of Language'), and Peter Collins's on modals in different varieties of English ('Modality across World Englishes: The Modals and Semi-Modals of Prediction and Volition'). The contributions to this volume illustrate compellingly the importance of considering the interface between grammar and discourse, as well as of examining grammar in interaction.

Metapragmatics in Use, edited by Wolfram Bublitz and Axel Hübler, consists of a number of chapters which examine the role of metapragmatic utterances in communicative practice. Each of the chapters is concerned with metapragmatics in the sense of the 'reflexive management of ongoing discourse' (p. 7). In their introduction, the editors begin by exploring relevant concepts discussed by Roman Jakobson, Gregory Bateson, Michael Silverstein, and John A. Lucy, and then draw on Claudia Caffi's [1994] work to define metapragmatics. The introduction is followed by the first of three parts, 'Metapragmatics in Everyday Use'. Highlights in this section include Sanna-Kaisa Tanskanen's investigation of 'Metapragmatic Utterances in Computer-Mediated Interaction', in which the author explores various writers' purposes for using metapragmatic utterances in asynchronous computer-mediated communication (CMC), and Axel Hübler's chapter, which explores the metapragmatic functions of different types of gesture in conversation. The second part of the book, 'Metapragmatics in Educational Use', includes chapters which explore the role of metapragmatics in a variety of educational settings. For example, Sara Smith and Xiaoping Liang examine 'Metapragmatic Expressions in Physics Lectures', and find that, in their data, the physics instructor used metapragmatic expressions to integrate various representations of related phenomena to guide students' processing strategies, and to assign participant roles to students. The volume's third section, 'Metapragmatics in Specialized Use', highlights some of the specific functions of metapragmatic utterances in different institutional contexts. For example, in '"So your story now is that...': Metapragmatic Framing Strategies in Courtroom Interrogation', Richard Janney uses excerpts from a US civil jury trial to illustrate how prosecuting attorneys use metapragmatic utterances strategically to frame a defendant's testimony as 'vague, misleading, evasive, uncooperative, or deceptive' (p. 231). Janney argues that these metapragmatic framing strategies play a major role in the jury's construal of how credible or co-operative a defendant is. In another chapter of this section, 'A Metapragmatic Examination of Therapist Reformulations', Peter Muntigl examines both the forms and functions of reformulations in a number of couples' therapy sessions. It includes an interesting analysis which compares the grammatical structures of client formulations and the subsequent therapist reformulations. Because there has only been one other volume on this topic (Adam Jaworski et al., *Metalanguage: Social and Ideological Perspectives* [2004]), *Metapragmatics in Use* is a most welcome addition to this area of discourse analysis.

In her monograph *Creativity and Convention* Rosa Vega Moreno examines figurative language in everyday speech. Moreno takes a relevance-theoretic approach to account for how we understand metaphors and, more generally, idiomatic speech. A fascinating and clearly written work, Vega Moreno's book opens with a chapter which provides background on cognition and selective processing. This is followed by a second chapter which presents an introduction to relevance theory. Chapter 3 discusses other approaches and theories of metaphor-processing. Chapters 4 and 5 apply relevance theory to metaphor interpretation, and chapters 6 and 7 address issues of analysability, transparency and pragmatic inference in idiom comprehension. The final chapter closes with a discussion of how metaphor interpretation relies on a balance of creativity and convention.

As is explained in the book's preface, the multiple authors represented in *Discourse on the Move: Using Corpus Analysis to Describe Discourse Structure* edited by Douglas Biber, Ulla Connor and Thomas Upton, share a mutual interest in examining discourse structure and organization from a corpus linguistic perspective. Approximately half of the book's chapters used the notion of 'vocabulary-based discourse units' to describe the text structure of different registers, such as biology research articles (James Jones), or university class sessions (Eniko Csomay). The other half of the book includes chapters which combine corpus linguistics techniques with Swalesean move analysis to describe genres such as biochemistry research articles (Budsaba Kanoksilapathom) and fundraising letters (Douglas Biber, Ulla Connor and Thomas Upton).

Cross-Cultural Pragmatics and Interlanguage English, edited by Bettina Kraft and Ronald Geluykens, provides a glimpse into the current state of research in cross-cultural, intercultural and inter-language pragmatics. The book is divided into three sections: the first includes chapters which focus on theoretical issues; the second includes studies which investigate face-threatening acts in elicited data (i.e. DCTs, or discourse completion tasks);

and the third part consists of chapters focusing on pragmatic issues found in interactional data. In their opening chapter, 'Defining Cross-Cultural and Interlanguage Pragmatics', the editors first define the terms 'cross-cultural pragmatics', 'intercultural pragmatics', 'contrastive pragmatics' and 'interlanguage pragmatics', and then provide a focused discussion of areas of overlap among these terms. This discussion helps set the stage for their central argument, which is that 'cross-cultural pragmatics' should be used as a cover term for all of these various, yet interconnected, strands of research. The chapter concludes with an overview of the rest of the volume. In addition to this introductory chapter, perhaps the other most useful contribution is the subsequent chapter by Geluykens, entitled 'On Methodology in Cross-Cultural Pragmatics'. In it Geluykens, making reference to numerous relevant studies, examines the strengths and limitations of various research methodologies used to investigate cross-cultural phenomena. He concludes by arguing for the need for more truly mixed-method, or multi-method, studies in the field. The second part of the volume consists of four chapters that focus on the following speech-acts: requests, apologies, complaints and responses to threats. Among the topics explored here are gender variation, variation in BrE and AmE, and variation between native speakers and language learners. The third part of the book includes four chapters which examine interactional data, such as, for example, speakers' use of coherence devices in a corpus of English as a Lingua Franca (ELF) conversation ('Coherence Devices in the Englishes of Speakers in the Expanding Circle' by Christiane Meierkord), and differences in patterns of discourse organization between speakers of Hong Kong English and native speakers of English ('Discourse Patterns in Intercultural Conversations' by Winnie Cheng).

Another collection focusing on communication across cultures is *Beyond Misunderstanding*, edited by Kristin Bührig and Jan D. ten Thije. Ten Thije begins his introductory chapter by explaining that the essays in the volume challenge a few dominant assumptions in work on intercultural interactions, which include an emphasis on the frequency of miscommunication, and the belief that intercultural communication is 'solely constituted by the fact that individuals from different cultural groups interact' (p. 1). Instead, the perspective of the authors featured here is that 'interculturality' is something that may—or may not necessarily—be relevant when speakers from different language background interact. The first set of chapters focuses more on theoretical issues—for example Georges Lüdi's 'Multilingual Repertoires and the Consequences for Linguistic Theory', which explores the complex relationships between multilingualism, communicative competence, code-switching, and 'translinguistic markers'. The second portion of this eclectic collection includes a number of analyses of intercultural discourse, such as Claudia Bubel's chapter, which analyses small-talk sequences in British–German telephone sales, and Lise Fontaine's study on the construction of an intercultural community in an online environment.

Dialogue and Culture, edited by Marion Grein and Edda Weigand, is a collection which explore the relationships between language, culture and nature. A number of authors represented in this volume use Weigand's 'dialogic action game' model in their analysis of dialogic interaction. The volume is divided into three broad sections. The first part provides some background on the 'language instinct debate', the second presents different theoretical positions and the third includes a number of empirical studies. The volume opens with a spirited chapter by Geoffrey Sampson, 'Minds in Uniform: How Generative Linguistics Regiments Culture, and Why It Shouldn't', in which Sampson raises a number of arguments against the non-empiricist side of the 'language instinct debate' and makes the case for his own empiricist position. This is followed by Weigand's 'The Sociobiology of Language', in which she presents her dialogic action game, or mixed game, model. Essentially, this framework conceptualizes 'language as dialogue'; in Weigand's terms, this 'is an open concept that copes with ever-changing empirical performance as well as with rules and conventions' (p. 38). Part II includes chapters on topics such as the interface between linguistic typology and dialogue linguistics (by Walter Bisang), and a cross-cultural study of gestural regulators and how they are used by speakers of English, French and Japanese (by Caroline Nash). The final part features a number of empirical studies, such as a cross- cultural examination of the speech-act of greeting (by Sebastian Feller) among speakers of English, German and Spanish. Although the scope of the volume as a whole is quite broad, many individual chapters represent rather standard types of pragmatics research, for instance, by drawing on speech-act theory, politeness theory, making reference to the Cross-Cultural Speech Act Realization Project (CCSARP) and using discourse completion tests (DCTs) to collect data.

   Context and Appropriateness, edited by Anita Fetzer, addresses context and appropriateness from various theoretical and applied perspectives. Following Fetzer's introduction, part I of the volume, 'Bridging Problems between Context and Appropriateness', includes three theoretical papers, including one (by Etsuko Oishi) which explores the concept of appropriateness from a speech act theoretic perspective. Part II, 'Bridging Problems between Communicative Action and Appropriateness', includes three chapters with a more applied focus, for example Lawrence Berlin on 'Cooperative Conflict and Evasive Language' found in the 9/11 US congressional hearings, and Annette Becker on 'The Appropriateness of Questions' in political media interviews. Finally, part III, 'Bridging Problems Between Micro and Macro', includes two chapters which offer analyses of the conditional and contrastive markers in two different sets of Italian interaction.

   Wallace Chafe's latest work, *The Importance of Not Being Earnest*, examines the connections between laughter, humour and what he terms 'the feeling of nonseriousness'. Opening chapters discuss the physical properties of laughter—such as vowel quality, pitch contour, pulses, inhalations/exhalations—and include spectrographic representations of various laughter types. Subsequent chapters address different reasons for laughter, different types of humour (unplanned, jokes, humour in writing), and humour in various cultures (e.g. Japanese, Navajo, Iroquois). In addition to a final coda, the book concludes with Chafe's reflections on how other authors (starting from Plato) have addressed the topics of humour and laughter. Chafe includes examples of humour from casual conversations and from literary texts, as well as from jokes. This is an interesting book, focusing on elements of discourse (i.e. laughter and humour), which are, in fact, pervasive in much of our talk, and yet have not been the main focus of many discourse analytic works.

Axel Hübler's *The Nonverbal Shift in Early Modern Conversation* offers a fascinating multidisciplinary historical account of how the uses of gesture for communication gradually became supplanted by prosodic means in sixteenth- and seventeenth-century England. Hübler draws on multiple historical documents from this period, including published 'courtesy books', which prescribe appropriate behaviour, as well as texts such as letters, diaries and chronicles, which document observations and provide commentaries on gestural behaviour during the same period. This historical anthropological approach is complemented by an analysis of concurrent developments in the English lexicon. Specifically, Hübler illustrates a gradual increase in verbal substitutes for gestures, and he also argues that the rise of lexical expressions related to prosodic characteristics indicates a shift away 'from kinesic gesturing to prosodic forms' (p. 214). In addition to chapters which focus on the aforementioned topics, the book also includes a helpful overview of different types of gesture, as well as a discussion of cognitive theories which address the interaction between the verbal and nonverbal in utterance production.

Irony in Language and Thought: A Cognitive Science Reader, edited by Raymond Gibbs and Herbert Colston, is an impressive volume of over 600 pages, which brings together authors who study irony from various perspectives and disciplines, including pragmatics. Each of the chapters has been previously published elsewhere, either in books or journals. The volume is framed by the editors' introductory chapter, 'A Brief History of Irony', and their concluding chapter, 'The Future of Irony Studies', where they point to broadening the scope of study to include examinations of irony in art, literature and music. The remaining twenty-two chapters are organized around five major themes: theories of irony, context in irony comprehension, the social functions of irony, development of irony understanding and situational irony. The first of these sections (i.e. theories of irony) includes a paper by Herbert Clark and Richard Gerrig, which provides an overview of some of the major theories of irony (pretence theory, mention theory and psychological approaches), a paper by Dan Sperber and Deirdre Wilson, which sketches out different types of verbal irony, and a paper by Salvatore Attardo, which conceptualizes irony as 'relevant inappropriateness'. The next section, focusing on irony comprehension, includes a number of experimental studies examining factors such as response times in irony-processing, discourse factors influencing irony comprehension, and irony comprehension in brain-damaged patients. The following section, on the social functions of irony, includes chapters which explore the vocal patterns of irony, and responses to irony in different types of spoken discourse (conversation, mass media, etc.). The next section takes a developmental perspective and includes various studies of how children perceive, recognize and comprehend irony. The volume's final section includes chapters which address different aspects of situational irony.

In *The Golden Silence: A Pragmatic Study on Silence in Dyadic English Conversation*, Yan Zuo examines an often neglected aspect of conversation—silence. Specifically, Zuo merges cognitive and CA approaches to come up with a framework for investigating silence in conversational interaction (i.e. data from three corpora of dyadic conversations). Zuo's study indicates that there is much more discourse analytic work that remains to be done on this topic.

Additionally, the following three titles on relevant topics may also be of interest to scholars of discourse and pragmatics. First, Daniel Chandler's *Semiotics: The Basics* (second edition) offers quite an accessible introduction to a very complex topic. Clearly written, and filled with examples, Chandler's book covers models of the sign, and notions such as codes and textual interactions. The appendix includes a list of 'Key Figures and Schools' of semiotics, a list of suggested readings for semiotics in different fields of study (for example advertising, cinema and architecture) and a glossary of terminology. Next, Richard Dimbleby and Graeme Burton's *More Than Words: An Introduction to Communication* is a very introductory-level text that focuses on communication as social interaction, covering topics such as interpersonal communication, communication in organizations and mass communication. The book's clear and direct writing style, plentiful examples and chapter-final summaries, discussion questions and exercises indicate that it would be an appropriate textbook for undergraduate students new to communication studies. Finally, Martin Conboy's *The Language of the News*, is another introductory-level text, and one which focuses on the language of journalism, specifically newspaper language. The opening chapters, which draw on critical linguistics (specifically, on the work of Gunther Kress and Robert Hodge), introduce readers to various 'analytic tools' and present examples of how nominalizations and transitivity function in newspaper reporting. Subsequent chapters focus more at the macro-levels of newspaper discourse (i.e. rhetorical and semiotic) and explore issues such as gender, exclusion and language ideology. Some of the useful features of the book include text boxes with activity ideas (which provide excellent ideas for instructors using the book in a course), as well as many excerpts from actual newspapers, which are also set apart in text boxes. However, the majority of the examples in the book come from British newspapers (with considerably fewer examples from Australian or US newspapers) and the book therefore appears to assume a primarily British readership.

12. Stylistics

At the inaugural conference of the International Society for the Linguistics of English (ISLE, Freiburg, 8–11 October 2008), Elizabeth Closs Traugott remarked in her presidential address on the renewed popularity that stylistics is now enjoying after a considerable period in the academic wilderness. Those who specialize in stylistics would say that it never actually went away. There is, after all, a specialist society for stylistics (the international Poetics and Linguistics Association, or PALA), as well as numerous journals focused on this area of language study (including PALA's own *Language and Literature*). Nonetheless, what was striking at the ISLE conference was the breadth and depth of interest in matters stylistic among those linguists who would not necessarily be found at a dedicated stylistics conference. In addition to a named strand in stylistics, there were, scattered around the conference, a large number of papers dealing with aspects of style in language, from reported discourse in Middle English to corpus-based analyses of lexico-grammatical features of style and their influence on identity construction. This is heartening, since it demonstrates that stylistics encompasses much more than the linguistic analysis of literary texts (a narrow conception of the discipline that is sometimes off-putting to language scholars working in other areas), and that its remit is wide and its methodologies varied. What it also demonstrates is that stylistics is unremittingly linguistic in nature. It shares with linguistics what Mick Short described at the conference as 'an attitude of mind'. That is, it proceeds on such principles as rigour, detail, replicability, falsifiability and objectivity. All of these traits were very much in evidence in the best work in stylistics from 2007.

Of all the stylistics publications in 2007, easily the most influential is the second edition of Geoffrey Leech and Mick Short's *Style in Fiction: A Linguistic Introduction to English Fictional Prose*. The extent of this book's influence may be seen from its 30,000+ sales and also by the fact that the first edition was recognized by members of PALA as the most influential publication in stylistics in the first twenty-five years of its existence. This prize was awarded in 2005 in celebration of PALA's twenty-fifth anniversary, and the appearance of the second edition two years later met an unremittingly enthusiastic reception. Wisely, Leech and Short avoided the temptation to substantially revise the book, since it would no doubt have been difficult to integrate new stylistic approaches into its already successful structure. Instead, the book has been updated by the addition of two additional chapters. In the first of these—'Stylistics and Fiction 25 Years on'—Leech and Short consider how stylistics has developed as a subdiscipline since the book's original publication. In so doing, the authors review issues concerning plot, fictional worlds and characterization. In the second—'The Bucket and the Rope'— Leech and Short bring together these new analytical methods and frameworks in an analysis of a complete short story by T.F. Powys, taking into account corpus and cognitive stylistic approaches, while also considering the value of these new techniques. These new chapters clearly confirm their authors' standing as two of the foremost stylisticians of the twentieth and twenty-first centuries, and this is a book that belongs on the shelf of any serious practitioner of stylistics. Following these two new chapters is a useful annotated list of further reading that takes particular account of more recent work. (As a minor aside, it is interesting to note that the revision of the book even extends to the foreword by Randolph Quirk; while the first edition referred to Leech and Short as 'men who are undoubtedly (but certainly not solely) linguists', new linguistic sensibilities have clearly motivated the change of this description to '*scholars* who are . . . linguists'. Even this small change is a measure of the stylistic sensitivity to be found in this new edition of the book!)

That *Style in Fiction* should occupy such an important place in the stylistics bibliography is apparent from the work that it has influenced on the stylistics of prose. In 2007 some excellent work was carried out on the stylistics of prose fiction, much of which was influenced—at least in some way—by the analytical models proposed originally by Leech and Short. Reiko Ikeo (*L&L* 16[2007] 367–87), for example, investigates the notion of ambiguity in free indirect speech and thought presentation (FIS and FIT respectively) in an analysis of the Lancaster Speech, Writing and Thought Presentation corpus (compiled by Short and a project team at Lancaster University). Her analysis is focused on explaining how prototypical FIS/FIT can be distinguished from examples that are ambiguous between FIS/FIT and narration. As a result of this analysis, she suggests that prototypical FIS/FIT is marked by the 'consistent management of a reported speaker's viewpoint' (p. 386). Ambiguous cases, on the other hand, are marked by unstable viewpoint shifts. Her corpus stylistic approach to the issue generates a number of other insights which would be unavailable using a qualitative methodology—for instance, that cases of FIS that are ambiguous with 'narration' (Ikeo's term for parts of the text that do not constitute discourse presentation) are to be found more often in journalistic prose than in fiction. Ikeo's analysis further refines the work on discourse presentation initiated by Leech and Short in *Style in Fiction*.

Joe Bray (*L&L* 16[2007] 37–52) also investigates free indirect discourse, though from a different perspective. Bray is interested in whether readers really do construct a dual voice when they read free indirect discourse (as critics such as Monika Fludernik have suggested), and how readers identify point of view. Bray reports on a small empirical study designed to investigate these two questions. Respondents were asked to read passages from Jane Austen's *Pride and Prejudice* and Charlotte Smith's *Marchmont* before answering a multiple-choice question concerning whose speech and whose viewpoint was represented in the extract. From this experiment, Bray concludes that to claim that readers do indeed construct a dual voice when they encounter free indirect discourse is perhaps rash. This was not the experience of many of his informants; fewer than half identified both Elizabeth's and the narrator's voice in the *Pride and Prejudice* example. Bray suggests instead that the effects of free indirect discourse are perhaps more easily recognized when one is already familiar with the nature of free indirect discourse. One issue with Bray's experiment (which he readily acknowledges) is that a far greater number of informants would be needed before such findings could be verified statistically. Nonetheless, this small-scale study does point towards some interesting hypotheses which could be tested in a larger experiment. One of the most successful aspects of Bray's article is his effort to make connections between his empirical findings and cognitive stylistic theories of text comprehension. All too often, cognitive stylistics proceeds without empirical verification, and Bray's work demonstrates that it is perfectly possible to test some of its key ideas.

The long arm of *Style in Fiction* also extended its reach to a special issue of the journal *Style* (41[2007]). The issue consists of papers from the *Style in Fiction* symposium, held at Lancaster University in March 2006 to commemorate the award of the PALA twenty-fifth anniversary book prize to Geoffrey Leech and Mick Short. The issue includes papers by all the plenary speakers from the symposium. Geoffrey Leech's opening article, 'Style in

Fiction Revisited: The Beginning of *Great Expectations*' (*Style* 41[2007] 117–33), discusses how topics from *Style in Fiction* have been further explored in the years since its publication. Leech then demonstrates some of the advances that have been made in an analysis of the opening of Dickens's *Great Expectations*. The analysis is a tour de force of stylistic detail and would make an excellent article to have undergraduate students of stylistics read, not least because of the clarity of the writing and thought. What I also particularly appreciated was its grounding in the formal features of the text and its focus on the concept of foregrounding and how an interpretation of the text 'grows' out of this. That Leech is then able to connect such concepts to recent developments in cognitive stylistics clearly demonstrates why he has achieved such eminence in the field. Barbara Dancygier's article, 'Narrative Anchors and the Processes of Story Construction: The Case of Margaret Atwood's *The Blind Assassin*' (*Style* 41[2007] 133–52) focuses on blending theory and explores how the concept of narrative anchors (defined by Dancygier as textual devices that prompt the emergence of narrative spaces) might be used to explain the construction of stories. Dancygier postulates that stories are complex blends arising out of the integration of narrative spaces. Although this is an interesting idea, one issue I have with Dancygier's article concerns the replicability of her analysis (and, indeed, of analyses generally that make use of blending theory). It is difficult to see the criteria by which blends are identified, though this issue does raise the possibility of doing some interesting empirical work. Following Dancygier, Elena Semino also takes a cognitive stylistic approach in her analysis of mind style and the advances that have been made in this area since the publication of *Style in Fiction* ('Mind Style Twenty-Five Years On', *Style* 41[2007] 153–73). Semino explores how cognitive theories such as schema theory and cognitive metaphor theory can be applied in the analysis of mind style, as well as pragmatic theories such as Gricean theory and politeness theory. Semino ends by considering the value of corpus linguistic methodologies. This move towards a computational method is the starting point for David Hoover's article, 'Corpus Stylistics, Stylometry, and the Styles of Henry James' (*Style* 41[2007] 174–203). This paper focuses on stylometric techniques for exploring authorial style variation. Interestingly, both Hoover's and Leech's articles in this issue involve returning to core principles of stylistics, though armed with contemporary analytical tools. This is also the case in 'Stylistics Meets Cognitive Science: Studying Style in Fiction and Readers' Attention from an Interdisciplinary Perspective', by Catherine Emmott, Anthony J. Sanford and Eugene J. Dawydiak (*Style* 41[2007] 204–26). This fascinating article reports on a study testing whether stylisticians' intuitive notions of what constitute foregrounded parts of a text have any reality in the experiences of other readers. To do this, the authors use a psychological framework that measures depth of processing. Their article is the result of an interdisciplinary collaboration between linguists and psychologists and demonstrates well the capacity that stylistics has for absorbing ideas and methods from other disciplines. Finally, Mick Short's article, 'Thought Presentation Twenty-Five Years On' (*Style* 41[2007] 227–41), discusses issues arising from the corpus-based investigation of discourse presentation that he and Elena Semino (and others) have been involved in since the early 1990s. This work was aimed initially at testing the model of speech and thought presentation outlined in *Style in Fiction*, and Short's article on the subject here demonstrates the value of this corpus-based approach. For example, the exhaustive annotation of around 250,000 words of text for categories of speech, writing and thought presentation has led to insights into the forms and functions of discourse presentation that would have been unlikely to have been discovered through qualitative analysis of specially selected examples. For instance, Short describes in his article how analysis of the Lancaster corpus has led to a question mark over the status of internal narration as a thought-presentation category. There is a clarity to Short's writing that belies the complex subject matter, and the article is a useful addition to the growing body of work on discourse presentation.

In the same way that the *Style* special issue returned to some of the key elements of stylistics, so too did the special issue of *Language and Literature* on 'Foregrounding', edited by Willie van Peer. Van Peer's preface, 'Introduction to Foregrounding: A State of the Art' (*L&L* 16[2007] 99–104), introduces the seven articles that comprise the issue, which are followed by van Peer's review article of Marisa Bortolussi and Peter Dixon's *Psychonarratology* (*L&L* 16[2007] 214–24). The first article in the issue is Olívia da Costa Fialho's 'Foregrounding and Refamiliarization: Understanding Readers' Response to Literary Texts' (*L&L* 16[2007] 105–24), in which he demonstrates empirically, through a study of humanities students' and engineering students' responses to a short story, that response to foregrounding in texts is independent of literary training. Jèmeljan Hakemulder's 'Tracing Foregrounding in Responses to Film' (*L&L* 16[2007] 125–39) reports on an experiment to discover whether foregrounding theory can predict audiences' responses to films in the same way that it can predict readers' responses to literary texts. Hakemulder finds evidence to support the view that it can, and his work will have resonance for anyone interested in multimodal stylistics (indeed, this careful empirical work is exactly what cognitive stylisticians should be taking account of as they construct elaborate theories of reader responses to multimodal texts). Colin Martindale's 'Deformation Forms the Course of Literary History' (*L&L* 16[2007] 141–52) explores the hypothesis that by investigating the way in which readers conceive of novel word combinations, it is possible to predict the direction of literary change. Martindale's hypothesis is fascinating, though readers may find it necessary to read his article in conjunction with some of his earlier work (for which see the references to Martindale's paper) in order to be firmly convinced. Following this, David Miall's study, 'Foregrounding and the Sublime: Shelley in Chamonix' (*L&L* 16[2007] 155–68), explores the notion of the sublime being an effect of defamiliarization, while Yeshayahu Shen's 'Foregrounding in Poetic Discourse: Between Deviation and Cognitive Constraints' (*L&L* 16[2007] 169–81) examines potential constraints on linguistic deviations. In ' "Creation from Nothing": A Foregrounding Study of James Joyce's Drafts for *Ulysses*' (*L&L* 16[2007] 183–96), Paul Sopcák applies foregrounding analysis to *Ulysses* in an effort to see whether foregrounding theory can account for effects in a longer and more complex text than the poems or straightforward narratives that are usually the material of analysis for foregrounding scholars. In this respect, Sopcák follows

Hakemulder's lead in testing the limits of foregrounding theory. The final article in this special issue is 'Lines on Feeling: Foregrounding, Aesthetics and Meaning' (*L&L* 16[2007] 197–213) by Willie van Peer, Jèmeljan Hakemulder and Sonia Zyngier. In this, the authors explore the relationship between deviation and aesthetic experience and find some evidence for a connection between the two. Overall, the issue is a well put together volume clearly covering the state of the art in what must be seen as a linchpin in the stylistics machinery. Readers interested specifically in empirical stylistics will also enjoy Willie van Peer, Jèmeljan Hakemulder and Sonia Zyngier's *Muses and Measures: Empirical Research Methods for the Humanities*, an ambitious textbook that aims to introduce empirical research methods not just to literary critics but to humanities students and scholars generally. This is a very valuable book for students, with much practical advice concerning experiment design, using SPSS and presenting results at conference. The book also includes a CD-ROM with helpful exercises and self-tests.

Concerning work in genre-based stylistics, a key publication in 2007 was Marina Lambrou and Peter Stockwell's edited collection of essays, *Contemporary Stylistics*. The innovative feature of this book is that chapters are written by more recent scholars of stylistics and introduced by established stylisticians. This is a thoughtful and successful way of presenting new research, and one of the book's most useful features is the fact that all the chapters demonstrate the practice of stylistic analysis—a feature that will make it particularly attractive to new students of stylistics. The book is divided into three sections: 'Stylistics of Prose', 'Stylistics of Poetry' and 'Stylistics of Dialogue and Drama'. Each section contains a wealth of practical stylistic analysis, and while there are too many chapters to discuss each in turn, I can perhaps single out Michael Burke's ' "Progress is a comfortable disease": Cognition in a Stylistic Analysis of e.e. cummings' (pp. 144–55), Violeta Sotirova's 'Woolf's Experiments with Consciousness in Fiction' (pp. 7–18) and Dany Badran's 'Stylistics and Language Teaching: Deviant Collocation in Literature as a Tool for Vocabulary Expansion' (pp. 180–93) as being exemplars of the excellent work to be found in the book. The only surprise is that Continuum has not yet seen fit to produce a paperback version of the volume, since this is a book that would surely sell well to undergraduate students.

Turning specifically to the stylistics of prose fiction, Nina Nørgaard's 'Disordered Collarettes and Uncovered Tables: Negative Polarity as a Stylistic Device in Joyce's "Two Gallants" ' (*JLS* 36[2007] 35–52) explores the meaning-making potential of negative propositions such as 'He approached the young woman and, without saluting, began at once to converse with her' (Joyce, quoted in N. Nørgaard, p. 43). Nørgaard argues that the negative propositions in 'Two Gallants' are not defamiliarizing but are more semantically loaded than their positive counterparts.

This concentration on small-scale linguistic features of a text is character-istic too of Christiana Gregoriou's first book, *Deviance in Contemporary Crime Fiction*, a study of linguistic, social and generic deviation in one particular literary genre. Gregoriou examines the work of such contemporary crime novelists as James Patterson, Michael Connelly and Patricia Cornwell, and explores such notions as mind style, demonstrating the linguistic make-up of the criminal in the texts she analyses, and how this differs from what we might perceive to be a norm. In so doing she provides a linguistic perspective on a genre that tends to be approached primarily from a non-linguistic, literary-critical angle (though 2007 also saw the publication of John Douthwaite's study, 'Using Speech and Thought Presentation to Validate Hypotheses Regarding the Nature of the Crime Novels of Andrea Camilleri', in Hoover and Lattig, eds., *Stylistics: Prospect and Retrospect*, pp. 143–68). Gregoriou's book has already been nominated for two awards from within the crime-writing community, but it is perhaps a shame that it appears in a series (Crime Files) that is not specifically linguistic or stylistic in nature, since it deserves the attention of this specialist readership.

The edited collection, *Stylistics and Social Cognition* by Lesley Jeffries, Dan McIntyre and Derek Bousfield is a volume of papers selected from the twenty-fifth annual PALA conference held at Huddersfield University in 2005, and focused around the theme of that conference: social cognition. David Hoover and Sharon Lattig's edited volume *Stylistics: Prospect and Retrospect* is the preceding volume in the series of which Jeffries et al.'s book is a part, and collects together some of the best papers from PALA's 2004 conference in New York. Both books are peer-reviewed collections which demonstrate the broad spectrum of current research in stylistics. Stand-out chapters in Hoover and Lattig's volume include Violeta Sotirova's 'Historical Transformations of Free Indirect Style' (pp. 129–42) and Mick Short's analysis of the speech-act of apology in the film *A Fish Called Wanda* (pp. 169–89). In Jeffries, McIntyre and Bousfield the stand-out chapters for me were David West's appraisal of I.A. Richards as a proto-cognitivist (pp. 1–18), Matt Davies's non-literary stylistic analysis of the effects of constructed oppositions in news texts (pp. 71–101) and Larry Stewart's 'You Must Alter Your Style, Madam: *Pamela* and the Gendered Construction of Narrative Voice in the Eighteenth-Century British Novel' (pp. 141–52).

Continuing the genre-based approach to stylistics, Susan Mandala's *Twentieth-Century Drama Dialogue as Ordinary Talk* is a welcome addition to the slowly growing body of work on the stylistics of drama. It would be easy to criticize this book for being a fairly workaday application of some basic stylistic and pragmatic frameworks to the analysis of dramatic texts, were it not for the rigour with which Mandala analyses her data. In this respect, the book is an exemplar of the stylistic method and should serve as a model for both students and professional academics of what doing objective analysis really means. Although the basic premise of the book is not in itself strikingly original (the notion that techniques from conversation analysis and pragmatics may be applied in the analysis of fictional dialogue is, after all, something that Deirdre Burton was demonstrating in 1980), where Mandala does add something new is in her admirably thorough consideration of how such stylistic analysis can augment literary-critical approaches to the texts she analyses—by either supporting or undermining them. In terms of its coverage of stylistic frameworks, this is a slim volume, which would have benefited from added consideration of more recent advances in stylistics and pragmatics; for example, Mandala's approach to linguistic politeness focuses almost exclusively on the Stephen Brown and Penelope Levinson model [1987] which, given its pre-eminence within pragmatics, is perfectly reasonable. Nonetheless, considerable advances have been made in recent years in the study of impoliteness, which has itself had an effect on the way in which the Brown and Levinson model should be viewed. Consideration of this factor would have improved the book substantially. Despite this shortcoming, however, let me reiterate that this book is an excellent exemplification of the rigorous application of analytical frameworks to a text, and for this reason I recommend it strongly.

Other work on the stylistics of drama in 2007 can be found scattered widely across a number of books and journals. Derek Bousfield's analysis of impoliteness in *1 Henry IV* (in Lambrou and Stockwell, eds., pp. 209–20) is a case in point regarding the advances in pragmatics alluded to in the previous paragraph. In the same volume (pp. 232–43), Beatrix Busse provides an admirably thorough analysis of address forms, metaphor and foregrounding in *The Reign of King Edward III* while Craig Hamilton takes a cognitive approach to explaining why Arthur Miller's *The Crucible* is often interpreted as a parable (pp. 221–31). Mandala herself further demonstrates her interest in applying sociolinguistic principles in the analysis of drama, by investigating the use and function of the -*y* suffix in characters' dialogue in the television series *Buffy the Vampire Slayer* (*L&L* 16[2007] 53–73). Mandala makes use of social network theory to suggest that the morphological ending in question is a marker of in-group identity for a core few of the main characters. She also suggests that the application of sociolinguistic models in the analysis of drama needs to take account not just of the realism of dramatic talk, but also 'thematically motivated divergence' from dramatic norms (p. 66).

In genre-based stylistics, of course, drama tends to be the poor relation to prose and poetry, and so it is encouraging that so much work was produced in this area in 2007. It is also the case that work on the stylistics of drama can be found outside the mainstream journals, if one knows where to look. As an example, Jeremy Munday's excellent study, *Style and Ideology in Translation: Latin American Writing in English*, contains a number of sections dealing specifically with film drama. The book is an extremely thorough investigation of stylistic issues in translating Latin American writers, and its appeal should go beyond those interested specifically in translation studies, precisely because it is so focused on what might be seen as a core principle of stylistics—the notion of style arising from motivated choice. Chapter 7 of the book, 'Style in Audiovisual Translation', is well worth the attention of those scholars currently working on multimodal issues in stylistics.

Of work in non-literary stylistics, Lesley Jeffries's *Textual Construction of the Female Body: A Critical Discourse Approach* demonstrates well how stylistics can be used to engage with such issues as ideology and identity construction. Jeffries investigates the ways in which magazines for teenage girls project often unattainable conceptualizations of the female body, which have the potential to be extremely damaging for their target readers. Jeffries's findings are based on the qualitative analysis of a corpus of texts, and the book includes analysis of nominalization, transitivity patterns and pragmatic issues, among numerous other aspects. Jeffries also engages with recent work in cognitive stylistics, which is especially appropriate given her concern with the ways in which readers react to the texts she analyses. With regard to this aspect of the book, it could have been made clearer that texts *project* identities while it is readers who *construct* them, though the book as a whole is a model of the kind of rigour and replicability that we should strive for in all stylistics research. Indeed, the clarity with which Jeffries presents her methodology, analysis and results makes this a project that might easily be replicated using a corpus linguistic methodology, which would have the potential to provide quantitative support for Jeffries's findings.

In a similar vein, Louise Mullany's *Gendered Discourse in the Professional Workplace* is an extremely thorough study of how workplace inequalities can be exacerbated through gendered discourses. Mullany takes an ethnographic approach to the issue and analyses a wide variety of data, from transcriptions of audio-recorded business meetings to written documents and notes on informal talk. Although sociolinguistic and discourse-analytic in nature, there is enough here concerning the matter of style for this book to be of interest to stylisticians, and it is particularly good to see linguistics generally being used for such a practical purpose.

Another work in non-literary stylistics deserving attention is Astrid Ensslin's *Canonizing Hypertext: Explorations and Constructions.* Ensslin focuses specifically on literary hypertext, which she defines as 'a specific form of literature that combines modern hypermedia with an at once "traditional" and innovative approach to reading' (p. 2). She concludes that integrating such hypertexts into the UK National Curriculum may well have the effect of making literature more relevant to contemporary readers who are increasingly familiar with computer technology, though she adds the cautionary note that to do so would involve rethinking our concept of literature and literary competence. For readers with a particular interest in new media, it is also well worth seeking out David Machin and Theo van Leeuwen's *Global Media Discourse: A Critical Introduction*, a textbook focused on how to analyse the impact of globalization on the discourses of global media industries, incorporating both linguistic and multimodal analysis. The analysis of news discourse is also the focus of Martin Conboy's textbook, *The Language of the News* (reviewed in the previous section) while Martin Montgomery's *The Discourse of Broadcast News: A Linguistic Approach* deals with the same topic but with the increased detail to be expected of a monograph. Montgomery's book is groundbreaking in its integration of linguistic, multimodal and socio-cultural analytical techniques and deserves to be read widely.

Finally, with regard to non-literary work, it is important to mention Malcolm Coulthard and Alison Johnson's excellent *An Introduction to Forensic Linguistics: Language in Evidence.* Although it covers numerous aspects of linguistics (for example, morphology, syntax and phonology), it also includes significant coverage of stylistic issues and their importance to the practice of forensic linguistics. Coulthard and Johnson draw on their combined experience to provide a fascinating discussion of issues such as authorship attribution, register and idiolect and how these are often key in the forensic analysis of texts. In so doing, the authors discuss examples such as the plagiarism accusation brought against Dan Brown for his thriller *The Da Vinci Code* and the supposedly verbatim statement made by Derek Bentley following his arrest for the murder of a policeman. The book is an excellent exemplar of the practical value of language analysis of all kinds, and is highly recommended.

Turning now to the issue of cognition, the surge of interest in recent years in cognitive poetics means that this area of stylistics was amply represented in 2007. Joanna Gavins's *Text World Theory: An Introduction* provides an admirably clear and succinct introduction to Paul Werth's hugely influential theory concerning how readers construct fictional worlds. Although intended as a textbook, the book is not merely a simplified reformulation of Werth's work, but suggests substantial revisions to 'Text World Theory'—such as the concept of world switches—in order to address defects in Werth's original concepts and to make it a more applicable theory analytically. One of the book's real strengths is its breadth of interesting analyses, which demonstrate well the value of Text World Theory. These are especially welcome, since without such exemplification there is a danger that new students may see Text World Theory as a simple descriptive account of the reading process which has little to say about the stylistic effects associated with the construction of fictional worlds. Gavins's book is an excellent counter to this danger.

For scholars of metaphor, 2007 was a bumper year. Two major publications were Gerard Steen's *Finding Metaphor in Grammar and Usage* and Andrew Goatley's *Washing the Brain: Metaphor and Hidden Ideology*. Steen's book is an admirably rigorous discussion of Cognitive Metaphor Theory and the evidence for the convergence of metaphor in language and thought. One of the most useful aspects of his book is the methodology that he outlines for the identification of conceptual metaphors, a process which will be of substantial value to stylisticians. This methodology is derived from the work of the Pragglejaz Group, an international association of metaphor scholars of which Steen is a member, and the methodology itself can also be found in the group's jointly authored publication 'MIP: A Method for Identifying Metaphorically Used Words in Discourse' (*Met&Sym* 22[2007] 1–39). Goatley's book is similarly impressive, and provides a wealth of examples of how conceptual metaphors can be culturally relative with significant consequences for the way in which we perceive our societies. Both books are highly recommended. Much shorter but no less rigorous is Jonathan Picken's *Literature, Metaphor and the Language Learner*. Picken's book is written primarily for L2 teachers who may want to include literature in their teaching. Picken provides much practical advice for such teachers, all of which is based on his own empirical research into readers' responses to metaphor and literature in the foreign language classroom. The clarity of Picken's writing, however, means that the book should reach a wider readership than its primary intended one. In addition to this wealth of research into the nature of conceptual metaphors, 2007 saw the publication of Mark Johnson's *The Meaning of the Body: Aesthetics of Human Understanding*, which provides much food for thought concerning the nature of embodied meaning and how the body is able to convey meaning even before the development of self-conscious thought.

One area of stylistics that is growing significantly is that which has come to be known as corpus stylistics. Over recent years the application of corpus linguistic techniques in stylistic analysis has been shown to be of immense value, especially when it comes to the analysis of long texts such as novels. The year 2007 saw the publication of a number of extremely insightful articles about this developing methodology, though some of these are in specialist corpus linguistics publications which stylisticians may not necessarily stumble across. Nonetheless, I would urge all stylisticians to seek these out, since they exemplify the corpus stylistic approach and demonstrate well its value. Among these publications are Keiran O'Halloran's 'The Subconscious in James Joyce's "Eveline": A Corpus Stylistic Analysis which Chews on the "Fish Hook"' (*L&L* 16[2007] 227–44) and his 'Corpus-Assisted Literary Evaluation' (*Corpora* 2[2007] 33–63). In the first of these, O'Halloran treats Joyce's short story 'Eveline' as a corpus and uses various pieces of software to examine its linguistic properties. For instance, he investigates the keywords of the text and intrinsic parallelisms (for example the pronoun 'her' followed by a body-part noun). The analysis is centred around demonstrating that Stanley Fish's (in)famous criticisms of stylistics as arbitrary and circular are unfounded, since it is possible using a corpus linguistic methodology to identify patterns and foregrounded features in a text in an objective way. In his second article, O'Halloran takes a slightly different approach and, rather than treating the literary text as a corpus, he uses the Bank of English to investigate what constitutes the 'normal' language against which Fleur Adcock's poem 'Street Song' deviates. What makes O'Halloran's work particularly successful is his concern to connect his corpus-assisted approach to the cognitive theory of schemata and the notion of literary reading. Corpus stylistics is sometimes dismissed as a mechanistic approach that disregards the experience of readers, though this is not an accusation that could be levelled at O'Halloran.

Further corpus stylistic work is to be found in *Language, People, Numbers: Corpus Linguistics and Society*, a Festschrift for Michael Stubbs edited by Andrea Gerbig and Oliver Mason. Stubbs, of course, is well known for his work in corpus-assisted discourse analysis and stylistics, and appropriately, corpus stylistics is represented in this volume published to mark his sixtieth birthday. In his chapter, 'The Novel Features of Text: Corpus Analysis and Stylistics' (pp. 293–304), Henry Widdowson follows up Stubbs's own corpus stylistic analysis of Conrad's *Heart of Darkness* (*L&L*[2005] 5–24) by subjecting the novel to his own corpus-based analysis. Unlike O'Halloran, however, Widdowson believes that corpus stylistics is circular in method and hence open to the criticisms of Stanley Fish. This, he argues, is because corpus stylistics proceeds on the basis of interpretations and hunches about a text that are then followed up by, say, examining wordlists or concordances. Widdowson claims that *Heart of Darkness* 'can only be subjectively interpreted' and that because of this 'what counts as evidence for interpretation can never be objectively determined' (p. 303). It would be possible to argue against Widdowson's position by, for instance, considering the notion of literary competence and what counts as a sensible interpretation, but for the stylistician in a hurry, a quick fix solution to this thorny problem is simply to read Widdowson's chapter and follow it up by reading O'Halloran (*L&L* 16[2007] 227–44). Other chapters in Stubbs's Festschrift that include discussion of corpus stylistics and stylistic issues generally are Guy Cook's 'Hocus Pocus or God's Truth: The Dual Identity of Michael Stubbs' (pp. 305–27) and Wolfgang Kühlwein's 'The Semiotic Pattering of Cædmon's Hymn as "Hypersign"' (pp. 99–128).

The year 2007 also saw the publication of *Text, Discourse and Corpora: Theory and Analysis* by Michael Hoey, Michaela Mahlberg, Michael Stubbs and Wolfgang Teubert. Naturally, given its authors, this is a book which contains significant insights into corpus stylistics. Mahlberg's own work on Dickens (*Corpora* 2[2007] 1–31; and in Lambrou and Stockwell, eds., pp. 19–31) is also well worth seeking out, exploring as it does the local textual functions of five-word clusters—in effect, a kind of parallelism. Elsewhere, articles on corpus stylistics can be found in the *International Journal of Corpus Linguistics*, wherein some of the most insightful are Paul Thompson and Alison Sealey's 'Through Children's Eyes? Corpus Evidence of the Features of Children's Literature' (*IJCL* 12[2007] 1–23) and Michael Toolan's 'Trust and Text, Text as Trust' (*IJCL* 12[2007] 269–88). The latter article is from a special issue entitled 'Words, Grammar, Text: Revisiting the Work of John Sinclair', published to mark Sinclair's untimely death. Sinclair, of course, remained interested in stylistics throughout his long career, and most of the articles in the issue are relevant—even if only indirectly—to stylistic analysis. Dan McIntyre's review article published in the following issue (*IJCL* 12[2007] 563–75) considers Sinclair's work in relation to stylistics specifically. Other noteworthy work from 2007 on corpus stylistics includes George L. Dillon's 'The Genres Speak: Using Large Corpora to Profile Generic Registers' (*JLS* 36[2007] 159–88), Rosamund Moon's 'Words, Frequencies, and Texts (Particularly Conrad): A Stratified Approach' (*JLS* 36[2007] 1–34), and Doug Biber's chapter, 'Corpus-Based Analyses of Discourse: Dimensions of Variation in Conversation' (in Bhatia, Flowerdew and Jones, eds., *Advances in Discourse Studies*, pp. 100–14).

I will end this review by mentioning some of the excellent textbooks that were produced in 2007, since these are the books that inspire new generations of scholars to produce the kind of work described elsewhere in this article. The third edition of the successful *Working with Texts: A Core Introduction to Language Analysis*, by Ronald Carter, Angela Goddard, Danutah Reah, Keith Sanger and Nikki Swift, includes significant coverage of stylistic issues, as does *Redesigning English*, edited by Sharon Goodman, David Graddol and Theresa Lillis, part of a series of introductory Open University books. Lesley Jeffries's chapter in this volume is the most obviously stylistic in nature, as may be apparent from its title: 'What Makes Language into Art?' (pp. 5–42). In it, Jeffries discusses such concepts as rhyme and alliteration, simile and metaphor, collocation and iconicity in poetry, and plot, dialogue and vernacular language in prose fiction and drama. Elsewhere in the book are other chapters dealing with familiar issues to the stylistician—for example, Alan Bell on 'Text, Time and Technology in News English' (pp. 79–112) and Collin Gardner on 'English and New Media' (pp. 205–42)—always in a clear and accessible manner. Lastly, Kim Ballard's second edition of

The Frameworks of English provides a clear and thorough introduction to the formal aspects of language study that underpin all stylistic analysis. In short, the plethora of publications from 2007 demonstrate clearly that stylistics is in good health and moving beyond the unfairly narrow preconception that others often have of it as the study of the language of literature. It goes without saying that this review is no more than a snapshot of a fast-developing area. For a discussion of other related work in stylistics from 2007, readers are referred also to Peter Stockwell's review of 'The Year's Work in Stylistics 2007' (*L&L* 17[2008] 351–64).

Books Reviewed

Aarts, Bas, and April McMahon, eds. *The Handbook of English Linguistics*. Blackwell. [2006] pp. xviii + 806. £99.99 ISBN 1 4051 1382 0.

Adger, Carolyn Temple, Walt Wolfram and Donna Christian. *Dialects in Schools, and Communities*, 2nd edn. Erlbaum. [2007] pp. xi + 226. hb £75 ISBN 9 7808 0584 3156, pb £21.99 ISBN 9 7808 0584 3163.

Aloni, Maria, Alastair Butler and Paul Dekker, eds. *Questions in Dynamic Semantics*. Elsevier. [2007] pp. xiv + 344. £73.95 ISBN 9 7800 8045 3477.

Anderson, John M. *The Grammar of Names*. OUP. [2007] pp. xi + 375. £85 ISBN 9 7801 9929 7412.

Ansaldo, Umberto, Stephen Matthews and Lisa Lim, eds. *Deconstructing Creole*. Benjamins. [2007] pp. xi + 290. €115 ($173) ISBN 9 7890 2722 9854.

Armstrong, David F., and Sherman E. Wilcox. *The Gestural Origin of Language*. OUP. [2007] pp. 168. £23.99 ISBN 9 7801 9516 3483.

Aurnague, Michel, Maya Hickmann and Laure Vieu, eds. *The Categorization of Spatial Entities in Language and Cognition*. Benjamins. [2007] pp. viii + 371. €120 ($180) ISBN 9 7890 2722 3746.

Baca, Keith. *Native American Place Names in Mississippi*. UMP. [2007] pp. xx + 143. $50 ISBN 1 5780 6955 6.

Ballard, Kim. *The Frameworks of English*. Palgrave. [2007] pp. xiv + 353. pb £17.99 ISBN 9 7802 3001 3148.

Bamberg, Michael, ed. *Narrative: State of the Art Narrative*. Benjamins. [2007] pp. vi + 270. €95 ($143) ISBN 9 7890 2722 2367.

Bamberg, Michael, Anna De Fina and Deborah Schiffrin, eds. *Selves and Identities in Narrative and Discourse*. Benjamins. [2007] pp. x + 355. €90 ($135) ISBN 9 7890 2722 6495.

Baptista, Marlyse, and Jacqueline Guéron, eds. *Noun Phrases in Creole Languages: A Multi-Faceted Approach*. Benjamins. [2007] pp. ix + 493. €125 ($188) ISBN 9 7890 2725 2531.

Barker, Chris, and Pauline Jacobson, eds. *Direct Compositionality*. OUP. [2007] pp. vii + 439. hb £75 ISBN 9 7801 9920 4373, pb £27.50 ISBN 9 7801 9920 4380.

Bartels, Anke, and Dirk Wiemann, eds. *Global Fragments: (Dis)Orientation in the New World Order*. Rodopi. [2007] pp. xx + 358. €76 ($110) ISBN 9 7890 4202 1822.

Bauer, Laurie. *The Linguistics Student's Handbook*. EdinUP. [2007] pp. ix + 387. hb £45.00, ISBN 978 0 7486 2758 5, pb £14.99, USBN 978 0 7486 2759 2

Baxter, Judith. *Positioning Gender in Discourse: A Feminist Methodology*. Palgrave Macmillan. [2007] pp. 215. pb £16.99 ISBN 9 7802 3055 4320.

Bayley, Robert, and Ceil Lucas, eds. *Sociolinguistic Variation: Theories, Methods, and Applications*. CUP. [2007] pp. xvi + 405. hb £55 ISBN 9 7805 2187 1273, pb £19.99 ISBN 9 7805 2169 1819.

Beard, Adrian. *Language Change*. Routledge. [2004] pp. ix + 114. hb £45 ISBN 9 7804 1532 0559, pb £19.99 ISBN 9 7804 1532 0566.

Bhatia, Vijay K., John Flowerdew and Rodney H. Jones, eds. *Advances in Discourse Studies*. Routledge. [2007] pp. ix + 262. pb £22.99 ISBN 9 7804 1539 8107.

Biber, Douglas, Ulla Connor and Thomas Upton. *Discourse on the Move: Using Corpus Analysis to Describe Discourse Structure*. Benjamins. [2007] pp. xii + 289. €105 ($158) ISBN 9 7890 2722 3029.

Biggam, Carole P., and Christian J. Kay, eds. *Progress in Colour Studies*, (vol 1: *Language, and Culture*. Benjamins. [2006] pp. xii + 223. €95 ISBN 9 7890 2723 2397. Also available as a set with C.P. Biggam and Nicola J. Pitchford, eds. *Progress in Colour Studies*, (vol 2: *Psychological Aspects*. Benjamins. [2006] pp. xiv + 237. €190 ISBN 9 7890 2723 2410.

Boeckx, Cedric. *Linguistic Minimalism: Origins, Concepts, Methods, and Aims*. OUP. [2006] pp. x + 246. hb £60 ISBN 9 7801 9929 7573, pb £18.99 ISBN 9 7801 9929 7580.

Bolton, Kingsley, and Braj B. Kachru, eds. *Asian Englishes*, vols. 1–5. Routledge. [2007] pp. xxxiii + 396, v + 300, vii + 410, v + 449, vii + 515. £725 ($1, 450) ISBN 9 7804 1537 4866 (set).

Borg, Emma. *Minimal Semantics*. OUP. [2006] pp. x + 288. £22 ISBN 9 7801 9920 6926.

Boškovic, Željko, and Howard Lasnik, eds. *Minimalist Syntax: The Essential Readings*. Blackwell. [2007] pp. xiv + 449. hb £60 ISBN 0 6312 3303 2, pb £26.99 ISBN 0 6312 3304 0.

Brewer, Charlotte. *Treasure-House of the Language: The Living OED*. YaleUP. [2007] pp. xiv + 334. £25 ISBN 9 7803 0012 4293.

Breznitz, Zvia, ed. *Brain Research in Language*. Springer. [2007] pp. 282. €106.95 ISBN 9 7803 8774 9792.

Brinton, Laurel J., and Leslie K. Arnovick, *The English Language: A Linguistic History*. OUP. [2006] pb £45.99 ISBN 9 7801 9542 2054.

Britain, David, ed. *Language in the British Isles*. CUP. [2007] pp. xii + 508. hb £53 ($101) ISBN 9 7805 2179 1502, pb £19.99 ($37.99) ISBN 9 7805 2179 4886.

Bublitz, Wolfram, and Axel Hübler, eds. *Metapragmatics in Use*. Benjamins. [2007] pp. vii + 301. €105 ($158) ISBN 9 7890 2725 4092.

Bührig, Kristin, and Jan D. ten Thije, eds. *Beyond Misunderstanding*. Benjamins. [2007] pp. vi + 339. €115 ($173) ISBN 9 7890 2725 3873.

Bunt, Harry, and Reinhard Muskens, eds. *Computing Meaning* (vol 3. Springer [2007] pp. vi + 477. €149.75 ISBN 9 7814 0205 9568.

Butler, Christopher, Raquel Hidalgo Downing and Julia Lavid, eds. *Functional Perspectives on Grammar and Discourse: In Honour of Angela Downing.* Benjamins. [2007] pp. xxx + 481. €125 ($188) ISBN 9 7890 2723 0959.

Cameron, Deborah. *The Teacher's Guide to Grammar.* OUP. [2007] pp. 176. pb £10.99 ISBN 9 7801 9921 4488.

Cappelen, Herman, and Ernie Lepore. *Language Turned on Itself: The Semantics and Pragmatics of Metalinguistic Discourse.* OUP. [2007] pp. x + 169. £19.99 ISBN 9 7801 9923 1195.

Carter, Ronald, Angela Goddard, Danutah Reah, Keith Sanger and Nikki Swift. *Working with Texts: A Core Introduction to Language Analysis.* Routledge. [2007] pp. xxii + 264. pb £16.99 ISBN 9 7804 1541 4241.

Chafe, Wallace. *The Importance of Not Being Earnest.* Benjamins. [2007] pp. xii + 167. €99 ($149) ISBN 9 7890 2724 1528.

Chandler, Daniel. *Semiotics: The Basics,* 2nd edn. Routledge. [2007] pp. xviii + 307. pb $17.95 ISBN 9 7804 1536 3754.

Conboy, Martin. *The Language of the News.* Routledge. [2007] pp. x + 229. pb £18.99 ISBN 9 7804 1537 2022.

Considine, John, and Giovanni Iamartino, eds. *Words and Dictionaries from the British Isles in Historical Perspective.* Cambridge Scholars Publishing. [2007] pp. xviii + 225. £34.99 ISBN 9 7818 4718 1688.

Coulthard, Malcolm, and Alison Johnson. *An Introduction to Forensic Linguistics: Language in Evidence.* Routledge. [2007] pp. xi + 237. pb £20.99 ISBN 9 7804 1532 0238.

Coupland, Nikolas. *Style: Language Variation, and Identity.* CUP. [2007] pp. xiv + 209. pb £17.99 ($34.99) ISBN 9 7805 2161 8144.

Culicover, Peter W., and Ray Jackendoff. *Simpler Syntax.* OUP. [2005] pp. xvii + 589. hb £84 ISBN 9 7801 9927 1085, pb £24.99 ISBN 9 7801 9927 1092.

Dehé, Nicole, and Yordanka Kavalova, eds. *Parentheticals.* Benjamins. [2007] pp. xi + 314. €115 ($173) ISBN 9 7890 2723 3707.

Denning, Keith, Brett Kessler and William R. Leben. *English Vocabulary Elements,* 2nd edn. OUP. [2007] pp. 336. pb £10.99 ISBN 9 7801 9516 8037.

Dent, Susie. *The Language Report: English on the Move 2000 + 2007.* OUP. [2007] pp. x + 166. £10.99 ISBN 9 7801 9923 3885.

Dessalles, Jean-Louis. *Why We Talk: The Evolutionary Origins of Language.* OUP. [2007] pp. xi + 395. £37 ISBN 9 7801 9927 6233.

Dimbleby, Richard, and Graeme Burton. *More Than Words: An Introduction to Communication.* Routledge. [2007] pp. xv + 283. pb $32.95 ISBN 9 7804 1530 3835.

Eguren, Luis, and Olga Fernández Soriano, eds. *Coreference, Modality, and Focus.* Benjamins. [2007] pp. xii + 239. €110 ($165) ISBN 9 7890 2723 3752.

Ehland, Christoph, ed. *Thinking Northern: Textures of Identity in the North of England.* Rodopi. [2007] pp. 448. €90 ISBN 9 7890 4202 2812.

Enfield, N.J., and Tanya Stivers, eds. *Person Reference in Interactions: Linguistics, Cultural, and Social Perspectives.* CUP. [2007] pp. x + 358. £55 ($105) ISBN 9 7805 2187 2454.

Englebretson, Robert. *Stancetaking in Discourse.* Benjamins. [2007] pp. vii + 323. €105 ($158) ISBN 9 7890 2725 4085.

Ensslin, Astrid. *Canonizing Hypertext: Explorations and Constructions.* Continuum. [2007] pp. vii + 197. £65 ISBN 9 7808 2649 5587.

Evans, Vyvyan. *A Glossary of Cognitive Linguistics.* EdinUP. [2007] pp. 256. pb £11.99 ISBN 9 7807 4862 2801.

Facchinetti, Roberta, ed. *Corpus Linguistics 25 Years On.* Rodopi. [2007] pp. 392. €80 ISBN 9 7890 4202 1952.

Fanselow, Gisbert, Caroline Féry, Ralf Vogel and Matthias Schlesewsky, eds. *Gradience in Grammar: Generative Perspectives.* OUP. [2006] pp. x + 405. £80 ISBN 9 7801 9927 4796.

Fetzer, Anita, ed. *Context and Appropriateness.* Benjamins. [2007] pp. vi + 265. €105 ($158) ISBN 9 7890 2725 4061.

Fetzer, Anita, and Gerda Lauerbac. *Political Discourse in the Media: Cross-Cultural Perspectives.* Benjamins. [2007] pp. vii + 379. €110 ($165) ISBN 9 7890 2725 4030.

Fiengo, Robert. *Asking Questions: Using Meaningful Structures to Imply Ignorance.* OUP. [2007] pp. xiii + 179. £34 ISBN 9 7801 9920 8418.

Fine, Kit. *Semantic Relationism.* Blackwell. [2007] pp. viii + 146. £45 ISBN 9 7814 0510 8430.

Fischer, Olga. *Morphosyntactic Change: Functional and Formal Perspectives.* OUP. [2007] pp. xviii + 378. hb £60 ISBN 9 7801 9926 7040, pb £21.99 ISBN 9 7801 9926 7057.

Fitzpatrick, Eileen, ed. *Corpus Linguistics Beyond the Word: Corpus Research from Phrase to Discourse.* Rodopi. [2007] pp. vi + 277. €58 ISBN 9 7890 4202 1358.

Freeborn, Dennis. *From Old English to Standard English: A Course Book in Language Variation across Time,* 3rd edn. Palgrave. [2006] pp. xxiii + 446. pb £20.99 ISBN 1 4039 9880 9.

Games, Alex. *Balderdash, and Piffle. BBC Books.* [2007] pp. 240. £12.99 ISBN 9 7818 4607 2352.

Gaskell, Gareth, ed. *The Oxford Handbook of Psycholinguistics.* OUP. [2007] pp. xiii + 600. £52 ISBN 9 7801 9956 1797.

Gavins, Joanna. *Text World Theory: An Introduction.* EdinUP. [2007] pp. x + 193. pb £19.99 ISBN 9 7807 4862 3006.

Geeraerts, Dirk, and Hubert Cuyckens, eds. *The Oxford Handbook of Cognitive Linguistics.* OUP. [2007] pp. 1,364. £85 ISBN 9 7801 9514 3782.

Georgakopoulou, Alexandra. *Small Stories, Interaction and Identities.* Benjamins. [2007] pp. ix + 185. €99 ($149) ISBN 9 7890 2722 6488.

Gerbig, Andrea, and Oliver Mason, eds. *Language, People, Numbers: Corpus Linguistics and Society.* Rodopi. [2007] pp. 327. €65 ISBN 9 7890 4202 3505.

Gibbs, Raymond, and Herbert Colston, eds. *Irony in Language and Thought: A Cognitive Science Reader.* Erlbaum. [2007] pp. x + 607. pb $34.95 ISBN 9 7808 0586 0627.

Goatley, Andrew. *Washing the Brain: Metaphor and Hidden Ideology.* Benjamins. [2007] pp. xvi + 431. pb €36 ISBN 9 7890 2722 7201.

Gonzalez-Marquez, Monica, Irene Mittelberg, Seana Coulson and Michael J. Spivey, eds. *Methods in Cognitive Linguistics*. Benjamins. [2007] pp. xxviii + 452. €130 ISBN 9 7890 2722 3715.

Goodman, Sharon, David Graddol and Theresa Lillis, eds. *Redesigning English*. Routledge. [2007] pp. iii + 302. pb £20.99 ISBN 9 7804 1537 6891.

Gorji, Mina, ed. *Rude Britannia*. Routledge. [2007] pp. xii + 147. pb £16.99 ISBN 9 7804 1538 2779.

Gregoriou, Christiana. *Deviance in Contemporary Crime Fiction*. Palgrave. [2007] pp. x + 178. pb £18.99 ISBN 9 7802 3000 3392.

Greimann, Dirk, and Geo Siegwart, eds. *Truth and Speech Acts*. Routledge. [2007] pp. ix + 389. £65 ISBN 9 7804 1540 6512.

Grein, Marion, and Edda Weigand, eds. *Dialogue and Culture*. Benjamins. [2007] pp. xi + 262. €105 ($158) ISBN 9 7890 2721 0180.

Griffiths, Patrick. *An Introduction to English Semantics and Pragmatics*. EdinUP. [2006] pp. xii + 193. hb £54 ISBN 9 7807 4861 6312, pb £15.99 ISBN 9 7807 4861 6329.

Grygiel, Marcin, and Grzegorz A. Kleparski. *Main Trends in Historical Semantics*. Wydawnictwo Uniwesytetu Rzeszowskiego. [2007] pp. 143. pb 15 zloty ISBN 9 7883 7338 3128.

Haegeman, Liliane. *Thinking Syntactically: A Guide to Argumentation and Analysis*. Blackwell. [2006] pp. xii + 386. pb £17.99 ISBN 1 4051 1853 9.

Halliday, Michael A.K., and Colin Yallop. *Lexicology: A Short Introduction* Continuum. [2007; 1st edn. 2004] pp. vi + 117. £12.99 ISBN 9 7808 2649 4795.

Harley, Heidi. *English Words: A Linguistic Introduction*. Blackwell. [2006] pp. xvii + 296. hb £55 ISBN 0 6312 3031 9, pb £17.99 ISBN 0 6312 3032 7.

Hartmann, Reinhard Rudolf Karl. *Interlingual Lexicography: Selected Essays on Translation Equivalence, Contrastive Linguistics and the Bilingual Dictionary*. Niemeyer. [2007] pp. xii + 246. pb €96 ISBN 9 7834 8439 1338.

Haumann, Dagmar. *Adverb Licensing and Clause Structure in English*. Benjamins. [2007] pp. ix + 438. pb €125 ISBN 9 7890 2723 3691.

Hedberg, Nancy, and Ron Zacharski, eds. *The Grammar–Pragmatics Interface: Essays in Honor of Jeanette K. Gundel*. Benjamins. [2007] pp. viii + 343. €110 ($165) ISBN 9 7890 2725 3989.

Heine, Bernd, and Tania Kuteva. *The Genesis of Grammar: A Reconstruction*. OUP. [2007] pp. 352. £80 ISBN 9 7801 9922 7761.

Hepburn, Alexa, and Sally Wiggins, eds. *Discursive Research in Practice: New Approaches to Psychology and Interaction*. CUP. [2007] pp. x + 322. pb $39.99 ISBN 9 7805 2161 4092.

Hickey, Raymond. *Irish English: History and Present-Day Forms*. CUP. [2007] pp. xx + 524. £60 ISBN 9 7805 2185 2999.

Hidalgo, Encarnación, Luis Quereda and Juan Santana, eds. *Corpora in the Foreign Language Classroom: Selected Papers from the Sixth International Conference on Teaching and Language Corpora (TaLC 6), University of Granada, Spain, 4–7 July, 2004*. Rodopi. [2007] pp. xiv + 362. €76 ($103) ISBN 9 0420 2142 X.

Hinzen, Wolfram. *An Essay on Names and Truth*. OUP. [2007] pp. vii + 244. hb £60 ISBN 9 7801 9927 4420, pb £20.99 ISBN 9 7801 9922 6528.

Hodson, Jane. *Language and Revolution in Burke, Wollstonecraft, Paine and Godwin*. Ashgate. [2007] pp. x + 226. £50 ISBN 9 7807 5465 4032.

Hoey, Michael, Michaela Mahlberg, Michael Stubbs and Wolfgang Teubert. *Text, Discourse and Corpora: Theory and Analysis*. Continuum. [2007] pp. 264. pb £27.99 ISBN 9 7808 2649 1725.

Hogg, Richard M., and David Denison, eds. *A History of the English Language*. CUP. [2006] pp. xiii + 495. hb £80 ISBN 9 7805 2166 2277, pb £23.99 ISBN 9 7805 2171 7991.

Holm, John, and Peter L. Patrick, eds. *Comparative Creole Syntax: Parallel Outlines of 18 Creole Grammars*. Battlebridge. [2007] pp. xii + 404. £24.99 ($45.95) ISBN 9 7819 0329 2013.

Holt, Elizabeth, and Rebecca Clift, eds. *Reporting Talk: Reported Speech in Interaction*. CUP. [2007] pp. xvii + 287. £60 ($110) ISBN 9 7805 2182 4835.

Hoover, David, and Sharon Lattig, eds. *Stylistics: Prospect and Retrospect*. Rodopi. [2007] pp. xxi + 212. pb €47 ISBN 9 7890 4202 3307.

Hough, Carole, and John Corbett. *Beginning Old English*. Palgrave. [2007] pp. xii + 251. hb £45 ISBN 1 4039 9349 1, pb £15.99 ISBN 1 4039 9350 5.

Howard, Martin. *Language Issues in Canada: Multidisciplinary Perspectives*. Cambridge Scholars. [2007] pp. vi + 217. £34.99 ISBN 9 7818 4718 2036.

Hübler, Axel. *The Nonverbal Shift in Early Modern Conversation*. Benjamins. [2007] pp. ix + 278. €115 ($173) ISBN 9 7890 2725 3972.

Hudson, Richard. *Language Networks: The New Word Grammar*. OUP. [2007] pp. xii + 275. hb £70 ISBN 9 7801 9926 7309, pb £21.99 ISBN 9 7801 9929 8389.

Humphrys, John. *Beyond Words: How Language Reveals the Way We Live Now*. H&S. [2007; 1st edn. 2006] pp. 240. pb £7.99 ISBN 9 7803 4092 3764.

Hundt, Marianne. *English Mediopassive Constructions: A Cognitive, Corpus-Based Study of their Origin, Spread, and Current Status*. Rodopi. [2007] pp. xv + 222. €50 ($68) ISBN 9 0420 2127 6.

Hundt, Marianne, Nadja Nesselhauf and Carolin Biewer, eds. *Corpus Linguistics and the Web*. Rodopi. [2007] pp. vi + 305. €65 ($94) ISBN 9 0420 2128 4.

Hurford, James R., Brendan Heasley and Michael B. Smith. *Semantics: A Coursebook*. CUP. [2007] pp. xiii + 350. pb £17.99 ($32.99) ISBN 9 7805 2167 1873.

Hutchby, Ian. *The Discourse of Child Counselling*. Benjamins. [2007] pp. xii + 144. €95 ($143) ISBN 9 7890 2721 8599.

Ingram, John C.L. *Neurolinguistics: An Introduction to Spoken Language Processing and its Disorders*. CUP. [2007] pp. xxi + 442. pb £25.99 ISBN 9 7805 2179 6408.

Jeffries, Lesley. *Textual Construction of the Female Body: A Critical Discourse Approach*. Palgrave. [2007] pp. xiii + 212. £48 ISBN 9 7803 3391 4519.

Jeffries, Lesley, Dan McIntyre and Derek Bousfield, eds. *Stylistics and Social Cognition*. Rodopi. [2007] pp. xvii + 277. pb €60 ISBN 9 7890 4202 3123.

Johnson, Mark. *The Meaning of the Body: Aesthetics of Human Understanding*. UChicP. [2007] pp. xvii + 308. pb £13 ISBN 9 7802 2640 1935.

Kaplan, Robert B., and Richard B. Baldauf Jr, eds. *Language Planning and Policy in Africa*, vol 2: *Algeria, Côte d'Ivoire, Nigeria and Tunisia*. MIM. [2007] pp. v + 307. £39.95 ($79.95) ISBN 9 7818 4769 0111.

Katamba, Francis, and John Stonham. *Morphology*, 2nd edn. Palgrave Macmillan. [2007] pp. xvii + 382. hb £55 ISBN 1 4039 1643 8, pb £19.99 ISBN 1 4039 1644 6.

Kaunisto, Mark. *Variation and Change in the Lexicon: A Corpus-Based Analysis of Adjectives in English Ending in -ic and -ical*. Rodopi. [2007] pp. x + 364. €75 ISBN 9 7890 4202 2331.

Kayne, Richard S. *Movement and Silence Oxford Studies in Comparative Syntax*. OUP. [2005] pp. xv + 376. pb £23.99 ISBN 9 7801 9517 9170.

Kouega, Jean-Paul. *A Dictionary of Cameroon English Usage*. Lang. [2007] pp. 202. €48.70 ($75.95) ISBN 9 7830 3911 0278.

Kövecses, Zoltán. *Metaphor in Culture: Universality and Variation* 2nd edn. CUP. [2007; 1st edn. 2005] pp. xv + 314. pb £17.99 ISBN 9 7805 2169 6128.

Kraft, Bettina, and Ronald Geluykens, eds. *Cross-Cultural Pragmatics and Interlanguage English*. LINCOM. [2007] pp. 260. pb €73.20 ($107.60) ISBN 9 7838 9586 7767.

Lambrou, Marina, and Peter Stockwell. *Contemporary Stylistics*. Continuum. [2007] pp. xiv + 287. £85 ISBN 9 7808 2649 3859.

Leech, Geoffrey, and Mick Short. *Style in Fiction: A Linguistic Introduction to English Fictional Prose*, 2nd edn. Pearson Education. [2007] pp. xv + 404. pb £19.99 ISBN 9 7805 8278 4093.

Leitner, Gerhard, and Ian G. Malcolm, eds. *The Habitat of Australia's Aboriginal Languages: Past, Present and Future*. MGruyter. [2007] pp. xii + 385. €98 ($137) ISBN 9 7831 1019 0793.

Lenker, Ursula, and Anneli Meurman-Solin, eds. *Connectives in the History of English*. Benjamins. [2007] pp. viii + 318. €115 ISBN 9 7890 2724 7988.

Llamas, Carmen, Louise Mullany and Peter Stockwell, eds. *The Routledge Companion to Sociolinguistics*. Routledge. [2007] pp. xix + 271. hb £55 ($110) ISBN 9 7804 1533 8493, pb £14.99 ($26.95) ISBN 9 7804 1533 8509.

Machin, David, and Theo van Leeuwen. *Global Media Discourse: A Critical Introduction*. Routledge. [2007] pp. viii + 188. pb £18.99 ISBN 9 7804 1535 9467.

Mandala, Susan. *Twentieth-Century Drama Dialogue as Ordinary Talk: Speaking Between the Lines*. Ashgate. [2007] pp. xiii + 138. pb £45 ISBN 9 7807 5465 1055.

Matthews, Peter H. *The Concise Oxford Dictionary of Linguistics*, 2nd edn. OUP. [2007] pp. 464. pb. £10.99 ISBN 9 7801 9920 2720.

McColl Millar, Robert. *Northern and Insular Scots*. EdinUP. [2007] pp. vii + 178. hb £50 ISBN 9 7807 4862 3467, pb £16.99 ISBN 9 7807 4862 3174.

Meyer, Antje, Linda Wheeldon and Andrea Krott, eds. *Automaticity and Control in Language Processing*. Psychology Press. [2007] pp. xiii + 304. £49.95 ISBN 9 7818 4169 6508.

Miller, Alexander. *Philosophy of Language*, 2nd edn. Routledge. [2007] pp. xviii + 416. pb $31.95 ISBN 9 7804 1534 9819.

Miller, D. Gary. *Latin Suffixal Derivatives in English and their Indo-European Ancestry*. OUP. [2006] pp. xxxvi + 386. £55 ISBN 9 7801 9928 5051.

Miyoshi, Kusujiro. *Johnson's and Webster's Verbal Examples: With Special Reference to Exemplifying Usage in Dictionary Entries*. Niemeyer. [2007] pp. xiv + 222. pb €84.95 ISBN 9 7834 8439 1321.

Montgomery, Martin. *The Discourse of Broadcast News: A Linguistic Approach*. Routledge. [2007] pp. xvii + 246. pb £24.99 ISBN 9 7804 1535 8729.

Morrish, Liz, and Helen Sauntson. *New Perspectives on Language and Sexual Identity*. Palgrave Macmillan. [2007] pp. xi + 223. £45 ISBN 9 7814 0393 7964.

Mukherji, Nirmalangshu, Bibudhendra Narayan Patnaik and Rama Kant Agnihotri, eds. *Noam Chomsky: The Architecture of Language*. OUP. [2000] pp. 106. pb £4.99 ISBN 9 7801 9568 4469.

Mullany, Louise. *Gendered Discourse in the Professional Workplace*. Palgrave. [2007] pp. xii + 236. £53 ISBN 9 7814 0398 6207.

Mund, Jeremy. *Style and Ideology in Translation: Latin American Writing in English*. Routledge. [2007] pp. xvii + 261. £70 ISBN 9 7804 1536 1040.

Nikolaeva, Irina, ed. *Finiteness: Theoretical and Empirical Foundations*. OUP. [2007] pp. xiv + 537. pb £27.50 ISBN 9 7801 9921 3740.

Penke, Martina, and Annette Rosenbach, eds. *What Counts as Evidence in Linguistics: The Case of Innateness*. Benjamins. [2007] pp. ix + 297. €95 ISBN 9 7890 2722 2374.

Pennycook, Alastair. *Global Englishes and Transcultural Flows*. Routledge. [2007] pp. viii + 189. hb £70 ($125) ISBN 9 7804 1537 4804, pb £19.99 ($35.95) ISBN 9 7804 1537 4972.

Pérez-Guerra, Javier, Dolores González-Álvarez, Jorge L Bueno-Alonso and Esperanza Rama-Martínez, eds. *'Of Varying Language and Opposing Creed': New Insights into Late Modern English*. Lang. [2007] pp. 455. pb €66.80 (£50.10, $103.95) ISBN 9 7830 3910 7889.

Peters, Pam. *The Cambridge Guide to English Usage*. CUP. [2004] pp. 620. £28 ISBN 9 7805 2162 1816.

Picken, Jonathan. *Literature, Metaphor and the Language Learner*. Palgrave. [2007] pp. xiii + 174. £48 ISBN 9 7802 3050 6954.

Pietarinen, Ahti-Veikko, ed. *Game Theory and Linguistic Meaning*. Elsevier. [2007] pp. xi + 246. £74.95 ISBN 9 7800 8044 7155.

Pinker, Steven. *The Stuff of Thought: Language as a Window into Human Nature*. Penguin. [2007] pp. 512. pb £9.99 ISBN 9 7801 4101 5477.

Plag, Ingo, Maria Braun, Sabine Lappe and Mareile Schramm. *Introduction to English Linguistics*. MGruyter. [2007] pp. 246. pb €19.95 ISBN 9 7831 1018 9698.

Pöchhacker, Franz, and Miriam Shlesinger, eds. *Healthcare Interpreting*. Benjamins. [2007] pp. vii + 155. €80 ($120) ISBN 9 7890 2722 2398.

Radden, Günter, and René Dirven. *Cognitive English Grammar*. Benjamins. [2007] pp. xiii + 374. hb €110 ISBN 9 7890 2721 9039, pb €33 ISBN 9 7890 2721 9046.

Radden, Günther, Klaus-Michael Köpcke, Thomas Berg and Peter Siemund, eds. *Aspects of Meaning Construction.* Benjamins. [2007] pp. x + 287. €110 ($132) ISBN 9 7890 2723 2427.

Ramchand, Gillian, and Charles Reiss, eds. *The Oxford Handbook of Linguistic Interfaces.* OUP. [2007] pp. xv + 640. £95 ISBN 9 7801 9924 7455.

Randall, Mick. *Memory, Psychology and Second Language Learning.* Benjamins. [2007] pp. x + 220. hb €105 ISBN 9 7890 2721 9770, pb €36 ISBN 9 7890 2721 9787.

Rasinger, Sebastian M. *Bengali-English in East London: A Study in Urban Multilingualism.* Lang. [2007] pp. 270. €47.60 ($73.95) ISBN 9 7830 3911 0360.

Rehbein, Jochen, Christiane Hohenstein and Lukas Pietsch, eds. *Connectivity in Grammar and Discourse.* Benjamins. [2007] pp. viii + 465. €80 ($120) ISBN 9 7890 2721 9251.

Reich, Peter, William J. Sullivan, Arle R. Lommel, and Toby Griffen, eds. *LACUS Forum 33: Variation.* Houston. LACUS. [2007] .

Ritchie, L. David. *Context and Connection in Metaphor.* Palgrave Macmillan. [2006] pp. xiv + 248. £50 ISBN 9 7814 0399 7661.

Roberts, Ian. *Diachronic Syntax.* OUP. [2007] pp. xiv + 508. hb £75 ISBN 9 7801 9928 3668, pb £26.99 ISBN 9 7801 9925 3982.

Sauerland, Uli, and Penka Stateva. *Presupposition and Implicature in Compositional Semantics.* Palgrave Macmillan. [2007] pp. ix + 285. £55 ISBN 9 7802 3000 5334.

Saul, Jennifer. *Simple Sentences, Substitution, and Intuitions.* OUP. [2007] pp. xiv + 176. £32 ISBN 9 7801 9921 9155.

Saussure, Louis de, Jacques Moeschler and Genoveva Puskás, eds. *Recent Advances in the Syntax and Semantics of Tense, Aspect and Modality.* MGruyter. [2007] pp. 253. €98 ISBN 9 7831 1019 5255.

Schegloff, Emmanuel. *Sequence Organization in Interaction: A Primer in Conversation Analysis,* vol. 1. CUP. [2007] pp. xvi + 300. pb $38.99 ISBN 9 7805 2153 2792.

Schmitter, Peter, ed. *Sprachtheorien der Neuzeit III/2: Sprachbeschreibung und Sprachunterrricht,* vol. 2. Narr. [2007] pp. 434. € 84 ISBN 3 8233 5010 2.

Schneider, Edgar W. *Postcolonial English: Varieties around the World.* CUP. [2007] pp. xvi + 367. hb £60 ($115) ISBN 9 7805 2183 1406, pb £21.99 ($39.99) ISBN 9 7805 2153 9012.

Schwarz-Friesel, Monika, Manfred Consten and Mareile Knees, eds. *Anaphors in Text: Cognitive, Formal and Applied Approaches to Anaphoric Reference.* Benjamins. [2007] pp. xv + 282. €110 ($165) ISBN 9 7890 2723 0966.

Sharifan, Farzad, and Gary B. Palmer, eds. *Applied Cultural Linguistics: Implications for Second Language Learning and Intercultural Communication.* Benjamins. [2007] pp. vii + 175. €95 ($143) ISBN 9 7890 2723 8948.

Sica, Giandomenico, ed. *Open Problems in Linguistics and Lexicography.* Polimetrica. [2006] pp. 372. pb €30 ISBN 9 7888 7699 0519. Also available free as an Open Access Publication: ISBN 9 7888 7699 0564.

Skandera, Paul, ed. *Phraseology and Culture in English.* MGruyter. [2007] pp. vi + 505. €98 ($137) ISBN 9 7831 1019 0878.

Smit, Ute, Stefan Dollinger, Julia Hüttner, Ursula Lutzky and Gunther Kaltenböck, eds. *Tracing English through Time: Explorations in Language Variation*. Braumüller. [2007] pp. xviii + 416. pb. €32.90 ISBN 9 7837 0031 6138.

Snyder, William. *Child Language: The Parametric Approach*. OUP. [2007] pp. 224. pb £19.99 ISBN 9 7801 9929 6705.

Späth, Andreas, ed. *Interfaces and Interface Conditions*. MGruyter. [2007] pp. xv + 377. €98 ISBN 9 7831 1019 5477.

Stanley, Jason. *Language in Context: Selected Essays*. OUP. [2007] pp. viii + 264. hb £58 ISBN 9 7801 9922 5927, pb £19.99 ISBN 9 7801 9922 5934.

Steen, Gerard. *Finding Metaphor in Grammar and Usage*. Benjamins. [2007] pp. xii + 430. €110 ISBN 9 7890 2723 8979.

Swan, Michael. *Practical English Usage*, 3rd edn. OUP. [2005] pp. xxx + 658. £29.85 ISBN 9 7801 9442 0990.

Taiwo, Rotimi, Akin Odebunmi and Akin Adetunji, eds. *Perspectives on Media Discourse*. LINCOM. [2007] pp. xv + 325. €69.20 ($96.88) ISBN 9 7838 9586 4759.

Tenbrink, Thora. *Space, Time and the Use of Language: An Investigation of Relationships*. MGruyter. [2007] pp. viii + 345. €88 ISBN 9 7831 1019 5200.

Teubert, Wolfgang, ed. *Text Corpora and Multilingual Lexicography*. Benjamins. [2007] pp. ix + 159. €80, $120 ISBN 9 7890 2722 2381.

Trask, R.L. *Language and Linguistics: The Key Concepts*, 2nd edn., ed. Peter Stockwell. Routledge. [2007] pp. xxi + 367. pb $26.95 ISBN 0 4154 1359 1.

Tsui, Amy B.M., and James W. Tollefson, eds. *Language Policy, Culture, and Identity in Asian Contexts*. Erlbaum. [2007] pp. ix + 283. hb £75 ($115) ISBN 9 7808 0585 6934, pb £22.99 ($36.50) ISBN 9 7808 0585 6941.

Turell, M. Teresa, Maria Spassova, and Jordi Cicres, eds. *Second European IAFL Conference on Forensic Linguistic / Language, and the Law*. Barcelona: Universitat Pompeu Fabra Institut Universitari de Lingüística Aplicada. [2007] pp. 358. ISBN 8 4967 4228 8.

Van Langendonck, Willy. *Theory and Typology of Proper Names*. MGruyter. [2007] pp. xvi + 378. €137 ISBN 9 7831 1019 0861.

Van Peer, Willie, Jèmeljan Hakemulder and Sonia Zyngier. *Muses and Measures: Empirical Research Methods for the Humanities*. Cambridge Scholars Press. [2007] pp. xx + 366. hb price £39.99 ISBN 9 7818 4718 1701.

Vega Moreno, Rosa. *Creativity, and Convention: The Pragmatics of Everyday Figurative Speech*. Benjamins. [2007] pp. xi + 249. €105 ($158) ISBN 9 7890 2725 3996.

Watts, Victor. *The Place-Names of County Durham*. EPNS. [2007] pp. xxv + 284. $29.99 ISBN 9 7809 0488 9734.

Wilson, Andrew, Dawn Archer and Paul Rayson, eds. *Corpus Linguistics around the World*. Rodopi. [2006] pp. viii + 233. €55 ($69) ISBN 9 7890 4201 8365.

Wurff, Wim van der, ed. *Imperative Clauses in Generative Grammar*. Benjamins. [2007] pp. viii + 352. €120 ISBN 9 7890 2723 3677.

Yong, Heming, and Jing Peng. *Bilingual Lexicography from a Communicative Perspective*. Benjamins. [2007] pp. x + 229. €99 ISBN 9 7890 2722 3333.

Zuo, Yan. *The Golden Silence: A Pragmatic Study on Silence in Dyadic English Conversation*. LINCOM. [2007] pp. v + 187. pb ISBN 3 8958 6676 8.

II

Early Medieval

STACY S. KLEIN AND MARY SWAN

This chapter has ten sections: 1. Bibliography; 2. Manuscript Studies, Palaeography and Facsimiles; 3. Social, Cultural and Intellectual Background; 4. Literature: General; 5. The Exeter Book; 6. The Poems of the Vercelli Book; 7. The Junius Manuscript; 8. The *Beowulf* Manuscript; 9. Other Poems; 10. Prose. Sections 1, 2 and 3 are by Mary Swan; sections 4, 8 and 9 are by Stacy Klein with contributions by Mary Swan; sections 5, 6 and 7 are by Stacy Klein; section 10 is by Mary Swan with contributions by Stacy Klein.

1. Bibliography

Old English Newsletter 40:i (Fall 2006) was published in 2007. It includes notes on forthcoming conferences and workshops, news of publications, reports and essays. The reports are 'Fontes Anglo-Saxonici: Twenty-First Progress Report', by Peter Jackson (*OENews* 40:i[2007] 20), 'Dictionary of Old English: 2006 Progress Report', by Joan Holland (*OENews* 40:i[2007] 21–5) and '2006 Summer Seminar on Medieval Manuscript Studies at the University of New Mexico', by Timothy C. Graham (*OENews* 40:i[2007] 26–7). Essays in this volume are 'Typing in Old English since 1967: A Brief History', by Peter S. Baker (*OENews* 40:i[2007] 28–37), 'Old English Studies in Spain: Past, Present and...Future?', by Juan Camilo Conde-Silvestre and Mercedes Salvador (*OENews* 40:i[2007] 38–58) and 'Circolwyrde 2006: New Electronic Resources for Anglo-Saxon Studies', by Edward Christie (*OENews* 40:i[2007] 59–62).

Volume 40:ii (Winter 2007) contains the Year's Work in Old English Studies 2005. Volume 40:iii (Spring 2007) includes news of conferences and publications and calls for conference papers. Patrick Styles offers 'Joan Turville-Petre: A Bibliographical Appreciation' (*OENews* 40:iii[2007] 24–6). The eighth annual report on the Anglo-Saxon Plant Name Survey is provided by C.P. Biggam (*OENews* 40:iii[2007] 27), and three essays are included: 'Old English Studies in France', by André Crépin, with Leo Carruthers (*OENews* 40:iii[2007] 28–30); Mary Clayton's extremely useful 'Letter to Brother Edward: A Student Edition' (*OENews* 40:iii[2007] 31–46); and 'Old English

Year's Work in English Studies, Volume 88 (2009) © *The English Association; all rights reserved*
doi:10.1093/ywes/map017

Textbooks in the 21st Century: A Review of Recent Publications', by Andrew
Scheil (*OENews* 40:iii[2007] 47–59). This volume of *OEN* also contains
Abstracts of Papers in Anglo-Saxon Studies. Volume 40:iv (Summer 2006)
contains the Old English Bibliography for 2006 and the Research in
Progress listings.
ASE 36 (2007) 235–330 includes the bibliography for 2006.

2. Manuscript Studies, Palaeography and Facsimiles

Manuscript studies has a prominent place in number of collections of
essays published this year. *Space, Text and Margin in Medieval Manuscripts*,
edited by Sarah Larratt Keefer and Rolf H. Bremmer Jr, contains several new
studies of Anglo-Saxon manuscripts. William Schipper's 'Textual Varieties in
Manuscript Margins' (pp. 25–54) includes discussion of British Library, Royal
4. A. xiv, fos. 107–8^v and Cambridge, Corpus Christi College 41. Catherine E.
Karkov's 'Margins and Marginalization: Representations of Eve in Oxford,
Bodleian Library, Junius 11' (pp. 57–84) reads across text and images to argue
that Eve is brought in from the margins so that 'her actions and her body' can
be understood 'as the assurance that paradise lost is Anglo-Saxon history
found' (p. 71). Sarah Larratt Keefer writes on 'Use of Manuscript Space for
Design, Text and Image in Liturgical Books Owned by the Community of
St Cuthbert' (pp. 85–115), with reference to Durham, Cathedral Library A. II.
17, B. III. 32, and A. IV. 19, and charts Anglo-Saxon re-use of older liturgical
material. Phillip Pulsiano's 'Jaunts, Jottings and Jetsam in Anglo-Saxon
Manuscripts' (pp. 119–33), originally published in *Florilegium* 19 [2002], but
not reviewed in *YWES*, is reprinted here in re-edited form. Its main examples
are drawn from a variety of Anglo-Saxon manuscripts, including glossaries,
the Paris Psalter and the Sherborne Pontifical. Karen Louise Jolly writes
'On the Margins of Orthodoxy: Devotional Formulas and Protective Prayers
in Cambridge, Corpus Christi College MS 41' (pp. 135–83), and provides
a case-study in approaches to this complex manuscript with particular focus
on the relationship between its margins and main texts and, as an appendix,
a very helpful chart of the uses of its margins.

*Text, Image, Interpretation: Studies in Anglo-Saxon Literature and its Insular
Context in Honour of Éamonn Ó Carragáin*, edited by Alastair Minnis and Jane
Roberts, includes contributions on topics ranging from art to prose, which are
reviewed in the appropriate sections below. The essays which take manuscripts
as their focus are M.B. Parkes's 'History in Books' Clothing: Books as
Evidence for Cultural Relations between England and Continent in the
Seventh and Eighth Centuries' (pp. 71–88), which uses as its opening examples
Cambridge, Corpus Christi College MS 286 and Oxford, Bodleian Library MS
Auct. D. 2. 14, both of which are Italian gospel books associated with
Augustine which travel to England. Parkes goes on to track textual references
to the transmission of books between England and mainland Europe and
evidence for the copying in England of imported books and in mainland
Europe of books exported from England. Michelle P. Brown writes on 'The
Barberini Gospels: Context and Intertextual Relationships' (pp. 89–116),

comparing the mix of cultural references in this early insular gospel book to the Lindisfarne Gospels, investigating its range of influences and what these might signal about their place and time of production, and suggesting Peterborough or a related location around the year 800 as one possibility. Brown then turns to a detailed analysis of the manuscript decoration, in terms of its symbolic meaning and exegetical references, noting that 'The Fens and East Anglia were the *fons* of the European visionary genre of marvellous creatures and demons which developed in response to the eastern hagiography relating to St Anthony and other desert fathers' (p. 116). Catherine Karkov's focus is 'Text and Image in the Red Book of Darley' (pp. 135–48)— Cambridge, Corpus Christi College MS 422—which she compares with the Ruthwell monument in its 'complex interactions of the visual and verbal...and conscious effort to unite the reader or viewer with the text or object' (p. 135). Through a detailed study of the opening sequence of pages, Karkov shows how the book works to construct an intimate relationship between reader, word and image.

Under the Influence: The Concept of Influence and the Study of Illuminated Manuscripts, edited by John Lowden and Alixe Bovey, contains two essays on Anglo-Saxon manuscripts. Michelle P. Brown alerts us to 'An Early Outbreak of "Influenza"? Aspects of Influence, Medieval and Modern' (pp. 1–10). Brown first considers the uses and implications of the term 'influence', and highlights its links to the notion of external influence on human will, and thus to medieval interest in astronomy and astrology. Her discussion includes the Harley, Ramsey, Utrecht and Vespasian psalters and the Lindisfarne Gospels. George Henderson's 'Insular Art: Influence and Inference' (pp. 11–20) draws on examples from stone sculpture and metalwork in comparison with book painting to discuss the influence of Roman *tituli* and classical painting and sculpture on Anglo-Saxon inscriptions and images.

As part of the August 2007 biennial conference of the International Society of Anglo-Saxonists a manuscript exhibition was held at Lambeth Palace Library, and its catalogue has been published. *Lambeth Palace Library and its Anglo-Saxon Manuscripts*, edited by David Ganz and Jane Roberts with Richard Palmer, contains an essay by Palmer on 'Lambeth Palace Library and its Early Collections' (pp. 6–16), an 'Editors' Note' on the exhibition (pp. 17–23) and descriptions, some with illustrations, of the manuscripts exhibited, which date from the tenth century to the sixteenth; the later examples include rolls from the household of Archbishop Matthew Parker, one of which names Joscelyn.

Work on individual manuscripts supplements these broader studies. Michèle Bussières addresses 'The Controversy about Scribe C in British Library, Cotton MSS, Julius E. VII' (*sic*) (*LeedsSE* 38[2007] 53–72). The focus is on the break in handwriting on folio 117, and Bussières provides a very close analysis of the variations in the hands of Scribes A and C, supported by graphs tracking letter shapes and frequencies, orthography, accents and spellings. The conclusion is that Scribes A and C are a single individual.

Tracey-Ann Cooper adds to the growing interest in lay devotion in 'Lay Piety, Confessional Directives and the Complier's Methods in Late Anglo-Saxon England' (*Haskins Society Journal* 16[2006] 47–61), in which she makes a case for the analysis of manuscript compilation as a key to understanding the intended function of pastoral care texts. Her particular focus is British Library Cotton Tiberius A. iii, which contains confessional directives and other texts which highlight the importance of confession, and she shows that this manuscript reflects a 'dynamic and responsive' (p. 60) religious culture by 'melding, however incompletely, the internal piety of the reformed church and the external piety of the high-status laity' (p. 61). For a review of an earlier article by Cooper on this manuscript, see *YWES* 87[2008] 174.

Several manuscript-based articles in Lendinara, Lazzari and D'Aronco, eds., *Form and Content of Instruction in Anglo-Saxon England*, are reviewed in section 3 below, and other relevant items are reviewed in sections 4–10.

3. Social, Cultural and Intellectual Background

The vibrant wider field of Anglo-Saxon studies offers those who work on textual culture the chance to understand how this works in the world and to root their research in a range of contexts. Several sections of *The Cambridge History of Libraries in Britain and Ireland*, volume 1, edited by Elisabeth Leedham-Green and Teresa Webber, focus on Anglo-Saxon England, and together they constitute an important overview of a topic central to our understanding of institutional, intellectual and textual cultures. In the introductory section of the volume, 'The Physical Setting', Richard Gameson's survey of 'The Medieval Library (to c.1450)' (pp. 13–50) opens with the important reminder that 'Most "medieval libraries" were not a single physical entity: rather they comprised a number of collections, often physically discrete, whose contents might shift from one to another, or be reconfigured, in response to changing needs and local conditions' (p. 13). Gameson examines evidence for arrangements for book storage, and includes Anglo-Saxon examples in his discussion. Two essays in the first main part, 'The Medieval Library', are of particular relevance. In 'Anglo-Saxon England' (pp. 91–108), David Ganz echoes Gameson's emphasis on the lack of 'certainties about what libraries may have been' (p. 91) in the pre-Conquest period, considers the relevant terminology in Latin and Old English and then turns to examine sources of information about libraries and their holdings, in particular manuscripts and booklists. He contrasts the relatively meagre scale of the English evidence with that from mainland Europe, and concludes that a wider range of Latin 'and especially patristic, literature appears only to have become more widespread among even the larger religious houses and cathedrals in England from the final decades of the eleventh century' (p. 108). Teresa Webber's 'Monastic and Cathedral Book Collections in the Late Eleventh and Twelfth Centuries' (pp. 109–25) picks up on this picture of growth in the scale of institutional book collections at the end of the Anglo-Saxon period. The focus of her essay is on the post-Conquest period, but her overview of the book holdings of late eleventh-century religious institutions is important as context for our understanding of continuities and discontinuities in copying and reading across 1066.

Rosamond McKitterick's 'The Migration of Ideas in the Early Middle Ages: Ways and Means' (in Bremmer and Dekker, eds., *Foundations of Learning: The Transfer of Encyclopaedic Knowledge in the Early Middle Ages*, pp. 1–17) has a wide geographical span, and includes examples of the production and use of books in Anglo-Saxon religious houses, in Anglo-Saxon missionary centres in mainland Europe, and by Alcuin. In the same volume, Rolf H. Bremmer Jr writes further on 'The Anglo-Saxon Continental Mission and the Transfer of Encyclopaedic Knowledge' (pp. 19–50), and focuses in particular on establishing what sorts of books Anglo-Saxon missionaries might have taken with them. Bremmer surveys the evidence for Frisia and Utrecht and then considers the sorts of books in question, and concludes that Anglo-Saxon missionaries brought with them not only key texts of Christian learning, but also the 'didactic tools with which to read, interpret and understand' them. (p. 38). An appendix to the article lists over a hundred eighth-century manuscripts with an English origin and mainland European provenance.

A storehouse of exciting new work on Anglo-Saxon schoolroom textual culture is published this year. *Form and Content of Instruction in Anglo-Saxon England*, edited by Patrizia Lendinara, Loredana Lazzari and Maria Amalia D'Aronco, is organized into three sections. The first, 'Manuscripts', consists of László Sándor Chardonnens's 'London, British Library, Harley 3271: The Composition and Structure of an Eleventh-Century Anglo-Saxon Miscellany'; 'The Transmission of Medical Knowledge in Anglo-Saxon England: The Voices of Manuscripts', by Maria Amalia D'Aronco; 'Instructional Manuscripts in England: the Tenth- and Eleventh-Century Codices and the Early Norman Ones', by Patrizia Lendinara; Alexander M. Rumble's 'Cues and Clues: Palaeographical Aspects of Anglo-Saxon Scholarship'; and 'The Drawing on the Margin of Cambridge, Corpus Christi College 206, f. 38r: An Intertextual Exemplification to Clarify the Text?', by Loredana Teresi. Part II, 'Texts and Glosses', is made up of 'Remigius' Commentary to the *Disticha Catonis* in Anglo-Saxon Manuscripts', by Filippa Alcamesi; 'Learning Latin Through the *Regula Sancti Benedicti*: The Interlinear Glosses in London, British Library, Cotton Tiberius A. iii', by Maria Caterina De Bonis; Claudia Di Sciacca's 'An Unpublished *Ubi sunt* Piece in Wulfstan's "Commonplace Book": Cambridge, Corpus Christi College 190, pp. 94–96'; 'An Unpublished *De lapidibus* in its Manuscript Tradition, with Particular Regard to the Anglo-Saxon Area', by Concetta Giliberto; Joyce Hill's 'Ælfric's Grammatical Triad'; Loredana Lazzari's 'The Scholarly Achievements of Æthelwold and his Circle'; 'Of the Choice and Use of the Word *Beatus* In the *Beatus quid est*: Notes by a Non-Philologist', by Ignazio Mauro Mirto; and Hans Sauer's 'A Dialectic Dialogue in Old and Middle English Versions: The Prose *Solomon and Saturn* and the *Master of Oxford's Catechism*'. Part III, 'Texts and Contexts', contains 'Teaching Medicine in Late Antiquity', by Isabella Andorlini; 'Medical Training in Anglo-Saxon England: An Evaluation of the Evidence', by Anne Van Arsdall; Luisa Bezzo's 'Parallel Remedies: Old English "paralisin þæt is lyft adl"'; 'Possible Instructional Effects of the Exeter Book "Wisdom Poems": A Benedictine Reform Context', by Michael D.C. Drout; 'Master–Student Medical Dialogues: The Evidence of London, British Library, Sloane 2839', by Florence Eliza Glaze; and Daniele

Maion's 'The Fortune of the *Practica Petrocelli Salernitani* in England: New Evidence and Some Considerations'. Indices of manuscripts and of late antique and medieval authors and works are supplied for the whole collection.

Loredana Teresi looks at 'Anglo-Saxon and Early Anglo-Norman Mappaemundi' (in Bremmer and Dekker, eds., pp. 341–79), situating their production firmly within monastic schools and identifying a number of coexisting models for representing the earth: schematic T-O maps, list maps, T-O maps in wind diagrams, T-O maps in computus diagrams, Jerusalem T-O maps, non-schematic tripartite maps, macrobian zonal maps, and maps with the five zones in projection.

Many aspects of ecclesiastical culture have yielded new work of relevance this year. Susan Wood's major study, *The Proprietary Church in the Medieval West*, has much to interest Anglo-Saxonists, including vital studies of the Roman and post-Roman situation, and of areas of mainland Europe with strong Anglo-Saxon links. Of specific relevance are the sections which examine Anglo-Saxon evidence for the situation in sixth- and seventh-century kingdoms, patterns of family interest in monasteries, noble founders and their heirs, and proprietors' arrangements with their priests.

The Augustinian conversion has received much scholarly attention in recent years. Roy Fletcher's 'Dagán, Columbanus, and the Gregorian mission' (*Peritia* 19[2005] 65–90), not previously reviewed in *YWES*, outlines the biography of the Irish bishop who encountered the Gregorian missionaries after their arrival in Canterbury. *Journeys from Jarrow*, Richard Morris's 2004 Jarrow Lecture, draws on textual, archaeological and landscape evidence to map long-distance travel in the early Middle Ages and in particular that of religious communities in the time of Bede, and to suggest a route for the early stages of Ceolfrid's journey towards Rome in 716. Flora Spiegel's 'The *Tabernacula* of Gregory the Great and the Conversion of Anglo-Saxon England' (*ASE* 36[2007] 1–13) shows that, in encouraging the building of *tabernacula*—small huts—by Anglo-Saxon Christian converts, Gregory is echoing traditions concerning the biblical conversion of the Israelites, and suggests that such structures were built in England, and that, at Yeavering at least, pre-Christian ritual structures may have been modified to make them.

Michael Lapidge re-examines 'The Career of Aldhelm' (*ASE* 36[2007] 15–69), focusing on his links with West Saxon and Northumbrian royalty and the effects and length of the time he spent with Theodore and Hadrian, and suggesting that in 688 he accompanied his relative Ceadwalla to Rome, where he studied Latin inscriptions. An appendix provides a new chronology of his Latin writings. For more new work on Aldhelm, see section 9 below.

New work on, and resources for the study of, individual Anglo-Saxon ecclesiastical centres continues to add detail to our understanding of the institutional landscape. In terms of resources, vital documentary evidence for the Anglo-Saxon diocese whose bishop remains in post longest after the Conquest is made available this year in the *English Episcopal Acta* volume for *Worcester 1062–1185*, edited by Mary Cheney, David Smith, Christopher Brooke and Philippa M. Hoskin. An introduction sets out important contextual topics, including bishops' households, diplomatic and seals, and appendices give further information on the early archdeacons of the see of

Worcester and the beginning of the year at Worcester in the twelfth and thirteenth centuries, and list the itineraries of the bishops of Worcester, 1062–1185. This collection will no doubt inform further work on the questions of continuity and change from the Anglo-Saxon to Anglo-Norman period of the 'long twelfth century'. John Hudson edits and translates *'Historia Ecclesie Abbendonensis': The History of the Church of Abingdon*, volume 1, a narrative account probably written in the mid-twelfth century, and introduces the text with thorough coverage of its manuscript witnesses, associated sources and structure, the key individual actors in its story, and the monastery's endowment and administration, buildings and monastic life. An appendix supplements the main contents most usefully by commenting on relevant Anglo-Saxon charters. In ' "Ad sedem episcopalem reddantur": Bishops, Monks, and Monasteries in the Diocese of Worcester in the Eighth Century' (in Cooper and Gregory, eds., *Discipline and Diversity*, pp. 114–29), Martin Ryan draws on charter evidence to explore the implications of the strategy of reversion of monasteries to diocesan ownership for the former owners of the institutions in question and to emphasize the importance of understanding a specific local context.

Lisa Weston's 'The Saintly Female Body and the Landscape of Foundation in Anglo-Saxon Barking' (*MFF* 43.2[2007] 12–25) draws on Bede's *Ecclesiastical History*, which conflates two separate accounts, the Hodilred Charter and archaeological evidence for the settlement at Barking and shows how Ethelburga is deployed as mediator between this world and the next and between earthly citizens, whether through male kinship lines or female liturgical figures.

Mary Frances Giandrea's study of *Episcopal Culture in Late Anglo-Saxon England* opens with a reminder that, although our knowledge of the tenth and eleventh centuries 'is due primarily to English churchmen, who, for all intents and purposes, maintained the institutional memory of the English people' (p. 1), we still do not have a clear understanding about key elements of ecclesiastical life in this period, including the development of the parish system and the effect of monastic reform, and that post-Conquest narratives have hugely coloured our view. Giandrea aims to provide a wide-ranging overview of her topic, via chapters focusing on history-writing, the relationship of episcopal and royal power, cathedrals, pastoral care, episcopal wealth (with an appendix table of episcopal holdings) and community and authority. She stresses the impact of individual bishops and the dynamism of the English Church at this period. Catherine Cubitt shares some of Giandrea's interests, as is seen in her 'Bishops and Councils in Late Saxon England: The Intersection of Secular and Ecclesiastical Law' (in Hartmann, ed., *Recht und Gericht in Kirche und Welt um 900*, pp. 151–67). The focus here is on the evidence provided by lawcodes and diplomatic anathemas for the relationship between ecclesiastical and secular law, especially on the topic of excommunication, and from this Cubitt concludes that councils and bishops maintain influence and significance in both ecclesiastical and royal affairs through this period.

Tom Licence examines 'Evidence of Recluses in Eleventh-Century England' (*ASE* 36[2007] 221–34), first by surveying relevant terminology in England and mainland Europe, and then by turning to look in some detail at eight case-studies from the textual record: six from the writings of Goscelin, one from William of Malmesbury and one from Herman. Licence concludes that reclusion grew more popular in the third quarter of the eleventh century.

New work on saints' cults and their development makes an interesting counterpart to the studies of individual hagiographic texts reviewed in section 10 below. 'Tradition and Transformation in the Cult of St. Guthlac in Early Medieval England', by John R. Black (*HeroicA* 10[2007] 35 paras), compares textual and iconographic accounts of Guthlac's Life to chart the development of the central figure from ascetic *miles Christi* in the early Middle Ages, to a more worldly figure and back again in the later medieval period. Clare Downham investigates 'St Bega—Myth, Maiden, or Bracelet? An Insular Cult and its Origins' (*JMH* 33[2007] 33–42). The geographical and temporal scope of the study is wide, the former including Ireland, Britain and Scandinavia. Of particular relevance to Anglo-Saxonists are the references to St Bees and Bassenthwaite in Cumberland, an argument against the theory that Bega's name derives from Old English *bēag*, and a discussion of the relationship of Bega to the Begu named in Bede's *Ecclesiastical History*.

Christine Walsh's study of *The Cult of St Katherine of Alexandria in Early Medieval Europe* includes a discussion of its introduction into England from around 1030. Walsh categorizes the development of Katherine's cult as atypical of England, primarily because it is not relic-focused; the English cult begins with liturgical veneration and then develops into a hagiographical tradition, and Walsh notes its potential resonances with other Anglo-Saxon lives of female, royal virgin saints. Three of the five chapters in *Signs of Devotion: The Cult of St. Æthelthryth in Medieval England, 695–1615*, by Virginia Blanton, will be of particular interest to Anglo-Saxonists. The first discusses Bede's treatment of Æthelthryth in the *Historia Ecclesiastica*, the second 'The Ideology of Chastity and Monastic Reform', and the third tracks the cult on into the post-Conquest period from 1066 to *c*.1113. An appendix to the volume provides very useful lists of images of Æthelthryth from 970 onwards, categorized by type of object.

Popular belief and its relationship to other forms of knowledge is the subject of some interesting work this year. Ann Lawrence-Mathers addresses 'The Problem of Magic in Early Anglo-Saxon England' (*RMSt* 40[2007] 87–104) via a survey of scholarly approaches to the topic, with a focus on the lack of a clear consensus in definitions of magic and of the distinction between magic and religion. She then turns to consider penitentials as evidence to assess whether early Church Council pronouncements on magic are being applied, and argues that the *Penitential of Theodore* 'used categories of paganism, medicine and magic which were flexible but clearly separate' (p. 100). Alaric Hall, in addition to his monograph on elves (reviewed in **section 4** below), publishes on 'The Evidence for *Maran*, the Anglo-Saxon "Nightmares"' (*Neophil* 91[2007] 299–317). His focus is linguistic, and he offers his methodology of reassessing the data as an example of how future similar investigations might be structured. Conclusions from his study include the identification of a gloss probably deriving from Isidore's *Etymologiae*, and the female gendering of the supernatural being it refers to. Philip Shaw re-evaluates the question of 'The Origins of the Theophoric Week in the Germanic Languages' (*EME* 15[2007] 386–401), and argues that a process of transfer in an early medieval scholarly Christian environment is more likely than a direct borrowing during fourth-century interactions between Roman and Germanic cultures.

Guy Halsall's *Barbarian Migrations and the Roman West 376–568* offers a closely argued account of current thinking on this period so crucial for the formation of the early Anglo-Saxon kingdoms. Halsall's geographic perspective is wide, which allows for a presentation of the specifics and complexities of cultural shifts and transmissions, and his approach to matters Anglo-Saxon (concentrated on pp. 311–19 and 357–68) identifies the significant gaps in evidence for the period from the mid-fifth to late sixth centuries, evaluates the evidence for disruption to settlement and organizational patterns and of shifts of power and rightly calls for more interaction with scholarship on western Britain and mainland Europe. Matthew Innes's *Introduction to Early Medieval Western Europe, 300–900: The Sword, the Plough and the Book* is an authoritative study which ranges across the whole of the West from the transformation of the Roman world to the end of the Carolingian empire, and which includes a chapter on 'Britain and Ireland: Kings and Peoples' (pp. 315–95). Lynette Olson's *The Early Middle Ages: The Birth of Europe* will give students and scholars new to comparative issues a wide-ranging and informative overview of the topic. Sections whose focus is Anglo-Saxon England are those on the Augustinian conversion, Alfred and the Norman Conquest.

New work on political and administrative issues key to the Anglo-Saxon period includes *Britons in Anglo-Saxon England*, edited by N.J. Higham, which offers a rich range of approaches to this important issue for the formation of the early Anglo-Saxon cultural landscape as viewed through early medieval and later lenses. The collection is divided into two parts, preceded by 'Britons in Anglo-Saxon England: An Introduction', by Nick Higham. Part I, 'Archaeological and Historical Perspectives', consists of 'Anglo-Saxon Attitudes', by Catherine Hills; 'Forgetting the Britons in Victorian Anglo-Saxon Archaeology', by Howard Williams; 'Romano-British Metalworking and the Anglo-Saxons', by Lloyd Laing; 'Invisible Britons, Gallo-Romans and Russians: Perspectives on Culture Change', by Heinrich Härke; 'Historical Narrative as Cultural Politics: Rome, "British-ness" and "English-ness" ', by Nick Higham; 'British Wives and Slaves? Possible Romano-British Techniques in "Women's Work" ', by Gale R. Owen-Crocker; 'Early Mercia and the Britons', by Damian J. Tyler; 'Britons in Early Wessex: The Evidence of the Law Code of Ine', by Martin Grimmer; 'Apartheid and Economics in Anglo-Saxon England', by Alex Woolf; 'Welsh Territories and Welsh Identities in Late Anglo-Saxon England', by C.P. Lewis; and 'Some Welshmen in Domesday Book and Beyond: Aspects of Anglo-Welsh Relations in the Eleventh Century', by David E. Thornton. Part II, 'Linguistic Perspectives', is made up of 'What Britons Spoke Around AD 400', by Peter Schrijver; 'Invisible Britons: The View from Linguistics', by Richard Coates; 'Why Don't the English Speak Welsh?', by Hildegard Tristram; 'Place-Names and the Saxon Conquest of Devon and Cornwall', by O.J. Padel; and 'Mapping Early Medieval Language Change in South-West England', by Duncan Probert.

'Reluctant Kings and Christian Conversion in Seventh-Century England' (*History* 92[2007] 144–61), by Damian Tyler, re-examines the idea that early Anglo-Saxon kings benefited from the conversion to Christianity by exploring the effect of the conversion on pre-existing social and political traditions. Tyler stresses the risk posed by the introduction of Christian customs to the vital but complex relationship between a king and elite groups in his kingdom. This year sees two further studies of Edgar's meeting with other kings at Chester. In 'Edgar at Chester in 973: A Breton Link?' (*NH* 44:i[2007] 153–7), Andrew Breeze proposes that Hywel and 'Iuchil' or 'Judethil' are not 'obscure Welsh princes' (p. 157) as formerly assumed, but rather the counts of Nantes and Rennes. S.J. Matthews offers another angle, in 'King Edgar, Wales and Chester: The Welsh Dimension in the Ceremony of 973' (*NH* 44:ii[2007] 9–26), with particular reference to Welsh sources for the meeting and to the political concerns which might have informed Edgar's going to Chester.

Steven Bassett's 'Divide and Rule? The Military Infrastructure of Eighth- and Ninth-Century Mercia' (*EME* 15[2007] 53–85) reveals the fortification and organization of a network of royal settlements across Mercia in these centuries, and proposes that this constitutes 'an embryonic burghal system' (p. 84). Stephen Baxter's *The Earls of Mercia: Lordship and Power in Late Anglo-Saxon England* presents a case-study in lay power and piety and in the social structures and relationships of this part of the period. Baxter tracks the trajectory of the House of Leofwine from the late tenth century to 1071, with discussions of the nature of its power, its landholdings, relationships with monasteries, lordship and downfall.

Two essays in Wormald and Nelson, eds., *Lay Intellectuals in the Carolingian World*, treat late Anglo-Saxon secular culture and its connections with learning. In '"Stand strong against the monsters": Kingship and Learning in the Empire of King Æthelstan' (pp. 192–217), Michael Wood opens with an analysis of a Latin poem written at the end of Alfred's reign and addressed to a prince whose identity is accepted as Æthelstan, and then turns to a wider investigation of signs of an overall strategy in Æthelstan's initiatives and to an exploration of his role as patron of letters. Scott Ashley's 'The Lay Intellectual in Anglo-Saxon England: Ealdorman Æthelweard and the Politics of History' (pp. 218–45) reassesses what Æthelweard's aims might have been in producing his *Chronicon*, and how these relate to his familial and political circumstances and his patronage of monastic reform. Ashley argues for the influence of a European context, and positions the *Chronicon*, along with the work of Bede and Alfred, as 'the central triptych in the early history of "Englishness" '(p. 245).

In *Viking Kings of Britain and Ireland: The Dynasty of Ívarr to A.D. 1014*, Clare Downham provides a useful comparative overview of the reigns of Anglo-Scandinavian kings and stresses the extent of the influence of Ívarr's dynasty. Her second and third chapters focus on England from the conquest of York to the Danish conquest, and draw on sources including the *Anglo-Saxon Chronicles*, Asser's *Life of Alfred*, Æthelweard's *Chronicon*, royal diplomas, hagiography, English, Irish and British historical narratives and numismatic evidence.

A section of *NMS* 51[2007] is devoted to 'Selected Papers in Memory of Christine Fell': 'Women in Anglo-Saxon England and Impact of Christine Fell', by Christina Lee and Jayne Carroll (*NMS* 51[2007] 201–5); 'Women and the Law in Seventh-Century England', by Carole Hough (*NMS* 51[2007] 207–30); '"To have and to hold": The Bridewealth of Wives and the *Mund* of Widows in Anglo-Saxon England', by Anne L. Klinck (*NMS* 51[2007] 231–45); and 'Ælfgifu of Northampton: Cnut the Great's "Other Woman"', by Timothy Bolton (*NMS* 51[2007] 247–68). In 'The King's Wife and Family Property Strategies: Late Anglo-Saxon Wessex, 871–1066' (*ANStu* 29[2007] 84–99), Ryan Lavelle draws on a range of textual sources, including lawcodes, wills, Domesday Book, and charters, and supports Pauline Stafford's earlier argument for the existence of 'a corpus of queenly lands' (p. 95), with the qualification that such lands are not exclusively the property of queens, but that of people for whom the king needed to make provision. Helen M. Jewell's *Women in Dark Age and Early Medieval Europe c.500–1200* offers students a concise but wide-ranging introduction to this large topic and to the recent scholarship on it. Many English examples are worked into the chapters, which cover issues including women in rural and urban communities, women and power, and women and religion.

'Demonstrative Behaviour and Political Communication in Later Anglo-Saxon England' is the focus of Julia Barrow's study (*ASE* 36[2007] 127–50) of tenth- and eleventh-century English examples, in the light of considerable scholarly work on Ottonian and Salian Germany. Barrow concludes that it is possible to identify two phases of intensification in such behaviours—including proskynesis to obtain pardon, formalized greeting conventions and crown-wearing—in England in the period before the Norman Conquest, and that the influence of mainland Europe is discernible in different ways at different stages. Paul Dalton explores 'Sites and Occasions of Peacemaking in England and Normandy, c.900–1150' (*Haskins Society Journal* 16[2006] 12–26), noting the focus on rivers and on Advent and Christmas and other Church feast days.

Simon Keynes considers the interactions of 'An Abbot, an Archbishop, and the Viking Raids of 1006–7 and 1009–12' (*ASE* 36[2007] 151–220). The individuals in question are Ælfric and Wulfstan, and Keynes re-examines responses to Viking activities in their writings and analyses key examples of political responses, in the form of Æthelred's programme of prayer, the *Agnus Dei* coinage, and chrismons in charters. A proposal for dating the composition of Wulfstan's *Sermo Lupi ad Anglos* to these years is put forward. An appendix provides a checklist of the *Agnus Dei* pennies.

The scope of Len Scales's 'Bread, Cheese and Genocide: Imagining the Destruction of Peoples in Medieval Western Europe' (*History* 92[2007] 284–300) is very wide, but encompasses Anglo-Saxon examples, including the St Brice's Day massacre and aspects of the writings of Gildas and Bede.

Art in its various forms looms large in this year's work on material culture. Éamonn Ó Carragáin's 'At Once Elitist and Popular: The Audiences of the Bewcastle and Ruthwell Crosses' (in Cooper and Gregory, eds., *Elite and*

Popular Religion, pp. 18–40) explores the arrangement of images and inscriptions on these monuments in the context of specific theological and ecclesiastical developments. Ó Carragáin suggests Acca's knowledge of Rome and his links with Wilfred as the most likely contexts for the Bewcastle monument and the Marian panels on the Ruthwell monument, and argues that the latter monument responds to the former.

Several of the essays in the Festschrift for Ó Carragáin, *Text, Image, Interpretation*, edited by Minnis and Roberts, offer new analyses of art and artistic culture. Carol A. Farr's '*Bis per chorum hinc et inde*: The "Virgin and Child with Angels" in the Book of Kells' (pp. 117–34) opens by setting the hymn praising the Virgin by Cú Chuimne, an eighth-century monk at Iona, alongside the Book of Kells Virgin and Child image, and goes on to make a case for the image 'evoking the heavenly and earthly liturgy, perhaps even referring to the community—one within the *familia* of St Columba and most likely at Iona—for which the Book of Kells was made, probably in the late eighth century' (p. 118). Anna Maria Luiselli Fadda examines 'The Mysterious Moment of Resurrection in Early Anglo-Saxon and Irish Iconography' (pp. 149–67), using the eighth- to ninth-century ivory panel of probable Northumbrian manufacture now in the Victoria and Albert Museum, as the English example. Charles D. Wright tells us 'Why Sight Holds Flowers: An Apocryphal Source for the Iconography of the Alfred Jewel and the Fuller Brooch' (pp. 171–86). The source in question is a version of a tradition transmitted in the Book of the Secrets of Enoch, which describes God as creating Adam's eyes from flowers. Wright shows that this version was available, and relatively popular, in Anglo-Saxon England, notes in relation to the Alfred Jewel the etymology of *episcopus* as 'overseer', and concludes by putting forward the hypothesis that the Fuller Brooch might have been made for Plegmund, Alfred's Archbishop of Canterbury. Elizabeth Coatsworth's 'Text and Textiles' (pp. 187–207) examines inscriptions on early medieval western European embroideries, which she divides into four categories: those commemorating donors or commissioners or makers or owners; those which identify something in or on the textile; those which tell a story; and those which make a statement. Further new work on textiles is reviewed elsewhere in this section. Ó Carragáin and Carol Neumann de Vegvar also publish a collection of essays this year on *Roma Felix—Formation and Reflections of Medieval Rome*, whose contents focus on saints' cults, architecture and related religious and cultural traditions in Rome. The whole is of enormous interest to Anglo-Saxonists concerned with *romanitas* in English culture.

Unsurprisingly, given the impact of Ó Carragáin's work on Anglo-Saxon stone sculpture, four of the essays in Minnis and Roberts, eds., *Text, Image, Interpretation*, treat this body of material. Carol Neuman de Vegvar's 'Converting the Anglo-Saxon Landscape: Crosses and their Audiences' (pp. 407–29) investigates the questions of original location and intended function, considering possibilities including weather magic in rural settings and stations for Rogationtide processions. A useful table sets out details of non-figural crosses/shafts decorated primarily with vegetal motifs. 'Gregory and Great and Angelic Meditation: The Anglo-Saxon Crosses of the Derbyshire Peaks' (pp. 431–48), by Jane Hawkes, notes similarities and differences amongst these monuments, and sets out the context for their interest in angels, stressing the sophisticated ecclesiastical milieu of their production and the ways in which they 'integrated the contemplative with the active and the pastoral' (p. 448). Richard N. Bailey contemplates 'The Winwick Cross and a Suspended Sentence' (pp. 449–72), on this tenth-century transom of the largest surviving Anglo-Saxon cross, on the modern Lancashire–Cheshire border. Bailey revises his former interpretation of Face B as depicting the death of Isaiah to a soul in hell, and then proceeds to evaluate the relationship of this scene to the Celtic west and to patristic and apocryphal texts. In 'The Representation of the Apostles in Insular Art, with Special Reference to the New Apostles Frieze at Tarbat, Ross-shire' (pp. 472–94), George Henderson surveys a range of representations in manuscript and sculptural art and their scriptural bases and then scrutinizes the Tarbat Frieze to stress its fluent adaptation of mainland European models and to show its importance for our understanding of the widespread devotion to the apostles in the Insular Church.

Fred Orton and Ian Wood, with Clare Lees, publish *Fragments of History: Rethinking the Ruthwell and Bewcastle Monuments*, a thoughtful and thought-provoking collaborative meditation on these two so often studied monuments as 'two material forms or fragments of ideology' (p. 203). The wide-ranging discussion includes consideration of what can be ascertained of the history of the Ruthwell monument from the mid-seventeenth century onwards, detailed study of the nature of the stones and the scenes and text carved onto them, and their position at the frontiers of Christianized Northumbria in landscapes being remapped by powerful alliances of royalty and monasticism. The authors conclude that 'no refined and spiritual things, like the Bewcastle and Ruthwell monuments, could exist were it not for the struggle for the crude and material things' (p. 203).

An important resource for work on Anglo-Saxon stone sculpture is published this year. *A Corpus of Early Medieval Inscribed Stones and Stone Sculpture in Wales* is divided into two volumes: the coverage of volume 1, *South-East Wales and the English Border*, by Mark Redknap and John M. Lewis, includes Herefordshire and Shropshire. Volume 2, *South-West Wales*, by Nancy Edwards, provides useful comparative material for Anglo-Saxonists, and such comparative work is greatly facilitated by the fact that the format of entries in both volumes matches that of the *Corpus of Anglo-Saxon Stone Sculpture* series and by the excellent illustrations of all monuments included.

The sources studied in Alfred Bammesberger's 'Old English Runic Inscriptions: Textual Criticism and Historical Grammar' (in Sauer and Bauer, eds., *Beowulf and Beyond*, pp. 69–87) are the Harford Farm Brooch, the Brandon Antler, the Overchurch Stone and the Ruthwell Monument inscription. Bammesberger examines earlier reconstructions of the inscriptions and offers corrections and suggestions.

Luxury goods and their Anglo-Saxon uses are popular themes this year. Thomas Green's 'Trade, Gift-Giving and *Romanitas*: A Comparison of the Use of Roman Imports in Western Britain and Southern Scandinavia' (*HeroicA* 10 [2007] 40 paras) sets out the distribution of Roman artefacts and reinforces our understanding of the relationship of such luxury imports to assertions of power, and of the organized system in place for their trading. In 'Acquiring, Flaunting and Destroying Silk in Late Anglo-Saxon England' (*EME* 15[2007] 127–58), Robin Fleming examines physical, textual and artistic evidence in order to emphasize the quantity of silk in England during this late period, its great potential for carrying symbolic meanings, and its use in secular and ecclesiastical dress and decoration and as wrapping for relics and as shrouds. Her striking conclusion is that 'pre-Conquest England was awash with silk' (p. 128).

The study of Anglo-Saxon textiles will be greatly facilitated by the publication of Elizabeth Coatsworth and Gale R. Owen-Crocker's *Medieval Textiles of the British Isles AD 450–1100: An Annotated Bibliography*. Introductory sections set out the range of items, the context and conditions of their survival and their use as evidence, and discuss details of textile production. The main bibliography spans almost 100 pages, and is followed by lists of find sites and present locations of the textiles and of textile tools. Lists of garments and non-clothing items attested among the textiles and of historical persons associated with them are also provided, along with a general index. The organization and range of supporting material make this an eminently useful reference work.

The Archaeology of Kent to AD 800, edited by John H. Williams, gives a beautifully illustrated survey of the development of this important Anglo-Saxon kingdom, via chapters on palaeolithic, prehistoric and Roman evidence and a study of 'Anglo-Saxon Kent to AD 800' (pp. 187–248).

Feasting the Dead: Food and Drink in Anglo-Saxon Burial Rituals by Christina Lee draws on a range of archaeological evidence from funerary contexts, including animal bones and cooking and eating utensils, and also textual and artistic depictions and discussions of wakes, to explore the ways in which feasting the dead functions as a tool for memory. Hirokazu Tsurushima looks at 'The Eleventh Century in England through Fish-Eyes: Salmon, Herring, Oysters, and 1066' (*ANStu* 29[2007] 193–213), and provides a study of fish culture in late Anglo-Saxon England which draws on Domesday Book, Ælfric's *Colloquy* and charters.

New work on place-names deepens our understanding of Anglo-Saxon landscapes, their histories and their conceptualization. Bethany Fox's 'The P-Celtic Place-Names of North-East England and South-East Scotland' (*HeroicA* 10 [2007] 25 paras) reveals how common such toponyms are in this area and proposes a 'synthesis of mass-migration and elite-takeover models' as the likeliest scenario for this and for the relationship of these names to Old English ones. Sarah Semple's task is 'Defining the OE *hearg*: A Preliminary Archaeological and Topographic Examination of *hearg* Place Names and their Hinterlands' (*EME* 15[2007] 364–85). Semple argues that this rare place-name element, usually translated to mean a religious site associated with pagan practice 'distinctively Anglo-Saxon and newly established in the fifth or sixth centuries' (p. 383), in fact indicates longstanding, continuing cult practice which is at its strongest from the late Iron Age to Romano-British period and which is significantly reduced by the early Anglo-Saxon period. In 'The Pre-English Name of Dorchester-on-Thames' (*SCel* 40[2006] 51–62), Richard Coates suggests that this is a Britonic descendant of a name like *Durocuccium* ('boat fort'), and possibly a fifth-century borrowing into Old English. Carol Hough investigates the semantic field of 'hill' in 'Old English *weargbeorg*' (*N&Q* 54[2007] 364–5) and suggests that the place-name of her title, which is recorded from a charter in the *Textus Roffensis*, might mean 'wolf hill' rather than 'gallows hill'.

Anglo-Norman Studies continues to advance our understanding of 1066 and its aftermath. This year, two new articles discuss the Battle of Hastings and its political and military effects: John Gillingham's R. Allen Brown Memorial Lecture, ' "Holding to the Rules of War (*Bellica Iura Tenentes*)": Right Conduct Before, During, and after Battle in North-Western Europe in the Eleventh Century' (*ANStu* 29[2007] 1–15), and S.D. Church's 'Aspects of the English Succession, 1066–1199: The Death of the King' (*ANStu* 29[2007] 17–34). Two further articles focus on the Bayeux Tapestry: Michael John Lewis's 'Identity and Status in the Bayeux Tapestry: The Iconographic and Artefactual Evidence' (*ANStu* 29[2007] 100–20), and Gale R. Owen-Crocker's 'The Interpretation of Gesture in the Bayeux Tapestry' (*ANStu* 29[2007] 121–44).

David Roffe's *Decoding Domesday* offers Anglo-Saxonists a reassessment of this important representation of England around the Conquest. Roffe discusses the shifting interpretations of the Domesday process since it took place, the nature of the inquest and the resulting texts and the relationship between them, and the ways in which scholarly interpretations of Domesday Book have influenced understandings of English society before 1066. Roffe argues that the book is driven by different aims than those which governed the inquest which preceded it, and that 'All of what we want Domesday Book to be—a register of title, a terrier, an index of wealth, a topography of power—it is not' (p. 319).

The year 2007 sees the publication in paperback of Christopher Harper-Brill and Elisabeth Van Houts, eds., *A Companion to the Anglo-Norman World*, an overview of the cultural transition at the end of the Anglo-Saxon period from the point of view of politics, social organization, territory, church architecture, language and textual culture. The hardback version of the collection was published in 2002, and it would be good to see this and the paperback version updated to incorporate new work on the topic.

Further work on post-Conquest transmission of Anglo-Saxon textual traditions is reviewed in section 10, below.

4. Literature: General

The year 2007 has seen the publication of a number of texts and materials that will be useful for teaching purposes. Carole Hough and John Corbett's *Beginning Old English* is a very basic textbook designed for beginning students with little to no knowledge of linguistics. This impressively lucid guide to Anglo-Saxon language, literature, and culture contains four Old English texts: *Cynewulf and Cyneheard*, *Beowulf* (excerpt), *Battle of Maldon*, and *The Dream of the Rood*. *Beginning Old English* also works to illustrate connections between Old and Modern English. Bruce Mitchell and Fred C. Robinson's classic teaching text, *A Guide to Old English*, has appeared this year in a seventh edition. The new edition contains minor variations and alterations, as well as two new texts: *Sermo Lupi ad Anglos* and the Cotton Gnomes or Maxims. Peter Baker's *Introduction to Old English* has appeared in a second edition. The new edition includes an expanded anthology and new glossary.

John D. Niles' *Old English Heroic Poems and the Social Life of Texts* is a collection of his essays unified by its attention to the mythic qualities of Old English poems, and the 'contribution of poetry to the evolving consciousness of the Anglo-Saxons during an era of nation-building and ethnopoesis' (p. 1). Two of the chapters in the volume are new; the rest have appeared elsewhere. The previously published essays are: 'Locating *Beowulf* in Literary History', '*Widsith*, the Goths, and the Anthropology of the Past', 'The Myth of the Anglo-Saxon Oral Poet', '*Maldon* and Mythopoesis', 'Byrhtnoth's Laughter and the Poetics of Gesture', 'True Stories and Other Lies', and 'Bede's Cædmon, "The Man Who Had No Story" (Irish Tale-Type 2412B)'. The first new chapter of the volume, 'Anglo-Saxon Heroic Geography: How (on Earth) Can It Be Mapped?' (pp. 119–40), explores the challenges of producing a map that would accurately represent how the Anglo-Saxons conceived of their ancestral lands, eastward of Britain. By examining information gleaned from four texts—*Beowulf*, *Widsith*, the Old English Orosius, and the Old English Bede—Niles reflects on the 'geographical consciousness' exhibited in these texts. The chapter concludes with a pictorial map that is intended 'to convey one scholar's impression of how the world of Beowulf might have been imagined through tenth-century English eyes' (p. 138). The second new chapter of Niles' volume, 'Heaney's *Beowulf* Six Years Later', is reviewed in section 8 of this chapter. In addition, the volume contains several brief chapters in which Niles reflects on his earlier essays.

Richard North and Joe Allard, eds., *Beowulf and Other Stories: A New Introduction to Old English, Old Icelandic and Anglo-Norman Literatures*, contains fifteen reader-friendly chapters that are suitable for introducing beginning students to Old English literature and its linguistic and cultural contexts. The volume's contents are: 'An Introduction to this Book', by Richard North, David Crystal, and Joe Allard; 'Old English Influence on *The Lord of the Rings*', by Clive Tolley; 'Beowulf and Other Battlers: An Introduction to *Beowulf*', by Andy Orchard; 'Old English Minor Heroic Poems', by Richard North; 'Joyous Play and Bitter Tears: the *Riddles* and the *Elegies*', by Jennifer Neville; '*The Dream of the Rood* and Anglo-Saxon Northumbria', by Éamonn Ó Carragáin and Richard North; 'Cædmon the Cowherd and Old English Biblical Verse', by Brian Weston Wyly; 'Monasteries and Courts: Alcuin and Offa', by Andy Orchard; 'Old English Prose: King Alfred and his Books', by Susan Irvine; 'The Old English Language' by Peter S. Baker; 'Viking Wars and *The Anglo-Saxon Chronicle*', by Jayne Carroll; 'Viking Religion: Old Norse Mythology' by Terry Gunnell; 'Sagas of Icelanders' by Joe Allard; 'Prose Writers of the Benedictine Reform', by Stewart Brookes; 'Anglo-Norman Literature: The Road to Middle English', by Patricia Gilles; and 'Epilogue: The End of Old English?', by David Crystal.

Another collection that contains a wealth of essays on Old English literature and its contexts is Alastair Minnis and Jane Roberts, eds., *Text, Image,*

Interpretation: Studies in Anglo-Saxon Literature and its Insular Context in Honour of Éamonn Ó Carragáin. The volume's contents are: 'Bede on Seeing the God of Gods in Zion', by Jennifer O'Reilly; 'Martyr Cult within the Walls: Saints and Relics in the Roman *Tituli* of the Fourth to Seventh Centuries', by Alan Thacker; 'History in Books' Clothing: Books as Evidence for Cultural Relations between England and the Continent in the Seventh and Eighth Centuries', by M.B. Parkes; 'The Barberini Gospels: Context and Intertextual Relationships', by Michelle P. Brown; '*Bis per chorum hinc et inde*: The "Virgin and Child with Angels" in the Book of Kells', by Carol A. Farr; 'Text and Image in the Red Book of Darley', by Catherine E. Karkov; 'The Mysterious Moment of Resurrection in Early Anglo-Saxon and Irish Iconography', by Anna Maria Luiselli Fadda; 'Why Sight Holds Flowers: An Apocryphal Source for the Iconography of the Alfred Jewel and Fuller Brooch', by Charles D. Wright; 'Text and Textile', by Elizabeth Coatsworth; 'The Third Voyage of Cormac in Adomnán's *Vita* Columba: Analogues and Context', by Diarmuid Scully; 'Bede's Style in his Commentary *On I Samuel*', by George Hardin Brown; 'The Form and Function of the Vercelli Book', by Elaine Treharne; '*The Dream of the Rood* as Ekphrasis', by Paul E. Szarmach; '*The Dream of the Rood* and *Guthlac B* as a Literary Context for the Monsters in *Beowulf*', by Frederick M. Biggs; 'The Solitary Journey: Aloneness and Community in *The Seafarer*', by Hugh Magennis; '*Staþol*: A Firm Foundation for Imagery', by Eric Stanley; 'Intoxication, Fornication, and Multiplication: The Burgeoning Text of *Genesis A*', by Andy Orchard; 'Understanding Hrothgar's Humiliation: *Beowulf* Lines 144–74 in Context', by Jane Roberts; 'Image and Ascendancy in Úlfr's *Húsdrápa*', by Richard North; 'Converting the Anglo-Saxon Landscape: Crosses and their Audiences', by Carol Neuman de Vegvar; 'Gregory the Great and Angelic Mediation: The Anglo-Saxon Crosses of the Derbyshire Peaks', by Jane Hawkes; 'The Winwick Cross and a Suspended Sentence', by Richard N. Bailey; 'The Representation of the Apostles in Insular Art, with Special Reference to the New Apostles Frieze at Tarbat, Ross-shire', by George Henderson; 'A Suggested Function for the Holy Well?', by Niamh Whitfield; 'Sacred Cities?', by Michael Ryan; 'Nineteenth-Century Travellers to Early Christian Sites in Co. Derry', by Elizabeth Okasha; and 'Éamonn Ó Carragáin: A Bibliography', compiled by Tomás Ó Carragáin. Essays in this volume that focus on individual texts are reviewed in the appropriate sections below. [MS]

The first three chapters of Seth Lerer's monograph, *Inventing English: A Portable History of the Language*, discuss Anglo-Saxon material. This highly readable book examines language change and usage in a manner that will interest beginning and more advanced scholars alike. Individual chapters are intended to be read as part of an 'episodic epic', with each chapter recalling a moment 'when a person or a group finds something new or preserves something old' (p. 2). Chapter one, 'Caedmon Learns to Sing: Old English and the Origins of Poetry', discusses how early English poets adapted Germanic verse to Christian concepts. Chapter two, 'From *Beowulf* to Wulfstan: The Language of Old English Literature', offers an overview of Old English literature, with attention to issues such as vocabulary, syntax, and sound. Chapter three, 'In This Year: The Politics of Language and the End of

Old English', focuses on changes that Old English underwent in the aftermath of the Norman Conquest.

Key Concepts in Medieval Literature, by Elizabeth Solopova and Stuart D. Lee, includes an introductory discussion of the Anglo-Saxon period, a substantial section on Old English, divided up by textual genre, as well as consideration of the Old English literary tradition after the Norman Conquest and a concluding discussion of approaches, theory and practice.

Several new monographs will enrich our understanding of Anglo-Saxon literature and its contexts. Alaric Hall's *Elves in Anglo-Saxon England: Matters of Belief, Health, Gender and Identity*, sheds welcome light on the many textual references to the elf-figure in Anglo-Saxon England. By integrating philology, textual analysis, history, folklore, and comparative material from medieval Ireland and Scandinavia, Hall is able to piece together a detailed study that greatly expands our understanding of the semantics of *ælf*, as well as the social, cultural, and religious functions that the elf-figure may have served in Anglo-Saxon England. Hall focuses in particular on the cultural significance of elves as an alleged cause of illness, on the Scandinavian magic of *seiðr*, and on the complex connections among elf-beliefs and Anglo-Saxon constructions of sex and gender. Martin K. Foys' *Virtually Anglo-Saxon: Old Media, New Media, and Early Medieval Studies in the Late Age of Print* begins from the premise that, while medievalists have welcomed new software and databases as aids to scholarly study, few have investigated the ways in which digital technology (or even print) shapes critical understandings of medieval expressions—literary, artistic, or otherwise. Foys sets out to show how print technology shaped scholarly interpretation of Anglo-Saxon texts, objects, and ideas, and then works to apply precepts of New Media theory to objects, texts, and cultural expressions from the Anglo-Saxon and early post-Conquest periods. Individual chapters focus on Anselm of Canterbury's devotional writings, the Bayeux Tapestry, the Cotton *Mappamundi*, and the Anglo-Scandinavian Nunburnholme Cross.

The first two chapters of Heather Blurton's monograph, *Cannibalism in High Medieval English Literature*, focus on Anglo-Saxon material. Blurton explores representations of cannibals and cannibalism in a range of medieval English texts, with particular attention to the complex ways in which discourses of cannibalism were implicated in the formation of personal, national, religious and social identity from approximately 950 to 1250AD. She begins from the literary critic Claude Rawson's claim that cannibalism, understood as the ingestion of one human being by another, has a unique metaphoric ability to function as a trope for other forms of incorporation, and proceeds to show that imaginative renditions of cannibalism were integral to the construction of national and cultural identity during the high Middle Ages. Chapter one, 'Self-Eaters: The Cannibal Narrative of *Andreas*', offers a reading of cannibalism in *Andreas* as a complex literary response to Viking incursions, in which the anonymous poet 'transforms the genre of hagiography...in order to conceptualize a new kind of narrative about the cultural politics of invasion' (p. 10). Chapter two, '*Eotonweard*: Watching for Cannibals in the *Beowulf*-Manuscript', seeks to show how representations of cannibalism and other kinds of monstrous consumption in such texts as the

Life of Saint Christopher, *Wonders of the East*, *Letter of Alexander to Aristotle*, and *Judith* create an interpretative context for reading *Beowulf* in the light of charged political issues such as conquest, colonization, and conversion. The introduction and first two chapters of John William Sutton's *Death and Violence in Old and Middle English Literature*, with a foreword by Sarah L. Higley, discuss Old English texts. Sutton's focus is on the death scene and on the performative elements of gender, heroism, and personal character that may be glimpsed in the final moments of a warrior's life. Texts discussed include *The Battle of Maldon*, *Beowulf*, and the anonymous verse *Judith*.

Nicholas Howe's important essay, 'Two Landscapes, Two Stories: Anglo-Saxon England and the United States' (in Paolo Squatriti, ed., *Natures Past: the Environment and Human History*, pp. 214–39), focuses on representations of the landscape of early medieval England and contemporary America to consider such issues as the aestheticization of the landscape as national myth, the symbolic mechanisms that allow landscapes to represent the beliefs of people who live and work within them, and the complex relations among landscapes, stories, and human lives. Howe draws on a range of Anglo-Saxon texts, including Bede's *Ecclesiastical History of the English People*, Anglo-Saxon charters, *The Ruin*, *Maxims II*, and also on modern writings and cultural productions such as Herman Melville's novel *Redburn* (1849) and the photographs of Robert Adams and Ansel Adams, and argues that 'the profound differences of topography and use in the landscapes of Anglo-Saxon England and the United States are all the more intriguing... precisely because the dominant culture of each located a common core of memory in its story of migration and exodus' (p. 218).

Christine B. Thijs studies 'Early Old English Translation: Practice Before Theory?' (*Neophil* 91[2007] 149–73). Thijs' goal is to provide a stronger understanding of the principles and aims underlying early English translation, with particular attention to theories of translation that may have informed King Alfred the Great's translation program. Thijs concludes that the tension between freedom and fidelity informs all theories of translation, regardless of language, culture, or purpose. Dolores Fernández Martínez proposes 'A Critical Religious Approach to the Study of the Old English Text as a Strategic Heterogenous Discourse Type' (*NM* 108[2007] 553–66). Martínez argues for 'an interdisciplinary and intertextual approach that rejects a strict distinction between literary and non-literary texts' (p. 554), and that is informed by insights from the area of study commonly known as 'Religion and Literature'. Robert D. Stevick reflects on 'Diagramming Old English Sentences' (in Noel Harold Kaylor, Jr. and Richard Scott Nokes, eds., *Global Perspectives on Medieval English Literature, Language, and Culture*, pp. 229–59), and argues that diagramming can serve as an effective peda-gogical tool for teaching the language of the Anglo-Saxons and their history.

Christine Thijs publishes a second essay on translation this year: 'Close and Clumsy or Fanatically Faithful: Medieval Translators on Literal Translation' (in Cawsey and Harris, ed., *Transmission and Transformation*, pp. 15–39). Here, Thijs opens with a reminder of the importance of seeking to understand the intended aim of a translated work, surveys early and later medieval translators' statements about their work, and then focuses on the example of the Old English translation of Gregory's *Dialogues* to compare the translation strategies evident in this work with those at play in the Old English translator of the *Rule of Chrodegang*, and to argue that 'the medieval landscape of translated literature also reserved a significant area for close and faithful translation' (p. 36). The Appendix to the article provides comparative examples from the Latin *Dialogues* and *Rule of Chrodegang* and the different manuscript versions of the Old English translations of them. [MS]

Richard Sowerby considers 'Hengest and Horsa: the manipulation of history and myth from the *adventus Saxonum* to *Historia Brittonum*' (*NMS* 51[2007] 1–29), with reference to Gildas, Bede and the Anglo-Saxon Chronicle, as well as to the *Historia Brittonum*. He concludes by identifying distinct uses of the episode, and by emphasising Bede's desire to compare the Anglo-Saxons to the Israelites. [MS]

Hugh Magennis offers a dazzling new study of 'Imagery of Light in Old English Poetry: Traditions and Appropriations' (*Anglia* 125[2007] 181–204). After a brief survey of light imagery and symbolism in the early church, Magennis investigates the use of light symbolism in Old English poetry, with particular attention to hagiographical verse. Magennis argues that, while Anglo-Saxon religious poets typically used light imagery to evoke sanctity, heavenly glory, and Christian truth, they were also aware of another, more secular and world-affirming use of light symbolism, and he examines the rich interplay between the two different traditions. Susan Button's '*þystro ealle geondlyhte*: Illumination in *The Gospel of Nichodemus*, *The Phoenix*, and *Christ and Satan*' (*InG* 27[2007] 55–66), also focuses on light imagery, and argues that light is used in these texts to symbolize Christ's triumph over Satan, and hence to provide solace for Christian readers.

Another tranche of the major project *Sources of Anglo-Saxon Literary Culture* is published this year in the form of *The Apocrypha*, edited by Frederick M. Biggs. This brings up to date the entries in the 1990 SASLC *Trial Version* volume (which was not reviewed in *YWES*), and will immediately be a crucial point of reference for Anglo-Saxonists working on all aspects of the availability and use of apocryphal texts and traditions. [MS]

Two essays in the 2006 volume of *NML* treat Old English poetry. Patricia Dailey's 'Questions of Dwelling in Anglo-Saxon Poetry and Medieval Mysticism: Inhabiting Landscape, Body, and Mind' (*NME* 8[2006] 175–214) is a study of 'points of resistance to, or the limits of subjectivity' (p. 175) which includes discussion of *Beowulf* and *The Ruin*, which she compares with writings of late medieval Beguines which also deploy landscape and dwelling-places as a central concepts. Emily V. Thormbury's 'Admiring the Ruined Text: The Picturesque in Editions of Old English Verse' (*NME* 8[2006] pp. 215–44) uncovers the effect of the aesthetic assumptions of mid-nineteenth-century editors of Old English poetry, and explores future directions for editorial work. Appendices reproduce Thorpe's edition of *The Ruin* and Kemble's *Remarks on the Text of Beowulf*. [MS]

R.D. Fulk studies 'Old English Meter and Oral Tradition: Three Issues Bearing on Poetic Chronology' (*JEGP* 106[2007] 304–24). Fulk begins by pointing out that metrical conservatism does not unambiguously point to archaic composition, and that oral tradition must always be taken into account when dating Old English poems. He then sets forth some possible metrical criteria for establishing a poetic chronology, and tries to illustrate the limits of the role of oral tradition in preserving archaic linguistic features. Don Chapman and Ryan Christensen examine 'Noun-Adjective Compounds as a Poetic Type in Old English' (*ES* 88[2007]447–64). They begin by observing that, while compounding has long been recognized as a characteristic device of Old English poetry, few scholars have attempted to identify formal classes of compounds, such as Noun-Noun or Noun-Adjective, that are more characteristic of poetry than prose. Their aim in this study is to 'show that at least one formal class of compounds—the Noun-Adjective compounds like *lof-georn* "praise-eager" and *hilde-hwate* "battle-brave"—is used proportionately much higher in Old English poetry than other classes of compounds, and is in that sense a poetic type' (p. 447).

Sara M. Pons-Sanz provides 'An Etymological Note on Two Old English Medical Terms: *ridesoht* and *flacg*' (*SN* 79[2007] 45–53). She argues that 'there is no need to rely on Norse parallels to explain either of them or to attribute the lemmata and their glosses to different semantic fields' (p. 45). William Sayers studies 'The Old English Antecedents of *ferry* and *wherry*' (*ANQ* 20[2007] 3–8), and proposes that the obscure English term *wherry*, designating a slim light boat used to ferry people or goods across rivers, derives from an Anglo-Saxon term first used to characterize British coracles and similar craft.

Several of the essays in the 2006 volume of *Poetica* use linguistic analysis to shed light on Anglo-Saxon concepts: Małgorzata Fabiszak and Anna Hebda's 'Emotions of Control in Old English: Shame and Guilt' (*Poetica* 66[2006] 1–35), Michiko Ogura's 'Old and Middle English Verbs of Emotion' (*Poetica* 66[2006] 53–72), and Eric G. Stanley's "FEAR Chiefly in Old English' (*Poetica* 66[2006] 73–114). Hans Sauer's study of 'Ælfric and Emotion' in this volume is reviewed in section 10, below. [MS]

Joyce Hill reports on some 'Dialogues with the Dictionary' (in Healey and Kiernan, ed., *Making Sense*, pp. 23–39) – the dictionary in question being the *Dictionary of Old English*. Hill emphasizes the 'galvanising effect' on Anglo-Saxon studies (p. 25) of the *DOE*, and demonstrates its scholarly rewards through case-studies on the Old English translation of the *Regularis Concordia* and a gloss in the *Durham Ritual*. [MS]

Michael Lapidge's chapter 'Old English' (in Alan Deyermond, ed., *A Century of British Medieval Studies*, pp. 363–81), will interest scholars of Anglo-Saxon literature. Lapidge examines contributions to the field of Old English studies made by Fellows of the British Academy who are no longer living, and then situates these contributions in the wider context of Old English studies worldwide, both in the twentieth century and before the foundation of the Academy in 1902.

5. The Exeter Book

The Exeter Book poetry typically generates a good deal of fine criticism, and this year is no exception. Johanna Kramer writes on ' "ðu eart se weallstan": Architectural Metaphor and Christological Imagery in the Old English

Christ I and the Book of Kells' (in Wright, Biggs, and Hall, eds., *Source of Wisdom: Old English and Early Medieval Latin Studies in Honour of Thomas D. Hill*, pp. 90–112). In this impressive interdisciplinary study, Kramer traces the biblical and exegetical sources of the *Christ I* poet's use of architectural metaphors and Christological imagery, and then contextualizes her findings in relation to the illuminated page from the Book of Kells known as 'The Temptation of Christ'. She pays particular attention to the *Christ I* poet's description of Christ as a *weallstan* and as a *lapis angularis/caput anguli*, and argues that the poet could have reasonably expected Anglo-Saxon audiences to appreciate and perhaps to visualize at least some of the typological implications of these metaphors. Kramer concludes that the poet's symbolic use of space in literary and artistic expression 'constructs a multi-faceted representation of Christological teachings in poetic form that . . . reverberates with imagery more broadly current in insular cultures at the time' (p. 91). Timothy D. Arner and Paul D. Stegner study ' "Of þam him aweaxeð wynsum gefea": The Voyeuristic Appeal of *Christ III*' (*JEGP* 106[2007] 428–46), with particular attention to the ways in which the *Christ III* poet figures the complex relations among vision, pleasure, interpretation and reading. They examine patristic and Anglo-Saxon treatments of 'voyeuristic pleasure', and contend that 'the key innovation of *Christ III* is the implication that the pleasure derived from the act of reading is continued in the afterlife' (p. 429).

The Exeter Book elegies continue to inspire new work. Alice Sheppard's important new essay, 'A Word to the Wise: Thinking, Knowledge, and Wisdom in *The Wanderer*' (in Wright, Biggs, and Hall, eds., pp. 130–44), greatly enriches our understanding of both *The Wanderer* and the genre of 'wisdom poetry'. Sheppard focuses on the Old English *gyd* as a sapiential form, with particular attention to the diverse meanings of *gyd*, whether as a poem of personal experience, an enigmatic text with riddlic qualities, or a proverb or wise saying. She explores the Wanderer's journey from sorrowing *anhaga* to one who is *snottor on mode*, and considers how this journey is inflected by the Wanderer's understanding of proverbs. Sheppard contends that 'at the end of the poem, the speaker's apparently pain-free existence is not so much a function of what he has learned from the individual proverbs as it is a marker of his ability to acknowledge the importance of thinking through and beyond proverbs, without necessarily applying their specific teachings' (p. 131). She concludes that *The Wanderer* bridges the gap between those poems in the Exeter Book that celebrate the mysteries of Christianity and those that focus on the mundanities of human existence, and that 'in teaching its readers how to handle wisdom, it asks them to interpret generalities in even the most personalized of narratives, and in so doing, it takes its place literally and conceptually at the centre of the Exeter Book' (p. 141). Scott Gwara examines '*Forht* and *Fægen* in *The Wanderer* and Related Literary Contexts of Anglo-Saxon Warrior Wisdom' (*MS* 69[2007] 255–98). Gwara contends that the warning not to be *to fægen* in *The Wanderer* should be understood as an effort to ward off over-confidence and to prevent reckless behaviour. He contends further that this reference does not parallel the Stoic doctrine of *apatheia*, but is instead correctly understood as relating to a 'native heroic pretense, a definition of courage regulated by warrior "wisdom" ' (p. 257).

Hugh Magennis offers an important new interpretation of 'The Solitary Journey: Aloneness and Community in *The Seafarer*' (in Minnis and Roberts, eds., pp. 303–18), and sheds fresh light on pre-modern understandings of subjectivity. By contextualizing *The Seafarer*'s treatment of earthly life in relation to discussions of this topic in other Exeter Book religious poems, such as *The Wanderer*, *Resignation*, and *The Riming Poem*, Magennis explores how ideas and images from secular heroic verse are reinterpreted in *The Seafarer* in spiritual and eschatological terms. Magennis concludes that *The Seafarer* is a highly unusual Old English poem, in that it depicts Christian identity as an individual rather than a communal phenomenon, with death as the distillation of physical, individual experience. This essay enriches our understanding of the diverse ways in which interiority was understood in early medieval literature and culture.

Sachi Shimomura's essay, 'Remembering in Circles: *The Wife's Lament*, *Conversatio*, and the Community of Memory' (in Wright, Biggs, and Hall, eds., pp. 113–29), provides a fascinating new reading of the complex relationships between self and community in *The Wife's Lament*. Through careful attention to the poet's treatment of time, Shimomura shows that the poem effects a move from individual to social memory, in which the Wife undergoes a kind of socializing conversion—moving beyond immersion in her own personal past and memory and arriving at a more generalized, communal (and gnomic) understanding of her situation. Sung-Il Lee examines 'The Identity of the "Geong Mon" (Line 42) in *The Wife's Lament* (or, "The Lament of an Outcast")' (in Kaylor and Nokes, eds., *Global Perspectives on Medieval English Literature, Language, and Culture*, pp. 175–93). Lee presents a new translation of *The Wife's Lament*, and contends that the speaker in the poem is correctly understood as a young man who has been exiled from his warlord. Sonja Daniëlli writes on '*Wulf, Min Wulf*: An Eclectic Analysis of the Wolf-Man' (*Neophil* 91[2007] 505–24). She considers references to the wolf figure in a range of texts, including the *Völsungasaga*, the *Elder Edda*, Old Norse myths, and Norse and Anglo-Saxon legal writings, and concludes that 'the kenning *Wulf* stands for war, violence, treason, crime, cruelty, blood revenge, shape shifting, and bestial behaviour' (p. 522). This essay was reviewed in *YWES* 87[2008], but its publication details were mistakenly given as *Neophil* 90[2006].

The year 2007 has seen a great deal of new work on the Exeter Book riddles. Melanie Heyworth has produced two essays this year that shed light on specific riddles. In 'Perceptions of Marriage in *Exeter Book Riddles 20* and *61*' (*SN* 79[2007] 171–84), Heyworth examines the complex ways in which Riddles 20 and 61 may reveal and/or engage with literary and/or social attitudes towards sexuality and marriage in Anglo-Saxon culture. In 'The Devils in the Detail: A New Solution to Exeter Book Riddle 4' (*Neophil* 91[2007] 175–96), Heyworth provides a detailed lexicographical analysis of Riddle 4, and contends that many of the words in this riddle are frequently found in Anglo-Saxon penitentials and homilies. Heyworth argues that the religious contexts evoked by Riddle 4 direct the audience to a solution of 'devil' and that the purpose of the riddle is thus to remind Christians of the need for continual vigilance against devilish temptation.

Patrick J. Murphy's study, '*Leo ond beo*: Exeter Book Riddle 17 as Samson's Lion' (*ES* 88[2007] 371–87), sheds new light on Riddle 17, as well as on the pair of runes, *lagu* (L) and *beorc* (B), found between Riddles 16 and 17 on folio 105ʳ of the Exeter Book. Murphy reviews previous attempts to solve Riddle 17 as 'siege-engine', 'fortress', 'forge', 'oven', 'inkwell', 'phallus', 'quiver' and 'bee-hive'. By looking at a set of metaphors concerning bees, honey and hives, and by exploring the biblical Samson's fierce encounter with the lion, whose carcass is ultimately occupied by a swarm of bees, Murphy ultimately seeks to show that Riddle 17 is correctly solved as 'Samson's lion'. Jennifer Neville's 'Fostering the Cuckoo: *Exeter Book* Riddle 9' (*RES* 58[2007] 431–46), takes the anthropomorphism of the cuckoo in Riddle 9 as a disguise for concealing social commentary on Anglo-Saxon practices of human fosterage. She contends further that 'solving' Riddle 9 is only a starting point for interpretation and that this text requires a different understanding of the riddle-genre itself' (p.431). Jerry Denno studies 'Oppression and Voice in Anglo-Saxon Riddle Poems' (*CEA* 70[2007] 35–47), focusing in particular on riddles that employ images of bondage, captivity, enslavement, or entrapment: Riddle 58 (reed pen), Riddle 19 (plough), Riddle 51 (battering ram), Riddle 12 (oxhide leather) and Riddle 50 (flail). Denno contends that because these riddles include represented voices of the enslaved they offer us a distant, poeticized resonance of voices that are typically suppressed in Anglo-Saxon literature and culture.

Scott Gwara proposes 'A "Double Solution" for Exeter Book Riddle 51, "Pen and Three Fingers"' (*N&Q* 54[2007] 16–19). By focusing on the phrases *feower eallum, winnende wiga*, and *fæted gold*, Gwara seeks to show that Riddle 51 yields a double solution, 'Pen and Three Fingers/Scribe (Writing the Gospels)' and 'Priest Performing Mass', and also to lend further support to the idea that some riddle writers intended double solutions. Eric Stanley investigates '*Staþol*: A Firm Foundation for Imagery' (in Minnis and Roberts, eds., pp. 319–32), with particular interest in shedding light on how the term *frumstaþol* should be understood in Riddle 60, the riddle which immediately precedes *The Husband's Message*. For an introductory essay on the riddles and the elegies, see Jennifer Neville's 'Joyous Play and Bitter Tears: the *Riddles* and the Elegies' (in North and Allard, eds., *Beowulf and Other Stories: A New Introduction to Old English, Old Icelandic and Anglo-Norman Literatures*, pp. 130–59)

Michael D.C. Drout has produced two essays this year on Exeter Book poems. Drout examines 'Possible Instructional Effects of the Exeter Book "Wisdom Poems"' (in Lendinara, Lazzari, and D'Aronco, eds., pp. 447–66). By providing textual analysis of *The Gifts of Men, Precepts, The Fortunes of Men*, and *Maxims I*, and by examining the circumstances in which the Exeter Book may have been copied and compiled, Drout seeks to show that the Exeter Book 'wisdom poems' were intended to teach novice and reform monks how to understand secular culture in relation to monastic life. In '"The Partridge" is a Phoenix: Revising the Exeter Book *Physiologus*' (*Neophil* 91[2007] 487–503), Drout contends that the poem about a bird on folios 97ᵛ–98ʳ of the Exeter Book is unlikely to be about the partridge and more likely to be about the phoenix. Drout bases his claim on three main points: that the structure of the Anglo-Saxon *Physiologus* is likely to conclude with a poem about Christ's resurrection, symbolized by the phoenix; that the appearance of a marvellous odour in the other two *Physiologus* poems (*The Panther* and *The Whale*) suggests that such an odour would have appeared in the third poem; and that the presence of the two words *hweorfan* and *cyrran* in the homiletic passage on folio 98 supports the link with the phoenix. Drout concludes that the use of animal exempla for didactic purposes links the *Physiologus* poems to other poems in the Exeter Book, such as the riddles, as well as to the cultural concerns of the Benedictine Reform. For further discussion of *The Phoenix*, see Susan Button's '*þystro ealle geondlyhte*: Illumination in *The Gospel of Nichodemus, The Phoenix*, and *Christ and Satan*' (*InG* 27[2007] 55–66), reviewed in **section 4** of this chapter.

Christopher Abram studies 'The Errors in *The Rhyming Poem*' (*RES* 58[2007] 1–9), and argues that these errors suggest that the poem was not always copied out as a continuous block (as it appears in the Exeter Book), but that it was once written down according to the conventions of Latin scribal culture. Abram concludes that the use of this kind of formatting is a reflection of *The Rhyming Poem*'s stylistic affinities with Anglo-Latin poetry. Mary R. Rambaran-Olm provides 'Two Remarks Concerning Folio 121 of the Exeter Book' (*N&Q* 54[2007] 207–8) that will be of interest to scholars working on *The Descent into Hell*. She argues that the missing word(s) in line 93b may be either [*modi*]*gust* or [*mod*]*gust* and she confirms scholars' earlier assertions that the three letters before the syllable -*lum* on folio 121ᵛ are in fact the letters *eng-*.

6. The Poems of the Vercelli Book

The poems in the Vercelli Book continue to stimulate new scholarship, with much of this year's work focused on *The Dream of the Rood*. María Beatriz Hernández Pérez writes on 'Elene as an Agent of Torture: An Anglo-Saxon Depiction of Sanctity' (in Brito and González, eds., *Insights and Bearings: Festschrift for Dr. Juan Sebastián Amador Bedford*, pp. 221–32), with an emphasis on the complex intertwining of torture and revelation in Cynewulf's *Elene*. She notes Cynewulf's reversal of hagiographical gender norms in his depiction of a woman as an agent rather than a victim of torture, and concludes that the poem states the superiority of Christianity to both Judaism and paganism and attempts to justify Christian violence through the august figure of the queen mother.

Two of the essays in Minnis and Roberts, eds., *Text, Image, Interpretation*, focus on the Vercelli Book and its poetry. Elaine Treharne considers 'The Form and Function of the Vercelli Book' (pp. 253–66), by comparing it to other late tenth- and early eleventh-century manuscripts containing Old English religious prose. Treharne offers the intriguing argument that the Vercelli Book was a deliberately constructed set of pastoral and devotional texts for a prelate and that, given the book's probable origin at St Augustine's, Canterbury, this prelate was likely a bishop or abbot. In this same volume, Paul E. Szarmach examines '*The Dream of the Rood* as Ekphrasis' (pp. 267–88). After reminding us of the definition of ekphrasis as 'the verbal representation of the visual', Szarmach explores the divergent attitudes towards art and its teaching by writers such as Augustine, Gregory the Great, Bede, and Ælfric. Szarmach then uses these ideas about art to read *The Dream of the Rood*, with particular attention to how the poem conjoins beauty, narrative, and meaning. Szarmach concludes that *The Dream of the Rood* poet's efforts to elicit emotion render the poem highly unusual in relation to contemporary understandings of the art object's functions.

Two of the essays in Wright, Biggs, and Hall, eds., *Source of Wisdom*, focus on *The Dream of the Rood*. James W. Earl studies 'Trinitarian Language: Augustine, *The Dream of the Rood*, and Ælfric' (pp. 63–79), with an emphasis on the talking cross and on the theological implications of prosopopoeia. Earl argues that Augustine's theory of language as a sign of the Word and an interface between ideas and the world (*De trinitate* 9.7–11) provides a useful means of understanding the rhetorical trope of talking objects. James W. Marchand focuses on 'The Leaps of Christ and *The Dream of the Rood*' (pp. 80–9). Marchand's goal is to show that the poet's repeated use of the verb *-stigan* (*gestigan/gestah*; ll. 34b, 40b) is an allusion to the motif of a leaping Christ, familiar to scholars from *Christ II*.

Barbara C. Raw's 'The Cross in *The Dream of the Rood*: Martyr, Patron and Image of Christ' (*LeedsSE* 38[2007] 1–15), is an important interdisciplinary study that examines the opening lines of *The Dream of the Rood* in the light of early medieval art-historical evidence, such as the cross in the apse mosaic of S. Apollinare in Classe, Ravenna. Raw contends that the cross in *The Dream of the Rood* functions in a manner very similar to crosses in medieval art: it does not simply imitate Christ but also serves to represent the relics of the cross, to identify Christ as the Tree of Life, and to symbolize Christ himself.

Carole Hough examines 'Old English *fea* in *The Dream of the Rood* 115b and *The Paris Psalter* 134:18' (*NM* 108[2007] 325–37), the two instances in Old English in which *fea* is generally taken to represent an adverb meaning 'little' as opposed to an adjective or an adjectival noun meaning 'few'. Hough contends that in both cases an interpretation as an adjectival noun is more appropriate, and that there is no evidence for an adverb *fea* in Old English. Hough concludes by proposing the following reading of *The Dream of the Rood*, lines 115–16: 'But they will then be afraid, and few (i.e. none) will think of what they should begin to say to Christ' (p. 337). For an introduction to *The Dream of the Rood* in its cultural and historical contexts, see '*The Dream of the Rood* and Anglo-Saxon Northumbria', by Éamonn Ó Carragáin and Richard North (in North and Allard, eds., pp. 160–88).

7. The Junius Manuscript

A small but noteworthy amount of scholarship has appeared this year on the poetry in the Junius manuscript. Two important essays are published on *Genesis A*. Heide Estes writes on 'Abraham and the Northmen in *Genesis A*: Alfredian Translations and Ninth-Century Politics' (*M&H* 33[2007] 1–13). Estes finds striking parallels between the language and cultural politics of

Genesis A and texts associated with the Alfredian translation programme. She contends that the resonances of the poem with events of the late ninth century suggest that *Genesis A* may have been copied and adapted in Alfred's circle, with specific details in the poem echoing contemporary events. Andy Orchard reflects on 'Intoxication, Fornication, and Multiplication: The Burgeoning Text of *Genesis A*' (in Minnis and Roberts, eds., pp. 333–54). In this characteristically detailed essay, Orchard examines how the *Genesis A* poet transformed his Latin sources, and considers whether the literary influence of *Genesis A* can be detected in any extant Old English poems. Orchard concludes by suggesting that the *Judith* poet may have borrowed directly from *Genesis A*, and that 'for later Anglo-Saxon authors, as for us, the antiquity and artistry of *Genesis A* were indeed a continuing revelation' (p. 347).

P.S. Langeslag's brief but illuminating study of 'Doctrine and Paradigm: Two Functions of the Innovations in *Genesis B*' (*SN* 79[2007] 113–8), contends that the *Genesis B* poet worked to emphasize the subtlety of the temptation, and also to bring Adam and Eve's behaviour more into accordance with their role in salvation history. Langeslag concludes that, in order to achieve these two aims, the poet has to abandon Eve's pride as an occasion for the Fall and also to neglect the theological differentiation between the sexes. Catherine E. Karkov's essay on Eve in Junius 11 is reviewed in section 2 above.

Alfred Bammesberger writes on 'Old English *Læste Near* (*Exodus*, Line 308b)' (*N&Q* 54 [2007] 357–9). He argues that *near* is to be understood as the adverbial comparative of *neah* 'nigh, near', and that lines 307–9 of the manuscript reading of *Exodus* do not require emendation. Susan Button's '*þystro ealle geondlyhte*: Illumination in *The Gospel of Nichodemus, The Phoenix*, and *Christ and Satan*' (*InG* 27[2007] 55–66) contains a brief discussion of *Christ and Satan*, and is reviewed in **section 4** of this chapter.

8. The *Beowulf* Manuscript

The year 2007 has been extremely fruitful for *Beowulf* studies. Several texts and materials have been published that are well suited for teaching purposes. Harold Bloom, ed., *Beowulf, Updated Edition*, brings together eleven previously published essays on *Beowulf*, along with a new introduction by Bloom. The volume's contents are: 'Introduction', by Harold Bloom; 'The Structure and the Unity of *Beowulf*', by Arthur Gilchrist Brodeur; 'Succession and Glory in *Beowulf*', by Richard J. Schrader; 'Locating *Beowulf* in Literary History', by John D. Niles; 'Grendel's Glove', by Seth Lerer; 'Psychology and Physicality: The Monsters of *Beowulf*', by Andy Orchard; 'Christian and Pagan Elements', by Edward B. Irving Jr; 'Myth and History', by John D. Niles; 'Theorizing Irony in *Beowulf*: The Case of Hrothgar', by Scott DeGregorio; 'Cycles and Change in *Beowulf*', by Phyllis R. Brown; 'The Fourth Funeral: Beowulf's Complex Obsequies', by Gale R. Owen-Crocker; and 'Launching the Hero: The Case of Scyld and Beowulf', by Judy King. Andy Orchard's 'Beowulf and Other Battlers: An Introduction to *Beowulf*' (in North and Allard, eds., pp. 63–94), provides a reader-friendly introduction to *Beowulf*, with attention to the role that violence plays in Anglo-Saxon literature.

The question of *Beowulf*'s grounding in a real-world locale receives substantial attention in *Beowulf and Lejre* by John D. Niles, with contributions by Tom Christensen and Marijane Osborn, and translations by Faith Ingwersen, Carole E. Newlands and William Sayers. This important interdisciplinary study focuses on two major archaeological excavations undertaken in 1986–8 and in 2004–5 at Lejre, on the Danish island of Zealand, the location that is often assigned to the Danish episodes of *Beowulf*. The book reports on the two hall-complexes unearthed in these excavations and on their significance with respect to the buildings depicted in *Beowulf*. Medieval sources relating to the legendary history of Lejre are edited and translated, and accompanied by analysis and commentary. The modern pseudo-scholarly 'myth of Lejre' is also discussed.

Three of the essays in Wright, Biggs, and Hall, eds., *Source of Wisdom*, discuss *Beowulf*. Joseph Harris investigates 'Beasts of Battle, South and North' (pp. 3–25), and contends that a full grasp of the symbolism of beasts of battle in Old English poetry must move beyond purely formal contexts. Harris argues that 'only ultimately religious roots can account for the persistent supernatural features, connections with the future and death, and the survival into later folklore ... these roots establish the most meaningful way of relating the Germanic materials to the overrich Celtic analogues, most conspicuously among them the avian-form war goddesses' (p. 15). James H. Morey focuses on 'The Fates of Men in *Beowulf*' (pp. 26–51), with particular attention to the different modes of death for each of the successors to the various thrones in the poem. Morey argues that, while Geatish and Swedish royals tend to meet violent deaths, many Danish potential claimants die in non-violent, or at least in unexplicit, mysterious circumstances. He claims further that the unambiguous circumstances of the deaths of Beowulf's predecessors facilitate Beowulf's succession to the Geatish throne without taint of treachery, while kin-slaying, namely the fratricide that Morey suspects may have cleared Hrothgar's path to the throne, is the 'dark family secret' (p. 44) that haunts Hrothgar and the Danes in the form of Grendel. Frederick M. Biggs reconsiders 'Folio 179 of the *Beowulf* Manuscript' (pp. 52–9) in order to shed fresh light on Kevin Kiernan's claim that folio 179 is a palimpsest. Biggs argues that most of the damage to the folio is accidental, and that the folio is not a revision in progress but an imperfect scribal record of the poet's intentions.

Two of the essays in this year's *Anglo-Saxon England* focus on *Beowulf*. Walter Goffart reconsiders 'The Name "Merovingian" and the Dating of *Beowulf*' (*ASE* 36[2007] 93–101). Goffart's main goal is to argue against Tom Shippey's claims that the dynasty name 'Merovingian' was condemned to oblivion soon after the dynasty was deposed (AD 751) and that the *Beowulf* poet's use of the name 'Merovingian' in line 2921 can thus be used as a basis for attributing an early date to the poem. Goffart demonstrates that, although the Merovingian dynasty was indeed deposed in 751, the Carolingians took pains to affirm continuity with their predecessors, and that the name 'Merovingian' was still well known in the ninth century. Goffart concludes that the *Beowulf*-poet's use of the term 'Merovingian' most likely does not provide firm ground on which to date the poem. Daniel Anlezark's essay, 'Poisoned Places: The Avernian Tradition in Old English Poetry'

(*ASE* 36[2007] 103–26), sheds new light on the question of whether or not *Beowulf* reflects the influence of classical Latin literature. Anlezark examines the motif of the 'poisoned place', most famously represented by Lake Avernus in the *Aeneid*, in texts such as *Beowulf* and *Solomon and Saturn II*. He contends that 'the Avernian tradition was known in Anglo-Saxon England not only wherever Isidore's *Etymologiae* were studied, but also through Latin epic poetry' (p. 126), and that the study of the Latin poetry of antiquity—and Lucan in particular—may have contributed to the genesis of vernacular epic poetry in Anglo-Saxon England.

Michael D. C. Drout examines 'Blood and Deeds: The Inheritance Systems in *Beowulf*' (*SP* 104[2007] 199–26), in order to understand the two main systems in the poem by which kingly power and identity pass from one man to another: inheritance-by-blood and inheritance-by-deed. Drout explores the social processes and dynamics of succession in both the poem and Anglo-Saxon culture, with particular attention to the ways in which different systems of inheritance may benefit different social and gender groups. He concludes that while 'blood-only replication leads to extinction[,] deeds-only replication leads to uncontrollable violence . . . [and] that the system leads inexorably to its own destruction' (p. 226). Karl P. Wentersdorf examines 'The *Beowulf*-Poet's Vision of Heorot' (*SP* 104[2007] 409–26). Wentersdorf reviews textual and archaeological evidence for Germanic royal halls, and contends that the *Beowulf*-poet's vision of Heorot was remarkably realistic, with the exception of one notable detail: the poet's repeated assertions that the *dryhtsele* was a golden or shining building. Wentersdorf argues that this unrealistic detail is meant to evoke the Roman tradition of gilded roofs, and that the poet introduced this architecturally incongruous feature to underscore the idea that the obsession with the acquisition of gold, shared by both Germanic and Roman cultures, was morally and politically hazardous.

The monsters in *Beowulf* continue to generate new scholarship. Frederick M. Biggs considers '*The Dream of the Rood* and *Guthlac B* as a Literary Context for the Monsters in *Beowulf*' (in Minnis and Roberts, eds., pp. 289–301). In this essay Biggs expands upon his earlier work, in which he proposed that the monsters in *Beowulf* function as a means for the poet to explore different models of succession. By examining the complex ways in which poems such as *The Dream of the Rood*, *Guthlac B*, and *Beowulf* elicit similar audience response, Biggs contends that monastic meditative reading provides a possible source for the construction and reception of *Beowulf*. Alexander Bruce writes on 'Evil Twins? The Role of the Monsters in *Beowulf*' (*MedFor* 6[2007] no pagination). He begins from the well-accepted premise that the *Beowulf*-poet highlights similarities between Beowulf and the monsters, and argues that the poet worked to equate hero and monster in order to show that humans may occupy both roles at the same time. Renée R. Trilling's 'Beyond Abjection: The Problem with Grendel's Mother Again' (*Parergon* 24[2007] 1–20), examines Grendel's mother as a 'nexus for the representation of the many dialectical tensions—male/female, human/monster, hall/wilderness, feud/peace, symbolic/semiotic—that both underwrite and critique the poem's symbolic order' (p. 1). Trilling argues that, while the poet manages to repress Grendel's mother by cloaking her in masculine pronouns and eventually

killing her off, the 400-odd lines detailing her actions return again and again to
horrify readers, both modern and medieval, by underscoring the terrifying fact
that there is no such thing as a unified, coherent identity.

William Cooke sheds light on 'Who Cursed Whom, and When? The Cursing
of the Hoard and Beowulf's Fate' (*MÆ* 76[2007] 207–24). Through careful
analysis of the various passages in *Beowulf* that deal with a curse or spell laid
on the dragon's treasure hoard, Cooke considers whether there is any evidence
for viewing the curse as heathen in nature and for seeing Beowulf as damned
by its workings. Cooke concludes that references to the treasure as a 'heathen
hoard' and as 'heathen gold' do not refer specifically to the curse laid on the
treasure but to the heathen men who originally fashioned it, and that 'the
terms of the curse that Beowulf's henchmen utter over the hoard are consistent
with the poet's portrayal throughout the poem of his "good" characters
as believers in a single, or at least a supreme, good God, and certainly not
"heathen"' (p. 219).

The dating of *Beowulf* continues to stimulate important new work. Roberta
Frank's 2007 presidential address at the annual meeting of the Medieval
Academy of America, 'A Scandal in Toronto: *The Dating of "Beowulf"* a
Quarter Century On' (*Speculum* 82[2007] 843–64), sheds fresh light on the 1980
Toronto conference on the dating of *Beowulf*, and on the subsequent
conference proceedings: *The Dating of 'Beowulf'*, ed. Colin Chase, Toronto
Old English Series 6 (Toronto, 1981), reprinted in 1997, with an afterword by
Nicholas Howe. Frank also considers what the dating of *Beowulf* has meant
for Anglo-Saxonists and for Anglo-Saxon studies. For further discussion of
the dating of *Beowulf*, see R.D. Fulk's 'Old English Meter and Oral Tradition:
Three Issues Bearing on Poetic Chronology' (*JEGP* 106[2007] 304–24),
discussed in **section 4** of this chapter.

This year, Frank also ponders '*F*-Words in *Beowulf*' (in Healey and
Kiernan, eds., *Making Sense: Constructing Meaning in Early English*, pp. 1–
22), with reference to the new *f*-fascicule of the *Dictionary of Old English*, and
notes many intriguing details in passing—not least 'The juxtaposition in
Beowulf 697–8 of a rather old-fashioned if not pagan-sounding formulation
("weavings of war-victories") and Benedictine Reform vocabulary (*frofor ond
fultum*)' (pp. 20–1). [MS]

R.D. Fulk has produced three essays this year that focus specifically on
Beowulf. Fulk examines 'Old English *þa* "Now That" and the Integrity of
Beowulf' (*ES* 88[2007] 623–31). He explores instances in Old English verse and
prose in which *þa* is correctly rendered 'now that' and finds that, with the
exception of the occurrences in *Genesis A* and *Beowulf*, causal *þa* is quite rare.
Fulk contends that the use of *þa* in the sense 'now that' in these two poems
may well be explained as an archaism. He concludes that the fact that the use
of *þa* in this manner is distributed widely throughout the portions of *Beowulf*
set in Denmark and Geatland may add to the degree of probability that these
two portions are in fact a single composition. Fulk also proposes 'Some
Emendations and Non-Emendations in *Beowulf* (Verses 600a, 976a, 1585b,
1663b, 1740a, 2525b, 2771a, and 3060a)' (*SP* 104[2007] 159–74), in order to
explain the reasoning behind some of the textual and interpretative choices
adopted in the revised issue of Klaeber's *Beowulf*. In 'The Textual Criticism of

Frederick Klaeber's *Beowulf* (in Wawn, ed., *Constructing Nations, Reconstructing Myth: Essays in Honour of T.A. Shippey*, pp. 131–53), Fulk reflects on Klaeber's textual and editorial principles, and offers some broader thoughts on textual editing. This same collection also contains John Hill's '*Beowulf* Editions for the Ancestors: Cultural Genealogy and Power in the Claims of Nineteenth-Century English and American Editors and Translators' (pp. 52–69). Hill examines a number of nineteenth-century editions and translations of *Beowulf*, and concludes that 'the reproduction or else the translation of an antiquity in modern, scholarly form is like a ritual sacrifice that would draw down for oneself powers and virtues projected into the ancestral past and its objects' (p. 69).

The enigmatic nature of the dragon continues to generate interest. Thomas Klein writes on '*Stonc æfter stane* (*Beowulf*, l. 2288a): Philology, Narrative Context, and the Waking Dragon' (*JEGP* 106[2007] 22–44), and focuses on the meaning of the verb *stincan* in line 2288a. Klein reviews the different meanings that have been attributed to *stincan* in this context—'to perceive a smell', 'to give off a smell', 'to leap', 'to move quickly', 'to rise up by smoke'—and concludes that 'to sniff' is the most logical choice in this context. Klein argues that the meaning of the term *stincan* is important 'because it conditions our perception of the dragon as a creature, rather than simply an elemental force' (p. 22).

InG 27[2007] is dedicated to the memory of Raymond P. Tripp, Jr, and contains four essays, three of which discuss *Beowulf*. Benjamin Slade examines '*Untydras ealle*: Grendel, Cain, and Vṛtra. Indo-European *śruti* and Christian *smṛti* in *Beowulf*' (*InG* 27[2007] 1–32). He examines Christian allusions in *Beowulf*, and argues that '*Beowulf* is essentially a "Germanic" story representing a pre-Christian world-view' (p. 1). J.D. Thayer writes on '*Nealles*: The "Not at all" of Experimental Elegy in *Beowulf*' (*InG* 27[2007] 33–53). Thayer examines elegiac passages in *Beowulf*, and argues that 'the poet creates ... negation so complete that ... [it] underscores the desperation of the lamenters and disallows the glimmers of hope that appear in other Old English elegies' (p. 34). The final essay in the collection (published posthumously) is Tripp's 'The Restoration of *Beowulf* 2221b: *Wyrmhorda cræft* and the Identity of the Thief' (*InG* 27[2007] 67–92). Tripp contends that the conventional view of the dragon as having been robbed and angered by a human thief needs to be corrected, and that 'the thief was indeed once human, and a prince, but now is a monstrous Dragon-King on the loose' (p. 69). *InG* 27 concludes with a bibliography of Tripp's publications on *Beowulf* (pp. 86–92).

The complex relationships among *Beowulf* and modern literature and film continue to attract attention. Marijane Osborn writes on 'Manipulating Waterfalls: Mythic Places in *Beowulf* and *Grettissaga*, Lawrence, and Purnell' (in Glosecki, ed., *Myth in Early Northwest Europe*, pp. 197–24). Osborn examines two landscape features that appear in both *Beowulf* and *Grettissaga*: the distance to the monster's lair and the description of the lair itself. She considers the possible relationship between these two medieval texts in the light of the provable relationship between two modern texts, D.H. Lawrence's story 'The Woman Who Rode Away' and Idella Purnell's novel *The Forbidden City*, and argues that the relationship between *Beowulf* and *Grettissaga* must

remain an open question. Kathleen Forni examines 'Graham Baker's Beowulf:
Intersections Between High and Low Culture' (*LFQ* 35[2007] 244–9), with a
particular interest in exploring 'how high art is made accessible and appealing
to a mass audience' (p. 244). Forni contends that 'although radically
transformed, the film nonetheless shares some thematic subtexts with the
original poem—most importantly, the equation of familial and communal
dysfunction and the suggestion that domestic discord poses a fundamental
threat to stable community' (p. 244).

Robin Norris's welcome new study of 'Mourning Rights: *Beowulf, the Iliad,*
and the War in Iraq' (*JNT* 37[2007] 276–95), brings together modern critical
theory, classical and Anglo-Saxon literature, politics and current events to
illuminate the myriad ways in which heroic poetry gives readers, both modern
and medieval, a means to process and to mourn the magnitude of the loss
of human life entailed in war. Norris reflects briefly on the psychological
processes of mourning as discussed in contemporary critical theory, and then
considers the final scenes of mourning in *Beowulf* alongside one modern
example of female mourning—Cindy Sheehan's response to losing her son
Casey in the war in Iraq. Manfred Malzahn writes on '*Beowulf* in Arabia:
Teaching Heroic Poetry in a Post-Heroic Age' (in Sauer and Bauer, eds.,
pp. 1–15). Malzahn contends that Anglo-Saxon and classical Arabic literature
can be productively studied and taught comparatively, and that 'works such as
Beowulf should be seen as having their rightful place in English curricula
especially in Arab countries, where the discussion of Old English literature
can be integrated very well into a contemporary cultural debate' (p. 1).

Seamus Heaney's 1999 translation of *Beowulf* continues to inspire critical
responses. Alison Finlay's 'Putting a Bawn into *Beowulf*' (in Crowder and
Hall, eds., *Seamus Heaney: Poet, Critic, Translator*, pp. 136–54), examines
how Heaney's personal history, academic experience, poetic habits, and
linguistic heritage, particularly the Scots-derived Irish dialect of his childhood,
inflect his *Beowulf* translation. Finlay explores words and phrases in Heaney's
Beowulf that resonate with the dialectal distinctness of his own Northern
Irish milieu, and concludes that 'Heaney's reduction of the particularities of
Germanic heroic culture shows his determination to find in this alien and
forgotten world the universal elements that will resonate in a modern,
mechanized, literate culture as well as reflecting the specifics of his individual
background' (p. 152). The second chapter of John D. Niles's volume, *Old
English Heroic Poems and the Social Life of Texts*, focuses on 'Heaney's
Beowulf Six Years Later'. Niles reviews critical responses to Heaney's
translation, with particular attention to Heaney's 'credentials' for taking on
such a momentous translation. Niles concludes that, at the time Heaney
undertook this project, he was one of the best-equipped writers for the task,
and that the question worth asking is not whether the translation is true to the
original poem, but 'is it true to human experience, and is it true to its own
mode of being as a lavish fiction set in the antique past?' (p. 352).

The enigmatic character names in *Beowulf* continue to intrigue scholars.
Gale R. Owen-Crocker writes on 'Beast Men: Eofor and Wulf and the Mythic
Significance of Names in *Beowulf*' (in Glosecki, ed., pp. 257–80). By exploring
the rich associations of these figures in Norse legend, poetry, and place-names,

Owen-Crocker seeks to show that, when viewed in their literary contexts, 'the figures of Beowulf... and to an even greater extent Wulf and Eofor, are men not beasts... [and are] inspired by ideals which are the products of human intellectual and emotional development, not animal instinct' (p. 277). Stefan Jurasinski considers 'The Feminine Name *Wealhtheow* and the Problem of *Beowulf*ian anthroponymy' (*Neophil* 91[2007] 701–15). Jurasinski contends that the different interpretations ascribed to the name *Wealhtheow* all begin from the shared assumption that names were in fact meaningful in the era *Beowulf* describes, and that Wealhtheow's name thus provides a clue to her personal history. By careful examination of both literary and onomastic scholarship regarding the meanings of names in early medieval literature and culture, Jurasinski seeks to show that Wealhtheow is not a dithematic name like Ælfgifu or Hildeburh and that no meaning can be construed correctly for it.

Analogues and parallels to *Beowulf* continue to generate new scholarship. Thomas D. Hill investigates 'Beowulf's Roman Rites: Roman Ritual and Germanic Tradition' (*JEGP* 106[2007] 325–35). Hill begins by reviewing the well-known similarities between Beowulf's funeral and the account of the funeral of Attila the Hun preserved in Jordanes' *Getica*, and subsequently observes that the funeral of Beowulf accords even more closely with the tradition of Roman military/imperial funerals than Attila's does. Hill provides three possible reasons for these textual parallels between Roman and Germanic military funerary rites: continuity of tradition between the late Roman and early Germanic world; the transmission of historical information about the Roman world to Anglo-Saxon poets through oral, written, or visual sources (for example Roman or Romano-British sarcophagi); or that the funerary rites given to both Attila and Beowulf were not originally Roman but rather Germanic rituals that were assimilated into Roman military practice. Hagop Gulludjian writes 'On Armenian Parallels to *Beowulf*' (*Journal of the Society for Armenian Studies* 16[2007] 73–87), with particular attention to similarities between *Beowulf* and the *Sasma Dzrer* epic cycle, an originally oral composition that has survived in oral form to the present day.

The complex relationships between *Beowulf* and Old Norse literature continue to inspire new scholarship. Geoffrey Russom looks 'At the Center of *Beowulf*' (in Glosecki, ed., pp. 225–40), and finds that the overall structure of *Beowulf* corresponds very closely with the structure of Norse mythic history. Both Norse myth and *Beowulf*, Russom contends, centre on a long-lasting feud with otherworldly creatures who threaten human society. In Russom's reading, Grendel's mother serves to create a narrative structure that is intended to underscore the terrible persistence of feud. This same collection of essays features John M. Hill's 'Gods at the Borders: Northern Myth and Anglo-Saxon Heroic Story' (pp. 241–56), in which Hill 'dwell[s] on the reflexes of old legend in Anglo-Saxon poetry and story, especially the survival of [the Norse war-god] Tyr's attributes and functions in the actions and status of the Germanic hero' (p. 241).

ANQ 20:iii[2007] is a '*Beowulf* Theme Issue', and contains modern English translations of Old and modern Icelandic analogues to *Beowulf*, with a focus on legends of the Skjöldung (Scylding) dynasty. Part I, 'Fragments of

Danish History' (*ANQ* 20:iii[2007] 3–33), presents the first continuous and complete translation of the initial Skjöldungr portion of Arngrímur Jónsson's *Rerum Danicarum Fragmenta* [1596], based on a now lost manuscript of *Skjöldunga saga*, an Old Icelandic saga about the Scylding kings. The translation has been prepared by Clarence H. Miller and is accompanied by an introduction by Paul Acker and notes by Bjarni Guðnason (translated by Sif Rikhardsdóttir). Part II, 'Beyond the Mere: Other Versions of Beowulfian Stories' (*ANQ* 20:iii[2007] 33–77), is devoted to Icelandic texts, both modern and medieval, that have not previously been widely available in English or that have not been gathered in this 'Skjöldung' context. A brief introduction to these texts has been prepared by Marijane Osborn.

Cruces in *Beowulf* continue to provide material for new studies. Oren Falk offers an important new reading of 'Beowulf's Longest Day: The Amphibious Hero in his Element (*Beowulf*, ll. 1495b-96)' (*JEGP* 106[2007] 1–21). Falk revisits the difficult question of how Beowulf is able to remain under water for *hwil dæges* 'the space of a day', and precisely what site is denominated by the term *grundwong*. By examining the nineteen different occurrences of the term *grund* throughout the poem, Falk seeks to show that lines 1495b–96 are correctly rendered as follows: 'Then it was the space of a day before he [Beowulf] might look on dry land'. Falk concludes that the poet's intention in these lines is to highlight Beowulf's longed-for return to the *grundwong*, the realm proper to humankind, as opposed to his immersion in the water-laden *mere*, the realm of monstrous life.

J.R. Hall studies '*Beowulf* 2009a: *f ... bifongen*' (*JEGP* [2007] 417–27), in order to shed light on the unreadable word in line 2009a that Beowulf uses to characterize Grendel's race. Hall reviews possible emendations for line 2009a, proposes the restoration *fære* as the most sensible solution, and concludes that this half-line is correctly understood as *fære befongen* 'entrapped in terror'. Alexander Bruce considers '*Beowulf* 1366a: *Fyr on flode* as the *Aurora Borealis*?' (*Archiv* 159[2007] 105–9). Bruce examines the description of Grendel's mere in lines 1357b–1366a, and suggests that the image of a *fyr on flode* may refer not only to a Christian depiction of Hell but also to the Northern Lights, and that this may be a moment in *Beowulf* when the poet has incorporated both pagan and Christian images. Jane Roberts writes on 'Understanding Hrothgar's Humiliation: *Beowulf* Lines 144–74 in Context' (in Minnis and Roberts, eds., pp. 355–67), and sheds new light on the difficult *gifstol* passage and on Hrothgar's humiliation.

As in past years, Alfred Bammesberger offers a number of short essays that help to illuminate difficult lines and phrases. In 'Grendel Enters Heorot' (*N&Q* 54[2007] 119–20), Bammesberger examines *Beowulf*, lines 721b–724a, in which Grendel touches, and easily swings open, the door to Heorot. Bammesberger argues that *muþan* in line 724a ought to be understood as a dative of place and that lines 721b–724a are correctly translated as 'The door strong with bars forged by fire opened immediately when he touched it with his hands; intent on evil, enraged as he was, he started up (= charged forth) at the entrance to the hall' (p. 120). In 'A Note on *Beowulf*, Lines 642–51a' (*N&Q* 54[2007] 359–61), Bammesberger seeks to show that the personal pronoun *hie* in line 648a refers to both Beowulf and Grendel. Bammesberger also investigates

'*Ealond Utan* at *Beowulf*, Line 2334a' (*N&Q* 54[2007] 361–4), and suggests that the phrase originally read *innan ond utan*, and that the actual reading of *eal ond utan* may be due to eye-skip. In Bammesberger's view, lines 2333–2335a are correctly translated as 'The fire-dragon had destroyed the people's stronghold, this fortress with flames from within and from without (= completely)' (p. 364). Chapter 2 in John William Sutton's *Death and Violence in Old and Middle English Literature* discusses *Beowulf* and *Judith*, and is reviewed in **section 4** of this chapter.

9. Other Poems

Chris Altman's 'Making Use of the Terrain: Byrhtnoð's Strategy in "The Battle of Maldon"' (*ANQ* 20[2007] 3–8) investigates *The Battle of Maldon* as an account of an actual historical battle, and seeks to show how Byrhtnoð employed the topographical setting of the causeway to maximize Viking enemy casualties, even as his plans ultimately went awry. Chapter 1 of Sutton, *Death and Violence in Old and Middle English Literature*, reviewed in **section 4** of this chapter, discusses *The Battle of Maldon*. Richard North's 'Old English Minor Heroic Poems' (in North and Allard, eds., pp. 95–129), contains an introduction to both *Waldere* and the Finnsburg Fragment.

Kazutomo Karasawa provides 'A Note on the Old English Poem *Menologium* 3b *On þy Eahteoðan Dæg*' (*N&Q* 54[2007] 211–15). Karasawa begins from the observation that the *Menologium*-poet typically omits the start day when calculating the number of days between two feasts, and that one would thus expect the poet to give seven rather than eight as the number of days between Christmas (25 December) and the Circumcision (1 January). The fact that the poet calculates the Circumcision as having taken place *on þy eahteoðan dæg* has perplexed many scholars and even led some to think that the poet viewed the Nativity as taking place on 24 December. Karasawa contends that the phrase *on þy eahteoðan dæg* is a set phrase used for the Circumcision and that in this instance the poet adopted the conventional phrase rather than following his own way of calculating the number of days between feasts.

The *Anglo-Saxon Chronicle* poems continue to generate a small but noteworthy amount of scholarship. Jayne Carroll focuses on '*Engla Waldend, Rex Admirabilis*: Poetic Representations of King Edgar' (*RES* 58[2007] 113–32). Carroll reads the vernacular versions of *The Coronation of Edgar* and *The Death of Edgar*, found in manuscripts ABC of the *Chronicle*, alongside Æthelweard's Latin adaptations of these poems, and concludes that the English and Latin verses present very different constructions of Edgar, each tailored to serve a particular context. Thomas A. Bredehoft sheds light on 'OE *Yðhengest* and an Unrecognized Passage of Old English Verse' (*N&Q* 54[2007] 120–2). He points out that Old English *yðhengestas* is a *hapax legomenon* occurring only in *Anglo-Saxon Chronicle* annal 1003, and that this rare poetic word is correctly understood as a kenning for 'ships'. Bredehoft argues that when this poetic word is considered in conjunction with the *Chronicle* writer's employment of alliterative patterns, as well as parallels to other annals such as 1011CDE, it creates a strong case for reading the entire final section of annal 1003 as an instance of late Old English verse. Sara Pons-Sanz's study of Wulfstan and *Chronicle* poetry is reviewed in section 10 below.

Allen J. Frantzen and John Hines, eds., *Cædmon's Hymn and Material Culture in the World of Bede*, contains six essays that will enrich our understanding of Cædmon's *Hymn* and its social and cultural contexts. Daniel P. O'Donnell focuses on 'Material Differences: The Place of Cædmon's Hymn in the History of Vernacular Poetry' (pp. 15–50). By examining analogues to Bede's account of Cædmon, O'Donnell makes the case that Cædmon was in fact a very traditional poet, valued mainly for his formal skill. Scott DeGregorio turns to 'Literary Contexts: Cædmon's Hymn as a Center of Bede's World' (pp. 51–79), and contextualizes the *Hymn* in the light of Bede's exegetical writing and views on monastic reform. Faith Wallis's essay, 'Cædmon's Created World and the Monastic Encyclopedia' (pp. 80–110), takes the history of early medieval science as a context for understanding the *Hymn* and its account of Creation, and argues for Bede's indebtedness to architectural metaphors and the encyclopedia of monastic scriptural allusions. Allen J. Frantzen writes on 'All Created Things: Material Contexts for the Story of Cædmon' (pp. 111–49), with a focus on understanding Bede's miracles in relation to the material contexts and everyday objects found in Book 4 of Bede's *Ecclesiastical History of the English People*. Christopher Loveluck's 'Cædmon's World: Secular and Monastic Lifestyles and Estate Organization in Northern England, A.D. 650–900' (pp. 150–90), situates Bede's narrative and the *Hymn* within archaeological contexts, and in so doing troubles any clear distinction between secular and monastic contexts. 'Changes and Exchanges in Bede's and Cædmon's World' (pp. 191–220), is the subject of John Hines's fine interdisciplinary study, which concludes the volume. For an introduction to Cædmon's *Hymn* and its various contexts, see Brian Weston Wyly, 'Cædmon the Cowherd and Old English Biblical Verse' (in North and Allard, eds., pp. 189–218).

Two essays this year shed light on the Old English metrical charms. Stephen O. Glosecki writes on 'Stranded Narrative: Myth, Metaphor, and the Metrical Charm' (in Glosecki, ed., pp. 47–70). Glosecki begins from the premise that mythic approaches to literature tend to focus on larger narrative forms, often overlooking texts such as charms, recipes and ritual prescriptions. Glosecki argues that 'myth is somehow more elemental than what we usually think of as a story' (p. 50), and he provides examples from charms such as the *Æcerbot* charm, *The Nine Herbs Charm*, *Wið Færstice* and *Wið Dweorh*. Marie Nelson and Caroline Dennis write on 'The Nine Herbs Charm' (*GNR* 38[2007] 5–10), with particular attention to understanding the charm's directions for assuming power. They note the personification of the herbs that appear in the charm, and explore how the charm 'call[s] upon a sense of the power that lies in the language of men of the church' (p. 9).

Anglo-Latin poetry continues to inspire exciting new work. Emily V. Thornbury sheds welcome light on 'Aldhelm's Rejection of the Muses and the Mechanics of Poetic Inspiration in Early Anglo-Saxon England' (*ASE* 36[2007] 71–92). Thornbury points out that, in the metrical preface to his *Enigmata*, Aldhelm briefly invokes the Muses and then rejects them, subsequently declaring David and Moses as models for his own poetic song. By tracing the 'rejection of the Muses' topos in Christian Latin poetry, and its roots in ancient literary thought, Thornbury seeks to show that Aldhelm's *Enigmata* draws upon a native Germanic tradition of poetry that valued technical skill over lofty subject matter. She concludes that, by portraying the Muses as useless rather than dangerous figures, Aldhelm enabled his literary successors to employ the Muses, and other classical allusions, as harmless decorative elements in their work.

'Book-Worm or Entomologist? Aldhelm's *Enigma* XXXVI', by Helen Foxhall Forbes (*Peritia* 19[2005] 20–9), not previously reviewed in *YWES*, examines possible natural and textual sources for this riddle, whose solution is *scnifes*, a small variety of fly, and argues in favour of the influence of book-learning. Filippa Alcamesi's 'The *Sibylline Acrostic* in Anglo-Saxon Manuscripts: The Augustinian Text and the Other Versions' (in Bremmer and Dekker, eds., pp. 147–73) notes the striking English interest in this originally Greek text on Christ's second coming: four different versions of it survive in a total of six Anglo-Saxon manuscripts. Alcamesi compares the versions to show that they indicate two lines of transmission of the Augustinian version, both of which were available in Canterbury from the ninth century. Patrizia Lendinara publishes two essays on *De die iudicii* this year. In 'The *Versus de die iudicii*: Its Circulation and Use as a School Text in Late Anglo-Saxon England' (in Bremmer and Dekker, eds., pp. 175–212), she analyses the evidence for the manuscript transmission of this text on good conduct and penitence, and argues from this and from the textual layout that it was used in schoolroom contexts in late Anglo-Saxon England. Appendices give details of all the relevant manuscripts. [MS]

Lendinara's second essay on this text is 'Translating Doomsday: *De die iudicii* and its Old English Translation (*Judgment Day II*)' (in Sauer and Bauer, eds., pp. 17–67). By exploring differences between *De die iudicii* and *Judgment Day II*, Lendinara seeks to show that, while *Judgment Day II* is a fairly literal translation, it nevertheless makes room for imaginative variations.

Roberta Frank writes on 'The Lay of the Land in Skaldic Praise Poetry' (in Glosecki, ed., pp. 175–96). Frank's detailed study of the complex relations among female sexuality, violence and political conquest as depicted in the verse of Norse court poets sheds light on a range of topics, including sacral kingship, marriage, eroticism, and the problematics of relating poetry and culture, and will interest many scholars of early medieval poetry.

10. Prose

Schoolroom texts of all kinds are growing in popularity amongst scholars, and new work on them fits well with the continuing stream of interest in glossing. Three of the essays in Bremmer and Dekker, eds., *Foundations of Learning*, offer new studies of Anglo-Saxon glossaries and glossing. Loredana Lazzari explores 'Isidore's *Etymologiae* in Anglo-Saxon Glossaries' (pp. 63–93), and concludes that the *Etymologiae's* influence is stronger than previously assumed, and that it increases in the tenth and eleventh centuries, partly as a result of the Latin scholarship of the Benedictine reform. Claudia Di Sciacca's 'The Manuscript Tradition, Presentation and Glossing of Isidore's *Synonyma* in Anglo-Saxon England: The Case of CCCC 448, Harley 110 and Cotton Tiberius A. iii' (pp. 95–124) assesses whether the *Synonyma* were used in Anglo-Saxon schoolrooms. The first two manuscripts under examination contain copies of the text glossed in Old English, and Tiberius A. iii includes a vernacular epitome of it. Di Sciacca's analysis of Tiberius A. iii strengthens the case for associating this manuscript with the writer Ælfric Bata, and she shows how central the *Synonyma* were to the Benedictine Reform movement. In 'The Canterbury Psalter's Alphabet Glosses: Eclectic but Incompetent' (pp. 213–51), Alan Griffiths focuses on the Vespasian Psalter (or 'Canterbury Psalter', as he prefers to call it) and argues that many of its glosses which have usually been seen as idiosyncratic have their roots in Hebrew traditions. Tables summarize aspects of the manuscript contents.

In addition, Joseph P. McGowan writes 'On the "Red" Blickling Psalter Glosses' (*N&Q* 54[2007] 205–7). These late eighth- or early ninth-century glosses to MS New York, Morgan Library M.776 have been edited and corrected on several occasions, and McGowan offers further corrections to two of the readings in the most recent edition. Hans Sauer looks at 'Old English Words for People in the *Épinal-Erfurt Glossary*' (in Sauer and Bauer, eds., pp. 119–81), with particular reference to their etymology, morphology and meaning, to argue that they show 'a rich internal structure and subdivision' (p. 162).

Peter A. Stokes offers a study of part of an eleventh-century Psalter manuscript in 'The Regius Psalter, Folio 198^v: A Reexamination' (*N&Q* 54[2007] 208–11). The folio in question is the final leaf of the manuscript, and contains two short additions. Stokes proposes a new interpretation of parts of the additions, puts forward palaeographic and textual evidence which links the additions and a third Old English note on the same folio to Christ Church, Canterbury, and to the first half of the eleventh century, and raises the question of whether the additions are connected with the drafting of the charter S.1471 from Christ Church.

László Sándor Chardonnens publishes two works on prognostics this year. 'Context, Language, Date and Origin of Anglo-Saxon Prognostics' (in Bremmer and Dekker, eds., pp. 317–40) provides an overview of the transmission of these texts in later Anglo-Saxon England, emphasizes the importance of studying them in their manuscript contexts, and offers a model for the manuscript-focused analysis of other 'peripheral texts' (p. 317). An appendix sets out a list of the texts in their manuscripts. Chardonnens' second publication on this topic is *Anglo-Saxon Prognostics, 900–1100: Study and Texts*, a monograph based on his doctoral thesis. The book divides into two parts: the first provides a thorough analysis of the prognostics, with a particular focus on the manuscripts in which they are recorded and their late Anglo-Saxon contexts and uses. The second offers editions of the texts. Appendices include a handlist of prognostics in ninth- to twelfth-century English manuscripts and a concordance to them.

Further essays in Bremmer and Dekker, eds., *Foundations of Learning*, expand our understanding of schoolroom texts. Kees Dekker examines

'Anglo-Saxon Encyclopaedic Notes: Tradition and Function' (pp. 279–315). Dekker identifies these notes as part of a group of texts which occur, in English and in Latin, in several Anglo-Saxon manuscripts. He edits the notes from manuscript CCCC 183, with translation and commentary, and then explores the manuscript context, genre and function of the notes as they transmit through the period and as their role changes from 'a hermeneutical to a heuristic tool' (p. 280) which also served 'a hermeneutical purpose by pointing the reader to a Christian world view' (p. 313). Concetta Giliberto looks at a tradition which entered England via the Canterbury school of Theodore—'Stone Lore in Miscellany Manuscripts: The Old English Lapidary' (pp. 253–78)—with particular reference to the codicological context of Tiberius A. iii, the sole surviving copy of this text. Giliberto provides an edition and translation of the text, and concludes that it was used in monastic schoolrooms. Rauer's study in the same collection of the Old English Martyrology is reviewed below. For other essays in the collection, including two on poetic schoolroom texts, see sections 3 and 9 of this chapter.

Rebecca Stephenson has been 'Reading Byrhtferth's Muses: Emending Section Breaks in Byrhtferth's "Hermeneutic English"' (*N&Q* 54[2007] 19–22). The passage in question includes words taken from Aldhelm glosses, and its inclusion in the *Enchiridion* has been the subject of much scholarly puzzlement. Stephenson identifies a problem with its position in the most recent edition of the text, and proposes that it should be seen not as forming the end of a chapter, but instead as opening a discussion on the divine inspiration of poetry.

In 'The *Revelationes* of Pseudo-Methodius and Scriptural Study at Salisbury in the Eleventh Century' (in Wright, Biggs and Hall, eds., pp. 371–86) Michael W. Twomey opens up the study of late Anglo-Saxon use of this anti-Islamic text, surveys a range of evidence for its availability in England from the later Anglo-Saxon period, and shows its influence on the study of biblical history. Several of the essays in Lendinara, Lazzari and D'Aronco, eds., *Form and Content of Instruction in Anglo-Saxon England*, deal with Anglo-Latin and Old English prose schoolroom texts. The whole collection is reviewed in section 3 above.

Bede studies continue apace, and this year include two essays in Minnis and Roberts, eds., *Text, Image, Interpretation*. Jennifer O'Reilly's 'Bede on Seeing the God of Gods in Zion' (pp. 3–29) refers to Numbers 33.1–49 and to *De mansionibus filiorum Israel*; a letter Bede wrote in response to a query from Acca, bishop of Hexham, about the Israelites' journey to the Promised Land. O'Reilly shows how Bede constructs a highly complex interpretation, drawing on specific traditions and textual references. George Hardin Brown examines 'Bede's Style in his Commentary *On I Samuel*' (pp. 233–51), and maps out the use of a range of styles in this single work which are 'all representative of Bede's mature and later exegesis in their complexity and sophistication' (p. 246). The appendix to Brown's article gives a translation of extracts from the commentary.

Tristan Major proposes '1 Corinthians 15:52 as a Source for the Old English Version of Bede's Simile of the Sparrow' (*N&Q* 54[2007] 11–16) and makes a case for the translator's alterations to the Latin *Historia Ecclesiastica* being driven by a desire for a readable English style, and for the fact that 'Through this biblical allusion, the Old English translator has heightened the craft of the simile beyond the original intentions of Bede' (p. 16). Wright, Biggs and Hall, eds., *Source of Wisdom*, also includes a study of Bede. Danuta Shanzer writes on 'Bede's Style: A Neglected Historiographical Model for the Style of the *Historia Ecclesiastica*?' (pp. 329–52). Via a close examination of the nature of the style of the *Historia Ecclesiastica*, Shanzer makes a case for the influence of Orosius and of Rufinus.

Bede features centrally in Emily V. Thornbury's ' "Ða Gregorius gamenode mid his wordum": Old English Versions of Gregory's Bilingual Puns' (*LeedsSE* 38[2007] 17–30), a study of the accounts of Gregory's encounter with the Anglian slave-boys in the Old English *Historia Ecclesiastica*, Ælfric's retelling of the story, and other Old English texts which exploit the range of associations of *dēore/Dēre/de ira*. Thornbury explores the strategies used by writers of Old English, and by the author of the Middle English *South English Legendary*, to present the bilingual wordplay of the exchange.

Alfredian prose has generated plenty of new scholarship too. In an article not previously reviewed in *YWES*, Bryan Carella investigates 'The source of the Prologue to the Laws of Alfred' (*Peritia* 19[2005] 91–118), and in particular those underlying the translation of Exodus which precedes the lawcode. Carella re-evaluates differing scholarly views, and concludes that it is reasonable to assume that Alfred knew the *Liber ex lege Moysi*.

Malcolm Godden throws into question the very category of Alfredian prose as he asks 'Did King Alfred Write Anything?' (*MÆ* 76[2007] 1–23). He concludes—after examining the internal evidence for Alfred's personal production of the translations attributed to him, and noting both the prevalence of texts written in the voice of another person and the clear critique of kingship in the English additions to the translation of the *Consolation of Philosophy*—that the answer is 'No', and that the Preface and main text of the *Pastoral Care* were issued with Alfred's authorization; the Old English *Consolation and Soliloquies* had no direct connection with him; the lawcode was written by others in the king's name; and that there is no evidence for authorship of the Old English Psalms. On the way to these conclusions, Godden suggests that Æthelweard's *Chronicon*, even if composed in English by its named author, was translated into its current Latin form by a cleric. David Pratt, too, is preoccupied by 'Problems of Authorship and Audience in the Writings of King Alfred the Great' (in Wormald and Nelson, eds., pp. 162–91), and also offers an assessment of the likelihood of a single authorial identity behind the texts principally associated with Alfred. His conclusion is that Alfred is strongly identified and identifiable as the texts' author.

Antonina Harbus investigates 'Metaphors of Authority in Alfred's Prefaces' (*Neophil* 91[2007] 717–27). Whether or not the reader, in the light of Godden's argument, accepts Harbus's assumption that Alfred did compose the Prefaces to the Old English translations in question, her study of the ways in which they present secular, textual authority is revealing of the implications of the association of wisdom and physical strength and of the role constructed for Alfred in the Prefaces, which combine to 'package his texts as securely authorised transmissions rather than as the textual adaptations they seem to us to be' (p. 726).

'God's Co-Workers and Powerful Tools: A Study of the Sources of Alfred's Building Metaphor in his Old English Translation of Augustine's *Soliloquies*', by Valerie Heuchan (*N&Q* 54[2007] 1–11), focuses on this distinctive Anglo-Saxon addition to the *Soliloquies* and proposes that its sources include 1 Corinthians 3.9–14 and also a more extensive portion of Aldhelm's *De Virginitate* than had been suspected. The potential English connections of manuscript Vatican City, Biblioteca Apostolica, MS lat. 3363, are further examined in Andrew Breeze's 'The Old Cornish Gloss on Boethius' (*N&Q* 54[2007] 367–8). The Cornish gloss *ud rocashaas* to *peorsa* ('loathing') in this manuscript was brought to Anglo-Saxonists' attention by the work of the UK Arts and Humanities Research Council-funded Alfredian *Boethius* project, co-directed by Malcolm Godden and Susan Irvine. Breeze translates it as 'she hated the land', suggests that it might have been written in the manuscript by a Cornish scribe at Alfred's court, and reminds us of his earlier suggestion that such a person might also have produced the Old English Orosius. Joseph Wittig offers further work on 'The "Remigian" Glosses on Boethius's *Consolatio Philosophiae* in Context' (in Wright, Biggs and Hall, eds., pp. 168–200), a topic of interest to students of the Old English *Consolation* and of the transmission of gloss and commentary traditions into England, in the form of an overview of the glosses in question and a questioning of the ascription of the commentary tradition from which they stem to Remigius of Auxerre. Specific examples from the manuscript tradition are summarized and a selection of glosses examined in some detail, and Wittig concludes that the glosses indicate 'much active involvement with Boethius's text, by many individuals, in many centres of learning' (p. 183). An appendix to the essay lists additions and corrections to Courcelle's 1967 list of manuscripts containing all or some of the 'Remigian' commentary.

Two of the essays in Healey and Kiernan, eds., *Making Sense*, stem from the current large-scale projects on the Alfredian *Consolation*. Kevin Kiernan describes the process of 'Remodeling Alfred's *Boethius* with the *tol ond andweorc* of Edition Production Technology (EPT)' (pp. 72–115) from the unique manuscript version of the Old English prose and verse *Consolation* in MS British Library, Cotton Otho A. vi, for the *Electronic Boethius* project, and concludes by suggesting that the all-prose version of the Old English *Consolation* in Oxford, Bodleian Library, Bodley 180 is 'a post-Alfredian creation of an all-prose version, made by scholars in Anglo-Saxon times who simply wanted a better text for philosophical inquiry than the Old English verses supplied' (p. 115). Malcolm Godden's 'King Alfred and the *Boethius* Industry' (pp. 116–38) discusses the industry in question from the ninth to eleventh and from the nineteenth to twentieth centuries from the perspective of Godden's own co-direction of the Alfredian *Boethius* project. Godden situates the Alfredian *Consolation* as the starting-point for a tradition of English work on the text, and characterizes this Old English prose translation as a move to make the text's ideas more widely available, and the Old English verse version as 'something quite different, a literary imitation of the Latin text in English' (p. 138).

Philip Edward Phillips's 'King Alfred the Great and the Victorian Translations of his Anglo-Saxon *Boethius*' (in Kaylor and Nokes, eds., pp. 155–73), discusses nineteenth-century translations of the Old English Boethius (both prose and metrical versions), and considers these texts as 'part of the Alfred mania that swept the mid- to late nineteenth century' (p. 171). [SK]

Two further essays in Wright, Biggs and Hall, eds., *Source of Wisdom*, focus on Alfredian texts. Paul E. Szarmach examines 'Alfred's Nero' (pp. 147–67), as presented in the Old English *Consolation*, and shows how this translation is informed by the commentary tradition. David F. Johnson asks 'Why Ditch the *Dialogues*? Reclaiming an Invisible Text' (pp. 201–16). Opening by quantifying and lamenting the scholarly neglect of the Old English *Dialogues*, Johnson contextualizes this in questions of canon formation and orthodoxy and notions of 'literary worth' and the lack of a suitable edition.

There is some new work this year, also, on political and administrative prose texts. Julian Harrison considers 'William Camden and the F-Text of the *Anglo-Saxon Chronicle*' (*N&Q* 54[2007] 222–4) and adds to Peter Lucas's earlier study (see *YWES* 82[2003] 20) by arguing strongly for Camden having owned the A-text and several other parts of manuscript Cotton Domition A. viii. Scott Thompson Smith's 'Of Kings and Cattle Thieves: The Rhetorical Work of the Fonthill Letter' (*JEGP* 106[2007] 447–67) takes a literary approach to this important tenth-century document to show how it deploys the figure of Alfred to underscore the legitimacy of the West Saxon royal house.

Ecclesiastical genres are the focus, as usual, of many individual essays. 'Usage of the *Old English Martyrology*', by Christine Rauer (in Bremmer and Dekker, eds., pp. 125–46), assesses the likelihood of this text having a role in ceremonial liturgical observances. Rauer notes its similarities with the liturgical calendar in terms of its non-hagiographical content, examines the use of the *Martyrology* by late Anglo-Saxon homilists, and concludes that it 'combines the characteristics of a martyrology, calendar, legendary, homiliary and encyclopedia' (p. 144). An appendix lists manuscripts of the *Martyrology*.

Allen J. Frantzen's online electronic edition of the Anglo-Saxon penitentials is now available at http://www.anglo-saxon.net/ It is a treasure-trove of materials for research and teaching, with editions and translations of all surviving texts and contextual discussions of the manuscripts and the history of penance, a 'cultural index' to the topics in the penitentials, and an unpublished essay by Frantzen, 'The "Literariness" of the Penitentials', and a bibliography. Frantzen draws on his work on the electronic edition to publish another article on penitentials this year: 'Sin and Sense: Editing and Translating Anglo-Saxon Handbooks of Penance' (in Healey and Kiernan, eds., pp. 40–71), which focuses on the issue of translation, both in the production of the Anglo-Saxon texts and in subsequent scholarly presentations of them.

The study of Anglo-Saxon homiletics has been gathering momentum for many years. A major new collection of work is produced this year by Aaron J. Kleist, whose *The Old English Homily: Precedent, Practice, and Appropriation* reflects the vibrancy and breadth of this field of study and serves as a good benchmark of how far it has come, and as a prompt to new directions.

The collection is divided into two parts. The first, 'Precedent', focuses on sources and influences and the Anglo-Latin tradition, and is made up of 'Old English Homilies and Latin Sources', by Charles D. Wright; 'Ælfric's Manuscript of Paul the Deacon's Homiliary', by Joyce Hill; 'The Carolingian *De festiuitatibus* and the Blickling Book', by Nancy Thompson; 'The Old Testament Homily: Ælfric as Biblical Translator', by Rachel Anderson; 'The Liturgical Context of Ælfric's Homilies for Rogation', by Stephen J. Harris; 'Reading the Style and Rhetoric of the Vercelli Homilies', by Samantha Zacher; 'The Codicology of Anglo-Saxon Homiletic Manuscripts, Especially the Blickling Homilies', by M.J. Toswell; 'Latin Sermons for Saints in Early English Homiliaries and Legendaries', by Thomas N. Hall; 'Homiletic Contexts for Ælfric's Hagiography: The Legend of Saints Cecilia and Valerian', by Robert K. Upchurch; 'Ælfric's or Not? The Making of a *Temporale* Collection in Late Anglo-Saxon England', by Loredana Teresi; and 'Wulfstan as Reader, Writer, and Rewriter', by Andy Orchard. The second part, 'Appropriation', tracks homiletic production and the reuse of homiletic material from the late Anglo-Saxon to Tudor periods. It consists of 'Old Wine in a New Bottle: Recycled Instructional Materials in *Seasons for Fasting*', by Mary P. Richards; 'The Circulation of the Old English Homily in the Twelfth Century: New Evidence from Oxford, Bodleian Library, MS Bodley 343', by Aidan Conti; 'Preaching Past the Conquest: Lambeth Palace 487 and Cotton Vespasian A. xxii', by Mary Swan; 'Anglo-Saxon Homilies in their Scandinavian Context', by Christopher Abram; and 'Anglo-Saxon Homiliaries in Tudor and Stuart England', by Aaron J Kleist. An appendix summarizes the contents of Anglo-Saxon homiliaries as identified by N.R. Ker in his *Catalogue of Manuscripts Containing Anglo-Saxon*, and an index enables searching by theme, text, genre and manuscript, amongst other possibilities.

Charles D. Wright publishes more work on homiletic prose this year, in the form of 'A New Latin Source for Two Old English Homilies (Fadda I and Blickling I): Pseudo-Augustine, *Sermo* App. 125, and the Ideology of Chastity in the Anglo-Saxon Benedictine Reform' (in Wright, Biggs and Hall, eds., pp. 239–65). As well as a very welcome addition to the corpus of Latin sources for Old English homilies, Wright offers an acutely perceptive analysis of the implications of vocabulary choice for ideological affiliation, and a persuasive argument that, of the cases under scrutiny, Fadda I aligns itself with the sorts of Benedictine Reform-affiliated interpretations of chastity seen in the works of Ælfric and Wulfstan, whilst Blickling I does not.

Thomas N. Hall ponders a striking detail in a little-studied text in 'Christ's Birth through Mary's Right Breast: An Echo of Carolingian Heresy in the Old English *Adrian and Ritheus*' (in Wright, Biggs and Hall, eds., pp. 266–89). Hall identifies and discusses several examples of Carolingian assertions of a similar nature, all connected to debates about the virgin birth of Christ, and reminds us that 'even the most aberrant strains of early medieval religious thought tend to operate according to a sound and internally consistent logical economy' (p. 280).

New work on Ælfric this year spans a wide range, from blood to animals, and includes Robert K. Upchurch's very welcome edition of *Ælfric's Lives of the Virgin Spouses*, which opens up the study of the texts in question—the

Lives of Julian and Basilissa, Cecilia and Valerian, and Chrysanthus and
Daria—to students and more experienced scholars. Editions of the Old
English texts and their Latin sources are presented with modern English
parallel-text translations. Introductory material covers the Latin legends,
Anglo-Saxon treatments of them and Ælfric's versions, and the texts are
supported with a glossary.

Mary Clayton writes on 'Blood and the Soul in Ælfric' (*N&Q* 54[2007]
365–7), with reference to a range of Ælfrician texts, including his key
statement on these two concepts in his *Letter to Wulfgeat*, and also *Lives of
Saints* and *Catholic Homilies*, and makes a careful case for Ælfric interpreting
blood as the soul but not claiming that the one equals the other. Hans Sauer's
theme is 'Ælfric and Emotion' (*Poetica* 66[2006] 37–52), and he explores it
with reference to Ælfric's *Grammar* and its treatment of 'I love' and
interjections, and the descriptions of saints and their enemies in the *Lives
of Saints*.

Two essays in Wright, Biggs and Hall, eds., *Source of Wisdom*, treat
Ælfrician topics. E. Gordon Whatley's 'Hagiography and Violence: Military
Men in Ælfric's *Lives of Saints*' (pp. 217–38) notes the good number of
examples of soldier-characters in the *Lives*, examines Ælfric's attitude to the
question of whether monks should be exempt from military service, and
suggests that Ælfric's depiction of war 'embodies an Augustinian ideal of
dispassionate warfare and rulership' (p. 229). James W. Earl's essay in this
collection—'Trinitarian Language: Augustine, *The Dream of the Rood*, and
Ælfric'—is reviewed in section 6 above.

Letty Nijhuis's ' "Sumum menn wile þincan syllic þis to gehyrenne": Ælfric
on Animals—his Sources and their Application' (in Cawsey and Harris, eds.,
Transmission and Transformation in the Middle Ages: Texts and Contexts,
pp. 65–76) shows that Ælfric conforms to a general pattern of use of animals
in homiletic and hagiographic compositions but also underlines his careful and
wide-ranging use of sources.

Sara Pons-Sanz publishes more work on Wulfstan this year, in the form of
'A Reconsideration of Wulfstan's Use of Norse-Derived Terms: The Case of
þræl' (*ES* 88:i[2007] 1–21). Through an overview of the chronology of the
works of Wulfstan which include Norse-derived terms, Ponz-Sanz shows that
Wulfstan is already making substantial use of Norse-derived terms before his
association with Cnut. She then turns to a detailed analysis of his use of *þræl*,
and argues that its selection is driven by a desire to stress the concept of
slavery, as opposed to the more generalized notion of service. Pons-Sanz's
second article on Wulfstan this year is 'A Paw in Every Pie: Wulfstan and the
Anglo-Saxon Chronicle Again' (*LeedsSE* 38[2007] 31–52); a re-examination
of the case for Wulfstan's authorship of the poems in annals 959 in the D- and
E- texts of the *Chronicle*. Pons-Sanz sets out a revised methodology for this
and proceeds to make a detailed analysis of expressions in the poems in
relationship to Wulfstan's known writings. As a result she is able to narrow
down the possible scenarios for the composition of the 959 poems to three:
that both are by Wulfstan; that only that in the D-version is by Wulfstan; that
both are by a composer very familiar with Wulfstan's lexical traits.

Melanie Heyworth reassesses Wulfstan's links with 'The "Late Old English Handbook for the Use of a Confessor": Authorship and Connections' (*N&Q* 54[2007] 219–22). The handbook in question is extant in different forms in a total of six manuscripts, three of which are identified as Wulfstan 'commonplace books'. Heyworth gives an overview of the ways in which the six handbook manuscripts connect to Wulfstan, either through Wulfstanian textual traditions or links to Worcester or sources. and concludes that 'It seems almost certain that Wulfstan himself read the "Handbook", and it appears likely that he annotated or edited it, whether or not he was its original composer' (p. 222). Renée R. Trilling relates 'Sovereignty and Social Order: Archbishop Wulfstan and the *Institutes of Polity*' (in Ott and Jones, eds., *The Bishop Reformed: Studies in Episcopal Power and Culture in the Central Middle Ages*, pp. 58–85) with particular reference to Wulfstan's reforming strategies as set out in the *Institutes*, where he positions the bishop as the key figure in the English state. Trilling concludes by noting the lack of transmission of Wulfstan's legislative stance into later medieval England, as seen in the continuing centrality of the king to lawgiving.

Another Wulfstan-related topic is addressed by Sarah Hamilton in 'The Anglo-Saxon and Frankish Evidence for Rites for Reconciliation of Excommunicants' (in Hartmann, ed., pp. 169–96). The Anglo-Saxon evidence is in the form of three manuscript copies of the English Rite: Cambridge, Corpus Christi College 265; London, British Library, Cotton Vespasian D. xv; and Oxford, Bodleian Library, Barlow 37. Using these, Hamilton examines the structure of the English as compared to the Frankish rite and notes that, although the earliest of the English manuscripts is from the third quarter of the eleventh century, the rite itself may have earlier origins, and that its lifespan is strikingly long, with a copy in the twelfth-century Canterbury/Exeter pontifical. She then turns to the question of Wulfstan's connection with it and, although firm conclusions cannot be reached, is able to supplement the case for his having invented it. Appendices to the article include an edition of all three versions of the English rite.

The study of post-Conquest transmission of Anglo-Saxon texts and traditions continues to gather momentum. E.G. Stanley scrutinizes 'Lambeth Homilies: Richard Morris's Emendations' (*N&Q* 54[2007] 224–31), drawing on a 1985 University of Oxford doctoral dissertation by Sarah M. O'Brien and commenting on both Morris's and O'Brien's editorial decisions in their work on Lambeth Palace MS 487. Two further essays in Wright, Biggs and Hall, eds., *Source of Wisdom*, treat post-Conquest Old English texts. Andrew Galloway's focus is 'The Peterborough Chronicle and the Invention of "Holding Court" in Twelfth-Century England' (pp. 293–310). Galloway tracks backwards from the thirteenth century the abstract notion of 'the court' and the related phrase 'to hold court', notes that *healdan curt* is first attested in the Peterborough Chronicle entry for 1154, and analyses the work of the First and Second Peterborough Continuators, and of the Old English writer whose work must underlie theirs, for signs of the notion of the court. Susan E. Deskis finds 'Echoes of Old English Alliterative Collocations in Middle English Alliterative Proverbs' (pp. 311–25) and in Middle English sermons and English proverbs included (and not translated) in Anglo-Norman court reports, and shows how these are a key element of connection between the Old and Middle English traditions.

John Frankis is also interested in 'Languages and Cultures in Contact: Vernacular Lives of St Giles and Anglo-Norman Annotations in an Anglo-Saxon Manuscript' (*LeedsSE* 38[2007] 101–33). The manuscript in question is Cambridge, University Library Ii. 1. 33, a collection of Old English homilies and saints' lives written in the second half of the twelfth century, and Frankis's focus is on two contemporary French marginal annotations. He examines both of them, turns to a detailed exploration of the second, which is the earliest manuscript evidence for *La Vie de Saint Gilles*, and proposes that the marginal annotator is connected with the Augustinian Priory of St Andrew and St Giles at Barnwell, Cambridge.

Rolf H. Bremmer, Jr's 'The *Gesta Herewardi*: Transforming an Anglo-Saxon into an Englishman' (in Summerfield and Busby, eds., *People and Texts: Relationships in Medieval Literature. Studies Presented to Erik Kooper*, pp. 29–42) contrasts the sparse surviving pre-Conquest references to Hereward with the rapid production of accounts of his life after his death, and then explores the *Gesta*'s emphasis of an English ethnic identity in contrast to a Norman one, its references to English-language accounts of Hereward's life and to the linguistic situation of post-Conquest England, its relationship to the 'Matter of England' and its presentation of accommodation to the new English political order.

Last year, Elaine Treharne scrutinized 'Categorization, Periodization: The Silence of (the) English in the Twelfth Century' (*NME* 8[2006] 247–69), an analytical survey of English prose works produced between *c*.1100 and 1200 in their cultural contexts. Drawing on models from postcolonial theory, Treharne argues for a reconceptualization of English literary traditions in this period as acts of resistance to Norman dominance. This year, Treharne offers a study of 'Bishops and their Texts in the Later Eleventh Century: Worcester and Exeter' (in Scase, ed., *Essays in Manuscript Geography: Vernacular Manuscripts of the English West Midlands from the Conquest to the Sixteenth Century*, pp. 13–28), which sets out the evidence for manuscripts associated with the episcopacies of Wulfstan II of Worcester (1062–95) and Leofric of Exeter (1050–72). The unusually detailed picture these manuscript survivals allow us to construct of two major institutions at this critical time of change enables Treharne to address important questions about the circumstances for the production of books in English at this period and to argue that 'Copying English, in itself, represents the deliberately resistive ideology of those involved . . . one should regard this as a proactive politics of vernacularity' (p. 28). The next essay in the same collection, Mary Swan's 'Mobile Libraries: Old English Manuscript Production in Worcester and the West Midlands, 1090–1215' (pp. 29–42), picks up the story of Worcester from the end-point of Treharne's contribution, scrutinizes the security of the grounds on which manuscript production and provenance are localized, maps out evidence for the production of books containing English in the West Midlands and identifies signs of what might be a programme of gathering and remaking manuscripts containing English and Latin produced elsewhere. Swan's final example is Lambeth Palace MS 487, the Lambeth Homilies, the subject of E.G. Stanley's article reviewed above and also of the next essay in *Essays in Manuscript Geography*, Bella Millett's 'The Pastoral Context of the Trinity and Lambeth Homilies' (pp. 43–64), which argues that the five homilies shared by both collections are likely to draw on a common source dating from no earlier than the late twelfth century, and suggests that these collections are 'part of an active response to contemporary developments in preaching and pastoral care' (p. 64).

Books Reviewed

Baker, Peter S. *Introduction to Old English*, 2nd edn. Wiley-Blackwell. [2007] pp. 408. pb $42.95. ISBN 9 7814 0515 2723.

Baxter, Stephen. *The Earls of Mercia: Lordship and Power in Late Anglo-Saxon England*. OUP. [2007] pp. xviii + 363. £63. ISBN 9 7801 9923 0983.

Biggs, Frederick M., ed. *Sources of Anglo-Saxon Literary Culture: The Apocrypha*. MIP. [2007] pp. xx + 117. pb $12 ISBN 9 7815 8044 1193.

Blanton, Virginia. *Signs of Devotion. The Cult of St. Æthelthryth in Medieval England, 695–1615*. PSUP. [2007] pp. xvii + 349. $65 ISBN 9 7802 7102 9849.

Bloom, Harold, ed. *Beowulf, Updated Edition*. ChelseaH. [2007] pp. vii + 280. $45 ISBN 0 7910 9301 8.

Blurton, Heather. *Cannibalism in High Medieval English Literature*. Palgrave. [2007] pp. 202. $68.95 ISBN 1 4039 7443 8.

Bremmer, Rolf H. Jr, and Kees Dekker, eds. *Foundations of Learning: The Transfer of Encyclopaedic Knowledge in the Early Middle Ages*. Peeters. [2007] pp. xii + 393. €60 ISBN 9 7890 4291 9792.

Brito, M., and M. Martín González, eds. *Insights and Bearings: Festschrift for Dr. Juan Sebastián Amador Bedford*. Universidad de la Laguna. [2007] pp. 389. price n.a. ISBN 9 7884 7556 7134.

Cawsey, Kathy, and Jason Harris, eds. *Transmission and Transformation in the Middle Ages: Texts and Contexts*. FCP. [2007] pp. 212. €55 ISBN 9 7818 5182 9903.

Chardonnens, László Sándor. *Anglo-Saxon Prognostics, 900–1100: Study and Texts*. Brill. [2007] pp. xv + 605. €99 ($148) ISBN 9 7890 0415 8290.

Cheney, Mary, David Smith, Christopher Brooke and Philippa M. Hoskin. *English Episcopal Acta 33: Worcester 1062–1185*. OUP. [2007] pp. lxxii + 227. £45 ISBN 9 7801 9726 4188.

Coatsworth, Elizabeth, and Gale R. Owen-Crocker. *Medieval Textiles of the British Isles AD 450–1100. An Annotated Bibliography*. BAR British Series 445. Archaeopress. [2007] pp. xi + 201 + 13 colour plates. £36 ISBN 9 7814 0730 1358.

Cooper, Kate, and Jeremy Gregory, eds. *Discipline and Diversity. Papers Read at the 2005 Summer Meeting and the 2006 Winter Meeting of the Ecclesiastical History Society*. Boydell. [2007] pp. xix + 427. £45 $90 ISBN 9 7809 5468 0930.

Cooper, Kate, and Jeremy Gregory, eds. *Elite and Popular Religion: Papers Read at the 2004 Summer Meeting and the 2005 Winter Meeting of the*

Ecclesiastical History Society. Boydell. [2006] pp. xii + 441. £45 $90 ISBN 9 7809 5468 0923.

Crowder, Ashby Bland, and Jason David Hall, eds. *Seamus Heaney: Poet, Critic, Translator*. Palgrave. [2007] pp. xii + 214. $79.95 ISBN 0 2300 0342 7.

Deyermond, Alan, ed. *A Century of British Medieval Studies*. OUP. [2007] pp. xxi + 801. £70 ISBN 9 7801 9726 3952.

Downham, Claire. *Viking Kings of Britain and Ireland: The Dynasty of Ívarr to A.D. 1014*. Dunedin Academic Press. [2007] pp. xxii + 338. £19.50 ISBN 9 7819 0376 5890.

Edwards, Nancy. *A Corpus of Early Medieval Inscribed Stones and Stone Sculpture in Wales*, vol. 2: *South-West Wales*. UWalesP. [2007] pp. xix + 568. £70 ISBN 9 7807 0831 9635.

Foys, Martin K. *Virtually Anglo-Saxon: Old Media, New Media, and Early Medieval Studies in the Late Age of Print*. UPFlor. [2007] pp. xiv + 275. $59.95 ISBN 0 8130 3039 0.

Frantzen, Allen J. *The Anglo-Saxon Penitentials: An Electronic Edition* www.Anglo-Saxon.net.

Frantzen, Allen J., and John Hines, eds. *Cædmon's Hymn and Material Culture in the World of Bede*. WVUP. [2007] pp. v + 265. pb $45 ISBN 1 9332 0222 X.

Ganz, David, and Jane Roberts, with Richard Palmer. *Lambeth Palace Library and its Anglo-Saxon Manuscripts. Exhibition Mounted for the Biennial Conference of the International Society of Anglo-Saxonists*, 3 August 2007. Taderon Press. [2007] pp. 94. £10 ISBN 9 7819 0265 6754.

Giandrea, Mary Frances. *Episcopal Culture in Late Anglo-Saxon England*. Boydell. [2007] pp. xv + 245. £50 ISBN 9 7818 4383 2836.

Glosecki, Stephen O., ed. *Myth in Early Northwest Europe*. ACMRS/Brepols. [2007] pp. xli + 338. $47 (€55) ISBN 0 8669 8365 1.

Hall, Alaric. *Elves in Anglo-Saxon England: Matters of Belief, Health, Gender and Identity*. Boydell. [2007] pp. xi + 226. $95 (£50) ISBN 1 8438 3294 1.

Halsall, Guy. *Barbarian Migrations and the Roman West 376–568*. CUP. [2007] pp. xvii + 592. pb £21.99 $41.99 ISBN 9 7805 2143 5437.

Harper-Bill, Christopher, and Elisabeth Van Houts, eds. *A Companion to the Anglo-Norman World*. Boydell. [2007] pp. xix + 298. pb £19.99 ISBN 9 7818 4383 3413.

Hartmann, Wilfried, ed. *Recht und Gericht in Kirche und Welt um 900*. Oldenbourg. [2007] pp. ix + 249. €49.80 ISBN 9 7834 8658 1478.

Healey, Antonette diPaolo, and Kevin Kiernan, eds. *Making Sense: Constructing Meaning in Early English*. PIMS. [2007] pp. xi + 138. C$ 24.95 ISBN 9 7808 8844 9078.

Higham, N.J., ed. *Britons in Anglo-Saxon England*. Boydell. [2007] pp. xii + 253. £50 ISBN 9 7818 4383 3123.

Hough, Carole, and John Corbett. *Beginning Old English*. Palgrave. [2007] pp. 240. hb £50 ISBN 1 4039 9349 1, pb £16.99 ISBN 1 4039 9350 5.

Hudson, John, ed. and trans. *Historia Ecclesie Abbendonensis: The History of the Church of Abingdon*, vol. 1. Clarendon. [2007] pp. ccix + 437. £105 ISBN 9 7801 9929 9379.

Innes, Matthew. *Introduction to Early Medieval Western Europe, 300–900: The Sword, the Plough and the Book*. Routledge. [2007] pp. xvi + 552. £75 ISBN 9 7804 1521 5060.

Jewell, Helen M. *Women in Dark Age and Early Medieval Europe c.500–1200*. Palgrave. [2007] pp. vii + 175. pb £19.99 ISBN 9 7803 3391 2591.

Kaylor, Noel Harold, and Richard Scott Nokes, eds. *Global Perspectives on Medieval English Literature, Language, and Culture*. MIP. [2007] pp. xv + 310. $45 ISBN 8 7915 8044 1209.

Keefer, Sarah Larratt, and Rolf H. Bremmer Jr, eds. *Space, Text and Margin in Medieval Manuscripts*. Peeters. [2007] pp. viii + 319. €62 ISBN 9 7890 4291 9808.

Kleist, Aaron, ed. *The Old English Homily: Precedent, Practice, and Appropriation*. Brepols. [2007] pp. xiii + 532. €90 ISBN 9 7825 0351 7926.

Lee, Christina. *Feasting the Dead: Food and Drink in Anglo-Saxon Burial Rituals*. Boydell. [2007] pp. xiv + 176. £45 ISBN 9 7818 4383 1426.

Leedham-Green, Elisabeth, and Teresa Webber, eds. *The Cambridge History of Libraries in England and Ireland*, 3 vols. CUP. [2006] pp. xx + 688. £315 ISBN 9 7805 2185 8083.

Lendinara, Patrizia, Loredana Lazzari and Maria Amalia D'Aronco, eds. *Form and Content of Instruction in Anglo-Saxon England in the Light of Contemporary Manuscript Evidence*. Papers presented at the International Conference Udine, 6–8 April 2006. Brepols. [2007] pp. xiii + 539 + 4 pp. colour plates. pb €59 ISBN 9 7825 0352 5914.

Lerer, Seth. *Inventing English: A Portable History of the Language*. ColUP. [2007] pp. viii + 305. $24.95 (£16.95) ISBN 9 7802 3113 7942.

Lowden, John, and Alixe Bovey, eds. *Under the Influence: The Concept of Influence and the Study of Illuminated Manuscripts*. Brepols. [2007] pp. xiii + 234. €80 ISBN 9 7825 0351 5045.

Minnis, Alastair, and Jane Roberts, eds. *Text, Image, Interpretation: Studies in Anglo-Saxon Literature and its Insular Context in Honour of Éamonn Ó Carragáin*. Brepols. [2007] pp. xxiv + 574 + 16 pp. colour plates. €110 ISBN 9 7825 0351 8190.

Mitchell, Bruce, and Fred C. Robinson. *A Guide to Old English*, 7th edn. Blackwell. [2007] pp. xvi + 432. pb £42.95 ISBN 1 4051 4690 7.

Morris, Richard. *Journeys from Jarrow: Jarrow Lecture 2004*. St Paul's Church, Jarrow. [2007] pp. 31. £4 No ISBN.

Niles, John D. *Old English Heroic Poems and the Social Life of Texts*. Brepols [2007] pp. xiii + 372. €80 ISBN 9 7825 0352 0803.

Niles, John D., featuring contributions by Tom Christensen and Marijane Osborn. *Beowulf and Lejre*. [2007] pp. xiv + 512 + 48 pp. colour plates. $89 (€95) ISBN 9 7808 6698 3686.

North, Richard, and Joe Allard, eds. *Beowulf and Other Stories: A New Introduction to Old English, Old Icelandic and Anglo-Norman Literatures*. Pearson Education. [2007] pp. xi + 525. pb £ 16.99 ISBN 1 4058 3572 9.

Ó Carragáin, Éamonn, and Carol Neuman de Vegvar, eds. *Roma Felix— Formation and Reflections of Medieval Rome*. Ashgate. ACMRS/Brepols [2007] pp. xiii + 353. £60 ISBN 9 7807 5466 0965.

Olson, Lynette. *The Early Middle Ages: The Birth of Europe*. Palgrave. [2007] pp. xvi + 248. pb £19.99. ISBN 9 7814 0394 2098.

Orton, Fred, and Ian Wood, with Clare A. Lees. *Fragments of History: Rethinking the Ruthwell and Bewcastle Monuments*. ManUP [2007] pp. xviii + 279. pb £17.99 ISBN 9 7807 1907 2574.

Ott, John S., and Anna Trumbore Jones, eds. *The Bishop Reformed: Studies of Episcopal Power and Culture in the Central Middle Ages*. Ashgate. [2007] pp. xv + 280. £55 ISBN 9 7807 5465 7651.

Redknap, Mark, and John M. Lewis. *A Corpus of Early Medieval Inscribed Stones and Stone Sculpture in Wales*. vol. 1: *South-East Wales and the English Border*. UWalesP. [2007] pp. xxi + 632. £70 ISBN 9 7807 0831 9567.

Reinhardt, Tobias, Michael Lapidge and J.N. Adams. *Aspects of the Language of Latin Prose*. OUP. [2005] pp. xii + 497. £60 ISBN 9 7801 9726 3327.

Roffe, David. *Decoding Domesday*. Boydell. [2007] pp. xx + 374. £50 ISBN 9 7818 4383 3079.

Sauer, Hans, and Renate Bauer, eds. *Beowulf and Beyond*. Lang. [2007] pp. xx + 333. pb. €49.50 (£37.10; $76.95) ISBN 3 6315 5925 9.

Scase, Wendy, ed. *Essays in Manuscript Geography: Vernacular Manuscripts of the English West Midlands from the Conquest to the Sixteenth Century*. Medieval Texts and Cultures of Northern Europe 10. Brepols. [2007] pp. xii + 294. €60 ISBN 9 7825 0351 6950.

Solopova, Elizabeth, and Stuart D. Lee. *Key Concepts in Medieval Literature*. Palgrave. [2007] pp. xiii + 338. £13.99 ISBN 9 7814 0399 7234.

Squatriti, Paolo, ed. *Natures Past: The Environment and Human History*. UMichP. [2007] pp. viii + 358. hb $85 ISBN 0 4720 9960 4, pb $32 ISBN 0 4720 6960 8.

Summerfield, Thea, and Keith Busby, eds. *People and Texts: Relationships in Medieval Literature. Studies Presented to Erik Kooper*. Rodopi. [2007] pp. xi + 205 €44 ISBN 9 7890 4202 1457.

Sutton, John William. *Death and Violence in Old and Middle English Literature*. Mellen. [2007] pp. v + 229. $109.95 (£69.95) ISBN 0 7734 5469 1.

Upchurch, Robert, ed. *Ælfric's Lives of the Virgin Spouses*. ExeterUP. [2007] pp. xii + 297. pb £15.99 $29.95 ISBN 9 7808 5989 7792.

Walsh, Christine. *The Cult of St Katherine of Alexandria in Early Medieval Europe*. Ashgate. [2007] pp. xix + 222. £55 ISBN 9 7807 5465 8610.

Wawn, Andrew, with Graham Johnson and John Walter. *Constructing Nations, Reconstructing Myth: Essays in Honour of T.A. Shippey*. Brepols. [2007] pp. xvii + 382 + 2 pp. colour plates. €70 ISBN 9 7825 0352 3934.

Williams, John H., ed. *The Archaeology of Kent to AD 800*. Boydell. [2007] pp. xvi + 288. £25 ISBN 9 7808 5115 5807.

Wood, Susan. *The Proprietary Church in the Medieval West*. OUP. [2007] pp. xiii + 1,020. £120 ISBN 9 7801 9820 6972.

Wormald, Patrick, and Janet L. Nelson, eds. *Lay Intellectuals in the Carolingian World*. CUP. [2007] pp. xiii + 263. £55 $110 ISBN 9 7805 2183 4537.

Wright, Charles D., Frederick M. Biggs and Thomas N. Hall, eds. *Source of Wisdom: Old English and Early Medieval Latin Studies in Honour of Thomas D. Hill*. UTorP. [2007] pp. xxiii + 420. $75 ISBN 9 7808 0209 3677.

III

Later Medieval: Excluding Chaucer

JENNIFER N. BROWN, JURIS LIDAKA, KENNETH ROONEY, RALUCA RADULESCU, MICHELLE M. SAUER AND GREG WALKER

This chapter has ten sections: 1. General and Miscellaneous; 2. Women's Writing; 3. Alliterative Verse and Lyrics; 4. The *Gawain*-Poet; 5. *Piers Plowman*; 6. Romance; 7. Gower, Lydgate, Hoccleve; 8. Malory and Caxton; 9. Middle Scots Poetry; 10. Drama. Section 1 is by Juris Lidaka; sections 2 and 9 are by Jennifer Brown; sections 3 and 5 are by Michelle M. Sauer; section 4 is by Kenneth Rooney; sections 6 and 8 are by Raluca Radulescu; section 7 is by Juris Lidaka; section 10 is by Greg Walker.

1. General and Miscellaneous

Robert E. Lewis has produced the second edition of the *Middle English Dictionary: Plan and Bibliography*; he has revised the *Plan* and, with Mary Jane Williams and with the assistance of Marilyn S. Miller, revised the *Bibliography*. The original was issued in 1954, after the first fascicle [1952], which reminds us how long the *MED* took to prepare, although the web version appeared with commendable swiftness once the whole was complete, and then it was made public when the University of Michigan had recouped its expenses (http://quod.lib.umich.edu/m/med/). The discursive material covers the history and scope of the *MED*, the design of entries (headwords largely regularized to SE Midlands forms *c*.1400), and dialectal or regional areas. To the last is added lists of localized texts, of abbreviations, and of the fascicles published, and notes and references for the first portion. The bulk of this fascicle is the bibliography itself, with its own introduction discussing preferred manuscripts and editions, the thorny problem of manuscript vs. composition dates, manuscript redating over the decades of work, and brief comments on the entries before long lists of abbreviations for manuscript collections, manuscripts, journals, collections and other printed works. These are followed by the title and incipit 'stencils', which most would just take as items or entries. First-time users are likely to be confused by the entries, for

Year's Work in English Studies, Volume 88 (2009) © *The English Association; all rights reserved*
doi:10.1093/ywes/map016

although each begins with a date the actual order is determined by the author, title and other such information. A little browsing makes most of the abbreviations used pretty clear ('Elsm' is the Ellesmere manuscript, of course), and the rest are easily consulted in the preceding abbreviations. Even with the *MED* online, the printed version eases consultation and belongs on everyone's shelves.

Martha W. Driver and Michael T. Orr's *Index of Images in English Manuscripts from the Time of Chaucer to Henry VIII, c.1380–c.1509: New York City, Columbia University–Union Theological* is another of the many volumes in this valuable series. Seven New York public institutions' holdings are included (eight were surveyed), with the Morgan Library's being the most interesting, especially for a copy of John Gower's *Confessio Amantis*, one of the *Speculum humanae salvationis*, and a thunder prognostication roll. These and others have extensive images. The catalogue includes seventy manuscripts with an additional nine continental ones made for the English market, but some of the first seventy are wholly or partly the work of non-English hands, such as one made by a German student at Oxford. Texts of interest include John Trevisa's translation of Bartholomæus Anglicus' *De proprietatibus rerum*, the *Brut*, Geoffrey Chaucer, John Gower, John Lydgate, Nicholas Love, *Pore Caitiff*, Reginald Pecock, Richard Rolle, the *Romance of Titus and Vespasian*, and Stephen Scrope. Although only nineteen figures are presented, the detailed catalogue descriptions and the extensive index of pictorial subjects (and a separate one for the continental manuscripts) serve quite well to help users find themes of interest, while those interested in texts can learn swiftly from the catalogue descriptions how those texts are decorated.

Those interested in sermons will need to see Veronica O'Mara and Suzanne Paul's 'A Preliminary List of Patristic and Other Authors Cited in the Middle English Prose Sermon: An Introduction to an Online Resource in Progress' (*Medieval Sermon Studies* 51[2007] 41–79), that resource being at http://www.hull.ac.uk/middle_english_sermons. The citations have yet to be verified, so, for example, the seventeen or eighteen ascribed to Bartholomæus Anglicus or the dozens to Bede may easily change, but the proverbial quotations certainly deserve a look.

EETS have issued the second volume of the *Gilte Legende*, edited by Richard Hamer with the assistance of Vida Russell. To ease reference, it is paginated continuously from where the first volume left off (see *YWES* 87[2008] 220) and contains eighty-six narratives. Almost all of these are saints' lives, but some have slightly different natures: the Finding of St Stephen, the Assumption of the Virgin and her Nativity, the Exaltation of the Cross, the Translation of St Remy, All Saints and All Souls, and, at the end, the Dedication of the Church, Advent, the Conception of the Virgin, Adam and Eve, and the Five Wiles of Pharaoh (more sermon than story, actually). Of course, there are more: for example, with Adam and Eve, how could one not continue with Cain and Abel, with Seth and the oil of the Tree of Mercy, and with the biographies Seth wrote of his parents, in a secret script that much later was revealed to Solomon? As usual with modern EETS editions, the focus on scholarly editing produces a text often sprinkled with editorial marks representing emendations to a faulty text, substitutions to an illegible or missing one, and scribal corrections; as is also usual, expansions of abbreviations are silent, and selected textual variants are posited at the bottom. Side margins include folio references to the base manuscript (British Library MS Egerton 876) and line numbers for reference within each narrative. Let us hope the introductory volume will not be long in coming.

In addition, EETS have issued Ralph Hanna's edition of *Richard Rolle: Uncollected Prose and Verse with Related Northern Texts*. By 'uncollected' Hanna means items not in S.J. Ogilvie-Thomson's 1988 edition based on MS Longleat 29. Ogilvie-Thomson's edition does not include works elsewhere, such as in Robert Thornton's miscellany, and includes one poem surely not Rolle's (p. xii). The texts are grouped into four parts, the first of which consists of four prose works from Thornton's miscellany (Lincoln Cathedral Library MS 91): 'Oleum effusum', four exempla, 'The Ten Commandments', and 'The Seven Gifts of the Holy Spirit'. The second part offers seven poems from a Cambridge manuscript, one poem given in two parts because other copies place a preceding poem between those two parts, plus two more lyrics that seem very like Rolle's work. The third part has unedited texts ascribed to Rolle in other manuscripts: in English, 'The Lessouns of Dirige', corresponding to a Latin text ascribed to Rolle and quite possibly his own translation and revision; 'Diliges dominum deum tuum' in parallel from two manuscripts with very different texts, the longer of which ascribes it as 'aftur Seynt Richard'; 'Of thre wyrkyngs in mans saule' ascribed to Rolle for quite some time, and a short 'De contricione', appended in one of those manuscripts, which explicitly ascribes it to Rolle. The fourth part has three *Vitae patrum* translations from Huntington Library, MS HM 148: 'A Pistille of Saynt Machari', 'The epistle of St John the hermit', and 'Verba seniorum', all of which appear elsewhere but have interesting forms in Hanna's chosen manuscript. As with Hamer's EETS edition, reviewed above, many editorial markings are included, and the textual notes and commentaries are added at the end (in matching parts within each type of note), as well as a selected glossary. While on the subject of a Thornton manuscript, we might add that Michael Johnston presents 'A New Document Relating to the Life of Robert Thornton' (*Library* 8[2007] 304–13): a letter related to a suit in the Court of Chancery, datable *c*.1452–4.

TEAMS Middle English Texts have issued Tamarah Kohanski and C. David Benson's edition of a popular work, *The Book of John Mandeville*. They argue that it 'has tended to be neglected by modern teachers and scholars' (p. 1), which seems a bit surprising. They begin their introduction by noting the *Book*'s reception from extremely broad popularity to denunciations of mendacity to acceptance as fiction, and then move on to the author and authorial voice and its verisimilitude. One wonders how many took the protestations of veracity as Swiftean comedy: the variety of short texts and their placement into a frame of travelogue makes for a fascinating entertainment that can be read as a medieval *Ripley's Believe It or Not* or as a *Gulliver's Travels*. This edition elects to reproduce the text of MS Royal 17 C. xxxviii, one of the 'Defective' texts, because of its independent derivation from the 'Defective' archetype (according to Seymour); its slightly enhanced contents and its editorial attempts to produce a text that is smooth and easy to read, in a dialect not too different from Chaucerian London. The text is the usual TEAMS edition: nicely spaced and paragraphed, with glosses at the bottom, explanatory notes following (with a few too many external references instead of slightly fuller discussion, perhaps) and then brief textual notes, an appendix on sources (including minor or potential sources), a bibliography, and short glossaries of words and proper names. If the selections taught through common anthologies are not enough, the low price and high readability of this TEAMS edition highly commend its use.

William of Newburgh's *The History of English Affairs, Book II*, is now presented by P.G. Walsh and M.J. Kennedy, long after Book I, which was published in 1988. This volume spans 1154 to 1175, the rise of Henry II, including the murder of Becket, victory over William I the 'Lion' of the Scots, and Henry's defeat of his own son's rebellion. The edition is bilingual, with the Latin (essentially a classicized version of the 1884 Rolls series edition) on the left and an English translation on the right. The introduction is short, providing a brief summary, a short biography of what little is known of William, some discussion of sources, and a bit of appreciative evaluation. After the text is a short commentary, with references to sources, historians' discussions, some allusions, occasional language notes and such, and the volume closes with a short index. Whilst on the subject, we might note that Anne Lawrence-Mathers takes on 'William of Newburgh and the Northumbrian Construction of English History' (*JMH* 33[2007] 339–57), showing how the *Historia rerum Anglicarum* (William the Conqueror to 1197/8) and its Prologue criticizing Geoffrey of Monmouth depend on faith in Bede and on use of certain manuscripts with historical, geographical and theological works.

Editions published as articles continue apace. Delbert Russell and Tony Hunt present 'Two Anglo-Norman Inedita from MS Douce d.6' (*Florilegium* 24[2007] 55–79): a verse debate between Humility and Pride, which is unique, and a prose legend of Seth and the Holy Rood, the earliest of five known copies (MS Arundel 507 should also be added to Dean and Boulton's *Anglo-Norman Literature* §481). Mark Jones edits and briefly discusses 'The Life of St. Eustace: A Saint's Legend from Lambeth Palace MS 306' (*ANQ* 20:i[2007] 13–23), this life coming from the *Gilte Legende*. Noel Harold Kaylor, Jr and Philip Edward Phillips re-edit '*The Boke of Coumfort of Bois* [Bodleian Library, Oxford MS Auct. F.3.5]: A Transcription with Introduction' (in Kaylor and Phillips, eds., *New Directions in Boethian Studies*, pp. 223–79), an adaptation of Chaucer's *Boece* with commentary inserted; their original edition was Noel Harold Kaylor, Jr, Jason Edward Streed and William H. Watts, '*The Boke of Coumfort of Bois*' (*Carmen Philosophiae* 2[1993] 55–104). Michael J. Curley offers up 'The Miracles of Saint David: A New Text and its Context' (*Traditio* 62[2007] 135–205), compiled after August 1405 and surviving in one of William Worcester's notebooks, which also has material on St Nonita, another Welsh saint; Curley edits the Latin David miracle texts and adds modern English translations.

Work has continued to produce texts of *Fachliteratur*. According to M. Teresa Tavormina, 'The Middle English *Letter of Ipocras*' (*ES* 88[2007] 632–52) resembles its Latin cousins in its looseness, so she edits a few copies of the common form—a prose prologue (and appends one in verse), the prose treatises on humours and uroscopy—and adds a longer, related prose uroscopy. She omits the medical recipes from this treatise said to be sent by Hippocrates (Ipocras) to Caesar. David Scott-McNab adds another version to his *J.B. Treatise* by offering 'An Autonomous and Unpublished Version of the *J.B. Treatise* in Exeter Cathedral MS 3533' (*MÆ* 76[2007] 70–84), this manuscript being a legal miscellany with the text, which has an East Midlands look to it, added slightly later. And Peter Grund presents a new version of '*Sidrak and Bokkus*: An Early Modern Reader Response' (*Anglia* 125[2007] 217–38); this one was annotated as an alchemical text in Philosophica Hermetica, Amsterdam, MS M199, with comments showing knowledge of further Middle English readings.

The most important work this year for manuscript studies is Morgan and Thomson's *The Cambridge History of the Book in Britain* volume 2, covering the period 1100–1400. It is less technical than many might imagine, and as the three broad portions indicate, but well worth reading and referencing. The first part is 'The Roles of Books', made up of the overviews 'Books and Society', by Christopher de Hamel (pp. 3–21) and 'Language and Literacy', by Rodney M. Thomson and Nigel Morgan; (pp. 22–38). The second—more technical—is 'Book Production': 'The Format of Books—Books, Booklets and Rolls', by Pamela Robinson (pp. 41–54); 'Layout and Presentation of the Text', by M.B. Parkes (pp. 55–74); 'Technology of Production of the Manuscript Book' subdivided into Rodney M. Thomson's 'Parchment and Paper, Ruling and Ink' (pp. 75–84), Nigel Morgan's 'Illumination—Pigments, Drawing and Gilding' (pp. 84–95) and Michael Gullick and Nicholas Hadgraft's 'Bookbindings' (pp. 95–109); 'Handwriting in English Books', by M.B. Parkes (pp. 110–35); 'Monastic and Cathedral Book Production', by Rodney M. Thomson (pp. 136–67); and 'Urban Production of Manuscript Books and the Role of the University Towns', by M.A. Michael (pp. 168–94). The third and largest portion—'Readership, Libraries, Texts and Contexts'—turns to the texts: 'Library Catalogues and Indexes', by Richard Sharpe (pp. 197–218); 'University and Monastic Texts' comprising Jeremy Catto's 'Biblical Exegesis, Theology, and Philosophy' (pp. 219–29), Jan Ziolkowski's 'Latin Learning and Latin Literature' (pp. 229–44) and Michael Twomey's 'Encyclopaedias' (pp. 244–9); 'Law', by Nigel Ramsay (pp. 250–90); 'Books for the Liturgy and Private Prayer', by Nigel Morgan (pp. 291–316); 'Compilations for Preaching and Lollard Literature', being Alan J. Fletcher's 'Compilations for Preaching' (pp. 317–29) and Anne Hudson's 'Lollard Literature' (pp. 329–39); 'Spiritual Writings and Religious Instruction', by Alexandra Barratt (pp. 340–66); the tripartite 'Vernacular Literature and its Readership' with Tony Hunt's 'The Anglo-Norman Book' (pp. 367–80), Julia Boffey and A.S.G. Edwards's 'Middle English Literary Writings, 1150–1400' (pp. 380–90) and Daniel Huws's 'The Welsh Book' (pp. 390–6); 'History and History Books', by Geoffrey Martin and Rodney M. Thomson (pp. 397–415); 'Archive Books', by Nigel Ramsay (pp. 416–45); 'Scientific and Medical Writings' is subdivided into Charles Burnett's 'The Introduction of Scientific Texts into Britain, c.1100–1250' (pp. 446–53) and Peter Murray Jones's 'University Books and the Sciences, c.1250–1400' (pp. 453–62); 'Music', by Nicolas Bell (pp. 463–73); and 'Illustration and Ornament', by Martin Kauffman (pp. 474–87).

Wendy Scase's *Essays in Manuscript Geography: Vernacular Manuscripts of the English West Midlands from the Conquest to the Sixteenth Century* assembles essays from a 2003 conference regarding the online Manuscripts of the West Midlands catalogue (http://www.mwm.bham.ac.uk, which at time of writing redirects to http://www.sd-editions.com/AnaServer?MWMnew+0+start.anv). The collection is divided into four parts; the first covers the Early Middle English period, beginning with Elaine Treharne's 'Bishops and their Texts in the Later Eleventh Century: Worcester and Exeter' (pp. 13–28), the texts being late Old English but the manuscripts showing a contemporary cultural environment, not pre-Conquest. Similarly, Mary Swan takes up 'Mobile Libraries: Old English Manuscript Production in Worcester and the West Midlands, 1090–1215' (pp. 29–42), with the implications of mobile scribes and readers. Bella Millett, in 'The Pastoral Context of the Trinity and Lambeth Homilies' (pp. 43–64), shares this vision that local situations affected the copying and revision of works. The second part covers the early fourteenth century: first, Susanna Fein's 'Compilation and Purpose in MS Harley 2253' (pp. 67–94) suggests that one sequence in the manuscript reflects performance in a multilingual Shropshire milieu, while Carter Revard sees various 'Oppositional Thematics and Metanarrative in MS Harley 2253, Quires 1–6' (pp. 95–112). John J. Thompson shows the difficulties in 'Mapping Points West of West Midlands Manuscripts and Texts: Irishness(es) and Middle English Literary Culture' (pp. 113–28), with reference to two West Midlands manuscripts lying behind a Middle Hiberno-English one. In the third portion, on the fifteenth century and later, Ryan Perry asks how exemplars of texts were available in the production of one manuscript, in 'The Clopton Manuscript and the Beauchamp Affinity: Patronage and Reception Issues in a West Midlands Reading Community' (pp. 131–59). Martha W. Driver's 'Inventing Visual History: Re-presenting the Legends of Warwickshire' (pp. 161–202) continues the topic of social sharing within peer circles. And David Griffith follows 'Owners and Copyists of John Rous's Armorial Rolls' (pp. 203–28) from John Rous in the sixteenth into the nineteenth century. In the last part, on corpus studies, Rebecca Farnham describes the method, scope and functions of 'The Manuscripts of the West Midlands Catalogue Project' (pp. 231–38), Alison Wiggins uses the catalogue to study 'Middle English Romances and the West Midlands' (pp. 239–55), finding selected relationships between London and other areas, and Orietta Da Rold is 'Fingerprinting Paper in West Midlands Medieval Manuscripts' (pp. 257–71), by more than watermarks and offering potential uses of such a database. Derek Pearsall closes with an 'Epilogue' (pp. 257–76) giving a retrospect and prospects.

A.S.G. Edwards and Theresa O'Byrne announce 'A New Manuscript Fragment of the *Prick of Conscience*' (*MÆ* 76[2007] 305–7) from the middle of the fifteenth century, used apparently as a wrapper for a University of Notre Dame printed copy of Sir Thomas More's *Supplication of Souls* and now bound within it; the leaves have 136 lines from parts IV and V on Purgatory and the signs of Doomsday. Taking a quite different approach to manuscript studies in 'Manuscript Agency and the Findern Manuscript' (*NM* 108[2007]

339–49), Simone Celine Marshall applies the indeterminacy of New Philology to the development and use of this manuscript in the first century or so of its existence.

For twelfth-century literature, Gaimar has been on the mind of Paul Dalton. First, he reconsiders 'The Date of Geoffrey Gaimar's *Estoire des Engleis*, the Connections of his Patrons, and the Politics of Stephen's Reign' (*ChauR* 42[2007] 23–47), narrowing the date to *c*.1141–50, then casting some light on Gaimar's praise of certain aristocrats to whom his patrons were connected. Second, he finds connections between 'Geffrei Gaimar's *Estoire des Engleis*, Peacemaking, and the "Twelfth-Century Revival of the English Nation"' (*SP* 104[2007] 427–54), with Constance Fitz Gilbert as a patron who might act as a peacemaker in the unsettled time of Stephen, and heroic and especially chivalric exemplars being held up for emulation. In 'Adgar's *Gracial* and Christian Images of Jews in Twelfth-Century Vernacular Literature' (*JMH* 33[2007] 181–96), Jennifer Shea finds that William Adgar's miracles of the Virgin portray Christians and Jews using themes and language adopted from courtly romances, which also provided virtues and vices for these portrayals. Clare Downham's 'St Bega—Myth, Maiden, or Bracelet? An Insular Cult and its Origins' (*JMH* 33[2007] 33–42) looks at the curious rise of Bega's cult in the twelfth and thirteenth centuries in Ireland, England and abroad, centuries after her life.

Turning to Latin, Marcus Bull focuses in on 'Criticism of Henry II's Expedition to Ireland in William of Canterbury's Miracles of St Thomas Becket' (*JMH* 33[2007] 107–29), placing that criticism into an environment of current debates about the 1171–2 expedition and finding it subtly connected to Becket's murder. From his 1163–70 exile in France, John of Salisbury engaged the Bible as his sole weapon in letters written for the defence of Becket against Henry II, as we learn from Julie Barrau's 'La Conversio de Jean de Salisbury: La Bible au service de Thomas Becket?' (*Cahiers de civilisation médiévale* 50[2007] 229–44). Readers of his *Policraticus* will note the radical change of source material.

In the *Florilegium* Festschrift for Brian Merrilees, Margaret Burrell discusses 'Hell as a Geological Construct' (*Florilegium* 24[2007] 37–54) in Benedeit's *Le Voyage de Saint Brendan* and Marie de France's *L'Espurgatoire seint Patriz*; geographical matters are equally important, particularly as Icelandic eruptions figure largely in clues for the former and various locations of torment for both. After Russell and Hunt's inedita (above) appears Pierre Nobel's 'La Bible de Jean de Sy et la Bible anglo-normande' (*Florilegium* 24[2007] 81–107), the first being in MS BNF fr. 15397 from the mid-fourteenth century and not wholly independent of the Bible anglo-normande. David Trotter looks into 'Words, Words, Words... But What Exactly Is a "Word" in Anglo-Norman?' (*Florilegium* 24[2007] 109–23), pointing out that senses are often perceived as different words and variant prefixes need not make for different lexemes.

Sometimes everyone needs a friend—but what kind? H.M. Canatella analyses 'Friendship in Anselm of Canterbury's Correspondence: Ideals and Experience' (*Viator* 38:ii[2007] 351–67), finding that Anselm's friendships with Gundulf, bishop of Rochester, and Countess Ida of Boulogne were aligned with classical Christian models. On the other hand, Cary J. Nederman's 'Friendship in Public Life during the Twelfth Century: Theory and Practice in the Writings of John of Salisbury' (*Viator* 38:ii[2007] 385–97) finds John working from a Ciceronian model in both the *Policraticus* and his two letter collections.

Friendship leads to those things one does with friends and potential friends. Julie Kerr's 'Food, Drink and Lodging: Hospitality in Twelfth-Century England' (*Haskins Society Journal* 18[2006] 72–92) uses Daniel of Beccles' *Urbanus*, Robert Grosseteste, Bartholomæus Anglicus' *De proprietibus rerum*, Geoffrey Gaimar, Adam of Balsham's *De utensilibus*, courtesy materials and the like to describe briefly feast tables, the service, table conduct, decor, accommodation of guests, hospitality and post-prandial activities. Her '"Welcome the coming and speed the parting guest": Hospitality in Twelfth-Century England' (*JMH* 33[2007] 130–46) also uses Beccles and Grosseteste but adds Gerald of Wales, Walter Map, Jocelin of Brakelond, Chrétien de Troyes, Raoul de Cambrai and some others to describe how guests were to be treated and how they sometimes were treated, from arrival and at the threshold, through entrance to the household, to duration of visit, departure (perhaps with an escort) and reciprocation.

Moving to the thirteenth century, we find an article published to commemorate the 120th anniversary of the Modern Language Society, Helsinki: Margaret Laing's '*The Owl and the Nightingale*: Five New Readings and Further Notes' (*NM* 108[2007] 445–77), which suggests new words or meanings in the poem, based on palaeographical grounds and linguistic influence from Anglo-French, with careful and extensive discussion. Lynn Staley connects 'Susanna and English Communities' (*Traditio* 62[2007] 25–58) through Alan of Melsa's *Tractatus metricus de Susann*' from Beverley (*c*.1204–12?) and the much later 'Pistel of Susan', both of which put law rightly in the heart and paint her as actively defending true justice. Elizabeth Keen depicts 'A Peopled Landscape: Bartholomew the Englishman on the Properties of Daily Life' (*Parergon* 24:ii[2007] 7–22), focusing not so much upon the text but on the glosses (which may well be Bartholomew's, we should add) to show a spiritually nuanced world-view. Heather Blurton's 'From *Chanson de Geste* to Magna Carta: Genre and the Barons in Matthew Paris's *Chronica majora*' (*NML* 9[2007] 117–38) uses a tale of a loyal but dispossessed knight to show the complicated situation around Henry III's confirmation of the Magna Carta in 1253.

Nicola Masciandaro's *The Voice of the Hammer: The Meaning of Work in Middle English Literature* really focuses on the late fourteenth century with some forays into the fifteenth. This short work (a revised dissertation) has three basic chapters: one on the Middle English vocabulary for 'work', one on the reception of the idea of labour and one on Fragment VIII of Chaucer's *Canterbury Tales*. Though only five lexical items are surveyed—'travail', 'labour', 'swink', 'werk' and 'craft'—it is a 'fact that English takes from Anglo-French only words for work that are associated with servitude and pain' (p. 11); a broader analysis charts these in a semantic range across subjective effort or livelihood and objective production or product (p. 27), where we find that only 'swink', 'travail' and 'labour' share the sense of effort, while the latter two terms also extend into livelihood, and 'labour' alone of the three extends into the objective senses. Masciandaro follows that by looking at how late Middle English literature imagined the origins and history of work, basing this upon the Cooke manuscript's history of masonry (BL Add 23198), Gower's *Confessio Amantis* Book IV (ll. 2363–2700), and Chaucer's 'Former Age'. The *Second Nun's Tale* and the *Canon's Yeoman's Tale* are curious reflections on work as opposed to idleness with an odd mismatch between the intent of labour and its actual end.

The title of Isabel Davis's *Writing Masculinity in the Later Middle Ages* is a tad deceptive because its concern is more precisely identified early on as 'intersections between medieval masculine subjectivity and the ethics of labour and living' (p. 2), and the works discussed actually range just from *c*.1360 to *c*.1430. Langland's *Piers Plowman* is treated through a polarity of labour and marriage within lay and clerical spheres, with the B-text urging marriage over virginity (which the C-text qualifies), and men doing well by being fruitful. Thomas Usk's *Testament of Love* is, based on its imagery, keenly interested in 'the home, the household and both familial and conjugal affectivity' (p. 40) within an environment of bourgeois values that reject unbridled desire. Gower's *Confessio Amantis* is approached from a cartographic perspective, in which Book IV charts errant, slothful masculinity. Having an itinerant or transient lifestyle, but quite different nonetheless, is Chaucer's autobiographical Canon's Yeoman who—in accepting his busy apprenticeship—has embraced the very system to which he is subservient, yet has a peculiar sexual tension of his own. This leads, of course, to the autobiographical Thomas Hoccleve, seeking respect from his co-workers in the homosocial bureaucracy, binding writing and self, juxtaposing socially sanctioned misogyny with his transient relationships with women, and confronting new dress styles with his social mentality.

Similarly, S. Elizabeth Passmore and Susan Carter explore femininity and reactions to it in their collection of essays, *The English 'Loathly Lady' Tales: Boundaries, Traditions, Motifs*, including Irish hags. S. Elizabeth Passmore's 'Through the Counsel of a Lady: The Irish and English Loathly Lady Tales and the "Mirrors for Princes" Genre' (pp. 3–41) opens by taking the hag's habit of giving advice more seriously than normal in criticism, using the Irish Níall tales, Gower's 'Tale of Florent', Chaucer's *Wife of Bath's Tale*, 'The Wedding of Sir Gawain and Dame Ragnelle' and 'The Marriage of Sir Gawain'. Turning more closely to Florent and his bride, R.F. Yeager takes up 'The Politics of *Strengthe* and *Vois* in Gower's Loathly Lady Tale' (pp. 42–72), focusing on those terms with special attention to the rituals of queenship. Elizabeth M. Biebel-Stanley's 'Sovereignty through the Lady: "The Wife of Bath's Tale" and the Queenship of Anne of Bohemia' (pp. 73–82) has a similar theme, finding a political moral for Anne—not Richard II—in Alisoun's sovereignty tale, emphasizing Arthur's queen, silencing the offended maiden, and noting parallels among that queen, Anne and Alisoun. Susan Carter's 'A Hymenation of Hags' (pp. 83–99) ruminates upon the sexual activity (and virginity) of the Wife of Bath's hag, the Loathly Ladies in 'Carn Máil' and 'The Adventures of the Sons of Eochaid', and Dame Ragnelle. Russell A. Peck returns to Gower in 'Folklore and Powerful Women in Gower's "Tale of

Florent"' (pp. 100–45), taking folklore as his source. Paul Gaffney's 'Controlling the Loathly Lady, or What Really Frees Dame Ragnelle' (pp. 146–62) uses Barthes's *discours* to propose that the audience is given greater authority to determine meaning in 'The Wedding'. Comparing that text to its mutilated Percy Folio version in '"The Marriage of Sir Gawain": Piecing the Fragments Together' (pp. 163–85), Stephanie Hollis gives a hypothetical reconstruction of the ballad and its themes. Mary Edwards Shaner takes 'A Jungian Approach to the Ballad "King Henry"' (pp. 186–98), mainly in the Child version, placing at centre the scattered human personality typified by the *anima* and *animus* that need to be reintegrated. In 'Repainting the Lion: "The Wife of Bath's Tale" and a Traditional British Ballad' (pp. 199–212), Lynn M. Wollstadt points to parallels between Chaucer's tale and the several versions of 'The Knight and the Shepherd's Daughter'. The editors move backwards again with Mary Leech's 'Why Dame Ragnell Had To Die: Feminine Usurpation of Male Authority in "The Wedding of Sir Gawain and Dame Ragnell"' (pp. 213–34), which reads Ragnell as a Bahktinian grotesque affront to ideal social order. Finally, in 'Brains or Beauty: Limited Sovereignty in the Loathly Lady Tales "The Wife of Bath's Tale," "Thomas of Erceldoune," and "The Wedding of Sir Gawain and Dame Ragnelle"' (pp. 235–56), Ellen M. Caldwell observes how in all these the Loathly Lady has the upper hand until she gets what she wants, when she turns into a conventional wife.

Several studies link literature to various elements of society. Emily Steiner's 'Naming and Allegory in Late Medieval England' (*JEGP* 106[2007] 248–75) gives a quick overview of naming practices as social actions before noting how literary works appropriate them with reference to the N-Town Trial of Mary and Joseph, Piers Plowman, the 'literature of 1381', and especially Gower in the *Vox Clamantis*. Marion Turner's 'Usk and the Goldsmiths' (*NML* 9[2007] 139–77) takes the 'Testament of Love' and 'Appeal' in both narrow and wider senses as related to the material culture of the mercantile guilds whose scribes were involved in the copying and appreciation of works by Usk, Chaucer, Gower, Langland and others. Working on 'John Mirk's Holy Women' (*PLL* 43[2007] 339–62), Nancy E. Atkinson points out how Mirk directs his audience to images visible in wall paintings and statues: the parishioners, already knowing the symbols and their meanings, are less 'lewde' than they might have thought. Mary Dockray-Miller teases out the 'Historical Sources of the Middle English Verse Life of St. Æthelthryth' (*ANQ* 20:ii[2007] 8–11) as Trevisa's *Polychronicon*, not Higden's version, thus showing also that the translation was available to someone at Wilton just seventy miles from Berkeley about forty years after Trevisa finished it. David Moreno Olalla's '*The fautys to amende*: On the Interpretation of the *Explicit* of Sloane 5, ff. 13–57, and Related Matters' (*ES* 88[2007] 119–42) looks at the text and language of John Lelamour's herbal, noting what internal evidence can and cannot reveal about the translator/compiler and suggesting that the text may have been written in or around Hereford in 1373 but the sole manuscript obscured it with London-like language a century later.

Other articles are interested in political culture. David Matthews's 'Laurence Minot, Edward III, and Nationalism' (*Viator* 38:i[2007] 269–88) sees Minot's poems less as separate works than as 'an embryonic biography of Edward III' (p. 272) and ties the oeuvre to the origins of vernacularity (briefly) and to the reception of Minot's nationalism through to our times. In 'English Poetry July–October 1399 and Lancastrian Crime' (*SAC* 29[2007] 374–418), David R. Carlson teases out from five poems their signs of conspiracy in supporting Henry IV's version of Richard II's deposition: a Latin verse beginning *O deus in celis, cuncta disponens fideli* (text and translation appended), an English 'On King Richard's Ministers', *Richard the Redeless*, John Gower's *Cronica tripertita*, and a marginal English verse in a St Albans manuscript of Thomas Walsingham's *Chronica maiora*. In 'The Penitential Psalms: Conversion and the Limits of Lordship' (*JMEMS* 37[2007] 221–69), Lynn Staley surveys responses to the seven psalms (6, 31, 37, 50, 101, 129 and 142 in the Vulgate) by a number of writers—Richard Rolle, Richard Maidstone, Julian of Norwich, Thomas Brampton, Eleanor Hull, John Fisher and later ones. Her eye is on not just on their acceptance of God's authority but also on the limits of human authority.

Combining politics and religion is Emma Lipton's *Affections of the Mind: The Politics of Sacramental Marriage in Late Medieval English Literature*, which argues that several literary representations of sacramental marriage engage with questions concerning authority, a basically political position, thanks to the lay piety of the growing middle class which is eyeing its social superiors. In short, adopting a sacramental model of marriage meant viewing marriage as consensual with a degree of equality and respect through love, unlike the long-standing hierarchical model, which established a prerogative involving differing levels of power and authority based on sex. Chaucer's *Franklin's Tale* offers a view of such a marriage, using traits of the classical friendship tradition, and ends by offering mutual respect and equality among the Knight, Squire, and Clerk, whose social relationships are normally quite unequal and hierarchical; the Franklin here is, of course, representing the rising middle class and its novel interests, curiously shifting attention from what is happening in the marriage to the male bonding at the end of the tale. In the *Traitié pour Essampler les Amantz Marietz*, a series of eighteen *balades*, Gower transforms romance and sermon by reconstructing heroes' domestic lives to reveal their responsibility for sex relations and to enhance the value of marriage over that of chastity, effectively removing social class from the value system. Three of the N-town plays are relevant here: the 'Marriage' and 'Trial' of Joseph and Mary, and 'Joachim and Anna'. The first is notable in making marriage more a matter of the two individuals and God than of a priest, and the second sanctifies lay piety by finding Mary innocent of adultery through a verbal truth test. The third finds value not in priestly authority or hierarchy but in lay piety, perhaps enhancing the status of the enacting guild members. Finally, Margery Kempe's plea for a chaste marriage rules out the 'marriage debt' of the traditional marriage model and thus seriously questions clerical authority.

A broad political view from the late fourteenth century into the very early fifteenth appears in Matthew Giancarlo's *Parliament and Literature in Late Medieval England*. His thesis is that Richard II and Henry IV were key for deliberative parliament and literature, and that Agincourt is a convenient terminus for his investigation because it emboldened royal independence of parliament. Of course, Chaucer was MP for Kent, Gower had dealings with parliament and MPs, copies of *Piers Plowman* were owned by parliamentarians, Langland's later imitators put parliament in their works, and administrative scribes were not isolated from literary copying. Reviewing the development of parliament from the thirteenth century onwards, Giancarlo points to an early Arthurian mythical-historical dynamic visible in Peter Langtoft's *Chronicle* and Robert Mannyng of Brunne's translation, and even in several romances. Bills and complaints (for more on which see Wendy Scase, below) increased in the fourteenth century, with a concomitant growth in the influence of the Commons, neatly illustrated in the *Anonimalle Chronicle*'s account of the Good Parliament of 1376. Ineffective or toadying parliaments were criticized by Thomas Brinton and John Bromyard. John Gower's *Mirour de l'Omme* and *Cronica tripertita* assume a baronial parliament and lambast legal wrangling, parody reality through the Devil's parliament, and portray three parliaments to seek the *vox populi*. Giancarlo approaches Chaucer from two angles: a collocation between parliament and marriage, and the procedure for petitioning for redress; these are visible in Prudence and Melibee, in the *Parliament of Fowls*, and in the framing of the *Canterbury Tales*. Langland's *Piers Plowman*'s rodent parliament explicitly presents a deeper concern with parliamentary affairs, evidenced in the trial of Meed and the Barn of Unity. *The Crowned King*, *Richard the Redeless*, and *Mum and the Sothsegger* support an expanded Commons and more access for petitioners.

Since the Good Parliament of 1376 and its reportage has been brought up, it is convenient to note here more new work on it. In 'The First Political Pamphlet? The Unsolved Case of the Anonymous Account of the Good Parliament' (*Viator* 38:i[2007] 251–68), Clementine Oliver argues that the account was parliamentary reportage intended for independent circulation; a 'process', as mentioned in the *Westminster Chronicle*, originating perhaps in the Langlandian reading circles of civil servants. If this argument is accepted, more 'processes' might be discovered, leading to a deeper understanding of news before the newspapers. The political situation is also key to Douglas Biggs's 'Archbishop Scrope's *Manifesto* of 1405: "Naïve nonsense" or Reflections of Political Reality?' (*JMH* 33[2007] 358–71), which concludes from six of the ten charges that Richard Scrope was actually politically astute.

Jenni Nuttall's *The Creation of Lancastrian Kingship: Literature, Language and Politics in Late Medieval England* also looks to politics and the same basic time frame, starting from the deposition of Richard II and the paired coin heads of Richard's demerits and Henry's merits. Richard's immaturity, wilfulness and other charges from the deposition were rapidly employed in histories and chronicles, and in *Richard the Redeless*, which pays special attention to Richard's household's excessively lavish dress. While *Richard the Redeless* urged the Lancastrian government and household to fulfil expectations, the same author's *Mum and the Sothsegger* pointedly warns that they have not. The language used was transformed, Nuttall argues, so that Hoccleve's *Male Regle* and *Regiment of Princes* use the themes of *de casibus*, youth vs. maturity, misrule and even dress, as do Scogan's *Moral Balade* and

Gower's *To King Henry the Fourth in Praise of Peace*. Initial hopes for Lancastrian good fiscal management soon floundered; Hoccleve, of course, was keenly aware of this and wrote of many financial matters in terms that reflect both the complaints of mismanagement and the arguments of policy and exigency. A 'discourse of credit' in cash and citizens' loyalty continued in Hoccleve (using advice from the *Secreta secretorum*) and the alliterative *Crowned King*, which advises Henry V about mutual obligations of money and allegiance between the king and his subjects. The potential dangers when money and loyalty are at odds feature greatly in Hoccleve's *Regiment of Princes*. The conclusion surveys political and governmental connections to poets and their works, and adds some brief comments on another political poem of the time, *Dede is Worchyng*.

There are plenty of signs of continued interest in Wyclif and the Lollards. Ian Christopher Levy's 'John Wyclif and the Primitive Papacy' (*Viator* 38:ii[2007] 159–89) points to Matthew 16.18–19 and Galatians 2.11–14 as key texts for understanding Wyclif's ideal church, based on the apostolic community. He follows up with 'John Wyclif on Papal Election, Correction, and Deposition' (*MS* 69[2007] 141–85); these three matters help to identify how to distinguish between a true and a false pope, with theologians (not lawyers) guiding secular lords in calling clerics to account. Alexandra Walsham's 'Inventing the Lollard Past: The Afterlife of a Medieval Sermon in Early Modern England' (*JEH* 58[2007] 628–55) looks at mid-Tudor use of Thomas Wimbledon's famous 1387/8 sermon on *Redde rationem villicationis tue* at Paul's Cross, which was ascribed at times to Wyclif and printed up to 1635, and then again in the 1730s.

The major publication in this area for the year is no doubt Mary Dove's *The First English Bible: The Text and Context of the Wycliffite Versions*. She opens with 'The Bible Debate' from Henry Knighton's *Chronicle* and the Dominican Thomas Palmer against translation to Trevisa, an anonymous 'The holi prophete Dauid seiþ', Richard Ullerston and other anonymous tracts in favour. Arundel's *Constitutions* stopped this debate and began a period of 'censorship', which continued into Thomas More's *A Dialogue Concerning Heresies*. In 'The Translators', Dove includes Wyclif as initiator and supervisor and, of course, John Trevisa among the translators, but mostly reviews the various discussions of the issue. What they worked from is the question in 'The Canonical Scriptures': the canon is Jerome's, the order follows French bibles after *c.*1200, and the prologues resemble those of the Paris bibles, but with some changes, especially in the Later version. 'The English Prologues' following Jerome stop with Baruch in the Old Testament and are spotty in the New Testament; others are new, and in the later version the Isaiah prologue (in one section called the 'Prologue to the Prophets') is also a general one in addition to the 'Prologue to the Wycliffite Bible' (also called the 'General Prologue'). 'The text' leaps into concerns about books included or not amongst the versions, the coverage and comments of the prologues, individual readings, predictably overlapping scribal copying of versions, textual criticism, and more. The marginal and intratextual glossing and its underlining is discussed, with some distinctions offered between explanatory glosses, variant translations, and alternative meanings and some comments on the use of sources (mostly Nicholas of Lyra). Finally, 'The Effects' looks to the legacy from the sixteenth century on to Forshall and Madden's edition.

There is such a thing as 'gossip theory', one learns from Susan E. Phillips's *Transforming Talk: The Problem with Gossip in Late Medieval England*. Hers is that gossip is transformative, and that pastoral concern thus derided 'janglyng' and idle talk although, she suggests, preachers and moral poets themselves put jangling to work for them in (typically) the exemplum, even as they fought the gossip interrupting services (also typically through exempla). Examples include Robert Mannyng of Brunne, Langland and *Jacob's Well*. Poets could reshape janglers and to gossip to their ends, too. So Chaucer sketches his theory of it in the *House of Fame* and practises it in various ways in the *Canterbury Tales*. Jangling became more of a women's thing later, to judge by Dunbar's *Tretis of Twa Mariit Wemen and the Wedo*. Eventually, the Middle English gossip—godparents, or baptismal sponsors—turned to initiating young women into women's things, or the 'gossips' we think of; these are best seen in the *Gospelles of Dystaues* and the *Fyftene Joyes of Maryage*.

In the wide-ranging book *Visions in Late Medieval England: Lay Spirituality and Sacred Glimpses of the Hidden Worlds of Faith*, Gwenfair Walters Adams finds that post-biblical visions as disseminated by the church ('didactic visions') determined how the laity would behave when perceiving or reporting personal visions ('lay visions'). Through a variety of dynamics, the supernatural events or visitations taught in sermon exempla (such as in *Jacob's Well*, Mirk, and the *Speculum sacerdotale*), in hagiographic accounts (such as the *South English Legendary* and the *Golden Legend*), in chronicles, and elsewhere (such as *Dives and Pauper*, the *Pore Caitiff*, Robert Mannyng of Brunne's *Handlyng Synne*, and *The Prick of Conscience*) found a receptive audience in the laity, as witnessed by Margery Kempe's *Book*, the *Revelations* of Julian of Norwich, records of sightings of the dead King Henry VI or the ghosts at Byland Abbey, St Patrick's Purgatory and an anonymous woman's revelation of purgatory in the fifteenth century, and even Elizabeth Barton's revelations. The large number of visions thus available is discussed through a number of types, which are subdivided in various ways and illustrated from the sources—ghosts in this world or in purgatory helped the pious understand atonement and satisfaction, saints responded to individuals' devotional acts (case-studies on this are Henry VI and Margery Kempe), demonic spiritual warfare could easily be countered by the faithful, and visions helped visualize aspects of the liturgy and the sacrament. The typology is followed by a closing overview on the power and dynamic of visions, which lost effectiveness through the Reformation's emphasis on scriptural authority above all other.

The point of Michelle Karnes's 'Nicholas Love and Medieval Meditations on Christ' (*Speculum* 82[2007] 380–408) is that the inward devotion of these works was not associated with any personal liberation from the church. Karnes focuses on Love's *Meditationes* and *Mirror* but has an eye on the Wyclifite Bible and Margery Kempe, with a short but interesting discussion of medieval theories of the imagination. Martin Heale's 'Training in Superstition? Monasteries and Popular Religion in Late Medieval and

Reformation England' (*JEH* 58[2007] 417–39) observes how monasteries continued attracting lay piety, until reformers' hostility to pilgrimages became very vociferous. Larissa Tracy discusses 'The Middle English Life of Saint Dorothy in Trinity College, Dublin MS 319: Origins, Parallels, and its Relationship to Osbern Bokenham's *Legendys of Hooly Wummen*' (*Traditio* 62[2007] 259–84), tracing the Trinity text to a particular Latin life, and then proposing that Bokenham used the Trinity version (or something very like it) for his *Legendys* and the recently found *Legenda aurea*.

In *John Capgrave's Fifteenth Century*, Karen A. Winstead's dominant thrust is the interrelationship between faith, obligation to others and intellect, thus blending the social with the spiritual. The opening chapter on Capgrave's life and times draws attention to his mid-life shift from writing in Latin to writing in English, supporting lay theology in the vernacular amid shifting hopes with regard to support from Duke Humphrey. With this understanding, she lays out how Capgrave's lives of St Augustine of Hippo and St Katherine of Alexandria display the two sides of an intellectual's responsibility to others: Augustine learned to fulfil his responsibility, while Katherine avoided social obligations and expectations to follow her personal studies; these motifs reflect Capgrave's worries over contemporary eremeticism and anti-intellectualism. Reading the lives of St Cecilia and St Norbert, in addition to Augustine and Katherine, Winstead finds these worries a reaction like Reginald Pecock's against orthodoxy's repression of lay vernacular study of theology, which would work against the church's own interests. With regard to women, Capgrave apparently further believed in an anti-eremetical lifestyle wherein holy virginity would be eschewed in favour of active engagement with the social, Christian community; suffering wives, mothers and widows obtained his sympathy, perhaps more than virgins. Even so, Capgrave's virgins show a kind of worldly pragmatism in the *Solace of Pilgrims*, as do St Gilbert and St Katherine. Politically, too, withdrawal from the world struck Capgrave as unwise, as his *Liber de illustribus Henricis* [*c*.1446] reveals. Winstead reviews Capgrave's Katherine and Lydgate's *Lives of SS Edmund and Fremund* as reactions to Henry VI as ruler—political hagiography, in effect—with the *Liber* implying that Henry VI needed to focus more on the active life so that his future deeds could be memorialized, as well as the past deeds of all the other Henries.

If we tire of theology, we could turn to nature, as Gillian Rudd does in *Greenery: Ecocritical Readings of Late Medieval English Literature*, taking general readers on a ramble from 'Earth' to 'Trees', 'Wilds, Wastes and Wilderness', 'Sea and Coast', and finally 'Gardens and Fields'. Broadly, ecocriticism looks at literary reflections of nature, wherein nature could be symbolic or not, and thereby it examines artistic relationships with nature and its many elements. 'Earth' prefers to deal with lyrics, not surprisingly opening with the famous 'Erthe toc of erthe' quatrain and following the various threads of what 'erthe' could signify until they lead to other lyrics, some mentioning the earth, others wind, plants and birds. 'Trees' turns first to Chaucer and what he does with particular species and with groves or woods, principally in *The Knight's Tale*, including a digression on animals (Palamon the lion and Arcite the tiger fight as wild boars), and then to Malory, such as the tree planted by Eve after the Expulsion (in the 'Book of Sir Galahad') and Lancelot getting lost in the forest. 'Wilds, Wastes and Wilderness' takes not the safety of the forest but its danger and extends that to uncontrolled spaces, such as are found in *Sir Orfeo* and *Sir Gawain and the Green Knight*, both of which 'take us from an indoors human court to a wild outdoors terrain, to another, possibly supernatural court and back' (p. 109). 'Sea and Coast' examines the voyages and passage over water in Chaucer's Man of Law's and Franklin's tales, the Chester and Wakefield Noah plays, *Cleanness*, and *Patience*. 'Gardens and Fields' involve human endeavours, and we find them in *The Franklin's Tale*, *Pearl* and, of course, Langland's *Piers Plowman*, the last two in particular bearing elements from Latin predecessors. Gardens can offer refuge and privacy, but might not exclude unwanted elements and may even grow and develop as they wish, not as people might want; Langland's book of Kynde sees order and beauty even as it seeks to establish a greater order.

History does not determine what literature may say, but writers' social and historical environment may lead them to think in certain ways. Thus, Karen Elizabeth Gross's 'Hunting, Heraldry, and the Fall in the *Boke of St. Albans* (1486)' (*Viator* 38:ii[2007] 191–215) shows how notions of class prerogatives and social understandings are embedded in the *Boke*'s encyclopedic dictionary. In a different fashion, Christoph Houswitschka discusses how individual fortunes determine the way in which writers depict Fortune, in 'The Eternal Triangle of Writer, Patron, and Fortune in Late Medieval Literature' (in Kaylor and Phillips, eds., pp. 125–41), using the examples of Christine de Pisan, Thomas Hoccleve, John Lydgate, Alain Chartier, William of Worcester, and John Fortescue. More political or social matters feature in 'Jack Cade's Rebellion of 1450 and the London Midsummer Watch' (*NMS* 51[2007] 143–66), where Alexander L. Kaufman finds Cade's midsummer behaviour in London—as described in Robert Bale's *Chronicle* and the anonymous *English Chronicle 1377–1461*—not only usurping midsummer festivities but perverting them and thereby losing him public sympathy.

Daniel Wakelin's *Humanism, Reading, & English Literature 1430–1530* wishes to emphasize the literary producers' 'new interest in the [classical] original, and the sense of its novelty' (p. 16). Wakelin begins with Duke Humfrey's commissioned works, first John Lydgate's *Fall of Princes* and its marginalia as confirming the duke's humanist interests, then the translation *On Husbondrie*, which is far more humanistic in method and appearance. Humanists like Osbern Bokenham in *De Consulatu Stilichonis* and the writer of *Knyghthode and Bataile* used classical allusions and translations to flatter their betters. The latter approaches a republican view of the commonweal, which William Worcester expands in *The Boke of Noblesse*. Humanist books were imported from abroad; Caxton and his early competitors also printed books that used classical texts to teach Latin and Ciceronian stylistics in schools and to the reader seeking cultivation. Caxton's prologues and epilogues urge the common reader to learn from classical antiquity and become worthy of political empowerment, though he misreads *Caton* to do so. Rhetoric leads to declamations and thence to debates, which appealed to humanists, whose approaches differed in balancing style and substance. Henry Medwall's *Fulgens and Lucres* instructs in oratory and begins to play upon the theme of reason—a theme recurring in Medwall's psychomachia *Nature*. The humanists' self-consciousness in originality best appears in the early sixteenth century, when English printers also began to favour translations over Greek and Latin originals. By then, humanists such as Colet, More, Elyot and Lupset had grown less open-minded, rejecting books and thinking that do not appeal to them, often using an economic metaphor of unprofitability. Some of this may have been due to doctrinal shifts under Henry VIII and Cromwell, but some, like Elyot, distinguished between the texts and their readers. In a related but different light, Andrew Higl looks at publishers' and audiences' reactions to the great names in 'Printing Power: Selling Lydgate, Gower, and Chaucer' (*EssaysMedSt* 23[2006] 57–77), finding that changed situations made Chaucer marketable, but not the other two. To those three, C. David Benson's 'Some Poets' Tours of Medieval London: Varieties of Literary Urban Experience' (*EssaysMedSt* 23[2006] 1–20) adds Hoccleve, *London Lickpenny*, and William FitzStephen's short Latin prose *Description of London* from *c*.1174 in order to share delight in the variety displayed, and that similarity of subject can produce such different results.

For works that span larger periods, let us begin with Anthony Bale's *The Jew in the Medieval Book: English Antisemitisms, 1350–1500*, which is not a history of the Jewish minority but one of how it was perceived and portrayed, beginning a generation or so after the expulsion. Four stories are traced and used as categories: history, miracle, cult, and Passion. The first story is that of the Jew at Tewkesbury who died because he and a Christian lord revered their respective Sabbaths: he fell into a privy on Saturday and he would not labour to be removed, and the lord would not labour to remove him on Sunday. This is found in Ranulph Higden's *Polychronicon*, William Rishanger's chronicle, the *Gesta Romanorum*, and elsewhere, where specific environments alter reception of the story in details, not in broad strokes. Second is the miracle of 'Hugh of Lincoln', the boy who continued to sing a Marian hymn after Jews killed him for it, best known to us from Chaucer's *Prioress's Tale* and the key element of the Croxton *Play of the Sacrament*, and well known in Latin exempla collections. Third is the tale of Robert of Bury St Edmunds, whose following rose to a cult after his alleged murder by Jews in 1181 and continued until the Reformation. There were good political reasons for Bury to establish the cult, but Lydgate's 'Praier to St Robert' is an opening for communal worship and veneration. Last is the motif of the *Arma Christi*, verses and images of objects related to the Passion, which include a 'spitting Jew'. Bale finds this fundamental to understanding the ideas about Jews, for—lacking actual communities of Jews—English writers maintained those ideas, illustrating how 'the signifier can flourish without its signified' (p. 166). An earlier Latin tale is discussed in Harvey J. Hames's 'The Limits of Conversion: Ritual Murder and the Virgin Mary in the Account of Adam of Bristol' (*JMH* 33[2007] 43–59), written *c*.1280 but placed in Henry II's reign, in which a straying priest is corrected, the converted Jews are killed, but others neither convert nor are punished, and more general Jewish conversion is implied as unlikely.

A wider chronological range but narrower focus is found in *The Harrowing of Hell in Medieval England* by Karl Tamburr, who combines typology and chronology and employs literary and non-literary materials that are fruitful for a more complete cultural understanding. The opening chapter looks at visits to the underworld before Christianity, and the movement of this tradition from east to west by the fourth century, notes traditional associations with the Exodus and baptism, and points out related liturgical features, such as the ceremony described by Margery Kempe, and the fourteenth-century dramatic rendition at Barking Abbey. The second chapter examines Christ as warrior-king rescuing the righteous souls from Hell; both motifs appear in Old English visual art and writing. The third chapter views the Harrowing backwards, relating to Adam and Eve and all those who came before the event, and forwards, as signifying the coming Judgement, with reference to Bede, *Christ I* and *II*, the Exeter *Descent, Christ and Satan*, and several homilies. Fourth, Tamburr examines the *Gospel of Nicodemus* and its visual, plastic and written reflections: *Cursor Mundi*, the Middle English metrical *Gospel of Nicodemus* and *Harrowing of Hell*, several dramas and Langland's *Piers Plowman*. The fifth chapter goes further by turning to a Marian emphasis and Christ's humanity, typically by imagining his stepping out of the tomb; literary versions occur in the N-town cycle, William Dunbar, *St Erkenwald* and Julian of Norwich. Finally, the Reformation turned away from the Harrowing, which lacks scriptural authority, and the church concurred after a fashion, even placing the *Gospel of Nicodemus* on the *Index*; nevertheless, Spenser found the Harrowing allegorically useful, and others followed in allegorizing St George's slaying of the dragon as Christ's defeat of Satan at the end of time.

Mostly late medieval works are discussed by many authors in Amanda Hopkins and Cory James Rushton's *The Erotic in the Literature of Medieval Britain*, a compilation originating, we are told, in a bar. The editors' introduction, 'The Revel, the Melodye, and the Bisynesse of Solas' (pp. 1–17) provides a broad survey of medieval sexuality, largely through modern commentators, before Sue Niebrzydowski's ' "So wel koude he me glose": The Wife of Bath and the Eroticism of Touch' (pp. 18–26) covers somewhat the same ground and then turns to the Wife and to January and May—who, we are told, 'says nothing' upon January's accusation (p. 23)—to argue that Alisoun understood and appreciated foreplay and sensitive loving. Turning to a male figure, Cory J. Rushton surveys the tradition of 'The Lady's Man: Gawain as Lover in Middle English Literature' (pp. 27–37), finding the knight's English tradition not too different from the French, in the cases of Malory, several ballads, the *Avowyng of Arthur* and *Sir Gawain and the Green Knight*. Back to women: in 'Erotic Magic: The Enchantress in Middle English Romance' (pp. 38–52), Corinne Saunders assembles a number of otherworldly ladies from Marie de France's *Lanval*, Thomas Chestre's *Sir Laundevale*, *Partonope of Blois*, *Melusine*, *Sir Gawain and the Green Knight* and several other romances, where the enchantresses tend to initiate and actively pursue their desires, although Chaucer's typically subvert the norm. Amanda Hopkins takes a different approach in ' "Wordy vnthur wede": Clothing, Nakedness and the Erotic in some Romances of Medieval Britain' (pp. 53–70): well-chosen attire in *Lybaeus Desconus*, *Sir Gawain and the Green Knight* and elsewhere enhances attractiveness, while it aggravates unattractiveness (as in Gower's 'Tale of Florent'), and nudity in the versions of *Lanval* ranges from Marie de France's erotic scantiness to *Sir Lambewell*'s static nakedness. Temperature leading to partial nudity, which then leads further, in *Sir Launfal* prompts Robert Allen Rouse in ' "Some Like it Hot": The Medieval Eroticism of Heat' (pp. 71–81) to consider similar links between hot weather and desire in *The Book of Margery Kempe*, Malory and Hoccleve's *Compleinte and Dialogue*. Using only a single work in 'How's Your Father? Sex and the Adolescent Girl in *Sir Degarré*' (pp. 82–93), Margaret Robson explores the princess's ambiguous childish adulthood and relationships with the fairy knight and her father, noting briefly the how the romance's second part seems to set right the problems of the first. Anthony Bale looks into the several fantasies revealing 'The Female "Jewish" Libido in Medieval Culture' (pp. 94–104), notably Jewish daughters, using exempla in the English translation of the *Alphabet of Tales*, the *Gesta Romanorum*, and *Jacob's Well*, and Hugh of Lincoln ballads. Michael Cichon's point in 'Eros and Error: Gross Sexual Transgression in the *Fourth Branch* of the *Mabinogi*' (pp. 105–15) is that these become offences against society: Gilfaethwy's rape of Goewin, Aranrhod's deception about her virginity (and the possible incest involved), and Blodeuwedd's adultery with Gronw Pebr against Lleu—each engendering the next—all act as offences against the honour of king and kin and violate social order. Thomas H. Crofts 'Perverse and Contrary Deeds: The Giant of Mont Saint Michel and the Alliterative *Morte Arthure*' (pp. 116–31) traces the giant and his tradition from the Old Testament to Geoffrey of Monmouth's *Historia regum Britanniae*, Wace, Layamon, and Robert Mannyng of Brunne's *Chronicle* to the *Morte*, noting changes in the rape and diet that turn the giant into a 'fully articulated nightmare' (p. 129), effectively launching Arthur into empire. Kristina Hildebrand's 'Her Desire and His: Letters between Fifteenth-Century Lovers' (pp. 132–41) takes a different approach, combing through Paston, Stonor and Plumpton letters from the betrothed or the espoused, revealing that women's register is more formal and that both express slightly suppressed sexuality.

In 'Sex in the Sight of God: Theology and the Erotic in Peter of Blois' "Grates ago veneri" ' (pp. 142–54), Simon Meecham-Jones reviews discussions of the authorship of this late twelfth-century lyric and offers it as a sly depiction of Faith triumphing over experience; the poem and his translation are appended. In 'A Fine and Private Place' (pp. 155–63), Jane Bliss finds a number of hints in the *Ancrene Wisse* concerning masturbation and lesbianism, noting that the author probably did not wish to raise these ideas in his readers but felt obliged to forbid the activities. Finally, Alex Davis leaves England for the continent in 'Erotic Historiography: Writing the Self and History in Twelfth-Century Romance and the Renaissance' (pp. 164–75).

Somewhat later yet is Thomas H. Ohlgren's *Robin Hood: The Early Poems, 1465–1560. Texts, Contexts, and Ideology*, three of whose four chapters are revised from previous publications. The first concerns *Robin Hood and the Monk*, which, apart from a fragment in the Bagford Ballads, survives in Cambridge University Library MS Ff. 5. 48, a mid-fifteenth-century manuscript Ohlgren says was owned by Gilbert Pilkington, well known as the main scribe, about whom some biographical information is given amid a manuscript description. The secular works in the manuscript are explained as works a secular priest might have mined for exempla. Second is *Robin Hood and the Potter* in Cambridge University Library MS Ee. 4. 35, a 'household' miscellany much like Pilkington's 'clerical' miscellany, supposedly patronized and first owned by the Richard Call, who was the Pastons' chief bailiff for a while, and redated to 1468 to fit Call's life and a different royal wedding. The contents are largely for self-improvement in various fashions, including mercantilism, a cusp of *Robin Hood and the Potter*'s humour and theme. In the era of print, Robin Hood tales proved popular enough for the *Lytell Geste of Robyn Hode* to be published by at least seven printers, one in Antwerp. The last chapter covers the version of *A Lytell Geste of Robyn Hode* printed by Pynson, *c*.1495, which Ohlgren believes 'was originally commissioned in the mid-to-late fifteenth century' for a mayoral inauguration or 'possibly the Draper's Company' (p. 25). For that reason, a lot of background is presented on mercantilism, Jack Cade's rebellion, King Edward in Robin Hood tales, Sir Richard at the Lee and guilds and their patron saints, activities, regulations and entertainments.

Moving from the fifteenth into the sixteenth century, with an eye on politics, is Robert J. Meyer-Lee's *Poets and Power from Chaucer to Wyatt*, first establishing an idea of laureate poetics in Chaucer and then tracing this poetics from Lydgate to Wyatt. The starting point is a distinction between Ricardian and Lancastrian poetics: authorial self-representation bridging from Petrarch to Chaucer, whose self-representation is paralleled in Langland's Will and Gower's Amans. Painting with a broad brush, Meyer-Lee turns to Lydgate as a monastic historian who used a humility topos to serve the authorities who were learning how to use him for their own purposes. Hoccleve reacts to the same historical situation as a mendicant poet, instead resisting power and struggling with his low rank within the administration. As a result, their poetry aimed in different directions—Lydgate's largely extended beyond his personal status and needs, while Hoccleve's turned inward. Even in the *Regiment of Princes* the lengthy prologue's begging belies any laureate authority Hoccleve might obtain, as the *Series* attests. Between Lydgate and Caxton are Benedict Burgh's 'Letter to John Lydgate', which strives to walk in his master's footsteps, William de la Pole's 'Reproof to Lydgate', which hopes to replace Lydgate by criticizing him, and George Ashby, who is both Lydgatean and Hocclevean and thus 'special' (p. 140) in politicizing poetry while touting his self-interest. After this, Meyer-Lee poses, a commodification of cultural objects took place, first with Shirley and certainly Caxton, to whom patronage seemed to be a business. Later, John Skelton, Stephen Hawes and Alexander Barclay strove to be like Lydgate, but lived more like Hoccleve. Meyer-Lee concludes with Wyatt, who took subjectivity and immersed it into his poetics, a tradition continuing up through Wordsworth.

More narrowly political, in *Literature and Complaint in England, 1272–1553*, Wendy Scase takes the development of judicial *pleinte* as strongly influential literary development, although she admits that the most revealing texts are not considered mainstream. The tale begins with Edward I's legal reforms and the curious problem that plaintiffs could be peasants but peasants were basically not legal subjects. Those of higher social status imitated or reflected their voices in the macaronic *Poem on Disputed Villein Services*, the Anglo-Norman *Song of the Church*, and the Middle English *Satire on the Retinues of the Great* and *Song of the Husbandman*. As the legal system developed, 'clamour' provided satirists with material; thus the Latin *Song on the Venality of Judges*, the French *Trailbaston*, the Middle English *Song on the Times*, and a macaronic invective against Roger Beler laid groundwork for later complaints in English, such as the Mercers' petition against Nicholas Brembre, which includes a sharp pun on his name. From this arose a 'literature of clamour', clearly recognized from the Peasants' Revolt and Lollard writings (such as the *Twelve Conclusions* and the *Lollard Disendowment Bill*), spreading more broadly in the late fifteenth century. *Piers Plowman* has relevant passages, but more so are related works such as *Richard the Redeless* and *Mum and Sothsegger*. Later 'literature of clamour' includes bills and occasional verses related to Jack Cade's rebellion, the Wars of the Roses and later troubles. Being occasional, these complaints were largely ephemeral and rarely survive outside larger works, such as the *New Chronicles of England and France*. Reflecting legal formulae in the *artes dictaminis* and formularies, the English complaints provided a model for an English *dictamen* that appears in works by Chaucer, Usk, Gower and Hoccleve; it even appears in rubrics and side-notes of poems, signifying wider influence.

Noel Harold Kaylor, Jr, and Richard Scott Nokes's *Global Perspectives on Medieval English Literature, Language, and Culture* is a sort of Festschrift for Paul Szarmach's direction of the Medieval Institute at Western Michigan University and the long-running International Congress on Medieval Studies, the volume here emphasizing contacts with Korean and Polish scholars. Andrzej Wicher points to cosmology as providing 'Medieval Echoes in C.S. Lewis's *The Chronicle of Narnia* with a Special Emphasis on *The Voyage of the Dawn Treader*' (pp. 3–20). Liliana Sikorska sees elements of medieval drama transformed for 'Writing a New Morality Play: The Court as the World in John Skelton's *Magnyfycence* and John Redford's *Wit and Science*' (pp. 21–40). Ji-Soo Kang's 'Clerical Anxiety, Margery's Crying, and her Book' (pp. 41–58) argues that her crying threatens patriarchal power structures. According to Władysław Witalisz's ' "The blood I souke of his feet": The Christocentric Heritage of Medieval Affective Piety—A Historical Overview' (pp. 59–91), Christ's humanity grew in importance across the early Middle Ages. In 'Despotic Mares, Dirty Sows, and Angry Bitches: On Middle English Zoosemy and Beyond' (pp. 93–116), Grzegorz A. Kleparski gives examples of animal metaphors, which tended to be applied to women. An Sonjae (Brother Anthony of Taizé)'s 'No Greater Pain: The Ironies of Bliss in Chaucer's *Troilus and Criseyde*' (pp. 117–32) parallels Chaucer with Dante, while in 'Re-examining Geoffrey Chaucer's Work in an Age of Globalization: *Troilus and Criseyde* and Chaucer's Global Perspective' (pp. 133–53) Noel Harold Kaylor Jr finds the parallels with Dante reveal a marked shift in direction of gaze. In 'Global Literature, Medieval Literature, and the *Popol Vuh*' (pp. 261–74), Richard Scott Nokes proposes 'the study of global literatures through the study of manuscript literature' (p. 263), which lies between oral and printed materials.

Spanning many centuries, including several visual art pieces, and using both Middle English and Latin prose, verse and dramatic texts, Jacqueline Tasioulas briefly explores ' "Heaven and Earth in little space": The Foetal Existence of Christ in Medieval Literature and Thought' (*MÆ* 76[2007] 24–48), since medieval imagination about Christ began with the Annunciation, for the laity and scholars alike. In '*Wod* et *wode* dans la littérature médiévale ou l'espace de la folie' (*MoyA* 113[2007] 361–82) Marie-Françoise Alamichel scans quite a few Middle English works for descriptions of or references to madness, adding several Old English and Latin references. In a somewhat similar fashion, Merridee L. Bailey's 'In Service and at Home: Didactic Texts for Children and Young People, c.1400–1600' (*Parergon* 24:ii[2007] 23–46) surveys a good number of texts, with an eye on what they reveal about adults' thinking about the young. In 'Aesop, Authorship, and the Aesthetic Imagination' (*JMEMS* 37[2007] 579–94), Seth Lerer muses on the didactic and moral uses of Aesopica, ranging from classical Greece through the Middle Ages to Hamlet, with constant reminders of modern interpretations shaping reception of the fables. *New Medieval Literatures* 9 includes versions of talks on medievalism from the 2006 New Chaucer Society: Thomas A. Prendergast and Stephanie Trigg's 'What Is Happening to the Middle Ages?' (*NML* 9[2007] 215–29) and Carolyn Dinshaw's 'Are We Having Fun Yet? A Response to Prendergast and Trigg' (*NML* 9[2007] 231–41) both see-saw between medieval studies and medievalism, but seem to agree broadly that ages rewrite the past with the pens of the present.

An offering more related to language studies is David Postles's *The North through its Names: A Phenomenology of Medieval and Early-Modern Northern England*, not restricting itself to names as attested in the north but with emphasis on names reflecting northern origins, and extending into the eighteenth century and into the prickly problem of bastardy. Because areas themselves varied in naming practices, Postles looks into family names ending in *-son* (mainly north of the Wash) and similar family-related names, such as -*wif* and -*doghter* (for example Agnes Magotesdowter). The north also has a proclivity for names in *-man* (including *-servant*), *-thacker*, *-lister*, *-greave*, and a preference for voicing *w-* to *qu-*. Bynames include the well-known ending *-by* as well as *Fox* and *Todd*, variants such as *-man/mon* or *-bank/bonk*, and various forms of *Pinder*. Personal names seem to have a tradition different from those in the south, and it is a curiosity that hypercorisms were often Latinized and enrolled in documents. On the other hand, occupational bynames were largely vernacularized and lasted longer in the north, as did topographical names including the preposition *del* and a strong mixture of Brettonic, Scandinavian, and Old English names. Sexual, somatic, animal and other types of nicknames are well attested, some of them evidently of a 'flyting' nature, and these continued into early modern times. By then, of course, many dislocations had occurred due to late medieval social and pestilential causes, and the records belie many perceived memorializations. A number of these features do help to separate northern and southern naming habits, despite the problem of Scandinavian influences.

V.P. McCarren, Ashby Kinch and Sean Pollock present 'A Prologomena to the Stonyhurst *Medulla*: An Edition of the Letter "A" ' (*Archivum*

Latinitatis medii aevi [*Bulletin du Cange*] 65[2007] 47–116), the *Medulla Grammatice* being a Latin–English dictionary from the late fifteenth century. Before the text, they discuss the prickliness of Greek and Hebrew in England, and stress the corrections and additions a full edition would add to the *OED*, the *MED*, and the *Dictionary of Medieval Latin from British Sources*. This may be a tough slog for *YWES* readers, but it is well worth the effort.

Some student guides have appeared this year, whether for class use or for independent study. Thorlac Turville-Petre's *Reading Middle English Literature* is one of Blackwell 's Introductions to Literature series for students and, as such, aims to provide background information rather than specific readings of selected texts, although this is designed to accompany his *Book of Middle English*. Accordingly, chapters are devoted to broad subjects, though they rarely stray far from literary examples: 'The Use of English' in its trilingual environment, 'Texts and Manuscripts', 'Literature and Society', ranging from bond and free men to Arthur's court and Criseyde's palace, 'History and Romance' with *Erkenwald*, Arthur and fairyland, 'Piety', ranging widely, and 'Love and Marriage', with some close readings from a number of apt texts. A different student introduction is Andrew Galloway's *Medieval Literature and Culture*, a volume in Continuum's Introductions to British Literature and Culture. Galloway opens with a cultural and political overview which surveys the populations in different periods—Roman Britain and the Germanic invasions, Anglo-Saxon, late West Saxon, Anglo-Norman, and later medieval—and offers a medieval social division between the rulers, the clergy and learning, and the labourers, with many references to historical and literary works. He then provides an overview of the literature twice: first, an historical overview (Anglo-Saxon, Anglo-Norman and later), and secondly by genres also somewhat divided across those periods (epic and history, lyric, prose, romance, saints' lives, allegory, satire and drama). This is followed by a survey of how medieval English literature was studied from the Renaissance through to the eighteenth century, the nineteenth and mid-twentieth centuries and more recently. The final chapter offers a number of 'resources': a chronology of works, people and events; a very short glossary of terms and concepts; a table of kings and rulers; and a bibliography, followed by an index.

On a somewhat more advanced level is Paul Strohm's *Middle English*, an Oxford Twenty-First Century Approaches to Literature offering, for which the emphasis is on what is coming or yet to come (including a section on 'Further Reading'), and in which themes are examined rather than texts. In the first thematic section, 'Conditions and Contexts', Carol Symes's 'Manuscript Matrix, Modern Canon' (pp. 7–22) proposes that 'If a [manuscript] text is decorative, large, distinctive, or bizarre, it will be remarked...if...it is mutable, camouflaged, and chameleon-like, it may pass unnoticed' (p. 8) and gives *Beowulf* (not *Judith*) as an example of a remarked text, although it is 'obscure' (p. 10) and not Middle English. 'Fluidity' seems key to Robert M. Stein's 'Multilingualism' (pp. 23–37) and Christopher Baswell's 'Multilingualism on the Page' (pp. 38–50), while Henry Lovelich is the exemplar of 'Translation' for Michelle R. Warren (pp. 51–67). Joyce Coleman's 'Aurality' (pp. 68–85) uses pictures to explain how works by

Chaucer, Gower and Malory were good to read or hear. Alexandra Gillespie approaches the instability of 'Books' (pp. 86–103) through Chaucer's 'Adam Scriveyn', Adam Pinkhurst and *Mum and the Sothsegger*. In the second section, 'Vantage Points', Carolyn Dinshaw approaches 'Temporalities' (pp. 107–23) or 'time perception' through Margery Kempe; Diane Cady theorizes 'Symbolic Economies' (pp. 124–41), or money, with a bit of Langland; Emily Steiner confronts 'Authority' (pp. 142–59) with drama and Langland; D. Vance Smith imagines 'Institutions' (pp. 160–76) with Chaucer's *House of Fame*, Hoccleve and Wyclif; Christopher Cannon takes on 'Form' (pp. 177–90) in a Platonic sense, using Robert Mannyng of Brunne's *Handlyng Synne* and *Pearl*; Elizabeth Allen's 'Episodes' (pp. 191–206) touches on *Athelston*, *Sir Degaré*, *Beves of Hampton* and the *Seven Sages of Rome*; Maura Nolan examines 'Beauty' (pp. 207–21) through Chaucer's *Miller's Tale*; Nicolette Zeeman confronts 'Imaginative Theory' (pp. 222–40) with *chansons d'aventure*; Sarah McNamer gets in touch with 'Feeling' (pp. 241–57) with help from *Wooing of Our Lord* and *Sir Gawain and the Green Knight*; and Marion Turner deals with 'Conflict' (pp. 258–73) under Richard II.

In the third section, 'Textual Kinds and Categories', Alfred Hiatt looks at the mutability of 'romaunce', 'balade' and 'tragedye' in 'Genre Without System' (pp. 277–94); Bruce Holsinger examines the difficulties and importance of 'Liturgy' (pp. 295–314) to the whole culture and literature; Jessica Brantley uses only one picture for the interrelationships among 'Vision, Image, Text' (pp. 315–34); Karen A. Winstead questions 'Saintly Exemplarity' (pp. 335–51); Matthew Giancarlo's 'Speculative Genealogies' (pp. 352–68) concern the romances; Nancy Bradley Warren turns to Julian of Norwich, Langland and Chaucer for 'Incarnational (Auto)biography' (pp. 369–85); Sheila Lindenbaum takes 'Drama as Textual Practice' (pp. 386–400) from mundane affairs; Vincent Gillespie ranges widely, especially in the age of Arundel, to explore 'Vernacular Theology' (pp. 401–20); and Andrew Cole finds a shift between 'Heresy and Humanism' (pp. 421–37) across the central six or seven decades of the fifteenth century. In the fourth section, 'Writing and the World', Kellie Robertson's 'Authorial Work' (pp. 441–58) looks to the valuing of labour, especially Chaucer's *General Prologue*; Stephanie Trigg's 'Learning to Live' (pp. 459–75) turns to questions raised by conduct literature; Susan E. Phillips turns to the likes of Chaucer's Canon's Yeoman and Robert Mannyng of Brunne in 'Gossip and (Un)official Writing' (pp. 476–90); and Lisa H. Cooper imagines *Fachliteratur* as high art in 'The Poetics of Practicality' (pp. 491–505).

Another such offering is Peter Brown's *A Companion to Medieval English Literature and Culture, c.1350–c.1500*, a hefty tome opening with some general overviews on 'Critical Approaches', by David Raybin (pp. 9–24), 'English Society in the Later Middle Ages: Deference, Ambition and Conflict', by S.H. Rigby (pp. 25–39), 'Religious Authority and Dissent', by Mishtooni Bose (pp. 40–55), 'City and Country, Wealth and Labour', by Sarah Rees Jones (pp. 56–73), and 'Women's Voices and Roles', by Carol M. Meale (pp. 74–90), before moving to 'Manuscripts and Readers', by A.S.G. Edwards (pp. 93–106), 'From Manuscript to Modern Text', by Julia Boffey (pp. 107–22), and 'Translation and Society', by Catherine Batt (pp. 123–39), after which come 'The Languages of Medieval Britain', by Laura Wright (pp. 143–58) and Donka Minkova's 'The Forms of Speech' and 'The Forms of Verse' (pp. 159–75, 176–95). A section on 'Encounters with Other Cultures' includes England and France', by Ardis Butterfield (pp. 199–214), 'Britain and Italy: Trade, Travel, Translation', by Nick Havely (pp. 215–30), 'England's Antiquities: Middle English Literature and the Classical Past', by Christopher Baswell (pp. 231–46) and 'Jews, Saracens, "Black Men", Tartars: England in a World of Racial Difference', by Geraldine Heng (pp. 247–69).

A section on 'Special Themes' has 'War and Chivalry', by Richard W. Kaeuper and Montgomery Bohna (pp. 273–91), 'Literature and Law', by Richard Firth Green (pp. 292–306), 'Images', mostly in Gower and Hoccleve, by Peter Brown (pp. 307–21), and 'Love', by Barry Windeatt (pp. 322–38). 'Genres' includes 'Middle English Romance', by Thomas Hahn and Dana M. Symons (pp. 341–57), 'Histories and Chronicles' by Raluca L. Radulescu (pp. 358–73), 'Dream Poems', by Helen Phillips (pp. 374–86), 'Lyric', with a good number of examples, by Rosemary Greentree (pp. 387–405), 'Literature of Religious Instruction', by E.A. Jones (pp. 406–22), 'Mystical and Devotional Literature', by Denise N. Baker (pp. 423–36), 'Accounts of Lives', by Kathleen Ashley (pp. 437–53), 'Medieval English Theatre: Codes and Genres', by Meg Twycross (pp. 454–72), and 'Morality and Interlude Drama', by Darryll Grantley (pp. 473–87). The final section of 'Readings' varies between broad introductions and more specific investigatory approaches to selected works or authors. The introductory type includes Pamela King's 'York Mystery Plays' (pp. 491–506), Ruth Evans's 'The *Book of Margery Kempe*' (pp. 507–21), Santha Bhattacharji's 'Julian of Norwich' (pp. 522–36), Stephen Kelly's '*Piers Plowman*' (pp. 537–53), Nicholas Perkins's 'Thomas Hoccleve, *La Male Regle*' (pp. 585–603) and Kevin Gustafson's '*Sir Gawain and the Green Knight*' (pp. 619–33). The investigatory type includes Mark Miller's 'Subjectivity and Ideology in the *Canterbury Tales*' (pp. 554–68), J. Allan Mitchell's 'John Gower and John Lydgate: Forms and Norms of Rhetorical Culture' (pp. 569–84), R. James Goldstein's 'Discipline and Relaxation in the Poetry of Robert Henryson' (pp. 604–18) and Catherine La Farge's 'Blood and Love in Malory's *Morte Darthur*' (pp. 634–47).

2. Women's Writing

The year 2007 was another big one for work on women's writing or medieval texts concerning medieval women. Before turning to this, the section will begin with an overdue review of the 2005 volume, *Intersections of Sexuality and the Divine in Medieval Culture: The Word Made Flesh*, edited by Susannah Mary Chewning. The collection, divided into four sections—'Secular Literature and Drama', 'Romance and Narrative', 'Saints and Religious Women' and 'Visionaries and Mystics'—contains many individual essays, particularly in the latter two sections, that are useful for scholars of women and gender in the medieval literature of England. Margery Kempe is the focus of Liz Herbert

McAvoy's 'Virgin, Mother, Whore: The Sexual Spirituality of Margery Kempe' (pp. 121–38). This chapter forms part of McAvoy's 2004 monograph *Authority and the Female Body in the Writings of Julian of Norwich and Margery Kempe* (*YWES* 85[2006] 195–6) and deftly brings together and analyses the paradoxes of Kempe's social and spiritual gender roles. Julie E. Fromer's 'Spectator of Martyrdom: Corporeality and Sexuality in the *Liflade ant te Passiun of Seinte Margarete*' (pp. 89–106) looks at the Katherine Group's St Margaret legend and argues that the text is constructed in such a way as to create an awareness of the readers' corporeality over that of the saint herself. The Katherine Group's sister text is the subject of Michelle M. Sauer's 'Cross-Dressing Souls: Same-Sex Desire and the Mystic Tradition in *A Talkyng of the Loue of God*' (pp. 157–81). Sauer discusses the *Talkyng* in light of its deviations from its sources in the Wohunge Group: *Þe Wohunge of ure Laured* and *On Uriesun of ure Lourede*, arguing that the changes translate an originally female-directed text into one that plays with gender and its inversions. Chewning herself looks at the *Wohunge* in ' "Mi bodi henge / wið þi bodi": The Paradox of Sensuality in *Þe Wohunge of Ure Lauerd*' (pp. 183–96), exploring how the physical and erotic metaphors of the text conflict with the spiritual and devotional concepts they are meant to represent for its readers. The virtues of the volume include its expansive definitions of eroticism and spirituality and the wide variety of texts covered (including, among others, the York cycle, conduct literature and Chaucer), demonstrating how firmly integrated devotion and its often gendered language was in the fabric of medieval literary culture.

A Companion to Medieval English Literature and Culture c.1350–c.1500, edited by Peter Brown, has several articles of note to scholars of medieval women's writing, touching upon the works of Marie de France, Julian of Norwich, Margery Kempe and the Paston family, as well as important female-centred texts like the *Ancrene Wisse*. Carol M. Meale's 'Women's Voices and Roles' (pp. 74–90) begins with the question with which scholars of medieval women's history and literature must constantly contend: 'did [medieval women] internalize [the] gendered construct, promulgated by a masculine elite; or did they negotiate with it, thus enabling mental and physical space through which to express themselves, their needs and their desires?' (p. 75). Meale's excellent article, which also serves as a small survey of women writers and readers in medieval England, approaches questions of women's literacy in medieval England, their influence and patronage. Ardis Butterfield's 'England and France' (pp. 199–213) looks at, among other texts, the prologue Marie de France wrote to her *lais*, arguing that it 'encapsulates the relations between England and the French' (p. 201), and brings to the forefront issues of both linguistic and cultural translations.

In 'Mystical and Devotional Literature' (pp. 423–36), Denise N. Baker gives an overview of the genre of Middle English mysticism, including the works of Richard Rolle, Walter Hilton, Julian of Norwich and Margery Kempe. Baker helpfully defines the terms of her title, and how they are both used and misused, before discussing the works themselves in more detail. Ruth Evans tackles Kempe more closely in 'The *Book of Margery Kempe*' (pp. 507–21) warning against a tendency in Kempe scholarship to reduce both the book and its protagonist to 'what is immediately familiar and comprehensible' (p. 507) when they defy this categorization. She looks closely at the vision Margery describes of looking for her name in the Book of Life, using this moment to clarify other themes in the *Book* and Margery's devotional practices, as well as to address questions of reading, writing and authority that the *Book* raises. 'Julian of Norwich', by Santha Bhattacharji (pp. 522–36), fittingly follows Margery Kempe. Bhattacharji begins the chapter with the claim that Julian is often considered 'ground-breaking where she is conventional' (p. 522) and ignored when she is truly revolutionary in her thought and theology. She contrasts Julian to Margery, situating Julian's approach in the context of the mystical, devotional landscape of fifteenth-century England. Bhattacharji ends the article with an entry into the debate about the dating of the Short and Long texts, somewhat challenging the dominant view that the Short precedes the Long by several years.

The year also saw several monographs take the subject of medieval women as their sole focus. Sandy Bardsley's *Women's Roles in the Middle Ages* is part of the relatively new Women's Roles through History series by Greenwood Press, and as such is a broad overview directed at a wide audience. Bardsley immediately acknowledges the problem with such an overview in her introduction: that 'discussing medieval women as a group implies that they saw they had something common' (p. 3), when in fact class and religion drastically divided medieval women from one another. The book reads like an introductory textbook in many places, defining important terms such as prosopography, and containing chapters that discuss women's roles in medieval religion, work, family, law, culture and power. The temporal and geographical range is sweeping, from the early Middle Ages to the late and from Byzantium to England. As far as English women writers go, Margery Kempe, Julian of Norwich and Margaret Paston all make several appearances. Because of the broad nature of the text, and the goals of the series, it would work very well as an introduction to the subject for a class, but is probably not as useful to more specialized scholars.

Helen M. Jewell's *Women in Late Medieval and Reformation Europe 1200–1550* is in Palgrave's European Culture and Society series, and is both more geographically and temporally limited than Bardsley's, focusing on the Latin West in the high and later Middle Ages. As with Bardsley, Margery Kempe and Julian of Norwich are well represented in the section entitled 'Women and Religion' (pp. 104–32). Both Bardsley and Jewell are historians, and they both contextualize Kempe and Julian from a historical perspective rather than a literary one but, given the interdisciplinary work so many medievalists do, that contextualization may be helpful indeed. Jewell's slim volume also feels like a nice introduction or accompaniment to a class on the subject of medieval women, but less helpful for a specialized reader.

In Diane Watt's *Medieval Women's Writing*, we have a literary critic's take on many of the same women that Bardsley and Jewell assess in their books. Watt's book is also directed at a broad audience, but her chapters are more specific and therefore nuanced than most introductory texts. Each chapter would be of interest to scholars of women in medieval England, in particular those who work on Christina of Markyate, Marie de France, legends and lives of women saints, Julian of Norwich, Margery Kempe and the Paston letters. The chapter on Christina deftly elucidates the problems of hagiography, where a woman's voice is filtered and mediated through that of the male author. Watt also discusses the wide range of cultural and linguistic traditions (French, Latin and Anglo-Saxon) surrounding Christina's life, positing that it represents a kind of hybrid textuality. In her chapter on Marie de France, Watt examines her hybridities as French/English/Anglo-Norman and as a translator/writer. Looking at the *Lais*, the *Fables*, and *Saint Patrick's Purgatory*, Watt makes a case for Marie's writing as a voice searching for definition and identity, one distinctly aware of gender and language. In the chapter on saints' lives, Watt returns to the story of Christina of Markyate, as well as other legends and saints' lives concerning local English saints, but also looks closely at Clemence of Barking's *Life of St. Catherine*. This chapter discusses the differences between translation and invention, and shows how Catherine (as well as Marie de France) navigates these same waters. Watt's chapter on Julian of Norwich certainly goes beyond introductory material as it seeks to evaluate the writing, reception and transmission of Julian's texts, which Watt—after Nicholas Watson and Jaqueline Jenkins's 2006 edition of Julian (*YWES* 87[2008] 236–7)—distinguishes as the *Vision* and the *Revelation*. Watt's chapter on Margery Kempe is likewise nuanced, also looking closely at the production and audience of Kempe's *Book*. This chapter easily pulls in elements of the prior ones, looking at saints' lives, especially that of Christina of Markyate, as well as Julian's writings. Watt closes with a chapter on the Paston letters, looking at both the lives and the words of the Norfolk Paston family's nearly fifty years of correspondence, much of it by women. The chapter appropriately problematizes the notion of women's authorship when it comes to letters, parsing out the relationship between the letter-writer and 'subjects, patrons, secretaries and readers' (p. 156) which certainly influenced what was written and by whom. Watt's fine volume concludes with an extremely useful bibliography and list of suggested readings.

The hefty volume *The Power of a Woman's Voice in Medieval and Early Modern Literatures* by Albrecht Classen has a few chapters that deal with medieval England, although the book also addresses continental literature such as that by Hildegard von Bingen and Christine de Pizan. Marie de France is the subject of two chapters, the first 'Women's Secular and Spiritual Power in the Middle Ages' (pp. 105–34), where Classen examines Marie's prologues and epilogues, and argues that the self-conscious nature of Marie's writing has much to say about her understanding of herself as a female author and authority. He then goes on to look at the women in Marie's *lais*, arguing that Marie's female characters have a power and autonomy normally missing from the romance tradition. Finally, Classen concludes the chapter by bringing Marie into dialogue with Hildegard von Bingen, arguing that 'neither Hildegard nor Marie specifically criticize the patriarchal structure of their societies, but implicitly they clearly staked their individuality and independence within a male-dominated world' (p. 133).

Marie also appears in the lengthily named chapter 'Domestic Violence in Medieval and Early-Modern German, French, Italian, and English Literature

(Marie de France, Boccaccio, and Geoffrey Chaucer)' (pp. 187–230). The title of the chapter is odd, however, because so many writers are mentioned other than the three named ones, who do not even make up the majority of the texts discussed. Marie's section is brief, touching on brutality in 'Guigemar', 'Equitan' and 'Yonec'. Classen devotes an entire chapter to Margery Kempe in 'Margery Kempe as a Writer: A Woman's Voice in the Mystical and Literary Discourse' (pp. 271–308). He begins by addressing the question of whether Kempe's book should be considered a text of mystical autobiography, or something else altogether, as well as what a reader can take as 'literary' from her idiosyncratic text. The rest of the chapter attempts to address these questions in relation to Margery, her text, and her social, religious and literary context. Classen ultimately views Margery's text as a compilation of dialogue, genre and visions—a kind of experimental discourse of the late Middle Ages. Overall, the book is scrupulously footnoted and researched, the bibliography alone will be of interest to scholars of medieval woman, but so much is packed into the text that one wishes points and examples were expanded upon.

Rounding out the monographs on medieval women and their texts is Jane Chance's *The Literary Subversions of Medieval Women*. Like Classen, Chance surveys both English and continental women's writing. Marie de France, Margery Kempe and Julian of Norwich are all well represented, as is the Middle English version of Catherine of Siena's *Dialogue*, *The Orchard of Syon*. Using postcolonial concepts of marginalization and otherness, Chance states that her purpose is to 'define a medieval feminist pattern of literary strategies of subversion in which women writers, resisting the repressions of a patriarchy that demanded a silencing of the female voice, express their alterity within the dominant tradition by rewriting conventions, and thereby, establishing authority as female' (p. 17). In her chapter on Marie, 'Marie de France versus King Arthur: Lanval's Gender Inversion as Breton Subversion' (pp. 41–61), Chance looks closely at Marie's *lai*, *Lanval*, and argues that Lanval—in his outsider, feminized and initially powerless state—mirrors Marie's own position as a woman in the English court, satisfying Marie's fantasy when he rejects the chivalric world of Arthur's court for a realm ruled by a fairy queen. She turns to Margery Kempe in 'Unhomely Margery Kempe and St. Catherine of Siena: "Comunycacyon" and "Conuersacion" as Homily' (pp. 99–126). In this chapter, Chance discusses the way in which Margery turns her unconventional and aberrant behaviour to advantage when dealing with charges of Lollardy and heresy—drawing on her presumptive powerlessness and marginality to counter such accusations. The only problem with this interesting chapter, and the important parallels that Chance draws between Margery's *Book* and Catherine's *Dialogue*, is that Chance refers to and uses the Middle English *Orchard* as if this is Catherine's own text, rather than the *Dialogue*. Chance's conclusion, 'Toward a Minor Literature: Julian of Norwich's Annihilation of Original Sin' (pp. 127–33), takes up Julian's *Revelations* and her feminized theology therein. Chance argues that all of the women writers she discusses, exemplified in Julian, create a 'minor literature' (p. 127) that is opposed to the dominant generic expectations and texts of the larger body of medieval literature, drawing on their own outsider status and marginal position in order to do so.

Palgrave's New Middle Ages series, in which Chance's book appears, published many useful books this year on the subject of gender. One volume in the series is the collection *Women and Medieval Epic: Gender, Genre, and the Limits of Epic Masculinity*, edited by Sara S. Poor and Jana K. Shulman. While most of the essays deal with Norse and German literature, the first essay, 'Winning Women in Two Middle English Alexander Poems', by Christine Chism (pp. 15–40), deals with women in the Middle English *Kyng Alisaunder* and *Wars of Alexander*. Another book in the same series, Valerie Allen's *On Farting: Language and Laughter in the Middle Ages*, deftly (and humorously) looks at the literature, etymology and history of farts, as well as other bodily functions, in the Middle Ages. Margery Kempe makes a few important appearances, most notably in her disgust at having to clean up after her sick and incontinent husband. Finally, Albrecht Classen's *The Medieval Chastity Belt: A Myth-Making Process* will also be useful to scholars of gender in the Middle Ages, especially those interested in medievalism or medieval myths in today's culture. As part of his study Classen looks at medieval texts, including Marie de France's *Guigemar*, which have been used (or misused, as Classen argues) in support of the idea of a chastity belt.

Another of the many interesting volumes to come out of Palgrave's New Middle Ages series this year is Cary Howie's *Claustrophilia: The Erotics of Enclosure in Medieval Literature*. Although the title seems to indicate that the book will focus on an anchoritic tradition, it is in fact a discussion of the idea of enclosure in many forms and its manifestation in primarily continental medieval literature. However, the chapter entitled 'Nothing Between' is largely devoted to the insular texts of Julian of Norwich and Marie de France. In his discussion of Marie's *Yonec* and *Guigemar*, Howie touches on the 'enclosed' women (both locked up against their will) of these *lais* and suggests that the texts demand of their readers and characters both a forced intimacy and a separation. Julian, Howie argues, takes enclosure not only as the material reality of her life but also as the foremost trope of her *Revelations*. Both Marie and Julian are concerned with defining space and proximity of the self to the other, be it human or God. Overall, Howie's text is more concerned with the theoretical implications of enclosure and eroticism than how these play out in specific medieval texts.

Kaylor and Nokes, eds., *Global Perspectives*, has two essays of particular interest here. The first, '"The blood I souke of his feet": The Christocentric Heritage of Medieval Affective Piety—A Historical Overview' (pp. 59–92) by Władysław Witalisz looks at the evolution of worship related to Christ's humanity, a movement towards an understanding of Christ that culminates in the mystical authors of the later Middle Ages such as Julian of Norwich and Margery Kempe. Beginning with the early Church Fathers and ending with the Middle English authors, Witalisz gives a comprehensive survey of complex theological issues and controversies. Margery Kempe is also the subject of Ji-Soo Kang's 'Clerical Anxiety, Margery's Crying, and her Book' (pp. 41–58). Here, Kang discusses the accusation and reality of Kempe's Lollardy and other suspected heresies, focusing on Kempe's relationship to the clergy and how this intersects with Lollard beliefs (real and imagined) about clerical authority.

Another book that offers useful essays to the scholar of medieval women writers is Hopkins and Rushton, eds., *The Erotic in the Literature of Medieval Britain*. In Kristina Hildebrand's essay 'Her Desire and His: Letters Between Fifteenth-Century Lovers' (pp. 132–41), the Paston, Stoner and Plumpton papers are looked at closely, revealing the erotic desire of the mostly private correspondence. Hildebrand acknowledges the difficulty of reading between the lines and lacunae of the texts, but argues that, upon examination, desire (and gendered differences among that desire) can be discerned through the husband–wife correspondence in these family papers. Jane Bliss's 'A Fine and Private Place' (pp. 155–63) also takes up a question of hidden eroticism in her reading of lesbian desire in texts as diverse as the *Ancrene Wisse* and Gower's *Confessio Amantis*.

Kathryn Kerby-Fulton's *Books under Suspicion: Censorship and Tolerance of Revelatory Writing in Late Medieval England* (*YWES* 87[2008] 286–7) was the subject of a series of responses in the *Journal of British Studies*, several which touched on women's writing—as did Kerby-Fulton's book, with its specific look at Julian of Norwich, Margery Kempe and the Middle English translation of Marguerite Porete's *Mirror*. John Arnold's 'Comment: Social Contexts of Censorship and Power' (*JBS* 46[2007] 748–52) brings historical and literary research on revelatory writing into dialogue, arguing that Kerby-Fulton's book should open the door to similarly sweeping research on the texts of countries other than England. Dyan Elliot, in 'Comment: English Exceptionalism Reconsidered' (*JBS* 46[2007] 753–7), remarks that Kerby-Fulton's book opens up the traditional understanding of heretical inquisition in late medieval England to more scrutiny. Anne Hudson also responds to Kerby-Fulton in 'Comment: Senses of Censorship' (*JBS* 46[2007] 758–61). Hudson complicates and questions the term 'censorship' as it is used in *Books under Suspicion*, arguing that our understanding of what censorship is and entails in late medieval England needs to be further parsed. Scott Lucas closes the comments by placing Kerby-Fulton's claims in relation to early modern England in 'Comment: The Visionary Genre and the Rise of the "Literary": *Books under Suspicion and Early Modern England*' (*JBS* 46[2007] 762–5). Kerby-Fulton herself closes this discussion with 'Response: *Books under Suspicion* and Beyond' (*JBS* 46[2007] 766–73). She takes up the criticisms (particularly those raised by Hudson) and compliments of the commentaries, responding to specific points and raising broader questions and avenues of enquiry. In the entire round-table discussion (a format, I would add, that is exceedingly provocative and rich and that *JBS* among other journals should continue), the texts of Margery Kempe and Julian of Norwich are both at its centre and on the margins.

D.H. Green tells his audience in the introduction to *Women Readers in the Middle Ages* that the book is written by a Germanist, even though it is surveying women's reading practices (and representations of these practices) in France and England, in addition to Germany. This information is valuable and sheds light on the approach taken throughout the book, which has more of a philological outlook than a theoretical one. A survey of the primary medieval texts cited and discussed in the book yields more German than any other language, but French and English texts are still well represented. In the section entitled 'Categories of Women Readers' Green gives a general survey of evidence of laywomen, nuns, recluses, semi-religious women and 'heretics' (in which category he looks at Lollardy, as well as accusations against Margery Kempe and Mechthild von Magdeburg). He also looks at some centres of women's reading, particularly convents, such as Barking, Syon and Helfta. I found myself wanting the book to focus on one of the many areas that Green covers: fictional characters, 'real' women readers, or other ways of reading. While Green has delivered a very astute, encompassing look at reading in the Middle Ages and then more closely at women's reading in the Middle Ages, it is one that ultimately provides a survey (as he himself calls it) rather than an in-depth study.

Catherine Sanok also takes up questions of reading, and in particular women's reading, in *Her Life Historical: Exemplarity and Female Saints' Lives in Late Medieval England*. Sanok argues that female saints' lives functioned as a kind of historical knowledge for their readers, encouraging a different kind of exemplarity than imitation of the life of the saint, and rather designed to help the reader to understand herself ethically in relation to both her gender and her community. The majority of Sanok's book focuses on the vernacular saints' lives themselves, but a good part of the text uses both Julian of Norwich and Margery Kempe (among others) as evidence for how these saints' lives may have been read or understood by its medieval readers. Sanok looks closely at Julian's imitation of St Cecelia, especially in her desire for three wounds, and also at how she shifts some of the physical torment and pain of the virgin martyr to those of a spiritual suffering. Sanok argues that this imitation 'shows how the exemplarity of hagiographic narrative could prompt an awareness of historical identity and location' (pp. 5–6). Kempe gets a more thorough treatment in the book, also in relation to St Cecelia (in particular the format of the virgin-martyr trial), as well as how she absorbs and integrates the legends of other female saints, especially Mary Magdalene, playing down those traditionally associated with Margery—such as Mary d'Oignies. Sanok's book calls attention to the number of vernacular female saints' lives in circulation in late medieval England, often under-studied in relation to audience, and urges medievalists to see exemplarity as a kind of medieval reading practice that both engaged and constructed a gendered audience. In turn, she argues that practice formulated a historical and ethical understanding of women and their relation to both community and God.

Reading is also central to Louise M. Bishop's *Words, Stones & Herbs: The Healing Word in Medieval and Early Modern England*. Bishop looks at healing both literally, as it is described in vernacular medical texts, and also metaphorically, as it is used in literary and devotional ones. As with Sanok's analysis of Kempe, Bishop brings Kempe into dialogue with Mary Magdalene, especially in relation to the *noli me tangere* theme and its use in medieval women's affective piety. This chapter, 'The Disease Called "Touch Me Not"' (pp. 153–88), which looks at the phrase in a fifteenth-century remedy book and its literal meaning (a skin disease) as well as its cultural connotations, and the chapter preceding it, 'Gendered Healing' (pp. 130–52), which looks at medicinal texts by and for women, as well as gendered metaphors, would be most useful to scholars of medieval women's writing.

Margery Kempe is an important element of Emma Lipton's *Affections of the Mind*. Lipton discusses Margery's *Book* in relation to the conflicting bourgeois marriage values of the day—on the one hand, marriage was virtuous but sex was not; on the other, sex was part of the marital contract. Margery is constantly trying to reconcile these opposites along with her desire to live a good and saint-like life. Lipton explores the values and identity of bourgeois marriage and the different ways in which it surfaces and defines Margery's spirituality and the text itself.

Mary Erler takes up Julian's *Revelations* as well as Margery Kempe's *Book* in relation to a fifteenth-century letter describing another revelation of an unnamed woman in ' "A Revelation of Purgatory" (1422): Reform and the Politics of Female Visions' (*Viator* 38[2007] 321–47), arguing that looking at this text will help place Kempe's and Julian's writing in a broader insular context, rather than simply the devotional landscape of the continent, to which they are often compared.

Margery Kempe's pilgrimages and their meanings are explored in Liliana Sikorska's 'Between Penance and Purgatory: Margery Kempe's *Pélérinage de la vie humaine* and the Idea of Salvaging Journeys' (in Sauer and Bauer, eds., *Beowulf and Beyond*, pp. 235–57). Sikorska looks at the literal and spiritual journeys that Margery takes and how they reflect on her own understanding of her piety. Rebecca Schoff Erwin looks at the textual tradition of Margery Kempe in 'Early Editing of Margery Kempe in Manuscript and Print' (*JEBS* 9[2006] 75–94), discussing the differences in the Wynkyn de Worde excerpts from the full manuscript, and how this may simultaneously silence Margery and allow her a voice. Erwin also looks at the manuscript itself and how it intersects with its marginal annotations.

Justine Semmens writes about Julian of Norwich's enclosure in 'Infinite "Becloseness" in Julian of Norwich's *A Revelation of Love*' (*MFF* 43[2007] 40–50), where she looks at spatial constructs, physical space and Julian's *Revelations*. Jay Ruud puts Julian in dialogue with Langland in 'Julian of Norwich and *Piers Plowman*: The Allegory of the Incarnation and Universal Salvation' (*SMART* 13[2007] 63–84), demonstrating ways in which the two sometimes alienating texts can be taught in a mutually illuminating way.

Last year, this section began to include works written by women in England in Latin and Anglo-Norman as well as in English. While no work on Latin texts written by women has come to my attention, this section has been greatly expanded by the addition of Anglo-Norman works, in particular those of Marie de France, as demonstrated by her many appearances so far. There are also three articles that take Marie as their main focus. The first, 'Treason and Charge of Sodomy in the *Lai de Lanval*', by Stefan Jurasinski (*RQ* 54[2007] 290–302), argues that critics have missed the point when discussing Guinevere's accusation of homosexuality directed at Lanval. Traditionally, scholars see the charge as a counter for Lanval's rejection of the queen's sexual proposition, but Jurasinski argues that the charge of sodomy would have been considered a kind of treason and that the queen had other motivations behind her remarks. Robert Clark also takes up traditional critical approaches to

Lanval and the question of homosexuality in 'The Courtly and the Queer: Some Like It Not' (in Rosenberg, Fresco and Pfeffer, eds., *Chanson Legie e a Chanter: Essays in Old French Literature in Honor of Samuel N. Rosenberg*, pp. 409–27). Clark argues that the episode needs to be read in the context of queer theory and history, in particular the question of the silencing and silence of Guinevere's accusation. Last, Michael Chernick, in 'Marie de France in the Synagogue' (*Exemplaria* 19[2007] 183–205), reads Marie's *Lais* against and in conjunction with a thirteenth-century Hebrew tale entitled 'King Solomon's Daughter'. Chernick suggests that a Hebrew translator familiar with Marie's works might have transmitted the story into the Jewish community, and that the connections between the two texts might suggest more cultural ties between Anglo-Norman England and continental Jews than previously believed.

Over the last decade or so, the Findern poems have increasingly received more critical attention and speculation as to female authorship for some of them. Ashby Kinch's ' "To thence what was in hir wille": A Female Reading Context for the Findern Anthology' (*Neophil* 91[2007] 729–44) speculates that the entire anthology indicates a female readership in its very layout, order and editing process.

3. Alliterative Verse and Lyrics

There was one significant publication in the area of Robin Hood studies this year. Thomas H. Ohlgren's *Robin Hood: The Early Poems, 1465–1560: Texts, Contexts, and Ideology* provides a thorough and much-needed examination of the original manuscripts against the social and cultural backgrounds in which they were produced. Ohlgren's work avoids questions of the 'real' or 'historical' Robin Hood in favour of examining the poems as material products of their own culture. He uses historical evidence combined with linguistic features, reception, manuscript collection and production in order to determine the cultural identity of the Robin Hood audience. Further, he suggests a revision in the way we look at Robin Hood scholarship by identifying the original owners of the two main Cambridge manuscripts. Each text he examines is situated historically, while questions of production, transmission and intertextuality are explored. Overall, this work is an essential cornerstone of Robin Hood studies, and should prove stimulating for scholars pursuing the field.

One other book-length publication came out this year, *Middle English Poetry in Modern Verse*, translated and edited by Joseph Glaser. It contains an odd assortment of Middle English works ranging from extremely short verses to whole romances. The introduction is brief and unsatisfactory, making sweeping generalizations such as 'the poems translated here appear to be the finished and accurate versions of what their authors intended' (p. ix), which implies a lack of knowledge about medieval writing practices. This is followed by a 'Note on Alliterative Verse' (p. xi) in which Glaser covers the principles of alliteration, albeit hurriedly. The contents are divided into five sections: 'Worldly Lyrics', 'Snatches', 'Religious Lyrics', 'Selections' and 'Narratives'.

The worldly lyrics include seventy-two verses of varying origin. To his credit, Glaser meticulously records the manuscript origins of each poem. Only a very few notes are included, and these merely to comment on supposed authorship. The introduction to the section is brief and reductive. This is followed by 'Snatches', which comprises mostly 'memory-joggers', and 'Religious Lyrics', which is self-explanatory, and even shorter introductions. The fourth section, 'Selections', is, perhaps, the most confusing. There appears to be no rhyme or reason to Glaser's choices for inclusion and the length to which these items are trimmed is mind-boggling; he includes 230 lines of *Piers Plowman*, 110 lines of *The Squire of Low Degree*, and 116 lines from Gavin Douglas's translation of Virgil's *Aeneid*, alongside Gower's *Tale of Ceyx and Alcyone* from the *Confessio Amantis*. The book closes with a selection of complete narratives, ranging from romances to beast fables. The limited bibliography contains mostly dated scholarship, though the list of first lines, sources and index numbers for the lyrics is useful.

'*Wynnere and Wastoure* 407–414 and *Le Roman de la Rose* 8813–8854' (in Summerfield and Busby, eds., *People and Texts: Relationships in Medieval Literature*, pp. 99–109), by Karen Hodder and John Scattergood, opens with a passage from *Wynnere and Wastoure* that has proved troublesome in previous scholarship, and goes on to suggest a reinterpretation based on a re-evaluation of punctuation practices. After covering the basics of editorial practice and reviewing those in existence, Hodder and Scattergood suggest a new reading combining repunctuating with cultural considerations of women's fashion. This leads to a comparison to a passage from *Le Roman de la Rose* that investigates the relationship between a husband and his fashionable wife. Fashion, satire and womanly wiles collide in an exploration of courtly gender that results in a reinterpretation of the passage in question.

Elsewhere, A.S.G. Edwards and Theresa O'Byrne note a significant discovery in 'A New Manuscript Fragment of the *Prick of Conscience*' (*MÆ* 76[2007] 305–7); 136 lines of the poem were discovered bound with a copy of Sir Thomas More's *Supplication of Souls* as part of the wrapper. Edwards notes that this version of the *Prick* 'follows the general sequence of the text with omissions and often quite extensive rewriting' (p. 306). While the authors provide a solitary example here, this discovery is sure to spark interest in the new fragment, and may uncover some intriguing new aspects of scholarship on the *Prick of Conscience*.

Another discovery is noted in 'A Previously Unrecorded Fragment of the Middle English *Short Metrical Chronicle* in Bibliotheca Philosophica Hermetica M199' (*ES* 87:iii[2007] 277–93) by Peter Grund. Grund both provides an edition of the piece and collates it with the other known version of the *Chronicle*. Because of the significance of the *Chronicle* this is a remarkable discovery, and a valuable edition. Grund begins with an overview of the manuscript itself, including a commentary on the scribal hand. He also discusses his theories behind the inclusion of the *Chronicle* in BPH M199, a primarily alchemical text. His ideas are intriguing and have merit. Focusing on the fragment's concern with the 'king's bath', Grund posits two theories: (*a*) the baths refer to alchemical tubs and properties; (*b*) the king refers to the philosopher's stone, or, possibly, gold, both of which have significant alchemical importance. This discussion is followed by the edition, collation and textual notes, along with a solid bibliography.

Ian Johnson examines a little-known text in '*Xpmbn*: The Gendered Ciphers of the *Book of Brome* and the Limits of Misogyny' (*Women* 18:ii[2007] 145–61). His analysis is sensitive to the overtly misogynist message present once the poem is deciphered. In the passages examined, women are described using the following terms: chatterers, frowners, shrews, angry creatures and things that take a beating. In all, women are disruptive annoyances of low moral character who are also consumable. Johnson contextualizes his discussion within the culture of medieval misogyny for a convincing argument, and also takes the time to explain cipher poems in the English tradition. Though he searches for a trace of redemption or resistance, Johnson is ultimately disappointed, and must conclude that it appears that most medieval consumers of this text enjoyed the prospect of denigrating women.

In 'Historical Sources of the Middle English Verse *Life of St. Æthelthryth*' (*ANQ* 20:ii[2007] 8–11), Mary Dockray-Miller asserts that 'historical source study of the last text in the composite manuscript London, BL Cotton Faustina B. iii can shed light on the transmission and use of chronicle texts and their translations in late medieval England' (p. 8). She examines the *Life of St. Æthelthryth* in connection to its Latin sources, in context of the scribal lists in the margins and in light of the variations from the *Polychronicon* to examine questions about Wilton's library and manuscript transmission.

'Line 33 of *St. Erkenwald*' (*N&Q* 54[2007] 124–5) by Helen Young examines the meaning of a line that focuses on Erkenwald's spiritual heritage. Young proposes that the standard interpretation—that Erkenwald inherited St Augustine of Kent's geographical location of authority—is a misinterpretation. Instead, she suggests that the line refers to Erkenwald's inheritance of Augustine's spiritual authority, promoting the importance of London through a lineage of power.

In '"The Beast Within": Animals and Lovers in Child's *The English and Scottish Popular Ballads*' (*Mosaic* 40:i[2007] 145–61), Goldie Morgentaler begins by acknowledging that the ballads were written down centuries after being created orally, and then proceeds to contextualize her discussion within the medieval tradition. In particular, she examines the beast fable tradition within the ballads, looking at those that contain 'animal lovers' and instances of sexual relationships between humans and animals. Far from being a study of medieval bestiality, this article provides an adroit analysis of animal–human interactions as a metaphor for the dual nature of humanity. Separating her discussion of animal lovers from the supernatural in general aids Morgentaler in this quest, as do her analyses of both positive and negative examples. Among the ballads she explores are 'The Earl of Mar's Daughter', 'The Three Ravens' and 'The Twa Corbies', though she intersperses numerous examples throughout. Finally, Morgentaler acknowledges the potential for monstrosity in human–animal reproduction, but further contextualizes this within the sexual culture of the day.

Richard J. Schrader's 'The Inharmonious Choristers and Blacksmiths of MS Arundel 292' (*SIP* 104:i[2007] 1–14) looks at two short alliterative poems added to a medieval miscellany on pages left blank by the original scribe. The first, 'A Complaint (or Satire) Against Blacksmiths', appears frequently in anthologies. The second, 'The Choristers' Lament', does not, as it requires extensive knowledge of musical terminology to read. Schrader suggests that these two should be read together because of their manuscript history, and proceeds to do so. They share some vocabulary choices and alliterative style, and also an affinity for violence. Some scholarship has linked 'Choristers' to *Piers Plowman* and the satirization of monastic clergy; Schrader posits a similar satirization in 'Blacksmiths', and further suggests that it mocks choirs in general with the hammering of the blows providing a diabolical 'music'. Thus, 'Blacksmiths' becomes 'an ironic compliment to "Choristers", forming a parody of the conventional dyad' (p. 14).

Two essays focus on MS Harley 2253 as a collection. In 'Compilation and Purpose in MS Harley 2253' (in Scase, ed., *Essays in Manuscript Geography*, pp. 67–94), Susanna Fein addresses previous scholarship that has attempted to determine the scribe's character by examining his or her selection and arrangement. There is some general consensus that the scribe was likely a trained cleric and a legal scribe, and was also familiar with Anglo-Norman. Fein then moves towards an examination of the Middle English lyrics within the text in order to uncover what this means about the scribe. Using linguistic cues, and an analysis of the compilation and verbal strategy, Fein ultimately suggests that he was also a type of professional *jongleur*.

Carter Revard, in 'Oppositional Thematics and Metanarrative in MS Harley 2253, Quires 1–6' (in Scase, ed., pp. 95–112) also focuses on the scribe's compilation choices. In outlining a speculative strategy for the early quires, Revard suggests that he will uncover a metanarrative by which the scribe ordered the entire text. The first four quires include all the lives of saints, setting the stage for quire 5, which Revard calls the 'key to the metanarrative' (p. 103); the underlying message is that the anthology was created to honour women. Yet their follies must be addressed too, and Revard demonstrates that the following quire reminds the female audience to be on their guard against particular downfalls, such as pride and greed, commonly displayed in fashion.

Finally, Eugene Green, in 'Civic Voices in English Fables: *The Owl and the Nightingale* and *The Nun's Priest's Tale*' (*AUMLA* 108[2007] 1–32), uses a comparison of beast fables to examine the conduct and style of debate, and the resultant effect on their audiences. He analyses each poem separately on points of diction for law, music, and gender in order to uncover what he calls 'civic ambiences' (p. 3). In *The Owl and the Nightingale*, the principal characters are written female both according to diction and according to subject matter. Further, the various words used for voice demonstrate a range of words that recall civic speech. A breakdown of patterns reveals that *The Owl and the Nightingale* has a high proportion of 'townspeople and others' who speak, whereas *The Nun's Priest's Tale* divides the diction more evenly among higher and lower classes. Still, Green states, 'the human voices enfolded into *The Owl and the Nightingale* bespeak a gamut of voices from unhappiness to joy associated with all the estates of medieval society' (p. 14). Ultimately he concludes that, though they appear centuries apart, both beast fables carry the same message to similar audiences—that debate, oral expression and community voices were an integral part of daily medieval life.

4. The *Gawain*-Poet

As is now perhaps customary, scholarship in 2007 on the putative author of the poems of British Library MS Cotton Nero A. x and (more putatively) *St Erkenwald*, can be divided into two categories: works on *Sir Gawain and the Green Knight*, and works on the other poems, with the former by far the more extensive category. *Gawain* continues to generate a wealth of responses—as only such an inexhaustibly rich narrative can—to its cultural contexts, matrices of production, putative influences and original reception, language and prosody. 2007 was a year, too, in which the *Gawain*-poet reached still wider audiences. If Sebastian Faulks was, with his newly published Bond novel *Devil May Care*, announced as 'writing as Ian Fleming', then it would seem too that, by sheer acclaim, Simon Armitage writes as the *Gawain*-poet, in his translation of *Sir Gawain and the Green Knight*, which offers a bravura imitation of the poem's original language and style. This translation, already appearing as an impeccably presented volume in its Faber livery (its cover depicting the mounted Gawain in his chivalric *Winterreise*), has had its overnight canonicity endorsed by the Folio Society, which has issued a beautiful illustrated version for 2008.

Armitage's translation comes just a year after the publication of fellow-poet and scholar Bernard O'Donoghue's muscular translation of *Gawain* for Penguin in 2006. This was not reviewed in *YWES* 87, but it is appropriate to consider both translations here now. It should be said at the outset that, as a potential first encounter with the poem for many new readers, it is a pity that neither publisher could find their way to presenting an edition of the full original Middle English text (O'Donoghue's provides a few lines), either to accompany the translation in parallel, or even as a supplement. The absence of an original text is some disappointment in O'Donoghue's volume, since his elegantly written introduction to his translation (pp. i–xix) is a little masterpiece of accessible scholarship, and would serve as an ideal guide to the poem for undergraduates. O'Donoghue discusses the manuscript, dialect, poetic art, genre, sources and analogues, and controversies of critical interpretation, as well as providing a detailed and stimulating translator's note (pp. xxii–xxvi), and appending a narrative account of further reading on pp. xx–xxi.

Armitage's volume benefits in its presentation from a policy to allocate a page to each stanza group; the poem is dispatched in 109 pages compared to O'Donoghue's 74. Yet Armitage's volume is ostentatiously devoid of anything resembling the (necessary) critical introduction or endnotes in O'Donoghue. This volume is decidedly Armitage's *Gawain*, almost abstracted out of time and context, save for his introductory translator's note which is in part an idiosyncratic sketch of the poem's character by one who must now know it as intimately as any of its editors or its best teachers.

To see the differing approaches of the translators let us examine a passage of the text (lines 1010–19) where the *Gawain*-poet's language and syntax are at their most modern, and least needful of any translation. In Armitage (p. 49) this passage is rendered as follows:

But I'm aware that Gawain and the beautiful woman
found such comfort and closeness in one another's company
through warm exchanges of whispered words
and refined conversation free from foulness
that their pleasure surpasses all princely sports
    by far.
Beneath the dins of the drums
men followed their affairs,
and trumpets thrilled and thrummed
as those two tended theirs

O'Donoghue (p. 33), offers:

But this much I know: Sir Gawain and the lady
took so much pleasure in each other's company
through the sweet endearments of their elegant words,
with proper speech, free of dishonour,
that their play surpassed any pastime of princes
    no doubt about it.
trumpets and kettledrums
and pipes rang out,
with each men set on pleasure,
as those two were on theirs.

Armitage attempts to reproduce the alliteration more systematically, where O'Donoghue prefers to discard alliteration but retain only the original stress patterns, as outlined in his introduction (p. xxiii). Neither translator, can, or perhaps ever could, accommodate 'þe wale burde'—'the lovely girl'—so familiar a Middle English epithet. The wheel, exhibiting, in the original, a silkiness of wit and diction, is more literally translated in Armitage; but, if the whole stanza is rendered more freely in O'Donoghue, then, we have an achievement of something closer to the desired spiciness of syntax and rhythm demanded by the Middle English when we turn to the wheel's quatrain: 'Trumpez and nakerys, / Much pypyng þer repayres; / Vche mon tented hys, / And þay two tented þayres'. If Armitage emulates the poet's language and prosody more closely, O'Donoghue, in phrases that are brazenly modern and colloquial ('no doubt about it'), achieves something closer to the wry, peppery cadences of the poet's original voice.

As if such prodigies of modernization were not enough, 2007 saw another translation of *Gawain* and its companion poems, with the appearance of the fifth edition of Malcolm Andrew and Ronald Waldron's *The Poems of the Pearl Manuscript*, long the standard edition of the four poems of Cotton Nero A. x. The major departure here is the provision of a full prose translation of the four texts on CD-ROM, from which the user retrieves a PDF file.

The same translation is provided also in a separate volume to be published in 2008. The fifth edition has been fully revised in its introduction, bibliography, annotation and glossary. The edited text has not been rekeyed, and retains its more conservative orthographical practice of not replacing Middle English letter-forms with their modern equivalents. The rewritten introduction organizes its discussion under the categories of 'manuscript', 'authorship' and an account of each poem. I missed the explicit description, in earlier editions, in each heading, of the genre of each poem—dream vision, exemplum, romance—something of the immediate sense of the manuscript as a varied anthology of genres and narratives is thereby lost, though it of course emerges perfectly in the discussion. The rewritten introduction emerges as painstakingly reshaped, ably poised in tone and material between what is expected of the standard scholarly edition and a student text. Together with its greatly expanded and reorganized bibliography, the introduction considers, more than prior editions could, recent critical interpretations of the poems to 2006. The fifth edition, overall, is a tremendous achievement, and secures Andrew and Waldron as the authoritative critical text and student edition of all these poems; a sixth will most likely not be needed for some time. The only way in which this edition could be improved would be (at great expense) to provide a digital manuscript facsimile (full or partial) in CD-ROM, or, at the very least, to provide colour reproductions of the manuscript illuminations in the edited text, so that the manuscript's status as an early complete illustrated book in English could be emphasized.

Let us turn now to individual studies of the poems, which, in 2007, are presented only in chapters and articles; there are no book-length studies. We begin with *Gawain*, before proceeding to the other poems. *A Companion to Medieval English Literature and Culture, c.1350–c.1500*, edited by Peter Brown, contains a chapter on *Sir Gawain and the Green Knight* by Kevin Gustafson (pp. 619–33). This essay is one of a series of chapter-length readings of set texts or text collections which concludes this theme-led critical anthology. Gustafson's lucid reading, designed as an introduction to the text, proceeds by way of generic definition through an appraisal of themes such as heroic identity, love and *trawthe*, and concludes with a consideration of gender identity and stereotyping.

Sir Gawain and the Green Knight is the 'control' text for modelling the development of Middle English alliterative prosody, in Geoffrey Russom's essay 'Evolution of the A-Verse in English Alliterative Meter' in Cain and Russom, eds., *Studies in the History of the English Language III* (pp. 63–8), a collection of essays on language change in English. Russom assesses the implication of language change on alliterative prosody over time, using models from Old Norse and Old English (runic inscriptions, the poetic *Edda*'s *Atlamál*; Sturlsson's *Háttatal*, *Beowulf*, and *The Battle of Maldon*), to arrive at his conclusions on *Gawain*.

A familiar crux in interpreting the *Gawain*-poet's word-hoard is revisited by Paul Battles in 'Sir Gawain's Bry3t and Broun Diamonds (*SGGK*, l. 618)' (*N&Q* 54[2007] 370–1), where he proposes a reversion to Tolkien and Gordon's glossing of *broun* as 'bright' in place of Davis's revision as 'brown' in his 1967 revision of their edition, one subsequently adopted by Andrew and

Waldron (and a reading not revised in their fifth edition, reviewed above). *Broun* as 'bright', far from being redundant, is merely the second component of an alliterative doublet, with both words signifying 'brightness' (p. 370). Battles demonstrates the attestation of this sense of the phrase by *The Middle English Dictionary* in its appearance in *Amis and Amiloun* and *Libeaus Desconus*.

We turn next to responses to problems of narrative, character and genre in *Gawain*. In 'The Convention of Innocence and Sir Gawain and the Green Knight's Literary Sophisticates' (*Parergon* 24:i[2007] 41–66), Bonnie Lander wishes to revise 'moralist, establishment criticism of the twentieth century' (p. 43) of the contest of Camelot and Hautdesert at the heart of the romance's moral enquiry. Lander's essay opens with a reading of Hautdesert as a site of 'terrorism' (p. 43), to define the process whereby Gawain is made to fear for his life. This gratingly contemporary language would have alarming implications if applied to the corpus of romance as a whole: does Lancelot, as it were, use extraordinary rendition upon Guinevere? The body of Lander's thesis, however, reads a 'Convention of Innocence' (p. 45) in the text, denoting Gawain's and Camelot's 'naïve' resistance to the implied (or 'metatextual', p. 46) interrogation by Hautdesert of the generic conventions of romance encoded in the conduct of Arthur and his court. Lander's essay concludes with a reading of the anti-feminist diatribe at the end of the poem as the one 'permanent and irredeemable failure' (p. 42) of Gawain: an index of a romance politics of scapegoating women for the disruptive consequences of the clash of heterosexual and homosocial allegiances encoded in the courtly ethos.

Gawain's affinities to other genres are the starting point of '*Sir Gawain and the Green Knight* and *St Patrick's Purgatory*' (*ES* 88[2007] 497–505), by Takami Matsuda, who, elsewhere, has written the most authoritative account of the reception of Purgatory in Middle English didactic writing. Here, Matsuda observes the generic and narrative proximity between *Sir Gawain and the Green Knight*, and the twelfth-century *Tractatus de Purgatorio Sancti Patricii*, which recounts the pilgrimage of a Sir Owein to the reputed earthly entrance to Purgatory in Lough Derg, County Donegal. This latter text spawned Middle English translations in prose and verse, as well as in other vernaculars, and was second only in popularity to *The Vision of Tondale* in ante-Dantean visionary writing. Similarly, it forms the kernel of a fascinating Catalan account of a journey to St Patrick's Purgatory which displays tempting narrative affinities with Gawain's voyage to the Green Chapel. Thus, in 1397, Raimon de Pellerós, set out, like Gawain, on All Soul's Day for Ireland via the English Channel, crossing Wales to Holyhead and thence the Irish Sea to the Uí Néill kingdom of Ulster, and, after surviving the Purgatory of Lough Derg, took in a visit to the relic of Gawain's head at Dover on the return journey. Both Gawain's journey-ordeal through the Welsh wilderness and Owein's and Raimon's journey towards, and sojourn in, Purgatory demonstrably reflect the impulses and motifs of both romance and didactic narratives. Matsuda's essay—ranging still further afield to the *ars moriendi* tradition and *The Awntyrs of Arthur*—is illuminating in its emphasis on the cross-currents of texts, genres, narratives and ideologies in medieval literature, while remaining appropriately restrained in its assertion of any demonstrable contact between the texts.

The interface of geography and devotion is also the focus of Andrew Breeze's erudite essay, 'The Gawain-Poet and Hautdesert' (*LeedsSE* 38[2007] 135–41). Breeze observes that, while much has been offered on the figure of Bertilak de Hautdesert, rather less has been said conclusively about the toponym 'Hautdesert' itself. Summarizing the different conclusions of various critics over the twentieth century—that the name should refer to the castle, not the chapel; thus 'high desert' is to be read as 'high 'wasteland', not 'high hermitage', or even 'high merit'—Breeze offers a corrective, reasserting the 'Celtic' ecclesiastical registers of 'desert-as-hermitage' proposed by Tolkien and Gordon in 1925 (but rejected by Burrow and Davis), by citing a preponderance of Welsh place-names verifiably attesting to the sense of 'desert-as-hermitage' in the region commensurate with Gawain's itinerary.

In 'Gawain's Family and Friends: *Sir Gawain and the Green Knight* and its Allusions to French Prose Romances' (in Summerfield and Busby, eds., pp. 143–60), Edward Donald Kennedy considers the potential for significant variations in how audiences' conventional and generic expectations of Gawain might have varied in accordance with the kinds of linguistic communities (French- or English-speaking) in which the text might have been encountered in England, and their commensurate knowledge of the French and English romance traditions in which the text is embedded.

In 'Galadriel and Morgan le Fey: Tolkien's Redemption of the Lady of the Lacuna' (*Mythlore* 25[2007] 71–89), Susan Carter explores, often wittily, an altogether more modern kind of intertextuality, by reading J.R.R. Tolkien's character of Galadriel from *The Lord of the Rings* against the similarly potent yet near-absent figure of Morgan le Fey in *Sir Gawain and the Green Knight*, and Tolkien's published criticism. Both are ladies 'of the lacuna': figures whose poetic force resides in their ambiguous and disproportionately limited presence in their narratives. Carter traces both women's lineage in a wide range of medieval texts and traditions in insular writings—*Thomas of Erceldoune*, the Irish sovereignty goddess (often familiar ground, as she admits)—and tests, in a sequence of close readings of Tolkien's fiction and *Gawain*, the narrative gestures which evoke these figures' significance for their audiences.

Staying with the ways in which texts, past and present, can engage in dialogue, the contemporary associations of *Sir Gawain and the Green Knight*, and its literary peers (specifically *Troilus and Criseyde*), form the basis of Sylvia Federico's 'The Place of Chivalry in the New Trojan Court: *Gawain*, *Troilus*, and Richard II' (*TennSL* 43[2007] 171–9). Here, *Gawain*'s narrative dilatoriness in the bedroom rather than the battlefield can be read as a mirror to complaints (in Walsingham's *Chronicle* and elsewhere) against Richard II's court as one comprised of Knights of Venus, and not Bellona (p. 172). In this reading the figure of the Green Knight himself becomes an 'extramasculine' rebuke—all beard and brawn—to the feyness of the Ricardian court encoded in the text's Camelot (p. 174).

The 'magic'—both extra- and intra-narrative—of *Gawain* is an unending source of responses. A recurring controversy of modern interpretation of the poem—its suggestiveness of attributes of extra-Christian cultures—is the subject of Larissa Tracy's 'A Knight of God or the Goddess? Rethinking Religious Syncretism in *Sir Gawain and the Green Knight*' (*Arth* 17[2007] 31–55). Citing, by way of analogue, the patterns of the medieval West's appropriation of classical and Islamic learning and philosophy, and the always imponderable question of pagan survivals, Tracy is firm in her thesis that *Sir Gawain and the Green Knight*'s art—bristling with what she contends to be pagan and Judaic symbols—is indebted to a culture less reflective of Christian hegemony than official medieval discourse (or even modern scholarship) would concede. This, of course, will remain a matter of ongoing debate, but Tracy's arguments are an important part of it. Her essay highlights the eloquence of the *Gawain*-poet's symbolic language, offering an erudite exposition of the symbolism of the pentangle (pp. 33–6) and the traces of perhaps irretrievable medieval cultural networks and influences encoded in the poem.

The fertility of such questions (often themselves concerning emblems of 'fertility') is indicated by a germane account in Jefferey H. Taylor's electronically published essay 'Semantic Social Games and the Game of Life in *Sir Gawain and the Green Knight* and Arrow-Odd's Saga' (*MedFor* 6[2007] no pagination) which explores—articulating sensible caveats, and offering an analysis of how symbols and beliefs can be reinterpreted over time—how the figure of the Green Knight might have been registered by late medieval audiences as a survival of a vegetation divinity or symbol. Taylor reads Gawain, 'tested', by nature, against an analogous figure from the late Norse romance *Arrow-Odd's Saga*, and with a wide range of references to Gower, *Sir Orfeo*, Ockham and Alanus de Insulis. His assessment of *Gawain* is as a text which, on a symbolic level, offers 'a critique of human perception' and social structures, while affirming the patterns of nature which facilitate the existence of human society.

Turning to poems other than *Gawain* (with *Pearl* apparently receiving no individual attention this year) the poem *Cleanness* is included for discussion in 'Heaven and Earth in Little Space: The Foetal Existence of Christ in Medieval Literature and Thought' (*MÆ* 76[2007] 20–48), by Jacqueline Tassioulas. The essay embeds the English poem in the perspectives afforded by a vast range of medieval texts and authors: Gertrude of Helfta, *The South English Legendary*, medieval embryological and gynaecological tracts, Bartholomeus Anglicanus, John Trevisa, Nicholas Love and the Chester and N-town mystery cycles. Tassiouslas adduces a reference in *Cleanness* (ll. 1085–8), which describes Christ's own physically 'clean' birth, and reads this against scenes of his birth in Gertrude, which is marked by the presence of a gleaming, divinely white afterbirth (p. 30), in an erudite essay which documents how medieval iconography and literature respond to a particular manifestation of the infant Christ: the foetal Christ—entering, or shown within, the Virgin's womb—at times represented in the art of the Annunciation.

Studies of *Cleanness* and *Patience* receive a significant new contribution in William Sayers's article 'Sailing Scenes in Works of the Pearl Poet (*Cleanness and Patience*)' (*ABäG* 63[2007] 129–55). Reading the maritime language of the Deluge in *Cleanness*, and of Jonah's voyage in *Patience*, Sayers observes its conventionality, and asserts the unlikelihood of these passages being inflected by the poet's theorized proximity to any coastal environment in the north-west Midlands. Illustrating his argument with extensive quotations and translations from the texts (as edited by Andrew and Waldron), he assesses these passages as 'narrativised catalogues', and explores the etymologies of specialized words and phrases describing 'naval architecture', 'sailing operations' and 'storms at sea', and their correlations in other texts and languages, going some way towards correcting and augmenting prior interpretations of the *Gawain*-poet's lexicon. He appends a table of nautical vocabulary used in the poems, classified as either native or international (p. 153).

In 'The Uneasy Orthodoxy of St Erkenwald' (*ELH* 74[2007] 89–115), Jennifer Sisk observes problems of generic expectation and theological interpretation in the text, and argues that the case for reading the poem's views on salvation as resolutely orthodox is less clear-cut than is generally held: the poem's art, rather, achieves an intended ambiguity and tension in the presentation of the implications of the heathen judge's post mortem baptism and salvation (p. 91). Sisk argues for a middle ground of interpretation, mandated by the poem's artistic ambiguity, which evokes 'an idiosyncratic position that uneasily negotiates the distance between orthodoxy and heterodoxy' (p. 108). The text, as saint's life, must, according to its genre, demonstrate the saint's unique powers as instrumental in its central miracle. This implies that the efficacy of the impromptu baptism depends on Erkenwald's own sanctity. But, as Sisk argues, medieval canon law excludes the possibility that any rite's efficacy resides in the status of the celebrant (p. 100). Therefore, Erkenwald should not himself have been needed to baptize the corpse and save its soul (even if it is his saintly virtue which revives the corpse in the first place). Furthermore, the baptism is unintentional, even if devoutly wished for (p. 101). These factors, Sisk argues, imply the ascription in the text of a sense of 'performativity' to the sacrament, indicating the rite's redundancy in the context of God's freely administered grace, and possibly aligning the problem with Wyclifite doubt on the necessity of the sacraments (p. 105). Yet, she concedes that the poet 'expresses traditional views [while being] driven by the energy of controversy' (p. 109).

Finally, Helen Young's note, 'Line 33 of St Erkenwald' (*N&Q* 54[2007] 124–5), glosses, in the line 'Now of this Augustynes art is Erkenwalde bischop', the word *art* not as 'territory' (attested only three times in the *Middle English Dictionary*), but as the more frequently attested 'body of knowledge, or learning'. The line is therefore to be read, she argues, with the sense that it is not Augustine's archiepiscopacy (Canterbury) but his learning that Erkenwald (Bishop of London) has inherited.

The year 2007, then, is far from a routine one for work on the *Gawain*-poet. Though no work on the four poems in their manuscript context (and therefore their relationships to each other) is forthcoming this year, and a striking inattentiveness to *Pearl* is observed, the more commonly neglected members of the putative poet's opus have not been ignored. *Gawain* continues to generate literature both for scholars and a wider audience, in the areas of language, genre, narrative art, intertextuality and reception, and, significantly, the poem (however transformed) reaches still newer audiences.

5. *Piers Plowman*

There was a great deal of activity in *Piers Plowman* scholarship this year, including a number of books as well as articles and essays. The first book of significance is the second volume in the Penn *Commentary* series, *The Penn Commentary on 'Piers Plowman'*, volume 5: *C Passus 20–22; B Passus 18–20*, by Stephen A. Barney. As before, this book collates the various versions of the poem and combines original reading with scholarly overview, although this volume seems more intent upon original close reading than scholarly overview, which Barney admits in his introduction. As such, with an emphasis on close reading, much of the evidence tends towards the linguistic and palaeographic, though certainly the cultural is not denied. Barney's comments are meticulous and detailed, providing cogent analyses of the work on both the microscopic and macroscopic levels. Overall, this resource is so important to modern scholarship that it cannot be overlooked.

Perhaps the most generally useful volume is Anna Baldwin's *A Guidebook to Piers Plowman*. This book is an invaluable resource for students reading *Piers Plowman* and for teachers alike. It opens with a section on 'Why Read *Piers Plowman*?', which is an eminently logical place to begin, especially when dealing with potentially reluctant students. From there, Baldwin moves adroitly into the rest of the introduction, which more than adequately covers the basics of both the poem and its medieval setting. The rest of the book is then divided into sections corresponding with each passus, with the chapters being grouped to correspond to the eight visions. Each chapter has the same contexts, including: genres and characters, close readings, commentary on relevant portions, study questions and sources for further reading. Each of these is contextualized according to the whole poem, as well as historically situated. Furthermore, boxes and side bars highlight specific line numbers, relevant lists (for example the seven deadly sins and the seven remedies), passages from other relevant literature and the occasional line drawing or other illustration. The only drawback is that the book is specifically keyed to follow A.V.C. Schmidt's 1995 parallel-text edition (*YWES* 76[1998] 145), so some specificity is lost for readers using other editions; however, this minor inconvenience is negligible.

Another major achievement is John Bowers's *Chaucer and Langland: The Antagonistic Tradition*. Here, Bowers tackles the two most important literary figures of the fourteenth century; moreover, he addresses the formation of the literary canon by interrogating the difference between immediate and long-standing influence. In particular, Bowers questions why Chaucer received the title 'father of English poetry' when Langland wrote his poem earlier and with clear and instant ramifications—*Piers Plowman* was widely disseminated and directly influential. In his investigation, Bowers considers factors such as education, court influence, literary heritage, audience appeal, theological orthodoxy and social reform. Though he bases much of his argument on socio-cultural evidence, Bowers does not neglect the manuscript tradition. He carefully negotiates the various editions to track the influence of both into the fifteenth century and beyond. Most intriguingly, Bowers demonstrates that Chaucer and Langland were rarely separated in literary history, and that constant interaction has almost demanded a 'victor'. Ultimately, Bowers concludes that Chaucer's patrons and connections, his literary heirs (for example Hoccleve and Lydgate), and his subtler satire, pitted against Langland's lower-class status and overt reform bent, secured Chaucer's place at the forefront of English poetry. Though this is the final conclusion, Bowers aptly demonstrates the process of marginalization and reclamation, as well as exposing the vital role Langland played in shaping English literature, society and religion.

The nature of allegory, vision and postmodern dialogic is interrogated in Madeleine Kasten's *In Search of 'Kynde Knowynge': Piers Plowman and the Origin of Allegory*. The work is divided into two parts. The first discusses the nature of allegory and dream poetry. Kasten deftly covers the classical background and medieval associations involved with dreams, then moves into a look at rhetoric and dreams in both Chaucer and Langland. She closes this section with an analysis connecting Walter Benjamin and allegorical dialectic (a tension between desire and frustration). The second part chronologically follows the eight visions of *Piers Plowman*. First she gives an excellent account of the background of the poem itself and its critical reception, including its various editions. She further analyses the dreams/visions themselves, focusing on the relationship between the dreamer and the divine, blurring the lines between art and doctrine and ultimately questioning the stance of postmodern theory and cultural historicism.

The *Yearbook of Langland Studies*, as always, has an interesting array of pieces, beginning with 'The Fortunes of *Piers Plowman* and its Readers' (*YLS* 20[2006] 1–42) by Maura Nolan. Nolan examines the audience of *Piers* by using the figure of Fortune and the discourse about it, both in *Piers* and in two poems not examined in this way before: 'How Myschaunce Regnythe in Ingeland' and 'A Complaint to Dame Fortune', collectively known as the Findern poems, so named for the manuscript in which they are found (Cambridge University Library, MS Ff. 1. 6). Nolan meticulously examines the instances of Fortune in all three poems, contextualizing them within the cultural and historical setting. Making good use of allusions among the works, she argues that the connections are clear. However, unlike *Piers*, the Findern poems, especially 'A Complaint', fail because of a (re)definition of Fortune as worldly goods rather than spiritual success.

In ' "As ploȝmen han preued": The Alliterative Work of a Set of Lollard Sermons' (*YLS* 20[2006] 43–65), Shannon Gayk examines the ploughing motif within the context of salvation, and especially within a set of Lollard sermons that resemble the 'moderacy' of texts like *Piers Plowman*. She discusses the formal Langlandian affiliations of the sermons, particularly the emphasis on manual and spiritual labour, to uncover a methodology for determining whether or not a text is working in what she calls a 'Langlandian mode'.

John Thorne, in 'Updating *Piers Plowman* Passus 3: An Editorial Agenda in Huntington Library MS Hm 114' (*YLS* 20[2006] 67–92), attempts to clarify what we know about the scribe of this manuscript, referred to as Ht. He further connects scribal practices with an emerging 'bigger picture' of manuscript production and late medieval culture, focusing on passus 3 where,

Thorne says, Ht's 'main editing methods and thematic interests become apparent' (p. 71).What follows is a comprehensive and detailed collation of Ht's activities in the various texts, wherein the A-text seems to trump the B-text, or at least equal it. His C-text passages, however, tend to use materials more selectively. Thorne then moves to Ht's motives, particularly reflecting on the scribe's apparent concern with prophecy, and his 'salvation' of the text from disarray.

The next article, '*Piers Plowman* and Tudor Regulation of the Press' (*YLS* 20[2006] 93–114) by Rebecca L. Schoff, discusses the fifteenth- and sixteenth-century reception of the poem. Schoff especially takes on the two traditional arguments regarding the 'troubled' relationship between *Piers* and the printing press—the poem was banned publicly, or the poem was aesthetically displeasing. Problematically, the poem was never officially banned, nor did it ever prove unpopular. Consequently, Schoff begins her search for a different reason for the late appearance of a printed version of the poem. She does this by first discussing the effects of Tudor regulation and censorship on poetic form, function and printing. Next, she contextualizes Crowley's edition within its own time and culture, demonstrating how it is particularly relevant and how it interacts with existing regulations. She concludes that Crowley preserves a voice for social reform, and this is partially due to the lapse of time between medieval manuscript and printed book.

'Langland, Wittgenstein, and the End of Language' (*YLS* 20[2006] 115–39) by Sarah Tolmie follows. She uses the philosophical principles of Ludwig Wittgenstein to explore language and function in *Piers*. Similar in nature to a post-structuralist analysis, Tolmie's study examines how Langland uses language to provoke thought—specific thought—to create certain representations. She focuses on personification as a vehicle for this exploration, as it factors 'verbal phenomena' and pre-existing thoughts. She argues that *Piers* is an apocalyptic poem but is not teleological in structure. The truth so longed for is never discovered, but the placement of the word will help with the continued search.

Traugott Lawler, in 'Harlots' Holiness: The System of Absolution for Miswinning in the C Version of *Piers Plowman*' (*YLS* 20[2006] 141–89), tackles Langland's approach to the 'corrupt system' wherein wrongdoers ('miswinners') are forgiven by means of a donation. He argues that 'the selling of absolution for miswinning' (p. 141), a form of avarice, is the most pernicious form, and the most prominent issue in *Piers Plowman*. Lawler situates his argument within a discussion of the medieval desire for salvation and fear of damnation to examine a system he agrees was probably less prevalent in real life than as portrayed in the poem. Nevertheless, its pre-eminence in the poem sends a message about salvation that is linked to extortion and greed, and the responsibility the community as a whole plays in the salvation of souls. Ultimately, of course, the friars and their abuse of the church systems are condemned as villainous. Lawler includes five appendices. The first contains analogues of texts concerned with absolution, miswinning, confession and so forth. The second is a chart tracking the development of absolution as a theme among the A, B, and C-texts. The third is a passage from the C-text that reflects non-clerical miswinning. The fourth more closely explicates a passage referred to in the essay, C.IX.256–80, which concerns bishops. The final appendix is a focused look at Conscience's feast, which is connected to what has been misowned.

In 'Retaining Men (and a Retaining Woman) in *Piers Plowman*' (*YLS* 20[2006] 191–214), Kathleen E. Kennedy examines Lady Meed's status as a lord of men and comments on lordship in general, and further looks at Meed and the Rat Parliament in terms of allegory and their historical settings in order to seek out criticisms of social institutions such as maintenance. Kennedy explores linguistic and cultural devices, including the range of formal terminology, to probe Langland's construction of these characters and their subsequent powerful messages. The message in the C-text is different than that of the B-text, more allegorically couched, and more politically expedient. This involves the acceptance by the lower classes of their status as 'potential retainers, but never those-who-retain' (p. 212). Still, however, both texts reflect the flexibility of maintenance relationships, and the importance of the social voice in political power.

Finally, Judith Bennett rounds out the volume with 'The Curse of the Plowman' (*YLS* 20[2006] 215–26). Here she focuses 'neither on the literary history of these many scripted plowmen nor on their meanings for late-medieval readers and listeners, but instead on the effect of all these plowmen on how modern literary scholars and historians have approached the late-medieval peasantry' (p. 217). In other words, the image of the ploughman presented in this literature has shaped how we view all medieval peasants—perhaps as much, or even more so, than the Victorian revisions. Bennett examines the historical roots of peasantry from varied sources, including historical, linguistic and artistic. Admitting that all sources have problems, Bennett urges us to at least be open-minded about the possibility of viewing medieval peasantry in a different manner. Not ignoring gender, Bennett further points out that the image of the ploughman is falsely profitable and falsely male, rendering disenfranchised people of both sexes and varying economic degrees silent. She closes with an exhortation to include all voices, not just the ones we have privileged, in our studies.

Several works focused almost exclusively on the theological aspects of *Piers Plowman*. C. David Benson's 'Salvation Theology and Poetry in *Piers Plowman*' (*ELN* 44:i[2006] 103–7) responds primarily to Nicholas Watson's arguments regarding Langland's role as a theologian, claiming that to see him strictly as such denies his poetic potential. Thus, Benson advocates a different vocabulary for discussing *Piers*, including 'visions' instead of 'theology' to emphasize the role of art. Generally in agreement with Watson's conclusions, Benson declares that the difference is in emphasis. For instance, Benson agrees that the hope of universal salvation is expressed; however, this desire is couched in poetic terms, not in theological ones. In fact, poetry can often do things—take chances—that theology cannot, which is a valuable lesson for the study of *Piers Plowman*.

In ' "Books ynowe": Vernacular Theology and Fourteenth-Century Exhaustion' (*ELN* 44:i[2006] 109–12), Katherine C. Little calls attention to the specific Englishness of the terms Dowel, Dobet and Dobest, and in doing so uses them to strengthen the link between *Piers Plowman* and vernacular theology. Moreover, Little claims, *Piers* is not only a work of vernacular theology, but also a meditation upon it—meaning that the search for a 'satisfying' conclusion must continue beyond the end of the text itself. She further contextualizes this 'experimentation' with varied forms of vernacular theological discourse within the post-Arundel era, citing the constitutions as a form of censorship, and *Piers* as a clever way around that.

'Langland and Chaucer' (in Hass, Jasper and Jay, eds., *The Oxford Handbook of English Literature and Theology*, pp. 363–81), by Nicholas Watson, begins with an introduction to medieval theology and the church before moving on to Langland, Chaucer and theology. On *Piers Plowman*, Watson claims that the 'convoluted narrative' is 'all about attempts to reform the church' (p. 366). Exploring *Piers* as a variety of genres, including the dream vision but focusing on vernacular theologies, Watson deftly moves into an examination of the prophetic qualities of the poem. This is highlighted by a difference in narratorial stance between Chaucer's works and Langland's— especially Langland's stance that society is in danger of imminent collapse. This apocalyptic viewpoint colours the entire poem and poetic vision, as well as the search for 'treuthe', making the critique of current theology necessary for salvation. Watson further reminds us that, while Langland makes some seemingly radical suggestions, he distances himself from them somewhat through personifications of formal theology (for example Holy Church) and always endorses the truth of Scripture and basic doctrine.

Finally, Mary Clemente Davlin contributes a fascinating piece: 'Devotional Postures in *Piers Plowman* B, with an Appendix on Divine Postures' (*ChauR* 42:ii[2007] 161–79). Here she examines the gestures and movements made within the poem as expressions of devotion, and how their presence affects the theological message and influence. At least twenty different postures are used in *Piers Plowman* as devotional mechanisms, while others are used in a satirical manner or as metaphors. Davlin discusses a range of these, including the more obvious ones such as waking, kneeling and standing. Walking is central to a poem that involves pilgrimage, of course, while kneeling signals penance and humility. More significantly, however, Davlin also demonstrates that the gestures under study are generally more communal ones rather than private ones. She lists other postures also, including sitting, lying down, rising and so on. Gestures that imply devotion are also addressed, including washing and being washed. References to ritualized and bodily forms of devotion connect the poem to the mystic tradition so popular during the fourteenth century without placing it among those texts. Davlin also points out that the absence of certain gestures is significant as well. For instance, there are no acts of extreme asceticism, and this provides a subtle critique of such devotional practices. Finally, Davlin reminds us that the devotional postures in *Piers Plowman* are indeed truly significant because they reflect the practices of the laity, not the clergy. From the poem, then, we can learn about communal postures and devotions.

Several texts discuss the impact of *Piers Plowman* on early modern English literature and society, with reference, especially, to Crowley's 1550 edition of the poem. In 'Langland, Apocalypse and the Early Modern Editor' (in McMullan and Matthews, eds., *Reading the Medieval in Early Modern England*, pp. 51–73), Larry Scanlon discusses Crowley as the 'first modern editor of *Piers Plowman*' because, he says, Crowley had goals closer to a modern editor's than to those of a religious reformer. Nevertheless, Crowley also, Scanlon believes, uses *Piers* to advance a religious cause that Langland himself may not have promoted. In particular, Scanlon suggests that Crowley uses Langland's poetic authority to squeeze out more conservative forms of Protestantism, especially through the apocalyptic and penitential aspects of the work. Both are aspects of poetry, not theology, and as such Langland's Catholicism can be transcended to fit Crowley's message regarding works and grace, social sanction and individual conscience.

In 'Medieval Harrowings of Hell and Spenser's House of Mammon' (*ELR* 37[2007] 175–92), Christopher Bond investigates the connection between the Harrowing of Hell scene in *Piers* and Spenser's version of those events in the *Faerie Queene*. First Bond confirms Spenser's familiarity with *Piers*, examining the history of Crowley's 1550 edition and its impact on Protestant sensibilities. Bond further suggests that Spenser was familiar with the mystery plays as well as *Piers*, and proceeds to connect the two through the versions of the Harrowing of Hell. In particular, he examines the image of Christ as a chivalric knight, such as those found in Spenser's epic. From there, Bond moves to what he sees as the central connection—the interaction between Guyon and Mammon—and how over-confidence, corruption and redemption work together in a complex relationship to justify Christ's binding of Satan and salvation of the lost souls. Bond concludes by clarifying what we learn from Spenser's reworking of *Piers*: Spenser aptly combines humour and theology and he demonstrates that humans can be shielded from beguilement. More significantly, however, he managed to disguise inclusion of materials that radial Protestants would find objectionable in a 'peculiarly English' manner, thereby lending a nationalistic bent to the theological impact.

Chapter 5 of Matthew Giancarlo's *Parliament and Literature in Late Medieval England*, entitled 'Parliament, *Piers Plowman*, and the Reform of the Public Voice' (pp. 179–208), also opens with a reference to Crowley's 1550 edition. Here, this edition, and references to the early modern *Piers* pamphlets, are used as framework for the heart of the discussion, which concerns the relationship between *Piers Plowman* and parliament. The parliamentary elements of *Piers* are, in Giancarlo's words, 'undeniable, intrusive, and challenging' (p. 181). He bases this conclusion on the compositional strategy of *Piers*, which, he claims, incorporates both baronial elements and community assembly. In particular, the question of how a critical social voice might result in actual reform is tantamount. Along the way, Giancarlo addresses a possible model for Lady Meed (Alice Perrers) and the historical Good Parliament of 1376, including the role of Sir Thomas Hoo, and their reflections in the parliamentary trial of Meed in passus 2–4. Parliamentary process, inquiry, and setting are investigated, with an ultimate conclusion that while *Piers* is not a parliamentary poem in the narrow sense, it is a model for commons speaking and the idea of social reform through public voice.

Aside from these scholarly trends this year, there is a flurry of activity on *Piers Plowman* in a more general way also. Stephen Kelly provides an excellent overview in his chapter entitled 'Piers Plowman' (in Brown, ed., pp. 537–53). Kelly focuses on the historicity of Piers Plowman, assessing it as a product of its culture, while suggesting that it might be better explored outside traditional approaches. He begins by addressing theories of authorship, reminding readers that we know little beyond Langland's name that does not come from the poem itself, and examining the 'author function', by itself and in connection to editions. From there, he moves to the invention of Piers as both a medieval and a modern text, looking at the multiple versions/editions of the poem that have always existed, with and without 'sanction'. Kelly notes that even reading itself is work in the world of Piers Plowman, but that's as it should be. Will provides a defence of poetry within his quest alongside presenting religious reform possibilities. Kelly closes with a look to the future of Piers studies. He advocates evaluating the success of the poem after a personal decision is made—will the scholar examine the text as the work of a scholar or as the product of historical/textual culture?

Daniel M. Murtaugh, in ' "As myself in a mirour": Langland between Augustine and Lacan' (Exemplaria 19[2007] 351–85), presents a rather convoluted argument connecting Lacan's reliance upon Augustine to an explanation of Piers Plowman. The underlying connection is scepticism of language on a fundamental level. Murtaugh argues that the Augustinian notion of the 'Real' is recapitulated by Langland as nominalism, which in turn provides a space for Lacanian analysis, focusing on the search for the Word through sign and signifier. Further, Piers, as a reflection of Christ's humanity, has the power to fulfil Will's quest in a way that is reminiscent of jouissance.

In 'The Two Ploughs of Piers Plowman (B XIX 430)' (N&Q 54[2007] 123–4), J.A. Burrow re-evaluates the assumption that the two ploughs mentioned in the final passus of Piers Plowman refer to the two harrows given to Piers by Grace. While agreeing that the identification is tempting, Burrow suggests that the passage instead refers to the two ploughs Piers uses during the course of the poem. This interpretation puts Piers in the position of providing for Christian bodies and souls.

In 'Kinsman as "Redeemer" in Piers Plowman, Passus 18' (MES 14:i[2006] 87–114), Horace Jeffrey Hodges examines what he believes is an Anglo-Saxon attitude towards kinship in Langland's poem. He adopts this attitude in order to avoid censorship for his risky support of universal salvation. The idea of universal salvation stems from the early Church Fathers yet was condemned by the fourteenth century. Langland sidesteps criticism by having Christ allude to multiple reasons for saving humanity: common law, royal prerogative and kinship. It is this last that Hodges asserts is the key. This idea of claiming kinship refers back to both Anglo-Saxon tradition, making it particularly English, and to Greek Stoicism, making it especially learned. Hodges goes on to explicate passages from the poem and the New Testament in order to demonstrate Christ's kinship with humankind, and to assert Christ's right to souls during the Harrowing of Hell.

'Church Reformers' Ideas of Warfare and Peace in Fourteenth-Century England: William Langland' (MES 14:i[2006] 115–37) by Dongchoon Lee addresses Langland's attitude towards warfare in general, but in particular religious war, such as the Crusades. Lee asserts that Langland is primarily critical of war, especially against 'heathens', but does not deny its necessity, and goes on to discuss Langland's attitude, as demonstrated in *Piers Plowman*, within the context of his ideas about salvation and conversion. Langland criticizes the Crusades through allusion, not directly, especially through his treatment of the Saracen emperor, Trajan, who insists that he found salvation through the open invitation from Christ, not through the pope's force. Thus Langland, who asserts that the unbaptized have a faith, and that they may be saved through the word of God, since they were led into wrong through deception and misunderstanding. In spite of this negative attitude towards the Crusades, however, Langland accepts the knightly and kingly duties of war as defence, a way of protecting both the spiritual and the body politic. Moreover, secular might can protect justice.

'"He knew not Catoun": Medieval School-Texts and Middle English Literature' (in Mann and Nolan, eds., *The Text in the Community: Essays on Medieval Works, Manuscripts, Authors, and Readers*, pp. 41–74), by Jill Mann, discusses the influence of medieval school-texts on later medieval literature, especially Chaucer's *Canterbury Tales* and *Piers Plowman*. While a good portion of her discussion focuses on various classical antecedents, which are outlined in a medieval school-text called the *Facetus*, Mann centres her connection to *Piers* around the teaching of proverbs and the rendition of the Harrowing of Hell. The former demonstrate wisdom; the latter is preceded by a debate, and could have been used to teach the form. Both result in something Mann calls the 'union of the clerkly and the experiential' (p. 66).

In 'Middle English as Foreign Language, to "Us" and "Them" (Gower, Langland, and the Author of *The Life of St. Margaret*)' (*SMART* 14:i[2007] 89–102), Andrew Galloway looks at the idea of Middle English as a 'foreign' language to the writers who used it, and then relates that concept to the teaching of these texts to students today, who also view the language as 'foreign'. Galloway reminds his audience that all medievalists who teach are teachers not only of literature or history, but also of language. The article opens with Galloway's pedagogical strategy—requiring students to translate and then meditate upon small passages of Middle English. As a routine assignment, this familiarizes them with rhythm, glossing, translation, and linguistic exercise, alongside interpretation. The bulk of the article, however, is devoted to exploring the connection between this pedagogical strategy and literary and cultural context. By focusing on individual words and their multiple meanings, Galloway believes the trilingual aspects of Middle English, as well as the foreignness of the writers' own language, reveals a great deal about medieval society to students in a way they might not have considered previously. For instance, in *Piers Plowman*, 'English words are often objects of keen historical, social, and intellectual scrutiny' (p. 97). Beyond the role of writer, historical and religious significance, and archival benefit, such studies also reveal linguistic shaping.

Lawrence Warner, in 'The Ending, and End, of *Piers Plowman* B: The C-Version Origins of the Final Two Passus' (*MÆ* 76:ii[2007] 225–50), claims that the 'nearly identical appearance of "Dobest" in B and C came about because these passages entered the former's manuscript tradition from the latter's, rather than the other way around' (p. 225), as has been traditionally assumed in scholarship. This is a controversial claim, and Warner sets about supporting it in infinite detail, including evidence from the narrative, the linguistic elements, scribal behaviour, and the cultural tradition. Figures trace the origins and patterns of the various manuscripts, demonstrating the possibility of reverse origins. The article is thought-provoking and opens up a great deal of room for scholarly debate, not only concerning the origins of *Piers* B and C, but also regarding late medieval English culture.

In '"Truthe is therinne"': The Spaces of Truth and Community in *Piers Plowman B*' (in Howes, ed., *Place, Space, and Landscape in Medieval Narrative*, pp. 141–54), Kari Kalve capitalizes on the recent scholarly trend of spatial criticism to examine the ideas of truth and heaven in *Piers*. In particular, she focuses on the tensions between private (inside) and public (outside) spaces and the social ramifications thereof. Kalve states upfront that the 'inside of people—their hearts' is far more important to Langland than the inside of buildings (p. 143). Further, Will wanders only outside, never inside. Nevertheless, Kalve proposes that the interior of heaven looms as an ideal space despite the ultimate failure of the poem to demonstrate the benefits of interiority. The essay is somewhat unsatisfying in this regard, as it tends towards a collection of, a listing of, Will's movements.

Simon Horobin and Daniel W. Mosser tackle scribal practice in 'Scribe D's SW Midlands Roots: A Reconsideration' (*NM* 106[2006] 32–47). The authors re-examine the evidence regarding Scribe D, the copyist responsible for the Ilchester manuscript of the C-text. Though previous scholarship has placed him as hailing from Worcestershire, Horobin and Mosser believe he was a native Londoner who used examples from south-west Midlands tradition, thus obscuring his real origins.

Finally, several pieces this year featured *Piers Plowman* as a primary example in a discussion of a broader subject. Diane Cady's 'The Gender of Money' (*Genders* 44[2006] 29 paras) explores just that. Despite the assumption that money is genderless, Cady proposes that, in the Middle Ages, money had a unique relationship with women. Women and money shared three vital characteristics: passivity, instability and exchangeability. Indeed, money is often personified as a woman in medieval texts (for example Lady Meed in *Piers Plowman*). Cady uses Lady Meed as an example to illustrate how important the connection between gender and money is to the future of medieval studies. Lady Meed is omnipresent in the text, and her foibles and instabilities affect the overall outcome. She is particularly unsettling because of her fickleness—just like money, Meed is 'freely circulating' her favours, sharing indiscriminately. Another text cited by Cady is *Sir Launfal*, wherein she further compares Guinevere to Lady Meed, focusing particularly on capricious behaviours. Ultimately, the essay urges others to continue exploring the connection between economy and gender.

Alan J. Fletcher's 'The Criteria for Scribal Attribution: Dublin, Trinity College, MS 244, Some Early Copies of the Works of Geoffrey Chaucer, and the Canon of Adam Pynkhurst Manuscripts' (*RES* 58[2007] 597–632) contains several brief mentions of *Piers Plowman* not in terms of literature, but rather as part of the scribal canon of Adam Pynkhurst. Examining some of the flourishes in the Trinity *Piers Plowman* helps identify the manuscript in question as being written by Pynkhurst, and helps to establish the Trinity *Piers* as one of his earliest productions. Overall, this additional finding categorizes him as one of the greatest scribes of the late fourteenth century.

Ralph Hanna devotes a chapter to *Piers Plowman* in his book *London Literature 1300–1380* (pp. 243–304). He begins with a discussion of the B-text's circulation in London, relying on manuscript evidence to trace its movements. He argues that the poem is primarily Edwardian in focus, basing this on its retrospective historicism. From here, Hanna moves into a discussion of the links between *Piers* and the romance tradition, with connections to popular devotions as well, in order to demonstrate the work's innate 'Londonness'.

In *Books under Suspicion*, Kathryn Kerby-Fulton uses various versions of *Piers Plowman* as case studies within her larger project. Case study 1, of 'Dangerous Reading among Early *Piers* Audiences', involves the 'York Austins and the "Kingdom of the Holy Spirit" in Cambridge University Library Dd.i.17'. Referencing historical scholarship on the Joachite 'trinitarian' patterns, and the search for such in *Piers*, Kerby-Fulton here examines how manuscript evidence illuminates the text's possible connections to radical and/or suspect thought. In other words, this text becomes radical when we examine what it was read with—and here in particular Kerby-Fulton looks at the Latin pieces, including poems, treatises and broadsides. These include works with possible Joachite leanings, and prophetic exegesis. Kerby-Fulton also argues that apocalypticism was a deliberate choice for Langland—it was not a safe one, but one he found appealing because of its being a tool of the powerless, and a reforming passion. Case study 2 concerns the 'Anglo-Irish Anti-Joachimism in the Cotton Cleopatra B.II Manuscript and a New *Piers* Tradition Poem(?)'. Here she focuses on the fragmentary poems that are anti-mendicant in nature in order to investigate how Joachite and other prophetic texts were infiltrating the Wyclifite movement. The third poem— cancelled in the manuscript—contains what appear to be several allusions to (or borrowings from) *Piers Plowman* and, if this is the case, these are the earliest. Ultimately, however, Kerby-Fulton declares 'these three poems, copied by a Hiberno-English scribe', to be a 'mystery' (p. 184). Finally, Case study 3 examines 'Arundel's Other Constitutions and Religious Revelation as Refuge for Political Protest in *Piers* Manuscript Bodley 851'. The third audience Kerby-Fulton sees as having a 'taste for dangerous reading' is the Benedictine readership of Bodley 851. This manuscript contains the Z-text of *Piers*, but also a Latin poem that scathingly denounces King Henry IV for his execution of Archbishop Scrope. Included are stanzas considered so offensive they were suppressed with the help of Archbishop Arundel; in fact this manuscript contains the only uncensored version of the poem. Thus, a version of *Piers* is collected with material under royal censorship, and read by Benedictine monks, testifying to the power and independence of the religious orders, as well as to the importance of local cults, especially to the increasingly disenfranchised north of England.

Of further interest is the reissue of James Simpson's *Piers Plowman: An Introduction*. While the bulk of the text remains unchanged, the discussion has been revised to include recent scholarship not covered in the previous edition.

His work is based on the B-text, and structurally follows the eight visions. Revisions also include an updated bibliography.

Unavailable for review was volume 21 of the *Yearbook of Langland Studies* (Brepols [2007]).

6. Romance

This has been a very fruitful year for Middle English romances, which receive treatment in a plethora of new articles as well as chapters in major edited volumes. Among the latter, 'England's other Arthur, his legend England's most successful romance' (p. xv of the Editorial Introduction), in other words *Guy of Warwick*, finally receives the extensive treatment it deserves, both in its Anglo-Norman and Middle English romance versions, in a very welcome volume, *Guy of Warwick: Icon and Ancestor*, edited by Alison Wiggins and Rosalind Field. This collection brings together twelve essays on topics ranging from manuscript and early print versions to translation, popularity and the role of women in the romance. Judith Weiss assesses *Gui de Warewic*'s position among its Anglo-Norman romance contemporaries, its ambitious spread, both geographical and historical, to encompass two empires and its links with English realities, in '*Gui de Warewic* at Home and Abroad: A Hero for Europe'. Marianne Ailes and Alison Wiggins provide two very useful and detailed reviews of the manuscript situation for the Anglo-Norman versions and the Middle English ones respectively, in '*Gui de Warewic* in its Manuscript Context' and 'The Manuscripts and Texts of the Middle English *Guy of Warwick*', including the manuscript contexts in which these appear, and the relevance of those contexts to the understanding of the romance variants. The importance of the process of translation and adaptation from the Anglo-Norman to the Middle English versions is examined by Ivana Djordjević in '*Guy of Warwick* as a Translation', and the process by which Gui became Guy and thus a popular hero is amply demonstrated by Rosalind Field in 'From *Gui* to *Guy*: The Fashioning of a Popular Romance'. As Field notes, the popularity of the hero in Middle English is partly justified by the possibilities his Anglo-Norman counterpart opens up; Gui is, in Field's words, a figure of 'individualistic fulfilment with a remarkable lack of responsibility' whose 'voluntary travels and pilgrimage are not really exile and the return is not dynastic', and who thus enjoys the appeal of the 'freelance, the free-wheeler, the mercenary' (p. 47). The context in which romance versions of this hero developed is dealt with by A.S.G. Edwards in an analysis of the devotional versions of the Guy tradition surviving in *Speculum Guy de Warwick* and Lydgate's *Guy of Warwick* ('The *Speculum Guy of Warwick* and Lydgate's *Guy of Warwick*: The Non-Romance Middle English Tradition'), while Robert Rouse investigates the local, national and international attributes of the legendary hero that helped transform the English Guy into a 'medieval culture-hero' in 'An Exemplary Life: Guy of Warwick as Medieval Culture-Hero'.

Other chapters in the collection deal with the surviving illustrations accompanying Guy in various manuscript contexts—David Griffith,

'The Visual History of Guy of Warwick'—and in the early prints—Siân Echard, 'Of Dragons and Saracens: Guy and Bevis in Early Print Illustration', and the representation of women in the variants—Martha W. Driver, ' "In her owne persone semly and bewteus": Representing Women in Stories of Guy of Warwick'. The collection ends with two essays on Guy's continuing appeal in the early modern period: in Spenser's *Faerie Queene*—Andrew King, '*Guy of Warwick* and *The Faerie Queene*, Book II: Chivalry through the Ages'—and in other early modern texts, including the *Tragical History of Guy of Warwick* and a poetical work, Samuel Rowlands's twelve-canto *Famous Historie of Guy of Warwick* in Helen Cooper's 'Guy as Early Modern English Hero'. Complete with a short and a detailed summary of the Middle English version, and a number of appealing black and white illustrations, this volume will undoubtedly serve not only as a pointer to further Gui/Guy research but also as a much-needed guide for all studying medieval popular romance.

Guy of Warwick is also examined by Alison Wiggins in her substantial study of 'A Makeover Story: The Caius Manuscript Copy of *Guy of Warwick*' (*SP* 104[2007] 471–500); through detailed codicological, palaeographical and dialectal, as well as comparative, analysis, Wiggins makes a persuasive case for the concern to 'update and refine the text' (p. 488), which is also evident in its attractive visual appearance in the manuscript. This leads Wiggins to suggest the possible patronage of the Beauchamp family, earls of Warwick, who may well have wanted a 'modernized, sanitized and ultimately more chivalrous version of the romance' (p. 492). Extant marginalia substantiate this claim; Wiggins also includes an analysis of this manuscript's ownership and circulation and of the fascinating connection between the Knyvett and Calthorp gentry families (mentioned in the marginalia) and the Pastons, leading to interesting new possibilities of uncovering new cultural circles.

Another edited volume, *The Erotic in the Literature of Medieval Britain*, edited by Amanda Hopkins and Cory James Rushton, unsurprisingly contains a good number of chapters dedicated to the study of this theme in medieval romance. Cory Rushton, in 'The Lady's Man: Gawain as Lover in Middle English Literature' (pp. 27–37), addresses Gawain's popularity as lover in Middle English popular romance, with references to a wide range of Gawain romances and the ballad tradition (*The Greene Knight*); Corinne Saunders's 'Erotic Magic: The Enchantress in Middle English Romance' (pp. 38–52) traces the erotic magic through the figure of the enchantress in romances such as Thomas Chestre's *Sir Launfal* and *Lybeaus Desconus, Partonope of Blois*, as well as *Sir Orfeo* and *Sir Degarré*. Amanda Hopkins's ' "Wordy vnthur wede": Clothing, Nakedness and the Erotic in some Romances of Medieval Britain' (pp. 53–70) continues the study of the erotic in romance by looking at detailed instances of clothing and nakedness in *Emaré*, *Lybeaus Desconus* and *The Weddyng of Syr Gawen and Dame Ragnell*, in particular offering a detailed and stimulating discussion of the theme in *The Erle of Tolous. Sir Launfal* is also discussed by Robert Allen Rouse in ' "Some Like it Hot": The Medieval Eroticism of Heat' (pp. 71–81), in which parallels are drawn between the sexual experiences presented in the romance and those described in several contemporary texts, among which is Margery Kempe's own account of her husband's sexual desire for her. Margaret Robson's 'How's Your Father?

Sex and the Adolescent Girl in *Sir Degarré* (pp. 82–93) looks at adolescent female sexual desire in *Sir Degarré*, in particular the troubled issue of incest, and Thomas H. Crofts returns attention to the alliterative *Morte Arthure* and the sexual licence given to the Giant of Mont St Michel in 'Perverse and Contrary Deeds: The Giant of Mont Saint Michel and the Alliterative *Morte Arthure*' (pp. 116–31).

Lybeaus Desconus once again attracts scholarly attention, as is evident in the new article by James Weldon, '"Naked as she was bore": Naked Disenchantment in *Lybeaus Desconus*' (*Parergon* 24:i[2007] 67–99). In this substantial study Weldon sheds light on Thomas Chestre's bold use of nakedness and female speech, which are especially linked to contemporary expressions of marital consent in contemporary law contracts and associated literature. Implicitly Weldon also takes a stance against earlier criticism of the romance, which has been seen by leading critics as an inferior production of the minstrel tradition.

In a new article on the identity of Robert Thornton, the well-known compiler of romances, Michael Johnston's 'A New Document Relating to the Life of Robert Thornton' (*Library*, 7th series, 8[2007] 304–13), draws attention to a series of events in the gentry environment in which Thornton led his career and to how legal struggles in his native North Yorkshire influenced his interest in the romances he copied, such as *Sir Eglamour* and *Sir Degrevant*, in which 'knightly—but definitely not magnatial' heroes successfully oppose the 'aggression of an earl' (p. 311).

The 2006 *Literature Compass* annual graduate prize, medieval section, was won by Alex Mueller's 'Linking Letters: Translating Ancient History into Medieval Romance' (*LitComp* 4:iv[2007] 1017–29), which contains a new examination of the fourteenth-century romance *Destruction of Troy* in the light of its author's attempt to use an alternative text than Geoffrey of Monmouth's *Historia regum Britanniae*, instead using Guido delle Collone's *Historia destructionis Troiae*. Another staple of romance teaching and criticism, the Anglo-Norman *Romance de Horn*, also receives fresh attention in Laura Ashe's provocative new book, *Fiction and History in England, 1066–1200*. The discussion of *Horn* is part of chapter 3, 'Historical Romance: A Genre in the Making' (pp. 121–58, esp. pp. 121–4 and 146–58), in which Ashe proposes a new and challenging interpretation of the text as the result of an 'insular cultural programme which seizes divine meaning to itself' (p. 158); by using the *Roman d'Eneas* as a contrastive piece representative of continental writing, Ashe redirects attention to the 'deep correspondence with contemporary insular chronicles' (p. 151) that she sees as evident in *Horn*.

Geoffrey of Monmouth and his work also make an appearance in several articles and chapters this year. Anke Bernau reviews the myths of origin incorporated in the *Historia* in her 'Myths of Origins and the Struggle over Nationhood in Medieval and Early Modern England' (in McMullan and Matthews, eds., pp. 106–18), while foundation myths and the alliterative *Morte Arthure* are also discussed in the introduction to Christopher Baswell's chapter, 'England's Antiquities: Middle English Literature and the Classical Past' (in Brown, ed., pp. 231–46). In the same volume Geraldine Heng's 'Jews, Saracens, "Black Men", Tartars: England in a World of Racial Difference' (pp. 247–69) draws attention to a link between Geoffrey of Monmouth's *Historia* and the First Crusade. Geoffrey of Monmouth's *Historia* also appears in the context of a broader discussion of *Normanitas* and Wace's construction of the concept of *Engleterre* in his *Roman de Rou*, in chapter 1 of Laura Ashe's *Fiction and History in England*, 'The Normans in England: A Question of Place' (pp. 28–80, esp. pp. 60–4).

Anne Lawrence-Mathers's 'William of Newburgh and the Northumbrian Construction of English History' (*JMH* 33[2007] 339–57) explores Newburgh's attack on Geoffrey's *Historia*, in particular its extensive treatment of King Arthur's reign; Newburgh thus justified his own *History of the English*, an encyclopedic work in Bede's tradition, from which King Arthur is evidently left out.

Other Middle English romances are mentioned in articles on broader topics, for example Norris J. Lacy's 'Perceval on the Margins: A Pan-European Perspective' (*ArthL* 24[2007] 1–14), in which the gradual marginalization of Perceval in favour of Gawain is examined in a number of texts in French, Norse, German, Dutch, Italian and English. Similarly wide-ranging, but largely drawing on examples from romance, is Richard W. Kaeuper's 'Literature as Essential Evidence for Understanding Chivalry' (*Journal of Medieval Military History* 5[2007] 1–15), in which a variety of texts, including *The Tale of Gamelyn*, *Havelok*, *Awntyrs of Arthur* and Malory's *Morte Darthur*, are employed to reveal the importance of imaginative literature for an understanding of the secular outlook of medieval knightly piety.

Middle English romance also features throughout Gillian Rudd's monograph *Greenery*, in particular in the chapter on 'Wilds, Wastes, and Wilderness' (pp. 91–132), which is largely divided between an analysis of *Sir Orfeo* and of *Sir Gawain and the Green Knight*. Somewhat surprising is the absence of romance from chapters like 'Sea and Coast' and 'Gardens and Fields', although admittedly the volume's aim is to cover a wide range of genres and to open up new directions in ecocriticism, which it successfully achieves.

Sir Orfeo is returned to academic scrutiny by Ellen M. Caldwell, 'The Heroism of Heurodis: Self-Mutilation and Restoration in *Sir Orfeo*' (*PLL* 43[2007] 291–311), in which our attention is directed to the political and psychological implications of the heroine's disfiguring wounds in the light of a range of parallels, among which are the 'loathly lady' motif, the martyred virgin, and the political associations with Edward III and Queen Isabel already noted by such critics as Oren Falk and Edward Kennedy; the latter are further expanded by Caldwell, who draws on the later ballad tradition in which this association is made explicit (pp. 306–8).

Two edited collections, one a guide, the other a companion, address topics directly relevant to romance studies. As expected, Middle English romances are discussed in several chapters in *Middle English*, edited by Paul Strohm; the collection as a whole attempts to point out new directions in research rather than offer authoritative surveys of themes and topics. Michelle R. Warren's chapter, 'Translation' (pp. 51–67), contains a fresh look at Henry Lovelich's translations, the *Holy Grail* and *Merlin*, from his civic perspective as a London skinner. Warren notes how, in Lovelich's use of terms such as 'shewing' and 'pageants', his narrative 'becomes a landscape of social transactions' (p. 54), while Lovelich's choice to associate 'Logres', the Arthurian kingdom, with Locrinus, Brutus's son, and London, and to place Logres at the centre of Arthur's world, 'urbanizes the romance landscape, turning royal Arthurian history into a civic chronicle' (p. 57). This section of the chapter marks fruitful avenues for future research, including the suggestion of a possible 'mirror book' in Oxford, Bodleian Library MS Douce 178. In the same volume Elizabeth Allen, 'Episodes' (pp. 191–206), reviews theories about the episodic nature of romance and other medieval narratives, in particular reminding us that 'episodic form functions as a method for anticipating and shaping audience response' (p. 191); she uses this to examine 'the link between narrative incoherence and dynastic discontinuity'. Deploying Bakhtinian theory, Allen calls attention to the irresoluteness of the story in *Athelston*, in which the eponymous character's violence remains unpunished and oblique inheritance is indicative of continuing challenges to continuity of power. The lay of *Sir Degare* is examined in the context of anxieties over social continuity and order in terms of the 'generational coherence' of 'marrying one's own kin' (p. 196).

Alfred Hiatt's 'Genre without System' (in Strohm, ed., pp. 277–94) also touches on the controversial debate on the nature and definition of romance; Hiatt uses the well-known romance lists from *Cursor Mundi* and the *Laud Troy Book*, and also discusses the fluid boundaries between medieval 'romance' as genre and language, ballad, tragedy and other related genres. Another chapter in the same collection, 'Speculative Genealogies' (pp. 352–68), is contributed by Matthew Giancarlo, who summarizes the romance and chronicle tendency to fictionalize genealogy, and moves on to an examination of 'childish romances'. Several rather brief and insufficiently argued cases are made for *Athelston*, *Gamelyn* and *Gowther* and later in the chapter for the pairing of *Sir Launfal* and *Sir Amadace* in terms of domestic loss and gain.

The second edited collection is Peter Brown's *Companion to Medieval English Literature and Culture c.1350–c.1500*, in which several chapters are dedicated to Middle English romance. Thomas Hahn and Dana M. Symons review work on the corpus in their 'Middle English Romance' chapter (pp. 341–57), in particular with reference to the popular romances, though briefly sketching reviews of the traditional canon (Malory, the alliterative *Morte Arthure* and *Sir Gawain and the Green Knight*). Hahn and Symons draw attention to the popularity of romance and its attributes; for example, *Sir Tristrem* is used to exemplify the appeal of 'an episodic narrative that thrives on lively dialogue, quick-paced action, bloody battles or other spectacular scenes, while avoiding any kind of inner turmoil or tension about meaning' (p. 350). By using examples such as this one and the previously less-studied Charlemagne romances, the contributors call attention to the exotic, while in the family romances, including *Sir Orfeo*, the magical and supernatural elements are examined. The trend in redirecting attention to the Charlemagne romances is continued in Richard W. Kaeuper and Montgomery Bohna's 'War and Chivalry' (pp. 273–91) in the same volume. The authors make use of Middle English romances in their exploration of the main attributes of prowess in arms and courtesy, behaviour in love and the display of piety. Abundant examples from a welcome range of very different texts include some from the little-studied *Prose Merlin* and from *Lybeaus Desconus*.

7. Gower, Lydgate, Hoccleve

(a) Gower

The 2006 Sir Israel Gollancz Memorial Lecture was James Simpson's 'Bonjour Paresse: Literary Waste and Recycling in Book 4 of Gower's *Confessio Amantis*' (*PBA* 151[2007] 257–84). Simpson argues that Genius' under-readings of old tales serve Amans' erotic passions, not his education, and Genius effectively works against that which he claims to work for. Continuing the examination of this topic, in 'Chamberlain Danger: The Social Meaning of Love Allegory in the *Confessio Amantis*' (*MÆ* 76[2007] 49–69), Elliot Kendall compares the Daungier in the *Roman de la Rose* and elsewhere with Gower's to observe how the wild servant is transformed into an aloof, capable figure serving and defending the power of social renewal ideally inherent in a great aristocratic household.

Does Gower succeed in his intentions for the *Confessio Amantis*? John M. Ganim's 'Gower, Liminality, and the Politics of Space' (*Exemplaria* 19[2007] 90–116) concludes that narrative settings and language relating to place and space make it quite hard for Gower to reconcile all his agendas. However, Misty Schieberle's ' "Thing which a man mai noght areche": Women and Counsel in Gower's *Confessio Amantis*' (*ChauR* 42[2007] 91–109) finds a key link between gender and counsel that points to Gower's subordinate role in his royal advice, which has women always advising princes well, most clearly in Peronelle's counselling her father and King Alphonse in 'Humility and the Tale of Three Questions'. Continuing this focus on gender, in 'Newfangled Readers in Gower's "Apollonius of Tyre" ' (*SAC* 29[2007] 419–64), Elizabeth Allen sees an imaginative exploration of the relationships between ruler and subjects, with the kings' daughters as the 'newfangled readers' who 'reinterpret in order to reaffirm monarchical power' (p. 419), and Amans who fails to see how the tale is personally relevant. The same tale with a different emphasis is used in 'Educating Richard: Incest, Marriage, and (Political) Consent in Gower's "Tale of Apollonius" ' (*Anglia* 125[2007] 205–16), where Sebastian I. Sobecki argues that the fact that consent is highly advisable in both politics and marriage is a point of constructive criticism for the young king.

David R. Carlson's 'Gower on Henry IV's Rule: The Endings of the *Cronica Tripertita* and its Texts' (*Traditio* 62[2007] 207–36) takes a hard look at the manuscripts to conclude that the unique ending in G (BL Harley 6291) must be Gower's final word, disillusioned no doubt by the king's execution—or murder—of Archbishop Richard Scrope. To help establish 'A Rhyme Distribution Chronology of John Gower's Latin Poetry' (*SP* 104[2007] 15–55), David R. Carlson examines internal and terminal rhymes, arguing for placement of loosely dated poems within a broader continuum; at the end, he adds short statistical tabulations of dactyl/spondee distribution and of line-initial monosyllables and line-final mono- and polysyllables.

R.F. Yeager's *On John Gower: Essays at the Millennium* is the third of his volumes of papers originally presented at the International Congress on Medieval Studies in Kalamazoo, Michigan, over more than two decades. Steven F. Kruger's 'Gower's Mediterranean' (pp. 3–19) explores Christian merchants confronting non-Christians (particularly Jews) when travelling abroad, though Gower's Mediterranean is largely adopted from his sources, as in the 'Tale of Constance'. Winthrop Wetherbee's 'Rome, Troy, and Culture in the *Confessio Amantis*' (pp. 20–42) finds that Gower tends to associate justice and wise government with Rome and chivalry with Troy, but he does not explicitly identify those cities as embodying the concepts. In 'Fraud, Division, and Lies: John Gower and London' (pp. 43–70), Craig E. Bertolet extracts from Gower's three major works and documentary materials a picture of how Gower sees London as a network of regulations among its citizens, ensuring prosperity and common profit. Also using Gower's three major works, in '*Principis Umbra*: Kingship, Justice, and Pity in John Gower's Poetry' (pp. 71–103), Yoshiko Kobayashi traces Gower's shifting examination of how justice ought to be administered, with a balance between tyranny and mercy. In ' "A bok for King Richardes sake": Royal Patronage, the *Confessio*, and the *Legend of Good Women*' (pp. 104–22), Joyce Coleman first reminds us how prioritizing the Henrician version of the *Confessio Amantis* leads us to dismiss Richard II's patronage and the original creation, and then offers reasons to believe that Gower's and Chaucer's (and Clanvowe's?) poems were parallel in origin and purpose, perhaps with the hand of Anne of Bohemia enrolling them into the cult of the Flower and the Leaf.

Eve Salisbury's 'Violence and the Sacrificial Poet: Gower, the *Vox*, and the Critics' (pp. 124–43) looks at the poet's 'sacrificial discourse' with regard to the Peasants' Revolt. In 'From Head to Foot: Syllabic Play and Metamorphosis in Book I of Gower's *Vox Clamantis*' (pp. 144–60), Kim Zarins focuses on metamorphoses in Gower and how he likes to play with words—even parts of them—for fun. According to Michael P. Kuczynski's 'Gower's Virgil' (pp. 161–87), Gower advertised himself as England's epic poet through the *Eneidos Bucolis* and partly echoed Virgilian lines. In 'Holy Fear and Poetics in John Gower's *Confessio Amantis*, Book I' (pp. 188–215), Claire Banchich looks to the register of *timor dei* or humility as modulated to upset Pride and express the poet's attitudes. Georgiana Donavin's ' "When reson torneth into rage": Violence in Book III of the *Confessio Amantis*' (pp. 216–34) is about wrath and gender, wherein social taboos about their association need to be opened up in order to reach peace.

(b) Lydgate

This year sees only one edition of John Lydgate's work: J. Allan Mitchell's edition of *The Temple of Glass*, the un-monastic, somewhat mystifying dream vision wherein two lovers are brought together by Venus. The lady's situation truly varies in a dream-like mode—first apparently unable to follow her heart or marry, later quite free once the man offers his devotion—and the occasion of the commissioned work cannot be identified, despite several attempts.

As Mitchell observes, the various textual states may well belie the idea that one occasion suffices to 'explain' *The Temple of Glass*; the shifts between couplets and rhyme royal are easily understood, though it is not explained why the narrative is also in rhyme royal near the end. The text is basically that of MS Tanner 346, modernized and regularized as is usual with TEAMS Middle English Texts. After a good introduction, the text appears with marginal glosses for difficult words and short phrases, then rather detailed explanatory notes, highly abbreviated textual notes, a bibliography and a glossary.

In 'Brunhilde on Trial: *Fama* and Lydgatean Poetics' (*ChauR* 42[2007] 139–60), Mary C. Flannery shows that the conceptual range of 'fame', 'rumour', or 'reputation' was shared by legal and literary thought, and then considers its force when Brunhilde and Bochas meet in the *Fall of Princes* IX, as well as in wider Middle English poetry. Nicole Nolan Sidhu's 'Henpecked Husbands, Unruly Wives, and Royal Authority in Lydgate's *Mumming at Hertford*' (*ChauR* 42[2007] 431–60) views the mumming as a gender comedy designed to show that both husbands and wives need to restore social hierarchical order and thereby join family and society in a more general unification; this results in creating a space for women in the social fabric. E.G. Stanley detects 'Malaria in Lydgate's Troy Book' (*N&Q* 54[2007] 239–40), or rather 'wikked eyr' in II.762, taken not from personal experience in the Mediterranean but from Guido delle Colonne's *Historia destructionis Troiae*. William Kuskin places Caxton's and de Worde's prints of 'The Churl and the Bird' into 'The Archival Imagination: Reading John Lydgate toward a Theory of Literary Reproduction' (*ELN* 45[2007] 79–92).

For Lydgate as a sort of poet laureate, see Robert J. Meyer-Lee's *Poets and Power from Chaucer to Wyatt*, discussed in section 1, above.

(c) Hoccleve

Two articles this year concern Hoccleve's 'profession'. First, Linne R. Mooney casts 'Some New Light on Thomas Hoccleve' (*SAC* 29[2007] 293–340), having found nearly 150 documents (most quite short) written by him between 1391 and 1425, largely Privy Seal records, as would be expected, including his receipt for his annuity, with his personal seal attached, reproduced as the volume's colour frontispiece. Mooney finds that his work favours 1415–16 for his 'wyld infirmyte', and one document may confirm his personal acquaintance with Chaucer. Second, in a different sense, Sarah Tolmie's 'The Professional: Thomas Hoccleve' (*SAC* 29[2007] 341–73) wishes to show Hoccleve trying to make himself out to be a professional secular poet, neither courtly nor clerical, as shown through the *Male Regle*, particularly in his prologue and his exemplum against tavern sins, when it is contrasted with Chaucer's and Langland's. Had he succeeded, he might have been a kind of poet laureate, as discussed by Robert J. Meyer-Lee's *Poets and Power from Chaucer to Wyatt*, for which see section 1, above.

In 'John Bale, Thomas Hoccleve, and a Lost Chaucer Manuscript' (*N&Q* 54[2007] 128–31), Nicholas Perkins explains how, while working on Hoccleve, Bale or an informant took *The Knight's Tale* to be Hoccleve's in the *Index*

Britanniae scriptorum, and ignored or corrected that in the *Scriptorum illustrium maioris Brytannie*.

8. Malory and Caxton

(a) Malory

As ever, Thomas Malory's *Morte Darthur* has attracted attention in a variety of new and interesting articles, which this year seem to fall mostly into two categories: love and piety, and love and women. Elaine of Ascolat, Malory's popular heroine, already featured in last year's monograph by Karen Cherewatuk, is this year the centre of Sue Ellen Holbrook's 'Emotional Expression in Malory's Elaine of Ascolat' (*Parergon* 24:i[2007] 155–78). Holbrook revisits Elaine's two shrieks and the moan expressed in her letter against the background of gendered reactions in Malory's work, in particular Lancelot's own shriek when wounded. These emotional reactions are reviewed in the context of contemporary lyrics and other texts, while the format of Elaine's letter—part complaint, part request for reparation—is identified as much in the same format as bills submitted to law courts (p. 170). Love and its effects in Malory's world are also explored in a review chapter by Catherine La Farge, 'Blood and Love in Malory's *Morte Darthur*' (in Brown, ed., pp. 634–47). Here La Farge revisits the connections between love and blood in the tales of Gareth and Lancelot and Guenevere, respectively.

Women's role in love relationships and their agency in shaping chivalric action are addressed by Amy Kaufman in two articles this year. In 'Between Women: Desire and its Object in Malory's "Alexander the Orphan"' (*Parergon* 24:i[2007] 137–54); Kaufman returns critical attention to the neglected aspect of female power in this tale, and suggests that 'the traditional love object may also be read as the desiring subject, and the traditional exchanger is himself exchanged' (p. 141). Gender theory is used to cast light on several episodes in this tale where male heroes have to turn to female support, for example King Mark's recourse to Morgan le Fay's network of power; female agency is thus shown to provide a more fruitful approach to this previous 'failure' of a story than the patriarchal views of chivalry. One of Kaufman's conclusions is that the ' "feminization" of its primary male character [Alexander]...might be read as a transformative act of gender resistance' (p. 153).

In a second article published this year, 'The Law of the Lake: Malory's Sovereign Lady' (*Arth* 17:iii[2007] 56–73), Kaufman proposes a new reading of Nynyve as 'a sovereign in her own right...a figure through which we can reread Malory's feminine without the distortion of a patriarchal lens' (p. 57); by analysing relevant episodes in the *Morte*, Kaufman suggests that there are other ways for Malory's heroines to fully realize themselves apart from those ancillary to chivalry—and that Nynyve is the best example of one such character who manages to 'be the law and to break it' (p. 67).

A broader discussion of Malory's sources and analogues is contained in 'About the Knight with Two Swords and the Maiden under a Tree' (*Arth* 17:iv[2007] 29–48), in which Helmut Nickel investigates a vast array of European parallels to motifs in Malory's story of Balin. In the same volume a brief contribution also examines Malory's Balin; Sarah Stanbury, in her 'Embarrassments of Romance' (*Arth* 17:iv[2007] 114–16) reads the scenes when swords are revealed as secret codes to voyeuristic pleasure. Also in the same volume Janet Jesmok, 'The Double Life of Malory's Lancelot du Lake' (*Arth* 17:iv[2007] 81–92), expands on Felicity Riddy's identification of the dark 'Other' in Lancelot's persona and uses close readings of episodes in the 'Tale of Sir Launcelot', that of Sir Tristram and the last tale to explore Lancelot's unchivalric, almost villainous, behaviour. Her view of Melleagaunt as Lancelot's double, who makes public the repressed desires of Malory's best knight (p. 87), is particularly interesting.

In 'Haunting Pieties: Malory's Use of Chivalric Christian Exempla after the Grail' (*Arth* 17:ii[2007] 28–48) Kenneth Hodges explores the possibility that the 'Poisoned Apple' and 'The Healing of Sir Urry' episodes can be read as exempla in which Malory responds to the religiosity and authority of the Grail quest narrative he inherited. Provocative, yet not entirely convincing, is the suggestion that in the first episode Lancelot's championing of Guenevere signifies Christ's fight to save a lady as encountered in a number of religious (and one chivalric) texts. Similarly, it remains debatable whether Malory or his gentle contemporaries would have been read texts such as *Disciplina Clericalis*, as Hodges seems to suggest (p. 30).

Malory's Gareth attracts renewed attention in two pieces this year. Kenneth J. Tiller re-examines 'The Rise of Sir Gareth and the Hermeneutics of Heraldry' (*Arth* 17:iii[2007] 74–91), starting from Bonnie Wheeler's earlier study of alchemy and colours. Tiller suggests that 'colours in *Gareth* mark the introduction of a heraldic system, and with it, of chivalric ethics into the narrative' (p. 77). Tiller explores the heraldic significance of the different colours (black, green, red, white) both in the encounters with different knights and in Gareth's colourful disguise at the final tournament. This noticeable development can be read as 'Gareth's quest into a progression through a symbolically charged landscape that signifies virtues and values of knighthood' (p. 86).

Carol Kaske, in 'Malory's Critique of Violence Before and Just After the Oath of the Round Table' (in Sauer and Bauer, eds., pp. 259–70), briefly uses the stories of Balin and the Roman war, then the character of Sir Brian of the Isles, to document Malory's inconsistent view of violence as a result of his possible ambivalent attitude to it.

References to Malory's *Morte* also appear in wider-ranging articles by Pierre Vitoux, 'The Mode of Romance Revisited' (*TSLL* 49[2007] 387–410), and Stefano Mula, 'Dinadan Abroad: Tradition and Innovation for a Counter-Hero' (*ArthL* 24[2007] 50–64), in which the development of Dinadan's character is followed in the context of other texts such as the prose *Tristan*, its adaptations and the *Tavola Ritonda*, alongside Malory. References also appear in Stephanie Trigg, '"Shamed be...": Historicizing Shame in Medieval and Early Modern Courtly Ritual' (*Exemplaria* 19[2007] 67–89), where Malory's text features among other sources used in an investigation of the enduring influence of the pair shame–honour in a chivalric context, in particular in the Order of the Garter practices.

In a brief note, 'Malory's Sir Garethis Tale of Orkney that was Callyd Bewmaynes by Sir Kay' (*Explicator* 65[2007] 66–8), James Simmons hurriedly suggests that the ongoing debate about Sir Gareth's nickname, Beaumains, results simply from Sir Kay's repeated naming of the unknown Gareth (seven times), which once again shows his uncouth nature. Kylie Murray, in 'Kingship in Malory's *Morte Darthur* and the Scots *Lancelot of the Laik*' (*MedFor* 6[2007] no pagination), reviews previous Malory criticism (only partly acknowledged in the body of the article) on Arthur's kingship and counsel in order to provide a background for a discussion of shared features, as well as different, more positive views of Arthur in the Scottish piece, in particular in relation to the wisdom of contemporary *speculum principis* literature.

Finally, it is good to see that Malory's work, and in particular the challenges posed by new critical studies linking the *Morte* with contemporary texts and the re-emerging interest in knightly piety, form the topic of two short pedagogical articles this year: Kate Dosanjh writes 'Rest in Peace: Launcelot's Spiritual Journey in Le *Morte Darthur*' (*Essential Teacher* 4[2007] 63–7) (note that an article with the same title and author was reviewed in last year's *YWES* 87[2008] 261), and Alexander L. Kaufman publishes 'Teaching Malory's *Morte Darthur* with Chronicles' (*Academic Exchange Quarterly* 11:i[2007] 41–5).

(b) Caxton

This year Caxton is present in research articles connected with printing, but his work is referred to only in passing; most studies are exclusively concerned with Chaucer's work, with two exceptions: Alison Wiggins, 'A Makeover Story: The Caius Manuscript Copy of *Guy of Warwick*' (*SP* 104[2007] 471–500), reviewed in section 6 above, and William Sayers's 'Chaucer's Description of the Battle of Actium in the Legend of Cleopatra and the Medieval Tradition of Vegetius's *De Re Militari*' (*ChauR* 42:i[2007] 79–90). Other articles that focus on Chaucer's work and at the same time make reference to Caxton's editions are Kathryn L. Lynch, 'Dating Chaucer' (*ChauR* 42:i[2007] 1–22); Stephen Bradford Partridge, 'Wynkyn de Worde's Manuscript Source for the *Canterbury Tales*: Evidence from the Glosses' (*ChauR* 41:iv[2007] 325–59); and Daniel Wayne Mosser, 'The Manuscript Glosses of the *Canterbury Tales* and the University of London's Copy of Pynson's [1492] Edition: Witness to a Lost Exemplar' (*ChauR* 41:iv[2007] 360–75).

9. Middle Scots Poetry

Middle Scots poetry appears still to be a marginalized field of study in 2007, with Henryson standing out as the most represented poet. In the expansive tome *A Companion to Medieval English Literature and Culture c.1350–c.1500*, edited by Peter Brown, only one of the thirty-eight chapters is solely dedicated to a Scots poet, and the few others that are mentioned get short billing in relation to other—often more obscure—English writers of the time. R. James Goldstein's 'Discipline and Relaxation in the Poetry of Robert Henryson' (in Brown, ed., pp. 604–18) looks closely at *The Morall Fabilis* and *The Testament of Cresseid*, and argues that, although Henryson might appear to be making 'gestures of deference' (p. 604) to the culturally powerful institutions and morals of his time, his poetry in fact subverts these norms and resists many of these authoritative structures. In the same collection, James I's *Kingis Quair* and Dunbar's *Golden Targe* get a nod in Helen Phillips's 'Dream Poems' (pp. 374–85), and his poem 'The Tabill of Confession' is examined in E.A. Jones's 'Literature of Religious Instruction' (pp. 406–22). Finally, Nick Havely discusses Douglas's translation of the *Aeneid* and his *Palice of Honour* in relation to Italian influences in 'Britain and Italy: Trade, Travel, Translation' (pp. 215–30).

Henryson's *Testament of Cresseid* is discussed in Roger Apfelbaum's '"Made and molded of things past": Intertextuality and the Study of Chaucer, Henryson, and Shakespeare' (in Pugh and Weisl, eds., *Approaches to Teaching Chaucer's 'Troilus and Criseyde' and the Shorter Poems*, pp. 122–6), where Apfelbaum discusses teaching Chaucer's *Troilus and Criseyde* and Shakespeare's *Troilus and Cressida* in conjunction with Henryson's major poem. Richard Utz also takes up Henryson's poem in relation to Chaucer's in 'Writing Alternative Worlds: Rituals of Authorship and Authority in Late Medieval Theological and Literary Discourse' (in Havsteen, Peterson, Schwab and Ostrem, eds., *Creations: Medieval Rituals, the Arts, and the Concept of Creation*, pp. 121–38). Utz argues that Henryson sees his poem as a Christian corrective to the secular attitudes towards courtly love and its repercussions that Chaucer puts forth in his poem.

Only one of the essays in the volume *England and Scotland in the Fourteenth Century: New Perspectives*, edited by Andy King and Michael A. Penman, really deals with literature, although many of the essays will be useful to scholars of the period and its texts. Michael A. Penman's '*Anglici caudate*: Abuse of the English in Fourteenth-Century Scottish Chronicles, Literature and Records' (pp. 216–35) begins by looking at the language against the Scots employed by English historians and churchmen, predominantly in the fourteenth century, and then turns to the contemporary Scottish chronicles and histories, in particular John Barbour's *Bruce*, John of Fordun's *Chronicle of the Scottish Nation*, and Andrew Wyntoun's *Original Chronicle*, ending with Blind Hary's *Wallace*.

The concern and question of nation and medieval Scotland show up in other articles this year. David Matthews writes, in 'Laurence Minot, Edward III, and Nationalism' (*Viator* 38[2007] 269–88), that Minot's fourteenth-century poems show a type of nationalism that many scholars believe is absent in the Middle Ages; of course, Minot's nationalism was English despite his Scottish heritage. Thea Summerfield addresses the Scots' view of England in 'Teaching a Young King about History: William Stuart's Metrical Chronicle and King James V of Scotland' (in Summerfield and Busby, eds., pp. 187–98), where she looks at Stuart's translation of Hector Boece's *Historia Gentis Scotorum* and discusses some of the pro-Scottish changes that Stuart highlights, such as questioning King Arthur's right to reign. Nation holds centre stage in Alan MacColl's 'The Meaning of "Britain" in Medieval and Early Modern England' (*JBS* 45[2006] 248–69). The article looks at the idea of 'Britain' through medieval English, Welsh and Scottish texts.

Katie Stevenson takes up the Scottish court of James I in ' "Recreations to refresh the spirits of his followers": Walter Bower's Revelations on Cultural Pursuits at James I of Scotland's Court' (*RANAM* 40[2007] 9–23), suggesting that a close study of Bower's *Scotichronicon*, particularly in relation to its artistic and literary pursuits, will give important insight into the court and culture of the *Kingis Quair* author. The court is also important in Elizabeth Ewan's ' "Tongue, you lied": The Role of the Tongue in Rituals of Public Penance in Late Medieval Scotland' (in Craun, ed., *The Hands of the Tongue*, pp. 115–36). Ewan looks at 'The Flyting of Dunbar and Kennedy', as well as texts by Henryson, Douglas and Lyndsay in order to examine public penance, literature regarding sins of the tongue and the 'tongue, you lied' ritual of medieval Scotland.

Dunbar gets a quick study in Andrew Breeze's contribution, 'Dunbar's *Brylyoun, Carrybald, Cawandaris, Slawsy, Strekouris,* and *Traikit*' (*N&Q* 54[2007] 125–8), where he looks at some of Dunbar's unusual vocabulary and parses out some possible etymologies and meanings. Henryson's language is likewise examined in Christian Sheridan's 'The Early Prints of the Testament of Cresseid and the Presentation of Lines 577–91' (*ANQ* 20[2007] 24–9), where Sheridan looks at Cresseid's actual 'testament' in Henryson's poem and how it is laid out in its early textual tradition.

John J. McGavin's *Theatricality and Narrative in Medieval and Early Modern Scotland* is the only monograph of 2007 that deals specifically with Scottish literature. McGavin is not exactly looking at medieval Scottish theatre, but at the ways in which the theatrical is portrayed and used in medieval Scottish literature. To this end, he examines chronicles, performances, travel journals, preaching and, not least, dramatic texts. There are many of the usual suspects here among the chronicles: Walter Bower and his *Scotichronicon*, John of Fordun's *Chronica Gentis Scotorum* and Andrew Wyntoun's *Original Chronicle*. For our purposes, the chapter that is most directly related to Middle Scots literature is chapter 4: 'From David Lindsay to Skipper Lindsay' (pp. 85–108), where McGavin reads Lindsay's *Satyre of the Thrie Estatis* in relation to the late sixteenth-century Revd James Melville's *Diary* and the story of Skipper Lindsay, 'a reputed madman, who intruded his own display into the public space which a royal play was supposed to fill' (p. 85). While other Scots writers, such as Gavin Douglas, are drawn on, mainly to illustrate the uses and understanding of vocabulary, most of McGavin's book is interested in how narrative and theatrical techniques are incorporated into the fabric of the non-literary writings of late medieval and early modern Scotland.

10. Drama

With authors and publishers alike eager to meet the 31 December 2007 deadline, before which work qualifying for the latest round of the all-consuming Research Assessment Exercise in the UK had to be published, it is perhaps no surprise that this year should be a bumper one in terms of the publication of monographs and essay collections. But even given this obvious pragmatic stimulus for publishing, it is remarkable just how much work has appeared this year in the field of early drama studies.

One very welcome publication focused on the secular moral drama is the splendid collection, *Interludes and Early Modern Society: Studies in Gender, Power and Theatricality*, edited by Peter Happé and Wim Hüsken. The volume, as Happé's introduction (pp. 7–21) makes clear, reflects the breadth and depth of interests that the interlude genre can address, from matters of taste, decorum and morality (both ethical and sexual) to politics, economics and religion, and the range of audiences and environments that could produce and witness such plays. Opening the series of uniformly impressive essays is 'Complicity and Hierarchy: A Tentative Definition of the Interlude Genre' (pp. 23–42) by the redoubtable French scholar Jean-Paul Debax. He casts an eye over questions of definition and form, sketching out the often contested and fractured nature of the interlude as a genre, and the nature of the Vice characters in particular. Lynn Forest-Hill's essay, 'Maidens and Matrons: The Theatricality of Gender in the Tudor Interludes' (pp. 43–69), explores the representation of women in the interludes, as wives, daughters, mothers and lovers, examples of virtue and representations of bawdy and vice, suggesting how they can contest as well as conform to stereotypes of gendered difference. John Skelton's only surviving interlude is the subject of Peter Happé's own chapter, 'Skelton's *Magnyfycence*: Theatre, Poetry, Influence' (pp. 71–94). As Happé ably demonstrates, the play is a prodigious example of the dramaturgical and prosodic sophistication of which the form was capable, as well as one of its earliest extant examples. As he also suggests, it set a theatrical agenda which later writers, most notably perhaps John Heywood and John Bale, seem to have been aware of and variously inspired by.

Mike Pincombe's chapter, 'Comic Treatment of Tragic Character in *Godly Queen Hester*' (pp. 95–116), explores those generic and tonal elements of the play which contain and inflect its potentially tragic material into more comic channels, ensuring that its representation of 'sadness' implies 'seriousness' rather than the kind of 'sorrow' that would be the kernel of the later tragic drama. *Godly Queen Hester* is also the subject of a second essay here (to have two chapters addressing this oft-neglected gem is surely a record for any essay collection), Janette Dillon's excellent 'Powerful Obedience: *Godly Queen Hester* and Katherine of Aragon' (pp. 117–39), which worries productively about the play's formal oddities, especially those surrounding Hardy-Dardy and the Vices, suggesting that their explanation lies in the fine detail of the political and gendered context of the fall of Cardinal Wolsey and Queen Catherine's resistance to Henry VIII's divorce campaign. Bob Godfrey's theme is also female representation. His chapter, 'Feminine Singularity: The Representation of Young Women in Some Early Tudor Interludes' (pp. 142–62), focuses especially on Melebea in *Calisto and Melebea* and Loved-Not-Loving in John Heywood's *Play of Love*, and argues that these characters offer a blueprint—conflicted though it might be—for the representation of female characters with a degree of the kinds of agency and intellectual credibility that are usually denied them in more heavily moralized representations of the 'saint or sinner' kind.

David Mill's chapter, 'Wit to Woo: The Wit Interludes' (pp. 163–90), examines the slightly incestuous trio of 'education' plays, *Wit and Science*, *The Marriage of Wit and Science* and *The Marriage Between Wit and Wisdom*, charting both their differences and similarities with characteristic wry wit. Dermot Cavanagh's theme in 'Reforming Sovereignty: John Bale and Tragic Drama' (pp. 191–209) is more sombre, but no less engaging. A further outcome of his ongoing re-evaluation of tragedy as a genre and mode in the sixteenth century, the essay fruitfully reads Bale's interlude, *King Johan*, through the lens provided by Walter Benjamin's discussion of the *Trauerspiel* or 'mourning play'. Two essays in the volume examine the complex politics of Sir David Lindsay's magnificent *Satyre of the Thrie Estaitis*. Greg Walker's 'Flytyng in the Face of Convention: Protest and Innovation in Lindsay's *Satyre of the Thrie Estaitis*' (pp. 211–38) deals with the formal innovations evident in the play, and interprets them as both a cause and a consequence of the play's rootedness in the urban communities which produced it. John J. McGavin's 'Working Towards a Reformed Identity in Lindsay's *Satyre of the Thrie Estaitis*' (pp. 239–60) focuses on the religious politics of the play, and productively takes issue to a degree with Walker's reading of the significance of the roles of Rex Humanitas and Divine Correctioun. Paul Whitfield White's chapter, 'The *Pammachius* Affair at Christ's Church Cambridge in 1545' (pp. 261–90), looks at Thomas Kirchmeyer's controversial polemical reformist play in both its material and its controversial contexts. Less contentious, but no less interesting dramatically, is *Impatient Poverty*, which is the subject of Roberta Mullini's essay, '*Impatient Poverty*: The Intertextual Game of Satire' (pp. 291–314), which draws out the ways in which this later interlude both conforms to and deviates from the norms of the genre. Peter Thomson's 'Sound City Jests and Country Pretty Jests: *Jack Juggler* and *Gammer Gurton's Needle*' (pp. 315–30) uses the terminology of the pamphlet *Tarlton's Jests* to explore the comic, performative elements of his chosen interludes, seeing them as, in part at least, vehicles for contests of clowning tailor-made for gifted comic actors. Alice Hunt's chapter, 'Legitimacy, Ceremony and Drama: Mary Tudor's Coronation and *Respublica*' (pp. 331–51), takes a more regal subject, suggesting the ways in which the coronation ceremonials and Nicholas Udall's interlude variously enact and represent the succession of a queen regnant. Finally, in 'Staging the Reformation: Power and Theatricality in the Plays of William Wager' (pp. 353–80), David Bevington explicates the theatrical and political implications of *The Longer Thou Livest* and *Enough is as Good as a Feast*, elegantly rounding off this excellent volume. The only flaw in such a copious collection is its lack of an index to aid readers in navigating more readily through its riches, but this is a minor complaint set against the quality of the volume as a whole.

Always much to be welcomed is the publication of a new edition in the Records of Early English Drama series, especially when it is such a monumental achievement as the two-volume *Cheshire Including Chester*, edited by Elizabeth Baldwin, Lawrence M. Clopper and David Mills. This new, combined, edition is, as the title suggests, both a republication, in revised and expanded form, of Clopper's *Chester* records, first published in 1979 and now long out of print, and the new volume of material from the county of Cheshire edited by Baldwin and Mills. As with all REED volumes, the scholarly apparatus is exemplary, combining an account of the geography and history of the city and region with a lively discussion of the local 'Drama, Music and Popular Customs' (pp. xxxiii–lxxxii), and a detailed introduction to the nature and scope of the wide range of documentary sources consulted. The records themselves then follow, divided between volume 1, which has the records from the Province of York archive and Diocese of Chester, and then records from the 'Townships, Parishes and other Localities' of Cheshire listed alphabetically from Acton to Chester c.1624. Chester 1624–5 to Wybunbury follows in volume 2, accompanied by noble and aristocratic household records, county records from the Great and Quarter Session books, and so on. The familiar and copious REED appendices give details of undated records, of royal and noble visits to Chester, John Payne Collier's account of the letter describing a lost 'Play of Robert of Sicily' played in Chester (taken from his *History of Early Dramatic Poetry* [1830]), the breviaries of archdeacons Robert Rogers and David Rogers, an account of the development of the Chester plays, a selective list of musicians and musical performers in the region, a list of saints' days and festivals, translations of all the records not originally in English, detailed end-notes and the usual excellent glossaries of Latin and English terms, provided by Abigail Ann Young.

Although primarily focused on the playhouse period, Gina Bloom's *Voice in Motion: Staging Gender, Shaping Sound in Early Modern England* has interesting implications for the theory and practice of theatrical acoustics across the periods, especially in the discussion of the capacities and potential of the human voice, the performances of boy actors, and the discussion of some of the central aspects of performativity theory on a more general level which early drama scholars may find useful. Readers with interests in the potential hermeneutic and cultural implications of the transformation of dramatic texts from scripts for performance to printed playbooks for sale might also profitably consult Rebecca L. Schoff's *Reformations: Three Medieval Authors in Manuscript and Moveable Type*, which, while it focuses chiefly on Chaucer's *Canterbury Tales*, the *Book of Margery Kempe* and *Piers Plowman* rather than the drama per se, has a number of interesting suggestions to make regarding the 'authorizing' and canonizing implications of print culture that might apply also to drama publishing in the sixteenth century. Similarly interested in the interaction between manuscript hands and printed books is William Sherman's *Used Books: Marking Readers in Renaissance England*, which ponders profitably the notes, annotations and various marks that Renaissance readers have left in the margins and across the pages of their books. Sherman ably demonstrates the manifold 'uses' to which texts as various as the Bible and Shakespeare might be put by pious and impious readers in the period.

Among the figures discussed in Elizabeth Salter's short, eclectic collection of biographical sketches, *Six Renaissance Men and Women: Innovation, Biography and Cultural Creativity in Tudor England, c.1450–1560*, two have dramatic connections through their service as Masters of the Chapel

Royal: Gilbert Banaster and William Cornish. Banaster appears largely as a poet and composer of courtly music, but Cornish (the younger) is considered in his guise as a designer of, and participant in, royal pageants. These productions are described by Salter, along with a discussion of his disputed authorship of 'A Ballad of Information', the satire of Empson, and the musical setting of 'Woefully Arrayed'. Anyone interested in the material fabric of Henrician court culture will also learn much from Maria Hayward's lavishly illustrated study, *Dress at the Court of King Henry VIII*. Drawn from a range of contemporary sources—Great Wardrobe accounts and warrants, inventories, chronicles, letters, and visual representations of all kinds—the study is a comprehensive guide to the substance, styles and functions of royal dress throughout the reign. Also included is a scholarly edition of John Worsley's Wardrobe Books for 1516 (BL Harley MS 2284) and 1521 (BL MS Harley 4217), accompanied by a useful account of the history and function of the Great Wardrobe as an institution. Readers anxious to discover the difference between a partlet and a placard, a brigandine and a base coat, need look no further for illumination, as each aspect of the dress of the king, his wives and children, servants and courtiers, is lovingly and informatively catalogued herein.

The activities of the early Tudor humanists, and Sir Thomas More in particular, receive considerable illumination in Peter Iver Kaufman's perceptive study, *Incorrectly Political: Augustine and Thomas More*, which examines the mingling of spiritual, ecclesiastical and political themes in the writings of these two monumental, and deeply theatrically informed, Catholic authors. John Parker's bold, provocative monograph, *The Aesthetics of Antichrist from Christian Drama to Christopher Marlowe* begins and ends with Marlowe, but traverses a good deal of earlier territory in between. His central thesis is that Marlowe did not offer a radical, Protestant, secularizing (or even atheist) critique of the Christian drama of the previous two centuries, but rather that medieval religious drama was always already 'Marlovian', if by that we mean sceptical, worldly, even decidedly 'dodgy' (p. viii) in its discussions of Christianity and Christian themes. This was nowhere more obvious than in the drama's treatment of that most theatrical and deceptive, but also theologically necessary and so paradoxically welcome manifestation of the Last Days, Antichrist. The book is punctuated by a number of powerful, contentious claims, not least the suggestion that the kind of terror inspired by the Crucifixion pageants at York and Chester was 'wholly artificial, far closer to the campy fun of a horror flick than to real trauma' (p. 70), which invite scholars of the early theatre to re-examine some of our most cherished assumptions about the texts we study and the culture(s) which produced and sustained them.

Also focused on a single, complex theme is Fiona S. Dunlop's *The Late Medieval Interlude: The Drama of Youth and Aristocratic Masculinity*. Concentrating primarily on the clutch of 'youth' interludes produced in the first third of the sixteenth century, Rastell's *Nature*, Medwall's *Fulgens and Lucrece*, the anonymous *Calisto and Melebea* and *The World and the Child*, and *The Interlude of Youth* itself, but drawing on a wider range of dramatic and non-dramatic material, Dunlop valuably explores the ways in which such plays variously performed, inflected and problematized models of late medieval aristocratic masculine identity and the processes of experience and education by which they were brought into being. What emerges is a more coherent sense of the nature of 'youth' as both a form of identity and a social and moral problem in the aristocratic culture of late medieval England, and also an appreciation of the often sophisticated ways in which these ostensibly fairly simple plays were able to address the issues to which the subject gave rise.

Christina M. Fitzgerald's *The Drama of Masculinity and Medieval English Guild Culture* is, as its title suggests, similarly concerned with issues surrounding masculine identities, although in this case the dramatic texts at the centre of her critical attention are the urban religious plays of Chester and York. The great northern cycles are read by Fitzgerald as largely male projects, not simply incidentally or pragmatically, but fundamentally, as they are 'dramas of masculinity', 'specifically and self-consciously concerned with the fantasies and anxieties of being male in the urban, mercantile worlds of their performance' (p. 1). Alive to the complex, multiple and potentially conflicted models of masculinity exposed in these plays, she nonetheless offers some bold, contentious readings of key elements in their dramaturgy, notably perhaps that the figure of Christ performed there is 'more distant, more silent, and less immediately present for affective, psychologically intense devotion' (p. 1) than that represented in other devotional forms; a reading which, if accepted, would alter fundamentally the way that, for example, the York *Crucifixion* pageant is conventionally understood. For Fitzgerald, these plays enact, and so strive to bring into being, a sense of masculine, 'guild' identity that is itself, to a degree, deliberately culturally and emotionally detached from conventional familial and friendship ties, characterized by a sense of idealized social responsibilities centred on sacrificial service and self-denial, setting it apart from the close, mundane, affective links constitutive of other forms of contemporary male and female identity.

This year also sees the publication of a clutch of excellent studies of early drama in France, each of which is well worth bringing to readers' attention. Sara Beam's *Laughing Matters: Farce and the Making of Absolutism in France* is an engaging analysis of the political culture of satirical and bawdy drama in the sixteenth and seventeenth centuries which presents a persuasive account of the steadily increasing policing and censoring and the gradual marginalization of the subversive, critical aspects of public comic theatre by local urban officials keen to ingratiate themselves with the increasingly absolutist institutions of royal power after the Wars of Religion. The slow strangulation of satirical farce and the feisty, carnivalesque culture that it embodied, Beam argues, was not so much a consequence of absolutism, but a constituent element in its creation, a claim that perhaps bears consideration in relation to the similar processes at work in England, which led to the suppression of the civic cycle plays at roughly the same time. Virginia Scott and Sara Sturm-Maddox's interdisciplinary study (duo-graph?), *Performance, Poetry and Politics on the Queen's Day*, similarly examines the complex intersections between politics, culture and dramatic performance. Focusing on the Fêtes de Fontainebleau, two courtly performances commissioned by Catherine de

Médicis for 13 February 1564, the study suggests how the productions of Pierre de Ronsard's dramatic eclogue, the *Bergerie* and the tale of 'La Belle Genièvre', taken from Ariosto's *Orlando Furioso*, counselled for the reconciliation of the factional differences exposed during the first French War of Religion and the accession of the weak child-king Charles IX.

The third, but by no means least, of the French books is Carol Symes's *A Common Stage: Theater and Public Life in Medieval Arras*, a substantial archival study of the performance texts and performance history of the secular plays of the Picardian city of Arras. These plays, surviving from the thirteenth century—*The Play of St. Nicholas, The Courtly Lad of Arras, The Boy and the Blind Man, The Play of the Bower* and *The Play about Robin and Marion*—are the earliest extant secular dramatic texts so far discovered in western Europe, and, Symes argues, each represents a forum for discussion and negotiation of contemporary events and aspects of cultural life. Each, she suggests, is also marked by an 'extreme topicality' (p. 2) growing from local personalities, scandals, or social concerns. Thanks to the 'precocious' (p. 3) habit of record-keeping locally, Symes is able to suggest the ways in which the drama created a kind of nascent public sphere for cultural debate for the citizens of Arras. Although it is, perhaps, a little over-zealous in its claim that 'the inseparability of premodern theatre history from the history of communities' is 'an important discovery' to be announced here (pp. 6–7)—much recent work on the English, Scottish and Burgundian drama (some of which Symes indeed cites) has been based on precisely this premise—this book is nonetheless a stimulating and valuable expansion of our knowledge of early theatre in France, and provides a useful case study of drama's interactions with other authoritative and authorizing forms of performative culture in a complex urban environment.

Lynette Muir's *Love and Conflict in Medieval Drama: The Plays and their Legacy*, a companion volume to her earlier survey, *The Biblical Drama of Medieval Europe* (CUP [1995]), is published in 2007, the year in which she died. It covers what she describes as the 'serious', non-biblical plays of western Europe from the tenth to the sixteenth centuries. Following the weight of the extant sources, it draws most of its evidence from France and Italy, but also has things to say about northern Europe, Germany, Britain and the Netherlands in particular, and Spain. The subjects of these plays are mainly saints' lives, miracles, romances and epic narratives, although the occasional comic play and biblical drama not covered in the earlier volume also sneaks in at times. Scholars and students seeking a sense of the breadth and scope of medieval European theatrical activity would do well to start with this concise, engaging survey.

Peter Happé's latest monograph, *The Towneley Cycle: Unity and Diversity*, focuses, as its title suggests, upon a single dramatic text, the religious pageants contained in the Towneley manuscript (Huntington Library MS HMI). In recent years the Towneley plays (as they are now usually called) have been the centre of a lively and ongoing critical debate, which has left much of what we thought we knew about them once more open to contention. What we once thought we knew was that the Towneley manuscript contained the text of the Wakefield cycle of late medieval religious pageants, a cycle performed on wagons on the streets of Wakefield by craft guilds, much in the same manner as the nearby York cycle, with which it shared a number of pageants. Thanks to the work of Barbara Palmer, Garret Epp and others, many of these seemingly secure assumptions have been thrown into doubt. The text, it transpires, could well be an eclectic collection of pageants gathered from many sources by a scribe associated with the Lancashire Recusant family, the Towneleys, in the middle of the sixteenth century, with little or no connection with Wakefield to unite them. So perhaps what we thought was the medieval Wakefield cycle is not medieval, not from Wakefield, and not a cycle at all. Peter Happé's contribution to this continuing debate attempts, if not to pour oil on troubled waters, at least to seek some common ground among the contending arguments. While acknowledging the lack of a clear Wakefield pedigree, and the good grounds for doubting the single, unified origins of the pageants (hence the 'diversity' in his title) he nonetheless argues that what we have before us—the Towneley manuscript—does give the collection its own kind of unity, even if it exists as a composite text to be read rather than a single script that was ever performed. And, in compiling the manuscript, the Towneley scribe must clearly have been working with a sense of a single narrative, a cycle of stories, in mind. So, although the text might not be the authentically grounded, medieval Wakefield cycle that we once thought, it is nonetheless a cycle of sorts, and a dramatic composition worthy of our consideration alongside the plays of York, Chester and (most obviously) the similarly problematic N-town, with which it seems to have a good deal in common. Indeed, the lasting impression created by this book—and probably its greatest achievement—is not so much the diplomatic care with which it seeks to tread among the various scholarly landmines strewn in its path, but the author's obvious admiration for the Towneley plays as works of literary and dramatic craft. As Happé shows, these are undeniably good plays, and their quality extends well beyond the clutch of pageants traditionally attributed to that acknowledged dramaturgic genius, the so-called Wakefield Master.

The cultural contexts in which the drama of moral and political counsel was created and performed are admirably illustrated in the collection of essays edited by John F. McDiarmid under the title, *The Monarchical Republic of Early Modern England: Essays in Response to Patrick Collinson*. Variously expanding upon, refracting and negotiating with the ideas originally advanced in Collinson's hugely influential article 'The Monarchical Republic of Queen Elizabeth I' (*BJRL* 69[1987] 394–424), the essays range over the literature (especially *The Mirror for Magistrates*), the drama (most notably Shakespeare's first tetralogy) and political writings of the Tudor century and beyond. A characteristically perceptive and wide-ranging end-word from Collinson himself neatly rounds off the volume with reflections on the state of scholarship since the first appearance of his essay. Scholars of drama and literature alike will also welcome the publication of a new edition of George Puttenham's *The Art of English Poesy*, edited by Frank Whigham and Wayne A. Rebhorn. Accompanied by a critical introduction to Puttenham's life, sources and style, *en face* and endnotes, name glossary, word glossary and index of first lines of illustrative quotations, the book is a comprehensive, lucid and eminently useful scholarly and pedagogical edition of this seminal Tudor text. Although explicitly concerned with the playhouse drama of the early seventeenth century, Jean E. Howard's *Theater of a City: The Places of London Comedy, 1598–1642* deals with synergies between performance, history, urban politics and social geography that have considerable relevance for the earlier period too. Many of the aspects of metropolitan spread, population and economic growth, cultural flux and ferment described by Howard as aspects of Jacobean and Caroline London, for example, can be detected, albeit in slightly muted or mutated forms, a century or more earlier, and can be seen to inform plays such as *Wisdom, Hickscorner* or Skelton's *Magnyfycence* as well as the later City comedies. Similarly, the account of the London whorehouses used to illuminate the analysis of the later plays might have implications for our understanding of the city moralities of the early Tudor period, especially *Wisdom* and *Hickscorner*.

Those readers stuck for inspiration when teaching the Morality plays or *The Second Shepherds' Play* will find some pedagogical notes and sample teaching questions in a new reference work, *The Christian Tradition in English Literature: Poetry, Plays, and Shorter Prose*, edited collectively by Paul Cavill, Heather Ward, Matthew Baynham and Andrew Swinford, with additional contributions by John Flood and Roger Pooley. Within its pages can be found, alongside short sections on *Everyman* and the Towneley plays, brief descriptive entries on texts from Bede and *Beowulf* to Beckett's *Endgame*. Those more interested in the 'spectatorial turn' in early drama studies, and with renewed interest in the phenomenological aspects of dramatic reception, might find fruitful matter in *The Beholder: The Experience of Art in Early Modern Europe*, edited by Thomas Frangenberg and Robert Williams. Most relevant in the current context is probably David Summers's short chapter, 'The Heritage of Agatharcus: On Naturalism and Theatre in European Painting' (pp. 9–36, with fifteen pages of illustrations) which follows E.H. Gombrich in analysing the 'scenic' aspects of perspectival painting and geometric optics through theatrical models. Heather Hill-Vásquez's *Sacred Players: The Politics of Response in the Middle Ages* is also interested in drama and spectatorship, focusing specifically on the religious cycle plays. Her subject is the durability and flexibility of the religious cycles, and in particular that self-reflexive, responsive quality that allowed them to outlive the 'medieval' Catholic religious culture and sensibility that spawned them and meet new audience needs through the very different confessional climates of the middle third of the sixteenth century. This 'second life', as Hill-Vásquez terms it, of the plays at Chester and York, and of an eclectic miracle drama such as the Croxton *Play of the Sacrament*, involved—and was to an extent enabled by—an explicit and fundamental attentiveness in the plays themselves to audience response, which could be readily adapted to the new 'Protestant' imperatives of the later period and so be used to redirect audiences towards what the new regimes saw as a 'proper' response to such material. Daniel Eppley's *Defending Royal Supremacy and Discerning God's Will in Tudor England* also charts the shift from Catholic to reformed religious practices in the turbulent years of the later sixteenth century, focusing on the writings of two apologists for royal authority in matters of religion, the Henrician lawyer

Christopher St German and the Elizabethan ecclesiast Richard Hooker. Readers interested in tracing the shifts in possible audience response to questions of divine will and royal authority in the religious plays will find the account of the public positions of these two problematic, semi-official writers offered by Eppley helpful and informative.

The latest issue of the always excellent *Medieval English Theatre* (*METh* 27 [2007 for 2005]) contains the usual breadth and depth of material on the drama of the early period. In this issue, *METh* stalwart David Mills looks at the social, spatial and geographical sweep of the York and Chester cycles in 'I Know My Place: Some Thoughts on Status and Station in the English Mystery Plays' (*METh* 27[2007 for 2005] 5–15). Peter Happé considers what may have prompted Jasper Heywood to translate Senecan drama in the later sixteenth century in ' "The restless mind that would never raging leave": Jasper Heywood's *Thyestes*' (*METh* 27[2007 for 2005] 16–33). In addition, a cluster of the essays in this issue are taken from the 2007 Medieval English Theatre conference held at the University of Sheffield, where John Skelton's interlude *Magnyfycence* was the focus of attention, and an innovative, partially abridged production of the play directed by Elizabeth Dutton was performed. Among these articles is John Scattergood's ' "Familiar and Homely": The Intrusion and Articulation of Vice in Skelton's *Magnyfycence*' (*METh* 27[2007 for 2005] 34–52), which re-examines the treatment of the Vices, their names (real and adopted), appearance and cultural implications, in Skelton's highly politicized text. In 'Skelton's *Magnyfycence* and Tragic Drama' (*METh* 27[2007 for 2005] 53–68), Dermot Cavanagh offers a powerful and challenging re-reading of the play, which helpfully brings its *de casibus*, tragic elements to the fore. Elizabeth Evershed's 'Meet for Merchants?: Some Implications of Situating Skelton's *Magnyfycence* at the Merchant Tailors' Hall' (*METh* 27[2007 for 2005] 69–85), explores the practical and cultural contexts that would have surrounded the play had it indeed been performed for the Merchant Tailors Company of London, as the reference to 'The Tailors' Hall' within it might perhaps suggest.

Staying with the early Tudor interludes, but moving away from *Magnyfycence*, Thomas Betteridge and Greg Walker's article, 'Performance as Research: Staging John Heywood's *Play of the Weather* at Hampton Court Palace' (*METh* 27[2007 for 2005] 86–104), reports on some of the outcomes of their Arts and Humanities Research Council-funded project to perform sections of that play with professional actors in the great hall at Hampton Court, and discusses the respective implications of striving, or not striving, for 'authentic' productions of early drama in historical spaces. Also concerned with modern productions of early plays is Pamela King's article, 'Twentieth-Century Medieval-Drama Revivals and the Universities' (*METh* 27[2007 for 2005] 105–30), which draws heavily and fruitfully on the archival resources of the University of Bristol Theatre Collection to describe the pioneering work of Glynne Wickham and others in reviving medieval plays in contemporary academic productions. Finally, a short communication from Elizabeth Baldwin, 'A Note on the Chester Pageant Route' (*METh* 27[2007 for 2005] 131–2), offers a promising suggestion regarding the identity of the 'St. Tola's Lane' mentioned in the records of the pageant route, while Pamela King provides a review of 'The Mysteries' performed at Coventry Cathedral by the Belgrave Theatre Company in August 2006 (*METh* 27[2007 for 2005] 133–6).

Katie Normington's short monograph, *Modern Mysteries: Contemporary Productions of Medieval English Cycle Drama*, also focuses on modern revivals of medieval plays, seeking to explore the current fascination with the expansive, spectacular, religious projects in what we are frequently told is a minimalist, secular and postmodern age, and one habitually uncomfortable with the kind of teleological grand narratives that are the very substance of the cycle drama. Normington deploys a number of theoretical models to account for the disjunctions and reconnections between the medieval works and their modern/postmodern reworkings, but at the heart of the book is a series of examinations of individual productions, ranging from the familiar candidates (the Bill Bryden and Tony Harrison *Mysteries* at the National Theatre, Katie Mitchell's RSC cycle, and Greg Doran's *Millennium Mysteries* at York) to less well known ventures such as the Coventry *Millennium Mysteries* (also discussed in Pam King's *METh* review article cited above) and the annual play at Worsborough, with many of the reviews usefully informed by valuable new interviews with participants.

The latest issue of *Early Theatre* (*ET* 10:ii[2007]) is largely devoted to the Caroline theatre, and to the work of Richard Brome in particular, but Leanne Groeneveld's article, 'A Theatrical Miracle: The Boxley Rood of Grace as Puppet' (*ET* 10:ii[2007] 11–50), is squarely concerned with the earlier period. Its subject is the mechanical rood (crucifix) at Boxley Abbey in Kent, which evangelical and later Protestant reformers denounced as an example of all that was fraudulent and idolatrous about late medieval Catholic devotion—and especially monastic devotion—and all that was gullible about popular, traditional worshippers. The Boxley rood, Henry VIII's commissioners reported in 1538, was made, through wires manipulated by a hidden monastic operator, to roll its eyes, move its mouth and weep and nod in response to priestly or parishioners' devotions. In reconsidering such performances in the light of contemporary—and slightly later—descriptions and understandings of puppetry, Groeneveld suggests that, rather than being an exercise in deception, the 'miraculous' rood would have been understood by its devotees as a mechanical aid to genuine worship—a perceptive sophistication elided by its critics for polemical effect.

Puppets also make a brief appearance in Clifford Davidson's *Festivals and Plays in Late Medieval Britain*, in allusions to marionettes and images associated with Easter sepulchre devotions and the Three Kings of Cologne respectively. But the bulk of the book is a collection of six linked essays surveying the connections between dramatic and quasi-dramatic performances and the feast of the ritual year, with detailed discussion of aspects of the York plays and the festival plays for Good Friday and Easter Day in Bodleian Library MS e. Museo 160. Overall the study presents a clear sense of the performative aspects of British festive and ritual culture across the late medieval and (very) early modern period. Also interdisciplinary in approach, drawing upon architectural, visual and liturgical material as well as literary and dramatic texts, is Karl Tamburr's illuminating study, *The Harrowing of Hell in Medieval England*. By tracing the sources and themes of the Harrowing through time, Tamburr valuably adds complexity and nuance to our understanding of a motif and narrative trope seemingly familiar from ecclesiastical imagery and the mystery cycles alike. He shows how it might be inflected in different ways by authors and artists to reflect upon either Christ's humanity or his divinity, his majestic power and authority or his corporeal vulnerability, to allude to baptism or burial, the beginnings of life or its end, in the period up to and including the Protestant reinterpretation of the theme in the sixteenth century.

Books Reviewed

Adams, Gwenfair Walters. *Visions in Late Medieval England: Lay Spirituality and Sacred Glimpses of the Hidden Worlds of Faith*. Brill. [2007] pp. xxiv + 274. €99 ($129) ISBN 9 7890 0415 6067.

Allen, Valerie. *On Farting: Language and Laughter in the Middle Ages*. Palgrave. [2007] pp. xiii + 239 £22.99 ($74.95) ISBN 9 7803 1223 4935.

Andrew, Malcolm, and Ronald Waldron, eds. *The Poems of the Pearl Manuscript*, 5th edn. ExeterUP. [2007] pp. x + 373. £16.14 ISBN 9 7808 5989 7914.

Armitage, Simon, trans. *Sir Gawain and the Green Knight*. Faber. [2007] pp. xii + 116 £12.99 ISBN 9 7805 7122 3275.

Ashe, Laura. *Fiction and History in England, 1066–1200*. CUP. [2007] pp. xii + 244. £50 ISBN 9 7805 2187 8913.

Baldwin, Anna. *A Guidebook to Piers Plowman*. Palgrave. [2007] pp. xvi + 295. £16.99 ISBN 0 2305 0715 8.

Baldwin, Elizabeth, Lawrence M. Clopper and David Mills, eds. *Records of Early English Drama: Cheshire Including Chester*, 2 vols. UTorP. [2007] pp. 1231. £195 ISBN 9 7808 0200 3264.

Bale, Anthony. *The Jew in the Medieval Book: English Antisemitisms, 1350–1500*. CSML 60. CUP. [2006] pp. xiv + 266. £48 ($96) ISBN 9 7805 2186 3544.

Bardsley, Sandy. *Women's Roles in the Middle Ages*. Greenwood. [2007] pp. xxi + 231. £34.95 $59.95 ISBN 9 7803 1333 6355.

Barney, Stephen A. *The Penn Commentary on 'Piers Plowman'*, vol. 5: *C Passus 20–22; B Passus 18–20*. UPennP. [2006] pp. 328. $65. £42.50 ISBN 9 7808 1223 9218.

Beam, Sara. *Laughing Matters: Farce and the Making of Absolutism in France*. CornUP. [2007] pp. 268. £34.50 ISBN 9 7808 0144 5606.

Bishop, Louise. *Words, Stones, & Herbs: The Healing Word in Medieval and Early Modern England*. SyracuseUP. [2007] pp. xiv + 276. £21.50 ($59.95) ISBN 9 7808 1563 1248.

Bloom, Gina. *Voice in Motion: Staging Gender, Shaping Sound in Early Modern England*. UPennP. [2007] pp. 288. £39 ISBN 9 7808 1224 0061.

Bowers, John M. *Chaucer and Langland: The Antagonistic Tradition*. UNDP. [2007] pp. xii + 406. $45 ($28.45) ISBN 0 2680 2202 X.

Brown, Peter, ed. *A Companion to Medieval English Literature and Culture, c.1350–c.1500*. Blackwell. [2007] pp. xviii + 668. £85 ($158.95) ISBN 9 7806 3121 9736.

Cain, Christopher M., and Geoffrey Russom, eds. *Studies in the History of the English Language III*. Mouton. [2007] pp. xiv + 301 £86.58 (€98) ISBN 9 7831 1019 0892.

Cavill, Paul, Heather Ward, Matthew Baynham and Andrew Swinford, eds. *The Christian Tradition in English Literature: Poetry, Plays, and Shorter Prose*. Zondervan. [2007] pp. 512. pb £14.99 ISBN 9 7803 1025 5154.

Chance, Jane. *The Literary Subversions of Medieval Women*. Palgrave. [2007] pp. xiii + 215. £40 ($68.95) ISBN 9 7814 0396 9101.

Chewning, Susannah, ed. *Intersections of Sexuality and the Divine in Medieval Culture: The Word Made Flesh*. Ashgate. [2005] pp. xii + 213. £55 ($120) ISBN 0 7546 4065 5.

Classen, Albrecht. *The Medieval Chastity Belt: A Myth-Making Process*. Palgrave. [2007] pp. 453. £40 ($74.95) ISBN 9 7814 0397 5584.

Classen, Albrecht. *The Power of a Woman's Voice in Medieval and Early Modern Literatures*. Gruyter. [2007] £91.14 ($157) ISBN 9 7831 1019 9413.

Craun, Edwin D., ed. *The Hands of the Tongue: Essays on Deviant Speech*. MIP. [2007] pp. xviii + 213. hb $40 pb $20 ISBN 9 7815 8044 1148, pb $20 ISBN 9 7815 8044 1155..

Davidson, Clifford. *Festivals and Plays in Late Medieval Britain*. Ashgate. [2007] pp. 216. £50 ISBN 9 7807 5466 0521.

Davis, Isabel. *Writing Masculinity in the Later Middle Ages*. CSML 62. CUP. [2007] pp. xiv + 226. £48 ($91) ISBN 9 7805 2186 6378.

Dove, Mary. *The First English Bible: The Text and Context of the Wycliffite Versions*. CSML 66. CUP. [2007] pp. xvi + 314. £55 ($99) ISBN 9 7805 2188 0282.

Driver, Martha W., and Michael T. Orr. *An Index of Images in English Manuscripts from the Time of Chaucer to Henry VIII, c.1380–c.1509*. New York City, Columbia University–Union Theological, gen. ed. Kathleen L. Scott. HM. [2007] pp. 176. pb €55 ($81) ISBN 9 7819 0537 5226.

Dunlop, Fiona S. *The Late Medieval Interlude: The Drama of Youth and Aristocratic Masculinity*. York Medieval Press. [2007] pp. 141. £45 ISBN 9 7819 0315 3215.

Eppley, Daniel. *Defending Royal Supremacy and Discerning God's Will in Tudor England*. Ashgate. [2007] pp. 243. £55 ISBN 9 7807 5466 0132.

Fitzgerald, Christina M. *The Drama of Masculinity and Medieval English Guild Culture*. Palgrave. [2007] pp. xiii + 214. £40 ISBN 9 7814 0397 2774.

Frangenberg, Thomas, and Robert Williams, eds. *The Beholder: The Experience of Art in Early Modern Europe*. Ashgate. [2007] pp. 233. £55 ISBN 9 7807 5460 6796.

Galloway, Andrew. *Medieval Literature and Culture*. Continuum. [2007] pp. vi + 154. hb $77 ISBN 9 7808 2648 6561, pb $16.95 ISBN 9 7808 2648 6578.

Gavin, John J. *Theatricality and Narrative in Medieval and Early Modern Scotland*. Ashgate. [2007] pp. xi + 160. £50 ($99.95) ISBN 9 7807 5460 7946.

Giancarlo, Matthew. *Parliament and Literature in Late Medieval England.* CSML 64. CUP. [2007] pp. xiv + 290. £50 ($95) ISBN 9 7805 2187 5394.

Glaser, Joseph, trans. and ed. *Middle English Poetry in Modern Verse.* Hackett. [2007] pp. xiv + 234. hb $39.95 ISBN 9 7808 7220 8803, pb $12.95 ISBN 9 7808 7220 8797.

Green, D.H. *Women Readers in the Middle Ages.* CUP. [2007] pp. xi + 296. £50 ($95) ISBN 9 7805 2187 9422.

Hamer, Richard, ed., with the assistance of Vida Russell. *Gilte Legende*, vol. 2. EETS Os 328. OUP. [2007] pp. 500. £65 ($199) ISBN 9 7801 9923 4394.

Hanna, Ralph. *London Literature 1300–1380.* CUP. [2005] pp. 384. $110 ISBN 0 5218 4835 0.

Hanna, Ralph, ed. *Richard Rolle: Uncollected Prose and Verse with Related Northern Texts.* EETS Os 329. OUP. [2007] pp. lxxviii + 234. £65 ($199) ISBN 9 7801 9923 6145.

Happé, Peter. *The Towneley Cycle: Unity and Diversity.* UWalesP. [2007] pp. 290. £60 ISBN 9 7807 0832 0488.

Happé, Peter, and Wim Hüsken, eds. *Interludes and Early Modern Society: Studies in Gender, Power and Theatricality.* Rodopi. [2007] pp. 380. €76 ISBN 9 7890 4202 3031.

Hass, Andrew, David Jasper and Elisabeth Jay, eds. *The Oxford Handbook of English Literature and Theology.* OUP. [1979] pp. 908. £85 ISBN 9 7801 9927.

Havsteen, Sven Rune, Nils Holger Peterson, Heinrich W. Schwab and Eyolf Ostrem, eds. *Creations: Medieval Rituals, the Arts, and the Concept of Creation.* Brepols. [2007] pp. 269. £40 ($87) ISBN 9 7825 0352 2951.

Hayward, Maria. *Dress at the Court of King Henry VIII.* Maney Publishing. [2007] pp. 458. hb £118 ISBN 9 7819 0435 0705, pb £48 ISBN 9 7819 0598 1410.

Hill-Vásquez, Heather. *Sacred Players: The Politics of Response in the Middle Ages.* CUAP. [2007] pp. 229. £39.95 ISBN 9 7808 1321 4979.

Hopkins, Amanda, and Cory James Rushton, eds. *The Erotic in the Literature of Medieval Britain.* Boydell. [2007] pp. xii + 182. £45 ($80) ISBN 9 7818 4384 1197.

Howard, Jean E. *Theater of a City: The Places of London Comedy, 1598–1642.* UPennP. [2007] pp. 312. £36 ISBN 9 7808 1223 9782.

Howes, Laura L., ed. *Place, Space, and Landscape in Medieval Narrative.* UTennP. [2007] pp. 208. $43 ISBN 1 5723 3586 6.

Howie, Cary. *Claustrophilia: The Erotics of Enclosure in Medieval Literature.* Palgrave. [2007] pp. xii + 196. £40 $74.95 ISBN 9 7814 0397 1975.

Jewell, Helen M. *Women in Dark Age and Early Medieval Europe c.500–1200.* Palgrave. [2007] pp. vii + 175. pb £19.99 ISBN 9 7803 3391 2591.

Jewell, Helen M. *Women in Late Medieval and Reformation Europe 1200–1550.* Palgrave. [2007] pp. viii + 171. hb £55 ($99.95) ISBN 9 7803 3391 2560, pb £18.99 ($31.95) ISBN 9 7803 3391 2577.

Kasten, Madeleine. *In Search of 'Kynde Knowynge': Piers Plowman and the Origin of Allegory.* Rodopi. [2007] pp. 257. €52 ($75) ISBN 9 0420 2173 X.

Kaufman, Peter Iver. *Incorrectly Political: Augustine and Thomas More.* UNDP. [2007] pp. 279. £23.50 ISBN 9 7802 6803 3149.

Kaylor, Noel Harold, Jr. and Richard Scott Nokes, eds. *Global Perspectives on Medieval English Literature, Language, and Culture*. MIP. [2007] pp. xv + 310. £30 $45 ISBN 9 7815 8044 1209.

Kaylor, Noel Harold, Jr, and Philip Edward Phillips, eds. *New Directions in Boethian Studies*. SMC 45. MIP. [2007] pp. xviii + 295. $45 ISBN 9 7815 8044 1001.

Kerby-Fulton, Kathryn. *Books under Suspicion: Censorship and Tolerance of Revelatory Writing in Late Medieval England*. UNDP. [2006] pp. 616. $50 ISBN 0 2680 3312 9.

King, Andy, and Michael Penman, eds. *England and Scotland in the Fourteenth Century: New Perspectives*. [2007] pp. xi + 269. £45 ($80) ISBN 9 7818 4383 3185.

Kohanski, Tamarah, and C. David Benson, eds. *The Book of John Mandeville*. TEAMS Middle English Texts. MIP. [2007] pp. viii + 184. pb $14 ISBN 9 7815 8044 1131.

Lewis, Robert E., Mary Jane Williams and Marilyn S. Miller. *Middle English Dictionary: Plan and Bibliography*, 2nd edn. UMichP. [2007] pp. viii + 174. pb $24.50 ISBN 9 7804 7201 3104.

Lipton, Emma. *Affections of the Mind: The Politics of Sacramental Marriage in Late Medieval English Literature*. UNDP. [2007] pp. x + 246. pb £27.50 ($32) ISBN 9 7802 6803 4054.

Mann, Jill, and Maura Nolan, eds. *The Text in the Community: Essays on Medieval Works, Manuscripts, Authors, and Readers*. UNDP. [2006] pp. xvi + 296. $37 ISBN 0 2680 3496 6.

Masciandaro, Nicola. *The Voice of the Hammer: The Meaning of Work in Middle English Literature*. UNDP. [2007] pp. xii + 212. pb $25 ISBN 9 7802 6803 4986.

McDiarmid, John F. ed. *The Monarchical Republic of Early Modern England: Essays in Response to Patrick Collinson*. Ashgate. [2007] pp. 320. £60 ISBN 9 7807 5465 4346.

McMullan, Gordon, and David Matthews, eds. *Reading the Medieval in Early Modern England*. CUP. [2007] pp. xiv + 287. £50 ISBN 9 7805 2186 8433.

Meyer-Lee, Robert J. *Poets and Power from Chaucer to Wyatt*. CSML 61. CUP. [2007] pp. xii + 238. £50 ($96) ISBN 9 7805 2186 3551.

Mitchell, J. Allan. ed. *The Temple of Glass* by John Lydgate. TEAMS Middle English Texts. MIP. [2007] pp. viii + 96. pb $12 ISBN 9 7815 8044 1179.

Morgan, Nigel J., and Rodney M. Thomson, ed. *The Cambridge History of the Book in Britain*, vol. 2: *1100–1400*. CUP. [2007] pp. xxiv + 616 + 82 plates. £95 ($190) ISBN 9 7805 2178 2180.

Muir, Lynette. *Love and Conflict in Medieval Drama: The Plays and their Legacy*. CUP. [2007] pp. xv + 294. £50 ISBN 9 7805 2182 7560.

Normington, Katie. *Modern Mysteries: Contemporary Productions of Medieval English Cycle Drama*. Brewer. [2007] pp. 190. £30 ISBN 9 7818 4384 1289.

Nuttall, Jenni. *The Creation of Lancastrian Kingship: Literature, Language and Politics in Late Medieval England*. CSML 67. CUP. [2007] pp. x + 190. £45 ($90) ISBN 9 7805 2187 4960.

O'Donoghue, Bernard, trans. *Sir Gawain and the Green Knight*. Penguin. [2007]pp. xxvi + 94. £8.99 ISBN 9 7801 4042 4539.

Ohlgren, Thomas H. *Robin Hood: The Early Poems, 1465–1560: Texts, Contexts, and Ideology*. UDelP. [2007] pp. 278. £37.50 ($55) ISBN 9 7808 7413 9648.

Parker, John. *The Aesthetics of Antichrist from Christian Drama to Christopher Marlowe*. CornUP. [2007] pp. xi + 252. £20.50 ISBN 9 7808 0144 5194.

Passmore, S. Elizabeth, and Susan Carter, eds. *The English 'Loathly Lady' Tales: Boundaries, Traditions, Motifs*. SMC 48. MIP. [2007] pp. xx + 272. hb $40 ISBN 9 7815 8044 1230, pb $20 ISBN 9 7815 8044 1247.

Phillips, Susan E. *Transforming Talk: The Problem with Gossip in Late Medieval England*. PSUP. [2007] pp. x + 238. £29.40 ($45) ISBN 9 7802 7102 9948.

Poor, Sara S., and Jana K. Schulman, eds. *Women and Medieval Epic: Gender, Genre, and the Limits of Epic Masculinity*. Palgrave. [2007] pp. xii + 299. £45 ($79.95) ISBN 9 7814 0396 6025.

Postles, Dave. *The North through its Names: A Phenomenology of Medieval and Early-Modern Northern England*. English Surnames Survey 8. Oxbow. [2007] pp. xii + 244. £35 ($70) ISBN 9 7818 4217 1769.

Pugh, Tison, and Angela Jane Weisl, eds. *Approaches to Teaching Chaucer's 'Troilus and Criseyde' and the Shorter Poems*. MLA. [2007] pp. 217. hb £45 ($37.50) ISBN 9 7808 7352 9969, pb £19.75 ISBN 9 7808 7352 9976.

Rosenberg, Samuel N., Karen Louise Fresco and Wendy Pfeffer, eds. *Chançon Legiere a Chanter: Essays in Old French Literature in Honor of Samuel N. Rosenberg*. Summa. [2007] pp. xix + 479. ISBN 1 8834 7954 1.

Rudd, Gillian. *Greenery: Ecocritical Readings of Late Medieval English Literature*. ManUP. [2007] pp. viii + 222. £50 ($74.95) ISBN 9 7807 1907 2482.

Salter, Elizabeth. *Six Renaissance Men and Women: Innovation, Biography and Cultural Creativity in Tudor England, c.1450–1560*. Ashgate. [2007] pp. 167. £55 ISBN 9 7807 5465 4407.

Sanok, Catherine. *Her Life Historical: Exemplarity and Female Saints' Lives in Late Medieval England*. UPennP. [2007] pp. 256. £30.50 ($55) ISBN 9 7808 1223 9867.

Sauer, Hans, and Renate Bauer, eds. *Beowulf and Beyond*. Lang. [2006] pp. 354. £44 ($55.95) ISBN 0 8204 8751 1.

Scase, Wendy, ed. *Essays in Manuscript Geography: Vernacular Manuscripts of the English West Midlands from the Conquest to the Sixteenth Century*. Medieval Texts and Cultures of Northern Europe 10. Brepols. [2007] pp. xii + 296. €60 (£44.27, $87) ISBN 9 7825 0351 6950.

Scase, Wendy. *Literature and Complaint in England, 1272–1553*. OUP. [2007] pp. xii + 216. £50 ($95) ISBN 9 7801 9927 0859.

Schoff, Rebecca L. *Reformations: Three Medieval Authors in Manuscript and Moveable Type*. Brepols. [2007] pp. xvi + 231. €60 ISBN 9 7825 0352 3163.

Scott, Virginia, and Sara Sturm-Maddox, eds. *Performance, Poetry and Politics on the Queen's Day*. Ashgate. [2007] pp. 278. £55 ISBN 9 7807 5465 8399.

Sherman, William. *Used Books: Marking Readers in Renaissance England.* UPennP. [2007] pp. 280. £29.50 ISBN 9 7808 1224 0436.

Simpson, James. *Piers Plowman: An Introduction*, 2nd edn. UExe. [2007] pp. vii + 248. $32.50 (£16.99) ISBN 0 8598 9802 4.

Strohm, Paul, ed. *Middle English.* Oxford Twenty-First Century Approaches to Literature. OUP. [2007] pp. xii + 524. £89 ($218.90) ISBN 9 7801 9928 7666.

Summerfield, Thea, and Keith Busby, eds. *People and Texts: Relationships in Medieval Literature. Studies Presented to Erik Kooper.* Rodopi. [2007] pp. xi + 205 pp. €44 ($64) ISBN 9 7890 4202 1457.

Symes, Carol. *A Common Stage: Theater and Public Life in Medieval Arras.* CornUP. [2007] pp. xix + 335. £25.50 ISBN 9 7808 0144 5811.

Tamburr, Karl. *The Harrowing of Hell in Medieval England.* Brewer. [2007] pp. xii + 212. £50 ($85) ISBN 9 7818 4384 1173.

Turville-Petre, Thorlac. *Reading Middle English Literature.* Blackwell. [2007] pp. x + 212. hb £50 ($74.95; A$165) ISBN 9 8706 3123 1714, pb £17.99 ($29.95; A$55.95) ISBN 9 7806 3123 1721.

Wakelin, Daniel. *Humanism, Reading, and English Literature 1430–1530.* OUP. [2007] pp. xii + 254. £53 ($110) ISBN 9 7801 9921 5881.

Walsh, P.G., and M.J. Kennedy, eds. *William of Newburgh: The History of English Affairs, Book II.* Aris & Phillips. [2007] pp. viii + 208. hb £40 ($80) ISBN 9 7808 5668 4739, pb £18 ($36) ISBN 9 7808 5668 4746.

Watt, Diane. *Medieval Women's Writing.* Polity. [2007] pp. viii + 208. £16.99 $69.95 ISBN 9 7807 4563 2551.

Whigham, Frank, and Wayne A. Rebhorn, eds. *The Art of English Poesy* by George Puttenham. CornUP. [2007] pp. 498. pb £12.50 ISBN 9 7808 0148 6524.

Wiggins, Alison, and Rosalind Field, eds. *Guy of Warwick: Icon and Ancestor.* CUP. [2007] £50 ISBN 9 7818 4384 1258.

Winstead, Karen A. *John Capgrave's Fifteenth Century.* UPennP. [2007] pp. xiv + 234. £36 ($55) ISBN 9 7808 1223 9775.

Yeager, R.F., ed. *On John Gower: Essays at the Millennium.* SMC 46. MIP. [2007] pp. x + 242. $40 ISBN 9 7815 8044 0981.

IV

Later Medieval: Chaucer

VALERIE ALLEN AND MARGARET CONNOLLY

This chapter is divided into four sections: 1. General; 2. *Canterbury Tales*; 3. *Troilus and Criseyde*; 4. Other Works. The ordering of individual tales and poems within the sections follows that of the Riverside Chaucer edition. With thanks to Wan-Chuan Kao of the Graduate Center, City University of New York, for his editorial assistance.

1. General

Mark Allen and Bege K. Bowers continue to provide a valuable service in compiling 'An Annotated Chaucer Bibliography 2004' (*SAC* 29[2007] 565–660); for the electronic version see the New Chaucer Society webpage: http://artsci.wustl.edu/~chaucer/or directly at http://uchaucer.utsa.edu. In 'Chaucer as a London Poet: A Review Essay' (*EssaysMedSt* 24[2007] 21–9), David Raybin surveys critical opinion on the topic, starting with David Wallace's influential argument that London is present by its absence and including Marion Turner's work (*YWES* 87[2008] 279–80) and Ardis Butterfield's recent collection (*YWES* 87[2008] 282–4).

David Wallace gives the presidential address to the New Chaucer Society (*SAC* 29[2007] 3–19), in which he ranges broadly over the ways in which Chaucer lives on in and is reimagined by popular culture and contemporary literature, as in Ted Hughes's *Birthday Letters*. Popular culture, including (among many others) Baba Brinkman's *Rap Canterbury Tales* and Peter Ackroyd's *Clerkenwell Tales*, mixes Chaucer into the here and now in provocative ways. Wallace has most to say about Marilyn Nelson's *Cachoeira Tales*, which formally models itself on Chaucer's poem. Richly allusive yet radically different, this poem glosses the *Canterbury Tales* and harnesses their canonicity to explore the unfamiliar. As if to verify the legacy of the poet, a short poem entitled 'Chaucer Authors the Distance' is published by Joshua A. Ware (*NOR* 33:ii[2007] 20). Karla Taylor offers a nuanced reading of Chaucer's literary legacy from Dante and Ovid in 'Chaucer's Volumes: Toward a New Model of Literary History in the *Canterbury Tales*' (*SAC* 29[2007] 43–85), where she gathers together critical words and

Year's Work in English Studies, Volume 88 (2009) © *The English Association; all rights reserved*
doi:10.1093/ywes/map015

images—*volume*; Jankyn's torn book; Dante's scattered leaves of the universe bound into a volume (*Paradiso* xxxii); turning over the *leef*; and Midas's wife telling tales. Taylor centres much of her essay on the Introduction to the *Man of Law's Tale* (a passage that has received some attention this year), where she portrays the pilgrim as a disgruntled reader, resistant to the precedent of Chaucerian and poetic tradition. This resistance is ironically enfolded into Chaucer's own authorial design.

In 'Chaucer's Man Show: Anachronistic Authority in Brian Helgeland's *A Knight's Tale*' (in Ramey and Pugh, eds., *Race, Class, and Gender in 'Medieval' Cinema*, pp. 183–97), Holly A. Crocker shows how, in the final version, Chaucer is less important to William's identity than the outtakes would suggest. In the outtakes, it is Chaucer who really authors the transformation of peasant William into knight Ulrich. 'Geoff's' verbal dexterity exposes the rhetorical, public and performative construction of identity. Tellingly, Geoff's first appearance is as a blank corpus, stark naked. Despite his poetic accomplishments, he cannot in the final cut elevate William; only the Black Prince can do that. Chaucer's authority is decentred in favour of a transcendent masculine nobility.

Candace Barrington's *American Chaucers* considers how Chaucer has figured in US popular culture over the last two hundred years. The first chapter discusses his impact via nineteenth-century poetry anthologies, a period when the US was transforming from colonized to colonizer. By explicitly appealing to family, sanitized to suit public morality, and eventually by being modernized, such anthologies appropriated Chaucer's poetry for American middle-class values. In the next chapter Barrington details a late nineteenth-/early twentieth-century stage dramatization of Chaucer, Percy MacKaye's *The Canterbury Pilgrims*, which depicts the poet as both the king's man and a man of the people who mediates between classes through art. In protest at the commercialism of the popular stage, and driven by a belief in civic art, MacKaye (never with notable success) reincarnated the play in various guises tailored to performance in factories, schools and universities, as pageant and finally as opera libretto. Chapter 3 tracks a First World War pilot, James Hall, and the copy of the *Canterbury Tales* he encountered as a German prisoner of war. Hall subsequently published his 'Prisoner's Tale' memoir, *Flying with Chaucer*. Through Chaucer's poem, particularly the *Knight's Tale*, Hall explores the losses and failed intentions of the Great War. The topic of chapter 4 is women's marginalized but important role in disseminating Chaucer: May Day pageants of the *Canterbury Tales* at Wheaton College, a women's liberal arts school in Massachusetts; adult education opportunities and women's clubs throughout the country; and a one-woman travelling show for women of recitations from Chaucer. The last chapter deals with Brian Helgeland's *A Knight's Tale*, which has already received considerable attention from Holly Crocker this year. Barrington considers the film's 'distinctly American ethos' (p. 143) of risk for gain and upward social mobility. In her postscript Barrington explains how her *American Chaucers* took liberties with the Chaucerian original that, however unscholarly, kept the poet alive in the popular imagination—a point to consider in our classrooms.

For Helen Phillips, writing about 'Nature, Masculinity, and Suffering Women: The Remaking of the *Flower and the Leaf* and Chaucer's *Legend of Good Women* in the Nineteenth Century' (in Costambeys, Hamer and Heale, eds., *The Making of the Middle Ages: Liverpool Essays*, pp. 71–92), the late Middle Ages demonstrates a 'new feminism' (p. 73) that deploys courtly rather than theological persuasions. Nineteenth-century appropriations of Chaucer represent him in tune with that interest in the courtly, affective feminine while at the same time they insist on the poet's healthy and wholesome masculinity, at one with nature. Chaucer maintains a low-key if frequent presence in Michael Alexander's *Medievalism: The Middle Ages in Modern England*. Where romance for the eighteenth century defined the Middle Ages, Chaucer is seen to have a problematic and self-conscious relationship with romance, tending to undercut it either egregiously, as he does in *Thopas*, or on a smaller scale, as he does at moments in *Troilus and Criseyde*. Despite this, Chaucerian romance, especially *the Knight's Tale*, influenced Walter Scott, who occupies his own chapter where Alexander offers some close comparisons between the Canterbury pilgrims and Scott's characters. Chaucer's poetry often offered models of supposed real life to eighteenth- and nineteenth-century writers. In the darker art of modernism, Alexander also considers T.S. Eliot's refashioning of Chaucer's pilgrim theme from the *General Prologue* and hence with the whole poetic tradition in the opening of *The Wasteland*. Some discussion of Chaucer in art is also offered, and an illustration of the attractive *Pardoner's Prologue* [1924] by Harry Mileham is included, as is Ford Madox Brown's *The Seeds and Fruits of English Poetry*. Chaucer figures indirectly in Scott Freer's 'The Mythical Method: Eliot's "The Waste Land" and *A Canterbury Tale*' (*Historical Journal of Film, Radio and Television* 27[2007] 357–70). This film, released in 1944 by director Michael Powell, employs the 'mythical method', Eliot's phrase for the synchronizing of past and present in a web of allusion and cross-reference. Both film and Eliot's poem articulate cultural disconnection from the present.

Seth Lerer has a chapter on Chaucer's English in his *Inventing English: A Portable History of the Language*. For Lerer, Chaucer's strength lay in realizing and expanding the possibilities of English in terms of grammatical complexity, register, dialect, idiom, stylistic range and semantic nuance. He is also important in making English itself the theme of much of his commentary on his own poetic craft. Lerer takes the opening to the *General Prologue* as an extended illustrative example, but his consideration moves beyond the *Canterbury Tales* (of which he mentions a number) to include *Troilus*, *Boece*, and the *Treatise on the Astrolabe*. Although the whole book is well worth reading, this short chapter stands alone as an excellent introduction to Chaucer's language, and one that is more student-friendly than the section on Language and Versification in the Riverside Chaucer.

For a book-length study of *Chaucer's Language* pitched at the same level, Simon Horobin delivers a smart, short monograph that is both accessible and informative. The first chapter explains how many Middle English words (*buxom, fre, corage*) prove false friends if understood in the same sense as their modern counterparts. A second chapter maps the state of the English language in Chaucer's time, explaining the intricate relations between English, Latin,

Norman and French. The chapter skims over major events that shaped language directly or indirectly (the Hundred Years War, the Peasants' Revolt, Lollardy), mentions key works already shaping the literary horizon (*Ancrene Wisse*, the *Brut*, etc.), and, drawing on political events such as Henry III's Proclamation of 1258, raises the critical question of Chaucer's national consciousness, if any. Chapter 3 tackles dialects, the importance of which is shown by the care with which Chaucer used speech difference in *the Reeve's Tale*. A stanza of *Sir Gawain and the Green Knight* both offers contrast to Chaucer's dialect and affords Horobin the opportunity to elaborate on the difference between the dialect of Chaucer and that of his scribes. Spelling and pronunciation are covered in the next chapter, with brief discussion of the Great Vowel Shift, and comparison between Middle English and modern vowels. The material in chapter 5, on Chaucer's lexicon, is perhaps harder to teach in that it requires the student to appreciate the French and Latin origins of many of his English words. Chapter 6, on grammar, returns to linguistic features such as strong and weak adjectives that are probably unfamiliar to the average student. Despite the technicality, the analysis keeps to essentials and clearly explains the material. The last two chapters, on style and on pragmatics, bring the discussion to the level of discourse analysis and construction of discursive meaning. The collection concludes with an appendix of sample texts (five from the *Canterbury Tales*, one from *Troilus*), and a short glossary of linguistic definitions.

Linne Mooney's identification of Chaucer's scribe (*YWES* 87[2008] 278) has energized the study of Chaucer's manuscripts, and this year Alan Fletcher seeks to add further to the corpus associated with Adam Pynkhurst by offering a long discussion of 'The Criteria for Scribal Attribution: Dublin, Trinity College, MS 244, Some Early Copies of the Works of Geoffrey Chaucer, and the Canon of Adam Pynkhurst Manuscripts' (*RES* 58[2007] 597–632). Fletcher combines both palaeographical and linguistic evidence to argue that part of Dublin, Trinity College, MS 244 is the work of Pynkhurst, or at least a scribe of his school. Fletcher further argues that the language of 'Scribe P', as he calls him, dates from the 1380s since it contains features of both 'Type II' and 'Type III' London English. This would locate the production of this collection of Wyclifite prose texts to Pynkhurst's earlier career, and would make him the earliest identifiable London-based copyist of Lollard material; if accepted, Fletcher's discovery has important ramifications for our understanding of Chaucer's association—via his principal scribe—with fourteenth-century religious radicalism.

Martha W. Driver and Michael T. Orr catalogue all manuscripts housed in New York City libraries that are written by an English scribe and decorated in an English style in *An Index of Images in English Manuscripts from the Time of Chaucer to Henry VIII c.1380–c.1509*. Seven institutions are referenced: Columbia University, General Theological Seminary, the Grolier Club, the Morgan Library, the New York Academy of Medicine, the New York Public Library, and the Union Theological Seminary. Three manuscripts containing Chaucer's works are listed: Plimpton MS 254 (containing the *Treatise on the Astrolabe* and held in Columbia University); Morgan 249 (containing the *Canterbury Tales*); and Morgan 817 (containing *Troilus and Criseyde*).

For anyone, resident or visitor, wanting to avail themselves of all the city's resources, this is an immensely useful catalogue.

Orietta Da Rold explores 'The Significance of Scribal Corrections in Cambridge, University Library MS Dd.4.24 of Chaucer's *Canterbury Tales*' (*ChauR* 41[2007] 393–438), a manuscript best known for its misogynistic additions to the *Wife of Bath's Prologue*. Using data assembled by the *Canterbury Tales Project* Da Rold carefully reassesses the work of the Dd scribe (a long appendix provides details of the three different groups of corrections that she describes). Unlike previous commentators Da Rold finds that the Dd scribe was a well-practised and thoughtful corrector, who respected the authority of the text and copied what was in front of him. She also challenges the traditional view of this scribe as an amateur, citing various different indications of his professionalism, and suggesting that he worked in the London-Westminster area rather than Oxford, as has previously been supposed. In conclusion she calls for greater study of the scribal practice of correction in the later medieval period, claiming that the benefits would be an improved knowledge of scribal training and additional evidence for the provenance of manuscripts. In ' "Here's one I prepared earlier" ': The Work of Scribe D on Oxford, Corpus Christi College, MS 198' (*RES* 58[2007] 133–53) Estelle Stubbs offers the physical state of the Corpus manuscript (Cp) as a key to correspondences between four early manuscripts: Hengwrt, Ellesmere, Harley 7334, and Cp. Parts of Cp, argues Stubbs, may have been copied earlier than Hengwrt and may thus give a clue to Chaucer's own involvement with both manuscripts. She points to vellum substitutions made visible only during Cp's latest rebinding in 1987, which suggest that tales were copied individually in loose quires, available for cutting and pasting. Cp's Scribe D and Adam Pynkhurst and maybe even Chaucer himself seemed to have worked in tandem.

A pair of articles published in the same issue of *Chaucer Review* ponder the codicological implications of extratextual features such as glosses. In the first, Stephen Partridge reconsiders 'Wynkyn de Worde's Manuscript Source for the *Canterbury Tales*: Evidence from the Glosses' (*ChauR* 41[2007] 325–59). Wynkyn de Worde's main exemplar for his 1498 edition of the *Tales* was William Caxton's second edition of 1482, but scholars increasingly believe that de Worde also relied upon a manuscript. In a detailed discussion Partridge shows that de Worde used this manuscript source for aspects of *ordinatio*, in particular for the glosses in the *Tale of Melibee* and the *Parson's Tale*. In doing so he reveals a very close affiliation between de Worde's edition and Trinity College Cambridge MS R.3.15, and concludes that both must have shared a lost exemplar that was related to the earliest surviving manuscripts of the *Canterbury Tales*. In the second article Daniel W. Mosser writes about 'The Manuscript Glosses of the *Canterbury Tales* and the University of London's Copy of Pynson's [1492] Edition: Witness to a Lost Exemplar' (*ChauR* 41[2007] 360–92). Mosser examines an extensive set of glosses (presented in a long appendix) that were added to a copy of Richard Pynson's 1492 edition of the *Canterbury Tales* by a hand contemporaneous with the book's production date. Pynson also used Caxton's second edition of the *Tales* as his base text, but Mosser finds that the content of the glosses closely accords with those examined by Partridge, concluding that both the handwritten glosses in this copy of Pynson and those in Wynkyn de Worde's edition must have derived from the same exemplar (though since this copy of Pynson is imperfect, lacking the *Parson's Tale*, the argument cannot be conclusively followed through). Mosser has also written this year on 'Dating the Manuscripts of the "Hammond Scribe":, What the Paper Evidence Tells Us' (*JEBS* 10[2007] 31–70), using watermark evidence to propose a sequence of production for this scribe's output; four of the manuscripts attributed to the 'Hammond scribe' contain works by Chaucer, including several of the shorter poems and two copies of the *Canterbury Tales*.

Nicholas Perkins connects 'John Bale, Thomas Hoccleve, and a Lost Chaucer Manuscript' (*N&Q* 54[2007] 128–31), to suggest that Bale knew of a manuscript, now no longer extant, which contained both *The Regiment of Princes* and the *Knight's Tale* (and possibly even the whole of the *Canterbury Tales*). Although this combination of texts exists in MS British Library Harley 7333, Perkins dismisses the possibility that this might have been the volume referred to by the sixteenth-century antiquary. In 'Father Chaucer and the Vivification of Print' (*JEGP* 106[2007] 336–63) Louise M. Bishop argues that the efforts of early print editors to present Chaucer as living and as father had the effect of vivifying the book itself, as if in refusal of its status as inert commodity. While there is no dispute with Bishop's identification of a paternal, animated Chaucer, her fundamental opposition between the dead print of a book and the 'living' manuscript seems questionable, and the animal providing the parchment would probably agree. More finely tuned distinctions between print and scribal culture on the one hand and between paper and parchment on the other are called for. David Matthews writes about the ways in which Thomas Speght also participates in a remembrance of the long-dead poet in 'Public Ambition, Private Desire and the last Tudor Chaucer' (in McMullan and Matthews, eds., *Reading the Medieval in Early Modern England*, pp. 74–88). Speght's aspiration to a near-personal relationship works alongside and perhaps in tension with his philological recuperation of a writer of an antique English. Matthews traces the ways in which Speght fashions Chaucer as a modern poet, thereby ensuring more than any other editor that he would be read throughout the seventeenth century.

Martha Dana Rust focuses on books produced in England and Scotland between 1400 and 1490 in her elegant description of *Imaginary Worlds in Medieval Books: Exploring the Manuscript Matrix*. Rust acknowledges her borrowing of the term 'manuscript matrix' from Stephen G. Nichols, but defines her use of it as more liminal than material: 'the manuscript matrix is an imagined, virtual dimension in which physical form and linguistic content function in dialectical reciprocity . . . in one overarching, category-crossing metasystem of systems of signs' (p. 9). After the introduction her book is divided into three chapters and an afterword organized according to the material constituents of the book: alphabetical characters, pages, and page design. The first chapter focuses on Middle English alphabet poems or *abecedaria*, which are divided into two rough categories: primer *abeces* on devotional themes, and *abeces* of morality or proper conduct. In the second chapter Rust moves seamlessly from considering alphabetical letters to actual missives, focusing on Criseyde's signature ('le vostre C') as it is represented in some manuscripts of *Troilus and Criseyde*, especially Oxford, Bodleian Library MS Arch Selden B. 24. Her study of medieval epistolary practices leads her to suggest an alternative view of Criseyde's notorious duplicity in love. In the third chapter Rust turns to an examination of marginal commentary and the marginal narratives in Gower. Finally she offers an afterword on the descriptive script and scrollwork of Ricardus Franciscus, a scribe whose work is identifiable in nine volumes. Two sections of this book have already appeared recently in other guises: part of chapter 1 was previously published in Daniel Kline's *Medieval Literature for Children* (*YWES* 85[2006] 168), and chapter 2 builds upon Dane's contribution to *New Perspectives on Criseyde*, edited by Cindy L. Vitto and Marcia Smith Marcez (Pegasus Press [2004], unaccountably missed by this chapter). Rust admits that some readers may find her work 'impressionistic' (p. 29), even 'quixotic' (p. 30), but it is at least copiously illustrated with more than thirty black and white plates, though the small-scale reproduction of these makes them less useful than they might have been.

Kathryn L. Lynch raises the question of 'Dating Chaucer' (*ChauR* 42[2007] 1–22), and in doing so calls attention to just how little we really know about this issue. Her article is seriously destabilizing, in that it identifies quandaries in dating almost all of Chaucer's poems; those that receive particular attention are the *Book of the Duchess*, the *House of Fame*, and *Anelida and Arcite*. Lynch shows that most dates and chronologies for Chaucer are based on assumptions and speculations rather than facts: 'Chaucer studies suffer from a general willingness to entertain unproven theories about date' (p. 9). No proofs are offered here either, and instead her rather defeatist advice is that the issue be abandoned as unhelpful and irresolvable. R.F. Yeager asks to what extent 'Chaucer Translates the Matter of Spain' (in Bullón-Fernández, ed., *England and Iberia in the Middle Ages, 12th–15th Century: Cultural, Literary, and Political Exchanges*, pp. 189–214). Acknowledging the absence of hard evidence that Spanish literature influenced or was even read by Chaucer, Yeager nonetheless argues for the strong possibility that he picked up some Spanish on his trip (of unknown duration) to Navarre when in his twenties, and that he read at least the tale collections of Petrus Alfonsi and Don Juan Manuel, whose narrative skill would have made Chaucer receptive to Boccaccio's tale collection, encountered subsequently.

Matthew Giancarlo has a chapter on Chaucer in his monograph *Parliament and Literature in Late Medieval England*. For Giancarlo, parliament or *parlement* is all about mediation, a concept that preoccupies Chaucer (himself a mediator) throughout his work, whether in the form of pleading, go-betweens, debate, social classes of middling means or marriage—a frequent item on parliamentary agendas. Indeed, in so far as both deal with representation, it can become difficult to distinguish literature from parliament. The *Parliament of Fowls* understandably figures large in the chapter, the procedural rituals and terminology of which Giancarlo carefully scrutinizes in light of parliamentary process: *pleyn eleccioun, presente, assented*. Chaucer's interest, both in the *Parliament* and in *Melibee*, lies in testing the boundaries of community.

The Oxford Handbook of English Literature and Theology, edited by Andrew W. Hass, David Jasper and Elisabeth Jay, offers fifty thematically arranged essays, two of which deal, to different extents, with the *Canterbury Tales*. Nicholas Watson compares the theology of 'Langland and Chaucer' (pp. 363–81), first likening the intellectual and cultural authority of theology in the fourteenth century to that of modern science, and drawing a careful distinction between theology and the institution of the church. Watson characterizes *Piers Plowman* as offering a critique of formal theology, but finds that the *Canterbury Tales* effectively divests itself of any claim to theological authority by presenting itself as the product of a specifically secular view of Christian society. After some consideration of the potential ramifications of the term 'host' (used to refer to the tavern keeper, Harry Bailey, but commonly signifying the body of Christ), Watson considers the tales of the Knight, Miller and Clerk, and most fully the *Tale of Melibee*, which he regards as 'the nearest thing to a theological centre' in the poem (p. 377). The brief section on Chaucer in David Scott's chapter 'Pastoral Tradition in Religious Poetry' (pp. 726–41) deals only with the portrait of the Parson from the *General Prologue*.

Frances McCormack puts the Parson and his tale at the centre of her discussion of *Chaucer and the Culture of Dissent*, identifying him from the start as deliberately evocative of Lollard idealizations of priesthood, an argument she tracks throughout the book as she picks her way between the *General Prologue*'s portrait, the Parson's own tale, and the epilogue to the *Man of Law's Tale*, each written at different points during the politically volatile years of the late fourteenth century, and each subject to its own treatments in the various manuscript witnesses. In chapter 1 she questions Chaucer's own affiliations, noting his connections with the Lollard Knights (Sir Lewis Clifford, Sir William Beauchamp, Sir Richard Sturry, et al.), the similarities between the *Parson's Tale* and Sir John Clanvowe's *The Two Ways*, and speculating that Chaucer 'may well have been a Lollard' (p. 15). McCormack recognizes the slipperiness of Lollard sectarian discourse, of which contemporary writers accused the Wycliffites. Identifying this Lollard lexicon is not as easy as flagging individual words; it is recognizable rather by its preoccupations with topics such as dominion and lordship, its quotation of Scripture, and its polarizing, essentializing rhetoric. The overall effect, however, is unmistakable for McCormack, who examines in chapter 2 the Parson's Lollard tongue. Exploring questions also posed by Fehrman, below, chapter 3 makes the case for the interrelationship between the Wycliffite Bible and the *Parson's Tale*. In chapter 4 McCormack considers broader rhetorical connections between Lollard and Chaucerian language, in particular the ambiguous overlaps between heterodox and orthodox discourse that make it ultimately impossible to identify the Parson definitively in sectarian terms. McCormack's study nonetheless makes a plausible case for the Parson's subtle affinities with Lollardy.

By the end of his article, 'Did Chaucer Read the Wycliffite Bible?' (*ChauR* 42[2007] 111–38), Craig T. Fehrman has revised his question to ask instead whether the Wycliffite Bible influenced Chaucer's translations. Having found his initial question impossibly encumbered by modern conceptions of reading and sources, he finds it easier to answer the second, stating that Chaucer absorbed and then applied the Wycliffite Bible's praxis and phrases as part of his interaction with Wycliffite vernacularity. To support his argument Fehrman compares translations from the *Canterbury Tales* (principally from the *Parson's Tale*), the later version of the Wycliffite Bible, and other contemporary works, especially Chaucer's *Boece*, within the context of the Wycliffite theory of 'opin' translation (p. 112). Translation is also a concern of Dan Wakelin's monograph *Humanism, Reading and English Literature 1430–1530*. Wakelin traces the development of vernacular humanism during the fifteenth century by analysing not only the texts of this period but also the evidence of readerly activity in those texts, as preserved in the form of notes and glosses. Technically Chaucer's writing falls outwith the date span of this study, but 'Chaucer's relationship to humanism is a vexed question' (p. 10), and Wakelin justifies his inclusion by claiming that various translations of classical texts such as Boethius and Vegetius are the obvious precedents for fifteenth-century humanism. In the first chapter *Boece* is considered alongside Walton's translation of Boethius, with the afterlife of Chaucer's version among annotating readers such as William Worcester receiving special attention.

A series of overviews of works of English literature that reflect and perpetuate the Christian tradition is offered in *The Christian Tradition in English Literature: Poetry, Plays, and Shorter Prose*, by Paul Cavill and Heather Ward. Chaucer gets his own short chapter on the *Canterbury Tales*, in which the Wife of Bath and Pardoner enjoy the limelight, although how they reflect the book's theme better than, say, the Parson, is not clear. Unsurprisingly the problematic status of the Pardoner's sexuality and his relationship to the Summoner are not debated. The *Nun's Priest's Tale* also figures in a different chapter on the medieval beast fable. The book itself only contains summaries and brief discussion points, being designed for reading alongside canonical texts appearing in the Blackwell, Norton, and Oxford anthologies of literature. In *Envisaging Heaven in the Middle Ages*, edited by Carolyn Muessig and Ad Putter, Elizabeth Archibald considers 'Chaucer's Lovers in Metaphorical Heaven' (pp. 222–36), where heaven is taken as a metaphor for marital bliss. As we might expect, Chaucer's use of the metaphor is deeply ironic, whether satirically so (in the *Merchant's Tale*) or tragically so (in *Troilus and Criseyde*). Tom Shippey reviews the life and work of Chaucer ('Tom Shippey on Geoffrey Chaucer' in Epstein, ed., *Literary Genius: 25 Classic Writers Who Define English & American Literature*, pp. 8–15). There is not much one can achieve in so few pages, particularly since three of them comprise quotations and a picture, but nonetheless Shippey concisely conveys something of Chaucer's complexity.

John M. Fyler describes his monograph *Language and the Declining World in Chaucer, Dante and Jean de Meun* as a book 'long in the making' (p. ix), and acknowledges that some of his ideas on this topic have appeared in print before, but these have been thoroughly revised to produce this coherent and elegant account of how medieval writers participated in debates about the history of language. A long opening chapter explores the biblical history of language, from its perfect initial state as God's true Word to its fallen depraved diversity post-Babel. Fyler summarizes patristic, rabbinic and medieval Christian commentaries on language as it is depicted in the book of Genesis and later in the New Testament, after Pentecost and in anticipation of the apocalypse. Turning then to medieval poets, Fyler first considers Jean de Meun's discussion of language and its relation to love in the *Roman de la Rose*, revealing the French poet's dependence on both Ovid and the Augustinian tradition. There is a great deal of incidental reference to Chaucer's works (principally the dream visions) in this chapter, as there is in the next, which is ostensibly focused on Dante. Here Fyler outlines Dante's Augustinian review of linguistic history in *De Vulgari Eloquentia* and the *Commedia* before considering the way that Chaucer exploits the ambiguities of fallen language in the *House of Fame*. In the final chapter linguistic degeneration is traced in the *Canterbury Tales* from the *Second Nun's Tale* to the *Canon's Yeoman's Tale*. Overall this is a scholarly and informative book, its long chapters supported by seventy pages of notes, and its wide-ranging research evident from the substantial list of primary sources and extensive bibliography.

In *Venus' Owne Clerk: Chaucer's Debt to the Confessio Amantis*, B.W. Lindeboom argues that Chaucer changed the design of the *Canterbury Tales* in direct response to the challenge laid down by Gower in his *Confessio Amantis*. That change of design is well known: from the initial scheme of four tales per teller on the outward and homeward return to Southwark to one tale per teller, ending at Canterbury with the *Parson's Tale*. In brief (it is a long book, extended across eight chapters), Lindeboom's thesis runs thus: Chaucer's Sergeant of Law is modelled on the real-life example of Gower, whom we assume had some legal training. Gower then responds in the *Confessio* with the challenge to Chaucer *to sette an ende of alle his werk* and to write a testament of love. Chaucer experiments first with rewriting the *Legend of Good Women* but then switches to the *Canterbury Tales*. Four figures in the poem yield critical evidence. In the prologues and tales of the Parson, Pardoner, Wife of Bath and Man of Law, Chaucer creates a *confessio amantis* in microcosm that displays the same dual theme of temporal and spiritual love. In the Parson's discourse, we see the founding structure of the Seven Deadly Sins. The *Pardoner's Tale* exemplifies them as a sermon. In the *Wife of Bath's Prologue*, Chaucer creates a new form of characterization, conflating sermon and confession in her autobiographical narrative. Her tale, of course, answers to Gower's tale of *Florent*. The *Pardoner's Prologue* also dilates the theme of confession and foregrounds spiritual love where the Wife foregrounded temporal. In the enigmatic passage in the Introduction to the *Man of Law's Tale* where the Man of Law comments on Chaucer's work, Chaucer explicitly answers Gower, and Lindeboom considers in detail the correspondences between the Man of Law's allusions and the sometimes discrepant evidence offered in the *Legend* and the *Confessio*. As in Terry Jones's *Who Murdered Chaucer* (*YWES* 84[2005] 224–5), Lindeboom's theory ultimately strains credulity, but its elaboration yields occasional intriguing possibilities.

Andrew Galloway debunks 'Gower's Quarrel with Chaucer and the Origins of Bourgeois Didacticism in Fourteenth-Century London Poetry' (in Harder, MacDonald and Reinink, eds., *Calliope's Classroom: Studies in Didactic Poetry from Antiquity to the Renaissance*, pp. 245–67) and explores the two poets' different conceptions of political morality. Galloway's argument focuses on how both poets deal with myth, with particular reference to the stories of Jephtha and Lucrece (in the *Confessio Amantis* and, respectively, the *Physician's Tale* and the *Legend of Good Women*). His analysis of the debate between self-interest and self-sacrifice leads him, via the seventeenth-century political theory of John Locke and Thomas Hobbes, to the conclusion that, while the *Confessio Amantis* is Gower's answer to the absolutist social didacticism of the *Legend of Good Women*, in the *Canterbury Tales* Chaucer offers mature consideration of the problems of individual absolutism, in which self-sacrifice is not a solution but a further sign of the universe of absolutist, ungovernable self-interest.

Scott Lightsey has two chapters on Chaucer in *Manmade Marvels in Medieval Culture and Literature*, one of which has already appeared in print (*YWES* 82[2003] 211). Lightsey's theme is the materialization of the marvellous in romance, where supernatural devices descend to the mundane level of mechanical curiosities, in which there flourished a booming commerce. In his third chapter, Lightsey turns to the question of technology. The anxiety provoked by the question manifests itself in various ways: the fragile distinction between body and machine; the tyranny of clock time; the idolatrous representation of man-made objects. Beginning his discussion with a consideration of the *Former Age*, Lightsey presents Chaucer as a conservative, sceptical of the redemptive possibilities of technology. That scepticism is given comic treatment in the *Nun's Priest's Tale*: here Chaunticleer and the mechanical clock are identified with each other in a world where empirical explanation increasingly replaces divine cause. In the *Canon's Yeoman's Tale*, the scepticism deepens as the idealism of alchemy is exposed as materialist in the most disenchanted and duplicitous of senses.

Raising similar concerns, Nicola Masciandaro considers Chaucer's contribution to *The Meaning of Work in Middle English Literature*, ranging from the meditative primitivism of the *Former Age* to the sweaty basics of *swynk*. Offering no agenda of reform, the *Former Age* seems a bleak indictment of a technocratic modernity with which the author nonetheless shows himself throughout the rest of his corpus to be complicit. The poem's nostalgia seems to have more in common with that of Gower for a time past when peasants knew their place, and seems likewise to depict labour as the cause rather than consequence of degeneration. Masciandaro complicates this apparent stance, showing how the primitivism is implausibly presented, and suggesting that Chaucer's sympathies are ultimately anti-primitivistic, and that an atechnic past is barbaric. Labour then arises from need rather than greed, and the *Former Age* is a 'reductio ad absurdum of primitivist nostalgia' (p. 115). Chapter 3, on *swynk* in the *Canterbury Tales*, centres on Fragment VIII, which constitutes for Masciandaro an emphatic assertion of the value of work as a subjective necessity, self-fulfilling and self-objectifying. The Second Nun's discourse on *bisynesse* as antidote to *ydelnesse* moves increasingly towards an acceptance of the objective value of work. And alchemy, the preoccupation of the *Canon's Yeoman's Tale*, itself raises the theme of transformation at all levels, most particularly, of the Canon's Yeoman's own transformation from empty drudge to creative individual.

'Chaucer, Technology and the Rise of Science Fiction in English' are considered by Helen Conrad-O'Briain (in Coleman, ed., *On Literature and Science: Essays, Reflections, Provocations*, pp. 27–42), who finds in the flying horse of the *Squire's Tale*, the machinations of the Clerk of Orleans in the *Franklin's Tale* and the alchemical experiments in the *Canon's Yeoman's Tale* an abiding interest in the fine line between 'the possible and the not necessarily impossible' (p. 42), that is, in science fiction by another name.

Marion Turner's interesting monograph *Chaucerian Conflict: Language of Antagonism in Late Fourteenth-Century London* is concerned with discourse and the urban environment, and uses Chaucer's writings as its linchpin. In her first chapter Turner reads the *House of Fame* alongside the *Mercers' Petition*, noting that both use the same phrasing, and reminding us of the intriguing possibility that both might have been written out by the hand of Adam Pynkhurst. The *Mercers' Petition* is a litany of complaints against Nicholas Brembre, in particular his harsh punishment of dissenters. Speech then is construed as dangerous, as in Chaucer's poem, which, Turner notes, consistently compares speech, slander and noise to violence and war. Chapter 2 continues to focus on the same historical moment—1380s London—this time comparing ideas of division and betrayal in *Troilus and Criseyde* with two letters written in 1382 that accused three London aldermen of betraying the city to the rebels during the revolt of the previous year (a version of this chapter previously appeared in *SAC* 25[2003], see *YWES* 84[2005] 250). The following chapter explores the different ways that *Troilus and Criseyde* and other late fourteenth-century texts about New Troy (Gower's *Vox Clamantis, St Erkenwald*, and Richard Maidstone's *Concordia*) deal with the conflict between an awareness of social fragmentation and a desire for social stability. Chapter 4 focuses on the writings of Thomas Usk, himself a reader of Chaucer's poetry (part of this chapter previously appeared in article form, see *YWES* 83[2004] 219). The Chaucerian focus tightens in the final two chapters, which consider parts of the *Canterbury Tales*. In the penultimate chapter Turner compares the poem with guild returns of 1388–9, demonstrating how associations and confederacies of all types were typically viewed with suspicion at this time. While the Canterbury fellowship is generally now interpreted as an essentially positive model of community, Turner finds it instead to be a conflicted gathering, citing the *Pardoner's Tale* as particular evidence. Finally, the last substantial chapter approaches the concept of antagonism from a different angle, asking what happens when authors explicitly try to write about peace. The texts used here are Philippe de Mézières' *Letter to Richard II* and the *Tale of Melibee*, the latter suggesting that reconciliation can at most be a temporary state of affairs. Turner's central thesis, that late fourteenth-century producers of texts were profoundly concerned with problems of civic dissent and social division, is amply defended in this clear exploration of the ways in which social antagonism was articulated and addressed in Chaucer's textual environment. Her equal consideration of what she terms 'feted' and 'sidelined' texts (p. 7) has produced a stimulating discussion that extends our understanding of medieval culture, and which is a pleasure to read.

Alfred Thomas describes his book, *A Blessed Shore: England and Bohemia from Chaucer to Shakespeare*, as a demonstration of the significance of political, diplomatic and cultural links between England and Bohemia in the pre-modern period. Although he focuses mainly on the fifteenth century, Thomas also devotes a good deal of time to the reign of Richard II, and in particular to assessing the role of Richard's first wife, Anne of Bohemia, as a cultural and religious mediatrix between the two countries. The opening chapter discusses English artistic and poetic reactions to Anne, including of course Chaucer's *Parliament of Fowls* and the *Legend of Good Women*, with some mention also of *Troilus and Criseyde*; Thomas further suggests that Anne might have inspired both Thomas Usk's *Testament of Love* and perhaps even *Pearl*, though he stops short of suggesting direct patronage. Other poems such as *Sir Gawain and the Green Knight* are discussed in the following chapter, along with the Wilton Diptych and Richard and Anne's double tomb in Westminster Abbey, as Thomas charts Richard's imperial desires. Anne's possession of versions of the New Testament in Czech, German and Latin provided English reformers with justification for the vernacular translation of the Bible, and religious issues are brought to the fore in the book's middle section, where Thomas considers the Bohemian reception of John Wyclif's theological and political ideas; his discussion reveals both differences and affinities between Wycliffism and Hussitism, though by the early fifteenth century these were more or less synonymous terms. Thomas also pays specific attention to the situation of women in medieval Bohemia, using misogynistic satirical texts such as 'The Beguines' and 'The Wycliffite Woman'. Other sections of the book cover fifteenth-century diplomatic contacts between the two countries, the emigration of English recusants to Bohemia in the sixteenth century, and the fortunes of English Catholics and Protestants in Renaissance Prague, as Thomas seeks to explain the utopian representation of Bohemia in Shakespeare's *The Winter's Tale*. Thomas's belief 'that Chaucer's and Shakespeare's Bohemia is neither simply a geographic place nor an English misrepresentation of it, but a fascinating intermingling of the real and the imaginary, fact and fiction' (p. 17) has led him to produce an interesting book that should help to rescue pre-modern Bohemian culture and history from relative neglect.

Louise M. Bishop's interdisciplinary study *Words, Stones, & Herbs: The Healing Word in Medieval and Early Modern England* offers an analysis of both poetic and medical texts in order to explore the cognitive and physical effects of words in relation to the healing process. Bishop demonstrates how medicine is the vehicle for epistemological, lexical and pious analysis in a range of later medieval texts including *Piers Plowman*, the *Canterbury Tales*, the Anglo-Norman *Livre de seyntz medicines* and Reginald Pecock's *Donet*. It is scarcely surprising to meet Chaucer's pilgrim physician in this book; what is surprising is that we do not encounter him more often, since much greater attention is devoted to other parts of the *Canterbury Tales*, specifically the tales of the Second Nun, the Canon's Yeoman, and the Manciple. Bishop traces ideas of translation and transformation through these narratives in part of her fourth chapter, 'Vernacular Science, Vernacular Poetry', interrogating particular terms such as 'conclusion', 'multiply' and 'lewd' to show how, in the context of orthodoxy and Lollardy, 'reading is materially dangerous: translation, like alchemy, is materially volatile' (p. 112). An alternative viewpoint, offered earlier in the volume, praises the material health benefits of reading, as exemplified by the narrator in the *Book of the Duchess*.

Transmission and Transformation in the Middle Ages: Texts and Contexts, edited by Kathy Cawsey and Jason Harris, contains ten new essays prefaced by a very brief introduction that identifies an overarching concern with cultural change and textual transformation. Two of the five contributions that deal with Middle English texts focus on Chaucer. Brendan O'Connell studies the incorporation of scientific ideas and images into literature in quite a long essay, '"Ignotum per ignocius"': Alchemy, Analogy and Poetics in Fragment VIII of *The Canterbury Tales*' (pp. 131–56), looking particularly at Chaucer's use and abuse of alchemical language and learning in the *Canon's Yeoman's Tale*, and arguing that by this representation of the failure of alchemy Chaucer was directly addressing the late medieval attack on analogical thought. In '"The venym of symony"': The Debate on the Eucharist in the Late Fourteenth Century and *The Pardoner's Prologue and Tale*' (pp. 115–30), Niamh Pattwell demonstrates how and to what extent Chaucer exploited the religious discourse—both heterodox and orthodox—of his day, and draws some compelling connections between the action of the tale, the role of the clergy in the mass, and the benefits or 'meeds' of the eucharist (p. 123). Pattwell's thorough grasp of medieval eucharistic practices illuminates the narrative of the three revellers, and her focus on the Pardoner's religious (as opposed to sexual) mutability is refreshing. Chaucer also features briefly in Kathy Cawsey's essay, '"I Playne Piers" and the Protestant Plowman Prints: The Transformation of a Medieval Figure' (pp. 189–206), where the apocryphal 'Plowman's Tale' forms part of her analysis of how sixteenth-century printers translated the figure of the medieval ploughman to a Reformation context.

Holly A. Crocker links medieval theories of vision with Chaucer's construction of gender in her short monograph *Chaucer's Visions of Manhood*. She acknowledges that her selection of texts comprises 'a much weirder kettle of fish' (p. 16) than those usually invoked in gender-focused studies, but argues: 'I chose the poems included here because the strategies for gender formation involving visibility are less moderate... Fantasies linking vision, agency, and masculinity are more extreme... more excessive' (p. 16). Her first evidence in fact is drawn from the prose *Tale of Melibee*, which she reads in conjunction with medieval optical theory, offering first a survey of the most relevant theories of sight and then a more extended examination of Roger Bacon's optical theory. She argues that Bacon's synthesis of competing theories of sight in accordance with a wider understanding of Christian metaphysics offers insight into Chaucer's construction of a masculinity that depends on the invisibility of feminine agency. Subsequent chapters do indeed deal with Chaucer's poetry, respectively the *Physician's Tale*, the *Book of the Duchess*, and the *Shipman's Tale*. In the second chapter, 'Portrait of a Father as a Bad Man', Crocker argues that in telling the story of Virginia, Chaucer investigates the limits of feminine exemplarity in order to expose the disfiguring violence of gender's ocularity, and relates the tale's advice to parents and governesses to a contemporary scandal: the elopement of Elizabeth of Lancaster with John Holland. In the following chapter we take a break from the *Canterbury Tales* to consider visual impact in the *Book of the Duchess* and the effects of growing iconoclasm on memorial practice, but chapter 4 returns us to the *Shipman's Tale*, which Crocker finds to be 'Chaucer's most radical investigation of the ways that men and women use invisibility to negotiate their exchanges of agency and passivity without regard for the borders a gender binary would impose' (p. 107). Her final chapter unexpectedly takes a more codicological approach by considering MS British Library Harley 7333, a large fifteenth-century anthology that contains the *Canterbury Tales* and, in the same section of the manuscript, a unique collection of thirteen proverbs attributed 'Quod Impingham'. In showing how these proverbs echo various Chaucerian poems Crocker also demonstrates the ways in which later audiences make Chaucerian masculinities visible.

Sylvia Federico begins her short essay on 'Chaucer and the Masculinity of Historicism' (*MFF* 43:i[2007] 72–6) thinking about the constructedness of gender, demonstrated at the end of *Troilus and Criseyde* in Troilus's sudden role switch from effeminized lover to virile warrior. Thence she turns to the constructedness of our roles as custodians of the past, that is, as historians. Taking issue with Lee Patterson's disavowal of psychoanalysis (*YWES* 82[2003] 215), she argues for the possibility of being both historicist and (psychoanalytically) feminist. 'The archive is not our enemy, and neither is Freud' (p. 75). M.M. Sauer asks '"Where Are the Lesbians in Chaucer?"': Lack, Opportunity and Female Homoeroticism in Medieval Studies Today' (*JLS* 11[2007] 331–45). The question is pointedly ironic, as the answer is that there aren't any, Chaucerian queer studies being predominantly a boys' club, Sauer notes. In search of the medieval lesbian, she finds herself faced with the theoretically impossible task of uncovering that which does not officially exist. Her review essay raises important questions about how academic periodization works to police the rules of permissible historical 'evidence'. Juliette Dor, in 'Caroline Spurgeon and her Relationship to Chaucer: The Text of her Viva Presentation at the Sorbonne' (in Summerfield and Busby, eds., *People and Texts: Relationships in Medieval Literature*, pp. 87–98) edits and translates the original text of Spurgeon's doctoral defence, Spurgeon being awarded her doctorate in 1911 and publishing her *Five Hundred Years of Chaucer Criticism and Allusion 1357–1900* fourteen years later. It is an interesting text, showing Spurgeon's acute awareness of how the meaning of Chaucer resides in the history of the meaning of Chaucer. Dor's researches draw from the Spurgeon archives held at Royal Holloway College, University of London.

Susan E. Phillips has a chapter entitled 'Chaucerian Small Talk' in her book *Transforming Talk: The Problem with Gossip in Late Medieval England*. For Phillips, gossip is a critical element of Chaucerian poetics, ultimately epitomizing poetry's ability to achieve narrative transformation. Various instances serve her purpose: the discussion of idle talk in the *House of Fame* and in the figures of Host and Wife of Bath in the *Canterbury Tales*. In each instance, gossip appears to be castigated yet that castigation is performatively contradicted. In the *House of Fame*, gossip forms the basic matter of tales, hiding, amplifying and distorting tradition to enable the poet to negotiate his position within it. Even as he warns against idle speech, the Host enacts it with ribaldry, swearing and gossip, all of which blur the boundaries between prologue and tale, fabliau and exemplum. Through the Host's interventions throughout the poem, Phillips gets to consider a range of tales and narrative moments. She concludes her chapter with a consideration of the Wife of Bath as gendered personification: gossip is a woman. Linked to the Midas story and to the transmutation of hag into beautiful woman at the end of the tale, the Wife's gossip is a powerful device of narrative transformation.

Corinne Saunders briefly considers Chaucer at the end of her essay on 'Erotic Magic: The Enchantress in Middle English Romance' (in Hopkins and Rushton, eds., *The Erotic in the Literature of Medieval Britain*, pp. 38–52). The enchantress is often a seductress, intriguing in actively pursuing her desire, although she is not necessarily a demonic figure. Chaucer plays both comically and seriously on the motif of the otherworldly lady when Arcite sees Emelye as a goddess and Troilus fails to see Criseyde as earthly and flawed. The *Wife of Bath's Tale* also plays with the convention, when the knight lies glumly in bed on his wedding night. Although the enchantress becomes a desirable woman in the end, her final act of enchantment paradoxically returns her to the human condition. Dana M. Symons writes about 'Comic Pleasures: Chaucer and Popular Romance' (in Hordis and Hardwick, eds., *Medieval English Comedy*, pp. 83–109), finding that the comic is as historically contingent and socially constructed as any other genre rather than a universal constant. She reviews various theorists of taste and humour, including Bakhtin, who offers us the idea that humour critiques the straightforward. She considers *Thopas* as well as the maligned Middle English *Sir Tristrem*. Humour is not natural or self-evident or given but acquired. She argues that *Thopas* undermines the horizon of expectations of romance. It is possible that some saw *Thopas* as a 'straight' romance.

Kenneth Bleeth ranges through *Troilus and Criseyde* and the tales of the Knight, Merchant and Franklin in considering 'Chaucerian Gardens and the Spirit of Play' (in Howes, ed., *Place, Space, and Landscape in Medieval Literature*, pp. 107–17). In each case the garden, however apparently secluded it might be, is closely linked to the world outside. Likewise what occurs in the garden has consequences that extend beyond the confines of its walls.

A special issue of *Exemplaria* celebrates the work of Sheila Delany. Three articles pertain to Chaucer, two discussed here and the third in the section on the *Canterbury Tales*. Laurie A. Finke writes about 'The Politics of the Canon: Christine de Pizan and the Fifteenth-Century Chaucerians' (*Exemplaria* 19[2007] 16–38). Despite the fact that Chaucer died before the heyday of Christine de Pizan's career, Finke nonetheless argues for a kind of reversed chronology of influence, namely, that without the multiple translations of Christine's work into English throughout the fifteenth century Chaucer would never have achieved the status he did as a quintessentially English poet. It was through encountering Christine's realization of the rhetorical possibilities of French that English writers such as Hoccleve (in his 'Letter to Cupid') recognized Chaucer's achievements in their own language. Finke's article deftly illuminates the constructedness of both nationalism and the literary canon. Jenna Mead follows with 'Chaucer and the Subject of Bureaucracy' (*Exemplaria* 19[2007] 39–66), in which she questions the impulse of Chaucerian historians to attribute to him a biographical subjectivity woven out of the fragments of bureaucratic memoranda. The Chaucer that emerges out of these memoranda is as much a rhetorical construct as any of his fictional characters. The most notorious memorandum of course has to do with Cecily Chaumpaigne, and in questioning the rhetorical relationship between the biographical Chaucer and the defendant of the *raptus* case, Mead salutes Delany's groundbreaking essay 'Slaying Python: Marriage and Misogyny in a Chaucerian Text' (*YWES* 66[1988] 179).

Chaucer Review has a special issue on the legacy of E. Talbot Donaldson, who for some time now has embodied the spirit of New Criticism. Donaldson's objective is to explain the text on its own terms, for its own sake and as an artistic totality. His method is close reading, a practice that apparently presents itself as untheorized and untheorizable. Journal editors David Raybin and Susanna Fein introduce the issue and its guest editors, Bonnie Wheeler and Carolynn Van Dyke, who open the discussion with 'The Legacy of New Criticism: Revisiting the Work of E. Talbot Donaldson' (*ChauR* 41[2007] 216–24). They explain how the collection arose out of three sessions organized in 2005 at the International Congress of Medieval Studies at Kalamazoo, and provide an overview of Donaldson's life, noting how instrumental he was in introducing a literary Middle Ages to the student curriculum. Reading Donaldson heightened their own senses of prose style— no small legacy. What emerges as indisputable is that New Criticism, in so far as it can be defined by Donaldson's practice, is a hermeneutic activity founded upon and inseparable from philological precision. There is nothing sloppy or impressionistic about Donaldsonian New Criticism.

Marie Borroff opens the essay collection proper with 'Donaldson and the Romantic Poets' (*ChauR* 41[2007] 225–30), in which she defends Donaldson's *Speaking of Chaucer* despite its political gender incorrectness, at least judged by modern standards. David Lawton turns to the important topic of 'Donaldson and Irony' (*ChauR* 41[2007] 231–9), showing how Donaldsonian irony keeps the reader in touch with the text in a way that allegory often does not, although allegory also is attuned to rhetorical inflection. Lawton laments current uninformed representations of New Criticism as a reactionary ideology, which misrepresent the New Critics' attempts to demystify and democratize the study of literature. Ralph Hanna finds Donaldson the superior theorist in 'Donaldson and Robertson: An Obligatory Conjunction' (*ChauR* 41[2007] 240–9). Hanna presents Robertsonian criticism, perhaps unfairly, as a clunky and predictable method derived mechanically from first principles, and the Donaldsonian 'system' as strategically unsystematic, having the ability to fit the rule to the occasion rather than vice versa.

With 'Amorous Behavior: Sexism, Sin, and the Donaldson Persona' (*ChauR* 41[2007] 250–60), Carolynn Van Dyke conjoins Robertson and Dinshaw in their accusations, variously argued but convergent in conclusion, that Donaldsonian New Criticism is guilty of self-love; that in studying medieval literature, it is really studying itself; that an apparent interest in the (implicitly feminized) medieval object masks a seeking out of the (masculinized) same. The accusation is almost correct, argues Van Dyke, but in overlooking Donaldson's ironic self-consciousness it misses the point. For Robert W. Hanning there is 'No [One] Way to Treat a Text: Donaldson and the Criticism of Engagement' (*ChauR* 41[2007] 261–70). Engagement with the text on its own terms is the signature of Donaldsonian criticism and is exactly what is lacking in exegetical 'one size fits all' criticism (p. 262). Moreover, engagement with the text is an intellectually disinterested practice that underlies his rhetorical stance of what Dinshaw calls 'reading like a man'. Judith H. Anderson comes next, 'Commenting on Donaldson's Commentaries' (*ChauR* 41[2007] 271–8), in particular his commentary on Dorigen's complaint in the *Franklin's Tale*. Echoing Van Dyke's line of argument, Anderson suggests that Donaldson's readings have been badly flattened by modern critics; their irony and nuance ignored. Elizabeth D. Kirk warmly recollects 'Donaldson Teaching and Learning' (*ChauR* 41[2007] 279–88), also noting the inability of modern feminist criticism to register his irony. Thomas J. Farrell attests to 'The Persistence of Donaldson's Memory' (*ChauR* 41[2007] 289–98), meaning the ways in which modern theoretical positions (especially on the topic of the Chaucerian narrator) articulate ideas that lurk within Donaldson's arguments as implied possibilities. In ' "The least innocent of all innocent-sounding lines" ': The Legacy of Donaldson's *Troilus* Criticism' (*ChauR* 41[2007] 299–310), Gretchen Mieszkowski reviews how criticism subsequent to Donaldson is shaped implicitly or explicitly by his work. Finally, in 'Revaluating "Chaucer the Pilgrim" and Donaldson's Enduring Persona' (*ChauR* 41[2007] 311–23), Geoffrey W. Gust argues for the continued relevance of Donaldson's famous piece in light of more modern theorizations of authorial function.

Visual representations of Chaucer's characters continue to intrigue critics. In 'A Note on the Urry-Edition Pilgrim Portraits' (*ChauR* 41[2007] 455–6) Betsy Bowden corrects Stephen R. Reimer's attribution of these pictures to George Vertue (see *YWES* 87[2008] 292), having recently discovered twelve of the original drawings, signed by the artist 'J. Chalmers', at the British Museum. Maidie Hilmo offers an ingenious interpretation of 'The Clerk's "Unscholarly Bow": Seeing and Reading Chaucer's Clerk from the Ellesmere MS to Caxton' (*JEBS* 10[2007] 71–105). Caxton's woodcut illustration of the Clerk shows the pilgrim carrying a bow rather than the expected book, a representation that has been dismissed as erroneous. Hilmo suggests instead that the bow is emblematic of the Clerk's status as a moral satirist, and cites contemporary parallels from manuscripts of Gower's *Vox Clamantis*, which frequently contain illustrations of an archer with a longbow (the moral satirist aiming his arrows at the world); eleven black and white figures, generously reproduced, substantiate her points about visual iconography. Charles LaPorte writes about 'Morris's Compromises: On Victorian Editorial Theory and the Kelmscott *Chaucer*' (in Latham, ed., *Writing on the Image: Reading William Morris*, pp. 209–19). Morris and Burne-Jones shared a belief that an illuminated edition without editorial apparatus established the most immediate connection between edition and medieval past. Their attempt, however, is monumental and unifying in a way that medieval editions of Chaucer's poetry are not. Victorian discomfiture with Chaucerian self-contradiction is evident in Morris's editing of the *Retraction*, hidden away on a verso folio amidst a series of minor lyric poems. Another unifying indication is

Morris's capitalization of *Lord Jhesu Crist* and spelling in full of religious formulae where the manuscripts themselves use lower case and abbreviations. *A Companion to Medieval English Literature and Culture c.1350–c.1500*, edited by Peter Brown, is the latest in a seemingly endless production of comprehensive guides to reading medieval literature, 'medieval' in this instance signifying Middle English only. The volume's seven sections funnel information from the general to the particular. The first section gives overviews of, for example, critical approaches, by David Raybin (pp. 9–24), and of English society, by S.H. Rigby (pp. 25–39), while the seventh section contains readings of specific authors, such as Gower and Lydgate by J. Allan Mitchell (pp. 569–84), and individual texts, for example *Piers Plowman*, by Stephen Kelly (pp. 537–53). In this seventh section Mark Miller's essay, 'Subjectivity and Ideology in the *Canterbury Tales*' (pp. 554–68), divides Chaucer's work into convenient slices to exemplify matters of class, economy and gender (the Knight and Wife of Bath), and to encompass ecclesiastical structures and religious authority (the Pardoner and Parson); further considerations of ethical perfection and moral purity unify this analysis. We also meet Chaucer a lot in the fourth section, which is devoted to 'Encounters with Other Cultures' (p. 197). Here Ardis Butterfield discusses the *Legend of Good Women* in her survey of 'England and France' (pp. 199–214), and Nick Havely's account of 'Britain and Italy: Trade, Travel and Translation' (pp. 215–30) is positively saturated with Chaucerian reference. It is not surprising to find Chaucer also popping up in Christopher Baswell's discussion of Middle English and its classical sources (pp. 231–46), nor that the Prioress is implicated in Geraldine Heng's survey of Jews and other aliens (pp. 247–69). The Prioress is also invoked in Laura Wright's account of 'The Languages of Medieval Britain' (pp. 143–58), and Donka Minkova grants a special slot in her survey of 'The Forms of Verse' (pp. 176–95) to Chaucer's metrical innovation of iambic pentameter. Readers will also find much material on Chaucer in the chapter on dream poems, contributed by Helen Phillips (pp. 374–86), and briefer reference to *Troilus and Criseyde* in the chapter on Middle English romances by Thomas Hahn and Dana M. Symons (pp. 341–57). Elsewhere Chaucer is frequently used as a touchstone for the work of other writers, even though one suspects that an 'anything but Chaucer' brief may have been given to the contributors. In the 'Special Themes' section, Barry Windeatt's chapter on 'Love' (pp. 322–38) uses *Troilus and Criseyde* as a backdrop to discussion of a number of non-Chaucerian texts; Peter Brown's own section on 'Images' (pp. 307–21) focuses on Gower and Hoccleve, but ends up considering the image of Chaucer in *The Regiment of Princes*; and the essay on 'War and Chivalry' by Richard W. Kaeuper and Montgomery Bohna (pp. 273–91) has a brief paragraph on Chaucer, though (and this is a surprise), they make no mention of the Knight. The editor's opening assertion that 'a volume such as this would have been impossible ten years ago' (p. 1) is doubtful, and readers might challenge his claim that late medieval English literature now has a 'new map' (p. 3), since there is definitely much of the old map of the subject in evidence here in the familiar sections on language, genres (including romance, lyric, dream, drama) and themes such as chivalry and love. Yet despite these caveats it must be acknowledged that there is much in this collection that will assist students at all levels.

Editor Paul Strohm gathers together thought-provoking essays into a collection that only looks like a companion, he notes in the introduction to his *Middle English* in the Oxford Twenty-First Century Approaches to Literature series. Rather than summing up already well-recycled knowledge, the essays seek to open new avenues of thought, and certainly the topics are not the usual expected fare. This review does not consider the collection systematically but only in so far as it extensively discusses Chaucer, whose presence nonetheless inhabits to varying degrees the entire collection. Christopher Baswell, speaking about 'Multilingualism on the Page' (pp. 38–50), considers the Latin marginalia of Chaucerian manuscripts, Ellesmere offering particularly rich illustrations of how Latin frames and organizes the vernacular text. In Michelle R. Warren's 'Translation' (pp. 51–67) Chaucer emerges as a writer deeply conscious of his role as a translator, whether he translates directly from another language or monolingually, by using words modelled on Latin and French forms. 'Aurality', a theme treated by Joyce Coleman (pp. 68–85), means 'the shared hearing of written texts' (p. 69), and is central to Chaucer's poetry, which is consistently directed to a live listening audience even as it consciously alludes to the act of reading books. Alexandra Gillespie opens her discussion about 'Books' (pp. 86–103) with Chaucer's *Wordes unto Adam, His Own Scriveyn* in order to make the point that instability and fluidity apply as much to the early modern book as they do to the medieval manuscript, that it is in the very nature of the book to be a mutable form and that it is far from incarnating fixed, ideal text. Christopher Cannon finds Chaucer intensely curious about 'Form' (pp. 177–90), and builds his discussion around the passage in *Troilus and Criseyde* that itself draws from Geoffrey of Vinsauf (the necessity of having a plan or archetype for building a house). In quest of 'Beauty' (pp. 207–21), Maura Nolan returns to the Miller's portrait, finding it a satisfying balance of the natural and artificial. The role coins play in the portrait is essential and suggests for Nolan that, like money, Chaucerian beauty possesses the intrinsic capacity to mediate. In 'Authorial Work', Kellie Robertson (pp. 441–58) notes the significance of Chaucer's choice to explore the relation between work and individual identity in the liminal, busy but non-labouring space of pilgrimage rather than in the secluded retreats of, for example, pastoral. Casting himself ironically as a bad labourer, Chaucer shows himself deeply conscious of the disjunctions and proximities between identity and objective labour. Susan E. Phillips continues her interest this year in 'Gossip and (Un)Official Writing' (pp. 476–90), in particular relation to the *Canon's Yeoman's Tale*, concluding as in her book that gossip and (the alchemy of) narrative transformation are intimately linked.

Elizabeth Solopova and Stuart D. Lee offer a survey of *Key Concepts in Medieval Literature*, ambitiously aiming to provide information about texts, themes, terminologies and methods relating to the study of English literature from the thousand years before the sixteenth century. In one small volume this is a tall order, and the discussion is inevitably rather superficial. The first section stresses the importance of context, defined here in terms of historical events, the development of society, and key religious and philosophical ideas;

separate sections dedicated to Old and Middle English follow, covering the usual ground. Chaucer is allocated a dozen pages in which the standard overview of his works and development is given and then destabilized by the editors' final comment that 'the chronology of Chaucer's works is known only approximately, the attribution of some works is disputed, and even the earliest copies of his poems vary in textual detail and contain evidence of scribal error and textual editing' (pp. 203–4). The last section of the book, a mixed bag of 'Approaches, Theory and Practice' is the most thought-provoking; here the book's imagined audience would seem to be that of the graduate beginner, rather than the undergraduate, but both categories will find this a useful introduction.

Gail Ashton, Louise Sylvester and seven other contributors offer help in *Teaching Chaucer*, focusing mostly on models for undergraduate courses. By way of introduction Gail Ashton gives an overview of institutional contexts and a summary of factors that influence the current teaching of medieval literature: a modern culture predominantly televisual; the prevalence of translations and modernizations; and the ubiquity of e-learning with all its advantages and dangers. The first four contributors draw upon the experience of teaching Chaucer in North America. Peggy Knapp recommends 'Chaucer for Fun and Profit' (pp. 17–29), beginning by describing some of the hermeneutic thinking she has found useful, notably Raymond Williams's historicism, Immanuel Kant's aesthetics, and Georg Gadamer's hermeneutics, before turning to the specific classroom techniques that she employs to put these historical and aesthetic ideas into practice. Steven F. Kruger describes 'A Series of Linked Assignments for the Undergraduate Course on Chaucer's *Canterbury Tales*' (pp. 30–45), stressing the value of 'low-stakes' mini-assessments on which beginners can cut their teeth. More imaginative styles of assessment are proposed by Fiona Tolhurst in her essay 'Why We Should Teach—and Our Students Perform—*The Legend of Good Women*' (pp. 46–64). Tolhurst recognizes the dangers of relying exclusively on the *Canterbury Tales* and instead uses this only as a starting point before presenting her students with several of Chaucer's dream vision poems. A distinctive feature in her course is her requirement that students devise performances of individual stories from the *Legend of Good Women*; the value of this is that students have to interpret the text actively, edit it for performance, and study it for sound and sense, as well as memorize verse—creative work that constitutes truly student-centred learning; some illuminating student testimonies about the benefits of this course are included. Moira Fitzgibbons also asks her students to work creatively, and in her contribution, ' "Cross-Voiced" Assignments and the Critical "I" ' (pp. 65–80), she records how the requirement that they take on a fictional voice and write imaginatively as a Chaucerian character ('a pretty weird assignment' (p. 79) to quote one of her students), helps them to develop a firmer sense of the stratagems, risks and evasions operating with any given speaker's 'I'.

The remaining contributions stem from UK educational contexts. In 'Teaching the Language of Chaucer' (pp. 81–95) Louise Sylvester problematizes the idea of teaching Chaucer's language, noting that many courses fail to deal explicitly with language, and that some which do 'do not give any suggestions about how an understanding of Middle English is to be achieved' (p. 84). She also finds a widespread assumption that engagement with language will be unwelcome to students and must therefore be clandestine. Simon Horobin however, is overt about the value of 'Teaching the Language of Chaucer Manuscripts' (pp. 96–104) and describes the way in which he introduces students to important concepts such as linguistic variation and the differences between fifteenth-century manuscripts and modern printed editions. Horobin uses the various CD-ROMs that have originated from the *Canterbury Tales* Project in his teaching, as well as various databases such as the Middle English Compendium. Other contributors have gone further in their harnessing of technologies. Gail Ashton describes her use of WebCT in 'Creating Learning Communities in Chaucer Studies: Process and Product' (pp. 105–19), though a postscript sadly notes the subsequent demise of her course from the syllabus. Philippa Semper also writes about the merits of using a virtual learning environment (VLE) in ' "The wondres that they myghte seen or heere": Designing and Using Web-Based Resources to Teach Medieval Literature' (pp. 120–38). Finally, Lesley Coote's contribution, 'Chaucer and the Visual Image: Learning, Teaching, Assessing' (pp. 139–52) puts the emphasis on visual rather than textual possibilities in using VLEs, describing techniques and methodologies borrowed from film studies. Many of the contributors to this volume voice the same desiderata—that students should read Chaucer's text in its original language, engage in historically grounded research, and read widely amongst good quality secondary criticism. All reject a top-down authoritative model for teaching, preferring to imagine the teacher as a guide, facilitating a hands-on supported learning that takes place in dialogue with active learners. Although some of the contributions read rather like samples of work from teaching portfolios, collectively these essays represent an exchange of ideas of good practice between committed teachers.

Still on the subject of teaching Chaucer, Gregory M. Sadlek explains the logistics of a student mock-trial in 'Chaucer in the Dock: Literature, Women, and Medieval Antifeminism' (*SMART* 14:i[2007] 117–31). The charge was medieval anti-feminism—an undecidable that offers a possibility for nuance on both sides. Eighteen students were equally divided into three groups— Prosecution, Defence, and Jury. One class was devoted to preparation of the case, another to the trial itself, and the Jury posted its deliberations on Blackboard software. Each group received a block grade. One student (whose side lost) later remarked on the usefulness of learning how to argue differently from her own convictions. In the same issue, Dana Symons challenges the inertia of canonicity and suggests how to contextualize Chaucer in 'Long-Lasting Love: Teaming Chaucer with *The Trials and Joys of Marriage*' (*SMART* 14:i[2007] 133–46). Teaching Chaucer alongside excerpts from the TEAMS edition, Symons emphasizes how unrepresentative he is of English medieval literature, and how important it is to train students on a broader literary spectrum. In her own example, she teaches a theme-based rather than single-author-based course. (An additional advantage of her sample assignment—having the students find their own points of connection between Chaucer's work and the anthology—is that it discourages plagiarism.) Tom Liam Lynch, a high school teacher in New York City, used to introduce students to the canonical by means of the popular, but explains how he reversed the process in 'Illuminating Chaucer through Poetry, Manuscript Illuminations, and a Critical Rap Album' (*EJ* 96:vi[2007] 43–9). The students began by studying Chaucer's poetics, then compared them with Eminem. Doing so opened up sophisticated appreciation of assonance, and end, internal, and slant rhymes. The students then composed their own rap lyrics that explicitly allude to Chaucer on some contemporary political issue. The work was then recorded and the lyrics published to look like a Chaucerian manuscript. Alfred Odierno exhorts us not to forget the joy of teaching, claiming that 'Chaucer Knows Best' (*Momentum* 38:ii[2007] 6–7) in depicting a pilgrim Clerk who 'gladly' taught.

David Williams writes about *Language Redeemed: Chaucer's Mature Poetry*. His introduction makes claims for Chaucer as a realist, although elaboration of the argument and evidence are both lacking. The discussion of *Troilus and Criseyde* proceeds book by book, the close reading occasionally indistinguishable from plot summary, translations substituted for the Middle English original, and the author engaging with no critical opinion other than his own. All this clearly suggests that the intended audience is popular rather than scholarly, but whoever the intended reader, more searching analysis is called for. It is not really explained on what basis the *General Prologue*, the *Wife of Bath's Prologue and Tale*, the *Pardoner's Prologue and Tale* and the *Nun's Priest's Tale* are selected by Williams for discussion, but, together with *Troilus and Criseyde*, they apparently support the claim that Chaucer's poetry is realist, by which is meant that it celebrates truths independent of the words that articulate them. Williams is eager to defend Chaucer from the dangerous taint of nominalism, which in his view leads inexorably to relativism and thence to nihilism.

Jamie C. Fumo continues the anti-nominalist strain in 'Chaucer as *Vates*? Reading Ovid through Dante in the *House of Fame*, Book 3' (in Smarr, ed., *Writers Reading Writers*, pp. 89–108). He disagrees that Chaucer's engagement of *Paradiso* I in his poem represents any undercutting of the grandeur of Dante's allusions and suggests that Chaucer shares with Dante a vision of the poet as *vates*, a vessel of prophetic inspiration. In arguing this position, Fumo disagrees with the dominant critical trend that characterizes Chaucer's poetics as essentially nominalist. Contrast the nominalism-informed perspective of Richard Utz, who challenges the legitimacy of Foucault's sweeping claim that medieval authors were anonymous, and argues for a medieval sense of authorial sophistication in 'Writing Alternative Worlds: Rituals of Authorship and Authority in Late Medieval Theological and Literary Discourse' (in Havsteen, Petersen, Schwab and Strem, eds., *Creations: Medieval Rituals, the Arts, and the Concept of Creation*, pp. 121–38). Utz's test cases are Chaucer's *Troilus and Criseyde*, Henryson's *Testament of Cresseid*, and John Metham's *Amoryus and Cleopes*, and his driving idea the nominalist concept of *potentia absoluta* in so far as it relates to the providential designs of God and poet. The ending of *Troilus and Criseyde* shows Chaucer experimenting with an authorial role that explicitly parallels that of the divine creator.

2. Canterbury Tales

Another overview of Chaucer's longest work is supplied by Gail Ashton's *Chaucer's 'The Canterbury Tales'*. The first chapter considers Chaucer's personal life (including the Cecily de Chaumpaigne *raptus* case) against the general background of the time—the Black Death, the Peasants' Revolt, the Hundred Years War, the Papal Schism, Lollardy—and against the literary background of manuscript production. Discussion questions follow at the end of every chapter. Things literary receive closer scrutiny in chapter 2, in which pronunciation is briefly surveyed, the vernacularity of England discussed, and the unstable order of the *Tales* is considered along with the poem's varied genres. A longer chapter on how to read the poem advises on how to navigate the welter of narrators and to deal with the critical stumbling-block of the *Retraction*. A medley of critical issues follows: queer readings, dominant themes, narrative devices of contrasts, repetitions and endings. A fourth chapter summarizes the trajectory of critical reception and publication of Chaucer's *Canterbury Tales*, opening up at the end to discuss different theoretical isms, leaving one wondering whether queer readings might be better placed in this chapter. A final chapter considers the ways in which Chaucer lives on in popular adaptations, and the book closes with some suggested further reading.

Valerie Allen's *On Farting: Language and Laughter in the Middle Ages* touches *passim* on many aspects of Chaucer, but the *Summoner's Tale* recurs consistently throughout the book in relation to different points—the division of a fart, music, the demonic and alchemy (in its affinities with the *Canon's Yeoman's Tale*). The tale is invoked to contribute to one of the central arguments, namely that the sacred and the profane can no longer be thought of in terms of opposing principles juxtaposed in medieval art as contraries. Rather, the sacred resides within the profane, manifesting itself in the act of desecration, or of brokenness, whether the breaking of bread or of a deer, or the broken air of a fart. The desecrations of the *Summoner's Tale* are effected not only by it being a parody of Pentecost but also in the punning language (*fundament, ferthing*) that insistently debases the apparent literal meaning. The tale also is mentioned briefly in the third section of the book, a case study of an apparently historical figure called Roland the Farter from Suffolk, who delivered annual performance farts for the King of England as his feudal service. Speculating on the material conditions under which Roland might have performed his annual feat, Allen points to how the cartwheel solution to the division of the fart that ends the *Summoner's Tale* carries many of the features of organized manorial entertainment. The *Miller's Tale* is also considered in relation to the discussion of the structure of jokes, and the *Merchant's Tale* figures in a consideration of the dangerous doubleness of the privy as place of sanctuary and entrapment, self-reflection and sedition, desire and disgust.

Susan Yager charts the common ground shared by 'Howard's *Idea* and the Idea of Hypertext' (*MedFor* 6[2007] no pagination), giving a brief overview of Donald R. Howard's *The Idea of the Canterbury Tales*, first published in 1976 (*YWES* 57[1978] 90–1), which identifies elements that parallel and anticipate concepts in hypertext theory.

Mass Market Medieval: Essays on the Middle Ages in Popular Culture, edited by David W. Marshall, contains much food for thought but, surprisingly, only one contribution that deals with Chaucer. This is Kevin J. Harty's account of 'Chaucer for a New Millennium: The BBC *Canterbury Tales*' (pp. 13–27), which offers a description of each of the six stand-alone telefilms first broadcast in 2003 and an assessment of how they relate (or fail to relate) to their Chaucerian originals. Harty's essay is informative, but short on critical analysis. Jonathan Bate and Susan Brock describe their most effective study day, on the *Canterbury Tales*, in 'The CAPITAL Centre: Teaching Shakespeare (and More) through a Collaboration between a University and an Arts Organization' (*Pedagogy* 3[2007] 341–58). CAPITAL stands for Creativity and Performance in Teaching and Learning, a grant-funded initiative between the Royal Shakespeare Company and the University of Warwick. Seminar discussion included issues such as what parts of the poem were easily dramatized and what were not; the relationships between the pilgrims; and the place of 'bad' poetry (the *Squire's Tale* and *Thopas*).

Spinning off last year's *Chaucer, Ethics, and Gender* (*YWES* 87[2008] 292–3) Alcuin Blamires thoughtfully offers some 'Philosophical Sleaze? The "Strok of Thought" in the *Miller's Tale* and Chaucerian Fabliau' (*MLR* 102[2007] 621–40). Too often regarded as a haven of temporary truancy from seriousness, or as naturalistic writing that has nothing to do with morality, the fabliaux rejoice in a series of apparently disconnected and spontaneous actions that nonetheless disclose an implicitly providential design. The convergence of plots (flood and arse-branding) in the *Miller's Tale* shows how things providentially knit together into a climactic 'knot' in which one understands the connection between things in a single *strok of thought*.

Chapter 4 of Isabel Davis's *Writing Masculinity in the Later Middle Ages* is on Chaucer, in which she takes the Canon's Yeoman as her primary study although the *Miller's Tale*, *Wife of Bath's Prologue* and *Cook's Tale* also figure because they feature apprentices. In an interesting conjunction that makes the Canon's Yeoman appear as a vulnerable and exploited apprentice rather than as a dangerous destabilizer, she places labour and masculinity in dialogue with each other. Labour rather than sexuality articulates the anxieties and subjectivity of masculinity. Nicolette Zeeman considers a range of male singers in the *Canterbury Tales* in 'The Gender of Song in Chaucer' (*SAC* 29[2007] 141–82) and, in doing so, notes many similarities among them. Nicholas, Absolon, Januarie, the *litel clergeon* and Chanticleer (to name only a few) are comically drawn to the point of caricature, yet also exhibit feminine, childlike qualities, and a self-preoccupation (even narcissism) that renders them vulnerable to the danger around them. Caught in the fantasy of their own song, they offer a commentary on art that for Zeeman reflects on Chaucer's own poetic practice and produces in Chaucer 'an anxious and aggressive self recognition' (p. 155).

R. James Goldstein seeks to replace the concept of a 'marriage group' with a 'perfection group' in 'Future Perfect: the Augustinian Theology of Perfection and the *Canterbury Tales*' (*SAC* 29[2007] 87–140). Emphasizing the abiding influence of Augustine on the fourteenth-century theology of grace, Goldstein presents the Wife of Bath and Custance as figures who epitomize the theological tensions of the time: where the Wife, a vernacular theologian, embraces the secular life with all its attendant temptations, Custance transcends temptation, being predestined for grace. Goldstein's reading takes issue with the recent essay by Nicholas Watson (*YWES* 86[2007] 299), which identifies Chaucer as a mediocritist rather than a perfectionist.

A fine essay is offered by Shayne Aaron Legassie, 'Chaucer's Pardoner and Host—On the Road, in the Alehouse' (*SAC* 29[2007] 183–223), who reconsiders how masculinity is performed in the social space of pilgrimage. The theory of pilgrimage as classless, liminal space (Victor Turner et al.) is insufficient to explain the interaction between medieval sedentary and ambulatory lives. The fixed space of the alehouse is the site through which pilgrims on the road pass. By balancing the pilgrimage frame with the interactions between the two pilgrims, Legassie shows how the Host's seemingly straightforward masculinity is produced by the very same fetishistic fantasies he attempts to expose in the Pardoner's unclear masculinity. Kathryn L. Lynch considers nature and culture in the distance 'From Tavern to Pie Shop: The Raw, the Cooked, and the Rotten in Fragment I of Chaucer's *Canterbury Tales*' (*Exemplaria* 19[2007] 117–38). This stimulating study applies Claude Lévi-Strauss's well known 'culinary triangle' to Chaucer, where the raw denotes nature and the cooked culture, and rotten undoes the distinction between them. Lynch tracks the ubiquitous food imagery and references throughout the fragment, and in the discussion of milling opens up the exegetic and hermeneutic meaning entailed in processing the raw.

Thomas J. Farrell deliberates on the metrics of 'The Prioress's Fair Forehead' (*ChauR* 42[2007] 211–21), and, after reviewing Middle English use of the word *spanne*, affirms the conclusions of Stephen Knight (*YWES* 49[1970] 104) that her forehead measures about four inches, rather than the eight inches frequently invoked by commentators. Thomas Carney Forkin considers Roger the pilgrim cook and urban food regulations in '"Oure Citee": Illegality and Criminality in Fourteenth-Century London' (*EssaysMedSt* 24[2007] 31–41). Chaucer demonstrates a consciousness of the city's seamy side that is as sharp as his sense of gentler sensibility. Norman Klassen suggests 'Two Possible Sources for Chaucer's Description of the Pardoner' (*N&Q* 54[2007] 233–6): Sallust, the *War with Catiline* and Aulus Gellius, *Attic Nights*. Gellius mentions how Sallust links avarice and effeminacy, a conjunction not usually made in medieval penitential literature. Both authors were known of and read in medieval England and their works could well have been available to Chaucer.

Excessiveness is the besetting failing of Palamon and Arcite, respectively expressed as amorousness and martiality, notes Ilan Mitchell-Smith in '"As olde storeis tellen us": Chivalry, Violence, and Geoffrey Chaucer's Critical Perspective in the *Knight's Tale*' (*FCS* 32[2007] 83–99). Mitchell-Smith finds Chaucer's narrative treatment leaning in favour of disengagement and temperance as both Arcite and Troilus finish their lives understanding the futility of earthly over-indulgence. James J. Paxson writes about the cinematic quality of the ekphrastic description of the temple of Mars in 'The Anachronism of Imagining Film in the Middle Ages: Wegener's *Der Golem* and Chaucer's *Knight's Tale*' (*Exemplaria* 19[2007] 290–309). Pressing the metaphor hard to demonstrate the 'sensory phenomenology' (p. 305) of the tale, Paxson shows how Chaucer's description pans, tilts, tracks, zooms and offers snapshots and close-ups. Contrasting the *Der Golem* with the *Knight's Tale*, Paxson notes a certain lack of facility in the latter, which sets up for the author speaking resonances with the 'body without organs' as elaborated by Deleuze and Guattari.

In 'From Snickers to Laughter: Believable Comedy in Chaucer's *Miller's Tale*' (in Hordis and Hardwick, eds., pp. 195–208) Peter G. Beidler compares the tale to the Middle Dutch *Heile van Beersele*. Where the Middle Dutch story has unexplained elements, Chaucer unites details of the story better into foreshadowing, and fleshes out characters more skilfully. For example, in the Dutch version it is too dark to direct the hot poker accurately at the priest's anus, while in the English version Nicholas's fart gives Absolom the perfect target (and also humiliates the squeamish man). Instead of merely snickering, we laugh outright at the story that is better told and is more believable.

Holly A. Crocker analyses gender relations in 'Affective Politics in Chaucer's *Reeve's Tale*: "Cherl" Masculinity after 1381' (*SAC* 29[2007] 225–58). *Cherl* masculinity spins on the theory of Lee Patterson's 'peasant consciousness' and is marked by the familial government of women, where women are simply instruments for social gain among a marginal and dispossessed peasantry. The representation of Sympkyn implies a domestic order maintained by the threat of immoderate violence. Women, as household governance books show, represent the 'sensitive' aspects of the man's domestic body, but Sympkyn's women, despite their compliance with his governance, undo his domestic authority.

In 'Adventurous Custance: St. Thomas of Acre and Chaucer's *Man of Law's Tale*' (in Howes, ed., pp. 43–59) Lawrence Warner notes a fusion of the mercantile and the military. The crusading Order of St Thomas of Acre, whose patron saint was Thomas à Becket, would have been known to Chaucer through its headquarters in London. Warner links an emergent militarism in martyr ideology with a shift in the meaning of 'adventurer' from passive undergoer of events to active quester of 'adventure'. Chaucer's tale highlights both merchant adventuring and a crusading element in Custance's adventures.

Sue Niebrzydowski considers the Wife's pleasure in Jankyn, who was 'so fresh and gay' in bed, in ' "So wel koude he me glose": The Wife of Bath and the Eroticism of Touch' (in Hopkins and Rushton, eds., pp. 18–26). The argument begins with a broad consideration of orthodox church opinion on the dangers of sight, groping and any sexual positions other than the missionary. Running counter to that view is the medical belief that a woman's pleasure aided conception. Jankyn's 'glosing' of the Wife suggests that he used erotic speech, and 'read' his wife's body as closely as a parchment, fashioning her into a pleasured and pleasure-giving body much as Pygmalion fashioned Galatea. Edwin D. Craun contributes an essay, ' "Allas, allas! That evere love was synne'": Excuses for Sin and the Wife of Bath's Stars', in his own edited anthology, *The Hands of the Tongue: Essays on Deviant Speech* (pp. 33–60). In confessional discourse, the penitent's self-deceiving excuses were a well-known trope: appeal to external cause such as the *cours of kynde* was nothing other than evil freely chosen masquerading as extenuating circumstance. Craun's analysis draws from many such discussions, including Augustine's *Enarrationes* and Thomas of Chobham's *summa* on preaching. In claiming astral influence, Craun argues, the Wife counters the constructed voluntarism of clerical discourse. Rafal Borysławski's essay 'Sirith-na-Gig? *Dame Sirith* and the fabliau hags as textual analogues to the Sheela-figures' (in Krygier and Sikorska, eds., *To Make his Englissh Sweete upon his Tonge*, pp. 121–33) touches briefly on the *Wife of Bath's Tale* as it proposes a correlation between medieval grotesque carvings of women and the hags of the fabliau tradition.

Carla Arnell considers the medieval inspiration of a modern novelist in 'Chaucer's Wife of Bath and John Fowles's Quaker Maid: Tale-Telling and the Trial of Personal Experience and Written Authority' (*MLR* 102[2007] 933–46). Fowles read the *Canterbury Tales* only late in his career, and Arnell argues for its explicit shaping of *A Maggot*. Beyond structural resemblances between the novel and Chaucer's poem, Fowles's protagonist, the 'Quaker Maid', and the Wife of Bath both draw from personal experience as a legitimate source of knowledge, despite being circumscribed by the textual authority of old books.

Brantley L. Bryant takes a closer link at the prevailing contemporary climate of concern about official corruption in ' "By extorcions I lyve": Chaucer's *Friar's Tale* and Corrupt Officials' (*ChauR* 42[2007] 180–95). Bryant shows how Chaucer inserts into his character portraits 'curious bureaucratic digressions' (p. 181) which have no origin in the tale's known sources and analogues, and which most likely arise from Chaucer's first-hand experience as an urban dweller and comptroller of customs.

John Finlayson considers the shift in critical understanding of 'Chaucer's *Summoner's Tale*: Flatulence, Blasphemy, and the Emperor's Clothes' (*SP* 104[2007] 455–70), in which clever scurrility is now seen as more radical theological statement. Finlayson considers in particular the possibility of a blasphemous analogy between the gift of a fart and God's gift of the Ten Commandments, the offence of which is only barely placed on the shoulders of narrators internal to the poem.

Susan Crane gives the biennial Chaucer lecture 'For the Birds' (*SAC* 29[2007] 23–41), which focuses on the *Squire's Tale* and inter-species difference, or what Chaucer would call difference of *kynde*, a topic that romance, with its capacious appetite for the marvellous, well facilitates. Drawing from anthropological analysis of the symbolic value of animals and from Jacques Derrida's essay 'Hostipitality', and pressing the question of charity to its limit, Crane asks about the ethics of showing compassion to a bird. This is an elegantly wrought essay that stays close to Chaucer's text while opening it up to large questions. Lindsey M. Jones turns to 'Chaucer's Anxiety of Poetic Craft: The *Squire's Tale*' (*Style* 41[2007] 300–18), finding in the tale a self-aware meditation on the poetic craft. As in *Thopas*, the poor prosody of the *Squire's Tale* draws attention to form, while the mature poetics of the *Knight's Tale* poses a strong contrast and brings the relationship between the

Knight and Squire to bear upon the matter of artistic control, or lack of it. The Squire is not in control of his rhymes, while the Knight is, employing caesurae in his tale with variety and grace.

The *Franklin's Tale* and the marriage debate are revisited by Emma Lipton in *Affections of the Mind: The Politics of Sacramental Marriage in Late Medieval English Literature*. Rather than seeing the tale articulate Chaucer's ideal notion of marriage, as Kittredge argued, Lipton sees marriage in the tale articulating the Franklin's class-based political ideals. Reading against the grain of much contemporary opinion of the tale, Lipton affirms the values of free choice and mutuality, and does not read them as cynically or ironically made. Rather, they are particularly appropriate for the gentle but unaristocratic status of the Franklin. Those values of marital friendship belong to the ideology of the middle political stratum. The political outworking of marital mutuality shares much with what David Wallace calls the 'associational ideology' of the *Canterbury Tales* (*YWES* 78[2000] 40–1). In keeping his abandonment of mastery a private arrangement, Arveragus reflects in his behaviour the incompatibility between the romantic values of *fin amour* and sacramental marriage. That tension between public reputation and private friendship mounts in the crisis of the tale, the resolution of which is found, however, in the bond forged between three men rather than between man and wife. That said, the homosocial bond is forged only through the commitment to heterosexual marriage.

Michael Calabrese looks beyond the obvious Boccaccian analogues to the *Franklin's Tale* to consider a much wider range of correspondences in 'Chaucer's Dorigen and Boccaccio's Female Voices' (*SAC* 29[2007] 259–92), and finds that Dorigen speaks recklessly to Aurelius, out of keeping with her status, wrapping a no in a seeming yes. Her verbal excess, both in the oath and in her lament, brings to mind the exhortation to conciseness in female speech made by Boccaccio's Pampinea. Dorigen's challenge to Aurelius sets in motion a competitive one-upmanship between men that does but did not have to resolve itself happily. For Kurtis B. Haas, in '*The Franklin's Tale* and the Medieval *Trivium*: A Call for Critical Thinking' (*JEGP* 106[2007] 45–63), Dorigen and Arveragus lack the critical thinking skills bestowed by even the sketchiest familiarity with the medieval *trivium*, and therefore are unable to see through the Orleans clerk's corruptions of the *quadrivium*. Through the Franklin as flawed narrator, for whom the *trivium* is mere troping and the *quadrivium* mere magic, Chaucer reveals the dependence of ethical action on proper consideration of concepts. The interdependence of word and praxis is elaborated through the work of Paolo Freire. Although the tale's interest in rhetoric and logical dilemma is evident, there remains something of a plausibility gap in Haas's argument between the main characters and the likelihood of their familiarity with the university *trivium*.

'Wardship and *Raptus* in the *Physician's Tale*' (in Rosenthal, ed., *Essays on Medieval Childhood: Responses to Recent Debates*, pp. 108–23) for Daniel T. Kline bring a critical element of family law to the tale and implicitly question the rights of Virginius. Bad intentions aside, Claudius pleads a suit against Virginius that at least seems colourable in terms of late medieval law on wardship. A man of means, Virginius had various non-violent options in countering Apius's fraudulent judgement, but instead he simply accepts the *sentence*, rendering his slaying of Virginia all the more disturbing for its unnecessariness. John Michael Crafton takes a closer look at biblical analogy in ' "The Physician's Tale" and Jeptha's Daughter' (*ANQ* 20:i[2007] 8–13), and finds it ironic in two ways: first in that Jeptha's daughter laments dying a virgin; second, in that her sacrifice is unnecessarily caused by Jeptha's foolish vow. Citing contemporary sermons, Crafton finds Jeptha's daughter an exemplum of foolish virginity and of indecorous wandering.

John Block Friedman moves away from Faux Semblant in the *Roman de la Rose* as the usual prototype for the Pardoner to medieval French travelling salesmen and in particular two satiric Old French trade poems (both rendered at the end into modern English), in 'Chaucer's Pardoner, Rutebeuf's *Dit de l'Herberie*, the *Dit du Mercier*, and Cultural History' (*Viator* 38:i[2007] 289–318). Friedman demonstrates broad similarities of characterization between the three poems and suggests a model for the Pardoner's sexual condition in one of the spices flogged by the Mercer of the *Dit du Mercier*, galenga (as in the Cook's *galyngale*), which in the Old French poem is said to emasculate clerics in minor orders.

Christian Sheridan contributes an intelligent piece about 'Funny Money: Puns and Currency in the *Shipman's Tale*' (in Hordis and Hardwick, eds., pp. 111–23). For Sheridan the tale's commodification impulse brings the comic and the commercial into a special relationship. This is achieved through puns. Where puns threaten language with meaninglessness, money threatens value with relativity. Both puns and money require circulation for meaning and belong to a system of signification in which value is relational rather than intrinsic. The hundred franks, which we never see spent, evaporate into fiction, a figure of speech, or in economic terms ghost money. Robert W. Hanning looks in depth at Boccaccio's tales in 'Before Chaucer's *Shipman's Tale*: The Language of Place, the Place of Language in *Decameron* 8.1 and 8.2' (in Howes, ed., pp. 181–96). He thinks about how place (urban Milan and the Tuscan countryside) variously mediates cultural and symbolic meaning and the tensions between town and country. Chaucer receives no direct consideration and although some comparisons might profitably be made with the *Shipman's Tale*, Hanning leaves them for the reader to pursue.

In an interesting essay, William Orth considers contemporary and medieval meanings of 'perform': 'The Problem of the Performative in Chaucer's Prioress Sequence' (*ChauR* 42[2007] 196–210). In Middle English, one might make or perform a thing (a promise, a bed), but there is no locution that enables the modern formulations of performing gender, or performing well or badly. Drawing from the work of J.L. Austin and John Searle, Orth then analyses the Prioress's reference to God's praise being *perfourned* (VII. 453–9) and finds that the Prioress, from the *General Prologue* and her tale, exhibits a close attention to performed acts; to the fashioning of self through acts performed in and as if in the eyes of others.

Eugene Green compares 'Civic Voices in English Fables: *The Owl and the Nightingale* and the *Nun's Priest's Tale*' (*AUMLA* 108[2007] 1–32), finding, despite their chronological distance from each other, a similarity of audience and of preoccupation with status as well as a sharing of the formal genre of beast fable. Taking etymological and lexicographical evidence into account, Green studies the distribution of words indicating speech and song in both poems, and finds that Chaucer's poem exhibits an increased showiness in the display of learning—an effect, he argues, of increased urbanization. Tom Mason compares 'Dryden's *The Cock and the Fox* and Chaucer's *Nun's Priest's Tale*' (*T&L* 16[2007] 1–28), defending the former for the liberties he took with Chaucer in a manner usually deemed patronizing by medievalists. Dryden effects a transformation rather than a translation of Chaucer, to which he brought a wealth of contemporary allusion and philosophical consideration of what makes bare, two-legged man distinctive in creation. None epitomizes this question better than Chaunticleer. In preferring Pertelote over his own intuitions, Dryden's Chaunticleer sums up the dilemma of Milton's Adam. Mason's essay is welcome in better explaining Dryden's intentions.

Echoes of Chaucer are noted by Peter Grund in '*Sidrak and Bokkus*: An Early Modern Reader Response' (*Anglia* 125[2007] 217–38). This Middle English verse dialogue, printed in the 1530s, was revised by the late sixteenth-/early seventeenth-century copyist/annotator of the alchemical miscellany, Bibliotheca Philosophica Hermetica, Amsterdam, MS M199. Most of Grund's essay comprises a detailed comparison of the manuscript and printed version. In the marginalia, the annotator makes some rather idiosyncratic connections with Chaucer: two to the *Monk's Tale* and one to the *Canon's Yeoman's Tale*. The citations suggest that the annotator used the third edition of William Thynne's *Canterbury Tales*.

3. Troilus and Criseyde

Tison Pugh and Angela Jane Weisl offer guidance on *Approaches to Teaching Chaucer's Troilus and Criseyde and the Shorter Poems*. This slim volume is divided into two unequal sections. Part I, written by the editors themselves, offers a useful survey of the materials required by students: editions, translations, anthologies, secondary reading, electronic and multimedia resources, and a note also of what should be on the instructors' library shelves. In part II the editors then introduce no fewer than thirty contributions outlining teaching strategies designed to incorporate works other than the *Canterbury Tales* into the classroom. This section is further subdivided into three unequal parts, the first of which, 'Teaching the Backgrounds', is concerned with the literary, historical and cultural contexts of Chaucer's works; ten essays explore this in different ways. First up is William A. Quinn, who pays particular attention to Chaucer's use of genre in 'The Short Poems: Sources, Genres, and Contexts' (pp. 27–32), noting especially the deployment of multiple generic tropes within a single text. The next three contributions variously concern themselves with Chaucer's indebtedness to European literature. Karla Taylor looks at 'Chaucer and the French Tradition' (pp. 33–7); Warren Ginsberg writes about 'Boccaccio's *Il Filostrato*, Chaucer's *Troilus and Criseyde*, and Translating the Italian Tradition' (pp. 38–42); and Noel Harold Kaylor Jr offers a diagrammatic analysis of 'Boethius, Dante, and Teaching Aspects of Chaucer's Tragedy' (pp. 43–9).

The equally important influence of Chaucer's English poetic contemporaries is the topic of Susannah Mary Chewning's essay, 'Chaucer and Vernacular Writing' (pp. 50–5), while in 'Troilus and Criseyde and Chaucer's Shorter Poems: Paleography and Codicology' (pp. 56–60), Julia Boffey shows how an awareness of the material circumstances governing medieval book production can illuminate modern textual analysis. A concern with the matter of history informs both Scott Lightsey's contribution, 'The Pagan Past and Chaucer's Christian Present' (pp. 61–5), and Alison A. Baker's account of 'Contemporary English Politics and the Ricardian Court: Chaucer's London and the Myth of New Troy' (pp. 66–70). The final two essays in this section demonstrate how ideological constructions of gender influenced Chaucer's literature and continue to influence today's readers. In 'Trust No Man But Me: Women and Chaucer's Shorter Poetry' (pp. 71–5) Lynn Arner discusses ways of teaching students how Chaucer's narratives reflect and subvert tropes of medieval misogyny, and in 'Teaching Masculinities in Chaucer's Shorter Poems: Historical Myths and Brian Helgeland's A Knight's Tale' (pp. 76–80), Holly A. Crocker offers an analysis of male homosociality in order to enlighten students' conceptions of medieval masculinities.

By far the largest subsection of the volume, with fifteen contributions, is 'Teaching the Poems'. William A. Quinn gets the privileged opening slot once again and offers 'Suggestions for Rehearsing the Short Poems in Class' (pp. 81–6). Glenn A. Steinberg calls attention to differences in modern and pre-modern reception in 'Chaucer and the Critical Tradition' (pp. 87–91), while Carolynn Van Dyke offers a series of exercises based on the shorter poems in 'Small Texts, Large Questions: Entering Chaucerian Poetics through the "Miscellaneous" Poems' (pp. 92–6). Moving on to the dream poems, Myra Seaman outlines the pedagogical challenges of 'Teaching Chaucer's Postmodern Dream Visions' (pp. 97–100), paying particular attention to the ways in which postmodern literary theories can enlighten these texts, and Michael Calabrese offers a series of practical suggestions in 'A Guide to Teaching The Legend of Good Women' (pp. 101–6). Two further essays tackle Troilus and Criseyde: Clare R. Kinney considers how genre and generic expectations influence interpretations of the poem in 'Chaucer's Dialogic Imagination: Teaching the Multiple Discourses of Troilus and Criseyde' (pp. 107–11), and Peggy A. Knapp investigates the complex relation between 'Philology, History, and Cultural Persistence: Troilus and Criseyde as Medieval and Contemporary' (pp. 112–16); both of these contributions are alert to the ways in which dialogic perspectives (both Chaucer's and the reader's) structure our understanding of the Chaucerian canon.

Several essays explore the pedagogical ramifications of recent trends in literary theory that have created new perspectives on medieval literature. The editors themselves consider 'Chaucer and Gender Theory' (pp. 117–21); Roger Apfelbaum charts the literary development of the Troilus legend in ' "Made and molded of things past": Intertextuality and the Study of Chaucer, Henryson, and Shakespeare' (pp. 122–6); and James J. Paxson assesses the benefits of using multiple theoretical approaches in teaching Chaucer in 'Triform Chaucer: Deconstruction, Historicism, Psychoanalysis, and Troilus and Criseyde' (pp. 127–33). Another clutch of essays focuses on techniques for reading and comprehending Chaucer's language. Martha Rust is concerned primarily with reading in 'A Primer for Fourteenth-Century English and Late Medieval English Manuscript Culture: Glossing Chaucer's "An ABC"' (pp. 133–7), while Alan T. Gaylord focuses on speaking in 'Two Forms, Two Poetic Stages, Developing Voices: *The Romaunt of the Rose* and *The Parliament of Fowls*' (pp. 138–43). Verbal translation is the topic of Barbara Stevenson's essay, '"In forme of speche is chaunge": Introducing Students to Chaucer's Middle English' (pp. 144–8), while Glenn Davis advocates the importance of 'Visual Approaches to Chaucer' (pp. 149–53). Conversely, Jean-François Kosta-Théfaine makes the case for using non-translated texts in the classroom, in 'Teaching Chaucer without (or with) Translations: An Introduction to Othon de Grandson's "Les cinq balades ensuivans" and Chaucer's "The Complaint of Venus"' (pp. 154–8).

The third subdivision of the 'Approaches' section is entitled 'Course Contexts' and contains four contributions that are closely concerned with pedagogical practice. Jenifer Sutherland offers the reflections of a novice instructor in 'Notes on a Journey: Teaching Chaucer's Short Poems and *Troilus and Criseyde* for the First Time' (pp. 159–64), whereas student novices are the subject of Marcia Smith Marcez ('Overcoming Resistance to "That Old Stuff": Teaching *Troilus and Criseyde* through Journaling and Debate', pp. 165–9) and Adam Brooke Davis ('"Diverse folk diversely they seyde": Teaching Chaucer to Nonmajors', pp. 170–4), both of whom present strategies for engaging readers who are unfamiliar with medieval literature. At the other end of the spectrum Lorraine Kochanske Stock concerns herself with the next generation of medievalists, in 'Chaucer's Early Poetry in Graduate Seminars: Opportunities for Training Future Chaucer Teachers and Molding "Yonge, Fresshe Folkes" into Publishing Scholars' (pp. 175–9). Finally, Alan T. Gaylord offers an appendix with 'Suggestions for Reading Chaucer Out Loud in the Teaching of Chaucer's Poetry' (pp. 180–3). The very high number of contributions to this volume means that individual essays are necessarily rather brief, but they are nevertheless packed with information; teachers of Chaucer, of whatever vintage, will find plenty of interest in this stimulating collection.

Apologies are owed to Gerald Morgan for omitting last year to include a review of volume 2 of his *The Tragic Argument of Troilus and Criseyde*. At the time of covering volume 1 (*YWES* 87[2008] 303–4), the reviewer mistakenly thought volume 2 to be still forthcoming. Continuing its pagination and chapter numbers from the previous book, volume 2 picks up the narrative at chapter 8, 'The Pain of Separation', and includes two more chapters. Chapter 8 looks in detail at Troilus's despair, which is deranged on account of the irrationality of his love for Criseyde; at Criseyde's sorrow; and at her descent by the end of Book IV to 'fraudulence and treachery' (p. 459). Chapter 9 charts at length 'The Timetable of Betrayal': Criseyde's initial good intentions, the advent of Diomede, her failure to return at the appointed time, Diomede's suit, her acceptance of Diomede as lover, Troilus's dream and letter and the proof of betrayal. The last chapter, 'The End of the Affair', moves towards some conclusions in asserting the absoluteness of divine love that contrasts with the deeply flawed love of Troilus. Morgan's book is hard to summarize as an argument in that it is essentially a 700-page close reading that sticks faithfully to the text and that neither engages with current critical debate nor comments on its own critical method. In his reading the poem emerges as an integrated artistic whole, driven by a morally coherent vision founded on love as expounded by scholastic philosophy and mediated by Dante. While Morgan's reading will offer the reader little by way of explicit critical positioning it offers much by way of close textual exegesis.

In ' "Of your herte up casteth the visage": Turning Troilo/Troilus's Eyes to God' (*Hortulus* 3[2007] no pagination) Jenny Lee takes medieval optical theory as the starting point for her sustained comparison of *Troilus and Criseyde* and *Il Filostrato*. She argues that Chaucer develops and transforms Boccaccio's conventional trope of the lover's gaze in order to reveal the inadequacy of corporeal love and the transcendence of the love of God. Lee focuses on the character of Troilus, but indicates that a similar investigation based on Criseyde might illuminate the complex gender dynamics within the poem's interlocking trajectories of gazes. Josephine A. Koster reassesses Criseyde *in situ* in 'Privitee, Habitus, and Proximity: Conduct and Domestic Space in Chaucer's *Troilus and Criseyde*' (*EssaysMedSt* 24[2007] 79–91). A consideration of Criseyde's setting shows that she is not as isolated and vulnerable as she is sometimes made out to be. As a wealthy woman surrounded by watchful companions, she would not have experienced much *privitee*. Her garden is a social place, not designed for solitude. Koster convincingly shows how little is private in Criseyde's world and, following through the logic of how one's character is defined by daily *habitus*, she explains Criseyde's subsequent infidelity in terms of her radically changed environment in the Greek camp.

Noh Kyung Lee's study of 'Acedia as a Motive in Trolius's Tragedy' (*JMEMS* 15[2007] 271–87), which is in Japanese, is noted. In a short essay Harold Kaylor draws close connections between 'Chaucer's *Troilus and Criseyde* and Boethius's *Consolation of Philosophy*' (in Krygier and Sikorska, eds., pp. 111–19), arguing that the poem's structure depends upon Boethius's four-level system of epistemology: sense-knowing, image-knowing, reason-knowing and intelligence-knowing. To make this fit more conveniently with the poem's five-part organization Kaylor subdivides the third level into positive (Book III) and negative (Book IV) arguments about love. Elsewhere Kaylor ponders the difference between Dantean and Chaucerian world-views in a contribution to his own co-edited collection, 'Re-Examining Geoffrey Chaucer's Work in an Age of Globalization: *Troilus and Criseyde* and Chaucer's Global Perspective' (in Kaylor and Nokes, eds., *Global Perspectives on Medieval English Literature, Language and Culture*, pp. 133–53). During that stretch of the greater part of the fourteenth century between the completion of Dante's *Commedia* and the commencement of Chaucer's *Troilus* Kaylor sees a shift of belief from moral absolutism to relativism. For Dante, there are two distinct realms of reality; for Chaucer, the two realms cannot easily be distinguished. At the end of his essay, Kaylor connects Chaucer's convergent worlds to Einstein's quantum world of space-time.

In the same collection, An Sonjae (Brother Anthony of Taizé), in 'No Greater Pain: The Ironies of Bliss in Chaucer's *Troilus and Criseyde*' (in Kaylor and Nokes, eds., pp. 117–32), draws our attention to the ironic allusions to both Boethius and Dante's Francesca (*Inferno* V) in Pandarus's phrase. Only too late does Troilus see that his romantic love is really *blinde lust*. Unlike An Sonjae, who assumes that Troilus's ultimate destination is Limbo, Karen Elaine Smyth proposes a different destination in 'Reassessing Chaucer's Cosmological Discourse at the End of "Troilus and Criseyde" (c.1385)' (*FCS* 32[2007] 150–63). Examining closely the description of Troilus' passageway into the next world, Smyth argues that Chaucer is vague about which numerical sphere his hero enters, but that it is logical to assume that Troilus moves first into the eighth sphere of fixed stars and then into the ninth sphere of the *primum mobile*; a helpful skymap (p. 161) illustrates this progression. Troilus's final resting place is therefore also a place of continual motion, and this non-closure accords with the poem's fundamental preoccupation with worldly change and instability.

4. Other Works

Kathryn L. Lynch edits *Dream Visions and Other Poems: Geoffrey Chaucer* in the Norton Critical Editions series. Lynch takes the unusual step of using Skeat's 1894 edition as her base text, albeit carefully checked against other more recent editions and individual manuscripts as well as heavily glossed and, where needed, modernized. Pointing out how the *Canterbury Tales* and *Troilus and Criseyde* fare better than the minor poems in terms of having manuscript witnesses much closer to Chaucer's own lifetime, Lynch registers the difficulty of reconstructing Chaucer's own orthography and metrical phrasing. A quick introduction to Chaucer's language, squeezed into four pages, follows, and then the text of the poems, first dream visions, then the minor poems, is given. Excepting the short poems, which are gathered under a single introduction, each poem receives a three- to four-page overview that explains historical context, genre and so on, as well as introducing discussion points. Lynch's next section, 'Contexts', excerpts relevant sources and analogues, and is cleverly introduced by means of an excerpt from Ruth Evans's 'Chaucer in Cyberspace' (*YWES* 82[2003] 220–1), in which Chaucer appears at his keyboard with multiple windows open on his screen—an image of poetic compositing. The final section showpieces a sampler of critical readings that overlap with each other in interesting ways: Charles Muscatine, from *Chaucer's Early Poems*; A.C. Spearing, from *Medieval Dream Poetry*; R.T. Leneghan, from 'Chaucer's Circle of Gentlemen and Clerks' (*YWES* 64[1986] 145); Richard Firth Green, 'Chaucer's Victimized Women' (*YWES* 69[1991] 180); Elaine Tuttle Hansen, 'The Feminization of Men in Chaucer's *Legend of Good Women*' (*YWES* 70[1992]); and Steven Kruger, from 'Medical and Moral Authority in the Late Medieval Dream' (*YWES* 80[2001] 191). Redressing a balance conventionally tilted in favour of Chaucer's two longest poems, this is a handy student textbook.

Disagreeing with modern editors and siding with Walter Scott's original judgement, Cedric D. Reverand II, in 'Dryden's "To the Duchess of Ormond": Identifying her Plantagenet Predecessor' (*N&Q* 54[2007] 57–60), argues that Dryden's allusion to 'the fairest Nymph' refers to Blanche, wife of Gaunt. The allusion comes in the opening poem of his *Fables Ancient and Modern*, which is addressed to Mary Somerset, duchess of Ormond, direct descendant of John of Gaunt. In it he establishes a poetic genealogical link between Chaucer and himself, heir to the tradition he is redefining in the act of translating Chaucer.

Elizabeth Eva Leach makes occasional mention of the *Parliament of Fowls* in *Sung Birds: Music, Nature, and Poetry in the Later Middle Ages*. The roundel at the end of the poem marks the cycle of the seasons and the seasonal mating of the ordinary birds. For the noble birds, refusing to mate is a noble decision, yet it draws attention to the tension within human society between natural compulsion and rational choice. In 'A Place among the Leaves: The Manuscript Contexts of Chaucer's *Parliament of Fowls*' (*Comitatus* 38[2007] 69–86) Todd Preston revokes David Lorenzo Boyd's contention that the poem's physical contexts direct us to read the text in terms of common profit or courtly love (see *YWES* 73[1995] 167–8). Unlike Boyd, who considered only three manuscripts, Preston assesses all fourteen, finding that most are not compilations concerned with readerly control but author-anthologies or miscellanies, each governed by its own organizational principles; this is a timely reminder that the implications of manuscript context are best assessed individually. Such is the approach adopted by Ashby Kinch, whose codicological study of Cambridge University Library MS Ff. 1. 6, '"To thenke what was in hir wille": a female reading context for the Findern anthology' (*Neophil* 91[2007] 729–44), contends that interpretative control was exercised over the manuscript's construction by its readers and compilers. Citing evidence of the selective editing of texts by female scribes, Kinch finds that various themes inform the volume as a whole, notably the power of female eloquence, and the tension between female choice and social compulsion, but this argument is based on only a selection of the contents of Ff. 1. 6, including relevantly here the *Parliament of Fowls*, *The Complaint of Venus* and excerpts from *Anelida and Arcite* and the *Legend of Good Women*.

In 'A Camp Wedding: The Cultural Context of Chaucer's "Brooch of Thebes"' (in Howes, ed., pp. 27–41), William R. Askins reviews the evidence for the theory that the *Complaint of Mars* and *Complaint of Venus* form a single poem or diptych. Askins suggests it was composed on the occasion of the wedding in 1386 at Plymouth between John Holland and Elizabeth of Lancaster, second daughter of Blanche and John of Gaunt, arguing that Chaucer witnessed this marriage via the involvement of his wife, Philippa, in Gaunt's household (see above on Holly Crocker's *Chaucer's Visions of Manhood*, chapter 2). The wedding both occasioned the first epithalamium in English literature and was the last time Chaucer saw his wife alive.

Framing her claims more carefully than Lindeboom (see above), Joyce Coleman covers similar terrain in '"A bok for King Richardes sake": Royal Patronage, the *Confessio*, and the *Legend of Good Women*' (in Yeager, ed., *On John Gower*, pp. 104–23). The consequences of Macaulay's selection of Gower's third recension as his base text have relegated 'Gower's first version of the text to a variant of the third' (p. 104), thereby throwing a shadow across the first version's story of Richard's commissioning of the *Confessio* from the poet. Coleman claims strong internal and external evidence for the story, not least the parallel treatments of royal patronage and Flower and Leaf motif in both Gower's poem and the F version of the *Legend of Good Women*.

Amanda Holton explores rhetorical techniques in 'Chaucer and *Pronominatio*' (*RMSt* 33[2007] 69–86), finding that, although Chaucer generally prefers direct naming techniques, he exceptionally uses *pronominatio* when relying on Virgil as a source in the *Legend of Good Women* and the *House of Fame*. She also demonstrates how Chaucer exploits the negative possibilities of *pronominatio* in the *Prioress's Tale* and *Troilus and Criseyde*.

Ian Johnson's essay 'The Ascending Soul and the Virtue of Hope: The Spiritual Temper of Chaucer's *Boece* and *Retracciouns*' (*ES* 88[2007] 245–61) seeks to analyse both Chaucer's attitude to the workings of the soul in stirring itself towards God and his representation of this process. The discussion focuses on two interrelated concerns: a Boethian conception of how the soul rises towards the divine, and a more official Christian theological understanding derived from the mainstream pastoral tradition of rudimentary instruction. Noting that the citation of Romans 15.4 in the *Retraction* is paralleled in Nicholas Love's *Mirror of the Blessed Life of Jesus Christ*, Johnson argues that this biblical text imbues Chaucer's closing words with a sense of hope.

William Sayers finds a close correspondence between 'Chaucer's Description of the Battle of Actium in the *Legend of Cleopatra* and the Medieval Tradition of Vegetius's *De Re Militari*' (*ChauR* 42[2007] 76–90), but suggests that Chaucer's technical descriptions of shipboard weapons and his general familiarity with maritime combat should be attributed not to a single manuscript source but to the general medieval culture of war at sea. This battle and legend also receive some attention in Laura J. Getty's more wide-ranging article, ' "Other smale ymaad before": Chaucer as historiographer in the *Legend of Good Women*' (*ChauR* 42[2007] 48–75). Getty argues that the constituent parts of the poem form a coherent whole because the legends construct metaphors about the dangers of writings from sources, and thus may be seen as the practical application of concerns voiced in the Prologue.

In 'Chaucer and Friends: The Audience for the *Treatise on the Astrolabe*' (*ChauR* 41[2007] 439–44) Edgar Laird explores the tradition of writing such technical works as an obligation of friendship, noting this motivation in other astrolabe treatises by Ascelin of Ausburg and Adelard of Bath. He further suggests that Chaucer wrote the treatise to help readers of the *Canterbury Tales* interpret its astronomical references correctly.

Two publications not available in time for review this year will be covered in next year's *YWES*: Peter Brown, *Chaucer and the Making of Optical Space* (Lang [2007]) and T.L. Burton and Peter Goodall, *Chaucer's Monk's Tale and Nun's Priest's Tale: An Annotated Bibliography* (University of Toronto Press [2007]).

Books Reviewed

Alexander, Michael. *Medievalism: The Middle Ages in Modern England.* YaleUP. [2007] pp. xxviii + 306. £25 ISBN 9 7803 0011 0616.

Allen, Valerie. *On Farting: Language and Laughter in the Middle Ages.* Palgrave. [2007] pp. xii + 239. $74.95 ISBN 9 7803 1223 4935.

Ashton, Gail. *Chaucer's 'The Canterbury Tales'.* Continuum. [2007] pp. v + 121. hb £50 ISBN 9 7808 2648 9357, pb £15.99 ISBN 9 7808 2648 9364.

Ashton, Gail, and Louise Sylvester, eds. *Teaching Chaucer.* Palgrave. [2007] pp. xi + 167. pb £16.99 ($29.95) ISBN 9 7814 0398 8270.

Barrington, Candace. *American Chaucers.* Palgrave. [2007] pp. xiv + 224. £40 ($74.95) ISBN 9 7814 0396 5158.

Bishop, Louise M. *Words, Stones, & Herbs: The Healing Word in Medieval and Early Modern England.* SyracuseUP. [2007] pp. xiv + 276. £18.50 ($24.95) ISBN 9 7808 1563 1248.

Brown, Peter, ed. *A Companion to Medieval English Literature and Culture, c.1350–c.1500.* Blackwell. [2007] pp. xvii + 668. £85 ISBN 9 7806 3121 9736.

Bullón-Fernández, María, ed. *England and Iberia in the Middle Ages, 12th–15th Century: Cultural, Literary, and Political Exchanges.* Palgrave. [2007] pp. x + 250. $74.95 ISBN 9 7814 0397 2248.

Cavill, Paul, and Heather Ward. *The Christian Tradition in English Literature: Poetry, Plays, and Shorter Prose.* Zondervan. [2007] pp. 512. pb $24.99 ISBN 9 7803 1025 5154.

Cawsey, Kathy, and Jason Harris, eds. *Transmission and Transformation in the Middle Ages: Texts and Contexts.* FCP. [2007] pp. 212. €55 (£50, $60) ISBN 9 7818 5182 9903.

Coleman, Philip, ed., *On Literature and Science: Essays, Reflections, Provocations.* Four Courts. [2007] pp. 270. €49.50 ISBN 9 7818 4682 0717.

Costambeys, Marios, Andrew Hamer and Martin Heale, eds. *The Making of the Middle Ages: Liverpool Essays.* LiverUP. [2007] pp. x + 252. £50 ISBN 9 7818 4631 0683.

Craun, Edwin D., ed. *The Hands of the Tongue: Essays on Deviant Speech.* SMC 47. MIP. [2007] pp. xviii + 214. hb $40 ISBN 9 7815 8044 1148, pb $20 ISBN 9 7815 8044 1155.

Crocker, Holly A. *Chaucer's Visions of Manhood.* Palgrave. [2007] pp. xiii + 250. £40 ($74.95) ISBN 9 7814 0397 5713.

Davis, Isabel. *Writing Masculinity in the Later Middle Ages.* CSML 62. CUP. [2007] pp. 240. £50 ISBN 9 7805 2186 6378.

Driver, Martha W., and Michael T. Orr, eds. *An Index of Images in English Manuscripts from the Time of Chaucer to Henry VIII c.1380–c.1509.* HM. [2007] pp. 176. pb £93.95 ISBN 9 7819 0537 5226.

Epstein, Joseph, ed. *Literary Genius: 25 Classic Writers who Define English and American Literature.* Paul Dry Books. [2007] pp. 246 hb $34.95 ISBN 9 7815 8988 0399, pb $18.95 ISBN 9 7815 8988 0351.

Fyler, John M. *Language and the Declining World in Chaucer, Dante, and Jean de Meun.* CUP. [2007] pp. xii + 306. £50 ($101) ISBN 9 7805 2187 2157.

Giancarlo, Matthew. *Parliament and Literature in Late Medieval England.* CUP. [2007] pp. xiii + 289. £53 ISBN 9 7805 2187 5394.

Harder, Annette, Alasdair A. MacDonald and Gerrit J. Reinink, eds. *Calliope's Classroom: Studies in Didactic Poetry from Antiquity to the Renaissance.* Peeters. [2007] pp. x + 323. €60 ISBN 9 7890 4291 8085.

Hass, Andrew W., David Jasper and Elisabeth Jay, eds. *The Oxford Handbook of English Literature and Theology.* OUP. [2007] pp. xvii + 889. £85 ISBN 9 7801 9927 1979.

Havsteen, Sven Rune, Nils Holger Petersen, Heinrich W. Schwab and Eyolf Strem, eds. *Creations: Medieval Rituals, the Arts, and the Concept of Creation.* Brepols. [2007] pp. 269. €60 ISBN 9 7825 0352 2951.

Hopkins, Amanda, and Cory James Rushton, eds. *The Erotic in the Literature of Medieval Britain.* Brewer. [2007] pp. viii + 182. £45 ISBN 9 7818 4384 1197.

Hordis, Sandra M., and Paul Hardwick, eds. *Medieval English Comedy.* Brepols. [2007] pp. 230. €55 ISBN 2 5035 2427 6.

Horobin, Simon. *Chaucer's Language.* Palgrave. [2007] pp. x + 198. hb $84.95 ISBN 9 7814 0399 3557, pb $26.95 ISBN 9 7814 0399 3564.

Howes, Laura L., ed. *Place, Space, and Landscape in Medieval Narrative.* Tennessee Studies in Literature 43. UTennP. [2007] pp. xiv + 208. $43 ISBN 9 7815 7233 5868.

Kaylor, Noel Harold, and Richard Scott Nokes, eds. *Global Perspectives on Medieval English Literature, Language, and Culture.* MIP. [2007] pp. xv + 310. $45 ISBN 9 7815 8044 1209.

Krygier, Marcin, and Liliana Sikorska, eds. *To Make his Englissh Sweete upon his Tonge.* Medieval English Mirror 3. Lang. [2007] pp. 133. pb €27.70 (£20.80; $42.95) ISBN 9 7836 3156 2857.

Latham, David, ed. *Writing on the Image: Reading William Morris.* UTorP. [2007] pp. xii + 254. $50 ISBN 9 7808 0209 2472.

Leach, Elizabeth Eva. *Sung Birds: Music, Nature, and Poetry in the Later Middle Ages.* CornUP. [2007] pp. xiii + 345. $55 ISBN 9 7808 0144 4913.

Lerer, Seth. *Inventing English: A Portable History of the Language.* ColUP. [2007] pp. vii + 305. hb $24.95 ISBN 9 7802 3113 7942, ebook (price not available) ISBN 9 7802 3151 0769.

Lightsey, Scott. *Manmade Marvels in Medieval Culture and Literature.* Palgrave. [2007] pp. xv + 212. $68.95 ISBN 9 7814 0397 4419.

Lindeboom, B.W. *Venus' Owne Clerk: Chaucer's Debt to the Confessio Amantis.* Rodopi. [2007] pp. 477. €100 ($140) ISBN 9 7890 4202 1501.

Lipton, Emma. *Affections of the Mind: The Politics of Sacramental Marriage in Late Medieval English Literature.* UNDP. [2007] pp. x + 246. $32 ISBN 9 7802 6803 4054.

Lynch, Kathryn L., ed. *Dream Visions and Other Poems: Geoffrey Chaucer.* Norton. [2007] pp. xx + 396. pb $15 ISBN 9 7803 9392 5889.

Marshall, David W., ed. *Mass Market Medieval: Essays on the Middle Ages in Popular Culture.* McFarland. [2007] pp. x + 205. pb £29.95 ($35) ISBN 9 7807 8642 9226.

Masciandaro, Nicola. *The Meaning of Work in Middle English Literature.* UNDP. [2007] pp. xii + 209. $25 ISBN 9 7802 6803 4986.

McCormack Frances. *Chaucer and the Culture of Dissent.* Four Courts. [2007] pp. 252. €45 ISBN 9 7818 4682 0496.

McMullan, Gordon, and David Matthews, eds. *Reading the Medieval in Early Modern England.* CUP. [2007] pp. xiv + 287. £53 ISBN 9 7805 2186 8433.

Morgan, Gerald. *The Tragic Argument of Troilus and Criseyde*, vol. 2. Mellen. [2005] pp. 376. $119.95 (£74.95) ISBN 9 7807 7345 9366.

Muessig, Carolyn, and Ad Putter, eds. *Envisaging Heaven in the Middle Ages.* Routledge. [2007] pp. x + 258. hb £75 ISBN 9 7804 1538 3837, ebook (price not available) ISBN 9 7802 0396 6211.

Phillips, Susan E. *Transforming Talk: The Problem with Gossip in Late Medieval England.* PSUP. [2007] pp. x + 238. $45 ISBN 9 7802 7102 9948.

Pugh, Tison, and Angela Jane Weisl, eds. *Approaches to Teaching Chaucer's Troilus and Criseyde and the Shorter Poems.* MLA. [2007] pp. viii + 217. hb £45 ($37.50) ISBN 9 7808 7352 9969, pb $19.75 ISBN 9 7808 7352 9976.

Ramey, Lynn T., and Tison Pugh, eds. *Race, Class, and Gender in 'Medieval' Cinema.* Palgrave. [2007] pp. vii + 228. $69.95 ISBN 1 4039 7427 6.

Rosenthal, Joel Thomas, ed., *Essays on Medieval Childhood: Responses to Recent Debates.* Shaun Tyas. [2007] pp. 180. £24 ISBN 9 7819 0028 9788.

Rust, Martha Dana. *Imaginary Worlds in Medieval Books: Exploring the Manuscript Matrix.* Palgrave. [2007] pp. xii + 290. £40 ($74.95) ISBN 9 7814 0397 2224.

Smarr, Janet Levarie, ed. *Writers Reading Writers: Intertextual Studies in Medieval and Early Modern Literature in Honor of Robert Hollander.* UDelP. [2007] pp. 255. $51.40 ISBN 9 7808 7413 9761.

Solopova, Elizabeth, and Stuart D. Lee, eds. *Key Concepts in Medieval Literature.* Palgrave. [2007] pp. xiii + 338. pb £13.99 ($24.95) ISBN 9 7814 0399 7234.

Strohm, Paul, ed. *Middle English.* OUP. [2007] pp. 576 £93 ISBN 9 7801 9928 7666.

Summerfield, Thea, and Keith Busby, eds. *People and Texts: Relationships in Medieval Literature. Studies Presented to Erik Kooper.* Rodopi. [2007] pp. vi + 205. €44 ISBN 9 7890 4202 1457.

Thomas, Alfred. *A Blessed Shore: England and Bohemia from Chaucer to Shakespeare.* CornUP. [2007] pp. xi + 239. $45 ISBN 9 7808 0144 5682.

Turner, Marion. *Chaucerian Conflict: Languages of Antagonism in Late Fourteenth-Century London.* OUP. [2007] pp. viii + 213. £59 ISBN 9 7801 9920 7895.

Wakelin, Daniel. *Humanism, Reading, and English Literature 1430–1530.* OUP. [2007] pp. xi + 254. £56 ISBN 9 7811 9921 5881.

Williams, David. *Language Redeemed: Chaucer's Mature Poetry.* Sapientia. [2007] pp. viii + 133. $18.95 ISBN 9 7819 3258 9351.

Yeager, R.F., ed. *On John Gower: Essays at the Millennium.* SMC 46. MIP. [2007] pp. x + 241. hb $40 ISBN 9 7815 8044 0981, pb $20 ISBN 9 7815 8044 0998.

V

The Sixteenth Century: Excluding Drama after 1550

ROS KING AND JOAN FITZPATRICK

This chapter has three sections: 1. General; 2. Sidney; 3. Spenser. Section 1 is by Ros King; sections 2 and 3 are by Joan Fitzpatrick.

1. General

It is not often that the writer of this section of *Year's Work* on the 'sixteenth century excluding drama after 1560' has the opportunity to review work that includes theatre. This is not simply because the drama before 1560 is still neglected rather more than is warranted, but that despite the evident theatricality and display of the culture of the entire period, and the fact that it is now fifty years since Erving Goffman invited us to think about the ways in which theatricality participated in everyday life, the everyday in this period has seemed hard to penetrate. Eyewitness accounts are of course few and far between (although not nearly so rare as we have assumed), but we have also tended to ignore evidence that might be useful to us because so much of it is not literary in any conventional sense. Even more of a difficulty is that the documentary basis for history-writing means that scholars find themselves at a loss in knowing how to deal with gaps in that evidence. There has been a tendency to assume that if no evidence remains for an event, it cannot be talked about, which means effectively that we treat it as if it never took place. The problem with this approach is that it tends to falsify the evidence that remains, and which we do talk about. There is, in short, a lacuna in the way we customarily view and write about the period, which the books under discussion this year, in their different but mostly interdisciplinary ways, are each seeking to fill.

Charles Whitney's book *Early Responses to Renaissance Drama* for example, announces its intention to look for evidence of the drama in places where it has never been sought before, in expressions of reception found from 'commonplace book to verse to memoir to tossed-off allusion in the course of speaking and writing...as myriad-minded audiences discover the copious resources of

Year's Work in English Studies, Volume 88 (2009) © *The English Association; all rights reserved*
doi:10.1093/ywes/map014

performance or text for their diverse purposes, lessons, and interests' (p. 1). This is indeed fertile ground. A keyword search on EEBO for 'Tamburlaine' or for 'Faustus', for example, throws up hundreds of hits in dozens of works of history, religion and literature. One can only imagine how many more there might be in other works that have not yet been transcribed and which therefore cannot be included in this remarkable research tool. In both these cases, a few examples are directly related to Marlowe's plays in performance, usually in the form of an assumption that the reader will have knowledge of what those performances looked and sounded like, in order to make a comparative, usually satirical, point about something else entirely. The remainder provide us with a salutary reminder that the written drama that has generated so much modern research publication represents merely a fraction of the resonance of those two names for sixteenth-century auditors and readers. Both figures warrant biographical entries in English publications before and after Marlowe, and both are also used as types for comparison. Faustus, however, was also the name of the Manichaean philosopher magician exposed by St Augustine and the bête noire of William Fulke, a popular Calvinist preacher and vice chancellor of Cambridge when Marlowe was a student. In short, the ways in which the popular drama grew from and fed into contemporary culture and non-dramatic writing is a topic that goes far beyond traditional source study. In his section on *Dr Faustus*, Whitney, however, concentrates on an autobiography written in the mid-seventeenth century by the navigator Richard Norwood, which includes fascinating references to his time as an out-of-work apprentice in London, frequenting performances by Prince Henry's men at the Fortune in 1611. Although Whitney does not know whether Norwood ever saw or read the play, he 'could' have done so, and this experience 'could' have contributed to his readiness to explore science. He could indeed. Whitney never closes the circle of his argument, however, because of the assumptions he makes about what he repeatedly and without much examination calls the 'protestant aesthetic'. Adopting a writing style that has unfortunately become increasingly prevalent in the last few years, he makes multiple impressionistic quotations from other modern critics in a display of erudition, but falls short on any rigorous analysis of the struggles, which are everywhere reflected in print during the period, of the movement which we tend to label uniformly (and misleadingly) as 'protestantism'. Whitney's choice of examples in his chapter on *Tamburlaine* seems arbitrary, and he does not sufficiently distinguish between post-play references that must relate directly to the play and those that owe more to the historical tradition. More discussion is needed on the extent to which the later ubiquitous references to Tamburlaine's infamous colour-coded tents stem from Marlowe's play or directly from the historical sources, or the ways in which the play and the histories might reinforce each other in the public imagination. I am glad, however, to have had my attention drawn to two poems from *Wittes Pilgrimage* by John Davies of Hereford—one where he mentions Tamburlaine by name, and another in which he recounts his experience, safely leaning against a 'pillar' in the 'middle room' at the playhouse, gazing down at the representation of the rise and fall of great ones on the stage. But I would be loath to put the chapter in the hands of students. In both poems Davies celebrates his own status in the 'mean'; Whitney interprets 'mean' as lowly 'groundling' (p. 43) when the reference is clearly to that of someone secure in his middle-ranking status in the middle gallery.

Davies was in fact an enthusiastic networker, as the dedications to the king and other great ones in the prefaces to his books make clear. As Brian Vickers puts it in *Shakespeare, 'A Lover's Complaint', and John Davies of Hereford*, 'Few other poets of this period can have addressed so many poems to prominent people' (p. 34). Davies sought employment as writing master and even moral tutor to a number of aristocratic households, but Vickers is more concerned with the ways in which his work as a scribe could have brought him into contact with the greatest literary figures of the late sixteenth century—which is again why it is legitimate to review the book here. Vickers's thesis is that the long poem 'A Lover's Complaint' that appears in the 1609 edition of Shakespeare's sonnets, and which is explicitly attributed to Shakespeare in that book, was added so as to 'conveniently fill the book's eleven remaining pages' (p. 7), and that far from being a juvenile Shakespeare's attempt to imitate Spenser, as has often been assumed, the poem is in fact by Davies. Vickers adduces voluminous evidence of the poem's borrowings from Spenser, Daniel, Shakespeare and others of images and collocations of words. Perhaps more convincingly, he supplies statistical evidence on the frequency in this poem of the word 'all', which lies within the range of its usage in Davies's other longer poems, occurring 'twice as often' as in other poems more firmly attributed to Shakespeare (p. 239). Vickers has an illuminating chapter on the relationship of this poem to the genre of 'female complaint', and for me the most persuasive aspect of his argument is his consideration of the general approaches to moral problems typically displayed by the various writers under discussion. For all his linguistic borrowings, Vickers finds Davies 'normative' (pp. 104, 105, 109)—a quality likewise found in this particular poem. By contrast, Daniel's *Rosamund* 'endorses such attitudes while insisting that erring women be treated with compassion', while Shakespeare's use of the genre elsewhere 'enlarges the necessary compassion for women to a denunciation of men, who are to blame for corrupting them' (p. 117). Traditional forms do not necessarily demand traditional attitudes or responses. Vickers clearly demonstrates that whereas Davies borrows, Shakespeare transforms.

John McGavin's *Theatricality and Narrative in Medieval and early Modern Scotland* is an illuminating short study of brief moments in the cultural and political history of Scotland from the fourteenth to the early seventeenth century. It opens and closes with personal reflection on how theatre impinges on the everyday, and both recounts McGavin's own experience of being a witness to an act of violence and reflects on the processes involved in recalling and retelling such incidents. The historical witnesses to actions and events in his book are all 'at least one remove from any theatrical act; they are substitutes, allusions, reports and attempts to recreate theatricality so as to harness its power for new purposes' (p. 141). The historical events he has chosen, presumably because they are colourful enough to bear recounting now, were clearly anomalous in some way: 'Chroniclers were attracted to occasions on which the genres of public action were misapprehended, manipulated, made ambiguous, bypassed, argued over or revealingly carried through', and in this he persuasively finds evidence for a 'common drive towards theatricality' and a 'common desire' for its pleasures of display (pp. 142–3). Much of the book is devoted to a number of instances of displays of assumed, counterfeit, or contested identities recorded in legal and other public archives, and one chapter is devoted to 'the story of Skipper Lindsay, a reputed madman, who intruded his own display into the public space which a royal play was supposed to fill' (p. 85). But there are also accounts of designated shows, in particular an analysis of what McGavin calls the 'theatre of departure', the semiotics of the way in which towns bade farewell to a visiting monarch. These might be less elaborate than the shows staged to welcome a monarch (and have therefore attracted less scholarly attention), but since they 'adumbrated the final break which would come with death' they tended to be more concerned with the monarch's 'enduring reputation' (p. 64). As well as any scripted or planned ceremonies, descriptions of public acts of petition (for instance by a 'poor widow' or other type whose bills for supplying the royal retinue remained unpaid) symbolized the king's responsibility for 'good norms of behaviour and good relations with his subjects' (p. 67). We may not be able to tell whether the 'widow's' consciousness of her act and what she meant by it differed from the intention of the person who chronicled the event, but by foregrounding these acts in the non-theatrical record, McGavin has also brought new light to bear on the structure, significance and metatheatricality of plays such as Lyndsay's *Satyre of the Thrie Estaitis*.

An interdisciplinary collection of essays edited by Jayne Elisabeth Archer, Elizabeth Goldring and Sarah Knight entitled *The Progresses, Pageants and Entertainments of Queen Elizabeth I* performs the useful task of synthesizing the explosion of work in this area that has appeared in the last ten years. It had its inception in the Elizabethan Progresses Conference in Stratford-upon-Avon in 2004, and is the companion volume to the ongoing project to edit the monumental and bibliographically complex work of the printer and publisher John Nicols. Nicols's various *Progresses* (published between 1788 and 1823) have often been the starting point (and sometimes, given the intervening loss of manuscripts, the finishing point) for research in the performative culture of sixteenth-century England. The keynote chapter by Mary Hill Cole, 'Monarchy in Motion', is a synthesis of her book *The Portable Queen: Elizabeth I and the Politics of Ceremony* [1999] and a consummate demonstration of the importance of integrating literary texts and historical, particularly financial, archive material. She demonstrates that 'By going on progress with all the expense and difficulty, the Queen dodged decision, delayed commitments, and cultivated her authority through the disorder of travel' (p. 45). Felicity Heal in 'Giving and Receiving on Royal Progress' explores the gift culture that progresses represent, while several essays draw out the ways in which the body of the queen (with all that that concept represents in terms of political symbol and actual virginity) was implanted and integrated on the land through which she passed. In wanting to stress Cole's thesis of movement, Archer and Knight (in 'Elizabetha Triumphans') perhaps go a little far in reading the representation of Elizabeth in the famous Ditchley portrait as hovering 'on pointed, dancing toes, over the land' (p. 7). Other commentators have seen her firmly planted in Sir Henry Lee's homeland area in the heart of Britain, with the pointy feet being perhaps a question of perspective. Patrick Collinson ('Pulling the Strings: Religion and Politics in the Progress of 1578') demonstrates that the politics of progress itself demonstrate the difficulty of establishing a single point of view concerning the nature of Elizabethan government: 'did the Queen take her court and Council to East Anglia [in 1578] or did they take her?' (p. 125). Coming down on the side of the Council, he observes that this was still a 'region of delicate instability': 'The Queen was lodged, it might have seemed indiscriminately, in the houses of Protestants, Catholics, and crypto-Catholics. But that did not mean that her government intended to be religiously neutral: quite the opposite' (p. 126). His analysis of various documentary witnesses to the discovery of an image of the Virgin in the barn at Euston Hall and its burning in front of the queen at the end of a set of 'country dances' is not dissimilar to John McGavin's approach to similar events in Scotland (above). Both he and Elizabeth Heale ('Contesting Terms: Loyal Catholicism and Lord Montague's Entertainment at Cowdray, 1591') ask whether this real-life event was in fact staged for the queen's benefit and evidence of a Privy Council plot hatched in London (pp. 130, 191). David Bergeron's account of the Norwich entertainments on that same progress ('The "I" of the Beholder: Thomas Churchyard and the 1578 Norwich Pageant') is a more traditionally literary analysis of two published accounts—Churchyard's *A Discourse of the Queenes Maiesties entertainment in Suffolk and Norfolk* and Bernard Garter's *The Ioyfull Receyuing of the Queenes most excellent Maiestie into hir Highness Citie of Norwich*, both published by Henrie Bynneman in 1578. Bergeron is interested in the authorial and authoritative 'I' of Churchyard's account of his activities as author, actor and presenter, and also makes a useful observation on the typographical performativity of Churchyard's printed text. Julian Pooley, in 'A Pioneer of Renaissance Scholarship', closes the book with a fascinating account of Nicols's working practices. Nicols regularly posted notices in his publication, the *Gentleman's Magazine*, under a variety of aliases, both to recruit correspondents with knowledge of or access to original documents from amongst the readership, and to review the results. His ultra-quick turnaround time, the resulting unreliability in both transcription and presentation, and his practice of issuing material in separate sequences mean that his volumes, though a godsend to modern researchers, are also something of a nightmare. The problem is demonstrated, although not consistently remarked upon in this volume. For instance, Cole, citing Nicols's transcription of Anthony à Wood, states unbelievably that it was the Christ Church stage that collapsed in 1566 killing three Oxford residents (p. 30). Later in the volume, Siobhan Keenan ('Spectator and Spectacle: Royal Entertainments at the Universities in the 1560s') correctly states that it was the staircase wall that did the damage, the queen sending out to see if any help could be offered, although none of this much delayed the performance. The plays performed during that progress have now been treated on a couple of occasions with some disagreements as to the significance of the evidence, but Keenan, while citing these works, does not explore their differences.

As the books reviewed here this year demonstrate, anyone who works on historical performance, whether in life or in the theatre, is aware of the problems of piecing together an idea of what happened, and how it might have been perceived at the time from the variety of incomplete surviving evidence: the documentation in account books of expenditure on props or the material for costumes; the occasional literary text or description of proceedings; the form of the buildings or spaces in which such events took place; the cultural and political context. Sometimes it is a matter of inferring the missing evidence from the perceived effect of the event on other events or writings. The process involved for the literary-historical critic is not unlike that of the archaeologist, although this is not often acknowledged. Philip Schwyzer's *Archaeologies of English Renaissance Literature* tackles this similarity head on, before exploring a number of instances of medieval and early modern archaeological encounters with the Roman, Saxon and, more recently, Roman Catholic past. Schwyzer's introduction picks out the words commonly used to describe the act of literary criticism: 'We *dig down* though textual *levels* or *layers* to *excavate* the *subtext* or *unearth* hidden meanings', pointing out that these are all examples of '*buried metaphors*' (p. 6; his emphases), although the treasure-hunting implication of meaning-finding is a sin to which no modern archaeologist or critic will want to admit. The recurring theme is Sir Mortimer Wheeler's: 'the archaeological excavator is not digging up *things*, he is digging up *people*' (quoted p. 20). It is the traces of people too that we find in literary texts, but it is the act of exhumation that enthrals Schwyzer. Successive chapters deal with the medieval poem *St Erkenwald* about the Anglo-Saxon bishop's baptism through a single tear of the miraculously preserved body of an ancient British lawgiver, which had been found while digging the foundations of St Paul's; the ruins of monastic buildings encountered in Elizabethan poetry; Irish rebels presented in Spenser's *Faerie Queene* as if rising from bogs and caves as troops of the undead; fear of the charnel house in both Shakespeare's works and his infamous tomb inscription; and the gruesome mysticism associated with mummies and mummy-eating in a variety of early seventeenth-century literature. In many respects this is an attempt to put flesh, so to speak, on Stephen Greenblatt's contention that his *Will in the World* is an attempt to 'speak with the dead'. Provided one can stomach the similarly groan-inducing puns (the chapter headings 'Charnel Knowledge' and 'Readers of the Lost Urns' for instance), this is a very provocative and stimulating book, which has interesting things to say about the ways in which many of the texts under discussion participate in a form of 'colonial archaeology' in their representations of the past. Just as the twelfth-century discovery of bodies taken to be King Arthur and Queen Guinevere at Glastonbury may have been a useful tool to the English in demonstrating the very deadness of British Arthur, so Thomas Browne's almost deliberate refusal to see the cremated remains buried in urns near Walsingham as Anglo-Saxon is an attempt to prevent these remains as being hailed as the direct ancestors of modern inhabitants of Norfolk, and therefore 'safe from the proprietary claims of a single ethnic group' (p. 190).

Those of us who want to imagine the culture of the first half of the sixteenth century in terms of what people looked like will be grateful for Maria Hayward's magnificent *Dress at the Court of King Henry VIII*. Textiles and clothing have traditionally been regarded as of marginal and/or female interest. But when we are dealing with an age when dress was not just conspicuous consumption or even royal magnificence, but an expression of political, religious and social allegiances, and of moral values, this is another lacuna in scholarship. Unless too we realize that clothing was regularly given in recompense or in lieu of payment for services rendered, as a means of ensuring adequate display for diplomats travelling abroad, or as a mark of especial favour to courtiers and visiting foreigners alike, we cannot begin to understand the political and cultural life of the sixteenth century. Hayward presents her project as a modest homage to Janet Arnold's *Queen Elizabeth's Wardrobe Unlock'd* (Leeds [1988]), and as an edition of 'The Wardrobe Book of the Wardrobe of the Robes' and an 'Inventory', both prepared by James Worsley, yeoman of the robes, in 1516 and 1521 respectively, but this does not do justice to the results. The bulk of this lavishly illustrated volume is devoted to Hayward's analysis of (among other things) the function of the great wardrobe, the various divisions of the king's household and other royal households, the court, the creation of knights, the ritual year and life events from christening, via coronation, to funeral. Her research correlates analysis of the financial records with evidence from portraiture, tied in with expert understanding of the construction of the few extant garments. With its indexes to the wardrobe accounts listing garment types, makers, objects and personnel, this is a tremendous resource for researchers in many fields, as well as the interested general reader, who may note, for example, amongst the myriad items of cloth of gold and of silver, the expenditure of 4*s.* on a pair of football shoes. The publishers too must be commended for the quality of production and the extensive illustration.

Finally this year comes a book which actively seeks to both enhance and complicate the way we view the early modern period. *Vanities of the Eye: Vision in Early Modern European Culture*, by Stuart Clark, starts by defining the physiology of sight as it was understood in the light of classical natural philosophy, and goes on to explore changing notions of the hierarchy of the senses and of the fallibility of the eyes as that physiology rubbed up against ideas of religious reformation, scepticism, magic and demonology. He then discusses ideas about imagination or fantasy and early understanding of the working of the brain, before devoting a chapter to 'prestiges' or magic illusion. Here, he includes the use of proportion in the construction of perspective, and the concomitant paradox that 'For perspective to be what its early users took it to be means paying attention to their reliance on the fallibility of the eyes', since of course, in the words of the 'fifteenth-century sculptor and architect Antonio Filarete . . . "it shows you a thing that is not" ' (p. 86). Clark stresses, however, 'that the endless statements—clichés, in effect—about perspective tricking the eyes need not be read literally but rather as expressions of a sentiment about perception itself' (p. 90). Subsequent chapters are headed 'Glamours: Demons and Virtual Worlds', 'Images', 'Apparitions', 'Sights' (which explores 'King Macbeth' in the light of the story of 'King Saul'), 'Seemings', 'Dreams' and 'Signs'. The apparent similarity of many of these terms, the overwhelming detail culled from a bewildering range of historical sources which are not treated chronologically or systematically does, however, add to a sense of 'equivocation', 'confusion and circularity' (p. 255) in the argument as well as in the subject matter. On page 350, for instance, we are told that 'To depend on sense impressions was thus to be like the inhabitants of Plato's cave, condemned to perceive only shadows' and may feel no further forward than we were on page 21, where 'The figure of Plato loomed especially large' in the 'doubts and hesitations of the ancients regarding the errors and uncertainties of sensory perception'. There is a great deal of material in this book, but it is not nearly as 'accessible' as it claims on the cover.

2. Sidney

A number of valuable journal articles on Sidney appeared this year, although there were fewer than in previous years and there were no monographs to consider. Additionally, this year's *Sidney Journal* was devoted entirely to Philip's younger brother, Robert Sidney, and so will not be discussed in this review.

In an original and convincing article, Garrett A. Sullivan traces the manner in which Sidney associates sleep with the passions and transformation in *The Old Arcadia* ('Romance, Sleep, and the Passions in Sir Philip Sidney's *The Old Arcadia*', *ELH* 74[2007] 735–57). He compares Sidney's text with Plato's *Republic*, noting that 'Many of *The Republic*'s themes—sleep, transformation, erotic desire, government of both self and polity, and indeed tyranny—are crucial for *The Old Arcadia*' (pp. 738–9). In both texts training the body is inseparable from training the mind: it is when one is asleep that the passions might well gain control over the body, but this will only occur in those whose waking behaviour is immoderate. Two characters who sleep in Sidney's romance, Pyrocles and Basilius, are transformed, and this transformation is associated with geographical change, which Sullivan argues is typical of Sidney's text, creating what Sullivan terms 'a landscape of the passions' (p. 740). From the outset of *The Old Arcadia* Sidney emphasizes the significance of bodily self-regulation. Sullivan cites early modern dietaries by Andrew Boorde, Thomas Cogan and William Bullein, all of which contain warnings against immoderate sleep, specifically midday sleep: the damage caused by immoderate sleep 'is not merely physical, for such sleep is also associated with various forms of sinful, hedonistic behavior, including lust and gluttony' (p. 741). The association of sleep with sin is hinted at in Sidney's representation of Dametas, a sloth-like figure who sleeps on his stomach, a posture considered harmful by the early moderns. Sullivan contends that the genre of romance 'flourishes where bodies succumb both to their (sometimes enchanted) environments and to corrupting pleasures or habits—lust, intoxication, indolence, immoderate sleep' (p. 746). Both Sleep and desire are powerful threats to identity, as in the case of Verdant in Book II of *The Faerie Queene*, who lies slumbering with his discarded armour nearby. The most significant example of sleep in *The Old Arcadia* is that induced by Basilius's consumption of a magical drink. His greedy consumption indicates moral weakness but he is, upon awaking, a wise ruler and thus a powerful example of the transformative power of sleep.

Tracey Sedinger builds upon the work of recent historians who have indicated that for the early moderns republicanism or a mixed constitution, one that would keep the monarch in check, was considered a viable form of government ('Sidney's *New Arcadia* and the Decay of Protestant Republicanism', *SEL* 47[2007] 57–77). The Ciceronian humanism that dominated Tudor humanist political discourse reinforced the acceptability of an advisory body that was compatible with monarchy, specifically a monarchical republic. A Protestantism that perceived England and the monarch as under constant threat only added to the sense that the Privy Council might be endowed with the Crown's authority. Sedinger claims that Philip Sidney's conflicts with the queen—disagreements that centred on his disapproval of her proposed marriage to d'Anjou and her refusal to aid the Protestant rebels in the Netherlands, and thus his military career—led him to consider what a good citizen can do when their monarch refuses to follow good counsel. By examining key episodes from Sidney's *New Arcadia*, specifically the addition of the helots' revolt, Sedinger traces evidence of a shift in Sidney's attitude towards counsel in the poem's revised version. The *Old Arcadia*, suggests Sedinger, is an effort to counsel, a kind of position paper and literary intervention into political debates over England's role in the Netherlands. In the *New Arcadia* the narrator is less intrusive and it becomes a multivocal piece where disengagement or rebellion is the only recourse left to a people who feel that they have no voice.

Staying with the political ramifications of Sidney's *Arcadia*, Richard Wood proposes that the *New Arcadia* is closer to the spirit of Philip Sidney's political philosophy than its predecessor, the *Old Arcadia* ('The Representing of so Strange a Power in Love: Philip Sidney's Legacy of Anti-Factionalism', *EMLS* 13:ii[2007] 1–21). Wood notes that Sidney's early editor, Fulke Greville, chose to connect the *Arcadia* with the Essex circle, a prominent faction of the 1590s. Where this emphasized the divisiveness of the romance, as Joel Davis observed, Mary Sidney based her later edition of the text on an anti-factionalist agenda. Wood usefully outlines the distinctions between the two editions and, citing Davis, notes that Greville's editorial practices served to highlight similarities between himself and Sidney, thus casting the poet as a courtier-soldier who rejects the effeminacy of pastoralism for a stoic moral and political philosophy. Via detailed reference to the text Wood suggests that Philip would have been more sympathetic to Mary's focus on factionalism as corruptive and her positioning of its female characters at the very heart of a conciliatory trajectory.

An essay from this year's *Spenser Studies* is worth mentioning here. Rebeca Helfer provides a welcome analysis of Spenser's rather neglected poem *The Ruines of Time*, specifically in its memorial to Philip Sidney ('Remembering Sidney, Remembering Spenser: The Art of Memory and *The Ruines of Time*', *SSt* 22[2007] 127–52). She traces a dialogue within Spenser's work about Cicero's art of memory 'that reforms fictions of permanence through a narrative of change, contingency, and continuity' and that venerates Sidney as 'the epitome of deathless poetry' (p. 129). Poetry as the art of memory, via the immortal poet, is reinforced by *The Ruines of Time*, which looks back to Sidney's *Defense of Poetry*, a work that itself looks back to *The Shepheardes*

Calender. The title of Spenser's later poem locates the work within time and history and thus creates what Helfer terms 'a memory theatre' for Sidney and England 'which explores how poetry builds and rebuilds immortality from and within the ruins of time' (p. 148).

There were a few essays on Sidney's sonnet sequence. Focusing on sonnets by Petrarch, Sidney and Spenser, Danijela Kambasković-Sawers argues that the 'sequentiality' of the sonnet sequence is often neglected by critics, and detects in this sequentiality a precursor of the novel form (' "Never was I the golden cloud": Ovidian Myth, Ambiguous Speaker and the Narrative in the Sonnet Sequences by Petrarch, Sidney and Spenser', *RS* 21[2007] 637–61). These sonneteers share 'the development of a fictive first-person narrative voice based on the self' (p. 637) and this voice is ambiguous. All three sonneteers are, argues Kambasković-Sawers, influenced by Ovid's myths. The first part of the essay is concerned with Petrarch's *Il Canzoniere*, part II with Sidney's *Astrophil and Stella* and part III with Spenser's *Amoretti*. In the section on Sidney, Kambasković-Sawers argues that Sidney uses Petrarchan ambiguous first-person fictionalization via revised Ovidian myth, introspection and societal observation in order to create meanings that 'temper and cancel each other' (p. 648). The sequence thus reveals to the reader Astrophil's 'emotional and authorial ambivalence' (p. 649) whereby shifting meanings interrogate gender roles and ethical and social concerns.

In a rather short piece, Maura Grace Harrington provides a close reading of Sonnet 59 from Sidney's *Astrophil and Stella*, where the speaker is dismayed that Stella should demonstrate more affection for her dog than for him ('Astrophil the Super Dog: Sidney's *Astrophil and Stella*', *Expl* 65[2007] 130–3). As an demonstration of how to read a sonnet this is a readable and engaging essay, with attention given to Sidney's use of alliteration, imagery and so on, but it amounts to little more than might be expected from a good undergraduate essay. There is no engagement with any criticism on the sonnet form, Sidney's engagement with it, or the use of animals in literature.

This year's *Notes and Queries* saw only one piece on Sidney (Guillaume Coatalen 'Shakespeare, Sidney and Du Bellay's Winters', *N&Q* 54[2007] 265). Noting that Sonnet 69 from Sidney's *Astrophil and Stella* ('Gone is the winter of my misery / My spring appears') is often considered a source for the opening lines of Shakespeare's *Richard III* ('Now is the winter of our discontent / Made glorious summer'), Coatalen suggests that both are derived from works by Du Bellay, a poet with whom Sidney, and perhaps Shakespeare also, was familiar.

3. Spenser

Two monographs published this year were devoted entirely to Spenser, with two others including one or more chapters on his work. Andrew Zurcher's *Spenser's Legal Language: Law and Poetry in Early Modern England* is a welcome study that is attentive to not only Spenser's understanding of legal process but also his linguistic dexterity and curiosity. In chapter 1, which forms the introduction to his book, Zurcher argues that although early modern poets, including Spenser, expected their readers to be alert to the linguistic elements in their verse and regarded this as key to interpretation, editions of Spenser and critical commentary on his works do not return the compliment. Chapter 2, ' "Pleasing Analysis": Renaissance Hermeneutics, Poetry, and the Law', explores the reading practices into which Spenser's poetry was first received and relates Spenser's own theory of interpretation to that evident in early modern English legal writing and practice, for example his use of precedent, authority and so on. In chapter 3, 'Results: A Survey of Spenser's Legal Diction', Zurcher provides an overview of Spenser's use of legal diction in all his writings, with words divided into subdivisions that discuss legal topics such as 'Feudal Law, Land Tenure, and Real Property', 'Contract, Covenant, and Assumpsit', 'Justice, Mercy, Equity, and Jurisdiction'. This important chapter also includes three lists: the first compares the number of times selected legal terms occur in Spenser, Chaucer, Sidney, Harington, and Fairfax; the next two reveal legal diction shared by *The Faerie Queene* and *A View of the Present State of Ireland* (which might prove useful in studies of authorial attribution) and legal diction shared by Spenser's autograph diplomatic letters and *The Faerie Queene*. It strikes this reviewer that this chapter might usefully be expanded into a dictionary of Spenser's legal language or the legal language used by Spenser and the others considered in this chapter, where the many words listed might be given a fuller treatment than is possible in a monograph of this kind (this is not a criticism of Zurcher, who notes in his introduction that his work is 'an avowedly preliminary' (p. 9) consideration of Spenser's language, but a suggestion for how this valuable study might be expanded upon). The next four chapters use the evidence gathered in chapter 3 to provide thorough readings of the second half of *The Faerie Queene*: chapter 5 is entitled 'Justice, Equity and Mercy in the Legend of Artegall'; chapter 6, 'Courtesy and Prerogative in the Legend of Sir Calidore'; and chapter 7 'The Composition of the Work: Managing Power in the Two Cantos of Mutabilitie'. The study also includes a chapter tracing the influence of Spenser's *Amoretti* and *Epithalamion*, 'Lyric Opposition in Spenser, Shakespeare, and Donne', in which Zurcher argues that all three authors were interested in the relation between lyric poetry and contemporary law, legal theory and legal readers. A minor criticism from this reviewer is that Zurcher includes a select bibliography when a fuller one would have been welcome.

Much has already been written about Ireland as a context for the writings of Edmund Spenser and although interest in the topic has waned, perhaps precisely because so much has been written, it has not altogether disappeared. Thomas Herron's monograph on the subject, *Spenser's Irish Work: Poetry Plantation and Colonial Reformation*, provides commentary on those aspects of Spenser's Irish context that have not yet been discussed at great length. The study is divided into three parts. Part I considers the subject of colonizing Ireland in English writings, position papers as well as poetry. In chapter 3 Herron considers the impact of various colonial treatises, by Edward Walshe, Thomas Smith and Richard Robinson, tracing their rhetorical strategies, with appeals to Roman imperial precedent from Walshe, the first direct appeal to enterprise and colonizing as a business venture from Smith and the use of biblical providential language from Robinson. In chapter 4 Herron's focus is the influence Spenser's writings had on his fellow planters who had poetic and political aspirations, specifically Ralph Birkenshaw and Parr Lane, two figures who have been hitherto neglected by Spenserians. In part II of the study Herron explores the influence of Virgil's *Georgics* on Book I of *The Faerie Queene* and how this text, and English translations of it, shaped Spenser's view of the English colonist as heroic husbandman. Part III identifies an Irish context for some of the characters that populate Spenser's epic, for example the villainous Souldan who appears in Book V and who is usually read as representing the might of Spain, but who Herron argues was likely inspired by a legend closer to home: that of the ancient Irish hero Cúchullain. Herron's study is alert to the work that has gone before him, and indeed chapter 1 is a detailed survey of the criticism on Spenser and Ireland that has preceded this study. But it is more than a mere survey since Herron engages with the difficult questions critics have posed about Spenser's political views, his religion and the degree to which he felt alienated in Ireland. This last point is an important one for Herron, who argues that previous critics have not recognized the degree to which Spenser set an agenda for the New English around him in Ireland and those further afield who supported the colonial project.

In a study focusing on Spenser and others, *Tradition and Subversion in Renaissance Literature*, Murray Roston argues that postmodern critics have been too negative in their view that there is an undecidability at the core of every text. The exception to such negativity, argues Roston, is Mikhail Bakhtin, who in his theory of the dialogic imagination 'defines multiplicity not as a disqualification but as a positive value' (p. x). Yet, as Roston notes, Bakhtin allows this only for the novel, arguing that it reveals two primary forces, the 'centripetal', which reinforces traditional linguistic and cultural patterns, and the 'centrifugal', which challenges or subverts them. Bakhtin is less positive in his view of poetry, the epic and drama. For Bakhtin poetry is univocal because the poet is immersed in his or her own language; the epic is so traditional a form that it does not allow for open-endedness; and drama, especially tragedy, is centripetal, underlining the dominant contemporary ideology. Roston's study presents a powerful argument against such views which, unfortunately, are all too common in some university English departments, where students are still encouraged to believe, for example, that the dramatic depiction of one bad marriage is typical of its age. Chapters 1 and 2 are devoted to Shakespeare's plays, *The Merchant of Venice* and *Hamlet* respectively. Chapter 4 deals with Jonson's *Volpone* and chapter 5 with Donne's religious verse. It is chapter 3, entitled 'Spenser and the Pagan Gods', that will be of most interest to Spenserians. In it Roston argues that, despite efforts by critics to account for numerous religious references in *The Faerie Queene*, Spenser's biblical references are 'meager' (p. 88), whereas there are numerous and overt allusions to classical sources. Unlike many of his contemporaries Spenser did not use classical allusions to present Christian ideas, ideas that were considered vaguely apparent to the pagan unbelievers, nor did he invoke Old Testament figures as 'models for contemporary Protestant behavior' (p. 108). His epic has a religious purpose and he makes use of pagan mythology throughout but, and this is Roston's main point, 'there is no attempt to merge those disparate elements' (p. 132). The reason for this, Roston claims, lies in Spenser's divergence from the Catholic notion that observation could provide the observer with truths, as is clear from Chaucer's habit of indicating character via mode of dress. Royston suggests that, for Spenser, wariness and suspicion replace mere observation. Spenser's refusal to merge the disparate elements of his poem is an example of 'intertextuality', the implanting of one text within another, and, argues Roston, it is this hybrid form that makes Spenser's poetry both rich and unique. This is a well-written, clearly argued and admirably researched study that should appeal to all early modern scholars. The only minor criticism from this reviewer is that a list of all the works cited rather than bibliographical endnotes and a selected bibliography would have been welcome.

The topic of Christopher Tilmouth's monograph *Passion's Triumph over Reason: A History of the Moral Imagination from Spenser to Rochester* is the passions and governance over them, specifically literary constructions of self-control and the philosophical and religious ideas that informed this subject between 1580 and 1680. The book begins with a useful survey tracing classical, religious and ethical traditions that informed early modern views about the passions and self-governance: those offered by Socrates and the Stoics, various forms of Aristotelianism, and Calvinism. Chapter 2 narrows the focus to Spenser's *Faerie Queene*. The first section considers the depiction of carnality in the poem, beginning with Redcrosse and his abandonment of Una, which triggers his 'complicity with fleshliness' via Duessa (p. 39). Tilmouth traces examples from the poem where Spenser shows 'a stabilizing distinction' (p.40) between lust and chaste love, for example in the Garden of Adonis episode, but elsewhere the distinction 'proves fractious' (p. 41), as when Amoret, who has been rescued by Chastity, is captured by Lust. Tilmouth argues that in the *Faerie Queene* the passions are out of control and the negative effects of them are typified not only in lust but also in pity and anger. Perhaps not surprisingly for a book focusing on the passions, Tilmouth moves on to the depiction of temperance in Book II of the *Faerie Queene* in the second section of this chapter. He argues that Spenser here presents 'a constant flexing of reason in opposition to incessantly rebellious passions' (p. 52), and traces a causal relationship between incontinence and intemperance. Tilmouth also traces Guyon's association with shame, a condition that encourages virtue even though it is not a virtue itself, and concludes that Spenser offers the reader 'what is primarily a humanist and rationalist vision of self-governance' (p. 72) even though his heroes sometimes require the support of grace, an element of the poem that is Calvinist. Subsequent chapters include studies of *Hamlet*, Renaissance tragedy, Augustinian and Aristotelian influences from Herbert to Milton, Hobbes, the Restoration and libertinism, and Rochester.

This year's *ELR* produced a number of excellent essays on Spenser. The dangers of monarchical absolutism that Tracey Sedinger considered in 'Sidney's *New Arcadia* and the Decay of Protestant Republicanism' (*SEL* 47[2007] 57–77), discussed in the section above on Sidney, are also at the core of Melissa E. Sanchez's essay, which considers Book IV of *The Faerie Queene* via Book III ('Fantasies of Friendship in *The Faerie Queene*, Book IV', *ELR* 37[2007] 250–73). Sanchez argues that chastity, a virtue applicable to both men and women, was considered an essential attribute by classical and Renaissance thinkers, who equated sexual licence with imperial tyranny. The altruism that is involved in controlling one's erotic desires is, argues Sanchez, crucial to the friendship of Book IV, which Spenser (following Aristotle, Cicero and Thomas Elyot) depicts as a model of political allegiance based on love. Sanchez notes that although critics have tended to examine gender in Spenser's poem, they have overlooked 'the extent to which female characters . . . represent not only actual women but also political subjects' (p. 252), which allows Spenser to consider issues such as hierarchy and consent in the context of debates surrounding the relationship between monarch and subject. Thomas Elyot, amongst others, described the proper relation between ruler and ruled as a union with the ruler's will curbed by council. Near the beginning of Elizabeth I's reign John Alymer attempted to assuage concerns over a female monarch by reference to the checks and balances of mixed polity, which he, like others, compared to marriage. The second half of Elizabeth's reign saw a move towards what her critics regarded as an absolutist sovereignty and away from a mixed polity based on council and consent. Amongst those alarmed by this development were the Sidney–Essex circle, of whom Spenser was a member, who feared for the future of the nobility and Protestantism. Sanchez argues convincingly that the 1596 *Faerie Queene* (containing Books IV, V and VI and the incomplete Book VII) 'mourns the not so distant past' (p. 255) when those Spenser supported at court could inform policy. For Sanchez, distinctions between the 1590 and 1596 endings for Book III are telling: where in the former Scudamour and Amoret merge into a hermaphrodite figure 'of mutual desire and devotion' (p. 256) this is replaced by Scudamour's suspicion and despair and the continued misery of Amoret. Instead of the union there is a series of erotic tests culminating in the flashback to a rape, which, Sanchez argues, shows 'parity and consent' replaced with 'hierarchy and conquest' (p. 257). The friendship Amoret and Scudamour apparently exemplify may be no more than a fantasy, with Amoret complicit in her own abuse. Sanchez suggests that, for Spenser, Amoret represents the people who have allowed themselves to become the victims of tyranny. In Busirane's masque, Amoret is similarly a passive object and the masque typifies the idolatry and delusion on which tyranny depends.

Wendy Beth Hyman explores the critical crux that is the Bower of Bliss episode from Book II of *The Faerie Queene* ('Seizing Flowers in Spenser's Bower and Garden', *ELR* 37[2007] 193–214). As Hyman rightly notes, the climactic lyric in the Bower of Bliss episode (beginning 'Gather the Rose of loue, whilest yet is time, / Whilest louing thou mayest loued be with equall crime') has been neglected by critics. Hyman is interested in the discrepancy between the lyric's urge to 'seize the day', what she terms a '*carpe diem* moment' (p. 194), and the Bower as a never-changing place without the presence of decay. She reads this moment as an important link between Books II and III because the problems of erotic desire evident in the Bower are not eradicated by Guyon but recur in the Garden of Adonis. Hyman considers two other episodes in Book II, which she argues prefigure what occurs in the Bower of Bliss: the moment when Cymochles confronts Phaedria in canto vi and the description of the Porter at the entrance to the Bower of Bliss.

It is ironic that the flowers should encourage Cymochles to cease his toil since Phaedria 'has expended great effort to display a spectacle of false ease' (p. 198); so, far from encouraging Cymochles to relax, this floral display should provoke him to be even more alert. As in the Bower of Bliss episode, there is 'an association between lyric and flowers, and the proximity of both of these to the threat of entrapment and even death' (p. 198). So too the Porter, Agdistes, is decked with flowers that symbolize concupiscence. The *carpe diem*-themed song in the Bower of Bliss is the final of three 'dangerous and misleading songs' that occur in canto xii. The Bower of Bliss is three times compared to Eden and the narrator is apparently unequivocal in his praise for it, yet the flowers are referred to as corruptive in their abundance. As Hyman points out, there is no reason why Guyon should be told to 'seize the day' because there is no decay in the Bower, but that he does so suggests that it is he who introduces death into the Bower and thus 'acts not as an exemplar of Temperance, but of Time' (p. 203). In destroying the Bower Guyon unwittingly becomes an agent of the materialism he abhors, which Hyman reads as a kind of rape: he literally 'deflowers' the Bower. The episode suggests the difficult balance to be struck between action, not least the action of the quest, and deliberation, when a thoughtful appraisal of the situation is called for. The Garden of Adonis in Book III is apparently sanctified, but there are striking similarities between it and the Bower of Bliss, specifically in the depiction of Adonis, that complicate any simplistic dichotomizing.

Another difficult episode from Book II of *The Faerie Queene* is the focus of Christopher Bond's essay: Guyon's visit to the House of Mammon ('Medieval Harrowings of Hell and Spenser's House of Mammon', *ELR* 37[2007] 175–92). Bond builds upon the notion that Guyon's descent into Mammon's cave is analogous to Christ's Harrowing of Hell and argues that its debt to a number of medieval sources provides real insight into Spenser's theology and his attitude towards his literary predecessors. Bond focuses specifically on Langland's *Vision of Piers Plowman* (*c*.1365–86) and the mystery cycles. As Bond notes, critics have tended to focus on connections between Langland's proto-Protestant allegory and Book I of *The Faerie Queene*, which is centred on Holiness. Yet Langland's work includes a lengthy account of Christ's Harrowing of Hell, based on a seventh-century Latin apocryphal book of the Bible, the Gospel of Nicodemus, and its thirteenth-century Middle English translation. It is already accepted that Spenser knew Langland, but here Bond makes a case for his familiarity also with the mystery cycles, despite their official suppression. Spenser could have seen these plays as a child or young man, and they formed an important part of the English cultural memory. It is therefore likely, argues Bond, that Spenser was indebted to three of the four mystery cycles that tell the story of Christ's Harrowing and are, in turn, indebted to the seventh-century work and, in at least one case, probably also Langland. One similarity between Spenser and his sources is the conception of Christ as a knight who does battle with the forces of the underworld, but the most important similarity, argues Bond, is that each of two figures (Guyon and Mammon/Satan and Christ) 'believes he knows his own powers and tries to assess the powers of his opponent, and each attempts to outwit the other' (pp. 180–1). Critics usually read Guyon as over-confident and thus deserving of his physical collapse but, notes Bond, they tend to ignore Mammon's point of view; his arrogance in his belief that he can entrap Guyon; and, crucially, the humour of the episode, which Bond suggests is taken directly from Spenser's sources. Guyon's humanity makes him vulnerable to Mammon, but it also empowers him and, as in the sources with Satan and Christ, Mammon's confidence is undermined and he is outwitted by Guyon. Bond concludes that Spenser's use of his sources in this episode reveals that he was not averse to combining low humour with high theology even when the episode concerned was deemed a 'Popish fiction' (p. 191) by a number of his Protestant contemporaries. It also reveals Spenser's belief that human nature, imbued with the spirit of Christ, might contribute to its own redemption.

Staying with the influence of older writings on Spenser, William Kuskin traces what he terms 'a textual culture of contingency' (p. 11) whereby sixteenth-century works owe a debt to fifteenth-century literary culture, a debt usually disavowed by critics who claim for sixteenth-century writers a material and intellectual break with the past ('"The loadstarre of the English language": Spenser's *Shepheardes Calender* and the Construction of Modernity', *TC* 2:ii[2007] 9–33). Reading the prefaces to Spenser's *Shepheardes Calender* [1579] and Thomas Speght's *Works of Chaucer* [1598] against John Lydgate's *Fall of Princes*, Kuskin argues that authority is presented via literary precedent. In *The Shepheardes Calender* E.K. cites Lydgate, a poet who is keen to underline his links with the literary past and who writes in a distinctly Chaucerian style. In Speght's edition of Chaucer the reader is offered not only Chaucer's works but those of other fifteenth-century poets, Speght's own work and that of other sixteenth-century writers. As Kuskin points out, literary history does not develop in a linear fashion but, rather, emerges from the past by engaging with it.

Kreg Segall suggests that in Spenser's *Shepheardes Calendar* a dominant theme is anxiety over the meaning of the poet ('Skeltonic Anxiety and Rumination in *The Shepheardes Calender*', *SEL* 47[2007] 29–56). Although critics have considered what Segall terms 'the nature of Colin's fractured self' (p. 29), by reference to Spenser's shifting relationship to Virgil and debates surrounding the pastoral and age versus youth, Segall traces the poet's identity via comparison with John Skelton, another 'equally anxious self-created poet' (p. 29). The poet as a marginal figure is a concern of both Skelton and Spenser, and of the pastoral genre. Segall argues that both poets create poetic figures onto which they can project, or in which they can locate, their own problematic selves within their own poetry. This explains Spenser's affinity with Skelton and his 'Collyn Cloute', from whom Spenser's poetic figure derives. Segall traces the problems faced by Skelton and Spenser in trying to accommodate the public and private aspects of the role of poet since both 'alternately seek to embrace and to break free of the "poetic vocation" and so do their author figures' (p. 37). Spenser's debt to Skelton is to represent the poet figure within a fractured and multivocal text. Segall traces Colin's development throughout the poem: he seems to become disgusted with himself as a character in January; is absent in October, April and August; performs for payment in November, and finally, his poetic voice is strongest in December, just before it is silenced.

James Holstun concentrates on John Heywood's interlude *Of Gentylnes and Nobylyte* (*c.*1525) and the episode from *Faerie Queene* V.ii, featuring Artegall and the giant ('The Giant's Faction: Spenser, Heywood and the Mid-Tudor Crisis', *JMEMS* 37[2007] 335–71). Holstun is interested in what these texts can tell us about the estates debate, 'a literary encounter between nobility, clergy, and commoners aimed at establishing the proper place and function of each' (p. 335). He argues convincingly that Spenser's poem in general reveals his desire to end debate, which is evident in his knights answering any debate, metaphorical or verbal, 'with literal assault and battery' (p. 337), thus invoking the word's origins in *battere*, 'to beat, knock'. Indeed the debates, by which individuals test institutions, are replaced by trials, where the opposite is the case. Holstun argues that the episode featuring Munera and Pollente in Book V of *The Faerie Queene* informs the subsequent one featuring Artegall and the Giant. Munera suggests the wealth of the church, and Pollente that of the secular power of the state, specifically poll tax and decapitation; the death of the tyrant and his daughter evokes the mid-Tudor commonwealth tradition with its sympathy for the poor and attacks on those who oppress them. The spirit of this episode is contradicted by the next episode, where the people denounce their oppressors in a gathering that resembles the Irish and ancient English folk motes. Artegall debates with the Giant, but the arguments of the former prove contradictory and their debate is ended by a literal attack upon the Giant by Talus. The people defended indirectly in the Pollente and Munera episode are conveniently turned into a rebellious rout and 'can be killed with heroic good conscience' (p. 343) since their desire to hold on to some of their wealth, via the Giant, has become a lust for riches.

In an important contribution to the study of Spenser, Benjamin P. Myers builds upon previous criticism on gender and Ireland by arguing that there is a significant yet hitherto overlooked connection between Spenser's engagement with gender, the Irish landscape, and Petrarchanism ('Pro-War and Prothalamion: Queen, Colony, and Somatic Metaphor among Spenser's "Knights of the Maidenhead"', *ELR* 37[2007] 215–49). A key concept for Myers is 'frowardness', whereby Spenser's portrayal of the queen as a Petrarchan lady who frowardly refuses to accept her lover is related to her frowardness in refusing to properly fund the Irish wars. Spenser presents an anti-Petrarchan critique, argues Myers, in which he privileges marriage over 'the danger of a frozen virginity' (p. 232), as evident in the episode featuring Britomart by the sea's edge. The problem of Elizabeth's refusal to take a husband parallels the problem of a land without husbandry: her frustrating refusal to marry is part of the same froward urge that marks her refusal to spend money on the Irish wars. The knights who fight frowardness in all forms throughout Spenser's poem, 'The Order of the Knights of the Maidenhead', indicate the link between sexual conquest and actual conquest with 'a masculinist ethic of frowardness that endorses both versions of conquest as it reiterates the Protestant commitment to action in the world' (p. 237). In Book V, Arthur's liberation of Belge reveals the benefits of decisive military action, while Flourdelis' rejection of her king, 'with all the pride of a Petrarchan mistress', reveals that 'Political allegiance and sexual allegiance . . . adhere to the same code of ethics' (p. 246). Both these episodes lead to the liberation of Irena (Ireland), where the sexualized image of a female land awaiting the male conqueror reinforces the fusion between sexual and colonial conquest.

David Scott Wilson-Okamura discusses the rather neglected topic of Spenser's use of rhyme ('The French Aesthetic of Spenser's Feminine Rhyme', *MLQ* 68[2007] 345–62). He begins by pondering why Spenser chose to use so many feminine rhymes in the second part of *The Faerie Queene* published in 1596. He notes that feminine rhymes are often associated with comic effect, as in Marlowe's *Hero and Leander*, and some of the examples from Spenser fall into that category, but this does not fully explain what is going on. Citing Maureen Quilligan, he argues that the use of feminine rhymes can be read as a comment on gender, but the examples discussed by Quilligan account for only a fraction of those used by Spenser. For Wilson-Okamura the key lies in considering how feminine rhyme was discussed in the period and what it was used for. It seems that in the 1590s many poets were moving away from feminine rhymes, so why did Spenser use more? Wilson-Okamura argues that Spenser was less influenced by the fashions adopted by his fellow-poets than by his reading, specifically his reading of vernacular poetry from Italy and France. Spenser's debt to the Italian poet Tasso is referred to, but detailed analysis is given of Spenser's use of Du Bellay since, as Wilson-Okamura puts it, the former 'would have softened him on feminine rhyme, but nothing more' (p. 360), Du Bellay inspired him to use a specific kind of feminine rhyme known as *rime léonine*, an exaggerated form of *rime riche*.

Moving from rhyme to language, Daniel Fried considers the significance of the name 'Calepine', the knight who appears in Book VI of *The Faerie Queene* ('Defining Courtesy: Spenser, Calepine and Renaissance Lexicography', *RES* 58[2007] 229–4). As Fried points out, names are telling in Spenser's epic poem, and Spenserians are keen to engage meanings they can tease from the text, but Calepine has hitherto received less attention in this regard that the poem's other heroes. Fried argues that the name would have been well known to a sixteenth-century reader because it is the anglicized version of Ambrogio Calepino, editor of the first and very popular early modern polyglot dictionary. The lexicographical associations are important, argues Fried, since the character Calepine 'highlights a concern for the semiotics of personhood, which has broader implications for understanding literati experiences of the patronage systems in which they operated' (p. 230). Fried provides a detailed analysis of the role of Calepino's dictionary in early modern culture before turning back to Book VI of Spenser's poem and the poet's choice of the name Calepine. Fried notes that Book VI is 'permeated by questions of linguistics and lexicography, arrayed about the central tension: how ought one to understand the true meaning of "courtesy"?' (p. 237). According to Fried, courtesy is the only virtue that is 'fundamentally semiotic' (p. 237), and this is crucial in terms of patronage in a way that holiness, temperance and chastity are not. While the other virtues are internalized, and recognized by God, courtesy is displayed; in order to benefit from patronage one must know how to present the correct signs and thus encourage the proper reading of those signs by others.

Spenser's shorter poems also received some attention this year. M.L. Stapleton traces Spenser's efforts to reconcile the erotic and earthly with the sacred throughout his career but specifically in his late sonnets ('Devoid of Guilty Shame: Ovidian Tendencies in Spenser's Erotic Poetry', *MP* 105[2007] 271–99). Spenser's debt to Ovid's *Metamorphoses* has been recognized by critics but, as Stapleton points out, little has been made of his debt to Ovid's *Amores*, the most important model for the Renaissance sonnet sequence. Stapleton considers the ironic distance between author and speaker in Ovid and Spenser, and concludes that the *Amoretti* persona is most like that in Ovid's *Amores* since both are unreliable and given to self-delusion (p. 279). Similarly, Spenser's lover, like Ovid's, criticizes himself for finding fault with his lady, and Spenser 'seems all too aware of the foolishness of the Ovidian lover' (p. 284). For Spenser, Ovidian lust becomes honest desire, but it is important 'to avoid compulsive fornications' (p. 285) as in the episode that takes place in Castle Joyeous in Book III of *The Faerie Queene*, although Malecasta's erotic escorts, among them Gardante (gazing), Iocante (playing) and Basciante (kissing), 'could serve as outline for the sacred courtship and marriage' that he outlines in his sonnet sequences (pp. 286–7). The attempt to distinguish between sacred and profane love in the *Amoretti* does not quite work, and both are informed by desire, but where Ovid stresses 'the adulterous pagan ethos' Spenser's focus is on 'the One Flesh model of Christian marriage' (p. 298).

As noted in section 2 above, Kambasković-Sawers's essay on the 'sequentiality' of the sonnet sequence as a precursor of the novel form includes sections on Petrarch, Sidney and Spenser (' "Never was I the golden cloud": Ovidian Myth, Ambiguous Speaker and the Narrative in the Sonnet Sequences by Petrarch, Sidney and Spenser', *RS* 21[2007] 637–61). In the section on Spenser, Kambasković-Sawers argues that Spenser's sonnet sequence is different from its predecessors in that it celebrates marriage and not 'the traditionally Petrarchan poetics of permanent frustration' (p. 655); the sequence has two readers: Elizabeth Boyle (Spenser's betrothed) and the wider audience. The reader is aware of a growing sense of expectation and also of voyeurism as the wider audience read what was meant for one pair of eyes only. As Kambasković-Sawers points out, this challenges not only the reader's ethical views but his or her preconceived notions of genre. The figure of Cupid is elided with the speaker, and his 'various guises project the conflicting nature of the speaker's desire' (p. 656), whereby the speaker becomes morally ambiguous and the wider audience more fully immersed in the story. Drawing on Ovidian mythical examples, Kambasković-Sawers shows how the speaker shifts from frustration to admiration for the lady. Sexuality is explored in the context of power before a conclusion where the lady is won but the reader is left eager for the denouement that will be found in the *Epithalamion*.

Judith Owens is concerned with the relationship between the heroic and the commercial in Spenser's *Prothalamion* ('Commerce and Cadiz in Spenser's *Prothalamion*', *SEL* 47[2007] 79–106). Owens's focus is the poem's refrain 'Against the Brydale day, which is not long: / Sweet Themmes runne softly till I end my Song', which she argues is a call for the busy London streets—full of noise and commerce—to become silent. Spenser's reference in the poem to the 'siluer streaming Themmes' provokes associations between silver and alchemy, and also commerce: the silver to be gained from expeditions such as that in Cadiz, from which Essex benefited. Owens states that in the *Prothalamion* 'this mercenary potential of "siluer streaming" [is] transmuted into quite another register, one provided by ... alchemical imagery in the poem' (p. 87), which provides an analogy for the poetic imagination. Spenser distinguishes between what he regards as the real alchemy of poetry, on the one hand, and the false promises of alchemical experience and commerce on the other. It is not the case, argues Owens, that Spenser denies the necessity of money or commerce, but that he objects to 'the conflation of honour with monetary or commercial gain' (p. 88), a point also developed in the Mammon episode from Book II of *The Faerie Queene*. In the *Prothalamion* Spenser presents Essex as a heroic knight, but only by denying the commercial and mercenary concerns with which he was connected by the expedition to Cadiz.

This year's *Spenser Studies* is a special volume consisting of selected papers from the conference 'Spenser's Civilizations' held in Toronto in May 2006. As the editors of the volume point out (David Galbraith and Theresa Krier, 'Spenser's Book of Living', *SSt* 22[2007] 1–4), the collection reveals a 'focus on conditions of embodiment, the energies of bodily life, affect and sympathy and less emphasis on the love poetry, eros, and gender politics than in earlier Spenser scholarship' (p. 1). Also notable is the shift away from Spenser and Ireland, a dominant issue for Spenserians in the 1990s and the early part of the first decade of the twenty-first century. *The Faerie Queene*, of course, remains of key interest but the elegiac poems too receive attention. Also apparent is a renewed interest in rhetoric and ethics.

Paul Stevens considers the role Protestantism, and specifically its engagement with grace, played in British imperial expansion ('Spenser and the End of British Empire', *SSt* 22[2007] 5–26). Via the analysis of empire made by Joseph Schumpeter and David Armitage he argues that Spenser's view of empire is not spatial but temporal and is driven by a culture's desire for its own permanence. Judith Owens's focus is the Ruddymane episode in Book II of *The Faerie Queene* ('Memory Works in *The Faerie Queene*', *SSt* 22[2007] 27–45). As Owens points out, the usual focus of interest for critics who consider this episode is the significance of the bloody hands of Ruddymane, the baby left orphaned by Acrasia, but Owens explores the neglected facts that Guyon becomes the executor of Amavia's will and that he establishes terms of wardship for the baby when he places him in Medina's care. For Owens the episode indicates the significance of family and memorializing in early modern culture, and how wardship was considered crucial to the effective maintenance of the commonwealth.

Richard A. McCabe considers the theme of friendship in a number of works that explore the delicate relationship between poet and patron (' "Thine owne nations frend / And patrone": The Rhetoric of Petition in Harvey and Spenser', *SSt* 22[2007] 47–72). The tension between the patron as friend in an idealized relationship and the patron as a figure to whom the poet was obligated is considered in works by Harvey, Churchyard and Ralegh, as well as Spenser's *Faerie Queene*. In the proem to Book IV of Spenser's poem McCabe detects a debt to Horace in Spenser's efforts to ingratiate himself with

Elizabeth having fallen out with her secretary of state and favourite, Burghley. James M. Nohrnberg reads some episodes from Spenser's *Faerie Queene* and Shakespeare's *A Midsummer Night's Dream* against important early modern political events ('Alençon's Dream/Dido's Tomb: Some Shakespearean Music and a Spenserian Muse', *SSt* 22[2007] 73–102). He draws parallels between Malecasta's attempts to seduce Britomart in Book III and the activities of Mary Stuart and the northern rebels, both of which threatened Protestant rule, while the episode featuring Busirane and Amoret, also from Book III, is compared to Queen Elizabeth's feelings about her possible marriage to the French duke of Alençon.

Gordon Teskey's focus is on Spenser's poetic thinking in *The Faerie Queene*—his creative process, his use of the past and so on—and he interrogates what this can tell us about Spenser's allegory ('Thinking Moments in *The Faerie Queene*', *SSt* 22[2007] 103–26). Teskey considers philosophical views on thinking and poetry and what previous readers and critics, including C.S. Lewis, have had to say about Spenser's epic. Moments from the poem considered in detail by Teskey include the Castle of Medina in Book II and the Mutabilitie Cantos. As noted in section 2 above, Rebeca Helfer's essay provides a welcome analysis of Spenser's rather neglected poem *The Ruines of Time*, specifically in its memorial to Philip Sidney ('Remembering Sidney, Remembering Spenser: The Art of Memory and *The Ruines of Time*', *SSt* 22[2007] 127–52). She traces a dialogue within Spenser's work about Cicero's art of memory 'that reforms fictions of permanence through a narrative of change, contingency, and continuity' and that venerates Sidney as 'the epitome of deathless poetry' (p. 129). Poetry as the art of memory, via the immortal poet, is reinforced by *The Ruines of Time*, which looks back to Sidney's *Defense of Poetry*, a work that itself looks back to *The Shepheardes Calender*. The title of Spenser's later poem locates the work within time and history and thus creates what Helfer terms 'a memory theatre' for Sidney and England 'which explores how poetry builds and rebuilds immortality from and within the ruins of time' (p. 148).

Andrew Wallace argues convincingly that the spirit of E.K., the commentator who is a dominant presence in Spenser's pastoral poems, is evident in the *Faerie Queene* ('Edmund Spenser and the Place of Commentary', *SSt* 22[2007] 153–70). E.K.'s influence can be found, argues Wallace, in the repeated encounters between the curious and puzzled observer or interpreter and the bewildering spectacle or work of art, a process clearly evident in the House of Busirane episode in Book III of Spenser's epic poem. Busirane also comes up in Lindsay Ann Reid's essay on the influence of Ovid on Spenser's depiction of this enchanter in Book III of *The Faerie Queene* ('*Certamen*, Interpretation, and Ovidian Narration in *The Faerie Queene* III.ix–xii', *SSt* 22[2007] 171–84). She argues that in this episode there are three Ovidian voices that interpret the narrative: those of Paridell, Busirane and the narrator. Reid acknowledges the influence of Lauren Silberman in reading the Busirane episode as 'a battle of interpretation' (p. 172), arguing that interpretations of Busirane and Paridell can be read via Ovid's story of Arachne and Minerva. Paridell lacks Arachne's 'critical sensibility and sense of irony' (p.174) and Busirane, who like Arachne creates a work of art, 'does not share in Arachne's critique of divine eros' (p. 177) and does not problematize lust. The narrator, argues Reid, is a truly Ovidian creature, where parody dominates and the irony that escapes both Paridell and Busirane is used 'to deflate and critique' (p. 181) their interpretations.

Andrew Escobedo investigates the distinction between 'will' and 'choice' in *The Faerie Queene*, specifically what it means to state that a character 'wills' but does not 'choose' something ('Daemon Lovers: Will, Personification, and Character', *SSt* 22[2007] 203–26). Tracing the views of many critics, he considers how far allegory and personification exert a constraining or deadening pressure on the poem's characters. Focusing on the episode that takes place in Busirane's castle (an episode that has been of interest to quite a few Spenserians this year) he notes that here 'Spenser's characters express their wills ... deliberately and voluntarily, without exactly choosing' (p. 221). Possession by something, for example love or a divine force, 'compromises our volition's independence' but does not kill it, and 'can serve as the basis of immensely powerful exertions of the will' (p. 221), as in the case of Britomart, where although she is not free of the allegory of love she can will it to positive ends and thus undermine the destructive impulse of Busirane.

Of particular interest in this year's volume of *Spenser Studies* were several essays with a focus on ecology, an area that has remained relatively neglected by Spenserians. The influence of Virgil's *Georgics* on Book I of Spenser's *Faerie Queene* and *A View of the Present State of Ireland* is the topic of Linda Gregerson's essay ('Spenser's Georgic: Violence and the Gift of Place', *SSt* 22[2007] 185–202). Gregerson considers Spenser's debt to Virgil in his contemplation of a conundrum: 'the difficult ethics of habitation in a household or *oikos* built on earth' (p. 186), specifically whether human beings should coexist peacefully with nature or impose upon it their will, the latter following the biblical concept of natural 'rule'. To impose human will is an act of violence, but it is one that Spenser seems to endorse in the *View*, where 'Irenius is unblinking about those violent impositions he construes as necessary to the work of civilization' (p. 189). In Book I, Redcrosse's name 'Georgos' signifies the ploughman's labour and he is 'taught to think ecologically' (p. 197), that is he is trained in 'the system-thinking of intricately balanced interdependent obligations and imperatives' (p. 198). For both Virgil and Spenser, human beings are stewards of the earth but human will must not reign unchecked.

A focus on the relationship between humans and animals emerged in a few essays. Elizabeth Jane Bellamy's piece considers how *The Faerie Queene* relates to classical, early modern and modern views of human/animal difference ('Spenser's "Open"', *SSt* 22[2007] 227–41). Bellamy begins by tracing the history of philosophical thinking in this area: Aristotle saw kinship between the human and the animal, but Descartes saw the animal as a machine, and Heidegger's 'theoretical biology' was 'the most notorious effort to separate the animal from the human' (p. 228). Heidegger's assertion, in his 1929–30 Freiburg lectures on biology, that animals have no consciousness or selfhood was anticipated by William Perkins's *A Discourse of Conscience* [1596], in which he noted that because animals 'want true reason, they want conscience also'. Heidegger rarely considers mammals but focuses on insects and thus, argues Bellamy, his lectures 'can provide a useful backdrop for probing the mysteries of Spenser's insect worlds' (p. 229). Via reference to Spenser's early poem *Virgil's Gnat*, Bellamy explores the pastoral gnat simile of the Errour episode from Book I of *The Faerie Queene*, where the monster's young swarming around Redcrosse's legs are compared to gnats. Heidegger denied the possibility that animals were capable of what he termed 'world-forming' abilities. For Heidegger all animals, including insects, were 'dazed, stupefied, 'benumbed . . . capable of "perishing", but never of attaining a state of "being-toward-death"' (p. 230). However for Spenser, argues Bellamy, the gnats and flies of his similes provide his readers 'with tantalizing naturalist glimpses into the realities of insect experience, an interest for its own sake *in what insects do*' (p. 235). In effect, they become more than a mere source of annoyance, their 'marred murmurings' causing the reader to question whether they inhabit a state beyond the 'benumbed'.

Elizabeth D. Harvey considers John Donne's debt to Spenser in the former's fragmentary poem *Metempsychosis*, or *The Progress of the Soul*, but of specific interest to Spenserians is her focus on Spenser's representation of the soul in the Castle of Alma, from Book II of *The Faerie Queene* ('Nomadic Souls: Pythagoras, Spenser, Donne', *SSt* 22[2007] 257–79). Harvey traces early modern attitudes to the soul, including the doctrine of reincarnation, which raises difficult questions about relations between humans and animals such as 'if the rational soul is unique to human beings, can it be translated into a vegetable or animal body?' and if it is translated 'does it retain memory and consciousness of its earlier life but without the power to articulate it?' (pp. 259–60). Part III of Harvey's essay concentrates on the Castle of Alma, an important source for Donne, and she here argues that Spenser's depiction of the soul is influenced by Platonic psychology, specifically in his *Timaeus*, but is Aristotelian in some respects, specifically 'in its insistence on the geometrical expression of the soul's immortal dimension and on the moral governance of the appetitive souls' (p. 272). The episode featuring Grill (or Grylle), the man turned pig in Book II of *The Faerie Queene*, is also of interest to Harvey since it is 'the most dramatic encounter of the animal–human interface' (p. 274) and engages with many of the questions raised by Renaissance debates about the soul and its relation to the animal and human.

Joseph Loewenstein argues that Spenser is not really interested in animals but that there are moments in *The Faerie Queene* revealing kinship between certain humans and certain animals ('Gryll's Hoggish Mind', *SSt* 22[2007] 243–56). The moments considered are those involving Grylle in Book II of the poem and the lion that attends to Una in Book I. Loewenstein focuses on the pig as a philosophical totem and points to Plutarch's *Moralia* and his unfinished *Beasts Are Rational*, otherwise known as the *Gryllus*, a dialogue that comes up late in the *Moralia*. This work of philosophical scepticism performs two critical functions: the denigration of human reason and insistence on the animal nature of the human. Loewenstein notes that the disputes provoked by Renaissance scepticism were once notorious; among the more notable is Gassendi's argument in his *Meditations* that animals think, and Montaigne's comments on the dignity of animals in *The Apology for Raymond Sebond*, which was influenced by Plutarch; in both texts the possibility is raised that animal intelligence is superior to human intelligence. Montaigne tells an anecdote from Diogenes Laertius about a superior pig who, unlike the humans around him, was unconcerned about a storm raging around him. The serenity of the pig 'models *ataraxia*, the tranquility of skeptical indifference' and is 'the product of that philosophical discipline which leads to *epoche*, or suspension of judgment' (p. 249). Also relevant to Spenser's Grylle is Gianbattista Gelli's *Circe*, which adds to the *Gryllus* by having dialogues between Ulysses and several animals. In the episode featuring Guyon and Grylle, Spenser seems to follow Plutarch and Gelli by asserting human/animal differentiation, but his innovation is to silence the men who have become beasts and thus focus on human–animal continuity. Moving on to Una's lion, Loewenstein argues that this episode 'depends on the skeptical principle of species continuity, of a fellow-feeling almost inconceivable, given the apparent alterity of animals' (p. 252). It is such fellow-feeling that Guyon lacks as he makes his way through Acrasia's Bower.

This year's volume of *Spenser Studies* is concluded by Garrett A. Sullivan, Jr, who draws on his experiences teaching Shakespeare and Spenser to consider how each differs in his conception of the human ('Afterword', *SSt* 22[2007] 281–7). Focusing on Book II of the *Faerie Queene*, Sullivan notes that Shakespeare is a poet of subjectivity but Spenser 'tends to approach the question of what it is to be human from the perspective of the vitality of all forms of life' (p. 283). Sullivan provides two examples, both involving sleep: the blurring between man and beast that occurs during Guyon's sleep, and the indeterminacy evident in the description of the sleeping Verdant, 'who exists at the intersection of the animal, vegetable and human' (p. 284). Sullivan concludes that, where Shakespeare might be considered to have invented the human, Spenser is responsible for problematizing it.

There was only one article on Spenser in this year's *Notes and Queries*. Tom MacFaul traces Spenser's influence on Donne ('Donne's "The Sunne Rising" and Spenser's "Epithalamion"', *N&Q* 54[2007] 37–8). He argues that Donne's poem is indebted to Spenser's since both share the theme of comparing marriage to the culture of the court. Both see 'an intruder in the bedroom' (p. 3), and for Spenser this is the feminine figure of Cynthia, signifying the moon, but also of Elizabeth I, rather than the masculine sun, who for Donne represents King James. Although the gender of the intruder is not the same, both poems, according to MacFaul, share a sense of privacy invaded by royal power.

Books Reviewed

Archer, Jayne Elisabeth, Elizabeth Goldring and Sarah Knight. *The Progresses, Pageants, and Entertainments of Queen Elizabeth I*. OUP. [2007] pp. xiv + 310. £53 ISBN 9 7801 9929 1571.
Clark, Stuart. *Vanities of the Eye: Vision in Early Modern European Culture*. OUP. [2007] pp. xi + 415. £35 ISBN 9 7801 9925 0134.

Hayward, Maria. *Dress at the Court of King Henry VIII*. Maney. [2007] pp. xviii + 458. hb £118 ISBN 9 7819 0435 0705, pb £48 ISBN 9 7819 0598 1410.

Herron, Thomas. *Spenser's Irish Work: Poetry Plantation and Colonial Reformation*. Ashgate. [2007] pp. 268. £50, ISBN 9 7807 5465 6029.

McGavin, John J. *Theatricality and Narrative in Medieval and Early Modern Scotland*. Ashgate. [2007] pp. xi + 160. £58 ISBN 9 7807 5460 7946.

Roston, Murray. *Tradition and Subversion in Renaissance Literature*. MRLS. Duquesne. [2007] pp. 258. £39.99 ISBN 9 7808 2070 3909.

Schwyzer, Philip. *Archaeologies of English Renaissance Literature*. OUP. [2007] pp. xii + 227. £53 ISBN 9 7801 9920 6605.

Tilmouth, Christopher. *Passion's Triumph over Reason: A History of the Moral Imagination from Spenser to Rochester*. OUP. [2007] pp. 414. £71 ISBN 9 7801 9921 2378.

Vickers, Brian. *Shakespeare, 'A Lover's Complaint' and John Davies of Hereford*. CUP. [2007] pp. xii + 329. £50 ISBN 0 5218 5912 3.

Whitney, Charles. *Early Responses to Renaissance Drama*. CUP. [2006] pp. xi + 341. £54 ISBN 0 5218 5843 7.

Zurcher, Andrew. *Spenser's Legal Language: Law and Poetry in Early Modern England*. Brewer. [2007] pp. 312. £55 ISBN 9 7818 4384 1333.

VI

Shakespeare

GABRIEL EGAN, PETER J. SMITH, ELINOR PARSONS,
JONATHAN HARTWELL, ANNALIESE CONNOLLY,
RICHARD WOOD, STEVE LONGSTAFFE,
JON ORTEN AND EDEL LAMB

This chapter has four sections: 1. Editions and Textual Studies; 2. Shakespeare in the Theatre; 3. Shakespeare on Screen; 4. Criticism. Section 1 is by Gabriel Egan; section 2 is by Peter J. Smith; section 3 is by Elinor Parsons; section 4(b) is by Jonathan Hartwell; section 4(c) is by Annaliese Connolly; section 4(d) is by Richard Wood; section 4(e) is by Steve Longstaffe; section 4(f) is by Jon Orten; section 4(g) is by Edel Lamb.

1. Editions and Textual Studies

One major critical edition of Shakespeare appeared in 2007: Katherine Duncan-Jones and H.R. Woudhuysen edited *Shakespeare's Poems: Venus and Adonis, The Rape of Lucrece and the Shorter Poems* for the Arden Shakespeare series. An edition of the *Complete Works of Shakespeare* by Jonathan Bate and Eric Rasmussen appeared from an alliance of the Royal Shakespeare Company and Macmillan, but is of little scholarly interest. The parts of the Oxford *Collected Works of Thomas Middleton*, edited by Gary Taylor and John Lavagnino, that overlap with the concerns of this review are of considerable scholarly interest and will be noticed. Uniquely for an Arden edition, Duncan-Jones and Woudhuysen's book is comprised of two major works, *Venus and Adonis* and *The Rape of Lucrece*, and they think that Shakespeare might well have conceived of them as a pair, albeit perhaps not until he began the second one. The title-page epigraph of *Venus and Adonis* is a quotation from Ovid about cheap shows pleasing the crowds, and this Duncan-Jones and Woudhuysen think might be an allusion to Shakespeare's theatre work in an effort to distance the present book from it (pp. 11–13). There is an allusion to the story of Venus and Adonis in the induction to *The Taming of the Shrew* and it catches a moment very like one caught in the Venus and Adonis sonnets in *Passionate Pilgrim* [1599], so perhaps these were early

Year's Work in English Studies, Volume 88 (2009) © *The English Association; all rights reserved*
doi:10.1093/ywes/map019

stabs at the theme done around 1590 when Shakespeare was writing
The Taming of the Shrew (pp. 18–19). The titles of the narrative poems were
attractive in indicating that they are about women, and in his early plays
Shakespeare was daring in his representation of women, especially the active
and devilishly attractive Katherine of *The Taming of the Shrew* and Margaret
of Anjou in the Henry VI plays. Duncan-Jones and Woudhuysen ingeniously
suggest that having his women be active and masculine was Shakespeare's
way of overcoming the limitations of the boy actors (pp. 31–2). They see
Shakespeare pondering republicanism in the waning years of Elizabeth's reign:
not only *The Rape of Lucrece* (which shows the events that led to Rome's
change from having kings to having consuls) but also *Julius Caesar*. In
Shakespeare's poem, unlike his sources, Adonis is really just a boy and not
ready for love, and Venus is scarily blind to that fact.

The publishing history and significance of *The Passionate Pilgrim* is
discussed by Duncan-Jones and Woudhuysen (pp. 82–91). This book of
sonnets appeared in octavo in 1599 with Shakespeare's name on the title page,
although of its twenty poems only five are by Shakespeare and of these three
were from *Love's Labour's Lost*, which was already available in print. A third
edition appeared in 1612 with some extra non-Shakespearian poems by
Thomas Heywood that had been published by William Jaggard in 1609, and
Heywood added an epistle to his *Apology for Actors* [1612] in which he wrote
that Shakespeare was annoyed with Jaggard for pirating his (Shakespeare's)
sonnets, which had appeared in a good edition in 1609. Duncan-Jones and
Woudhuysen think it quite likely that Romeo appeared disguised as a pilgrim
at the Capulets' feast, giving force to *The Passionate Pilgrim*'s appearance as
a kind of spin-off: one of its poems seems to give the reader Romeo's thoughts
on the way back from the Capulet house after his first meeting with Juliet.
Duncan-Jones and Woudhuysen discuss the biographical links that might
connect people involved in *The Passionate Pilgrim* and Shakespeare, and how
far Shakespeare might have been actively involved in the project, but on the
possible manuscript copy for *The Passionate Pilgrim* Duncan-Jones and
Woudhuysen defer to Colin Burrow's Oxford edition of 2002 (reviewed in
YWES 83[2004]). The discussion of *The Phoenix and the Turtle* puts the poem
into a detailed context of what the book it appeared in, Robert Chester's
collection *Love's Martyr* [1601], was trying to do for its dedicatee John
Salusbury (pp. 91–123). Duncan-Jones and Woudhuysen reject the idea that
The Phoenix and the Turtle was about the execution of Catholic Anne Lyne,
since Salusbury would not have welcomed such sympathies expressed in his
name; they offer extensive new material on Salusbury and his connections with
Shakespeare (especially via the Middle Temple) and his attempts to enter
parliament (pp. 95–111). Perhaps, they suggest, the Phoenix is Elizabeth 1
and the Turtle is Salusbury. The introduction to this edition ends with the
reflection that apart from the works already discussed, *Venus and Adonis*, *The
Rape of Lucrece*, the bits of *The Passionate Pilgrim* by him, and *The Phoenix
and the Turtle*, plus of course the sonnets, Shakespeare left us no substantial
poetry.

So, to the texts themselves. There is little emendation to comment upon
because Fields's editions of *Venus and Adonis* and *The Rape of Lucrece* were

well printed and Duncan-Jones and Woudhuysen do not claim any startling new emendations. In *Venus and Adonis* they print 'And whe're he run or fly they know not whether' (line 304) in place of Q's 'And where he runne, or flie, they know not whether'. This is Edmond Malone's emendation for the sake of metre and sense, with *whether* meaning 'which of the two'. Oddly, there's a textual note justifying this emendation, but it has no preceding asterisk so it is hard to know just how big a change in meaning is necessary to warrant one. (Like all the current Arden series, the prefatory material promises that 'Notes preceded by ∗ discuss editorial emendations . . .' (p. xiii).) There is an asterisked note drawing attention to their printing of 'But blessed bankrupt that by loss so thriveth' (line 466) where Q has 'But blessed bankrout that by loue so thriueth', saying that *loue* was picked up from its use two lines earlier. The first edition to emend thus was Henry N. Hudson's American edition of 1886, based on a conjecture by Sidney Walker. There is an asterisked note too for 'With purple tears, that his wounds wept, was drenched' (line 1054) where Q has 'With purple tears that his woûd wept, had drencht'. This is an emendation (*had* to *was*) that first appeared in Q7. Duncan-Jones and Woudhuysen are not sure about it: Q's *had* 'may be correct', they write, if, as Richard Proudfoot suggests, the line was originally 'W^{ch} purple tears that his woûd wept, had drencht' and *W^{ch}* was misread as though it were *Wth*, or if the first word was *The*, as in 'The purple tears that his woûd wept, had drencht'.

The text of *The Rape of Lucrece* shows rather more intervention, and again the use of asterisks to highlight the relevant notes is either irregular or follows a system that this reviewer cannot infer. Duncan-Jones and Woudhuysen print 'As is the morning silver melting dew' (line 24) where the uncorrected state of Q (hereafter Qu) has 'As is the morning siluer melting dew' and the corrected state (Qc) has 'mornings'. Duncan-Jones and Woudhuysen see this as a miscorrection: the word is fine as an adjective, as in Qu. Another miscorrection explains their 'What needeth then apology be made' (line 31) where Qu has 'What needeth then Appologie be made' and Qc has instead 'Apologies'. At line 55 Duncan-Jones and Woudhuysen defend their changing Q's *ore* to *o'er*, which was first actioned in Q5 but is really just a modernization of spelling. The real reason for their asterisked note at this point is that Malone wanted to emend here (to *or*, the heraldic name for gold) and they want to resist him. Further miscorrection explains why they print 'And every one to rest himself betakes, | Save thieves and cares and troubled minds that wakes' (lines 125–6) where Qu has 'And euerie one to rest himself betakes, | Saue theeues, and cares, and troubled minds that wakes' and Qc has 'And euerie one to rest themselues betake, | Saue theeues, and cares, and troubled minds that wake'. Punctiliously, at line 147 Duncan-Jones and Woudhuysen give an asterisked note to explain that *altogether* (Q's reading) and *all together* (their preference, from Q8) have different meanings now even though they were not carefully distinguished when this poem was written. And yet they offer no note for their admittance of Q's 'To dry the old oaks' sap and cherish springs' (line 950), where most editors have wanted to do something with the last two words so that the springs are harmed, emending to such things as 'perish springs' or 'blemish springs'. Three readings from the corrected state of

Q follow: 'Which by him tainted shall for him be spent' (line 1182) where Qu has 'Which for him . . .', 'As lagging fowls before the northern blast' (line 1335) where Qu has 'northern blasts', and 'Even so this pattern of the worn-out age' (line 1350) where Qu has *this* and *the* the other way around. Unsurprisingly, Duncan-Jones and Woudhuysen accept Walker's justly celebrated conjecture and print 'With sad-set eyes and wreathed arms across' (line 1662), where Q has 'wretched armes'. They accept too Edward Capell's conjecture (adopted by Malone) and print 'The face . . . | . . . carved in it with tears' (lines 1712–13) where Q has 'caru'd it in with tears'. In the last line of the poem, Duncan-Jones and Woudhuysen punctuate to indicate the 'TARQUINS' everlasting banishment' whereas most editors make it a singular punishment (*Tarquin's*). As they rightly point out, even leaving known history aside for a moment the poem's Argument indicates that the whole family has to go.

There are no further emendations to discuss, although the remainder of this long edition (nearly 600 pages) has much more to say about the texts. Duncan-Jones and Woudhuysen's treatment of *The Passionate Pilgrim* (pp. 385–418) reproduces the two sonnets later to appear in Shakespeare's *Sonnets* [1609], plus two sonnets that had already appeared in *Love's Labour's Lost* [1598], plus one non-sonnet poem from *Love's Labour's Lost*. Duncan-Jones and Woudhuysen do not attempt major editorial work but rather their collations and notes aim to highlight the differences between the versions presented in *The Passionate Pilgrim* and the versions as they appeared elsewhere. This makes sense, as the differences are by no means certain to be printing errors that need correction: they might be authorial tweaks. Duncan-Jones and Woudhuysen have each edited one of the other books that these poems appear in (*Sonnets* and *Love's Labour's Lost* respectively) so there is little remaining editorial work to be done. Although they print all the other poems in *The Passionate Pilgrim*, Duncan-Jones and Woudhuysen do not engage directly with the detail of the arguments for attributing some of them to Shakespeare, but simply refer the reader elsewhere. For the Shakespearian verses in *Love's Martyr* (that is, *The Phoenix and the Turtle*, pp. 419–28) Duncan-Jones and Woudhuysen reproduce only the parts of the book thought to be by Shakespeare and there are no important textual matters to discuss. The last section of the edition that reproduces the poetry itself covers 'Attributed Poems' (pp. 429–69), meaning those that Duncan-Jones and Woudhuysen do not guarantee are by Shakespeare. The first eleven are early attributions, starting with 'Shall I Die?', about which the editors declare themselves convinced by Brian Vickers that it is not Shakespeare. They are less explicit about 'Upon a Pair of Gloves', but do not sound convinced that it is authentic. Going into some considerable detail, Duncan-Jones and Woudhuysen are in favour of accepting 'Verses on the Stanley tomb at Tong' because, when added to other circumstantial evidence, the fact that Milton's poem in the preliminaries to the Second Folio [1632] seems to allude to these verses 'strongly suggests that they may be by Shakespeare' (p. 445). Strangely, they do not give an explicit opinion on the four-line poem 'On Ben Jonson', but sound sceptical. The 'Inscription for the coat of Shakespeare's arms' (that is, the three words *Non sans droict*) is of course genuine.

Duncan-Jones and Woudhuysen are avowedly undecided on 'An epitaph on Elias James' while accepting that the two epitaphs on John Combes might be genuine. Regarding 'Upon the King', Duncan-Jones and Woudhuysen report that Vickers will in a forthcoming *Notes and Queries* article give this to John Davies of Hereford, but they hold the matter to be still open. (That article did not appear in 2007 or 2008.) The motto that Shakespeare wrote for the Rutland impressa is of course lost, and that Shakespeare wrote the curse upon his tomb in Stratford-upon-Avon strikes Duncan-Jones and Woudhuysen as 'plausible'. Turning to the modern attributions, Duncan-Jones and Woudhuysen start with 'The Lucy Ballad' and point out that Mark Eccles observed that Sir Thomas Lucy did not have a deer park at Charlecote (it was elsewhere) and that the story does not actually say Shakespeare stole deer, only that he fell in with a group that did and that he robbed a park. Presumably, if it is true, Shakespeare robbed Lucy's rabbit warren at Charlecote. Duncan-Jones and Woudhuysen are unconvinced that there is anything in the various seventeenth- and eighteenth-century ballads that are supposed to record the event in the oral tradition. The 'Skipworth verses' are now known to be not Shakespeare's but William Skipworth's and are not printed here. What Duncan-Jones and Woudhuysen call 'the Stanford poem' is the epilogue that Juliet Dusinberre thinks is Shakespeare's and belongs to *As You Like It*, but Duncan-Jones and Woudhuysen 'are not convinced' and it is not printed here. Everyone knows that 'A Funeral Elegy' is definitely not Shakespeare, and it is not printed here. Finally, of 'Tom O'Bedlam's song to King James' they give no view but mention that Stanley Wells rejected the attribution, and it is not printed here.

The appendices to the edition are substantial and deal with the textual situation of each of the major works included (*Venus and Adonis, The Rape of Lucrece, The Passionate Pilgrim* and *The Phoenix and the Turtle*) and provide the sources (extracts from Ovid and Livy), and also a photofacsimile reproduction of the part of *Love's Martyr* where *The Phoenix and the Turtle* appears. Duncan-Jones and Woudhuysen accept the view of the Oxford *Complete Works of Shakespeare* that *Venus and Adonis* and *The Rape of Lucrece* were well printed by Richard Field in 1593 and 1594, quite possibly from authorial papers. Field's printer's copy for two of John Harington's works survives, so we can get a sense of what his compositor(s) did but should be careful applying that knowledge to Shakespeare: Harington's poetry differs from Shakespeare's and his books were in folio and octavo while Shakespeare's were in quarto (p. 472). The compositor(s) of *Venus and Adonis* seem(s) different from the compositor(s) of *The Rape of Lucrece*, and indeed different from the compositor(s) of Harington's *Ariosto*, to judge by spelling and typographical preferences listed here (pp. 473–6). *Venus and Adonis* was entered to Richard Field in the Stationers' Register on 18 April 1593 and the Bodleian Library copy of Q1 printed later that year is the only extant exemplar. One of the problems that the text gave the printer was that the indentation of the last two lines of each stanza sometimes made a line that would exceed the measure if remedial steps were not taken. From the substitutions from other-sized founts, it looks like the printer was short of certain sorts, especially upper-case V. There are two sets of running titles, distinguishable by an oversize V that first appears in the head title on B1r and recurs in the running title on each 2r in sheets B–F but then (presumably because the two skeletons were swapped) on G4r. Duncan-Jones and Woudhuysen conclude that it is at present impossible to tell whether the printer's copy was autograph or scribal copy.

The Rape of Lucrece was entered to John Harrison in the Stationers' Register on 9 May 1594, and thus while Field printed and published *Venus and Adonis*, for *The Rape of Lucrece* he printed for another man, Harrison, who was its publisher. Duncan-Jones and Woudhuysen note that when, as here, Field was printing for another man he tended to use arabic rather than roman numerals for signatures. There are ten copies plus one fragment of the book extant. Running-title evidence suggests two skeleton formes, one used for the inner and outer formes of sheets B, D, F, H, K and the other used for the inner and outer formes of sheets C, E, G, I, L (with M, the last full gathering, and the half-sheet N both being anomalous). Press variants were collated by Hardy M. Cook in an article reviewed in *YWES* 86[2007]. One forme, I(o), survives in two states of correction. The press corrections cannot, write Duncan-Jones and Woudhuysen, be 'firmly attributed to Shakespeare' (p. 485). I think they mean we cannot be sure that they were made by reference to copy: the idea of the author being responsible for them does not, I think, extend to agency beyond the manuscript. As in *Venus and Adonis*, there was a problem getting the verse lines into the measure (especially in the indented final couplet of each stanza) and the same expedients of turn-over and turn-under and abbreviation were resorted to. Because B(i) is anomalous in its avoidance of capitals and small capitals for proper nouns, Duncan-Jones and Woudhuysen think it was probably set first, when the compositor(s) had not established the practice then followed throughout the rest of the book (p. 486). As with *Venus and Adonis*, the printer was short of certain capital letters, which led to inconsistent capitalization and substitution of different sized sorts, and as before we cannot tell whether the printer's copy was autograph or scribal copy.

The Passionate Pilgrim first appeared in an edition, O1, of which only a fragmentary exemplar survives, giving eleven leaves from what were probably twenty-eight. There was no Stationers' Register entry for it and the printer was perhaps William Jaggard working perhaps in the year 1599; the missing title page makes it hard to know. O2 appeared in 1599, printed by Thomas Judson for Jaggard and sold by William Leake, and it survives in one fragment and two complete exemplars. Collation of O2 shows minor variants on D1r and D3r, and the recurrence of the 'flowers' ornaments in *The Passionate Pilgrim* can be treated like headline recurrence, giving a pattern that strongly suggests that O1 was set by formes (p. 493). Duncan-Jones and Woudhuysen assert that O1's unknown printer was not the Thomas Judson who printed O2, but they omit to tell the reader how they know that; the English Short Title Catalogue speculates that Judson did set O1 (p. 494). Again, recurrence of the ornaments suggests O2 was also set by formes. It emerges by implication—Duncan-Jones and Woudhuysen do not spell it out—that O2 was not a reprint of O1. In 1612 Jaggard printed O3 as a reprint of O2, but the two surviving exemplars show two states of the title page, and it seems that the first state (naming Shakespeare) was cancelled and the second (omitting him) was its replacement.

Notoriously, O3 also included some of Thomas Heywood's poems to which Jaggard had the rights, but to which Heywood objected the same year (1612) in his *An Apology for Actors*. Duncan-Jones and Woodhuysen try to untangle just what Heywood's objection should tell us, but do not get very far (pp. 497–8). *Love's Martyr* was not entered in the Stationers' Register but was first printed (Q1) in 1601 by Richard Field for Edward Blount, and a reissue of the unsold sheets with a new title page and new preliminaries was published in 1611 by Matthew Lownes; it is not clear how he got the sheets. It survives as two complete and one fragmentary Q1, and just one Q2. With one exception, the Attributed Poems have not survived in manuscripts or printed books before the 1630s, and Duncan-Jones and Woodhuysen do not think it worth hazarding guesses about their early transmission.

A brief section of this first appendix explains Duncan-Jones and Woodhuysen's editorial practices (pp. 504–14). The first printings of *Venus and Adonis*, *The Rape of Lucrece* and *Love's Martyr* were carefully done and present no problems; they are the bases of the poems presented here. *The Passionate Pilgrim* and the attributed poems are trickier. Duncan-Jones and Woodhuysen present a surprisingly long disquisition on the typographic feature of capitalization and on the modernization of punctuation and spelling, and how the early printings and previous editions are inconsistent in these matters. This edition uses initial capitals 'only when a personification seems to be clearly intended' (p. 505). Duncan-Jones and Woodhuysen explain why they have retained in *The Rape of Lucrece* the quotation marks that begin lines of *sententiae*, even though they cannot be shown to be authorial: 'it seems possible Shakespeare would have known that they played a part in the volume' (p. 509). It is noticeable that Duncan-Jones and Woodhuysen do not make clear whether Shakespeare knew beforehand about this feature and went along with it, or found out after and did not mind; there is subtly distinct agency at work in each case. In the event, they are so lightly marked in this edition—by an opening and closing pair of quotation marks rather than one at the start of each line—that a reader might easily miss them. Likewise, they retain *The Rape of Lucrece*'s use of small capitals for proper nouns since Shakespeare might have approved their use, and having decided to retain them they naturally have to apply the feature consistently even where the early printing did not. Duncan-Jones and Woodhuysen permit themselves a little self-deprecating irony in calling this 'a bold and probably controversial decision' (p. 510). *The Passionate Pilgrim* is printed here from O1 where possible and where not then O2.

The Royal Shakespeare Company *Complete Works* is edited by Jonathan Bate and Eric Rasmussen, with two dozen others acknowledged in various roles that contributed to the 'fifteen person-years of editorial labour' that made the book (p. 6). The edition is based on the 1623 Folio, and as if to forestall the obvious criticism that this foundational decision was bound to attract, Bate published an article in the *Times Literary Supplement* explaining the edition's rationale ('The Folio Restored: Shakespeare "Published According to the True Originall Copies"', *TLS* 5429(20 April)[2007] 11–13). The fundamental objection to be overcome is that one ought not to base an edition on a mere reprint of an extant book but rather prefer the original over its derivative. For several plays, the Folio essentially reprints a surviving quarto, albeit with sporadic additional independent authority because its copy was first improved by consultation of an authoritative manuscript. It is the absence of evidence for extensive and consistent additional authority that makes editors prefer the quarto over the Folio for certain plays, and not (as Bate claims) their slavish adherence to an absurd rule that 'the earliest surviving text must be the one closest to the original authorial manuscript'. Instead of arguing case by case, Bate attributes to the Folio a general and thoroughgoing theatrical authority deriving from the actors Heminges and Condell working on it. In truth we do not know that they worked on the book, only that they signed an address to the reader at the front. All else is speculation. Thus while the Folio is a fascinating 'socialized' text embodying multiple labours, it is not the best text for every play. We get closer to Shakespeare (as writer and as sharer in the leading acting company) by choosing the most authoritative surviving text on a play-by-play basis.

A longer article on the same topic appeared on a website to accompany the edition (Jonathan Bate, ' "The Case for the Folio": An Essay in Defence of the RSC Shakespeare' [2007] online at http://www.rscshakespeare.org). After a (not entirely up-to-date) survey of the editorial problem in Shakespeare, Bate gets to his defence of editing from the Folio. Here a basic fact of printing is wrongly stated: type is not placed in the stick 'upside down and back to front' (p. 37) but upside down only; were it back to front, it would be impossible to work from left to right through each line of the copy. Considering the evidence that for certain plays the quarto used as printer's copy for the Folio was itself first annotated by reference to an authoritative manuscript, Bate assumes that this was done out of respect for the theatrical manuscripts (p. 38). Perhaps, but it might also have been to evade the accusation of copyright infringement that might follow from reprinting someone else's book. Having established that the Folio is theatrically enhanced by this process of manuscript consultation, Bate leaps to the conclusion that 'It surely follows that a Folio-based' edition will be the more theatrical (p. 41). This does not follow: one needs to pick out the bits that are theatrical enhancements from the bits that are debasements, such as the untheatrical massed entry stage directions inserted by the scribe Ralph Crane making copy for the Folio. Bate is fully aware of the objection to the basis of his edition: 'The accusation is that the Folio should not be used when its copy-text is a derivative quarto, since it suffers from an accumulation of errors evolving through several quartos. The riposte is that it also has the benefit of accumulated improvements evolving through several quartos' (p. 52). The reply to this riposte is that where one thinks that these 'improvements' take us closer to Shakespeare, one should import them into an edition based on the earliest substantive text, rather than accept them all as a batch and thereby risk treating as Shakespearian things that are just artefacts of the reprinting process. Bate is forearmed for this answer too: 'We must cut the Gordian knot here. It is best not to over-fetishize the source of individual corrections' (p. 52). It is hard not to read this as a fancy way of saying that the editor cannot be bothered to make the distinctions on a case-by-case basis and would rather press on and get the work done. The result is an edition that does not warrant close attention to the thinking that went on in those fifteen person years.

The *Collected Works* of Thomas Middleton, edited by Gary Taylor and John Lavagnino, was also a collaborative work, with sixty-one senior scholars listed as contributors to the project (p. 5). Only three plays in this edition are of relevance to this review: *Timon of Athens*, *Macbeth* and *Measure for Measure*. *Timon of Athens*, described as being by Shakespeare and Middleton (pp. 467–508), is edited and annotated by John Jowett and introduced by Sharon O'Dair. O'Dair's introduction is largely concerned with the relative lack of productions and the problems of the script, which co-authorship does not dissolve. She wants us to understand *Timon of Athens* in its own time and not as a simple lesson that the older ways of doing things (Timon's ways before his fall) are better ways: the play does not idealize Timon. In the text of the play, the notes are all explicatory, not textual. There is nothing in the text to mark the transition from the bits Shakespeare wrote to the bits that Middleton wrote. The text seems much as Jowett's 2004 Oxford Shakespeare *Timon of Athens* (reviewed in *YWES* 85[2006]), although stage directions that are simply given in the Oxford Shakespeare edition are here marked in square brackets as editorial additions, reflecting the editions' different rules on marking intervention. Also, the odd stage direction is phrased slightly differently and decisions on scene breaks have been revised. For example, the direction at 14.538 (equivalent to 14.536 in the Oxford Shakespeare) is rephrased and is also the end of scene 14 here while in the Oxford Shakespeare the scene carries on. It is a matter of staging, for F has a stage direction exit which implies that Timon goes back into his cave—he does not leave the stage—which the Oxford Shakespeare respects by sending him into his cave, while the Middleton edition emends to 'Exeunt' and is thereby obliged to start a new scene.

The edition of *Macbeth* is described as a 'Genetic' text and is edited by Gary Taylor and introduced by the late (and sorely missed) Inga-Stina Ewbank (pp. 1165–1201). Ewbank notes that 11 per cent of the words of the Folio text are Middleton's, and he might also have cut about 25 per cent or more of the Shakespearian words. Ewbank starts with the point that it is only our post-Romantic conceptions that make us see what Middleton did to the play as adulteration: back then it was normal. On the evidence of Simon Forman's eyewitness account and Raphael Holinshed's chronicles, Ewbank concludes that the weird sisters were quite possibly a lot less weird in Shakespeare's version of the play. Ewbank finds the addition of songs and dances to be an intelligent reworking, taking attention from Macbeth's self-destruction and celebrating the witches' relative autonomy and their subversive, liberatory anarchism. Moreover the songs and dances make *The Witch* an intertext of *Macbeth*: audiences would have seen the same actors in both and understood them as alternative 'takes' on the same phenomena. In the text of the play, passages added (or moved to their present location) by Middleton are in bold typeface and bits he cut (or moved from their present location) are in greyed-out type. Thus passages that have been moved appear twice: once in grey where they used to be and once in bold where they ended up. To see how these distinctions were arrived at one must go to the edition's Textual Companion, reviewed below.

The edition of *Measure for Measure* is also described as a 'Genetic' text and is edited and introduced by John Jowett (pp. 1542–85). His introduction repeats the well-known argument from *Shakespeare Reshaped* that the song 'Take, O take' was brought in from *Rollo, Duke of Normandy*, that the 'O place and greatness' speech that covers the time in IV.i during which Isabella talks Mariana into sleeping with Angelo used to be at the end of Act III and the 'He who the sword of heaven will bear' speech at the end of Act III used to cover the time while Isabella talks Mariana into the plot, and that the first telling of Claudio's arrest (by Mistress Overdone to the gentlemen) was Middleton's interpolation intended to replace Shakespeare's dialogue (a little later in F) in which Pompey tells Mistress Overdone the same news. Since we know of these major changes, we have to suppose that there are others that are not so obvious, and Jowett lists what he thinks these are. Bringing Juliet on in two scenes where she has nothing to say might be one: she acts as 'silent moral comment' (p. 1543). Jowett does not say here why he thinks that silent moral comment was not part of the original composition but of the revision. Some of the Provost's lines in II.ii were given to Lucio, who also had new ones written for him by Middleton to make him more cynical and detached. Mistress Overdone was probably just called Bawd in the original: Overdone is a name that Middleton liked, and wherever it occurs in dialogue there is a disruption symptomatic of intervention. As mentioned in the Textual Companion, Pompey's speech about the inhabitants of the prison (in which Mistress Overdone is also mentioned) is a Middleton interpolation. Escalus's surprisingly intolerant assertion that Claudio needs to die (at the end of II.i) is another Middleton interpolation: it is entirely detachable, brings in a character (Justice) with no other purpose in the play, and it serves only a Calvinist point about the need to regulate behaviour. Jowett outlines the evidence that the play was originally set in Ferrara, and that to cover his tracks Middleton cut dialogue references to the Italian names Vincentio and Francisca. In the text of the play, greyed-out type and boldface are again used as in *Macbeth* to represent the changes made by Middleton in revision.

As with the Oxford *Complete Works of Shakespeare*, this Middleton edition wisely prints all the textual scholarship unpinning the work in a separate volume (*Thomas Middleton and Early Modern Textual Culture: A Companion to the Collected Works*). For the three plays that concern this review, the parts of interest are the relevant portions of the section 'Works Included in This Edition: Canon and Chronology' (pp. 335–443) and the textual introductions to each play. Starting with the first of these, the section on *Timon of Athens* written by John Jowett (pp. 356–8) is essentially the same as the argument in his 2004 Oxford Shakespeare edition. The section on the adaptation of *Macbeth* in autumn 1616, written by Taylor, seeks to explain point by point how the adaptation occurred and how Taylor's edition of the play represents the 'before' and 'after' versions (pp. 383–98). Taylor's disentangling of the Shakespeare and Middleton parts is based on pursuing the logic of the definitely added Hecate material and the song-and-dance routines—that is, the dialogue and staging consequences of these additions—filtered through knowledge of what kinds of phrasing, staging and source reading (especially Holinshed, of which Middleton seems ignorant) are typically Shakespearian and typically Middletonian. Taylor is uniquely well placed to make these calls, and does not pretend that there is any certainty in them. A distinctive Middleton habit is stage directions taking the form 'Enter X, meeting Y' which Shakespeare never used.

The adaptation of *Macbeth* must follow the writing of *The Witch* in spring 1616, but since that latter play was suppressed the reuse of its songs right away would make sense. (Obviously, the very latest they could have been added to *Macbeth* is shortly before the printing of the Folio in spring 1623.) Once it is admitted that Middleton worked on the play, the judgement of how much of it is his can proceed on the internal evidence. If the Folio text of *Macbeth* is all that Shakespeare wrote plus what Middleton added, then Shakespeare wrote what was for him an extraordinarily short tragedy; more likely Middleton cut lines that we will now never see. By comparison with the average lengths of his other plays, Taylor reckons that 700–1,200 lines of the Shakespearian play were cut by Middleton. Where there is a Middletonian 'Enter X, meeting Y' direction (as in 'Enter Duncan... meeting a bleeding captain', I.ii.0) an editor is entitled to suppose that what follows has been touched by Middleton too. Picking apart I.ii (because of its opening direction), Taylor finds plenty that echoes Middleton elsewhere and not Shakespeare. The Middleton bits cluster in lines 8–9, 15, 22, 27–9, and since dramatists were by the 1610s thinking battle scenes a bit old-fashioned, it is likely that the first thirty lines of I.ii (which tell the outcome of a battle) are Middleton's rewriting of an opening in which the battle itself was depicted.

Taylor reprints all of Forman's account of a performance of the play, and wonders if its reference to Macbeth and Banquo 'riding through a wood' means that in the original play at the Globe they were on horseback in I.iii and that Middleton cut this because the Blackfriars theatre had a smaller stage. One of Taylor's two pieces of evidence for horses, real or property, being used on the stage is the entrance of the apparently dead D'Alva 'carried vpon a horse couvered with blacke' in *A Larum for London* (B1v). In fact, it is clear from the ensuing action that this is not a horse but a hearse (presumably spelt *herse* and misread by someone as *horse*). The second bit of evidence is that the skimmington in *The Witches of Lancashire* is 'on a horse', which is not terribly convincing as the whole point of such a procession is mockery and hence we should not imagine it as anything grand enough to be suitable for Macbeth and Banquo. For this evidence Taylor relies on the entry for 'horse' in Alan Dessen and Leslie Thomson's *A Dictionary of Stage Directions in English Drama, 1580–1642*, and indeed they have misread the *A Larum for London* stage direction.

Taylor notes that the casting needs of the 1623 text are heavy on boys: scene III.v needs three witches, three spirits, Hecate and a boy-as-cat (that makes eight), as does IV.i. It seems that adding the Hecate material made impossible demands on the cast if the witches were played by boys, and since Forman's account suggests that the witches are female and attractive Taylor proposes that Middleton, in adapting the play, changed these nymphs into gender-indeterminate hags by adding Banquo's reference to their beards (in I.iii). That would save three boy actors by allowing adult men to play the witches. The bit after the witches leave in IV.i, in which Macbeth is surprised that Lennox did not see the witches pass him, is problematic as it ought not to surprise Macbeth that they vanish: he has seen them do that before. But this exchange with Lennox has an exact parallel in the Middleton canon and Taylor thinks it is his. By adding Hecate to this scene (IV.i) with a song and dance after the show of eight kings, Middleton prevented the exit of two boy actors needed for Lady Macduff and her son at the start of the next scene, so he had to write extra dialogue at the end of the scene—about the witches passing Lennox unseen and about his own intention to act without hesitation in future and about surprising Macduff's castle—to give these two boys time to change into Macduff's wife and son. The inclusion of Banquo in the show of eight kings is oddly phrased in F—'A shew of eight Kings, and Banquo last, with a glasse in his hand', yet the dialogue makes clear that the eighth king, not Banquo, has the glass—and Taylor thinks that 'and Banquo' was a Middletonian marginal addition. After all, nothing else in the play suggests that the witches have power over the dead. In that case, Macbeth's lines of horror at seeing Banquo ('Horrible sight!...is this so?') are also Middleton's interpolation.

Taylor finds the three apparitions rising from the cauldron in IV.i suspect too: Shakespeare originally had the witches speak the prophecies. Adding the apparitions required an extra boy or two to perform inside the cauldron. The show of kings was changed by Middleton: Shakespeare had them arise from the trap and go back that way. This effect Middleton transferred to the apparitions he invented, and that meant that in order to avoid an anticlimax (he could not have it come up the trap too) the show of kings had to be made into a parading across the stage. Perhaps the plan to surprise Macduff's castle, now stated in the soliloquy at the end of IV.i, was originally Macbeth's response to the scene's first prophecy ('beware Macduff'). This would make sense of his 'Then live Macduff' as a response to the second apparition (about no man of woman born hurting him): Macbeth changes his mind. In other words, the extra dialogue Middleton added to the end of the scene (to enable a couple of boys to double) was plundered from Shakespeare's original response of Macbeth to the first prophecy. Scene III.vi is sometimes said to have been moved from elsewhere, not least because it reports that Macbeth knows that Macduff has fled to England, and yet at the end of IV.i Macbeth receives news of that flight and reacts violently to it. But that bit at the end of IV.i is a Middletonian interpolation, so in fact III.vi is fine where it is and the problem has been created solely by Middleton's work on IV.i. Probably all or part of III.vi was meant by Middleton to be cut, and the 1623 printers ought not to have included it. Cutting III.vi would also remove a reference to Edward the Confessor, as Calvinist Middleton would no doubt have wanted to do. There probably was also a scene later for Edward the Confessor, turned by Middleton into an onstage report.

The phrase 'how wilt thou do for a father' is said twice, twenty-three lines apart, by Lady Macduff in IV.ii, and this is a known sign of insertion or deletion. For insertion, the logic is that the inserted material ended with a repetition of the next line of the original that should follow after the insertion, but the printer included that line from the original before starting the insertion and included it again as the last line of the insertion. For deletion, the logic is that someone copied out at the start of the deletion the line that should follow next after the deleted material had been removed, but the deletion was not actioned and this line was printed before the stuff that was meant to be deleted (but was not) and printed it again after the stuff that was meant to be deleted. At least, this was W.W. Greg's view of how so-called 'repetition brackets' came about. In the present case, Lady Macduff's repetition in IV.ii, the material in between is Middletonian, most clearly because in it the words *i'faith* and *'em* collocate closely (thirteen words apart) and no one does this collocation as often as Middleton. Other collocations confirm the attribution. (This part of Taylor's argument demonstrates admirably just what a transformation of the field of attribution studies has been enacted by the creation of the Literature Online database.) The inserted lines allude quite clearly to the Overbury plot (topical in 1616 but not in 1606), and faults in the lineation just before and just after the alleged insertion are consistent with there being an insertion at this point. Finally, Taylor thinks that the witches calling to familiars (Greymalkin and Paddock) in I.i is Middleton. The names are Middletonian, and without these calls the women retain their ambiguity— it is not entirely clear what they are—whereas Middleton makes them unambiguously witches. On this point, one small note of disagreement creeps in. Whereas Ewbank had argued that Middleton's addition of songs and dances allowed celebration of the witches' freedom, Taylor thinks that the witches' new references to their 'masters' makes them less autonomous than Shakespeare's women (p. 391). Perhaps Middleton gave with one hand and took with the other.

For the 'Canon and Chronology' section on the adaptation of *Measure for Measure* in October 1621 (pp. 417–21), Jowett is able to draw on his body of published research showing that the 'war news' material in I.ii makes no sense in 1603–4 when Shakespeare wrote the play but perfect sense in 1621 when Middleton adapted it. That aside, the case for Middleton doing the adaptation was already made in Taylor and Jowett's book *Shakespeare Reshaped* [1993], and Jowett does not have to argue that matter point by point as Taylor did for *Macbeth*. Jowett revises the view given in *Shakespeare Reshaped* that the lines after the song in IV.i were by John Webster. Reconsideration of the evidence (and especially a realization that Crane himself turned *has* into *hath* without authority, and that therefore one cannot rely on this word as a test of authorship) changed Jowett's mind, and he now gives those lines back to Middleton. Likewise Pompey's speech (about the population of the prison) at the start of IV.iii.

With so much of the textual evidence covered in the 'Canon and Chronology' section, there is little left to be dealt with in the textual introduction to each of the Shakespeare plays. For *Measure for Measure* (pp. 681–9), Jowett argues that there would be no point just representing the adapted version, since that is what every Shakespeare edition already has. This insight warrants boldness, and Jowett summarizes the new advances (beyond those in the Oxford *Complete Works* of 1986 and *Shakespeare Reshaped* of 1993) that are embodied in this edition, and tells the reader that the evidence is in the Critical Introduction and the commentary. It is nonetheless odd that Taylor decided to put his argument in the 'Canon and Chronology' section while Jowett puts his into the Critical Introduction and commentary; on the face of it this makes the edition seem inconsistent. Equally, if *Macbeth* and *Measure for Measure* are parallel cases (as their shared designation as 'Genetic' texts and shared use of boldface and greyed-out type suggest) it is odd that they treat modernization in differing ways, as we shall see.

In the textual introduction to *Macbeth* (pp. 690–703), Taylor argues that the case for Middletonian adaptation is widely accepted and need not be presented afresh here. (It is in any case fully presented in the 'Canon and Chronology' section, as we have seen.) Taylor has decided to remove capitals from the beginnings of lines and to remove punctuation, since that is how both dramatists wrote their plays. Because 'speech directions' ('aside', 'To X' and so on) are rare in manuscripts from this period they are omitted here. Spelling is trickier as an editor cannot just leave it out, so because there is no authority to recover—we do not know Shakespeare's spelling and Middleton was not the main author—the least intrusive thing to do is to use modern spelling. This is defensible because modern spelling is standardized, so it does not draw attention to itself, and its use 'removes meaningless arbitrary variation' (p. 691). This seemingly counter-intuitive point is exceptionally well made by Taylor. And yet Taylor has chosen to add stage directions where necessary (marked by square brackets) and to emend F where he thinks it in error. This strange mix of editorial choices Taylor defends by pointing out that there is no shortage of editions of Shakespeare's *Macbeth*, so one has no obligations to fulfil in preparing a new one and can instead 'deliberately' set out to make something 'alien and alienating' (p. 692). Here the lack of an overall editorial policy is most clearly marked, for if the case of *Measure for Measure* is parallel to that of *Macbeth*, as the edition seems to insist, it is peculiar that Jowett's *Measure for Measure* capitalizes the first letters of verse lines and deploys modern punctuation. Finally, for this edition, John Jowett's textual introduction for *Timon of Athens* (pp. 704–11) indicates that he has not started from scratch but only revisited his Oxford *Complete Works* text and that the textual notes are 'skeletal' as it has all been said in the Textual Companion to that edition.

The most important monograph this year is Sonia Massai's *Shakespeare and the Rise of the Editor*, and its thesis is striking. Massai sets out to challenge the idea that until Nicholas Rowe's 1709 edition each new edition of Shakespeare was just a reprint with errors and hence inherently worse than its predecessor. Massai is not referring to the injection of new authority into a reprint by the printer's copy (a previous edition) being first annotated by reference to an authoritative manuscript, but rather the idea that early readers could do such annotation using just their own wits. Necessarily, Massai needs to qualify her terms: their idea of 'authority' is not ours, and their editorial practices were different too (p. 2). We need, she argues, to widen our perspectives on seventeenth-century textual practices. The 1679 edition of the Beaumont and Fletcher Folio (a reprint of the first edition of 1647) contained a note saying that the publisher had got hold of a copy of the first edition that had been annotated by someone who knew the authors and had attended early performances, and Massai notes that they called 'perfecting' the act of improving a manuscript or printed book so that it may serve as printer's copy for a reprint (pp. 4–5). In the preliminaries to the 1623 Folio, Heminges and Condell write that 'it hath bin the height of our care ... to make the present worthy ... by the perfection', which suggests that they did not (as they stated earlier) just collect them.

Massai implies that where a reprint has substantive variants, including in the case of Q2 *Richard III* (a reprint of Q1) a couple of lines not in the book being reprinted, we should suspect editorial improvement (in this case an injection of fresh authority from a manuscript). But what about the possibility that the Q1 used as printer's copy had press variants no longer witnessed in surviving exemplars? There are only four exemplars of Q1 *Richard III* in the world, after all. Massai finally admits this possibility when attributing the insight to Peter Davison in 1977 (p. 219 n. 5), but she rejects the objection as 'reductive' because Davison 'focused solely on press variants' (p. 219 n. 5). This is poor logic: the objection is not reductive, but rather Davison pointed out one vector by which reprints might differ from what we think is their copy. That Massai thinks she has found another possible vector does not invalidate his. A surviving exemplar of Q2 *The Contention of York and Lancaster* has proof marks on B(o) and they are concerned only with accidentals, so Massai takes this as evidence that proof-readers did not bother with the substantives (p. 12). Annotations of printed books for use in performance (of which there are a couple of examples) show that they did not bother normalizing speech prefixes or stage directions or altering dialogue unless they wanted to make a big change in the action, and we know from William Long's work that theatre people did not tidy their manuscripts for use in performance. Yet from readers' annotations of printed plays for reading purposes we find the errors in speech prefixes and stage directions corrected (p. 14). (It is awfully hard to say for sure that these printed books were annotated for reading rather than for performance, and Massai does not explain how she differentiates these classes of evidence.)

Massai notes that recent work by scholars such as Zachary Lesser and Gary Taylor has turned attention away from the author and towards publisher-centred approaches that consider how the publisher shaped meanings by functioning as a guarantor of quality in his specialized field. Yet, she argues, we have not taken on board the role of the publisher as the person who maintained that quality by perfecting copy or by securing copy that had been perfected (pp. 33–5). She begins her examination of this role by looking at John and William Rastell as early sixteenth-century publishers committed to humanist pedagogy through their association with Thomas More and his circle, which was itself shaped by continental publishing practice and the work of Erasmus (pp. 41–68). This fascinating section of her book has little relevance to this review, but it is worth noting that evidence derived from the printing of *Utopia* and Erasmus's role in it as editor or even co-author ought to be treated with circumspection. After all, the textual authority of the entire project (with Raphael Hythloday as its point of origin) is entirely a fabrication. Moreover, some of the principles she draws from the evidence seem peculiar.

For example, More came to prefer print over oral or handwritten communication because it was harder for others to misuse it: a speech might be misreported, a handwritten letter might be altered by others and then published, but a printed book cannot be interfered with without the reader spotting it, since handwritten alterations stand out (pp. 56–7). One might reasonably conclude from this that the marginalia in a book are of less value than the words printed in it, which is almost exactly the opposite of Massai's general view.

Having established that John and William Rastell's editions of More's work are punctilious, Massai hopes to show the same principle (punctiliousness) in the Rastells' publications of interludes, which comprise 'three quarters of the extant printed interludes from the period' (p. 58). Thus stated as a fraction, the Rastells' domination of the market seems significant, but when we realize that Greg's chronological *Bibliography of the English Printed Drama* (*BEPD*) has by this point (the mid-1540s) reached only play number 21, the total population of printed plays seems too small for us to make much out of the relative proportions by publisher. In the midst of this discussion of punctiliousness, Massai's book itself becomes surprisingly inaccurate (p. 60). Quoting the title page of John Rastell's *The Four Elements*, where the reader is told how it may be cut for shorter performance time, Massai fails to distinguish ordinary *p* without a bar (also used in the same sentence in *parte*) from the *p* with a bar that the printer uses as an abbreviation for *par*, as in 'the messengers p < ar > te': she just gives 'pte', using one modern sort for what in the book are two distinct sorts. Yet earlier (p. 7) she was conservative enough to preserve an early printer's use of two letters *v* to make a *w* in *vvho*). Also, she transcribes *playd* or *playde* or *playdt*—it is not clear which it is but editors usually choose the first as the last letter is indistinct and might not be meant to be there at all—as *plydt* which is definitely wrong in dropping the *a*. There are other mistranscriptions in quoting from this book: *matter* where the book has *mater* and *wyse* where the book has *wyle* (both on signature E6v but wrongly given by Massai as C6v). Massai quotes Roger Coleman claiming that the printing of music with movable type in one impression shown in *The Four Elements* had not yet been invented when this book was printed, which is clearly impossible and cannot be what Coleman meant (p. 61). Greg in *BEPD* dates the play after 1525 precisely because of the music thus printed. Massai reads the movement of speech prefixes from a central to a left-marginal position as indicating the temporary misrule of the disruptive characters (beginning with the entrance of Sensual Appetite) and the return of centred prefixes as indicating the containment of these subversives. By comparison, the interludes printed by Wynkyn de Worde are less sophisticated in *mise-en-page*, and that early readers cared about such things is shown by marginal annotations that correct Rastell's few printing errors (pp. 62–4).

In a chapter on 'Italian Influences on the Publication of Late Tudor Drama' (pp. 69–87), Massai reads the dearth of published plays in the middle of the sixteenth century as arising from a general decline in performed drama towards the end of Henry's reign, whereas in the second half of the century well-printed Italian plays by the likes of Ariosto and Cinthio began to come into England with the flood of Protestant exiles from the

Counter-Reformation. In these books, the level of editorial intervention and care was deliberately foregrounded as a selling point. She outlines the career of the publisher John Wolfe, the man mainly responsible for bringing Italian Renaissance texts to London readers and employer of 'correctors' (especially Gabriel Harvey) to improve copy before printing, and his use of false continental imprints to give his books extra kudos. She also describes the career of Richard Jones, who printed *Tamburlaine* and addressed its reader with a note about the 'fond and frivolous gestures' in the play as he received it and that he omitted. (This last point rather undercuts Massai's argument that he was a conscientious 'corrector': from our point of view he was a meddling busy-body who should have printed what he received.) Massai suggests that Jones also lightly annotated his printed copy for *Tamburlaine* before reprinting it (so that the variants between the first three editions are not authoritative), and in this it feels like she is fighting her primary materials: she wants to suggest that printers were doing something to add authority and her evidence keeps contradicting her.

Massai's study of Andrew Wise is, as she indicates, central to her argument (pp. 91–105). Although not the first to publish Shakespeare, Andrew Wise was the first to seriously invest in publishing him and had a series of hit Shakespeare books in the 1590s: two editions of *Richard III* and three each of *1 Henry IV* and *Richard II*. Massai asks, 'can we assume that Shakespeare himself corrected the texts of his popular history plays when Wise decided to, or was prompted to, reprint them? Or, are we to assume that he entrusted Wise with their transmission into print?' (p. 91). She senses a means to test the New Bibliography, and claims that 'The Wise Quartos, in other words, represent an ideal study case [*sic*] to test Pollard, McKerrow and Greg's optimistic assumption that a direct line of transmission connected authorial manuscripts to the so-called "good" quarto editions of Shakespeare's works, without any significant "interference" from the non-authorial agents involved in their publication.' In fact, this last sentence is not the previous point (about the authority of reprints) expressed 'in other words' but rather concerns the New Bibliographical assumption that the copy for the first printing was a manuscript in Shakespeare's hand rather than a theatrical document or a scribal transcript, which assumption in turn arises from prior assumptions about the textual economy of the early modern playhouse, and in particular the desirability of there existing no more than two manuscripts of each play, the author's foul papers and the promptbook.

There is a way to link New Bibliography and the reprints that Massai is interested in, but it is not via the first-generational work of Pollard, McKerrow and Greg as she claims but rather in the compositor studies that began in the 1950s and to which she turns. Alan E. Craven used the evidence of how a particular compositor changed a text as he reprinted it from known printed copy to work out the compositor's general habits. Massai is not convinced that compositors could make changes of the kind Craven attributed to them. For example, Craven claimed that for Valentine Simmes's Compositor A to fix a faulty speech prefix in scene V.iii of *Richard II* Q1 (in which York rather than King Henry is made to say 'Good aunt stand up') requires him to have 'worked out the degree of kinship and power relations among the four speakers in this exchange' (p. 93). In fact it only requires him to follow the action and notice that York ought not to call his own wife 'Good aunt'. Massai objects that Craven assumed that the variants between Q1 *Richard II* and its reprint Q2 are all down to the compositor, but since she cannot show another vector she ought to be obliged on principle not to multiply the agents by speculation.

Massai summarizes Wise's career and speculates about how he came to publish three Chamberlain's men smash-hit plays. She reckons the link was that Wise knew writers under George Carey's patronage, which included Shakespeare (pp. 92–5). She makes the common mistake of giving the date that George Carey was made Lord Chamberlain as 17 March 1597, but in fact it was, as Greg long ago pointed out, actually 17 April 1597 (p. 100). Massai offers as one possible reason for the Chamberlain's men selling Wise the copy for three plays in 1597–8 their needing money to pay rent at the Curtain as the expiry of the lease on the Theatre drew near (p. 101). Since the company was in any case paying the Burbage family rent on the Theatre, it presumably made no difference to the company—only to the Burbages—if they moved to the Curtain and paid rent there. Moreover, they did not move to the Curtain when the lease expired but rather hung on at the Theatre for more than a year, and in any case it is likely that the Burbages owned the Curtain too.

In order to show that someone annotated the printed copy for Wise's Shakespeare quartos before he reprinted them, Massai starts with the line 'As thought on thinking on no thought I thinke' from II.ii in Q1 *Richard II* which was reprinted as 'As though on thinking on no thought I thinke' in Q2. She comments that the fact that some editors adopt Q1's reading and some Q2's shows that 'intervention in Q2 was not determined by an obvious misreading in Q1' and she gives as an example of a modern editor going for Q1's reading Charles Forker's Arden3 edition (p. 102). (Massai's bibliography entry for this edition wrongly gives the date as 1998 and the publisher as Athlone: it was 2002 and Thomson Learning.) Importantly, Forker himself was only repeating the reading from the Oxford *Complete Works*, which was the source of the innovation: no previous edition had gone for Q1's reading. Massai thinks this the kind of 'textual variation which seems to stem from light annotation' but she has not eliminated other reasonable possibilities. Obvious examples are that Q2 was printed from an exemplar of Q1 that had *though* as a press correction, or that the compositor of Q2 just missed off the terminal *t* by accident, or that the compositor read the Q1 line and believed it to be in error and tried to fix it. The variants of Q1–Q2 *1 Henry IV* are outlined by Massai, and she admits that scholars generally agree they are the kinds of things that can happen in the printshop, yet instead of offering reasons why that explanation must be abandoned she simply says she is 'more inclined' to the view that they require an understanding of 'the fictive world of the play' that was beyond a compositor's ken and thus they are more likely to be the work of an annotator (pp. 102–3). At this point argument becomes sheer assertion, and by referring the reader back to her introduction Massai gives the impression that the present example is the reinforcement of a case already made. But in fact the introduction promised that the case would be made here, so the rhetoric is circular.

Regarding the variants in Q1–Q2–Q3 *Richard III* Massai rather unfairly claims that John Jowett 'attributes them to [the printer Thomas] Creede' (p. 103) when the passage she quotes only says 'Q2 may...have been corrected' from the copy for Q1 retained by Creede. The bigger problem, not addressed by Massai, is that in the edition she is quoting, the Oxford Shakespeare text, Jowett wrongly claimed that Q1 and Q2 were published by Creede (p. 153 n. 102), but in fact Creede only printed (did not publish) Q2 and Q3 and Peter Short and Valentine Simmes printed Q1 *Richard III*. It is clear that a simple typo explains all this: Jowett meant to say that Wise published Q1 and Q2 (but he accidentally typed 'Creede') and that hence it is possible that Q2 benefits from a reading in the manuscript copy for Q1 that Wise retained. Massai points out that Wise the publisher and not Creede the printer would have held the manuscript copy for Q1, which is true and is exactly what Jowett wrote elsewhere in the same edition (p. 116 n. 3). Out of Jowett's typo Massai constructs a straw man. Rather than offer a new theory, Massai picks holes in Jowett's narrative and constructs a paragraph-long explanation of Creede's generally not being a careful man and hence not likely to introduce the small and unobvious corrections in *Richard III*, and concludes that without Creede in the frame we are left with the agency of either Wise or Shakespeare in making the improvements. A more generous approach would have been to ask Jowett to clarify the glaring contradiction in his edition, but this would have denied Massai her straw man.

Massai's chapter on the Pavier quartos of 1619 (pp. 106–35) does, however, offer a new and plausible interpretation of the facts. The standard narrative is that the letter of the Lord Chamberlain (William Herbert) to the Stationers' Company of May 1619, in which it was ordered that no King's men's play was to be published without the players' consent, was directed at suppressing Thomas Pavier's plan for a collected Shakespeare, perhaps because the 1623 Folio was already in planning. Indeed Lukas Erne argued that Pavier's quartos (and not the bad quartos) were the ones complained of by the Folio preliminaries. Massai is not buying this: the company order of 1619 was not directed at Pavier at all. The printers of the Pavier quartos were William and Isaac Jaggard, and it was Isaac—thus inspired by Pavier's vision of a collected Shakespeare—who persuaded the King's men to get the order stopping other stationers (not Pavier) from securing copy for the as yet unpublished Shakespeare plays. And it was Isaac who persuaded Pavier to falsify the title-page dates so that his partial collection (sold together or individually) would seem like a gathering of old and new material and thus 'whet, rather than satisfy, readers' demand' for a collected Shakespeare (p. 107). Working with Jaggard and the players this way, Pavier got their protection and got to make money lending his rights to the Folio syndicate.

Massai thinks that her narrative answers previously hard-to-answer questions, such as why Pavier made such a poor attempt to fake title pages from twenty years earlier, and it also explains why Pavier was not punished by the Stationers' Company for breaking its order (p. 108). (I would have thought that Pavier's falsified title pages were fairly convincing, since it took Greg's celebrated detective work with watermarks to reveal them.) To bolster her narrative, Massai looks to later repetitions of the Lord Chamberlain's intervention. In June 1637 and again in August 1641, successive Lords Chamberlain (Philip Herbert, William's brother, and then Robert Devereux) wrote to the Stationers' Company, invoking William Herbert's letter of 1619 as a precedent, asking it to protect court-patronized players from publication of their plays. The letter of 1637 asks the company to check with the players that for any of their plays already entered in the Stationers' Register they are content to have the play printed, and to do this for any more of their plays that come into Stationers' Hall for entry, but nowhere does it mention taking action against stationers who have already printed plays. The letter of 1641 lists plays that had never been printed. Thus, argues Massai, the two letters suggest that the players were not able to prevent the reprinting of plays, only to keep their as yet unprinted plays out of print (p. 109).

Thus, on the evidence of these letters, we cannot assume that the 1619 order was supposed to cover reprints (and of course all of Pavier's quartos were reprints) and hence the 1619 letter might not have been aimed at Pavier at all. A potential objection that Massai might have forestalled is that we cannot apply the 1637 and 1641 letters to the lost 1619 letter in this way because of what had happened in the meantime: the Folio had been published in 1623. This clarified and established the rights for virtually the whole Shakespeare canon, and the letters of 1637 and 1641 are thus clearly concerned with the non-Shakespearian plays of the companies named. In 1619 the rights to the Shakespeare canon had not been clearly established—as indeed the printing schedule of the Folio seems to show, with disruptions apparently due to disputes over rights—and the Lord Chamberlain's letter might well for that reason have had quite a different intent from the later letters. Massai points out that we can tell that the letter of 1637 had an effect because in the five years before the letter thirteen Queen's men's plays were published, of which seven were new (in the sense of being previously unpublished), while in the five years after the letter twenty were published, of which only two were new. For the King's men, the rates are seven plays published in the five years before the letter, of which three were new, while in the five years after the letter eight plays were published, of which only one was new. So, the letter did have the affect of keeping unpublished plays out of print (p. 110).

Massai reckons that it was the dramatists, such as Thomas Heywood, who seemed to want their stuff published and against whom the Lord Chamberlain's letter of 1637 was written. Massai admits a problem in applying the 1637 letter to the 1619 conditions, since in fact there had been a slump in the publication of previously unpublished plays in the 1610s (so there was little for him to prevent), and indeed the same was true in the later 1630s, just ahead of the letter of 1641. That the 1641 letter lists old unpublished plays to be protected presumably indicates that the players were planning a collection of previously unpublished plays and wanted to stop anyone pre-empting it, and indeed that may have been what the 1619 letter did, with even a similar list attached (pp. 111–12). Greg's claim that Pavier broke the Stationers' Company order of 1619 by his quartos, and that this is why he gave them false imprints, is undermined by the fact that of the ten plays (nine quartos, *The Whole Contention* being two plays in one) he owned the rights to five of them, that he worked closely with the owners of the rights to three of them, and that the rights to the other two were derelict. Moreover two of the ones with false dates are ones Pavier himself owned the rights to (pp. 113–14). It was not the other stationers nor the actors Pavier wanted to deceive, it was the readers: he wanted to look like he had gathered some old printings with some new ones for a 'nonce' collection. Other 'nonce' collections had mixed title-page dates in them, and Pavier was successfully imitating those. Why do it? As a promotional build-up to the 1623 Folio.

We usually give Edward Blount the credit for coming up with the idea for the Folio, but the Jaggards had connections with the King's men, and that Blount came into the project late is suggested by his name not appearing alongside Isaac Jaggard's in the mention of the Folio in the Frankfurt book fair catalogue of 1622. Blount had the rights and the money, but Isaac Jaggard had the idea and got it from his father William's involvement with Pavier in 1619 (pp. 117–18). Isaac persuaded Pavier to make his quartos collection look like a 'nonce' work 'as a pre-publicity stunt' for the Folio and to diminish its directly competing with the Folio when that came out. What would Pavier get out of it? By offering his quartos as both individual plays and a 'nonce' collection, Pavier would hedge his bets, and he would be able to lend his rights to the Folio consortium for a fee; he might even have been a potential member of that consortium (p. 119). That cashing in on the planned Folio was seen as a potential opportunity explains Matthew Law's reprints of *Richard III* and *1 Henry IV* in 1622. The undated reprint of *Romeo and Juliet* in 1622 by John Smethwick, one of the Folio consortium, shows that he wanted to get a general Shakespeare boom going but not to compete with his other project, the Folio. (This reprint is now confidently dated to 1623—see below—but that does not harm Massai's argument.) Thomas Walkley's 1622 *Othello* was probably also permitted pre-publicity for the Folio: after 1619 it is hard to see Walkley getting away with printing a previously unpublished Shakespeare play without the syndicate's agreement (p. 120).

Thus Massai makes a plausible and nuanced case that the Pavier quartos were not piratical but part of a careful plan and that is why their corrections of their printer's copies are so good. Massai shows that, when taken as a group, the Pavier reprints show certain patterns of editorial improvement, with certain directions being amplified or clarified and others (especially those useful to actors rather than readers) cut. There is an overall tendency to make the things more literary and less theatrical. As before, Massai asserts but does not prove that the changes made to the copy happened before the copy was submitted to the printshop: she assumes that no one in the printshop was smart or careful enough to do it. Massai claims that there are similarities in the ways that stage directions are rephrased across eight of the ten plays and quotes a few examples, but without stating what she thinks is common in them; I cannot see a similarity (p. 124). In further examples, one habit is clear: the removal of redundantly repetitive *and*s in stage directions, but of course this is pretty easily attributed to an observant compositor. In the Pavier reprint of *Oldcastle* some lines amounting to a page and a half are omitted, and Massai reads this as an adjustment made to allow more white space around stage directions in order to make a prettier page. She argues that the cuts are clever in that they do not disrupt the sense, but is it really plausible that someone who tweaked stage directions to make them read better would also countenance such massive cuts for the sake of a good-looking page? The major example of editing of the copy for a Pavier reprint is his Q3 *The Contention of York and Lancaster* which is based an edited form of Q1 in which York's mangled account of his own genealogy is unmangled (pp. 126–8). True, but this has long been recognized. Compared to other reprints of the period, Pavier's are in many ways improved over the books they reprint, so we should not consider his project shady (p. 132). He seems to have put money into perfecting his copy, but who did the perfecting?

On the evidence of his reprint (Q3, 1602) of *A Looking Glass for London and England*, it was Pavier himself. There too, as in the Pavier 1619 reprints of *A Yorkshire Tragedy* and *The Merchant of Venice*, the reprint adds pronouns to clarify and improve stage directions: 'Embrace him' becomes 'She imbraceth him', 'spurns her' becomes 'He spurns her', and 'open the letter' becomes 'He opens the letter'. (Since these are simply changes from the imperative to the indicative mood I cannot see the improvement, and even if we accept that the parallels—Massai has fifteen in all—are compelling evidence of the same man at work, why does it have to be Pavier rather than a man he hired in 1602 and again in 1619?) *Henry V* Q1 was reprinted in 1602 by Pavier (Q2) and again by Pavier from Q1 in 1619 (Q3), and the pattern of improvements each time was the same. What Pavier had done to improve the play for his Q2 he had done again independently to improve it for Q3 (rather than reprinting directly from Q2). Thus the same man was involved both times (in 1602 and in 1619) and the obvious candidate is Pavier himself (p. 134). Again, this we may call 'editing' after a fashion, but if it does not involve access to additional authoritative documents it does not transform the textual situation in the way that Massai seems to think: a clever guess by someone from Shakespeare's own time is still just a guess. For Massai, Pavier has thus been shown to be 'an integral part of the editorial tradition', and in the limited sense of 'editorial' she is right, since after all Nicholas Rowe's 1709 Shakespeare is typically called 'edited', although he too used only his own wits.

Massai turns next to the plays for which the 1623 Folio reprints an existing quarto (pp. 136–79). Massai thinks that the editors of the Oxford *Complete Works* of 1986 indulged in wish-fulfilment in their belief that the theatrical origins of certain Folio texts' departures from their printed Q copy were caused by annotation of that copy by reference to a promptbook. Why would a publisher collate his printed copy against the theatrical manuscript (one not known to be radically different from it) only to recover a handful of readings? We know that, for the purpose of printing, authors such as John Lyly cut out the songs and dumbshows, and that the first publisher of *Tamburlaine* removed what he thought were theatrical frivolities for the sake of his readership. So why would the Shakespeare Folio syndicate bother to make their copy 'better' by reference to a theatrical document? This rhetorical question of Massai's, and the analogues on which it is thus based, skate over some important differences that are worth pursuing for a moment. Where it is claimed that the Folio copy was a quarto that was first annotated by reference to a manuscript, the idea is to undo the harm done by the first printer. Richard Jones's printing of *Tamburlaine*, on the other hand, was made from manuscript copy. Where the Folio is printed from foul papers and is our only text of the play (as in *All's Well That Ends Well*), no one supposes that these papers were made more theatrical by reference to a theatrical document, although if they were it is hard to see how we would be able to tell this kind of subsequent annotation apart from simple annotation of those papers for use in the theatre. Also, to annotate the printed copy by reference to the promptbook takes the Folio text away from being a simple reprint of a quarto, and this might be helpful if the publisher of that quarto were thought likely to claim that his rights were being infringed. For the Folio project the theatre texts were the authorities, but since it is easier to set type from printed copy it would have been handier to use that authority by having it modify an easily purchased quarto. In any case, the licensed theatrical texts ought not to be allowed out of the theatre.

Massai compares the Folio variants from its own printed copy with the kinds of annotation made by readers in a couple of quartos, and as they are unalike she concludes that annotation of the printer's copy quarto is not the cause of the Folio variants. However, she deals only with John Dover Wilson's claim that the quarto of *Love's Labour's Lost* used to print the Folio had itself once been the promptbook and had annotations for performance on it. She does not address the Oxford editors' claim that the quarto used as printer's copy was annotated by reference to a promptbook in order to bring it into alignment with that promptbook. Massai says she will show that the Folio departures from its printed copy in *Romeo and Juliet* and *Love's Labour's Lost* are not because Q was marked up for performance, but again no one since Dover Wilson has made that claim. Only after disposing of straw man Dover Wilson does she turn to the Oxford claim of quartos marked up by reference to a promptbook, although she is careful to choose as a test case a play about which the Oxford editors were uncertain and admitted alternative possibilities, such as the annotator of *Romeo and Juliet* having only his recollections of performance to guide him. Militating against the hypothesis that a theatrical manuscript or recollections of performance were use to improve Q3 *Romeo and Juliet* before it was used as copy for F is the fact that on a couple of occasions it worsens the stage directions, making them less accurate an account of what must have happened on stage. Likewise, the Folio flattens out the speech prefixes of the musicians from 'Fidler' and 'Minstrels' in Q3 to just 'Mu[sician]', thus reducing detail, not enhancing it, and on some occasions the Folio gets speeches wrong that Q3 gets right, or at least more right than the Folio does in any case. Massai lists some more things that this putative annotator must have got wrong, and agrees with S.W. Reid (albeit he does not say this on the page she cites) that the Folio departures from Q3 cannot be put down solely to a Folio compositor. But she cannot accept either—because of the textual harm that would have to be attributed to him—that the annotator's authority was either a promptbook or his memory of performance. This is straining at gnats, for the Oxford editors readily conceded that if the Q3 copy for Folio *Romeo and Juliet* was improved by consultation of an authoritative manuscript, the process was not thorough.

Regarding *Love's Labour's Lost*, Massai points out that John Kerrigan and Stanley Wells disagree on why the annotation of Q1 to make copy for F did not produce a better text than we have: Kerrigan says the annotator was slovenly and Wells says the manuscript used for the annotation was not good. (This is something of a false opposition, for Wells too argues that the annotator was slovenly.) Massai deals with the tangled speech prefixes that conceal which lord will pair off with which lady in the story (pp. 147–8), but without mentioning Manfred Draudt's argument that these couples are supposed to switch partners early on in the play because these people are like that. Massai simply asserts that the Folio departures from its Q copy are largely a matter of that Q having been sporadically annotated by a reader using nothing but his wits, but she is forced to concede that the intrusion in F of the speech prefix 'Prin.' halfway through a speech already assigned to the Princess of France in II.i cannot be explained that way and must be as Wells describes it, the effect of looking at a different textual witness in which the first twenty lines of her speech were marked for omission (pp. 148–9). (Of course, having conceded that point there is no reason for her to persist in positing an additional vector of annotation since this one alone can account for all the problems.) Looking across the Folio texts printed from existing quartos, Massai notices that the variants are not of the same kind in each case, suggesting to her that they do not all come from the same process by the same people, the putative Folio editors. Some of them (such as the part-lines added to *1 Henry IV* and *2 Henry IV* when reprinted in F from quarto copy) look like the things she has previously observed as the habits of annotating readers (pp. 151–8). There is here much repetition of arguments made earlier, but now taking as a starting point certain moments from—not comprehensive surveys of—Folio texts printed from quarto copy and arguing that they are better explained as the effect of readers annotating their copy (to improve it) than as someone sporadically collating F's printed quarto copy with a manuscript.

Massai revives Eleanor Prosser's claim that an anonymous editor added bits to Q1 *2 Henry IV* before it was used to make F (p. 153), and describes the annotator working on copy for Folio *Much Ado About Nothing* as someone intent on removing unnecessary characters from stage directions, and going too far in some places and not far enough in others. Massai makes the mistake of claiming that 'Leonato's wife ... is only mentioned once in the opening stage direction of both editions [Q and F]' (p. 157), but in fact she is mentioned again, in both editions, in the opening stage direction for the second act. If the F variants from its printed Q copy are all due to the prior-to-printing annotation of Q by comparison with an authoritative manuscript, why are the outcomes so different for different plays? Why is profanity based on the name of Jesus removed from *1 Henry IV* but allowed to stand in *Romeo and Juliet*? For Massai, this indicates different annotators with different tastes (p. 158), but of course it could just as easily reflect differences in the authoritative manuscripts, such as one being made for first performance or revival before the ban on stage oaths and one being made for a revival after the ban.

To discover which member of the Folio consortium engaged the annotator(s), Massai surveys each man's other projects (pp. 159–79). Edward Blount's 1632 edition of six Lyly plays, all reprints, shows no sign of this activity. To see if Isaac Jaggard might have engaged an annotating reader Massai goes on a fairly lengthy detour through the works of, and attitude towards print held by, Thomas Heywood solely to evaluate if the Jaggard editions of *A Woman Killed with Kindness* [1607, 1617] show such a person at work. Answer: no. William Aspley gets the same treatment and answer, leaving just John Smethwick. Massai relies on Lynette Hunter's essay 'Why Has Q4 *Romeo and Juliet* Such an Intelligent Editor?' (reviewed in *YWES* 82[2003]) and agrees that an annotator was at work on the copy for Q3 *Romeo and Juliet* and for Q4 *Romeo and Juliet*, but unlike Hunter she does not think the same person was that annotator in both cases. Thus rather than being the annotator, Smethwick probably just engaged an annotator when he printed Q3 and Q4, and presumably he did the same as part of the Folio consortium.

The first half of Massai's last chapter, 'Perfecting Shakespeare in the Fourth Folio (1685)' (pp. 180–95), is a condensed reprint of her article ' "Taking just care of the impression": Editorial Intervention in Shakespeare's Fourth Folio, 1685' reviewed in *YWES* 83[2004], and the second part is an argument for relative continuity between the seventeenth-century 'editors' of Shakespeare that she has identified—her annotating readers—and their eighteenth-century successors such as Alexander Pope and Thomas Hanmer. The conclusion (pp. 196–205) observes that correcting did not end with the printing of the book: readers were enjoined to carry on the process by correcting their books. Massai ties this to the idea of the text as infinitely perfectible, fluid and unstable. What are the consequences for editing? Massai finds fault with the New Bibliography and the recent campaign for un-editing, since both treat the book as a static object, which she thinks is an anachronistic approach since early moderns saw the book as an ongoing process. The important thing, she asserts, is to be historical about all this. Her own question remains unanswered, however, since she does not say what this historical approach would mean for editing.

John Jowett's book *Shakespeare and Text* displays its author's extraordinary capacity for explaining complex textual problems, and his solutions of them, in terms that anyone can understand and then drawing out the subtle philosophical correlatives that go with his approaches. He neatly sums up recent developments by observing that in general we used to think that Q1 and Folio *King Lear* were imperfect witnesses to a singular antecedent authorial version, and now we are in danger of deluding ourselves that they are perfect witnesses to two equally viable authorial versions, whereas in fact the truth lies between these positions: authorial revision and corruption separate these printings (p. 3). The work of Lukas Erne has clearly moved Jowett's position somewhat, for he writes that Shakespeare 'might have anticipated' that his plays would be printed but there is 'little evidence that he was actively concerned' with printing (p. 4). Jowett's first chapter, 'Author and Collaborator' (pp. 6–26), is a survey of the primary evidence and the recent stylometric discoveries. Throughout, the book is studded with insights that only someone stepping back from a long and close engagement with the textual detail is able to offer, as when observing that the attack on Shakespeare in *Greene's Groatsworth of Wit* is necessarily a compliment too, since it does not name him directly and hence assumes that Shakespeare was well enough known that readers could identify him merely by allusion (p. 7). Not every point need receive assent. Jowett claims that the spelling of *scilens* (for *silence*) in Hand D of *Sir Thomas More* is not known in any un-Shakespearian text 'of the period' (p. 13), but that rather depends how flexible you are about the period: it was an accepted late medieval spelling and is found in John Lydgate's poetry. The chapter 'Theatre' (pp. 27–45) is a survey of the textual economy of the theatre, including the creation and purposes of plots and parts and how revision and adaptation occurred. There is an odd slip here: quoting Arthur Brown on Heywood's *The Captives*, Jowett reports that the manuscript was annotated to guide the scribe 'for whom' the official 'book' was to be made, but of course Brown wrote 'by whom' (p. 28). Jowett reads the Master of the Revels Henry Herbert's demand (written into the licence for *The Launching of the Mary*) for 'fair copy hereafter' as meaning 'of this play', but since it can also be read as meaning 'in future send me fair copy' it would have been useful to know why Jowett excludes this possibility (p. 29).

Jowett urges textual scholars to retain the term 'promptbook' in favour of more recently proposed terms such as 'playbook' that are less loaded with nineteenth-century theatrical assumptions because it suggests the active connection with what is happening, minute by minute, on the stage. This he thinks these documents really are concerned with, especially as witnessed in their 'readying' notes, examples of which he usefully lists (pp. 32–5). He points out that taking the reference in *Romeo and Juliet* to 'two-hours traffic' as an indication of how long the performance will run is a bit over-literal, since after all no one would think that *Henry V* lasts sixty minutes because the Prologue says the events have been compressed into an 'hourglass' (p. 36). Jowett does not accept the recently floated idea that bad quartos are performance texts and the good quartos and Folio texts are authorial. Not only Shakespeare but also Jonson, Webster and Fletcher tended to write long plays whose early printings—*Every Man Out of His Humour* [1600], *The Duchess of Malfi* [1623] and Humphrey Moseley's preface to the 1647 Beaumont and Fletcher Folio—indicate that the author's text was cut for performance. Thus Folio *Hamlet* or *Henry V* may still represent the full author's script, as represented in the promptbook, from which the actors cut a few scenes to make their performances (p. 37). Regarding the purposes for which playhouse 'plots' were created, Jowett quotes David Bradley's interpretation (that they are casting documents) as an alternative to Greg's (that they were a backstage 'cheat sheet' for forgetful performers), but Bradley's quotation is assigned to his page 120 when it in fact appears on his page 126 (pp. 40, 206 n. 18).

In his chapter 'The Material Book' (pp. 46–68) Jowett explains the appearance of the long s as like 'f' without a forward crossbar', which is a little confusing for the reader as while the book-opening he presents in facsimile (from Q1 *Troilus and Cressida*) has long s as he describes it (with a crossbar to the left of the stem but not to the right of it) the modern typeface with which Oxford University Press has represented this sort has no crossbar at all (p. 48). Jowett offers a neat and succinct summary of the process of entry in the Stationers' Register, although he once (p. 51) treats 'authority'—which the entry for *Troilus and Cressida* needs more of—as a matter of 'trade regulation' rather than ecclesiastical permission; elsewhere he follows Peter Blayney's accepted distinction of *allowance* = *authority* (= external approval from the church) and *licence* (= internal approval from the Stationers' Company). Jowett reckons that Blayney's estimates for the profitability of printing a play are a bit low: it cannot be the case that first editions did little more than break even, and all the profits were in reprints, since only 50 per cent of books achieved reprints (p. 53). Under these conditions, who would bother doing a first edition if there were a less than even chance of eventually making a profit on it? (I am not sure I agree with this logic: with nearly half the gambles paying off and the rest not losing any money, most gamblers would be happy to keep taking a chance.) Jowett makes the excellent point about the practice of compositors setting by formes rather than seriatim, and—one I have not heard before—that this brings about the completion of a quarto forme at regular time intervals (one after every four pages are set) whereas seriatim work completes them unevenly (one after seven pages, and then after one, and then seven, and so on). Jowett explains the workings of a printing press well, but the description is let down by a picture of a press that has no frisket in place so it is not clear just how this operates as a mask to keep unwanted ink off the sheet to be printed (p. 55).

In his chapter 'The First Folio' (pp. 69–92), Jowett gives an account of the Pavier quartos of 1619, including a reference to Massai's account of them but not crediting her with the new idea that Pavier was in league with the Folio syndicate: Jowett sticks to the old story that Pavier was working against their interests, but then at the end wonders if Pavier was, perhaps inadvertently, helping to get the Folio project started by showing what was possible in republishing Shakespeare. (For Massai, as we have seen, Pavier was doing just this intentionally.) Jowett makes the familiar assertion that without the Folio we would not know of sixteen of Shakespeare's plays, but actually this counterfactual is not necessarily so straightforward. If no one had thought to make the Folio then it is possible that publishers might have issued the unpublished plays in individual quartos over the succeeding years; after all, *The Two Noble Kinsmen* did not get its first quarto until 1634. Jowett's claim about the book's influence is well made, however. As he points out, as recently as Peter Alexander's 1951 *Complete Works*, *The Tempest* was printed as the first play for no other reason than that the Folio had it so. In 'Mapping the Text' (pp. 93–114) Jowett makes the point that the character commonly called Lady Capulet is merely an editorial invention: the Capulets are not aristocrats; he is just Capulet and she is his wife (p. 99). Editors could, he argues, synthesize the view of Barbara Mowat that editions should be concerned primarily about the needs of the reader (not so much the author) with Greg's distinction between the accidentals and the substantives, and so produce texts in which 'matters of incidence and presentation would be ceded to the interests of the reader, while the substantives of the text would be recognized as having integrity in terms of their origin' (pp. 113–14).

Jowett's chapter on 'Emendation and Modernization' (pp. 115–35) offers an excellent example of the obligation to undo assumed censorship even where we have no access to the uncensored version other than by inference. When Angelo says 'heauen in my mouth, | As if I did but onely chew his name' in Folio *Measure for Measure*, he must originally have been given the line

'God in my mouth'. Jowett concedes that there is idealism in emending in 'pursuit of a prior text', meaning the author's manuscript, but rightly insists that this is less pernicious than the idealism of being willing only 'to correct the errors in a document to no other criterion than an ideal version of itself' (p. 116). This prior manuscript was not necessarily a perfect expression of the mind creating it: Jowett gives examples of Hand D of *Sir Thomas More* not writing what he meant, as when making slips and also when forcing two verse lines into one because he has reached the end of the page and has no more room (pp. 117–18). Regarding 'Versification and Stage Directions' (pp. 136–57), Jowett makes the important point that, when originally written, the stage directions were meant to determine what would happen on the stage, while in a modern edition they are attempting to account for what might or must have happened on the stage, and hence these two kinds of writing are 'ontologically distinct' (p. 149). He might nonetheless be overstating the case. We could say that the modern stage directions are showing what the original ones would have looked like if the original writers and readers, the actors, had our modern sense of how much you need to tell someone about the action. Looked at in this way, old and modern stage directions belong in the same ontological category, and we can proceed by analogy with the modernization of spelling and punctuation.

There has been a recent demand that editors cease making explicit what they think the stage action should be, should cease being prescriptive in their invented stage directions, and should retain the multitude of possibilities latent in the incomplete or missing directions in the early printings. Jowett offers the splendid rejoinder that this view overlooks the distinct possibility that rather than experiencing such moments as a range of performance possibilities the unaided reader might well simply have no idea what is happening on the stage (p. 155). Jowett ends this chapter by quoting the opening moments of *Timon of Athens* from the Oxford *Collected Middleton* (reviewed above), but unfortunately not entirely accurately in terms of typography. The indenting of the second part of the split verse line is not properly aligned in the last line of the quotation. The fact that the Oxford *Collected Middleton* puts the speech prefix on a line of its own for a speech of verse (except where someone else completes a split verse line) is misrepresented. In the quotation here the speech prefix is on the same line as the first word of the speech, and indeed that is the cause of the misalignment of the final split verse line. A pair of square brackets around an editorial stage direction is italicized in the quotation and should not be for the brackets are not italicized in the Oxford *Collected Middleton*. Another slip: 'As noted in Chapter 5, John Dover Wilson's Cambridge series employed quotation marks to identify wordings taken from the base text' (p. 156) but in fact there is no such point made anywhere earlier in this book, so presumably this is a relic from an earlier state of the text. Jowett's last chapter, 'Texts for Readers' (pp. 158–69), is largely a survey of the digital future, especially the Internet Shakespeare Editions project.

Thomas Merriam's book *Co-authorship in King John* has the same thesis as his previous one on *Henry VIII* (reviewed in *YWES* 86[2007]): the play was co-authored and Shakespeare did not write the anti-Catholic bits. Merriam reports that most people accept that *King John* is based on the anonymous

two-part play *The Troublesome Reign of King John.* John Bale's *King Johan*
and *Troublesome Reign* make John seem a proto-Protestant and portray
Catholicism as bad, but Shakespeare seems to have evened the balance
somewhat. Yet there remain three pro-Protestant speeches in *King John* and
they are all in III.i, and also distinctly Catholic sentiments remain. Critics have
seen this as another demonstration of myriad-minded Shakespeare seeing
both sides of an argument, but for Merriam the contradiction comes
from co-authorship. Merriam begins with a postulate: in a study of relative
frequency of words by an author, the median frequency should be close to the
mean frequency (p. 15). This principle is refreshingly well explained by
Merriam, which is not always the case with such research. Merriam provides a
table of the relative frequency of the word *and* in twenty-seven plays of
undisputed Shakespearian sole authorship, ranked from *Henry V* (the highest,
in which 3.7 per cent of all words are *and*) to *The Two Gentlemen of Verona*
(where only 2.35 per cent of all words are *and*), and as expected the mean
frequency (about 2.8 per cent) is close to the median frequency (held by *Romeo
and Juliet*, fourteenth out of twenty-seven plays in the list, with an *and*
frequency of about 2.8 per cent) (p. 16). This principle of symmetry (median
equalling mean) in relation to one word's relative frequency should exist too in
the subdivisions of a play if it is all by one hand. Merriam divides *King John*
into twenty-seven sections and puts each section into his ranking order table
for twenty-seven plays. The outcome is that ten chunks of *King John* use *and*
way more often than the Shakespeare play that uses *and* the most, which is
Henry V, and thereby upset the median/mean symmetry (pp. 17–18). Likewise
for the pronoun *I*, the adverb *not*, and the pronoun *it*, which are all used way
too little in *King John* (pp. 19–24). Moreover, for these four tests (*and*, *I*, *not*,
it) it is the same subsections of *King John* that are the outliers: the prime cases
at the tops of the tables being units 1, 11a, 17 and 19 and at the bottoms being
14, 18 and 20. This suggests dual authorship. To refine the technique, Merriam
brings in a further seventeen such test words and makes a combined table of all
twenty-one test words' results, to which he applies Principal Component
Analysis. This confirms that certain bits of *King John* are much unlike the rest
of Shakespeare (pp. 25–6). Interestingly, the bits of *King John* that critics
have praised as its core great scenes are well within the Shakespeare norm, and
the really strong outlier is the crucial hinge speech of twenty lines by
the Bastard in IV.iii, where he seems to take on responsibility for the future
well-being of England. Take out the fifteen outliers (representing half the play)
and the remaining chunks fit perfectly well into the Shakespeare profile
(pp. 27–8).

Then comes a new approach to the problem (pp. 29–34). Merriam takes
ninety-two words that occur 781 times in *Tamburlaine* but only eighty-three
times in *As You Like It* and takes 104 words that occur 693 times in *As You
Like It* but only thirty times in *Tamburlaine*. (Here Merriam makes the types/
tokens distinction but does not explain it. A simple illustration is that this
review contains 30,952 words (tokens) in total, but many of them are
repetitions such as *and* and *the*, so that the number of different words (types) is
only 4,428). Thus the *Tamburlaine* set comprises words favoured by Marlowe
(and a lot of them seem to be about power), and the *As You Like It* set

comprises words favoured by Shakespeare. The words chosen for these two sets are not the usual filler words (like *and*), so we need to check if they are subject to authorial influence (one writer to another) or vary by a play's subject matter. Merriam does this by showing that for twenty-seven Shakespeare plays, three Marlowes, and three Peeles, the Shakespeare words occur way more often in the Shakespeare plays (always more often than they occur in the Marlowe or Peele) and the Marlowe words occur way more often in the Marlowe plays (always more often than in the Shakespeare or the Peele). Thus the frequency with which these words appear is a good discriminator of these authors. Merriam also puts usage of *and* in the same table and it follows the same pattern: all the Shakespeares (except *Henry V*) use *and* less often than the Marlowes and Peeles do. Apply the same test with the twenty-seven subsections of *King John* described above and they more or less fall into two camps: the sections that the previous tests suggested were Shakespeare are at the top of the table (with lots of uses of the Shakespeare words) and the non-Shakespeare sections are down the bottom because using lots of the Marlowe words, albeit two sections of each type are in the wrong camps. E.A.J. Honigmann noticed that the word *right* occurs more often in *King John* than any other Shakespeare play (*3 Henry VI* is next in rank), and using this instead of *and* in the comparison of the twenty-six sections of *King John* with the twenty-seven Shakespeare canon plays the same general outcome appears: mostly the non-Shakespearian sections are at the top (heavy users of *right*), then come the twenty-seven Shakespeare plays, then the Shakespearian parts of *King John* down at the bottom as infrequent users of *right*. In previous tests it was twenty-seven sections of *King John* not twenty-six, and the difference is that one of those twenty-seven was itself a sub-subsection, 11a, that Merriam has now left out of the argument without saying why. On page 17 Merriam promised he would later explain this 11a sub-subsection, but in fact the reason for its existence is never made explicit.

Merriam then turns from numbers to language, and especially the varieties of irony (pp. 35–44). Some ironies are hard to make sense of: the Bastard speaks favourably of the French war to support Arthur's claim while himself following King John loyally, he rails on commodity and then says he will follow it too, and he mocks Hubert's bombast and then emulates it. These incoherent ironies might come from co-authorship, while other ironies Merriam finds coherent as perhaps allusions to Elizabeth I's own official bastardy and suggesting little Arthur as a kind of Mary Queen of Scots figure. John is like Shakespeare's Richard III in being a younger brother claiming the throne at the expense of his nephews, and Shakespeare emphasized the link by making Arthur, who is a young man in Holinshed and in *Troublesome Reign*, into a child, and by making him (like Prince Richard in *Richard III*) be 'rhetorically precocious' (p. 42). Also, the suborning of Hubert is like the suborning of Tyrrell. All this is very daring on Shakespeare's part since it makes John look especially bad, whereas Holinshed made John an innocent victim of Rome and Bale made him a hero. The anti-Catholicism of *King John*, which is greatly attenuated from the source play *Troublesome Reign*, is concentrated in III.i.61–105, the arrival of the papal legate Cardinal Pandolf and his abuse by John (p. 45), and Merriam thinks it significant that some particularly anti-Catholic lines in III.i were struck out in a copy of the second Folio used at the English Jesuit college at Valladolid in Spain (pp. 46–7). Merriam explains the Catholic distinction between a pardon (a release from the guilt of a sin) and an indulgence (a release from the temporal punishment for an already forgiven sin), and observes that section 11a of *King John* (III.i.91–3) mixes up these ideas. So too does *Doctor Faustus* when referring to 'some ghost, newly crept out of Purgatory, come to beg a pardon of your Holiness' since ghosts in Purgatory have already been forgiven.

Merriam thinks both this section of *King John* and *Doctor Faustus* mix up the idea in order to blackguard Catholicism by suggesting that the Roman Church sells forgiveness, which it does not. Round about the same part of *King John* there are words borrowed from John Foxe's *Book of Martyrs*, which itself may have got its account of King John from Bale, author of *King Johan*. Why would Shakespeare be Protestant around a time when he was also mocking Oldcastle? He would not: this bit is the work of another dramatist (pp. 47–54). The same bit of the play, Pandolf's threat to John, contains an apparent advance promise of forgiveness (indeed, even canonization) for the sin of regicide, which is just what the Protestant extremists (and *Troublesome Reign*) claimed that Catholics were promised, but which in fact the Pope (in declaring her subjects' duty to Elizabeth to be void in 1570) specifically avoided promising. The Pope did not call for regicide, only disobedience. That Pandolf in *King John* offers as reward for regicide the chance to be 'worshipped as a saint' (III.i.103) itself echoes anti-Catholic wilful confusion of the matter, for of course saints are venerated not worshipped, a distinction that Shakespeare himself makes in *The Two Gentlemen of Verona* (II.iv.142–51). Moreover, there is ample evidence in other plays that Shakespeare knew all these theological niceties backwards and forwards. (pp. 54–74). Merriam's last chapter (pp. 75–83) is a response to Roland Mushat Frye's *Shakespeare and Christian Doctrine* [1963], which claimed that Shakespeare's art is essentially secular. Frye assumed that Elizabethans were by default Protestants and adherents of the ideas of Martin Luther and John Calvin, but Eamon Duffy has overturned this assumption. Frye relied upon the expurgation of a second Folio in Valladolid, which attended to theological matters clustered in *Henry VIII* and *King John*, but in both cases it was the non-Shakespearian bits (as established for the former by James Spedding and for the latter by this study) that attracted the Roman Catholic blue pencil. There's also the deletion of a bit of *1 Henry VI*, but it is a bit that Gary Taylor attributes to Nashe. Also gone are the conjuring scene and the unmasking of Simpcox's supposed miracle in *2 Henry VI*, which latter Merriam suspects is not by Shakespeare. Merriam's conclusion is that in general *King John* is less anti-Catholic than *Troublesome Reign*, but in specific bits it is much more anti-Catholic, which is just the kind of evasion recusants had to practice. That is to say, co-authorship was a way to state your view without equivocation, since the other writer could give the opposing view. This sensible and well-argued ending is to my mind spoilt by a pointless application of Bayes's Theorem to test the likelihood that *King John* is co-authored, based on plucking from the air certain variables such as 0.7 being the consensus likelihood of single authorship and $< = 0.5$ being the likelihood that

Heminges and Condell were telling the truth in describing the Folio as the works of one man.

The last relevant monograph this year is Brian Vickers's *Shakespeare, 'A Lover's Complaint', and John Davies of Hereford*. This is a study of Davies himself as a poet, and of the scholarship that has (wrongly) confirmed the attribution of *A Lover's Complaint* to Shakespeare, especially that done by Kenneth Muir and MacDonald P. Jackson. Refuting those, and introducing a battery of tests that show *A Lover's Complaint* to be typical of Davies but wildly untypical of Shakespeare, Vickers expands upon an argument first made in an article called 'A Rum "Do"' in the *Times Literary Supplement* in 2003 and reviewed in *YWES* 84[2005]. The book-length version uses literary-critical skills where the stylometric case is not proven, and as such can only deal in probabilities and need not detain us here. Three book-format collections of essays contain matter relevant to this review. The most important is Andrew Murphy's *Shakespeare and the Text*. Helen Smith's essay 'The Publishing Trade in Shakespeare's Time' (in Murphy, ed., pp. 17–34) is a fine introduction to the background for our topic, but has nothing new of direct concern to this review. In 'Reading and Authorship: The Circulation of Shakespeare 1590–1619' (in Murphy, ed., pp. 35–56) Peter Stallybrass and Roger Chartier track the popularity of Shakespeare as an author (especially of poetry) in his life and shortly thereafter, recording who bought what and what they said about him. They claim that the publishing of *The Rape of Lucrece* in octavo in 1598 was probably a way of signalling its high status, since a quarto was considered ephemeral whereas an octavo had class. (Actually, this is a tricky argument to make, since Stallybrass and Chartier stress Shakespeare's being known in print more as a poet than a dramatist; they ought not to remain silent on the fact that his *Richard Duke of York*/*3 Henry VI* appeared in octavo in 1595.) Stallybrass and Chartier repeat approvingly de Grazia's claim (from *Shakespeare Verbatim*) that 'Renaissance "quotation marks"' were the opposite of modern ones: they marked public property whereas ours mark private property. They ought to acknowledge Paulina Kewes's and Edmund G.C. King's independent demonstrations that in fact the use of the symbols in the modern way was common long before 1800, which is when de Grazia—for whom they exemplify the emergence of the Foucauldian 'author-function' around 1800—dates the change.

In 'Shakespeare Writ Small: Early Single Editions of Shakespeare's Plays' (in Murphy, ed., pp. 56–70), Thomas L. Berger reports that the word *promptbook* is not recorded before 1809, which is indeed what the print and old CD-ROM versions of the *OED* indicate, but in fact the online version now has examples from 1768 and 1772 (p. 65). Likewise Berger says that *prompter* in the theatrical sense is first used in *Othello*, but online *OED* has a use from 1585. Strangely, Berger here repeats, as if he accepts them, a number of putative rules about early modern performance that are not universally agreed upon: that the prompter sat on the stage, that entrances and exits were anticipatorily marked in the promptbook, and that only the first and last words of letters spoken on stage were recorded in the promptbook. Berger wrongly gives the date of the expiration of the lease on the site of the Theatre: it was 1597 not 1598 (p. 66). Anthony James West's 'The Life of the First Folio in the Seventeenth and Eighteenth Centuries' (in Murphy, ed., pp. 93-108) is a history of the owners of the book, and includes a lament about the loss through theft of the exemplar with the longest recorded provenance, the Durham University copy. Since the publication of this essay that exemplar has been recovered and returned. In his 'The Birth of the Editor' (in Murphy, ed., pp. 93–108) Andrew Murphy implicitly rejects Sonai Massai's argument (reviewed above) by insisting that the editing of Shakespeare changed radically in the early eighteenth century, which development he reviews. Paul Werstine's ironically titled essay 'The Science of Editing' (in Murphy, ed., pp. 109–27) begins by pointing the reader to the few occasions when the Cambridge/Macmillan edition [1863–6] speculates about the printer's copy. In fact, Werstine's page-number references do not work for the 1863–6 edition, and he must be working from a reprint that repaginated the texts. His references fit the 1891 reprint so maybe Werstine used that without realizing that the pagination had changed from the first edition. Werstine thinks that in the first half of the twentieth century it was by no means agreed that there was a new and unified approach to Shakespearian bibliography: only retrospectively did it seem like a 'new' bibliography. (Werstine believes that the term New Bibliography came into being with F.P. Wilson's 1942 talk on the topic, but in fact Greg himself used it as early as 1919.) Werstine usefully surveys the disagreements within early New Bibliography, including Greg's later realization that his own 'memorial reconstruction' theory for Q1 *Merry Wives of Windsor* does not fit all the evidence perfectly. A.W. Pollard and John Dover Wilson's alternative and convoluted explanations of the origins of bad quartos (based on multiple revisions), outlined in 1919, were swept away by Peter Alexander's demonstration of memorial reconstruction lying behind *The Contention of York and Lancaster* and *Richard Duke of York*, for which Werstine here neglects to give a date: it was 1924.

Werstine credits E.K. Chambers with being the first to spot that Pollard was wrong about the relationship between non-entry in the Stationers' Register and publication of a bad quarto, although he gives the wrong reference: it is pages 186–7 of the second volume of *The Elizabethan Stage*. Strangely, Werstine declares himself convinced by Blayney's argument that playbooks were not terribly popular (and so were not worth a stationer's getting himself into trouble over by piracy) despite Alan Farmer and Zachary Lesser's demolition of it (reviewed in *YWES* 86[2007]). Werstine rehearses his familiar objection to the hypothesis that Hand D of *Sir Thomas More* is Shakespeare's, and renews his long-running attack on the means by which Greg derived the category 'foul papers'. Greg compared Edward Knight's transcript of John Fletcher's play *Bonduca* to the printed text and decided that certain differences (such as reordering of lines) were created by the difficulty Knight had in reading what must have been (Greg inferred) crabbed authorial papers. In rejecting Greg's article on *Bonduca* for publication in *The Library* (it did not reach print until 1990), Pollard rightly pointed out that we cannot extrapolate from *Bonduca* to anything else as it seems unique, especially since comparison of other two-text plays never produces the kinds of misplaced lines seen in *Bonduca*. Werstine rightly dates the entry of the word *promptbook* into the language to the late eighteenth century, and it is a pity that Murphy, as editor of the volume, did not notice that this contradicts what Berger wrote earlier (p. 65) about its first being recorded in the early nineteenth century.

Leah Marcus's essay 'Editing Shakespeare in the Postmodern Age' (in Murphy, ed., pp. 128–44) is a loosely linked collection of assertions about how postmodernism's approval of everything discontinuous, inconsistent, fragmented, impure, unruly, borrowed and imbricated chimes well with how we now think about Shakespeare. From an editing point of view, this offers the fashionable nonsense that we should leave speech prefixes unregularized, not mark speeches as 'aside', and leave stage directions incomplete or productively imprecise. The speech prefix for Edmund in Q1 *King Lear* is uniformly some shortened version of *Bastard* so Marcus thinks that this 'almost nameless' character is 'chastely regularized' in modern editions that make him uniformly *Edmund* (p. 134). In pursuit of this postmodern anonymity, Marcus overlooks the fact that not only is he called *Edmund* in the stage directions but his name is uttered thirty times by characters on stage, including more than once by Edmund himself. In theatre someone's name is precisely what is spoken, not what is written in the script and least of all what is written in the speech prefixes. Another ironic slip is that Marcus quotes, she says, from the Folio *Hamlet* the lines 'whose griefes | Beares such an Emphasis? Whose phrase of Sorrow' and that thus 'unemended by modern editors' these lines display what we would think of as bad grammar (p. 138). If fact her quotation is emended, for in F it is 'whose phrase' not 'Whose phrase'. Marcus or a copy-editor or printer, presumably under the pressure of modern norms (in which an exclamation point ends a sentence and hence must be followed by a capital letter), has unconsciously emended.

In 'Shakespeare and the Electronic Text' (in Murphy, ed., pp. 145–61) Michael Best gives a history of electronic Shakespeares and a survey of some current projects, plus an indication of the current technical limitations. A small slip is that he claims that the Oxford *Complete Works* came out on CD-ROM in 1988 (p. 147), but in fact it was on what are now almost unreadable 5.25 inch floppy disks. Regarding the technical means for preventing users copying material that one makes available to them over the internet, Best notes that 'video clips can be streamed rather than downloaded' (p. 150). As the YouTube generation is well aware, streaming stops only the naive beginner from copying the stuff. The internet offers many pieces of software that will capture an incoming video stream and turn it back into a single file that can be saved and reused when offline. David Bevington's 'Working with the Text: Editing in Practice' (in Murphy, ed., pp. 165–84) surveys the textual problems of *1 Henry VI* (which he concludes are essentially intractable) and then *Othello* and *Troilus and Cressida*. Bevington thinks that in *1 Henry VI* Beaufort (the Bishop of Winchester) makes his 'first appearance, as he enters with his men to forbid access to the Tower of London' in I.iv (p. 169), but in fact he is already bickering with Gloucester in the play's opening scene. In a book aimed at textual non-specialists, it is confusing to write (of *Troilus and Cressida*) that editors have disagreed 'whether the quarto or the Folio text was derived, with changes, from the other' (p. 177) since the non-specialist is going to ask herself how a quarto made in 1609 could possibly derive from a Folio made in 1623.

Bevington is referring to the underlying manuscripts of these printings, and it is a shame to confuse the non-specialist by omitting to say so.

Sonia Massai's 'Working with the Texts: Differential Readings' (in Murphy, ed., pp. 185–203) is a history of *King Lear* editions from the seventeenth century to the present, and thus is somewhat repetitious of the historical narrative offered in Murphy's chapter. Samuel Johnson, she notes, thought that Shakespeare revised the text underlying Q1 *King Lear* to make the text underlying the Folio version, and yet, like R.A. Foakes in his 1997 Arden3 edition, Johnson kept in his edition things that he thought Shakespeare was quite right to cut when turning whatever underlay Q into whatever underlay F. Massai says that we have Rowe to thank, via a scene location note, for the 'heath' that people imagine Lear being mad upon. Or rather, Rowe probably got it from Nahum Tate's adaptation (represented in his 1681 edition) that first set Lear on a 'heath', which Rowe presumably saw in performance. (Perhaps I am underestimating the Restoration theatre's realism, but I have trouble imagining so distinctive a landscape as to permit the word 'heath' to travel, as it were, by sight; why might not Rowe simply have read Tate's text?) The last essay is Neil Rhodes's 'Mapping Shakespeare's Contexts: Doing Things with Databases' (in Murphy, ed., pp. 204–20), which explains how to teach using large-text corpora and does not really fit with the rest of the book except near the end, when Rhodes lists some of the outcomes of teaching projects, which are mini-surveys of the books that name Cuthbert Burby and Peter Short in their imprints. It also contains a couple of errors: the date of Q2 *Romeo and Juliet* is given as 1589 instead of 1599, and the printer of Q1 *Romeo and Juliet* is given as just John Danter despite the certainty that Edward Allde printed some of the sheets, as established by Chiaki Hanabusa in 1997.

Afterwords to collections of essays are usually innocuous and easily ignored, but John Drakakis's (in Murphy, ed., pp. 221–38) stands out for a number of reasons. It starts with irrelevant reflections on the recent interest in objects instead of subjects in early modern literary studies (deriving from the work of Hugh Grady and Jean Howard, whom Drakakis does not mention) and then turns to book history. Drakakis's attempts to weave a sentence or two about each of the preceding chapters into his own tedious account of textual variation is so clumsy as to constitute an insult to the contributors. Particularly egregious is the way that Anthony James West's work is tacked on to a point being made by Drakakis (p. 230), and with one essay Drakakis simply gives up and admits he can find no connection at all: 'But this is a different kind of epistemological discourse from that traversed by Michael Best, who in chapter 8 above is concerned to identify what is available electronically to readers of Shakespeare's texts.' Even on its own terms (that is, aside from the duty to argue for the chapters' coherence), Drakakis's argument is weak, and he gets wrong simple things like the Marxist notion of a commodity (p. 225). He thinks that it is the fact of being produced in order to be exchanged for money that makes something a commodity (and thus early books qualify), whereas in truth it is the attribute of being indistinguishable from another of its kind, as with, say, the notional barrel of Brent crude oil that is traded around the world. This matters because it is the realization that early books are not identical even within a single edition (because of press variants) that has recently brought postmodernists and post-structuralists into the discipline.

Drakakis gets wrong the title of Honigmann's *The Stability of Shakespeare's Text* (p. 228), and surprisingly, having just glanced at Werstine's essay in this book in which the history of Greg's invention of the category 'foul papers' is given and Greg is shown to have extrapolated much too far from one document (the transcript of *Bonduca*), Drakakis nonetheless shamelessly uses the term 'foul papers' to describe the likely printer's copy for Q1 *The Merchant of Venice*. Drakakis bemoans the fact that no one has had the courage to print a modern edition of *The Merchant of Venice* with variable speech prefixes for *Jew* and *Shylock* as in the early printing, and claims that this is because we labour under 'some stable conception of dramatic "character"' (p. 229). Of course, he ought to know that dramatic characters are stable—not once is a character in an early modern play supposed to be played by more than one actor—and that this stability is reified in the single actor's 'part' for each character. The postmodern approach cannot destabilize the author and his characters at once, as Tiffany Stern's anti-authorial, 'part'-centred, research shows. Drakakis implicitly insults his fellow contributor Marcus by silently modernizing her American spelling when quoting her book *Unediting the Renaissance* and dropping a couple of her words ('to its'), and he seems to think that the Arden3 edition of *Hamlet* contains four texts: the edited one plus Q1, Q2 and F (p. 231). In fact it contains edited versions of Q1, Q2 and F.

Drakakis gives the date of 1594 for *Famous Victories of Henry V* but in fact it was published in 1598 and first performed 1583–8 according to Alfred Harbage's *Annals* (p. 233). He also seems to totally misunderstand the argument for putting Oldcastle into speech prefixes in *1 Henry IV* and he absurdly wonders aloud if Shakespeare's manuscript had 'Falstaff' in speech prefixes but that in writing the dialogue Shakespeare tried to gesture towards 'the model', that is the Lollard martyr. Drakakis gives a quotation about the Oldcastle controversy supposedly from the Textual Companion to the Oxford *Complete Works* of Shakespeare but it is not on the page he cites (p. 509), which is about *King Lear*. More misquoting follows (p. 234), this time of Greg ('comes so glibly' rendered as 'comes glibly'), and with the end of his contribution in sight he is not even grammatical: 'all the inconsistencies … is because' (p. 235). (In the ellipsis was a singular noun and that seems to have distracted him.) In a single sentence Drakakis manages to get wrong the working practices of the early modern printshop and of modern cinema in imagining compositors leaving sheets on the printshop floor just as directors leave rushes on the floor (p. 237). Of course, compositors did not handle sheets (that was the work of pressmen) and rushes are not discarded but used to make a workprint to be edited; only then are bits discarded, and by editors not by directors. In the bibliography to the book I noticed only one error: on page 254 there is a typo in the URL for the Text Encoding Initiative's wiki entry on how to deal with non-hierarchical textual structures. It should be < http:// www.tei-c.org/wiki/index.php/SIG:Overlap > not < http://www.teic.org/wiki/ index.php/SIG:Overlap > .

The annual *Shakespeare Yearbook* was this year themed *The Shakespeare Apocrypha* and contains essays relevant to this review. The title of John Jowett's essay, 'Shakespeare Supplemented' (in Brooks, Thompson and Ford, eds., pp. 38–73), comes from Jacques Derrida's work, and he shows how high French literary theory can illuminate textual studies. Jowett begins with Erne's point that for Heminges and Condell to be castigating the bad quartos in their Folio preliminaries would be odd, since none had appeared for a long time, but that they might be referring to the recent Pavier quartos. Jowett gives the narrative and chronology of the Pavier quartos which, because the seriously fake imprints begin only part-way through the manufacture of the collection, looks like a reaction to the Stationers' Company receipt of a letter from the Lord Chamberlain preventing publication of King's men's plays without the players' consent. Here, as in *Shakespeare and Text* reviewed above, Jowett considers the possibility that the players knew of Pavier's project and even tacitly approved for their own reasons. Jowett investigates just why seven more plays were added to the second issue of the third Folio [1664] and gives a history of the Shakespeare apocrypha in the eighteenth century, and then the nineteenth century (when a whole new slew of apocrypha was added by the work of Ludwig Tieck), and on into the twentieth century. His main point is that the hard boundaries of the canon are made by book production, not theatrical production, and that we do not need to accept them. Since we are sceptical of binaries such as good/bad quarto and foul papers/fair copy, why not the binary of 'canonical and' (p. 68)? That is how Jowett's essay ends, with what I take to be a Derridean joke, although it would be equally amusing if Jowett's typescript put the last words 'under erasure' and someone misread this as simple deletion.

Michael Egan's 'Woodstock's Golden Metamorphosis' (in Brooks, Thompson and Ford, eds., pp. 75–115) is literary criticism, based on Egan's false attribution of the play to Shakespeare; it reads a bit oddly coming as it does after Jowett's masterful account of the categorization of the apocrypha. Richard Preiss's 'A Play Finally Anonymous' (in Brooks, Thompson and Ford, eds., pp. 117–39) is a work about the theatre and publishing history of Anonymous's play *Mucedorus*. Likewise, 'A Fear of "Ould" Plays: How *Mucedorus* Brought Down the House and Fought for Charles II in 1652' (in Brooks, Thompson and Ford, eds., pp. 141–66), by Victor Holtcamp, explores Rowe's account of an illicit performance of this play (in which the floor gave way) in 1652. Scott Maisano's 'Shakespeare's Dead Sea Scroll: On the Apocryphal Appearance of *Pericles*' (in Brooks, Thompson and Ford, eds., pp. 167–93) is a literary-critical essay arguing that Q1 *Pericles*'s being a bad quarto is actually part of what the play dramatizes, its own status as a recollection, a retelling of sources. Paul Edmondson's ' "Beyond the Fringe"? Receiving, Adapting, and Performing *The London Prodigal*' (in Brooks, Thompson and Ford, eds., pp. 195–221) is literary criticism and theatre history of this play. In 'The Actors in *Sir Thomas More*' (in Brooks, Thompson and Ford, eds., pp. 223–40) Tom Rutter argues that, just as in other Munday plays (he considers *John a Kent and John a Cumber* and *The Downfall of Robert Earl of Huntingdon*), *Sir Thomas More* shows just how bad amateur actors are in order to show how good the professionals putting on the play are (as indeed *The Taming of A Shrew* and *A Midsummer Night's Dream* do).

The significance of Gerald Downs's essay is clear from its title, 'A Question Not to be Askt: Is Hand D a Copy?' (in Brooks, Thompson and Ford, eds., pp. 241–66). Downs revives some old claims that features of Hand D can be explained by eye-skip of a copyist and he works through each piece of evidence. Downs thinks it unlikely that the deletion in 'nor that the elament*es* | wer not all appropriat to ~~ther~~ yor Comfort*es*' is authorial (p. 246), but it seems to me that the author has forgotten that he is in the subjunctive mood (what if your case was as the strangers' case?) and thinks for a moment he is describing the strangers' case directly. Downs considers it quite impossible for an author to write 'ymagin that yo^u see the wretched straingers | their baby*es* at their back*es*, ~~and~~ w^t their poor lugage | plodding tooth port*es* and cost*es* for transportacion' since luggage cannot plod (p. 247), but surely the subject (strangers) can be separated from the verb (plodding) by this parenthetical clause without damage to the meaning. Downs works through Giorgio Melchiori's readings of the evidence for *currente calamo* correction and tries to undermine each one (p. 248). Of course, this becomes a matter of how convincing one finds Downs's hypotheses versus Melchiori's, for neither has an absolutely irrefutable piece of evidence. If Hand D is a transcription, it is surely not one by which a scribe would want to advertise his work.

As for who actually composed the words, Downs thinks that styolmetry cannot go to work on a piece this short (p. 251). This is not so: MacDonald P. Jackson's 'The Date and Authorship of Hand D's Contribution to *Sir Thomas More*: Evidence from "Literature Online"' (reviewed in *YWES* 87[2008]) established conclusively that, leaving aside who owns the handwriting, the words in Hand D's contribution to the play were composed by Shakespeare. Perhaps, since they are not very different, Hands C and D are the same hand? If so, asks Down, why did the same man come back to his own writing (at line 237) to delete two and a half lines and replace them with a simple bridge 'tell me but this'? Because he realized he had botched the copying in the first place (pp. 252–3). As before, Downs's hypothesis relies on this being the work of an especially slovenly scribe. Throughout Downs's essay are infelicities of layout, such as the mechanical starting of a new paragraph after each inset quotation, even where there is no new idea but rather the continuation of an old one. Also, the occasional quotation of the manuscript in modernized form is unhelpful, as is the failure to mention that when quoting from Greg's Malone Society Reprints edition of the play, the corrections identified by Harold Jenkins in the 1961 reissue of that edition have been applied. It is hard to know to whom one should attribute these infelicities, as Downs himself is publicly on record as being in dispute with the journal *Shakespeare Yearbook*, which he claims published the article without his authority after it was accepted elsewhere and which did not give him the opportunity to make corrections in proof.

The remainder of the book contains essays of only tangential relevance to this review. In 'Apocryphal Agency: *A Yorkshire Tragedy* and Early Modern Authorship' (in Brooks, Thompson and Ford, eds., pp. 267–91), Michael Saenger offers literary criticism of the play, and its relation to the construction of authorship via title pages. Jeffrey Kahan's 'Canonical Breaches and Apocryphal Patches' (in Brooks, Thompson and Ford, eds., pp. 293–316) is a tour through others' arguments about attribution, picking holes in them by selective quotation; it becomes increasingly bizarre as it progresses and ends with the suggestion that *Edward III*'s entry into the canon was a reaction to the attacks of September 11, 2001, which made it topical. Nicola Bennett and Richard Proudfoot write about the Royal Shakespeare Company production of the same play, and the ways in which it failed to help make the case for Shakespearian authorship (' "Tis a rightful quarrel must prevail": *Edward III* at Stratford', in Brooks, Thompson and Ford, eds., pp. 317–38).

Colin Burrow, whose Oxford Shakespeare edition of the sonnets was reviewed in *YWES* 83[2004], offers a defence of modern editing, as opposed to the fashionable un-editing, 'Editing the Sonnets' (in Schoenfeldt, ed., *A Companion to Shakespeare's Sonnets*, pp. 145–62). Burrow provides an excellent guide to the textual situation of the 1609 quarto and Benson's 1640 edition, and makes a convincing argument that Malone's driving impulse was not so much 'proud discovery of the biographical foundations of the sonnets' or anything else to do with the works themselves but rather the 'correction of the work of others' (p. 152). The un-editors (he identifies Margreta de Grazia and Randall McLeod) are too unsympathetic to the ordinary reader, who wants to hear the poetry without having her sense of what constitutes a sentence challenged by unfamiliar typography, orthography and punctuation. In the process they make a fetish of the object instead of a fetish of authorial intention, which is what they accuse their opponents of doing. McLeod's argument for retaining the reading 'They had still enough your worth to sing' (Sonnet 106) instead of the usual emendation to 'skill enough' was made on the basis of the *st* ligature—a compositor cannot select a *t* instead of a *k* by accident since they are linked to the *s*—but it overlooks the obvious objection that a compositor could simply have misread his copy, and in any case *skill* is the reading in early seventeenth-century manuscript copies that may descend independently of Q. In the same collection, Arthur F. Marotti, 'Shakespeare's *Sonnets* and the Manuscript Circulation of Texts in Early Modern England' (pp. 185–203). deals with the copying of sonnets from printed texts (especially the 1609 quarto and Benson's edition of 1640) into commonplace books, which happened rather less frequently for Shakespeare's poems than it did for others'. Interestingly, the abstractions or decontextualizations frequently left off the poet's name, giving credence to the idea that literary authorship was less important to the early moderns than it is to us.

So to the journal articles. The most important article this year is R. Carter Hailey's demonstration that Q4 *Romeo and Juliet* can be confidently dated 1623 and Q4 *Hamlet* can be certainly dated 1625 ('The Dating Game: New Evidence for the Dates of Q4 *Romeo and Juliet* and Q4 *Hamlet*', *SQ* 58[2007] 367–87). Of all the early printings of Shakespeare, only these two lack a date on the title page, and of course scholars want to know if they were printed early enough to be available to use in the setting of the Folio in 1623. Both were printed by William Stansby for John Smethwicke, which was a longstanding partnership; Stansby's initials are on Q4 *Hamlet* and his role as printer of Q4 *Romeo and Juliet* is inferred from the presence of one of

Stansby's ornaments. Hailey gives the history of the attempts to date these books (pp. 369–72), including Lynette Hunter's demonstration that George Walton William's dating of *Romeo and Juliet* on the basis of a deteriorating tailpiece was faulty, and Rasmussen's recent similar work dating *Hamlet* by deterioration in the title-page device (both reviewed in *YWES* 82[2003]). The key to Hailey's discoveries is that paper moulds lasted about twelve months, that paper made from a particular mould is detectable in surviving books, and that paper was bought for each printing job and rapidly consumed rather than held on to. Thus if one can show that two books are printed on the same stock of paper (that is, from the same mould) then they were printed no more than a year apart (p. 372). Hailey has been measuring the spaces between successive chain lines in a series of books, so for each stock of paper he has a 'fingerprint' of spacings, as well as his 'mugshots' of the watermarks. Having established his 'fingerprint' and 'mugshot' for Q4 *Romeo and Juliet*, Hailey went looking for other books using the same paper stock, starting in the likeliest year (1622) and looking at other books by the same publishing pair. He soon hit on the 1623 edition of Thomas Lodge's *Euphues Golden Legacie*. Stansby is not named as the printer of this Smethwicke book, but shared ornaments and distinctive type between this book and known Stansby books prove it is his work. Since in multiple copies of this book the watermarks from Q4 *Romeo and Juliet* appear only in sheet A, the obvious inference is that there was a little of this stock of paper left over from the printing of *Romeo and Juliet*, thus we can date *Romeo and Juliet* to just before the printing of *Euphues* in 1623.

Q4 *Hamlet* was a much harder case. It was printed from a mixed stock of two papers, both poor quality and so hard to see through. In nine Folger Library exemplars, sheets D, G and L were all printed on one of the papers and A and N were (almost) all printed on the other paper, with the other sheets being mixed in the sense that in some exemplars a given sheet was from one paper and in other exemplars the same sheet was from the other paper. With only nine exemplars this could happen by chance: in the whole print run the pattern may not have held. That is to say, the sheets that Hailey has identified (from nine exemplars) as being printed on either one or other of the papers might in fact have been printed from mixed stock, with the surviving exemplars (a random subset of the print run) just happening to all show one stock of paper for one set of sheets and the other stock of paper for the other set of sheets. Hailey found the same two papers in *Usury Arraigned and Condemned* [1625], which also has the same setting of type as Q4 *Hamlet* used for the imprint. Thus this imprint was kept as standing type, and therefore *Usury Arraigned and Condemned* must have been printed consecutively or concurrently with Q4 *Hamlet*. So how did Rasmussen get it wrong? He did not examine enough copies to properly establish progressive deterioration of the printer's ornament: Hailey shows that even in exemplars from the same edition the 'break' in the ornament comes and goes according to inking and press-pull variation. We can now say for sure that Q4 *Hamlet* had no effect on the Folio, but could itself have been influenced by the Folio, which would explain their occasional agreements against other witnesses. With a date of 1623 now established for Q4 *Romeo and Juliet*, it was probably not available before the

Folio text of that play was typeset. Hailey ends by answering the question 'What is the significance of these Q4s appearing without dates?' Answer: probably nothing, as 15 per cent of all books did.

In the same journal, Brian Vickers argues that only three dramatists, not four as Gary Taylor thought, composed *1 Henry VI*, and that the shares are not quite as Taylor divided them ('Incomplete Shakespeare: Or, Denying Co-authorship in *1 Henry VI*', *SQ* 58[2007] 311–52). Vickers begins with a summary of the state of the art of co-authorship studies and makes a (rather long-winded) analogy between collaborative playwriting and collaborative Renaissance art. Using C.J. Sisson's account of the lost play *Keep the Widow Waking*, and the evidence of Henslowe's Diary, Vickers gives an account of a typical coming together for collaborative playwriting, the dividing up of shares in the work, and of how the 'author-plot' was used to pitch the project to the players and to control the collaboration. The unit of collaboration seems to be the act (measured in sheets, each being a folio folded in the middle to give two leaves and four pages) and the prime-mover dramatist in a group seems to be the one who writes the first act. Vickers's history of Shakespearian stylometry includes the clearest account I have read of Marina Tarlinskaya's analysis of proclitic and enclitic microphrases.

One way to explain the inconsistencies in *1 Henry VI* is to say that it was rushed out to capitalize on the success of *2 Henry VI* and *3 Henry VI*, but Vickers thinks that co-authorship, with imperfect agreement between the shares, is another. These are not mutually exclusive possibilities, of course, and indeed Taylor, cited here by Vickers as a supporter of the 'prequel' theory, also argues for co-authorship to (p. 325 n. 1). Taylor's essay itself is wrongly cited as appearing in 1993 but it was in fact 1995. As examples of the chaos in *1 Henry VI* Vickers cites the poor placing of act intervals in the Folio and the confusion over whether Winchester is a bishop or a cardinal, but could not the former simply indicate that it was not written for intervals and had them imposed when printed? The latter was explained as no crux at all by Karl Wentersdorf in an article reviewed in *YWES* 87[2008]. In his history of attempts to work out who wrote what in *1 Henry VI*, Vickers charts the emergence of Thomas Nashe as prime candidate, and the clincher is that the sources of certain phrases are shown to be ones that Shakespeare nowhere else drew on, but that Nashe used in his published works. Turning again to Taylor's article (and giving it the right date this time), Vickers is full of praise for its rightly using previous work that showed Nashe's hand in *1 Henry VI* but castigates it for applying a set of inappropriate tests that led Taylor to posit two other hands too. Vickers agrees with Taylor that Act I is Nashe and that II.iv, IV.ii, IV.iii, IV.iv and IV.v are Shakespeare, but disagrees about IV.vi and IV.vii.1–32 which he sets out to show are not Shakespeare. In IV.v, Talbot Senior uses *thou* to address Talbot Junior, who replies with *you* as we would expect of a familiar father and a respectful son. But in IV.vi Talbot Junior starts to *thou* his father, which is wrong and un-Shakespearian, as is some particularly poor choice of words. Act IV, scene vi, is like IV.vii in its diction ('bookish', 'portentous gestures and linguistic display') and in its clumsy verse, and each contains a mention of Icarus, who is unknown elsewhere in Shakespeare (p. 342).

Tarlinskaya's work—which rejects Taylor's divisions and just has Act I
Nashe, II.iv and IV.ii–IV.v Shakespeare, and the rest Y—shows that Nashe
averages ninety-three enclitics per thousand lines while Shakespeare averages
fifty-five per thousand lines, and Y just fifteen. Corroborating this are three
clearly distinct rates of using feminine endings in these three shares in the play.
All that remains to be done is find out who Y is (pp. 344–5). Vickers ends
surveying the recent editions of Shakespeare and ranking them according
to how open-minded they are about the facts of co-authorship. Andrew
Cairncross's Arden2 *1 Henry VI* was particularly cavalier in its complex
hypotheses about interference from scribes and others, and the wild cutting
that followed, to avoid admitting co-authorship. At the close Vickers
acknowledges Wentersdorf's article on the Winchester-as-bishop-or-cardinal
crux, but only to say that it has no bearing on matters of authorship. In
fairness he ought to have acknowledged that Wentersdorf argues that there
simply is no crux at all, since once we properly appreciate the history being
depicted there is no contradiction in the play as it reads in F.

In the same journal, Denise A. Walen argues that the Folio text of *Othello*
IV.iii represents the original staging at the Globe playhouse while the shorter
version in the 1622 quarto represents the scene as cut for the Blackfriars
('Unpinning Desdemona', *SQ* 58[2007] 487–508). The Willow Song is absent
from Q, and Walen reckons it was used to cover the action of unpinning
Desdemona, which refers not to her hair but to her clothes. This took a while,
and if the two minutes or so of stage time allowed by the text of the Willow
Song as we have it was not enough then the actor was to sing as many extra
verses as were needed to get the job done. This version of the scene gives
a reflective pause before the final violent action, but such a long pause was not
needed at Blackfriars because there was an act interval (with its own music to
replace the Willow Song) right after this scene, so IV.iii got cut down for
the Blackfriars, whence Q.

Nina Levine offers a literary-critical reading of *Sir Thomas More* that tries
to make analogies between the collective enterprises in the play (the outraged
Londoners coming together to do something) and the collective enterprise of
the dramatists writing it ('Citizens' Games: Differentiating Collaboration
and *Sir Thomas More*', *SQ* 58[2007] 31–64). The play gives the 'mob' a lot of
individuation, including personal names, and it was presumably in objection to
this that censor Edmund Tilney crossed out the speech prefixes at the start of
the play. (Well, he crossed out De Barde's as well as Doll's, which does not fit
this supposed anti-rebels explanation.) Hand C reassigns to Lincoln
specifically the line '[we will] by ruld by yoᵘ master moor yf youle stand our
| freind to procure our pardon' that Hand D gave to 'all', and this makes
Lincoln's execution (which is like More's at the end) all the more ironic, since
he is the only rebel not to be pardoned. Equally, Hand C (whom McMillin
says we should treat as a collaborator with D, maybe even the same man)
individuates the speakers that Hand D leaves as 'others'. The last piece of
relevance from this volume of *Shakespeare Quarterly* is by Stephen Orgel ('The
Desire and Pursuit of the Whole', *SQ* 58[2007] 290–310), and it offers a short
summary of the size and shape of the Shakespeare canon in print up to present
day, literary-critical points about the plays themselves being not 'complete',

nor the performances, and a description of the Cranach Press edition of
Hamlet of 1929.

Papers of the Bibliographical Society of America published three essays
relevant to this review. In the longest and least rewarding, Lynette Hunter tries
to explain the differences between Q1 and Q2 *Romeo and Juliet* by positing a
whole set of slightly different manuscript readings arising over time as
theatrical needs demanded ('Adaptation and/or Revision in Early Quartos of
Romeo and Juliet', *PBSA* 101[2007] 5–54). It is tempting to stop reading
Hunter's article when she lays her cards on the table about her approach to
textual scholarship and says she 'does not seek truth or authorial intention'
(p. 6). Hunter reports that all quotations will be from the edition of *Romeo and
Juliet* that she and Peter Lichtenfels published with Ashgate in 2007, but
neither the British Library, nor Amazon, nor indeed the Ashgate website, has
any record of this book, although there is a similar-sounding title from Hunter
and Lichtenfels forthcoming from Ashgate in 2009. The agenda set for this
essay is to bring together the theatrical and the bibliographical, but Hunter
immediately begs the question of agency by calling the differences between
Q1 and Q2 'changes' (p. 7). To see why this is a logical error, one has only
to imagine someone calling the differences between two photographs of the
Empire State Building 'changes'. Certainly, the building might have changed
in the interval between the taking of the first picture and the second, but this is
not the only possibility: the pictures could differ merely because of different
lighting, time of day and means of reproduction. Equally, in textual
scholarship an argument about 'change' has to be made, not assumed.

A foundational hypothesis of the essay is that Q1 and Q2 *Romeo and Juliet*
'stem from an earlier manuscript' but via 'scripts for theatre production' (p. 8),
meaning that there were multiple manuscript versions between composition
and printed book; this is not a new hypothesis but it is one that is very hard to
prove. Having noted that although an exemplar of Q1 was somewhat used in
the printing of Q2 it cannot have been the main copy as there are far too many
differences between Q1 and Q2 for them all to have been written onto an
exemplar of Q1, Hunter out of the blue, and with no prior justification for it,
simply prints her own proposed stemma with seven distinct manuscript
versions leading in two lines of descent to Q1 and Q2 (p. 13). She uses a bizarre
system of notation in which, for example, Q2P, Q2Pb and Q2C are three
different manuscripts that lead eventually to the printing of Q2. Aside from
any other objection, this requires that three intervening transcripts (intervening between the author's papers and the printed book) prior to Q2 failed to
remove the very obvious false-start duplications whereby first Friar Laurence
and then Romeo describe the dawn in precisely the same terms, and whereby
Romeo gets to repeat himself at length in his soliloquy before dying.

Hunter wants to reject the commonly accepted idea that Q2 was set from
foul papers, so she asserts that 'there is no evidence of the existence of
Shakespeare's "foul papers"' (p. 14). However, since she must accept that
there was at some time a first complete script in Shakespeare's hand (unless
like Barbara Cartland he composed by dictation) then the point stands: Q2
shows no sign that it is based on an intervening transcript, since the
duplications that seem plausibly part of authorial papers (but not plausibly

part of a transcript) are in Q2. One-quarter of the way into this long article, Hunter has not brought one new idea to the debate, nor adduced one new piece of evidence; she just keeps asserting things like 'Q2 itself may well have been affected by rehearsal' (p. 14) without a shred of evidence or argument to support it. Now Hunter starts to read Q1 and Q2 for theatrical differences, and observes that Q1 'is one of the earliest printed texts of Shakespeare's plays to present the part of a woman on stage alone' (p. 16). Indeed, but since the only printings of Shakespeare's plays before Q1 *Romeo and Juliet* were *2 Henry VI*, *3 Henry VI* and *Titus Andronicus*, this is the first of his plays with a woman in the title to be printed. It ought to be no surprise that it gives a female character significant stage time. Juliet has a lot more to say and do in Q2 than in Q1, so Hunter ponders whether a change in the personnel (the loss or acquisition of a good actor) caused this difference, and she quotes Q1 and Q2 to make an argument about cutting but using a modernized text of each. This modernized text is particularly unhelpful in that Hunter is trying to find evidence in Q1 of a rupture marking a cut, and such evidence is much easier to see if one has not first modernized the thing.

Hunter notices that many of the things that Q2 has that Q1 lacks 'occur at the end or toward the end of scenes' and (without saying why) she asserts that 'It is unlikely that an actor, dramaturge, or manager would have added this material to produce a script behind Q2' (p. 21). She seems ignorant of Scott McMillin's demonstration, given in his work on *Sir Thomas More*, that padding out the end of a scene is precisely what early modern actors would want to facilitate a reduction in casting, for it gives other actors a chance to change for the next scene. Hunter finds some things absent from Q1 and present in Q2 that are hard to explain as additions in the latter but easy to explain as omissions in the former, which is of course what the memorial reconstruction hypothesis was based upon. Regarding the moment in Q2 where Romeo and Friar Laurence describe the dawn in precisely the same terms, Hunter toys with the idea that the lines were for the Friar but someone accidentally added them to the part for Romeo. (Surely that would have been noticed once they started speaking their parts in rehearsal, and thereafter fixed.) Then she offers Randall McLeod's implausible suggestion that the repetition is intentional (p. 24). Nothing Hunter has written so far justifies her stemma that posits seven manuscript versions of the play, and all she has done is evaluate the evidence in Q1 and Q2 for what it would tell us about her stemma if indeed that stemma were correct. This is not scholarship but self-indulgent speculation. Amongst a group of things present in Q2 and consistently absent from Q1 is the act of retelling a story, and a slew of small references to law and justice; it is hard to see why these would be cut (or forgotten) so Hunter assumes they were added to the play. (Such cases can almost always be argued either way, and what is wanted to settle the matter is a conclusive example that everyone will agree goes only one way.) As well as shortenings in Q1 of what is longer in Q2, Hunter finds a few things expanded or adapted in Q1 from what Q2 has, but not done well enough to warrant the hand of a dramatist; therefore she says that 'managers, [or] actors' did them (pp. 29–32). Hunter looks at a long list of small variants where single words are altered, and reckons she can tell those that probably are important enough to be the work of a dramatist and those that are not and hence are probably the work of 'an actor or a scribe or a compositor' (p. 36).

Hunter explores the possibilities for a memorial reconstruction explanation, on the basis of the main recollectors being the actors of Romeo, Mercutio and Paris (as Kathleen Irace conjectured) and including the possibility that there were other recollectors (maybe the whole company) recalling a different version of the play, and she repeats the old and inaccurate saws about Q1 being more suited to touring than Q2 because it is shorter and simpler. By this point, three-quarters of the way into the article, the hypotheses are so complex and so laboured that is almost impossible to discern what Hunter is arguing. For example, she writes that there is 'evidence for manuscript copy for Q1' (p. 41), but unless someone were to be arguing for the existence of a lost Q0 that served as copy for Q1, what else could be the printer's copy but a manuscript? She genuinely seems to consider the possibility that the actors entered the printshop as a troupe and recited the play to the compositor, only to reject it: 'the text was not directly memorially transmitted at the printing house'. Apart from anything else, we know that Q1 was set by formes, so there had to be a written version for the printer to cast off. Against the argument for memorial reconstruction being the basis of Q1, she writes, is the fact that Q1 has extensive stage directions derived from dialogue in Q2. (Actually, that shows the weakness of her attack on memorial reconstruction on this score, since while actors trying to recall their performances are not likely to remember the precise wording of stage directions they certainly should remember instructions embedded in the dialogue.)

Not satisfied with her seven-manuscript stemma, Hunter hypothesizes some more manuscripts: a whole line of them from $Q1P^1$ to $Q1P^n$. Actually, it has never been clear by these notations whether Hunter is referring to distinct manuscripts or distinct states of the same manuscript (as in Wilson and Pollard's notion of 'continuous copy'), but now the possibility emerges that a single manuscript might, without being changed at all, appear with different notations in Hunter's system (and occupy different places in her stemma) just because it is used for two productions: 'a text from one performance (say $Q1Pb^1$) may be in fact the same text used by the next production of the play $(Q1P^2)$' (p. 42). More utterly implausible ideas are then considered, such as the printer being willing to accept (and the company being willing to hand over) the bundle of actors' parts as the basis for printing Q1, or his sending off to the company to find someone who could remember a scene that is present in Q2 but absent from Q1 (p. 43). Hunter harbours bizarre misunderstandings of the basic hypotheses at work in these problems, displayed when she writes that 'there are several bibliographical indications that Q2 was set from manuscript rather than from actors speaking the scripts' (p. 44). Of course no one supposes that the actors spoke their lines directly to the compositors; the memorial reconstruction hypothesis explains how the printer's copy manuscript was made and is not an alternative to there being such a manuscript. Hunter also knows little about printing, for she says that Q2's having 'Nerona' where 'Verona' is clearly the right word might be because the printer had printed, or would print, that same year a story with a character 'Neronis' in it. More plausibly, of course, a letter 'N' had fallen into the 'V' compartment (directly below it) in the capitals typecase. Surely someone at the journal could have told her this and saved her from making a silly suggestion. To establish that Q2 was not based on memorial reconstruction, Hunter locates in it things that memorial reconstruction would not produce. This is the wrong method: one needs to find things that only transcription could produce, for the things she has found might exist even in the printed version of a script recovered by memorial reconstruction.

When Hunter gets to the (ample) evidence for the copy for Q2 being authorial, she gives Randall McLeod rather than R.B. McKerrow the credit for noticing that the speech prefix variation for Capulet's Wife reflects her differing social function in different scenes (pp. 44–7). In a section of the article called 'Theatre Practice' Hunter argues that Q2 has post-theatrical elements, but she is relying almost entirely on hunches about such things as certain lines being improvisations and the guess that deliberate mislineation of verse as prose marks it off as lines that actor has been given licence to adapt. Hunter assumes that the actor playing Nurse was a specialist in 'straight comedy' and hence that the additional lines in Q2 (over what the Nurse has to say in Q1) were added by this comic. She seems unaware that this part must have been played by an apprentice, not a clown. The self-confusion that was bound to emerge from clumsy nomenclature is apparent in Hunter's claim that 'Q2 is not working [typeset] directly from Q1 but from Q2C' (p. 48). Since in her notation Q2C is defined as the printer's copy for Q2—that is what she means by this siglum—this claim is tautologous. She concludes that the Acts V of Q1 and Q2 show equally viable variants (as opposed to say Q1 just lacking something in Q2), so it looks like revision as well as garbling separate Q1 and Q2. This is not news: most cases of what used to be explained solely as memorial reconstruction are now treated as more likely to be cases of revision as well as memorial reconstruction. This entire article is weak in its logic and lacking in basic theatrical and bibliographical knowledge, and does harm to the reputation of the scholarly journal that elected to publish it.

In the same journal, Arthur Sherbo continues his work on Malone's textual scholarship with two pieces ('Restoring Malone', *PBSA* 101[2007] 125–48; 'Edmond Malone and the Johnson-Steevens 1778 *Shakespeare*', *PBSA* 101[2007] 313–28). In the first he records that Malone's debut publication as a Shakespeare editor was a 1780 two-volume supplement to the 1778 edition by Samuel Johnson and George Steevens, and that in 1783 Malone supplemented this supplement with what he called the *Second Appendix*. This was unknown to the New Variorum editors, as was part of the supplement, and only where bits of these made it into George Steevens's 1793 Shakespeare are they widely known to modern scholarship. The rest of the article is devoted to explaining exactly what Malone was up to in these books, reprinting the otherwise hard-to-find notes, and pointing out which notes the various Variorum editors missed. (An odd slip that someone ought to have caught in proofs is the reference to Shakespeare's play '*4H4*' (p. 128).) The second article is similar to the first, pointing out that there are lots of notes by Malone in the Steevens ten-volume edition of 1778 itself, and these too are largely unknown to modern editors because they turn to later books in the false assumption that all of Malone's notes were copied forward. Sherbo reprints in an appendix all the ones connected to the plays; the ones for the poems are to come elsewhere.

The Review of English Studies published two pieces of interest to this review. In the first Christine Cornell and Patrick Malcomson argue that the Q2 ending of *Titus Andronicus* (four extra lines usually dismissed as non-Shakespearian patching to cover a lacuna in its copy text, Q1) is worth restoring as it might have had a place in early performances ('The "Stupid" Final Lines of *Titus Andronicus*', *RES* 58[2007] 154–61). The standard view is that Q1 *Titus Andronicus* was reprinted as Q2 but, because the exemplar of Q1 was imperfect, with a number of guessed readings and with four spurious lines at the end where the last leaf was mutilated. Q2 was reprinted as Q3 and F was set from an exemplar of Q3 that had been annotated by reference to a playhouse manuscript, hence the 'fly' scene, III.ii, was added for F. Modern editors use Q1 as their authority for the play except for III.ii, for which F is the authority. Cornell and Malcolmson see an illogicality in accepting F's authority for III.ii but not for the extra four lines added in Q2. (Putting it like this muddies the waters somewhat, since even if the lines are admitted as authentic, F itself cannot be the authority for them as it is only a reprint of a reprint; if we think the lines are genuine, Q2 would be our authority.) According to Cornell and Malcolmson, the four lines tacked on the end are, in Q2, Q3 and F: 'See Justice done on Aaron that damn'd Moore, | From whom, our heavy happes had their beginning: | Then afterwards, to Order well the State, | That like Events, may ne're it Ruinate' (pp. 155–6). They are mistaken, and this is not the ending in any of the texts: they have quoted from the execrable Applause modern-type edition of F, which illogically retains capitalization and punctuation, but modernizes u/v and i/j spellings and removes emphatic italics. Moreover, F is substantively different from Q2 and Q3, which have 'By whom[e]' not 'From whom'. It is sloppy of Cornell and Malcomson to get this wrong.

Cornell and Malcomson ask why, if Greg was right that a copy of Q2 was used as a promptbook, were the offending four lines not deleted from it? That is to say, how come they got into Q3 and F? The right answer, of course, is that no one is claiming that the particular exemplar of Q2 used as a promptbook—supposing for a moment that this indeed happened—was the one used to print Q3: the book-keeper could have struck them out in his exemplar of Q2 and they would still appear in a reprint of this edition. Cornell and Malcolmson try to defend these four added lines by pointing out that *ruinate* is used in *3 Henry VI* in a scene, V.i, that also mentions the chopping off of hands (p. 157). Also, supposedly corroborating the 'mutilation' hypothesis is the fact that where Q2 reprints what would have been the other side of the supposedly damaged bottom of the last leaf of Q1, it has substantial rewording too. But this rewording Cornell and Malcolmson also think intelligent and appropriate, and it has a phrase, 'tender spring', used by Shakespeare in *Venus and Adonis* and *The Rape of Lucrece* around the same time as *Titus Andronicus*. Their suggestion is that 'someone who knew the play well wrote the lines, which were then generally accepted' (p. 158). This last clause they put in, I think, to explain why the lines are in Q3 and F, but of course that does not indicate acceptance by the company. Here they also mix up their terminology, calling

Q1 'the manuscript [that] was damaged'. Their main point, though, is that even if we accept that Q1 was damaged that does not mean the lines invented have no place in the canon: the company might have accepted them into the play as performed. Cornell and Malcomson address Eugene Waith's rejection of Greg's claim that an exemplar of Q2 was used as the promptbook. How come, they ask, if the exemplar of Q3 used to make printer's copy for F was first collated with the promptbook, the spurious last four lines of Q3 were not deleted as being not found in the promptbook, and yet a missing line in I.i was recovered from the promptbook? It is possible to defend the added lines: they shift attention away from Tamora (on whom Q1 ends) and towards Aaron and towards the wider political scene, promising stability, and in particular seeming to hint at constitutional change so that the likes of Aaron will never succeed again.

The second article from *RES* is Roger Stritmatter and Lynne Kositksy's attempt to show that the Strachey Letter was, contrary to the date given upon its first publication, written later than *The Tempest* and therefore not a source for it ('Shakespeare and the Voyagers Revisited', *RES* 58[2007] 447–72). Malone thought that *The Tempest* was based on Sylvester Jourdain's *Discovery of the Bermudas* [1610] but this has been discredited: it was Henry Howard Furness who popularized the idea that *The Tempest* was based on a manuscript version of William Strachey's *True Reportory* [1625], the Letter, and hence must postdate the shipwreck that Strachey describes. As Stritmatter and Kositsky point out, we have no evidence that Strachey's text circulated in manuscript before publication, nor that if it did Shakespeare would have had access to it. Strachey's account seems to draw on other books that it is hard to imagine him having access to in Bermuda or Virginia, and it is hard to see how the account would have got back to London from the New World in time for *The Tempest*. Indeed, Stritmatter and Kositsky think that Strachey's Letter is most plausibly read as his response to a letter to him of 14 December 1610 from the Virginia Company asking for news, for Strachey seems to answer their questions in the Letter. Moreover, Strachey seems to describe the voyage back to London of Thomas Gates beginning on 15 July 1610, which is the one by which Strachey's account is itself supposed to have reached London, and this is logically impossible. In 1612 Strachey wrote of an as yet incomplete work about Bermuda that he was producing, and the logical referent of that is the *True Reportory*. Also, *True Reportory* seems to plagiarize books not published until November 1610 or later, and if it does it is too late to be a source for *The Tempest*.

At this point (p. 455), Stritmatter and Kositsky start to quote the parallels that they think prove Strachey a plagiarist, and indeed the same stories are told (of certain fruit and plants) but the wording is not close at all: these could be stories that were routinely circulating amongst the travellers. But for Stritmatter and Kositsky this 'borrowing', which required access to a library, must have been done after Strachey returned to London from Jamestown, and hence the Letter was not available to influence *The Tempest*. Indeed, since several works (including *The Tempest*) that were published before *True Reportory* have strong parallels with it, it were better not to assume that Strachey (in manuscript) was their source but that Strachey borrowed from these works. Stritmatter and Kositsky quote the strong parallel between *True Reportory* and *True Declaration of the Estate of the Colony of Virginia* (entered in the Stationers' Register on 10 November 1610), but they acknowledge that the standard explanation is that this was added to Strachey's Letter before it was published in 1625 even though it was not part of the original writing (p. 457). Other examples of Strachey's alleged plagiarism depicted here are weak: they would not get a modern undergraduate into much hot water. At the close, Stritmatter and Kositsky mention the fatal flaw in their position: when first published (in Samuel Purchas's *Hakluytus Posthumus or Purchas His Pilgrimes* [1625]), the Strachey Letter is given the date 'July 15, 1610'. They simply assert that Purchas is not to be relied upon for this date. For an unexplained reason, their article is signed by Stritmatter but not Kositsky.

Carl D. Atkins makes a study of Benson's 1640 edition of Shakespeare's sonnets as a reprint of the quarto of 1609 ('The Importance of Compositorial Error and Variation to the Emendation of Shakespeare's Texts: A Bibliographic Analysis of Benson's 1640 Text of Shakespeare's *Sonnets*', *SP* 104[2007] 306–39). Benson's edition was the basis for subsequent editions in the eighteenth century. As we have the quarto that it reprints (albeit with editorial changes) we can learn about printing habits from Benson's edition. Atkins offers an appendix listing all the variants between the two, categorized by kind. Benson's compositor corrected almost all the obvious misprints of Q, missing only *emnity*, which Atkins says should be *enmity*. (In fact Literature Online contains thirteen occurrences of *emnity* in printings from the sixteenth and seventeenth centuries, so we might almost say that this counts as a minor alternative spelling although *OED* does not list it.) Using what he has learnt from Benson's compositor's mistakes, Atkins turns to the problem of emending *Sonnets* where Q seems in error. This is not a sound methodology: better to learn from other reprints, where we can compare source and output to infer habits and characteristic slips, produced around the time of Q and preferably coming from the same printshop and so likely to have been worked upon by the same people. Strangely, Atkins rejects Duncan-Jones's claim that the misprint in Q of having *lack* (where editors agree the word needed is *latch*) comes via the spelling variant *lach* because, he says, the *OED* gives no examples of that spelling (p. 137). It does: Wyclif's Bible has one. The date of Duncan-Jones's Arden3 *Sonnets* is here given as 1977 but should be 1997. Naseeb Shaheen makes a surprisingly belated claim for the Q1 *Henry V* deriving from a memorial reconstruction ('*Henry V* and its Quartos', *ShN* 57[2007–8] 43–4, 48). He summarizes the textual situation of *Henry V* and says that there are two main views of Q1: that it is a memorial reconstruction, or James Shapiro's new idea that it is a sanitized, depoliticized version put out by the players when they realized that the original was too politically provocative. Shaheen does not specify whether he means 'out on the stage' or 'out into print', and he does not address Andrew Gurr's argument that Q1 represents the simplified stage version, the 'minimal' text, nor Richard Dutton's recent argument (reviewed in *YWES* 86[2007]) that F represents revisions of the Q1 version in the light of events of 1601. Shaheen decides that Shapiro is wrong and Q1 *Henry V* is based on a memorial reconstruction because there are things missing in it that no one would deliberately leave out in a process of sanitizing the play. This article is intellectually underpowered and widely ignorant of the state of the textual debate about this play.

Finally, to the round-up from *Notes and Queries*. Guillaume Coatalen points out that as a source for 'Now is the winter of our discontent | Made glorious summer' (*Richard III*), Philip Sidney's Sonnet 69 from *Astrophil and Stella* is usually cited ('Gone is the winter of my misery | My spring appears'), but that in fact both might come from the French poet Joachim du Bellay (*c.*1522–60), who in different works refers to 'l'hiver de mes douleurs' and 'l'hyver de mes ennuis' ('Shakespeare, Sidney and Du Bellay's Winters', *N&Q* 54[2007] 265). John Peachman thinks that *The Two Gentlemen of Verona* was written in 1597 or 1598, draws on Nashe, and alludes to the *Isle of Dogs* scandal ('Why a Dog? A Late Date for *The Two Gentlemen of Verona*', *N&Q* 54[2007] 265–72). The only sure thing about the date of *The Two Gentlemen of Verona* is that is was completed before Francis Meres referred to it in *Palladis Tamia* (entered in the Stationers' Register on 19 October 1598), and the view that it is early is based on subjective interpretation of its weaknesses. J.J.M. Tobin pointed out *The Two Gentlemen of Verona*'s borrowing from Nashe's *Have With You to Saffron-Walden* [1596], including the names of seven characters, and Tobin produced a list of significant collocations that the works share and that Peachman reproduces. This list has lots of commonplace words that really count for nothing except where they closely collocate, such as *cur*, *tongues* and *forest*. Peachman picks on a particular collocation that he thinks significant: ' "puling" is in close proximity to "wench" ' in only one play of the period, according to Literature Online, and that is *The Two Gentlemen of Verona* (p. 267). Peacham is mistaken about this: there is also Samuel Daniel's *The Queen's Arcadia* [1605]: 'there shall be found Fantasticke puling wenchnes in the world'.

It seems that Peachman does not know how to search Literature Online properly, and this exposes one of the dangers of this kind of work. The evidence on which his assertion rests is negative, that there are no other examples of X, but one is always afraid that what is really meant is 'I failed to find other examples of X', and that the scholar simply overlooked them. That Peachman thinks that the thing to search for is a play indicates another weakness in his methodology, since he should be searching all kinds of writing to see if these are common phrases in the literary-dramatic culture. A second collocation that Peachman thinks decisive is 'water cast in an urinal' in Nashe and 'water in an urinal' in *The Two Gentlemen of Verona* (p. 267). In fact, collocations of *water*, *cast* and *urinal* are not hard to find: there is 'an urinall . . . you cast | The water' in Dekker and 'Casting their Water in his Vrinalls' in John Davies of Hereford. And if we drop the word *cast* (since it is not in *The Two Gentlemen of Verona*) then there are over a dozen collocations including the perfect match 'water in an Vrinall' in John Day's play *Law Tricks* [1604]. The warnings about the evidential weakness of simple verbal parallels given by Muriel St Clare Byrne seventy-five years ago are still not being heeded. Peachman has several more one-word parallels but they prove nothing. He explains the presence in *The Two Gentlemen of Verona* of a scandalous dog who is dry-eyed when he should be weeping and peeing when he should not be as an allusion to the play *The Isle of Dogs* by Nashe and others in 1597, named after the wet peninsula in the Thames. Convinced he has got a 'hit', Peachman then reads *The Two Gentlemen of Verona* for its set of allusions to *The Isle of Dogs*, and finds a bit of Jonson's stubbornness in Crab too. He ends on even more tenuous links between *The Two Gentlemen of Verona* and the publication of Marlowe's *Hero and Leander* in 1598 and Jonson's *Every Man Out of His Humour* with its dog-related imagery.

Thomas Merriam, in a point also made in his book reviewed above, notes that *King John* is like *Richard III* in being about uncles ordering the deaths of their dispossessed nephews ('Parallel Nephews, Parallel Uncles', *N&Q* 54[2007] 272–4). Wolfgang Riehle thinks that Lysander's name in *A Midsummer Night's Dream* is an allusion to the story of Hero and Leander and also a pun on 'lie-sunder', meaning sleep apart, as Hermia insists they do in the woods ('What's in Lysander's Name?', *N&Q* 54[2007] 274–5). Alan J. Altimont has a Hebraic source for the same play, since Nedar means 'absentee' in Hebrew, which suits this character—he is not there to prevent Demetrius breaking faith with Helena—and also means 'pledge, vow' ('The Meaning of *Nedar* in *A Midsummer Night's Dream*', *N&Q* 54[2007] 275–7). That *A Midsummer Night's Dream* has a source in the Talmud does not, Altimont reassures us, require that we imagine Shakespeare reading Hebrew: he might just have heard about it. According to Beatrice Groves, the idea of the wall between families coming down (as it does metaphorically in *Romeo and Juliet* and literally in *A Midsummer Night's Dream*) derives from the Bible, Ephesians 2, where it refers to the union of gentiles and Jews ('"The Wittiest Partition": Bottom, Paul, and Comedic Resurrection', *N&Q* 54[2007] 277–82). A.B. Taylor notes that Bottom's allusion to the Bible, 1 Corinthians 2.9— 'The eye of man hath not heard, the ear of man hath not seen, man's hand is not able to taste, his tongue to conceive, nor his heart to report what my dream was' (*A Midsummer Night's Dream* IV.i.208–11, wrongly given as Act V in this article)—was not the first time that Pyramus and 1 Corinthians 2.9 had been linked: John Gower did it in *Confessio Amantis* ('John Gower and *Pyramus and Thisbe*', *N&Q* 54[2007] 282–3). Also, Shakespeare borrowed from Gower the reference to a lion 'in wild rage' and there being a hole in the wall; in Ovid it is only a crack. Matt Baynham explains that Portia's calling mercy 'twice blest' (*Merchant of Venice* IV.i.183) alludes to the biblical Sermon on the Mount, for there only the merciful receive what they give; the peacemakers do not get peace, for example ('Why is Mercy "Twice Blest"?', *N&Q* 54[2007] 285).

Anthony Miller finds sources for the pointless war over a tiny patch of ground in *Hamlet* IV.iv, and for the reflections on a 'buyer of land' in *Hamlet* V.i, and for Lear's 'we came crying hither' (*King Lear* IV.v) in Pliny's *Naturalis historia* ('Fortinbras' Conquests and Pliny', *N&Q* 54[2007] 287–9). Thomas Festa thinks that Hamlet's comment that his father was a man 'take him for all in all' (I.ii.186) echoes the 'all in all' from the biblical Corinthians that was prescribed reading in the Book of Common Prayer for the burial of the dead ('"All in all": The *Book of Common Prayer* and *Hamlet*, I.ii.186', *N&Q* 54[2007] 289–90). David Lisle Crane notes that, when Angelo asks incredulously if Isabella is talking about the Duke's deputy, and says 'The prenzie, *Angelo*?' (*Measure for Measure* III.i.92), *prenzie* is obviously wrong. Crane reckons that a *u* before the *p* might have been mistaken by the

compositor for a flourish and that the word really was *upright* here, and three
lines later when Isabella repeats it (*'Measure for Measure* III.i.93, 96: Prenzie',
N&Q 54[2007] 292). Andrew Hadfield claims that Isabella in *Measure for
Measure* is a novice because she is meant to be like the St Ursula who had the
same dilemma about choosing between life and virginity in the book *The
Golden Legend* by Jacobus de Voragine. ('Isabella, Marina, and Saint Ursula',
N&Q 54[2007] 292–3). He thinks the conversion of brothel-goers in *Pericles*
might also be indebted to this account of St Ursula. Hadfield is right that *The
Golden Legend* went through many editions, but the latest of those was in 1527
so was not quite so 'hard to avoid' (p. 293) in 1603 as Hadfield suggests.
Rodney Stenning Edgecombe thinks that Othello's reference to being roasted
in sulphur (*Othello* V.ii) has its source in Ovid's account in *Metamorphoses* of
Phaeton's end being the reason that Ethiopians are black, and that this also
was in Shakespeare's mind when Othello refers to 'medicinable gum' in the
'pearl away' speech, for Phaeton's sisters in Ovid weep tears that turn to amber
that is later made into jewellery ('Ovid and the 'Medicinal Gum' in *Othello*
V.ii', *N&Q* 54[2007] 293–4). David Womersley claims that certain passages
from Heywood's *2 If You Know Not Me* (Stationers' Register entry 14
September 1606) echo *Macbeth*, which must therefore have been completed
and performed by this date in order for Heywood to use it ('Heywood's *2
If You Know Not Me* and the Date of *Macbeth*', *N&Q* 54[2007] 296–8).
Extraordinarily, Womersley quotes nothing from *Macbeth* to support this,
apparently thinking the parallels so obvious that the relevant textual details
need not be given. He also assumes, without giving reasons, that Shakespeare
was the lender not the borrower.

According to Juan Christian Pellicer, the servant's word *saltiers* in *The
Winter's Tale* IV.iv is not a rustic mangling of *satyrs* but a learned Latin
coinage (to convey leaping satyrs) perhaps prompted by the phrase 'saltantis
satyros' in Virgil's *Eclogues* ('Shakespeare's "Saltiers"/Satyrs in *The Winter's
Tale* and Virgil's *Saltantis Satyros*', *N&Q* 54[2007] 303–4). MacDonald P.
Jackson has a new way to date *Sir Thomas More* ('A New Chronological
Indicator for Shakespeare's Plays and for Hand D of *Sir Thomas More*', *N&Q*
54[2007] 304–7). Using software that 'analyses various structural features',
Hartmut Ilsemann has counted the length of speeches in Shakespeare and
noticed that they get shorter over his career. Jackson does not say so, but
presumably the point about analysing structural features means that the
software does not just rely on punctuation to determine where speeches end,
otherwise the method would be counting data from the printing/editorial
processes, not from Shakespeare himself. Unfortunately, in a footnote citing
Ilsemann's work, the URL—given twice albeit with the same real address, for
the tilde is once given its ASCII code instead—points to a page no longer
available on the worldwide web. Ilsemann's method more or less corroborates
the Oxford *Complete Works* chronology, although *The Two Gentlemen of
Verona* and *The Taming of the Shrew* seem on this evidence to be later than
usually thought. (If accepted, this would corroborate John Peachman's article
reviewed above.) On this evidence, Hand D of *Sir Thomas More* was
composed around 1603–4, and the two halves of *Pericles* are once again shown
to be highly distinct. Kevin Curran finds that Cleopatra's aversion to the

messenger's 'but yet' (leading up to the news of Antony's marriage) is an idea borrowed from Samuel Daniel's *The Tragedy of Philotas* ('Shakespeare and Daniel Revisited: *Antony and Cleopatra* II.v.50–4 and *The Tragedy of Philotas* V.ii.2013–15', *N&Q* 54[2007] 318–20). Finally for this section, Arthur Sherbo reprints some notes by George Steevens and Edmond Malone (from Steevens's 1793 edition) that ought to have appeared in the New Variorum editions of *Poems* [1938] and *Sonnets* [1944] by Hyder Edward Rollins, and many of them are about bits of the plays that are illuminated by usages in the sonnets and the narrative poems ('Corrections and Additions to Professor Rollins's Editions of Shakespeare's *Sonnets* and Poems', *N&Q* 54[2007] 483–90). I assume that this fulfils the promise made by Sherbo in his longer article reviewed above, but the textual situation is so tangled and the notes are coming out in such short bursts and in so many different places that it is hard to be entirely sure.

2. Shakespeare in the Theatre

While the title of Simon Palfrey and Tiffany Stern's collaborative *Shakespeare in Parts* acknowledges the canonical dismemberment of the supreme Bard on the one hand, it deftly engages with the excavation of 'original practice' theatre on the other. The 'parts' that it exhumes for autopsy are the constituent organs of the Shakespearian play-text: the individuated 'sides' (also 'lengths'), each separate speech of which is prefixed by a two- or three-word cue. Each role was physically a roll, committed to memory linearly, conned in isolation. None of the actors would, in advance of its first performance, have a detailed overall sense of what the play was about, how they fitted into its narrative nor even when or from whom their next cue was about to come. The advantage was a sense of spontaneity, a sustained engagement with the other actors prompted by an intense concentration on what was happening on stage: 'Because the cue just *might* come from anyone, the actor must always remain "on cue"' (p. 93).

Palfrey and Stern are adamant that the shared intimacy of actors and playwright was more than sufficient to compensate for this lack of ensemble rehearsal as well as the absence of the guiding presence of a director: 'Shakespeare really knew these actors; he worked with some of them for thirty years' (p. 41). The rapidly revolving repertory necessitated short runs so that the similitude of imminence which, in the modern theatre, paradoxically necessitates repetitive rehearsal over a sustained period, was, in the theatre of Shakespeare's time, less of an illusion than an actuality: one of the benefits of part-learning is the 'drip-feeding to the actor [of] strictly limited amounts of contextual information' (p. 134).

The authors are deft, sometimes over-ingenious, interpreters, proposing that minor cues provide the actor with intimations of his situation. In the case of the incarcerated Malvolio (pp. 111–13) they isolate c(l)ues such as 'darke'; 'obstruction'; 'fogge' (but they overlook 'Parson', 'fowle', 'opinion'). Most compelling is their exploration of 'repeated cues' which may bring other actor(s) in early and especially in crowd scenes, 'can be a useful means of creating the required polyphony' (p. 164). There are excellent readings of

The Merchant of Venice and *Macbeth*. Shylock's repeated cues invite others to talk over him and so demonstrate his 'refusal to listen' (p. 201), while Macbeth's part 'fastidiously places the actor in uncertainties' (p. 488). Occasionally the perspicacious engagement with the prosody and arrangement of parts yields far-fetched psycho-biography: as Prospero tells Miranda to 'awake', the cue becomes a 'psychic chamber beyond capture or apprehension' (p. 281). Elsewhere the prioritization of vocabulary can lead to strained readings: 'Helena's pointed repetition of "I die"/"let me die" [constitutes] a "shared" and "perfect" rhyme that is at once bold, ominous, and an impudent invitation to imagine mutual orgasm' (p. 430). But in the main this is a lucid and persuasive study which successfully infuses academic Shakespeare with the vibrancy and insecurity of live performance: 'Shakespeare's actors had to play their parts *now*, perilously in the present' (p. 491).

Kent R. Lehnhof's 'Performing Woman: Female Theatricality in *All's Well, That Ends Well*' (in Waller, ed., *All's Well, That Ends Well: New Critical Essays*, pp. 111–23), confronts the exclusion from theatre history of 'early modern female performance' (p. 111). He claims that while women were absent from the professional stage, they frequently appeared in mountebank shows across Renaissance Europe, and he goes on to propose that there is a particular relevance in considering the similarity of Helena to 'a number of actual early modern female mountebanks' (p. 113). While Lehnhof considers the medical nature of Helena's role as making her a suitable parallel, he also stresses that both she and the mountebank enact forbidden or censored kinds of female sexual autonomy. While noting that the female mountebank was often associated with an erotic openness, he explores the equation of a 'woman's willingness to perform dramatic roles with a willingness to perform sexual ones' (p. 115). Indeed, the analogy of Helena and the mountebank allows one to 'begin to make sense of the strangely erotic nature of her characterization and comportment in the court of the King' (pp. 117–18). He concludes by alluding to David McCandless's proposal to cast two actors as Helena—'a woman to perform the passages when Helena displays desiring independence, and a man in drag to enact the "hyperfeminine" episodes when Helena adopts an idealized posture of meekness and subservience' (p. 122). Lehnhof asserts that such a double casting would have the virtue of complicating 'the concept of stable sexual identity by implying that masculinity and femininity are a function of costume, comportment, and custom' (p. 122).

Peter Holland moves us from the early modern theatre to that of the eighteenth century. In 'Hearing the Dead: The Sound of David Garrick' (in Cordner and Holland, eds., *Players, Playwrights, Playhouses: Investigating Performance, 1660—1800*, pp. 248–70), he sets out to redress an imbalance in the prevailing method of performance history. The discipline is, he opines, 'tied to the visual rather than the aural' (p. 249) and he sets out in a mischievous parody of Stephen Greenblatt not to speak with but rather to listen to the dead, particularly David Garrick. The contemporary fad for original practices/original pronunciation such as that practised at the Southwark Globe will not do: 'I do not want to hear someone pretending to be Garrick; I want to hear Garrick' (p. 251). Inevitably, Holland has to admit that such an aspiration is 'doomed to failure...hopeless' (p. 248).

What Holland does produce, however, is an extraordinarily detailed set of contemporary audience responses which analyse Garrick's treatments of lines and even individual words. Thomas Sheridan (who went on to coach Sarah Siddons), John Henderson, J.W. Anderson, Roger Pickering et al. commented directly on Garrick's pronunciation and pitch as well as speed of delivery. Holland argues that Sheridan, in particular, brings 'an awareness of character and imagination to bear on processes of rhythm and emphasis' (p. 256). Joshua Steele actually drew up a notation, similar to sheet music, for documenting Garrick's delivery of specific speeches. Of course, without any independent evidence, such responses have to be taken on trust. Nonetheless, for all its incertitude, Holland is able to impute various qualities to the oral aspect of Garrick's performances: 'Difficult and abstruse though Steele's system may be, it is the most complex and considered notation of a moment of theatre speech available and Garrick's lightness and speed are conspicuously apparent' (p. 259). Holland concludes that in spite of the inherently capricious quality of such responses and their notations, 'Garrick's form of speaking allowed for multiple and complex emotions both to succeed each other rapidly and to co-exist within a single moment' (p. 267).

In 'Sowing the *Dragon*'s Teeth: Amateurism, Domesticity, and the Anglophone Audience for Shakespeare, 1607–2007' (*Gramma* 15[2007] 27–45), Michael Dobson juxtaposes three canonical and three non-canonical moments from the long history of Shakespeare in performance. Alongside the publication of F1 in 1623, he places the first recorded amateur performance of a Shakespeare play, a production of *Henry IV* at the house of Sir Edward Dering. The year 1774 saw the publication of the first academic monograph on Shakespeare: William Richardson's *A Philosophical Analysis and Illustration of Some of Shakespeare's Remarkable Characters*. Dobson notes that the same year saw the first recorded all-female production of a play by Shakespeare— *The Winter's Tale*. And while 1932 is best remembered in Shakespearian circles as the year which saw the opening of the Folger Shakespeare Library in Washington, DC, as well as the Shakespeare Memorial Theatre in Stratford-upon-Avon, Dobson reveals that the same year saw the inauguration of the first playhouse to be designed and owned by a woman (Rowena Cade): the Minack in Cornwall. In making these comparisons, Dobson implies that the history of amateur Shakespeare is at least as important as that of its professional (scholarly and performative) counterpart. He asserts that amateur Shakespeare remains 'massively under-studied' (p. 43) and yet oddly empathic with Shakespeare's art. For instance, he notes that 'Shakespeare's own work never depicts professional playwrights but only schoolmasters who compose dramatic entertainments for particular groups and occasions' (p. 44). Indeed, with a remarkable degree of equanimity, he self-consciously suggests that even so-called professional scholarship is really nothing more than a kind of glorified amateurism: '*Shakespeare Survey* and *Shakespeare Quarterly* are only fanzines, and even the most august international Shakespeare conferences are only social gatherings of people who choose to participate in doing Shakespeare in whatever manner or capacity; people who, if they were primarily interested in making money or serving the status quo, would surely do something else instead' (pp. 44–5). In this way, Dobson neatly debunks the dour materialist orthodoxy that Shakespeare is a bastion of cultural capital which acts as a bulwark in the defence of a capitalist or patriarchal hegemony: perhaps, he concludes, 'the history of this business called Shakespeare has all along been a story about amateurs' (p. 45).

Bridget Escolme's 'Living Monuments: The Spatial Politics of Shakespeare's Rome on the Contemporary Stage' (*ShS* 60[2007] 170–83) is an account of her direction of *Coriolanus* for Flaneur Productions in Minneapolis and Rochester, Minnesota, in April 2006. She reads her own production against Deborah Warner's *Julius Caesar* (Barbican, 2005) finding and condemning in the latter an over-eager search for parallels between the civil strife in Shakespeare's play and the contemporary crisis in Iraq. While such analogies are inevitable, Escolme is impatient with the ways in which the presentation of Warner's production (including photographs in the programme) shoe-horned audience reaction into a single and specific response. Preferable, she maintains, is the seeking of analogy through the art of others. For instance, she refers to the work of Minnesota photographer Paul Shambroom, who documented a series of council meetings of small towns across the States (three of his pictures are reproduced for us). Escolme explains that, for her, they capture 'how supremely unglamorous the workings of government are, how hedged about with contingency and tedium' (p. 178). Escolme is refreshingly candid about the contingencies of performance and the coincidental quality of many of her production's best effects. For instance, her actors were assembled in front of a row of TV sets which suggested the televisual quality of politics, although the presence of these televisions 'was entirely fortuitous: they were part of an artist's installation on display at the Art Center at the time' (p. 180). Elsewhere Coriolanus confronted Menenius in front of the American flag (which the gallery happened to have flying at the time). While in no way rejecting conventional theatre seating, Escolme is keen to foreground 'the live encounter between text, space, human figures acting and human figures recalcitrantly being themselves' in order to animate the relationship between the plays and 'our own political crises and concerns' (p. 183).

3. Shakespeare on Screen

The year 2007 marked a significant increase in the number of book-length publications which engage with Shakespeare on screen. Perhaps the December 2007 deadline for submissions from British universities for their Research Assessment Exercise offers a partial explanation for the greater quantity of material? Three monographs and one collaboratively authored book deal exclusively with Shakespearian film and television productions. A further four monographs and one edited collection embrace screen versions within performance-orientated studies. Both *The Cambridge Companion to Shakespeare in Popular Culture* and *The Cambridge Companion to Literature on Screen* include essays which relate to Shakespeare on screen. The inclusion of three articles in *The Literature/Film Reader: Issues in Adaptation* signals the place that Shakespeare versions occupy within broader studies of cinematic adaptations. One edited collection (*Shakespeare and Childhood*, edited by

Kate Chedgzoy, Susanne Greenhalgh and Robert Shaughnessy) ranges beyond performance-orientated enquiries and embraces within its enquiry two essays analysing Shakespearian screen versions.

A significant contribution to screen-related reference material is made this year with two encyclopedic publications. Richard Burt's multi-volume *Shakespeares after Shakespeare: An Encyclopedia of the Bard in Mass Media and Popular Culture* combines detailed filmographies and interpretative essays. The listings in John O'Connor and Katharine Goodland's *A Directory of Shakespeare in Performance: 1970–2005, volume 1: Great Britain*, embrace stage, television and film versions. The arguments presented in several journal articles focus on Shakespeare on screen, with the greatest number appearing in the customary 'Shakespeare on Film' issue of *Literature/Film Quarterly* (*LFQ* 35[2007]).

The three Shakespeare on screen monographs published this year vary significantly in their approach and content. While part of the impulse behind Russell Jackson's *Shakespearean Films in the Making: Vision, Production and Reception* might be the author's experience as textual adviser on Kenneth Branagh's film sets, it is just briefly in the introduction that Jackson makes reference to personal experience in relation to *Hamlet* [1996]. The book's three chapters centre upon films which hold an acknowledged place in the canon of Shakespearian film versions. Chapter 1 focuses on Reinhardt's *A Midsummer Night's Dream* [1935], chapter 2 analyses Olivier's *Henry V* [1944] and chapter 3 focuses on three versions of *Romeo and Juliet*: MGM [1936], Castellani [1954] and Zeffirelli [1968]. Identifying the Reinhardt–Dieterle *Dream* through the name of the theatre director, Max Reinhardt, signals the interest that Jackson shows in the film's theatrical context. In contrast, connecting the 1936 *Romeo and Juliet* with the production company rather than George Cukor, the director, demonstrates Jackson's interest in the influence of 'the studio's self-image' (p. 4) alongside that of the director, the producer and the scriptwriter. A sense of each film's priorities is established through a detailed exploration of scripts and other production materials. Jackson seeks to assess the 'significance of the works for their makers (both corporate and individual) and the audiences of their own time' (p. 1). The approach is explicitly historical, and 'reception' does not, therefore, embrace later critical perspectives on the films. Jackson's exploration is strengthened by extensive quotation of promotional materials and reviews. The inclusion of twenty-two illustrations helps underpin the book's desire to temper a text-centred analysis with an awareness of these versions as motion pictures.

An interest in commercial pressures on film reinterpretations of Shakespeare's plays is shared by Mark Thornton Burnett. His *Filming Shakespeare in a Global Marketplace* considers the way that 'the films reveal themselves as acutely responsive to their own marketplace location' (p. 3). Burnett analyses a broad range of Shakespeare on film material. He chooses to begin with film and television productions which 'construct the enduring stability of Shakespearean theatre' (p. 4). The first chapter focuses upon *In the Bleak Midwinter* (Branagh [1995]), *Beginner's Luck* (Callis and Cohen [2001]), BBC2's *Indian Dream* [2003] and the Miramax teen picture *Get Over It* (O'Haver [2001]). The examples are used to consider 'vexed and unresolved attitudes towards the relations between cinema, theatre and the global scene' (p. 8). While the four films construct theatre as 'a site of refinement, reformation and possibility' (p. 16), they also suggest that 'past beliefs and conventions have a niche in the present landscape' (p. 27).

Chapter 2 focuses on *Much Ado About Nothing* (Branagh [1993]) and *A Midsummer Night's Dream* (Hoffman [1999]). Burnett builds on recognized connections between the two films and he argues that Hoffman's film might productively be seen as a sequel to Branagh's *Much Ado*. The identification of a line of influence between the films produces the concluding suggestion that Hoffman's film 'gravitates back, ironically underscoring the limitations of the comedic form' (p. 46). Chapter 3 considers conversations between Shakespearian films with reference to versions of *Hamlet* and *Macbeth*. The plays are linked through location rather than genre, and the analysis considers ideas of what 'local' means in relation to a Shakespearian film. Chapter 4 investigates *Othello* (Parker [1995]) and *O* (Nelson [2001]) and considers race in relation to globalization. The historical and political implications of the more recent *The Merchant of Venice* (Radford [2004]) are considered in detail in chapter 5. The sixth chapter considers systems of belief and ideological implications of *Macbeth in Manhattan* (Lombardo [1999]) and *The King Is Alive* (Levring [2000]). Chapter 7 analyses twenty-first-century screen versions, and Thornton Burnett identifies a group of parodic versions: *The Street King* (Bedford [2002]), *In Othello* (Abel [2003]) and *Romeo and Juliet* (Lachapelle [2005]).

Maurice Hindle's *Studying Shakespeare on Film* focuses on films which have retained Shakespeare's dialogue, with exceptions made for silent films and Kurosawa's *Throne of Blood* [1957]. The study is divided into five parts, within which are multiple sub-sections. Hindle's organization of his material, the accessible style and the inclusion of a 'glossary of terms' (pp. 255–60) reinforces a sense of the text being targeted towards students studying Shakespeare's work. Part I considers 'Shakespeare and the Language of Film'. Brief introductory sections chart familiar Shakespeare-on-screen territory with consideration of the tension between theatre and cinema, the differences between the respective kinds of audience experience and the use of verbal and visual imagery in film. Part II moves chronologically through 'The History of Shakespeare on Film 1899–2005'. The section presents an annotated list of films, and while priority is given to films 'which at the time of writing are available on DVD or video' (p. xvii) some reference is made to less easily accessed versions, such as Charlton Heston's *Antony and Cleopatra* [1972]. Hindle supports his judgements of the film versions with reference to a range of critical voices. In Part III he self-consciously follows Jorgens's technique of identifying 'modes of representation' (p. 68). Subsections order brief descriptions of the respective style and offer examples which seem to fit within the theatrical mode, the realistic mode, the filmic mode and, finally, the periodizing mode. The concluding section of part II establishes the importance of film genre, but the rapid movement between examples prevents sustained analysis. The section ends with analysis of Kurosawa's *Macbeth* version, *Throne of Blood*. Hindle labels the film as a 'cross-cultural...adaptation' (p. 99), and makes a short examination of the film in the context of Noh theatre and the samurai movie.

The fourth part of Hindle's monograph seems perhaps most clearly student-focused. Fourteen short essays are offered on the best-known Shakespearian film adaptations. The essays are grouped by the play's genre. Three adaptations are analysed: *Much Ado About Nothing* (Branagh [1993]), *A Midsummer Night's Dream* (Noble [1996]) and *A Midsummer Night's Dream* (Hoffmann [1999]). Four essays focus on what Hindle labels as 'histories': *Henry V* (Olivier [1944]), *Henry V* [1989], *Richard III* (Olivier [1955]) and *Richard III* (Loncraine [1995]). The section culminates with seven separate essays on tragedies: *Romeo and Juliet* (Zeffirelli [1968]), *William Shakespeare's Romeo + Juliet* (Luhrmann [1996]), *Hamlet* (Olivier [1948]), *Hamlet* (Branagh [1996]), *Hamlet* (Almereyda [2000]), *Macbeth* (Welles [1948]) and *Macbeth* (Polanski [1971]). Part V marks a separation between types of screen Shakespeare by engaging with 'Shakespeare on Television'. Hindle states explicitly a dissatisfaction with the term, 'screen', because film and television 'differ greatly' (p. 221). One section engages with the BBC-TV Shakespeare, and that is followed by 'hybrid' stage-to-screen versions (p. 233). Here there is brief engagement with a couple of adaptations, including Andrew Davies's modernization of *Othello* (Sax [2001]).

While Thomas Cartelli and Katharine Rowe's *New Wave Shakespeare on Screen* seems to be similarly student-centred, their study benefits from a sharper focus. Their exploration focuses on work released in the past fifteen years and that enables more in-depth exploration of their chosen texts. They use 'screen' self-consciously because, they suggest, it 'marks the convergence of film and other audio-visual media . . . includ[ing] not just film, television, video, and DVD, domestic and global, but also web-based and cellular media, delivered via desktop, laptop and hand-held means' (p. x). Cartelli and Rowe give attention to their decision to label recent Shakespearian work on film as 'new wave'. Their primary justification is that of the experimental nature of recent screen Shakespeares and of recent scholarship. They organize their material into seven chapters. Chapter 1 signals the movement 'Beyond Branagh and the BBC'. The analysis focuses on Branagh's *Henry V* [1989] and *William Shakespeare's Romeo + Juliet* (Luhrmann [1996]). Chapter 2 engages with 'Adaptation as a Cultural Process', and the films explored include *Richard III* (Loncraine [1995]), *Conte d'hiver* (Rohmer [1992]) and *Prospero's Books* (Greenaway [1991]). Chapter 3 focuses on '*Hamlet* Rewound' and, accordingly, engages with Almereyda's 2000 film version of *Hamlet* and then rewinds to consider Olivier's 1948 version of the same play. Chapter 4 focuses on 'Colliding Time and Space' in *Titus* (Taymor [1999]). Chapter 5 uses three American adaptations to explore 'Vernacular Shakespeare': *Looking for Richard* (Pacino [1996]), *The Street King* (Bedford [2002]) and *Scotland, PA* (Morrissette [2001]). The penultimate chapter analyses Andrew Davies's adaptation of *Othello* (Sax [2001]). The representation of race on screen leads to the suggestion that 'performances of Othello "channel" a prevailing racial construction as much as they do a dramatic persona' (p. 121). The final chapter looks at *The King Is Alive* (Levring [2000]) as evidence of 'Surviving Shakespeare'. Cartelli and Rowe's organization of their material ensures that films with an established place in Shakespeare-on-screen scholarship are productively set against those that are more recent or less well known.

John O'Connor and Katharine Goodland jointly compiled *A Directory of Shakespeare in Performance*. So far, just volume one has been published and this text focuses on performances in Great Britain between 1970 and 2005. The introduction establishes the rationale behind what are acknowledged to be choices affected by 'a degree of subjectivity' (p. xii). The decision not to include versions which might be described as 'modern English adaptations, [and] spin-offs' (p. xii) justifies some omissions. Adopting the same typographical style and layout for the records of the screen versions and the theatrical productions helps signal a desire to move away from established oppositions between theatre and film. Richard Burt's *Shakespeares after Shakespeare* marks a neat contrast with the O'Connor and Goodland directory. Burt proclaims his interest in 'eccentric Shakespeare materials' (p. 5) and he seeks to establish his approach in contrast to that adopted by Rothwell and Melzer in the key reference work for *Shakespeare on Screen*. The ambitious publication is part edited collection of essays and part bibliography (or perhaps more accurately mass media-ography). The contributors include Michael P. Jensen, Courtney Lehmann, Douglas Lanier, Wes Folkerth, Annalisa Castaldo, Ellen Joy Letostak, Susanne Greenhalgh, Amy Scott-Douglass, Minami Ryuta and Fabio Ciaramaglia. The volume seeks to challenge established approaches to Shakespearian adaptation with the order of its nine chapters. The volumes are organized by type of cultural product and so chapter 1 engages with 'Cartoons and Comic Books' and 'Theater' provides the focus of chapter 9.

In contrast, David Bevington signals his priority is theatre in the title of his monograph. *This Wide and Universal Theater: Shakespeare in Performance Then and Now* does, however, embrace film and television work within its definition of 'performance'. The book seeks to engage with the original theatrical world of the plays and to relate those ideas to more recent performance choices. The pace is rapid, and so moments from screen productions are briefly sketched and set alongside choices made in productions staged in London, Stratford and regional theatres in England. The eclectic mix makes the book entertaining but, at times, frustrating when there is so little space to give any context for the chosen version's choices. In considering 'Stage Business in the Comedies', chapter 3 touches on a range of versions of *Shrew*: *Kiss Me Kate* [1953], *10 Things I Hate About You* [1999], Sam Taylor's film [1929], Zeffirelli's version [1967] and Miller's television production [1981]. Branagh's *Love's Labour's Lost* [2000] is commended and has the distinction of being accompanied with a double-page photograph by way of illustration. The following chapters are organized broadly by genre, and there is a similarly broad range of reference. The dominance of examples from television and film makes the language of Bevington's conclusion seem peculiar. He ends his survey by suggesting that it has provided evidence to affirm 'the theatrical world to which [Shakespeare's dramatic characters] belong and where they eternally dwell' (p. 224).

Lena Cowen Orlin and Miranda Johnson-Haddad's *Staging Shakespeare: Essays in Honor of Alan C. Dessen* combines essays which study Shakespeare on stage and on screen. The three essays relevant to 'Shakespeare on Screen' are grouped in part III, 'Recordings'. Edward L. Rocklin considers the 1964 screen record of Richard Burton's performance as Hamlet: ' "That his heels may KICK at heaven": Exploring *Hamlet* through the Prompt-Script, Film, and Audio Recordings of the Gielgud–Burton Production' (in Orlin and Johnson-Haddad, eds., pp. 133–56). Rocklin explores the variations between the versions of the 1964 production. The discussion destabilizes discussions of 'a' production with details about the making of the screen record of the production. Burton's performances were recorded on three successive evenings with fifteen cameras. Rocklin analyses the film in relation to the studio-made audio recording of scenes and soliloquies, the introduction to the Folio Society's *Hamlet* [1954] and the stage production's Prompt Script.

In 'Fooling with Matches in Trevor Nunn's *Twelfth Night*: Or, Lines, Women, and Song' (in Orlin and Johnson-Haddad, eds., pp. 183–96), Caroline McManus makes the broad statement that there is an 'affinity between women and fools' within 'the canon as a whole' (p. 183). It seems strange that briefly sketched observations about a proposed 'Shakespearean paradigm' (p. 183) are then proven by applying them to a film version of *Twelfth Night*. The excisions and revisions in Nunn's screenplay are given little attention. McManus draws attention to the film's connections between Feste, Olivia, Maria and Viola. Nunn is unproblematically celebrated as 'an astute reader' (p. 183) and McManus seems on uncertain territory with a conclusion which suggests ideas of improvements for the film. She would have preferred the film to end with 'one more shot . . . to suggest that Illyria has not lost its truth-telling androgynous fool' (p. 195).

Michael D. Friedman focuses more explicitly on cinematic Shakespeare: ' "This fearful slumber": Some Unacknowledged Sources of Julie Taymor's *Titus*' (in Orlin and Johnson-Haddad, eds., pp. 157–81). Friedman moves beyond the sources acknowledged in Taymor's numerous interviews and commentaries and identifies unacknowledged borrowings from Jane Howell's *Titus Andronicus* (BBC [1985]) and Adrian Noble's film (deriving from his stage production) of *A Midsummer Night's Dream* [1996]. Taymor's 1999 film follows both of these earlier Shakespearian adaptations by sifting the action through the consciousness of a child. The points of connection between the three screen versions are traced with close and detailed analysis of specific choices made by Taymor. Friedman concludes by suggesting that Taymor 'adopts the dreaming boy from Howell, refines him through Noble, and places him at the heart of her indictment of institutionalized violence in the postmodern world' (p. 176).

An interest in the role that children have played (and might potentially play) in performance is explored at more length in Carol Chillington Rutter's monograph, *Shakespeare and Child's Play: Performing Lost Boys on Stage and Screen*. Rutter is 'asking questions about the cultural location and valuation of children (then, now) . . . wondering what we "mean" by children in Shakespeare—and what children in Shakespeare "mean" by us' (p. xv). It is Rutter's second chapter which focuses in the most sustained way on one specific film version. The chapter explores *Titus Andronicus* and how, specifically 'in Taymor, young Lucius's looking frames the story' (p. 69). In the context of Michael Friedman's article, it is perhaps relevant to note the absence of any reference to Jane Howell's earlier screen version. Chapter 4 gives some attention to the British television film *Macbeth on the Estate* (Woolcock [1997]). The Weird Sisters become Weird Children, and that decision gives them a peculiar potency.

The collection of essays edited by Kate Chedgzoy, Susanne Greenhalgh and Robert Shaughnessy has a wide-ranging interest in *Shakespeare and Childhood*. A couple of essays in part II explore most directly the implications of an interest in 'childhood' for Shakespeare-on-screen scholarship. Susanne Greenhalgh's essay centres upon one play: 'Dream Children: Staging and Screening Childhood in *A Midsummer Night's Dream*' (in Chedgzoy, Greenhalgh and Shaughnessy, eds., pp. 201–17). Her argument seeks to explore the paradox that 'child performance becomes both the quintessence of artificiality and manipulation, and a fulfilment of adult desire to surrender to the pleasures of dramatic illusion' (p. 202). Greenhalgh focuses on the Dieterle–Reinhardt *A Midsummer Night's Dream* [1935] and *The Children's Midsummer Night's Dream* (Edzard [2001]). Detailed studies of both films are offered, and Greenhalgh identifies their choices as representative of different periods and cultures. The implicit comparison allows 'differences within and between historical childhoods [to] come into sharper focus' (p. 214).

Richard Burt's 'Shakespeare 'tween Media and Markets, in the 1990s and Beyond' (in Chedgzoy, Greenhalgh and Shaughnessy, eds., pp. 128–232). Burt's piece is characteristically eclectic and he identifies childhood-related Shakespearian examples in a range of advertisements, PBS puppet shows, cartoons, 'family' films, television film retellings of fairy tales, books and toys. The integration of children's Shakespeare into the Shakespeare industry is coupled with the place that Shakespeare has in the American education system. He focuses upon child-related 1990s and millennial films and television shows 'from a perspective derived from deconstruction and media theory' (p. 219). The edited collection is marked apart from other monographs and collections this year with its unusually helpful appendices. Appendix 1 is provided by Mark Lawhorn: 'Children in Shakespeare's Plays: An Annotated Checklist' (in Chedgzoy, Greenhalgh and Shaughnessy, eds., pp. 233–49). Lawhorn gives a play-by-play account of children's parts, and his introduction to the list prompts consideration of how performance choices (both on stage and screen) complicated the process of list-making. Chedgzoy, Greenhalgh and Edel Lamb provide, in appendix 2, a 'Bibliography of Shakespeare and Childhood in English' (pp. 233–49). Part III provides details of a useful collection of audio-visual resources.

Julie Sanders's study *Shakespeare and Music: Afterlives and Borrowings* directs attention to the often neglected audio element of films. Her study ranges between 'classical symphonies, operas, ballets, musicals, and film scores'. The fourth chapter considers 'contemporary' musical adaptations, and reference is made to the films of *Kiss Me Kate* [1953] and *West Side Story* [1961]. At times, there seemed a need for greater clarity about whether Sanders's analysis was of the stage musical or the film version, and distinctions between stage and screen versions were blurred in the 'Shakespeare at the Ballet' chapter too. One chapter is dedicated to 'Symphonic Film Scores', and Sanders draws attention to established collaborative relationships between Nino Rota and Zeffirelli, and Patrick Doyle and Branagh.

The Reinhardt–Dieterele film of *A Midsummer Night's Dream* [1935] receives attention in relation to its score, and its choreography is considered in the earlier chapter on dance versions. Sanders makes sustained reference to music in films in her penultimate chapter: '"You know the movie song": Contemporary and Hybrid Film Scores'. The chapter considers the compilation soundtracks of *William Shakespeare's Romeo + Juliet* (Luhrmann [1996]), *O* (Nelson [2001]) and *10 Things I Hate About You* (Junger [1999]).

The journal *College Literature* provides an article which seeks to yoke an academic approach to Shakespeare on screen with practical guidance on teaching strategies. Martine van Elk's 'Criticism, Pedagogy and *Richard III*' (*CollL* 34:iv[2007] 1–21) outlines an approach which focuses on identity in Shakespeare's early tragedy. Historical contextual material is used to inform analysis of three screen versions: Olivier [1955], Jane Howell's BBC Shakespeare [1983] and Richard Loncraine [1995]. The article suffers from confused distinctions between the versions—it is suggested that Howell's television production is a stage version. Martine Van Elk's claims that her ideas draw together historicist and performance-oriented approaches seem overstated.

The special Shakespeare issue of *Literature/Film Quarterly* includes eight essays which, in contrast with previous special issues, have no controlling theme or approach. An interest in genre emerges in several of the pieces, and it is perhaps Yvonne Griggs's two studies of *King Lear* films which demonstrate an engagement with cinematic genre most comprehensively. Griggs analyses two American films, Edward Dmykryk's *Broken Lance* [1954] and Jocelyn Moorhouse's *A Thousand Acres* [1997] in '*King Lear* as Western Elegy' (*LFQ* 35:ii[2007] 92–100) and ' "All our lives we looked for each other the way that motherless children tend to do": *King Lear* as Melodrama' (*LFQ* 35:ii[2007] 101–7), respectively. The analysis of *Broken Lance* directs deserved attention to a much-neglected cinematic reworking, and Griggs argues persuasively for the rewards of seeing the film in the context of the Western. The article signals that analysis of the film in relation to its genre helps identify its 'commentary on the hypocrisy, racism, and opportunism at the core of post-war America' (p. 93). A similarly complex perspective is prompted in Griggs's second article, which analyses the more recent *A Thousand Acres*. The piece makes connections with the melodrama genre by drawing specific links with Douglas Sirk's *Written on the Wind* [1955].

Kirk Melnikoff moves earlier in American cinematic history to analyse the Shakespearian allusions in Tay Garnett's film in 'Wartime Shakespeare: The Strange Case of *Bataan* (1943)' (*LFQ* 35:ii[2007] 129–39). The article is self-confessedly exploratory. *Bataan* is connected to *Hamlet* through its protagonist, Sergeant Bill Dane. The character's name and his contemplation in a graveyard at the end of the film signal Shakespearian connections which, Melnikoff suggests, contribute to the film's 'artistry' and its ability to 'develop complex themes' (p. 136). *Macbeth* features in the film too, and through the career of the film's writer, Robert Hardy Andrews, Melnikoff makes persuasive connections with Orson Welles's 1936 'Voodoo' stage production of the play. The analysis of *Bataan* helps qualify ideas that Shakespeare was

shunned by Hollywood in the 1940s, and instead Melnikoff suggests that his
work 'was essentially repacked' (p. 136).

Elsewhere in the journal attention is directed towards the responses that
Indian cinematic tradition provides to Shakespeare's work. In ' "Filmi"
Shakespeare' (*LFQ* 35:ii[2007] 148–58), Poonam Trivedi offers an overview of
a recurring use of Shakespeare by Indian film directors. The breadth of the
enquiry is ambitious, and consequently brief attention is given to Sohrab
Modi's *Khoon-ka Khoon* (*Hamlet* [1935)], Kishore Sohn's *Hamlet* [1954],
Gulzar's *Angoor* (*The Comedy of Errors* [1981]) and Jayaraaj's relocation of
Othello to rural Kerala in *Kaliyattam* [1998]. More sustained analysis is given
of *Maqbool* [2004], and Trivedi suggests that this film signals a more recent
trend to 'play around' (p. 153) with Shakespeare. Her final, evocative image,
is of a cultural practice which in the 'act of devouring is both a violation
and an act of homage' (p. 157).

Alexander McKee seeks to establish a relevant historical context in his
exploration of Peter Greenaway's 1991 cinematic reinterpretation of *The
Tempest* in 'Jonson vs. Jones in *Prospero's Books*' (*LFQ* 35:ii[2007] 121–8).
McKee makes reference to the Renaissance debate between Ben Jonson and
Inigo Jones about the relative merits of the word and of spectacle in order to
offer a perspective on the film's concern with 'the unstable relationship
between word and spectacle' (p. 121). McKee offers brief analysis of
Shakespeare's text before he considers *Prospero's Books*. In his discussion of
the film, McKee shifts from identifying a tension between 'word' and
'spectacle' to consider 'text' and 'image'. Reference to Greenaway's later film
The Pillow Book [1995] helps elide these two labels, and it seems surprising
that McKee's analysis resolutely seeks to apply a perceived dichotomy to
Greenaway's *Prospero's Books* and ultimately suggests that the film succeeds
in 'refusing to allow either text or image to take precedence' (p. 127).

Simon J. Ryle's article also focuses on one film: 'Filming Non-Space: The
Vanishing Point and the Face in Brook's *King Lear*' (*LFQ* 35:ii[2007] 140–7).
His analysis of Brook's 1971 *Lear* follows critical tradition by focusing on the
Dover cliff scene. Ryle acknowledges the debate between Catherine Belsey and
Graham Holderness and pays tribute to Jack Jorgens's evocative description
of this sequence in the film. Following Jorgens's lead, Ryle focuses on the
camera's concentration on Gloucester's face (Alan Webb). Emmanuel
Lévinas, Erwin Panofsky and André Bazin are deployed to help shape a
complex argument about 'the potential of the face to encode the vanishing
point ... of Edgar's non-cliff of "proximity" with the infinity of the face'
(p. 146).

In 'Michael Radford's *The Merchant of Venice* and the Vexed Question of
Performance' (*LFQ* 35:ii[2007] 108–10), Laury Magnus explores 'what works
and does not work' in the 2004 film (p. 108). The judgement of degrees of
success in the film's choices seems to need more explicit explanation of the
author's rationale. Magnus articulates an interest in the extent to which the
film seeks to give an 'authentic' reading of the text, and this approach is
contextualized through recent productions on original practice stages: the
Blackfriars Playhouse in Staunton, Virginia, and the London Globe. Gaps
between those theatrical experiments and early modern theatrical practice

could perhaps have been articulated more explicitly. Questions about the *mise-en-scène*, the actors' cinematic personae and the cutting of the text could perhaps have been pursued more persuasively.

L. Monique Pittman considers the same film in a more focused way: 'Locating the Bard: Adaptation and Authority in Michael Radford's *The Merchant of Venice*' (*ShakB* 25:ii[2007] 13–33). Her analysis of the 2004 film suggests that the version marks a cinematic 'return . . . to period setting and costuming' (p. 1). That observation establishes an engagement with authenticity, authority and legitimacy which acknowledges a debt to W.B. Worthen's analysis of the authority of performance. While Pittman laments the film's failure to problematize notions of 'authority', the emphasis she places on Radford's attitudes (in the DVD commentary and interview) seems to endorse rather than unsettle the importance of the 'author function' (p. 15). Olwen Terris's 'The Forgotten *Hamlet*' (*ShakB* 25:ii[2007] 35–9) draws attention to the potential for fascinating discoveries in research. The article discusses a 1956 live broadcast of Peter Brook's *Hamlet* performed at the Phoenix theatre, with Paul Scofield in the title role. An industrial dispute in February 1956 meant that the *TV Times* was not published, and researchers have therefore erroneously cited *The Comedy of Errors* as the first broadcast of a play by Independent Television. Terris's engagement with cultural context allows her to explore 'the friction between culture and commercialism in the very early days of ITV' (p. 37). Terris's article makes a persuasive case for an ambitious Arts and Humanities Research Council-funded project to create an International Database of Shakespeare on Film, Television and Radio, administered by the British Universities Film and Video Council. Terris's fascinating piece includes extensive quotation from reviews of the television broadcast. Ivor Jay, the *Birmingham Evening Despatch* reviewer, was disappointed by Scofield's performance because 'he is a most masculine actor and there is so much in Hamlet that is feminine' (p. 37).

Interpretations of Hamlet's gender are explored in greater detail in Tony Howard's monograph, *Women as Hamlet: Performance and Interpretation in Theatre, Film and Fiction*. Howard begins his introductory chapter with the observation that 'The first Hamlet on film was a woman, Sarah Bernhardt (1900)' (p. 1). He is concerned to explore the different ways of, and the different reasons behind, artistic exploration of 'the femininity of Hamlet' (p. 1). The examination ranges between stage performances, representations in art and screen versions. Sarah Bernhardt's performance is analysed in chapter 4, but instead of considering the reception of the film, Howard focuses on responses to her on stage and makes extensive use of detailed reviews from the London press. Chapter 5 gives brief attention to Bernhardt on screen and then directs more sustained attention towards Sven Gade's 1920 film: ' "I am whom I play": Asta Nielsen'. Howard considers the relationship between the film and E.P. Vining's theory that Hamlet is really a woman, and observes that, rather than offer 'an act of male impersonation, Nielsen played a woman trapped in a life-long masquerade' (p. 140). Howard's celebration of the remarkable film concludes by suggesting that Nielsen's performance demonstrates 'the inseparability of gender politics from the political upheavals' of the time (p. 157). Howard returns to the 1920 film in chapter 9,

'Films and Fictions: Hamlet, Men's Eyes, and the Ages of Woman'. The chapter engages with the responses of American critics to Nielsen's performance and then progresses to consider a 'sub-genre of fiction films, chinese-box dramas about women who wished to play the Prince, or became him' (p. 240). Howard gives greatest attention to Katharine Hepburn's performance as Eva Lovelace in the early US sound film, *Morning Glory* [1933].

The concluding sequence of journal articles features in the British Shakespeare Association's journal, *Shakespeare*. Five essays deal exclusively with Shakespeare on screen and the journal's final issue of the year centres around the idea that 2007 marks a centenary no less important than 1999's commemoration of Beerbohm Tree's pioneering *King John* film. Judith Buchanan's 'Introduction' (Shakespeare 3.iii[2007] 283–92) refers to the release in 1907 of Méliès's *Hamlet* and *Shakespeare Writing Julius Caesar* and *Othello* from Italian production company Cines. Buchanan argues that these versions marked a shift by offering 'a sequentially unfolding Shakespearean narrative' (p. 283). The articles in this issue seek to direct attention towards Shakespeare in the cinema at the beginning of the twentieth-century. The publications in 2007 give weight to the issue's suggestion that early film is still a neglected area of screen scholarship.

James Ellison's '*King John* (1899): A *Fin-de-Siècle* Fragment and its Cultural Context' (*Shakespeare* 3:iii[2007] 293–314) provides a fascinating, detailed and provocative analysis of the layers of context behind the earliest surviving fragment of film. He asserts the importance of viewing the fragment in its theatrical context, in the historical context of the second Boer War and the Dreyfus affair and, most intriguingly, in a commercial context. Ellison suggests that the screening in London of the American-owned Biograph Company's short film, *The Kissing Scene between Trilby and Little Billee* [1897], might have articulated the potential power (and profit) posed through cinematic performance. Beerbohm Tree had enjoyed considerable success as Svengali in his own stage version of *Trilby* just two years earlier. Judith Buchanan's article also invokes Beerbohm Tree's theatrical reputation. She focuses on the Clarendon silent film of *The Tempest* [1908]. Her piece presents a detailed account of theatrical choices made by Beerbohm Tree in 1904/5 and seeks then to relate these choices to the Clarendon *Tempest*. The article offers a convincing account of the way the inner conflict between theatrical influences and cinematic possibilities ensures that the film 'plays host to a set of tensely revealing antagonisms' (p. 333).

Luke McKernan's '"A complete and fully satisfying art on its own account": Cinema and the Shakespeare Tercentenary of 1916' (*Shakespeare* 3:iii[2007] 337–51) argues persuasively for the importance of 1916 in Shakespearian cinematic history. McKernan analyses the form and function of films which featured within events commemorating the tercentenary of Shakespeare's death. At the Coliseum in March J.M. Barrie offered, as part of a variety of entertainments, a comic interpretation on film of *Macbeth: The Real Thing at Last*. The piece began with the actors in the film performing on stage and marked, therefore, a playful mixing of theatre and cinema. A royal gala performance in May at Drury Lane used dumb-show sequences, showed an awareness of its star names and used music in such a way as to show 'its unconscious alliance with strategies of the silent film' (p. 343). The reception of Beerbohm Tree's *Macbeth* film is analysed, and McKernan also engages with America and seeks to evaluate responses to Fox and Metro's competing feature-length versions of *Romeo and Juliet*. All three of these films are lost, and McKernan recognizes that this presents difficulties in judging their 'artistic worth or place in the filmed Shakespeare pantheon' (p. 347).

In 'Sex, Lies and Videotape: Representing the Past in *Shakespeare in Love*, Mapping a Future for Presentism' (*Shakespeare* 3:i[2007] 40–62) Cary DiPietro seeks to counter established notions of conflict between presentist interpretative styles and approaches adopted in historicist, materialist and postmodernist criticism. Some reference is made to Baz Luhrmann's *William Shakespeare's Romeo + Juliet* [1996], but greatest attention is directed towards Madden's *Shakespeare in Love* [1998]. Di Pietro traces a line of connections between Stephen Greenblatt, the two scriptwriters Marc Norman and Tom Stoppard, James Joyce, Freud and Shakespeare, and argues that these 'narrative encounters...produce a literary sedimentation that resonates through the film' (p. 47). Presentist readings are shown to complement rather than negate other theoretical approaches.

James Welsh and Peter Lev edited a collection of essays, *The Literature/Film Reader: Issues of Adaptation*, and three Shakespeare-focused pieces appear in part II, 'Classic and Popular Literature'. James M. Welsh asks 'What *Is* a Shakespeare Film Anyway?' (in Welsh and Lev, eds., pp. 105–14). His article offers a direct challenge to recent trends in Shakespeare-on-screen scholarship and labels 'adaptations that ignore Shakespeare's language while exploiting his plots and characters' as 'misguided and corrupt' (p. 105). Welsh objects to serious study of cinematic reinterpretations such as *Joe Macbeth* (Hughes [1955]), *A Thousand Acres* (Moorhouse [1997]) and *Jubal* (Daves [1956]). He suggests that being influenced by Shakespeare ought not to qualify these versions as Shakespearian films. The article concludes with the assertion that 'A film that presumes to adapt poetic drama should at the very least be "poetic" in style and substance' (p. 112). Yong Li Lan offers a perspective upon the closing shot of four films in 'Returning to Naples: Seeing the End in Shakespeare Film Adaptation' (in Welsh and Lev, eds., pp. 115–24). The essay focuses on *Hamlet* (Branagh [1996]), *William Shakespeare's Romeo + Juliet* [1996], *Shakespeare in Love* (Madden [1998]) and *Prospero's Books* (Greenaway [1991]). Lan gives some consideration to 'looking structures in...situations of cinematic watching', but the analysis of a gap between the spectator's perspective and the camera's eye could be applied more directly to the chosen case studies. Elsie Walker's article gives more sustained treatment to the 1996 *Romeo + Juliet*: 'Pop Goes the Shakespeare: Baz Luhrmann's *William Shakespeare's Romeo + Juliet*' (in Welsh and Lev, eds., pp. 125–48). Her argument centres upon the 'film as a kind of social document'. Walker explores the film's intertextuality and celebrates the film's ability 'to make strange the familiar' (p. 143).

Two essays in *The Cambridge Companion to Literature on Screen*, edited by Deborah Cartmell and Imelda Whelehan, focus on Shakespeare. Douglas Lanier considers 'William Shakespeare, Filmmaker' (pp. 61–74). His essay identifies the idea of Shakespeare as 'composer' with 'an imagination fundamentally visual not verbal' (p. 61) in Méliès's *La Mort de Jules César* [1907] and Madden's *Shakespeare in Love* [1998]. The essay then pursues a broader enquiry into the position of the Shakespearian film in popular culture. Lanier considers the way screen versions of the plays are used in the classroom, and worries that 'textual fidelity remains a primary concern' (p. 68). Lanier explores his suggestion with reference to two adaptations of *Romeo and Juliet*: *Tromeo and Juliet* (Kaufman [1996]) and *Shakespeare in Love* (Madden [1998]). The analysis underlines the importance of 'the ideological implications of film adaptation' (p. 73).

The Cambridge Companion to Shakespeare in Popular Culture contains four essays to relevant to Shakespeare on screen. Barbara Hodgdon considers 'Shakespearean Stars: Stagings of Desire' (in Shaughnessy, ed., pp. 46–66). Her study crosses between film, television, stage and public roles in a consideration of what makes an actor a 'Shakespearean star'. The study begins with Michael Gambon and moves then to more detailed study of Laurence Olivier's 'ownership of Shakespearean roles' and the ones Hodgdon lists are, tellingly, those preserved on film: 'Henry V, Hamlet, Richard III and Othello' (p. 56). Branagh's career is considered, but it is suggested that he has not inherited Olivier's 'star status' (p. 59). Hodgdon interrogates the term 'Shakespearean star' and asks, in her study of Ian McKellen, 'what is the position, place and work of the star in the age of digital reproduction?' (p. 61). Brief reference to Patrick Stewart helps articulate the cross-over between status on stage, in Shakespearian films and more commercially successful ventures such as *Star Trek*. Douglas Lanier expands Hodgdon's consideration of a range of types of media in his engagement with Shakespeare and biography: 'Shakespeare™ Myth and Biographical Fiction' (in Shaughnessy, ed., pp. 93–113). Of interest to Shakespeare-on-screen scholars is Lanier's engagement with Al Pacino's *Looking for Richard* [1996] and 'the first talkie featuring Shakespeare as a character, *The Immortal Gentleman* (1935)' (p. 101). Lanier suggests that the latter film has its roots in nineteenth-century bardolatry. *Shakespeare in Love* [1998] gives evidence of 'how powerfully Shakespeare identifies with and functions as a mainstream icon for heteronormative sexuality' (p. 103). The characterization of Shakespeare in relation to Christopher Marlowe is explored in a brief analysis of ATV's 1978 TV mini-series *The Life of Shakespeare*.

Emma Smith directs attention to a neglected 1960 BBC television series: 'Shakespeare Serialized: *An Age of Kings*' (in Shaughnessy, ed., pp. 134–49). Smith seeks to start with the fifteen-episode series and use it to examine 'the functions of serial narrative in Shakespeare's play' (p. 134). While Smith makes the point that *An Age of Kings* has not been preserved, the language used in her analysis conceals that absence of direct contact with the production: 'Viewing *An Age of Kings* now...' (p. 136). More explicit engagement with the sources used might have helped create a more transparent sense of Smith's imaginative reconstruction of the broadcast. ITV's broadcast of *Coronation Street* in the same year shapes an exploration of the way that both series share 'narrative structures' and 'characterizations' (p. 141). The article seeks, therefore, to situate *An Age of Kings* in the context of other television broadcasts, and Smith's final suggestion is that television is 'the medium that above all has defined the notion of "popular culture".' (p. 147). It is perhaps fitting to conclude with W.B. Worthen's 'Performing Shakespeare in a Digital Culture' (in Shaughnessy, ed., pp. 227–47). Worthen considers the way that performance can now be viewed on 'the digital screen, the same screen that most of us use for reading and writing' (pp. 227–8). He focuses his analysis on Shakespeare on DVD, and suggests that the format 'paradoxically offers a considerably more bookish engagement with Shakespearean drama than earlier recording technologies' (p. 232). The DVD play-text might be identified as an edition and, as such, can be situated with the 'cultural framework of print' (p. 233). The limits imposed by region codes and subtitle language choices maintain another 'symmetry with print' (p. 239). Worthen's ideas help expand concepts about the types of cultural production that might be embraced within studies of Shakespeare on 'screen'.

4. Criticism

(a) General

Reviews of general Shakespeare work published in 2007 will appear in the entry in next year's *YWES*.

(b) Comedies

A Midsummer Night's Dream seems a good place to start this year, as it offers my only book-length study devoted to a single play, Henry S. Turner's *Shakespeare's Double Helix*. I deliberately avoid the term 'monograph', as Turner's study forms part of a series, Shakespeare Now!, which likes to think of itself as offering rather 'minigraphs'—short studies designed to fall somewhere between the standard academic article and monograph in both length and style, and which aim to be open-ended, alive, exciting, innovative and very much of the moment. Turner's volume certainly responds to this particular brief, not least through its title, which is both an eye-catching attempt to assert Shakespearian contemporaneity and a genuine reflection of aspects of the volume's content. The blurb on the back of my paperback edition grandly claims that 'this book focuses on one of the key questions for culture and science in both Shakespeare's time and our own', namely, 'What does it mean to make life?'. Turner's own opening gambit states slightly more prosaically that 'this book reads Shakespeare's *A Midsummer Night's Dream* in order to explore the nature of creativity and experimentation in literature and in scientific research' (p. x). There is, as it were, a doubly double focus here, on science and literature, and on Shakespeare's time and our own. Thus the content of the book explores the influence of scientific developments on literature as well as the creative dimensions of scientific activity and discourse, while at the same time drawing parallels between the 'new science' of the Renaissance/early modern period and the latest scientific developments of modern genetics and genetic engineering.

All of these elements are consciously figured in the title's invocation of the double helix, which serves as an image not only for the doubly interweaving themes of the book, but also for its very structure. For to quote Turner's own description, his book 'consists of two separate but related essays that run parallel to one another on facing pages' (p. xii). The essays are said to wrap around each other like the double helix, available for reading in turn one at a time, or simultaneously with 'the eye wandering across the divide of the page to make spontaneous graftings among ideas and to generate new and entirely unanticipated arguments with each reading and re-reading' (pp. xii–xiii). There is in itself, of course, nothing particularly new in such structural experimentation, but it has to be acknowledged that it has a definite novelty value in the context of Shakespearian criticism, and it is raised above the merely gimmicky here by the highly apposite image that Turner finds for his title. Having said this, in the end the double helix of the study seems to me more Turner's than Shakespeare's. And having chosen for my purposes to read each essay separately in turn, which essentially creates the effect of having to read through the book twice, I felt little inclination or incentive in the process to let my eyes stray across the gutter to the other side, on either my first or second passage through.

The left-hand pages provide the more conventional literary-critical part of the volume, offering an essay focusing on the play itself, addressing issues relating to its literary and theatrical techniques and content, but pursuing throughout the idea that, read through 'the contemporary eye', *A Midsummer Night's Dream* offers us 'startlingly familiar scenes, organized around problems that continue to drive the scientific thought of our own era' (p. 2). The right-hand essay, distinguished by a different typeface, 'advances a series of arguments about *mimesis* in science, about language and naming, about the nature of experiment and how scientific knowledge gets produced, and about how contemporary biotechnology forces us to reconsider our normative definitions of the human and our ideas about life in general' (p. xii). This is not to say that the content of the two halves remains entirely distinct, for plenty of references to *Dream* find their way into the right-hand essay, and themes of metamorphosis, hybridity and so on are pursued throughout the discussion specifically focused on the play. I found the right-hand essay fascinating in many places, but ultimately a little unsatisfying. Turner provides what seems to me, writing as someone with little background in the subject, a very readable, clear and informative quick overview of the development of modern genetic research, covering the discovery of DNA through to current practices and ideas in the area of hybridization. There is an evident timeliness to Turner's work, with its links to ecocriticism and contemporary theories and philosophies of the post-human and the non-human, and his tracking of appearances of *A Midsummer Night's Dream* within the realm of contemporary genetic research is fascinating and entertaining. But other elements of the essay, such as his whistle-stop tour of textual instability in Shakespeare (pp. 71–85) or perfunctory invocation of the art/nature debate from *The Winter's Tale* (pp. 89–93), are rather more humdrum. And I would have preferred a little more engagement with or acknowledgement of some of the ethical and political dimensions and controversies of modern genetic science.

Yet there is much of interest here, crowded into a short space, and occasional moments startle with a penetrating turn of expression or juxtaposition of ideas.

The left-hand essay, too, with its more direct focus on Shakespeare's play, has plenty of interest in it, not least some of the extended discussions of particular passages, such as Titania's speech about the seasons. Themes relating to nature, metamorphosis, translation, magic and mimesis are all effectively pursued. I have to say, though, that the overall effect is partly spoiled for me by a certain carelessness in quotations and references; lines from Shakespeare lose or gain syllables (immediately noticeable in blank verse), while references assign quotations to the wrong scene, give completely wrong line numbers, or provide a range of line numbers far greater than the number of lines actually quoted (various examples can be found on pp. 38, 46, 60, with some of the errors congregating together). It's a minor point, but it nags, and of course might make one wonder about the accuracy of some of Turner's other quotations that are not so easily traceable to be checked. But despite such reservations, there is much interesting and stimulating comment in Turner's study, and the book itself is undeniably memorable and thought-provoking.

Certainly, moving from Turner's book to Stuart Sillars's '"Howsoever, strange and admirable:" *A Midsummer Night's Dream* as *via stultitiæ*' (*Archiv* 244[2007] 27–39) is like entering another critical world. Sillars's main concern is in elucidating the traditions of 'a vision other than the intellectual' (p. 30) that were available to Shakespeare and his audience, ranging from Ficino through to Julian of Norwich. The play's elevation of the idea of the *via stultitiæ*, 'the way of the foolish' (p. 29), or in a different formulation, of 'idiocy as a higher form of understanding' (p. 30), is allied to gender power struggles, figured particularly through Hippolyta's account in V.i of the events of the wood and the rejection of Theseus' intellectualizing position which this is seen to embody. Sillars has some useful things to say on the play's biblical and Erasmian intertexts and potential intertexts. But I would question the implicit assumption that the play-text or the dramatic action necessarily ratify Hippolyta's interpretation of events over that of Theseus. I also find problematic Sillars's virtually untrammelled confidence (doubt briefly emerges at one point) that the play's 'original performance' was 'at an aristocratic wedding' (p. 28), and his reliance on this idea to posit a particular audience for and reading of the play.

Tom Pettitt's '"Perchance you wonder at this show": Dramaturgical Machinery in *A Midsummer Night's Dream* and "Pyramus and Thisbe"' (in Butterworth, ed. *The Narrator, the Expositor, and the Prompter in European Medieval Theatre*, pp. 211–34) seems to me a rather more successful piece of work. Pettitt's study is built around exploring some of the metadramatic elements of the play, and particularly the 'inwardly orientated procedures' of the dramatic action (p. 211), such as cues, internal prompts, entrance and exit directions etc., that contribute to making the drama 'work'. Connected to this approach is an emphasis on the 'Pyramus and Thisbe' playlet as 'essentially a revels interlude which (at least in rehearsal) is also associated with certain aspects of the Elizabethan stage', and on *Dream* itself as 'an Elizabethan stage-play to which is also attributed certain features of medieval household revels' (p. 214). In this respect, for Pettitt, *A Midsummer Night's Dream* emerges as 'emphatically a stage-play' (p. 215), but one which 'successfully constructs for itself, within the playhouse, the ambience of aristocratic wedding revels it creates for "Pyramus and Thisbe" within its play world'; or to put it another way, 'revels are effectively the *implied* auspices of *A Midsummer Night's Dream*' (p. 216). This seems a much more profitable and nuanced approach than the assumption that the play must have been written for performance at a wedding.

The main body of Pettitt's essay is divided into sections discussing issues such as prompting, getting on (entrances), in-performance direction, getting off (exits), presentation, explication, narrative and taking leave. Most of these basic elements, inherent to the fabric of stage drama, are of course represented explicitly on stage during the course of the play through the rehearsal process for 'Pyramus and Thisbe'. Pettitt also takes pains to trace some of their antecedents in earlier forms of drama, though I think perhaps he overdoes references to folk-play traditions. There is much sensitive discussion of particular moments in the dialogue, with an awareness of the actions that might go with them, or the problems they might pose (or solve) for the actors themselves. Attention is drawn particularly to the way the 'junior' fairies seem to be stage-managed or overtly directed within the dialogue itself, in a way that is matched elsewhere in *Dream* only in the dialogue of 'Pyramus and Thisbe'. Pettitt also notes how devices that appear in crude form in the play-within-the-play are given more sophisticated treatment elsewhere in the drama. So whereas 'Pyramus and Thisbe' includes obvious exit lines for its performers, some apparent exit lines within the main action are actually '*misleading* exit signals' (p. 225). This leads to the suggestion that 'it would not be incompatible with Shakespeare's often playful dramaturgy for the "false" scripted directions... to be inserted deliberately to test, or demonstrate, his company's skills' (p. 226).

There has also been something of a spate of notes on *A Midsummer Night's Dream* this year. I found Steven J. Doloff's 'Bottom's Greek Audience: *I Corinthians* 1.21–5 and Shakespeare's *A Midsummer Night's Dream*' (*Expl* 65[2007] 200–1) anything but convincing in its attempt to suggest a further biblical context for Bottom's famous soliloquy at the end of IV.i, beyond its obvious associations with 1 Corinthians 2. The suggestion coming out of the perceived allusion is that the Greek foolishness Paul speaks of in chapter 1 of his epistle might be meant to reflect back on the Greek audience of the mechanicals' play in Act V of *Dream*. Wolfgang Riehle's discussion of 'What's in Lysander's Name?' (*N&Q* 54[2007] 274–5) quickly dismisses earlier comment on this subject with the confident assertion that, based on allusions to *Hero and Leander* in the play, 'there can be no doubt that the name Lysander is supposed to allude to Leander' (p. 275). Shakespeare apparently changed 'Leander' to 'Lysander' to allow a pun, 'lie asunder', in Lysander's and Hermia's dialogue as they lie down to sleep in the forest (as Hermia actually asks Lysander to 'lie further off' it is perhaps no surprise this pun has been missed by earlier commentators). And secondly, the change is seen to reflect another aspect of Shakespeare's fusion of English and classical elements in the play.

Also ultimately perhaps rather strained in the argument it has to offer is Alan J. Altimont's contribution, following immediately on in the same volume, 'The Meaning of *Nedar* in *A Midsummer Night's Dream*' (*N&Q* 54[2007] 275–7). Altimont is aware of Terence Hawkes's discussion of this name in his *Meaning by Shakespeare* [1993], but is unconvinced by Hawkes's attempts there at identifying a possible source for the name. For someone aware of Hawkes's comments, though, Altimont is surprisingly confident in the identification of Nedar as 'the name of Helena's father' (p. 275). Altimont turns for an explanation to Hebrew, where *nedar* 'exists as a verb meaning "was missing; was absent", as an adjective meaning "missing, absent", and as a noun meaning "absentee"' (p. 275). Pursuing further possible allusions, the name is also tentatively connected to the Hebrew plural *neder*, deriving from a noun meaning 'pledge' or 'vow'. Additional connections lead to the *Nedarim Tractate* of the Babylonian Talmud. The arguments are far from compelling, but at the same time the possibilities are intriguing, and Altimont may have a case in his closing statement that the issue is 'worthy of further scholarly interest' (p. 277).

Still on *Dream*, Rodney Stenning Edgecombe has a very brief note exploring a potential pun on 'tire' as in tiring house/attire ('A Player's Pun in *A Midsummer Night's Dream* III.1' (*N&Q* 54[2007] 275). Beatrice Grove's ' "The wittiest partition": Bottom, Paul, and Comedic Resurrection' (*N&Q* 54[2007] 277–82) leads back again to Bottom's dream, and its intertextual Pauline and Erasmian associations. There are some good comments here on the physicality of Bottom and the mechanicals, their concern with the realm of the material— props, clothing, the constituents of their presented wall, etc. The focus of the discussion becomes Bottom-as-Pyramus's 'resurrection' after the play within the play to assure his audience that 'the wall is down' that parted the dead lovers' fathers. It is argued that the phrase used here is an echo of Ephesians 2. Finally in this group, A.B. Taylor's 'John Gower and "Pyramus and Thisbe" ' (*N&Q* 54[2007] 282–3) has another take on the antecedents of Bottom's dream, claiming a previously unrecognized debt in Shakespeare to Gower's version of the Pyramus and Thisbe story in Book III of the *Confessio Amantis*. Gower is seen to have pre-empted Shakespeare in echoing 1 Corinthians 2.9 in connection with a Pyramus figure, and the detail is also picked up that there is a hole in the wall in Gower's version that is not described in quite the same terms in Ovid or other recognized sources for this sequence.

Staying with notes leads me on to *The Merchant of Venice*. Matt Baynham's 'Why is Mercy "Twice Blest"?' (*N&Q* 54[2007] 285) also claims to find an echo not noted in any previous edition of the play, seeing an allusion in the phrase under discussion to the beatitude about the merciful in Matthew 5.7. Charles R. Forker's 'Marlowe's *Edward II* and *The Merchant of Venice*' (*ShN* 57[2007–8] 65, 70), despite its title, actually spends a lot of its time noticing echoes of Marlowe in the Shakespeare canon in general, and particularly *Richard II*. The echo argued for with respect to *Merchant* links one of Gratiano's speeches in II.ii with an exchange between Spencer Junior and Baldock in II.i of Marlowe's play. To my mind, Forker sees a 'probable indebtedness' (p. 65) where his evidence suggests more an interesting parallel. Staying with notes, a quick mention for Richard Levin's 'Launcelot's and Huck's Moral Dilemmas' (*ShN* 56[2006–7] 83), which draws a parallel (not necessarily one of influence) between Gobbo's debate with himself about whether he should leave his master and a similar moment in Mark Twain's *Huckleberry Finn*. For Levin, both writers are making a serious point about attitudes to 'the subjugation of servants and slaves'.

Turning to more substantial studies of *The Merchant of Venice*, Jonathan Gil Harris's 'The Time of Shakespeare's Jewry' (*ShakS* 35[2007] 39–46) packs a wide range of reference—George Herbert, John Stow, Richard Hakluyt, John Dee, Hegel, St Paul, Alain Badiou, Dipesh Chakrabarty, the Bush administration and the *Left Behind* Christian apocalyptic novel series—into not many pages, with Shakespeare and the London district of Old Jewry in there as well, along with reflections on the nature of typological cosmopolitanism. In the end, there's not actually all that much of Shakespeare or *The Merchant of Venice* here, though the paragraph on the play's interest in typology (p. 42) is at the core of the argument, which takes off from the notion that this play 'makes explicit the workings of what we might call typological cosmopolitanism' (p. 42). Those workings are then pursued through explorations of the traces of the old Jewish community in the London of Shakespeare's time, at both a literal and a figurative level, and their possible implications for the present day. For according to Harris, 'we ignore at our peril the troublesome histories of the cosmopolitan if we understand it only in spatial and secular terms', because alongside these, 'in a literal as well as figurative way, it is about time' (p. 46).

M. Lindsay Kaplan's 'Jessica's Mother: Medieval Constructions of Jewish Race and Gender in *The Merchant of Venice*' (*SQ* 58[2007] 1–30) is an essay of a rather more conventional type than Harris's, but none the worse for that. Kaplan takes as a way into her subject the neglected figure of Leah and her significance in the play, leading on from here into a discussion of the relevance of gender and constructions of gender to the play's racial politics and its presentation of Jessica. Much of the essay is devoted to presenting material on medieval constructions of Jewishness, leading to the conclusion that 'the three central elements of modern racist thinking are present in medieval constructions of a Jew as an inferior religious and physical other whose nature, as his immunity to conversion testifies, is determined by his body, not his belief' (p. 13). But the key element in the argument is the influence of gender issues on this discourse, and the idea that gender prejudices, as it were, outweighed racial prejudices in relation to Jewish women.

The idea that comes out of all this is that, for the period, 'the Jewish woman is whiter in both flesh and blood than the Jewish man' (p. 20). This argument is reinforced by discussion of the theory of 'maternal imprinting', seen to be exemplified in the story of Jacob's sheep, which is used to illustrate the cultural lack of importance assigned to the mother figure (as evidenced by the case of Leah) in the creation/construction of the newborn child. Patriarchal prejudices and cultural beliefs mean that anxieties about Jewishness cluster much more around men than women—which for Kaplan is a factor that may be reflected in Jessica's particular discomfort with her masculine attire. In line with this overall approach, Kaplan seeks to challenge critical readings that see Jessica at the end of the play as unassimilated into the Christian community, as retaining a 'racial residue' (p. 26). Racial anxieties are bypassed in the culture of Venice with respect to Jessica, due to the view that, 'as a woman she is "whiter" than her Jewish brethren and that as a mother, she contributes nothing to the race of her child' (p. 27).

Douglas A. Brooks's ' "I'll mar the young clerk's pen"': Sodomy, Paternity and Circumcision in *The Merchant of Venice*' (in Moncrief and McPherson, eds., *Performing Maternity in Early Modern England*, pp. 225–37) is a dense essay with a wide frame of reference that seeks to examine the way this play 'contributes to the project of reformulating traditions associated with Judaism, circumcision, paternal authority and maternity—a project that has been central to Christianity' (p. 225). Circumcision is a particular focus, located in the play primarily through an invocation of its images of paternity and cutting. There is a lot of historical and anthropological background invoked here, but there also seems to me a great deal of strain in the effort to apply much of this material to the play itself. So we learn, for example, in a line of reasoning that is not untypical, that when the main source for the play 'was first published in Italy, Jewish loans, sexual favors, sodomy and Christian marriage had all come to be part of a metonymic chain in which earrings linked circumcised Jewish financiers with pierced Christian prostitutes'. The application to *Merchant* is that being 'an avid cultural materialist, Shakespeare uses rings in the last scene of the play to rehearse these correspondences' (p. 231). Obviously, I am providing a very bald summary of a dense argument here, but on the face of it, it is hard to know how seriously one is meant to take such a comment. Yet a sense of humour is not one of the most obvious elements displayed by this article.

In many ways, Brooks's essay feels like an attempt at a form of bravura performance, linking together some of the standard themes of New Historicism, gender criticism and queer theory, picking up in particular on recent work on *Merchant* coming out of these traditions, and the insights they have provided, and pushing these themes and ideas in new directions or extending their frames of reference. But there is something in the application that just doesn't hold together. The arguments seem to be too divorced from the action of the play itself, too dependent on reading one thing as implying another as implying another and so on, and in the end the whole process seems to spiral out of control in the effort to pack too much in or to be too clever. Indeed, the essay quite literally goes out of control towards the end, where a bizarrely mangled sentence in the antepenultimate paragraph ends up saying that the Jason of Euripides' *Medea* was taught to read Latin aloud by George Buchanan during the reign of Henry VIII (see p. 236). I can't even work out what this sentence was trying to say. And in its final paragraph the essay then goes off on a completely new tangent with a sudden discussion of Joseph Papp's views on the play.

Of a very different nature is Mark Bayer's '*The Merchant of Venice*, the Arab–Israeli Conflict, and the Perils of Shakespearean Adaptation' (*CompD* 41[2007–8] 465–92). This is essentially an exploration of aspects of the afterlife of the play, and particularly how it has figured to competing ends in literary

adaptations and cultural discourse on either side of the Arab–Israeli conflict
during the twentieth century. In this respect, Bayer's work largely falls outside
my remit, as most of the literary comment here is directed at texts that are
appropriating Shakespeare. But there is some useful discussion of the nature of
literary appropriation in relation to Shakespeare's play here, and the essay
offers a reminder of the way this play interacts with discourses that can lead
far away from literary criticism.

Staying briefly in this area, the online *Journal for Cultural and Religious
Theory* devotes an entire edition (8:iii[2007]) to *The Merchant of Venice* in
relation to continental philosophy, following on from a symposium held at
Pomona College in November 2006. The nature of the journal and the focus
taken by the essays again puts much of this work outside, or at least on the
very edge of, English studies. But it seems worth recording that the papers
include: Zdravko Planinc, 'Reading *The Merchant of Venice* through Adorno'
(25 paras); Arthur Horowitz, 'Shylock after Auschwitz: *The Merchant of
Venice* on the Post-Holocaust Stage—Subversion, Confrontation and
Provocation' (32 paras); Julia Reinhard Lupton, 'Shylock between
Exception and Emancipation: Shakespeare, Schmitt, Arendt' (19 paras);
Paul A. Kottman, 'Avoiding Tragedy in *The Merchant of Venice*' (47 paras);
Ken Jackson, 'Shylock: The Knight of Faith?' (40 paras); Oona Eisenstadt,
'Heart's Blood: Derrida and Portia on Translation' (24 paras); and a response
to the symposium by J. Aaron Kunin (12 paras). Perhaps not surprisingly
given the nature of the journal concerned, the issue of Shylock's forced
conversion provides a major focus for discussion in most of these essays.

A collection of essays entitled *The Law in Shakespeare*, edited by Constance
Jordan and Karen Cunningham, inevitably yields a number of contributions
relating to *The Merchant of Venice*. First up is Charles Ross's 'Avoiding the
Issue of Fraud: 4, 5 Philip & Mary c.8 (the Heiress Protection Statute), Portia,
and Desdemona' (pp. 91–108). This explores the legal issue of 'fraudulent
conveyances' in the period in relation to both *Merchant* and *Othello*, with
a specific focus on the law surrounding 'the conveyance of women' and
the statutes in place 'against seducing women for their money' (p. 92). In
discussing *Merchant* from this perspective, Ross obviously focuses on the
situation in Belmont and the Portia–Bassanio relationship. For Ross, 'part of
the problem of understanding Portia is finding the right frame of reference
for her'. He offers the suggestion that at least part of the appropriate frame
of reference lies in the play's interest in 'the ethics of and remedy for financial
fraud'—for Portia, as Ross neatly puts it, 'is always on the verge of fraud'
(p. 98). Examples include the possible manipulation of Bassanio's choice of
caskets through the song, quibbling over the meaning of the pound of flesh,
threatening to give away Bassanio's money and so on. Ross also tries to tease
out the implications of what Portia could do with her money after Bassanio
has chosen correctly, arguing that the law of the time might have given her
more power over disposing of her own money than is often assumed, or than
she chooses to use.

Thomas C. Bilello's 'Accomplished with What She Lacks: Law, Equity, and
Portia's Con' (in Jordan and Cunningham, eds., pp. 109–26) offers a rather
more negative reading of Portia's character. According to Bilello, 'by inserting

herself by artifice into the legal proceedings to enforce the bond, Portia converts the law into an instrumentality of her will', thereby managing to appropriate to her own ends 'the mechanisms of the court' (p. 110). Analysis of Portia's role is initially conducted through an exploration of 'the notion of equity as understood in sixteenth-century England' (p. 110). However, the subject of equity is found to be 'conspicuously absent' from the play (p. 114), replaced by an emphasis on mercy in the trial scene. Bilello goes through the process of attempting to locate the play's action, and specifically the trial sequence, in relation to the law of the period. But he is also sensitive to the fact that if legal equity is actually absent, 'it should be remembered that this play is more about a sublegal desire for revenge than about the legal process that constrains and controls that desire; the legal process merely acts to mediate the desire' (p. 120). Revenge is the motivation all round, with legal processes serving as a cover for this according to how they can be used. And this does not just apply in relation to Shylock. For Bilello, analysis suggests that 'Portia's bias reduces the Venetian court to a forum of revenge rather than law' (p. 124).

Finally in this group, and on this play, there is Luke Wilson's 'Drama and Marine Insurance in Shakespeare's London' (in Jordan and Cunningham, eds., pp. 127–42), one of the more unlikely essay titles one might expect to encounter, but a fascinating essay nonetheless. Wilson starts off by analysing Antonio's sadness at the beginning of the play, which is interpreted as 'the wrong affect'—he seems sad when he should be fearful over the fate of his ships (p. 128); or is he 'sad because he is not fearful'? (p. 129). One of Wilson's suggestions here is that Antonio does not properly understand risk. This leads into a discussion of questions relating to marine insurance, picking up on an earlier comment from Marc Shell [1982] wondering why Antonio has not insured his ships. Wilson offers one possible explanation for this with the argument that Antonio 'has no insurance because he is sad—because, that is, he is unable to understand risk except as something wholly unmanageable' (p. 129).

It is only a tentative suggestion, and Wilson is well aware that questions of marine insurance may simply be outside the play's frame of reference or interest (see p. 130). But he uses the idea that a lack of insurance is actually 'the enabling condition of the play' (p. 131) to justify pursuing the issue further. If Antonio had insurance, he would have no problem paying his bond (though if one wants to pursue verisimilitude to this level, one might suggest that delays in paying up on that insurance could still have led him into difficulties with Shylock). Much of the rest of the essay discusses the enabling conditions of different types of marine insurance, including an interest in the subject of 'the evaluation of risk in relation to the probability of reports', an issue crucial to the maritime insurance business and also a subject in which Shakespeare was very much interested, 'especially when it came to maritime adventures' (p. 135). This leads in turn to an interrogation of the final report about the safe arrival of Antonio's ships in harbour—why does this information come to Portia, is the report necessarily true given that earlier reports of their miscarrying were assumed to be true, how much does any of this register with an audience, is there 'the generic equivalent of an insurance policy' (p. 136) going on? If nothing else, marine insurance and the theatre of the time are seen to come together in their need for 'a sophisticated appreciation of risk and probability' and a shared focus on the business of calculating 'the probability of human testimony' (p. 138).

Staying on the subject of law and in the same collection leads me on to *Much Ado About Nothing*. Cyndia Susan Clegg's 'Truth, Lies, and the Law of Slander in *Much Ado About Nothing*' (in Jordan and Cunningham, eds., pp. 167–88) sets out in part to explore 'the complex legal and social dimensions of slander and libel in late Elizabethan England that inform Shakespeare's play' (p. 167). Clegg starts by citing case examples and general practice from the period to illustrate aspects of that legal background, including its gender expectations and topical resonances, which she sees as informing the play's engagement with issues of slander and defamation. The play's demonstrable interest in exploring issues relating to 'slander and the law that seeks to contain it' leads her to the idea that *Much Ado* seems almost to have been 'conceived, like a legal fiction, as an imaginative construction designed to clarify legal principles' (p. 170). Even the characters are seen to share an interest in legality, with Clegg suggesting that Don John's 'defamation displays a subtle knowledge of slander's legal definition that nearly allows his scheme to succeed' (p. 170).

In pursuing this idea, Clegg turns first not to perhaps the most obvious area of the slander against Hero, but to 'the slander Don John directs at Claudio' (p. 171), arguing that this is conducted with legal precision. She emphasizes the extent to which Claudio, within this particular culture of male honour, is actually himself being slandered through the imputation of cuckoldry that is inherent in the accusations against Hero. In this respect, 'Claudio's actions become if not justifiable at least understandable' (p. 173). Clegg also draws attention to the nature of slander's relationship to the law, through the idea, as evidenced in the play, that 'slander works immediately to destroy the fabric of social relationships; legal remedies for slander take time' (p. 174). And there is no guarantee that law can do much to remedy the effects of slander: the evidence against Hero is clear-cut for those who want to believe it, and Leonato's assurance that Claudio and Don Pedro would not lie on such a matter points to the difficulties of remedying such an issue. The problem of slander, then, 'is not the lie alone, but the readiness with which hearers, based on their cultural and social perspectives, embrace lies' (p. 176). In a sense, by providing for a particular social contextualization for their behaviour, Clegg is seeking to excuse or palliate the condemnation modern audiences tend to feel towards Claudio and Don Pedro for their public exposure of Hero.

The discussion moves on to address the way 'the relationship between truth, lies, and slander' (p. 176) is also interrogated in the play's two 'subplots'. Clegg notes, for example, that Benedick expressly articulates a fear of being cuckolded, and Beatrice a fear of being accused of infidelity (see pp. 176–9). There is also interesting comment on the language of the play here, the way Dogberry's malapropisms, while deriving from almost the opposite linguistic impulse or character traits to Beatrice and Benedick's controlled war of wits, still produce a form of linguistic humour that 'requires a similar effort on the audience's part' (p. 178). In this respect, Dogberry offers a lesson in linguistic competence to the audience, and the play 'concerns itself less with mistaking words than with discerning their legitimate meaning' (p. 179). What Dogberry and the Watch do not do, however, is offer any grounds for confidence in the law and institutionalized legal proceedings. Rather, the play is said to find greater hope for resolution in the ecclesiastical courts than in the temporal courts, and in doing this, to be intervening in contemporary debates on this issue. Thus resolution in the play comes initially through the Friar, to be reinforced through the penance and ritual of the tomb scene. In this respect, *Much Ado* is seen as offering an essentially conservative, backward-looking solution to slander, 'that reaffirms both chivalric honor and the older, more traditional ecclesiastical jurisdiction as the appropriate venue for mitigating slander's damage' (p. 184).

Similar aspects of the play are addressed in Nancy E. Wright's 'Legal Interpretation of Defamation in Shakespeare's *Much Ado About Nothing*' (*BJJ* 13[2006] 93–108), an article carried over from last year. Wright's premise is that 'study of characters' use of judicial genres, rules, and norms to interpret utterances explains how Don John *in absentia* is condemned as "the author of all"' (p. 93). There is a strong overlap of theme here with Clegg's essay, though the approach and focus actually end up quite different. What Wright particularly seeks to negotiate around is the dissatisfaction that modern audiences and critics tend to feel with 'the exculpation of Claudio and Don Pedro' (p. 95) that is one of the consequences of shifting all the blame on to Don John. Guilt of defamation is seen to depend upon intentions, and the Friar decides that the intentions of Don Pedro and Claudio were honourable, whereas those of Don John are not. In this play, 'intentions, whether honorable or malicious, are known only by means of interpretation in both judicial and extrajudicial contexts' (p. 96). This is seen precisely as a legal problem, with the play demonstrating that legal rules 'cannot resolve alternative interpretations of an utterance or the speaker's intention' (p. 98). Wright cites various instances from the text to illustrate this, particularly the dialogue in III.ii between Margaret and Hero, with Margaret's accusation that Hero has placed an 'illegitimate construction' upon her words. She also traces various references to slander throughout the dialogue, and indeed, pays rather closer attention to the textual fabric of the play than Clegg does, with some telling comment on Hero's role in the deception of Beatrice, or on Antonio's challenge to Don Pedro and Claudio.

Next, Hugh Macrae Richmond's 'The Two Sicilies: Ethnic Conflict in *Much Ado*' (*ShN* 57[2007–8] 17–18), which draws attention to the historical background of the play (both the Sicilian Vespers and the career of Don John of Austria) and 'Shakespeare's awareness of the multi-ethnic nature of Sicilian history resulting from the island's position as a meeting point of Mediterranean cultures and styles'. For Richmond, the early scenes set up an opposition between 'the archaic chivalric values of Spain' and 'the skeptical views of ironic Italians' (p. 17). Emphasizing the importance of the historical background and the play's concerns with ethnic identity leads to an interpretation of *Much Ado About Nothing* as presenting a world where 'the confrontation of two equally incomplete ethics' creates the necessity for compromise 'for mutual survival' (p. 18). Richmond then touches on the possible implications of such a reading for contemporary performance, for example in the context of modern California.

Moving on now to *As You Like It*, I am afraid I can find little of value in Wendell Berry's 'The Uses of Adversity' (*SR* 115:ii[2007] 211–38). For me, this essay highlights by default many of the virtues of the mainstream critical tradition and the conventions of academic writing, because coming in from the outside, as it were, Berry seems all at sea. There is an unfortunate amateurism at work here, illustrative of someone writing outside their own field, which in this case is not compensated for by any freshness of vision that might come from offering a new perspective. Knowledge of the recent critical tradition would prevent or challenge many of the comments made. Berry begins from the position that he has found it useful 'to think of *As You Like It* and *King Lear* as versions of the same archetypal story belonging to human experience both before and after the plays' (p. 211). And this opening gambit seems to carry some promise. Coming out of this, though, what we are offered is a straightforward progress through the action of each play, read through the light of Berry's own particular philosophies and with characters and actions judged and interpreted according to these standards. It doesn't help that most of the comments and arguments advanced are little more than trite. So we learn, for example, that 'by the play's end all of its principal characters have been changed, and for the better, by their time in the forest', and that 'Shakespeare saw, and wants us to see, that the forest can be corrective and restorative to disordered human life' (p. 223).

Much Ado About Nothing and *As You Like It* are brought together, along with *Twelfth Night*, in Carolin Biewer's 'The Semantics of Passion in Shakespeare's Comedies: An Interdisciplinary Study' (*ES* 88[2007] 506–21). Biewer's approach is to try to locate the contemporary Elizabethan 'semantic fields' and resonances for Shakespeare's language of passion in the comedies. This involves an extended discussion of the theory of humours and ideas relating to the location of passion within the body, and the vocabulary associated with these topics. Particular semantic fields discussed include '*passion, organs, eyes* and *humours*', with examples cited as appropriate from the three plays concerned, in an approach that is said to give 'insight into how Shakespeare uses language to create different characters of lovers who represent three different types of love' (p. 520). In the end, though, interesting ideas and comment on individual sequences lead to some fairly dull conclusions, and again there is a sense of somebody writing outside the main critical tradition, in a way that is limiting rather than liberating. This outsider status is reflected, if nowhere else, in Biewer's use of the (surely now largely outmoded and certainly unhelpfully ambiguous) term 'late comedies' to describe the three plays on which she focuses.

Staying with general studies on the comedies leads me on to Loreen L. Giese's monograph, *Courtships, Marriage Customs, and Shakespeare's Comedies*, which though it carries a publication date of 2006 seems actually to have first appeared only early in 2007. Giese's title promises rather more than it delivers, because she actually focuses on only two of Shakespeare's comedies, *Twelfth Night* and *The Two Gentlemen of Verona*. The basis of her study is her work on court depositions from the period, specifically cases from the London Consistory Court relating to courtship and marriage customs. Giese presents a wealth of details from the records she has consulted, illuminating many aspects of courtship, marriage and sexual behaviour and conventions from the period, in ways that often work against what casual assumption might have taken to be the case. Her approach is to focus on different aspects of behaviour across different chapters, and then to use the second half of each chapter to relate the issues raised to the situations found in *Two Gentlemen* and *Twelfth Night*.

Individual chapters cover topics related to choosing a spouse, determining marital suitability, courting behaviour (including a consideration of talking, tokens and touching) and the making of contracts (covering issues such as vows, hand-holding and gift-giving). These four principal chapters are bookended by an introduction and postscript setting out the general situation, explaining the nature of the records consulted and how they have been used, and providing some brief concluding comments. Much of the work on the records themselves and the cases described is fascinating stuff, and Giese's attention to detail is very impressive in these sections. At times, her knowledge of the material she is dealing with can lead her to expect too much familiarity from her audience, as she has a casual ease which doesn't always help the reader to remember the case concerned. But this is a minor cavil. When it comes to the discussion of the two Shakespeare plays themselves, however, I must admit to finding the book a little disappointing. There is obviously material that can illuminate the plays here, but the application becomes repetitive after a while, and a wider focus, taking in more of the comedies, might have helped to ameliorate this. Much of the time, Giese is reduced to virtually formulaic contrasts—one play does this, the other does that, and so on. And her conclusions are often just bland, as in: 'the differences in the kinds of marriage arrangements that the plays under discussion exemplify suggest we cannot make any definitive statements regarding Shakespeare's portrayal of marital forms, apart from acknowledging the emphasis that seems to be placed on the reciprocal consent of individuals as the basis of marriage' (p. 157). Giese does have some interesting things to say about both *The Two Gentlemen of Verona* and *Twelfth Night*—with the latter, I particularly liked the focus on Olivia's role that comes out of the approach adopted—but her engagement with the historical records is much the more valuable part of her study.

Continuing with work on *Twelfth Night*, Laura Sarnelli's 'Staging the Space of Desire: A Queer Reading of *Twelfth Night*' (*Textus* 20[2007] 617–32) does live up to the expectations raised by its title. Sarnelli's is essentially a straightforward, albeit fairly derivative, reading of *Twelfth Night* as a play where 'homosocial and homoerotic relationships alternate in a dynamic interplay according to the contingent identifications characters take on' (p. 630). Sarnelli begins by providing an overview of the broad trends of feminism, gender criticism and queer theory in Shakespeare studies in recent years (i.e. the 1990s onwards), with a particular focus on cross-dressing. For me, the length of this section rather overbalances the rest of the essay, and Sarnelli is led at times into questionable generalizations about Renaissance thought, such as the idea that 'sexual behaviours were considered as acceptable only insofar as they did not compromise patriarchal power-structures' (p. 619). The broad sweep of this idea may hang true, but expressed in these terms I would say it oversimplifies the situation rather. And it is against a background of certainty about what the period believed that Sarnelli is able to pursue the idea of how the theatre of the time, 'in both its literary and meta-dramatic dimension, becomes a powerful space of desire which resists and transgresses the contained, oppressive discourses of patriarchy and social norms' (p. 623).

Sarnelli moves from this background to the play itself through the argument that '*Twelfth Night* is the Shakespeare comedy that best illustrates the thematic and dramatic convention of the boy heroine in male disguise' (p. 623). Yet it is tempting to suggest that what she actually means is that *Twelfth Night* is the play where the treatment of the disguised heroine best lends itself to her particular concerns. Which is not necessarily the same thing at all. A similar tone of definitiveness mars other elements of the essay for me. Certain standard emphases of gender-based approaches to this play recur here— reading Antonio as displaying an 'exclusive homoerotic attraction to Sebastian' (p. 625), making great play out of the fact that Viola is still dressed in male attire at the end. But they are taken as givens, applied with a lack of subtlety. So while the readings put forward are entirely plausible and can be made to signify in all sorts of interesting ways, they are not the only readings available, and a greater sensitivity to the possibilities of interpretation would have helped. Without this, the essay becomes in the end, for me, very much reading by numbers.

Working in a similar area is Nancy Lindheim's 'Rethinking Sexuality and Class in *Twelfth Night*' (*UTQ* 76[2007] 679–713). In general, I much preferred Lindheim's article to Sarnelli's, and this essay, though in the end it probably fails to live up to its initial promise, does cover some of the areas that are missing from Sarnelli's approach. Lindheim sets out to explore the ways in which 'Shakespeare's calculations in *Twelfth Night* are geared throughout towards the formal need for a comic ending plausible enough to be satisfying, yet still sensitive to the erotic and social problems his fable creates'. And she specifically sets out to interrogate some of the recent orthodoxies behind many of the recent gender-based studies of this play, but to what I would see as at least initially positive ends. In Lindheim's words, 'although my argument tactically sets itself against certain critical positions for purposes of clarity, its aim is a more inclusive understanding of the play' (p. 679).

Lindheim starts with the final scene, and seeks to set out the elements in this that work towards satisfactory generic closure, emphasizing for example the similarities Shakespeare creates between Sebastian and Viola, even down to their parallel modes of speaking, which render more plausible the love between Sebastian and Olivia. There is also good analysis of the Antonio–Sebastian relationship here, its potential erotic dimensions and its potential non-erotic dimensions. In Lindheim's words, '*Twelfth Night* gives strong, sympathetic expression to Antonio's passion—especially when he feels that it has been abused—without necessarily sexualizing it' (p. 691); and as she also notes, at the end, 'Antonio need not be desolate and is certainly not excluded from the feast' (p. 693). Similarly, Antonio's silence after his reconciliation need not be significant—I liked Lindheim's suggested comparison here of Antonio's silence to that of Florizel after V.i in *The Winter's Tale*. Similarly, Lindheim seeks to emphasize that the dominant audience experience in the period in relation to the boy player was to accept 'women characters as female' (p. 695), suggesting that the claim that the presence of the boy-player beneath the female character is always a factor in the dramatic action is a distortion of that dominant experience. Thus the fact that Viola is still dressed as Cesario at the end of the play need not be a 'sexual issue' (p. 694); indeed, as Lindheim points out, it has a dramaturgical explanation deriving from the action relating to Antonio and Malvolio.

The tone of Lindheim's approach, then, is to question just how much certain elements in the play, now almost conventionally read as 'disturbing', really work to compromise the generic movement to a happy ending. She extends this to discussing two elements more related to class issues than gender issues, 'Malvolio's angry refusal of a comic resolution, and the marriage between Maria and Sir Toby' (p. 696). The argument questions the extent to which the subplot characters can be thought of as 'lower class', given the 'claim to gentility' of most of them (p. 698). Malvolio emerges from this reading as a carefully delineated character, who does not conform to any of the obvious types—servant, Puritan, social upstart—that seem to circulate round him. He is also seen to be obviously balanced against Sir Toby, in a reading which highlights the unsavoury aspects of the latter's character and teases out a possible path to reformation. Lindheim also questions readings of Maria that interpret her marriage as 'a triumph of the scheming female underclass' (p. 704). In the end, the argument, or the presentation of the argument, goes much too far in the other direction. Lindheim's initial claim to be setting herself against certain positions for tactical reasons seems to disappear, so that what we are actually given comes close to being an old-fashioned straightforward reading of *Twelfth Night* as a comedy with no problematic elements in it at all. Where Lindheim is questioning the way certain 'new' readings of the play have established themselves as orthodoxies, I find her work a valuable corrective; but when it can seem that she is essentially looking to debunk or 'contain' such new readings, that becomes much more problematic.

Finally on this play, we have Gabriel Josipovici's 'The Opinion of Pythagoras' (in Poole and Scholar, eds., *Thinking with Shakespeare: Comparative and Interdisciplinary Essays for A.D. Nuttall*, pp. 23–32). Josipovici's essay sites itself as part of an old philosophical debate, pursuing the idea that works of art can help bridge the gap between life and thought, 'and so help us in our philosophical task of understanding ourselves and the world'. *Twelfth Night* again emerges here as an exemplary text in the Shakespeare canon, 'the play that shows up, perhaps more so than any other he wrote, the difficulty discursive thought has when faced with a work of art' (p. 23). The difficulties lie not in our immediate response to the play, but in how we try to make sense of the experience after the event. Much is made of Shakespeare's transformation of his sources, his ability to create protean characters, or to shift into another gear. And there are recurrent comparisons of Shakespeare to Mozart that are obviously meant to be meaningful but really just serve to obscure. Occasional passages spark interest, such as the comparison of the sequence of dialogue that furnishes Josipovici's title to a moment from the world of Ionesco or Pinter. But the essay does little to justify its own premise, because in the end it has little to say about the vision the play offers beyond superficialities or obscure images, such as the comparison of Feste's closing song to a firework that 'rises up into the sky and then spreads, as it falls, over the whole of the play we have just experienced'. In the end, what this work of art can apparently contribute to philosophy is the ability to make us realize 'the possibilities of human life, more fully and with more intensity than ever before or after' (p. 31).

I turn back now to the other play discussed in Giese's monograph, *The Two Gentlemen of Verona*, and, first of all, Stephen Guy-Bray's 'Shakespeare and the Invention of the Heterosexual' (*EMLS* 13:ii[2007] 28 paras). This opens with the statement that 'the currently conventional view of heterosexuality typically presents it as the happy ending of a narrative beginning with an infant's attachment to his or her mother and progressing from close attachments to members of the same sex to a single attachment to a member of the opposite sex' (para. 1). Some framework would have been helpful here to indicate where this currently conventional view is coming from, and which particular discourse or whose particular attitudes Guy-Bray is invoking—it's not exactly a dictionary definition that he's presenting. This description of the heterosexual norm is then contrasted to the situation in the Renaissance, presented as a culture where male–male friendships/bonds were regarded as those of full maturity, and where effectively 'homosociality' was 'more important than married love' (para. 2). Guy-Bray sets out to challenge what he sees as the typical view that Shakespeare's plays support 'a view of mixed-sex affection as the most important affective bond in a person's life', with *The Two Gentlemen of Verona* invoked as a play that 'makes such an interpretation problematic' and that 'presents heterosexuality as something that is made up, rather than as something that is an essence or as something that the characters naturally do' (para. 5). Issues given prominence in the course of the argument are the idea of sexuality as a form of performance, of heterosexuality as a kind of prosthesis, and a view of character and selfhood as something that is always in process. Attention is also given to the prominence of letters and the theme of substitution within the play. The overall conclusion is that 'Shakespeare's achievement in *The Two Gentlemen of Verona* is to produce a narrative in which same-sex and mixed-sex relationships can co-exist' (para. 28).

Next an article that seeks to call into question the very name by which we know this play. David M. Bergeron's 'Wherefore Verona in *The Two Gentlemen of Verona*?' (*CompD* 42[2007–8] 423–38) takes Shakespeare's titles in general, particularly the titles of the comedies, as the basis for an argument that this play 'has an inappropriate title, based on a faulty location' (p. 423). I say Shakespeare's titles, but as Bergeron comments, 'if we think about the matter, we have to admit that we do not know where the plays' titles come from' (p. 423). Yet Bergeron is surely on a hiding to nothing when he attempts to suggest that Francis Meres's mention of Shakespeare's '*Gentlemen of Verona*' in his *Palladis Tamia* [1598] is not actually a reference to the play we now know as *The Two Gentlemen of Verona*. The suggestion is made, perhaps not entirely seriously, that Meres is actually referring to *The Taming of the Shrew*, not otherwise included in his list of Shakespeare's plays.

Of course, there is a well-known problem with location in *Two Gentlemen*, and Bergeron pursues all the evidence relating to this, not just the few (and occasionally problematic) references to Verona within the dialogue, but also, perhaps most interestingly, moments where Verona is not named in the dialogue when one might expect it to be. This leads to some interesting comments on the role of 'home' in the play, but the main conclusion drawn from such moments is that Shakespeare had not actually decided where Valentine and Proteus were from at the time of writing. In this respect, '*The Two Gentlemen of Verona* is the story of a playwright who has not made up his mind' (p. 436). Yet Bergeron himself seems to struggle to make up his own mind about what his actual theory is here. He has apparently dropped the *Shrew*-as-*Two-Gentlemen* argument entirely when he writes, with a logic that escapes me, 'I think that Shakespeare included Verona in the title because he had not yet decided what to call the city from which the characters move.' In the end, the essay seems to come down to the fact that Bergeron just doesn't like the Folio title, and would prefer something like '*The Two Gentlemen FROM Verona*' (p. 436). Any possible reason for challenging the Folio title is invoked, even where those reasons are mutually incompatible.

From a challenge to conventional naming to a challenge to conventional dating. John Peachman's 'Why a Dog? A Late Date for *The Two Gentlemen of Verona*' (*N&Q* 54[2007] 265–72) claims that the date of this play 'is one of the most uncertain in the canon' (p. 265). This is something of an exaggeration given that, *pace* Bergeron, a clear *terminus ad quem* is established by Meres's reference to the play in 1598, whereas of course other plays (*All's Well*, *Timon of Athens*) offer no external evidence at all for dating before their appearance in the First Folio. Peachman, obviously aware of Meres's comments, seeks to place *Two Gentlemen* around 1597, and therefore make it not anticipatory of works such as *Romeo and Juliet* or *The Merchant of Venice*, but borrowing from them. The theory turns on reviving an old argument about the influence of Thomas Nashe's *Have with You to Saffron-Walden* on Shakespeare's play, particularly on its names. The key point here is that Nashe's work was first printed in 1596, though the possibility (mentioned by William C. Carroll in his Arden3 edition [2004], p. 128) that it might have circulated earlier in manuscript is not considered by Peachman.

Another note provides the only contribution on *Love's Labour's Lost* to have come my way this year (I have not seen Juliet Dusinberre's '*Love's Labour's Lost* and the Pursuit of Fame' (*ShStud* 45[2007] 1–25)). Gillian Woods's 'The Contexts of *The Trial of Chivalry*' (*N&Q* 54[2007] 313–18) is largely a discussion of this anonymous dramatic romance, printed in 1605, but gains a place here through the connections it seeks to draw between this play and *Love's Labour's Lost*. The comparison is based not so much on the idea of a direct or conscious influence (though Woods seems to want to keep this option open), but more on the notion of the 'timeliness' of their connections. In terms of Shakespeare's play, Woods picks up in particular on the potential topical relevance of the names of the male characters, especially that of Navarre, a name that also figures in *The Trial of Chivalry*. Woods places the date of *The Trial of Chivalry* in the late 1590s, and pursues some tenuous connections between this date and the first printing of *Love's Labour's Lost*, as well as between the publication of *The Trial of Chivalry* and the recorded performance of *Love's Labour's Lost* at court in 1604–5. Rather more interesting is the exploration of the potential historical 'timeliness' of both plays in relation to French politics and English topical interest in French affairs.

Staying with the early comedies, we come next to *The Comedy of Errors*, and Kent Cartwright's 'Language, Magic, the Dromios, and *The Comedy of Errors*' (*SEL* 47[2007] 331–54). This is another article interested in aspects of experience beyond the rational, which argues specifically that 'words and thoughts in *The Comedy of Errors* unexpectedly acquire a certain magical agency and that the magical and the fantastical also acquire a certain potential for truth' (p. 331). Cartwright obviously has a firm textual basis to work from here with the various references to magical experience made during the course of the action and the appearance of Doctor Pinch. Against this background, he focuses particularly on three aspects of magic, 'sympathy, language, and possession' (p. 332). Ideas of demonic possession, sympathy of experience, the way language seems to take on a magical life of its own as words and images 'migrate and double' (p. 334), are all pursued across the different strands of the action. Cartwright also seeks to draw a correspondence between the realm of magic and ideas of *copia* and amplification, as reflected in particular in images of doubling, clowning, festive misrule and linguistic exuberance.

While the principal focus for the discussion becomes the Dromio twins, the way in which words seem to move between characters and get picked up on again from earlier scenes is explored across the whole cast. Cartwright is sensitive to the fact that he could just be picking up on a standard Shakespearian technique of verbal reiteration here, but the way he connects that technique to the thematic relevance of magic is totally plausible. And his work here is a reminder of the richness of the verbal texture of this play that is so often dismissed as *just* a farce. In the end, it is the Dromios that best exemplify the elements of the play that Cartwright is seeking to emphasize, for they 'evince the wildest imaginations', 'enlarge the imaginative dimension of the play' (p. 345) and respond to events through 'two seemingly contradictory mentalities: realism and fantasticality' (p. 344). Enchantment for the Dromios breeds 'the unexpected correlative of excitement, intensity, and vividness, a new immediacy of experience that might be taken as a value in its own right' (p. 346). In this respect, they come to symbolize the recuperative energies of farce, for which they are 'the prime agents' (p. 348) in *The Comedy of Errors*.

Also covering this play is Marissa Greenberg's essay, 'Crossing from Scaffold to Stage: Execution Processions and Generic Conventions in *The Comedy of Errors* and *Measure for Measure*' (in Cohen, ed., *Shakespeare and Historical Formalism*, pp. 127–45). This picks up on issues relating to the correlation 'between theatrical representations and their real-word counterparts' (p. 127), as Greenberg tries to 'formulate a response to the question of the theater's distinctiveness by focusing on the interaction of generic and punitive forms—specifically, on what happens when Shakespeare's comedies represent execution processions' (pp. 127–8). Greenberg is concerned with the nature of forms, the familiarity they create, and what happens when that familiarity is reproduced on stage. *Measure for Measure* is given the more extended treatment, in a section of the essay that falls outside my remit. The discussion of *The Comedy of Errors* inevitably focuses primarily on the frame-story, with the opening entry of the play read specifically as 'an execution procession' (p. 132). I.i is seen to present 'juridical sentences in conjunction with generic clues' (p. 133), so that an expectation of extenuation is created. This process is paralleled in the final scene, where repeated delays to the execution procession 'signal and draw out the shift from deferral to pardon' (p. 134), and theatrical and generic momentum takes over to sweep aside the power of the law.

Helga Ramsey-Kurz's 'Rising Above the Bait: Kate's Transformation from Bear to Falcon' (*ES* 88[2007] 262–81) begins its discussion of *The Taming of the Shrew*, like so many other essays, with Katherine's 'obedience speech' (p. 262), emphasizing its potential for ambiguity and irony. Ramsey-Kurz is concerned particularly with the idea of taming as a form of performance, 'a performance undertaken to coerce further performance' (p. 263). And she seeks to distinguish between different forms of taming, contrasting the more 'gentle' approach required in taming falcons, for example, with the more extreme or cruel methods required for the kind of 'animal subjection underlying the wild-beast shows which formed an integral part of [the] Elizabethan entertainment industry' (p. 263). Ramsey-Kurz writes well on the play's interest in performativity and its various uses of disguise and show. I also like the idea that Petruchio's appearance alters Kate's dramatic status, changing her from an obstruction to the marriage plot to 'the cardinal cause of every subsequent major action' (p. 272). Kate's progress through the action becomes one of learning that she is performing in a play in which Petruchio belongs to the same cast, and this collaborative, learning process is felt to elevate her 'taming' from its more brutal, more beastly associations. Their relationship is ultimately imaged, positively within the context of the essay, in the 'bond between falconer and falcon'. Productions and readings that emphasize Petruchio's brutality in his taming methods 'routinely ignore that the manning methods applied in falconry were devised in the interest of the bird, to reduce the stress of captivity, protect the raptor from self-injury, and, most importantly, to preserve its predatory instincts' (p. 278). I doubt I am the only one who would find in this description images of captivity and exploitation that are far more disturbing when applied to women than to falcons. I would also note that the essay is slightly marred by inaccuracies in citing critics' names ('Jeane Howard' (p. 265) and 'Jeane Addison Roberts' (p. 279) both make an appearance).

Still on *Shrew*, Patricia Parker's 'Construing Gender: Mastering Bianca in *The Taming of the Shrew*' (in Callaghan, ed., *The Impact of Feminism in English Renaissance Studies*, pp. 193–209) concerns itself with the role of Bianca rather than that of Katherine. Parker's principal focus is the scene between Bianca and the disguised Lucentio and Hortensio in III.i; the use of the phrase 'preposterous ass' in this scene will strike immediate resonances with anyone familiar with Parker's earlier work, and the ramifications of this phrase are certainly explored. But Parker is also concerned with the rivalry of the arts (*ars*) that is being evoked at this point, suggesting that the way 'the proper ordering of rival arts appears to be the subject of the debate in this scene is consistent with the emphasis on arts and learning that pervades *The Taming of the Shrew*', an emphasis, as Parker notes, that has often been submerged under a reading of the play as 'simply an early Shakespearean farce' (p. 194). Tracing the background to this sequence, including contemporary theories of music and teaching, and noting its echoes of the ceremony of matrimony, provides Parker with a way of teasing out important thematic significances present in this part of the action. In a scene where Bianca starts to emerge more fully as a rounded dramatic character, gender structures are overturned as she becomes 'not a submissive female but director of both masters' (p. 200).

This overturning is played out very precisely through the pedagogical sequence of the mock-construal of lines from Ovid's *Heroides*, where Bianca offers her own construing that redefines the terms of the pedagogical situation and deliberately eschews a subordinate position within the dialogue. The final section of the paper pursues the 'intertextual markers' (p. 202) that have frequently gone unnoticed in this section, even by feminist critics (a point Parker rather unnecessarily repeats a couple of times). Parker pursues in detail the implications of the citation from Ovid, the fact that the text from which this comes is 'Penelope's anything but submissive or silent complaint against her own husband and master for taking so long to return home' (p. 203). She also notes the presence of the *Metamorphoses* behind the dialogue that follows on from the construing of the quoted Ovidian text, arguing that Bianca again comes out best from this exchange with her 'master'. For Parker then, this scene is a key moment in the characterization and presentation of the younger sister, as we already see her emerging here as a 'much less tractable figure' than the 'wifely ideal' she is initially perceived to be by her various suitors (pp. 205–6).

Patricia Parker's work in general provides a link that leads me on to the final play in my group, *The Merry Wives of Windsor*, and Will Stockton's article, avowedly influenced by Parker's work on this play and elsewhere, ' "I am made an ass": Falstaff and the Scatology of Windsor's Polity' (*TSLL* 49[2007] 340–60). Stockton takes exploration of the bodily and scatological punning of this text to new lengths (or perhaps that should be new depths!). And, as his work clearly shows, the many different strands of puns and the acts of humiliation that run throughout this play all interlink in a wide network of associations and signifying chains. Stockton's principal focus is on the ramifications of the word 'ass' and its various applications, and the process by which Falstaff ends up as the butt of everyone's joke, the ultimate 'ass'. As always in discussions that seek to pull out hidden meanings, the occasional suggestion of a buried pun can seem to go a little too far down the path of implausibility, but at the same time the sheer linguistic richness and exuberance of this play, demonstrated time and again through Stockton's careful analysis, can indeed give the impression that anything goes.

Stockton's work is not just an exploration of linguistic exuberance and excess. These themes are also very much related to issues of class, social cohesion, scapegoating, national differences, gender and so on, as part of a general process of exploring the nature of the Windsor community that Shakespeare creates. In this respect, his essay has some similarities to Michael Steppat's 'In Mercury's Household: *The Merry Wives of Windsor*' (*CahiersE* 72[2007] 9–19), though whereas the density of Stockton's prose generally serves the purposes of his argument, Steppat's writing style (and the length of some of his paragraphs) seems to me too often to obscure what he is trying to say. Steppat's primary concerns relate to issues of property and the domestic, and what he sees as a theatrical interrogation of 'a middle-class obsession with matters of ownership' (p. 9), in contrast to the celebration of middle-class values he feels earlier critics have tended to find in the play. He also discusses in some detail aspects of the overlap between property and desire in the *Merry Wives*, finding a locus for this theme in the Latin language scene, amongst other places. In the end, though, Steppat almost seems to resist the seriousness of his own approach, suggesting disappointingly for me that perhaps one should not try to read too much into the 'playful mood' (p. 14) of *Merry Wives*, and not look for it to be 'overly profound' (p. 17).

Finally this year we have Timothy Billings's 'Masculine in Case: Latin and the Construction of Gender in *Hic Mulier* and *The Merry Wives of Windsor*' (in Huang, Wang and Theis, eds., *Class, Boundary and Social Discourse in the Renaissance*, pp. 63–86). This begins by discussing Walter Ong's famous 1959 article on Latin pedagogy, using this to lead into a discussion of the language lesson in *Merry Wives* as 'based on a logic of exclusion that would have affected audience members who had not been "initiated" into the male community of grammar school' (p. 65). From here, Billings goes on to discuss in rather more detail *Hic Mulier* and *Haec Vir*, in sections of the essay that I shall not review. Much of what Billings has to say about the Latin lesson in *Merry Wives* is familiar from other treatments, notably the work of Elizabeth Pittenger and (again) Patricia Parker. And he also is touching on areas covered by Stockton and Steppat. What perhaps most characterizes Billings's approach to the language scene is an emphasis on the sense of exclusion that it creates, as reflected in his suggestion that while no knowledge of Latin is required to appreciate the bawdy humour of the scene, knowledge of the Latin meanings can allow a sense of superiority for those who have it over those without such privileged access. In this respect, the scene would function to interpellate the initiated spectator into a position of superiority to all four characters on stage (see pp. 69–70). The final dimension of the sequence that Billings seeks to emphasize is its transvestism (even to the extent of claiming that 'Evans as an actor' is in 'effeminating Welsh drag' (p. 72)), and the various gender issues and sexual anxieties this can set off or put into play. And Billings is adamant, to bring me back finally to a recurring issue in this year's work, that this 'sexualization of the scene' is not something that can 'simply be dismissed as conventionally irrelevant' (p. 73).

(c) Problem Plays

The only book-length study of the problem plays this year was Ira Clark's *Rhetorical Readings, Dark Comedies and Shakespeare's Problem Plays*.

This work is an example of an emerging critical trend in literary studies which has been labelled 'historical formalism' and attempts to combine consideration of form and genre with historicist criticism. Although Clark does not use this label himself, his introductory comments indicate this critical affiliation: 'In pursuit of the potential contribution to the study of literature and culture that understanding the forms of figures and stylistic traits might make, I take comfort in a recent resurgence of rather formal analyses of literature that make use of the many gains of historicist projects of the last quarter century' (pp. 2–3). This critical position is reflected in the book's organization, as it begins with a chapter which considers the problem plays and their stylistic features in the context of other contemporary examples of comedy, while surveying the critical history which has attempted to account for the particular qualities of Shakespeare's late comedies. The chapters on each of the plays focus on a specific rhetorical device, including chiasmus in *Measure for Measure*, aphorism in *All's Well That Ends Well* and wit and reflexivity in *Troilus and Cressida*.

This year the play which received the most attention individually was *All's Well That Ends Well*, having been the subject of four essays. Three of the four essays examine questions about female agency in the play from a number of different critical perspectives. The first of these is Kathryn M. Moncrief's '"Show me a child begotten of thy body that I am father to": Pregnancy, Paternity and the Problem of Evidence in *All's Well That Ends Well*' (in Moncrief and McPherson, eds., pp. 29–43). This fascinating collection focuses on the cultural representation of maternity between 1540 and 1690, and Moncrief reads Helen's presentation of her pregnant body against contemporary guides to midwifery and gynaecological manuals. The over-riding attitude expressed towards pregnancy in these manuals is one of uncertainty and that both the body and the pregnant woman herself are unreliable sources of information regarding the pregnancy or the paternity of the child. Moncrief argues that Bertram's scepticism towards Helena and her claim that he is the father of her child, rather than simply characterizing Bertram as an unfeeling cad reflects a cautious, even prudent, attitude, in the light of the problematic evidence he is presented with. Moncrief concludes that Helena's pregnancy should signal uncertainty rather than point to Bertram's reformation and closure: 'When viewed through the lens of pregnancy and its ambiguities, the neat conclusion upon which the title of the play depends remains elusive—the promised happy ending that Helena and the audience desire still to be delivered' (p. 43). The second essay '"One that's dead is quick": Virgin Re-birth in *All's Well That Ends Well*' is to be found in another important edited collection, Buccola and Hopkins, eds., *Marian Moments in Early Modern British Drama* (pp. 35–46). Here Alison Findlay considers the play's Marian allusions, specifically the role of Helena as mediatrix and the roles of the Countess and the widow as intercessors, to argue that 'moments which celebrate virginity and maternity can be read as a secular refashioning of the cult of relics, images, and rituals in which Mary had assumed a tangible authority of her own in the lives of Christians' (p. 37). Meanwhile, in '"My intents are fix'd": Constant Will in *All's Well That Ends Well*' (*SQ* 58[2007] 200–27), Katherine Schwartz returns to an aspect of the play which continues to exercise critics: Helena's pursuit of Bertram. Schwartz argues that it is Helena's quality of devotion or constancy to Bertram that strains the limits of both genre and gender since it is not merely a passive virtue 'Constancy intervenes into masculine homosocial privilege in a way at once vital and unsettling, its guarantees securing a hierarchy that they expose as a structure of need. Aggressively directed to an admirable end, Helena's unruly virtue reveals a patriarchal ideology both functional and contingent, its efficacy as practice articulated through women's work and will' (p. 201).

The final essay which deals exclusively with *All's Well* is Maurice Hunt's article ' "O Lord Sir!" in *All's Well That Ends Well*' (*ES* 88[2007] 143–8), which examines the editorial gloss for Lavatch's phrase 'O Lord Sir!' deployed by the Clown in a series of exchanges with the Countess in Act II, scene ii, as he demonstrates 'an answer [that] will serve all men'. Hunt explains that the phrase 'O Lord Sir!' had a specific stage history, having been employed by Ben Jonson in *Every Man Out of His Humour*. In Jonson's play the phrase 'identifies a courtier simpleton, a fool for whom the phrase becomes a knee jerk response covering ignorance' (p. 145). Hunt reads Shakespeare's use of the phrase in *All's Well* in the wider context of Jonson's attacks upon Shakespeare in *Every Man*, to suggest that in the problem play Shakespeare capitalizes upon Jonson's use of the phrase and that its inclusion provides Shakespeare with 'another opportunity for transcending the limits of Jonsonian satire' (p. 146). This point is demonstrated by examination of the way the phrase is subsequently given to Parolles when sentenced to death for his treachery, 'who unintentionally reclaims the significance of a virtually meaningless faddish utterance, informing it with its original prayerful meaning' (pp. 146–7).

Martha Widmayer's essay ' "To sin in loving virtue": Angelo of *Measure for Measure*' (*TSLL* 49:ii[2007] 155–80) reads Shakespeare's characterization of the play's precise deputy against the details of a specific lawsuit found in the Essex Records Office in 1578. The Records Office outlines a dispute between two justices of the peace, Lord Morley and Mr Leventhorpe. Morley had intervened on behalf of his tenant, a man called Smith who had fathered a child by Morley's maidservant. The woman had been sent away to a village which came under Leventhorpe's jurisdiction, but she had been returned to Morley since the villagers refused to support the woman and her child. Morley used a warrant to send the woman back again to the village of Ashwell, but here Leventhorpe intervened, refusing to honour Morley's warrant and in effect forcing Morley and Smith to support the maidservant. Widmayer uses this legal dispute to frame her discussion of Angelo, whose behaviour she argues 'bears a striking resemblance to godly magistrates like Leventhorpe' (p. 156). A second essay on *Measure* by Marissa Greenburg also begins by considering the play's depiction of the law and the punitive measures it performs. 'Crossing from Scaffold to Stage: Execution Processions and Generic Conventions in *The Comedy of Errors* and *Measure for Measure*' (in Cohen, ed., pp. 127–45) considers two plays which both begin with a condemned character crossing over the stage and conclude with the thwarting of the death sentence. The comparison between *Errors*, as an early comedy, and *Measure*, a later 'dark comedy', permits discussion of the ways in which each of the plays introduces and subverts the audience's punitive and generic expectations.

There were two notes on *Measure for Measure* this year. In '*Measure for Measure* III.i.93, 96: Prenzie' (*N&Q* 54[2007] 292) David Lisle Crane offers a solution to the crux in this scene by suggesting that the word 'Prenzie' is in fact a misreading by the compositor of the secretary hand with the flourish used to denote the 'P' in fact a 'u'; he argues that consequently it is possible to read 'Prenzie' as 'Upright'. In the second note (*N&Q* 54[2007] 292–3) 'Isabella, Marina, and Saint Ursula' Andrew Hadfield considers the story of St Ursula found in Jacobus de Voraigne's *Golden Legend* [*c.*1260] as a possible source for Isabella in *Measure for Measure*, and accounts for her depiction as a novice in the play. Hadfield also suggests that stories about the saint may have influenced the brothel scenes in *Pericles*.

The only work dealing exclusively with *Troilus and Cressida* can be found in *The Whirligig of Time: Essays on Shakespeare and Czechoslovakia* by the Czech Shakespearian scholar Zdeněk Stříbrný. The essay, 'Time in *Troilus and Cressida*', was first published in 1976 and together with essays on the history plays and *The Winter's Tale* explores the concept of 'double time', the different speeds at which simultaneous dramatic events take place. In the problem play Stříbrný examines the ways in which Shakespeare complicates the relationship between the love story and account of the Trojan War through the time-frames he employs. The collection provides fascinating insights into life in Czechoslovakia under the Russian regime and the way it shaped Shakespeare's place in that society.

(d) Poems

Two major publications on Shakespeare's sonnets (an essay collection and a single-authored volume) and one on Shakespeare's poetry in general were published in 2007: *A Companion to Shakespeare's Sonnets*, edited by Michael Schoenfeldt; Dympna Callaghan's *Shakespeare's Sonnets*; and *The Cambridge Companion to Shakespeare's Poetry*, edited by Patrick Cheney. The first of these, *A Companion to Shakespeare's Sonnets*, is divided into nine sections. Each section contains between two and four essays by leading scholars in their chosen subjects. They vary from original readings to provocative surveys of a particular field of scholarship. The volume serves as an authoritative first port of call for students of Shakespeare's sonnets. Without discussing every one of the twenty-five essays, what follows will give an indication of the importance of this collection. The first section, entitled 'Sonnet Form and Sonnet Sequence', contains two essays that have been published previously (an excerpt from *An Essay on Shakespeare's Sonnets* [1969] by Stephen Booth and another from *The Art of Shakespeare's Sonnets* [1997] by Helen Vendler) and two essays composed specifically for this volume. James Schiffer's contribution, 'The Incomplete Narrative of Shakespeare's Sonnets' (pp. 45–56), assumes, for the purposes of his essay, that the sonnets were shaped into a collection and that the narrative structure is as the author intended. He then addresses the following question, based on A.C. Bradley's assessment of the poems (*Oxford Lectures on Poetry* [1909]), 'why did Shakespeare present in the sonnets' "final form" the story of and behind these poems...in an "obscure," at times "unintelligible," inconsistent, incomplete, unsatisfying...way?' This 'anti-narrativity', as Schiffer terms it, might have been the result of one of several literary motivations, all of which are discussed: 'dramatic effect', 'voyeuristic pleasure', 'pleasures of detection and invention', 'replication' and 'deflection'. The other essay in this section, Margreta de Grazia's 'Revolution in *Shake-speares Sonnets*' (pp. 57–69), reads the 1609 quarto containing the sonnets and *A Lover's Complaint* according to the putative tripartite structure which separates Sonnets 153 and 154 from the previous 152 on the basis of their peculiarly epigrammatic character. According to de Grazia, the 152 sonnets, the epigrammatic pair and the *Complaint* all 'rehearse programs of return'. The sonnets are 'stuck in the cycle of hating-after-loving and loving-after-hating'; the epigrams are locked in a round of 'rekindling-after-quenching and quenching-after-rekindling'; and the *Complaint* cannot escape from 'perversion-after-reconciliation and reconciliation-after-perversion'. The second section, entitled 'Shakespeare and his Predecessors', contains three essays. Richard Strier's essay, 'The Refusal to be Judged in Petrarch and Shakespeare' (pp. 73–89), highlights significant dissimilarities between Petrarch and Shakespeare in terms of their poetic representation of the relationship between the physical and spiritual. Nevertheless, Strier's main contribution to this area of scholarly debate is in his elucidation of the 'continuity between Petrarch's sonnets and some of Shakespeare's' on such issues. Heather Dubrow's essay from the same section, ' "Dressing old words new"? Re-evaluating the "Delian Structure" ' (pp. 90–103), turns, like de Grazia, to the tradition (nominally associated with Samuel Daniel's collection, *Delia*) of the tripartite structure: a sonnet sequence followed by a short poem, often in tetrameters, followed by a longer poem, often a complaint. Dympna Callaghan ('Confounded by Winter: Speeding Time in Shakespeare's Sonnets', pp. 104–18) addresses Shakespeare's 'accelerated sonnet temporality' and notes that, again relative to Petrarch, he brings a new contemporariness to the previously timeless lyric. Part III, entitled 'Editorial Theory and Biographical Inquiry: Editing the Sonnets', contains Stephen Orgel's piece, previously published in the *London Review of Books* [8 August 2002], 'Mr. Who He?' (pp. 137–44), as well as new essays by Richard Dutton ('*Shake-speares Sonnets*, Shakespeare's Sonnets, and Shakespearean Biography', pp. 121–36), Colin Burrow ('Editing the Sonnets', pp. 145–62) and Lars Engle ('William Empson and the Sonnets', pp. 163–82). Dutton surveys recent changes (from the 1970s onwards) in the mutual relationship between biographical and literary-critical responses to Shakespeare's sonnets, ending with a brief assessment of the consequences for our view of Shakespeare's 'life' of Patrick Cheney's work (*Shakespeare, National Poet-Playwright* [2004]) on what may be more narrowly termed his 'literary career'. Burrow's essay is similarly constructed as a survey of his chosen topic over time, culminating with a cautionary passage subtitled, 'A Very Woe: Editing the Sonnets Today'. Burrow would prefer that editors 'regard themselves as part of a conversation about a text that will continue after they are dead' rather than anything more definitive. Engle charts the relationships between William Empson's readings

of the sonnets and those of Laura Riding, Robert Graves, Stephen Booth and
Helen Vendler, before reflecting, like Dutton, on the area of 'speculative
biography'. There are two essays, by Arthur F. Marotti and Marcy L. North,
in a section headed 'The Sonnets in Manuscript and Print' (pp. 183–222).
Part V, 'Models of Desire in the Sonnets' (pp. 223–90), includes four essays,
written by Douglas Trevor, Bradin Cormack, Rayna Kalas and Jyotsna G.
Singh, that touch on the anti-Platonic nature of the sonnets, offer a reading of
their Latinity based on Colin Burrow's reading of the Latinate vocabulary of
the plays ('Shakespeare and Humanistic Culture', in Martindale and Taylor
(eds.), *Shakespeare and the Classics* [2004]), expand on the significance of the
curved brackets (or lunulae) at the end of Sonnet 126 and view Shakespeare's
sonnets through the prism of 'early modern taxonomies of passion and
affection', respectively. The remaining four parts, VI–IX, deal with 'Ideas of
Darkness in the Sonnets', 'Memory and Repetition in the Sonnets', 'The
Sonnets in/and the Plays', and 'The Sonnets and *A Lover's Complaint*', the last
of which is discussed below with other publications dealing with the *Complaint*.

Dympna Callaghan's *Shakespeare's Sonnets* is another invaluable guide to
the sonnets that includes several features that will be of particular help to
students daunted by the complexity of an early modern sonnet sequence.
The introductory chapter deals with the collection in its literary and historical
context, examining the issues of authorization, publication and the identity of
the sonnets' addressees. Callaghan then in a further five chapters seeks
'to engage the poems themselves and to clarify and elucidate the most
significant interpretive ideas that have circulated around these complex poems
since their first publication'. The chapter on 'Identity' expands on the ideas
discussed in the introduction around the 'love triangle' of personae in the
sonnet sequence. In sections with the sub-headings, 'Lyric Identity', 'Who's
That Lady?' and 'My Lovely Boy', the author discusses the issue in both
literary and biographical terms. The chapter on 'Beauty' emphasizes
the 'unequivocally . . . masculine' nature of the ideal beauty presented in the
sonnets. This idealization is not without 'a twist', for Callaghan, in that 'the
beautiful young man looks like a woman'. A chapter entitled 'Love' charts
the 'sexual, complicated, messy, and unsettling' course of love in the poems,
culminating with a discussion of venereal disease. Further chapters discuss
'Numbers' and 'Time' in the sonnets, and the volume concludes with a
particularly useful appendix, 'The Matter of the Sonnets', in which Callaghan,
while recognizing that the 'sonnets cannot and should not be *reduced* to their
paraphrasable content', offers the reader what is indeed a paraphrase of all 154
poems. The author, 'without trying to force the sonnets into a definitive
pattern', shines a guiding light on the still contestable sequence.

The Cambridge Companion to Shakespeare's Poetry, another volume that
will be of importance to new (not to mention older) students of Shakespeare,
has fourteen chapters and an introduction (by the editor, Patrick Cheney) that
together tackle the poetry of William Shakespeare in all its forms, whether in
the poems or the plays. Each chapter is written by a leading international
scholar, but these essays, rather than offering original readings of the texts
under discussion (as is often the case with the Blackwell collection discussed
above), conform to the rubric of a general companion volume. Organized

along similar lines to other volumes in the same series, it has three informally differentiated sub-sections dealing with, in turn, the literary and cultural foundations on which Shakespeare was building, the poetry itself (including its contribution to the culture discussed in earlier chapters), and, in the third section, a more wide-ranging discussion of the ways of reading the poetry and its themes, as well as chapters on its reception and life in performance. Michael Schoenfeldt (the editor of the Blackwell *Companion to Shakespeare's Sonnets* discussed above) contributes the chapter on the sonnets. There are also authoritative chapters on *Venus and Adonis* (by Coppélia Kahn), *The Rape of Lucrece* (by Catherine Belsey), *The Passionate Pilgrim* and 'The Phoenix and Turtle' (by James P. Bednarz), and *A Lover's Complaint* (by Katherine Rowe). There are also select reading lists for all the chapters, together with a chronology and a notably up-to-date list of reference works on Shakespeare's poetry.

Of the articles dealing specifically with Shakespeare's sonnets, five restrict their discussion to a single sonnet. Amy D. Stackhouse, in her article, 'Shakespeare's Half-Foot: Gendered Prosody in Sonnet 20' (*Expl* 65:iv[2007] 202–4), highlights the significance of the sonnet's feminine endings, adding an extra unstressed half-foot, for reading the sexual ambiguity of the poem's theme, made more explicit in the twelfth line: 'By adding one thing to my purpose nothing'. McDonald P. Jackson, 'Shakespeare's Sonnet CXI and John Davies of Hereford's *Microcosmos* (1603)' (*MLR* 102:i[2007] 1–10), finds a notable literary 'occasion' on which Shakespeare might have been provoked to write his Sonnet 111. The 'long and tedious poem', *Microcosmos*, by John Davies of Hereford (whose credentials as the author of *A Lover's Complaint* are discussed below), appears, in the light of Jackson's article, to have 'touched a nerve' with Shakespeare sufficient for a shorter and less tedious poetic reply. An unusual reading of Sonnet 129 forms part of Kit Fryatt's article, 'Shakespeare and Berryman: Sonnet 129 and Dream Song 1' (in Coleman and McGowan, eds., *'After Thirty Falls': New Essays on John Berryman*, pp. 81–6). Following the Jewish hermeneutic tradition of midrash, which emphasizes non-literal interpretations (highlighted by Deborah L. Madsen in her work, *Re-reading Allegory: A Narrative Approach to Genre* [1995]), Fryatt argues that a 'mood of perversion and illogic...and erotic anger' is present in both Shakespeare's sonnet and Berryman's 'Song'. Regula Hohl Trillini's article, 'Tom, Dick and...Jack in the *OED* and in "Sonnet 128"' (*ShJW* 143[2007] 177–9), suggests a fortieth entry in the *OED* for the meaning of the word *jack*, not least on the grounds that it 'completely determines Shakespeare's "Sonnet 128"'. The jack in question is an 'upward-thrusting' wooden object attached to the back of the key-lever of a virginal or harpsichord, and has no little part to play in Shakespeare's lines: 'Do I envy those jacks that nimble leap, | To kiss the tender inward of thy hand' (ll. 5–6). A more substantial article by Alan Sinfield, 'Coming on to Shakespeare: Offstage Action and Sonnet 20' (*Shakespeare* 3:ii[2007] 108–25), offers the reader a new interpretation of the speaker, in Sonnet 20, who 'suddenly [finds it] necessary...to clarify...his relation to the Boy's gender, gender in general and the Boy's penis in particular'. For once, as Sinfield suggests, the 'queer-identified critic' may be considered the 'ideal reader'. He posits an offstage encounter between the speaker and the Boy in which the latter 'has claimed the "active" role' and provoked the former into his hasty clarification.

Lynne Magnusson, in 'A Pragmatics for Interpreting Shakespeare's Sonnets 1–20: Dialogue Scripts and Erasmian Intertexts' (in Fitzmaurice and Taavitsainen, eds., *Methods in Historical Pragmatics*, pp. 167–83), makes a specific case for the interpretation of certain linguistic features within Shakespeare's Sonnets 1–20. In particular, Magnusson plots the *thou/you* shifts in the sonnets relative to a 'dialogue script' that Shakespeare imitates and transforms: Erasmus's *De conscribendis epistolis*, a textbook in use in sixteenth-century English grammar schools. Beatrice Groves reads Shakespeare's sonnets in parallel with the marginalia of the Geneva translation of the Bible, drawing inspiration from their shared readerly character. Groves's article, 'Shakespeare's Sonnets and the Genevan Marginalia' (*EIC* 57:ii[2007] 114–28), turns up such gems as the Genevan annotator's gloss on Psalm 77: God is found culpable for the psalmist's loss of sleep, but the annotator, 'unwilling to blame God for his wakefulness', glosses 'thou Keepest mine eyes waking' and declares that 'his sorrowes were as watchmen'. This adds new meaning to Shakespeare's Sonnet 61: 'It is my love that keeps mine eyes awake' (l. 10). Danijela Kambasković-Sawers, in an essay entitled, ' "Three themes in one, which wondrous scope affords": Ambiguous Speaker and Storytelling in Shakespeare's *Sonnets*' (*Criticism* 49:iii[2007] 285–305), eschews 'the current scholarly debate' on the sonnets' 'Delian' structure (that is present in other works discussed here) in favour of a discussion of certain cohesive aspects of the sonnet sequence, especially the role of ambiguous characterization. This feature, Kambasković-Sawers argues, is central to reader involvement and the 'perception of [Shakespeare's] sequence as an integral work'. Sasha Roberts's essay, 'Shakespeare's *Sonnets* and English Sonnet Sequences' (in Cheny, Hadfield and Sullivan, eds., *Early Modern English Poetry: A Critical Companion*, pp. 172–83), is the first of three on Shakespeare's poetry from this collection. Roberts places Shakespeare's sequence 'against' the sonnet tradition in terms of his 'sonnet mistress', who is 'notoriously attainable', and in terms of the 'unconventional' relationship of the male speaker and the male beloved, before anatomizing the sonnets' wit and their relationship with 'the last English sonnet sequence to be published in the Elizabethan-Jacobean period', Mary Wroth's *Pamphilia to Amphilanthus*. In the Ashgate collection, *Shakespeare and Historical Formalism*, edited by Stephen Cohen, R.L. Kesler, in 'Formalism and the Problem of History: Sonnets, Sequence, and the Relativity of Linear Time' (pp. 177–93), otherwise concerned with history, formalism and the English poetic form in general, describes Shakespeare's particular innovations in 'a field crowded with competition'. By extending the limits of the sonnet sequence, however, Shakespeare is, in Kesler's reading, 'hastening its decline' by superseding and 'undermin[ing] the functional credibility of the older form'. In a discussion with a very different methodology from that of Kesler, Patricia Phillippy, 'Procreation, Child-Loss and the Gendering of the Sonnet' (in Chedgzoy, Greenhalgh and Shaughnessy, eds., pp. 96–113), compares the sonnet sequence, the 'Foure Epytaphes', attributed to Anne Cecil de Vere, countess of Oxford, and published in John Soowthern's *Pandora* [1584], with

Shakespeare's 'procreation sonnets'. As memorials to Anne's son, who died in 1583, the 'Foure Epytaphes' 'construct gender as predicated upon procreation and child-loss' and serve as a sequence of notable comparison for Shakespeare's sonnets, that, in Phillippy's terms, construct gender along similar lines.

In another essay from *Early Modern English Poetry: A Critical Companion*, Patrick Cheney draws on his recent larger work, *Shakespeare, National Poet-Playwright* [2004]. In this shorter work, 'Shakespeare's Literary Career and Narrative Poetry' (pp. 160–71), he posits 'a historical model' for Shakespeare's career that has the poet-playwright mapping an 'aesthetic opposition' between the rival career models of Marlowe (following Ovid) and Spenser (following Virgil) onto the erotic, political and religious conflicts of his narrative poems: *Venus and Adonis, The Rape of Lucrece*, and *A Lover's Complaint*. The first of these poems, according to Cheney, provides the outline, the second the development and the third the crystallization of this model. In a series of dense readings, Cheney argues that the erotic, political and religious conflicts the poems interrogate are unified by the poet's preoccupation with 'the Protestant queen's Cult of the Virgin'.

A further essay from *Early Modern English Poetry* discusses 'The Phoenix and the Turtle'. Lynn Enterline, in ' "The Phoenix and the Turtle", Renaissance Elegies, and the Language of Grief' (in Cheney, Hadfield and Sullivan, eds., pp. 147–59), places Shakespeare's poem in the contexts of Renaissance humanist pedagogy, the long history of elegiac forms and the history of grief, including pertinent religious controversies. Enterline concludes that the poem engages with the Erasmian precept which puts words before truth. In doing so, the poem stakes a claim for the poet's skill in 'eternizing' the poem's subjects, before 'turn[ing] the elegy's symbolic labor over to its readers' and inaugurating a new 'proto-secular' form of prayer for the dead.

Judith Luig's article, 'Sonic Youth—Echo and Identity in *Venus and Adonis*' (*Wissenschaftliches Seminar Online* 5[2007] no pagination), is a Lacanian reading of Echo in Shakespeare's poem, in which the author coins the term 'echo stage' as an equivalent to Lacan's mirror stage of psychological development. Shakespeare's Venus, at least before the verses in which Echo is heard, is compared to a child prior to the mirror stage, lacking in a coherent, though alienating, identity; when the goddess 'starts beating her breast and venting her frustration merely with an acoustic element, for the first time in the poem she gets some lasting satisfaction'. The echoing of Venus's moans is, for Luig, the 'echo stage': 'Passion on passion deeply is redoubled' (line 832). Nevertheless, Echo, 'the mythological archetype of scorned female wooers', provides a less than satisfactory metamorphic identity for Venus, a merely imitative poetic voice that also brings the author's vanity of poetic achievement into question. Susan C. Staub, in an essay from a collection she also edits, ' "My throbbing heart shall rock you day and night": Shakespeare's Venus, Elizabeth, and Early Modern Constructions of Motherhood' (in Staub, ed., *The Literary Mother: Essays on Representations of Maternity and Child Care*, pp. 15–32), sees Shakespeare's Venus as a paradoxically constructed, both benevolent and malevolent, mother figure.

Eschewing the modern theories that have been previously employed to examine Venus's 'maternal aspect', Staub shows that the Venus of the poem reflects the early modern 'ambivalent construct of maternity', the threatening combination of maternal nurturance and female authority being complicated by an aggressive erotic desire. For Staub, Venus is a troubling figure, especially when occasionally seen as a ' "refracted" vision of Elizabeth'. The monarch's adoption of the metaphorical role of mother to the nation, to justify her rule and mitigate any perceived threat to male hegemony, is undermined by Shakespeare's construction of an overtly sexualized Venus as sometime mother to Adonis.

Kenji Go had two significant essays on *A Lover's Complaint* published in 2007. The first of these, 'Samuel Daniel's *The Complaint of Rosamond* and an Emblematic Reconsideration of *A Lover's Complaint*' (*SP* 104[2007] 82–122), as well as 'propos[ing] an emblematic reinterpretation of *A Lover's Complaint*', also 'presents a fresh case for its Shakespearean attribution'. Engaging with the recent work of Brian Vickers, Go rejects the charges that the poem contains a 'grotesque episode', is psychologically improbable and bears 'a confused narrative line'. Central to this reappraisal is the seemingly grotesque scene in which the love tokens that the young seducer has acquired from earlier conquests are given to the maid he now pursues. Go places this episode in the context of 'the pervasive religio-cultural influence of Scripture and the emblem in Shakespeare's England', and, in doing so, uncovers its 'covert emblematic significance' and its centrality to the poem's 'intricately wrought [hitherto confused] narrative line'. For Go, the tokens allude to the biblical 'parable of the talents', which suggests one or two significant parallels between *A Lover's Complaint* and Samuel Daniel's *Rosamond* (Daniel being an author to whom Shakespeare is significantly indebted in general), as well as providing a means for rehabilitating the poem's apparent grotesquerie and justifying the maid's psychologically improbable fall. During this reading, Go also finds several correspondences between *A Lover's Complaint* and Shakespeare's other works, including the sonnets (with which it was collected in the quarto of 1609), *Cymbeline*, *Othello* and *Macbeth*, before concluding that this 'quite weighty' evidence substantiates the attribution of the poem to Shakespeare. In ' "Religious Love" and Mocking Echoes of the Book of Common Prayer in *A Lover's Complaint*' (*N&Q* 54[2007] 298–303), Kenji Go continues his insightful critical engagement with *A Lover's Complaint*, this time focusing on the seducer's tale of his seduction of a nun. Here, the critic expands on John Kerrigan's gloss (in Kerrigan ed., *The Sonnets and 'A Lover's Complaint'* [1986, 1995, 1999]) of the seducer's reference to the 'Religious love put out religion's eye' (line 250). Kerrigan notes the 'tasteless quibble . . . Not the *eternal love* of line 238 but secular love that is *Religious* in the sense devoted, committed, assiduous'. Go, in a similar critical move to that achieved in his *SP* essay, also sees the seducer as invoking the biblical epistles of St Paul and St John, 'as read in the Book of Common Prayer', to disguise his profane love as genuinely Christian in origin. Go's reading encompasses the seducer's whole argumentative strategy for concealing the true nature of his love, and, as in his other essay, includes arguments in favour of attributing the poem to Shakespeare. The stylistically 'weak', repeated use of ' 'gainst' in line 271 has led critics to doubt the conventional attribution, but Go persuasively points to Paul's letter (Ephesians 6), in which the saint declares that 'wee wrestle not *against* flesh and blood, but *against* rule, *against* power, *against* worldly rulers', in order to strengthen his argument. Moreover, for Go, an allusion to Ephesians brings to mind *The Comedy of Errors*, a play set in Ephesus that is also profitably read in the light of Scripture, and was, appropriately for Go's purposes, written by Shakespeare.

The same year also saw the publication of a book-length work in which the author argues for John Davies of Hereford's authorship of *A Lover's Complaint*. Brian Vickers's *Shakespeare, A Lover's Complaint, and John Davies of Hereford* is divided into two parts, the first of which, entitled 'Background', is further subdivided into three chapters, dealing sequentially with the life and work of John Davies, the Spenserian nature of the *Complaint* (which, Vickers contends, favours Davies's authorship above that of Shakespeare) and the poetic tradition of 'Female Complaint'. In the chapter on John Davies's life, Vickers does a thorough job of placing what he terms a 'mediocre poet' in the literary and social context of the late Elizabethan and Jacobean periods. Among numerous other instances, Davies appears in the historical record, in 1599, as the calligrapher commissioned by the countess of Pembroke to make a copy of the Sidney Psalms for presentation to Elizabeth, and, in 1609, publishing a volume of poems addressed to Algernon, Lord Percy, to whom he was tutor, and living in the Tower with his pupil's father, Henry (ninth earl of Northumberland), who was imprisoned on suspicion of complicity in the Gunpowder Plot. Vickers's aim is to reconstruct a milieu for Davies that makes the inclusion of a poem by him, 'presumably by mistake', in the same volume as Shakespeare's sonnets less unlikely than it first appears. Davies, Vickers argues, was much more of a Spenserian than Shakespeare, and the chapter on the *Complaint's* Spenserian nature is intended to further the former's claim to authorship. The chapter on the 'Female Complaint' identifies the 'simultaneously moralizing and misogynistic' character of *A Lover's Complaint*, and finding such attitudes absent from Shakespeare's work but pervasive in Davies's, again rules in Davies's favour. The second part of the book, 'Foreground', contains two chapters, one making the case against Shakespeare, the other the case for Davies. The first of these looks in detail at the diction, use of rhetorical figures (and one trope, metaphor), syntax and verse form of the poem. The choices on all these counts are found to differ from Shakespeare's usual preference. The chapter which follows includes a similar exercise, finding a close correspondence with Davies's practice on this occasion. Indeed, Vickers presents a great deal of evidence linking Davies's poetic habits to the text of *A Lover's Complaint*, and, similarly, shows the poem to be outside Shakespeare's favoured method, at least in terms of the chosen parameters. Nevertheless, there remains sufficient room for other scholars, Kenji Go perhaps, focusing on other criteria and other aspects of either author's works, to reach different conclusions. Vickers also includes appendices containing the text of *A Lover's Complaint* and six uncollected examples of poetry attributed to Davies.

A Companion to Shakespeare's Sonnets, edited by Michael Schoenfeldt (discussed in more detail above), also contains two essays that discuss

A Lover's Complaint. Margaret Healy's essay, '"Making the quadrangle round": Alchemy's Protean Forms in Shakespeare's sonnets and *A Lover's Complaint*' (pp. 405–25), connects the sonnets with the *Complaint* through the suggestion that the youth of the latter corresponds with the 'lovely Boy' of the former. Healy highlights the continuation of alchemical language (associated with the analogous characters) from the sonnets into the *Complaint*, and, as such, provides another counterpoint to Vickers's arguments against their common authorship. It must be emphasized, however, that this essay, along with the other essays in this collection, does not engage with Vickers's book directly, probably due to the collection's earlier date of publication. Catherine Bates, in her essay, 'The Enigma of *A Lover's Complaint*' (pp. 426–40), discusses the authorship question, but, less interested in deciding the issue, she investigates what 'nags, troubles, and complains—that piques and irritates' critics about the poem such that they continually return to the question of its status. She ultimately concludes that the answer lies in psychoanalytic theory. More specifically, she draws attention to 'recent developments... which suggest that an originary masochism is constitutive of all human subjectivity', and that 'the poem begins to make sense when it is seen to anticipate recent suggestions that the figure of the seduced girl might, perhaps, be the prototype of all human sexuality, "male" no less than "female"'. This approach allows Bates to draw an illustrative parallel between the *Complaint* and another early modern text: Sir Philip Sidney's *New Arcadia*. In Bates's reading of Sidney's romance, more specifically the story of Dido and Pamphilus from Book II, 'a group of women are driven to erotic frenzy by a callous youth who manipulates them in exactly the same way as the youth of the complaint: in "the stirring of our own passions"'. Sidney's women (and by extension, the women of the *Complaint*), despite being fully aware of the youth's duplicity, 'enter [masochistically] with full gusto and enthusiasm into the spirit of the game'.

In an essay, 'The Rape of Clarissa and *The Rape of Lucrece*: The Performance of Exemplarity and the Tragedy of Literary Allusion from Dramatic Poem to Dramatic Narrative' (*Textus* 20:iii[2007] 581–602), which elucidates Samuel Richardson's debt to Shakespeare's *The Rape of Lucrece* in his novel *Clarissa*, Sylvia Greenup reinforces the earlier criticism of Katharine Eisaman Maus on Shakespeare's dramatic poem. Greenup sees Richardson drawing on the misogyny and brutality revealed, by Shakespeare, at the heart of courtly love poetry for his representation of the rape of Clarissa. In what in places amounts to a parallel reading of both texts, Greenup contributes to the study of Shakespeare's literary reception as well as to the study of the history of the novel.

(e) Histories

A.D. Nuttall's *Shakespeare the Thinker* is a book for when you think you are bored with Shakespeare: beautifully written, ranging widely across the canon, intelligent and alert. The early histories are read for themselves ('the closer one comes to the human material, the more it shimmers') and proleptically, as part of defining the 'Shakespearian' (or proto-Shakespearian). There are vividly mediated engagements with scenic architecture and artistry—the 'astonishing thing' of the rose scene in *1 Henry VI*, the 'unexpectedly believable' scene between Anne and her husband's killer at the opening of *Richard III*, from which the 'abrupt movements of Richard's mind, oscillating between smart denial and horror' in his despair before Bosworth 'derive, with a coherence that is frightening'. The chapter on the major histories includes an assessment of Richard II as 'a man with ideals but no convictions, a walking congeries of images, poses, pretences, who, because he is intelligent, ironically perceives what is afoot, but from the side, in narrative profile. This contemplative observer is really at the heart of the action, is its sacrificial victim.' Nuttall contrasts Richard's 'high-fantastical' player-king with the 'great study of *invisible acting*' in the Henriad. In Hal/Henry V, Shakespeare moves away from the notion of historical causation as a 'nexus of relations' dissolving 'central agency' towards this distinctive personality as '*central*, unified cause'. However, this unification is never either complete or secure; Nuttall's blow-by-blow account of the Williams episodes draws out the ways in which even Henry's acting can go wrong. The major histories are much-worked-over territory, and Nuttall's work here contains few surprises; you should read it not for decisive interventions in individual debates but because, like the best monographs of recent years on the histories (Holderness, Grady, Goy-Blanquet), it combines fascinating close reading of individual scenes with an original synoptic overview.

The most substantial full-length work this year on the histories is Catherine Grace Canino's monograph *Shakespeare and the Nobility*, which begins from the insight that 'virtually every English character in the plays is the ancestor of descendants living in Shakespeare's time', whether directly or through conferred title. This is not simply a matter of avoiding upsetting the powerful, à la Oldcastle affair; Canino points out that the family histories of the powerful potentially offered a challenge to the top-down Tudor myth of the chronicle, both in their alternative perspective on winners and losers and their refusal of the reign as the building block of history. So in providing not merely regnal but family histories in the first tetralogy, Shakespeare was entering sensitive territory requiring attention to both chronicle 'source' and contemporary social rankings. Canino argues that he 'consistently modified and revised the portrayal of . . . ancestors with the status of their descendants in mind . . . deliberately and carefully [creating] individuals who, in some way, reflected the position or activities of their Elizabethan descendants'. There then follow chapters on the Staffords, the dukes of Suffolk, the Nevilles, the Talbots, the Cliffords, the Stanleys and 'the gentry' (via Lord Saye). The chapters offer detailed cameos of the relevant Elizabethans, as well as considering a variety of chronicle and other portrayals of the families; Canino's typical approach is to look at the changes Shakespeare made to his sources and investigate a possible relation—not always approbatory—to the contemporary bearers of the name. However, though the parallels explored are frequently fascinating, and persuasive with regard to Shakespeare's compositional processes, the conclusions are frustratingly limited to Shakespeare personally, so that the positive representation of the Stanleys 'may well have been Shakespeare's acknowledgement of sympathy for the Stanley family', for example. Shakespeare may well, to an extent under-appreciated heretofore, 'use the plays to comment on the status and activities of descendants', but the status of that comment itself awaits another investigation.

Lorna Hutson's wide-ranging *The Invention of Suspicion: Law and Mimesis in Shakespeare and Renaissance Drama* proposes a relationship between 'popular legal culture' and popular dramaturgy. Quintilian's and Cicero's rhetoric addresses not simply arguments, but judicial (or forensic) ones; Hutson argues that legal rhetoric's concern with probabilities and likelihoods was incorporated into late sixteenth-century developments in dramaturgy. In particular, Shakespeare's 1590s plays incorporate a sense of speeches as 'attempts to prove a set of dubious "facts", or to test one's suspicions about the motives of others', consequently allowing an audience, via inference, to imagine what they cannot see, and thus promoting a drama of 'inwardness'. This is especially true of histories, which refer not merely 'offstage', but 'back' to events of previous plays. Hutson demonstrates this by comparing *2 Henry IV* with its source-play, the Queen's men's *Famous Victories of Henry V*, noting that the former play involves 'less action as such than a series of diagnoses, or conjectures' involving inferences about the minds of those who in their various ways are pursuing power. This in turn leaves us in the place of Hal, the arch-anticipator and suspector, so that 'we are complicit in the process that produces his friends as "shallow", easily-sounded'.

Hutson then turns to *The Contention*, a play which features more than one investigative 'case', with Eleanor's magic forming part of the case against Duke Humphrey, as does the Simpcox episode; Humphrey's death in turn links to Cade's 'legal carnival' (Craig Bernthal's phrase) which parodies the corrupt forensic strategies of legal procedures on display earlier in the play. The first half of the play, in fact, is a sequence of 'cynical manipulations of judicial procedure', interrupted by the 'popular forensic activity' initiated by Humphrey's death, after which the commons are themselves constructed as 'an audience capable of judging', and rumour is turned into 'a forensic scenario'. As these are Hutson's last words in the chapter, it seems that this positive construction of the commons survives the Cade scenes themselves. There is significant overlap between this material and Hutson's chapter 'Noises Off: Participatory Justice in *2 Henry VI*' (in Jordan and Cunningham, eds.).

Oliver Arnold considers the representation of parliament in the first tetralogy in *The Third Citizen: Shakespeare's Theater and the Early Modern House of Commons*. Three parliaments are crucial: in London at *1 Henry VI* III.i, Henry restores Richard Plantagenet's lands and titles; again in London (in *3 Henry VI*), he bars Edward Plantagenet from the succession; and at Bury St Edmunds in *2 Henry VI* ('the king's Waterloo') he allows the arrest of Duke Humphrey by Suffolk before allowing the parliament to continue without him. Arnold argues that in doing so Henry (a 'serial abdicator') transforms himself into a commoner, satisfactorily present through his representatives, by splitting the king's two bodies. For Tudor constitutionalists, as (perhaps) to commonsensical laymen, this assumption could not work. Jack Cade's claim that his mouth shall be the parliament, just a few scenes later, ironically reunites the body politic and body natural Henry had sought to sunder (and in terms used by both Wat Tyler and Richard II in his tyrannical phase).

This in turn confirms Cade's ambition to himself become king, as his 'Ricardian usurpation of Parliament simultaneously conjures up both the tyranny of absolute monarchism and of absolute representation'. Arnold is more positive about Salisbury's representation of the national mood over Suffolk—though he notes that Shakespeare elides the role of the House of Commons in pursuing him—but also points out that the question of representation never comes up regarding Cade, because he rests 'entirely and openly on the people's support' rather than ventriloquizing their concerns, practising a 'politics of total presence'.

Simon Barker's wide-ranging and lucid study of *War and Nation in the Theatre of Shakespeare and his Contemporaries* includes a chapter on Shakespeare's histories as a 'kind of compendium of conflict'. Even the many guises of Richard III are bookended by those famous opening words—for Barker the classic theatrical articulation of masculine militarism's position on the decadence of peace—and Richard's final reinscription as a soldier on the battlefield. The militarism Richard embodies—at these moments, at least—had, in theory been swept aside by the eirenic Tudors, making its links to contemporary advocates of 'English remilitarization' all the more unsettling. Richard's pre-Bosworth speech ticks many of the boxes recommended by conservative military theorists—contrasting the Breton 'vagabonds' in Richmond's army with the 'yeomen' in Richard's, like Richmond appealing to God and St George, informal and colloquial.

More straightforward critiques of militarism are found elsewhere in the histories. Barker points out that the doubled father/son scene in *3 Henry VI* ends with the dead son returning to the private sphere, with the obsequies—winding sheet, sepulchre, funeral bell—provided by the father; there is no formulaic tragic public remembrance to gloss over wasteful death. *Richard II* too critiques militarism's 'waning chivalric code'. *King John* provides an 'excessive display of war's moral ambiguity and susceptibility to fortune'. Hal leaves 'civilian life' when he returns to his father's court, and Henry's later Harfleur rhetoric (invented, as the killing of the French prisoners at Agincourt was not, by Shakespeare) shows the distance between military conflict and civilian ethics.

Michael Harrawood, in 'High-Stomached Lords: Imagination, Force and the Body in Shakespeare's *Henry VI* Plays' (*JEMCS* 7:i[2007] 79–95), begins from the five uses of the word in *1* and *2 Henry VI* by the mayor of London, Henry (twice), Talbot and Cade to consider 'digestion and alimentation'. The stomach was not only seen as the body's 'cook' (in its relation to food), assimilating the world into itself, but as jockeying for primacy amongst the other organs, drawing food to itself. So 'high stomachs' seek, as it were, to draw others into them. There is a lot about early modern digestive theory in this piece, and it does successfully demonstrate that, as Empson would have it, 'stomach' is a complex word.

Jean Howard's 'Stage Masculinities, National History, and the Making of London Theatrical Culture' (in Orlin and Johnson-Haddad, eds., pp. 199–214) sees the early histories as in a sense workshop pieces, during the course of which Shakespeare was learning 'how to create compelling and diverse stage masculinities'. The 'problem' was exacerbated, Howard reminds us, by the very high number of men in them (*3 Henry VI* has forty-two men and three women). Henry VI is the 'foil' for a variety of opposing masculinities, including the 'warrior hero' Talbot. Suffolk in *2 Henry VI* represents the 'masculinity of modernity', here cast as mastery of Castiglione's arts of the courtier. Cade's 'artisanal physical vigor' distinguishes him from both, and Richard is 'the medieval vice refashioned to encompass the skills and glamour of the modern tragedian'. In the same volume, Raphael Falco provides a fascinating and persuasive account of 'Charisma and Institution-Building in Shakespeare's Second Tetralogy' (pp. 215–37). Falco's central point is that the *Henry IV* plays show the failure of personal charismatic authority to build or sustain institutions, or indeed social order. However, he also proposes *Henry V* as a 'proof text' of those revisions of the original Weberian charismatic hypothesis, taking it away from its focus on the founding 'missionary moment' into a vision of 'normal' charisma as 'attenuated and dispersed'. Falco argues, challenging David Scott Kastan in *Shakespeare After Theory*, against the comic flexibility/charismatic kingship binary many critics see behind the subversiveness of Falstaff. In fact, the still overlapping elements of charisma (personal/lineage/office) deny the notion, which Falstaff's prominence in many accounts demands, of Henry V's kingship as 'a petrified set of charismatic symbols'.

Mary Polito, on the other hand, begins not from Weber but from the use of Shakespeare by a variety of business 'self-fashioning' handbooks, in ' "Warriors for the working day": Shakespeare's Professionals' (*Shakespeare* 2:i[2006] 1–23). She proposes that this is not appropriation so much as recognition: Henry V *is* 'a liberal subject and a pastoral governor who is learning to perform his profession as he works to teach others to do so as well'. Polito compares a modern 'Shakespeare self-help' book with Elyot's *Governor* as 'catalogues of secular virtue', and proposes the readers of the former as 'liberal descendants' (immune to irony, it seems) of the readers of the latter; Falstaff, of course, resists both productivity (through pastoral self-government) and professionalism of any kind, preferring to labour in his vocation. Ewan Fernie, too, addresses, as does Polito, the 'uses' of *Henry V*, here specifically in regard to contemporary military self-fashioning, in 'Action! *Henry V*' (in Grady and Hawkes, eds., pp. 96–120). Hal's 'I know you all' speech is a specimen of 'fiercely concentrated agency', opposing a 'nonchalantly incorruptible, absolute will' against (our) consciousness of identity as historically/culturally determined. What this 'fierce agency' means for others is not worked out on the battlefield; rather, it is in Falstaff's 'suffering' and death that heroic agency's characteristic of severing itself from 'unnecessary' relationships is anatomized. Henry's wooing of Katherine, though it has plenty of improvisational brio, is 'a form of instrumental action rather than exploratory, self-extending play'. There isn't much 'action' in the play, though; Fernie notes that *Henry V* tends to 'freeze the horrible flux of war into strangely still, heightened images' rather than descriptions (still less, representations) of actual violence. Action itself, Fernie argues, does not signify; only when shaped by the 'muse of fire' does it, as it were, 'find the name' of action. But Henry's agency still holds because it stands, in concentrated form, for 'the sovereign human subject's desire and power to act'. John S Mebane's ' "Impious war"': Religion and the Ideology of Warfare in *Henry V* (*SP*[2007] 250–66) sees the play as working to undercut the cultural work of 'making warfare acceptable to Christians' (by which he means New Testament-focused Christians). Shakespeare does this by ironically deflating patriotic rhetoric, providing in the Chorus and other characters a comic parody of chauvinism, and by juxtaposing pro-war statements with antithetical biblical/theological allusions. Where this leaves nationalism, however, is unclear, and Mebane doesn't engage with Norman Rabkin's 'duck/rabbit' reading of the play in order to demonstrate how such deflation, parody and juxtaposition would neutralize those other elements of the play Rabkin, and many others, have seen as working against this.

Steve Sohmer's *Shakespeare for the Wiser Sort* ingeniously proposes a variety of 'esoteric' allusions in the plays. These include 'tributes' to William Brooke in *Henry V* and Henry Carey in *King John*. The Brooke 'allusion' seems to me to be weak; its strongest point is that both Brooke and Falstaff died at the same time during the night, and that the description of Falstaff's death appears in Shakespeare's play at the point at which a marginal note alluding to Oldcastle (Brooke's ancestor) appears in Holinshed. This allusion was made for a 'coterie' consisting of those present at, or with exact knowledge of, Brooke's death. Sohmer suggests that *King John* was written in 1596 to commemorate the death of Henry Carey, but the 'minute details' and 'barely detectable nods' again seem slight. Sohmer traces the name of Lady Falconbridge's companion 'Gurney' to 'the Normandy, the ancestral home of the Careys'; Prince Henry's reference to a cygnet mourning a swan is a reference to Carey's son mourning his father (whose crest was a swan). If these are problems, they are scarcely susceptible to only one interpretation, as Sohmer acknowledges. More interesting is his demonstration that Constance's lament, at the start of Act III, is placed on a solstice day, when 'the glorious sun | Stays in his course'; and the Magna Carta was signed on the longest day of 1215—15 June. Constance's anger, then, is a buried allusion to the Magna Carta. Given the inexhaustibility of Shakespeare's language, it would be foolish to dismiss out of hand Sohmer's work, but his picture of a Shakespeare writing for the 'wiser sort' depends on a repressive and detailed censorship regime which would be unrecognizable to those acquainted with the recent work of Clegg or Dutton on the topic. The persuasiveness of Sohmer's points depends to a large extent upon the persuasiveness of the contexts he produces for them, and the book does not present compelling evidence that such coteries existed—in other words, just because it's 'barely detectable' doesn't mean that it's a 'nod'.

Rebecca Lemon reads *Richard II* alongside Persons's and Hayward's representations of that king in *Treason by Words: Literature, Law, and Rebellion in Shakespeare's England*. Richard in Shakespeare's play, Lemon argues, functions as a kind of ham-fisted Hal, producing, and (crucially) exonerating, the opposition which will actually topple him; he has a 'perverse productivity in generating traitors'. This agency means that 'sanctified' readings of Richard's position as monarch never really take hold. Though the play argues against both tyranny and armed resistance, giving us both a culpable tyrant and a martyred anointed king, Lemon sees it as coherent rather than fractured, a 'meditation on rulership itself'; the alternative, she implies, is a polemic along the lines of Persons's *Conference* which polemically misreads multivalent chronicle accounts in the service of a definite political thesis on deposition. The play's complex shifting of sympathies is closely delineated, and Lemon's exploration of the role of York as (further) distraction from Bolingbroke, even as he achieves power, shows that this switching between positions continues right up to the play's end. Robert M Schuler's 'Holy Dying in *Richard II*' (*Ren&R* 30:iii[2006/7] 51–88) continues his engagement with the 'demonically inflected' elements in the play begun in his 2005 *Exemplaria* article. I still find his insistence on the specifically demonic nature of inversion in the play unconvincing—for example, that Richard's 'sacrilegious' oath-giving and his 'blasphemous' reversal of the prayer for the dying 'exemplify the demonic politics of his upside-down world', that his pride is 'Luciferan', and so on. As with the earlier article, along with the broad-brush reading of intellectual and cultural history which enables such confident generalizations about the place of the 'demonic' in the world, there is some subtle and perceptive close reading, particularly of Richard's progress towards a truly 'holy dying'.

Charlotte Scott finds in *Richard II* Shakespeare's most complicated 'idea of the book' in her monograph on *Shakespeare and the Idea of the Book*. At the heart of Richard's reign is 'the book of heaven', which he 'harnesses . . . to his body'. Scott insists that 'Richard's rather nebulous identification with the book becomes central to how he isolates and represents his own narrative of meaning', as 'Richard projects himself on to the idea of the book'. Thankfully, the chapter then moves into the far less nebulous territory of a sequential consideration of the play's direct and indirect deployments of the book as both metaphor and object, initially by Mowbray ('the book of life') and Gaunt ('inky blots and rotten parchment bonds'). Richard's focus on substance and shadow, word and image, Scott argues, has as its basis the ineffable truth of the 'heavenly ledger' (Scott's phrase) to which he later explicitly refers. But the book was a particularly charged Reformation symbol, and Scott interestingly teases out the ways in which Richard's 'book' partakes of both a pre-Reformation 'celebrating and defending the divine right of kings' and a post-Reformation 'inward and protective faith' with a particular relationship to subjectivity, contextualizing the image of the book using a variety of religious writings. Richard eventually claims he is his own book, 'where all my sins are writ', calling for a glass in which to read himself (and the audience can see neither Richard's heavenly book nor his reflection). The self-deposed king's shattering of the mirror divorces symbolic from bodily self. Scott gives us close reading of a particularly intense kind, moving between literal reference to books and the larger semantic fields of making meanings of which the book is part, and a fresh approach to the worked-over topic of the king's several 'bodies'. Philip Lorenz also approaches the nature of Richard's sovereignty in ' "Christal mirrors": Analogy and Onto-Theology in Shakespeare and Francisco Suarez' (*R&L* 38:iii[2006] 101–19). Both Suarez and Shakespeare prefigure a new ontology of sovereignty; in Shakespeare's play this is especially noted in the Queen's tears in II.ii, and Richard's destruction of the mirror which 'marks the end of a world order built on analogical correspondence'.

The historical claims in the article are based on a broad-brush approach to intellectual history; whether this 'ontology' is new or not, and whether a few key moments in Shakespeare's play can be said to mark it, needs more argument for this reader.

Sandra Logan spends a lot of time in her *Texts/Events in Early Modern England* on various representations of the reign of Richard II. Her perspective on Shakespeare's play is thus informed by its differences from and similarities to other accounts. For example, Shakespeare's vision of Richard's 'unnatural' relationship differs from *Woodstock*'s—which is predicated on Richard's 'foreignness'—in its use of a variety of maternal imagery (including some from Richard). Logan does tend towards descriptive-assertive writing, and though her account of the play is coherent it does not appear to offer anything new on such topics as Richard's loss of monarchical authority (his dismissal of the law has destabilized society), his unsuitability as a moral model (which Logan says was the 'usual perception' of the monarch), or the function of the garden scene (which again inverts the 'traditional assumption' of Richard's level of society being seen as a moral model, with the formality of their speech ensuring any social inversion is mitigated).

Ava Zilberfain's chapter on *Richard II* in *Stealing the Story: Shakespeare's Self-Conscious Use of the Mimetic Tradition in the Plays* is also predominantly descriptive-assertive, and appears to come from a parallel universe in which it is the first critical attempt to engage with the play. It is entirely ignorant of critical work (referencing only one book article and one book chapter, both from two decades ago), and thus devotes a great deal of energy to arriving at a station most people will have started from. While it could function adequately as an introduction to the play, its usefulness even here is vitiated by its lack of critical sophistication and sometimes clunking style ('Against history, Shakespeare's tragic depiction of structural demolition speaks volumes for revision over deconstruction', p. 74). In similar vein, Kristin Smith's 'Martial Maids and Murdering Mothers: Women, Witchcraft, and Motherly Transgression in *Henry VI* and *Richard III*' (*Shakespeare* 3:ii[2007] 143–60) discusses the representation of 'corrupt femininity' in Joan and Margaret, and the redeeming masculinity of Richmond, without once mentioning Rackin and Howard's great book on the histories—indeed it is not even in her bibliography. For those of us who have read this groundbreaking work (published now more than a decade ago) Smith's reinvention of the wheel has nothing to offer.

Beatrice Groves's *Texts and Traditions: Religion in Shakespeare 1592–1604* includes, as well as a slightly revised version of the piece on Hal and the Harrowing of Hell published in *Shakespeare Survey* in 2004, a chapter on religious imagery and succession in *King John*. Her central point is, *pace* those insisting on John's status as proto-Protestant assassinee, that Arthur, not John, is the 'locus of holiness' in the play, the subject of a 'relocation of religious imagery from the king to the child'. This is not because Shakespeare challenges the conventional linkage between divinity and royalty, but because John has, effectively, lost his royalty. In earlier representations such as Foxe's or Bale's, John's death had taken on sacrificial, Christlike, aspects, which in Shakespeare's play are transferred to Arthur. This realignment of sacredness with powerlessness is in itself a critique of conventional royal panegyric. Groves shows how Shakespeare reshaped the characters inherited from *The Troublesome Reign* to bulk out Arthur's importance relative to John (for example, by his focus on Constance), and carefully delineates the typological resonances (principally to Isaac, and therefore to Christ) of Arthur's victim status, particularly in his 'near-blinding' scene with Hubert. Groves writes clearly and persuasively, and her comparative method helps bring these aspects of Shakespeare's play more clearly into view.

Ken Jackson covers similar ground in '"Is it God or the sovereign exception?": Giorgio Agamben's *Homo Sacer* and Shakespeare's King John' (*R&L* 38:iii[2006] 85–100). Jackson begins from the contemporary Italian philosopher's exploration of *Homo Sacer*, the sacred man; counter-intuitively, this designation is legal rather than religious, referring to a figure who may be killed outside the law with impunity but whom human and religious law cannot touch, 'a form of bare life . . . exposed to the violent force of sovereign power outside both human and religious law' (and hence analogous to the modern 'refugee'). Arthur's actual death (as opposed to the much more obviously sacrificial 'persuasion' scene before it) is a 'thwarted or failed sacrifice', visible only to the audience, and thus 'outside the particular juridical-political world order of the play', which inscribes him as *Homo Sacer*. Agamben's analysis of sovereignty suggests a trans-historical grounding for it in acts of structural exclusion and inclusion, linking the Greeks, early modern/medieval 'sacred' kingship, and the present day, and Jackson's article concludes with the suggestion that this aspect of Shakespeare's play suggests to us 'our disturbingly and apparently timeless political situation'. Joseph Campana's 'Killing Shakespeare's Children: The Cases of *Richard III* and *King John*' (*Shakespeare* 3:i[2007] 18–39) is much more sceptical about Arthur, and about critics, arguing that a 'pervasive sentimentality' covers up 'complex and often discomfiting erotic and emotional investments in childhood innocence'. Campana doesn't attend to the religious/sacrificial reading noted above, seeing Arthur's impact as due to adult fantasies about childhood (he is a child, not a child-king, for Campana). John's suborning of Hubert is an 'erotic pact'; Arthur 'seduces him away from his intent' into an 'erotic compact' based on the 'magnetism associated with physical care'. Arthur is subject, rather than object, in this process; however, Constance's speeches grieving for him show perverse and unmanageable affect, revealing more about her than him, and spreading to other characters via 'affective contagion'. *Richard III*, on the other hand, while it too displays the unmanageability of affect in respect of children, counterweights it with Richard's utter detachment from the 'childish foolish'.

Anny Crunelle-Vanrigh writes on '*Henry V* as a Royal Entry' (*SEL* 47[2007] 355–77). She is committed to an evolutionary model of the drama, and therefore is puzzled by Shakespeare's use of an 'outdated dramatic form' like the chorus in an 'otherwise groundbreaking play'. She rescues the bard from this by proposing that the choruses 'originate' in the non-dramatic form of the royal entry (oddly, choosing a very old royal entry—Elizabeth's into London in 1558/9—as her example of the presumably non-outdated alternative origin, to which she traces several features of the play). If the play is a royal entry, then the choruses, structurally, are 'the textual equivalent of a triumphal arch', and the presence of so many national voices/accents mimics the allegorical figures of a royal entry. She then goes on to consider the ways in which the play contains 'antipageantry' (in a phrase which makes perfect sense but has a wonderfully surreal quality, 'the plot has its own ducks to marshal against the rabbits that the Chorus and the king so deftly conjure out of their hats'), but the 'royal entry' trope commits her to a fairly swift dismissal of it. I find the parallels between *Henry V* and Elizabeth's entry (a recently republished account of which would have been available to Shakespeare) to be rather weak, and can't see how a royal entry from the 1550s is an adequate model for Shakespeare when a play from the 1580s using a chorus isn't. Nonetheless, this new perspective does allow some interesting interpretations of scenes, and offers an addition to the many Foucauldian readings of the play.

Literary critics may consider themselves close readers, but they have nothing on stylisticians. Two extremely interesting books devoted themselves more or less to Shakespeare's use of one kind of word—Beatrix Busse's massive *Vocative Constructions in the Language of Shakespeare* and Penelope Freedman's *Power and Passion in Shakespeare's Pronouns: Interrogating 'You' and 'Thou'*. Freedman's is the easier read, Busse's the more profound in coverage, but both books offer extremely detailed narratives of shifting usage within and between scenes and characters—the shift between 'thou' and 'you', for example, requires a sophisticated sense of which of the many different usages of both is being brought into play. Busse's focus on vocatives extends this analysis to all sorts of ways of addressing others. I found the level of detail, particularly in Busse's work, astounding, and there is plenty in both books to stimulate Shakespearians for some time to come.

The representation of commoners in *2 Henry VI* continues to attract a great deal of attention. William Leahy focuses on the constant threat (and frequent use) of violence against commoners in ' "For pure need": Violence, Terror and the Common People in *Henry VI, Part 2*' (*ShJE* 143[2007] 71–83). However, Leahy's analysis is not particularly original ('it is possible that many [of the audience] would have found Cade a sympathetic character to some extent'), features some circular reasoning ('he is violent, angry and forceful as well as being articulate, rational and charismatic, because this would, in all probability, represent a believable character to Shakespeare's audience'), and is based on some rather sweeping statements about what all previous criticism has missed. Maya Mathur writes on the Cade scenes in a more nuanced fashion in 'An Attack of the Clowns: Comedy, Vagrancy, and the Elizabethan History Play' (*JEMCS* 7:i[2007] 33–54. Mathur finds in scenes of commons rebellion 'strategic jesting' seeking to blur social borders, and that unmasking the roguish protestors' imposture simply confirms them as 'victims of economic inequality'. Unlike many writers on the scenes, Mathur sees Cade's linkage between the articulation of dearth and comedy as destabilizing neo-classic didactic theories on the laughable rather than undermining his 'social criticism' function. She points out that Iden kills Cade for trespass rather than for his political actions (he does not know who Cade is until he is dead). Simon C Estok's 'Theory from the Fringes: Animals, Ecocriticism, Shakespeare' (*Mosaic* 40:i[2007] 61–78) claims the play 'participates in and subverts a popular radical vegetarian environmentalist ethic and offers "the garden" as part of a continuum of social control', but also offers the familiar line that once Cade turns up we are left with the contained comic and carnivalesque. To call Cade vegetarian is stretching it a bit, though it does enable Estok's interesting contrast between Cade's end and the butchery metaphors (and stagings) earlier in the scenes; the notion of Cade's death as a kind of pruning is also thought-provoking. Nina Levine's 'Citizens' Games: Differentiating Collaboration in *Sir Thomas More*' (*SQ* 58[2007] 31–64) stresses that the early scenes of the play offer an 'individuated commonality' engaged in the 'shared labour of protest'; this sense of 'horizontal' commonality is the basis for More's successful appeal to their sympathies for the 'strangers' case', though only once the vertical link to the monarch (hence, nation) has been removed by 'banishment'. But, Levine points out, this commonality has a deeply compromised past.

Stephen Dickey teases out the meanings of a variety of props in 'The Crown and the Pillow: Royal Properties in *Henry IV*' (*ShS* 60[2007] 102–17). These include Falstaff's cushion-crown (nicely topsy-turvy, not least because the crown is usually placed on a cushion), his sceptre/dagger (the violence Henry IV must rely on to rule), and his throne/tavern chair. Crown and pillow, crown and mock-crown, reappear in Act IV of *2 Henry IV*; though Hal's choice is long since made, 'the moment registers that action as the ghost of a chance, the road not taken'. Hal's taking the crown, though, bequeaths his father the pillow—fittingly, in a sense, as Henry is, according to Dickey, one of 'the parade of false or surrogate kings to be purged on behalf of Henry V'. The actor playing Falstaff, like the cushion, is stuffed. Dickey's fascinating article also brings to bear a sensitivity to the structural parallels, particularly around crowning, within the play. Frances K. Barasch (in Marrapodi, ed., *Italian Culture in the Drama of Shakespeare and his Contemporaries: Rewriting, Remaking, Refashioning*) begins from Quickly's 'harlotry players' to suggest the influence of the harlequin and other elements of *commedia all'improvviso*. Falstaff himself recalls *commedia*'s Capitano, and his 'play extempore' resonates with one of the stock scenes collected in Flaminio Scala's early seventeenth-century *Scenarios*; harlequin's links to the devil also echo with the 'white bearded Satan'. Ellen Caldwell, in a scholarly and careful analysis, '"Banish all the wor(l)d": Falstaff's Iconoclastic Threat to Kingship in *1 Henry IV*' (*Renascence* 59:iv[2007] 219–45), proposes Falstaff's subversiveness as a proto-Protestant distrust of and scorn for ceremony and image, offering 'Reformationist commentary' rather than carnivalesque subversion. Princely power is 'representational, iconic, and false', and here the state is the 'false religion' targeted by reformers. Others have seen Falstaff as a satirical attack on Puritanism; Caldwell, while not directly engaging with this argument, offers a range of quotations from Reformation figures to show the (proto-)orthodoxy of Falstaff's position. Jessika Wichner's 'The Flying Falstaff' (*Folio* 14:i[2007] 37–43) attempts to understand one M. Prosser's peculiar eighteenth-century project to construct a giant balloon in the shape of Falstaff. The only evidence for this project is the 1785 call for subscriptions, complete with illustration, and Wichner thinks this means the project did not come off. She goes on to explore the ways in which the character of Falstaff is balloon-like (hot air and the like) before pointing to the ways in which the union flag wielded by the balloon-buffoon blurs the boundary between Falstaff and John Bull.

Joel Elliott Slotkin proposes a new approach to *Richard III* in 'Honeyed Toads: Sinister Aesthetics in Shakespeare's *Richard III*' (*JEMCS* 7:i[2007] 5–32). Audience identification with the evil Richard is enabled by a 'sinister aesthetics' rather than the character's deceptiveness or, indeed, a moral flaw in themselves. Seeking to avoid this demonization/pathologization of audience response, Slotkin proposes a poetics of malevolent theatricality and deformity to explain characters who see Richard's evil 'yielding' to him anyway (and, therefore, an audience doing the same thing). Much of the article provides close readings of the 'seduction' of Anne as emblematic of the whole process. This relies on the 'ironic effect' of 'the spectacle of a villain who has mesmerized his victim so completely that he can provide her with the means to defeat him, and urge her to do so, knowing that she will not listen'. However, Slotkin seems to contradict this at a later point when he grants Anne much more agency, claiming that Anne's 'erotic attraction' to Richard is generated by 'the dark, ironic beauty of Richard's carefully constructed self-presentation as a creature of deceptive malevolence'. Slotkin claims that the entire political realm follows Anne's example, and that though Richard is destroyed, the play 'makes no serious attempt to repress or refute the sinister poetics that make Richard such a powerful figure in the first place, allowing them to persist beyond his death'. It's a bold claim, and certainly enables a fresh look at the play, but the focus on seduction and (erotic) attractiveness does seriously underplay the operations of political power within the play for this reader; the focus on Richard 'in quest to have' underplays 'this hell' the nation soon finds itself in. Murray Levith, in *Shakespeare's Cues and Prompts*, suggests that monstrosity of Richard allows the play to draw on the 'St George and the dragon' myth for its closure.

Christopher J. Cobb's *The Staging of Romance in Late Shakespeare: Text and Theatrical Technique* includes some short considerations of *Henry VIII*. The opening scenes in this and other late plays (*The Tempest*, *Two Noble Kinsmen*) do not introduce the story, and thus are more likely to be seen (and ironized) as theatrical spectacle. The Field of the Cloth of Gold evokes romance only to bring it swiftly into contact with a suffering with which it has no transformative relationship. Spectacle in this play is the grounds for Cobb's claim that it, along with *Two Noble Kinsmen*, is Shakespeare's 'least dramatic but most theatrical' play. The coronation scene has a set-up and postscript which discourage an audience from seeing it as a romance plot climax; however, it functions to 'order the realm' via a kind of gift-exchange between citizens and royalty, and the display of nobility around the monarch. This disjunction between the function of the coronation within the play world, and as a plot element within the play itself, is 'a test of romance ... for which the play provides no answer key'.

Finally, to student-focused work and reprints. Warren Chernaik's *The Cambridge Introduction to Shakespeare's History Plays* is a clear survey of all the Folio histories. Those new to the histories will find it contains plenty of useful narrative; though it does not dwell overmuch on particular critical approaches, it is imbued with a sure sense of what critics have found to talk about over the years. Jonathan Baldo's 'Forgetting Elizabeth in *Henry VIII*' (in Hageman and Conway, eds., *Resurrecting Elizabeth I in Seventeenth-Century England*) is a shorter version of his 2004 *ELR* essay on the play, placing it as part of a patron-sensitive attempt to manage the memory of Elizabeth and other Reformation figures. Kevin Ewert's volume in the student-focused Shakespeare Handbooks series on *Henry V, A Guide to the Text and its Theatrical Afterlife*, does several jobs very well, offering commentary on the play itself, an introduction to key modern productions and films, and a guide to contemporary critical thinking and Shakespeare's own theatrical and cultural contexts. Ewert is particularly interesting on performance, and his lucid and stimulating prose manages to be both accessible and challenging.

(f) Tragedies

The year 2007 has been an active one in Shakespeare scholarship. Writers on Shakespearian tragedy continue to develop old and explore new avenues to the dramatic texts. It is not only the 'great' tragedies that attract scholarly attention. Several impressive analyses deal with texts that earlier received little attention, such as *Titus Andronicus* and *Coriolanus*. The increased interest spurred by the RSC's devotion to the complete works of Shakespeare, both theatrically and editorially, may have increased the focus on texts that naturally include the tragedies. *The RSC Shakespeare*, edited by Jonathan Bate and Eric Rasmussen, is a major new edition of the complete works which is of particular interest in that it is the first edition to be based on a modern-spelling version of the 1623 first Folio. The following survey of publications on Shakespeare's tragedies starts with the more general studies, and studies covering more than one play, before dealing with particular tragedies in the order in which they are thought to have appeared.

Surveying the field of Shakespearian tragedy, one should include Jennifer Wallace's *The Cambridge Introduction to Tragedy* in the Cambridge Introductions to Literature series, as chapter 2 of the book devotes some twenty pages to Shakespeare. In her discussion, Wallace notes the sense of mystery that critics tend to find in Shakespeare, and that makes it easier to consider the various tragedies than to find their quintessential components. She suggests that the difficulty in defining Shakespearian tragedy could stem from the fact that all Shakespeare's tragedies challenged existing generic conventions. Another reason why writing about Shakespearian tragedy is complicated is that Shakespeare combined tragedy and comedy in his plays. Finally, critics find it difficult to write about Shakespeare's tragedies because of the at once creative and destructive vision which inheres in the language of the plays. Characters create what *Coriolanus* calls a 'world elsewhere'. The author finds, however, that it is in these difficult areas in Shakespeare that we paradoxically see the source of his power. 'It is in the nature of his tragic sense to defy explanation and to confound categorisation' (p. 44). In her discussion, Wallace relates Shakespeare's challenge to the traditional concept of tragedy to transformation on the political, religious and philosophical scene of his day.

The Cambridge Introduction to Shakespeare, by Emma Smith, has also appeared in Cambridge Introductions to Literature. This relatively short book is packed with useful information and is divided into seven subject-based chapters devoted to character, performance, texts, language, structure, sources and history. According to the author, each chapter includes a range of examples with a focus on the plays most frequently studied. As to the tragedies, they are all referred to at some point, but it is partly for its introduction to the dramatic world of Shakespeare, and partly for the more extensive references to the 'great' tragedies that the book is useful reading to the student of Shakespearian tragedy. The first chapter starts out, invitingly, at Juliet's balcony in Verona. Among many interesting observations on the tragedies, one can note valuable commentary on several characters, including Hamlet, Macbeth and Othello. Importantly, the emphasis of the book is less on facts than on critical approaches. 'Where Next?' sections at the end of each chapter are encouraging guides to further reading. As a general introduction to Shakespeare's work, with an emphasis on making readers meet his plays, Emma Smith's book forms a firm basis for further study.

In 2007 yet another relevant study appeared in Cambridge Introductions to Literature, namely Janette Dillon's *The Cambridge Introduction to Shakespeare's Tragedies*. The book includes a separate chapter on tragedy before Shakespeare, which points out classical influences, the mixed tradition of early English tragedy, the influence of Kyd and Marlowe, and comments on Elizabethan tragic practice and theory. The plays covered are those placed in the group named 'Tragedies' in the first Folio, with the exception of *Cymbeline*. As Dillon observes, at least three of the tragedies, *Titus Andronicus*, *Timon of Athens* and *Macbeth*, 'have possible links with other dramatists' (p. 6). Interestingly, Shakespeare's first tragedy, *Titus Andronicus*, and his last, *Coriolanus*, receive slightly more attention than the others. One of the approaches in the book is to give close analysis of particular moments, sometimes peripheral ones, to show how they reveal the play's particular concerns. In the case of *Romeo and Juliet*, the core scene commented on is I.v, a feast scene bringing together the comic dimension and lurking tragedy, in *Othello* it is the willow scene (IV.iii), and in *King Lear* it is the blinding of Gloucester (III.vii). The author argues that Shakespeare's approach to tragedy was experimental, that he set himself new challenges in each play. In her study, Dillon seeks to explore Shakespeare's range of experimentation and to give room for the distinctiveness of each play. Admittedly, it is a daunting task in a book of limited length to try to cover ten plays so much discussed in earlier publications. It is to the credit of the author that she gives insightful background information while revealing specific concerns in each of the tragedies.

Daniella Jancsó's *Excitements of Reason: The Presentation of Thought in Shakespeare's Plays and Wittgenstein's Philosophy* is a study of moments of uncertainty in Shakespeare's plays. In doing this she draws on the philosophy of Ludwig Wittgenstein. The reason for using Wittgenstein is that he ascribes importance to the moment of uncertainty and wonder, the state of being at a loss. Wittgenstein's philosophical activity is construed as an ongoing attempt at achieving clarity. In this respect Jancsó finds it instructive to focus on the study of *Hamlet* and *Macbeth*, as well as *Much Ado About Nothing* and *The Tempest*. The author sees the opening of the night scene in *Hamlet* as being dominated by a figure of uncertainty, the ghost, while the day scene begins with the entrance of a figure of certainty, Claudius. In his oration (I.ii.1–17), Claudius establishes an opposition between culture and nature, or, in Wittgenstein's terminology, a language game in which he plays the part of the ruler, while automatically casting the others in the role of the ruled. To Jancsó, Hamlet's inability to act and Wittgenstein's observations on the interconnection between thoughts, doubts and action lead to the realization that, in the moment of action, thinking must be suspended. To Wittgenstein, thinking comes to a halt when previous problem-solving strategies fail. In Jancsó's view, such moments of confusion in Shakespeare are mainly evoked by figures of uncertainty, such as ghosts, fairies and witches. In Hamlet's case, he acts when he is overpowered by fear and astonishment, when he is in a state of shock. In her analysis of *Macbeth*, the author sees the play as developing from a godless rite and presenting a world from which the divine has been eliminated. Just as in *Hamlet*, the beginning of the play displays figures of uncertainty. The Wittgenstein-inspired discussion of *Macbeth* involves the question of free will and the philosophical problem of causality. The interpretation involves the role of figures of uncertainty, the lack of objective certainty and the plight created by mental operations in the God-forsaken world of the play. The book is an intriguing study of ways in which Wittgenstein's style of reasoning resembles Shakespeare's thinking in drama. It is also enlightening for readers who struggle with the question why Shakespeare's plays, as well as Wittgenstein's philosophical writings, continue to generate such contradictory interpretations.

Shakespeare in Parts by Simon Palfrey and Tiffany Stern is a stimulating in-depth study combining a consideration of actors' parts and the vertiginous dramatic moment. The book is divided into four main parts, the first dealing with the actors and their parts and with rehearsing and performing, the second with interpreting cues, the third considering repeated cues, and the fourth discussing aspects of dramatic prosody. Of the tragedies, *Romeo and Juliet* is seen as having perhaps the most extravagant use of repeated cues in all of Shakespeare. The scene of mistaken mourning for the presumed-dead Juliet is considered tragedy with a twist, mixing pathos with bathos. In Shakespeare's mature tragedies, the authors contend, repeated cues are employed at the moment of the most serious or terrifying or finest climax, such as at the time of Desdemona's murder, the sleep-walking of Lady Macbeth, the reconciliation of Lear and Cordelia, the exit of the mad Ophelia and so on. In *Julius Caesar* such repeated cues are used to evoke popular turbulence, for example when Mark Antony inflames the Roman crowd, and to call forth subjective loneliness when Brutus is preparing for death. In *Hamlet*, the leave-taking of the mad Ophelia receives detailed comment, in which she is regarded as the chief subject of the climactic echoing cue. In their discussion of *Othello*, the authors focus particularly on the time preceding Desdemona's murder, showing that in the frantic exchange over the handkerchief, she struggles for entrance into her husband's foreclosed mind. What marks the tragedy at this point is the impossibility of Desdemona getting a word in. The mutual isolation of Othello and Desdemona can truly be felt only by separating them into a 'linear' exchange. In *Macbeth*, Lady Macbeth's final scene is considered 'perhaps the most striking instance where the premature cue is used as a sign of existential separation' (p. 237). As the authors point out, *King Lear* uses repeated cues throughout and is a good example of Shakespeare's manipulation of cues, for example in Gloucester's early scenes. Similarly, different kinds of echoing cues are commented on in Edgar's 'part within the part' of Poor Tom, when Gloucester enters and seems to prompt another of Edgar-Tom's horrid repeated cues, and when the repeated cue is described as being used by Shakespeare to represent the 'mad' Lear in particular ways. The quite extensive discussion of *King Lear* includes references to repeated cues in Cordelia's speech, with informative comments on differences between the Folio and the quarto. Many of the uses of cues in the play recur in the scene of Lear's death, where repeated cues or repeated 'refused' cues abound. In the authors' view, the echoing repetitions are designed to enable, protect and strengthen Lear's state of grief. All in all, the book represents a fresh view in an exciting field of Shakespeare study. It reveals how intimate and important working in parts is to Shakespeare's recurring preoccupations.

Shakespeare Quarterly (58:iii[2007]) is a special issue devoted to the RSC's *Complete Shakespeare*. Among its interesting articles, we note Stephen Orgel asking, in 'The Desire and Pursuit of the Whole' (pp. 290–310), whether we now really have The Complete Works. As he observes, 'Surely the impulse to conflate quarto and folio texts of *King Lear, Hamlet, Troilus and Cressida*, and *Othello* springs from a conviction that none of the individual texts is complete. *Macbeth* is obviously incomplete, indicating several of its witches' songs only as incipits ("Come away, come away &c."; "Blacke spirits &c.")' (pp. 292–3). Orgel also has many pertinent observations concerning *Hamlet* as, for example, 'The play has often been felt to be incomplete, despite its immense length' (p. 307). He further observes that while it has been frequently argued that Hamlet is the first dramatic character with a genuine psychology, his motivations are missing. Orgel notes that it increasingly became the task for the actor to provide that part of Hamlet's psychology.

'From Revels to Revelation: Shakespeare and the Mask' is Janette Dillon's contribution to *Shakespeare Survey*'s volume on 'Theatres for Shakespeare' (*ShS* 60[2007] 58–71). She initially observes that Shakespeare's late plays are frequently said to be influenced by masque, the context for such influence being the sumptuous Jacobean masque encouraged by Queen Anne from 1604. This type of masque is linked with the literary and classically inspired writing of, for example, Ben Jonson. As Dillon notes, the influence of this form of masque on Shakespeare is often associated with the King's men's move to the Blackfriars in 1609. She interestingly maintains that Tudor mask has been the poor relation in Shakespeare studies as well as in studies of court theatre more widely. The distinction in spelling ('mask' versus 'masque') seems to signal a felt need to distinguish a boundary between Tudor mask and the newer masque, the latter implicitly being associated with greater sophistication. Rather than overlooking the influence of Tudor mask on Shakespeare,

Dillon makes an attempt at giving it the place it deserves. As she suggests, Shakespeare's knowledge of masking could have come from a variety of written sources, including Hall's *Chronicle* and possibly anecdotal reports from people travelling in Europe. Masking elements might also be suggested by the plays' immediate source, such as in the case of *Romeo and Juliet*. To show the influence of mask, Dillon considers scenes from several early Shakespearian plays, including *Titus Andronicus*, V.ii and *Romeo and Juliet*, I.iv and v. *Timon of Athens* is also briefly considered. Dillon's view of the use of masking in Shakespeare is that the distinction between 'mask' and 'masque', i.e. between the Elizabethan and Jacobean forms of this type of court entertainment, cannot be absolute. It follows that there can be no clear separation between Shakespeare's early and later uses of the form.

ELR (37:iii[2007] 337–59) contains an article by Richard Levin on 'Protesting Too Much in Shakespeare and Elsewhere, and the Invention/ Construction of the Mind'. Levin takes as his point of departure *The Murther of Gonzago*, during which Gertrude protests that 'The lady doth protest too much, methinks' (III.ii.230), one of the best lines in *Hamlet*. The statement reflects ironically on Gertrude's own behaviour. Levin goes on to comment on the literary tradition of over-protesting and then succumbing widows going back 'at least as far as Petronius' tale of the Ephesian widow' (p. 337). The author's succeeding comments include references to several plays, such as Chapman's *The Widow's Tears*. Levin also mentions *The Puritan, or The Widow of Watling Street*, 'an anonymous play once attributed to Shakespeare' (p. 339). References to Shakespeare's tragedies include *King Lear*, in which a serious example of over-protesting is evident in the love test at the play's beginning, where Goneril and Regan express their devotion to their father in hyperbolic terms. Levin further notes that over-protesting is not limited to women. In *Romeo and Juliet*, Romeo's behaviour is described by Benvolio and Montague as a kind of over-protesting, even before the audience see him. From his survey of twenty-one characters who exhibit over-protesting, Levin finds certain shared characteristics. Their over-protesting is shown early in the play, it is always exhibited in the presence of other characters, and their over-protesting collapses suddenly and completely. Following this, they take an action directly opposed to it—the widows quickly remarry, the daughters spurn their father, the Petrarchan lovers fall out of love, and so on. Further commenting on *Hamlet*'s Gertrude, Levin notes that while we initially are led to believe that Gertrude is just another of the over-protesting and then succumbing widows, it soon becomes clear that her show of love for her husband was dissembled, causing the Ghost to call her 'my most seeming virtuous queen' (I.v.46).

In *Shakespeare Newsletter* (57:ii[2007] 43, 48, 52, 58, 60) David Thatcher, in ' "The manner of their deaths": Causality in *Romeo and Juliet* and *Antony and Cleopatra*', initially reminds the reader that in Shakespeare's time medical knowledge was still in its infancy. Some explanations ask for the willing suspension of disbelief. As Thatcher remarks, *Hamlet* provides several examples of confusion and ambiguity on the subject, for example when Laertes returns from France vowing revenge for his father's death before he knows how he died (IV.v.131). In his discussion Thatcher makes reference to several Shakespeare plays, noting that there are many cases in Shakespeare's work where the cause of death is not initially communicated or requested. His comments on *Romeo and Juliet* in this respect are quite extensive. Turning to *Antony and Cleopatra*, the author notes the fact that this play represents death coming to a generation older than Romeo and Juliet. In its attempts to clear up mysteries, Thatcher shows, *Antony and Cleopatra* in its denouement structurally resembles the ending of *Romeo and Juliet*, with Octavius replacing Prince Escalus as principal investigator. Indifference to the causes of Fulvia's death and the supposed death of Cleopatra is now replaced by a determination to establish the whole truth. In the author's view, Shakespeare chose to omit or suppress, until the denouement, enquiries into the cause of death in order to exploit the gulf between what the audiences know and what knowledge the characters get access to. It is through laborious (re)construction or misconstruction that the characters seek the truth.

Rebecca Ann Bach has written a special kind of book, *Shakespeare and Renaissance Literature before Heterosexuality*. Its main argument is that the playwright has been misread as having modern ideas about sex and gender. In her study Bach attempts to show how Shakespeare's plays, among others, were rewritten and adapted editorially in the Restoration and the eighteenth century to make them conform to modern views, or to what she terms an emerging heterosexual imaginary. The reason why Shakespeare's plays and Renaissance literary culture are the object of the book's primary discussions is that those plays have been considered to reveal natural human behaviour, and this would include what has been regarded as natural male–female sexual relations. In Bach's view, the homosocial imaginary gradually lost its dominance from the Restoration until the end of the eighteenth century. During the years following the early modern period, Bach maintains, Shakespeare's texts, among others, were rewritten and edited. This was the formative period for heterosexuality, and writers and editors considered the homosocial, aristocratic values of the past to be primitive. According to Bach, it became imperative to erase the traces of the homosocial past in plays, including Shakespeare's. Of Shakespeare's tragedies, Bach's study includes comments on *King Lear*, *Antony and Cleopatra* and *Othello* and portrays a world before heterosexuality. The author's chapter-long discussion of *King Lear* builds on the view that the play evokes chastity as an ideal, possibly the only ideal that is kept unpolluted throughout the play, and at a time preceding the valorization of lust and greed its hatred of male–female sex is pervasive. In the three following chapters, Bach focuses on aspects of Restoration Shakespeare, including effects on the plays of an emerging heterosexuality, and including in her analysis references to several of the tragedies. The fifth chapter is devoted to *Othello* as it was regarded in the seventeenth and eighteenth centuries, and it explores the colonial origins of heterosexuality. Bach's study presents insight into a field seldom discussed in Shakespeare studies. The book demonstrates discerningly how criticism and revisions of Renaissance drama helped the emergence of heterosexuality. According to Bach, changing views on status, friendship, adultery and race represented aspects of that emergence.

Richard Levin makes some comments (*N&Q* 54[2007] 294–5) on the stereotype that he calls 'The Lady and her Horsekeeper', the idea that some upper-class women were attracted to lower-class men. Levin's application of this stereotype includes the relationship of Tamora, the newly crowned queen, to Aaron the Moor in *Titus Andronicus*. Although Aaron is not a manual labourer, he is connected to the stereotype as a 'coloured' man. In *Titus Andronicus*, Levin points out, Tamora's adultery with a 'coloured' man is considered a sign of her shameless lust. This is focused on in II.ii.10–29, where she invites Aaron to their sexual 'pastimes' and he puts her off. Levin also finds race to be crucial in linking this stereotype to the relationship between Desdemona and Othello at the beginning of the play. While our initial impression is that the marriage of Desdemona and Othello is another version of 'The Lady and her Horsekeeper', this stereotype is decisively rejected when the truth about their marriage is finally established at the end of Act I.

Comments on *Titus Andronicus* are numerous this year. In a lengthy article, 'Racial Impersonation on the Elizabethan Stage: The Case of Shakespeare Playing Aaron' (*MRDE* 20[2007] 17–45), Imtiaz Habib refers to Donald Foster's stylometric SHAXICON test concerning specific roles Shakespeare may have played, with special focus on the roles of Aaron in *Titus Andronicus*, Morocco and Antonio in *The Merchant of Venice* and Brabantio in *Othello*. The author argues that a consideration of the psychosocial transactions involved in such possibilities may give new insight into the complexities of racial discourse in Shakespeare. In his discussion, Habib points out that 'Shakespeare's racial impersonation in his playing of Aaron may issue from an obscure instinct of racial solidarity but may also involve an instinct of racial critique deployed across the triple agendas of ethnic control, surveillance, and programming' (p. 27). He finds that *Titus* possibly may constitute a more complex case of impersonation than *Othello* and even *Antony and Cleopatra*. But the question whether Shakespeare actually played the role of Aaron cannot be answered.

Christopher Crosbie has an article on 'Fixing Moderation: *Titus Andronicus* and the Aristotelian Determination of Value' (*SQ* 58[2007] 147–73). He observes that *Titus Andronicus* has elicited criticism for being 'excessive in its sensationalism yet lacking in its stylistic organization' (p. 147). Crosbie asks several questions concerning the basis for the criticism of Titus's excesses, and questions whether the reason for such views lies in a chaotic internal structure. Crosbie argues that the play's excesses 'signal instead the play's use of extremity to define the ethical, a representational strategy that exhibits sophistication and nuance amid, even through, sensational display' (p. 147). As Crosbie maintains, excess and moderation, themes present throughout *Titus Andronicus*, were established conceptual categories in early modern England. Situating the play within Aristotelian ethical theory of the late 1590s reveals a coherent underlying structure. What follows in Crosbie's article is a rereading of *Titus Andronicus* based on the view that the ethical mean allows a theoretical range of action as 'moderate', depending upon the circumstances. The result of the argument is flexible rigidity, which helps place Titus as noble yet savage, horrifying yet just. While the play causes us to consider the moral ambiguities inherent in the conflict between Roman and Goth, its Aristotelian framework also prompts us to contemplate ethical values through its constant appeal to equity.

Being devoted to one tragedy only, Marvin W. Hunt's volume on *Looking for Hamlet* is of particular interest. The author initially notes that Hamlet is an unlikely masterpiece, ungainly and extremely long if uncut. Moreover, there is little action in it until the end. Hunt further observes that the artistic merits of the work have been questioned, not least by T.S. Eliot, who failed to find any objective correlatives in it. Yet reality refutes all complaints against it, since *Hamlet* is the most frequently staged play in any language. Hunt argues that Shakespeare's greatest tragedy acts out an extreme and extraordinary internalization of reality. He then 'attempts to show how the resulting sense of a palpable interiority has reflected and shaped the intellectual history of the West, making *Hamlet* the single most important work in constructing who we are, especially in how we understand our psychological, intellectual, and emotional beings' (pp. 7–8). This is a daunting task. He starts by exploring the sources of the play, before considering its complex printing history. As Hunt notes, *Hamlet* appeared in three different versions. Two of them (in 1603 and 1604) were printed during the playwright's lifetime, while the third did not appear until 1626. These three versions coalesced into the relatively stable version of *Hamlet* published and produced since. Next Hunt discusses the great fifth act, trying to demonstrate why *Hamlet* is such a central work. In Hunt's view, the play takes reality from outside the human mind to within it, relocating us from an anterior and objective medieval mindset to an early modern outlook that largely sees reality as a function of subjective experience. The result of this new belief is the realization that what goes on inside our heads is, in the final analysis, real. The rest of Hunt's study presents a history of reception, noting that while the play should seem quite old, even antiquated, with the swordplay, the Ghost and the ornate language, it really, from most perspectives, defies ageing. In Hunt's view, *Hamlet* is currently more central to the world than ever. He argues that Hamlet the character 'is the collective dead son of Western history, the lost child that haunts our culture, perpetually killed and resurrected again in each performance before succeeding generations' (p. 9). The reader may or may not embrace every bit of Hunt's appreciative wording; however, he nevertheless presents a fresh, incisive and greatly informative study of this unique play.

In '"But I have that within which passeth show": Shakespeare's Ambivalence toward his Profession' (*ShN* 56[2006–7] 85–6, 100, 106, 110, 116–17), R.W. Desai argues that there is evidence in the sonnets to suggest that Shakespeare disliked his profession as actor and playwright. Corroborative evidence, especially from *Hamlet*, 'might help to explain why the three tragedies written after *Hamlet* are so different from *Hamlet*' (p. 85). Desai's argument is that although *Hamlet* is a unique theatrical success, it encapsulates a conflict within the author and marks the turning point towards tragedies with a different direction. In Desai's view, all the great tragic figures following Hamlet—Othello, Macbeth, Antony, Cleopatra, Lear, Timon and Coriolanus—are 'simple-minded, non-intellectual, non-complex characters' (p. 85). To Desai Hamlet is Shakespeare's alter ego, the critic concealed within the dramatist. He further comments on Hamlet's scathing critique of the contemporary stage. In Desai's view, Shakespeare's drama after *Hamlet* takes a turn towards a direct, less complex style with mass appeal, a repudiation of Hamlet's ideal critic.

Antony Miller, in his article 'Fortinbras' Conquests and Pliny' (*N&Q* 54[2007] 287–9), quotes *Hamlet* IV.iv.15–26 and remarks that Hamlet's incredulous exchange with the Norwegian captain has been compared with two passages in Montaigne. Miller quotes from the essay 'Of bad meanes employed to a good end' (II.xxiii), in which Montaigne considers the behaviour of Roman gladiators, who killed each other to instruct the Roman people in valour and contempt for death. To Montaigne, the willingness of men to die in this manner is strange and incredible. Miller points out that although there is a general similarity between Montaigne's thought and that of Hamlet, 'their tenor is quite different' (p. 287). Miller also refers to Montaigne's essay 'How one ought to governe his will' (II.x). To Miller, Montaigne's examples, like the war in *Hamlet*, are all instances of trivial causes giving rise to great effects. To the author, Pliny's *Naturalis historia*, which was familiar to Renaissance schoolboys, represents a closer parallel to the passage in *Hamlet* than either of Montaigne's passages. Pliny discusses the limits set on human habitation by the earth's climate and then reflects on the melancholy fact that it is on the *mundi puncto* that men seek glory and power.

In *Shakespeare Survey* (*ShS* 60[2007] 223–36) Graham Holderness comments on '"I covet your skull"': Death and Desire in *Hamlet*'. The article focuses on the appearance of the skull in *Hamlet*. This human skull, also known as Yorick's skull, is not merely an anonymized object serving to create a memento mori, lamentation or satire, but an individualized skull, the remains of a known and loved person. Skulls on stage are awesome or weird because of the oscillation between subject and object. In Holderness's view, Hamlet's commentary is at once scientific, religious, sceptical and Protestant as well as Catholic.

Notes and Queries (*N&Q* 54[2007] 289–90] has an article by Thomas Festa on 'All in All: The Book of Common Prayer and *Hamlet*, I.ii.186'. According to Festa, the precise meaning of Hamlet's reply to Horatio's recollection of Old Hamlet following Hamlet's first soliloquy has not yet been understood, due to a misconception about the source and function of Hamlet's idiom. Scholars and critics have missed the primary allusion, in Festa's view. He argues that Hamlet's phrase alludes to a verse from the first epistle to the Corinthians: 'When all thynges are subdued vnto hym, then shall the sonne also hym selfe be subiect vnto hym that put all thynges vnder hym, that God may be all in all' (1 Cor. 15.28). The likelihood that Shakespeare had this text in mind when writing this line is increased by the fact that it was a part of the lesson read during the ceremony for the burial of the dead in the Book of Common Prayer.

Gene Fendt discusses '"The time is out of joint": Medieval and Roman History and Theology in *Hamlet*'s Act I Temporal Disturbances' (*N&Q* 54[2007] 290–2). Seeing the Ghost as both *res* and *signum*, Fendt initially describes it as the dark sacrament of the play. Act I of *Hamlet* closes with Hamlet, disturbed by the ghost of his father, considering its presence a sign of the disturbance of the temporal order. Fendt questions whether the darkness is in the sacrament or in the times, and refers to saints behind the names of the central characters in Act I, Francisco (St Francis) and Barnardo (Bernard of Clairvaux), and two martial names from earlier Roman history, Marcellus and Horatio. In Act I, the author sees history as reversing itself and flowing backwards to a time before the empire (Marcellus), past the earliest republic (Horatio). 'Marcellus presents, as the first act's first disturbances wash over us, the counter-image of . . . time at peace as the Eternal enters it at the season of our Saviour's birth' (p. 291). However, *Hamlet*'s Horatio does not come from Rome but from Wittenberg, and he does not believe in ghosts. In Fendt's view, the question of the Ghost's true nature divides Hamlet from Horatio, until the latter at the end seems to have been converted to Hamlet's view.

In a short article entitled 'Shakespeare's *Hamlet*' (*Expl* 65:ii[2007] 68–71) David McInnis comments on the royal plural in III.ii.324–5. McInnis discusses this occurrence of the royal plural salutation and comments on several critical interpretations by different scholars. The author further explores the thematic implications of the royal plural.

' "Try what repentance can": *Hamlet*, Confession, and the Extraction of Interiority', by Paul D. Stegner (*ShakS* 35[2007] 105–29), uses Kenneth Branagh's inclusion of the confessional in the film adaptation of *Hamlet* [1996] as a starting point for a discussion of ritual confession and the problem of assurance in early modern England. Stegner goes against the Foucauldian emphasis on the connection between confession and social control. Rather, in his essay he posits that confessional rituals and language indicate the diffuse tension between traditional rituals and inwardness persisting throughout the early modern period and enacted on the English stage. Stegner seeks to demonstrate that *Hamlet* reveals changes taking place in confessional practices by providing Catholic as well as Protestant confessional rites that promise consolation and reconciliation, while indicating that in the theological world of the play these promises cannot be realized. The author examines the changes in penitential practices during the early modern period. Hamlet's role as confessor is a reminder of the ongoing theological and theatrical problem of deciding the authenticity of another's confession. Stegner discusses in what ways Hamlet's role as confessor complements his position as avenger and influences his approach to the tensions between thought and action. Hamlet's attempts at taking on the role of father confessor are part of his efforts to avenge the crimes against his father and himself.

In *Interpretation* (34:iii[2007] 207–74) Mark A. McDonald has written a lengthy article entitled 'On *Hamlet* and the Reformation: "To show the very age and body of the time his form and pressure" '. To the author *Hamlet* is a tragedy about a thinker. While *The Tempest* is the autobiographical play, the author sees a possible autobiographical element in *Hamlet* in that the play exemplifies what people, including Shakespeare, might have become had they not avoided a tragic alternative. Another autobiographical element, according to McDonald, may be represented by Horatio, who tells the story of Hamlet to the world, and who also relates to the theatre. The author sees in *Hamlet* an analogy between the action and the crisis in the ordering of the West around the Reformation. This analogy represents the foundation for the meaning of the play. In the author's analysis, Shakespeare rejects the Lutheran response to the Reformation while favouring a more remote, independent response.

The Wittenberg response to the crisis is regarded as noble yet tragic, but the response to the disturbance in the soul of the West is with philosophy and drama.

Medieval and Renaissance Drama in England (*MRDE* 20[2007] 111–35) contains an article by Alison A. Chapman on 'Ophelia's "Old Lauds": Madness and Hagiography in *Hamlet*'. Chapman initially notes that recent scholarship shows that *Hamlet* raises questions about early modern religion. She finds, however, that recent critics have mainly attached the religious questions of the play to the character of Hamlet. But Shakespeare did not limit himself to Hamlet's character when probing religious questions. As Chapman argues, 'Ophelia's ravings also display a complex awareness of England's medieval Catholic past' (p. 111). In Chapman's view, Ophelia's network of religious allusions is not in conflict with the sexualized nature of her madness. Ophelia finds herself caught between two models of female behaviour: one, embodied by the girl of the song, is both realistic and tragic. The other, represented by St Charity, is unrealistic and yet empowering. Both positions are equally untenable. The task of accommodating the two irreconcilable religious positions of English Protestantism and Catholicism can result in madness, according to Chapman. In the play, Hamlet and Ophelia reconcile the religious past and present in different ways, Hamlet seemingly shaking free of the spectre of Catholic purgatory, Ophelia seeming to slip entirely into the past.

Turning to *Othello*, we find John Drakakis's article '*Othello* and the Barbarians' (*RCEI* 54[2007] 101–17), which analyses the role of 'barbarians' in a civilization's definition of itself. The author is concerned 'with the ways in which particular texts negotiate the difficult territories of 'self' and 'other' (p. 104). He notes that, in the case of Shakespeare, a number of texts have appeared fruitful to postcolonial studies, including *The Tempest, Antony and Cleopatra* and *Othello*. Barbarians are at the same time 'other' and symbolically central to the process of self-definition, being 'outside' as well as 'within' society. In Drakakis's view, this dynamic can be explored in a comparison between Shakespeare's *Othello* and J.M. Coetzee's *Waiting for the Barbarians*. The author makes these two texts, which are chronologically and culturally wide apart, part of a discussion on empire and colonization. Drakakis concludes that Shakespeare's *Othello* is at the beginning of a process of historicization that ideologically preserves boundaries, while Coetzee's *Waiting for the Barbarians* represents complexities inherent in the uncritical dissolution of boundaries. Both texts prompt fundamental questions of identity.

Explicator (*Expl* 65:iv[2007] 197–9) has a commentary by C. Harold Hurley on 'Shakespeare's *Othello*, IV.iii.60–105'. The author discusses the integration and influence of Christopher Marlowe's poem 'The Passionate Shepherd to his Love' in *Othello*. C. Harold Hurley describes the references to chief motives found in Marlowe's poem in Act IV, scene iii, of *Othello* and analyses the implications of the theme for Desdemona's and Emilia's ethical standards.

Rodney Stenning Edgecombe has commented on 'Ovid and the "Medicinal Gum" in *Othello* V.ii' (*N&Q* 54[2007] 293–4). The author considers *Othello* V.ii.347–52 and notes the presence of *Metamorphoses* 64, a resemblance that according to Stenning Edgecombe has so far not been remarked. He further observes that the *Liebestod*-type speech that is uttered over the corpse of Desdemona (V.ii.280–2) ends in imagery as much Phaeton-like as hellish. Admitting that commentators are right in focusing on Pliny when expounding the medicinal gums as coming from myrrh trees, Stenning Edgecombe argues that the simile serves the idea of grief rather than healing. Being vague about the boundaries between Araby and Ethiopia, Shakespeare probably had *Metamorphoses* 64 in mind. In Stenning Edgecombe's view, Shakespeare would have assumed some sort of continuity between amber and myrrh in incense mixtures. 'He would also no doubt have known that Galen discoursed on the curative properties of the gem—hence "medicinal"' (p. 294).

A survey of studies of *King Lear* begins with a look at *CahiersE* (71[2007] 37–47), where David Stymeist writes on '"Fortune, that arrant whore, ne'er turns the key to th' poor": Vagrancy, Old Age and the Theatre in Shakespeare's *King Lear*'. The author notes that Shakespeare wrote in an era in which vagrancy was criminalized. In this light he considers *King Lear*, arguing that Shakespeare presents a radical deconstruction of the discourses of homelessness. Stymeist considers the tragedy a commercial exploitation of the social anxieties around homelessness and abandonment of the old. Still the play presents a public contestation of the governmental rhetoric employed to justify the persecution of vagrants. *King Lear* uncovers the social and economic roots of vagabondage, shows familial constructions that obscured vagrancy and parodies the stereotype of the dissembling beggar. In *King Lear* Shakespeare 'exposes vagrancy as "the classic crime of status, the social crime par excellence"' (p. 45). In Stymeist's view, Shakespeare's subversive representation of vagrancy was partly motivated by his concern to disconnect problematic links between players, the homeless poor and dissimulating rogues.

Religion and the Arts (*ReAr* 11[2007] 436–53) contains an article by Sean Benson entitled 'Materialist Criticism and Cordelia's Quasi-Resurrection in *King Lear*'. It is an examination of Lear's conviction that the dead Cordelia is resuscitated near the end of the play. This quasi-resurrection is included only in the first Folio [1623]. As Benson shows, some critics consider the moment to be delusion and others a moment of blessed release. The author then explores the materialist interpretations of Stephen Greenblatt and Jonathan Dollimore, who both insist that Cordelia's quasi-resurrection, as it is never realized, frustrates a religious interpretation of the play. To Benson, Cordelia's quasi-resurrection points towards a possible otherworldly redemption, while reminding the audience of the resurrection that cannot take place in Lear's pagan world.

Naomi Conn Liebler writes on 'Pelican Daughters: The Violence of Filial Ingratitude in *King Lear*' (*ShJE* 143[2007] 36–51). As she notes, Lear's 'pelican daughters' (III.iv.74), Goneril and Regan, pluck out the heart of their father. The death of the third daughter, Cordelia, breaks his heart, so unintentionally she too is one of the pelicans. The essay analyses different aspects of violence and cruelty in *King Lear* with reference to two of the most influential theatre critics of the twentieth century, Brecht and Artaud. Both called for a theatre that disturbed people's complacencies.

The political setting of *Macbeth* is approached in Sharon Alker and Holly Faith Nelson's article, 'Macbeth, the Jacobean Scot, and the Politics of the Union' (*SEL* (47[2007] 379–401). It is often argued that *Macbeth* presents a certain position on Anglo-Scottish politics that defines itself in relation to the belief system of one small political body. In opposition to this, Alker and Nelson present three models of the Union recorded in the pamphlet literature of the period and dramatized on the Jacobean stage. The overall construction of the drama, according to the authors, including character, form and genre, as well as the use of space, adds up to several competing positions on the Union. Macbeth thus 'leaves us with a sense of the contradiction and multiplicity of the discursive formation of the nation' (p. 396). The construction of *Macbeth* reflects the complexity of its relationship to the Court as well as to the marketplace.

Richard Wilson, ' "Blood will have blood" ': Regime Change in *Macbeth*' (*ShJE* 143[2007] 11–35), points out that *Macbeth*, which was first presented on 7 August 1606 in Hampton Court following the Gunpowder Plot, was considered a propaganda piece for King James. His image, distantly reflected, may have been mirrored in the masque. But in view of the ambiguity about which 'great king' the witches served to welcome, the presence of the witches may call for another reading, according to Wilson. In the background there is the anti-Catholic war on terror. The superimposition of Macbeth's face over that of James in the witches' ball would carry an ominous twist when the old agents of terror are unpunished in the new order. James may have seen his own head reflected beside Macbeth's, and the mirror masque might expose Macbeth as yet another Herod.

Jonathan Gil Harris's 'The Smell of *Macbeth*' (*SQ* 58[2007] 465–86) is an examination of gunpowder in *Macbeth*. The purpose is to cast light on ways in which smelly materials in early modern theatrical performances worked on their audiences, or their olfactors. According to Gil Harris, the smell of *Macbeth*'s 'thunder and lightning' was of theatrical importance and was of significance because of its visual and acoustic impact. Play-goers' responses to the odour of the squib were not just physiologically conditioned, but part of larger cultural syntaxes of olfaction and memory. The author is also interested in how the play's smells put pressure on the very notion of a self-identical moment as the true basis of historical interpretation. What he locates in smell he terms a polychronicity, i.e. a palimpsesting of diverse moments in time, as a result of which past and present coincide with each other. 'In the specific instance of Shakespeare's play, smell's polychronicity generates an explosive temporality through which the past can be made to act upon, and shatter the self-identity of, the present' (p. 467). As Gil Harris sees it, the stink of *Macbeth*'s squibs must have generated experiences on the part of the audience that to us are culturally elusive and not easily legible.

Turning to *Antony and Cleopatra*, we find an interesting article, 'Lives and Letters in *Antony and Cleopatra*' by Alan Stewart (*ShakS* 35[2007] 77–104). The essay is a literary criticism of the play which contests Linda Charnes's argument (in *Notorious Identity: Exceeding Reputation in 'Antony and Cleopatra'* [1993]) that the play represents the triumph of Octavius. According to Stewart, such a claim does not address the complexities involved in the characters' bids for posterity. The author argues that the play challenges the foundation of Roman historiography. However attractive the binary of letter-bound Rome versus oral Egypt may be, it is impossible to support strictly dichotomous models of message-bearing, since the carrying of messages is transactive, moving across the play's two cultures.

Kevin Curran writes on 'Shakespeare and Daniel Revisited: *Antony and Cleopatra* II.v.50–4 and *The Tragedy of Philotas* V.ii.2013–15' (*N&Q* 54[2007] 318–20). This is an intertextual short study on links between Shakespeare and Daniel, a connection that has been well documented. As noted by Curran, *Antony and Cleopatra* is of particular interest in that it shows borrowings in both directions. Daniel's closet drama *Cleopatra* [1594] influences *Antony and Cleopatra*, while Daniel's 1607 revised and expanded *Cleopatra* seems to have been influenced by Shakespeare's play. In his essay Curran explores another link, namely between *Antony and Cleopatra* and Daniel's Senecan political drama, *The Tragedy of Philotas* [1604–5]. He notes that Shakespeare's borrowing from *The Tragedy of Philotas* in II.v.50–4 of *Antony and Cleopatra* has so far gone unnoticed. Having particularly considered Act II, scene v, of Shakespeare's play, Curran concludes that if *Antony and Cleopatra* was composed between 1606 and 1607, he finds it plausible that the text of Daniel's *Cleopatra* that Shakespeare was influenced by was the one found in the collection *Certain Small Poems lately printed: with the tragedie of Philotas*. 'In this collection Shakespeare would not only have found *Cleopatra*, but also the first printed edition of *The Tragedy of Philotas*, which provided the source for *Antony and Cleopatra* II.v.50–4' (p. 320).

Mary Rosenberg has an article entitled 'She Here—What's Her Name?' (*ShN* 57[2007–8] 5–6). The author is puzzled by *Antony and Cleopatra* IV.xv and wonders why Antony, at a moment of great intimacy, twice addresses Cleopatra by the name of her country: 'I am dying, Egypt, dying.' In her discussion, Rosenberg remarks that even at this final moment the lovers are not alone. But, as she notes, these lovers seldom are alone. She observes, though, that this is not the only occasion on which Cleopatra is identified with her country. To herself she is 'Egypt's queen'. As the author observes, Egypt to uncomfortable Romans is a place of soft licentiousness. But it is also a place of beauty and delight, as well as mystery and domination. The significance of the term depends on the user and the context. While Antony is clear about Cleopatra's royal status, he is angry with her and disgusted with himself when he first addresses her as 'Egypt' (III.xi) after his defeat at sea. And in III.xiii, when finding Cleopatra submitting to the courtesies of the messenger Thidias, Antony offers cruel lines that strip her of both title and identity: 'what's her name | Since she was Cleopatra?' As Rosenberg points out, the complete lack of confidence is heartbreaking. Antony fears the loss of Roman authority, being at this moment all Roman, while Cleopatra has become the representative of opposing values. Perhaps the fact that Antony lashes out at the woman closest to him is a token of his love, the author suggests. To the dying Antony, Cleopatra is simple woman, 'sweet' and 'gentle', as well as Egyptian queen, 'Egypt'.

A study of *Coriolanus*, by Anita Pacheco, has appeared in the Writers and their Work series. In a limited space the author manages to give an interesting

introduction to Shakespeare's last play. *Coriolanus* is placed within its proper
historical period in a chapter on antique Romans in Renaissance England. The
author then considers the way class conflict is represented in the play. Pacheco
notes that Shakespeare departs from Plutarch's 'Life of Caius Martius
Coriolanus', as translated by North, in ascribing military service primarily
to the patrician class, and that Coriolanus's martial prowess is exaggerated.
In a chapter on contradictions in the concept of honour, she points out that
Shakespeare deviates from North's description of Coriolanus as a political
animal in that he is happy only in battle and is dissatisfied with Roman civic
life. A separate chapter discusses the mother and son dichotomy, with the
play's portrait of Volumnia as Martius's principal teacher. The study finally
considers later appropriations of the play. Pacheco's *Coriolanus* is an
informative guide to the play. It clearly displays Shakespeare's craft of
reworking the source material to make it suit his purposes. The study is
admirably suitable as a first introduction to the play.

Coriolanus is also approached in James Kuzner, 'Unbuilding the City:
Coriolanus and the Birth of Republican Rome' (*SQ* 58[2007] 174–99).
According to Kuzner, much recent criticism is involved with the degree to
which early modern texts can be considered republican. A case in point would
be Annabel Patterson's reading (recuperation) of *Coriolanus* (in chapter 6 of
her *Shakespeare and the Popular Voice* [1989]), in which she sees the play as
one that avoids absolutism and advocates an English republic that would
encourage bounded and discrete subjects. Kuzner questions such a reading of
Coriolanus, both with a view to textual accuracy and its attention to bounded
selfhood. Many recent theoretical works have noted dangers inherent in the
idea of personal boundaries central to republican arguments. Kuzner argues
that Shakespeare represents the birth of Roman republicanism as the birth of a
state that uses law to place people outside the law. Life within the city thus
becomes life that can be killed without the use of ordinary legal channels.
Accordingly, *Coriolanus* cannot be read as a pro-republican document, but the
play may still be politically appealing. Kuzner's subsequent analysis involves,
among other aspects, a discussion of *Coriolanus* in relation to early modern
concepts of the bounded self, recent theory and forms of self-undoing, the
Rome of the play as the state of exception, and the Coriolanian being seeking
self-undoing.

It is somewhat surprising that there was no work this year focusing solely on
Romeo and Juliet, *Julius Caesar* or *Timon of Athens*. And it is striking that
many critics have given *Titus Andronicus* a great deal of critical attention. The
types of critical approaches to Shakespeare found in these texts are truly
manifold.

(g) Late Plays
Of the work on Shakespeare's late plays in 2007, one of the most substantial
and notable studies is one that, in fact, claims not to be a book about
Shakespeare's late plays. Instead, Gordon McMullan's *Shakespeare and the
Idea of Late Writing: Authorship in the Proximity of Death* is a book 'about a

particular critical *idea* of Shakespeare's late plays and, by extension, about the late work of a highly select cohort of writers, artists and composers' (p. 5). This book thus insists on the necessity of considering what we mean when we use the term 'late' Shakespeare to refer to the playwright's late romances or tragicomedies. This term, McMullan points out, does not simply affirm chronology or reflect a creative process that Shakespeare would have been familiar with; nor is it a concept that applies only to Shakespeare. It invokes, McMullan claims, 'a general history of critical analysis, a history that starts with the establishment of style as the organic product not of an epoch but of the life and will of a given artist. (p. 2). This book is about this approach to late style across the disciplines, and it aptly demonstrates its interdisciplinary approach by moving fluently between analyses of the emergence of the idea of late work in musicology, art history and literary studies. McMullan's central argument is that it is impossible to separate late Shakespeare from this wider concept of lateness, which, despite being perceived as transcultural and transhistorical, is a critical construct. *Shakespeare and the Idea of Late Writing* thus offers a detailed examination of the place of an understanding of 'late Shakespeare' in this critical history.

Although McMullan emphasizes that this could be 'a book about any given set of plays as they are assessed in relation to period of the playwright's life in which they were written' (p. 6), in choosing Shakespeare's late plays as a case study to interrogate this discourse, he provides a comprehensive and lively evaluation of the reception history of the late plays. Commenting on the tendency of criticism to focus on *Pericles, The Winter's Tale, Cymbeline* and *The Tempest* and to exclude *Henry VIII, Cardenio* and *The Two Noble Kinsmen* which postdate them, McMullan demonstrates the limitations of critical approaches to these plays. He revisits debates on the dating and evidence on the material production of the plays. Yet, instead of suggesting conclusive new groupings, he demonstrates the problematic critical assumptions that underpin such conclusions. Arguing that the late plays have become associated with the aesthetic at the expense of the historical, McMullan reintroduces a historical element to the discourse of lateness by combining a consideration of the way in which an understanding of late style has emerged historically with an evaluation of attitudes towards lateness, last words and endings of lives in early modern England and the contexts of production in early modern theatre. Through an analysis of role of the acting company and collaborative authorship in the production of early modern play texts, he offers a fresh consideration of the collaboratively authored late plays and convincingly illustrates the ways in which an ascription of late style 'misunderstands the conditions of production for early seventeenth-century theatre' (p. 225). This book thus exposes the limitations of the tendency of the majority of studies of late Shakespeare that utilize, to some extent, a biographical approach and insists upon the necessity of rethinking the plays in their historical and institutional contexts. McMullan also offers an interesting analysis of the ways in which old-age style and late style have been conflated in Shakespearian criticism, and explores the subsequent interpretation of *King Lear* as a late play. Noting the connections between this play and *The Tempest* sustained by theatrical performances, McMullan proceeds to demonstrate the ongoing utility of the idea of 'late Shakespeare', particularly in recent films and performances of the latter. This is achieved through an examination of the ways in which Sir John Gielgud and Mark Rylance have deployed Prospero as 'a figure both of late Shakespeare and of the late career in general' (p. 320), and the study thus concludes with a new analysis of performances of *The Tempest* and the ways in which it has been appropriated in the twentieth and twenty-first centuries.

In critically re-examining the concept of 'late Shakespeare', McMullan's study raises important questions about Shakespeare's late plays, their original theatrical contexts, and responses to them, as well as about early modern attitudes to old age and the ending of lives and the construction of an idea of late style, late writing or late work across the disciplines of musicology, art history and literary studies. Above all, *Shakespeare and the Idea of Late Writing* insists upon a new critical awareness when thinking about and using the terminology of 'lateness' in relation to the plays known as Shakespeare's late work. It is, therefore, with caution that I proceed to look at the other work on Shakespeare's 'late' plays this year.

This includes Christopher Cobb's ambitious study of the power of performance to bring about change in Shakespeare's romances, *The Staging of Romance in Late Shakespeare: Text and Theatrical Technique*. Positing a fundamental relationship between dramatic technique, performance and personal and social change, Cobb argues for the 'power and value of staging romance' (p. 13), which in the late plays, he suggests, brings characters, actors and audiences to the 'boundary between humanly producible transformations and supernatural ones, exploring the extent to which human change can be understood as a theatrical event' (p. 12) and ultimately effects 'human transformations' (p. 11). Cobb makes his case persuasively through a close analysis of *The Winter's Tale*. While providing examples from Shakespeare's other late plays, and indeed some non-Shakespearian romances, he suggests that a detailed case study is the most effective way of demonstrating the transformative power of the genre and that *The Winter's Tale*, as a turning point in the history of the staging of romance and in Shakespeare's engagement with this genre, is the most appropriate example. The centrality of *The Winter's Tale* to the genre of romance is further conveyed through the structure of Cobb's book, which moves between detailed case study and a broader survey of the genre. Chapters 3 and 6 look at a range of other plays, offering an interesting context for the original and thorough readings of *The Winter's Tale* in the other chapters. Chapter 2 offers a detailed account of the potential interpretations of Act I, scene ii, in terms of how the characters, and the audience, are offered various methods of dealing with Leontes' uncertainty. Beginning with close textual analysis of this example, Cobb then moves fluently to a consideration of the staging of this scene in the 1994 Royal Shakespeare Company performance directed by Adrian Noble, and in the 1988 National Theatre production directed by Peter Hall. Chapter 4 focuses on the dramatized response of onstage audiences in the play to the destructive force of Leontes' jealousy, and chapter 5 explores the play's attempt to redirect the audience through a series of interpretative challenges. As the title and these chapter synopses suggest, the history and possibilities of the genre of romance are central to the book's examination of the late plays, as is the representation of theatricality. Indeed, *The Staging of Romance in Late Shakespeare* engages intriguingly with more general questions of theatrical mimesis, early modern acting techniques and the relationship between the audience and the performance, and sheds new light on these issues through the example of *The Winter's Tale*. In Cobb's own words, the book examines 'the transactions between artists—playwrights, actors and characters—and their observers' (p. 13) and contends that through such transactions characters, and even the audience, gain a 'power of action' and 'find themselves changed' (p. 201). While this is an ambitious claim for the power of theatre, Cobb's carefully informed and detailed account of genre, language, theatricality and performance convinces.

In contrast to this focus on genre and performance, the third book-length study of Shakespeare's late plays in 2007, Raphael Lyne's *Shakespeare's Late Work*, takes a thematic approach to the plays. As part of the Oxford Shakespeare Topics series, Lyne's book addresses a range of issues pertinent to the late plays in an accessible and lively manner. Focusing on *Pericles, Cymbeline, The Winter's Tale* and *The Tempest*, Lyne's aim is 'to characterize and analyse the similarities between the four romances, but also to open up the idea of late Shakespeare and thereby to consider a wider range of works' (p. 11). He begins by emphasizing that Shakespeare's metamorphosis into a new style in his late years can be and has been overstated, and while this book highlights some distinctive features of these plays, Lyne's approach is largely comparative in order to demonstrate the ways in which the key interests of many of Shakespeare's earlier works are reworked in the late plays. The book opens with a useful overview of some of the recurrent features of the late plays (romance, irony and metatheatricality), a brief critical history and an account of textual production. The remaining chapters are dedicated to examinations of particular features or themes in the late plays and consider how these relate to other early modern and earlier literature. This includes an examination of the interactions between seeing and believing in *The Tempest, The Winter's Tale* and *Cymbeline* in comparison with *Antony and Cleopatra*; a reading of the themes of finding and discovery in *The Tempest, Pericles* and *The Winter's Tale* alongside *Hamlet*, early modern poetry, classical literature and the Bible; a comparison of the relationships between fathers and daughters in the late plays, and of family bonds, in *Hamlet, Romeo and Juliet, King Lear* and *Othello*; the parallels and alternatives to James I's promotion of his family as the new dynasty offered by the conservative endings of the romances; and an analysis of non-Shakespearian literature to assess the extent to which the late plays re-present older tales. Through this approach, Lyne provides useful insights for students into the key themes of Shakespeare's work, the development of these themes across his plays and fresh readings of the late work's thematic concerns. In addition, Lyne offers an interesting examination of collaborative authorship in the late plays and extends this to a consideration of the ways in which Thomas Middleton and John Fletcher used similar styles in their own drama as a further basis for considering late Shakespeare as part of 'a wider cultural tendency' (p. 137).

The diverse approaches taken in these three new monographs on Shakespeare's late work build on Russ McDonald's 2006 study, *Shakespeare's Late Style*, not included in last year's review. McDonald begins, as this year's studies do, by clarifying what he interprets as Shakespeare's late plays. He includes all of the plays post-1607, and, in contrast to Lyne, emphasizes the distinct elements of this group. His argument is that 'late Shakespeare' defines a particular style of writing which is the product of 'Shakespeare's increasingly sophisticated way of thinking about the world' (p. 32). This is different from McMullan's concept of the idea of late writing put forward in his 2007 study. Indeed the two books' differing approaches to the concept of a late style are complementary. McMullan himself draws attention to this, distinguishing between his recognition of a stylistic shift in late Shakespeare that stems from and produces an overarching understanding of late style and McDonald's focus on the minutiae of style (p. 7). McDonald clarifies his own approach claiming that he begins with the specific, with 'microscopic units such as syllables and lines' (p. 2), rather than trying to characterize plays according to theme or genre, before 'moving outward' in order to 'define the principle properties' of the style adopted by Shakespeare in his late plays and to 'explore the relation of that style to the dramatic forms it was devised to serve' (p. 2). McDonald achieves this by first evaluating the origins of this style in *Macbeth*, *Coriolanus* and *Antony and Cleopatra*, and then through a detailed analysis of the use of ellipsis, syntax and repetition in Shakespearian drama post-1607. In doing this, he comments on the compression of complex ideas into a few words as the most distinctive feature of Shakespeare's late style; notes the correspondences between the structure of the sentences of Shakespeare's dramatic verse and the dramatic action and the ways in which sentences become a kind of 'miniature romance' (p. 169) in these plays; examines the musical effects of the auditory combinations in the plays; and explores the ways in which Shakespeare's poetry promotes uncertainty and ambiguity. Ultimately, McDonald addresses the question of how an acquaintance with these technical features helps us to understand the plays, and in the book's final chapter he reviews some commonly addressed themes with the advantage of his detailed attention to style.

The publication of these four monographs on late Shakespeare indicates, perhaps, a revived interest in Shakespeare's late works, and, through their different approaches and alternative readings, these texts demonstrate the continuing significance of the plays as sites for revisiting questions of genre, style, performance and history. This is further evidenced by the attention given to Shakespeare's late plays in another two monographs in 2007. Gina Bloom's *Voice in Motion: Staging Gender, Shaping Sound in Early Modern England* and Michael Witmore's *Pretty Creatures: Children and Fiction in the English Renaissance* both include lengthy chapters on the late plays. Bloom offers an entirely fresh reading of Shakespeare's late plays, and particularly of the female characters, in a chapter at the centre of her innovative study of the voice as a literary, historical and performative motif in early modern English drama and culture. In this material history of the voice and of how early moderns represented its production, transmission and reception, Bloom ably demonstrates that the human voice is represented as possessing material attributes in early modern culture through an analysis of a range of texts, including medical treatises, song books, pronunciation manuals, acoustic studies, religious sermons and plays. Chapter 3, which focuses on the late plays, is one of a number of chapters that look at play texts and performance contexts, from boy actors' unmanageable voices to the differences between the written text and live performance in George Gascoigne's treatment of Echo in his entertainments at Kenilworth Castle. This chapter examines the representation of ears and hearing in early modern texts, or, as Bloom states, considers 'what happens to vocal communication when the voice reaches its most unpredictable destination, the listener' (p. 18). In a theoretically-engaged analysis, Bloom marks out her unique critical position in attending to gender in this context, an issue that is not considered in previous work on hearing and sound in early modern culture. While recent critics have argued for a relationship between sound and subjectivity, the emergent subject's relationship to sound is, Bloom points out, often figured as one of subordination. Yet, when these models of acoustic subjectification are applied to *Cymbeline*, *Pericles*, *The Winter's Tale* and *The Tempest*, as they are in this study, their limitations become evident. The late plays, Bloom claims, 'explore most intently the transformative power of hearing' (p. 122). She demonstrates this through an analysis of the representation of receptive ears as crucial for salvation and of open ears as a liability in Protestant sermons. A reading of the late plays alongside these texts leads to an original interpretation of the salvation of the male characters in the late plays. In *Cymbeline*, Bloom argues, auditory acts induce the collapse and the restoration of the king's family and state; in *Pericles* and *The Winter's Tale*, the male protagonists undergo the process of salvation through aural receptivity. However, it is Bloom's analysis of the female characters of the late plays in these terms that it is most significant and interesting. Engaging with the critical tendency to focus on the late plays' valorization of feminine and maternal virtues and on female speech, Bloom questions the extent to which these signify a more generous portrayal of women. Stating that 'although Marina, Innogen and Paulina speak persuasively at crucial moments, their vocal power has diminished currency in plays that figure salvation as aural, rather than oral' (p. 132), Bloom points out that while aural openness signifies heroic capacity for the men in the late plays, it signifies lasciviousness for the women. Hearing therefore, Bloom suggests, functions as a site of gender differentiation in the late plays. Yet she goes on to argue convincingly that this does not mean that women are denied power; rather, the plays dramatize a provocative model of female agency, albeit one that locates agency in aural acts. Bloom utilizes the theories of Judith Butler and Pierre Bourdieu to argue that the plays illustrate the potential transformation of constructive aural defence into disruptive deafness. In other words, if female auditors are expected to practise aural defence, then it is possible that they will use these skills when they should be listening, and Bloom explores the relationship between Prospero and Miranda as a key example. Ultimately, she extends this exploration of listening in the late drama to consider an audience who may also choose not to listen. Concluding with an entirely new slant on *The Tempest*'s representation of the power of the theatre, Bloom suggests that if Miranda resists Prospero's performance this problematizes the play's representation of the spellbinding effect of theatre. This original examination of the late plays thus offers a fresh interpretation of the plays' representations of gender, subjectivity and of theatre itself.

A chapter on Shakespeare's late plays is also central to Michael Witmore's study of the child as a metaphor for, and producer and consumer of, fiction and the imagination in *Pretty Creatures*. Noting the ways in which scholars have associated Shakespeare's late plays with childhood, Witmore offers a fascinating interpretation of one of Shakespeare's most famous child characters, Mamillius, and delivers a new reading of Shakespeare's meditation on his art in his late career through a lively analysis of childhood and storytelling in *The Winter's Tale*. Positioned within the wider exploration offered by Witmore's study of the associations between the child, imagination and fiction in the period, this chapter draws 'Shakespeare and his late writing into the larger conversation about children and fictional agency in the seventeenth century' (p. 138). Beginning with a brief survey of the function of child characters in Shakespeare's earlier work, Witmore argues that the Shakespearian child often symbolizes the origin of a story or serves as a medium of exchange between adults, and that Shakespeare turns more intently to nature and children in his late plays to interrogate methods of storytelling and the nature of his art. He reads the representation of childhood, storytelling and the imagination in *The Winter's Tale* as exemplary of the late plays in order to get a 'more precise sense of their dramaturgy and distinctive representation of the agency of fiction' (p. 140), and suggests that a consideration of these motifs in this play provides a fresh perspective to debates on Shakespeare's interrogation of his own art. His analysis of Mamillius's dramaturgical role in carrying the story, of his associations with origins and imaginative generativity and of the links between this child figure and Autolycus in the representation of storytelling constitutes a novel examination of the representation of fiction and theatre in the late plays, moving away from the usual focus on the play's statue scene. In contrast to the common conclusions of critical examinations of the representation of art in the late plays, Witmore concludes that *The Winter's Tale* stands as one of the most focused explorations of the nature of fiction, and that the 'writer of the late plays was not so much interested in explaining the causes of the theatre's power as he was in illustrating its effects' (p. 170).

Shakespeare's late plays are also used to explore further questions of genre in two edited collections this year. In *Early Modern Tragicomedy*, edited by Subha Mukherji and Raphael Lyne, Gordon McMullan returns to the question of the terminology used to describe this group of plays, querying the neutrality of the term late and comparing it to other tags such as romance and tragicomedy. This essay, ' "The Neutral Term": Shakespearean Tragicomedy and the Idea of the "Late Play" ' (pp. 115–32), as its title suggests, extends the arguments of McMullan's monograph to explore tragicomedy as a 'late' genre in theatrical history. He interestingly considers Shakespeare's late works in conjunction with those of John Fletcher and Ben Jonson, reaching the conclusion that tragicomedy is 'a logical corollary of and development from...the primitive forms of tragedy and comedy' (p. 132). This is one of four essays on Shakespeare's late plays in this collection of work that consider concepts of tragicomedy from Aristotle to early modern Irish theatre. Ros King's contribution, 'In Lieu of Democracy, or How Not to Lose Your Head: Theatre and Authority in Renaissance England' (pp. 84–100), considers the political import of tragicomedy. It reads *Cymbeline* as an example of this genre alongside *Damon and Pythias*, *The Comedy of Errors* and *Dr Faustus*, and focuses on the duality within these plays and the careful balancing of tragedy with comic moments. One of most interesting aspects of this essay is its analysis of specific moments in *Cymbeline* and its readings of the potentially different generic effects of these moments on those watching the play in contrast to those reading it. One example is King's account of Imogen's clasping of the headless body. When reading the play, she suggests, this is a tragic moment, with the emphasis on the pathos of the speech. However, in performance the audience might be reminded that Imogen has got the wrong person and this has the potential, King proposes, to function as a comic moment as the intensity of character's emotions becomes embarrassing and liable to provoke laughter. According to King, therefore, this play's balance of tragedy and comedy may depend on the presentation medium.

Another essay in this collection, 'Taking *Pericles* Seriously' by Suzanne Gossett (pp. 101–14), focuses on Francis Beaumont and John Fletcher's attempts at tragicomedy in the context of the development of the genre in the early years of the seventeenth century. *Pericles* is central to this discussion as Gossett insists on its popularity and points to repeated productions of the play to argue for its influence on the work of Beaumont and Fletcher, particularly *Philaster*, *A King and No King*, *Cupid's Revenge* and *The Faithful Shepherdess*. Rather than the archaic flavour, episodic sweep or language of Shakespeare's late play, 'what the young collaborators modelled from *Pericles* as they moved to the King's Men', Gossett argues, 'was the power of sexuality to disturb the state, the mixture of social classes, the strong, virtuous heroine, and most of all the ability to move audiences' (p. 114).

Michael Witmore and Jonathan Hope's essay in this collection, 'Shakespeare by Numbers: On the Linguistic Texture of the Late Plays' (pp. 133–53), takes an unusual but intriguing approach in the writers' account of their attempts to make quantitative assessments about the late plays, or to do Shakespeare by numbers. In this essay they outline their methodology in using a computer text analysis tool, Docuscope, to analyse this group of late plays, romances or tragicomedies in an effort to identify linguistic features that might be used to separate this group from the tragedies, comedies and histories and to define a fourth Shakespearian genre. Their findings include interesting original evidence on the linguistic differences between the late plays and other genres, such as an increase in direct representations of the past. They acknowledge that language in the theatre is influenced by material factors, such as the number of actors, the size of stage and staging technologies, and note that when counting the use of linguistic features it is necessary to account for the degree to which 'texts of plays are saturated with dramaturgical exigencies—the need to do something with language in a particular way in a particular set of circumstances' (p. 152). Nonetheless, their conclusion that genre is a 'coordinated pattern of various types of dramaturgical and linguistic effects' (p. 152) that might be defined through this form of statistical analysis not only sheds new light on the features and linguistic composition of the late plays but also gestures towards the potential impact of computer text analysis on our understanding of genre.

Genre is also a key issue in the examination of Shakespeare's late plays in two essays included in *Shakespeare and Historical Formalism*, edited by Stephen Cohen. Emphasizing the displacement of an examination of formal techniques in New Historicism, the essays in this collection exemplify a new body of work that returns to matters of form but also retains the theoretical and methodological gains of historicism and they thus 'fulfil the promise of a historical formalism' (p. 3). Shakespeare's late plays figure prominently in part I of this volume, specifically in Heather Dubrow's ' "I would I were at home": Representations of Dwelling Places and Havens in *Cymbeline*' (pp. 69–93) and Christopher Cobb's 'Storm versus Story: Form and Affective Power in Shakespeare's Romances' (pp. 95–124). Dubrow's chapter is a lively exploration of the interplay of generic norms and cultural tensions in *Cymbeline*. Comparing Shakespeare's play with contemporary cinema, especially the films of the Coen brothers, Dubrow suggests that these performances share a delight in parody and an emphasis on the centrality of dwelling places, and she explores the ways in which the invasion of spaces perverts and pays homage to traditional structures, specifically generic types. Dubrow moves fluently between an outline of the potentialities of the genres of romance and pastoral for exploring the loss and recovery of dwellings and an investigation of historical context, specifically of the significance of dwellings, Wales and coinage in early modern culture, and she brings both to bear on *Cymbeline* through close textual analysis. The essay's main argument is that the genres of romance and pastoral become metagenres in this play, as Shakespeare subjects their conventions to ironic critique, and it offers an interesting insight into this possibility. However, Dubrow concludes that, in spite of the play's reinterpretation of the genres, its final scene returns to a traditional use of the forms.

Christopher Cobb's excellent essay is a version of chapter 6 of his monograph discussed above. It begins with a comparison between the features of romance used to open the three early late plays (*Pericles*, *Cymbeline* and *The Winter's Tale*) and those used to open *The Tempest*, *Henry VIII* and *The Two Noble Kinsmen*. The former group, he argues, emphasize narrative forms of romance, while the latter, on which he focuses here, use elaborate theatrical spectacles of the romance genre that are also employed in forms of political theatre. Cobb's essay offers a dense analysis of the ways in which Shakespeare's late plays become overtly involved in theatrical politics via this use of the romance genre. Examining how these plays ironically represent the pretensions of royal spectacle and undermine the power of such spectacles to induce belief, this is a welcome engagement with *Henry VIII* and *The Two Noble Kinsmen*. Furthermore, as one of many studies of the representation of theatre in *The Tempest*, this is innovative and moves forward from previous work on this topic. To comment on the use of masque in the play as means of affirming power or the monarch, Cobb acknowledges, would be nothing new; but what he offers is a consideration of the ways in which the use of masque is interrupted by a range of theatrical forms, including the techniques of the public theatres, which results in a tension between the representation of the theatrical means used and the desired political ends. This reading of Shakespeare's late plays also has wider implications for theoretical approaches to drama, as Cobb illustrates how a careful consideration of the romance framework of these plays can 'reveal aspects of the politics of these forms inaccessible to intertextual and topical studies enabled by New Historicist methodologies' (p. 96) and proposes that, in order to reconsider forms of romance in the theatre, it is necessary to reconsider form, especially theatrical form, in historicist methodology.

Performance contexts of *The Tempest* form the basis of further studies of this late play this year. It is considered in relation to music in Daniel Albright's *Musicking Shakespeares: A Conflict of Theatres*. The introduction to this noteworthy study of the ways in which composers have responded to the distinctive features of Shakespeare's plays includes an analysis of the music in the original Jacobean performances of *The Tempest* and in Restoration operatic appropriations. Outlining the types of music and songs incorporated by the playwright into his drama, Albright suggests that at the end of his career, and illustrated by *The Tempest*, Shakespeare's attitude to the dramatic possibilities of music changed. Via an examination of the play's text, Albright comments, as others have, on the influence of the court masque on the play and the cues given by the stage directions for dances, music and singing. However, Albright goes further than other commentaries on this topic and considers two songs written for the play by Robert Johnson. Examining the extant manuscript copies of these songs from *c*.1660, Albright imagines a 'nonexistent *Tempest* opera that might have been produced in James I's or Charles I's England' (p. 16) before looking at Restoration operatic versions of the play. He is thus in a position to suggest new ways in which the play might be read as a meditation on the technical evolution of the stage and fresh interpretations of the masque-like structure of the play. Arguing that *The Tempest* calls for a sophisticated code of analysis, Albright uses this example to establish his method of reading opera and drama in this study. This method collapses the boundaries between the two performance forms to offer innovative readings of Shakespearian appropriations by Purcell, Berlioz, Verdi and Britten which, Albright convincingly argues, push the boundaries of theatre and the operatic medium.

This reading of *The Tempest* develops a critical interest in the play's musical elements also evident in David Lindley's 2006 study, *Shakespeare and Music*. This introductory guide evidently offers less specialist analysis, but nonetheless provides a comprehensive commentary on the potential use of music in the play in Shakespeare's time. Arguing that musical moments in Shakespearian drama can only be fully comprehended when located in a wider cultural concept of music in the early modern period, Lindley considers the various musical moments of the play in this context. In the final chapter he reads the play alongside *Twelfth Night*, commenting on how the music and songs might have been performed and on their effects, and suggesting ways in which songs explore the limits of Shakespeare's art.

Another student guide to *The Tempest* is Trevor Griffith's *The Tempest: A Guide to the Text and its Theatrical Life*, included in Palgrave's new series, The Shakespeare Handbooks. Like the other books in this series, this is a detailed examination of the play's text, original performance conditions, appropriations on stage and screen and critical history, and includes a scene-by-scene commentary. This focused analysis highlights a range of potential readings of the play for students, and, in addition to the necessary comments on action, language and dramatic structure, offers informative remarks on staging issues. The section on sources and cultural contexts also includes some interesting information on the contexts of the Sea Venture, representations of the New World, slavery and early modern concepts of genre, and provides relevant extracts from contemporary documents, making this a particularly useful source for the classroom. Teachers and students will appreciate the well-presented insights into the play and its historical, performance and critical contexts.

The Winter's Tale is, as usual, also considered in a number of other books and journals this year. Catherine Belsey's captivating study, *Why Shakespeare?*, examines the play in the context of tale-telling and oral culture in Renaissance England. Belsey explains the play's unlikely occurrences by approaching it as 'an old wives' tale, although one with a considerable difference in the telling' (p. 67), and contrasts the realism of the first three acts with the fairy-tale elements of Perdita's story. Highlighting the significance of changing costume and adopting new identities with ease for Perdita's character, Belsey suggests that 'like any fairytale princess, Shakespeare's figure has no identity, only a succession of identifications, and she inhabits each of them without indications of serious anxiety' (p. 79). Belsey also identifies fairy-tale elements to Hermione's story, but, arguing that this is a mimetic representation with elements of folk tale while Perdita's is predominantly a fireside tale with elements of realism, she asks: 'what are we to make of the moment when the two stories converge?' (p. 79). Having worked through the potential interpretations of the statue scene in the context of this combination of realism and fairy tale, Belsey concludes that to settle on one reading of the final scene does an injustice to a play that sustains its own mystery. The effect of this, she proposes, is a generic undecidability that leaves play's happy ending in question. What initially appears to be a gentle interpretation of the play as fairy tale, therefore, is in fact a serious theoretical analysis of the complexities of play's final moments, which exposes the darker undercurrents of the play's apparently happy ending. Of course, we would expect nothing less from Belsey's study, and this is typical of the book as a whole. *Why Shakespeare?* attempts to answer the momentous question of why Shakespeare continues to be so popular, and proposes that one reason is the way in which his plays rewrite familiar stories that have always held a wide-ranging appeal, especially fairy tales. Through this examination of the fairy-tale heroine in *The Winter's Tale*, of the relationship between folk tales and *As You Like It*, of fairies in *A Midsummer Night's Dream*, of riddles in *Twelfth Night*, of riddles and villains in *The Merchant of Venice*, of ghosts and fools in *Hamlet*, and of fathers and daughters in *King Lear*, Belsey offers a close analysis of language and carefully theorized readings of the plays that introduce questions of identity and gender in an accessible manner for students, and gives a lively and convincing account of the position of Shakespeare's plays in a history of storytelling and popular culture.

A reading of *The Winter's Tale* is also provided in the final chapter of David Hillman's *Shakespeare's Entrails: Belief, Scepticism and the Interior of the Body*. Drawing on psychoanalytic, philosophical, historicist and literary-critical methodologies, this book examines the emergence of modern subjectivity in relation to changing attitudes towards the interior of the human body in the Renaissance and the connections between embodiment, knowledge and acknowledgement in *Troilus and Cressida, Hamlet, King Lear* and *The Winter's Tale*. In the example of *The Winter's Tale*, Hillman examines the images of the interior body, specifically Hermione's pregnant body and its depiction of the possibility of bodily inhabitation, Leontes' reading of his wife's body as his own, his desire to purge his body and the imagery of eating and breathing. Relating Leontes' scepticism to these representations of the body, this chapter examines the gendering of scepticism in the play and in this culture to offer a detailed examination of Leontes from a psychoanalytic perspective. Hillman additionally reads the play through an original manner through a comparison with *King Lear*; indeed, his overall argument is that this late Shakespearian play might be interestingly re-read as a return to *King Lear* and 'an attempt to revisit, and to escape from, the intensity of that play's engagement with the terrors and hopes regarding who or what can inhabit the human body' (p. 153). Through this approach he offers new interpretations of oft-examined lines and moments in *The Winter's Tale*.

Finally, Ros King's 'Reading Beyond words: Sound and Gesture in *The Winter's Tale*' (*Pedagogy* 7:iii[2007] 385–400) also focuses on *The Winter's Tale* and addresses the topics of oral and aural culture in relation to the late plays—topics that are, of course, central to Bloom's study discussed above. However, in contrast to Bloom's focus on early modern concepts of the voice, King addresses the importance of reading aloud in her article on teaching the aural aspects of Shakespeare. Demonstrating the ways in which close attention to sound might alter the way we critically approach the late plays and outlining the implications for teaching Shakespearian drama, King concludes with a case study of *The Winter's Tale*, indicating some ways in which it might be read and taught with an emphasis on speaking, silence and listening that offers a creative interpretation of Leontes' jealousy.

Books Reviewed

Albright, Daniel. *Musicking Shakespeare: A Conflict of Theatres*. URP. [2007] pp. x + 317. £45 ISBN 9 7815 8046 2556.

Arnold, Oliver. *The Third Citizen: Shakespeare's Theater and the Early Modern House of Commons*. JHUP. [2007] pp. xiv + 308. £36.50 ISBN 0 8018 8504 3.

Bach, Rebecca Ann. *Shakespeare and Renaissance Literature before Heterosexuality*. Palgrave. [2007] pp. xi + 243. $74.95 ISBN 1 4039 7654 6.

Barker, Simon. *War and Nation in the Theatre of Shakespeare and his Contemporaries*. EdinUP. [2007] pp. viii + 239. £50 ISBN 9 7807 4862 7653.

Bate, Jonathan, and Eric Rasmussen. eds. *The Complete Works (The Royal Shakespeare Company Complete Works)*. Macmillan. [2007] pp. 2,576. £35 ISBN 9 7802 3000 3507.

Belsey, Catherine. *Why Shakespeare?* Palgrave. [2007] pp. xii + 190. £9.99 ISBN 9 7814 0399 3205.

Bevington, David. *This Wide and Universal Theater: Shakespeare in Performance Then and Now*. University of Chicago Press [2007] pp. 256. hb $25. ISBN: 0 2260 4478 5.

Bloom, Gina. *Voice in Motion: Staging Gender, Shaping Sound in Early Modern England*. UPennP. [2007] pp. 277. £39 ISBN 9 7808 1224 0061.

Brooks, Douglas A., Ann Thompson and John Ford, eds. *Shakespeare Yearbook 16: The Shakespeare Apocrypha*. Mellen. [2007] pp. 568. $140 ISBN 0 7734 5421 7.

Buccola, Regina, and Lisa Hopkins, eds. *Marian Moments in Early Modern British Drama*. Ashgate. [2007] pp. 177. £50 ISBN 9 7807 5465 6371.

Burnett, Mark Thornton. *Filming Shakespeare in a Global Marketplace*. Palgrave Macmillan. [2007] pp. 227. hb £45 ISBN 1 4039 9215 0.

Burt, Richard, ed. *Shakespeares after Shakespeare: An Encyclopedia of the Bard in Mass Media and Popular Culture*, 2 vols. Greenwood Press. [2007] pp. 888. hb $299.95 ISBN 0 3133 3116 2.

Busse, Beatrix. *Vocative Constructions in the Language of Shakespeare*. Benjamins. [2006] pp. xviii + 525. £117 ISBN 9 0272 5393 5.

Butterworth, Philip ed. *The Narrator, the Expositor, and the Prompter in European Medieval Theatre*. Brepols. [2007]

Callaghan, Dympna. *Shakespeare's Sonnets*. Blackwell. [2007] pp. 176. £15.99 ISBN 1 4051 1398 7.

Callaghan, Dympna ed. *The Impact of Feminism in English Renaissance Studies*. Palgrave. [2007]

Canino, Catherine Grace. *Shakespeare and the Nobility*. CUP. [2007] pp. x + 266. £50 ISBN 9 7805 2187 2911.

Cartelli, Thomas, and Katherine Rowe. *New Wave Shakespeare on Screen*. Polity Press. [2007] pp. 201. hb £55, pb £16.99. ISBN 0 7456 3392 7, 0 7456 3393 5.

Cartmell, Deborah, and Imelda Whelehan, eds. *The Cambridge Companion to Literature on Screen*. Cambridge UP. [2007] pp. 288. hb £48, pb £15.99. ISBN 0 5218 4962 4.

Chedgzoy, Kate, Susanne Greenhalgh and Robert Shaughnessy, eds. *Shakespeare and Childhood*. Cambridge UP. [2007] pp. 296. hb £50 ISBN 0 5218 7125 5.

Cheney, Patrick, ed. *The Cambridge Companion to Shakespeare's Poetry*. Cambridge UP. [2007] pp. 316. £16.99 ISBN 0 5216 0864 3.

Cheney, Patrick, Andrew Hadfield and Garrett A. Sullivan, Jr, eds. *Early Modern English Poetry: A Critical Companion*. OUP. [2007] pp. xxiii + 342. £21.99 ISBN 9 7801 9515 3873.

Chernaik, Warren. *The Cambridge Introduction to Shakespeare's History Plays*. CUP. [2007] pp. ix + 210. £11.99 ISBN 9 7805 2167 1200.

Clark, Ira. *Rhetorical readings, Dark Comedies, and Shakespeare's Problem Plays*. UPFlor [2007] pp. 144. £54.62 ISBN 978-0813030401.

Cobb, Christopher J. *The Staging of Romance in Late Shakespeare: Text and Theatrical Technique*. UDelP. [2007] pp. 304. £51.50 ISBN 9 7808 7413 9716.

Cohen, Stephen, ed. *Shakespeare and Historical Formalism*. Ashgate. [2007] pp. ix + 252. £50 ISBN 9 7807 5465 3820.

Cordner, Michael, and Peter Holland, eds. *Players, Playwrights, Playhouses: Investigating Performance, 1660–1800*. Palgrave. [2007] pp. xiii + 300. £50 ISBN 9 7802 3052 5245.

de Grazia, Margreta. *'Hamlet' without Hamlet*. CUP. [2007] pp. 280. $91 ISBN 0 5218 7025 9.

Dillon, Janette. *The Cambridge Introduction to Shakespeare's Tragedies*. CUP. [2007] pp. vi + 169. £11.99 ISBN 9 7805 2167 4928.

Duncan-Jones, Katherine, and H.R. Woudhuysen, eds. *Shakespeare's Poems: Venus and Adonis, The Rape of Lucrece and the Shorter Poems*. Thomson. [2007] pp. 593. £9.99 ISBN 9 7819 0343 6875.

Ewert, Kevin. *Henry V: A Guide to the Text and its Theatrical Afterlife*. Palgrave. [2006] pp. vii + 166. £9.99 ISBN 9 7814 0394 0773.

Freedman, Penelope. *Power and Passion in Shakespeare's Pronouns: Interrogating 'You' and 'Thou'*. Ashgate. [2007] pp. xiv + 294. £50 ISBN 9 7807 5465 8306.

Fryatt, Kit. 'Shakespeare and Berryman: Sonnet 129 and Dream Song 1', pp. 81–86. In Coleman, Philip, ed. and introd., McGowan, Philip, ed. and introd., Kelly, Richard J., preface. *'After Thirty Falls': New Essays on John Berryman*. Amsterdam: Rodopi, 2007.

Giese, Loreen L. *Courtships, Marriage Customs, and Shakespeare's Comedies*. Palgrave. [2006] pp. xiii + 217. £38.99. ISBN 0 3121 6604 5.

Grady, Hugh and Hawkes, Terence, eds. *Presentist Shakespeare*. Routledge. [2007] Hb £60 ISBN 0 415 38528 8 Pb £18.99 ISBN 0 415 38529 6.

Griffiths, Trevor. *The Tempest: A Guide to the Text and its Theatrical Life*. Palgrave. [2007]. pp. xi + 160. £9.99 ISBN 978 1 4039 3478 9.

Groves, Beatrice. *Texts and Traditions: Religion in Shakespeare, 1592–1604*. OUP. [2007] pp. 244. $55 ISBN 0 1992 0898 0.

Hageman, Elizabeth H., and Conway, Katherine, eds. *Resurrecting Elizabeth I in Seventeenth-Century England*. FDUP. [2007] pp. 292. £46.95 ISBN 9 7808 3864 1156.

Hillman, David. *Shakespeare's Entrails: Belief, Scepticism and the Interior of the Body*. Palgrave. [2007] pp. xiii + 263. £50 ISBN 9 7814 0394 2678.

Hindle, Maurice. *Studying Shakespeare on Film*. Palgrave Macmillan. [2007] pp. 272. hb £50. pb £16.99. ISBN: 1 4039 0673 4, 1 4039 0672 6.

Howard, Tony. *Women as Hamlet: Performance and Interpretation in Theatre, Film and Fiction*. Cambridge UP. [2007] pp. 341. hb £50, pb £16.99. ISBN 0 5218 6466 6.

Huang, Alexander C.Y., I-Chun Wang and Mary Theis, eds. *Class, Boundary and Social Discourse in the Renaissance*. National Sun Yat-Sen University, Kaohsiung, Taiwan. [2007]

Hunt, Marvin W. *Looking for Hamlet*. Palgrave. [2007] pp. vi + 230. £27.95 ISBN 1 4039 7036 X.

Hutson, Lorna. *The Invention of Suspicion: Law and Mimesis in Shakespeare and Renaissance Drama*. OUP. [2007] pp. x + 382. £50 ISBN 9 7801 9921 2439.

Jackson, Russell. *Shakespearean Films in the Making: Vision, Production and Reception*. Cambridge UP. [2007] pp. 292. hb £50. ISBN 0 5218 1547 9.

Jancsó, Daniella. *Excitements of Reason: The Presentation of Thought in Shakespeare's Plays and Wittgenstein's Philosophy*. Winter. [2007] pp. 257. ISBN 9 7838 2535 4107.

Jordan, Constance, and Cunningham, Karen, eds. *The Law in Shakespeare*. Palgrave. [2007] pp. x + 286. £53 ISBN 1 4039 9214 2.

Jordan, Constance and Karen Cunningham, eds. *The Law in Shakespeare*. Palgrave. [2007]

Jowett, John. *Shakespeare and Text*. OUP. [2007] pp. 229. £12.99 ISBN 9 7801 9921 7069.

Kathryn M. Moncrieff and Kathryn R. McPherson, eds. *Performing Maternity in Early Modern England*. Ashgate. [2007]

Lemon, Rebecca. *Treason by Words: Literature, Law, and Rebellion in Shakespeare's England*. CornUP. [2006] pp. ix + 234. £28.50 ISBN 9 7808 0144 4289.

Levith, Murray. *Shakespeare's Cues and Prompts*. Continuum. [2007] £45 ISBN 0 8264 9597 4.

Lindley, David. *Shakespeare and Music*. Arden. [2006]. pp. xii + 284. £22.99 ISBN 9 7819 0343 6189.

Lloyd, Megan S. *Speak It in Welsh: Wales and the Welsh Language in Shakespeare*. Lexington. [2007] pp. 209. $60 ISBN 0 7391 1760 2.

Logan, Sandra. *Texts/Events in Early Modern England*. Ashgate. [2007] pp. viii + 360. £50 ISBN 9 7807 5465 5862.

Lyne, Raphael. *Shakespeare's Late Work*. OUP. [2007] pp. 173. £12.99 ISBN 9 7801 9926 5954.

Magnusson, Lynne. 'A pragmatics for interpreting Shakespeare's Sonnets 1–20: Dialogue scripts and Erasmian intertexts', pp. 167–83. In Fitzmaurice, Susan, ed. and introd., Taavitsainen, Irma, ed. and introd. *Methods in Historical Pragmatics*. Berlin: Mouton de Gruyter, 2007.

Marrapodi, Michele, ed. *Italian Culture in the Drama of Shakespeare and his Contemporaries: Rewriting, Remaking, Refashioning*. Ashgate. [2007] pp. 302. £55 ISBN 9 7807 5465 5046.

Massai, Sonia. *Shakespeare and the Rise of the Editor*. CUP. [2007] pp. 266. £50 ISBN 9 7805 2187 8050.

McDonald, Russ. *Shakespeare's Late Style*. CUP. [2006] pp. x + 260. £54 ISBN 9 7805 2182 0684.

McMullan, Gordon. *Shakespeare and the Idea of Late Writing: Authorship in the Proximity of Death*. CUP. [2007] pp. xii + 402. £55 ISBN 9 7805 2186 3049.

Merriam, Tom. *Co-authorship in King John*. RenI. [2007] pp. 92. No price, no ISBN.

Moncrief, Kathryn M, and Kathryn R. McPherson eds. *Performing Maternity in Early Modern England*. Ashgate. [2007] pp. 247. £50 ISBN 9 7807 5466 1177.

Mukherji, Subha, and Raphael Lyne, eds. *Early Modern Tragicomedy*. Brewer. [2007] pp. x + 216. £50 ISBN 9 7818 4384 1302.

Murphy, Andrew, ed. *Shakespeare and the Text*. Blackwell. [2007] pp. 280. £55 ISBN 9 7814 0513 5283.

Nuttall, A.D. *Shakespeare the Thinker*. YaleUP. [2007] pp. xiv + 428. £19.99 ISBN 9 7803 0011 9282.

O'Connor, John, and Katharine Goodland, *A Directory of Shakespeare in Performance 1970–2005*, vol. 1: *Great Britain*. Palgrave Macmillan. [2007] pp. 1760. hb £140. ISBN 1 4039 1734 5.

Orlin, Lena Cowin, ed. *Center or Margin: Revisions of the English Renaissance in Honor of Leeds Barroll*. SusquehannaUP. [2006] pp. 318. £46.95 ISBN 978 1 57591 098 7.

Orlin, Lena Cowen, and Miranda Johnson-Haddad, eds. *Staging Shakespeare: Essays in Honor of Alan C. Dessen*. UDelP. [2007] pp. 274. hb $53.50. ISBN 0 8741 3987 2.

Pacheco, Anita. *William Shakespeare: Coriolanus*. Northcote. [2007] pp. viii + 120. £12.99 ISBN 9 7807 4631 1478.

Palfrey, Simon, and Tiffany Stern. *Shakespeare in Parts*. OUP. [2007] pp. xiv + 545. £20 ISBN 9 7801 9927 2051.

Poole, William, and Richard Scholar, eds. *Thinking with Shakespeare: Comparative and Interdisciplinary Essays for A.D. Nuttall*. Legenda. [2007] pp. 200. $38 ISBN 1 9043 5084 4.

Poole William, and Richard Scholar, eds. *Thinking with Shakespeare: Comparative and Interdisciplinary Essays for A. D. Nuttall*. Legenda. [2007]

Rutter, Carol Chillington. *Shakespeare and Child's Play: Performing Lost Boys on Stage and Screen*. Routledge. [2007] pp. 250. hb £65, pb £19.99. ISBN 0 4153 6518 X, 0 4153 6519 8.

Sanders, Julie. *Shakespeare and Music: Afterlives and Borrowings*. Polity. [2007] pp. 248. hb £50, pb £15.99. ISBN 0 7456 3296 3.

Schoenfeldt, Michael, ed. *A Companion to Shakespeare's Sonnets*. Blackwell. [2007] pp. 536. £85 ISBN 1 4051 2155 6.

Scott, Charlotte. *Shakespeare and the Idea of the Book*. OUP. [2007] pp. 216. £53 ISBN 9 7801 9921 2101.

Shaugnessy, Robert, ed. *The Cambridge Companion to Shakespeare and Popular Culture*. CUP. [2007] pp. 304. hb £45, pb £15.99. ISBN 0 5216 0580 6.

Smith, Emma. *The Cambridge Introduction to Shakespeare*. CUP. [2007] pp. 176. $20 ISBN 0 5216 7188 4.

Sohmer, Steve. *Shakespeare for the Wiser Sort*. MUP. [2007] pp. xv + 192. £50 ISBN 9 7807 1907 6671.

Staub, Susan C. '"My throbbing heart shall rock you day and night": Shakespeare's Venus, Elizabeth, and Early Modern Constructions of Motherhood', pp. 15–32. In Staub, Susan C, ed. *The Literary Mother: Essays on Representations of Maternity and Child Care*. McFarland: Jefferson, NC, 2007.

Stephen Cohen, ed. *Shakespeare and Historical Formalism*. Ashgate. [2007]

Stříbrný, Zdeněk. *The Whirligig of Time: Essays on Shakespeare and Czechoslovakia*. UDelP. [2007] pp. 258. £44.95 ISBN 9 7808 7413 9563.

Taylor, Gary, and John Lavagnino, eds. *The Collected Works*, by Thomas Middleton. OUP. [2007] pp. 2,018. £89 ISBN 9 7801 9818 5697.

Taylor, Gary, and John Lavagnino, eds. *Thomas Middleton and Early Modern Textual Culture: A Companion to the Collected Works*. OUP. [2007] pp. 1,184. £105 ISBN 9 7801 9818 5703.

Turner, Henry S. *Shakespeare's Double Helix*. Shakespeare Now! Continuum. [2007] pp. xiii + 129. £50. ISBN 0 8264 9119 0.

Vickers, Brian. *Shakespeare, 'A Lover's Complaint', and John Davies of Hereford*. CUP. [2007] pp. 342. £50 ISBN 9 7805 2185 9127.

Wallace, Jennifer. *The Cambridge Introduction to Tragedy*. CUP. [2007] pp. viii + 243. £15.99 ISBN 9 7805 2167 1491.

Waller, Gary, ed. *All's Well That Ends Well: New Critical Essays*. Routledge. [2007] pp. xx + 258. ISBN 9 7804 1597 3250.

Welsh, James M. *The Literature/Film Reader: Issues of Adaptation*. Scarecrow. [2007] pp. 392. pb $45 ISBN 0 8108 5949 1.

Witmore, Michael. *Pretty Creatures: Children and Fiction in the English Renaissance*. CornUP. [2007]. pp. ix + 233. £20.50 ISBN 978 0 8014 4399 2.

Zilberfain, Ava. *Stealing the Story: Shakespeare's Self-Conscious Use of the Mimetic Tradition in the Plays*. Continuum. [2007] pp. 181. £58 ISBN 9 7808 2641 7367.

VII

Renaissance Drama: Excluding Shakespeare

SARAH POYNTING, PETER SILLITOE, PETER J. SMITH,
ANDREW DUXFIELD AND MATTHEW STEGGLE

This chapter has three sections: 1. Editions and Textual Scholarship;
2. Theatre History; 3. Criticism. Section 1 is by Sarah Poynting; section 2 is
by Peter J. Smith; section 3(a) is by Peter Sillitoe; section 3(b) is by Andrew
Duxfield; section 3(c) is by Matthew Steggle.

1. Editions and Textual Scholarship

There can be no doubt about the major event of the year for this section: the
publication of the long-awaited *Thomas Middleton: The Collected Works*, with
its textual companion *Thomas Middleton and Early Modern Textual Culture*.
This is, in every sense, a massive achievement, and Gary Taylor and the
associate editors (MacDonald P. Jackson, John Jowett, Valerie Wayne and
Adrian Weiss) are to be congratulated on it; John Lavagnino, the second
general editor, is responsible for the supporting website now in development
(http://thomasmiddleton.org). So many scholars contributed to the content of
these volumes that it is impossible to name them all or to review every text
and essay, so my apologies to those who go unmentioned here.

That said, this is not an edition without problems, the most obvious being
its ease of use, which is connected to the rationale behind the decisions made
on the form it should take. The polemical opening of Gary Taylor's
introductory essay 'Thomas Middleton: Lives and Afterlives' makes it clear
that Middleton is being set up as Shakespeare's equal and rival, the only other
writer of the period to have 'created plays still considered masterpieces in four
major dramatic genres' (which provokes the response: considered by whom?).
Part of the reason for his not being seen as such is the lack of an equivalent of
the First Folio, or Jonson's 1616 *Works*: so this is explicitly 'the Middleton
First Folio' (p. 58), necessitating the inclusion in one volume of everything it
can be established that he wrote (as well as a good deal that he didn't). One
result of this is that the first volume alone has over 2,000 pages in double

Year's Work in English Studies, Volume 88 (2009) © *The English Association; all rights reserved*
doi:10.1093/ywes/map013

columns: though it's undoubtedly good value for the quantity of material and the text is never too small to be readable in reasonable comfort, on a purely practical level it's too big, too heavy to lug around and too expensive for students. This brings me to the second issue I have with it concerning use: the intended readership. In 'How To Use This Book', the modernized spelling is explained as aiming 'to make Middleton accessible to anyone interested in literature and drama' (p. 21), while the three essays introducing volume 1 have their source citations in volume 2, 'minimizing the distraction caused to ordinary readers by the courtesy rituals of academic culture' (p. 22). This seems to assume that only academics are interested in sources, but I should have thought that any 'ordinary readers' willing to fork out for this much Middleton might well take an interest in where the writers of these essays got their information, and might be a little irritated to find that they would need to stump up a good deal more to find out. There are a number of quotations, too, in both 'Lives and Afterlives' and Paul S. Seaver's 'Middleton's London' that are not individually referenced at all; this is surely unsatisfactory, and not just as a matter of a 'courtesy ritual'. The essays in this volume are presumably directed towards this readership, as, while some of the specific detail on Middleton is fascinating, much of the contextual material and the ideas informing it will be familiar to the academics who I find it hard to believe will not be the edition's main constituency.

The other major result of the 'First Folio' principle is that, like the Oxford Shakespeare, all textual information is in the companion volume; not only that, but in two different places. 'Works Included in This Edition: Canon and Chronology' provides details on authorship, publication and dating, with texts organized chronologically as they are in volume 1 (allowing readers to gain an impression of Middleton's development through time); 'The Texts' supplies all other textual information, with works listed in order of the earliest surviving witness; moreover, the use of the name of the printer or printers by which to cite early modern editions, while more precise than the usual 'Q1' or 'F2', can be confusing. Altogether, it's not the simplest arrangement that can be imagined.

In 'Lives and Afterlives', Taylor establishes the community and class into which Middleton was born, both temporally and geographically, siting him within a network of relationships, institutions and moments in history, both national and local. Of particular interest is the information on his mother Anne Snowe and the legal cases in defence of her property in which she became embroiled; as a young man Middleton acquired, through no fault of his own, a good deal of experience of the law courts. The comparison of her with Elizabeth I is a bit of a stretch, though, and the description of both women's 'wrinkled parsimonious stubbornness' as being unattractive to the young Middleton is both odd and unnecessary (p. 38). Where detail about Middleton himself is lacking, the gap is filled with what he is likely to have experienced: not knowing when or where he went to school, for example, Taylor tells us about Elizabethan grammar school education and its likely effect on Middleton's writing. It is hard to imagine Taylor's account of his career as an author within the Elizabethan and Jacobean worlds of publishing, theatre, the city of London and the marketing of literature being bettered, but there are times when his passion for his subject makes him dismissive of other playwrights. Middleton's most common collaborators, Rowley and Dekker, are dealt with generously, but there is rarely a good word for Jonson and one of Middleton's publications is referred to, rather coyly, as 'the imposing large folio which included *The Life of Timon of Athens*', while the treatment of Massinger is frankly bizarre. Taylor suggests that we can discover the reason for their perhaps surprising lack of collaborative work—or any that has survived—from posthumous engravings of them, neither of them of great quality, in which he sees Middleton as stylishly dark, Massinger as stolid and pasty, too contrasting to make a successful partnership (unlike the podgy Rowley, presumably). A very different reading of the Middleton engraving can be found in John H. Astington's 'Visual Texts: Thomas Middleton and Prints' in volume 2. There is a similar lack of logic in the assertion that Middleton's wife made a 'sound enough' choice in accepting 'a man remarkable for his representations . . . of a masculinity defined by non-violence' (p. 38); one might equally argue that she made a dangerous choice in accepting a man remarkable for his depictions of murderous lechers.

The delineation of Middleton's posthumous reputation sometimes has a slightly embittered tone. The English civil war (its causes neatly summarized in a paragraph) is held responsible both for the loss of a substantial proportion of his writing—it is suggested that as much as two-thirds of it may have been destroyed—and for determining 'how and by whom he would be interpreted', unlikely to appeal to any of its participants. In particular, Taylor suggests, 'it is hard to imagine' Charles I reading Middleton while in prison (p. 50), a statement that seems neither wholly relevant, nor, indeed, necessarily accurate, given that at the time the king was attempting to organize an adulterous liaison; *A Chaste Maid in Cheapside* could have been just the thing. But this is reflective of a strategy throughout the essay of associating Middleton with those considered sufficiently interesting (Hogarth, Caravaggio), and dissociating him from the less worthy. Not until the nineteenth century did the fragmentation of the Middleton canon begin to be repaired, since when his 'status has continued to rise', but it took many decades for 'the larger problem of the canon itself' to be solved (p. 55), making possible a fuller understanding of the range of his work, pamphlets, poems and pageants as well as plays: and so we reach the Middleton 'First Folio'. I have already mentioned the practical problem arising from this, but there is a more serious one as well. The edition pulls in two different directions: much is made of the 'play of diversity', of Middleton as a collaborative writer, but the determination to place Middleton alongside Shakespeare as an *individual* genius, to establish his 'canon', militates against this, tending at times to flatten out the importance of his co-authors. A last, perhaps pedantic, point arising from this essay: in an edition coming from Oxford, I should have thought someone would know how to spell Duke Humfrey's.

'Lives and Afterlives' is followed by Seaver's 'Middleton's London', in which he describes London through Middleton's lifetime from his birth in 1580, with its rapid population growth, hundreds of churches, incomers looking for work from country districts and abroad, and 'appalling mortality rates' (p. 61). Middleton may have died at the early age of 47, but Seaver suggests that survival for this long 'itself was a minor miracle', largely because of frequent outbreaks of the plague. The development of trade and manufacturing is analysed in some detail, along with the ways in which the consequent rise in merchant communities affected the social structure of the capital, with status becoming ever more complex. The hierarchy and duties of the government of the City of London and of the livery companies are clearly outlined, together with Middleton's family links to the latter. The post-Reformation parish structure and the nature of the London clergy, the lawyers, gentry and landed elite all find a place here. It is a useful and interesting survey.

The third essay in this volume is 'Middleton's Theatres' by the late Scott McMillin, a relatively brief account of the state of the theatre/theatres, mainly from 1601, though the Lord Chamberlain's Men's building of the Globe from the timbers of the Theatre gets a mention. (Is it really true that 'Lovers of Shakespeare do not often dwell on this piece of commercial aggression and questionable legality' (p. 75)? It always goes down well with students.) McMillin compares the public and private theatres and their playing companies, and discusses which of them Middleton, as a young playwright, might have preferred to work for, and why. The Chamberlain's Men would have seemed well established but old-fashioned (yet another Shakespeare history play?), unlike the children's companies with their 'satirical and avant-garde' productions (p. 76), or the Admiral's Men at the Fortune, with their stable of established playwrights from whom Middleton could not only learn, but with whom he could write. His plays for both the children and for the Fortune are considered, as well as the nature of the theatres—audiences, physical layout and location—in which they were performed, and the ways in which they could be staged. This is accompanied by the usual illustrations (de Witt, Inigo Jones's designs), nicely reproduced, as all the images are in the edition. The possible use of stage space is explored in relation to *The Witch*, *Women Beware Women*, *Michaelmas Term*, and *The Patient Man and the Honest Whore*, though I'm not persuaded by the suggestion that modern audiences find fluid, non-realist Elizabethan concepts of staging difficult to grasp because of our experience of film and realist theatre. McMillin concentrates on Middleton's work for the theatre, but also gives a short account of the city pageants in which he was involved, as well as of the masques that are embedded in his plays, pointing out that future developments in the theatre lay less in the kinds of theatres for which Middleton wrote, or in the city streets, than in the expensive experiments with movable perspective scenery and sophisticated technology being made at court.

More specialized essays are to be found in volume 2, examining a wide range of the cultural influences within which Middleton was working. Of these, MacDonald P. Jackson's 'Early Modern Authorship: Canons and Chronologies' is essential reading. In establishing the works written by Middleton, or in which he had a hand, Jackson attacks the idea made popular by postmodern theory that this is in some way a pointless or even an illegitimate exercise, declaring unequivocally that the plays 'result from the workings of his own creative imagination within a social, literary, and philosophical milieu. They bear the stamp of his distinctive genius . . . Renaissance writers were real people too' (p. 80). He argues that it matters who the real person behind any text is: the facts cannot always be easily established, but 'we have an obligation to get them as right as we can'. Mistaken attribution leads to misrepresentation. Jackson reiterates the importance of the Shakespeare First Folio to our sense of his achievement, comparing it with both Jonson's *Works* and the 1647 'Beaumont and Fletcher' folio, the three collections making their authors pre-eminent after the Restoration; the scattered and often anonymous or misattributed plays by Middleton led to his virtual disappearance (clearly there is an overlap here with Taylor's essay in volume 1). He discusses briefly the editions of Middleton's plays by Dyce [1840] and Bullen [1885–6], both of which excluded some of his best work, and included plays for which he was not responsible.

There is an overview of the kinds of evidence, internal and external, that can support an attribution to Middleton (or any early modern writer), and an assessment of their varying degrees of reliability, with a survey of the history of 'attribution studies'. The method of analysing inconsequential linguistic habits and patterns (introduced by Cyrus Hoy and familiar over recent years from Jackson's own articles) is described to demonstrate how decisions were reached as to the contents of the canon, testing the results from such analysis against external evidence. The same process is employed to distinguish between different writers within any play. The canon not only gains but loses plays through this analysis: *The Honest Whore, Part II* and *Blurt, Master Constable* become Dekker's alone, *The Family of Love* Lording Barry's. Jackson challenges Jeffrey Masten's view on the social production of collaborative texts, arguing that our understanding of such production is increased 'by any information we can glean about the ways in which collaborating playwrights divided their labours' (p. 87), and that the obstacles to doing so can be overcome. He gives the example of *The Roaring Girl*, arguing that the division of work between Dekker and Middleton, contrary to the claim of the New Mermaid editor, can be firmly established, though it is unclear whether Coppélia Kahn, the play's editor in the *Collected Works*, fully concurs with this judgement. Significantly, Jackson recognizes that 'the compound of two authors may produce an effect different than the work of either author in isolation', and that this mutual influence must be taken into account in authorship analysis, but that 'to take no interest in "who wrote what" would be to lack historical curiosity' (p. 88). However, as Jackson notes, the kind of linguistic patterning that provides sound proof of authorship for drama is less helpful in the other literary forms to which Middleton contributed. The problems involved in investigating the authorship of anonymously printed prose pamphlets are outlined, the reliability of the use of 'parallels' such as rare phrases being particularly considered. Jackson's conclusion is that while the 'dramatic canon seems relatively fixed; his non-dramatic canon may not be' (p. 90).

Linguistic details may be used not only to establish authorship, but also to examine the development of a writer's style, and hence to suggest a chronology of his work. Jackson discusses the way in which this practice has been applied to the Shakespeare canon, but points out that work in this field with regard to Middleton has hardly started. He outlines such analysis as has been carried out on Middleton's verse, seeing him as a 'strikingly original' metrist, though mainly after 1611 (p. 92); his increasing idiosyncrasies in metre and syntax are summarized, as well as Ants Oras's computer analysis of 'pause patterns' in early modern drama.

A final defence of attribution studies points out that critical commentary ranging over a century on plays thought to be by other dramatists nevertheless associates them with each other in terms of the qualities found within them, in some cases being found 'Middletonian', even while ascribing them to Tourneur, or wholly to Shakespeare. These have now been established as being 'Middletonian' in fact, not merely in style, Middleton's 'authorial personality' having manifested itself to the critics: 'authors, however circumscribed their autonomy, are agents to be reckoned with' (p. 95). Regrettably, the logic isn't flawless, since the argument, of course, ignores plays described as 'Middletonian' that are not by him, but I'm in sympathy with the sentiment.

Another essay I particularly like is Maureen Bell's 'Booksellers Without an Author, 1627–1685', which, while being concerned with exactly what the title implies, is not limitingly specialist, but relevant to anyone with an interest in the seventeenth-century history of the book; it is both scholarly and entertaining. As she says, there are gaps in book trade records, especially for the period 1640–60, which render problematic the investigation of the posthumous publication of Middleton's plays (and this is entirely about his dramatic output), but this is admirably addressed.

Bell begins by outlining the legal position as regards copyright, and the distinctions (or not) between printer, publisher and bookseller, before tabulating printed editions of the plays from the death of Middleton in 1627 to that of Charles II in 1685. In view of the length of time (sometimes more than half a century) between first performance and first edition, or between first and second editions, she raises the question of why, given the commercial marketplace in which printers and booksellers were operating, they should have chosen to publish these at all. She explores posthumous publication before the civil war, only two of his plays appearing for the first time in this period (*Chaste Maid* in 1630 and *The Bloody Banquet* in 1639), while there were six new editions of plays published in his lifetime (including *Timon of Athens* and *Macbeth*). The evidence for claims of any kind of updating—for presenting the plays as 'current', rather than appealing to nostalgia—is examined, finding a trend during the 1630s towards presenting the editions as being aimed at a 'discriminating readership, elaborating the bare play text into a literary product' (p. 265). She then moves on to the 1650s and early 1660s, when there was something of a boom in Middleton publication of elaborate quartos 'designed to appeal both to a nostalgia for performance and to an interest in the plays as literary artefacts', the acting companies and theatres of the 1630s being repeatedly mentioned on title pages. The books also became a marketing tool, carrying advertisements for other plays published by the bookseller. Turning back to the 1640s, when no editions of Middleton's plays appeared, Bell enquires why this should be, and why the situation then changed, relating her questions to broader issues of readership, the status of printed plays, and the bookselling market. She records the way in which rights to his plays changed hands between booksellers in this decade, focusing in detail on the career of Humphrey Moseley and his publication of the 1647 Beaumont and Fletcher folio, and examining how this came to contain two unattributed Middleton plays. The 'new market in "old" plays' is discussed, with booksellers' catalogues suggesting that there was a 'specific play-buying market' by the mid-1650s (p. 271). Bell considers Moseley's innovations in marketing, along with his interest in publishing contemporary poetry, often by royalists, and asks what place Middleton has in this programme. She finds part of the answer in the evidence that Moseley bought up the rights of every pre-war play that he could, often 'in job lots...from acting companies' or other booksellers (p. 273). In marketing Middleton's plays, Moseley presented them in accordance with his buyers' interests, in effect co-opting him 'into the myth of cavalier sensibility' and myth-making, and also issuing three 'woman' plays in 1657, perhaps conscious of the greater public presence of women at this period (pp. 274–5).

The competition to Moseley is assessed, particularly in the post-Restoration confusion, when Francis Kirkman began to publish plays to which he did not own the rights, establishing himself with a deliberately unpretentious style by comparison with Moseley (whose work was continued by his wife and daughter after his death in 1661), in a bid, perhaps, to widen the market. Kirkman lost heavily, however, when the Stationers' Company moved in to assert itself. Bell re-examines what is known of the book trade in relation to authors, the market, and booksellers in the years 1660–85, discussing the damaging effect of the emergence of a canon of dramatists on future Middleton publication.

Also excellent are the volume's essays on music and illustration, 'Middleton, Music, and Dance' by Gary Taylor and Andrew J. Sabol, and John H. Astington's 'Visual Texts: Thomas Middleton and Prints'. In the former, Taylor and Sabol draw attention to the fact that the first Middleton publication, *Wisdom of Solomon*, in 1597, interpolates a variety of musical forms into its verse paraphrase, music remaining a significant feature of his drama. They discuss the publication of contemporary music and the centrality of music and dance to leisure activity, together with developments in the notation of both. Use of music and dance in the theatre in general and Middleton's drama in particular is considered before a final section which prints all the music—songs and instrumental—that can be identified with his work. Astington's suitably well-illustrated article looks closely at the only 'supposed likeness' of Middleton, which he finds a not 'particularly accomplished engraving' (p. 226), examining the evidence for its artist. He describes the techniques for reproducing illustrations in print, comparing the style of woodcuts with engravings and etchings, and discusses the ways they were used in editions of early modern drama. He suggests that 'Middleton seems to have been particularly interested in the visual presentation of his own published work' to a greater extent than other playwrights (p. 230), including title pages with original decorative woodcuts in three of his plays, and engravings in *A Game at Chess*, as well as further illustrations in his non-dramatic publications, all of which are analysed in detail.

John Jowett's 'For Many of your Companies: Middleton's Early Readers' is also enlightening, if at times unavoidably speculative. The article's aim is 'to provide a map, albeit merely a sketch-map, of the circulation of [his] works in the seventeenth century' (p. 286), while recognizing that many of his readers may not have been aware that they were reading Middleton at all. Jowett considers the general problems in conducting readership analyses in the early modern period, before engaging specifically with Middleton's texts. He examines the notional reader envisaged by prefatory epistles and dedications, these 'collective readers . . . [being] constituted as a homogeneous group that is an idealized simplification of any actual readership' (p. 288). He suggests that Middleton 'shows himself to be unusually aware of the reader', invoking a 'diversity of assumed book-buyers' in line with the range of his writing (p. 289). Print-runs provide further evidence of readership in terms of numbers, while the cost and even the typeface of editions can suggest the intended market. Having discussed these issues in relation to particular texts, Jowett goes through the sequence of readers encountering any individual piece such as collaborators, actors and others involved in the processes of bringing it on to the stage or into multiple copies (manuscript and print). The work of scribes as editors as well as copyists in manuscript production is illustrated by the journey of the song 'Hence, all you vain delights' through verse miscellanies and songbooks: 'readership and transmission become two aspects of a single activity' (p. 297). The role of publishers and booksellers in 'constructing a readership' is examined, especially in relation to commendatory material in posthumous publications. The presence of Middleton's works in early modern book collections, the ownership of complete manuscripts, and seventeenth-century readers' responses as found both in rare marginalia and external commentary are all described in detail, before appendices which list publishers of his texts, dedications and prefaces, songs in miscellanies that can be identified with an owner or scribe, and readers' interventions in printed books, including such minutiae as owners' signatures or initials, underlining, and marginal crosses.

The longest essay in this volume is 'The Order of Persons' by Gary Taylor, assisted in his research by Celia R. Daileader and Alexandra G. Bennett, which aims to 'analyse a textual culture by looking at how it represents relations between persons', while avoiding 'the anecdotalism that has dominated Renaissance studies for the last quarter century' (p. 31). (New Historicism does not do well in the essay.) This is done by investigating different kinds of 'lists' from genealogies and baptismal registers to lists implying economic relationships such as Henslowe's diary, the Stationers' Register, and membership of occupational communities such as livery companies. As Jackson does in his essay, Taylor attacks the idea that authorial agency was unknown in the early modern period, examining the inclusion of authors' names on title pages. He considers 'hierarchies of value' in both society and text ('T.M. Gent.'), looking at 'competing claims to textual value' to assert that 'the theatrical popularity of Shakespeare, Fletcher, or Middleton soon encouraged publishers to use their names to market printed books' (pp. 45–6). Jonsonians may not entirely relish this section.

After this exploration of lists of real people, Taylor goes on to analyse the development of 'Lists of Virtual Persons', or what he terms 'identification tables': cast lists (though the term is, in the main, strenuously avoided), title-page character illustrations, the naming of acting companies, the description of scenic location. Again, he considers the organization of hierarchy within tables, which may 'privilege the order of time' (order of appearance) or 'reflect hierarchies that exist outside the theatre' in terms of gender or social status (pp. 66–7). Those which have mixed hierarchies, like *The Roaring Girl*, whose list is organized by household, raise questions about social perceptions of significance which are answered in different ways. Taylor looks in detail at the increasing tendency to list casts by gender, arguing that 'It may not be accidental that 1629, the beginning of Personal Rule, was also the first year when gendered tables began appearing in significant numbers', which suggests a good deal of prescience on the part of publishers. The uniformity that came to characterize cast lists, however, was absent from 'the four early tables which seem closest to Middleton himself', which lack any formula that would allow us to construct them in reference to each other (p. 76). Their diversity is at odds with the predictability and invisibility that Taylor sees as desired by editors, who suffer from an illusion that they can 'remove the evidence of their own inevitable mediation between author and reader'. The slightly anti-climactic main point of this attack on the self-awareness of editors is that casts lists in the edition are not harmonized.

This decision is associated with editorial practice as a whole: the edition 'aims to make a virtue out of multivocality, illustrating a range of possible approaches', calling 'attention to the ways in which annotation itself shapes our experience of a text' (vol. 1, p. 18). The diversity of Middleton's publications is signalled through typography—a sans serif font is used to represent black-letter print—and running titles, which vary both typographically and in content, reflecting both the material state of his works and their variant titles (so the *Masque of Heroes* appears on one verso under its subtitle *The Inner-Temple Masque.*—with long 's'—but otherwise as MASQVE OF HEROES.). The idea is to remind readers of the variety of original documents underlying the texts, and that we are 'reading a text that has been modernized' (p. 21). The representation in the titles of a variety of early modern hands for plays surviving in manuscript is especially irritating; I imagine the effect intended was wittily playful, but I found it messily patronizing. Despite all this, the vast majority of texts have been edited and presented according to perfectly orthodox practices. Editors of a number of them state their intention of concentrating on a particular facet of the text in their commentary (*Michaelmas Term*: 'This commentary pays special attention to sexual innuendo'; *A Trick to Catch the Old One*: 'foregrounds issues relating to women, marriage, social class, and sexual commerce'; *The Revenger's Tragedy*: 'focuses particularly upon verbal imagery and linguistic play'), but in no case did this seem to be to the detriment of other elements that one would hope to find in the commentary, which is throughout much fuller than might be expected of a one-volume edition.

There are a small number of exceptions to this orthodoxy, some more successful than others. The late Julia Briggs's immaculate edition of *The Lady's Tragedy* (which used to be known as *The Second Maiden's Tragedy*) has parallel texts showing the censorship the play incurred in manuscript, revealing with great clarity the changes that were made to it. Given that collations and textual information are in volume 2, this is particularly helpful. Variant versions of *The Nightingale and the Ant*, on the other hand, edited by Adrian Weiss, are printed consecutively 'to illustrate its evolution from manuscript to the final printed form' (p. 149), rendering comparison between the two much more difficult. Moreover, the 'manuscript version' is in itself a reconstruction (there is no surviving manuscript), so its printing in a single typeface to 'to recreate (to a limited extent) the "manuscript reading experience" ' seems a rather questionable exercise, apart from the fact that I would never have guessed that this was the purpose of the typeface; no manuscript was ever so dull and uniform in appearance. It is, however, an interesting attempt to demonstrate the problematic development of the texts Weiss is dealing with, unlike Jeffery Masten's treatment of *Old Law* (whether prefixed by *A* or *The*), which strikes me as not only self-indulgent, but at odds with the desired aim of the *Collected Works* to reach 'ordinary readers'. A textual introduction notes the departure from protocol in including textual notes (not a collation) within the commentary, detailing emendations and modernizations, in preference to having this textual information in volume 2. This ought to make the reader's life easier, since chasing these details in two different places in the textual companion is time-consuming and frustrating; however, that is not the purpose of the exercise. Rather, Masten wishes to make plain 'the multiple interventions the editorial process makes in the text' to enable readers to experience its plurality (p. 1335). In practice, this means printing the commentary randomly beneath, on either side of, or above the text; and once, both above and below it. This is tiresomely distracting, not merely making the editorial process visible, but making the editor more visible than the play or its author. It is all the more regrettable in that the commentary itself is really good, and I do find it helpful to have emendations discussed on the same page as the text (as is normal in, say, a Revels edition, without making quite such a song and dance about it). Clearly to have done so for every play, though, would have meant abandoning the 'First Folio' concept, and splitting the texts between two or more volumes.

The texts that have inevitably attracted most attention are those that we normally regard as being by Shakespeare: *Timon of Athens*, *Measure for Measure* and *Macbeth*. These are dealt with in rather different ways, the two latter being printed with 'genetic texts' while *Timon* is presented in an altogether more straightforward way. In the case of *Macbeth* (edited by Gary Taylor with an introduction by Inga-Stina Ewbank), 'Passages apparently added or rewritten by Middleton are printed in bold type; passages apparently deleted or intended for deletion are printed in grey; transposed passages are printed in grey where Shakespeare probably placed them, and in bold where Middleton apparently moved them' (p. 1170); the remainder (and majority) of the text is in normal type. This would not make for an easy read even without the decision, for which I could find no persuasive reason, to print the play entirely unpunctuated, except, oddly, for the use of apostrophes (one of the least used punctuation marks of the early modern period), hyphens and accents to mark metre. As can be seen, there are a great many 'apparentlys': Middleton comes out of it with slightly more than the Hecate scenes, and is seen as responsible for shortening the play, but this is essentially

Shakespeare's *Macbeth*. The excellent introduction (by another much-missed scholar) comes as close as I think is possible to persuade of the merit of Middleton's additions and alterations, examining them in relation to *The Witch* and the dancing witches in Jonson's *Masque of Queens*; but losing chunks of Shakespeare to gain Hecate still doesn't strike me as an entirely fair bargain. A similar editorial process (though not the loss of punctuation) is used in John Jowett's edition of *Measure for Measure*, which aims to show the play in transition between Shakespeare's 'reconstructed' original and Middleton's 1621 adaptation (p. 1547); so every mention of 'Vienna' is in bold, preceded by 'Ferrara' in grey, with a very brief explanation for the choice of Ferrara in the introduction. Scenes are again printed twice, once in their First Folio position in bold, and again in the place it is thought they may have occupied in the original in grey. Conjectural Shakespearian profanities, thought to have been expurgated, are also supplied in grey ('in faith' for 'indeed', 'Fore God' for 'Why' in Lucio's speeches in III.i, for example), the 'purity of diction [being] implausible for a Shakespeare play of 1603–4' (p. 1542). The historical relevance of Vienna in 1621, but not to the earlier period, is argued both here and in more detail in the 'Canon and Chronology' section in the textual companion, where we also find that the case for Middleton as sole reviser cannot be demonstrated with the absolute certainty that it is presented as having elsewhere. The commentary for the play concentrates on 'providing further detail in support of the Middleton context' rather than glossing the text (p. 1546); anyone wanting both will have to use a Shakespeare edition alongside this.

The case for including *Timon* is quite different: Jowett's account of the text in volume 2, drawing on the work of Holdsworth, Lake and Jackson, suggests a real collaboration, with Middleton responsible for about one-third of the play, especially the 'early-middle scenes', with the opening being a joint venture and the rest mostly Shakespeare's. 'Shakespeare gave the play its schematic structure, and gave Timon his inspired, misanthropic, universalizing rage. Middleton added comic social nihilism, but also introduced some brief moments that question Timon's later cynicism about human worth' (pp. 357–8). What neither this nor Sharon O'Dair's critical introduction appears to query is how successful a collaboration this was: what has frequently been seen as an unsatisfactory play, on stage as on the page, does not cease to be so because of Middleton's involvement; however, given the division of labour, we may note that it is the Shakespearian scenes that have attracted most criticism. The text itself is conventionally presented, and anyone interested in who wrote what will need to consult the textual companion.

There are, of course, plenty of readily available editions of these three plays. Where the *Collected Works* really wins is in its inclusion and full editing of texts often only to be found otherwise in EEBO. Prose and poetry do not, strictly speaking, come under the remit of this section, but the variety of the former in particular is revelatory to anyone (like myself) not already familiar with it. The dramatic works written not for the stage, but for the city streets, are equally remarkable. The first of these, *The Whole Royal and Magnificent Entertainment of King James through the City Of London, 15 March 1604*, *with the Arches of Triumph*, contains only one speech of sixty lines by Middleton (it is otherwise by Dekker and Jonson, with triumphal arches designed by Stephen Harrison), but is nonetheless very welcome. The splendid introduction by its editor, R. Malcolm Smuts, vividly depicts the experience of viewers of the event, and how far this would have differed from that of readers. Smuts discusses the history of the royal entry and the development of accompanying pageants before exploring James's entry in detail. This focuses on the iconography and symbolism employed by Dekker, Jonson and Harrison, whose finely engraved arch designs are reproduced alongside the text of the pageant performed at each site. He distinguishes between the work of Dekker and Jonson, the former weaving 'descriptions of the watching "world of people" into his narrative', while Jonson 'subsumes the crowd within his visual and poetic invention', taking, it will come as no surprise to learn, 'every opportunity to parade his scholarship' (p. 221). Middleton, Smuts suggests, is sited somewhere between the two, emerging 'as a poet less interested than Jonson in intricate classical learning, but more adept than Dekker at integrating iconographic imagery into a lucid and decorous speech' (p. 222): a skill that would stand him in good stead in his later career as city chronologer. The text that follows is a reconstruction, merging the separate accounts of the event by its three major creators, presenting a record of the event not only 'more cohesive . . . than any spectator could have achieved', but than was available to contemporary readers. Jonson's learned notes are printed alongside his text; the commentary is as good as the introduction, though brief compared with that for Middleton's own *Triumphs of Honour and Industry* [1617], edited by David M. Bergeron, with annotations and introduction by Kate D. Levin, who similarly compares Middleton's narration of his pageant with regard to audience with that found in the writing of Jonson and Munday. The commentary—longer than the text itself—is very informative, in particular providing details about the event's costs and about trading relations with the countries represented in it. By contrast, *The Triumphs of Truth* has a somewhat meagre commentary, needing greater explication of its emblems, but in his introduction to it David Bergeron (responsible for much of the work on the pageants) provides a helpful history of the mayoral pageant. This might, though, have been more logically placed preceding the first of the events, or even better in a separate survey of Middleton's work in this field. Indeed, given the unfamiliarity of much of the material in the *Collected Works*—theatrical as well as non-dramatic—generic introductions to Middleton's corpus would have been useful, rather than tucking them away in critical introductions to texts, like Bergeron's to the pageant or Paul Yachnin's to the 'mock-almanac' before his text of *Plato's Cap*. The only general surveys of this kind are 'Lost Plays: A Brief Account' by Doris Feldmann and Kurt Tetzeli von Rosador (placed oddly between *The Patient Man and the Honest Whore* and *Michaelmas Term*), and Thomas Cogswell's 'Lost Political Prose, 1620–27: A Brief Account' (after the last of the pageants and before *Juvenilia*), both necessarily speculative. Middleton's output as a writer of masques was considerably less substantial than that for the city or the non-court theatre, but his two complete texts (*Masque of Heroes* and *The World Tossed at Tennis*), as well as *Masque of Cupids*, of which only two short songs survive, all attract full and enlightening coverage (indeed, a bit overwhelming in the case of the last given how little actual text there is to discuss).

However, as the useful 'Index of Titles by Genre' makes clear, Middleton's dramatic work was dominated by comedy, and especially city comedy (a fact made even more obvious when Shakespeare's plays are taken into account in the tragedy and tragicomedy lists), though some of the tragedies are without doubt among the finest and most distinctive plays of the Jacobean period. Much valuable work has gone into the analysis and comparison of these comedies, restoring to our attention a number of long-ignored plays, even if some editors exude more enthusiasm than others (*Your Five Gallants* attracts the somewhat half-hearted comment from Ralph Alan Cohen on the basis of a university production that it 'plays better than it reads' (p. 594)). What does become evident in working through the first volume is the length of the period over which it has been assembled: Kahn's reference to recent essays on *The Roaring Girl*, for example, lists nothing later than 1993, and she writes of 'the decade since 1983', while elsewhere articles and books published in 2006 are cited. In an edition that should be standard for many years to come, and which will have the benefit of a supporting website where updates can be made, this is not a major issue; but it is disconcerting to read a critical introduction to a play published in 2007 that was written more than ten years before.

Finally (because one has to stop somewhere), it is impossible to ignore the feat of scholarship that is Gary Taylor's *A Game at Chess*, with textual notes alone amounting to 278 pages. Two complete versions of the play are printed, *An Early Form* printed in old spelling with a primarily historical commentary, and *A Later Form* in modern spelling with notes focusing on literary and theatrical issues. The former 'attempts to reconstruct a particular lost manuscript, the author's first complete draft of the play... determinedly authorial in its substance and presentation', reproducing features of early modern manuscripts. The latter is an eclectic text, seeking to 'reconstruct, not only the play as collaboratively produced and performed in August 1624, but a *reading text* which could effectively represent those performances', with Taylor as the last in a long line of revisers and editors, from Ralph Crane onwards (vol. 2, pp. 847–8). In doing so, he has to take on his own position in relation to the two versions of *King Lear*, arguing that there are essential differences between Shakespeare and Middleton that make this a theoretically acceptable exercise. This one should run and run.

The Middleton edition wasn't the only one to come to fruition this year: the third and final volume of the Cambridge old-spelling *Works of John Webster*, which I thought was complete as far as plays were concerned in 2003, in fact contains a substantial amount of dramatic material; like volume 2, this was edited by David Gunby, David Carnegie and the apparently tireless MacDonald P. Jackson. As well as Webster's poetry and prose, we are given the Lord Mayor's pageant *Monuments of Honour*, additions to Marston's *The Malcontent* and the comedy *Anything for a Quiet Life* (dated to 1621–2), which, being written with Middleton, makes its second appearance in a major collection in one year, despite having been hardly the most glorious achievement in either playwright's career.

Jackson provides a reassessment of the Webster canon which supplements his articles published in *Notes and Queries* in 2006. He explains the decision to exclude from it the four-page authorial draft of a scene contained in the Melbourne manuscript, which was discovered in 1986 and advertised at auction as *The Duke of Florence* by Webster. When the first volume of the *Works* was published in 1995, it was intended that the scene should be included, but Jackson's analysis of it finds the attribution to Webster unconvincing, while failing to identify a probable author with any confidence, though he does not wholly discount James Shirley, who used the scene in *The Traitor*. Jackson also suggests on the basis of linguistic evidence that a date in the 1630s may be more likely than the previously proposed 1606–9. Other variously plausible suggestions for inclusion in the canon reconsidered and rejected by him are the additions to *The Spanish Tragedy*, the Hand D 'Shakespeare' passage of *Sir Thomas More* and a collection of model letters, *A Speedy Post*. He remains uncertain, however, about the possibility of Webster's having made a contribution to *The Honest Man's Fortune* (published in the Cambridge Beaumont and Fletcher), Rowley's *The Birth of Merlin*, and *The Valiant Scot*, a tragedy about William Wallace published in 1637 as by 'J.W., Gent'. The last of these attracts particular attention, Jackson coming to the conclusion that no 'compelling case' has been made for its inclusion while clearly feeling that it merits further investigation. He ends this section wistfully, in the hope that the canon might be augmented if a copy of the lost *Guise* is gathering 'dust in some obscure repository—perhaps on the same shelf as Shakespeare's *Love's Labour's Won*'.

The critical introduction to *Anything for a Quiet Life* (as to the volume's poetry and prose) is by David Gunby, who attempts to rescue the play from F.L. Lucas's damning judgement in 1927 that it had given him no pleasure to edit it, and he would have been happy to suppress it. Later criticism, surveyed by Gunby, is hardly more favourable, the denouement, in which Lady Cressingham is revealed as having behaved outrageously in order to rescue her husband from his obsessions with alchemy and gambling, coming in for particular opprobrium; the equally sudden revelation of Lord Beaufort's page as George Cressingham's wife is found similarly unconvincing. Nevertheless the dramatic structure, with its cleverly interlinking plots, has been praised. The division of the play between the two dramatists is seen by the editors as clear, with Middleton developing the three essentially comic intrigue plots following Webster's establishment of all four plots, and the latter remaining responsible for the more serious, perhaps tragicomic, Cressingham strand of the play. Gunby goes through it scene by scene, demonstrating ways in which the playwrights draw on Jacobean sexual stereotypes, especially concerning marriage between an elderly widower and a 15-year-old girl, and the expected relationships between young courtiers and citizens' wives. He shows how, through the juxtaposition of stereotypes, it becomes difficult for the audience to judge the characters both individually and in relation to each other, though this can result in confusion rather than interesting ambiguity. Lines are teased out that may hint at the problematic revelations of the denouement, but it is recognized that some of the questions raised by it (was Lady Cressingham always acting honourably? why did George Cressingham's wife go into service as a page to Lord Beaufort?) are unanswered and unanswerable. However, Gunby sees the real difficulty of the ending as lying in the uncertain moral status of Lord Beaufort in view of his 'presiding role' over the play's resolution, which is combined with his being 'the one transgressor who is not brought to book' and who never admits his fault in attempting the seduction of Sib Knaves-bee (p. 21).

This is followed, as in previous volumes, by a generous theatrical introduction by David Carnegie, which concentrates on the possibilities for a modern production rather than analysing its likely contemporary staging, noting of the latter only that the acting resources of the King's Men at the Blackfriars would not have been unduly stretched by it. He focuses especially on the problems of the play's locale, showing that any attempt to create realist locations would fall victim to its shifting and sometimes uncertain settings. The importance of costume 'as an indicator of both fortune and moral standing' is emphasized (p. 28), in discussing which Carnegie refers—as does Gunby—to Leslie Thomson's introduction to *Anything for a Quiet Life* in the Middleton *Collected Works*, in which she argues that it is the play's central metaphor. Carnegie looks in some detail at the demands made on the actors, giving advice as to how they should interpret their characters, and where they may find moments of outstanding comedy or of unexpected seriousness, drawing, as always, on his experience of producing the play with his own students.

Jackson's textual introduction considers the problems raised by the paper-saving strategies of its first printer in 1662, Thomas Johnson, who determinedly set the entire play as prose apart from the prologue, epilogue and the odd couplet. Hence lineation presents major problems, especially in view of the flexibility of both playwrights' iambic pentameters, and Middleton's easy shifting between verse and prose. However, previous editors, including Leslie Thomson, have come to much the same conclusions about it, and this edition does so too; any variations are recorded following the play (pp. 133–5). Jackson also analyses the printing process, looking, without conclusive success, for patterns that might help distinguish different compositors, a task rendered more difficult by Johnson's practices in the workshop. He describes the quarto's 'features suggesting that it was printed from a theatrical script usable as a seventeenth-century "promptbook"' (p. 46), and lays out, relatively briefly, his findings on the division of labour between Middleton and Webster, a subject which he addressed in rather more detail in one of his 2006 *Notes and Queries* articles.

As in earlier volumes, the collation is at the foot of each page, while the commentary is printed as endnotes—the only really unsatisfactory decision made about the layout of the Webster *Works*. Both again make reference to Thomson's edition, which the editors clearly had the considerable benefit of seeing well before publication. As always the notes are admirably full and informative. Following the commentary, there is a brief discussion of sources, drawing particular attention to similarities between the Chamlet scenes and the Candido scenes in *The Honest Whore*, Middleton being the author of both.

The grand pageant for the Lord Mayor in 1624, *Monuments of Honour*, has an excellent introduction by David Carnegie (though the year goes unmentioned until some twenty pages in), which looks at the occasion both in general and in particular, examining the five shows 'that constitute the spectacular highpoints of the procession and establish the thematic narrative' (p. 225) in the context of the history of the event and contemporary descriptions of other such pageants. Carnegie is unfortunate in not having any designs to draw on (as for *The Whole Royal and Magnificent Entertainment of King James* in the Middleton *Works*), but makes good use of a few images from other shows to depict what it may have looked like. Following a lively evocation of the event, Carnegie provides a briefer exploration of possible interpretations of *Monuments of Honour*, examining the exact historical moment in which it occurred and the significance that may be placed first on the historical figures that Webster has chosen to represent, and then on the tribute to Prince Henry (d. 1612) in the final pageant, which seems to suggest that his younger brother might do well to emulate him.

The text is based on the single surviving copy now at the Huntington Library, which, as Jackson notes, 'contains errors and ignorant misspellings' obviously emended in the edition. The text itself consists of Webster's quite short dialogue and speeches, combined with longer prose descriptions of the 'Spectacles', with identifications of the figures portrayed and a brief explanation of the 'conceite' (pp. 255–6), to which the admirable commentary adds more detail—indeed it is substantially longer than the text itself.

Webster's Induction and additional passages for *The Malcontent* constitute the final dramatic material in the volume, again introduced by David Carnegie. He considers the theatrical purpose and self-reflexiveness of the Induction, noting that its 125 lines 'constitute well over five per cent of the length of the boys' version of the play', and that this 'warm-up act' would have made an enjoyable substitute for the music played by the children's company but jettisoned in the move of *The Malcontent* to the King's Men (p. 299). There is a separate discussion of the five additional scenes written for it by Webster, with their introduction of the wholly new character, Passarello; he finds the argument that the part was written for Robert Armin persuasive. Jackson, in the textual introduction, also looks at the purpose of the expansion of the play, as well as the 'mysterious' acquisition of the play by the King's Men; he is more critical than Carnegie of the Passarello scenes ('not well integrated into the play, in terms of either characterization or action', p. 310). He lays out the linguistic evidence for authorship of the play's eleven additional scenes, arguing that the six written by Marston himself are not necessarily related to the King's Men's 'appropriation' of his play (p. 312). Jackson's conclusion is that while nothing can be proved, it seems more likely that Webster and Marston did not collaborate on their respective additions.

I see from the Cambridge University Press website that the three volumes of *The Works of John Webster* are now available as a paperback set. It is still not especially cheap, but while I haven't always agreed with all the decisions taken by the editors, I wouldn't be without my copies; I recommend it very highly. Fredson Bowers's *Complete Works of Christopher Marlowe* has also been reissued by Cambridge in paperback.

There were two interesting editions from Manchester University Press this year, one a full Revels, and the other a Revels Student edition. The former is Philip Massinger's *The Roman Actor*, edited by Martin White. As he remarks, Massinger has been 'ignored more or less entirely', excluded even from university curricula (not to say mocked by Gary Taylor); one suspects that the RSC's wonderful production of the play in 2002 has done little to change this situation if the 1976 five-volume edition of his works by Philip Edwards and Colin Gibson failed to do so. Given this neglect, the introductory section on Massinger's life and works is more than usually helpful. It is a regrettable indication of the facts of life for the early modern playwright that the first reference to Massinger as a dramatist comes in 1613, when he, Nathan Field and Robert Daborne wrote to Henslowe to ask him to put up the money to get them out of debtors' prison (he appears to have done so). Their letter's mention of the new play they have jointly authored also introduces us to Massinger's career as a collaborative dramatist, and especially his association with John Fletcher, whom he succeeded as chief playwright to the King's Men, and in whose grave he is believed to have been buried. White assesses Massinger's reputation and status in the 1630s in the light of a row between professional and courtly writers sparked by the failure of Davenant's *The Just Italian* at the Blackfriars in 1629, as well as the blow given to his critical reputation in the twentieth century by T.S. Eliot's dismissal of his work as merely bland.

This introduction is followed by a judicious account of Massinger's sources for *The Roman Actor*, both classical and contemporary. White finds that, in addition to classical historians, Massinger turned to Juvenal's *Satires* for both detail and tone, and also owed a considerable debt to Jonson's *Sejanus* in theme, structure and language. *The Roman Actor* was first performed in late 1626 and published in 1629: the editor gives us a detailed analysis of the precise contexts of both years, looking particularly at Charles's accession in 1625 and the implications of the cancellation of his royal entry into London, as well as at his relationship with parliament both as prince and king, and how this was affected by his closeness to Buckingham. *The Roman Actor* is seen persuasively in the light of resistance to the 1626 Forced Loan, fears concerning over-weening use of the royal prerogative, and the overwhelming unpopularity of the duke, providing 'any spectator who wished to see it with an image of his or her own times' (p. 18). The use of Roman analogies, both by dramatists wishing to explore sensitive political issues and by the early Stuart kings, is briefly but pertinently addressed. Events between performance and publication would, White argues, only have underlined its topicality; indeed, he suggests that it may even have been amended by Massinger to maintain its immediate relevance following the murder of Buckingham and the 1629 dissolution. There is, however, some rather less convincing reading from hindsight, the play being seen as proleptic of Charles's execution two decades later. This whole discussion is so interesting that it is unfortunate that there are a couple of lapses in accuracy: Laud did not become an archbishop until 1633, although referred to as such in the 1620s, and the description of Charles's Shakespeare folio as 'well-marked' is a decided exaggeration, given his light annotation of its contents page alone (pp. 17, 19).

The discussion of the play itself is as good as the previous sections. Given *The Roman Actor*'s own focus on the nature of performance, White's concentration on its theatricality is a natural one, but he also continues to examine contemporary relevance by picking up on the textual detail that supports it. The structure of the play, and the development of the characters within it, especially Domitian, Paris and Domitia, are analysed, the editor drawing together its political and performative aspects to demonstrate how 'Massinger addresses some potent issues concerning the nature and role of theatre' within his society (p. 44). White challenges previous critical arguments that the three inset plays reveal the early modern theatre as lacking political or social influence, arguing that they rather demonstrate that spectators must take responsibility for learning from what they see on stage. As a whole, he asserts, *The Roman Actor* shows that 'at its best theatre can have the power to transform and to teach' (p. 46).

The stage history of the play includes a detailed description of its Blackfriars production and the likely stage settings, effects and properties employed, as well as a consideration of the relationship between action and audience. Later revivals, including the use of excerpts from the play staged in the eighteenth and nineteenth centuries, are discussed, along with substantial reviews of late twentieth-century and twenty-first-century productions, including White's own by the University of Bristol Drama Department, and the RSC production starring Sir Antony Sher, an interview with whom is included as an appendix. Having seen the latter myself, I fully support White's claim that *The Roman Actor* has 'vibrant *theatrical* qualities' (p. 8).

The textual discussion of the play is also to be found in two appendices, but this relegation does not, fortunately, signal a diminution in information. In appendix 1, White describes the 1629 quarto which is necessarily his own copy-text, there being no other seventeenth-century printings. Of special interest is the 'Harbord' copy now at the Folger Library, in which *The Roman Actor* was once bound together with a number of other plays by Massinger himself, and which contains corrections that have been accepted as his own (recognizable from the autograph manuscript of *Believe As You List*). White has incorporated in his edition all the substantive alterations made by Massinger (listed in the collation), but not all those made to punctuation, which he finds 'idiosyncratic' (p. 207). There are further manuscript corrections found in other copies of the quarto, the most extensive being in a copy at King's College, Cambridge, the emendations to which are listed in appendix 2. In the first appendix White also describes Massinger's hand and orthography, and the effect these may have had on the accuracy of the printer, and discusses the status of the manuscript from which the quarto was printed. Appendix 3 includes biographical sketches of the actors as listed in the 1629 quarto.

The critical commentary is as full and helpful as one expects from a Revels edition, being particularly strong on Massinger's use of his source material, though there is an inconsistency in citations from other early modern plays, lines from them sometimes being quoted and sometimes given only as a reference. This does not seem to bear any relationship to the length of the quotation (at V.i.52–4, for example, two lines from *Catiline* are referred to for comparison but not quoted), and I would have liked to see all such lines in full. This is, nevertheless an excellent addition to the Revels series, and I sincerely hope that it may be made available in paperback.

Also from Manchester University Press this year was Kristen McDermott's very useful collection *Masques of Difference: Four Court Masques by Ben Jonson*. The masques in question are *The Masque of Blackness*, *The Masque of Queens*, *The Irish Masque at Court*, and *The Gypsies Metamorphosed*. Given that this is now the only reasonably priced collection of masques in print it is very welcome, though it is perhaps regrettable that space wasn't found for *The Masque of Beauty* to round off *Blackness*. The rationale for McDermott's choice of texts is set out in her thoughtful introduction, in which she explains that she sees each as engaging with 'a critical moment in English political and cultural identity' (true, I should have thought, of every masque). 'Difference' is defined as elements in the masques which may be seen as oppositional to the royal ideology they purport to convey, as well the inclusion in them of 'a marginalized or "othered" population': Ethiopians, witches, Irishmen and gypsies (p. 5). She is especially interested in ideas of unity, reconciliation and exclusion; of sexual identity; and of political order.

For a student edition, there is an unusually long and thorough introduction of over seventy pages. It contains a brief account of James VI and I after his arrival in England: his desire to create a kingdom of 'Great Britain', his pacifist European policies, and—picking up the theme of 'difference'—his 'Scottishness'. In this there is a faintly worrying identification of inherent traits in the nature of the Scots, who are apparently pugnacious, frugal and humorous, amongst other things; greater clarity is needed as to whether these are early modern stereotypes or not. This is followed by a sketch of Jonson's life and character, and a comparison of him with James (both stubborn with a weakness for drink). McDermott suggests that just as Jonson 'often suffers in comparison to Shakespeare' in the hands of critics (surely no longer the case?), so James's reputation 'still suffers by comparison with ... Elizabeth, and his martyred successor, Charles I'. That, I think, would come as a surprise to anyone who works on Charles. There is, though, a good assessment of the conditions within which masques were performed, and the factional and individual competitiveness they engendered, including the potential rivalry between the courts of James himself, Anna of Denmark and Prince Henry, both of whom are also considered in relation to Jonson as well as to the king. The art of Jonson's masques and his own attitude towards them are discussed at some length, looking at the imagery and philosophy of the main masque, and purpose and development of the antimasque, which McDermott sees as a mechanism allowing Jonson to address the complexities of the court. Masque staging, dance and music are described in a valuable summary for students, before analyses of the individual masques which discuss their performances, themes and action, as well as any contemporary commentary on them and recent criticism. The historical moments in which they occurred are outlined, like, for example, the diplomatic negotiations between Spain and the Netherlands prior to *The Masque of Queens*, though students would need to follow up elsewhere what the truce between them involved. McDermott gives close attention to the representation of the witches in *Queens*, and to what, combined with the queens themselves, the masque suggests about the construction of feminine identity. The section on *The Irish Masque* provides a usefully detailed explanation of the events that led to Jonson's choice of the Irish as its focus and examines the language and costume in which they were presented. She argues that the dialect form used by Jonson suggests that 'the language and culture the masque attempts to "efface" are as stubbornly resilient as the Irish people themselves', creating a subversive subtext to the prevailing orthodoxy (p. 53).

The longest section of the introduction is given over to *The Gypsies Metamorphosed* (logically in view of the comparative lengths of the texts). While seeing this as one of Jonson's most obviously satirical masques, McDermott points out that the object of the satire is uncertain, partly because the gypsies—the masque's 'other'—were played by courtiers led by Buckingham, about whom McDermott provides biographical details (though it is not true that the king had made him a duke by 1617—that did not happen until 1623; he was a marquis at the time of the masque). Her exploration of the nature of the gypsies is not entirely consistent: having argued that the 'gypsy in early modern England bears little resemblance to the romantic image of the . . . nomad of modern song and story', being viewed with suspicion as thieves and vagabonds, she then goes on to suggest that, within the masque, they are portrayed as having 'the romantic charisma of the gypsy [which] has been legendary for as long as they have existed' (pp. 56–7). This may support her point about the masque's ambiguity, but here it feels self-contradictory.

The three locations where variant performances of the masque took place in 1621 (Buckingham's estate at Burley-on-the-Hill, Belvoir Castle, the home of his father-in-law, and Windsor Castle) are linked to landmarks and names specified in the text, and the significance of its references to Wales and to the Devil's Arse cave in the Peak District is explored. McDermott also considers the different audiences present at these performances, and the effect of these on the masque's reception, particularly with regard to how Buckingham, as James's powerful favourite, may have been perceived in his unprecedented performance as the light-fingered gypsy Captain. She queries whether *The Gypsies Metamorphosed* may have offended influential courtiers, however much it may have pleased the king, arguing that the masque appears to mark a high point in Jonson's relationship with the court. (Again, there is a slight inaccuracy in this account: Jonson was never 'named' as poet laureate.) The presence in the audience, especially at Windsor, of potential patrons with competing agendas, she suggests, must have made it impossible to please them all. Nevertheless, she sees it as revealing 'as complex a psychological portrait of the relationship between monarch, favourite, and a poet as is possible to imagine' (p. 70).

The introduction is followed by a useful explanatory list of further reading. This being a student edition, there is no specific textual information, though some is provided in the introduction to each masque. McDermott has drawn on both Herford and Simpson and Stephen Orgel's Yale edition, *Ben Jonson: the Complete Masques*, though in giving precedence to the text from the latter for *Gypsies Metamorphosed*, she has 'silently added' material from the second folio of Jonson's works published in 1640–1 omitted both by Orgel and by Herford and Simpson. It would be nice to know what this is; even without a textual apparatus, the information could have been provided in the commentary. However, the text of the masque does supply useful parallel passages from the three different performances, making the revisions to it on its travels very clear. The commentary itself is helpful, explaining problematic vocabulary, classical and contemporary references, and moments of stage action. Some of Jonson's annotations in the autograph copy of *Queens* he presented to Prince Henry are excerpted or summarized; the Irish dialect in the *Irish Masque* is explicated (with a 'translation' into standard English provided in an appendix), as is the fairly mild thieves' cant in *Gypsies*. Two other appendices supply biographical details of the masquers in *Blackness* and *Queens*, in the case of the former also supplying interpretations of the names of the women's roles and of the symbols carried by them.

Somewhat to my relief, articles of textual interest were thin on the ground this year, and the first is anyway poised on the border between article and critical edition: in 'George Chapman's *Masque of the Twelve Months* (1619)' (*ELR* 37[2007] 360–400), Martin Butler presents an edited text of the masque, as well as an account of it. As he explains, there has always been a gap for winter 1618/19 in the records for masque performances at court, the year when Jonson was in Scotland. He proposes that 'the missing text has been in the public domain for over 150 years, but unidentified, and that the poet responsible was Chapman'. The text was first printed in 1848 in an edition of five masques published by the deeply dodgy John Payne Collier from a manuscript supposedly in his possession, but not since discovered. Because of Collier's reputation, its authenticity has been doubted, but Butler argues that the very confusion of the text as printed is a sign that it is genuine: it would not have been so muddled, had Collier invented it rather than failing to understand the order of the manuscript he was copying. As it was, he printed it 'bizarrely inside-out'. There is also good 'internal and external evidence relating to authorship and dating' in support of the masque's authenticity, with echoes in the text of works by Chapman and references to recognizable astronomical phenomena, as well as a more recently discovered description of the performance that provides confirmation for the date. Collier clearly did not spot the former, and had no access to the latter.

Butler makes the case for the masque's authorship (first proposed by Kenneth Muir in 1950) on the basis of passages having 'intricate parallels' in other works by Chapman, of which, obviously, he gives the details, as well as of linguistic habits that point towards him; he also deals with problems arising from the attribution of a masque to him in this period. The date and time of year of the masque are considered, external confirmation of internal evidence being provided from the reports of Gabaleone, the duke of Savoy's agent at court, who sent back a detailed, if not wholly accurate, account of the event which Butler analyses in relation to the masque text. Further support is provided by three of Inigo Jones's sketches, which Butler demonstrates are identifiable with the masque, linking both to the text and to Gabaleone's report.

Following these persuasive arguments, Butler discusses the action of *The Masque of the Twelve Months*, contrasting its episodic structure with Jonson's masques: 'Chapman strives for pleasing variety, not ethical confrontation.' Unity is found in the performance of Prince Charles as chief masquer, but while there are reminiscences of Prince's Henry's masques, Charles is seen as a 'figure of generational restoration', lacking the sense of confrontation with his father engendered by his elder brother. Members of the audience would, Butler argues, have recognized within the masque anxiety concerning the need to negotiate a marriage for the prince, particularly in view of the unsettled political situation in Europe. Chapman linked a celebration of the 'bond between father and son' to an understanding of 'dynastic priorities'.

Butler has necessarily used Collier's text in editing his own, rearranging the muddled sections to produce a logical sequence with the aim of producing a readable modernized version that 'represents the masque as it would have been seen in performance'; this he has certainly succeeded in doing. A collation records departures from Collier, and there is a full commentary; altogether an admirable and convincing article.

In 'Who Wrote *The Christmas Ordinary*?' (*RES* 58[2007] 657–68), Matthew Steggle examines evidence relating to the Oxford University comedy printed anonymously in 1682, which G.E. Bentley dated to the mid-1630s. Steggle suggests that it deserves to be better known, being more 'anarchic and . . . consciously irresponsible' than most other comedies of the period. A partial manuscript of it in the British Library (in which its prose has been turned into unconvincing verse) attributes it to 'H.B.', argued to be Dr Henry Birkhead. The date proposed by Bentley is found persuasive, the text having an allusion to Prynne's *Histrio-mastix*, and making reference to a continuing and lengthy period of peace. Putting together all the biographical evidence that can be adduced from a number of sources, Steggle finds that Birkhead, a student at Trinity College with a later reputation as a 'poet, scholar, and wit' and known to have written at least one other play, matches all the necessary criteria. Both *The Christmas Ordinary* and *The Female Rebellion* (H.B.'s other play) 'celebrate drink and male bonding as a resistance against authority and Puritanism', with more specific scenic parallels supporting Birkhead's reuse of lines from the former in a Latin drinking song as evidence of his authorship. More precise dating is suggested from Birkhead's presence at Trinity in 1633–6, and the play's possible imitation of William Cartwright's *The Ordinary*. Steggle discusses the play as a reflection on undergraduate life in the period, and in terms of its literary influences, primarily Jonson, Cartwright and Jasper Mayne. Birkhead is now primarily remembered as founder of the Professorship of Poetry at Oxford; this article gives us an excellent introduction (an introduction for me, anyway) to Birkhead as an author in his own right.

Ben Jonson makes his second appearance (other than as a presence haunting the work of other writers) in Peter Happé's 'Printing the Third Volume of Jonson's *Works*' (*BJJ* 14[2007] 21–42), a detailed and technical analysis of its subject. The third volume having appeared posthumously, printed in 1639–41, it presents different issues from the first two: Happé considers how far it reflects Jonson's wishes and whether it could in part have been set from autograph or corrected copy, as well as analysing the production process and describing watermarks and type. He looks at other work produced by the printer John Dawson, his association with the bookseller Thomas Walkley, for whom the volume was printed, and Dawson's legal dispute with John Benson as to copyright which affected its production. The composition of different parts of the book is analysed, along with the 'rather crude' attempts to unify it, and both departures from and conformity with Jonson's practices with regard to layout, punctuation and spelling in the 1616 folio are recorded. Happé suggests that the copy used by Dawson was 'of very mixed quality', including some that had already been printed with Jonson's authority (though with some revision), and manuscripts by or approved by him. Watermark distribution and evidence of change in the skeletons used help to establish the chronology of the printing process, with interruptions to the printing of *Discoveries* and *The Sad Shepherd*: a summary narrative is provided based on these. Compositorial work and the extent of stop-press corrections are outlined, the latter indicating a greater degree of concern for accuracy than Dawson has always been credited with; Happé examines these in relation to the different sections of the volume and the problems faced by the compositors. He finds the resulting folio 'workmanlike', but not always successful in coping with the problems with which the printer was presented.

Richard Wood considers 'A Source for Bertha and Parallels with Henrietta Maria in *The Queenes Exchange*' (*N&Q* 252[2007] 391–2), proposing that Holinshed was the source for Brome's Saxon queen Bertha in the play performed *c*.1633. In the fifth book, Holinshed writes of a French king's daughter (named by Bede as Bertha) married to Ethelbert, king of Kent, whose marriage was dependent on her being allowed to continue to practise her religion with a bishop provided for that purpose. The parallels with Charles's wife are striking, he argues, while Osriick's fool may be based on Jeffrey Hudson. In 'One *Osmond the Great Turk*, Not Two' (*N&Q* 252[2007] 35–6), Friederike Hahn takes issue with Elsie Duncan-Jones's 1961 claim that there were two early modern plays with this title, arguing that there is no reason to suppose that the play licensed in 1622 and Lodowick Carlell's published in 1656 are not the same work: the murder of Sultan Osman, a recent event in 1622, is echoed, if not directly represented, in Carlell's play.

Finally, Andrew Duxfield examines authorship evidence in ' "That horse that runnes vpon the toppe of powles": Middleton, Dekker and the Anonymous *The Fatal Marriage*' (*N&Q* 252[2007] 264–5). Referring back to an earlier article in which he argued that the play was written in the 1590s and later revised, not written in the 1620s as previously thought, he looks at a speech by Jacomo in which he talks of a horse running along the roof of St Paul's. A prose pamphlet by Dekker dates this odd event to 1600, of which there are only nine other mentions in works of the period, all but one of which (and that much later) occur in the writing of Dekker or Middleton. Their authorship of the play, he suggests tentatively, may be worth further consideration: a thought to bring joy to the hearts of the editors of *Thomas Middleton: The Collected Works*.

2. Theatre History

Matthew Steggle has formulated the year's most tantalizing title: *Laughing and Weeping in Early Modern Theatres*. One's instinctive reaction is 'How can we ever know?' While the idea of the signification of an inward emotion sounds as though it is raising the old chestnut of the existence or otherwise of an early modern self—a self which must feel in order to cry or laugh—Steggle deftly sidesteps such imponderables, relying instead upon a wide sample of dramatic examples and contemporary responses. While insistent that 'even emotions have cultural histories' (p. 1), he is refreshingly uninterested in the consequences of audience response as evidence for early modern subjectivity. The book is much more practically engaged, which seems all the more justified in the light of the evidence Steggle adduces that weeping and laughter were thought of as being physical responses rather than the 'symptoms of spiritual passions' (p. 86), much closer to a corporeal and probably involuntary reaction rather than the manifestation of a psychological condition. What Steggle is concerned to trace are 'explicit allusions to a visible and audible phenomenon, rather than any indication of mental state' (p. 93). Thus while neatly avoiding the mire of New Historicist controversy, Steggle is far from nonchalant about historical difference, insisting that laughter and weeping are far 'from being unhistorical absolutes [rather] they are enmeshed within a whole set of Renaissance debates about the nature of the human animal; the relationship between man and God; and the ways in which society works or should work' (p. 22). Along the way there are some powerful insights on 'the infectiousness of emotions' (p. 7); the capacity of the 'frenetic carnage' (p. 123) of the more extreme revenge tragedies to incite audience laughter and the hostility of early modern anti-theatricalists to shared audience laughter. In spite of the persuasiveness of his criticism, Steggle is candidly beaten at points: an incisive enquiry into how naturalistic or realistic Elizabethan tears may have been is 'unanswerable' (p. 43). Moreover, just occasionally one is not convinced: Steggle seems sure that 'ha ha ha' was a stage direction for the actor to enact laughter rather than pronounce the utterance 'ha ha ha'. While probable, this is by no means certain—compare Lear's 'Howl, howl, howl' which is more often than not spoken rather than howled. Steggle's finest chapter is his last, which insists on the mutuality of weeping and laughter in Shakespeare's theatre: 'weeping and laughter are fundamentally interchangeable in a universe poised between those two actions' (p. 137). For its subtlety and sophistication, and its attention to the usually elusive 'acoustic texture of the theatre' (p. 30), this volume deserves a wide readership.

Two essays underline the links between early modern theatre professionals and the court. In ' "Rejoice ye in us with joy most joyfully": John Heywood's Plays and the Court' (*CahiersE* 72[2007] 1–8), Peter Happé reads what are traditionally thought of as light-hearted comedies as serious political allegories. He notes that while the 'occasion, location and nature of the performances cannot be documented' (p. 1) for any of the surviving plays, their publication—by William Rastell in 1533 and 1534—coincided with the rise of Queen Anne (who was married secretly to Henry on 25 January 1533). Happé finds in the plays an intention to sway 'royal opinion by comic and indirect means' (p. 2). For instance, he reads *The Pardoner and the Friar* as a 'microcosm of conflict' which deals with 'the power and the danger of heresy and folly' (p. 3). Drawing on a tradition of ecclesiastical satire which goes back to the *Canterbury Tales*, Heywood's work fits into a contemporary set of concerns that was involving such luminaries as More and Erasmus. Happé suggests that either Heywood enjoyed immunity from attack as a result of his position at court as 'a kind of allowed fool' (p. 4) or that the plays were performed away from court beyond the reach of Henry. In this neatly balanced essay, Happé shows how Heywood's drama and poetry both celebrate royal authority and discourage tyranny.

The relationship of the individual and the court is also the topic of S.P. Cerasano's 'Philip Henslowe and the Elizabethan Court' (*ShS* 60[2007] 49–57). She proposes that Henslowe's 'court career was much more central to his ambitions than we have previously realised' (p. 51). Indeed she goes on to propose that 'it would appear that the Rose, as well as Henslowe's other businesses, were *funding* his career at court' (p. 53). By tracing mentions of Henslowe through the business accounts of the court as well as examining entries in the *Diary*, Cerasano demonstrates that both he and Edward Alleyn had serious commitments at court in terms of their official duties and their finances; Henslowe seems to have been there between the early 1590s and 1611. Both of them enjoyed gentry status, unlike James or Richard Burbage, for instance. Thanks to this essay, a much fuller picture of Henslowe emerges than the received image of him as 'a Scrooge-like playhouse manager who sat in the theatre and watched every penny cross his desk' (p. 53).

3. Criticism

(a) General

Beginning as usual with single-authored monographs, an excellent place to start appears to be Peter Womack's introduction to early modern theatre, *English Renaissance Drama*. This fine book should prove to be an influential reference point for scholars and postgraduates working in the field, and will hopefully be seen as a vital primer for undergraduates new to the area of early modern theatre. The title begins with a helpful timeline of texts and key events, before moving through—and explaining—a rich variety of contextual themes, including the emergence of the first public theatres in 1570s London, religious discourses, court, city, actors and the stage. The study then helpfully surveys some of the main approaches to the drama in terms of familiar topics, including useful discussions of allegory, language, genre and history, together with slightly surprising entries including medicine and festival. Furthermore, the book offers introductory biographies on all of the major Renaissance playwrights, before offering casebook studies of various plays, including Thomas Kyd's *Spanish Tragedy*, several plays by Shakespeare, Marlowe and Jonson, alongside readings of Thomas Dekker's *Shoemakers' Holiday*, John Marston's *Dutch Courtesan*, Francis Beaumont's *Knight of the Burning Pestle* and his *Maid's Tragedy* (with John Fletcher), Dekker and Thomas

Middleton's *Roaring Girl*, Middleton's *Chaste Maid in Cheapside*, John Webster's *Duchess of Malfi*, Philip Massinger's *Roman Actor*, Thomas Heywood's *The Fair Maid of the West*, John Ford's '*Tis Pity She's a Whore*, and Richard Brome's *A Jovial Crew*. Crucially, then, the monograph gives a reasonable amount of space to Caroline drama, continuing the rebirth of interest in the later period begun two decades earlier by Martin Butler. The study concludes with a lively section on 'Actions that a Man Might Play', including 'Conjuring', 'Going Mad' and 'Swaggering', and it is this enthusiastic approach to the topics that will help university teachers to enthuse undergraduates with a sense of the excitement of Renaissance drama throughout the reigns of all three monarchs.

Another significant 'textbook' has emerged this year in the shape of Sandra Clark's *Renaissance Drama*. This monograph also employs a thematic and chronological approach to the drama of the period by surveying most of the key dramatists and applying to their works a strong sense of cultural contexts and the theorized approaches of modern criticism. Owing to this structure, Clark's study, like that of Womack, should be of immense usefulness to scholars and students alike. Moving through the chapters in order, the introduction glosses the emergence of public theatre in the mid-Elizabethan period while introducing the reader to the more famous anti-theatrical texts and their impact on the stage and wider culture. Chapter 2 looks at monarchical authority in various plays, including Sackville and Norton's *Gorboduc*, Shakespeare's *Richard II*, Middleton's *A Game at Chess*, *The Isle of Dogs* by Nashe and Jonson, and Marston's *Malcontent*, while the chapter also introduces students to the cult of Elizabeth, and the two later Stuart courts. The third chapter views the staging of domestic issues of sex, family and marriage in plays such as Marston's *Dutch Courtesan* and various works by Middleton and Webster. Of particular interest should be the chapter on what Clark usefully terms 'journalistic plays', by which she refers to plays that 'centre on the lives of the non-elite' (p. 63), including the anonymous *Arden of Faversham* and *The Witch of Edmonton*. Furthermore, relatively neglected texts are discussed, including a useful pause on *The Miseries of Enforced Marriage* by George Wilkins. Further chapters explore more familiar genres, including an excellent discussion of history plays that moves well beyond the usual Shakespearian interpretation to consider various other works, together with a lively discussion of 'Tragedies of Tyrants'. Before discussing Shakespeare in a separate chapter, the book journeys towards a close with a fascinating discussion of the discourse of revenge on the Renaissance stage, from Kyd's early *Spanish Tragedy*, all the way through to Caroline drama such as Shirley's *Cardinal*, before going on to dedicate an entire chapter to city comedy, including the appropriate plays by Jonson. This is a detailed and thought-provoking study which should prove to be of immense value to all, particularly undergraduate students encountering the period for the first time.

Moving away from undergraduate-based texts, we come to an interestingly original approach to Renaissance drama by Sandra Logan. In her *Texts/ Events in Early Modern England: Poetics of History*, Logan attempts to read various literary and dramatic works alongside, or even against, the 'true' historical event being recorded textually. As Logan puts it herself,

'Considering a range of events—historical moments, theatrical performances, public presentations, and individual actions—and the texts that record them, this book engages with current scholarly attention to Elizabethan political culture, understood as the contested territory of social, religious, economic, and political formations of Elizabethan England' (pp. 1–2). Owing to this approach, the monograph offers an excellent discussion of Elizabeth's 1558 coronation, arguing that it was 'no more elaborate or coherent than other examples of the genre, but...was represented in the primary written account in such a way that the *text/event*, with its particular interests and agenda, has displaced and come to stand in for the event itself' (p. 35). Furthermore, argues Logan, we can begin to realize that Mulcaster's printed account actually offered a 'Protestantization' of the ceremony, as opposed to the 'true' religious politics of the event. Similarly, a key chapter on the 1575 Kenilworth festivities will be of interest to all those working on the Elizabethan progresses and their accompanying pageantry, particularly as Logan takes the helpful step of reading the two printed accounts side by side. Thus the monograph offers insightful work on Robert Laneham's *A Letter* and George Gascoigne's *Princely Pleasures* with a persuasive and sophisticated critical methodology.

Our last monograph this year is a detailed study of early Stuart masquing culture from Barbara Ravelhofer. *The Early Stuart Masque: Dance, Costume, and Music* builds upon the groundbreaking interdisciplinary work of James Knowles, Clare McManus and Karen Britland in order to view the surviving textual accounts of the court masques in light of performance theory, gender studies, architecture, history of art, costume and music. Indeed, the book is particularly good on the European contexts of many of the entertainments, and offers insightful material on the sense of spectacle that the texts evoke. The study surveys various European and English sources on dance and display, as well as including an entire section devoted to the neglected topic of masquing costume. Finally, the last movement of the book offers detailed case studies of Jonson's *Masque of Queens* and the later *Oberon*, as well as *Coelum Britannicum* and the Constantinople masque. Overall, this is an excellent read for scholars of early Stuart theatre, particularly those interested in highly interdisciplinary work on the English court. The book benefits from a number of colour illustrations and plates, allowing the intended emphasis on visual and material culture to flourish beside the given readings of key texts. Furthermore, the study moves into relatively unexplored material relating to movement and dance and yet still manages to offer a coherent and well-structured argument. Indeed, it will be particularly interesting to view the monograph alongside the forthcoming studies of Martin Butler and James Knowles.

Staying with the theme of courtly ritual and display allows us to move on to edited collections, and, in particular, one work of great importance that should have been featured last year. *The Progresses, Pageants, and Entertainments of Queen Elizabeth I*, edited by Jayne Archer, Elizabeth Goldring and Sarah Knight, arises out of the huge undertaking of the John Nichols Project at the University of Warwick, and will eventually be viewed as a critical companion to the edited collection of entertainments, due out next year from the same team. The collection of essays continues the historical work of Mary Hill Cole on the Elizabethan progresses, but, like Ravelhofer's discussion of the later masquing culture, the studies are interdisciplinary and extremely wide-ranging. For instance, the useful introduction by Archer and Knight contextualizes the progresses in terms of Elizabethan political, courtly, urban and aristocratic cultures, while a chapter by Cole builds upon and expands on her earlier work. Furthermore, Felicity Heal looks at the concept of gift-giving on the progresses, Hester Lees-Jeffries examines the coronation entry of 1559, Siobhan Keenan offers an excellent discussion of entertainments for the queen at the universities and C.E. McGee allows us a fascinating glimpse of the civic aspects of city entertainments for the queen. Likewise, Patrick Collinson offers a persuasive account of the politics behind the 1578 progress alongside a usefully detailed account of the 1578 Norwich entertainments by David Bergeron. The fully interdisciplinary nature of the collection emerges through intriguing essays by Elizabeth Goldring on portraiture, on literary and historical perspectives on the Cowdray entertainment of 1591 by Elizabeth Heale, on gender and authorship by Peter Davidson and Jane Stevenson, and a fascinating discussion of the manuscript culture that helped to circulate the texts by Gabriel Heaton. Lastly, this brilliant collection of essays concludes by moving beyond the Elizabethan period, as James Knowles expertly examines Jonson's later appropriation of the Kenilworth entertainments for Charles I, while Julian Pooley looks at John Nichols himself, the earlier editor of so many of these surviving texts. Taken as a whole, the collection offers the definitive word on the progresses, and should prove particularly enjoyable when read alongside the forthcoming freshly edited dramatic texts.

Another edited collection that covers a wide variety of themes and topics has emerged this year from Ashgate. *Italian Culture in the Drama of Shakespeare and his Contemporaries*, edited by Michele Marrapodi, takes the view that far more work is to be done on Italianate aspects of the drama. Because much of the collection is concerned with plays by Shakespeare, these essays sadly fall beyond the scope of this particular review. However, important scholars give detailed and insightful responses to various Shakespearian works in terms of Italian influence, while two essays move beyond the bard in order to examine Marston and Middleton respectively. First, in an excellent eleventh chapter entitled 'Re-make/Re-model: Marston's *The Malcontent* and Guarinian Tragicomedy', Jason Lawrence argues a very persuasive case for the neglected importance of Italian influence upon the play. As the author puts it himself, it is 'clearly significant that Marston chooses to borrow extensively from . . . Battista Guarini's *Il pastor fido* (first printed in 1590)' (p. 155). Also in the same collection, Celia R. Daileader, in her 'The Courtesan Revisited: Thomas Middleton, Pietro Aretino, and Sex-phobic Criticism', argues for a feminist reassessment of the playwright's long-supposed misogyny, particularly in terms of his presentation of sexually active female characters. As the author makes clear, her essay seeks 'to defend Middleton against these recurrent charges of misogyny by calling attention to a shared network of assumptions that have prevented an appreciation of his more progressive gender politics' (p. 224). Thus, argues Daileader, we can trace the influence of Aretino on Middleton's forward-looking dramatic project.

Turning our attention to shorter studies of Renaissance drama in scholarly journals, a sensible place to start chronologically is Peter Happé's overview of the career of John Heywood. In ' "Rejoice ye in us with joy most joyfully": John Heywood's Plays and the Court' (*CahiersE* 71[2007] 1–8), Happé offers a useful summary to this key early dramatist and his continued involvement with the various Tudor courts, pointing out that Heywood was at court as early as 1519 and yet was also present during Elizabeth's reign. Furthermore, alongside this historical chronology Happé expertly traces records of the dramatist's changing focus in terms of the theatrical production of the six plays that we still have with us today.

A useful place to continue in terms of chronology comes in the shape of a recent article by Ineke Murakami on mid-Tudor drama. Her 'Wager's Drama of Conscience, Convention, and State Constitution' (*SEL* 47[2007] 305–29) helpfully examines early modern drama before the emergence of the public theatres in London in the 1570s, and so argues that 'William Wager serves as an ideal test case for thinking about convention in moral drama' (p. 306). In light of this, the author tackles *The Longer Thou Livest, the More Fool Thou Art* [c.1559–68] as well as Wager's later play, *Enough Is as Good as a Feast* [1571]. Murakami goes on to argue that, in his plays, Wager 'deploys convention to mask social critique' (p. 306), and that we can view him as evidence of theatrical commentary on societal events much earlier than had previously been thought.

Also of interest to scholars of the earlier part of our period will be an engaging article by Christine M. Neufeld. In 'Lyly's Chimerical Vision: Witchcraft in *Endymion*' (*FMLS* 43[2007] 351–69), the critic contextualizes Lyly's significant work (c.1585–8) alongside the witchcraft statute of 1562, arguing that the play 'communicates a profound anxiety about the monstrous shadow cast by the Virgin Queen' (p. 352). Importantly, the article goes on to highlight textual references and moments of classicism in order to argue that the text's discussion of witchcraft 'disrupts the play's Neoplatonic structure . . . [and so] blurs the boundary between the monstrous witch and the divine queen' (p. 352).

Moving on to the birth of the public theatre in the 1570s and 1580s, we come to an intriguing discussion of vengeance and religion from Thomas Rist. In 'Memorial Revenge and the Reformation(s): Kyd's *The Spanish Tragedy*' (*CahiersE* 71[2007] 15–25), Rist comments on the neglect of funeral rites in the earliest surviving revenge tragedy and neatly situates this fact within contemporary religious debates. As the critic makes clear, 'In an age in which . . . Reformers confronted and reduced traditional acts of memorial for the . . . dead, *The Spanish Tragedy* emphasizes that diminished funerary memorial is incomplete and a cause of revenge' (p. 20). From this perspective, Rist concludes that the play might be viewed as an anti-Reformist play rather than an anti-Catholic propaganda. Staying with Kyd's play, we also have Rebekah Owens's important 'Parody and *The Spanish Tragedy*' (*CahiersE* 71[2007] 27–36), in which she revisits the anonymous *The First Part of Jeronymo*. Owens argues that the numerous parodies of this text in more familiar works can be seen as evidence for the wide appeal of the play as well as its enduring legacy and influence. As the critic makes clear, 'one can disregard the implication that parody is mockery and instead view any parodic . . . material as a commentary on *The Spanish Tragedy*' (p. 29). Indeed, the article then traces the various parodies of the play in other dramatic works and so argues for the importance of both the anonymous text and the famous play by Kyd, thus urging critics to move away from Jonson's view of *The Spanish Tragedy* as old-fashioned and uninspiring.

Mark Hutchings, 'The "Turk Phenomenon" and the Repertory of the Late Elizabethan Playhouse' (*EMLS* SI 16[2007] 10.1–39), demonstrates, by means of an impressive table, just how much in vogue the motif of Turkishness was in late Elizabethan drama: and not merely in plays which explicitly staged Turkishness (although there were plenty of them) but in plays which alluded to Turks. Although Hutchings does offer readings of particular plays—notably Marlowe's *Tamburlaine*—the co-ordinates of his approach are informed by repertory studies, and he is particularly interested in the interchange of Turkish motifs in plays staged by different companies in this period. For Hutchings, the companies' use of Turkish themes in this period constitutes 'a halfway house, as it were, between collaboration and competition' (p. 39). Hutchings's work is a good companion piece to Annaliese Connolly's article 'Peele's *David and Bethsabe*: Reconsidering Biblical Drama of the Long 1590s' (*EMLS* special issue 16[2007] 9.1–20), which also uses tables to demonstrate the extent of another now largely overlooked genre on the late Elizabethan stage: the biblical drama, of which at least thirteen were commissioned between 1590 and 1602 but of which only two survive. Peele's play, Connolly demonstrates, is indebted to *Tamburlaine* in interesting ways, and also interacts with Elizabethan representations of David as a military leader.

Andrew Gurr, 'The Work of Elizabethan Plotters and *2 The Seven Deadly Sins*' (*EarT* 10:i[2007] 67–88), is a detailed consideration of the enigmatic 'plot' of the article's title, with particular reference to what little is known about the business of 'plotting' and its importance for Elizabethan theatre companies. Disagreeing, in particular, with the arguments of David Kathman, who dates the *Sins* plot to 1598, Gurr makes the case that it must have been prepared for Lord Strange's Men in the early part of 1591. Further progress on the same issue is provided by Lawrence Manley, in a note, 'Thomas Belte, Elizabethan Boy Actor' (*N&Q* 54[2007] 310–13). Manley locates the baptismal record for Thomas Belte, named in the 'plot' and identified by Kathman, and shows that he was born in Norwich in 1579. While this might, on the face of it, seem to be evidence in favour of the proposed later date for the plot, there is good evidence that boy actors were, by today's standards, remarkably young. Manley argues that there is reason to think that Belt could well have acted the parts attributed to him as a boy actor at the age of 13.

One intelligent and persuasive article is difficult to place chronologically as it approaches Renaissance drama thematically and covers much ground. In ' "Ick verstaw you nict": Performing Foreign Tongues on the Early Modern Stage' (*MRDE* 20[2007] 204–21), Andrew Fleck shows us that 'playwrights would try to represent linguistic difference' in order to please the expectations of the London audiences (p. 205). In doing so, argues Fleck, the drama 'signalled the emergence of English and cosmopolitan London on the metaphorical stage of European events' (p. 205). In light of this thesis, the article explores a number of key plays, including *The Spanish Tragedy*, Shakespeare's *Henry V*, William Haughton's *English for my Money* and Marston's *Dutch Courtesan*, as well as various plays by Dekker.

Moving on to the Jacobean stage we have a detailed discussion of mercantile credit by Aaron Kitch. In 'The Character of Credit and the Problem of Belief in Middleton's City Comedies' (*SEL* 47[2007] 403–26) Kitch 'suggest[s] how several of Middleton's city comedies apply the logic of the commercial theatre to the economic and theological problem of credit in early modern England' (p. 403). As a result of this approach the critic also dips into Middleton's own biography as well as including a fascinating discussion of Calvin's use of 'debt' as a metaphor, in order to intellectually contextualize the plays of Middleton. Thus the article offers detailed readings of *The Roaring Girl* and *A Mad World, My Masters*, as well as of *A Trick to Catch the Old One*, in order to 'see how credit determines the social fantasies of mercantile London' (p. 422). Mark Hutchings, 'Mary Frith at the Fortune' (*EarT* 10:i[2007] 89–108), is concerned with Middleton and Dekker's *The Roaring Girl*, and with the question of how, exactly, Moll Frith took part in the play. In particular, he suggests, 'she may well have been a much less willing collaborator in Middleton and Dekker's version of her life than the quarto's closing advertisement suggests' (p. 90). On other recorded occasions, Hutchings argues, Frith sought to subvert the state's attempts to discipline and punish her: perhaps the same is true of her involvement, whatever it was, in a performance of the play recorded in *The Consistory of London Correction Book*, and usually taken to indicate her enthusiastic participation in the life-writing of her undertaken by Middleton and Dekker's comedy.

Staying with Middleton for one more piece, we have Ceri Sullivan's excellent, thought-provoking discussion of 'Thomas Middleton's View of Public Utility' (*RES* 58[2007] 162–74). In this article, Sullivan examines Middleton's *A Chaste Maid at Cheapside, His Lordship's Entertainment at the Running Stream* and *The Triumph of Truth* in order to articulate a convincing case for the works 'as commentary on the market in water made by his patrons the Myddeltons in 1613, in strong preference to a feminist reading of flows in the city comedy' (p. 162). Sullivan goes on to read the civic entertainments alongside the public drama and offers the context of London's problematic water supply, thus reconsidering the texts in light of this neglected economic and social sphere.

One particularly enlightening article emerged this year on Jacobean tragedy and, in particular, on Webster's drama. In 'The Domestication of Religious Objects in *The White Devil*' (*SEL* 47[2007] 473–90) Elizabeth Williamson offers a strong case for the importance of the appearance of crucifixes in the revenge play. As she makes clear, 'The controversial nature of the crucifix might lead us to conclude that all such objects were necessarily absent' (p. 473). However, argues the critic, such an object appears in Webster's play in the fifth act as the possession of Cornelia, and Webster actually makes sure that the object 'is positively inflected as a key element of a family unity' (p. 477). Also on Webster is a note on *The Duchess of Malfi*, glossing the passage where the Duchess tells a story comparing herself to a salmon being persecuted by a dogfish. James T. Bratcher, in 'Fishermen's Lore and the

Salmon-Dogfish Fable in Webster's *The Duchess of Malfi*' (*N&Q* 54[2007] 324–5), quotes Erasmus Darwin's account of the beliefs of eighteenth-century fishermen in Scarborough: they too believe that dogfish persecute other fish.

In terms of Jacobean drama, 2007 also offered an intriguing article by Marina Hila entitled 'Dishonourable Peace: Fletcher and Massinger's *The False One* and Jacobean Foreign Policy' (*CahiersE* 71[2007] 21–30). In this piece, Hila reads the play in light of Ralegh's execution and the accompanying Spanish–English religious politics. As Hila states, 'the play is a response to the contemporary controversy surrounding King James's pacifist and Hispanophile foreign policy, echoing the concerns voiced in the anti-Spanish, anti-Catholic pamphlets of the early 1620s' (p. 21). Thus, the article delves into Thomas Scott's *Vox Populi* in order to freshen our understanding of the contemporary anxiety that may have framed the play's cultural presentation and reception.

Work on Caroline drama this year includes Erin Obermueller's article, '"On cheating pictures": Gender and Portrait Miniatures in Philip Massinger's *The Picture*' (*EarT* 10:ii[2007] 87–108). This reads the eponymous miniature of Massinger's play in terms of the history of Renaissance miniature portraits, in particular in terms of their construction of gender. For Obermueller, 'a common rubric of gender ideology' (p. 89) links the aesthetics of portrait miniatures and of drama. Massinger's play, she argues, constitutes a meditation upon, and a challenge to, such conventional constructions of gender. *Early Theatre* also contains several short essays on Richard Brome, linked by an introduction by Eleanor Lowe, 'Offstage and Onstage Drama: New Approaches to Richard Brome' (*EarT* 10:ii[2007] 109–16). Eleanor Collins, 'Richard Brome's Contract and the Relationship of Dramatist to Company in the Early Modern Period' (*EarT* 10:ii[2007] 116–28), challenges the usual reading of Brome's contract (as evidenced at second hand by his legal dispute with Richard Heton) as paradigmatic of the lost contracts which bound other Renaissance dramatists to their companies. Rather, she observes, the very fact that this contract led to a lawsuit suggests that it may be untypical of wider practice. '"Now mark that fellow; he speaks extempore": Scripted Improvisation in *The Antipodes*' (*EarT* 10:ii[2007] 129–40), by Karen Kettnich, compares Brome's play to Beaumont's *The Knight of the Burning Pestle* in terms of its interest in and techniques for creating the illusion of on-stage improvisation. Noting that Brome's plays come from 'a culture replete with improvisational theatre' (p. 130), Kettnich's article raises the fascinating, and by definition almost unanswerable, question of how much 'real' improvisation there was on the Renaissance stage.

Farah Karim-Cooper, '"This alters not thy beauty": Face-Paint, Gender, and Race in *The English Moor*' (*EarT* 10:ii[2007] 140–8), offers a detailed investigation of the connections between cosmetics, gender and race on the Renaissance stage, as manifested in a play which, chronologically at least, is the successor to *The Antipodes*. Karim-Cooper observes the contemporary suspicion of make-up in general—'of the devil's invention and never of God's teaching' (p. 141)—and suggests that the central motif of Brome's play, in which a calumniated woman is made to disguise herself as a moor before a return to whiteness which triumphantly vindicates her chastity, reflects not just contemporary attitudes towards race but also ideas of female virtue. And that theme—of concerns about female virtue transferred into surrogate objects—comes up again in Mimi Yiu's 'Facing Places in *The Weeding of Covent Garden*' (*EarT* 10:ii[2007] 149–57). In Brome's place-realism play, the character Dorcas turns out not, in fact, to be a notorious Venetian whore displaying herself on the facades of the new buildings of Covent Garden, but a wronged English girl in disguise. 'casting aside her foreign identity like an ill-fitting, ill-proportioned façade', writes Yiu, 'This putative Venetian *puta* returns to the fold...[but] Brome's text itself seems unable to eliminate the spectre of femininity that perverts its very structure' (p. 155). Also on Brome, Eleanor Lowe's note 'Confirmation of Richard Brome's Final Years in Charterhouse Hospital' (*N&Q* 54[2007] 416–18) finds new Brome signatures in the archives of Charterhouse, where he died in 1652. These are of interest in filling in the picture of Brome's final years, and valuable too as an undoubted example of Brome's autograph, with potential implications for other manuscript documents which have been connected to Brome.

Finally, 2007 was a good year for important scholarship on the masque and other courtly entertainments. Scholars of progress entertainments and courtly masques should consider an important recent discussion by Markus Klinge. Although his 'Triumphal Shews: German and English National Identity in Weckherlin's 1616 Stuttgart Triumph' (*SC* 22[2007] 201–24) does not deal exclusively with British drama in our period, the article can be usefully read alongside other discussions of English ceremonial court culture and does ask why there was an English translation of this theatrical event abroad in the first place. Lastly, in 'The Wisdom of their Feet: Meaningful Dance in Milton and the Stuart Masque' (*ELR* 37[2007] 74–99), Blair Hoxby examines the Ludlow masque (*Comus*) in terms of the employment of dance and spectacle alongside other more 'courtly' masques performed for Charles I at Whitehall Palace in the 1630s and early 1640s, pointing out both differences and similarities in their uses of dance.

(b) Marlowe

The year 2007 saw the publication of two monographs dealing with the work of Christopher Marlowe. John Parker's *The Aesthetics of Antichrist: From Christian Drama to Christopher Marlowe* is a study of broad scope and notable complexity, tracing the notion of Antichrist from early Christian writing through to Marlowe's plays via medieval Christian drama. Parker, as critics such as David Bevington and Ruth Lunney have done before, sets out to demonstrate a continuity between medieval drama and the new commercial theatre spearheaded by Marlowe, but does so from a different perspective; rather than detecting residual elements of a unilaterally pious Christian drama in Marlowe's more morally ambiguous work, Parker argues that the continuity between the two apparently opposing forms suggests that our view of the earlier drama has been too simplistic. 'If Marlowe preserves certain elements of medieval drama,' he argues, 'should this not...be allowed to imply that his medieval predecessors achieved by means of the Bible a drama almost as dodgy as his?... A medieval Marlowe, I want to say, should allow us to see all the better how Marlovian the middle ages were' (p. viii). After the book's introduction and opening three chapters, which discuss early Christianity and medieval drama and which accentuate the paradoxically close proximity between Christ and Antichrist and between Christian worship and theatre, the discussion in the final chapter moves on to Marlowe's work. This chapter begins by setting up a dialectical opposition between Marlowe and his fellow Cambridge student and eventual denigrator Thomas Beard. As elsewhere in the book, Parker demonstrates ways in which the apparently stark opposition between the playwright and the polemicist dissolves into similarity upon inspection, identifying a distinctly Marlovian flair for cruelty in Beard's work, and in his iconoclastic dismissal of superstitions a resonance with Marlowe's scoffs as reported in the Baines note. The chapter then moves on in a similar vein to a reading of three of the major plays alongside figures from Christian history, pairing Barabas with Barabbas, Tamburlaine with the apostle Paul, and Faustus with Simon Magus. In each case Parker demonstrates the parallels between the Marlovian protagonist and a figure who hovers on the boundary between Christ and Antichrist.

Robert Logan's *Shakespeare's Marlowe: The Influence of Christopher Marlowe on Shakespeare's Artistry* sets out to expand on the discussion of Marlowe's influence on Shakespeare in a number of ways. First, it is notable that the plays of Shakespeare discussed in the volume run to as late as *The Tempest*; rather than simply manifesting itself by way of veiled allusions and linguistic echoes in Shakespeare's early work, Logan sees Marlowe's influence as having 'rooted itself in Shakespeare and developed, for it continued to thrive for 18 years after Marlowe's death' (p. 8). Secondly, Logan refigures the nature of that influence, consciously moving away from the notion that the two playwrights were rivals in a sense of the word that implies hostility, and aiming at looking beyond exclusively literary aspects to 'theatrical practices', by which he means 'those strategies that Shakespeare devised to give the production of his plays maximum effectiveness, whether measured *pragmatically*, by the plays' degree of commercial success, or *aesthetically*, by such ingredients as conflict and tension, spectacles... and climactic moments' (p. 2). Thus the book considers not just the thematic and syntactic influence, but also the dramaturgical influence of Marlowe's plays on Shakespeare. Logan goes on to offer chapters analysing the relationship of influence in *The Massacre at Paris*, *Titus Andronicus* and *Richard III*; *Hero and Leander* and *Venus and Adonis*; *Edward II* and *Richard II*; *The Jew of Malta* and *The Merchant of Venice*; The *Tamburlaine* plays and *Henry V*; *Dido, Queen of Carthage* and *Antony and Cleopatra*; and finally *Doctor Faustus*, *Macbeth* and *The Tempest*. Artistic influence is the topic of another piece which discusses Marlowe, albeit indirectly. In 'Shakespearean Seductions, or, What's with Harold Bloom as Falstaff?' (*TSLL* 49:ii[2007] 125–54), Alan D. Lewis critiques Harold Bloom's theory of influence, and his formulation of Shakespeare's liberation from the influence of Marlowe enacted by the creation and rejection of Falstaff. Bloom's thesis, Lewis contends, relies on a questionable conception of Shakespeare's work as 'spiritual autobiography', and ultimately contributes to the ongoing reproduction of the 'authentic Shakespeare' (p. 125).

Marlowe biography continues to provoke discussion, with two articles surfacing on this topic. Arata Ide's 'Christopher Marlowe, William Austen, and the Community of Corpus Christi College' (*SP* 104:i[2007] 56–81) examines the social networks likely to have been active at Corpus Christi (and Cambridge in general). Focusing first on the networks of contact between students and the people of the town, Ide discusses the case of William Austen, who was brought before a university tribunal for failing to pay for food given to him on credit by a local victualler named Richard Gee. Austen was apparently accompanied on his fateful trip to see Gee by one Christopher Morley. From this episode, and related anecdotes, Ide draws suggestions of close-knit communities of contact and friendship throughout Cambridge life, and hence the danger of damaging rumours such as those that were suggested by the famous Privy Council note of 1587 to have been spread about Marlowe. In these circles, Ide suggests, reputation is vital, particularly to poorer scholars such as William Austen and Christopher Marlowe, who must rely on it in securing patronage should they decline to take up holy orders. Much like Lukas Erne in 2005, J.A. Downie, in his article 'Marlowe, May 1593, and the 'Must-Have' Theory of Biography' (*RES* 58[2007] 245–67), takes aim at the recent industry of Marlowe biography, much of the intrigue of which surrounds accounts of the dramatist's activities as a government intelligencer and of the events surrounding his death in May 1593. Downie highlights the paucity of documentary evidence concerning Marlowe's life, and challenges what he calls the 'must-have' approach to biography (i.e. Marlowe must have done this, or must have done that), which he argues has governed the majority of studies of Marlowe's life. Downie first argues that the Privy Council note of 1587 detailing a correspondence with Cambridge University which implies some kind of service to the country on Marlowe's part, provides no evidence as to the nature of that service. As this document is taken as the primary piece of evidence for Marlowe's espionage activity, all subsequent discussion of the dramatist as an intelligencer is based on assumption. Downie goes on to make similar arguments regarding the perception of the playwright's death as having resulted from a conspiracy involving influential courtiers, or even the queen herself; the speculations over the nature of Marlowe's death, he suggests, arise from equally questionable speculations over his activities during his lifetime.

Each of the plays in the Marlowe canon received critical attention in 2007. Starting with *Dido*, Lucy Potter's 'Marlowe's *Dido* and the Staging of Catharsis' (*AUMLA* 107[2007] 1–23) pays particular attention to Aeneas's narrative of the sacking of Troy, and in doing so argues that the play ultimately valorizes its hero and endorses the Virgilian version of events, as opposed to the more standard critical position that Marlowe represents Aeneas ironically, in a more Ovidian spirit. Taking Else's idea of Aristotelian catharsis as something that occurs throughout the framework of a drama rather than simply as a result of it, Potter argues that Aeneas's response to telling the story is a cathartic one; he experiences pity and fear in the telling of it, and the relief he derives from it lifts the emotional paralysis with which he has been beset up until this point. That this cathartic effect is achieved,

Potter suggests, is confirmation of the tragic dignity of the tale being told, and, ultimately, of its teller.

The *Tamburlaine* plays have been the works to provoke the most comment, with four essays discussing them. In 'Tamburlaine's Domestic Threat' (in Moncrief and McPherson, eds., *Performing Maternity in Early Modern England*, pp. 211–23), Mary Stripling's reading of the plays focuses specifically on the relationship between the conqueror and his wife, and on the threat that she, and her maternal influence, pose to his campaign. Tamburlaine, Stripling argues, subdues Zenocrate's maternal identity by describing her in desexualized and virginal terms (as Marlowe subdues it by leaving the birth of her three sons in the gap between the two plays) and ultimately destroys it by murdering Calyphas, the son who most reflects the characteristics of his mother. Bernhard Klein's '*Tamburlaine*, Sacred Space and the Heritage of Medieval Cartography' (in McMullan and Matthews, eds., *Reading the Medieval in Early Modern England*, pp. 143–58) looks at the *Tamburlaine* plays in the context of the development of cartography from the medieval *mappa mundi* tradition to the early modern 'New Geography' practised by the likes of Gerard Mercator and Abraham Ortelius. Klein draws a parallel between Tamburlaine's campaign and the New Geography's stripping away of the *mappa mundi*'s religious symbolism and association with the body in favour of maps as secularized navigational tools; as the plays' geographical scope widens, 'Tamburlaine's fury only increases, generating images of a disembodied and desacralised landscape that has lost all regard for authority or tradition' (p. 152). The new cartography's disregard for the body perhaps comes back to haunt Tamburlaine, Klein suggests, when he surveys his map on his deathbed and realizes that the abstract map 'dislodges everyone . . . Even world conquerors have only particular bodies' (p. 158). Claudia Richter, in her essay 'Performing God's Wrath: *Tamburlaine*, Calvinism and the Phantasmata of Terror' (*ShJE* 143[2007] 52–70), reads the *Tamburlaine* plays against the background of the Calvinist-infused environment in which Marlowe's plays were conceived, written and performed. The emphasis on prophecy in the plays, Richter argues, aligns them with the doctrine of predestination which was central to Calvinism and which doubtless featured heavily in the blood-and-thunder sermons of the streets of London. The essay goes on to compare the tone of the play with a selection of psalms in which, Tamburlaine-like, a vengeful God promises the destruction of his enemies. Clayton G. MacKenzie provides the remaining work on *Tamburlaine* in 'Marlowe's Grisly Monster: Death in *Tamburlaine, Parts One and Two*' (*DR* 87:i[2007] 9–24). This essay employs as a context the theatrical, artistic and cultural tradition of the *danse macabre*, which generally employed the figure of Death in a scene which demonstrated the inescapability of mortality, regardless of one's social standing. Against this background, MacKenzie provides a study of the representation of Death in the Tamburlaine plays. Tamburlaine's cruelty, he argues, is highlighted by the presence in the play of notions of desirable or gentle death, notions which are starkly contrasted by the merciless and turbulent brand dealt out by the conqueror. Similarly, while his apparent hesitation implies a certain gravitas in Tamburlaine, the eventual visitation of

Death upon him ultimately demonstrates, in the tradition of the dance of death, that nobody can escape the inevitability of their demise.

MacKenzie also provides a similar reading of *The Massacre at Paris*. Like his essay on *Tamburlaine*, 'The Massacre at Paris and the Danse Macabre' (*PLL* 43:iii[2007] 311–34) studies Marlowe's play in the context of the dance of death tradition. The mocking skeletons of the *danse macabre*, who emphasize the certainty and indiscriminateness of death by leading away individuals from every section of society to their graves, are reflected in the routine killings of *The Massacre at Paris*, each performed on a person of a distinct social position and each accompanied by some appropriate jest. Taking the parallel further, MacKenzie argues that rather than representing a piece of Protestant propaganda, the play indulges in a typically Marlovian trick by having King Henry, once in power, become as cruel as the Guise, and ultimately to die a similarly pointless death.

Doctor Faustus is the subject of two pieces of work. Andrew Duxfield's ' "Resolve me of all ambiguities": *Doctor Faustus* and the Failure to Unify' (*EMLS* special issue 16[2007] 7.1–21) argues that Faustus's main project in the play is the pursuit of unified knowledge, a project characterized by his stated desire to be resolved of all ambiguities. The play's tragic effect, Duxfield contends, is in large part brought about by the tension between Faustus's unifying desire and the ambivalent nature of the playworld in which he exists; the generic structure of the play, which allows it to be read as a morality play or a tragedy, is resistant to any unifying tendencies. In the note 'Wise Blood: *Aeneid* 3.22–57 and Marlowe's *Doctor Faustus*' (*N&Q* 54[2007] 248–9), Arnd Bohm identifies a resonance between the apparent sentience of Faustus's blood in the bond-signing scene and the passage in the *Aeneid* in which a sapling which Aeneas has pulled from the ground begins to ooze blood. In both cases, the appearance of the blood is accompanied by a warning to flee.

Anna Beskin provides the only work to concentrate solely on *The Jew of Malta*, in the shape of her note 'From Jew to Nun: Abigail in Marlowe's *The Jew of Malta*' (*Expl* 65:iii[2007] 133–6). Beskin argues for the tragic status of Abigail's murder, challenging the position of Bartels and others who argue that it is simply a symptom of the play's descent into farce. Beskin highlights also that Abigail's young age—she is barely 14—is also significant; Barabas's child murder, she suggests, fulfils yet another sinister anti-Semitic stereotype in the play.

In 'To Sodomize a Nation: *Edward II*, Ireland, and the Threat of Penetration' (*EMLS* special issue 16[2007] 11.1–21), Marcie Bianco sets out to state the case for a reading of *Edward II* that acknowledges Ireland as a significant presence in the play. This essay identifies a resonance between the threat of physical sodomy and the threat to the body politic of penetration 'from behind', a threat which Ireland was characterized as representing in Marlowe's time. This resonance, Bianco argues, is foregrounded in the play by the metonymic relationship between Gaveston and Ireland that is established when the king's favourite is created governor of that land during his exile. The insidious threats of the sodomite and of the Irish nation inform each other in this play, and provide another aspect of its interweaving of the private and the political spheres.

Hero and Leander is the only non-dramatic work to have prompted discussion; in 'Hero's Afterlife: *Hero and Leander* and "lewd unmannerly verse" in the Late Seventeenth Century' (*EMLS* 12:iii[2007] 4.1–24), Roy Booth provides a survey of responses to and rewritings of *Hero and Leander*, suggesting that, in contrast to common consent, Marlowe's influence was alive during the Restoration. Wycherley's burlesque version, Booth argues, is more sympathetic than it is critical, and in any case the knowledge that the Restoration parodists had of the Elizabethan poems they mocked meant that essential spirit of the original was kept alive by their rewriting. Wolfgang Riehle's note, 'What's in Lysander's Name?' (*N&Q* 54[2007] 274–5), argues that Lysander's name constitutes an allusion to Leander, in line with *A Midsummer Night's Dream*'s other gestures to the poem. The alteration in the name, Riehle suggests, allows for an extended series of puns on the word 'lie', and is also consistent with the play's blending of classical and English traditions.

The final two items covered in this entry apply more generally to Marlowe's work as a whole. Kirk Melnikoff's ' "Iygging vaines" and "riming mother wits": Marlowe, Clowns and the Early Frameworks of Dramatic Authorship' (*EMLS* special issue 16[2007] 8.1–37) questions the widespread reading of the prologue to *Tamburlaine, Part I* as a dismissal of the popular theatre that preceded it and the announcement of the sudden arrival of a loftier kind of drama. In presenting this thesis, Melnikoff looks at evidence of the robust health of clownage in *The Jew of Malta* and *Doctor Faustus*. Ithamore, he contends, represents a clown figure, albeit one whose role has developed into a slightly less prominent and absurd one. Similarly, the renowned comic scenes in *Faustus*, combined with the many instances of spectacle that infuse the play's tragic material and which seem to derive directly from medieval pageantry, show that Marlowe's drama is at a stage of development whereby it incorporates both the visual spectacle of popular drama and the high astounding terms of the more script-based drama that will evolve more fully on the Elizabethan stage after his death. Thomas Healy's 'Marlowe and Shakespeare' (in Hass, Jasper and Jay, eds., *The Oxford Handbook of Literature and Theology*, pp. 382–97) examines the relationship between theology and theatre in early modern England. In it, he emphasizes the ambiguous nature of this relationship. Having identified that distinctions between the myriad religious categories available to the Elizabethans were less than clear, he goes on to discuss why critics have been able to see evidence of apparently mutually exclusive religious positions in Marlowe's and Shakespeare's work. Pointing out the ambiguity of Renaissance drama, Healy argues that the vagaries of early modern text and the context of performance ensure that, while Shakespeare and Marlowe engage with contemporary theological concerns, they never do so unilaterally.

(c) Jonson

We begin this year's *YWES* entry on Jonson with a monograph. Heather C. Easterling's *Parsing the City: Jonson, Middleton, Dekker, and City Comedy's*

London as Language offers much of interest to Jonson scholars. Easterling 'would argue that city comedy not only represents but interrogates the language of Jacobean London in plays that regularly stage the city precisely as language or languages' (p. 1). Easterling suggests that the plays she focuses on display 'London as a landscape of language', participating as they do so in contemporary debates about the status of the vernacular (p. 4). *Epicoene*, *Bartholomew Fair*, and Middleton and Dekker's *The Roaring Girl* are the three plays which receive detailed discussion, but the implications spread far and wide across the Jonson canon. An introduction persuasively argues that the Jacobean era was one of linguistic fragmentation and linguistic self-consciousness, of which one obvious marker is the proliferation of 'grammars, orthographies, and other language-manuals' (p. 13) that appeared in print in that period. In such a setting, while *Epicoene* and *The Roaring Girl* struggle, in different ways, with ideas of gendered language and gendered order, *Bartholomew Fair* depicts a world in which order seems impossible and language is explicitly reduced to a game.

Matthew Greenfield's essay, 'Trial by Theater: Jonson, Marston, and Dekker in the Court of Parnassus' (in Kezar, ed., *Solon and Thespis: Law and Theater in the English Renaissance*, pp. 19–39), is concerned with the courtroom scene in *Poetaster*, compared to the legal practice of Jonson's England and to the equivalent scene in Dekker's *Satiromastix*. Greenfield sees Jonson's scene, in particular, not merely as knockabout comedy, but as a sustained meditation on issues of moral agency and social responsibility, especially as they pertain to writers. Jonson's scene, he observes, appears to be governed by Roman law, while Dekker's takes place within the world of English law and includes a jury. Also on *Poetaster* and the law, broadly defined, is Charles Cathcart's excellent '*Poetaster* and the Prince of Love: A Note' (*BJJ* 14[2007] 206–17), which reads *Poetaster* in the light of its dedicatee Richard Martin. In particular, Cathcart draws attention to the dynamics of the feud between Richard Martin and John Davies recorded in Benjamin Rudyerd's account of the Prince of Love revels, *Le Prince D'Amour* [1660]. In the end, Cathcart suggests, both the feud and Jonson's play address a nexus of issues around wit, collaboration, social rejection and violence: Davies, Cathcart concludes, is in some ways a 'suppressed icon for the young Ben Jonson' (p. 214).

Cynthia Bowers, in ' "I will write satires still, in spite of fear": History, Satire, and Free Speech in *Poetaster* and *Sejanus*' (*BJJ* 14[2007] 153–72), reads *Poetaster* and its successor, *Sejanus*, in terms of late Elizabethan censorship, especially the Bishops' Order of 1599 targeting satires and histories. It is a pity this essay seems not to have come across Tom Cain's essay on *Poetaster* in Sanders, Chedgzoy and Wiseman, eds., *Refashioning Ben Jonson: Gender, Politics and the Jonsonian Canon* [1998], with which it shares some interesting concerns. On the other hand, there is also a thought-provoking overlap with Ali Chetwynd's article ' "He that lends you pity is not wise": Rereading *Sejanus* for Pity and Terror' (*BJJ* 14[2007] 43–60). The articulate but ineffective Arruntius, who observes but cannot stop the evil at Tiberius's court, is often regarded as the nearest that *Sejanus* has to a normative figure. But Chetwynd sees in Jonson's tragedy a play which denies a single moral viewpoint, and implicitly criticizes Arruntius for his lack of pragmatism. Arruntius, for Chetwynd, should be considered like Surly in *The Alchemist*: one who fails to achieve. Chetwynd writes well about the ways in which Arruntius's certainties misdirect the audience, leading up to the shocking denouement of the account of Sejanus's death.

Moral complexity, guilt, and not a little pity and terror come up too in Frances Teague's essay 'Ben Jonson and London Courtrooms' (in Kezar, ed., pp. 64–77). *Volpone* has often been seen as a play which should be linked somehow to the Gunpowder Plot, but Teague draws attention specifically to the parallels between the courtroom scenes displayed in the play and the trials of the Gunpowder Plotters. Also on *Volpone* this year, Purificación Ribes writes on 'Stefan Zweig's *Volpone, eine lieblose Komödie* on Stage in Austria and Germany (1926–1927)' (*BJJ* 14[2007] 61–77). Zweig's free adaptation of the play introduced a fair amount of onstage violence and bawdy language (as well as a happy ending). It enjoyed astonishing success, not just in German, but also in French, Spanish and English translations: she records runs of 160 nights in New York, and 250 performances in Paris. But the main subject of Ribes's article is the play's success in Vienna and in Germany, which she explores with the aid of prompt-books and original performance records. It is fascinating to see Jonson's play, complete with anti-Jewish jokes left intact by the Jewish adaptor, playing in Dresden, Berlin, Frankfurt, Hamburg and Munich in the winter of 1926/7: Ribes does an excellent job of putting this interesting text in a wider cultural context.

Epicoene, which features heavily in Easterling's book, is also prominent in the year's periodical literature. Mark Albert Johnston writes on 'Prosthetic Absence in Ben Jonson's *Epicoene*, *The Alchemist*, and *Bartholomew Fair*' (*ELR* 37[2007] 401–28), with the bulk of the time being spent on the first of these three Jacobean city comedies. He is interested in Jonson's 'play with gender prostheses' (p. 403) in these plays: by gender prostheses Johnston means, not just women's clothing, but equally, and in strange parallel to it, the male beard, which signifies both in its presence and in its absence, and which is frequently referred to within, for instance, *Epicoene*. This gives an interesting perspective on Jonson's comedy, argues Johnston: 'the insistence with which the play asserts the prosthetic construction of femininity operates superficially to conceal an anxiety about the possibility that masculinity and its prerequisite privileges are also prosthetically constructed and inherently artificial' (p. 413).

The gender paradoxes of *Epicoene* also concern Mimi Yiu in her article 'Sounding the Space between Men: Choric and Choral Cities in Ben Jonson's *Epicoene; or, The Silent Woman*' (*PMLA* 122[2007] 72–88). This lively and learned piece takes in Platonic concepts of space, acoustic approaches to London's cities, and *The Matrix* to read Morose as 'a paternalistic icon of resistance to the city changing around him' (p. 78), whose misanthropy is defined by his refusal to enter the communal matrices of sounds and celebrations, and who instead attempts to cultivate a private space, only for this space to be queered—rendered epicene—by the very efforts to preserve it.

Epicoene was featured in two other pieces of work this year. Barbara Sebek's short article 'Morose's Turban' (*ShakS* 35[2007] 32–8) uses Morose's links to Turkishness as a springboard for exploring how merchant and aristocratic elites in this period regarded foreign practices and customs: in particular, their reaction, she demonstrates, was not always the knee-jerk xenophobia one might naturally expect. Secondly, Dennis McCarthy contributes a note arguing for personation in the play: 'Sir Thomas North as Sir John Daw' (N&Q 54[2007] 321–4). As is often the case with such allegations of personation, not all of the details alleged are equally impressive, but McCarthy's best piece of evidence—that Sir John Daw mentions by name Doni's *Philosophy*, which North translated—is hard to argue with.

Paul Cantor, 'The Law Versus the Marketplace in Jonson's *Bartholomew Fair*' (in Kezar, ed., pp. 40–63), is a development of the same author's article from *BJJ* 8[2001] 23–64. For Cantor, *Bartholomew Fair* is bound up with questions of the government regulation of free markets, and thus reflects (among other things) on the conditions of professional drama, that highly entrepreneurial yet also highly regulated sector of the early modern economy. Kezar reads the play using Friedrich Hayek's theory of spontaneous ordering within economic systems, and studies its overlapping and competing economic and legal systems in areas from retailing to prostitution.

Rebecca Yearling discusses 'Ben Jonson's Late Plays and the Difficulty of Judgment' (*BJJ* 14[2007] 192–205). In particular, she draws attention to what previous critics have generally identified as a flaw in these plays: the 'sense of a conflict between cynicism and idealism' (p. 200) in their loose ends and slightly hollow-seeming happy endings. For Yearling, this is not a flaw but a feature: she notes that 'Jonson had always been interested in problematizing audience response' (pp. 200–1), and reads these plays as challenging the audience to think, and to reconsider their attitudes to the social problems described in the play and 'the contradictions and paradoxes of human behavior and society' (p. 203). It is good to see Jonson's late plays getting further scholarly attention, and a pity that Yearling's work is not yet in dialogue with, for instance, Julie Sanders's analyses of them: clearly more remains to be done on what used to be called Jonson's 'dotages'.

Martin Butler, 'Jonson's Fant'sy' (*BJJ* 14[2007] 1–19), is an excellent piece of old-school scholarly work: a close reading of one of the most mystifying passages in Jonson, Fant'sy's monologue from the *Vision of Delight*. This appears, to most readers, to be utter nonsense from start to finish, with its strings of phantasmagorical imagery including (in the space of a representative ten lines) puddings, bellows, bagpipes, squirrels, dogs, dreams, windmills, bells in a beard, boots on a head, whales and mousetraps. So far only Stephen Orgel has attempted to offer a detailed explication of the imagery. Butler builds on Orgel's work, but whereas Orgel believes that the solutions to the passage depend on an assumed familiarity on the part of the audience with Ripa and other emblem-books, Butler takes a simpler, more literal approach and sets about disentangling the grammar of Fant'sy's language. 'It seems to me, then', concludes Butler, 'that insofar as a rational meaning can be made out of Fant'sy's monologue—and I readily admit that the imagery has many other possible associations that my paraphrases fail to accommodate—the underlying drift is an endorsement of the value of court festivity and the legitimacy of pleasure' (p. 15).

Also on the masques is Molly Murray's article 'Performing Devotion in *The Masque of Blacknesse*' (*SEL* 47[2007] 427–49). Murray starts by putting the masque in the context of the uncertainties about devotional practices at James's court, with particular regard to the (correct) rumours that his wife Anne had already converted to Catholicism. Her central argument is that the African exotic of *The Masque of Blackness*, usually discussed in terms of ideas of race and colonialism, is also, on one level, a metaphor for Catholic devotional practices. To a text where race and religion are already intertwined in such complex ways—above all, through the master image of the black body being turned white—Murray's argument, soberly made and well documented, adds a new level of complexity.

Melissa Hudler studies 'Dance: The "Speaking Body" in Jonson's *Pleasure Reconciled to Virtue*' (*BJJ* 14[2007] 173–91). Hudler surveys Renaissance theories of how bodily movements could create meaning, with particular reference to the dancing-manuals of Thoinot Arbeau and Fabritio Caroso. I particularly enjoyed Caroso's discussion of how even doffing a hat can create a range of meanings, depending on how it is done, and his warning that a gentleman should be very careful in doing so not to expose onlookers to the 'indecent and repulsive sight' of the sweaty headband inside it (p. 180). Having developed this model of the Renaissance understanding of dance and meaning, Hudler proceeds to read *Pleasure Reconciled* in the light of it, and finds it full of playful awareness of 'the cognitive effect of spectacle' (p. 185).

One final piece of work on the masques this year is Alison V. Scott's article, 'Jonson's Masque Markets and Problems of Literary Ownership' (*SEL* 47[2007] 451–73). Scott is concerned here with Jonson's decisions to print his masques in quarto and folio forms, decisions which would seem to threaten the very status of the masque as a luxury product which performs its work precisely by being both ephemeral and exclusive. Scott explores the intellectual paradoxes attendant upon this project, relating them to both seventeenth-century and more contemporary writings on concepts of luxury, commodity, ownership and learning.

In 'Mary and Bedford Jonson: A Note' (*BJJ* 14[2007] 78–87) Tom Cain draws attention to what may well be a baptism register entry, on the very day of the Essex rebellion, for the Jonsons' short-lived daughter Mary, immortalized by her father's delicate lyric on her death. Even more tantalizingly, Cain finds later references in the same parish to a 'Bedford Jonson' (b. 1616), who is very plausibly a hitherto unknown son of the playwright, named after Jonson's major patrons the earl and countess of Bedford. Bedford himself went on to father, in 1638, a son of his own, christened Benjamin.

The *Ben Jonson Journal* continues its policy of publishing 'Jonson and his Era: Overviews of Modern Research', short and pithy guides to the current state of scholarship in specific areas. This year brings Richard Harp on both 'Catholicism' (*BJJ* 14[2007] 112–16) and 'Christianity' (*BJJ* 14[2007] 116–21); Claude J. Summers on '*Epicoene*' (*BJJ* 14[2007] 233–54); and Bruce Boehrer on both ' "Inviting a Friend to Supper" ' (*BJJ* 14[2007] 255–8) and 'Martial' (*BJJ* 14[2007] 259–62).

Books Reviewed

Archer, Jayne, Elizabeth Goldring and Sarah Knight, eds. *The Progresses, Pageants, and Entertainments of Queen Elizabeth I*. OUP. [2006] pp. 352. £56 ISBN 0 1992 9157 8.

Clark, Sandra. *Renaissance Drama*. Polity. [2006] pp. 232. £50 ISBN 0 7456 3310 2.

Easterling, Heather C. *Parsing the City: Jonson, Middleton, Dekker, and City Comedy's London as Language*. Routledge. [2007] pp. xii + 197. £65 ISBN 0 4159 7950 1.

Gunby, David, David Carnegie and MacDonald P. Jackson, eds. *The Works of John Webster*, vol. 3. CUP. [2007] pp. xli + 533. £116. ISBN 9 7805 2126 0619.

Hass, Andrew, David Jasper and Elisabeth Jay, eds. *The Oxford Handbook of Literature and Theology*. OUP. [2007] pp. 720. £85 ISBN 0 1992 7197 6.

Kezar, Dennis, ed. *Solon and Thespis: Law and Theater in the English Renaissance*. UNDP. [2007] pp. 352. £31.95 ISBN 0 2680 3313 7.

Logan, Robert A. *Shakespeare's Marlowe: The Influence of Christopher Marlowe on Shakespeare's Artistry*. Ashgate. [2007] pp. 251. £50 ISBN 0 7546 5763 9.

Logan, Sandra, *Texts/Events in Early Modern England: Poetics of History*. Ashgate. [2007] pp. 360. £50 ISBN 0 7546 5586 5.

Marrapodi, Michele, ed. *Italian Culture in the Drama of Shakespeare and his Contemporaries*. Ashgate. [2007] pp. 300. £55 ISBN 0 7546 5504 0.

McDermott, Kristen, ed. *Masques of Difference: Four Court Masques by Ben Jonson*. ManUP. [2007] pp. viii + 214. pb £5.99 ISBN 9 7807 1905 7540.

McMullan, Gordon, and David Matthews, eds. *Reading the Medieval in Early Modern England*. CUP. [2007] pp. 302. £50 ISBN 9 7805 2186 8433.

Moncrief, Kathryn M., and Kathryn R. McPherson, eds. *Performing Maternity in Early Modern England*. Ashgate. [2007] pp. 262. £50 ISBN 0 7546 6117 2.

Parker, John. *The Aesthetics of Antichrist: From Christian Drama to Christopher Marlowe*. CornUP. [2007] pp. 252. £20.50 ISBN 0 8014 4519 1.

Ravelhofer, Barbara. *The Early Stuart Masque: Dance, Costume, and Music*. OUP. [2006] pp. 336. £67 ISBN 0 1992 8659 0.

Steggle, Matthew. *Laughing and Weeping in Early Modern Theatres*. Ashgate. [2007] pp. 172. £45 ISBN 9 7807 5465 7026.

Taylor, Gary, and John Lavagnino, eds. *Thomas Middleton: The Collected Works* and *Thomas Middleton and Early Modern Textual Culture*. 2 vols. Clarendon. [2007] vol. 1 pp. 2,016, £105 ISBN 9 7801 9818 5697; vol 2 pp. 1,183, £89 ISBN 9 7801 9818 5703; 2-vol. set £158 ISBN 9 7801 9922 5880.

White, Martin, ed. *The Roman Actor: a Tragedy* by Philip Massinger. Revels. ManUP. [2007] pp. xxiv. 246. £55 ISBN 9 7807 1907 7036.

Womack, Peter. *English Renaissance Drama*. Blackwell. [2006] pp. 336. £21.99 ISBN 0 6312 2630 3.

VIII

The Earlier Seventeenth Century: General

JOHN BURTON, LISA WALTERS AND SUZANNE TRILL

This chapter has two sections: 1. General; 2. Women's Writing. Section 1 is by John Burton; section 2 is by Lisa Walters and Suzanne Trill.

1. General

In studying the early modern writer's preoccupation with the self and their relationship to the increasingly explored world about them, one can hardly avoid the growing interest in environmental and ecological studies. The associated somatic impact of environment and travel form the basis for a collection of essays edited by Mary Floyd-Wilson and Garret A. Sullivan, Jr, entitled *Environment and Embodiment in Early Modern England*, in which scholars handle the Renaissance anxiety over ecological relations of the body. While the volume concerns itself with a wide range of early modern texts, of particular note for this section is David J. Baker's study '"My Liquid Journey": The Frontispiece to *Coryat's Crudities* (1611)' (pp. 118–136). Lamenting the lack of interest by many scholars in William Hole's engraved frontispiece, Baker interprets the text through the lens of the prefacing artwork, in which Coryate's travels are depicted through the medium of bodily function and movement—with Coryate's own body both the recipient and transmitter of bodily function and fluids on his journeys. Vomit is both spewed by him and upon him, and the entire piece, Baker convincingly asserts, constitutes a fluid 'circulatory apparatus' with Coryate's corporeal humours sloshing to and fro with the motion of his European tour. The impact of changing environment upon the body is referred to within the text, and here Baker suggests that early modern readers would have readily recognized and interpreted his somewhat bizarre approach to his literature as part of a system of 'geo-somatic exchanges' relevant to his relationship to the world and his reading public. This relationship is tested at times by Coryate's marketing and self-promotion tactics (Baker observes Coryate's role as a father of modern tourism), but it is the ruthless use of his own body as part of the negotiation with his reading public that interests Baker. For Coryate not only centred his text on the humoral impact of his travels upon the restless body, but also

Year's Work in English Studies, Volume 88 (2009) © *The English Association; all rights reserved*
doi:10.1093/ywes/map012

returned to present himself as a celebrity clown in a shamelessly entrepreneur-ial enterprise designed to promote both his book and the possibility of experi-encing the bodily escape from domestic quarters European travel offered.

Coryate was not unfamiliar with using his body for public entertainment, as Michelle O'Callaghan reports in *The English Wits: Literature and Sociability in Early Modern England*. In her exposition of the social clubs and groups of the period, Coryate makes an appearance as the buffoon at the Mitre club, attended regularly by John Donne, Inigo Jones and others. Coryate's seemingly natural sense of witty self-promotion fits well with the verbal duelling and political satire that could be heard across the dining tables of London's elite clubs. Indeed, it is Coryate's letter from India to the 'Sireniacal Gentlemen' of one of the Bread Street clubs that opens the work.

Any study of literary sociability in London will of necessity take into account the Inns of Court, parliament, and the numerous civic and social clubs, but it is the part played by the lawyer-wits themselves, their convivial and experimental use of provocative and occasionally volatile language, that really interests O'Callaghan. Working from Coryate's letters from Ajmer in India, from the abundance of prefatory material in his *Crudities*, from Jonson's many references to taverns, clubs and metropolitan social groupings, the manuscript poem 'Convivium Philosophicum', and several other sources, O'Callaghan draws a fascinating outline of London's social arena centring on the 'Wits', the elite community of urbane gallants who founded a new sense of literary play and the sociability of text amid the emerging culture of fraternity.

Several studies have emerged this year demonstrating how the body has captured a lively interest among critics of the period. A special edition of *Trivium* entitled 'The Nature and Culture of the Human Body' arises both from an open lecture series on the body at the University of Wales, Lampeter, and an exhibition of anatomical and other works related to the human body from Lampeter's Founder's Library. Of particular interest in this section is Peter Mitchell's 'Living Anatomy in Renaissance Culture' (*Trivium* 37[2007] 65–92) and Helen Vella-Bonavita's 'Body of Evidence: Witchcraft and the Signs of Guilt' (*Trivium* 37[2007] 211–22). Peter Mitchell's article explores the curious question of those anatomical diagrams of the period that display the animated flayed body or skeleton as a living being among the flora and fauna of a world they appear to inhabit. His chief concerns are how such depictions are to be understood, and what these depictions imply about the early modern concept of the body. Concluding that the anatomical subject was 'the disclosure of the human body' as a divinely created 'vehicle for the soul' (p. 83), Mitchell uses five explanations; an interest in physiology, rationalism, artistic influence, 'professional dignity', that is, a desire among anatomists to gain social acceptance, and the reflection of Christian ethics in the prints.

Helen Vella-Bonavita explores the complex issue of the bodily evidence of witchcraft, and argues that the body of the witch forms a significant material point of tension in the period, held between empirical notions of external evidence and the view that 'the material world reflects the eternal truths of the immaterial one' (p. 214). Her discussion includes references to *Macbeth*, *The Witch of Edmonton* and textual references to the case of Jane Wenham, the final witch trial in England.

There are few more obvious signs of maturity and socio-economic standing among early modern men than the beard. The presence of facial hair not only imbued the wearer with a vague but discernible air of wisdom and patriarchal privilege, but it also specifically signalled the status of freeman, the completion of an apprenticeship, and thus the freedom to marry. But what does early modern society make of the bearded woman? Mark Albert Johnston considers references to beards and bearded women in 'Bearded Women in Early Modern England' (*SEL* 47[2007] 1–28). Johnston considers the cultural implications of beards in texts from the 1570s to the late seventeenth century, including Shakespeare, diary entries and European depictions in print and paint, concluding that the presence of the bearded woman in early modern culture poses a symbolic threat to the economy of patriarchy.

While notions of the body as reflected in literature interest many scholars, Katharine A. Craik turns her attention to the impact of literature upon the body in *Reading Sensations in Early Modern England*. In examining the relationship between book and body, Craik's opening chapter discusses two texts that consider the effects of reading and writing upon the body's systems, Thomas Wright's *The Passion of the Minde in Generall* [1601], and Henry Crosse's *Vertues Commonwealth* [1603]. While Crosse and Wright concerned themselves with the bodily dangers of secular literature, particularly that of a passionate nature, Craik explores the extent to which Sir Philip Sidney and George Puttenham posited the opposite; the view that emotionally charged literature actively improved the reader. Picking up the question of anger, with its attendant somatic responses, she continues to explore Sidney's works and addresses the question of whether Sidney changed his views on the ethics of anger aroused in readers of poetry. Considering the emotion of despair and the elegies of John Donne, Craik moves on to the playfulness of Coryate's *Crudities*, a text which, it is argued, manipulates 'connections between reading, writing and sensory indulgence' (p. 114). The ethics of bodily sensation prompted by reading and writing provocative literature is of continuing concern in the book. Closing the work with a chapter on the physical and emotional arousal induced by pornography, Craik again explores both sides of the divide, with Richard Braithwait's *The English Gentleman and A Nursery for Gentry* vying for attention alongside Thomas Cranley's *Amanda: Or, the Reformed Whore* [1638], arguing that the notion of pornography emerged in the period as gentlemen read in a way that involved the loss of reason and self-control. Writers like Cranley achieved this, it is argued, by largely blurring the division between fiction and reality.

Indeed, the position of the book and the act of reading gave rise to a number of valuable studies this year. Naomi Conn Liebler's collection of essays, *Early Modern Prose Fiction: The Cultural Politics of Reading* approaches the early modern print revolution as a 'reading revolution', a suggestion Liebler takes from Stephen Orgel, and one which is explored with great insight and care. Liebler's opening chapter performs more than an introductory role; it examines the socio-political culture of reading, the economics of print, and the ways in which it could be said that printing and reading the printed word (specifically prose fiction) constructed a social and economic arena—a virtual 'marketplace of ideas and entertainments' (p. 7). Three chapters on Nashe indicate a sustained interest in his role in producing literature that defied generic and literary classification, but of particular relevance to this section, I turn my attention to Constance C. Relihan's 'Fishwives' Tales: Narrative, Agency, Female Subjectivity, and Telling Tales Out of School', in which she examines the social implications of the narrative framework of *Westward for Smelts*. Understood to have been published in 1620, the anonymous work consists of six Boccaccian tales each told by a fishwife and set in England. Relihan is concerned with the female working-class voice in constructing an appropriate standard of conduct, a combined voice that exemplifies 'an ideological position at odds with the dominant cultural constructions of social order' (p. 58).

How should one read a royal book? That is, a book written by a monarch, as Jane Rickard investigates in *Authorship and Authority: The Writings of James VI and I*. Rickard begins her study with James's poetry at the end of the sixteenth century, and expands it to encompass his theological and political writings, printed speeches, his *Workes* of 1616, and his involvement with the Authorized Version of the Bible published in 1611. As the title suggests, of chief concern is the fascinating question of authorship and authority in the writings of a king, and Rickard reveals James as an author who endeavoured to exercise authorial and royal control over his readership while trying to establish both his political and literary authority. It is her assertion that, despite his best efforts to the contrary, James's writings amplify and expose oppositional forces between author and authority.

The monarch was frequently figured as the father of an offspring nation, and the metaphor of the family in period is considered in Su Fang Ng's *Literature and the Politics of Family in Seventeenth-Century England*. Considering a wide range of political and literary texts throughout the period, including authors on both sides of the civil wars, Ng explores the contested position of the family and its head, competing notions of patriarchy and the relationship between politics and the figure of the family.

The polemical writings of Peter Heylyn come under scrutiny in Anthony Milton's *Laudian and Royalist Polemic in Seventeenth Century England*. As the title suggests, the dual focus of Heylyn's works, Laudianism and royalism, reveals a more fractured and self-opposing author than has customarily been portrayed. Milton examines Heylyn's works from the 1630s to the late seventeenth century, and although it is written from the perspective of a historian his book illuminates the sometimes contradictory nature of one of the period's chief polemicists.

C.S. Lewis famously lamented that 'rhetoric is the greatest barrier between us and our ancestors', a concern readdressed by Brian Vickers in the 1980s. Since then a number of works have endeavoured to bridge the gap, and this year a significant advance was made with the publication of *Renaissance Figures of Speech*, edited by Sylvia Adamson, Gavin Alexander and Katrin Ettenhuber, a collection of thirteen essays, each on a figure of speech common in a range of works from the end of the sixteenth to the later seventeenth century, and the first modern study to focus solely on the figures. While the book does explore the extent to which early modern theories of rhetoric developed, and to some extent how specific figures of speech evolved, moving in some cases from one class to another, at its heart is the notion that authors of the period used rhetorical figures on paper and in thought; 'simultaneously thinking with the figure and about the figure' (p. 9). Each chapter forms a useful stand-alone reference for such figures as synonymia, periodos, puns, ekphrasis, metalepsis, hyperbole and prosopopoeia. In addition the unattributed introduction (perhaps all three editors shared the task) provides a framing structure within which the figures can be contextually understood, and while each chapter demonstrates the extent to which specific authors of the period concerned themselves with the use and placement of rhetorical devices, the collection as a whole serves to illustrate the wider cultural concerns of early modern society.

The general shift from outward representations of faith to an inward belief forms a necessary background to the rise of the astrological almanac in the early modern period, according to Alison A. Chapman, who examines the curious cultural position of astrology in 'Marking Time: Astrology, Almanacs, and English Protestantism' (*RenQ* 60[2007] 1257–90). Establishing the popularity of the astrology and the almanac in the sixteenth and seventeenth centuries (Chapman tells us over one million copies were printed in a two-year period in the latter half of the seventeenth century), she infers that the almanac responded to the dislocation of space and time from public devotion, the Protestant elimination of the notion of sacred places and the reduction in holy days in mainstream religious culture giving rise to a taste for the local almanac with its characteristic regional data and calendars. The organizing principle in the almanac is of course astrology, and with it the 'assumption that time and place mattered in a larger celestial sense' (p. 1260). As Chapman is keen to point out, despite Calvinist opposition and the rise of empirical science astrology held a significant place in the minds of an early modern public eager to perceive the protection and providence of a divine hand, who were conscious of celestial rather than occult significance, and who desired to regain a sense of space and time. Readers gained an awareness of how the cosmos could reflect in their local village, and interestingly, Chapman moves her discussion to the point at which cosmic signifiers meet the most localized of spaces—that of the human body itself (with the moon affecting menstruation and hair and nail growth), and the astrological diary in which one recorded how cosmic forces influenced daily events in a person's life (some almanacs offered blank pages for this). Chapman leaves us comparing spiritual diaries with astrological diaries, noting the strong appeal for specific time and place in the latter. Drawing on examples from Milton, Donne and John Dee, and a sample of the many almanacs of the period, Chapman outlines a fascinating approach to the early modern interest in stellar and planetary influences.

The cultural implications and interpretations of celestial phenomena guide James Doelman's study in 'The Comet of 1618 and the British Royal Family' (*N&Q* 54[2007] 30–5). Both King James and the young Prince Charles composed poems marking the event amidst a series of texts that variously interpret the phenomenon as a commentary upon the royal family. The death of Queen Anne appeared to add credence to the belief that the 'blazing star' was a portent. It is the seeming competition between Jacobean monarchic authority and celestial omen that forms the basis of Doelman's study of cultural responses to the event, which continued well into the 1620s and re-emerged with the death of James in 1625.

Two valuable smaller entries in *Notes and Queries* fill gaps in knowledge, with Reid Barbour identifying smallpox as the subject of Sir Thomas Browne's dissertation for his MD at Leiden University, a disease that appears to have revisited his mind as it raged in Norwich in the final year of his life (*N&Q* 54[2007] 38–9), and Emilio Sergio's work to identify the likely date of Thomas Hobbes's manuscript containing his *De Motibus Solis* (*N&Q* 54[2007] 54–6).

A study of the early modern letter, in particular the correspondence between Francis Bacon and the earl of Essex, leads Andrew Gordon to consider how such texts were composed and used to establish reputation and allegiance (*ELR* 37[2007] 319–36). Essex's fall from grace following his early return from Ireland led to a series of events catastrophic for his position at court, in which Francis Bacon found himself among those advisers who determined the fate of his former patron. Gordon considers the 'afterlife' of the letters, in which they emerge from their apparently private sphere into a public realm, where they are used as evidence in proceedings and circulated in an effort to accrue social and political leverage. But what is most stimulating is Gordon's consideration of the texts themselves, their emergence in manuscript form, the competition between versions of the same letters, and the rhetorical mechanics by which the letters aim to establish both personal standing and social order.

While witch literature has attracted considerable interest among scholars in recent years, Anna Bayman places the Elizabethan and Jacobean witch pamphlet in the context of the pamphleteering trade (*L&H* 16[2007] 26–45). The culture of the pamphlet, she argues, with concerns of commercial success and moral position, threw up a series of interesting challenges for early modern writers, and gives the modern reader a fascinating glimpse into early modern print culture. Witch pamphlets vary widely in length and in overall aim. Some are more didactic and moral in their approach, and Bayman notices the specific challenges facing those writers who chose to moralize in a medium known for its titillating and voyeuristic mode. Others took a lighter approach, preferring to entertain rather than inform, and here Bayman positions the witch pamphlet in line with other rogue pamphlets in which the use of 'the comic and the titillating to bolster scepticism is a distinctive feature of the pamphlet culture' (p. 31). Concluding that cheaply printed and therefore mass-produced witch pamphlets served to undermine the public and legal discourse of witches and witch detection, Bayman senses that a lasting shadow of scepticism was in part inaugurated by the use of the pamphlet in examining the social and moral implications of witches.

2. Women's Writing

While the material published this year covers a wide range of authors, genres and critical debates, the two areas which predominate are autobiography/life-writing (in both critical discussion and critical editions) and a renewed engagement with the question of women's political agency. With regard to the study of individual writers, there is an unusual scarcity of studies relating to Aemilia Lanyer; by contrast, however, there has been a significant rise in discussions of Lady Mary Wroth and Elizabeth Cary.

(a) Autobiography

The vexed issue of what constitutes the early modern 'self' and which texts can be defined as autobiographical was drawn attention to last year in two collections of essays: Ronald Bedford, Lloyd Davis and Philippa Kelly, eds., *Early Modern Autobiography: Theories, Genres, Practices*, and *Recording and Reordering: Essays on Seventeenth- and Eighteenth-Century Diary and Journal*, edited by Dan Doll and Jessica Munns. While the Bedford collection is particularly welcome for its varied approach to potential theoretical models for approaching this subject, both collections play an important part in extending our awareness of often neglected texts in this area. However, only two of the essays in each volume are specifically concerned with women's writing. As Jean E. Howard's contribution to the Bedford collection focuses on Isabella Whitney, only Nancy E. Wright's 'Accounting for a Life: The Household Accounts of Lady Anne Clifford' (in Bedford, David and Kelly, eds., pp. 234–51) is directly relevant to this chapter. While most critics have so far concentrated on Clifford's early battles to secure her inheritance, Wright chooses to focus on Clifford's later life, particularly as represented in two of her account books, *The Expenses of My House* and *The Expenses of My Private Purse* (p. 235), and her will. Wright argues that 'the production and circulation' of these texts 'represent her life as a woman of property' which modify our expectations of such genres as Clifford's interventions within them can be aligned with her *Diaries* and other autobiographical projects. Wright concludes that such materials 'provide a means to evaluate Charles Taylor's suggestion that in the early modern period self-identity is "oriented in moral space" (p. 28)' (p. 249). Effie Botonaki's 'Early Modern Women's Diaries and Closets: "Chambers of choice Mercies and beloved retirement' (in Doll and Munns, eds., pp. 43–64) offers an abbreviated version of her earlier book *Seventeenth-Century English Women's Autobiographical Writings: Disclosing Enclosures* [2004]. In 'Women's Diaries of Late Stuart England; An Overview' (in Doll and Munns, eds., pp. 65–101), Ava Kauffman argues that 'all Protestant Stuart women diarists write within a prescribed range of established contexts and conventions' (p. 65). While Kauffman's observation that 'diarists wrote in the context of community' (p. 73) is helpful, it seems rather odd to discuss the self-confessed Church of England devotee Anne, Lady Halkett with reference to Puritan journals (pp. 79–80, see also the discussion of Trill, ed., and Lamb below).

This year has seen been a number of publications which primarily focus on early modern women's autobiographical writings. As Michelle Dowd and Julie Erkerle, the editors of *Genre and Women's Life Writing in Early Modern England*, state, this is indeed the 'first critical collection that focuses exclusively on women's life writings' (p. 1) in the early modern period. The 'focus on genre' is intended to counter 'the tendency to read these texts as unmediated representations of the experiences of "real" women' (p. 2), and the majority of the essays make important contributions to the theorization of early modern women's life-writings. Unfortunately, the organization of the volume implicitly posits a teleological view of the 'formal and cultural developments' (p. 5) of this genre as the subjects of the essays move from 'manuscript fragments' to the novelistic ' "women's defense-narrative" ' (p. 10). That aside, however, this collection is an invaluable addition to the field which contains some outstanding individual contributions.

One of the highlights is Margaret J. M. Ezell's 'Domestic Papers: Manuscript Culture and Early Modern Women's Life Writing' (in Dowd and Erkerle, eds., pp. 33–48), which addresses the crucial question of the material production of these documents. Ezell analyses how our understanding of genre might be altered by focusing primarily on 'the mode of their textual creation and transmission'; that is, she asks 'what, if any, difference might it make to our understanding of the authorial practices of life writing to look at the texts which existed as part of a manuscript culture, rather than a print one' (p. 33). To do so, Ezell examines both manuscript and printed texts side by side, with the latter primarily being funeral sermons. Ezell notes that in general the women monumentalized in such texts are 'average'; importantly, one of their shared characteristics includes the daily practice of reading and writing. Thus, in a significant challenge to the by now all-too-familiar image of the early modern woman as chaste, silent and obedient, Ezell concludes that 'manuscript sources make it clear that life writing of a spiritual nature was not frowned upon by friends, family, or the culture at large' (p. 45). Ezell's observations are reinforced in ' "Many hands hands": Writing the Self in Early Modern Women's Recipe Books' (pp. 49–63) by Catherine Field which draws attention to the different kind of self constructed in predominantly collaborative manuscript texts. In contrast to the negative sense of self so often found in spiritual forms of self-expression, Field argues that these texts enabled 'women to construct themselves as "expert" on anything having to do with the body under their care' (p. 54). As these books were frequently passed down to the next generation, Field concludes that they allowed women to 'imagine' both body and soul 'as a healable whole and not just as a leaky vessel' (p. 58). A variety of manuscript sources are also the subject of Megan Matchinske's insightful 'Serial Identity: History, Gender, and Form in the Diary Writing of Lady Anne Clifford' (pp. 65–80). Building on recent articles by Elizabeth Chew and Mihoko Suzuki, and Kathleen Osler Acheson's recent critical edition of Clifford's 1616–19 *Diary*, Matchinske explores the significance of space and temporality in both the form and the content of Clifford's writing. Central to Matchinske's argument is the question of why Clifford continued writing 'even *after* Clifford's estate is securely in her hands' (p. 68). When answering this question Matchinske convincingly asserts that 'in the *Diaries*, origin promises futurity' (p. 70) and concludes that 'regardless of secure status or achieved success, [Clifford's] then is a history of anxious possibility' (p. 76). The final manuscript source discussed in this volume is the subject of Mary Ellen Lamb's 'Merging the Secular with the Spiritual in Lady Anne Halkett's Memoirs' (pp. 81–96). Here, Lamb astutely argues that Halkett's *Memoirs* can be seen to have been shaped by a specific 'form of spiritual analysis'; that is, 'a series of cases of conscience' (p. 84). This insightful observation facilitates a careful re-reading of Halkett's romantic and political exploits. In conclusion, Lamb forcefully reminds us that 'instead of a locus of arid doctrines, religion constituted a form of desire, fully compatible with sexuality, capable of generating an extraordinary diversity of variously nuanced subjectivities' (p. 94). Complementing such arguments is Victoria E. Burke's compelling case for the need to 'pay attention to [the] material characteristics' of a text which 'not only enriches our understanding of content' but 'sometimes affects what that content is' in 'Let's Get Physical: Bibliography, Codicology, and Seventeenth-Century Women's Manuscripts' (*LitComp* 4:vi[2007] 1667–82).

  Genre and Women's Life Writing moves on to address primarily printed materials. Appropriately, this shift is marked by Julie A. Eckerle's examination of the 'unique textual space' (p. 97) of the preface in 'Prefacing Texts, Authorizing Authors, and Constructing Selves: The Preface as Autobiographical Space' (pp. 97–113) Further attention to such paratextual material is evident in Michelle M. Dowd's 'Structures of Piety in Elizabeth Richardson's *Legacie*', when she discusses the importance of the text's dedication to Richardson's four daughters. Dowd's analysis offers a fresh account of the significance of the genre of mothers' legacies which disputes the prevailing critical assumption that the genre of the 'Mother's Legacie' developed partly because married women were unable to write a will. The next two essays focus on Margaret Cavendish (see section 2(*e*) below). While Cavendish is briefly discussed in the final essay in the collection, ' "That all the world may know": Women's "Defense-Narratives" and the Early Novel' (pp. 169–82) by Josephine Donovan, more attention is paid to Mary Frith and Elizabeth Cellier. Here Donovan builds upon her discussion of women and casuistry in *Women and the Rise of the Novel, 1405–1726* to suggest that, ultimately, the female agency expressed in these earlier texts is contained when the form is appropriated by Defoe in *Moll Flanders* and *Roxanna*.

  In what is arguably an unfashionable move, in *Early Modern English Lives: Autobiography and Self-Representation 1500–1660*, Ronald Bedford and Philippa Kelly emphasize that a 'feature that emerges again and again in the diaries of this period' is 'the expression of an "I" as bequeathed by God, and thus experienced, as it were, in the third person' (p. 3). While well aware of the significance of multiple subjectivities and a lack of distinction between the 'private "I" and the social role permitted to the "I" ' (p. 4), Bedford and Kelly produce a nuanced introduction which balances the demands of the 'sacred' and the 'secular'. While Bedford and Kelly are not only interested in women's autobiographical writings in this period, they devote two chapters specifically to such issues: chapter 7, 'A Gendered Genre: Autobiographical Writings by Three Early Modern Women', and chapter 8, 'Women's Wills'. The title of chapter 7 is somewhat misleading in so far as the three writers discussed (Lady Grace Mildmay, Lady Margaret Hoby and Lady Anne Clifford) are, in fact, 'three well-known female *diarists*' (p. 164, my emphasis). Furthermore, the authors justify their self-confessedly conservative choice in this selection on the basis that it is not their intention to uncover new writers 'but rather to examine new possibilities for writing widely acknowledged to be exemplary artifacts [*sic*] from the period' (p. 164). There are some insightful moments in this chapter, perhaps most notably the following comparison between Mildmay and Hoby's writings; for example, when examining Hoby's 'anxious self-scrutiny', the authors argue that Hoby's 'is not (as with Lady Grace) a piety that *proves* her worth before God, but a piety that *seeks* worthiness in God's eyes' (p. 181, original emphasis). Less convincing is the turn to Lady Anne Clifford, who is positioned as motivated by 'an unashamedly secular interest' (p.185). The discussion of 'Women's Wills' is more robust, and complicates our understanding of the genre by exploring its contingency. Importantly, the authors note that 'wills are at once highly private and public texts' which perform multiple functions: 'a will signifies the past, present and future agency of its author. It exemplifies the remarkable power of texts to mean and do things for oneself and for others, and thereby underscores the capacity for social action that rests with a speaker or author' (p. 210). This is amusingly evidenced by one Elizabeth Condell, who leaves 'her "goodes" to her daughter Elizabeth ffinch and £50 to her granddaughter Elizabeth Cundall. She then declares, "I doe intend the same as that my said sonne in lawe Mr herbert ffynch shall neuer have possession of the same", and "I would have no parte of my state neither prodigally spent, nor lewdly wasted" by her son, Willam Cundall' (p. 211). As Bedford and Kelly persuasively argue, this is but one example of how 'wills disclose the potential impact of women's moral judgments in the familial and social spheres' (p. 212).

Complementing the increase in critical and theoretical discussions concerning early modern women's autobiography/life-writing, this year also sees the publication of three welcome additions to Ashgate's The Early Modern Englishwoman 1500–1700: Contemporary Editions series (general editors Betty S. Travitsky and Anne Lake Prescott). These are Nicky Hallet's *Lives of Spirit: English Carmelite Self-Writings of the Early Modern Period* and *Witchcraft, Exorcism and the Politics of Possession in a Seventeenth-Century Convent*, and Suzanne Trill's *Lady Anne Halkett: Selected Self-Writings*. As the titles of Hallet's two editions indicate, these volumes provide a much-needed selection of early modern Catholic women's self-writings which should help to challenge the notion that 'self-writing' arose as a result of Protestantism. Both editions draw on an astonishing array of materials originally written by about sixty English nuns and lay sisters at the Carmelite convents in Antwerp and Lierre. *Lives of Spirit* provides selections from forty of these texts. This collection is, perhaps not unsurprisingly, highly generically diverse: texts range from letters and ephemera to 'more or less sustained autobiographical or biographical accounts contained either in individual Lives or in official histories and necrologies' (p. 8). Significantly, both the ordering of the archive and the contents of the texts militate against Gusdorf's famous assertion that autobiographical materials privilege the ' "conscious awareness of the singularity of each individual life" (Gusdorf, 1980, 29)' (p. 28). For 'not only do individual Lives relating to one particular person sometimes exist in various locations, but the women themselves also often express a sense of dissipated selfhood that derives in part from mnemonic systems practised within a contemplative tradition that aspired to self-forgetfulness' (p. 8). Furthermore, these writers often self-consciously patterned their own lives on those of their ancestors as 'some of the nuns quite transparently base their accounts on Teresa de Jesus' *Book* . . . and she, in turn, had quite clearly modelled hers on other writers such as Catherine of Sienna' (p. 28). Thus, Hallet argues, these texts 'demonstrate how much "community" (literally and metaphorically) is central to personal construction' (p. 28).

The materials reproduced here in original spelling vary in size according to the length of the original text, with the shortest being chapter 25, 'Mary of St Barbara: The Life of an Oblate from the Coffee-house', which is only one page long (p. 129), whereas the longest, chapter 28, 'Mary Xaveria of the Angels: Her Illness, Miraculous Cure and Her Spiritual Favours Before and After Death', occupies twenty-six pages (pp. 135–61). Collectively, these fascinating texts attest to both the shared assumptions and diverse experiences of the women in these two convents. Importantly, their contents not only challenge the concept of the individuality of the subject but also undermine our expectation of linear chronology. The women whose lives are recorded here variously lived from 1588 to 1777, but Hallet's edition follows the original organization of their narratives, which was not chronological. Frustratingly, Hallet acknowledges that 'some Lives have simply been omitted' (p. 31), but she does not tell us which ones or why. Presumably, however, some of these materials are included in her other volume *Witchcraft, Exorcism and the Politics of Possession in a Seventeenth-Century Convent.* While *Lives* seeks to reveal the differences between the inhabitants of the convent, *Witchcraft* facilitates a more in-depth analysis of the various accounts of two women's experiences of possession, exorcism and recovery: that is, the Mostyn sisters Margaret and Elizabeth, who became known as Margaret of Jesus and Ursula of All Saints. Although this material has never been published before, this edition reproduces ten different accounts of their experiences, ranging from 'Sister Margaret's Spiritual Confessions: her pre-exorcism diary' and Father Edmund Bedingfield's 'account of their exorcism', to 'Sister Ursula's tribute' to her sister and 'accounts of Margaret of Jesus by other nuns'. This astonishing array of materials provides a detailed insight into the complicated issues surrounding possession and exorcism during this period, which will undoubtedly enable scholars interested in this area to nuance their understanding of these processes. Astonishingly, the apparent success of the exorcism is attested to by the fact that, successively, Sister Margaret and Sister Ursula became prioress at Lierre. While there is some overlap between the two volumes (with extracts of the Lives of Margaret of Jesus, Ursula of All Saints, and Edmund Bedingfield appearing in both) as the *Lives'* extracts are in original spelling and those in *Witchcraft* are modernized, they provide access to different readerships.

The life-writings of Lady Anne Halkett, written between 1658 and 1699, are explored in Suzanne Trill's *Lady Anne Halkett: Selected Self-Writings.* The edition includes ten chapters, nine of which provide lengthy chronological excerpts from *Meditations*, a text which has received little scholarly attention. Chapter 5 includes Halkett's *Autobiography*, written between 1677 and 1678. Trill's introduction persuasively demonstrates how the edition challenges critical assumptions of Halkett on many levels. For example, although critics tend to focus on her romantic intrigues, the writings in the edition instead portray how Halkett attempted to construct a self-image that accords with a more solemn, biblical example of widowhood to defend herself against scandals. The writings also portray her profound engagement with social, religious and political change alongside her changing and developing subjectivity. The texts illustrate how, as a committed Episcopalian in a predominantly Presbyterian region, her allegiance was frequently a source of communal conflict and dissent. Also, her staunch support for James VII/II positioned her as a Jacobite, which was seditious. Trill argues that the 'focus on her autobiography, and especially upon her romantic intrigues, has divested her work of its political and religious commitments while simultaneously erasing its Scottish dimensions'. Although most scholarship understands Halkett as an English royalist and Halkett identifies herself as English, she was Scottish by blood, living in Scotland, and her writings are often predominantly concerned with Scottish affairs. Consequently, the edition provides 'a unique opportunity to examine the complexity of early modern national identities'. Significantly, Halkett's writings, which cover a wide range of subject matter, increasingly become more autobiographical, evolving into a form that is similar to what we would now identify as diary entries. Providing an innovative approach to the texts, the edition attempts to capture the materiality and organization of the original manuscript. Trill replicates the original marginal glosses and provides a photograph of each relevant volume at beginning of each chapter. The size, dimensions, ink and corrections are further described, along with a brief account of the subject matter of the volume as a whole, while old spellings, grammar, colloquialisms and abbreviations are retained as much as possible. Also, the edition contains a detailed bibliography of primary and secondary sources and a helpful list of Bible references made by Halkett in her writings. Overall this welcome and timely edition gives access to Halkett's lesser-known writings, which will provide an opportunity to reassess her literary and historical significance. Both Hallet and Trill's definition of self-writing is intentionally broad and inclusive, in part because the materials they are presenting complicate modern concepts of what constitutes 'autobiography'. Together with the essays in *Genre and Women's Life Writing in Early Modern England*, these editions open up this specific area of study and bear testimony to Ashgate's position as a leading force in the publication of high-quality research in the field of early modern women's writing.

(b) Women and Politics

Kate Chedgzoy's *Women's Writing in the British Atlantic World: Memory, Place and History, 1550–1700* offers a new perspective on the study of the politics of early modern women's writing. Focusing on women's memorial practices, Chedgzoy explores how they engage with geographical space and how this, in turn, helps them to shape and reflect on their own sense of history. In the process, she produces new evidence of women's engagement with contemporary political affairs, and broadens our awareness of Scottish, Irish and Welsh women's writing in a variety of languages. Significantly, this study demonstrates that the much-debated topic of the 'British problem' needs to be inflected with questions of gender to nuance our understanding of the issues involved. By simultaneously setting such debates within the broader context of Atlantic and archipelagic studies, Chedgzoy's study certainly offers 'a more capacious, diverse and inclusive history of early modern British women's writing than has previously been attempted' (p. 14). In doing so, Chedgzoy also succeeds in her self-conscious aim to 'contribute to the feminist scholarly project of recollecting women's forgotten contributions to the cultural past' (p. 69). Overall, this book presents a challenging template for future work in this field. By illuminating the significance of women's voices and experiences in areas usually associated predominantly with men, Chedgzoy's book marks an important shift, which brings the study of women's writing out from the margins of Renaissance and early modern studies and challenges scholars in that wider field to take women's writing more seriously.

This year sees the appearance of the impressive four-volume series of *Women's Political Writings, 1610–1725*, edited by Hilda L. Smith, Mihoko Suzuki and Susan Wiseman. The general introduction, written by Smith and Suzuki, explains the historical scope of the project and the focus on political texts which explore 'topics relating to the power and legitimacy of the state, the most effective forms of government, and the relative power of rulers and their subjects or citizens' (vol. 1, p. xiii). The editors acknowledge that 'the difficulty of defining politics itself' (vol. 1, p. xiii) in this context. They argue that whereas this term is presently 'most readily associated with the operations of government . . . in . . . the early modern period, politics would have been more associated with the authority and advancement that came from personal relationships' (vol. 1, p. xiii) whether that be one's position at court, one's relationship to influential town officials, or, in the countryside, one's connections with 'a Justice of the Peace, or to the local squire or his representatives' (vol. 1, p. xiii). The next section, 'Political Realities and Women's Intellect' counters the 'underlying (if sometimes unspoken) assumption that "women don't" or "women can't" when it comes either to holding political office, exercising political rights, or, just as significantly, writing political works' (vol. 1, p. xvi). This is followed by 'Early Modern Politics', which further dismantles the notion that even when early modern women did participate in politics in some way their efforts had no lasting effect or influence. By contrast, the editors trace how women's involvement in the civil wars can be seen to set the path for the future; importantly, of course, a significant factor in the civil wars was the relationship between religion and the organization of the social and political order. From Anna Trapnel through Margaret Fell to Mary Astell, a woman's religious beliefs enabled her to participate in political debates. This section also highlights the fact that female political (activists) were not only to be found among the aristocracy.

In outlining their 'Principles of Selection' Smith et al. consciously aim to alter our perception of women's writings by, for example, shifting 'the current scholarly emphasis on Mary Astell's feminist thought in *A Serious Proposal to the Ladies* [1694] and *Reflections Upon Marriage* [1706] to a focus on her more strictly political works defending the reign of Charles I and the institutional foundation of the Church of England' (vol. 1, p. xx; see also vol. 4). While the decision not to reproduce materials which are currently available elsewhere is to be welcomed, the exclusion of 'works that focus solely on what might be characterized as "feminist" arguments not having to do with women's relation to the state or society' (vol. 1, p. xxi) is rather more contestable. 'Feminist' is defined here as 'those [texts] concerning the relationship between the sexes or the subordination of women in the family' (vol. 1, p. xxi): given the importance of the family to the organization of early modern society, this is a potentially false dichotomy.

The potential difficulty of such a distinction is immediately apparent in Wiseman's specific introduction to the first volume. Wiseman directly addresses the question of what is meant by 'politics' in the early modern period and highlights 'the need to think outside modern paradigms' to recognize it. However, Wiseman also touches on the problem of distinguishing between the 'personal' and the 'political': 'Given women's position as excluded from the political realm, it is not always possible to draw a clear distinction between political writing as an aspect of familial politics and political writing which concerns polis, government and public good' (vol. 1, p. xxviii). Wiseman suggests that 'it is productive to consider where and how a distinction' of these issue might be made. To address this question, Wiseman turns to Harley's letters and insightfully argues that 'in Harley's political thinking what sometimes seems to us to separate women from politics—household, marriage, wifely obedience—are key parts of what enables her to act and write politically. Harley saw no need to resolve what seem, to us, to be contradictions, even paradoxes' (vol. 1, p. xxix). Clifford also poses some problems as Wiseman admits 'it would be hard to trace in her writings articulations of political involvement' (vol. 1, p. xxxi). However, Suzuki's headnote to 'the great Book' succinctly manages to justify the inclusion of Clifford's genealogical history as this plays a vital role in her battle to regain her lands and inheritance. The inclusion of this particular text is greatly to be welcomed. Although occasionally mentioned by critics, it has been generally ignored, and this publication will help to further our understanding of Clifford's writing life.

The introduction to the second volume provides a concise account of women's increasing participation in the production of pamphlets and petitions during the civil wars. There is also an indication of the politics of contemporary women's poetry, with a brief selection of texts by An Collins and Anne Bradstreet. As promised in the general introduction, the vast majority of the material included in this volume has not been reproduced in modern editions before. Particularly welcome is the reproduction of ten pamphlets by or about women from 1641 to 1653, and the broad selection of sectarian women writers (including Mary Cary, Mary Howgill and Priscilla Cotton). Less convincing is the decision to include Anna Trapnel's *The Cry of a Stone* and *Strange and Wonderful Newes from White-Hall* when both are already accessible in modern editions. This is particularly regrettable given that the headnote includes references to *A Legacie for Saints* which, like the *Report and Plea*, is not available in a full-length modern edition. It is perhaps also a missed opportunity that the volume does not include any examples of explicitly royalist women's writing; however, the inclusion of Elizabeth Poole, Mary Pope and Sarah Jinner allows for some insight into the complexities of political identifications during this period. Furthermore, royalist positions are abundantly apparent in the third volume, which covers the period 1660–1700. That said, approximately a third of this volume consists of a series of texts by Quaker women writers. In addition to the well-known Margaret Fell, this volume also includes materials by Elizabeth Hooton, Dorothy White, Joan Vokins, Anne Dowcra, Mary Smith, Judith Boulbie and Margaret Braister. Whereas these texts are predominantly in prose, the most obviously royalist writers in this volume are poets: that is, Katherine Philips, Rachel Jevon, Elizabeth Singer Rowe and Elizabeth Johnson. The connection between support for the Church of England and a predilection for monarchy is also testified to here in the writings of Elinor James, Alicia D'Anvers and Joan Whitrowe. But perhaps the most interesting text included here is Elizabeth Cellier's *Malice Defeated* [1680]. Most recently discussed as an example of a case of conscience and linked with the rise of the novel, Cellier's account of her alleged involvement with the 'Meal-Tub Plot' is a superb text for exploring the intense complexity of women's religious and political affiliations in the late seventeenth century.

While the first three volumes are clearly related to the editors' organizing principles, and are either chronologically or alphabetically arranged, these matters are less clear in the final volume. In her specific introduction, Smith suggests that there were 'fewer writings [which] linked women's own standing in society to an understanding of its political structure, whether from a royalist or Tory perspective, or a revolutionary or sectarian one' in the late seventeenth century (vol. 4, p. vii). This is said to be caused by 'the growing influence of ideas associated with sensibility and a glorification of the young, delicate female' (vol. 4, p. vii). In addition, the satirizing of women's political engagement was replaced by 'romance and procreation', which 'drive [women's] goals in life and their underlying value-systems' (vol. 4, p. vii). This appears unnecessarily teleological and, ultimately, unnecessarily defeatist. There are also indications that the potential false dichotomy mentioned above re-emerges here. For example, Smith claims that Astell's *Reflections upon Marriage* [1700] was 'the last of her works to be devoted centrally to women's issues', yet then continues that *The Christian Religion, as Profess'd by a Daughter of the Church of England* [1705] 'is less a polemical attack against her religious and political adversaries and more a lengthy defence of Anglicanism grounded once again in a strongly feminist framework' (vol. 4, p. viii). Despite such issues, these volumes represent a much-needed extension to the 'canon' of early modern women's writing. Unfortunately at £350 for the set, these materials will have limited use in the classroom but are highly recommended for library acquisition.

In *Rhetoric, Women and Politics in Early Modern England*, the editors Jennifer Richards and Alison Thorne also address the question of how we can 'conceive of early modern women as politically active' (p. 1). Unlike Smith et al., Richards and Thorne *do* point to the politicized nature of the 'domestic' realm. They suggest that 'Women's domestic roles were generally recognized as already possessing an inherently political dimension' (p. 8), which is reinforced by citing William Gouge's acknowledgement that women's '"household duties...may be accounted a publicke worke"' because 'the family was a "little commonwealth"' (p. 9). Moreover, they demonstrate how women used this connection to enable and justify their collective petitioning of parliament. Further, the editors argue that, just as the 'political' has needed reconsideration, so too do we need 'to expand our understanding of the terms "rhetoric" and "rhetorical"' (p. 10). They suggest that when rhetoric is reconceptualized as 'the study of "eloquence", the development of which depends on "practice", in a variety of contexts rather than technical training and scholarly regimens, then it is possible to begin to extend its exercise to women of all ranks' (p. 12). They also note that rhetorical skills could be acquired in a number of ways—from 'attending a play, reading a letter or listening to a sermon' (p. 12). But a crucial question remains: 'how did [women] establish their *ethos*, that is, an authoritative and trustworthy rhetorical persona from which they could persuasively intervene in "public" debate?' (p. 13). Noting that the use of the humility topos and the genre of complaint may make 'uncomfortable reading' for modern feminists, the editors point out that such positions share many conventions with the contemporary deliberative oration, or 'language of entreaty'. Significantly, Richards and Thorne point out that such orations were categorized by both Erasmus and Thomas Wilson 'as a form of deliberative speech that seeks to persuade or dissuade an audience from taking a specific course of action' (p. 15).

The collection has 'two broad aims, first, to reflect on the many different ways in which female eloquence is represented in this period and, second, to explore some of the forms it took in practice' (p. 18). Of the eleven essays included in this volume, only three are properly relevant to this chapter: Danielle Clarke, 'Speaking Women: Rhetoric and the Construction of Female Talk' (pp. 70–88); Susan Wiseman, 'Exemplarity, Women and Political Rhetoric' (pp. 129–48); and Hilary Hinds, 'Embodied Rhetoric: Quaker Public Discourse in the 1650s' (pp. 191–211). Clarke focuses on the 'ambiguous legacy of the myth of Echo' (p. 87) which '"can augment and trope the utterance it echoes, as well as reduce and ridicule" (Hollander 1981: 31)' (p. 84). Clarke explores the 'transformative capacity' of Echo primarily in relation to the figure of Eve in *Paradise Lost*; however, she concludes with a reference to the opening sonnet of the *Urania*, which invokes the figure of Echo while mourning the 'loss of her [Urania's] *self*' (p. 87, original emphasis) in which Echo is no longer 'a form of containment, but a model for intervention and authorship' (p. 87). Susan Wiseman discusses how references to early modern exemplary figures, including Arria, Cornelia, Esther and Lucretia, work to position women politically as 'indices of political virtue' (p. 132). She then examines how Aemilia Lanyer deploys discourses of exemplarity to political ends in her patronage poems and argues that this serves three functions: to provide 'a renovatory politics in terms of both the gender and political hierarchy'; to indicate 'a regrouping or reworking of the politics of patronage'; and to move beyond 'a specifically feminist politics' as it 'articulates an understanding of politics in terms of poet–patron relations, wealth and biblical hierarchy' (p. 143).

Another exemplary female figure is the focus of *The Good, the Bold, and the Beautiful: The Story of Susanna and its Renaissance Interpretations* by

Dan. W. Clanton. As this book appears in the Library of Hebrew Bible/Old Testament Studies it provides some useful scholarship relating to the variant versions of Susanna's story; however, the focus of its 'Renaissance interpretations' is primarily on visual art rather than literary texts.

Hilary Hinds's continuing contribution to our understanding of women's participation in public, political affairs is evidenced both by 'Embodied Rhetoric' (in Richards and Thorne, eds., pp. 191–211) and 'The Paratextual Profusion of Radical Sectarian Women's Writing of the 1640s' (*PSt* 29[2007] 153–77). In the former, Hinds explores whether 'we can begin to think of a Quaker "art" of persuasion, a distinctive Quaker rhetoric' (p. 194). Hinds concludes that the Quaker preaching was perceived as threatening because it went 'beyond a rhetorical equivalence of the doctrine they preached and moved instead into its rhetorical embodiment' (p. 210). In the latter, paying particular attention to Gérard Genette's concept of the 'peritextual', Hinds explores the gendered dynamics of the prefatory materials to printed texts by Katherine Chidley and Mary Cary. Ultimately, Hinds suggests that the proliferation of such prefatory materials validated women's engagement with public affairs by positioning their texts as communal utterances. In the same volume, Catie Gill examines how Anna Trapnel negotiated contemporary codes of masculinity and femininity in the public and private spheres to express her revolutionary message, in ' "All the Monarchies of this World are going down the Hill": The Anti-Monarchism of Anna Trapnel's *The Cry of a Stone* (1654)' (*PSt* 29[2007] 19–35). Trapnel is also alluded to in 'Scriptural Exegesis, Female Prophecy, and Radical Politics in Mary Cary' by David Loewenstein (*SEL* 46[2006] 133–53). Loewenstein aims to redress the lack of scholarly attention paid to Cary's writing. Concentrating on *The Little Horns Doom & Downfall* and *A More Exact Mappe*, both of which were dedicated to women with parliamentary connections, Loewenstein persuasively argues that Cary's careful and extensive exegetical works 'helped shape and articulate the radical religious politics of Fifth Monarchist discourse' (p. 148) in a rather different manner than that of the more sensational Trapnel.

(c) Lady Mary Wroth

Of the many essays and articles devoted to Lady Mary Wroth this year, Edith Snook's 'The Greatness in Good Clothes: Fashioning Subjectivity in Mary Wroth's *Urania* and Margaret Spencer's Account Book (BL Add. MS 62092)' (*SC* 22[2007] 225–59) is outstanding. Building upon recent studies on the materiality of clothes and clothing, Snook juxtaposes the semiotics of Nereana's clothes in the *Urania* with Margaret Spencer's expenditure on clothing to demonstrate how upper-class women's clothing reveals a conflict between the demands of early modern gender hierarchies and the class structure. In both cases, Snook argues that this conflict enables women to 'articulate a non-subordinate social position' (p. 242). This fascinating article concludes with an eight-page transcription of Spencer's expenditure 'on labour for the production of clothing (not including laundry)' (pp. 252–9)

By contrast "What is my nation?"': Lady Mary Wroth's Interrogations of Personal and National Identity' by Sheila T. Cavanagh (in. Liebler, ed., *Early Modern Prose Fiction*, pp. 98–114) is a rather uneven essay. Although Cavanagh insightfully observes that 'personal lineage is more important than country of origin for most of the figures at the center of this narrative' (pp. 110–11), she digresses into a discussion of Wroth's 'narrative perambulations' and classifies her prose style as 'undeniably infuriating at times' (p. 113). Importantly, however, she concludes that as an 'early look at the globalization...the *Urania* promotes unity among distinct peoples, as it submerges differences apart from religion' (p. 114). The question of religion is usually sidelined in discussions of the *Urania* because, of course, it is generically defined as a romance. However, as Melissa E. Sanchez points out in 'The Politics of Masochism in Mary Wroth's *Urania*' (*ELH* 74[2007] 449–78), despite the critical predilection for focusing on Pamphillia 'the title situates Urania—the name for the muse of heavenly contemplation—as the central character' (p. 457). Sanchez's main interest here, though, is how Wroth's romance 'indicates the necessity of relinquishing romanticized notions of absolute rule in favour of a more compromised vision of mixed monarchy' (p. 450). Sanchez's nuanced reading moves the discussion of Wroth's romance beyond simplistic binaries and idealizations. While Sue P. Starke, in *The Heroines of English Pastoral Romance*, also notes that the character of Urania embodies the wisdom associated with heavenly geometry and provides sage advice, she nevertheless suggests that 'Candiana's story...reaffirms the central value of female constancy in the romance and provides an example of cosmic justice toward inconstant men' (p. 141).

In chapter 5 of *Women Writers and Familial Discourse in the English Renaissance: Relative Values*, Marion Wynne-Davies discusses Wroth (' "As I, for one, who thus my habits change", Mary Wroth and the Abandonment of the Sidney/Herbert Familial Discourse'). Summing up the family connections, Wynne-Davies acknowledges the formative influence of Sir Philip Sidney but seeks to 're-contextualise Wroth as an independent author within the history of Early Modern European literature' (p. 90). Wynne-Davies's approach clearly challenges the tendency for critics to reinforce the concept of the Sidneian 'family romance' and argues against straightforward biographical readings of her texts as the 'duplication and conflation' of characters and 'familial allegory' undercut 'fixed identities and any implied certainty of interpretation' (p. 91). To further her argument, Wynne-Davies focuses on *Love's Victorie* and makes a convincing case for its political allegorization of the betrothal and marriage of Princess Elizabeth to Frederick, Count Palatine. Less convincing, given the reception of the later *Urania*, is the description of Wroth's 'confident incursion into the most fraught political issues of the period' (p. 103). Wynne-Davies concludes that '*Love's Victorie* must be read as both a culmination of and as a radical challenge to the Sidney/Herbert familial discourse' (p. 103). The influence of family ties on Wroth's and other women writer's texts is also discussed by Theresa D. Kemp in 'Women's Patronage-Seeking as Familial Enterprise: Aemilia Lanyer, Esther Inglis, and Mary Wroth' (*LitComp* 4:ii[2007] 384–406). Questioning the prevalent critical practice of 'applying anachronistic notions of "friendship" based on equity'

(p. 386) to an imaginary unified, female early modern community, Kemp focuses on the way in which 'women's interests might also be *tied to* rather than *in conflict with* those of male relatives and peers' (p. 387).

While Kemp briefly mentions Lanyer, the only essay to focus on her this year is 'Aemilia Lanyer and the Virgin's Swoon: Theology and Iconography in *Salve Deus Rex Judaeorum*' by Gary Kuchar (*ELR* 37[2007] 47–73). This impressive piece eruditely dismantles the presumption of a specifically 'Protestant Poetics' in Lanyer's poetry by tracing her depiction of Mary to medieval art and iconography. Importantly, Kuchar concludes that Lanyer's representation of Mary as a 'physically real, emotionally expressive, and intellectually engaged exemplum of female spiritual power' (p. 73) not only relocates Mary as an active agent in the process of redemption but offers a vision of her which 'was not available in either of the official doctrines... in Post-Reformation Europe' (p. 73).

(d) Elizabeth Cary

Heather Wolfe begins her introduction to *The Literary Career and Legacy of Elizabeth Cary, 1613–1680* with the recognition that 'once relegated to the status of a nearly forgotten playwright and eccentric Roman Catholic convert, Elizabeth Cary (1585?–1639) is now increasingly appreciated as a Renaissance woman historian, playwright, translator, and poet' (p. 1). Importantly, given that 'Cary figures so prominently in the inclusive literary landscape of male *and* female writers', Wolfe poses the question: 'where do we go from here?' (p. 1). Excitingly, this collection actively moves beyond the current critical focus on Cary's best-known dramatic texts and extends our knowledge of Cary's productivity by exploring both printed and manuscript texts. In parts I and II of the collection this facilitates some lively reassessments of *The Tragedy of Mariam* and *The History of... Edward II*; it is, however, part III. 'Other Writings'. and part IV. 'Literary Patronage and Legacies'. which are properly of interest in this current context. Part III opens with Karen L. Nelson's '"To informe thee aright": Translating Du Perron for English Religious Debates' (pp. 147–63). As Nelson admits, *The Reply... to the Answeare of the most Excellent King of Greate Britaine* (Douai [1630]) is 'an often over-looked element of Cary's canon' (p. 147). Whereas Perron's text was directed to James VI/I, Nelson convincingly argues that the timing of Cary's translation represents a direct intervention in contemporary religious controversies, as it ultimately suggests that, in spiritual terms, an earthly ruler should be subject to the pope's authority. Drawing upon the work of the historians Kevin Sharpe and Jonathan Scott, Nelson produces a timely deconstruction of Dolan's depiction of Cary as 'a lone figure of Catholic rebelliousness' (p. 149). In the next chapter, 'Elizabeth Cary and the Great Tew Circle' (pp. 165–82), R.W. Serjeantson also addresses Cary's controversial contribution to 'the lively debate over conversion to the Roman Catholic Church' (p. 165). However, unlike the '500-page, folio-sized volume' (p. 147) discussed by Nelson, Serjeantson begins his contribution with the apparently paradoxical admission that it 'is about a piece of writing by Elizabeth Cary that no longer exists' (p. 165). Ultimately however, by re-examining the 'intellectual concerns' (p. 167) of the so-called 'Tew Circle', Serjeantson suggests that, via Jean Daillé's *Traicté de l'employ des saincts pères* [1631], Cary's translation of Du Perron was a significant influence upon William Chillingworth's *The Religion of Protestants* [1638]. Another form of author-ship question is the subject of the final contribution to this section, ' "Reader, stand still and look, lo here I am": Elizabeth Cary's Funeral Elegy "On the Duke of Buckingham"' by Nadine N.W. Akkerman (pp. 183–200). Here, of course, the issue is attribution. Akkerman achieves her aim of 'bring[ing] together sufficient evidence to support the attribution to Cary' (p. 185) and helpfully includes a transcription of both the epitaph and the elegy in an appendix (pp. 195–6).

Part IV opens with ' "A more worthy patronesse": Elizabeth Cary and Ireland', by Deana Rankin (pp. 203–21). Rankin sets out to explore the 'much-neglected interlude in Cary's life: her four brief years in Dublin' (p. 204). In so doing, she draws attention to the politics of Richard Belling's dedication of his *Sixth booke of the Countesse of Pembroke's Arcadia* [1624] to Cary and complements Chedgzoy's argument (above) by suggesting that Cary needs to be resituated 'as a writer who moves and thrives between [the] worlds and cultures' (p. 205) of the Three Kingdoms. It concludes with ' "To have her children with her": Elizabeth Cary and Familial Influence' (pp. 223–41), in which Marion Wynne-Davies charts the different ways in which Cary's children (Anne, Lucy, Patrick and Lucius) engaged with the 'discourses of faith and conversion, which had been initiated by their mother, in their own textual productions' (p. 223). An extended version of this argument also appears in chapter 6 of *Women Writers and Familial Discourses*.

(e) Margaret Cavendish

A very welcome contribution to Cavendish scholarship is provided in chapter 6 of Su Fang Ng's *Literature and the Politics of Family in Seventeenth-Century England*. Ng examines the complexities of Cavendish's political theories in the *Blazing World*, arguing that the text depicts Caroline values in order to critique Restoration sexual and state politics. Ng argues that the Empress of the *Blazing World* is a figuration of Henrietta Maria, and that an unstable, corporate body of women functions as a substitute for the ideal relationship between king and marginalized Cavaliers. Cavendish's politics are also explored in Hilda Smith's 'Margaret Cavendish and the False Universal' (in Broad and Green, eds., *Virtue, Liberty, and Toleration: Political Ideas of European Women, 1400–1800*, pp. 95–110). Drawing on examples from *Orations, Sociable Letters* and Cavendish's own life experiences, Smith argues that Cavendish is unique because she does not perceive women as having a distinct nature or place in society, and further judges women by the same standards of power, authority, personal development and public recognition that apply to men.

In chapter 3 of *Sociable Criticism in England 1625–1725*, Paul Trolander and Zeynep Tenger argue that Cavendish 'reversed the conventional practices of sociable criticism' in her earliest frontpieces as she presented herself as the judge and editor of her own works. The pressures of coterie critical traditions influenced her as she later identified herself with family and husband, but they ultimately did not shape her singular authorial self-identity. Contrasting views are expressed in the two essays in *Genre and Women's Life Writing*. In 'Intersubjectivity, Intertextuality, and Form in the Self-Writings of Margaret Cavendish' (in Dowd and Erkele, eds., pp. 131–50), Elspeth Graham argues that, for this writer, 'autobiography is not an occasional form of output ... but is intrinsic to the whole project of her writing' (p. 133). This position is reinforced by Lara Dodds, 'Margaret Cavendish's Domestic Experiment' (in Dowd and Erkele, eds., pp. 151–68), who likewise suggests that 'for Cavendish ... life writing became a space in which to express her lifelong experiment with genre and through which she explored her philosophical interest in the problems of experience' (p. 164).

Three articles explore Cavendish's science this year. A wide range of Cavendish's scientific texts is adeptly explored in Karen Detlefsen, 'Reason and Freedom: Margaret Cavendish on the Order and Disorder of Nature' (*AGP* 89[2007] 157–91). Detlefsen argues that Cavendish portrays the natural world as rational and perceptive as part of a theory of the ubiquitous freedom of nature: a theory which accounts for both the order and disorder in nature and human behaviour. Jacqueline Broad examines correspondences between Cavendish and Joseph Glanvill in 'Margaret Cavendish and Joseph Glanvill: Science, Religion, and Witchcraft' (*SHPS* 38[2007] 493–505). As Cavendish argues against the existence of witches, she demonstrates how Glanvill's arguments about witchcraft betray his own rigorous standards of scientific enquiry. Cavendish's responses suggest that the principles of early modern science could "promote a healthy scepticism toward the existence of witches". In ' "English them in the easiest manner you can": Margaret Cavendish on the Discourse and Practice of Natural Philosophy' (*RhetR* 26[2007] 268–85), Denise Tillery examines how Cavendish's inclusive and subjective under-standing of plain style relates to her scientific practices as portrayed in *Observations*. Cavendish's discussion of plain style further explicitly and implicitly challenges the discursive and experimental practices of the Royal Society, particularly questioning the assumption of objectivity in language as well as knowledge.

Cavendish is also discussed by Marion Wynne-Davies in the final chapter of *Women Writers and Familial Discourse*. As one might expect in this context, Cavendish's individual writings are relocated within the context of materials produced by her siblings. Wynne-Davies highlights 'the marked continuity of thematic and generic elements' (p. 169) within the Cavendish family's diverse literary productions. To understand this, Wynne-Davies argues that such writings 'must ... be set against the material upheavals of the [English civil] war, and it is precisely this axis that determined the mutating nature of the Cavendish familial discourse' (p. 169). Throughout this book, Wynne-Davies lucidly argues for a reappraisal of the significance of familial discourses for early modern women's writing. She argues that familial location 'enable[d] women to write, not because of a sheltered, nurturing environment, but because of gaps in the patriarchal boundaries that appeared when the ideological apparatus became fractured through external disorder' (p. 173). It is pleasingly fitting to conclude this year's review, which overall signals a far more nuanced approach to early modern women's individual and political subjectivity and agency, with reference to Wynne-Davies's assertion that, 'by tracing the way in which early modern families enabled women to write, this book argues that women did benefit from a "Renaissance" ' (p. 172).

Books Reviewed

Adamson, Sylvia, Gavin Alexander and Katrin Ettenhuber. *Renaissance Figures of Speech*. CUP. [2007] pp. 306. £55 ISBN 0 5218 6640 5.

Bedford, Ronald, Lloyd Davis and Philippa Kelly, eds. *Early Modern Autobiography: Theories, Genres, Practices*. UMichP. [2006] pp. x + 309. £59.50 ISBN 9 7804 7209 9283.

Bedford, Ronald, and Philippa Kelly, eds. *Early Modern English Lives: Autobiography and Self-Representation 1500–1660*. Ashgate. [2007] pp. vi + 250. £50 ISBN 0 7546 5295 5.

Broad, Jacqueline, and Karen Green, eds. *Virtue, Liberty, and Toleration: Political Ideas of European Women, 1400–1800*. Springer. [2007] pp. xxii + 211. £79 ISBN 1 4020 5894 3.

Chedgzoy, Kate. *Women's Writing in the British Atlantic World: Memory, Place and History, 1550–1700*. CUP. [2007] pp. viii + 267. £53 ISBN 9 7805 2188 0985.

Clanton, Dan. W. *The Good, the Bold, and the Beautiful: The Story of Susanna and its Renaissance Interpretations*. Clark. [2006]. pp. x + 213. £65 ISBN 0 5670 2991 3.

Craik, Katharine A. *Reading Sensations in Early Modern England*. Palgrave Macmillan. [2007] pp. 200. £47 ISBN 1 4039 2192 X.

Doll, Dan, and Jessica Munns, eds. *Recording and Reordering: Essays on the Seventeenth- and Eighteenth-Century Diary and Journal*. BuckUP. [2006]. pp. viii + 248. £40.50 ISBN 0 8387 5630 1.

Dowd, Michelle M., and Julie A. Erkerle, eds. *Genre and Women's Life Writing in Early Modern England*. Ashgate. [2007] pp. xii + 212. £50 ISBN 9 7807 5465 4261.

Floyd-Wilson, Mary, and Garret A. Sullivan, Jr, eds. *Environment and Embodiment in Early Modern England*. Palgrave. [2007] pp. 240. £47 ISBN 1 4039 9774 8.

Hallet, Nicky, ed. *Lives of Spirit: English Carmelite Self-Writing of the Early Modern Period*. Ashgate. [2007] pp. xi + 299. £55 ISBN 9 7807 5460 6758.

Hallet, Nicky, ed. *Witchcraft, Exorcism and the Politics of Possession in a Seventeenth-Century Convent: 'How Sister Ursula was once Bewitched and Sister Margaret Twice'*. Ashgate. [2007] £55 ISBN 0 7546 3150 8.

Liebler, Naomi Conn, ed. *Early Modern Prose Fiction: The Cultural Politics of Reading*. Routledge. [2007] pp. xii + 185. £18.99 ISBN 0 4153 5840 X.

Milton, Anthony. *Laudian and Royalist Polemic in Seventeenth Century England*. ManUP. [2007] pp. 288. £55 ISBN 0 7190 6444 9.

Ng, Su Fang. *Literature and the Politics of Family in Seventeenth-Century England.* CUP. [2007] pp. viii + 236. £53 ISBN 0 5218 7031 3.

O'Callaghan, Michelle. *The English Wits: Literature and Sociability in Early Modern England.* CUP. [2007] pp. 234. £45 ISBN 0 5218 6084 9.

Richards, Jennifer, and Alison Thorne, eds. *Rhetoric, Women and Politics in Early Modern England.* Routledge. [2007] pp. x + 254. £60 ISBN 0 4153 8526 1.

Rickard, Jane. *Authorship and Authority: The Writings of James VI and I.* ManUP. [2007] pp. 256. £50 ISBN 0 7190 7486 X.

Smith, Hilda L, Mihoko Suzuki and Susan Wiseman, eds. *Women's Political Writings, 1610–1725,* 4 vols. P&C. [2007] pp. 1600. £350 ISBN 1 8519 6792 3.

Starke, Sue P. *The Heroines of English Pastoral Romance.* Brewer. [2007] pp. ix + 246. £45 ISBN 9 7818 4384 1241.

Trill, Suzanne, ed. *Lady Anne Halkett: Selected Self-Writings.* Ashgate. [2007] pp. xlii + 226. £50 ISBN 0 7546 5052 2.

Trolander, Paul, and Zeynep Tenger. *Sociable Criticism in England 1625–1725.* UDelP. [2007] pp. 233. £42.50 ISBN 0 8741 3969 4.

Wolfe, Heather, ed. *The Literary Career and Legacy of Elizabeth Cary, 1613–1680.* Palgrave. [2007] pp. xiii + 258 £47.50 ISBN 1 4039 7016 5.

Wynne-Davies, Marion. *Women Writers and Familial Discourse in the English Renaissance: Relative Values.* Palgrave. [2007] pp. viii + 209. £48 ISBN 1 4039 8641 X.

IX

Milton and Poetry, 1603–1660

DAVID AINSWORTH, HOLLY FAITH NELSON, PAUL DYCK AND ALVIN SNIDER

This chapter has four sections: 1. General; 2.Donne; 3. Herbert; 4. Milton. Section 1 is by David Ainsworth; section 2 is by Holly Faith Nelson; section 3 is by Paul Dyck; section 4 is by Alvin Snider.

1. General

The year 2007 saw rather little published on those poets represented by the general category, but most of what appears offers broader application to the study of poetry, both within and beyond the immediate period of 1603–60. In the spirit of comprehensive complexity, Su Fang Ng's *Literature and the Politics of Family in Seventeenth-Century England* mixes historicist and materialist approaches to texts with discourse theory to argue for a dynamic association between family structures and political structures in England. Ng suggests that the language of family associated itself with political discourse in contentious ways, complicating patriarchal interpretations of this discourse by arguing that the language of family can undermine as well as reinforce kingship. While Ng focuses on prose works and masques, she also considers the poetry of John Dryden, James I and John Milton. Her presentation of familial discourse as a common language of political disagreement could open up interpretative possibilities in readings of other poets and poems in the period. In particular, her attentiveness to social dimensions, class concerns and religious discourse might productively propagate itself into narrower readings of poets in the period.

Several articles in Nicola Royan, ed., '*Langage cleir illumynate*': *Scottish Poetry from Barbour to Drummond, 1375–1630*, remind the reader that English poetry was never written in a vacuum. Within the 1603–60 period, Katherine McClune's 'The Scottish Sonnet, James VI, and John Stewart of Baldynneis' argues that Scottish poets reject the sonnet form as a particularly romantic or love-focused kind of poetry, instead employing it for a range of political and religious purposes (pp. 165–80). McClune focuses on the relationship between reader and author, arguing that James VI counters the threat that his readers

Year's Work in English Studies, Volume 88 (2009) © *The English Association; all rights reserved*
doi:10.1093/ywes/map011

might pose to his power by inscribing himself as author within his poems as a paradigmatic reader. John Stewart, following James's lead, explores issues of poetic authority by playing out a literary self-consciousness within his poetry. In both instances, the attempt to construe poetic authorship as a form of moral self-interpretation draws upon yet deflects the model of sonnets as encapsulated desire. McClune focuses on developing an understanding of Scottish literary concerns, but her article does suggest room for productive work relating these trends in Scottish poetry with the changing employment of sonnets in England. Two articles consider William Drummond's poetry. David Atkinson, in '*Flowres of Sion*: The Spiritual and Meditative Journey of William Drummond', relates that work of poetry to a personal and meditative mode of thought, arguing that Drummond's poetry reflects on Christian themes of resurrection and hope and expresses the creative tension between the desire for worldly experience of God and the *ars moriendi* theme (pp. 181–91). Michael Spiller's ' "Quintessencing in the finest substance": The Sonnets of William Drummond' examines Drummond's remarks on Petrarchanism in English poetry generally and considers too Drummond's thoughts on poets such as Sir Philip Sidney and Samuel Daniel (pp. 193–205). Spiller suggests that Drummond's own poetry consciously imitates Petrarch in an attempt to carry out Drummond's argument that English poets write and represent the most distilled version of Petrarch in all of Europe.

Spiller's essay might usefully be related to Stefan Hawlin's 'Epistemes and Imitations: Thom Gunn on Ben Jonson' (*PMLA* 122[2007] 1516–30). Hawlin discusses *imitatio* as a concept crossing period boundaries through translation or adaptation. Although primarily tracing Gunn's adaptation of Jonson's poems ('To Sir Robert Wroth') and funerary elegy ('Elegie on the Lady Jane Pawlet'), Hawlin also problematizes historicist accounts to demonstrate that repetition can also make things new, both drawing a trope or form into a given historical moment and asserting connections with past moments. The common concerns re-envisioned through this repetition might profitably be traced back to reveal aspects of Jonson's poems. *Imitatio* thus offers a reinterpretative structure for Jonson via Gunn.

David Landrum, in 'Robert Herrick and the Ambiguities of Gender' (*TSLL* 49[2007] 181–207), argues for a Herrick who interrogates and critiques gender standards of his day. Landrum suggests that Herrick sets Neoplatonic conceptions of women against contemporary customs. He interprets 'A nuptiall Song, or Epithalamie, on Sir Clipseby Crew and his Lady' as investing the lady with divine attributes set against the crude male lust directed at her to suggest the degrading effects of patriarchal power wielded in this way. Customary female subservience in marriage thus comes into question, as the propriety of patriarchal power structures conflicts with the prurient male desire which those structures reinforce. According to Landrum, Herrick's poetic persona must be distinguished from the man himself; he critiques psychoanalytic interpretations of Herrick's poetry. Landrum argues that the Herrick in Herrick's poetry is a character, reading the Herrick in *Hesperides* as denied sexual access by an authoritarian Venus coded as chaste and unwilling to reveal herself sexually to him. The inaptness of the Herrick persona for love thus disrupts and parodies poetic conventions regarding gender, especially poetic relationships with erotic muses, but also with the imaginary mistresses of *Hesperides*.

Denise Inge's 'Thomas Traherne and the Socinian Heresy in *Commentaries of Heaven*' (*N&Q* 54[2007] 412–16) contextualizes Traherne's poetry within his defence of orthodox Christianity against heresy, although Inge concentrates on Traherne's religious writing. David McInnis, in 'The Golden Man and the Golden Age: The Relationship of English Poets and the New World Reconsidered' (*EMLS* 13:i[2007] 1.1–19), considers poems by Chapman and Marvell but also Drayton's 1606 'To the Virginian Voyage'. He argues that it presents Virginia in Ovidian terms, offering the place as a prelapsarian landscape. He also seeks a balance between propaganda and classical appropriation in the poem. Henry Power's '"Teares breake off my verse": The Virgilian Incompleteness of Abraham Cowley's *The Civil War*' (*T&L* 16[2007] 141–59) discusses the unfinished epic poem *The Civil War*, abandoned in 1643, as an imitation of Virgil which breaks down as it crosses the line between epic and elegy, drawing upon a strict imitation of Virgilian half-lines to do so. The implication is that epic triumph cannot be complete or filled out in a civil war; success must also inevitably figure failure. David M. Schiller, in '"O false, yet sweet contenting": John Coprario's Songs for Penelope Rich on the Death of Lord Mountjoy' (*JDJ* 26[2007] 241–68), discusses the songs in *Funeral Tears* as epideictic rhetoric deigned to re-create Mountjoy's persona subsequent to his death. The lyrics cast Penelope as the performer of the songs and reference her role in *Astrophil and Stella* in order to transfer authority to Penelope. Penelope as speaker then addresses Mountjoy, creating him anew. Schiller concentrates on the musical composition of the *Funeral Tears* but also reads some of the prefatory poems.

2. John Donne

While scholarly energies in John Donne studies continue to expand and diversify, as is evident in the many articles, book chapters, and monographs published this year, Donne's 'afterlife' in Britain, North America and beyond was a subject of particular fascination in 2007, as scholars worked to trace his sometimes elusive presence in arts, culture and the academy across space and time (Dayton Haskin, *John Donne in the Nineteenth Century*, p. xxii).

The *John Donne Journal* dedicated a section of its twenty-sixth volume to the identification and analysis of the 'voiceprint' of Donne in the poetry of twentieth-century writers (p. 269). In 'Tracking the Voiceprint of Donne' (*JDJ* 26[2007] 269–82), Judith Scherer Herz considers the manner in which Donne's language is 'breathed through' or translated into 'modern idiom' in the poetry of Paul Muldoon, Mark Jarman, Michael Symmons Roberts and Carl Phillips (p. 292). Herz claims that Muldoon 'swallow[s] Donne whole', Jarman effortlessly mingles the voices of George Herbert and Donne in his *Unholy Sonnets*, and both Roberts and Phillips engage with the erotic and sacred 'corporeality' of Donne's verse (pp. 270, 276). In 'Donne, Discontinuity, and the Proto-Post Modern: The Case of Anthony Hecht' (*JDJ* 26[2007] 283–94), Jonathan F.S. Post argues that Donne taught Hecht how to shape his ideas in verse. Donne's representation of human experience in the language of rupture and discord, Post speculates, provided Hecht with a way both to comprehend the 'discontinuities and dissonances' of existence and to 'organize in verse what was discontinuous in life' (pp. 292–3).

In 'A "Re-vision" of Donne: Adrienne Rich's "A Valediction Forbidding Mourning"' (*JDJ* 26[2007] 333–62), Helen B. Brooks maintains that in 'A Valediction Forbidding Mourning', Rich reads Donne's poem of the same name in opposing ways: as a vessel of patriarchal discourse and aesthetic patterns and as an unorthodox, even revolutionary, poetic space. As a result, Rich's feminist re-reading and reimagining of Donne's 'A Valediction Forbidding Mourning' in her own poem involves 'her combined adherence to and departure from' the antecedent text according to Brooks (p. 360).

In 'Registering Donne's Voiceprint: Additional Reverberations' (*JDJ* 26[2007] 295–312), Raymond-Jean Frontain, drawing on the research of Walter Ong, insightfully theorizes the concept of voiceprint, demonstrating that the term is much broader and less constrictive than the categories of quotation, reference, or even allusion. In exploring the flexibility and fluidity of the Donnean voiceprint, as well as the difficulty of mapping such a 'richly amorphous artifact', Frontain identifies Donne's influence on the development of the dramatic monologue in modernist texts; the treatment of the sexual and sacred in the works of Tennessee Williams and D.H. Lawrence; the expression of 'the paradoxes of desire' in the poems of Edna St Vincent Millay; and the conceptualization of sexuality in the poetry of Allen Ginsberg (pp. 295, 305). Frontain contends that Donne's voiceprint is present even in lyrics composed in languages other than English, pointing to the work of Rabindranath Tagore, whose exposure to Herbert J.C. Grierson's edition of *The Poems of John Donne* during his residence in London led to frequent Donnean references in his Bengali poetry, prose and songs.

Donne's indirect influence on later writers is also addressed in 'Deaths and Entrances' (*BS* 32[2007] 138–44), in which Paul Dean Daniggelis considers the influence of a passage from Donne's best- known sermon, *Deaths Duell*, on Martha Graham's enigmatic ballet *Deaths and Entrances*, which opened in Vermont in 1943 and was most recently staged in 2005. Dean believes that Graham accessed Donne's phrase indirectly through Dylan Thomas's poem 'Deaths and Entrances' and concludes that the aesthetic energies of Donne and Thomas enrich the thematic concerns of death, resurrection and eternal life in Graham's ballet.

Traces of the imagined voices of Donne, Ann More and their children are also to be found in *Conceit*, a novel on the life of Margaret (Pegge) Donne by the Canadian writer Mary Novik. In her 'Valediction' to *Conceit*, Novik invokes John Donne's dictum, 'I did best when I had least truth for my subjects', and it is important to keep this maxim in mind when reading the novel. Fact and fiction are often unpredictably merged in this narrative centred on the unyielding desire of Pegge Donne for Izaac Walton, a desire that is juxtaposed with the ardent love of John Donne and Ann More. While Novik draws on historical material she does not wish to be limited by it, reminding her readers that she has 'invented joyfully and freely' as she created her own version of life in seventeenth-century London (pp. 401– 2).

Donne's influence in Britain and abroad is no doubt linked to the ways in which he has been represented and 'packaged' during the process of canonization. In 'Anthologizing Donne in the Twentieth Century: Integrating Jack and John?' (*Anglistik* 18[2007] 9–26), Jochen Petzold reviews the reception of Donne, surveying early modern miscellanies as well as nineteenth- and twentieth-century anthologies, particularly versions of the *Norton Anthology of English Literature* issued between 1962 and 2000. Petzold's findings confirm that while Donne's contemporaries were highly receptive to 'Jack Donne', most nineteenth- and twentieth-century anthology editors have found 'Dr Donne' more palatable. However, Petzold describes the tendency of editors from the 1960s on to anthologize Donne's more sexually explicit poems alongside those deemed transcendent, which he attributes to the evolving social mores in America and to a growing body of criticism on the body and sexuality in literature.

Dayton Haskin's *John Donne and the Nineteenth-Century*, an impeccably researched, intellectually stimulating, and elegantly written monograph, sketches the reception of Donne in Britain and the Americas from the 1820s to the 1890s, although Haskin moves back and forward in time where necessary to contextualize his claims. The manuscript and printed materials upon which he draws could have easily led a less accomplished scholar to write a dull and pedestrian account of Donne among the Victorians. Yet Haskin brings these artefacts to life, generating a rich and lively narrative of Donne's 'afterlife' in the period, while remaining fully committed to the facts of history. While Haskin explains that the Donne Variorum project had a significant role to play in this study, he recognizes that Variorum editions cannot assimilate 'textual, critical, and biographical perspectives' on the transmission and reception of Donne. He therefore takes up this challenge in *John Donne and the Nineteenth Century*, successfully cataloguing and assessing 'the modes of assimilating Donne that were prevalent in nineteenth-century literary culture' (p. xx).

Haskin begins the volume by establishing the principal role played by Walton's *Lives* in the reception of Donne in the first half of the nineteenth century and by examining the tendency of Wordsworth and Coleridge to read Donne in 'religious... terms' or with a 'religious imagination' (pp. 25, 45). He concludes by comparing the reception of Donne in the academy with that of the wider artistic community at the fin de siècle. Between these chapters, Haskin examines too much to recapitulate here. However, it can be said that he assigns an important place to Henry Alford's edition of *The Works of John Donne* [1839] in his account of the 'First Revival' of Donne (p. 13); highlights the popularity of Donne's letters in the mid-nineteenth century and explores the skill and sensitivity of some of their readers; considers the significance of Alexander B. Grosart's *The Complete Poems of John Donne* [1872–3] and traces the struggle of Grosart and other editors and critics to deal with the sensual or sexual elements of Donne's works; examines attempts of Victorian biographers to merge Walton's and Grosart's versions of Donne; and details the complex reception of Donne in New England, emphasizing the critical part played by Le Baron Russell Briggs, whose lectures on Donne at Harvard University were highly influential in the resurrection of Donne in the academy.

Haskin's study, without a doubt, demonstrates that 'T.S. Eliot did not invent Donne' (p. 269).

The reception of Donne in China is outlined by Kui Yan in 'A Glory to Come: John Donne Studies in China' (*JDJ* 26[2007] 313–32). Yan describes the process by which Donne's works came to be increasingly valued in Chinese universities, remarking on the significance of the lectures given at Peking University by William Empson, Robert Winters and Harold Acton in the 1930s. Yan attributes the mounting popularity of Donne to the growing number of translations of his works into Chinese, though he notes that nearly all of Donne's prose awaits translation. Donne's fate in China, Yan explains, was linked to the nation's political state, and Donne's reputation could only be established 'once the Republic decided to implement its opening and reform policies' (p. 318). Yan identifies the principal academic players in Donne's reception in China between the 1980s and the present day, evaluating their contribution to the field, and concludes by describing developments that will ensure the continued growth of Chinese scholarship on Donne.

The stress placed on Donne's 'afterlife' and enduring 'voiceprint' this year is complemented by an emphasis on his negotiation of past works and traditions. In her monograph, *Divine Deviants: The Dialectics of Devotion in the Poetry of Donne and Rūmī*, Manijeh Mannani reads the poetry of Donne alongside that of the Persian medieval mystic Rūmī, situating the lyrics of both men within the broader mystical tradition. The chief arguments of *Divine Deviants* are that the aesthetically innovative and deeply metaphysical poems of Rūmī and Donne treat in a similar fashion a series of interrelated themes on sin, salvation, eternal life and earthly love; operate within an intellectual framework while remaining sensitive to the reality of daily life; resist religious orthodoxy; and privilege philosophy over poetry. Mannani initially distinguishes the mystical pantheism of Rūmī from the philosophical mysticism of Donne. She then explains that the sense of '[r]eligious obligation and the great passion to be forgiven' in Donne's poems is alien to Rūmī, who feels 'so drowned in the ocean of God's love he could barely think of anything else including himself, his life, and his sins' (pp. 49, 64). Mannani next stresses that while Donne is more 'meticulous a thinker' than the Persian poet, he is also less visionary (p. 100). Mannani concludes with an examination of embodied love and erotic desire in the poems of Donne and Rūmī.

Divine Deviants undertakes a laudable task: to uncover in Islamic and Christian devotional poetry spiritual ways of being and knowing that cross geographical, cultural and temporal boundaries. However, Mannani's portrayal of a mystical Donne is not fully convincing since the differences she discovers in the poetry of Donne and Rūmī could be ascribed to the possibility that Donne is not a mystic, a point she comes very close to making herself (p. 64). Further, Mannani appears to have a limited knowledge of the 'contextual specificities' of Donne's works and of early modern devotional texts more generally (p. 159). Nevertheless, the comparison of 'Islamic and Christian mystical systems' through representative figures is certainly a subject worthy of study (p. 30).

In *Tradition and Subversion in Renaissance Literature: Studies in Shakespeare, Spenser, Jonson, and Donne*, Murray Roston cogently and fruitfully applies Mikhail Bakhtin's theory of dialogism and heteroglossia in the novel to early modern dramatic, poetic and meditative prose texts. He theorizes that a 'creative tension' between 'tradition and subversion' in *The Faerie Queene*, *The Merchant of Venice*, *Hamlet*, *Volpone* and Donne's devotional prose is both 'animating' and 'profoundly enriching', resulting in a plenitude of meaning that does *not* lead to interpretive paralysis, as the postmoderns suggest (pp. xii-xiii). In the fifth chapter of *Tradition and Subversion*, 'Donne and the Meditative Tradition', Roston argues that a principally Protestant theology is shaped by a definitively Catholic 'process of thought' in Donne's devotional works, and this merger of 'traditional and innovative elements' renders them more aesthetically and spiritually potent (p. 180).

Donne's creative reworking of the meditative tradition is also briefly explored by A.D. Cousins and R.J. Webb in 'Donne's Annunciation' (*Expl* 65[2007] 136–7). Cousins and Webb note that in the 'Annunciation', Donne's speaker does not engage in orthodox Ignatian meditative practices in which the self becomes passive witness in the presence of the holy, but rather works to dramatize the self. Cousins and Webb find that, in the last ten lines of the sonnet, the persona conjures up a sacred landscape only to transform it into a stage on which he can perform the role of devout spiritual tutor of both the reader and, more shockingly, the Virgin Mary.

Sarah Powrie locates Donne in the tradition of the medieval Neoplatonic epic in 'The Celestial Progress of a Deathless Soul: Donne's *Second Anniuersarie*' (*JDJ* 26[2007] 73–101). Powrie envisions the *Second Anniversary* as an early modern version of the *Paradiso* of Dante Alighieri or the lesser-known *Anticlaudianus* of Alan of Lille, 'philosophical epic[s]' in which '[c]osmographic material and personal meditation' merge and 'complement each other in creative dialogue' (pp. 75, 82). By recourse to the syncretistic Neoplatonic thought embedded in this tradition, Donne is able to suture together the broken body of the universe. Therefore, the Neoplatonic narrative of 'progress and integration' that Donne generates, Powrie argues, challenges Baconian philosophy which fragments or shreds the universe, the very philosophy Donne satirized in *The First Anniversary* (p. 79).

Donne's relation to the Spenserian tradition is explored by Tom MacFaul in 'Donne's "The Sunne Rising" and Spenser's "Epithalamion"' (*N&Q* 54[2007] 37–8). MacFaul claims that in 'The Sunne Rising' Donne refers to Spenser's marriage hymn because he finds in it a fitting attitude towards the monarch. In both poems, the ruler is figured in solar terms in order to convey 'the pervasive power of royalty' to penetrate the private moments of its citizens (p. 37). However, MacFaul suggests that the borrowing is not a straightforward one, because while Spenser makes the intrusive figure 'the paradoxical guarantor of generation', Donne 'only wants the sun to *warm* him and his lady', which signifies Donne's 'request for royal favour' (p. 38). Regardless of this distinction, MacFaul believes that both Spenser and Donne intimate that the sovereign must 'supply his or her poets for their private lives' (p. 38).

In 'Nomadic Souls: Pythagoras, Spenser, Donne' (*SSt* 22[2007] 257–79), Elizabeth D. Harvey also situates Donne in the Spenserian tradition. Taking note of the adaptation of the Spenserian stanzaic form in *Metempsychosis*,

Harvey proposes that Donne's borrowing here betrays his interest in Spenser's treatment of the soul and body in the *Complaints* and the second book of *The Faerie Queene*. Harvey views *Metempsychosis* as a 'space of poetic cohabitation' in which the encounter between Spenser and Donne clarifies the classical and contemporary philosophical sources, as well as the moral implications, of their ideas on the spirit and the flesh (p. 259).

The nature of the flesh, or embodiment, in the works of Donne is also the subject of three articles and a book chapter this year, all of which focus on the significance of the diseased, ageing, or decaying body of the writer or subject. In 'A Donne Deal' (*BMJ* 335 [11 Aug. 2007] 307), Theodore Dalrymple very briefly reflects on Donne's conception of disease in the *Devotions upon Emergent Occasions* and in 'Why doth the Poxe so much affect to undermine the nose?' Dalrymple proposes that Donne's view of humans as 'great self-destroyer[s]' in the *Devotions* anticipates modern medical perspectives on disease; so too, he finds that the sentiment that disease disturbs 'the most eminent and perspicuous part' of the body and assails 'the most eminent and conspicuous men' expressed in 'Why doth the poxe' resonates with modern attitudes towards victims of disease (p. 307).

The decaying body is also explored in Margaret Maurer's 'Poetry and Scandal: John Donne's "A Hymne to the Saynts and to the Marquesse Hamilton"' (*JDJ* 26[2007] 1–33) and Christopher Martin's 'Fall and Decline: Confronting Lyric Gerontophobia in Donne's "The Autumnal"' (*JDJ* 26[2007] 35–54). Maurer considers Donne's poetic response to the scandal that surrounded the death, and unnaturally swift decomposition of the body, of the second marquis of Hamilton. Aware that the rate at which the corpse putrefied was being attributed to Hamilton's papist leanings, Donne guides his readers away from 'scandalous' ruminations on Hamilton's spiritual state at death and offers up a 'consoling vision of celestial reunion of all who loved the deceased' (p. 33). Martin addresses Donne's preoccupation with the passage of time and bodily decay in 'The Autumnal'. He finds that opposing views on ageing collide in this elegy, since Donne both censures and reinscribes 'gerontophobic prejudice' in the poem (p. 40). This ambivalence towards the ageing body serves Donne's twin purpose, which is, Martin conjectures, 'to console and chasten' his readers 'with the prospect of time's effect on sexuality, prestige, and the self-image grounded in these social experiences' (p. 51).

In her well-researched and convincing monograph, *Reading Sensations in Early Modern England*, Katharine A. Craik produces a nuanced reading of the connection between the male gentlemanly body and literary texts in the early modern period. She begins by analysing this connection in Thomas Wright's *The Passions of the Minde in Generall* and Henry Crosse's *Vertues Commonwealth*, before turning to the works of George Puttenham, Sir Philip Sidney, John Donne, Thomas Coryat, Richard Braithwait and Thomas Cranley. In the fourth chapter of the volume, '"These spots are but the letters": John Donne and the Medicaments of Elegy', Craik argues that Donne does not simply accept the orthodox view that elegiac literature is therapeutic to both the mind and body of the grieving subject. Focusing on Donne's *Anniversaries*, she speculates that Donne did not believe that his 'elegies could mend the distressing symptoms of despair' because of his sinful, infected writerly body

(p. 8). While Donne is unable to accomplish this task in *The Anniversaries*, however, Craik claims that the case is different when he is writing from his seriously ailing body in *Devotions Upon Emergent Occasions*, because in this medical condition he can 'achieve a powerfully restorative, confessional voice' (p. 75).

Craik's attention to the *Devotions Upon Emergent Occasions* is shared by four members of the John Donne Society, whose colloquium presentations on the *Devotions* at the annual meeting were published in the *John Donne Journal* this year. Their four articles are introduced by Kate Gartner Frost, who provides a brief background on the *Devotions* (*JDJ* 26[2007] 363–4). Brooke Conti, in 'The *Devotions*: Popular and Critical Reception' (*JDJ* 26[2007] 365–72), then traces the response to the *Devotions* from the date of first publication until the twenty-first century; highlights the absence of editions for two centuries after the issuing of the 1638 edition; reviews recent critical debates on its formal features, literary and spiritual antecedents, and political significance; and considers the shift in interpretative approaches to the work. In 'Theology, Doctrine, and Genre in *Devotions Upon Emergent Occasions*' (*JDJ* 26[2007] 373–80) R.V. Young argues that the *Devotions* are, theologically speaking, moderate and inclusive. He demonstrates that the literary genres on which Donne relies and the doctrines that he invokes in the *Devotions* were popular with both Catholics and Protestants.

Mary A. Papazian contends in '"No man [and nothing] is an *Iland*": Contexts for Donne's "Meditation XVII"' (*JDJ* 26[2007] 381–5) that Donne's *Devotions* must be read as an unfolding narrative composed in specific personal and political circumstances. Papazian explains that when Donne composed the *Devotions*, he was, despite his sickness, at the height of his success; she therefore believes we must look to the political context to understand the anxiety recorded in the work, particularly in terms of Donne's reaction to Stuart policies on the 'Bohemian cause', the proposed match between Prince Charles and the Spanish Infanta, and the growing authority of Archbishop Laud (p. 383). Papazian concludes that it is Donne's dissatisfaction with political realities that lead him to gesture away from the material realm and to focus on the sphere of the eternal in the *Devotions*.

In the final contribution to the colloquium on the *Devotions*, '"Was I not made to *thinke*?": Teaching the *Devotions* and Donne's Literary Practice' (*JDJ* 26[2007] 387–99), Helen Wilcox identifies and responds to the five most common questions posed by her students on the *Devotions*. These questions relate to generic influences; the tripartite form of each devotion; the frequency and function of tropes, especially metaphor, in the text; the overarching movement and purpose of the volume; and the significant presence of 'apparent contradictions' or opposing elements in the *Devotions* (p. 397). Wilcox is convinced that in responding to these questions teachers will be able to convey key features of the Donnean aesthetic.

Robert Jungman is also concerned with a section of the *Devotions* in 'Mining for Augustinian Gold in John Donne's *Meditation 17*' (*ANQ* 20[2007] 16–20). Acknowledging that two of the three dominant figures (the tolling bell and the work of translation) in *Meditation 17* have received substantial critical attention, he turns to the third, the act of mining for gold, which he believes has neither been fully grasped nor suitably linked with the other two metaphors. Jungman posits that Donne borrows the figures of textual translation and gold-mining from a passage in the second book of *On Christian Doctrine* in which Augustine defends the use of unearthing and appropriating pagan knowledge for the Christian cause. Jungman theorizes that this allusion allows Donne to justify the 'proper use' of another man's death in *Meditation 17*, which requires those who hear the toll of the bell to translate the sound into a spiritual message on their own mortality (p. 18).

Donne's sermons received as much scholarly attention this year as his *Devotions*. Three articles in the *John Donne Journal* address aspects of Donne's sermonic rhetoric or context: Robert A. Guffey's 'Parabolic Logic in John Donne's Sermons' (*JDJ* 26[2007] 103–25), Katrin Ettenhuber's '"Take heed what you heare": Re-reading Donne's Lincoln's Inn Sermons' (*JDJ* 26[2007] 127–57) and John N. Wall's 'Situating Donne's Dedication Sermon at Lincoln's Inn, 22 May 1623' (*JDJ* 26[2007] 159–239). Guffey discovers in Donne's sermons a form of logic characteristic of the parables of the New Testament. The rhetorical sophistication of Donne's sermons, Guffey believes, is partially due to this 'figurative technique', by which the expectations associated with a 'familiar and predictable' image are transgressed or challenged to ensure the spiritual awakening and transformation of his audience (pp. 104, 107).

Ettenhuber spotlights the intersection of legal and religious concepts in a single Donne sermon preached on Genesis 18.25 at Lincoln's Inn in 1620. She explores the merging of the legal conception of equity and the ethical notion of charity in this Trinity Sunday sermon on 'appeal and judgment' in order to demonstrate Donne's overarching desire in the Lincoln's Inn sermons to link 'pulpit and lawcourt, Church and State' (pp. 138, 155). Ettenhuber believes that Donne accomplishes this end by promoting 'equitable and charitable exegesis' in matters of judgment; interrogating the prerogative justice of the sovereign; and defending the need for active 'civil engagement' in the political realm (pp. 153, 130).

While also attending to one sermon preached at Lincoln's Inn, John Wall dwells on the reconstruction of the ecclesiastical space rather than the substance of that sermon. After drawing an analogy between preaching a sermon and performing a play, Wall argues that we must become familiar with the script, set, players and costumes available to Donne at Trinity Chapel for the consecration service at Lincoln's Inn on 22 May 1623. Wall relies on a bill from a joiner and a description of the consecration translated from a Latin manuscript to demonstrate that the 'architectural design' of Trinity Chapel on the day of Donne's sermon followed, in certain respects, the 'fashion' in 'new church construction' at this time (pp. 177, 210). The design included a 'centrally located pulpit', multiple stained-glass windows and a flexible choir or chancel area in which Holy Communion could be taken (p. 207). These and other facts lead Wall to conclude that Trinity Chapel was a 'building for a time of transition' and that it therefore 'looks both forward and backward' in time (p. 216).

Roberta Albrecht also attends to the sermons of Donne, though her focus is on the potency of visual signs in two churching sermons. In 'Addressing Fear and Grief: Llullian Mnemotechnics and Alchemico-Llullian Signs in Donne's Sermon(s) for the Churching of the Countess of Bridgewater' (*CatR* 20:i[2006] 9–37), Albrecht argues that Donne deploys Llullian 'spiritual logic' and alchemical figures in his churching sermons, specifically the signs of 'the ark, the rainbow, and *rest*', to invite members of competing 'political and religious factions', adept decoders of such ciphers, 'to discover therein their own particular dove of peace, offering them, as it were, an olive branch' in turbulent times (pp. 13, 14, 22).

The scholarly attention paid to the *Devotions* and sermons this year reflects, to some extent, a broader concern with the nature and role of religion and religious imagery in Donne's works, subjects explored in a series of publications this year. In 'Herbert and Donne', the twenty-fourth chapter of Andrew Hass, David Jasper and Elisabeth Jay, eds., *The Oxford Handbook of English Literature and Theology*, Helen Wilcox describes the distinct religious contexts or 'devotional cultures' in which Herbert and Donne lived and wrote; sketches the intricate connection between the aesthetic and the theological in their texts; examines how their works were 'read...theologically' by their contemporaries; and argues that it is not possible to interpret their works without recourse to theology even in modern times (pp. 398, 401). Wilcox also considers how readers over the past three centuries have made different 'theological use[s]' of the writings of Herbert and Donne (p. 409).

In 'Donne's Religious Poetry and the Trauma of Grace' (in Cheney, Hadfield and Sullivan, eds., *Early Modern English Poetry: A Critical Companion*, pp. 229–39), Achsah Guibbory argues that the devotional verse of Donne inscribes what she calls the 'trauma of grace', a trauma generated by the emergence of Protestant churches alongside the Church of Rome and by the rival soteriologies set forth as undisputed truth by these churches (p. 230). Guibbory reminds us that the intensity of this trauma was especially profound for Donne because he personally abandoned the Catholic faith to serve in the Protestant church. While the 'spiritual crisis' in the life of Donne is made manifest in his devotional poetry, it is expressed, as Guibbory shows, with the same 'wit and passion' that we find in his secular love lyrics (p. 238).

Donne's fixation on the notion of martyrdom may have been sparked, in part, by the 'trauma of grace' he endured. In '*Apologia Pro Vita Sua*: Martyrdom in Donne's Prose' (*PSt* 29[2007] 378–93), Neal E. Migan undertakes a psycho-biographical reading of the motif of martyrdom in Donne's prose works. Migan believes that Donne, fuelled by *thanatos* or a death-drive, constitutes himself as a kind of living martyr in his prose. He is convinced that Donne ultimately engages in the act of 'passive suicide', writing 'significant portions of himself to death' (p. 380). In this way, Migan argues, Donne was able gradually to eliminate 'the psychic portions of his ego' that blocked his 'path to glory', rendering him worthy of the name martyr because he had endured a 'psychological...death' (pp. 381, 389).

The figure of the martyred Christ in a sonnet of Donne is the subject of Kirsten Stirling's 'Lutheran Imagery and Donne's "Picture of Christ Crucified"' (*JDJ* 26[2007] 55–71). Stirling suggests that the convergence of the cross and the Last Judgement in the visual culture of pre-Reformation England explains the presence of 'rood and doom' in Donne's Holy

Sonnet 9 (p. 57). The ambivalent treatment of these visual objects in Holy Sonnet 9, Stirling claims, calls to mind Luther's 'equivocal position' on religious images, especially the 'internal crucifix' which figures prominently in Donne's sonnet (p. 63). Stirling theorizes that Donne, like Luther, summons the image of the cross in his writings to confront 'the iconography and the doctrinal implications of the Last Judgment' (p. 65). However, Stirling recognizes that even the 'internal crucifix' cannot entirely eradicate the speaker's fear in Holy Sonnet 9 of his final encounter with God.

The relation between Donne's life and art was raised in three articles this year. In 'Autobiographical Reference in John Donne's "Nature's Lay Idiot"' (N&Q 54[2007] 36–7), Kate Shuttleworth argues that the phrase 'Chafe wax for others' seals' in line 29 of Donne's Elegy 12 should be interpreted as a personal allusion to the Lord Keeper of the Great Seal, Sir Thomas Egerton, uncle to Ann More. In 'John Donne, Travel Writer' (HLQ 70[2007] 61–85), Antony Parr complicates the relation between Donne's actual travel experience at sea in the final decade of the sixteenth century and the representation of travel and 'reportage of travel' in his works at a time when map-making was flourishing and tourism expanding (p. 66). In 'Donne's Songs and Sonets and Artistic Identity' (in Cheney, Hadfield and Sullivan, eds., pp. 206–16), Andrew Hadfield considers the blurring of boundaries between authorial self and poetic persona in Donne's lyrics. While recognizing that Donne's works are autobiographical on occasion, Hadfield emphasizes that, for the most part, there is only a 'tangential relationship' between 'an external reality' and the substance of Donne's poetry (p. 207). He maintains, therefore, that the Songs and Sonets should be read as a textual site on which Donne fashions a witty, dramatic, impudent and sometimes misogynistic 'poetic identity' for himself (p. 215).

While formalist readings of Donne's works are rare this year, several articles do attend to his poetry in terms of its organization or structure of thought. In 'Formalism and the Problem of History: Sonnets, Sequence, and the Relativity of Linear Time' (in Cohen, ed., Shakespeare and Historical Formalism, pp. 177–93), R.L. Kesler explores the connection between history and literary form, relating the evolution of the early modern English sonnet to the 'familiar modern narrative of sequential history' (p. 179). Within this context, Kesler argues that Donne fundamentally re-forms and renews the English sonnet, 'destabilizing' it in a 'developing environment of commercial printing', thereby extending the life of the genre (pp. 187, 179).

In 'Donne's Epigrams: A Sequential Reading' (MP 104:iii[2007] 329–78), Theresa M. DiPasquale contends that the Variorum editions of Donne's poems prove that he was fully involved in revising and organizing his works, self-consciously emending individual poems and altering the order of poems published in sequence. In this landmark study, DiPasquale considers three major sequences of Donne's epigrams identified by the editors of the Variorum edition (the early, intermediate and late sequences, containing nine, twenty, and sixteen epigrams respectively) and determines that, despite the association of epigrams with closure and finality of thought, they are composed in such a way as to inspire intertextual connections between poems in each sequence and to invite interpretative openness.

While the penchant for interpreting seventeenth-century texts through the lens of postmodern literary theory appears to be on the decline, in *English Renaissance Literature and Contemporary Theory: Sublime Objects of Theology*, Paul Cefalu argues for its value as an exegetical tool. Cefalu is a methodical scholar who makes every effort to demonstrate that the writings of Jacques Lacan, Slavoj Žižek, Giorgio Agamben and Eric Santner illuminate Donne's conception of the relation between himself and the divine. With respect to political theology, Cefalu argues that the Reformed Donne eliminates 'sovereign-subject distinctions' and experiences sovereignty within (p. 41). Because this leads to the idolatrous adoration of the interior 'king of kings', it results in backsliding (a spiritual 'state of emergency'), divine intervention and, paradoxically, the animation and restriction of 'the otherwise arbitrary nature of the Godly state of exception' (pp. 42, 17, 44). Cefalu then turns his focus to the treatment of idolatry in 'The Cross' and 'Good Friday'. Cefalu claims that the speaker of 'The Cross' cannot 'move from a state of *being* to one of *having* the cross', exists as no more than an 'objectified idol' to satisfy the divine, and thus becomes a 'hysterical subject' (pp. 51, 18, 52). In contrast, the speaker of 'Good Friday, 1613. Riding Westward' is diagnosed by Cefalu as a 'perverse' and 'masochistic' subject who is denied access to 'the symbolic' because of 'Christ's failure to establish paternal law' (pp. 53, 18). Cefalu, however, does find in the Holy Sonnets an interaction between the human and the divine that is rooted in 'agape or divine love' and which operates as 'the very expression of law' (p. 55).

While Cefalu's reading of Donne's political theology does, as he hopes, present an intelligent challenge to Deborah Kuller Shuger's vision of Donne's absolutism, too many fragments of theoretical texts are uneasily patched together in his analysis of the relation of sovereign and subject in Donne's writings. Further, the intersecting theories introduced into the analysis often unnecessarily weigh down and marginalize the language and belief systems of Donne's own time.

A monograph on the major themes in the works of Donne, Richard Sugg's *John Donne*, made its appearance this year. Sugg introduces his subject by engaging in imaginative exercises, inviting his readers to inhabit early modern London by referring to them in the second person: 'Little flurries of filthy and underfed children break like human surf around your knees; women carrying baskets of oranges cry their wares in an accent resembling nothing you have ever quite heard. Beggars rot in the mouths of alleyways' (p. 14). He describes Donne in equally vivid Dickensian prose, identifying him as 'one who lives on wits, nerves and charm all ground and polished by the gritty frictions of life outside the recognized social world' (p. 9). While these rhetorical strategies deviate from orthodox historiographical methods, they are clearly intended to draw the reader in, and the volume as a whole is comprised of a series of perceptive investigations of six central concerns in Donne's works: subjectivity or selfhood; gender and sexual politics; religious belief; natural philosophy; colonial discovery; and death and eternal life.

Sugg first explores the proto-modern 'oppositional self-hood' forged by Donne in his poetry, particularly in reaction to the Petrarchan lyric subject (p. 55). Sugg then considers how this Donnean self negotiates same-sex and opposite-sex relationships, concluding that all intimate liaisons for Donne are characterized by a 'fiercely personal emotion' regardless of whether the object of love is 'abused or elevated' (p. 93). Sugg next considers Donne's conception of sinfulness and 'spiritual inferiority', identifying it as largely Protestant in nature, though he points to the instability of Donne's religious leanings in other areas (p. 98). Sugg dissects the 'obsessive science of sin' in the early modern period to explain the 'intense personal drama' of transgression and deliverance in Donne's writings (pp. 105, 106). Sugg perceives in Donne's writings a tension between committed religious belief and compulsive intellectual inquisitiveness that leads Donne to ponder the ontological and theological implications of new discoveries in the field of anatomy. While Donne is drawn to anatomy, however, Sugg maintains that he cannot help but resist its 'aggressively demystifying power' (p. 141).

Sugg moves from science to colonialism in the sixth chapter of *John Donne*, where he traces Donne's diverse and shifting reactions to the Americas and records the 'powerful . . . restless, psychic pressure' that informs Donne's imaginative engagement with the New World, a terrain understood in gendered terms (p. 168). Sugg concludes the volume by remarking upon Donne's obsession with death and 'death-in-life', demonstrating that for Donne the annihilation of the self in death is simply a means to recover 'his full self' in eternity (pp. 191, 196)

A new Norton Critical Edition of *John Donne's Poetry*, edited by Donald R. Dickson, was issued this year. This volume benefits greatly from the work completed thus far on the Donne Variorum, an ongoing editorial project in which Dickson is involved. Dickson takes as his copy-text the Westmoreland manuscript, but is not bound by it where he finds authorial readings in other reliable manuscripts and, to a lesser degree, seventeenth-century printed editions. Dickson's careful delineation of the manuscripts and printed editions he has consulted, in addition to his precise recording of substantive variants for many of the 125 poems included, is extremely useful for scholars and students interested in the transmission of Donne's poetry. Although Dickson does not explain his selection process, the judiciously annotated poems included in the volume represent many of the poetic genres favoured by Donne: satire, elegy, verse letter, hymn, song, sonnet, lament and epithalamion. The volume contains nearly 250 pages of criticism on, for example, Donne's metaphysical poetics, ecclesiastical allegiances, professional identity, generic innovation, spiritual sensibility and sexual politics. Dickson's new edition will certainly help to ensure that Donne's 'voiceprint' continues to resonate with students, scholars and creative writers in the twenty-first century, thereby extending the 'afterlife' of John Donne.

3. Herbert

The most notable contribution to Herbert studies this year is Helen Wilcox's annotated edition *The English Poems of George Herbert*. Wilcox's stated aim is to make Herbert paradoxically clear and complex poetry available to the twenty-first-century reader. She does so with remarkable grace, combining vast knowledge with admirable clarity and conciseness. One senior Herbertian has nicknamed the book, not unjustly, 'the Wilcox Wonder'. Wilcox provides commentary on a wide range of subjects, including the intertextual relationships between the poetry and the Bible and the liturgy as well as the poetry of predecessor and contemporary poets, the poetry's relation to contemporary theological and political debates, and the forgotten meanings of the deceptively simple words that the poems employ. Among the tools she has included are a chronology and a glossary as well as an index of biblical references. The core of the book, though, is Wilcox's multi-part commentary on each poem, which addresses texts and sources, gives a short essay summarizing modern criticism of that poem, and then gives multiple pages of notes keyed to line numbers. Wilcox's ability to home in on key ideas and quotations from multiple scholars produces a lively sense of the debate surrounding the poems and makes her edition the natural starting point for anyone working on Herbert, from undergraduates to senior scholars. The only problem with her accomplishment is that it, naturally, does not extend into the future, and its fullness may inadvertently tempt readers to stop with her account. At the same time, her bringing to light of the history of Herbert criticism easily outweighs this limitation. Readers should also see Wilcox's article on Herbert and Donne, reviewed in the preceding Donne section.

Michael Schoenfeldt's 'George Herbert, God, and King' (in Cheney, Hadfield and Sullivan, eds., pp. 264–77) introduces readers to Herbert as 'a religious poet for readers who hate religious poetry, and for those who love it' (p. 264). His essay accomplishes with admirable breadth and insight a whirlwind tour of Herbert's poetry and why it matters. Schoenfeldt credits Herbert with writing a devotional poetry that is socially resonant and thus authentic, a divine poetry that is fully engaged with the world. Schoenfeldt begins by parting Herbert from his reputation as a poet of sweetness and light, pointing to his first 'Affliction' poem for evidence that Herbert's spiritual insight comes only through an ironic struggle with physical and spiritual grief. The passions of this poem lead to Schoenfeldt's observation that Herbert is 'a great poet of rebellion' (p. 267). He also points out Herbert's unusual awareness of the internal complications of praising God with art, noting his skill in exploring this problem through verse itself. At the same time, he credits Herbert as having 'a fuller and more inventive sense of the resources of lyric form than any previous writer in English', noting particularly Herbert's skill in making 'form an integral conceptual part of the poem' (p. 269). He demonstrates this skill in both Herbert's innovative forms (such as in 'The Collar' and 'Easter-wings') and in his reinvigoration of conventional forms such as the sonnet (noting the very different 'Prayer [I]' and 'Redemption'). Schoenfeldt then turns to the structure of *The Temple* as a whole, describing it as 'one of the most carefully constructed volumes of poetry published in its day' (p. 274). He concludes, appropriately, by observing that while Herbert's courtly and aesthetic accomplishments are great, he is remarkable as a poet of everyday life, most starkly in his poem 'Sion', in which the 'inglorious utterance of authentic emotion' bests the most glorious of temples as 'musick for a king' (p. 275).

The 2007 volume of the *George Herbert Journal* (dated 2004–5) published three articles as well as reprinting a popular early twentieth-century short story about Herbert with a new scholarly introduction. Of the three articles, two deal with the recurring quality of affliction in Herbert's poetry, albeit from two distinct—though both material—vantage points. Sarah Skwire, in 'George Herbert, Sin, and the Ague' (*GHJ* 28[2004–5] 1–27), argues that while Herbert's attention to bodily disease has been generally recognized by scholars, his particular naming of the disease as 'ague' in 'The Sinner' and 'Affliction [I]' has not until now been adequately explored. Significantly, ague was a malaria-like disease that, then as now, could not be entirely cured, but that dwelt in the body permanently, receding then recurring at intervals. Herbert's poetic figuring of ague as analogous to sin relies for its full effect upon the reader's familiarity with this inescapable and dire recurrence, a quality shared by the Calvinist category of sin. Herbert thus establishes the word as a signal for an inextricably tied bodily and spiritual suffering.

In ' "Thou didst betray me to a lingring book": Discovering Affliction in *The Temple*' (*GHJ* 28[2004–5] 28–46), Paul Dyck deals with the recurrence of affliction bibliographically, arguing that Herbert ordered his poetry to deliberately baffle his reader. In the manuscripts and early editions, the five 'Affliction' poems were not numbered as they are in modern editions, nor otherwise distinguished from each other. These poems, distributed through the first half of *The Temple*, confound a linear progression through the book by forcing the reader to identify and compare them. These recurring 'Afflictions' shape reading itself as an affliction, which Herbert teaches in the poems themselves, is a necessary experience for spiritual growth. Herbert thus connects the practice of gathering commonplaces with the bodily and spiritual subject of those commonplaces.

In ' "Light thy darknes is": George Herbert and Negative Theology' (*GHJ* 28[2004–5] 47–64), Hillary Kelleher effectively argues for the importance of Dionysius and the tradition of negative theology for Herbert's poetry. In a wonderfully economical article, Kelleher explains the relationship of the *via positiva* and the *via negativa* and shows them operating in *The Temple*, offering a coherent account of Herbert's ability, at times, to praise God and his realization, at other times, of the inadequacy of language. Her account of analogy as the figure of a positive identification of God with his work and paradox as the figure of divine otherness from the created order provides a generative way of understanding both figures in Herbert's poetry.

Frances M. Malpezzi's 'The Parson Fictionalized: A Reprise' (*GHJ* 28[2004–5] 65–86) reintroduces Margery Bowen's short story 'Holy Mr. Herbert', first published in *Harper's* in 1910. Bowen was one of many pen names of Margaret Gabrielle Vere Campbell Long, a self-educated and amazingly prolific writer of stories and novels. Malpezzi highlights Bowen's use of Izaac Walton's *Life of Herbert* for her characterization of the poet, which emphasizes his courtliness and humility. The tale features a newly married couple who have come, through trial, to fractious disagreement, and whose chance encounter with Herbert indirectly leads to reconciliation. While the tale presents a simplified Herbert who ministers chiefly through a natural sweetness and displays none of his reputed temper when interrupted in his work, it does have the virtue of demonstrating, in this Herbert's actions, some of the virtues he describes in his *Country Parson*. Here is the legendary ideal parson that might drive real parsons mad, in all his romantic glory.

In 'The Roman Steps to the Temple: An Examination of the Influence of Robert Southwell, SJ, upon George Herbert' (*Logos* 10[2007] 131–50) Gary M. Bouchard finds in Southwell a source for Herbert's mission to convert poetry to the service of God, and a source for some of Herbert's most memorable images, such as the heart as an altar. This argument is weakened, however, by a tendency to loosely attribute images and poetic movements to Southwell when they have a broader cultural prominence, for example the common trope of Christ as a 'sweet and saving wine' (p. 143). To his credit, though, Bouchard tells a vivid and generally creditable story of Southwell's cultural influence and likely influence on the younger poet, accounting well for the silence of this influence. He also uses the connection to draw out important differences between the poets, thus avoiding making too large a claim on Herbert and also putting the relationship to productive use.

Eric B. Song, in 'Anamorphosis and the Religious Subject of George Herbert's "Coloss. 3.3"' (*SEL* 47[2007] 107–21), works with Stanley Fish's reading of the poem, agreeing with Fish's conclusion that the double motion of the text, through its disruptive effect, gives the reader an experience of the elusive reality that is divine truth. Song accounts for this conclusion by drawing upon theories of anamorphosis from Baltrušaitis to Lacan to Kierkegaard, arguing that Herbert employs anamorphosis, disrupting the unity of apprehension to enact a body/spirit dualism. With particular attention to how the poem's diagonal text repeats and modulates the epigraph, which itself alters the biblical text to which the poem's title refers, Song argues that the poem does not, *contra* Fish, see the uniting of the speaker's voice with God's, but rather with the reader, in a common downward experience of human division and fallenness. Finally, though, the poem makes a third motion, from the central word *Him* up to the word Christ in the epigraph, inviting the reader to finish reading and to look at the poem as a unifying image of incarnation and resurrection that takes up and overcomes the haunting effects of anamorphosis.

In ' "This is the famous stone": George Herbert's Poetic Alchemy in "The Elixir" ' (in Linden, ed., *Mystical Metal of Gold: Essays on Alchemy and Renaissance Culture*, pp. 301–24), Yaakov Mascetti argues that Herbert uses alchemical language and method in 'The Elixir' to overcome a common theological dualism, and in the process fashion 'a new concept of metaphor, and of poetic text' (p. 305). Mascetti traces Herbert's revisions of this poem, which is available to us in three versions, from its dependence on organic metaphors to alchemical ones. He points out the theological problems of the earlier metaphors, in particular their suggestion of the efficacy of human works, as well as the early poem's fixity on human awareness. Alchemical modes of operation, Mascetti argues, allow Herbert to 'prepossess' a consciousness of God's grace and to thereby transmute the dross of human will into the gold of God's will (p. 304). In arguing for the alchemical operations of the poem, however, Mascetti reads the poetic act itself, rather than the earlier 'clause'—'All may of thee partake' (l. 13) as the 'famous stone/That turneth all to gold' (ll. 21–2). In so doing, he risks giving alchemical discourse priority and, in overcoming an allegedly dualistic and imprisoning theological discourse, reinscribing Herbert's celebration of common action as an esoteric operation.

Shiao C. Chong, in 'Interpreting the Self and George Herbert: Modern, Post-Modern and Biblical Alternatives' (in Bowen, ed., *The Strategic Smorgasbord of Postmodernity: Literature and the Christian Critic*, pp. 206–24), locates Herbert and representative Herbert criticism within a brief history of the self. He identifies Terry Sherwood and Helen Vendler as working respectively within rational and expressive versions of the modern accounts of the autonomous self, and Stanley Fish and Michael Schoenfeldt as working respectively within 'deconstructed' and 'pragmatic' versions of postmodern accounts of the contingent self. Chong finds both the optimism of modern accounts and the pessimism of postmodern accounts unsatisfactory, preferring instead a biblical account that would have been more familiar to Herbert: the self that exists on the condition of its relationship to the divine Other, and that becomes most fully itself as that relationship is more fully realized. Chong addresses the postmodern potential of this account by exploring its development in the work of Mikhail Bakhtin, and reading 'The Clasping of Hands' and 'Love' (p. 3) in terms of a conflict between the dialogical and the monological.

Material missed last year includes Sharon Achinstein's article 'Reading George Herbert in the Restoration' (*ELR* 36[2006] 430–65). Achinstein sheds light on Herbert's paradoxical status as a central figure of both Restoration Anglicanism and of nonconforming churches, which were at times bitterly opposed to each other. She argues that the former drew upon Herbert as a resource in politics and ecclesiology while the latter drew upon him in poetics and theology. Achinstein traces these uses of Herbert through the later seventeenth-century editions of his work, demonstrating how the poems 'Superliminare' and 'The Altar' were, in the 1674 edition, changed from textual pictures—things themselves—to engraved pictures of Restoration churches, pictures that relegate the poems to 'visual clues' (p. 434), firmly locating the poetry within an orthodox ecclesiology. She next traces Herbert's central place in the narration of the Restoration church, examining how Oley, Howell and Walton found in Herbert's ministry the ideal point of continuity between the pre-war church and the restored version: Achinstein points out particularly how Walton's pastoral account of Herbert's life functioned as the gentle counterpart to the harsh Second Conventicle Act (both 1670), at worst a nostalgic cover for a persecuting church. Against these uses of Herbert, Achinstein reads the Nonconformist John Bryan's sermons, published as *Dwelling with God*, also in 1670. Bryan made extensive use of Herbert, not as a figure of holiness, but as an experimentalist, whose poetry seeks God's presence within the heart, not within external structures such as those of the 1674 'Altar'. Achinstein shows how both Walton and Bryan omitted parts of Herbert's texts to achieve their ends (Walton, Herbert's love of Scripture; Bryan, Herbert's references to the propitiatory sacrifice of Christ and the ceremonial cup of the Eucharist), but more generally demonstrates the viability of the Nonconformist reading of Herbert, which she argues, has not been given its due.

A.W. Barnes, in 'Editing George Herbert's Ejaculations' (*T & C* 1[2006] 90–113), asserts a tension within the first edition of *The Temple* between its devotional and its poetic natures. While, on the one hand, Herbert reportedly asked Nicholas Ferrar to publish the book only if he thought 'it might turn to the advantage of any dejected poor soul', on the other Ferrar claimed in his preface to the book 'to leave it free and unforestalled to every man's judgement' (p. 90). In the first, Barnes finds an anxiety of Herbert's to 'restrict readership to the Anglican faithful' as a devotional text (p. 91), while in the second he sees an invitation on the part of Ferrar to offer the text to all for their judgement of it as poetry. That the claims coexist he attributes to the unstable printing history of the early seventeenth century, a instability that is expressed particularly in the volume's subtitle: 'Sacred Poems and Private Ejaculations'. Barnes goes on to trace the text's reception by later poets William Cowper and Samuel Taylor Coleridge (who both came to see a union of its poetic and devotional qualities) and then to examine the treatment of its subtitle in nineteenth- and twentieth-century editions, concluding that the frequent dropping of the subtitle limits the ability of modern readers to understand the original reception of the book. Barnes's argument would be stronger if he explained his repeated assertion that Herbert's desire to reach 'any dejected poor soul' meant a wish to restrict his audience, how Ferrar's invitation foregrounds poetry over devotion, and how 'ejaculations' encodes the conflict Barnes sees between the two.

Anne-Marie Miller Blaise, in 'Beauté et iconicité dans *The Temple* de George Herbert: "If I but lift mine eyes" ' (*EA* 59[2006] 131–44), deals with the problematical status of beauty—especially that of art—for a Christian poet such as George Herbert. In the light of the theology of icons which was elaborated by the Greek Fathers, it attempts to show how the visual qualities of Herbert's poems become the tool for reconciling worldly and divine beauties. By truly teaching the reader how to see properly, they pre-empt both the typically baroque threat of shapelessness and the risk of idolatry which was such a strong concern in seventeenth-century England.

Andrew Mattison, in ' "Keep your measures": Herrick, Herbert, and the Resistance to Music' (*Criticism* 48[2006] 323–46), takes on Walter Pater's truism that 'all art constantly aspires to the condition of music'. In his close reading of several poems of Herbert and Herrick, Mattison argues, rather, that in this moment of the development of lyric poetry, poetic references to music accomplish not aspiration but resistance. Mattison reads Herbert's 'Grief', 'Deniall' and 'Church Music', demonstrating that these poems' musical references and self-conscious experiments in rhythm and rhyme do not attempt a mimesis of sounded music, but refer rather to an ideal music, the music of proportion theorized by Pythagoras and Plato. To prove his point, which seems to rely upon Herbert's suspicion of the body, Mattison points to Herrick, who robustly celebrates the body. Mattison finds in Herrick's poems 'To Music' and 'To M. *Henry Lawes*' celebrations of an ideal that performed music cannot achieve. In both poets, then, he reads the difference between the form of the poem and form of the music the poem describes not as a failure of poetry, but as the grounds of poetry's ability to do what music cannot.

Gregory Kneidel's 'Herbert and Exactness' (*ELR* 36[2006] 278–303) does the difficult but rewarding work of placing Herbert's parson within the theological-rhetorical nuances of the seventeenth century. Kneidel takes on recent work on the *Country Parson*, acknowledging the value of its counter-hagiography, but critiquing its identification of courtesy and entrepreneurial literature as the primary models for Herbert's work. Rather, he argues, we should take seriously Herbert's own stated model for the ideal parson: not Christ the Good Shepherd, but Christ the crucified Son of God. Kneidel takes up the language of Herbert and others to describe the afflictions of Christ for the body of Christ that is the church, examining in particular the debate over the exactness of Christ's affliction: the question of whether, as Catholics argued, Christ's suffering was inexact and excessive and continued into the present-day meritorious suffering of the church, or whether Christ paid an exact price, a satisfaction of sin that requires nothing more for completion. In his careful reading of 'Dialogue', Kneidel finds a drama in which the Catholic idea of a treasury of grace is replaced with a double-entry balance sheet. In his poetry, then, Herbert rejects the idea of a meritorious imitation of Christ while having the speaker complete the already completed work of Christ. His idea of the priest takes up this completing of the already completed. Working from Colossians 1.24, in which Paul 'fills up that which is behind of the afflictions of Christ' (p. 279), Herbert develops a model of the parson's exact affliction, an affliction of the parson as the parson embodies the congregation. The parson exercises self-control and thus authority not as a proto-panopticon, but as Christ on the cross, afflicted and afflicting, reproving his church not as an end but as the means to the life of the body. It is precisely this Protestant emphasis on collective religious experience that has been obscured by the current critical preoccupation with introspective individualism.

4. Milton

The pace of scholarly production focused on John Milton's poetry and prose shows no sign of decreasing as we approach the 400th anniversary of Milton's birth in 2008. Along with a year's worth of exhibitions, lectures and performances presented at Christ's College, Cambridge, the New York Public Library, the Morgan Library and Museum, the Bodleian Library and elsewhere, we soon can expect to see a flood of celebratory publications. The pre-quadricentennial year of 2007 brings us several single-author studies and editions likely to enjoy a shelf-life that could extend for decades, if not centuries; on the distant horizon looms a new complete edition of Milton published by Oxford University Press under the general editorship of Thomas Corns and Gordon Campbell, with the first volume, *De Doctrina Christiana*, slated to appear in 2008.

The authorship of the *De Doctrina* manuscript continues to provoke debate, and the first fruits of this fresh bout of editorial labour appear in *Milton and the Manuscript of 'De Doctrina Christiana'*, a collaborative effort by Campbell, Corns, John K. Hale and Fiona J. Tweedie. The ascription of *De Doctrina* resurfaced as an issue in the 1990s, when William B. Hunter argued for identifying its author as one of Milton's students, an unknown writer whose choice of authorities rarely overlaps with the theologians upon whom Milton usually relied. Denying Milton the authorship of the treatise sometimes joins with a recuperative effort to bring him back into the fold of religious orthodoxy. However we choose to understand the intentions of participants in the authorship debate, much of the evidence against ascribing it to Milton remains convincing. The authors of this study muster support from the study of the manuscript's transmission and method of composition, from computer-assisted stylometrics and the study of the treatise's Latinity, to conclude that, 'if one adopts a nuanced sense of what constitutes authorship in a genre (that of systematic theology) with strict conventions that make many examples seem remarkably similar, then Milton may be said to be the author of the treatise' (p. 3). In a telling sentence, the study pronounces the theology of *De Doctrina* 'unexceptionable', apart from 'a small number of doctrines, some central (e.g. Christology), some peripheral (e.g. the creation) and some immensely contentious in the seventeenth century (e.g. mortalism)' (p. 92). Numerous small revelations appear in chapter 2, which traces the history of the manuscript in its journey from Milton's house in Bunhill Fields to the Old State Paper Office at Whitehall, where it turned up in 1823. The chapter weaves a compelling narrative from biographical information about two early scribes of *De Doctrina*—Jeremie Picard and the slightly disreputable Daniel Skinner—stories that have all the telling incidental detail of good fiction. Evidence for the manuscript's provenance, however, no matter how deftly handled, can settle nothing conclusively, and irrefutable proof of Milton's authorship has yet to emerge. Even at this late date, the problems have not yielded to a battery of approaches, or to the collective theological, archival, linguistic, stylistic, classical and bibliographical expertise deployed here.

Another crack team of Miltonists, William Kerrigan, John Rumrich and Stephen M. Fallon, have produced a single-volume rival, *The Complete Poetry and Essential Prose of John Milton*, to what many still consider the gold standard: Merritt Y. Hughes 1957 *Complete Poems and Major Prose*. This new edition makes available all the poetry and most of the prose studied in undergraduate classes, packaged in a judiciously edited, modernized edition of 1,365 pages. Instructors will find the excerpts from the controversial prose adequate for most purposes, and the brief introductions models of economy, insight and stylish writing. Only the list of Works Cited strikes me as flawed, that is, insufficiently selective, somewhat dated and organized on no principle other than alphabetical order.

With Barbara Lewalski's militantly unmodernized version of *Paradise Lost*, Blackwell has published the first of a three-volume student edition of the complete poetry and major prose. Lewalski's decision to preserve the spelling, italicization and punctuation of the epic proceeds on the ground that 'the characteristic light punctuation of the 1674 edition builds up and maintains an energetic, pulsating tempo that pushes the reader through the verse paragraphs', and that modernizing punctuation 'often breaks rhythmic patterns readers are intended to hear and can learn pretty quickly how to read' (p. xxxiii). The real strength of the text comes in the annotations, which Lewalski supplies sparingly but with unwavering good judgement and profound erudition. The approach here recalls Lewalski's editorial work, with Andrew J. Sabol, some three decades ago in *Major Poets of the Earlier Seventeenth Century* (Odyssey Press [1973]), another textbook that adapted current scholarship to the needs of undergraduate readers without ever condescending to them.

A useful pedagogical aid for undergraduate teachers of Milton is Margaret Olofson Thickstun's *Milton's 'Paradise Lost': Moral Education*, which leans on developmental psychology to outline a reading of the poem that places moral development at its centre. Attention to 'teachable moments' found in the poem fuses seamlessly with current Milton scholarship and psychological research on adolescent quandaries involving God the Father, peer pressure, parents, relationships, work and self-determination. A middle-aged professor who raises these issues with 18-year-olds does so at the risk of coming off a bit like Dr Phil, dispensing well-meaning advice about life strategies. Yet Thickstun teaches us how to navigate these dangerous shoals, approaching moral issues intelligently and with admirable aplomb.

A fairly specialized and very welcome *Paradise Lost* appears in John T. Shawcross and Michael Lieb's version of the 1667 first edition, a volume based on a fresh examination of the sources and buttressed with a detailed textual apparatus but no annotations. This text represents a considerable advance over the frequently consulted (but unreliable) facsimiles by Harris Francis Fletcher [1945] and the Scolar Press [1968], and provides able guidance to the early publishing history of the poem. Lieb and Shawcross have also collected ten essays in a companion volume to supplement their new edition, all of which attempt to breathe new life into the classic by approaching it through 'the contemporary political, social, religious, biographical, and literary contexts' from which it emerged (pp. vii–viii). Lieb's own essay in the collection, 'Back to the Future: *Paradise Lost* 1667', offers 'a reading in which the first edition is viewed as a work at once fully in command of its own destiny, distinguished by its own shape, its own integrity, its own sense of beingness' (p. 3), without having it supersede the canonical work to come. Stephen B. Dobranski's 'Simmons's Shell Game: The Six Title Pages of *Paradise Lost*' focuses on a key detail and analyses the six different title pages issued by the publisher Samuel Simmons between 1667 and 1674. Dobranski sets out to answer the obvious yet perplexing question of why Simmons went to the trouble of updating the title page in the same edition. The essay provides some very concrete discussion of Simmons's customary marketing strategies and the practices of booksellers and compositors, thus effectively situating the poet in a seventeenth-century milieu of authors, readers and printers to which be belonged. Joseph Wittreich's '"More and more perceiving": Paraphernalia and Purpose in *Paradise Lost*, 1668, 1669' also pays close attention to the materiality of the book and the semiotics of the paratext. The same Milton who wrote in *Areopagitica* of five imprimaturs 'seen together dialogue-wise in the Piatza of one Title page, complementing and ducking each to other' very likely maintained some level of involvement in the typography and design of his books. Wittreich concerns himself with the process of 'accretion' that transformed an unadorned book into the swollen, formal-dress productions of the eighteenth century: thus, 'a look at the first edition of *Paradise Lost* in its various states forecasts a larger history' (p. 34). Achsah Guibbory's 'Milton's 1667 *Paradise Lost* in its Historical and Literary Contexts' situates the poem in relation to Charles II's restoration, High Church apologetics, experimental philosophy, and to younger writers such as John Dryden. Richard J. DuRocher's 'The Emperor's New Clothes: The Royal Fashion of Satan and Charles II' argues that 'Milton's references to Satan as a "great Sultan", or Muslim tyrant, ominously reflect the king's chosen style of dress between 1666 and 1670–2, specifically his brief adoption of the so-called Persian vest as a distinguishing feature of his court' (p. 100). Charles gave up on affecting Middle Eastern style (if not imperial grandeur) by 1672. Yet Milton's description at the opening of Book II of Satan sitting exalted on a 'Throne of Royal State, which far/Outshone the wealth of Ormus and of Ind' subtly underlines a resemblance between the fallen angel and the restored monarch. Two other contributions—by Laura Lunger Knoppers and Bryan Adams Hampton—also explore Milton in the context of Restoration public culture, and Phillip J. Donnelly and Michael Bryson write on the philosophical and theological aspects of the epic. Closing out the volume, John T. Shawcross contributes an essay that reiterates some of the larger themes that animate the project as a whole.

A commitment to bringing current Milton scholarship into the undergraduate classroom gathered new momentum in 2007. One valuable pedagogical tool, a sort of how-to manual that dispenses excellent advice for anyone daunted at the prospect of venturing beyond *Paradise Lost* at a state or redbrick university, has appeared with the latest entry in the MLA series on teaching world literature, Peter C. Herman, ed., *Approaches to Teaching Milton's Shorter Poetry and Prose*. Some thirty-seven Miltonists explore approaches to general subjects such as Milton and nationalism (Andrew Escobedo), Milton and Hebraism (Jason P. Rosenblatt) and Milton and textual studies (Stephen B. Dobranski), and also provide valuable guidance for teaching specific texts: Elizabeth Sauer writes on two political sonnets, Richard Rambuss on 'On the Morning of Christ's Nativity', David Loewenstein on *Samson Agonistes*, Laura Lunger Knoppers on *Eikonoklastes*, and so forth. In comparison to the 1986 *Approaches to Teaching Milton's 'Paradise Lost'*, edited by Galbraith M. Crump, the methods here gravitate towards offering practical suggestions, providing resources and sharing tactics for overcoming anticipated obstacles. Many of the pieces carry the subtext that teachers of Milton can expect some level of resistance to these reading assignments. As the editor, Peter C. Herman, notes: 'There are few prose stylists as difficult as Milton. His verse often participates in genres that have become alien to contemporary culture, and his prose often concerns issues and controversies far from the "knowledge base" of most contemporary students' (p. xi). Yet the effect of reading through these short contributions is oddly reassuring, something like taking part in a roundtable discussion with our most intellectually generous and pedagogically innovative colleagues.

The 'road map' they provide charts a vast portion of a terrain both varied and 'ferociously difficult' (p. 17) for those who venture on it.

Designed for students themselves rather than their teachers, *A Concise Companion to Milton*, edited by Angelica Duran, joins Blackwell's much bulkier *Companion to Milton* [2001] and surveys many of the topics that routinely turn up in survey courses. Among the distinguished contributors we find Robert Thomas Fallon, John T. Shawcross, Annabel Patterson, Paul Alpers, Achsah Guibbory and others. In his brief survey of three centuries of Milton criticism, Flannagan identifies 'interest in Milton's science', combined with 'an ecological perspective' (p. 56), as a notable trend in the Milton criticism of the twenty-first century, and Juliet Lucy Cummins contributes a chapter on 'The Ecology of *Paradise Lost*' that attempts to institutionalize an ecocritical approach, in a manner analogous to the way in which topics such as Milton and the Bible and Milton and gender functioned for earlier generations. Indeed, a wave of recent work explores Milton not only as an Edenic pastoral poet but as a green writer, a poet conscious of seventeenth-century natural philosophy who responded to the scientific revolution in a manner rightly considered 'ecological'.

In *Milton's Uncertain Eden: Understanding Place in 'Paradise Lost'* Andrew Mattison argues that 'Milton's descriptions of place work to unite the poem's preplasarian and postlapsarian sections, while simultaneously taking part in trans-historical textual interchanges that blur the poem's relationship to the historical conditions of its production' (p. 5). In other words, Mattison contends that topical descriptions in the poem, our sense of Eden's landscape (and Adam's, too) undermine Milton's theodicy, that the problem of understanding the surrounding environment becomes central to the meaning of the Fall at a time when the discussion of place has given way to an abstract conception of space as extension. To put the problem in slightly different terms, the reader and Adam share the difficulty of locating themselves in respect to their surroundings in *Paradise Lost*, and this difficulty works within the poem to disrupt any attempt to make sense of it in exclusively theological terms. The struggle to understand place remains constant before and after the Fall. Understanding the epic in terms a poetics of space, Mattison maintains, shifts the burden of interpretation away from theological and historical considerations, the dominant modes of Milton criticism, and on to theory. Still, Mattison's quarrels are mainly with other Miltonists and he begins the study with a chapter that reinstates Virgilian pastoral as a primary context for Milton's epic, focusing on transactions with the landscape in which characters seek consolation yet fail to find it. Chapter 2, 'The Environs of Imagination: *Paradise Lost* 7 and 8', explores the difficulty Adam and Raphael encounter in describing place, and concludes, in a mildly deconstructive spirit, that any recourse to locality intended to 'create certainty' finds itself inevitably undermined by an uncertainty inherent to environment. To summarize in a nutshell: 'Raphael's predicament shows the power of place: the indescribability of Eden presents a serious obstacle to a discourse of the human condition and the Fall' (p. 79). Two more chapters take up Books IX and X of *Paradise Lost*, and further explore the insurmountable problems of conceptualizing place outside of time before the Fall, or of coming to terms with it after the Fall, with both activities being constrained by the limitations of language. The same Edenic landscape that functions as a site of human labour and physical interaction continues to serve in the postlapsarian world as a place rather than a state of being or abstract idea.

John Gillies, in 'Space and Place in *Paradise Lost*' (*ELH* 74[2007] 27–57), cites Edmund S. Casey's *The Fate of Place*, as does Mattison, on how 'space and place had decisively parted company in scientific and philosophical discourse of the period, with place being supplanted from physics and metaphysics alike by space' (p. 27). Gillies argues that Milton accommodates the new scientific thought by conceptualizing place in terms of the body rather than the mind, and by mediating the opposition between space and place in terms of 'a third domain: room' (p. 32). Reading Milton as a 'profoundly corporeal and correspondingly placial' writer (p. 39), Gillies pictures the Miltonic 'room' as a physical and metaphysical environment, less a given place than a moral and spiritual centre. Bodies and places undergo a subtle sort of fusion in Milton's physicalist theology, and the motif of room comes to sustain his imagining of heaven and hell at a time when science has stripped place of much of its traditional meaning.

Similarly influenced by Edmund Casey's work but reaching different conclusions, Maura Brady's 'Space and the Persistence of Place in *Paradise Lost*' (*MiltonQ* 41[2007] 167–82) holds that the modern idea of space does not appear full-blown in Isaac Newton's *Principia Mathematica*, but that 'emergent notions about space were in play with other, older ways of conceiving the physical world' (p. 167), a study of which reveals how Milton's epic participated in the early modern production of space. Brady situates *Paradise Lost* on the cusp of modernity, at a historical moment before space enters Western consciousness as something absolute and inert, linking Milton's conception of an animate, sensate space to the work of Thomas Campanella. The spaces through which Satan travels in his flight from Hell anticipate modern astronomy, with its innumerable worlds and distant stars. The cosmic emptiness of *Paradise Lost*, however, does not serve as an inert medium for planetary motion but as an actively productive force in its own right: hovering on the brink of modernity, 'the poem registers emergent features of modern space, but also their disruption by the persistence of place' (p. 178).

The two phrases that together comprise the title of Angelica Duran's *The Age of Milton and the Scientific Revolution* might look like strange bedfellows as well as problematic in their own right. To view the intersection of science and poetry in the seventeenth century through the prism of a single author— one whose career, especially towards the end, kept him remote from the networks of knowledge production associated with the Royal Society— presents a formidable challenge. In recent years Harinder Marjara, John Rogers, Stephen Fallon, Denise Albanese, Karen Edwards and others have attempted, in various ways and with considerable success, to close the gap between Milton's theocentric views and scientific materialism, and to account for his seemingly sceptical treatment of experimental science in *Paradise Lost*. Duran overcomes the difficulty of this task by writing a book more about educational theory and humanist practice than on relations between scientific and literary cultures in Milton's day, while reiterating versions of her 'belief that by joining literary studies to scientific scholarship we may grapple—if not elegantly, at least honestly—with the extent to which Milton's poetic lines work in conjunction with mathematical lines and scientific texts to sketch out a responsible moving image of the compatible role of the literary and the scientific' (p. 19). To portray Milton as 'deeply engaged with the chief concerns of his scientifically minded contemporaries' (p. 1) requires some sleight of hand since Milton tends not to name his scientific sources, yet Duran reminds us in her first chapter of Milton's contacts with the circle around Samuel Hartlib, with Henry Oldenburg, Robert Boyle and others (pp. 38–48). Chapters 3 and 4 deal with the archangels as practitioners of the new scientific method of experimentation and as teachers of natural history. Chapter 5 gives an 'account of some of the features of curricular changes in seventeenth-century England and Milton's role in them' (p. 114), and chapter 6 looks at shifts in disciplinary knowledge during the period as witnessed in *L'Allegro*, *Il Penseroso* and *Comus*. The next chapter, on the curricular reform described in *Of Education*, lays the groundwork for a chapter on 'The Sexual Mathematics of *Paradise Lost*', which concentrates on scenes of instruction in Books IV and VIII where 'Milton incorporates the new mathematical universe into a productive, human worldview' (p. 180). Although these chapters teem with fascinating quotation, the analysis of scientific thought can appear quite thin, and Duran makes guarded use of the history of mathematics or astronomy. Four vigorously argued chapters bring *Comus*, *Paradise Regained* and *Samson Agonistes* into conjunction with the intellectual ferment precipitated by the new science, winding the discussion around to educational theory and the Baconian advancement of learning, without, however, saying much about the specific scientific disciplines that informed contemporary understandings of nature.

Diane McColley's *Poetry and Ecology in the Age of Milton and Marvell* depicts Bacon as an apostle of instrumental reason against whom she pits a view of language and of nature associated with seventeenth-century poets who responded to the aspirations of the new science and technology with moral critique. McColley joins literary scholars, feminist historians of science and other critics of modernity in claiming that Bacon's scientific programme demanded unequivocal language and the domination of nature—language Adam himself seems to echo in Book IV when he speaks of the 'power and rule/Conferred upon us, and dominion giv'n/Over all other creatures that possess/Earth, air, and sea' (pp. 207–8). McColley unearths in the writing of several poets a vein appropriately described as 'ecological' in its concern for humanity's systematic depredations of nature. In her extended discussion of 'Milton's Prophetic Epics' in chapter 7, McColley proposes that Milton embraces a theology that charges human beings, 'the species gifted with discursive reason, articulate speech, and a capacity for magnanimity', with a custodial function she calls 'earth-care' (p. 197). Characterizing the wounding of the earth at the Fall as 'an ecological disaster', McColley makes a case for environmental stewardship as a moral imperative. In God's judgement, 'the pleasant task of dressing and keeping the earth becomes the necessity of tilling the soil by the sweat of one's brow; original responsibility now becomes regenerative necessity' (p. 223). It is Milton the monist and vitalist who shines through most clearly in this study, not the patriarchalist and staunch monotheist of earlier criticism but a devotee of Gaia. Commenting on the language of the Creation in Book VII, McColley observes: 'For Milton, Earth, like a woman, is not merely a vessel. Earth's womb is the soil in and from which lives are formed, and animals' energies are self-activated in the process of emergence' (p. 161). Milton, along with George Herbert, Henry Vaughan, Thomas Traherne and Margaret Cavendish, 'confront[ed] the new philosophy and technology in language that asserts the life of nature and promotes the life of words that are rooted in the natural world as well as the human community' (p. 62); theology served them well in their resistance to Baconian materialism.

Catherine Gimelli Martin's chapter 'Rewriting the Revolution: Milton, Bacon, and the Royal Society Rhetoricians' (in Cummins and Burchell, eds., *Science, Literature and Rhetoric in Early Modern England*, pp. 102), casts Milton's Baconianism in a somewhat different light, following in the footsteps of a earlier generation of scholars for whom Bacon's influence went almost without saying. Milton's understanding of language, Martin writes, aligns Milton with Royal Society stalwarts such as Abraham Cowley, Thomas Sprat and John Wilkins, 'who commonly believed that the knowledge of God and his laws must first be grounded in a concrete knowledge of language and nature, not vice versa', even though Milton placed greater emphasis on rhetoric and logic than they did. In making the case for Milton's intellectual affiliation with the virtuosi, figures ordinarily identified with the Restoration court and royal patronage, Martin underlines Milton's disenchantment with the political and religious views of the Puritan establishment, particularly in the matter of 'Milton's dedication to full religious toleration' (p. 115). Noting a resemblance between Satan and the Calvinist saints, Martin sees in Milton's rhetoric a repudiation of obscurantist mysticism and the embrace of ideals now associated with Enlightenment rationalism.

Milton and Toleration gathers fifteen essays, along with an afterword and introduction, of consistently high quality and sharp focus on this issue, which combine to make the volume one of the most rewarding and provocative collections on Milton to appear in many years. Considering the importance of the topic, not only to Miltonists but also to political scientists, historians, theologians and researchers in other disciplines, the volume fills a substantial gap and should provide a starting point for future investigations of Milton's putative liberalism. The co-editors, Sharon Achinstein and Elizabeth Sauer, offer in part I a revisionist view of Whiggish and progressivist accounts of Milton's and England's role in disseminating tolerationist theories: Nigel Smith writes on toleration's broader European contexts, David Loewenstein on 'Toleration and the Specter of Heresy in Milton's England', Thomas Corns on Milton's relation to Roger Williams (author of *The Bloudy Tenent, of Persecution*) and Nicholas von Maltzahn on religious tolerance in Milton and Marvell. These rigorously historicist contributions set the question of Milton's position in multiple frameworks and resist a simplified narrative where the poet figures as a precursor of John Locke and herald of Enlightenment thinking. As the editors remind us, Milton does not always appear in his writing as a defender of liberty of conscience and implacable foe of religious persecution. Another, less tolerant, Milton 'restricted his appeal to civil liberties and freedoms of the press to Protestants, with the Roman Church ever vilified for its tyrannies; this Milton was largely silent on the proposed readmission of the Jews in 1655; this Milton championed Cromwell's campaign against the Roman Catholic Irish in the 1649 *Observations*; and this Milton spattered his writings across his career with anti-Catholic satire and invective. His last pamphlet, *Of True Religion*, protested against the toleration of Roman Catholics when English political leaders were considering a Catholic Indulgence' (p. 2).

Rather than substituting an image of an intolerant, bigoted Milton for a formerly liberal one, the collection demonstrates how the poet engages other modern discourses that intersect tolerationism, including 'liberty of conscience, natural law, equity, materialism, libertinism, rhetoric, secularism, even literature itself' (pp. 3–4). Part II, 'Philosophical and Religious Engagements', features James Grantham Turner on libertinism (with glances towards Giordano Bruno and Pietro Aretino), Jason P. Rosenblatt on natural law (Hugo Grotius, John Selden, Locke etc.), and Victoria Silver on legal theory. Martin Dzelzainis and Andrew Hadfield round out this section in essays that deal, respectively, with Milton in relation to antitrinitarianism and Roman Catholicism. Literature comes to the fore in Part III, with Sauer's essay on 'Toleration and Nationhood in the 1650s: "Sonnet XV" and the Case of Ireland', which explores the relation between toleration and imperialism during the Interregnum. Achinstein incisively and very astutely confronts a problem in Milton's poetry with her 'Toleration in Milton's Epics: A Chimera?'. Noting the absence of a utopian ideal of toleration in the major poems, she shows how 'Milton presents a vision of tolerance from within Christianity' (p. 242), where it serves mainly to safeguard the conscience and combat superstition. In his 'Intolerance and the Virtues of Sacred Vehemence', Paul Stevens points out an apparent discontinuity in Milton's writing between competing drives towards toleration and exclusion, and explains how Milton's 'rhetoric of violence seems to develop into something less obviously at odds with his rival commitment to liberty of conscience' (p. 248). Lana Cable's contribution explores links between secularism and republicanism, and Gerald MacLean adds to a growing body of recent scholarship on relations between the Ottomans and Christian Europe in the early modern period, revealing a series of unsuspected affinities between the English poet and thinkers in the Muslim world. The range and diversity of the insights afforded by this tightly interwoven book of essays discourage any attempt at brief summary, and each of them adds something substantial to a conversation that has implications for political philosophy and postcolonial theory.

Melissa M. Caldwell, 'Minds Indifferent: Milton, Lord Brooke, and the Value of *Adiaphora* on the Eve of the English Civil War' (*SC* 22[2007] 97–123), describes a historical moment before the outbreak of civil war when the principles of toleration and moral obligation came into conflict, and Robert Greville, second Baron Brooke, and Milton both considered the doctrine of *adiaphora* (indifference to matters external to moral law) as a justification for limiting freedom of conscience, Milton only to reject it. Caldwell concludes that Milton later returned to the doctrine in *Areopagitica*, which contrasts 'tolerated Popery' with indifferent matters that need not provoke strife (pp. 117–18). Following a similar drift in recent scholarship, Christopher N. Warren, 'When Self-Preservation Bids: Approaching Milton, Hobbes, and Dissent' (*ELR* 37[2007] 118–50), returns to the historical conjuncture of the Restoration and discovers an overlap between Hobbes's thought on religious toleration and Milton's. Assembling evidence of a tolerationist strain in the *Leviathan*, Warren goes on to read *Samson Agonistes* as Milton's confrontation with certain aspects of Hobbesian theory, and to treat the political dynamic of the 1660s as riven by ideologies more various and complicated than republicanism versus royalism, which had the effect of landing the ostensible antagonists Hobbes and Milton in the same anti-clerical camp.

Not all of this year's work on *Samson* follows a political bent. Ever since the discoveries several years ago that John Milton Senior served as a trustee of the Blackfriars playhouse (located close to the Miltons's house in Bread Street) and may have contributed a commendatory poem to Shakespeare's First Folio, conventional wisdom concerning Milton's attitude towards the theatre has needed re-evaluating. In its opening chapter Timothy J. Burbery's *Milton the Dramatist* explores Milton's experience as a theatre-goer and as a reader and annotator of drama. Burbery finds in the references to play-going in *Elegia Prima* and *L'Allegro* evidence of Milton's attendance at the theatre, specifically at a 1626 production of Ben Jonson's *The Staple of News*. The argument seems plausible, if impossible to prove, and helps to explain Jonsonian borrowings in Milton's early writings, which receive far less critical notice than his Shakespearian debts. The movement from *Arcades* to *Comus*, Burbery argues, traces an arc of artistic development as the young Milton mastered masque conventions and then tried his hand at dramatic forms. In another chapter Burbery lays out the case for Milton as a foe of the anti-theatrical prejudice, and finds in *The Reason of Church-Government*, published around the time of the closing of the theatres, a powerful argument for elevating the standards of the public entertainment. Milton's jottings in the Trinity manuscript, the projected tragedies based on the Bible or British history, suggest that he continued to think about the possibilities of the stage throughout the 1640s. In these fragments 'we see a playwright at work, selecting subjects, experimenting with titles, writing down personae lists, outlining plots, and confronting problems of physical staging and characterization' (p. 67). The logic of his position, which to this point has leaned heavily on plausible scenarios (formulae such as 'it is even possible' do some heavy lifting) shifts in two chapters on *Samson Agonistes* and its performance history. Here he depends on a conceptual split between genuine drama and mere poetry. Burbery reminds us that the closing of the theatres in 1642 and Milton's blindness a decade later certainly put a damper on his enjoyment of theatrical spectacle. In addition, he very reasonably holds that 'Milton's unwillingness to put *Samson* on stage stemmed principally from his lack of significant personal contact with the theater of his day, and from the fact that he would have had little control over production details' (p. 96). Burbery treats Milton as a writer who strives throughout his career to overcome the problems that mar his early work as a dramatist and sees in *Samson* the realization of this promise, the culmination of his talent in a work that rivals its Greek models. Burbery concludes his useful study with an aesthetic judgement, that 'while the overall dramatic achievement of Milton' does not match that of Jean Racine, his biblical and neoclassical drama compares very favourably to two works in the same vein, *Athalie* and *Phèdre* (pp. 170–4).

Burbery paints Milton as a patron of the theatre who found himself, after 1660, understandably scandalized by the Restoration stage, someone who 'never intended' (as he phrased it the prefatory epistle to *Samson Agonistes*) to stage his work in a space he would have to share with the likes of William Wycherly and other libertine playwrights. Christopher D'Addario's *Exile and Journey in Seventeenth-Century Literature*, which devotes a chapter to Milton, sees the poet as living in far more straitened circumstances between 1660 and 1667. Reading *The Readie and Easie Way* and *Paradise Lost* along with Thomas Hobbes, John Dryden and other writers who found themselves on the losing side of seventeenth-century political conflicts, he finds Milton struggling with the defeat of revolutionary hope and seeking 'to counteract the specific exigencies of political and religious displacement and his marginalization as a writer through the formulation of new modes of speaking as well as transformations of old' (p. 88). Driven into internal exile after the reversals of 1660, removed from social contact and public spaces, D'Addario registers the distance of Milton's art and language from the dominant discursive modes of the time: 'Milton, blind, briefly imprisoned and otherwise sequestered, would have heard keenly the drunken shouts for Charles Stuart around the bonfires that burned calves' rumps in effigy of the Rump Parliament, as well as the reports of attacks on Puritan ministers, the burning of the Commonwealth's arms and the extravagant pageantry of the king's return' (p. 7). Milton and the other exiles who had little appetite for Restoration culture and literature retreated to idiosyncratic forms of self-expression and uses of language. D'Addario considers Milton's apparent isolation from contemporary events a mode of engagement: despite the occasional acknowledgement of the pressure of Restoration culture and politics on *Paradise Lost*, 'Milton, at specific junctures in the poem, presents himself and his creative efforts as sequestered from the public world in which he so recently had participated' (p. 103).

The distinguished historian Blair Worden believes that academic literary criticism, despite the historicist work of the last three decades, resists placing *Samson Agonistes* in the context of contemporary political developments. The title of his most recent book, *Literature and Politics in Cromwellian England*, makes his basic claim explicit, and in ten chapters approaches Milton biographically and politically. The study as a whole paints a triptych that considers the careers of Milton, Andrew Marvell and Marchamont Nedham in conjunction. Worden's periodic reminders that we should not detach Milton from the world he inhabited might seem superfluous, even quaint, to a generation reared on new historicism, but Worden weaves together the prose writings of Milton and his contemporaries with particular care for the resemblances and divergences among them. Showing how Cromwellian rule tutored Milton in 'the uses of oblique political commentary' (p. 385) prepares the ground for a topical re-reading of the major poems, yet these sections appear as something of an afterthought. In a chapter on *Samson Agonistes*

Worden provides a relatively sustained analysis of the drama against the events and ideas of 1660–2, a few years earlier than most literary scholars would place it, a conclusion more or less determined by the chronological focus of the study. Worden proceeds to map his finely detailed knowledge of the period's controversies on to *Samson*, detecting a correspondence between the argument between Samson and Manoa and a debate among commonwealth men such as Edmund Ludlow, Algernon Sidney and Sir Henry Vane. Any literary scholar naive enough to treat biblical analogies in poetry as evidence of timeless transcendence will learn that Scripture can take on political coloration, that 'any Puritan reader of a poem about Samson—with whom Milton had earlier compared first Charles I and then the nation which opposed him—would have read it with an eye to the present' (p. 361), or that the Satan who appears early in *Paradise Lost* has affinities with Oliver Cromwell (pp. 344–7). Yet Worden puts substantial flesh on the bones of such familiar insights, and in the pages that cover Milton's attitude towards Cromwell, the debates over the constitution and republicanism, Milton's collaboration with Nedham on the *Mercurius Politicus*, and the *Defensio Secunda* and Milton's other prose writings, we see how micropolitical analysis, when skilfully employed, can still yield new knowledge of canonical texts.

We find a very different approach to the study of political thought in Su Fang Ng's *Literature and the Politics of the Family in Seventeenth-Century England*, which focuses on parallels between the family and the state in several seventeenth-century writers, Milton among them. In the prose of the 1640s, Ng argues, Milton established a gendered discourse of freedom that associated liberty with virility and imagined the church as a Christian fraternity or 'band of brothers' (pp. 54–5). Reading *Paradise Lost* together with Genesis and patriarchalist theory, Ng treats the epic as continuous with the prose tracts and their construction of society as a sort of family. As God the Father rules in heaven, Adam and Eve serve as 'our first Parents' down below. With the figure of Nimrod, the architect of the tower of Babel who appears in Book XII as an 'execrable Son' set on usurping the authority of his brothers, Milton further adapts the familial metaphor to a political meaning. The family and political hierarchies that pervade *Paradise Lost* appear fluid, meritocratic and subject to alteration: 'Milton's dynamic and flexible family dismantles hierarchies and undermines traditional authorities, especially the authority of the father but also that of the elder brother, both of which are resonant metaphors for royalists in justifying the monarchy' (p. 150). Ng looks at several key episodes in *Paradise Lost* and judges them unencumbered by conventional notions of patriarchal hierarchy, arguing that the poem reverses the gendered notion of a male community of believers by making Eve responsible for the foundation of civil society and the efflorescence of religious fraternity (pp. 165–6).

Similarly focused on communities of believers, Ken Simpson's *Spiritual Architecture and 'Paradise Regained'* explores Milton's 'literary ecclesiology', his engagement in church reform and the construction of a religious brotherhood based on the authority of Scripture. He sees in *Paradise Regained*'s battle between Jesus and Satan 'a contest between the true and false church, Jesus' victory standing as an ecclesiological ideal for persecuted Nonconformists of the 1670s, and as a strident warning for the established church' (p. xi). The image of church-building alluded to in the book's title comes from *Areopagitica*, and Simpson develops this notion of spiritual architecture as the establishment of a textual community, which, he argues, served as a foundational principle of Milton's ecclesiology throughout his career (p. 24). Simpson borrows the notion of textual community from Brian Stock's work on medieval literacy and orality, but applies it more narrowly to encompass truth-seeking members of the visible church united 'by virtue of the clarity of Scripture and the illumination of the Holy Spirit' (p. 139). Church membership, according to this model, depends on the act of reading, and in Simpson's account encounters with the Word possess an almost mystical character. In particular, chapter 3, on 'The Priesthood of Believers and the Vocation of Writing', regards reading as a type of devotional practice guided by the Holy Spirit, and writing as a 'ministry in poetry' (p. 67), the visible testimony of one's spiritual gifts. Simpson puts it thus: 'Believing himself called to serve the church and to write sacred poetry, when God called him to write controversial prose in 1640, Milton did not abandon his ministerial vocation; his ministry simply changed from an ordinary to an extraordinary, inspired ministry of the Word' (pp. 71–2). This line of analysis goes well beyond affirming the study of sacred texts as a substitute for ritualism to treat poetry as a force more efficacious than preaching in expressing the Word. Poetry, in other words, 'performs a ritual function in Milton's literary ecclesiology', and *Paradise Regained* takes on the office of 'an act of worship' (p. 106). We can agree that Milton drew no firm line between his religious and poetic vocations, and that poetry had a liturgical value for Protestants who looked upon ritual observances with suspicion. Yet this elevation of reading also limits its possibilities in a seventeenth-century context. The son of a London scrivener, a translator of diplomatic correspondence, a journalist and (on Blair Worden's account) a sort of propagandist, Milton's relation to books was complicated by many factors. Simpson's ecclesiological model hardly exhausts Milton's experience of reading and writing but rather constricts it by removing it from the circumstances of textual production and the actual practices of literate Protestants. For all its emphasis on sacred verse and Scripture, the study reaches towards a kind of discourse that transcends human language altogether. Simpson points out that silence is a recurrent theme in *Paradise Regained*, reaching its apogee in the pinnacle scene where Jesus rebuffs Satan's temptation, cites Scripture, keeps his counsel, and stands firm. Simpson comments: 'the silence on the pinnacle is two-sided: on the one hand, it authorizes and redeems language for the proclamation of the Word by the Word; on the other hand, as a minimal image of the Father's ineffable glory, it is also a reminder that such glory is never fully present in words or the Word' (p. 35). Language fails in its attempt to represent the Incarnation, and seeks shelter in the unsayable.

For another approach to the interplay of silence and speech in Milton, we can page forward to the concluding chapter of Terry G. Sherwood's *The Self in Early Modern Literature: For the Common Good*. Reading Milton's formal prose defences, and the companion poems *Paradise Regained* and *Samson Agonistes*, 'Milton: Self-Defense and the Drama of Blame' notes that avoiding temptation can mean not succumbing to the guilty pleasure of vociferous over-reaction. Jesus easily can avail himself of the resources of 'protracted argument' but the brevity of his disdainful response in Book IV of *Paradise Regained* avoids the trap of turning righteous scorn into 'prideful, obsessive defensiveness' (p. 306). Samson's angry defensiveness, Sherwood avers, dramatizes this 'disposition to prideful excess' (p. 319), the raging self-esteem that Milton mistrusted in his own nature. From Sherwood we can take the larger point that Milton's characteristic posture of aggressive defensiveness connects closely to his sense of self-esteem and belief in serving 'the common good', or entering the public sphere. In the great poems of his maturity Milton retreats from what some might construe as the overbearing, wordy defensiveness of his younger self, a stance necessitated by his enlisting in the pamphlet wars but also by his temperament and peculiar habits of mind.

A study of Milton's representation of the self throughout his career, Stephen M. Fallon's *Milton's Peculiar Grace: Self-Representation and Authority* 'attempts a *literary* biography of the *autobiographical* Milton' (p. xi), in other words, it reads Milton's construction of a self through his writings. Aware of the theoretical problems such an agenda entails (but undeterred by the difficulty of speaking of the self as something that exists outside of and prior to the act of representation), Fallon first turns to the 1633 'Letter to a Friend' as a document that closely foreshadows later developments. As Fallon points out, the letter 'embodies a recurrent pattern in Milton's writing, one in which the author scrutinizes himself, finds nothing amiss, and asserts his innocence' (pp. 21–2). Moving chronologically, Fallon traces a course that takes Milton from relatively straightforward affirmations of himself, to expressions of something resembling self-doubt, and finally to the more ambiguous and uncertain self-portraits of his later career. As he launches himself as a writer, Milton ascribes to himself, Fallon convincingly argues, a sort of sinlessness or exemption from the universal fallen nature of mankind. Fallon treats the *Apology for Smectymnuus* as of a piece with his earlier texts in its drawing virtue and eloquence together and its insistence on 'the continuity between a virtuous interior, a name, and a reliable self-representation' (p. 109). For various reasons (among them Milton's own problem of admitting no distinction between the self and its textual representation) this hyperbolic manoeuvre becomes impossible to sustain. Milton's strain of spiritual perfectionism suggests a connection to radical sectarianism that clearly puts him at odds with Calvinists, who tended to revel in acknowledging their own sinfulness. By the time of the divorce tracts, Milton at least can entertain the possibility of his own imperfection, yet his habitual self-regard continues to run through autobiographical channels. Milton's *Second Defence* takes on the anxious, self-defensive tone that Sherwood also notes in his book, and in it, as in *Areopagitica*, Milton 'writes from a keen sense of personal grievance and personal prerogative' (p. 171). In his later chapters Fallon identifies a drive to self-representation everywhere in the major poems, populating them with ghostly holograms of the poet and detecting Miltonic preoccupations in almost every character. Milton's 'identification with the Son in the brief epic is the culmination or apotheosis of this strain of self-presentation' (p. 238), by which Milton exempts himself from the consequences of the fall, while in *Samson* 'Milton comes closest to acknowledging the possibility that he has himself faltered' (p. 250). Poets of the self (Walt Whitman also comes to mind in this respect) tend to invite psychobiographical attention, and Fallon here uses Milton's career-long project of self-representation to illuminate some larger issues in seventeenth-century literature and theology. The spotlight, however, mostly stays trained on Milton as author and recipient of peculiar grace, a towering figure whose creative genius vindicates his self-promotion and sometimes staggering presumption.

Feisal G. Mohamed, 'Reading *Samson* in the New American Century' (*MiltonS* 46[2007] 149–64), explores how Milton criticism after 9/11 has experienced a deepening discomfort with this anxiously contested text, how recent events have 'raised the stakes of a heated literary debate', loading criticism 'with the possibility of unsettling real world implications' (p. 161). *Milton Studies* for 2007 includes two other essays on Milton's politics, Clay Daniel's 'Royal Samson' (*MiltonS* 46[2007] 123–47), which advances the thesis that 'Samson is a royal figure and that the dramatic poem's strongest political messages warn against restoring the monarchy' (p. 124); and James Egan, '*Areopagitica* and the Tolerationist Rhetorics of the 1640s' (*MiltonS* 46[2007] 165–90), which belongs together with Achinstein and Sauer's collection discussed above, and places *Areopagitica* alongside tracts written in the 1640s in order to register stylistic and structural echoes among the texts. Egan sees the emergence of a republican aesthetic in the creative process whereby Milton 'inventoried a range of popular toleration texts before settling on the structure and styles of *Areopagitica*, thereby legitimating the democratic, allegedly ephemeral idiom of the political tract' (p. 185). In 'Milton, the Gunpowder Plot, and the Mythography of Terror' (*MLQ* 68[2007] 461–91) Robert Appelbaum reads 'In Quintum Novembris' and *Paradise Lost* as meditations on terrorism *avant la lettre*. Appelbaum sees in the former a study of how 'evil is directly if perversely caused by the strength and virtue of the targets of violence', and, symmetrically, in the latter how 'evil is directly if perversely caused by the innocence of its targets, who are undeserving of evil in themselves but then are seduced into becoming deserving of it' (p. 490). In a sense Appelbaum's pursuit of a parallel between 9/11 and the Gunpowder Plot instantiates the critical tendency against which Mohamed warns, that of invoking terrorism so as to confirm the assumptions of Western liberal humanism and obfuscate the political and religious views of one of the tradition's great exemplars, whose attitude towards religious violence does not entirely match our own.

A novel and even startling approach to religion and literature is much in evidence in Kent R. Lehnhof 's 'Scatology and the Sacred in Milton's *Paradise Lost*' (*ELR* 37[2007] 429–49), which studies the presence of excremental imagery in Milton's heaven and hell. Lehnhof concludes that *Paradise Lost* forges 'meaning out of the body's scatological modalities as well as its sexual ones', that in the same way that his predecessors use erotic desire as an analogy for religious feeling, 'Milton makes similar connections by way of the body's evacuative experiences' (p. 449). Pitt Harding, 'Milton's Serpent and the Birth of Pagan Error' (*SEL* 47[2007] 161–77), connects Milton's understanding of error to early Christian apologetics, in particular to Lactantius, whose moral critique informs the serpent's approach to Eve in *Paradise Lost*. Treating the temptation scene as 'the culmination of a consistently organized genealogy of error', Harding argues that allusions to the serpent recall denunciations of imperial Rome's cultural corruption, and that 'the project of converting the pagan epic to a Christian theme commits Milton to revive issues raised in the early encounter between the church and the classical order in which it emerged' (p. 162). A second article on Milton and religion in the same number of *SEL*, William Walker's 'On Reason, Faith, and Freedom in *Paradise Lost*' (*SEL* 47[2007] 143–59), takes up the contention of Stanley Fish (and others) that for Milton religious faith operates independent of reason. According to Walker, Milton grounds human freedom in a rationalist, not a voluntarist, theology, and avoids representing the Fall as a lapse of faith and free will. Attending to the theory of reason, faith and freedom presented in the epic, Walker sees Milton's thought as falling in step with a rationalist argument, 'versions of which were propounded by Hugo Grotius, Samuel von Pufendorf, and John Locke against voluntarists such as Martin Luther, John Calvin, and Thomas Hobbes' (p. 152)

The breadth and depth of Milton criticism make it impossible to sound far below the surface of so much scholarly writing, even for a single year, and for reasons of space I have had to omit summaries of several articles that deserve careful consideration. From this admittedly partial survey we can detect a groundswell of interest in Milton's biography, which likely will crest in the coming year; an extension of work on Milton, early modern science and ecology; and continuing engagement with the central themes of seventeenth-century religion and politics that figure so prominently in Milton's writings and those of his contemporaries.

Books Reviewed

Achinstein, Sharon and Elizabeth Sauer, eds. *Milton and Toleration*. OUP. [2007] pp. x + 320. $99 ISBN 9 7801 9929 5937.

Bowen, Deborah, ed. *The Strategic Smorgasbord of Postmodernity: Literature and the Christian Critic*. Cambridge SP. [2007]. pp. 340. $79.99 ISBN 9 7818 4718 1619.

Burbery, Timothy J. *Milton the Dramatist*. Duquesne. [2007] pp. xviii + 206. $58 ISBN 9 7808 2070 3879.

Campbell, Gordon, Thomas N. Corns, John K. Hale and Fiona J. Tweedie. *Milton and the Manuscript of 'De Doctrina Christiana'*. OUP. [2007] pp. xii + 240. $110 ISBN 9 7801 9929 6491.

Cefalu, Paul. *English Renaissance Literature and Contemporary Theory: Sublime Objects of Theology*. Palgrave. [2007] pp. ix + 217. $68.95 ISBN 9 7814 0397 6697.

Cheney, Patrick, Andrew Hadfield and Garrett A. Sullivan, Jr, eds. *Early Modern English Poetry: A Critical Companion*. OUP. [2007] pp. xxiii + 342. £21.99 ISBN 9 7801 9515 3873.

Cohen, Stephen, ed. *Shakespeare and Historical Formalism*. Ashgate. [2007] pp. ix + 242. $99.95 ISBN 9 7807 5465 3820.

Craik, Katharine A. *Reading Sensations in Early Modern England*. Palgrave. [2007] pp. xi + 200. $79.95 ISBN 9 7814 0392 1925.

Cummins, Juliet, and David Burchell, eds. *Science, Literature and Rhetoric in Early Modern England*. Ashgate. [2007] pp. xiii + 241. $99.95 ISBN 9 7807 5465 7811.

D'Addario, Christopher. *Exile and Journey in Seventeenth-Century Literature*. CUP. [2007] pp. viii + 199. $96 ISBN 9 7805 2187 0290.

Dickson, Donald R., ed. *John Donne's Poetry*. Norton. [2007] pp. xiv + 439. $15.65 ISBN 9 7803 9392 6484.

Duran, Angelica. *The Age of Milton and the Scientific Revolution*. Duquesne. [2007] pp. xii + 349. $58 ISBN 9 7808 2070 3862.

Duran, Angelica, ed. *A Concise Companion to Milton*. Blackwell. [2007] pp. xiv + 274. $84.95 ISBN 9 7814 0512 2719.

Fallon, Stephen M. *Milton's Peculiar Grace: Self-Representation and Authority*. CornUP. [2007] pp. xx + 274. pb $24.95 ISBN 9 7808 0147 4859.

Haskin, Dayton. *John Donne in the Nineteenth Century*. OUP. [2007] pp. xxv + 315. £66 ISBN 9 7801 9921 2422.

Hass, Andrew, David Jasper and Elisabeth Jay, eds. *The Oxford Handbook of English Literature and Theology*. OUP. [2007] pp. 889. £85 ISBN 9 7801 9927 1979.

Herman, Peter C., ed. *Approaches to Teaching Milton's Shorter Poetry and Prose*. MLA. [2007] pp. xii + 284. pb $37.50 ISBN 9 7808 7362 5947.

Kerrigan, William, John Rumrich and Stephen M. Fallon, eds. *The Complete Poetry and Essential Prose of John Milton*. Modern Library. [2007] pp. xxxiv + 1,365. $55 ISBN 9 7806 7964 2534.

Lewalski, Barbara K., ed. *Paradise Lost*. Blackwell. [2007] pp. xxxvi + 351. $31.95 ISBN 9 7814 0512 9299.

Lieb, Michael, and John T. Shawcross, eds. *'Paradise Lost: A Poem Written in Ten Books': Essays on the 1667 First Edition*. Duquesne. [2007] pp. xi + 288. $60 ISBN 9 7808 2070 3930.

Linden, Stanton J. *Mystical Metal of Gold: Essays on Alchemy and Renaissance Culture*. AMS. [2007]. pp. 435. $94.50 ISBN 9 7804 0462 3425.

Mannani, Manijeh. *Divine Deviants: The Dialectics of Devotion in the Poetry of Donne and Rūmī*. Lang. [2007] pp. ix + 181. $64.95 ISBN 9 7808 2048 8592.

Mattison, Andrew. *Milton's Uncertain Eden: Understanding Place in 'Paradise Lost'*. Routledge. [2007] pp. ix + 190. $110 ISBN 9 7804 1598 1347.

McColley, Diane Kelsey. *Poetry and Ecology in the Age of Milton and Marvell*. Ashgate. [2007] pp. 252. $89.95 ISBN 9 7807 5466 0484.

Ng, Su Fang. *Literature and the Politics of Family in Seventeenth-Century England*. CUP. [2007] pp. viii + 236. £45 ISBN 0 5218 7031 3.

Novik, Mary. *Conceit: A Novel*. Doubleday. [2007] pp. 402. $29.95 ISBN 9 7803 8566 2055.

Roston, Murray. *Tradition and Subversion in Renaissance Literature: Studies in Shakespeare, Spenser, Johnson, and Donne*. Duquesne. [2007] pp. xiii + 258. $60 ISBN 9 7808 2070 3909.

Royan, Nicola, ed. *'Langage cleir illumynate': Scottish Poetry from Barbour to Drummond, 1375–1630*. Rodopi. [2007] pp. 222. £31.43 ISBN 9 0420 2319 8.

Shawcross, John T., and Michael Lieb. *'Paradise Lost: A Poem Written in Ten Books:' An Authoritative Text of the 1667 First Edition*. Duquesne. [2007] pp. xvi + 456. $68 ISBN 9 7808 2070 3923.

Sherwood, Terry G. *The Self in Early Modern Literature: For the Common Good*. Duquesne. [2007] pp. viii + 384. $60 ISBN 9 7808 2070 3954.

Simpson, Ken. *Spiritual Architecture and 'Paradise Regained': Milton's Literary Ecclesiology*. Duquesne. [2007] pp. xiii + 256. $58 ISBN 9 7808 2070 3916.

Sugg, Richard. *John Donne*. Palgrave. [2007] pp. xv + 251. pb $32.95 ISBN 9 7814 0399 5100.

Thickstun, Margaret Olofson. *Milton's 'Paradise Lost': Moral Education*. Palgrave Macmillan. [2007] pp. xiv + 184. $68.95 ISBN 9 7814 0397 7571.

Wilcox, Helen. *The English Poems of George Herbert*. CUP. [2007] 740 pp. $189.99 ISBN 9 7805 2186 8211.

Worden, Blair. *Literature and Politics in Cromwellian England: John Milton, Andrew Marvell, Marchamont Nedham*. OUP. [2007]. pp. xv + 458. $49.95 9 7801 9923 0815.

X

The Later Seventeenth Century

NOAM REISNER, LESLEY COOTE, HELEN BROOKS AND
JAMES OGDEN

This chapter has three sections: 1. Poetry; 2. Prose; 3. Drama. Section 1 is by
Noam Reisner; section 2 is by Lesley Coote; section 3(a) is by Helen Brooks;
section 3(b) is by James Ogden.

1. Poetry

The year 2007 was a lean one for Marvell studies, but it has seen the
publication of a number of interesting articles and one related monograph. In
all of these, the usual concern with the indeterminacy of Marvell's poetic
personae and his political loyalties, on the one hand, and with the difficult
relationship between his biography and art, on the other, continue to generate
vibrant critical debates. In all of these, the poems that continue to draw the
most critical attention are 'Upon Appleton House' and the 'Horatian Ode'.

In Diane Kelsey McColley's *Poetry and Ecology in the Age of Milton and
Marvell*, Marvell features centrally together with Milton, alongside several
other important authors from the period, as a proto-ecological poet.
McColley's definition and analysis of what might constitute ecological
poetry in the seventeenth century is rich with detail and learning, always
interesting, and on the whole convincing, despite the fact that the differences
between ecological concerns today and Marvell's time are far greater and have
far more implications than McColley allows. Nevertheless, what McColley
detects in Marvell, Milton and some of their contemporaries is a heightened
sympathy with all living beings, and an animist-vitalist concern for the
integrity of natural habitats and the myriad life forms they sustain. McColley
distinguishes in the period between economical concerns which seek to manage
and control natural resources and ecological ones which call for a responsive
meditation on the natural world through a celebration of 'delight, gratitude,
the interplay of the untamable energies of nature, imagination, and language'
(p. 37). Throughout the study, McColley links the common ecological
concerns she detects in the poetry chiefly of Milton and Marvell with a vitalist-
monist world-view, a political concern for liberty and the belief in a fully

Year's Work in English Studies, Volume 88 (2009) © *The English Association; all rights reserved*
doi:10.1093/ywes/map010

immanent and passible God as opposed to an impassible, absolutely transcendental deity. Unfortunately, McColley's ecological enthusiasm occasionally tends to simplify these complicated ideas and elides in these sections of the book the necessary distinction between the two poets' world-views. While Milton was certainly a vitalist-monist (or animist-materialist), the claim that Marvell, a Platonic idealist, was also a monist who shared these views is highly contentious and requires adequate demonstration, not to mention that their respective political ideologies were also marked by subtle yet clear differences. For McColley, however, the ecological sensitivity of Marvell, Milton and many of their contemporaries (including Herbert, Vaughan, Traherne, Cowley, Cavendish and others) and their regard for the animist integrity and sanctity of the life-giving earth and its habitats transcends political and partisan loyalties and accounts for their individual linguistic and poetic inventiveness. Submitting many poems from the period to detailed close readings, McColley highlights the connectivity between ecological empathy and linguistic creativity, where, for example, the richness of the natural landscape depicted in Marvell's 'Upon Appleton House' or 'The Garden', or Milton's Eden in *Paradise Lost*, 'complicate and delight our sense of connections by the woven processes of language they lead us through' (p. 50). McColley plots her survey through a number of ecological themes, ranging from the perception of habitats, through earth and mountain theology, air, water and wood imagery, to poems about plants, animals and birds, concluding the book with a reflection on the ecologically prophetic epics of Milton. For Marvell scholars, however, the first chapter of the book, on the perception of habitats, will prove the most useful. In this chapter, McColley offers an extended close reading of 'Upon Appleton House' as the poem of ecological habitat *par excellence*. Whether or not readers will agree with McColley's ecological thesis, her analysis of what she terms the 'sensuous reciprocity' of Marvell's celebrated estate poem is engrossing and itself so rich with detail and insight that its sheer energy at least vindicates the merit of reading some seventeenth-century English poetry through ecological eyes.

If McColley elides the differences in political and intellectual outlook between Milton and Marvell in the interests of her ecological reading, Catherine Gimelli Martin dwells on these important differences in the interests of a political reading in 'Rewriting Cromwell: Milton, Marvell, and Negative Liberty in the English Revolution' (*ClioI* 36[2007] 307–33). Martin makes a compelling case for viewing Milton's and Marvell's subtly different views about liberty in secular rather than religious terms. Looking in particular at their respective portrayals of the Lord Protector, Martin traces the roots of Milton's and Marvell's views for or against 'negative' liberty—that is, liberty which insists on an individual's absolute freedom from governmental control as opposed to an individual's freedom to attain personal and societal prosperity—to their respective reactions to Hobbes and Machiavelli, and their different interpretations of classical humanist republicanism. Unlike Milton, argues Martin, Marvell shared Hobbes's admiration for the idea of the sovereign as a guardian of individual and societal liberties and so was a keen supporter of Cromwell at the height of his executive power and later of Charles II as well. But since his view of liberty in the state was far more negative than Milton's, he eventually found himself increasingly disillusioned with the royal government under the restored monarchy. Martin then traces these subtle differences and nuances in Milton prose, sonnets and *Paradise Lost* on the one hand, and Marvell's 'Horatian Ode' and 'First Anniversary' on the other.

Two more articles offer an indirect counter-argument to McColley's ecological thesis. In 'Eros and Abuse: Imagining Andrew Marvell' (*ELH* 74[2007] 371–95), co-authors Derek Hirst and Steven Zwicker offer a comprehensive reassessment of Marvell's 'The Unfortunate Lover'—one of his most enigmatic and bizarre poems—and through it a reassessment of the prevalent notion that Marvell's poetry offers no coherent script of selfhood. According to Hirst and Zwicker, 'The Unfortunate Lover' encodes and animates a story of selfhood and artistic singularity which can then be traced coherently through all of Marvell's major poems. What emerges is a 'narrative of abusive, sustained, and yet pleasurable and deeply guilty violation' (p. 376) where nature and the human condition it foregrounds, far from offering a source of animist inspiration and creativity, shape 'the conditions of disaster and dependence' (p. 375) in which the shipwrecked unfortunate lover hovers between life and death and from whose imagined plight Marvell's singularity as a poet is born. Hirst and Zwicker then trace this narrative as it bubbles to the surface in many of Marvell's major poems, including 'Upon Appleton House' and 'To His Coy Mistress'.

John Faust's 'Blurring the Boundaries: *Ut pictura poesis* and Marvell's Liminal Mower' (*SP* 104[2007] 526–55), next offers an interesting analysis complementary to that of Hirst and Zwicker but from a very different perspective. Far from being a product of his sympathy with the vital energies of natural habitats, Faust sees Marvell's enigmatic creativity and interests in poetic and meta-poetic liminality arising from his appreciation of contemporary painting techniques. Faust detects behind Marvell's poetry the shadowy *chiaroscuro* of Italian and Dutch painting which influenced Jacobean tastes for the heightened realism of mood and perspective in landscape and portraiture art. Holding up Marvell's Mower figure as his most enigmatic and liminal persona, Faust analyses the four Mower poems for their shadowy liminality, where all conventional generic boundaries and expectations are blurred. Marvell's Mower, argues Faust, much like the unfortunate lover, 'cannot reconcile nature and the art that derives from human nature' and so remains, like a shadowy figure, 'out of focus' (p. 545).

Yet another article which explores the fertile correspondence in the period between poetry, science, and politics is Jonathan Sawday's ' "The chief mystery of the seminall business": Andrew Marvell, William Harvey, Abraham Cowley and the Politics of Fertility in the Seventeenth Century' (*English* 56[2007] 107–25). Sawday explores a tantalizing link between the politics of William Harvey's scientific treatise on generation, *De generatione*, and an emerging 'language of psychosexual recuperation' (p. 122) in the poetry of Marvell, using Cowley's 'Ode upon Doctor Harvey' as a link between the two. Sawday analyses Marvell's 'Horatian Ode' for its uses of psychosexual images of emasculation and fertility, first in its depiction of the executed monarch, and then in the rampant figure of Cromwell. Sawday argues that the royalist appropriation of the tropes offered up by Harvey's scientific excursions into the mysteries of seminal generation, referred to by Marvell in *The Rehearsal Transpros'd* as 'the chief mystery of the seminall business', legitimated a broad range of such images in the political and poetic language of the day, both before and after the Restoration.

An interesting theoretical article which illuminates the method of the articles cited so far in relation to Marvell is Paul Alpers's 'Renaissance Lyrics and their Situations' (*NLH* 38[2007] 309–31). Although the very inclusion of this article in a review of Marvell criticism perhaps defeats its generalizing purpose, Alpers's analysis of George Gascoigne's 'Woodmanship' and Marvell's 'Horatian Ode' as two case studies in what he calls, following Kenneth Burke, poems which encompass a 'situation' is interesting not just for the presented theory but for the insights it offers into both poems. Seeing in these poems a series of lyric scenes, or 'events', which also have a contextual corollary as biographical-historical events, Alpers calls for a balance in the literary criticism of Renaissance lyrics between purely formalist and purely historical-contextual readings. According to Alpers, a Renaissance poem's engagement with specific historical 'situations' or 'events' is often transmuted aesthetically into a series of internal poetic 'scenes' and 'situations' which ought to direct our attention, so Alpers argues, 'to the possibility of purposive utterance' (p. 328). In the case of Marvell's 'Horatian Ode' such a strategy allows Alpers to show how the poem's 'poise and equilibrium are due to rhetorical devices that align the lyric speaker with other agents in [the historical] events [it represents]' (p. 327).

One scholar who does not toe the Alpers line is Martin Dzelzainis, who contributes to the bibliographical study of Marvell in 'Andrew Marvell and the Restoration Literary Underground: Printing the Painter Poems' (*SC* 22[2007] 395–410). Using his archival detective skills, Dzelzainis reconstructs the printing history of the satirical 'Advices to a Painter' poems, two of which (the third and second 'Advices') are widely presumed to be the work of Marvell. Tracking the movement of the scandalous 'Advice to a Painter' poems from manuscript to contraband print, and sorting out fact from fiction in the received wisdom about the provenance of the extant editions of these poems, Dzelzainis sheds light on the murky world of rogue printers and booksellers, government spies and double agents, secret print houses and government raids, and one conspicuously absent figure—that of Marvell himself. As Dzelzainis concludes, Marvell, 'like Macavity... is never there' (p. 405). It seems that if, as is widely assumed, Marvell was indeed the author of two of these scurrilous attacks on the duke of York and the king's person, which he then circulated in manuscript, he was very good at covering his tracks when these manuscript poems 'happened' to find their way to the printing presses.

Marvell also features this year in a number of interesting notes. In ' "Allies" and "Alleys": An Unexplored Crux of Marvell's "Upon Appleton House", line 289' (*N&Q* 54[2007] 45–6), Vitaliy Eyber takes issue with all previous editors of Marvell who have either glossed or amended the word 'allies' in line 289 to 'alleys' and argues that the context of stanza 37 in which the word appears—a stanza describing bees inseminating flowers in the Fairfax garden—plainly implies that the word should be read and glossed as 'allies' in a military sense and therefore referring to the flowers, not to the man-made paths between them.

In what is more of an article than a note, 'Marvell's "Horatian Ode" and "The City": An Alternative Interpretation' (*N&Q* 54[2007] 46–54), Ian C. Parker challenges claims made by John McWilliams in a previous *N&Q* contribution regarding Marvell's possible familiarity with an anonymous royalist broadside, 'The City', published in Oxford in early 1643. Parker contests McWilliams's claims that the apparent echoes of the broadside in the 'Horatian Ode' indicate that Marvell had read the broadside in 1643 and remembered it when he came to write the ode many years later. Agreeing with McWilliams that there are resemblances between the two texts, Parker offers a different interpretation of these echoes. Parker demonstrates that the resemblances between the two texts may be accounted for not by assuming that Marvell read the broadside, but by identifying 'probable proximate sources that resemble elements in Marvell more closely than do those in "The City"' (pp. 46–7). Unpicking carefully each of the passages identified by McWilliams, Parker shows how in each case a nearer and more plausible source for Marvell's imagery and word-choice may be produced.

In 'The Apples in Marvell's "Bermudas"' (*N&Q* 54[2007] 418–19) David McInnis reflects on the word 'apples' in Marvell's lines from 'Bermudas': 'apples plants of such a price/No tree could ever bear them twice' (pp. 23–4). After producing contextual evidence to support his claim, McInnis argues that, contrary to Nigel Smith's gloss of these lines in his edition, Marvell is referring here to a pineapple, not an apple, and is therefore invoking New World imagery and associations, and not the poetry of Virgil as a previous critic opined.

In 'Playing on Absent Words in Andrew Marvell's "Upon Appleton House"' (*N&Q* 54[2007] 420–1) Vitaliy Eyber provides two examples of puns on absent words in Marvell's 'Upon Appleton House'. Eyber points out that stanza 62, which compares the trees of the Fairfax wood to the genealogical trees of the Fairfax and Vere families, forms an 'unmade' pun on the term 'family tree' which does not appear in the stanza itself (having discounted the word 'pedigree' as a likely connotation). Then, in stanza 75, Eyber concludes that the absent word at the centre of the stanza's punning energy is 'fan'. In another note, '"Liberty" in Line 100 of Marvell's "Upon Appleton House": The Meaning and the Context' (*N&Q* 54[2007] 421–2) Eyber dwells on the word 'liberty' in line 100 of 'Upon Appleton House' and teases out its many possible contexts and connotations as a further demonstration of what he calls the 'unobserved, unostentatious notional complexity and inter-connectedness of "Upon Appleton House"' (p. 422).

Finally, in 'Marvell's Use of Nedham's Selden' (*N&Q* 54[2007] 422–5), Andrew Fleck argues that Marvell's knowledge and use of Nedham's translation of Selden's *Mare Clausam*, a disputation against Hugo Grotius's theory of maritime commerce, is apparent in several allusions to the translation in Marvell's satirical 'The Character of Holland'.

As with Marvell, studies of Dryden's poetry have produced a relatively slim yield in 2007. Christopher D'Addario's monograph, *Exile and Journey in*

Seventeenth-Century Literature, includes a revised republication of an article from 2004 which analyses Dryden's later works as 'exile literature'. D'Addario defines in this case 'exile literature' as literature which negotiates 'distance and loss' and which often 'evokes both nostalgia and continued attachment' to a lost homeland (p. 133), or in Dryden's case, to the loss of a familiar political and religious world. Although the material here is not new, readers might well appreciate the wider context into which D'Addario casts the older article. With new material on New England literature, Hobbes and Milton's epics preceding it, the analysis of Dryden's literary engagement and disengagement from past masters (Milton, Virgil) as well as from a lost ideological world gains added point and depth.

Erik Bond's 'Historicizing the "New Normal": London's Great Fire and the Genres of Urban Destruction' (*Restoration* 31[2007] 43–64) explores the uses of literary genre as a 'formal tool' to 'enact healing' (p. 44) after the urban trauma of the devastation caused by the Great Fire of 1666. Analysing, side by side, Pepys's *Diary* and Dryden's *Annus Mirabilis* for their literary treatment of the Great Fire, Bond draws the links between the generic implications of each literary work to strategies of psychological and public healing following the traumatic event, when Londoners, much like New Yorkers after 9/11 as Bond suggests, had to confront the unspeakable urban void created by the catastrophe. Unlike Pepys, who attempts to 'discipline' trauma, Bond argues that Dryden seeks to nurture through the formal use of trauma-encoding repetition and the generic cues inserted into the prefatory material 'an imaginative, contemplative space above the quotidian' (p. 57) where Londoners may confront and then overcome their grief.

The growing trend of reclaiming Dryden's translations at the centre of his poetic oeuvre continued in 2007. In a thought-provoking essay, 'Translating toward Eternity: Dryden's Final Aspiration' (*PQ* 84[2005] 49–75), Melissa Pino reflects on the sincerity of Dryden's religious conversion and argues for a link between the growing seriousness of Dryden's religious thought and his theories of translation. Singling out and analysing religious and biblical metaphors in Dryden's prefaces, dedications and literary criticism, Pino concludes that Dryden's movement in his later translations away from the practice of the 'metaphrase' (as practised for example in the translation of Ovid's *Epistles*) towards looser forms of what he himself had defined in the preface to the *Epistles* as 'imitation' can be explained in terms of his change in religious outlook and his growing quarrel with Protestant theories of biblical exegesis and religious sensibility. According to Pino, by rejecting the Protestant obsession with the literality of the Scriptures, and by extension of all literary texts, the Catholic Dryden came to view himself as the 'inspired caretaker' of ancient texts who held a 'direct communion with the ancient authors he revealed to the English people' (p. 66). While Pino's mixing of religious and literary terms (for example, describing Dryden's later methods of translation in terms of transubstantiation as opposed to the Lutheran idea of consubstantiation) is at times confusing and depends more on loose association than concrete demonstration, her thesis is sure to intrigue Dryden scholars and stir debate.

Closely related in theme to Pino's essay is Tom Mason's 'Dryden's *The Cock and the Fox* and Chaucer's *Nun's Priest's Tale*' (*T&L* 16[2007] 1–28). Whereas Pino theorizes about the conceptual reasons behind Dryden's drive towards looser forms of translation, Mason explores in great detail the intellectual and literary currents which cause Dryden's mind to drift from his source in specific moments in his *The Cock and the Fox*, a loose translation from *Fables* of Chaucer's *Nun's Priest's Tale*. Mason shows how, whenever a moral topic or a particular Chaucerian sensibility appeals to Dryden, his mind drifts to a wider range of other literary sources, including his own earlier work. The next article in the same volume, Adam Rounce's 'Eighteenth-Century Responses to Dryden's *Fables*' (*T&L* 16[2007] 29–52), then shows how Dryden's *Fables* themselves were to become a focal point for literary inspiration, debate and imitation in the works of such eighteenth-century poets and authors as Jabez Hughes, Joseph and Thomas Warton, Richardson in his *Clarissa*, the satirist Charles Churchill, William Hayward Robert and Mary Wollstonecraft, among others. Again, Rounce stresses that such eighteenth-century luminaries responded chiefly to the striking individuality and inventive singularity of Dryden's later translations.

With regard to the *Fables*, Dryden scholars are sure to appreciate the first publication of the late C.P. Macgregor's previously unpublished essay, 'Dryden's *Alexander's Feast*'. The context for the unusual publication of an essay which is after all well over twenty years old is a volume of commemorative essays, *Sustaining Literature: Essays on Literature, History, and Culture, 1500–1800*, assembled in memory of Simon Varey, and edited by Greg Clingham. As Clingham observes in his introduction to Macgregor's essay, the 'continuing freshness' of Macgregor's historicist reading of the poem merits and justifies its long-overdue publication.

On the bibliographical front, there were two articles of note in 2007 which address Dryden's poetry. In 'Fixity versus Flexibility in "A Song on Tom of Danby"' and Dryden's *Absalom and Achitophel* (in Baron, Lindquist and Shevlin, eds., *Agent of Change: Print Culture Studies after Elizabeth L. Einstein*, pp. 140–55) the late Harold Love engages with the question of what constitutes 'fixity' of texts in transmission from manuscript to print. Love approaches the question from his own eminently learned familiarity with scribal, mostly satirical, Restoration literature. After contesting in general terms the notion that the processes associated with bringing a manuscript to print in the early modern period conferred greater authorial fixity on a text than scribal transmission, Love than goes against his own argument and provides two examples which precisely prove the opposite. He compares the rate of textual 'mutation' in two Restoration political satires, 'A Song on Tom of Danby' from 1679, which circulated entirely through manuscript copies, and Dryden's *Absalom and Achitophel* from 1681, which circulated wholly through the press. Having shown that the manuscript poem was subject to far more mutations than Dryden's printed poem, Love concludes that the graphical and authorial fixity of Dryden's printed satire accounts for our treatment of it as 'literature' and our corresponding dismissal of such manuscript lampoons as 'A Song on Tom of Danby' as 'evanescent popular culture' (p. 152). He then finally adds that Dryden deliberately exploited the fixity of the printing press to anchor the 'shiftiness' of his satire, which in turn is rooted in the printed fixity of the Bible itself.

Another article which in its own ways reinforces Love's claims about the peculiar fixity of the printed text in the later seventeenth century is John Barnard's 'Creating an English Literary Canon, 1679–1720' (in Eliot, Nash, and Willison, eds., *Literary Cultures and the Material Book*, pp. 307–21). Barnard makes a compelling case for considering the influence of the book trade and its practices when theorizing about the emergence of an English literary canon in the course of the eighteenth century. To demonstrate his point, Barnard explores the 'mutually beneficial relationship' between the publisher Jacob Tonson and, first, Dryden and, later, Congreve, in establishing a ' "polite" canon of poetry and drama between 1679 and 1720' (p. 307). In Dryden's case, Barnard considers the collaboration with Tonson on Dryden's *Miscellanies* and later on the translations of Virgil. In both cases, Barnard highlights the ways in which the collaboration of both men—Whig printer and Jacobite poet-critic—established the norms of non-partisan contemporary literary canonicity. This reflection then also extends to Tonson's publication of Congreve's *Works* in 1710.

Indeed much in Barnard's essay chimes with another piece this year by Harold Love, 'Dryden's Dorset: How Poet and Patron Overcame their Differences to Create a National Literature' (*TLS* 25 May[2007] 12–13). Love devotes his essay to the literary influence of Charles Sackville, sixth earl of Dorset, who was one of the most powerful and influential literary patrons in Restoration England. Love focuses especially on Dryden's complex and often fraught relationship with the earl, who despite falling out with Dryden over the latter's unrepentant Catholic conversion and Tory politics (it was Dorset who, as Lord Chamberlain, stripped Dryden of his laureateship and pension), seemed to have mended the relationship in later years, as indicated by Dryden's dedication of the 'Discourse on the Original and Progress of Satire' of 1693 to Dorset. The profuse eulogy of Dorset in the dedication, argues Love, is indicative of the mutual desire of both men, via the efforts of the printer Tonson, to 'encourage the birth of a recognized national literature' transcending 'divisions of party and religion' (p. 13).

Outside studies devoted to either Marvell or Dryden, undoubtedly the most important publication of 2007 for the later seventeenth century is the magisterial two-volume edition of *Plays, Poems and Miscellaneous Writings associated with George Villiers, Second Duke of Buckingham*, co-edited by Robert D. Hume and Harold Love. This far ranging, comprehensive edition is important in several respects, but chiefly because it offers a miscellany of Restoration plays, poems and squibs which, when read in sequence, say far more about the culture which produced them than about the outrageous court wit associated with them. Indeed, the key word in Hume and Love's title is 'associated'. Following on from Harold Love's equally definitive edition of Rochester's works in 1999, the editors of the present two-volume edition make no attempt to resolve questions of attribution and authorship which are largely insoluble, especially in the case of the twenty-two poems included in the edition, most of which were circulated scribally and never printed in Buckingham's lifetime. Rather than fretting over the question of a canon,

the editors have opted for an inclusive, bibliographical approach supported by
detailed notes and lengthy appendices, as if to set before the reader the known
facts about any given text previously or recently attributed to Buckingham
and allow readers to decide for themselves on matters of authorship. As a
consequence, the question of authorship is rightly relegated to the margins and
what remains is essentially a vibrant collection of Restoration texts gathered
under the colourful biographical aegis of George Villiers, the second duke of
Buckingham, who may or may not have been the author or co-author of many
of the literary works associated with him in this edition, but who, along with
Rochester, best embodies the temperament and wit of his social milieu and
Restoration court culture more generally.

Similar concerns about reputation and attribution dominate the only article
this year devoted to Rochester's poetry, Nicholas Fisher and Matt Jenkinson's
'Rochester and the Specter of Libertinism' (*HLQ* 70[2007] 537–52). Fisher and
Jenkinson submit to close analysis the emerging spectre of Rochester's
contemporary atheist and libertine reputation in three 'ghosted' poems written
in Rochester's voice and published well after his death. Fisher and Jenkins
demonstrate that all three 'ghost' poems—the anonymous 'Rochester's Ghost
addressing it self to the Secretary of the Muses' and 'Rochester's Farewell',
and Thomas D'Urfey's 'A Lash at Atheists'—were in fact written in
Rochester's lifetime and reflect, each in its own peculiar way, the political
divisions between emerging Whigs and Tories in the wake of the Popish Plot
and the Exclusion crisis. As Fisher and Jenkinson demonstrate, Rochester's
contemporary reputation as an effective and witty satirist, as well as a
notorious and then repentant libertine, was readily appropriated by individual
writers and readers, then as now, wishing to paint the late repentant earl into a
specific (usually Whiggish) political and moral corner.

Alan De Gooyer offers a rare analysis of the much-neglected Edmund
Waller in 'Edmund Waller on St. James's Park' (*Restoration* 31[2007] 47–60).
De Gooyer analyses the subtle politics and ironies of Waller's panegyric 'On
St. James's Park' and in the process challenges in more general terms Waller's
reputation today as a poet prone to 'lofty banality' (p. 49) and a slavish and
even trite reliance on literary conventions and formulae. Although it is
doubtful whether De Gooyer's efforts can mend the reputation of a poet who
writes of the animals in the St James's Park menagerie, 'All that can, living,
feed the greedy eye/Or dead, the palate, here you may descry' (lines 41–2), this
article does offer sound proof that Waller was capable of deeper poetic
intelligence than he is often given credit for.

Finally, scholars of the later seventeenth century are sure to be pleased with
a new and long-overdue collection of critical essays on the life, thought and
work of Mary Astell, *Mary Astell: Reason, Gender, Faith*, edited by William
Kolberner and Michael Michelson. As is to be expected, the majority of the
essays in this collection engage with Astell's philosophical and political prose
works, but one article, Claire Pickard's ' "Great in humilitie": A Consideration
of Mary Astell's Poetry' (pp. 115–26) offers an interesting reflection on Astell's
small volume of devotional poems addressed in 1689 to William Sancroft,
archbishop of Canterbury. While Pickard reserves judgement on the artistic
merit of Astell's small collection of religious verses, she does show how Astell's

techniques of 'transference', similarly employed in the prose, allow her to argue for gender equality in the spiritual life of the hereafter, if not in the physical life of the here and now. Pickard argues that Astell's religious poems, 'by focusing solely upon spiritual rather than earthly solutions to questions of gender inequality, elaborate her own feminine conception of other-worldly martyrdom and heroism' (p. 117).

2. Prose

John Parkin's *Taming the Leviathan: The Reception of the Political and Religious Ideas of Thomas Hobbes in England 1640–1700* provides a very scholarly, in-depth study of the reception of Hobbes's work in England in the seventeenth century. The title bears witness to ultimate lack of clarity over who or what was *Leviathan*—the book, or Hobbes himself. Parkin charts the reception of Hobbes's developing theories in his own country from the philosopher's early work to the years immediately following his death (at 91 years of age) in 1679. Attitudes to Hobbes and his work were never simple, never unified, and in many cases they bore little relation to the actual intent of the writer. However, the writer himself was, like his audience, deeply affected by the social and political contexts in which his works took shape. Parkin's research, and his exposition of his subject, reveals not only a great deal about the nature of reputation-building (and destroying) through the period, but along the way much also about the nature of the later seventeenth-century book trade, friendships and patronage politics, political and social networks, together with a penetrating insight into how these interacted with one another. The book is extremely pleasurable to read, despite the depth of the scholarship involved and the apparent (rather than real) dryness of its subject. The chronological divisions make sense, in addition to splitting the volume into easily digestible sections. The volume reveals many interesting characters beside the philosopher himself, and successfully conveys the life and thought of seventeenth-century intellectuals. Parkin charts the means by which criticism of Hobbes developed into 'Hobbism', and how this became by turns a weapon, a definition, or an 'other' by which opponents might be denigrated. Interestingly, he also demonstrates how Hobbism, like Hobbes's ideas themselves, could be shifting and dangerous, a useful tool at one moment and an accusation which stuck the next. Hobbes and the civil war, Hobbes and the Protectorate, Hobbes and the Restoration, Hobbes and Exclusion, Hobbes and the Glorious Revolution, are all analysed, and all are revealed in a different light by this analysis. Parkin does what he sets out to do, and a great deal more besides.

The thought of a book on philosophy does not always fill everyone with excitement, but the essays in *The Concept of Love in 17th and 18th Century Philosophy*, edited by Gábor Boros, Herman de Dijn and Martin Moors, offer insights into some important aspects of moral, social, religious and political thought from Descartes to Locke. Who we love, the nature of how we love, the opposite of love, how we can or cannot love God, the people, the nation, form the bedrock of religious and political thought in an age of 'amateur'

philosophers. In religious terms, the essays also deal with concepts central to
Protestant theology, such as whether it is morally right or wrong to love
people and/or things in this world while claiming, or seeking, to fully love
God. Deeper insights are offered into the political, social and philosophical
ideas of Thomas Hobbes, in relation to a background which ranges from
Descartes to Locke, with many others (Spinoza, Malebranche, Bossuet, Liebniz
and many more, including work by Catherine Wilson on women and
philosophical discussion) in between. Can we feign a moral appearance while
inwardly harbouring desires for personal ambition, money and lust of the flesh?
The issues discussed carried considerable weight in the period covered, and the
book itself repays careful attention in respect of the insights it offers, and the
bibliographical and textual reference information associated with them.

There is more work on Descartes in Christopher Tilmouth's article,
'Generosity and the Utility of the Passions: Cartesian Ethics in Restoration
England' (*SC* 22[2007] 144–67), this time centring on the French philosopher's
less well-known work, *Les Passions de l'âme* [1650], and the level of
engagement with this work in Restoration England. The relationship of soul
and body, and the theory of their connection via the pineal gland or cornarius,
was a topic of some debate at the time, and Descartes deals with this in his
book. After evaluating Descartes's ideas in some detail, Wilson notes their
(provable) influence upon some important writers in Restoration England,
notably John Smith, William Ramesey and Walter Charleton. He demonstrates how these ideas were also used in conjunction with, or refutation of,
those of Thomas Hobbes. He pays particular attention to similarities and
influences in ideas concerning the nature and meaning of 'generosity', and in
conclusion interestingly points to the use of this word by others, such as its use
by John Wilmot, Earl of Rochester, in his poetry. This seems to suggest that
there may be much more in the way of Cartesian influences yet to be
discovered; there will doubtless be much 'following up' of these leads.

In his work on *Exile and Journey in Seventeenth-Century Literature*,
Christopher D'Addario also discusses the work of Thomas Hobbes. It is
D'Addario's overall contention that, despite much authoritative modern work
on exile (for example, that of the late Edward Said), we have not yet related
this to the idea and experience of exiles in less recent history. The experience of
exile, he says, involves the need for private space, while conveying a sense of
loss, uprootedness and provisionality, all of which must be negotiated in text.
This partial alienation from the 'now' occasions a fall from mimetic language
into allegory (see Machosky's article below, on Bunyan's 'fall into allegory'),
and the use of language to carry forward traditions and cultural identity.
There is a distance between the exile's own and hegemonic, accepted forms of
discourse. These elements create a nervousness over the fixity of language, the
importance of public gesture and performance in the constitution of the self.
Hobbes is seen as an exile, his work demonstrating all of these characteristics,
arguably even after his return to England. D'Addario argues that there were
many in Hobbes's audience who did not see themselves as exiles but as
belonging to the established order, who yet found sympathetic voices and ideas
in apparently oppositional writing. In addition to these extremely important
observations, not only on Hobbes but maybe on all English writers after 1640,

D'Addario's work on Hobbes also provides a very interesting and valuable vignette of the book trade—traffic, publication, dissemination and its problems—in the period. This is really significant work.

Three articles concern the writings of John Bunyan. Beth Lynch conducts a very interesting textual and rhetorical examination of the relationship between Bunyan's works and the *Anatomie of Abuses* by sixteenth-century writer Philip Stubbes ('Uses and Abuses: John Bunyan, Philip Stubbes, and the Ambiguity of Literary Influence', *SC* 22[2007] 283–304). Bunyan acknowledged his debt to Arthur Dent's *The Plaine Man's Path-way to Heaven*, a bestseller in his own day, which in turn owed much to Stubbes, but Lynch explores the similarities between Bunyan's work and the Stubbes original with a view to determining whether Bunyan's knowledge of Stubbes is entirely due to Dent's mediation. Did Bunyan actually use the Stubbes original, without acknowledgement? After admitting the difficulty of the task she has set herself, Lynch concludes that, although rhetorical similarities between, in particular, the *Anatomie* and *The Life and Death of Mr Badman* could result from a familiarity with Dent and literary/cultural traditions of his own time and religion, there is sufficient evidence to be drawn from, for example, the 'traveller' characters in the two books for at least a tentative conclusion that Bunyan did also know Stubbes's own work. In any case, says Lynch, this has further eroded the claim, widely believed and advanced by Bunyan himself, that his learning and his sources were very limited.

In her article, 'As Blood Is Forced out of the Flesh: Spontaneity and the Wounds of Exchange in *Grace Abounding* and *The Pilgrim's Progress*' (*ELH* 74[2007] 271–99), Lori Branch examines the influence of economic and legal discourses of salvation on John Bunyan, as evidenced in his self-fashioning in *Grace Abounding*, and in *Pilgrim's Progress*. This is evident, says Branch, in Bunyan's suspicion of his own assurances of salvation. The writer of *Grace Abounding* and *Pilgrim's Progress* ultimately finds reassurance in what amounts to a rejection of the economic and legal bases of Puritan ideas of salvation, in favour of a simple 'letting go', irrationally placing his entire trust in a God of whose favour he realizes he can never be sure. In the course of her argument Branch notes and examines the effects of the Puritan conversion experience (the acknowledgement of Christ's death as payment for an individual's sins) on *Pilgrim's Progress*, in which this forms part of the narrative, as well as on Bunyan himself. The idea of the roll as a proof of salvation is evidence of a 'desperation for certification', and the Puritan desire for certainty of election for paradise. The commerce of Vanity Fair is denigrated, but the same commercial imperative lies at the heart of the writer's own religious faith.

'Trope and Truth in *The Pilgrim's Progress*' (*SEL* 47[2007] 179–98) discusses Bunyan's use of allegory. Brenda Machosky begins her examination with Bunyan's statement in the preface that he 'fell' into allegory while attempting something else, and he then found it difficult, even impossible, to control. Using the idea of the link between allegory and the Baroque allegory of the emblem, Machosky offers the 'fall into allegory' as evidence for her argument that the second part of *Pilgrim's Progress*—Christiana's journey— explains and expands the first part—Christian's pilgrimage to the Holy

City—into an emblem. The first part, which was increasingly open to mis-reading as time went on, could be explained correctly, according to Bunyan's original intent. Christiana is an example of a 'right reader' of the first part of *Pilgrim's Progress*, through the remains/landscape of which she and her fellow pilgrims move. In the course of her article Machosky compares seventeenth-century allegory and emblem with medieval allegory, and concludes with a comparison between the ending of Bunyan's story and Dante's *Divine Comedy*. Instead of merging with the divine, she maintains, the writer/reader of *The Pilgrim's Progress* retains only a glimpse of heaven before 'falling' away again into the allegory of the world. This world is the truly allegorical and unreal, while the seemingly dreamlike is actually the real. This article gains a great deal from being read in conjunction with D'Addario's introductory chapter.

More general in intent and content is Vivasvan Soni's article, 'Trials and Tragedies: the Literature of Unhappiness (a Model for Reading Narratives of Suffering)' (*CL* 59[2007] 119–39). Soni seeks a general methodology and critical language for the study of 'tragedy' and 'trial' narratives. This, Soni says, is lacking but necessary if we are to understand these types of literature, then goes on to propose that this should be grounded not in unhappiness, but in a 'hermeneutic of happiness'. The importance of the question of happiness for the protagonist in a narrative can reveal the differences between trial and tragedy. Is the question of happiness relevant to the life of the protagonist for the duration of the narrative? Questions of differences and similarities between the tragic and the trial begin with classical examples, ending with more contemporary Holocaust narrative. *The Pilgrim's Progress* is considered alongside the story of Job, *Pamela*, *Paradise Lost* and the New Testament story of Christ's temptation. This is all very general, a bit over-general really, but it does contain some interesting ideas which could undoubtedly be noted and developed—like John Aubrey's 'hints' (see the article by Kate Bennett below). I am not sure that the theories expounded actually help with an understanding of Bunyan, but some of the 'hints' might be usefully developed.

Contextualizing the work of Bunyan and other nonconforming writers of the day, William Gibson's 'Dissenters, Anglicans and the Glorious Revolution: *A Collection of Cases*' (*SC* 22[2007] 168–84) asks why the Dissenters made common cause with the Anglican clergy in 1688, rather than accepting the overtures made to them by James II. Gibson studies *The Collection of Cases and other Discourses, lately written to recover Dissenters to the Church of England, by some Divines of the City of London* and its contributors, in order to provide some answers. He discovers that the London clergy involved were a mixture of Presbyterian sympathizers and opponents, but their publication represents a significant movement towards reconciliation with the ejected Nonconformists in the 1680s. By this time, Dissenters had acquired a much more unified identity as a group, in contrast to the fragmented group of sects and 'churches' which existed immediately after the Restoration, and there was considerable sympathy for a reconciliation among Anglican clergy. Thus, nonconforming groups who had been prepared to accept and benefit from Charles II's 1672 Declaration of Indulgence were far more inclined to ally with sympathetic Anglicans in 1688.

Further insight into Protestant literary culture in early modern England is provided by Alison Chapman in her article 'Marking Time: Astrology, Almanacs and English Protestantism' (*RQ* 60[2007] 1257–90). Chapman notes the popularity of the astrological almanac in the seventeenth century, and its reconciliation with earlier Protestant beliefs about faith, time and place. Astrology was both current and credible at this time, although it was called into question by Protestant beliefs that God was everywhere, not specially in one particular place, such as a shrine or church. At the same time, God did not work specially powerfully at a particular time, such as a saint's day or other liturgical festival. Gradually, the Protestant church became aligned with the requirements of popular belief/superstition which would not go away—over one million copies of almanacs were sold, Chapman tells us, between 1664 and 1666 alone. The stars and planets continued to be read as signs placed in the heavens by God, and astrology was seen as an aid to understanding divine handiwork. The heavens were God's book. Chapman notes the increasing trend towards 'newness' of almanacs (rather than perpetual calendars) in the seventeenth century, and their increasing association with particular places and times. Astrological diaries became very popular, some written on blank leaves placed for this purpose in almanacs themselves, an interesting reminder that culture in later seventeenth-century England had many different aspects.

Hobbes's friend and biographer John Aubrey is the subject of Kate Bennett's article 'John Aubrey, Hint-Keeper: Life-Writing and the Encouragement of Natural Philosophy in the Pre-Newtonian Seventeenth Century' (*SC* 22[2007] 358–80). Beginning with Samuel Butler's statements about hint-keeping by the Royal Society in his *Occasional Reflection on Dr Charleton's Feeling a Dog's Pulse at Gresham College*, Bennett examines both Aubrey's own life and his *Brief Lives* for possible answers. The progress of stories such as Isaac Newton's 'discovery' of the forces of gravity by the fall of an apple, and Aubrey's championship of amateur practitioners and researchers such as Francis Potter is used to demonstrate the initial purpose of the pre-Newtonian Royal Society. This consisted of taking ideas, or 'hints', recording and passing them on for testing, to see if they could be of use, and offering a supportive and encouraging environment to those from whom these, frequently very diverse, hints originated. The conflict between this and the idea of the scientist as a single-minded, methodical individual is what essentially lies behind the disputes between Newton and Robert Hooke. Along the way, Bennett opens very interesting doors on the nature of patronage and preferment in the seventeenth century, which invites much further discussion.

The art of occasional meditation itself is explored in 'Redeeming Parcels of Time: Aesthetics and Practice of Occasional Meditation' by Marie-Louise Coolahan (*SC* 22[2007] 124–43). This form of writing, indeed of self-discipline, was developed with the purpose of preventing 'mental meandering' which might lead to sin. Random events or sights might be the occasion for meditation on the spiritual and the divine, which was in its turn both self-improving and useful for others. This type of meditation was a feature of seventeenth-century Protestantism, and often found a literary outlet in spiritual diaries and prayers, usually in prose but sometimes in verse. The occasional meditation was not to be rhetorically complex, and was particularly suitable for women and the less educated lower classes. It could take place in leisure time, or during the working day. Later, says Coolahan, the occasional meditation was appropriated by intellectuals such as Robert Boyle, as a language for natural philosophy. It was Boyle's use of the genre which led to satirical attacks by Butler and Jonathan Swift, but this was not its original form, or its original intention.

Guyla Armstrong examines the progress of a text in 'Paratexts and their Functions in the Seventeenth-Century English Decamerons' (*MLR* 102[2007] 40–57), by means of the paratextual elements of editions of Boccaccio's *Decameron*. The ensuing editions of the 1620 'full text' translation of this Italian medieval classic [1625, 1634, 1657 and 1684] used paratext to place the text within English/Italian/French cultural, literary and linguistic interchange, to situate it within the tastes and understandings of their changing audience, and to make it cater for the requirements of an intended reading public. At the same time, Armstrong offers a view (through a small window) of the book trade, its imperatives and its developments, through this period. By the time the text was edited in 1702, Armstrong notes, the removal of any frame narrative made it possible to read the stories as not being parts of a single work, maybe even without realizing it was a translation at all. How a book is read may be largely conditioned by the manipulation of its paratextual elements.

As David E. Shuttleton's *Smallpox and the Literary Imagination 1660–1820* has not been covered in a previous volume, I will review it here, in the light of the fact that it is an important study which should be brought to potential readers' attention. The book deals with the medical scourge of the 'long eighteenth century', a disease which was important in historical and political terms (as Shuttleton points out) in that it carried off several important members of the Stuart royal family, not least Queen Anne's only surviving heir. The disease is described within its medical context, charting its development from a childhood disease akin to chickenpox, which was fatal in a small number of cases, to a highly contagious killer from the mid-century onwards. Also noted, and extremely important, is smallpox's relationship to the 'great pox' or syphilis. Another major issue is the distance, cultural and social, between the ideal of smooth, white skin and classical beauty and the reality of fever, smell and contagious, suppurating pustules. A social leveller, in that class was not a factor (but was a cultural issue) in who succumbed, the book also pays considerable attention to the accounts of survivors. In this respect, some little-known and highly significant works are critically evaluated, with more valuable information in the bibliography. Shuttleton also discusses the idea of disease as metaphor, and associated moral dilemmas such as whether this terrible illness is a punishment, and whether disease comes from inside or outside a human being. Another extremely interesting issue is the gendering of smallpox, and its cultural association with the sinning female, its semantic relationship with sexually transmitted diseases. Following on from these, another major issue discussed is the gendering of socio-political responses to the scarring left by smallpox. As might be expected, the effect on men in social terms was less than that upon women. This is a lively, well-written and scholarly book, dealing with some of the period's major issues from an interesting and original standpoint, covering more than 'just' the literary.

3. Drama

(a) Restoration Drama

Two strands are apparent in the material covered this year. A focus on staging and the performance experience features prominently, whilst concerns over politics and identity, and in particular masculine and feminine identities, are central to a range of material.

In *Shakespeare and Renaissance Literature before Heterosexuality* Rebecca Ann Bach examines the part played by long eighteenth-century adaptations of Shakespearian plays in shaping what she describes as the 'heterosexual imaginary' (p. 2). Bach argues that there was a progressive shift away from the homosocial framework in which Renaissance plays were written, and through a nuanced comparison of a selection of Shakespearian tragedies with long eighteenth-century adaptations of them, she reveals the ways in which traces of the homosocial past were erased from plays from 1660 onwards. Offering new readings of both Renaissance and Restoration texts, Bach highlights the ways in which the dominance of the heterosexual imaginary has led to misreadings of Renaissance texts by modern scholars. Focusing, in chapter 2, on revisions to characters in Restoration adaptations of *Antony and Cleopatra* and *Timon of Athens* in particular, Bach finds new male and female sexual positions being written and expressed. With the rise of hetero/sexualized masculinity and the reshaping of political and military homosocial bonds as bonds of sexual honour in the heterosexual imaginary, she finds a necessity for the new English female identities of the 'mistress true' and desexualized wife. Focusing closely upon the changing usage and meanings of female descriptors, Bach charts shifting identities for women. In her third chapter she focuses on the reshaping of Shakespearian villains as libertines, and the changing relationship between sexual behaviour and class. She finds that Restoration adaptations show both continuities and differences in sexual ideologies, thereby offering glimpses of emergent heterosexuality. As such, she concludes, these plays and their characters mark a short but important moment of transition from the homosocial to the heterosexual imaginary.

The formation of masculine gender identity is also central to D. Christopher Gabbard's essay 'Clashing Masculinities in Aphra Behn's *The Dutch Lover*' (*SEL* 47[2007] 557–72). Gabbard is interested in Behn's treatment of masculine identities, arguing that the play complicates notions of contemporary masculinity through dramatizing its various subject positions on a spectrum from 'warlike' to 'effeminate'. He concludes that Behn elevates a masculine heroism built on wit and spirit. In 'Aphra Behn's *The City Heiress:* Feminism and the Dynamics of Popular Success on the Late Seventeenth-Century Stage' (*CompD* 41[2007] 141–66) Robert Markley sees Behn treating wit rather differently. He suggests that Behn's regendering of desire and ironic reversals offer one resolution to the difficulty of aligning her commercial success with her protests against anti-feminism. Through an examination of Behn's economic status and earning power, and a nuanced reading of *The City Heiress*, Markley concludes that the play is an ironic treatment of Restoration wit, which challenges both patrilinear society and moral coercion.

Kathleen Leicht's essay 'Dialogue and Duelling in Restoration Comedy' (*SP* 104[2007] 267–80) also focuses upon comedy. Leicht examines comic representations of duelling in a range of plays performed between 1664 and 1707, and in doing so demonstrates the distinctive and diverse ways in which theatrical duels reflected late seventeenth-century social anxieties. From illustrating the ways that changing structures of authority were impacting on individuals and reflecting concerns over the shift from a courtly to a civil society, to offering comments on the performative nature of human interaction and identity and functioning as a means of class identification, the duel's function is demonstrated to be diverse.

In 'Dryden and Lee's *Oedipus*: A Probable Performance in January or February 1697/98' (*TN* 61[2007] 32–4) John D. Baird argues that the preface to George Granville's tragedy *Heroick Love* suggests that *Oedipus* was being performed at Lincoln's Inn Fields in early 1698. In the same issue Tim Keenan takes issue with Colin Visser's influential model of Restoration staging. In 'The early Restoration Stage Re-Anatomized: *The Adventures of Five Hours* at Lincoln's Inn Fields, 1663' (*TN* 61[2007] 12–31) Keenan argues that Visser's model demands unusually long periods of scenic disparity—where the fictional location of the scene and the images on the wings and shutters are at odds—and that evidence from foreign visitors praising scenery for its flexibility and changeability makes these levels of scenic disparity unlikely. A more likely model of scenic arrangement, Keenan argues, is offered in his 2006 essay, 'An Early English Restoration Theatre: Modelling the Lincoln's Inn Fields Stage (1661–74)' (in Tabata ed., *Chikamatsu, Osaka, and the World: Cultural Exchange in Drama between East and West*). Applying this model to the particular demands of staging Sir Samuel Tuke's *The Adventures of Five Hours*, Keenan demonstrates how the otherwise apparently enigmatic stage action might be clarified without rejecting the text's staging information, or demanding a special mode of audience perception.

The staging of *The Adventures of Five Hours* is also examined by Richard Kroll in *Restoration Drama and 'The Circle of Commerce: Tragicomedy, Politics and Trade in the Seventeenth Century*. Kroll draws together theories of economic circulation and trade with early modern ideas on the circulation of blood and bodily fluids, and argues that the concept of circulation informs the objects, characters and plot devices in Restoration tragicomedy. The first half of his study centres around Restoration drama's role as a prime vehicle of political debate. Kroll proposes that tragicomedies were, with their inbuilt indeterminacies and like Davenant's masques of the 1630s, forms of advice to the monarch rather than instruments of Stuart absolutism. Exemplifying, for Kroll, the significant continuities between early and late Stuart drama, which he argues must be considered on a continuum, Davenant and his fondness for Fletcher feature as a touchstone throughout the study. The middle part is devoted to charting Davenant's development from the 1630s through to his collaboration with Dryden on *The Tempest*. The exploration of staging, and in particular of the perspectival stage's role in the thematic argument of a play, is demonstrated to be central to Davenant's progression, and to have culminated with this production. In the final section of the book Kroll examines six Restoration plays, from *Marriage à la Mode* through to *The Way of the World*, concluding that Restoration drama as a whole functioned as a form for authoritative political debate and analysis of society.

Drama's role in social and political debate, and dramatic continuities across the seventeenth century are also central themes for Matthew Birchwood. In *Staging Islam in England: Drama and Culture, 1640–1685* Birchwood traces the changing significance and dramatic treatment of Islam at a time of revolutionary change for the English and Ottoman empires, demonstrating the intensity of dramatic recourse to Islam at points of national crisis. Arguing that English national identity was shaped through its cultural encounters with Islam throughout the period, Birchwood proposes that Islam was a central construct by which national identity, authority and religion were debated in the highly politicized dramas of the middle decades of the seventeenth century. Charting this debate, Birchwood concludes that the instability of Islam as a touchstone explains its popularity with writers of diverse political allegiances.

The diversity of essays and material covered in Daniel Ennis and Judith Slagle's edited collection *Prologues, Epilogues, Curtain-Raisers, and Afterpieces: The Rest of the Eighteenth-Century London Stage* offers a valuable picture of the wider theatrical experience in the long eighteenth century. Other than Chloe Wigston Smith's essay, 'Dressing Up Character: Theatrical Paintings from the Restoration to the Mid-Eighteenth Century' (pp. 70–105), the essays dealing with Restoration performance focus largely on prologues and epilogues. Smith's essay, however, looks at the new mode of theatrical painting in the Restoration and argues that audiences read stage costume through a lens of portraiture. She charts the shifting visual codes by which character was marked across the period, demonstrating the differences in representations of actors and actresses until the early eighteenth century. The celebrated Restoration actresses Anne Oldfield and Nell Gwynn are the focus of Diana Solomon's essay, 'Tragic Play, *Bawdy* Epilogue?' (in Ennis and Slagle, eds., pp. 155–78). Solomon argues for the bawdy epilogue as a uniquely female form of performance, merging character and persona and creating a state of 'betweenness'. In this way, she argues, bawdy epilogues challenged Restoration notions of unity and generic integrity, undermining audiences' investment in character and plot. She concludes that this sacrifice of role and genre in the epilogue functioned to return the actress to her position as (lower-class) whore, and satisfied audience demands for the actress's sexual display. The display of actresses' sexuality is also a theme in Paul McCallum's essay, 'Cozening the Pit: Prologues, Epilogues and Poetic Authority in Restoration England' (in Ennis and Slagle, eds., pp.33–69), where he argues that such displays appeal to the 'pit's collective sexual ego' (p. 42). McCallum is interested in the different ways that playwrights used prologues and epilogues between 1667 and 1677 to cozen the pit into embracing an identity which would ultimately undermine their public authority during the twin crises of the Popish Plot and Exclusion. As well as charting the shift in the tone of prologues and epilogues in the early 1680s McCallum concludes that long-term cozening was a central means by which Restoration playwrights located themselves and their stage as prominent political and social authorities. Robert Sawyer offers a different perspective on the function of the prologue and epilogue in his essay on Dryden's contributions to the form, 'Prologues and Epilogues: Performing Shakespearean Criticism in the Restoration' (in Ennis and Slagle, eds., pp.135–54). Sawyer suggests that by considering Dryden's prologues and epilogues as a unique example of dramatic criticism in performance we can untangle his apparently conflicted relationship to Shakespeare. Drawing on Bakhtin in his detailed analysis of the prologues and epilogues, Sawyer concludes that the works cumulatively offer a picture of a writer wrestling with the most significant figure in the canon in order to shape his own identity as a playwright.

Susanna Centlivre's prologues are the focus of Rivka Svenson's essay, '"A soldier is her darling character": Susanna Centlivre, Desire, Difference, and Disguise' (*JNT* 37:i[2007] 65–87). As well as drawing attention to features and strategies within a range of Centlivre's prologues Svenson pays particular attention to the prologue for *A Bold Stroke for a Woman*. She is particularly interested in moving beyond the subject/object discourse in exploring the relationship between author and spectator within prologues, and concludes that Centlivre's prologues challenge such dichotomies as male and female, and self and other, working instead to cultivate exchange between the theatrical parties.

The Man of Mode, or Sir Fopling Flutter, edited and introduced by Trevor R. Griffiths, is a good-value, student-friendly edition based on the quarto of 1676. It includes a concise introduction to Etherege, Restoration theatre, key themes and the play in performance.

(b) Dryden

Richard Kroll's *Restoration Drama and 'The Circle of Commerce'* is mainly about seventeenth-century tragicomedies or double-plot plays. Kroll argues that they offered constructive criticism of the Stuart monarchy; he begins with Davenant and concludes that both he and Dryden were loyalists who 'consistently urged their royal audiences to examine and so justify, rather than merely assert, the grounds of their power'. Discussion then focuses on six representative plays: *Marriage à la Mode*, *The Plain Dealer*, *The Rover*, *All for Love*, *Don Sebastian* and *The Way of the World*. These are chosen partly because 'they are good plays too infrequently performed', though Kroll doubts whether *Don Sebastian* would work on the stage today. I would think a similar claim might be made for the Dryden–Davenant *Tempest* and some other plays which would work on the stage, but not that it could be substantiated in a book that so learnedly relates them all to seventeenth-century natural and political philosophy, and to political and commercial history. Shakespeare's and the Dryden–Davenant *Tempest* are found to be 'starkly different' because the former sees 'real evil' in Caliban, while the latter sees 'political immaturity' in Hippolito, who somewhat resembles Charles II. Hobbes is brought to bear on the problems of *Marriage à la Mode*, where the low plot commends marriage more persuasively than the high plot supports monarchy. In *All for Love* Dryden offers Charles the bad example of Antony and the good one of Octavius, whom Antony characteristically dismisses as a mere tradesman. In *Don Sebastian* Dryden's 'double thesis' is that 'actual kings are highly problematic, not to say self-defeating', while the ideal king is absent, 'the transcendental signifier for the system, securing but not disrupting it'. I notice that this chapter reprints Kroll's *HLQ* article (*YWES* 82[2003] 471), including his own memorable signifier, 'an experiential disequilibrium that catapults one historical moment into the next, so weaving the web by which we recognize "history"'.

I noted three articles in learned journals. The one of most general interest was James A. Winn's '"Thy wars brought nothing about": Dryden's Critique of Military Heroism' (*SC* 21[2006] 364–82). Winn argues persuasively that, despite his 'dutiful gestures' in support of the militant but not triumphant activities of Charles II and his brother James, Dryden throughout his career showed 'a healthy scepticism about warfare and a deep distaste for violence'. Evidence comes from many sources; in his drama, his adaptation of *Troilus and Cressida*, his embarrassments over the heroic plays and *Amboyna*, the opera *King Arthur*, and of course *The Secular Masque*. Michael Burden's '"To repeat (or not to repeat)?"': Dance Cues in Restoration English Opera' (*EMu* 35[2007] 397–417) concludes that in performances 'there was more dancing than even the already copious amounts suggested by the printed sources'. Students, and especially producers of *King Arthur* and other Restoration operas, will profit from reading this well-illustrated essay. John D. Baird's 'Dryden and Lee, *Oedipus*: A Probable Performance in January or February 1697/8' (*TN* 61[2007] 32–4) reports 'circumstantial' evidence that this play was revived at that time, probably by Betterton's company. Certainly there are references to *Oedipus* in two 1698 publications, and Dryden's 'noble and sublime Thoughts and Expressions' are contrasted with Lee's 'Rants and Fustian'.

Books Reviewed

Bach, Rebecca Ann. *Shakespeare and Renaissance Literature before Heterosexuality*. Palgrave. [2007] pp. ix + 243. £45. ISBN 9 7802 3060 3639.

Baron, Sabrina Alcorn, Eric N. Lindquist and Eleanor F. Shevlin, eds. *Agent of Change: Print Culture Studies after Elizabeth L. Einstein*. UMassP. [2007] pp. vii + 442. ISBN 9 7815 5849 5920.

Birchwood, Matthew. *Staging Islam in England: Drama and Culture, 1640–1685*. Brewer. [2007] pp. viii + 200. £50. ISBN 9 7818 4384 1272.

Boros, Gábor, Herman de Dijn, and Martin Moors, eds. *The Concept of Love in 17th and 18th Century Philosophy*. LeuvenUP. [2007] pp. 269. €34.50. ISBN 9 7890 5867 6511.

Clingham, Greg, ed. *Sustaining Literature: Essays on Literature, History, and Culture, 1500–1800, Commemorating the Life and Work of Simon Varey*. BuckUP. [2007] pp. 352. £56.95 ISBN 9 7808 3875 6560.

D'Addario, Christopher. *Exile and Journey in Seventeenth-Century Literature.* CUP. [2007] pp. 208. £47 ISBN 9 7805 2187 0290, e-book ISBN 9 7805 1128 2287.

Eliot, Simon, Andrew Nash and Ian Willison, eds. *Literary Cultures and the Material Book.* BL. [2007] pp. xix + 444. £45 ISBN 9 7807 1230 6843.

Ennis, Daniel James, and Judith Bailey Slagle. *Prologues, Epilogues, Curtain-Raisers, and Afterpieces: The Rest of the Eighteenth-Century London Stage.* UDelP. [2007] pp. ix + 260. $47.50. ISBN 0 8741 3967 8.

Griffiths, Trevor R., ed. *The Man of Mode, or, Sir Fopling Flutter,* by George Etherege. Hern. [2007] pp. v + 138. pb £3.99. ISBN 9 7818 5459 9650.

Hume, Robert D., and Harold Love. *Plays, Poems, and Miscellaneous Writings associated with George Villiers, Second Duke of Buckingham,* 2 vols. OUP. [2007] pp. lxii + 752, x + 403. £110 ISBN 9 7801 9812 7611 (set).

Kolbrener, William and Michal Michelson, eds., *Mary Astell: Reason, Gender, Faith.* Ashgate [2007] pp. x + 219. ISBN 0754652645.

Kroll, Richard. *Restoration Drama and the 'Circle of Commerce': Tragicomedy, Politics, and Trade in the Seventeenth Century.* CUP. [2007] pp. vii + 312. £55 ISBN 9 7805 2182 8376.

McColley, Diane Kelsey. *Poetry and Ecology in the Age of Milton and Marvell.* Ashgate. [2007] pp. 252. £55 ISBN 9 7807 5466 0484.

Parkin, John. *Taming the Leviathan: The Reception of the Political and Religious Ideas of Thomas Hobbes in England 1640–1700.* CUP. [2007] pp. 472. £63 ISBN 9 7805 2187 7350.

Shuttleton, David E. *Smallpox and the Literary Imagination 1660–1820.* CUP. [2006] pp. 264. £50 ISBN 9 7805 2187 2096.

Tabata, ed., *Chikamatsu, Osaka, and the World: cultural exchange in drama between East and West,* Osaka: Osaka City University, 2006.

Chapter XI

The Eighteenth Century

STEVEN LYNN, ELLES SMALLEGOOR, DAVID SHUTTLETON AND MARJEAN PURINTON

This chapter has four sections: 1. Prose and General; 2. The Novel; 3. Poetry; 4. Drama. Section 1 is by Steven Lynn; section 2 is by Elles Smallegoor; section 3 is by David Shuttleton; section 4 is by Marjean Purinton.

1. Prose and General

To begin at the beginning, Kevin Cope's *In and After the Beginning: Inaugural Moments and Literary Institutions in the Long Eighteenth Century* is this year's most challenging and stimulating, most brilliant and daring, book. What comes 'in and after the beginning' is ostensibly everything, and Cope's book, which begins with a chapter on the amalgamative rhetoric of the Restoration, is itself an amalgamative organism, swallowing the entire long eighteenth century. Cope asserts that he is focusing on works 'that take as their focus the *convergence* of disparate parts into what authors proclaim to be a purportedly new social institution' (p. 14), but these convergent starting points, Cope says, are also the 'beginnings for divergence', and the expanse of works that fit into his topic is mind-boggling. Cope juxtaposes Bunyan and Royal Society experiments, Shaftesbury's *Characteristics* and Defoe's *Robinson Crusoe* (the notion of Crusoe's 'one-man club' is delightful); he deals with texts as varied as Samuel Hartlib's *The Reformed Virginian Silkworm* and Cowper's *The Task*. Cope's essay is more of an inspired meditation on 'perpetual beginning' than a thesis-driven analysis. His interest in 'garbology', the 'throw-away detail' that is introduced for no reason, is fertile, but is a kind of new beginning in itself, as well as an illustration of itself. Whatever the reader's interests, Cope will provide some entertaining and unexpected insights, as well as some engaging conversation-starters.

Conversation figures crucially in Paul Trolander and Zeynep Tenger's *Sociable Criticism in England, 1625–1725*, which opens up new resources and new ways of thinking about the history of literary criticism. By focusing on published criticism, Trolander and Tenger argue, we have missed a whole world of 'sociable' criticism that circulated largely in oral discussions and

Year's Work in English Studies, Volume 88 (2009) © *The English Association; all rights reserved*
doi:10.1093/ywes/map009

private documents. The purpose of this criticism was social and political, not aesthetic or interpretative, as authors collaborated with friends and relatives to shape the reception of their work, advance their personal careers or reputation, cultivate favour, create affiliations and much more. Lively chapters on Katherine Philips, Margaret Cavendish, Dryden, *The Rehearsal*, religious reform and John Dennis lead up to the climactic chapter on the literary criticism in Addison's *Spectator*. Katherine Philips and her sociable circle, for instance, provide Trolander and Tenger with a compelling case, illustrating how the manuscript reception of her writing was guided by influential criticism. The social connections created by the discussion of her poetry assisted Phillips in attempting to recover family property, rehabilitate the family's reputation, and relocate from Dublin to London. Trolander and Tenger not only identify this rich resource of sociable criticism, based on the ideals of conversation and mutual benefit, but they also explain how it was supplanted. John Dennis's *Impartial Critick* attempted in 1693 to displace this private coterie criticism with public objectivity, but Dennis seemed ill-natured, unfriendly, repulsive in his strictures. Dryden's *Essay of Dramatic Poesy*, violating the rules of small-group discussion, friendship and patron–client relationships, was judged imprudent and rude. Addison, however, successfully adopted a rhetorical stance that synthesized the writer's concerned friend with the impartial guardian of social and literary standards. The shift, Trolander and Tenger convincingly conclude, marks a crucial turn for literary criticism, as 'the social context that had once bound closet readers and writers had been renegotiated to bind print readers and print writers' (p. 175).

A different perspective on conversation is taken by Ann Dean in *The Talk of the Town: Figurative Publics in Eighteenth-Century Britain*, which focuses on two simple and fascinating questions: 'What does a good political discussion sound like? How can that sound be represented in print?'. The answers are important because the development of a republican government, according to Kant and Habermas, depends upon informed public opinion, which results from open and reasonable discussion. Did the British have such discussions in the eighteenth century? British writers, as Dean shows us, 'frequently reported that they had participated in such discussions, locating them in spaces that were neither universally accessible nor reasonable—private parties, male-only urban coffee houses, the King's Drawing Room' (p. 11). In eighteenth-century Britain, Dean argues, 'the public sphere was a figure of speech'. People who were not physically present at conversations nonetheless imagined them and understood their own sociable interactions as extensions of these represented discussions. Thus writing and printing helped to create the sense of people talking: in coffeehouses, in drawing rooms, in civic meetings. Dean is not positing one huge textual coffeehouse that gave the illusion of a public discourse, but she is instead drawing our attention to 'hundreds of coffeehouses with people and language circulating among them' (p. 16). Although eighteenth-century writers might refer to 'the nation' or 'the people', they located political talk in 'representative coffeehouses, drawing rooms, or meetings' (p. 17).

Dean's extensive and imaginative research draws especially on letters, memoirs and newspapers (especially the *London Chronicle* and *Public*

Advertiser). Separate chapters are devoted to coffeehouse talk in the *Spectator* and its heirs, to the language of court politics, to the political 'clamour' depicted in the newspapers, and to the 'candid debate' described in parliament. In the wake of the *Spectator*, coffeehouses were often described in newspapers, books and letters as 'schools of democracy', places where a cobbler and a peer of the realm 'could share a newspaper and a political discussion' (p. 21). Thus, as coffeehouse conversations were taking place in London, Birmingham, Philadelphia and Kingston, the public sphere could be imagined as a local and familiar social space. The courtly sphere was also represented in print for a growing public audience, amplifying a network of manuscripts and gossip. The newspapers also helped to create the sense of a national conversation through, as Dean puts it, 'a bewildering array of literary devices, including dialogues, narratives, lectures, prophetic dreams, overheard coffeehouse conversations, observations of fictional visitors from Asia or Europe, and various combinations of the above' (p. 22). The legalization of parliamentary reporting in 1771, Dean notes, had of course a dramatic effect on the way parliament was depicted. Opening up parliament, exposing its 'free and candid debate', encouraged other bodies to emulate, including debating societies, charities and civic associations. Dean's topic ultimately is the question—as important today as it was in the eighteenth century—of 'how a republican government derives legitimacy, of what makes an opinion or a discussion public, and of how actions by the state are understood and judged by citizens' (p. 24). The 'figurative publics' that she identifies clearly played a key role. Although no one would be surprised by the assertion that Addison and Steele promoted Augustan values of decorum, good sense and politeness, we still may wonder why characters who exemplify these values are almost completely absent from their work. Anthony Pollock argues, in 'Neutering Addison and Steele: Aesthetic Failure and the Spectatorial Public Sphere' (ELH 74[2007] 707–34), that 'the ideal of spectatorial neutrality or of "standing Neuter" is central to Addison and Steele's cultural project', and their papers 'stage the failure of their public engagement in order to enable a privately-conducted neutralization...of their audience's impulse to make ethics public' (p. 707).

If national identity was in some degree a matter of talking, it was also a matter of feeling, as Evan Gottlieb finds in *Feeling British: Sympathy and National Identity in Scottish and English Writing, 1707–1832*. Gottlieb wants to consider how the discourse of sympathy relates to the formation of national identity, and he finds that sympathy both advances and complicates the notion of 'feeling British'. Beginning with 1707 and the Act of Union, Gottlieb considers how the literary public sphere contributed to the harmonizing and unifying efforts of government policy. Gottlieb's introduction, '"Union and No Union": Feeling British in the Long Eighteenth Century', focuses on the Scottish Enlightenment's understanding of sympathy, the sharing of emotions between people. 'Union and No Union' is of course Defoe's title for his 1713 pamphlet, which assesses 'the Grievances of the Scots'. While Defoe acknowledges the legitimate complaints all around, he nonetheless argues vigorously for the rightness of the Union. Defoe understood that changing the way people felt about each other—their sympathy for one another—would be crucial to fostering a sense of unity. Gottlieb does not argue that Britishness was invented in the eighteenth century, or that being British precluded the Scots from self-identifying in many other ways (including gender and class), but he does claim that 'a more secular, more popular, and therefore more modern form of Britishness' emerged, and that 'the discourse of sympathy... was central to the formation of this new identity' (pp. 14–15).

Gottlieb also examines David Hume and Adam Smith's different theories of moral sympathy and considers their implications for the project of 'feeling British'. For Hume, Gottlieb says, 'sympathy is a nonrational, involuntary mechanism by which people take on each other's emotions and even opinions', whereas for Smith, sympathy is 'a voluntary, "achieved" state of emotional harmony capable of actively uniting disparate peoples' (p. 22). Gottlieb finds that Smollett's work stages a debate between Hume and Smith's theories, and his chapter on Boswell and Johnson reads Johnson's *Journey* as a failed effort to connect sympathetically with the Scots, whereas Boswell creates an adaptable national identity for himself and for Lowland Scots generally. Chapters on Romantic poetry and Scotland and on Scott's Waverley novels show how the centrality of sympathy in advancing national feeling evolves into a more imperial orientation. This is a lively and deftly argued book, yet another benefit from the foundation provided by Linda Colley. A nice companion to *Feeling British* is provided by Leonard Tennenhouse in *The Importance of Feeling English: American Literature and the British Diaspora, 1750–1850*. The link between America's desire for national identity and the emergence of American literature, Tennenhouse observes, has seemed so obvious as to require no analysis. But the first American authors, writing of course in the context of pre-existing British models, were also influencing British writers, and Tennenhouse points to the impact of Timothy Dwight, Philip Freneau, William Hill Brown and Charles Brockden Brown upon Jane Austen, Horace Walpole and others. By rethinking American literature as 'a literature of diaspora', drawing attention to American writers' efforts to embody Englishness in their works, Tennenhouse thus challenges the concept of 'American literature' as well as expanding our notions of British literary history. The English were, as Tennenhouse says, 'just one among several such groups who attempted to make a home in an utterly alien place', but the English Americans were able to transform the culture they inhabited by reproducing language and form associated with 'Englishness'. In this transformation, which certainly included the participation of many other groups (but which was initiated by the English Americans), the Americans, Tennenhouse concludes, 'not only ceased to be diasporic but ceased to be English as well' (p. 128).

Another perspective on the complex issue of 'being British' is offered by Nick Harding in *Hanover and the British Empire, 1700–1837*. Harding argues that our political and intellectual history has underestimated the importance of the connection between Great Britain and Hanover between 1714 and 1837, and he highlights the European influences in British imperial thinking, focusing on the nature of 'empire' as it was conceived in Britain. Hanoverian mercenaries were often used by the British, and Hanover often found that the British were not serving them well. By complicating and enriching our sense of Hanover's place in British history, Harding is especially interested in fostering a greater appreciation of 'Britain's European identity' (p. 14). A 'unique window on Britain's history between 1750 and 1850' is presented in John Severn's *Architects of Empire: The Duke of Wellington and his Brothers* (p. xii), which ambitiously tells the story of five brothers, focusing on Wellington but richly amplified by this larger familial context. An alternative approach to national identity is presented by Leanne Maunu's excellent study, *Women Writing the Nation: National Identity, Female Community, and the British–French Connection, 1770–1820*, which challenges the emerging emphasis on nationalism and political theory derived from Linda Colley's landmark work, *Britons: Forging the Nation 1707–1837*. In her *Letters on the Female Mind, its Powers and Pursuits*, Laeticia Matilda Hawkins imagined a female community, a society of women living in comfort and safety, creating their own small paradise. Such a vision, Maunu notes, was shared by many British women around the time Hawkins was writing in 1793. It was a defining moment for British national identity, and Colley's argument in part is that competition with France, a common enemy, united disparate Britons: England after all had been at war with France off and on since 1689, and declared war yet again in 1793. What the British had in common was that they were not the French, and they therefore imagined themselves as a community. They were a single people, as Colley puts it, 'not because of any political or cultural consensus at home, but rather in reaction to the Other beyond their shores' (quoted p. 15). What Maunu wishes to add to this project is a deeper consideration of how women contributed to the creation of national identity. So far, Maunu notes, work has concentrated on women's gender politics and their contribution to literature. But nationalism was 'entrenched in their very beings' (p. 14), and so Maunu wants to remedy the lack of attention given by Colley and others to the 'often conflicting demands that exist between gender and national identity' (pp. 16–17).

Focusing particularly on Frances Burney, Charlotte Smith and Mary Wollstonecraft, Maunu makes the case that if we look more closely at late eighteenth-century women writers, 'it was often not their *national* identity that these women used to be heard, but rather their *gender* identity': 'British women took advantage, as it were, of the nationalist discourses dominating the political landscape to promote their own gender politics' (p. 17). They mimicked a national imagined community, imagining within the imagined community of Britons a subgroup of women, united by gender as much as by national affiliation. For men, in other words, the common bond is Britishness; for women, it is gender identity within a British context. But women typically envisioned an inclusively gendered and nationalist community, one that would welcome women who were undetermined or evolving in their national identity. If the national identity of men included the assumption that anyone who is not one of Us is one of Them, women typically had a different view, according to Maunu's research, tending to accept that another woman in a politically liminal state might become one of Us. There were vast differences to be sure in the way women imagined these communities, ranging from Mary Wollstonecraft and the 'protolesbian space' in her unfinished work on 'The Wrongs of Woman', to Laeticia Hawkins, who worried about women being too close to each other, in part because they might lose the protection of men.

But throughout a wide range of women writers, nationalism and gender were 'ideologically and rhetorically intertwined with each other' (p. 20).

Nationalism, gender and sexual orientation have all been viewed in essentialist or constructionist terms. As Chris Mounsey and Caroline Gonda observe in *Queer People: Negotiations and Expressions of Homosexuality, 1700–1800*, social constructionists have arrived at the point at which it is possible to ask whether 'homosexuals existed in history'. Lisa Jardine and Alan Stewart for instance seem uninterested in the question of Francis Bacon's sexuality because 'the homosexual is a modern construct and cannot be located in the Renaissance' (p. 11). Although essentialists can easily counter by saying that of course we can identify people who lived then whose status as homosexuals would be recognizable today, the question still remains of where we should be positioned as students of culture and history. In terms of where we actually are positioned, Rictor Norton's *The Myth of the Modern Homosexual*, as Mounsey and Gonda point out, argues for the essential historical reality of same-sex desire. Similar divisions exist in our understanding of lesbianism (Emma Donoghue's essentialism versus Harriette Andreadis's social constructionism, for instance). Mounsey and Gonda's goal in this collection is to demonstrate 'that both approaches have their strength, and that neither, on its own, encompasses all the subtleties needed for the analysis of homosexuality' (p. 11). They say, in other words, that there is no principled reason 'why social constructionist strategies should preclude historical understanding, or why historical contextualization should preclude social constructionism'. But what about the principle that these two views are based on mutually contradictory assumptions, as Diana Fuss's *Essentially Speaking* argues? Mounsey and Gonda are able to propose drawing on both ways of seeing by setting aside the most basic assumptions of a sexual dichotomy. This opening, acknowledging that there is instead a continuum of sexualities, allows each theory to contribute substantially. This way forward seems thoroughly persuasive, consistent for instance with some sociologists' notion that nature (essence) might contribute 60 per cent, and nurture (construction) might contribute 40 per cent of a person's individuality, as Mounsey and Gonda note, although the idea of a continuum still may seem, in some respects, too simple for the multi-vectored complexity that is human sexuality.

Mounsey and Gonda provide an unusually rich discussion of how the collection's essays fit into the ongoing scholarly discussions. In the initial essay, Ellen Harris sets up the problem by discussing the problematic public reaction to her biography *Handel as Orpheus* (pp. 41–66). Harris's book, even before it was published, was announced with banner headlines 'Handel Was Gay', which misrepresents her work in several ways. The subsequent essays illustrate the various benefits of a more sophisticated critical approach, one that embraces both essentialist and social constructionist views. In this group of excellent and engaging essays, several seemed especially resonant: Thomas King's 'How (Not) to Queer Boswell' (pp. 114–58) looks carefully at the evidence and the frameworks for reading it and weighs the gains and losses of describing Boswell as homosocial or homoerotic, and of declining to do so: 'by assuming the identity of males', King says, we 'naturalize modern genders and repeat the erasure of an early erotic economy that was not based only in the gender of its subjects' (p. 146). Also, Joseph Campana's witty 'Cruising Crusoe: Diving into the Wreck of Sexuality' (pp. 159–79) convincingly argues that 'the sodomite' as a critical category is worn out and useless. Caroline Gonda's 'Queer Doings in Oxford: *The Christian's New Warning Piece* (1753)' (pp. 261–73) explores this work's dramatically explicit sexual satire in the context of the failure of the Jew Bill and the fear of mass circumcision. Gonda exposes some fascinating ambiguities of sexual potency and hetero- versus homoeroticism. An interestingly related model for 'a theory of the self' is explored in Rebecca Tierney-Hynes's 'Hume, Romance, and the Unruly Imagination' (*SEL* 47[2007] 641–58). Tierney-Hynes argues that Hume's thoughts on popular romance influence his theory of sympathy; focusing on his essays and his *Treatise of Human Nature* [1739], Tierney-Hynes concludes that 'the imagination in contact with literature is Hume's model for his theory of the self' (p. 645).

Although Katherine Crawford's *European Sexualities, 1400–1800* may not advance our understanding substantially, Crawford nonetheless deftly synthesizes a great deal of material. Crawford's History 221 students are thanked in the acknowledgements, and this book would work well as a core text for any course dealing with the history of sexuality. One of Crawford's unifying concerns, at times fading far to the background, is the story of how sexuality became, quite recently, 'the preeminent personal referential frame' (p. 3): 'Sexual identity', Crawford observes, 'worked rather differently before 1800' (p. 2). The book is also about the essentialist versus social constructionist view of sexuality, which Crawford frames succinctly in this way: 'On the one hand, essentialist thinking allowed that "deviance" would have to be accepted as innate. On the other hand, constructionists felt that even the most persistent sexual prejudices might be reconstructed' (pp. 4–5). Like Mounsey and Gonda, Crawford believes that both positions 'have merit', and her study also tries 'to negotiate between them', taking account of both lived experience and its representations (p. 5).

Crawford devotes comprehensive chapters to 'Marriage and Family: The Nexus of the Sexual', 'Religion and Sexuality', 'The Science of Sex', 'Sex and Crime' and 'Deviancy and the Cultures of Sex', and in her 'Conclusion: Regimes of Sexuality' Crawford asks 'Why was (is) there so much anxiety about sex?' (p. 232). Obviously interpersonal reasons (fears of encountering or losing intimacy, jealousy) and cultural reasons (religious prohibitions, disease) were important, but Crawford finds that 'one historical answer stands out: anxiety about sex was anxiety about procreation' (p. 232). But this anxiety about procreation was also layered onto other meanings and issues: power, pleasure, social status, communal organization, intimacy, affection. 'The earlier layers did not disappear', Crawford maintains (p. 233), and she concludes her book with a whirlwind recap of how sex was perceived from ancient Greece through to the Enlightenment. In a book that tries to accommodate the spectrum of approaches across a daunting historical expanse, Crawford ends by asserting the paradoxical nature of the current centrality of sexual identity, which 'denies and enables personal specificity; denies and enables the hegemony of the "normal" relative to the "deviant";

denies and enables the layers of history that provided possibilities from which sexual identity could be claimed or fashioned' (p. 237).

It's not exactly Indiana Jones, but Hal Gladfelder's 'In Search of Lost Texts: Thomas Cannon's *Ancient and Modern Pederasty Investigated and Exemplify'd*' (*ECLife* 31[2007] 22–38) does add to our understanding of sexuality in this period, telling the fascinating story of a missing text, a circuitous search, and an apparent recovery: mostly. From a mysterious notice in 1749 in the *Gentleman's Magazine*, through various clues, to the King's Bench court records, Gladfelder explains how he recovered an apparently truncated version of Cannon's text, which is 'significant as the most extensive and varied treatment of male same-sex desire in all of eighteenth-century literature' (pp. 34–5). The text itself is presented, edited by Gladfelder, in 'The Indictment of John Purser, Containing Thomas Cannon's *Ancient and Modern Pederasty Investigated and Exemplify'd*' (*ECLife* 31[2007] 39–61), and it is both intriguing and amusing to see how the text pretends to be criticizing the sexuality presented, but is obviously actually celebrating and luxuriating in the acts described.

Identity in a different sense is the key issue in 'Olaudah Equiano and the Eighteenth-Century Debate on Africa' (*ECS* 40[2007] 241–55) by George Boulukos. Why, Boulukos asks, does Olaudah Equiano define his national identity as British rather than Igbo or Beninite in *The Interesting Narrative* [1789]? The answer, Boulukos says, can be found in a debate involving William Snelgrave, Anthony Benezet and others who would have portrayed Africans as brutal or corrupted, thus leading Equiano to present a different persona. The struggle to negotiate identity is also key to Mary Peace's 'The Magdalen Hospital and the Fortunes of Whiggish Sentimentality in Mid-Eighteenth-Century Britain: "Well-Grounded" Exemplarity vs. "Romantic" Exceptionality' (*ECent* 48[2007] 125–48). Peace considers the evolution of the sentiments that led to the founding of the Hospital for Penitent Prostitutes, and she argues that it is 'the cultural high-water mark of the earlier sentimental, Whiggish discourse of improvement' (p. 125). In this origin Peace finds 'the seeds of its . . . decline in the 1780s' into a 'sanctimonious sweatshop'. In '"Callico Madams": Servants, Consumption, and the Calico Crisis' (*ECLife* 31[2007] 29–55), Chloe Wigston Smith examines the depiction in 1719–21 of 'Indian textiles as a national threat to English trade and gender roles' (p. 29). Defoe, Steele and others wrote pamphlets and tracts supporting the wool trade and attempting to control the sexuality, consumption and appearance of working women. But by focusing so much upon 'the sartorial transgressions of servants, the anti-calico pamphleteers betray their own ends, criticizing working women for their inability to refrain from buying calico, while at the same time confirming the power of servants to express themselves in the marketplace' (p. 29).

A more startling view of women and control emerges in Anne-Marie Kilday's *Women and Violent Crime in Enlightenment Scotland*, which is the first substantial study of Scottish women's involvement in crime during the pre-modern period. Consider: between 1750 and 1815, some 4,223 people from Lowland Scotland were indicted at the Justiciary Court (p. 147). Women comprised 23 per cent (967) of this group. A stunning percentage of these women were indicted for violent offences: 72 per cent (696 out of 967), compared to 40 per cent of the men (1,294 out of 3,256). This finding obviously challenges the commonly held opinion that women were very rarely brought to court on violent charges during this period. It is also striking that none of these women was described as being drunk at the time of her offence, although the men were often involved in random drunken disputes. Very few of the women appeared to commit violent acts as the result of mental illness. The women's violent acts were 'habitually premeditated' and many were involved in family-related violence (p. 148).

With chapters devoted to Scottish crime and women, Scots law, homicide, infanticide, assault, popular disturbances and robbery, Kilday's book convincingly challenges previous feminist perspectives that have seen women as victims of male violence, male institutions and male-controlled economies. But why were Lowland Scottish women so violent, much more than in other European countries? Kilday's speculations include the recognition that there were fewer barriers to Lowland Scottish women entering the world of commerce and work. Women were thus more likely to achieve economic independence, more likely to be outside the home, more likely to see themselves as equal to men and more willing to believe that they needed to protect themselves or look out for their own interests. Kilday notes also that Scottish women have a long history of involvement in resistance to oppression. Their religious fervour, Kilday says, might also have made them more willing to act in righteous vengeance or self-defence, as they perceived it. Or perhaps Scottish judges were just more willing to make an example of them. Whatever the reason, Kilday's chronicling of the 'active agency' of these women is an important contribution to cultural and criminological history.

Our understanding of women's non-lethal agency in the period is advanced by William Kolbrener and Michal Michelson's collection, *Mary Astell: Reason, Gender and Faith*. This strong group of essays opens up new topics regarding Astell's politics, faith and philosophy, and also presses the case for considering Astell a major figure. Sharon Achinstein argues that 'one would be hard pressed to call [Astell's philosophy] feminism' (p. 24) because it is rooted in obedience, otherworldliness, and what Achinstein terms a 'master/slave' orientation towards God. Hilda Smith offers the opposite point of view, and Anne Jessie Van Sant acknowledges Astell's commitment to obedience but asserts that she was also 'profoundly committed to women's equality' (p. 129). E. Derek Taylor discusses the epistemological foundation of Astell's educational theory, questioning, like Mark Goldie, the widespread assumption that Astell is constantly setting herself up to oppose Locke. Melinda Zook places Astell's feminism within the context of her Tory politics, and Hannah Smith uses the framework of Anglicanism. William Kolbrener draws upon Platonist metaphysics to explain Astell's understanding of feminine friendship, while Claire Pickard explores the significance of the idea of martyrdom in Astell's early unpublished poems. For Jacqueline Broad, Descartes's ethical theory of judgement helps us to understand Astell's second *Serious Proposal*, a view supported also by Eileen O'Neil's essay.

Women's issues illuminate John Locke in Nancy Hirschmann and Kirstie McClure's stimulating group of essays, *Feminist Interpretations of John Locke*.

The contributors engage the persistent question in feminist scholarship regarding whether Locke was a feminist or a sexist, considering gender, femininity, masculinity, the state and the law as Locke understood them. The volume includes classic and new essays and deals with a wide range of Locke's writings. Mark Goldie's edition, *John Locke: Selected Correspondence*, also promises to expand our understanding of Locke, supplementing Roger Woolhouse's fine biography that appeared last year. Goldie gathers 245 letters to and from Locke, selected from over 3,600 letters connecting Locke to correspondents in China, India, North America and all over Europe. This selection of letters underscores Locke's vast interests and wide range of friends and relationships.

Susan Manly traces Locke's influence in *Language, Custom and Nation in the 1790s: Locke, Tooke, Wordsworth, Edgeworth* (discussed further in Chapter XII). It is an interesting grouping: Locke and the Edgeworths' *Practical Education* [1798], Wordsworth's *Lyrical Ballads* [1798] and Tooke's linguistic speculations and political activism. By breaking the link between words and things, Locke encouraged various thinkers to consider how words had developed and the political significance of grammar and meaning. Tooke undermined the status quo by attacking the language it was built upon; the Edgeworths exposed the illogic and oppression embedded in grammatical teaching; Wordsworth celebrated the simple language of ordinary people. Manly's work thus ranges over a wide variety of texts and genres in a compelling and engaging argument. In *Locke, Language, and Early-Modern Philosophy*, Hannah Dawson also takes up the 'problem with language' debate with regard to Locke's *Essay*. Although there are passages that allow one to place Locke on both sides of the argument over the efficacy of language, Dawson argues that Locke ultimately sides with those who were sceptical about language. Locke does conclude the *Essays*, to be sure, by talking about remedies, but he is making the best of a bad linguistic situation, as Dawson sees it. Locke shares 'the anxiety that characterizes so much early-modern treatment of language, that fuels so many of the reformatory plans with which we are familiar' (p. 5), Dawson says, and he identifies the extraordinary power of words 'to disrupt truth and society' when people do not recognize 'their fragile relation to the concepts and things to which they were supposed to be fixed'. Dawson situates Locke's views of language in the trivium of logic, grammar and rhetoric in her first three chapters, focuses on the philosophical background in her next three chapters, and concludes with four chapters focused upon 'Locke on Language'. Where Locke leaves us, and where Dawson leaves us, is with an acute sense of how we are 'mired in false opinions and brutish passions', betrayed by language, and yet even so 'we can work at reason': 'Bravely treading the path between hope and experience, Locke shows us that though we are proud, unfaithful, and insular, *still* we must judge, trust, and interact' (p. 304).

A much more optimistic (and often amusing) stance is highlighted in Rhodri Lewis's *Language, Mind and Nature: Artificial Languages in England from Bacon to Locke*. Lewis offers the most complete study of a fascinating topic, the seventeenth-century artificial language movement, in which the brilliant and learned, eccentric and disturbed, aimed to connect words and things in some direct and powerful way. Lewis builds on much good research in this area, giving particular attention to the language planners' theological beliefs. Lewis also illuminates the interplay of occult and mainstream natural philosophies. The instability of language is also the subject of Christina Lupton's 'Sincere Performances: Franklin, Tillotson, and Steele on the Plain Style' (*ECS* 40[2007] 177–92). Lupton uses three texts that are ostensibly concerned with 'plain and sincere' language but in reality, Lupton argues, are more engaged with the performance of truth than conventional treatments of Enlightenment ideology suggest. Linguistics, ontology and epistemology are also at the heart of Helen Thompson and Natania Meeker's special edition of *The Eighteenth Century* devoted to 'Empiricism, Substance, Narrative' (*ECent* 48[2007] 183–6). Most of the essays deal with fiction, but a worthy exception is Wolfram Schmidgen's essay, 'The Politics and Philosophy of Mixture: John Locke Recomposed' (*ECent* 48[2007] 205–23), which takes on the difficult question of how Locke's politics relate to his ontology and epistemology. Schmidgen traces the idea of 'mixture' through Locke's view of species, identity and the origins of political thought. 'Mixture' allows Locke to 'project a profoundly interconnected world in which identity, freedom, and knowledge are communal effects', thereby linking the *Essay* and *Two Treatises* (p. 205). Berkeley's dramatically more radical view of the communal effects of knowledge are addressed in Talia Mae Bettcher's *Berkeley's Philosophy of Spirit: Consciousness, Ontology and the Elusive Subject*. Noting that Berkeley's ideas about consciousness have long been kicked around, 'relegated to virtual ignominy' (p. 1), Bettcher reminds us that Berkeley lost the manuscript of the Second Part of his *Principles of Human Knowledge*, and that he claimed to have made 'considerable progress' on it, and was therefore unwilling (as he put it) 'to do so disagreeable a thing as writing twice on the same subject' (quoted p. 1). The easy conclusion is that Berkeley actually did not rewrite his manuscript because his thinking was incoherent, but Bettcher's purpose is 'to vindicate Berkeley's conception of spirit', arguing that he was neither 'blundering or duplicitous': 'Far from incoherent', Bettcher says, 'Berkeley's philosophy of spirit reflects an important transition from the older notion of a subject as supporter of accidents to the more modern notion of subject (as opposed to object)' (p. 2). What this means is that Berkeley's philosophy of spirit anticipates and illuminates modern understandings of subjecthood, making Berkeley therefore 'a great early modern figure in issues concerning self and self-consciousness', joining Descartes, Locke, Hume and Kant. Bettcher's rehabilitative effort, taking Berkeley seriously, is rigorous and thoughtful, and it does lead us to a different source point for the contemporary sense of an elusive subject. Bettcher's final chapter, entitled 'The Elusive Subject', may be sufficient for those not in departments of philosophy and willing to forgo the journey and simply enjoy the destination.

Literal travel and ontology figure prominently in *A Cruising Voyage Round the World* [1712], in which Woodes Rogers insists upon the accuracy of his description, in contrast to the tales of some other travellers. Readers, as Jason Pearl says in 'Woodes Rogers and the Boundary of Travel Facts' (*ECLife* 31[2007] 60–75), were increasingly sceptical, as fiction writers were employing the conventions of fact, and modern critics have generally acknowledged that the lines between truth and fiction were often blurry or non-existent. Pearl argues that Rogers, however, had a very clear strategic and stylistic line that defined for him how the truth should be presented: 'Truthfulness required ... explicitly repressing the passions, the imagination, and even interpretation. If truthful testimony was not necessarily unadulterated truth, it was at least a kind of information that seemed plain enough to be honest—or plain enough to be an unimaginative lie' (p. 60). One of the century's most famous and important travellers is the subject of Harriet Guest's *Empire, Barbarism, and Civilisation: Captain Cook, William Hodges, and the Return to the Pacific*, which focuses primarily on the second voyage (1772–5), and on the interesting role played by the artwork of William Hodges, who accompanied Cook. Cook's three voyages (1768–80) took place during the challenging period of the war with the American colonies and the Wilkite riots, and the voyages both captured the British imagination and bolstered national confidence and self-image. Hodges' work, Guest says, 'is central to what might be described as the philosophical project of the voyage' (p. 13): painting the Easter Island monuments, the fleet of Otaheite war canoes, various landscapes, indigenous people, historical moments and more: Hodges shapes how the voyage is understood, especially with his exhibition in London in 1794. Guest gives us insightful readings of many of Hodges' works, placing them within a rich intellectual, historical and artistic context: the interaction of gender and exoticism, the philosophy of Adam Smith and John Millar, the significance of tattoos in various portraits, how the British represented cannibals, how representations of Cook relate to Britain's conception of itself as a colonial power: in short, the moral and political significance of Hodges' art. This is a beautiful book, with eighty-two illustrations (fifty colour plates), and a fascinating array of topics, including how Hodges' 'grandly ambitious' paintings were appropriated by other artists (p. 193).

Appreciating these artists includes not only sweeping arguments but also illuminating details and allusions. Elise Lawton Smith argues, for instance, in '"The aged pollard's shade": Gainsborough's *Landscape with Woodcutter and Milkmaid*' (*ECS* 41[2007] 17–39) that the two prominent oaks signify different views of England's future, consistent with John Barrell's identification of 'complementary pairs' in Gainsborough. Regarding Gainsborough, David Fallon argues in '"That angel who rides on the whirlwind": William Blake's Oriental Apotheosis of William Pitt' (*ECLife* 31[2007] 1–28) that Blake's strange painting of Pitt was 'much more understandable and politically resonant to an informed contemporary audience than has hitherto been recognized' (p. 1). Blake drew upon the London art world's absorption in commemorative projects, upon models taken from ancient Hindu sculpture and upon a specific satirical vocabulary to appeal to radical factions within the Royal Academy. Unfortunately, the most influential reviewer of the exhibition 'recognized neither the aesthetic nor the radical political appeal of the image' (p. 26), lacking apparently the necessary oriental reference points. Although the Orient was for many in the century fascinating, James Watt suggests how its materials might be put to more insular uses in 'Thomas Percy, China, and the Gothic' (*ECent* 48[2007] 95–109). Although Percy issued the first translation of a Chinese novel in a European language, *Hau Kiou Choaan*, *or, The Pleasing History* [1761], as well as a collection of *Miscellaneous Pieces Relating to the Chinese* [1762], Watt revealingly relates these efforts to Percy's more familiar project of advancing the native Gothic genius and rejuvenating British literature.

An ambitious effort to reveal how Europeans understood themselves in relation to the greater world is mounted by Charles W.J. Withers in *Placing the Enlightenment: Thinking Geographically about the Age of Reason*. Rather than 'What was it?', or 'When was it?', or 'How has it persisted or passed away?', Withers asks 'Where was the Enlightenment?'. The meaning of space was redefined for Europeans during this period, Withers argues, and he focuses on the circulation of geographical information and mapping projects. This shift to geography highlights the transnational nature of the Enlightenment, as travel accounts, geological theories, climactic theories and natural histories oriented readers to a viewpoint transcending national boundaries. Withers's beautifully illustrated and richly documented book shows how geographical matters link together a number of Enlightenment networks, with few degrees of separation between Royal Society members in London and Native American elders. Withers surveys deftly the English, Dutch, German, Italian and French understandings of people and places. The book is thus inevitably also about the print culture surrounding geographical knowledge: the maps, books, institutions, publishing houses, booksellers and so forth that distributed the geographical Enlightenment. Of course, the knowledge that many in the eighteenth century desired to distribute was religious in nature, and Margaret Connell Szasz's *Scottish Highlanders and Native Americans: Indigenous Education in the Eighteenth-Century Atlantic World* tells two intimately related yet distant stories of these efforts: how the Society in Scotland for the Propagation of Christian Knowledge (SSPCK), founded by Scottish Lowlanders, sought to educate the Scottish Highlanders; and at the same time how the SSPCK sought to educate the indigenous peoples of the New World: the Iroquois, Algonquin and various south-eastern Native Americans. The two stories have striking and illuminating parallels, contributing substantially to the emerging interest in comparative education and cross-cultural history. The Highlanders, the SSPCK fully believed, spoke the wrong language, followed the wrong faith and embraced the wrong politics. They needed to be converted from the Gaelic to English, from Episcopalianism to Presbyterianism, from Jacobitism (latent or actual) to loyalty to the British Crown. The Native Americans were similarly unenlightened. Szasz compares Native American and Highland cultures prior to 1700 in order to describe the SSPCK's impact on these cultures, drawing interesting connections between the way each culture absorbed and resisted the effort to educate and save it. She also studies the function of 'the cultural intermediary': Dugald Buchanan for the Highlanders, Samson Occom for the Native Americans. As these fascinating stories unfold, especially in this intertwined fashion, they become increasingly ambiguous as the lines blur between charity and colonialism, saving and destroying, intention and consequence, good and evil. There were losses large and small, as the Highlanders gave up their folk music, destroyed their fiddles (the 'instrument of the devil'), and widely lost the Gaelic language. Today Highland music is most preserved in Nova Scotia, and Gaelic speakers are located in Glasgow and the Hebrides. Even Occom's own wife thought he had betrayed his people's traditions, but Occom saw himself as protecting Native culture by adapting the power of the Europeans. Szasz's half-full conclusion is that 'the indigenous people of North America and the Highlands of Scotland chose selectively' from the colonialist ventures they encountered, 'accepting what they believed was best for themselves and their communities' (p. 13).

A surprising number of people in the twenty-first century are still struggling to accept the brilliant insights of Darwin: Erasmus Darwin, I mean, the visionary grandfather of Charles. In the mid-1790s Erasmus, widely acknowledged to be the leading medical man of his day, published a theory of evolution that was in fact more visionary than his grandson's theory, articulated fifty years later, as Desmond King-Hele points out in his edition of *Collected Letters of Erasmus Darwin*. Charles's grandfather, King-Hele notes, 'was the first to tell us where we came from (microscopic specks), how we got here (via gradual evolution, with no supernatural help), and how long it took (hundreds of millions of years, not the orthodox 6000 years)' (p. x). Erasmus Darwin provided the first description of photosynthesis in plants; he presented a Big Bang description of creation, and a black hole ending in which star after star will 'headlong extinct to one dark centre fall' (p. xi). He thought that the moon was formed violently out of the earth, a theory that has recently become widely accepted among astronomers. He articulated the biological origins of oil, and he suggested that the earth has a liquid core composed mostly of iron. In 1762 he explained the ideal gas law. His prediction of powered flight inspired the aeroplane's inventor, Sir George Cayley. He designed a new method of steering a carriage and tested it over 20,000 miles; most early modern cars, including the Model T, used the same method. He invented a mechanical copying machine that produced perfect copies, an astonishing speaking machine, a multi-mirror telescope (which would not be constructed until 1979), the hydrogen-oxygen rocket motor and much more (at least forty-four other inventions). In addition to all this, in the 1790s he was widely recognized as the leading poet of his age. As a framework for the 460 letters that he gathers, King-Hele's introduction is thus quite enticing. King-Hele's 1981 edition of Erasmus's letters contained only 220, and over half of those in this new edition are previously unpublished. The notes are generous, and King-Hele, author of an award-winning biography of Darwin in 1999, provides thorough and deft guidance. Few letters are boring, and many offer intriguing glimpses into the daily life of a scientific genius: wondering if Josiah Wedgwood really ought to be eating soap in order to lose weight, and how Wedgwood might deal with his missing leg's phantom-limb pain, for instance. Erasmus recounts his efforts to treat a women with leprosy with 'a gruel made with inner bark of elm' (p. 308); he asks Joseph Banks and Linneaus if they'll do some proofreading for him. He partners James Watt to try to raise money for a Pneumatic Institution, where patients might be cured of disease by breathing medicinal gases. His patience in responding to requests for medical advice is impressive; his efforts to imagine how various illnesses are being caused and what might be done are indefatigable. And yet the scientific understanding of the age is such a dim light, so riddled with mistaken assumptions about the balance of the body's humours, that many of these letters must elicit enormous pity.

More pitiful and appalling of course is the monster of slavery in the period, which is explored in Brycchan Carey and Peter J. Kitson's impressive collection, *Slavery and the Cultures of Abolition: Essays Marking the Bicentennial of the British Abolition Act of 1807*. 'It is no longer possible in 2007, as it was even a mere decade ago', Carey and Kitson write, 'to teach or to research eighteenth and early nineteenth-century literature without paying attention to issues of race and empire' (p. 7). This wide-ranging collection of essays certainly advances that effort. A highlight of the collection is Deirdre Coleman's commentary and transcription of Henry Smeathman's 'Oeconomy of a Slave Ship', which was written sometime after 1775. The intriguing nature of Smeathman's work is perhaps suggested by Coleman's assertion that it is underpinned by Hobbesian theories of nature and Linnean ideas about the essential place of insects in the great scheme of nature. Focusing on eighteenth-century Islamic slavery in the tales we know as the *Arabian Nights*, Felicity Nussbaum examines one of the most influential tales, which is also one of the least authentic, and finds that the portrayal of Africans and slaves 'do[es] not fit easily into the concerns of abolitionist discourse'.

The church played a crucial role not only in slavery and its abolition, but also in the broader expansion of empire, which is the focus of Rowan Strong's *Anglicanism and the British Empire, c.1700–1850*. Strong's purpose is not 'a history of missions, or of the Anglican missionary societies whose publications are used here; nor is it a history of the colonial development of the Church of England in North America, Bengal, Australia, or New Zealand' (p. 7). Instead, Strong tells the story of how Anglican Christian belief shaped the various identities of people in North America, Bengal, Australia and New Zealand. Christian belief was a lens through which one might understand the colonizing and the colonized. Tony Claydon, in *Europe and the Making of England, 1660–1760*, questions the notion that England was insular and xenophobic, arguing instead that the English were engaged with Europe, seeing themselves as part of Christendom as a whole and the Protestant reformation in particular. It was not an age of secularization, Claydon says, an assertion supported by W.M. Jacob's *The Clerical Profession in the Long Eighteenth Century, 1680–1840*, which is especially concerned with the myriad and various ways that parish clergy were interwoven into the economies and communal lives of their parishes. They needed an understanding of local markets, agriculture and manufacturing to serve most effectively, and they played a key role in educating poor children. Revitalizing the church was the life's work of Thomas Secker (1693–1768), who is the subject of Robert Ingram's rigorously researched *Religion, Reform and Modernity in the Eighteenth Century: Thomas Secker and the Church of England*. Secker's life, Ingram argues, 'possesses a seismographic quality', providing a fresh way to think about some key aspects of eighteenth century society (p. ix). Orthodox church reform has been under-appreciated in two respects particularly, Ingram says: first, most reformers, like the Renaissance humanists, believed the answers for the future were in the past; and second, what eradicated this mindset was war, not any social, economic or cultural development.

Ingram's first chapter makes the case for thinking of the eighteenth century as an age of reform, and the next two chapters place Secker within that context, narrating his abandonment of Dissent and embrace of the established Church of England. Chapters 4 to 8 focus on particular themes: the church and the Enlightenment, the church and parishioners, the church and the state, the church and America, the church and churches abroad. Ingram's argument runs against the 'master-narrative' of English religious history that assumes secularization is inevitable. Eighteenth-century England, Ingram insists, 'remained a religious society to the marrow of its bones', but the recurrent wars it fought 'nevertheless chipped away at the foundations of the confessional state' (p. 286).

A very different religious figure is glimpsed in the fifth volume of the *Selected Spiritual Writings of Anne Dutton*, edited by JoAnn Ford Watson. This volume, *Miscellaneous Correspondence*, further contributes to our understanding of how Dutton's writings influenced the evangelical movements in England and the colonies. Anne Dutton was a remarkably long-lived (1692–1795) and prolific Baptist theologian, who established in 1743, in *A Letter to Such of the Servants of Christ, who May have any Scruple about the Lawfulness of PRINTING any Thing written by a Woman*, that it was biblical for her to be an authoress. Dutton wrote theological tracts, usually presented as letters, on a wide range of controversial topics: Sabellianism, antinomianism, the Holy Spirit, election, justification, grace and other topics related to the growth of Baptist congregations and beliefs. Our sense of the religious foundation of the century is also expanded by Andrew Starkie's *The Church of England and the Bangorian Controversy, 1716–1721*: what J.C.D. Clark calls 'the most bitter domestic ideological conflict of the century'. So why is Starkie's book 'the first extensive account' of this controversy (p. 1)? The controversy is so extensive and complicated, as Starkie and Clark both maintain, 'that historians have been deterred from tackling it' (quoted p. 1). Starkie tries to help us understand why the debate was so intense, and why so many people were involved: 'high churchmen, nonjurors, orthodox whig churchmen, heterodox low churchmen and those deemed "Freethinkers"' (p. 2). Starkie explains how the controversy was ostensibly about the relationship between church and state, stemming from a sermon preached by Benjamin Hoadly, the low church bishop of Bangor, on 31 March 1717. Hoadly's sermon endorsed the power of the state over the church, drawing attacks upon him from orthodox churchmen of both the Whig and Tory parties. But the controversy was also the site for a more complex political struggle. Starkie's claim is that understanding this controversy will help us to understand religious history in particular and intellectual history in general, and it is, in many ways, an intriguing story. This is a work of careful and diligent scholarship: Starkie's 'Pamphlet Map', which describes in nine pages the incredible number of pamphlets and their relationships, is in itself an impressive work of reconstruction.

The reconstruction of a conference, reconstructing Johnson's reconstruction of Shakespeare, gives us one of the year's most delightful books. The papers from this unusual symposium are presented in Eric Rasmussen and Aaron Santesso's collection, *Comparative Excellence: New Essays on Shakespeare and Johnson.* Five leading Shakespearian scholars and five leading Johnsonian scholars gathered at the University of Nevada and Squaw Valley, California, and they considered a variety of relationships between their major figures. The essays are stunningly good: the notion that these scholars drawn together might inspire and press each other was obviously confirmed. An introduction would have been welcome, as would an index sufficiently detailed to capture the richness of the essays. Peter Holland writes on 'Playing Johnson's Shakespeare' (pp. 1–23), and finds that 'Johnson's Shakespeare resists performance', although his edition would prove useful for other people's visions (p. 20). Robert DeMaria's essay on 'Samuel Johnson and the Saxonic Shakespeare' (pp. 25–46) reveals the evolution of Johnson's approach to Shakespeare's language, which is towards depressing the 'obsolete, the obscure, and the singular—in sentiment and in language...in favor of the known, the common, and the received' (p. 43). In 'Shakespeare's Ghost: Johnson, Shakespeare, Garrick, and Constructing the English Middle-Class' (pp. 47–69), Nicholas Hudson considers how the canonizing of Shakespeare, which is in no small part the result of Johnson's editorship and praise, 'is related to the social revolution occurring during the same time—which is sometimes, misleadingly, called "the rise of the middle class"' (p. 47) Part of the explanation, Hudson argues, has to do with 'a disinterest in exploring the possible contradictions' in the categories of 'natural' and 'authentic' as these played out in Shakespeare, the theatre and social interactions (p. 64). Tiffany Stern's '"I do wish that you had mentioned Garrick": The Absence of Garrick in Johnson's Shakespeare' (pp. 71–96) persuasively argues that Johnson's *Shakespeare* 'is shaped by the absence of David Garrick'. The reasons are personal and complex, but also temperamental, as Shakespeare at one point at least 'irritates Johnson—by being theatrical', and Garrick finds Johnson incapable of understanding Shakespeare—because he has read too many books (pp. 88, 89).

Jack Lynch, in 'The Dignity of an Ancient: Johnson Edits the Editors' (pp. 97–114), expands our appreciation of Johnson's responses to previous editors of Shakespeare, something that is unavoidably occluded in the Yale *Johnson on Shakespeare.* Shakespeare's obscurity, Anne McDermott notes, especially inspired those in the eighteenth century who wanted to settle and fix the language to prevent further deterioration and decline. In 'Johnson's Editing of Shakespeare in the *Dictionary*' (pp. 115–38), McDermott argues that Johnson 'is as much a textual critic in the *Dictionary* as he is a lexicographer', and that these two activities are richly intertwined (p. 135). As a critic, Johnson's judgements were more often conjectural than 'authoritative, dogmatic, and prescriptive' (p. 136), leaving the reader to judge for him or herself. In 'The Siren Call of Earlier Editorial Practice; or, How Dr. Johnson Failed to Respond Fully to his Own Intuitions about the Principles of Textual Criticism and Editing' (pp. 139–60), David Bevington takes Johnson to task for not following his own theories of editing in handling *Richard III.* Bevington ponders why Johnson failed to follow his own principles, and acknowledges that 'his editing of some other plays gives a better representation of Johnson's acuity', but the case is convincingly made that Johnson's critique of Pope and Theobald in his Preface is not supported by his own work (p. 159).

Aaron Santesso explores 'the precise nature' of Johnson's feelings for London, with connections to Shakespeare woven in, in 'Johnson as Londoner' (pp. 161–79), and Stephen Orgel imaginatively focuses on 'Johnson's Lear' (pp. 181–202), especially his remarkable and famous preference for Nahum Tate's happy ending. Orgel argues that Tate's version is, in fact, quite good ('clear, well paced, dramatically effective'), and Johnson is also considering the audience's response as 'an essential element in the action' (p. 201). Finally, Claude Rawson closes this outstanding volume with 'Cooling to a Gypsy's Lust: Johnson, Shakespeare, and Cleopatra' (pp. 203–38), which argues intriguingly that Johnson's moral disapproval of the play drove him 'to avoid expressions of either praise or censure that risked conferring on the play the kind of attention, however hostile, that might permit a glimpse of its power' (p. 232).

Shakespeare without Johnson, but with artists, is the subject of *Painting Shakespeare*, Stuart Sillar's excellent work from last year on how eighteenth-century artists interpreted Shakespeare. Sillar's work is followed this year by William L. Pressly's *The Artist as Original Genius: Shakespeare's 'Fine Frenzy' in Late-Eighteenth-Century British Art*, which inverts the argument in a way. If, as Sillar argued, eighteenth-century artists offered readings of Shakespeare in their art, Pressly finds that Shakespeare provided a characterization of the artist that was adopted in the late eighteenth century. Pressly notes that many of these artists produced influential images of the plays, but his concern is with the notion of the 'original genius' portrayed in Shakespeare, and performed by the artists in their lives and their works. The 'fine frenzy', from Theseus' speech at the close of *Midsummer Night's Dream*, is a crucial passage which is linked to John Hamilton's *Shakespeare Heads* and other works.

Johnson's relationship to another major figure is explored in Katherine Mannheimer's superb essay, 'Personhood, Poethood, and Pope: Johnson's Life of Pope and the Search for the Man Behind the Author' (*ECS* 40[2007] 631–49). Mannheimer observes that, 'while Johnson may continue assiduously to separate out public and private, professional and domestic, writer and man, the example of Pope's letters declares the undertaking doomed from the outset' (p. 640). Johnson is intent on finding the 'real individual' that is Pope, focusing on Pope's body and its physical reality: his crooked spine, his love of 'meat highly seasoned', his 'bodice made of stiff canvas', his 'three pair of stockings'. But just as Johnson 'seems to be exposing Pope's most hidden and vulnerable body, that body turns out to be constructed as much from text as from flesh and blood' (p. 645), and in the end Johnson gives up and resigns himself to the poet, whose life remains mysterious, 'unbiographable' (p. 646). An intriguingly similar theme emerges in Raymond Stephanson's '*Letters of Mr. Alexander Pope* and the Curious Case of Modern Scholarship and the Vanishing Text' (*ECLife* 31[2007] 1–21). Stephanson notes that 'almost no one studies Pope's correspondence as it was intended to be read in the 1730s when it was first published'; Pope managed, deceiving Curll, a 'remarkable self-promotional feat' (p. 3), replacing 'the nasty images of Pope the hunchback, Pope the sexless fumbler or horny bachelor, Pope the wasp or monkey or *durgen*, Pope the malevolent satirist . . . with portraits of him as loyal friend, devoted son, charming gallant, favorite of elder statesmen of wit, and man of conscience' (p. 18). Stephanson explains how this neglect occurred, and what we might gain by remedying it. If Curll and Pope have seemed to this point forever intertwined, with Curll a footnote to Pope, Paul Baines and Pat Rogers have shifted the spotlight with *Edmund Curll, Bookseller*. 'There will never be another Curll', Rogers and Baines conclude (p. 319), and no one reading this engaging volume would disagree. Not only did Curll occupy a unique niche at a singular moment, slipping in between the transition from the age of patronage to the age of commercial booksellers, taking advantage of the decaying regulatory power of the Stationers' Company, Curll possessed an amazing energy and appetite for controversy. Curll makes Larry Flynt and *The National Inquirer* seem complacent and unimaginative, pioneering in the publication of pornography, scandalous gossip, stolen and unauthorized papers, reckless political attacks, instantaneous (and often erroneous) obituaries and much, much more. Baines and Rogers spend, as we might expect, much time illuminating Curll's battle with Pope, but Curll was of course much more than the victim of Pope's satire and emetic. In this biography, the first since Ralph Straus's *Unspeakable Curll* in 1927, much is still not known, but Baines and Rogers have done a masterful job of illuminating Curll and his work in publishing.

The Age of Johnson continues to be a major publishing event in Johnson and related studies, especially this year with a memorial volume dedicated to Paul J. Korshin, the founding editor of the journal. As such, the essays were solicited from friends, colleagues and former students of Korshin—a departure from the series' usual peer review—and their outstanding quality amply honours that magnificent Johnsonian's memory. It would be difficult to pick out highlights here. Robert Folkenflik adds new insights to the discussion of the politics embedded in Johnson's *Dictionary*. Thomas Curley illuminates Johnson's relationship with William Shaw, who was an important figure in the debate over Macpherson's *Ossian*. Arthur Cash adds to his already large contribution to our understanding of John Wilkes and his relationship with Johnson, considering the politics and the reasons that led Boswell to stage the famous dinner with the Dilly brothers. Howard Weinbrot identifies 'meeting the monarch' as a hitherto neglected (because unrecognized) genre, which features of course Johnson in one of the most important royal meetings. Philip Smallwood considers a global Johnson, considering his work in the shifting context of world literature. James Cruise deals with hieroglyphics, drawing on Korshin's interest in secret languages, and Maximilian Novak looks at *Robinson Crusoe*, print history and epistemology. Jack Lynch's essay on the problems of identifying forgery has fascinating implications for Johnson. James Gray ponders the acting theories of Diderot and Garrick; Lisa Berglund examines various editions of Hester Thrale Piozzi's *Anecdotes*; Mona Scheuermann analyses social class in Austen's *Mansfield Park*. George Justice considers a nineteenth-century novel, *Reginald Dalton*, and Gloria Sybil Gross offers an intriguing study of Stanley Kubrick's approach to the eighteenth century. The volume concludes with a bibliography of Korshin's work, followed by various memories from friends, students and colleagues, and then the usual richly stocked smorgasbord of book reviews.

Mark Wildemuth is concerned with the undecipherable in 'Samuel Johnson and the Aesthetics of Complex Dynamics' (*ECent* 48[2007] 45–60). Wildemuth looks for a way to get beyond both a progressive reading of Johnson (Bate, Hagstrum, Greene) and a post-structuralist reading (Deutsch, Reinert, Lynn), and he makes a surprisingly persuasive argument that Johnson is 'an early modern chaologist', whose 'extraordinary grasp of the intimate relation between order and disorder in complex systems of literature...prefigures current developments in critical theory and the study of chaos or complex dynamics' (p. 46). A tool useful for understanding Johnson and others has been left to us by the late historian C. Helen Brock in *The Correspondence of Dr William Hunter*, a definitive edition of these previously uncollected letters. Hunter (1718–83) was a prominent anatomist and obstetrician, Royal Society member (elected in 1767), and astute collector. The Hunterian Museum at the University of Glasgow preserves his specimens and treasures. This edition, containing all of his known correspondence, includes letters to and from Joseph Banks, Benjamin Franklin, David Garrick, Edward Gibbon, David Hume, John Hunter, Samuel Johnson, William Pitt, Joseph Priestley, John Pringle, Joshua Reynolds, William Smellie, Queen Charlotte and George III. A more general tool for understanding the period as a whole is offered in Elaine M. McGirr's *Eighteenth-Century Characters: A Guide to the Literature of the Age*. McGirr is serious about her subtitle: she really does aim to provide an introduction to the eighteenth century and its literature through the lens of a baker's dozen of different characters: the rake, the fop, the country gentleman and the Cit; the wife, the coquette and the prude; the country maid and the town lady, the learned ladies and female wits, the Catholic Other, the Protestant Other and the British Other (the Scot). Suitable for undergraduates, the discussions are wide-ranging and informed, explaining for example why the rake evolved from a kind of hero in the Restoration to insignificance by the late eighteenth century. An extensive chronology and further readings for each chapter enhance this volume's practical value. Another useful survey is William Kupersmith's *English Versions of Roman Satire in the Earlier Eighteenth Century*, which considers Pope's *Imitations of Horace*, Samuel Johnson's *The Vanity of Human Wishes* and various other examples of the genre by Swift, Fielding, Smart and others, illuminating each work in various contexts.

The essays collected in *Studies in Eighteenth-Century Culture* are also always of general usefulness and value, and this year's volume, edited by Jeffrey Ravel (*SECC* 36[2007]), is no exception. James Swenson argues vigorously in 'Critique, Progress, Autonomy' (*SECC* 36[2007] 1–11) that these three terms powerfully illustrate the relevance of the eighteenth century for our age, as the same issues that animated debate then have persisted. Eve Tavor Bannet's excellent study of 'Printed Epistolary Manuals and the Rescripting of Manuscript Culture' (*SECC* 36[2007] 13–34) finds that letter-writing manuals were adapted to local conditions, as letters were based in conversation and often read aloud, linking textual and oral discourse. Madeleine Forrell Marshall also deals with orality and literacy in her essay on 'Late Eighteenth-Century Public Reading, with Particular Attention to Sheridan's *Strictures on Reading the Church Service* (1789)' (*SECC* 36[2007] 35–54). The most interesting direction here is that ministers should emulate the cadence and speech of their illiterate parishioners rather than their elitely educated colleagues. Daniel Rosenberg identifies the inventor of the timeline in 'Joseph Priestley and the Graphic Invention of Modern Time' (*SECC* 36[2007] 55–103), and examines how Priestley's innovation was received. The most dramatic medical breakthrough figures in David Shuttleton's *Smallpox and the Literary Imagination, 1660–1820*, which covers canonical and non-canonical works by Dryden, Johnson, Steele, Goldsmith and of course Lady Mary Wortley Montagu. Epidemics were certainly influenced by the distribution of the population, and the skyrocketing growth in the number of people living in cities, between 1750 and 1914, is the concern of Andrew and Lynn Hollen Lee's *Cities and the Making of Modern Europe, 1750–1914*. Lee and Lee seek to show how and why people congregated together at so rapid a pace, and why this physical and demographic shift mattered so much. The obvious driving force, industrialization, and the not so obvious consequence, democratization, are part of the answer, but 'new forms of transportation, communication, employment, family life, governance, and leisure' were also 'closely linked to urban development' (p. 1).

At the opposite end of the spectrum from urban growth is the *World of Toil and Strife: Community Transformation in Backcountry South Carolina, 1750–1805*. In this innovative work, Peter Moore sets out to understand why Agnes Richardson, a young widow in 1771, was forced to prove, by touching his decomposing corpse, that she had not murdered her husband. That quest led Moore to a detailed study of the community Agnes inhabited, in the Waxhaws in backcountry South Carolina. The resulting book not only makes for fascinating reading, but it also reveals the dynamic changes under way in this predominantly Scots–Irish settlement well before the growth of cotton planters. Moore illuminates the impact of the Great Revival, Indian conflicts, slavery and much more. South Carolina benefited substantially from its relationship with Great Britain during this period, and so the dispute over the 'rights of Carolina Englishmen', the struggle between imperial control and self-rule, was especially intense. Jonathan Mercantini, in *Who Shall Rule at Home? The Evolution of South Carolina Political Culture, 1748–1776*, considers the South Carolinians' hard-headed strategies of resistance, which involved a consistent avoidance of compromise, an all-or-nothing strategy that reflected both the character of the people and their assessment of the high stakes involved. In a different sense, the question of who shall rule at home drives 'A Jewel in the Crown? Indian Wealth in Domestic Britain in the Late Eighteenth Century' (*ECS* 41[2007] 71–86) by Tillman W. Nechtman. Nechtman considers how the British public viewed the wealthy nabobs, employees of the East India Company, when they returned home rich. Britons blamed them for increasing prices, and pointed in particular to Indian diamonds as tangible proof of the connection between the nabobs' wealth and inflation. And Julie Murray, in 'Company Rules: Burke, Hastings, and the Specter of the Modern Liberal State' (*ECS* 41[2007] 55–69), considers Edmund Burke's prosecution of Warren Hastings and argues that Burke actually offers a harsh criticism of Britain's feudal logic, and not an apology as is usually assumed. Edmund Burke is also the source of trouble for

Mary Wollstonecraft, and Alex Schulman in 'Gothic Piles and Endless Forests: Wollstonecraft between Burke and Rousseau' (*ECS* 41[2007] 41–54) considers how Wollstonecraft embraces a contradictory stance, between Burke and Rousseau, between sense and sensibility, in order to support the French revolutionaries.

Having begun at the beginning, we might perhaps end at our eventual and inevitable ending, as human machines (many of us already have various devices implanted replacing knees, hips, heart valves, teeth and more). The most intriguing title this year is *The Enlightenment Cyborg: A History of Communications and Control in the Human Machine, 1660–1830*, in which Allison Muri declares in the first sentence that 'there is no such thing as the Enlightenment cyborg'. So what, one may wonder, is this book about? Muri is interested in how postmodern scholars have neglected or misunderstood Enlightenment conceptions of the body as a self-regulating homeostatic machine, and machines as bodies. Muri's lively and insightful readings of Thomas Willis, La Mettrie, Boyle, Descartes, obscure iatromechanists, Swift, Smollett and others expose the simplistic and uninformed views of man-machines circulating in the postmodern, post-human, cyborgian discourse. But I will end instead with the obvious observation that many scholars perform valuable service reviewing books and clusters of books (and also reading manuscripts of books and articles, and tenure and promotion files, and some sort of assessment and budget plan that was due last Tuesday), without a whole lot of glory. Reviews of the year's works usually overlook other reviews, but they are a crucial part of the work that we do, and in closing this section, I would like to mention one excellent essay review here as a kind of acknowledgement of all the others. In 'Reconfiguring the Idea of Eighteenth-Century Literature in a New Epoch: Moving from the Augustan to the Menippean' (ECLife 31.2[2007] 83-95), John J. Burke reviews two books by Howard Weinbrot published in 2005, *Menippean Satire Reconsidered: From Antiquity to the Eighteenth Century*, and *Aspects of Samuel Johnson: Essays on his Arts, Mind, Afterlife, and Politics*. Burke uses this occasion to assess Weinbrot's eleven major books over an illustrious forty years of first-rate work, and it is a pleasure and inspiration to contemplate Weinbrot's amazing achievement through the lens of Burke's review.

2. The Novel

This year saw a growing critical interest in eighteenth-century mind–body connections. One of a number of articles on contemporary emasculation fears is Deborah Needleman Arminor's 'The Sexual Politics of Microscopy in Brobdingnag' (*SEL* 47[2007] 619–40), which investigates the 'intersection between anxieties over the popularization of the microscope and contempora-neous anxieties over the dildo' (p. 632) in *Gulliver's Travels*. While fully endorsing Marjorie Nicolson's emphasis on the importance of microscopy in Swift's work, Needleman Arminor challenges this critic's view that Gulliver symbolizes the eighteenth-century microscopist, arguing that his lack of 'power to pick and choose the objects of his magnified gaze' and his ultimate role as 'miniature woman-owned seeing object' (p. 620) and 'phallic prop' (p. 632) make him more an emblem of the microscope itself than of its user. By depicting in detail Gulliver's discomfort at being transformed from a powerful male subject into a helpless commodified object, she suggests, Swift becomes 'a sexual satirist exposing the gynophobia latent in Enlightenment science's aversion to the new consumerism' (p. 623). Continuing interest in anthropomorphism and hybridity is evident in Ann Kline Kelly's 'Gulliver as Pet and Pet Keeper: Talking Animals in Book 4' (*ELH* 74[2007] 323–49), which examines Swift's representation of 'interspecies amity' (p. 332) in *Gulliver's Travels*. Its main purpose is to challenge readings that emphasize Gulliver's insanity and/or extreme individualism at the end of Book IV, arguing that he 'ends up relatively sane and sociable' (p. 324).

The intersection between genre, gender and Enlightenment thinking is explored in *Gender and Utopia in the Eighteenth Century: Essays in English and French Utopian Writing*, edited by Nicole Pohl and Brenda Tooley. This rich collection of essays is informed by contemporary feminist thought that acknowledges 'postmodernism's usefully corrosive exploration of western liberal feminism's limits' (p. 3) but nevertheless embraces utopianism as an essential part of its theory and practice. The editors aim to complement existing studies of utopianism that have either overlooked or marginalized both eighteenth-century utopias in general and eighteenth-century utopias written by women in particular. In chapter 2, Lee Cullen Khanna examines gender as 'an aspect of the playful negotiation of difference' (p. 19) in Margaret Cavendish's *The Blazing World*, Aphra Behn's *Oroonoko*, and Sarah Scott's *Millenium Hall* and *Sir George Ellison*. In chapter 3, Joseph F. Bartolomeo investigates Sarah Fielding's treatment of the domestic utopian space in *David Simple*, concluding that 'in terms of representation, [it] is destined to remain nowhere' (p. 52). The reliance of the utopian community on its dystopian 'other' is highlighted in chapter 4, in which Brenda Tooley presents the convent in Ann Radcliffe's *The Italian* as a feminine space that 'comments upon the exercises of power surrounding it' (p. 53). In chapter 5, Caroline Weber reads Isabelle Charrière's *Letters from Mistress Henley Published By Her Friend* as a 'forceful and unmistakable critique' (p. 73) of Jean-Jacques Rousseau's *Julie, or, The New Héloïse*, as it transforms Rousseau's idealized image of enlightened domesticity into 'a soul-deadening dystopia' (p. 73). In the next chapter, Mary McAlpin examines the role of the seraglio in Montesquieu's *Lettres persanes*, focusing in particular on Letter 141 in order to shed light on the novel's juxtapositions of male and female sexuality, orientalism and occidentalism, utopia and reality. In chapter 7, Ana M. Acosta offers an insightful analysis of the parallels between Sarah Scott's *Millenium Hall* and the Marquis de Sade's *The 120 Days of Sodom*, arguing that 'both propose radical social alternatives, and both are deeply invested in the Enlightenment ideology of transparency' (p. 107). The 'critical voyage utopia' (p. 121) in Ellis Cornelia Knight's *Dinarbas* is under scrutiny by Nicole Pohl in chapter 8, while in chapter 9 Elizabeth Hagglund and Jonathan Laidlow investigate questions of colonialism, gender and race in Robert Paltock's Robinsonade *The Life and Adventures of Peter Wilkins*, in which the eponymous hero marries a woman with wings. Seth Denbo considers the limits of 'a sexual utopia where paternity is always knowable' (p. 161) in Henry Neville's *Isle of Pines* in chapter 10. In the final chapter, Alessa Johns makes a case for the study of eighteenth-century women's utopianism, arguing it may be a valuable source of inspiration for academic feminists struggling to determine the future shape of the women's movement.

Observing stricter generic boundaries, Maximillian E. Novak, 'Edenic Desires: *Robinson Crusoe*, the Robinsonade, and Utopias' (in Clymer and Mayer, eds., *Historical Boundaries, Narrative Forms: Essays on British Literature in the Long Eighteenth Century in Honor of Everett Zimmerman*, pp. 19–36), points to 'distinctions between the quest for utopia, the interest in an earthly paradise, and the fervid fascination for the Robinsonade' (p. 20) in the period. Discussing Defoe's novel in order to ascertain why the latter category became most popular from the eighteenth century onwards, Novak concludes that it is because of its open acknowledgment of 'the imperfection of reality' (p. 33).

Oxford University Press has produced a new Oxford World's Classics edition of Daniel Defoe's *Robinson Crusoe*, edited and introduced by Thomas Keymer, with notes by Keymer and James Kelly. Based on J. Donald Crowley's 1972 first-edition text, this scrupulously annotated edition includes a select bibliography, textual notes, a contemporary map of the world, a glossary of terms, the frontispiece and preface to *Serious Reflections* (appendix 1) and chronologies of both Daniel Defoe and his novel (the latter in appendix 2). The introduction takes us carefully through the work's reception history, showing the 'rich interpretative possibilities' (p. vii) and ongoing appeal of Defoe's novel.

Set against the backdrop of ongoing critical discussion about the relationship between the novel and Enlightenment aesthetics, Jesse M. Molesworth's '"A dreadful course of calamities": *Roxana*'s Ending Reconsidered' (*ELH* 74[2007] 493–508) argues that Defoe 'scrutinizes his entire fictional corpus in the final scenes of *Roxana*' (p. 497) by introducing Susan as a disturbing presence in, and competing narrator of, her mother's story, thus undermining 'the fantasy of a single-character plotline' (p. 505). Julie Crane's 'Defoe's *Roxana*: The Making and Unmaking of a Heroine' (*MLR* 102:i[2007] 11–25) initially raises the reader's curiosity by claiming that H.F. 'can be seen as a significant precursor' (p. 11) of Roxana, but offers little comparative analysis in the body of the article, which consists mostly of conventional reflections on the heroine's narratorial voice. In ' "The rage of the street": Crowd and Public in Defoe's *Moll Flanders*' (in Clymer and Mayer, eds., pp. 73–86) Carl Fisher analyses Moll's encounters with street throngs in order to demonstrate that 'Defoe stands out as an anomaly in eighteenth-century fiction for his representation of crowds' (p. 76). Whereas most authors of the period imagine the crowd as an abstract, emotional and potentially dangerous mass, Fisher argues, Defoe gives it a 'neutral quality' and 'practical dimension' (p. 77).

This year saw two new additions to revisionist studies of Ian Watt's account of the 'rise' of the English novel. Katherine E. Kickel's *Novel Notions: Medical Discourse and the Mapping of the Imagination in Eighteenth-Century English Fiction* establishes a link between developments in late seventeenth- and early eighteenth-century medicine and changing ideas about literary composition in the field of eighteenth-century prose fiction. Kickel relates how Enlightenment medical scientists and philosophers increasingly conceptualized the imagination as 'a discernible, working, organic entity' rather than 'a mysterious flight of "fancy"' (p. 2) and thereby fuelled widespread interest in, and debate about, its mechanisms. '*Novel Notions*', she explains in her introduction, 'tells the story of how the medical community's investigation of the imagination's "authoring" (i.e. its functional operations) soon translated into a fascination with literal "authoring" in the English novel's form and content' (p. 3). The first chapter offers a framework for the four case studies that are to follow and focuses on the work (and rhetoric) of four physicians who questioned teleological, Galenic ideas about the relationship between body and mind. Chapter 2 scrutinizes the trope of inexpressibility in Daniel Defoe's *A Journal of the Plague Year* and links it to growing scientific interest in 'the effects of... disease on the human voice' (p. 64). As H.F. comes to realize that there are no words to express the horrors of the plague, he registers only its sounds, thus not only finding a creative way out of 'a community's massive speech disorder' (p. 50) but also moving beyond traditional associations of the imagination with vision (pp. 40–1). Though perceptive in its analysis, the chapter (containing no references to other early 1700s novels) is too limited in scope to substantiate Kickel's more general claims about 'authoring' concerns in 'early English novels' (p. 4). Moving to 'a second phase of mapping the imagination in the English novel' (p. 67) in chapters 3 and 4, Kickel investigates how Henry Fielding's *Tom Jones* and Laurence Sterne's *Tristram Shandy* draw attention to both 'the power of the created object' (p. 67) and the reader's imaginative needs. She discusses Fielding's anxieties about the mutable relationship between the author, his literary creation and the reader in the context of scientific debates about 'embryonic formation' (p. 72) between pre-formationists and epigenesists, and then proceeds to examine the character of Partridge as both a troubled father-figure and an uneducated 'reader'. Laurence Sterne's play with the reader's sensual experiences is presented as 'a creative enactment of the medical community's curiosity about synaesthesia' (p. 90), a 'condition' whereby 'sensory reactions often occur simultaneously across more than one sense domain' (p. 93). Kickel discusses the various ways in which the author stimulates and manipulates the reader's multiple senses, arguing that the novel reveals 'that imagining is not only intellectual, but also perceptual and emotional' (p. 110). In the last chapter, Kickel examines Emily St Aubert's developing vision in Ann Radcliffe's *The Mysteries of Udolpho* in the light of George Berkeley's *A New Theory of Vision*, a contemporary work that put unprecedented emphasis on the subjectivity of sight.

In a *YWES* section that is traditionally based on an Anglocentric understanding of the eighteenth-century novel, it is hard to do justice to a revisionist study that challenges such an understanding. Jenny Mander, ed., *Remapping the Rise of the European Novel*, is a collection of twenty-two essays that offers an entirely new perspective on the history of the novel by acknowledging 'the sort of traffic between different languages and geographical spaces that would seem to have been integral to the genre' (pp. 3–4), as well as the fact that, in Andrew Hadfield's words, 'the rise of the novel was a contingent and discontinuous process' (p. 27). Broadening its perspective both temporally and geographically, and devoting special attention to the subjects of translation, empire, travel, 'bibliometrics' (p. v) and consumption, this exciting collection incorporates studies of classical texts such as Heliodorus's *Aethiopica* as well as German, Russian, English, French, Italian and Spanish fiction from the period between 1500 and 1800, including William Baldwin's *Beware the Cat* [1552], Miguel de Cervantes' *Persiles y Sigismunda* [1617] and Wilhelmina Karoline von Wobeser's *Elisa oder das Weib wie es sein sollte* [1795]. For those keen to explore the eighteenth-century English novel in its continental context, this is definitely a work worth reading.

The struggling female voice is examined in Thorell Porter Tsomondo's *The Not So Blank 'Blank Page': The Politics of Narrative and the Woman Narrator in the Eighteenth- and Nineteenth-Century English Novel*, of which two chapters will be discussed in this section. In an erudite if rather theoretical and densely written introduction, Tsomondo elucidates the different elements of her title, demonstrating that Izak Dinesen's short story 'The Blank Page' can be a valuable point of departure for the critic wishing to describe the conflicted nature of the feminocentric narrative, and arguing that the novels under discussion—Daniel Defoe's *Moll Flanders*, Charlotte Lennox's *Harriot Stuart*, Mary Hays's *Emma Courtney*, Charlotte Brontë's *Jane Eyre* and Charles Dickens's *Bleak House*—point to 'a textual dynamic that speaks to the absence or unavailability of any uncompromised narrative operational space' (p. 11). The first chapter, 'Concerning Leave to Speak: Moll Flanders' Suit', usefully reminds the reader that Moll's narrative is framed by the male editorial voice, which, it is argued, acts as 'a running check' to Moll's 'appeal' for narrative authority (p. 14). Fully engaging with earlier studies of the novel, Tsomondo concludes that 'Defoe's authorial stance is less that of masquerader as or appropriator of a feminine persona than it is of male authority engaging in ideological debate with what the writer as well as his society constructs as female' (p. 19). The second chapter, 'Speaking of Chastity, Virtue, Honor: The Life of Harriot Stuart Written By Herself', contributes to established critical views that characterize the eighteenth-century woman narrator as both conservative and subversive. Tsomondo argues that the confessional voice of the autobiographer Harriot is defined by struggle, because 'the narrative space she outlines is overshadowed by the speaker's concern in the present of her narration with the possible effect that her tale could have on her reputation' (p. 44).

Tonya Moutray McArthur's 'Jane Barker and the Politics of Catholic Celibacy' (*SEL* 47[2007] 596–618) investigates the Jacobite and Catholic framework of Barker's first novel *Love Intrigues* [1713], focusing in particular on Barker's treatment of female monasticism, which, McArthur argues, is presented as 'a viable and first-rate choice for women who have been exiled or abandoned by disingenuous lovers or because of their politico-religious affiliations' (p. 206). The article concludes with a discussion of the ideologically significant revisions that Barker made to the 1719 edition. Julie McGonegal's 'The Tyranny of Gift Giving: The Politics of Generosity in Sarah Scott's *Millenium Hall* and *Sir George Ellison*' (*ECF* 19:iii[2007] 291–306) examines Scott's representation of the gift through the lens of

Pierre Bourdieu's social theories, showing that, in the two novels, the act of giving serves as a means through which the female protagonists can both uphold and subvert existing power relations.

Samuel Richardson's allusive intentions in his portrayal of Lovelace in *Clarissa* are under renewed examination in Adam Rounce's 'Eighteenth-Century Responses to Dryden's *Fables*' (*T&L* 16[2007] 29–52), while Adam Budd's 'Why Clarissa Must Die: Richardson's Tragedy and Editorial Heroism' (*ECLife* 31[2007] 1–28) revisits Richardson's steadfast refusal to add a happy resolution to his second novel. Budd offers a thoughtful contribution to debates about the novelist's generic innovations and convictions about the didactic function of literature, and draws deserved attention to that other 'editorial hero' (p. 16), Mr Belford, whose 'moral reformation', Budd argues, 'is the single most important event in *Clarissa*' (p. 19). Hobbesian and Lockean notions of property and selfhood are foregrounded in Ann Louise Kibbie's Gothic reading of Richardson's *Clarissa* in 'The Estate, the Corpse, and the Letter: Posthumous Possession in *Clarissa*' (*ELH* 74[2007] 117–43). The 'essentially gothic' element of the novel, Kibbie suggests, is 'the battle between the living and the dead' (p. 124), which originates with grandfather Harlowe's contested will and is fuelled by Clarissa's own 'posthumous agency' (p. 125). Kibbie concludes by explaining why the novel's final preoccupation with literary ownership—that is, the heroine's wish to publish her tragic history, to possess her own text—is its 'logical end point' (p. 137).

Five chapters in *The Cambridge Companion to Henry Fielding*, edited by Claude Rawson, are devoted exclusively to the author's novels. All contributors assume the reader's basic familiarity with the plots. Thomas Lockwood's '*Shamela*' (pp. 38–49) celebrates Fielding's playful experimentation with the narrative voice of the eponymous heroine, arguing that it offers the reader 'a vital if not fully legible record' (p. 39) of how the playwright turned novelist. Paul Baines's '*Joseph Andrews*' (pp. 50–64) is predominantly concerned with Fielding's literary self-consciousness, first concentrating on Parson Adams's relationship to classical and religious texts, and then broadening its scope to discuss the distinctions between Fielding and Defoe and Richardson, covering subjects such as sexuality, place (geographical and social), morality, law and authority. In '*Jonathan Wild*' (pp. 65–79) Jenny Davidson uses close reading to define Fielding's role as criminal biographer, concluding that, unlike Defoe, he wishes 'to expose the general tendencies of human nature rather than to detail the particulars of the actual thief-taker's method and practices' (p. 67). Nicholas Hudson's '*Tom Jones*' (pp. 80–93) points to the complexities underlying the seeming simplicity of Fielding's novel by showing its sophisticated and often deeply ironic interrogation of the socio-political, cultural and ideological changes of its time. Finally, a considerable part of Peter Sabor's '*Amelia*' (pp. 94–108) is devoted to the novel's reception history, highlighting the dissatisfaction of the eighteenth-century public with the noseless heroine and the "lowness" of scenes and characters. Sabor takes the reader through both the weaker and stronger (or at least compelling) parts of the novel, drawing attention to Fielding's puzzling treatment of gender identities, his 'disturbing' (p. 105) allusions to violence, and the occasional 'failure of tone' (p. 105) in the novel. For those interested in *Amelia*, Sabor recommends the unbowdlerized first-edition text.

Spatial and human containment form the subject of Christopher Parkes's '*Joseph Andrews* and the Control of the Poor' (*SNNTS* 39:i[2007] 17–30), which examines Fielding's novel alongside the author's two pamphlets on poor relief. The novel's questioning of the reliability of traditional, local benevolence and its movement towards the social reintegration of the wanderer Joseph, Parkes suggests, is analogous to Fielding's promotion of institutional forms of charity whereby vagrants are transformed into valuable labour assets for the nation. E.M. Langille's somewhat speculative article 'La Place's *Histoire de Tom Jones; ou, L'Enfant trouvé* and *Candide*' (*ECF* 19:iii[2007] 267–89) develops Manfred Sandmann's 1973 claim that Fielding's *Tom Jones* may have been a powerful source of influence for Voltaire's *Candide*, methodically enumerating the parallels (and differences) in character, style and form between La Place's 'highly personal' (p. 268) and 'curious' (p. 270) French translation of Fielding's novel and Voltaire's philosophical tale.

The intersection between empiricism and religion in the eighteenth century forms the subject of Treadwell Ruml's 'The Boundaries of Bishop Burnet's *History* and Henry Fielding's Fiction' (in Clymer and Mayer, eds., pp. 37–55), which is a study of genre that compares Fielding's voice and narrative method to those of historian and autobiographer Gilbert Burnet in *A History of My Own Time*, assessing the ways in which both writers utilize 'a historical method to produce a providential design' (p. 52). Also of interest to Fielding scholars is Roberta Ferrari's succinct and lucid article ' "A foundling at the crossroads": Fielding, Tradition(s) and a "Dantesque" Reading of *Tom Jones*' (in Littlejohns and Soncini, eds., *Myths of Europe*, pp. 101–11) which contends that we can find clear echoes of Dante's *Divine Comedy* in the central six books of Fielding's novel. Ferrari states that both Dante and Fielding are concerned with 'structural balance and numerological symbology' (p. 109) and the development of the comic, and argues persuasively that Partridge is an ironic version of Virgil, that Mazard Hill is an adaptation of the Mountain of Purgatory, that the Man of the Hill is modelled on Cato and that Mrs Waters, 'the only depository of memory' (p. 108) in the novel, is a personification of Dante's two rivers of forgetfulness and remembrance, Lété and Eunoé.

Stephen Ahern's well-written *Affected Sensibilities: Romantic Excess and the Genealogy of the Novel 1680–1810* can be read as another reassessment of the history of the novel, but it is characterized as a reformulation of 'the history of sensibility' (p. 15) which is usually said to have its origin in the mid-eighteenth century. Approaching sensibility primarily as 'a literary ideal' (p. 11) that both reflected and reinforced wider cultural changes in English society, Ahern traces its beginnings back to the Restoration period, when the writers of amatory prose fiction transformed existing romance narratives and developed 'an aesthetic of excess' (p. 13) that insisted on the intensity of feeling. It is this excess, both emotional and rhetorical, Ahern argues, that serves as 'a substantive connection' (p. 13) between the amatory, the sentimental and the Gothic novel: 'they are all sensibility narratives and thus are in important ways all of a piece' (p. 12). The first chapter is devoted to a critical investigation of existing studies of sensibility (deploring the much-overlooked influence of mid-seventeenth-century French romance fiction) and a detailed explanation of the methodology and terminology used (emphasizing, amongst other things, the need 'to rethink the distinction between novel and romance' (p. 27)). The book is then divided into three parts to indicate that, despite discernible connections, there is development in the ways novelists of the three subgenres give shape to the discourse of sensibility. The ten contemporary book illustrations found throughout the book nicely offer visual testimony to this notion of change within continuity. Part I, 'Amatory Fiction', examines Aphra Behn's *Love-Letters Between a Nobleman and his Sister* and Eliza Haywood's *Love in Excess*. Ahern points to the tension that exists between Behn's 'essentialist royalist conservatism' (p. 53) and her progressive acknowledgement of 'the contingent status of social norms and beliefs' (p. 53) and argues that her characters reflect this tension because 'they promote an ideal of sensibility that celebrates both libertine self-indulgence and sentimental self-sacrifice' (p. 54). Discussing the epistolary style of Philander and Silvia in the context of the plot, Ahern shows how Behn reveals the slipperiness of the language of 'affective intensity' (p. 54), forcing the reader to ask: when are expressions of love and desire authentic and when artificial? *Love in Excess*, Ahern argues, also points to the problematic theatricality of romantic communication. He defines Haywood's novel by an 'erotics of sympathy' (p. 74) and sees it as a transitional work between earlier amatory novels and later sentimental novels, as it still relies on Restoration libertinism but also expresses discomfort with the pursuit of pleasure (p. 87). Part II, 'Sentimental Fiction', continues to investigate the complex interplay between affection and affectation by discussing the ways in which Laurence Sterne explores the limits of sentimental idealism through the character of Yorick in *A Sentimental Journey*, and by analysing Henry Mackenzie's 'constant preoccupation with the performative nature of the individual's dealings with the public world' (p. 119) in *The Man of Feeling*. In Part III, 'Gothic Fiction', Ahern examines the ambivalent role of memory in Ann Radcliffe's *The Mysteries of Udolpho* and shows how it is linked to the novel's uneasiness about the reliability of sensual perception and 'the dream of virtue grounded in a disembodied reason' (p. 152). In a discussion of Ambrosio's struggle between passion and reason in Matthew Lewis's *The Monk*, Ahern challenges critics who do not discern a 'moral ethos' (p. 181) in the novel and examines Lewis's 'frank treatment of the power dynamics underlying the plot of sentiment and seduction' (p. 197). In the 'Epilogue', Ahern turns to Jane Austen's *Sense and Sensibility* to contend that the 'domestication of romantic excess' (p. 206) at the end of the eighteenth century was never quite successful.

Pearson Longman has published a Longman Cultural Edition of Horace Walpole's *The Castle of Otranto* and Henry Mackenzie's *The Man of Feeling*, edited by Laura Mandell. It is, she writes, the 'focus on emotion—emotion as the means for knowing, judging, and ultimately understanding the world' (p. xv) that brings these ostensibly disparate works together. Students will find much to explore in this annotated edition; it includes a short general introduction that defines Gothic and sentimental modes of writing, eight illustrations (most of them of Walpole's Gothic villa Strawberry Hill), a list of important dates and a selection of contemporary reviews, as well as a 'Contexts' section that covers subjects such as Gothic architecture, conduct literature, the sublime, and 'cultures of feeling' (p. 250). These are elucidated by extracts of works from a total of twenty-nine contemporary writers (somewhat disappointingly, though, only two are women), amongst whom Francis Hutcheson, Samuel Johnson, Edmund Burke, Walter Scott and Clara Reeve all feature.

Cynthia Wall's engaging article, '*The Castle of Otranto*: A Shakespeareo-Political Satire?' (in Clymer and Mayer, eds., pp. 184–98) addresses the puzzling presence of 'gigantic Things' (p. 196) in Walpole's novel, inviting us to relish them as satirical 'exaggerations of the giant things in culture—politics, patriarchy, bardolatry' (p. 196). Combining biographical criticism with incisive close reading, Wall presents Walpole as a writer who pokes fun at romance conventions by subtly portraying the seeming hero Theodoro as 'an incompetent ass' (p. 189), and who exploits the subterranean and supernatural qualities of the Gothic to deride not only 'overt political authority' (p. 193) but also popular attempts to transform Shakespeare into a 'Sacred National Object' (p. 193).

In 'Between *Version* and *Traduction*: Sterne's *Sentimental Journey* in Mid-Nineteenth-Century France' (*T&L* 16[2007] 53–65) Susan Pickford examines 'the sudden rash of new translations' (p. 55) of Sterne's work in France in 1841, concluding that 'The paradigm of translation practice . . . corresponds neatly in each case to the editorial identity of the volume, and likewise to its putative readership.' (p. 64). *Tristram Shandy* is one of the key texts in Carol Watts's *The Cultural Work of Empire: The Seven Years' War and the Imagining of the Shandean State*, which is a dual exploration of the potent cultural 'climate' (p. 293) of Britain's mid-century conflict and 'the writerly dilemmas of Sterne's narratives' (p. 293). This is not always an easy read. Watt uses complex and at times repetitive diction, and meanders through an over-whelming number of topics (amongst which are commerce, invasion, patriotism, masculinity, bastardy, Filmerism, slavery, sublimity, the home, friendship and duration) that occasionally cause the reader to lose sight of the book's larger picture. However, for those willing to appreciate its somewhat disorienting design as a deliberate attempt to capture what Watts calls Sterne's 'curious writerly liberation' and 'wavy trajectories' (p. 293), for those willing to follow with Watts 'a Shandean route to the understanding of the formation of imperial subjectivity in eighteenth-century Britain' (p. 57), this is a work that will inspire.

Mary Douglas's thought-provoking book *Thinking in Circles: An Essay on Ring Composition* includes a short chapter called '*Tristram Shandy*: Testing for Ring Shape' (pp. 85–100), which investigates structural parallelisms in Sterne's novel to ascertain whether it conforms to an 'ancient literary form' (p. 1) called the ring composition. Though it does so only partly, Douglas shows that despite its 'incessant ups and downs', the book is 'skillfully contrived' and has 'a crystalline structure' (p. 96). Drawing on eighteenth-century and contemporary 'theories of tool use' (p. 696), William C. Mottolese, 'Tristram Cyborg and Toby Toolmaker: Body, Tools, and Hobbyhorse in *Tristram Shandy*' (*SEL* 47[2007] 679–701), draws attention to the machine imagery in

Sterne's novel, discussing the ways in which the hobbyhorse in *Tristram Shandy* can act as a kind of mechanical mediator, bridging 'th[e] large gap or discontinuity between an active and productive mind and a limited body' (p. 681). Using Sterne's black page as a point of departure, James Kim, '"Good cursed, bouncing losses": Masculinity, Sentimental Irony, and Exuberance in *Tristram Shandy*' (*ECent* 48:i[2007] 3–24), examines the novel's 'wilful mixtures of the satirical and the sentimental' (p. 5) in the context of eighteenth-century attitudes to masculinity. Wide-ranging in scope, the article carefully moves from critical debates about the relationship between gender and sensibility to the idea of 'phallic loss' (p. 6), from the Freudian distinction between mourning and melancholia to the early modern propensity for theatrical self-fashioning, from the early-century mock-epic to a mid-century 'aesthetics of exuberance' (p. 6), arguing that Sterne's generic hybrid is best understood as 'the effort to overcome loss that joyously reproduces loss' (p. 14).

Emasculation anxieties are the subject of William Gibson's well-researched 'Tobias Smollett and Cat-for-Hare: The Anatomy of a Picaresque Joke' (*ECS* 40[2007] 571–86). The article aims to enhance our understanding of Smollett's place within the picaresque tradition by scrutinizing a practical joke in *Peregrine Pickle*, in which a group of men vomit after having been tricked into believing they have eaten cat meat. Gibson reveals the etymological and intertextual richness of Smollett's emetic prank, showing not only its connection to 'the taboo of cunnilingus' (p. 580) but also, more generally, 'a movement away from the disgust of the stomach into a masculine anxiety about one's standing in the social realm' (p. 577).

Gibson also shows us that there is more to Smollett than the picaresque, in *Art and Money in the Writings of Tobias Smollett*, which is a book-length study of the author's critical and imaginative engagement with the increasingly commercialized art world of his time. It analyses, amongst other things, the ways in which Smollett gives shape to the emerging profession of the cultural critic through his position as art reviewer in *The Critical Review* (1756–63), and offers insight into the author's attitude to the liberal arts, which, Gibson explains, 'was defined by the popular notion of a sympathetic interaction between an art object and a spectator' (p. 12). Very valuable in this respect is appendix 1, which is an annotated collection of Smollett's articles on fine art, 'printed', as Gibson informs us, 'in their entirety for the first time since their original publication' (p. 13). Of special interest for this section are chapters 4 and 6, which focus respectively on the characters of Layman Pallet in *Peregrine Pickle* and Matthew Bramble and Lydia Melford in *Humphry Clinker*. Gibson argues that the 'bumbling, accident-prone painter' (p. 81) Pallet is a complex comic figure whose function goes beyond mere entertainment, as his would-be connoisseurship and lack of artistic originality allow Smollett 'to raise specific issues regarding the value of viewing art on the Grand Tour and the place of Continental art in the English aesthetic he wished to see created' (p. 82). Gibson also discerns a shift from mockery to sympathy in the novel as Pallet returns to England, arguing that the change of tone reveals Smollett's anxieties about the socio-economic vulnerability of the artist in the domestic marketplace. In his discussion of *Humphry Clinker*, Gibson looks at 'the short bursts of aesthetic criticism' (p. 137) found throughout the novel, most notably those of Bramble on Mr T's landscape painting and John Wood's Palladian-style architecture, which he connects to the novel's 'derision not only of middle-class taste, but also of the commercial art market that was driven by that taste' (p. 151). He also draws attention to Lydia's 'sense of awe' (p. 154) at Bath's architectural design and argues that her response echoes Smollett's own in his *Essay on the External Uses of Water*, thus concluding that the novel contains the author's 'disparate voices' (p. 137) about the function and future of the liberal arts.

The growing interest in Smollett seems to run parallel with the comeback of biographical criticism in literary studies. In the introduction to *Tobias Smollett, Scotland's First Novelist: New Essays in Memory of Paul-Gabriel Boucé*, editor O.M. Brack Jr argues that, in Smollett's novels at least, 'it is impossible to ignore the author's life' (p. 16), although he warns against what Boucé has termed 'inverted autobiography' (p. 15), the questionable method of equating Smollett with his fictional characters in order to construct his biography. Preceded by a brief career survey of 'PGB' (as Boucé was called by intimates), written by Serge Soupel, this collection of essays highlights the different ways in which Smollett's novels are informed by the author's career in medicine, his health problems, his work in journalism, translation, political propaganda and historiography, his professional rivalries and his personal friendships and animosities. Brack Jr revisits questions of authorship in *Peregrine Pickle*, demonstrating that Smollett played a 'considerable' (p. 48) role in the composition of the 'Memoirs of a Woman of Quality', while in 'When Smelfungus met Yorick' Ian Campbell Ross persuasively argues that 'the role of the discontented traveller, grumbler and philistine both, more properly belonged not to Tobias Smollett but to Laurence Sterne' (p. 78). Robert A. Erickson provides a fine analysis of *Humphry Clinker*, connecting Smollett's *Essay on the External Uses of Water* to the 'thematic image-cluster of water' (p. 100) in the novel. He also gives an interesting new reading of Smollett's last novel, suggesting that in this work, the author 'is exploring his own biographical, creative, and linguistic "origins"' (p. 95). Also focusing on *Humphry Clinker*, Allan Ingram examines Dr Lewis's epistolary silence in the light of 'Georgian expectations of medicine and cure' (p. 122). Gerald J. Butler traces the development of Boucé's criticism of *Roderick Random*, and discusses this alongside the late scholar's appreciation for the works of twentieth-century French novelist Louis-Ferdinand Céline. Linda Bree judiciously probes Smollett's supposed personal and professional antagonisms against Henry Fielding, while Elizabeth Durot-Boucé discusses the frequently over-looked Gothic characteristics of *Ferdinand Count Fathom*. Leslie A. Chilton deplores the 'critical abuse' (p. 192) of Smollett's translations, arguing that they reveal not only the author's qualities as translator but also his indebtedness to the writers he translated, amongst whom were Cervantes, Le Sage and Fénelon. Smollett's imaginative engagement with contemporary politics in *The History and Adventures of an Atom* is under scrutiny by Walter H. Keithley, while the last two essays by Ian Simpson Ross and James E. May examine Smollett's historical writings, the latter providing a useful descriptive bibliography of the various editions of the *Complete History*.

Frances Burney's four novels receive two full chapters and frequent mention throughout others in *The Cambridge Companion to Frances Burney*, edited by Peter Sabor. Jane Spencer's '*Evelina* and *Cecilia*' (pp. 23–37) is an excellent introduction to the author's first two novels. In clear and lucid prose, Spencer offers plot summaries, enlightens the reader on Burney's position (as a woman) in the field of eighteenth-century authorship, and considers her distinctive contribution to the development of the novel. In her discussion of *Evelina*, Spencer describes Burney as 'an economical epistolary writer' (p. 27) who, unlike Richardson, limits the number of letter-writers in the novel to only a few characters. She rightly sees the exclusion of Madame Duval's voice as a reflection of the novel's 'ambivalen[ce] about the matriline' (p. 27), but such a gender-centred reading is of course only part of the story considering Madame Duval's lower-class origins: significantly, the correspondents are either professional (clergyman Mr Villars) or of gentle birth (Lady Howard, baronet's daughter Evelina). In her examination of *Cecilia*, Spencer analyses the Johnsonian elements of the novel and challenges critics who have deplored Johnson's influence on Burney. By drawing on philosophical tales such as *Rasselas*, Spencer argues, 'Burney was raising the well-known plot of a young lady's entrance into the world from mere romantic story to the status of serious morality' (p. 30). Moreover, she adds, the author developed her own independent style through her experimentation with free indirect discourse and reliance upon dialogue and speech differentiation (p. 37). Sara Salih's '*Camilla* and *The Wanderer*' (pp. 39–53) is somewhat less accessible for readers unacquainted with these two still fairly unfamiliar novels. Nevertheless, it provides valuable insight into the ways in which Burney connects identity (be it gender, class, race, moral, religious or national) to notions of performance and theatricality. *Camilla*, Salih argues, is concerned with gender ambiguities, and reveals 'that men, no less than women in the novel, are acting, dissembling, engaging in social theatre—except when they cannot help involuntarily stepping out of character' (p. 43). In her discussion of Burney's last novel, Salih draws attention to 'the doubling that informs *The Wanderer* thematically, formally and ideologically' (p. 46). Drawing useful comparisons to other contemporary novelists such as Austen, she analyses Juliet's role as Lady Townly, her 'sequential acts of racial, gendered and social transvestism' (p. 50) and Elinor's dramatic behaviour, concluding with the 'profoundly unstable' (p. 52) quality of Burney's fictional social worlds.

Patricia L. Hamilton's 'Monkey Business: Lord Orville and the Limits of Politeness in Frances Burney's *Evelina*' (*ECF* 19:iv[2007] 415–40) analyses the complex role of the 'male paragon' (p. 417) in Burney's first novel. After discussing the ways in which Orville's behaviour conforms to an early, rather than a late, eighteenth-century exemplary model of the gentleman, Hamilton uncovers Burney's characteristically 'divided' treatment of this model, arguing convincingly that her novel 'endorses a value system it reveals to be largely ineffectual' (p. 433).

The genre of the novel figures prominently in *On Second Thought: Updating the Eighteenth-Century Text*, edited by Debra Taylor Bourdeau and Elizabeth Kraft, which looks at 'revisions, revisitings, reimaginings, parodies, transmutations, transplantations, intertextualities, recontextualizations, reinterpretations, and adaptations' (p. 11) of eighteenth-century literary works (as well as one visual artwork by Hogarth). The essays in the first part, 'The Eighteenth Century', focus on authors from the period in question who have either 'updated' their own writings or those of their contemporaries. Two contributions relevant to this section are Allen Michie's 'Far From Simple: Sarah Fielding's *Familiar Letters* and the Limits of the Eighteenth-Century Sequel' (pp. 83–111) and W.B. Gerard's ' "Betwixt one passion and another": Continuations of Laurence Sterne's *A Sentimental Journey*, 1769–1820' (pp. 123–38). In a celebratory essay on Sarah Fielding's playful experimentation with literary form, Michie draws attention to the author's neglected 'miscellany of moral anecdotes' (p. 108) and undertakes 'to reconsider it seriously *as a sequel*' (p. 84) to *David Simple*. He stresses the need for critics to acknowledge that eighteenth-century sequels did not necessarily 'stay within the same stylistic boundaries as the original' (p. 108), a view familiar in Defoe studies. Published three years after *David Simple* and six years before *Volume the Last*, *Familiar Letters* is presented by Michie as a text that should be seen as part of a 'trio' of novels, whose author consciously presents readers with 'the full range of sentimentality, didacticism, and tragedy' (p. 100). W.B. Gerard demonstrates that sequels of *A Sentimental Journey* 'tend toward blatant indulgence of either the pathetic or the erotic, unalloyed with the delicately crafted ambiguities of the original' (p. 136). The second part of the book, 'The Twentieth Century', concentrates on authors and artists who have made creative use of eighteenth-century texts in the recent past, thereby offering new insights not just into questions of intertextuality, authorship and literary innovation, but also into the original texts used. Six essays in this part focus on the novel. In 'Writers that Changed the World' (pp. 141–57), Elizabeth Kraft presents Upton Sinclair's *Another Pamela* as a text that enables us to appreciate even more fully Richardson's skilful 'literary strategies of social reform' (p. 141). Defoe's complex and sensitive treatment of colonialism in *Robinson Crusoe* is uncovered in Brett C. McInelly's 'Remaking Crusoe in Derek Walcott's *Pantomime*' (pp. 158–73), while the attractions of *Tristram Shandy* to postcolonial writers are the subject of Michael Hardin's 'Nativity and Nationhood: Laurence Sterne's *Tristram Shandy* and Carlos Fuentes's *Christopher Unborn* as Critiques of Empire' (pp. 174–92). In ' "Dizzy with the beauty of the possible": *The Sot-Weed Factor* and the Narrative Exhaustion of the Eighteenth-Century Novel' (pp. 193–209), Robert Scott explores the idea of 'literary exhaustion' (p. 204) in John Barth's scintillating book, a work greatly indebted to the fiction of Fielding, Smollett and Sterne, which, Scott argues, 'is to offer within its structure both a novel and a critique of the novel form' (p. 206). Finally, in 'Rewriting Sentimental Plots: Sequels to Novels of Sensibility by Jane Austen and Another Lady' (pp. 210–44), Tamara Wagner offers a guide through the maze of Jane Austen sequels, concluding that 'the less imitative and repetitive a sequel becomes, the less successful it will be in fulfilling the expectations it has raised *as* a sequel' (p. 239).

Unfortunately, Paul Baines's *Daniel Defoe: Robinson Crusoe and Moll Flanders* (Reader's Guides to Essential Criticism), Judith Broome's *Fictive Domains: Body, Landscape, and Nostalgia, 1717–1770* and *A Celebration of*

Frances Burney edited by Lorna Clark, Paul Stepanowsky and Peter Sabor were not received in time for review but will be covered in next year's *YWES*.

3. Poetry

This year saw relatively few full-length studies of eighteenth-century poetry, with work in the field largely represented by a diverse range of essays addressing individual poets or particular themes. When read collectively, these reveal a continuing trend towards consolidating recent moves to reassess or widen the existing canon. Scholarly editions were also scarce, a worthy exception being Clare Brant and Susan E. Whyman's excellent volume *Walking the Streets of London, Gay's Trivia (1716)* (hitherto only accessible to students and general readers in anthologized extracts). With so much attention being given in recent years to Gay's mock-heroic pedestrianism, this is a most welcome appearance, not least because in addition to providing a well-annotated edition of the entire 1716 edition of the poem (including the original footnotes and index), Brant and Whyman also include their own substantial introduction along with no less than nine contextual and interpretative critical essays by others: Philip Carter on 'Faces and Crowds', Alison Stenton on 'Spatial Stories' (cultural geography), Tim Hitchcock on *Trivia* and 'public poverty', Mark Jenner on 'Pollution, Plague, and Poetics', Margaret R. Hunt on gender, Aileen Ribero on dress, and Susanna Morton Braund on 'Walking the Streets of Rome'. Two additional essays are by the volume's editors. These short but engaging essays not only bring into clearer focus recently established critical debates, including the question of how we are to read the persona of 'The Walker' as he shifts between gestures of disgust and fascination, but they also serve to deepen our understanding of some important topographical, cultural and generic contexts. This is an attractively produced volume, generously illustrated with ten black and white plates including a contemporary map and various views of the city by Hogarth and others, and it will be of lasting value to both scholars and students alike (it will be available in paperback in 2009).

Roger Lonsdale's four-volume, Clarendon Press edition of Samuel Johnson's *The Lives of the Most Eminent English Poets* [2006], as discussed earlier (*YWES* 87[2008] 638), is the subject of a substantial review essay by Greg Clingham ('Samuel Johnson, Another and the Same', *EIC* 52:ii[2007] 186–94). Clingham opens his judicious assessment with a fulsome acknowledgement of the editor's scholarly achievement; 'Roger Lonsdale has surveyed all of the primary material from China to Peru, and produced a magnificent and monumental work that may become the standard edition for the next century' (p. 187). A detailed summary of the edition's extensive scholarly apparatus (in which Clingham identifies only a few minor omissions, inconsistencies and typos), concludes with the observation that Lonsdale's 'commentary provides us with a cornucopia of eighteenth century biography (as witnessed by the hundreds of proper names in the index), and with information sufficient to recover the canons for drama, epic, odes, masques, the heroic couplet, blank verse, the sonnet, satire, aesthetics, art history, criticism, and literary history for the years from the English Civil War to the early nineteenth century' (p. 188). Clingham's only substantial criticism—more a case of regret than outright complaint—is that while the edition's 'vast commentary impl[ies] critical as well as scholarly comprehensiveness' yet 'the general critical understanding of the *Lives of the Poets* in this edition does not reflect most of the new work on Johnson over the last twenty years', with the result that 'Lonsdale's introduction, though providing an excellent survey, does not balance the minuteness of the commentary with a more imaginative account of how Johnson thinks critically and biographically' (p. 190). In pursuing this argument Clingham provides his own summary of recent Johnson studies before concluding with some speculations on how the long-awaited Yale edition will make up the loss.

The Cambridge Companion to Alexander Pope, edited by Pat Rogers, is the year's most substantial and important collection of essays devoted to a major poet. Introducing the volume, having considered how, despite the attempts of late Victorians to see him 'dead and buried' Pope has simply 'refused to lie down', Rogers explains that the 'reason why the *Companion* is organized in part around issues such as identity, gender, the body, the history of the book, crime, and the other, goes back to a simple fact; Pope's work raises these issues in a peculiarly direct and pervasive way' (p. 2). In the event, such an approach—which certainly reflects the direction of Pope studies over the last twenty or more years—seems fully justified. Rogers has managed to rally a most impressive cast of contributors who, taken collectively, represent many of the very best of current Pope scholars. For practical reasons I do not propose discussing all seventeen essays in any detail, and while I do not wish to isolate particular essays for special praise in such a representative, uniformly well-written, lively volume, it is inevitable that the following, largely descriptive, summary, should betray some of what proved of particular interest to the present reader on a first reading. Helen Deutsch's opening essay on 'Pope: Self and World' (pp. 14–24) is one of two contributions to place particular emphasis upon how Pope's physical deformities served to shape his social and poetic persona. The other is George Rousseau writing on 'Medicine and the Body' (pp. 210–21) which opens with what is probably the most definitive summary to date of what we can actually ascertain regarding the nature of Pope's deformities; curvature of the spine, stunted stature and the unspecific genito-urinary problems stemming from a childhood injury which may have left him impotent. While carefully avoiding any crass retrospective psycho-analytical diagnosis, Rousseau explores how Pope's physical otherness and long-term ill health must have all had a psycho-sexual impact. In 'Pope's Friends and Enemies: Fighting with Shadows' (pp. 25–36) David Nokes is one of several contributors to emphasize the importance of homosociality in Pope's poetic career, including the early role of his older male mentors, William Trumball, William Wycherley and Thomas Betterton, as well as the Scriblerians. John Sitter, in 'Pope's Versification and Voice' (pp. 37–48), alerts us to the rewards of listening carefully to the differing registers of what he describes as Pope's 'many voices'. Steven Shankman on 'Pope's Homer and his Poetic Career' (pp. 63–75) not only addresses the Homeric influence upon the major poems, but also, despite the title, takes in the later Horatian imitations.

Howard D. Weinbrot, on 'Pope and the Classics' (pp. 76–88), and David Fairer, on 'Pope and the Elizabethans' (pp. 89–104), are valuable accounts, the former ending with a most lucid summary of what 'the classics' meant to Pope, while the latter openly invites us to give much more attention to Pope's engagement with Spenser, Jonson and Donne. In two particularly original contributions, Cynthia Wall's 'Poetic Spaces' (pp. 49–62) and Pat Rogers's 'Pope in Arcadia: Pastoral and its Dissolution' (pp. 105–17), we are alerted to the importance of considering the matter of rural and urban topography, both geographical and cultural, when reading Pope. Wall emphasizes the strong visual element in Pope's poetry (as informed by his study of the classical conventions regarding poetic *descriptio* and easel painting) before mapping the poet's own use of 'dramatic spatial gestures' (p. 49). Rogers considers how the Berkshire countryside of the poet's childhood spent at Binfield and Chiswick informed the *Pastorals* and *Windsor Forest*: 'With very little exaggeration we could say that the region created as potent an imaginative matrix for his work as Cumbria did for Wordsworth, Wessex for Hardy, or the Mississippi for Faulkner' (p. 106). Pope's marginalized social standing as a Catholic, and his role as an oppositional political poet, are the concerns of complementary essays by Brian Young, on 'Pope and Ideology' (pp. 118–33), which explores 'cultural politics', and Howard Erskine-Hill, on 'Pope and the Poetry of Opposition' (pp. 134–49). In the latter Erskine-Hill outlines the debate over Pope's active Jacobitism in order to raise the wider question of how we are to separate out 'cultural' from 'political' politics in any such discussions. He eventually brings these questions into focus around the unresolved matter of Pope's later dealings with Robert Walpole and his administration. Drawing upon manuscript sources, Erskine-Hill examines how William Fortescue's attempts to forge a rapprochement between Walpole and the poet might be brought to bear upon our reading of *The Dunciad Variorum* and the satires of the 1730s. Both these essays bring into sharper focus what Erskine-Hill describes as the 'blurred edges' (p. 135) of what might otherwise be deemed a now broad consensus regarding Pope's oppositional political stance. They sit comfortably next to Paul Baines on 'Crime and Punishment' (pp. 150–60), Malcolm Kelsall on 'Landscapes and Estates' (pp. 161–74) and Catherine Ingrassia on 'Money' (pp. 175–85). Baines argues that, while Pope often justified his satirical practice through invoking the established judicial metaphor of 'the lash', the poetry confirms that the poet's attitude 'to crime and the law was actually more complex' and the early works in particular are often marked by 'considerable tolerance towards transgressors, especially female sexual delinquents' (p. 150). Kelsall begins by outlining Pope's 'fundamental influence on the development of the late eighteenth-century picturesque garden', and his important role in establishing principles of taste, before seeking to negotiate the marked tensions between those who read the 'expression of these principles in his writings' as emphatically 'setting the highest standards of taste', and those who view 'the whole landscape movement with which he is associated' as being 'exploitative and a mystification of power' and thus cast Pope as merely 'a lackey of the rich and apologist for the dark side of British politics' (p. 161). If Kelsall goes on to largely disregard the latter position, certainly his attention to Pope's ethical concern with country-house landscapes as symbols of 'the right use of riches' leads directly on to Ingrassia's opening remarks upon how Pope lived through an era in which 'the economic landscape of England changed dramatically, moving from a traditional land-based model of wealth to a world shaped by the possibilities and contingencies of "paper credit"', a transition from a culture which, 'in idealized representations, embodied a devotion to a patrician ethos of generosity and morality to a financially driven, avaricious society where "A man of Wealth is dubb'd a Man of worth"' (p. 176). Her essay explores how friendship, words and money—and their relative values— represent three central 'currencies' that are 'deeply imbricated and mutually reinforcing' as 'Pope's professional success increased, aided in part by an ad hoc system of patronage and his savvy determination to control the publication of his texts' (p. 175). This latter aspect of Pope's career is the focus of 'Pope and the Book Trade' (pp. 186–97), by James McLaverty, who is very well qualified to give a succinct overview of the recent work in a field to which he has himself made major contributions. Valerie Rumbold's essay takes on the sometimes contentious question of 'Pope and Gender' (pp. 198–209). The balanced nature of her essentially biographical and historicist approach is reflected in her opening observation that 'Pope's work was both energized and constrained by gender; but evaluating its effects is far from straightforward, since gender in Pope's time was neither a monolithic system nor an entirely stable one' (p. 198). Rumbold asks us to consider how 'Pope's combination of civil and medical disabilities entailed restrictions in many ways close to those within which women had to operate; but he also lived strenuously, in so far as his health permitted, as a member of a masculine cultural and intellectual world' (p. 199), before going on to provide succinct readings of how such constraints and tensions around gender inform several of the major poems. Last, but far from least, Laura Brown addresses 'Pope and the Other' (pp. 222–36). She opens with a lucid explanation of what is meant by 'the other' in contemporary critical studies, before offering a close analysis of the passage on the 'poor Indian' in the first epistle of Pope's *Essay on Man* which 'stands as an example of the status of native Americans in the early-eighteenth century' (p. 222). This essay is exemplary in the way it illustrates the application of current feminist and postcolonial concerns with 'alterity' (and associated theoretical models) through a practical exercise in close reading. Taken as a whole, the *Companion*'s well-organized thematic structuring around 'issues' and 'contexts' is far from tending to the exclusion of poetry. Many essayists offer valuable close readings and it is easy to use the index to trace contrasting approaches to the same poem (there is also a summary bibliography). The expert contributors to *The Cambridge Companion to Alexander Pope* not only provide a series of well-informed, summary insights into the state of current scholarship and criticism, but their original essays often point us in the direction of fresh critical pathways. This is an excellent addition to an excellent series, and one that will be warmly welcomed by academics, students and the general reader alike.

Appearing in late December 2006, Louise K. Barnett's well-received study *Jonathan Swift in the Company of Women* might have fallen through the net, but although it is not exclusively concerned with the poetry it certainly deserves passing notice here. Barnett does not merely revisit the perennial question of Swift's misogyny, but draws upon recent developments in women's history to address the whole matter of how women shaped Swift's life and writing career in multifarious roles as mothers, nurses, intimate friends, social acquaintances, the targets of satire and critics.

Last year's entry first drew our attention to Bill Overton's 'uncompromisingly empirical' work on the verse epistle as presented by his contribution to the *Blackwell Companion to Eighteenth-Century Poetry* (*YWES* 87[2008] 648). This year saw the publication of his full-length study *The Eighteenth-Century British Verse Epistle* which can justly claim to provide the first detailed, wide-ranging survey of what is shown here to have been a statistically significant genre yet—with a few notable exceptions such as Pope's *Eloisa to Abelard*—one that has often been ignored. Taking advantage of current facilities for undertaking detailed title and other word searches of existing electronic databases—principally Chadwyk-Healey's *Literature Online* and Gale's *Eighteenth-Century Collections Online*—Overton's study is based upon his ability to trace the frequency of poems with a claim to be called 'epistles' or 'letters' appearing in print between 1700 and 1800 (his search criteria and methods being meticulously set out in an appendix). The opening chapters address wider question concerning generic definition—both in the period itself and amongst modern critics—as well as the matter of frequency. Further chapters examine the particular kinds of verse epistle available under the thematic category headings 'Familiar and Humorous', 'Discursive', 'Heroic and Amatory' and 'Satirical and Complimentary'. These findings justify Overton's opening claim that 'the verse epistle was a key form in eighteenth-century Britain' (p. ix), by showing how such poems range in form and content well beyond the popular Ovidian heroic epistle and the Horatian verse letter or verse essay. An appendix provides a collated list of the verse epistles to be found in John Dryden's *Miscellany Poems*, Robert Dodsley's *Poems by Several Hands* and George Pearch's *Collections of Poems by Several Hands*, as well as Roger Lonsdale's two modern collections, the *New Oxford Book of Eighteenth-Century Verse* [1984] and *Eighteenth-Century Women Poets; An Oxford Anthology* [1989]. This is at heart an unapologetic, self-consciously empiricist exercise in descriptive bibliography, presenting 'a survey rather than an argument', but despite Overton's prior warning that this will 'involve more use of statistics than is common in critical studies' (p. ix), his descriptive accounts do much to expand our awareness of a genre which served a diverse range of writers, including many women and poets of both sexes writing from a labouring-class position. Overton's painstaking work of recovery and taxonomy provides a sound basis for further, more overtly critical, studies.

Turning to essays in edited volumes, when attention was first drawn to the Lorna Clymer's edited essay volume *Ritual, Routine and Regime: Repetition in Early Modern British and European Cultures*, under heading 'Prose and General' (*YWES* 87[2008] 623), it was concluded that 'these essays are discernibly influenced by Derrida and Deleuze, but in the final analysis most people will seek out this volume for its individual essays' (p. 623). In retrospect, it is worth drawing closer attention to the two valuable essays in this volume which are devoted exclusively to eighteenth-century poetry.

The first is Chris Mounsey's contribution on 'Christopher Smart's Lyrics: Building Churches in the Air' (pp. 132–50), which addresses the neglected theme of Anglican hymnology. Mounsey considers the apparent anomaly that, while many orthodox Anglicans of the eighteenth century 'saw the hymn as the uncontrolled outburst of enthusiasm' and therefore a 'political blight' belonging to the previous century to be 'looked upon with horror', yet some orthodox Anglicans, including Christopher Smart and William Cowper, were themselves hymn-writers. Largely focusing on Smart, a High Anglican, in this richly contextual account Mounsey extends an argument he first mounted in his earlier biography of the poet *Christopher Smart; Clown of God* [2001] by seeking to untangle previous critical confusions which have often invited us to read the 'mad' poet's 'enthusiastic' hymn-writing as merely a matter of personal pathology, rather than, as is argued for here, as 'a guard against Dissenting enthusiasm . . . consonant with non-juring Anglican ideas' (p. 137).

The second essay of interest in Clymer's volume is David Fairer's '"The Year's Round": The Poetry of Work in Eighteenth-Century England' (pp. 153–71). Fairer's characteristically lucid, well-informed essay uses the volume's thematic concern with patterns of time and ritual to examine 'The Poetry of Work' between 1700 and 1760, and in so doing successfully draws together 'two aspects of eighteenth-century poetry that have been usually kept apart; the georgic and the poetry of the labouring classes' (p. 155). In the context of the models set by Hesiod and Virgil, Fairer launches into a series of deftly handled close readings of some now familiar poems by Stephen Duck and Mary Collier, alongside less familiar ones by Robert Tatershall, poet of *The Bricklayer's Miscellany* [1734–5] (looking forward to the factory system of the early Victorian era, he frames this discussion with a reading of 'The Song of the Shirt' by Thomas Hood). Along the way Fairer's wide-ranging analysis manages to take in related passages on repetitive work rituals in other georgic poems, including John Philips's *Cyder* [1708], James Thomson's *The Seasons*, Christopher Smart's *The Hop-Garden* [1743–4], John Armstrong's *The Art of Preserving Health* [1774], James Grainger's *Sugar-Cane* [1753] and John Dyer's *The Fleece* [1757]. Having anticipated finding a simple contrast between idealized georgic celebrations and labouring-class denunciations of the repetitious rituals of work, Fairer uncovers a far more complex relationship between poetics, ergonomics and politics in the actual poems.

Two general essay volumes (only reaching my desk too late for any detailed discussion) deserve mention. The essay by Jonathan Lamb, entitled 'The Rape of the Lock as Still Life' appearing in Mark Blackwell's edited volume *The Secret Life of Things: Animals; Objects, and It-Narratives in Eighteenth-Century England*, might otherwise be overlooked by anyone interested in Pope. The essay volume *On Second Thought: Updating the Eighteenth-Century Text*, edited by Debra Taylor Bourdeau and Elizabeth Kraft, also includes an essay on Pope's *Rape of the Lock*, '"An inviolate preservation": Immortalizing the Ephemeral Lock', by Emily Hipchen. The same volume also provides two further essays on authorial revisions; one by Sandro Jung on 'Updating Summer' in James Thomson's *The Seasons* and the other by John Adrian comparing John Gay's 'First and Second Series of Fables'.

Turning to essays in journals, these covered a diverse range of writers, poetic forms and thematic topics, including a small flush of mainly short essays addressing the mixed reputation of William Collins (1721–59). In the most substantial, 'Odes of Absorption in the Restoration and Early Eighteenth Century' (*SEL* 47[2007] 659–78) Margaret Koehler sets out to complicate the commonplace story of how, with William Collins and Thomas Gray, we find 'Restoration histrionics give way to midcentury meditations' as the ode supposedly shifts register 'from public to private, panegyric to introspection, real persons to personified abstractions' (p. 659). While not wholly rejecting this 'broad arc', Koehler challenges the idea of any 'instantaneous' change of direction around 1740 by illustrating how examples of 'interiority' occur in the earlier phase. Starting with a comparison of the visual tropes at work in Abraham Cowley's 'To Dr Scarborough', first published in the *Pindarique Odes* [1707–11] and Collins 'Ode to Fear' [1746], she goes on to analyse further contrasting uses of the Pindaric by John Dryden, William Congreve, Anne Finch, John Dennis and John Pomfret. Koehler concludes that any move towards the blurring of 'calling voice and invoked object' that we traditionally associate with mid-century practice comes about more gradually in a more evolutionary process (p. 659).

In 'William Collins and the Goddess Natura' (*ANQ* 20:iv[2007] 17–23) Sandro Jung argues for reading Collins's notoriously obscure use of personifications in his *Odes on Several Descriptive and Allegoric Subjects* [1746] in the context of a far more fundamental concept of invoking the deity ('Natura' or 'Physis') to found in the hymnal ode of classical antiquity, which sought to encapsulate the 'elementary religious essence that depicted man's encounter with the spiritual presence of the personified deity' (p. 18). Carson Bergstrom's no-nonsense title 'William Collins and Personification (Once Again)' heads a cogent essay which also begins by drawing attention—in a succinct critical survey—to the marked contrast between the often positive contemporary responses to Collins's *Odes* and the largely negative verdict of modern critics (*ANQ* 20:iv[2007] 29–39). Bergstrom argues that many modern charges against the poet's persistent use of personification rest upon some rather simplistic, under-theorized, definitions of the workings of metaphor. He goes on to provide a lucid exposition of recent, more sophisticated, accounts of metaphor by such cognitive linguists as George Lakoff, Mark Turner and Zotàn Zövecses which, contrary to earlier accounts of it being merely a rhetorical device which simply forges connections 'between things', wish to emphasize that metaphor is a more fundamental element in everyday speech and thus essential to the way we comprehend embodied life. One only regrets that this relatively brief essay does not allow Bergstrom much room to apply these interesting developments in linguistics to sustained readings of Collins's actual poetry. The same journal issue also includes a short note on 'William Collins and the Gaze Beyond' by Raffaella Antinucci (*ANQ* 20:iv[2007] 39–44).

Another essay by Sandro Jung, entitled 'William Collins, Grace and the "cest of amplest power"' (*Neophil* 91:iii[2007] 539–54) seeks to address eighteenth-century understandings of 'grace' as an aesthetic concept of equal, if not more, importance for reading Collins and the Burkean sublime. Jung traces how 'grace' functions in the ethical and literary critical writings of, amongst others, Shaftesbury, William Warburton, John Gilbert Cooper and Schiller, and how these writers provide a context for reading Collins's 'Ode on the Poetical Character' [1746]. Jung's analysis comes into focus around the image of the 'cest of amplest power' (Spenser's *cestus* of chastity) which Sandro claims provides Collins with the 'the medium through which poetic inspiration can be conferred on the supplicating poet' (p. 539). Jung concludes on the importance of comprehending this aesthetic conception of 'grace' as the essential idea informing Collins's significant 'rewriting and inverting of traditional (creation) gender stereotypes, [in] the ambivalent mythological figure of Aphrodite, [and] Spenser's Florimel episode' (p. 554).

Michael Tomko's essay 'Abolition Poetry, National Identity, and Religion: The Case of Peter Newby's "The Wrongs of Almoona"' (*ECent* 48[2007] 25–43), offers a contextual analysis of a somewhat neglected though substantial abolition poem by Peter Newby (1745–1827), a prominent philanthropic Roman Catholic schoolmaster, if more diffident poet, who published his *The Wrongs of Almoona, or, The African's Revenge* [1788], dedicated to William Cowper, over the pseudonym 'A Friend to All Mankind'.

Murray Pittock's substantial essay 'Allan Ramsay and the Decolonisation of Genre' (*RES* 58[2007] 316–37), provides an important reassessment of Ramsay's poetic practice as well as his influential role as both a collector and adapter of native Scottish songs. Pittock's essay fully justifies his characteristically well-informed opening argument for the value of revisiting early twentieth-century accounts which began to recognize Ramsay's importance as 'an avatar of Romantic practice' (p. 317). In his own re-evaluation, Pittock stresses Ramsay's promotion of a distinctive Scottish public sphere and 'Scots mindset', not least through his influential inflections of genre; a project consciously 'designed to protect and promote a distinctive national voice by transforming English uses of literary kinds, not surrendering to them' (p. 316). Paying particular attention to Ramsay's adaptations of elegy and pastoral into a vernacular register, Pittock offers some informative close readings of specific poems. He concludes by suggesting how Ramsay, by rewriting 'his inheritance in broadside and popular poetry', was able to enact a 'decolonization of genre' which liberated Scottish verse from the tyranny of the deadening, English, metropolitan, linguistic standards which subsequently meant that 'Wordsworth's "real language of men in a state of vivid sensation" could never be Cumbrian speech or any representation of it' (p. 319). In the process Pittock expands our understanding of the local (Edinburgh), political (Jacobite) and wider cultural contexts within which to read Ramsay's lively, and still unjustly neglected, poetry.

English chapbook ballads and popular song lyrics form a significant part of the evidence analysed in Robin Ganev's essay 'Milkmaids, Ploughmen and Sex in Eighteenth-Century Britain' (*JHSex* 16:i[2007] 40–67). In what is primarily an exercise in social history, Ganev addresses the conventional portrayal of lusty ploughmen and lascivious milkmaids in songs and other popular verses of the long eighteenth century, where such figures are frequently positively contrasted with a sexually debilitated urban aristocracy. By reading this often bawdy material in the context of contemporary concerns regarding sexual vigour, health, luxury and population growth this study expands our understanding of the cultural significance of these popular pastoral lyrics. In particular Ganev examines how traditional conceptions of uninhibited rural heterosexuality were being countered by anxieties concerning rustic stupidity, illegitimacy, overpopulation and moral decline.

In the field of translation studies, William Kupersmith's *English Versions of Roman Satire in the Earlier Eighteenth Century* addresses the well-known imitations by Pope and Johnson, alongside lesser-known examples by Swift, Henry Fielding and Christopher Smart, to provide students with a useful overview of the genre. Adam Rounce's essay 'Eighteenth-Century Responses to Dryden's Fables' (*T&L* 16[2007] 29–52) serves to reinforce recent moves to re-evaluate the central importance of John Dryden's translations for the immediate generations after his death in 1700. Rouse provides a necessarily selective study in the reception of *The Fables Ancient and Modern* of 1700 by concentrating upon examples where later writers display a marked critical engagement with this very popular work. In particular Dryden's reworkings of Chaucer (*Palamon and Arcite*) and Boccaccio (*Sigismonda and Guiscardo* and *Cymon and Iphegenia*), were appreciated for their 'individuality' as, in effect, original works in their own right. Rouse's analytical survey covers a wide range of responses, stretching from that of the relatively obscure translator and poet Jabez Hughes (1684/5–1731)—in a very appreciative poem penned in 1707 (published 1721) describing in glowing terms his warm response to first reading the *Fables*—through Charles Churchill's invocation, in his *Epistle to William Hogarth* [1763], of Dryden's high poetic achievement in the *Fables* to denigrate the latter's print 'Sigismonda Mourning over the Heart of Guiscarda' to related poetic tributes by Thomas Gray and William Hayward Roberts. Rouse also addresses the later comments, in prose, of the likes of Samuel Johnson, William Godwin, Mary Wollstonecraft and William Hazlitt. Of particular note is the detailed attention afforded in this essay to Samuel Richardson's often pointedly moral use of allusions to the *Fables* in his novel *Clarissa* [1748–9].

Continuing with the matter of translation, last year's entry on eighteenth-century poetry closed with a brief mention of Stuart Gillespie's editing of some previously unknown translations of Juvenal's Satires VI and X by William Popple (1700–64) found in two related manuscript books held by the Bodleian and the British Library (*T&L* 15[2006] 47–96). It seems fitting therefore to end by reporting that in 2007 Gillespie was able to supplement these findings by publishing a further, related discovery in the Osborn collection of the Beinecke Rare Book and Manuscript Library at Yale (*T&L* 16[2007] 205–35). This consists of two thick, folio-size volumes matching those already located in London and Oxford, which when taken together to make up 'a complete verse translation of Horace, in rhyming couplet for the *Satires*, *Epistles*, and *Ars Poetica*, and for the *Odes*, *Epodes*, and *Carmen Sæculare* in largely stanzaic rhyming verse' (pp. 205–6). Popple, who served as governor of the Bermudas in 1745, has hitherto only been known as a minor playwright. As published in 1753 his sole published translation, Horace's *Art of Poetry* carried no explanatory preface, but, as Gillespie explains, one of the Yale volumes contains a substantial preface in which Popple explains his reasons for undertaking these translations in what now looks like a substantial long-term project. This preface, which Gillespie reproduces here alongside some specimen poems from the newly unearthed volumes, is of particular interest for the attention Popple gives to Pope's Horatian imitations, which he acknowledges as a major inspiration but which he is not afraid to criticize. All Gillespie's findings regarding these now dispersed manuscript volumes certainly seems to support his highly plausible suggestion that this eager translator had prepared a 'Poems and Translations of William Popple' which for some unknown reason never reached print.

4. Drama

This year's work in eighteenth-century British drama falls into five discernible categories: actors and performance history, specific authors (Henry Fielding, Aphra Behn, Thomas Southerne, Thomas Durfey and Eliza Haywood), dramatic ephemera, cultural traditions and editions of plays. The direction of this year's work in eighteenth-century British drama demonstrates the ways in which performance studies and theatrical matters are informing scholarship. Work on Joanna Baillie is discussed below in Chapter XII.

Two important collections of essays which reflect the diverse ways in which performance history is becoming integral to eighteenth-century drama studies were published this year, Michael Cordner and Peter Holland's *Players, Playwrights, Playhouses: Investigating Performance, 1660–1800* and *Prologues, Epilogues, Curtain-Raisers, and Afterpieces: The Rest of the Eighteenth-Century London Stage*, edited by Daniel James Ennis and Judith Bailey Slagle. Robert D. Hume's essay 'Theatre History, 1660–1800: Aims, Materials, Methodology' (in Cordner and Holland, eds., pp. 9–44) challenges scholars to enrich their interpretations of dramatic texts within their historical performance circumstances. He encourages scholarship that demonstrates the connections between the writing and reception of plays based on what can be learned of their performances. Hume reminds us that, during the long eighteenth century, plays were rarely regarded as literature. Instead, it was primarily their performance that audiences valued. Hume questions the habit of twenty-first-century scholars of ignoring or diminishing the theatrical terms of the plays in favour of their published forms. Much theatre history is lost by focusing only on published texts, and Hume illustrates this by pointing out that, between 1660 and 1800, 2,400 new plays were professionally staged in London, and of those, about twenty-five have received serious scholarly attention. London staged a large amount of fringe theatre, some printed and some not, and much stage ephemera has been ignored. Hume correctly concludes that we should utilize more of the performance-based materials available to us in our analytical work on eighteenth-century drama.

Taking up Hume's challenge, Judith Milhous turns to the performance-based materials of account books and financial documents for the patent theatre of eighteenth-century London in 'Reading Theatre History Account Books' (in Cordner and Holland, eds., pp. 101–31). Her fascinating essay surveys the extant materials, explains how budgets and financial records worked in eighteenth-century London theatres and reviews some questions these resources have helped us answer, such as the size, shape and managerial operations of the theatres. Milhous shows us how to read an account book, and surveys bookkeeping practices that illuminate the underlying process of theatre accounting. Her theatrical accounting analysis of six brief cases reveals, for example, that the patent theatres were stable, enduring enterprises and that the salary scale for performers and stagecraft members demonstrate a brutally clear hierarchy. Because accounting books shed light on box-office results, additional analysis may help us to learn more about audience preferences and how money conditions theatrical art.

In 'Theatre for Nothing' (in Cordner and Holland, eds., pp. 175–88), Michael Dobson examines how non-professional theatre changes perceptions of the place of drama in eighteenth-century culture. Dobson points out that the boundaries between professional and non-professional theatrical economy were blurred and permeable. Actors worked for the patent theatres and for wealthy patrons, for example, and both amateur and professional theatres were involved in the economics of charity performance. Private theatricals, expanded dramatic parlour games, such as that performed by the Harris family of Salisbury in 1774, contributed to anxiety about the proliferation of non-professional shows, as Richard Cumberland's 1788 essay 'Remarks upon the Present Taste for Acting Private Plays' attests. Cumberland was particularly concerned about those productions in which well-bred young women (such as Laetitia Wyndham) displayed themselves on private stages as a public exhibition of marital eligibility. The cross-class activity promoted by theatrical performances may have been a source of anxiety, Dobson concludes, but it represents the vital economic and anthropological role that theatre played in eighteenth-century culture.

In 'The Visibility of the Theatre' (in Cordner and Holland, eds., pp. 271–93), Shearer West turns to the rise of the theatrical celebrity in the eighteenth century as a dimension of performance that can enrich our understanding of drama from the eighteenth century, a transitional time when the visual culture of celebrity, West argues, functioned creatively. Portraits of theatrical performers reflected and affected the way the public engaged with their leisure and social world. From 1760, the increasing 'culture of visuality' moved theatre and art close together, opening onto what West terms an 'intermedial' relationship, characterized by distancing and ambiguity, between the object and the audience (pp. 272, 280). West illustrates this visual reading with Joshua Reynolds's portrait *Mrs Siddons as the Tragic Muse* [1784], Thomas Gainsborough's *Mrs Siddons* [1785] and James Gillray's *Melpomene (Mrs Siddons)* [1784]. Chole Smith Wigston, in 'Dressing Up Character: Theatrical Painting from the Restoration to the Mid-Eighteenth Century' (in Ennis and Slagle, eds., pp. 70–105), argues that the representation of clothing and the meaning of character dramatically changed as a result of the depiction of theatrical costuming in portraits of stage performers. Smith Wigston traces the evolution of portraiture from a Restoration aesthetic that marks character with sweeping strokes to a mid-eighteenth-century layering of details from past and present. According to Smith Wigston, the portraiture of the 1750s requires more engagement from the viewer than the stock figures of the Restoration.

Illustrations and discursive discussions include Sir Godfrey Kneller's portrait of Thomas Betterton and John Greenhill's black and red chalk drawing of Betterton as Soloyman from *The Siege of Rhodes*; John Michael Wright's portrait of John Lacy in the title character in *Sauny the Scot*, as Monsieur Gailliard in *The Variety* and as Scruple from *The Cheats*; Sir Peter Lely's portrait of Mary (Moll) Davis; and John Smith's portrait *Anne Bracegirdle as the Indian Queen*. Chloe Smith astutely observes that, by the early eighteenth century, new styles of acting were demanding new styles of pictorial representation so as to convey character as a concept open to multiplicity. Illustrations and discursive discussions include Giuseppe Grisoni's portrait of Colley Cibber in the role of Lord Foppington from *The Relapse; or, Virtue in Danger*; William Hogarth's depictions of Dryden's *The Indian Emperor*, Act IV; and John Faber's portrait of Margaret (Peg) Woffington as Mrs Ford in *The Merry Wives of Windsor*.

If West and Smith Wigston's essays are concerned with how the eighteenth century read theatrical icons, then Peter Holland's discussion is interested in trying to recapture the sound of eighteenth-century performers. In 'Hearing the Dead: The Sound of David Garrick' (in Cordner and Holland, eds., pp. 248–70), Holland explores the conflicting accounts of exactly what Garrick sounded like when, as King Lear, he cursed Goneril. Holland responds to Robert D. Hume's challenge to explore performance aspects of drama by pursuing the histories of phonology and elocution, the aural dimension of performance that is sorely under-studied. Using Garrick as his case study, Holland gathers evidence from letters to Garrick critical of his performance delivery. Holland pays close attention to clues about Garrick's phoneme, speed, silence and syntax as interpretative lenses. His study reveals that Garrick's speech may have had some Lichfield tinges to particular words, that his speed and energy of delivery were both praised and denigrated and that he sometimes paused too long or in the wrong place, as he was wont to mis-accent a line. Coached by Charles Macklin, Garrick electrified audiences with his horrific curse from *King Lear* for over thirty years. Holland concludes that the conflicting accounts of the performance may in fact point to the strengths of Garrick's abilities to show multiple and successive emotions rapidly or simultaneously.

Erin J. Smith looks to the contribution of dance to the eighteenth-century stage in 'Transitional Performances: Eighteenth-Century London Theater and the Emergence of Professional Dance' (in Ennis and Slagle, eds., pp. 106–18). Attempting to fill in the gap in dance history from *ballet d'action* in the early to mid-eighteenth century to the professional dance troupes of the early nineteenth century, Smith points out that dances included in the mainpieces were fundamentally different from the dances specifically devised as an *entr'acte*, which were supplemental to the mainpiece. In the 1780s and 1790s dance had not completely broken free from theatre and opera, but it began to replace operatic singing as a conventional *entr'acte* entertainment because it was seen as a less threatening and less culturally specific art form. Smith speculates that in the last two decades of the eighteenth century, theatrical dance, caught between Enlightenment and Romantic ballet, was therefore not appreciated for its role in the evolution of profession dance, criticized as it was for its deterioration into circus-like spectacles and oddities.

Reiko Oya's monograph *Representing Shakespearean Tragedy: Garrick, the Kembles, and Kean* (also discussed in Chapter XII) examines the performances of these tragedians as crucial to our understanding of eighteenth-century drama, and he maintains that, to understand their performances, we must look at the total theatrical milieu in which they occurred. Oya notes, for example, that Garrick corrected what some considered a defective delivery of King Lear and in the process created an innovative acting style, psychological realism, a performance delivery that Holland's essay (discussed above) explores. According to Oya, Garrick based his impersonation of Lear on an actual distracted gentleman he often visited and imitated. Garrick's 1752 performance gave rise to Joseph Warton's 1753 essay on the madness of Lear in the *Adventurer* and Arthur Murphy's 1754 essay in the *Gray's-Inn Journal* as well as a host of other writings speculating on the cause of Lear's madness and Garrick's interpretation of madness. Garrick responded to the critical essays with his orchestration of the Stratford Jubilee in 1769, his Jubilee Ode, his self-caricature and self-promotion in the 1765 anonymous pamphlet *The Sick Monkey: A Fable*, and his afterpiece *The Jubilee*. Garrick frequently performed the mad Lear as a parlour entertainment. In other words, Garrick's performances took on more forms and manifestations than in those roles he enacted upon the stage. If *King Lear* was the defining Shakespearian tragedy for Garrick, then *Macbeth* fulfilled that function for John Philip Kemble and Sarah Siddons. Their performances, like those of Garrick, were based on character studies that explored the dark psychology of guilt, terror and anguish. Like Garrick, they too wrote essays on their characters. Kemble exaggerated supernatural effects of his performance of Macbeth with hallucinatory noises and visions. In the 1794 production he eliminated the stage ghost and impelled the audience to imagine it as he spoke to a vacant stool on stage. After mixed audience responses, Kemble restored the ghost. Oya concludes that John Boydell's gallery of Shakespearian paintings, like the discursive character analyses, transformed ephemeral stage performances into visual permanence, as in Joshua Reynolds's *Mrs Siddons as the Tragic Muse*.

Other performance studies look at the eighteenth-century actress. Two essays from *The Cambridge Companion to the Actress*, edited by Maggie B. Gale and John Stokes, show how the problematic public figure of the actress evolved throughout the long eighteenth century. In 'Spectacle, Intellect, and Authority: The Actress in the Eighteenth Century' (pp. 33–51), Elizabeth Eger traces the positive moral shift in the reputation of the actress after women pushed against social and political boundaries that sought to contain them. Actresses such as Charlotte Charke, Hanna Pritchard, Lavinia Fenton and Sarah Siddons developed new styles of performance that endeared them to the public. These successful performers broke away from formulaic acting manuals to create new modes of dramatic expression. Other actresses, such as Hannah Pritchard, Dora Jordan and Charlotte Charke, played breeches roles that enabled them to compete with men for key roles. Susannah Centlivre, Charlotte Charke, Catherine Clive, Elizabeth Griffith, Eliza Haywood, Elizabeth Inchbald, Susanna Rowson, Sarah Siddons and Mary Robinson were among those actresses whose self-invention included their own writing in various genres. Eger makes clear that publicity could be manipulated for and against women of the theatre. The visibility of actresses captured in portraits by Reynolds, Gainsborough, Romney and Hamilton improved these women's social status and reputation for virtue.

Similarly, Viv Gardner traces the now familiar path of plight negotiated by the eighteenth-century actress in her essay 'By Herself: The Actress and Autobiography, 1755–1939' (in Gale and Stokes, eds., pp. 173–92). In this discussion, Gardner shows how Charlotte Charke, George Anny Bellamy, Mary Robinson and Sarah Siddons used their own life stories to shape public perceptions of the woman on stage. A more detailed discussion of the power of autobiography in shaping public opinion of female celebrity appears in chapter 7 of Robert L. Mack's monograph *The Genius of Parody: Imitation and Originality in Seventeenth- and Eighteenth-Century English Literature.* Charlotte Charke's *A Narrative of the Life of Mrs Charlotte Charke* appeared in April and May 1755 in eight weekly instalments, and it is one of those performance-based materials that Robert D. Hume claims to be so important to our analytical work on eighteenth-century drama. The story of Colley Cibber's daughter records or fictionalizes much behind the scenes theatre lore as well as being a personal account of one theatre celebrity. Mack identifies *A Narrative* as a parody of Cibber's *The Provok'd Husband*, and so the autobiography is a theatricalized family tragedy that sheds light on controversial aspects of Cibber's career as well as on spectacular features of Charke's habits and behaviour. Mack challenges feminist readings of *A Narrative* as partial and fractured, overtly polemical and uncompromising in their zeal to see Charke as a transgressive and subversive figure. His reading of the autobiography perceives the ventriloquism of Charke, her poking fun at her multiple selves (male and female), as the manifest disguise for the serious subtext of familial reconciliation.

As these studies in eighteenth-century performance demonstrate, theatre and drama do not occur in a vacuum, and in fact, theatre is so culturally integrated that we must consider its multiple dimensions. Several essays in Ennis and Slagle's *Prologues, Epilogues, Curtain-Raisers, and Afterpieces* examine those theatrical ephemera that have escaped close scholarly consideration. The introduction (pp. 13–29), co-authored by Ennis and Slagle, declares that the collection of essays represents acts of recovery of tertiary forms and dramatic components relegated to the margins by contemporary scholarship. They maintain that illegitimate forms were sites of dramatic invention, and afterpieces gained increasing influence during the eighteenth century and so should occupy an important space in cultural and dramaturgical understandings. In 'Cozening the Pit: Prologues, Epilogues, and Poetic Authority in Restoration England' (in Ennis and Slagle, eds., pp. 33–69), Paul McCallum demonstrates how these short dramatic pieces are key to our comprehending the relationship between playwright and audience. In fact, these short dramatic interludes were the site for stage–audience interactions. Writers of these pieces, McCallum points out, cozened their audiences; in other words, they lured and tricked adversarial audience members into a psychologically exposed and rhetorically vulnerable position so that they could influence political and social commentary. Often, these writers used these pieces to flatter fools in their folly, give them the superficial fare they craved and then cozen them into utter disrepute. Among his many examples, McCallum examines Dryden's epilogue to *Aureng-Zebe*, delivered by Michael Mohun in November 1675 at Drury Lane.

According to Robert Sawyer, 'Prologues and Epilogues: Performing Shakespearean Criticism in the Restoration', we can better understand Restoration responses to Shakespeare by examining Dryden's pithy prologues and elegant epilogues (in Ennis and Slagle, eds., pp. 135–54). Using the lens of Mikhail Bakhtin's theories of the speaking person and authoritative discourse, Sawyer explores the dramatic criticism and critical theory written into these short pieces. Dryden's conflicted response to Shakespeare often appears in the dialectic between a prologue, citing and praising the Bard, and then in the main play, challenging and rebuking him. Dryden's debate with Shakespeare was as much on stage as it was in his formal critical writing, and it is in the stage pieces that we find Dryden's most significant Shakespearian criticism. Diana Solomon continues this line of investigation about the dialectical relationship between epilogue and main play by questioning the kind of influence a bawdy epilogue would have on a tragedy. Does a tragedy that is followed by a bawdy epilogue lose its integrity of character and genre? What happens when the heroine of the tragedy speaks the bawdy epilogue? In 'Tragic Play, Bawdy Epilogue?' (in Ennis and Slagle, eds., pp. 155–78), Solomon concludes that playwrights and theatre managers seemed less concerned about the moral integrity of the actress's role and genre in order to accommodate audience desire to experience the actress's sex comedy, the epilogue's sexually comic reinterpretation of the play's tragic content. Solomon illustrates this with Joseph Addison's bawdy epilogue to Ambrose Philips's tragedy *The Distrest Mother* [1712], one of the most popular tragedies of the eighteenth century, starring Anne Oldfield. The epilogue converts the suffering heroine into a figure of cunning and lust, but audiences demanded revivals of the play that included this epilogue and its sanctioned indecency. It was the epilogue that ensured the popularity of the tragedy, performed at least on fifty-one different occasions. Additionally, the epilogue was seen as an occasion when Oldfield could play herself, a bonus for the audience, given the ironic context of her celebrated life and her affair with Arthur Maynwaring.

In 'Invasion of the Afterpieces: Richard Brinsley Sheridan and Frederick Pilon, 1778–1779' (in Ennis and Slagle, eds., pp. 214–37), Daniel J. Ennis examines afterpieces written by Sheridan and Pilon during the height of British anxiety about loss of rule on the seas and concerns about French invasions. According to Ennis, Sheridan and Pilon's short dramatic pieces had to reconcile Britain's legendary maritime security, a function of innate British virtue, with the nation's actual peril. Ennis's analysis is indebted to the work of Gillian Russell on the period's war dramas. Sheridan's *The Camp: A Musical Entertainment* is a satiric afterpiece of England's hurried preparations for an invasion, and it was the most produced dramatic piece in London during the 1778 season. It critiques the fashionable English who flock to see the preparatory camps as though they were exhibits at Vauxhall. Sheridan's

The Critic, performed in late October 1779, can also be seen in this military context with its absurd Spanish Armada scene and its eighteenth-century patriotic songs. Pilon's *The Invasion; or, A Trip to Brighthelmstone* is an afterpiece that parodies military preparations under the leadership of the well-intentioned but ineffectual patriot Sir John Evergreen. Like Sheridan's successful afterpiece at Drury Lane, Pilon's satire ran for twenty-four nights at Covent Garden, beginning in early November 1778. Opening in April 1779, Pilon's afterpiece *Illumination; or, The Glaziers Conspiracy* ran for nine nights at Covent Garden. An invasion-inspired farce, it was performed as a curtain-raiser as well as an afterpiece, and was inspired by the 1778 court martial of Admiral Augustus Keppel. While both Sheridan and Pilon were writing topical afterpieces, Ennis claims that they achieved their governmental satire in different ways: Sheridan relies more on the conflation of the theatrical and real worlds so as to present a complicated critical position; Pilon embraces and announces theatre's artifice, its separation from real-world events.

Jack Rochi explores Mathew Lewis's monodrama *The Captive*, an afterpiece, after the play and before the farce, performed on 23 March 1803 at Covent Garden. For Rochi, Lewis's afterpiece represents the masculine Gothic in its appropriation of the feminine as spectacle. In 'A Feminine Spectacle: The Novelistic Aesthetic of Matthew Lewis's *The Captive*' (in Ennis and Slagle, eds., pp. 238–52), Rochi argues that both dramaturgy and audience expectations by the end of the eighteenth century expected a Gothic masculine ideology on the stage that was present in many Gothic novels. Lewis shocks his audience with graphic manipulation of the horrifying female spectacle and with pathetic music. Rochi challenges feminist readings of *The Captive* by Jeffrey N. Cox and D.L. Macdonald by maintaining that the captive is powerless to alter her circumstances and is therefore an agent for pure aesthetic terror. Whatever interaction she receives is torment rather than salvation. The denouement of the afterpiece is a lengthy pantomime in which the woman no longer speaks because she has become a captive of her own objectification, a mere picture.

Angela Escott looks at the theatrical parody offered by pantomime, frequently considered low drama and used as a term of critical abuse, in her essay ' "Gorgons hiss, and dragons glare": *Lady Fashion's Rout*—the First Speaking Pantomime and *The Ton*' (in Ennis and Slagle, eds., pp. 198–213). The focus of Escott's discussion is Charles Dibdin's pantomime *The Touchstone; or Harlequin Traveller*, performed in January 1779 following George Lillo's *The London Merchant*, and described by Dibdin as an 'operatical pantomime' and a 'speaking pantomime' (p. 198). It was a popular afterpiece, performed forty-two times in the first season. Hannah Cowley contributed two scenes in its revival performances, one substituting Lady Fashion's home for the gambler's scene which became known as 'Lady Fashion's Rout' (p. 199). Relying on the work of John O'Brien on pantomime, Escott points to the importance of *The Touchstone* in the evolution of eighteenth-century pantomime and its role in the generation of other speaking pantomimes in major and minor theatres. Dibdin and Cowley brought innovations to the dramatic form: Dibdin's *commedia dell'arte* characters interacted with his newly created characters; Cowley refined the satire on polite society and its misuse of language.

While Rochi's analysis of *The Captive* and Escott's discussion emphasize the visibility of the spectacle, Ruth Smith, in 'Love between Men in Jennens's and Handel's *Saul*' (in Mounsey and Gonda, eds., pp. 226–45), turns to the often dismissed tertiary form of dramatic music, the oratorio. According to Ruth Smith, the relationship between David and Jonathan has never been explored in libretti of this pathetic drama about patriarchy. Smith traces the revolutionary music drama from its theatrical lineage, Shakespeare's *The Merchant of Venice* and George Granville's *The Jew of Venice* [1701], as well as its Old Testament lyrics and Cicero's dialogue on virtue in friendship, *De Amicitia*. Smith argues that, while David is the touchstone of virtue in *Saul*, the oratorio does not identify virtue with the rising bourgeois, as do many eighteenth-century dramas. The chief source of David's virtue is spirituality, and *Saul* depicts virtue with and without sexual desire. This analysis, with its attention to music theatre, like others that address tertiary dramatic forms discussed above, contributes to our understanding of eighteenth-century dramatizations of the passions.

I will now turn to scholarship that addresses drama in more familiar and canonized forms by looking at essays that focus on single authors, Henry Fielding, Aphra Behn and Eliza Haywood. Rawson, ed., *The Cambridge Companion to Henry Fielding* (also discussed in section 2 above), includes two essays relevant to this section. Linda Bree's 'Henry Fielding's Life' (pp. 3–16) offers a brief listing of Fielding's major theatrical writings, and maintains that it was the 1737 Stage Licensing Act that ended Fielding's career as a dramatist. In 'Fielding's Theatrical Career' (pp. 17–37), however, Thomas Keymer cautions against considering Fielding's theatrical career through the lens of the Licensing Act. Both Bree and Keymer agree that Fielding was the most popular and influential London dramatist of the early eighteenth century, and Keymer gives a more detailed analysis of key plays, as well as an impressive list of statistics that account for Fielding's dramatic success. Keymer attributes Fielding's unprecedented success to a number of factors: he wrote furiously and quickly; he exploited the talents of star actors, such as Kitty Clive; he monitored the vogue for spectacular pantomime and made creative use of afterpieces; and he responded to audience demands, remaining flexible and ready to improvise and revise. According to Keymer, Fielding's dramas revolve around a stable thematic core: all human transactions are commercial propositions. Fielding self-consciously implicated himself in that commercial world, embracing opportunities to reinvent his authorial self throughout his career, and not only when he turned from writing plays to writing novels. According to Carl Fisher, Fielding's afterpieces were an important aspect of his entire drama output. In 'Pleasing the Public: Fielding's Afterpieces as Satyr Plays' (in Ennis and Slagle, eds., pp. 119–31), Fisher points out that several of Fielding's main plays and much of his fame were derived from his afterpieces, which are spaces in which Fielding could be innovative and satirical. Arguing that Fielding's afterpieces function as satyr plays in their critique of disorder and base appetites, Fisher maintains that Fielding turned to the rehearsal format in his afterpieces, where he could cloak his criticisms.

Besides exposing theatrical politics, Fielding also used his afterpieces to encourage audiences to attend an evening's entire programme.

Aphra Behn is the subject of two articles: Leah Lowe's 'Gender and (Im)Morality in Restoration Comedy: Aphra Behn's *The Feigned Courtesans*' (*Theatre Symposium* 15[2007] 92–106), and Michael Cordner's 'Sleeping with the Enemy: Aphra Behn's *The Roundheads* and the Political Comedy of Adultery' (in Cordner and Holland, eds., pp. 45–77). Lowe examines Behn's representations of gender differences in the context of prevailing Restoration moral codes in the 1679 marriage-plot comedy *The Feigned Courtesans; or, A Night's Intrigue* and argues that the play upholds the values of its patriarchal social system despite its internal contradictions and ambivalence about feminine agency and desire. Her feminist analysis questions how much autonomous feminine desire the narrative mechanics of the romantic comedy can endorse, and she concludes that Behn undermines Restoration society's glorification of feminine chastity and sexual passivity in the liminal representation of her heroines (disguised as prostitutes) and exposes the social limitations that shape feminine sexual subjectivity in a world where women are economically dependent on men. The liminal space points to the potential of breaking gender conventions, but ultimately the social order is resolved to patriarchal control. Cordner examines Behn's *The Roundheads; or, The Good Old Cause* [1681–2], the first post-1660 play to bring on stage Interregnum military commanders under their own names, and argues that the play revives political memory so as to critique the restored monarchy for its inadequate resistance to enemy threats. Behn entwines political and sexual intrigue in ways unprecedented in Restoration comedy with the play's cuckolding plot involving Oliver Cromwell in Act IV. *The Roundheads* is indebted to mid-century plays, Tatham's *The Rump; or, The Mirror of the Late Times*, Howard's *The Committee* and Cowley's *Cutter of Coleman Street*, all helpful to Behn in constructing communal memory of earlier political events.

In 'Comical Satire Alive and Well after the Glorious Revolution' (in Clingham, ed., *Sustaining Literature: Essays on Literature, History, and Culture, 1500–1800. Commemorating the Life and Work of Simon Varey*, pp. 85–107), J. Douglas Canfield maintains that comical satires do appear after 1688, and that these satires attack predatory libertinism and conspicuous consumption. He illustrates this position with two cases, Thomas Southerne's 1691 corrective satire *The Wives' Excuse; or, Cuckolds Make Themselves* and Thomas Durfey's 1694–5 three-part Menippean satire *The Comical History of Don Quixote*. Southerne's bourgeois play paints a predatory world in which women and sex are commodities. Durfey's play is a potpourri of folk farce that ends in deconstructive absurdity. According to Canfield, after the Restoration not all comedy closure is comic, a reminder that comic closure is itself a social construction.

Patsy S. Fowler considers Eliza Haywood's self-representation as an extension of Behn's demand for authorial equality in 'Rhetorical Strategy and the "Dangerous Woman-Poet": Eliza Haywood and the Politics of Self-Promotion' (in Ennis and Slagle, eds., pp. 179–97). Fowler examines Haywood's dedication to *The Fair Captive* as a statement defining the role of effective critics while censuring malicious ones. The dedication also details the plight of women writers who are denied the advantage of men. Haywood's prologue to the 1721 play creates a patriotic paradigm in the face of the financial crisis of the South Sea Bubble as it feigns a feminine need for acceptance and pity. Haywood's prologue to her only comedy, *A Wife to Be Lett*, promotes herself as a female author deserving public respect. In the 1723 prologue she refers to herself as 'a dangerous woman-poet' who fears no critic (p. 187). Haywood's preface to her final play, *Frederick, Duke of Brunswick-Lunenburgh*, defends the merits of her work despite the play's lack of success. Fowler's analysis of Haywood's self-representation is indebted to Catherine Burroughs's work on Romantic women dramatists and their drama theory.

Another categorical grouping of this year's work on eighteenth-century drama involves various kinds of cultural traditions and underpinnings that inform our readings. Two articles follow the oriental tradition in the drama. Chapter 4 of Bernadette Andrea's monograph *Women and Islam in Early Modern English Literature* traces the genealogy of feminist orientalism in some of the forty or more plays by women for the London stage between 1660 and 1714. Pointing to the uneven articulation between feminism and orientalism during this theatrical period, Andrea explains that women playwrights vacillate between the consolidation of feminist orientalism (complicit with Anglocentric discourse of empire) and counter-orientalist challenges from within the feminist camp. For example, Aphra Behn, Susanna Centlivre, Mary Pix and Catharine Trotter depicted Western fantasies about the Ottoman sultan's seraglio. According to Andrea, however, Delarivier Manley's *The Royal Mischief* is an example of counter-orientalist intervention as it features an Eastern heroine's struggle for personal, political and sexual agency. In this play, Manley deconstructs the traditional opposition between the proper fair woman and the suspect dark woman upon which feminist orientalism depends. Manley provided the first full English translation of the Arabic *1001 Nights: Almyna; or, The Arabian Vow* in 1706, and Andrea points to the near-anagram of Almyna/Manley, which links the English woman playwright with the proto-feminist Muslim woman narrator, Scheherazade, on whom she models her title character. Andrea asserts that Manley's dramatic work presents the most sustained articulation of the strained relationship between feminism and orientalism during the eighteenth century: 'Rather than using orientalist tropes to displace oppressive patriarchal practices such as domestic immurement and polygamy into eastern cultures, Manley in her plays . . . situated these practices squarely within her own culture' (p. 104).

Mita Choudhury's essay 'Universality, Early Modernity, and the Contingencies of Representing Race' (in Cordner and Holland, eds., pp. 231–47) argues that the most forceful evidence of the insularity of eighteenth-century British theatre lies in the infrequent appearance of the Black, the Jewish, the West Indian and the Other character, whose presence could only have been marginal. Eighteenth-century playwrights followed the pattern of universalist logic that repressed Otherness so as to create box-office appeal. Choudhury asserts that the practical consequence of David Garrick's playing Othello or Oroonoko, for example, was not that of emphasizing race but of presenting universal themes and emotions that would appear 'natural' to spectators (p. 242). The presence of the subaltern on the eighteenth-century stage, Choudhury insists, was not to subvert the forces of the normative but to facilitate European benevolence. Choudhury's analysis is shaped by the feminist and postcolonial theories of Judith Butler and Gayatri Spivak, and takes issue with scholarship by Elizabeth Kowaleski Wallace and Jessica Munns, who read the Other characters of eighteenth-century drama as subversive and transgressive figures.

Two essays trace the development of Irish cultural traditions in eighteenth-century drama. In 'Mixed Marriage: Sheridan, Macklin, and the Hybrid Audience' (in Cordner and Holland, eds., pp. 189–212), Susan Cannon Harris demonstrates how intertwined the marriage plot, literary plagiarism and Irishmen were in the eighteenth-century international theatrical marketplace. For Harris, the marriage plot helped to transform the stage Irishman and conceptions of national identity being contested on London and Dublin stages, as she illustrates with Richard Sheridan's *The Brave Irishman* and Charles Macklin's *Love à la Mode*. Marriage became one of the dominant metaphors for representing England's complicated relationship with its British colonies. Furthermore, forced marriage in Ireland was political and racial, a means to recoup land and status lost under British penal laws, as Captain O'Blunder, the Irish fortune hunter, represents in *The Brave Irishman*. For English audiences, *The Brave Irishman* foreshadowed transformations, such as forbidding private marriage, that would be codified in the 1753 Marriage Act. Macklin's *Love à la Mode* [1759] features O'Brallaghan as a domesticated Irishman, exotic and erotic, but matrimonially appropriated in a plot about reformed marriage regulations.

Helen Burke's essay, 'Country Matters: Irish "Waggery" and the Irish and British Theatrical Traditions' (in Cordner and Holland, eds., pp. 213–28), points to the frequent crossings between Irish popular performances and British theatre in the unorthodox, so-called 'waggery' of the upper gallery in Dublin's theatre and in Oliver Goldsmith's 1773 comedy *She Stoops to Conquer*. Burke asserts that these two performance sites were points of transfer between the anti-bourgeois popular performance tradition of rural Ireland and the theatre proper. By the mid-eighteenth century, the Dublin upper gallery had developed forms of behaviour uncommon in London playhouses that were read as evidence of Irish recidivism: passing jests, singing out the names of the elite as they entered the house and joking with the performers during performances. Yet mocking play was regularly deployed in the Gaelic tradition to enforce customary norms, and it emerged in theatres at the time when Dublin was evolving from a primarily Protestant to a primarily Catholic city. These gestures were therefore charged with the political power of disturbing Dublin theatre's imbrication in the colonial system. *She Stoops to Conquer* has its roots in this Irish popular tradition of mocking play. The interaction between stage and audience performances and the Irish entertainer's ability to move between social contexts and cultural traditions (for example John O'Keeffe), Burke argues, suggest that eighteenth-century theatre was a 'travelling' rather than a 'rooted' culture (p. 226).

In their discussion of William Congreve's *The Way of the World*, in *The Christian Tradition in English Literature: Poetry, Plays, and Shorter Prose* (pp. 203–5), Paul Cavill and Heather Ward trace its Christian underpinnings as a morality play reinterpreted for the eighteenth century. The 'world' of the play is ruled by lust for power, money and sensual gratification, while its 'way' is to make human beings wolves to one another, transforming social life into a predatory game. In this allegorical reading, Fainall is the vice figure, Witwould epitomizes vanity and Sir Wilful acts as an impetuous child. These characters have lost their moral compass. Millamant and Mirabell, on the other hand, are the figures of love, wit and integrity. In its happy ending, goodness triumphs over evil, human folly and a disorderly society. This interpretation, intent on finding a Christian vision and biblical lessons in Congreve, has the unfortunate tendency of reminding one of students' blundering attempts to find Christian sources in literary texts, including the obligatory biblical citations taken wholly out of context. Conrad Brunström's brief discussion of Frances Burney's *The Witlings* in 'Sex and Shopping with Frances Burney' (in Mounsey and Gonda, eds., pp. 86–98) identifies economics as the prevailing cultural underpinning of the comedy. The 'world' of the Witlings club, asserts Brunström, is a 'queer' one in which all value is relative (p. 91). Paula R. Backscheider's essay 'Shadowing Theatrical Change' (in Cordner and Holland, eds., pp. 78–100) examines the frequent inclusion in eighteenth-century novels of the set piece involving a young heroine with her friends absorbed in a play. Backscheider argues that these often overlooked scenes should be considered in the context of the teaching of correct cultural consumption and studied as significant interventions in theatrical controversies. She convincingly makes her case with examples from Sarah Fielding's *The Adventures of David Simple*, Tobias Smollett's *Peregrine Pickle*, Oliver Goldsmith's *The Vicar of Wakefield*, Frances Burney's *Evelina* and Samuel Richardson's *Pamela II*. David Garrick's innovative performances and actors' performance styles are described in various novels. Because England was a 'drama-mad' nation, the vocabulary and theories of acting were integrated into novels along with easily recognizable references and allusions to the theatre (p. 94).

The issue of censorship is another cultural tradition influencing eighteenth-century drama scholarship. In 'Jeremy Collier and the Politics of Theatrical Representation' (in Cordner and Holland, eds., pp. 135–51), Lisa A. Freeman looks at William Congreve's 1700 play *The Way of the World* as a response to Jeremy Collier's 1698 pamphlet *A Short View of the Immorality and Profaneness of the English Stage*. According to Freeman, Congreve's drama asserts that comedic representation could provide effective moral instruction by reflecting the word as it is, a corrective to Collier's depiction of the theatre as a source of social debauchery. What lies at the heart of the anti-theatrical disputes at the beginning of the eighteenth century, Freeman argues, is a struggle over the character of the body politic that governs a nation and the bodies public that represent the nation. For Freeman, Collier's attack on the stage was a political event, evidenced by its concern with loss of authority in the body politic, and the stage was a cultural site functioning as a competing source of political and religious authority in the public sphere. Freeman also examines the anti-theatricality debate expressed in George Ridpath's 1698 play *The Stage Condemned* and the anonymous pamphlet *The Stage Acquitted*. Matthew J. Kinservik's essay 'Reconsidering Theatrical Regulation in the

Long Eighteenth Century' (in Cordner and Holland, eds., pp. 152–71) seeks a richer understanding of the Stage Licensing Act 1737 and its place in the larger history of theatrical regulation. Kinservik reminds us that the Licensing Act was not a product of the 1730s alone and that it was not merely an anti-theatrical measure. Proposals of regulation emanated from the early seventeenth century through the 1730s, with the Licensing Act a part of this tradition of philo-theatrical regulatory schemes. During the 1730s there were several proposals for a censorial committee, based on French models, to regulate the stage. Writers such as Thomas Rymer, Charles Gildon, John Dennis and Aaron Hill believed that theatre could only flourish under the careful stewardship of the state. Proponents of regulation advocated state oversight and limiting the number of theatrical venues to ensure quality control. They sought to rid theatres of crudely commercial and senseless drama and to restore the stage to the glory days of Athenian and Roman drama. The Licensing Act was more modest in its regulatory power than many of the proposals that preceded it, and so Kinservik positions it as more philo-theatrical than anti-theatrical.

Three editions of eighteenth-century drama are a part of this year's work. Thorton Wilder and Ken Ludwig's adaptation of George Farquhar's *The Beaux' Stratagem* revives a project that Wilder began in 1939 but never completed. Ludwig finished the adaptation, and it was performed in 2006 by the Shakespeare Theatre Company in Washington, DC. The edition is definitely an acting or classroom text, as it offers no line numbers, no notes, no critical apparatus and no variant manuscripts for the 1707 play. Christine A. Colón's edition of Joanna Baillie's *Six Gothic Dramas* is also a teaching text based on the 1851 edition of the plays from the *Dramatic and Poetical Works of Joanna Baillie*. In her note on the texts, Colón asserts that her goal was to make the plays available and affordable, four of the plays never having been reproduced since the 1851 edition. One of the plays in the collection is *De Monfort*, and in her introduction to the play Colón maintains that Baillie uses the Gothic to illustrate how a dysfunctional character can threaten social order at a time when that society is undergoing transformation. Derek Hughes's edition *Visions of Blackness: Key Texts on Slavery from the Seventeenth Century* includes Aphra Behn's 1676 *Abdelazer* and Thomas Southerne's 1696 adaptation of *Oroonoko*. In the introduction to the collection Hughes maintains that neither Behn nor Southerne is interested in the economic genesis and basis of slavery. According to Hughes, Behn wrote a play about an individual not a racial type, and Southerne deplored the excesses of slavery rather than the institution of slavery itself. The editions of the plays include the appropriate critical apparatus for scholarly as well as classroom use.

One other edition deserves mention: Ben P. Robertson's three-volume edition of *The Diaries of Elizabeth Inchbald*. The first volume, *The Early Years on the Stage: Scotland, France, and the Provinces and London* includes Inchbald's diaries of 1776, 1780 and 1781. The edition makes the diaries, housed at the Folger Shakespeare Library in Washington, DC, accessible to scholars, students and performers what Robertson identifies as the single most important repository of information about Inchbald and her circle. The 1776 diary details Inchbald's acting with West Digges's company in Edinburgh, her beginning studies in French, her constant reading, and her bumpy relationship with Joseph Inchbald. The 1780 diary records Inchbald's first acting experiences in London and her early efforts at writing her own drama. Inchbald's friendships with the marquis of Carmarthen and Dr Brodie, following her husband's death, her acting schedule at Covent Garden and her writing and revising of her own drama appear in the 1781 diary. In this meticulous scholarly edition, we have an exceptional addition to the extra-literary and theatre-based materials which Robert D. Hume challenges us to use in our work on eighteenth-century drama in his essay 'Theatre History, 1660–1800: Aims, Materials, Methodology' (in Cordner and Holland, eds., pp. 9–44), discussed above.

Books Reviewed

Ahern, Stephen. *Affected Sensibilities: Romantic Excess and the Genealogy of the Novel 1680–1810*. AMS. [2007] pp. 239. $82.50 ISBN 9 7804 0463 5497.

Andrea, Bernadette. *Women and Islam in Early Modern English Literature*. CUP. [2007] pp. x + 185. $85 ISBN 9 7805 2186 7641.

Baines, Paul, and Pat Rogers. *Edmund Curll, Bookseller*. Clarendon. [2007] pp. x + 390. £30 ISBN 9 7801 9927 8985.

Barnett, Louise K. *Jonathan Swift in the Company of Women*. OUP. [2007] pp. xi + 225. £38.99 ISBN 9 7801 9518 8660.

Bettcher, Talia Mae. *Berkeley's Philosophy of Spirit: Consciousness, Ontology, and the Elusive Subject*. Continuum. [2007] pp. 173. $120 ISBN 9 7808 2648 6431.

Blackwell, Mark. ed. *The Secret Life of Things: Animals; Objects, and It-Narratives in Eighteenth-Century England*. BuckUP. [2007] pp. 365. $62.50 ISBN 0 8387 5666 9.

Bourdeau, Debra Taylor, and Elizabeth Kraft. eds. *On Second Thought: Updating the Eighteenth-Century Text*. UDelP. [2007] pp. 304. $57.50 ISBN 9 7808 7413 9754.

Brack, O.M. Jr, ed. *Tobias Smollett, Scotland's First Novelist: New Essays in Memory of Paul-Gabriel Boucé*. UDelP. [2007] pp. 320. $63.50 ISBN 9 7808 7413 9884.

Brant, Clare, and Susan E. Whyman. eds. *Walking the Streets of London; John Gay's Trivia (1716)*. OUP. [2007] pp. x + 256. $120 ISBN 9 7801 9928 0490.

Brock, Helen C., ed. *The Correspondence of Dr William Hunter*, 2 vols. P&C. [2007] pp. 800. $350 ISBN 9 7818 5196 9043.

Carey, Brycchan, and Peter J. Kitson, eds. *Slavery and the Cultures of Abolition: Essays Marking the Bicentennial of the British Abolition Act of 1807*. Brewer. [2007] pp. viii + 232. $55 ISBN 9 7818 4384 1203.

Cavill, Paul, and Heather Ward. *The Christian Tradition in English Literature: Poetry, Plays, and Shorter Prose*. Zondervan. [2007] pp. 512. pb $24.99 ISBN 0 3102 5515 5.

Claydon, Tony. *Europe and the Making of England, 1660–1760*. CUP. [2007] pp. 386. $100 ISBN 9 7805 2185 0049.

Clingham, Greg, ed. *Sustaining Literature: Essays on Literature, History, and Culture, 1500–1800. Commemorating the Life and Work of Simon Varey.* BuckUP. [2007] pp. 325. $59.50 ISBN 0 8387 5656 5.

Clymer, Lorna. ed. *Ritual, Routine, and Regime; Repetition in Early Modern British and European Cultures.* UTorP. [2006] pp. 256. $60 ISBN 0 8020 9030 3.

Clymer, Lorna, and Robert Mayer, eds. *Historical Boundaries, Narrative Forms: Essays on British Literature in the Long Eighteenth Century in Honor of Everett Zimmerman.* UDelP. [2007] pp. 268. $53.50 ISBN 9 7808 7413 9396.

Colón, Christine, ed. *Six Gothic Dramas.* Valancourt Books. [2007] pp. xxxvii + 415. pb $16.99 ISBN 0 9792 3320 8.

Cope, Kevin L. *In and After the Beginning: Inaugural Moments and Literary Institutions in the Long Eighteenth Century.* AMS. [2007] pp. 384. $93.50 ISBN 0 4046 4857 2.

Cordner, Michael, and Peter Holland, eds. *Players, Playwrights, Playhouses: Investigating Performance, 1660–1800.* Palgrave. [2007] pp. xiii + 300. $84.95 ISBN 9 7802 3052 5245.

Crawford, Katherine. *European Sexualities, 1400–1800.* CUP. [2007] pp. 258. $75 ISBN 9 7805 2183 9587.

Dawson, Hannah. *Locke, Language and Early-Modern Philosophy.* CUP. [2007] pp. xi + 361. $90 ISBN 9 7805 2185 2715.

Dean, Ann C. *The Talk of the Town: Figurative Publics in Eighteenth-Century Britain.* BuckUP. [2007] pp. 152. $41.50 ISBN 9 7808 3875 6720.

Douglas, Mary. *Thinking in Circles: An Essay on Ring Composition.* YaleUP. [2007] pp. 169. $35 ISBN 9 7803 0011 7622.

Ennis, Daniel James, and Judith Bailey Slagle, eds. *Prologues, Epilogues, Curtain-Raisers, and Afterpieces: The Rest of the Eighteenth-Century London Stage.* UDelP. [2007] pp. 263. $47.50 ISBN 0 8741 3967 8.

Gale, Maggie B., and John Stokes, eds. *The Cambridge Companion to the Actress.* CUP. [2007] pp. xxi + 345. pb $31.99 ISBN 0 5216 0854 6.

Gibson, William L. *Art and Money in the Writings of Tobias Smollett.* BuckUP. [2007] pp. 227. $49.50 ISBN 9 7808 3875 6379.

Goldie, Mark, ed. *John Locke: Selected Correspondence.* OUP. [2007] pp. 320. pb £19.99 ISBN 9 7801 9920 4304.

Gottlieb, Evan. *Feeling British: Sympathy and National Identity in Scottish and English Writing, 1707–1832.* BuckUP. [2007] pp. 280. $52.50 ISBN 0 8387 5678 2.

Guest, Harriet. *Empire, Barbarism, and Civilisation: James Cook, William Hodges, and the Return to the Pacific.* CUP. [2007] pp. xx + 249. £55 ISBN 9 7805 2188 1944.

Harding, Nick, *Hanover and the British Empire, 1700–1837.* B&B. [2007] pp. 296. $105 ISBN 9 7818 4383 3000.

Hirschmann, Nancy J., and Kirstie M. McClure, eds. *Feminist Interpretations of John Locke.* PSUP. [2007] pp. 352. $80 ISBN 9 7802 7102 9535.

Hughes, Derek, ed. *Visions of Blackness: Key Texts on Slavery from the Seventeenth Century.* CUP. [2007] pp. xxxiii + 381. pb $23.99 ISBN 9 7805 2168 9564.

Ingram, Robert G. *Religion, Reform and Modernity in the Eighteenth Century: Thomas Secker and the Church of England.* B&B. [2007] pp. 336. $90 ISBN 9 7818 4383 3482.

Jacob, W.M. *The Clerical Profession in the Long Eighteenth Century, 1680–1840.* OUP. [2007] pp. 350. $85 ISBN 9 7801 9921 3009.

Keymer, Thomas, ed. *Robinson Crusoe,* by Daniel Defoe. OUP. [2007] pp. lii + 321. pb £4.99 ISBN 9 7801 9283 3426.

Kickel, Katherine E. *Novel Notions: Medical Discourse and the Mapping of the Imagination in Eighteenth-Century English Fiction.* Routledge. [2007] pp. 185. $110 ISBN 9 7804 1597 9481.

Kilday, Anne-Marie. *Women and Violent Crime in Enlightenment Scotland.* RHS. [2007] pp. 200. $95 ISBN 9 7808 6193 2870.

King-Hele, Desmond. *The Collected Letters of Erasmus Darwin.* CUP. [2007] pp. 666. $197 ISBN 9 7805 2182 1568.

Kolbrener, William, and Michal Michelson, eds. *Mary Astell: Reason, Gender, and Faith.* Ashgate. [2007] pp. 230. $99.95 ISBN 9 7807 5465 2649.

Kupersmith, William. *English Versions of Roman Satire in the Earlier Eighteenth Century.* UDelP. [2007] pp. 271. $54.50 ISBN 9 7808 7413 9600.

Lee, Andrew, and Lynn Hollen Lee. *Cities and the Making of Modern Europe, 1750–1914.* CUP. [2007] pp. xii + 300. $80 ISBN 9 7805 2183 9365.

Lewis, Rhodri. *Language, Mind and Nature: Artificial Languages in England from Bacon to Locke.* CUP. [2007] pp. xvi + 262. $90 ISBN 9 7805 2187 4755.

Littlejohns, Richard, and Sara Soncini, eds. *Myths of Europe.* Rodopi. [2007] pp. 295. pb €60 ISBN 9 7890 4202 1471.

Mack, Robert L. *The Genius of Parody: Imitation and Originality in Seventeenth- and Eighteenth-Century English Literature.* Palgrave. [2007] pp. vi + 285. $79.95 ISBN 0 2300 0856 4.

Mandell, Laura, ed. *The Castle of Otranto,* by Horace Walpole, and *The Man of Feeling,* by Henry Mackenzie. Pearson Longman. [2007] pp. xxvi + 292. pb $16.95 ISBN 9 7803 2139 8925.

Mander, Jenny, ed. *Remapping the Rise of the European Novel.* SVEC. [2007] pp. ix + 344. pb £65 ISBN 9 7807 2940 9162.

Manly, Susan. *Language, Custom and Nation in the 1790s: Locke, Tooke, Wordsworth, Edgeworth.* Ashgate. [2007] pp. 212. $99.95 ISBN 9 7807 5465 8320.

Maunu, Leanne. *Women Writing the Nation: National Identity, Female Community, and the British–French Connection, 1770–1820.* BuckUP. [2007] pp. 312. $57.50 ISBN 9 7808 3875 6706.

McGirr, Elaine M. *Eighteenth-Century Characters: A Guide to the Literature of the Age.* Palgrave. [2007] pp. x + 214. $30.95 ISBN 1 4039 8558 3.

Mercantini, Jonathan. *Who Shall Rule at Home? The Evolution of South Carolina Political Culture, 1748–1776.* USCP. [2007] pp. 336. $49.95 ISBN 9 7815 7003 6545.

Moore, Peter N. *World of Toil and Strife: Community Transformation in Backcountry South Carolina, 1750–1805.* USCP. [2007] pp. 176. $34.95 ISBN 9 7815 7003 6668.

Mounsey, Chris, and Caroline Gonda, eds. *Queer People: Negotiations and Expressions of Homosexualities, 1700–1800*. BuckUP. [2007] pp. 305. $65 ISBN 0 8387 5667 0.

Muri, Allison. *The Enlightenment Cyborg: A History of Communications and Control in the Human Machine, 1660–1830*. UTorP. [2007] pp. x + 310. $60 ISBN 0 8020 8850 3.

Overton, Bill. *The Eighteenth-Century British Verse Epistle*. Palgrave. [2007] pp. xiv + 299. £53 ISBN 9 7814 0394 1701.

Oya, Reiko. *Representing Shakespearean Tragedy: Garrick, the Kembles, and Kean*. CUP. [2007] pp. xii + 244. £53 ($100) ISBN 9 7805 2187 9859.

Pohl, Nicole, and Brenda Tooley, eds. *Gender and Utopia in the Eighteenth Century: Essays in English and French Utopian Writing*. Ashgate. [2007] pp. 206. £50 ISBN 9 7807 5465 4353.

Pressly, William L. *The Artist as Original Genius: Shakespeare's 'Fine Frenzy' in Late-Eighteenth-Century British Art*. UDelP. [2007] pp. 236. $80 ISBN 9 7808 7413 9853.

Rasmussen, Eric, and Aaron Santesso, eds. *Comparative Excellence: New Essays on Shakespeare and Johnson*. AMS. [2007] pp. viii + 248. $76.50 ISBN 9 7804 0464 8527.

Rawson, Claude, ed. *The Cambridge Companion to Henry Fielding*. CUP. [2007] pp. xv + 202. pb $31.99 ISBN 0 5216 7092 6.

Robertson, Ben P., ed. *The Diaries of Elizabeth Inchbald*, vol. 1: *The Early Years on the Stage: Scotland, France, and the Provinces and London*. P&C. [2007] pp. xlv + 373. $495 ISBN 9 7818 5186 8688.

Rogers, Pat. ed. *The Cambridge Companion to Alexander Pope*. CUP. [2007] pp. xiii + 255. £45 ISBN 9 7805 2184 0132.

Sabor, Peter, ed. *The Cambridge Companion to Frances Burney*. CUP. [2007] pp. 214. pb £18.99 ISBN 9 7805 2161 5488.

Severn, John. *Architects of Empire: The Duke of Wellington and his Brothers*. UOklaP. [2007] pp. 602. $37.50 ISBN 9 7808 0613 8107.

Shuttleton, David E. *Smallpox and the Literary Imagination, 1660–1820*. CUP. [2007] pp. 264. $85 ISBN 9 7805 2187 2096.

Starkie, Andrew. *The Church of England and the Bangorian Controversy, 1716–1721*. B&B. [2007] pp. 274. $95 ISBN 9 7818 4383 2881.

Strong, Rowan. *Anglicanism and the British Empire, c.1700–1850*. OUP. [2007] pp. 288. $90 ISBN 9 7801 9921 8042.

Szasz, Margaret Connell. *Scottish Highlanders and Native Americans: Indigenous Education in the Eighteenth-Century Atlantic World*. UOklaP. [2007] pp. 304 $34.95 ISBN 9 7808 0613 8619.

Tennenhouse, Leonard. *The Importance of Feeling English: American Literature and the British Diaspora, 1750–1850*. PrincetonUP. [2007] pp. xii + 162. $35 ISBN 9 7806 9109 6810.

Trolander, Paul, and Zeynep Tenger. *Sociable Criticism in England, 1625–1725*. UDelP. [2007] pp. 240. $49.50 ISBN 0 8741 3969 4.

Tsomondo, Thorell Porter. *The Not So Blank 'Blank Page': The Politics of Narrative and the Woman Narrator in the Eighteenth- and Nineteenth-Century English Novel*. Peter Lang. [2007] pp. ix + 149. $61.95 ISBN 9 7808 2047 6490.

Watson, JoAnn Ford. *Selected Spiritual Writings of Anne Dutton: Eighteenth-Century, British-Baptist, Woman Theologian*, vol. 5: *Miscellaneous Correspondence*. MercerUP. [2007] pp. lviii + 417. $50 ISBN 9 7808 8146 0292.

Watts, Carol. *The Cultural Work of Empire: The Seven Years' War and the Imagining of the Shandean State*. EdinUP. [2007] pp. 352. £60 ISBN 9 7807 4862 5642.

Wilder, Thornton, and Ken Ludwig, eds. *The Beaux' Stratagem*. Samuel French. [2007] pp. 97. pb $16.99 ISBN 9 7805 7365 0536.

Withers, Charles W.J. *Placing the Enlightenment: Thinking Geographically about the Age of Reason*. UChicP. [2007] pp. 336. $45 ISBN 9 7802 2690 4054.

XII

Literature 1780–1830: The Romantic Period

ORIANNE SMITH, GAVIN BUDGE, DAVID STEWART,
ANA ALICIA GARZA, JASON WHITTAKER,
FELICITY JAMES AND JEREMY DAVIES

This chapter has five sections: 1. General; 2. Prose; 3. Poetry; 4. The Novel; 5. Drama. Section 1 is by Orianne Smith; section 2 is by Gavin Budge; section 3 is by David Stewart, Ana Alicia Garza (Romantic women poets) and Jason Whittaker (Blake); section 4 is by Felicity James; section 5 is by Jeremy Davies.

1. General

Mary Wollstonecraft, William Godwin and their daughter, Mary Shelley, are perhaps the most mythologized family of writers in England. It is hard to resist the telling and retelling of the story of the teenage Mary Shelley reading her mother's books by her mother's grave, which was also allegedly the scene of the consummation of her youthful affair with the dashing poet Percy Shelley. The anecdotal stories that surround this family, especially the women, are often implicated in critical interpretations of their written work. Biographical readings are a vexed issue in general for scholars who work on women writers, whose literary efforts are often read against their life narratives. Yet to deny the relevance of the personal lives of writers is to cut off a potentially fruitful way of understanding the genesis and the socio-historical contexts of their literary endeavours. One of the most significant books published this year in the area of general Romanticism, Julie A. Carlson's *England's First Family of Writers: Mary Wollstonecraft, William Godwin, Mary Shelley*, is an attempt to address precisely this issue. As Carlson persuasively argues, the lives and writings of Wollstonecraft, Godwin and Shelley were inextricably connected. Our cultural fascination with the personal lives of these writers is the consequence of their own deliberate attempts to blur 'the boundaries between person and text, private and public, living and writing, works of literature and works of mourning' (p. 3). Carlson's use of the term 'life/writing' throughout this book to describe the oeuvre of this family reminds us of this fact, and

Year's Work in English Studies, Volume 88 (2009) © *The English Association; all rights reserved*
doi:10.1093/ywes/map008

provides us with a useful point of departure to begin to trace the complex relations between life, death and the literary act in their written work.

England's First Family of Writers is divided into two three-chapter sections, 'Revising Family' and 'Life Works'. Familial themes and the critique of these conventions within the work of these three writers is the subject of the first section. The first chapter, 'Making Public Love', provides an extended discussion of heterosexual love in Wollstonecraft's *Maria, or The Wrongs of Woman* [1798] and Godwin's *Fleetwood* [1805]. Even before they knew each other, both writers were sharply critical of passion between the sexes, with Wollstonecraft arguing that passion prevented women from being treated or thinking of themselves as autonomous individuals and Godwin strenuously objecting to institutions (such as marriage, property and inheritance laws) rather than the experience of love itself. Where they both agreed, however, was in their mutual emphasis on the significance of reading in the process of courtship: Maria falls in love with Darnforth when she reads his marginal notes to Rousseau in *The Wrongs of Woman* and Godwin paints a glowing picture of the act of reading together as an amorous activity in *Fleetwood*. The next chapter, 'Forms of Attachment', focuses on Godwin's concern that familial bonds interfere with individual autonomy and substitute sentiment for rational judgement. Whilst many scholars have pointed to Godwin's coldness in his critical assessment of the significance of family, Carlson argues that his views on this subject should be contextualized within his ongoing attempts to extricate attachment from the purely sentimental realm and reconnect it with a sense of responsibility to the community at large. The third chapter, 'Family Relations', focuses on Mary Shelley's revisions of her parents' beliefs regarding the role of domestic affections in her novels. A particular strength of this chapter is Carlson's in-depth discussion of Shelley's later novels, which tend to be written off as capitulating to a more conservative 'Victorian' view of familial responsibilities and traditions. As Carlson persuasively demonstrates, Shelley's last two novels, *Lodore* [1835] and *Falkner* [1837], are sustained attempts to bridge the gap between realism and romance by injecting the narratives of courtship and love in each novel with a healthy dose of realism.

The second part of *England's First Family of Writers* is entitled 'Life Works', which is somewhat of a misnomer given its preoccupation with death, tragedy and trauma. 'Fancy's History' discusses how fancy becomes a conduit for this family of Romantic writers to go beyond the realm of the imagination (and its limitations) to explore death and magic as necessities of life that cannot be repressed. 'Living Off and On: The Literary Work of Mourning' establishes Godwin's *Essay on Sepulchres* as a foundational text in Mary Shelley's approach to death and mourning in her works. 'A Juvenile Library; or, Works of a New Species' investigates how Wollstonecraft, Godwin and Shelley take the standard trope of the book as child and, each in their own way, explore the sense of responsibility that an author or parent has (or should have) towards his or her literary and biological offspring. *England's First Family of Writers* concludes with an epilogue on Percy Shelley. 'On Percy's Case' is a thoughtful discussion of Percy Shelley's work within the framework of this family, revealing how the various legends of Shelley have tended to elide his indebtedness to the 'life/writings' of his illustrious in-laws.

Life, death and literature are the subjects of another excellent book published this year in the area of general Romanticism. Mark Canuel's *The Shadow of Death: Literature, Romanticism, and the Subject of Punishment* is an original and elegantly written contribution to our understanding of the connections between Romantic-era debates about the death penalty and modern notions of political sovereignty. The opposition to the death penalty gained significant momentum during the Romantic period, when legal reformers such as Samuel Romilly argued passionately against its use in *Observations on the Criminal Law of England* [1811] and other works. Canuel argues that many Romantic writers, including William Wordsworth, Jane Austen, Samuel Taylor Coleridge and Percy Bysshe Shelley, participated in these debates over capital punishment, and articulated in their literary works many of the underlying contradictions regarding the use of capital punishment that continue to haunt our own debates on this deeply problematic issue. Although there were attempts in the eighteenth century to reform the penal system, what set the Romantic response apart was how writers and thinkers represented appropriate forms of punishment as negotiations between conflicting perspectives rather than a seamless whole. As *The Shadow of Death* demonstrates, these justifications were the impetus behind a wide range of literary as well as political texts in the Romantic era.

The first chapter provides an overview of the Romantic opposition to the death penalty as a series of efforts to redefine the relationship between political subjects and legal structures or, more generally, the definition of punishment itself. Chapter 2 focuses on the works of Hannah More, and the ways in which her didactic works, such as the *Cheap Repository Tracts* [1795–8], *Strictures on the Modern System of Female Education* [1799] and *Coelebs in Search of a Wife* [1809], dramatize the struggle between secular and religious beliefs that informed contemporary opinion regarding penal reform as well as More's own ambivalence on this subject. As Canuel notes, the ambivalence registered by More stemmed from her belief that capital punishment threatens the authority and the wisdom of Providence. The source of Wordsworth's simultaneous resistance and attraction to the death penalty is somewhat different, as suggested in chapter 4. Canuel argues that the two opposing views on capital punishment in *Salisbury Plain* [1793–4] and *Sonnets upon the Punishment of Death* [1841] mirror the attempts by Romantic reformers to contain and limit the use of the death penalty in the penal system.

One of the most compelling and thought-provoking chapters in *The Shadow of Death* is chapter 5, 'Jane Austen, the Romantic Novel, and the Importance of Being Wrong'. Whereas Wordsworth looked to a future in which the death penalty would no longer be necessary, Austen creates a world in *Mansfield Park* [1814] that asserts the positive aspects of punishment as a means for defining the limitations of selfhood and an individual's relationship to society. As Canuel astutely notes, Fanny's preference for the privations at Mansfield over and above the misery she suffers at Portsmouth is not simply a case of newly acquired snobbery: 'The Mansfield household provides not just a static emblem of upper-class taste or sensibility but a technology of classification.

With her wealthier relations, she always knows where she stands' (p. 86). Above and beyond material possessions and luxury, what Mansfield provides Fanny is a sense of identity.

Chapter 6 continues to investigate the psychological implications of punishment in the works of Coleridge and Shelley. Coleridge's drama *Osorio* [1797] and Shelley's *The Triumph of Life* [1822] both explore the relationship between aesthetic representation and the poetics and politics of conscience. Whereas Coleridge's drama asserts the primacy of remorse as the key ingredient for a more humane version of social justice, Shelley's poem reveals the power of poetry itself as an agent of shame. The final chapter investigates the rationale in the Romantic period for linking the abolition of slavery to the abolition of the death penalty, demonstrating how the rhetoric of abolition of slavery depended upon the discourse of penal reform and its appeal to sympathy for the criminal. *The Shadow of Death* is recommended reading not only for scholars of the Romantic period but also for scholars interested in the history of penal reform as well as the philosophical and socio-historical background of current thinking on the death penalty and the nature of punishment.

Another very good book published this year in the crimes and misdemeanours category of general Romanticism is Tilar J. Mazzeo's *Plagiarism and Literary Property in the Romantic Period*. Mazzeo's book seeks to answer what appears to be a relatively straightforward question: what did the accusation of plagiarism mean at the end of the eighteenth and the beginning of the nineteenth centuries? As Mazzeo demonstrates, however, what the Romantics described as plagiarism bears very little or no resemblance to what we think of as plagiarism now. For the Romantics there were two very distinct types of plagiarism: 'culpable' plagiarism, which had a moral component akin to our own contemporary repugnance at the thought of stealing another's literary property, and 'poetic' plagiarism, in which the author plagiarized but did not improve upon or acknowledge the original author. In the case of the latter, the plagiarist was guilty of nothing more than bad writing. With the exception of a few celebrated cases, Romantic authors were seldom indicted for 'culpable' plagiarism, which was very difficult to prove. The debates over 'poetic' plagiarism, however, were a different story. Many of the canonical writers that we associate with Romanticism were accused—in their time and, in the case of Coleridge, our own—of liberally borrowing from their predecessors and contemporaries. The first chapter of *Plagiarism and Literary Property* provides a helpful overview of the terms of plagiarism as they were used in the Romantic period, and contrasts the set of circumstances under which a Romantic writer would have been charged with plagiarism to our current ideas concerning what constitutes plagiarism. Coleridge's liberal borrowings are perhaps the most familiar instances of plagiarism to Romantic scholars, and chapter 2 begins on this familiar ground, with a discussion of why Coleridge's plagiarisms have been singled out for particular notice over the past 200 years. Chapter 3 discusses the Romantic-era rationale for the appropriation of what were considered non-literary texts: journals, folk tales, legends, ballads and popular print culture. This chapter introduces the historical connections between gender and literary plagiarism, although Mazzeo does not venture too far down this path, confessing at the outset that it is her belief that issues of genre were more significant than issues of gender in the context of literary plagiarism. Some scholars who work on gender in the Romantic period might object to what seems to be an unnecessary distinction: why must one category matter more than another? Fortunately, this somewhat arbitrary pronouncement does not interfere with the very useful discussions that follow of Coleridge's borrowings from the German poet Sophie Christiane Friederike Brun and his poetic dialogue with Mary Robinson, and the ways in which Dorothy Wordsworth's observations in her journals were routinely recycled by her brother and Coleridge.

The second half of *Plagiarism and Literary Property in the Romantic Period* considers the plagiarisms of Byron, Percy Shelley and Wordsworth, respectively. Chapter 4 focuses on the accusations of plagiarism levelled at Byron by Wordsworth and his friend Henry Taylor. This conflict between a first- and second-generation Romantic revealed the stark contrast between the aesthetics of these two very different poets and their very different ideas concerning their relationship to their work. Whereas Wordsworth thought of his poetry as an extension of himself and as his sole property, Byron tended to think of his literary work as a multiplicity of imagined subjectivities. The debate between Wordsworth and Byron was well known to their contemporaries, played out as it was in the print media. Percy Shelley's lesser-known plagiarism is the subject of chapter 5, which focuses in particular on his fear that he might be accused of plagiarizing travel writing, and more generally on the generic ambivalence of travel writing as it was perceived during this period. Travel narratives were both literary and non-literary: travel writing was unique as a genre in that it bridged the gap between fact and fiction, between impartial observation and subjective experience. As Mazzeo points out, its ambiguous position made appropriation an aesthetic risk—one that poets such as Shelley had to circumnavigate with care. *Plagiarism and Literary Property* concludes with a discussion of Wordsworth's representation of his poetry as literary and personal property within the larger context of the perceived connections between literary and real property during the early nineteenth century.

Scholars interested in the war of words generated in England by the French Revolution will be pleased to note the publication this year of several excellent books on this subject. Kevin Gilmartin's *Writing Against Revolution: Literary Conservatism in Britain, 1790–1832*, discussed in several sections this year, calls into question the tendency of recent historical scholarship to identify sympathy with the French Revolution with the rise of Romanticism and to privilege the progressive ideology of Romantic-period literature and culture over and above the conservative reaction in Britain to the events across the Channel. As Gilmartin demonstrates in his nuanced exploration of the counter-revolutionary movement in the Romantic era, this binary opposition of conservatives and radicals is reductive at best, eliding the complex ways in which conservative writers engaged with print culture in order to wage an active campaign against what they believed to be the destructive forces unleashed by the revolution. Not all conservative thinkers fell in step with the nostalgic conservatism typically identified with Edmund Burke. On the contrary, many counter-revolutionary writers believed, along with their radical counterparts, in the necessity of utilizing print communication as an impetus for change. Indeed, as Gilmartin points out, the tendency in recent scholarship to cast Burke as the representative voice of the conservative movement over-emphasizes his influence in the period. Drawing upon the pamphlet campaigns of the loyalist Association movement and the Cheap Repository, as well as periodical review and anti-Jacobin fiction, *Writing Against Revolution* goes well beyond the Burkean model to reveal the diversity and range of counter-revolutionary expression in the culture of the Romantic period.

The first chapter investigates the rhetorical crisis of loyalism exemplified by the attempts of John Reeves's Association for Preserving Liberty and Property against Republicans and Levellers to align itself with its readership as well as the authority of the government. Meeting at the Crown and Anchor tavern, the association, formed at the end of 1792 by a group of men claiming to be private citizens, galvanized the loyalist movement by creating a robust network of affiliates who vigorously participated in the distribution of conservative pamphlets and loyalist speeches. As Gilmartin points out, precisely the same tools were employed by the radical movement. The association therefore found itself in a paradoxical situation, on the one hand engaging in the kind of activism espoused by the radical London Corresponding Society, and on the other attempting to uphold the authority of the government against precisely this kind of public protest. Chapter 2 provides another example of what Gilmartin describes as 'counterrevolutionary enterprise' in Hannah More's *Cheap Repository Tracts* [1795–8] and some lesser-known works by More such as the *History of Tom White the Postilion* and its sequel, *The Way to Plenty* [1795]. In each case what begins as a moral parable inevitably gives way to a fictional representation of the public arena in which More could stage her counter-revolutionary efforts at moral reform.

Although the controversy over the French Revolution in Britain has been characterized as a pamphlet war (initiated by Burke's *Reflections on the Revolution in France* and Paine's *Rights of Man*), very little attention has been paid to the ways in which conservative periodicals contributed to the revolutionary debate. The third chapter of *Writing Against Revolution* deepens our understanding of the critical strategies engaged in by conservative periodicals, from the *Anti-Jacobin Review* and the *Quarterly Review* to more obscure organs such as William Blair's *The Loyalist*. Chapter 4 explores how the satirical plots of anti-Jacobin novels enabled their authors to participate in the counter-revolutionary movement through fictional representations of the dangerous consequences of radicalism. Appearing in the late 1790s and during the first decade of the nineteenth century, anti-Jacobin novels were latecomers to the revolutionary controversy. Like the loyalist pamphlets and periodicals earlier in the period, however, they too were experiments in public reform that attempted to negotiate the shifting terrain of print culture. *Writing Against Revolution* concludes with an investigation of the attempts of Robert Southey and Samuel Taylor Coleridge to distance themselves from the anti-Jacobin movement of the 1790s as well as from their own earlier participation in the radical movement.

Representing the opposite end of the political spectrum, Susan Manly's *Language, Custom and Nation in the 1790s: Locke, Tooke, Wordsworth, Edgeworth* probes the tremendous influence of John Locke on Romantic-era radicalism. In this well-written and well-researched book, Manly points out that most contemporary scholarship casts revolutionary thinking in the Romantic period as either a response to the American and French revolutions or to the influence of the radical philosophy of Rousseau. *Language, Custom and Nation in the 1790s* traces the roots of British radicalism even further back to Locke's discussion of 'arbitrary' language and tyranny. The first half of the book traces the trajectory of the influence of Locke's arguments on language and thought in the eighteenth century in general, and in particular its impact on the radical philology of John Horne Tooke. As Manly points out, Locke conceived of language as metaphorical leaps of the mind impelled by the need to communicate as well as the need to strengthen a sense of community and a common fund of knowledge. Locke's emphasis on the creation of language as a collective enterprise is what gave it the political freight that revolutionary thinkers at the end of the eighteenth century used to underwrite their belief in the constitutional right of the people to depose unrepresentative rulers. The first chapter provides an overview of Tooke's radical philology, including a discussion of his etymological treatise, the *Diversions of Purley* [1786–98]. In *Diversions of Purley*, Tooke argues along with Locke that language is fundamentally metaphorical. Tooke, who thought of his etymological project as a continuation of Locke's exploration of words and ideas, pushed Locke's notion of the communal power of language even further to examine the political abuses and misuses of rhetoric by those invested in the status quo. Chapter 2 provides a survey of the debate in the 1790s on the political power of language by a wide range of conservative and radical thinkers, concluding with an in-depth exploration of John Thelwall's *The Rights of Nature Against the Usurpations of Establishments* [1796] and his assertion of the subversive potential of popular eloquence. The second half focuses on the responses by Wordsworth and Maria Edgeworth to these debates on language and power after Tooke published the second—and much more explicitly politicized— edition of *Diversions of Purley* in 1798. The period 1798–1802 was significant for both Wordsworth and Edgeworth: these were the years in which *Lyrical Ballads* appeared in three editions and in which Ireland experienced a near-revolution, which prompted Edgeworth's *Essay on Irish Bulls* [1802]. As Manly points out, although Wordsworth and Edgeworth both focused on the necessity of a common language, Wordsworth confined his democratization of language to literary endeavour whereas Edgeworth used Locke's theory of government to suggest, in *Practical Education* [1798], that children should be treated as rational beings by adults, and to argue against anti-Irish stereotyping in her *Essay on Irish Bulls*. *Language, Custom and Nation in the 1790s* will appeal to Romanticists who are interested in the intersection between 1790s radicalism and philology, women's writing during the period and the troubled relations between Ireland and Britain at the end of the eighteenth century.

Jane Hodson's *Language and Revolution in Burke, Wollstonecraft, Paine, and Godwin* utilizes modern stylistic analysis (including lexical analysis software) in her exploration of the relationship between politics, literary style and linguistic theory in the pamphlet wars in England. Hodson focuses specifically on four influential and widely read texts: Burke's *Reflections on the Revolution in France* [1790], Wollstonecraft's *Vindication of the Rights of Men* [1790], Paine's *Rights of Man* [1791] and Godwin's *Enquiry Concerning Political Justice* [1793]. The fundamental differences between Hodson's approach to this subject and the arguments of two influential scholars on the politics of language during this period are addressed in the first chapter. Whilst Hodson's book builds upon James Boulton's *The Language of Politics* [1963] and Olivia Smith's *The Politics of Language* [1984], she argues that both scholars err in their adherence to a strict understanding of the terms 'radical' and 'conservative' in relation to linguistic theories circulating in the Romantic era. Hodson approaches each of the texts in her study from the point of view of a linguist rather than a literary scholar. Although this approach may be unfamiliar to many literary critics, Hodson's methodology yields some interesting results. In the chapter on Wollstonecraft's *Vindication*, for instance, Hodson examines Wollstonecraft's deliberate use of exclamation marks, question marks and dashes to indicate strong emotion. As Hodson points out, this was a strategic choice and not symptomatic of poor writing, as Godwin hinted and other more recent scholars have suggested: Wollstonecraft's emotional and emotive style was an implicit attack on the studied eloquence and artificiality of Burke's rhetoric. *Language and Revolution in Burke, Wollstonecraft, Paine, and Godwin* will generate interest amongst historians of language and linguistics as well as literary scholars of the Romantic period.

The language of the marketplace is the subject of another very good book published this year. John Strachan's *Advertising and Satirical Culture in the Romantic Period* provides us with a fascinating glimpse of one area of material culture that has been largely ignored by scholars of the Romantic period: the discourse and cultural resonance of advertising in the late eighteenth and early nineteenth centuries. This lively account of Romantic-era advertisers such as Robert Warren, who hawked his 'Matchless Blacking' in comic verse, and George Packwood, who cleverly marketed his Razor Strops, reveals the close family relationship between their advertisements and literary Romanticism. These proprietors and others often adopted the persona of the 'author' in their advertisements, and attempted to align their sales pitches to the literary taste of the age. Much of this was tongue in cheek. As Strachan demonstrates, advertising and satire were inextricably linked during this period, with parodists revelling in the genre of advertising as a satirical medium and copywriters engaging in a similar parodic appropriation of a wide variety of literary and non-literary genres of writing. The fodder for advertisers ranged from elevated verse to Socratic dialogues, picaresque travel narratives, and mock-playbills. The similarities between Romantic ad copy and Romantic literature did not go unnoticed by the literary figures of the age: Strachan includes in his discussion the responses of writers such as George Crabbe, Thomas Hood, Lord Byron and the youthful Charles Dickens to the commercial culture around them. During the 1820s and 1830s many writers fretted that books were being hawked in the same manner as other, more pedestrian, products such as blacking, hair oil or lottery tickets.

As commercial culture became more aestheticized in the period, the reverse was happening as well: books by popular authors such as Byron and Scott were commodified for the reading public. As Strachan persuasively argues, 'Romanticism is ineluctably involved with marketing and an author's original and individual genius is sold along the same lines as Robert Warren's "original matchless BLACKING"' (p. 269).

The past few years have witnessed an increasing interest in the influence of religion in the Romantic period, calling into question the argument that Romantic-era poetry and prose marked the beginning of the erosion and internalization of religious belief assumed by M.H. Abrams and others. Colin Jager's *The Book of God: Secularization and Design in the Romantic Era* is an important contribution to this branch of Romantic studies. *The Book of God* is a study of the argument from design that emerged in the Romantic era. Drawing upon a wide range of philosophical, theological and literary texts, Jager explores the question of secularization in England by tracing the idea of design in the works of many of the writers we associate with Romanticism. As Jager points out, the enduring influence of design at the end of the eighteenth century challenges the notion that religion during this period gave way to a secularized modernity. The first two chapters provide a historical framework for Jager's thesis by considering Blake's critique of Deism and David Hume's emphasis on design as a lived practice. The four chapters that follow alternate between literary and philosophical thinking on this subject, tracing the argument for design in the poetry and prose of Barbauld, Wordsworth and Austen as well as in the philosopher William Paley's influential *Natural Theology* [1802] and Immanuel Kant's *Critique of Judgment* [1790]. The book concludes with two chapters that consider the transformation of evil from a metaphysical to a moral category in Wordsworth's *Ruined Cottage* and the issues that confront contemporary scholars who bring criticism to bear on the study of religion. The afterword provides us with a particularly bracing and incisive discussion of the modern debate surrounding intelligent design and evolution.

Essaka Joshua's *The Romantics and the May Day Tradition* explores the persistence of folklore and folk tradition in the Romantic period, focusing on the connections between the customs associated with May Day and Romantic poetry. As Joshua notes, scant attention has been paid by scholars to the ways in which Romantic poets situated their poetry within regional traditions, including the celebration of May Day. According to Joshua, the theme of May Day, perhaps more than most folkloric rituals, resonates with many issues of interest to scholars today, touching upon contemporary beliefs regarding the natural world, city life, the pastoral, the past, regional and national identities, popular culture and how diverse social groups interacted within the public sphere. Building upon Jürgen Habermas's influential account of the emergence of the bourgeois public sphere, Joshua introduces a new term to describe the space in which folkloric traditions were enacted: the common sphere. This common sphere was characterized by its sense of community and regional differences as well as its detachment from the world of commerce by many Romantic writers, including Wordsworth, Southey, Leigh Hunt, Clare and Blake. As Joshua points out, the notion of the common sphere introduced a mythical space in which bourgeois writers and their readers could interact with rural subjects. The first chapter provides an overview of the rise of folklore and the history of the May Day tradition in England. The Lake Poets and their reliance on representations of folkloric ritual as a means to challenge public authority are discussed in chapter 2. Chapter 3 explores Leigh Hunt's assertion that May Day celebrations dissolved class boundaries and thus provided an antidote to the poisonous influence of urban commercialism. Blake's use of the urban May Day ritual was different from his contemporaries (who tended to focus on rural May Day celebrations) but, as chapter 4 demonstrates, in *Songs of Innocence and Experience* he uses the May Day celebration to contrast the rural, pastoral innocence that figures the liberation of the chimney sweeps with the corruption of the city festival. The concluding chapter discusses John Clare's deployment of the May Day theme as a means of pointing out the dangers of enclosure and the disappearance of the common space.

Nicholas Halmi's *The Genealogy of the Romantic Symbol* poses this question: what intellectual and social purposes did the idea of the symbol serve for the Romantics? Halmi's innovative study reveals how the idea of the Romantic symbol was an attempt to counter the alienation experienced by humankind in the wake of the scientific revolution by engendering a sense of unity between the human mind and nature. Seeking 'to effect a re-enchantment of the world by reforming perception' (p. 24), Romantic symbolism became the conduit for the transformation of human understanding of the external world for philosophically inclined poets and theorists in Britain and Germany. The symbol to which Halmi refers has nothing to do with poetic imagery (for example, the albatross in *The Rime of the Ancient Mariner*). It was a theoretical construct that was both infinitely meaningful but resisted being reduced to a singular meaning. Although many critics have dismissed this effort by the German Idealists and British poets such as Coleridge as a futile attempt to counteract Enlightenment thinking and its investment in rationality and scientific progress, Halmi argues that the idea of the Romantic symbol took one of the products of the Enlightenment—the aesthetic—and attempted to preserve it from the corrosive effects of scepticism. Halmi's genealogical methodology clearly demonstrates the positive relationship and connections between the rise of Romantic symbolism and the Enlightenment, and enables him to pursue his line of enquiry in a broader and more wide-ranging context than previous studies of this topic. The result is a brilliant and original study that is essential reading for scholars of the Romantic period.

Recent studies such as Gerard Carruthers and Alan Rawes's *English Romanticism and the Celtic World* [2003] and Leith Davies, Ian Duncan and Janet Sorenson's *Scotland and the Borders of Romanticism* [2004] have deepened our understanding of the complexities of regional and national identities in the Romantic era. Scholars interested in exploring the Romanticisms of the four nations will welcome the publication this year of *Wales and the Romantic Imagination*, a wide-ranging and diverse collection of essays edited by Damian Walford Davies and Lynda Pratt. Michael J. Franklin's 'The Colony Writes Back: Brutus, Britanus and the Advantages of an Oriental Ancestry' (pp. 13–42) investigates the complex genealogy of the myth-making that associated the Welsh with ancient Britons, Trojans and Phoenicians during a period of imperial expansion. In 'From the See of St. Davids to St. Paul's Churchyard: Joseph Johnson's Cross-Border Connections' (pp. 43–64), Helen Braithwaite explores the fascinating connections between Wales and the cause of dissent in the catalogue of publications by the radical publisher Joseph Johnson. Mary-Ann Constantine's ' "A subject of conversation": Iolo Morganwg, Hannah More and Ann Yearsley' (pp. 65–85) discusses Iolo, a stonemason by trade who was attempting to establish himself as a labouring poet along the lines of Yearsley, and the differences and similarities between his relationship with More and More's patronage of Yearsley. In 'Southey in Wales: Inscriptions, Monuments and Romantic Posterity' (pp. 86–103), Lynda Pratt probes Southey's Welsh connections and their contribution to what he had hoped to be his magnum opus, *Madoc*. Andrew Davies's ' "Redirecting the attention of history": Antiquarian and Historical Fictions of Wales from the Romantic Period' (pp. 104–21) supplies a useful overview of representations of Welsh history in Romantic fiction, and argues these fictional narratives helped to conceptualize issues of national identity in Wales and the rest of Britain. In ' "The fostering aid of a sister country": Wales in Irish Novels, 1796–1810' (pp. 122–40) Jim Shanahan continues this discussion of representations of Wales in Romantic fiction, focusing in particular on the significance of Wales in Irish fiction during the period of the Irish rebellion. David Chandler's 'Walter Savage Landor and Wales in the 1790s' (pp. 141–60) explores the Romantic poet's ambivalent attitude towards this country and its people. In ' "That deathless wish of climbing higher": Robert Bloomfield on the Sugar Loaf' (pp. 161–79), John Goodridge discusses the reasons why the English labouring-class writer Robert Bloomfield believed that his ascent of the Sugar Loaf mountain in 1807 was one of the most momentous events of his life. Percy Shelley's articulation of 'the Welsh sublime' in a series of poems written in 1811 and 1812 is addressed in Cian Duffy's ' "One draught from Snowdon's ever-sacred spring": Shelley's Welsh Sublime' (pp. 180–98). Damian Walford Davies's ' "Sweet sylvan routes" and Grave Methodists: Wales in De Quincey's *Confessions of an English Opium-Eater*' (pp. 199–227) emphasizes the importance of Wales as an idyll that contrasts with the sordid metropolitan setting of De Quincey's *Confessions*, but also as a troubling and ambiguous site with hitherto unrecognized connections to the more famous nightmarish scenes of addiction. Felicia Hemans, who spent most of her adult life in Wales, is the subject of Diego Saglia's ' "Harp of the mountain-land": Felicia Hemans and the Cultural Geography of Romantic Wales' (pp. 228–42), which explores Hemans's articulation of the cultural geography of Wales through an elaboration of sounds and images. The final essay in this collection, Jane Moore's ' "Parallelograms and circles": Robert Owen and the Satirists' (pp. 243–67), discusses the elision of Owen's Welshness by his satirists as the consequence of a general cultural blindness in the Romantic period to the influence of Enlightenment thinking in Wales.

Romanticism and Form, edited by Alan Rawes, builds upon the revival of interest in form in Romantic studies in the 1990s and the first few years of this century. The writers in this volume include many of the authors or editors who have broken new ground in recent years with 'New Formalism', providing a historically nuanced attention to form that is influenced more by deconstruction than New Criticism with its emphasis on fragmentation, instability and openness. The first chapter, Paul M. Curtis's 'Romantic Indirection' (pp. 1–22), explores the pleasures of maladjustment in reading Romantic poetry in the context of significant changes in poetical and philosophical attitudes to the sequence of ideas in the mind. In '"Conscript fathers and shuffling recruits": Formal Self-Awareness in Romantic Poetry' (pp. 23–39), Michael O'Neill investigates the formal decisions of Romantic poets, including Wordsworth's blank verse and Byron's ottava rima, and the decidedly un-Augustan couplets of Keats, Hunt, Shelley and Thomas Lovell Beddoes. Gavin Hopps's 'Romantic Invocation: A Form of Impossibility' (pp. 40–59) contends that the uncertainty registered in Romantic invocation was the result of conflicting impulses rather than disbelief or a rejection of the possibility of transcendence. The posthumous exchange between deceased poet and future reader is the subject of Mark Sandy's '"Ruinous perfection": Reading Authors and Writing Readers in Romantic Fragments' (pp. 60–77). In 'Combinatoric Form in Nineteenth-Century Satiric Prints' (pp. 78–94), Steven E. Jones argues that the relation between images and text in satiric prints is 'modular' in that they are separable units that are artfully juxtaposed and deliberately draw attention to the multiple possibilities for combining and recombining verbal and visual representations. Alan Rawes's 'Romantic Form and New Historicism: Wordsworth's "Lines Written a Few Miles above Tintern Abbey"' (pp. 95–115) argues that we reread the poem in light of Wordsworth's famous note that places it within the tradition of the canonical ode, a form that has typically been used to introduce contradictory or opposing ideas. Rawes argues that a close reading of the odal form of 'Tintern Abbey' challenges the New Historicist readings (by Jerome McGann, Marjorie Levinson and Kenneth Johnston amongst others) that point to the poem's displacement of political and social tensions. In 'Southey's Forms of Experiment' (pp. 116–37), Nicola Trott explores the ways in which Southey can be described as an experimental poet and a keen satirist, whose experiments with form and diction were quite different from those practised and endorsed by Wordsworth and Coleridge. The next essay, Bernard Beatty's 'Believing in Form and Forms of Belief: The Case of Southey' (pp. 138–53), probes the ways in which Southey's long poems embody religious forms of insight. Jacqueline M. Labbe's 'The Seductions of Form in the Poetry of Ann Batten Cristall and Charlotte Smith' (pp. 154–70) investigates how these two poets utilize form in order to explore the nature of poetic subjectivity. In '"Seldom safely enjoyed by those who enjoyed it completely": Byron's Poetry, Austen's Prose and Forms of Narrative Irony' (pp. 171–91), Caroline Franklin argues that Byron and Austen pioneered narrative forms of irony which were designed to point out the limitations of the Romantic paradigm as well as to dispel its validity. Co-written by Jane Stabler, Martin H. Fischer, Andrew Michael Roberts and Maria Nella Carminati, '"What constitutes a reader?"' *Don Juan* and the Changing Reception of Romantic Form' (pp. 192–212) explores the reception of Byron's use of ottava rima in his own day and now from the point of view of an interdisciplinary research project that uses the methodology of cognitive psychology to gather empirical data regarding readers' responses to Romantic and late twentieth-century poetry. *Romanticism and Form* concludes with a thought-provoking afterword by Susan J. Wolfson that contextualizes the arguments of the contributors to this collection within the framework of a renewed appreciation for the formal qualities of Romantic poetry in Romantic scholarship today.

2. Prose

Reflecting the continuing impact of the Bollingen collected edition, this year saw the publication of a number of major studies of Coleridge as a prose writer which in various ways took issue with received critical views of the Coleridgean intellectual legacy. In his monograph *Coleridge and the Crisis of Reason*, Richard Berkeley addresses what he characterizes as 'the central weakness in Coleridge studies: the persistent failure to grasp the full significance of the pantheism controversy for Coleridge's poetry and thought' (p. 1), arguing that Thomas McFarland's classic study *Coleridge and the Pantheist Tradition* [1969] distorts Coleridge's engagement with the question of Spinozism by presenting 'the image of Spinoza as a settled one' (p. 1) which can be made the subject of a straightforward influence study (p. 11), whereas in Berkeley's view Spinoza represents for Coleridge a more general intellectual crisis characterized by 'the recognition that the project of rational metaphysics (and by implication science) is leading to the surrender of the humanistic soul, to a world of mechanical sterility' (p. 38) which can only be adequately studied by adopting a Gadamerian methodology focusing on the 'hermeneutic circle operating between Coleridge's religious concepts and the texts of the pantheism controversy' (p. 11). Berkeley draws attention to the duality of the role Spinoza plays in the *Pantheismusstreit*, where he is 'variously interpreted as a mystical or rationalistic thinker' (p. 32), in order to emphasize his centrality to the Coleridgean preoccupation 'with the attempt to carve out a conception of reason that would somehow combine a determinate rational universe with freedom, consistency with creativity, personality with infinity' (p. 210) and thus the continuing relevance of the pantheism controversy to 'Coleridge's final Trinitarian position' (p. 165). The book highlights the importance of F.H. Jacobi's 'anti-rationalism' (p. 90) for Coleridge's understanding of the issues raised by pantheism, and examines 'the complexity of Coleridge's understandings of Schelling's texts' (p. 108) as evidenced in Coleridge's 'ongoing transformation of his conceptions of reason, being and God' (p. 108), in an argument that has important implications for critical attempts to situate British Romanticism within the intellectual context of German Idealist thought.

Ben Brice, in *Coleridge and Scepticism*, also identifies theological questions as central to Coleridge's reception of German thought, providing a fresh perspective on the well-rehearsed debate amongst modern scholars about the relationship of the Coleridgean symbol to the concept of allegory (p. 180). Brice's point of departure is Coleridge's 'privately expressed doubts' (p. 2) about his sacramental account of symbolism, which he sets in the context of what, following Nicholas Wolterstorff, he calls 'epistemological piety' (p. 49), exemplified by Boyle, Locke and Newton (p. 7), in which is stressed 'the weakness, blindness, and "tendency to error"...innate in human reason' (p. 38), and the allied intellectual tendency to 'theological voluntarism' (p. 5) characteristic of Calvinism, which contradicted the tradition of natural theology by insisting that 'the physical universe is just one arbitrary and contingent expression of God's will...[which] can yield no reliable knowledge of its creator' (p. 31). Brice argues that Hume's *Dialogues Concerning Natural Religion* made use of these positions to set revealed and natural religion in conflict, establishing that 'the respective grounds for their belief in God are mutually exclusive rather than—as was traditionally conceived— supplementary arguments that should be advanced in tandem' (p. 73), a contradiction which the theory of the symbol presented in Coleridge's later thought struggled, and ultimately failed, to address (p. 154). For Brice, 'Kantian aesthetics acted as a kind of "Trojan Horse" through which Coleridge was forced to confront Humean scepticism' (p. 83), in that Kant's account of the sublime highlighted the issue of anthropomorphism, or idolatry, inherent in natural theology's claims to identify a relationship of analogy between the natural world and the mind of God (p. 80), and he suggests that this persistent tension in Coleridge's thought, which exhibits an 'ambivalent loyalty to both analogy and disanalogy' (p. 196), is the source of that slipperiness and instability in the distinction between symbol and allegory which modern criticism has identified.

In *Coleridge and German Philosophy: The Poet in the Land of Logic*, Paul Hamilton likewise addresses the vexed relationship between symbol and allegory in Coleridge's later thought, taking the strikingly original approach of reading the *Biographia Literaria*, the 1818 recension of *The Friend* and the *Opus Maximum* from a perspective suggested by Schelling's late work, a deliberately anachronistic procedure for which Hamilton cites in justification Schelling's own reading of Coleridge (p. 105) and the need to situate Coleridge in the 'Hegelian picture' (p. 7) of post-Kantian philosophy. Central to Hamilton's reading is the Coleridgean concept of 'tautegory', defined as a 'repetition of sameness with a difference' (p. 59) which, in the form of 'historical reinterpretation allows the same event to develop more of itself across time in art and history' (p. 59); viewed in this way, Coleridgean 'tautegory' licenses Hamilton's own anachronistic interpretative procedure in which Coleridgean thought is characterized as one articulation of the basic 'speculative problem' (p. 10) underlying German Idealism. Hamilton identifies the notion of 'tautegory' with Coleridge's account of a desynonymizing process in language which 'respects the difference necessary for a truth to reproduce itself in history, under different historical circumstances' (p. 84), finding in the 'apparently divergent volumes' (p. 104) of the *Biographia Literaria* an example of this desynonymizing and tautegorical mode of repetition in which 'at the levels both of...the philosophical understanding of life and the literary understanding of poetic expression' (p. 103) a Schellingian 'process of individuation' (p. 103) is at work. Going against the trend of recent politically orientated criticism, Hamilton argues that the Coleridgean symbol is not necessarily reactionary, in that, as a form of 'tautegory', it is inherently open to the possibility of reinterpretation in a way which undermines the monolithic Enlightenment certainties of an allegorical hermeneutic (p. 108), testifying to 'our production by language' (p. 109).

A number of articles investigate the relationship of Coleridgean thought to philosophy, with Ayon Roy's 'The Specter of Hegel in Coleridge's *Biographia Literaria*' (*JHI* 68[2007] 279–304) taking an approach comparable to Hamilton's in locating Coleridge within a Hegelian intellectual framework despite Coleridge's own 'curiously willed ignorance of Hegel' (p. 279), although Roy interprets the 'radically self-undermining text' (p. 280) of the *Biographia* as approaching a Hegelian critique of Schelling's 'foundationalist intuitionism' (p. 280) without ever quite committing itself to 'the decisive Hegelian step of repudiating the category of intuition altogether' (p. 290). Alan Barnes, on the other hand, in 'Coleridge, Tom Wedgwood and the Relationship between Time and Space in Midlands Enlightenment Thought' (*BJECS* 30[2007] 243–60), calls into question the received critical narrative of Coleridge's engagement with Kantian thought by producing fresh evidence from the Wedgwood Archive to show that Coleridge's 1801 philosophical letters respond to topics discussed with Tom Wedgwood, rather than reflecting any particular study of Kant (p. 252). In 'Coleridge and the "More Permanent Revolution"' (*ColB* 30[2007] 1–16) Gregory Leadbetter disputes the common depiction of 'Coleridge as a "conservative" apostate to his earlier "radicalism"' (p. 1), arguing for a view of Coleridge as a 'precursor to the present-day philosophy known as "social idealism" as developed by the British jurist Philip Allott' (p. 4). Joel Faflak's 'Philosophy's Debatable Land in Coleridge's *Biographia Literaria*' (in Lamont and Rossington, eds., *Romanticism's Debatable Lands* pp. 136–47) explores the relationship between Coleridge's philosophy and nationalism, arguing that Coleridge's fascination with mesmerism is due to the way it suggests 'an *interpenetration* of minds and bodies that transgresses subject boundaries' (p. 142) and so undermines the 'actively self-commanding and managerial' (p. 144) imperial subject the project of whose fashioning Coleridge inherits from Scottish Enlightenment philosophy.

The connection between Coleridge's philosophical preoccupations and his medical interests also forms the subject of a number of other essays. Neil Vickers, in the closely related articles 'Coleridge and the Idea of "Psychological" Criticism' (*BJECS* 30[2007] 261–78) and 'Coleridge, Moritz and the "Psychological" Case History' (*Romanticism* 13[2007] 271–80), links Coleridge's development of new kind of psychological analysis of literary characters such as Hamlet to his friendship with the Bristol doctor and renowned Germanist, Thomas Beddoes. Gavin Budge's 'Indigestion and Imagination in Coleridge's Critical Thought' (in Budge, ed., *Romantic Empiricism: Poetics and the Philosophy of Common Sense*, pp. 141–81) examines the relationship between Romantic-period medical theories linking indigestion with hallucination and Coleridge's ideas about the imagination, particularly as exemplified in *The Friend*'s discussion of Luther's vision of the Devil (p. 162). The relationship between medical theory and the Coleridgean imagination is also the focus of Kiran Toor's ' "Offspring of his genius": Coleridge's Pregnant Metaphors and Metamorphic Pregnancies'

(*Romanticism* 13[2007] 257–70), which suggests that Coleridge's significantly twofold definition of imagination is designed to resolve 'the antinomy . . . between determinism and freedom' (p. 263) which characterized medical debates over preformationism and epigenesis as accounts of embryonic development. Toor draws attention to the crucial role played in this controversy by the polyp's ambiguous status between vegetable and animal kingdoms (p. 264), a topic which is explored in more depth by Deirdre Coleman in ' "Aetherial journeys, submarine exploits": The Debatable Worlds of Natural History in the Late Eighteenth Century' (in Lamont and Rossington, eds., pp. 223–36).

Coleridge's influence on European literature is comprehensively surveyed in *The Reception of S.T. Coleridge in Europe*, edited by Elinor Shaffer and Edoardo Zuccato (discussed in more detail in section 3(a)), in which Michael John Kooy's 'Coleridge's Early Reception in France, from the First to the Second Empire' (pp. 27–60) innovatively argues for the important contribution made by Coleridge to 'the culture in which Baudelaire, and later Symbolism, would flourish' (p. 57). Laura George explores an aspect of Coleridge's contribution to the Anglo-American literary critical tradition in ' "The *technique* of ordinary poetry": Coleridgean Notes toward a Genealogy of *Technique*' (*ERR* 18[2007] 195–203), which examines the way in which the Coleridgean concept of poetic technique 'continues to function as a placeholder for what true poetry must leave behind or outgrow' (p. 201).

Studies of Coleridge dominated the field this year, but other Romantic prose writers also received scrutiny. In 'The Man of Feeling History: The Erotics of Historicism in *Reflections on the Revolution in France*' (*ELH* 74[2007] 829–57), Mike Goode suggests that Burke 'grounds historical epistemology in manly feeling while also grounding that manly feeling in what he takes to be a true sense of history' (p. 831) in a way that is not necessarily 'heteronormative' (p. 846). Melissa Schwarzberg, in 'Jeremy Bentham on Fallibility and Infallibility' (*JHI* 68[2007] 563–85), examines the origins of J.S. Mill's democratic 'arguments for fallibility and against the assertion of infallibility' (p. 565) in Bentham's linked 'challenges to natural religion and to legal immutability' (p. 572), while David Collings's 'The Discipline of Death: Knowledge and Power in *An Essay on the Principle of Population*' (*ERR* 18[2007] 223–30) challenges the Foucauldian emphasis on the centrality of Bentham in 'the shift to a modern disciplinary regime' (p. 229), arguing that the way Malthus makes disaster 'the basis of a social analysis' (p. 224) represents a 'crucial step from eighteenth-century to nineteenth-century political economy' (p. 226) in that it 'regards society as expressing a deeper logic whose laws must be reconstructed through disciplinary knowledge' (p. 224).

The genre of travel-writing continued to attract scholarly attention, although from widely differing perspectives. Following on from a number of recent studies of Romantic colonialism, Peter J. Kitson's *Romantic Literature, Race and Colonial Encounter* provides a nuanced approach to the emergence of the category of race in the Romantic period, situating it within the context of the continuing power of other 'stalwarts of identity formation, religion, class, gender and nation' (p. 2). Kitson emphasizes the importance of the comparative anatomy of Blumenbach (p. 32) and John Hunter (p. 62) in the development of the scientific forms of racism that came to predominate in the later nineteenth century, while downplaying the importance of racism to the legitimation of slavery, noting that 'the race idea flourishes most *outside* the contact zone of transcultural exchange' (p. 93) and as a consequence tends to assume greater prominence in abolitionist writing than it does in pro-slavery writing (p. 104). An innovative feature of Kitson's book is its discussion of reactions to the South Seas, where he argues that 'the figure of the cannibal becomes key to effecting a racist division between the fair and the dark-skinned inhabitants of the Pacific' (p. 124), and the change in attitude towards China during the Romantic period, when 'an Enlightenment Universalist discourse of ethnological relativism' is replaced by 'an emergent British nationalism' (p. 165). Kitson's very scholarly account is accompanied by discussions of Coleridge, Byron, De Quincey and Mary Shelley's *Frankenstein* which situate these literary texts within the complexities of the development of racist discourses. An article by Kitson, 'Debating China: Romantic Fictions of the Qing Empire, 1760–1800' (in Lamont and Rossington, eds., pp. 211–22) is closely related to material covered in the book. A more conventional colonialist perspective is taken in Kari J. Winter's 'Jeffrey Brace in Barbados: Slavery, Interracial Relationships, and the Emergence of a Global Economy' (*NCC* 29[2007] 111–25), which examines an early nineteenth-century slave narrative in the context of the period's 'increasingly transnational economy' (p. 123).

Carl Thompson's *The Suffering Traveller and the Romantic Imagination* (also covered in section 3(a)), on the other hand, uses the 'hugely hetero-geneous genre' (p. 14) of travel-writing to provide an unusual perspective on issues in Romantic poetics, emphasizing its role in creating 'contemporary expectations that pertained to a range of misadventures or "romantic situations" that seem to have been especially attractive to the Romantic traveller, and that he accordingly either sought out in his actually travelling, or at least laid claim to in his self-fashioning *qua* traveller' (p. 11). Thompson follows Marlon Ross and Anne Mellor in regarding ' "Romanticism" . . . as very much a masculine agenda' (p. 6), so that the paradoxical Romantic 'scripting' of travel as characterized by unforeseen accidents (p. 19) becomes definitive of a masculinity which is opposed to the modernity represented by the figure of the tourist (p. 41), especially 'the programmatic aspect of picturesque tourism' (p. 53). In an examination of the 'convergence of shipwreck narrative and Puritan spiritual autobiography' (p. 78) Thompson makes a convincing case for regarding Coleridge's *Ancient Mariner* as an exploration of tensions in the 'providential perspective' (p. 100) of these narratives, which he suggests were politically ambiguous, exhibiting 'a distinctly patriotic and nationalistic tendency . . . bound up with . . . a subtly authoritarian agenda' (p. 115) which could nevertheless be interpreted against the grain by 'readers of a radical or liberal disposition' (p. 125), being problematized by a focus on 'moments of apparent insubordination, even mutiny' (p. 125). Thompson argues that this ambiguity accounts for the prominent role played by 'shipwreck, mutiny and other stock situations of maritime literature as part of the "tropological dynamic" of Wordsworth's early poetry' (p. 127), contrasting this with Byron's more relativistic use of tropes and situations from the literature of travel (p. 241).

Complementing the rise of Southey studies in other areas, David M. Craig, in *Robert Southey and Romantic Apostasy: Political Argument in Britain, 1780–1840*, discussed further in section 3(a), offers a historical survey of the development of Southey's thinking which takes issue with 'the whole tradition of "apostasy" which views the lake poets as passing from "Jacobin radicalism" to "Tory conservatism"' (p. 7). Craig argues that the continuity in Southey's thought turns on his religious position, which 'remained remarkably consistent throughout his life and would have been recognized easily by a Unitarian' (p. 212), characterizing his later Anglicanism as essentially a continuation of eighteenth-century latitudinarianism (p. 191), and his later conservatism as, paradoxically, a development of Godwinian emphasis on the power of institutions, since 'if it was accepted that institutions shaped manners, and also that the populace became deeply attached to those which were familiar, it followed that any radical alteration of those institutions was hazardous' (p. 213). Craig develops a nuanced account of Southey's nationalism which stresses its intimate connection with a providential view of history (p. 125), and emphasizes the political complexity of Southey's relationship with the *Quarterly Review*, where his 'pro-war and pro-reform' (p. 49) agenda led him to align himself against the 'pro-reform but . . . anti-war stance' (p. 50) of the *Edinburgh Review*, providing a useful contextualization which has significant implications for critical understanding of Coleridge and Wordsworth. Southey's nationalism is also the subject of Jen Hill's 'National Bodies: Robert Southey's *Life of Nelson* and John Franklin's *Narrative of a Journey to the Shores of the Polar Sea*' (*NCL* 61[2007] 417–48), which analyses Southey's use of the Arctic to legitimize a 'rugged, even reckless individualism [which] served national goals without threatening social order at home' (p. 418), testifying to an 'intense and persistent ideological investment attached to male bodies' (p. 420) responsible for shaping the reception of Franklin's potentially much more problematic narrative of the hardships of Arctic exploration.

A number of articles make use of a focus on non-canonical writers as a means of exploring issues central to Romanticism. Nigel Leask, in the two closely related articles 'Robert Burns and Scottish Common Sense Philosophy' (in Budge, ed., pp. 64–87) and ' "The Shadow Line": James Currie's "Life of Burns" and British Romanticism' (in Lamont and Rossington, eds., pp. 64–79) analyses the contribution of Currie's 1800 biographical account of Burns to the arguments of Wordsworth's Preface to *Lyrical Ballads*. Brian McGrath's 'Thomas De Quincey and the Language of Literature: Or, on the Necessity of Ignorance' (*SEL* 47[2007] 847–62) explores the context of De Quincey's formulation of the category of the 'literature of power' within a discussion of information overload (p. 852) while Philip Flynn, in 'Early Blackwood's and Scottish Identities' (*SiR* 46[2007] 43–56), describes *Blackwood's* Romantic reaction against 'the secular rationalism, smug modernism, and disdain for Scotland's past . . . from the time of Hume to the time of Jeffrey and the *Edinburgh Review*' (p. 52). Periodical culture is also an important point of reference in Marcus Tomalin's ' "Vulgarisms and broken

English": The Familiar Perspicuity of William Hazlitt' (*Romanticism* 13[2007] 28–52), which examines Hazlitt's *New and Improved Grammar of the English Tongue* as a defence of the validity of the 'familiar style' (p. 28) against linguistically orientated attacks (p. 30) which draws on the linguistic theory of Horne Tooke (p. 49).

Interpretative issues surrounding canonicity are central to Kenneth R. Cervelli's short monograph *Dorothy Wordsworth's Ecology*, discussed further in section 3(b), which examines the paradoxical place of Dorothy Wordsworth in literary studies, given that 'we are now in the curious position of knowing more about Dorothy and her work than her contemporaries did' (p. 1). Cervelli takes issue with conventional feminist approaches to Dorothy Wordsworth, which in his view make interpretation of her work over-reliant on its relationship to William Wordsworth's poetry and so tend 'to distort both figures' (p. 7), as well as ignoring inconvenient features such as 'how easily and naturally she gravitates towards domestic environments' (p. 42) in her writing. Cervelli proposes instead a 'holistic approach' (p. 88) in which her work is considered 'as a kind of ecosystem in which even the most seemingly innocuous elements . . . contribute to its health and vitality' (p. 88), an interpretative stance which is remarkably close to nineteenth-century conceptions of female 'influence'. A comparable investigation of the intellectual basis for a conservative conception of feminism can be found in Fiona Price's essay, 'Elizabeth Hamilton's *Letters on Education*: Common Sense Alternatives to Scepticism and their Aesthetic Consequences' (in Budge, ed., pp. 88–111), which examines the context of Hamilton's critique of political radicalism, as expressed in her theories of education, in the philosophy of Dugald Stewart and the Common Sense school.

3. Poetry

(a) General

Most work on Romantic poetry this year focuses closely on the specific and the contextual, preferring to create a series of detailed miniatures rather than the grander macroscopic perspectives of an older type of criticism. Adam Potkay's *The Story of Joy: From the Bible to Late Romanticism* is in this respect a blast from the past. Potkay traces the evolution of a concept, 'joy', across an at times bewildering spread of texts, taking in troubadour ballads, twentieth-century advertising and the Everly Brothers. The book is of particular relevance to students of Romantic poetry, as Wordsworth, Coleridge, Blake and Shelley are 'the rock on which this study is built' (p. xi). Potkay begins by distinguishing joy from happiness, a state that 'elevates inner integrity, constancy and wisdom', unlike joy, which is 'an expansion and at least partial loss of self' (p. 3), and ecstasy, which consists not of 'fullness but rather of absence' (p. 20), a complete surrender. Joy is a will towards 'blissful totality and undemarcated awareness' (p. 76), a loosening of the bounds of self that may be, paradoxically, also a form of self-exaltation. Eighteenth-century aesthetics, for Potkay, concentrated on the ethics of joy;

Wordsworth retreats from ethical action, but in doing so forms a 'Green' ethics which takes issue with mankind's 'increasingly irresponsible stewardship of the earth' (p. 122). Central to Potkay's reading of Coleridgean joy is the 'Dejection' ode. Coleridge retains a theological 'framework of grace', but he insists, unlike Christian thought, on 'joy as an interior event'. Discussion of Schiller, Blake and Shelley moves towards 'post-Christian' writers whose work nevertheless depends on a similar structure. In *Prometheus Unbound* Shelley insists on forgiveness as a key principle by which humanity can return to a state that is at once godlike and childlike in its innocent perception. It is the book's very scale that underlines its significance, and yet one cannot help at times feeling disappointed that we do not hear more of Wordsworth or Coleridge and other poets, such as Hemans, whom Potkay is obliged to sweep past. That such a book was tenable in these times seemed unlikely; that Potkay succeeds to such an extent is a tribute to his scholarship.

Similar in some respects is Michael O'Neill's *The All-Sustaining Air: Romantic Legacies and Renewals in British, American, and Irish Poetry since 1900*, which continues his commitment to the importance of close reading and sustained attention to the detail of poetics. The book opens with a superb chapter that takes the Romantic use of 'air' and runs with it, diving in and out of poetry by Yeats, Rich, Bishop and Stevens, interweaving allusions and echoes to Shelley, Keats, Byron, Blake, Coleridge and Wordsworth. Yeats, the editor of Blake and idolizer of Shelley, is a good place to start. As O'Neill demonstrates, Shelley remained 'both double and anti-self' in mid- to late Yeats. O'Neill's prose proves remarkably supple as he draws out the relationship: at one point, gloriously, 'the swan of the second and third stanzas [of 'Coole and Ballylee, 1931'] has flown straight in from the pages of Shelley's *Alastor*' (p. 51). O'Neill flits through poetry by Auden, Spender, Wallace Stevens and a range of poems by Northern Irish poets including a superb chapter on Paul Muldoon's *Madoc*. T.S. Eliot's 'overt hostility to Romanticism' seems to pose a harder case, but it is in opposition to the Romantics that O'Neill finds the most fruitful connections, with Eliot giving 'a new start to English Romanticism by reminding the reader of the persistent obduracy of the longings and desires it dramatizes and analyses' (p. 74). This is a key phrase; for O'Neill, Romanticism is an incomplete project. The Romantics' voices do not 'vanish', but enter 'the minds of their readers' (p. 191), allowing ever more renewals and re-evaluations. The book is as important for Romanticists who neatly divide their own period from what follows as it is for twentieth-century scholars who too lazily read the work of modern poets as rejecting a conservative or bombastic Romantic paradigm. The myth that the modernists threw off the influence of the Romantics is also cogently challenged by Ben Coffer's 'The "Hyperions" and "Hugh Selwyn Mauberley": The Common Historiographic Approach in Keats's and Pound's Fragment Poems' (*KSR* 21[2007] 46–55).

Discussion of Romantic poetry continued to be dominated, however, by an interest in history and context. Carl Thompson's *The Suffering Traveller and the Romantic Imagination* (also discussed in section 2 above) is an important, ambitious book that seeks to account for the literary vogue for particularly unpleasant travel in the Romantic period. Much of the material discussed is not directly literary (shipwreck narratives and travel books feature widely), but Thompson treats literary and non-literary texts alike, as both create culturally prevalent set narratives, 'scripts' or 'topoi' (p. 10) that are followed by writers and readers in search of similar misadventure. Having set out the cultural ground, Thompson proceeds to explore four touristic 'scripts' followed in the period. The first two are largely cultural, and stem from maritime adventure. Romantic readers were 'steeped in accounts of shipwreck' (p. 62), and these printed accounts provided a distinct mode of experiencing wrecks, such that even 'participants in a wreck...carried in their heads a very clear story of how such disasters were likely to unfold' (p. 66). These narratives often offered providential causes for wrecks, and Thompson argues that the moral instability of the *Ancient Mariner* can be traced to its uncertain appropriation of such source material. The political implications of maritime travel models are fully discussed, before two chapters which describe how Wordsworth and Byron were influenced by these cultural narratives, and how they influenced their own Wordsworthian and Byronic models of travelling. Thompson places Wordsworth, perhaps a little simplistically, as a walker in service of 'nationalist and imperialist agendas' (p. 220). But if Wordsworth offers moral certainty achieved through strenuous experience, Byron, the hero of Thompson's book, revels in the possibility of instability, travel constantly offering an 'opening-up of the self' (p. 240). *Don Juan* and *The Island* are read in the context of a reworking of the shipwreck narrative, suggesting that Byron offers an oceanic mobility, a restlessness that is both politically and textually liberating. Also worth mentioning in this section is Thompson's edition of *Romantic-Era Shipwreck Narratives*. This superb volume contains eight of these immensely popular accounts, annotated and introduced by Thompson, including an account of the wreck of the *Earl of Abergavenny* in which Captain John Wordsworth lost his life. The Romantic period was a time when, as Thompson points out, the navy was the 'single greatest employer in the country' (p. 5), and this edition, along with Thompson's book, should begin a period of sustained interest in the sea in Romantic scholarship.

Peter Melville's *Romantic Hospitality and the Resistance to Accommodation: Rousseau, Kant, Coleridge, and Mary Shelley* occupies a similar critical terrain, but he approaches it from a quite different theoretical perspective. Melville mobilizes the 'Derridean commentary' (p. 13) on hospitality in a range of Romantic-period texts, in Rousseau, Kant, Coleridge and Mary Shelley. All of these texts, for Melville, offer 'various scenes of reading strangers and/or foreigners' (p. 7) so all might be considered 'literary' in the sense that they all self-consciously focus on the nature and structure of reading. Melville is clearly well versed in Derrida, and this is an unusually subtle use of his work. For Derrida, 'hospitality is structurally impossible', offering at once an invitation and a recognition of exclusion. Melville's work is important not only for historicizing and contextualizing this thesis in the late eighteenth and early nineteenth centuries, but also for the ambitious argument that these Romantic writers anticipate Derrida, or indeed 'exceed' his work in problematizing 'its own impossibility' (p. 13). Of greatest significance to this section is an excellent chapter on Coleridge. Rousseau and Kant's 'unsettled' and 'conflicted' scenes of hospitality are reconfigured by Coleridge, who sees a competitiveness in the act of welcome which renders impossible the hospitable act. *Christabel* in particular is read as 'a kind of microcosm for the recurring pattern of failed hospitable encounters in Coleridge's poetry' (p. 114). It is a bracing, theoretically astute read.

John Strachan's *Advertising and Satirical Culture in the Romantic Period*, also discussed in section 1, treats much ephemeral poetry on the margins of print culture. Advertising culture, he argues, can be seen as a worryingly close flip-side of Romantic culture as a whole, but Strachan is not primarily concerned with tracing the similarities between Day and Martin and *Don Juan*. Rather, this is an account of advertising which takes the topic as an end in itself. He shows a thorough awareness not only of an extraordinary range of Romantic-period poetry (particularly neglected writers like Leigh Hunt and Thomas Hood), periodical writing, novels, drama and other forms, but also the Popean and classical satirical formats that advertising writers often invoked. The case of J.R.D. Huggins, poet and barber, is particularly intriguing. One poem mocks a rival barber, invoking Pope's *Rape of the Lock*, but also quoting from Southey's anti-Della Cruscan satires of 1799, themselves a response to William Gifford's *Maviad* and *Baviad*. Huggins 'borrows a parodic attack upon poetic over-elaboration and the bejewelled celebration of triviality and co-opts it to sell hair-pieces' (p. 245). At its most complex, advertisers such as Huggins achieve a density of poetical reference that suggests a picture of the Romantic age that is much less monolithic than that which the traditional canon assumes. Strachan rereads Coleridge's 'To Fortune' as less biographical than self-parodic (pp. 186–8), placing it alongside lottery ads, which, Strachan suggests, mirror Coleridge's visionary verse in their 'appeal to the human capacity for dream and revelry' (p. 203), though in a rather more 'democratic' manner. It is an entertaining study, and should prove a rich source book for those interested in rediscovering poetry that is as enjoyable as it is ephemeral.

The vexed relationship between Romantic poetics and the burgeoning visual culture of the period has been the subject of a number of significant studies recently, and Sophie Thomas's *Romanticism and Visuality: Fragments, History, Spectacle* is an important addition. The book is interdisciplinary, incorporating chapters on Keats, Shelley and Coleridge alongside chapters on phantasmagoria and dioramas. One of the most innovative aspects of the study is Thomas's sense of the interpenetration of these cultural spheres. Both 'visual and literary culture', she argues, engage with 'what is inherently imaginative, and with what borders on the invisible' (p. 7). The concept of the invisible, the attempt to view that which is beyond the limits of the visible, is an important structuring concept. The fragment, 'that which challenges and indeed deforms form' (p. 21), becomes a central trope, both as a poetic 'form' and as a subject for poetry. Keats's dependence on metaphors of sight in his visionary poetics underlines a complex doubling of the visionary and the visible. The possibility of a visionary poetics is undermined by its dependence on the visible, just as the hope for the elusive whole is undermined by the formal dependence on the fragmentary. The tension between the idealized and the material is further explored in discussion of *The Prelude*, Shelley's 'Mont Blanc' and Coleridge's 'Hymn Before Sun-rise, in the Vale of Chamouni'.

These poets are confronted by an experience not of the real, but of a 'vacancy' (p. 112) that exceeds the visible, haunting the 'debate about the status and function of the imagination' (p. 113). The study closes with readings of Coleridge's *Remorse*, a play that, Thomas argues, relies heavily on the spectacular, and Shelley's engagements with artistic representations of Medusa. The border between the visible and the invisible produces, for Shelley, an oscillation between 'horror' and 'grace' (p. 153); and it is a similar uncertainty that Thomas shows operating in the Romantic engagement with the visual.

Edward Larrissy's *The Blind and Blindness in Literature of the Romantic Period* offers an important survey of blindness as a literary trope across a wide array of texts. The connections between literature and medicine have been discussed with increasing frequency recently, but Larrissy does not follow this route, offering instead a meditation on how writers used the idea of blindness. Larrissy begins with a discussion of Enlightenment ideas of blindness and education alongside a consideration of seers and blind harpers in the Scottish Highlands in the eighteenth century. The Gaelic tradition of considering poetry in terms of loss following eighteenth-century suppression of the Gaels constructs a paradigm in which 'something is exchanged, in the progress of society, for abstraction and commerce' (p. 47). Larrissy discusses Wordsworth's accounts of blindness, but also his accounts of 'exchanges' where 'visionary intensity is renounced in favour of the world of habit and custom' (p. 103). The chapter on Wordsworth is the strongest in the book, as Larrissy considers the poet's work as a series of 'unstable transitions between one perspective and another' (p. 138). There is also an excellent discussion of Keats's combination of the visual and the spoken, the way blindness 'lays bare the complexity of the links between the aesthetic and the political' (p. 172) in Byron, and sustained discussion of Shelley, Blake and Mary Shelley. Larrissy is thoroughly acquainted with a wide range of literary figures—Thomas Blacklock, Thomas Moore, Leigh Hunt, Felicia Hemans and others mingle with the visionary company—yet despite that range, or perhaps because of it, the book tends to lack focus at times. The prose can be rather clumsy, with sections apparently thrown together with little thought to their fitness. Yet this is a valuable book, and an important consideration of Romantic poetics.

James Robert Allard's *Romanticism, Medicine and the Poet's Body*, however, offers just such an analysis of literature's connection with medicine. Allard enters a busy field, but he makes a significant contribution. He focuses on the body in the period (the period being the new-fangled 'Romantic Century', 1750–1850) in which medicine professionalized and literature Romanticized. He surveys the changes in medical theory in the period, in which the body became a kind of text which was examined and tested for causes beneath the surface. The second chapter focuses on Wordsworth and Joanna Baillie, contextualizing their work with reference to the emergent discourse of the body. The best part of the book, though, is the second section, which considers a fascinating hybrid, the 'Poet-Physician', in discussion of John Thelwall, Keats and Thomas Lovell Beddoes, all of whom received a medical training, such that they were uniquely placed to discuss the 'interpenetration of poetry and medicine' (p. 16). Thelwall's astonishingly diverse career as poet, politician and medical man allows him to examine the body politic as well as the body poetic. The discussion of Keats is largely about his oddly bodily afterlife in critical dissections of his poetic corpus, and the book ends with a discussion of Beddoes's self-conscious theorization of the link between poetry and medicine. Allard's prose is sprightly, and he puns and alludes most merrily. But of greatest importance here is the understanding that he develops that these disciplines were never coherently distinct in a period in which categorization began to seem increasingly important.

Romantic poets, and Wordsworth and Coleridge in particular, are often blamed for creating a model of authorship that opposed the autonomy of the genius with money-making and professionalism. It is the contention of Brian Goldberg's *The Lake Poets and Professional Identity* that the developing eighteenth-century notion of the professional, most clearly found in the law and medicine, was in fact a formative influence on Coleridge, Southey and Wordsworth's conception of poetic identity. Goldberg begins by providing a reorientation of the concept of the professional in the long eighteenth century, discussing the cultural contexts that fed into the thinking of the Lakers, particularly with regard to earlier models of the professional writer such as Edward Young, Richard Savage, David Hume, Samuel Johnson and James Beattie. Savage's career is typically taken to be a significant step in the movement from patronage into autonomy, and Goldberg's discussion of him as a 'visionary' who foretold later developments is original and sprightly. Beattie's *Minstrel* provides a development of the model, which Goldberg reads as an assault on Hume's scepticism, before the Lake Poets take up these wandering, autonomous figures in their 1790s verse. These early experiments with such figures often end in disaster, but, for Goldberg, they provide a negative image out of which the more positive models follow. *The Ancient Mariner*, *Peter Bell* and *Madoc* are discussed in detail, showing how Cowper's influence helped the Lakers rehabilitate the itinerant model. Goldberg moves from textual examples to public debates in the book's final section, which delicately threads through the contradictions and difficulties encountered in Southey and Wordsworth's attempts to make public claims for the poet as an autonomous and honourable cultural labourer. This is a hugely ambitious book, but that ambition is well supported with a wealth of knowledge both poetical and contextual. While it attacks a central prop of constructions of the Romantic (the opposition to professions), the book's real value is contained in the detail and the breadth of its argument about the evolution of a cultural concept across a century.

Andrew Franta's *Romanticism and the Rise of the Mass Public* argues that awareness of the emergence of a mass reading public produced a formative effect on Romantic poetry that was not simply negative. Rather, an awareness of the changed nature of reception becomes an element internal to the act of poetic creation. Franta is not concerned with recovering the audiences that Romantic poetry may have reached or did reach, but with how the poems themselves register the idea of audience, and how a concern with reception shapes those poems. Franta's conception of the relationship between poem and audience differs from the work of Lucy Newlyn [2000] in that he challenges the idea that the relationship between poet and mass market was typically anxious. For Franta reception is structured in terms not of anxiety but of collaboration. Franta offers a series of readings of the way that reception is incorporated into poetic production in Wordsworth, Keats and Shelley that is not always wholly convincing, but can frequently illuminate particular poems. Shelley recognizes the way in which his poetry cedes agency to future readers, allowing a collaborative production of meaning, while Keats recognizes the significance of reviews as mediators between poet and public, even as he resists the coterie factionalism of reviewing culture. One would assume that a book with this title might be placed alongside the growing interest in contemporary reading audiences, but Franta is interested not in concrete specifics and empirical facts, but in poetic ideas. The book is only the more compelling because of it.

A book which helpfully reflects on the politics of Romanticism is Kevin Gilmartin's *Writing Against Revolution: Literary Conservatism in Britain, 1790–1832*. Romanticists have had a tendency to focus on radicalism at the expense of other political perspectives, and indeed to denigrate the conservative writers of the period. Gilmartin's critical focus is admirably non-sectarian, aiming as he does to 'recover for literary studies the range and complexity of counterrevolutionary expression, and to demonstrate the enterprising and productive (rather than merely negative or reactive) presence of counterrevolutionary voices in the culture of the romantic period' (p. 9). The book has an importance to students of Romantic poetry primarily for the attention Gilmartin pays to the later careers of Coleridge and Southey, but his repositioning of the culture of the period as a whole will benefit Romantic studies. Gilmartin takes the conservatism of Coleridge and Southey seriously, developing a sophisticated argument about their developing political beliefs in relation to the changing social pressures in the period. Rather than viewing their anti-radical sentiments simply in negative terms, Gilmartin aims to fully understand their complex positions. Coleridge and Southey, Gilmartin shows, defended a conception of the political community that gradually became irrelevant.

Beyond historicism, different types of theory continued to prove interesting to Romantic scholars. 'Psycho-analytical', as Joel Faflak points out in *Romantic Psychoanalysis: The Burden of the Mystery*, was a Coleridgean neologism. Faflak takes this fact and runs with it: for him, 'Romantic poetry, by confronting the unconscious of philosophy, *invents* psychoanalysis' (p. 7). This is at first sight an unlikely claim. Psychoanalysis is typically used as a key with which critics unlock Romantic poems: as Faflak puts it, these critics 'oppose Romantic literary blindness to the theoretical insights of psycho-analysis' (p. 11). Wordsworth and Coleridge are both taken, perhaps a little simplistically, as poets with a clear sense that they may come to fully know their own minds (that this knowledge is 'terminable'). But, in poems such as *Christabel*, 'The Ruined Cottage' and *The Prelude*, the spectre of interminability raises its head. These investigations of self and trauma, visited through primal scenes (or 'spots of time') are perhaps best represented as modes of frustrated completion. Both *The Recluse* and the *Magnum Opus* remained unfinished, and both writers return to this failure compulsively in their careers. The final chapter considers Keats's *Endymion*, *Hyperion* and *The Fall of Hyperion*. The dreamy qualities of these poems are considered in terms of Keats's 'fancy', a feminized response to the masculine 'imagination', but which ultimately destabilizes gender categories. Faflak's account will seem insufficiently historicized to many, but this is a question Faflak pre-empts, offering not a 'cultural' but a 'psychological history of psychoanalysis as it emerges in Romanticism' (p. 4). That said, there are a few fairly broad stretches, not least in the rather formulaic discussion of Enlightenment philosophy. But this is a book that ought to attract substantial interest, not simply amongst Romanticists interested in psychoanalysis, but also amongst those interested in the literary basis of psychoanalysis. Steven Groarke's 'Rycroft and the Romantic Imagination' (*AI* 64[2007] 457–83) covers similar ground. Groarke assesses the contribution of Charles Rycroft to the Independent tradition of British psychoanalysis, arguing that his ideas are deeply indebted to Wordsworth and Coleridge, particularly in his understanding of symbolism, interpretation and the primary and secondary imaginations.

One of the more significant contributions to Romantic studies this year, though only fitfully concerned with poetry, was two special editions of *Studies in Romanticism* devoted to revisiting Derridean criticism. David L. Clark's 'Lost and Found in Translation: Romanticism and the Legacies of Jacques Derrida' (*SiR* 46[2007] 161–82) opens the collection, and notices that Derrida had relatively little to say about British Romanticism. But Clark goes on to argue that his intervention in the academic postmodern is such that he remains a constant presence. In 'Derrida's Ghosts: The State of our Debt' (*SiR* 46[2007] 183–201) David Simpson provides an elegant account of the way Derrida shapes and unsettles Romantic literary criticism, specifically with regard to *Specters of Marx*. Orrin N.C. Wang takes this discussion a step further, proposing a spectral 'ghost theory' with regard to the work of and the work in mourning, in 'Ghost Theory' (*SiR* 46[2007] 203–25). Marc Redfield's 'Aesthetics, Theory and the Profession of Literature: Derrida and Romanticism' (*SiR* 46[2007] 227–46) finds that one of Derrida's legacies was a 'romanticism that claims him even as it disowns or tries to ignore him' (p. 246). Sara Guyer's 'The Rhetoric of Survival and the Possibility of Romanticism' (*SiR* 46[2007] 247–63) looks at legality and punishment with regard to Derrida's later work, moving through work by Shelley and Wordsworth on the death penalty. Theresa M. Kelly's 'Reading Justice: From Derrida to Shelley and Back' (*SiR* 46[2007] 267–87) considers Derrida's later work, which challenged the notion that deconstruction has nothing to do with justice, in relation to Shelley's *Prometheus Unbound*. Kelly is confessedly rather impatient with Shelley's idealism, but the essay is a superb treatment of both Derrida and Shelley that interrogates notions of justice, law, force and undecidability. David Farrell Krell's 'Two Apothecaries: Novalis and Derrida' (*SiR* 46[2007] 289–309) notes how the Romantic view of nature was commonly 'as threatening as it was propitious' (p. 291) before arguing that both Novalis and Derrida should be considered as apothecaries, relating Novalis's 'pharmaceutical principle' to Derrida's 'Plato's Pharmacy'. Tilottama Rajan's 'First Outline of a System of Theory: Schelling and the Margins of Philosophy, 1799–1815' (*SiR* 46[2007] 311–35) has less to say about Derrida, but nonetheless offers a compelling argument about Schelling's development of a 'psychoanalysis of philosophy' (p. 312). In 'Singularities: On a Motif in Derrida and Romantic Thought (Kant's Aesthetics, Rousseau's Autobiography)' (*SiR* 46[2007] 337–60), Ian Balfour takes an unlikely topic for the philosopher of différance, singularity. Like many of the contributors, Balfour focuses on writers whom Derrida himself commented upon, thus restricting the possibility of references to British Romantic poets. Yet these issues suggest that, while Derrida remains at something of a remove from much Romantic criticism, his presence in other strains of criticism is remarkably potent, not to say complex. Particularly pleasing is the range of Derridean texts covered by some very accomplished scholars.

Robert Mitchell and Ron Broglio guest-edit a special edition of *Romantic Circles Praxis Series*, entitled 'Romanticism and the New Deleuze'. The work of Gilles Deleuze has not had quite the impact on Romantic studies that one might have expected, and this collection of essays ought to prompt further investigation. Mitchell opens the collection with 'The Transcendental: Deleuze, P.B. Shelley, and the Freedom of Immobility' (*RCPS* [2007] 27 paras), which uses Deleuze's understanding of Kant's use of rhythm to return to Shelley's 'Mont Blanc'. Mitchell offers a surprisingly formal reading of the poem, brilliantly showing how its rhythmic structure connects with its thematic content, and how that process commands readers' sensations. David Collings extends this essay in a response to Mitchell, 'Rhyming Sensation in "Mont Blanc": In Response to Rob Mitchell' (*RCPS* [2007] 12 paras). Collings takes Mitchell's model a step further, arguing that 'complex ironies of [Shelley's] embrace of the sublime' add another layer of 'discordant harmony' to the Deleuzian/Kantian pattern in the poem. Ron Broglio's 'Wandering in the Landscape with Wordsworth and Deleuze' (*RCPS* [2007] 10 paras) uses Deleuze to show how the 'privileged interiority of the subject is just another surface without depth', 'flattening' Romanticism in the process. One wonders whether Deleuze is necessary to complete a process that most Romanticists would agree has already happened, but the interest in bodies, monstrosity and madness that Broglio develops is truly fascinating.

Toby Benis introduces an edition of *The Wordsworth Circle* in honour of Karl Kroeber. Kroeber's interest in the connections between ecology and the humanities is well served in a number of essays collected. Carl Woodring's entertaining 'Centaurs Unnaturally Fabulous' (*WC* 38[2007] 4–12) tracks the use of centaurs in literature through Keats, Shelley and Hunt up to the twentieth century. James C. McKusick follows the 'jug-jug' of the nightingale through literary history, from Ovid to the Romantics, in 'The Return of the Nightingale' (*WC* 38[2007] 34–40), mobilizing Kroeber's ecocriticism to read the nightingale as both a 'literary *topos*' and 'a biological organism that thrives in a specific habitat' (p. 34). Joseph Viscomi's 'Wordsworth, Gilpin and the Vacant Mind' (*WC* 38[2007] 40–9) offers a reading of 'Lines left upon a Seat in a Yew-tree'. It is vital, Viscomi argues, that we understand the lines as written, not spoken. Wordsworth, as Viscomi's elegant piece shows, was seeking a perspective distant from Burke's sublime and Gilpin's picturesque. Mark Jones picks up on Kroeber's term 'population thinking' in a discussion of Keats's romance plots in ' "Population Thinking": Keats and the Romance of Public Thinking' (*WC* 38[2007] 63–70). Jones subtly threads through Keats's expressions of contempt for public opinion in the form of reviews, but notes that he is just as capable of a 'quixotic, self-enabling "ardour"' (p. 69) with regard to the public determination of credit. In a wonderfully wide-ranging essay, 'From the Fossils to the Clones: On Verbal and Visual Narrative' (*WC* 38[2007] 77–83), Marilyn Gaull discusses the 1790s in terms of a relationship with time and orality. 'Romantic writers and thinkers, painters and shopkeepers were the first generation to live in a world that contained fossils and clones' (p. 82) and we, as she demonstrates, are very much their heirs. David Simpson's essay on Southey is discussed below.

Sound in Romantic poetry was discussed in four very different essays in *The Wordsworth Circle*. Michael O'Neill provides an elegant musing on Romantic poets' use of sound patterns and their possible connection with sense in ' "Driven as in surges": Texture and Voice in Romantic Poetry' (*WC* 38[2007] 91–3). Jeffrey C. Robinson's 'Romantic Poetry: The Possibilities for Improvisation' (*WC* 38[2007] 94–100) sees poets such as Byron, Shelley, Keats, Beddoes, Barry Cornwall and others engaging with the '*improvvisatore*' to place this ephemeral art at 'the center of Romantic concerns' (p. 94). In a subtle, culturally informed piece, Robinson discusses such writers' engagement with the tropes of improvisation in a written form. Terence Hoagwood's 'The Textualizing of Sound: Romantic-Period Pseudo-Songs' (*WC* 38[2007] 100–4) argues that a new interest in typography in the period changed the way songs were understood. Hoagwood's important article focuses on Moore's *Irish Melodies* and Scott's *Minstrelsy of the Scottish Border*, exploring the ways in which they 'simultaneously perpetrate and lament, exploit and criticise' (p. 102) the loss of orality that typography introduced. Morton D. Paley also considers sound effects in Coleridge, returning to the borrowings from *Christabel* in Scott's *Lay of the Last Minstrel* in a pleasant article entitled 'Coleridge, Scott, and "This mescolanza of measures"' (*WC* 38[2007] 104–7).

Jennifer Davis Michael's 'Ocean Meets Ossian: Staffa as Romantic Symbol' (*Romanticism* 13[2007] 1–14) considers the frequent representations of Staffa in Romantic poetry and contemporary travel writing. In discussion of Wordsworth, Keats and J.M.W. Turner, she produces an excellent reading of the site's significance in the history of nineteenth-century conceptions of the natural and the artificial. Those interested in the afterlife of the Romantic poets may be interested in Jeffrey Meyers's ' "Daisy Miller" and the Romantic Poets' (*HJR* 28[2007] 94–100), which tracks Henry James's numerous references to Byron, Keats and Shelley, all poets who died abroad. Also worth considering in this section, though largely of interest to educationalists rather than Romanticists, is David Halpin's *Romanticism and Education: Love, Heroism and Imagination in Pedagogy*. Halpin shows the continuing relevance of Romantic ideas to modern culture, studying the work of Wordsworth, Coleridge, Blake and Hazlitt, arguing that their conception of 'childhood, heroism, love, imagination and criticism' (p. 10) ought to influence and shape contemporary pedagogy.

Worth commending here is Uttara Natarajan's *The Romantic Poets: A Guide to Criticism*. The book aims to survey the highly complex development of criticism of Romanticism for the uninitiated undergraduate, providing a view of the 'field at a glance' (p. 2). The story of Romantic criticism is, of course, the story of the Romantic canon, and Natarajan quite properly accords a chapter to each of the 'Big Six', poets who continue to dominate the field even if only as a dominant discourse against which canon-busting critics define themselves. The chapter on Wordsworth is exemplary. Natarajan opens with the full text of Hazlitt's wonderfully ambivalent *Spirit of the Age* portrait, and also discusses important contemporary criticism in the *Edinburgh Review* and *Blackwood's Magazine*. The narrative then threads through Matthew Arnold and A.C. Bradley, leading up to Geoffrey Hartman's seminal account of the Simplon Pass episode. This is accompanied by a superbly annotated list of criticism in this tradition. From here things get more complicated, but Natarajan covers the ground dispassionately and elegantly. Alan Liu's revision of Hartman is rightly described as 'the *tour de force* of the new historicist criticism of Wordsworth' (p. 90), and it is balanced by a selection from David Bromwich's 'restitution and reclamation' (p. 105) of the poet. Clearly, covering all of the complexities of critical opinion regarding these poets would be impossible, but Natarajan usefully points the interested student in ecocritical, oriental and gendered directions. The book ends with an important, though perhaps underplayed, discussion of the expanding canon, particularly with reference to Clare and women poets. This is a truly useful addition to scholarship, and ought to assist the next generation of Romantic scholars for some time to come.

Wordsworth studies benefited this year from a number of theoretical approaches. Simon Jarvis, in *Wordsworth's Philosophic Song*, presents a significant argument not simply about Wordsworth, but about the way literary critics connect philosophy with literature. Many critics have seen Coleridge's suggestion that Wordsworth write a great philosophical epic as a stultifying burden that we can only be glad Wordsworth failed to complete. Wordsworth's best poetry, in this view, is completed in spite of his (or Coleridge's) philosophical ambitions. Others have explored Wordsworth's attachment to Godwinian and Coleridgean philosophies, seeing Wordsworth as a systematic thinker. Both perspectives, as Jarvis observes, maintain an opposition between poetry and philosophy that Wordsworth may not himself have held. Jarvis returns to *The Recluse*, Wordsworth's promised but incomplete 'philosophic song', to suggest that 'the song itself, *as song*, is philosophic... that instead of being a sort of thoughtless ornament or reliquary for thinking, verse is itself a kind of cognition, with its own resistances and difficulties' (p. 4). A particularly innovative element is Jarvis's deliberate habit of not giving the names of the theorists and critics he refers to except in footnotes. This lends a fluidity to the book, but it also importantly changes the way that the argument functions. The names of Adorno, Derrida, Foucault and others often act as a kind of benediction in literary criticism, a guarantor of theoretical sophistication without any need to engage with the ideas of these writers. Jarvis's technique allows his book to engage with the theories of these theorists, which is the more appropriate given that it is the work of precisely such writers which has done so much to question the monolithic authority of authorship and names. The first half, 'Counter-Spirits', acts as a philosophical introduction which questions many of the assumptions made by literary scholars and by Romanticists in particular. With remarkable clarity, Jarvis shows how critics have misread Marx's conception of 'ideology', particularly in 'materialist' critiques of Wordsworthian escapism. Jarvis attacks much New Historicist criticism, but he does so from an unusually strong position. Much literary scholarship includes references to philosophical and theoretical texts that are slight or even tokenistic, but Jarvis immerses his discussion of Wordsworth in a formidably vast volume of reading across several centuries. As important as the idealism/materialism binary is the distinction between the mind and the body. It is refreshing to read literary criticism that goes beyond the more fashionable twentieth-century philosophers and fully elucidates complex aspects of Augustine, Descartes and Malebranche. The poetry itself risks getting lost amid so much philosophy, but Jarvis makes use of some superb close readings of early drafts towards *The Recluse*, the 'Intimations' ode and *The Prelude*. These are remarkably subtle and pay the serious attention to the complexity of Wordsworth's language that it warrants.

Andrew Bennett's *Wordsworth Writing* takes issue with one of the most pervasive myths about Wordsworth, that he composed as he walked, and indeed that he was a poet 'who, paradoxically, doesn't write poetry' (p. 4). Wordsworth's apparent opposition to the physical act of inscription, as Bennett argues, is tied to a conception of his verse as 'natural', free and unfettered by technologies of writing. The book is largely concerned to investigate the relationship between writing and speech. The work of Jacques Derrida is a constant presence, and Bennett also draws on the work of David R. Olsen and Roy Harris to argue that 'the integration of speech with writing irreversibly transforms' (p. 62). Wordsworth, he argues, is indeed a poet who wrote, but of greater importance is the idea that he is a poet for whom the nature of writing was an integral part of his poetry. For Wordsworth, writing is traumatic. The pain which produces his best work should not be located in his biographical past (as in psychoanalytic criticism) or in political history (as in the dominant mode of Romantic criticism), but in the act of writing itself. Where much criticism has taken writing as a psychological cure of a more or less political nature, Bennett suggests that, rather than leading to 'certainty, fulfilment and resolution', expression leads to 'an eventual refusal or rejection of writing itself' (p. 150). Wordsworth's infamous creative 'falling-off' from 1805 to 1850 is explained, for Bennett, by his retreat from writing, his refuge in poetic convention (those endless sonnets) and amanuenses. It is a compelling thesis, but an uneven book. Bennett's theoretically informed concern with speech and writing is refreshing and convincing, and he produces a number of excellent readings of major poems including 'Tintern Abbey' and *The Prelude*. Yet he takes rather a long time knocking down critical commonplaces, and accordingly a number of these readings lack the full and rounded discussion that Bennett's theoretical apparatus merits. But this important study should prompt much criticism that begins again to take seriously the nature of writing.

A related but ultimately quite different book is Peter Simonsen's *Wordsworth and Word-Preserving Arts: Typographic Inscription, Ekphrasis and Posterity in the Later Work*. Bennett challenges the myth that Wordsworth did not write; Simonsen challenges the myth that Wordsworth did not print. We typically think of Wordsworth as opposed to the emergent mass print market and its 'reading public', preferring to circulate his works in manuscript amongst a coterie of friends and family that he knew intimately. Yet, as Simonsen demonstrates, Wordsworth grew increasingly interested in the visual, printed nature of his work as his career progressed (connecting his work to that of Franta, discussed above). Through some ingenious close readings of neglected verse such as the *River Duddon* sonnet sequence, *Yarrow Revisited* and his inscriptions, Simonsen proposes a model of 'visual poetry', a kind of poetry that combines the verbal with the physical. Wordsworth's interest in typography in these years led him to use the physical nature of words as part of their meaning. Simonsen draws attention to Wordsworth's increasing interest in ekphrasis, particularly in his friendship with Sir George Beaumont, and in the visual culture of an age that was increasingly influenced by the newly public nature of art. Yet if this Wordsworth seems daringly modern, he was also in this period becoming both politically and aesthetically conservative, and Simonsen does not neglect this. Wordsworth began fully articulating, in the face of the growth of the print audience, his theory of the poet's true audience being one in posterity. Simonsen argues that the poet writing for a posthumous audience must find a durable form for his poetry, hence his interest in print. To appreciate this late poetry is to appreciate its placement in a different culture to that of the 'great decade', and Simonsen does well not to attempt to 'save' Wordsworth from his conservative self. This is a compelling read, and an eloquent call for fuller attention to be paid to both late Wordsworth and the literary culture of the 1820s and 1830s. Simonsen covers the same territory in article form in 'Italic Typography and Wordsworth's Later Sonnets as Visual Poetry' (*SEL* 47[2007] 863–80).

The later Wordsworth was in fact well served this year, despite the critical neglect that Simonsen notes. In 'Wordsworth's *Excursion* in Romantic Philanthropy' (*ERR* 18[2007] 43–68), J. Andrew Hubbell reassesses the politics of a poem that, while its poetics have been considered in a more positive light, remains under a weight of opprobrium as the first major fruit of Wordsworth's newly Tory political stance. Hubbell asks us to reconsider this view, arguing that Wordsworth's interest in philanthropy might not be as conservative as once thought. Stephen Gill's 'Wordsworth and *The River Duddon*' (*EIC* 57[2007] 22–41) considers Wordsworth's dedicatory 'To the Rev. Dr. W –', arguing that it is 'delicately connected' (p. 22) to the *River Duddon* volume as a whole. Gill's elegant and hugely well-informed piece importantly discusses the sonnet sequence both as a cultural artefact that placed Wordsworth emphatically amid his native Lakes and as a literary document of real merit.

Wordsworth's ambition to reject a sterile 'poetic diction' in favour of a language 'really spoken by men' has been chewed over long and hard since 1798, but in an excellent study by Susan Manly, *Language, Custom and Nation in the 1790s: Locke, Tooke, Wordsworth, Edgeworth* (also discussed in section 1), the full political resonance of such attempts is fully evaluated. Language, as Romanticists are often keen to point out, had a keen political significance in the period. But what has been missed, Manly argues, is the central significance of the work of John Locke to this tradition. For Locke, language was significant as a collectively produced enterprise, and this collectivity gave a political charge to the way in which it was mobilized by the likes of John Horne Tooke in the 1790s. The first half of the book establishes this intellectual tradition, but the second, which concentrates on Wordsworth and Edgeworth, is of greatest interest to this section. It is Edgeworth, and not the young Wordsworth, who emerges as the more consistent inheritor of Locke and Tooke's radical linguistics. The Lockean tradition of 'egalitarianism and communitarianism' (p. 105) combines in Wordsworth with a Burkean insistence on continuity and a resistance to novelty. It is a far less radical Wordsworth that Manly offers, one whose Burkean conservatism ultimately undermines the radical thrust of his appeal to common language. Given the significance of Wordsworth's statements on language, and the continuing interest in the politics of language, it is an analysis that should not be ignored.

Christopher R. Miller takes issue with the use of the word 'epiphany' to describe Wordsworthian moments of interruption and revelation in 'Wordsworth's Anatomies of Surprise' (*SiR* 46[2007] 409–31), proposing instead a new term: 'surprise'. Miller carefully threads a path through the intricacies of poems such as 'Surprised by Joy' and the 'Matthew' poems, elucidating the cognitive elements that allow such moments to become both events and contemplations of those events such that 'the poem formally enacts the feeling of surprise for the reader' (p. 425). *The Prelude*, as usual, received a great deal of attention. Noel Jackson's 'Archaeologies of Perception: Reading Wordsworth after Foucault' (*ERR* 18[2007] 175–85) argues that Wordsworth's critique of French sensationalist psychology in *The Prelude*, along with its representation of psychology as subject to historical change in Book II of the poem, signifies an anticipation of Foucault's insight that the category of 'man' emerged in historically specific conditions. Ross Hamilton's 'Deep History: Association and Natural Philosophy in Wordsworth's Poetry' (*ERR* 18[2007] 459–81) reworks Roland Barthes's idea of understanding the incorporation of earlier texts in a text, but moves beyond 'influence' into 'concepts so thoroughly absorbed that they resonated within the vocabulary of everyday life' (p. 460). Hamilton performs a remarkable work of excavation in key passages of *The Prelude* to work out Wordsworth's complex absorption of the collision between Newtonian and Enlightenment ideas. Kelly Grovier's 'Dream Walker: A Wordsworth Mystery Solved' (*Romanticism* 13[2007] 156–63) convincingly offers John 'Walking' Stewart, philosopher of tennis balls and cosmology, as the source for the rambler in the Arab dream passage that opens Book V of *The Prelude*. In an elegant short piece, 'Readable Cities' (*PMLA* 122[2007] 306–9), Rachel Bowlby uses Wordsworth's *Prelude* Book VII to show why the phrase 'reading the city' has such a remarkable currency. As Bowlby points out, in the early nineteenth century, 'more and more urban reading crossed the quotidian path of the city dweller' (p. 308) such that nineteenth-century walkers saw the city with 'reading eyes' (p. 309).

Tom Duggett considered Wordsworth's Gothicism in three articles. 'Celtic Night and Gothic Grandeur: Politics and Antiquarianism in Wordsworth's *Salisbury Plain*' (*Romanticism* 13[2007] 164–76) describes how Wordsworth abandoned the Celtic radicalism he had adopted on his return from France in 1792. The turn to a specifically English interest in the past should be considered evidence not of a reactionary turn, however, but a commitment to a distinct tradition of Gothic radicalism. Wordsworth's 1809 prose pamphlet *The Convention of Cintra* is considered in 'Wordsworth's Gothic Politics and the Convention of Cintra' (*RES* 58[2007] 186–211). The pamphlet, for Duggett, moves between the poet's past radical and future conservative political positions by adopting a 'Gothic' standpoint influenced by the 1790s debates over the French Revolution, particularly in the writing of Edmund Burke and John Thelwall. In ' "A poet and an Englishman": The *Gentleman's Magazine* and the Gothic Style of *The Recluse*' (*WC* 38[2007] 211–14), Duggett argues that the 'Gothic church' allusion in *The Recluse* continues the tenor of these debates, but that, post-Napoleon, to deny that Gothic was English was to 'side with the defeated Napoleonic regime' (p. 213). Wordsworth's refusal in *The Excursion* to outline a poetical 'system' might be considered a deliberate mirroring of debates over the unwritten British constitution.

Quentin Bailey, in ' "Dangerous and suspicious trades": Wordsworth's Pedlar and the Board of Police Revenue' (*Romanticism* 13[2007] 244–56), fleshes out the historical context behind Wordsworth's choice of a pedlar as the hero of *The Ruined Cottage*, written in a period in which pedlars had become the subject of attempts to control their movements. Wordsworth's politics were also discussed by Paul Christian Jones in 'The Politics of Poetry: The *Democratic Review* and the Gallows Verse of William Wordsworth and John Greenleath Whittier' (*AmPer* 17[2007] 1–25). Jones considers how the populist New York *Democratic Review* made Wordsworth a device through which it prosecuted its aim of insisting on poetry as a politically liberal tool by discussing his *Sonnets upon the Punishment of Death*. Mark Canuel's *The Shadow of Death: Literature, Romanticism, and the Subject of Punishment*, discussed in detail in section 1, also considers these sonnets, placing them in contrast with the *Salisbury Plain* poems. Both discuss capital punishment, the earlier opposing it, the latter defending it. But these poems mirror the contending forces within penal reform. The Salisbury Plain poems 'oppose the penalty of death at the same time as they reinforce it with displays of violence' while the *Sonnets* 'can only regard the horror of judicial murder itself as a threat to the poet's imagination and as an insult to his readership' (p. 80).

Joshua Gonsalves's 'Reading Idiocy: Wordsworth's "The Idiot Boy" ' (*WC* 38[2007] 121–30) seeks to correct a too-simplistic reading of the pleasure Wordsworth took in rereading 'The Idiot Boy'. Gonsalves mounts a three-pronged recontextualization, opening up the poem by adducing Enlightenment understandings of idiocy, Platonic philosophy and Southey's understanding of the topic in 'The Idiot', to produce a temperate and subtly expressed reading of the issues. Wordsworth's interest in children was usefully contrasted with Blake's by Galia Benziman in 'Two Patterns of Child Neglect: Blake and Wordsworth' (*PAns* 5[2007] 167–97), also discussed below. Benziman challenges the idea that Puritan and Romantic notions of the child form a neat opposition, arguing instead that Puritan and catechetical thinking forms a residue in the Romantic period. Also worth mentioning here is Arnd Bohm's 'Borrowing from Robert Merry in *Descriptive Sketches* (1793)'

(*WC* 38[2007] 147–8), which is particularly significant not so much for clearing up an editorial issue as for proving that Wordsworth had direct knowledge of the Della Cruscans. Bohm also discusses Wordsworth's afterlife in a Herman Melville short story in 'Wordsworth in Melville's "Cock-a-doodle-do"' (*Leviathan* 9[2007] 25–41). Melville's complex reinterpretation of 'Resolution and Independence' depends, for Bohm, on a 'cynical caricature' of Wordsworth driven by a 'profound critique of Wordsworth's theory of language' (p. 27) and politics. Worth noting here is Robert Hemmings's 'Landscape as Palimpsest: Wordsworthian Topography in the War Writings of Blunden and Sassoon' (*PLL* 43[2007] 264–90), a fine article which insists on the importance of Wordsworth's sense of landscape to the poetry of Siegfried Sassoon and Edmund Blunden. An ambitious article that goes beyond the bounds of Wordsworth studies is Ortwin de Graef's 'Grave Livers: On the Modern Element in Wordsworth, Arnold, and Warner' (*ELH* 74[2007] 145–69). De Graef begins with Wordsworth's conception of 'low life' as 'real life' in 'Resolution and Independence' before constructing a rather ambitious argument which seeks to pin down the modern condition. Michael Ferber offers translations and a brief discussion of Charles-Augustin Sainte-Beuve's two imitations of Wordsworth sonnets in 'Sainte-Beuve's "Imitations" of Two Sonnets by Wordsworth' (*WC* 38[2007] 215–17). Ian H. Thompson's 'William Wordsworth, Landscape Architect' (*WC* 38[2007] 196–203) continues the efforts of those who have sought to remake Wordsworth as ecowarrior, arguing that his interest in landscape gardening (particularly as expressed in his prose works) suggests he is an important intellectual precursor of those gardeners 'who have incorporated ecological insights into their design philosophies' (p. 196). Deborah Kennedy's 'Wordsworth's *Poems* of 1807 and the Haunting Cry of Alice Fell' (*WC* 38[2007] 203–8) takes the bicentenary of Wordsworth's collection to insist on the importance of reading the poems in their original context. In a rather subtle short piece, 'Wordsworth's "A Slumber Did My Spirit Seal"' (*Expl* 65[2007] 71–5), John Hughes reads the poem in terms of Wordsworth's loss of his mother, but he also considers why it is that the poem engages readers to ponder in this way.

The *Charles Lamb Bulletin* published a selection of lectures from the Wordsworth Winter School. Michael O'Neill's '"The tremble from it is spreading": A Reading of Wordsworth's "Ode: Intimations of Immortality"' (*ChLB* 139[2007] 74–90) superbly argues for the 'cultural' significance of the poem, revising Harold Bloom's reading of it as a 'crisis poem', while also providing a remarkable celebration of Wordsworth's artistry. David Chandler's 'Life Writing in Wordsworth's 1807 *Poems in Two Volumes*' (*ChLB* 139[2007] 91–106) argues that the poems in this volume are 'framed' by the problems Wordsworth encountered when revising *The Prelude*. Felicity James's 'Re-reading "Resolution and Independence"' (*ChLB* 139[2007] 107–21) uses Lewis Carroll's parody quite brilliantly to help open up the troubling nature of response in and to the poem and concludes, nicely, that Wordsworth 'ends with the last laugh' (p. 121) against his materialist critics. '"Moods of my own mind": Wordsworth and the Spontaneous' (*ChLB* 139[2007] 122–33) by Sally Bushell looks at the idea of spontaneity and the effect it has on Wordsworth's creativity with regard to the 1807 *Poems*, and the collection concludes with George Soule's highly enjoyable '"The Solitary Reaper" and other Poems "Written During a Tour of Scotland"' (*ChLB* 139[2007] 134–44). Also on the subject of Wordsworth and Scotland was Fiona Stafford's '"Inhabited solitudes": Wordsworth in Scotland, 1803' (in Duff and Jones, eds., *Scotland, Ireland and the Romantic Aesthetic*, pp. 93–113). Stafford explores the sense of disappointment and emptiness expressed in the Intimations ode, suggesting that Scottish tradition, literature and landscape provided something of a creative catalyst.

The publication of *Faustus, from the German of Goethe. Translated by Samuel Taylor Coleridge*, edited by Frederick Burwick and James McKusick, was undoubtedly the most talked about event in Coleridge studies in 2007. The reviews of the volume have been mixed, to say the least. The most strident critique is that offered by Roger Paulin, William St Clair and Elinor Shaffer (*'A Gentleman of Literary Eminence': A Review Essay*), although others have been rather more positive, notably Susanne Schmid (*WC* 38[2007] 157–8). The debate will doubtless roll on, but it should not obscure the remarkable work of textual and cultural scholarship that the volume represents. Given Coleridge's reputation, then and now, for promising more than he could deliver, it has been easy to dismiss as naive Goethe's claim that Coleridge was at work on a translation of his *Faustus*. Coleridge had begun work on a translation for John Murray in 1814, only to abandon it. But in the early 1820s, following the publication of de Staël's *De l'Allemagne* and a series of illustrations from *Faustus*, publishers realized that the time was ripe for a full translation. Coleridge provided it for Boosey and Sons in 1821. The translation, primarily in blank verse, but with prose plot summaries of around half of the play, is presented with full annotation alongside other contemporary translations by de Staël, George Soane, Daniel Boileau, John Anster and Lord Francis Leveson-Gower, and the illustrations by Moritz Retsch that accompanied the volume. The volume concludes with a stylometric analysis performed by McKusick which compares Coleridge's translation with *Remorse* and texts by other likely candidates.

Burwick's introduction goes well beyond attempting to prove that Coleridge was the author (although this is the primary aim), providing a thorough and comprehensive discussion of the cultural mechanics behind the production of the text. Burwick also provides excellent close readings of different versions of the play which speak of an extraordinary immersion in British and German Romantic writing. What Burwick shows most convincingly is that this translation is certainly the best. The blank verse, as he puts it, moves 'freely and yet with... harmony and coherence' (p. xlvi) while the translation displays an understanding of the complex philosophical influences that Goethe adduced. Given this, Coleridge seems a likely author, and Burwick's argument is thorough and forceful. Yet one of the more productive suggestions put forward by Paulin, St Clair and Schaffer is the notion that the translation 'could have been presented as a matter on which questions of attribution are more open' (p. 31). The question of Coleridge's authorship is doubtless intriguing to Coleridgeans, but as Romantic scholarship moves increasingly in the direction of the history of the book and an interest in the materiality of printed texts, such strenuous debating over authorship seems a little passé.

Indeed, one of the major contributions of this volume is the knowledge Burwick and McKusick provide of the textual history of the translation and the way in which Goethe's text entered the British public sphere.

The case for the defence was sharpened by Burwick in a follow up, 'On Coleridge as Translator of *Faustus: From the German of Goethe*' (*WC* 38[2007] 158–62). Burwick dismisses convincingly the (admittedly unlikely) claim by Paulin et al. that George Soane is the better candidate, and concludes with some aplomb that 'All evidence points to Coleridge as the translator of *Faustus from the German of Goethe*. No evidence points elsewhere' (p. 161). Burwick's 'Coleridge's Art of Translation' (*WC* 38[2007] 108–12) offers an elegant reading of a wide variety of translations by Coleridge, concentrating on the difference Coleridge saw between a 'translation' and a 'transferred' work, closer to a retelling. Yet as Burwick shows, this distinction was never wholly maintained: Coleridge produced a range of strategies for coping with the untranslatable, involving 'varying degrees of appropriation and intervention' (p. 112).

The Reception of S.T. Coleridge in Europe, edited by Elinor Shaffer and Edoardo Zuccato, is the latest in an important series of books which address the Europe-wide reception of major literary figures. The book begins with a superb timeline compiled by Paul Barnaby, opening in 1772, sweeping across Romanian, Italian, Hungarian, Slovenian and other editions, translations and monographs, and concluding with the publication of *Faustus* in 2007. One of the strengths of Burwick and McKusick's edition is the attention it pays to Coleridge's two-way connections with German literature, and this work is extended significantly in this hugely important volume. Coleridge's poetical influence is studied, but he is also placed as a significant part of a 'Europe-wide intellectual movement' (p. 2). Seamus Perry opens the volume with a discussion of his English reception amongst a tradition of poet-critics such as Arnold and Eliot, but the majority of the volume focuses further afield. The importance of Gustave Doré's illustrations of the *Ancient Mariner* to French interpretations is discussed by Gilles Soubigon, who sees in the relationship a 'great mutual enrichment' (p. 87), while Michael John Kooy ably discusses the complexities of Coleridge's pre-Doré French reception. Coleridge's German reception pre-war is discussed by Frederick Burwick, after which Hans Werner Breunig picks up the baton, and there are chapters on the Italian, Portuguese, Czech, Polish and Russian receptions. Reception takes fascinating, unexpected forms: Spanish liberal exiles in London in the nineteenth century took to Coleridge; he became popular as a poet in twentieth-century Italy (unlike Wordsworth) while having a complex place in Italian Idealist and aesthetic philosophy, while Czech critics often found him too airy and visionary. Discussion of René Wellek's interest in Coleridge is a good example of the critical methodology employed: Wellek's Coleridge 'cannot be fully understood without reference to the culture in which [he was] educated' (p. 11). This is, accordingly, a hugely ambitious book, tracing not simply Coleridge's afterlives, but also the developmental causes behind those versions of the poet. As such, it is an incomplete project, but the book is intended as a prompt to further scholarship as much as anything, and it will assuredly provide that.

Much of the work on Coleridge focused on his philosophical prose writings, and this element of his work is discussed in section 2 above. Of particular relevance to his poetry are Paul Hamilton's *Coleridge and German Philosophy: The Poet in the Land of Logic* and Ben Brice's *Coleridge and Scepticism*. Brice's book offers a notably graceful account of Coleridgean religion which was, indeed, something of a hot topic in 2007. Peter Larkin's 'Repetition, Difference and Liturgical Participation in Coleridge's "The Ancient Mariner"' (*L&T* 21[2007] 146–59) is a remarkably imaginative treatment of the troubling matter of the moral in the poem. Larkin begins with the Welsh poet David Jones, who saw the poem's failure to reach a coherent moral conclusion as a failure of imagination, before considering the mariner's narrative telling and its divergence from 'reality' in terms of postmodern theology. *The Ancient Mariner* is also considered in theological terms by Thomas Dilworth in 'Spatial Form in *The Rime of the Ancient Mariner* and the Problem of God' (*RES* 58[2007] 500–30). Dilworth's essay is an intriguing meditation on what he sees as two major symbolic patterns: the shooting of the albatross and the blessing of the water snakes. This patterning of the events in the Mariner's narrative has gone unnoticed until now, and the 'concentric pairings of images' (p. 500) that Dilworth uncovers with remarkable dexterity are certainly worthy of our attention. Dilworth also discusses the poem in 'Parallel Light Shows in Coleridge's *The Rime of the Ancient Mariner*' (*Expl* 65[2007] 212–15), in which he discovers an unexpected thematic significance in the connection between the maritime 'corposant' effect and the Southern Lights. William A. Ulmer's 'The Rhetorical Occasion of "This Lime-Tree Bower My Prison"' (*Romanticism* 13[2007] 15–27) argues that Coleridge's poem offers not so much self-consolation for the loss of 'promised good', but consolation to Charles Lamb that is 'less imaginative than theological' (p. 15), and, specifically, Unitarian. Too often Unitarianism is used as a shorthand for political dissent, but Ulmer's thorough understanding of the theological issues produces a much more rounded perspective. Ulmer's '*Christabel* and the Origin of Evil' (*SP* 104[2007] 376–407) also considers Coleridge's Unitarianism. Coleridge planned to write a poem on the origin of evil, a poem that Ulmer speculates ultimately became *Christabel*. For Unitarians, original sin was a 'state of guiltless corruption' (p. 377), a moral ambivalence which Coleridge dramatizes in the poem. Gregory M. Leadbetter's recondite 'Coleridge and the Languages of Paganism' (*WC* 38[2007] 117–21) takes Ronald Hutton's *The Triumph of the Moon* [1999] to task for insufficiently recognizing Coleridge's paganism. The four languages of a contemporary paganism that Hutton uncovers are all to be found in Coleridge, but Coleridge does not simply give voice to them; he uses them to forge his own language. Coleridge's symbolism was discussed this year by Kazuko Oguro in 'From Sight to Insight: Coleridge's Quest for Symbol in Nature' (*ColB* 29[2007] 74–80).

Two superb articles addressed Coleridge in *Studies in Romanticism*. 'Shakespeare, Coleridge, Intellecturition' (*SiR* 46[2007] 77–104) finds Theodore Leinwand enraptured in the complex of exclamations and qualifications in Coleridge's lectures on and annotations to Shakespeare. Leinwald insists that Coleridge's Shakespeare 'always exercises judgement'

(p. 79): that is, he is a philosophical poet. Leinwald's excellent essay engages with Coleridgean thinking about thinking, placing this habit of writing in the context of his need to keep talking. Robert Mitchell's 'The Fane of Tescalipoca: S.T. Coleridge on the Sacrificial Economies of Systems in the 1790s' (*SiR* 46[2007] 105–27) is a subtle, original take on an oft-discussed topic, Coleridge's interest in systems. This interest has been widely discussed in relation to German philosophy, but Mitchell shows how important (in the 1790s at least) Adam Smith's *Theory of Moral Sentiments* was to Coleridge. This enormously refreshing essay argues for a reconfiguration of the political, reading poems such as 'Recantation: An Ode' and the *Ancient Mariner* in terms of their ability to 'stage multiple, and contradictory, moral and political systems' (p. 127).

Thomas Pfau's 'The Philosophy of Shipwreck: Gnosticism, Skepticism, and Coleridge's Catastrophic Modernity' (*MLN* 122[2007] 949–1004) covers bewilderingly complex philosophical ground with Pfau's customary surefooted ease. The focal point is Coleridge, but Pfau's interest is much wider, showing how understandings of knowledge in modernity (specialized, sceptical) by Blumenberg, Heidegger and others are underpinned by Gnosticism. For Coleridge, modernity is not simply a set of political problems, but a 'metaphysical catastrophe' (p. 951), and in this he unwittingly echoes the original Gnostic problem. An article for specialists, perhaps. The 'Dejection' ode is considered in an essay by Andrew Keanie that puns a pun it seems astonishing has not been punned before: 'Coleridge's Capable Negativity in "Dejection: An Ode"' (*Romanticism* 13[2007] 281–92). The ode is typically taken as a melancholy paradox, a great poem lamenting Coleridge's inability to write great poetry. But Keanie proposes the novel notion that it is the first of many poetical writings which make literary capital out of an insistent negativity. The poet in him was not dead, but had moved into other paths. Peter Larkin looks at sound in Coleridge's conversation poems in 'Coleridge Conversing: Between Soliloquy and Invocation' (*WC* 38[2007] 113–17). Larkin draws on contemporary philosophy to understand the mode as something 'looser than a genre', 'an unstable tonal register which dreams of embodying a vocal register' (p. 114).

Worth mentioning here is an excellent article (discussed in more detail in Chapter XIII) by Lauren Caldwell, 'Truncating Coleridgean Conversation and the Revisioning of "Dover Beach"' (*VP* 45[2007] 429–45). Caldwell notes how closely Coleridge's career (as a great poet who gave up poetry to be a greater critic) foreshadows Matthew Arnold's. Coleridge also stands as a ghostly foreshadowing of a present troubled self for T.S. Eliot according to Peter Lowe's 'Life as a "Ruined Man": Samuel Taylor Coleridge and T.S. Eliot's Marital Crisis' (*ES* 88[2007] 298–319). This is, for Lowe, a more 'biographical' than literary 'affinity' (p. 298): as Eliot began to face a turbulent personal life while lecturing on literary history, the figure of a poet and lecturer similarly 'ruined' seemed uncannily present. Tim May fills a scholarly gap with 'Coleridge's Slave Trade Ode and Bowles's "The African"' (*N&Q* 54[2007] 504–9) by showing that Coleridge certainly did read William Lisle Bowles's 'The African' as he prepared his Cambridge ode on the slave trade. Coleridge's critique of David Hartley's associationist philosophy is given a modern twist by Alexandra Neel in ' "A *something-nothing* out of its very contrary": The Photography of Coleridge' (*VS* 49[2007] 208–17). Neel writes clearly and sharply, arguing that Coleridge's interest in the camera obscura (all sight and no thought) is used to criticize Hartley's philosophy in the *Biographia*, which can be used to explain the tyranny of an 'I' by the 'eye' in *The Ancient Mariner*. Laura Mandell's 'Imaging Interiority: Photography, Psychology, and Lyric Poetry' (*VS* 49[2007] 218–27) (discussed in section 3(c) below) also covers photography and interiority in relation to Romantic poetry, arguing that if Gothic anticipates film, the lyric anticipates the photographer's desire to capture inner states. The lyric's deployment of typography and the mourning in print of lost sound is compellingly linked to further technological developments in the nineteenth century.

In ' "Desultory Fragments" or "Printed Works"? Coleridge's Changing Attitude to Newspaper Journalism' (*PLL* 43[2007] 24–44) Nikki Hessell continues her investigation of Coleridge's vexed understanding of the relationship between the newly emergent category of 'literature' and the newly degraded category of hack journalism. This important work is continued by Hessell in 'Coleridge and the "Rhapsody on Newspapers": A New Intertext for "Fears in Solitude" ' (*ColB* 30[2007] 27–38), which discovers a *Monthly Magazine* parody of newspaper reading and asks for a consideration of Coleridge's poems as providing 'a perspective on the nature of contemporary interpretations' (p. 27). Richard Lines's 'Coleridge and Charles Augustus Tulk' (*ChLB* 140[2007] 167–79) fills in a biographical gap with regard to the Swedenborgian Tulk. James Vigus, in 'Did Coleridge Read Plato by Anticipation?' (*ColB* 29[2007] 65–73), writes very well indeed about Coleridge's growing appreciation of Plato, puzzling through his sense of 'anticipation' and situating his thought in the context of Platonic philosophy. Barry Hough and Howard Davis present some important research with regard to Coleridge's time in Malta in 'Coleridge's Malta' (*ColB* 29[2007] 81–95). Peter Heymans's 'Reading the Animal: An Ecocritical Approach to the Discourse of the Sublime in "The Ancient Mariner" ' (*ColB* 30[2007] 17–26) juggles a remarkable array of critical balls: multiplicity and oneness, attraction and repulsion, politics and the sublime.

The Robert Southey renaissance continued apace this year, with two important books devoted to the apostate laureate. The first, David M. Craig's *Robert Southey and Romantic Apostasy: Political Argument in Britain, 1780–1840*, also discussed in section 2, shows more of an interest in Southey's political writings than in his poetry, but the thoroughgoing and complexly rendered analysis that Craig offers will be of interest to all Southeyans. Southey has been criticized both in his own lifetime and more recently for turning against his early republicanism, becoming instead a conservative, imperialistic prop of Tory despotism. Craig problematizes this narrative of 'apostasy', but he goes further than this too. Southey stands as an example of a far more complex history of ideas than has typically been allowed. Rather than simply a rejection of Enlightenment individualism in favour of Burkean Romantic collectivism, Craig suggests that the cultural picture was far less simply defined. Craig finds continuities between Southey's 1790s republicanism and his later faith in church and state that belie the caricatures so often foisted on him. This is a significant work of scholarship, using material from right across Southey's vast corpus of reviews at the *Edinburgh Annual Register*, the *Quarterly Review* and in innumerable other sources that ought to change the way Romanticists see not just Southey, but the political map of the early nineteenth century.

But if Southey is coming back into critical favour it is often in spite of his political positions. Craig points out that he was 'passionately attached to the idea of a civilising mission to the uncivilised world' (p. 142) in his writings on empire, and it is such troubling territory that Carol Bolton explores in *Writing the Empire: Robert Southey and Romantic Colonialism*. Bolton's impressively broad book makes a significant claim for Southey as one of the key thinkers on 'non-European cultures and societies during the Romantic period' (p. 3). Central to this is his poetry, for, as Bolton demonstrates, Southey offers 'an imaginative engagement with the issues of colonialism, in that Southey's responses were literary (rather than political)' (p. 11). It is this literary, imaginative spirit that ultimately proves unsettling in the narrative Bolton pursues: the very poetical nature of these engagements often betokens a certain loss of control over the subject matter, and a descent into some rather lurid fears and anxieties about colonial 'others'. Bolton takes a different colonial area for each chapter, opening with an excellent discussion of Southey's influential, if complex, engagement with slavery from the 1790s into his conservative later years. Southey's Welsh/American epic, *Madoc*, is again considered as a vexed combination of radical and conservative ideas, in which Southey (like Wordsworth) lays claim to the landscape by naming it, an impulse Bolton '[traces] back to the radical inscriptive poetry he wrote in the late 1790s' (p. 70). *Thalaba* is discussed as a 'paradoxical' (p. 168) poem that mounts a critique of Arabian morality from a British perspective, but which ultimately undermines the British perspective as thoroughly as the Arabian one, while in *The Curse of Kehama* empire again comes home, as Southey's account of despotism reflects back on his fears over Napoleon and anxieties about British India. This is a deeply literary analysis of Southey's poetry, but like much recent criticism of the poet laureate, this is not a defence of his literary technique: Southey is 'often moralizing, didactic and preachy, or overly sentimental' (p. 204). Instead, it is at once the influence of such 'preaching' and the instability of his ideas (their 'paradoxical' nature) that has proved most interesting. As Bolton ably shows in this subtle and perceptive study, if Southey careers between extremes or shows signs of bewilderment, that might make him the more telling sign of his times.

Southey's colonial interests preoccupied a number of critics this year, although there was a degree of dissent as to quite how progressive those interests were. Andrew Rudd's ' "Oriental" and "Orientalist" Poetry: The Debate in Literary Criticism in the Romantic Period' (*Romanticism* 13[2007] 53–62) describes Southey's faithful delineation of Hindu customs as opposed to other poems which offered Eastern luxury as a commodity to be consumed by Western customers, such as Moore's and Byron's Eastern Tales. These poems, however, as Rudd carefully notes, offered a 'compromise' necessary to 'penetrate European literary markets, not an arbitrary move designed to belittle other cultures' (p. 61). An excellent article by David Simpson,

'Romantic Indians: Robert Southey's Distinctions' (*WC* 38[2007] 20–5), sees Southey's interest in other nations, pursued across several lengthy poems and histories, as evidence not simply of imperialism but of one 'compulsively given to the personae and performance of cosmopolitanism' (p. 21), particularly in *A Tale of Paraguay*, producing a sensitive, temperate reading. Southey's colonial interests were also considered in a piece by Jen Hill, 'Robert Southey's *Life of Nelson* and John Franklin's *Narrative of a Journey to the Shores of the Polar Sea*' (*NCLE* 61[2007] 417–38), discussed in section 2. Walter Savage Landor's *Gebir* has garnered a little attention lately as an early Eastern Tale known to have influenced Southey in particular, and one which is representative of the imperialist politics readily found in the genre. But Humberto Garcia, in 'The Hermetic Tradition of Arabic Islam and the Colonial Politics of Landor's *Gebir*' (*SiR* 46[2007] 433–59), argues that Landor's radical Protestant interest in biblical chronology suggests that his use of the narrative of a thirteenth-century Arabian romance in *Gebir* produces a 'radical hermetic critique of Anglican-British imperialism' (p. 436). Southey and Landor were both discussed in a Welsh context in Damian Walford Davies and Lynda Pratt's *Wales and the Romantic Imagination*. Pratt's 'Southey in Wales: Inscriptions, Monuments and Romantic Posterity' (pp. 86–103) considers Southey as a Welsh poet, discussing his inscriptions written for Daniel Stuart's *Morning Post* alongside *Madoc*. Southey's 'radical patriotism' for Wales, in opposition to England, was such that Pratt imagines Southey's memorial being moved from Keswick to Wales, the place he had hoped might be his spiritual home. Walter Savage Landor is distinguished, as David Chandler argues, as having 'the distinction of having had most to do with Wales' (p. 141) in 'Walter Savage Landor and Wales in the 1790s' (pp. 141–60). Chandler discusses Landor's disappointment with a country whose inhabitants did not meet his expectations when he set up an estate there, before concluding with a superb discussion of Landor's 'Verses, Written Near the Sea', a poem which offers a meditation on the 'pre-industrial landscapes around Swansea' (p. 154) quite distinct from the picturesque tradition and Romantic philosophizing. There were two other important essays on Southey's poetry, both included in Alan Rawes's *Romanticism and Form*. Nicola Trott's 'Southey's Forms of Experiment' (pp. 116–37) discovers a lively, formally fresh Southey in the early work, while Bernard Beatty's 'Believing in Form and Forms of Belief: The Case of Robert Southey' (pp. 138–53) is a superbly punchy chapter, discussing Southey's religion and arguing for him as a 'good negative example of form' (p. 138).

The Palgrave Advances series is intended to provide a metacritical overview of the most innovative recent scholarship, and Jane Stabler's *Palgrave Advances in Byron Studies* admirably achieves that aim. The twelve essays included are by leading Byronists, which, on top of the 'state of the art' statements they provide, often present significant arguments in their own right. *Don Juan* has usurped the Eastern Tales and *Childe Harold* as the dominant text in Byron studies of late, and it dominates here with five of twelve essays. Byron studies, as Stabler's excellent introduction argues, have benefited more than most from the fact that 'the academy is seriously interested in bread and circuses' (p. 5). If Byron suffered under the reign of the New Critics, the 'vitality of a revisionary "pull of the peripheral"' (p. 12) currently dominating Romantic studies has worked in his favour. Indeed, the major schools of critical and theoretical thought that have shaped the field in recent years are all represented here: orientalism, discussed by Peter Kitson, psychoanalytic criticism (Pamela Kao and David Punter), intertextuality (Nanora Sweet), queer studies (Steven Bruhm), ecocriticism (Timothy Morton) and gender studies (Susan Wolfson). But the glamour of 'history' has had the biggest pull of all. Philip Shaw provides a fascinating account of Byron's connection with war through *Childe Harold's Pilgrimage* 1, and Caroline Franklin ably demonstrates 'the centrality of history to virtually everything [Byron] wrote' (p. 85). It is a wide-ranging collection, critically and theoretically current, and it is especially timely in its discussion of Byron, as it seems that, for the time being at least, where Byron studies lead, Romantic studies follow. Similar, though aimed at those beginning study of Byron, is Caroline Franklin's *Byron*, an instalment in the Routledge Guides to Literature series. It begins with a concise and useful 'sketch of Byron's life as a *writer*' (p. 1) followed by discussions of his major publications that set those works in historical and poetic context, and a final section on critical approaches to Byron from his contemporaries up to the present. Franklin is the ideal choice to present such a guide, as one who has been with Byron since the start of his critical resurgence. She offers a clear-sighted appraisal of the major critical viewpoints in Byron studies, from Brougham in the *Edinburgh Review* to the present array of psychoanalytic, historicist and formalist views, that stays refreshingly clear from ideological finger-wagging. *Byron* is definitely worth recommending to the promising but puzzled undergraduate.

One of the most stimulating books written on Romantic poetry this year was Tom Mole's *Byron's Romantic Celebrity: Industrial Culture and the Hermeneutic of Intimacy*. Byron's celebrity status has been covered before, but Mole's theoretical aims are much broader than his topic suggests. Celebrity, for Mole, is a 'cultural apparatus' consisting of 'relations between an individual, an industry and an audience' (p. xi). Earlier figures had achieved fame, but Mole argues that Byron was the first who could properly be called a celebrity: 'although the self-presentation of individuals such as Sterne and Garrick included celebrity characteristics, it required the growth of a modern industry of production, promotion and distribution, and a modern audience— massive, anonymous, socially diverse and geographically distributed—before these elements combined to form a celebrity culture in the modern sense' (p. 10). Mole follows up his theoretical argument with seven case studies. He shows how Byron's celebrity made *Hebrew Melodies* a curiously composite work, intended to represent a religiously serious change in direction. But John Murray clearly wanted more of the same, and, through clever manipulation of print production techniques, managed the poem in such a way as to suggest a formal continuity with his earlier work. Throughout, Mole is strong on the way that 'Byron' emerged through a complicated cultural mechanism involving poet, publishers, printers, advertisers, reviewers, other writers, painters and the reading public. Yet Byron was not simply a passive victim of these cultural conditions. Not only did he exploit them, he made them part of his work. In a superb closing chapter, Mole shows how *Don Juan* adopts an anachronistic conception of subjectivity as a direct critique of the celebrity culture that Byron had helped instigate. Romantic celebrity, for Mole, helped in the development of modern ideas of selfhood as deep and developmental. The genius of *Don Juan* is that it undermines these assumptions from the inside. It is a fitting conclusion to an excellent book. Mole's 'Impresarios of Byron's Afterlife' (*NCC* 29[2007] 17–34) focuses on the way Byron's posthumous cultural existence continued as a visual, as well as a textual, phenomenon. Visual artists, as Mole shows, were able to continue Byron's cultural impact in two distinct areas: they sustained 'Byron's posthumous existence as a celebrity while also securing his canonicity' (p. 20).

Of particular interest to Byronists this year is Andrew Nicholson's elegantly presented edition of every (extant) letter sent to the poet by John Murray. The letters cover an eleven-year spell, from Murray's first commendation of 'so beautiful a poem' as *Childe Harold* in September 1811, to the recriminations in November 1822 that led Byron to threaten to go public about Murray's treatment of him, and caused Murray to protest that Byron's complaints were 'as groundless as they are unworthy of you' (p. 461). The letters, almost wholly unpublished prior to this edition, give a remarkable insight into one of the most significant literary relationships of Byron's career. They consist initially of respectful promptings about publishing matters and careful, enthusiastic literary criticism, but soon come to suggest a real intimacy. Murray acts as a kind of literary gossip, keeping Byron up to date about the latest literary happenings, while Byron sends back suggestions for future publications by the Murray imprint. Both Byron and Murray were deeply immersed in a publishing world of sales figures, ephemeral magazines, newspapers, travel books, political pamphlets and poetasters. This atmosphere makes the letters peculiarly vivid accounts of their age, but they are also hard to read. Nicholson's voluminous notes display a profound understanding of the complex literary culture of the period. The edition also comes with three useful appendices: an account of how Murray came to be Byron's publisher, transcriptions of attacks on Byron in newspapers following the 1814 publication of 'Lines to a Lady Weeping' and a rare copy (housed in the Murray archive) of the sale catalogue for Byron's library dating from his departure for the continent.

The apparent opposition between art and politics is of central importance to Romanticism, both as a principle which began to take its modern shape in the period and as a key feature of current criticism. It is an opposition that Matthew Bevis skilfully deconstructs in *The Art of Eloquence: Byron, Dickens, Tennyson, Joyce* (also discussed in Chapter XIII). Bevis's broader argument is about the difference between writing and speech, set in the context of the rise of parliamentary oratory as a kind of theatrical spectacle. The insistence on the importance of this historical context is a vital part of Bevis's work—Byron's Eastern Tales 'need to be considered as a particular kind of reaction to the parliamentary process and to certain forms of public speech' (p. 49)—but Bevis goes much further, offering a polemic against polemicism: a call to reread the 'literary' and 'political' fields in terms other than opposition. Bevis mounts a strong critique against an Eagletonian 'hermeneutics of suspicion' (p. 11) which seeks to condemn writers for their retreat from left-wing politics, instead adopting an approach which takes that very opposition as its subject. Rather than trying to find out which side a writer is batting for, Bevis invites us to consider the way in which writers explored writing as a field in which such polemical opposition might be questioned. Byron, a poet whose masterpiece asks 'if a writer should be quite consistent, | How could he possibly show things existent?', is the obvious choice to explore this thesis, and Bevis uses the poet's interest in the 'richness and responsibility of unsettled thinking' (p. 39) to excellent effect. Bevis's readings of Byron's poems can become a little strained at times, but they are in general subtle and eloquently expressed. But it is his theoretical contribution that ought to be taken most note of by Romanticists of any persuasion: this is an intelligent and significant incursion into the debates which have dominated the field over the past thirty years.

Andrew Nicholson discusses the textual history of Byron's translations of Martial in 'Nauseous Epigrams: Byron and Martial' (*Romanticism* 13[2007] 76–83). Nicholson uncovers a number of textual allusions to Martial which are not accompanied by quotation marks, 'partly it seems because they are woven into the fabric of his thought' (p. 80). Adam Komisaruk's ' "That imperious passion": Self as Vortex in *Don Juan*'s Russian Affair' (*NCC* 29[2007] 219–35) looks at the 'Siege of Ismail' passage in *Don Juan*. The political backdrop (an expansionist venture intended to produce Russia as a Westernized capitalist economy) becomes, for Komisaruk, part of Byron's critique of sexuality. Byron's 'orientalist' writings were reconsidered by Tatiana Kuzmic in 'Childe Harold's Pilgrimage in the Balkans' (*CCS* 4[2007] 51–65). Kuzmic questions Edward Said's critique of Byron, arguing that through his interest in Albania, the 'geographically circumscribed' (p. 52) Balkan region, Byron in fact engages a discourse that muddles conventional binaries between West and East. Two essays in the *Keats–Shelley Journal* looked at 'Regency Travel and Tourism' in Byron. In ' "Almost as far as Petersburg": Byron and the Russians' (*KSJ* 56[2007] 52–77) Richard Landsdown and Dosia Reichardt attempt to get beyond questions of the extent of Byron's influence in Russia, arguing instead that 'it is in ideological terms rather than strictly literary ones' (p. 54) that we should consider the relationship. In a similar vein, Catherine B. O'Neill's 'Childe Harold in Crimea: The Byronic Sea Voyage in Russian and Polish Romanticism' (*KSJ* 56[2007] 78–99) provides a fascinating account of Byron's continuing cultural prevalence. It is worth mentioning here Colin D. Dewey's ' "The hint of style": Byron, John Hookham Frere, and Melville's Marginalia in William Tennant's *Anster Fair*' (*Leviathan* 9[2007] 25–41), which discusses Herman Melville's ongoing literary relationship with Byron with reference to recently discovered marginal comments by Melville in a copy of Tennant's *Anster Fair*. Byron's literary afterlife in South Africa was ably discussed by Kai Easton in 'Coetzee's Disgrace: Byron in Italy and the Eastern Cape c.1820' (*JCL* 42[2007] 113–30). Easton looks at J.M. Coetzee's deployment of Byron in Italy in *Disgrace*, arguing that Coetzee offers a radical Romanticism, destabilizing the canonical version deposited at the Cape in 1820. Peter Cochran is on wonderfully sardonic form as he challenges the host of myths regarding Byron's relationship with Islam in 'Byron and Islamic Culture' (*KSR* 21[2007] 65–78). Malcolm Kelsall's erudite and challenging

'Byronic Homer' (*ByronJ* 35[2007] 1–10) treats the relationship as offering mutually 'new interpretive possibilities'. Vitana Kostadinova's elegant article, 'Byronic Ambivalence in *Childe Harold's Pilgrimage* IV' (*ByronJ* 35[2007] 11–18) finds a *Don Juan*-like uncertainty, a 'multiple oneness' (p. 17), rather than binary oppositions in the final instalment of *Childe Harold*, while Andrew Nicholson's scholarly piece, 'Byron's copy of *Childe Harold* IV: Emendations and Annotations' (*ByronJ* 35[2007] 19–25), adds to our knowledge of it. Tony Howe mobilizes a wealth of scholarship to argue that *Don Juan* 'alters significantly in tone and style' (p. 27) following Shelley's 1818 visit, in 'Shelley and the Development of *Don Juan*' (*ByronJ* 35[2007] 27–39). Jonathan Gross finds some unlikely parallels between Byron and Thomas Jefferson in 'Flyting in *The Declaration of Independence* and *The Vision of Judgment*' (*ByronJ* 35[2007] 41–51). The second volume of the *Byron Journal* is dedicated to Jerome McGann on the occasion of his seventieth birthday. Alice Levine's 'Byronic Annotations' (*ByronJ* 35[2007] 125–36) discusses Byron's note-taking, an insight garnered from McGann's editorial 'attentiveness not just to poems but to publications' (p. 134). Peter W. Graham's 'Byron and the Artifice of Sincerity: "To the Po" and its Epistolary Analogues' (*ByronJ* 35[2007] 137–50) styles itself a 'shoutout' to McGann, and provides a close reading of sincere insincerity in 'To the Po' and letters to Teresa Guiccioli.

One of the more enjoyable books published this year was Sally West's *Coleridge and Shelley: Textual Engagement*. West's study of influence between the two poets is a swerving from Harold Bloom's model of anxious misreading by insisting on the importance of history. For Bloom, whether one poet has read his precursor's work is of little interest, but for West 'a "strong" poet from our point in literary history may not be the same "strong" poet from the historical point of view of the ephebe under examination' (p. 4). The book moves largely chronologically, charting Shelley's developing textual relationship with the older poet. Shelley's poetical relationship with Southey is given a new significance, as Southey becomes a model for the way Shelley conceived of Coleridge and Wordsworth. West considers Shelley's disappointment in Coleridge in more detail, arguing that Coleridge might be considered a model for the *Alastor* poet, one who has turned solipsistically inwards having failed to connect the mind's imaginings with the outer world. West depends here, as elsewhere, on a combination of biographical reconstruction and sensitive close reading, opening up those areas of influence in which she sees the Bloomian model failing. It is not enough that 'O! there are spirits' contains echoes of Coleridge: West also demonstrates the likelihood that Shelley had read the relevant passage of *The Friend* based on letters and Shelley's reading lists. She follows a similar process in a wonderful chapter which argues for 'Mont Blanc' as a reworking of 'Hymn Before Sun-rise' and which recognizes the 'submerged fear' in the Coleridgean original to produce a poem that confronts the 'fear of nothingness' to discover 'a source of poetic and visionary strength' (p. 73). West sees Shelley reworking the Coleridgean anxiety about the primacy of language over thought and tracks the evolution of Shelley's engagement with the Ancient Mariner in *Prometheus Unbound*. The book concludes with a consideration of metaphor, in which West argues that the themes of 'community and regeneration' (p. 15) that Shelley develops in

Prometheus Unbound find their most complete expression in Shelley's own co-operative and mutually sustaining engagement with Coleridge.

Michael A. Vicario's *Shelley's Intellectual System and its Epicurean Background* treats Shelley's philosophical writings with extraordinary seriousness. For Vicario, Shelley is interesting in an explication of the history of philosophy, not, as is more common, the other way around. Vicario places Shelley as a 'Platonizing atomist' (p. 21), and as a significant development of an intellectual tradition that includes Bacon, Gassendi, Cudworth, Malebranche, Drummond and Hume. Central to the thesis is the challenge to the likes of Terence Alan Hoagwood and Jerrold E. Hogle who, in different ways, have placed Shelley as a sceptic. His scepticism is, for Vicario, 'a mere tool within a more comprehensive and more centrist system' (p. 7), which system is 'an ancient and modern edifice built by many hands' that is 'squarely at the center of seventeenth- and eighteenth-century debate over the empirical, sensuous foundation of all our ideas' (p. 8). The book is primarily philosophical (there is an entire chapter devoted to Gilbert Wakefield), and although there are some eye-opening readings of 'Mont Blanc' and *Prometheus Unbound*, it will find a readership primarily amongst those who see Shelley as a thinker rather than a poet or politician.

Thomas R. Frosch's *Shelley and the Romantic Imagination: A Psychological Study* is a detailed and intensive study of Shelley's poetry. If Romanticism was once synonymous with the word 'imagination', the term has slipped from view of late. Frosch's study is, indeed, rather traditional, offering an investigation of Shelley's poetics indebted to Harold Bloom, M.H. Abrams and Geoffrey Hartman that is largely insulated from recent debates about radical politics, Peterloo and the Corn Laws. But it is none the less rewarding for that, as Frosch sensitively and subtly explores the philosophical and psychological complexities of Shelley's verse. Too often psychoanalysis tends to overpower poetry, but here it is used appropriately, gently opening up key ideas. Frosch's knowledge is clearly very deep, going well beyond Freud and Lacan to include contemporary theorists such as Heinz Hartman and Margaret Mahler. The crux of the study is an opposition that Frosch draws from Milton, between an aggressive, narcissistic Satanic impulse and an 'Adamic' outgoing impulse that searches for ideal completion. The book leads us through Shelley's career, with the first section focusing on *Alastor* and an '*Alastor* complex' (p. 59) in Shelley's poetry more widely. A desire for an 'ideal completion' will most likely lead to disappointment, but if Wordsworth can be satisfied with 'abundant recompense', Shelley remains unsatisfied, if idealistic about the possibility of such satisfaction. The second section takes as its text *Prometheus Unbound*, charting Shelley's wrestle with a troubling imaginative source in Satanic aggression in which he ultimately goes beyond reason into romance. The final section challenges the idea that Shelley became less idealistic as he grew older, arguing that in *The Triumph of Life* Shelley further explores this visionary idealism. A mystic Shelley would be a problem to many contemporary critics, but not so for Frosch. Shelley the idealizer and mythologizer is brought vividly back into the critical eye in an eloquent study, if one that would have benefited from a little editorial pruning.

The influence of German Romanticism on its British counterpart has been rather better considered than the cultural traffic moving in the opposite direction, and Susanne Schmid's *Shelley's German Afterlives: 1814–2000* is accordingly a significant contribution. Schmid follows Jerome McGann's principles of textual criticism, recognizing the instability of the material text and the multiple acts of interpretation that the materiality of the text allows. Schmid traces Shelley's influence in magazines, travel books, anthologies, often widely different translations, socialist songs and a great variety of ephemeral artefacts. Given this variety and the historical scope of Schmid's research, it is perhaps not surprising that she uncovers a range of versions of Shelley, as different readers adopted different texts and were influenced by different interpretative traditions. Often these marginal sites of reception proved greatly significant. Shelley's female readers were particularly important: as Schmid notes, 'Louise von Ploennies, a translator, anthologist, and salonnière, influenced the German Shelley reception much more than Goethe ever did' (p. 17). Yet certain paradigms recur as frequently in Germany as they have done in Britain. Schmid recognizes three in particular: the 'lyrical, revolutionary, and Faustian' (p. 20). Shelley emerges as a poet with a peculiar cultural hold on his readers. Schmid's erudite and theoretically astute study, alongside Shaffer and Zuccato's work discussed above, ought to influence further investigation of the varied reception of Romantic texts in Europe. Further evidence of Shelley's relationship with European culture is found in Oskar Nellens's 'Shelley in the Netherlands: A Comprehensive List of his Dutch Translations' (*KSR* 21[2007] 97–114).

A special issue of the *European Romantic Review* on 'Romanticism and the Law' produced two articles on Shelley and legality. Alex J. Dick's remarkably subtle 'The Ghost of Gold: Forgery Trials and the Standard of Value in Shelley's *The Mask of Anarchy*' (*ERR* 18[2007] 381–400) focuses on the paper money debates of the early 1820s. Where Cobbett and Wooler disputed the government's mandate to impose a standard of value, Shelley instead proposes a literary standard in which the economic field is regulated not by the invisible hand but by the unseen legislator, the imaginative genius. Melynda Nuss's 'Prometheus in a Bind: Law, Narrative and Movement in *Prometheus Unbound*' (*ERR* 18[2007] 417–34) places Shelley between two competing understandings of punishment, one Platonic, the other deriving from Aeschylus. Nuss is ultimately pessimistic about the play's ability to resolve the question of whether punishment can be reformative without acquiescing to the authority of the punisher. It has become something of a critical commonplace that Shelley's poetry was intended to have a direct impact on contemporary events; Michael Rossington's ' "The destinies of the world": Shelley's Reception and Transmission of European News in 1820–1' (*Romanticism* 13[2007] 233–43) shows just how intensively Shelley pursued that aim. Shelley positioned himself as a disseminator of news from Europe, particularly Italy, in a period of anxious political crisis, allowing him to address audiences that his poetry would not let him. Kelvin Everest's 'Shelley's *Adonais* and John Keats' (*EIC* 57[2007] 237–64) is an extended excursus in praise of both poets, which elucidates the allusions to the Greek pastoral poems of Bion and Moschus in *Adonais*. The elaborate classicism of the poem is read by Everest as an attempt to celebrate Keats's classical ambitions, ambitions for which he was amusingly mocked in *Blackwood's Magazine*. Everest argues that *Adonais* is the 'grandest of the many compliments paid to Keats as a poet' (p. 259); this finely wrought essay might be considered a fitting tribute to the tribute.

In a piece well informed by linguistic theory, 'Foregrounding and the Sublime: Shelley in Chamonix' (*L&L* 16[2007] 155–68), David S. Miall considers linguistic foregrounding in Shelley's treatment of the sublime in 'Mont Blanc'. Miall moves from a thorough linguistic analysis of the poem, discussing defamiliarization, disruptive syntax, sense under pressure and the merging of mind with nature, to produce a fascinating ecocritical reading of the poem. A special issue of *Romantic Circles Praxis Series* on Romanticism and Buddhism, edited by Mark Lussier, contained much of general interest and John Rudy's 'Shelley's Golden Wind: Zen Harmonics in *A Defence of Poetry* and "Ode to the West Wind"' (*RCPS* [2007] 22 paras). For Rudy, Shelley's sense of the imagination in the moment of creation might be considered not as an affirmation of self, but as a 'self-emptying exposure to a prior Buddhistic oneness with all beings'. It is an intriguing argument, but it is based on a little too much conjecture to make a connection, rather than simply a parallel, between Shelley and Buddhism. In biographical vein, Donald B. Prell's 'The Sinking of the *Don Juan* Revisited' (*KSJ* 56[2007] 136–54) reconsiders the seaworthiness of the fateful Shelleyan boat. Nicholas A. Joukovsky adds some important scholarship to Shelley studies in 'Contemporary Notices of Shelley: Addenda to *The Unextinguished Hearth*' (*KSJ* 56[2007] 173–95). Cian Duffy investigates Shelley's early attachment to Wales, particularly in 'On Leaving London for Wales' in ' "One draught from Snowdon's ever-sacred spring": Shelley's Welsh Sublime' (in Walford Davies and Pratt, eds., pp. 180–98). The essay (also noticed in section 1 above) is largely biographical, but it includes an excellent discussion of the increasingly political resonance Shelley gave the natural sublime following his Welsh adventures.

It is also certainly worth mentioning an important new biography of Shelley by Ann Wroe, *Being Shelley: The Poet's Search for Himself*. The book confesses itself to be 'an experiment' (p. ix), not so much a biography as an account of the development of a poetic free spirit. Rather than life events, Wroe gives us moments of vision, dangerous enthusiasm, imagined encounters with words and mountains. Two samples of her prose give the tone and the method: 'a calm wide eye, carefully drawn and shaded, presided over these words as he first wrote them' (p. 349); 'he might live, and soar on, towards the fire' (p. 289). The book is as much about Wroe as it is about Shelley, a passionate encounter inscribed in awed tones, but Shelleyans are advised to dip into it, if only to remind themselves what it is about Shelley that proves so entrancing.

It was a very quiet year in Keats studies, but a number of significant articles were published. Foremost amongst these was Emily Sun's 'Facing Keats with Winnicott: On a New Therapeutics of Poetry' (*SiR* 46[2007] 57–75), which takes Keats's conception of the therapeutic function of poetry to explore his understanding of the relationship between aesthetics and ethics. Sun's use of

D.W. Winnicott's psychoanalysis tends to get in the way of some really rather subtle textual criticism, but this is an ambitious step forward. Arnd Bohm's excellent 'Just Beauty: Ovid and the Argument of Keats's "Ode on a Grecian Urn"' (*MLQ* 68[2007] 1–26) discusses Keats's attempt to find consolation, first in nature, then in art, in a world shorn of religious faith. Bohm's thorough understanding of Keats's Latin sources allows him to produce a fascinating interpretation of the poem, suggesting ultimately a Shaftesburyian humanism behind Keats's sense of beauty and truth. John Barnard's largely biographical '"The busy time": Keats's Duties at Guy's Hospital from Autumn 1816 to March 1817' (*Romanticism* 13[2007] 199–208) gives some intriguing insights into the nature of medical training in the period. Further discussion of Keats's medical background and its influence on his work is found in Akiko Okada's erudite 'Keats's Use of Scientific Words' (*KSR* 21[2007] 79–96). Clayton G. MacKenzie's 'John Keats and the River Teign' (*N&Q* 54[2007] 141–2) shows that Keats's 1818 poem written to B.R. Haydon maintains a regular rhyme scheme throughout: Keats was echoing the differing local pronunciations of 'Teign'. In a sprightly piece, 'Who Killed John Keats?' (*ChE* 53:xix[2007] 27 paras), Amy Leal considers Keats's paranoid suspicions about his death, arguing that these suspicions may help inform us about his methods of thinking, his negatively capable habit of remaining in 'mysteries, doubts'. Thomas Dilworth and Betsy Keating's 'Keats's "On Sitting Down to Read King Lear Once Again"' (*Expl* 65[2007] 78–82) considers two problematic images in the text, both connected with death: Romance as a 'syren' and the 'phoenix wings' of desire, subtly threading through the significance of the terms. Also worth mentioning here is Jack Stillinger's discussion of the 'psychic links' that he forged between himself and Keats in his editing work on the poet: 'Keats and Me' (*WC* 38[2007] 139–43). Alison Pearce's '"Magnificent mutilations": John Keats and the Romantic Fragment' (*KSR* 21[2007] 22–34) positions Keats in a 'period of aesthetic and ideological instability' following the cultural response to the Elgin Marbles, particularly with regard to *Hyperion: A Fragment*. A.D. Harvey discusses why Keats was interested in Wordsworth's vernacular experiments in 'Keats, Wordsworth, Burns and the Real Language of Men' (*KSR* 21[2007] 115–21). In an elegant piece, Daniel Pollack-Pelzner discusses Dante's influence on Keats's Chapman Sonnet: 'Revisionary Company: Keats, Homer, and Dante in the Chapman Sonnet' (*KSJ* 56[2007] 39–49).

Paul Chirico's *John Clare and the Imagination of the Reader* is a major study of the poet that seeks to emphasize his cultural ambition, his canny understanding of the literary market, and in the process restore 'the suppressed history of his cultural pragmatism' (p. 1). Earlier studies of Clare have positioned him as a victim of the publishing market, but Chirico emphasizes Clare's understanding of these conditions and his complex acts of self-positioning in relation to an emergent mass market. Chirico places Clare as a collaborative poet in two senses, both with his readers and with his fellow writers. His writing 'directs the responses of its readers; its linguistic artifice constructs the eccentric experience of its implied audience' (p. 18). In a series of superb close readings of Clare's poems, Chirico reconstructs Clare's attempts to direct and relate to an audience he cannot understand in anything but a mediated way. Chirico focuses on Clare's 'creative redeployment of existing texts from other sources' (p. 29), creating a 'textual sociability' (p. 32) with writers like Anna Adcock, Robert Bloomfield and, most intriguingly of all, John Keats. Chirico picks up on the largely unnoticed connection between Keats and Clare, but that connection is only ever textual: it is a 'largely fantasised social interaction with other writers whom he admired' (p. 46). Throughout this study, Clare is revealed as a poet who sees nature as a textual construct. We are used to positioning Clare as the only truly 'natural' poet in an age of affected rurality, one whose genuine connection with the earth allows him to comment critically on city poets finding nightingales in Shoreditch. Yet, as Chirico subtly elucidates, Clare is frequently interested in natural images rather than natural objects. 'The terrain which the poet habitually describes is itself a cultural construct' (p. 20), a product of Clare's often unacknowledged quotations from other poets. This is a diverse, culturally aware and critically subtle Clare, one interested in textual commodities, contemporary poets, antiquarian research and the print market as much as foraging off the beaten track for pettichaps' nests. Chirico's analysis of Clare is learned and precise, but it is also remarkably alive to the psychological subtleties of Clare's verse, and to the complexities of his cultural positioning.

'"Making myself a soldier": The Role of Soldiering in the Autobiographical Work of John Clare' (*Romanticism* 13[2007] 177–88), by Neil Ramsay, posits the remarkable body of narratives published by labouring-class soldiers as an important context to open up Clare's poetry. The connection between politics and linguistic choices in Clare's verse was explored in a fine, theoretically informed piece by Andrew Cooper, '"Landscapes of language": John Clare and the Cultural Politics of Language Theory, 1820–1850' (*TPr* 21[2007] 433–55). Cooper historicizes Clare's interest in dialect use, placing his work in the context of publications such as Cobbett's writings on grammar. Clare's challenge to linguistic propriety is, for Cooper, 'actually produced by the poems' protest against the appropriation of land' (p. 437). Cooper's aims are ultimately much broader (he insists on the significance of literary texts to theories of the politics of language), but this is a salutary reappraisal of Clare's dexterous, playful linguistics. In a pleasant short piece, 'John Clare: "Searching for Blackberries"' (*WC* 38[2007] 208–11), Eric Robinson sheds further light on the historical context of Clare's semi-legal gathering of berries and wood in the wasteland near Helpstone. Vincent Newey's 'Existing at the Margins: A Double Echo of Cowper in Clare' (*N&Q* 54[2007] 148–9) points out just how well Clare knew Cowper, noting a double echo in 'St Martin's Eve' of *The Task*. The *John Clare Society Journal* had a number of notable articles. Simon White, whose work on Bloomfield is discussed below, contributes a fine piece on community, hawthorns and May Day rituals (connecting usefully with Essaka Joshua's work, discussed in section 1), 'Landscape Icons and the Community: A Reading of John Clare's "Langley Bush"' (*JCSJ* 26[2007] 21–32). Mick Shrey discusses Clare's 'truly serene' later poetry on the death of infants in '"Infant graves are steps of angels": Childhood Mortality as a Recurrent Theme in Clare's Poetry' (*JCSJ* 26[2007] 33–59). Simon Kövesi's 'Beyond the Language Wars: Towards a Green Edition of John Clare' (*JCSJ* 26[2007] 61–75) attempts to move beyond the notorious debates over Clare's spelling and his editors, old and new, proposing an original, 'ecologically informed' (p. 74), solution that draws on the work of Gilles Deleuze.

Clare's fellow labouring-class poet Robert Bloomfield seems to be on the verge of a real critical resurgence. Simon J. White's *Robert Bloomfield, Romanticism and the Poetry of Community* is the first major monograph on the poet, and it is a very good one. The book begins with the striking, counter-intuitive claim that Wordsworth was writing in a Bloomian '"shadow" of Bloomfield rather than vice versa' (p. 1). White offers something of a polemic, a strident call for a reorientation of Romantic studies that foregrounds labouring-class poets, shifting away from a Wordsworthian/Coleridgean paradigm. Certainly Bloomfield was more popular than Wordsworth, so he reached more readers. But White goes further, arguing that Bloomfield offers a model of poetry that is poetically and politically *better* than Wordsworth's. Wordsworth's *Prelude* saw the poet finding a 'calling [that] set him apart from the rest of humankind' so it is unsurprising, for White, that he should patronize the rural poor, whereas Bloomfield is interested in 'interactions with others in close and supportive communities' (p. 30) in *The Farmer's Boy*. White then moves on to Bloomfield's ballads and tales, which are again contrasted favourably with Wordsworth's vernacular affectations, redolent for White of 'property-orientated bourgeois morality' (p. 3) rather than Bloomfield's communitarianism. The focus on community ties White's work to an important current in Romantic studies, and White follows the likes of Jeffrey Cox in seeing a politically liberating element in that community spirit. Bloomfield and Wordsworth's parallel lyrics on the Wye valley are compared, with Bloomfield able to comment tellingly on contemporary sociological and political issues. White also sheds significant light on Bloomfield's relationship with Capel Lofft. The book concludes with Bloomfield's 'manifesto' for the intellectual emancipation of the labouring poor's poets, allowing them to get into print, unlocking their potential. White's book aims to provide something of the same function within Romantic studies. The attacks on Wordsworth get a little too close to a hatchet job, but this is nonetheless a call for Bloomfield's poetic importance that should not go unheeded.

Bloomfield was also discussed this year by John Goodridge, who builds on Tim Burke's recent revival of interest in Robert Bloomfield's *The Banks of the Wye*, focusing on Bloomfield's engagement with a textual Scotland through the figure of Burns in his ascent of Sugar Loaf mountain in '"That deathless wish of climbing higher": Robert Bloomfield on the Sugar Loaf' (in Walford Davies and Pratt, eds., pp. 161–79). Community in Romantic poetry was also considered in Daisy Hay's wonderfully sprightly 'Musical Evenings in the Hunt Circle' (*KSR* 21[2007] 122–34), which fleshes out the sociable context to Leigh Hunt's 'cheerful' philosophy, particularly in relation to Vincent Novello. It is also worth mentioning Essaka Joshua's *The Romantics and the May Day Tradition*, discussed in detail in section 1. Joshua's study has a wide relevance for the writers in this section, but her focus on folklore, the local and the communal has a particular relevance to poets such as Clare, Bloomfield and Leigh Hunt. Hunt's hilarious description of Italian poetry as 'truly a lump of sunshine on my shelves' (p. 77) provides the crux to Joshua's account of his engagement with Maying. Hunt sees nature and culture in close and mutually sustaining contact; he is 'interested in how culture influences the way we think about the seasons' (p. 75). Joshua suggests that Hunt's interest in reviving such celebrations is more than mere nostalgia. Rather, he 'looks to the past in order to move forward' (p. 87), hoping to remodel human society on more communal, friendly grounds. Joshua takes issue with the 'polarization' predominant in Clare studies between high culture and folk culture, insisting instead on the 'complexity of Clare's cultural position' (p. 116), which chimes with Paul Chirico's argument, discussed above.

An excellent book that studies the work of another neglected poet is Sara Lodge's *Thomas Hood and Nineteenth-Century Poetry: Work, Play and Politics*. Lodge clearly feels that Hood has been neglected unjustly, and her book is an eloquent call for his reappraisal. Yet she is carefully attuned to recent debates about the nature of canonicity, arguing that 'looking at his work should encourage us to reconsider the "minor" as a deliberate stance and a quality to be celebrated, rather than redeemed' (p. 7). Hood falls between a number of critical stools: writing primarily between 1824 and 1840 he is what Richard Cronin has called a 'Romantic Victorian'; writing primarily comic verse he has been excluded from a canon of writers that prides itself on its seriousness, and writing in a number of aesthetic formats he is not ever strictly a poet. Yet it is his very in-betweenness that makes Hood such a valuable figure. Lodge places Hood's poetry in a vivid metropolitan print context, amidst advertising, lottery puffs and washerwomen. Born the son of a publisher, Hood was intimately acquainted with the material underpinnings of literary work, and, as Lodge shows, that context allowed Hood to question the transcendental direction of much of the work of his contemporaries. Hood's career incorporated a vast variety of genres and artistic modes, from comic verse to puns, from woodcuts to protest poems. Underpinning all of these is what Lodge calls Hood's 'play', his delight in exposing 'plural interpretation' (p. 4), whether it be in the jarring doubleness of a pun or in poems which, as Lodge convincingly demonstrates, are important precursors to the dramatic monologues of Browning and Tennyson. Hood has typically been dismissed for lacking seriousness, yet Lodge shows how influentially political he was in the 1820s, 1830s and 1840s, and moreover how 'the inextricability of Hood's play and protest poetry' (p. 185) means that he can be at his most political when he is most playful. Hood emerges from Lodge's study as an important figure, worthy of rescuing from his current neglect, precisely in so far as he resists the critical commonplaces which have ensured his non-canonical status. Elsewhere in Hood studies, Rodney Stenning Edgecombe continues his fine work on Hood's letters in ' "Lightography" in a Letter by Thomas Hood' (*N&Q* 54[2007] 140–1), noting this 'micro neologism' for photography which failed to catch on.

Another writer whose work interestingly resists generic and period definition, Thomas Lovell Beddoes, benefited from a new book in 2007. *The Ashgate Research Companion to Thomas Lovell Beddoes*, edited by Ute Berns and Michael Bradshaw, arrives at an exciting time for Beddoes studies. The editors note the commonplace, if seemingly paradoxical, appreciation of him as, in Ian Jack's words, 'a man of genius who wrote nothing that is commonly remembered' (p. xvii). This certainly seemed to be Beddoes's position, but the past five years or so have seen a resurgence in interest in the poet, politician, playwright and physician. This *Companion* is an important collection of thirteen essays by major scholars from a wide variety of theoretical and literary perspectives that, rather than signalling a call for renewed attention to a neglected author, is evidence of the flourishing state of the field. Much of the book is concerned with Beddoes's drama, and it is discussed in more detail in section 5.

There were three excellent essays on political poetry in the 1810s and 1820s. In a joyous article titled 'Thomas Brown [alias Thomas Moore], Censorship and Romantic Cryptography' (*ERR* 18[2007] 187–94), Jane Moody argues that in Moore's *Intercepted Letters: or, the Twopenny Post-Bag* the poet's satirical persona, Thomas Brown, became 'a form of Regency counter-intelligence' (p. 188). The essay puts Moore's superbly subversive collection in the context of government surveillance, but suggests that in the post-bag, 'the squib is a poem turned weapon' (p. 189) in which Moore turns the state's own weapons against it. Moore was also discussed by Jane Moore in 'Thomas Moore as Irish Satirist' (in Duff and Jones, eds., *Scotland, Ireland and the Romantic Aesthetic*, pp. 152–71), which calls for a reassessment of Moore's Irishry, moving away from the regrettable melodic sentimentalist towards the fearsome, witty satirist of the *Twopenny Post-Bag*. John Gardner returns to the well-trodden ground of Peterloo in 'The Suppression of Samuel Bamford's Peterloo Poems' (*Romanticism* 13[2007] 145–55). Bamford's poems, unknown to literary critics and suppressed by their author, reveal a remarkably active voice in the contemporary political scene, one closer to revolutionary than reformist sentiments. Gardner notes that 'as a poet Bamford seems to have influenced no one' (p. 153), but his vigorous involvement in the politics of the period, now revealed by Gardner, ought to reshape conceptions of both Bamford and the Peterloo debates.

(b) Women's Poetry

An invaluable addition to studies in this category is *Romantic Women Poets: Genre and Gender*, edited by Lilla Maria Crisafulli and Cecilia Pietropoli, which takes as its focus the self-conscious poetic styles at work in Romantic women's poetry. The essays in this collection are thoughtful and elegant studies which aim to re-evaluate the assumptions often made about the role these women played in the construction of a Romantic poetics and culture. The first essay, 'Anna Seward and the Dynamics of Female Friendship' (pp. 11–22), by Stuart Curran, traces how same-sex relationships in the eighteenth century were treated by twentieth-century critics. Turning to the celebrity of the Ladies of Llangollen (Lady Eleanor Butler and Sarah Ponsonby), Seward's 'Llangollen Vale' [1796], and the posthumously published 'A Farewell to the Seat of Lady Eleanor Butler and Miss Ponsonby', Curran argues that the emotional power which she applies to these poems is seen also in her earlier poems dealing with her relationship with Honora Sneyd, writing that the poems are 'a counterpart to and an enactment of the relationship two women may hold outside the normative social structures defined by patriarchy' (p. 20). Next, Jane Stabler's '"Know me what I paint": Women Poets and the Aesthetics of the Sketch 1770–1830' (pp. 23–34), draws attention to women poets' ambivalence towards visual art, and the ways in which they portray it both as a liberating activity and as an activity that contributes to feminine bondage. Stabler argues that this ambivalence is seen in the poets' tendency to blend the quotidian with imagination, fancy and the sublime in their verse, and in the ways in which they negotiate between flights of fancy and descriptions of visual art. This 'aesthetic indeterminacy' is explored in poems by Anne Radcliffe, Charlotte Smith, Dorothy Wordsworth, Amelia Opie, Mary Robinson and Mary Scott. Lilla Maria Crisafulli's 'Within or Without? Problems of Perspective in Charlotte Smith, Anna Laetitia Barbauld and Dorothy Wordsworth' (pp. 35–62) argues against the notion of a high, or 'vertical' Romanticism, which is public and masculine, and a low, 'horizontal' Romanticism, which is domestic and feminine. As her title suggests, Crisafulli considers this to be an opposition between the 'within' and the 'without' of poetic subjectivity. She focuses on Anna Laetitia Barbauld, Charlotte Smith and Dorothy Wordsworth, and traces the ways in which they negotiate between both perspectives in their work. Anna Laetitia Barbauld's and Charlotte Smith's poetic personae, she argues, position these subjectivities against each other— one representing an ethical sentimentality and the other an unjust rationality— while Dorothy Wordsworth's journals reveal a profound interest in and knowledge of the natural world, which seems to blur the divide between what is internal and external, familiar and foreign. In 'Helen Maria Williams: The Shaping of a Poetic Identity' (pp. 63–78), Lia Guerra considers Williams's introduction to her 1823 collection against the backdrop of her development as a writer who was comfortable working with different genres. Guerra considers Williams's apologetic introduction as a bringing together of her younger and more mature authorial selves.

Timothy Webb's enlightening essay in this collection, 'Listing the Busy Sounds: Anna Seward, Mary Robinson and the Poetic Challenge of the City' (pp. 79–113), explores the ways in which Anna Seward and Mary Robinson responded to an increasingly urbanized landscape. Examining Seward's 'To Colebrook Dale' [1799] and 'Colebrook Dale' [1810], Webb explores her ambivalence towards industrialization and urbanization and her engagement with ' "the industrial sublime" ', while Mary Robinson is seen as embracing the sounds and sights of London in 'London's Summer Morning'. Next, 'Joanna Baillie's Embarrassment' (pp. 113–36), by Dorothy McMillan, remarks on the role of Scotland and Scottish identity in Romantic culture. McMillan explores Baillie's attempts to preserve her Scottish identity while not denouncing her adopted country and then focuses on the problems of Scottish representation in the performance and publication of Baillie's *The Family Legend* [1810].

In the same collection, Beatrice Battaglia, in 'The "Pieces of Poetry" in Anne Radcliffe's *The Mysteries of Udolpho*' (pp. 137–52), considers the often overlooked poems in the novel, and the ways in which they work alongside the prose to evoke a neoclassical sublime. In these poems, Battaglia argues, the poet and nature become one, and they serve to create an almost musical atmosphere that evokes the power of the unconscious. Diego Saglia's 'Ending the Romance: Women Poets and the Romantic Verse Tale' (pp. 153–68) explores the ways in which Felicia Hemans's *The Abencerrage* and Letitia Landon's *The Improvisatrice* both accepted and reshaped the structures and themes of the verse narrative as used traditionally by men such as Southey, Byron and Scott. Saglia's careful study looks at the similarities and differences between the male and female poets' treatment of the genre, focusing specifically on lack of closure and the romantic 'trace' or revenant. Serena Baiesi, in 'Letitia Elizabeth Landon's *The Improvisatrice*: The Fatal Combination of Gender and Genre' (pp. 169–84), shows how the female heroine is both subject and object in this poem, which brings together the epic, the lyric and drama. Baiesi proposes that Landon revises the masculine Romantic epic with its traditional male narrator and instead creates a heroine who speaks for herself and for other women, and who brings together Italian and English characteristics. In 'Anna Laetitia Barbauld's Ethics of Sentiment' (pp. 185–96), Donatella Montini considers the poet as a literary critic who argued against the absolutist idea that poetry has a greater emotional effect on readers and that novels, as opposed to romance, should take place in the quotidian sphere rather than the fantastical world of the romance epic.

In the same collection Cecilia Pietropoli argues, in 'Women Romantic Writers: Mary Tighe and Mary Hays' (pp. 197–208), that the distinction between history (the domain of men) and popular romance (the domain of women) resulted in the creation of sub-genres, such as Gothic parody. Pietropoli considers Tighe's *Psyche* and Mary Hays's 'A Fragment, in the Manner of the Old Romances' as examples of two different responses to women's traditional roles in romances. Pietropoli shows the ways in which these poets reinforced and readapted different romantic tropes in order to create their own versions of a suitable romantic ending. In an excellent essay, 'Felicia Hemans, Letitia Landon, and "Lady's Rule"' (pp. 209–40), Richard Cronin argues against modern criticism that looks for subversive undertones in Hemans's poetry. She must be read in the light of her popularity during her life, he argues, and in the light of the values her readers cherished. Cronin complicates Hemans's legacy, however, by drawing attention to the discrepancies between the power and geographical range of many of her poems and her role as an icon of femininity and domesticity. His study of Landon's poetry shows how her treatment of thwarted love and abandonment displays a self-reflexivity which highlights the poet's own feminine vulnerability. Finally, he shows how the young Tennyson imitates this vulnerability through the adoption of the female voice. The last essay in this admirable collection, Gioia Angeletti's 'Women Re-Writing Men: The Examples of Anna Seward and Lady Caroline Lamb' (pp. 241–58), aims to position these two poets within the context of the literary canon by showing how they appropriate and subversively manipulate the style and tropes of male Romantic writers. Focusing on the relationship between Seward and Erasmus Darwin, Caroline Lamb and Lord Byron, Angeletti argues that Lamb imitates his narrative persona and 'deploys his satirical style in order to turn it against him' (p. 253).

Seward's 'Colebrook Dale' is also discussed in ' "Pond'rous engines" in "outraged groves": The Environmental Argument of Anna Seward's "Colebrook Dale" ' by Sharon Setzer (*ERR* 18[2007] 69–82). Setzer argues that identifying the poem's imagery primarily with a masculine sublime fails to recognize 'the trauma that one might expect a female poet to associate with a "violated" female landscape' (p. 73). She compares Seward's poetic response to Colebrook Dale with that of Milton, Pope and Erasmus Darwin to show how male accounts did not see industrialization there as damaging to nature. For Setzer, this makes Seward's rape imagery all the more striking. Masae Kawatsu's 'Romantic Friendships in Anna Seward's *Louisa*' (*SEL* 47[2006] 45–63) argues against what she calls a 'strong heterosexual bias', which, in her view, has dominated previous readings of the poem. Focusing on the relationship between Louisa and Emma in the narrative, she questions the supposed binary opposition between eighteenth-century romantic friendships and 'sapphism', to argue that Seward's poem strikes a balance between a romantic female relationship and heterosexual love. Also on Seward, Adeline Johns-Putra's 'Anna Seward's Translations of Horace' (in Dow, ed., *Translators, Interpreters, Mediators: Women Writers 1700–1900*, pp. 111–29), argues that Seward's translations can more aptly be labelled 'paraphrases'. Not only was English her only language but, as this essay argues, Seward privileged poetic spirit and sentimentality over literal translations. Johns-Putra's thoughtful study shows how her letters to friends and her prefaces reveal a conviction that 'a masculine classical education does not make men better translators of poetry' (p. 118).

Charlotte Smith received much critical attention this year. In 'Varieties of Privacy in Charlotte Smith's Poetry' (*ERR* 18[2007] 483–502), Sarah Zimmerman invokes two models of solitary reading—by Roger Chartier and Jürgen Habermas—in order to argue that Smith's definition of privacy changes throughout her career from the solitary in *Elegiac Sonnets* to the intimate in *Beachy Head*. In an enlightening comparison between the tone of *Beachy Head* and letters Smith wrote to her friend Sarah Farr Rose, whom she never met, Zimmerman concludes that 'the sonnets emphasize a private encounter between the reader and the book; in *Beachy Head*, written verse mediates a relationship between the poet and the reader' (p. 498). A chapter on Charlotte Smith in Susan Rosenbaum's *Professing Sincerity: Modern Lyric Poetry, Commercial Culture, and the Crisis in Reading*, argues that Smith's elegiac poetry negotiated between the sincerity readers demanded from poets and her well-known financial hardships. That death is presented as an escape in poems such as 'Death the Leveller' and 'Written in a Churchyard at Middleton in Sussex', Rosenbaum argues, signals a social critique not present in the traditional elegy. The chapter argues that 'by de-forming her elegiac lyrics, Smith criticizes the moral assumptions that support a sincere ideal, and attempts to re-form sympathy to levelling ends' (p. 109). Stephen Bernstein's essay, ' "Nature seem'd to lose her course": Crisis Historiography and Historiographic Crisis in Charlotte Smith's *The Emigrants*' (in Felber, ed., *Clio's Daughters, British Women Making History, 1790–1889*, pp. 29–42), considers the problems of Smith's cyclical representations of nature and linear representation of history in *The Emigrants*. Finally, the first chapter in Amy

Christina Billone's *Little Songs: Women, Silence, and the Nineteenth-Century Sonnet*, 'Breaking "The silent sabbath of the grave": Romantic Women's Sonnets and the "Mute arbitress of grief"', compares Smith's *Elegiac Sonnets* to those of Thomas Gray and William Lisle Bowles. Billone also considered the complicated friendship between Smith and Helena Maria Williams and Anna Maria Smallpiece. Another essay on Mary Tighe, Allison Hobgood's 'The Bold Trespassing of a "Proper Romantic Lady": Mary Tighe and a Female Romantic Aesthetic' (*ERR* 18[2007] 503–19), focuses on *Psyche* and contends that Tighe's poetry creates a new female Romantic aesthetic 'through a shrewd refusal to take up the gaze structure as a poetic technique in her poem' (p. 505). Tighe does this, Hobgood says, by using blindness to privilege other ways of knowing, such as touch and speech. In so doing, the poetess 'cultivates instead a specifically female, Romantic aesthetic grounded in embodiment and the corporeality of experience as opposed to a literal or philosophic mind's eye' (p. 515).

Nanora Sweet's essay, 'Byron and Intertextuality: Laureate Triumph in *Childe Harold* IV: Staël, Hemans, Hobhouse, Byron' (in Stabler, ed., *Palgrave Advances in Byron Studies*, pp. 234–56, discussed in section 3(a)), offers a thorough survey of recent work which has explored the poetic relationships between these writers. Sweet identifies further similarities in language to argue that 'Byron did not carry the voices of male precursors only' (p. 235). Sweet also deals with de Staël, Hemans and Italy in '"Those siren-haunted seas besides": Naples in the Work of Staël, Hemans, and the Shelleys' (in Lamont and Rossington, eds., pp. 160–71), where she focuses on the writers' poetic responses to Naples. Finally for Hemans, an excellent essay by Diego Saglia, '"A deeper and richer music": The Poetics of Sound and Voice in Felicia Hemans's 1820s Poetry' (*ELH* 74[2007] 351–71). Saglia's essay 'seeks to reconstruct and assess the pervasive presence of sounds and voices in Hemans's output in order to reveal the carefully orchestrated, as well as consistently situated, nature of her poetry' (p. 352).

A chapter on Barbauld appears in Colin Jager's *The Book of God* (also discussed in section 1). In 'Theory, Practice, and Anna Barbauld', Jager focuses on 'A Summer Evening's Meditation' to consider her religious scepticism and shows how her use of the language of fancy and analogy enables her to negotiate between the self, nature and God. Jager's chapter also explores some of the ways in which her poetry responds to Milton and Priestley. There are also chapters on Barbauld in Natasha Duquette's *Sublimer Aspects: Interfaces Between Literature, Aesthetics, and Theology*—'Anna Barbauld and Mary Anne Schimmelpenninck on the Sublimity of Scripture'—and in number 336 of the *Dictionary of Literary Biography*, *Eighteenth-Century British Historians*, edited by Ellen J. Jenkins, where Ancilya Hancock-Barnes offers a brief biography and a bibliography of Barbauld's published works. Vassiliki Markidou's '"Bubbles" and Female Verse: A Reading of Anna Laetitia Barbauld's "Washing Day"' (*CS* 19[2007] 19–33), focuses on the 'contradictory politics' of gender in the poem. Arguing that Barbauld's poem exists in a liminal space between feminism and middle-class conservatism, Markidou reads the passing down of folk tales as signifying 'an alternative type of inheritance to legal partrilineage, namely, cultural matrilineage' (p. 24). The essay argues also that this is reinforced by the intertextual links between the poem and Shakespeare's *As You Like It* and Pope's *The Dunciad*. There is also a chapter on Barbauld in Susan B. Rosenbaum's *Professing Sincerity*, which considers the 'doubleness of language' in her essays about Joseph Priestley. In 'Nature, Nation, and Denomination: Barbauld's Taste for the Public' (*ELH* 74[2007] 909–30), Emma Major studies Barbauld's poetic response to the preservation of the Corporation and Test Acts and positions her educational writings for children within the context of Dissenting texts and, in particular, in relation to other Warrington writers.

In addition to the essays on Mary Robinson in *Romantic Women Poets*, Emily Allen's 'Loss Incommensurable: Economies of Imbalance in Mary Robinson's *Walsingham*' (*ECN* 5[2006] 67–92) considers 'the question of the stance that female Romantic poets adopted towards male Romantic aesthetics, and of how their own aesthetic view elaborated its own vision, challenging and in many ways even influencing that of men' (p. 39). Kevin Gilmartin studies Hannah More's Cheap Repository Tracts [1795–8] in *Writing Against Revolution: Literary Conservatism in Britain, 1790–1832*, which, along with another essay on More, Eileen Cleere's 'Homeland Security: Political and Domestic Economy in Hannah More's *Coelebs in Search of a Wife*' (*ELH* 74[2007] 1–25), is reviewed in section 4 below. In 'Helen Maria Williams's Personal Narrative of Travels from *Peru* [1784] to *Peruvian Tales* (1823)' (*NCGS* 3:ii[2007] 24 paras), Jessica Damián explores the significance of the poems' shift in focus from nature and mining to accounts of the human cost of imperial expansion in Williams's revision of *Peru*. Damián argues that the revision is anti-commercialist and signals a disagreement with the commercial motives behind Britain's support of South American autonomy. The essay explains that 'The landscape aesthetics of *Peru* had no "place" in the *Peruvian Tales* since the discourses of nature had become complicit with the project of British expansion in the Andes'. Juan Sánchez's essay, 'Helen Maria Williams's *Peru* and the Spanish Legacy of the British Empire' (in Lamont and Rossington, eds., pp. 172–85), highlights the role of Spain in the creation of a British imperial ideology through Williams's *Peru*. For Sánchez, the tensions and ambiguities in Williams's account of imperial prowess uphold the imperial fantasy of empire expansion without blood-letting through the lurid descriptions of Spanish violence which served to invalidate their evangelical motives. Yet Williams's position is complicated somewhat since she accepts violence in a revolution but not for a conquest.

Angela Esterhammer's essay, 'The Improvisatrice's Fame: Landon, Staël, and Female Performers in Italy' (in Bode and Neumann, eds., *British and European Romanticisms*, pp. 227–37), compares the reception of two female *improvisatrice*, Corilla Olimpica in the eighteenth century, and Rosa Taddei in the nineteenth, to draw attention to the shift between performer as embodiment of inspiration and enthusiasm in the eighteenth century to 'the spectacle of the suffering [female] body and the attenuated spirit' in the nineteenth (p. 230). These contradictions between public and private, conventional and spontaneous, Esterhammer argues, are played out in

Landon's 'Erinna' [1826] and 'A History of the Lyre' [1828], which offer a 'self-conscious reflection on the psychology of the female performer' (p. 234).

Dorothy Wordsworth received much critical attention this year. First, Kenneth Cervelli's excellent monograph, *Dorothy Wordsworth's Ecology*, argues that 'to read her work ecologically, then, is to consider it as a totality—to consider it, that is, as a kind of ecosystem in which even the most seemingly innocuous elements (such as her children's poems) contribute to its health and vitality' (p. 88). Cervelli does this by studying the interrelatedness of the often fragmented entries in the Grasmere Journals, the relationship between tourism and the environment in *Recollections of a Tour Made in Scotland*, the relationship between Wordsworth's journals and her poetry and, finally, the relationship between her poetry, death and her daily experiences of nature, focusing on *A Narrative Concerning George and Sarah Green of the Parish of Grasmere*. Next, in 'Dorothy Wordsworth's Experimental Style' (*EIC* 57[2007] 325–49), Lucy Newlyn offers a thoughtful and enlightening exploration of Wordsworth's Alfoxden and Grasmere journals. As Newlyn shows, these journals can be read not only as accounts of daily life and descriptions of landscape and nature, but also as careful experiments with narrative and poetic prose styles. This essay considers the various narrative plots in the journal to argue that they were carefully crafted and deliberate. To consider the similarities between Wordsworth's journals and novels of sensitivity as coincidences is, for Newlyn, 'to miss the way that her awareness of genre shapes her experience and perception of reality' (p. 337). Instead, Newlyn considers the significance of Wordsworth's process of selection and the metrical patterns in her writing. A chapter entitled 'Dorothy Wordsworth, Natural History, and the Web of Nineteenth-Century Topography', in Mary Ellen Bellanca's *Daybrooks of Discovery, Nature Diaries in Britain, 1770–1870*, suggests that Wordsworth's Alfoxden and Grasmere journals embody a 'diversified practice' in which her recorded observations of nature, records of domestic life and lists of scientific facts are interlaced with 'the linguistic experiments of a creative writer' (p. 115). Bellanca explains that 'indeed, all these ways of interaction are interrelated and subsumed in one total enterprise, the building and writing of a relationship with nature and a sense of place-as-home' (p. 126). In this way, Bellanca argues, Wordsworth's journals are doubly domestic because they record the landscape around their house and because they also bring nature inside the house, thus treating 'the life found outside human-built walls as one with the life of household and human bonds' (p. 141). Finally for this section, Pamela Woof offers a biographical sketch of Wordsworth's life, focusing on her education and the period during which she wrote the Alfoxden and Grasmere journals, in 'Dorothy Wordsworth as a Young Woman' (*WC* 22[2007] 130–8).

(c) Blake

The year 2007 was the 250th anniversary of the birth of William Blake and saw a glut of (often fairly opportunistic) publications to celebrate the event. Most of these were reprints of editions of Blake's verse, such as the ongoing

Kessinger Publishing series and almost innumerable editions of *Songs of Innocence and of Experience*. Of critical work published during the year, as well as traditional fare for Blake scholars considering socio-historical contexts and Blake's crafts as an engraver, there was also a substantial number of publications that dealt with his influence on later generations.

Robert Rix has been engaged in researching radical Christian sects and Blake for several years now, and 2007 saw the publication of his book, *William Blake and the Cultures of Radical Christianity*. This section has frequently provided updates of various papers and articles published by Rix, and so it is with some pleasure that I was finally able to read a sustained account of how Blake interacted with some of the more esoteric and outré fringe figures who mixed religion, politics and more bizarre interests during the 1790s. Of course, important work has been done in this field by scholars such as Jon Mee and Marsha Keith Schuchard, but Rix's book will also stand on its own as a significant contribution. *Cultures* begins with two contextualizing chapters that place Blake within a more general milieu. The first deals with general religious themes, in particular analysing Blake's interests as part of speculative Protestantism of the more theosophical variety, the important point being made that, in the late eighteenth century at least, this type of mysticism did not see itself as being in retreat from the world but, by contrast, engaged with social and political matters as well as religious interests. One insight offered by Rix stems from the observation that Blake—a brief flirtation with Swedenborgianism aside—managed to avoid the sectarianism that was rife in those millenarian days, although for many fellow travellers 'religious loyalties were often fickle and ideas were received secondhand' (p. 2). Rix, then, sees Blake drawing upon such ideas as Moravian notions of universal love or Familist traditions that had gained ground since the seventeenth century, which, drawing upon work by David Worrall, Morton Paley and E.P. Thompson as well as Mee and Schuchard, he mingled with other libertarian ideals that gained currency during the 1790s.

The core of the book deals with Swedenborgianism: in recent years, Blake's relationship with Swedenborgianism has retreated somewhat in Blake studies compared with various other sects with which he or his family had potential links. As Rix reminds us, however, 'Swedenborg presented a radical form of ultra-evangelism in his reading of the Bible' (p. 57), one which had great appeal to Blake even when he took it upon himself to attack the church set up by the Swedish mystic (the satirical purpose of *The Marriage of Heaven and Hell* being the theme of a later chapter). Swedenborgianism itself, however, took a more conservative course as the eighteenth century progressed, and so Rix charts such elements as connections with the illuminati and radical preachers such as Richard Brothers that continued a more radical Christian line during the volatile final decade of the century. At all times, however, it is those important links forged via Swedenborgianism which give Blake his entry into this esoteric underworld, and this book provides exhaustive, detailed and fascinating analysis of those cults and cultures that provide a focus for Blake's religious and political ideas.

Political and religious radicalism in the 1790s is the starting point for the edited collection *Blake, Modernity and Popular Culture*, edited by Steve Clark and Jason Whittaker, although the focus of this collection is really the reception of Blake from the late Victorian period until the first decade of the twenty-first century. Continuing work begun in *Radical Blake: Influence and Afterlife from 1827* [2002], the collection explores the uses and abuses of Blake in both high and low culture, with a collection of essays by European and North American scholars. The first two chapters, G.A. Rosso's 'Popular Millenarianism and Empire in Blake's *Night Thoughts*' (pp. 12–25) and David Worrall's 'Blake in Theatreland: Fountain Court and its Environs' (pp. 25–38), place Blake firmly in the turbulent upheaval of the late eighteenth and early nineteenth centuries, each of them concerned to focus on how popular and nascent mass culture influenced Blake's art and thinking at this time. The next six chapters, by Colin Trodd, Shirley Dent, Edward Larrissy, Steve Clark, James Keery and Mark Douglas, focus on what could loosely be called Blake's contribution to modernist and high cultural forms, tracking through the reception of Blake during the Victorian period and ending with Jarman's queer aesthetic as a final flourish to the careers of Auden and Benjamin Britten. What is remarkable about the reception of Blake in the early part of the twentieth century is just how prevalent this neglected poet was, a point made admirably by Edward Larrissy in 'Blake: Between Romanticism and Modernism' (which covers similar ground to his recent *Blake and Modern Literature* [2006]). It is also significant that, while the late Victorians responded most acutely to Blake's painting, for the modernists and their immediate successors it was the poetry that was most resonant.

The final seven chapters move into the latter half of the twentieth century and blur the boundaries between high and popular culture. Matt Green and Christopher Ranger deal with two more literate writers, Salman Rushdie and Angela Carter, while the contributions by Mark Lussier, Michelle Gompf and Jason Whittaker deal with a variety of mass media forms, whether the graphic novels of Alan Moore, the use of Blake in the advertising and other industries, or the Hannibal Lecter series of novels and films. High points of this part of the book are Wayne Glausser's thoughtful take on both psychiatry and the complications of Blake studies in 'What Is It Like To Be a Blake? Psychiatry, Drugs and the Doors of Perception' (pp. 163–78), and Susan Matthews's 'Fit Audience tho Many: Pullman's Blake and the Anxiety of Popularity' (pp. 205–20). As Matthews remarks, 'For many academic critics, huge sales are a sign of danger, suggesting ideological complicity' (p. 211): Blake's isolation during his lifetime may have preserved him from such corruption, but as this collection demonstrates, the 'Blake brand' has had a remarkable impact in the past hundred years or so.

Coinciding with an exhibition that celebrated the bicentenary of the abolition of the slave trade as well as the anniversary of Blake's birth was the catalogue to *Mind-Forg'd Manacles: William Blake and Slavery*, edited by David Bindman. Although there has been a scattering of articles on Blake and slavery this was, as the curators point out in the foreword, the first substantial publication and display of Blake's work devoted to that subject. A sceptic would perhaps consider the relative paucity of references beyond the famous Stedman illustrations and 'The Little Black Boy' as reason why Blake has not featured so heavily in critical discussions of slavery during the Romantic period, at least with regard to the Atlantic trade. However, as Bindman points out in his introductory essay, images and allusions to slavery are endemic to Blake's art, and the artist's parallels between African slavery and the slavery of men and women bound to the wheels of Albion's machinery are more than mere opportunism. As such, 'Blake's responses to slavery are then somewhat apart from and more radical than the more "respectable" abolitionists of his time' (p. 20). As part of the context of more orthodox abolition movements, an essay by Darryl Pinckney offers a brief introduction to the themes and ambitions of the movement that culminated in the 1807 Act.

One slightly curious slim volume published in this year was '*Wheels Within Wheels': William Blake and Ezekiel's Merkabah in Text and Image* by Christopher Rowland. Concentrating on how Ezekiel informs Blake's art, Rowlands notes that there have been many discussions of cabbalistic doctrine in his works, but argues that it is Ezekiel 1 that was of specific interest to subsequent generations of Christian artists and scholars. Of particular importance is the influence of *merkabah* mysticism (from the Hebrew word for chariot), with Jewish mystics from the first century CE onwards seeking in Ezekiel's evocative description at the beginning of the prophetic book bearing his name an explanation of the secrets of creation. Rowlands makes the important point that 'we cannot . . . [suggest] that Blake was influenced by *merkabah* mysticism itself, though he was deeply indebted to the prophetic inspiration of Ezekiel. What is not in doubt, however, is that Ezekiel's *merkabah* has a prominent place in Blake's work, forming the inspiration of his major poetic work *The Four Zoas*' (p. 22). While very good on providing a context for *merkabah* mysticism, '*Wheels Within Wheels*' sometimes falls a little flat in terms of analysis of Blake's texts themselves. Thus his summary of *The Four Zoas* as 'essentially an exploration of human psychology in which each creature becomes a multi-faceted aspect of the human personality' (p. 32) is a fair but rather uninspiring exposition of Blake's most ambitious, sprawling, frustrating and challenging work, the confusing and unfinished nature of which prevents other scholars from making glib assertions as to its intent. Likewise, assertions such as 'William Blake was a visionary who communed with angels and even his dead brother regularly' (p. 17) does not provide much of a critical insight into what such visionary communication meant. However, when it comes to a reading of the biblical tradition, Rowlands really does provide some excellent material that can be used for an exegesis of Blake's texts, such as Jacob's dream of angels descending from and ascending to heaven. This is made even more important by the fact that biblical criticism is often overlooked in favour of other political, social and cultural contexts, yet was a tradition in which Blake was very deeply involved. At the Blake 250 conference in York, Andrew Lincoln stated that theological contexts for the study of Blake were a much-neglected area: Rowlands's book does not display the best critical thinking with regard to Blake's life and works, but is an important indication of how attention must be returned to this cornerstone of the artist's thinking.

While the majority of books published on Blake tend to concentrate on his literary productions, Martin Myrone's *The Blake Book* takes as its central point Blake's art. Part of the Tate Essential Artists series, this follows the standard format of the series in providing an authoritative guide to the life and career of artists in an accessible format. Myrone's book begins with contextual information on Blake's life and times, and the author's position as curator at Tate Britain with a specialism in eighteenth- and nineteenth-century art places him in a good position to offer crucial insights into Blake's relations with his contemporaries such as Fuseli and Flaxman. The book also draws on recent scholarship that concentrates on Blake's innovative engraving techniques, while not ignoring the illustrations done by Blake to Milton, the Bible and Dante among others. This is more a digest of work done in the past two decades or so exploring Blake's artistic achievements, and so is aimed at the general public more than art historians per se. It is, however, admirable in its clarity and presentation, and highly recommended also for literary scholars who need to catch up quickly with Blake's visual work. Another title for more general readers, although one focused on Blake's verbal rather than visual art, was Jonathan Roberts's *William Blake's Poetry: A Reader's Guide*. Part of the Continuum Reader's Guide series, this is really aimed at undergraduates rather than scholars so, in contrast to Myrone, there is not that much that will appeal to anyone researching Blake, although Roberts does a good job of providing some context to thematic approaches to the poet (such as religious, political or social) before considering some of Blake's texts in detail.

More interesting was the chapter, 'Escape from Repetition: Blake versus Locke and Wordsworth' by Laura Quinney (in Clymer, ed., *Ritual, Routine, and Regime: Repetition in Early Modern British and European Cultures*, pp. 36–79), which considered Blake's approaches to subjectivity and its relation to the natural world in *The Four Zoas*, contrasting this to an empirical attitude espoused by Locke in his *Essay Concerning Human Understanding* and to what Blake saw as a fatal repetition of this stance in Wordsworth's poetry. Before going on to consider journal articles published in 2007, a minor footnote should be made of two close readings of Blake's poems, 'A Dream', provided by Isabelle Keller-Privat, and the 'Introduction' to *Songs of Innocence*, by Françoise Besson (in Doumerc and Harding, eds., *An Introduction to Poetry in English*, pp. 94–8). These are both fairly straightforward, if brief, guides to the poems as part of a more general and wide-ranging introduction.

Of articles published in *Blake: An Illustrated Quarterly* during 2007, the winter edition saw another of the fruits of Keri Davies's labours on the Moravian background of the Blake family with 'Jonathan Spilsbury and the Lost Moravian History of William Blake's Family' (*Blake* 40:iii[2007] 100–9). A minute particular, it is part of the ongoing project that is helping gradually to contextualize the religious background of Blake and correct a few of the heresies that gained ground in the 1990s following the rather unfortunate suppositions made by E.P. Thompson in *Witness Against the Beast: William Blake and the Moral Law* [1993]. The Moravian tradition was likewise the subject of Marsha Keith Schuchard's 'Young William Blake and the Moravian Tradition of Visionary Art' (*Blake* 40:iii[2007] 84–100). Again drawing on the voluminous materials around the Moravians that formed the basis for her *Why Mrs Blake Cried* [2006], Schuchard argues for the importance of spiritual vision as part of a family tradition that could have been influential on Blake as a young boy and as a man.

The following issue of *Blake* saw Robert Essick's yearly round-up of sales in 'Blake in the Marketplace, 2006' (*Blake* 40:iv[2007] 116–46), although probably the biggest news of that year was something of a damp squib as the controversial sale of Blake's illustrations to Blair's *The Grave* failed to reach their estimate of $12–$17 million. This was then followed by another round-up, this time G.E. Bentley's familiar 'William Blake and his Circle: A Checklist of Publications and Discoveries in 2006' (*Blake* 41:i[2007] 4–43), the rest of each of these two issues including little more than minor notes and queries. More substantial was Joseph Viscomi's 'Blake's "Annus Mirabilis": The Productions of 1795' (*Blake* 41:ii[2007] 52–83), which concentrated on *The Song of Los*, *The Book of Ahania* and *The Book of Los*. The most startling aspect of Viscomi's work (more clearly visible in the digital reconstructions provided by him at http://www.rochester.edu/College/ENG/blake/1795/1795/index.html) is the way in which he shows that Blake originally conceived the now separate plates of *The Song of Los* as one visual artefact, later dividing them to construct his book. This allows him to make concrete and very convincing arguments as to Blake's printing process, the culmination and perfection of his printing experiments that began in 1789.

One of the most interesting publications of 2007 was a special edition of *ImageTexT* (http://www.english.ufl.edu/imagetext/archives/v3_2/), the journal of interdisciplinary comics studies, devoted to Blake and entitled *William Blake and Visual Culture*. Edited by Roger Whitson and Donald Ault, Whitson's introduction begins with the installation by David Burrows based on 'The Sick Rose' as one of the many examples of 'just how pliable William Blake's images remain' (para. 2), this 'pliability' being the subject of the intriguing essays contained in this edition. Arkady Plotnisky's 'Minute Particulars and Quantum Atoms: The Invisible, the Indivisible, and the Visualizable in William Blake and in Niels Bohr' begins with Blake's 'The Vision of the Last Judgement' as an 'initial configuration' of vision that is meant to 'infinitely expand . . . into ever larger assemblages . . . [a] dynamically expanding array of minute particulars' (para. 1). Blake's concept of minute particulars is related by Plotnisky to a quantum view of the atom proposed by Bohr that replaced the older, mechanical model that had its roots in Democritus. Although any hypothesis that Blake was a quantum physicist before Bohr should be viewed suspiciously (as with other claims such as that he was a psychoanalyst before Freud, as Plotnisky points out clearly), the article offers an interesting (if also slightly impish) take on Blake's anti-Newtonian philosophy of science that insists on the importance of observation of phenomena as a conscious act. Fascinating and probably more than a little confusing for the general humanist scholar.

Such a reader will be on more familiar ground with Nelson Hilton's 'Wordsworth Illustrates Blake ("All light is mute amid the gloom")', which argues that Blake's engraving for 'Holy Thursday' were influenced by Wordsworth's first book, *An Evening Walk*, published by Joseph Johnson in 1793 at the height of Blake's involvement with the radical publisher. This is a tightly argued and convincing piece, in contrast to Ron Broglio's 'William Blake and the Novel Space of Revolution' (*ImageTexT* [2007] 3.ii paras 1–24), which is much more ambitious but also sometimes rather vague in its argument. The following essay, 'Panelling Parallax: The Fearful Symmetry of William Blake and Alan Moore' (*ImageTexT* [2007] 3.ii paras 1–24), by Roger Whitson, is much more compelling. Moore has frequently laid claim to Blake's influence: 'Alan Moore's anxiety over his status as someone who must commodify his identity as a radical visionary artist in order to have a distinct audience of fans finds its expression in his obsession with William Blake' (para. 9). The clearest example is in *From Hell* (only discussed incidentally here), but a series of parallels between Blake and graphic novels, *Watchmen* in particular, makes for a significant contribution to the reception of Blake.

As well as these critical essays, the special edition includes an account by Matthew Ritchie of his Blake-inspired installation, 'The Universal Adversary', an interview with Bryan Talbot, author of the graphic novel *Alice in Sunderland*, a collage by John Coulthart based on the poetry reading, 'The Tygers of Wrath' that involved Billy Bragg, Iain Sinclair and others, and a graphic novel entitled 'Mr Blake's Company'. While the overall theme of this special edition of *ImageTexT* (ostensibly Blake's contribution to graphic novels) was watered down by some of the contributions and deserved a slightly clearer focus—there are not a few graphic artists who see in *Jerusalem* and *Milton* the precursors to their own art—it is intriguing and valuable in terms of demonstrating Blake's ongoing influence as a living artist.

Jeffrey Kripal's 'Reality against Society: William Blake, Antinomianism, and the American Counterculture' (*CK* 13:i[2007] 98–112) is another article concentrating on the reception of Blake's work, this time as part of a counter-culture that concentrates on Allen Ginsberg, Aldous Huxley and Theodore Roszak. The focus ends up being fairly narrow in terms of Blake's influence on figures from this time, but Kripal has some interesting comments on how Blake was incorporated, often anachronistically, into a revived interest in Asian religion and mysticism. Dealing not so much with reception as with potential correlations of ideas, Louise Economides takes a very different approach in 'Blake, Heidegger, Buddhism and Deep Ecology', published in Mark Lussier's 'Romanticism and Buddhism', part of the *Romantic Circles Praxis Series* (*RCPS* [2007] 17 paras). With a focus on *Milton*, Economides has some extremely pertinent remarks to make about the contribution of deep ecological thinking in terms of both identification and différance and in terms of our understanding of other life forms; what she finds in Blake is the importance of identification with the other that, alongside Heidegger's philosophy, recognizes the limitations of such identification, building on previous work done by Lussier. A different take on the role of Blake in terms of influencing subsequent artists was offered by Laura Mandell in 'Imaging Interiority: Photography, Psychology, and Lyric Poetry' (*VS* 49[2007] 218–27), also discussed in section 3(a). The central point of Mandell's extremely interesting thesis is that 'the romantic lyric anticipates the photograph' (p. 218). This assertion in its strong form appears ultimately flawed, yet Blake's *Songs* and Wordsworth's 'Tintern Abbey' (the central texts in Mandell's discussion) do seem to be good examples of how later Victorian photographers framed their subjects.

Although the question of reception in some shape or form featured largely in works published in 2007, there were plenty of other articles that dealt with the artist in the context of either Romanticism or Blake's own response to earlier aesthetic or philosophical principles. One example of the latter was Russell Prather's 'William Blake and the Problem of Progression' (*SiR* 46[2007] 507–40). Considering the dismissive remarks by the poet in *The Marriage of Heaven and Hell*, Prather takes a more contentious line that Blake was more influenced by Aristotelian logic than may at first appear. I am not sure I agree with all of Prather's assertions (for example, the almost throwaway remark on Blake viewing marriage as 'utterly crippling' appears too strong an assertion of the poet's position), but he is correct in his assessment of at least some of the origins of Blake's dialectical vision.

Important historical context for Blake's writing is provided by Mark L. Barr's 'Practicing Resistance: Blake, Milton, and the English Jury' (*ERR* 18[2007] 361–79), which takes the 1804 trial of Blake as a central point for understanding his poem *Milton*. The poet's experience of that trial, argues Barr, encourages 'readerly revolt' against any authorial, dictatorial power that is analogous to rebellions by 'pious' jurors against the legal authorities of the early 1800s. A later edition of the *European Romantic Review* provided another article that places Blake in historical contexts, this time the 1790s. In 'Blake, the Famine of 1795, and the Economics of Vision' (*ERR* 18[2007] 597–622) Dennis M. Welch provides solid cultural and economic background for the 1795 prophecies against a backdrop of widespread famine that increased political unrest during that year. Blake, argues Welch, took the sense of conspiracy and paranoia surrounding fears over the manipulation of food prices and reinterpreted these in spiritual terms as the deceptions of Urizen and Fuzon. Against the selfish materialism of such figures, Blake's own proto-socialist economic vision emphasized brotherhood, and Welch's paper is a useful reminder of Blake's intense interest in not just the politics but also the economics of his day.

Galia Benziman's 'Two Patterns of Child Neglect: Blake and Wordsworth' (*PAns* 5[2007] 167–97) (also discussed in section 3(a)) uses these two poets to challenge any simplistic opposition between Romantic and Puritan concepts of childhood. Both Blake and Wordsworth attempt to subvert authoritative and catechetical thinking that silences the child yet, Benziman argues, their poems tend not to liberate child narrators but instead subsume them in their own adult discourses. This act of 'poetic ventriloquism' even goes as far as maintaining precisely the authoritative frameworks they ostensibly reject, constituting 'a sacrifice of the child's difference and uniqueness' (p. 194). Childhood is considered from a different perspective in Debbie Lee's 'Lost Girls, Lost Women: Foundlings in the Art and Poetry of William Blake' (*Prism(s)* 15[2007] 129–53). While dealing with Blake's early poetry in particular, especially that of the *Songs*, Lee provides sympathetic and detailed contexts for the treatment of foundlings at the very end of the eighteenth century, and which was part of a wider discourse of social concern that Blake would have encountered on a daily basis. A very different type of context, but one increasingly familiar to anyone working in Blake studies, is provided by G.E. Bentley Jr in 'Blake's Heavy Metal: The History, Weight, Uses, Cost, and Makers of his Copper Plates' (*UTQ* 76:ii[2007] 714–70), a carefully detailed account of the materials used by Blake in his engraving work. As with the majority of Bentley's work over the past half-century, this article is meticulous and provides another set of minute particulars concerning the conditions affecting Blake's work as a printmaker.

There were also individual articles that concentrated on various textual aspects of Blake's work. 'A Voice without Form: Blake's Book of Ahania and Song of Solomon' by James Mulvihill (*ES* 88[2007] 522–30) considered the Old Testament Song as one of the sources for Blake's text, one of those that receives much less critical attention than contemporary prophetic works such as *The Book of Urizen* (although *Ahania* did also feature in Joseph Viscomi's treatment of Blake, as mentioned above). As such, this article provides a welcome reading of a marginalized text, but also has perceptive insights into the eroticism of Blake's poetry. '"That angel who rides on the whirlwind": William Blake's Oriental Apotheosis of William Pitt' (*ECLife* 31:ii[2007] 1–28) presents a close analysis of the portrait of William Pitt by David Fallon. As part of Blake's 1809 solo exhibition, Fallon begins with the observation that this painting (along with that of Nelson) would have been confusing to many contemporaries, and that Blake was aware of this, but as the article goes on to suggest quite clearly this was part of a discourse on tyranny that the audience would have been familiar with. Kelly Aitken's 'Wonder; No Wonder: William Blake's Illustrations to the Book of Job' (*QQ* 114:iv[2007] 571–5), meanwhile, is a short, more subjective piece on the author's responses to Job.

4. The Novel

This year was marked by a close attention to reception history, and to patterns of creativity, exchange, and influence amongst different groups and families, as well as repeated interrogations of national identity. *The Reception of Jane Austen in Europe*, edited by Anthony Mandal and Brian Southam, part of the Continuum series on the reception of British and Irish authors in Europe, is a work of serious scholarly exchange and an invaluable broadening of our commonly anglocentric view of Austen reception. Has Austen's Englishness, the book asks, 'abetted or hindered her transmission across national borders and cultural boundaries?' (p. 1). As the editors point out, despite the current lively interest in Austen's critical fortunes, there has been little systematic consideration of her European reception. Moving across seventeen countries, the volume addresses three key periods: a fallow time of little widespread recognition during the nineteenth century; a change in fortunes through the period 1901–90; and the surge of widespread 'Austenmania' during 1991–2005, which the editors describe as 'pan-European' (p. 2).

The volume begins with a timeline showing the steady arc of Austen translation and critical recognition across the continent, beginning as early as 1813 when the first extracts from *Pride and Prejudice* appeared in French translation in a Genevan journal. France and Switzerland led the way in publishing translations; between 1815 and 1824 all six novels were translated. Yet, as Isabelle Bour notes, 'there was not a single review of any of the translations' (p. 12). In the first three chapters, she traces the consequences of this apparent contradiction, outlining the different trajectories of the novel in

England and France through the nineteenth century, and meticulously outlining the context of reception for British fiction across the Channel. Looking not only at the translations and adaptations but also at editorial decisions, contemporary guidebooks and excerpts in periodicals, she repeatedly asks just what continental readers might have *expected* of Austen. Isabelle de Montolieu's translations, for instance, presented Austen's work in the context of novels of sensibility, 'heightening' emotional scenes, flattening her ironies and ignoring her humour and, most importantly, altering her narrative voice and largely erasing the use of free indirect speech. Like the fainting heroines of Austen's own *Juvenilia*, Montolieu 'rarely misses an opportunity to have characters cry and fall into each other's arms' (p. 23). Towards the latter part of the nineteenth century, however, Bour shows a gradual recognition of Austen as 'a humorist and a stylist' (p. 34), and suggests that analysis of her narrative strategies and handling of voice now occupies a significant place in French higher education. Yet Bour concludes that her work is still best known in France through the altered medium of the films, which—like those anonymous early translations—are not always connected to Austen herself. Bour's complex analysis in the first three chapters sets the tone for the volume, which shows the enormous difficulty of assessing the impact and interpretation of Austen's original versions in varying cultural contexts. Annika Bautz's comments on the different reception of Austen in East and West Germany offers a particularly good example. 'The schism between East and West is striking', she notes, 'West Germans see her as socially critical but not as emancipated, whereas East Germans see her as socially uncritical but as a pioneer of emancipation' (p. 106). In Finland, similarly, Austen's presentation of class—her depiction of 'the self-important petty-bourgeois social circle of the good old days' (p. 177)—has historically proved a stumbling block. What is immediately noticeable, however, from Spain to Serbia and from Holland to Russia, is that this is a time of unprecedented interest in Austen. Fuelled by film adaptations, this has nevertheless resulted in a boom in translations, popular and academic: from Gallimard's Pléiade series to mass reprints in Spanish. This makes this important volume especially timely. To explore her Russian reinterpretation as 'a sort of *Eugene Onegin* on British soil' (p. 349), or her presence in Romanian gender studies criticism opens up a new field for Austen reception history and promises, as the editors conclude, 'a vibrant and long-lived future for Jane Austen in Europe as the twenty-first century unfolds' (p. 3).

This is borne out by a strong collection of articles and studies of Austen this year. Anthony Mandal's *Jane Austen and the Popular Novel: The Determined Author* strikingly recontextualizes Austen in light both of recent developments in bibliographical studies and of a trend towards more nuanced political readings. Like Roger Sales and Peter Knox-Shaw, Mandal argues that we need to be wary about critical tendencies to situate Austen—both in literary and political terms—too firmly in the 1790s. Instead, he seeks to set Austen's ambitions during that decade in dialogue with her success in the 1810s, and to make the case for the Regency period as a 'vibrant and receptive market for women writers' (p. 4). Thus the first half of the study looks in detail at Austen's intentions and aims in the 1790s, setting these in the context of a booming marketplace for the novel: the 'halcyon period during 1788–96' (p. 17). But this boom time was followed, he suggests, by a period of indirection later in the 1790s, and it was not until the 'overlooked 1810s' that a subsequent generation of female novelists really began to enjoy success. Mandal's careful and thorough uncovering of the fluctuating dynamics of the fiction market allows a rereading of Austen's negotiations with her publishers. Why, for instance, did Cadell and Davies reject *First Impressions*? Mandal acknowledges specific reasons—the inadequacies of George Austen's letter for a start—but suggests other possibilities, showing that 'the conditions of the publishing season 1797–8 were clearly different from those of spring 1795' (p. 60). Wary of a genre which had started to attract political and moral opprobrium, respectable publishers had begun to back away from the novel, allowing their publication of fiction to decrease. Austen's output, Mandal argues, was deeply and directly informed by the contemporary publishing context, and the changing conditions of the 1790s had a formative influence on her first three works. The later novels, similarly, 'belong categorically to the 1810s' (p. 88). *Mansfield Park* is read as a response to evangelical fiction and contemporary models such as Mary Brunton's *Self-Control*; *Emma*, marking Austen's move to the high-profile John Murray, is shown to engage with national fictions, *Persuasion* to challenge the Waverley novels. Austen was, Mandal concludes, neither 'hermetically sealed within a single epoch nor entirely self-referential' (p. 216). Although it might have been good to see more of the period between this 1790s/1810s division, Mandal's study affords a new and thorough reading of Austen's contemporary context; his clear use of complex bibliographical data also points up new critical possibilities.

Michael Kramp's *Disciplining Love: Austen and the Modern Man* begins with a discussion of modern men's movements, from evangelical meetings to 'Iron John ceremonies'. Kramp explores what happens to masculinity—perceived to be in crisis—and suggests how Austen's men successfully negotiate their own post-revolutionary uncertainties. From Henry Tilney's 'masculinity of restraint' (p. 36) to Marianne Dashwood's desire for a passionate lover, Kramp discusses the ways in which men in Austen's novels might discipline and regulate their emotions; he also discusses issues of social and economic security, exploring Bingley and Gardiner as representatives of a new 'trade class'. Kramp's study asks how the 'modern man' might be constructed, addressing different models of masculinity in the Regency period, as well as different critical approaches including Gilles Deleuze and Michel Foucault. Austen, he argues, repeatedly demonstrates that 'post-Revolutionary English society desires carefully disciplined masculine subjects who will assume the responsibility of guiding England through its post-Revolutionary transformation' (p. 70). Elizabeth Sabiston's *Private Sphere to World Stage from Austen to Eliot* also addressed gender politics in Austen. Sabiston's passionate defence of the novelist as conscious artist in the face of 'critics who patronize Austen' seems a little dated now; there are few critics who still adhere to the Henry James line of her 'composing in the drawing room in the intervals of dropped stitches' (p. 5). Using *Northanger Abbey* to argue that 'Jane Austen was an artist who knew exactly what she was doing' seems a well-trodden path (p. 14), and the whole premise that these nineteenth-century women novelists, including Austen, Brontë and Gaskell, were operating by stealth on a male 'world stage' is strongly reminiscent of older criticism such as *The Madwoman in the Attic*, despite footnotes to recent critical studies. However, Sabiston has an engaging, individual voice, and her readings of Charlotte Lennox's *The Female Quixote* as a parallel to *Northanger Abbey* are especially involving. Emily Auerbach's *Searching for Jane Austen*, reprinted this year, provides an overview of new critical trends and a humorous take on the problems of teaching Austen in the face of new readerly expectations, shaped by film adaptations. Her portrayal of a subversive Austen is not quite as 'revolutionary' as the blurb claims, but she gives a lively account of contemporary appropriations of Austen. William Baker's substantial essay-review, 'Jane Austen Once More' (*SNNTS* 39:iii[2007] 357–67) also gives an overview of recent developments in Austenian reception criticism, enthusiastically responding to Kathryn Sutherland's *Jane Austen's Textual Lives* [2005] and dissecting the power of the 'Janeite' legacy.

Valerie Wainwright, *Ethics and the English Novel from Austen to Forster* (also discussed in Chapter XIII) offers a discussion of Victorian morality through novels which place emphasis on fulfilment and happiness, and on virtue as 'anchored to conceptions of rewarding lives' (p. 3). Wainwright explores Austen as part of a broad sweep of novelists across the nineteenth and early twentieth centuries, including Gaskell, Dickens, George Eliot, Hardy and Forster, all of whom are fascinated by the moral identity of the individual. Her discussion of Austen centres on *Mansfield Park*, asking us to reconsider the portrayal of Fanny as a figure of 'moral rectitude' (p. 67), and challenging the widespread critical notion of her as a model of exemplary behaviour. Wainwright analyses several moments where Fanny's behaviour might have 'troubling implications'—particularly in her dealings with the Crawfords—and suggests that Austen is deliberately inviting the reader to question the 'picture of good' with which the novel closes. If we no longer accept Fanny as moral arbiter, argues Wainwright, we have also to reread her happy ending, and the ethical stance of the novel is thus more complex and challenging. Margaret Watkins Tate, 'Resources for Solitude: Proper Self-Sufficiency in Jane Austen' (*P&L* 31:ii[2007] 323–43) also explored the nature of virtue in Austen's heroines, although she did not touch on Fanny Price. Watkins Tate investigates Austen's portrayal of the struggle against 'mundane evils' faced by Emma or Anne—isolation or ennui—to construct a concept of 'flourishing' which is based on 'self-sufficiency'. Stefanie Markovits, in 'Jane Austen and the Happy Fall' (*SEL* 47[2007] 779–97), discusses Austen's 'understanding of falling': not simply in the physical sense, from the Cobb or from horseback, but from a moral perspective. She suggests that the 'moral fall' helps us understand Austen's attitude to happiness—a concept which, for Austen, 'embraces movement and change, not stillness' (p. 784). Michael J. Stasio and Kathryn Duncan offered a very different view of Austen's ethics in 'An Evolutionary Approach to Jane Austen: Prehistoric Preferences in *Pride and Prejudice*' (*SNNTS* 39:ii[2007] 133–46). This attempted to link the shift towards companionate marriage in the eighteenth century and interest in evolutionary psychology with the rise of the novel. However, the link between the concepts remains slightly obscure, and this dogged reading of the novel as a textbook on 'mate choice' seems determined to overlook its status as fiction. Darcy's first attraction to Elizabeth's 'pair of fine eyes', for instance, draws the solemn comment that 'in early ancestral environments, cloudy or dull eyes may have been a sign of disease or bad genes'—save for some minor environmental differences, there is little to choose between Austen and her 'Pleistocene ancestors'.

A clutch of articles dealt specifically with language in Austen. Janine Barchas, in 'Very Austen: Accounting for the Language of *Emma*' (*NCF* 62:iii[2007] 303–38), dealt with the 1,212 uses of the word 'very' in the novel—a higher rate than any other Austen text. Is this repeated use simply an 'unconscious filler'? Barchas argues that it represents the 'impact that isolation exerts upon speech patterns', showing not only the isolated, repetitive nature of Highbury life but also Austen's own keen attention to linguistics. Massimiliano Morini, in 'Say What You Mean, Mean What You Say: A Pragmatic Analysis of the Italian translations of *Emma*' (*L&L* 16:i[2007] 5–19), similarly paid close attention to the language of *Emma*, using examples of its translation into Italian to demonstrate the importance of pragmatics for translation analysis. In 'The "Dual Voice" of Free Indirect Discourse: A Reading Experiment' (*L&L* 16:i[2007] 37–52), Joe Bray used cognitive poetics to 'test how readers respond to free indirect discourse' in *Emma*, exploring the effect of point of view on perception. Terence Murphy, in 'Monitored Speech: The "Equivalence" Relation between Direct and Indirect Speech in Jane Austen and James Joyce' (*Narrative* 15:i[2007] 24–39), explored the role of the reader in utilizing 'examples of monitored speech to devise directly quoted speech paraphrases of their own' (p. 28), showing how this might work in examples ranging from *Mansfield Park* to 'The Dead'. In ' "What Edward promises he will perform": "How to do things with words" in *Sense and Sensibility*' (*TPr* 21:i[2007] 113–34) Edward Neill also focused on Austen's slippery language games. Neill begins by suggesting that Austen pre-empts her later namesake, J.L. Austin, in exploring the subtle uses of 'our ordinary words' (p. 114); he then draws a parallel between Austin's interest in the 'performed' and 'performative language' and the many instances of promises and performance in *Sense and Sensibility*. Lorri G. Nandrea, in 'Difference and Repetition in Austen's *Persuasion*' (*SNNTS* 39:i[2007] 48–64), looks closely at the narrative structure of the novel and argues that it experiments with 'the formal principles of "origin and ending" ', replacing them with 'difference and repetition' (p. 55). Austen constantly alerts the reader to the possibility of different outcomes, different trajectories, which are intricately connected to acts of persuasion within the novel; Nandrea shows how these narrative complexities might open up larger questions of gender and history.

There were two nice readings of Austen and Byron. Sarah Wootton's 'The Byronic in Jane Austen's *Persuasion* and *Pride and Prejudice*' (*MLR* 102[2007] 26–39) puts forward a fresh and thoughtful perspective on the 'deep Romantic undercurrents' between the two authors. Both interrogate and seek to redefine heroism—as well as responding to Gothic villainy—and Wootton persuasively argues for a rereading of Darcy as Byronic hero. Peter Robinson, 'Captain Benwick's Reading' (*EIC* 57[2007] 147–70) offers a sympathetic approach to Benwick's fondness for poetry, often critically dismissed as a sign of self-indulgent mourning. 'Could the usual disapproval of Benwick's reading and change of fiancée', asks Robinson, 'be connected with the domestic reputation of *The Corsair*'s author?'. He asks us to reconsider and rehabilitate Benwick's character, and to ponder the complex ways in which *Persuasion* might engage with Romantic poetry on several different levels.

Alexander Bove, in 'The "Unbearable Realism of a Dream"': On the Subject of Portraits in Austen and Dickens' (*ELH* 74[2007] 655–79), seeks to complicate the critical claim that Austen may be seen as developing 'the aesthetic of mimetic characterization', through an exploration of the doubts and anxieties over representation present in the portrait scene of *Pride and Prejudice*. He compares and contrasts this with Dickens's treatment of portraits in *David Copperfield*, concluding that both authors 'frame their portrait scenes in terms of different responses to the same crisis of representation' within the novel (p. 677). Meanwhile, Karen Valihora in 'Impartial Spectator Meets Picturesque Tourist: The Framing of *Mansfield Park*' (*ECF* 20:i[2007] 89–114) considers perspectives from another angle: that of the picturesque tourist. Picturesque theory gives Valihora a way of exploring an engaged way of seeing analogous to the immersive reading experience created by Austen; 'picturesque aesthetics', she argues, 'are predicated not on distance, but on absorption' (p. 91). She then deftly draws parallels between the picturesque prospects in which Fanny finds herself and Austen's manipulation of narrative viewpoint. Ann Bermingham, in her essay 'The Cottage Ornée: Sense, Sensibility, and the Picturesque Cottage' (in Clymer and Mayer, eds., pp. 215–24), also addresses the picturesque. She relates contemporary aesthetic dilemmas over the picturesque cottage—which to be truly picturesque must be dilapidated and opposed to modern convenience—to Austen's opposition between sense and sensibility. The Regency 'cottage ornée' is, she concludes, a 'triumph of sense *and* sensibility', a romantic compromise similar to that made by Marianne when she plumps for the flannel-waistcoated Brandon.

Over a century's-worth of striking essays on *Emma* are presented by Fiona Stafford in her *Jane Austen's Emma: A Casebook*. This is a good updating of the casebook format, a useful and relevant collection of pieces which form a good starting point for students interested in Austen's reception history. Stafford's introduction is clear, thoughtful and gives a good summary of changes in critical perception of Austen, the way in which, in Lionel Trilling's words, 'the opinions which are held about her work are almost as interesting, and almost as important to think about, as the work itself' (p. 3). Her introduction to the evolution of these opinions is a strong framework for the essays which follow, beginning with Jane Austen's own attentive comments on readers' responses to the work and Walter Scott's *Quarterly* review—although this last is discussed in the introduction, its original source could have been flagged up a little more in the body of the text. We then move on to some classic essays from the 1950s from Trilling and Wayne C. Booth; responses to feminist criticism represented by Claudia L. Johnson and Joseph Litvak; John Wiltshire's discussion of health and Brian Southam on patriotism. There are also essays on the novel's interpretation through film—Linda Troost and

Sayre Greenfield—and in postcolonial criticism (Gayle Wald). Frances Ferguson's formalist discussion closes the volume.

The JASNA journal (*Persuasions* 29[2007]), also focused this year on *Emma*. Many of the essays took as their starting point Emma's moment of Highbury observation, waiting outside Ford's for Harriet, her eye falling 'on the butcher with his tray . . . two curs quarrelling over a dirty bone', and discussed different aspects of Emma's community, local and literary. Janet Todd's opening piece, for instance, discussed the class anxieties and 'linguistic uneasiness' of *Emma* and its minute description of the 'constant flow of commonplace social intercourse' (p. 25), and Phyllis Ferguson Bottomer speculated on the view a speech language pathologist might take of Highbury. Juliet McMaster discussed the psychological geography of the novel; more literal geographies of Highbury were explored by Barbara Britton Wenner and Tara Ghoshal Wallace. There was a nod to the Vancouver setting of the JASNA AGM with Jean Barman's exploration of 'British Columbia in Jane Austen's Time', but elsewhere the attention was firmly on local detail, as in Shannon E. Campbell's vindication of Jane Austen's knowledge of late-flowering apple varieties. Alice Marie Villaseñor placed the novel in the context of Edward Austen Knight's Godmersham library, and Jane Fairfax was set in a broader literary tradition by Jocelyn Harris's discussion of *Jane Eyre* and Penny Gay's analysis of 'She-Tragedies' of the eighteenth century, with Theresa Kenney re-examining Mr Knightley. Douglas Murray noticed portraits of the Prince Regent in the novel, and Palma Bjarnason analysed its dance scenes. There are too many pieces to be discussed in full detail, but the journal is always a good-humoured forum for Austen scholarship. Meanwhile, its online edition (*PersuasionsO* 28:i[2007]) provides a supplement to these conference papers, with discussions of *Emma* as detective fiction, and its film adaptations. The first volume (*PersuasionsO* 27:ii[2007]) offers a collection of essays on different aspects of Joe Wright's 2005 adaptation, *Pride & Prejudice*.

Annika Bautz's *The Reception of Jane Austen and Walter Scott: A Comparative Longitudinal Study* is a careful and useful guide to the changing fortunes of the literary reputations of Austen and Scott across the centuries, divided into three parts: contemporary, Victorian and later twentieth-century response. The disparity between Scott as the bestseller who is now hardly read and the extraordinary contemporary popularity of Austen offers a highly interesting case study of the factors which determine literary reception. Bautz gives an account of functions of the periodical and reviewing in the Romantic period, as well as uncovering the contemporary responses of individual readers in letters and diaries. She then moves on to a section on Victorian reception, outlining editions as well as reviews and criticism; the closing section discusses twentieth-century responses, critical and cultural. Newspaper and film reviews are discussed—Austen emerged from the *Guardian*'s overheated commentary as the 'Quentin Tarantino of the middle classes'; for the optimistic *Independent* she united 'the literati and the lads' (pp. 128–9)—and data such as visitor numbers to her house at Chawton are analysed. She concludes this thoughtful overview of reception patterns by assessing the impact of postcolonial and politicized readings of Scott and Austen.

The Reception of Sir Walter Scott in Europe, edited by Murray Pittock, also part of the Continuum Reception of British Authors in Europe series, contains essays on Scott's French, Spanish, Catalan, German, Hungarian, Czech, Polish, Russian, Slovene, Danish, Norwegian and Swedish reputations, and closes with chapters tracing his impact on European poetry, opera, art and cultural tourism. Pittock's introduction reminds us of the complexities of Scott's fictionalization of Enlightenment historiography. While it might have been understood as relatively conservative in Great Britain, 'in societies struggling for independence against regional powers or colonial oppressors, with suppressed languages, disordered civic societies and no historiography save that of native resentment and patriot resistance, the radical undertow in Scott's writing could seem more prominent' (p. 5). While giving a very thorough overview (including an extensive chronology) of Scott's translations and adaptations, the study also shows the startling range of these manipulations and reinterpretations. The book opens with two essays tracing his reception in France which give us a good idea of the range and style of the volume. The first, by Richard Maxwell, shows the importance of French literature and history in Scott and traces the way in which, in turn, the French absorbed the Waverley novels 'with dazzling speed' (p. 12): from Emma Bovary dreaming over 'guardrooms, old oak chests and minstrels' (p. 23) to Marcel Proust's college student in *Sodome et Gomorrhe* who has not yet realized that what 'he desires is Rob Roy and not Diana Vernon' (p. 11). Paul Barnaby's chapter focuses on how Scott's influence was framed, with a close reading of Auguste-Jean-Baptiste Defauconpret's translations. Long supposed to be 'colourless but essentially accurate', Barnaby shows how in fact Defauconpret tailored 'the Waverley novels to a Legitimist, Catholic, post-Napoleonic readership' (p. 32). From the start, then, we have a sense of the complex double movement of the study: it shows both how Scottophilia, in many different forms, shapes the literature of Europe, and how Europe's writers and readers, in their turn, shape Scott. We encounter a Catalan Ivanhoe and a Transylvania 'analogous to Highland Scotland' (p. 153): detailed statistics uncover different afterlives for Scott in East, West and reunified Germany. Moreover, we have a larger sense of the way in which Scott pulses through the great writing of the nineteenth century—Hugo, Dumas, Balzac, Pushkin, Tolstoy, the early Mickiewicz—as well as its poetry, its opera and its art.

Four major studies take Scott as their focus this year, all, in different ways, exploring how we might reread Scott's engagement with Scottish national identity. Andrew Lincoln's *Walter Scott and Modernity* insists on the contemporary relevance of Scott's novels. In Scott's hands the historical novel, with its careful negotiations between present and past, offered 'an imaginative space' in which his contemporary readers, still reeling from continuing conflicts and threats to national security, 'could encounter their own anxieties while appearing to escape from them' (p. 2). Moreover, argues Lincoln, Scott's strategies are still useful for an understanding of modernity, and particularly our attitudes to liberalism. Scott's historical fiction, by confronting the modern liberal individual with attitudes from the past they are by now supposed to have renounced, 'enables an unprecedented fictional engagement with some of the enduring moral, social, and political problems bequeathed by the emergence of liberalism' (p. 151). Lincoln's study opens by showing how Scott's novels anticipate current debates, including the consequences of abrupt regime change and the political role of the individual. He begins by reading the poetry—still, as he points out, decidedly neglected— and *Waverley* in the context of Scott's conception of 'the artist as agent of national reconciliation', transforming a disrupted and conflicted past into 'a usable heritage in the modern state'. This is an attentive reading of Scott's self-conscious negotiations with history; like Caroline McCracken-Flesher in her 2005 study, *Possible Scotlands*, Lincoln argues against a purely nostalgic, myth-making Scott. Rather, he highlights Scott's use and transformation of history, as in his rereading of *Ivanhoe* and *Kenilworth* alongside Scott's management of George IV's ceremonial visit to Edinburgh, when Scott's fascination with pageantry is reinterpreted not simply as antiquarian game-playing, but as part of 'a heightened sensitivity to the political and communal function of spectacle' (p. 67). The chapter places this, interestingly, in the context of contemporary British spectacle, such as the 2002 Golden Jubilee: heritage fantasies which point up the ongoing significance of Scott's reflections on nation-building and national storytelling. Elsewhere in the book, Lincoln discusses Scott's attitude to the Orient through *Guy Mannering* and *The Talisman*, arguing—much like Julia M. Wright's study, *Ireland, India, and Nationalism in Nineteenth-Century Literature*, discussed later in this section— that his awareness of English behaviour towards the Scots shaped his outlook on imperial projects. A similarly complex attitude is analysed in Scott's treatment of commercial interests in *Rob Roy* and *The Legends of Montrose*, and Lincoln closes the volume with a discussion of Scott's engagement with views of liberalism. This is both intellectual history and literary criticism; it offers a strong argument for the continued rereading of Scott, not only in relation to Scottish national identity, but also in terms of modern liberal consciousness.

Ian Duncan, in *Scott's Shadow: The Novel in Romantic Edinburgh*, looked in detail at Scott's literary and historical context, by giving a portrait of the Scots literary scene between 1802—the year of the founding of the *Edinburgh Review*—and 1832, the year of Scott's death. This was a boom time for Edinburgh as a literary and cultural metropolis, and for Scottish fiction in general, centring around Scott himself. 'Scott's shadow', as Duncan terms it, refers to Scott's overwhelming dominance of the literary scene in Edinburgh, a 'force field' of influence which shaped Scottish Romanticism and exerted a powerful effect on those writers around him. 'Scott's shadow' also refers to the diffuse identity of Scott himself, and his 'veiled', elusive authorial persona (pp. xii–xiii). Duncan begins with an exploration of the lively Edinburgh literary scene, replete with civic confidence, newly pictured by Turner and described in contemporary prints as a *Modern Athens* (p. 10). He shows how its transformation into a thriving commercial marketplace may be seen as representative of the birth of modern literary culture, and deftly shows the many different strategies employed by Scottish writers to exploit their situation, and to create their own fictions.

Within this flourishing context, Duncan shows how Scott produced a new type of fiction. Like Lincoln, he rejects a reading of the Waverley novels which would flatten them 'into a pageantry of Tory prejudice'. Rather, he argues, Scott tries to open up new forms for debate. His novels had a 'national representativeness' which reviews and magazines lacked (p. 30), and prompted a very blizzard of other Scotch novels, inciting other novelists to enter the field. Duncan's analysis of these competing fictions is excellent, giving a real sense of patterns of influence and reception across a range of novels, from Susan Ferrier to John Galt. As we see, for instance, Mr Ramsay in Ferrier's *The Inheritance* becoming addicted to Scott, 'completely absorbed' in *Guy Mannering*, we realize the ways in which novelists attempted to read their rivals. The study is thus divided between a study of Scott himself and his wider context and reception. In the five chapters of the first half Duncan argues for the importance of our own attentive reading of Scott within different cultural contexts in the 1810s and 1820s. These include 'Edinburgh, Capital of the Nineteenth Century', 'The Invention of National Culture' and 'Economies of National Character', which shows how novelists such as Hamilton dealt with such questions as Scottish 'dirt' and nastiness. Duncan concludes the section by arguing for an appreciation of the Humean underpinning of Scott's novels. He then moves on to focus on other Scots authors and their rival regional and national projects: in particular, he directs us to the writings of James Hogg and John Galt, for whose fiction he makes a compelling argument. He concludes with a look ahead to Thomas Carlyle, and what he sees as the disintegration of Scottish Romanticism in *Sartor Resartus*. This is a very detailed and dense study, which will have an impact on readings of Scottish Romanticism for many years.

Kenneth McNeil, in *Scotland, Britain, Empire: Writing the Highlands, 1760–1860*, also thinks deeply about Scott's complex negotiations with Scottish collective identity. Beginning with an account of the formation of the Highland Society of London in 1778, McNeil's study assesses the part Highland culture might have played in shaping Scottish national culture, and the role of the Highlands 'as a site for the Scottish negotiation of national identity in an age of empire' (p. 7). He argues for a particular attention to detail, to the 'complexities of identity and difference that are visible in Scottish writing on the Highlands' (p. 3), and in Highland writing itself. This includes Macpherson's translation of Ossian, with which the study begins, as well as lesser-known works such as David Stewart's *Sketches of the Highlanders* [1822]. In the centre of the study McNeil places two chapters rereading Scott's portrayal of a 'fake Highlands', which he initially puts forward as part of a larger 'ideological project of consolidating Scotland's absorption into an Anglo-dominated Great Britain'. Scott, argues McNeil, packaged and commodified the Highlands into a distinctive but inert, lifeless, historical identity, which he sees as culminating in Scott's 'gaudy overuse of "tartanry" ' (p. 52) during the 1822 royal visit, an event he reads alongside *Rob Roy*. But, having mooted this argument, McNeil shows how we might place a more sympathetic interpretation on Scott's desire to 'articulate a Scottish solidarity', a collective identity which might perform its own resistance (p. 81). The focus moves outwards, to show the ways in which narratives of the Highlands might become incorporated into imperial and national projects. McNeil discusses Edward Waverley's perceptions of the Highland warrior, and shows how the ideal of the Highland soldier-hero served an important purpose in British military rhetoric. He concludes with a study of a different type of imperial narrative: Queen Victoria's Highland diaries, which he sets alongside Anne Grant's travelogues. Scott's reading of the Highlands is thus placed in a broader Romantic and Victorian landscape.

The year also saw a paperback issue of Julian Meldon D'Arcy's *Subversive Scott: The Waverley Novels and Scottish Nationalism* first published in 2005. This revisits seminal views of Scott formed in the 1950s by David Daiches and Duncan Forbes, exploring his divided allegiances to Scots nationalism and Hanoverian Britain. Instead of the 'Daichean model', Meldon D'Arcy puts forward a Scott whose attraction to Scottish nationalism is much more complex and deep-rooted. It manifests itself, he argues, in a hidden 'Scots' version of the text which might easily be missed by English readers; in his use of dialect, and his versions of Scots history, Scott is writing for a 'dual readership' (p. 43). In a re-evaluation of the Waverley novels, Meldon D'Arcy analyses Scott's manipulation of narrative endings, imagery and metaphors, suggesting that they create a 'dissonant discourse' (p. 230) which critiques the Union and English imperial policy.

If Tony Blair has, on several occasions, declared Ivanhoe to be his favourite novel, Ruth Clayton Windscheffel, in 'Gladstone and Scott: Family, Identity, and Nation' (*ScotHR* 86:i[2007] 69–95), reveals an earlier political admirer. Tracing the pervasive, life-long influence of Scott on William Ewert Gladstone, Windscheffel notes that Scott's were 'amongst the earliest texts' Gladstone read. He enthusiastically 'imbibed' and appropriated Scott's views, which helped to shape his 'developing sense of identity and nationality' and his 'conceptualisation of the status and future of the Scottish political nation' (p. 70). Windscheffel uses Gladstone's reading diary to demonstrate his long history of repeated engagement with Scott's works at times of heightened emotion—he courted his wife with *Kenilworth*, and 'read Marmion to her' on their wedding night (and, adds Windscheffel, the succeeding day). At a time when Scott's own relationship with Scottish nationalism is being debated, it is salutary to be reminded of the ways in which Gladstone was using him—particularly during his Midlothian campaigns—to evoke a Scottish collective identity. In uncovering a personal reading history, Windscheffel revealingly demonstrates the long reach of Scott's public influence.

There were several pieces which considered the generic experimentation of Scott, and the possible effect on his readership. Catherine Jones's 'Scott, Wilkie, and Romantic Art' (in Duff and Jones, eds., pp. 208–35), links David Wilkie's artistic experimentation—combining genres, depicting ordinary lives, thinking about national history—to the influence of Scott. Looking closely at David Wilkie's technique and at Scott's own practices of representation, Jones shows how different genres might fruitfully be read together. Ayse Çelikkol's 'Free Trade and Disloyal Smugglers in Scott's *Guy Mannering* and *Redgauntlet*' (*ELH* 74[2007] 759–82) also reflects on genre. Using the imagery of smuggling as a way of understanding early nineteenth-century debates on free trade, Çelikkol also shows how the smuggler as a romance figure might help towards an understanding of Scott's use of the romance genre. Ralph Stewart, in 'The Devil Takes a Hand: Daniel Webster, Wandering Willie, and Lord Balmerino' (*SSR* 8:i[2007] 9–16), traces the unacknowledged influence of a tale included in Scott's *Redgauntlet* (itself drawing on narratives of a trial held in Scotland in 1635) on Stephen Vincent Benet's 1924 story 'The Devil and Daniel Webster'. The tale, revolving around a trial featuring the Devil, is thus shown to cross historical and national boundaries. Two pieces tackled Scott as editor. Victor Sage, in 'The Author, the Editor, and the Fissured Text: Scott, Maturin and Hogg' (in Hadjiafxendi and Mackay, eds., *Authorship in Context: From the Theoretical to the Material*, pp. 15–32), explores the various framing devices used by all three authors. His reading argues that Scott tries to create a stable relationship between reader and text, a unified narrative. The 'fissures' and parodies employed by Maturin and Hogg, on the other hand, Sage sees as expressing both their complicated literary relationship with Scott and their willingness to allow for rhetorical—and political—instability in their works. Robert Mayer, in 'Authors and Readers in Scott's Magnum Edition' (in Clymer and Mayer, eds., pp. 114–37), left more room for Scott's self-consciousness and knowingness as editor. Mayer discusses the forty-eight-volume edition produced between 1829 and 1833, with its elaborate paratext of notes and prefaces, as opening up the very 'fissures' which Sage denies. Packaging the Waverley novels as commodities, Mayer shows, Scott also theorized his fictional practice, and put forward 'complex versions of authorship and readership' (p. 132).

While plenty of criticism touched on Hogg in relation to other authors, the outstanding single contribution to Hogg studies this year was Gillian Hughes's biography, *James Hogg: A Life*. As the general editor of the Edinburgh University Press volumes of Hogg's collected works, Hughes has done much to confirm Hogg as an important presence in Romantic fiction. Her biography draws on years of Hogg scholarship and mobilizes a deep understanding of his work and culture. The biographer's is a difficult task, since Hogg's origins are uncertain. As Hughes notes, his is a story of striking transition, from the remote clay-built cottage of Ettrickhall and his boyhood life as a cowherd to *Blackwood's* author. His own dissembling 'Memoir of the Author's Life' and 'Reminiscences of Former Days' complicate the narrative still further. Nevertheless, Hughes does a remarkable job of outlining the socio-economic conditions which fostered Hogg's career, filling in the kinds of reading material which might have been available to him, for instance, and suggesting his early identification with different religious groups. In terms of his social rise and development as an author, she draws perceptive parallels both with Burns and—further away—with Dickens, who was similarly shaped by childhood trauma and family upheaval (p. 10). This is not wholly a story of triumph, of course; Hughes discusses the darker legacies of his early years, and the problems and difficulties of his identity as 'The Shepherd'. His complicated literary allegiances—his fictional characters and his fictional characteristics—are sensitively and clearly explored. Hughes's painstaking account of Hogg thus nicely complements Ian Duncan's *Scott's Shadow*, allowing a larger and more precise understanding of Scottish literary identity. She ends with a celebration of new readings of Hogg, suggesting that the 'instabilities and uncertainties of his work' make him increasingly attractive, and pointing out his continuing influence, ending with a tantalizing reminder that Alice Munro is a physical, as well as a literary, descendant of Hogg (p. 304). Hogg's presence on the wider literary scene was also evoked in an essay by Susan Mitchell, 'Dark Interpreter: Literary Uses of the Brocken Spectre from Coleridge to Pynchon' (*DR* 87:ii[2007] 167–87). This set Hogg's treatment of the apparition in *The Private Memoirs and Confessions of a Justified Sinner* in a wider literary context, ranging from Coleridge's 'Constancy to an Ideal Object', to De Quincey's *Suspiria de Profundis* and, most surprisingly, Pynchon's *Gravity's Rainbow*.

Alongside the works which reinterpret the national identity of Scott and Hogg, we should place several rereadings of women's writing in relation to national and racial difference. Clíona Ó Gallchoir's 'Celtic Ireland and Celtic Scotland: Ossianism and *The Wild Irish Girl*' (in Duff and Jones, eds., pp. 114–30), reflects on Celtic identity in recent criticism. She suggests that current academic understanding of Celticism, filtered through Linda Colley's influential study, *Britons*, relates it to British rather than Irish nationalism. The article instead argues for a revived appreciation of a 'Scoto-Irish' context, suggesting how Owenson's construction of Ireland draws heavily upon Ossianic Celticism, despite seeming overtly to deny its Scottish influence. This double movement, she argues, 'makes it an instructive text for those interested in establishing an archipelagic critical practice' (p. 128). Mark Mossman, 'Disability, Ireland, and *The Wild Irish Girl*' (*ERR* 18[2007] 541–50) uses recent work in disability studies to look closely at the character of the Prince of Inismore, Glorvina's father in *The Wild Irish Girl*. Mossman links the strategies used to represent physical difference with the portrayal of Ireland's national differences.

Julia M. Wright, in *Ireland, India, and Nationalism in Nineteenth-Century Literature* (also mentioned in Chapter XIII), also discusses complex engagements with national and colonial identity in the work of Owenson and Edgeworth, amongst others. Wright's comparative analysis is interested in the ways in which writers from colonized nations—in this case, Ireland—tackled the subject of colonization, drawing on their own responses to British imperial projects and foreign invasion. She explores Irish and British writing about Ireland and India, although not Indian writing about Ireland or Britain. Enlightenment sensibility, she shows, is key to an understanding of these responses. She begins by showing it at work in Charles Hamilton Teeling's 1828 account of the 1798 Irish uprising, showing how Teeling strove to arouse the sympathies of readers for Ireland; her second chapter then traces this move through fiction, showing sensibility at work in the national tale, such as *The Wild Irish Girl*, and in Edgeworth's writing, including the *Essay on Irish Bulls*, 'Lame Jervas' and *Ennui*. The themes of marriage and fostering are discussed as potent ways of figuring colonial relationships. She then discusses several important representations of India by Irish writers, including Morgan's *The Missionary*, Moore's *Lalla Rookh*, and writing by William Hamilton Drummond, which offer uneasy imagery of the cultural alienation suffered by religious converts. In the second half of her study, Wright focuses less on the sentimental and more on the commercial, discussing the driving economic forces behind colonization. Edgeworth's 'Lame Jervas' is discussed alongside Lewis's 'The Anaconda' from his *Romantic Tales* [1808], a marvellous tale of— in Wright's reading—colonial trauma and guilt. Lewis's main character, Everard, is employed by the plantation owner Seafield, who is unfortunately killed by an anaconda, which Everard pursues and eventually manages to kill. Inheriting Seafield's wealth, Everard then falls under suspicion of having killed not an anaconda, but a Miss Anne O'Connor. Wright nicely brings out how the spiralling narrative confusion points to 'a traumatized nation, haunted by the terrors which shadow colonial wealth' (p. 131). This is one example of her good close engagement with narrative forms and colonial discourses. She also discusses the 'embedded tales' and fragmentary narratives of Maturin, and then, in the closing chapters, moves further into the nineteenth century with an analysis of Oscar Wilde's *The Picture of Dorian Gray*, Bram Stoker's *The Lair of the White Worm* and *The Lady of the Shroud*, and Rudyard Kipling's *Kim*, reinterpreted as a 'wild Irish boy'.

Rather more conventional treatments of women writing about racial difference were offered by Susan B. Iwanisziw, 'Intermarriage in Late-Eighteenth-Century British Literature: Currents in Assimilation and Exclusion' (*ECLife* 31:ii[2007] 56–82) and George Boulukos, 'The Horror of Hybridity: Enlightenment, Anti-Slavery and Racial Disgust in Charlotte Smith's *Story of Henrietta* (1800)' (in Carey and Kitson, eds., *Slavery and the Cultures of Abolition: Essays Marking the Bicentennial of the British Abolition Act of 1807*, pp. 87–109). Iwanisziw explores the shifting portrayal of interracial marriage in three late eighteenth-century British texts by George Colman the Younger, John Gabriel Stedman and Edgeworth. She discusses the revision of the Juba–Lucy marriage in *Belinda* as evidence of a growing national distrust of interracial union, and offers a perhaps slightly one-dimensional account of Edgeworth's 'condescending', 'patronizing' portrayal of racial difference. George Boulukos similarly reads Smith's pessimistic novel *Story of Henrietta* as marking 'the transition from discomfort with the concept of race in the eighteenth century to ever more pronounced belief in racial difference in the nineteenth century'. He reads Henrietta's disgust at encountering her 'sisters by the half blood' as demonstrating Smith's horror at the thought of 'hybridity': any contact between the races might carry contaminating danger.

The difficulty of defining and gendering identity in the period was discussed in a series of articles on women writers. Scott A. Nowka, in 'Materialism and Feminism in Mary Hays's *Memoirs of Emma Courtney*' (*ERR* 18[2007] 521–40), draws on the developing critical interest in the connections between religion and feminism, furthering and complicating recent readings of Hays's Dissenting allegiances. He situates Hays's feminism in the context of her connections with Joseph Priestley and her readings of David Hartley, as well as Locke and Helvetius, showing the crucial importance the concepts of materialism and necessitarianism assumed in Hays's philosophical development. Nowka locates this as the main difference between the thought of Hays, Godwin and Wollstonecraft; for Hays, he suggests, 'necessitarianism can make feminism not only conceivable but also unavoidable' (p. 524). Martha Musgrove, in 'Relocating Femininity: Women and the City in Mary Brunton's Fiction' (*ECF* 20:ii[2007–8] 219–44), also highlights Brunton's religious, evangelical identity. Instead of the regional focus discussed by Ian Duncan, Musgrove offers a different reading of place in Brunton, emphasizing the importance of metropolitan identity in *Self-Control* and *Discipline*. Giving some nice close readings of Brunton's heroines being buffeted in London printshops and auction rooms, Musgrove makes the case that Brunton's novels engage forcefully with the city and with the problems of negotiating a gendered identity in an urban setting. Eileen Cleere, in 'Homeland Security: Political and Domestic Economy in Hannah More's *Coelebs in Search of a Wife*' (*ELH* 74[2007] 1–25), suggested that instead of reading More as part of a larger feminist narrative we should explore the 'historically specific' conservative agenda of her novel. Pointing to Lucilla Stanley's busy cultivation of apple-trees in her orchard grounds, Cleere identifies her as a 'practitioner of enclosure', participating in a national agricultural movement. Learning how to read the political meanings of *Coelebs*, she argues, allows us access to the 'discourses of internal management in wartime' and of women's role in furthering national ideology (p. 23).

Kevin Gilmartin's *Writing against Revolution: Literary Conservatism in Britain, 1790–1832* also presents a lively reassessment of More, arguing for the important role of counter-revolutionary print forms in the Romantic period. Overturning the often prevalent connection between literary and imaginative expression and revolutionary sympathy, Gilmartin demonstrates the 'productive role of conservative movements in the political culture of the period' (p. 1). This involves a range of genres and forms, from pamphlets and tales to critical views and novels. He devotes a chapter to a close analysis of the narrative energies of Hannah More's 'Cheap Repository Tracts' and her lesser-known pamphlets, such as her *History of Tom White the Postilion* [1795], a moral parable narrating Tom's temptation away from rural virtue by the lure of the 'Bath road' taverns. Through this pamphlet and its sequel Gilmartin traces More's development of narrative form, from 'conventional parable to a more ambitious fictional synthesis of the whole machinery of moral reform' (p. 59). He shows how, over and above her often noted 'social realism'—her desire to portray ordinary life—More is interested in the ways in which fiction might affect this ordinary village life. This interest in the complex ideological work done by fiction is extended in his chapter on novels; the Anti-Jacobin novel, he suggests, was one of the most experimental of counter-revolutionary forms. Building on M.O. Grenby's study, *The Anti-Jacobin Novel* [2001], Gilmartin explores a range of novels by Elizabeth Hamilton, George Walker, Henry James Pye and Jane West, putting forward the concept of a 'hybrid' form which united the domestic romance and the picaresque in order to speculate on the nature of home and nation.

There were several thoughtful treatments of Maria Edgeworth, including Julie Nash's *Servants and Paternalism in the Works of Maria Edgeworth and Elizabeth Gaskell*. Nash explores how the two novelists both viewed servants as 'essential characters for examining the tensions produced by social transformation and conflicting values' (p. 2); both, she shows, used their servant characters to question paternalistic values. From Fowler in *Harrington*—sinister, threatening, the instigator of Harrington's early fears—to *Belinda*'s loyal Juba and powerful Marriott, Nash shows how

Edgeworth often toys with stereotypes but ultimately gives her servants 'a sympathetic voice and a dynamic role in a changing social order' (p. 51). Gaskell, she argues, takes Edgeworth's subversive implications even further, frequently arguing for servants as the true protectors and parents of families. The links between the two authors are revealingly drawn out in terms of literary affinities and echoes, biographical overlaps and critical parallels. Both, for example, have had their responses to social change played down in favour of their 'feminine charm' (p. 8). Though they did not know one another personally, there were multiple intersections: Gaskell was raised on *Practical Education*, and Edgeworth kept up correspondence with Gaskell's relatives the Hollands. Both authors were 'immersed in the same intellectual atmosphere' (p. 3), as Nash outlines at the start of the book. It would have been good to know still more about these overlaps, and the precise nature of this similar 'intellectual atmosphere', running from the eighteenth to the nineteenth centuries. However, it is very welcome to see a full-length comparative study of the two, so often separated into strictly demarcated 'Romantic' and 'Victorian' periods. Nash's focus on the changing status of—and changing attitudes towards—servants through the long nineteenth century allows her study to move across period boundaries in a rewarding way.

Susan Manly's reading of Edgeworth similarly defied boundaries of period—and also of genre. Her study *Language, Custom and Nation in the 1790s* (discussed widely in this chapter) looks to John Locke to understand fully both 'radical "Jacobin" poetics of the 1790s, and the concept of a "revolutionary" poetry' in the 1790s (p. 1). Moreover, she argues for Edgeworth as the chief Romantic exponent of the radical linguistic tradition initiated by Locke—she retains the 'anti-authoritarianism' of Locke and Tooke, while Wordsworth—who also draws on this tradition—is revealed to have dodged the full implications of 'a language "really spoken by men"' (p. 3). Manly supports this in the fourth chapter of her study through a close focus on *Practical Education* and an analysis of its politics of language, reading the work alongside *Lyrical Ballads* in its attention to real language and conversation, but also in terms of its 'less authoritarian approach to children's language acquisition' (p. 151). She moves on to discuss Edgeworth's *Essay on Irish Bulls*, again suggesting the ways in which conventional authority structures might be contested. Manly's striking intellectual history does not directly analyse Edgeworth's better-known fiction, which is in some ways regrettable, but her argument is rich in implications for our understanding of the novels.

In *Opening the Field: Irish Women, Texts and Contexts*, edited by Patricia Boyle Haberstroh and Christine St Peter, Edgeworth is placed in a context of Irish women's writing through the centuries. An essay by the poet Eilean Ni Chuilleanain, one-time editor of *Belinda*, pays close attention to the evolution of the young man, Ormond. She suggests that Edgeworth is responding not only to her own father's life and fiction, but also to models of masculinity put forward by Fielding, whose *Tom Jones* and *Charles Grandison* Ormond reads eagerly. Deborah Weiss, 'The Extraordinary Ordinary Belinda: Maria Edgeworth's Female Philosopher' (*ECF* 19:iv[2007] 441–61) argues for a radical, reformist Edgeworth. Rereading Harriet Freke as a false philosopher, set alongside Belinda as a true one—an everywoman who has been transformed from within—Weiss argues for a new understanding of Edgeworth's 'innovative theories of sex and gender' as a significant 'contribution to Enlightenment moral philosophy' (p. 443).

An interesting new take on gender studies is offered by Jane Hodson in 'Women Write the Rights of Woman: The Sexual Politics of the Personal Pronoun in the 1790s' (L&L 16:iii[2007] 281–304). Using the textual analysis program WordSmith, Hodson investigates the use of personal pronouns in four pamphlets of the 1790s—Wollstonecraft's A Vindication, Hays's An Appeal to the Men of Great Britain, Mary Robinson's Letter to the Women of England and Mary Anne Radcliffe's The Female Advocate. Hodson's very interesting study shows the embedded ways—for instance, through the use of a religious register—in which these women carve out an identity for themselves in a male-dominated world of political pamphleteering, when 'even apparently gender-neutral pronouns such as I, we and you were in fact covertly gendered'.

Meanwhile, in studies on the Godwin–Shelley circle it is not so much gender as the family which seems to be the focus of critical debate. Familial relations are the subject of two engaging studies, Julie A. Carlson's England's First Family of Writers (discussed in section 1) and Sharon Lynne Joffe's The Kinship Coterie and the Literary Endeavors of the Women in the Shelley Circle. Both books deal with the dynamics of family creativity and the ways in which the Shelley circle attempted to formulate and practise particular theories of the family. Carlson begins by meditating on the continuing power of the Shelley family myth, contending that 'the lives of this family embody some of our best information on the psychosocial dynamics of being a writer and the attractions, even sexiness, of a life devoted to mental pursuits' (p. 2). She points to the persistent return to the theme of family in their writings, and the repeated explorations of family reform, marital relations and domestic affections from Godwin and Wollstonecraft to Mary and Percy Shelley to show how life and writing were intimately interconnected for these 'public intellectuals' (p. 4). As she comments, this study is not intended to replace William St Clair's biography of the family, nor as a purely literary-critical study, but rather to probe biographical, literary and cultural interconnections (p. 13). It is a detailed and full study, which moves through the family circle chronologically. The first half—'Revising Family'—deals with the struggles of Godwin and Wollstonecraft, and then Mary Shelley, to articulate and to rewrite the sentiments of family life in their political, literary and private writings, from the Vindication to Frankenstein. The second—'Life Works'—looks closely at the darker side of family life, exploring the ways in which each member of the circle dealt with tragedy, trauma, and mourning, shaping the past through acts of memorialization such as Godwin's Essay on Sepulchres. It also looks at attempts—such as the Juvenile Library—to shape the future. The study as a whole explores the delicate boundaries between life and writing, and between fiction and life-writing, questioning the public and private legacies of this writing family.

Carlson's study is not only important for scholars of the Godwin, Wollstonecraft and Shelley circle; it also raises very interesting questions about new directions in Romantic criticism. Authorship, in her reading, emerges not as individual or collaborative but 'collective', making this less a study of influence than of 'transference'. The study thus connects with a growing interest in patterns of Romantic creativity which centre around the sociable and familial, which interest themselves in the group or the network rather than the solitary writer. Indeed, as Carlson comments, 'the number of collective projects in the period makes one wonder how the cult of the isolated genius ever became associated with this age' (p. 14). This is echoed by Joffe's study which, similarly, 'contests the Romantic ideal of solitariness...and promotes instead the idea that the writer belongs to, and creates within, a specific community' (p. x). Joffe carefully builds up the concept of a 'kinship coterie' amongst the Shelley women, bound together familiarly and intellectually, developing and sharing views. Like Carlson, she is struck by the way in which 'shared family experience became the impetus for, and the very subject of, the group's writing' (p. 4). Her emphasis, however, is more squarely on maternity, and she focuses on women members of the circle to suggest the powerful, lingering influence of Wollstonecraft as author and mother. Her reading of *Valperga*, for instance, finds echoes of Wollstonecraft's depictions of maternity and sorority in *Maria*. Perhaps most striking—and welcome—are Joffe's efforts to broaden our understanding of the Shelley family circle through her thoughtful analysis of its less frequently considered members. She gives a full account of Fanny Imlay's letters and her part in conversations and literary exchanges, and chapter 6 is devoted to Claire Clairmont's life-writing, correspondence and the short story, 'The Pole', begun by her and probably completed by Mary Shelley. There is also a rare discussion of Maria James Reveley-Gisborne as part of the circle, her friendship with Mary Shelley cast as a potential surrogate mother–daughter relationship. Joffe's concept of 'kinship coterie' thus works inclusively, and she ends the study with an attempt to show this model working in other contexts. It may be transferred, she argues, to other literary families, such as the Brontës, or even, she speculates, Charles and Mary Lamb. Joffe's sprightly and accessibly written study is a topical and lively contribution to a developing strand of Romantic criticism.

The lasting power of Wollstonecraft's biography is also addressed by Patricia A. Matthew in 'Biography and Mary Wollstonecraft in *Adeline Mowbray* and *Valperga*' (*WW* 14:iii[2007] 382–98). Like Joffe, she sees *Valperga* as engaging with Wollstonecraft's life and writing, particularly with *A Vindication*; so too, she argues, is Amelia Opie's *Adeline Mowbray*. Matthew, too, is interested by the patterns of female influence through familial and friendly relations, and the ways in which biography might be used—by women writers and by the critic—to 'offer destabilizing views of the roles women hold in Romantic-era culture' (p. 383). Interest in family creativity is also evident in Ranita Chatterjee's 'Filial Ties: Godwin's *Deloraine* and Mary Shelley's Writings' (*ERR* 18[2007] 29–41). Chatterjee explores Godwin's last—and rarely discussed—novel *Deloraine*, setting it in dialogue with Shelley's *Mathilda*, 'The Mourner', and *Falkner* to analyse the father–daughter relationship in intertextual and biographical terms. Chatterjee argues for the concept of 'psychonarration' as a means of understanding Romantic collaboration and authorial identity within the family. Peter Melville, in

'The Problem of Immunity in *The Last Man*' (*SEL* 47[2007] 825–46), also interests himself in the family as a theme in Shelley's writing. He discusses the 'unresolved' problem of Lionel's resistance to the plague, rereading his encounter with the 'negro half clad' and giving a thorough account of critical perceptions of this scene. Melville's own analysis reinforces his own strong reading of the novel as, essentially, a 'family drama'. Lionel's rejection of the black man, he argues, marks 'the ideological limits and defensive strictures of a family survival story' (p. 837). Melville expands his treatment of the novel in his full-length study, *Romantic Hospitality and the Resistance to Accommodation* (also discussed in section 3), placing it in the broader context of Romantic attitudes to the stranger, and the ambiguous relationship of host and guest, subject and other. In texts from Barbauld to Rousseau to Coleridge as well as *The Last Man*, Romantic hospitality becomes 'a figure for the contradictory responses of a subject who both fears *and* sympathizes with spectres of alterity and difference' (p. 21). The final chapter of Edward Larrissy's study *The Blind and Blindness in Literature of the Romantic Period* (discussed fully in section 3) also presents a novel reading of three Shelley works within the context of Romantic fascination with the figure of the blind bard and the inward revelations blindness might bring. Representations of blindness, suggests Larrissy, help us understand Romantic historical self-consciousness and negotiations with the concept of inwardness. From De Lacey in *Frankenstein* to the blind old man in *The Last Man* who listens to his daughter playing Haydn, Larrissy explores how literal blindness in Mary Shelley's novels points up the 'figurative blindness' of others. Blindness, too, helps us understand her viewpoint on science, and of seeing 'beyond pre-established modes of understanding even in modernity' (p. 201).

As these examples show, there was a welcome attention to Mary Shelley's less well known novels this year although *Frankenstein* does feature in several essays, the most interesting being unusual contextual studies by Karen Piper and Patrick Vincent. Piper's 'Inuit Diasporas: *Frankenstein* and the Inuit in England' (*Romanticism* 13[2007] 63–75) sets Shelley's novel in the context of North Pole explorations of 1818, suggesting that *Frankenstein* might have capitalized on the 'suspense and widely popular appeal' of these journeys, which Shelley eagerly read about in the *Quarterly Review*. In ' "This wretched mockery of justice": Mary Shelley's *Frankenstein* and Geneva' (*ERR* 18[2007] 645–61), Patrick Vincent discusses the political and legal context of Justine Moritz's trial, arguing that Shelley's portrayal of the city-republic of Geneva in the 1790s might be seen as a response to her views of British repression in 1817–18. Vincent's close attention to the novel's setting extends our under-standing of Shelley's political engagement, and her deep suspicion of arbitrary law. Meanwhile, the continuing power of *Frankenstein* as science fiction was discussed in two essays by Cary Jones and Jason P. Vest (in Yang, ed., *The X-Files and Literature: Unweaving the Story, Unravelling the Lie to Find the Truth*).

Elsewhere, it was *Valperga* and *Lodore* which attracted scholars. Adam L. Mekler's 'Broken Mirrors and Multiplied Reflections in Lord Byron and Mary Shelley' (*SiR* 46[2007] 461–80) finds a source in Byron's writing for Euthanasia's image of the multiple reflections offered by a broken mirror.

Mekler uses this as a starting point for a larger discussion of the 'professional relationship' between Byron and Mary Shelley, emphasizing her allusive and conceptual sophistication as a writer and her willingness to critique male authors. In the same issue, in '"Do you then repair my work": The Redemptive Contract in Mary Shelley's *Valperga*' (*SiR* 46[2007] 481–505) Sharon M. Twigg also focuses on Mary Shelley's critique of male-authored theories. Highlighting the 'rhetoric of bargain, promise, and exchange' as a key to understanding female characters within the novel, she goes on to link this to Shelley's interest in economic thought, notably her highly critical reading of Malthus, arguing that *Valperga* offers a sustained challenge to the Malthusian 'ideology of contract and redemption' (p. 501). Finally, Nicholas M. Williams, in 'Angelic Realism: Domestic Idealization in Mary Shelley's *Lodore*' (*SNNTS* 39:iv[2007] 397–415) addresses some of the reasons for the neglect of *Lodore*. Is it, Williams asks, a text of retreat, even of ideal feminine self-sacrifice? He attempts to complicate our readings by paying close attention to Shelley's self-conscious authorial work; admitting the importance of idealization in the novel, he maintains that it also concerns itself with the 'strains of the idealizing process' (p. 413), and the power of the author.

There were also several essays which focused specifically on Wollstonecraft and on Godwin. Daniella Mallinick, 'Sublime Heroism and *The Wrongs of Woman*: Passion, Reason, Agency' (*ERR* 18[2007] 1–27) discusses Wollstonecraft's engagement with the aesthetic of the sublime, which she sees as constructed differently from that of both Kant and Burke. *Maria*, Mallinick suggests, traces a sublime which is 'regulated by reason, and grounded in religious conviction', based on the strength and heroism of her female characters; yet, she concludes, Wollstonecraft is also uneasily aware of the shortcomings and problems her own model posed for readers, an uncertainty we can perhaps detect in the work's Preface. This is also the starting point for Lisa Plummer Crafton's '"Stage Effect": Transgressive Theatricality in Wollstonecraft's *Maria, or the Wrongs of Woman*' (*WW* 14:iii[2007] 367–81). Picking up the mention of 'stage-effect' in the Preface, Crafton traces different aspects of theatricality in Wollstonecraft's work, from allusions to plays and mentions of Mrs Siddons to the staging of public spectacles such as the trials. Although wary of the power exerted by such spectacles, concludes Crafton, Wollstonecraft did perceive 'theatricality as a subversive and transgressive mechanism' (p. 377).

Nicolle Jordan, in 'The Promise and Frustration of Plebian Public Opinion in *Caleb Williams*' (*ECF* 19:iii[2007] 243–66), tackles the questions raised with regard to public opinion in the novel, particularly popular or plebeian opinion. She argues for an understanding of the novel as portraying 'both the promise and the threat posed by an expansive public sphere' (p. 266), fluctuating between optimism and unease about the power of the crowd's opinion. Andrew Franta's 'Godwin's Handshake' (*PMLA* 122[2007] 696–710) also deals with the political ambiguity of *Caleb Williams*. He sees the importance of the handshake in the novel as pointing to the gradual emergence of commercial society, something perhaps at odds with conventional readings of politics within the novel. If Franta looks to a social and behavioural context for an understanding of *Caleb Williams*, Ingrid Horrocks, in 'More Than a

Gravestone: *Caleb Williams, Udolpho*, and the Politics of the Gothic' (*SNNTS* 39:i[2007] 31–47) explores its literary connections. Suggesting that Godwin was meeting and actively rereading Anne Radcliffe when composing the novel, Horrocks points to his adoption and exploitation of Gothic modes to sustain mystery and highlight oppression. She is particularly interested in the interpretative possibilities of the novel's two endings, which, she argues, delicately balance Godwin's optimism and sense of hopelessness, and show him unwilling to close down political alternatives. The mystery, uncertainty and contradiction of Radcliffean Gothic, she suggests, may have influenced his attraction towards the ambiguous ending.

Dale Townshend's *The Orders of Gothic: Foucault, Lacan and the Subject of Gothic Writing, 1764–1820* gives a detailed discussion of how we might theorize the modernity of the Gothic. Townshend argues for the ways in which eighteenth- and early nineteenth-century Gothic might be fruitfully read alongside the New Historicism of Foucault and the revisionist psychoanalysis of Lacan, which he images as 'knotted or yoked together in a supplementary relation of addition and replacement, extension and substitution' (p. 8). He admits that these might be seen as 'strange theoretical bedfellows', but suggests that they help us to appreciate the multiple shifts and transformations of the Gothic. He gives a full account of critical understandings of psychoanalytic theory as applied to the Gothic, and then moves into a good range of readings of specific authors, including Walpole, Maturin, Lewis and Dacre. He traces repeated patterns of particular themes and fascinations within Gothic writing: patricide, incest, torture and darkness. Of particular interest for this section is his chapter on 'Gothic Paternity from Ann Radcliffe to Mary Shelley', which gives a strong reading of *Udolpho* and *The Romance of the Forest*, inflected by Locke and Rousseau, before moving on to trace portrayals of paternal tyranny in Wollstonecraft's *Maria*, and the questioning, uncertain attitude to fatherhood in *Frankenstein*.

Other work on the Gothic included Scott R. Mackenzie's 'An Englishwoman's Workhouse Is her Castle: Poor Management and Gothic Fiction in the 1790s' (*ELH* 74[2007] 681–705). This looks closely at the ways in which debates surrounding the poor and their treatment are refracted in Gothic fiction of the 1790s, particularly in Radcliffe's *Romance of the Forest*. He also suggests the ways in which Gothic fiction might have had a corresponding influence on the debates themselves. Beatrice Battaglia, 'The "Pieces of Poetry" in Ann Radcliffe's *The Mysteries of Udolpho* (in Crisafulli and Pietropoli, eds., pp. 137–51), analyses *Udolpho*'s particular brand of 'romance narrative', and the part played by its interspersed verses, discussing their particular appeal to a female reading audience and demonstrating how they are 'organically bound' to the narrative. Brenda Tooley's 'Gothic Utopia: Heretical Sanctuary in Ann Radcliffe's *The Italian*' (in Pohl and Tooley, eds., *Gender and Utopia in the Eighteenth Century: Essays in English and French Utopian Writing*, pp. 53–68), is covered in Chapter XI. Beatriz González Moreno's 'Gothic Excess and Aesthetic Ambiguity in Charlotte Dacre's *Zofloya*' (*WW* 14:iii[2007] 419–34) argued for the challenging power of Dacre's writing. Beginning by exploring the tensions over femininity and the Gothic inherent in Dacre's pen-name 'Rosa Matilda', Moreno shows the ways in which Dacre might have used the Gothic to interrogate different models of female behaviour and female authorship.

5. Drama

David Worrall's *The Politics of Romantic Theatricality, 1787–1832: The Road to the Stage* is a major new study of London's non-patent theatres. Densely researched and intricately argued, it seeks to show how licensing laws and intrusive censorship determined the character of the Romantic-period stage. While the two patent theatres preserved the spoken-word literary heritage that looked above all to early modern tragedy, the non-patent theatres—where speaking on stage was forbidden by law—saw the development of a highly distinct plebeian public sphere and dramatic tradition. The legal status of speech was of more fundamental concern than questions of genre, and it was not melodrama, Worrall argues, but burletta and pantomime that became the major locus of popular theatrical creativity. Worrall's sympathies are with the apprentices and clerks whose fondness for amateur theatricals caused consternation to their masters, and with those theatres that in amongst their ready stereotyping and equestrian spectacles successfully embodied a working-class identity on stage. He also, though, includes a chapter to show that the patent theatres were sometimes allowed by the censor to respond to contemporary events, as with Robert Merry's reflection on the 1791 Birmingham riots in *The Magician no Conjurer* [1792]. His third chapter distinguishes the traditions of representation of black characters on the British stage from those of North American minstrelsy. It contrasts the (West End) Haymarket's 'essentially anti-abolitionist' (p. 94) *The Benevolent Planters* with *Harlequin Mungo*, produced in London's racially mixed docklands. The latter saw the blackface character Mungo transformed into the black-*masked* Harlequin, who marries a white woman. 'Everything suggests', Worrall writes, 'that pantomime could take greater risks, be more culturally adventurous, than spoken drama' (p. 102). The next chapter sees William Henry Ireland's Shakespeare forgery *Vortigern* as a response to the difficulty of getting original spoken drama on to the stage, and describes how Ireland later found his real vocation as a satirist. The fifth chapter sees the burgeoning Cockney theatre culture that was the context for *Blackwood's* notorious attack on the Cockney poets, and especially William Thomas Moncrieff's hit *Giovanni in London*, which in 1817 coincided with a post-war boom in popular culture. The last two chapters deal with the popular *Tom and Jerry* burlettas spun off from Pierce Egan's 1820 novella *Life in London*. These sophisticated portrayals of 'flash' slang and the revelries of London's aristocrats and low life not only give evidence of a culture of striking racial tolerance among the metropolitan working class, but 'mark the maturity of a genuine public plebeian sphere located at the heart of London' (p. 206).

Reiko Oya's *Representing Shakespearean Tragedy: Garrick, the Kembles, and Kean* (also discussed in Chapter XI) defines itself against studies of eighteenth-century Shakespeare that describe the reception of his texts as an 'anonymous' and 'impersonal' process of cultural appropriation. Oya seeks to recast this history 'in more intimate, personal terms', with a relaxed narrative of the individuals who did most to mould perceptions of the major tragedies (pp. 4–5). She declares an interest not only in the 'appropriation' of Shakespeare but also in how individual critical intelligences found that his texts resisted appropriation. The first chapter deals with David Garrick's revolutionary naturalism in playing King Lear, and the contrasting perspectives on Shakespeare of Samuel Johnson and Elizabeth Montague. The second is organized around John Kemble's and Sarah Siddons's collaboration in *Macbeth* and their innovative psychologizing of the lead roles—a sympathetic understanding of the couple that translated only indirectly into their stage performances—although it proves to be most deeply interested in Joshua Reynolds's paintings of Shakespearian scenes, and closes with a section on theatricality in Burkean aesthetics. These various topics are tied together by Oya's interest in the sublime, and by the intriguing question of how to represent supernatural objects on stage and canvas. The last chapter draws a vivid contrast between Kemble's and Edmund Kean's portrayals of Hamlet, before a final discussion of Coleridge and Keats's attempts to write for the stage. Oya explores the influence of *Hamlet* on Coleridge's *Remorse*, and argues that the writing process that Keats adopted for *Otho the Great* was modelled on his understanding of Kean's acting technique.

In one of the year's most ambitious and stimulating essays, 'British Romantic Drama in a European Context' (in Bode and Neumann, eds., pp. 115–30), Jeffrey N. Cox ranges over three national theatrical traditions to describe the emergence of 'a trans-European drama of subversion and seduction, a jacobinical drama that arises in England, is transported to Germany, and that returns to England filled with notions borrowed from revolutionary France' (p. 122). The emergence of an equally transnational melodrama seemed to present an alternative to this Jacobin aesthetics, Cox argues, but in the end could only offer its audiences a fantasy of universal reconciliation. Cox looks instead to 'a dramaturgy of the moment, of separable dramatic gestures, motifs, movements, tactics' (p. 128): the Romantic drama of Byron, Shelley and Hunt, understood as 'a European drama' that only 'happens to be written in English' (p. 126). Also among the most significant new work on Romantic drama this year was a remarkable group of three essays by Nathaniel Leach, drawing on the work of Emmanuel Lévinas to develop readings of Baillie, Byron and Beddoes. In 'Joanna Baillie's "Great Moving Picture" and the Ethics of the Gaze in *De Montfort*' (*ERR* 18[2007] 623–42), Leach describes how Joanna Baillie's dramatic theory is challenged and disrupted by her own stagecraft. The benevolent, disinterested 'sympathetick curiosity' with which her audience should scrutinize the passions is revealed to be itself a potentially dangerous form of passion. A penetrating reading of *De Montfort* concludes that even after his death De Monfort's body is a Gothic excess that can only be recognized by the way in which it exposes the inadequacy of each successive attempt to give an account of it. In 'Historical Bodies in a "Mental Theatre": Byron's Ethics of History' (*SiR* 46[2007] 3–19), Leach's reading of *Marino Faliero* and *The Two Foscari* shows how these historical tragedies that appeal to the conventions of both physical staging and silent reading uncover an excess or alterity in the very notion of the performance of history. Leach concentrates on the two doges: Faliero 'places his faith in the power of history' (p. 12), whereas Foscari 'endorse[s] a fatalistic resignation to alterity' (p. 16), but both seek to mobilize those veils and silences that cannot be contained by the oppressive power of the state. Finally, 'Between the "hostile body" and the "hieroglyphic human soul": The Ethics of Beddoes's "mental theatre" ' (in Berns and Bradshaw, eds., pp. 123–33) sees *Death's Jest-Book* as radicalizing many of the preoccupations of Baillie's and Byron's mental theatre in the self-conscious artificiality with which it stages the body, and in its obsession with death as that which lies beyond representation. The similarity between the three titles reflects accurately how single-minded Leach is in his methodological focus, but the readings that he develops are consistently incisive and enlightening.

The *Companion to Thomas Lovell Beddoes* in which Leach's essay appears is also discussed in section 3(a), but equally it makes one of the year's most valuable contributions to the study of Romantic drama. The editors describe the collection as a whole as seeking to move beyond the traditional focus on Beddoes's lyrics and to acknowledge instead that dramatic form was central to his work. A crucial chapter in this respect is Ute Berns's 'Performing Genres in *Death's Jest-Book*: Tragedy as Harlequinade' (pp. 135–52), which maintains that 'Beddoes, up to the completion of the first manuscript version of *Death's Jest-Book*, did intend the play for the stage' (p. 138). Berns argues for the influence of the 'illegitimate' London theatre on the play, comparing it persuasively to contemporary pantomime and harlequinade, as part of a broader argument that the text refashions revenge tragedy by making the body politic rather than the monarch the avenger's target. Conversely, Alan Halsey's 'Beddoes and the Theatre of Cruelty; or the Problem of Isbrand's Sister' (pp. 153–63) suggests that with *Death's Jest-Book* Beddoes tried and failed to move completely beyond existing tragic structure and 'the established forms of drama' (p. 157), comparing his dramatic theory to that of Artaud. The collection concentrates on *Death's Jest-Book*—it concludes with an informal 'Epilogue' (pp. 241–7) by Jerome McGann and Frederick Burwick describing their inaugural staging of the play in 2003—but also contains groundbreaking analysis of his other dramas, notably Shelley Rees's '*The Brides' Tragedy* and the Myth of Cupid and Psyche' (pp. 193–205), on the cruelties of male Romantic fantasies of androgyny.

There were two publications this year on the scientific contexts of Joanna Baillie's plays. Victoria Myers's 'Joanna Baillie and the Emergence of Medico-Legal Discourse' (*ERR* 18[2007] 339–59) discusses the emergent disciplines of forensic medicine and psychology, and their influence on legal findings of guilt and diminished responsibility, then reads *De Monfort* and *The Homicide* in terms of their shifting assessments of legal and ethical culpability. Nathan Elliot, in ' "Unball'd sockets" and "The mockery of speech": Diagnostic Anxiety and the Theater of Joanna Baillie' (*ERR* 18[2007] 83–103), maps Baillie's theatrical technique on to the concerns of her uncles, William and John Hunter, who worried about the difficulty of deriving securely grounded scientific generalizations from individual anatomical specimens. For Elliot, the Gothic marks the moments of hermeneutic crisis in Baillie's attempt to represent scientifically the physiological conditions of passion. Her increasing 'diagnostic pessimism' (p. 85) means that Gothic tropes come to the fore in her development from *De Monfort* to *Orra*; in the latter play, Radcliffean realism is no longer able to overcome Gothic horror. Dorothy Macmillan takes up the question of Baillie's Scottishness in 'Joanna Baillie's Embarrassment' (in Crisafulli and Pietropoli, eds., pp. 113–34), also discussed in section 3(b). The two plays Baillie set in Scotland both imply delicate negotiations about national identity and cross-border relations, but while the Ossianic Highland romance of *The Family Legend* engages in 'the packaging of Scotland into a manageable idea' (p. 131), the late, neglected, *Witchcraft* emerges as the more interesting text, giving a central place to 'one of the first of these persistent nineteenth-century "madwomen in the attic"' (p. 133). Regina Hewitt's 'Improving the Law: Property Rights and Self-Possession in Joanna Baillie's *The Alienated Manor*' (*WC* 38[2007] 50–5) reads the play as 'an indictment of existing laws based on possessive individualism and a call for improved laws based on the common good' (p. 50). After an absorbing account of the theory of property law, she shows how individualistic legal principles manifest themselves in the self-destructive personality of Baillie's central character. Christine A. Colón's edition of Joanna Baillie's *Six Gothic Dramas* is discussed in Chapter XI.

A group of three essays on the 'low culture' of the Romantic stage in *European Romantic Review* begins with Julie A. Carlson's 'New Lows in Eighteenth-Century Romantic Theater: The Rise of Mungo' (*ERR* 18[2007] 139–47). Isaac Bickerstaff's comic opera *The Padlock* [1768] introduced the enduringly popular figure of the black servant Mungo. For all the crudity of his characterization, Carlson argues, this farcical figure came to hold emancipatory possibilities, especially when the role was taken on by the first black tragedian, Ira Aldridge, immediately after his great performance of Othello. In 'Bread: The Eruption and Interruption of Politics in Elizabeth Inchbald's *Every One Has His Fault*' (*ERR* 18[2007] 149–57), Daniel O'Quinn describes the play—which opened eight days after the execution of Louis XVI—as turning on its audience's most immediate political concerns: the scarcity that would be brought about by war, and the question of whether the middle classes would rise against aristocratic authority. Ultimately, though, domestic class antagonism is trumped by the traumas of imperial desire. Finally, Jim Davis's 'The Sublime of Tragedy in Low Life' (*ERR* 18[2007] 159–67) discusses the reception of the Covent Garden actor John Emery. A Yorkshireman, he played tragic and tragicomic rustic parts, and Davis's title comes from Hazlitt's description of his acting at its best. Davis elucidates the valences of Hazlitt's phrase, and gathers reviews of Emery by Leigh Hunt and others. Emery was credited with tragic intensity, but, as a genre actor, his work was seen as imitative and particular rather than creative and universal.

Celestine Woo compiles for the first time the extant data on Sarah Siddons's nine or more appearances as Hamlet between 1775 and 1805, in 'Sarah Siddons's Performances as Hamlet: Breaching the Breeches Part' (*ERR* 18[2007] 573–95). Rather than a titillating 'breeches' role, Woo claims, this was 'a harbinger of [the] protean, ambiguously gendered Hamlet' of Coleridge and Hazlitt (p. 582), one that invited spectators to become conscious of the artificiality of constructions of gender. In 'Borderline

Engagements: The Crusades in Romantic-Period Drama' (in Lamont and Rossington, eds., pp. 186–97), Diego Saglia brings together three historical dramas about inter-religious warfare in the Mediterranean that show that the Crusades still helped to shape Western identity in the early nineteenth century. Baillie's *Constantine Paleologus* demonstrated that broken physical defences against the East (here, the walls of Constantinople) could be redefined as cultural and ethical ones, and Richard Lalor Sheil's *Bellamira* gave a patriotic historical context to contemporary British interventions in North Africa. Hemans's *The Siege of Valencia*, though, suggests that Christian as well as Islamic militarism is dangerously antithetical to feminine affective values. Amy Garnai's 'Radicalism, Caution and Censorship in Elizabeth Inchbald's *Every One Has His Fault*' (*SEL* 47[2007] 703–22), the year's second discussion of the play, begins by showing how successfully Inchbald evaded theatrical censorship throughout her career, and goes on to describe *Every One Has His Fault* as fundamentally pessimistic: benevolence and idealistic truthfulness must ultimately submit to 'the immovable patriarchal presence' (p. 716).

Drawing upon a close scrutiny of the manuscripts of Shelley's unfinished *Charles the First*, Nora Crook argues persuasively, in 'Calumniated Republicans and the Hero of Shelley's "Charles the First"' (*KSJ* 56[2007] 155–72), that the republican martyr Henry Vane the Younger was intended to have been the hero of the play. She goes on to make the case that the play was intended firmly for the stage, not the closet, and that the chaotic state of the draft does not show Shelley's inability to work with his historical sources but simply his characteristic writing practices. Simon Hull places Charles Lamb's writings on the theatre in the context of the theatricalized London crowds and their politically unsettling love of ever more extravagant spectacle. In 'The Ideology of the Unspectacular: Theatricality and Charles Lamb's Essayistic Figure' (*RoN* 46[2007] 22 paras) he argues that, although the pre-Elian Lamb joined the other canonical Romantic critics in seeing the stage as inherently incapable of representing Shakespearian profundity, in the Elia essays Lamb uses theatricality as a way of introducing imaginative complexity into the act of reading. A fascinating essay by Luisa Calé distinguishes between the abstract and transnational community of sympathy that is postulated by the sentimental novel and the localized, embodied collective identity established among theatrical audiences. 'Sympathy in Translation: *Paul et Virginie* on the London Stage' (*RoN* 46[2007] 23 paras) maps this distinction on to Bernardin de Saint-Pierre's *Paul et Virginie*, a sentimental tale of the colonial encounter, and its adaptation by James Cobb into the comic opera *Paul and Virginia*. Cosmopolitan sympathy is replaced by a patriotic, ameliorist perspective on slavery and Creole identity in the West Indies.

Volume 29 of the *Coleridge Bulletin* was largely given over to Coleridge and drama. Jim Mays asks 'Are Coleridge's Plays Worth the Candle?' (*ColB* 29[2007] 1–16). He answers that we should learn to appreciate the plays on their own terms, as works that embrace the constraints imposed on them by the popular stage; he focuses on *Zapolya*, 'the most satisfactory play Coleridge wrote' (p. 6). R.A. Foakes, in '"Daubed landscapes": Coleridge and Dramatic Illusion' (*ColB* 29[2007] 17–30), explores Coleridge's conviction that even the most elaborate of the scenic illusions being developed on the contemporary stage could not serve as a substitute for the spectator's willed acceptance of dramatic illusion. Joyce Crick's wide-ranging account of the German Romantic theatre introduces a subtle analysis of Coleridge's translation of Friedrich Schiller's *Wallenstein*, showing how the translation reconfigures and brings to the fore the Shakespearian elements of Schiller's work, in 'Something on William Shakespeare Occasioned by *Wallenstein*' (*ColB* 29[2007] 31–42). A short paper by John Beer, 'Coleridge's Dramatic Imagination' (*ColB* 29[2007] 43–9), calls attention to Coleridge's instinct for dramatization and dialogue in all of the forms in which he wrote, and particularly in his engagement with the poetry of George Herbert. Chris Murray's 'Coleridge and "Real Life" Tragedy' (*ColB* 29[2007] 50–64) explores Coleridge's changing view of the relationship between historical fact and tragic structure. Murray analyses the generic and rhetorical instabilities in *The Fall of Robespierre*, the 'Monody on the Death of Chatterton' and the later writings against revolution, all in the light of Coleridge's belief that real life is a privileged source of tragic narrative and that tragedy is under a special obligation to point towards resolutions for real social problems. Elsewhere, Michael Tomko's 'Politics, Performance and Coleridge's "Suspension of Disbelief"' (*VS* 49[2007] 241–9) tests Coleridge's commitment to the willing suspension of disbelief in aesthetic judgement against his response to Maturin's Jacobinical drama *Bertram*. Coleridge's hostility to the play's politics makes him react to it with abrupt sarcasm rather than with the 'generous and genial experimental faith' (p. 248) that he thought a critic should display. His 'complicated aesthetic approach' (p. 246) proves unable to negotiate such intense ideological difference.

Books Reviewed

Allard, James Robert. *Romanticism, Medicine and the Poet's Body*. Ashgate. [2007] pp. viii + 166. £50 ISBN 9 7807 5465 8917.

Auerbach, Emily. *Searching for Jane Austen*. UWiscP. [2007] pp. 358. $21.95 ISBN 9 7802 9920 1845.

Bautz, Annika. *The Reception of Jane Austen and Walter Scott: A Comparative Longitudinal Study*. Continuum. [2007] pp. x + 198. £60 ISBN 9 7808 2649 5464.

Bellanca, Mary Ellen. *Daybooks of Discovery: Nature Diaries in Britain, 1770–1870*. UPVirginia. [2007] pp. 248. £48.40 ISBN 0 8139 2612 2.

Bennett, Andrew. *Wordsworth Writing*. CUP. [2007] pp. xi + 249. £50 ISBN 9 7805 2184 199.

Berkeley, Richard. *Coleridge and the Crisis of Reason*. Palgrave. [2007] pp. xii + 231. £45 ISBN 9 7802 3052 1643.

Berns, Ute, and Michael Bradshaw, eds. *The Ashgate Research Companion to Thomas Lovell Beddoes*. Ashgate. [2007] pp. xviii + 273. £60 ISBN 9 7807 5466 0095.

Bevis, Matthew. *The Art of Eloquence: Byron, Dickens, Tennyson, Joyce*. OUP. [2007] pp. viii + 302. £50 ISBN 9 7801 9925 3999.

Billone, Amy Christine. *Little Songs: Women, Silence, and the Nineteenth Century Sonnet.* OSUP. [2007] pp. 232. £22.91 ISBN 0 8142 1042 2.

Bindman, David. *Mind-Forg'd Manacles: William Blake and Slavery.* Hayward Publishing. [2007] pp. 147. £14.99 ISBN 9 7818 5332 2594.

Bode, Christoph, and Fritz-Wilhelm Neumann, eds. *British and European Romanticisms: Selected Papers from the Munich Conference of the German Society for English Romanticism.* Trier. [2007] pp. 283. pb £23 ISBN 9 7838 8476 9591.

Bolton, Carol. *Writing the Empire: Robert Southey and Romantic Colonialism.* P&C. [2007] pp. x + 332. £60 ISBN 9 7818 5196 8633.

Brice, Ben. *Coleridge and Scepticism.* OUP. [2007] pp. x + 229. £50 ISBN 9 7801 9929 0253.

Budge, Gavin, ed. *Romantic Empiricism: Poetics and the Philosophy of Common Sense, 1780–1830.* BuckUP. [2007] pp. 202. £40.50 ISBN 0 8387 5712 3.

Canuel, Mark. *The Shadow of Death: Literature, Romanticism, and the Subject of Punishment.* PrincetonUP. [2007] pp. xiii + 206. £19.95 ISBN 9 7806 9112 9617.

Carey, Brycchan, and Peter J. Kitson, eds. *Slavery and the Cultures of Abolition: Essays Marking the Bicentennial of the British Abolition Act of 1807.* Brewer. [2007] pp. viii + 227. £30 ISBN 9 7818 4384 1203.

Carlson, Julie A. *England's First Family of Writers: Mary Wollstonecraft, William Godwin, Mary Shelley.* JHUP. [2007] pp. xii + 328. $50 ISBN 9 7808 0188 6188.

Cervelli, Kenneth. *Dorothy Wordsworth's Ecology.* Routledge. [2007] pp. 116. £60 ISBN 0 4159 8037 2.

Chirico, Paul. *John Clare and the Imagination of the Reader.* Palgrave. [2007] pp. xi + 222. £45 ISBN 9 7802 3051 7639.

Clark, Steve, and Jason Whittaker, eds. *Blake, Modernity and Popular Culture.* Palgrave. [2007] pp. x + 240. £45 ISBN 9 7802 3000 8441.

Clymer, Lorna, and Robert Mayer, eds. *Historical Boundaries, Narrative Forms: Essays on British Literature in the Long Eighteenth Century in Honor of Everett Zimmerman.* UDelP. [2007] pp. 268. £45.50 ISBN 9 7808 7413 9396.

Craig, David M. *Robert Southey and Romantic Apostasy: Political Argument in Britain, 1780–1840.* Boydell. [2007] pp. xiv + 236. £50 ISBN 9 7808 6193 2917.

Crisafulli, Lilla Maria, and Cecilia Pietropoli, eds., *Romantic Women Poets: Genre and Gender.* Rodopi. [2007] pp. 280. £40 ISBN 9 7890 4202 2478.

Dow, Gillian, ed. *Translators, Interpreters, Mediators, Women Writers 1700–1900.* Lang. [2007] pp. 268. £33 ISBN 3 0391 1055 1.

Duff, David, and Catherine Jones, eds. *Scotland, Ireland, and the Romantic Aesthetic.* BuckUP. [2007] pp. 296. $55 ISBN 9 7808 3875 6188.

Duncan, Ian. *Scott's Shadow: The Novel in Romantic Edinburgh.* PrincetonUP. [2007] pp. xx + 388. £23.95 ISBN 9 7806 9104 3838.

Duquette, Natasha. *Sublimer Aspects: Interfaces Between Literature, Aesthetics and Theology.* CambridgeSP. [2007] pp. 240. £34.99 ISBN 9 7818 4718 3361.

Faflak, Joel. *Romantic Psychoanalysis: The Burden of the Mystery*. SUNYP. [2007] pp. xiv + 319. $85 ISBN 9 7807 9147 2699.

Felber, Lynette, ed. *Clio's Daughters: British Women Making History, 1790–1889*. UDelP. [2007] pp. 310. £46.50 ISBN 0 8741 3981 3.

Franklin, Caroline. *Byron*. Routledge. [2007] pp. 144. pb £14.99 ISBN 9 7804 1526 8561.

Franta, Andrew. *Romanticism and the Rise of the Mass Public*. CUP. [2007] pp. 245. £50 ISBN 0 5218 6887 4.

Frosch, Thomas R. *Shelley and the Romantic Imagination: A Psychological Study*. UDelP. [2007] pp. 359. £44.50 ISBN 9 7808 7413 9785.

Gilmartin, Kevin. *Writing Against Revolution: Literary Conservatism in Britain, 1790–1832*. CUP. [2007] pp. xii + 316. £50 ISBN 0 5218 6113 6.

Goldberg, Brian. *The Lake Poets and Professional Identity*. CUP. [2007] pp. viii + 297. £50 ISBN 9 7805 2186 6385.

Haberstroh, Patricia Boyle, and Christine St Peter, eds. *Opening the Field: Irish Women, Texts and Contexts*. CorkUP. [2007] pp. vii + 181. €39 ISBN 9 7818 5918 4103.

Hadjiafxendi, Kyriaki, and Polina Mackay, eds. *Authorship in Context: From the Theoretical to the Material*. Palgrave. [2007] pp. xii + 236. £45 ($65) ISBN 9 7814 0394 9011.

Halmi, Nicholas. *The Genealogy of the Romantic Symbol*. OUP. [2007] pp. x + 206. £47 ISBN 0 1992 1241 5.

Halpin, David. *Romanticism and Education: Love, Heroism and Imagination in Pedagogy*. Continuum. [2007] pp. 161. £75 ISBN 0 8264 8472 7.

Hamilton, Paul. *Coleridge and German Philosophy: The Poet in the Land of Logic*. Continuum. [2007] pp. ix + 175. £55 ISBN 9 7808 2649 5433.

Hodson, Jane. *Language and Revolution in Burke, Wollstonecraft, Paine, and Godwin*. Ashgate. [2007] pp. ix + 216. £50 ISBN 0 7546 5403 2.

Hughes, Gillian. *James Hogg: A Life*. EdinUP. [2007] pp. 320. £25 ISBN 9 7807 4861 6398.

Jager, Colin. *The Book of God: Secularization and Design in the Romantic Era*. UPennP. [2007] pp. xi + 272. £39 ISBN 0 8122 3979 2.

Jarvis, Simon. *Wordsworth's Philosophic Song*. CUP. [2007] pp. 267. £48 ISBN 9 7805 2186 2684.

Jenkins, Eileen J. *Eighteenth-Century British Historians*. Gale. [2007] pp. xix + 491. £140 ISBN 0 7876 8154 7.

Joffe, Sharon Lynne. *The Kinship Coterie and the Literary Endeavors of the Women in the Shelley Circle*. Lang. [2007] pp. xvi + 206. £35 ISBN 9 7808 2049 5064.

Joshua, Essaka. *The Romantics and the May Day Tradition*. Ashgate. [2007] pp. ix + 153. £45 ISBN 0 7546 5774 3.

Kitson, Peter J. *Romantic Literature, Race and Colonial Encounter*. Palgrave. [2007] pp. 280. £42.50 ISBN 1 4039 7645 7.

Kramp, Michael, *Disciplining Love: Austen and the Modern Man*. OSUP. [2007] pp. xvi + 202. $37.95 ISBN 9 7808 1421 0468.

Lamont, Claire, and Michael Rossington, eds. *Romanticism's Debatable Lands*. Palgrave. [2007] pp. xi + 251. £48 ISBN 9 7802 3050 7852.

Larrissy, Edward. *The Blind and Blindness in Literature of the Romantic Period.* EdinUP. [2007] pp. viii + 232. £50 ISBN 9 7807 4863 2817.

Lincoln, Andrew. *Walter Scott and Modernity.* EdinUP. [2007] pp. x + 250. £50 ISBN 9 7807 4862 6069.

Lodge, Sara. *Thomas Hood and Nineteenth-Century Poetry: Work, Play and Politics.* ManUP. [2007] pp. xvi + 216. £55 ISBN 9 7807 1907 6268.

Mandal, Anthony. *Jane Austen and the Popular Novel: The Determined Author.* Palgrave. [2007] pp. xii + 253. £50 ISBN 9 7802 3000 8960.

Mandal, Anthony, and Brian Southam, eds. *The Reception of Jane Austen in Europe.* Continuum. [2007] pp. xxxvi + 428. £160 ISBN 9 7808 2646 9328.

Manly, Susan. *Language, Custom and Nation in the 1790s: Locke, Tooke, Wordsworth, Edgeworth.* Ashgate. [2007] pp. vii + 204. £50 ISBN 0 7546 5832 0.

Mazzeo, Tilar J. *Plagiarism and Literary Property in the Romantic Period.* UPennP. [2007] pp. xiv + 236. £36 ISBN 0 8122 3967 9.

McNeil, Kenneth, *Scotland, Britain, Empire: Writing the Highlands, 1760–1860.* OSUP. [2007] pp. 280. $41.95 ISBN 9 7808 1421 0475.

Meldon D'Arcy, Julian, *Subversive Scott: The Waverley Novels and Scottish Nationalism.* IcelandUP. [2007] pp. 294. pb $40 ISBN 9 9795 4666 2.

Melville, Peter. *Romantic Hospitality and the Resistance to Accommodation: Rousseau, Kant, Coleridge, and Mary Shelley.* WLUP. [2007] pp. viii + 199. £35.99 ISBN 9 7808 8920 5178.

Mole, Tom. *Byron's Romantic Celebrity: Industrial Culture and the Hermeneutic of Intimacy.* Palgrave. [2007] pp. xiv + 227. £45 ISBN 9 7814 0399 9931.

Myrone, Martin. *The Blake Book.* Tate. [2007] pp. 224. £16.99 ISBN 9 7818 5437 7272.

Nash, Julie. *Servants and Paternalism in the Works of Maria Edgeworth and Elizabeth Gaskell.* Ashgate. [2007] pp. x + 130. £45 ISBN 9 7807 5465 6395.

Natarjan, Uttara, ed. *The Romantic Poets: A Guide to Criticism.* Blackwell. [2007] pp. xii + 359. £55 ISBN 9 7806 3122 9315.

Nicholson, Andrew, ed. *The Letters of John Murray to Lord Byron.* LiverUP. [2007] pp. xxxi + 576. £25 ISBN 9 7818 4631 0690.

O'Neill, Michael. *The All-Sustaining Air: Romantic Legacies and Renewals in British, American, and Irish Poetry since 1900.* OUP. [2007] pp. 208. £14.99 ISBN 9 7801 9929 9287.

Oya, Reiko. *Representing Shakespearean Tragedy: Garrick, the Kembles, and Kean.* CUP. [2007] pp. xii + 244. £53 ($100) ISBN 9 7805 2187 9859.

Paulin, Roger, William St Clair and Elinor Shaffer. *'A Gentleman of Literary Eminence': A Review Essay.* Institute of English Studies, School of Advanced Studies, ULondon. [2007] pp. 35. http://ies.sas.ac.uk/Publications/stc-faustus-review.pdf.

Pittock, Murray, ed. *The Reception of Sir Walter Scott in Europe.* Continuum. [2007] pp. lxxiv + 406. £150 ISBN 9 7808 2647 4100.

Pohl, Nicole, and Brenda Tooley, eds. *Gender and Utopia in the Eighteenth Century: Essays in English and French Utopian Writing.* Ashgate. [2007] pp. 206. £50 ISBN 9 7807 5465 4353.

Potkay, Adam. *The Story of Joy: From the Bible to Late Romanticism.* OUP. [2007] pp. xiii + 304. £55 ISBN 9 7805 2187 9118.

Rawes, Alan, ed. *Romanticism and Form.* Palgrave. [2007] pp. xv + 231. £46 ISBN 1 4039 9472 1.

Rix, Robert. *William Blake and the Cultures of Radical Christianity.* Ashgate. [2007] pp. ix + 230. £55 ISBN 9 7807 5465 6005.

Roberts, Jonathan. *William Blake's Poetry: A Reader's Guide.* Continuum. [2007] pp. 124. £10.99 ISBN 9 7808 2648 8602.

Rosenbaum, Susan B. *Professing Sincerity: Modern Lyric Poetry, Commercial Culture, and the Crisis in Reading.* UPVirginia. [2007] pp. 320. £33.95 ISBN 0 8139 2610 6.

Rowland, Christopher. 'Wheels Within Wheels': William Blake and the Ezekiel's Merkabah in Text and Image. MarquetteUP. [2007] pp. 43. $15 ISBN 9 7808 7462 5875.

Sabiston, Elizabeth, *Private Sphere to World Stage from Austen to Eliot.* Ashgate. [2007] pp. ix + 224. $99.95 ISBN 9 7807 5466 1740.

Schmid, Susanne. *Shelley's German Afterlives: 1814–2000.* Palgrave. [2007] pp. xi + 243. £40 ISBN 9 7814 0397 7502.

Shaffer, Elinor, and Edoardo Zuccato. *The Reception of S.T. Coleridge in Europe.* Continuum. [2007] pp. lx + 403. £125 ISBN 9 7808 2646 8451.

Simonsen, Peter. Wordsworth and Word-Preserving Arts: Typographic Inscription, Ekphrasis and Posterity in the Later Work. Palgrave. [2007] pp. x + 216. £45 ISBN 0 2305 2481 8.

Stabler, Jane, ed. *Palgrave Advances in Byron Studies.* Palgrave. [2007] pp. xii + 287. £62 ISBN 9 7814 0394 5938.

Stafford, Fiona, ed. *Jane Austen's Emma: A Casebook.* OUP. [2007] £17.99 ISBN 9 7801 9517 5318.

Strachan, John. *Advertising and Satirical Culture in the Romantic Period.* CUP. [2007] pp. xii + 353. £55 ISBN 0 5218 8214 9.

Thomas, Sophie. *Romanticism and Visuality: Fragments, History, Spectacle.* Routledge. [2007] pp. xvii + 227. £60 ISBN 9 7804 1596 1189.

Thompson, Carl, ed. *Romantic-Era Shipwreck Narratives.* Trent Editions. [2007] pp. 226. £9.99 ISBN 9 7818 4233 1293.

Thompson, Carl. *The Suffering Traveller and the Romantic Imagination.* OUP. [2007] pp. ix + 299. £45 ISBN 9 7801 9925 9984.

Townshend, Dale. *The Orders of Gothic: Foucault, Lacan, and the Subject of Gothic Writing, 1764–1820.* AMS. [2007] pp. x + 366. $87.50 ISBN 9 7804 0464 8541.

Vicario, Michael A. *Shelley's Intellectual System and its Epicurean Background.* Routledge. [2007] pp. xii + 303. £50 ISBN 9 7804 1598 1439.

Wainwright, Valerie. *Ethics and the English Novel from Austen to Forster.* Ashgate. [2007] pp. vi + 218. $99.95 ISBN 9 7807 5465 4322.

Walford Davies, Damian, and Lynda Pratt, eds. *Wales and the Romantic Imagination.* UWalesP. [2007] pp. xi + 285. pb £16.99 ISBN 0 7083 2066 2.

West, Sally. *Coleridge and Shelley: Textual Engagement.* Ashgate. [2007] pp. xii + 197. £50 ISBN 9 7807 5466 0125.

White, Simon J. *Robert Bloomfield, Romanticism and the Poetry of Community.* Ashgate. [2007] pp. ix + 171. £50 ISBN 9 7807 5465 7538.

Worrall, David. *The Politics of Romantic Theatricality, 1787–1832: The Road to the Stage*. Palgrave. [2007] pp. 266. £50 ISBN 0 2305 1802 8.

Wright, Julia M. *Ireland, India, and Nationalism in Nineteenth-Century Literature*. CUP. [2007] pp. viii + 272. £50 ($95) ISBN 9 7805 2186 8228.

Wroe, Ann. *Being Shelley: The Poet's Search for Himself*. Jonathan Cape. [2007] pp. xii + 452. £25 ISBN 9 7802 2408 0781.

Yang, Sharon R. ed., *The X-Files and Literature: Unweaving the Story, Unravelling the Lie to Find the Truth*. CambridgeSP. [2007] pp. xxv + 378. $79.99 ISBN 9 7818 4718 2395.

DUBLIN BUSINESS SCHOOL LIBRARY

XIII

The Nineteenth Century: The Victorian Period

WILLIAM BAKER, LINDA REINERT, ANNA BARTON,
ALEXIS EASLEY AND DAVID FINKELSTEIN

This chapter has five sections: 1. Cultural Studies and Prose; 2. The Novel; 3. Poetry; 4. Drama; 5. Periodicals and Publishing History. Sections 1 and 2 are by William Baker and Linda Reinert; section 3 is by Anna Barton; section 4 is by Alexis Easley; section 5 is by David Finkelstein.

1. Cultural Studies and Prose

(a) General

A broad historical perspective on the Victorian period is the focal point for several intriguing studies published in 2007. Simon Joyce's *The Victorians in the Rearview Mirror* considers twentieth century reactions to and reimaginings of the Victorian period. Joyce analyses literature, politics, film and visual culture to uncover the ways in which the Victorian period has been represented, as well as various aspects of twentieth-century cultural conditions which are conducive to interpretations of this era. This is an in-depth study of how the twentieth century reacted to and refashioned the previous century, through the examination of heritage culture, politics and imitations of Dickens's fiction. Joyce shows, for instance, how the Bloomsbury Group reinterpreted the intellectual legacy of their parents and denied Dickensian networks of social sympathy in favour of individualism and interiority. An interesting article on neo-Victorian writing appeared in the fall issue of *The Victorian Newsletter*: Jill E. Wagner's 'Class Consciousness, Critter Collecting, and Climatic Conditions: Post-Victorian Existentialism in the "Morphing" Victorian Scientist' (*VN* 112[2007] 32–50). Wagner's focus is John Fowles's *The French Lieutenant's Woman* [1969] and A.S. Byatt's novella 'Morpho Eugenia', from *Angels and Insects: Two Novellas* [1992]. She argues that both depict a 'vehement nineteenth-century philosophical battle and an emerging quasi-triumphant existentialist viewpoint through the figure of the Victorian scientist in their postmodern Victorian novels'. Wagner adds that 'this figure

Year's Work in English Studies, Volume 88 (2009) © *The English Association; all rights reserved*
doi:10.1093/ywes/map007

analytically explores evolution and religion while faced with social temptations and the result and ramifications of subsequent moral and ethical decisions' (p. 33). Jonathan Loesberg's 'The Afterlife of Victorian Sexuality: Foucault and Neo-Victorian Historical Fiction' (*CLIO* 36:iii[2007] 361–89) also discusses works of twentieth-century Victorian fiction, including *The French Lieutenant's Woman* and *Possession*.

Similarly focused on new and changing perceptions of the Victorian period, *The Victorian Studies Reader*, edited by Kelly Boyd and Rohan McWilliam, is a compilation of previously published articles which provides a picture not only of present-day views of Victorian literature and culture, but also of those held over the past century. International writings come together to present perspectives on familiar aspects such as parliamentary reform and poverty, as well as diverse subjects such as the mesmerist, barmaid and cosmopolitan man, as well as the Chartist, the British empire and Darwinian evolution, plus Victorian religion, morality and hypocrisy. Each of the fourteen sections features an introduction on the topic, with a total of twenty-nine chapters. In addition to the editors' contribution, 'Rethinking the Victorians' (pp. 1–48), contributions range from Richard Price's 'Should We Abandon the Idea of the Victorian Period?' (pp. 51–66) to Gertrude Himmelfarb's 'In Defense of the Victorians' (pp. 209–20), Gillian Beer's seminal 'Darwin's Imagination' (pp. 282–7) and Catherine Hall's 'Bringing the Empire Back In' (pp. 413–30).

In an important study, *A Half-Century of Greatness: The Creative Imagination of Europe, 1848–1883*, Frederic Ewen completes his magnum opus which began with *Heroic Imagination* published in 1984. *A Half-Century of Greatness* emphasizes the 1848 revolution, and vividly describes the effects of its failure on Romantic and Victorian literary figures as it depicts the creative thought of mid to late nineteenth-century Europe. Ewen uncovers surprising connections among novelists, poets and philosophers from England, Germany, Austria, Hungary, Russia and Ukraine, especially Dickens, Carlyle, Mill, the Brontës and George Eliot; Hegel, Strauss, Feuerbach, Marx, Engels, Wagner and several German poets; the Hungarian poet Sandor Petofi; Gogol, Dostoevsky, Bakunin and Herzen in Russia, and the great Ukrainian poet Shevchenko. This volume was reconstructed and edited by Jeffrey Wollock from Ewen's manuscript. Ewen's reference citations are found throughout the text, there is a reconstructed bibliography and an updated further reading list. These two volumes navigate a panorama of the social, political and artistic aspects of European Romanticism, foreshadowing and augmenting recent work on the relation of Marxism to Romanticism. Joanne Parker, in her *'England's Darling': The Victorian Cult of Alfred the Great*, explores the Victorian fascination with King Alfred. Parker states that her aim is to offer a broad account of the nineteenth-century cult of King Alfred and in doing so answer the modern tendency to focus exclusively on Arthur, and to attend to a void in criticism on nineteenth-century medievalism. Particularly enlightening chapters include 'The Hero as King: Alfred and Nineteenth-Century Politics' (pp. 82–127), ' "The root and spring of everything we love in church and state": Alfred and Victorian Progress' (pp. 128–67), ' "The most perfect character in history": Alfred and Victorian Morality' (pp. 167–99) and '"Never to be confused with King Arthur": Alfred After Victoria' (pp. 200–18).

Marion Thain's 'Modernist Homage to the Fin de Siècle' (*YES* 37:i[2007] 22–40) urges a more nuanced and complex model for viewing the *fin de siècle*, while Nicholas Shrimpton's '"Lane, you're a perfect pessimist": Pessimism and the English Fin de Siècle' (*YES* 37:i[2007] 41–57) also adds to changing perspectives on these decades. A number of contributions published in 2007 focus on the intellectual thought of the period more broadly. H.S. Jones, in *Intellect and Character in Victorian England: Mark Pattison and the Invention of the Don*, provides a fascinating account of Mark Pattison, who has been mistakenly noted as the prototype for Mr Casaubon from *Middlemarch*. Pattison is known as a proponent of Germanic concepts of the university, as a follower of Newman, and as an agnostic and thoroughly secular intellectual. Frequently disagreeing with his contemporaries on the subject of the academic's vocation, Pattison became one of the most interesting Oxford dons of the Victorian period. In his introduction, Jones remarks that Pattison would have perceived contemporary pragmatic compromises in higher education as a betrayal of the academic need for thought. Consequently, Pattison would have been an ineffective reformer, yet his ideas still resonate today. In *Anglo-French Attitudes: Comparisons and Transfers between English and French Intellectuals since the Eighteenth Century*, editors Christophe Charle, Julien Vincent and Jay Winter bring together a collection of essays written by scholars from a variety of disciplines and addressing a broad range of issues. These include the international circulation of economic, political and literary ideas, the translation and reception of authors in various contexts, and the concepts of 'Englishness' or 'Frenchness'. The Anglo-French relationship is employed as a starting point for an examination of the conflicting demands that intellectual life should be trans-national and cosmopolitan, and that intellectuals should represent their national mind. The contents of the volume include: part I, 'Towards A Reflexive History Of Intellectuals', with 'The Intellectuals: A Prehistory' (pp. 25–44) by Jean-Philippe Genet; 'British Exceptionalism Re-considered' (pp. 45–62) by Stefan Collini; in part II, 'An Anglo-French Republic of Letters?', with 'The Royal Society and the Académie des Sciences in the First Half of the 18th Century' (pp. 63–77) by Pascal Brioist; 'The English in Paris' (pp. 78–97) by Daniel Roche; 'The French Republic of Letters and English Culture, 1750–1790' (pp. 98–124) by Lawrence W.B. Brockliss; part III, 'Cultural Transfers', with 'Reconstructing Ruins And Revolution: Towards a History of the Volney Vogue In England' (pp. 125–46) by Alexander Cook; 'Mid-Nineteenth Century "Moral Sciences" Between Paris and Cambridge' (pp. 147–72) by David Palfrey; part IV, 'The Internationalisation of Intellectual Life', with 'Literary Import into France and Britain around 1900: A Comparative Study' (pp. 173–93) by Blaise Wilfert; 'The Commerce of Ideas: Protectionism and Free Trade in the International Circulation of Economic Ideas in Britain and France around 1900' (pp. 194–213) by Julien Vincent; 'The Ibsen Battle: A Comparative Analysis of the Introduction of Henrik Ibsen in France, England and Ireland' (pp. 214–34) by Pascale Casanova; part V, 'Intellectuals, National Models and the Public Sphere', with 'French Intellectuals and the Impossible English

Model at the End of the 19th Century' (pp. 235–55) by Christophe Charle; 'An English Crisis in French Thought? French Intellectuals Confront England at the Time of Fashoda and the Boer War' (pp. 256–70) by Christophe Prochasson; 'Homosexual Networks and Activist Strategies from the Late Nineteenth Century to 1939' (pp. 271–83) by Florence Tamagne; and 'Ironies of War: Intellectual Styles and Responses to the Great War in Britain and France' (pp. 284–98) by Jay Winter. This is a far-reaching and useful study.

The assessment and legacy of the famed Crystal Palace is featured in *Victorian Prism: Refractions of the Crystal Palace*, edited by James Buzard, Joseph W. Childers and Eileen Gillooly. Part I, 'Exhibitionary Aims and Anxiety', includes 'Rhetorical Remedies for Taxonomic Troubles: Reading the Great Exhibition', by Eileen Gillooly (pp. 23–39) and 'Conflicting Cartographies: Globalism, Nationalism, and the Crystal Palace Floor Plan' by James Buzard (pp. 40–54); part II, 'Exhibition Viewing', includes 'Languages of Glass: The Dreaming Collection' by Isobel Armstrong (pp. 55–83) and 'This Sublime Museum: Looking at Art at the Great Exhibition' by Rachel Teukolsky (pp. 84–122); part III, 'Exhibiting Publics', includes 'Mayhew, the Prince, and the Poor: The Great Exhibition of Power and Dispossession' by Karen Chase and Michael Levenson (pp. 123–37); ' "A palace for the people"? The Crystal Palace and Consumer Culture in Victorian England' by Peter Gurney (pp. 138–50) and 'Distracting Impressions and Rational Recreation at the Great Exhibition' by Andrea Hibbard (pp. 151–70); part IV, 'Others on Exhibit', includes 'Exhibiting American: The Native American and the Crystal Palace' by Kate Flint (pp. 171–85); '*Jerusalem, My Happy Home*: The Palestine Exhibition and the Limits of the Orientalist Imagination' by Eitan Bar-Yosef (pp. 186–202) and 'A Gothic Class Case in the Tropical Forest: The First Venezuelan National Exhibition of 1883' by Beatriz González-Stephan (pp. 216–32). Lastly, part V, 'Afterlives', includes 'The Great Exhibition and Modernization' by John R. Davis (pp. 233–49); ' "A dark exhibition": The Crystal Palace, *Bleak House*, and Intellectual Property' by Clare Pettitt (pp. 250–70) and 'Paxton's Legacy: Crystal Palace to Millennium Dome' by Jay Clayton (pp. 271–90). As with any such collection by diverse hands, some contributions are more opaque than others.

Amongst political biographies, Richard Shannon's *Gladstone: God and Politics* is of interest to literary scholars. In addition to offering a general readership the narrative of Gladstone's life, through emphasis on the statesman's strivings to realize God's purposes in his public service and an examination of the relationship between Gladstone's image as a Liberal along with his heritage as a disciple of his mentor Sir Robert Peel, Shannon draws upon Gladstone's prolific prose. It would be an understatement to add that Gladstone's prose is not the only instance of Victorian politicians' prose that has been woefully neglected by literary historians and critics.

There are quite a number of fresh contributions to Victorian cultural readings in science, including an intriguing and innovative study, Jonathan Taylor's *Science and Omniscience in Nineteenth-Century Literature*. Taylor ventures from mathematical and physical sciences to literature, philosophy, history, theology and music in order to illuminate connections as well as debates among thinkers in these fields. Taylor's central issue is 'omniscience', which is universally viewed as a fragile subject and therefore fertile ground for assumptions concerning epistemological confidence in the Victorian era. Through an exploration of the history of intellectual insecurity, this book offers a substantial contribution to our comprehension of Victorian culture. Of the three major sections of the book, the initial one, 'On History, Chaos and Carlyle' (pp. 11–101), is devoted to Carlyle. Taylor's afterword has a distinct focus on Dickens studies: 'On Demonic Omniscience and Dickens' (pp. 148–62) concentrates specifically on *The Old Curiosity Shop* [1840–1].

In *Herbert Spencer and the Invention of Modern Life* Mark Francis utilizes archival material and contemporary printed sources to produce a fascinating portrait of Spencer, who attempted to explain modern life through a unique philosophical and scientific system that bridged the gap between empiricism and metaphysics. In addition to England, Spencer's influence pervaded the United States and Asia. Though Spencer achieved success in the realm of ideas he was an unhappy individual, feeling crippled by the Christian values of his childhood and incapable of romantic love, as evidenced in his relationship with George Eliot. In another study of interest to students of Spencer, 'Of Beasts and Boys: Kingsley, Spencer, and the Theory of Recapitulation' (*VS* 49[2007] 583–609), Jessica Straley argues that Spencer's proposal of scientific pedagogy is a reflection of Kingsley's *The Water Babies*. Another intriguing cultural study drawing upon a scientific field is Stuart Clark's *The Sun Kings: The Unexpected Tragedy of Richard Carrington and the Tale of How Modern Astronomy Began*. This study concerns the nineteenth-century scientific controversy about the sun's hidden influence over the earth. Clark retraces the events surrounding the mysterious explosion on the sun in September 1859, which caused a gigantic cloud of gas, a blood-red aurora which erupted across the planet, and related crashes of telegraph systems, with electrical shocks rendering operators unconscious. Only amateur astronomer Richard Carrington realized the cause of these phenomena. Clark brings to life the scientists who rejected and embraced Carrington's discovery of solar flares, as well as the scandal that destroyed Carrington's reputation and his 1875 suicide. In *Space and the 'March of Mind'*, Alice Jenkins analyses the ways in which literary and scientific writers grappled with similar political and intellectual concerns, such as the regulation of access to knowledge, the organization of knowledge in productive ways and the formation of relationships between old and new knowledge. Poetry, essays and fiction, as well as scientific papers, textbooks and journals support her assertions of the relationships between various genres of writing and the physical sciences. The seven chapters are divided into two sections, 'Thinking with Space' and 'Thinking about Space'. Patricia Murphy's *In Science's Shadow: Literary Constructions of Late Victorian Women* reverses the stereotypical history of scientific theories of women's nature. Instead, Murphy analyses Victorian literary images of women as scientists and allies these results to historical debates concerning women's intellectual and biological capacities. The book begins with a historical perspective concerning women and science, and continues with a chapter of close readings on poet Constance Naden, botanical painter Marianne North and novelists such as Charles Reade, Wilkie Collins and

Thomas Hardy. Several of Murphy's conclusions are intriguing, for instance her observations on how Wilkie Collins's *Heart and Science* [1883] favours the passive female patient over the more threatening and forceful scientist, and on the manner in which Naden manoeuvres poetic forms as a means of dramatizing woman's omission from greater scientific discussion.

Deborah Denenholz Morse and Martin A. Danahay's *Victorian Animal Dreams: Representations of Animals in Victorian Literature and Culture* brings together fourteen diverse essays organized under three main themes: animals and Victorian scientific controversies, the division between humans and animals and animals as scapegoats. Beginning with part I, 'Science and Sentiment', chapters include: 'Animal Angst: Victorians Memorialize their Pets' by Teresa Mangum (pp. 15–34); 'Victorian Beetlemania' by Cannon Schmitt (pp. 35–52); 'Killing Elephants: Pathos and Prestige in the Nineteenth Century' by Nigel Rothfels (pp. 53–64); 'Designs after Nature: Evolutionary Fashions, Animals, and Gender' by Susan David Bernstein (pp. 65–80) and 'Dying Like a Dog in *Great Expectations*' by Ivan Kreilkamp (pp. 81–94). Part II, 'Sex and Violence', includes the following chapters: 'Nature Red in Hoof and Paw: Domestic Animals and Violence in Victorian Art' by Martin A. Danahay (pp. 97–120); ' "The crossing o' breeds" in *The Mill on the Floss*' by Mary Jean Corbett (pp. 121–44) and 'Pacific Harvests: Whales and Albatrosses in Nineteenth-Century Markets' by Anca Vlasopolos (pp. 167–78). The third and final part includes: ' "The Mark of the Beast": Animals as Sites of Imperial Encounter from *Wuthering Heights* to *Green Mansions*' by Deborah Denenholz Morse (pp. 181–200); 'Beastly Criminals and Criminal Beasts: Stray Women and Stray Dogs in *Oliver Twist*' by Grace Moore (pp. 201–14); 'The Sins of Sloths: The Moral Status of Fossil Megatheria in Victorian Culture' by Alan Rauch (pp. 215–28); 'Tiger Tales' by Heather Schell (pp. 229–48) and 'The Empire Bites Back: The Racialized Crocodile of the Nineteenth Century' by Mary Elizabeth Leighton and Lisa Surridge (pp. 249–70).

Maureen Moran's 2006 *Victorian Literature and Culture: A Student Guide*, part of the Introductions to British Literature and Culture series, usefully offers sections on such areas as 'Historical, Cultural and Intellectual Context', 'Literature in the Victorian Period', 'Critical Approaches' and 'Resources for Independent Study'. In *Adventures in Realism*, edited by Matthew Beaumont, the objective of the sixteen essays by prominent scholars is, as expressed in the title to the introduction, 'Reclaiming Realism'. This collection provides historical, cultural, intellectual and literary contexts essential to the understanding of developments in realism, and incorporates artistic mediums and technologies such as painting and film that have helped shape the way we perceive reality; it also investigates literary and visual sub-genres such as naturalism and socialist realism. Chapters include: 'Introduction: Reclaiming Realism' by Matthew Beaumont (pp. 1–12); 'Literary Realism Reconsidered: "The world in its length and breadth" ' by George Levine (pp. 13–32); 'Realist Synthesis in the Nineteenth Century Novel: "That unity which lies in the selection of our keenest consciousness" ' by Simon Dentith (pp. 33–49); 'Space, Mobility, and the Novel: "The spirit of place is a great reality" ' by Josephine McDonagh (pp. 50–67); 'Naturalism: "Dirt and horror pure and simple" ' by

Sally Ledger (pp. 68–83); 'Realism Before and After Photography: "The fantastical form of a relation among things"' by Nancy Armstrong (pp. 84–102); 'The Realist Aesthetic in Painting: "Serious and committed, ironic and brutal, sincere and full of poetry"' by Andrew Hemingway (pp. 103–24); 'Interrupted Dialogues of Realism and Modernism: "The fact of new forms of life, already born and active"' by Esther Leslie (pp. 125–41); 'Socialist Realism: "To depict reality in its revolutionary development"' by Brandon Taylor (pp. 142–57); 'Realism, Modernism, and Photography: "At last, at last the mask has been torn away"' by John Roberts (pp. 158–76); 'Cinematic Realism: "A recreation of the world in its own image"' by Laura Marcus (pp. 177–92); 'The Current of Critical Irrealism: "A moonlit enchanted night"' by Michael Löwy (pp. 193–206); 'Psychoanalysis and the Lacanian Real: "Strange shapes of the unwarped primal world"' by Slavoj Žižek (pp. 207–23); 'Feminist Theory and the Return of the Real: "What we really want most out of realism ..."' by Helen Small (pp. 224–40); 'Realism and Anti-Realism in Contemporary Philosophy: "What's truth got to do with it?"' by Christopher Norris (pp. 241–60) and 'A Note on Literary Realism in Conclusion' by Fredric Jameson. This collection, with contributions from highly distinguished hands, includes a brief bibliography and suggestions for further reading at the end of each section.

Given current fashions colonialism is, predictably, the subject of much work. Christopher Herbert's *War of No Pity: The Indian Mutiny and Victorian Trauma* focuses on a single incident, that of 11 May 1857, when Hindu and Muslim sepoys massacred British residents and native Christians in Delhi. This initiated a maelstrom of similar violence that engulfed Bengal in the following months. In Britain, this uprising was often portrayed as a clash of civilization and barbarity demanding merciless retribution. Herbert examines Victorian domestic perceptions of the mutiny. He draws on largely overlooked nineteenth-century texts, including memoirs, histories, letters, works of journalism and novels. Chapters include: 'Introduction: Jingoism, Warmongering, Racism' (pp. 1–18); 'Diabolical Possession and the National Conscience' (pp. 19–57); 'Three Parables of Violence' (pp. 58–98); 'The Culture of Retribution: Capital Punishment, Maurice Dering, Flotsam' (pp. 99–133); 'The Mutiny in Victorian Historiography' (pp. 134–204); 'The Infernal Kingdom of *A Tale of Two Cities*' (pp. 205–38); '*Lady Audley's Secret*: The Mutiny, the Gothic, and the Feminine' (pp. 239–72) and the epilogue, 'Fiction Fair and Foul: Novels of the Mutiny' (pp. 273–88). Georgina Howell's *Gertrude Bell: Queen of the Desert, Shaper of Nations* is a biography of the British traveller, poet, historian, mountaineer, photographer, archaeologist, gardener, cartographer, linguist, servant of the state and intelligence agent. Bell's (1868–1926) letters, diaries and writings, largely to be found today in the University of Newcastle upon Tyne Library, are integral to Howell's text, along with her presentation of the role Bell played in the creation of Iraq and the establishment of a monarchy with Faisal upon the throne. A recommended new study is Jane Stafford's *Maoriland: New Zealand Literature*, which re-evaluates the writings of nine later nineteenth- and early twentieth-century writers who fell out of favour largely because of their apparent adherence to colonialist methods of representation, including the racial romance. Authors included are Alfred Domett, Jessie Mackay, Henry Lawson, A.A. Grace, Katherine Mansfield, Edith Searle Grossmann, Blanche Baughan and William Satchel, concluding with a chapter on early Maori writer Apirana Ngata.

Julia M. Wright, in *Ireland, India, and Nationalism in Nineteenth-Century Literature* (also discussed in Chapter XII), investigates how authors from colonized nations wrote about colonization outside their own borders. In doing so, Wright's study encompasses a discussion of hitherto largely neglected texts. Chapters include: 'Introduction: Insensible Empire' (pp. 1–28); part I, 'National Feeling, Colonial Mimicry, and Sympathetic Resolutions', with ' "National Feeling": The Politics of Irish Sensibility', including Teeling's memoir of the 1798 Uprising (pp. 29–52); 'Empowering the Colonized; or, Virtue Rewarded', including Lady Morgan's *Wild Irish Girl* (pp. 53–80); and 'Travellers, Converts, and Demagogues', including Morgan's *The Missionary* and Thomas Moore's *Lalla Rookh* (pp. 81–118). part II, 'Colonial Gothic and the Circulation of Wealth', includes 'On the Frontier: Imitation and Colonial Wealth in Edgeworth and Lewis', encompassing a discussion of Edgeworth's fiction concerning foster-children, the notion of 'Going Native' and Matthew Lewis's 'Anaconda' (pp. 119–41); ' "Some neglected children": Thwarted Colonial Genealogies', including Morgan's 'Absenteeism', Charles Maturin's *Melmoth the Wanderer*, and MacCarthy's 'Afghanistan' (pp. 142–81); and 'Stoker and Wilde: All Points East', including *The Picture of Dorian Gray*, *The Lair of the White Worm* and *The Lady of the Shroud* (pp. 182–210). In a related article, 'The City of London, Real and Unreal' (*VS* 49[2007] 431–56), Garrett Ziegler tracks how mid-century writers promoted and grieved for the loss of private space in favour of commercial space. Harriet Ritvo's 'Manchester v. Thirlmere and the Construction of the Victorian Environment' (*VS* 49[2007] 457–82), chronicles the controversy created by the proposed conversion of Thirlmere, in the Lake District, into a reservoir for Manchester, an event which continued to be challenged after the reservoir opened in 1894.

There are a number of book reviews of literature concerning colonialism worth recording, all in the spring issue of *Victorian Studies*: A. Martin Wainwright's reviews of *Edge of Empire: Lives, Culture, and Conquest in the East, 1750–1850* by Maya Jasanoff and *The Ruling Caste: Imperial Lives in the Victorian Raj* by David Gilmore (*VS* 49[2007] 555–8); Stephen Heathorn's review of *The Discovery of Islands: Essays in British History* by J.G.A. Pocock (*VS* 49[2007] 560–2); Patrick Brantlinger's reviews of *Empire and Superempire: Britain, America and the World* by Bernard Porter and *Colonialism in Question: Theory, Knowledge, History* by Frederick Cooper (*VS* 49[2007] 562–5); Mary Ellis Gibson's review of *Epic and Empire in Nineteenth-Century Britain* by Simon Dentith (*VS* 49[2007] 565–7), and Bruce J. Hunt's review of *Predicting the Weather: Victorians and the Science of Meteorology* by Katharine Anderson (*VR* 33:ii[2007] 137–8).

Robert Sulcer writes, in 'Ungentlemanly Scholars' (*VIJ* 35[2007] 137–70), of the alleged affair of William Money Hardinge and Walter Pater, as well as other homosexual affairs, and how various scholars treated the subject well before Oscar Wilde's conviction for sodomy. Jean-Michel Rabaté's *1913: The Cradle of Modernism* expands the analysis of artistic events with analysis of canonical texts in one critical year, 1913. Rabaté analyses a variety of simultaneous artistic, literary and political endeavours from Yeats, Pound, Joyce, Du Bois and Stravinsky. Chapters include 'Introduction: Modernism, Crisis, and Early Globalization' (pp. 1–17); 'The New in the Arts' (pp. 18–45); 'Collective Agencies' (pp. 46–71); 'Everyday Life and the New Episteme' (pp. 72–95); 'Learning to be Modern in 1913' (pp. 96–117); 'Global Culture and the Invention of the Other' (pp. 118–40); 'The Splintered Subject of Modernism' (pp. 141–63); 'At War with Oneself: The Last Cosmopolitan Travels of German and Austrian Modernism' (pp. 164–84); 'Modernism and the End of Nostalgia' (pp. 185–207) and the conclusion, 'Antagonisms' (pp. 208–16).

In 'Culinary Utilitarian: Ideology in the Work of Alexis Benoît Soyer' (*VIJ* 35[2007] 171–208), Paul Thomas Murphy offers intriguing information on a seldom studied subject: the philosophy of the most famous chef in Victorian England. James Gregory's *Of Victorians and Vegetarians: The Vegetarian Movement in Nineteenth-Century Britain* contains three parts. Part I provides a history of the vegetarian movement through a survey of activity from 1840 to 1846. The main features of the movement are identified and analysed in terms of location, institutions and activity. Part II investigates the varieties of vegetarianism, devoting a chapter to physical Puritanism, the relationship to medical orthodoxy, the animal welfare movement, religious dimensions and relationships with spiritualism and radicalism. The third part of the book is concerned with vegetarian dietetic practice in public and private, vegetarianism in the press and the movement's social bias.

A welcome study in the realm of the Victorian arts is Jason Rosenfeld and Alison Smith's *Millais*, with 180 colour and twenty black and white illustrations. In the book's foreword Stephen Deuchar, director of Tate Britain, notes that a recent exhibition was the first since the Royal Academy retrospective of 1898 to present an overview of Millais's works, but that Millais was featured in three recent exhibitions: *The Pre-Raphaelites* in 1984, *Ruskin, Turner, and the Pre-Raphaelites* in 2000 and *Pre-Raphaelite Vision* in 2004. Among the chapters in this study are: 'Millais in His Time and Ours' by Jason Rosenfeld (pp. 10–13); '"The poetic image": The Art of John Everett Millais' by Alison Smith (pp. 14–19); and the catalogue, from Pre-Raphaelitism to 'The Late Landscapes' as well as a chronology by Heather Birchall and Jason Rosenfeld (pp. 246–9). In addition, this excellent collection contains notes, a bibliography, a list of exhibitions, exhibited works, lenders and credits and a detailed index. Carol Jacobi's *William Holman Hunt: Painter, Painting, Paint*, offers a discriminating view of Hunt's life, focused on his memoirs, while navigating Hunt's involvement in the publicity-conscious realm of Victorian art. It examines the probability of fictionalization in Hunt's autobiography, resulting in innovative interpretations of his paintings. Also on the Pre-Raphaelites, Brian Donnelly offers 'Sensational Bodies: Lady Audley and the Pre-Raphaelite Portrait' (*VN* 112[2007] 69–90).

In *The Making of English Photography: Allegories*, Steve Edwards traces the central role England played in revolutionizing the production of images, chronicling the development of English photography as an industrial, commercial and artistic enterprise from the first negative by William Henry

Fox Talbot in Wiltshire's Lacock Abbey in 1835. Across the first decades of photography's history, Edwards tracks the pivotal discernment between art and the document as it emerged in the writings of scientists and professional photographers, suggesting that this key difference is rooted in the social fantasies of the worker. Through close readings of the photographic press in the 1860s, Edwards reconstructs the ideological world of photographers and utilizes the unstable category of photography to cast light on art, class and industrial knowledge. In this fascinating study, Edwards draws upon early photographs, recent historical and theoretical scholarship, and extensive archival sources.

Sharon Aronofsky Weltman's *Performing the Victorian: John Ruskin and Identity in Theater, Science, and Education* (also discussed in section 4), is a study of Ruskin's writing on the theatre. Weltman examines Ruskin's discriminating eye for spectacle in opera, theatre, pantomime and dance, as well as Ruskin's search for transcendence of self, which emerges in his Winnington Hall lectures for girls. In *Facing the Late Victorians*, Margaret D. Stetz provides an intriguing study of portraits of artists and writers featured in the Mark Samuels Lasner collection at the University of Delaware. Stetz concentrates her study on how and why representations of artists' and writers' faces were published in the periodical press, exhibitions in London and book publishing, and then examines the variety of ways in which audiences learned to read those faces for signals about masculinity, femininity and class status, and especially for an understanding of what genius comprised. Writers and artists of the last two decades of the nineteenth century are the subjects of this excellent study, with especial concentration on Oscar Wilde as the consummate manipulator of a new market for portraits in order to advance his own career. A wider variety of writers and artists are incorporated into the study as Stetz examines the broader topic of writers' and artists' faces as objects of idealization, caricature and close study by the general public. Of special interest to *YWES* readers may be the portraits and commentaries concerning poet and journalist William Allingham (pp. 24–5), W.B. Yeats (p. 132), and 'Cope's Christmas Card' (p. 136), December 1883, which served as advertisement in its depiction of such figures as J.M. Whistler, Oscar Wilde, Robert Browning and Matthew Arnold in a panoramic watercolour card, sent free upon request to its customers.

The first issue of a new journal focusing on a neglected area of investigation, the *Journal of Illustration Studies*, contains articles on the Victorian period. These include David Skilton's 'The Centrality of Literary Illustration in Victorian Visual Culture: The Example of Millais and Trollope from 1860 to 1864' (*JOIS* [2007] 25 paras); Julia Thomas's 'Reflections on Illustration: The Database of Mid-Victorian Wood-Engraved Illustration (DMVI)' (*JOIS* [2007] 26 paras); and Paola Spinozzi's 'Interarts and Illustration: Some Historical Antecedents, Theoretical Issues, and Methodological Orientations' (*JOIS* [2007] 43 paras). The journal is available on an open-access basis and is an important contribution to our understanding of Victorian culture and taste and to a hitherto largely ignored area of study generally. Rosemary Hill's *God's Architect: Pugin and the Building of Romantic Britain*, is the first modern biography tracing one of Britain's greatest architects over his brief career,

Born in 1812, Pugin worked for King George IV at Windsor Castle, but by the age of 21 he had been shipwrecked, bankrupted and widowed, and he died nineteen years later, insane, but having changed the face of British architecture. Pugin authored the first architectural manifesto. Before turning 30 he had designed twenty-two churches, three cathedrals, six outstanding houses and a Cistercian monastery. For eight years he worked with Charles Barry (1795–1860), creating the luxurious interiors at the Palace of Westminster and the House of Lords, and Big Ben. He is known as the first architect-designer to cater for the middle classes, creating utilitarian objects from plant pots to wallpaper and early flat-pack furniture. Hill's account draws upon thousands of unpublished letters and drawings. *Hidden Burne-Jones: Works on Paper by Edward Burne-Jones from Birmingham Museums and Art Gallery, with essays by John Christian, Elisa Korb and Tessa Sidey*, edited by Tessa Sidey, John Christian and Elisa Korb, includes a catalogue of 'Edward Burne-Jones: Drawings, Watercolours, Prints and Archive Material at Birmingham Museums and Art Gallery'. Chapters included are: 'The Compulsive Draughtsman' by John Christian (pp. 7–16), 'Colour Plates' (pp. 17–27), 'Models, Muses and Burne-Jones's Continuous Quest for the Ideal Female Face' by Elisa Korb (pp. 28–33) and 'Public Patronage: The Burne-Jones Collection in Birmingham' by Tessa Sidey (pp. 34–8), plus two further chapters by Korb and Sidey, 'Exhibits' (pp. 39–40) and 'Edward Burne-Jones: Catalogue of Drawings, Watercolours, Prints and Archive Material at Birmingham Museums and Art Gallery' (pp. 62–94).

Jeremy Dibble, in his *John Stainer: A Life in Music*, tells the story of one of the most important musicians of the Victorian era, John Stainer (1840–1901), the composer of Anglican liturgical music and of secular works, a brilliant organist, fine scholar, theorist, pedagogue and teacher. Stainer's life is also a story of extraordinary social mobility, as he rose from lowly origins to become organist of St Paul's Cathedral and Professor of Music at Oxford. He achieved wide popularity with works such as 'I Saw the Lord' and *The Crucifixion*. Replete with musical and photographic illustrations including material drawn from the archives of the Stainer family, Dibble's book illuminates an important aspect of a key figure in the Victorian musical world, some of whose music is still performed today. Dibble demonstrates convincingly that more of it should be performed and that there are neglected masterpieces from Stainer's hand. In short, this is a well-written and richly documented biography. It concludes with an annotated 'List of Stainer's Works' (pp. 316–38), a detailed enumerative bibliography and a useful index (pp. 339–62).

Edward Elgar and his World, edited by Byron Adams, provides a comprehensive study of Elgar and his age, including twelve chapters, organized in four parts. The first, 'Worcester', includes Charles Edward McGuire, 'Measure of a Man: Catechizing Elgar's Catholic Avatars' (pp. 3–38), Mathew Riley on 'Elgar the Escapist?' (pp. 39–58), Byron Adams on 'Elgar and the Persistence of Memory' (pp. 59–96) and Daniel M. Grimley on '"The spirit-stirring drum": Elgar and Populism' (pp. 97–126). The second, 'Documents', includes early reviews of *The Apostles* from British periodicals, selected, introduced and annotated by Aidan J. Thomson (pp. 127–72) and 'Charles Sanford Terry and

Elgar's Violin Concerto' (pp. 173–92). The third section, 'London', includes Aidan J. Thomson on 'Elgar's Critical Critics' (pp. 193–222), Sophie Fuller on 'Elgar and the Salons: The Significance of a Private Musical Works' (pp. 223–48), Nalini Ghuman's 'Elgar and the British Raj: Can the Mughals March?' (pp. 249–86), Deborah Heckert's 'Working the Crowd: Elgar, Class, and Reformulations of Popular Culture at the Turn of the Twentieth Century' (pp. 287–316), and Rachel Cowgill's 'Elgar's War Requiem' (pp. 317–64). In the fourth section, 'Summation', Leon Botstein writes on 'Transcending the Enigmas of Biography: The Cultural Context of Sir Edward Elgar's Career' (pp. 365–408), concluding with a helpful index and notes on contributors. Although some of the contributions are more readable than others, and not all of Elgar's career is thoroughly examined, the volume offers much to students of late Victorian and Edwardian culture, and of course will be devoured eagerly by Elgar lovers.

Also related to music in Victorian studies is a review of William Weber's *The Musician as Entrepreneur, 1700–1914: Managers, Charlatans, and Idealists*, by Jeremy Dibble (*VS* 49[2007] 534–6). Other reviews related to books dealing with art and music include the following from the spring issue of *Victorian Studies*: Leo Costello's review of *Turner as Draftsman*, by Andrew Wilton (*VS* 49[2007] 527–9); Frank M. Turner's review of *Painting the Bible: Representation and Belief in Mid-Victorian Britain*, by Michaela Giebelhausen (*VS* 49[2007] 529–30); Leah Price's review of *The Look of Reading: Book, Painting, Text*, by Garrett Stewart (*VS* 49[2007] 531–2); and Michael Pickering's review of *Visual Delights Two: Exhibition and Reception*, edited by Vanessa Toulmin and Simon Popple (*VS* 49[2007] 532–4).

Anthony Trollope's *The Eustace Diamonds* [1871] and Wilkie Collins's *The Moonstone* [1868] are discussed at some length in John Plotz's chapter 'Discreet Jewels' (in Blackwell, ed., *The Secret Life of Things*, pp. 329–54), though most of this edited volume is devoted to writings of the eighteenth century. In *Magical Objects: Things and Beyond*, edited by Elmar Schenkel and Stefan Welz, there is an interesting contribution of note from the pre-eminent German Victorianist Paul Goetsch. His 'Uncanny Collectors and Collections in Late-Victorian Fiction' (pp. 67–87) illustrates how the theme of collecting was used to express late Victorian concerns. Goetsch's examples are gathered into four categories: those relevant to high capitalism in the world of art; post-Darwinian nature; evolutionary anthropology and imperialism and the civilized and primitive in Europe. A well-written and useful study concerning Victorian female writers and education was published in 2006: Isobel Hurst's *Victorian Women Writers and the Classics: The Feminine of Homer*. Hurst analyses the role of women writers in the Victorian vision of ancient Greece and Rome, revealing that they exhibited more imaginative interpretation of classical literature than has been previously acknowledged, and that their educational constrictions may have resulted in more open interpretations of classical literature. She asserts that the Victorian reworking of classical texts validated women's claims to authorship, expedited demands for access to education, highlighted feminist issues through heroines in ancient tragedy and helped to repudiate the warrior ethos of ancient epic. A wide variety of both canonical and little-examined writers is drawn upon.

Simon Morgan's *A Victorian Woman's Place: Public Culture in the Nineteenth Century* draws upon private as well as public documents to argue that women played an important role in the formation of the public identity of the Victorian middle class. While the image of bourgeois Victorian women as angels in the house, isolated from the world in private domesticity, has long been dismissed as an unrealistic ideal, according to Morgan women have remained marginalized in many recent accounts of the public culture of the middle class. Morgan attempts to redress the balance by drawing on a variety of sources. Through their support for cultural and philanthropic associations and their engagement in political campaigns, he argues, women developed a nascent civic identity, which for some informed their later demands for political rights. Carolyn W. de la L. Oulton's *Romantic Friendship in Victorian Literature* revisits the logic by which nineteenth-century authors presented the ideal of same-sex romantic friendships. Oulton focuses on both male and female friendships, pinpointing similarities indicated in works by Mary Elizabeth Braddon, Charlotte Brontë, Dickens, Disraeli and Tennyson, as well as in religious treatises, conduct manuals and periodicals from mid-century to the *fin de siècle*. Oulton challenges authors who have presented friendships of this period as innocent and uncomplicated. From a more limited territorial perspective, but nonetheless valuable, is Jane Aaron's *Nineteenth-Century Women's Writing in Wales*. Aaron argues that the way in which women came to perceive and represent themselves as Welsh was greatly affected by the gender ideology of the Romantic and Victorian periods. Aaron introduces the reader to a number of critically neglected Welsh women authors at work during the years 1780 to 1900, tracing the development of the Welsh nation as its women, in particular, imagined and helped to create it. Focusing on the rediscovery and inclusion of many forgotten writers, Aaron analyses the development of Welsh literature, and her study will be of interest to scholars of gender and nationalism and literary historians alike.

Anti-Feminism in Edwardian Literature, edited by Lucy Delap and Ann Heilmann, reprints the works of authors who opposed at least some feminist ideas in early twentieth-century England. This expensive six-volume set includes some pieces later than the Edwardian period (from the 1920s) and offers generally available items such as Mrs Humphry Ward's novel *Daphne* (all of volume 1), and Arnold Bennett's essay *Our Women*, which takes up all of volume 6. Other not inaccessible materials such as a satirical skit by W.H. Mallock and essays by Frederic Harrison are included, as well as more difficult to find materials, such as essays by Marie Corelli and Belford Bax, books by C. Gasquoine Hartley, Arabella Kenealy, and Ardeshir Ruttonji Wadia, as well as a West Indian newspaper's didactic dialogues. *Victorian Honeymoons: Journeys to the Conjugal*, by Helena Michie, brings together recent interests in Victorian travel and sexuality. Michie traces the popularity of honeymoons across the Victorian period, when going on honeymoon became common practice for all but the poorest classes. Sources for this study include the letters and diaries of sixty-one Victorian couples and excerpts from novels such as *Frankenstein* and *Middlemarch*. Michie's study leads from ideas of the centrality of the honeymoon to evolving notions of conjugality, as well as the notion of the married couple as primarily a social entity.

Claudia Nelson's *Family Ties in Victorian England* is a well-written and thoroughly researched sociological study in which Nelson draws upon Victorian nineteenth-century fiction and non-fiction. Chapters are presented on the format of familial roles, such as husband and wife, mother and father and children and siblings, in addition to extended, foster-, and stepfamilies. Nelson addresses both the historical facts of Victorian domestic life and conflicting images in texts of the time, all in search of how such familial roles, with their co-ordinating domestic duties, served national interests.

Literature and place once again became the focus of several studies. A highly recommended 2006 contribution is Nicola J. Watson's *The Literary Tourist: Readers and Places in Romantic and Victorian Britain*. Watson goes beyond recent books on the subject as she explores theoretical issues such as the disruption of intimacy between reader and writer, the falsification of tourist sites, and the domination of elements of commerce at the expense of artistic concerns. Poet's Corner in Westminster Abbey, the grave sites of Percy Bysshe Shelley, Thomas Gray and John Keats, Stratford-Upon-Avon, Robert Burns's birthplace, Walter Scott's Abbotsford, the Haworth of the Brontës and other spots are examined in detail. *Literature and Place: 1800–2000*, edited by Peter Brown and Michael Irwin, offers ten original essays centred on a wide variety of locations such as islands, countries and cities, topoi used to evoke place, such as maps, ruins, landscape and history and their manifestations in biography, travel writing, fiction and poetry. Authors established and new write about places in England, Scotland, Ireland, France, Germany, the United States and the South Pacific. In addition to Michael Irwin's initial chapter, 'Maps of Fictional Space' (pp. 25–48), of particular interest to readers concerned with Victorian issues are 'The English Cottage as Cultural Critique and Associationist Paradigm' by Malcolm Andrews (pp. 49–68), 'Urban Labyrinths: Dickens and the Pleasures of Place' by Murray Baumgarten (pp. 69–86), 'Scott, Cartography, and the Appropriation of Scottish Place' by David Blair (pp. 87–108) and 'Proust, Ruskin, Stokes, and the Topographical Project' by Stephen Bann (pp. 129–46).

Robert MacFarlane's clearly written and well-argued *Original Copy: Plagiarism and Originality in Nineteenth-Century Literature* documents and examines the dramatic reassessment of literary originality and plagiarism that occurred during the nineteenth century, from the 1820s through the writings of Oscar Wilde and Lionel Johnson. George Eliot, Dickens, Reade, Pater, Wilde and Johnson are formative to MacFarlane's discussion of how notions of originality and plagiarism were founts of creative resource. Mary Anne Gillies's *The Professional Literary Agent in Britain, 1880–1920* initiates an important investigation into the study of British literary culture during a crucial transitional period. The emergence of the professional literary agent in Britain around 1880 accompanied and accelerated the transformation of both publishing and authorship. Rather than providing a broad overview of the period, Gillies focuses on a specific figure, the professional literary agent, and on two agents in particular. The first is A.P. Watt, widely acknowledged as the first professional literary agent, who founded his agency in 1875 and saw himself as an honest broker between author and publisher. Watt's clients were generally established writers such as Kipling, Rider Haggard and

Conan Doyle. The second is J.B. Pinker, the leading figure in the second wave of the agent business, whose approach was that of discoverer and champion of new writers such as James Joyce and Katherine Mansfield. Gillies's chapters include 'Why Did the Professional Literary Agent Emerge in the 1880s?' (pp. 12–26); 'A.P. Watt: Professional Literary Agent' (pp. 27–39); 'Establishing the Agency Model: George Macdonald and Watt' (pp. 40–63); 'Testing the Agency Model: "Lucas Malet" and Watt' (pp. 64–86); 'The Second Wave of Agenting: J.B. Pinker' (pp. 87–110); 'The Agent and Popular Literature: Somerville and Ross and Pinker' (pp. 111–35); and 'Building a Career: Joseph Conrad and Pinker' (pp. 136–66).

Religion and spiritual concerns were the focus of several studies in 2007. *The New Encyclopedia of Unbelief*, edited by Tom Flynn, is a comprehensive reference work on the history, beliefs and thinking on aspects of atheism, agnosticism, secular humanism, secularism and religious scepticism. Topics include morality without religion, unbelief in the historicity of Jesus, critiques of intelligent design theory, unbelief and sexual values and summaries of the state of unbelief around the world. More than 100 authoritative contributors have written in excess of 500 entries. The volume includes connections between unbelief and the social reform movements of the nineteenth and twentieth centuries, the labour movement, female suffrage, anarchism, sexual radicalism and feminism. There are substantial entries on, for instance, Marian Evans (George Eliot) (pp. 299–301) and other major Victorian figures. Nadia Valman's *The Jewess in Nineteenth-Century British Literary Culture* is a well-written examination of stories about Jewish women that proliferated in nineteenth-century Britain as debates about the place of the Jews in the modern nation raged. Valman argues that the Jewess as virtuous, appealing and sacrificial brings to light how hostility towards Jews was joined to pity, identification and desire. Utilizing sources from popular romance to the realist novel, Valman investigates how the complex figure of the Jewess brought to the fore questions of race, religion and national identity. Tracing the narrative of the Jewess from its beginnings in Romantic and Evangelical literature, and reading canonical writers including Walter Scott, George Eliot and Anthony Trollope alongside minor figures such as Charlotte Elizabeth Tonna, Grace Aguilar and Amy Levy, Valman demonstrates the remarkable persistence of the narrative and its myriad transformations across the century. This is a highly original and recommended study on a complicated issue that includes perceptive critical readings of hitherto neglected works. Timothy Larsen's *Crisis of Doubt: Honest Faith in Nineteenth-Century England* demonstrates that, in contrast to the common discourse concerning loss of religious faith in writers such as George Eliot, there were also freethinking and secularist leaders who came to faith during this period. These sceptics were exposed to the latest ideas that seemed to undermine faith and yet, after experiencing a crisis of doubt, they defended the intellectual clarity of Christianity. After addressing the topic 'Crisis of Faith' in chapter 1 (pp. 1–17), Larsen goes on to discuss the following reconverts: 'William Hone' (pp. 18–49); 'Frederic Rowland Young' (pp. 50–71); 'Thomas Cooper' (pp. 72–108); 'John Henry Gordon' (pp. 109–35); 'Joseph Barker' (pp. 136–72); 'John Bagnall Bebbington' (pp. 173–96); and 'George Sexton' (pp. 197–227). In the final chapters Bagnall considers 'How Many Reconverts Were There?' (pp. 228–38) and 'Crisis of Doubt' (pp. 239–53).

Sarah A. Willburn's *Possessed Victorians: Extra Spheres in Nineteenth-Century Mystical Writings*, published in 2006, analyses nineteenth-century spiritualism in its connections with such conventional concerns as Marxism and Darwinism. The first section forges direct connections to the literary world with analyses of *Daniel Deronda* and *Villette* as well as the work of Marie Corelli. Various aspects of spiritualism, including spirit photography and spiritual evolution through sex, as well as the animate séance table, are examined in the other chapters. This study also includes chapters on 'Harriet Martineau and Mesmeric Cure' and 'Florence Marryat: The Professional Medium and Promiscuous Community'. Linda M. Austin's *Nostalgia in Transition, 1780–1917* chronicles the development of nostalgia from the eighteenth-century perception of it as memory disorder to Victorian notions of memory as a pleasing pastime. Austin traces notions of nostalgia in a variety of poems by Arnold, Tennyson, Hardy and Emily Brontë, as well as novels by Hardy, and illustrations by Kate Greenaway and Helen Allingham and on to late Victorian cultural histories of the cottage as an example of public remembering. Dedicated readers are investigated in *The English Cult of Literature: Devoted Readers, 1774–1880*. In this clearly written study, William McKelvy challenges the assumption that England's literary tradition grew from Christianity's lost hold on the imagination and the political realm. McKelvy uses a series of case studies, as well as a wide variety of writings, to shift the focus from literary critics to the historical role of religious professionals in the formation of and debate over authority in print matter. This study is based on recent investigations in book history and newer historiographies which challenge conventional secularism.

Those book reviews concerning Victorian culture in general that we have identified for particular attention are: David Andrews's review of *The Natural Origins of Economics* by Margaret Schabas (*VR* 33:ii[2007] 134–6); Jordanna Bailkin's review of *The Ideas in Things: Fugitive Meaning in the Victorian Novel* by Elaine Freedgood (*VS* 49[2007] 507–8); Fred Wilson's review of *Reforming Philosophy: A Victorian Debate on Science and Society* by Laura J. Snyder (*VS* 49[2007] 515–16); David Weinstein's review of *The 'Puritan' Democracy of Thomas Hill Green* by Alberto de Sanctis (*VS* 49[2007] 517–18); Hugh McLeod's review of *Rural Society and the Anglican Clergy, 1818–1914: Encountering and Managing the Poor* by Robert Lee (*VS* 49[2007] 518–20); Emma Mason's review of *The Victorians and the Eighteenth Century: Reassessing the Tradition*, edited by Francis O'Gorman and Katherine Turner (*VS* 49[2007] 537–9); and David Bivona's review of *Epic and Empire in Nineteenth-Century Britain* by Simon Dentith (*NCL* 62[2007] 127–9). Further *Victorian Studies* reviews include: Laura L. Peters's review of *Imagined Orphans: Poor Families, Child Welfare, and Contested Citizenship in London* by Lydia Murdoch (*VS* 50[2007] 112–14); Patrick Scott's review of *A Catholic Eton? Newman's Oratory School* by Paul Shrimpton (*VS* 50[2007] 116–18); Mark Knight's review of *Catholicism, Sexual Deviance, and Victorian Gothic Culture* by Patrick R. O'Malley (*VS* 50[2007] 118–20); Allison Pease's review of *The Traffic in Obscenity from Byron to Beardsley: Sexuality and*

Exoticism in Nineteenth-Century Print Culture by Colette Colligan (*VS* 50[2007] 120–2); Jonathan Rose's reviews of *Bound for the 1890s: Essays on Writing and Publishing in Honor of James G. Nelson*, edited by Jonathan Allison, and *Print Culture and the Blackwood Tradition, 1805–1930*, edited by David Finkelstein (*VS* 50[2007] 122–4); Margaret D. Stetz's review of *Reading, Publishing and the Formation of Literary Taste in England, 1880–1914* by Mary Hammond (*VS* 50[2007] 123); Joseph Bristow's review of *Writers, Readers, and Reputations: Literary Life in Britain 1870–1918* by Philip J. Waller (*VS* 50[2007] 126–8); Kevis Goodman's review of *Nostalgia in Transition, 1780–1917* by Linda Marilyn Austin (*VS* 50[2007] 130–3); José Ramón Bertomeu Sánchez's review of *Poison, Detection, and the Victorian Imagination* by Ian A. Burney (*VS* 50[2007] 133–5); Barry S. Godfrey's reviews of *The Golden Old Days: Crime, Murder and Mayhem in Victorian London* by Gilda O'Neill, and *Poisoned Lives: English Poisoners and their Victims* by Katherine Watson (*VS* 50[2007] 135–6); Jordi Cat's review of *When Physics Became King* by Iwan Rhys Morus (*VS* 50[2007] 138–9); Amanda Gilroy's review of *Victorian Fiction and the Cult of the Horse* by Gina Dorré (*VS* 50[2007] 140–1); Sonya O. Rose's review of *The Culture of History: English Uses of the Past 1800–1953* by Billie Melman (*VS* 50[2007] 142–3); Timothy Carens's review of *Ethnicity and Cultural Authority from Arnold to DuBois* by Daniel G. Williams (*VS* 50[2007] 143–5); Walter L. Arnstein's review of *Politics and Culture in Victorian Britain: Essays in Memory of Colin Matthew*, edited by Peter Ghosh (*VS* 50[2007] 145–7); Timothy L. Alborn's review of *Creating Capitalism: Joint-Stock Enterprise in British Politics and Culture, 1800–1870* by James Taylor (*VS* 50[2007] 147–9); Janice Helland's review of *Representing Female Artistic Labour, 1848–1890* by Patricia Zakreski (*VS* 50[2007] 149–51); Jason Rosenfeld's *Time Present and Time Past: The Art of John Everett Millais* by Paul Barlow (*VS* 50[2007] 151–3); Laura Vorachek's review of *The Musical Crowd in English Fiction, 1840–1910: Class, Culture and Nation* by Phyllis Weliver (*VS* 50[2007] 152–5); Susan Wollenberg's *Europe, Empire, and Spectacle in Nineteenth-Century British Music*, edited by Rachel Cowgill (*VS* 50[2007] 155–7); Julie F. Codell's review of *Media and the British Empire*, edited by Chandrika Kaul (*VS* 50[2007] 157–60); Nupur Chaudhuri's *The Harem, Slavery and British Imperial Culture: Anglo-Muslim Relations in the Late Nineteenth Century* by Diane Liga Robinson-Dunn (*VS* 50[2007] 160–1); Bradley Deane's review of Kaori Nagai's *Empire of Analogies: Kipling, India and Ireland* (*VS* 50[2007] 162–3); Mridu Rai's review of *The Scandal of Empire: India and the Creation of Imperial Britain* by Nicholas B. Dirks (*VS* 50[2007] 164–6); and Regenia Gagnier's review of *Imperial Masochism: British Fiction, Fantasy, and Social Class* by John Kucich (*VS* 50[2007] 166–8). Norman Vance reviews Michael Wheeler's *The Old Enemies: Catholic and Protestant in Nineteenth-Century English Culture* (*NCL* 61[2007] 510–13). A review focused on elements of aestheticism is Leonee Ormond's discussion of *Continental Crosscurrents: British Criticism and European Art 1810–1910* by J.B. Bullen (*YES* 37:i[2007] 245–6). Kristine Swenson reviews *Victorian Literary Mesmerism* and *Mesmerists, Monsters, and Machines: Science Fiction and the Cultures of Science in the Nineteenth Century*, edited by Martin Willis and Catherine Wynne (*NCL* 62[2007] 288–93). In an essay review entitled

'Past and Present: Two Studies of British *Fin-De-Siècle* Culture' (*VIJ* 35[2007] 281–9), Elizabeth J. Deis examines *Imperial Masochism: British Fiction, Fantasy, and Social Class* by John Kucich and *The New Woman and the Empire* by Iveta Jusová. In a review concerning women writers, A.A. Markley offers a review of *Victorian Women Writers and the Classics: The Feminine of Homer* by Isobel Hurst (*VS* 50[2007) 110–12). A number of books related to gender and feminist studies in the area of Victorian studies were reviewed in the spring issue of *Victorian Studies*. They include Moira Martin's review of *Women, Welfare and Local Politics, 1881–1920: 'We Might Be Trusted'* by Steven King (*VS* 49[2007] 520–1); Lucy Bland's review of *The Long Sexual Revolution: English Women, Sex, and Contraception* by Hera Cook (*VS* 49[2007] 521–3); Arlene Young's review of *Gender at Work in Victorian Culture: Literature, Art and Masculinity* by Martin Danahay (*VS* 49[2007] 523–5); and Janice Helland's review of *History's Beauties: Women and the National Portrait Gallery, 1856–1900* by Lara Perry (*VS* 49[2007] 525–7). T. Johnson Woods reviewed *The London Journal 1845–83: Periodicals, Production and Gender* by Andrew King (*NCC* 29:i[2007] 55–6).

(b) Prose

A useful addition to prose studies for the Victorian period is the eminent Gertrude Himmelfarb's edited collection *The Spirit of the Age: Victorian Essays*. Seventeen essays focus on figures such as Carlyle, Mill, Macaulay, Thackeray, Dickens, George Eliot, Bagehot, Ruskin, Newman, Arnold, Acton, Gladstone, Huxley and Wilde, with a few lesser-known writers such as Beatrice Webb (1858–1943) and the English suffragist and feminist Millicent Fawcett (1847–1929). In selecting these essays spanning a variety of subjects and sixty-four years, Himmelfarb employs Mill's well-known phrase 'The Spirit of the Age' emphasizing the Victorian predisposition to ponder the dominant trends of the time, usually involving themes such as change, progress and anxiety, with morality as an overarching concern. Himmelfarb explains how the essay genre became the distinctive mode of discourse for the period. Talia Schaffer's *Literature and Culture at the Fin de Siècle* features well-known works by *fin-de-siècle* authors alongside non-canonical stories, poems and articles. Organized into four thematic units, 'Aestheticism', 'New Women', 'Mind and Body' and 'England and its Others', this text delves into the provocative topics relevant to this literary era. This collection seems to be the first undergraduate reader devoted to the *fin de siècle*, and offers famous poems, popular fiction and controversial journalism, along with rare non-canonical texts, to suit broad surveys and single-topic seminars alike. The readings provide a wide representation of well-known and lesser-known authors, including Oscar Wilde, Rudyard Kipling, Walter Pater, A.E. Housman, Alice Meynell, Arthur Symons and Una Ashworth Taylor. Innovative juxtapositions of material offer a fresh perspective on well-known texts. Headnotes, footnotes and unit introductions supply brief, readable explanations to support and contextualize the readings.

Irish Literature: The Nineteenth Century (volumes 2 and 3), edited by the late A. Norman Jeffares and Peter Van De Kamp, includes forewords by Conor Cruise O'Brien and Bruce Arnold. These volumes follow the first [2005] and complete the Irish Academic Press series on Irish literature of the eighteenth and nineteenth centuries. The second volume encompasses the middle decades of the period, including the Great Famine, with first-hand accounts as well as *Jail Journal*, by John Mitchel; the rise of cultural nationalism with Davis, Mangan and Lady Wilde as contributors to *The Nation*; and the Irishness of Unionist intelligentsia in the *Dublin University Magazine*. This volume also places the authentic Gaelic voices in translation of Ferguson and Walsh against those of Mangan and 'Father Prout' and chronicles the rise of Fenianism through Charles Kickham and others, as well as presenting the emergence of new literary confidence in the works of Sigerson and Todhunter. The third volume encompasses the final thirty years of the century, including the emergence of the Land League, the dynamiting campaign of the Fenians and the career of Charles Stewart Parnell, along with the changes in literary genres which accompanied these events: Standish James O'Grady's affirmation of Gaelic Ireland's literary heritage, Douglas Hyde's promotion of Irish language and culture via the Gaelic League, writers associated with the Irish Literary Society, a new interest in Celticism, the development of Irish mythology and legend through W.B. Yeats's *The Wanderings of Oisin* and on into *The Secret Rose* and *The Wind Among the Reeds*. Oscar Wilde on decadence, George Bernard Shaw on social hypocrisy, the influence of Ibsen, and George Moore's combination of Zola's naturalism with *Totalkunst*'s synaesthesia, are also central to this volume. In short, these meticulously annotated volumes are the completion of a long-needed project providing rich sources for the study of well-established and lesser-known authors alike.

Harriet Martineau's *Autobiography*, edited by Linda H. Peterson, is the first comprehensively annotated edition of the text since it was originally published in 1877. Martineau's life-story involves her experiences as a reviewer and journalist after her family's fortune had collapsed, the publication of her best-selling series, *Illustrations of Political Economy* [1832–4], her disability following a hearing loss, her reputation as literary lion in London society, her tour of the US, explorations of North Africa and the Middle East, her publication of editorials on slavery for the *London Daily News* and her role as a commentator on public issues such as politics, history and religion. The useful appendices include illustrations from the *Autobiography*, a private memorandum from June 1829, letters from Martineau to her mother of 22 January 1830 and 'Letter to the Editor of "Men of the Time" (22 March 1856)', as well as 'Appendix D: Contemporary Reviews', including 'Margaret Oliphant', *Blackwood's Edinburgh Magazine* (April 1877) (pp. 673–704), 'John Morley', *Macmillan's Magazine* (May 1877) (pp. 705–24), and 'W.R. Greg', *The Nineteenth Century* (August 1877) (pp. 725–37). In 'Open Accounts: Harriet Martineau and the Problem of Privacy in Early-Victorian Culture', Aeron Hunt discusses Martineau's novel *Deerbrook* [1839] and its tense efforts to square claims of privacy with the author's social, intellectual and political commitments to free circulation (*NCL* 62[2007] 1–28). The important five-volume *The Collected Letters of Harriet Martineau*, edited by Deborah Anna Logan, provides a long-awaited scholarly edition of the extant letters. These magnificently edited volumes bring together letters formerly scattered throughout the United States and United Kingdom. Almost all of the upwards of 2,000 letters in the collection have never before been published. The letters extend from Martineau's early years through to just before her death, and include family letters and publishing correspondence relating to most of her work. They reveal, for instance, her coming of age as an intellectual young woman, her development as a self-supporting writer, her trials and tribulations, her friendships and much more.

Richard Reeves's *John Stuart Mill: Victorian Firebrand* is an engagingly written biography of a relatively neglected Victorian. The fifteen chapters include: 'An Unusual and Remarkable Education (1806–20)' (pp. 1–10); 'A Dismal Science? (1848–52)' (pp. 204–37); '*On Liberty* (1859)' (pp. 262–306); and 'The Father of Feminism' (pp. 413–48). As noted in Reeves's prologue, reasons for a study of Mill include his instructiveness for modern readers on the regulation of such subjects as gambling, smoking, drinking and prostitution, avenues for education provision, justifications for foreign intervention, women's rights and models for capitalism. This biography also addresses Mill's views on the uneasy balance between individual rights versus collective action, 'how to build democratic and civic institutions which "empower" . . . and how to honour authority while encouraging dissent' (p. 8). The book jacket uses the striking image of Mill in G.F. Watt's painting. Janice Carlisle and James R. Simmons Jr, in *Factory Lives: Four Nineteenth-Century Working-Class Autobiographies*, present a sampling of working-class biographies from the Victorian period. John Brown's *A Memoir of Robert Blincoe*, William Dodd's *A Narrative of the Experience and Sufferings of William Dodd*, Ellen Johnston's *Autobiography* and James Myles's *Chapters in the Life of a Dundee Factory Boy* are the autobiographies presented, discussed and set in context. Appendices include contemporary responses to the autobiographies, debates on factory legislation, transcripts of testimony given before parliamentary committees on child labour and excerpts from literary works on factory life by Harriet Martineau, Frances Trollope and Elizabeth Barrett Browning, as well as others.

The spring issue of *Victorian Studies* features a 'Forum of the South Seas' in which Anna Johnston's 'The Strange Career of William Ellis' (*VS* 49[2007] 491–501) examines the relatively short tenure of William Ellis in the mission field (1816–25), during which he carefully documented his interactions with peoples and cultures in the extremely diverse geographical regions, concentrated on the Pacific region, opened during early nineteenth-century imperialism. *The Travel Journals of Robert Hyde Greg of Quarry Bank Mill* has come to publication through the editorship of Beryl and Allen Freer. Robert Hyde Greg was the son of the founder of Quarry Bank Mill at Styal, near Wilmslow in Cheshire, which was one of the largest cotton mills of Europe during the late eighteenth and nineteenth centuries. Greg travelled in Scotland, Spain, Portugal and then on the Grand Tour through France, Italy, Greece and the Ottoman empire between 1814 and 1817, before he joined the family cotton mill concern. Greg's manuscript journals of these travels are now published, and contain much which will be of interest to social and economic historians. His travels were interrupted by the threat of Napoleon's restoration to power. Greg also made intelligent social observations and survived adventures in the company of the prince of Hess Homburg. Drawings, as well as contemporary illustrations from other sources, some in colour, are also included in this intriguing set of journals, plus sixty-four pages of photographic plates.

The year 2007 saw the publication of several useful new studies dealing with Victorian prose in scientific fields, including James Mussell's *Science, Time and Space in the Late 19th-Century Periodical Press*. Recent theoretical debates on scientific writing form a framework from which Mussell proposes a new methodology for the comprehension of nineteenth-century scientific debate. As part of this, he argues that a new perspective on print culture within its wider cultural context is also in order. He employs historical accounts of scientific controversy, documentation of references to time and space in the periodical press, and new discoveries about the dissemination and distribution of periodicals, authorship and textual authority. A discussion of recent debates concerning digital publication adds an extra dimension to Mussell's research. Chapters include 'Introduction: "Movable Types"' (pp. 1–2); part I, 'Spaces: Astronomy and the Representation of Space' (pp. 27–8); 'The Spectacular Spaces of Science and Detection in the *Strand Magazine*' (p. 61); part II, 'Times: Representing the Present' (p. 91); 'Discovery and the Circulation of Names' (pp. 121–7); 'Periodicity and the Rhythms of 19th-Century Science' (pp. 147–51); 'Conclusions: 19th-Century Electricity in the Electronic Age' (pp. 183–5); and a useful bibliography. Anne Stiles's edited collection, *Neurology and Literature, 1860–1920*, is organized into four sections: 'Catalysts', 'Diagnostic Categories', 'Sex and the Brain' and 'The Traumatized Brain'. These demonstrate how late Victorian and Edwardian neurology and fiction shared philosophical concerns and rhetorical strategies. In the years 1860–1920 Americans such as Silas Weir Mitchell and Oliver Wendell Holmes wrote poignantly on the subject of neurology, while novelists such as H.G. Wells and Wilkie Collins frequently employed fiction to dramatize neurological discoveries and their consequences. Over the six decades there was unprecedented interdisciplinary collaboration between scientists and artists, who discovered common ground in their ambivalence towards the prevailing intellectual climate of biological determinism. The first section, 'Catalyst', contains Laura Otis's 'Howled Out of the Country: Wilkie Collins and H.G. Wells Retry David Ferrier' (pp. 27–51) and Don La Coss's 'Our Lady of Darkness: Decadent Arts & the Magnetic Sleep of Magdeleine G.' (pp. 52–76). Section 2, 'Diagnostic Categories', consists of Andrew Mangham's 'How Do I Look: Dysmorphophobia and Obsession at the *Fin de Siècle*' (pp. 77–96) and Kristine Swenson's 'Doctor Zay and Dr. Mitchell: Elizabeth Stuart Phelps's Feminist Response to Mainstream Neurology' (pp. 97–118). Section 3, 'Sex and the Brain', contains Randall Knoper's 'Trauma and Sexual Inversion, circa 1885: Oliver Wendell Holmes's *A Mortal Antipathy* and Maladies of Representation' (pp. 119–40) and James Kennaway's 'Singing the Body Electric: Nervous Music and Sexuality in *Fin de Siècle* Literature' (pp. 141–62). Section 4, 'The Traumatized Brain', has

Jill Matus's 'Emergent Theories of Victorian Mind Shock: From War and Railway Accident to Nerves, Electricity and Emotion' (pp. 163–83) and Mark S. Micale's 'Medical and Literary Discourses of Trauma in the Age of the American Civil War' (pp. 184–206).

In a special issue of *Victorian Studies* based on papers and responses from the third annual conference of the North American Victorian Studies Association, held jointly with the North American Society for the Study of Romanticism annual meeting, also discussed in Chapter XII, the 'Matters of Memory' section includes Athena Vrettos's 'Displaced Memories in Victorian Fiction and Psychology' (*VS* 49[2007] 199–207), in which she examines literary, psychological and parapsychological writings by Thomas Hardy, Arthur Conan Doyle, George Henry Lewes, Samuel Butler and F.W.H. Myers, as well as a response by Deirdre Lynch (*VS* 49[2007] 228–32); plus a section entitled 'Form at the Limits', including 'Pursuing Proper Protocol: Sarah Bowdich's Purview of the Sciences of Exploration' (*VS* 49[2007] 277–85), in which Mary Orr highlights the work of scientist, artist and writer Mrs Sarah Bowdich (1791–1856), who utilized biography to overcome obstacles that discouraged women from entering scientific disciplines; '"A dim world, where monsters dwell": The Spatial Time of the Sydenham Crystal Palace Dinosaur Park' (*VS* 49[2007] 286–301), by Nancy Rose Marshall; and 'Liberalism and the Time of Instinct' (*VS* 49[2007] 302–12), by Walter Bagehot, followed by responses to each article by Cannon Schmitt (*VS* 49[2007] 313–24).

The great Duke–Edinburgh edition of *The Collected Letters of Thomas and Jane Welsh Carlyle* continued in 2007 with the publication of volume 35, January–October 1859. This volume includes 'Letters to the Carlyles' (pp. xxvii–xxviii) and a 'Chronology, January–October 1859' (pp. xxix–xxxiv) in addition to the letters of the Carlyles themselves. Duke University Press has made the *Carlyle Letters* available to all, and they are now online at carlyleletters.org. Brent E. Kinser is the co-ordinating editor. *Carlyle Studies Annual* for 2007 opens with a moving tribute by Rodger L. Tarr to Georg Bernhard Tennyson (*CStA* 23[2007] 3–6). The issue continues with the late Ruth Roberts's '"The lore of Heaven, the speech of Earth": Carlyle, Mahomet, and Islam' (*CStA* 23[2007] 7–12); David R. Sorensen's '"Une religion plus dogne de la Divinité": A New Source for Carlyle's Essay on Mahomet' (*CStA* 23[2007] 13–42); 'Appendix 2: Audiffret and Sacy's Entry on Mahomet' (*CStA* 23[2007] 43–74); 'Appendix 2: Thomas Carlyle to G.F. Watts' (*CStA* 23[2007] 75–8); Owen Dudley Edwards's 'Carlyle and Catholicism, Part I: Hilaire Belloc and *The French Revolution*' (*CStA* 23[2007] 79–104), along with 'Appendix: Hilaire Belloc's 1906 Introduction to Carlyle's *The French Revolution*' (*CStA* 23[2007] 105–18); David R. Sorensen's 'Thomas Carlyle's MS Notes for "The Diamond Necklace"' (*CStA* 23[2007] 119–24); 'Transcription of Carlyle's MS Notes' (*CStA* 23[2007] 125–46); 'Digital Facsimile of Carlyle's MS Notes' (*CStA* 23[2007] 147–156); Brent E. Kinser's 'Rebecca Buffum Spring and the Carlyles' (*CStA* 23[2007] 157–68); and Stuart Wallace's '*Blethering Blackie* and Thomas Carlyle' (*CStA* 23[2007] 169–86). The spring issue of *Victorian Studies* includes John D. Rosenberg's review of the Chris R. Vanden Bossche, Joel L. Brattin and D.J. Trela edition of

Past and Present by Carlyle (*VS* 49[2007] 547–49). In the spring/fall issue of *Nineteenth-Century Prose* are the following: a lovely tribute to Cecil Y. Lang, 'In Memoriam: Cecil Y. Lang', by Lawrence W. Mazzeno (*NCP* 34:i–ii[2007] 1–8); Clinton Machann's 'Introduction: Arnold's Prose Today' (*NCP* 34:i–ii[2007] 9–24); Linda Ray Pratt's 'Passionate Reporting: Arnold on Elementary Schools, Teachers, and Children' (*NCP* 34:i–ii[2007] 25–58); Ignacio Ramos Gay's 'Matthew Arnold on Victorian Theatre' (*NCP* 34:i–ii[2007] 59–88); Katherine Bahr's 'The Function of Matthew Arnold's Criticism: Resolution and Independence' (*NCP* 34:i–ii[2007] 89–114); Julie Carr's 'Matthew Arnold's Pregnancy' (*NCP* 34:i–ii[2007] 115–42); Mark Allison's 'Prematurity, Periodicity, and Agency in "The Function of Criticism at the Present Time"' (*NCP* 34:i–ii[2007] 143–62); Frances Frame's 'Arnold and the Irish Question: Anticipating Communitarianism' (*NCP* 34:i–ii[2007] 163–90); Joe Phelan's 'The Language of Criticism in Arnold's Religious Writings' (*NCP* 34:i–ii[2007] 191–210); Brian Crick's 'Henry James and "the critical arms of Matthew Arnold": "Restoring the perverted balance of truth"' (*NCP* 34:i–ii[2007] 211–36); Michael DiSanto's 'Matthew Arnold under Conrad's Eyes: *Lord Jim* as Literary Criticism' (*NCP* 34:i–ii[2007] 237–56); Ranjan Ghosh's 'A Reading in Comparative Aesthetics: Arnold as Indian Sage?' (*NCP* 34:i–ii[2007] 257–82); and Roger L. Brooks's 'The Advertisement to Dr. Arnold's Fragment on the Church: A Misascription to Mathew Arnold' (*NCP* 34:i–ii[2007] 291–4). Some of the contributions are more readable than others.

Gowan Dawson's *Darwin, Literature and Victorian Respectability* argues that the fashioning of respectability concerning sex was neither straightforward nor unproblematic, with Darwin and his principal supporters facing accusations of encouraging sexual impropriety. Integrating contextual approaches to the history of science with literary studies, Dawson sheds new light on debates over evolution by examining them in relation to the murky underworlds of Victorian pornography, sexual innuendo, unrespectable free thought and artistic sensualism. Chapters include: 'Introduction: Darwinian Science and Victorian Respectability' (pp. 1–26); 'Charles Darwin, Algernon Charles Swinburne and Sexualized Responses to Evolution' (pp. 27–81); 'John Tyndall, Walter Pater and the Nineteenth-Century Revival of Paganism' (pp. 82–115); 'Darwinism, Victorian Freethought and the Obscene Publications Act' (pp. 116–61); 'The Refashioning of William Kingdon Clifford's Posthumous Reputation' (pp. 162–89) and 'T.H. Huxley, Henry Maudsley and the Pathologization of Aestheticism' (pp. 190–221).

The revival of interest in Walter Pater, once a neglected figure, is partly due to the efforts of the *Pater Newsletter* and its editors. The first issue of 2007 'A Queer Theory Roundtable', includes the following articles: Stefano Evangelista's 'Walter Pater: The Queer Reception' (*PaterN* 52:i[2007] 19–24); Heather Love's 'Exemplary Ambivalence' (*PaterN* 52:i[2007] 25–30); Dennis Denisoff's 'Walter Pater and the Queer Sympathies of Today's Paganism' (*PaterN* 52:i[2007] 31–6); Megan Becker-Leckrone's 'Same-Sex and the Second Sex in "Style"' (*PaterN* 52:i[2007] 37–44); Michael Davis's 'The Sexual Position of Walter Pater' (*PaterN* 52:i[2007] 45–51); Thomas's Albrecht's 'The Queer Poetics of Pater's "Leonardo Da Vinci"'

(*PaterN* 52:i[2007] 52–63); and Vincent A. Lankewish's 'Walter Pater, Queer Aesthete: Now Playing at Your Local High School' (*PaterN* 52:i[2007] 64–72). The full text of W.T. Stead's *The Maiden Tribute of Modern Babylon* has been reprinted for the first time since its original publication in the *Pall Mall Gazette* [1885] by the True Bill Press. The Criminal Law Amendment Bill— designed to raise the age of female consent to 16 and make brothels more susceptible to legal jurisdiction—which languished in parliament for several years, was given crucial support at a critical time by the publication of *The Maiden Tribute*. This serialized, sensational report documented the complexity and breadth of organized prostitution as well as the sophisticated techniques used in the entrapment of young girls into prostitution. Though details were inaccurate and the text was poorly written, its influence is thought to have led to the most far-reaching piece of British legislation related to sexuality and its exploitation. It represents a major primary source on Victorian attitudes towards female sexuality. Antony E. Simpson's annotations identify people and places specified by Stead. Simpson's introductory essay is especially useful for historical context as it traces efforts to combat organized prostitution from the 1820s onward. Beyond prostitution in general, Simpson's essay addresses the Labouchère Amendment, which led to easier prosecution of consensual homosexual activity and remained the principal legal means for harassing homosexuals over the ensuing eighty years. His edition initiates a valuable contribution to Victorian studies, with promised further reprints of primary sources to come from True Bill Press.

Guy Arnold, in his *In the Footsteps of George Borrow: A Journey through Spain and Portugal*, visits the same places where Borrow attempted to distribute Protestant Testaments in fiercely Catholic Spain from 1835 to 1840, and about which Burrow created the classic travel adventure *The Bible in Spain*, which is still in print. A century and a half later, staying where possible in the same inns, and taking the same roads, Arnold explored the varied landscapes and cities of the Iberian peninsula in a journey that took him through Madrid, Lisbon, Toledo, Seville, Cadiz, Salamanca and Segovia as well as many small towns and villages. Guy Arnold also considers Borrow's ambiguous religious beliefs, his taste for the social low life and a mysterious liaison with a widow from Norfolk. Modern Spain is also compared with that of Borrow's time, and Arnold reveals that little seems to have changed. The spring 2007 edition of the *George Borrow Bulletin* contains the following: 'Manuscrit trouvé à Pétersbourg (Part 2)' by Peter Missler (*GBB* 34:ii[2007] 6–14); 'Owlglass in Peking: Father Hyacinth Bichurin' by Michael Rawbone (*GBB* 34:ii[2007] 15–24); 'John Bowring's Memoirs and their History, with Special Reference to A Chapter on Denmark' by Inge Kabell (*GBB* 34:ii[2007] 25–30); 'Notes and Queries: (1) George Borrow and Sir Walter Scott: Two Heads Compared by the Phrenologists' by Iain Gordon Brown (*GBB* 34:ii[2007] 31–4); 'Two English Eccentrics: George Borrow (1803–1881) and John Cowper Powys (1872–1963)' by Jacqueline Peltier (*GBB* 34:ii[2007] 49–61); '"Is it possible that I am under the roof of an author?"': Borrow's Treatment of the Creative Sensibility in *Lavengro*' by Clive Wilkins-Jones (*GBB* 34:ii[2007] 62–71); 'The Texts in Borrow's Texts; or, Borrow the Borrower' by Ann Rider (*GBB* 34:ii[2007] 72–82); 'The Fourth Fraser

Memorial Lecture: Shorsha Borrow's Tipperary Experience' by Martin Murphy (*GBB* 34:ii[2007] 83–95); and 'A Tailpiece: She *Asked* Me about Dickens...I *Told* her about Borrow, 9 February 2007' (*GBB* 34:ii[2007] 98–102) by John Hentges. The fall issue offers 'The Father of the Novel and the Mother of the Waters' by Peter Missler (*GBB* 35:ii[2007] 10–20); '*Almaraz: The Relics of the Wolf* by David Fernández de Castro' translated by Peter Missler (*GBB* 35:ii[2007] 21–33); 'Borrow as Muse, his Impact on Paul Nash' by Norrette Moore (*GBB* 35:ii[2007] 34–41); '... and in the Right Corner We Have...? (The Continuing Saga of John Greaves of Ponterwyd)' by John Hentges (*GBB* 35:ii[2007] 42–54); 'Mrs. Borrow's Account Book: The Borrows' Lodgings in Yarmouth' by Phyllis Stanley (*GBB* 35:ii[2007] 77–81); 'The Fifth Fraser Memorial Lecture: The Elusive George Borrow' by Guy Arnold (*GBB* 35:ii[2007] 82–7); and 'The Bitter End: Borrow's Lost Job Opportunity and its Impact on *The Romany Rye*' by Ann M. Ridler (*GBB* 35:ii[2007] 88–101).

A shifting of emphasis towards a long overdue focus on Victorian prose work is reflected in the extent of recent reviews of work focusing on prose and other genres. They range from Ruth Livesey's review of *Victorian Interpretation*, by Suzy Anger (*VS* 49[2007] 325–7); Mary Ann O'Farrell's review of *Common Scents: Comparative Encounters in High-Victorian Fiction* by Janice Carlisle (*VS* 49[2007] 328–9); Joseph A. Kestner's review of *The Imagination of Class: Masculinity and the Victorian Urban Poor* by Daniel Bivona (*VS* 49[2007] 329–31); Melissa Valiska Gregory's review of *Bleak Houses: Marital Violence in Victorian Fiction* (*VS* 49[2007] 331–3); Paul R. Deslandes's review of *Hard Men: Violence in England since 1750* by Clive Emsley (*VS* 49[2007] 333–5); James H. Mills's *The Victorians and Sport* by Mike Huggins (*VS* 49[2007] 335–6); Neal Garnham's review of *The Irish Policeman, 1822–1922* by Elizabeth Malcolm (*VS* 49[2007] 337–8); Joanne Shattock's review of *Women Making News: Gender and Journalism in Modern Britain* by Michelle Elizabeth Tusan (*VS* 49[2007] 338–40); Peter W. Sinnema's review of *Images at War: Illustrated Periodicals and Constructed Nations* by Michelle Martin (*VS* 49[2007] 340–2); Panikos Panayi's review of *Gypsies and the British Imagination, 1807–1930* by Deborah Epstein Nord (*VS* 49[2007] 342–3); Daniel Bivona's review of *Outlandish English Subjects in the Victorian Domestic Novel* by Timothy L. Carens (*VS* 49[2007] 344–5); Tony Ballantyne's review of *The Holy Land in English Culture 1799–1917* by Eitan Bar-Yosef (*VS* 49[2007] 346–7); Jeffrey Cox's *Converting Women: Gender and Protestant Christianity in Colonial South India* by Eliza F. Kent (*VS* 49[2007] 348–9), Anna Johnston's review of *Nature and Godly Empire: Science and Evangelical Mission in the Pacific, 1795–1850* by Sujit Sivasundaram (*VS* 49[2007] 349–51); A.J.C. Mayne's review of *Inventing Pollution: Coal, Smoke, and Culture in Britain since 1800* by Peter Thorsheim (*VS* 49[2007] 352–3); Deborah Brunton's review of *The Western Medical Tradition, 1800–2000* by W.F. Bynum (*VS* 49[2007] 354–5); Christopher E. Forth's review of *Nervous Conditions: Science and the Body Politic in Early Industrial Britain* by Elizabeth Green Musselman (*VS* 49[2007] 355–7); David Wright's review of *Madness at Home: The Psychiatrist, the Patient, & the Family in Madness in England* by Akihito Suzuki (*VS* 49[2007] 357–9); Alison Bashford's review of *Dangerous*

Motherhood: Insanity and Childbirth in Victorian Britain by Hilary Marland (*VS* 49[2007] 359–60); Frank A.J.L. James's review of *Karl Pearson: The Scientific Life in a Statistical Age* by Theodore M. Porter (*VS* 49[2007] 360–2); Suzy Anger's '*The Busiest Man in England': Grant Allen and the Writing Trade, the Fin de Siècle* by Peter Morton (*VS* 49[2007] 362–5); Ruth Y. Jenkins's review of *More Usefully Employed: Amelia B. Edwards, Writer, Traveler and Campaigner for Ancient Europe* by Brenda E. Moon (*VS* 49[2007] 365–7); Jane De Gay's review of *Graham R.: Rosamund Marriott Watson, Woman of Letters* by Linda K. Hughes (*VS* 49[2007] 367–8); Valerie Sanders's review of Gillian Sutherland's *Faith, Duty and the Power of Mind: The Cloughs and their Circle 1820–1960* (*VS* 49[2007] 369–70); Sara Haslam's review of *Ford Madox Ford and the Regiment of Women: Violet Hunt, Jean Rhys, Stella Bowen, Janice Biala* by Joseph Wiesenfarth (*VS* 49[2007] 370–2); Nick Groom's review of *John Payne Collier: Scholarship and Forgery in the Nineteenth Century* by Arthur Freeman and Janet Ing Freeman (*VS* 49[2007] 372–4); Jason B. Jones's review of *The Apostle of the Flesh: A Critical Life of Charles Kingsley* by J.M.I. Klaver (*VS* 49[2007] 377–9); Lindy Stiebel's *H. Rider Haggard on the Imperial Frontier: The Political and Literary Contexts of his African Romances* by Gerald Cornelius Monsman (*VS* 49[2007] 379–80); Sally Ledger's review of *The Victorian Novel* by Louis James (*VS* 49[2007] 380–2); Stacy Gillis's review of *Detective Fiction* by Charles J. Rzepka (*VS* 49[2007] 382–4); Michael Pickering's review of *The Circus and Victorian Society* by Brenda Assael (*VS* 49[2007] 384–6); Renata Kobetts Miller's review of *Women's Theatre in Victorian Britain* by Katherine Newey (*VS* 49[2007] 386–7); Lene Østermark-Johansen's review of *Alfred Gilbert's Aestheticism: Gilbert amongst Whistler, Wilde, Leighton, Pater and Burne-Jones* by Jason Edwards (*VS* 49[2007] 388–9); and Elizabeth K. Helsinger's review of *Desire and Excess: The Nineteenth-Century Culture of Art* and *Haunted Museum: Longing, Travel and the Art-Romance Tradition*, both by Jonah Siegel (*VS* 49[2007] 389–92). The following issue's reviews include: Sarah J. Heidt's review of *Life Writing and Victorian Culture* edited by David Amigoni (*VS* 49[2007] 539–41); Margaret Flanders Darby's review of '*The Busiest Man in England': A Life of Joseph Paxton, Gardener, Architect & Victorian Visionary* by Kate Colquhoun (*VS* 49[2007] 541–3); and Ann-Barbara Graff's *Deciphering Race: White Anxiety, Racial Conflict, and the Turn to Fiction in Mid-Victorian English Prose* by Laura Callanan (*VS* 49[2007] 558–60). Frank M. Turner reviews *The Letters of Matthew Arnold*, edited by Cecil Y. Lang (*VIJ* 35[2007] 251–80). Judith Stoddart offers a review of David Melville Craig's *John Ruskin and the Ethics of Consumption* (*VS* 50[2007] 106–8).

2. The Novel

(a) General

The fashion for placing fiction in Victorian settings is continued with D.J. Taylor's splendid *Kept: A Victorian Mystery*, which offers a fascinating tale featuring a failed landowner who dies in a riding accident, his wife's subsequent disappearance and the hideous Baskerville-style death of his friend, a famous naturalist. The novel moves between the beautifully evoked English countryside, mid-century London and Canada. Taylor creates a wonderful swirl of historical fact and homage to the Victorian novel. Tamara Wagner, in her 'Lost in a Good Book: Remapping the Victorian Novel in Post-Millennium Britain' (*VIJ* 35[2007] 81–108), offers useful insights on neo-Victorian novels such as James Wilson's sequel to *The Woman in White*, entitled *The Dark Clue* [2001], Michel Faber's *The Crimson Petal and the White* [2002], and Jasper Fforde's series which began with *The Eyre Affair* [2003]. Several other publications this year discussed neo-Victorian texts or issues, and these are discussed above in the general section.

To shift gears, Julian Wolfrey's *Writing London*, volume 3: *Inventions of the City* continues his extensive explorations focusing on interventions and invention between 1880 and 1930. Neglected authors of the period and key literary texts are subtly explored, with sharp distinctions made between modernity and modernism. Extensive readings of works by Richard Marsh, Amy Levy, Arnold Bennett and T.S. Eliot are included in the following chapters: 'Introduction: Of Invention and the Singularities of the City Of London' (pp. 1–7); 'The Hieroglyphic Other: *The Beetle*, London, and the Anxieties of Late Imperial England' (pp. 8–36); 'The "tortuous geography of the night world": The "productive disorder" of the Noctuary Text' (pp. 37–62); 'Between Seeing and Knowing: Amy Levy, Arnold Bennett and Urban Counter-Romance' (pp. 81–134); '"All the living and the dead": Urban Anamnesis in John Berger and Iain Sinclair' (pp. 159–90); and '"Concatenated words from which the sense seemed gone": *The Waste Land*' (pp. 191–246). Wolfreys deals with complicated ideas and occasionally his prose tends to become rather prolix. On the whole, however, it is remarkably clear and at times contains flourishes worthy of poetry.

The prolific Wolfreys's *Dickens to Hardy, 1837–1884: The Novel, the Past, and Cultural Memory in the Nineteenth Century* focuses on readings of such novels as Elizabeth Gaskell's *Cranford*, Wilkie Collins's *The Moonstone*, George Eliot's *Middlemarch* and Thomas Hardy's *A Laodicean* and *Desperate Remedies*. Wolfreys questions how the Victorian middle classes identified themselves in their modernity and discusses how literature mediated the construction of identities through notions of cultural memory. In addition to the examination of the novels, two chapters focus on the Gothic and the political. Part I, 'Cultural Memory', includes '"The same story…with a difference": *The Pickwick Papers* (1836–7)' (pp. 13–50) and '"Our society": *Cranford* (1853)' (pp. 51–80); part II, 'Questions of Englishness: Being and Historicity', includes '"The English mind": The Moonstone (1868)' (pp. 81–125) and '"Minutely and multitudinously scratched in all directions": *Middlemarch* (1871–1872)' (pp. 126–92); part III, 'The Next Generation', includes '"The modern flower in a medieval flowerpot": The Example of Thomas Hardy' (pp. 193–252). Also included are a selective chronology covering 1832–84, an annotated bibliography (pp. 274–8) and a useful index of names and another of subjects. In short, there are some fascinating insights and interconnections to be found in Wolfreys's work.

Frank Christianson's *Philanthropy in British and American Fiction: Dickens, Hawthorne, Eliot and Howells* suggests that the early high capitalism which England and America shared during the Victorian period grew into a new kind of cosmopolitanism in the age of literary realism, and argues for the necessity of a transnational analysis based upon economic relationships of which people on both sides of the Atlantic were increasingly conscious. The connecting point of this exploration of economics, aesthetics and moral philosophy is philanthropy. This book explores questions of the nature of philanthropy shared by both countries. Christianson explores the relationship between philanthropy and literary realism in novels by Charles Dickens, Nathaniel Hawthorne, George Eliot and William Dean Howells, and examines how each used literary figures of philanthropy to redefine social identity and refashion his or her aesthetic practices. Chapters include: 'From Sympathy to Altruism: The Roots of Philanthropic Discourse' (pp. 31–74); 'Dickensian Realism and Telescopic Philanthropy' (pp. 75–103); 'Hawthorne's "Cold Fancy" and the Revision of Sympathetic Exchange' (pp. 104–38); 'Altruism's Conquest of Modern Generalisation in George Eliot' (pp. 139–69); and 'William Dean Howell's "Altrurian" Aesthetic in the Modern Marketplace' (pp. 171–93).

Valerie Wainwright's *Ethics and the English Novel from Austen to Forster* traces an ethical perspective that favours lifestyles that are worthy and fulfilling as well as admirable and rewarding. With fresh research into the ethical debates in which her chosen authors participated, Wainwright reveals the ways in which the ideas of Kant, F.H. Bradley and John Stuart Mill, along with little-known writers such as the priest Edward Taggart, the preacher William MacCall and philanthropist Helen Dendy Bosanquet, were appropriated and reappraised. Wainwright also places these novelists in the wider context of modernity and proposes that their responses can be linked to ongoing discussions characteristic of modern moral philosophy. Contents include part I, 'What Matters (Most)', including 'Modes and Sensibilities: Varieties of Ethical Thought' (pp. 21–44) and 'Narrative Perspectives' (pp. 45–58); part II, 'Ethical Designs', including 'On Being Un/reasonable: *Mansfield Park* and the Limits of *Persuasion*' (pp. 59–84); 'Discovering Autonomy and Authenticity in *North and South*: Elizabeth Gaskell, John Stuart Mill, and the Liberal Ethic' (pp. 85–104); 'On Goods, Virtues and *Hard Times*' (pp. 105–22); 'Anatomizing Excellence: *Middlemarch*, Moral Saints and the Languages of Belief' (pp. 123–42); 'The Magic in *Mentalité*: Hardy's Native Returns' (pp. 143–60); and '*Howards End* and the Confession of Imperfection' (pp. 161–82).

Laurence Talairach-Vielmas's *Moulding the Female Body in Victorian Fairy Tales and Sensation Novels* is more interesting than its title suggests. It investigates Victorian representations of femininity in fairy tales by George MacDonald, Lewis Carroll, Christina Rossetti, Juliana Horatia Ewing and Jean Ingelow, and in addition sensation novels by Wilkie Collins, Mary Elizabeth Braddon, Rhoda Broughton and Charles Dickens. Talairach-Vielmas contends that feminine representation is actually presented in a hyper-realistic manner in anti-realistic genres such as children's literature and sensation fiction. Chapters include: 'Introduction: Femininity through the Looking-Glass' (pp. 1–16); '"That that is, is": The Bondage of Stories in

Jean Ingelow's *Mopsa the Fairy* (1869)' (pp. 17–32); 'Macdonald's Fallen Angel in "The Light Princess" (1864)' (pp. 33–48); 'Drawing "Muchnesses" in Lewis Carroll's *Alice's Adventures in Wonderland* (1865)' (pp. 49–66); 'Taming the Female Body in Juliana Horatia Ewing's "Amelia and the Dwarfs" (1870) and Christina Rossetti's *Speaking Likenesses* (1874)' (pp. 67–88); 'A Journey through the Crystal Palace: Rhoda Broughton's Politics of Plate Glass in *Not Wisely But Too Well* (1867)' (pp. 89–112); 'Investigating Books of Beauties in Charles Dickens's *Bleak House* (1853) and M.E. Braddon's *Lady Audley's Secret* (1862)' (pp. 113–32); 'Shaping the Female Consumer in Wilkie Collins's *No Name* (1862)' (pp. 133–46); 'Rachel Leverson and the London Beauty Salon: Female Aestheticism and Criminality in Wilkie Collins's *Armadale* (1864)' (pp. 147–58) and 'Wilkie Collins's Modern Snow White: Arsenic Consumption and Ghastly Complexions in *The Law and the Lady* (1875)' (pp. 159–72).

In 2006's suggestively entitled *The Dangerous Lover: Gothic Villains, Byronism, and the Nineteenth-Century Seduction Narrative* (discussed last year in Chapter XII), Deborah Lutz adopts a philosophical, rather than feminist, perspective on the dangerous lover. Lutz traces the literary figure from sources such as Richardson's *Pamela*, *The Picture of Dorian Gray* and *Don Juan*, as well as in works by Ann Radcliffe, Jane Austen, the Brontë sisters and Dickens, and on into the twentieth century. This monograph claims to be the first book-length study of the pervasive literary hero, and it disputes the tendency of sophisticated philosophical readings of popular narratives and culture to focus on male-coded genres. Arguing for the dangerous lover's central influence not only in literature but also in the history of ideas, this book somewhat ironically positions such a figure within the philosophy of Martin Heidegger, the modernism of Georg Lukács and Roland Barthes's theories on love and longing. Lutz draws on the works of canonical authors such as Ann Radcliffe, Charles Maturin, Lord Byron, Charles Dickens, George Eliot and Oscar Wilde, as well as non-canonical texts such as contemporary romances. John Gibson's *Fiction and the Weave of Life* offers a novel and intriguing account of the relationship between literature and everyday life, and shows how literature offers an understanding of our world without literally being about our world.

Great Victorian Lives: An Era in Obituaries, edited by Andrew Sanders, documents the lives of the great and the good through obituaries, the first of which appeared in *The Times* during the Victorian era. Obituaries of some of the most significant and influential scientists, social reformers, composers, writers and politicians of the nineteenth century are gathered in this intriguing volume, including Charles Dickens, William Gladstone, Karl Marx, Louis Pasteur, Christina Rossetti, Thomas Cook and Oscar Wilde. Insightful commentary has been added to highlight the subtexts and omissions from the original texts. Arranged according to the date of death and illustrated with rare pictures from *The Times* archive, these lives offer a fascinating perspective on the society, people and values of the Victorian period. Rachel Sagner Burma's 'Anonymity, Corporate Authority, and the Archive: The Production of Authorship in Late-Victorian England' (*VS* 50[2007] 15–42) examines the notion that late Victorian readers and writers held a more flexible notion of authorship than do present-day readers and writers. The neglected Mary Elizabeth Hawker's pseudonymously published novel *Mademoiselle Ixe*, along with related author–publisher correspondence, is used as a case in point.

Karl Kroeber's *Make Believe in Film and Fiction: Visual vs. Verbal Storytelling* surveys a wide variety of literary types and explores the cultural and historical developments of the novel form itself, while it poses questions pertaining to money, capitalism, industry, race and gender and, at the same time, to formal issues, such as plotting, perspective and realism. Kroeber analyses classic films and novels as he argues for the benefits of the visual simultaneously with the imaginative power of the verbal. Kroeber writes persuasively about the basic differences between seeing and reading, as well as about the different forms of imagination that fine films and books elicit. He describes in detail exact differences between the psychological experience of reading a novel and watching a film, elucidating how a film's unique magnification of movements produces stories especially powerful in exposing hypocrisy, the spread of criminality in contemporary society and the relation of private experience to the natural environment. By contrasting novels with visual storytelling, this book explicates how fiction facilitates the sharing of subjective fantasies, frees the mind from limiting spatial and temporal preconceptions and dramatizes the ethical significance of even trivial and commonplace behaviour, while intensifying a reader's consciousness of how he or she thinks and feels. Of special interest to readers of Victorian studies will be chapter 8, 'Madame Bovary: Linguistic Figurings of Imaginative Corruption' (pp. 93–106); chapter 9, '*Rahomon* and *Wuthering Heights*' (pp. 107–24); and chapter 12, '*Great Expectations*: Insights from the Impossibility of Adaptation' (pp. 163–78).

The annual account would somehow be bereft without mention of a work from the hand of the prolific John Sutherland, who in his very succinct *Bestsellers: A Very Short Introduction*, examines lists of all-time best-selling novels to reveal what bestsellers have been read and why. Sutherland argues that bestseller lists monitor one of the strongest pulses in modern literature and are therefore worthy of serious study. Exploring the relationship between bestsellers and the fashions, ideologies and cultural concerns of the day, this book includes short case-studies and very lively summaries of bestsellers through the years, from *In His Steps*, the biggest all-time bestseller between 1895 and 1945, to *Gone With the Wind* and *The Da Vinci Code*. Focusing on classic as well as contemporary novels, Sutherland puts the bestseller industry under a microscope, revealing what constitutes a bestseller and what separates bestsellers from canonical, mostly Victorian, fiction. Sutherland always has something interesting to say, expressed at times in a startling way.

Maurizio Ascari's *A Counter-History of Crime Fiction: Supernatural, Gothic, Sensational* aims at a reassessment of assumptions about the origins of detective fiction, presenting an evolution of crime fiction from the Middle Ages up to the early twentieth century, when the genre was first termed detective fiction. Considering 'criminography' as a system of interrelated sub-genres, Ascari explores the connections between modes of literature such as revenge tragedies and providential fictions, the Gothic and the ghost story, urban mysteries and anarchist fiction, with consideration of the influence of pseudo-sciences such as mesmerism and criminal anthropology. In the comparative approach which underlies the study, Ascari cites examples of crime fiction from Great Britain, the United States, France and Italy. Highlights of the text's sections and chapters include: 'Revising the Canon of Crime and Detection' (pp. 1–11); part I, 'Supernatural and Gothic', including 'Detection before Detection' (pp. 17–40), with attention to 'Ghosts, Politics, and Revenge' (pp. 21–5) and 'The *Newgate Calendars*' (pp. 34–6); 'Persecution and Omniscience', including 'Victorian Ghosts and Revengers' (pp. 55–65) and 'Pseudo-Sciences and the Occult' (pp. 66–92); part II, 'Sensational', including 'The Language of Auguste Dupin', with 'The Strange Case of Wilkie Collins and M. Forgues' (pp. 103–5); 'On the Sensational in Literature' (pp. 110–32), including 'Women as Sensation Writers and Readers'; 'London as a "Heart of Darkness"' (pp. 133–44) and 'The Rhetoric of Atavism and Degeneration' (pp. 145–55), as well as the 'Conclusion: The Age of Formula Fiction', including 'The Sherlock Holmes "Myth"' (pp. 156–8), as well as other topics. Ascari's extensive bibliography should not be ignored.

   Rachel Ablow's *The Marriage of Minds: Reading Sympathy in the Victorian Marriage Plot* presents innovative and convincing perspectives on canonical works of the Victorian period. Ablow uncovers the representation of sympathy along with its psychic, political and ethical consequences. She interprets this sympathy as a common element in married life. *The Marriage of Minds* initiates a bridge between eighteenth-century philosophical conceptions of sympathy and twentieth-century psychoanalytical notions of identification and examines various ways in which novels were understood to educate or reform readers in the mid-nineteenth century. Ablow's study also demonstrates how the form of the Victorian novel, as well as the experience resulting from the form, was associated with ongoing debates about the nature, function and law of marriage. Chapters include 'Labors of Love: The Sympathetic Subjects of *David Copperfield*' (pp. 17–44), 'The Failure of *Wuthering Heights*' (pp. 45–69), 'George Eliot's Art of Pain' (pp. 70–94), 'Good Vibrations: The Sensationalization of Masculinity in *The Woman in White*' (pp. 95–117), and 'Anthony Trollope and the Pleasures of Alienation' (pp. 118–43). Molly Youngkin, in *Feminist Realism at the Fin de Siècle: The Influence of the Late-Victorian Woman's Press on the Development of the Novel*, argues for the influence of a late Victorian 'feminist realist aesthetic' on narrative techniques of modern fiction. This influence emitted from novelists and book reviewers— especially from reviewers in *Shafts* and *The Woman's Herald*, late nineteenth-century feminist journals—who developed a model of women's agency based on 'consciousness', 'spoken word' and 'concrete action'. A chapter of the book is devoted to each of these aspects, drawing upon analysis of works by neglected and better-known novelists, including Mona Card, Ménie Dowie (1867–1945), the writer and traveller George Gissing, Sarah Grand, Thomas Hardy, George Meredith, George Moore and Henrietta Stannard. In the concluding chapter Youngkin argues that Stannard's *A Blameless Woman* [1894], which she regards as an exemplary work of feminist realism, was ignored by Moore's contemporaries because of its conventional romance tropes in favour of Moore's *Esther Waters* [1894].

Claudia Nelson analyses a wide variety of examples of 'The Child-Woman and the Victorian Novel' (*NCStud* 20[2006] 1–12). She investigates child-women as objects of vision and spectacle, child-women and agency, and the child-woman's meaning as orphan, with references to *David Copperfield*, *Olive*, *The Woman in White* and *Adam Bede*. Gregory F. Tague's *Character and Consciousness: George Eliot, Thomas Hardy, E.M. Forster, D.H. Lawrence*, was published in 2005. It examines the concepts of character and consciousness through an interdisciplinary reading relying primarily on philosophical ideas and a genealogy of the idea of character from Victorian novelists to the modern writers. Philosophical approaches, including the metaphysics of Schopenhauer, the phenomenology of Merleau-Ponty, and the hermeneutics of Gadamer, are applied to major British authors to analyse various levels of consciousness: of the body, metaphysical and ethical. This work is a direct contribution to the emerging field of consciousness studies as it offers a fresh definition of consciousness for literary criticism in a philosophical rather than a psychological way. Tague incorporates philosophies from the pre-Platonic to Schopenhauer and Nietzsche, as well as contemporary literary criticism as applied to characters. Chapters include 'George Eliot: *Middlemarch* and Character as Marble' (pp. 27–68), 'Thomas Hardy: *Tess of the D'Urbervilles*, *Jude the Obscure*, and Character in Nature' (pp. 69–118), 'E.M. Forster: *Where Angels Fear to Tread*, *A Room with View*, *Howards End*, *A Passage to India*, and Character Connecting to Consciousness' (pp. 119–69), as well as two chapters on D.H. Lawrence. At times, Tague's monograph is hard going, but it has interesting things to say.

Kevin Mills's *Approaching Apocalypse: Unveiling Revelation in Victorian Writing* relates the Victorian novel to science. This study is less about biblical matter than Darwin's *Origin of Species*. Mills examines apocalypse, both in earnest and in parody, through overt allusion to Revelation as well as less obvious thematic echoes. Hardy's *Far from the Madding Crowd* and Charlotte Brontë's *Jane Eyre* are frequently drawn upon. Suzanne Keen's *Empathy and the Novel* presents a comprehensive account of the relationships among novel reading, empathy and altruism. Though readers' and authors' empathy certainly contributes to the emotional resonance of fiction and its success in the marketplace, Keen finds the case for altruistic consequences of novel reading inconclusive. She offers a detailed theory of narrative empathy, with proposals about its deployment by novelists and its results in readers. *Empathy and the Novel* engages with neuroscience and contemporary psychological research on empathy, bringing affect to the centre of cognitive literary studies' scrutiny of narrative fiction. Drawing on narrative theory, literary history, philosophy and contemporary scholarship in discourse-processing, Keen brings together resources and challenges for the literary study of empathy and the psychological study of fiction reading. Empathy robustly enters into affective responses to fiction, but its proper role in shaping the behaviour of emotional readers has been debated for three centuries. Keen surveys these debates and offers a series of hypotheses about literary empathy, including narrative techniques inviting empathetic response. She argues that above all readers' perception of a text's fictiveness increases the likelihood of empathy, by releasing readers from their guarded responses to the demands of real others. Keen suggests that if narrative empathy is to be better understood, then women's reading and popular fiction must be accorded the respect of experimental enquiry.

Contextualization and close reading are to the fore in John Glendening's *The Evolutionary Imagination in Late Victorian Novels: An Entangled Bank*. Glendening continues conversations initiated by Gillian Beer and George Levine, but relocates the focus onto late Victorian fiction. Glendening's chapters include '"Green confusion": Evolution and Entanglement in Well's *The Island of Dr. Moreau*' (pp. 39–68); 'The Entangled Heroine of Hardy's *Tess of the D'Urbervilles*' (pp. 69–106); 'What "modernity cannot kill": Evolution and Primitivism in Stoker's *Dracula*' (pp. 107–36); and 'Death and the Jungle in Conrad's Early Fiction' (pp. 137–84). *Troubled Legacies: Narrative and Inheritance*, edited by Allan Hepburn, examines narratives of inheritance in Irish and British fiction from 1800 to the present. Essays in this compilation set legal and novelistic dialogue side by side. This interpretation of literature in the context of law yields fascinating and provocative assertions about the specific relationship between novels and inheritance. The contributors argue that novels reinforce property law, an argument made with examples of women, workers and Jewish and Irish dispossession of rights and cultural inheritance. Major segments of this study of special interest to Victorian students include: 'Introduction: Inheritance and Disinheritance in the Novel' by Allan Hepburn (pp. 3–25); 'Owenson's "Sacred union": Domesticating Ireland, Disavowing Catholicism in *The Wild Irish Girl*' by Patrick R. O'Malley (pp. 26–52); 'The Nation's Wife: England's Vicarious Enjoyment in Anthony Trollope's Palliser Novels' by Sara L. Maurer (pp. 53–86); 'Ghostly Dispossessions: The Gothic Properties of *Uncle Silas*' by Ann Gaylin (pp. 87–108); 'The Englishness of a Gentleman: Illegitimacy and Race in *Daniel Deronda*' by Natalie Rose (pp. 109–36); and 'A Battle of Wills: Solving *The Strange Case of Dr Jekyll and Mr Hyde*' by Carol Margaret Davison (pp. 137–62).

Colonialism and the novel was inevitably the focus of a number of the studies published in 2007. Yumna Siddiqi's *Anxieties of Empire and the Fiction of Intrigue* examines late nineteenth- and twentieth-century stories of detection, policing and espionage by British and South Asian writers. Siddiqi presents a compelling exploration of the cultural anxieties created by imperialism. She indicates that while colonial writers use narratives of intrigue to endorse imperial rule, postcolonial writers turn the generic conventions and topography of the fiction of intrigue on its head, instead launching a critique of imperial power that makes the repressive and emancipatory impulses of postcolonial modernity visible. Initial portions of the book are devoted to colonial fiction by Arthur Conan Doyle and John Buchan, in which the British regime's preoccupation with maintaining power found its voice. The rationalization of difference, pronouncedly expressed through the genre's strategies of representation and narrative resolution, helped to reinforce domination and, in some cases, allay fears concerning the loss of colonial power. In the second portion, Siddiqi argues that late twentieth-century South Asian writers also underscore the state's insecurities, yet, unlike British imperial writers, they take a critical view of the state's authoritarian tendencies. Such writers as Amitav Ghosh, Michael Ondaatje, Arundhati Roy and Salman Rushdie use the conventions of detective and spy fiction in creative ways to explore the coercive actions of the postcolonial state and the power dynamics of a postcolonial New Empire. Drawing on the work of leading theorists of imperialism such as Edward Said, Frantz Fanon and the subaltern studies historians, Siddiqi reveals how British writers express the anxious workings of a will to maintain imperial power in their writing. She also illuminates the ways in which South Asian writers portray the paradoxes of postcolonial modernity and trace the ruses and uses of reason in a world where the modern marks a horizon not only of hope but also of economic, military and ecological disaster. Siddiqi has interesting things to say. Unfortunately, at times, perhaps inevitably given the nature of her discourse, the style is rather opaque.

John Kucich's *Imperial Masochism: British Fiction, Fantasy, and Social Class* explores the pivotal role of the forms of masochism played out in British thinking about imperial politics and class identity, as exhibited in the writings of Robert Louis Stevenson, Olive Schreiner, Rudyard Kipling and Joseph Conrad. Kucich draws on recent psychoanalytic theory to define masochism in terms of narcissistic fantasies of omnipotence rather than sexual perversion. The book contains four central chapters: 'Melancholy Magic: Robert Louis Stevenson's Evangelical Anti-Imperialism' (pp. 31–85); 'Olive Schreiner's Preoedipal Dreams: Feminism, Class, and the South African War' (pp. 86–135); 'Sadomasochism and the Magical Group: Kipling's Middle-Class Imperialism' (pp. 136–95); and 'The Masochism of the Craft: Conrad's Imperial Professionalism' (pp. 196–246). Peter Childs's *Modernism and the Post-Colonial: Literature and Empire, 1885–1930*, analyses and clarifies a variety of ways in which literary works from 1885 to 1930 conveyed anxieties and ambivalence concerning imperialism. Each of the central chapters discusses a variety of authors, including Conrad, Lawrence, Eliot, Woolf, Joyce, Kipling, Conrad, Doyle and Haggard. Chapters include 'Sons and Daughters of the Late Colonialism' (pp. 26–44); 'The Anxiety of Indian Encirclement' (pp. 45–63); 'Mongrel Figures Frozen in Contemplative Irony' (pp. 64–83); 'Naked and Veiled Geographical Violence' (pp. 84–100); 'The Materialized Tower of the Past' (pp. 101–17); and, in conclusion, 'Peripheral Vision into the 1930s' (pp. 118–29).

Kenneth McNeil's *Scotland, Britain, Empire: Writing the Highlands, 1760–1860* examines James Macpherson's *Ossian*, national origins, the difficulties of 'translating' Highland legends, the distortion of Highland reality in Sir Walter Scott's *Rob Roy* (as a question of respect for George IV's visit to Scotland in 1822) and Scott's appealing portrayal of Highland masculinity through *Waverly*, as well as David Stewart's *Sketches of the Highlanders of Scotland*, plus the exemplary conduct of the Highland soldiers during the Indian Mutiny of 1857, and the burgeoning importance of women's travel writing as exemplified in Ann Grant's *Letters from the Mountains* and Queen Victoria's *Leaves from the Journal of Our Life in the Highlands*. McNeil's fascinating monograph challenges early literary representations of Scotland through postcolonial studies. Diane Simmons's *The Narcissism of Empire: Loss, Rage, and Revenge in Thomas De Quincey, Robert Louis Stevenson, Arthur Conan*

Doyle, Rudyard Kipling, and Isak Dinesen examines the lives of these authors, all of whom were concerned with empire, revealing their deeply scarred pasts and linking these to their fragile emotional state, a supposed cause of bolstering their fantasies of empire. She looks not only at the youthful experiences of the writers themselves, but also at child-rearing attitudes during the British imperial period. Simmons utilizes the theories of Heinz Kohut, W.R.D. Fairbairn and D.W. Winnicott in her argument that all five of her chosen authors were trapped between victorious and pessimistic imperialisms, and that all five exhibited psychopathic or neurotic behaviour. Kurt Koenigsberger's *The Novel and the Menagerie: Totality, Englishness, and Empire* is a pioneering study of the relation of collections of imperial beasts to narrative practices in England. Koenigsberger argues that domestic English novels and zoos, circuses, travelling menageries and colonial and imperial exhibitions share important aesthetic strategies and cultural logic. Readings of novels by authors such as Charles Dickens, Virginia Woolf, Salman Rushdie and Angela Carter are employed alongside analyses of ballads, handbills, broadsides and the memoirs of showmen.

Ronald Paulson's *Sin and Evil: Moral Values in Literature* draws upon Dickens and, to a lesser degree, Thomas Hardy, Joseph Conrad and Conan Doyle. Central to Paulson's study is his differentiation between religion, sin, moral transgression and evil, as distinguished by the denotation of sin as a construct derived from tradition and situation. Marjorie Garson's *Moral Taste: Aesthetics, Subjectivity, and Social Power in the Nineteenth-Century Novel* offers a diverse collection of readings on Austen, Dickens, Charlotte Brontë, Gaskell and Eliot. Chapter titles include: 'The Discourse of Taste in *Waverley*' (pp. 39–72); 'A Room with a Viewer: The Evolution of a Victorian Topos' (pp. 73–113); 'Resources and Performances: *Mansfield Park* and *Emma*' (pp. 114–72); 'J.C. Loudon and Some Spaces in Dickens' (pp. 173–238); 'Charlotte Brontë: "Sweetness and Color"' (pp. 239–89); '*North and South*: Stately Simplicity' (pp. 290–329) and 'The Importance of Being Consistent: Culture, Commerce in *Middlemarch*' (pp. 330–67). The prolific George Levine made another important contribution to the study of Victorian writers and culture. His *How to Read the Victorian Novel* surveys a wide spectrum of literary types while exploring the cultural and historical developments of the novel. Chapter titles include: 'What's Victorian about the Victorian Novel?' (pp. 1–36); 'The Beginnings and *Pickwick*' (pp. 37–54); '*Vanity Fair* and Victorian Realism' (pp. 55–80); 'Jane, David, and the *Bildungsroman*' (pp. 81–99); 'The Sensation Novel and *The Woman in White*' (pp. 100–25); and '*Middlemarch*' (pp. 126–67). As usual, Levine's work contains interesting and challenging insights into Victorian fiction and ideas. Vicki Mahaffrey's *Modernist Literature: Challenging Fictions* is a well-argued monograph which redefines the word 'modern' to connote literature that challenges readers through its complexity, originality, transgressive nature or obscurity. Mahaffrey maintains that, through reading modernist literature, one learns to challenges aesthetic and moral conservative cultural assumptions. Mahaffrey begins with a discussion of writers such as Oscar Wilde, new women authors and the Decadents. Arthur Conan Doyle's Sherlock Holmes epitomizes for Mahaffrey the role of the good reader who detects hidden meanings. 'Narratives and Eustace Diamonds, Rorschach, Victorian Diamond' is a chapter in *The Secret Life of Things*, by Mark Blackwell, which discusses diamond narratives in works by Wilkie Collins and Anthony Trollope.

Book reviews regarding the novel include the following from the spring issue of *Victorian Studies* [2007]: Judith Wilt reviewing *Nation and Novel: The English Novel from its Origins to the Present Day* by Patrick Parrinder (*VS* 49[2007] 505–7); Jennifer Ruth's review of *Patent Inventions—Intellectual Property and the Victorian Novel* by Clare Pettitt (*VS* 49[2007] 509–11); Gowan Dawson's review of *Mesmerists, Monsters, and Machines: Science Fiction and the Cultures of Science in the Nineteenth Century* by Martin Willis (*VS* 49[2007] 513–15); Alistair M. Duckworth's review of *An Imaginary England: Nation, Landscape and Literature, 1840–1920* by Roger Ebbatson (*VS* 49[2007] 551–3); and Laurie Langbauer's review of *Talking Animals in British Children's Fiction, 1786–1914* by Tess Cosslett (*VS* 49[2007] 553–5). The third issue of *Cambridge Quarterly* for 2007 includes David Gervais's review of *Nation and Novel: The English Novel from its Origins to the Present Day* by Patrick Parrinder (*CQ* 38[2007] 284–91). John Kucich reviews Carolyn Lesjak's *Working Fictions of the Victorian Novel* (*VS* 50[2007] 104–6). Other reviews concerning the novel include S. McPherson's review of *Literary Secretaries/Secretarial Culture* by Leah Price and Pamela Thurschwell (*NCC* 29:i[2007] 57–8) and V. Warne's review of *Grant Allen: Literature and Cultural Politics at the Fin de Siècle*, edited by William Greenslade and Terence Rodgers (*NCC* 29:i[2007] 61–2). Paul A. Westover reviews *The Literary Tourist: Readers and Places in Romantic and Victorian Britain* by Nicola J. Watson (*VS* 50[2007] 128–30). John R. Reed reviews Kimberly Harrison and Richard Fantina's *Victorian Sensations: Essays on a Scandalous Genre* (*VIJ* 35[2007] 308). Ann Rowell Higginbotham reviews *Christianity and Social Service in Modern Britain: The Disinherited Spirit* by F.K. Poschaska (*VS* 50[2007] 114–16). In reviews of works concerning women and the novel, Richard Dellamora, Laura E. Nym Mayhall, and Martha Vicinus explore issues raised in Sharon Marcus's *Between Women: Friendship, Desire, And Marriage in Victorian England*, with a response by Sharon Marcus (*VS* 50[2007] 67–98). Michael Kramp reviews Deborah Epstein Nord's *Gypsies and the British Imagination, 1807–1930* (*VIJ* 35[2007] 291–3), and Leila S. May reviews Carolyn Lesjak's *Working Fictions: A Genealogy of the Victorian Novel* (*VIJ* 35[2007] 299–301).

(b) Authors

The neglected W. Harrison Ainsworth's *Jack Sheppard*, initially published in 1839, tells the tale of a criminal more famous for his escapes from prison than for his crimes. The novel is set in eighteenth-century London, where Jonathan Wild rules as criminal mastermind and government agent. Ainsworth is remembered today largely for this novel, as well as his other 'Newgate novel', *Rookwood*, which tells the story of highwayman Dick Turpin. This reprint of *Jack Sheppard* is presented with the original illustrations by George Cruikshank. Ainsworth was prolific and it is perhaps too much to hope that a revival will one day be on the way. Pickering & Chatto's *Lives of Victorian Literary Figures V*, volume 1: *Mary Elizabeth Braddon*, edited by Andrew Maunder, was published in 2007. The volume is packaged with volumes 2, *Wilkie Collins*, and 3, *William Thackeray*, discussed below. The collection is a fine assortment of primary sources valuable to students of Victorian studies. Along with introductions, bibliography, chronology, copy-texts and abbreviations, documents are gathered into the following categories: 'Braddon the Actress' (pp. 1–20); 'Braddon the Novelist' (pp. 21–42); 'Braddon's Relationships with John Gilby and John Maxwell' (pp. 43–52); Margaret Oliphant, 'Novels', *Blackwood's Edinburgh Magazine* (p. 53); 'Braddon as Thief' (pp. 67–70); 'Recollections of John Maxwell' (pp. 73–120); 'Braddon's Social Networks' (pp. 121–54); 'Profiles and Interviews' (pp. 155–208); 'Matilda Betham Edwards, *Mid-Victorian Memories*' (pp. 209–16); 'Young Admirers' (pp. 217–28); 'Ford Maddox Ford (Hueffer), *It was the Nightingale*' (pp. 229–32); 'Obituaries and Tributes' (pp. 233–54). Also pertinent to Braddon studies (currently undergoing something of a revival), Lyn Pykett reviewed *From Sensation to Society: Representations of Marriage in the Fiction of Mary Elizabeth Braddon, 1862–1866* by Natalie Schroeder and Ronald A. Schroeder (*NCL* 61[2007] 533–5). Ernest Bramah, creator of *The Wallet of Kai Lung* and *The Eyes of Max Carrados*, is the subject, for the first time, of a biography. Aubrey Wilson has thoroughly researched his life for a decade and produced *The Search for Ernest Bramah*, on the elusive writer of short stories, humour, a new style of 'Mandarin English', novels and articles. Bramah's political philosophy, literary development and literary reception are integral to Wilson's important labours.

Marianne Thormählen, in *The Brontës and Education*, presents a compelling and important study of the Brontës' education, treated contextually. Though the Brontë novels feature education as a fundamental theme, this is the first full-length book on the subject. Fictional teachers and schools are featured, along with a wealth of documentary evidence about educational theory and practice in the lifetime of the Brontës. This is an important study and Thormählen writes clearly, with critical acumen, and with erudition. Margaret Smith's major and pioneering work is reinforced by a welcome *Selected Letters of Charlotte Brontë*. This brings together early letters full of vivacity, letters to her master, the Belgian schoolteacher Constantin Heger, which reveal intense, obsessive longing, and moving letters relating to the agony of Charlotte's loss at her brother's and sisters' deaths. In the process of reading these letters, Charlotte's progress in writing and the success of *Jane Eyre*, as well as her contacts with her publishers, are revealed. Other letters offer glimpses into visits to art galleries, operas and the Great Exhibition of 1851 at the Crystal Palace. Dramatic letters from December 1852 portray the emotional storm brought on by curate Arthur Nicholls's proposal of marriage to her and her father's violent reaction, along with glimpses into her happy marriage up to her death in March 1855. This volume is a tribute to the significance of Margaret Smith's monumental *The Letters of Charlotte Brontë* [1995–2004]. All Victorian scholars owe her an enormous debt of gratitude. *A Brontë Encyclopedia*, by Robert Barnard and Louise Barnard, signals the continued interest in the writers. Their 347-page volume provides a comprehensive guide to the Brontës and encompasses approximately 2,000 alphabetical entries, including significant people and places of influence on the family, descriptions and definitions concerning fictional characters and settings, original literary commentaries and coverage of Charlotte's unfinished novels, as well as her and Branwell's juvenilia and illustrations. However, it is no replacement for Christine Alexander and Margaret Smith's fine, scholarly, *Oxford Companion to the Brontës* [2006].

Patsy Stoneman, in *Jane Eyre on the Stage, 1848–1898*, has brought together all eight dramatic versions of *Jane Eyre* which had appeared in England, America and continental Europe by 1900. The collection makes for fascinating reading, though most versions were not performed. They remain fascinating at least in part because Victorian playwrights observed no reverence for the text. In one version, the story contains a sidekick-like cast of comic characters who follow Jane Eyre from Lowood to Thornfield, while in another the identity of the madwoman is revealed as the sister-in-law of an innocent Rochester and in yet another Blanche Ingram is reduced to a fallen woman who is seduced and then abandoned by John Reed. Stoneman's introduction discusses the theatrical, social and political contexts of the plays. The plays include John Courtney's *Jane Eyre or the Secrets of Thornfield Manor* [1848] (pp. 17–64); John Brougham's *Jane Eyre* [1849] (pp. 65–108); the anonymous *Jane Eyre* [1867] (pp. 109–36); Charlotte Birch-Pfeiffer's *Jane Eyre or The Orphan of Lowood* [1870] (pp. 137–98); Mme von Heringen Hering's *Jane* Eyre [1877] (pp. 199–267); James Willing's *Jane Eyre or Poor Relations* [1879] (pp. 267–336); T.H. Paul's *Jane Eyre* [1879] (pp. 337–72); and W.G. Wills's *Jane Eyre* (pp. 373–428). Each play includes editor's notes, background on the playwright, the theatre(s) and performance(s), reception of the play and distinctive features of the play. Stoneman has contributed a fascinating study. In 'Unsuspecting Storyteller and Suspect Listener' (*ArielE* 37:ii–iii[2007] 1–32), Carine M. Mardorossian argues that *Jane Eyre* challenges male colonial discourse as expressed in Rochester's actions and replaces it with an alternative form of female power. Beth Newman has edited a new edition of *Wuthering Heights* [1847] based on the first edition as its copy-text. This edition corrects the first edition's obvious misspellings and misprints, as well as taking liberties with older punctuation patterns. The introduction and appendices to this Broadview edition, which place Brontë's life and novel in the context of the developing 'Brontë myth', explore the impact of industrialization on the people of Yorkshire, consider the novel's representation of gender and survey the way contemporary scholarship has sought to account for Heathcliff, open up multiple contexts within which *Wuthering Heights* can be read, understood and enjoyed.

Also of interest in Brontë studies are the following: Alison Hoddinott's 'Reading Books and Looking at Pictures in the Novels of Charlotte Brontë' (*BS* 32:i[2007] 1–10); Shanyn Fiske's 'Between Nowhere and Home: The Odyssey of Lucy Snowe' (*BS* 32:i[2007] 11–20); Sandro Jung's 'Charlotte Brontë's *Jane Eyre*, the Female Detective and the "Crime" of Female

Selfhood' (*BS* 32:i[2007] 21–30); Lakshmi Krishnan's ' "It has devoured my existence": The Power of the Will and Illness in *The Bride of Lammermoor* and *Wuthering Heights*' (*BS* 32:i[2007] 31–40); Graeme Tytler's 'The Role of Religion in *Wuthering Heights*' (*BS* 32:i[2007] 41–56); and Michael Walker's 'J.B. Leyland: Sculptor and Friend of Branwell Brontë' (*BS* 32:i[2007] 57–70). Of further interest in the July issue of *Brontë Studies* are Brian Wilk's 'A Bishop, Bed and Breakfast, A Mystery Dessert and a Poignant Letter: Material Found Among the Papers of Dr. Charles Longley, Archbishop of Canterbury' (*BS* 32:ii[2007] 91–5); James Phillips's 'The Two Faces of Love in *Wuthering Heights*' (*BS* 32:ii[2007] 96–105); Laura Selene Rockefeller's '*Shirley* and the Politics of Personal Faith' (*BS* 32:ii[2007] 106–15); Ian and Catherine Emberson's 'A Missing Link: The Brontës, the Sowdens and the Listers' (*BS* 32:ii[2007] 116–24); Robert D. Butterworth's ' "If this be all" and the Poetry of Statement' (*BS* 32:ii[2007] 125–31); Lee A. Talley's 'The Case for Anne Brontë's Marginalia in the Author's Own Copy of *The Tenant of Wildfell Hall*' (*BS* 32:ii[2007] 132–6); Paul Dean Daniggelis's 'Deaths and Entrances' (*BS* 32:ii[2007] 138–44); Wendy Anne Powers's 'Emily Brontë and Emily Dickinson: Parallel Lives on Opposing Shores' (*BS* 32:ii[2007] 145–50); Polly Salter's 'Exciting Recent Acquisitions at the Brontë Parsonage Museum: Letters Bought by the Brontë Society on 4 July 2006' (*BS* 32:ii[2007] 151–4); Bob Duckett's delightful tribute to former *Brontë Society Transactions* editor Charles Lemon, in 'Charles Lemon, BCE (1914–2007)' (*BS* 32:ii[2007] 155–6), and James Ogden's 'A Brontë Reading List' (*BS* 32:ii[2007] 157–64).

Completing a most productive year in Brontë studies, articles in the November 2007 *Brontë Studies* issue include the following conference proceedings: Stephen Whitehead's 'The Haworth the Brontës Knew' (*BS* 32:iii[2007] 181–92); Bob Duckett's 'Where Did the Brontës Get their Books?' (*BS* 32:iii[2007] 193–206); Ian M. Emberson's ' "The likeness of a kingly crown": John Milton's Influence on Charlotte Brontë' (*BS* 32:iii[2007] 207–16); Yukari Oda's '*Wuthering Heights* and the Waverley Novels: Sir Walter Scott's Influence on Emily Brontë' (*BS* 32:iii[2007] 217–26); Elizabeth Leaver's 'Why Anne Brontë Wrote as She Did' (*BS* 32:iii[2007] 227–44), Tom Winnifrith's 'The Church Census and the Brontës' (*BS* 32:iii[2007] 245–52) and Tonya Edgren-Bindas's 'The Cloistering of Lucy Snowe: An Element of Catholicism in Charlotte Brontë's *Villette*' (*BS* 32:iii[2007] 253–60). Linda Gill offers 'The Princess in the Tower: Gender and Art in Charlotte Brontë's *Jane Eyre* and Alfred Lord Tennyson's "The Lady of Shalott" ' (*VIJ* 35[2007] 109–36). Charlotte Brontë plays a major role in Laura Green's 'Wishing to be Fictional' (*VIJ* 35[2007] 217–28), in which Green investigates the ambivalent awareness of the reader's desire to enter the fictional world; in the same issue, Grace Moore and Susan Pyke offer 'Haunting Passions: Revising and Revisiting *Wuthering Heights*' (*VIJ* 35[2007] 239–50). In 'Authorizing Emily: The Production of an Author-Function in Charlotte Brontë's 1850 Edition of *Wuthering Heights* and *Agnes Grey*' by Augustin Trapenard (*EA* 60:i[2007] 15–28), the author reconsiders the 'Biographical Notice' as part of a text which was written and orchestrated by Charlotte Brontë in the 1850 edition of *Wuthering Heights* and *Agnes Grey*. This was a new title advertised as containing Currer Bell's editing. The edition also included Ellis and Acton Bell's unpublished poetical works, reworked and prefaced.

A much-neglected figure, Samuel Butler, is the subject of an interdisciplinary collection of thirteen essays that provides a critical overview of his career: *Samuel Butler: Victorian Against the Grain*, edited by James G. Paradis. Essays are organized in three parts: 'New Zealand and Early London Years, 1860', including 'From Canterbury Settlement to Erewhon and Antipodean Counterpoint' by Roger Robinson (pp. 21–44); 'Butler, Memory, and the Future' by Gillian Beer (pp. 45–57); and 'The Ironies of Biblical Criticism: From Samuel Butler's "Resurrection" Essay and *The Fair Haven* to *Erewhon Revisited*' (pp. 58–90). Part II, 'Evolutionist, 1874–1886', includes '"The written symbol extends infinitely": Samuel Butler and the Writing of Evolutionary Theory' by David Amigoni (pp. 91–112); '"A conspiracy of one": Butler, Natural Theology, and Victorian Popularization' by Bernard Lightman (pp. 113–42); 'Evolutionary Psychology and *The Way of All Flesh*' by Sally Shuttleworth (pp. 143–69); 'Samuel Butler as Late-Victorian Bachelor: Regulating and Repressing the Homoerotic' by Herbert Sussman (pp. 170–94); and 'Mind Matters: Butler and Late Nineteenth Century Psychology' by Ruth Parkin-Gounelas (pp. 195–222). Part III, 'On the Margins: 1887–1902', includes 'Samuel Butler, Local Identity and the Periodizing of Northern Italian Art: The Travel Writer-Painter's View of Art History' by Clarice Zdanski (pp. 223–50); 'Samuel Butler's Photography: Observation and the Dynamic Past' by Elizabeth Edwards (pp. 251–86); 'Butler's "Narcissus": A Tame Oratorio' by Ellen T. Harris (pp. 287–316); 'Why Homer Was (Not) a Woman: The Reception of the Authoress of the Odyssey' by Mary Beard (pp. 317–42); and 'Butler after Butler: The Man of Letters as Outsider' by James G. Paradis (pp. 343–70).

An exciting and valuable new collection of primary source materials concerning Wilkie Collins has been released as part of a three-volume set from Pickering & Chatto: *Lives of Victorian Literary Figures V*, volume 2: *Wilkie Collins*, edited by William Baker and Andrew Gasson. This anthology of contemporary biographical material on Wilkie Collins illuminates the processes at work in the establishment of a public image and a critical reputation. Each facsimile page is digitally enhanced, improving on the quality and legibility of the original, and as for each volume, full editorial notes include a substantial general introduction, introductions to each volume, bibliographies, chronologies, headnotes and endnotes. Primary documents include the following: '[George Makepeace Towle], "Wilkie Collins", *Appleton's Journal* [1870]' (pp. 1–6); 'James Payn, *Some Literary Recollections* (1885)' (pp. 7–10); 'Personal Recollections of Wilkie Collins' (pp. 11–26); '[Meredith White Townsend], "Wilkie Collins", *Spectator* [1889]' (pp. 27–30); 'Hall Caine, "Wilkie Collins. Personal Recollections" [*The Globe*, 1889]' (pp. 31–6); 'Algernon Charles Swinburne, "Wilkie Collins" [*Fortnightly Review*]' (pp. 37–50); 'Andrew Lang, "Mr Wilkie Collins's Novels" [*Contemporary Review*, 1890]' (pp. 51–62); 'Edmund Yates and the *World* (1889)' (pp. 63–76); 'Horatio Noble Pym, *A Tour Round My Bookshelves* (1891)' (pp. 77–92); 'Harry Quilter, *Preferences in Art, Life and Literature* (1892)' (pp. 93–128); '[Nathaniel Beard], "Some Recollections of Yesterday",

Temple Bar (1894)' (pp. 129–56); 'Mary Anderson, *A Few Memories* (1896)' (pp. 157–68); 'William Tinsley (1900) & Edmund Downey (1905)' (pp. 169–78); 'Arthur Waugh, "Wilkie Collins: And his Mantle. A Personal Predilection," *Academy and Literature*' (pp. 179–82); 'Lewis Melville, *Victorian Novelists* (1906)' (pp. 183–206); 'Wybert Reeve, "Recollections of Wilkie Collins", *Chamber's Journal* (1906)' (pp. 207–12); 'William Winter, Old Friends (1909)' (pp. 213–34); 'Marie and Squire Bancroft, The Bancrofts: *Recollections of Sixty Years* (1909)' (pp. 235–46); 'Arthur Compton-Rickett, "Wilkie Collins", *The Bookman* (1912)' (pp. 247–56); 'Frank Archer, *An Actor's Notebooks* (1912)' (pp. 257–72); and 'Lucy Bertha Walford, *Memories of Victorian London* (1912)' (pp. 273–88).

Recommended too is *The Cambridge Companion to Wilkie Collins*, edited by Jenny Bourne Taylor. This contains Bourne Taylor's thorough introduction covering Collins's rise in critical attention (pp. 1–6), followed by thirteen essays, including the following: 'Collins's Career and the Visual Arts' by Tim Dolin (pp. 7–22); 'The Early Writing' by Anthea Trodd (pp. 23–36); 'Collins's Shorter Fiction' by John Bowen (pp. 37–49); 'Collins and the Sensation Novel' by Lyn Pykett (pp. 50–64); 'The Moonstone, Detective Fiction and Forensic Science' by Ronald R. Thomas (pp. 65–78); 'The Later Novels' by Jenny Bourne Taylor (pp. 79–96); 'The Professional Writer and the Literary Marketplace' by Graham Law (pp. 97–111); 'The Marriage Plot and its Alternatives' by Carolyn Dever (pp. 112–24); 'Collins and Victorian Masculinity' by John Kucich (pp. 125–38); 'Collins and Empire' by Lillian Nayder (pp. 139–52); 'Disability and Difference' by Kate Flint (pp. 153–67); 'Collins and the Theatre' by Jim Davis (pp. 168–80); and 'The Afterlife of Wilkie Collins' by Rachel Malik (pp. 181–93). Some of the contributions are more valuable than others, some retread hallowed ground, others investigate new territory in Collins study, and some are very difficult to read.

Another highly recommended source for research in Wilkie Collins studies is William Baker's *A Wilkie Collins Chronology*. This valuable source draws upon recently published editions of Collins's letters to provide the first comprehensive source of the facts of Wilkie Collins's mysterious life. The chronology begins in 1740, with the birth of Collins's grandfather, and ends in 2005 with the publication of the four-volume *Collected Letters*. The work is organized chronologically, even down to the day of the week, and includes contemporary reactions, as well as circumstances of publication for each work, Collins's travels, comments on some of the works as they were being composed and excerpts and memoirs. Use of the index is especially well facilitated by the organization into 'Works by Wilkie Collins' (including plays, articles and novels), 'People' and 'Places'. Credits noted in the introduction assist greatly in mapping out the most valuable sources for Collins research. A discovery is revealed in the *Wilkie Collins Society Newsletter* for winter 2007, which presents as an accompanying pamphlet 'The New Dragon of Wantley: A Social Revelation'. This Graham Law reveals to be a yet unidentified story by Wilkie Collins. Utilizing evidence from the *Collected Letters* and computer analysis of phrases in the text, Law establishes that the story, published in *The Leader* on 20 December 1851, is conclusively by Collins. Law's analysis of the evidence, along with a new assessment of Collins's contributions to *The Leader*, is published with the twenty-page story.

Yet another welcome and intriguing addition to Wilkie Collins studies for 2007 is *Wilkie Collins: Interdisciplinary Essays*. This includes essays on previously neglected works as well as fresh interpretations of Collins's canonical works. Andrew Mangham edited this collection of sixteen essays arranged in five parts, including part I, 'Collins in Context': ' "Too absurdly repulsive": Generic Indeterminacy and the Failure of *The Fallen Leaves*' by Anne-Marie Beller (pp. 10–21); 'A Distaste for Matrimonial Sauce: The Celebration of Bachelorhood in the Journalism and Fiction of Collins and Dickens' by Holly Furneaux (pp. 22–36); and 'Parallel Worlds: Collins's Sensationalism and Spiritual Practice' by Tatiana Kontou (pp. 37–55). Part II, 'Collins and Art', contains 'Text and Image Together: The Influence of Illustration and the Victorian Market in the Novels of Wilkie Collins' by Clare Douglass (pp. 56–73) and 'The Face of the Adversary in the Novels of Wilkie Collins' by Aoife Leahy (pp. 74–89). Part III, 'Collins and Medicine', includes 'Mental States: Political and Psychological Conflict in *Antonina*' by Andrew Mangham (pp. 90–106); 'Reading Faces: Physiognomy and the Depiction of the Heroine in the Fiction of Wilkie Collins' by Jessica Cox (pp. 107–21); 'Questioning Moral Inheritance in *The Legacy of Cain*' by Amanda Mordavsky Caleb (pp. 122–135); 'Habituation and Incarceration: Mental Physiology and Asylum Abuse in *The Woman in White* and *Dracula*' by William Hughes (pp. 136–48); and '*Heart and Science* and Vivisection's Threat to Women' by Greta Depledge (pp. 149–65). Part IV, 'Collins and the Law', contains 'The Scotch Verdict and Irregular Marriages: How Scottish Law Disrupts the Normative in *The Law and the Lady* and *Man and Wife*' by Anne Longmuir (pp. 166–77); 'Collins on International Copyright: From "A National Wrong" (1870) to "Considerations" (1880)' by Graham Law (pp. 178–94); and 'The Dangerous Brother: Family Transgression in *The Haunted Hotel*' by Lynn Parker (pp. 195–207). Part V, 'Collins, Theatre, and Film', incorporates ' "Twin Sisters" and "Theatrical Thieves": Wilkie Collins and the Dramatic Adaptation of *The Moonstone*' by Richard Pearson (pp. 208–21); 'Sensation Drama? Collins's Stage Adaptation of *The Woman in White*' by Janice Norwood (pp. 222–36); 'Detecting Buried Secrets: Recent Film Versions of *The Woman in White* and *The Moonstone*' by Stefani Brusberg-Kiermeier (pp. 237–49); and an afterword by Janice M. Allan. Inevitably, in such a varied collection from experienced and relatively novice hands, there will be diversity in quality. The essays in this volume testify to the revival of interest in Collins's life and work. Some of the contributions reflect contemporary fashionable critical modes and some at times are very difficult to read. In spite of such caveats, Mangham has brought together many useful differing perspectives upon a great writer woefully neglected and living in Dickens's shadow for almost a century. And finally, in a very productive year for Collins studies, Neil Hultgren, in 'Imperial Melodrama in Wilkie Collins's *The Moonstone*' (*VIJ* 35[2007] 53–80), considers melodrama, linking theatre and novels to the Orient, in order to illuminate *The Moonstone*.

Perhaps the most challenging contribution to Dickens studies in 2007 is Rosemarie Bodenheimer's *Knowing Dickens*. Bodenheimer follows a similar procedure to the one she used in *The Real Life of Mary Ann Evans: George Eliot, her Letters and Fiction* [1994]. In other words, she draws upon an author's letters to illuminate their work. *Knowing Dickens* utilizes the twelve volumes of the magnificent Pilgrim Edition of *The Letters of Charles Dickens* and *The Dent Uniform Edition of Dickens' Journalism* in order to cast fresh light upon the letters, the novels and the journalism. Each of Bodenheimer's six chapters 'juxtaposes letters, stories, articles and sections of novels that bear on its subject area, discovering patterns that are common to the life and the writing'. Although 'chronological sequences appear within each chapter, the chapters themselves do not trace out the course of Dickens's career from beginning to end' (pp. 14–15). Bodenheimer's approach reveals much about Dickens's life and work.

Oxford University Press's *A Christmas Carol & Other Christmas Books* includes all of the original illustrations for *A Christmas Carol*, along with Dickens's four other Christmas books, *The Haunted Man*, *The Chimes*, *The Cricket on the Hearth* and *The Battle of Life*. Robert Douglas-Fairhurst supplies the introduction. *Dickens and the Popular Radical Imagination*, by Sally Ledger, pioneers a compelling investigation into the extent to which Dickens's fiction and journalism sprouted from and continued to nurture popular radical culture of the time. Regency radicals, such as William Hone and William Cobbett, and mid-century radical writers, such as Douglas Jerrold and the Chartists Ernest Jones and G.W.M. Reynolds, are central to Ledger's clearly written monograph. Significant and innovative readings of works from *Pickwick* to *Little Dorrit* reveal that Dickens's populism bridged eighteenth- and nineteenth-century notions of the popular. This study is generously illustrated with twenty-four illustrations reproduced from nineteenth-century pamphlets and periodicals, accentuating the interplay between Dickens's writings and popular graphic art, by George Cruikshank, Robert Seymour, C.J. Grant and others. Another fine addition to Dickens studies is Paul Davis's *Critical Companion to Charles Dickens*. Davis's volume contains a concise biography of Dickens and synopses and critical assessments of Dickens's major and minor works, along with portraits of Dickens characters, historical and thematic information essential to understanding Dickens's fiction, and analyses of Dickens's cultural context. A chronology of Dickens's life, 116 illustrations and a bibliography of primary and secondary sources will prove useful as well. Donald Hawes's clearly written *Charles Dickens*, part of the Writers' Lives series, is an unpretentious, introductory-level source featuring a concise biography of Dickens's life, and equal numbers of chapters concerning Dickens's works and their contexts. Of the twenty-one chapters, contexts include such subjects as 'Dickens's London', 'Prison and Crime', 'Medicine, Doctors, Nurses, and Hospitals' and 'Dickens and Animals'. A most refreshing aspect of Hawes's book is that it eschews the almost obligatory (though often valuable) reference to critical theory when it is not necessary.

As usual, *The Dickensian* offers much of interest. The first issue for 2007 features Leon Litvack's '*Dickens's Dream* and the Conception of Character' (*Dickensian* 103:i[2007] 5–36). Litvack discusses in detail 'an unfinished watercolour which came to be known as *Dickens's Dream*' hanging in the Charles Dickens Museum. Litvack's analysis is accompanied by twelve illustrations.

The watercolourist is in fact the artist Robert William Buss (1804–75), who had illustrated Dickens's 'A Little Talk about Spring and the Sweeps' which appeared in Chapman & Hall's *Library of Fiction* in 1836. Litvack's is a fascinating account of an unfinished painting that conveys 'a sense of fulfilment of Dickens's works' (p. 31). This article is followed by Angus Easson and Margaret Brown's 'The Letters of Charles Dickens: Supplement VII' (*Dickensian* 103:i[2007] 37–59). Easson and Brown's invaluable contribution provides corrigenda, additional annotations and newly discovered Dickens letters to the great twelve-volume Pilgrim Edition of *The Letters of Charles Dickens*. Robert Giddings, in his 'Boz on the Box: A Brief History of Dickens on British Television' (*Dickensian* 103:ii[2007] 101–15), provides exactly what its title says it will. Beryl Gray's 'Man and Dog: Text and Illustration in *The Old Curiosity Shop*' (*Dickensian* 103:ii[2007] 125–43) is accompanied by illustrations that illuminate the 'collaboration of artist with author', the artists primarily being George Cattermole and Hablot K. Browne (Phiz). One wonders when Beryl Gray is going to exhaust her discussions of the significance of the canine in Dickens and George Eliot: perhaps she will make a welcome return to her musical explorations in Victorian fiction! Wendy S. Jacobson's illuminating 'The Muddle and the Star: *Hard Times*' (*Dickensian* 103:ii[2007] 144–56) 'moves from the generally accepted thesis, that the circus in *Hard Times* is set up to counter Gradgrindery, in order to argue that what is hidden . . . in the characters of Stephen Blackpool, and also Rachel, leads from the circus/Gradgrindery dichotomy to another conclusion about the novel's purpose' (p. 144). Peter Orford's 'An Italian Dream and a Castle in the Air: The Significance of Venice in *Little Dorrit*' (*Dickensian* 103:ii[2007] 144–65) draws attention to the use of venues other than London in *Little Dorrit*. David Paroissien's 'Affecting Tales in *David Copperfield*: Mr. Peggotty and *The Man of Feeling*' (*Dickensian* 103:iii[2007] 197–202) is an all too brief disquisition on the significance of Henry Mackenzie's novel *The Man of Feeling* to sections of *David Copperfield*. John Bowen's short note, 'Dickens, Bret Harte and the Santa Cruz Connection' (*Dickensian* 103:iii[2007] 203–5), highlights a mid-nineteenth-century connection between Dickens, Bret Harte and Santa Cruz in California. Angus Easson and Margaret Brown, with Leon Litvack and Joan Dicks, 'The Letters of Charles Dickens: Supplement VIII' (*Dickensian* 103:iii[2007] 206–33), continues the important augmentation of the Pilgrim Edition of *The Letters of Charles Dickens*. Particular attention should be paid to a lengthy letter to Edmund Phipps, dated 12 June 1848. The Dickens holograph letter is today in the MS Kunstsammlungen der Veste Coburg. Phipps (1808–57) was a provincial barrister and recorder active in the north of England. The letter throws light upon a proposed 1848 theatrical performance by Macready (pp. 212–13). In addition to a letter to Elizabeth Gaskell dated 18 March 1852 (pp. 223–4), an incomplete Dickens text to William Woodley Frederick de Cerjat (d. 1869) a 'member of an old Vaudois family' is published in its entirety, its holograph having emerged from special collections at Lehigh University (pp. 227–30). Each issue contains interesting reviews of books and theatrical, radio and television performances, plus other items of interest to Dickensians. There are also obituaries, including one by Michael Hollington of Professor Sylvère Monod (1921–2006), 'quite simply

the finest and most influential Dickensian France has ever produced'
(*Dickensian* 103:iii[2007] 283).

Dickens Studies Annual features David McAllister's ' "Subject to the scepter
of imagination": Sleep, Dreams, and Unconsciousness in *Oliver Twist*' (*DSA*
38[2007] 1–18); Leona Toker's '*Nicholas Nickleby* and the Discourse of Lent'
(*DSA* 38[2007] 19–34); Albert D. Pionke's 'Degrees of Secrecy in Dickens's
Historical Fiction' (*DSA* 38[2007] 35–54); Alan P. Barr's 'Matters of Class and
the Middle-Class Artist in *David Copperfield*' (*DSA* 38[2007] 55–68); Shari
Hodges Holt's 'Dickens from a Postmodern Perspective: Alfonso Cuaron's
Great Expectations for Generation X' (*DSA* 38[2007] 69–92); Clay Daniel's
'Jane Eyre's *Paradise Lost*' (*DSA* 38[2007] 93–114); and Thomas Recchio's
'Toward a Theory of Narrative Sympathy: Character, Story, and the Body in
The Mill on the Floss' (*DSA* 38[2007] 114–42). The issue also includes a list
of recent Dickens studies for 2005, compiled by Diana C. Archibald (*DSA*
38[2007] 143–204); 'Recent Studies in Robert Louis Stevenson; Survey
of Biographical Works and Checklist of Criticism—1970–2005', compiled by
Roger G. Swearingen (*DSA* 38[2007] 205–98); and 'Dickens's Christmas
Books, Christmas Stories, and Other Short Fiction: An Annotated
Bibliography, Supplement I: 1985–2006', compiled by Ruth F. Glancy (*DSA*
38[2007] 299–496).

The first issue of *Dickens Quarterly* for 2007 contains John R. Reed's
'Dickens and Personification' (*DQu* 24:i[2007] 3–17). Reed demonstrates that
Dickens blends personification with de-animation in order to emphasize
how human existence may be seen as hyper-real, and thereby illustrating
a resistance to the realist movement. Trey Philpotts's 'Dickens, Invention, and
Literary Property in the 1850s' (*DQu* 24:i[2007] 18–26), argues that Dickens
would have resisted any simplistic connection between copyrights and patents.
Chris Louttit's 'Lowell Revisited: Dickens and the Working Girl' (*DQu*
24:i[2007] 27–36) adds Louttit's point that women are a key element in the
fourth chapter of *American Notes* to the earlier contrasting interpretations of
this chapter by Meckier and McKnight, also presented in *Dickens Quarterly*.
The second issue of *Dickens Quarterly* for 2007 features the following articles:
'Mourning Becomes David: Loss and the Victorian Restoration of Young
Copperfield' by Alan P. Barr (*DQu* 24:ii[2007] 63–77); 'The Book of Jasper',
by Bert Hornback (*DQu* 24:ii[2007] 78–85); and 'The Drood Remains
Revisited—The Sapsea Fragment', by Arthur J. Cox (*DQu* 24:ii[2007] 86–102).

In the third issue of the year, George Goodin elucidates 'The Uses and
Usages of Muddle' (*DQu* 24:iii[2007] 135–44), the first of a two-part study;
Barry Tharaud presents 'Form as Process in *The Pickwick Papers*: The
Structure of Ethical Discovery' (*DQu* 24:iii[2007] 145–58); Robert Tracy offers
insights into the life of Dickens's good friend in 'W.C. Macready in *The Life
and Adventures of Nicholas Nickleby*' (*DQu* 24:iii[2007] 159–66); and Stephen
Bertman draws intriguing parallels in 'Dante's Role in the Genesis of
Dickens's *A Christmas Carol*' (*DQu* 24:iii[2007] 167–74). This issue also
includes a lovely tribute to the eminent Dickensian Philip Collins (*DQu*
24:iii[2007] 186–7). The December issue of *Dickens Quarterly* includes the
second in George Goodin's two-part article, 'The Uses and Usages of Muddle'
(*DQu* 24:iv[2007] 201–10); Eleanor McNess's 'Reluctant Source: Murray's

Handbooks and *Pictures from Italy*' (*DQu* 24:iv[2007] 211–29); and John M.L. Drew's 'Picture from *The Daily News*: Context, Correspondents, and Correlations' (*DQu* 24:iv[2007] 230–46). Continuum's Reader's Guides series offers Ian Brinton's *Dickens's 'Great Expectations'*. Sections include: 'Contexts' (pp. 1–16); 'Language, Form and Style' (pp. 17–32); 'Reading *Great Expectations*' (pp. 33–80); 'Critical Reception and Publishing History' (pp. 81–96); 'Adaptation, Interpretation and Influence' (pp. 97–110); and 'Works Cited and Further Reading' (pp. 111–22). *Nineteenth Century Contexts* features 'Consuming the Family Economy: Tuberculosis and Capitalism in Charles Dickens's *Dombey and Son*' by K. Byrne (*NCC* 29:i[2007] 1–16) and 'Professions of Labour: *David Copperfield* and the "Dignity of Literature"' by R. Salmon (*NCC* 29:i[2007] 35–52).

Shanyn Fiske's 'Sati and *Great Expectations*: Dickens in the Wake of the Indian Mutiny' (*VIJ* 35[2007] 31–52) treads upon some familiar territory. In the special section, 'Our Imaginary Friends' Leslie Haynsworth offers, 'Mrs. Jellyby and Me: 21st-Century Reverberations of Victorian Social Critique' (*VIJ* 35[2007] 209–16). *Nineteenth-Century Literature* for September 2007 features 'Charles Dickens's Families of Choice: Elective Affinities, Sibling Substitution, and Homoerotic Desire' (*NCL* 62[2007] 153–92) by Holly Furneaux. This article presents the fruitful strategy, in-lawing, through which Dickens and his contemporaries expressed queer possibilities in the assumedly heterosexual family. In-lawing involved denial of desire for a member of the same sex and redirecting that desire to an opposite-sex sibling. Furneaux specifies examples in Dickens's early career, *The Pickwick Papers*, *Nicholas Nickleby* and *Martin Chuzzlewit*, which expose both male and female homoerotic motivations, reflecting and contributing to more pervasive contemporary literary and biographical discussions about the assimilation of homoerotic desires into the Victorian family. The fall 2007 issue of *The Victorian Newsletter* features 'John Opie's Lectures to the Royal Academy and *Little Dorrit*' (*VN* 112[2007] 91–100), by the prolific Rodney Stenning Edgecombe. Helen Groth's 'Reading Victorian Illusions: Dickens's Haunted Man and Dr. Pepper's Ghost' (*VS* 50[2007] 43–6) examines John Henry Pepper's successful 1862 adaptation of Charles Dickens's Christmas story. So, all in all, another most productive year for Dickens studies with important monographs and articles.

Andrew Lycett's *The Man Who Created Sherlock Holmes: The Life and Times of Sir Arthur Conan Doyle* includes detailed descriptions of the Doyle family tree as he delves into the origins of the famous detective's name (fellow student Patrick Sherlock and Oliver Wendell Holmes) and Conan Doyle's associations with everyone from Oscar Wilde to Harry Houdini. It is pleasant to record that Megan Early Alter contributes 'A Perilous Performance: Aestheticizing Fetishism in *Trilby*' (*Genre* 39:i[2007] 1–28) as a George Du Maurier revival is long overdue. Jan Jędrzejewski has written a comprehensive, highly recommended and clearly written introductory survey, *George Eliot*. There are three sections: 'Life and Contexts' (pp. 1–31), 'Works' (pp. 32–96) and 'Criticism' (pp. 97–149), along with a 'Chronology' (pp. 150–5), and 'Further Reading', including 'Editions' and 'Critical Studies of Individual Texts' (both on p. 156), as well as 'Collections of Critical Essays' (pp. 157–8), and a brief bibliography (pp. 159–60). Jędrzejewski's discussion encompasses Eliot's poetry, along with her important periodical contributions, as well as the fiction. He makes some fine critical distinctions in his third chapter on 'Criticism' (pp. 97–149), which is comprehensive and judicious. The *George Eliot Review* contains Rosemary Ashton's 'Glimpses of Life at 142 Strand'. This constitutes 'The Thirty-Fifth George Eliot Memorial Lecture, 2006' (*GER* 37[2007] 7–23) and treads some very familiar territory, some of which is not always acknowledged. Melissa Raines writes on 'Awakening the "Mere pulsation of desire" in *Silas Marner*' (*GER* 37[2007] 24–30). Margaret Harris draws upon the *Coventry Herald* and other provincial printed sources in her interesting account of 'The George Eliot Centenary of 1919' (*GER* 37[2007] 32–48). There are also the usual book reviews and parochial notes. *George Eliot–George Henry Lewes Studies* opens with Ernest Fontana's investigation of 'Gentleman as Signifier in *Middlemarch*' (*GEGHLS* 52–3[2007] 1–8), in which he reveals the various ways in which Eliot mines ambiguity in the term 'gentleman' across the novel. The issue continues with Alain Barrat's 'The Representation and Thematic Function of Vegetation in George Eliot's *Adam Bede*' (*GEGHLS* 52–3[2007] 9–18); Gary Scharnhorst's essay on American journalist, actor, lecturer and travel writer Kate Field in 'Kate Field on George Eliot and G.H. Lewes' (*GEGHLS* 52–3[2007] 19–27); Martin Bidney's ' "The Legend of Jubal" as Romanticism Refashioned: Struggles of a Spirit in George Eliot's "Musical Midrash" ' (*GEGHLS* 52–3[2007] 28–59), which presents a fascinating exploration of a little-read poem by Eliot which is based on one line of Hebrew Scripture involving Jubal, who is traditionally credited with inventing the art of music. The poem presents the origins of a myth which Eliot creates as an avenue of expressing her own artistic goals. The issue continues with David McGlynn's 'Transfusing the Secret in George Eliot's "The Lifted Veil" ' (*GEGHLS* 52–3[2007] 60–75); Moira Gatens's thorough 'George Eliot's Incarnation of the Divine in *Romola* and Benedict Spinoza's "Blessedness": A Double Reading' (*GEGHLS* 52–3[2007] 76–92); and Paul Goetsch's extensive 'German-Language Publications on George Eliot, 1980–2004' (*GEGHLS* 52–3[2007] 105–22).

Maria La Monaca imagines Dorothea Brooke's concerns in her ' "An occupation for Bedlam": Some Reflections on the Academic Life, Inspired by Dorothea Brooke' (*VIJ* 35[2007] 229–38). The September 2007 issue of *Nineteenth-Century Literature* includes Jules Law's 'Transparency and Epistemology in George Eliot's *Daniel Deronda*' (*NCL* 62[2007] 250–77). Law examines the epistemology and figurative representations through which Eliot's politics are elaborated and the figure of transparency and the thematics of political vocation, concluding in the figure of the spectral Jew. *Cambridge Quarterly* features in its initial issue for 2007 'The Spoiled Child: What Happened to Gwendolen Harleth?' (*CQ* 38[2007] 33–50), by Margaret Loewen Reimer. The third issue of *Cambridge Quarterly* for 2007 features ' "The sensitive author": George Eliot' (*CQ* 38[2007] 250–72). 'Translating Authority: *Romola*'s Disruption of the Gendered Narrative' (*VN* 112[2007] 6–18) comes from Lesa Scholl. In the online journal *Nineteenth-Century Gender Studies* Catherine A. Civello, in 'The Ironies of Widowhood: Displacement of Marriage in the Fiction of George Eliot' (*NCGS* 3:iii[2007] 29 paras), presents a well-defended argument for George Eliot's use of feminist irony in placing widowhood, not marriage, at the fore of *Middlemarch, Daniel Deronda* and *Romola*. She argues that such a plan disturbs cultural and literary idealization of marriage, thereby also challenging assumptions about the configuration of irony in women's fiction. On the whole, then, a useful year for George Eliot studies.

The *Gaskell Society Journal* continues to produce articles of considerable interest. The 2007 issue is no exception. It contains Nils Clausson's 'Romancing Manchester: Class, Gender and the Conflicting Genres of Elizabeth Gaskell's *North and South*' (*GSJ* 21[2007] 1–20); Kamilla Elliott's 'The Romance of Politics and the Politics of Romance in Elizabeth Gaskell's *Mary Barton*' (*GSJ* 21[2007] 21–37); Caroline P. Huber's '"Heroic pioneers": The Ladies of *Cranford*' (*GSJ* 21[2007] 38–49); Lacy L. Lynch and Susan E. Colón's 'A Weakness, a Sin, or a Mind Diseased: A New Assessment of Cynthia Kirkpatrick' (*GSJ* 21[2007] 50–64); the indefatigable Graham Handley's '"A Dark Night's Work" Reconsidered' (*GSJ* 21[2007] 65–72); and Rebecca Styler's '"Lois the Witch": A Unitarian Tale' (*GSJ* 21[2007] 73–85). These articles are followed by 'Notes' that include: Tatsuhiro Ohno's 'Dramatic Irony in *Ruth*' (*GSJ* 21[2007] 86–90); Maurice Milne's 'The Changing Title of *Mary Barton*' (*GSJ* 21[2007] 91–4); and John Chapple's 'A "tangled bank": Willets, Wedgwood, Darwin and Holland families' (*GSJ* 21[2007] 95–9). There is in addition an impressive roster of reviewers of recent Elizabeth Gaskell studies, including John Chapple on volumes 4, 6, 8, 9 and 10 of the Pickering Edition of *The Works of Elizabeth Gaskell* (*GSJ* 21[2007] 100–13), Elizabeth Williams on Fran Baker's fascinating edition of Gaskell's *The Ghost in the Garden Room* (*GSJ* 21[2007] 114–15) and, to mention one other review, Graham Handley writes succinctly on *The Cambridge Companion to Elizabeth Gaskell* (*GSJ* 21[2007] 120–2).

Tracy Hargreaves's 'Nostalgic Retrieval: Sexual Politics, Cultural Aesthetics and Literary Form in John Galsworthy's *The Forsyte Saga*' (*English* 56[2007] 127–46), also discussed in Chapter XIV, is devoted to the long-neglected writer Galsworthy, and specifically *The Forsyte Saga* [1922] and *A Modern Comedy* [1929]. Hargreaves places these novels within the twentieth-century family saga and in the transitional literary context of the Victorian, Edwardian and modernist periods. The article argues that the cultural schism between property and art, worked out in the saga-like feud between Soames and Young Jolyon, operates as a measure of how to negotiate and represent sexual relations and a cultural aesthetic, which characterizes what is transitional about the move from Victorian to modernist sensibility. Jill L. Matus's *The Cambridge Companion to Elizabeth Gaskell* has twelve chapters that revolve around three themes in Gaskell's work: gender and family, social transformation, and Unitarianism. As a text the essays dispel critical myths that Gaskell's writings are consistent in their exploration of conflict between the classes and relations between the sexes, but instead highlight the ambiguities of personal and private history. Following Matus's introduction addressing the complexity of emotion in Gaskell's writing and negating characterizations of Gaskell's work as sentimental, are 'The Life and Letters of E.C. Gaskell' by Deirdre D'Albertis (pp. 10–26); '*Mary Barton* and *North and South*' by

Jill L. Matus (pp. 27–45); '*Cranford* and *Ruth*' by Audrey Jaffe (pp. 46–58); 'Elizabeth Gaskell's *The Life of Charlotte Brontë*' by Linda H. Peterson (pp. 59–74); '*Sylvia's Lovers* and other Historical Fiction' by Marion Shaw (pp. 75–89); '*Cousin Phillis, Wives and Daughters*, and Modernity' by Linda K. Hughes (pp. 90–107); 'Elizabeth Gaskell's Shorter Pieces' by Shirley Foster (pp. 108–30); 'Gaskell, Gender, and the Family' by Patsy Stoneman (pp. 131–47); 'Elizabeth Gaskell and Social Transformation' by Nancy Henry (pp. 148–63); 'Unitarian Dissent' by John Chapple (pp. 164–77); and 'Gaskell Then and Now' by Susan Hamilton (pp. 178–91). Some very eminent hands have contributed to this welcome volume.

In 'Elizabeth Gaskell's *Wives and Daughters:* Professional and Feminine Ideology' (*VIJ* 35[2007] 7–30) Susan E. Colón broadens the discussion of Molly Gibson's acquiescence beyond gender and into considerations of class dynamics, which allow for her emergence into a professional economy. In 'The Return of the "Unnative": The Transnational Politics of Elizabeth Gaskell's *North and South*' (*NCL* 61[2007] 449–78), Julia Sun-Joo Lee sees another 'North and South' through Frederick Hale's profession as sailor, which connects the cotton-producing American south to the cotton-manufacturing of the British north, and then goes on to consider the implications of Frederick's cosmopolitanism and suggest that this link anticipates Gaskell's agony over the American Civil War. '"Have at the masters?": Literary Allusions in Elizabeth Gaskell's *Mary Barton*' by Joanne Wilkes (*SNNTS* 39:ii[2007] 147–60) shows how numerous 'high-culture' literary allusions are aimed to appeal to middle- and upper-class readers. Clearly, Gaskell studies are undergoing a long-awaited revival.

A Man of Many Parts: Gissing's Short Stories, Essays and Other Works, edited by Barbara Rawlinson, traces the development of Gissing's writing from its early stages in the more individual tales to his American period, with its accumulation of themes which were refined and adapted, with causality emerging as the predominant voice. The volume continues chronicling Gissing's work with his return to England and his shifting political and philosophical beliefs as shown in his non-fiction, which, in turn, impacted his short fiction, as well as looking at the part played by realism in his short stories and his writings on Dickens, which added a dimension to his works in their entirety. Barbara Rawlinson's *A Man of Many Parts* provides a comprehensive view of the scope of George Gissing's career. From his year in America, the origin of so many themes he would later revisit, to his return to England and his changed political and philosophical beliefs reflected in his non-fiction and short fiction, to the role of realism in his short stories and writings on Dickens, and on to the last period of Gissing's development, Rawlinson, in this important contribution to Gissing studies, traces each stage with careful attention and thorough scholarship. The initial instalment of the *Gissing Journal* includes: '"A crazy idea . . . All gone off in smoke": George Gissing and Miss Curtis, Part Two, *The Curtis Family*' by Markus Neacey (*GissingJ* 43:i[2007] 1–22) and 'The Gissings's Wakefield Circle, IV: The Hick Family' by Anthony Petyt (*GissingJ* 43:i[2007] 23–32). Volume 43's third instalment contains Ryan Stephenson's 'Mr. Baker and Miss Yule: Mass Literacy and the Complexity of Reading and Writing in George Gissing's *New Grub Street*'

(*GissingJ* 43:iii[2007] 3–25); and M.D. Allen's ' "Feeble idyllicism" ': Gissing's Critique of *Oliver Twist* and *Ryecroft*' (*GissingJ* 43:iii[2007] 26–31). The fourth instalment of the *Gissing Journal* includes Roger Milbrandt's 'How Poor Was George Gissing? A Study of Gissing's Income between 1877 and 1888' (*GissingJ* 43:iv[2007] 1–16); M.D. Allen's '*Bleak House* and *The Emancipated*' (*GissingJ* 43:iv[2007] 17–26); Bouwe Postmus's 'The Peregrinations of a Preston Traveller' (*GissingJ* 43:iv[2007] 27–32); and Anthony Petyt's 'The Gissings' Wakefield Circle: V: The Mackie Family' (*GissingJ* 43:iv[2007] 33–40).

A second edition of Thomas Hardy's *Tess of the D'Urbervilles*, edited by Sarah E. Maier, offers a wealth of contextual materials and contemporary reviews, as well as extracts from Hardy's notebooks. These sources include debates about women. This text also reprints two separately published stories, 'Saturday Night in Arcady' and 'The Midnight Baptism', which were salvaged from the expurgated text published in the *Graphic*, later to be reinstated in the three-volume edition of 1891. In addition to the chronology and the text, appendices include appendix A, 'General Preface to the Wessex Edition of 1912' (pp. 397–401); appendix B, 'Bowdlerized Passages from the *Graphic*' (pp. 402–13); appendix C, 'Hardy's "Saturday Night in Arcady" (1891) and "The Midnight Baptism" (1891)' (pp. 414–27); appendix D, 'Hardy's Map of Wessex (1895)' (p. 428); appendix E, 'Hardy's "Tess's Lament" (1911)' (p. 429); appendix F, 'Contemporary Reviews' (pp. 431–48); appendix G, 'Contemporary News' (pp. 449–50); appendix H, 'Contemporary Debates on Women, Sexuality, and Fiction' (pp. 451–64); appendix I, 'Hardy's "Candour in English Fiction" (1890)' (pp. 465–70); and appendix J, 'Excerpts from Hardy's Autobiography' (pp. 471–4). Ralph Pite's *Thomas Hardy: The Guarded Life* is a biography focusing on the youthful Hardy. Pite argues that, in contrast to Hardy's own two-volume *Life*, there was a more vibrant and unpredictable Hardy who struggled with the urban and rural worlds as well as the proximity of failure to success in authorship. Pite's work is a worthy contribution to Hardy studies, revitalizing perceptions of Hardy in contrast to those previously thought of as authentic in his autobiography.

Another important contribution to Hardy studies is Martin Ray's edited and annotated collection of significant literary and biographical pieces concerning Hardy. Ray's *Thomas Hardy Remembered* brings together 150 annotated interviews and recollections of Hardy, most of which are reprinted for the first time. Close personal reflections by old friends include those by Sir George Douglas, J.M. Barrie and Edmund Gosse. Part I focuses on interviews; part II focuses on Hardy's boyhood; part III focuses on his courtship; part IV's concentration is on the 1880s; part V's on the following decade; part VI's on the 1900–10 period; part VII encompasses the years 1911–17; part VIII deals with two years, 1918–20; part IX the years 1921–5; and part X the final two years, 1926–8. Martin Ray notes that this collection of memoirs and diaries with the publication of personal letters would have been disliked by Hardy, 'averse as he was to personal comment and the unsanctioned recording of his conversation' (p. 2). Ray also observes that his book complements James Gibson's *Thomas Hardy: Interviews and Recollections*, although the majority of items do not overlap. Pamela Gossin brings an astronomical perspective to

Hardy studies with the first book-length study of such an approach in her *Thomas Hardy's Novel Universe: Astronomy, Cosmology and Gender in the Post-Darwinian World*. Gossin presents her eight chapters in two sections: part I, 'Critical Methodology, Literary and Historical Background', containing 'Introduction: "Convergences of the Twain": A Personal Perspective on the Interdisciplinary Study of Literature and Science' (pp. 3–20); 'Literary History of Astronomy and the Origins of Hardy's Literary Cosmology' (pp. 21–56); and 'The *Other* "Terrible Muse"': Astronomy and Cosmology from Prehistory through the Victorian Period' (pp. 57–104), and part II, 'Reading Hardy's Novel Universe', containing 'Hardy's Personal Construct Cosmology: Astronomy and Literature Converge' (pp. 105–22); 'Celestial Selection and the Cosmic Environment: *A Pair of Blue Eyes*, *Far from the Madding Crowd*, and *The Return of the Native*' (pp. 123–54); 'Universal Laws and Cosmic Forces: The Tragic Astronomical Must in *The Woodlanders* *Tess of the D'Urbervilles*, and *Jude the Obscure*' (pp. 197–228); and 'Conclusion: Moral Astrophysics: Myth, Cosmos, and Gender in Nineteenth-Century Britain and Beyond' (pp. 229–50).

Sophie Gilmartin and Rod Mengham's *Thomas Hardy's Shorter Fiction: A Critical Study* offers a complete rendering of the guiding preoccupations and recurring writing strategies across Hardy's works, along with detailed readings of multiple individual texts. Also emphasized are the formal choices forced on Hardy in his capacity as contributor to *Blackwood's Magazine*, as well as other periodicals. This is one of the few books providing comprehensive criticism of Hardy's complete short stories and it includes detail on the background of social and political unrest in Dorset only partially revealed in his version of Wessex. In ' "The actual sky is a horror": Thomas Hardy and the Arnoldian Conception of Science' (*NCL* 61[2007] 479–506), Anne De Witt sets Hardy's novel *Two on a Tower* [1882] in the context of astronomy and contemporary thermodynamics. Damon Franke writes on 'Hardy's Ur-Priestess and the Phases of a Novel' (*SNNTS* 39:ii[2007] 161–76). John Sutherland has contributed another fascinating and fun quiz book in his *So You Think You Know Thomas Hardy?*, published in 2005. Starting with easy, factual questions that test how well you remember a novel and its characters, the quizzes progress to a level of greater difficulty, demanding close reading and interpretative deduction. The questions evolve to a higher level of interpretation, but are all designed to amuse and divert as the questions and answers take the reader on an imaginative journey into the world of Thomas Hardy, where hypothesis and speculation produce fascinating and unexpected insights.

Gerald Monsman's *H. Rider Haggard on the Imperial Frontier: The Political and Literary Contexts of his African Romances*, published in 2006, presents eight chapters arranged chronologically. Haggard's relevance to a modern audience is promoted through citations of travel writing, history, psychology and anthropology. Deborah Mutch's 'A Working Class Tragedy: *The Fiction of Henry Mayers Hyndman*' (*NCStud* 20[2006] 99–112) discusses aspects of socialist narratives in fiction, and leadership and duty in Tory socialism. *Emily Lawless 1845–1913: Writing in Interspace*, by Heidi Hansson, addresses a critical period in women's writing in Ireland. Hansson borrows Lawless's own term, 'interspace', to describe the Anglo-Irish Protestant Lawless, who was set on avoidance of the nationalist–unionist tensions of her time. Delving into her life and works, Hansson centres her study on the theme that Lawless fails to take a stand and so speaks simultaneously in political and apolitical voices. This circumstance creates difficulty for feminist interpretations of her work. Hansson has written a well-researched study on a subject little investigated.

Kaori Nagai, in *Empire or Analogies: Kipling, India and Ireland*, adds to the postcolonial debate between those who emphasize Irish involvement in British imperialism and others who emphasize Irish national resistance. Nagai focuses on Kipling's Irish characters as they move from national to imperial identities. This book is arranged chronologically in three parts, from the 1880s when Kipling lived in India, to the 1890s when he gained international fame, and on into the Boer War years. Sumangala Bhattacharya offers 'Coding Famine: Famine Relief and the British Raj in Rudyard Kipling's "William the Conqueror"' (*ClioI* 36:iii[2007] 333–60). The winter 2007 *Kipling Journal* features articles including 'A Matter of Identity' by Jane Keskar (*KJ* 81:cccxxiv[2007] 8–11); 'Rudyard Kipling and the Commemoration of the Dead of the Great War' by Michael Aidin (*KJ* 81:cccxxiv[2007] 12–30); 'Rudyard Kipling and History' by Hugh Brogan (*KJ* 81:cccxxiv[2007] 31–40); 'Gribayedoff Portrait of Kipling' by Roger Ayers (*KJ* 81:cccxxiv[2007] 40–1); 'An Unfamiliar Kipling Story' by Thomas Pinney (*KJ* 81:cccxxiv[2007] 42–6); 'A Drawing of a Tiger's Head' by the Editor (*KJ* 81:cccxxiv[2007] 47–8); and 'Edward Kay Robinson' by Janette Kay Robinson (*KJ* 81:cccxxiv[2007] 49–51). John McGivering and the editor of the *Kipling Journal* include the following reviews for December 2007: *Rudyard Kipling: The Books I Leave Behind* by David Alan Richards (*KJ* 81:cccxxiv[2007] 52); *Rudyard Kipling*, by Jan Montefiore (*KJ* 81:cccxxiv[2007] 53–5); *The Narcissism of Empire*, by Diane Simmons (*KJ* 81:cccxxiv[2007] 55–6, 60); and *The Dangerous Book for Boys*, by Conn Iggulden and Hal Iggulden (*KJ* 81:cccxxiv[2007] 63).

James Walton's *Vision and Vacancy: The Fictions of J.S. Le Fanu* emphasizes how vision brings Le Fanu protagonists to discover a void in their lives, which hints that many emotional/spiritual issues are voids in themselves, though they may at first seem to signal guidance. Kristin Mary Mahoney reviews *Vernon Lee: Decadence, Ethics, Aesthetics*, edited by Catherine Maxwell and Patricia Pulham (*VS* 50[2007] 108–10). Madeleine Humphreys's *The Life and Times of Edward Martyn: An Aristocratic Bohemian*, traces the life of Galway-born Edward Martyn, who became the author of a utopian novel, a playwright for over thirty years, the patron of the great Dublin choir and, along with Thomas MacDonagh and Joseph Plunkett, the founder of the Irish Theatre in Hardwicke Street. Humphreys draws on previously unpublished and unknown documents, memoirs, letters and journalism. *Writing on the Image: Reading William Morris*, edited by David Latham, is a collection of essays featuring the varied canon of William Morris, from his editorship of *The Commonweal* for the Socialist League in the 1880s, along with his lectures at political rallies, to his leadership as founder of the Kelmscott Press in 1891, with his Kelmscott *Chaucer*. His authorship of eight prose romances in the 1890s is featured as well. Richard Dellamora's

'Female Adolescence in May Sinclair's *Mary Olivier* and the Construction of a Dialectic Between Victorian and Modern' (*NCStud* 20[2006] 171–82) is a welcome addition to the analysis of a forgotten author. Linda Lear's *Beatrix Potter: A Life in Nature* deftly traces more than the life of the writer for children's books. Potter's life as a successful landowner, farm manager and sheep breeder is also discussed. Lear focuses on the settings behind Potter's books and on her personal evolution as a shrewd businesswoman and devoted preservationist of the rural landscape of her beloved Lake District, where she left vast holdings of land and property to the National Trust. The social settings and circumstances of Potter's early life as a Victorian child of privilege are traced. Jed Esty's 'The Colonial Bildungsroman: *The Story of an African Farm* and the Ghost of Goethe' (*VS* 49[2007] 407–30) examines characterization, plot structure and figurative language in Olive Schreiner's *The Story of an African Farm*.

In *The Irish Scene in Somerville and Ross*, Julie Anne Stevens examines Edith Somerville and Violet Martin, who wrote together under the name Martin Ross. The writers are here viewed from a number of perspectives, among them Somerville's production of artwork for children's and sporting publications and the influence of history, landscape and imagination on the two writers' works. In contrast to most other critics, Stevens also investigates the authors' engagement with the lower classes. In part I, 'The Colonial Vision', the 'Land: *Naboth's Vineyard* and the Colonial Nightmare' is featured (pp. 13–49), along with 'Religion: *The Real Charlotte* and the Colonial Dream' (pp. 49–90). Part II, 'Contexts of *The Irish RM*', includes chapters on 'Money: The Business of Being Irish in the Periodical Press' (pp. 91–126) and 'Law: Marlequin in Ireland' (pp. 127–60). In part III, 'Landscaping in *The Irish RM*', the sections are 'History: Picturing the Past' (pp. 161–88) and 'Sport/Politics: The Treasure in the Bog' (pp. 189–223). Flora Annie Steel's *On the Face of the Waters*, originally published in 1896, is offered in a new edition for 2007. Steel was the wife of a British officer, had a wide circle of Indian friends and had lived in India for twenty-two years. The subtitle of *On the Face of the Waters* is 'The Great Novel of the Indian Mutiny, Based on Accounts of Those who Lived Through It'. It is set in the Delhi of 1857, while the city was under siege. The story sketches the romance of Major Erlton and Alice Gissing, the uprising and their separation, and the coming together of Mrs Erlton and James Greyman.

Thomas L. Reed Jr traces clues that indicate Stevenson intended alcohol as the elixir central to Dr Jekyll's transformation in *The Transforming Draught: Jekyll and Hyde, Robert Louis Stevenson and the Victorian Alcohol Debate*. Reed's evidence grows from the shadowy presence of alcohol in Stevenson's life and proceeds across various aspects of the novel, including its patterns of language, plot, characterization and imagery. Period concerns about alcohol and references in other works by Stevenson feature in the argument as well. An interesting fifteen-page appendix traces Stevenson's references to alcohol across his works. In a refreshingly innovative study of the influence of travel on Robert Louis Stevenson's writing from the beginning to the end of his career, Oliver S. Buckton showcases juvenile fiction and travel writing in *Cruising with Robert Louis Stevenson: Travel, Narrative, and the Colonial Body*.

In this thoroughly researched and long-needed work on Stevenson, Buckton argues that Stevenson's revolutionary critiques of European colonialism take shape amidst alluring Polynesian island landscapes. Buckton situates cruising as a critical term, linking Stevenson's leisurely method of travel with the jarring narrative motifs of disruption and fragmentation that characterize his writings. Buckton traces the development of Stevenson's career from his early travel books to show how his major works of fiction, such as *Treasure Island*, *Kidnapped* and *The Ebb-Tide*, are built from innovative techniques and materials Stevenson gathered in his global travels. Section topics include 'Travel and the (Re)animated Body', 'Mapping the Historical Romance', Stevenson's complicated relationship between colonialism and anti-colonialism, in which Samoan and Highland cultures are compared in their searches for independence, the failure of Stevenson's ambition to produce a masterpiece on the traditions, culture and history of the islands and Stevenson's treatment of racial differences challenging any simplistic 'white' and 'native' categories. Multiple critical perspectives of 'the body', gender theory, queer theory and postcolonial studies permeate this valuable study.

Glenda Norquay's *Robert Louis Stevenson and Theories of Reading: The Reader as Vagabond* features a unique combination of literary history and reception theory. From Stevenson's fiction and literary essays Norquay argues that Stevenson both exemplified tensions inside the literary market of his time and foreshadowed developments in reading theory. Jane Lilienfeld writes a review of *The Transforming Draught: Jekyll and Hyde, Robert Louis Stevenson and the Victorian Alcohol Debate*, by Thomas L. Reed (*VS* 50[2007] 136–8), and Oliver S. Buckton reviews *Robert Louis Stevenson, Science, and the Fin de Siècle* by Julia Reid (*NCL* 62[2007] 133–6). Erin Hazard writes ' "A realized day-dream": Excursions to Nineteenth-Century Authors' Homes' (*NCStud* 20[2006] 13–33), in which she traces the origins of literary tourism in Great Britain as evident in the building of Abbotsford, in the travels of Washington Irving and in William Howitt's *Homes and Haunts of the Most Eminent British Poets* [1847]. David Farrier's *Unsettled Narratives: The Pacific Writings of Stevenson, Ellis, Melville and London* features chapters on 'The Written Pacific' (pp. 1–14); ' "Talk languished on the beach": The Possibility of Reciprocity in Robert Louis Stevenson's *In the South Seas*' (pp. 15–72); and ' "These words are so changed in a native's mouth": Contested Frames in William Ellis's *Polynesian Researches*' (pp. 73–116).

Dracula's Guest and Other Weird Stories, by Bram Stoker, follows the text of the first edition, collated by Florence Stoker and published in London in April 1914 by George Routledge and Sons Ltd and the first edition of *The Lair of the White Worm*, published in London in November 1911 by William Rider and Son Ltd. This new 2007 edition is edited with an introduction by Kate Hebblethwaite. *Bram Stoker: A Literary Life*, by Lisa Hopkins, is dominated by Stoker's *Dracula*, but Hopkins repeatedly emphasizes Stoker's seventeen other books, as well as his reputation as manager of Sir Henry Irving's Lyceum Theatre. These lesser-known aspects of Stoker's life include his educational experiences, travels and personal relationships. Critical evaluation of *Dracula*, as well as *The Lady of the Shroud*, *The Lair of the White Worm* and *The Mystery of the Sea*, as well as other novels, is mixed with Stoker's life, characterized by love of travel, a deep knowledge of the theatre and his passion for esoteric knowledge. Hopkins writes clearly and perceptively and her discussions encompass many of his hitherto neglected writings. In 'Productive Fear: Labor, Sexuality, and Mimicry in Bram Stoker's *Dracula*' (*TSLL* 48:ii[2006] 145–70), E.K.W. Yu significantly revises and develops the 'productive fear' thesis which connects vampire fighters to the rise of professionalism.

A major contribution to Thackeray studies is part of the three-volume set, *Lives of Victorian Literary Figures V*. Beyond the introduction, bibliography, chronology, copy-texts and abbreviations, the following documents have been reproduced in *William Thackeray*, edited by Judith L. Fisher: 'School Days: Thackeray at Charterhouse' (pp. 1–36); 'The "Set": The 1840s' (pp. 37–62); 'Henry Vizetelly, *Glances Back through Seventy Years*' (pp. 63–74); 'The Author as Artist and Art Critic' (pp. 75–92); 'The Author as Editor' (pp. 93–120); 'Thackeray in the United States' (pp. 121–90); 'James T. Fields, *Yesterday with Authors*' (pp. 191–218); 'Richard Bedingfield, "Recollections of Thackeray, by his Cousin", *Cassell's Magazine*' (pp. 219–26); '*Letters of Elizabeth Barrett Browning to Richard Hengist Horne*' (pp. 227–38); 'George Hodder, *Memories of My Time*' (pp. 239–54); 'Frederick Locker-Lampson, *My Confidences*' (pp. 255–68); '[John Brown and Henry Lancaster], "Thackeray", *North British Review*' (pp. 269–72); 'Jane Townley Pryme and Alicia Bayne, *Memorials of the Thackeray Family*' (pp. 273–96). In spite of this, it is sad to record yet another very thin year for Thackeray studies.

A similar situation is regrettably to be recorded for Anthony Trollope studies. Clara Claiborne Park's 'Grease, Balance, and Point of View in the Work of Anthony Trollope' (*HudR* 60:iii[2007] 435–45) presents a surprising example of his writing beyond the characteristic balances in characters' pluses and minuses—his point of view on colonization in Australia and New Zealand. The fall 2007 issue of *The Victorian Newsletter* features 'Against "All that roudy lot": Trollope's Grudge against Disraeli' (*VN* 112[2007] 55–68), by Karen Kurt Teal. 'The Fact of a Rumor: Anthony Trollope's *The Eustace Diamonds*' (*NSL* 62:i[2007] 88–120), by Ayelet Ben-Yishai, features a consideration of facts and fact-making in *The Eustace Diamonds*, revealing their unstable nature, and therefore urging a reconsideration of the epistemology of realist form and novelistic probability.

There are two articles to record in H.G. Wells studies. R. Person offers 'Primitive Modernity: H.G. Wells and the Prehistoric Man of the 1890s' (*YES* 37:i[2007] 58–74) and the fall issue of the *Victorian Newsletter* contains 'The Anarchist and the Detective: The Science of Detection and the Subversion of Generic Convention in H.G. Well's "The Thumbmark"' (*VN* 112:iii[2007] 19–31), by Nils Clausson. There is a different situation in the world of Oscar Wilde studies. *The Complete Works of Oscar Wilde*, volume 3: *The Picture of Dorian Gray, the 1890 and 1891 Texts*, edited by Joseph Bristow, is the third volume in the Oxford English Texts edition of the works of Oscar Wilde. This definitive variorum edition of Wilde's *The Picture of Dorian Gray* reprints the thirteen-chapter and twenty-chapter versions of this famous story as separate works. The volume provides readers with the most detailed account available of the considerable changes that Wilde made to a controversial narrative that appeared in two very different editions in 1890 and 1891 respectively. *The Complete Works of Oscar Wilde: Criticism*, volume 4: *Historical Criticism, Intentions, The Soul of Man*, edited by Josephine M. Guy, reproduces only critical pieces which were published in book form in Wilde's lifetime, as well as the graduate essay which was presented in three fair-copy quarto notebooks when Wilde submitted it for the Chancellor's English Essay Prize at the University of Oxford in 1879. Guy and Bristow are to be complimented on their introductions and erudite scholarship.

Angela Kingston's inventive and valuable *Oscar Wilde as a Character in Victorian Fiction* presents Oscar Wilde through the lenses of his contemporaries and beyond as they trace his career through the 1880s and 1890s. Significant details and links are revealed as Kingston utilizes unused primary and secondary sources. Wilde's willingness to be portrayed in both caricature and parody is represented across the three sections of the book. The first section is concerned with Wilde as aesthete from 1877 to 1890. The second section features those who portrayed Wilde as the decadent (1891–5) and in the final chapter Kingston presents portrayals of Wilde as pariah through works by Leverson, Le Gallienne, Praed and others. The thirteen-page appendix specifies portrayals of Wilde across the twentieth century and on into 2007. Four photographs and four illustrations are included as well.

3. Poetry

What's the Import? Nineteenth-Century Poems and Contemporary Critical Practice, by Kerry McSweeney, is a trenchant and provocative book that seeks to 'restore a balance to the critical study of nineteenth-century poetry' (p. 7) by proposing an aestheticist methodology in opposition to what McSweeney sees as an academy dominated by theoretical and cultural studies. Although there has been an interest in the recovery of New Criticism in the development of new/cultural formalism in the last few years, McSweeney's is the first monograph to pose a direct challenge to cultural theory and New Historicism by asserting literary value as something separate from other cultural and textual materials, which can be studied on its own terms. As such, questions about the quality of individual poems ('Is it any good?') become central, whereas cultural/historical categories (Victorian, Romantic, British, American) are of less interest, and so McSweeney privileges a transatlantic nineteenth century. The book's ten short chapters all perform affective close readings of one or two well-known nineteenth-century poems. In chapter 2 McSweeney compares 'The Solitary Reaper' and 'Tears, Idle Tears', poems that frame or are framed by song, offering an alternative to the deconstructionist critique of J. Hillis Miller by demonstrating how the poems achieve or perform the lyric affect of the songs they describe. Chapter 3 looks at Victorian poems on paintings, a theme that is taken up by much of this year's work in Victorian poetry, taking in the ekphrastic lyrics of Michael Field, Dante Gabriel Rossetti and Swinburne as examples of different types of aesthetic engagement. Chapter 4 takes two poems that have been hostages to various theoretical fortunes, 'Childe Roland' and 'Goblin Market', again taking an anti-interpretative stance and drawing attention to the aesthetic resolution achieved by both of these ambiguous narratives. Hopkins is the last British Victorian to be addressed by McSweeney in a chapter that seeks to counterbalance the dominant Christian interpretative discourse by drawing attention to the human value of the poems. McSweeney's lively and accomplished readings develop out of the identification, by Isobel Armstrong, Kirstie Blair and others, of affect and the aesthetic as central to nineteenth-century poetics, transforming them into twenty-first-century methodological practice. This short book could prove to be an important intervention in the field.

Little Songs: Women, Silence and the Nineteenth Century Sonnet by Amy Christine Billone continues the work of other recent publications on the nineteenth-century sonnet (Joseph Phelan [2006] and John Holmes [2005]), approaching the form from a feminist perspective and drawing on the work of critics such as Alison Chapman and Tricia Lootens, who highlight the significance of silence to a nineteenth-century feminine poetic. Like McSweeney, Billone takes a long nineteenth-century perspective. Beginning with Charlotte Smith and concluding with the modernist rejection of the sonnet, she charts the development of the tradition over the course of the century. In chapter 2, Billone links Elizabeth Barrett Browning's use of the sonnet to the silence of grief. She compares the poet's inability to express her feelings about the death of her brother with her concurrent poetic productivity and argues that Barrett Browning develops an understanding of the lyric as textual silence. In a thoughtful close reading of Barrett Browning's sonnet 'Grief' as a subversion of the Wordsworthian sonnet, she suggests that the poet sublimes absence and makes poetic failure visible. Barrett Browning is then seen as a point of departure for Christina Rossetti, whose sonnets are represented as covert celebrations of the self; Rossetti and Barrett Browning together are figured as muses for Isabella Southern, Dora Greenwell and Michael Field, who give their mute muses a voice, challenging their poetic of silence. The lineage that Billone traces, whereby female sonneteers are shown to respond to their poetic mothers and grandmothers, further establishes the importance of the feminine tradition in Victorian poetry and introduces writers whose work is as yet not widely recognized to readers of Rossetti and Barrett Browning.

Andrew Radford's wide-ranging study, *The Lost Girls: Demeter–Persephone and the Literary Imagination*, contains a rich chapter on Victorian poetry's appropriation of the Persephone myth that takes in the work of Jean Ingelow, Dora Greenwell, Mary Shelley, Barrett Browning, Swinburne, Dante Gabriel Rossetti, George Meredith, Tennyson, Helen Hunt Jackson, Caroline FitzGerald and Mathilde Blind. Radford's knowledgeable discussion demonstrates the various interventions 'divine mother and maid' make in feminist, pagan, aesthetic, secular materialist and patriarchal domestic poetic discourses.

Matthew Arnold attracted only a small amount of critical attention in 2007. Lauren Caldwell's article, 'Truncating Coleridgean Conversation and the Revisioning of Dover Beach' (*VP* 45:iv[2007] 429–45) is a suggestive essay that approaches the poetic doubt which Arnold expresses in 'Dover Beach' through the work of Coleridge, understanding both poets as readers who are, to a greater or lesser extent, troubled by the relationship between language and the world. For Caldwell, Arnold is a post-Romantic Coleridge whose solipsism does not even have the consolation of faith in his own poetic vision. She rehearses arguments that have categorized 'Dover Beach' as either a dramatic monologue or a dramatic lyric, and makes a case for it as a conversation poem that ultimately succeeds in finding a way of writing with a broken language. Similar concerns are at the heart of E. Frances Frame's nice reading of 'Sohrab and Rustum', 'Shaping the Self: Critical Perspective and Community in "Sohrab and Rustum"' (*VP* 45:i[2007] 17–28). As Frame shows, this poem explores the tension between the ambition of the individual and the achievement of human community through a dramatization of the struggle to achieve critical perspective. In the context of Hegel's master–slave dialectic and Arnold's own critical prose, Frame suggests that the battle between the poem's eponymous protagonists is the battle between the critic and the philistine. Donald Mackenzie's article, 'Two Versions of Lucretius: Arnold and Housman' (*TL* 16:ii[2007] 16–77), pairs Arnold's *Empedocles on Etna* with *A Shropshire Lad*, setting up a fruitful comparison that explores Housman's reversals of Lucretius alongside Arnold's appropriation of the classical poet in his 'georgic of the mind' (p. 160), and argues that Arnold uses Lucretius in his work both to exemplify and to cure the disenchanted modern consciousness. David Rampton's article, 'Back to the Future: Lionel Trilling, "The Scholar Gypsy", and the State of Victorian Poetry' (*VP* 45:i[2007] 1–15) offers an account of 'The Scholar Gypsy' and its critical heritage as a way into a wider discussion about how best to approach Victorian poetry and the decades of critical discussion that surround it. The article writes in defence of Lionel Trilling's study, *The Opposing Self*, and constitutes a reassessment that might be viewed as timely in the light of recent academic trends that seek to re-embrace the formalist methodologies of the 1950s.

Janet Gezari breaks new ground with *Last Things: Emily Brontë's Poems*, the first book-length study of Brontë's poetry and a valuable contribution to the field. The book offers 'new ways to read Brontë's poems and new reasons for wanting to read them' (p. 1) and seeks to amend the omission of Brontë from the canon, which Gezari argues is the result of Brontë's failure to contribute to the shared identity and shared concerns of nineteenth-century women writers. For this reason Gezari avoids applying what she sees as a problematic gender poetics to Brontë and instead leads the reader to focus on the poet's ends and endings in a discussion of lyricism and temporality that shares many of the concerns of Thain's study *'Michael Field'* (discussed below). Refusing to draw a distinction between Brontë's 'Gondal' poems and her personal lyrics, Gezari organizes her study around the themes of remembrance, narrative, fragmentation, death and Brontë's posthumous life in the hands of Charlotte: different ways in which Brontë's poetry ends and fails to end. In a fascinating reading of 'Remembrance', she draws on Freud's essay 'On Mourning and Melancholia' and nineteenth-century definitions of remembrance and recollection in order to suggest forgetting as a form of suppression that ensures the preservation of memory; whereas in a chapter that considers Emily's poetry in the context of her own death, death is figured as a process that worries at temporality and at the separation between this world and the next. Throughout, Gezari offers insightful readings of the poems, many of which are reproduced in full, and the book provides an excellent introduction to readers and critics new to Brontë's poetic corpus. Gezari also sets up a rich network of intertexts, including the work of Keats, Wordsworth, Coleridge, Plath, Hughes and Carson, as well as Brontë's own *Wuthering Heights*, demonstrating Brontë's relevance to a broad range of critical study. This is the only work to be published this year on the Brontës' poetry, which remains an underdeveloped area of study despite two fairly recent collected editions of Emily's poetry.

Following Elizabeth Barrett Browning's bicentenary in 2006, the Brownings continue to attract a wealth of interest. A new literary biography of Robert Browning, *The Dramatic Imagination of Robert Browning: A Literary Life*, begun by Richard S. Kennedy and completed by Donald Hair, sets the tone for much of this year's work on Browning, focusing as it does on Browning's development of the dramatic monologue. Kennedy's lucid and sympathetic account of Browning's life and work places emphasis on Browning's fascination with the stage, giving new importance to the poet's relationship with William Macready (also the subject of Thomas C. Crochinus's essay, see below) and to productions of Browning's own plays. New life is given to the dramatic monologue by this theatrical context and Kennedy proposes a more expansive appreciation of Browning's use of the dramatic, preferring the term 'monodrama' as one that might include soliloquies, dramatic narratives, dramatic monologues and dramatic lyrics. A change in emphasis is perceptible in the section written by Hair, who discusses the dialogic and interpretative frameworks that inform Browning's later works, drawing attention to the relationship between human thought and action that they interrogate. This biography, which includes accessible close readings of some of Browning's major poems, also points the reader towards more detailed critical studies and provides overviews of critical debates and reception history. It is a worthwhile introduction to the poet. John Woolford's book, *Robert Browning*, another addition to the Writers and their Work series published by Northcote House, provides an introduction to Browning of a very different kind. The brevity that Northcote House demands of its authors means that these critical introductions often have little room for biographical description and critical overview, and the most successful numbers are those that address their subject from a single, often original, perspective. Woolford's deft study is exemplary in this regard, comprising an extended essay on Browning and the grotesque. Taking early twentieth-century representations of Browning as odd, barbaric and ungentlemanly as its starting point, the book separates Browning from the Oxbridge urbanity of Tennyson, Arnold, Clough and FitzGerald, suggesting a fascination with grotesquery that has more in common with the work Victorian novelists than poets. Theories of the grotesque are contextualized and historicized through neat explications of Kant, Ruskin, Hugo and Bagehot, which characterize the grotesque and therefore Browning as particularly Victorian, sceptical of the Romantic sublime and fascinated by the embodiment of paradox. Browning's grotesquery is identified as by turns ludic and terrible, and Woolford ably demonstrates how his poetry keeps returning to the paradox of body and mind, showing the material of the body, including the words that it speaks or writes, to be an inadequate limit for the ambition of the mind.

'Winking through the Chinks: Eros and Ellipsis in Robert Browning's "Love Among the Ruins"'' (*VP* 45:iv[2007] 349–68), by Peter Merchant, reads Browning's poem after the tradition of the eighteenth-century ruin poem, developed in the Romantic period by Wordsworth and Shelley. Suggesting the influence of nineteenth-century travel-writing and particularly the work of Charles Fellows, Merchant identifies the ruins as those of an ancient city dedicated to Aphrodite, which prompts a reconsideration of the poem's representation of love. David Sonstroem's essay, 'The Poison Within: Robert Browning's "The Laboratory"' (*VN* 112[2007] 29–47), also reassesses the poem's relationship to its historical context. Sonstroem argues against prevailing readings of Browning's dramatic monologue that cast the speaker as a revolutionary sans-culotte and suggests instead that she is a figure of the *ancien régime* itself, which becomes a place of dangerous beauty, poisoned from within. The identity of another of Browning's speakers is at issue in Heather Morton's article, '"A church of himself": Liberal Skepticism and Consistent Character in *Bishop Blougram's Apology*' (*VP* 45:i[2007] 29–47), which offers a nice comparison of the poem's reception history and contemporary readings by Newman and Wiseman and reads Browning's poem in the context of nineteenth-century suspicion of the Tractarian desire to reunite the church as a single authority. In this light, the poem becomes a problematization of the relationship between speech and inner life that demonstrates the paucity of public language as a means of revealing anything meaningful about the self. In 'Browning, Grief, and the Strangeness of Dramatic Verse' (*CQ* 36[2007] 155–73) Francis O'Gorman considers the possibilities of the dramatic monologue form. Beginning with the observation that Browning's verse is uniquely distanced from the theme of mourning amongst its Victorian contemporaries, he describes Browning as a 'resurrectionist poet' (p. 159) whose dramatic monologues replace sorrow with vitality and embody the poet's sincere faith in an aesthetic afterlife, employing a fine reading of 'Fra Lippo Lippi' to illustrate his argument. Peggy Dunn Bailey's article, 'Robert Browning's Dramatic Dialogue' (*PR* 33:ii[2007] 23–36), proposes the speakers of 'By the Fireside' and 'Any Wife to Any Husband' as dramatizations of Romantic and Victorian world-views, reading against biographical interpretations of the poems. Dunn Bailey's close readings draw out the opposing ideologies of the two speakers, demonstrating the male speaker's recapitulation of the egotistical sublime that denies the woman a voice and the female speaker's Victorian scepticism, which brings its male auditor into sharp, real focus. 'Literary Homosociality and the Political Science of the Actor's Closet' by Thomas C. Crochunis (*VS* 49[2007] 258–67) (also discussed in section 4) takes a rare look at Browning's plays in a discussion of his relationship with William Macready and the production of *A Blot in the'Scutcheon*. Michael Ackerman's essay, 'Monstrous Men: Violence and Masculinity in Robert Browning's *The Ring and the Book*' (in Bienstock, ed., *Horrifying Sex: Essays on Sexual Difference in Gothic Literature*, pp. 122–34), is interested in Gothic rather than dramatic traditions as a context for Browning's poetry. His accessible discussion of 'Browning's Gothic Masterpiece' (p. 123) identifies its male speakers as Gothic villains and focuses on the representation of Count Guido, arguing that his villainy is a response to a disenfranchised male patriarchy.

The *Browning Society Newsletter* published a collection of articles that concentrate on the Brownings' life in Italy. ' "Oh, a day in the city square, there is no such pleasure in life!": Robert Browning's Portrayal of Contemporary Italians' (*BSNotes* 32[2007] 4–17) considers Browning's observation and interpretation of the Italian national character and suggests the influence of Romantic theories of political oppression and Victorian cultural histories that drew a distinction between the northern European and Mediterranean character, arguing that Browning understood himself as the English poet of Italy's poetry. Maurizio Masetti's article, 'Lost in Translation: "The Italian in England" ' (*BSNotes* 32[2007] 17–27) further interrogates Browning's English appreciation of Italian politics through a carefully historicized close reading of Browning's 1845 poem about the struggle for Italian independence, which was translated by Mazzini. Agreeing with contemporary reviews of the poem that identified the speaker as Mazzini, Masetti explores the acquaintanceship of the two men, makes a good case for their friendship and mutual regard and charts Browning's changing attitude to Mazzini's politics after his marriage to Elizabeth. The different attitudes towards Italy held by husband and wife that Massetti infers are discussed in relation to the upbringing of their son in Christopher M. Keirstead's article, ' "He shall be a 'citizen of the world' ": Cosmopolitanism and the Education of Pen Browning' (*BSNotes* 32[2007] 74–83), which observes the ways in which the Brownings' concerns about national, gender, public/private and political/aesthetic boundaries, which they wrote about in their poetry, were also brought to bear on Pen's childhood. Using an account of Pen's early education, gleaned from Elizabeth Barrett Browning's journals and letters, Keirstead identifies Pen's childhood identity as liminal, occupying the space between different poles of identity, and suggests that he is a figure who deserves greater critical attention in Browning studies.

Three other articles in the volume focus on the work of Elizabeth Barrett Browning. 'The Home Front in Elizabeth Barrett Browning's "Mother and Poet" and "The Runaway Slave at Pilgrim's Point" ' (*BSNotes* 32[2007] 27–55) by Sandra Donaldson compares these two poems in which Barrett Browning deals with feminine complicity in acts of war and oppression, and suggests both poems are performances of reparation. The two remaining articles deal with Barrett Browning's relationship with other women poets and painters in Italy. Simon Avery's article, 'Casa Guidi Neighbours: Eliza Ogilvy, Elizabeth Barrett Browning and the Poetry of the Risorgimento' (*BSNotes* 32[2007] 55–74), revisits the relationship between Barrett Browning and Ogilvy, which began in Italy and continued via frequent correspondence. Avery looks at Ogilvy's contribution to the posthumous reconstruction of Barrett Browning's poetic persona and draws attention to Ogilvy's own poetic output and its close relationship to Barrett Browning's Risorgimento poetry, making a claim for the need for further study of the role of women in the politics of Risorgimento Italy. By contrast, 'Ottocento Spiritualism: From Elizabeth Barrett Browning to Evelyn de Morgan' (*BSNotes* 32[2007] 83–97), by Judy Oberhausen and Nic Peters, is concerned with Florence as an important location for nineteenth-century spiritualism, and compares spiritualism's influence on Barrett Browning and Evelyn Pickering de Morgan, making a connection between the two women via their shared interest in Swedenborgian thought.

Haunted becomes enchanted in Alison Chapman's absorbing chapter, '"I think I was enchanted": Elizabeth Barrett Browning's Haunting of American Woman Poets' (in Frank, ed., *Representations of Death in Nineteenth Century Writing and Culture*, pp. 109–24), which reads a number of poems written in praise of Elizabeth Barrett Browning by American woman poets (Emily Dickinson, Anne C. Lynch Botta, Sarah Helen Whitman and Lilian Whiting) whose poems balance the traditional elegiac trope of feminine spirituality with an insistence on the poet's corporeal materiality. Chapman's chapter, which continues the work of her 2000 monograph on Christina Rossetti, suggests the poems are literary ghostings that body forth the feminine spirit, potential sites of erotic encounter where literary possession implies possession by a foreign body. Another article to address Barrett Browning's American readership is Cheryl Styles's '"Different planes of sensuous form": American Critical and Popular Responses to Elizabeth Barrett Browning's *Aurora Leigh* and *Last Poems*' (*VPR* 40:iii[2007] 239–55), which provides succinct summaries of previously unrecorded reviews of Barrett Browning published in American periodicals between 1856 and 1862, made available as part of the electronic database, *American Periodicals Series*. In '"La Prude Angleterre": Elizabeth Barrett Browning's Cultural Relativism' by Berry Chevasco (in Dow, ed., *Translators. Interpreters, Mediators: Women Writers 1700–1900*, pp. 209–23), Barrett Browning's work is placed again in its European context through a discussion of the poet's prose translations of Balzac and Eugène Sue. In Karen Dielman's article, 'Elizabeth Barrett Browning's Religious Poetics: Congregationalist Models of Hymnist and Preacher' (*VP* 45:ii[2007] 135–57), the figure of the Congregationalist preacher is offered as a more appropriate means of understanding Barrett Browning's responsibility to her readership than a masculine 'sage discourse'. Dielman provides a lucid account of Elizabeth Barrett Browning's Congregationalist faith that highlights its democracy, social awareness and intellectual rigour and begins to reassess the poet's early hymns, the religious dramatic lyrics published mid-career and *Aurora Leigh* in this new context. *King Lear* is found to be an important intertext for *Sonnets from the Portuguese* in the first section of James Hirsh's article, 'Covert Appropriations of Shakespeare: Three Case Studies' (*PLL* 43:i[2007] 45–67), an illuminating demonstration of Barrett Browning's appropriation of Goneril's insincere profession of filial love in Sonnet 43.

The only monograph to be published on the poetry of the *fin de siècle* in 2007, Marion Thain's *'Michael Field': Poetry, Aestheticism and the Fin de Siècle*, is also the first single-author study of 'Michael Field'. Thain's absorbing book makes a persuasive case for the importance of Bradley and Cooper by moving the focus away from the eccentricities of their shared life and onto their poetry; by broadening their poetic associations to include poets of both sexes from both their own historical moment and earlier in the period, as well as other *fin-de-siècle* woman poets, and by placing new emphasis on the work that the pair produced after their conversion to Roman Catholicism. Thain's central thesis is that the aesthetic of the *fin de siècle* can be understood to be motivated by a paradoxical drive to reconcile the synchronic with the diachronic, and this dualism is one of a number that Thain finds to be important to the work of 'Michael Field'. Her close readings also draw out the relationship between the economic and the aesthetic, the pagan and Christian, history and modernity and masculinity and femininity. An important trope for Thain's study is that of the fetish, adopted from Freudian discourse as a materialization of difference and employed by Thain in discussions of historicity, the lyric and the pseudonym. Although the book interrogates the implications of the Michael Field pseudonym in detail, it does not let the multiple identities of the two poets complicate the study, dealing only with works published by Bradley and Cooper as Field. After an initial chapter that engages with the diaries of Bradley and Cooper in the context of late Victorian theories of history and the legacy of Carlyle and Pater, each subsequent chapter deals with a single volume of Bradley and Cooper's poetry. Chapter 2, a reading of *Long Ago*, tackles the questions of gender and sexuality, arguing that this collection of Sapphic lyrics relocates Field's lyric voice to a distant past that can refuse sexological discourse of the late Victorian present. Chapter 3 further contributes to this year's work on ekphrastic verse, reading *Sight and Song* as a collection that interrogates the temporal and spatial paradoxes that the ekphrastic lyric, and the lyric more broadly, embody. Chapter 4 looks back to Metaphysical definitions of the lyric in order to discuss the lyrics published in *Underneath the Bough*, which occupy and describe the space between two speaking subjects. Chapters 5 and 6 concentrate on Michael Field's religious work, which seeks to reconcile pagan and Christian discourses in poetry that looks towards the modernism of the next century. This comprehensive, lucid and original book is a significant scholarly achievement that successfully relocates the work of Katherine Bradley and Edith Cooper at the centre of the *fin-de-siècle* aesthetic project.

Apart from Andrew Radford's discussion of new woman appropriations of the Demeter–Persephone myth (addressed above), Jean Ingelow and Mary E. Coleridge were the only *fin-de-siècle* woman poets to receive any critical attention in 2007. Maura Ives's article, ' "Her life was in her books": Jean Ingelow in the Literary Marketplace' (*VN* 111[2007] 12–19), attempts a recovery of Ingelow's poetry through an account of her publication history, focusing on three significant moments in her publishing career. In this context Ingelow is portrayed as an ambitious and savvy publisher whose career might be fruitfully compared with earlier career-poets such as Hemans and Landon. ' "Set the crystal surface free!" Mary E. Coleridge and the Self-Conscious Femme-Fatale' by Heather L. Braun (*WW* 14:iii[2007] 496–507) interrogates Coleridge's conservative approach to the gender politics of the new woman by exploring representations of the dread experienced by, rather than of, the femme fatale and suggesting that she becomes a figure of silence and social exclusion that Coleridge seeks to overcome.

The year 2007 also saw relatively little work on male poets of the *fin de siècle*. Mark Llewelyn's article, ' "Pagan Moore": Poetry, Painting and Passive Masculinity in George Moore's *Flowers of Passion* (1877) and *Pagan Poems*

(1881)' (*VP* 45:i[2007] 77–91), proposes that Moore's first collection of poems was formative of the poet's 'pagan' authorial identity and considers his representation of masculinity in crisis in poems that engage with and subvert masculine fantasies represented in the work of Swinburne, Rossetti, Manet, Degas and Renoir by problematizing masculine desire via the challenging gaze of the woman. Traugott Lawler's brief article, ' "Charade": A New Verse Note by Kipling from 1892' (*KJ* 81[2007]35–40), reports the discovery of a charade in verse by Kipling, one of a handful of brief signed verse epistles that the poet addressed to friends and acquaintances. 'Dowson's "Cynara", Stanza Three' by Stephen E. Tabanick (*Anglistik* 65:iii[2007] 160–2) draws attention to the grammatical and syntactic difficulty of the most famous lines of Dowson's poem, suggesting that they are a proto-stream-of-consciousness fragmentation, modelled on French Symbolist poetics and pre-empting modernist forms.

Publication on Gerard Manley Hopkins continues to thrive, with two major monographs on the poet appearing in 2006/7. The substantial body of this year's work on Hopkins is characterized by a recontextualization of a poet, and a number of critics do valuable work labouring against the common assumption that Hopkins is a law unto himself. *Hopkins's Poetics of Speech Sound: Sprung Rhythm, Lettering, Inscape* by James I. Wimsatt, missed last year, is a study of Hopkins's prose writings. By collecting together Hopkins's discussions of poetic theory in essays, letters and journals, Wimsatt elucidates and expands on the vexed question of the Hopkins poetic, achieving a holistic account out of an array of fragments and a variety of literary-theoretical contexts. The chapters tackle Hopkins's familiar, baffling terminology. Sprung rhythm is shown to offer an objectification of the natural rhythms of speech, a materialization of sound that is discussed in terms of Aristotle's analysis of rhetoric and brought into conversation with modern linguists such as Saussure and Kristeva. Their dialogic understanding of language, Wimsatt contends, speaks directly to Hopkins's belief in the inscape of sound. In a chapter on 'lettering' Wimsatt compares Hopkins's understanding of the phonic patterns of poetry in relation to poetic unity and in comparison to the poetry of T.S. Eliot, Wordsworth and Frost, while his discussion of inscape continues to stress the importance of Scotistic philosophy to Hopkins's metaphysics. Although Wimsatt employs examples from Hopkins's poetry to illustrate his argument at certain points, the poetry is not his central concern in this study. It goes against the grain to decentralize Hopkins's poetry in this way, but by characterizing Hopkins as a literary theorist, Wimsatt is successful in bringing new relevance to his work.

Gerard Manley Hopkins and the Victorian Visual World, by Catherine Phillips, is concerned with Hopkins's poetry only as part of a meticulous and lively study of Hopkins's experience of and engagement with Victorian visual art. Taking Hopkins's rich artistic inheritance as her starting point, Phillips addresses the visual worlds of his childhood, his life at university and his mature religious life, always with an eye on the developing technology and emergent professionalization of the art world in the nineteenth century. Phillips draws on a wide variety of sources, underlining the significance of visual culture for the Victorians in general as well as for Hopkins in particular. Hopkins's personal inheritance is the subject of the first chapter, which places

834 THE NINETEENTH CENTURY: THE VICTORIAN PERIOD

Hopkins's work as an artist and his contributions to the growing number of illustrated periodicals at the centre of a discussion of his wide network of family influences: brothers, sisters, aunts and uncles working in the fields of photography and lithography as well as painting and sketching. Chapter 2, which provides a detailed study of visual and verbal description in Hopkins's own sketchbooks and suggests the influence of Ruskin's *Elements of Drawing* on his work, and chapter 3, which considers the poet's appreciation of Gothic architecture, both emphasize the fascination with colour and pattern that has direct implications for Hopkins's poetry as well as demonstrating that the poet was also an artist of considerable talent. Chapters 4 and 5 deal with the professional art world in discussions of nineteenth-century art criticism and the illustrated periodical press. Phillips's account of the exhibitions that Hopkins attended and his debates with friends such as F.T. Palgrave about what he saw there show the extent of Hopkins's knowledge of and enthusiasm for the visual arts, and her contextualized close reading of *The Wreck of the Deutschland* demonstrates his engagement with contemporary print culture. Final chapters deal with the New Sculpture and the visualization of religious belief. Throughout, Hopkins is presented as an artist and poet who was unmistakably Victorian in his aesthetic concerns. This is an important, thorough book, and a significant contribution to Hopkins criticism.

Hopkins's eccentricity is still preserved, however, in articles that find it necessary to coin new terminology in order to get to the bottom of his poetry. One such article is Dennis Sobolev's 'Semantic Counterpoint and the Poetry of Gerard Manley Hopkins' (*VLC* 35:i[2007] 103–19), which proposes a new model of interpretation that refuses both the semantic unity of New Criticism and the dissemination and fragmentation of deconstructionists. Identifying counterpoint as a neglected concept in the work of Hopkins, Sobolev employs the term 'semantic counterpoint' to explore the tension between the intellectual and the limits placed on the intellect by the existential in 'Thou art indeed just, Lord' and *Wreck of the Deutschland*. In a similar vein, ' "Gliding": A Note on the Exquisite Delicacy of the Religious Glissade Motif in Hopkins's "The Windhover" ' by Nathan Cervo (*VN* 111[2007] 29), offers a Hopkinsian reading of 'The Windhover', tracing the development of the word 'glide' through the poem in the light of its Danish and Anglo-Saxon roots. 'Brooding over the "bent world": An Ecopoetics of Gerard Manley Hopkins' by Kim Won-Chung (*NCL* 11:i[2007] 59–81) is one of a handful of publications that explore Hopkins's work from a scientific angle, addressing the poet's scientific and theological concerns in order to make a case for the work's eco-critical credentials. 'Darwinism, Doxology, and Energy Physics: The New Sciences, the Poetry and Poetics of Gerard Manley Hopkins' by Marie Banfield (*VP* 45:ii[2007] 175–94) addresses Hopkins's struggles with and attraction to the new materialism of the nineteenth-century natural world and the challenge that his poetry presents to it. Making a good case for what she describes as his 'passive interest' in Darwinism (p. 178), she provides a useful recapitulation of recent literary-scientific readings of Hopkins, and a survey of the presence of scientific nature in his major poems, focusing on the materiality and energy of his own poetic language. Mary Ellen Bellanca's book, *Daybooks of Discovery: Nature Diaries in Britain, 1770–1870*, contains a chapter on the subject of Hopkins's Swiss travel journal and the 'poetics of natural history' (p. 200). This chapter has much in common with both Wimsatt's and Phillips's monographs, focusing as it does on Hopkins's prose descriptions of nature, which are at once a 'means of encounter' (p. 201) and its limitation. Bellanca's interest in Hopkins as nature diarist, like Phillips's and Wimsatt's respective interests in the poet as visual artist and literary theorist, further anchors Hopkins to his period, while remaining aware of his distinctiveness.

Hopkins's classicist credentials are explored in Frederic W. Schlatter's extensive essay, 'Hopkins and Virgil' (*HQ* 34:i–ii[2007] 17–53), which details Virgil's influence on the development of Hopkins's early poetic theory in a further attempt to make it more intelligible. Schlatter gives an account of Hopkins's early experience of classical translation and his use of Virgil's pantheon to evaluate classical and contemporary poets in the context of a wider discussion of Virgil's significance for the Victorians as a figure that represented Victorian literature's own view of itself as secondary. Hopkins's engagement with the language and literature of his period is the subject of an interesting article, 'Philological Nationalism: Bridges, Hopkins and the Society for Pure English' by Jude V. Nixon (*HQ* 34:iii–iv[2007] 65–78), which sheds light on Hopkins's involvement in a society set up by Robert Bridges to promote responsibility towards the English language and draws connections between the work of the society and Hopkins's interest in Anglo-Saxon philology. Interest in Hopkins as a religious poet remains keen. Aakanksha J. Virkar's article, 'Gerard Manley Hopkins and the Song of Songs' (*VP* 45:ii[2007] 195–207) focuses on the representation of the heart as fount and vessel of holy water in the Old Testament, which is reiterated throughout *Wreck of the Deutschland* and is employed by Hopkins to allude to baptism, configured as marriage to Christ. Joshua King's article, 'Hopkins' Affective Rhythm: Grace, Intention in Tension' (*VP* 45:ii[2007] 209–37), returns to the theme of sprung rhythm, arguing that it was the means by which Hopkins sought to offer the reader an affective experience of grace. In this case, Hopkins is read as anti-Darwinian in his employment of the incarnation of Christ as a model for the incarnation of the Spirit's energies in human language. The physicality of language is also the theme of Dennis Sobolev's Lacanian reading of Hopkins, 'The Dismemberment: Hopkins' Representations of the Body and the Ideas of Jacques Lacan' (*HQ* 34:iii–iv[2007] 79–101). Sobolev looks at the literal and metaphorical bodies that Hopkins's poetry bodies forth via Lacan's theories of fragmentary reality versus imaginary unity. Characterizing instances of bodily alienation and dissolution in Hopkins's poetry as fragmentation, Sobolev argues against a masochist reading of Hopkins and towards an appreciation of the authentic physical and psychological subjectivity of his work. In its discussion of directed energies, King's article has interesting implications for the theme of human will and Victorian poetry. A final essay, '"Meaning motion": Reclaiming the Dynamic Poetics of Hopkins' (*HQ* 34:i–ii[2007] 3–16), returns us to more well-trodden paths within the field in its discussion of the active performativity of the poetry, highlighting Hopkins's frequent use of the participle and arguing that inscape is more properly understood as a verb than a noun, in readings of the some of his best-known poems.

Andrew Radford's discussion of George Meredith's representations of the Demeter–Persephone myth, included as part of the chapter discussed above, is one of only two publications to address Meredith's work. The other is Nicholas A. Joukovsky's article, 'George Meredith's Early Verse: A New Manuscript in his First Wife's Hand' (*VP* 45:iii[2007] 257–62), which takes on the neglected area of Meredith's juvenilia: poems that he sought to distance himself from after the failure of his first marriage. The article uncovers some previously unpublished poems and fragments transcribed by his first wife, which it reproduces in full.

Work on Christina Rossetti dominated the field of Pre-Raphaelite studies in 2007. The emphasis remained on Rossetti as a Victorian woman poet, but questions of gender and poetic production were enriched and broadened by discussion of the poet's religious identity, which in turn highlighted the importance of gender to the growing debate surrounding Victorian poetry and Victorian religion. These concerns are at the heart of Dinah Roe's *Christina Rossetti's Faithful Imagination: The Devotional Poetry and Prose*, unavailable for review last year, which sets out to 'demonstrate the effects of religious reading on Rossetti's poetry and thought' (p. 2), reassessing the perceived incompatibility of Victorian ideas of femininity and theological study by placing new emphasis on Rossetti's later work and insisting that the devotional prose can be approached as an object of literary study. Roe's timely study makes a critical intervention into the feminist construction of Rossetti, seeking to resolve the conflicts of faith, gender and creativity that have been identified therein, in a study that views her, first and foremost, as an artist whose art is successful in its synthesis of a variety of secular and sacred influences. These influences are given generous coverage in Roe's study, which draws out the subtleties of Rossetti's religious poetic, making a strong case for the value of an exegetical reading of her work, in opposition to critics such as Jerome McGann and Germaine Greer, who have been influential in the lack of emphasis given to scriptural intertextuality in Rossetti scholarship up to this point. In early chapters that cover Rossetti's relationship with the Tractarian movement, her negotiation of Keatsian notions of melancholy and earthly mortality, and Dante's longing for Beatrice via the Christian doctrine of resurrection and expressions of spiritual longing, Roe's agile and detailed close readings suggest the network of cultural discourses that inform and are transformed by Rossetti's poetry. Questions of authorial responsibility are addressed in the second half of the book, which considers Rossetti's growing awareness of her audience and her continuing desire to reflect her own individual relationship to her faith, suggesting that she is both poet and preacher by exploring the intersections between the poetry and the prose of her later works. Throughout, Roe's engaging account offers us a poet of impressive and subtle intellect who was both self-assured and humble in her faith.

John Bunyan, a source of religious influence not considered by Roe, is the subject of Simon Humphries's article, 'Who Is the Alchemist in Christina Rossetti's "The Prince's Progress"?' (*ELH* 74[2007] 684–97). Humphries answers his own question by suggesting that the alchemist is 'a representation of false religion' (p. 688), a figure drawn from images of Jewishness in both the

Bible and Gothic literature. Reading the poem as an ironic recapitulation of *Pilgrim's Progress*, Humphries, like Roe, brings biblical, literary and popular sources to bear on Rossetti's poem and suggests a close relationship between literary and scriptural interpretation. In a second article, 'The Uncertainty of Goblin Market' (*VP* 45:iv[2007] 391–413), Humphries again emphasizes the importance of historicist theological approaches to Rossetti while at the same time emphasizing the non-Christian world that Laura and Lizzie inhabit. As such, Humphries argues, 'Goblin Market' is a poem that accommodates doctrinal uncertainty: the goblin fruit is both damning and redemptive because, as material of the fallen world, it can only be transformed through God's grace. The poem having received so much attention in 2006, it is perhaps unsurprising that only one other brief article about 'Goblin Market' was published in 2007. 'Subversive Ecology in Rossetti's "Goblin Market"' by Heidi Scott (*Anglistik* 65:iv[2007] 219–22) takes as its starting point the observation that, whereas the goblin men of the poem exhibit animal characteristics, the two sisters are consistently compared to plants. In light of this fact, new significance is given to Lizzie's consumption of the goblin fruit, which for Scott represents a reversal of the natural order. 'Grafted Warmth: Rossetti's "English May" and the Spiritual-Sensual Aesthetic' by Heather McAlpine (*Anglistik* 65:iii[2007] 151–4) returns to the theme of religion with a nice reading that invokes Isobel Armstrong's discussion of the Victorian double poem in order to suggest the tensions between paganism and Christian spirituality, the body and the soul, contained within the image of the hawthorn tree and the concept of grace, the two figures on which Rossetti's poem turns. Anthony H. Harrison's article, 'Christina Rossetti: Illness and Ideology' (*VP* 45:iv[2007] 415–27), offers a Marxist feminist account of Christina Rossetti and Victorian religion that contrasts sharply with the work of Roe and Humphries. Harrison approaches the subject of Rossetti's own physical and mental illness in the context of representations of the indulgence of sexual desire, often expressed as an illness or addiction causing malaise or death, in her poetry. By arguing that the poet was subject, in both her life and her poetry, to the ideologies of Victorian patriarchy and Puritan religion, Harrison represents Rossetti, the victim of both illness and ideology, as a poet markedly less robust than Roe's Christian intellectual, and his article provides a useful counter-argument to Roe, demonstrating that there is still room for debate concerning Rossetti's religious identity.

One final article on Christina Rossetti, 'Imagining *Ophelia* in Christina Rossetti's "Sleeping at Last"' (*VN* 111[2007] 8–9), by Mary Faraci, provides a new biographical interpretation of Rossetti's last poem, usually understood to be about Rossetti's own mortality. Instead, Faraci links the poem to Millais's painting of Ophelia and to his model for the painting, Elizabeth Siddal. Faraci's short article suggests links between Rossetti's poem and two poems by Siddal herself, and she is one of a couple of critics to address Siddal's work as part of the Pre-Raphaelite corpus. Elsewhere Laurence J. Starzyk, in 'Elizabeth Siddal and the "Soulless Self-Reflection of Man's Skill"' (*JPRAS* 16[2007] 8–26), makes a strong claim for Siddal's relevance to current trends in the field, while at the same time finding little artistic value in either her poetry or her paintings. Starzyk's study of ekphrasis in Siddal's work, which ranges from considerations of Shelley's Romantic doubt to comparisons with the ekphrastic art of Dante Gabriel Rossetti to the paintings of Magritte, concludes that Siddal's work, in its movement between image and text, finally reveals the inadequacy of both.

Ekphrasis was the subject of two articles on Dante Gabriel Rossetti in 2007. Carolyn F. Austin's thoughtful essay, 'Mastering the Ineffable: Dante Gabriel Rossetti's "The Vase of Life" and the Kantian Sublime' (*VP* 45:ii[2007] 159–73), offers a gendered reading of the Kantian notion of the sublime and its relation to time and space, which Austin applies, in a reading of Rossetti's 'The Vase of Life' and Keats's 'Ode on a Grecian Urn', to the relationship between poetry and visual art, arguing that ekphrastic art is that which asserts the subliming power of the temporal over the threatening infinity of the special. 'Double Transgenerity: Narrating Pictures in Poems' by Peter Hühn (*Anglistik* 18:ii[2007] 43–61) takes Rossetti's poem, 'For "Our Lady of the Rocks" by Leonardo Da Vinci' as the starting point for his wide-ranging discussion of the relationship between visual art, poetry and narrative, which takes in ekphrastic works by living poets such as Thom Gunn, Eavan Boland and Paul Muldoon. A discussion of D.G. Rossetti's painting of the kiss of Paolo and Francesca prefaces D.M.R. Bentley's article, '"La bocca mi baciò": The Love Kiss in the Works of Dante Gabriel Rossetti' (*JPRAS* 16[2007] 31–44), which revisits Robert Buchanan's attack on the Pre-Raphaelite school in his 1871 article 'The Fleshly School of Poetry'. Buchanan's article focuses its displeasure on Rossetti's poem, 'Nuptial Sleep', one of his 'House of Life' sonnets, and Bentley locates the cause of this displeasure in the poem's representation of the erotic kiss. Bentley makes a good case for Rossetti's interest in this trope, tracing it through its multiple representations in his poetry and its erasure from the poet's later, more respectable, collections. Andrew M. Stauffer's article, 'Dante Rossetti's "The Burden of Nineveh": Further Excavations' (*JPRAS* 16[2007] 45–59), points towards the implications of digital archives for scholarship in the field. Stauffer's article corrects his earlier interpretation of the poem using new material made available by Jerome McGann's online Rossetti Archive, as well as the new edition of the Rossetti correspondence, to reassess its textual history.

The final member of the Pre-Raphaelite circle to be addressed in 2007 is William Morris, whose poetry receives attention in two articles. '"Honourable and noble aventures": Courtly and Chivalric Idealism in Morris's Froissartian Poems' by Richard Frith (*JWMS* 17:iii[2007] 13–29) is a persuasive article that seeks to recover the idealism of Morris's poetry, most often characterized as starkly realist. Frith reads Morris's Froissartian poems in the context of earliest prose romances, Froissart's chronicles and the visual art of Rossetti and Burne-Jones in order to draw out Morris's belief in the idealism and romance of death in battle and the honour of self-sacrifice which, Frith argues, is not compromised by Morris's brutal representations of the reality of the battlefield. Todd O. Williams's article, 'Teaching Morris's Early Dream Poems through the Three Registers' (*JWMS* 17:ii[2007] 99–114), part of a special issue on teaching Morris, describes his use of Lacan's three registers as a method of teaching poems that 'confound linguistic meaning' (p. 100). Williams's method might be described as ekphrasis in practice. Inspired by Dante Gabriel Rossetti's dictum that art is best criticized with art, it requires students to respond imaginatively to the non-linguistic elements of Morris's poetry.

Swinburne received very little attention in 2007 and is the subject of only two brief articles. 'Will Drew and Phil Crewe and Frank Fane: A Swinburne Enigma' (*BC* 56:i[2007] 31–3), by Terry L. Meyers, uncovers a literary joke that was the work of Cecil Y. Lang and John S. Mayfield, who produced a forgery of Swinburne in the 1960s. Rodney Stenning Edgecombe's article, 'Swinburne's *Tristram of Lyonesse* and Woolf's *To the Lighthouse*' (*Anglistik* 66:i[2007] 11–15), considers a genuine Swinburne legacy in his discussion of Virginia Woolf as a reader of Swinburne. He argues that the famous 'Time Passes' section of *To the Lighthouse* is inspired by Swinburne's account of the burial of Tristram, and that both Victorian poet and modernist author subvert the topos of natural decay that provides consolation within pastoral elegy through descriptions of vast and random geological forces, the patterns of which are beyond human comprehension.

Kathryn Ledbetter's *Tennyson and Victorian Periodicals: Commodities in Context* was the only single-author study of Tennyson to be published in 2007. Claiming Tennyson as 'the first media poet', Ledbetter identifies Tennyson's relationship with the nineteenth-century periodical press as an important and neglected area of Tennyson scholarship. With a focus on poems by Tennyson that were published, with or without the poet's permission, in Victorian journals, gift books and newspapers on both sides of the Atlantic, Ledbetter gives new significance to some of his minor poems. Her book is the first cultural materialist study of Tennyson to be published since Alan Sinfield's 1985 study of the poet, the first to deal in detail with his relationship with his publishers since June Steffensen Hagen's *Tennyson and his Publishers* [1979], and the first rigorous assessment of Tennyson's laureate verse since Valerie Pitt's *Tennyson, Laureate* [1963]. Her study offers a careful working through of the intricacies of Tennyson's dealings with the periodical press, and with nineteenth-century copyright law in particular, and offers a convincing portrait of Tennyson as a consumer and producer of a variety of print media. Ledbetter is interested in the poetry as cultural artefact, the aesthetic value of which is irrelevant, and so her chapters deal with neither Tennyson's best nor his best-known poems. It is a book that seeks to put Tennyson in his place, both as cultural icon and therefore also as a writer absolutely subject to the cultural ideology of his period. According to Ledbetter, Tennyson's poems do not speak for themselves, but are part of a Bakhtinian heteroglossia, made up of his own voice and those of editors, illustrators and journalists. The book spans Tennyson's career. Its first chapters discuss his early contributions to periodicals and deal with the tension between Tennyson's famous disavowal of gift-book culture and the role the gift book played in the poet's professional success. Central chapters address Tennyson's political poetry and his role as laureate, and a final chapter explores his reception in America, providing a helpful comparison of British and American publishing practices and demonstrating the importance of periodical publications to American cultural identity, an identity that was negotiated, in part, through an appropriation of Tennyson's poetry. The book contains rich contextual detail throughout, including appendices that summarize Tennyson's periodical publications in both Britain and America, and its argument stands in interesting opposition to McSweeney's aestheticist approach (discussed above).

Further work on Tennyson and print culture is carried out by Lorraine Janzen Kooistra's article, 'Poetry in the Victorian Marketplace: The Illustrated *Princess* as Christmas Gift Book' (*VP* 45:i[2007] 49–76), which offers an insightful account of the significance of Maclise's illustrations to a reading of the poem. The article, which takes Tennyson's well-known dislike of illustrated versions of his own poems as its context, ably demonstrates how the drawings pre-empt the reader's interpretation and wrest authority from the poet. A second article on Tennyson's first published narrative poem, 'Nursery Poetics: An Examination of Lyric Representations of the Child in Tennyson's *The Princess*' by Anna Barton (*VLC* 35:ii[2007] 489–500), argues for the significance of 'The Losing of the Child' (a lyric omitted from published versions of *The Princess*) to an understanding of the poem's representation of childhood, and suggests lyricism itself as an embodiment of childlike inarticulacy. Lyricism is also the subject of John Hughes's article, '"Hang there like fruit, my soul": Tennyson's Feminine Imaginings' (*VP* 45:ii[2007] 95–115), which finds new significance in the scene from *Cymbeline* that Tennyson held open on his death-bed. Hughes's thoughtful and engaging reading aims to overcome what he sees as problematic categories of gender and sexuality and sheds new light on questions of gender and the lyric, suggesting that Tennyson's lyrics enabled the poet to divest himself of the disguise of masculine selfhood. A second article by Barton, 'Lyrical and Responsible Names in Tennyson's *Maud*' (*TRB* 9:i[2007] 43–59), again addresses the relationship between the lyric and Tennyson's longer poems, this time as part of a discussion of Tennyson's attitude to anonymity and signature. Reading *Maud* in the context of its anonymous attackers in the periodical press, Barton suggests that the ravings of the poem's anti-hero constitute an anonymous poetic from which he can only be rescued by resolving to make his name.

The theme of Tennyson and nationhood is addressed in two very different articles. '"Akbar's Dream": Moghul Toleration and English/British Orientalism' (*MP* 104:iii[2007] 379–411), by Paul Stevens and Rahul Sapra, is a difficult but rewarding postcolonial critique of Akbar's dream, read as a trope of the Victorian imperial dream of India. Tennyson's description of the dream is placed in the context of seventeenth-century historical representations of Akbar's empire in order to draw out the relationship between ideas of religious toleration and transculturation. The article's discussion of the impact of Indian religion on late eighteenth-century orientalists and its threat to history's emergent hegemony contributes to wider debates about Eurocentricity and the production of a history of modernity. Ayse Celikkol's article, 'Dionysian Music, Patriotic Sentiment and Tennyson's *Idylls of the King*' (*VP* 45:iii[2007] 239–56), employs Victorian ideas about the place of music in society, both as a civilizing and an uncivilized influence, to foreground a discussion of music in the *Idylls*, arguing that, in Tennyson's

Camelot, spontaneous, passionate music, in the Dionysian tradition, is redeployed as an expression of patriotism, while still maintaining the power to subvert. As Celikkol suggests, her reading has interesting implications for Tennyson's own role as laureate and the relationship between his laureate and non-laureate verse. Camelot is again read as a figure for Victorian Britain in Sally Hinton's article, 'The Pursuit of Wandering Fires: Religious Controversy and "The Holy Grail"' (*TRB* 9:i[2007] 3–21), which reads the Grail Quest as a quest for a false idol in which Percivale is represented as a High Church fop who fails to understand or participate in the broad church Anglicanism represented by Arthur's Camelot.

Tennyson is discussed alongside Byron, Dickens and Joyce in Matthew Bevis's impressive multi-author study, *The Art of Eloquence*, which explores the developing relationship between literature and political speech during the long nineteenth century (also discussed in Chapter XII). Bevis gives a nuanced account of Tennyson's engagement with the public voices that informed his work. He questions the distinction drawn by Mill between poetry and eloquence that is reiterated in Arthur Hallam's early review of Tennyson, and demonstrates that Tennyson was part of a generation of poets increasingly aware of the presence of a listener. His wide-ranging discussion traces the multi-vocal appeal of Tennyson's early poetry, his eloquent representation of Hallam as an aspiring orator, the tension between 'outspoken eloquence' and 'unspoken limitations' (p. 172) in his dramatic monologues, the negotiation between the individual and the civic voice in *Maud* and the oratory of Arthur in the *Idylls*.

'Tennyson and Creation' by Dennis R. Dean (*TRB* 9:i[2007] 22–41) is the only article on Tennyson and the natural sciences to be published in 2007. The article is an addendum to his 1985 monograph, *Tennyson and Geology*, following the subsequent publication of the second and third volumes of Tennyson's letters, and lists geological references made in Tennyson's later letters. Its focus is a letter from Tennyson to naturalist and poet Cuthbert Collingwood, in which Tennyson expresses interest in Collingwood's *A Vision of Creation*, a poem which attempts to reconcile scientific and scriptural creation narratives. Dean draws attention to Collingwood's poem as important for the study of literature and science and suggests its influence on some of Tennyson's later poems. John Batchelor's '"Keep nothing sacred": Tennyson and Biography' (*TRB* 9:i[2007] 60–76) is a second article in anticipation of Batchelor's forthcoming biography of the poet, which again argues the case for a biographical understanding of the poems and reflects on the anxiety of biographical inheritance when dealing with a poet whose life has been written and rewritten over the course of more than a century. Finally, 'Appreciating Memorialization: *In Memoriam A.H.H.*' (*TRB* 9:i[2007] 77–95), by Jane Wright, is a sensitive reading of Tennyson's early sonnet 'As when with downcast eyes' and *In Memoriam* which charts the differences between a poem that memorializes a living friend and one that commemorates the same friend after death, carefully tracing the metaphors and similes from sonnet to elegy and demonstrating patterns of departure and return.

4. Drama

Recent scholarly work in the field of Victorian drama demonstrates a fascination with the behaviors and critical viewing practices of spectators during theatrical performances. Scholars also explored the economic context of Victorian theatre, examining the role of economically marginalized members of the theatrical community as well as the role of risk and competition within the theatre industry. The central importance of melodrama within Victorian theatrical culture was of particular interest to critics this year, as was the study of children's involvement in the theatre as readers and performers. This year also saw the publication of essays illuminating the role of theatre and performance in the works of major literary figures: John Ruskin, Robert Browning, Matthew Arnold and Wilkie Collins.

The publication of Tracy Davis's and Peter Holland's collection of essays, *The Performing Century: Nineteenth-Century Theatre's History*, was one of the highlights of this year's work in Victorian drama. The volume is divided into three sections: 'Performance Occasions', which includes essays by Jim Davis, Tracy Davis, Emily Allen and Thomas Postlewait; 'Performance Anxieties', which includes essays by Heidi Holder, Jane Moody and Mark Phelan; and 'Repertoires', which includes essays by Jeffrey Cox, Gilli Bush-Bailey, Edward Ziter, Catherine Burroughs, Richard Schoch and Jacky Bratton. These essays explore a variety of performers, performance venues and audiences that have previously been neglected in histories of nineteenth-century theatre. For example, Jim Davis, in his essay 'Boxing Day' (pp. 3–31), explores the important role of Boxing Day pantomimes in the Victorian theatrical calendar. In particular, he examines press coverage of the unruly audiences that attended these post-Christmas spectacles. He concludes that 'far from merely enabling a saturnalian inversion of everyday life, the Boxing Day performances of the nineteenth-century British pantomime were repeatedly the site for a celebration of disorder, self-regulation and power by a crowd, which, however out of control it might seem, was far more in control than the press accounts imply' (p. 30).

Emily Allen's 'Communal Performances: Royal Ritual, Revolution and National Acts', also published in *The Performing Century* (pp. 60–79), examines press coverage of the 1871 wedding of Princess Louise, a state event celebrated as a series of public spectacles. The image of the adoring British crowd stood in marked contrast to press coverage of the French civil war, where mobs were depicted as being both chaotic and barbarous. These alternative representations of public behaviour in the popular press 'provided a tutorial in aggregate identity, a tutorial that continued in other guises as these national events were merchandized to a public hungry both for collective experience and the experience of collecting' (p. 72). By collecting mementos commemorating the royal marriage and the destruction of Paris, the British public 'created its own form of exclusive populism, one that discriminated itself from the disastrous populism of France' (p. 76). In this way, they participated in mass rituals that enabled them to join in the broader project of imagining British nationhood.

Jennifer Hall-Witt's *Fashionable Acts: Opera and Elite Culture in London, 1780–1880* similarly addresses the important role of British audiences in shaping theatrical performance. She does so by examining the history of public reception of the opera, particularly the transformation of audience behaviour from the Georgian to the Victorian periods. In the 1780s the opera house was a site of privilege and aristocratic patronage; however, by the 1880s it was a venue dominated by the middle classes. The aristocratic audiences of the earlier period viewed themselves as active participants in the onstage spectacle, jeering, cheering, ogling and otherwise taking part in performative spectatorship. In the later period, audiences were more likely to listen silently to operatic productions, acting as a decorous example to other members of the assembly. This led to greater veneration of the operatic text and score as well as the canonization of composers and their work. The increased appreciation for opera as high art was also facilitated by critical reviewing practices, which influenced the behaviour of spectators and shaped conceptions of the new 'elite' audience for operatic performance. Hall-Witt concludes the volume with useful appendices listing the prices of opera tickets and subscriptions from 1780 to 1880.

Musical theatre is also the focus of David Haldane Lawrence's essay, '"Such a humble branch of our art": The Victorian Theatre Orchestra' (*TN* 61:i[2007] 40–55). In this study, Lawrence explores the vital yet underappreciated role of theatre musicians in a wide range of theatrical productions during the Victorian era, including opera, melodrama and West End plays. He provides background on the hardships faced by theatre musicians, who often endured deplorable working conditions. They were not only poorly paid but were often at the mercy of hostile actors, directors and audiences. The location of musicians beneath the stage or in an orchestra pit symbolized their low status within the theatrical hierarchy. Yet theatre musicians were crucial to the success of the productions they accompanied. For example, when accompanying melodrama, musicians were responsible for cueing the entrances and exits of actors from the stage. Even in the more respectable theatres, such as Henry Irving's Lyceum, rank-and-file musicians were often subject to long hours and low pay. Lawrence speculates that this hostility may have been caused by cultural xenophobia since many of the musicians were foreign-born. He also suggests that theatre-goers may have believed that the musical score was less important than the written text in theatrical performances.

The harsh economic realities faced by those involved in the Victorian theatre industry are also the subject of two essays published in Francis O'Gorman's collection of essays, *Victorian Literature and Finance*. Jane Moody's 'The Drama of Capital: Risk, Belief, and Liability on the Victorian Stage' (pp. 91–109) demonstrates how nineteenth-century plays made implicit and explicit references to capitalism: financial investment, liability, risk and speculation. Focusing on several plays, including George Henry Lewes's *The Game of Speculation* [1851], Moody draws attention to affinities between the worlds of theatre and capital. The theatre and the capitalist economy, she notes, both rely upon 'belief, confidence, faith, and trust' and share a concern with the ways in which economic relationships succeed and fail (p. 94). Particularly fascinating is Moody's examination of the ways in which sexual narratives are entwined with stories of financial anxiety and risk. Also published in *Victorian Literature and Finance*, Catherine Seville's essay, 'Edward Bulwer Lytton Dreams of Copyright: "It might make me a rich man"' (pp. 55–72), examines Lytton's efforts towards securing national and international authorial copyright protection for British writers, including playwrights. These efforts were directly related to Lytton's ambivalent relationship to the literary marketplace. Lytton desired maximum profit from his literary undertakings, yet, as suggested in his comedy *Money* [1840], he was at the same time repelled by the idea of greed and mass-market popularity.

The economic context of Victorian drama is further illuminated by Ignacio Ramos Gay in his essay, 'Matthew Arnold on Victorian Theatre' (*NCP* 34:i–ii[2007] 59–87). Gay examines the contradictory role of French theatre in British culture during the last quarter of the nineteenth century. French plays and actors were wildly popular, their success eclipsing the accomplishments of British theatre companies during the same time period. Yet many critics expressed anxiety about the French cultural invasion, which motivated British production companies to compete by emphasizing profit over quality. The result, many critics believed, was a degraded British theatre. Unlike many of his fellow critics, Arnold saw the success of French theatre as an opportunity to revitalize the dramatic arts. In his essay, 'The French Play in London' [1879], Arnold praised the Comédie-Française, a French performance company that had taken London by storm in the 1870s. Arnold called for the establishment of a similar British national theatre company that would revitalize drama as public art addressed to all classes of society. Public funding for a national theatre would enable the company to place educational and aesthetic concerns above monetary necessity, thus ensuring the production of high-quality contemporary and classic plays. Gay concludes by noting that Arnold's vision of a national theatre anticipated the development of the Royal Shakespeare Company and the National Theatre.

The important role of theatre criticism in Victorian intellectual history is similarly addressed in Sharon Aronofsky Weltman's *Performing the Victorian: John Ruskin and Identity in Theater, Science, and Education*. Weltman examines the relationship between Ruskin's work as a theatre critic and his own conflicted sense of identity as performance. Ruskin's writing about contemporary theatre reveals his fascination with the fluidity of the self, especially where issues of gender and sexuality are concerned. Indeed, Ruskin imagines an 'ever-changing fluid self, one that always has the potential to crystallize through performance of an action, then to melt back again' (p. 8). His shifting, contradictory view of identity carries over into his scientific and educational writings, which meditate on notions of indeterminacy and change. Ruskin thus offers 'twenty-first-century readers a radical take on the instability of epistemological and ontological categories as he grapples with his own anxiety about how they shift' (p. 115).

Thomas Crochunis's 'Literary Homosociality and the Political Science of the Actor's Closet' (*VS* 49[2007] 258–67) also investigates the link between Victorian theatricality and masculinity. Crochunis examines the tense exchange between William Macready and Robert Browning prompted by the creation and 1843 staging of Browning's *A Blot in the 'Scutcheon*. From the time that Macready first received a draft of the play in 1841 there was tension between the two artists that led to mutual slights and insults, including Macready's unwillingness to read the script aloud to his production company and Browning's decision not to cast Macready as the lead actor in the play. These mutual hostilities are reflected in the content of the play itself, which highlights masculine insecurities and conflicts in homosocial relationships. As Crochunis puts it, the 'history of dramatic writing and literary acting is, in part, marked by moments such as these, when relationships, institutions, and sociability crack under the strain of opposing purposes and stylistic commitments' (p. 266).

Gender issues in the production and reception of Victorian theatre are also the subject of two essays published in *Shakespeare and Childhood* edited by Kate Chedgzoy, Susanne Greenhalgh and Robert Shaughnessy. Kathryn Prince's 'Shakespeare in the Victorian Children's Periodicals' (pp. 153–68) explores the ways in which boys' and girls' periodicals appropriated Shakespeare and contributed to the formation of English national identity during the Victorian period. Inevitably, these adaptations were focused on reinforcing gender-specific virtues. In periodicals such as the *Boys' Own Paper* and *Boys of England*, Shakespeare is depicted as the epitome of the British self-made man. These periodicals also included illustrations and scripts that could be used by boys to stage their own productions of Shakespeare's plays. Girls' periodicals also participated in the widespread veneration of Shakespeare as an exemplary moralist. Periodicals such as the *Girls' Own Paper* depicted Shakespearian heroines as models of moral behaviour and feminine virtue. Other periodicals for girls, such as *Atalanta*, encouraged a more intellectually engaged response from young readers.

Pascale Aebischer's essay, 'Growing Up with Shakespeare: The Terry Family Memoirs', also published in *Shakespeare and Childhood* (pp. 169–83), examines Ellen Terry's account of her early exposure to Shakespeare in her 1908 memoir *The Story of My Life*. The memoir demonstrates how Terry devoted herself to reading and performing Shakespeare during her formative years as an actress. When her autobiography turns to a discussion of her disastrous romantic relationships with George Watts and Edward Godwin, Shakespearian narratives become subtext, informing her interpretation of these early traumas. Through indirect references to Ophelia, she signals her refusal to assume the role of the fallen woman, instead asserting her own independence as a woman and artist. Later her son, Gordon Craig, also referenced *Hamlet* as a way of describing his difficult relationship with his mother. His memoirs depict Terry as a Gertrude figure who abandons her husband and son, instead focusing on her own ambitions. Such personalized adaptations of *Hamlet* in memoir led to a more 'intellectualized, problematic Shakespeare . . . that has predominated in the twentieth century' (p. 181).

An essay recently published in *New Theatre Quarterly* also illuminates the history of childhood and the Victorian theatre. In 'Locating Never Land: *Peter Pan* and Parlour Games' (*NTQ* 23:iv[2007] 393–402), Anne Varty explores the ways in which J.M. Barrie's 1904 play alludes to Victorian children's games, including kite-flying, play-acting, shadow pantomimes and blind man's buff.

In the process, she draws attention to the ways in which the play emphasizes the playful sense of time and myth-making associated with children's games, a fascination with children's culture that lends the play a sense of 'structural and ideological cohesion' (p. 393). These games thus evoked the 'Victorian notion of the "children's hour"', which 'facilitated an easy rapport between the play and its early audiences' (p. 402). Another article published in *New Theatre Quarterly* explores the racial context of *Peter Pan*. In '*Peter Pan* and the White Imperial Imaginary' (*NTQ* 23:iv[2007] 387–92), Mary Brewer examines the play's treatment of racial difference, arguing that it relies upon late Victorian discourse on otherness as a way of reinforcing white patriarchal cultural authority.

The topic of racial difference is also the subject of Hazel Waters's *Racism on the Victorian Stage: Representation of Slavery and the Black Character*. Focusing primarily on representations of race in British theatre in the first half of the nineteenth century, Waters illuminates the history of racial stereotyping from a variety of illuminating perspectives. For example, she includes a chapter on Ira Aldridge, a black actor who performed on the British stage from the 1820s to the 1860s. Press reaction to Aldridge's performances was generally hostile, but he nevertheless was able to extend his repertoire beyond stock roles and thus undermined 'ingrained notions of black inferiority' (p. 89). However, with the rising influence of American 'Jim Crow' comedy on British theatrical culture came a corresponding proliferation of racial stereotypes in blackface minstrelsy and racist comedy routines popularized by comic actors T.D. Rice and Charles Matthews. Waters also explores the mania surrounding the adaptations of Harriet Beecher Stowe's *Uncle Tom's Cabin* that were staged in London beginning in the 1850s. Far from representing an advancement from the racist theatre of earlier decades, *Uncle Tom* plays 'validated the status of the black as a comic, even grotesque figure or, at best, as a nonentity, from whom all threat had gone' (p. 177).

Victorian melodrama was the subject of a number of other fascinating studies this year. Ankhi Mukherjee's *Aesthetic Hysteria: The Great Neurosis in Victorian Melodrama and Contemporary Fiction* traces the role of hysterical subjectivity and excess in several Victorian melodramas, including *Lady Audley's Secret* [1863], the *Bells* [1871] and Arthur Wing Pinero's *The Second Mrs. Tanqueray* [1893]. Through an investigation of these and other texts, Mukherjee argues that 'Victorian melodrama teems with subjectivities trapped in the discontinuity between the imaginary and the real, mad women and sometimes men suffering from unfixable desires or living out traumas' (p. xiii). With the production of *The Second Mrs. Tanqueray* hysteria was not only figured in 'mute, material signifiers' but in a 'tremendous range of mental states' (p. 42).

In his book *The Wonderful and Surprising History of Sweeney Todd: The Life and Times of an Urban Legend*, Robert Mack also addresses the importance of melodrama as a dramatic form during the nineteenth century. As part of his wide-ranging study, Mack includes a chapter on theatrical adaptations of the Sweeney Todd narrative, which was first published in Edward Lloyd's *The People's Periodical and Family Library* in 1846–7. Mack includes extensive discussion of the first of these adaptations,

George Dibdin Pitt's *The String of Pearls; or, the Fiend of Fleet Street*, which was first performed at the Britannia Theatre, Hoxton, in March 1847. Because the venue was considered less than respectable, Victorian critics paid little attention to Pitt's production, which nevertheless 'flourished in innumerable and constantly changing "versions" for many years' (p. 212). There is little documentation of these early productions; however, Thomas W. Erle fortunately recorded his impressions of the play in his 1880 memoir, *Letters from a Theatrical Scene-Painter*, thus providing a valuable, if largely disdainful, account of the Britannia's production. Mack makes references to other versions of the play, including Frederick Hazleton's *Sweeney Todd the Barber of Fleet Street; or, the String of Pearls*, which premiered at the Old Bower Saloon, Lambeth, in 1865. Mack concludes the volume with a timeline tracing the various theatrical and other adaptations of the Sweeney Todd legend during the nineteenth and twentieth centuries.

Another sensationalist hero of melodrama was the Tichborne Claimant: an Australian butcher who claimed to be English aristocrat Sir Richard Tichborne. In his study of the case, *The Tichborne Claimant: A Victorian Sensation*, Rohan McWilliam provides detailed analysis of the two high-profile trials resulting from the case, including the public's reaction to the claimant's conduct. During the trials, the Tichborne Claimant became the subject of a variety of pantomime and musical theatre productions, appearing alternately as a 'victim of injustice, a villain and an opportunity for vulgarity' (p. 212). The Claimant was also the subject of a variety of popular songs, including many broadside ballads. In addition, several melodramas inspired by the case appeared on the London stage, including *The Two Mothers* [1877] and *The Lost Heir and the Wreck of the Bella* [1872]. Indeed, coverage of the Tichborne case in the press relied on melodramatic conventions—including the use of stock characters, plot devices and dramatic dialogue in newspaper accounts of the trials. 'Ultimately', McWilliam concludes, 'the Tichborne case was melodramatic in that it was a form of street theatre' (p. 269). As working-class crowds came to the defence of the Claimant, they imagined themselves 'locked in combat with authority and in terms derived from melodrama' (p. 270).

Two recent essays published in Andrew Mangham's *Wilkie Collins: Interdisciplinary Essays* (discussed above) explore Collins's uneasy relationship to Victorian melodrama as a genre. In his essay ' "Twin Sisters" and "Theatrical Thieves": Wilkie Collins and the Dramatic Adaptation of *The Moonstone*' (pp. 208–21), Richard Pearson argues for more serious scholarly attention to be paid to Collins's work as a dramatist, a career which extended over four decades. Although Collins was very successful as a playwright, he nevertheless felt an anxiety of authorship as he contemplated his own 'interventions in an illegitimate area of dubious respectability' (p. 211). These anxieties haunted his adaptation of *The Moonstone*, which premiered at the Olympic theatre in 1877. Pearson highlights the changes that Collins made to the fictional narrative when adapting it to a theatrical context, noting its 'softening' of the novel's sensational content, converting it to 'realist drawing room drama' (pp. 217, 218). These changes were in part motivated by Collins's concern for his own reputation as a novelist, which might have been compromised by a more sensationalized production.

Collins's 1871 theatrical adaptation of *The Woman in White* also down-played the sensational content of its fictional source. In her essay 'Sensation Drama? Collins's Stage Adaptation of *The Woman in White*' (in Mangham, ed., pp. 222–36), Janice Norwood demonstrates how Collins downplayed the most shocking scenes in the novel, going so far as to eliminate the first meeting between Walter Hartright and the Woman in White from the play script. Norwood points out that the toned-down content was reflected in the illustrations of 'contemplative' or 'static' scenes from the play that were published in periodicals such as the *Graphic* and the *Illustrated London News* (p. 228). As Norwood points out, Collins's 'contemplative' adaptation of *The Woman in White* is difficult to place within the sensation drama genre. Instead, it anticipates the psychological drama that would soon dominate British theatre.

5. Periodicals and Publishing History

This year saw the publication of hefty tomes covering national book histories. Of note were Ulrike Stark's study of the Naval Kishore Press, an Indian-based publishing giant whose nineteenth-century origins owed a great deal to its links to British colonial authorities. In *An Empire of Books: The Naval Kishore Press and the Diffusion of the Printed Word in Colonial India*, Stark delves comprehensively into fifty years of this Lucknow-based enterprise, started in 1858 by Naval Kishore. For the next forty years, the Naval Kishore Press would dominate printing in the Indian subcontinent, publishing an estimated 5,000 titles in Hindi, Urdu, Persian and Sanskrit languages covering literary, prose, religious and educational subjects, and taking on coveted government contracts for educational, legal and general texts. Naval Kishore also diversified the press's activities to include the editing and production of weekly and daily newspapers and monthly literary journals, started a paper mill to ensure a reliable supply of raw material and set up distribution networks across the Northwest and Oudh provinces to reach both an urban and a rural readership. Ulrike Stark tells in exhaustive detail the story of Naval Kishore's rise to print prominence as a means of demonstrating the manner in which indigenous Indian enterprises such as the Naval Kishore Press appropriated and adapted Western technology to service and foster local needs. It is an important story, and Stark does full justice to the subject, despite the lack of extant publishing archive material. Stark reminds us through her detailed and well-documented study of the press's many activities that a holistic approach to publishing history is needed to account for the industry's impact in both social and economic terms.

Such holistic approaches mark two other volumes dealing with national book history, Bill Bell's edited volume *The Edinburgh History of the Book in Scotland: Ambition and Industry 1800–1880*, and David Finkelstein and Alistair McCleery's *The Edinburgh History of the Book in Scotland: Professionalism and Diversity, 1880–2000*. These linked volumes, the final two of a projected four-part series, track the evolution of the Scottish book trade's dominance in the wake of the Industrial Revolution, its expansion outwards into all corners of the English-speaking world through publication and promotion of literary, educational, religious, medical, cartographic and legal texts, among many others, and the inevitable challenges that industry and print faced in the twentieth century. The two volumes contextualize the form and function of books and print in economic, social and cultural terms, following models of interdisciplinary analysis now becoming familiar to those engaged in similar national studies.

Further general insights into transnational book history are collected in Simon Eliot, Andrew Nash and Ian Willison's edited essay collection *Literary Cultures and the Material Book*. The contributions emanate from a conference on the subject of international book history held in London in 2004, and draw in topics as diverse as sixteenth-century Japanese print culture, pre-colonial Indian writing and oral performance and the form in which old print centres such as Paris and London affected the shaping of textual transmission and literary canon formation in Australia, Quebec and South Africa. In 'Towards a History of the Book and Literary Culture in Africa' (pp. 121–32) Isobel Hofmeyr presents a compelling case for contemplating South African book and print culture history as a process of absorption of text technology into existing African intellectual traditions and oral transmission; thus the spreading of Protestant evangelical and Bible texts across South Africa in the nineteenth century incorporated and interpreted visual imagery drawn from African contexts while relying heavily on technology and printing techniques pioneered and imported from Britain and elsewhere. A study of South African national book history cannot therefore be undertaken, she notes astutely, without considering transnational dimensions. John Barnes makes a similar point in his piece exploring the links between Australian literary pioneers at the start of the twentieth century and the Australian and British publishers who published and recirculated their works throughout Australia, focusing on the experiences of five writers: 'Steele Rudd' (A.H. Davis), 'Tom Collins' (Joseph Furphy), Henry Lawson, Miles Franklin and Barbara Baynton. Equally thoughtful pieces on the national and transnational shaping of nineteenth- and early twentieth-century bibliographical traditions and the study of the book as material artefact feature in Richard Landon's '"The elixir of life": Richard Garnett, the British Museum Library and Literary London' (pp. 343–54) and Stephen Bury's 'The Tradition of A.W. Pollard and the World of Literary Scholarship' (pp. 355–66).

Finally, the same volume has a short but telling piece by Michael Winship on the transnational and multi-media dimensions to the nineteenth-century reception of Harriet Beecher Stowe's *Uncle Tom's Cabin*: 'In the Four Quarters of the Globe, who Reads an American Book?' (pp. 367–78). Its success as a novel was exponentially increased by its recirculation as a Christmas illustrated edition, as song sheet, poem, play, burlesque, melodrama, puzzle, game, postcard, ephemeral knick-knacks and eventually as a silent short film in 1903. The history of its production, consumption and reception is also told in Claire Parfait's extensively researched monograph *The Publishing History of Uncle Tom's Cabin, 1852–2002*. Parfait draws on a multitude of sources to demonstrate eruditely how this key nineteenth-century American text was exported and then recirculated and re-presented to succeeding generations of readers in the US and elsewhere. Its value and use shift as issues such as copyright concerns, production activity and cultural assessments affect its presentation and reception: yet another good example of an iconic text contextualized within transnational print culture history.

How interdisciplinarity can inform more focused enquiries is apparent in James Raven's finely balanced and astute study *The Business of Books: Booksellers and the English Book Trade*. Raven's work is more of a synthesis history, guiding us through the revolution in print undergone in the capital of British book production from the mid-fifteenth to the mid-nineteenth centuries. But this is a synthesis benefiting from new research in such areas as economic history and cultural geography. Particularly telling is Raven's use of material drawn from projects mapping the changing geography of book trade activity in London from the fifteenth century onwards, demonstrating how remarkably continuous key areas remained central to London print culture dissemination from an early period in its history. Raven also dedicates time to such subjects as advertising, the rise of the British consumer society and its effect on book production, and the technological innovations that powered London's dominance in the book trade both at home and abroad.

Books on the Move: Tracking Copies through Collections and the Book Trade, edited by Robin Myers, Michael Harris and Giles Mandelbrote, looks at a different aspect of print culture, namely the history of book-collecting. Covering several hundred years of book-collecting activity, the case studies in this volume draw on an inventive range of research techniques to bring their subjects to light, ranging from physical inspections of volumes in arcane libraries through to searches of printed catalogues, auction records and correspondence files. Of nineteenth-century interest is Pierre Delsaerdt's piece, 'Bibliophily and Public–Private Partnership: The Library of Gustave van Havre (1817–92) and its Afterlife in Antwerp Libraries' (pp. 133–52). The case study is an exemplary piece that draws attention to the shift from private book collections to well-funded public institutions and repositories that occurred across Europe as the nineteenth century drew to a close, with in this case a significant national Belgian book collection saved through the timely intervention of civic-minded patrons.

Works that cross over disciplinary boundaries significantly mark out this year's offerings in publishing and periodical studies. A case in point is Gerry Beegan's *The Mass Image: A Social History of Photomechanical Reproduction in Victorian London*. This is an excellent, in-depth yet broad-ranging study of the way changes in illustration and image reproduction affected the production of mass-media journals in London and environs over the nineteenth century. Though Beegan focuses on illustration in the 1890s, he also ranges widely across issues related to technology, print culture and readership. In doing so he breaks genuinely new ground while complementing existing work on photography, illustrated magazines and technological innovation in the nineteenth century. The book tackles the periodical press in the sense that it locates periodicals at the very centre of cultural discourses at the end of the century, paying extensive attention to a range of titles in the process.

Feminist accounts of Victorian periodical press activity remain a strong presence in critical discussions this year. Molly Youngkin contributes to this theme with *Feminist Realism at the Fin de Siècle: The Influence of the Late-Victorian Woman's Press on the Development of the Novel*, also discussed in section 2. The book addresses the way the periodical press helped to develop a distinct feminist aesthetic at the end of the century. Though well written, there is little engagement with the periodical form per se, as Youngkin is really more interested in the development of the novel as constructed in magazines than in magazines. Her use of periodicals tends to be confined to mining them for relevant, contemporary book reviews to support her discussions about periodical reception of fiction.

In contrast, Kathryn Ledbetter ranges more successfully across disciplines in *Tennyson and Victorian Periodicals: Commodities in Context*, also discussed in section 4. An excellent reading of Tennyson's placement in various periodical formats, this focused study draws on a wide range of subject areas—book history, print culture, biography, construction of authorship and readership, the history of ideas and themes, transatlantic receptions, the negotiations of time and space, UK and US rhythms, the debates about science and faith and the efforts to fit print context to poetic content—to craft a fine exemplar of periodical studies work.

Two useful pieces on nineteenth-century editorial constructions of authors and journals can be found in Kyriaki Hadjiafxendi and Polina Mackay's edited collection *Authorship in Context: From the Theoretical to the Material*. Hadjiafxendi contributes an effective piece on George Eliot, ' "George Eliot", the Literary Market-Place and Sympathy' (pp. 33–55), charting how the transition she undertook from journalism to literature, from reviewing and editing to writing novels, shaped her conception of art 'as an extension of solidarity' and shaped her response to publishing negotiations in particular with the Edinburgh-based Blackwood publishing firm (p. 33). The aesthetic themes of empathy and the value of personal relationships that thread their way through her work are also reflected in the business approaches adopted by her and her long-term partner George Henry Lewes. As Hadjiafxendi concludes, 'Eliot's attempt to balance the literary and economic value of her work was integral to her promotion of sympathy as a Blackwood author' (p. 55). The same volume features an exemplary piece by Helen Small on the early editorial careers of John Morley and James Knowles ('Liberal Editing in the *Fortnightly Review* and the *Nineteenth Century*', pp. 56–74). Small draws attention to the material constraints binding editors in their work—the office space, printing house, accountant's room—as examples of the forces editors had difficulty managing as they attempted to steer journals along politically and socially liberal lines. The editorial decisions they made were strongly influenced, and sometimes dictated, by market forces and publishing contexts over which they had little control, an important point for researchers into nineteenth-century periodicals to note, particularly those accustomed solely to analysing the surface text of literary journals for intended editorial meaning.

Winnie Chan shifts attention to the final decade of the nineteenth century in *The Economy of the Short Story in British Periodicals of the 1890s*. In three long chapters and an introduction, she focuses on the *fin-de-siècle* publications the *Strand Magazine*, the *Yellow Book* and *Black and White*, exploring the relationship between the content of periodicals and their format and materiality. Her writing is clear and original, though there is some repetition between chapters, as if each had been written to be published as a separate article. By far the most original section is that dedicated to discussing *Black and White*, particularly as little has been written previously on its place in periodical and literary history. Three useful appendices list all short stories published in these three journals between 1891 and 1900.

More on Victorian periodical management is in evidence in articles published in *Publishing History* this year. Susan Drain discusses the history of *Aunt Judy's Magazine*, a family edited monthly aimed at children and published by the London publishers Bell and Daldy (later George Bell and Sons Ltd), in 'Family Matters: Margaret Gatty and *Aunt Judy's Magazine*' (*PubH* 61[2007] 5–45). The journal, edited first by Margaret Gatty from its launch in 1866 to her death in 1873, then by her daughter Horatia from 1873 until her untimely death in 1885, was best known for publishing the works of Hans Christian Andersen and Lewis Carroll, though it also served as a space for featuring Gatty family material. Among the latter was Margaret's daughter Juliana Horatia Ewing, who would find literary success with her tales for youngsters published as *Aunt Judy's Tales* [1859] and *Aunt Judy's Letters* [1862]. The magazine served for over twenty years as a family-run enterprise, its content dominated by fiction, poetry, science material, games and historical pieces intended for families who read together.

Kate Macdonald and Marysa Demoor undertake an interesting study of a later example of a family-based journal in 'The *Dorothy* and its Supplements: A Late-Victorian Novelette (1889–1899)' (*PubH* 61[2007] 71–101). Issued weekly between 1889 and 1899, the journal featured a full-length story or novelette, complemented by letters pages, serialized material, and supplements on fashion, giveaway illustrations, and sheet music. The journal has been little studied, but analysis of its 450 issues shows it to be an exceptionally good example of a periodical that consciously studied and adapted its material to reach a mass-market audience ignored by general literary journals of the period.

An intelligent and long-overdue appraisal of visual culture and popular representations of dustmen can be found in Brian Maidment's *Dusty Bob: A Cultural History of Dustmen, 1780–1870*. It is an excellent piece of work that examines general popular visual print culture, including pamphlets, plays, novels and newspaper reportage, and contrasts their representations with those found in such mainstream periodical sources such as the *Illustrated London News* and *Punch*. The book is replete with illustrations that thoroughly enhance the reading experience.

The place of print culture in the Romantic period is explored in Tom Mole's study of Byron and celebrity culture in *Byron's Romantic Celebrity: Industrial Culture and the Hermeneutic of Intimacy* discussed at length in Chapter XII. Though most of the book is on Byron's work and the process by which he was turned into a commodified celebrity, Mole does devote space to Byron's conscious utilization of technology to reach a reading audience more efficiently and quickly. The Koenig steam press, adopted in 1814 around the time of Byron's ascendancy to iconic status, revolutionized the manner in which literary producers like Byron were able to produce their work. Byron, urged to 'write by steam', became one of the most visible beneficiaries of the Industrial Revolution, despite his own misgivings about its potentially destructive role in British society.

Andrew Franta takes the argument further in *Romanticism and the Rise of the Mass Public* (also discussed in Chapter XII), arguing for the inclusion of close studies of the arc traversing the space between the Romantic poet and his (in the case studies chosen by Franta) reader. The place of publicity and public opinion, authors' perceptions of their intended audience and publishing contexts of the circuit on which poetic texts operated in the early nineteenth century underpin Franta's case studies of Wordsworth, Keats, Shelley and Byron. While some material proves abstruse, of note is the chapter exploring how copyright and libel laws could entangle authors within a web of authorial creation, retention of intellectual rights and the press's power to create alternative readings of texts that threatened authors politically and financially.

Science and its popularization in nineteenth-century culture is the focus of several works out this year. The dissemination of science in periodical publications is addressed in James Mussell's *Science, Time and Space in the Late 19th-Century Periodical Press*. This study draws on funded research into science publications and offers a sophisticated and innovative analysis of the materiality of their subject matter, both through time and space, attempting to link conditions of book and journal publication with the reception of science in contemporary culture. It is a complex topic, and some chapters seem better positioned than others in the intellectual range and depth of arguments presented. Nevertheless the work as a whole adds a great deal to our knowledge of how science began to be woven into the general cultural framework of the periodical press.

Continuing this theme is Bernard Lightman, who contributes a multifaceted study of the publishers, journals and key actors who played a significant part in spreading scientific knowledge in nineteenth-century British culture in *Victorian Popularizers of Science: Designing Nature for New Audiences*. Lightman draws on recent work by John Topham, James Secord, Aileen Fyfe, Leslie Howsam and other exponents of book history, print culture and periodical studies to explore how interlinked networks of men and women science writers, publishing opportunities and the development of new journal sources for discussing science in popular terms encouraged changes in the way scientific knowledge was communicated and consumed throughout the nineteenth century. Particularly interesting are the sections on the masters of the lecturing circuit, whose showman style and dramatic declamations captivated large audiences and shaped public understanding of geological, material and astrophysical phenomena.

Samantha Matthews gives some important insight into the autographic volumes that were printed for readers in the mid- to late nineteenth century for use as scrapbooks and personal annotation in 'Gems, Texts and Confessions: Writing Readers in Late-Victorian Autographic Gift-Books' (*PubH* 62[2007] 53–80). Marketed at young middle-class women readers, these elaborate gift-books were used in ways ranging from confessional and literary notebooks to religious diaries and text records. Matthews uses interesting archival examples to explore issues of reader identity and reading response.

Mass-market texts of a different sort are featured in J. Cowan and Mike Paterson's edited selection of Scottish chapbooks, *Folk in Print: Scotland's Chapbook Heritage 1750–1850*. A strong introduction contextualizes what is known about early Scottish cheap pamphlet and chapbook printing—'the people's print' as such texts were commonly called—followed by extensive selections of primary texts. These texts are divided into themes ranging from trades and occupation to love, drink, sailors, soldiers and adventurers. Also included are examples demonstrating the artificiality of anglicized or broad Scots reinterpretations of Gaelic material. Rich in primary examples, the work is an interesting text, but those interested in a full discussion of chapbook printing will have to turn to other sources such as the late John Morris's detailed contribution on 'The Scottish Chapman' (in Myers, Harris and Mandelbrote, eds., pp. 159–86). The same volume also features an interesting piece by Michael Harris, 'The Book Trade in Public Spaces: London Street Booksellers, 1690–1850' (Myers, Harris and Mandelbrote, eds., pp. 187–211), documenting the shaping of London's urban landscape throughout the eighteenth and nineteenth centuries by permanent and ambulatory street booksellers and book stalls.

Market forces and their place in literary culture and publishing practices form cornerstone issues in present-day book history studies. Some exemplary work on literary agency and copyright history has been published this year, not least Mary Ann Gillies's *The Professional Literary Agent in Britain, 1880–1920*. The first significant study on British literary agency history since James Hepburn's short yet groundbreaking work of the 1960s, Gillies's book taps primary and secondary sources to map out the early history of the insertion of the literary agent into the publishing process. She intersperses welcome insight into the activities of early agents such as A.P. Watt and J.B. Pinker with strong case studies on the handling of the intellectual property of George MacDonald, 'Lucas Malet', Somerville and Ross and Joseph Conrad. Catherine Seville looks at similar issues in 'Edward Bulwer Lytton Dreams of Copyright: "It might make me a rich man"' (in O'Gorman, ed., pp. 55–72), providing a historically informed analysis of Edward Bulwer-Lytton's lobbying efforts for stronger mid-nineteenth-century copyright protection, and his successes and struggles over financial recompense for his novels and plays. Her insights into the tension between Bulwer Lytton's quest for literary respect and his close attention to copyright management and financial rewards offer an exemplary model of interdisciplinary approaches to textual production.

The effects that the Berne Convention on copyright in 1886 would have on the subsequent career of artists and authors are materially demonstrated by Robert Montgomery and Robert Threlfall's *Music and Copyright: The Case of Delius and his Publishers*. Delius's musical career developed most fully in the first two decades of the twentieth century. Nevertheless, as a useful case study into the opportunities to benefit materially from music performance and publication royalties as a result of the Berne Convention, this thorough and detailed study of Delius's business relations with his British and European publishers draws on and reproduces primary sources (letters, contracts, royalty summaries) to contextualize music publishing in a way few others have done in the past.

Distribution networks and the business of publishing during the nineteenth century are the topics of two important articles issued this year. In 'Bankrupt Books? The Aftermath of the 1825–1826 Crash and the British Book Trade' (*PubH* 62[2007] 41–52), Ross Alloway modifies our general understanding of the British book trade crisis of 1825–6 through careful use of statistical details drawn from official announcements of bankruptcies in the Edinburgh and London *Gazettes*. The new material uncovered offers a valuable insight into the extent to which the financial crash affected Scottish and English trades differently. While the negative impact on the British book trade of the crash of the English financial market during this period has long been taken for granted, data demonstrates that in Scotland the book trade did not suffer as greatly as previously suggested. Nevertheless, contractions in both English and Scottish book production show how interlinked the financial markets and book-production activity were during this period. Frederick Nesta makes a revisionist argument for revisiting the significance of Mudie's Circulating Library in maintaining the three-volume format favoured by publishers from the 1830s to the 1890s in 'The Myth of the "Triple-Headed Monster": The Economics of the Three-Volume Novel' (*PubH* 61[2007] 47–69). Nineteenth-century book distribution in the UK was long said to be dominated by the London-based Mudie's Circulating Library, with Mudie's guaranteeing of a level of purchases for his library sufficient to create demand for three-volume novel publications. New archival analysis suggests, however, that this was not the case—that in fact three-volume publications often lost money for the publisher, and that readers were likely to buy books in different formats when the price was affordable enough, countering general arguments and perceptions about the Victorian readership's tastes and interests.

Newspaper press historians do not often draw attention to unusual readership groups. *Politics, Religion and the Press: Irish Journalism in Mid-Victorian England* by Anthony McNicholas proves an exception, focusing on a close reading of the history of three London-based, Irish migrant press titles in the mid-nineteenth century: the *Universal News*, the *Irish Liberator* and the *Irish News*. It complements existing work on the Irish press, and is an in-depth, solid study of a neglected series of titles produced between 1860 and 1869, a particularly turbulent decade of Irish political struggle and debate.

More on the press and media publications from a transatlantic perspective is on display in Joel H. Wiener and Mark Hampton's edited collection *Anglo-American Media Interactions, 1850–2000*. The volume places nineteenth-century periodicals in a global context, with about 40 per cent of the contributions (six of fourteen pieces) dedicated to specifically British titles of the period. The work as a whole is a very strong contribution to media history, dealing with the complexity of media networks from mid-century onwards, and inserting the periodical press into a general media infrastructure that was increasingly framed within expansionary political, imperial and communication aspirations and networks. The introduction by Wiener and Hampton is particularly good in reviewing past work in the area and setting the agenda for future developments. Of particular relevance to nineteenth-century specialists are the following contributions: Richard D. Fulton, 'Sensational War Reporting and the Quality Press in Late Victorian Britain and America' (pp. 11–31); Matt McIntire, 'Embracing Sporting News in England and America: Nineteenth-Century Cricket and Baseball News' (pp. 32–47); '"Get the News! Get the News!"—Speed in Transatlantic Journalism, 1830–1914' (pp. 48–66); Christopher Kent, 'Matt Morgan and Transatlantic Illustrated Journalism, 1850–90' (pp. 69–92); and Michael de Nie, 'The London Press and the American Civil War' (pp. 129–54).

Journal articles that have appeared this year with relevance to periodical and publishing history studies include the following: Jane E. Brown and Richard Samuel West, 'William Newman (1817–70): A Victorian Cartoonist in London and New York' (*AmPer* 17:ii[2007] 143–83); James Gregory, 'Eccentric Biography and the Victorians' (*Biography* 30:iii[2007] 342–76); Richard Yeo, 'Lost Encyclopedias: Before and After the Enlightenment' (*BoH* 10[2007] 47–68); Keri A. Berg, 'Contesting the Page: The Author and the Illustrator in France, 1830–1848' (*BoH* 10[2007] 69–102); Solveig C. Robinson, '"Sir, it is an outrage": George Bentley, Robert Black, and the Condition of the Mid-List Author in Victorian Britain' (*BoH* 10[2007] 131–68); Megan Smitley, 'Feminist Anglo-Saxonism? Representations of "Scotch" Women in the English Women's Press in the Late Nineteenth Century' (*CSH* 4:iii[2007] 341–59); Sally Ledger, 'Wilde Women and the Yellow Book: The Sexual Politics of Aestheticism and Decadence' (*ELT* 50:i[2007] 5–26); Kathryn Gleadle, 'Charlotte Elizabeth Tonna and the Mobilization of Tory Women in Early Victorian England' (*HistJ* 50:i[2007] 97–117); Simon J. Potter, 'Webs, Networks, and Systems: Globalization and the Mass Media in the Nineteenth- and Twentieth-Century British Empire' (*JBS* 46:iii[2007] 621–46); Peter Garside and Iain Gordon Brown, 'New Information on the Publication of the Early Editions of Waverley' (*JEBibliog* 2[2007] 11–22); Katie Halsey, '"Critics as rare as donkeys": Margaret Oliphant, Critic or Common Reader?' (*JEBibliog* 2[2007] 42–68); Catherine Waters, '"Fashion in undress": Clothing and Commodity Culture in *Household Words*' (*JVC*12:i[2007] 26–41); Alexis Weedon, 'The Economic Life of the Author' (*JVC* 12:i[2007] 97–101); Leslie Howsam, Christopher Stray, Alice Jenkins, James A. Secord and Anna Vaninskaya, 'What the Victorians Learned: Perspectives on Nineteenth-Century Schoolbooks' (*JVC* 12:ii[2007] 262–85); Jo Aitken, '"The horrors of matrimony among the masses": Feminist Representations of Wife Beating in England and Australia, 1870–1914' (*JWH* 19:iv[2007] 107–31); Randolph Ivy, 'M.E. Braddon in the 1860s: Clarifications and Corrections' (*Library* 8:i[2007] 60–9); M.O. Grenby, 'Chapbooks, Children, and Children's Literature' (*Library* 8:iii[2007] 277–303); Priti Joshi, 'Mutiny Echoes: India, Britons, and Charles Dickens's "A Tale of Two Cities"' (*NCL* 62[2007] 48–87); Jason David Hall, 'Popular Prosody: Spectacle and the Politics of Victorian Versification' (*NCL* 62[2007] 222–49); Christopher Pittard, '"Cheap, healthful literature": *The Strand Magazine*, Fictions of Crime, and Purified Reading Communities' (*VPR* 40:i[2007] 1–23); Margaret D. Stetz, '"Can anyone picture my agony?": Visualizing Gender, Imperialism, and Gothic Horror in the *Wide World Magazine* of 1898' (*VPR* 40:i[2007] 24–43); David E. Latané Jr, 'Charles Molloy Westmacott and the Spirit of the Age' (*VPR* 40:i[2007] 44–71); Linda K. Hughes, 'What the *Wellesley Index* Left Out: Why Poetry Matters to Periodical Studies' (*VPR* 40:ii[2007] 91–125); Julia M. Chavez, 'Wandering Readers and the Pedagogical Potential of *Temple Bar*' (*VPR* 40:ii[2007] 126–50); Christopher Banham, ' "England and America against the world": Empire and the USA in Edwin J. Brett's *Boys of England*, 1866–99' (*VPR* 40:ii[2007] 151–71); Arlene Young, 'Ladies and Professionalism: The Evolution of the Idea of Works in the *Queen*, 1861–1900' (*VPR* 40:iii[2007] 189–215); ' "The life of a bachelor girl in the big city": Selling the Single Lifestyle to Readers of *Woman* and the *Young Woman* in the 1890s' (*VPR* 40:iii[2007] 216–38); Cheryl Stiles, ' "Different plans of sensuous forms": American Critical and Popular Responses to Elizabeth Barrett Browning's *Aurora Leigh* and *Last Poems*. Annotated Bibliography American Periodicals, 1856–62' (*VPR* 40:iii[2007] 239–55); Ewen A. Cameron, 'Journalism in the Late Victorian Scottish Highlands: John Murdoch, Duncan Campbell and the *Northern Chronicle*' (*VPR* 40:iv[2007] 281–306); John B. Osborne, ' "Governed by mediocrity": Image and Text in *Vanity Fair's* Political Caricatures, 1869–1889' (*VPR* 40:iv[2007] 307–31); Gary Simons, 'Thackeray's Contributions to the *Times*' (*VPR* 40:iv[2007] 332–54); Lorraine Janzen Kooistra, 'Poetry in the Victorian Marketplace: The Illustrated Princess as a Christmas Gift Book' (*VP* 45:i[2007] 49–76); and Rachel Sagner Buurma, 'Anonymity, Corporate Authority, and the Archive: The Production of Authorship in Late-Victorian England' (*VS* 50[2007] 15–42).

Books Reviewed

Aaron, Jane. *Nineteenth-Century Women's Writing in Wales*. UWalesP. [2007] pp. 256. $35 ISBN 0 7083 2060 0.

Ablow, Rachel. *The Marriage of Minds: Reading Sympathy in the Victorian Marriage Plot*. StanfordUP. [2007] pp. 248. $55 ISBN 0 8047 5466 7.

Adams, Byron, ed. *Edward Elgar and his World*. PrincetonUP. [2007] pp. 426. $22.95 ISBN 0 6911 3445 6.

Ainsworth, W. Harrison. *Jack Sheppard*. Traviata. [2007] pp. 565. £12 ISBN 9 7819 0533 5091.

Arnold, Guy. *In the Footsteps of George Borrow: A Journey through Spain and Portugal*. Signal Books. [2007] pp. 326. £14 ISBN 1 9049 5537 1.

Ascari, Maurizio. *A Counter-History of Crime Fiction: Supernatural, Gothic, Sensational*. Palgrave. [2007] pp. 240. $69.95 ISBN 0 2305 2500 8.

Austin, Linda M. *Nostalgia in Transition, 1780–1917*. UPVirginia. [2007] pp. 248. $39.95 ISBN 9 7808 1392 5981.

Baker, William. *A Wilkie Collins Chronology*. Palgrave. [2007] pp. 236. $80 ISBN 1 4039 9481 1.

Baker, William, Judith L. Fisher, Andrew Gasson and Andrew Maunder, eds. *Lives of Victorian Literary Figures V: Mary Elizabeth Braddon, Wilkie*

Collins and William Thackeray by their Contemporaries, 3 vols. P&C. [2007] pp. 1,072. $485.67 ISBN 1 8519 6819 9.

Barnard, Robert, and Louise Barnard. *A Brontë Encyclopedia*. Blackwell. [2007] pp. 347. £60 ISBN 1 4051 5119 6.

Beaumont, Matthew ed. *Adventures in Realism*. Blackwell. [2007] pp. 280. $95.99 ISBN 1 4051 3577 8.

Beegan, Gerry. *The Mass Image: A Social History of Photomechanical Reproduction in Victorian London*. Palgrave. [2007] pp. 302. £55 ISBN 9 7802 3055 3279.

Bell, Bill. *The Edinburgh History of the Book in Scotland: Ambition and Industry, 1800–1880*. EdinUP. [2007] pp. 576. £95 ISBN 9 7807 4861 7791.

Bellanca, Mary Ellen. *Daybooks of Discovery: Nature Diaries in Britain, 1770–1870*. UPVirginia. [2007] pp. 248. £50 ISBN 0 8139 2612 2.

Bevis, Matthew. *The Art of Eloquence: Byron, Dickens, Tennyson, Joyce*. OUP. [2007] pp. viii + 302. £50 ISBN 9 7801 9925 3999.

Bienstock Anolik, Ruth, ed. *Horrifying Sex: Essays on Sexual Difference in Gothic Literature*. McFarland. [2007] pp. 281. £29 ISBN 0 7864 3014 7.

Billone, Amy Christine. *Little Songs: Women, Silence and the Nineteenth-Century Sonnet*. OSUP. [2007] pp. 199. $40 ISBN 0 8142 1042 2.

Blackwell, Mark. *The Secret Life of Things: animals, objects and it - narratives in eighteenth-century England*. Bucknell UP. [2007] pp. 365. $62.50 ISBN 9 7808 3875 6669.

Bodenheimer, Rosemarie. *Knowing Dickens*. CornUP. [2007] pp. 256. $30 ISBN 9 7808 0144 6146.

Boyd, Kelly, and Rohan McWilliam, eds. *The Victorian Studies Reader*. Routledge. [2007] pp. 432. $41.95 ISBN 0 4153 5579 6.

Brinton, Ian, ed. *Dickens's Great Expectations: A Reader's Guide*. Continuum. [2007] pp. 144. $16.95 ISBN 0 8264 8858 7.

Bristow, Joseph, ed. *The Complete Works of Oscar Wilde*, vol. 3: *The Picture of Dorian Gray, the 1890 and 1891 Texts*. OUP. [2005] pp. 534. $278.50 ISBN 0 1981 8772 6.

Brown, Peter, and Michael Irwin, eds. *Literature and Place: 1800–2000*. Lang. [2006] pp. 235. $50.95 ISBN 3 9067 5862 1.

Buckton, Oliver S. *Cruising with Robert Louis Stevenson: Travel, Narrative, and the Colonial Body*. OSUP. [2007] pp. 354. $44.95 ISBN 0 8214 1756 8.

Burne-Jones, Edward, John Christian and Elisa Korb, eds. *Hidden Burne-Jones: Works on Paper by Edward Burne-Jones from Birmingham Museums and Art Gallery*. D. Giles. [2007] pp. 96. $32.95 ISBN 1 9048 3230 X.

Buzard, James, Joseph W. Childers and Eileen Gillooly, eds. *Victorian Prism: Refractions of the Crystal Palace*. UPVirginia. [2007] pp. 356. $45 ISBN 9 7808 1392 6032.

Carlisle, Janice, and James R. Simmons Jr, eds. *Factory Lives: Four Nineteenth-Century Working-Class Autobiographies*. Broadview. [2007] pp. 498. $21.95 ISBN 1 5511 1272 8.

Chan, Winnie. *The Economy of the Short Story in British Periodicals of the 1890s*. Routledge. [2007] pp. 236. £45 ISBN 0 4159 7733 9.

Charle, Christophe, Vincent Julien and Jay Winter, eds. *Anglo-French Attitudes: Comparisons and Transfers Between English and French*

Intellectuals since the Eighteenth Century. ManUP. [2007] pp. 336. $85 ISBN 0 7190 7537 8.

Chedgzoy, Kate, Susanne Greenhalgh and Robert Shaughnessy, eds. *Shakespeare and Childhood*. CUP. [2007] pp. 284. £50 ISBN 9 7805 2187 1259.

Childs, Peter. *Modernism and the Post-Colonial: Literature and Empire, 1885–1930*. Continuum. [2007] pp. 164. $110 ISBN 0 8264 8558 8.

Christianson, Frank. *Philanthropy in British and American Fiction: Dickens, Hawthorne, Eliot and Howells*. EdinUP. [2007] pp. 256. $90 ISBN 0 7486 2508 9.

Clark, Stuart. *The Sun Kings: The Unexpected Tragedy of Richard Carrington and the Tale of How Modern Astronomy Began*. PrincetonUP. [2007] pp. 236. $24.95 ISBN 0 6911 2660 7.

Cowan, Edward J., and Mike Paterson. *Folk in Print: Scotland's Chapbook Heritage, 1750–1850*. John Donald. [2007] pp. 438. £25 ISBN 9 7819 0460 7519.

Davis, Paul. *Critical Companion to Charles Dickens*. FOF. [2007] pp. 512. £51.77 ISBN 0 8160 6407 5.

Davis, Tracy, and Peter Holland, eds. *The Performing Century: Nineteenth-Century Theatre's History*. Palgrave. [2007] pp. 271. £55 ISBN 0 2305 7256 1.

Dawson, Gowan. *Darwin, Literature and Victorian Respectability*. CUP. [2007] pp. 298. $96 ISBN 9 7805 2187 2492.

Delap, Lucy, and Ann Heilmann, eds. *Anti-Feminism in Edwardian Literature*, 6 vols. Continuum. [2006] pp. 2,356. $1,150 ISBN 1 8437 1150 8.

Dibble, Jeremy. *John Stainer: A Life in Music*. Boydell. [2007] pp. 384. $55 ISBN 1 8438 3297 6.

Douglas-Fairhurst, Robert, ed. Charles Dickens. *A Christmas Carol & Other Christmas Books*. OUP. [2008] pp. xlviii + 438. £6.99. ISBN 9 7801 9280 6949.

Dow, Gillian E., ed. *Translators. Interpreters, Mediators: Women Writers 1700–1900*. Lang. [2007] pp. 268. £33 ISBN 3 0391 1055 1.

Edwards, Steve. *The Making of English Photography: Allegories*. UPennP. [2007] pp. 358. $94 ISBN 0 2710 2713 4.

Eliot, Simon, Andrew Nash and Ian Willison, eds. *Literary Cultures and the Material Book*. BL. [2007] pp. 444. £45 ISBN 9 7807 1230 6843.

Farrier, David. *Unsettled Narratives: The Pacific Writings of Stevenson, Ellis, Melville and London*. Routledge. [2006] pp. 288. $110 ISBN 0 4159 7951 X.

Finkelstein, David, and Alistair McCleery, eds. *The Edinburgh History of the Book in Scotland: Professionalism and Diversity, 1880–2000*. EdinUP. [2007] pp. 544. £95 ISBN 9 7807 4861 8293.

Flynn, Tom, ed. *The New Encyclopedia of Unbelief*. Prometheus. [2007] pp. 897. $199 ISBN 1 5910 2391 2.

Francis, Mark. *Herbert Spencer and the Invention of Modern Life*. CornUP. [2007] pp. 434. $45 ISBN 0 8014 4590 6.

Frank, Lucy, ed. *Representations of Death in Nineteenth Century Writing and Culture*. Ashgate. [2007] pp. 50. £50 ISBN 0 7546 5528 8.

Franta, Andrew. *Romanticism and the Rise of the Mass Public.* CUP. [2007] pp. 245. £50 ISBN 0 5218 6887 4.

Freer, Beryl, and Allen Freer, eds. *The Travel Journals of Robert Hyde Greg of Quarry Bank Mill: Travels in Scotland, Spain and Portugal, France, Italy, and the Ottoman Empire, 1814–17.* Shaun Tyas. [2007] pp. 271. £30 ISBN 1 9002 8988 1.

Garson, Marjorie. *Moral Taste: Aesthetics, Subjectivity, and Social Power in the Nineteenth-Century Novel.* UTorP. [2007] pp. 483. $75 ISBN 0 8020 9138 5.

Gezari, Janet. *Last Things: Emily Brontë's Poems.* OUP. [2007] pp. 183. £22 ISBN 0 1992 9818 1.

Gibson, John. *Fiction and the Weave of Life.* OUP. [2007] pp. 234. $75 ISBN 0 1992 9952 8.

Gillies, Mary Ann. *The Professional Literary Agent in Britain, 1880–1920.* UTorP. [2007] pp. 247. £42 ISBN 9 7808 0209 1475.

Gilmartin, Sophie, and Rod Mengham. *Thomas Hardy's Shorter Fiction: A Critical Study.* EdinUP. [2007] pp. 208. $90 ISBN 0 7486 3265 4.

Glendening, John. *The Evolutionary Imagination in Late Victorian Novels: An Entangled Bank.* Ashgate. [2007] pp. 225. $99.95 ISBN 9 7807 5465 8214.

Gossin, Pamela. *Thomas Hardy's Novel Universe: Astronomy, Cosmology and Gender in the Post-Darwinian World.* Ashgate. [2007] pp. 300. £47.50 ISBN 0 7546 0336 9.

Gregory, James. *Of Victorians and Vegetarians: The Vegetarian Movement in Nineteenth-Century Britain.* Tauris. [2007] pp. 313. $79.95 ISBN 9 7818 4511 3797.

Guy, Josephine M., ed. *The Complete Works of Oscar Wilde: Criticism,* vol. 4: *Historical Criticism, Intentions, The Soul of Man.* OUP. [2007] pp. 800. $185 ISBN 0 1981 1961 5.

Hadjiafxendi, Kyriaki, and Polina Mackay, eds. *Authorship in Context: From the Theoretical to the Material.* Palgrave. [2007] pp. 231. £45 ISBN 9 7814 0394 9011.

Hall-Witt, Jennifer. *Fashionable Acts: Opera and Elite Culture in London, 1780–1880.* UNewHampshireP. [2007] pp. 390. £36.50 ISBN 1 5846 5625 5.

Hansson, Heidi. *Emily Lawless 1845–1913: Writing the Interspace.* CorkUP. [2007] pp. 234. $49 ISBN 9 7818 5918 4134.

Hawes, Donald. *Charles Dickens.* Writers' Lives. Continuum. [2007] pp. 167. $21.95 ISBN 0 8264 8964 8.

Hebblethwaite, Kate, ed. *Dracula's Guest and Other Weird Stories with The Lair of the White Worm,* by Bram Stoker. Penguin. [2006] pp. 336. £8.99 ISBN 9 7801 4144 1719.

Hepburn, Allan, ed. *Troubled Legacies: Narrative and Inheritance.* UTorP. [2007] pp. 336. £32 ISBN 0 8020 9110 5.

Herbert, Christopher. *War of No Pity: The Indian Mutiny and Victorian Trauma.* PrincetonUP. [2007] pp. 352. £19.95 ISBN 9 7806 9113 3324.

Hill, Rosemary. *God's Architect: Pugin and the Building of Romantic Britain.* Allen Lane. [2007] pp. 601. $45 ISBN 0 7139 9499 1.

Himmelfarb, Gertrude, ed. *The Spirit of the Age: Victorian Essays.* YaleUP. [2007] pp. 327. $35 ISBN 9 7803 0012 3302.

Hopkins, Lisa. *Bram Stoker: A Literary Life*. Palgrave. [2007] pp. 208. $65 ISBN 1 4039 4647 7.

Howell, Georgina. *Gertrude Bell Queen of the Desert, Shaper of Nations*. FS&G. [2007] pp. 512. $27.50 ISBN 0 3741 6162 3.

Humphreys, Madeleine. *The Life and Times of Edward Martyn: An Aristocratic Bohemian*. IAP. [2007] pp. 286. $55 ISBN 0 7165 2923 8.

Hurst, Isobel. *Victorian Women Writers and the Classics: The Feminine of Homer*. OUP. [2006] pp. 272. £49 ISBN 9 7801 9928 3514.

Jacobi, Carol. *William Holman Hunt: Painter, Painting, Paint*. ManUP. [2007] pp. 288. $80 ISBN 0 7190 7288 3.

Jędrzejewski, Jan. *George Eliot*. Routledge. [2007] pp. 171. $90 ISBN 9 7804 1520 2503.

Jeffares, Norman A., and Peter Van De Kamp, eds. *Irish Literature: The Nineteenth Century*, vol. 2. IAP. [2007] pp. 534. $37.50 ISBN 9 7807 1653 3344.

Jeffares, Norman A., and Peter Van De Kamp, eds. *Irish Literature The Nineteenth Century*, vol. 3. IAP. [2007] pp. xxii + 535. $37.50 ISBN 9 7807 1653 3580.

Jenkins, Alice. *Space and the 'March of Mind'*. OUP. [2007] pp. 257. $95 ISBN 0 1992 0992 8.

Jones, H.S. *Intellect and Character in Victorian England: Mark Pattison and the Invention of the Don*. CUP. [2007] pp. 294. $101 ISBN 9 7805 2187 6056.

Joyce, Simon. *The Victorians in the Rearview Mirror*. OSUP. [2007] pp. 211. $22.95 ISBN 0 8214 1762 2.

Keen, Suzanne. *Empathy and the Novel*. OUP. [2007] pp. 274. $65 ISBN 0 1951 7576 X.

Kennedy, Richard S., and Donald Hair. *The Dramatic Imagination of Robert Browning: A Literary Life*. UMissP. [2007] pp. 492. £43 ISBN 0 8262 1691 9.

Kingston, Angela. *Oscar Wilde as a Character in Victorian Fiction*. Palgrave. [2007] pp. 320. $79.95 ISBN 0 2306 0023 9.

Kinser, Brent (co-ordinating editor), et al. *The Carlyle Letters Online* (Thomas and Jane Welsh Carlyle). DukeUP. [2007] http://carlyleletters.dukejournals.org/.

Koenigsberger, Kurt. *The Novel and the Menagerie: Totality, Englishness, and Empire*. OSUP. [2007] pp. 278. $41.95 ISBN 0 8142 1057 0.

Kroeber, Karl. *Make Believe in Film and Fiction: Visual vs. Verbal Storytelling*. Palgrave. [2007] pp. 240. $69.95 ISBN 1 4039 7279 6.

Kucich, John. *Imperial Masochism: British Fiction, Fantasy, and Social Class*. PrincetonUP. [2007] pp. 270. $37.50 ISBN 0 6911 2712 3.

Larsen, Timothy. *Crisis of Doubt: Honest Faith in Nineteenth Century England*. OUP. [2006] pp. 336. $125 ISBN 0 1992 8787 2.

Latham, David, ed. *Writing on the Image: Reading William Morris*. UTorP. [2007] pp. 254. $50 ISBN 0 8020 9247 0.

Lear, Linda. *Beatrix Potter: A Life in Nature*. St Martin's. [2007] pp. 608. $30 ISBN 0 3123 6934 4.

Ledbetter, Kathryn. *Tennyson and Victorian Periodicals: Commodities in Context*. Ashgate. [2007] pp. 231. £50 ISBN 0 7546 5719 4.

Ledger, Sally. *Dickens and the Popular Radical Imagination*. CUP. [2007] pp. 314. $99 ISBN 0 5218 4577 7.

Levine, George. *How to Read the Victorian Novel*. Wiley-Blackwell. [2007] pp. 200. $26.95 ISBN 1 4051 3056 3.

Lightman, Bernard. *Victorian Popularizers of Science: Designing Nature for New Audiences*. UChicP. [2007] pp. 545. £26 ISBN 9 7802 2648 1180.

Logan, Deborah Anna, ed. *The Collected Letters of Harriet Martineau*, 5 vols. P&C. [2007] pp. 2,036. $795 ISBN 9 7818 5196 8046.

Lutz, Deborah. *The Dangerous Lover: Gothic Villains, Byronism, and the Nineteenth-Century Seduction Narrative*. OSUP. [2006] pp. 117. $42.95 ISBN 0 8142 1034 1.

Lycett, Andrew. *The Man who Created Sherlock Holmes: The Life and Times of Sir Arthur Conan Doyle*. FreeP. [2007] pp. 576. $30 ISBN 0 7432 7523 3.

Mack, Robert. *The Wonderful and Surprising History of Sweeney Todd: The Life and Times of an Urban Legend*. Continuum. [2007] pp. 375. £25 ISBN 9 7808 2649 7918.

Mahaffrey, Vicki. *Modernist Literature: Challenging Fictions*. Blackwell. [2007] pp. 242. $89.95 ISBN 0 6312 1307 4.

Maidment, Brian. *Dusty Bob: A Cultural History of Dustmen, 1780–1870*. ManUP. [2007] pp. 251. £50 ISBN 9 7807 1905 2835.

Maier, Sarah E. ed. *Tess of the D'Urbervilles*, by Thomas Hardy. Broadview. [2007] pp. 522. $22 ISBN 1 5511 1066 0.

Mangham, Andrew, ed. *Wilkie Collins: Interdisciplinary Essays*. CambridgeSP. [2007] pp. 284. £34.99 ISBN 9 7818 4718 1091.

Matus, Jill L., ed. *The Cambridge Companion to Elizabeth Gaskell*. CUP. [2007] pp. 211. $29.99 ISBN 9 7805 2160 9265.

MacFarlane, Robert. *Original Copy: Plagiarism and Originality in Nineteenth-Century Literature*. OUP. [2007] pp. 244. $60 ISBN 0 1992 9650 2.

McKelvy, William. *The English Cult of Literature: Devoted Readers, 1774–1880*. UPVirginia. [2007] pp. 322. $45 ISBN 0 8139 2571 1.

McNeil, Kenneth. *Scotland, Britain, Empire: Writing the Highlands, 1760–1860*. OSUP. [2007] pp. 280. $41.95 ISBN 9 7808 1421 0475.

McNicholas, Anthony. *Politics, Religion and the Press: Irish Journalism in Mid-Victorian England*. Peter Lang. [2007] pp. 370. $84.95 ISBN 9 7830 3910 6998.

McSweeney, Kerry. *What's the Import? Nineteenth-Century Poems and Contemporary Critical Practice* McG-QUP. [2007] pp. 177. £52 ISBN 0 7735 3202 1.

McWilliam, Rohan. *The Tichborne Claimant: A Victorian Sensation*. Hambledon. [2007] pp. 363. £25 ISBN 1 8528 5478 2.

Michie, Helena. *Victorian Honeymoons: Journeys to the Conjugal*. CUP. [2007] pp. 288. £50 ISBN 0 5218 6874 2.

Mills, Kevin. *Approaching Apocalypse: Unveiling Revelation in Victorian Writing*. BuckUP. [2007] pp. 228. $49.50 ISBN 9 7808 3875 6270.

Mole, Tom. *Byron's Romantic Celebrity: Industrial Culture and the Hermeneutics of Intimacy*. Palgrave. [2007] pp. 227. £45 ISBN 9 7814 0399 9931.

Monsman, Gerald. H. *Rider Haggard on the Imperial Frontier: The Political and Literary Contexts of his African Romances.* ELT. [2006] pp. 294. $40 ISBN 0 9443 1821 5.

Montgomery, Robert, and Robert Threlfall. *Music and Copyright: The Case of Delius and his Publishers.* Ashgate. [2007] pp. 410. £25 ISBN 9 7807 5465 8467.

Moran, Maureen. *Victorian Literature and Culture: A Student Guide.* Continuum. [2006] pp. 184. $17.95 ISBN 9 7808 2648 8848.

Morgan, Simon. *A Victorian Woman's Place: Public Culture in the Nineteenth Century.* Tauris. [2007] pp. 256. £57.50 ISBN 1 8451 1210 5.

Morse, Deborah Denenholz, and Martin A. Danahay, eds. *Victorian Animal Dreams: Representations of Animals in Victorian Literature and Culture.* Ashgate. [2007] pp. 281. $94.95 ISBN 9 7807 5465 1145.

Mukherjee, Ankhi. *Aesthetic Hysteria: The Great Neurosis in Victorian Melodrama and Contemporary Fiction.* Routledge. [2007] pp. 121. £60 ISBN 9 7804 1598 1408.

Murphy, Patricia. *In Science's Shadow: Literary Constructions of Late Victorian Women.* UMissP. [2006] pp. 239. $39.95 ISBN 0 8262 1682 X.

Mussell, James. *Science, Time and Space in the Late 19th-Century Periodical Press.* Ashgate. [2007] pp. 237. £50 ISBN 9 7807 5465 7477.

Myers, Robin, Michael Harris and Giles Mandelbrote, eds. *Books on the Move: Tracking Copies through Collections and the Book Trade.* OakK and BL. [2007] pp. 164. £25 ISBN 9 7815 8456 2191.

Nagai, Kaori. *Empire or Analogies: Kipling, India, and Ireland.* CorkUP. [2007] pp. 185. $39 ISBN 1 8591 8408 1.

Nelson, Claudia. *Ties in Victorian England.* Praeger. [2007] pp. 216. $39.95 ISBN 0 2759 8697 7.

Newman, Beth, ed. *Wuthering Heights,* by Emily Brontë. Broadview. [2007] pp. 400. $14.95 ISBN 1 5511 1532 8.

Norquay, Glenda. *Robert Louis Stevenson and Theories of Reading: The Reader as Vagabond.* ManUP. [2007] pp. 204. $74.95 ISBN 0 7190 7386 3.

O'Gorman, Francis, ed. *Victorian Literature and Finance.* OUP. [2007] pp. 201. £56 ISBN 9 7801 9928 1923.

Oulton, Carolyn W de la L.. *Romantic Friendship in Victorian Literature.* Ashgate. [2007] pp. 178. £50 ISBN 9 7807 5465 8696.

Paradis, James G. ed. *Samuel Butler: Victorian against the Grain. A Critical Overview.* UTorP. [2007] pp. 416. $70 ISBN 0 8020 9745 6.

Parfait, Claire. *The Publishing History of Uncle Tom's Cabin, 1852–2002.* Ashgate. [2007] pp. 269. £55 ISBN 9 7807 5465 5145.

Parker, Joanne. *'England's Darling': The Victorian Cult of Alfred the Great.* ManUP. [2007] pp. 256. £55 ISBN 9 7807 1907 3564.

Paulson, Ronald. *Sin and Evil: Moral Values in Literature.* YaleUP. [2007] pp. 432. $42 ISBN 0 3001 2014 1.

Peterson, Linda, ed. *Autobiography,* by Harriet Martineau. Broadview. [2007] pp. 744. $29.95 ISBN 1 5511 1555 7.

Phillips, Catherine. *Gerard Manley Hopkins and the Victorian Visual World.* OUP. [2007] pp. 303. £32 ISBN 0 1992 3080 8.

Pite, Ralph. *Thomas Hardy: The Guarded Life*. YaleUP. [2007] pp. 522. $35 ISBN 9 7803 0012 3371.

Rabaté, Jean-Michel. *1913: The Cradle of Modernism*. Blackwell. [2007] pp. 246. $34.95 ISBN 9 7814 0515 1177.

Radford, Andrew. *The Lost Girls: Demeter–Persephone and the Literary Imagination, 1850–1930*. Rodopi. [2007] pp. 356. £50 ISBN 9 7890 4202 2355.

Raven, James. *The Business of Books: Booksellers and the English Book Trade*. YaleUP. [2007] pp. 493. £35 ISBN 9 7803 0012 2619.

Rawlinson, Barbara, ed. *A Man of Many Parts: Gissing's Short Stories, Essays and Other Works*. Rodopi. [2006] pp. 288. $93 ISBN 9 0420 2085 7.

Ray, Martin, ed. *Thomas Hardy Remembered*. Ashgate. [2007] pp. 338. $99.95 ISBN 9 7807 5463 9732.

Reed, Thomas L. Jr. *The Transforming Draught: Jekyll and Hyde, Robert Louis Stevenson and the Victorian Alcohol Debate*. McFarland. [2006] pp. 268. $35 ISBN 9 7807 8642 6485.

Reeves, Richard. *John Stuart Mill: Victorian Firebrand*. Atlantic. [2007] pp. 620. £30 ISBN 1 8435 4643 4.

Roe, Dinah. *Christina Rossetti's Faithful Imagination: The Devotional Poetry and Prose*. Palgrave. [2006] pp. 220. £45 ISBN 0 2300 0507 5.

Rosenfeld, Jason, and Alison Smith. *Millais*. Tate. [2007] pp. 272. £42.99 ISBN 1 8543 7667 5.

Sanders, Andrew ed., *Great Victorian Lives: An Era in Obituaries*. HC. [2007] pp. 704. $24.95 ISBN 0 0072 5973 5.

Schaffer, Talia, ed. *Literature and Culture at the Fin de Siècle*. Longman. [2006] pp. 606. $32 ISBN 0 3741 6162 3.

Schenkel, Elmar and Stefan Welz, ed. *Magical Objects: things and beyond*. Berlin, Germany: Galda, Wilch Verlag. [2007] pp. 205. ISBN 9 7819 3125 5196.

Shannon, Richard. *Gladstone: God and Politics*. Continuum. [2007] pp. 550. $130 ISBN 1 8472 5202 8.

Siddiqi, Yumna. *Anxieties of Empire and the Fiction of Intrigue*. ColUP. [2007] pp. 305. $45 ISBN 0 2311 3808 3.

Simmons, Diane. *The Narcissism of Empire: Loss, Rage, and Revenge in Thomas De Quincey, Robert Louis Stevenson, Arthur Conan Doyle, Rudyard Kipling, and Isak Dinesen*. SussexAP. [2007] pp. 148. $57.50 ISBN 1 8451 9156 0.

Simpson, Antony E., ed. *The Maiden Tribute of Modern Babylon: Report of the Secret Commission*, by W.H. Stead. True Bill Press. [2007] pp. 207. $65 ISBN 0 9791 1160 9.

Smith, Margaret, ed. *Selected Letters of Charlotte Brontë*. OUP. [2007] pp. 350. $49.95 ISBN 0 1992 0587 6.

Stafford, Jane. *Maoriland: New Zealand Literature*. UVict. [2006] pp. 350. $24.95 ISBN 0 8647 3522 7.

Stark, Ulrike. *An Empire of Books: The Naval Kishore Press and the Diffusion of the Printed Word in Colonial India*. Permanent Black. [2007] pp. 586. Rs795 ISBN 9 7881 7824 1968.

Steel, Flora Annie. *On the Face of the Waters*. Traviata. [2007] pp. 552. $26 ISBN 9 7819 0533 5084.

Stetz, Margaret D. *Facing the Late Victorians: Portraits of Writers and Artists from the Mark Samuels Lasner Collection*. AUP. [2007] pp. 158. $49 ISBN 0 8741 3992 9.

Stevens, Julie Anne. *The Irish Scene in Somerville and Ross*. IAP. [2007] pp. 287. $75 ISBN 0 7165 3366 9.

Stiles, Anne, ed. *Neurology and Literature 1860–1920*. Palgrave. [2007] pp. 240. $69.95 ISBN 0 2305 2094 4.

Stoneman, Patsy. *Jane Eyre on Stage, 1848–1898: An Illustrated Edition of Eight Plays with Contextual Notes*. MPG Books. [2007] £55 ISBN 9 7807 5460 3481.

Sutherland, John. *Bestsellers: A Very Short Introduction*. OUP. [2007] pp. 127. $11.95 ISBN 0 1992 1489 1.

Sutherland, John. *So You Think You Know Thomas Hardy? A Literary Quizbook*. OUP. [2005] pp. 214. $11.95 ISBN 0 1928 0443 X.

Tague, Gregory F. *Character and Consciousness: George Eliot, Thomas Hardy, E.M. Forster, D.H. Lawrence (Phenomenological, Ecological, and Ethical Readings)*. Academica. [2005] pp. 281. $74.95 ISBN 1 9309 0191 7.

Talairach-Vielmas, Laurence. *Moulding the Female Body in Victorian Fairy Tales and Sensation Novels*. Ashgate. [2007] pp. 220. $99.95 ISBN 0 7546 6034 6.

Taylor, D.J. *Kept: A Victorian Mystery*. Vintage. [2007] pp. 480. £7.99 ISBN 9 7800 9948 8743.

Taylor, Jenny Bourne. *The Cambridge Companion to Wilkie Collins*. CUP. [2007] pp. 207. $85 ISBN 9 7805 2184 0385.

Taylor, Jonathan. *Science and Omniscience in Nineteenth-Century Literature*. SussexAP. [2007] pp. 202. $ 69.50 ISBN 9 7818 4519 1252.

Thain, Marion. *'Michael Field': Poetry, Aestheticism and the Fin de Siècle*. CUP. [2007] pp. 270. £50 ISBN 0 5218 7418 2.

Thormählen, Marianne. *The Brontës and Education*. CUP. [2007] pp. 304. $95 ISBN 0 5218 3289 6.

Valman, Nadia. *The Jewess in Nineteenth-Century British Literary Culture*. CUP. [2007] pp. 288. $91 ISBN 0 5218 6306 6.

Wainwright, Valerie. *Ethics and the English Novel from Austen to Forster*. Ashgate. [2007] pp. vi + 218. $99.95 ISBN 9 7807 5465 4322.

Walton, James. *Vision and Vacancy: The Fictions of J.S. Le Fanu*. UCDubP. [2007] pp. 229. $44.95 ISBN 9 7819 0455 878 79 8.

Waters, Hazel. *Racism on the Victorian Stage: Representation of Slavery and the Black Character*. CUP. [2007] pp. 243. £50 ISBN 0 5218 6262 0.

Watson, Nicola J. *The Literary Tourist: Readers and Places in Romantic and Victorian Britain*. Palgrave. [2006] pp. 244. $65 ISBN 1 4039 9992 9.

Weltman, Sharon Aronofsky. *Performing the Victorian: John Ruskin and Identity in Theater, Science, and Education*. OSUP. [2007] pp. 177. £20.99 ISBN 0 8142 1055 4.

Wiener, Joel H., and Mark Hampton, eds. *Anglo-American Media Interactions, 1850–2000*. Palgrave. [2007] pp. 309. £50 ISBN 9 7802 3052 1254.

Willburn, Sarah A. *Possessed Victorians: Extra Spheres in Nineteenth-Century Mystical Writings*. Ashgate. [2006] pp. 169. $89.95 ISBN 0 7546 5540 7.

Wilson, Aubrey. *The Search for Ernest Bramah*. Creighton and Read. [2007] pp. 261. £18.99 ISBN 0 9553 7530 4.

Wimsatt, James I. *Hopkins's Poetics of Speech Sound: Sprung Rhythm, Lettering, Inscape*. UTorP. [2006] pp. 162. £28 ISBN 0 8020 9154 3.

Wolfreys, Julian. *Dickens to Hardy, 1837–1884: The Novel, the Past, and Cultural Memory in the Nineteenth Century*. Palgrave. [2007] pp. 293. $90 ISBN 0 3336 9623 9.

Wolfreys, Julian. *Writing London*, vol. 3: *Inventions of the City*. Palgrave. [2007] pp. 256. $69.95 ISBN 0 2300 0895 X.

Wollock, Jeffrey, ed. *A Half-Century of Greatness: The Creative Imagination of Europe, 1848–1883*, by Frederic Ewen. NYUP. [2007] pp. 571. £36.50 ISBN 0 8147 2236 9.

Woolford, John. *Robert Browning*. Northcote. [2007] pp. 106. hb £40 ISBN 0 7463 1043 9, pb £13 ISBN 0 7463 0981 3.

Wright, Julia M. *Ireland, India, and Nationalism in Nineteenth-Century Literature*. CUP. [2007] pp. vii + 272. £50 ($95) ISBN 9 7805 2186 8228.

Youngkin, Molly. *Feminist Realism at the Fin de Siècle: The Influence of the Late-Victorian Woman's Press on the Development of the Novel*. OSUP. [2007] pp. 216. £26.86 ISBN 0 8142 1048 1.

XIV

Modern Literature

NICK BENTLEY, MATTHEW CREASY, MARY GROVER,
REBECCA D'MONTÉ, ANDREW HARRISON, AARON JAFFE,
JUSTIN QUINN, ANDREW RADFORD, BRYONY RANDALL
AND GRAHAM SAUNDERS

This chapter has seven sections: 1. General; 2. Pre-1945 Fiction; 3. Post-1945 Fiction; 4. Pre-1950 Drama; 5. Post-1950 Drama; 6. Pre-1950 Poetry; 7. Irish Poetry. Section 1 is by Aaron Jaffe; section 2(a) is by Andrew Radford; section 2(b) is by Mary Grover; section 2(c) is by Andrew Harrison; section 2(d) is by Bryony Randall; section 3 is by Nick Bentley; section 4 is by Rebecca D'Monté; section 5 is by Graham Saunders; section 6 is by Matthew Creasy; section 7 is by Justin Quinn. The sections on James Joyce and post-1950 poetry have been omitted this year. Publications from 2007 in these areas will be reviewed in *YWES* 89.

1. General

In 1989 Peter Keating could write: 'At present, several of literary theory's proliferating strands are even more aggressively ahistorical than the literary criticism they are displacing...the study of literary literature in the present century has been, in effect, de-historicised' (The Haunted Study, p. viii). In the intervening twenty years, literary studies has so thoroughly tunnelled into the historical archive and what Franco Moretti has called 'the large mass of facts' that it has sometimes lost its theoretical bearings (p. 3). Paradoxically, one of the side-effects of all this historical burrowing has been a dwindling of the self-evident logic of chronology and grand periodization in structuring the field itself. Denis Donoghue, for example, describes recent curriculum reforms to the English major at Harvard as an exercise in diminishing 'the role of chronology as the absolute, as the only organizing rubric...to combine it with genres and with geography as equally viable ways of thinking about literature and studying literature' (*Inside Higher Ed* [2008]). Indeed, it is perhaps stating the obvious to observe that little history is now the rule for synthetic and synchronic studies of twentieth-century literature: little histories

Year's Work in English Studies, Volume 88 (2009) © *The English Association; all rights reserved*
doi:10.1093/ywes/map006

of genre—mostly concerning narrative and the novel—and local histories of literary geography and various other small-bore rubrics predominate. Various gravitational fields continue to exert their sway: a new transatlanticism, evidenced in a useful new reader, *Transatlantic Literary Studies: A Reader*, edited by Susan Manning and Andrew Taylor, but also in a number of studies that usefully cross borders to combine British, Irish and North American cases into a new Anglo-American orientation (albeit an orientation more presumed than discussed), new 'modernisms' with increasingly expanded reference, postcolonialism alloyed with cosmopolitanism and continued attention to the relations between literature and other media, cultural forms, material culture and institutions. The sense of an ending to academic interest in 'postmodernism' and 'theory' continues to be as prevalent as it is premature—a received idea as facile as the common theory/history opposition—but there are undeniable elegiac undertones when these words appear now.

While the scholarly monograph remains decisive in advancing literary-critical work and knowledge, edited collections of essays continue to be a vital way for scholars to balance the thematic complexity of the field, the demand for specific forms of expertise and erudition and the desire for provisional versions of the *longue durée*, the big picture or the view from above. One such collection that garnered a lot of attention is the magisterial two-volume *Modernism*, edited by Astradur Eysteinsson and Vivian Liska, including sixty-five essays by as many international scholars, the breadth of which seeks to do justice, in the editors' words, to the current sense that 'the very limits of modernism have been shifting and expanding, including an even greater number of registers, stylistic forms, genres, participating agents and locations' (p. xi). Another less monumental but still timely collection that appeared is *Little Magazines and Modernism: New Approaches*, edited by Suzanne W. Churchill and Adam McKible. Churchill and McKible's book considers the role of periodical culture in enabling a thicker description of modernism as 'an odd and absorbing concourse' (p. 5) for shifting and shuttling 'experimental works or radical opinions of untried, unpopular or under-represented writers' (p. 6). *Poetry, The Dial, The Little Review, The Egoist, Others, Ebony, Topaz, Rogue, Midland, The Soil* and *Rhythm* are given substantial examinations in individual chapters. For the most part, these titles were incredibly short-lived, but they supplied quick and dirty publication venues very good at putting out a variety of heteroclite literary goods. What's more, they comprised a complex constellation of institutions that gave precarious modernist cultures a small but influential foothold on both sides of the Atlantic. As Faith Binkes writes in her excellent essay on John Middleton Murry and Michael Sadleir's *Rhythm*, 'how the modernist "renaissance" would develop within the little magazine field had a lot to do with who would succeed in establishing... cultural capital, rather than who would win the battle for higher circulation or sales' (p. 24). The essays collected here show how much can be learned when the magazines are scrutinized as critical objects themselves. Mark Morrison, who has blazed the trail in this area, writes a fitting preface to the volume that includes a brief but useful overview of the recent turn to material culture in modernist studies initiated by the likes of Michael North, Jennifer Wicke, Kevin J.H. Dettmar, Stephen Watt, Janet Lyon, Alan Golding (also represented in the collection) and others: 'Rather than interpreting little magazines simply as useful anthologies of modernist material, scholars have begun to frame the magazines themselves as primary texts. Recent studies analysing modernism's relationship to its long-ignored parent, modernity, have engaged with little magazines; the rehistoricizing of twentieth-century print culture, including modernist magazines, has again brought public-sphere theory to the fore' (pp. xv–xvi).

The availability of archival materials and reprint runs in libraries and web-based initiatives, such as the Modernist Journals Project led by Sean Latham and Robert Scholes (who wrote a methodologically suggestive afterword to this volume), also helps facilitate a bloom in this kind of research into an alternative public sphere. At its best, this work does more than rescue new masterpieces from oblivion. It provides new ways of writing and thinking about literature, critical new consideration of the original scene of the presentation of modernist value as a product of complex editorial choices, negotiations and controversies.

Isolated and atomized, a typical little magazine hardly seems to speak for more than a hobby concern: in Golding's words, 'it was programmatically non-commercial, lived constantly on the edge of bankruptcy, could not pay its contributors, and . . . had a small circulation of never more than two thousand and probably closer to one' (p. 69). Yet, in practice—as Golding shows in his examination of *The Little Review* and *The Dial*—the aggregation of these venues formed a mutually productive network for all involved, a small virtual world of sorts. Many journals had explicit political orientations, or, like *The Egoist*, formerly *The New Freewoman*, had evolved out of vestigial organs designed for political causes, and some of the lessons of solidarity built through activist networking were retained: 'the office of the *Liberator*, a leftist political magazine, provided a place for Mike Gold, a budding Communist from Jewish streets of the Lower East Side, to overhear the Baroness Elsa von Freytag-Loringhoven, a wildly eccentric German immigrant, recite her Dadaist poetry to Claude McKay, a Jamaican sonneteer with connections to radical political organizations in England and a growing prominence in the flourishing Harlem Renaissance' (p. 4). In Churchill and McKible's account, this scene of modernist communitarianism (which McKible discusses in his contribution) provides a congenial and pluralist image for their collection that belies something of its factionalist origins: 'a "great party" model [of modernism] that duly recognizes the era's sense of urgency, mechanization, and conflict but also addresses modernism's spirit of creativity, conviviality, and playfulness' (p. 13).

This commitment to modernist pluralism and collaboration is also evident in *Gender in Modernism: New Geographies, Complex Intersections*, edited by Bonnie Kime Scott. This isn't merely a reissue of the groundbreaking *The Gender of Modernism*—assembled in 1990 by Scott and 'a team of collaborators', editors and anthologists—as one might expect from the title (p. 1). Instead, it represents both a sequel and a reboot for the project, accounting for changes in modernist studies, new theoretical conceptions of gender and the shifting conditions for feminist literary scholarship. There is, of course, a newly thematically organized—rather than author-oriented—table of contents, providing a storehouse of archival goodies: 'The organization of [the predecessor volume] by author betrays how important the challenge to the canon and recuperative work were . . . Once assembled, however, a rich set of connections and common concerns among the selected authors became obvious. An illustration from the introduction, titled "A Tangled Mesh of Modernists," has been one of the most frequently cited aspects of the book . . . Further tangling has become the order of the day for [this book, its successor]' (p. 14).

In this recombinant tangle of modernist others and contemporary gender critics, Scott proposes the confluence of their shared interests in networking: "in the first decade of the twenty-first century, gender is most interesting as a system connected with and negotiated among cultural identifiers' (p. 2). Following a balanced but finally ambivalent overview of the changing critical climate of the last two decades (about the emergence of critical work on masculinities, for instance, she detects 'the spectre of male co-option, or reinforcement of contentious lines of opposition', p. 4), Scott doubles down on the sober assessment that, for second-wave feminist literary scholarship, opening up the modernist archive is and remains one of its durable accomplishments (a 'retro-prospective' gain in her phrase). Indeed, on the crucial matter of modernist women, material culture and literary work, the chapters grouped as 'Issues of Production and Reception' maintain the important critical continuity with Shari Benstock's decisive *Women of the Left Bank* [1976], for newer concerns with literary cultures, readers, access, markets and cultural administration without question owe much to a decidedly feminist literary critical genealogy.

Among the fascinating materials anthologized in the book as a whole one finds Hope Mirrlees's *Paris: A Poem*, an expansive gathering of documents connecting early modernism to suffragism and progressive politics and a selection of alternative genres such as manifestos, participatory journalism and proto-film criticism. Sonita Sarker's chapter, 'Race, Nation, and Modernity: The Anti-Colonial Consciousness of Modernism'—with selections by Behramji Merwanji Malabari, Victoria Ocampo and Cornelia Sorabji, as well as Jean Rhys and Gertrude Stein, who were both, of course, represented in the predecessor—advances this line of argument by insisting that a modernist canon merely pluralized to include other voices doesn't work: the 'expansion of the term [international modernism] is not performed by adding South American and Asian regions to the more frequently employed Western European–North American connections . . . these geographies and their respective histories are mutually formative, even within imbalances of power' (p. 473). In other words, thinking back to the most profound lessons of this and its processor volume, modernity itself can no longer be simply adduced from which modernist masterworks survived, even if this habit is still with us. The recent addition of 'new geographies' to modernist concerns, evidenced by Sarker's section and the book's subtitle, necessarily adds the problem of linguistic difference and translation—matters which historically have been the purview of comparative literature—to this productive mix.

Mary Ann Gillies's *The Professional Literary Agent in Britain: 1890–1920* offers the kind of focused approach to the study of material cultures and practices only a monograph can handle. Her topic, the rise of the professional literary agent, cuts across the late nineteenth and early twentieth centuries. On the whole, this project, which draws considerably on book history and the new bibliographic studies, is a historical narrative about the emergence of professionalization as an intermediation between authors and publishers. The figure of the professional literary agent—who synthesized the skill sets of publisher's reader, literary journalist, bookkeeper, copyright lawyer and editor—promised the author expert knowledge in different horizontal publishing niches, the so-called 'planes' of publishing (a term Gillies takes from Janice Radway, who in turn repurposed it from an essay by Henry Seidel Canby, the critic and founding editor of the *Saturday Evening Post*). Rather than borrowing from esoteric cosmology, it may make more sense to think of this knowledge as market expertise. The powers of agents as intermediaries between authors and the publishers rested on their demonstrated knowledge in creating value through publication and publicity in different markets delivering different literary demographics, on the one hand, and maintaining a stable of talented and reliable authors on the other. Agents were proficient not just in securing favourable book deals but also in slicing up the burgeoning periodical marketplace for their clients, making serialization deals and, perhaps most critically, knowing how to navigate the benefits of complex new copyright laws for their clientele.

The two main protagonists of the study are A.P. Watt, the first professional agent, who was active from the 1880s until his death in 1914, and J.B. Pinker, who was active from the mid-1890s until his death in 1922. Watt, who essentially invented the professional protocols (such as the 10 per cent commission), departed from the man-of-leisure amateurism that predominated in literary culture; his bullpen included only established late Victorian literary reputations of authors such as George MacDonald, Rudyard Kipling, Marie Corelli and Arthur Conan Doyle. Pinker's speciality was assisting authors with emerging reputations and riskier, more original output—Arnold Bennett, Joseph Conrad, Henry James, D.H. Lawrence, James Joyce and Katherine Mansfield. With Conrad (who, with MacDonald, provides one of the two authorial axes of Gillies's book), Pinker, in effect, tried to discipline his client's unruly business practices, renegotiating contracts and repurchasing copyrights when necessary, 'consolidating management of all of Conrad's literary property ... finding markets for new works; and working with Conrad to raise his public profile' (p. 145). The idea, Gillies argues, was to centralize and stabilize Conrad's literary livelihood through a more regular income of residuals, advances and even loans until his ship came in. In this sense—and noting Pinker's obvious affection for his client—Gillies characterizes Pinker's function as 'patron-investor', borrowing Lawrence Rainey's term (p. 99). Yet, for Pinker, the emphasis should be more on investor than patron, an investor choosing high-potential yields on risky long-term literary stocks in emerging markets. His advice to the prolific Bennett, for example, was to slow down publication output so as not to dilute his brand precipitously. With Lawrence, the risk didn't pay out; after years of loans and exertions, the author severed ties with the agent, several hundred pounds in hock. Still, Pinker's successes depended on his reputation as a literary risk-taker and talent-spotter, and, for that, the occasional eccentric failure (gossip that he was a 'little parvenu snob of a procurer of books', p. 100) did no harm. It may have been less lack of professionalism (as Gillies emphasizes) than impatience that led Lawrence, Joyce and, at first, Conrad to pursue side dealings—such as Joyce's famous publishing experiment with Sylvia Beach—an impatience which could easily be read in terms of a superior grasp of the still inchoate modernist scene. Indeed, *pace* Gillies and Rainey, the evidence here is not of patronage 'disguised as something else' but exactly the opposite, something else, something instrumentally related to making a scene, occasionally disguised in the costume of patronage and coterie.

Vicki Mahaffey's *Modernist Literature, Challenging Fictions* situates itself as something of a field guide to modernism's readers (or 'learners', as she prefers) about unfamiliar literary terrain. Consequently, it is pitched at level suitable for advanced undergraduates. The first section of the book is also a long essay about an expressive link—a kind of felt pedagogical actuality—between reading modernist fiction today and the notion that 'Modernist literature emerged out of [a] drive for a freer, less socially conservative form of education' (p. vii). The essay begins with a consideration of Stanley Milgram's experiments about social obedience and authoritarianism, connecting these studies with the habituated cruelties of the ordinary enablers of the Nazi regime. Mahaffey argues that challenging modernist fiction seeks to forgo this perilous dynamic of identification: 'To the extent that reading promotes emotional identification with people of different backgrounds, it may interrupt the distancing mechanisms that are necessary to obey authority' (p. 36). Texts like *The Waste Land, Ulysses, The Waves*, the *Cantos*, Beckett's trilogy and *The Sound and the Fury*, she writes later, 'are designed not to help readers identify with some ideal of virtue, but to restore an awareness of the interconnectedness of things. Instead of gratifying our desires and allaying our fears, they work to expose the interdependence of desire and fear, good and evil and a host of other oppositions. These works reward those who are looking for a comprehensive and dynamic view of reality from which neither the reader nor the author is exempted by privilege or excellence' (p. 56).

'Hypocrite lecteur!—mon semblable,—mon frère!' In times when there is much written about modernism's bads, its ugly feelings and violent affect, Mahaffey's is an apologia—a refreshing defence of the possibilities of profounder modernist benefits, a defence that leads her in the end to expand the actuality of a modernist scene far beyond the familiar 1890–1940 purview she initially proposes: 'If . . . we understand modernism to designate an attempt to grapple more immediately with an increasingly dynamic and contradictory reality, then modernism is very much alive' (p. 67). The persistence of the same impulse to recuperate modernism's aesthetic also motivates Kevin Bell's contrarian and theoretically incisive *Ashes Taken for Fire: Aesthetic Modernism and the Critique of Identity*, which, like Mahaffey's book, is concerned with a salutary conjunction of modernism's literary powers and its potential for conceptualizing and—in Bell's argument—critiquing identity formation. His study concerns familiar figures from the new modernist studies—Conrad, Woolf, Ralph Ellison, William Faulkner, Nathanael West and Chester Himes—but his Anglo-American congregation is interesting, if somewhat unexplored. What makes the book specifically contrarian in this light is its lack of interest in an account of modernism informed by historical and historicist modes of criticism, other than the pertinent modernist reflexive 'event' of its 'giving of language itself'—a move usually more typical in books about modernist and avant-garde poetics (p. 5). Yet it is Bell's version of a *poetics* of modernist fiction that entails profound implications for the subject of race and gender; the modernist aesthetic experiment in fiction, he argues, 'thematizes both the profound absence prior to language and the strategic concealment of that void by language' (p. 1).

'Always historicize', Fredric Jameson wrote. With this imperative in mind, here's the first stanza of Henry Reed's poem 'Chard Whitlow', written in 1941 in what was then the late Eliotic idiom:

As we get older we do not get any younger.
Seasons return, and to-day I am fifty-five,
And this time last year I was fifty-four
And this time next year I shall be sixty-two.
And I cannot say I should like (to speak for myself)
To see my time over again—if you can call it time:
Fidgeting uneasily under a draughty stair,
Or counting sleepless nights in the crowded tube.

How did modernism age? Did all that seemed terribly new circa 1910 (or 1914 or 1922), age well circa 1941 (or 1945)? How does the Second World War—one of the hard-landscape features of twentieth-century history more generally, and of British social and cultural history in particular—implicate conceptions of the modernist achievement? These are some of the questions that resonate after reading Marina MacKay's provocative *Modernism and World War II*. The expressed subject is re-examining 'late' British modernism—late work by Eliot, Woolf and Rebecca West, supplemented by Evelyn Waugh and Henry Green—in conjunction with the various modes of social, cultural, and political disruptions and settlements represented by the Second World War. The familiar relations of the First World War and modernism's origins have been far more thoroughly hashed over, from Paul Fussell to Vincent Sherry. The role of the 'sequel' on conceptions of modernism's ends, 'its realisation and its dissolution', in MacKay's phrase, is a particularly interesting and under-examined topic (p. 1). MacKay is interested in what this second, very different experience of England at war (or being besieged at home) did to the politics of literary modernism, from the ageing first-wave modernists Eliot and Woolf 'forced . . . belatedly to scrutinise their own social and political investments' (p. 4) to the subsequent—if not terribly young— second-generation modernists forced to ask 'how the consensus politics of the Second World War [could be] productive of acutely self-aware literary forms' (p. 14). The abstraction of the latter war into a kind of cultural-historical caesura in literary history has proven as stubbornly distortional as the effects of the former. A critique of the unreflective, teleological commonplaces of modernist studies is one of the most welcome implications of this book, focused, like Tyrus Miller's *Late Modernism* [1999] before it, on

'longer outcomes rather than [modernism's] notional origins' (p. 15).
MacKay's work is a vigorous reappraisal of a truly under-theorized and
under-historicized concern. Rethinking literary periodizations also demands
consideration of the limits necessarily imposed by the generational lifespan of
authors. In 1941, when Woolf died, she was 59 (Joyce, who died two short
months before, was 58). That year, Eliot was 52 (not 55, as Reed has it) and,
among the 'younger' modernists (p. 10) of MacKay's study, West was 48,
Waugh was 37 and Green was 35. Just for contrast, William Golding was 29,
Reed was 27, Muriel Spark was 23 and Keith Douglas was 21.

Continuing in this vein, Peter Kalliney's *Cities of Affluence and Anger: A
Literary Geography of Modern Englishness* looks at twentieth-century English
literary history with a different, even more expansive, periodizing lens in order
to revisit the increasingly vexed and vexing issues of nationality and identity.
Like Jed Esty's *Shrinking Island*, a predecessor in this regard, it sets in motion
an account of English literature that is ambitiously congruent across the mid-
century ('reaccess[ing] the dividing line of World War II' in particular (p. 111))
without sealing off such international tendencies as modernism, cosmopolitanism, migration and postcolonialism as non-nativist. Indeed, like Esty,
Kalliney accepts the necessary challenge and cultural implications of 'the
long durée of imperial contraction' in crafting an unrestricted account of
English/British literature (p. 6), but also does so in a way that largely ignores
MacKay's caveat about the Second World War as a crucial aspect of
England's 'diminution' (p. 17). For an organizing logic, Kalliney turns to
London itself, arguing that, in the twentieth century, its symbolic capacity for
conveying Englishness supplanted the countryside as a dominant setting
and resource for reimagining national identity with a series of new settlements
regarding class, ethnicity and economics, building on Raymond Williams's
The Country and the City. His chapter on E.M. Forster's *Howards End* and
Waugh's *Brideshead Revisited* recount the crisis and ruin of the country house
(initiated as much by the rise of the parodic imitation in suburbia as anything
else) as a failure of a social order based on the prerogatives of a privileged few
and the cultural invisibility of the rest. For Kalliney, these novels recount
through a doubled nostalgia the failure of 'a "real" literary place . . . through
which the pastoral could perform substantive political and cultural work'
(p. 73). Woolf's *Mrs Dalloway* and a brief consideration of Sam Selvon's
Lonely Londoners let Kalliney discuss the formation of new literary places as
modernist interventions in busy commercial cultures ('tacky, cacophonous,
ostentatious', p. 75) and with a high communitarian potential for new
political, social and sexual awareness experienced outdoors, especially in
public parks. The middle section on John Osborne's *Look Back in Anger*
and Alan Sillitoe's *Saturday Night and Sunday Morning*—which provides the
keywords of the book's title—allows the author to go inside the postwar urban
dwelling and explore the literary and cultural politics of the welfare state. The
last chapters on Doris Lessing's *The Golden Notebook* and Salman Rushdie's
The Satanic Verses take this 'literary home anthropology' (p. 143) outward by
considering the postwar transformation of domesticity in the context of
postcolonial literature and migration narratives for a globalized cosmopolity.

Replete with fascinating archival research, Kalliney's book, in effect, tells the story of the literary legitimation of new kinds of urban space.

In *Novels, Maps, Modernity: The Spatial Imagination, 1850–2000*, Eric Bulson pursues the spatial analysis of literature from a different angle. He examines changes in literary spaces of modernity by exploring 'the concept of "location" ' (p. 24) for readers via representations of the phenomena of orientation and disorientation in novels. Not only is there a long history of printing maps of literary places—real or imagined—in the front and back matter of novels, but, also, there was a certain literary motive in the origins of travel guidebooks and their reception and evolution. Literary pilgrimages and literary sightseeing 'were at once conceived as guides to the "holy sites" of literary personages and secularized reading tools that enabled readers to confirm or detract from the authenticity of poems and novels' (p. 26). Of particular interest for Bulson is the rise of what he calls 'travelling for the plot', which connects paradigmatically with Dickens, and an impulse which 'tore readers from their armchairs and created a set of sightseeing detours across England and the continent . . . to break from the routine of more well-trodden itineraries' (p. 26). Rapidly changing urban spaces created new difficulties for such tourist-readers, trained on a certain realist exactitude of detail. This change, in part, led to the emergence of modernist modes of literary orientation and disorientation which he calls 'mapping the plot': 'What made the modernist urban novel of the 1920s so remarkably different was the fact that the city was renamed more than it was described' (p. 31). In this context, literary mapping is as troublesome as it is instrumental: 'Like the novel, they can create effects of simultaneity, produce the illusion of reality, and even give shape and meaning to something as abstract as a nation' (p. 41). Building on Walter Benjamin, Henri Lefebvre, Guy DeBord and Franco Moretti, Bulson provides an intriguing blueprint for 'a materialist history of novelistic space' (p. 41); his relatively small book concentrates on just three admittedly expansive novels—*Moby-Dick, Ulysses* and *Gravity's Rainbow*—all of which supply textually specific mapping conundrums. His chapters make use of interesting contextual materials such as the likely cartographical source materials for each work and attempts by commentators on these novels to render supplemental maps of their represented spaces, as well as such primary map-making materials as the Ordnance Survey.

A third book interested in the cultural phenomenology of space in modernity is David L. Pike's *Metropolis on the Styx: The Underworlds of Modern Urban Culture, 1800–2001*. It begins with a congenial description of Pike's own childhood home in Louisville, Kentucky, 'a three-story Victorian-style house, built in 1879', with a terrifying, filthy and nearly incomprehensible 'netherworld' of an unfinished cellar (pp. xiii–xiv). The futile attempt to make rational sense and use of this area as a workshop or a playroom is a familiar enough enterprise to this reviewer and a fitting emblem for the infernal and uncanny aspects of the inevitable dark places of modernity and its cities. *Metropolis on the Styx* is a compendious successor to—and continuation of—Pike's last book, *Subterranean Cities: The World beneath Paris and London, 1800–1945* [2006]. Whereas *Subterranean Cities* focused on the subway, the cemetery and the sewer, this one turns to new underworldly constellations, representations of commingling bodies, seemingly subterranean dwellers in tenements, mineral mines, arcades and railway arches, the trenches of First World War warfare and darkened movie theatres. With a subject like 'the vertical city, its twin modes of perception—the view from above, the view from below—and the unstable thresholds between them', the author quite rightly sees a need for 'interdisciplinary and eclectic' methodological invention (p. xv). One of his most generative axioms is that 'When interpreting the under-ground . . . whatever the form it takes, it always includes a displaced vision of something that poses a crisis of representation in the world above' (p. 2). Not surprisingly, this is an account of modernity that gives pride of place to certain 'texts'—Paris, London, Baudelaire, Benjamin, Hollywood film noir, Satanism, the nineteenth century—but it is a noteworthy achievement to analyse the phantasmagoria of so many semiotically overdetermined sites with theoretical acuity and simultaneously to provide an archivally rich (not to mention engrossingly illustrated) take on the Industrial Revolution.

Elisabeth Ladenson's *Dirt for Art's Sake: Books on Trial from Madam Bovary to Lolita* asks, 'how does an "obscene" book become a "classic"?'. What transmogrifies literary dirt into the stuff of 'required reading lists' (pp. xv–xvi)? Pursuing this question, she insists on an understanding of censorship history as not peripheral but central to the study of such famous censored works as *Madame Bovary*, *Fleurs du mal*, *Ulysses*, *The Well of Loneliness*, *Lady Chatterley's Lover*, *Tropic of Cancer* and *Lolita* (each gets a chapter). Her study emphasizes the implications of various legal proceedings and attendant controversies alongside fraught publication histories and literary publicity campaigns to comment on the works themselves, their reception and adaptation into film and the evolving social and political context of censorship in modern France, England and the United States. The eight novels and one book of poetry she examines became what they are (in her assessment, five or six classics still held in the highest regard, one classic of the gay and lesbian canon, one or two uneven curiosities) not in spite of their difficulties with the censor but because they solicited such difficulties: 'nine examples of works that were banned or prosecuted, or both, when they first appeared and have since achieved, in one way or another, "classic" status' (p. xiii). As her scare quotes indicate, 'classic' is not a word used much today, after the canon wars, without a degree of irony—long after Frank Kermode's and, further back, Eliot's mediations; at the same time, neither is the word 'obscene'.

Still, if academics and scholars have given up on conferring the former appellation, and literary prosecutors the latter, where do they come from? Literary journalists? In effect, censorship—and, perhaps more vitally, a work's capacity to invite and then to withstand the charge of indecency or obscenity—is for certain works a key ingredient to subsequent dissemination, interpreta-tion and, in many cases, materiality as a text, becoming less a published work than a perennial survivor (of the slaughterhouse). Legal histories stick to these texts like lamprey fish. Flaubert, for example, hired a private stenographer to record the trial of *Madame Bovary* and included the transcripts in the published version. This framework then became essential to the novel's adaptation in the 1949 Vincente Minnelli film, which is framed by a fictionalized version of the trial. In a sense, Flaubert's awareness of the paradoxical sanction provided by legalistic censure not only influenced his novel's reception and fame but also, in effect, is implicated in his initial choice to represent (and, thinking of Dominick LaCapra's argument, represent without explicit censure) the moral hazards of a bored female petit bourgeois. As other scholars on this topic have shown—LaCapra, Adam Parkes, Alison Pease and Celia Marshik—the implications of analysis of censorship, obscenity and pornography for literary criticism and theory are rich; aside from a drive-by acknowledgement of Michel Foucault in the preface, this book is not so much devoid of theory as content to leave jargon to one side in favour of a tone that is all too deceptively breezy. Nonetheless, the book remains highly suggestive in this vein. For example, one of the reasons Ladenson suggests that past censorship continues to add interpretive frisson for present-day readers is that it supplements reading classics with requisite reading: the bad-faith interpretative choices of the past's literary litigators. Ladenson is careful to argue against what she calls 'chronological chauvinism', a kind of Whig history of obscenity and censorship in which the enlightened present redeems the benighted past, but notes an important hangover of literary nostalgia for times when a book could be considered subversive and cause a public stir. Another key thread running through the book is how—beginning in Paris in 1857, the year of the Baudelaire and Flaubert trials, which inspired the British obscenity laws, it seems—the agents of censorship were intertwined with the critical legacies concerning realism (the case that diverse forms of sexuality, moral hazards for lower-class women, excrement, profane language etc., are realistic parts of the human condition and thus virtuous to represent) and the process by which art for art's sake becomes a transparent, received ideology. Despite its early emphasis on France, the core of this book, in fact, centres on anglophone writers of the modernist period—Joyce, Lawrence and Radclyffe Hall—and two uniquely cosmopolitan American late modernists— Henry Miller and Nabokov. Thus it should be of special interest for twentieth-century transatlanticists, in particular those interested in what Colin MacCabe has called 'the complicated interrelations between the worlds of literature and film' (p. x).

This quote from MacCabe, in fact, is referring to David Trotter's *Cinema and Modernism*, in his foreword to that outstanding book, which provides a compelling account of these interrelations. 'It is no exaggeration', MacCabe writes, 'to say that [Trotter's book] is the most important book on this topic yet written' (p. x). What makes his assessment right is the theoretical acuity and historical purchase one comes to expect from Trotter, coupled with his crucial insight that cutting through the fog on this topic first depends on recognizing that modernism and cinema did not evolve in hermetically sealed universes, but with—again to borrow from MacCabe—a 'certain aesthetic convergence' of purpose (p. xi): 'There is a history . . . to literature's affinities with cinema . . . such affinities should only be established—and put to use in literary criticism—on the basis of what a writer might conceivably have known about cinema as it was at the time of writing' (p. 2). A principled aversion to anachronism and analogy is a healthy corrective to tendencies in the respective histories of literature and film to over-represent and over-sample their avant-garde teleologies (healthy, if a bit draconian—surely creative anachronism and analogy have a heuristic role). One of Trotter's real achievements is to recognize that Woolf, Eliot and Joyce were indeed 'folk' theorists of the cinema in their own time, and so too were D.W. Griffiths and Charlie Chaplin theoretical *bricoleurs*, cobbling together working philosophies and approximations of literary technique.

2. Pre-1945 Fiction

(a) British Fiction, 1900–1930
Like previous years, 2007 continues to offer formally attentive and intellectually capacious accounts of the early twentieth-century British novel, not only in terms of how it evolved in myriad forms, or why it retains the power to disrupt our sentimental and generic expectations, but also through its tendency to amplify or complicate what Jessica Berman calls 'Modernism's Possible Geographies'. Since the publication of Gaonkar, ed., *Alternative Modernities* [2001], scholars have evinced a keen fascination with 'the cultural and political discourses of global modernity' and the 'linguistic and national boundaries' it traverses (p. 8). This trend is noticeable not only in the voluminous postcolonial research dedicated to perennially popular literary figures such as Joseph Conrad and E.M. Forster, but also in punchy and wide-ranging surveys of the period geared towards a university readership, such as Pericles Lewis's *Cambridge Introduction to Modernism*, Morag Shiach, ed., *The Cambridge Companion to the Modernist Novel*, Leigh Wilson's succinct *Modernism* and David Punter's richly multiplicitous concept of *Modernity*.

Lawrence Phillips, ed., *A Mighty Mass of Brick and Smoke*, Peter Brooker's *Bohemia in London: The Social Scene of Early Modernism* and David L. Pike's *Metropolis on the Styx* are all admirably attuned to the recent emergence of a vibrant interdisciplinary field of urban socio-cultural studies (for example, Alev Çinar and Thomas Bender, eds., *Urban Imaginaries: Locating the Modern City*). Phillips's collection prompts us to enquire whether Edwardian depictions of London might be construed in terms of a 'grid structure'—a template of visual and material patterning reinforced across 'legible spaces' from the visual-textual integration of the printed page' to the design of elegant metropolitan thoroughfares (p. 11). Nicholas Freeman's *Conceiving the City: London, Literature, and Art 1870–1914* engages in the most productive mode of literary analysis, one whose breadth of attention is fused with deep, discipline-specific close reading of narrative strategies. Freeman probes the ways in which writers and artists approached the representation of London between the death of Charles Dickens in 1870 and the outbreak of the Great War. During these years, London was the most densely populated city in the world, and one whose physical and psychological limits seemed 'all but impossible to demarcate' (p. v). Freeman perhaps underestimates the role maps, guides and commercial directories played in the lived experience of the capital, and more could have been said about the tangle of race, class and gender politics imbuing George Sims's *Devil in London* [1908]. Nevertheless, Freeman's carefully argued study functions especially well through unorthodox but compelling figures such as Arthur Machen, whose stories evoke the capital as a locus of concealed rooms, shadowy enclaves and arcane rituals.

As Freeman's *Conceiving the City* acknowledges, Machen's fiercely eclectic and controversial corpus rarely features in the master-narratives of literary modernism. Indeed, some of the most trenchant research in 2007 counsels the continuing value of uncovering modernisms in improbable but provocative places, surveying those British novelists—such as John Galsworthy, H.H. Munro (Saki), Mary Butts and the Powys brothers—who have been frequently overlooked or misconstrued by commentators eager to keep the literary canon 'high' and 'narrow'. Tracy Hargreaves's 'Nostalgic Retrieval: Sexual Politics, Cultural Aesthetics and Literary Form in John Galsworthy's *The Forsyte Saga*' (*English* 56[2007] 127–46) raises lively questions about how architecture operates as a complex meeting point of the opposed tenets of art and property that imbue the rancorous personal feuds of the Forsyte clan. Kurt Koenigsberger's *The Novel and the Menagerie: Totality, Englishness, and Empire* charts the degree to which exhibitions of zoological exotica have generated and mingled with a series of memorable narratives of England and contested ideologies of Englishness. This ambitious enterprise incorporates not only fascinating literary oddities like Rebecca West's London fantasy *Harriet Hume* [1929], but also Arnold Bennett's best-known novel, *The Old Wives' Tale* [1908], which portrays how a travelling menagerie of the 1860s subverts the stultifying rhythms of regional existence.

Sandie Byrne's *The Unbearable Saki: The Work of H.H. Munro* argues that Saki's writing was no nostalgic rendering of a lost golden age of patrician power, patronage and privilege, and the study brings a welcome focus to novels largely forgotten today, such as *When William Came* [1913], which problematizes the cosmopolitan insouciance of his short stories. In his novels Saki intimates a fear that male energies might be stifled by the homogenizing force of consensus in the cheerless English suburbs, which invites detailed comparison with E.M. Forster's account of debilitating domesticity in *The Longest Journey* [1907]. Byrne's scrutiny of short stories sometimes oversimplifies the slyly sardonic play of Saki's wit. Moreover, Byrne's habit of utilizing selected tales to illuminate the numerous unknown facets of Saki's career while simultaneously excavating the life for a key to unlock the mysteries of his 'fictional craft' (p. 39) creates structural awkwardness. Byrne is most perceptive in chapter 7, which canvasses Saki's mordant rendering of the atavistic forces that threaten to erupt in the midst of a staid bourgeois hinterland.

That John Cowper Powys has never garnered the acclaim he deserves as one of the twentieth century's most idiosyncratic storytellers is unsurprising, according to Morine Kristdóttir in *Descents of Memory: The Life of John Cowper Powys*. This is the first comprehensive biography of a novelist who seemed to revel in his position on the outer margins of academic and literary kudos. Until he was nearly 60, Powys earned his living as an itinerant lecturer, much of the time in America. Kristdóttir ventures a convincing and textured reading of Powys's novels that attempts to put his sizeable oeuvre on the map of twentieth-century literary history, while indicating why he so often goes unread. Kristdóttir's searching account also throws into sharp relief the sensuous immediacy and intellectual scope of the unjustly neglected early fictions *Wood and Stone* [1915] and *Rodmoor* [1916], as well as the 'Wessex novel' that many pundits hail as his crowning achievement, *Wolf Solent* [1929].

Andrew Radford addresses the Edwardian regional novelist Mary Webb in 'Hardy's *Tess*, Mary Webb and the Persephone Myth' (THY 35[2007], 55–72). Webb's *Gone to Earth* [1917]—selected by Rebecca West as 'Novel of the Year'—was filmed in 1950 by Michael Powell and Emeric Pressburger, and much of her fiction remained in print for years before Virago initiated a more methodical policy of reprints in the 1970s. In Radford's study Webb is construed as an 'imaginative archaeologist', committed to salvaging the mental and physical heirlooms of an endangered 'West Country' tradition.

Like John Cowper Powys and Mary Webb, Mary Butts is identified as a 'West Country' author whose fiction, especially *Armed with Madness* [1928], utilizes occult tropes to restore a forgotten legacy, the myth of matriarchal origins. In striking contrast to Virginia Woolf, D.H. Lawrence and James Joyce, who generate impressive cottage industries in academic circles, Butts remains an obscure and equivocal presence. For Angela Kershaw and Angela Kimyongür, eds., *Women in Europe between the Wars: Politics, Culture and Society*, this erasure of women's novels from literary and cultural history is ideologically motivated and far from accidental. However, over the past decade Mary Butts has become the recipient of subtle and sophisticated criticism, thanks largely to Jane Garrity, whose *Step-Daughters of England: British Women Novelists and the National Imaginary* [2003] remains essential reading for anyone interested in the intricate racial and class politics imbuing interwar women's fiction. Laura Doan and Jane Garrity, eds., *Sapphic Modernities: Sexuality, Women and National Culture*, explores how the Sapphic figure, in her varied and contradictory guises, 'refigures the relation' (p. 1) between public and private space within literary modernity. Like Georgia Johnston's *The Formation of 20th-Century Queer Autobiography* and Catherine Maxwell and Patricia Pullman, eds., *Vernon Lee: Decadence, Ethics, Aesthetics*, *Sapphic Modernities* gauges with rigour myriad constructions of a transgressive or oppositional femininity. Garrity's deeply pondered essay on 'Mary Butts's "Fanatical Pédérastie": Queer Urban Life in 1920s London and Paris' reveals an elliptical and shifting queer selfhood at the core of Butts's epistolary novel *Imaginary Letters* [1928].

George M. Johnson's scrupulously researched essay on Algernon Blackwood's psychic detective, Dr John Silence [1906–7] (in Fox and Melikoglu, eds., *Formal Investigations: Aesthetic Style in Late-Victorian and Edwardian Detective Fiction*, pp. 76–91) will be of considerable interest to scholars of Mary Butts, on whose high modernist fiction Blackwood's tales exerted a signal influence. Johnson proposes that Blackwood's detective tales comprise a vibrant proto-modernist exploration of the aesthetic potential of the new psychology and more esoteric mystical lore. Johnson's fluent and timely contribution is one of a number of conceptually assured essays in *Formal Investigations* which underscore how much our comprehension of the Edwardian detective genre owes to the impact of mass culture on the establishment of literary hierarchies. *Formal Investigations* nicely complements

Sarah Dillon's *The Palimpsest: Literature, Criticism, Theory*, which provides a resourceful reading of Arthur Conan Doyle's 1904 Sherlock Holmes story 'The Adventure of the Golden Pince-Nez'.

The troubling contradiction at the heart of Butts's non-historical fiction, which Garrity addresses with rare insight—the tendency to deploy a paranoid, punitive and even anti-Semitic rhetoric while simultaneously lauding facets of modernism's cosmopolitan panache—is also probed by Maren Tova Linett's *Modernism, Feminism, and Jewishness*. Linett assesses the aesthetic and political roles performed by Jewish characters in interwar British women's fiction. Linett argues that Jean Rhys, Sylvia Townsend Warner and Dorothy Richardson each enlist 'a multifaceted vision of Jewishness' (p. 18) to help them shape fictions that are thematically bold and formally stringent. Linett shows well Richardson's simultaneous identification with and edgy distancing from members of this ethnic group, which generates an enigmatically ambivalent perspective in which Jews function on occasions as standard-bearers for the author's crusading aesthetic, and at times foils against which her stylistic repertoire is defined.

Howard Finn's essay 'Writing Lives: Dorothy Richardson, May Sinclair, Gertrude Stein' (in Shiach, ed., pp. 191–205) is particularly astute in delineating the centrality of the autobiographical dimension in Richardson's *Pilgrimage* and also in the ways in which modernist formal innovations and stylistic choices are 'bound up' in her fiction with the endeavour both to express and to repudiate 'traumatic material' in the process of chronicling a life (p. 191). The second chapter of Scott McCracken's *Masculinities, Modernist Fiction and the Urban Public Sphere*, which fuses urban cultural history, gender studies and critical theory in its analysis of Dorothy Richardson and the New Woman novelists, is effective in showing how *Pilgrimage* as a text repudiates the 'fixity of secure boundaries for identity' (p. 20). The metropolis in McCracken's shrewd analysis of Richardson's fiction emerges as a field of experience or process that may often be as 'aesthetic' as it is 'concrete' (p. 21).

As Vicki Mahaffey posits in *Challenging Fictions*, Dorothy Richardson's *Pilgrimage*, through its 'discomfiting insights' and its 'strong emotional undercurrents', provokes readers to interrogate the brittle 'fictions' that they live by (p. 52). To read *Pilgrimage* in a way that unlocks its acerbic humour, Mahaffey suggests, we must be both receptive and resistant to the author's textured perspective, actively testing it with our own experience, knowledge and sensibilities. Richardson also features prominently in Laura Marcus's *The Tenth Muse: Writing about Cinema in the Modernist Period*, which charts the author's energetic responses to the new medium of cinema, its techniques and exhibition, giving an enriched understanding of the ways in which her film articles located discursive strategies adequate to the representation of the technology, with its unprecedented powers of movement.

Bryony Randall's *Modernism, Daily Time and Everyday Life* proposes that Dorothy Richardson's oeuvre confronts and calibrates the nature of quotidian experience and diurnal social reality in terms of the modernist misgivings that Randall ascribes to such contemporaneous influences as feminism, developments in psychical research and the seismic social and psychological impact of the First World War. Randall's chapter on Richardson scrutinizes *Pilgrimage* through the lens of Gilles Deleuze, usefully linking its disruptive narrative strategies to a more thoroughgoing and stringent 'critique of everyday life' (p. 14). While not immediately allying the quotidian with specifically feminine experience, Randall nevertheless, and confidently, indicates that Miriam's bitter struggles as a woman in reconciling the 'weekday' self with 'mystical' promptings outside the brutality of the normal disclose not only that the everyday consists of both, but also that the professional role and the dissident numinous self are mutually 'imbricated'.

Although this reviewer would have preferred more sustained engagement with the novel form itself as a collection of diurnal imaginative practices, a notable marker of taste and class for a bourgeois audience that inhabits a 'commonplace' milieu (p. 20), Randall offers a judicious Marxist analysis of how ideologies of work and leisure actively shaped concepts of everyday life in the early twentieth century. These insights are extended by Jean-Michel Rabaté in *1913: The Cradle of Modernism*, whose third chapter gauges formulations of diurnal existence in the last year of peace before the eruption of the First World War. How did publishing and distribution practices impinge upon reader choice before the outbreak of conflict? And who determined whether or not a book was a 'classic' (p. 35)? Rabaté's lively approach, along with that of Mary Hammond and Shafquat Towheed, eds., *Publishing in the First World War: Essays in Book History*, sheds light on the institutions and ideologies that largely determined a text's accessibility and circulated format, and thus its mode of address to specific readerships. Moreover, Elizabeth Darling and Lesley Whitworth, eds., *Women and the Making of Built Space in England, 1870–1950*, elucidates the links between gender, the diurnal, homemaking and participatory citizenship by bringing together a diverse range of scholars operating in literary, architectural, urban, design, labour and social history.

Catherine Clay's *British Women Writers 1914–1945: Professional Work and Friendship* is anchored in vivid literary-historical case studies that weigh the practices, meanings and effects of friendship within a network of British women writers, who were all loosely affiliated with the feminist weekly periodical *Time and Tide*. This is a significant project, since seminal historical approaches to male literary collaboration and camaraderie—Wayne Koestenbaum's *Double Talk* [1989], Jack Stillinger's *Multiple Authorship and the Myth of Solitary Genius* [1991] and Jeffrey Masten's *Textual Intercourse* [1997]—only gesture tentatively towards collaborative efforts between women writers. Clay methodically canvasses the correspondence and journals, as well as fiction, poetry and memoirs, of authors such as Vera Brittain, Winifred Holtby and Storm Jameson. Clay assesses these women's friendships in connection with a couple of key contexts: the multiple resonances of early twentieth-century feminism, as a generation of young women tried to fashion themselves as professional writers (a phenomenon also delineated by Lucy Delap's *The Feminist Avant-Garde: Transatlantic Encounters of the Early Twentieth Century*), as well as the profound historical shifts in the cultural appraisal of lesbianism crystallized by *The Well of Loneliness* trial in 1928.

As Elisabeth Ladenson shows in *Dirt for Art's Sake*, the circumstances surrounding the publication of Radclyffe Hall's controversial novel forcibly remind us of literary modernism's status as 'a revolution of the word' (p. 56) and the committed experiments with genre, language and representation carried out by Hall and many others led to prosecution under the law of obscenity. Clay follows Allison Pease's *Modernism, Mass Culture, and the Aesthetics of Obscenity* [2000] and Kieran Dolin's *Critical Introduction to Law and Literature* in adumbrating how the 'shocks' of metropolitan modernity were brought to the courtroom and engendered innovative modes of legal creativity. Clay makes a telling contribution to the growing critical literature on the interrelations between censorship and sexual representation in late nineteenth- and early twentieth-century British literature. While her study offers solid evidence of the pivotal function close and enduring friendships played in women's professional lives, it also reveals the postures, concealments, nagging insecurities and denials of these relationships. Her percipient account of *Time and Tide* can be read alongside Churchill and McKible, eds., *Little Magazines and Modernism*, which reflects the primacy of little magazines as a vital critical tool for canvassing the local and material conditions that shaped British fiction from this period.

The year 2007 proved to be a remarkable one for scholarship devoted to E.M. Forster. David Bradshaw, ed., *The Cambridge Companion to E.M. Forster*, contains conceptually ambitious and incisive readings of every facet of his wide-ranging career. The sheer breadth and range of this sixteen-chapter volume permits us to appreciate Forster's achievement from a fresh perspective. Instead of following the drably predictable path of many literary companions—the author's biography plus a cagey chronological assessment of the canonical fiction—Bradshaw's collection supplies an appealing range of frequently overlooked topics, among these 'Forster as a Literary Critic', 'Filmed Forster' and 'Forster's Life and Life-Writing'. Rather than rehearsing the familiar thesis that Forster was cosily ensconced within the intellectual and artistic milieu of Bloomsbury, David Medalie's essay 'Bloomsbury and Other Values' (pp. 32–46) convincingly argues that Forster's relationship with this coterie was far from straightforward and his fiction can be more productively scrutinized as a record of uneasy adjustment and tense negotiation, even a searching critique of this clique's values. Peter Morey's 'Postcolonial Forster' (pp. 254–73) methodically situates the author in relation to a tendency towards more globalized readings of Euro-American canonical works, events and discourses, as well as an expansion of the canon itself beyond its Euro-American focus—as part of that 'scramble for planetarity', to adopt Spivak's memorable phrase. As Morey shows, the intellectual project of postcolonial studies has long interrogated the hegemony of canonical modernist texts and writers in twentieth-century literature and has also exhaustively theorized the relations of writers such as Conrad, Forster and others to the postcolonial texts that would later 'appropriate and subvert' them (pp. 267).

Peter Morey's essay links up effectively with Robert P. Marzec's *An Ecological and Postcolonial Study of Literature: From Daniel Defoe to Salman Rushdie*, which affords a historically sensitive account of Forster's *Howards End* in terms of inhabiting land in the age of empire and how imperial geography and spatiality resonate in *A Passage to India*. Marzec is responsive to Forster's quirky and protean narrator in *Howards End*, and his examination throws into relief the intricate verbal texture of this novel, which blends spry comedy of manners with scathing social satire; at once facetious and brooding, celebratory and pensive. This formally astute approach is amplified by Brian May's essay on 'Romancing the Stump: Modernism and Colonialism in Forster's *A Passage to India*' (in Begam and Valdez Moses, eds., *Modernism and Colonialism: British and Irish Literature, 1899–1939*, pp. 136–61).

Gail Fincham's essay on 'Space and Place in the Novels of E.M. Forster' (in De Lange Fincham, Hawthorn and Lothe, eds., *Literary Landscapes: From Modernism to Postcolonialism*, pp. 38–57) contends that in *Howards End* and *A Passage in India* the novelist disavows a belief in the possibility of that bracing 'free space' privileged and prioritized by his earlier social comedies. In Forster's last two novels, Fincham claims, the political economy of capitalism crowds out the possibility of a liberal humanist world-view and its belief in a redemptive rustic hinterland to which the beleaguered individual can retreat. So while in the earlier novels movement from one geographical locale to another—from stuffy suburban England to the lush Italian countryside for example—can mirror a movement from rigid class stratification to bold social mixing, in *Howards End* the combined effects of capitalist commodification and imperialist rapacity preclude opportunities for such enabling modes of 'escape' (p. 39).

Valerie Wainwright's *Ethics and the English Novel from Austen to Forster* discerns a new orientation towards an expansive ethics of flourishing or living well in *Howards End*. Wainwright connects Forster's thinking to the ongoing and animated discussions that characterize modern moral philosophy. This rigorous work canvasses the ways in which ideas of major theorists such as Kant, F.H. Bradley or John Stuart Mill, as well as those of now little-known cultural commentators such as the priest Edward Tagart, the preacher William MacCall and philanthropist Helen Dendy Bosanquet, were appropriated and reappraised in the imaginative patterns of Forster's major fiction.

Amardeep Singh's 'Reorienting Forster: Intimacy and Islamic Space' (*Criticism* 49[2007] 35–54) documents the key impact of recent readings of Forster's later fiction, such as Stuart Christie's *Worlding Forster* [2006], which profitably explicate key continuities in the different genres of Forster's writing on race and empire and its grievous discontents. Like Antony H. Copley in *A Spiritual Bloomsbury: Hinduism and Homosexuality in the Lives and Writing of Edward Carpenter, E.M. Forster, and Christopher Isherwood*, Singh approaches the question of Forster's lifelong fascination with the numinous and the arcane, and, more particularly, the question of how his move to another religion and culture was a way of dealing with his homosexuality. Singh is acutely responsive to the tension between Forster's brittle yet enduring liberal humanism, his belief in substantive personal relationships, his interest in multiplied or heightened perception and the ways in which his sexual frustration is inextricably tied to notions of spiritual release. However, Singh also probes the ostensible gap between Forster's liberal and progressive public writings and the more vexed, unsettling fantasies of dominance over (and sometimes submission to) Indian and African men, many of them of Islamic heritage, that feature in Forster's posthumously published writings.

Singh's essay demonstrates that, in his various colonial writings, Forster refines a unique concept of intimacy in threshold Islamic spaces, at the border of public and private, which enables him provisionally to overcome the obstacles introduced by the grotesque imbalance of power between Caucasian colonizer and subjugated 'Other'. Singh's account of Forster's interest in Islamic space, as both a mode of knowledge and an intense structure of feeling, represents a discourse that is at once more personal and less monolithic than Edward Said's orientalist thesis.

Jesse Matz's 'Masculinity Amalgamated: Colonialism, Homosexuality, and Forster's Kipling' (*JML* 30:iii[2007] 31–51) explicates E.M. Forster's 1909 lecture on Rudyard Kipling, which ascribes Kipling's reputation to fantasies about homoerotic primitivism and extrovert virility, and proposes to affirm instead a Kipling whose manliness is 'amalgamated' with other qualities. As the lecture on Kipling finally develops an anti-imperial critique, Matz posits that Forster's homosexuality entailed a postcolonial mindset. Michael Lackey's 'E.M. Forster's Lecture "Kipling's Poems": Negotiating the Modernist Shift from "the Authoritarian Stock-in-Trade" to an Aristocratic Democracy' (*JML* 30:iii[2007] 1–30) also canvasses Forster's incisive lecture about Kipling, and the politically debilitating and dangerous aspects of his aesthetic. Central to Forster's critique, according to Lackey, is the conviction that contemporary culture is and should be moving from inflexible autocratic models to a vision of peace anchored in spirited democratic debate and easy-going tolerance—a project of meaningful integration that might fuse differences without removing them.

Allan Hepburn, ed., *Troubled Legacies: Narrative and Inheritance*, contains a perceptive essay by Jay Dickson on 'E.M. Forster's *The Longest Journey* and the Legacy of Sentiment' (pp. 163–90). Andrew Shin's 'The English Patient's Desert Dream' (*LIT* 18:iii[2007] 213–36) measures Forster's *A Passage to India* against Anthony Minghella's film adaptation of Michael Ondaatje's novel *The English Patient* and investigates how crucial questions of national identity and colonialism are raised in each. Laurie Kaplan's essay 'Forster, Scott, and Stoppard and the End of Empire' (in Usandizaga and Monnickendam, eds., *Back to Peace: Reconciliation and Retribution in the Postwar Period*, pp. 34–48) compares the treatment of British imperialism and social clubs in *A Passage to India* with similar episodes in Paul Scott's *Raj Quartet* [1976] and Tom Stoppard's *Indian Ink* [1995].

The questions of space, place and national belonging in the context of writing in the twilight of empire, broached in recent studies such as Ian Baucom's *Out of Place* [1999], Jed Esty's *A Shrinking Island* [2004] and Kurt Koenigsberger's *The Novel and the Menagerie* [2007], also imbue Christine Berberich's *The Image of the English Gentleman in Twentieth-Century Literature: Englishness and Nostalgia*. Berberich notes that studies of the English gentleman have tended to focus mainly on the nineteenth century, encouraging the implicit assumption that this influential literary trope has less resonance for Edwardian and modernist fiction. Berberich debunks this notion by showing that the English gentleman has proven to be a remarkably adaptable and relevant ideal that continues to influence not only literature but other forms of representation, including the media and advertising industries.

Berberich's monograph invites us to revisit Ford Madox Ford's scrutiny of the political and moral claims of insular nationality in *The Good Soldier* and in his masterpiece *Parade's End*. Paul Skinner, ed., *Ford Madox Ford's Literary Contacts*, is the fifth collection in the International Ford Madox Ford Studies series. Founded in 1997 in the wake of Max Saunders's magisterial biography *Ford Madox Ford: A Dual Life* [1996–7], the series reflects the recent resurgence of interest in him as a major presence in early twentieth-century literature. Like Ruth Livesey's *Socialism, Sex, and the Culture of Aestheticism in Britain, 1880–1914*, Skinner's collection demonstrates that one of the most arresting facets of Ford's career is his close involvement with many of the key international literary groupings, coteries and urgent causes of his time. Ford was a tireless promoter of younger writers, reading manuscripts and recommending them to publishers. Previous annuals in this series have dealt with Ford and metropolitan modernity, as well as history and representation in his writings. The present volume contains twenty-one essays and notes on 'contacts', flexibly construed so as to include creative friendships, editorial involvements and seminal biographical encounters, and they comprise the most substantial, central section on 'Contemporaries and Confreres'. This grouping covers Edward Garnett, Marie Belloc Lowndes (Hilaire's sister), John Cowper Powys, Oliver Madox Hueffer (Ford's brother), Rebecca West and Herbert Read. Skinner's collection makes a compelling case for Ford's centrality on the literary scene during the Edwardian period and for a good twenty years after it.

Of particular note is Seamus O'Malley's disciplined and penetrating piece on the use of pastoral in *Parade's End* and Rebecca West's novel *The Return of the Soldier* [1918], while John Coyle profitably compares Marcel Proust and Ford. The annual's utility would have been greatly strengthened had it featured an index; given the dazzling array of writers mentioned and the numerous Ford works and topics dealt with, this type of apparatus becomes essential. Ford Madox Ford's memoir *It Was the Nightingale* has been reissued by Carcanet, edited by John Coyle. Ford evokes the literary milieus of London, Paris and New York between the wars, and Coyle's judicious introduction explores how recollections range across time in a highly subtle and flexible narrative that fuses fiction and autobiography. Coyle evokes Ford's status as a 'ghost-seer' in this text: preserving for posterity the survivals of a bygone generation. At the core of these memoirs is a period of three weeks of which Ford's memory is completely lost, and it is this 'blank' which forms the basis for *Parade's End*. Indeed, Coyle shows that the genuine purpose of *It Was the Nightingale* emerges as a companion volume to *Parade's End*, reiterating the key concerns of the tetralogy with renewed urgency and panache, while supplementing its portrayal of a society gone to seed by the use of a fluid and relativizing first-person perspective, reminiscent of *The Good Soldier*.

As Peter Childs's *Modernism and the Postcolonial* suggests, scholars and journalists continue to view contemporary issues of globalization and the 'new world order' (p. 11) as foreshadowed by the concerns of much of Joseph Conrad's fiction: dislocation, homelessness, cultural clash, atrophy of personal vision and the atavistic eruptions of the irrational. As Natalie Melas also indicates in her chapter 'Ungrounding Comparison: Conrad and Colonial Narration' in *All the Difference in the World: Postcoloniality and the Ends of*

Comparison, radical ambivalence, precariousness and irreconcilable antagonisms are central to Conrad's aesthetic repertoire, and numerous commentators in 2007 traced Conrad's political and ideological development as an evolving response to his unease about capitalist modernity. According to Childs, the quality of Conrad's engagement with his day—one very much like our own—permits him, as both literary model and stringent cultural commentator, to continue to haunt us today. This 'haunting' also proves richly suggestive for John G. Peters in his *Cambridge Introduction to Joseph Conrad* [2006] as well as for Sanjay Krishnan in *Reading the Global: Troubling Perspectives on Britain's Empire in Asia*, whose final chapter canvasses 'Animality and the Global Subject in Conrad's *Lord Jim*'.

Childs gauges the notable shifts in aesthetic representation over the period 1885–1930 that coincide with both the rise of literary modernism and imperialism's apex. Childs argues that modernist literary writing should be read in terms of its response and relationship to events overseas, moving towards an emergent postcolonialism instead of grappling with a residual colonial past. Beginning by offering an analysis of the generational and gender conflict that spans art and empire in the period, Childs uses Joseph Conrad to assess the modernist expression of 'a crisis of belief in relation to subjectivity, space and time' (pp. 1–15).

Begam and Moses, eds., *Modernism and Colonialism*, treats major works written or published between 1899 and 1939, the boom years of literary modernism and the period during which the British empire reached its greatest geographical expanse. Moses's essay 'Disorientalism: Conrad and the Imperial Origins of Modernist Aesthetics' (pp. 43–69) is shrewd in its reading of *Lord Jim* as a dissection of the experience of a European consciousness confronting a profoundly alien culture at the periphery of empire, and how it played a key role in generating formal modernism. Challenging the view that modernist innovation explicitly lauded the larger enterprise of colonialism, Moses demonstrates that Conrad's canny manipulation of avant-garde literary tactics—for instance anachrony and perspectivism—transmuted and debunked the Victorian imperial romance. Conrad's narrative risk-taking, as Adrian Hunter also evinces in his *Cambridge Introduction to the Short Story in English*, is geared towards disorienting the reader, thus showing British imperialism not as a buoyant narrative of progressive enlightenment but as a cultural catastrophe.

Jeremy Hawthorn's *Sexuality and the Erotic in the Fiction of Joseph Conrad* presents 'a sustained critique' of the interlinked (and contradictory) views that Conrad's fiction is 'largely innocent' of any fascination with sexual imperatives and that when Conrad does attempt to depict 'erotic excitement' it results in clumsy or facile writing (pp. 7–8). As in his excellent chapter on 'Joseph Conrad's Half-Written Fictions' (in Shiach, ed., pp. 151–64), Hawthorn argues that the comprehensiveness of Conrad's vision includes an abiding concern with the sexual and the erotic, not as separate spheres of human life, but as elements dialectically related to those matters public and political that have always been affirmed as core components of Conrad's fictional achievement. Hawthorn's work on *The Shadow-Line* and *Under Western Eyes* also opens

Conrad's narrative tactics to readings informed by the insights of theorists associated with gender studies and postcolonialism.

Hawthorn's enterprise also irradiates John Kucich's salutary and persuasive discussion of Conrad's 'Imperial Professionalism' in *Imperial Masochism: British Fiction, Fantasy and Social Class*. Despite its 'shadowy critical status', Kucich argues that 'masochistic fantasy' is a 'primary organizing structure' in Conrad's oeuvre (p. 197). How did the language of wilful self-martyrdom, evangelism and atonement function to secure empire? For Kucich, a self-destructive energy is not merely at the centre of Conradian thematics, but it also underpins his 'self-consuming practices' as a writer (p. 198). Kucich not only elucidates the role masochistic fantasy plays in identity formation beyond the field of sexuality, but also discloses 'the social purposes' of such fantasy in British culture, thus recuperating 'for historicist studies both the category of social class and the domain of the psychological' (p. 248). To Kucich, masochism is a psychosocial language, not a rigid repertoire of behavioural tics, and masochistic fantasy is a catalyst for social action, not a specific act in itself. Class in Conrad's fiction class is 'a symbolic medium' of conflict 'rather than an economic or political category'—in which conceptions of social identity are framed. Conrad, 'predictably the subtlest of imperialists' imported elements of masochistic self-consciousness that subverted the 'chivalric' aims he hopelessly opposed to capitalism's deleterious 'excesses' (p. 248). In Kucich's rigorously theorized account Conrad, contrasting mariners to other social groups, vouchsafes a critique of imperialism, but one that remains cagey and conservative, since it could not appeal to a predominantly bourgeois readership.

Fiona Becket and Terry Gifford, eds., *Culture, Creativity and Environment: New Environmentalist Criticism*, provides an effectual lens through which to inspect Conrad's evocation of Africa in *Heart of Darkness* as a space for violence against animals, a negative projection screen for a series of hallucinatory white European fears. Helga Ramsey-Kurz's *The Non-Literate Other: Readings of Illiteracy in Twentieth-Century Novels in English* shows that Conrad's *Heart of Darkness* reflects a growing insecurity concerning the possibilities of meaningful representation, an insecurity engendered by the realization that the uses to which the English language, and with it, alphabetic writing had come to be put in the course of the colonial enterprise was barely conducive to a genuinely sympathetic comprehension of the varieties of otherness encountered outside Europe. Ramsey-Kurz argues that the images evoked in *Heart of Darkness* mainly serve to conjure 'voices rather than visions' (p. 15), moments of subjective experiencing rather than actual events, a talking self rather than the tangible milieu that self once encountered. The penultimate chapter of John Glendening's *The Evolutionary Imagination in Late-Victorian Novels: An Entangled Bank* also focuses on *Heart of Darkness*. Not only does Conrad confront Darwinian complications, Glendening proposes, but also the contingencies, uncertainties and confusions generated by evolutionary theory, interacting with multiple cultural influences, which thoroughly permeate the early fiction and its descriptive and thematic fabric.

Rodopi, in association with the UK Joseph Conrad Society, has published posthumously Martin Ray's *Joseph Conrad: Memories and Impressions—An Annotated Bibliography* that is the first in a series intended to make available rare, out-of-print or newly unearthed fragments of Conradiana. Ray's annotated bibliography aims to identify those reflections of the author by those who knew him or met him. This volume has its origin in Ray's earlier projects *Joseph Conrad and his Contemporaries* [1988] and *Joseph Conrad: Interviews and Recollections* [1990]. The latter is an illuminating anthology that affords the general reader with a portrait of Conrad in sixty or so telling snippets. That Ray chose to organize this present volume by alphabetical order of contributor instead of chronologically or thematically will, I suspect, prove awkward for the newcomer or non-specialist. However, Ray's enterprise— which boasts extensive annotation for nearly all the entries—undoubtedly benefits from the publication of *The Collected Letters of Joseph Conrad* in recent years.

Veteran Conrad scholars may well judge Mary Ann Gillies's *The Professional Literary Agent in Britain, 1880–1920* a serious letdown. Gillies reacts to the long-standing demand for a detailed social history charting the rise of literary agents in England towards the close of the nineteenth century and their signal impact on 'the emergence of literary modernism'. Gillies analyses only a couple of eminent agents, A.P. Watt and J.B. Pinker; the latter's list of clients represents a pantheon of the literary elite from this era: Stephen Crane, Arnold Bennett, Ford Madox Ford, Henry James, John Galsworthy and Katherine Mansfield. Even James Joyce conjured his name in the Circe episode of *Ulysses*. The account of Conrad's long career, so vigorously enabled by Pinker's unflagging industry and verve, is sketched in disappointingly broad brushstrokes here, as is Pinker's desire adventurously to seek out untested new talent, defending it in 'a crowded literary marketplace' (p. 59). And for all Gillies's eloquent insistence on surveying the most astute secondary scholarship, Linda Marie Fritschner's essay 'Literary Agents and Literary Traditions', which punctiliously comments on Pinker (in Balfe, ed., *Paying the Piper* [1993]), is oddly missing from the bibliography. As Mary Hammond suggests in *Reading, Publishing and the Formation of Literary Taste in England, 1880–1914*, which skilfully fuses the methodologies of sociology, literary studies and book history, the question of *exactly where* the agent pursued business opportunities is surely 'of fundamental importance' (p. 6). McCracken's *Masculinities, Modernist Fiction and the Urban Public Sphere* recognizes the function of teashops and cafes in the emergence of a new literary climate at the start of the twentieth century. Gillies could have said much more about the placement of Pinker's offices in Arundel Street just off the busy Strand, which were within walking distance of 'typing agencies, the popular press and the thriving financial sector' (p. 45). Pinker believed that authorship merited the highest professional acumen and scrupulous management; like banking, it was dependent upon a network of supplementary services, including the restaurants clustered in the vicinity where clients could be entertained and sounded out.

Allan H. Simmons and J.H. Stape, eds., *The Secret Agent: Centennial Essays*, reconsiders one of Conrad's most important political novels from a variety of critical perspectives and presents a useful documentary section as well as specially commissioned maps and new contextualizing illustrations. Much fresh research is provided on the novel's sources. David Punter indicates that the Professor from *The Secret Agent* is 'an early avatar of the suicide bomber' (p. 201) in Jo Collins and John Jervis, eds., *Uncanny Modernity: Cultural Theories, Modern Anxieties*. Richard Littlejohns and Sara Soncini, eds., *Myths of Europe*, contains an essay by Mario Curelli which identifies some of the qualities of classical heroism that contribute to the construction of gender in the 1903 volume *Typhoon and Other Stories*. Other perspicacious contributions published in 2007 include Jennifer Turner's 'The "Passion of Paternity"—Fathers and Daughters in the Works of Joseph Conrad' (*Conradiana* 39:iii[2007] 229–47); Yael Levin's 'The Moral Ambiguity of Conrad's Poetics: Transgressive Secret Sharing in *Lord Jim* and *Under Western Eyes*' (*Conradiana* 39:iii[2007] 211–28); Michael DiSanto's 'Matthew Arnold under Conrad's Eyes: *Lord Jim* as Literary Criticism' (*NCP* 34:i–ii[2007] 237–55); Joshua Esty's 'The Colonial *Bildungsroman*: The Story of an African Farm and the Ghost of Goethe' (*VS* 49[2007] 407–30).

Lee Oser's *The Return of Christian Humanism: Chesterton, Eliot, Tolkien, and the Romance of History* contains a thought-provoking chapter on G.K. Chesterton, which situates his fiction among the prominent intellectual debates of the early twentieth century, especially the literary clash between a dogmatically relativist modernism and a robust revival of Christian humanism. Oser avers that Chesterton's Christian humanism encourages a genuine diversity of thought based on cool rationality, nature and accomplishments of artistic genius. Chesterton's Christian humanist thought occupies the 'radical middle' between church and state, past and future, faith and reason; and Oser makes a robust case for reconsidering how this movement imbues interwar British fiction, especially the historical novel, with fabulous and visionary romances.

Alison Milbank's *Chesterton and Tolkien as Theologians* takes Chesterton's 'natural theology' as part of a sober intellectual attempt to show that numinous modes of thinking are ingrained in the very roots of our metaphysical assumptions, an enterprise also delineated by Gregory Erickson in *The Absence of God in Modernist Literature*. Milbank vouchsafes a nuanced and thorough treatment of Chesterton's writing in the first decade of the new century, which sought to refine surprising fictional modes to irradiate the strange contours of diurnal life. *The Club of Queer Trades* [1905] shows organized attempts to release the bored bourgeois from the lumpishness of daily routine by means of the 'Adventure and Romance Agency'; *The Man Who Was Thursday* [1908] restores sensation through 'dowsing' the startled reader in the genres of social comedy, black farce, thriller and fairy tale in quick succession; while *Manalive* [1912] focuses on the protagonist as 'performance artist'.

Finally, Valancourt Books has reissued Forrest Reid's *The Garden God: A Tale of Two Boys*, first published in 1905, and dedicated to Henry James (a gesture which incurred James's unwavering animosity). This is a timely reissue given the publication of Carol Mavor's study *Reading Boyishly*, which addresses another notable pre-war British novelist of boyhood, J.M. Barrie. Michael Matthew Kaylor's energetic introduction stresses the importance of *The Garden God* from a cultural standpoint, given its intimations of pederastic desire in the wake of the Oscar Wilde trial.

(b) British Fiction, 1930–1945

Many of the best studies weaken the binary oppositions which, until recently, have dominated our readings of fiction between the wars. Such studies serve to complicate our notions that fiction of this period is to be read as modernist or realist, sophisticated or merely middlebrow, radical or conservative, or bound by its genre categorization. New perspectives on familiar texts have been created by discussing them alongside texts outside this period, using a common thematic or conceptual link. A prevalent starting point for analysis is Freud on mourning, which still has the power to stimulate new readings. Most of the work reviewed helps modify notions of this period as a dreary hinterland of realism between the glittering uplands of the modernist and the postmodern.

The compilation of essays which most directly addresses fiction of this period is Chris Hopkins's *English Fiction in the 1930s: Language, Genre and History* [2006], which could not be reviewed last year. These essays deal with texts from a wide range of genres, many of which have, till recently, been marginalized in literary scholarship, in part because of their genre identification. Hopkins's essays are always informed by his extensive knowledge of the nature of leftist debates in this period, their urgency and the frequent contradictions inherent in the positions taken. The collection is organized into four sections. Part I, entitled 'Modernism and Modernity', deals first with Winifred Holtby, Storm Jameson and Phyllis Bentley. Hopkins argues that novels by these authors represent women rather than men as the 'true heirs' of progressive modernity, while fiction by leftist male novelists tends to represent the defeat of the values they sought to promote. The essay on Elizabeth Bowen is more concerned with stylistics and contains an interesting discussion of how Bowen employs modernist techniques associated with representing the subjective to dramatize a tragic absence of an inner life. The essays in part II, entitled 'Documentary and Proletarian Pastoral', deal with regional novels which respond to the historical and political events of the period. Particularly subtle is the analysis of the class dimensions of the various discourses in Walter Greenwood's *Love on the Dole* [1933] and then in texts termed 'leftist pastorals': Ralph Bates's *The Olive Field* [1936], Lewis Jones's *Cwmardy* [1937], Richard Llewellyn's *How Green Was My Valley* [1939] and James Hanley's *Grey Children: A Study in Humbug and Misery* [1937]. The curious interplay between the urge to both pastoral and documentary modes is demonstrated in Welsh constructions of an authentic regional identity. Part III, 'History and the Historical Novel', and part IV, 'Thrillers and Dystopias', deal with the ways in which popular genres are adapted to suit the political purposes of writers such as Naomi Mitchison, Rosamond Lehmann, Christopher Isherwood, Rex Warner, Eric Ambler, Robert Graves and Sylvia Townsend Warner. Instead of engaging in the old game of 1930s scholars of trying to assess the authenticity and leftist credentials of each of these writers, Hopkins examines how the kind of narrative strategies used in individual bids for authenticity are affected by an author's choice of genre. Particularly revealing is Hopkins's reconstruction of a set of arguments by 1930s Marxists such as Christopher Caudwell about the inauthenticity of the thriller. Hopkins analyses the traces of this complex generic argument in actual leftist thrillers.

Another book dealing with leftist literary culture of this period is Ben Clarke's *Orwell in Context: Communities, Myths, Values*. Whereas Hopkins's readings are contextualized in 1930s debates about cultural and political value, Clarke, at the outset, sets the way class, gender and Englishness are constructed by Orwell in the context of debates conducted by classic Marxist theorists about ideology and about the relation of the cultural critic to hegemonic values. His incisive delineation of the ways in which Marx, Engels, Althusser, Macherey and Barthes theorized ideology leads him to pose the key question which has haunted Orwell studies: can an intellectual construct notions of individual identity without rooting those notions in inherited ideologies? Though Clarke points out that Orwell's perception that Marxists dismiss the reality of 'superstructural' elements such as religion or nationhood is unfounded, he scrupulously avoids, throughout the book, alignment with those involved in the 'get Orwell' project. Each chapter seeks to establish the exact nature of the often ambiguous and self-contradictory ways in which Orwell developed key constructs, with extensive reference to the complete range of Orwell's writings. Barthes argued that to critique the values inherent in myth was to estrange the critic from the culture of which he was a part. However, Orwell operates his critique of ideology explicitly from within it, citing former kinds of 'Englishness' from which to measure the inadequacies of contemporary manifestations of which he was critical. Clarke is also illuminating about the ways in which Orwell's idealizations of masculine working-class culture intersect with the way he genders his own class. Indeed, all the constructs discussed are demonstrably interlinked. Clarke argues in opposition to those who accuse Orwell of 'regressive social patriotism' that 'his patriotism . . . is far from regressive. It is indeed integral to his vision of the future, and to a socialism inseparable from the commitment to both the "England beneath the surface" and the "future England" it will produce' (p. 146).

John Rodden's *The Cambridge Companion to George Orwell* contains a useful essay on Orwell's novels of the 1930s by Michael Levenson. Levenson's analysis of the first three of Orwell's novels of the 1930s engages with the issue sketched so clearly in the introduction to Clarke's book: the impossibility of establishing a realist literary mode when such modes have been devalued by their dependence on recognitions of authenticity that are complicit with dominant hegemonic values. It is Orwell's uneasy negotiations of a radical perspective which is also allied with the 'normal' and the 'decent' (notions which most Marxist critics would suggest were derivative 'false consciousness') that account, in Levenson's view, for Orwell's surreality and uneasiness of tone. 'A paradox inhabits these novels, which articulate an ethic of workaday routine that can only be understood through a radical recognition. The goal is to disclose the truth about a contemporary social emergency . . . but the disclosure can only take place through a collapse of routine' (p. 65).

John Baxendale's *Priestley's England: J.B. Priestley and English Culture* is, like Clarke's study of Orwell, as much a debate about the range of contemporary notions of Englishness and of literary culture as it is about a single author. As a historian, Baxendale examines the origins of judgements of literary value at this period. He points out, 'It can be argued that it was the "middlebrow" best-sellers who were providing the most consistent and widely read commentary on, as Priestley puts it, "man in the society he has created", just as their Victorian forebears had done. This raises important issues, still current in our own time, about the relationship between commerce and the public sphere, entertainment and information, pleasure and politics' (p. 2). Baxendale situates the position-taking of Virginia Woolf and George Orwell in the 'brow wars' and in relation to the social structures within which such positions were taken. The year 1932, that peculiarly intense year for the brow wars, saw, for example, Orwell's glaring misreading of Priestley's savage indictment of speculative capitalism, *Angel Pavement* [1930], as 'genuinely gay and pleasant' (p. 50). Such inaccuracy can only be understood, in Baxendale's opinion, by its context in the *Adelphi*, the readers of which would not have welcomed any attempt to modify their sense that Priestley's cultural value was irredeemably compromised by the vast commercial success and entertainment value of *The Good Companions* [1929]. In fact, as Baxendale demonstrates, novels such as *Wonder Hero* [1933] and, to a lesser extent, *Let the People Sing* [1939] dramatize the power of the mass media to distort ethical values and to divert readers from key political debates. Like Hopkins and Clarke, Baxendale's familiarity with the materials of cultural production, letters, journal articles and, in Baxendale's case, the popular press make all three books invaluable tools to deepen our understanding of the cultural context of fiction produced at this period.

Baxendale's study of the way in which Priestley was evaluated and the way he positioned himself is a salutary reminder to literary scholars that the canonical or most formally innovative texts of this period can distort our understanding of how the public sphere of debate in twentieth-century Britain operated. Like Clarke, Baxendale complicates received notions about his subject. He reveals as many ambiguities in Priestley's attitudes to popular culture as there are in Orwell's. On the one hand, Priestley, like Orwell, seems to identify 'authentic' popular culture with the 'gusto' of Edwardian forms of entertainment such as vaudeville, which he felt was threatened by commercial and American mass culture. On the other hand, he was often contemptuous of the amateurism of much of the entertainment put out by the BBC, contrasting the professionalism and 'pep' of the Jack Benny show with the bland and under-resourced English equivalent.

Baxendale from the outset aligns himself with scholars such as Nicola Humble, Chiara Briganti, Kathy Mezei, Dan LeMahieu and Alison Light, who are engaged in exploring the origins and nature of tastes disparaged as 'middlebrow'. Faye Hammill's *Women, Celebrity and Literary Culture Between the Wars* also contributes to this project. Hammill argues that 'what is needed is a concept of the middlebrow which allows for the slipperiness, complexity, and multiple satirical targets of texts such as *The Diary of a Provincial Lady* or *The Constant Nymph*, or journals such as *Time and Tide* or *Vanity Fair*, which dramatize their own cultural status by reflecting on and satirizing not only highbrow pretension and lowbrow entertainment but also the more limiting formations of middlebrow culture itself' (p. 208). Texts such as *The Constant Nymph* and *The Diary of a Provincial Lady* 'critique the commodification of art, yet as highly profitable commodities they become part of the cultural

battle which is dramatized in their pages' (p. 11). Some of the authors
discussed by Hammill are not British (Anita Loos, Dorothy Parker, Mae
West and L.M. Montgomery), but they are persuasively linked with British
authors (Margaret Kennedy, Stella Gibbons and E.M. Delafield) who shared
a celebrity status which complicated their cultural value for their contemporaries and possibly obscures the efforts of modern scholars to characterize
their fiction.

Hammill discusses the recurrence in all Margaret Kennedy's fiction of the
theme of celebrity, not only in her bestseller *The Constant Nymph* [1924].
She describes how *A Long Time Ago* [1932] parodies the way in which the
celebrity memoir commodifies the inner life of its subject and 'seeks to
establish the continuity of her public self with a supposed inner essence'
(p. 147). By introducing the dimension of celebrity identity into debates about
authorial self-positioning between the wars, Hammill deftly combines literary
analysis and cultural history and demonstrates that spectacular commercial
success often worked to limit a female author's autonomy, for the success of
these texts became both a problem and an opportunity for their authors.
It exposed them to the full force of gender assumptions about authorship. It
also meant that they and their texts became cultural markers in the market
whose vagaries and shifting values they so satirized so successfully in their
novels. These shifts are explored through examination of a huge range and
variety of print cultures, including the style magazine (on both sides of the
Atlantic), middlebrow magazines like *Time and Tide*, correspondence, life-
writings and the novels themselves. Hammill's gift for the brief illustrative
quotation communicates the wit and sharpness of the satire in these books,
often dismissed as not literature but 'sheer flapdoodle' in the words of Stella
Gibbons herself in the foreword to *Cold Comfort Farm* [1932]. Hammill
demonstrates the range and subtlety of Gibbons's several parodies in this text.
Canonical authors (Hardy and the Brontës), the highbrow (D.H. Lawrence),
the middlebrow (Mary Webb) and generic popular romances are all satirical
targets. The way in which the novel itself acquired an ambiguous cultural
status is illustrated by Hammill in her examination of the debates surrounding
Gibbons's success in winning the prestigious Femina Vie Heureuse in 1933
(as had the middlebrow Constance Holme and Webb before her). Hammill
demonstrates the power of parody to reinscribe texts (like Webb's) that would
otherwise leave no cultural trace.

Hammill's final analysis is of the reception and cultural politics of E.M.
Delafield's *Diary of a Provincial Lady*, published in book form in 1930 and
followed by three sequels in the 1930s. Just as William Faulkner patronizingly
told Loos, 'You have builded better than you knew', so Delafield was told,
'I don't suppose you have the least idea of why it's good' (p. 200), Hammill
demonstrates how artfully Delafield's air of artlessness was contrived and how
'Delafield's interlocutor constructs a route of communication between
a sophisticated text and a sophisticated reader which excludes the author'.
The four books reviewed set high standards for researchers of British print
cultures at this period. Hammill's book will direct scholars towards the
expanding fields of magazine and middlebrow culture as well as to the
neglected fields of comedy and satire in this period.

Another collection which groups together essays on individual authors is Marina MacKay and Lyndsey Stonebridge's *British Fiction after Modernism: The Novel at Mid-Century*. The project of this book, to find a way of describing fiction of the mid-twentieth century in terms that are not wholly circumscribed by the high value set on modernism, is timely. In grouping fictions either side of the Second World War, the editors hope to construct a focus which counters the tendency to value texts of this period only in terms of a vestigial modernism or a proleptic postmodernism. Elisabeth Maslen's 'The Case for Storm Jameson' (pp. 33–41) suggests that Jameson's fiction is informed by her sense that personal identity is dependent on the way in which we describe our pasts to ourselves. Maslen links this process with Jameson's work with refugees, whose adaptation to the present depended on their ability to describe a past from which they were irredeemably severed. Her project is, in part, to weaken the inevitability of the link between the two terms of the habitual and pejorative collocation of 'nineteenth century' with the term 'realist'.

James Wood calls his essay on the novels of Henry Green 'A Plausible Magic' (pp. 50–8), and his own eloquence evokes the poetry of Green's prose. Wood is perhaps over-anxious to set Green in a non-modernist genealogy while avoiding any identification of his narrative mode with realism. He revealingly sets Green in the tradition of Dickens and Hardy, who use representation of speech to suggest an interiority which appears to be garnered from the outside, the narrator as auditor. Thus, Green creates the illusion that the characters are the poets of themselves. As Wood puts it, 'Green's writing is both mimetic and magically artificial' (p. 57). He points the contrast between the apparently trivial puzzles which his characters are seeking to solve, 'plot enigma' and the deeper understanding of themselves and others that are constantly addressed by but constantly elude the questioner, the 'human enigma'.

John Mepham, too, focuses on talk, using a model derived from the works of linguists such as Howard Garfinkel, and of the philosopher Paul Grice. His linking of Patrick Hamilton and Elizabeth Bowen is entitled 'Varieties of Modernism, Varieties of Incomprehension' (pp. 59–76). Though chiefly concerned with Hamilton's Pinteresque and surreal dialogues, Mepham argues that the conversation taking place in the suburban fastness of the Kelways' home in Bowen's *The Heat of the Day* is reminiscent of those in Ivy Compton-Burnett's novels, in which families combine superficial politeness with deep malice, itself a form of what Woolf called 'domestic fascism'. Mepham is concerned with the coercive nature of dialogue in Hamilton's *Hangover Square* and also with the way in which Hamilton represents the internal monologue of a man with a split-personality syndrome which is linked to what might be called a form of autism, in which the pressure to focus on and control the movements of his own thoughts means he cannot hear what is meant in the speech of those around him. A free indirect style represents this abnormal state of an inner monologue so obsessive that it locks out the voice of any interlocutor. Mepham asks if this could be intended by Hamilton to be a critique of the implausibility inherent in representing interiority by attempted imitation of an imagined 'stream of consciousness'.

Gerard Barrett, too, is concerned with the surreal effects created by his subject, James Hanley. Interestingly, Barrett places the surreality and modernist nature of Hanley's narratives in the context of his resistance to the more privileged Joseph Conrad, another 'author of the sea' often described as an early modernist. His desire to represent the reality 'below deck' (psychologically and socially) drove him to evolve narrative techniques which ironically were better appreciated by upper-class writers such as Henry Green than they were by a proletarian readership. There are many prompts to further research into Hanley's work (no biography, for example, exists). In Barrett's reading of *No Directions* [1943], Hanley is suggesting 'that the artist's capitulation to the unconscious will ultimately lead him towards, rather than away from, the infernos that surround him'; images which seem to offer coherent patterns of signification are 'fraught with indeterminacy'. Unlike Hanley, Graham Greene claimed an affinity with Conrad. Andrzej Gasiorek argues that his surreal and often melodramatic effects derive from a similar sense that the visible is haunted by the invisible world.Also in this collection are essays on Howard Spring's 'northern camp' by Paul Magrs (pp. 42–9) and an essay by Sara Crangle entitled 'Ivy Compton-Burnett and Risibility' (pp. 99–120), which is a useful counterbalance to the otherwise vestigial attention given to comedy of this period.

Many essays on fiction of this period are to be found in collections with a thematic focus. There are two essays on British writers in Angela Kershaw and Angela Kimyongür's *Women in Europe between the Wars: Politics, Culture and Society*. Jennifer Birkett's '"The Spectacle of Europe": Politics, PEN and Prose Fiction. The Work of Storm Jameson in the Inter-War Years' (pp. 25–38) describes the interdependence in Jameson's writing between the aesthetic and the political. She argues that, in the *Mirror in Darkness* trilogy, in *In the Second Year* [1936] and *Europe to Let* [1940] Jameson sought to place England's social and political life alongside those of her European neighbours, viewed from a common perspective. In *Europe to Let* [1938], a tension is created between viewing the present terror as a product or a destruction of Europe's past. During the course of the narrative the historical context becomes inner landscape; community can only be born if the viewer empathizes with rather than objectifies what is perceived. Mary Anne Schofield's essay on the way in which British women writers addressed the rise of fascism deals with Jameson and also with Phyllis Bottome and Rebecca West.

Maren Tova Linett's monograph *Modernism, Feminism, and Jewishness* has three chapters dealing with Jean Rhys and Sylvia Townsend Warner in conjunction with others. Linett's contention that women projected their economic insecurity as writers and exclusion from the marketplace on the grounds of sex on to the figure of the Jew as capitalist is tested against readings of Rhys, Warner and Woolf. She contrasts the casual anti-Semitism of Woolf, in *The Years*, for example, with the figuring by Rhys and Warner of the Jew as artist, careless of money and generous. However, she acknowledges that, as 'in *Summer Will Show*, the generous Jew in *Good Morning Midnight* depends on readers' familiarity with its opposite' and so, to some extent, reinscribes an anti-Semitic stereotype.

In her nuanced and extended comparison between Woolf's and Warner's use of Jewish characters to comment on the promises and dangers of modernity, Linett distinguishes between the empathy Warner created towards her Jewish characters so that 'their deaths are used to reinforce a liberal-democratic commitment to the value of artistic autonomy even while the value of revolutionary self-sacrifice is asserted', and the use Woolf makes of her Jewish characters to represent the negative features of modernity. She concludes her chapter: 'Coinciding with the pervasive notion that Jews were quintessentially modern was a cultural association between Jews and the past, and between Jews and a racial continuity which brings that past into the present' (p. 109). In chapter 5, 'The "No time region": Time, Trauma, and Jewishness in Barnes and Rhys', Linett argues that in *Nightwood*, *Voyage in the Dark* [1934] and *Good Morning Midnight* [1939] the historical recurrence of anti-Semitism and its attendant psychological trauma induces a sense of timelessness because such individual and collective experience deeply disrupts memory and sense of chronology.

The concerns of this last chapter parallel those in Patricia Rae's *Modernism and Mourning*. These essays are concerned with the ways in which post-First World War modernist fictions tend to resist consoling versions of elegy. Rae's book acknowledges its debt to Jahan Ramazani's *The Poetry of Mourning: The Modern Elegy from Hardy to Heaney* [1994], itself derived from Freud's 'Mourning and Melancholia' [1917]. In the course of an incisive consideration of how Freud, Melanie Klein, Julia Kristeva and Judith Butler theorize mourning, Rae sketches the opposition between Freud's view that it is healing and desirable to return to the image of the lost to unlock it and release oneself from one's attachment to it, and the view that such consolations are unethically reconciling the elegist to what should not be accepted. Stacy Gillis argues that fiction such as that of Dorothy L. Sayers's *The Nine Tailors* [1934] and *Busman's Honeymoon* [1937] brings trauma and its aftermath into the drawing room rather than offering the consolation of a 'solution'. She suggests that it was part of the project of the Golden Age detective novel to represent mourning as a social responsibility to be shared: 'it became the work of everyone, both men and women, to work together to place a pattern of signs behind a corpse, to find out "whodunit"' (p. 187). She links this idea to Derrida's view that successful mourning depends upon accurately placing the body, asking 'who and where'. She also suggests that this is a kind of condition-of-England novel, and points out the ambiguities of making the traumatized Wimsey the epitome of traditional Englishness. She notes the ambivalence of Harriet Vane's declaration 'I have married England'.

Rae's essay on Orwell's *Coming up for Air*, 'Double Sorrow: Proleptic Elegy and the End of Arcadianism in 1930s Britain', is a fine addition to debates about Orwell's construction of Englishness and has interesting parallels with Hopkins's debates about proletarian pastoral. Rae argues that many 'proleptic elegists of the late 1930s seize on the image of an archetypal cycle that has been fractured and therefore rendered useless, or emphasize the redundancy of the experience they are about to undergo' (p. 32). She does not use the notion of the pastoral loosely, and her sense of its traditional uses underpins analysis of the way in which this genre was used and adapted by Orwell and contemporary poets. For example, she observes of the fishing image in both Stephen Spender's 'Three Days' and in Orwell's *Coming up for Air*, 'it is notable that they invoke piscatory eclogues: texts in which the nostalgic gaze fixes on the solitude and autonomy of the fisherman, rather than on the kind protectiveness embodied by the shepherd' (p. 217). Her conclusion is cogent: 'The world before this new war was an inappropriate object for future-nostalgia because it had *never been* a scene of carefree youth' (p. 224).

Rae's collection also contains an essay on Elizabeth Bowen by Eluned Summers Bremner. This, taken with Keri Walsh's essay on Bowen's surrealism, Maria DiBattista's on Bowen's modernism and the edition of *Modern Fiction Studies* devoted to Bowen, make this an important year for Bowen scholars. Summers-Bremner focuses on Bowen's 'Unhomely' sense of place and the way Bowen assigns a 'peculiar valency to nothing' (p. 262). Her perceptive reading of a short story, 'The Disinherited' [1934], shows how it dramatizes a number of losses or absences that are inexpressible. Developing Corcoran's characterization of Bowen's narrative mode, she argues that 'in the stories, the twin themes of urban specularity, associated with the cinema, the media and the masses, and the empty or haunted home, associated with the war and with women, take the place of what in the novels is arguably Bowen's strongest formal innovation: the use of ellipsis to structure plot and serve as placeholder for historical events that continue to resonate with unresolved meaning' (p. 267). Persuasive too is her conclusion that 'Bowen's landed antecedents, far from insulating her against the reality of urban change and postwar dispossession, instead provide her with a particularly charged version of it' (p. 269).

Susan Osborn has edited a special edition of *Modern Fiction Studies*, 'Elizabeth Bowen: New Directions for Critical Thinking' (*MFS* 53:ii[2007] 225–402). Bowen exerts an increasing fascination for the literary critic. As Osborn argues in her introduction, the difficulties of critics in categorizing her work and the lack of homogeneity in her literary modes lead us to question whether scholars have accepted too readily the terms in which Woolf and her contemporaries asserted the dichotomy between modernist and realist modes of representation. One of the key points made is that the shifting nature of Bowen's narrative mode from text to text and the way in which she draws attention to the limits of fictional representation, wilfully rendering speech inexpressive (see also Mepham's essay in MacKay's anthology), lead to comparison with Samuel Beckett. Whereas Beckett establishes a distinctive personal aesthetic, Bowen evades such stylistic consistency. Thus the study of Bowen serves the purposes of projects such as MacKay's which find the mapping of mid-century fictions between the polar opposites of high modernism and narrow realism unhelpful in understanding the nature of fiction at this period. Osborn describes how Bowen's 'stylistic and structural irregularities—including her weird and inconsistent mimeticism, the dramatizations of impasse and non- or dissolved presence, the elliptical dialogue and lacunae in plotting—often but not always efface areas of expected significance by unsystematically conferring onto the diverse narrative and formal elements of her narratives' unfamiliar, unexpected, and sometimes apparently arbitrary emphases and values' (p. 228). Osborn has selected essays which provide a wide range of distinct and distinctive strategies, and her introduction is an excellent introduction to Bowen scholarship.

In 'Unstable Compounds: Bowen's Beckettian Affinities' (*MFS* 53:ii[2007] 238–56), Sinéad Mooney reads *Eva Trout* as the 'proto-postmodernist younger sister' (p. 252) of Beckett's *Watt*, both of whom are estranged from the discourses they have inherited. Jed Esty's essay, 'Virgins of Empire: *The Last September* and the Antidevelopmental Plot' (*MFS* 53:ii[2007] 257–75), deals with the hybrid form of *The Last September* [1929], both a Gothic romance and *Bildungsroman*, and characterizes its formal experimentation as modernist. In a fruitful conjunction of psychoanalytic criticism and stylistic analysis, '"Something Else": Gendering Onliness in Elizabeth Bowen's Early Fiction' by Elizabeth Cullingford (*MFS* 53:ii[2007] 276–305) links the high-cultural complexities of Bowen's allusions to the ambiguous gendering of only children and siblings. Elizabeth Inglesby's 'Expressive Objects: Elizabeth Bowen's Narrative Materializes' (*MFS* 53:ii[2007] 306–33) links the strange relation of the inanimate world to the affective life of Bowen's characters.

The two final essays, Victoria Stewart's 'That Eternal "Now": Memory and Subjectivity in Elizabeth Bowen's *Seven Winters*' (*MFS* 53:ii[2007] 334–50) and Brook Miller's 'The Impersonal Personal: Value, Voice, and Agency in Elizabeth Bowen's Literary and Social Criticism' (*MFS* 53:ii[2007] 351–69), deal with two texts of non-fiction that have been neglected. Stewart analyses the way Bowen dramatizes how 'the real will always be transformed by the process of representation' (p. 348). Miller examines Bowen's delineation of her aesthetic in light of her awareness of its historical contingency. He points out that Bowen's aesthetic claims 'are articulated in a literary environment in which writers and critics [such as T.S. Eliot] demonstrate intensive interest in the ligature of national literary traditions' (p. 367).

Miller's essay is followed by a selected bibliography compiled by Marcia Farrell, supplementing J'nan M. Sellery and William O. Harris's comprehensive bibliography published in 1981. This will be invaluable in helping the scholar new to this field map the rapidly increasing and disparate work being done on Bowen.

Such work includes a chapter on Bowen in Richard Begam and Michael Valdez Moses's collection, *Modernism and Colonialism*. Maria DiBattista, in her account of Bowen's 'Troubled Modernism' (pp. 226–45), compares the complex Chekhovian nature of her friend Hubert Butler's response to the relationship between local and national identities with Bowen's representations of colonial Ireland in *The Last September*. She relates the shifting modes of narration to the conflicted nature of Bowen's attitudes to the sense of community born in the Anglo-Irish community during the Troubles.

Also published this year was Keri Walsh's 'Elizabeth Bowen, Surrealist' (*Éire* 42:iii–iv[2007] 126–47), which links in many ways with Inglesby's essay on the disjunction between the material and affective worlds in Bowen's work. It makes the point that for many surrealists Ireland was linked with surreality (though Irish modernists, such as Joyce, did not align themselves with the surrealists). Walsh claims that Bowen's collection of short stories *The Cat Jumps* [1934] is one of the first literary responses in English to the phenomenon of surrealism. Discussion focuses on 'The Tommy Crans' in which the effect of automatic writing is burlesqued. In this story, Bowen 'explores the semiotic disjunctions of surrealism' and 'considers its problematic assumptions', contesting the idealization of childhood that André Breton had emphasized in his 1924 'First Manifesto' (p. 132).

Perhaps the most penetrating essay of the year also deals with the relationship between European surrealism and the aesthetic of those whose cultural and geographical displacement has contributed to what Walsh calls the 'semiotic disjunctions of surrealism' (p. 132). It would be difficult to find a more persuasive conjunction of formal and cultural analyses than that of Christina Britzolakis in '"This way to the exhibition": Genealogies of Urban Spectacle in Jean Rhys's Interwar Fiction' (*TPr* 21:iii[2007] 457–82). Her multifaceted and cogent analysis sites Rhys's interwar fiction in the context of the surrealist, colonialist and anti-colonial exhibitions of Paris in the 1930s. Focusing on *Good Morning Midnight* [1939], Britzolakis argues that the 'exhibition . . . becomes a sign for the operation of commodity spectacle more generally. It provides a key articulation not only of Rhys's relationship to a more broadly conceived modernist project, but also for the terms of Euro-American modernism's encounter with the global horizon of an increasingly unstable late imperial world system' (p. 459).

Another essay on Rhys, though dealing with a short story not from this period, offers an insight into the way modernists responded to Rhys and her fiction at this period. Ulla Rahbek's 'Controlling Jean Rhys's Story "On Not Shooting Sitting Birds"' (in Rønning and Johannessen, eds., *Readings of the Particular: The Postcolonial in the Postnational*, pp. 107–18) takes as its starting point Stella Bowen's attempt to control and exploit Rhys's intermediate and ambiguous status as a creole who belongs not in the civilized and self-controlled world of the modernists but in a squalid and disordered subterranean world which was exoticized by an infatuated Ford Madox Ford.

Warner continues, like Bowen and Rhys, to attract scholars. Research into Warner is still dominated by 'transformative criticism', as Heather Love describes her project in the introduction to her monograph *Feeling Backward* (p. 1). Queer theorists and critics of the left alike focus on *Summer Will Show*. This novel and *After Don Juan* are also rich sites for examination of Warner's Marxism. However, Love maintains that it is important not to read these texts as progressivist because, she argues, Warner's queer politics, though working towards acceptance of same-sex desire, is linked to the impossibility of queer love being accepted and acceptable.

The Edwardians [1930] is the focus of Sophie Blanch's examination of Vita Sackville-West's constructions of the feminine in 'Contested Wills: Reclaiming the Daughter's Inheritance in Vita Sackville-West's *The Edwardians*' (*CS* 19:i[2007] 73–83). Blanch argues that the 'progresssion from a definition of femininity as an hereditary condition towards a social constructionist model is encapsulated here in evolving narratives of the mother–daughter dynamic' (p. 78).

Male novelists, apart from Priestley and Orwell, have received relatively little critical attention this year. There are three essays in the *Proceedings of the Anthony Powell Centenary Conference* which concern novels from this period: Lisa Colletta's 'Too, Too Bogus: The London Social Scene in the Early Novels of Powell and Waugh' (pp. 18–24), David F. Butler Hallett's 'Dance Steps: A Reassessment of Powell's Early Novels' (pp. 25–36) and Richard Canning's ' "[I]t would be a mistake to claim too much", or, the Author Who Wasn't Quite There: Anthony Powell's Ronald Firbank' (pp. 217–28). Hallett resists the tendency to read Powell's early novels as rehearsals for *Dance to the Music of Time*. He seeks to establish the serious melancholy beneath the comedy, reading the novels as dramatizations of many of the types of melancholy first figured by Robert Burton in *The Anatomy of Melancholy*. Canning compares the ways in which Evelyn Waugh, Gerald Berners, Jocelyn Brooke, Aldous Huxley and others are indebted to Firbank but seem loath to acknowledge that debt.

Evelyn Waugh's *Black Mischief*, the subject of Rita Bernard's essay, is to be found in Begam and Moses, eds., *Modernism and Colonialism*. In ' "A Tangle of Modernism and Barbarity" ' (pp. 162–82), Bernard refuses to be blinded, as others have been, by Waugh's savage frivolity and instead reads his contradictory but serious engagement with colonialism and modernity as 'a lucid understanding that modernism is best grasped as the culture of a wildly uneven but nonetheless singular process of global modernity' (p. 178).

Katherine Saunders Nash gives John Cowper Powys finer critical attention than he usually receives in her reading of *A Glastonbury Romance* (*Narrative* 15:i[2007] 4–23). She uses the engagement of Susan Winnett with the narratology of Peter Brooks to answer the question 'How does a narrative with no hermeneutic puzzle to decipher and no story-level problem to solve compel readers to keep reading to the end, particularly if it is over a thousand pages long?' (p. 5). She concludes that Powys 'separates the erotics of progression from the hermeneutics of progression, and does so without sacrificing narrativity' (p. 5).

The next set of texts requires no special pleading for their narrativity. Detective and domestic fiction are connected in Kathy Mezei's 'Spinsters, Surveillance, and Speech: The Case of Miss Marple, Miss Mole, and Miss Jekyll' (*JML* 30:ii[2007] 103–20). Mezei shows how the 'socially marginal but potentially transgressive' (p. 27) figure of the spinster is placed in a position of speculative power in these texts precisely because her status is indeterminate. There is an essay by B.A. Pike on Margery Allingham's short stories in *Clues* (25:iv[2007] 27–36).

Verena-Susanna Nungesser's 'From Thornfield Hall to Manderley and Beyond: *Jane Eyre* and *Rebecca* as Transformations of the Fairy Tale, the Novel of Development, and the Gothic Novel' (in Rubik and Mettinger-Schartmann, eds., *A Breath of Fresh Eyre: Intertextual and Intermedial Reworkings of Jane Eyre*, pp. 209–26), demonstrates that both novels 'fuse transformational and transpositional aspects in the Genettean sense in creating extended and multifaceted versions of fairy tales, turning the narration into a novel of development, and in making use of elements of the Gothic novel to portray the anxieties of female development and female authorship' (p. 224).

Though a collection of anecdotes and memories rather than a sustained study of reception, Paul Skinner's *Ford Madox Ford's Literary Contacts* offers material useful for study of reception of Ford in the 1930s. Bernard Bergonzi's discussion of Graham Greene's admiration for *The Good Soldier* also suggests possible directions for study of Greene's literary antecedents. It throws light on reception of Ford and on what his narratives, especially *The End of an Affair* [1951], were to owe to his admiration of *The Good Soldier*.

The selection of Huxley's letters in James Sexton's *Aldous Huxley: Selected Letters* includes his love letters to Mary Hutchinson, previously unpublished. Though a useful resource and one which demonstrates Huxley's generosity to aspiring writers, it is unfortunate that the index only contains references to recipients of letters, not to people referenced in the letters. More editorial comment would have been welcome.

(c) D.H. Lawrence

D.H. Lawrence criticism and scholarship continue to flourish. The year 2007 saw the publication of a collection of essays on Lawrence's European reception, a book charting his reception in South Africa, and three new critical monographs. Seven noteworthy essays on Lawrence were published in related monographs and edited volumes, and five articles appeared in non-specialist journals. In addition, the *D.H. Lawrence Review* made a welcome return after a period of dormancy; it supplements two new numbers of *Études lawrenciennes* and the latest issue of the *Journal of D.H. Lawrence Studies*. This year has also seen the publication of a new selection of Lawrence's poetry, a popular edition of *The Virgin and the Gipsy*, and another four titles in the new Penguin Classics edition of Lawrence's works.

The Reception of D.H. Lawrence in Europe, edited by Christa Jansohn and Dieter Mehl, is published as part of the Athlone Critical Traditions series, whose aim is 'to initiate and forward the study of the reception of British and Irish authors in continental Europe' (p. vii). It comes in the wake of *The Reception of D.H. Lawrence around the World* [1999], edited by Takeo Iida. Lawrence's critical fortunes across Europe are documented very fully in this latest volume (it takes stock of the fate of his works in the German-speaking countries, Italy, France, Spain, Portugal, Greece, Russia, the former Czechoslovakia, Bulgaria, Poland, Sweden, Norway and Denmark). There is an opening essay by Rick Rylance, in which he usefully discusses Lawrence's troubled relation to England and Englishness; then follow sixteen essays by international scholars, each tracing the historical development of Lawrence's reception in the specific countries, from contemporary times to the present day, paying particular attention to the various translations of his works. The book concludes with a chronological listing of these translations for each of the countries covered, and with separate national bibliographies of relevant critical works. The entries for Germany and Italy open the account, and because of Lawrence's special ties with these two countries they seem the most significant and interesting, but the long-overdue recognition recently given to Lawrence's intellectual cosmopolitanism, and his wider cultural importance, makes all these essays a welcome addition to the academic record.

On this same topic of Lawrence's international reception, the omission of South Africa from Iida's earlier book has been rectified with the publication of *D.H. Lawrence around the World: South African Perspectives*, edited by Jim Phelps and Nigel Bell. This handsome volume reprints essays which are past landmarks in D.H. Lawrence criticism in South Africa; it collects reminiscences from critics who first encountered Lawrence in South Africa (including H.M. Daleski, Mark Kinkead-Weekes and Christopher Heywood); it contains reflections on the teaching of Lawrence in the country's various universities; and it also includes new essays from a current generation of South African Lawrence scholars. There is even a listing of articles on Lawrence in South African journals, and a checklist of postgraduate theses written on Lawrence and submitted to South African universities between 1948 and 1999. The book has obvious archival importance as the record of a significant, but hitherto obscure, thread in the history of Lawrence criticism, but its account of the teaching of Lawrence in this former British dominion also casts a fascinating diagnostic light on academic developments back home, and the modern essays attest to the continuation of a strong interest in Lawrence, in spite of his regrettable absence from university reading lists.

Two of the three new monographs attempt to shed fresh light on Lawrence's relations with Italy and Germany. In *D.H. Lawrence's Italian Travel Literature and Translations of Giovanni Verga: A Bakhtinian Reading*, Antonio Traficante uses Bakhtin's concept of dialogism to explore the author's changing response to the 'Italian Other' (p. 2) in his three books of Italian travel writings, *Twilight in Italy*, *Sea and Sardinia* and *Etruscan Places*. Traficante traces an archetypal progression in these works from 'self-confident ignorance' (*Twilight in Italy*) to 'self-critical scepticism' (*Sea and Sardinia*) to 'self-knowledge' and 'authentic knowing' (*Etruscan Places*) (p. 147). Chapter 3, 'Translating the Other: Lawrence, Bakhtin and Verga', considers Lawrence's translations of Verga's novel *Mastro-Don Gesualdo* and his story collections, *Little Novels of Sicily* and *Cavalleria Rusticana and Other Stories*. The idea of examining Lawrence's approach to translation as a means of gauging the sensitivity of his response to Italian otherness is intriguing, but there is very little discussion here of Lawrence's actual word choices, and in the absence of a sufficiently rigorous theoretical model to account for his translations we are left with the disappointing (and wearyingly familiar) image of Verga as 'a kind of sacrificial lamb, placed upon the altar to serve Lawrence's chief god: his art' (p. 118).

Carl Krockel's *D.H. Lawrence and Germany: The Politics of Influence* seeks to locate Lawrence's works in the context of German culture, and especially of German Romanticism in its reaction against the classicism of Goethe and Schiller. Krockel discusses the full range of Lawrence's writings, reading them alongside the works and philosophies of (among others) Goethe, Schopenhauer, Wagner, Nietzsche, Martin Buber, Max and Alfred Weber, Gerhart Hauptmann, Wassily Kandinsky, Freud and his Austrian disciple Otto Gross, Alfred Rosenberg and Hermann Hesse. The background research for the book is impressive, and at its best it provides a suggestive cultural framework which really illuminates the underlying structure of Lawrence's works. The early chapters on *The White Peacock* and *The Trespasser* are particularly interesting: Krockel discusses Lawrence's developing idea of tragedy in relation to Schopenhauer, Nietzsche and Wagner. Lawrence read Schopenhauer in translation, though Krockel also suggests that Lawrence would have encountered his pessimistic philosophy in the novels of Thomas Hardy, and especially in *Jude the Obscure*. In his reading of *The White Peacock*, Krockel produces an interesting comparison with Goethe's *Die Wahlverwandtschaften*, arguing that this book's philosophy of attraction was mediated to Lawrence through George Eliot. The concept of mediation here is very germane and well handled. However, in other parts of the book there is a problem with the sheer proliferation of contextual sources; Krockel sometimes places enormous strain on isolated allusions, and his critical language often implies authorial intention where none is demonstrable. For example, Lawrence's reference to Gerald Crich in *Women in Love* as 'freer, more dauntless than Bismarck' provokes a comparison of his 'management of the mines to Bismarck's rule over Germany, to the modernization of the mining industry in Germany, and to the capitalist ideology of the Protestant ethic that Max Weber had analysed' (p. 163). Assertions of the following type abound: 'In *Sons and Lovers* Lawrence responded to Otto Gross' reading of Nietzsche in conjunction with Freud to affirm the liberation of the individual's unconscious energies' (p. 129); 'In Will [Brangwen] he combines the Romanticism of Novalis with a Nietzschean aggressiveness to evoke Marc's Expressionist vision of the war' (p. 129); 'While composing *Women in Love* Lawrence struggled between opposing Nietzsche and Freud to each other, and combining them' (p. 181). The comparative readings are interesting and fruitful, but the assumption of authorial intention is unconvincing. Krockel's anxiety on the topic of influence is felt in the frequency of his references to the possible and the likely: 'Lawrence may have picked up a line from *A Study of Wagner*, where Ernest Newman criticizes [a scene from *Parsifal*] as an extreme form of Wagner's idealism' (p. 105); 'it is highly probable that Lawrence was at least aware of the art of the Blaue Reiter' (p. 111); 'It is possible that Lawrence was aware of Goethe's first ending in *Wilhelm Meisters theatralische Sendung*' (p. 200). A more sceptical and disciplined handling of the boundaries between illuminating context and direct influence might have helped to preserve a greater sense of Lawrence's particular positioning in German culture.

Jae-kyung Koh's *D.H. Lawrence and the Great War: The Quest for Cultural Regeneration* sets out to explore 'the polymorphous effects, social, political, psychological, of the war, on and in Lawrence's work' (p. 15). Koh discusses Lawrence's sense that the Great War represented the end of a Christian civilization which had privileged the 'love-mode' at the expense of the 'power-mode', repressing pre-Christian pagan forces and unleashing destructive, reactive violence in the process. Lawrence is said to view destruction as a necessary prelude to a new mode of life and a new kind of being. This is the origin of a comparison Koh draws between Lawrence and Foucault: Koh claims that 'Lawrence's historical vision parallels Michel Foucault's paradoxical vision of historical development as an endlessly repeated movement of discontinuity and continuity' (p. 15). Lawrence's 'rejection of the idea of historical evolution and progress, and his view of history as an endless cycle of destruction and creation' is also found to 'echo Nietzsche's vision that everything is the expression of "will to power"' (p. 162). Koh is mostly content to summarize the Lawrentian position on a host of topics, from the European Christian tradition to instinct, history and mechanization; he is not really interested in historicizing Lawrence's views, nor in examining the social or political contexts to the author's pronouncements on the Great War. This lack of historical perspective is certainly evident in the limited range of texts he chooses to discuss. The major wartime essays—the 'Study of Thomas Hardy' and 'The Crown'—receive very little attention, as does Lawrence's short-lived but important friendship with the pacifist philosopher Bertrand Russell, with whom he planned to deliver anti-war lectures in London. Koh unaccountably omits any mention of 'With the Guns', the short piece on modern mechanized warfare which Lawrence published in the *Manchester Guardian* for August 1914; he does not refer to one of Lawrence's most disturbing war poems, 'Eloi, Eloi, Lama Sabachthani?'; and he simply overlooks two of the most revealing war stories, the 1915 version of 'England, My England' and 'The Thimble' (also of 1915: later revised as 'The Ladybird'). He also analyses the postwar *Women in Love*, when he might have referred to the 1916 *First 'Women in Love'*. *D.H. Lawrence and the Great War* is hamstrung by these omissions and oversights: it adds very little to our understanding of a crucial period in Lawrence's life and career.

Moving now to essays published in related monographs and edited volumes, Michael Bell is concerned with an aspect of the German philosophical context to Lawrence's works in '"The passion of instruction": D.H. Lawrence and "Wholeness" versus *Bildung*', a chapter in his latest book, *Open Secrets: Literature, Education, and Authority from J.-J. Rousseau to J.M. Coetzee* (pp. 165–92). The book's central theme is the relationship between the tutor or mentor figure and the pupil in the tradition of the European *Bildungsroman* and related philosophical writings. Bell identifies in this tradition a radical scepticism concerning the ability of the teacher to move beyond Gradgrindian fact to communicate the most important lessons in life. The increasingly self-reflexive treatment of this theme as we move from Rousseau to Laurence Sterne, C.M. Wieland and Goethe reflects a deepening scepticism, finding its apogee with Nietzsche, whose emphasis on kinds of being and experience implodes the whole idea of humanistic teaching, exposing it as a power struggle between tutor and tutee. Lawrence, not Thomas Mann, is said to be the true heir to this Nietzschean insight, since 'Mann is ultimately too decorous to be a fully adequate vehicle of Nietzschean thought', while 'Lawrence...has the visceral directness, self-exposure, and readerly discomfort that Nietzsche's thought properly entails' (p. 167). Stressing Lawrence's own experience as a schoolteacher in Croydon, 1908–11, and his reputation as a prophetic and didactic writer, Bell begins by examining a scene from the 'Class-room' chapter of *Women in Love*, in which Ursula Brangwen (a schoolteacher), Rupert Birkin (a school inspector) and Hermione Roddice discuss the value of different kinds of knowledge. Birkin, the most obviously Lawrentian figure of the three, surprisingly emphasizes the teaching of facts, while Hermione Roddice, in some respects the Lawrentian nemesis, stresses the importance of integrating the intellectual and emotional worlds.

Birkin attacks Hermione for uttering the right sentiments in the wrong spirit (for too consciously espousing the value of the holistic approach). Between the two positions we can detect an emphasis on 'wholeness' as the ultimate value of education and life; true knowledge will entail the right approach to ideas, and this in turn will require a constant adjustment to experience. As Bell notes, 'Vital truth of the kind in question here is not a proposition to be reached and retained so much as a constant momentary adjustment to the inner and outer worlds' (p. 175). The breach between utterance and intent, language and experience, is explored by Lawrence in his essays on American authors in *Studies in Classic American Literature*, where their words are said to skate over hidden symbolic depths, but Bell also wants to stress the structural importance of Lawrence's interest in wholeness to the way we approach the author's own didactic texts. Lawrence's discursive essays (for example, 'Education of the People') sometimes attract criticism and ridicule for their dogmatic and repetitive aspects, but the author's inconsistencies and excesses reveal an ongoing adjustment between the message and the manner of its articulation (what Lawrence termed the 'struggle into verbal consciousness'); we should attend to this continual adjustment and struggle, properly relativizing Lawrence's utterances, rather than taking him at his word. For Bell, 'What is distinctive in Lawrence resists recognition and dissemination as "thought" because it is so closely, and properly, tied to its occasions. As "thought" it is fatally vulnerable to banality' (p. 177). This is a rich and nuanced account of an important crux in Lawrence's writing.

Michael Freeman contributes an essay entitled 'Time and Space under Modernism: The Railway in D.H. Lawrence's *Sons and Lovers*' to *The Railway and Modernity: Time, Space, and the Machine Ensemble*, a book he co-edited with Matthew Beaumont (pp. 85–100). His piece draws on ideas in the work of Bergson and Henri Lefebvre, suggesting that the railway timetable is one of the most powerful reminders of the extent to which modernity affected our understanding of time and space. The commuter's internalization of the railway's timings and its spatial connections (of slow and express trains, and of disjointed journeys) demonstrates the 'very palpable disunities or disjunctures to the new space-time nexus' (p. 91). Applying this insight to the novel, Freeman contrasts the distinctive attitudes to train travel of Paul Morel and his mother. Where Paul 'is fully drilled in the workings of the railway as spatial practice, familiar with its timetables, its excursion bills and even many of its idiosyncrasies and incoherences of operation' (p. 99), Mrs Morel 'appears oblivious of differential spatial realms: [for her] every railway journey, whether quick or slow, forms a tedium, an irritation' (p. 94). While the observation is interesting as far as it goes, it is hardly groundbreaking; the same difference of attitude between the generations might have been observed in any number of sources, literary and otherwise. The insight does not lead to any more thorough analysis of *Sons and Lovers*, and Freeman does not refer to the importance of trains in Lawrence's other texts, so his use of the novel here seems rather random and opportunistic. Freeman's own essay ironically generates the experience of disunity which it identifies as a central feature of modernity; it fizzles out in several incoherent and wildly speculative biographical asides to Lawrence's broader travels in Europe and beyond.

Andrew Radford includes a long chapter on 'Lawrence's Underworld' in his book *The Lost Girls: Demeter–Persephone and the Literary Imagination* (pp. 224–73). His main theme is the engagement with, and transformation of, the Demeter–Persephone myth in English literature from Victorian to modernist times (from Thomas Hardy to Mary Butts, via Mary Webb, E.M. Forster and Lawrence). Radford begins by discussing different versions of the myth in antiquity, but he is particularly interested in English Hellenism and the work of Walter Pater, John Ruskin, John Addington Symonds and Jane Ellen Harrison. His anthropological approach also inevitably invokes E.B. Tylor, whose work *Primitive Culture* Lawrence read and admired, and J.G. Frazer. The specific focus of the chapter on Lawrence is *The Lost Girl*, which Radford reads as a subversive retelling of the Persephone story. Rebelling against the dull bourgeois values of her provincial English Midlands upbringing, Alvina Houghton gleans a new understanding of life's possibilities through her descent into the Throttle-Ha'penny pit. Where others might be frightened or repelled, Alvina undergoes a kind of awakening underground. The pattern of willing submission to dark subterranean forces is repeated when she joins a touring troupe of actors, trains to be a maternity nurse in run-down Islington, and then leaves England altogether to take up a bewildering new role as the wife of Ciccio Marasca in the remote and rural Califano, an Italian hamlet close to Pescocalascio (based on Picinisco). Radford contrasts Lawrence's treatment of Italy here to that of Forster: 'Unlike Forster's Italian fictions, in which characters only achieve any kind of self-realization once they have crossed the Channel, Lawrence shows Alvina embarking upon a number of both geographic and figurative migrations and returns within England itself, rehearsing an expatriate adventure that paradoxically carries her "home" to her "own true nature"' (p. 232). Like Persephone, Alvina is compelled at regular intervals to leave the comfortable surfaces of her customary life to experience imaginative or literal exile in some dark underworld. However, Alvina is not doomed to undergo the exile; she actively chooses it as a positive alternative to the sedate dullness of provincial English society. The focus on *The Lost Girl* as a retelling of the myth is interesting, and the argument is convincing enough, but the chapter would have benefited from more careful editing. At fifty pages it is far too long, and the repeated use of unnecessary alliterative phrases—e.g. 'subterranean site' (p. 226), 'existential experimentation' (p. 231), 'petty provinciality of the pinched Woodhouse' (p. 233), 'pale, passionless Persephone' (p. 243)—soon loses its charm.

Mary Bryden's *Gilles Deleuze: Travels in Literature* attempts to provide not 'a systematic introduction to the diverse ways in which Deleuzian analysis can apply itself to literature', but 'a series of close exposures to what Deleuzian analysis can give rise to when pursued along open-ended textual pathways' (p. 10). This strange formulation gives Bryden licence to wander from topic to topic in the works of T.E. Lawrence, Herman Melville, D.H. Lawrence, Michel Tournier and Samuel Beckett, directed only by her sense of Deleuze's interest in the material under discussion. In the chapter entitled 'Travelling Inwards: D.H. Lawrence' (pp. 50–83), Bryden focuses on Lawrence's approaches to leadership and power, journeying, psychoanalysis and desire, and becoming. In the opening pages of the chapter her language suggests an underlying wish to evaluate the nature and extent of Deleuze's engagement with Lawrence on these topics. She notes how Nietzsche is 'appropriately cited by Deleuze' in the preface he wrote to an edition of *Apocalypse* (p. 58), and she similarly observes that *The Man Who Died* (otherwise known as *The Escaped Cock*) is 'appropriately' used by Deleuze 'when considering the annexing of Christ's self-sacrifice by the evangelising fervour of John of Patmos' (p. 60). Bryden writes that throughout his work 'Deleuze . . . shows his familiarity with a wide generic range of Lawrence's writing, including essays, correspondence, poetry . . . theoretical writings . . . and novels' (p. 61). However, although she carefully notes instances where Deleuze draws appositely on Lawrence's writings, she seems less inclined to explore those cases where Deleuze forcefully appropriates the earlier writer's works; such cases are glossed as merely 'surprising' or 'curious'. At one point we are told that 'Deleuze, perhaps surprisingly, paraphrases Lawrence's constabulary description [in *Apocalypse*] without further comment, though within parentheses' (p. 55); elsewhere, Bryden notes how 'Curiously, while [in 'Chaos in Poetry'] Lawrence presents chaos as a fascinating, desirable, mercurial element to which all good poetry must open up, Deleuze and Guattari appear slightly to dilute the radical exuberance of his argument' (p. 70). The deceptive qualifications 'perhaps' and 'slightly' seem intended to preclude any further critical enquiry. The approach of the chapter is really broadly comparative, but the tendency to play down these areas of questionable appropriation removes any polemical tension from the account and so gives the essay a feeling of flatness. The continual asides to Deleuze seem to be offered in a spirit of largely uncritical appreciation, which has the effect of alienating the uninitiated reader still further from several of his more cryptic utterances on Lawrence, as translated by Bryden herself: for example, 'Red has become dangerous for mankind (and we must not forget that Lawrence is writing while spitting blood)' (p. 63). The chapter will probably appeal more to Deleuzians than Lawrence scholars.

Andrzej Gąsiorek adopts an explicitly comparative approach in 'War, "Primitivism", and the Future of "the West": Reflections on D.H. Lawrence and Wyndham Lewis' (in Begam and Valdez Moses, eds., *Modernism and Colonialism: British and Irish Literature, 1899–1939*, pp. 91–110). Gąsiorek notes the important difference between British colonial expansionism up to 1870 and subsequent imperial consolidation, marked by a questioning of colonialism's 'moral validity and economic viability' (p. 92). The sense of cultural crisis created by the Great War resulted in both a questioning of Europe's supremacy over its colonies and the creation of a reactionary discourse of 'East' and 'West', asserting the existence of a collective European cultural identity by mourning its gradual decline and imminent collapse. Lawrence and Lewis are discussed as writers preoccupied with the issue of European cultural decadence who nonetheless resist this colonialist tendency to mourn the 'decline of the West'. In spite of their similarities—they both 'criticized nationalism, imperialism, and materialism; questioned the benefits of democracy; favoured natural aristocracies; and urged the transformation of Western civilization' (p. 93)—the two writers viewed the European crisis very differently and advocated different routes to postwar cultural regeneration. While Lawrence is said to have 'turned for his vision of cultural rebirth to what he saw as the intuitive, animist view of life expressed in other cultures— principally the "Indians" of New Mexico and the ancient Etruscans' (p. 93), Lewis 'viewed the postwar turn to intuitionism as a disintegrative atavism' (p. 94), arguing that the legacy of Western art (and especially of pre-war avant-garde experimentalism) should be retained and renewed through exposure to anti-naturalistic, non-European influences. It is clear where Gąsiorek's own sympathies lie. He suggests that Lawrence's turn to other cultures in an attempt to rejuvenate a decadent Europe shows him using a 'homogenizing language' which discusses those cultures 'in terms of a unified worldview', presenting them as 'object[s] to be studied', or as merely antithetical to the dominant 'white' culture (pp. 103–4). Lewis, by contrast, 'was conscious of the ideological work performed by the discourses that sustained such oppositions', critiquing '*all* racialist rhetorics', and remaining sceptical of nationalism, even though he 'misread National Socialism so abysmally' (pp. 97–8). The comparisons are suggestive, though the account of racial or colonial discourse and its formation through the process of abjection is very familiar, and the critique of Lawrence it generates seems predictable and a little unquestioning. The essay concludes by noting that Lewis's dogged faith (*contra* Lawrence) in the Western intellectual tradition was, in any case, badly affected by the Second World War, which caused him to refer to 'Western Europe' as 'bankrupt, if possible more confused than ever, broken and apathetic' (p. 106).

Lawrence also features in two new books in the Cambridge Companions to Literature series. Hugh Stevens contributes an essay entitled 'D.H. Lawrence: Organicism and the Modernist Novel' to *The Cambridge Companion to the Modernist Novel*, edited by Morag Shiach (pp. 137–50). The focus here is on the essays Lawrence wrote on the art of the novel in 1923 and 1925: 'The Future of the Novel', 'Why the Novel Matters', 'The Novel', 'Morality and the Novel' and 'The Novel and the Feelings'. In 'The Future of the Novel', Lawrence attacks Joyce, Proust and Dorothy Richardson for what he considers to be their excessive self-consciousness and for the analytical quality of their works; in contrast, he stresses the importance of the novel as a form whose value resides in its capacity to enlarge and direct our sympathies. Stevens argues that Lawrence's 'aesthetic ideals for fiction have as much in common with Romantic organicism and Victorian realism...as with modernist radicalism' (p. 140), but he demonstrates this thesis not in a reading of *Women in Love* (arguably the author's most modernist novel) but *Lady Chatterley's Lover* (arguably his least modernist). Any student reading the essay could be forgiven for thinking that Lawrence is essentially a late nineteenth-century English writer with European cultural ties, whereas *Women in Love* would have confirmed the opposite view of him as a European modernist writer with important connections to England. Sandra M. Gilbert's treatment of 'D.H. Lawrence's Place in Modern Poetry' (in Corcoran, ed., *The Cambridge Companion to Twentieth-Century English Poetry*, pp. 74–86) also sounds a disappointing note of retrenchment. Where we might have expected a discussion of recent critical and theoretical approaches to the poetry, or an exploration of Lawrence's relation to modernist verse and his important influence on subsequent English poetry, we are given a peculiarly dated account dwelling primarily on his social background, his indebtedness to Whitman and Swinburne, and the rather prickly response of T.S. Eliot to Lawrence's poetry. For Gilbert, Lawrence's verse is shaped by 'an effort to find a style that would be free of what he considered verbal constraints': 'he fought to find a poetics adequate to his desire for a liberation of substantial being' (pp. 74–5). The terms of this argument would hardly have surprised readers in the 1960s. It is telling that Gilbert's few references to other critics all come from books published in the 1950s; it is the only essay in the volume which lacks a list of further reading.

In one of this year's journal articles, Nils Clausson takes a deconstructive approach to a Lawrence short story in 'Practicing Deconstruction, Again: Blindness, Insight and the Lovely Treachery of Words in D.H. Lawrence's "The Blind Man"' (*CollL* 34:i[2007] 106–28). This essay is framed as a practical riposte to the popular devaluation of deconstruction as an abstruse theoretical mode swathed in an impenetrable discourse lacking any sense of aesthetic or political conviction. Clausson notes Lawrence's famous dictum in *Studies in Classic American Literature*, 'Never trust the artist. Trust the tale', suggesting that 'Lawrence the critic seems to be cautioning us against finding in his stories the very doctrine that, paradoxically, Lawrence the prophetic artist presumably set out to put in them' (p. 110). His analysis identifies an opposition in 'The Blind Man' between a positive blind sensuality (Maurice Pervin) and a negative mental consciousness (Bertie Reid), but it goes on to show how Lawrence's treatment of his characters, his language, and his symbolism break down this binary opposition, leaving us uncertain whether Maurice's blind world is peaceful or violent, and whether Bertie Reid's horrified response to contact with him and his facial disfigurement is unreasonable or instinctive. The story's memorable ending, in which Maurice lays claim to a new bond with Bertie, is said to aim at exposing and ridiculing Bertie's 'insane reserve', where in fact it merely underscores the characters' shared isolation. In Clausson's analysis, 'Lawrence's story… becomes an allegory of (partial) authorial blindness: the blindness of Lawrence's blind man…is a figure for the blindness of Lawrence to those meanings that escape his conscious control' (p. 110). The reading of the story is detailed and convincing in its emphasis on the underlying instability of the text's 'message', and the clarity of the writing certainly puts paid to the claim that deconstructive analysis must always be opaque and obscure. The problem, however, lies in the essay's approach to the question of what, or who, is being deconstructed. Clausson correctly notes that 'the binaries in the story are in deconstruction' (p. 112), but he also clearly believes it is a case of the tale deconstructing the artist: of Lawrence setting out to valorize the body over the mind, but tripping himself up in the attempt. The argument repeatedly refers to 'Lawrence's assertion of the superiority of Maurice's blood-consciousness' and 'the Lawrentian ideal of blood-consciousness' (pp. 112, 117), where in fact any reader would be hard pressed to deduce the author's sympathies, or his attempt to inculcate a specific 'ideal', solely from a reading of the story itself. Clausson postulates a Lawrentian subtext, and then demonstrates how the story fails to support any such imposition. In arguing that the ambivalence of the story somehow defeats the intentions of its doctrinaire author, Clausson overlooks the fact that it is his own critical adherence to the concept of a Lawrentian doctrine which is being brought into question. He might more reasonably have concluded that the story reveals a self-reflexive authorial voice which resists any straightforward ideological reading, exposing the blindness of the predisposed critic in the process.

In '#$%ˆ&∗!?: Modernism and Dirty Words' (*Mo/Mo* 14:ii[2007] 209–23), Loren Glass compares Ernest Hemingway's negotiations with editor Maxwell Perkins over the excision of three dirty words from *A Farewell to Arms* to Barney Rosset's struggle to publish (and gain copyright for) an unexpurgated edition of *Lady Chatterley's Lover* in America. The essay makes several fascinating observations on the origin and social significance of swear words. Glass notes that the derivation of swear words, usually taken to be Anglo-Saxon, is in fact notoriously obscure; anthropologists have even suggested that expletives may have been among the earliest primitive utterances. Returning to the early twentieth century, the essay explores how swear words became a marker of anxiety about social change in the anglophone world. Traditionally linked to the exclusively male environments of the battlefield and the smoking room, their use by women signalled a challenge to male power and to the shaping values of a British empire in decline. Hemingway saw the censoring of his text as a kind of symbolic castration; Lawrence, meanwhile, defiantly put an aristocratic female character at the centre of his novel, and gave the dirty words a domestic (rather than a military) context. Rosset's success in the 1959 American trial of *Lady Chatterley's Lover* was won partly through his defence of Lawrence's claim that its intention was to cleanse or redeem the offending words, but Grove Press still had to fight the New American Library for the right to issue an unexpurgated text. In the end, the two came to an agreement and both editions appeared. While Hemingway's novel was sanitized for its appearance in *Scribner's Magazine*, Lawrence's swear words became his novel's scandalous selling point three decades later. The argument of the essay is interesting, if rather disparate; its ambition to 'establish the centrality of so-called dirty words ... not only for any understanding of Hemingway and Lawrence's considerably different styles but also of Anglo-American modernism more generally' (p. 210) is, however, quite absurd. One must also question how the article came to print containing several textual and bibliographical references to 'James Gordon Frazier' (pp. 214, 215, 222), the anthropologist better known to modernist scholars as J.G. Frazer, author of *The Golden Bough*.

John Lyon celebrates the restless quality of Lawrence's epistolary style in 'Going On: Lawrence's Cockney Letters' (*EIC* 57[2007] 1–21). Quoting Lawrence's letter to Edward Garnett of 22 April 1914, in which he defends himself against the charge that he is 'half a Frenchman and one-eighth a Cockney', Lyon argues that it is precisely Lawrence's Cockney vulgarity and refusal to take himself (or anyone else) too seriously which redeems his more portentous and didactic pronouncements. Lyon notes that 'Lawrence's intelligence was remarkably restless and at its most idiosyncratically weak when it allowed itself to come to rest' (p. 7). The letter form is particularly suited to Lawrence's creativity because 'the letter as a form is without the demands or temptations of completeness which, however construed, accompany other forms of writerly expression'; letters also 'bring with them an immediate and particular sense of address or audience and, with that, a self-awareness and mindfulness of especial value in the case of a writer such as Lawrence, too easily suspicious of self-consciousness and self-contradictingly hostile to thought and to the mind itself' (p. 9). Lyon contrasts two wartime letters, one of 10 August 1914 from Henry James to Rhoda Broughton, the other of 30 April 1915 from Lawrence to Lady Ottoline Morrell. Despite several similarities in tone and content, 'James's...is the voice and style of an older man and of an earlier generation; Lawrence's is astonishingly modern, almost negligent, manifesting an informality verging on formlessness' (p. 14). The article ends by underlining the importance of the provisional in Lawrence's writing: 'The "truth" of the letters is more provisional [than in his other writings], tied to the moment of their writing and to the continuing relation with particular interlocutors of which they are but a part' (p. 19).

The topic of violence in Lawrence's work has received much attention at recent conferences; it was the subject of a special number of *Études lawrenciennes* in 2004. Michael Squires argues for the central, and developing, role of violence in Lawrence's work in 'Modernism and the Contours of Violence in D.H. Lawrence's Fiction' (*SNNTS* 39:i[2007] 84–104). Squires argues that there are three periods in Lawrence's career when violence operates in distinctive ways: 'In his early phase (1905–1915), violence typically images the disruptive class differences that alter human relationships...In Lawrence's middle phase (1916–1924), violence illuminates characters caught in roles they must alter in order to attain personal and spiritual fulfilment...In Lawrence's final phase (1925–1930), violence, ever more verbal, generates fresh narrative risks and stirs characters...to dismantle social constraints in order to find sexual liberation' (p. 85). The examples for each phase are drawn from a broad selection of the short stories and novels, and Squires draws parallels with the different phases in Picasso's career, from his 1910 Cubist work to 'his female images of 1925 to 1930' (p. 99) and his 'paintings of violence (1925), the crucifixion (1930), and other forms of human destruction (e.g. *Guernica*, 1937)' (p. 89). Ultimately, Squires suggests that 'The contours of violence in Lawrence's fiction trace a Modernist sequence—emergent and marginal, inclusive and central, then infiltrative—that encodes disorder and culminates in multiple forms of dissonance' (p. 102).

Finally, in 'A Confederacy of Sons and Lovers: Similarities between *A Confederacy of Dunces* and *Sons and Lovers*' (*NConL* 37:ii[2007] 11–12), Bernard Lewis identifies 'a measure of similarity' between the portrayals of Paul Morel and Ignatius Reilly in John Kennedy Toole's novel, published in 1980. He notes that both characters have weak fathers and troublesome mothers, and that they have comparable problems with women: 'Ignatius is unable to find his own sexual identity—that is not to say, his gender identity, but his sexual identity in relation to another person' (p. 12). He fails to mention that, applying these same terms, we might compare *Sons and Lovers* to innumerable other works in the Western canon (and outside it). A specious argument is further undermined by calamitous mistakes: he erroneously refers to Paul's relationship with 'an older, *divorced* woman named Clara Dawes' (emphasis added) and, more egregiously, to 'William Morel and his son, Paul' (p. 12).

Lawrence scholars will welcome the return of the *D.H. Lawrence Review* after an extended period of dormancy. The latest issue (31:iii), was published in 2007 but backdated to 2003. It contains a tribute to the critic Mark Spilka (1925–2001) by Dennis Jackson; an essay by Tim Lovelace on a little-discussed poem, 'D.H. Lawrence's "The Combative Spirit": Tinkering with the Canon' (*DHLR* 31:iii[2003] 3–12); Andrew Nash's essay ' "At the Gates": New Commentaries on a Lost Lawrence Text' (*DHLR* 31:iii[2003] 13–23), first published in the *Review of English Studies* in 2005, which reproduces and contextualizes newly-discovered readers' reports relating to one of Lawrence's unpublished and now lost philosophical works; and a comparative piece by Douglas Wuchina entitled ' "My Heart's Desire": "Physical Passion" and "A New Sort of Love" in *Women in Love* and *The First "Women in Love"*'(*DHLR* 31:iii[2003] 25–42).

This year the two issues of *Études lawrenciennes*, volumes 36 and 37, were devoted to travel and movement. Volume 36, 'The Poetics of Travel and Cultural Otherness', contains eleven essays, including Peter Preston's 'Seeing Florence to Death: Lawrence in the City of David' (*EL* 36[2007] 73–90), Keith Cushman's 'Lawrence and Achsah Brewster in Ceylon: The Journey of Identity' (*EL* 36[2007] 91–117) and Neil Roberts's 'Recognising Otherness? The Place of *Mornings in Mexico* in Lawrence's Encounter with Native America' (*EL* 36[2007] 119–30). Volume 37, 'Shift, Movement, Becoming', contains thirteen essays, the most interesting being Michael Bell's 'Lawrence and Deleuze: De faux amis?' (*EL* 37[2007] 41–56), which provides an interesting counterpoint to other, less critical, discussions of the intellectual kinship between Lawrence and Deleuze, and Violeta Sotirova's 'Shifts in Point of View: From *Paul Morel* to *Sons and Lovers*' (*EL* 37[2007] 143–65), which analyses important narratological and stylistic changes in Lawrence's early work as a novelist.

The *Journal of D.H. Lawrence Studies* (1:ii[2007]), contains the 'Further Letters of D.H. Lawrence', edited by James T. Boulton, plus essays by Helen Baron, Boulton, N.H. Reeve, Paul Poplawski, Peter Preston and Keith Cushman, Sean Matthews, John Worthen and David Ellis. N.H. Reeve's piece on 'Editing "Wintry Peacock" ' (*JDHLS* 1:ii[2007] 59–69) deserves special mention for its sensitive response to one of Lawrence's most underrated short stories, written and revised between 1919 and 1921. The history of the story's composition, revision and publication is particularly complicated for so short a text, and Reeve's detailed work on the manuscript and typescript versions for the forthcoming Cambridge edition of *The Vicar's Garden and Other Stories* leads to some fascinating observations on its deep structure and the changing nature of Lawrence's engagement with its central themes.

Among the new editions of Lawrence's texts, Faber has published *D.H. Lawrence: Poems Selected by Tom Paulin*, a slim and very reasonably priced volume notable for the first reproduction on its front cover of a photograph of Lawrence in a trilby hat, taken in 1915 by Elliott & Fry. This photograph emerged from the same session as the famous one of him sitting at a table with a book (they may both have been author publicity images arranged by Methuen, the company that was poised to publish Lawrence's fourth novel, *The Rainbow*). Unfortunately the front cover is really the sole point of originality in the volume. Paulin's seven-page introduction is largely uninspiring, and the selection of poems, while serviceable for those new to Lawrence, contains no real surprises for the more knowledgeable reader.

Like last year, four new Penguin Classics editions of Lawrence's works were published during 2007: *D.H. Lawrence and Italy* (containing *Twilight in Italy*, *Sea and Sardinia* and *Sketches of Etruscan Places*), *The Rainbow*, *Selected Stories* and *Women in Love*. The volumes usefully reproduce the standard Cambridge texts. *Selected Stories*, edited by Sue Wilson, contains many of the classic tales, together with a few surprises (for example 'Vin Ordinaire', an early version of 'The Thorn in the Flesh'; and the shorter, 1915, version of 'England, My England'). In keeping with recent Penguin policy, each volume is introduced by a contemporary writer; these editions carry introductions by Tim Parks, James Wood, Louise Welsh and Amit Chaudhuri. James Wood is characteristically incisive and stimulating in his introduction to *The Rainbow*, countering popular criticism of Lawrence's repetitive style and doctrine in that novel by noticing 'the delicacy of Lawrence's metaphorical power' (p. xii) and examining in detail those moments when he is 'not at all schematic, and pushes beyond his announced "doctrine"' (p. xxvi). Unfortunately Wood's well-pitched essay is the exception rather than the rule. Tim Parks and Louise Welsh are never more than perfunctory in their observations on the Italian writings and the short stories, and Amit Chaudhuri is formless and unfocused in his rather too personal approach to *Women in Love* (one winces from his lengthy biographical note in the front of the book, which significantly occupies the same space as the notes on Lawrence himself).

Penguin also published *The Virgin and the Gipsy* as number fourteen in its nicely designed series of twenty short tales entitled 'Great Loves'. It is pleasing to see the story presented in this popular and affordable format, and intriguing to see Lawrence keep company with Abelard and Heloise, Boccaccio and Giacomo Casanova.

(d) Virginia Woolf

Mrs Woolf and the Servants by Alison Light is the book on Woolf published this year that will doubtless reach the widest audience. It combines rigorous historical research with moments of delicate textual analysis, producing a highly readable narrative beginning well before Woolf's birth, and extending beyond her death. This book provides a history of domestic service in the late nineteenth and the twentieth centuries; alongside this history, it produces another version of the life of Woolf. This version does not always present Woolf in the most sympathetic light, since her diaries and letters are famously replete with critical or downright offensive comments about her servants. Yet overall Light's careful consideration of the various factors—historical, economic, emotional, psychological—which come together in the intense relationship between mistress and servant balances her condemnation of the inequities perpetuated even in the relatively progressive Bloomsbury households. The book offers some suggestive insights into the realities of everyday life for Woolf and her servants, and those like them. Light notes, for example, that until 1929 the Woolfs 'had never been alone before in their own home' (p. 192), or, more broadly, that, even into the 1930s, 'giving or taking orders was the most common relationship between women' (p. 179)—both observations whose implications are ripe for further consideration. Light also gave 2007's Virginia Woolf Birthday Lecture, entitled 'Composing Oneself: Virginia Woolf's Diaries and Memories'.

Two monographs published this year, Emily Blair's *Virginia Woolf and the Nineteenth-Century Domestic Novel* and Steve Ellis's *Virginia Woolf and the Victorians*, focus on connections between Woolf and her Victorian literary and cultural heritage. Blair's book is something of a defence of earlier women writers, specifically Elizabeth Gaskell and Margaret Oliphant, against Woolf's faint praise (of Gaskell) or outright antipathy (towards Oliphant). Blair argues that nineteenth-century domestic discourse, which Woolf is largely held to have emphatically rejected in her murder of the Angel in the House, in fact informs and in some ways underpins Woolf's 'conceptions of female artistry' (p. 211); as Blair puts it, 'Woolf learns to live with The Angel in her house of fiction' (p. 213). This book becomes increasingly convincing as it progresses, moving through some close readings of Gaskell and Oliphant as well as Woolf, and the readings of *Mrs Dalloway* and *To the Lighthouse* at the end are particularly convincing in support of Blair's contention that Woolf's focus in these novels on the society hostess is entirely congruent with her 'modernist and feminist aims to depict "what is commonly thought small" ' (p. 230). Ellis's book argues that, rather than being primarily attached to the radical potential of the twentieth century, Woolf's texts display a profound ambivalence about modernity, and a greater nostalgia for Victorian culture and society than previous critics have allowed. *Night and Day* and *The Years* of course feature prominently; other chapters focus on *To the Lighthouse* and *Mrs Dalloway*. Ellis begins by positing Woolf as 'Post-Victorian', where 'Post [expresses] a complex relationship of difference and debt' (p. 1), and then argues that Woolf moves through various positions in relation to the Victorian in her work: reclamation, synchronicity, integration and disillusion and concluding with the incoherence (in this context) of the final works. Analyses of the visual feature strongly, as Ellis takes issue with previous work by critics such as Jane Goldman. Arguing, for example, that Woolf's visual schema tends to equate modernity with the harsh, unshaded electric lightbulb, emphasizing its negative qualities, Ellis suggests that by contrast the equivalent terms used to describe the Victorian period—shadow, penumbra and so on—frequently emerge as positive and contiguous with 'the value of "obscurity" to Woolf' (p. 30). One of Ellis's conclusions is, therefore, that 'Woolf's feminism . . . is not so much about embracing a visionary future as of attending to the past' (p. 168).

Joanne Campbell Tidwell's *Politics and Aesthetics in the Diary of Virginia Woolf* provides an overview of the diary and draws out some key features. A first chapter proposes a development in the diary's 'I'; the second chapter assesses the diary against two others proposed as paradigmatic, those of

Samuel Pepys and Anaïs Nin; the third chapter compares Woolf's diary with those of her contemporaries Katherine Mansfield and Vera Brittain; and a fourth chapter further contextualizes the diaries by considering the relationship between the diary and feminist-modernist aesthetics.

Anna Snaith, in her introduction to *Palgrave Advances in Virginia Woolf Studies*, states that the volume aims 'to aid readers in their engagement with [the] plethora of biographical, cultural and editorial work' produced on Woolf over recent years (p. 2)—an aim which the book ably achieves. The introduction provides a very helpful overview of Woolf's early reception, and later chapters, while inevitably paying closer attention to very recent developments, place these developments in literary-historical context. Chapters, many from major scholars in the field, range from the more familiar topics of narratological approaches (Melba Cuddy-Keane), modernist studies (Jane Goldman) and feminist approaches (Beth Riegel Daugherty), to the more obviously novel lesbian approaches (Diana L. Swanson), postcolonial approaches (Jeanette McVicker) and European reception studies (Nicola Luckhurst and Alice Staveley). However, familiar topics do not necessarily make for familiar readings, and these essays for the most part not only provide solid overviews of the critical field, but make room for their authors to express their own perspectives on Woolf's work, and work on Woolf. In some cases, this individual perspective loomed rather large, as in Pamela Caughie's chapter on 'Postmodernist and Poststructuralist Approaches', which was dominated by material drawn from her *Virginia Woolf and Postmodernism*, perhaps to the detriment of an overview of other recent work in the field. But overall this text is a much-needed addition to the field, and also provides a vivid sense of a community of Woolf scholars with a healthy sense of their need to be self-aware about their critical positions and their place within the vast landscape of Woolf studies.

Snaith is also co-editor, with Michael Whitworth, of *Locating Woolf: The Politics of Space and Place*, announced as 'the first book-length study of Woolf and place' (p. 4). The range of this collection is indicated in the editors' observation that 'While Woolf has long been placed in the context of urban modernity, we want to consider a range of spatial formations: broadcasting space, geopolitical space, rural space, imperial space' (p. 4). Thus this collection contributes to the current 'international Woolf' trend in Woolf studies, notably in essays by Kurt Koenigsberger, Suzanne Lynch, Nobuyoshi Ota and Ian Blyth. It also embraces such diverse approaches to the theme of space and place as Tracy Seeley's reading of the 'tropics of evasion and digression' (p. 2) in *A Room of One's Own*; Helen Southworth's Blanchot-informed exploration of the figure of interruption in *Between the Acts*; Linden Peach's work on the relationship between Woolf and Walter Sickert through their 'shared interest in the link between people and objects' (p. 66); and explorations of the imaginative possibilities (and indeed threats) posed by new technologies which modified conceptualizations of space, from Leena Kore Schröder, on Woolf and cars, and Jane Lewty, on Woolf and radio.

Georgia Johnston's *The Formation of 20th-Century Queer Autobiography: Reading Vita Sackville-West, Virginia Woolf, Hilda Doolittle, and Gertrude Stein* is perhaps misleadingly titled since it proposes that these authors produce a specifically lesbian autobiography, in texts which may or may not be traditionally recognized as autobiographical. Thus, while Johnston's chapter on Woolf does focus on 'A Sketch of the Past', it also begins with a brief consideration of *Orlando* as responding to, and countering, Sackville-West's sexological model of lesbianism in her novel *Challenge*. Johnston makes productive use of Cuddy-Keane's concept of the 'coercive text' (p. 73) to read 'Sketch' as adopting and adapting the Freudian case-study model in order to refute its premises. While the argument that this produces a specifically lesbian text involves the reader working 'Sketch' back through Johnston's unpicking of the Freudian family romance, it certainly captures the multiple position of the 'I' maintained in Woolf's autobiographical text—both ensnared within the web of family and coolly observing from the position of spectator, and refusing (as Freud's model would require) to 'reinterpret' the past, but rather 'reenter[ing]' it (p. 91).

Woolfian Boundaries: Selected Papers from the Sixteenth Annual International Conference on Virginia Woolf provides a lively selection of the papers presented at the 2006 conference held in Birmingham, UK. The editors have opted not to present the papers in subheaded sections, allowing readers to make their own connections between them, within and across boundaries. However, some clusters do emerge. The continued growth of ecocriticism as a theoretical approach is signalled in the fascinating group of papers on, broadly, Woolf and the natural world, by Ian Blyth (pp. 80–5), Richard Epsley (pp. 86–92), Christina Alt (pp. 93–9), Jane Goldman (pp. 100–7) and Bonnie Kime Scott (pp. 108–15). Epsley's paper on Woolf's relationship between Woolf and London Zoo was particularly intriguing, touching on Woolf's relationship with the bodily, her ambivalent engagement with classification and the way in which Woolf both uses and undermines the 'fallacy of animality' or 'attempts to perceive the world of the animal' (p. 86). As these papers indicate, the conference theme of boundaries was addressed in a wide variety of ways, not restricted to the geographical or spatial. Having said that, papers on the relationship between the Woolfs and the Birmingham Writers' Group of the mid-1930s (by Helen Southworth (pp. 43–50) and Lara Feigel (pp. 51–7)) obviously reflected the conference's physical location this year. Woolf and visual culture continued to feature strongly, with Maggie Humm's (pp. 150–6) paper continuing her valuable work on Stephen and Woolf family photography, here discussing the physical layout of the photographs in the family's albums in terms of a 'heterotopology', where 'physical, measurable space is interdependent with symbolic and imaginative spaces' (p. 153). Other notable papers were Katie Macnamara's (pp. 22–9) on the potential of the essay form to resist authoritarianism, discussing Woolf alongside Theodor Adorno and Montaigne and suggestively proposing that the essay form can be seen as productively 'passive-aggressive' (p. 23); Alyda Faber's (pp. 58–64) interdisciplinary reading of Woolf's correspondence with the Raverats, providing an interesting theological perspective on the famous 'shocks' described in 'A Sketch of the Past'; Thaine Stearns's (pp. 121–6) unearthing of Woolf's engagement with Pound's Imagism; and Wendy Parkins' (pp. 144–9) continuation of the critical focus on Woolf as cultural icon (inaugurated by Brenda Silver) in her entertaining and scholarly essay on Nicole Kidman's appearance as Woolf in the film version of Michael Cunningham's *The Hours*—with particular focus on 'the media fetishization of Woolf's nose' (p. 144). The collection was topped and tailed with, respectively, Ruth Gruber's (pp. vi–xiii) reminiscences on her meeting with Woolf in 1935 and Cuddy-Keane's (pp. 172–80) suitably expansive meditation on Woolf's 'ragged beginning[s]' (p. 172).

Suzette Henke and David Eberly's edited collection *Virginia Woolf and Trauma: Embodied Texts* demonstrates how much critical mileage remains in the strand of Woolf studies inaugurated by Louise DeSalvo's controversial work on Woolf's history of sexual abuse. However, not every essay in this collection focuses on this particular trauma, and many of the essays which do nevertheless present new and challenging positions that even the most strongly anti-DeSalvo reader should find productive. A shift in focus from content, which preoccupied earlier readings of trauma in Woolf's work, to form, emerges as a key theme. Jane Lilienfield's essay, for example, begins with an exemplarily careful discussion of the controversies surrounding the reading of trauma in Woolf's work, and opens onto a fascinating discussion of the narrative form of *To the Lighthouse* as itself linked to traumatic experience. Viewing this text as a kind of 'life-writing', Lilienfield 'challenges the book's recently established status as an icon of high modernist art' (p. 98). This challenge to 'modernism' is more emphatically articulated in Toni McNaron's essay, which invites readers to approach Woolf's aesthetic innovations not so much as part of a modernist project, but as a complex response to her experiences of incest and the silencing attendant upon it. Patricia Morgne Cramer's essay convincingly argues for the need to distinguish between Woolf's early work, primarily *The Voyage Out*, in which Woolf has not yet come to terms with her traumatic experiences, and later texts such as *The Years* which propose a 'lesbian "voyage out"'... of endless trauma reenactments' (p. 48). Other essays address a wide variety of 'traumas'. Henke's own essay proposes *The Waves* as ontological trauma narrative, in a reading which addresses the ultimate trauma, death, and its figuring in *The Waves*; the novel, she suggests, celebrates 'the unacknowledged heroism of speaking beings who continue to project meaning onto quotidian experience, despite psychological trauma and corporeal pain' (p. 146), drawing out the commingled melancholia and ecstasy of this text. Also on *The Waves*, Clifford Wulfman attempts to draw out the significance of its 'little language' as part of Woolf's attempt not simply to communicate but to transmit in her work, informed by the 'shock' following the transmission model set up in 'A Sketch of the Past'. David Eberly and Claire Kahane each provide a different perspective on *Between the Acts*: Eberly reads the text through Emmanuel Lévinas's concept of the 'face', focusing in particular on questions of audience, while Kahane draws out more emphatically the historical context of the novel to meditate on the trauma of war and the relationship between text and history. Holly Laird's essay contributes to the increasing interest in Leonard Woolf's own writing by analysing the last chapter of his autobiography, 'Virginia's Death', as a narrative riven at a textual level by the trauma of Woolf's suicide.

Also contributing to this strand in Woolf studies is Patricia Moran's book *Virginia Woolf, Jean Rhys and the Aesthetics of Trauma*. However, Moran's first two chapters on Woolf take a very broad view of what might constitute 'trauma', presenting intriguing and novel readings of Woolf's work. She discusses *A Room of One's Own* as a text written not, as it purports to be, for an audience of young women, but for an audience of Woolf's male peers—in particular, Desmond McCarthy, whose quarrel with Woolf in the pages of the *New Statesman*, and specifically its sexological foundation, Moran draws upon to explore how Woolf partly complies with, and partly rebuts, 'the misogynist arguments of sexology' (p. 44) in *A Room of One's Own*. A similar ambiguity, this time around the figure of hymeneal rupture, is explored in her third chapter; here, Moran sees Woolf moving from an early anxiety about women's writing as ruptured hymen to her 'fear that writing for women represents a kind of loss of chastity' (p. 53), in large part through her correspondence with the physically uninhibited, maternal figure of Ethel Smyth. Moran relies here on sustained readings of Woolf's figurative language rather than direct references to the ruptured hymen, and argues that the language Woolf uses about the hymeneal and the membrane interestingly anticipates the language of Luce Irigaray. In her final chapter on Woolf, Moran argues that Woolf's late work does analyse 'the sexual life of women', as Woolf apparently intended it to, but through writing its 'abrogation and subsequent attenuation' (p. 68) in *The Years* and *Between the Acts*. Trauma does feature centrally here, but, perhaps more importantly, Moran argues that 'Woolf's female characters—not just the traumatized Rose or Isa—exhibit classic symptoms of shame when female sexual experience or desire is at issue' (p. 69). Moran's conclusion draws together her work on Rhys and Woolf to explore the trauma of maternal absence and its effect on the aesthetic form of these writers' work.

In Maren Tova Linett's monograph *Modernism, Feminism and Jewishness*, Woolf features as one of Linett's five 'key authors [who] enlist a multifaceted vision of Jewishness to help them shape fictions that are thematically daring and formally experimental' (p. 2). Linett dissents from those critics who play down the anti-Semitic elements in Woolf's work, adducing evidence from *The Years*, *Three Guineas* and *Between the Acts* where Jewishness is evoked. Linett provides no easy answer to the question she herself poses, namely 'what does it mean when anti-Semitism stains the very feminist project we admire?' (p. 59), but she does provide a compelling account of Woolf's use of a range of negative Jewish stereotypes—some explicit, some covert—concluding that Woolf aligns Jewishness with threats to intellectual freedom.

Laura Marcus's chapter on Woolf in her important monograph *The Tenth Muse: Writing about Cinema in the Modernist Period* reveals the depth and complexity of Woolf's engagement with cinema. Beginning by noting the surprising paucity of Bloomsbury writings on film in its early decades, which she read as a 'necessary pause...by no means connot[ing] indifference' (p. 102), Marcus traces an intricate web of links between Woolf's writing on the cinema and that of her contemporaries, as well unpacking the 'cinematographic dimensions' of her novels; this fascinating chapter leaves us with a much fuller sense of Woolf's ambivalent relationship with cinematic aesthetics and its importance to her oeuvre.

Lee Oser's book *The Ethics of Modernism: Moral Ideas in Yeats, Eliot, Joyce, Woolf and Beckett* asserts that it is time to reconsider the role of 'human nature' in the humanities and specifically in literary criticism. In his chapter entitled 'Virginia Woolf: Antigone Triumphant', Oser observes a contradiction in Woolf's work between a post-Christian spiritualizing feminism and a refusal to 'preach doctrines' or a more purely artistic interest, and proposes that Woolf is able to reconcile these through G.E. Moore, whose insistence on the primacy of the thinking individual can be found in, for example, her assertion that 'we are the words; we are the music; we are the thing itself' in 'A Sketch of the Past' (p. 89). His argument about Woolf's aesthetic ethics is nimbly summed up in his reading of *The Waves*, where he asserts, 'The good of art transcends the negations of life simply by being good. Like Bernard, Woolf is saint and martyr for that goodness, which is her art' (p. 101).

Postcolonial approaches are represented in chapters by Jed Esty and Kurt Koenigsberger. Esty's chapter 'Virginia Woolf's Colony and the Adolescence of Modernist Fiction' (in Begam and Valdez Moses, eds., pp. 70–90) is a fast-paced and stimulating new reading of *The Voyage Out*, arguing that, in common with other modernist texts in colonial settings, the novel's rewriting of the *Bildungsroman* coincides with an implicit critique of colonial time, particularly in its deployment of an adolescent and fragmented protagonist whose eternal youth—the fantasy of modernity—resists assimilation into the completed, adult world of nationality and instead snaps into its 'obverse-sudden death' (p. 84). Koenigsberger's chapter on Woolf in his *The Novel and the Menagerie* explores Woolf's critical response to the 'imperial menagerie', the figuring of exotic beasts and monsters, in *The Years* and *The Waves*. His central section is particularly fascinating, reading 'Mr Bennett and Mrs Brown', 'Character in Fiction' and the less well-known 'Thunder over Wembley' through the Empire Exhibition of 1924, and drawing a provocative connection between the discourse of realism and that of the exhibition itself.

Marina MacKay's chapter on Woolf in her *Modernism and World War II* seeks, like a number of other works published this year, to reconsider the extent of Woolf's radical politics by suggesting that *Between the Acts* is more proximate than has previously been recognized to the communalizing and nostalgically pastoral discourse of wartime nationalism. Strong on historical and political context, this chapter suggests that by the time of Woolf's final novel 'the diffuseness and iconoclasm of high modernist mimesis have become sinister, threatening and suicidal' (p. 41).

A number of survey works published this year contain new material on Woolf. As one would expect, Woolf is a touchstone throughout *The Cambridge Companion to the Modernist Novel*, edited by Morag Shiach, but there is also a chapter by Meg Jensen devoted to Woolf. Entitled 'Tradition and Revelation: Moments of Being in Virginia Woolf's Major Novels' (pp. 112–25), this chapter provides snapshots of six novels, using the concept of the 'moment of being' to focus each summary and provide points of comparison between the novels. Though it is perhaps a result of limited space, it is nevertheless unfortunate that *Night and Day* and *The Years* are not mentioned, particularly given the increasing interest in these until recently critically neglected texts; their omission in a survey of Woolf's 'major novels' risks perpetuating this neglect. *The Cambridge Introduction to the Short Story in English* by Adrian Hunter includes a chapter on this still relatively neglected part of Woolf's oeuvre, providing an incisive reading of the short story as central to her 'revolutionizing [of] the theory and practice of "modern fiction"' (p. 63). Gill Plain and Susan Sellers, eds., *A History of Feminist Literary Criticism*, includes a chapter on 'The Feminist Criticism of Virginia Woolf' by Jane Goldman (pp. 66–84). A lively and incisive exposition of the range of Woolf's feminist thought, necessarily focusing on *A Room of One's Own* but also taking in *Three Guineas* and several other essays, this chapter opens by alerting the reader to the multitude of feminist writers contemporaneous with Woolf, cautioning against the image of Woolf as a lone voice implied by her subsequent canonization as 'the founder of modern feminist literary criticism' (p. 66).

The collection *Language and Verbal Art Revisited*, edited by Donna R. Miller, includes a chapter by Carol Taylor Torsello on 'Projection in Literary and Non-Literary Texts' (pp. 115–48). While the title and methodology may daunt the reader not trained in linguistic analysis—and indeed the significance of some of the detail here may elude the non-specialist—nevertheless Taylor Torsello's meticulous analysis of 'projection' (broadly, the reporting of speech or thought) provides concrete and precise examples of how Woolf achieves different effects, and for what purpose, in *A Room of One's Own*, *To the Lighthouse* and *Mrs Dalloway*. A similar approach is taken by Violeta Sotirova, whose chapter 'Woolf's Experiments with Consciousness in Fiction' (in Lambrou and Stockwell, eds., *Contemporary Stylistics*, pp. 7–18) draws on cognitive and cultural theory to articulate the 'mind-reading' implications of Woolf's experiments with narrative fiction, arguing that the interpenetration of consciousnesses articulated in her work may be closer to the way we actually function in relation to each other than might be expected.

The *Woolf Studies Annual* offered its usual showcase of scholarly approaches to Woolf. In '"Each is part of the whole: we act different parts but are the same": From Fragment to Choran Community in the Late Work of Virginia Woolf' (*WStA* 13[2007] 1–24), Emily Hinnov proposes a more optimistic reading of *The Waves*, *Three Guineas* and *Between the Acts* than that found in much critical work. Hinnov draws on Kristeva to elaborate the concept of the 'choran community', an interface between self and other in the context of a wider community which generates a 'potentially transformative aesthetic' in later Woolf (p. 21). Renée Dickinson's 'Exposure and Development: Re-Imagining Narrative and Nation in the Interludes of *The Waves*' (*WStA* 13[2007] 25–48) continues the productive strand of Woolf criticism engaged in postcolonial readings of *The Waves*; her welcome focus here is on the relatively neglected interludes, where, she argues, feminine images represent both the colonized and the colonizing. In 'Geometries of Time and Space: The Cubist London of *Mrs. Dalloway*' (*WStA* 13[2007] 111–36), Jennie-Rebecca Falcetta notes Roger Fry's early connection of Woolf's prose with Cubism; observing that critics have failed to pursue this connection in *Mrs Dalloway*, she produces a reading of that novel as an urban Cubist text. Jane Goldman's '"Ce chien est à moi": Virginia Woolf and the Signifying Dog' (*WStA* 13[2007] 49–86) hunts down Woolf's 'radically unstable canine metaphors' (p. 56), exploring the interrelated identities of dog, slave and woman in the narrator of *A Room of One's Own*, and continuing to a sustained reading of the contentious 'negress' passage in that text. Goldman's lively pursuit of the text's intertexts and their implications not only sheds important light on the proliferating meanings to be found in this particular passage, but reminds the reader how much Woolf's texts invite, and how well they respond to, such dogged readings. In '"Myself—it was impossible": Queering History in *Between the Acts*' (*WStA* 13[2007] 87–110), Erica Delsandro pursues the current critical thinking on 'queer' as 'as much about historical identity as it is about sexual identity' (p. 95) to articulate the temporal and historical disruptions enacted in *Between the Acts*. David Sherman's 'A Plot Unraveling into Ethics: Woolf, Lévinas and "Time Passes"' (*WStA* 13[2007] 159–80) draws on Lévinas's conception of the ethical as relationship with the other to offer a sustained and careful reading of the narrative voice and its temporality in the middle section of *To the Lighthouse* as a 'narrative poetics of alterity' (p. 160). Eve Sorum's 'Taking Note: Text and Context in Virginia Woolf's "Mr. Bennett and Mrs. Brown"' (*WStA* 13[2007] 137–58) provides an extremely valuable recontextualization, and indeed defamiliarization, of that familiar essay, tracing its early publication history to emphasize the different contexts in which it was deployed.

Lévinas and the ethical made another appearance in Rachel Hollander's essay, 'Novel Ethics: Alterity and Form in *Jacob's Room*' (*TCL* 53[2007] 40–66). Hollander engages a Lévinasian ethics of alterity to produce a reading of *Jacob's Room* emphasizing its insistence on the ultimate unknowability of the 'other'. Her essay concludes, most productively, with a discussion of Woolf's ambivalent treatment of Jacob's experience of education, affirming Woolf's interest in modes of pedagogy and coming to rest on a tentative suggestion of what this novel might itself 'teach' us.

Essays focusing on various aspects of national identity include 'Virginia Woolf's "Harum Scarum": Irish Wife: Gender and National Identity in *The Years*' (*CCS* 4:i[2007] 31–50), where Lisa Weihman focuses on Woolf's perhaps surprisingly critical portrayal of Delia Pargiter and her appropriation of the Irish nationalist cause (given Woolf's own support for Irish independence). Comparing Delia with her real female contemporaries in the Irish nationalist movement, Weihman argues that Woolf articulates a critique through Delia of the damaging ideologies of nationalism during the 1930s, in particular female complicity with these ideologies. Helen Southworth's 'Virginia Woolf's "Wild England": George Borrow, Autoethnography, and *Between the Acts*' (*SNNTS* 39:ii[2007] 196–215) is a fascinating reading of Woolf's last novel through the travel writer and 'autoethnographer' Borrow, whose work Woolf knew. Building on recent critical work on the '"anthropological turn" in English modernist writing of the late 1930s and 1940s' (p. 197)—in particular that of Jed Esty—Southworth challenges readings of *Between the Acts* as a novel about house-dwelling, stasis and nostalgia, and instead draws on Borrow's tropes of the nomadic, of vagabondage and of the strangeness, indeterminacy and multiplicity of Englishness, to show how these operate in Woolf's novel. Southworth's subtle analyses provide an exciting new way to think about Woolf's relationship with national identity in this and other late works.

Ray Monk's long and detailed essay, 'This Fictitious Life: Virginia Woolf on Biography and Reality' (*P&L* 31:i[2007] 1–40), asserts that the influence of Virginia Woolf's thinking about biography on 'contemporary theorizing about biography is, on the whole, a misfortune' (p. 1), and further, that 'when they are applied to biography, Virginia Woolf's thoughts about fiction reveal themselves to be fundamentally flawed' (p. 37). Monk is primarily a philosopher, whereas Woolf, ultimately, is not; thus, from a literary-critical perspective, the essay displays a problematic tendency to conflate Woolf herself with her narrative voice, a failure to consider the polemical qualities of a text such as 'Mr Bennett and Mrs Brown' (instead approaching it as a categorical statement of belief) and an insistence on the 'polarities that dominate Virginia Woolf's thinking about fiction' (p. 35), where Woolf critics have, on the contrary, found Woolf resisting binaries throughout her oeuvre.

A special issue of *Critical Survey* [Spring 2007] on history and the modernist woman writer featured three short articles on *Orlando*: on the role of the gypsy as 'floating signifier' in Woolf and in Brontë (Abby Bardi, 'In Company of a Gipsy': The "Gypsy" as Trope in Woolf and Bronte' (*CS* i[2007] 41–50); on buried connections between *Orlando* and Lady Mary Wortley Montagu's *Turkish Embassy Letters* (Alison Winch, '"In plain English, stark naked"': *Orlando*, Lady Mary Wortley Montagu and Reclaiming Sapphic Connections' (*CS* i[2007] 51–61); and on Woolf's implicit engagement with historians of the Renaissance, critiquing her father and John Ruskin, and affirming the approach taken by Walter Pater, John Addington Symonds and Vernon Lee (Jane de Gay, 'Virginia Woolf's Feminist Historiography in *Orlando*' (*CS* i[2007] 62–72).

Also taking a historical perspective, Ruth Livesey's 'Socialism in Bloomsbury: Virginia Woolf and the Political Aesthetics of the 1880s' (*YES* 37:i[2007] 126–44) sheds fascinating light on Woolf's politics and aesthetics in historical context. Woolf's readers are familiar with her apparently emphatic rejection of the generation of writers immediately before her own; Livesey draws our attention to Woolf's perhaps more problematic engagement, direct or otherwise, with an earlier generation of thinkers from the 1880s. Livesey observes continuities and discontinuities between their 'distinctively aesthetic politics of socialism' (p. 127) and Woolf's work, particularly in that politically fraught essay Woolf wrote as a preface to *Life As We Have Known It*. In the same issue, Wendy B. Faris's article 'Bloomsbury's Beasts: The Presence of Animals in the Texts and Lives of Bloomsbury' (*YES* 37:i[2007] 107–25) contributes to the growing body of work on Woolf and animals; here, Faris also includes Leonard Woolf and E.M. Forster in her discussion and suggests that animals in writing by the Bloomsbury set serve three main functions: they 'embody repressed emotions or unresolved social issues... represent revered feelings of connection with the cosmos [and construct a] web of communal feelings and mysterious connections that comprises Virginia Woolf's "luminous envelope" of life itself' (pp. 107–8).

Other essays on disparate topics indicate the range of preoccupations in this year's work. Barbara Caine's 'Stefan Collini, Virginia Woolf, and the Question of Intellectuals in Britain' (*JHI* 68:iii[2007] 369–73) draws on Cuddy-Keane's influential 2003 study *Virginia Woolf, the Intellectual and the Public Sphere* to take issue with Stefan Collini's 'gender blindness' in his *Absent Minds: Intellectuals in Britain*, asserting Woolf's identity as a major intellectual but operating within a very different model of the 'intellectual' from that put forward by Collini. Rishona Zimring's '"The dangerous art where one slip means death": Dance and the Literary Imagination in Interwar Britain' (*Mo/Mo* 14:iv[2007] 707–27) explores the significance of social, as opposed to performed, dancing, both in British culture as recorded by participants in Mass-Observation and as represented in Woolf's novels (or rather, as in cases such as *Mrs Dalloway*, as conspicuously absent). Zimring suggests that social dancing represented the possibility of a collective (national) identity, one which is, however, revealed in Woolf's work as evanescent and transitory. Indeed, dancing represented for Woolf, according to Zimring, a 'danger', complicating the received notion of dance as liberating and redemptive. Merry Pawlowski draws on archival material to further our understanding of the crucial visual aspects of *Three Guineas*, focusing in particular on Woolf's use of the Pauline 'veil', in her 'Virginia Woolf's Veil: The Feminist Intellectual and the Organization of Public Space' (*MFS* 53:iv[2007] 722–51). While much of Sophie Blanch's entertaining essay 'Taking Comedy Seriously: American Literary Humor and the British Woman Writer' (*STAH* 3:xv[2007] 5–15) is taken up with a discussion of the uses of humour by American suffragist writers, the connections made with Woolf's own use of humour (which is often, as the author notes, overlooked) are intriguing.

Christine Reynier begins her 'Virginia Woolf's Ethics of the Short Story' (*EtA* 60[2007] 55–65) with a clear, if possibly surprising, statement of her methodology, explaining that she turns to Woolf's 'essays, rather than her short stories, to see whether she had any theory of the short story' (p. 55). This makes for a very controlled and seductive argument, as Reynier draws the conclusion that a theory of the short story is indeed here discernible, if diffuse, and that it has three key elements: impersonality, proportion and emotion. Of particular interest is Reynier's use of the term 'bewilderment', drawn from Spinoza, to indicate the quality of leaving questions unanswered which Woolf admires in a short story. Thus, Reynier argues, we may make links from Woolf to later twentieth-century theoreticians of fiction such as Barthes. As Reynier invitingly concludes, 'What would remain to be seen is whether and how Woolf's short stories match up her theory' (p. 64).

The theme of unanswered questions is also central to Christopher J. Knight's sensitive essay '"The God of Love is full of tricks": Virginia Woolf's Vexed Relation to the Tradition of Christianity' (*R&L* 39:i[2007] 27–46). Knight moves on from Woolf's avowed anti-religious bias to attend to the language of religious and non- or anti-religious characters in Woolf's work, and argues that Woolf's fiction is characterized by 'a tone of inquiry, or questioning' (p. 31), of searching, which itself might be understood as having a religious dimension. Like Knight, Lambrotheodoros Koulouris begins with but moves on from biographical observations, here addressing the role of 'love' in Woolf's early life and work. '"Love unconquered in battle" and Other Lies: Virginia Woolf and (Greek) "Love"' (*IntLS* 8:ii[2007] 37–53) distinguishes from 'Hellenism' a specific kind of 'Greekness' found in Woolf's early work, a stance linked with the poetics of loss, informed by her early traumatic losses, which is in turn a key feature of Woolf's depictions of love—frequently associated with 'awkwardness, regret and consternation' (p. 39).

In 'Mr. Ramsay, Robert Falcon Scott, and Heroic Death' (*Mosaic* 40:iv[2007] 135–50), Allyson Booth makes a plea for attention to Mr Ramsay 'in his own right' (p. 136). Booth traces Mr Ramsay's personal trajectory in the novel through intertexts implicitly or explicitly evoked, from the 'heroic deaths' of Scott of the Antarctic and the Light Brigade to Sir Walter Scott's depiction of a non-heroic death, concluding with Cowper's shift of focus from heroism to the lonely individual. Booth argues that Mr Ramsay re-emerges at the end of the novel as, indeed, an explorer hero, but one whose move away from the militaristic models of heroic death evokes the sympathy from his children that has been otherwise unavailable to him, embodying a heroism 'that is not about dying well but about living well' (p. 148).

Among the varied reminiscences, essays and previously unpublished documents relating to Woolf in the three issues of the *Virginia Woolf Bulletin*, particularly noteworthy are Sayaka Okumura's (pp. 27–35) essay, 'Communication Networks: The Telephone, Books, and Portraits in *Night and Day*' (*VWB* 26[Sept. 2007]) and, in that same issue, Julia Paolitto's (pp. 9–18) 'Virginia Woolf, Desmond McCarthy and Literary Character: A Newly Discovered Woolf Letter' (*VWB* 26[Sept. 2007]), in which Paolitto comments on the light that this previously undiscovered letter (published here) sheds on Woolf's well-known debate with McCarthy, as 'Affable Hawk', in the pages of the *New Statesman*.

Two texts containing material already in circulation are nevertheless worth mentioning this year. Continuum has republished Winifred Holtby's 1936 monograph *Virginia Woolf: A Critical Memoir* with a brief but helpful new preface by Marion Shaw; the wider availability of this first major study of Woolf, whatever its shortcomings from a twenty-first-century perspective, will be welcomed by Woolf scholars interested in contemporary responses to her work. Finally, a new collection of work by Woolf also appeared this year, edited by S.P. Rosenbaum under the title *The Platform of Time: Memoirs of Family and Friends*. This collection of Woolf's biographical and autobiographical writing, consisting of memoirs, letters, obituaries, 'memoir fantasies' and other fragments (mainly by Woolf, but including some short pieces by members of her family), brings together material either scattered through other collections or, in some cases, not republished since their first appearance (the anonymous obituary letter written for Janet Case). It makes a most welcome complement to the longer pieces collected in *Moments of Being*.

3. Post-1945 Fiction

The year 2007 has been another productive one in the area of post-1945 fiction, with several monographs, introductory books, edited collections and essays in the field.

There have been two monographs this year focused on writing from the 1950s: one is Susan Brook's *Literature and Cultural Criticism in the 1950s: The*

Feeling Male Body, and the other is Nick Bentley's *Radical Fictions: The English Novel in the 1950s*. Brook's *Literature and Cultural Criticism in the 1950s* is a fascinating contribution to the field and is concerned to investigate the way in which masculinity is reconfigured in a series of works from the period including fiction, drama and texts associated with the British New Left. Her main argument relates to the way in which the 'feeling male body', as she calls it, is addressed in a number of texts and operates as an indicator of social and cultural concerns and anxieties informing the decade. In a very useful introduction she explains her focus on a shift in British fiction from sentiment to vitality in discussions of the male body, citing precursors of this trend in D.H. Lawrence and George Orwell, among others. She sees the Angry Young Men and writers associated with the New Left, such as Richard Hoggart and Raymond Williams, developing this trope in the 1950s. As Brook argues, this is related to issues around class and gender: 'the postwar feeling male body responds to waves of social change rippling through British society' (p. 5). She also stresses that the book's argument is literary-historical rather than theoretical and this forms the basis of the erudite and detailed close reading she undertakes of specific texts. One of the strengths of the book is the way it identifies tropes working across fiction and cultural theory, which adds weight to the socio-literary-historical argument. Chapter 1 concentrates on the writing that came out of the early New Left, looking at articles from *Universities and Left Review* (a key journal of the period), Hoggart's *The Uses of Literacy* and Williams's 1960 novel *Border Country*. Chapters 2 and 3 look at key texts by the Angry Young Men. Chapter 2 argues that both Kingsley Amis's *Lucky Jim* and John Osborne's *Look Back in Anger* emphasize an affective and emotional form of masculinity that in part offers a coherence for the male antagonists that is lacking in their contradictory response to the politics of class. Chapter 3 discusses Alan Sillitoe's *Saturday Night and Sunday Morning* and John Braine's *Room at the Top*. The analysis of Sillitoe's text is particularly interesting in that Brook argues that the concentration on the vitality and suffering of the male body in the novel reveals a masochism that is the result of the main character Arthur Seaton's negotiation of newer and older forms of masculinity. At the same time, this is read as a symptom of the need for a working-class male to reassert a sense of power in response to his subordinate position in class terms. This, in part, explains not only his masochistic tendencies but also his misogynist treatment of women. Chapter 4 extends the discussion to look at texts from the period by women writers: Lynne Reid Banks's *The L-Shaped Room* and Doris Lessing's *The Golden Notebook*. Her reading of *The Golden Notebook* makes a convincing case that the novel, in its experimentation with narrative form and structure, not only challenges conventional realism but does so in terms of the masculine ideologies that lay behind much of the Angry writing of the period. This flags up the uneasy relationship Lessing had with the New Left during the late 1950s and early 1960s. The last chapter moves out of the main period of the book to look at texts from the 1970s, 1980s and 1990s. Brook also moves from cultural criticism to fiction to film in a detailed analysis of texts by the cultural critics Dick Hebdige and Paul Willis, Martin Amis's *Money*, Irvine Welsh's *Trainspotting* (novel and film) and the popular 1990s British film *The Full*

Monty. In this chapter, she argues that the representation of the feeling male body persists from the 1950s into much more recent texts. There is also a short conclusion that addresses issues of narrative form in relation to the idea of the feeling male body, in particularly in terms of realism and postmodernism.

Bentley's *Radical Fictions* is also concerned with this period in British literature and shows the increased interest literary criticism is showing in that fascinating decade. (The present reviewer is the author of this book so what follows is informative rather than critical.) Like Brook, Bentley looks at both fiction and cultural criticism from the period. *Radical Fictions* challenges the prevailing reading of the 1950s English novel, which emphasizes an anti-experimentalism among the main writers of the period and a return to realist forms of narrative popular in the 1930s and before the modernism of the early twentieth century. By looking at canonical writers of the period as well as less well-known authors, Bentley argues that this prevailing reading of a return to realism in British fiction is limiting and not indicative of the wide range of styles and experiment carried out during the period. The introduction sets out the methodological approach the book takes, which is a combination of New Historicism with an analysis that borrows from narratology and post-structuralism. After this, the book is divided into two parts, the first of which contains three chapters on the cultural, social and political factors informing 1950s writing; the second has five chapters on selected fiction from the period. Chapter 1 identifies three important cultural and political factors informing the 1950s novel: discussion among literary commentators about the imminent demise of the novel; the shifting perceptions of Englishness caused by the loss of international power and the break-up of empire; and the crisis in left-wing and Marxist politics precipitated by Nikita Khrushchev's revelation of Stalin's purges and the Hungarian revolution. Chapter 2 focuses on the way in which literary forms and techniques of the period operated with respect to assumptions about the relationship between form and ideology and explains these in relation to important formal tropes during the period such as realism, experimentalism and the 'committed' novel. Chapter 3 discusses early New Left writing and in particular works by Williams, Hoggart and Stuart Hall. It investigates the preoccupation with cultural expressions of class in the New Left and how this tended to blind the discourse to other areas of cultural politics such as race, gender, sexuality and youth. Part II includes chapters on Kingsley Amis's *Lucky Jim* and John Wain's *Hurry on Down*; Muriel Spark's 1950s novels *The Comforters*, *Robinson* and *The Ballad of Peckham Rye*; Sillitoe's *Saturday Night and Sunday Morning* and *The Loneliness of the Long Distance Runner*; Colin MacInnes's exploration of youth and ethnicity in *City of Spades* and *Absolute Beginners*; and Sam Selvon's *The Lonely Londoners*. A short conclusion brings together these texts and discusses the preoccupation with identity politics they share as revealing of specific social and cultural anxieties in the 1950s.

Nicky Marsh's *Money, Speculation and Finance in Contemporary British Fiction* also has significant sections on 1950s writing but is much broader in scope, looking at fiction from each decade from 1950 to 2000. It offers close analyses of several contemporary novels, identifying their engagement with metaphors relating to money and economics. Marsh's main argument is that changes in the way money has been represented socially and politically have been dramatized in fiction of the period. As she argues in the introduction, 'fiction is an important site for disrupting the ideological naturalization of conventional economics that has successfully diminished the political analysis of the money economy in much cultural discourse' (p. 8). After a shortish introduction, the book has five chapters organized chronologically covering the period from 1945 onwards. The first chapter concentrates on money as a driving force in the postwar thriller and includes an excellent reading of Ian Fleming's *Goldfinger*, identifying Bond's conservative response to the cultural and social shifts of 1950s Britain. The next two chapters concentrate on fictional representations of 1980s economics. There's an excellent discussion of Thatcher's money rhetoric in the introduction to chapter 3, which sets up the discussion of a number of 1980s (and 1980s-set) novels in these two chapters, including insightful analysis of Martin Amis's *Money* and *London Fields*, Margaret Drabble's *The Radiant Way*, Fay Weldon's *Darcy's Utopia* and Jonathan Coe's *What a Carve Up!* Coe's novel, in particular, receives a perceptive analysis. Chapter 4 identifies the rogue trader in popular culture and fiction as a subversive figure that threatens to exploit the instability inherent in late capitalism and who acts in fictional representations as a potential catalyst to the breakdown of the financial system. Marsh extends her analysis in this chapter to cover some American novelists, including Paul Kiduff and Christopher Reich as well as the British writer Michael Ridpath, and explores the Anglo-American terrain of this trend in popular fiction. This chapter also includes an excellent discussion of Don DeLillo's *Cosmopolis*. The final chapter, 'Women, Work and Risk', focuses on the post-feminist 'sex and shopping' novels of Helen Fielding and Helen Dunne, and Lesley Campbell's financial thriller *Forged Metal*. Overall, Marsh offers an erudite and cogent analysis of the metaphorical and symbolic use of money in the contemporary novel.

Sarah Falcus's *Michèle Roberts: Myths, Mothers and Memories* is the first full-length monograph on a writer who has been on the margins of contemporary British fiction for a number of years but is now rightly gaining the critical recognition she deserves. Falcus writes cogently on several topics in Roberts's fiction, including her relationship to Second Wave feminism, her critical engagement with discourses of God, religion and particularly Catholicism, the importance of re-engaging with narratives of the past, and her experiments with fictional forms and techniques. Falcus concentrates on the novels and takes a broadly chronological approach, organized in six chapters. The first is an introduction, in which she identifies the main themes in Roberts's fiction and emphasizes her critical approach as 'an active engagement with theory' (p. 14). Falcus draws heavily on theories from Second Wave and French feminism, which produces insightful readings of Roberts's fiction against the work of Julia Kristeva and Luce Irigaray in particular. The second chapter develops this approach in relation to Roberts's first two novels and explores the way in which the novelist develops a critique of patriarchal structures by focusing on female relationships. Falcus shows how these 'female genealogies' are often problematic in the novels, but that they are exemplified in *A Piece of the Night* by the search for 'a language and basis for communication' between women (p. 49). This reading draws intelligently on critical theories around Kristeva and the concern in French feminism to explore the idea of a pre-Oedipal phase as it relates to mother–daughter relationships. The third and fourth chapters move from a chronological to a thematic analysis of Roberts's fiction during the period 1984–97. The first of these identifies Roberts's concerns with addressing theological and spiritual issues in four novels, *The Wild Girl* [1984], *The Book of Mrs Noah* [1987], *Daughters of the House* [1992] and *Impossible Saints* [1997]. Falcus shows how the investigation into the discourses of religion is always bound up for Roberts with feminist issues, teasing out the patriarchal structures at play in religious texts and scripture, and how these are played out in personal narratives. The fourth chapter concentrates on the experimental techniques Roberts deploys in *In the Red Kitchen* [1990] and *Flesh and Blood* [1994]. Falcus argues convincingly that the interweaving narratives in both these novels draws on her engagement with Kristeva's notion of cyclical time as a potentially subversive (feminist) space for fiction. The fifth chapter continues to explore Roberts's interest in feminist narratives in three novels from the last ten years, *Fair Exchange* [1999], *The Looking Glass* [2000] and *The Mistressclass* [2003]. A short sixth chapter brings the analysis of Roberts's fiction up to date with a discussion of her recent move to what can be described as a 'chick-lit' novel, *Reader, I Married Him*, but, as Falcus's knowledge of critical theory makes clear, is a complex and self-aware exploration of this genre. Overall, Falcus's book is an excellent close analysis of Roberts's fiction, grounded in intelligent and thought-provoking knowledge of relevant critical theory.

Another postwar writer who has received relatively little critical attention is Barbara Pym, but Orna Raz's *Social Dimensions in the Novels of Barbara Pym, 1949–1963* addresses this gap. Raz reads Pym as a realist writer, but one for whom realism is, as Raz puts it, 'never banal or "naïvely mimetic"' (p. 4). By making an analogy with Jan van Eyck's painting *The Arnolfini Marriage*, Raz argues that what lies behind the apparent transparency of Pym's writing is a glimpse of the author and the social contexts informing the way in which the characters interact. As Raz notes, 'Her seemingly random details create a subtext that ranges from classic literary allusions through Anglo-Catholic practices to cultural debates of the 1950s' (p. 3). This provides the basis for Raz's close analysis of Pym's novels. This analysis draws on a New Historicist approach signalled through reference to Clifford Geertz's concept of 'thick description' that emerges in her analysis. The book is divided into nine chapters, each of which takes an aspect of Pym's work as the focus. These include topics on Pym's representation of the postwar church (and Anglo-Catholicism and women in the church), women's roles in higher education and in domestic environments, the treatment of male sexuality and the friendships between women. There is a final interesting chapter on Pym's social commentary that identifies her as a conservative writer, but one who is sensitive to the benefits of certain aspects of the changing social and cultural climate of the 1950s, especially in relation to aspects of the welfare state.

Peter J. Kalliney's excellent *Cities of Affluence and Anger: A Literary Geography of Modern Englishness* is a well written and timely reassessment of the treatment of class in twentieth-century English fiction. Kalliney recognizes that class analysis has been a neglected area over the past thirty years or so in literary criticism, as it has been overshadowed by other aspects of cultural politics such as race, gender and sexuality. Kalliney draws on previous studies of class in literature but states his own position as an interest in the way twentieth-century English fiction 'consistently mobilizes class politics as a way of theorizing social difference and imagining political agency in a rapidly changing cultural context', and a 'tension between class as a material condition and class as an ideological disposition becomes manifest through symbolic apparatus, such as literary texts' (p. 4). He also makes the case for the specificity of the English class system and the impact it has, represented in literature, on both the imperial project of the early twentieth century and the subsequent reassessment of discourses of Englishness in later texts. In six chapters, Kalliney embarks on a fascinating close analysis of a number of twentieth-century writers, including E.M. Forster, Evelyn Waugh and Virginia Woolf, from the pre-war period. There are excellent discussions of the representation of the city and park spaces in Sam Selvon's *The Lonely Londoners* and the relationship between domesticity and class in Sillitoe's *Saturday Night and Sunday Morning*. There is also discussion of two postcolonial engagements with Englishness in the analyses of Lessing's *In Pursuit of the English* and *The Golden Notebook*, and Salman Rushdie's *The Satanic Verses*. Overall, *Cities of Affluence and Anger* advances the discussion of the importance of class in twentieth-century English fiction in interesting and critically engaged ways.

Richard Bradford's *The Novel Now: Contemporary British Fiction* is a lively survey of the British novel over the past forty years. Bradford's distinctive critical voice is sensitive to vicissitudes in the field over the period and is not afraid to identify the pretentiousness of certain writers, while making a clear case for those he admires. He is critical, for example, of 'the seminar-by-fiction' novels of writers such as Jeanette Winterson, Emma Tennant and Helen Fielding (p. 133), and he questions the motivations behind Ian McEwan's deployment of Freudian ideas in *The Cement Garden* in the following terms: 'In all probability the rather cumbersome exercise in Freudian coat-trailing was a reflection of McEwan's university experience' (p. 20). What drives Bradford's critical approach appears to be a suspicion regarding the way academic analysis of fiction has had, in his opinion, a negative effect on our engagement with the novel. As he makes clear in his conclusion: '[literary theory's] preoccupations have effectively alienated it from its alleged subject, literature and the body of individual readers who are that subject's lifeblood, intelligent ordinary readers' (p. 246). I'm not sure whether 'intelligent ordinary readers' can be homogenized in this way, but Bradford's provocative approach to the discipline can be refreshing. The book is divided into four parts in a commendable attempt to cover the vast terrain that is contemporary British fiction. Part I takes a formalist approach as the basis for an analysis of a range of fiction, the first section of which establishes Bradford's interest in discussing examples of contemporary fiction against the realism/modernism debate that it inherited from the 1950s, 1960s and 1970s. Bradford challenges the apparent simplicity of this critical dichotomy when applied to individual novels, shown in the analysis of the work of Martin Amis and Ian McEwan that follows this first section. Part II concentrates on two aspects of contemporary genre fiction: the 'new' historical novel, and crime and spy fiction, looking at works by writers such as Peter Ackroyd, Pat Barker, Sebastian Faulks and Jane Rogers in the former category, and by Bill James, Jake Arnott and P.D. James in the latter. Part III includes the intriguing headings 'Women', 'Men' and 'Gay Fiction' under the title 'Sex', and looks at the way in which gender and sexual politics have impacted on the contemporary literary scene. The longest, final, part of the book attempts to tackle the areas of 'Nation, Race and Place', and focuses on the national identities of Scotland, England, Wales and Northern Ireland, and the impact of writers from diverse ethnic backgrounds on British fiction. Bradford's book is ambitious in its coverage, and perhaps each of the many novels he covers only receives limited discussion, nevertheless, his lively prose style and his impressive overview of the fiction of the period make this an essential book for the 'interested ordinary reader' as well as anyone involved in the academic study of contemporary fiction.

There has been continued research into the place of contemporary popular literature this year, shown especially in Katarzyna Smyczyńska's *The World According to Bridget Jones*, which, as the title suggests, looks at chick-lit novels of the last twenty years. Smyczyńska is interested in the way that chick-lit constructs narratives of identity, mainly female but also male. The opening chapter draws on a variety of theoretical ideas related to the relationship between identity and narrative, including those of Roland Barthes, Stuart Hall, Stanley Fish, Jonathan Culler and Fredric Jameson. This confident introduction sets out a series of approaches to the way in which popular fiction engages with contemporary models of female identity. This is followed by five chapters, each of which investigates a sub-genre within chick lit. A chapter on the development of Harlequin and Mills & Boon romances investigates the contemporary status of such popular fiction in relation to postmodernism's blurring of 'high' and 'low' culture. Smyczyńska argues that *Bridget Jones* and other novels that came out in the late 1990s 'openly contest many traditional female behaviours promoted by category romances' (p. 58). This argument is developed in subsequent chapters to explore the way in which chick lit negotiates the potential for producing a radical discourse of contemporary identity and the 'normalisation of a so far marginalized voice through its assimilation into mainstream culture' (p. 59). Smyczyńska explores the Red Dress Ink series in the third chapter, suggesting that it pushed the boundaries of identity and behaviour in romance fiction. The fourth chapter looks at family relationships and the male Other in selected chick-lit novels. The last two chapters explore contemporary popular fiction with respect to postmodern models of identity. Overall, Smyczyńska produces a detailed and engaging exploration of the formal and cultural significance of chick lit.

The year 2007 has seen the first contributions to what promises to be an excellent series entitled New British Fiction, aimed primarily at the 'student reader'. The series is published by Palgrave, and edited by Philip Tew and Rod Mengham. Two books have come out in this series this year, Bradley Buchanan's *Hanif Kureishi* and Robert Morace's *Irvine Welsh*. Buchanan's book is grounded on a reading of Kureishi's fiction that stresses its theatricality and responds to some of the criticism the writer has received by emphasizing that his work moves away from 'transparent literary realism' (p. x). The book is divided into three parts that look in turn at biographical readings of Kureishi in his historical and cultural context, the major works of fiction, and criticism and contexts. In an erudite introduction that places Kureishi in historical and cultural context, Buchanan argues that the under-standing of the novelist as a postcolonial writer misrepresents his importance as a commentator on a range of contemporary British issues: 'the blurring of class boundaries, the rise of feminism, the emergence of gay and lesbian movements, and the institutionalisation and commercialisation of youth culture and popular music' (p. 14). Buchanan thus argues convincingly that Kureishi is central to contemporary British fiction, rather than a marginalized writer working on the peripheries, despite (and maybe because of) the fact that postmodern and marginalized models of identity form the bases of much of his narrative. The introduction goes on to provide a reading of Kureishi's fiction based on his biography, referring often to his 2004 memoir *My Ear at his Heart: Reading my Father*. This approach is useful in detailing Kureishi's background, family and personal relationships; however, the dangers of speculation that often attend author-centred reading are apparent. Thus, Kureishi's return to Oedipal themes in his fiction is problematically attributed to family and personal relationships, rather than signalling an intellectual and aesthetic interest in Freudian theory. Nevertheless, such an author-centred response is legitimate for an author who often relates his fiction to his own life. The second section includes three chapters on the major works. Chapter 3 discusses *The Buddha of Suburbia* and *The Black Album*. Chapter 4 looks at *Love in a Blue Time*, *Intimacy* and *Midnight All Day*. Chapter 5 tackles *Gabriel's Gift* and *The Body*. The analysis of the novels takes a broadly chronological approach, suggesting that the first two are similar in that they take young Asian British male characters on a series of picaresque adventures—a device that allows Kureishi to explore the political and social contexts informing 1970s and 1980s Britain. The middle three novels are read as an indication of Kureishi's outlook becoming 'more tragic and conflicted' (p. 91). The last two novels see Kureishi trying to regain a sense of optimism, but moving away from the concerns with social and political themes that marked out the earlier novels. The third section is designed for the student market and includes an interesting interview with Kureishi, an overview of his other writings, and a summary of some of the critical responses to his work.

Morace's *Irvine Welsh* is organized in the same way as Buchanan's book (and indicates the template for the New British Fiction series generally). The first section of Morace's book includes a timeline and an introduction that locates Welsh within his historical and cultural context, emphasizing the 'Welsh phenomenon' and how he influenced other writers during the period. Morace draws on a cultural materialist approach to Welsh's fiction, reading it against significant political and cultural contexts from the late 1970s through to the 1990s, including Thatcherism, youth (sub)cultures and cultural and political devolution in Scotland. Morace chooses not to emphasize the working-class contexts of Welsh's writing, although it is never far away from the analysis of individual texts. Morace also discusses the way in which Welsh negotiates trends in contemporary Scottish fiction. The 'Major Works' section of the book is divided into five chapters and offers accessible readings of the Welsh's novels. Chapters 2 and 3 concentrate on the novel *Trainspotting* and its 1996 film adaptation, respectively, emphasizing the impact both had on different areas of British cultural life. Chapter 4 analyses Welsh's subcultural novels *The Acid House*, *Ecstasy* and *Filth*, tracing in them a carnivalesque trip through club, rave and drug cultures. Morace is also keen to show the way in which what were perceived as the literary shortcomings of some of Welsh's works (such as *Ecstasy*) combined with his best-seller status to construct Welsh as a celebrity phenomenon that often detracted from a serious critical engagement with his fiction. Morace therefore tries to reclaim Welsh's writing from some of the harsh criticism it has received. The next chapter looks at the myth of the 'hard man' in *Marabou Stork Nightmares*. Chapter 6 discusses *Glue* and *Porno*, arguing that the former is Welsh's most mature and expansive work. The third section looks at some of Welsh's other writings and includes a summary of the critical reception of his works.

Another book of note out this year aimed primarily at the undergraduate student market is Helen Stoddart's *Angela Carter's Nights at the Circus*. This is part of a Routledge series of study guides on important literary works. Stoddart provides a well-written and comprehensive introduction to one of Carter's most important novels. The book includes an analysis of the important literary, cultural and political contexts informing Carter's novel, including discussion of Thatcherism in the 1980s and the influence of the cultural revolution of the 1960s on Carter's thinking and fiction. It also offers an extremely useful section that identifies a series of important theoretical contexts, including work by Benjamin, Foucault, Mulvey and Bakhtin, and issues related to postmodernism, magic realism and the performative in Carter's novel. This section provides an essential guide to a critical engagement with *Nights at the Circus*. Part II extends this critical focus by drawing on other relevant readings of the novel including the Frankfurt School, performativity, the grotesque, magic realism and the Gothic. The final part includes academic essays by Heather Johnson, Sarah Sceats, Jeanette Baxter and Stoddart herself.

There has been increased interest in Iris Murdoch this year, including a book of essays edited by Anne Rowe, and the publication of a second edition of Hilda D. Spear's excellent 1995 book on Murdoch. Rowe's collection aims to take a broad view of Murdoch's writing and to make interdisciplinary connections. The book has an intriguing preface by Peter J. Conradi that compares George Orwell's reading of Dickens with Murdoch's fiction, suggesting that both have limitations in terms of engagement with the political, a narrow social range and the use of stock characters, but that both are great because they produce memorable descriptions of people and places, and that both were 'utterly unlike their contemporaries' (p. xv). This sets the tone for the book as a whole as it attempts to reassess Murdoch's writing in fiction, philosophy and theology. The book is divided into six parts, some of which will be of more interest to literature scholars than others, although each offers insight into Murdoch's interdisciplinary corpus. Part I has essays on theology, while part II focuses on moral philosophy. Part III contains two essays on Murdoch's theological and philosophical work *The Saint and the Artist*, one of which, by Brian Nicol, compares it to her 1958 novel *The Bell*. Parts IV and V will be of most interest to literary scholars and students. Part IV, entitled 'Rereading Literature', includes four essays. The first is by Nick Turner and surveys the vicissitudes in the academic and popular response to Murdoch's fiction from the 1950s to the present, suggesting that the lack of recent interest in her work may be due to the fact that her writing appears to be too immersed in the historical context of its time to maintain a place in the canon of postwar British fiction. However, the essay ends on the positive, if somewhat self-reflexive, note that the edited collection under discussion suggests a continued interest in her work. Priscilla Martin discusses the influence of Henry James on Murdoch and argues convincingly that this influence is most pronounced in Murdoch's 1962 novel *An Unofficial Rose*, with its themes of 'the relationships between love, art, freedom and money, and between frustration and vicarious living' (p. 125). Alex Ramon investigates the idea of literary influence with another North American author, Carol Shields. Ramon identifies several themes they share, including 'the (often self-reflexive) portrayal of writer characters in their novels [and] their shared concern with the purging of authorial personality [and] a tension between pattern and randomness...[and] their close attention to details of the quotidian' (p. 137). Ramon produces a convincing argument that Murdoch has acted as a literary 'foremother' for Shields. Rowe completes the chapters on intertextual influence by comparing Murdoch's *The Black Prince* with McEwan's *Atonement*, identifying a similarity in the engagement with 'contemporary debates about authorship and the value of literature' (p. 148). Rowe argues convincingly that '*The Black Prince* and *Atonement* dramatize the epistemological problems encountered by writers who share a commitment to the moral function of literature yet write under the umbrella of postmodernism' (p. 150). Part V of the book contains essays on gender, sexuality and feminist issues in Murdoch's writing. Tammy Grimshaw discusses the importance of Platonism in Murdoch's representation of sexuality and explores this in her 1985 novel *The Good Apprentice*. Marije Altorf reads Murdoch with respect to feminist philosophy and attempts to gauge the influence feminism had on her fiction and philosophical writings. The final part focuses on the problems related to writing biographically on Murdoch. The volume as a whole is a valuable interdisciplinary reassessment of Murdoch's corpus, enhanced by Rowe's thorough and sensitive editing, noticeable in the links made between chapters.

Another second edition to note that has come out this year is Philip Tew's *The Contemporary British Novel*, the first edition of which came out in 2004. The new edition includes a revised introduction and a chapter on post-millennial fiction, in which Tew explores the idea of the 'traumatological', identified particularly in a series of post-9/11 novels, including David Peace's *GB84*, Alex Garland's *The Coma*, McEwan's *Saturday*, J.G. Ballard's *Kingdom Come* and Will Self's *The Book of Dave*. This chapter provides a valuable extension to an already engrossing account of the contemporary British fiction scene.

Some notable articles have come out this year, although lack of space dictates that these be listed rather than closely reviewed. Bentley's

'Re-writing Englishness: Imagining the Nation in Julian Barnes's *England, England* and Zadie Smith's *White Teeth*' (*TPr* 21:iii[2007] 483–504) offers a comparative analysis of the representation of national identity in these two novels, drawing on the theories of Lacan and Ricoeur. Niall O'Gallager's 'Alasdair Gray's *Lanark*: Magic Realism and the Postcolonial Novel' (*TPr* 21:iii[2007] 533–50) reclaims the radicalism of Gray's novel from its 'incorporation into existing critical narratives' by the prevailing literary criticism on the work to date. Daniel Lea and Aliki Varvogli have both written on British and American responses to 9/11 in fiction, Lea 'Aesthetics and Anaesthetics: Anglo-American Writers' Responses to 9/11' (*Symbiosis* 11:ii[2007] 3–26) and Varvogli 'Thinking Small across the Atlantic: Ian McEwan's *Saturday* and Jay McInerney's *The Good Life*' (*Symbiosis* 11:ii[2007] 47–59). Another journal article of note this year is Heta Pyrhönen's 'Imagining the Impossible: The Erotic Poetics of Angela Carter's "Bluebeard" Stories' (*TPr* 21:i[2007] 483–504).

The following books were published in 2007, but will be reviewed in next year's list: Sonya Andermahr (ed.) *Jeanette Winterson: A Contemporary Critical Guide* (Continuum); Brian Baker, *Iain Sinclair* (ManUP); Dominic Head, *Ian McEwan* (ManUP); and Simon Kövesi, *James Kelman* (Man UP).

4. Pre-1950 Drama

There has been a crop of theatrical biographies relevant to this period recently, including Elizabeth Schafer's *Lilian Baylis*, Laura Thompson's *Agatha Christie* and Terry Coleman's *Olivier*, as well as two studies of J.B. Priestley and a collection of Noël Coward's letters. Other critics have been concerned with reassessing British theatre in the first part of the twentieth century, showing it as being more varied, complex and experimental than was once thought, and there is also a growing interest in regional theatre.

Lilian Baylis managed the Old Vic theatre and Sadler's Wells, as well as being instrumental in the founding of the British National Theatre, the Royal Ballet and the English National Opera. Given her importance, it is surprising how little has been published on her, and so Schafer's book is to be commended. Shortlisted for the Theatre Book Prize in 2006, this is a well-researched piece of work which makes good use of Baylis's own autobiographical writings and other original material. Here, much is made of the way in which Baylis's early life was influenced by the suffrage movement, which helps to place her in the context of women like Cicely Hamilton and her aunt, Emma Cons, who represented radically different ways of living to a woman born during the Victorian era. Baylis took over the management of the Old Vic after the death of Cons in 1912 and continued there until 1937. During this time she developed opera alongside straight drama. While her heart lay with the former, she realized the importance of commerciality, and so ended up inadvertently championing the centrality of Shakespeare in the British theatre through production of nine-month seasons of his plays, as well as a complete cycle from 1914 to 1923. Baylis managed to solve the competing forces of both genres by opening a new theatre at Sadler's Wells in 1931. Much is made of

Baylis's formidable energy and vision, particularly during the 1920s, which was a time of national and international recognition for her work. Also, it is from the midpoint of the decade that Baylis starts to think of there being a 'natural growth of a National Theatre from the Old Vic' (p. 167), though with estimable foresight she questions the problems of 'a state-endowed playhouse', believing that it would end up being 'mainly supported by the intelligentsia' (p. 168). Like Joan Littlewood, herself stirred by Shakespearian productions at the Old Vic, Baylis believed in the non-elitism of art, whether that was opera, ballet or theatre. Schafer moves forward our understanding of Baylis's place in history, taking her from a rather comic and tangential figure to one who revolutionized many aspects of the British theatre.

Agatha Christie is so well known for her numerous detective novels and spin-off television productions with Hercule Poirot and Miss Marple that it is easy to forget that she was also a dramatist, writing the world's longest-running play, *The Mousetrap* [1952]. Laura Thompson's biography follows a conventional, chronological approach, and is none the worse for it. All aspects of Christie's life are covered, including, of course, her mysterious disappearance in 1926. Discussion of her theatrical work is embedded in this, starting with the way in which Christie was so irritated by an adaptation of *The Murder of Roger Ackroyd* [1926] as *Alibi* two years later that she wrote her first play, *Black Coffee* [1930]. Although this was a success, there were a number of false starts until *Ten Little Niggers* (renamed *And Then There Were None*) in 1943. This was followed by Christie's own adaptation of *Appointment with Death*, reopening the Piccadilly theatre after wartime bombing in 1945. As one would expect, each of her plays is mentioned, including adaptations of books (for example, *Murder on the Nile* [1946]; *The Hollow* [1951]), and original scripts (for example, *The Mousetrap* [1952]; *Witness for the Prosecution* [1953]; *Spider's Web* [1954]; *Verdict* [1958]). Because the focus of the book is on understanding Christie through relating her life, disappointingly little is made of her contribution to the theatre, or even of analysing the plays themselves. In fact, Thompson announces that 'Despite the extreme popularity of what she wrote... Agatha's plays were lightweight things on the whole', with only *Akhnaton* (written in 1937, but never produced at the time), about ancient Egyptian power politics, and *Verdict*, a psychological study of a crime of passion, having 'any real depth' (p. 360). The reader does get the impression, though, that Christie enjoyed writing for the theatre, finding that it varied her literary output, and was more than happy to go along to rehearsals. By 1960, however, audiences' expectations had changed, with *Go Back for Murder* shocking Christie with its bad reviews. Thompson is right in agreeing with Christie's belief that critics resented the phenomenal success of *The Mousetrap*, but there are two points that need further thought. First, although Thompson states that the reputation of Christie's books is quite different from that of the plays, no reason is given for *The Mousetrap*'s continued popularity, nor of the play's frequent revival by repertory and amateur companies. Even Thompson's belief that the plays 'do not endure in any meaningful sense' (p. 459) could have gained from awareness of a growing critical appreciation of how Christie's work responds to social and political changes in the 1940s and 1950s.

Coleman opens his life of Olivier with the claim that he 'was the greatest English actor and man of the theatre of the twentieth century' (p. 1). It is interesting, therefore, that the author's focus lies with the actor's life, rather than any careful analysis of his particular acting style. Nevertheless, there is much here on Olivier's chameleon-like ability to create personae for himself both on and off stage. This echoes other studies on him, such as Peter Holland's article in *Theatre and Celebrity in Britain, 1660–2000* [2005], and makes an illuminating interpretation of his personality, which relies on embellishment and obfuscation of the truth. Olivier once asked, 'What is acting but lying?' and the complexities raised by this question would have been fruitful for a theatre historian. The chronology of plays at the end of the book provides useful information, though, and reminds us of Olivier's vast body of work. There is also a real sense of the theatrical world of the twentieth century, with Olivier's career spanning its various forms, from the indignities of repertory to Shakespeare seasons at Baylis's Old Vic and commercial theatre to the 'angry young men' and beyond. While this is not an in-depth analysis of the intricacies of the theatre and Olivier's place in it, what we have here is a solid biography, based on unprecedented access to private papers.

Maggie Gale's book on J.B. Priestley has been published as part of the commendable Routledge Modern and Contemporary Dramatists series. The book is divided into three sections: life, politics and theory; themes in his plays; and a more detailed look at *The Good Companions, An Inspector Calls* and *Johnson over Jordan*. The titles of the latter sections could have been more distinctly focused, as section II is entitled 'Key Plays' and section III 'Key Plays/Productions'. That minor matter apart, Gale has put the case for Priestley's significance, outlining how the success of his novel *The Good Companions* [1929] gave him the financial stability to work full-time as a writer and broadcaster. During the interwar period Priestley wrote nearly thirty plays, a dozen of which were extremely successful and, as Stephen Daldry's revival of *An Inspector Calls* [1992] showed, relevant to the modern day. The consideration of individual plays and production history is particularly lucid. Explaining the seeming failure of the first production of *Johnson over Jordan* in 1939, for example, Gale explores its experimentalism, and how the play's suggestion that 'we might take more responsibility for our actions and better understand their impact on others' is 'in the original context of a country on the brink of war ... a challenging proposal' (p. 168). Priestley's work was wide-ranging in terms of genre, themes and dramatic technique, and, as Gale shows us, his own critical works did much to create a debate about the importance of 'popular' rather than commercial theatre, as well as the idea of theatre as a 'live art form' (p. 28). The point is made that it is difficult to pigeonhole Priestley's plays because of his movement between the theatrically conventional and unconventional, and the way in which he constantly returned to specific ideas. The role of the family and relationships between men and women appear across several decades, as with *Dangerous Corner* [1932], in which Priestley explodes the falsities perpetrated by the bourgeois family unit. His 'Time' plays are broken down into sections to show Priestley's 'interest in time as a fourth dimension' (p. 91). This is placed in its historical moment, to show how the merging of past, present and future is frequently used to demand 'an engagement with questions around "being" and "becoming", a self-reflection about individual and social actions and responsibility' (p. 92).

Of necessity, Gale concentrates on Priestley's contribution to the theatre. In contrast, John Baxendale's *Priestley's England* looks at his work more thematically, arguing that the view of Priestley as 'some kind of conservative ruralist' downplays his more complex engagement with nationhood (p. 1). In fact, he rejected the empire, ceremony and sentiment, instead being concerned with the future rather than the past, the urban landscape, not the countryside, and the common people instead of the privileged (p. 2). Here we can see how his plays strained to reflect social and political concerns, as with the rejection of pre-war ideas in *An Inspector Calls* and the play's attempt to reflect on what qualities were required in a postwar Britain. Obviously Baxendale's book is not designed to consider Priestley's plays in detail, but it is disappointing to find that only a couple of works are mentioned. However, Baxendale does much to give a sense of Priestley's influences, from Jung to Ouspensky, and from the Depression to the creation of a 'New Jerusalem' in the 1945 election.

The Letters of Noël Coward is a monumental work, handsomely illustrated throughout, and skilful at exposing Coward's process as a dramatist, director and actor. Barry Day's role as editor is intentionally much in evidence. Rather than having a light touch by simply adding explanatory footnotes about the people and events mentioned in the letters, Day evidently wanted a different approach. Here we have introductions to each section, as well as numerous comments throughout, and it is to Day's credit that he manages to let Coward's voice come through while still making sure that the reader does not lose his or her way in the mass of correspondence. The book is set chronologically, in four parts: Coward's early years, the period of his greatest prosperity in the 1920s and 1930s, wartime and the less commercially successful but still productive later years. Occasional breaks—rather whimsically called 'Intermissions'—give lengthier information about key figures in Coward's life, such as Gertrude Lawrence. As he was a prolific letter-writer from an early age, and expert in the social art of what we would now call 'networking', there are innumerable anecdotes, comic and otherwise, peppered throughout the book. Perhaps the best are those where Coward critiques the work of others, and while his views are astute, even he realizes that at times he has overstepped the mark. Asked by John Gielgud why he had walked out of *Musical Chairs* [1932], Coward remarked: 'I thought you were overacting badly and using voice tones to elaborate emotional effects, and as I seriously think you are a grand actor it upset me v. much' (p. 346). His admiration of W.S. Maugham's *Sheppey* in 1933, but not the production, led to 'Willie' responding, 'I sat in my box at the first night feeling like a disembodied spirit. I have done with playwriting...I do not myself think the theatre has much to offer the writer compared with other mediums in which he has complete independence and need consider no one' (p. 227). Sometimes this approach brought surprisingly odd friendships. John Osborne and Coward bonded when the representative of the younger generation asked that Coward stop criticizing his fellow writers to the media, and a friendship was forged with Harold Pinter when Coward wrote a fan letter after seeing

The Homecoming. Occasionally the tone of Coward's letters is grating; he indulges in pet names and baby talk, but, as he said of his wartime escapades as a spy, his 'disguise would be [his] own reputation as a bit of an idiot—a merry playboy' (p. 395). The overall impression at the end of this volume, though, is of a workaholic, always in 'a hurry to get on to the next thing and the next place' (p. 6), but a man whose energy, drive and ambition constantly pushed him to find a place in the literary world of the twentieth century.

As someone who has written reviews and theatre histories, as well as biographies of several actors, including Olivier, Ralph Richardson, Gielgud, and John Mills, Robert Tanitch is well placed to write on the *London Stage in the 20th Century*. From the outside, this looks like a coffee-table book. In fact, it is more useful than what this might imply. While it is of large format, and lavish in its use of illustrations, what we have here is an encyclopedia of productions on the West End stage. Of course, not all plays can be listed, but Tanitch has been judicious in his choices, presenting us with a representative sample from each year. Brief details under each entry draw on details about main actors, plot details, anecdotes and reviews, and there is a highlighted section on world premieres and historical facts. So we learn that in 1900 Gerald du Maurier and Mrs Patrick Campbell acted in Frank Harris's *Mr and Mrs Daventry* in which a wife tells her husband she is carrying her lover's child; a reviewer described it as 'the drama of the dustbin' (p. 5). For a critic seeing Sarah Kane's *Blasted* in 1995, it was 'like hanging your head down in a bucket of offal' (p. 284)—*plus ça change*. What Tanitch's approach loses in depth, it gains in range. Even if we just look at the period up until 1950, the reader immediately becomes aware that there is here a huge wealth of subject matter, genre and talent. It is not always remembered, for example, that British theatre during the Second World War did not just offer up the entertaining and cosy: in 1939 there might have been Flanagan and Allen in *The Little Dog Laughed* at the Palladium, but there was also Priestley's experimental morality play *Johnson over Jordan* at the New Theatre, Karel Capek's war allegory *The Mother* at the Garrick, and T.S. Eliot's modern tragedy *The Family Reunion* at the Westminster. Inevitably, in a work of monumental research and editing such as this, there are slips. The most obvious one is labelling a photograph of Dodie Smith's *Dear Octopus* [1938] as *Dear Brutus* (J.M. Barrie's play of 1917).

Heinz Kosok's excellent book *The Theatre of War: The First World War in British and Irish Drama* goes beyond stating which plays were produced between 1914 and 1918. Instead, as the full title of his book announces, his is an examination of the way in which the First World War has been represented in British and Irish drama. How ambitious this is can be seen by the chronology (helpfully compiled alphabetically and by date), which lists a huge number of plays written between 1909 (those which anticipate the war) and the 1990s (those which reference the war). Kosok even includes the last series of *Blackadder*, with its surprisingly poignant denouement. The myth that few dramatists tackled the subject during the war itself is exploded, with over sixty plays listed during this time. Again, while it might be expected that these would tail off at the beginning of the 1930s, the subject matter continued unabated until 1938, when it dwindled to two plays: Horace Flather's

Jonathan's Day and W.B. Auden and Christopher Isherwood's *On the Frontier*. The book is divided into several parts, which look at issues such as subject matter, dramatic technique and staging, authorial intent and reception. One of the strengths of this approach is the ability of the author to make references across temporal and contextual boundaries. Thus, a connection is made between George Bernard Shaw's *O'Flaherty V.C.* [1915] and Jennifer Johnston's *How Many Miles to Babylon?* [1993] in terms of their use of Anglo-Irish tensions, and the subtle complexities of terms such as 'realism' and 'reality' bring together R.C. Sherriff's *Journey's End* [1928] and William Douglas Home's *A Christmas Truce* [1989]. With over 200 plays listed, the question of choice becomes paramount. There are areas that could have been mentioned, such as the representation of the 'surplus' women in the 1920s and 1930s after the loss of a generation of young men, but Kosok has done well to set limitations on what can and cannot be included.

Anselm Heinrich's comparative *Entertainment, Propaganda, Education: Regional Theatre in Germany and Britain between 1918 and 1945* at first sight seems a rather strange linking together of subject and locality. Heinrich begins by outlining the way in which the theatre of Germany and Britain was generally seen as quite different in terms of theme, style and even at the level of institution: overseas, theatre was regarded with seriousness, and there was heavy state subsidy and a mix of classics like Schiller with the avant-garde; by contrast, it was thought that there was a lack of political and aesthetic import in British theatre, with commercial audiences attracted by lightweight comedies and melodramas. Heinrich challenges this view, stating that his researches show how the two countries 'became increasingly similar during the Second World War', with Britain wanting to 'adapt certain elements' from Germany (p. 2). But rather than finding that German influence made British plays more experimental, a typical season drawn from 1931 seems to consist mainly of comedies and melodramas, somewhat contradicting the author's earlier points. Again, he makes a strong case for focusing on the regions rather than the capital cities, but his reasoning for looking at only two areas, Yorkshire and Westphalia, is not entirely convincing. They have been chosen for their comparability in terms of geographical size and cultural significance, but it might have made a more rounded book to have included a range of places: the title certainly suggests that this is what is being done. Given this reservation, though, there is much here of use to scholars of regional theatre, looking at the relationship between city council and theatre, the repertory system, the impact of the Second World War and the founding of ENSA (the Entertainments National Service Association) and CEMA (Council for the Encouragement of Music and the Arts).

Mick Wallis's chapter on 'Drama in the Villages: Three Pioneers' (in Brassley, Burchardt and Thompson, eds., *The English Countryside 1918–39: Regeneration or Decline?*, pp. 102–15) also looks at regional theatre. Wallis explores the little-researched area of amateur theatre to show how it was used to 'regenerate village life; and to deliver adult education in rural areas' (p. 102). The examples given are fascinating, and show how individuals, councils and other bodies, like the Women's Institute, helped to foster drama during the interwar years. Such initiatives brought with them tensions between competing forces. So Gloucestershire Council's move towards a 'Countryside Drama Competition' (p. 105) sparked a national concern that it would pose a threat to the sense of community and 'festive spirit' (p. 106) created by village theatre. Here, Wallis only has room to sketch out three examples, but his point that the Village Drama Society (eventually subsumed into the British Drama League) covered over 600 villages by 1939 has great potential for future studies.

The continued reassessment of theatre in the first half of the twentieth century continues apace, as can be seen in Kosof's book, amongst others. Christopher McCullough looks to an earlier period for evidence of a radical past. In 'Harley Granville Barker: A Very English Avant-Garde' (*STP* 27iii[2007] 223–35), he shows how the dramatist/director's Shakespearian productions at the Savoy between 1912 and 1914 can be seen in this light. He connects the avant-garde with the late nineteenth-century *fin de siècle*, noting the irony in associating Shakespeare with these kinds of cultural movements. His central claim is that Granville Barker's 'rejection of the nineteenth century barnstorming styles of performing, as well as his abandonment of elaborate pictorial scenography and the haphazard cutting of received texts, may mark him out as a "modern" man, but his modernity was constructed, not innate' (pp. 224–5). McCullough shows how his productions of *The Winter's Tale* and *Twelfth Night* [both 1912] and *A Midsummer Night's Dream* [1914] draw on the visual arts movements of art nouveau, orientalism and Post-Impressionism. It is these changes in scenography, as well as the delivery and understanding of the text (fast-paced, and involving 'the modernist concept of interior character', p. 231), that marks Granville Barker out as radically moving forward the style of Shakespearian productions.

Critics such as Clive Barker, Maggie B. Gale and Dan Rebellato have all done much to counter the view that plays such as *Look Back in Anger* swept away the conservative and unimaginative drama prior to 1956. Luc Gilleman's article 'From Coward and Rattigan to Osborne, or the Enduring Importance of *Look Back in Anger*' (*MD* 51:i[2008] 104–25) begins rather crudely by rehashing the strong similarities of form, subject and character between John Osborne's play and Terence Rattigan's *The Deep Blue Sea* [1952], but does usefully include Coward's *The Vortex* [1924] as well. At the centre of the earlier plays 'is masculine bafflement at the enigma of woman . . . And as they move from complication to confrontation, the plays reveal their traditionally gendered understanding of the forces of order and disorder' (p. 113). Osborne's play also expresses this idea, but 'is less interested in analysing this male anxiety than in enacting and performing it in all its absurdity and inconsistency' (p. 119). For Gilleman, this marks the essential difference between pre- and post-1956 drama, with the latter focusing on ambiguity and 'existential uncertainty' (p. 123).

Finally, we have *The Cambridge Companion to the Actress*, edited by Gale and John Stokes. This adds to a growing body of material on this subject, including Tracy C. Davis's *Actresses as Working Women* [1991], Elizabeth Howe's *The First English Actresses* [1992], Sandra Richards's *The Rise of the English Actress* [1993] and the recent books by Stokes and Kirsten Pullen, *The French Actress and her English Audience* and *Actresses and Whores* [both 2005]. With *The Cambridge Companion*, Gale and Stokes continue to uphold the quality of this excellent series. Bringing together an estimable group of critics, the editors engage with Butlerian arguments about the performativity of the self, and Ellen Donkin's concern with how female performers have attempted to move from being (male-constructed) objects to (female-empowered) subjects. The book is not organized chronologically, as the editors did not want to suggest that the history of the actress unfolds in a developmental model. There are three sections: 'key historical moments', 'professional opportunities' and 'genre, form and tradition', and the subject covers a variety of media, including theatre, music hall, photography, cinema and music hall. Gale and Stokes are aware of the inevitability of lacunae in a collection of this nature. Nevertheless, they have achieved their goal of providing 'a preliminary survey of a rich and extraordinarily diverse history in which certain typical narratives might be usefully highlighted' (p. 11).

Some individual entries demand further comment in this part of *YWES*. In 'The Actress as Photographic Icon: From Early Photography to Early Film' (pp. 74–94), David Mayer explores how pictorial representations of the Victorian and Edwardian actress serve to expose the links between performance and celebrity. Mayer asks important questions about the relationship between sitter and photographer, actress and audience, and buyers and sellers. In all of this the role of actress as consumable becomes paramount. Generally speaking, stage photography only took place from the 1890s onward as lighting techniques became more advanced; before this, a 'simulacrum of the theatrical settings in which she [the actress] appeared at the theatre nearby' was set up in the photographer's studio (p. 80). With admirable research, Mayer has tracked down the leading photographers of the period and details the photographic techniques needed for these portraits.

Lucie Sutherland looks at 'The Actress and the Profession: Training in England in the Twentieth Century' (pp. 95–115), a topic that is intrinsic to the changing status of the actress. Sutherland describes the various ways in which women were offered support in the industry, from the Theatrical Ladies Guild in 1891, and the Actresses' Franchise League in 1908, to the founding of RADA and the Central School of Speech and Drama, and the increasing unionization of acting. Almost from the start, the disparity between the working conditions of men and women was obvious, and George Bernard Shaw is thought to be one of those who entered into the debate as author of *The RADA Graduates' Keepsake and Counsellor* [1941], a book which notes how actresses' wages were sometimes below subsistence rate, arguing that a fixed rate should be set by the British Actors' Equity Association. Shaw reasoned that this would help to dissipate the correlation made from the start between actress and prostitute, an area that could perhaps have been further developed by Sutherland. The author is particularly interesting, though, when relating how women often took positions of authority in the new acting schools—Irene Vanbrugh at RADA, for example, Elsie Fogerty, who founded CSSD, and Judith Gick, who taught at several of the leading academies. Athene Seyler, Sybil Thorndike and May Whitty also sat on various councils, helping to effect fundamental changes to the running of these places.

Elaine Aston's ' "Studies in Hysteria": Actress and Courtesan, Sarah Bernhardt and Mrs Patrick Campbell' (pp. 253–71) continues the link between

French actresses and the British stage brought out by Stokes's book last year. Aston juxtaposes two ideas about the actress in the late nineteenth and early twentieth centuries: that is, the link between acting and prostitution, and the negation of this through the celebrity accorded popular actresses like Ellen Terry, Bernhardt and Campbell.

Three other articles can also be mentioned. Viv Gardner's 'By Herself: The Actress and the Autobiography, 1755–1939' (pp. 173–92) takes up a theme that is current in early twentieth-century theatre history: the link between the public/private self and performance, also discussed in Aston's article. Common to both as well is Campbell, whose autobiography *My Life and Some Letters* was published in 1922. The form utilized by Campbell, consisting of chronological narrative and fragmentary recollection, is, Gale suggests, a reflection of Campbell's own life. In 'The Screen Actress from Silence to Sound' (pp. 193–214), Christine Gledhill continues her critically acute engagement with the cinema, particularly in relation to women's film history. Here she explores how actresses moved from stage to cinema, from silent films to 'talkies', and from Britain to America, thus demonstrating 'the potential exchange value of national character types and performance modes, and the discursive clashes and shifts around gender roles and definitions of femininity that take place in the process' (p. 211). Gale's 'Going Solo: An Historical Perspective on the Actress and the Monologue' (pp. 291–313) accesses a less explored area of the female monologist. While a successful form amongst Americans such as May Isabel Fisk, Ruth Draper and the British-born but American-domiciled Beatrice Herford, this form was also taken up by others in the United Kingdom. Joyce Grenfell, herself a distant cousin to Draper, made the monologue her speciality through the 1940s and 1950s.

5. Post-1950 Drama

Theatre writing since the 1990s has dominated several major studies this year. One of the most ambitious has been Steve Blandford's *Film, Drama and the Break-Up of Britain*. As the title suggests, the book analyses 'some of the ways that film and theatre... reflect and contribute to a Britain that is changing so rapidly... [that it] amounts to a break-up of the very idea of there being a meaningful British identity at all' (p. 1). Blandford draws the conclusion that by the end of the 1990s Northern Ireland, Wales and Scotland were looking to Europe, not only for funding in film and theatre projects, but also increasingly for a wider cultural identification. In terms of theatre, chapters on the work produced in England, Scotland, Wales and Northern Ireland allow the reader to make comparisons. Blandford's work is timely in that it provides an alternative reading to the predominant study of the period, Aleks Sierz's *In-Yer-Face Theatre: British Drama Today* [2001], which was almost exclusively concentrated on the young dramatists based around London in the relatively short period between 1994 and 1999. Blandford not only comprehensively looks at the whole decade but traces moments where a distinct mood emerged within a region, notably Scotland. The book also traces points of discomfiture and failure. These include England's schizophrenic and troubled relationship with its identity and Wales's relative failure—after several false dawns—to establish a convincing identity for itself in terms of new theatre writing. The book also offers excellent analysis on how each region has responded to the issue of multiculturalism through representation in film and theatre. Books such as this, which attempt a synthesis of different cultural forms within a specific historical period, are to be welcomed, and Blandford demonstrates an expertise and passionate engagement in the disciplines of both film and theatre studies.

Geraldine Cousin's *Playing for Time: Stories of Lost Children, Ghosts and the Endangered Present in Contemporary Theatre* is a far more subjective study in that it eschews historical analysis, opting instead for a series of case studies based on new plays, adaptations and revivals of classic twentieth-century drama in the period between 1990 and 2005. The theme of Cousin's book develops an observation Elaine Aston made in her earlier monograph, *Feminist Views on the English Stage* [2003], in which she locates 'an emergent urgency and concern for the child . . . at risk in the world' (p. 10) by a number of women dramatists in the 1990s. Similarly, Cousin points out that 'a key motif in the book is the "lost child"' (p. 11) as a real event, and sometimes as a form of ghostly return. Cousin's monograph is mainly a study of English playwrights, although there are sections on the work of Irish dramatists Conor McPherson and Marina Carr. The book starts with a chapter on Stephen Daldry's 1992 revival of *An Inspector Calls*, in which Cousin draws parallels with the production's novel device of a collapsing house as a prescient political metaphor for the events of 9/11 nearly a decade later. Subsequent chapters look at Tom Stoppard's *Arcadia* [1993], Michael Frayn's *Copenhagen* [1998], recent plays by Caryl Churchill and stage adaptations such as Philip Pullman's *His Dark Materials* [2003] and Helen Edmundson's *Coram Boy* [2005]. Like Blandford's study, which looks at film and theatre in the 1990s, Cousin at times looks at other cultural forms to complement her analysis of particular plays. For instance, in her discussion of Bryony Lavery's *Frozen* [1998] and Martin McDonagh's *The Pillowman* [2003], Cousin draws attention to both the media's obsession with murdered children and a number of novels that appeared at the time, including Alice Sebold's *The Lovely Bones* [2002], in which murdered children are the focus. Again, this approach, which considers work from a wider cultural and artistic sphere, is something to be welcomed. Cousin's analysis of the plays is also frequently original (especially on Churchill), although at times this subjective approach is a drawback. For instance, there is little attempt to historically contextualize the period covered and scant attention is paid to other major critical studies of the work discussed. Rather, secondary sources are mainly drawn from newspaper reviews. This might well have been a deliberate strategy, but acquaintance with significant examples of recent scholarship on the subject would have been welcome.

Christina Wald's *Hysteria, Trauma and Melancholia: Performative Maladies in Contemporary Anglophone Drama* also takes a number of plays from the 1990s as its focus. The study argues that, since the 1980s, a number of prevalent themes have emerged in British and American playwriting concerned with particular forms of mental illness: Wald categorizes these as 'The Drama of Hysteria', 'Trauma Drama' and 'The Drama of Melancholia' and argues that 'increasingly contemporary culture defines its own moment through hysteria, trauma and melancholia' (p. 1). This has often taken the form (bordering at times on the prurient) of child abuse as well as other examples of 'wound culture', exhibited through Gulf War syndrome and body dysmorphia. Wald provides historical accounts of how these conditions have come to be understood as types of mental pathology. These are followed by detailed readings, framed in places with recourse to aspects of Judith Butler's ideas about gender formation, on how such illnesses are presented theatrically in plays such as Terry Johnson's *Hysteria* [1993], Sarah Daniels's *Beside Herself* [1990] and Sarah Kane's *Cleansed* [1998]. This monograph is the first to explore in detail how these three forms of mental affliction have come to quite literally haunt the stage. It is a significant book, and will undoubtedly be followed by others on the subject. Partly this is to do with Wald's decision to concentrate on a relatively small number of plays from the 1980s and 1990s. Notwithstanding, she alerts the reader to a whole host of other contemporaneous plays that also explore the same territory. She is also aware of significant gaps: for instance, in her chapter on the drama of hysteria 'which historically has been subject to gendering...as a specific female malady' (p. 27) she points out that cases of 'male hysteria' manifest themselves just as frequently.

Rebecca D'Monté and Graham Saunders's edited collection, *Cool Britannia? British Political Drama in the 1990s*, assesses a range of engagements undertaken in the representation and discussion of politics in theatre from the last decade. The book is divided into three sections: the first, '"In-Yer-Face Theatre": A Reconsideration', challenges and assesses Sierz's influential reading of playwriting culture in the latter part of the 1990s. Indeed, the section opens with Sierz's '"We all need stories": The Politics of In-Yer-Face Theatre' (pp. 23–37), where he provides both a defence and a self-critical assessment of his work. Ken Urban's 'Cruel Britannia: In-Yer-Face Theatre, Nihilism and the 1990s' (pp. 38–55) also provides an interrogation of Sierz's terminology, and defends writers such as Sarah Kane and Mark Ravenhill from charges of political disengagement; rather, Urban sees their work as predicated on a form of nihilism that allows for the possibility of transformative change. Mary Luckhurst's 'Harold Pinter and Poetic Politics' (pp. 56–68) considers various responses from previous generations of writers, such as David Hare, Churchill and Pinter, during the 1990s. The second section, 'Thatcherism and (Post-)Feminism', also seeks to readdress the received view that the plethora of plays that dealt with various aspects of masculinity in crisis in the 1990s necessarily stifled the voices of female dramatists. D'Monté's chapter, 'Thatcher's Children: Alienation and Anomie in the Plays of Judy Upton' (pp. 79–95), argues that Upton's work during the 1990s provided a critical assessment of the political legacy of the 1980s. Lynette Goddard's 'Middle Class Aspirations and Black Women's Mental (Ill) Health in Zindika's *Leonara's Dance* and Bonnie Greer's *Munda Negra* and *Dancing on Blackwater*' (pp. 96–113) looks back to a style of writing in black women's drama during the 1980s that by 1997 had all but been rendered moribund. However, Goddard sees the situation improving for the millennial generation of young black women dramatists such as Dona Daly and Debbie Tucker Green. Elaine Aston's 'A Good Night Out, for the Girls' (pp. 114–30) looks at popular theatre from the 1990s to the present. While agreeing with those who detect a fragmentation in women's writing during the 1990s, the chapter looks at the popularity of shows such as Eve Ensler's *The Vagina Monologues* [1996], as well as Catherine Johnson's *Shang-a-Lang* [1998] and *Mamma Mia!* [1999], and suggests that these plays provide not only entertainment, but a sense of empowerment for their predominantly female audiences.

The last section, 'Nation, Devolution and Globalization', sees David Pattie, Roger Owen, Nadine Holdsworth and Wallace McDowell's assessments of Scotland, Wales and Northern Ireland, respectively. Dan Rebellato's '"Because it feels fucking amazing": Recent British Drama and Bodily Mutilation' (pp. 192–207) moves further, in concluding that the motif of bodily mutilation in plays such as Kane's *Cleansed* and Martin Crimp's *The Treatment* [1992] is representative of individuals' sense of powerlessness in the face of globalization. The final chapter, playwright David Greig's 'Rough Theatre' (pp. 208–21), assesses the impact of politics on 1990s drama, but also looks towards definitions and dramatic strategies for the millennial decade.

British theatre in the 1990s is also the principal theme of a collection of interviews conducted by Mireia Aragay, Hildegard Klein, Enric Monforte and Pilar Zozaya in *British Theatre of the 1990s: Interviews with Directors, Playwrights and Academics*. The book is divided into four categories, with the aim of providing comprehensive yet divergent readings of the 1990s in terms of the theatre produced. The interviews are wide-ranging and go beyond presenting familiar or received views of the decade. One of the major strengths of the collection is the detailed footnotes that accompany references to individual plays, specific productions or cultural events. Although interviews with the directors narrowly focus on Ian Rickson, Stephen Daldry and Max Stafford Clark, their accounts of running the Royal Court during the 1990s provide valuable new insights into the history and artistic policies of the theatre during this period. The range of playwrights interviewed is more diverse, ranging from Mark Ravenhill, who did much to establish a 1990s zeitgeist in theatre writing, to Kevin Elyot, who moved between work at the Royal Court, the Royal National Theatre and West End stages during the decade. There are also interviews with Neil Bartlett, Martin Crimp and Joe Penhall. The interviews with critics and academics also provide many points of departure. Sierz's interview is of particular interest, where he again both defends and points out the shortcomings of his term 'in-yer-face theatre'. Alan Sinfield also provides a useful overview of British culture during the 1990s through which to assess gay and lesbian drama. Overall, despite the very different agendas that all the interviewees present, the collection confirms the editors' belief that 'a consensus does seem to emerge that *something* was happening' during the 1990s' (p. 1). The collection will go some way to providing primary material for further reassessments of this important decade in British theatre.

Peter Billingham's *At the Sharp End* is another collection of interviews that privileges a number of dramatists who first came to prominence during the 1990s. These include Greig, Tanika Gupta and Ravenhill. The volume also includes interviews with David Edgar and, somewhat perversely, Tim Etchells, from the devised performance group Forced Entertainment, who might perhaps take umbrage at being associated with the culture of playwriting. However, the interviews conducted by Billingham are illuminating and are complemented by accompanying commentaries on the work of each writer that contextualizes the interview material.

Billingham also interviews the playwright Edward Bond in *PAJ: A Journal of Performance and Art* (*PAJ* 29:iii[2007] 1–14), while a previous issue contains Caridad Svich's interview with Greig (*PAJ* 29:ii[2007] 51–8). Bond's work for young people is also the subject of David Allen's ' "Going to the centre': Edward Bond's *The Children*' " (*STP* 27:ii[2007] 115–36), which interrogates Bond's notion of the 'the centre' in performance.

The special issue of *Modern Drama* [Fall 2007] entitled 'Recent British Drama' looked at the development and changes in British playwriting culture since the mid-1990s. Janelle Reinelt's 'Selective Affinities: British Playwrights at Work' (*MD* 50:i[2007] 303–45) and Christopher Innes's 'Towards a Post-Millennial Mainstream? Documents of the Times' (*MD* 50:i[2007] 435–52) provide excellent analysis and overview of recent developments, with both arguing for recognition of older dramatists. Innes makes a case for David Hare's recent docu-plays such as *The Permanent Way* [2003] as 'providing a model for younger playwrights' (p. 449). Reinelt sees the relationship between young and old as more complementary, not to say nurturing, and makes a convincing case for re-evaluating the importance in 2007 of two plays, Roy Williams's *Days of Significance* [2007] and *Catch* [2006], written by a group of women playwrights spanning the generations from April de Angelis to Stella Feehily, Chloe Moss and Laura Wade, as evidence of this mutually supportive writing environment. Other articles focus on the work of one writer or a significant work: Urban's 'Ghosts from an Imperfect Place: Philip Ridley's *Nostalgia*' (*MD* 50:i[2007] 325–45) considers Ridley's use of nostalgia in his work from the 1990s, Candice Amich's 'Bringing the Global Home: The Commitment of Caryl Churchill's *The Skriker*' (*MD* 50:i[2007] 394–413) locates the play as a dystopian vision of globalization, Harry Derbyshire's 'Roy Williams: Representing Multicultural Britain in *Fallout*' (*MD* 50:i[2007] 414–34) makes a case for the play as an important work that analyses the debates about causes of inner-city violence and black crime, Sierz's ' "Form follows function": Meaning and Politics in Martin Crimp's *Fewer Emergencies*' (*MD* 50:i[2007] 375–93) concentrates on Crimp's 2005 trilogy of short plays collectively entitled *Fewer Emergencies* as a radical way of using dramatic form to suggest new ways of analysing global politics, and Kim Solga's '*Blasted*'s Hysteria: Rape, Realism, and the Thresholds of the Visible' (*MD* 50:i[2007] 346–74) examines the use of rape through its non-representation in the play itself. Together, these contributions are exemplary in the detail and sophistication of their arguments and very much set a benchmark for current scholarship in British theatre.

Some of the work produced in 2007 has gone beyond the work of a single decade and taken a retrospective approach to British theatre history. The most comprehensive of these accounts is Michael Billington's *State of the Nation: British Theatre since 1945*, which won the Theatre Book Prize for 2007. Drawing on Billington's work as a newspaper theatre critic, this wide-ranging study manages to provide a useful historical overview of postwar British theatre that emphasizes the political and cultural events that informed the drama. Billington's main interest lies with playwriting culture, and he puts forward some interesting re-evaluations of the established canon. These include making a case for J.B. Priestley as every bit as angry a young man as Osborne, as well as being a far more experimental writer. The book also looks at the role of certain institutions and figures in shaping postwar theatre. These include the role of the Arts Council and the theatre impresario Hugh 'Binkie' Beaumont. While Billington's book contains few surprises in many of its assessments, it is an authoritative and informative overview of the period.

D. Keith Peacock's *Changing Performance: Culture and Performance in the British Theatre since 1945* is more of a specialized work in that it charts the slow awareness of European theatrical practice on postwar British theatre. Whereas existing studies such as Stephen Lacey's *British Realist Theatre* [1995] or Sierz's *In-Yer-Face Theatre* analyse events through specific plays, Peacock takes the emergence of different acting styles, often adapted from continental models, as his starting point. Crucially, this begins far earlier than either the 1956 watershed of *Look Back in Anger* or Peter Hall's production of *Waiting for Godot* [1955], locating the moment as Joan Littlewood's establishment of Theatre Workshop in 1945.

While he draws on many familiar secondary sources, Peacock usefully arranges this pre-existing material into a series of case studies, whereby a particular production, company or practitioner is examined in detail. These range from Peter Hall's production of *The Wars of the Roses* [1963] and Peter Brook's *Marat/Sade* [1964], via the emergence of the Royal Shakespeare Company, to Complicité's *The Three Lives of Lucie Cabrol* [1994]. Each example is analysed from a number of different criteria: these include the performance space or building and, most notably, the production process itself. Of particular interest are Peacock's discussions regarding specific economic criteria that eventually influenced crucial decisions relating to actual performance—most notably the role the Arts Council has played to date. Although Peacock sets out to show how British theatre underwent a slow transition from a time when actor training meant little more than exercises in deportment to the adoption of a more European model, the book slowly metamorphoses (much like its case study of Stephen Berkoff's best-known Kafka adaptation) into a more familiar account of postwar British theatre, drawing on familiar landmark productions (such as Terence Rattigan's *The Browning Version* [1948], Brook's *Marat/Sade* and Shelagh Delaney's *A Taste of Honey* [1958]) and figures (such as Brook, Simon McBurney and Peter Hall) who have emerged since 1945.

Throughout 2006 the Royal Court celebrated its fiftieth anniversary as the English Stage Company. Ruth Little and Emily McLaughlin's *The Royal*

Court Theatre: Inside Out continues this retrospective look at one of the most enduring and influential British theatre companies. The book is a lively historical account of the theatre from 1956 to 2007, and while it draws extensively on existing sources, such as Philip Roberts's *The Royal Court and the Modern Stage* [1999] and Richard Findlater's *At the Royal Court: 25 Years of the English Stage Company* [1981], it has the advantage of being able to continue the Royal Court's history, from the period of its renovation and temporary move to the West End during the late 1990s to its fortunes during the present decade. This is augmented with new interviews that draw on the experiences of playwrights, directors and technical staff who have been associated with the Royal Court from its inception to the present. The book is also beautifully illustrated, and while some of its photographs are well known, many are drawn from the personal collections of individuals as well as the Royal Court archives held at the V&A's Theatre Museum. These include fascinating items, such as Ian Rickson's performance schedule from 2001 and original design sketches for plays. As well as providing a historical account of the theatre, the book also looks at specific productions in detail. Again, this is most welcome in the attention given to more recent work such Churchill's *Drunk Enough to Say I Love You* [2006] and *My Name is Rachel Corrie* [2005]. While necessary attention is paid to historical landmark productions such as Osborne's *Look Back in Anger* and Bond's *Saved* [1965], it was also pleasing to gain new insights into less well-known productions such as N.F. Simpson's *A Resounding Tinkle* [1957] and David Cregan's *Miniatures* [1965].

Several collections this year feature essays on aspects of post-1950 drama. *Alternatives within the Mainstream II: Queer Theatres in Post-War Britain*, edited by Dimple Godiwala, revisits the period in terms of how theatre engaged with alternative sexualities: primarily, the essays concentrate on the depiction of and issues surrounding the performance of homosexuality in British drama. Despite its title alluding to theatre, as with Blandford's *Film, Drama and the Break-Up of Britain*, there is also a welcome section devoted to television drama. The best articles in the collection provide broad historical contextualization, yet do so without parroting received wisdom: these include Spilby's 'The Trouble with Queers: Gays in Plays 1945–1968' (pp. 12–35) and Kate Dorney's 'Tears, Tiaras and Transgressives: Queer Drama in the 1960s' (pp. 36–58), which makes good use of archival sources to argue that Joe Orton's work broke out of a tradition of depicting the melancholic and self-loathing homosexual. Dorney also makes a convincing queer reading of Pinter's *The Collection* [1962], as a precursor to later work based on exclusively male relationships such as *No Man's Land* [1975] and *Betrayal* [1978]. More specific but equally useful articles include Paul T. Davies's 'Loving Angels Instead: The Influence of Tony Kushner's *Angels in America* on 1990s Confrontational Drama' (pp. 59–82), which, as its title suggests, makes a strong case for the 1992 British premiere of Kushner's play acting as a catalyst for 'in-yer-face' playwrights such as Anthony Neilson, Kane and Ravenhill. Sarah Jane Dickenson also provides an interesting update on the work of Ravenhill and the 'omnipresent' (p. 124) figure of the vulnerable boy from early work such as *Shopping and Fucking* [1996] through to more recent work such as *Citizenship* [2004]. Dickenson maintains that 'Ravenhill's resilience as a writer stems from his ability to tap into the persistent anxiety connected to homosexuality' (p. 126), with *Citizenship* marking a breakthrough in terms of its wider dissemination via performances throughout many British schools. Selina Busby and Stephen Farrier, in 'The Fluidity of Bodies, Gender, Identity and Structure in the Plays of Sarah Kane' (pp. 141–59), like Wald's case-study of *Cleansed*, read Kane through the increasingly amorphous gender identities that preoccupy other late works such as *Crave* [1998] and *4.48 Psychosis* [1999]. Like Wald, they also take ideas from Judith Butler's theories about the construction and performativity of gender, in that 'Kane's work, like queer, is never finished . . . because it is not rooted to a particular ideological idea' (p. 145). While the collection overall sheds important new light on the ever-developing area of gender and representation in British drama, the volume is marred by being poorly edited and proof-read, as well as containing some major factual inaccuracies which detract from the originality and quality of many of the submissions.

There have been several other edited volumes of theatre essays in 2007 that contain chapters on British drama after 1950. For instance, Scott Magelssen and Ann Haugo's *Querying Difference in Theatre History* brings together work from a wide range of geographical locations, historical periods and particular styles and genres of theatre. The one chapter on recent British theatre is Sara Freeman's 'The Immigrant, the Exile, the Refugee in Wertenbaker's *Credible Witness*: A Poetics of Diaspora' (pp. 133–40), which argues that this figure not only informs all of Timberlake Wertenbaker's original plays, but is equally the principal subject of her work as a translator of Greek drama. Drawing on the ideas of Avtar Brah's 'disapora space', Freeman argues that Wertenbaker's 2001 play *Credible Witness* is an example of what she calls 'a poetics of diaspora', as 'drama built on the terms of displacement and estrangement', but, at the same time, 'reaching toward new formulations of home and citizenship' (p. 136). The article also shows that by setting part of the play in a British detainment centre the idea of diaspora space becomes contested, set against the resistance imposed through 'national space' (p. 137).

Elaine Aston and Sue-Ellen Case's *Staging International Feminisms* is a collection that reflects the ongoing work of the Feminist Research Working Group, which since 1994 has met at the annual International Federation of Theatre Research. As the title suggests, many of the articles are concerned with what Aston and Case call 'feminist critical navigations of the global arena' (p. 4) and 'feminist possibilities for change' (p. 5). Noelia Hernando-Real's 'Cultural Memory in *El Séptimo Cielo*: An International Staging of Caryl Churchill's *Cloud Nine*' (pp. 132–9) suggests that reasons for the poor reception of the 2004 Spanish production of Caryl Churchill's *Cloud Nine* [1979] arose from decisions made in its translation and staging. These amounted to what Hernando-Real calls 'a direct attack on Spanish cultural memory' (p. 132), where, instead of the Victorian values of nation and family that the play originally set out to critique, the Spanish production looked at the links between fascism and patriarchy as a legacy of General Franco's dictatorship.

Lynette Goddard's *Staging Black Feminisms: Identity, Politics, Performance* is a welcome monograph dedicated to the representation of black women on the British stage since the 1950s in terms of self-representation by others. Goddard stresses that 'it is not enough to locate all black women's work as feminist by virtue of its very existence' (p. 2), and argues that black women's performances entail a different series of feminist aesthetics which draws on African American and Caribbean literature (p. 4).The book is divided into sections on the work of playwrights such as Winsome Pinnock and Debbie Tucker Green, and sections on 'Performances' that draw on devised and physical theatre practice. The introductory chapter charts the emergence of black female theatre companies during the 1970s and 1980s and the subsequent struggles many had to contend with over funding. The 'History and Aesthetics' section contains a very useful overview chapter, charting an alternative history for black writers and performers in theatre (and television). The section 'Black Feminist Performance Aesthetics' looks at institutional policies since the 1990s whereby exclusively black women's theatre groups were eventually disbanded, in part as a result of theatre's embrace of multicultural practices. Goddard recognizes that this has boosted the profile of new black writers in recent years, yet, as she points out, it has benefited male dramatists more significantly. Slightly more problematic are Goddard's own 'suggestions for a progressive black feminist practice for the twentieth century' (p. 2). Here, she draws attention to the dearth of black lesbians represented onstage. Although she addresses and brings to light work in this area by Jackie Kay and Valerie Mason-John, at times one feels that Goddard writes about the kind of theatre she would wish to see rather than accepting and addressing the state of theatre as it exists.

The dramatist Howard Barker is even more excoriating in his assessment of the shortcomings of contemporary British theatre in *A Style and its Origins*. Adopting the persona of Eduardo Houth, the book is a faux biography whereby Barker is able to distance himself as a third-person subject. *A Style and its Origins* could very easily have been given the alternative title *My Way*, with Barker taking an almost perverse pleasure in depicting himself as the malcontent outsider. This feeling of estrangement includes the times in which he lives, his home in Brighton, critics, theatre audiences and the apparatus of British theatre itself—to which he gives the collective noun 'the dramaturgy'. Barker sees himself as an outcast prophet with a small but fanatically devoted cult of followers, and many will find both the style and tone of the book irritating. Comments such as 'Barker disliked compromise, and was reluctant to delegate. If theatre is a collective art, he brought to it a poet's innate self-reference, and pushed theatre nearer to the poem and the poem nearer to the stage' (p. 41), are bound to affront. Yet such provocations have always been part of Barker's theatre, and one of the many pleasures of *A Style and its Origins* are the shibboleths and conventions of liberal humanist theatre that Barker takes to task: here, its social mission is dismissed as 'patronising to the public and profoundly destructive to the nature of the theatre experience' (p. 55), while the politics of 'radical theatre' is dismissed by Barker through its 'preposterous claims to educate' and its 'subsequent grotesque simplifications' (p. 85). It is easy to see how Barker has effectively sent himself into exile in his home country when his views about the function of theatre are so removed from the consensus, yet iconoclasts such as Barker romantically compel. *A Style and its Origins* could easily have become an embittered rant if its arguments were not expressed with such sharp clarity and skill. Barker is as much an accomplished prose writer as he is a dramatist and poet. There is also much to stimulate and learn from in his self-assessments. For instance, he considers later plays such as *Und* [1999], *Gertrude—The Cry* [2002] and *The Fence in its Thousandth Year* [2005] to be his most accomplished, rather than earlier, better-known plays such as *The Castle* [1985] and *Scenes from an Execution* [1984]. Barker also gives fascinating accounts of how he began to direct and design his own plays, as well as the changing fortunes of the Wrestling School, the theatre company that exclusively performs his work.

The theme of censorship in British theatre has been a lively subject this year. David Thomas, David Carlton and Anne Etienne's *Theatre Censorship: From Walpole to Wilson* is a comprehensive study of state censorship from the mid-eighteenth century until its abolition in 1968. This is a readable and well-researched historical account that benefits from a long historical grasp, back to the origins of censorship in the English theatre in the eighteenth century. Another particular strength is the emphasis placed on both the political and legal mechanisms that sought to uphold the practice and those who attempted reform via a parliamentary system which seemed after 1945 to be increasingly archaic. This is an important approach to take, as much work up until 2003 has tackled the subject of theatre censorship with regard to how it directly affected theatres, playwrights and directors in terms of artistic policy adopted. The length of the book means that it cannot rival the detail and analysis of Steve Nicholson's ongoing three-volume series *The Censorship of British Drama, 1900–1968* [2003, 2005], and this is particularly the case with the last chapter, entitled 'The Aftermath: British Theatre Following the Abolition of Statutory Censorship' (pp. 225–55). While it attempts to discuss the many forms of direct and indirect theatre censorship since 1968, this chapter is the least successful because, while the account is informative, it simply attempts to cover too much material within the confines of a single chapter. Nevertheless, this excellent study traces and contextualizes an important area of theatre history.

Signs of the degree and complexity of current debates on indirect forms of theatre censorship can be found in the fourth issue of *Contemporary Theatre Review* (*ConTR* 17:iv[2007]). Arising out of a symposium entitled 'Gagging' that was held at the University of Hull in December 2006, this series of short articles considers the issues and implications of self-censorship within a number of recent theatre events. Elizabeth Wilson's 'Gender and Censorship' (*ConTR* 17:iv[2007] 518–24) provides an overview of self-censorship by artists in its consideration of religion as it relates to issues of gender. The article goes on to consider these questions in a theatrical context. The playwright David Edgar's 'From the Nanny State to the Heckler's Veto: The New Censorship and How to Counter It' (*ConTR* 17:iv[2007] 524–32) looks at how the problems of enactment are seen in some quarters as tantamount to condoning criticism on sensitive subjects such as child abuse. He considers whether a case can be made for theatres to offer protection against offending audiences

(p. 528) in plays such as Howard Brenton's *The Romans in Britain* [1980] and Gurpreet Kaur Bhatti's *Bezhti* [2004]. The *Behzti* affair is also considered in Helen Iball's 'Still My Mouth: Playing in the Face of Terror' (*ConTR* 17:iv[2007] 533–41) and Gabrielle Griffin's 'Gagging: Gender, Performance and the Politics of Intervention' (*ConTR* 17:iv[2007] 541–9). These articles also consider a range of other examples, such as the censorship issues that bedevilled Sarah Kane's *Blasted* [1995] and the New York production of *My Name is Rachel Corrie* [2005]. Mary Luckhurst's 'The D Word: New Writing Cultures in England' (*ConTR* 17:iv[2007] 549–66) considers negative perceptions of the dramaturge as a figure who censors the work of new playwrights, and how this attitude is in many respects mistaken. Together, these articles represent important new thinking on potentially worrying developments. Reinelt also adds to this debate in her article 'The Limits of Censorship' (*TRI* 32:i[2007] 3–15). Here, she discusses high-profile examples such as *My Name is Rachel Corrie* and *Bezhti*, but also sounds a word of caution in what has amounted to an application of the blanket term 'censorship' to such works. *Theater* contains a transcript from a panel discussion entitled 'Who's Afraid of *Rachel Corrie*?' (*Theater* 37:ii[2007] 55–65), where theatre director Gregory Mosher, playwright Christopher Shinn and academics including Marvin Carlson spoke at an event organized in April 2006 at Barnard College in America following the New York postponement of *My Name is Rachel Corrie*.

There have been several studies in 2007 devoted to the work of a single playwright. Richard Rankin Russell's edited collection *Martin McDonagh: A Casebook* builds on the 2006 collection *The Theatre of Martin McDonagh*. Both volumes continue the fierce debates concerning McDonagh's work. José Lanters's essay 'The Identity Politics of Martin McDonagh' (pp. 9–24) argues that the plays should be seen as examples of postmodern satire that seeks to destabilize grand narratives. In McDonagh's case, this applies specifically 'with the foundations of Irish nationalism' (p. 9), such as the stereotype of nationhood being portrayed through heroic women (p. 20). Joan Fitzpatrick Dean's 'Martin McDonagh's stagecraft' (pp. 25–40) observes that the plays' often controversial depictions of violence and Irishness mask an employment of the traditional form of the 'well-made play' in much of the work. McDonagh's borrowings from an extensive range of other genres are the subject of several essays. Laura Eldred's 'Martin McDonagh and the Contemporary Gothic' (pp. 111–30) considers the influence of contemporary horror films on McDonagh's work, and particularly the treatment of monsters shaped by societal forces. Patrick Lonergan's excellent essay 'Never Mind the Shamrocks: Globalizing Martin McDonagh' (pp. 149–75), which closes the volume, looks in some detail at specific films such as *Shallow Grave* [1996], and television soap operas that seem to have influenced the style of McDonagh's playwriting. Karen Vandevelde's 'Postmodern Theatricality in the Dutch/ Flemish Adaptation of Martin McDonagh's *The Leenane Trilogy*' (pp. 77–91) provides an interesting account of a 2000/1 production in the Netherlands, which not only staged the trilogy as one play but also moved away from the tradition of staging McDonagh's work realistically. The depiction of violence exercises several of the contributions. Marion Castleberry's 'Comedy and Violence in *The Beauty Queen of Leenane*' (pp. 41–59) and Maria Doyle's

'Breaking Bodies: The Presence of Violence on Martin McDonagh's Stage' (pp. 92–110) revisit this topic. Castleberry sees McDonagh's use of comic violence as the most recent within a long tradition of Irish literary and dramatic writing, while Doyle looks at both the calculated and the unexpected effects of violence in terms of the audience's reaction. Stephanie Pocock's 'The "ineffectual Father Welsh/Walsh"? Anti-Catholicism and Catholicism in Martin McDonagh's *The Leenane Trilogy*' (pp. 60–76) offers a detailed reading of Father Walsh in *The Lonesome West* [1997] and argues that, rather than simply functioning as a comic buffoon, he is one of the rare instances in McDonagh's work of a character who displays a complex and humane moral centre. Brian Cliff's '*The Pillowman*: A New Story to Tell' (pp. 131–48) also argues that amidst the dark subject matter lies a redemptive centre.

Richard Boon's editorship of *The Cambridge Companion to David Hare* succeeds in bringing together a highly imaginative range of academics and practitioners to provide a fulsome analysis and assessment of Hare's prolific career. This not only includes his activity as a writer in several mediums, but also as a director (and occasionally actor), together with his role as a 'public figure'. The first section, 'Text and Context', opens with Tony Bicât's memoir 'Portable Theatre: "Fine detail, rough theatre". A Personal Memoir' (pp. 15–30) and Boon's more scholarly 'Keeping Turning Up: Hare's Early Career' (pp. 31–48), that looks at the period from 1969 through to the 1970s. Lib Taylor's 'In Opposition: Hare's Response to Thatcherism' (pp. 49–63) charts and analyses Hare's work in theatre during the 1980s, while Les Wade's 'Hare's Trilogy at the National: Private Moralities and the Common Good' (pp. 64–78) is devoted to the three plays that for many represent Hare's best work to date—*Racing Demon* [1990], *Murmuring Judges* [1991] and *The Absence of War* [1993]. Duncan Wu's 'Hare's "Stage Poetry", 1995–2002' (pp. 79–91) follows on from these very 'public' plays to work that is more 'private' in tone, yet does not ignore the politics that define his work. The various forms that Hare's politics take in his drama are the subject of Peter Ansorge's '"Stopping for lunch": The Political Theatre of David Hare' (pp. 92–108). The next section, 'Working with Hare', begins with Cathy Turner's 'Hare in Collaboration: Writing Dialogues' (pp. 109–22), that not only considers Hare's more formal writing partnerships, such as his longstanding associations with Howard Brenton and Tariq Ali, but other 'collaborations', such as the recent engagement with documentary sources and testimonies dramatized in *The Permanent Way* [2003]. Bella Merlin's 'Acting Hare: *The Permanent Way*' (pp. 123–37) provides a fascinating account of her experience as an actress rehearsing and performing in *The Permanent Way*. Richard Eyre's 'Directing Hare' (pp. 138–52) is a similarly illuminating account of a partnership that began in 1972 with *The Great Exhibition*, and in which, to date, Eyre has directed a further five plays. The third section, 'Hare on Screen', looks at work in the media of film and television and is represented by John Bull's '"Being taken no notice of in ten million homes": David Hare's Adventures in Television' (pp. 153–68) and Boon's interview 'Hare on Film' (pp. 169–82). In the final section, 'Overviews of Hare', Steve Nicholson's '"To ask how things might have been otherwise …": History and Memory in the Work of David Hare' (pp. 183–99) and Reinelt's 'Performing

Histories: *Plenty* and A *Map of the World* (pp. 200–19) both examine the ways in which Hare incorporates historical success in his work. Michael Mangan's '"Marbled with doubt": Satire, Reality and the Alpha Male in the Plays of David Hare' (pp. 220–35) follows on from Taylor's examination of 'redemptive women' in Hare's stage plays of the 1980s, with Mangan looking at Hare's treatment of masculinity in the same period. The volume concludes with Chris Megson and Rebellato's '"Theatre and anti-theatre": David Hare and Public Speaking' (pp. 236–49), which critically interrogates the sometimes blurred line between the role of David Hare as a high-profile public figure and his work for theatre.

In *Theatre Writings by Kenneth Tynan*, Dominic Shellard brings together a collection of the celebrated critic's writings on theatre from 1951 to 1963. The volume succeeds in presenting the astonishing range of Tynan's writings on postwar drama. Included are not only celebrated reviews of individual plays, including Tynan's famous assessment of Osborne's *Look Back in Anger* (pp. 112–13), but also witty and at times caustic profiles of individual performers ('Profile of Vivien Leigh', pp. 21–4), and then current debates about theatre censorship ('The Royal Smut-Hound', pp. 245–58) and the triviality of much early 1950s drama ('Apathy', pp. 36–8). There are also a number of reviews on notable Shakespearian productions, such as Peter Brook's 1955 *Titus Andronicus* and *Hamlet*. The work is arranged chronologically, so that at a glance one can assess patterns in the output of drama in any given year. This allows the reader not only to quickly glance at notable theatre events that went before, but also to anticipate what was on the horizon. Another valuable aspect of the book is its blend of the familiar with the unfamiliar, so that frequently quoted reviews such as 'Dodging the Ban' (pp. 128–9) are mixed with less well-known gems such as 'Out of Touch' (pp. 175–6), which features Tynan's report on a 1957 lecture given by the playwright John Whiting. Not only is Shellard's choice of material for inclusion judicious, but he provides a very readable introduction that assesses not only Tynan's contribution as a theatre critic, but also his critical role as dramaturge in the early years of the National Theatre.

The work of Samuel Beckett continues to be well represented. Richard Cave and Ben Levitas's edited collection *Irish Theatre in England* includes an essay by the present reviewer, 'Reclaiming Sam for Ireland: The Beckett on Film Project' (pp. 79–96), which considers not only disputed claims for Beckett's nationality but his incorporation as an essentially Irish dramatist in the filming of his stage plays for the ambitious *Beckett on Film* [2001] project. The volume also contains two chapters on the work of Northern Irish dramatist Gary Mitchell. Tim Miles ('Understanding Loyalty: The English Response to the Work of Gary Mitchell', pp. 97–112) and Wallace McDowell ('Traditional Routes: Challenges and Re-affirmations in the Representation of the Ulster Protestant', pp. 113–28) cover, respectively, the rise and fall of Mitchell's career in England and his position in relation to dramatic representations of the sectarian struggle in Northern Ireland.

The March 2007 issue of the journal *Performance Research* is devoted to the work of Beckett and includes an eclectic range of topics ranging from Simon Jones's 'Beckett and Warhol, Under the Eye of God' (*PerfR* 12:i[2007] 94–102), that looks at Beckett's work in film and television, and Bill Prosser's 'Drawing from Beckett' (*PerfR* 12:i[2007] 86–93), that considers the doodles Beckett added as marginalia to his writings, to Kathy Smith's 'Abject Bodies: Beckett, Orlan, Sterlac and the Politics of Contemporary Performance' (*PerfR* 12:i[2007] 66–76), that draws comparisons between Beckett's view of the body in plays such as *Not I* [1972] and *Footfalls* [1975] in relation to 'performance art'. Anna McMullan looks at the adaptation of Beckett's prose texts in 'Mutated Bodies: Stage Performances of Beckett's Late Prose Texts by Mabou Mines (1984) and Gare St. Lazare Players, Ireland (2005)' (*PerfR* 12:i[2007] 57–65), while Sarah Jane Bailes draws comparisons between Beckett's dramaturgy and the American performance group Goat Island in 'Some Slow Going: Considering Beckett and Goat Island Performance Group' (pp. 35–49). Jonathan Kalb's 'American Playwrights on Beckett' (*PAJ* 29:i[2007] 1–20) presents a fascinating cross-section of interviews with playwrights including Richard Foreman, Kushner and Paula Vogel on their responses to the work of Beckett. *Modern Drama* also represents his work: Richard Begam's 'How To Do Nothing with Words, or *Waiting for Godot* as Performativity' (*MD* 50:ii[2007] 139–67) argues that the radical break in dramatic form in Beckett's best-known play lessens when considering the linguistic experiments of his work in poetry and fiction during the 1940s. Begam's article considers the work of J.L Austin and Ludwig Wittgenstein on Beckett's work in terms of performative pronouncements that *seem* to set things in motion. In the same issue, Jon Erickson's 'Is Nothing to be Done?' (*MD* 50:ii[2007] 258–75) returns to the question of how to read Beckett's plays through a political framework. The essay begins with Herbert Blau's assertion that *Waiting for Godot* [1953] superseded Arthur Miller's *The Crucible* [1954] as the key political dramatic work of the 1950s. The article goes on to test this belief in reading *Waiting for Godot* as 'the demand for justice and fairness' (p. 261). *Modern Drama* this year also contains Elinor Fuch's 'Waiting for Recognition: An Aristotle for "Non-Aristotelian" Drama' (*MD* 50:iv[2007] 532–44), which considers *Waiting for Godot* in terms of the precepts outlined in Aristotle's *Poetics*. Patricia Boyette and Philip B. Zarrilli's 'Psychophysical Training, Physical Actions, and Performing Beckett: "Playing chess on three levels simultaneously"' (*ConTR* 17:i[2007] 70–80) looks at ongoing research work investigating acting approaches to the work.

Other work in journals continues to provide an eclectic range of approaches to drama of the period. Bella Merlin's article, '*The Permanent Way* and the Impermanent Muse' (*ConTR* 17:i[2007] 41–9), provides an extensive account of Merlin's experiences in rehearsal for Hare's *The Permanent Way* [2004]. The title of Trish Reid's '"Deformities of the frame": The Theatre of Anthony Neilson' (*ConTR* 17:iv[2007] 487–98) is something of a misnomer as the article concentrates mainly on two recent plays—*The Wonderful World of Dissocia* [2004] and *Realism* [2006]—but it is no less welcome for that. Neilson has received woefully little critical attention of late, and Reid's article does much to reassess a playwright who is all too often still associated with the so-called 'in-yer-face' dramatists of the mid-1990s. Stephen Knapper's 'Peter Hall in Rehearsal' (*ConTR* 17:iv[2007] 578–81) is an account of Peter Hall's production of *Waiting for Godot* that is concluded by an interview with the celebrated director.

The introduction of the 'Backpages' section to *Contemporary Theatre Review* is a welcome development. Here, short and often polemical submissions provide up-to-date reports on issues in British theatre. Sierz's 'New Writing: The Old Guard Departs' (*ConTR* 17:iv[2007] 596–9) provides a much-needed assessment of the current state of new writing following the changeover of artistic directors at the Royal Court, the Royal National Theatre and the Bush Theatre. Sierz notes a lull in excitement and formal experimentation in many new plays being produced and a return to a director-led style of theatre, as well as a trend towards middle-class angst as a dominant theme in much new writing. The article is sharply critical but often incisive, and the running citation of lyrics from the beat group Babyshambles to comment on the state of British theatre writing once more demonstrates that Sierz remains the authentic youthful voice of theatre criticism. In the same issue, there is also a report on the symposium 'Theatre and Truth' (*ConTR* 17:iv[2007] 599–603) held at the University of Birmingham in September 2007. Here, short pieces of writing were presented by a number of playwrights and theatre practitioners who looked at issues concerning verbatim theatre and representation of documentary sources. Respondents such as Chris Thorpe, Alex Chisholm and Steve Waters discussed the sometimes precarious relationship that exists in the enterprise of presenting empirical events to the stage. The flurry of plays written after the events of 9/11 exercised several of the speakers and debate centred on presenting known events as against an approach that utilizes fiction. The issue concludes with Rebellato's considera-tion of Dennis Kelly (*ConTR* 17:iv[2007] 603–7), a playwright who since *Debris* [2003] has represented factual events in plays such as *Taking Care of Baby* [2007] for purposes Rebellato believes to be 'less for the sake of fidelity than estrangement' (p. 605).

Stephanie Pocock's ' "God's in this apple": Eating and Spirituality in Churchill's *Light Shining in Buckinghamshire*' (*MD* 50:i[2007] 60–76) looks at the rituals of eating and suggests that these motifs inform 'religious traditions and . . . characters' attitudes towards eating' (p. 61) across a spectrum of Churchill's writing. Robert Leach's 'The Short, Astonishing History of the National Theatre of Scotland' (*MD* 50:ii[2007] 171–83) analyses the innovative achievements of the National Theatre of Scotland since its inauguration in 2006. He concludes that in large part these arise from its decision to reject the need for a permanent theatre venue.

Kwame Kwei-Armah's ' "Know whence you came": Dramatic Art and Black British Identity' (*NTQ* 23:iii[2007] 253–63) is a wide-ranging interview with the playwright that also contains a short but useful background section by Deidre Osborne that frames the interview. *New Theatre Quarterly*'s fourth issue [November 2007] is mainly devoted to the work of the late theatre practitioner Clive Barker, and the articles give an indication of his wide range of interests. Alec Patton's 'Jazz and Music-Hall Transgressions in Theatre Workshop's Production of *A Taste of Honey*' (*NTQ* 23:iv[2007] 331–6) incor-porates interview material to argue that the live jazz band accompanying the celebrated Theatre Workshop production made an important contribution to breaking realist conventions operating in the theatre at that time through motifs borrowed from music hall. Phillip B. Zarrilli's 'Embodying, Imagining, and Performing Displacement and Trauma in Central Europe Today' (*NTQ* 24:i[2008] 24–40) documents his collaboration with the playwright Kaite O'Reilly and performers on *Speaking Stones*, a piece commissioned by Theatre Aou of Graz. David Barnett's 'When Is a Play Not a Drama? Two Examples of Postdramatic Theatre Texts' (*NTQ* 24:i[2008] 14–23) revisits Martin Crimp's *Attempts on her Life* [1997] and Sarah Kane's *4.48 Psychosis*, which stand as perhaps the best-known British examples of Hans-Thies Lehmann's term 'postdramatic theatre'.

The work of Hans-Thies Lehmann looms prominently in Christoph Henke and Martin Middeke's edited collection of papers from the annual *Contemporary Drama in English* conference, entitled *Drama and/after Postmodernism*. Lehmann provides the opening article, 'Word and Stage in Postdramatic Theatre' (pp. 37–54), where he sketches out his definition of postdramatic theatre and relates it to the late work of Kane. Brian Richardson's 'Plot after Postmodernism' (pp. 55–67) considers work such as Beckett's *Endgame* [1957], Churchill's *Traps* [1977] and Crimp's *Attempts on her Life* [1997] which 'subvert the classical conceptions of plot' (p. 55). Susan Blatte's 'Is the Concept of Character Still Relevant in Contemporary Drama?' (pp. 69–81) does the same with examples drawn from the work of Pinter, Churchill and Kane. Churchill also forms the subject of Siân Adiseshiah's 'Still a Socialist? Political Commitment in Caryl Churchill's *The Skriker* and *Far Away*' (pp. 277–92). Laurens De Vos's 'Stoppard's Dallying with Spectres: Rosencrantz and Guildenstern Live On and On' (pp. 106–25) is a highly theorized reading via Lacan and Derrida that offers the suggestion that Stoppard's protagonists' real fear resides not in their deaths, but in a constant return through the meta-performance of *Hamlet*. Sarah Heinz's ' "Funny thing memory, isn't it?": Deconstructing Remembered Identities in Michael Frayn's *Donkey's Years* and *Copenhagen*' (pp. 127–47), looks at ideas of cultural memory through Frayn's plays; Clara Escoda Agustí's ' "Head green water to sing": Minimalism and Indeterminacy in Martin Crimp's *Attempts on her Life*' (pp. 149–63) and Sierz's ' "The darkest place": Certainty and Doubt in Martin Crimp's *Fewer Emergencies*' (pp. 293–310) both look at the work of a writer who has often been associated with the term postmodernism. Michal Lachman's 'The Colours of History or Scenes from the Inquiry into Verbatim Drama' (pp. 311–25), and Markus Wessendorf's 'Postmodern Drama Post-9/11: Adriano Shaplin's *Pugilist Specialist* and David Hare's *Stuff Happens*' (pp. 325–50) both look at the uses made of documentary sources in recent plays. The volume concludes with a transcript of the playwright Richard Bean in conversation with Sierz (pp. 351–62.).

Jenny Spencer's 'Performing Translation in Contemporary Anglo-American Drama' (*TJ* 59:iii[2007] 389–410) considers a number of American, Irish and British plays, including David Edgar's *Pentecost* [1994] in terms of how it translates non-English cultures.

Finally, the recent work of Brenton is the subject of two journal articles this year. The prolific Janelle Reinelt's 'The "Rehabilitation" of Howard Brenton' (*TDR* 51:iii[2007] 167–74) considers Brenton's fall from favour during the

1990s and his re-emergence in the millennial decade with plays such as *In Extremis* [2006] and *Paul* [2006]. John H. Baker's 'Gospel Truth? Howard Brenton's *Paul* and the Bible' (*NTQ* 23:iii[2007] 264–71) provides a comparative analysis of Brenton's dramatic construction of Paul from biblical sources. The article also considers Brenton's motivation in writing the play and concludes that it is perhaps Paul's fundamentalism, and the currency this term holds today, that makes the subject a compelling one for Brenton.

6. Pre-1950 Poetry

The Cambridge Companion series continued to expand in 2007 with the *Companion to Modernist Poetry*, edited by Alex Davis and Lee Jenkins, and the *Companion to Twentieth-Century English Poetry*, edited by Neil Corcoran. Davis and Jenkins aim to reflect recent critical developments, including the 'new modernist studies' and widening critical canons of modernism. Their companion opens with four general essays on the background to modernism: David Ayers considers the development of the concepts of 'history' and 'poetry' from Aristotle, through Kant and Hegel, to Marx and then Freud (pp. 11–27); Paul Peppis surveys key movements such as Futurism, Imagism and the Harlem Renaissance and traces the role of small-scale periodicals in their development and dissemination (pp. 28–50); Peter Nicholls investigates modernist attitudes towards the sources of inspiration (pp. 51–67); and Cristanne Miller considers the role of gender and sexuality in modernist poetry, from the attitudes of male poets towards women to the work of female poets themselves (pp. 68–84).

A central section of the book is devoted to individual authors: Laurence Rainey assesses the relative claims of T.S. Eliot and Ezra Pound to be representative of modernism (pp. 87–113); Rachel Blau DuPlessis considers H.D. as a visionary poet, exploring her use of mythopoeia as a critique of hegemonic forms of myth (pp. 114–25); and Anne Fogarty explores Yeats's claim to be a modernist poet (pp. 126–46). There are also essays on individual American poets by Bonnie Costello (pp. 163–80), Mark Snoggins (pp. 181–94) and Sharon Lynette Jones (pp. 195–206), and an essay on postcolonial modernist poetry by Jahan Ramazani (pp. 207–21). Drew Milne considers the difficulties associated with British modernism in the light of the domination of Anglo-American figures such as Eliot and Pound (pp. 147–62), and Jason Harding provides a survey of the critical reception of modernism and the shifting inclusions and exclusions of its canonical authors (pp. 225–43).

The first half of Corcoran's volume on twentieth-century English poetry contains several essays relevant to this entry. Daniel Albright surveys the forms of modernist verse (pp. 24–41), demonstrating the influence of Old English, classical, Chinese and Japanese poetry upon the metres of Pound, H.D. and Eliot. Peter Howarth compares the work of A.E. Housman, Charlotte Mew, Thomas Hardy and Edward Thomas (pp. 59–73), discerning a common interest in 'division and constraint' and in 'ironis[ing] conventions of rural idyll' (p. 59). Sandra Gilbert starts with Eliot's mixed feelings about D.H. Lawrence, surveying Lawrence's progression towards freer forms of verse and arguing that his poetry may be understood in terms of Eliot's stated aim to get 'beyond poetry' (pp. 74–86). Corcoran centres his account of war poetry upon Wilfred Owen, but manages to encompass work by Edward Thomas, Siegfried Sassoon, Isaac Rosenberg and Ivor Gurney too (pp. 87–101). Michael O'Neill considers Auden's formal maturation during the 1930s, identifying the technical achievements of 'Lay your sleeping head' and 'September 1, 1939' with a resonant response to the tensions between poetry and propaganda (pp. 105–16). Adam Piette examines the 'looking-glass' experience of Keith Douglas during the Second World War (pp. 117–30) and concludes that the work of Douglas, Alan Lewis and Sidney Keyes constitutes an 'inaugural and collective response to the new war machine of the twentieth century' (p. 129). Edward Larrisey seeks the formal ties and influences that connect William Empson, Dylan Thomas and W.S. Graham (pp. 131–44).

Both of these Companion volumes are lacklustre in parts—a by-product of their role as introductory surveys. Still, they are likely to be serviceable to students dipping into individual essays. The best of these engage closely with the texture of their subject, as when Corcoran considers the loving, homoerotic gaze that Owen turns upon dead and dying fellow soldiers, when O'Neill examines the workings of Auden's poetry, or when Rainey makes detailed use of unpublished material in his account of Pound and Eliot.

Pericles Lewis's *Cambridge Introduction to Modernism* contains significant material relating to poetry: chapter 4 on modern poetry focuses mainly on *The Waste Land*, but elsewhere in the book Lewis draws attention to work by Eliot, Owen, Pound and the Imagists. This is an introductory overview for 'nonspecialists' (p. xvii), but the lists of standard critical works on modernism and some recent research will be useful to undergraduates and some postgraduates. Lewis unites his material by considering modernism as the period of 'a crisis of representation' (p. xviii). Although focusing on work in English and largely written in England, he sketches international movements of interest too, making a concerted effort to bring reference to the visual arts into his discussion.

Sharon Cameron devotes two essays in her collection *Impersonality* to Empson (pp. 1–20) and Eliot (pp. 144–79). Empson's fascination with representations of the face of the Buddha serves as a useful introduction to her interest in 'a subjectivity that isn't a subjectivity, a person who is impersonal or who aims, though cannot will, to be so' (p. 12). She concludes from Empson's unpublished science fiction, *The Royal Beasts*, that he found uncomfortable judgements 'about human value, about the value of being human' (p. 20) within the Buddha's gaze. Her essay on *Four Quartets* explores the way in which voices in Eliot's poem overlap and resist reduction to a single source. Cameron reads this as a 'disarticulation' that represents 'experience that is particularized without being particularized as someone's' (p. 149). She explores the criss-crossing allusive sources of Eliot's writing in relation to the persistence of identity after death in the form of voice, combining exposition of Eliot's literary sources with attention to the ambiguities surrounding the contexts of utterance in *Four Quartets*.

Robert Shaw's wide-ranging survey *Blank Verse: A Guide to its History and Use* incorporates reference to a number of the poets under consideration here in a chapter on 'Blank Verse and Modernism' (pp. 82–160). He finds Robert Frost's influence in Edward Thomas's rhythmic variation and considers the uses of blank verse for Robert Graves and Siegfried Sassoon in conveying the experience of war. Eliot receives more extended treatment: Shaw traces the 'ghost' of pentameter within revisions to *The Waste Land* (p. 126) and examines the impact of his rhythmic deviations from blank verse upon subsequent generations.

Two of the chapters in *The All-Sustaining Air: Romantic Legacies and Renewals in British, American, and Irish Poetry since 1900*, Michael O'Neill's study of filiations between Romantic poetry and twentieth-century poets, are relevant to this entry. O'Neill sketches the influence of Shelley upon Eliot (pp. 60–82), tracing local allusions as well as larger patterns. Poised between hope and despair, 'What the Thunder Said', he claims, adopts 'a characteristic Romantic stance' (p. 68). Eliot is, O'Neill argues, 'powerfully counter-Romantic' (p. 81), a formulation that suggests Eliot's critical reaction against Shelley was inseparable from his influence. O'Neill also finds that Auden 'works as a complicatedly post-Romantic poet' (pp. 83–104). Auden, he suggests, takes 'poetic bearings' from 'Romantic precursors' (p. 89), just as Stephen Spender's work contains a reconciling 'neo-Romantic idiom' (p. 103). These are fluent and lively readings with an ever-present grasp on the detail of poetic form.

The year 2007 also saw the first publication of a fully edited and annotated edition of Hope Mirrlees's *Paris: A Poem* in Bonnie Kime Scott's anthology *Gender in Modernism* (pp. 261–303), a volume which revises and complements Scott's previous collaborative anthology *Gender and Modernism* [1990]. *Gender in Modernism* gathers a range of neglected modernist texts and provides introductory essays by modern critics which broach important questions about gender and race. *Paris: a Poem* is introduced and extensively annotated by Julia Briggs, and its renewed availability is a significant achievement.

Eliot's understanding of tradition in 'Tradition and the Individual Talent' is a recurrent element of recent scholarship on him. Giovanni Cianci and Jason Harding bring together a variety of international scholars in *T.S. Eliot and the Concept of Tradition* to address this topic. Some readings are responses to Eliot's work by subsequent thinkers: Claudia Corti considers the influence of Eliot's essay upon 'receptionist' understandings of tradition in the work of Hans Blumenberg; Aleida Assmann argues that Eliot revises historical thinking about the canon, questioning 'obsolete dichotomies, such as tradition and innovation' (p. 22) in favour of the 'systemic'; Stan Smith reads the essay in relation to different kinds of frontiers in order to bring out a motif of transgression in Eliot's life and work.

Most of the contributions are fairly straightforward attempts at providing historical contexts to 'Tradition and the Individual Talent': Jewel Spears Brooker places it within the philosophical context of Eliot's studies in Kantian idealism at Harvard. Bernard Brugière considers it in relation to the critics and philosophers Eliot encountered in Paris before the First World War, identifying the influence of works such as Julian Benda's *Belphégor* and Charles Maurras's *L'Avenir de l'intelligence*. Jason Harding follows Eliot's career through his literary journalism: he claims that 'Tradition and the

Individual Talent' is 'a carefully deliberated polemic' (p. 98) and a rebuff to the nihilism of the Dadaists, rather than a break with tradition. Massimo Bacigalupo argues for the influence of Pound's *The Age of Romance* and the aesthetics of the early cantos upon Eliot's understanding of tradition. Giovanni Cianci examines contemporary debates within the pictorial arts and the avant-garde: Eliot's tradition, he argues, is a reaction against Futurism and part of a '*rappel à l'ordre*' after the chaos of the First World War (p. 123). Caroline Patey shows how Eliot's essay is 'profoundly enmeshed' (p. 162) in the anthropological writings of Lucien Lévy-Brühl, Émile Durkheim, E.B. Tyler and Wilhelm Wundt that Eliot read at Harvard and reviewed in journals. She identifies the Australian anthropology of Baldwin Spencer and Frank Gillen as an influence upon the desert landscapes of *The Waste Land*. Max Saunders contrasts Eliot and Ford Madox Ford. They shared, he suggests, an interest in the effacement of personality through art and a vision of tradition as dynamic rather than static.

The best of these essays, such as Brooker's or Patey's, generate a sense of paradigm shift as well as providing informative historical material. But there is also a strong whiff of deliberate paradox: Clive Wilmer contests Philip Larkin's claim to reject the influence of Eliot's modernism, tracing Eliotic personae in poems by Tom Gunn, Sylvia Plath and Geoffrey Hill; Marjorie Perloff discerns affinities between Eliot and Marcel Duchamp, identifying their shared interest in the artist as a medium and their drive to escape Romantic expressions of personality through art; Michael Hollington attempts to trace links between Eliot and Alois Riegl, by considering the direct influence of Wilhelm Worringer, T.E. Hulme and Herbert Read; Brett Neilson attempts to reconcile the Marxism of Walter Benjamin's 'Theses on the Philosophy of History' with Eliot's right-wing politics through their strategies of allusion and their dealings with the eclipse of history. Neilson's litotic observation that Eliot and Benjamin 'may not be wholly irreconcilable' (p. 207) indicates the shaky underpinnings involved in such controversialism.

Peter White tackles similar ground in ' "Tradition and the Individual Talent" Revisited' (*RES* 58[2007] 364–92). He discerns fluctuations within Eliot's attitudes by comparing essays and articles written immediately before and after 'Tradition and the Individual Talent', by discussing Eliot's correspondence in detail and by considering his debt to Clive Bell's 'Tradition and Movements'. White's interest in 'Modern Tendencies in Poetry', an article only published by Eliot in Madras, borders on obsession, but his familiarity with the detail of Eliot's writing career and its publishing contexts is impressive.

Rebecca Beasley's *Theorists of Modern Poetry* considers Eliot together with Pound and Hulme. It consists of six chapters: the first traces the origins of modernism as a reaction to aestheticism; the second explores the philosophical influence of Bergson and Bradley on modernism; the third chapter describes the anti-democratic politics of modernism, from Hulme and Eliot's fascination with the Action Française to Pound's individualism; the fourth chapter addresses the questions of tradition broached in Harding and Cianci's volume, evoking the influence of J.G. Frazer and of Ernest Fenollosa's Chinese scholarship; the fifth chapter considers *Cantos* and *The Waste Land* as war poems; the sixth chapter explores Pound and Eliot's social beliefs and their investment in Social Credit and Christianity, respectively. The book finishes with a brief treatment of the afterlife of modernism, concluding that the legacy of these poets and critics was a tradition of close reading. It is a tantalizing combination of scholarship and reduction, devoting only one page to the vexed issue of Eliot's anti-Semitic views and summarizing concepts such as 'existential historicism' in scant side-panels. Nevertheless, the informative material on the philosophical background of modernism make this a very useful volume for undergraduates.

In the *Yeats Eliot Review*, Kinereth Meyer discerns common ground among *Four Quartets*, St Augustine and Derrida in 'Between Augustine and Derrida: Reading T.S. Eliot's Poetry of Exile' (*YER* 24:ii[2007] 3–9). These writers, she argues, share an interest in spiritual exile and in language as a form of exile. In 'The Aristotelian Mr. Eliot: Structure and Strategy in *The Waste Land*' (*YER* 24:ii[2007] 11–23), John H. Timmerman argues that 'Eliot carefully adapts the philosophy of Aristotle to nuance his analysis of the modern human condition' (p. 12). In practice, this means that Timmerman discerns signs of a 'debased trinity' (p. 21) within *The Waste Land*, which he traces to Aristotle's analysis of the passions, his teleological philosophy and an interest in the *via negativa* of Aquinas. In 'Eliot's Shadows: Autography and Style in *The Hollow Men*' (*YER* 24:iv[2007] 12–24), Joseph Jonghyun Jeon interprets evasions and ambiguities in the language of *The Hollow Men* as a symptom of Eliot's difficulties in reconciling himself to an orthodox religious position. Identifying a process of 'echolocation' (p. 3), Chad Parmentier traces allusive interconnections between Eliot's poetry and the work of Yeats in 'Eliot's Echo Rhetoric' (*YER* 24:iv[2007] 2–12). Peter Lowe's article, 'Cultural Continuity in a Time of War: Virginia Woolf's *Between the Acts* and T.S. Eliot's *East Coker*' (*YER* 24:iii[2007] 2–19), attempts to tease out the links between Eliot's late poetry and Woolf's final novel. They share, he argues, a conception of history as pageant and an interest in the unifying power of music.

Elsewhere, Roger Bellin also scrutinizes the difficulties of *Four Quartets*, pointing out ambiguities within passages that seem deceptively clear in 'The Seduction of Argument and the Danger of Parody in the *Four Quartets*' (*TCL* 53:iv[2007] 421–41). There is a risk, Bellin argues, that such solemnity slips into parody, but this in turn may, he suggests, embody 'rigorous self-criticism' and Eliot's belief in 'the inadequacy of poetry to its goal' (p. 433). In 'Eliot's "Portrait of a Lady" Restored' (*EIC* 57[2007] 42–58), Derek Roper seeks to redress hostile accounts of the unnamed 'Lady' addressed in Eliot's poem. His is a sympathetic but curiously old-fashioned essay, which seeks to recuperate her character on the basis of hypothesis and character judgement rather than fresh textual or historical evidence. David Gervais claims that Racine deserves precedence over Dante in relation to Eliot in 'T.S. Eliot and Racine: Tragedy and Resignation in *Bérénice*' (*CQ* 36[2007] 51–70). *Bérénice*, he argues, models a mood of 'submission to suffering' (p. 55) and embodies chaste, classical formal values congenial to Eliot. K. Narayana Chandran's 'A Receipt for Deceit: T.S. Eliot's "To the Indians who Died in Africa"' (*JML* 30:iii[2007] 52–69) is severe on this neglected piece of occasional poetry. Chandran catches Eliot betraying 'imperialist biases' (p. 52), undervaluing the contribution of

Indian soldiers to Britain's imperial war effort and producing a piece of verse 'morally high-toned and rhetorically deceitful' (p. 60).

The title of Morag Shiach's essay, '"To purify the dialect of the tribe": Modernism and Language Reform' (*Mo/Mo* 14:i[2007] 21–34), indicates the prominent role she gives to Eliot when investigating the links between modernism and 'various projects of linguistic "purification"' (p. 21). Eliot's 'wrestle' with words in *Four Quartets* features alongside the Society for Pure English, Esperanto and Hugh MacDiarmid's experiments with Scots dialect. Paradoxically, Shiach concludes that Eliot's allusion to Mallarmé confirms how central the English language was to his poetry.

The only major difference between David Trotter's chapter on Eliot in *Modernism and Cinema* and his article 'T.S. Eliot and Cinema' (*Mo/Mo* 13:ii[2006] 237–65) reviewed last year (*YWES* 87[2007] 934) is the addition of four pages which argue for a distinction between cinematic forms of knowledge and Henri Bergson's theory of intuition. However, his attempt to extend critical thinking about the relationship between modernism and cinema remains an important intervention in Eliot studies and interdisciplinary work on film.

As well as in these journals, Eliot continues to receive significant critical attention within the scope of larger arguments about the period, such as Marina MacKay's *Modernism and World War II*. She considers the treatment of an older generation in Eliot's later poetry in relation to her claim that modernism found its 'end' in the Second World War. 'Gerontion' and the 'old men' of the *Four Quartets* are strikingly compared to Colonel Blimp and the political advocates of appeasement. MacKay argues generally that the decline of Britain's imperial holdings forced modernists 'to scrutinise the political and moral claims of insular nationality' (p. 2), and she traces a strange consonance between modernism's formal innovations and the shock to British public life brought by the war. Her aim is 'to give a context for experimental form and political impurity' (p. 14). As such, she reads *Four Quartets* as more cagey about the organicist, rural roots of culture than Eliot's public pronouncements in prose, and she reads the uncertainties generated by the form of these poems as 'situational thinking', apt to the uncertainties of the Blitz and the failings of some members of the political establishment. The connections she traces between form and historical or political context produce sometimes startling results: they're not always convincing, but they *are* thought-provoking.

MacKay's historical thesis is at odds with Vincent Sherry's contribution to *Modernism and Colonialism*, edited by Richard Begam and Michael Valdez Moses (pp. 111–35). Sherry locates the crisis of British imperialism at the beginning of the First World War, when Eliot moved to London. He treats the Easter Rising as representative and reads shifts of cadence within Eliot's quatrain poems as 'a rhythmical synonym for the dying fall of an older order of empire' (p. 120). Both MacKay and Sherry read formal effects within the verse as symptomatic of an engagement with wider historical and political forces. This indirect approach to political expression may help to account for their divergent understandings of history.

Lee Oser contrasts Eliot's engaged relationship to Aristotle with his rejection of Matthew Arnold in *The Ethics of Modernism*. His chapter on Eliot culminates with an affirmation of the 'moral coherence' (p. 64) of *The Cocktail Party* as part of the book's wider argument that the 'moral project' of modernism was 'to transform human nature through the use of art' (p. 2). Andrew Miller dedicates one and a half chapters of *Modernism and the Crisis of Sovereignty* (pp. 1–21, 89–128) to Eliot as part of his general argument that Eliot, Yeats and Woolf respond to 'a globally pervasive crisis of sovereignty' (p. xix) around the time of the First World War by cultivating a 'postnational' perspective (p. i). Miller argues that Eliot's theory of the 'dissociation of sensibility' is inseparable from anxieties relating to the effects of the American Civil War. Considering 'the metaphorical structure of Eliot's rhetoric' (p. 90), Miller identifies splits and tensions within Eliot's thought, which is, he argues, 'powerfully implicated in many persistent conflicts concerning the character of social, political and cultural sovereignty' (p. 90). *Modernism and the Crisis of Sovereignty* is dense with theories of statehood and identity, from Pierre Bourdieu and Foucault to Étienne Balibar and Giorgio Agamben. This reflects Miller's sense that the crises of modernism are pertinent to recent global developments.

Notes and Queries continues to provide snippets of scholarly findings relating to Eliot's work. A.V. Schmidt elaborates a pattern of allusion to John Davies's 'Orchestra' from *Ash Wednesday* to *Four Quartets* (*N&Q* 54[2007] 164–7), Derek Roper investigates the 'cracked cornets' from 'Portrait of a Lady', attempting to trace the exact kind of instrument Eliot had in mind (*N&Q* 54[2007] 167–9), and Peter White points out that Eliot's essay on George Wyndham, 'A Romantic Patrician', was first published during celebrations of Leonard da Vinci's quater-centenary (*N&Q* 54[2007] 173–5). Eliot's comparison between Wyndham and da Vinci, which has puzzled critics, turns out to be 'a thought-provoking topical aside' (p. 175).

The essays in *The International Reception of T.S. Eliot*, edited by Elisabeth Däumer and Shyamal Bagchee, look beyond Eliot's poetry to his influence on others and the response of subsequent generations to his work. Many of the essays focus on Europe: William Marx examines Eliot's relationship with the *Nouvelle revue française* and identifies a 'cultural misunderstanding' (p. 32) whereby the *NRF* was prepared to advocate avant-garde critical practice, but was less tolerant of iconoclastic creative practice. Däumer compares Eva Hesse's 'anagogic' readings and translations of *The Waste Land* with those of E.R. Curtius, raising questions about Eliot's sexuality as well as assessing his impact in Germany. Astradur Eysteinsson and Eysteinn Thorvaldsson consider Eliot's influence upon Icelandic literature, from the belated translation of *The Waste Land* in 1948 to the gradual accommodation of Eliot's poetics to traditional Icelandic forms. Stefano Maria Casella considers Eliot's reception in Italy through the critical work of Carlo Linati and Mario Praz and the poetry of Eugenio Montale and Mario Luzi. Santiago Rodriguez Guerrero-Strachan examines Eliot's reception in Spain through the critical responses of poets such as Juan Ramon Jiminez, Luis Cerruda and Jaime Gil de Biedma, and maps responses to Eliot against Spain's troubled political history. J.H. Copley charts Eliot's relationship with E.R. Curtius, examining the decline of their friendship in the 1930s and 1940s. Copley reads Curtius's criticisms of Eliot as '*ad hominem* attacks' (p. 248) in retaliation for Eliot's perceived resistance to the possibility of recuperating German influence within European culture after the Second World War.

But this collection also aims to diversify understanding of Eliot by considering his resonance beyond Europe: Juan E. De Castro links Borges's creative practice of allusion and literary re-creation to his reading of Eliot's ideas about tradition. Sean Cotter investigates Lucian Blaga's translation of 'Journey of the Magi' into Romanian, clarifying the political and cultural sensitivities of translation under Soviet rule. Magda Heydel describes Eliot as an enabling influence upon the work of Czesław Miłosz, concluding that his engagement with *The Waste Land* was 'creative, never purely imitative' (p. 240). Lihui Liu considers Eliot's influence upon modern Chinese literature, from translations in the 1930s to the influence of visiting academics and poets such as Empson and I.A. Richards. Liu also outlines Eliot's assimilation within the work of the 'nine poets' in the 1940s, his relative neglect under Maoism and more recent attempts to reassess his influence. Shunichi Takayanagi provides a similar history of Eliot's reception in Japan, describing Nishiwaki Junzaburō's experiences in England during the 1920s, the work of George Fraser and Edmund Blunden as 'cultural ambassadors' (p. 186), a burgeoning Anglophile enthusiasm for Eliot's work from the 1950s onwards and the influence of Eliot upon the work of Nobel prizewinner Ōe Kenzaburo.

Some of these readings have implications for postcolonial understandings of Eliot: Matthew Hart discusses Eliot's influence in the Caribbean and the value of his 'auditory imagination' for the poetry of Edward Kamau Brathwaite. He sees Brathwaite's verse as a 'respectful encounter' with Eliot (p. 21). Shirshendu Chakrabarti's account of Eliot's influence on Bengali poetry examines translations and assimilations of his work into the poetry of Samur Sen and Bishnu Dey, where Eliot acts as a 'submerged voice' (p. 99). Leonore Gerstein discusses Eliot's reception by Israeli poets, from T. Carmi's mythopoeic poetry to the 'unconscious affinity' with Eliot in the poetry and criticism of Natan Zach. Brian Trehearne considers the mixed inheritance that Eliot represented for Canadian poet A.J.M. Smith. Eliot's work on tradition aided Smith's developing aesthetic of allusion, but his influence may have contributed to accusations that Smith's work was derivative. Trehearne determines that Eliot's theory of poetic impersonality was the source for 'a kind of creative ethics' in Smith's work (p. 209)

The volume concludes in a peculiarly personal way with a series of autobiographical accounts of Eliot's impact: Meyer illustrates the difficulties of 'cross-cultural' readings of Eliot's work from her experiences of teaching both Arab and Jewish students at Bar-Ilan University in Israel, Srimati Mukherjee describes her encounters with Eliot from childhood in Bengal and study at Calcutta to teaching his work at American universities, and Sean Pryor charts his experiences as an Australian of the strangeness of Eliot's work.

Rachel Wetzsteon's study of Auden's sources, *Influential Ghosts*, is surprisingly short. It contains chapters on Auden's early interest in Hardy, on 'structural allusion', on Auden's reworking of the elegy and on his interest in Kierkegaard. The readings are lucid and thoughtful, but hardly groundbreaking. The chapters on Kierkegaard and Hardy trace a common pattern of infatuation followed by Auden's later decision to distance himself from the object of his affection. Wetzsteon's strongest line of argument is that Auden's allusive practice embodies a 'deeply ambivalent attitude toward the poetry of the past' (p. 32), but *Influential Ghosts* is strangely inconclusive and lacks a final chapter to bring together the intelligent material it gathers.

Auden also features prominently in *The Forms of Youth*, Stephen Burt's account of the representation of adolescence in twentieth-century poetry, forming a keystone in Burt's chapter on British modernism (pp. 44–82). This concentrates on the representation of school life in Auden's juvenilia, finding echoes of school in early works such as *The Orators* and *Paid on Both Sides*. Auden's poetry emerges as one of the 'inherited forms' by which Philip Larkin, Thom Gunn and Basil Bunting explore adolescence as 'a space for nonutilitarian, non-reproductive pleasure and for specialised verbal exchange, devoted to self-construction, meant to give pleasure, and defined (by others, from the outside) as immature' (p. 76).

Oxford University Press has served Empson well. Having published two volumes of biography and a selection of letters previously, it published Matthew Bevis's collection *Some Versions of Empson* in 2007. The volume is marked throughout by a curious sense that Empson constitutes some kind of special case: Seamus Perry's essay on Empson and Coleridge begins, 'One of the questions that most interests admirers of Empson' (p. 104), as if to acknowledge the existence of a group that shared a somewhat recherché taste. There are a number of recurrent themes in the volume, such as Empson's idiosyncratic style of 'argufying' and his obsessive denunciation of neo-Christian critics in the latter part of his career. Nevertheless, the topics covered are varied and wide-ranging. Deborah Bowman explores familial influences upon Empson through the allusive texture of his poetry. Adam Piette describes Empson's defence of the 'cool logic' associated with children's thought patterns as a form of sanity in the face of impending war. Peter Robinson tracks Empson's renunciation of writing poetry through his translations of the poems of a Japanese acquaintance. Jason Harding maps Empson's experiences in China before and after the war onto his intellectual output. Eric Griffiths identifies Empson's failure to attend to those aspects of Christianity which did not fit his argument that the crucifixion constituted torture-worship. Hugh Haughton explores Empson's abiding interest in nonsense through his criticism of the Alice books and through the unusual logic of his own metaphysical conceits. Matthew Creasy presents a paradoxical case for appreciating the tact of this famously brusque critic. Paul Fry addresses Empson's intervention in debates about the role and value of authorial intention in literary criticism. Christopher Norris suggests that *The Structure of Complex Words* sheds light on recent philosophical thinking about discrepant forms of linguistic usage such as malapropism. Katy Price maps the conceits of Empson's love poetry onto Arthur Eddington's scientific writings, revealing the ways in which scientific theories of the universe open up models for thinking about the possibility of knowing others or acknowledging their otherness. Susan Wolfson considers the gendering of Empson's critical language, and the volume concludes by reprinting a neglected interview with

Empson from the 1970s, edited by John Haffenden. Perry and Haughton's essays are the strongest and most lucid, but Bevis's introduction is excellent: filled with articulate insights, it communicates a genuine delight in reading Empson's critical prose.

There were no monographs on Kipling's poetry in 2007, but a special issue of the *Journal of Modern Literature* reprints Michael Lackey's transcription of E.M. Forster's 1909 lecture on Kipling's poetry (*JML* 30:iii[2007] 12–30), along with 'Masculinity Amalgamated: Colonialism, Homosexuality and Forster's Kipling' by Jesse Matz (*JML* 30:iii[2007] 31–51), which attempts to use Forster's lecture as proof that homosexuality 'entailed a postcolonial mindset' (p. 31). Forster's basic argument is that Kipling's poetry has been admired by the middle classes for its vital 'passion' (p. 14). He finds Kipling's representation of cockney speech unconvincing in parts and disdains the jingoism of Kipling's imperialism, before concluding with praise for the 'tender' wisdom of his poetry about children (p. 27). The editor of the *Kipling Journal* explores C.G. Leland's comic poems about Hans Breitmann and their influence upon Kipling's demotic language in the *Barrack-Room Ballads*, reprinting Kipling's parodic tribute from 1896, 'How Breitmann Became President on the Bicycle Ticket' (*KJ* 81:cccxxi[2007] 48–59). Traugott Lawler reproduces a 'Charade' by Kipling, pasted into a copy of *Original Charades* by L.B.R. Briggs, in '"Charade": A New Verse Note by Kipling from 1892' (*KJ* 81:cccxxii[2007] 34–9), supplementing this with a meditation upon this (now lost) genre of riddle.

YWES received no monographs on the poetry of Hardy either, but his work received significant coverage in journals. In 'Thomas Hardy and the Impersonal Lyric' (*JML* 30:iii[2007] 95–115), Susan Miller identifies Hardy's use of retrospect as the source of a split within the subjectivity of his lyric poems. His poetic narrators do not look back with sudden clarity, she observes: 'understanding is cumulative rather than momentary' (p. 101), and this generates a dissociation between the speaker and his experiences. The result is a 'surprisingly impersonal form of lyric' (p. 96) which she compares to the work of modernists such as Pound and Eliot. Hardy's poetry also features in Tim Armstrong's essay, 'Player Piano: Poetry and Sonic Modernity' (*Mo/Mo* 14:i[2007] 1–19). 'In a Museum' is used to illustrate 'the ontological realm of recorded music: music detached from its producer' (p. 9). Armstrong cites the philosophy of Schopenhauer and the musical theory of Hermann von Helmholz to explore the links between music and bodies, and then traces the consequences for the poetry of Hardy and Wallace Stevens.

In *With Poetry and Philosophy*, David Miller contrives critical dialogue between the Marxist theories of Theodor Adorno and Hardy's poetry (pp. 85–98). The possibility that poetry might achieve uplift by negation is, he argues, reduced by Hardy to the 'ghost or memory of the possibility of transcendence' (p. 85). Poems such as 'Channel Firing' and 'Memory and I' embody in their form, Miller claims, a 'sense of belated or dead voices' (p. 93) that anticipates Adorno's intimation of the impossibility of poetry in the wake of Auschwitz.

Sally Minogue argues that Hardy aimed to 'obliterate' class and sex distinctions within his poetry by incorporating demotic language ('The Dialect of Common Sense: Hardy, Language and Modernity', *THJ* 23[2007] 156–72).

She finds modernist ironies in 'Drummer Hodge' and the doubleness of *The Dynasts*, discovering 'the insignia of modernity' (p. 162) within the shifting perspectives, multiple ironies and textual reflexivity of Hardy's poetry.

Edward Thomas continues to garner critical response, as well as poetic tribute. *Branch-Lines: Edward Thomas and Contemporary Poetry*, edited by Guy Cuthburtson and Lucy Newlyn, brings together four essays on Thomas by Edna Longley (pp. 29–41), Jem Poster (pp. 43–50), Guy Cuthbertson (pp. 57–63) and Lucy Newlyn (pp. 64–82), with anecdotes and poems by fifty-four contemporary poets, including Seamus Heaney, Andrew Motion and Anne Stevenson. These writers respond to Thomas or describe poetic debts to his work. Longley rereads Thomas in relation to ecology, war and memory, reviewing his claim to 'adumbrate an aesthetic of war poetry' (p. 36) and identifying his poetry as 'a kind of memory bank' (p. 41). Jem Poster measures Thomas against the modernists, tracing links between Thomas and the novels of Woolf. Compared to Eliot, Thomas is, he suggests, 'similarly, if perhaps less knowingly, representative' of early twentieth-century uncertainties (p. 44). Cuthbertson reflects on Thomas's appeal to adolescents, tracing his influence upon Auden and Larkin. Thomas's poetry cultivates this appeal, he argues, without being adolescent in itself, and he suggests that Thomas's influence upon Auden lingered longer than Auden cared to admit. Newlyn describes the importance for Thomas of 'the rhythm, experience and literature of walking' (p. 67) as one source of 'measured, internal quietness' (p. 74) and a syntax which 'carries the freight of complex patterns of thought' (p. 75). Contemporary poets, she suggests, 'inhabit' this syntax—it is a significant part of his legacy. As well as these poetic and critical tributes to Thomas, the book itself is a glossy homage, filled with previously unpublished black and white photographs of the poet and facsimiles of his manuscripts.

Judy Kendall's *Edward Thomas's Poets* reproduces poems by Thomas and his literary acquaintance alongside letters to and from Thomas. Kendall's introduction (pp. xiii–xxvi) is strongly weighted towards the conditions under which Thomas composed poetry, both his physical location and the material arrangement of his drafts on the page. This is also reflected in an appendix consisting of extracts from Thomas's letters regarding the composition process. As a whole, the volume does a useful job of highlighting how important dialogue with his contemporaries was to Thomas and the relationship between his poems and the times and places where they were composed.

Modernism from the Margins by Chris Wigginton alternates chapters between Louis MacNeice and Dylan Thomas. The chapters on Thomas consider 'the life of the poem at the level of language' (p. 32), exploring an intractability in Thomas's use of metaphor which Wigginton compares to the cultivated difficulties of modernism. Citing the psychoanalytic theories of Freud and Kristeva, he discovers powerfully disruptive unconscious forces at work, significant to 'a semi-surrealized metaphysical mode' within Thomas's poetry, which, Wigginton argues, is 'forged . . . from a marginalised and . . . problematic Welsh modernism' (p. 50). Two subsequent chapters elaborate on these claims by examining Thomas's poems in relation to concepts of the monstrous and by considering their Welshness. Wigginton emphasizes Thomas's interest in 'ambiguous and fragmented identities' (p. 116), but the alternating structure of *Modernism from the Margins* itself fragments a thoughtful account of MacNeice and Thomas as marginalized poets from differing regional backgrounds, obscuring the thread of his argument at times.

Marion Eide's 'Witness and Trophy Hunting: Writing Violence from the Great War Trenches' (*Criticism* 49:i[2007] 85–104) surveys war poetry in Italian and German as well as the work of Gurney, Sassoon, Owen, Henri Gaudier-Brzeska and Richard Aldington. Eide discovers an impulse to bear witness to the horrors experienced by these soldier-poets together with a guilty violence within their poems. At worst, the violence amounts to trophy-hunting, she argues—at best, it forms part of the complexities of bearing witness to destruction. But Eide's article is eclipsed by the publication of *The Oxford Handbook of British and Irish War Poetry*, edited by Tim Kendall, which discusses related issues from a wide range of perspectives, in relation to a diverse collection of poets. This handbook is a major intervention in the scholarship of war poetry and a significant resource for students and teachers.

It begins with essays on poetry that preceded the twentieth century, including Matthew Bevis's essay on Victorian war poetry (pp. 7–33). Ralph Pite discusses Hardy, arguing against those critics who claim that Hardy's war poetry is 'inert' because it does not belong to a tradition which rejects Victorian certainties for horror and doubt (pp. 34–50). He discusses *The Dynasts* and poems relating to the Boer War and the First World War, disclosing the profound dejection Hardy felt at the First World War. Daniel Karlin reviews Kipling's war poetry, from the *Barrack Room Ballads* to his poems about the First World War (pp. 51–69). Karlin argues that Kipling's best war poetry 'is the product of a divided self' (p. 52), and he traces a split within the fabric of the poems, generated by Kipling's sympathies for the imperial project, for the fighting soldier and even for the enemy.

The collection then moves on to 'The Great War': Santanu Das considers the physical experiences of Owen and Isaac Rosenberg in the trenches (pp. 73–99) and argues that they embodied this in a 'sensuousness of poetic form' (p. 78). Stacey Gillis describes women poets of the First World War (pp. 100–13), addressing questions of gender which have affected the growth of the canons of war poetry and examining the work of individual poets, such as Jessie Pope and Nina Macdonald. Gillis identifies a variety of responses by women of various social classes to the war and calls for a complex critical response appropriate to this diversity. Mark Rawlinson begins by describing Owen's position within contemporary canons of war poetry, and then surveys his poetic output (pp. 114–33). Vivien Noakes appraises the careers of Rosenberg, David Jones and Gurney, identifying the 'timeless truths' (p. 189) embodied in their verse (pp. 174–89). Vincent Sherry (pp. 190–207) recapitulates his arguments in *The Great War and the Language of Modernism* [2004] (*YWES* 86[2007] 866), contending that works such as *Homage to Sextus Propertius* respond to the war by satirizing the language of the Liberal government's attempts to rationalize it. Fran Brearton describes the friendship between Graves and Sassoon (pp. 208–26), examining their close contact during the war and consequent poetic filiations. She documents the subsequent breakdown in their relationship due to tensions between their public and private lives.

A central section focuses upon 1930s poetry. Stan Smith reviews the role of the Spanish Civil War as a testing ground for the ideological and poetic commitments of Auden, Spender, MacNeice and Francis Cornford (pp. 245–63). Rainer Emig tackles similar issues in his discussion of Auden's 'Spain' (pp. 264–78). Revisions to this poem, he argues, constitute 'more than mere biographical and ideological turns' (p. 264); close reading of the poem, stanza by stanza, presents 'Spain' as an ethical poem, somewhat tainted by bourgeois liberal affiliations, but oriented towards the possibility of genuine moral responsibility. John Lyon's essay on Auden, Yeats and Empson bears only a tenuous relationship to the topic of war poetry (pp. 279–95) and concludes on a footnote, but this may be symptomatic of Lyon's argument, which concerns 'the tendency of poetry in the face of the extremities of war . . . to pursue evasiveness or trickery or even nonsense' (p. 294).

The volume gives due weight to the Second World War as well: Dawn Bellamy considers the relations between the poetry of the First World War and poets writing during the Second World War (pp. 299–314). She discusses poems by John Jarmain, Keith Douglas and Alan Lewis, arguing that their works were 'influenced, rather than silenced' (p. 314) by their precursors. Geoffrey Hill offers a considered account of Sidney Keyes's poetry (pp. 398–418), discovering 'the semantic record of an unusual intelligence' (p. 406) within poems such as 'The Buzzard' or 'Ulster Soldier'. Through finely tuned readings he reveals that Keyes was a 'minor poet with a potential for greatness, whereas Douglas is a major poet though on a smaller scale'. Nevertheless, Hill concludes by identifying his own 'immense debt' to Keyes (p. 418). Helen Goethals describes the conflicting demands of patriotism for poets of the Second World War, and the resistance of writers such as Jarmain and Douglas to writing propaganda (pp. 362–76). In her reckoning, poetry has failed to do adequate justice to civilian victims of the war.

These essays also look to wider themes, historical issues and questions of genre. Edna Longley examines varieties of pastoral within war poetry (pp. 461–82), describing how 'the war became paradoxical muse' to the 'poetic pastoral' of Edward Thomas (p. 466). She also discusses the 'inter-war eclogues' of Yeats, Auden and MacNeice and concludes by reviewing the response to conflict in Ireland in the poetry of Paul Muldoon and Heaney. Sarah Cole traces 'the searing pain that cuts through war verse' (p. 483) back to Homer's *Iliad* (pp. 483–503). Ranging across the twentieth century, she discerns 'a poetics of pain' (p. 503) in poems by Randall Jarrell, Yeats, Owen and David Jones. Peter Robinson considers responses to the bombing of civilians, from Picasso's *Guernica* to the Vietnam War (pp. 504–23). He discusses works by poets from Empson to Dylan Thomas and Roy Fisher in order to ask whether it is possible to create poetry from 'clumsy ineptitude or calculatedly casual killing' (p. 505). His essay closes with a pessimistic allusion to more recent civilian casualties.

As a collection, this handbook is least enlivened in its dealings with conventional war poetry of the First World War. Yet it exhibits clear leanings towards a broader understanding of the category, including essays on

Scottish and Welsh war poetry by David Goldie (pp. 153–73) and Gerwyn Williams (pp. 340–61), as well as extensive coverage of Irish poetry by Peter McDonald (pp. 377–97), Edna Longley (pp. 461–82), Paul Volsik (pp. 669–83), Brendan Corcoran (pp. 684–705) and April Warman (pp. 706–23). Gender is important to the perspectives offered too. In addition to Gillis's contribution, Simon Featherstone examines the writings of Mina Loy, Gertrude Stein and E.J. Scovell as responses to war (pp. 445–60). These women writers, he argues, were resistant to 'the subordination of poetic discourse to male experience' (p. 447). As a consequence, their work may be read as 'a way of thinking through war's experience and rhetoric by dealing with women's, not men's, bodies' (p. 460). Hugh Haughton examines anthologies of war poetry, tracing current canons back to the 1960s but also examining contemporary anthologies of poetry published during the First and Second World Wars (pp. 421–44). His essay might be read as a reflection upon the project of the *Handbook* itself, since he draws attention to the roots of 'our current ideologies of poetry and war' (p. 444).

The year 2007 was a good one for the critical fortunes of Isaac Rosenberg: in addition to the attentions of Neil Corcoran, Das and Noakes (discussed above), it saw the publication of his unpublished letters, in *Poetry Out of My Head and Heart*, edited and introduced by Jean Liddiard, and a monograph, *'Essenced to Language': The Margins of Isaac Rosenberg* by Nayef Al-Joulan. Liddiard explains that the letters were discovered in a box of documents relating to Laurence Binyan during the relocation of the British Library in 1995. Perhaps the most significant material is to be found in letters to Gordon Bottomley, which include earlier draft versions of key poems by Rosenberg. These have especial value since Rosenberg is one of the few poets to have written poems in the trenches.

Monograph studies of Rosenberg's work are scarce, but Al-Joulan is less interested in Rosenberg's role as war poet than his identity as a working-class Jew. Chapter 1 addresses questions of Jewish identity in relation to racial and national identities and considers the value of Zionism to Rosenberg's work. Chapter 2 discovers consonance between Freud's theory of the unconscious and Rosenberg's approach to poetic creativity, whereas chapter 3 examines Rosenberg's 'mythological fascinations' (p. 103) with archetypes such as David and Lilith and their relation to his 'Orphic vision' (p. 142). Chapters 4 and 5 emphasize Rosenberg's status as a working-class poet and the ways in which this has impacted his reception, and the book concludes with a study of the influence of Donne, Francis Thompson and Rosenberg's experiences of the visual arts upon his 'idea of "essencing" thought to sound' (p. 239). Al-Joulan emphasizes Rosenberg's 'uniquely disparate imagination' (p. 270) through a series of intricate close readings, but the book is overloaded with footnoted material that could have been lost in the transition from his doctoral thesis.

In 'Therapeutic Measures: The *Hydra* and Wilfred Owen at Craiglockhart War Hospital' (*Mo/Mo* 14:i[2007] 34–54), Meredith Martin explores the relation between the use of poetic composition as a therapeutic tool for shell-shocked soldiers and their prior training in metre. A tension emerges between the order required of disciplined soldiers and the disordered emotion and feelings associated with trauma. The article culminates in a detailed metrical reading of Owen's 'Dulce et Decorum Est' as haunted by a resistance to 'the coupling of military discipline and disciplined literary language' (p. 51).

7. Irish Poetry

The representation of ethnicity in American literature has an interesting and varied history. Of primary importance is African American literature, but the other ethnicities, for clear historical reasons, have not followed that particular dynamic. There has been much talk since the late 1960s of Asian American, Native American and Chicano literature, to name some of the more important. So when Daniel Tobin claims in his introduction to *The Book of Irish American Poetry* that Irish American literature has been neglected as a category, he is correct, because the Irish became part of the establishment earlier. His anthology of Irish American poetry, stretching from the eighteenth century to the present, is an interesting gambit and makes one wonder whether it attenuates or expands the categories of 'Irish literature' and 'American literature'. Certainly expansion is constitutive of the latter, but not the former. So does this anthology expand our ideas of Irish literature? The answer is no, and the main reason is that Tobin's criteria for inclusion are unpersuasive. In his introduction he calls 'the genetic formula' (the author having Irish forebears) 'specious', and yet that seems to be the only basis for including the likes of A.R. Ammons or Peter Cooley. The other criterion is subject matter: thus Czesław Miłosz is included because he has a poem about Robinson Jeffers that refers in passing to his 'Scotch-Irish' ancestry. Tobin makes the point that Irish American poets can be found across the whole stylistic range of twentieth-century American poetry, but for the most part the category is filled with misty-eyed tourist poems about the old country. Here it is worth noting that stylistically these poems are indistinguishable from the work of a lot of poetry from other American ethnicities: lots of autobiographical anecdote, and family reminiscence in generic free verse. No review of an anthology would be complete without a list of omissions: I can't see why Vona Groarke and Conor O'Callaghan, two Irish poets who have lived in and written about their time in the US, aren't here; Michael Longley has several excellent poems about America, and yet he is absent; Michael Hartnett has a vituperative poem entitled 'USA', also not here. Obviously Paul Muldoon is represented, but it is surprising to see him given less space than, say, Galway Kinnell and Thomas Lynch, and the same as Ben Howard. More than any other poet in the book, Muldoon has made Irish-America the subject of his poetry over the last two decades, exploring the hyphen in profound ways. Perhaps a monograph would have been a better way for Tobin to make his argument, through a more selective approach to the poetry. The anthology itself weighs in at just under 1,000 pages, and prompts the thought that Irish American poets, like the Irish themselves in America, are everywhere and really not there at all anymore.

The *Yeats Annual*, edited by Warwick Gould, continues to set a very high standard for scholarship of the poet. One of the highlights of this number is Edward Marx's essay about Yeats's involvement with Japan through the figure of Yone Noguchi. In a subtle cross-cultural case of 'influence and confluence' (the subtitle of the annual), Noguchi seems to have anticipated the Irish poet's interest in Japan, preparing the material carefully so it would strike the right chord. Deborah Ferrelli has an excellent essay on the personal and professional relationship of Yeats with Dorothy Wellesley. Other contributions include Neil Mann on Yeats's interest in the occult matter of the 'vegetal phoenix'; Anthony Cuda on the genealogy of the image of painted horses; Wayne K. Chapman on an unfinished play (a transcription of the manuscript is also published here); Derek Roper on the image of the Quattrocento used in 'Among School Children'; Sally Connolly on elegy in Yeats, Auden and Heaney; and essays by Rory Ryan and Brendan McNamee on *A Vision*.

Tim Kendall has gathered some fine essays in his *Oxford Handbook of British and Irish War Poetry*. This Oxford series would seem to be competing with Cambridge's Companions and Introductions, the difference being sheer size: whereas the latter publisher aims for a book of 200–300 pages, Oxford's series can only notionally be called 'handbooks'. Kendall's book ranges over the twentieth century and includes work by established reputations as well as doctoral students (some of these are among the best). The first essay on Irish poetry is by Marjorie Perloff, and one might question her suitability to examine 'Easter, 1916' in its historical context when she refers to James Connolly as 'an actor at the Abbey Theatre'. John Lyon discusses Yeats in the context of Auden's elegy, emphasizing what he sees as the contradictions in the Irish poet's attitude to war, especially in his final decade. Peter McDonald judiciously mixes biography and criticism in his account of Louis MacNeice during the Second World War, remarking that 'MacNeice did not approach the losses of the War in a shallowly journalistic spirit; on the contrary, he saw those losses as presenting a profound challenge to any writing which prioritized factual content over larger questions of meaning.' McDonald teases out the implications of this in some excellent close readings. Tara Christie's essay on responses to Isaac Rosenberg by Geoffrey Hill, Longley and Cathal Ó Searcaigh is one of the book's best, especially when she deals with Longley's complex imaginative reading of the English tradition. The book's final section deals with Northern Ireland. Paul Volsik's essay, subtitled 'Negotiating with the Epic in Northern Irish Poetry of the Troubles', deals mainly with Heaney and does not shed much new light on its subject; much the same might be said of Brendan Corcoran's essay, subtitled 'Heaney, Poetry, and War'. Paul Muldoon is considered as a war poet by April Warman through a comparison of his earlier work which dealt with Northern Ireland and a later poem, 'At the Sign of the Black Horse, September 1999', which addresses the Holocaust. She wonders 'how much Muldoon abandons when he exchanges the endlessly volatile (because incontrovertibly private) subtext of his own experience (including his experience of living in a time and place of violence) for the relatively stable (because fundamentally public) investigation of the individual's relation to twentieth-century history'. This is an interesting question which involves further questions about Muldoon's move to America and the implications of such hybrid poetry, as I indicated above, for our understanding of national canons.

Heidi Hansson's study of Emily Lawless, *Emily Lawless, 1845–1913: Writing the Interspace*, deals for the most part with the fiction, but because her reputation rests on her work as a poet rather than a novelist, and because there is one chapter on her poetry, the book should be noted here. The 'interspace' of the title is Lawless's term, and it allows Hansson to examine the way in which the work falls outside the usual categories. Not recuperable by nationalist or older feminist narratives, Lawless's work has fallen into neglect. Applying ideas of eco-feminism, Hansson seeks to redress this, first by exploring the writer's complex genealogy, and then her ambivalent attitude to the suffragette movement in England. Though some of the writing is theoretical boilerplate, for the most part the book is written in a clear fashion, and presents a strong case for Lawless's writing, if not for her poetry.

As a critic of poetry, Helen Vendler has few peers. Attentive to both contemporary production and the established canon, she always works close to the grain of the text, and is sensitive to the imaginative contours of poems. More than any other critic, she brings us close to what it must have been like to write some of the great poems of the English language—the formal choices involved, the progression of imagery, the tonal shifts, the resolutions and the irresolutions. So one expects much when she writes that 'There exists no general book examining the sorts of lyrics Yeats wrote, the imaginative impulses that dictated the choice of stanza for his subjects, the poet's development within particular formal genres . . . or the ideological meaning for him of certain rhythms of stanza forms.' *Our Secret Discipline: Yeats and Lyric Form* begins by dealing with the Byzantium poems, then turns to the two sequences 'Nineteen Hundred and Nineteen' and 'Meditations in Time of Civil War'. After this, she attends to the early poems, remarking that 'Yeats derived confident will from his accomplished formal intent.' This is to say that the magisterial voice of late Yeats came from his mastery of form, and not from his dominating voice in theatre business and the management of men. This is followed by a chapter on Yeats's treatment of the ballad form, and then by a chapter on his treatment of the sonnet.

This chapter, entitled 'Troubling the Tradition: Yeats at Sonnets', is perhaps the least convincing, as she tendentiously argues that Yeats was wary of the sonnet because the form was so central to the English (read: imperial) poetic tradition. Vendler here sounds very like one of the book's dedicatees, Heaney, when she talks of how he 'made [the sonnet] Irish'. To this dubious end, she searches out attenuated and truncated sonnets in the most unlikely of places. She builds up a long chapter on ideas of loyalty and disloyalty to Ireland relating to his avoidance of the Shakespearian sonnet, and then in an offhand way remarks, 'It may also be that he, like Keats, disliked the effect of the terminal couplet.' This amounts to saying that it may also be that the chapter is erroneous from start to finish.

Trimeter-quatrain poems, tetrameter lines, blank verse, ottava rima, long stanzas, and the rare form of terza rima: as Vendler teases out the modalities and valencies of Yeats's use of these forms, our sense of the poet's relish for and engagement with formal variety deepens. One is grateful for the range and richness of the readings, but it is a difficult book to read over a few days. The reader begins to miss the oxygen of other contexts, contexts that were so important to the poet himself. Of course, Vendler would argue that because those contexts have been elucidated so excellently, a formal approach is now required as complement. It will perhaps be most useful when consulted for readings of individual poems, and provide a healthy reminder to critics schooled in cultural theory of the particular resources and resonances of poetic discourse.

The editors of *Seamus Heaney: Poet, Critic, Translator*, Ashby Bland Crowder and Jason David Hall, are well aware that justification is required for yet another academic book on the Irish Nobel laureate. In their introduction they make their case, but unfortunately their book does not deliver. The authors are by no means uniform in their praise of Heaney—some are extremely negative—and that is a healthy sign. However, very few of the essays present original critical analyses or adduce new contexts or information about the poet. (If it weren't for Heather Clark's book *The Ulster Renaissance: Poetry in Belfast 1962–1972*, published last year, one might be tempted to think that subject of Heaney was exhausted. Her study demonstrated that the archives still hold much of interest concerning him and his coevals.) Stephen Regan deals with Heaney's handling of elegy. Richard Rankin Russell discusses politics in relation to Heaney's poetry and ends his essay with the sentence 'His poetic invitation to us is to join him at the frontier of writing, where hope, tempered by reality, awaits us.' Colleen McKenna discusses the symbol of trees in the poetry—trees are established, then their 'fixity and permanence' are 'challenged'. Sidney Burris takes a look at Heaney's criticism, and he remarks of it that it 'clears out an internal space for these contending discourses to thrive and have their day, and he is drawn to those authors whose writing arises from these contending points of view, whose achieved stance rests on the momentary resolution of hostile forces'. Michael Baron tries to get to the bottom of the negative reviews of Heaney's critical prose through a comparison with Geoffrey Hill. Daniel W. Ross's essay on the influence of Frost and Eliot on Heaney is a much weaker version of the argument that Rachel Buxton made in *Robert Frost and Northern Irish Poetry* [2004], to which Ross does not refer. To be sure, Buxton didn't cover Eliot, but then Ross's argument here is not persuasive in that matter. Paul Turner brings a classicist's eye to Heaney's version of *Philoctetes* (but not, strangely, *Antigone*), remarking that for Heaney, 'Sophocles's tragedy seems to have served mainly as a kind of literary knacker's yard, a handy source of raw material for a modern Muse.' Alison Finlay discusses his translation of *Beowulf*. Joseph Brooker deals with the theme of memory in *Station Island*. While the editors saw fit to get scholars of Greek and Old English to look, respectively, at Heaney's translations from those languages, they did not get anyone to look at his translations from arguably the most important language of all for Heaney (and the only language he speaks from among those from which he has translated), that is, Irish.

Three essays stand out. First is Jerzy Jarniewicz's on Heaney in relation to the postwar Polish poets, especially Zbigniew Herbert and Miłosz. Jarniewicz, a Polish poet as well as a critic, is sensitive to the ways in which Heaney shapes the oeuvres to his own needs; and this also provides insight into the kind of poet that Heaney *isn't*. That is, Heaney avoids a large European historical canvass in his poetry, perhaps because he has not experienced these events himself; in this he differs from Herbert especially, who showed no such reluctance. Most writing on Heaney's relation to the east European poets has, largely speaking, lacked critical distance. This is what Jarniewicz provides, though he is sympathetically engaged with the poetry. Second, Ruben Moi writes on the collection *Electric Light* [2001], with insight on the 'literariness' of the book and also more generally of the positions Heaney has taken up in relation to Irish politics, remarking: 'Heaney's continuous meditations risk blandness, but in a highly charged field where the extremes lay claim to the middle, they always constituted a radical position.' Third, and finally, Barbara Hardy writes trenchantly on Heaney's literary allusions, arguing that for the most part there is little subtlety or aptness in his use of the device. Most of Hardy's objections boil down to her preference for the source work as it was, and not how Heaney has mediated it, and if, ultimately, she is not persuasive, she succeeds in being provocative.

If the field of criticism on Heaney is crowded, the same cannot be said of that on Derek Mahon. Yet it remains difficult to say why exactly that should be so. When the dust settles, it is probable that readers will be puzzled about the differences in the reputations of Heaney, Mahon and Longley (Muldoon is now creeping up on Heaney in the US). Hugh Haughton's *The Poetry of Derek Mahon* is the first full-length study of the poetry (although there have been edited volumes on him, most notably *The Poetry of Derek Mahon*, edited by Elmer Kennedy-Andrews [2002]), and it is a splendidly written book. Haughton is sensitive to the poetry as well as to its changing biographical and historical contexts. Indeed, the development of Mahon's work is intimately connected with his travels—his movements between countries and continents—so that it takes a critic who is particularly fly to keep pace with him. The pleasure of reading his exegeses of the poems is seconded only by reading the poems themselves.

The importance of the book lies not in any new angle on Mahon, or the adduction of new information (although Haughton helps out with the sources of the poems 'Lives' and 'A Disused Shed in Co. Wexford'), but rather in its sustained, delicate attention to Mahon's poetry as a coherent oeuvre, through which it becomes possible to view afresh the history of Irish poetry over the last four decades and also, in subtle ways, the history of the island in that period. Mahon, through his very choice of marginality and a kind of exile, or emigration, through his very avoidance of the public stances of the kind taken by Heaney, provides an opportunity to tell a different story. What are the contours of that story? First, Mahon shows that to be an Irish poet does not mean that one must restrict oneself to Irish subject matter, but one can range through the world. Second, he shows that in choosing traditional forms one does not avoid engagement with the legacy of modernism. Third (this follows from the first point), he shows that translation does not necessarily have to be of texts with Irish or English provenance, with a postcolonial acoustic, but can range more widely (in Mahon's case, of francophone poets) and still profoundly affect the poet's original work. Also, Haughton's defence of *The Hudson Letter* [1995] and *The Yellow Book* [1997] will give pause to those readers who were persuaded by the many negative reviews of those books. It is hard to know how Haughton's book will be surpassed.

Gerald Dawe's *The Proper Word: Collected Criticism: Ireland, Poetry, Politics*, edited by Nicholas Allen, gathers essays and reviews spanning three decades. Some of these deal with general Irish cultural issues, others more specifically with the north of Ireland, others again with the relation between the writer and Ireland. (I should here disclose that its author taught me for several years at Trinity College, Dublin.) The most valuable and compelling chapters are those in which Dawe reviews the work of particular poets, some of them famous, some of them neglected. His essays on Padraic Fiacc, W.R. Rodgers, Charles Donnelly, John Hewitt and Brendan Kennelly will not cause any of these reputations to be raised, but they do provide nuanced, informed analysis of some of the prejudices and presumptions at work in Irish poetry criticism. Dawe is particularly alert to ideas of Irish poetry as overwhelmingly rural, and shows how the city of Belfast is a theme of some of the poets he admires. He has a fine essay comparing Longley and Mahon, and also excellent responses, individually, to Mahon, MacNeice, J.M. Synge and Heaney. He follows Mahon's line in asserting that he, Mahon, was never a member of Philip Hobsbaum's Belfast Group, but this surely is no longer tenable after the publication of Heather Clark's book, mentioned above, which demonstrates just how involved he was in the poetry scene in Belfast in the 1960s.

The most provocative, but also most frustrating, part of the book is the first section of over 100 pages, which deals with more general cultural issues. It is full of many refreshing and stringent moments, for instance when he remarks that 'the Protestants of Northern Ireland are peripheral since the critical focus of definition does not *involve* them'. This alerts us to a lack of synchronization between the big talk about Ireland (for example news reportage and literary journalism from abroad about its writers) and the situation on the ground. More generally, Dawe is wonderfully sensitive to such discrepancies. Beyond this section he asks, 'What is a "Protestant writer", after all? By what peculiar gestures, accents, manicure, or space between his eyes is this species known to man?' But Dawe frustrates because he does not begin to answer the questions he provokes. The tone is all brass tacks and sleeve-rolling, but he fails to follow up with detailed analysis in which names are named and developments are carefully contextualized. No doubt Dawe is trying to avoid the dryness of academic criticism, by sailing closer to literary journalism, but even journalism has to be more exact and exacting than this.

Applying ideas of translation to the subject of postcolonial poetry, Ashok Bery's *Cultural Translation and Postcolonial Poetry* examines the rich interfaces which empire creates between the poetries of different cultures and languages. He is aware that he is stretching the notion of translation to cover material which, for the most part, has little to do with literary transmission between languages; and, if he is ultimately not convincing in his use of the concept, he nevertheless provides some very lively discussion of several Irish poets, especially Heaney. If his choice of Heaney for his postcolonial credentials is predictable, his discussion of the poetry is not, especially where he counters the argument (expressed by Ciaran Carson in a review of *North* [1975]) that Heaney absconds from history to mythology. Here is Bery: 'the poem ['The Tollund Man'] arrives at an in-between space, a distance both from Ireland and Jutland, which serves as a location where critique (and through that, change) become possible. It is noticeable that the poem insists on its hypotheticality and futurity.' Also, MacNeice is a refreshing choice for a chapter in such a context, and might precipitate a reconsideration of poets such as Longley, Richard Murphy and Mahon, and thus complicate, in good ways, our ideas of Irish poetry and postcolonialism. There are also chapters on Judith Wright, Derek Walcott, Les Murray and A.K. Ramanujan.

Only three of eight chapters of Michael O'Neill's book, *The All-Sustaining Air: Romantic Legacies in British, American, and Irish Poetry since 1900*, are directly related to the subject of this section; others deal with Eliot, Wallace Stevens, Auden, Stephen Spender, Geoffrey Hill and Roy Fisher. Of these, Eliot and Stevens receive chapters to themselves (as does Yeats). It will come as no surprise to see these poets discussed in a post-Romantic context; Frank Kermode's *Romantic Image* and then later Harold Bloom's studies of Stevens and Yeats made it central to our understanding of their work. O'Neill does not present a particularly original reading of early twentieth-century poetry, but cross-hatches our received ideas with sensitive readings of poems, showing how Romanticism was read and misread by these later poets. At his best, he provides perceptive and delicate close readings; at his worst, his comments are anodyne, and one blandly agrees with them. Thus, towards the end of the chapter on Yeats, he says that 'it is important to note' that the poet 'does not return to the Romantics for a system of belief. But he draws on their practice for hints about how to dramatize conflict.' It is important, but most academic readers of Yeats will have done so a long time back.

Chapter 6 covers Patrick Kavanagh and Heaney (and, more cursorily, Mahon and Carson). He sees Byronic aspects in Kavanagh's rhymes and also asserts Romanticism to be 'born again' in the rapturous late work (in a borrowing from Antoinette Quinn's study of Kavanagh). In Heaney's poetry, he tentatively proposes, a 'longing for Romantic authority pervades [his] work, as does the ironic opposition to that longing'. Again, one agrees, if only because Heaney himself has proclaimed his debts to Romanticism so lucidly and at length in both his prose and poetry, constantly inflating and deflating his own lyric authority. The chosen thesis leads occasionally to strain, as when O'Neill suggests that 'it is Wordsworth who provides the steadiest Romantic focus for Heaney's thinking about the rival claims of poetry and politics'; perhaps 'the steadiest Romantic focus', but certainly not the 'steadiest focus', and O'Neill's elision of the Irish poet's debts in this matter to Osip Mandelstam is unhelpful. The chapter on Paul Muldoon's 'Madoc—A Mystery' is routine in its perceptions and does not exceed the work of Tim Kendall and Clair Wills on the subject. Thus, its final sentence: 'Yet Muldoon's post-Romantic irony in "Madoc" is generously accommodating; it includes in its range of effects the satirical and the elegiac, and its scepticism about language is inseparable from its relish for the proliferations of meaning.' Again, this is true, but the Romantic critical angle only leads to a widely accepted view of the poem.

Books Reviewed

Adamson, Walter L. *Embattled Avant-Gardes: Modernism's Resistance to Commodity Culture in Europe.* UCalP. [2007] pp. xii + 435. $45 ISBN 9 7805 2025 2707.

Al-Joulan, Nayef. *'Essenced to Language': the Margins of Isaac Rosenberg.* Lang. [2007] pp. 287. pb £35.50 ISBN 3 0391 0728 3.

Allen, Nicholas, ed. *The Proper Word: Collected Criticism: Ireland, Poetry, Politics,* by Gerald Dawe. CreighUP. [2007] pp. 365. pb $25 ISBN 1 8818 7152 5.

Andermahr, Sonya. Ed. *Jeanette Winterson: A Contemporary Critical Guide.* Continuum. [2007] pp. 177. £15.99. ISBN 978 0 82649 275 3.

Aragay, Mireia, Hildegard Klein, Enric Monforte, Pilar Zozaya, (eds). *British Theatre of the 1990s: Interviews with Directors, Playwrights, Critics and Academics.* Palgrave [2007] pp. 220. hb £45 ISBN 978 0 230 00509 9.

Aston, Elaine and Sue-Ellen Case, (eds) *Staging International Feminisms.* Palgrave [2007] pp. 250. hb £43 ISBN 978 1 4039 8701 3.

Ascari, Maurizio. *A Counter-History of Crime Fiction: Supernatural, Gothic, Sensational.* Palgrave. [2007] pp. 240. £45 ISBN 9 7802 3052 5009.

Baker, Brian. *Iain Sinclair.* Contemporary British Novelists. ManUP. [2007] pp. 192. £50 hb. ISBN 978 0 71906 904 8. £15.99 pb. ISBN 978 0 71906 905 5.

Barker, Howard, and Eduardo Houth. A Style and its Origins. Oberon Books [2007] pp. 119. pb £10 ISBN 1 84002 718 5.

Baxendale, John. *Priestley's England: Priestley and English Culture.* MUP. [2007] pp. 256. £50 ISBN 0 7190 7286 7.

Beasley, Rebecca. *Theorists of Modern Poetry: T.S. Eliot, T.E. Hulme, Ezra Pound.* Routledge. [2007] pp. ix + 144. £55 ISBN 0 4152 8540 7.

Beaumont, Matthew, and Michael Freeman, eds. *The Railway and Modernity: Time, Space, and the Machine Ensemble.* Lang. [2007] pp. 262. £34 ISBN 9 7830 3911 0247.

Beaumont, Matthew, ed. *Adventures in Realism.* Blackwell. [2007] pp. 320. £50 ISBN 9 7814 0513 5771.

Becket, Fiona, and Terry Gifford, eds. *Culture, Creativity and Environment: New Environmentalist Criticism.* Rodopi. [2007] pp. 260. £37 ISBN 9 7890 4202 2508.

Begam, Richard and Michael Valdez Moses, eds. *Modernism and Colonialism: British and Irish Literature, 1899–1939.* DukeUP. [2007] pp. 326. $89.95 ISBN 9 7808 2234 0195.

Begam, Richard and Moses, Michael Valdez, eds. *Modernism and Colonialism: British and Irish Literature 1899-1939.* DukeUP. [2007] pp. x + 326. hb $89.95 ISBN 0822340195. pb $24.95 ISBN 0 8223 4038 6.

Begam, Richard, and Michael Valdez Moses, eds. *Modernism and Colonialism: British and Irish Literature, 1899–1939.* DukeUP. [2007] pp. ix + 326. £14.99 ISBN 9 7808 2234 0386.

Bell, Kevin. *Ashes Taken for Fire: Aesthetic Modernism and the Critique of Identity.* UMinnP. [2007] pp. 240. £42 ISBN 0 8166 4900 6.

Bell, Michael. *Open Secrets: Literature, Education, and Authority from J.-J. Rousseau to J.M. Coetzee.* OUP. [2007] pp. x + 254. £53 ISBN 9 7801 9920 8098.

Bentley, Nick. *Radical Fictions: The English Novel in the 1950s.* Lang. [2007] pp. 330. £42. ISBN 978 3 03910 934 0.

Berberich, Christine. *The Image of the English Gentleman in Twentieth-Century Literature: Englishness and Nostalgia.* Ashgate. [2007] pp. ix + 207. £50 ISBN 9 7807 5466 1269.

Bery, Ashok. *Cultural Translation and Postcolonial Poetry.* Palgrave. [2007] pp. 240. £45 ISBN 1 4039 3310 3.

Bevis, Matthew, ed. *Some Versions of Empson.* OUP. [2007] pp. 342 + xiv. £50.00 IBSN 0 1992 8636 2.

Billingham, Peter. *At the Sharp End: Uncovering the Work of Five Leading Dramatists.* Methuen Drama [2007] pp. 272. pb £16.99 ISBN 978 0 7136 8507 7.

Billington, Michael. *State of the Nation: British Theatre since 1945.* Faber [2007] pp. 416. hb £25 ISBN 10 0571210341.

Blair, Emily. *Virginia Woolf and the Nineteenth-Century Domestic Novel.* SUNYP. [2007] pp. xii + 287. $75 ISBN 9 7807 9147 1197.

Blandford, Steve. *Film, Drama and the BreakUp of Britain.* Intellect [2007] pp. 206. pb £19.99 ISBN 978 1 84150 150 5.

Boon, Richard. *The Cambridge Companion to David Hare.* CUP[2003], pp. 286. pb £17.99 ISBN 978 0521615570.

Boussahba-Bravard, Myriam, ed. *Suffrage Outside Suffragism: Women's Vote in Britain, 1880–1914.* Palgrave. [2007] pp. 256. £56 ISBN 9 7814 0399 5964.

Bradford, Richard. *The Novel Now: Contemporary British Fiction.* Blackwell. [2007] pp. viii + 259. £50 hb. ISBN 978 1 40511 385 4. £16.99 pb. ISBN 1 4051 1386 3.

Bradshaw, David, ed. *The Cambridge Companion to E.M. Forster.* CUP. [2007] pp. xvii + 287. $24.95 ISBN 9 7805 2154 2524.

Brassley, Paul, Jeremy Burchardt and Lynne Thompson, eds. *The English Countryside between the Wars: Regeneration or Decline?* Boydell. [2006] pp. 280. £55 ISBN 1 8438 3264 X.

Brook, Susan. *Literature and Cultural Criticism in the 1950s: The Feeling Male Body.* Palgrave. [2007] pp. ix + 197. £45. ISBN 978 1 4039 4106 0.

Brooker, Peter. *Bohemia in London: The Social Scene of Early Modernism.* Palgrave. [2007] pp. 248. £55 ISBN 9 7802 3054 6929.

Bryden, Mary. *Gilles Deleuze: Travels in Literature.* Palgrave. [2007] pp. x + 184. £47 ISBN 9 7802 3051 7530.

Buchanan, Bradley. *Hanif Kureishi.* New British Fiction. Palgrave. [2007] pp. xii + 177. £42.50 hb. ISBN 978 1 40399 049 5. £9.99 pb. ISBN 978 1 4039 9050 1.

Bulson, Eric. *Novels, Maps, Modernity: The Spatial Imagination, 1850–2000.* Routledge. [2007] pp. 188. £55 ISBN 0 4159 7648 0.

Burrells, Anna, *et al.*, eds. *Woolfian Boundaries: Selected Papers from the Sixteenth Annual International Conference on Virginia Woolf.* Clemson University Digital Press. [2007] pp. xiii + 195. $19.95 ISBN 9 7809 7960 6618.

Burt, Stephen. *The Forms of Youth: Twentieth-Century Poetry and Adolescence*. ColUP. [2007] pp. 263 + vii. $36.50 ISBN 0 2311 4142 0.

Byrne, Sandie. *The Unbearable Saki: The Work of H.H. Munro*. OUP. [2007] pp. 288. £21 ISBN 9 7801 9922 6054.

Cameron, Sharon. *Impersonality: Seven Essays*. UChicP. [2007] pp. xx + 260. hb $65.00 ISBN 0 2260 9131 0. pb $25 ISBN 0 2260 9132 5.

Cave, Richard and Ben Levitas, (eds). *Irish Theatre in England*. Carysfort Press [2007] pp. 299. pb £14 ISBN 1 904505 26 0.

Çinar, Alev, and Thomas Bender, eds. *Urban Imaginaries: Locating the Modern City*. UMinnP. [2007] pp. xxvi + 290. $75 ISBN 9 7808 1664 8023.

Childs, Peter. *Modernism and the Post-Colonial: Literature and Empire 1885–1930*. Continuum. [2007] pp. 152. £60 ISBN 9 7808 2648 5588.

Churchill, Suzanne W., and Adam McKible, eds. *Little Magazines and Modernism: New Approaches*. Ashgate. [2007] pp. 276. £55 ISBN 9 7807 5466 0149.

Cianci, Giovanni and Jason Harding, eds. *T.S. Eliot and the Concept of Tradition*. CUP. [2007] pp. xv + 229. £53 ISBN 0 5218 8002 2.

Coleman, Terry. *Olivier: The Authorised Biography*. Bloomsbury. [2005] pp. 624. £20 ISBN 0 7475 7798 6.

Collins, Jo, and John Jervis, eds. *Uncanny Modernity: Cultural Theories, Modern Anxieties*. Palgrave. [2007] pp. viii + 234. £45 ISBN 9 7802 3051 7714.

Copley, Antony. *A Spiritual Bloomsbury: Hinduism and Homosexuality in the Lives and Writing of Edward Carpenter, E.M. Forster, and Christopher Isherwood*. Lexington. [2006] pp. xi + 397. £56 ISBN 9 7807 3911 4643.

Corcoran, Neil, ed. *The Cambridge Companion to Twentieth-Century English Poetry*. CUP. [2007] pp. xv + 268. £17.99 ISBN 9 7805 2169 1321.

Couperus, Stefan, et al., eds. *In Control of the City: Local Elites and the Dynamics of Urban Politics, 1800–1960*. Peeters. [2007] pp. xxii + 230. £35 ISBN 9 7890 4291 9419.

Cousin, Geraldine. *Playing for Time*. ManUP [2007] pp. 180. hb £50 ISBN 978 0 7190 6197 4.

Coyle, John, ed. *It Was the Nightingale, by Ford Madox Ford*. Carcanet. [2007] pp. xxiii + 354. £14.95 ISBN 9 7818 5754 9324.

Crowder, Ashby Bland, and Jason David Hall, eds. *Seamus Heaney: Poet, Critic, Translator*. Palgrave. [2007] pp. 240. £45 ISBN 0 2300 0342 7.

Cuthbertson, Guy and Lucy Newlyn, eds. *Branch-lines: Edward Thomas and Contemporary Poetry*. Enitharmon. [2007] pp. 264. £15.00 ISBN 1 9046 3435 5.

Darling, Elizabeth, and Lesley Whitworth, eds. *Women and the Making of Built Space in England, 1870–1950*. Ashgate. [2007] pp. 220. £55 ISBN 9 7807 5465 1857.

Däumer, Elisabeth and Shyamal Bagchee, eds. *The International Reception of T.S. Eliot*. Continuum. [2007] pp. xiii + 303. £80 ISBN 0 8264 9014 X.

Davies, Laurence, Owen Knowles, Gene M. Moore and J.H. Stape, eds. *The Collected Letters of Joseph Conrad*, vol. 9: *Uncollected Letters and Indexes, 1892–1923*. CUP. [2007] pp. xlviii + 383. $180 ISBN 9 7805 2188 1890.

Davis, Alex and Lee M. Jenkins, eds. *The Cambridge Companion to Modernist Poetry*. CUP. [2007] pp. xviii + 259. hb £47.00 ISBN 0 5218 5305 7. pb £18.99 ISBN 0 5216 1815 1.

Day, Barry, ed. *The Letters of Noël Coward*. Methuen. [2007] pp. 800. £25 ISBN 0 7136 8578 6.

De Lange, Attie, Gail Fincham, Jeremy Hawthorn and Jakob Lothe, eds. *Literary Landscapes: From Modernism to Postcolonialism*. Palgrave. [2007] pp. 248. £45 ISBN 9 7802 3055 3163.

Delap, Lucy. *The Feminist Avant-Garde: Transatlantic Encounters of the Early Twentieth Century*. CUP. [2007] pp. x + 357. $95 ISBN 9 7805 2187 6513.

D'Monte, Rebecca and Graham Saunders, (eds.) *Cool Britannia?: British Political Drama in the 1990s*. Palgrave [2007] pp. 251. pb £15.99 ISBN 978 1 4039 8813 3

Dillon, Sarah. *The Palimpsest: Literature, Criticism, Theory*. Continuum. [2007] pp. 164. £60 ISBN 9 7808 2649 5457.

Doan, Laura, and Jane Garrity, eds. *Sapphic Modernities: Sexuality, Women and National Culture*. Palgrave. [2007] pp. x + 261. £40 ISBN 9 7814 0396 4984.

Dolin, Kieran. *A Critical Introduction to Law and Literature*. CUP. [2007] pp. 272. £45 ISBN 9 7805 2180 7432.

Ellis, Steve. *Virginia Woolf and the Victorians*. CUP. [2007] pp. xi + 211. £45 ISBN 9 7805 2188 2897.

Erickson, Gregory. *The Absence of God in Modernist Literature*. Palgrave. [2007] pp. viii + 236. $65 ISBN 9 7814 0397 7588.

Eysteinsson, Astradur, and Vivian Liska, eds. *Modernism*, 2 vols. Benjamins. [2007] pp. 1,043. £217 ISBN 9 0272 3454 X.

Falcus, Sarah. *Michele Roberts: Myths, Mothers and Memories*. Lang. [2007] pp. 262. £33. ISBN 978 3 03911 054 4.

Fox, Paul, and Koray Melikoğlu, eds. *Formal Investigations: Aesthetic Style in Late-Victorian and Edwardian Detective Fiction*. Ibidem. [2007] pp. xii + 236. £20 ISBN 9 7838 9821 5930.

Freeman, Nicholas. *Conceiving the City: London, Literature, and Art 1870–1914*. OUP. [2007] pp. xii + 240. £50 ISBN 9 7801 9921 8189.

Gale, Maggie B. *J.B. Priestley*. Routledge. [2008] pp. x + 207. £55 ISBN 0 4154 0242 5.

Gale, Maggie B., and John Stokes, eds. *The Cambridge Companion to the Actress*. CUP. [2007] pp. 364. £45 ISBN 0 5218 4606 4.

Gillies, Mary Ann. *The Professional Literary Agent in Britain, 1880–1920*. UTorP. [2007] pp. xiii + 247. $65 ISBN 9 7808 0209 1475.

Glendening, John. *The Evolutionary Imagination in Late Victorian Novels: An Entangled Bank*. Ashgate. [2007] pp. vii + 293. £55 ISBN 9 7807 5465 8214.

Goddard, Lynette. *Staging Black Feminisms: Identity, Politics, Performance*. Palgrave [2007] pp. 238. hb £48 ISBN 978 1 4039 8640 5.

Godiwala, Dimple (ed.) *Alternatives within the Mainstream II: Queer Theatres in Post War Britain* [2007] pp.373. hb £39.99 ISBN 978 19047 18306 4.

Gould, Warwick, ed. *Influence and Confluence. Yeats Annual No. 17: A Special Number*. Palgrave. [2007] pp. 400. £65 ISBN 0 2305 4689 7.

Hammond, Mary, and Shafquat Towheed, eds. *Publishing in the First World War: Essays in Book History*. Palgrave. [2007] pp. xiv + 241. £47 ISBN 9 7802 3050 0761.

Hammond, Mary. *Reading, Publishing and the Formation of Literary Taste in England, 1880–1914*. Ashgate. [2006] pp. xii + 209. £50 ISBN 9 7807 5465 6683.

Hansson, Heidi. *Emily Lawless, 1845–1913: Writing the Interspace*. CorkUP. [2007] pp. 242. £35 ISBN 1 8591 8413 8.

Haughton, Hugh. *The Poetry of Derek Mahon*. OUP. [2007] pp. 384. £32 ISBN 0 1992 1544 8.

Hawthorn, Jeremy. *Sexuality and the Erotic in the Fiction of Joseph Conrad*. Continuum. [2007] pp. viii + 178. £60 ISBN 9 7808 2649 5273.

Head, Dominic. *Ian McEwan*. Contemporary British Novelists. ManUP. [2007] pp. 219. £50 hb. ISBN 978 0 71906 656 6. £14.99 pb. ISBN 978 0 71906 657 3.

Heinrich, Anselm. *Entertainment, Propaganda, Education: Regional Theatre in Germany and Britain between 1918 and 1945*. UHertP. [2007] pp. 256. £25 ISBN 1 9028 0674 3.

Henke, Christoph and Martin Middeke, (eds). *Drama and / after Postmodernism*. WVT Verlag Trier [2007] pp. 379. pb € 35 ISBN 978 3 88476 9362.

Henke, Suzette and David Eberly, eds. *Virginia Woolf and Trauma: Embodied Texts*. Pace UP. [2007] pp. 328. $30 ISBN 0 9444 7379 2

Hepburn, Allan, ed. *Troubled Legacies: Narrative and Inheritance*. UTorP. [2007] pp. viii + 297. $50 ISBN 9 7808 0209 1109.

Holtby, Winnifred. *Virginia Woolf: A Critical Memoir*. Continuum. [2007] pp. 206. £9.99 ISBN 0 8264 9443 9.

Hunter, Adrian. *The Cambridge Introduction to the Short Story in English*. CUP. [2007] pp. 302. £14.99 ISBN 9 7805 2168 1124.

Jansohn, Christa, and Dieter Mehl, eds. *The Reception of D.H. Lawrence in Europe*. Continuum. [2007] pp. xliv + 367. £125 ISBN 0 8264 6825 X.

Johnston, Georgia. *The Formation of 20th-Century Queer Autobiography: Reading Vita Sackville-West, Virginia Woolf, Hilda Doolittle, and Gertrude Stein*. Palgrave. [2007] pp. x + 203. $65 ISBN 9 7814 0397 6185.

Kalliney, Peter J. *Cities of Affluence and Anger: A Literary Geography of Modern Englishness*. UPVirginia. [2007] pp. viii + 266. $59.50 hb. ISBN 978 0 8139 2573 8. $22.50 pb. ISBN 978 0 8139 2574 5.

Kendall, Judy, ed. *Edward Thomas's Poets*. Carcanet. [2007] pp. xxx + 207. pb £14.95 ISBN 1 8575 4908 9.

Kendall, Tim, ed. *The Oxford Handbook of British and Irish War Poetry*. OUP. [2007] pp. xvi + 754. £89.00 ISBN 0 1992 8266 1.

Kendall, Tim, ed. *The Oxford Handbook of British and Irish War Poetry*. OUP. [2007] pp. 800. £93 ISBN 0 1992 8266 8.

Kershaw, Angela, and Angela Kimyongür, eds., *Women in Europe between the Wars: Politics, Culture and Society*. Ashgate. [2007] pp. xi + 249. £50 ISBN 9 7807 5465 6845.

Koenigsberger, Kurt. *The Novel and the Menagerie: Totality, Englishness, and Empire.* OSUP. [2007] pp. xvi + 278. $41.95 ISBN 9 7808 1421 0574.

Koh, Jae-kyung. *D.H. Lawrence and the Great War: The Quest for Cultural Regeneration.* Lang. [2007] pp. 237. £35.60 ISBN 9 7830 3910 9760.

Kosok, Heinz. *The Theatre of War: The First World War in British and Irish Drama.* Palgrave. [2007] pp. vii + 286. £50 ISBN 0 2305 2558 X.

Kövesi, Simon. *James Kelman.* Contemporary British Novelists. ManUP. [2007] pp. 204. £50 hb ISBN 978 0 71907 096 9. £14.99 pb. ISBN 978 0 71907 097 6.

Krishnan, Sanjay. *Reading the Global: Troubling Perspectives on Britain's Empire in Asia.* ColUP. [2007] pp. ix + 242. £24.50 ISBN 9 7802 3114 0706.

Kristdóttir, Morine. *Descents of Memory: The Life of John Cowper Powys.* Duckworth. [2007] pp. 480. £25 ISBN 9 7815 8567 9171.

Krockel, Carl. *D.H. Lawrence and Germany: The Politics of Influence.* Rodopi. [2007] pp. x + 333. £49.29 ISBN 9 0420 2126 8.

Kucich, John. *Imperial Masochism: British Fiction, Fantasy, and Social Class.* PrincetonUP. [2007] pp. x + 258. £50 ISBN 9 7806 9112 7125.

Ladenson, Elisabeth. *Dirt for Art's Sake: Books on Trial from Madame Bovary to Lolita.* CornUP. [2006] pp. 272. £34.50 ISBN 0 8014 4168 4.

Lambrou, Marina and Peter Stockwell. *Contemporary Stylistics.* Continuum. [2007] pp. 304. £85 ISBN 9 7808 2649 3859.

Lawrence, D.H. *D.H. Lawrence and Italy.* Penguin. [2007] pp. xxx + 495. £14.99 ISBN 9 7801 4144 1559.

Lawrence, D.H. *D.H. Lawrence: Poems Selected by Tom Paulin.* Faber. [2007] pp. 176. pb £3.99 ISBN 9 7805 7123 4912.

Lawrence, D.H. *Selected Stories,* ed. Sue Wilson. Penguin. [2007] pp. xxxviii + 353. pb £12.99 ISBN 9 7801 4144 1658.

Lawrence, D.H. *The Rainbow.* Penguin. [2007] pp. xxxiv + 492. pb £9.99 ISBN 9 7801 4144 1382.

Lawrence, D.H. *The Virgin and the Gipsy.* Penguin. [2007] pp. 119. pb £4.99 ISBN 9 7801 4103 2894.

Lawrence, D.H. *Women in Love.* Penguin. [2007] pp. xxxiv + 558. pb £9.99 ISBN 9 7801 4144 1542.

Lewis, Pericles. *The Cambridge Introduction to Modernism.* CUP. [2007] pp. xii + 276. hb £45.00 ISBN 0 5218 2809 0. pb £15.99 ISBN 0 5215 3527 4.

Lewis, Pericles. *The Cambridge Introduction to Modernism.* CUP. [2007] pp. xii + 276. $70 ISBN 9 7805 2153 5274.

Light, Alison. *Composing Oneself: Virginia Woolf's Diaries and Memories.* VWGB. [2007] pp. 23. £4 ISBN 9 7809 5388 6692.

Light, Alison. *Mrs Woolf and the Servants.* Fig Tree. [2007] pp. 376. £20 ISBN 9 7806 7086 7172.

Linett, Maren Tova. *Modernism, Feminism, and Jewishness.* CUP. [2007] pp. xi + 229. £53 ISBN 9 7805 2188 0978.

Linett, Maren Tova. *Modernism, Feminism and Jewishness.* CUP. [2007] pp. xi + 229. $95 ISBN 9 7805 1136 5294.

Little, Ruth and Emily McLaughlin. *The Royal Court Theatre Inside Out.* Oberon Books [2007] pp. 480 pb £20 ISBN 978 1 84002 763 1

Littlejohns, Richard, and Sara Soncini, eds. *Myths of Europe*. Rodopi. [2007] pp. 295. £33 ISBN 9 7890 4202 1471.

Livesey, Ruth. *Socialism, Sex, and the Culture of Aestheticism in Britain, 1880–1914*. OUP. [2007] pp. 230. £30. ISBN 9 7801 9726 3983.

Lusty, Natalya. *Surrealism, Feminism, Psychoanalysis*. Ashgate. [2007] pp. ix + 174. £50 ISBN 9 7807 5465 3363.

MacKay, Marina. *Modernism and World War II*. CUP. [2007] pp. viii + 192. £47.00 ISBN 0 5218 7222 7 / 9 7805 1127 0697.

Magelssen, Scott and Ann Haugo, (eds) *Querying Difference in Theatre History* Cambridge Scholars Publishing [2007] pp.199. hb £29.99 ISBN 1 84718 303 4.

Mahaffey, Vicki. *Modernist Literature: Challenging Fictions*. Blackwell. [2007] pp. 264. £55 ISBN 0 6312 1306 6.

Manning, Susan, and Andrew Taylor, eds. *Transatlantic Literary Studies: A Reader*. JHUP. [2007] pp. 336. $65 ISBN 0 8018 8730 5.

Marcus, Laura. *The Tenth Muse: Writing about Cinema in the Modernist Period*. OUP. [2007] pp. xv + 562. $65 ISBN 9 7801 9923 0273.

Marsh, Nicky. *Money, Speculation and Finance in Contemporary British Fiction*. Continuum. [2007] pp. vii + 162. £60. ISBN 978 08264 9544 0.

Marzec, Robert P. *An Ecological and Postcolonial Study of Literature: From Daniel Defoe to Salman Rushdie*. Palgrave. [2007] pp. vii + 200. £45 ISBN 9 7814 0397 6406.

Mavor, Carol. *Reading Boyishly: Roland Barthes, J.M. Barrie, Jacques Henri Lartigue, Marcel Proust, and D.W. Winnicott*. DukeUP. [2007] pp. x + 522. £16.99 ISBN 9 7808 2233 9625.

Maxwell, Catherine, and Patricia Pulham, eds. *Vernon Lee: Decadence, Ethics, Aesthetics*. Palgrave. [2006] pp. xx + 210. £47 ISBN 9 7814 0399 2130.

McCracken, Scott. *Masculinities, Modernist Fiction and the Urban Public Sphere*. MUP. [2007] pp. 208. £50 ISBN 9 7807 1904 4830.

Melas, Natalie. *All the Difference in the World: Postcoloniality and the Ends of Comparison*. StanfordUP. [2007] pp. xvi + 278. £35 ISBN 9 7808 0473 1980.

Milbank, Alison. *Chesterton and Tolkien as Theologians*. Continuum. [2007] pp. xvi + 184. £40 ISBN 9 7805 6704 0947.

Miller, Andrew John. *Modernism and the Crisis of Sovereignty*. Routledge. [2007] pp. xxx + 222. £60.00 ISBN 0 4159 5604 8.

Miller, David. *With Poetry and Philosophy: Four Dialogic Studies – Wordsworth, Browning, Hopkins and Hardy*. CScholP. [2007] pp. x + 119. £19.79 ISBN 1 8471 8250 0.

Miller, Donna R., ed. *Language and Verbal Art Revisited*. Equinox Publishing Ltd. [2007] pp. 287. £50 ISBN 9 7818 4553 0945.

Morace, Robert A. *Irvine Welsh*. New British Fiction. Palgrave. [2007] pp. xii + 180. £42.50 hb. ISBN 978 1 40399 675 6. £9.99 pb. ISBN 978 1 4039 9676 3.

Moran, Patricia. *Virginia Woolf, Jean Rhys and the Aesthetics of Trauma*. Palgrave. [2007] pp. viii + 217. $65 ISBN 9 7814 0397 4822.

Najder, Zdzisław. *Joseph Conrad: A Life*. CamdenH. [2007] pp. xxiv + 745. £50 ISBN 9 7815 7113 3472.

O'Neill, Michael. *The All-Sustaining Air: Romantic Legacies and Renewals in British, American, and Irish Poetry since 1900*. OUP. [2007] pp. 224. £47 ISBN 9 7801 9929 9287.

O'Neill, Michael. *The All-Sustaining Air: Romantic Legacies and Renewals in British American, and Irish Poetry since 1900*. OUP. [2007] pp. xii + 208. £47.00 ISBN 0 1992 9928 7.

Oser, Lee. *The Return of Christian Humanism: Chesterton, Eliot, Tolkien, and the Romance of History*. UMissP. [2007] pp. xi + 190. $37.50 ISBN 9 7808 2621 7752.

Oser, Lee. *The Ethics of Modernism: Moral Ideas in Yeats, Eliot, Joyce, Woolf and Beckett*. CUP. [2007] pp. ix + 186. £65. ISBN 9 7805 2186 7252.

Oser, Lee. *The Ethics of Modernism: Moral Ideas in Yeats, Eliot, Joyce, Woolf and Beckett*. CUP. [2007] pp. x + 188. £45.00 ISBN 0 5218 6725 8.

Peacock, D. Keith. *Changing Performance: Culture and Performance in the British Theatre since 1945*. Peter Lang [2007] pp. 284. £35 pb ISBN 978 3 03911 071 1.

Phelps, Jim, and Nigel Bell, eds. *D.H. Lawrence around the World: South African Perspectives*. Echoing Green. [2007] pp. xxii + 335. £35 ISBN 9 7809 8025 0114.

Phillips, Lawrence, ed. *A Mighty Mass of Brick and Smoke: Victorian and Edwardian Representations of London*. Rodopi. [2007] pp. 316. £45 ISBN 9 7890 4202 2904.

Pike, David L. *Metropolis on the Styx: The Underworlds of Modern Urban Culture, 1800–2001*. CornUP. [2007] pp. xvii + 377. $27.95 ISBN 9 7808 0147 3043.

Plain, Gill, and Susan Sellers, eds. *A History of Feminist Literary Criticism*. CUP. [2007] pp. 352. £70 ISBN 9 7805 2185 2555.

Poplawski, Paul, ed. *English Literature in Context*. CUP. [2007] pp. xx + 685. £45 ISBN 9 7805 2183 9921.

Punter, David. *Modernity*. Palgrave. [2007] pp. ix + 237. $84 ISBN 9 7803 3391 4564.

Rabaté, Jean-Michel. *1913: The Cradle of Modernism*. Blackwell. [2007] pp. 272. £19.99 ISBN 9 7814 0516 1924.

Radford, Andrew. *The Lost Girls: Demeter–Persephone and the Literary Imagination, 1850–1930*. Rodopi. [2007] pp. 356. £50 ISBN 9 7890 4202 2355.

Ramsey-Kurz, Helga. *The Non-Literate Other: Readings of Illiteracy in Twentieth-Century Novels in English*. Rodopi. [2007] pp. x + 506. £74 ISBN 9 7890 4202 2409.

Randall, Bryony. *Modernism, Daily Time, and Everyday Life*. CUP. [2007] pp. x + 222. £45 ISBN 9 7805 2187 9842.

Ray, Martin. *Joseph Conrad: Memories and Impressions. An Annotated Bibliography*. Rodopi. [2007] pp. x + 188. $60 ISBN 9 7890 4202 2980.

Raz, Orna. *Social Dimensions in the Novels of Barbara Pym, 1949-1963: The Writer as Hidden Observer*. Mellen. [2007] pp. vi + 213. £69.95. ISBN 978 0 7734 5387 3.

Rosenberg, Isaac. *Poetry Out of my Head and Heart*, ed. Jean Liddiard. Enitharmon. [2007] pp.150. £15.00 ISBN 1 9046 3438 4.

Rowe, Anne. Ed. *Iris Murdoch: A Reassessment*. Palgrave. [2007] pp. xix + 217. £45. ISBN 0 230 00344 6.

Russell, Richard Rankin. *Martin McDonagh: A Casebook*. Routledge [2007] pp. 208. hb $120 ISBN 978 0 4159 7765 4.

Schafer, Elizabeth. *Lilian Baylis: A Biography*. UHertP. [2007] pp. 320. pb £8.99. ISBN 1 9028 0664 6.

Scott, Bonnie Kime, ed. *Gender in Modernism: New Geographies, Complex Intersections*. UIllP. [2007] pp. xviii + 872. $95 ISBN 9 7802 5207 4189.

Scott, Bonnie Kime, ed. *Gender in Modernism: New Geographies, Complex Intersections*. UIllP. [2007] pp. xx + 872. hb $95.00 ISBN 0 2520 3171 7. pb $40.00 ISBN 0 2520 7418 9.

Shaw, Robert B. *Blank Verse: A Guide to Its History and Use*. OhioP. [2007] pp. xiv + 305. $36.99 ISBN 0 8214 1757 7.

Shellard, Dominic. *Kenneth Tynan: Theatre Writings*. Nick Hern Books [2007] pp. 278. hb £20 ISBN 978 1 85459 050 3.

Shiach, Morag, ed. *The Cambridge Companion to the Modernist Novel*. CUP. [2007] pp. xx + 252. £45 ISBN 0 5216 7074 8.

Shiach, Morag, ed. *The Cambridge Companion to the Modernist Novel*. CUP. [2007] pp. xx + 249. £18.99 ISBN 9 7805 2167 0746.

Simmons, Allan H. *Conrad's Heart of Darkness*. Continuum. [2007] pp. viii + 132. £10.99 ISBN 9 7808 2648 9340.

Simmons, Allan H., and J.H. Stape, eds. *The Secret Agent: Centennial Essays*. Rodopi. [2007] pp. 195. £35 ISBN 9 7890 4202 1761.

Skinner, Paul, ed. *Ford Madox Ford's Literary Contacts*. Rodopi. [2007] pp. 271. £38.57 ISBN 9 0420 2248 5.

Smyczyńska, Katarzyna. *The World According to Bridget Jones*. Literary and Cultural Theory. Lang. [2007] pp. 195. £28.80. ISBN 978 3 03911 054 4.

Snaith, Anna, and Michael Whitworth, eds. *Locating Woolf: The Politics of Space and Place*. Palgrave. [2007] pp. xi + 240. £47 ISBN 9 7802 3050 0730.

Snaith, Anna, ed. *Palgrave Advances in Virginia Woolf Studies*. Palgrave. [2007] pp. 328. £62 ISBN 9 7814 0390 4041.

Spear, Hilda D. *Iris Murdoch*. 2nd edn. Palgrave. [2007] pp. ix + 149. £14.99. ISBN 1 4039 8710 6.

Stoddart, Helen. *Angela Carter's Nights at the Circus*. Routledge Guides to Literature. Routledge. [2007] pp. xii + 152. £55 hb. ISBN 978 0 415 35011 2. £14.99 pb. ISBN 978 0 415 35012 9.

Tanitch, Robert. *London Stage in the 20th Century*. Haus. [2007] pp. 312. £30 ISBN 1 9049 5074 4.

Tew, Philip. *The Contemporary British Novel*. 2nd edn. Continuum. [2007] pp. xx + 257. £60 hn. 978 0 82649 319 4. £16.99 pb. ISBN 978 0 8264 9320 0.

Thomas, David, David Carlton, and Anne Etienne. *Theatre Censorship: From Walpole to Wilson*. OUP [2007] pp. 297. hb £53 ISBN 978 0 19 926028 7.

Thompson, Laura. *Agatha Christie: An English Mystery*. Headline. [2007] pp. 534. £20 ISBN 0 7553 1487 5.

Tidwell, Joanne Campbell. *Politics and Aesthetics in* The Diary of Virginia Woolf. Routledge. [2007] pp. vi + 120. £50 ISBN 9 7804 1595 8172.

Tobin, Daniel, ed. *The Book of Irish American Poetry: From the Eighteenth Century to the Present.* UNDP. [2007] pp. 925. $65 ISBN 0 2680 4230 6.

Traficante, Antonio. *D.H. Lawrence's Italian Travel Literature and Translations of Giovanni Verga: A Bakhtinian Reading.* Lang. [2007] pp. x + 206. £34.50 ISBN 9 7808 2048 8172.

Trotter, David. *Cinema and Modernism.* Blackwell. [2007] pp. 224. pb £17.99 ISBN 1 4051 5982 0.

Trotter, David. *Cinema and Modernism.* Blackwell. [2007] pp. xii + 205. £17.99 ISBN 1 4051 5982 1.

Usandizaga, Aránzazu, and Andrew Monnickendam, eds. *Back to Peace: Reconciliation and Retribution in the Postwar Period.* UNDP. [2007] pp 320. pb $35 ISBN 9 7802 6804 4527.

Vanheste, Jeroen. *Guardians of the Humanist Legacy: The Classicism of T.S. Eliot's Criterion Network and its Relevance to our Postmodern World.* Brill. [2007] pp. xviii + 542. €99.00 ISBN 9 0041 6160 3.

Vendler, Helen. *Our Secret Discipline: Yeats and Lyric Form.* OUP. [2007] pp. 428. £21 ISBN 0 1992 8186 6.

Wainwright, Valerie. *Ethics and the English Novel from Austen to Forster.* Ashgate. [2007] pp. vi + 216. £55 ISBN 9 7807 5465 4322.

Wald, Christina. *Hysteria, Trauma and Melancholia: Performative Maladies in Contemporary Anglophone Drama.* Palgrave [2007] pp. 297. hb £50 ISBN 978 0 230 54712 4.

Wetzsteon, Rachel. *Influential Ghosts: A Study of Auden's Sources.* Routledge. [2007] pp. xiv + 128 £45.00. ISBN 0 4159 7546 8.

Wigginton, Chris. *Modernism from the Margins: The 1930s Poetry of Louis MacNeice and Dylan Thomas.* UWalesP. [2007] pp. xi + 166. pb £18.99 ISBN 0 7083 1927 7.

Wilson, Leigh. *Modernism.* Continuum. [2007] pp. vi + 192. pb £10.99 ISBN 0 8264 8561 8.

Woolf, Virginia. *The Platform of Time: Memoirs of Family and Friends.* Ed. S. P. Rosenbaum. Hesperus Press Limited. [2007] pp. ix + 222. $16.95 ISBN 9 7818 4391 7113.

Zaylor, Michael Matthew, ed. *The Garden God: A Tale of Two Boys, by Forrest Reid.* Valancourt. [2007] pp. lvi + 100. pb $14.95 ISBN 9 7819 3455 5040.

XV

American Literature to 1900

CLARE ELLIOTT, ANNE-MARIE FORD AND
THERESA SAXON

This chapter has two sections: 1 General; 2. American Literature to 1900. Section 1 is by Theresa Saxon; section 2 is by Clare Elliott, Anne-Marie Ford and Theresa Saxon.

1. General

Key resources for scholars and those generally interested in American literature of the nineteenth century feature in the Book Reviews and Brief Mentions sections of the quarterly publication *American Literature* (*AL*). The full and detailed bibliographical listing of books, articles, review essays, notes and dissertations of the annual publication *Modern Language Association International Bibliography* (*MLAIB*) also consistently proves a useful resource for scholars. *American Literary Scholarship: An Annual* (*AmLS*) constitutes an exhaustive bibliographical survey of the year's critical writing; editor David Nordloh and the team of reviewers cover extensive ground in this valuable resource, which includes sections on Emerson, Thoreau, Fuller and transcendentalism; Hawthorne; Melville; Whitman and Dickinson; Mark Twain; Henry James; Wharton and Cather, as well as providing a general guide to scholarship on nineteenth-century literature. This year's edition [2007] covers critical material published in 2005. *American Literary History* (*ALH*) continues to offer a substantial range of resources for students and specialists in American literature; the four issues that form volume 19 [2007] incorporate multicultural and interdisciplinary studies of nineteenth-century literature relating to religious practices, print culture and journalistic literature, temperance, travel and the transatlantic; notable essays include Kendall Johnson, '1969—*Peace, Friendship, and Financial Panic: Reading the Mark of Black Hawk in* Life of Ma-Ka-Tai-Me-She-Kia-Kiak' (*ALH* 4[2007] 771–99), which traces the role of the Peace Medal in transferring the life of the 'Indian' to a metaphorical space, and the relationship between that shift from material to figurative in the lands claims of the early nineteenth century. Overall, the

Year's Work in English Studies, Volume 88 (2009) © *The English Association; all rights reserved*
doi:10.1093/ywes/map005

essays published throughout 2007 maintain an essential focus on the role of the literary voice in America's cultural output.

2. American Literature to 1900

Edited by Paula Bernat Bennett and Karen L. Kilcup, *Teaching Nineteenth-Century American Poetry* is a timely and valuable contribution to American studies, divided into four sections. Part I, 'Teaching Various Kinds of Poems', begins with Betty Booth Donohue's 'Oktahutchee's Song: Reflections on Teaching Nineteenth-Century American Indian Poetry'. She points out that Native American poetry is little known and offers a range of fascinating examples, with a particular focus on 'power' words which create an ironic double meaning, offering the possibility of a subversive speech, when delivered to different audiences. 'Teaching the Sorrow Songs', by Barbara McCaskill, engages with the spirituals of the African American and is succeeded by Karen L. Kilcup's '"Wild Nights"? Approaches to Teaching Nineteenth-Century Erotic Poetry'. In this section the poems of Walt Whitman, Emily Dickinson (one of whose poems contributed to the title of this essay), Alice Dunbar-Nelson, Frances Ellen Watkins Harper, Frances Sargent Osgood and Pauline Johnson are discussed in a lively and engaging tone. Turning in a different direction, Paula Bernat Bennett's 'Mill Girls and Minstrels: Working-Class Poetry in the Nineteenth Century' explores the poetics of the Lowell mill girls, and the development of minstrelsy in particular. This is followed by 'Reenacting American Civil War Poetry', in which Tyler Hoffman singles out for attention Herman Melville's *Battle-Pieces and Aspects of the War* [1866], by Sarah Piatt, whose work is now receiving considerable attention, and two African American poets, Frances E.W. Harper and Paul Laurence Dunbar. '"I looked again and saw": Teaching Postbellum Realist Poetry' is Elizabeth Renker's offering, and also discusses the compelling works of Melville and Piatt, as well as that of Edwin Arlington Robinson and William Dean Howells. The concluding chapter in this section is Angela Sorby's 'Teaching the Schoolroom Poets', in which she proposes that many popular writers of the time wrote poems that functioned as performance texts. She demonstrates this in a detailed discussion of the work of William Cullen Bryant, Oliver Wendell Holmes, James Russell Lowell, John Greenleaf Whittier and Henry Wadsworth Longfellow, so bringing the first section of the study to a close. Part II, 'Teaching Poets in Context', develops earlier themes, and begins with Paul Lauter's teaching of the works of Lydia Sigourney, in which he concentrates on her Native American poems. This is followed by '"The glorious secrets of sad love": The Development of Margaret Fuller's Poetry', by Jeffrey Steele, where another significant woman writer and her intellectual and poetic legacy are explored in a detailed and thoughtful piece. In 'Teaching African American Poetry of the Reconstruction Era: Frances E.W. Harper's "Moses: A Story of the Nile"', the two authors, Frances Smith Foster and Valerie L. Ruffin, demonstrate that before and after the Civil War, African Americans routinely compared their situation with that of the Hebrews enslaved in Egypt. This theme is developed in sparkling fashion, before merging effortlessly into Gregory Eiselein's essay on 'Emma Lazarus and Jewish Poetry'. The subsequent chapter, 'Charlotte Perkins Gilman's "Toolbox": The Value of Satiric Poetry and Social Reform', by Alfred Bendixen, focuses on a writer best known for her powerful short story 'The Yellow Wall-Paper' [1899]. He insists, however, that Gilman also deserves to be admired for her poetry, and recommends it as a teaching tool. The following essay, 'Paul Laurence Dunbar and Postbellum African American Poetry', by Nassim W. Balestrini, discusses Dunbar's poems, and those of other African American writers, in the historical context of a recently reunited country. Judith P. Saunder's 'Stephen Crane: American Poetry at a Crossroads', explores his oeuvre, and the power of just 136 short poems, written at the end of the nineteenth century, thus bringing the second section to a conclusion. Part III, 'Strategies for Teaching', begins promisingly with 'Poe, Women Poets, and Print Circulations', by Eliza Richards, followed by Katharine Rodier's 'Poetry and the American Renaissance: Another Reconsideration'. A lively period for narrative poetry is further discussed in ' "Told in story or sung in rhyme": Narrative Pairings in Prose and Verse', by Jane Donohue Eberwein. Elizabeth Petrino's 'Discordant American Vistas: Teaching Nineteenth-Century Paintings and Poetry', appears to pick up on the musical theme, but actually debates visual materials as effective tools in teaching poetry. This is succeeded by Elizabeth Savage's 'Understanding Sentimentalism', and Cheryl Lawson Walker's amusingly entitled 'Sex, Drugs, and Mingling Spirits: Teaching Nineteenth-Century Women Poets', in which she explores poetics with regard to the ecstatic. Returning to the practical is 'Teaching Nineteenth-Century American Poetry in the Community College', by Gregory Byrd and Nan Morelli-White. This section draws to a close, aptly enough, in Edward Brunner's 'In Newspaper, over Radio Waves, on Envelopes: Nineteenth-Century Poetic Discourse in the Early Twentieth Century'. The final part of this collection offers a wide-ranging selection of resources, organized by Philipp Schweighauser, which concludes an effective and innovative selection of materials designed to teach and mine the rich vein of American studies.

Mitchell Breitwieser, in *National Melancholy: Mourning and Opportunity in Classic American Literature*, inaugurates his study with a rider: 'classic' he argues does not equal 'aesthetically superior'; rather, the enduring popularity of his chosen texts—Anne Bradstreet's poetics, Thomas Jefferson's *Notes on the State of Virginia*, Walt Whitman's *Leaves of Grass*, Henry David Thoreau's *Cape Cod*, Sarah Orne Jewett's *Deephaven*, alongside F. Scott Fitzgerald and Jack Kerouac—mean that they merit definition as 'classic' in a more accommodating sense. The extended, detailed and wide-ranging introductory chapter (aligning Salman Rushdie's *Midnight's Children* with Walt Whitman's *Leaves of Grass*, for example), assesses the construction of nation seen from the perspective of the participant, 'or particle of' a nation, particularly a concept of nation that is inherently flawed and weak, producing a 'national melancholy' as a fantasy for the notion of nation. Mourning is a structuring feature of this study, as Breitwieser explores the various ways in which his writers find themselves struggling for expression, in a society where emotion is stemmed into a vehicle for communal requirements, boundaries and codes, which align mourning with the good of the nation, resulting in a fraudulent emotive state that exhausts and depresses. But, argues Breitwieser, these writers found a range of creative outlets for their emotions that did not capitulate to the social whole, instead reaching a gateway for a reinvigorated understanding of experience. In this searching and thoughtful study, Mitchell Breitwieser revisits the canon and resists canonicity.

In *American Elegy: The Poetry of Mourning from the Puritans to Whitman*, Max Cavitch explores the development of the American elegy—whose history, he contends, is difficult to trace; with its capaciousness and flexibility, the genre's ability to shift and respond in dynamic ways to loss and mourning, the genre is 'difficult to historicize', and in America has been 'virtually ignored'. Citing the examples of Benjamin Franklin and Mark Twain as satirists of elegies, Cavitch further argues that the history of American elegy has been subsumed by other literary models; his aim, in this book, is to reassert that history, and consider the ramifications of the diversity and dynamism of the elegy within American letters. At the same time, this historicist exercise attends to the deeply private and idiosyncratic elements inherent to the poetry of mourning. Rejecting the 'declension narrative' of the elegy, wherein Puritan culture of the eighteenth century renders the form irrelevant, Cavitch argues, through an exploration of the elegiac works of Cotton Mather, Benjamin Franklin, Richard Lewis, Annis Boudinot Stockton, Phyllis Wheatley and Philip Freneau, that the elegy became central to the shaping of local and national identities. The debate continues with a consideration of the plethora of elegies for George Washington, including works by famous literary figures such as Susanna Rowson and Charles Brockden Brown; a consideration of the elegy in relation to Jackson expansionism and the impact on Native Americans as can be seen in the writings of William Cullen Bryant; an exploration of the much-maligned and mocked 'child elegy', exemplified by Lydia Sigourney and Henry Wadsworth Longfellow and, perhaps inevitably, Ralph Waldo Emerson's 'Threnody', then moving into an account of African American elegiac responses to the conditions of slavery through to the Civil War, in the poetry of Phyllis Wheatley, George White, Julia Howard Ward and Frances Harper, amongst others. The book concludes with an account of the elegies to Abraham Lincoln, arguing that Whitman manages to produce a version of elegy free from 'deformation of grievance', against history. A study of a specific genre and an account of American poetics, this text will ably serve the community of critics.

Judy Cornes's *Madness and the Loss of Identity in Nineteenth Century Fiction* is a critical study of the works of such writers as Ambrose Bierce, Henry James, Charles Chesnutt and Lillie Devereux Blake. The iconoclastic American writer Bierce was among those wounded in the Civil War, and his world-view was to be dramatically altered by his personal wartime experiences. In all his stories, mingling the real with the surreal, identity becomes a quagmire in which characters disappear and are lost for ever. The nightmare worlds he creates are ones of horror and despair. The cynical Bierce rarely allows his characters much opportunity to enjoy love and romance; instead people move as though they are wandering on circular paths which, ultimately, result in the tragic. Shadows and substance merge in Bierce's writings, and the Fates play a terrible, cosmic joke on mankind. The chapter on Henry James begins with a quote from his 'The Art of Fiction' [1884], in which he explores the tension between the unseen and the seen. However, only one of James's texts is discussed, perhaps in view of the volume of work already devoted to his writings. As a result, chapter 2, 'Henry James and the Examined Life', is slighter than the other sections and feels more so, coming immediately after the detailed exploration of what Cornes describes as 'The Nightmare World of Ambrose Bierce'. 'Charles Chesnutt and the Despair of Blackness' represents in its title a powerful reference to racism; it contains fascinating excerpts and analysis of *Mandy Oxendine* [1896], the first extant novel written by black author Chesnutt, who was both a social historian and a psychological realist. In 'Lillie Devereux Blake and the Perilous Web of Sex', Cornes explores the ominously titled *Fettered for Life* [1874], in which the author often intrudes into her narrative in order to present a didactic speech on the evils men commit against women. Blake also uses a main character whom the reader knows as Frank Heywood, but, at the novel's end, realizes is actually a woman. Although much of *Fettered for Life* is heavy-handed in its long, polemical speeches about the need for women's suffrage, it is also effective in engaging the reader's attention regarding Heywood. His melancholy and gentle behaviour is touching, and from the outset we recognize something different about this character which entrances us. This critical study centres on preoccupations with vague, shifting and dualistic characterizations, and offers, especially in the discussions on Bierce, Chesnutt and Blake, valuable insights into nineteenth-century concepts of identity and selfhood.

If, as Gregg Crane insists, in *The Cambridge Introduction to the Nineteenth-Century American Novel*, American fiction could not help reflecting the turbulence and diversity of nineteenth-century life, then the reader may reasonably expect this study to be both rich and complex. It certainly does not disappoint, and is beautifully organized into a lively and detailed exploration of the literary, mirroring concerns about social stability, even as it embraces ideas of rapid change. He recounts the story of the novel from its beginnings in the early republic to the end of the nineteenth century, examining the genre's major themes, Crane discusses both famous and less well-known texts, as the novelists respond to their historical moment. Divided into three chapters, Crane's book begins by exploring the romances, through the fiction of Nathaniel Hawthorne, James Fenimore Cooper, Edgar Allen Poe, Harriet Beecher Stowe, Herman Melville, Lydia Maria Child and Catharine Maria Sedgwick. The ubiquity of the romance was such that, as Nina Baym in her 'Concepts of Romance', remarks, the terms 'novel' and 'romance' were used interchangeably in the antebellum era. The main types of romance were historical, philosophical and sensational, and claimed a common theme of deep significance, such as the fate of the nation, or the deformation of human nature in an urban environment. The historical romancers' transformation of history into legend is evident in Cooper's *The Last of the Mohicans*, or Hawthorne's *The Blithedale Romance* (although the author refers to this text throughout as *The Blithesdale Romance*). Crane develops his study of the sub-genre in tales of the plantation, race and republicanism, before debating the philosophical traits of texts through Poe's 'The Narrative of Arthur Gordon Pym' [1838], Hawthorne's *The Scarlet Letter* [1850] and Melville's *Moby-Dick* [1851]; he argues for the educative quality of such thought-provoking works, reflecting a nation experiencing vast social and cultural change. Finally, he explores the excesses of the sensational—focusing on shock, terror and intense excitement—before moving, in chapter 2, to 'The Sentimental Novel'. Here Stowe's *Uncle Tom's Cabin* [1852], Susan Warner's *The Wide, Wide World* [1850], Maria Cummins's *The Lamplighter* [1854] and Fanny Fern's *Ruth Hall* [1855], all bestsellers, are examined in detail. Crane elaborates, in this sub-genre, on texts as representative of a moment of conversion, when a flood of emotions transforms the individual. This, he suggests, reveals central moral truths and access to the values that give life meaning, which the reader of the time instinctively celebrates in actions of reform, change and development. Towards the conclusion of this section Crane deliberates on the move towards realism in literature following the Civil War. Here he introduces us to Rebecca Harding Davis and Elizabeth Stoddard as writers of the key texts in this drift towards realism. Davis's *Life in the Iron Mills* [1861] offers vivid images of the toil of the mill-workers, pushing for reform of industrial capitalism. Stoddard's *The Morgesons* [1862], meanwhile, breaks with conventions of sentimental fiction very differently. Written in the first person, it has a complex time structure and a heroine who seeks change, movement and continuing rupture with the past, without concern for the future. The third chapter develops this thread in 'The Realist Novel', in which Crane explores realist techniques and subject matter. He recognizes, too, the tensions and divergences in realist fiction in the work of William Dean Howells and Henry James, as well as the short stories of Sarah Orne Jewett and the fiction of Mark Twain. In conclusion, Crane includes detailed notes in his story of the American novel, a wide-ranging narrative, which offers scholars a rich resource.

Theo Davis, in *Formalism, Experience, and the Making of American Literature in the Nineteenth Century*, argues that American literature should not be regarded as an ongoing articulation of American identity, challenging one of the cornerstones of American literary criticism. Her study encompasses Ralph Waldo Emerson, Nathaniel Hawthorne and Harriet Beecher Stowe, as writers whose conception of experience manifests itself as an abstracted province of typicality rather than subjective and individuistic, demonstrating that the theoretical promise that history contributes to the shape of literary form is untenable. Rather than regarding experience as embodied within the textual weave, then, Davis contends that experience is an object of contemplation, an invention that emanates from the text, manifestly shaped and projected. In a lengthy and detailed introduction, Davis talks us through the development of deconstruction and New Criticism, forging a pathway through the distinctions and shared ground within these critical models, and demonstrates ways in which her own study departs from the conventional apprehension that we can see meaning as separate from experience, or that we see meaning as part of experience. Maintaining that 'experience has a form', Davis's study of the relationship between literary productions and experience will be of use to scholars keen to explore new ways of thinking about the literature of the nineteenth century.

Slumming in New York: From the Waterfront to Mythic Harlem, by Robert M. Dowling, explores the shaping of the city space through an examination of 'one of the most intriguing discourses to materialize form New York's tempestuous ascent'—the interaction between mainstream/outsider voices and marginalized/insider ones. In the process, Dowling inverts usage of these key terms, as 'insider' comes to stand for those who belong to smaller, marginalized districts within the city writ large, distinguishable from the standard sense of the 'marginal', who belong nowhere. This concept of the insider encompasses divergent perspectives dating from 1880 to 1930—a period of intense development within the city—addressing the East Side waterfront, the infamous Bowery, 'black bohemia', the Jewish Lower East Side and Harlem. through an engagement with competing outsider/insider voices in 'slumming' narratives, including Helen Campbell's *The Problem of the* Poor [1882], Stephen Crane's Bowery tale *George's Mother* [1896], Paul Laurence Dunbar's *The Sport of the Gods* [1902], Hutchins Hapgoods's *The Spirit of the Ghetto* [1902] and Carl Van Vechten's *Nigger Heaven* [1926]. Taking issue with the understanding of realist forms as a containment of the threat posed by marginalized voices, Dowling argues that the narrative dialogue between insider and outsider, as demonstrated within his chosen literary productions, offers an opportunity for us to challenge popular morality as well as the extent to which the outsider narrative penetrated the cultural consciousness of the insider. A fascinating study, which assesses the literary history of New York City crossing borders of class, race, ethnicity and locale as well as genre, interlacing reformist and sociological writings with fiction, this text will be of use to scholars keen to extend their New York knowledge.

In her introductory essay to *Representations of Death in Nineteenth-Century US Writing and Culture*, editor Lucy E. Frank clarifies an important distinction in this area of study, between 'death' as an end-of-life affair that was the experience of the socially privileged, and 'death' as an untimely fact of life and an everyday occurrence that was the pervading atmosphere for marginalized groups. With this in mind, the essays gathered together for this collection feature a range of canonical and non-canonical writers and tales, examining the diverse literature of death that emerged throughout the nineteenth century. The first section of essays deals with the relationship between death and political identities. In 'Chief Seattle's Afterlife: Mourning and Cross-Cultural Synthesis in Nineteenth-Century America', John J. Kucich examines the transcript of the speech made at Puget Sound in the 1850s to warn the white audience against land appropriation. Although the speech was ignored, contends Kucich, the 'afterlife' of its warning remained manifestly ever present to the invading white settlers, a statement of the resilience of Native American rituals and cultural forms even in the face of death. Jeffrey Steele, in 'Escaping the "Benumbing influence of a present embodied death": The Politics of Mourning in 1850s African-American Writing', looks at 1850s African American writers coming to terms with the emotional and physical damage of slavery, the loss of life alongside the 'deathly effect' of this permanent sense of loss. Dana Luciano's 'Representative Mournfulness: Nation and Race in the Time of Lincoln' argues that African American mourning placed Lincoln as an emancipator but avoided the mythologizing pitfall that swallowed up prevalent memorial discourse, resisting the urge to locate ideals of nation within a timeless, transcendental sphere that could avoid questions of culpability and blame. In ' "Stock in dead folk": The Value of Black Mortality in Mark Twain's *The Adventures of Huckleberry Finn*', Stephen Shapiro also examines Charles Chesnutt's *The Marrow of Tradition*, arguing that the sentimental mode, which perpetuates a particular image of death and public displays of mourning, acts to consolidate rather than override social frictions and dissonance. Grauke's ' "I cannot bear to be hurted anymore": Suicide as Dialectical Ideological Sign in Nineteenth Century American Realism', examines Rebecca Harding Davies's *Life in the Iron Mills*, where the act of suicide amongst marginalized working-class groups can be regarded as both self-affirming and self-destructive, reiterating a well-worn stereotype of the incapable class and its dependency on external order and control, in need of bourgeois reform. Joanne van der Woude's 'Rewriting the Myth of Black Morality: W.E.B. DuBois and Charles W. Chesnutt', the final essay of this section, examines how the escalating rate of death amongst black communities was linked, by DuBois and Chesnutt, to white racist ideologies about death in relation to the physical and moral violence enacted on the body of the black American. The second section of essays focuses on elegies and death. Alison Chapman's ' "I think I was enchanted": Elizabeth Barrett Browning's Haunting of American Women Poets' looks at the homage poems dedicated to EBB, exploring a transatlantic dialogue between women poets as a sub-genre of 'poetess praise poems', which act to render the poet both spiritually and materially, both mourned as gone yet erotically present and tangible, her influence leading to a poetics that transits from consolation to the political. Paula Bernat Bennett, in 'God's Will, Not Mine: Child Death as Theodicean Problem in Poetry by Nineteenth-Century American Women', examines the impact of high infant mortality rates on elegiac poetics, arguing that the apparently resigned tone of much of this poetry—written by the likes of Lydia Sigourney, Frances Harper, Emily Dickinson and Sarah Piatt— demonstrates an urge to resist consolation, challenging the sentimentalization of the dead infant. Jessica F. Roberts concludes this second section with ' "The little coffin": Anthologies, Conventions and Dead Children', which examines the marketing strategies for anthologies of elegies to dead children in the nineteenth century, featuring Henry Wadsworth Longfellow, Lydia Sigourney, James Russell Lowell, Ralph Waldo Emerson and Felicia Hemans— challenging the conventional view that the elegy, as a sentimental form, was predominantly the remit of women writers. The evocation of culture in ritual and mass phenomena and death forms the topic of the final section of essays in this volume. Ann Schofield's 'The Fashion of Mourning' examines the ritual of mourning that developed in the Victorian era as a gendered social performance intrinsically linked to the middle-class and feminine culture of sentiment, enacted on the body of the grieving woman, enabling an eroticized version of mourning that became populist by the end of the century. In ' "At a distance from the scene of the atrocity": Death and Detachment in

Poe's "The Mystery of Marie Rogêt" ', Elizabeth Carolyn Miller examines the public response to this infamous 'murder', arguing that Poe's disinterested narrative, while claiming opposition to the sentimental press, demonstrates a similar fascination with the case and an urge to capitalize on the commodification and erotics of violent death. Dassia N. Posner's 'Spectres on the New York Stage: The (Pepper's) Ghost Craze of 1863' examines a fleeting yet fervent fanaticism for spectral illusions on stage, charting the ingenuity of invention that corresponded to the increasing street rioting against the Civil War draft, the ghostly emanations offering rational explanation alongside the frisson of fear, a comfort for a generation attempting to come to terms with the inexplicable horror and death of war and inner-city mob violence. Ann Heilmann's 'Medusa's Blinding Art: Mesmerism and Female Artistic Agency in Louisa May Alcott's "A Pair of Blue Eyes; or, Modern Magic" ' focuses on Alcott's subversion of the conventional mesmeric relations—male mesmerist, female medium—in her ghostly tale of revenge haunting, a figurative exploration of the damage done to women controlled by injunctions imposed within a dominantly patriarchal social order. This collection concludes with Kelly Richardson's ' "To surprise immortality": Spiritualism and Shakerism in William Dean Howells's *The Undiscovered Country*', which addresses the compassion and ambivalence expressed by Howells in his consideration of the spiritualist urge to come to terms with bereavement, but cautions against untrammelled grieving and the thirst for 'knowledge' about the spiritual world. Individually, these essays explore their chosen writers and topics with intellectual clarity; taken together, the collection does indeed offer a fascinating insight into an era's preoccupation with death, mourning and the otherworldly.

George B. Handley's *New World Poetics: Nature and the Adamic Imagination of Whitman, Neruda and Walcott* embarks on a dialogue between postcolonialism and ecocriticism, constructing a comparative study of New World writers from the Americas North and South as well as the Caribbean. Taking Derek Walcott's 1974 essay 'The Muse of History' as a point of departure, Handley argues that ecocriticism can fulfil an important task in coming to terms with the New World in contemporary times, with its postlapsarian adamic (adamic in lower case) emphasis on the ramifications and depredations of colonialism in terms of both the 'human and natural' provinces of history, opening the door to a vision of the New World's nature as potentially redemptive, without resorting to expression of 'New World elation' as a capitulation to colonial discourses. With a broad focus on the New World as a product of the history of colonization, the American hemisphere is considered within the parameters of well-trodden ground— slavery, European settlements, the subjugation of Native Americans and the displacements of populations. The writers who address these issues— Whitman, Neruda and Walcott—all do so within 'epic' parameters, argues Handley, in attending to the 'cross-cultural and environmental' features that form the collective inheritance of this region. Three parts explore this ground in detail: the first sets out the parameters of the study, examining the relationship between ecology and literature; the second engages ecocritical approaches to a comparative study of the three poets; and the third, focusing on Walcott, sets out to explore the little-studied impact of the environment on his poetics. This book, which casts a redemptive light on the possibilities of the New World, as, according to Handley, is demonstrated in the environmental poetics of the region, constitutes an informed and detailed literary study, as well as appealing to our sense of human community and hope for continuity, and will be both of interest to scholars and deeply rewarding to the general reader in search of optimism.

Les Harrison's account of museum culture in America, *The Temple and the Forum: The American Museum and Cultural Authority in Hawthorne, Melville, Stowe and Whitman*, stems from Duncan F. Cameron's formulation of two types of museum: the temple, where we are guided by the curatorship of highest cultural value, and the forum, where we are involved in an experimental, dynamic model that echoes the showman exhibitionism of P.T. Barnum's mid-nineteenth-century American Museum. The apparent competition between these two models, argues Harrison, can be read as an emblem for the enactment of a series of binaries across American culture in the nineteenth century, the most notable, of course, being highbrow versus lowbrow. Such competing tendencies, we discover, are highlighted through a joint study of Hawthorne, who seems to have regarded museums as a repository of relics that formed an essential bridge between the present and the fleet-of-foot transient past, Melville and Whitman, who saw in museums a variety and breadth that could respond to the plenitude of America as a democratic nation, and Stowe, to whom a museum was a store for keeping an account of and interrogating a history of racial difference. Comparing literary attitudes to museums as curatorship or exhibitionism by exploring American writers alongside Charles Wilson Peale's Philadelphia Museum (1785–1843), P.T. Barnum's American Museum in New York City (1841–65) and the United States National Museum at the Smithsonian in Washington, DC, which opened its doors in 1879, Harrison demonstrates that the concept of competition between the temple and the forum is somewhat less than clear-cut. The museum, ultimately, argues Harrison, is less a repository of relics of America than part of an ongoing debate about the 'contents and contours' of American culture. Lucid and engaged, and supported by instructive illustrations, this book will serve the general reader as well as offering insights into nineteenth-century American literary culture for the specialist in that field.

Nine essays make up the body of *There Before Us: Religion, Literature, and Culture from Emerson to Wendell Berry*, supplemented by editor Roger Lundin's introduction and an afterword by Andrew Delbanco. While religion and religious beliefs exist at the core of American society, argues Lundin, critical exploration of the significant literary engagement with belief and faith remains 'an invisible domain'. The collection sets out to illuminate that domain, exposing what has been 'there before us' in American letters, examining the religious beliefs and impact of spirituality on the writing of several key American writers, and is based on work done by the American Literature and Religion Seminar, this volume's focus on Judaism and Christianity being a reflection, contends Lundin, of the spiritual influences enacted on major American writers. Inevitably, it might be suggested, the collection heads off with an account of Ralph Waldo Emerson, whose religious influences, one could quibble, are less than invisible in his writing. Certainly Emerson demonstrated a profound indifference to orthodox scriptural readings, but, as Lundin notes, this was made manifest in his writings as a keen interest in religious practices and spirituality. Barbara Packer's 'Signing Off: Religious Indifference in America' offers a broad outline of indifference as an intrinsic aspect of antebellum America's religious experience, as attention became riveted on social movements such as abolitionism, which performed as a site of 'moral clarity' for the congregation of like-minded 'believers'. John Gatta, in '"Rare and delectable places": Thoreau's Imagination of Sacred Space at Walden', argues that Thoreau's 'reading' of nature in *Walden* ran contrary to the Protestant biblical orthodoxy of the previous two centuries, shifting authority from text to space, and translating revelation from the 'visible facts of creation'. Michael Colacurcio's 'Charity and its Discontents: Pity and Politics in Melville's Fiction' finds a representation of Karl Marx's concept of religion as opium in Melville, but argues that, ultimately, Melville's literary theodicy made space for a politics that was partial, stopping short of revolutionary radicalism. Roger Lundin takes the task of Emily Dickinson and faith on his shoulders, in 'Nimble Believing: Dickinson and the Conflict of Interpretations', investigating her 'struggle with God' through an analysis of letters as well as poems, and drawing on theoretical paradigms engaging with our ongoing struggle to believe, particularly that proposed by Paul Ricoeur (*Freud and Philosophy*), to argue that Dickinson gave shape to debates that would resonate into the twentieth century. Katherine Clay Bassard, in 'Private Interpretations: The Defence of Slavery, Nineteenth-Century Hermeneutics, and the Poetry of Frances E.W. Harper', turns attention to African American traditions which locate Christianity as a source of power rather than a site of internal conflict, arguing that Harper's poetry developed a Christocentric vision that challenged the 'specifically racialized hermeneutic' that had structured readings of the Bible, circumscribed by slaving ideologies, in the early nineteenth century. The second half of this collection, as it moves towards the twentieth century, becomes less explicitly focused on Christianity, as did, according to Lundin, American culture more broadly, to think about 'religion' within less constrained boundaries. Harold K. Bush Jr, in 'Mark Twain's Lincoln as "Man of the Border": Religion, Free Thinking and the Civil War', argues that belief shifted from a focus on scriptured religion and faith to a secularized version of belief—in the nation itself—exemplified in the deification of Abraham Lincoln that can be seen in the writings of Southerner Mark Twain, whose conscious espousal of 'Northern' writings of the Civil War, one might argue, is echoed in his description of Lincoln as 'a man of the border', a figure to bring about the holy unity of that disjointed, warring America. In 'The Liberal Saint: American Liberalism and the Problem of Character', M.D. Walhout locates the later writings of William and Henry James, particularly *The Varieties of Religious Experience* and *The Wings of a Dove*, as interrogators of a type of liberal, individualist secular saintliness, and finds the inherent contradiction in the tragedy of being saintly and the need to celebrate success and victory within a society idealizing 'democratic perfectionism'. Moving into the twentieth century 'proper', Gail McDonald's 'A Homemade Heaven: Modernist Poetry and the Social Gospel' traces the socialization of the Gospels, moving from a consideration of the internalized religious experience to a more politicized liberal theology of the social gospel, through her examination of the divergent responses to Christian tradition, yet ultimate urge to make the 'gods' new—and in earthly communication—in Ezra Pound, H.D. and T.S. Eliot. Lawrence Buell's powerful 'Religion and the Environmental Imagination in American Literature' concludes this volume, with a sweeping and keen survey of nineteenth- and early twentieth-century attitudes towards religion, finding within American writings that the 'mystique of nature', forms a pervading influence, one which is consistently reworked and redrawn, pointing to a shared 'spiritual concern' within American letters for the destiny of our planet. A brief afterword by Andrew Delbanco, musing on the future direction of literary studies of religion and spiritual beliefs, completes this collection of rigorous and thoughtful essays, written in varying yet accessible formats, which provide food for environmental as well as spiritual thought for literary critics.

Incorporated within *This Watery World: Humans and the Sea*, edited by Vartan P Messler and Nandita Betra, are three essays that will be of interest to scholars of nineteenth-century American literature. The first, 'Madness and the Sea in the American Literary Imagination', by Ian D. Copestake, engages with the metaphorical value of the sea, assessing the transatlantic preoccupation with water and madness, particularly melancholia, that emerged within the American literary imagination, with particular emphasis, almost inevitably, on Herman Melville's *Moby-Dick; or, The Whale*. The other essays here discussed both base themselves on a study of Herman Melville, the sailor-writer. The first of these, Karen Lentz Madison's 'Tennyson's Maritime Influence on Melville's "John Marr"', takes a transatlantic glance at the synergies between *Enoch Arden* and Melville's sailor poetics, arguing that the 'language of isolation' demonstrated in both works indicates a desire for social interaction and a mourning for its loss when examined in terms of context and intellectual underpinnings. The other essay of relevance in this collection is Robert M. Madison's 'The Aviary of Ocean: Melville's Tropic-Birds and Rock Rodondo—Two Notes and an Emendation', which charts Melville's studied awareness of natural history, tracing the assessment of twentieth-century Melville critics, notably Mary K. Bercaw Edwards, back to the origin of and sources for Melville's body of works.

Joan Richardson's *A Natural History of Pragmatism: The Fact of Feeling from Jonathan Edwards to Gertrude Stein* examines the history of American pragmatism as a product of a 'thinking language', an organic entity subject to evolutionary principles, governed by the system of rules that applies to all life forms. Sharing with Darwin the trait of writerly revisionism, the subjects of this study—Jonathan Edwards, Ralph Waldo Emerson, William James, Henry James, Gertrude Stein and Wallace Stevens—all contribute to the language of pragmatism, argues Richardson, in their appropriation of compelling contemporaneous narratives of natural history, language theory and science, looked to ways in which, aesthetically in the first instance, to fill the void left by the dissolution of the Puritan semiotics of reading God. Drawing on current thinking about cybernetics as well as the performative in language, Richardson's study encompasses American religious and spiritual experience and scientific exploration within a study of a literary culture of pragmatism in the New World, a wide-ranging literary history that provides specialist resources to interdisciplinary scholars keen to expand their knowledge base.

Mary McCartin Wearn's *Negotiating Motherhood in Nineteenth-Century American Literature* begins, in '"Stronger than all was maternal love": Maternal Idealism in *Uncle Tom's Cabin*', by pointing out that the author of this seminal text, Harriet Beecher Stowe, was far from an example of typical motherhood herself. Having enjoyed a progressive education for a woman of her day, she was to quickly become the primary breadwinner of the family in a very public literary area. Nevertheless, no American novel more fully exploits or aggressively propagates sentimental maternity than Stowe's *Uncle Tom's Cabin*. In her novel she figures mothers as symbols of peace for a national family divided by race and slavery. One of her characters, Eliza Harris, a black slave, is at the centre of an escape narrative which sanctifies motherhood and demonstrates how the maternal can be translated into the public sphere. In a collaborative effort to aid Eliza, Stowe creates a network of benevolent mothers, who represent female opposition to the masculine, market-driven slave economy. The succeeding section of Wearn's study, 'No More "the pillow of affection": Deconstructing the "softening influence" of Motherhood in *The Scarlet Letter*', offers a detailed exploration of Hawthorne's nineteenth-century text, itself set in seventeenth-century Puritan New England. Deciphering Hawthorne's ambivalence towards Hester's maternity is complex, since through this wayward mother he creates a passionate and sympathetic image. However, Hester, despite her nurturing qualities, has a radicalism which is potentially dangerous. Wearn argues that, for those critics who read *The Scarlet Letter* as a paean to motherhood, the conclusion seems to validate this image. In the final tableau on the pillory, as Dimmesdale lies dying, Hester cradles his head in her bosom. This is not an act of motherhood as the man she embraces is her erstwhile lover; instead, it illustrates Hester's primary motivation, passion. Wearn's third chapter, '"Links…of gold": The Bonds of Motherhood in *Incidents in the Life of a Slave Girl*', is a study of Harriet Jacobs's tale of her own experiences of slavery and womanhood. While mothering and freedom are inextricably linked in this narrative, maternity is not the route to freedom the heroine desires. Realizing that her children will 'follow the condition of the mother', and become slaves, the slave mother is deeply ambivalent about motherhood. Wearn discusses Jacobs's experience of authorship and unsatisfactory appeal for Stowe's assistance, which represents a larger battle fought on the pages of the novel. While she chose to write her own narrative, Jacobs sought the editorial assistance of Lydia Maria Child, and in doing so accepted the sentimental expectations of that writer. Thematically constructed upon her maternity, then, the novel presents the heroine's own quest for freedom as a way of ultimately securing her children's liberty. The concluding section of Wearn's study, '"She has been burning palaces": The Maternal Poetics of Sarah Piatt', considers that motherhood is the poet's key preoccupation. Piatt's maternal poetics both originates in and challenges the tradition of sentimental motherhood. Providing an alternative to the devoted, selfless, middle-class Madonna, Piatt's poetry sympathetically treats women who fail to live up to the sanctified image of the maternal. Wearn includes excerpts from a wide range of Piatt's work and maintains the importance of her recovery to the study of nineteenth-century literature. Her poems offer us an opportunity to revisit conceptions of cultural norms in that period in their production of an alternative discourse which refused to participate in accepted notions of womanhood. A brief conclusion, detailed notes and bibliography complete this compelling study of literary negotiations of the maternal.

Kristianne Kalata Vaccaro opens the article '"Recollection...sets my busy imagination to work": Transatlantic Self-Narration, Performance, and Reception in *The American Female*' (*ECF* 20[2007–8] 127–50) by claiming that *The Female American* [1767] has alienated scholars since its publication. Vaccaro suggests that the unknown authorship of the novel, its unconventional narrative strategies, and the complex narrator-protagonist can account for the resistance of critics to its literary merits and wider cultural significance. Her article (which won the *Eighteenth-Century Fiction* Graduate Prize in 2006) unravels the complexities of the story to leave us with an intriguing and enlightening commentary on eighteenth-century American life. Vaccaro argues compellingly that the novel does not merely reflect its protagonist's life experiences (as with so many eighteenth-century novels) but rather '*performs* life experiences in order to reveal how the social systems informing them— namely, race, class, and gender—are constructed to support the cultural dominant of which Unca is not part'. Unca is not part of the cultural norm, as she has 'a hybridized Native American and British female self'. The article renews interest in a forgotten text which will be especially relevant for readers of early American literature and for those interested in its complex negotiations of gender, class and race.

A rewarding product of her research into Margaret Fuller's time at the Temple School, Karen English's *Notes of Conversations, 1848–1875: Amos Bronson Alcott* gathers together a collection of twenty-five records of A. Bronson Alcott's conversations, transcribed by himself from the records of conversations for adults by his faithful acolytes. Alcott had intended to produce a volume of these transcripts, which are annotated with notes and a record of attendants, but that never occurred in his lifetime, and only three have appeared in print that bear any resemblance to the archived collection of material. Three complete series exist, from 1848/9, 1850 and 1851, as well as a range of subsequent conversations which date to 1874. The editor's preface details the process of recovery and tracing copies to source, as well as recording methodology in the copying and reproduction of Alcott's words. An introductory essay details the background to Alcott's attitudes to conversation, and his transformation into one of the most famous speakers in America, giving us an insight into the oral culture of the mid-nineteenth century. This collection consists of ten sections, incorporating the Alcott design for three complete series, as well as transcripts accounting for his wide-ranging activities, such as his New England Women's Club Conversations and the Plato Club talks. Completed by a series of appendices and a glossary of

Alcott attendants, this volume offers a key insight into the development of oral culture in nineteenth-century America, as well as a fascinating account of one of America's most profound speakers.

Tracing the impact of Emerson's 'literary intellectual' on the development of critical approaches to American writing, Randall Fuller's *Emerson's Ghosts: Literature and the Making of Americanists* assesses the impact of essays, notably 'The American Scholar', on the production of the 'Americanist' literary critic. Fuller argues that critics looked to this essay specifically as the legitimation for their cultural project, collapsing the 'aesthetic energies' of Emerson within 'their own instrumental readings'. Why Emerson should have so haunted twentieth-century critics is a key issue of this study as Fuller examines previously unpublished material by critics such as Van Wyck Brooks, Perry Miller, F.O. Matthiessen and Sacvan Bercovitch alongside published texts, assessing the cultural production of 'Emerson' within literary criticism and also exploring in depth the development of literary scholarship in the twentieth century. Arguing that Emerson, far from supporting the critic's urge to look to an ideal future from a disillusioned present, haunts latter-day critics as an 'admonitory presence' that advises us, through a specifically literary language, that ideals run into pathology, and that historicized readings—the dominant mode of the American scholar—leave much unsaid about the text itself. Fuller's study, a historicized account of critical scholarship, and therefore, as he himself acknowledges, an account of white male academics, offers —apart form the closing chapter, which attempts to draw in some of the marginal areas of the academic institution—a rich resource for scholars of literary criticism. Shoji Goto's *The Philosophy of Emerson and Thoreau: Orientals Meet Occidentals* aims to redress a significant gap in current knowledge about Emerson and Thoreau's thoroughgoing acquaintance with, and love of, Eastern religion and philosophy. Emerson's 'Plato; or the Philosopher' noted the Plato's indebtedness to the religions of Asia, and Thoreau enthusiastically argued that the Bhagavad-Gita, along with Indian philosophy, would survive the dominion of the British imperial presence in India. Yet critics in the twentieth century focused on establishing the Americanness of these key transcendentalist writers. Arguing that the emergence of social Darwinism at the end of the nineteenth century disturbed what had been a genuine acceptance of Brahmanism and Chinese and Persian ethics in the nineteenth century, Goto, drawing on Wai Chee Dimock's 'Deep Time: American Literature and World History', enables readers to explore Emerson and Thoreau in the context of their extended reading of Oriental philosophy. The accessible style and the emotional as well as intellectual bond between Goto and his material make for an evocative study that will enhance the scholarship of Emerson and Thoreau, of twentieth-century criticism and of Oriental religious systems and beliefs. Ralph Waldo Emerson, albeit an American icon and a great writer and thinker, has rarely been considered as specifically heroic. Len Gougeon, in his critical biography *Emerson and Eros: The Making of a Cultural Hero*, does just that, examining the radical move from the epitome of convention and tradition to a 'revolutionary prophet', who has captured the imagination of generations of those who would 'unsettle all things'. Gougeon links Emerson's own concept of the development of the 'God within', a personal transcendence that was to become a key factor in a shifting social climate marked by an unsettled morality. Transcendentalism, a private philosophy, thereby became the catalyst for social change, argues Gougeon. Emerson's philosophies, infused with the dynamism of Eros's unifying cosmology, and his emergence as a major cultural hero, are here traced through a consideration of his role in the development of a 'psychomythic humanism' in the twentieth century. Gougeon contends that, while Emerson did demonstrably shift in terms of attitude, life and thinking, his understanding was seamlessly laced with a holistic and harmonized approach to reality and experience. A valuable contribution to Emersonian scholarship, this book, in its consideration of heroism in terms of psychomythism, also provides thoughtful matter for the construction of heroism in the contemporary era.

Spanning the entirety of Melville's oeuvre and arguing that the Pacific Ocean remained an enduring passion within his writing, the *'Whole Oceans Away': Melville and the Pacific*, edited by Jill Barnum, Wyn Kelley and Christopher Sten, examines the work of the man who lived among cannibals through the various critical lenses of linguistics, performance theory, popular culture and non-verbal cultural practices. The usual suspects appear—*Typee* and *Moby-Dick*—but the later Melville also comes under scrutiny as a writer whose response to the conditions of life for peoples of the Pacific region became complexly ambivalent. This volume, containing twenty-two essays, usefully divided into four parts—'Pacific Subjects', 'Colonial Appropriations and Resistance', 'Empire, Race and Nation' and 'Postcolonial Reflections'—emerges from a 2003 'Melville and the Pacific' conference that took place in Lāhaina, Maui, and consists of submissions from scholars from a range of backgrounds and disciplines. Thus, the book constitutes an exploration of 'transnational relations and cultural appropriation', from the perspective of Melville, but is also a repository of diverse scholarly thinking. Carefully conceived as a collection, the essays come together to give an overview of Herman Melville's literary evocation of the sea, as well as individually offering fascinating accounts of Melville's works. A revised edition of *Herman Melville A to Z* [2001], the *Critical Companion to Herman Melville: A Literary Reference to his Life and Work*, edited by Carl Rollyson, Lisa Paddock and April Gentry, builds on the strength of its original, and also features new critical commentary sections on short stories and poetry, and an expanded biography and updated bibliography. The first part of this companion offers an insight into Melville's personal life, assessing how key events influenced his development as a writer. The second part consists of concise yet comprehensive alphabetized entries on Melville's works, including novels, poems, short fiction and non-fiction pieces. The majority of these accounts are accompanied by a brief synopsis and examination of characters, and a description of their publishing and reception histories. The third part of the companion is devoted to an examination of people, places and topics that relate to Melville and his writing—for example, we are presented with brief accounts of Hawthorne and Hawaii, both of which exerted influence on the Melvillean writing style. The fourth part wraps up the companion, with a series of relevant appendices featuring a Melville chronology and an extensive bibliography of secondary resources, and reproduces some of the key reviews of his works as well as excerpts from his correspondence. Meat and drink to Melville scholars, this book will also introduce the uninitiated to the joys of reading the man who lived among cannibals.

Another volume in the Mark Twain and his Circle series from the University of Missouri Press (series editor Tom Quirk), John Bird's *Mark Twain and Metaphor* refreshes studies of an American writer through whose word usage, argues Bird, we have come to know. Revisiting Twain within the paradigm of metaphor theory enables us to read not just for style but for unconscious motives, and is particularly appropriate, contends Bird, to the analysis of a writer within whose literary output dreams and humour play such a key role, 'mere' humour forming an exploration of hidden desires and dreams—and the nightmare of the 'damned human race'. Bird's study, extending William M. Gibson's *The Art of Mark Twain* [1976] and I.A. Richards's work on metaphor theory, examines the figurative implications of 'Mark Twain' as a developmental pseudonym and a 'metaphorised self', also considering the figurative implication of the Mississippi river in *The Adventures of Tom Sawyer* and *The Adventures of Huckleberry Finn* and a selection of the shorter fiction, including 'A True Story' and 'The Man that Corrupted Hadleyburg'. It also assesses the darkness of texts from the end of Twain's writing career, particularly *A Connecticut Yankee in the Court of King Arthur*, suggesting that the despair clearly expressed in these later works enabled the production of some of the most creative and most affirmative metaphors. Concluding with an account of how the 'myth' of metaphor—a powerful weapon, with a 'blade' that 'strikes deep'—has played its part in the shaping, or misshaping, of our perception of Mark Twain, Bird's analysis is an invigorating reconfiguration of Twain writing, and one that provides insight into the reader's relationship with a celebrity writer. Another volume in the Cambridge Introductions to Literature series, which aims to introduce students to key authors, is Peter Messent's *The Cambridge Introduction to Mark Twain*, which focuses on the major works of this prolific writer, notably travel accounts *The Innocents Abroad*, *A Tramp Abroad*, *Roughing It* and *Life on the Mississippi*, alongside the novels *Tom Sawyer* and *Huckleberry Finn*. In line with the standard format, sections of this study are devoted to Mark Twain's life, the context of his writing, introducing students to the figure of Samuel Langhorne Clemens as well as Mark Twain. An account of the critical reception and the later works concludes this guide, which is written in an accessible style, and is supported by notes and a guide to further reading introducing students to the works of Mark Twain and also offering some useful ways to develop more complex interpretations of his writing. The latest volume in the noteworthy Mark Twain and his Circle series is Linda A Morris's *Gender Play in Mark Twain: Cross-Dressing and Transgression*. Locating Twain's literary evocation of cross-dressing as overt and manifest across the canon of his works, and informed by discourses of race as well as gender, Morris begins her thesis with an account of a theatrical tradition of cross-dressing, from Shakespeare to minstrelsy, noting that it was the famous staging of Sarah Bernhardt as Hamlet that informed the illustrations for *A Connecticut Yankee in the Court of King Arthur*, before moving on to a consideration of the 'New Sexuality'

of the late nineteenth century, which witnessed the publication of some
significant volumes on the subject of sex—or indeed the psychologizing of sex.
Morris also takes account of the impact of a relationship that development
between Mark Twain's daughter and a college friend as an exemplar of the
social history of women in the late nineteenth century. Drawing on the work of
Mikhail Bakhtin on the humour of the carnivalesque, Morris examines the
cross-dressing incidents in *Huckleberry Finn*, *Pudd'nhead Wilson*, *Personal
Recollections of Joan of Arc*, the short tale 'Hellfire Hotchkiss' and the stage
play *Is He Dead*, suggesting that Twain's fascination with the subversive
power of cross-dressing in terms of challenging conventional and comfortable
morality grew with his literary output. A stimulating look at oft-examined
texts, Morris's book will serve Twain scholars well. In a busy year for the
Mark Twain and His Circle series, series editor Tom Quirk's *Mark Twain and
Human Nature* sets itself the task of examining the author's abiding interest in
humanity, as it was expressed in his thinking and through his writing. Refusing
to negotiate the well-worn debate over cultural conditioning/genetic programming and stating baldly that the 'truth' of the 'concept of human nature lies
outside this study', Quirk instead faces the impact of reading Mark Twain on
developments in our ideas about human nature. Claiming that Twain, while an
intellectual, did not really foray into philosophy yet demonstrated a clear
faculty for philosophizing, this book focuses on humour—Twain's 'comic
"temperament"'—as it informed Twainian studies of human nature. Drawing
on the intellectual accounts of human capacity that abounded in the mid- to
late nineteenth century, from Thomas Paine to William James, Quirk's
chronological study assesses both major and minor shifts in Twain's attitudes
as they are demonstrated in his writing, his reflections on and responses to his
travels, and his various readings of contemporary history and scientific studies
and developments, as well as his complex relationship with politics. Drawing
on anecdotal accounts of Twain as well as published works, Quirk attends
to travel writing—notably *The Innocents Abroad*—and the key novels, *The
Adventures of Tom Sawyer*, *The Adventures of Huckleberry Finn* and
Pudd'nhead Wilson, as well as the lesser-known 1906 polemic *What Is Man?*
Concluding with an assessment of Twain's well-documented late-career
disillusion with the human species, but also the value of humour in redressing
that despair, Quirk's discussion of Twain's study of human nature is profound
and far-reaching, demonstrating a level of scholarship and an accessibility
of style that are gratefully accepted by this reviewer. Forrest G. Robinson's
The Author-Cat: Clemens' Life in Fiction argues that the American writer's
decision that his autobiographical dictations—over 250 in all—should be
published posthumously to ensure strict reliability revealed very little about
the author himself. More revelatory, contends Robinson, the fictional legacy
of Twain, which the writer himself claimed to be 'simply autobiographies'.
Acknowledging his debt to the plethora of Clemens biographies in circulation,
Robinson's study takes account of the well-documented sense of guilt that
hounded Clemens throughout his life and which culminated in his sense of
moral complicity in slavery. Torment and suffering, bad faith and guilt—all
facets of Clemens's character—are exposed to view through close examination
of his literary output, and Robinson probes this body of works for the ways in

which it explores and even transforms the history of the writer, particularly the products of the latter years, to get to a Samuel Clemens uninhibited by the veneer of autobiographical truth-telling. A fascinating study of the work of biographical readings of fiction, this text will serve the academic community, as well as providing insights for general readers wishing to acquaint themselves with Twain.

The latest volume in the Cambridge Introductions to Literature series is M. Jimmie Killingsworth's *The Cambridge Introduction to Walt Whitman*, focusing on the American poet through his most famous literary collection, *Leaves of Grass*. As with other editions in this series, the text is divided into key areas, exploring Whitman's life and the context of his writing—the key historical and cultural events that informed his works—then moving into a concise and informative study of his works: the development of his poetry both before and after the Civil War, and his prose writings, including the 1855 preface to *Leaves of Grass*, *Democratic Vistas* and *Specimen Days*, concluding with an account of the critical reception from 1855 to 2005. Accompanied by informative notes and a guide to further reading, this text will indeed introduce students and first-time readers to the writings and lively career of an American great.

Books Reviewed

Barnum, Jill, Wyn Kelley and Christopher Sten, eds. *'Whole Oceans Away':
Melville and the Pacific*. KSUP. [2007] pp. xxii + 350. $65 £44.50 ISBN 9
7808 7338 8931.

Bennett, Paula Bernat, Karen L. Kilcup and Philipp Schweighauser, eds.
Teaching Nineteenth-Century American Poetry. MLA. [2007] pp. 402. hb
£27.50 ISBN 9 7808 7352 8214, pb £15 ISBN 9 7808 7352 8221.

Bird, John. *Mark Twain and Metaphor*. UMissP. [2007] pp. xiv + 250. $39.95
£27.50 ISBN 9 7808 2621 7622.

Breitwieser, Mitchell. *National Melancholy: Mourning and Opportunity in
Classic American Literature*. StanfordUP. [2007] pp. xii + 324. $60 ISBN 9
7808 0475 5818.

Cavitch, Max. *American Elegy: The Poetry of Mourning from the Puritans to
Whitman*. UMinnP. [2007] pp. viii + 358. pb £14 ISBN 0 8166 4893 X.

Cornes, Judy, *Madness and the Loss of Identity in Nineteenth Century Fiction*.
McFarland. [2007] pp. 224. pb £34.50 ISBN 9 7807 8643 2240.

Crane, Gregg, *The Cambridge Introduction to the Nineteenth-Century
American Novel*. CUP. [2007] pp. 248. hb £38 ISBN 9 7805 2184 3256,
pb £14.99 ISBN 9 7805 2160 3997.

Davis, Theo. *Formalism, Experience, and the Making of American Literature in
the Nineteenth Century*. CUP. [2007] pp. vi + 216. $85 £45 ISBN 9 7805 2187
2966.

Dowling, Robert M. *Slumming in New York: From the Waterfront to Mythic
Harlem*. UIllP. [2007] pp. xii + 204. $35 ISBN 9 7802 5203 1946.

English, Karen. ed. *Notes of Conversations, 1848–1875: Amos Bronson Alcott.* FDUP. [2007] pp. 288. £37.50 ISBN 9 7808 3864 1187.

Frank, Lucy E., ed. *Representations of Death in Nineteenth-Century US Writing and Culture.* Ashgate. [2007] pp. xii + 236. £50 ISBN 9 7807 5455 5282.

Fuller, Randall. *Emerson's Ghosts: Literature and the Making of Americanists.* OUP. [2007] pp. xvi + 194. $55 ISBN 9 7801 9531 3925.

Goto, Shoji. *The Philosophy of Emerson and Thoreau: Orientals Meet Occidentals.* Mellen. [2007] pp. xii + 194. $109.95 (£69.95) ISBN 9 7807 7345 3517.

Gougeon, Len. *Emerson and Eros: The Making of a Cultural Hero.* SUNYP. [2007] pp. x + 268. £35 ISBN 9 7807 0147 0770.

Handley, George B. *New World Poetics: Nature and the Adamic Imagination of Whitman, Neruda and Walcott.* UGeoP. [2007] pp. xiv + 442. £27.50 ISBN 9 7808 2032 8645.

Harrison, Les. *The Temple and the Forum: The American Museum and Cultural Authority in Hawthorne, Melville, Stowe and Whitman.* UAlaP. [2007] pp. xxx + 274. £28.95 ISBN 9 7808 1731 5634.

Killingsworth, M. Jimmie. *The Cambridge Introduction to Walt Whitman.* CUP. [2007] pp. viii + 142. pb $21.99 ISBN 0 5216 7094 2.

Lundin, Roger, ed. *There Before Us: Religion, Literature, and Culture from Emerson to Wendell Berry.* Eerdmans. [2007] pp. xxii + 250. pb $18 (£9.99) ISBN 9 7808 0282 9634.

Messent, Peter. *The Cambridge Introduction to Mark Twain.* CUP. [2007] pp. xii + 138. hb $65 (£35) ISBN 0 5218 5445 8, pb. $19.99 (£10.99) ISBN 0 5216 7075 6.

Messler, Vartan P., and Nandita Betra, eds. *This Watery World: Humans and the Sea.* CambridgeSP. [2007] pp. xii + 228. £50 ISBN 9 7818 4718 6607.

Morris, Linda A. *Gender Play in Mark Twain: Cross-Dressing and Transgression.* UMissP. [2007] pp. xiv + 186. $34.95 (£25.50) ISBN 9 7808 2621 7592.

Quirk, Tom. *Mark Twain and Human Nature.* UMissP. [2007] pp. xviii + 290. $39.95 (£27.50) ISBN 9 7808 2621 7585.

Richardson, Joan. *A Natural History of Pragmatism: The Fact of Feeling from Jonathan Edwards to Gertrude Stein.* CUP. [2007] pp. xviii + 330. $96 (£45) ISBN 9 7805 2169 4507, pb $29.99 (£17.99) ISBN 0 521 6945 07.

Robinson, Forrest G. *The Author-Cat: Clemens' Life in Fiction.* FordUP. [2007] pp. xviii + 244. £30.95 ISBN 9 7808 2322 7877.

Rollyson, Carl, Lisa Paddock and April Gentry. *Critical Companion to Herman Melville: A Literary Reference to his Life and Work.* FOF. [2007] pp. vi + 394. £54.50 ISBN 0 8160 6461 X.

Wearn, Mary McCartin, *Negotiating Motherhood in Nineteenth-Century American Literature.* Routledge. [2007] pp. 168. £57 ISBN 0 4159 8104 2.

XVI

American Literature: The Twentieth Century

JAMES GIFFORD, JAMES M. DECKER, MICHAEL BOYD,
AMY M. FLAXMAN AND SARAH ROBERTSON

This chapter has five sections: 1. Poetry; 2. Fiction 1900–1945; 3. Fiction since 1945; 4. Drama; and 5. Native, Asian American, Latino/a and General Ethnic Writing. Section 1 is by James Gifford; section 2 is by James M. Decker; section 3 is by Michael Boyd; section 4 is by Amy M. Flaxman; and section 5 is by Sarah Robertson.

1. Poetry

The year 2007 saw a significant continuation of projects begun in the previous year. Lyn Graham Barzilai's *George Oppen: A Critical Study*, published in 2006, was followed by Peter Nicholls's very strong study *George Oppen and the Fate of Modernism* as well as Stephen Cope's critical edition of Oppen's *Selected Prose, Daybooks, and Papers*. This interest in Oppen covers his early and later works, including the significant mid-century gap in his career. The preponderance of Nicholls's work and Cope's edition discuss the latter portion of Oppen's career, though both give significant critical attention to the poet's early modernist ties and his objectivist interactions with William Carlos Williams, Louis Zukofsky, Lorine Niedecker and Charles Reznikoff. Nicholls's work is doubly significant in that it marks the first study of Oppen published by a university press and is likely to be the primary critical resource on Oppen for quite some time, even following as it does in the wake of Barzilai's monograph. Cope's work significantly expands critical interest in the recursive nature of Oppen's writings, and his focus on the daybooks from the 1950s to the 1970s prompts genetic studies of Oppen's work. The trend appears to be developing a major expansion of research on Oppen in general.

A significant innovation in genetic and archival studies of American poets was published in 2006 by ELS Editions (only available in 2007): Stephen Collis's *Through the Words of Others: Susan Howe and Anarcho-Scholasticism*. The anarchist philosophy of the book is enacted in its engagement with the

Year's Work in English Studies, Volume 88 (2009) © *The English Association; all rights reserved*
doi:10.1093/ywes/map004

archive as a collaborative activity, such that Collis's scholarly work is integrated into Howe's own exhumation of previous American poets and her correspondence with Robert Duncan, and also George Butterick with regard to his editorial work on Charles Olson's poetry. Both in method and erudition this is a striking volume that reinvigorates interest in archival work and the dialogic construction of scholarship. Collis is also persuasive in his positioning of Howe as a major voice in American poetry, and it seems likely that this text will prompt further critical engagement. Allan Antliff's *Anarchy and Art: From the Paris Commune to the Fall of the Berlin Wall* also develops an anarchist interpretation of Duncan's works. Antliff's monograph is largely focused on the visual arts, but American poets and networks significantly overlap with the anarchist visual arts he explores, and they are then taken up in tandem in Antliff's analysis. As with Collis, the political impetus is primarily toward anti-authoritarian activities in a general sense, rather than a specific and defined branch of anarchism. This, in purpose and function, allows for greater interpretative flexibility.

Other heavily politicized readings of American poetry include Rachel Potter's *Modernism and Democracy: Literary Culture 1900–1930*. Potter's express purpose is to interrogate the relationships that exist between democracy and Anglo-American poetry. Her choice of poetic subjects focuses on the most recognizable figures of the period: Ezra Pound, H.D., Mina Loy, T.S. Eliot and Richard Aldington. Some of her more interesting comparisons arise between feminism and the politics of modernism, in particular her insistence that female poets of the period were affiliated with anti-authoritarian views, and that this resistance to subjugation is mirrored in a critique of democracy in such works as 'The Love Song of J. Alfred Prufrock'. This interpretation places Potter in a unique position with regard to the frequent association of the 'Men of 1914' and modernist poetics in general with authoritarian or even fascist politics. This stance alone ensures that critics will rely on Potter, either agreeing or disagreeing with her, in order to articulate modernist politics. However, her monograph is also beneficial for the insights it gives into archival holdings of unpublished materials by Eliot, Loy, and H.D. in particular. John Lowney's *History, Memory, and the Literary Left: Modern American Poetry, 1935–1968* takes a similarly politicized approach to American literature, in many respects continuing the approach Potter has begun with the preceding generation. Whereas Potter aligns her readings with a loosely anti-authoritarian sense of resisting the tyranny of the majority, Lowney's focus is on overtly communist visions of six subjects in his case studies, though both authors privilege the role of gender in their approach. Lowney opens the volume with a contextual chapter that turns attention to the everyday in American poetry of the 1930s, and hence to the class preoccupations of contemporary communist movements. From this base, he moves into six chapters that explore his opening concern with the revolutionary potential of working-class lives, each chapter focused on a specific poet: Muriel Rukeyser, Elizabeth Bishop, Langston Hughes, Gwendolyn Brooks, Thomas McGrath and George Oppen. The final chapter on Oppen does not create a full sense of closure with regard to the volume's project, and it seems likely that readers will select individual chapters rather than reading the volume as an organic whole.

Philip Metres renders the most topical and broad investigation in 2007 of the political life of American poetry in *Behind the Lines: War Resistance Poetry on the American Home Front since 1941*. The position of the book is clear, though a broader range of nuanced pacifism would have helped to clarify its scope and intentions. Metres expressly limits his attention to pacifist poetry of the non-combatant, leaving war poetry per se to other projects. This serves to focus his attention on American anti-war poetry more sharply, since in contrast to most discussions or anthologies of war poetry, the poetry written outside the home nation garners the most attention. Metres divides the book into three events, and avoids the potentially expansive role of American military interventions in the twentieth century overall—he takes up only the Second World War, the Vietnam War, and the First Gulf War. The book is also confined to the twentieth century proper. With regard to sites of conflict and indigenous American resistance to armed action following 11 September 2001, only a short coda addresses contemporary poetic resistance. Metres's discussions of Robert Lowell and Denise Levertov are among the more effective in the volume. Robert Duncan and Allen Ginsberg are also discussed significantly but only intermittently. The book perhaps reads best for a more popular audience, though its argument and critical readings of specific poems will prove useful to scholars interested in these particular authors or in American anti-war poetry propaganda in general. The University of Iowa Press also released Joe Amato's *Industrial Poetics: Demo Tracks for a Mobile Culture*, which shares the same accessibility for a lay audience while offering flashes of strong interpretative insight. As with Metres's book, a broader explicit base in existing scholarly materials would make the book stronger from a critical perspective, but its readability and excitement derive from its quick flow and juxtapositions, which a more scholarly apparatus could not sustain.

Marina MacKay's exploration of late modernism as a period stands out this year as perhaps one of the most engaging volumes for general modernist studies: *Modernism and World War II* is sure to expand the increasingly late modernist concerns of studies in American poetry or of modernism in general. Though divided between British and American authors, her contextualization of late modernist preoccupations during and after the Second World War is effective and dispenses with lingering disputes over the appropriateness of regarding 1940s writing as part of a continuous whole centred on high modernism. In particular, her heavily political reading of Eliot's *Four Quartets* reinvigorates studies of Eliot's ideological concerns and critiques of his contemporaries. In this sense, MacKay's and Potter's volumes call out for a comparative study that might reconcile their differing yet equally convincing interpretations. In many ways, MacKay also continues, while redirecting, Jed Esty's influential *A Shrinking Island*.

For the high modernists, Rebecca Beasley's *Ezra Pound and the Visual Culture of Modernism* makes a major contribution to studies of Pound, in many respects initiating significant revaluations and new critical perspectives on the poet's works. This is certainly the most significant book dedicated to

Pound for quite some time, and it is likely to be one of the most influential single-author studies in American poetry of the year. As with so many other books discussed so far, Beasley's approach is heavily invested in the politics of modern American poetry, and she gives significant attention to anarchist activities, ties between literary and anarchist publishing networks and Pound's realpolitik affiliations with fascism. Her attention to the relationship between Pound's early poetry, as well as its politics, with his interests in the visual arts, is thoroughly convincing and makes a major contribution to critical views of Pound's works. This is further substantiated via Beasley's impressive use of Pound's unpublished early works. As with Antliff and Potter, her interpretations acknowledge the importance of anti-democratic and anti-authoritarian practices, tying the arc of Pound's rise and fall to the dominant currents in the visual arts of the same period. In this way, the movement from egoistic anarchism through anti-democratic values and finally to authoritarian fascism make greater sense. *Ezra Pound and the Visual Culture of Modernism* goes a long way to contextualizing Pound's influence and his otherwise erratic career. However, a stronger distinction from anti-authoritarian yet mutualist anarchism, the most prevalent general view of the period, would have been useful in this context, such as the forms of anarchism privileged by Antliff and Collis. Beasley's second volume in 2007 is equally impressive, though it will likely not have as significant an impact on its field as her first. Her *Theorists of Modernist Poetry: T.S. Eliot, T.E. Hulme and Ezra Pound* builds on the political approach in *Ezra Pound and the Visual Culture of Modernism*. It is no surprise that the chapter 'Anti-Democracy: The Politics of Early Modernism' is likely the strongest in the volume. Beasley unifies Eliot, Hulme and Pound as anti-democratic in their views, but she distinguishes among them, pointing most forcibly to Pound's uniqueness. She links Hulme and Eliot strongly with regard to classicism and the notion of a centralized state power. In contrast, the early Pound is presented through expressly anarchist descriptions, which reflect her discussions of Pound in *Ezra Pound and the Visual Culture of Modernism*. In this respect, Beasley's evidence and transparent diction are highly persuasive in presenting Pound as anti-democratic in the anarchist sense, though closely tied to Max Stirner's egoism and popular understandings of Nietzsche via Stirner at the time. While this view significantly contextualizes Pound's later sympathies for fascism, Beasley leaves the anti-authoritarian views less fully explored. This gives the impression of a rather impoverished form of anarchism, one that is primarily egoism or individualism, and only scant mention is made of the more dominant syndicalist and mutualist forms of anti-authoritarianism in general. Regardless, Beasley's articulation of the role of anti-democratic views in the development of Pound, Eliot and Hulme's modernism (and by extension that of most major modernist poets) is highly persuasive. The volume is also aided by clear summaries and definitions of terms, which will make it particularly useful in the classroom or for young scholars.

A. David Moody rounds out the year's major works on Pound with *Ezra Pound: A Portrait of the Man and his Work*, volume 1: *The Young Genius*. As this is the first in a multi-volume biography, there is much that must be held back for future evaluation. However, Moody is thorough in his scholarship and succeeds in generating a vision of the young Pound that will surely drive critics back to review his juvenilia and writings prior to the *annus mirabilis* for modernism, 1922. Moody suggests going back very early indeed, such that his comments on many works are the first to appear in print. Moreover, as a biography, this volume has the auspicious merit of taking the man with the work, rather than leaving critical analysis to another project. Moody avoids the potential for hero-worship or larger-than-life anecdotes, and instead renders a biography that brings attention to the writings. In doing so, he compellingly argues for the merits of Pound's early writings, not only as presaging the *Cantos* and his subsequent criticism, and not only based on his influence on other poets, but for their intrinsic value. That he succeeds so thoroughly makes the reader anticipate a swell in the number of articles that take up the finer details of Pound's early poetry.

Daniel Katz's *American Modernism's Expatriate Scene: The Labour of Translation* is largely dedicated to prose, but his two chapters on Pound and his final chapter on Ashbery, Schuyler and Spicer both suggest profitable ways of reconsidering expatriation in American poetry of the first half of the century. The general premise that expatriation is not a flight from 'home' bears more consideration, specifically Katz's argument that expatriation is a deep engagement with American identity, and even that expatriation is itself a form of American identity. Katz's argument draws significantly on psychoanalytic theories of identity and language, though his discussion of translation is not tied to Spivak's or to postcolonial studies in a systematic manner.

Eleanor Cook's *A Reader's Guide to Wallace Stevens* seems equally useful for the classroom in its scope and detail with regard to Stevens's poetry. The volume opens with a contextual biography, which offers a surprisingly lucid communication of its key points. The remainder relies heavily on 'glosses' of individual texts by Stevens, followed by a final chapter guiding students on 'how to read poetry'. On whole, the volume seems ideal for undergraduate use or for graduate students expanding their familiarity with Stevens but who require some guidance. Daniel Morris pursues a pedagogical project in *The Poetry of Louise Glück: A Thematic Introduction* in a similarly effective manner. The first five chapters give thematic overviews of the main concerns of Glück's oeuvre while the subsequent chapters discuss individual texts in the light of this thematic understanding. This is the first single-author work on Glück, and the reader will find that various potential interpretations are left unexplored, but as a guide to Glück's poetry one could ask for little more. Morris's readings are adroit and achieve their purpose: to bring Glück to a wider critical audience. The writing can at times become heavy, but for scholarship on Glück this book will be indispensable.

Shyamal Bagchee and Elisabeth Däumer's *The International Reception of T.S. Eliot* pursues a highly engaging series of questions surrounding Eliot's influence as well as how that influence was transformed in a variety of global receptions of his works. The editorial matter in the collection is minimal, and a stronger sense of continuity could have been provided by a more thorough introduction. The editorial contention that modernist scholarship tends to render communism, fascism and Nazism as 'non-western' is highly questionable and certainly idiosyncratic, especially in the light of the New Modernist studies, but the insistence on privileging 'other' receptions of Eliot is quite valuable nonetheless. Likewise, several of the contributions engage in a personal discussion of reception. The most engaging chapter in the collection is certainly Astradur Eysteinsson and Eysteinn Thorvaldsson's 'T.S. Eliot in Iceland: A Historical Portrait' (pp. 103–22), which implicates Scandinavian modernism more generally. Matthew Hart's 'Tradition and the Postcolonial Talent: T.S. Eliot *versus* Edward Kamau Brathwaite' (pp. 6–24) renders the most compelling discussion of empire in the dissemination of Eliot's works and merits mention here as well.

The year 2007 was particularly active for studies of Eliot. Giovanni Cianci and Jason Harding's critical collection *T.S. Eliot and the Concept of Tradition* returns to a standard approach to Eliot's works and poetic legacy. Marjorie Perloff's 'Duchamp's Eliot: The Detours of Tradition and the Persistence of Individual Talent' (pp. 177–84) is a strong contribution to the volume. The reader is less impressed by innovation here than by the careful exploration of Eliot's seminal 'Tradition and the Individual Talent'. Aleida Assman's 'Exorcising the Demon of Chronology: T.S. Eliot's Reinvention of Tradition' (pp. 13–25) opens the volume and immediately leads into a careful explication of Eliot's notion of tradition followed by an exploration of its implications in literary criticism. The strongest shadow in the volume is Harold Bloom's, and in many ways the collected essays look back rather than forwards to Eliot's influences on tradition. For an overview and detailed examination of this ubiquitous subject in Eliot and modernist poetry in general, *T.S. Eliot and the Concept of Tradition* is sure to be useful as a reference. This year also saw the paperback publication of Cassandra Laity and Nancy K. Gish's well-received *Gender, Desire, and Sexuality in T.S. Eliot*. This new format is more affordable, and the volume has been released as an e-book as well. Oxford University Press also reissued Louis Menand's classic study of Eliot, *Discovering Modernism: T.S. Eliot and his Context* in paperback.

Piotr Gwazda's *James Merrill and W.H. Auden: Homosexuality and Poetic Influence* completes a study of reception akin to that of Bagchee and Däumer. Taking Merrill's interpretations of and influence from Auden, he pursues a general project to articulate the nature of influence and reception in a specifically homosexual context. The result is compelling and is given added force by Gwazda's careful exploration of archival materials outlining Merrill's ongoing reactions to Auden, in *The Changing Light at Sandover* in particular.

Tony Trigilio offers the first lengthy and systematic attempt to understand Allen Ginsberg's poetry through his Buddhist practices. *Allen Ginsberg's Buddhist Poetics* remains primarily focused on productive ways of critically engaging with Ginsberg's works, and this respect it succeeds well. Trigilio's integration of post-structural and gender theory also suggests productive ways of expanding on the work begun in the book.

Amie Elizabeth Parry adopts a highly intriguing approach to internationalism and reception of modernist poetic texts, and she adeptly uses poetry in her postcolonial reading of relations between Taiwan and the USA. Her *Interventions into Modernist Cultures: Poetry from beyond the Empty Screen* states the express purpose of completing a comparative analysis of modernist poetry in the two nations, specifically drawing on their political contexts and aims. An intriguing part of her claim is that poetry is undervalued in contrast to prose in postcolonial studies in general. While one could certainly find individual instances in which this is not true, as a general trend her book begins a formidable and necessary corrective. Her formal and structuralist approach to the primary texts allows her to contend that their fragmented structural features demonstrate akin responses to their social contexts, and as such they merit comparison with regard to their political aims and activities. The familiar names from American modernism—Pound, Gertrude Stein and, to a lesser degree, H.D.—are profitably held up against the models developed by the Taiwanese writers Yü Kwang-chung, Hsia Yü and Theresa Hak Kyung. These comparisons provoke exciting new interpretations of American literature, not only with regard to its influence, but, more importantly, as a reassessment of the nature of its response to the political circumstances of the USA as a neocolonial military power. A more lengthy discussion of Robert Duncan, T.S. Eliot and Amy Lowell is left as a palpable possibility, but this certainly is not necessary for the purposes of the book. Likewise, a more extensive engagement with American late modernist poetry from the latter half of the century would have unified the time-frame, but this is secondary to Parry's primary aim. The book remains focused throughout, and its integration of gender and queer theory into its political discussion is welcome as well as highly productive.

Cristanne Miller approaches her study of three authors through an international and gendered conceptualization as well. *Cultures of Modernism: Marianne Moore, Mina Loy, and Else Lasker-Schuler* moves beyond a simple comparison or exploration of the three authors by seeking to situate and gender American modernist poetry in a comparative framework in contrast with that of Britain and Germany. The book begins by focusing on urban situatedness, but rapidly expands to question how gender dynamics differ based on the exigencies of place—in other words, how does urban space construct elements of engendered life, and how does gender influence the experience of varying urban locations in modernist poetry? Miller points out and expands on the way that sexuality, misogyny and women's responses to both vary from place to place as well as altering the nature of those engagements with each location. The closing contention of the book—that female modernist poets made their performance of sexuality and gender self-conscious while male authors did not—is open to some debate, and that debate is certainly active; however, Miller's analyses and her conceptualization of her project remain compelling and innovative. Her discussion of Moore is not likely to reorganize scholarly approaches to the poet, but she contributes meaningfully to how Moore is compared to her international contemporaries.

'Burning Interiors': David Shapiro's Poetry and Poetics, edited by Thomas Fink and Joseph Lease, makes a significant contribution to the poet's reputation and the availability of scholarship on his works. The contents are at times uneven, and the book gives the genuine sense of being a collection of scholarly work rather than a comprehensive study compiled for the purpose of exploring a single facet of the author's work. For Shapiro, however, this is what is actually needed. The chapters all range widely, and hence they provide a strong overview of the poet's oeuvre for the reader. All of the materials are

comprehensive and avoid needless jargon, although the concerns expressed are often those of the poet rather than those of the literary critic. Jeremy Gilbert-Rolfe's 'House Blown Apart' (pp. 154–62) is perhaps the strongest chapter in the collection, or at least the most direct in its aims and purpose in critically engaging with Shapiro. While several chapters turn to the abstract rather than establish a nuanced critical apparatus in existing scholarship, this develops a conversational tone in the text and prompts the reader towards a broader view of Shapiro's poetry. The volume prompts greater critical engagement with Shapiro's works and emphasizes the need for further scholarship.

Juan A. Suarez, in his *Pop Modernism: Noise and the Reinvention of the Everyday*, adopts ongoing theories of the everyday in tandem with a cultural studies approach in order to develop the thesis that the avant-garde was significantly engaged in a project to reinvent quotidian life. Interest in the everyday has increased in the past several years, but Suarez's contribution is unique in that he recuperates lesser modernist poets and artists as well as popular works, demonstrating the layers of allusion, citation and influence that bind them to established 'major' works of modernism. The overwhelming breadth of materials and references that Suarez manages is impressive, and simply as a resource for such matters the book is certain to be useful. Its more important contribution relates to his demonstration of the intricate ties between everyday materials and the major works that they engendered. The discussion of Charles Henri Ford is particularly good to see, and the links to Parker Tyler are highly effective. Suarez also expands on the long-acknowledged importance of gramophone recordings and song lyrics to Eliot's *The Waste Land* in a chapter dedicated to the topic.

With regard to general collections on the subject of American twentieth-century poetry, Viorica Patea and Paul Scott Derrick's co-edited *Modernism Revisited: Transgressing Boundaries and Strategies of Renewal in American Poetry* is particularly strong. Contributions by Marjorie Perloff and Charles Altieri provide bookends to round out the volume, but, between these, several chapters surprise in their innovativeness. Work on e.e. cummings, Pound, Williams, Eliot, Robert Creeley, Lowell and Stevens gives the volume range, but it also engages with the international nature of American writing during the century. Perloff's contribution is particularly useful for contextualizing the volume.

2. Fiction 1900–1945

Several new books appeared on Willa Cather in 2007, including *Violence, the Arts, and Willa Cather* edited by noted Cather critics Joseph R. Urgo and Merrill Maguire Skaggs. Drawing on revised papers from the 2005 International Willa Cather Seminar, the collection, which divides its essays between 'violence' and the 'arts', contains twenty-three contributions, including the introduction by Urgo, which focuses on Cather's alleged 'cosmos of existential terror'. Making a tenuous connection between Cather and 9/11, Urgo highlights Cather's representation of 'creative responses to the horror of human life'. The essays themselves cover a large swath of Cather's fiction, from *One of Ours* and 'Paul's Case' to *Death Comes for the Archbishop* and *O Pioneers!* In the 'violence' section, the topics range from violent death to sexual trauma, while the 'arts' segment tackles subjects such as choreography and gender identity. Unlike many collections based on a conference theme, this book provides a fairly coherent vision and, despite Urgo's somewhat forced connection between Cather and the so-called War on Terror, offers a challenging look at violence within the work of Willa Cather.

Among the stand-out essays in the collection is Margaret Doane's ' "Do talk to me": Violent Deaths and Isolated Survivors in Cather's Novels', a study that investigates the high frequency of 'particularly gruesome' deaths in Cather's canon. Doane looks at the grieving process and how Cather's characters often lack the opportunity to communicate their pain to others, a phenomenon that refigures them as 'emotional pariahs' who must face a well-meaning but incompetent community that places avoidance of pain above 'real emotional solace'. Timothy W. Bintrim and Mark J. Madigan present some exciting primary source material for one of Cather's strongest stories in their 'From Larceny to Suicide: The Denny Case and "Paul's Case" '. In their essay, the authors pursue an oft-discussed but unexamined factual basis for 'Paul's Case', and reprint numerous headlines about a Pittsburgh robbery that parallels Cather's fictional one. Bintrim and Madigan explore Cather's journalism experience and explain how she transformed the real incident via allusions to Goethe and Tolstoy and avoided the 'contagion of yellow newspaper fiction'.

In the same collection, J. Gabriel Scala focuses on sexual violence in ' "At the center of her mystery": Sexual Trauma and Willa Cather', an essay that examines *The Song of the Lark* through the lens of sexual abuse. Scala notes in the opening scene both a 'blatant sense of force' and 'clear evidence of the dissociation commonly described in victims of childhood sexual abuse'. While Scala's close reading is intriguing, less convincing is his effort to posit a link between the sexual trauma in the novel and an unrecoverable antecedent in Cather's life, as he relies solely on oblique metaphors. While somewhat tenuously connected to the volume's theme of violence, Wendy K. Perriman's 'Dancing behind the Veil: Willa Cather's Literary Choreography in *A Lost Lady*' provides a fascinating look at how Cather subtly infused imagery and themes drawn from dance into her narratives. Perriman reveals how dances as various as the Sioux Ghost Dance and the Nijinsky version of *Le Spectre de la Rose* impacted Cather and prompted her to 'highlight how patriarchal society (not Marian) is responsible for betrayal and...[show] the resilience of the human spirit'. One final essay of note from the collection is David H. Porter's 'From Violence to Art: Willa Cather Caught in the Eddy', which explains some connections between Cather and Christian Scientist Mary Baker Eddy. Porter, contrary to the critical consensus, avers that Eddy's influence on Cather may equal that of Sarah Orne Jewett, and suggests that Eddy functioned as a negative example, particularly with regard to Cather's views on sexuality. Porter further suggests that several of Cather's characters, most notably Thea Kronborg and Myra Henshawe, contain definite traces of Eddy's personality and philosophy. In all, the essay collection offers a series of new interpretative possibilities for Cather studies.

In *Axes: Willa Cather and William Faulkner*, Merrill Maguire Skaggs, a premier Cather critic, looks at the ways in which Willa Cather and William Faulkner engaged in a fictional dialectic of sorts that culminated in 'an homage to the other'. Despite admittedly thin biographical evidence, Skaggs, relying on close textual comparisons, charges that Cather and Faulkner consciously responded to each other's aesthetic and thematic assumptions, 'saluting the other, as well as revising the other and one-upping the other, while insistently rewriting the other'. Skaggs commences in 1921 and then quickly moves to 1922's *One of Ours*, which she convincingly demonstrates served as a model for several passages in later works by Faulkner, most notably *Soldier's Pay*. Skaggs teasingly suggests that Cather may have modelled her character Claude on Faulkner and intimates that the pair could have met in New York City, a detail that has hitherto escaped the biographers. Skaggs next argues that Cather's impact on Faulkner's *Mosquitoes* was even more dramatic, stating that the Southerner 'plundered thoroughly the salient possibilities he chose from Cather's *The Professor's House*'. Skaggs observes that Faulkner references many of Cather's 'characterizing details'. Skaggs indicates that Cather was furious at Faulkner's petty thefts, but she wonders why an established novelist such as Cather would care so much that a budding novelist (in a failed novel) had stolen her themes: Cather herself had appropriated Faulkner's poetry, as well as Phil Stone's preface, in 'Tom Outland's Story'. Skaggs states that Stone's preface gave Cather 'the sketch of a personality who is exactly the opposite Professor St. Peter'.

Skaggs suggests that, in *The Sound and the Fury*, Faulkner used details from at least four of Cather's novels. She further remarks that his use increased markedly in quality, and it also drew from Cather's narrative approach in addition to her prose style. Skaggs is meticulous in comparing passages and noting how Faulkner transforms his source, and the critic comments that Faulkner was 'as substantially perceptive and insightful a reader as [Cather] ever acquired'. For her part, Cather, according to Skaggs, included a sketch of Faulkner in *Death Comes for the Archbishop*. While intriguing, this speculation lacks a solid basis—such as a letter—for its hypothesis. However, as Skaggs points out with regard to *As I Lay Dying* and *Obscure Destinies*, 'The *textual* evidence, in contrast to the "known facts", might suggest that each was responding directly to the works of the other.' Skaggs claims that, while it seems nearly impossible that Faulkner read Cather's 'Neighbor Rosicky' before finishing *Light in August*, the latter almost systematically 'denie[s] or invert[s]' the former 'down to the metaphors'. Cather, Skaggs, notes, utilizes the plot of *Absalom, Absalom!* for her *Sapphira and the Slave Girl*, as well as many similar names and themes. Skaggs states that 'correspondences and anomalies occur in pairs'. She concludes her volume by examining Cather's story 'Before Breakfast', which she suggests explicitly examines Cather's textual relationship with Faulkner, who in turn responded in *The Reivers*. Individually, Skaggs's theories might be dismissed as coincidence, but collectively, they show a fine critical mind at work. *Axes: Willa Cather and William Faulkner* is an idiosyncratic, fun book that uses keen interpretative strategies.

Volume 7 of Cather Studies is entitled *Willa Cather as Cultural Icon*, and it offers numerous meta-examinations of Cather's status in the academy and the public at large. In his introduction Guy Reynolds claims that Cather 'was an icon discomfited by iconic status', yet 'her steady movement to the center of the twentieth-century U.S. literary canon' suggests that 'she has achieved a status that extends beyond the immediate community that works on her texts'. In addition to Reynolds's introduction, the volume includes twenty essays covering topics such as 'Advertising Cather', the Book-of-the-Month Club, and Cather's public. Unlike Urgo and Skaggs's collection (reviewed above), however, this one deviates from its stated goal with tenuous connections to Cather's iconic status in essays such as '"Have I changed so much?": Jim Burden, Intertextuality, and the Ending of *My Ántonia*', and 'Cather, Freudianism, and Freud', the latter of which explicitly acknowledges that it 'does not argue for or particularly examine Willa Cather's cultural iconicity'. Given that perhaps more of the essays fail to examine Cather through the lens of iconicity than accomplish the task, the book's title is somewhat misleading, and truly focused readings of this intriguing topic make up more of a 'cluster' than an integrated theme.

This quibble notwithstanding, several of the essays make a solid contribution to the crowded field of Cather studies. Joseph C. Murphy, for example, tackles 'Double Birthday', a less often studied Cather story, in his 'The Dialectics of Seeing in Cather's Pittsburgh: "Double Birthday" and Urban Allegory', which, while making a faint reference to Cather's iconicity in its opening paragraph, views the tale through the framework of Walter Benjamin's *The Arcades Project* and comments on how the narrative 'seeks a realignment of community and values within a city that is in various ways disintegrating'. Murphy applies a close reading to the story and discovers that 'Albert's vision, like Benjamin's, follows the oblique and shifting contours of a modern city where no overarching perspective, of time or space, is possible.' Another deft interpretation of Cather, and one much more on point, appears in Mark J. Madigan's 'Willa Cather and the Book-of-the-Month Club', a essay that reconstructs Cather's extensive relationship with the influential organization. Madigan, while observing the lack of extant official records, relies on letters from the novelist (and Cather friend) Dorothy Canfield Fisher, who served as a judge for the group, and various Book-of-the-Month Club reviewers to establish that the club emphasized the 'formal qualities and characterization' of Cather's books, 'while ignoring their tantalizing problems and complexities'. Although Madigan unfortunately fails to discuss the ramifications of his findings extensively enough, he does begin a dialogue on a forgotten chapter in the early reputation of Willa Cather.

In an essay that neglects the book's ostensible theme yet advances our understanding of Cather, Jonathan D. Gross's 'Recollecting Emotion in Tranquility: Wordsworth and Byron in Cather's *My Ántonia* and *Lucy Gayheart*' effectively demonstrates how Cather refigures several images and themes from her Romantic influences. Much as Skaggs does in *Axes*, Gross applies a nuanced close reading to Cather's narratives and teases out how she both admires and transforms the Romantics, ultimately 'show[ing] the limits of Wordsworthian complacency [and] Byronic egotism [and how they contrast] unfavorably with women like Ántonia and Lucy, who...face life squarely, despite setbacks'. Another interesting essay, and one more in tune with the book's central idea, is Robert Thacker's ' "A critic who was worthy of her": The Writing of *Willa Cather: A Critical Biography*', which examines E.K. Brown and Leon Edel's seminal biography of Cather, a book that Thacker describes as 'be[ing] a foundational act of Cather's establishment as a cultural icon'. Thacker is the first to plumb the archives for this story, and he makes excellent use of primary material in his investigation of the book's genesis and its importance in establishing Cather's posthumous reputation. Thacker states that the biography 'embodies in its provenance the issues that confront Cather critics still as scholars, and which confront especially any attempt to gauge Cather as a "cultural icon" '. Other essays of note in the collection include those by Erika Hamilton, Joseph R. Urgo and Steven Trout.

Another book that discusses Cather, although not exclusively, is Philip Joseph's *American Literary Regionalism in a Global Age*. Joseph acknowledges two key periods in his book, 1880–95 and 1920–39, during which main figures consciously joined a discussion on how 'rural hamlets and urban neighborhoods with marginal access to the centers of economic and political power' tied in with national and international progressive trends. Joseph views as a central interpretative issue the way(s) in which regionalists 'reconcile values like home, neighborhood, and locality with democratic ideals like freedom of movement, individual self-determination, collective empowerment, and open-ended debate'. Joseph employs central figures, rather than tangential or emerging ones, in his examination primarily because such luminaries function as 'active interlocutors in the contemporary context' whereas more forgotten writers generally fail do so. In Joseph's early group are Hamlin Garland, Sarah Orne Jewett and Abraham Cahan, while in the later period he considers Mary Austin, Willa Cather, Zora Neale Hurston and William Faulkner.

After chapters on Garland and Jewett and Cahan, Joseph turns to Mary Austin, whom he discusses in the context of her opposition to a planned 'Cultural Center for the Southwest'. While at first blush it might seem odd for Austin to oppose a celebration of south-western customs, Joseph points out that the writer felt that such a centre would serve as a magnet for 'Main Street America' and project a 'cheap imitation' of the local colour that attracted Austin to the region. Joseph argues that Austin's early work, such as *The Land of Little Rain*, failed to evince the social concerns of her 1920s narratives, such as *The American Rhythm*, which conveyed the idea that 'nationalization depends on a moment of rupture and cultural forgetting' but that also 'envisioned a diversity of...communities...distinguishable from one another by the influences of their respective local geographies'. Joseph further links her objections to Austin's 'protest against the circumscribed domestic space of the bourgeois family' represented by women's clubs. Joseph claims that for Austin such clubs, which enthusiastically backed the Center, endorsed a 'process of distortion and domestication'. Austin preferred that individuals should encounter indigenous cultures in their local contexts. In this way, Joseph argues, Austin felt that alienated modern citizens would be healed by the contact.

In the next chapter, Joseph discusses Willa Cather and her use of characters 'whose inner lives exceed their immediate physical surroundings and the communities in which they presently participate'. *Contra* Austin, Cather, according to Joseph, rejected the notion that proximity to native culture could act as a salve for the soul and instead heralded an image of the artist 'as a producer who is unrestricted by national or racial culture'. Joseph reads *Death Comes for the Archbishop* as a narrative in which Cather demonstrates that the artistic sensibility, while impacted by 'the generative conditions of collected life' is nonetheless 'freed from the obligation to serve a particular interest group'. Joseph avers that, for Cather, the 'cosmopolitan local subject', the 'psychic nomad', transcends the importance of any given region and that the 'meaningfulness of contemplation' supersedes traditional details.

The final two chapters deal with Hurston and Faulkner. With respect to Hurston, Joseph concentrates on her 'awareness that cultural workers have a role to play in repairing representational damage'. He views Hurston's repeated theme of justice, particularly racial and feminist justice, as one way in which she accomplishes the goal of correcting the damage of the earlier plantation tradition. Joseph examines a number of texts, including an extended discussion of *Jonah's Gourd Vine*, a novel that contemplates the merits of local connections versus the education afforded by travel (in this case to the North). He concludes, though, that neither travel nor community can fully heal the wounds of the past. He ends his study with a discussion of the transformation of regionalism and its literary reputation, and he employs Faulkner's Flem Snopes as a metaphor for the ways in which hitherto remote towns become linked to a larger system. The critic argues that 'Faulkner does not construct his community according to the belief that the more the community revises itself the more it ensures its survival.' In this remark, Joseph considers the idea of duration and how literary works are uniquely suited to visit and revisit the conflict between tradition and progress.

Chad Trevitte offered an additional discussion of Willa Cather in his 'Cather's *A Lost Lady* and the Disenchantment of Art' (*TCL* 53[2007] 182–211), which argues that the novel simultaneously employs nostalgia and suggests that nostalgia leads to 'blindness'. After placing the novel in an aesthetic context and examining it through the theoretical lens of Huyssen, Adorno and others, Trevitte concludes that 'By incorporating aesthetic disenchantment in her own ambiguous mode of narration, Cather not only participates in the modernist critique of illusion that informs the work of writers such as Flaubert, James and Conrad, but also addresses how the problem of artistic illusion is itself symptomatic of the uneasy relationship between autonomous art and commerce in industrialized modernity.'

Although requested, several books on William Faulkner were not received. Nevertheless, as usual, many articles on Faulkner appeared, including Thomas Fick and Eva Gold's ' "He liked men": Homer, Homosexuality, and the Culture of Manhood in Faulkner's "A Rose for Emily" ' (*EurekaStudies* 8[2007] 99–107), which argues that Homer Barron is 'combatively heterosexual'. The authors support their contention by examining the ways in which conceptions of heterosexuality have evolved and by arguing that the homosocial world that Homer inhabits in fact reinforces his masculinity and that his resistance to marriage reflects the 'perceived threat of being caught in a woman-controlled world where the purse (literal and Freudian) is both controlled and controlling'. Arguing that Faulkner's use of the prostitute, while rejecting nineteenth-century genteel values, reveals an essentially 'conservative, pre-modern conception of gender', Jeffrey J. Folks's 'William Faulkner and the Image of the Prostitute' (*ArkR* 38[2007] 31–41) suggests that the writer's frequent representation of prostitution served as a response to the perceived threat of the New Woman movement. Exploring prostitutes in various of Faulkner's novels, including *Sanctuary*, *The Reivers* and *Mosquitoes*, Folks claims that 'Faulkner's conflicted representation of the prostitute reflects, among other things, a questing for absolute freedom, including the male longing for female companionship and maternal attention free of spousal or filial commitments; the yearning for an idyllic, amoral acceptance of sexuality within a culture of rigid moral restrictions; and a prelapsarian fantasy of guiltless sexual play.'

In 'Freud, Faulkner, Caruth: Trauma and the Politics of Literary Form,' Greg Forter (*Narrative* 15[2007] 260–85) studies Faulkner via Freud and trauma studies and breaks with the typical use of Freud by trauma critics, employing earlier Freudian models that apply better to 'systemic traumatizations'. Analysing *Light in August* and *Absalom, Absalom!*, Forter concludes that 'Faulkner's generalization of trauma as the Truth of historical experience saves him from confronting the forms of guilt and responsibility that the history he anatomizes bequeathed to him. If we are "all" traumatized by virtue of suffering the movement of History, then there's nothing Faulkner can or need *do* to combat the legacy of slavery and patriarchy whose history his novel recounts.' Daniel Spoth compares Faulkner to W.B. Yeats in his 'The House that Time Built: Structuring History in Faulkner and Yeats' (*EJAC* 23[2007] 109–25), an article that reads *Absalom, Absalom!* and 'Meditations in Time of Civil War' and their negotiation of both the 'ancestral beauty' of the 'Big House' and its 'threatened decay'. Paying attention to architectural analogues as he comments on the works, Spoth views the authors' projects as constituting 'a calculated autoeradication of the structural model of history and its replacement with an authoritarian, parasitic, highly narrativized and reconstituted model'. In 'Coordination Problems in the Work of William Faulkner' (*PLL* 43[2007] 89–112), Michael Wainwright employs game theory—particularly as it relates to 'coordination problems', which are 'situations in which the actions of an individual depend on the behavior of others'—to such works as *Light in August*, *The Town* and *A Fable*. For each interpretation, Wainwright sets up a logical matrix and then proceeds to show how the narratives adhere to it. Pairing Faulkner and Balzac, David Walter's 'Strange Attractions: Sibling Love Triangles in Faulkner's *Absalom, Absalom!* and Balzac's *La Fille aux yeux d'or*' (*CLS* 44[2007] 484–506) posits that critics have generally ignored the French writer's influence on the Southerner's major works. Walter discovers unmistakable parallels between *Absalom, Absalom!* and Balzac's novella and argues that 'it is precisely when Faulkner abandons his self-conscious imitation of Balzac and finds his own voice that he remanifests his French master's themes in the deepest way'. Benjamin Widiss charts Faulkner's use of a linguistic 'play harnessed to the specific objectives not only of adding new layers to our understanding of particular moments in the narrative but also of stressing aesthetic qualities of the text that are not reducible to the representation of either particular moments or solitary psychologies' in his 'Fit and Surfeit in *As I Lay Dying*' (*Novel* 41[2007] 99–120). Widiss teases out how 'Faulkner facilitates and accentuates this developing acumen at the level of the individual word, encouraging a reading process that at last reaps from the vocabulary of loss a syntax of plenitude. This plenitude, predicated on a syntax that is the novel's rather than any single character's, constitutes an alternative emotional register, an invitation to indulge in aesthetic satisfactions denied to the characters—and thus an invitation that leaves us seesawing between an empathetic identification with the characters' plight and an intellectual and emotional pleasure that we share with the author, whose putative absence is, in fact, repudiated in this very fashion.'

Doreen Fowler's 'Beyond Oedipus: Lucas Beauchamp, Ned Barnett, and Faulkner's *Intruder in the Dust*' (*MFS* 53[2007] 788–820) investigates the novel's repeated trope of burial and reburial and finds a symbolic order in which Faulkner strives for 'an alternative model of signification that differentiates without dominating or discriminating'. While admiring Faulkner's project in *Intruder in the Dust*, Fowler observes that ultimately 'the text's critique of a repressive phallic authority is itself mired in repression, since its subversive content is buried under layer after layer of displacement and substitution'. In 'Taking "money right out of an American's pockets": Faulkner's South and the International Cotton Market' (*EJAC* 23[2007] 83–95), Taylor Hagood historicizes Yoknapatawpha County's link to the global commodities market and studies Faulkner's cognizance that Mississippi's 'transformation into a juggernaut of global capitalism—a transformation that all inhabitants of Faulkner's Mississippi apparently see as necessary for the state's political and economic future health, however destructive it may be to the land, the wilderness, or themselves'. Hagood ably studies contemporary resources in grounding his argument, and he looks at a variety of Faulkner's texts in concluding that, while the market may turn land and humans into commodities, it also allows the South to touch the world and the world to touch the South. Gary Harrington, in 'Faulkner's *The Sound and the Fury*' (*Expl* 65:ii[2007] 109–11), notes that *The Sound and the Fury*'s reference to the cotton market's opening value of 20.62 encodes Quentin's age at the time of his death as well as the month and day of his death. In his 'The Ghostly Voice of Gossip in Faulkner's "A Rose for Emily"' (*Expl* 65:iv[2007] 229–32) Thomas Klein cites the problematic nature of the pluralistic narration in Faulkner's story, and posits that the writer modelled it on 'the gossipy, first-person style of society columnists, especially that found in the "Talk of the Town" section of the *New Yorker*'.

Exploring the role of human diversity in Faulkner's novel, Avak Hasratian's 'The Death of Difference in *Light in August*' (*Criticism* 49[2007] 55–84) applies the work of anthropologist Giorgio Agamben to the book's dialectic over the destructive properties of finding kinship through exclusion. Hasratian shows how many of the novel's characters lack traditional bonds, but he opines that *Light in August* demonstrates that such a phenomenon privileges 'the living mass in its collectively generic rather than individually important "character"' as represented by potentially delimiting and prejudicial differences. Stephanie Li, in 'Resistance, Silence, and Placées: Charles Bon's Octoroon Mistress and Louisa Picquet' (*AL* 79[2007] 85–112), looks at *Absalom, Absalom!* and its treatment of Bon's lover and how she 'is at all times determined by the whims and desires of male narrative power'. Li studies *Louisa Picquet, the Octoroon* as a way of determining that Faulkner's strategies in describing Bon's mistress bespeak not characterization but 'the embodiment of conflicted desires and images'. At first blush the linking of 'A Rose for Emily', *Peyton Place* and *Psycho* might seem an odd one, but John A. McDermott makes the case, in '"Do you love mother, Norman?"': Faulkner's "A Rose for Emily" and Metalious's *Peyton Place* as Sources for Robert Bloch's *Psycho*' (*JPC* 40[2007] 454–67), that the resemblance is not coincidental but consistent. Ticien Marie Sassoubre's 'Avoiding Adjudication in Faulkner's *Go Down, Moses* and *Intruder in the Dust*' (*Criticism* 49[2007] 183–214) examines how, in Faulkner's early work, lynching sets up an extra-legal paradigm that 'does not threaten but rather coexists with the rule of law', but contends that in his later novels the perceived intrusion of federal law less tolerant of vigilante justice demands 'resisting federally imposed law by employing extralegal norms and practices in the place of official adjudication'. After extensively historicizing the struggle between federal and state law, Sassoubre suggests that both novels offer a cohesive investigation of the legal conflict, and shows how a conscientious and paternalistic local legal system could effectively 'moderate those elements of the community prone to violence' while still 'protecting community based norms' from federal encroachment.

The object of many biographies and memoirs, Ernest Hemingway's life hardly needs another rehearsal of the well-known facts. However, Linda Wagner-Martin ably condenses Hemingway's multifarious experiences into fewer than 200 very readable pages. Wagner-Martin traces the role that Hemingway's significant relationships with women played in his development as a writer and focuses on his 'fluidity'. After quickly but aptly describing Hemingway's boyhood and wartime experience, Wagner-Martin breezes through the young Hemingway's association with his nurse, Agnes von Kurowsky. She speculates, plausibly, that Ag's night shifts perhaps let 'woman and boy [share] confidences that would have been impossible during busy day duty'. The biographer finds evidence in existing letters between the two that bear out the passion that Hemingway had for the older woman, and she notes the 'many bitter letters' that the young man wrote in 'exorcis[ing] his love' for Ag, and the erratic behaviour that ensued after the nurse's engagement to an Italian officer. Wagner-Martin does not examine Hemingway's early work on the Toronto *Star Weekly*, but she does point out that Grace Hemingway felt writing to be a 'meaningless pastime', a view that vexed the 20-year-old. Wagner-Martin asserts that the anguish that Hemingway felt over the episode 'found its way into his mature fiction'. A particularly strong chapter on Hemingway's ambivalence over his impending marriage to Hadley Richardson makes excellent use of a letter from Hemingway to his sister, and the chapter further details Richardson's anger at a separation from Hemingway and her sadness at losing a valise full of her husband's manuscripts (an incident, Wagner-Martin reminds her readers, that would resurface in two of

Hemingway's posthumously published novels). In the next two chapters, Wagner-Martin ably examines *In Our Time* and links it with Hemingway's experiences in Oak Park and elsewhere. She then turns to Hemingway's relationship with Fitzgerald and Scribner's, as well as his novel *The Sun Also Rises* and his affair with Pauline Pfeiffer. She remarks that 'most of Hemingway's expatriate friends were bewildered about his divorce and remarriage', and she offers concise but solid readings of several of Hemingway's strongest stories as well as *A Farewell to Arms*.

The next three chapters tackle Hemingway's fame, as well as several of his most cherished avocations and metaphors: bullfighting, fishing and hunting. Hemingway's affairs also play a central role in the book's middle chapters, although, as with the rest of the narrative, the stories are quite truncated. Wagner-Martin characterizes Hemingway's marriage to Martha Gellhorn as 'wistful', and she notes an odd episode in which Hemingway outfitted the *Pilar* with guns, ostensibly to hunt submarines during the Second World War, and spent hours at sea drinking and carousing. She suggests that this was but one sticking point in his failing marriage with Gellhorn. The book's final chapters discuss Hemingway's fourth marriage, as well as his experiences in Cuba writing *The Old Man and the Sea*, and his African plane crash. Wagner-Martin discusses the balance of Hemingway's life in the final chapter. In all, she provides an admirable and well-written introduction to Hemingway's life, but the breakneck pace and the unavoidable omissions mean that serious students of Hemingway will continue to look to other sources for the day-to-day details of his biography.

Numerous articles on Hemingway's art and life appeared in 2007, including Ron Berman's 'Hemingway's Michigan Landscapes' (*HemRev* 27:i[2007] 39–54), which examines how the writer's use of painterly techniques in describing landscapes evolved. Berman employs a Hemingway observation about Cézanne to demonstrate how the writer moved from an unsophisticated realism and towards a less idealistic view that represents a Michigan wherein 'earth and water are mixed in the form of marsh and swamp; air and water combine to take the form of mist'. Via 'address, semantic congruence, off-color language, and representation of speech', Milton M. Azevedo compares multiple visions of Hemingway's *The Fifth Column* in 'Translation Strategies: *The Fifth Column* in French, Italian, Portuguese, and Spanish' (*HemRev* 27:i[2007] 108–28). Azevedo closely analyses representative passages from the book and illustrates how various translators add and subtract substantial elements, and how misunderstanding of Hemingway's historical context(s) can affect the translation's accuracy. Examining how the protagonist in Hemingway's 'Soldier's Home' 'becomes an outsider to what once was his life, and how his tragedy is brought about by the conflicting social norms that govern his behavior', Ruben de Baerdemaeker offers 'Performative Patterns in Hemingway's "Soldier's Home"' (*HemRev* 27:i[2007] 55–73). De Baerdemaeker engages Judith Butler's theories in exploring how Hemingway's story traces Harold Krebs's new paradigm of masculinity, one that causes him problems because he 'cannot translate his European war experiences into the pattern of Oklahoma'. Arthur F. Bethea inspects Raymond Carver for Hemingway's influence in 'Raymond Carver's Inheritance from Hemingway's

Literary Technique' (*HemRev* 26:ii[2007] 89–104) and finds that, while Carver 'consciously rejected Papa's gravitational force' in terms of theme, the later writer also 'followed [Hemingway] technically and echoed without derision'. Bethea looks at several Hemingway stories—most notably 'Hills like White Elephants'—to demonstrate how Carver appropriated Hemingway's technique of omission.

George Cheatham's 'The World War I Battle of Mons and Hemingway's *In Our Time* Chapter III' (*HemRev* 26:ii[2007] 44–57) contends that Hemingway's text 'deployed literal topical details and allusions not as mere counters in some archetypal pattern, but as significant organizers of culturally coded meaning'. Offering a detailed look at the battle and its contemporary significance Cheatham avers that, unlike the names of the war's other major battles, 'the name Mons evokes the official myth as a straight background against which the remainder of Hemingway's text can then develop an ironic counter-myth'. An under-studied story receives its due in Robert C. Clark's 'Papa y el Tirador: Biographical Parallels in Hemingway's "I Guess Everything Reminds You of Something"' (*HemRev* 27:i[2007] 89–106), which opines that the tale is 'a biographically-based narrative that exposes the complex emotions leading to the collapse of Gregory and Ernest's relationship'. Drawing on letters and other evidence, Clark reviews several incidents between father and son before turning to the story to puzzle out biographical antecedents and concluding that the narrative, with respect to Hemingway's treatment of Gregory, is 'dismissive and coldly absolute'. Studying Hemingway's novel for the ways in which it demonstrates that 'teaching can be a powerful source of learning for the teacher', Donald A. Daiker's 'The Pedagogy of *The Sun Also Rises*' (*HemRev* 27:i[2007] 74–88) claims that Jake Barnes's philosophy is predicated on the notion that learning is the pre-eminent goal of life. Daiker illustrates how Jake, while failing as an instructor, 'has so well internalized the lessons he had earlier tried to teach Brett that he lives them'. Applying theories from the emergent field of disability studies, Dana Fore, in 'Life Unworthy of Life? Masculinity, Disability, and Guilt in *The Sun Also Rises*' (*HemRev* 26:ii[2007] 74–88), states that 'Jake will never achieve the psychological stability he craves because he finally accepts prevailing social and medical philosophies about his injury—and these ideas, in turn, will always leave him vulnerable to the fear that he will "degenerate" into an invalid or a "pervert".' Fore sensitively re-examines the novel and demonstrates Jake's responses to various stereotypes about wounds and masculine power, concluding pessimistically that the character ultimately 'accept[s] the life society has mapped out for him as a disabled man'.

Jennifer Lester's 'Reading *For Whom the Bell Tolls* with Barthes, Bakhtin, and Shapiro' (*HemRev* 26:ii[2007] 114–24) analyses how Hemingway 'frames the imagery and narrative of war, creates layers of discourse to tell the story of war, and codes social experiences of war within the text'. Lester points out how Hemingway places images of war next to beautiful landscapes, compares various characters' feelings about war, and examines Robert Jordan's internal conflict over the war, and demonstrates how 'these elements allow us to think about war from phenomenological, linguistic, and structural perspectives'. In 'Hemingway and the *OED*' (*HemRev* 26:ii[2007] 105–13), Charles M. Tod

Oliver investigates the writer's 332 appearances in the online *Oxford English Dictionary*, including forty-six entries (compared to thirty-nine in the second printed edition) in which Hemingway is cited as the first author to use a word in print. Oliver lists a variety of words, such as 'bal musette', 'cojones' and 'bop', and he notes that the number of Hemingway's original uses exceeds Faulkner's twenty-five. *Kansas City Star* writer Steve Paul's ' "'Drive', he said": How Ted Brumback Helped Steer Ernest Hemingway into War and Writing' (*HemRev* 27:i[2007] 21–38) looks at a pivotal moment in the young Hemingway's career when he met Brumback, formerly an ambulance driver in the First World War. Paul relies heavily on Brumback's memoir of his time with Hemingway. Adding to the biographical knowledge of Hemingway, Anthony E. Rebollo, in 'The Taxation of Ernest Hemingway' (*HemRev* 26:ii[2007] 22–43), examines contemporary taxation principles and discusses the impact of tax rates in excess of 90 per cent on the writer. Using the IRS taxation code and other documents, Rebollo explains why writers were hit especially hard by existing rules and indicates various ways in which Hemingway could spread out his tax burden. Examining Hemingway's cinematographic 'multi-focal' aesthetic, Zoe Trodd's 'Hemingway's Camera Eye: The Problem of Language and an Interwar Politics of Form' (*HemRev* 26:ii[2007] 7–21) tries to determine how the writer attempted to overcome 'language's depleted capacity for expression'. Trodd claims that Hemingway would frequently subvert his 'one-shot photographic aesthetic' with linguistic strategies inspired by film. Looking at an under-studied aspect of Hemingway's canon, Verna Kale suggests, in 'Hemingway's Poetry and the Paris Apprenticeship' (*HemRev* 26:ii[2007] 58–73), that the author's poems may have 'functioned as experimental drafts of difficult prose exercises'. Kale traces how poems such as 'The Age Demanded' anticipated reformulations in novels such as *The Sun Also Rises*.

In 'Hemingway's "The Killers" and Heroic Fatalism: From Page to Screen (Thrice)' (*LFQ* 35[2007] 404–11), Philip Booth comments on how adaptations of the story treat the idea of Hemingway's ideal of a 'dignified, graceful acceptance of one's circumstances in the face of personal disaster'. Booth quickly interprets the story and then moves to a discussion of three screen versions, pointing out differences but refraining from evaluation, save the comment that 'The emotional impact on viewers of all three movie adaptations of "The Killers" matches the effect the original story has on readers.' In 'Justice for Ernest Hemingway' (*AR* 65[2007] 239–55), G.T. Dempsey considers Hemingway's post-1945 output, which he claims lacks the 'classical austerity, the purity of line, the narrative tension and muscularity' of his earlier prose. Dempsey argues that Hemingway's physical and mental deterioration contributed heavily to this artistic demise, and he calls for scholarly editions of Hemingway's posthumous work so that readers can see how parts of larger manuscripts were cannibalized for shorter narratives. Meg Gillette compares debates over whether or not to have an abortion in one of Hemingway's most famous stories and a once popular but now under-studied novel in 'Making Modern Parents in Ernest Hemingway's "Hills like White Elephants" and Viña Delmar's *Bad Girl*' (*MFS* 53[2007] 50–69). While suggesting that the radical stylistic innovations of Hemingway's story seem distant from Delmar's popular text, Gillette demonstrates that rhetorical breakdowns over whether or not to have a baby stand at the thematic centre of both narratives. In a spirited examination of how Hemingway and Claude McKay formed a complex intertextual relationship, Gary Edward Holcomb's 'The Sun Also Rises in Queer Black Harlem: Hemingway and McKay's Modernist Intertext' (*JML* 30:iv[2007] 61–81) avers that 'On the one hand, Hemingway's narrative of white modern expatriates entitled McKay to envision his black transnational, transgressive innovation; on the other hand, McKay's radical anastrophe enabled Hemingway to envisage the instability of the binary: modern/primitive.' Holcomb suggests both that Hemingway's novel could not have employed its 'primitives' without the fountainhead of the Harlem Renaissance and that McKay radically revised *The Sun Also Rises* through a queer perspective. Jeffrey Meyers, in 'Hemingway's Feasts' (*PLL* 43[2007] 426–42), studies how Hemingway's increasingly elaborate descriptions of food gesture towards the writer's decline in prose style. Oddly, Meyers, after showing how food functions in the earlier works, avoids extended discussion of cuisine in the later narratives, with the exception of *A Moveable Feast*, but he remarks that Hemingway's heroes treat food as a 'constant source of sensual pleasure'.

Edith Wharton's all-encompassing enthusiasm for applied aesthetics provides the impetus for *Memorial Boxes and Guarded Interiors: Edith Wharton and Material Culture*, a critical anthology edited by Gary Totten. Totten writes in his introduction that Wharton possessed a tremendous 'ability to perceive the deeper cultural significance of material phenomena', and he argues that examining the writer's texts without considering her integration of material culture 'limits our understanding of her artistic contribution'. Apart from the introduction, the collection consists of eleven essays on subjects such as body art, commodification and domestic technology. In general, the essays do not seek to examine such material culture in isolation but rather look at how Wharton infuses her characters and themes with an awareness of how external aesthetic features alter people's relationships to society and to themselves. The first two essays concern themselves with Wharton's reception, but the third, Jacqueline Wilson-Jordan's 'The Woman Writer and the Struggle for Authority in "Mr. Jones"', examines how Wharton employs Gothic elements, particularly the idea of the house as 'the locus of terror for a female heroine who is trapped inside'. Wilson-Jordan links this terror to depression and the house's (and the story's) 'ruling master, Mr. Jones', and ultimately asserts that 'a woman writer's bold attempts to assume authority over her house and its stories will not go unchallenged'.

One of the volume's most outstanding contributions is Emily J. Orlando's 'Picturing Lily: Body Art in *The House of Mirth*', an essay that compares Lily Bart's control over 'her objectification as a work of art' to a series of *tableaux vivants*. Orlando convincingly juxtaposes Wharton's descriptions of Lily to paintings such as Sir Joshua Reynolds's *Portrait of Joanna Lloyd of Maryland* and Dante Gabriel Rossetti's *Beata Beatrix*, a comparison that, Orlando suggests, demonstrates Wharton's critique of the objectification of women, as, for instance, in the case of the Pre-Raphaelite trope of 'position[ing] dead beautiful women as the subject of the gazes of men'. Another strong contribution is Jennifer Shepherd's 'Fashioning an Aesthetics of Consumption in *The House of Mirth*', which reveals how Wharton's novel 'obliquely figures the transition of not only the American caste system but also the contemporary fashion system'. Shepherd notes that older social markers, such as pedigree, are challenged by new ones, such as sumptuous (and expensive) clothing: the 'sartorial register'. Examining the numerous uses of fashion in *The House of Mirth*, Shepherd concludes that despite increased access to the sartorial register, 'women's specular gaze and fantasy life were still strongly subject to male control'. Totten's own essay, 'The Machine in the Home: Women and Technology in *The Fruit of the Tree*', is another helpful addition to Wharton studies, as it explores how turn-of-the-century 'cultural and technological transitions . . . were both exciting and threatening' for women, depending largely on social class. Using both contemporary sources and recent historical analysis, Totten considers the narratives of various characters in relation to the 'Machine-like language and images [that] demonstrate the complicated effects of the machine's intrusion into this domestic space'. For Totten, Wharton's use of such technological imagery problematizes the idea that machines would liberate women from drudgery by suggesting that the benefits of technology may come at the cost of 'personal happiness and cultural position'. In all, the volume stays true to its stated goal, and it provides strong readings of Wharton's works and use of material culture.

Janet Beer and Avril Horner consider how Wharton 'deliberately experiments with blurring genre boundaries, producing a new hybrid mode through which to critique the modern age', in 'Wharton the "Renovator": *Twilight Sleep* as Gothic Satire' (*YES* 37[2007] 177–92). The authors study various strategies within *Twilight Sleep* and determine that 'Through her skilful blending of generic opposites—the comic and the tragic, the satiric and the Gothic—Wharton is doing more than offering an analysis of post-war society; in this late novel she is critiquing the very nature of modernity.' 'Edith Wharton's Alchemy of Publicity' (*AL* 79[2007] 725–51), by Lorna Brittan, investigates Wharton's canon and claims that, 'Even as these texts point to the dangers of publicity for the individual, they simultaneously reveal skepticism that individuality can be fully articulated in a pure state of privacy.' Brittan looks at a variety of Wharton's texts, including *The Decoration of Houses* and *The House of Mirth*, in determining that 'For Wharton, publicity alchemistically transforms the breach of privacy into the rebirth of personality, upholding the distinct individual as the touchstone of worth even as it supports the crowd's will.' Jamil S. Selina, in 'Wharton's "Roman Fever"' (*Expl* 65:ii[2007] 99–101), looks at the image of knitting in Wharton's story and suggests that 'Cirace alone is the knitter because she alone acquires the grace with which to acknowledge the past and hence to see the connection between the present and the past.' In ' "A Journey": Edith Wharton's Homage to F. Marion Crawford's "The Upper Berth" ' (*SCR* 40[2007] 19–26), Terry W. Thompson looks at how Wharton's 'cumulative horror' nods admiringly to Crawford's tale via 'clear and numerous' similarities. Thompson compares both narratives and shows how Wharton 'creates a feminine companion piece of sorts to Crawford's touchstone tale'.

Joanne Marshall Mauldin explores Thomas Wolfe's last years in her biography, *Thomas Wolfe: When Do the Atrocities Begin?* While most biographies of Wolfe pay particular attention to the writer's formative years and the material that he would reshape in his fiction, Mauldin eschews a comprehensive approach for an in-depth look at Wolfe's activities in 1937 and 1938. The book lacks an introductory note that offers an explicit rationale for confining its discussion to the last two years (as opposed, say, to the last three or four) and dives right into the material, which offers an implicit reason: Wolfe's 'bone-weary' state of mind and his decision to journey home for the first time in over seven years. Mauldin writes very fluidly, and she establishes an effective narrative pace, which she punctuates with copious references to primary materials. Mauldin's microscopic approach enables readers to glean a dense idea of Wolfe's state of mind in his final years, and she does not shy away from the less savoury details of the writer's life, such as the 'two women [who] claimed that he had impregnated them during the year'. Unlike several comprehensive Wolfe biographies, this book has the luxury to tell its story in Wolfe-like detail, and readers discover a variety of facts about the author and the people he visited, such as the late afternoon when a very hungry Wolfe sat drinking highballs with Tom Polsky, Jane Whitson, Max Whitson, Tot Weaver and Jackie Reynolds before Wolfe and Max attempted to go to Ashville for steaks but were stopped by a sheriff, who subpoenaed Wolfe to appear as a witness in a murder trial. The stress of the trial caused Wolfe to '[pop] his cork', resulting in a disorderly conduct arrest and a jail-bound conversation about playwriting with a firefighter fan who heard that Wolfe was a captive audience.

Mauldin fills her book with delightful stories about Wolfe's encounters with figures famous (Clifford Odets and Sherwood Anderson, among many others) and unknown, and she does not neglect the prodigious author's writing habits either. One amusing anecdote involves Wolfe's beleaguered typist, Elizabeth Nowell, who, attempting to decipher the stacks of unnumbered manuscript pages, 'determined which page followed which by the degree that the careless writer's cigarette had burned through the paper'. In an intriguing move, Mauldin discusses the details of Wolfe's illness, death and funeral midway through her biography, devoting the second half of the book to the numerous remembrances and condolences that appeared after the writer's death. Further, she examines the 'bales of manuscript . . . stored in seven cardboard cartons' and totalling 'more than one million words'. Mauldin provides a fascinating look at Edward C. Aswell's editing of Wolfe's notoriously unwieldy manuscripts, remarking on how he 'added lines . . . created titles . . . bridged gaps . . . changed point-of-view . . . [and] standardized names' in addition to pruning potentially libellous material. The publication and reception of the resultant *You Can't Go Home Again* is given significant attention, as are other posthumous works, including *The Lost Boy* and various collections of letters, and significant memoirs of Wolfe. In all, this biography offers great insight into Wolfe's final days and his posthumous fiction.

James W. Clark, Jr, in 'Eugene Goes to Sydney' (*TWR* 31[2007] 37–46), explains that 'whenever Eugene Gant goes to Sydney in *Look Homeward, Angel* [1929] and *O Lost* [2000], he retraces trips to Raleigh that the author

Thomas Wolfe had made when he was a student at Chapel Hill between 1916 and 1920. Wolfe, so to speak, guides or mentors his leading character on these adventures.' In 'Mother vs. Daughter: The Relationship between Eliza and Helen in *Look Homeward, Angel*' (*TWR* 31[2007] 62–77), Elizabeth Crowder asserts, *contra* previous scholarship, that the characters of Eliza and Helen Gant 'are remarkably similar' in the ways in which they are detached from relationships, have trouble with communication, and 'suffer from compulsions and/or addictions'. Noting the ways in which the characters use each other for a support system despite their animosity, Crowder states that 'it is fitting that this remarkably similar mother and daughter provide each other some sympathy and companionship'. Shawn Holliday's 'And the Soul Shall Dance: Thomas Wolfe's Influence on Wakako Yamauchi' (*TWR* 31[2007] 11–21) explores the impact of Wolfe on the prizewinning playwright, particularly how the Southerner's novels offered Yamauchi an 'autobiographical template through which she explored the loneliness and nostalgia of Japanese Americans who experienced the disorienting cultural effects of hopeful immigration, failed assimilation, and forced internment during the first half of the twentieth century'. Holliday argues that, 'In Eugene Gant, Yamauchi found a fictional counterpart, an individual who also felt trapped within the confines of self and history.' Allison Kerns's essay, '"It was like a dream of hell": Gantian Dreams Deferred' (*TWR* 31[2007] 47–61), examines the failed aspirations of Wolfe's fictional family. Kerns claims that 'The narrative of *Look Homeward, Angel* is evidence of [Eugene Gant's] success, but he could not have succeeded without learning from his family's mistakes and their heartache over disastrous failures.'

In 'Journey to the Interior: The Influence of Xenophon's *Anabasis* on Thomas Wolfe's *O Lost*' (*TWR* 31[2007] 5–10) Lisa Kerr demonstrates that 'Wolfe titles the opening section of the prologue "Anabasis" to make undeniable the parallel to Xenophon's work, which combined history with autobiography to explore both the external and internal journeys of its characters, and, in doing so, constituted a new form of literature.' Kerr argues that Wolfe employs Xenophon to reveal a 'vision of himself as being, like Xenophon, both a social and personal historian'. 'Adrift in the "Life Sargassic": The Case of *Look Homeward, Angel*' (*TWR* 31[2007] 78–94), by Dan Latimer, offers an idiosyncratic look at Wolfe's novel and some of its influences, and asserts that 'The use that Wolfe makes of Wordsworth and Plotinus is to account for the intensity of being special, alone, of not belonging here below.' Ted Mitchell reprints a pair of letters to Wolfe and his mother from his brother in 'Brother Tom and the Moravians: Two Letters from Ben Wolfe' (*TWR* 31[2007] 126–30), and shows how the correspondence 'provides a biographical glimpse into the relationship of the two brothers that is eventually transmogrified into the close bond between Ben and Eugene Gant in *Look Homeward, Angel*'. The article provides the full text of the news-like letters. In his 'Thomas Wolfe in Nazi Concentration Camps' (*TWR* 31[2007] 22–36), Lawrence D. Stokes explores evidence that prisoners read Wolfe and suggests that 'it is conceivable that for a while it may have been easier to obtain Wolfe's books in a concentration camp than elsewhere in Germany' given the author's low reputation among the Nazis.

In her *The Making of a Counter-Culture Icon: Henry Miller's Dostoevsky*
Maria Bloshteyn delivers a long-needed investigation of Dostoevsky's
importance to Miller. Bloshteyn grounds her argument very effectively and
challenges many critical preconceptions, particularly those expounded by
Bakhtin and his followers. She contends that Miller viewed the Russian as a
source of 'transliterary' prose that 'would be liberated from the literary
constraints and conventions'. Starting with an examination of Dostoevsky's
critical reputation in the twentieth century, Bloshteyn suggests that the
Russian was subject to extreme interpretative distortion, particularly with
respect to his complex ideology. Bloshteyn next traces Miller's appropriation
of Dostoevsky as well as his indefatigable promotion of the writer to members
of the Villa Seurat circle, including Anaïs Nin and Lawrence Durrell. She
writes that, for Miller, Dostoevsky 'had achieved not only all that was possible
to achieve within the novel form but, indeed, all that was possible within the
confines of literature itself'. Bloshteyn discusses how Miller discovered
Dostoevsky, as well as the Russian's iconic status in Greenwich Village,
where she claims 'an openly and freely expressed love for Dostoevsky was an
identifying badge of true Greenwich Village Bohemians'. At the Villa Seurat,
Dostoevsky also functioned as a metaphor for subversion, although Bloshteyn
suggests that Miller, Durrell and Nin sought to transcend his model. In
looking at Dostoevsky's influence on Miller's texts, Bloshteyn discovers
numerous parodies and 'metatextual implications' stemming from the
American's transformation of the Russian's texts.

Bloshteyn also considers other influences on Miller and his circle, including
surrealism, but she returns to Dostoevsky's stylistic impact on Miller. She
contends that Miller first saw Dostoevsky as lacking form, but she observes
that he changed his mind and later saw in the Russian a 'sense of spontaneity
and immediacy' that affirmed life. Miller also decided that Dostoevsky's
example could lead him to a prose that exuded 'textual chaos' and reflected the
'disintegration of the world'. Nin also bristled at Dostoevsky's formal chaos,
according to Bloshteyn, but she, too, came to admire his style. In both cases,
the Villa Seurat writers felt that a spontaneous style could lead one out of
a thicket of fact and detail and into a realm of 'deeper reality'. Bloshteyn
devotes an entire chapter to the impact of *Notes from the Underground* on the
trio of writers, and suggests that the Villa Seurat interpretation—in which 'the
average man of the crowd...walks the streets...with secret hate and
loathing...hidden deep in his soul'—became 'inscribed into American
literature'. She concludes that, while Miller ignores many crucial spiritual
and ideological components of Dostoevsky's aesthetic, he (and others at Villa
Seurat) successfully employed the 'creative potential inherent in their wrestling
with their version of Dostoevsky's legacy'.

Another treatment of Miller's connection to Dostoevsky appears in Frank
Marra's 'The Dostoevsky/Miller Project: Investigations in Human
Consciousness and Doubt' (*Nexus* 4[2007] 120–49), which posits that 'In
broad terms both men's inquiries into the social world and human
phenomenon are directed at *de-centering the reader's conscious center*.'
Marra explains that, through his use of Dostoevsky, Miller 'illustrates how
the schizophrenic paradigm can be functional and how doubt...can lead to

the expansion of consciousness rather than the pitfalls of relativism or nihilism'. In ' "That crude mixture": How Theater Gives Shape to *Plexus*' (*Nexus* 4[2007] 105–19), Jeff Bursey declares that Miller's novel, which has been previously said to lack form, 'is constructed around the theater'. Bursey avers that '*Plexus*' multiplicity of media resembles, and requires, the elastic structure of theater, where everything and anything may be seen, from songs to skits to melodrama to bawdiness.' Karl Orend reveals, in 'The Observations Gathered Concerning his Morality and Probity Are Favorable: Henry Miller Glimpsed by the French Secret Service' (*Nexus* 4[2007] 181–93) that Miller 'was singled out for investigation because he was suspected of being a Nazi spy'. Showing how Miller was eventually cleared of suspicion, Orend incorporates several hitherto unpublished documents relating to the investigation, including one that states, 'Calling himself a reporter or journalist, Miller was frequently absent from home without explanation.'

Writing for advanced high schoolers and beginning undergraduates, Stephanie Buckwalter offers *A Student's Guide to Jack London*, a brief book that gives a glimpse at London's biography, themes and historical context, as well as readings of some of his more popular novels. Buckwalter does a good job of fleshing out London's biography with historical trends, and a series of marginal definitions of terms such as 'Yellow Peril' and 'Bildungsroman' serves as one of the more helpful features of the book. Buckwalter refrains from original interpretations and supplies students with consensus views of London and his texts. For instance, she explains that London's 'plain talk and direct, sometimes violent depictions of events contrasted sharply with the Victorian romance novel'. Buckwalter accompanies her readings with plot summaries, and she focuses on broad themes such as 'determinism' and 'the dominant primordial beast'. Buckwalter generally avoids critical disputes and posits her interpretations in a straightforward way. She also includes discussion of London's socialism, although she takes a very basic approach. Her choice of texts (beyond obvious choices such as *White Fang*) is somewhat uneven, as is the depth of her discussion (*People of the Abyss*, for instance, receives two pages of commentary while 'To Build a Fire', a story with arguably less need for contextualization, receives six). Those looking for more complex treatments of London should turn elsewhere, but Buckwalter's explications may prove useful for beginning students.

In addition to Buckwalter's book, four articles on London appeared, including Laura Bedwell's 'Jack London's "Samuel" and the Abstract Shrine of Truth' (*StudiesAmNaturalism* 2:ii[2007] 150–65), which, in contrast to most of the author's narratives, reveals 'admiration for the individual who upholds a personal, and deeply gratifying, vision of truth in the face of intense opposition from a community whose values are inimical to human freedom'. Bedwell reads the story as 'illustrat[ing] that when a community seeks refuge from a dangerous truth in lies that punish the innocent, the individual is better off alone with a tolerable truth'. 'Tracking Changes in Jack London's Representation of the Railroad Tramp' (*JamC* 30[2007] 175–86), by Christine Photinos, notes that London's later stories about tramps eliminated overt socialist tendencies and emphasized 'adventure and physical testing'. Photinos suggests that prior critics fail to recognize London's duelling portraits, and uses the writer's own diary to demonstrate that, in later tramp portraits, 'What the tramp diary points to is not so much London's attempt to conceal hardship as his attempt to romanticize it.' Adam Ruh and Gary Scharnhorst, in ' "Fifteen minutes on socialism with Jack London": A Recovered Interview' (*StudiesAmNaturalism* 2:i[2007] 66–77), reprint a November 1905 interview that highlights several aspects of London's role in the socialist movement. In the interview, London praises George Bernard Shaw, discusses socialist politics, advocates violence, derides American apathy, and denies the possibility of writing the Great American Novel: ' "This country is so vast, so cosmopolitan in its make-up," he said, "that it would be impossible for any writer to cover the ground thoroughly so that his work would be denominated the great American novel." ' In 'Talk about Real Men: Jack London's Correspondence with Maurice Magnus' (*JPC* 40[2007] 361–77), Louise E. Wright considers London's thoughts on homosexuality, as expressed in letters to Magnus, who had queried character Wolf Larsen's sexuality. The correspondence reveals that London, who is at first guarded, 'understood homosexuality not as an absolute preference but as a relative one', and Wright paraphrases London's comment that 'sexual desire diminished when a man engaged in strenuous activity, whether physical or mental'.

In *A Vocabulary of Thinking: Gertrude Stein and Contemporary North American Women's Innovative Writing*, Deborah M. Mix traces the impact of the notoriously difficult modernist's prose on several contemporary writers, including Harryette Mullen, Daphne Marlatt, Betsy Warland, Lyn Hejinian and Theresa Hak Kyung Cha. Mix begins by distinguishing Stein's innovation as one of vocabulary rather than definitions, which she claims '[emphasize] constraint, demanding narrowness and specificity' and don't allow 'much space for a reader to act in response'. In contrast, she views vocabulary as a 'tool of empowerment' that alters 'with the specific needs of the individual'. In this regard, Mix considers Stein's work not as a 'template...of a feminist experimental aesthetic' but as 'a way of thinking about contemporary linguistically innovative poetries'. Arguing that Stein saw 'language and literary form as primary sites for feminist and antiracist intervention', Mix claims that Stein's radical texts thwart 'reading strategi[es that] seek mastery' which 'will inevitably be frustrated'. Instead, Stein, 'through her radical unhinging of grammar, her remaking of narrative and generic structures, and her translation and transposition of identities...takes on the social constructions built by language and linguistic habits'. In addition, Stein 'destabilize[s]...the dualities of reader/writer and self/other'.

From this flexible starting point, Mix turns to a discussion of Mullen, who explicitly cites Stein as an influence. However, Mix notes that Mullen performs 'transracial signifying' on Stein's *Tender Buttons* (among other texts) and resists her inspiration's racial and class assumptions. Mix reviews Mullen's *Trimmings* and *S*PeRM**K*T* and contends that while they are 'closely linked to Stein's path-breaking experiments', they also 'offer critiques of a literary and cultural history' that attempts to obscure race and push readers beyond a 'consumer-driven culture'. In her next chapter, Mix looks at the collaborative work of Marlatt and Warland, maintaining that their *Double Negative* functions similarly to Stein's *Lifted Belly* in that it 'remake[s] the

[love] lyric such that it no longer serves the conservative, even reactionary politics and aesthetics of its old masters'. Rather, like Stein's (and Toklas's?) polyphonia in *Lifted Belly*, the authors employ 'double voicedness [to] immediately refus[e] the traditional subject/object dichotomy in favor of a more balanced relationship between two lovers who are, at the same time, two beloveds'. In so doing, Mix asserts that the poets 'delineat[e] a literal site... onto which the lesbian, the woman, the other can inscribe a self but within which she is not herself sited or sighted'. Turning to a discussion of autobiography, Mix next compares Stein to Lyn Hejinian, whom she claims similarly 'use the genre of autobiography not so much to reveal themselves as to meditate on the construction of identity'. Mix views Stein's major contribution as 'the potential to open up what has been an essentially closed genre by undermining the autobiographical pact and inviting the reader to question the authority of the person who is positioned as expert'. For Hejinian, the consciousness of 'inaccurate memories' highlights the mediated nature of autobiography and serves to 'authorize a new relationship not only between past and present but also between reader and author'. In her chapter on Theresa Hak Kyung Cha, Mix looks to Stein's *The Making of Americans* to show how both writers 'seek to disrupt the possibility of "unified" narratives and identities'. Cha's *DICTEE*, which Mix calls 'insistently unstable', tries 'to find a balance between... opposing forces, a balance that can best reflect the haunting experiences and the troubling dislocations of homes, languages, and identities that have been lost and cannot be reclaimed'. Mix's epilogue discusses the ways in which Stein and the other writers critically engage patriarchal traditions and 'prepar[e] the way for material intervention'.

Numerous articles on Stein appeared, such as Amy Feinstein's 'Gertrude Stein, Alice Toklas, and Albert Barnes: Looking Like a Jew in *The Autobiography of Alice B. Toklas*' (*Shofar* 25:iii[2007] 47–60), which claims that 'The shifts in Stein's writings about Jewish nature... illuminate the importance of her concrete ties to early social sciences of race and, later, alert us to the lingering racialism underlying an otherwise anti-essentialist view of human nature.' Feinstein notes the absence of overt references to Jews in *The Autobiography* and contends that the book's 'anecdote about Barnes exemplifies Stein's method of unmasking Jewish stereotype *as stereotype* instead of as racial type'. In 'Defamiliarizing the "Family": Gertrude Stein's *The Making of Americans* (1925)' (*ELN* 45[2007] 137–47), Catriona Menzies-Pike examines the Stein archive and hypothesizes that biographical and historical 'reference is refused at the level of both narrative and composition'. Menzies-Pike suggests that 'The utter incommensurability of the objective knowledge consolidated in *The Making of Americans* to that available in an archive strongly suggests that archival work must be informed by a consideration of a given text's attitude to the archive. To read Stein with respect, to take the text so scrupulously presented seriously, the opposition of the text to the use of archival and biographical material must be acknowl-edged.' 'Hermeneutic Resistance: Four Test Cases for the Notion of Literary Uninterpretability' (*JLS* 36[2007] 121–34), by Leonard Orr, looks at Stein—as well as James Joyce, Samuel Beckett and the Dadaists—and the notion of unreadability, a category that he maintains has shifted over the centuries.

In the Stein section, Orr suggests that the difficulty in interpretation arises because 'all outside references and allusions are detached from the texts, grammar is reformulated and classes of words, such as nouns and verbs, are exchanged in function'. Rebecca Scherr, in 'Tactile Erotics: Gertrude Stein and the Aesthetics of Touch' (*LIT* 18[2007] 193–212), argues that 'Stein's belief in the materiality of language, that is, in the "thingness" of language, inspired her to use words to mime what bodies and objects feel like, to get at the essence of what they do.' Scherr looks at *Tender Buttons* and *Lifting Belly* to conclude that 'textual tactility is never actual touch but rather an approximation of it as communicated in words and sounds, lending Stein's tactile aesthetic a melancholic quality'.

Mark Whalan pairs Sherwood Anderson and Jean Toomer in his *Race, Manhood, and Modernism in America: The Short Story Cycles of Sherwood Anderson and Jean Toomer*, a book that purports to study how 'both men presented a complex and in many ways complementary response to the temporal shocks, uncertainties, and possibilities of the period surrounding World War I'. Whalan avows that both writers familiarized themselves with numerous emerging movements, such as ethnography, machine technology and primitivism, in renegotiating their relationship with concepts such as race, gender and class. Taking a self-proclaimed interdisciplinary approach, Whalan stresses the connection between ideological proclivities and formal choices, remarking that 'rapidly developing fields of knowledge and aesthetics that related to gender and race were closely involved with the formal and generic choices of *Winesburg, Ohio* and *Cane*. Whalan views his project, moreover, as a partial corrective to the, in his eyes, misguided view that modernism and the Harlem Renaissance were utterly discrete literary movements. Whalan devotes two chapters to Anderson, three to Toomer, and one to both men's relationship with Waldo Frank.

Whalan notes Anderson's career-long preoccupation with gender relations, but he points out that *Winesburg, Ohio* transforms Anderson's awareness of the 'new forms that gay culture was taking in America's urban centers in the early twentieth century'. Arguing with those who view Anderson's appropriation of gay culture as a 'conflation of femininity with homosexuality', Whalan contends that the same-sex relationship in fact 'enables [the male–female] binary through the way it influences a wide range of social conduct'. For Anderson, who experienced homosexual solicitation in Chicago, 'keeping the figure of the "homo-sexual" visible in his work' demonstrated an attempt to 'prove the solidity of his own heterosexuality'. Whalan proceeds to examine some stories from Anderson's opus and notes that 'the pattern of a futile, masculinized search for order, significance, and the legible female body is staged repeatedly throughout *Winesburg, Ohio*' and that its 'only alternative is the marginalization of Wing Biddlebaum or the "half-insanity" brought about by being rejected by Belle Carpenter'. Whalan next moves to Anderson's treatment of race, which he also links to Anderson's gender politics, and the 'anxiety, envy, and celebration' that such attention entailed. Interestingly, Whalan views Anderson's preoccupation with African American culture as holding its 'significan[ce] ... as a vision of community founded on a laboring practice that, through integrating labor and cultural production, could guarantee the hegemony of patriarchal masculinity'. Whalan suggests that Anderson felt that American capitalism had an emasculating effect on alienated, poor white males and that a 'return to craft' could counteract the trend. Anderson further felt, according to Whalan, that ' "blackness" [was] performative both in its citationality and his conception of it as an act of display'. In this chapter, Whalan focuses mainly on *Dark Laughter*, although he does cite other works as well. In the chapter on Anderson, Toomer and Frank, Whalen identifies how Toomer would critique the Young Americans' conception of 'buried cultures'. Frank's *Our America* piqued the interest of both Anderson and Toomer, but while Anderson allied himself with Frank and felt that the African American South offered a 'storehouse of culture for the revitalization of the nation', Toomer ultimately rejected Frank, viewing his ideas as endorsing a problematic 'racial essence' that erased individual differences and communal interaction.

In turning to Toomer, Whalan considers the complicated political and aesthetic conflict inherent in *Cane*'s merger of Southern African American culture and high modernist poetics, a clash that 'surprised and disconcerted' Toomer. Whalan argues that *Cane* 'offers an interrogation of "authentic" black subjectivity rather than a celebration of it', and he observes that the 'veil' of race 'is language itself, the point at which transformation, translation, understanding, and segregation occur'. In learning more about Southern life, Toomer came to disregard Frank because of his 'tendency to discount individual variations within a culture', differences that often manifested themselves within language. Ultimately, Whalan contends, Toomer decided that Frank's notion of essentialized buried cultures 'would have to be killed off' before an intelligent discussion of race might occur. In the book's final two chapters, Whalan reads *Cane* through the perspectives of the body and form respectively. Whalan claims that Toomer identified racial identity as more a matter of 'design than determination' and indicates that, for Toomer, 're-creating the body as a method of re-creating identity' offered a lasting appeal. With respect to form, Whalan asserts that Toomer is conscious that 'discontinuity—between either identity groups or text units—is something that invites the application of cohering principles and collective address'. Thus, while Toomer seeks multiple audiences, he also 'produces tropes that unsettle [hegemonic] foundations'. Whalan's text offers a provocative new look at both writers, and it makes a convincing case for its thesis.

Joseph B. Entin offers another interdisciplinary study in his *Sensational Modernism: Experimental Fiction and Photography in Thirties America*. In this book Entin suggests that a group of modernists resisted the trend of depicting impoverished Americans in pitying, condescending, or sentimental ways and instead 'used striking images of pain, prejudice, crime, and violence to create avant-garde aesthetics of astonishment' designed to 'arouse in their audiences a new, more urgent understanding of poverty'. Entin notes that the rise of modernism paralleled the rise of sensational pop culture such as 'amusement parks, freak shows, tabloid newspapers, pulp magazines, and dime museums'. Using an array of primary texts, Entin reveals how the sensational modernists 'constitute a much more loosely formed tradition of artistic practice' than the avant-garde modernists. Entin focuses on documentary rather than avant-garde photography because, as he explains, the former allows the middle class to 'inspect' the poverty-stricken. Entin argues that 'sensational modernists...seize on what is usually submerged, using arresting and frequently disorienting images of bodily harm, sexual aggression, or racial prejudice'. Using an array of texts, from Fitzgerald's *The Great Gatsby* and Nathanael West's *Miss Lonelyhearts* to Pietro di Donato's *Christ in Concrete* and Richard Wright's *Native Son*, Entin explores numerous topics, such as Dalton Trumbo's 'repudiat[ion of] the logic of masculine, aesthetic heroism to which Hemingway's writing aspires' and Tillie Olsen's use of collage to subvert supposed journalistic objectivity. Other intriguing interpretations involve Faulkner's *As I Lay Dying*—which Entin views as 'privileging a chorus of working-class voices [that lent] working-class experience a layered depth and internal complexity'—di Donato's 'labor modernism'—which 'strips the description of work and the construction site of conjunctions and punctuations to craft crowded, confusing sentences that overwhelm standard syntax'—and Wright's *Lawd Today*—which 'allows readers surprisingly intimate access to Jake's inner thoughts'. In all, Entin covers an impressive number of texts and offers a viable explanation of one aesthetic alternative to avant-garde modernism.

No books on F. Scott Fitzgerald were received, but several articles appeared, including J.D. Thomas's 'Regarding Joyce's Manuscripts: A Letter from Sylvia Beach to F. Scott Fitzgerald' (*ANQ* 20:i[2007] 50–2). Thomas includes the entire, previously unpublished letter, and he contextualizes how Beach came to enlist Fitzgerald's help in locating a buyer for her Joyce collection. Comparing Nella Larsen and Fitzgerald in 'Babbled Slander where the Paler Shades Dwell: Reading Race in *The Great Gatsby* and *Passing*' (*LIT* 18[2007] 173–91), Charles Lewis discovers 'remarkably extensive and largely unrecognized' parallels between the two books. Lewis close reads the two novels and determines that, while Larsen does not technically plagiarize Fitzgerald, the resemblances in *Passing* 'underscore how passing functions both as a literal theme in the novels and as a figurative trope for reading them not only independently but also in relation to one another'. Chris McDonough's '"The starry heaven of popular girls": Fitzgerald's "Bernice Bobs her Hair" and Catullus's "Coma Berenices"' (*Expl* 65:iv[2007] 226–9) suggests that the name of Fitzgerald's heroine may allude to Catullus's character, particularly since the latter also regrets cutting her hair. Benjamin Schreier, in 'Desire's Second Act: "Race" and *The Great Gatsby*'s Cynical Americanism' (*TCL* 53[2007] 153–81), contends that previous readings of Fitzgerald's masterwork fail to notice that the novel rejects the 'recognizant expectation [of]...historicism' and heralds 'a more open and critical form of reading'. Schreier assesses recent 'visible' criticism on the novel and then offers an alternative reading and concludes that 'This novel is not about American identity; instead, it offers disappointed testimony to the impossibility that America can mean anything one wants it to mean.' In 'Fitzgerald's *The Great Gatsby* and "Babylon Revisited"' (*Expl* 65:iii[2007] 164–7), Brian Sutton points out that Fitzgerald returns to the themes of his 1925 novel in one of his best stories, a phenomenon that goes against the author's pattern of using his story material later in his novels.

Charlotte Perkins Gilman's disdain for sensationalist journalism prompts Sari Edelstein to show how the writer sought to expose patriarchal ideology and to create a female reading community that stood in staunch opposition to what she considered to be the menacing effects of the yellow press, in 'Charlotte Perkins Gilman and the Yellow Newspaper' (*Legacy* 24[2007] 72–92). Edelstein, while noting that the term 'yellow journalism' had not gained currency by the time that Gilman wrote 'The Yellow Wall-Paper', reads the story allegorically and discovers that it 'foregrounds competition among professional, political, and popular discourses, and . . . [shows how] the rise of yellow journalism exacerbated this discursive struggle through its influence on the literary marketplace'.

Christopher Taylor's ' "Inescapably propaganda": Re-Classifying Upton Sinclair Outside the Naturalist Tradition' (*StudiesAmNaturalism* 2:ii[2007] 166–78) reviews previous dismissals of Sinclair's aesthetic as too hinged to naturalist suppositions, and he argues that Sinclair, while admiring the naturalists, 'deliberately' wrote in the propagandist *roman à thèse* tradition. Taylor shows that because Sinclair abandons many of naturalism's central tenets—such as determinism—he may be more fairly evaluated via a different set of criteria, including 'the power to arouse readers' emotions and wills, the accuracy and fairness of the situations depicted, and the social value of the actions called for'.

Bobbi Olson, in 'The Ambiguities of Gender in Eudora Welty's "Petrified Man" ' (*EurekaStudies* 7:ii[2007] 143–51), argues that Welty's story 'blurs the distinction between genders' and problematizes the issue of Welty's feminism. Olson determines that 'Femininity is not restricted to adhering to concretely defined terms of "appropriate" gender behavior because the feminine gender role can be expressed across a much broader spectrum of human behavior.' In '(Silenced) Transgression in Eudora Welty's *The Optimist's Daughter*' (*Critique* 48[2007] 184–96), Daniel S. Traber contends that, *contra* previous readings, Fay plays a 'subversive role' in the novel. Traber claims that, while Fay's personality still may grate, it plays a key role in supporting Laurel's 'system of ethical and class distinctions'.

Ashley Craig Lancaster weighs in on Erskine Caldwell's appropriation of contemporary racial theories in his 'Weeding Out the Recessive Gene: Representations of the Evolving Eugenics Movement in Erskine Caldwell's *God's Little Acre*' (*SLJ* 39[2007] 78–99). Lancaster asserts that Caldwell enlarges the rubric of 'poor white' beyond economics, and looks at how Caldwell explored the concept of 'genetic inferiority' and performed a 'literary sterilization' that echoed eugenicists' arguments about the literal sterilization of supposedly inferior races.

In 'John Dos Passos in Mexico' (*Mo/Mo* 14[2007] 329–45), Rubén Gallo corrects previous dismissals of Dos Passos's travels to Mexico as insignificant and unearths the writer's link to the Estridentistas, an avant-garde movement for which he translated several works. In particular, Dos Passos admired the work of Manuel Maples Arce, with whom he had a 'fruitful intellectual exchange'.

3. Fiction since 1945

In their volume entitled *On Second Thought: Updating the Eighteenth-Century Text*, Debra Taylor Bourdeau and Elizabeth Kraft edit a collection of essays focused on uncovering literary connections between twentieth-century texts and the eighteenth-century texts which they 'expand, elaborate, and revise' (p. 9). For example in her chapter, Elizabeth Kraft examines Upton Sinclair's 1950 novel *Another Pamela* in relation to its 'point of origin', Samuel Richardson's *Pamela*. In the following chapter, Brett C. McInelly looks at Derek Walcott's *Pantomime* as a 'remake' of Defoe's *Robinson Crusoe*. Michael Hardin's chapter compares Carlos Fuentes's *Christopher Unborn* with Sterne's *Tristram Shandy*. Robert Scott finds a number of eighteenth-century connections in John Barth's *The Sot-Weed Factor*, and Tamara Wagner, in her chapter, explores a number of contemporary 'sequels' to the sentimental plots of Jane Austen's work.

Kyriaki Hadjiafaxendi and Polina Mackay's collection, *Authorship in Context: From the Theoretical to the Material*, examines the changing relationship between criticism and the author by looking, chronologically, at changing notions of authorship. Part I contains essays regarding the nineteenth-century literary marketplace, part II examines twentieth-century 'mythologies of authorship', and part III focuses on the role of criticism as it regards the author in postmodern culture. Highly theoretical, the essays collected in this volume are focused more on philosophical understandings of authorship in relation to material forces of production than they are on literary aspects of the texts they address. Nevertheless, Kathy Acker, Donald Barthelme and William S. Burroughs are among the authors mentioned in the book.

Marc Bosco and Kimberly Rae Connor's *Academic Novels as Satire: Critical Studies of an Emerging Genre* examines novels about academic life; they claim that this emerging genre is represented by works that 'once were mildly ironic novels about academe', but have 'become more satiric barbs' (pp. 2–3). Phillip Roth, Joyce Carol Oates, James Hynes, Richard Russo, John L'Heureux and Jane Smiley are mentioned in the introduction. Numerous additional authors are mentioned in the essays comprising the collection: Don DeLillo, William Gass, David Lodge and A.S. Byatt. While the essays cover a wide array of topics, they work together in an attempt to identify a kind of 'academic fiction' focused on fictional narratives of academe and the lives of academics professionals.

John Cant's *Cormac McCarthy and the Myth of American Exceptionalism* is an important and substantial contribution to the scholarship on McCarthy's literary career. Cant organizes his study into three sections; the first deals with biographical issues while the second and third deal with his Tennessee texts (*Wake for Susan*, *A Drowning Incident*, *The Orchard Keeper*, *Outer Dark*, *Child of God*, *Suttee*, *The Stonemason* and *The Gardener's Son*) and the Southwestern texts (*All the Pretty Horses*, *The Crossing*, *Cities of the Plain* and *No Country for Old Men*) respectively. Additionally, the appendices contain examinations of *The Sunset Limited* and *The Road*. Clearly Cant's aims in this book are ambitious; his intent is to 'identify themes that unify McCarthy's text' and 'trace lines of development' while dealing with each text on an individual basis (p. 3). In completing this project, Cant argues that McCarthy 'deliberately sets out to give his texts mythic form' to 'point out the destructive consequences of structuring the consciousness of individuals by means of powerful mythologies which they are not in a position to live out' (p. 9). Considered as a whole, according to Cant, McCarthy's work is a 'critique of the mythology that informs American culture' (p. 17).

In his article 'Cormac McCarthy's "World in its Making"': Romantic Naturalism in *The Crossing*' (*StudiesAmNaturalism* 2:i[2007] 46–65), Steven Frye begins by claiming that Cormac McCarthy's *The Crossing* 'explores the most essential of questions: the role of suffering in the material world and the fundamental nature of the divine' (p. 46). In arguing this thesis, Frye, using McCarthy's narrative, makes connections between naturalism and the 'romantic and idealist impulse' (p. 62).

David Brauner's *Phillip Roth* focuses solely on Roth's works, which according to the author are now receiving 'more critical attention within the academy than at any previous time in his career' (p. 3). In fact, in many ways, Brauner's goal may be to ensure that Roth's 'literary stock' (p. 4) continues to rise. Brauner posits that his goal in the book is not to 'defend the embattled author' but to identify and explore 'ambiguities, ambivalences, and paradoxes' in the works from the latter half of Roth's career. It is the last half of Roth's career that Brauner examines, and he does so by looking at three major questions. The first question aims to identify Roth's fiction as 'autobiographical fiction' or 'fictional autobiography'. The second asks if Roth is a Jewish American or an American Jew; the third asks if Roth is a conservative radical or a radical conservative. As is not hard to discern from the identified research questions, Brauner is intent to examine paradoxes and ambiguities as essential elements in Roth's fiction.

Brian Stableford's *Space, Time, and Infinity: Essays on Fantastic Literature*, is a patchwork of selections from his lectures and talks at public libraries and science fiction conventions. Each selection is formalized into essay form and encounters some aspect of contemporary science fiction and fantastical fiction. Perhaps the most interesting piece examines Adolf Hitler's effect on the economic history of science fiction magazines. Among the authors mentioned are Ursula K. LeGuin, Arthur C. Clarke, William Golding, H.G. Wells, Edgar Rice Burroughs, Ray Bradbury, L. Sprague de Camp and Jules Verne.

Sabine Heuser, in her essay '(En)gendering Artificial Intelligence in Cyberspace' (*YES* 37:ii[2007] 129–45), begins with the premise that one prevailing characteristic of the cyberpunk sub-genre is the presence of 'some version of virtual reality' and 'artificial intelligences' (p. 129). Her essay then explores the manner in which these artificial intelligences 'display gendered features or gender specific behaviour' (p. 129). Authors discussed are Pat Cadigan and William Gibson.

A number of essay-length works addressed DeLillo's fiction this year. Anne Longmuir's 'Genre and Gender in Don DeLillo's *Players* and *Running Dog*' (*JNT* 37[2007] 128–45) argues that DeLillo's two novels, *Players* and *Running Dog*, are not only companion pieces, but part of a 'continuous project' (p. 128). Further, her claim is that these novels demonstrate that gender 'plays a more central role' in DeLillo's work than has been previously conceived. For Longmuir, both the thriller and the Western genre operate under 'masculine ideology' and are 'fundamentally flawed' (p. 144). Her final conclusion is that 'it is only feminine subjects, who acknowledge the impossibility of achieving wholeness, who achieve any kind of agency' (p. 144). Chi-ming Chang, in 'Death as the Other in Don DeLillo's *White Noise*: From the Sensible Immediate to the Technologically Mediated' (*TkR* 37:iii[2007] 145–75), claims that DeLillo's treatment of Death as an 'ethical Other' (p. 146) in *White Noise* makes death a metaphor for 'ethical relationship(s) in the postmodern age' (p. 169). David Noon's 'The Triumph of Death: National Security and Imperial Erasures in Don DeLillo's *Underworld*' (*CRevAS* 37[2007] 83–110) is primarily a criticism of DeLillo's Underworld for what DeLillo does not say regarding the aftermath of the Cold War. According to Noon, DeLillo's novel is about the 'remnants of the cold war' and an obsession with 'waste and nuclear warfare'. Noon argues that DeLillo is 'unable to fully imagine the domestic consequences of the cold war' (p. 86) for the Native American communities 'who inhabit some of the most heavily and lastingly polluted regions of the nation' (p. 106). John Coyle's 'Don DeLillo, Aesthetic Transcendence and the Kitsch of Death' (*European Journal of American Culture* 26[2007] 27–39) examines aesthetic transcendence in DeLillo's fiction. According to Coyle, DeLillo has turned from narrative, in which simulacra are a 'scatterbrained distraction', to visual representation as a 'redemptive, transcendent aesthetic' (p. 27). Part of DeLillo's intention in doing this, Coyle argues, is to 'reaffirm certain properties more traditional to the novelist' (p. 29).

Timothy Jacobs's 'The Brothers Incandenza: Translating Ideology in Fyodor Dostoevsky's *The Brothers Karamazov* and David Foster Wallace's *Infinite Jest*' (*TSLL* 49:iii [2007] 265–92) posits a place for David Foster Wallace in the Dostoevskyan tradition. Although Jacobs begins by disagreeing with Marshall Boswell's contention that allusions to *Hamlet* in David Foster Wallace's *Infinite Jest* are more important than allusions to *The Brothers Karamazov*, Jacobs's primary contention is that *Infinite Jest* is a 'rewriting or a figurative translation' of Dostoevsky's novel (p. 265). Jacobs's primary thesis is that Wallace 'aligns himself with the Dostoevskyan tradition' (p. 266).

Beginning with an evocation of Freud, M. Cleveland's 'Truth Versus Knowledge: Laplanchean Afterwardsness and the Traumatic Memory of Chappaquiddick in Joyce Carol Oates' Black Water' (in Batra, Nadita, and Vartan P. Messier *Narrating the Past: (Re)Constructing Memory, (Re)Negotiating History*, pp. 38–48) examines the 'fictionalized account of Ted Kennedy's infamous incident at Chappaquiddick' found in Joyce Carol Oates's *Black Water*. In doing so, he hopes to examine the 'structural complexity of memory and the ambivalent character of truth' (p. 38). His analysis makes connection between Oates's narrative and Žižek's 'truth effect' (p. 47).

Although requested, a number of works were not received for review: Leland's *Why Kerouac Matters: Lessons of* On The Road *(They're Not What You Think)*, Dimock and Buell's *Shades of the Planet: American Literature as World Literature*, Gretlund and Westarp's *Flannery O'Connor's Radical Reality*, Kleppe and Miltner's *New Paths to Raymond Carver: Critical Essays on his Life, Fiction, and Poetry,* Hardy's *The Body in Flannery O'Connor's Fiction,* Cote, Day, and Peuter's *Utopian Pedagogy: Radical Experiments against Neoliberal Globalization,* Henninger's *Ordering the Façade: Photography and Contemporary Southern Women's Writing,* McMullen's *Inside the Church of Flannery O'Connor: Sacrament, Sacramental, and the Sacred in her Fiction,* and MacFarlane's *The Hippie Narrative: A Literary Perspective on the Counterculture.*

4. Drama

In *Student Companion to Eugene O'Neill,* Steven F. Bloom offers an overview of O'Neill's life, place in theatre history, and eight plays. Designed for undergraduates, the book opens by rehearsing key events in O'Neill's biography. While factually accurate, this chapter stays fairly close to the surface and generally avoids both specific anecdotes and excerpts from O'Neill's own accounts. Bloom next turns to a discussion of O'Neill's 'literary heritage', and he notes that the playwright had influences ranging from facile melodrama to Shakespeare and Strindberg. The result was plays that 'turned to some of the devices of melodrama to engage [the] audience in stories that were to reveal depth of character and provoke thought about timely social issues, as well as timeless universal questions about the human condition'. Bloom also considers how O'Neill's plays fit into the international tradition yet still reveal significant American tendencies. This chapter also links O'Neill with Nietzsche, Darwin, Marx and Freud. Bloom further shows O'Neill's influences on dramatists such as Tennessee Williams, Arthur Miller, Edward Albee and August Wilson.

Bloom's selection of plays is unsurprising, save for *Ah, Wilderness!,* which rarely makes its way onto undergraduate syllabi, and he includes early plays such as *Anna Christie, The Emperor Jones* and *The Hairy Ape* and later classics such as *The Iceman Cometh* and *Long Day's Journey into Night.* Each play receives its own chapter, and Bloom follows a pattern in which he examines 'setting and plot development', 'character development', 'thematic issues' and 'stylistic and literary devices'. The first two rubrics stay relatively on the surface, although the second two categories make helpful connections for undergraduates, such as the comment that *Long Day's Journey into Night* 'captures the essence of existential philosophy' or that the music in *Ah, Wilderness!* (a comedy) 'punctuate[s] the play with either sadness, tension, or both'. Each of these chapters also includes a brief 'alternative perspective' that reads the play through a critical lens. Examples include reader-response theory (*Anna Christie*), Freudian analysis (*Desire under the Elms*), and feminist criticism (*A Moon for the Misbegotten*). The readings hold few surprises, but they do adequately orient undergraduates and suggest ways 'into' the dramas. For instance, in his Marxist reading of *The Iceman Cometh,* Bloom argues that the characters have 'failed within the norms of capitalism and have now become unproductive, forgotten outsiders'. In his mythic reading of *The Hairy Ape* and *The Emperor Jones,* Bloom avers that 'O'Neill taps into the Jungian unconscious by using a creature that symbolizes primitive urges and impulses in human beings'. While hardly innovative, the book will certainly be of assistance for those unfamiliar with O'Neill and his critics.

John Patrick Diggins advances a more sophisticated analysis of O'Neill in his *Eugene O'Neill's America: Desire under Democracy*, which looks past the playwright's autobiographical focus and teases out the political aspects of his drama. Diggins examines numerous aspects of O'Neill's thought and influences, including his Irish heritage, and argues that 'it is difficult to separate the personal from the social' within the playwright's work—work that tackles a range of pressing issues, from race and gender matters to socialism and addiction. Painstaking in his research, Diggins engages not only O'Neill's plays but also the playwright's influences and reception, such as when he examines Mary McCarthy's scathing review of *The Iceman Cometh* or Oswald Spengler's impact on O'Neill's oeuvre. Diggins opines that O'Neill's politics, while at times crudely displayed early on, were 'skeptical of the radical dreams that drove the American Left of his era' and tempered with the realities of 'survivors'. Beyond providing the general context and philosophical implications, Diggins also intersperses insightful discussions of the plays. For instance, he examines *The Emperor Jones* and concludes that it 'may be less a study in racial atavism or in religious salvation than in social emulation, with Jones aping the worst aspects of the leisure class by assuming that money alone symbolizes that which is the highest and the best'. In another reading, Diggins views *The Iceman Cometh* as symbolizing a Hegelian 'end of history' wherein 'the characters prefer to sleep and pass out rather than to listen and learn'. Diggins perspective is fresh, and it invigorates our understanding of the plays.

In *Arthur Miller's Global Theater*, Enoch Brater collects a series of essays that tackle Miller's international reception as well as how various cultures have located significance within the plays. In addition to Brater's introductory essay, the volume contains twelve essays, ranging from Linda Ben-Zvi's 'Arthur Miller's Israel and Israel's Arthur Miller' and Robert Gordon's 'Guilty Secrets and Cultural Blind Spots: Miller's Plays in South Africa' to Matthew Martin's 'Arthur Miller's Dialogue with Ireland' and Laura Cerrato's 'Arthur Miller in Buenos Aires'. Brater's introduction poses a series of questions that the various authors begin to answer, among them 'What happens to the friction in a Miller work as it crosses linguistic and cultural borders?' and 'What does it mean for a playwright from imperial America to find a voice elsewhere?'. An example of the responses to such queries is Belinda Kong's 'Traveling Man, Traveling Culture: *Death of a Salesman* and Post-Mao Chinese Theater', which looks at Miller's 1983 production of his famous play. Kong finds that, despite overt imperialist impulses on Miller's part, the play's staging revealed 'some disturbing Orientalist accents in this comfortable dichotomy of knowledge between West (has) and East (has not)'. Another exemplar of the book's approach is Michael Raab's 'Not All One Song: Arthur Miller in the German Theater', which attempts to understand Miller's relatively low standing in the 'director-dominated' country. Raab discusses German theatre's emphasis on innovation and points out, for instance, that Miller's 'use of the epic narrator...looks hopelessly outdated and clumsy' and that 'his wish to not be too sophisticated...is held against [him]'. Collectively, the volume offers a fascinating look at the problems of cross-cultural adaptation and sheds light on many of Miller's overt and covert ideological facets.

Editor Robert Bray's *Tennessee Williams and his Contemporaries* proffers transcripts of eight panel discussions from the Tennessee Williams Scholars conference. Rather than providing essays on a given theme, the book highlights scholarly give and take on several broad topics, including 'The Early Plays', 'Teaching Tennessee', 'Williams and the Grotesque', and 'Lillian Hellman and Tennessee Williams', among others. While the discussions vary in quality, many are surprisingly coherent, and they offer some insightful information, such as Brian Parker's comments on the 'huge, *huge* pile of manuscripts' for *The Glass Menagerie* and Barbara Ewell's observation that Williams and Carson McCullers both consistently attempted to 'denaturaliz[e] heterosexuality'. Of particular interest is the chapter on 'The Unpublished Tennessee Williams', which asks a variety of Williams scholars for their thoughts on their recent examinations of the various manuscript archives. Allean Hale, for example, notes that Williams 'never let an idea die' and then traces the use of dance in the earliest extant work, *Beauty Is the Word*, through familiar plays such as *A Streetcar Named Desire*, to late plays and fragments such as *Cavalier for Milady*. While the volume does contain many such insights, the nature of the give and take unfortunately does not always allow for the various contributors to pursue their interesting ideas.

Annette Saddik's *Contemporary American Drama* explores the theatre scene from the Second World War to the present, although its main focus is post-1960 drama. Eight chapters deal with subjects such as 'African American Theatre: Voices from the Margins', 'The Politics of Identity and Exclusion' and 'The "NEA Four" and Performance Art: Making Visible the Invisible'. Saddik discusses the turn from realism and method acting to anti-realism, and she examines numerous trends and playwrights. For instance, she explains the innovations of Williams and Miller, particularly in regard to how they critiqued the American Dream and 'explore[d] issues of identity in terms of role playing and authenticity in American culture'. Of particular interest is Saddik's chapter on African American theatre, which comments on Amira Baraka, Ed Bullins, Adrienne Kennedy and Suzan Lori-Parks, among others. Saddik offers readings of a number of plays, including *Dutchman*, which she regards as 'highly symbolic [with] characters [that] are meant to be taken as representative of particular attitudes, social positions, or points of view, rather than as complex human beings'. The chapter on avant-garde theatre is also strong, with Saddik investigating the movement away from an emphasis on language to 'the visual and physical aspects of a play's production'. Saddik looks here at Jack Gelber's *The Connection* and writes that its 'structure...is essentially that of a play-within-a-play, blurring the line between actor and character, and aggressively breaking the fourth wall separating audience and performer'. Other chapters deal with postmodernism, identity, fragmentation and performance art.

Ilka Saal investigates the ways in which American political drama resisted the modernist tendencies of the international leftist tradition in her *New Deal*

Theater: The Vernacular Tradition in American Political Theater. Saal suggests that unlike, for example, Brecht, American directors and playwrights frequently retained the 'sentimental strategy of building up the human appeal of a story' and tapping into the audience's feelings of empathy. In her examples, Saal looks at works by a variety of both luminaries and lesser-known playwrights, such as Clifford Odets, Luis Valdez and Marc Blitzstein. Movements, such as agitprop and El Teatro Campesino are also discussed. Saal notes that the realism of the left dominated the stage in the mid- and late 1930s. She also, however, examines the amateur troupes that took 'their performances directly to the mines and factories, to union meetings and picket lines'. Saal discovers that, by the 1960s, the disjuncture between the avant-garde and the proletarian theatres had dissolved and that postmodern theatre draws on both traditions.

In *Angels in the American Theater: Patrons, Patronage, and Philanthropy*, Robert A. Schanke collects a series of essays on the private gifts that have shaped the American stage. The volume consists of Schanke's introduction and sixteen essays that focus on discussions of specific individuals—such as Theresa M. Collins's 'Modern Cosmopolitan: Otto Kahn and the American Stage' and Alexis Greene's 'Queen of Off Broadway: Lucille Lortel'. The essays chart the varied and evolving expectations that attend the large donations, and they explore the relationships between donors and artists. For example, in 'Raising the Curtain: Rockefeller Support for the American Theater', Stephen D. Berwind shows how the Rockefeller Foundation helped to expand university theatre programmes in the 1930s and asserts that the organization's strength lies in its 'willingness to take chances on emerging artists while loyally supporting established artists'. Early in the twentieth century individuals dominated theatre patronage, but later in the century foundations and corporations (such as Disney and Clear Channel) provided most of the theatre funding. The essays are consistent in their strength, and they offer numerous details that reveal the intersections between money and art.

Susan Harris Smith performs a much-needed survey in her *Plays in American Periodicals, 1890–1918*, a book that considers some seventy playwrights whose work appeared in American magazines and newspapers. Smith observes that while plays rarely appear in periodicals today, at the turn of the century the phenomenon 'played a significant role in the social constitution of the middle class as citizens and consumers'. Adopting a cultural studies approach and referring to such luminaries as Raymond Williams and Benedict Anderson, Smith notes that the ideological propensities of the periodicals drove the choice of plays that appeared. Smith is particularly adept at contextualizing her study and ranges through a panoply of historical and cultural happenings. While some international playwrights, such as George Bernard Shaw and John Galsworthy, many were of American heritage, such as Edith Wharton, Mary Wilkins Freeman, Hamlin Garland and William Dean Howells. Smith holds no illusions about the general quality of the plays, and she, perhaps predictably, holds that the strongest works came from the most recognizable figures. Other of her findings include the 'startling absence of African Americans as playwrights or characters' and the possibility that 'the readers of periodicals approached dramatic texts not as play scripts to be performed but more as "stories" in dramatic form amplified by illustrations and narrative stage directions'. Smith also argues that these plays form 'a separate canon'.

Smith examines the plays from a variety of angles and offers chapters such as 'Cultures of Social Distance and Difference', 'Women as American Citizens', 'Cultural Displacement' and 'Dis/Contented Citizens'. In addition to affording (brief) space to selected plays, Smith allows readers to see broad outlines, such as *Century*'s tendency to publish 'safe, "high culture" artifacts' in contrast to *Forum*'s reformist agenda. When she turns to her examples, such as the anonymously published *A Woman's Luncheon*, Smith goes beyond plot summary and makes critical observations, such as the work being 'similar in style and spirit to those of Howells, James, and Wharton'. Smith searches for patterns, such as the preponderance of plays that 'draw on myth, history, and the Bible ... to indulge in titillating subject matter under the rubric of "high art" and "high purpose"'. Smith concludes that the dramatic contributions to American periodicals 'participated instrumentally in furthering an American imperial agenda'. While one might wish for more extended discussion of Smith's examples, the book is a welcome addition to the critical literature.

The Enchanted Years of the Stage: Kansas City at the Crossroads of American Theater, 1870–1930, by Felicia Hardison Londré and David Austin Latchaw, establishes Kansas City as a microcosm of American theatre and the phenomenon of the roadshow. The study follows the impact of touring shows in Kansas City from the early influence of the Coates family (and their opera house) to the waning of vaudeville. The authors point out that the city 'craved cultural validation', and that numerous stellar actors played Kansas City, including Edwin Booth, James O'Neill, and Edwin Forrest. The book offers many stories of local politics, and it is meticulous in its reconstruction of the theatre scene as, for instance, when it discusses Thomas W. Keene's missing trunk (which contained his costumes) and how the Catholic Church came to the rescue with some of its robes. The book also looks at key personalities, such as Abraham Judah and H.D. Clark. The authors are careful to preserve the flavour of the theatre scene, and their descriptions of performances and stagings are colourful, as when they discuss the tunnel that led from the theatre to the Hotel Baltimore's lobby: 'With electric lights and a mosaic floor, the underground passageway proved popular, especially in winter when theatergoers could go out during intermission or for supper after the show without having to bundle up again.' In all, the book offers a delightful history of a long-forgotten chapter in American theatre.

Numerous books were requested but not received this year.

5. Native, Asian American, Latino/a and General Ethnic Writing

Native American and mixed-blood writers and their diverse, yet often intersecting, interests in place and space, take centre-stage in Helen May

Dennis's *Native American Literature: Towards a Spatialized Reading*. Dennis's text is the latest addition to the provocative Routledge Transnational Perspectives on American Literature series. Throughout this study Dennis interweaves detailed literary engagement with thoughtful deliberation on the strengths and limitations of Gaston Bachelard's *The Poetics of Space* [1958]. In the first half Dennis concentrates on Native women writers and the elements of second-wave feminism that intersperse with their tribal-influenced explorations of home and belonging. Borrowing Toni Morrison's account of 'inscape', Dennis considers both felicitous and infelicitous space in texts by Paula Gunn Allen, Leslie Marmon Silko, Linda Hogan and the less canonical writers Janet Campbell Hale and Betty Louise Bell. Occasionally Dennis's illuminating study is beset by an apologetic tone set to appease Native nationalist writers, such as Jace Weaver and Robert Warrior, who question non-Native readings. However, this is a considered approach that strikes a balance between applying Western readings and examining the 'imaginative universe of the tribal or mixed-blood author'. Dennis moves from Bachelard to William Bevis's account of the 'homing-in plot' in the latter half of the study, opening up Bevis's primarily male-authored approach to texts by both Louise Erdrich and non-Native writer Frank Waters. Louis Owen's *Dark River* [1999] also comes into play as Dennis reveals how these authors complicate 'the static, over-simplified, bipolar model of homing-in' by drawing on Bhabha's notion of the third space. Dennis's text contains informative readings that illuminate the works of both canonical and non-canonical authors, and it perhaps goes some way to achieving one of her initial objectives: to draw the Native American canon closer to the American literary canon.

Cross-cultural reflections and interdisciplinary methodologies form the basis of the ten stimulating essays collected in Angela L. Cotton and Christa Davis Acampora's *Cultural Sites of Critical Insight: Philosophy, Aesthetics, and African American and Native American Women's Writings*. Many of these essays tackle both the failure to address all aspects of African Native identities and the absence of sustained studies of African Native literature—issues astutely raised by Cotton in the introductory chapter. Barbara S. Tracy's fine analysis of the Cherokee strains in Alice Walker's *Meridian* [1976] traces the intertextual dialogue between Walker's novel and John Neihardt's *Black Elk Speaks* [1932]. As Tracy pays attention to the multi-voiced qualities of Walker's writing she pertinently employs Henry Louis Gates's concept of 'signifyin' to reveal the 'syncretism' between Native and African at play in the text. For other authors in the collection, Native American womanist issues offer postcolonial perspectives that enable forms of healing and self-discovery. Although AnaLouise Keating's study of Paula Gunn Allen's *Grandmothers of the Light* [1991] risks echoing the rhetoric of the self-help books to which she refers, the feminist theorization on offer as she debates 'womanist self-recovery' adds a crucial critical edge. Ellen L. Arnold expands the feminist slant of the collection with her adroit comparison of the similarities and disjunctures between Linda Hogan's *Solar Storms* [1995] and Margaret Atwood's *Surfacing* [1972], an essay that again brings the postcolonial into focus. Luci Tapahonso's Native reworking of Yeats's 'Leda and the Swan' in

'Leda and the Cowboy', and mothering and double consciousness in Zitkala-Sa's early twentieth-century writings, are the subjects of the closing arguments by Maggie Romigh and Margot R. Reynolds, respectively. Both critics grasp the concept of the gynocentric as they discuss female empowerment in Native communities. There is a great deal to recommend this text, not least its emphasis on cross-cultural rather than monolithic readings.

Alicia A. Kent, in challenging previous, myopic conceptions of modernity, also takes a cross-cultural approach in her excellent *African, Native, and Jewish American Literature and the Reshaping of Modernism*. Kent hopes to transform modernity as she discusses the critical role that ethnicity played in a rapidly modernizing America from the late nineteenth to the early twentieth centuries. Six case studies are positioned within detailed, if not always groundbreaking, socio-historical accounts of the migrations and exiles at the centre of Native, African and Jewish American experiences. The most interesting aspects of Kent's study emerge as she turns her attention to the novels: Charles Chesnutt's *Marrow of Tradition* [1901]; Zora Neale Hurston's *Their Eyes Were Watching God* [1937]; Mourning Dove's *Cogewea* [1927]; D'Arcy McNickle's *The Surrounded* [1936]; Abraham Cahan's *The Rise of David Levinsky* [1917] and Anzia Yezierska's *Bread Givers* [1925]. With separate chapters devoted to each ethnicity, it is through insightful intertextual comparisons across the chapters that Kent successfully echoes the cross-cultural exchanges that shape her understanding of modernism. Kent provides intriguing accounts of the various modes and methods by which her chosen authors intervened in predominantly white Euro-American discussions of modernity, ranging from discussions of genre to considerations of language and assimilation. It is rather disappointing, however, that Kent chose to turn so heavily to socio-historical contextualization over a wider range of literary texts. Regardless, Kent's eventual turn to the diasporic raises new and important questions about modernity that serve to open up future debates. This text reveals that cross-cultural approaches can be effective models for approaching the diverse yet often intersecting ethnicities within America.

Diversity in the form of handicrafts is the focus of Deborah Weagel's 'Elucidating Abstract Concepts and Complexity in Louise Erdrich's *Love Medicine* through Metaphors of Quilts and Quilt Making' (*AICRJ* 31:iv[2007] 79–95). Weagel's discussion shares similarities with discussions of quilting and quilt metaphors in black American fiction as she links these conjoined patterns with issues of wholeness, mixed-blood identities and the narrative structure of Erdrich's novel.

Hilary E. Wyss's 'Native Women Writing: Reading Between the Lines' (*TSWL* 26:i[2007] 119–25) looks back to the colonial period as she examines the impact of English literacy on the writing patterns of Native women. In a speculative yet interesting approach, Wyss asks many pertinent questions about the origins of Native women's writing.

In 'Remembering Migration and Removal in American Indian Women's Poetry' (*RMR* 61:ii[2007] 54–62), Amy T. Hamilton takes issues with the dominant preoccupation with the idea of place and placedness in American Indian literature. Through nuanced readings of poetry by Wendy Rose, Luci Tapahonso and Linda Hogan, Hamilton reveals the significance of walking and mobility when considering cultural identity. Place is also a central concern for Esther Belin in 'Contemporary Navajo Writers' Relevance to Navajo Society' (*WSR* 22:i[2007] 69–76). Belin details her own emergence as an Indian poet, considering as she does so the impact of both boarding school and higher education on Indians. The essay also draws on Sherman Alexie's reclaiming of the term 'Indian' in his poetry.

Scott Andrews's 'A New Road and a Dead End in Sherman Alexie's *Reservation Blues*' (*ArQ* 63:ii[2007] 137–52) reveals a frustration with the 'emptiness' that Andrews finds at the centre of the novel. The article neatly summarizes the novel's interest in the cross-cultural exchanges between African and Indian Americans, and its failure to develop those exchanges in productive ways for Alexie's Spokane characters. In contradistinction, the move from reservation to city is the focus of John Blair Gamber's '"Outcasts and dreamers in the cities": Urbanity and Pollution in *Dead Voices*' (*PMLA* 122:i[2007] 179–93). Gamber concentrates on the positive, futuristic vision of urban life detailed in Gerald Vizenor's *Dead Voices: Natural Agonies in the New World* [1992]. Gamber argues that Vizenor's employment of the trickster figure allows him to consider ways in which 'Native people can still be who they are, even in the city'.

Following the lead of Robert Warrior and Craig Womack, Roumiana Velikova's 'Will Rogers's Indian Humor' (*SAIL* 19:ii[2007] 83–103) expands the definitions of Native American literary history by incorporating the much-maligned figure of humorist Will Rogers. Velikova offers a compelling interpretation of Rogers's role in American political life.

The autobiographical impulse is under scrutiny in Tyra Twomey's 'More Than One Way to Tell a Story: Rethinking the Place of Genre in Native American Autobiography and the Personal Essay' (*SAIL* 19:ii[2007] 22–51). Twomey convincingly demonstrates the need to move away from applying Western notions of autobiography to the Native form, and the restrictive limits that such categories can create. In effect, Twomey calls for a transition from literary classification to forms of rhetorical action.

Activism and the responsibility of both author and reader form the basis of Lisa J. Udel's 'Revising Strategies: The Intersection of Literature and Activism in Contemporary Native Women's Writing' (*SAIL* 19:ii[2007] 62–82). Urdel primarily draws on the fiction of Winona LaDuke and Elizabeth Cook-Lynn, with Linda Hogan's novels offered as supporting texts. The argument adroitly considers the ideological demands made by these authors, although more time could have been devoted to the onus placed on the reader.

Edward Dauterich IV's 'Time, Communication, and Prophecy: Prodigious Unity in *Almanac of the Dead*' (*CLAJ* 50:iii[2007] 348–63) unpacks the vastness of Leslie Marmon Silko's novel in light of her 'gynocentric, Native American heritage'. For Dauterich, issues including time and alternative histories form the backbone of Silko's approach, and unify the diverse elements of the novel. Silko is again the focus of attention in Kimberly Roppolo's 'Vision, Voice, and Intertribal Metanarrative: The American Indian Visual-Rhetorical Tradition and Leslie Marmon Silko's *Almanac of the Dead*' (*AIQ* 31:iv[2007] 534–58). Roppolo turns to Silko after a lengthy opening discussion concerning Plains sign language, and turns that interest into a useful account of images in Silko's novel. Focusing particularly on the image of the snake, Roppolo considers the numerous traditions drawn on by Silko, including paintings.

Native American studies form the basis of two key articles: Jace Weaver's 'More Light than Heat: The Current State of Native American Studies' (*AIQ* 31:ii[2007] 233–55) and Duane Champagne's 'In Search of Theory and Method in American Indian Studies' (*AIQ* 31:iii[2007] 353–72). In Weaver's thoughtful account the future of Native American studies in the academy and Native rests in the interconnected relationship between the two. Weaver also provides a succinct summary of some of the most significant publications in the field, drawing particular attention to the intellectual intersections of *American Indian Quarterly*, *Wicazo Sa Review* and *American Indian Culture and Research Journal*. Champagne's study echoes Weaver's in its hope that American Indian communities will benefit from the work undertaken in the academy. For Champagne, the study of indigenous peoples warrants a greater expansion of specific Native American studies that cross theoretical boundaries.

Manifold interpretations are central to Sidner Larson's 'Multiple Perspectivism in James Welch's *Winter in the Blood* and *The Death of Jim Loney*' (*AIQ* 31:iv[2007] 513–33). Larson traces Welch's intricate mapping of 'the American Indian world in all its complexity', most pertinently by considering the impact of capitalism and colonization in the two texts.

For those new to recent Native American studies, or for teachers looking for a concise, student-friendly approach to the subject, Rebecca Tillett's *Contemporary Native American Literature* will be of particular interest. In six chapters Tillett follows the emergence of Native American writing through to the present day, including a key chapter on 'seminal writers', N. Scott Momaday, James Welch and Leslie Marmon Silko. In line with the title's contemporary focus, Tillett dedicates two chapters to the period from 1980 to 2000: one with a concentration on women writers, Louise Erdrich, Anna Lee Walters and Luci Tapahonso and the other concerning 'tricksters and critics', Simon Ortiz, Louis Owens and Gerald Vizenor. In the concluding chapter Tillett turns her attention to recent Native American writing, with a particular focus on Sherman Alexie. This is a useful survey of the field and is a worthwhile addition to the British Association of American Studies paperback series of guides for students of American studies.

Elvira Pulitano collects together the work of fourteen European scholars working in the field of Native American studies in her *Transatlantic Voices: Interpretations of Native North American Literatures*. In the introduction Pulitano regards these essays as routes between US and European Native American studies, and the impressive range of issues and Native authors covered in the collection certainly points to the dynamism of non-US scholarly investigations in the field. Separated into four parts, this text traverses issues of history, myth, memory and identity in interesting and illuminating ways. Helmbrecht Breinig provides a detailed account of how the concepts of transculturality and transdifference are pertinent to discussions of Native Americans. Breinig's focus on identity draws the other two essays of part one neatly together, since Hartwig Isernhagen's concern with storytelling and

Bernadette Rigal-Cellard's account of history and myth in Native American literature, revolve around the issues of identity and group formation. A discussion of 1930s novels by Native American writers John Joseph Mathews and D'Arcy McNickle and an overview of the various styles and concerns of contemporary Native American novels constitute a rather brief part II. In a more cohesive third section, essays by Deborah L. Madsen, Kathryn Napier Gray and Rebecca Tillett deal with issues of trauma and amnesia in works by Paula Gunn Allen, Wendy Rose and Leslie Marmon Silko respectively. Highlights of the final six essays that compose part IV include Mark Shackleton's work on cross-cultural symbolism in Louise Erdrich's *Love Medicine* [1984] and *Tracks* [1988], in which he convincingly conjoins irony and signification as he unpacks cross-cultural concerns. In the final essay of the collection, A. Robert Lee's study of Jim Barnes's poetry examines both the Native and European influences in Barnes's writing, and offers an engaging analysis of the poet that also draws together the collection's wider interest in crossovers and transatlantic exchanges.

Also of interest is Annette Trefzer's *Disturbing Indians: The Archaeology of Southern Fiction*. While Trefzer focuses solely on white writers of the Southern Renaissance, her wider concern is with Native American signifiers in their work. Reading the fiction of Andrew Lytle, Caroline Gordon, Eudora Welty and William Faulkner in light of the excavations of Native American sites in the 1930s, Trefzer argues that Native Americans are 'essential to the southern writers' understanding of region and nation'. Trefzer's balanced argument is pertinent reading for Native American studies scholars as well as those working on Southern literature and the idea of place.

Place is a crucial component of Jeffrey F.L. Partridge's *Beyond Literary Chinatown*, in which he deconstructs the ghettoization of Chinese American literature. Partridge provides an insightful critique of contemporary publishing practices and the role they play in forming readers' expectations of the Chinese American worlds they encounter in works by Chinese American authors. With emphasis on the authentic ethnicity of the authors, Partridge suggests that publishing houses present Chinese American authors as tour guides into the mysterious and hitherto closed space of Chinese communities in the US. In doing so, Partridge draws interesting analogies between the emergence of Chinatowns and the bracketing of Chinese American authors, both acts of containment that, for Partridge, are dispelled by the nuances of the literary texts themselves. As Partridge establishes a polycultural approach to Chinese American literature he explores a range of contemporary texts including work by Li-Young Lee, Shirley Geok-lin Lim, David Wong Luie, Shawn Wong and Gish Jen. From work on diaspora through to the role of baseball, Partridge provides fresh and stimulating insights into Chinese American writing. Accompanying these detailed analyses are pertinent and engaging discussions of Maxine Hong Kingston and Amy Tan. In particular, Partridge traces the common features that run through Tan's oeuvre, revealing how these traits, most notably the idea of 'enigma', have been marketed in ways that commodify ethnicity. Through his polycultural approach, Partridge offers a compelling account of how recent Chinese American authors have broken out of the borders of Chinatown, opening up new horizons that seek to interact with readers in new ways.

Displacement and disfiguration are central concerns for Sheng-mei Ma in his *East-West Montage: Reflections on Asian Bodies in Diaspora*. Ma homes in on the proliferation of bodies in the Asian diaspora, echoing the fluidity of the diaspora in a multi-disciplined approach that encompasses analyses of films, poetry, comics, plays and prose. Ma successfully avoids a one-dimensional understanding of the Asian body as he moves, in deliberately jarring fashion, from one body part and Asian body to another. With each section of the book entitled 'Intercuts', Ma slices through monolithic, Orientalist approaches to the Asian body to unravel a myriad of diasporic experiences, from those of Japanese Americans to Korean and Hmong refugees. From the outset Ma sets up a tension between Asian diaspora studies and Asian American studies that he carries through the work with interesting effect. Tensions are a key facet of the study, and are utilized to good effect in chapter 11, where Ma examines the varied depictions of disabled Chinese bodies in literature by Chinese and Chinese American authors. Here, Ma skilfully contrasts writers such as Ha Jin and Zhang Yimou with Maxine Hong Kingston and Amy Tan. While he sets up a dichotomy between the Oriental writers' Orientalist approach to the body and the Asian American writers' enabling depictions of disabled Chinese bodies, Ma works towards a more nuanced reading that allows scope for all these texts to 'exorcize the specter of Orientalism'. Alongside his account of 'camp scatology' in Japanese American literature dealing with internees in American camps during the Second World War, Ma also turns his attention to the story cloths created by Hmong refugees. For Ma, these tapestries undercut the 'post' of 'post-traumatic stress disorder' as they depict a continually traumatic refugee experience of relocation and assimilation. From trauma theory to theories of diaspora, this is a compelling text and an important intervention in Asian diasporic studies.

Ma's work also features in Joel Kuortti and Jopi Nyman's fascinating collection, *Reconstructing Hybridity: Post-Colonial Studies in Translation*. The essays gathered here investigate and galvanize Homi Bhabha's 'third space' as they explore the complex terrain of hybridity. The conceptual essays that make up the first half are neatly complemented by the textual readings of the latter section, with the depth and breadth of the entire study resulting in refreshing views of the hybrid self. Sabine Broeck raises the important question of where whiteness fits into discussions of hybridization, by examining what is entailed in acknowledging whiteness as a category. Broeck disrupts any homogenous notion of 'white' while David Huddart's rendering of Bhabha argues that hybridity, in terms of human rights, 'requires us to read *and* legislate with greater attentiveness to that which moves in between'. Provocatively, in the final essay of the theoretical section, Andrew Blake challenges the anti-Americanism he detects in Paul Gilroy's work by turning to the series of Matrix films. In part II, essays on Native and Asian American identities sit alongside studies of British and postcolonial writings by authors including Salman Rushdie and Hanif Kureishi. Zoe Trodd considers a selection of early autobiographies by Native American writers, with a primary focus on Charles Alexander Eastman's *From the Deep Woods to Civilization* [1916], William

Apess's *A Son of the Forest* [1829], *Black Elk Speaks* [1932] and Mary Crow Dog's *Lakota Woman* [1990]. Sheng-mei Ma turns the focus to Amerasians and the need to apply notions of mixed-blood identities to Asian American texts, while Jopi Nyman considers the Japanese American writer Cynthia Kadohata's novel *The Floating World* [1989]. Both Ma and Nyman's essays demand new ways of looking at Asian American subjects, something captured in Joel Kuortti's essay on Jhumpa Lahiri. There is much to recommend this text, from its rigorous assessment of theoretical paradigms to the detailed readings of literary texts.

Steven G. Yao's 'Toward a Prehistory of Asian American Verse: Pound, *Cathay*, and the Poetics of Chineseness' (*Rep* 99[2007] 130–58) considers the development of Chinese poetry during the modernist period. Yao contends that the 'poeticity of the Chinese written character played especially vital roles in the Anglo-American modernist poetic revolution'. Yao offers a detailed and rigorous account of the cross-cultural exchanges that took place during this period.

The position of unruly, humorous women, in terms of both authors and characters, occupies Margaret D. Stetz in '*Who's Hu?* And where Is the Asian American Women's Comic Tradition in Fiction?' (*Studies in American Humor* 15:iii[2007] 101–11). Stetz investigates the limited recognition of humour in texts by Asian American women, taking Lensey Namioka's *Who's Hu?* [1980] as her case study. Women are again the focus in Michelle Black Wester's 'The Concentric Circles of Dictee: Reclaiming Women's Voices through Mothers' and Daughters' Stories' (*JAAS* 10:ii[2007] 169–91). Wester suggests that Hak Kyung Cha's *Dictee* [1982], with its employment of the legendary Korean goddess Princess Pali, offers Korean Americans, and more particularly Korean American women, 'a dual history with which to identify'. The essay pivots around the connection between women's histories and the processes of imperialism.

Susie Lan Cassel's ' "... the binding altered not only my feet but my whole character": Footbinding and First-World Feminism in Chinese American Literature' (*JAAS* 10:i[2007] 31–58) considers the ways in which Chinese American literature, with its 'activist agenda', deals with the issue of footbinding through the lens of Western paradigms. Cassel challenges what she regards as the 'blind conviction' against footbinding in Chinese American fiction, taking the stance that within Chinese culture 'footbinding made perfect sense for women'. This provocative statement will surely pave the way for future work on the footbinding practice.

A refreshing account of the masculine position in Asian American writing can be found in Bonnie Zare's 'Evolving Masculinities in Recent Stories by South Asian American Women' (*JCL* 42:iii[2007] 99–111). Zare examines Jhumpa Lahiri's *Interpreter of Maladies* [1999] and Meera Nair's *Video and Other Stories* [2002], dealing with the complex position of the male characters. For Zare, men in South Asian texts have for too long been employed as one-dimensional representations of male power, yet, she contends, with the emergence of these novels, that position is shifting.

Rocío G. Davis takes another foray into Asian American studies with her *Begin Here: Reading Asian North American Autobiographies of Childhood.*

With a look at American and Canadian autobiographies from the late nineteenth century through to the present, Davis questions the impact of place and space upon autobiographical re-enactments of childhood as she turns to texts that focus on childhoods spent in either Asia or North America. Davis comes at these autobiographies from a number of angles, including a consideration of biracial childhoods, and in a surprising yet illuminating turn in the final chapter she turns to childhood autobiographies written for children. The real strength of this approach to ethnic autobiography rests with its attentiveness to these texts as literary productions as well as socio-historical documents. Through detailed and highly nuanced textual analysis, Davis debates the depictions of childhood in texts ranging from Yan Phou Lee's *When I Was a Boy in China* [1887] through to Quang Nhoung Huynh's *The Land I Lost: Adventures of a Boy in Vietnam* [1982]. Davis's focus on the varied experiences of the peoples who fall into the bracket of 'Asian American' is most pronounced when she explores the impact of wars and cultural revolutions on memories of childhood. In this chapter Davis considers the conflicts in China, Vietnam and Cambodia since the 1960s that have influenced North American Asian autobiographies. Indeed, Davis regards the 1960s as a watershed moment when the inception of the term 'Asian American' led to a more intricate 'perception of the relationship of an Asian past to an American present'. Davis's study will appeal to both ethnicity scholars and to those working in autobiographical studies, and is a key addition to Asian American studies.

The promising title of Sämi Ludwig's 'Ethnicity as Cognitive Identity: Private and Public Negotiations in Chang-rae Lee's *Native Speaker*' (*JAAS* 10:iii[2007] 221–42) is somewhat undercut by a central argument that implies that ethnicity does not in any way shape identity. This rudimentary approach should not, however, distract entirely from a competent examination of Lee's novel.

The ghostly is a shared interest for Lynn Ta and Monika Elbert in their individual contributions to Sladja Blazan's *Ghosts, Stories, Histories: Ghost Stories and Alternative Histories*. Ta provides a rigorous critique of global capitalism, the 'interstitial citizen' and the Chinese American experience in Fae Myenne Ng's *Bone* [1993]. For Ta, the exploitation of immigrant bodies in American sweatshops is inextricably tied to mourning and cultural haunting in Ng's novel. Ta reads the economic ghostly through the microcosm of Ng's Leong family. The family, in particular the relationships between mothers, daughters and the Chinese mother tongue, is the subject of Elbert's more pedestrian work on Amy Tan's *The Joy Luck Club* [1989] and Michelle Cliff's *No Telephone to Heaven* [1987].

The act of becoming historical, of writing the Latino body into American history, is the cornerstone of Lázaro Lima's *The Latino Body: Crisis Identities in American Literary and Cultural Memory*. In this excellent multidisciplinary examination of the Latino body, including analyses of literature, photography and film, Lima considers the ways in which the Mexican body has been rendered 'extranational' as it has been repeatedly written out of American notions of national identity. A particularly striking element of Lima's argument comes when he turns, in chapter 1, to two testimonials from

Hubert Howe Bancroft's History of California project [1884–9]. Lima's discussion of Eulalia Pérez's *Una vieja y sus recuerdos* (*An Old Woman and her Recollections*) provides an insightful account of the photograph of Pérez that accompanied her account, examining how the image was consumed and objectified by a mainstream white American audience. Lima turns from Pérez to Catarina Ávila de Ríos's *Recuerdos históricos de California por la Señora Catarina Ávila de Ríos* (*Memoirs of Doña Catarina Ávila de Ríos*) to reveal a more subversive testimony that sought to counter American cultural amnesia. Other topics of consideration in part I, entitled 'Longing History', include Ruiz de Barton's *The Squatter and the Don* [1885] and a detailed account of Tomás Rivera's ... *And the Earth Did Not Devour Him* [1971]. Part II, 'Postmodern Genealogies: The Latino Body, in Theory', begins with a somewhat familiar account of the place of Latino studies in the academy, although Lima does deliver a fine consideration of identity negotiations in Cabeza de Vaca's *Castaways* [1885]. Difficult forms of remembering and confrontational sexualities are the basis of Lima's final chapter, where he concentrates on Luz María's Umpierre's *Margarita Poems* [1987], Elías Miguel Muñoz's *The Greatest Performance* [1991] and Rafael Campo's *What the Body Told* [1996]. This is a stimulating study that highlights new and important questions for Latin American studies.

Marta Caminero-Santangelo probes the different languages, religions and cultures that serve to trouble the generic term 'Latino' in her *On Latinidad: U.S. Latino Literature and the Construction of Ethnicity*. In an engrossing introduction that raises the question 'Who Are We?', Caminero-Santangelo sets up the concept of difference that is crucial to her study and to her interest in pan-ethnicity. In part I, chapters on Rudolfo Anaya's *Bless Me, Ultima* [1972] and Piri Thomas's *Down These Mean Streets* [1967] allow Caminero-Santangelo to examine the socio-historical context of the Chicano movement. More pertinently, though, she skilfully contrasts the notions of ethnicity explored by both writers, to argue that 'essentialist myths are inexorable and necessary to a panethnic identity'. In part II, though, Caminero-Santangelo probes the notion of essentialism, weighing up its limitations as well as its possibilities in relation to Julia Alvarez, Achy Obejas and Christina García. Most notable in this section is the fine work on the violence of representing others in various works by Alvarez. As the study moves into the third and final section the focus shifts to the potential of pan-ethnicity and the changing notions of *Latinidad*. Alongside chapters on Ana Castillo's *So Far from God* [1993] and Demetria Martínez's *Mother Tongue* [1994], Caminero-Santangelo provides an interesting examination of writers, including Margarita Engle, Elías Miguel Muñoz and Alisa Valdes-Rodriguez. At the close of this illuminating study Caminero-Santangelo expresses her commitment to 'attending to the historical and present differences among Latinos' as well as to the solidarity among Latinos most apparent in the 'overlapping of analogous histories' shared by those with a South American heritage.

The complex formulations of the term 'Latino' are also explored in diverse and interesting ways in the twelve essays that comprise Carlota Caulfield and Darién J. Davis's *A Companion to US Latino Literatures*. In the introduction Caulfield and Davis offer a standard overview of the unstable notion of both a Latino collective and of the socio-economic position of Latinos in the US. For them, the collection 'provides a window into the vibrancy of contemporary Latino literature in the US'. As such, the essays provide insights into a range of Latino backgrounds, with chapters on Mexican, Cuban and Puerto Rican influences, while others deal with less recognized Latino identities, such as Argentinian, Central American and Brazilian cultures. Certainly, the strength of the collection lies in its range, as the essays deal with literature, theatre, autobiography, poetry and film. In addition, chapters by Armando González-Pérez on Afro-Cuban identities and Lydia M. Gil on 'Jewish-Latino Literature' further disrupt and expand the Latino umbrella. Of particular note are Patricia M. Montilla's 'The Island as Mainland and the Revolving Door Motif: Contemporary Puerto Rican Literature of the United States' and Sergio Waisman's 'Argentine Writers in the US: Writing South, Living North'. Both detail the ways in which the spaces and places are traversed, collided and merged in the literature of writers that share a dual vision, one that encompasses the land left behind and the land where the literary creation takes place. The collection ultimately introduces a range of different cultures into the Latino construct and the chapters' concern with issues such as border crossings and hybridity mark this as an important addition to the field of Latino studies.

Cross-cultural intersections are the subject of Helane Adams Androne's 'Revised Memories and Colliding Identities: Absence and Presence in Morrison's "Recitatif" and Viramontes's "Tears on My Pillow"' (*MELUS* 32:ii[2007] 133–50). Across both texts Androne maps the similarities between black and Chicano American notions of cultural memory as well as both writers' interest in mythology and identity. The cornerstone of the argument is the notion of absent/present mothering and its impact on the female protagonists of both texts.

For Raphael Dalleo and Elena Machado Sáez, in their *The Latino/a Canon and the Emergence of Post-Sixties Literature*, Latino/a literature of the latter half of the twentieth century and the beginning of the twenty-first has traditionally been categorized into two opposing groups. Writers of the 1960s and 1970s are, they argue, read as anti-colonialists whose work resonates with the political impact of the civil rights generation. In contradistinction, their successors have sacrificed the political to attain market success, falling into a 'sell-out' category. Dalleo and Sáez saliently challenge such readings as they employ Néstor García Canclini's work on the process of negotiation. For Dalleo and Sáez, binary categorizations of Latino/a literature are reductive, as they prove with their analysis of key authors and their work. In the first chapter they compare two poems by Pedro Pietri—an earlier poem 'Puerto Rican Obituary' [1973] and a more recent work 'El Spanglish National Anthem' [1993]—to show how Pietri's earlier anti-colonial, anti-marketplace stance has, in his later work, become less oppositional as it considers the intersections between Latino/a politics and the economic realities of the contemporary publishing world. This chapter allows Dalleo and Sáez to develop their argument, that echoes but does not engage Homi Bhabha in its call for a third space for literature where opposing anti-colonial and multicultural groupings of Latino/a literature can interact in more productive ways. They establish this approach through readings of fiction by Abraham Rodriguez, Ernesto Quiñonez, Junot Díaz, Angie Cruz, Christina Garcia and Julia Alvarez. In the conclusion, the authors turn away from their previous engagement with a 'New York-based Latino/a tradition' to focus on the impact of the marketplace on Nilo Cruz, Chantel Acevedo and Ana Menéndez, Cuban American writers from Miami. Ultimately this is an engaging study whose breadth and depth offer intriguing insights into the formation of, and future for, a Latino/a literary tradition.

The issue of multilingualism in the contemporary United States is a matter for debate in Lourdes Torres's 'In the Contact Zone: Code-Switching Strategies by Latino/a Writers' (*MELUS* 32:i[2007] 75–96). The non-translated, Spanish sections of Giannini Braschi's *Yo-Yo Boing!* [1998] and Susana Chávez-Silverman's *Killer Crónicas* [2004] are offered as forms of radical bilingualism, with questions raised about the inclusion/exclusion of readers and the movement towards an increasingly multilingual society.

An increasing interest in literary representations of ethnic cuisines is addressed in the year's final edition of *MELUS* (32:iv[2007]). Editors Fred. L. Gardaphé and Wenying Xu introduce seven essays 'that centralize the multivalent meaning of food in various ethnic literary traditions'. Asian American cuisine within a diasporic context features in both Anita Mannur's 'Culinary Nostalgia: Authenticity, Nationalism, and Diaspora' (*MELUS* 32:iv[2007] 11–31) and Laura Anh Williams's 'Foodways and Subjectivity in Jhumpha Lahiri's *Interpreter of Maladies*' (*MELUS* 32:iv[2007] 69–79). Both essays offer delectable accounts of the role of food in relation to identity. Mannur's work on nostalgia and imaginary (re)constructions of home in relation to, amongst others, Madhur Jaffrey's *An Invitation to Indian Cooking* [1975] is of particular note. Lorraine Mercer and Linda Storm continue the discussion of a culinary diaspora in their consideration of Arab American literature, 'Counter Narratives: Cooking Up Stories of Love and Loss in Naomi Shihab Nye's Poetry and Diana Abu-Jaber's *Crescent*' (*MELUS* 32:iv[2007] 33–46). Mercer and Storm convincingly claim that the shared meals and cross-cultural exchanges that appear in these texts can help to reconcile the exilic self with its present condition. Joanna Barszewska Marshall's '"Boast now, chicken, tomorrow you'll be stew": Pride, Shame, Food, and Hunger in the Memoirs of Esmeralda Santiago' (*MELUS* 32:iv[2007] 47–68) sets up notions of abjection and reconciliation that are echoed in the one essay that deals with a male author, Michele Fazio's '"Vomit your poison": Violence, Hunger, and Symbolism in Pietro di Donato's *Christ in Concrete*' (*MELUS* 32:iv[2007] 115–37). In light of the very different contexts of the Puerto Rican migrant and Italian immigrant experiences, Marshall and Fazio negotiate the wrought, complex relationships with food in terms of gender and class politics respectively.

Eric Estuar Reyes's 'American Developmentalism and Hierarchies of Difference in Zamora Linmark's *Rolling the R's*' (*JAAS* 10:ii[2007] 117–40) is 'concerned with the processes by which Filipino American writers challenge the politics of globalization'. While Reyes's argument details the impact of American imperialism in R. Zamora Linmark's fiction, he also casts a glance at other writers, including Carlos Bulosan. This nuanced essay carefully explores the issue of subject formation for the exiled self. Filipino American identity is also examined in Meg Wesling's 'Colonial Education and the Politics of Knowledge in Carlos Bulosan's *America Is in the Heart*' (*MELUS* 30:ii[2007] 55–77). Wesling points to the contradictions that lie at the centre of Bulosan's story of immigration and assimilation through detailed textual analysis.

David S. Goldstein and Audrey B. Thacker, in their *Complicating Constructions: Race, Ethnicity, and Hybridity in American Texts*, have collected together fourteen essays whose depth and breadth offer new ways of thinking about American literary production and canon formation from the nineteenth century to the present. Jesse Alemán's insightful account of María Amparo Ruiz de Burton's late nineteenth-century novels *Who Would Have Thought It?* [1872] and *The Squatter and the Don* [1885] establishes the ways in which Ruiz de Burton 'stretches the nation's geopolitical terrain of whiteness to include Californios' while also noting that the exclusion of other ethnic groups from her account ultimately limits the nature of whiteness in her novels. Other highlights amongst these theoretically adroit arguments include Sheree Meyer, Chauncey A. Ridley and Olivia Castellano's collaborative study of double consciousness and its shifty meanings. The three employ the notion of double consciousness alongside discussions of multiculturalism as they consider texts by Jewish American, Chicano and African American writers. Jewish American literature is also the focus for Joe Lockard and Derek Parker Royal, with Lockard taking on William Pierce's controversial *The Turner Diaries*, and Royal making a convincing case for the need to study the postmodern techniques and interests of contemporary Jewish American writing. Jeffrey F.L. Partridge investigates 'literary Chinatown' in an essay focusing on Gish Jen's *Mona in the Promised Land* [1996]. Noting the ways in which Chinese American ethnicity has been ghettoized by both mainstream white American culture and, to varying degrees, by Chinese American authors themselves (of which Partridge offers Amy Tan's *The Joy Luck Club* as an example), Partridge regards Jen's novel as breaking new ground for Chinese American ethnicity in its foregrounding of 'pan-ethnic interaction' and 'multicultural hybridity'.

In *From Shadow to Presence: Representations of Ethnicity in Contemporary American Literature*, Jelena Sesnic offers a heavily theorized consideration of American ethnicities since the 1960s. Sesnic's is the first publication in Rodopi's new series, Critical Approaches to Ethnic American Literatures, which promises to be an exciting addition to the field. Sesnic draws on a range of theoretical paradigms that she rigorously debates, including the use of psychoanalytical theory in relation to ethnicity and work on the diasporic condition. Gender is a key consideration for Sesnic as she negotiates the terrain of cultural nationalism in the post-civil rights era. In the first two sections Sesnic addresses key manifestos with distinctive masculine concerns, including *Aiiieeeee!* [1974], 'El Plan Espiritual de Aztlán' ('The Spiritual Plan of Aztlán) [1969] and Vine Deloria's *Custer Died for Your Sins: An Indian Manifesto* [1969]. She complements her theoretical treatment of these manifestos with literary analyses of both Shawn Hsu Wong's *Homebase* [1979] and the autobiographies of Oscar Zeta Acosta. While acknowledging the seminal position of these works, Sesnic takes issue with their predominantly masculine concerns as she explores the wider impact of the feminist movement in relation to ethnic women's writing, especially in regard to Toni Morrison and Maxine Hong Kingston. In the final sections of the study Sesnic deviates from her strongly gendered approach as she questions the ideas of borderlands and the diasporic in contemporary notions of ethnicity. One particularly perceptive discussion occurs in relation to Sherman Alexie's depictions of reservation life in both his poetry and his prose. Troubling straightforward readings of Alexie's postcolonial rhetoric allows Sesnic to move seamlessly on to the work of Denise Chávez and Rolando Hinojosa. She goes on to view diaspora through the terrains of Florida, Cuba and the Caribbean, making this a rounded treatment of post-1960s ethnicity.

The position and future of Arab Americans studies is the focal point of Steven Salaita's *Arab American Literary Fictions, Cultures, and Politics*. Salaita draws on the idea of creolization as he stresses the idea of communal uniqueness alongside larger ideas of an Arab diaspora. The text hinges on the overarching notion of an Arab-centric approach rather than 'an approach centered exclusively on Arabs' in order to demand recognition for Arab Americans as subjects rather than objects in discussions of American ethnicity. Salaita also questions the lack of Arab American studies in North American universities, arguing for their wider recognition and development and offering as he does so a blueprint for turning this ideal into a working reality. Salaita makes the interesting turn, in chapter 2, to the role of the Lebanese civil war in Arab American fiction, where the discussion rests at the level of the sociological and aesthetic, rather than on the specifics of Israel–Palestine conflict. Such a move underscores the text's opening references to the diverse nature of Arab American writing and the various political, religious and cultural influences on Arab American writers. In dealing with stereotypical misconceptions of Arab Americans Salaita concentrates, in chapter 3, on Norma Khouri's fraudulent *Honor Lost: Love and Death in Modern-Day Jordan* [2003]. Salaita suggests that American preconceptions about the treatment of women in Arab countries gave credence to a text that does little more than fall into 'an American tradition of ethnic impersonation and falsified personal narrative'. The final chapter engagingly focuses on the ways in which fiction can combat anti-Arab racism, with particular attention given to the fiction of Joseph Geha and Laila Halaby. Salaita's text unflinchingly deals with the contentious issue of what defines area studies, and his work acts as a crucial intervention in debates about the position of Arab American studies.

Worthy of mention here is Brinda Metha's *Rituals of Memory in Contemporary Arab Women's Writing*. Arabic women's writing from across the world features in Metha's text as she pertinently explores issues of identity, memory and the diasporic condition. Of relevance is the work on Diana Abu-Jaber's *Crescent* [2003], the topic of the book's final chapter. In this section Metha investigates the idea of culinary memory in relation to Abu-Jaber's protagonist, Sirine, whose cooking allows her to access both sides of her Iraqi American identity. As Metha traces the semiology of food in *Crescent* she proposes that culinary practices are one way of troubling multiculturalism by insisting on 'specificity within diversity'.

The golem and the act of creation are of central concern to Nicola Morris in her *The Golem in Jewish American Literature: Risks and Responsibilities in the Fiction of Thane Rosenbaum, Nomi Eve and Steve Stern*. Morris provides a sustained history of both the emergence and the evolution of the golem, and despite some abrupt shifts in focus, her links between creating the golem and notions of power and powerlessness in the wake of the Holocaust and the abuses of Israel are illuminating.

Maeera Y. Shreiber's *Singing in a Strange Land: A Jewish American Poetics* is a significant addition to studies of both Jewish American identity and the poetic form. Shreiber's argument rests on the relationship between Jewish American poetry and the exilic condition. Shreiber treats the poetic form as a disruptive force that explores not only questions of identity but also of gender politics in the Jewish American community. Throughout the study Shreiber tackles what she regards as a pervasive silence surrounding Jewish American poetry and as such she offers detailed readings of the 'aesthetic and formal concerns' of the selected poems in an attempt to 'generate a lexicon for Jewish American poetic practice'. The range of this study is impressive as it moves from poets such as Charles Reznikoff and Allen Ginsberg to Adrienne Rich and Irena Klepfisz, and as Shreiber investigates the treatment of issues including religion, gender and diaspora. In recent years there has been a significant increase in the critical attention given to ethnic American poetry and Shreiber's work is a valuable contribution to this area.

An interesting treatment of Italian American writing can be found in Kenneth Scambray's *Queen Calafia's Paradise: California and the Italian American Novel*. To date, many studies of Italian American literature have focused on the East Coast and the work of authors such as Don DeLillo. Here, Scambray draws attention to the Italian American communities spread over California through his concentration on six key writers: Jo Pagano, Lorenzo Madalena, P.M. Pasinetti, Dorothy Bryant, Steven Varni and John Fante. This is a wide-ranging exploration of both the many shared and the disparate experiences of Italian Americans in the region.

Francisco Cota Fagundes's 'Charles Reis Felix's *Through a Portagee Gate*: Lives Parceled Out in Stories' (*MELUS* 32:ii[2007] 151–63) traverses relatively new terrain in its focus on Portuguese American literature. Fagundes regards Felix's part-autobiographical, part-biographical text as a watershed moment for Portuguese American letters, placing emphasis on its embodiment of 'several interrelated subjectivities'. This essay serves to show that discussions of American ethnicities continue to expand in interesting directions.

Molly Crumpton Winter's *American Narratives: Multiethnic Writing in the Age of Realism* demands recognition for its attribution to ethnic writers of the development and expansion of American realism. In chapter 1 and the conclusion Winter ably sets up the multiple ways in which Mary Antin, a Russian-born Jewish American, the Sioux writer Zitkala-Ša, African American Sutton E. Griggs and Chinese American Sui Sin Far address realist concerns in their writing. Curiously, though, in the other four chapters, each dedicated to one of the four authors, very little mention is made of realism.

Instead, Winter offers socio-historical readings of the authors' lives and texts, incorporating as she does so notions of assimilation and multiculturalism that play more to an ethnic studies strand. Although the study borders on the repetitious at times, its strength lies in Winters's focus on overlooked writers and her attempts to test the boundaries of realism.

The graphic narrative's encounter with ethnicity shapes a special issue of *MELUS* (32:iii[2007]). In addition to Derek Parker Royal's editor's introduction, 'Coloring America: Multi-Ethnic Engagements with Graphic Narrative' (*MELUS* 32:iii[2007] 7–22), nine essays complete a collection that, in Royal's words, 'addresses the possibilities, and even the potential liabilities, of comics when representing ethnoracial subject matter'. Framing and the Asian American body in comic strips interest Sandra Oh in her 'Sight Unseen: Adrian Tomine's *Optic Nerve* and the Politics of Recognition' (*MELUS* 32:iii[2007], 129–51), while Japanese internment during the Second World War is the subject of Xiaojing Zhou's 'Spatial Construction of the "Enemy Race": Miné Okubo's Visual Strategies in *Citizen 13660*' (*MELUS* 32:iii[2007], 51–73). Corporeality is also at play in Menachen Feuer's 'Every*body* is a Star: The Affirmation of Freaks and Schlemiels through Caricature in the Comics of Drew and Josh Friedman' (*MELUS* 32:iii[2007] 75–101). Feuer considers both the difference of the Jewish body and the Friedman comics' 'democratic impulse' in the spaces they create for freaks to flourish. Jennifer Glaser's 'An Imaginary Ararat: Jewish Bodies and Jewish Homelands in Ben Katchor's *The Jew of New York*' (*MELUS* 32:iii[2007], 153–73) investigates Katchor's comic depiction of an imaginary community, one that, Glaser argues, does not romanticize a Jewish past but that attempts to explore a 'more "authentic" Jewishness'.

Books Reviewed

Amato, Joe. *Industrial Poetics: Demo Tracks for a Mobile Culture*. UIowaP. [2006] pp. 226. pb $29.95 ISBN 9 7815 8729 5010.

Antliff, Allan. *Anarchy and Art: From the Paris Commune to the Fall of the Berlin Wall*. Arsenal. [2007] pp. 224. $23.95 ISBN 9 7815 5152 2180.

Bagchee, Shyamal, and Elisabeth Däumer, eds. *The International Reception of T.S. Eliot*. Continuum. [2007] pp. 320. £75 ISBN 9 7808 2649 0148.

Barzilai, Lyn Graham. *George Oppen: A Critical Study*. McFarland. [2006] pp. 231. $45 ISBN 9 7807 8642 5495.

Batra, Nadita, and Vartan P. Messier. *Narrating the Past: (Re)Constructing Memory, (Re)Negotiating History*. Cambridge Scholars [2007] pp. 170. $69.99 ISBN 1847181145.

Beasley, Rebecca. *Ezra Pound and the Visual Culture of Modernism*. CUP. [2007] pp. 238. £47 ISBN 9 7805 2187 0405.

Beasley, Rebecca. *Theorists of Modernist Poetry: T.S. Eliot, T.E. Hulme and Ezra Pound*. Routledge. [2007] pp. 144. pb £12.99 ISBN 9 7804 1528 5414.

Blazan, Sladja, ed. *Ghosts, Stories, Histories: Ghost Stories and Alternative Histories*. CambridgeSP. [2007] pp. viii + 291. £39.99 ($79.99) ISBN 1 8471 8219 4.

Bloom, Steven F. *Student Companion to Eugene O'Neill*. Greenwood. [2007] pp. xiv + 205. $65 ISBN 0 3133 3431 5.

Bloshteyn, Maria. *The Making of a Counter-Culture Icon: Henry Miller's Dostoevsky*. UTorP. [2007] pp. xi + 261. $60 ISBN 0 8020 9228 1.

Bosco, Mark, and Kimberly Rae Connor, eds. *Academic Novels as Satire: Critical Studies of An Emerging Genre*. Mellen. [2007] pp. 165. $99.95 ISBN 0 7734 5418 7.

Bourdeau, Debra Taylor, and Elizabeth Kraft, eds. *On Second Thought: Updating the Eighteenth Century Text*. UDelP. [2007] pp. 301. $57.50 ISBN 0 8741 3975 9.

Brater, Enoch, ed. *Arthur Miller's Global Theater*. UMichP. [2007] pp. 168. $49.50 ISBN 0 4721 1593 6.

Brauner, David. *Philip Roth*. ManUP. [2007] pp. 272. pb $24.95 ISBN 0 7190 7425 8.

Bray, Robert, ed. *Tennessee Williams and his Contemporaries*. CambridgeSP. [2007] pp. 180. $59.99 ISBN 1 8471 8101 5.

Buckwalter, Stephanie. *A Student's Guide to Jack London*. Enslow. [2007] pp. 160. $28 ISBN 0 7660 2707 4.

Caminero-Santangelo, Marta. *On Latinidad: U.S. Latino Literature and the Construction of Ethnicity*. UFlorP. [2007] pp. x + 296. £51.50 ($59.95) ISBN 0 8130 3083 8.

Cant, John. *Cormac McCarthy and the Myth of American Exceptionalism*. Routledge. [2007] pp. 368. $95 ISBN 0 4159 8142 5.

Caulfield, Carlota, and Darién J. Davis, eds. *A Companion to US Latino Literatures*. Tamesis. [2007] pp. ix + 235. £50 ($85) ISBN 1 8556 6139 4.

Cianci, Giovanni, and Jason Harding, eds. *T.S. Eliot and the Concept of Tradition*. CUP. [2007] pp. 246. £53 ISBN 9 7805 2188 0022.

Collis, Stephen. *Through the Words of Others: Susan Howe and Anarcho-Scholasticism*. ELS. [2006] pp. 148. pb $18 ISBN 9 7809 2060 4960.

Cook, Eleanor. *A Reader's Guide to Wallace Stevens*. PrincetonUP. [2007] pp. 370. $35 ISBN 0 7806 9104 9830.

Cope, Stephen, ed. *Selected Prose, Daybooks, and Papers*, by George Oppen. UCalP. [2007] pp. 296. pb $19.95 ISBN 9 7805 2025 2325.

Cotton, Angela L., and Christa Davis Acampora, eds. *Cultural Sites of Critical Insight: Philosophy, Aesthetics and African American and Native American Women's Writings*. SUNY. [2007] pp. viii + 216. pb £14.49 ($24.95) ISBN 0 7914 6980 4.

Dalleo, Raphael, and Elena Machado Sáez. *The Latino/a Canon and the Emergence of Post-Sixties Literature*. Palgrave. [2007] pp. x + 205. £42 ($65) ISBN 1 4039 7796 0.

Davis, Rocío G. *Begin Here: Reading Asian North American Autobiographies of Childhood*. UHawaiiP. [2007] pp. xii + 234. £35.95 ($42) ISBN 0 8248 3092 2.

Dennis, Helen May. *Native American Literature: Towards a Spatialized Reading*. Routledge. [2007] pp. ix + 236. £70 ($140) ISBN 0 4153 9702 2.

Diggins, John Patrick. *Eugene O'Neill's America: Desire under Democracy.* UChicP. [2007] pp. 288. $29 ISBN 0 2261 4880 7.

Entin, Joseph B. *Sensational Modernism: Experimental Fiction and Photography in Thirties America.* UNCP. [2007] pp. 344. $59.95 ISBN 0 8078 5834 9.

Fink, Thomas, and Joseph Lease, eds. *'Burning Interiors': David Shapiro's Poetry and Poetics.* FDUP. [2007] pp. 186. $43 ISBN 9 7808 3864 1552.

Goldstein, David S., and Audrey B. Thacker, eds. *Complicating Constructions: Race, Ethnicity, and Hybridity in American Texts.* UWashP. [2007] pp. xxviii + 320. pb £14.99 ($25) ISBN 0 2959 8835 1.

Gwiazda, Piotr K. *James Merrill and W.H. Auden: Homosexuality and Poetic Influence.* Palgrave. [2007] pp. 216. $74.95 ISBN 9 7814 0398 4319.

Hadjiafxendi, Kyriaki, and Polina Mackay, eds. *Authorship in Context: From the Theoretical to the Material.* Palgrave. [2007] pp. 256. $69.96 ISBN 1 4039 4901 8.

Joseph, Philip. *American Literary Regionalism in a Global Age.* LSUP. [2007] pp. xii + 232. $45 ISBN 0 8071 3188 1.

Katz, Daniel. *American Modernism's Expatriate Scene: The Labour of Translation.* Edinburgh Studies in Transatlantic Literatures. EdinUP. [2007] pp. 208. £45 ISBN 9 7807 4862 5260.

Kent, Alicia A. *African, Native, and Jewish American Literature and the Reshaping of Modernism.* Palgrave. [2007] pp. x + 230. £42.50 ($65) ISBN 1 4039 7797 7.

Kuortti, Joel, and Jopi Nyman, eds. *Reconstructing Hybridity: Post-Colonial Studies in Translation.* Rodopi. [2007] pp. x + 330. £50 ($91) ISBN 9 0420 2141 9.

Laity, Cassandra, and Nancy K. Gish. *Gender, Desire, and Sexuality in T.S. Eliot.* CUP. [2007] pp. 280. pb $53 ISBN 9 7805 2103 9468.

Lázaro, Lima. *The Latino Body: Crisis Identities in American Literary and Cultural Memory.* NYUP. [2007] pp. 240. $70.00 ISBN 0814752144.

Londré, Felicia Hardison, and David Austin Latchaw. *The Enchanted Years of the Stage: Kansas City at the Crossroads of American Theater, 1870–1930.* UMissP. [2007] pp. 348. $34.95 ISBN 0 8262 1709 7.

Lowney, John. *History, Memory, and the Literary Left: Modern American Poetry, 1935–1968.* UIowaP. [2006] pp. 303. $39.95 ISBN 9 7815 8729 5089.

Ma, Sheng-mei. *East-West Montage: Reflections on Asian Bodies in Diaspora.* UHawaiiP. [2007] pp. xxiii + 302. pb £19.50 ($27) ISBN 0 8248 3181 3.

MacCay, Marina. *Modernism and World War II.* CUP. [2007] pp. 200. £46 ISBN 9 7805 2187 2225.

Mauldin, Joanne Marshall. *Thomas Wolfe: When Do the Atrocities Begin?* UTennP. [2007] pp. 361. $38 ISBN 1 5723 3494 0.

Mehta, Brinda. *Rituals of Memory in Contemporary Arab Women's Writing.* SyracuseUP. [2007] pp. x + 303. £30.95 ($45) ISBN 0 8156 3135 4.

Menand, Louis. *Discovering Modernism: T.S. Eliot and his Context.* OUP. [2007] pp. 240. pb $18.95 ISBN 9 7801 9515 9929.

Metres, Philip. *Behind the Lines: War Resistance Poetry on the American Home Front since 1941.* University of Iowa Press. [2007] pp. 298. $39.95 ISBN 9 7808 7745 9989.

Miller, Cristanne. *Cultures of Modernism: Marianne Moore, Mina Loy, and Else Lasker-Schuler.* UMichP. [2006] pp. 288. $24.95 ISBN 9 7804 7203 2372.

Mix, Deborah M. *A Vocabulary of Thinking: Gertrude Stein and Contemporary North American Women's Innovative Writing.* UIowaP. [2007] pp. 228. $39.95 ISBN 1 5872 9613 6.

Moody, A. David. *Ezra Pound: Poet. A Portrait of the Man and his Works,* vol. 1: *The Young Genius 1885–1920.* OUP. [2007] pp. 544. pb £25 ISBN 9 7801 9921 5577.

Morris, Daniel. *The Poetry of Louise Glück: A Thematic Introduction.* UMissP. [2006] pp. 274. $42.50 ISBN 9 7808 2621 6939.

Morris, Nicola. *The Golem in Jewish American Literature: Risks and Responsibilities in the Fiction of Thane Rosenbaum, Nomi Eve and Steve Stern.* Lang. [2007] pp. x + 147. $60.95 ISBN 0 8204 6384 1.

Nicholls, Peter. *George Oppen and the Fate of Modernism.* OUP. [2007] pp. 240. $99 ISBN 9 7801 9921 8264.

Parry, Amie Elizabeth. *Interventions into Modernist Cultures: Poetry from Beyond the Empty Screen.* DukeUP. [2007] pp. 200. pb $22.95 ISBN 9 7808 2233 8185.

Partridge, Jeffrey F.L. *Beyond Literary Chinatown.* UWashP. [2007] pp. xvii + 246. pb £17.99 ($24.95) ISBN 0 2959 8706 4.

Patea, Viorica, and Scott Derrick Paul, eds. *Modernism Revisited: Transgressing Boundaries and Strategies of Renewal in American Poetry.* Rodopi. [2007] pp. 252. $70 ISBN 9 7890 4202 2638.

Potter, Rachel. *Modernism and Democracy: Literary Culture 1900–1930.* OUP. [2006] pp. 208. £46 ISBN 9 7801 9927 3935.

Pulitano, Elvira, ed. *Transatlantic Voices: Interpretations of Native North American Literatures.* UNebP. [2007] pp. xxxv + 298. £43 ($55) ISBN 0 8032 3758 2.

Reynolds, Guy, ed. *Willa Cather as Cultural Icon.* Cather Studies 7. UNebP. [2007] pp. xi + 354. pb $35 ISBN 0 8032 6011 5.

Saal, Ilka. *New Deal Theater: The Vernacular Tradition in American Political Theater.* Palgrave. [2007] pp. 244. $74.95 ISBN 1 4039 7801 8.

Saddik, Annette. *Contemporary American Drama.* EdinUP. [2007] pp. 224. $120 ISBN 0 7486 2493 7.

Salaita, Steven. *Arab American Literary Fictions, Cultures, and Politics.* Palgrave. [2007] pp. 208. £40 ($65) ISBN 1 4039 7620 8.

Scambray, Kenneth. *Queen Calafia's Paradise: California and the Italian American Novel.* FDUP. [2007] pp. 211. £39.95 ($46.50) ISBN 0 8386 4117 0.

Schanke, Robert A., ed. *Angels in the American Theater: Patrons, Patronage, and Philanthropy.* SIUP. [2007] pp. 320. pb $35 ISBN 0 8093 2747 3.

Sesnic, Jelena. *From Shadow to Presence: Representations of Ethnicity in Contemporary American Literature.* Rodopi. [2007] pp. 285. pb £71 ($77) ISBN 9 0420 2217 1.

Shreiber, Maeera Y. *Singing in a Strange Land: A Jewish American Poetics.* StanfordUP. [2007] pp. xi + 287. £46.95 ($55) ISBN 0 8047 3429 5.
Skaggs, Merrill Maguire. *Axes: Willa Cather and William Faulkner.* UNebP. [2007] pp. xvii + 202. $40 ISBN 0 8032 1123 0.
Smith, Susan Harris. *Plays in American Periodicals, 1890–1918.* Palgrave. [2007] pp. 245. $74.95 ISBN 1 4039 7765 8.
Stableford, Brian. *Space, Time, and Infinity: Essays on Fantastic Literature.* Wildside Press. [2007] pp. 208. $35 ISBN 0 8095 0911 3.
Suarez, Juan A. *Pop Modernism: Noise and the Reinvention of the Everyday.* UIllP. [2007] pp. 336. pb $25 ISBN 9 7802 5207 3922.
Tillett, Rebecca. *Contemporary Native American Literature.* EdinUP. [2007] pp. 177. pb £16.99 ($34) ISBN 0 7486 2149 1.
Totten, Gary, ed. *Memorial Boxes and Guarded Interiors: Edith Wharton and Material Culture.* UAlaP. [2007] pp. 315. pb $34.95 ISBN 0 8173 5419 0.
Trefzer, Annette. *Disturbing Indians: The Archaeology of Southern Fiction.* UAlaP. [2007] pp. xii + 223. £26.50 ($38.50) ISBN 0 8173 1542 9.
Trigilio, Tony. *Allen Ginsberg's Buddhist Poetics.* SIUP. [2007] pp. 280. $45 ISBN 9 7808 0932 7553.
Urgo, Joseph R., and Merrill Maguire Skaggs. *Violence, the Arts, and Willa Cather.* FDUP. [2007] pp. 320. $61.50 ISBN 0 8386 4157 6.
Wagner-Martin, Linda. *Ernest Hemingway: A Literary Life.* Palgrave. [2007] pp. x + 201. $69.95 ISBN 1 4039 4001 0.
Whalan, Mark. *Race, Manhood, and Modernism in America: The Short Story Cycles of Sherwood Anderson and Jean Toomer.* UTennP. [2007] pp. 294. $43 ISBN 1 5723 3580 7.
Winter, Molly Crumpton. *American Narratives: Multiethnic Writing in the Age of Realism.* LSUP. [2007] pp. ix + 204. $36.50 ISBN 0 8071 3225 8.

XVII

New Literatures

FEMI ABODUNRIN, LEIGH DALE, CHRIS TIFFIN,
RICHARD LANE, SUZANNE SCAFE, CAROLINE HERBERT,
CATHERINE LEAN AND NELSON WATTIE

This chapter has six sections: 1. Africa; 2. Australia; 3. Canada; 4. The Caribbean; 5. The Indian Subcontinent and Sri Lanka; 6. New Zealand. Section 1 is by Femi Abodunrin; section 2 is by Leigh Dale and Chris Tiffin; section 3 is by Richard Lane; section 4 is by Suzanne Scafe; section 5 is by Caroline Herbert and Catherine Lean; section 6 is by Nelson Wattie.

1. Africa

(a) General

A History of Theatre in Africa, edited by Martin Banham, is a volume of historical and critical essays attempting the daunting task of chronicling the history of theatre in Africa. The volume uses the word theatre 'in a way that embraces a wide range of aspects of performance—in truth we use it in its largest and most inclusive sense' (p. xv). What is meant by Africa, by theatre and by history are clearly terms to be clarified. According to Banham, while what is meant by Africa is a straightforward choice between 'sub-Saharan Africa or the total continent including the Maghreb and Egypt', and bearing in mind that we are dealing with a continent the history of which all agree is not singular, it is the second term, 'theatre', that 'is more elusive and presents a greater problem. The variety of performance forms in African societies is immense, ranging from dance to storytelling, masquerade and communal festival, with a vibrant and generally more recent "literary" and developmental theatre' (p. xv). Kole Omotoso's opening essay, 'Concepts of History and Theatre in Africa' (pp. 1–12), fleshes out what is described as the 'various and varied rituals, festivals, demonstrations and performances' (p. 3) that are crucial to the formation of a theatre consciousness in the average African or 'the initial exposures of young ones to performance' (p. 4). Given that indigenous languages and indigenous environments are the most enduring aspects of theatre and performance in African countries, one of Omotoso's primary conclusions is that 'it would seem rather inadequate to speak of Francophone theatre or Anglophone theatre when speaking of the totality of theatre and performance experiences of the African peoples, of French colonial experience in west and central Africa, of the African peoples of English colonial Africa in west, east and southern Africa and of the African peoples of Portuguese colonial experience in west, east and southern Africa' (p. 4).

Thus, while the infamous language debate in African literature rages, the bulk of theatre and performance existing in African languages could guide the would-be researcher and student of African theatre to a true realization of the continent's theatrical resources. Omotoso's historical account examines the undeniable link between language and performance that begins with the daily and seasonal rituals of life; he observes further that, with the possible exception of the Arabic language and the Islamic religion, and their ubiquitous roles and dominance in North Africa, 'The dramas and performances linked to these rituals have become aspects of the cultures of many African countries and peoples' (p. 5). Omotoso links the whole notion of language and performance to the 'unwritten culture of oral tradition', in what many would regard as an endorsement of the Ngugi school of African literature over its Achebean counterpart. He suggests that it is only through translating foreign knowledge and foreign ideas into African languages that 'the African can begin to make genuine contributions to world knowledge and ideas ... Indeed, this is the only means by which the knowledge brought by the European languages of colonial experience can co-mingle and cross-fertilise one another' (p. 6). In theoretical terms, Omotoso insists on using the performances of his own Yoruba culture, history and rituals to demonstrate the quintessential differences between African theatre and its Euro-American counterparts, while noting that while the three major characteristics differentiating Yoruba theatre from Western forms may not be applicable to the theatre performance of other parts of the continent. He cites with relish the foremost scholar and critic of African theatre Professor Adedeji, who himself quotes Hubert Ogunde's observation that 'African theatre is a *celebration*. At the end of it, ensure that your audience show appreciation for the encounter and its experience with relish' (cited on p. 9, original italics). Furthermore, unlike its prose and poetry counterparts, African theatre and performance have remained, according to Omotoso, the only art forms insisting on 'the relevance of history to artistic endeavours': 'In the meantime, theatre, drama and performance will continue to assert that the holy places of African peoples are not in Jerusalem, not in Mecca and Medina, not in the consumer emporiums of London, Paris, New York and Tokyo. Rather, our performance traditions will continue to assert that our holy places are next door to us, in the affirmation of our tribal identity within the embrace of our modern African country's identity, and that our everyday sacred rituals continue in our indigenous languages' (p. 12).

Omotoso's largely essentialist argument and conclusions set the tone for the volume *A History of Theatre in Africa*. While he argues that the term 'post-tribal state', inaugurated at the Berlin conference of 1884–5, is the 'post' that best describes and approximates the contemporary African situation and history, he maintains simultaneously that 'Theater, drama and performance have been the instruments of the undermining of the post-tribal state or *status quo ante*' (p. 11) in Africa. With the exception of John Conteh-Morgan's lengthy 'Francophone Africa south of the Sahara' (pp. 85–137), Luis R. Mirtras's 'Theatre in Portuguese-Speaking African Countries' (pp. 380–97) and Osita Okagbue's 'Surviving the Crossing: Theatre in the African Diaspora' (pp. 430–47), all the other contributions are focused on the different regions of the continent and are discussed in their respective geographical sections below. Conteh-Morgan's contribution opens with the familiar language debate, branding the whole notion of francophone Africa as a contested term: 'With its emphasis on French and its place in Africa, and the new, French-derived culture to which this language has given rise, the word, it is claimed, marginalizes the numerous African languages and non-Francophone, that is non-French derived cultures in these countries' (p. 85). Perhaps the best way to realize the adjective francophone as applied to sub-Saharan Africa, which refers to a territorial unit of some twenty-one French-speaking countries, is through the dichotomous nature of the French language itself vis-à-vis its indigenous counterparts or the transactions between them. According to Conteh-Morgan, while the indigenous traditions of theatre cannot be said to enjoy the same recognition and status as their French-language counterparts, it is only by discussing 'The plurality of theatre forms in Francophone Africa (as distinct from Francophone theatre)— indigenous, urban-popular and literary . . . on their own terms (their contexts of performance, form and function), and not as constituting points of origin or arrival' (p. 87) that some of the most vital cultures of performance in Africa from 'the region of Africa now commonly described as "Francophone"' (p. 88), can be realized fully. Similar to Omotoso's observation that perhaps the cultural and historical issues at stake is the fact that, by the time the Europeans arrived in Africa, 'Their histories, their antecedents, their backgrounds of primitivism and pre-Christianity did not accompany them' (p. 5), Conteh-Morgan cites Jean Duvignaud's 'characterisation of medieval European societies as "*des sociétés visuelles*" (visual societies)' (p. 88). Thus, against the backdrop of two distinguishable broad categories of indigenous performance—the recreational and the devotional—one of Conteh-Morgan's primary conclusions is that if we take on board theatre critic Blandier's observation about these medieval societies—'tout s'y montre et tout s'y joue, les pratiques socials s'y jouent dans une dramatisation permanente' ('everything in them is displayed and performed, social practices are in a state of permanent dramatization'; cited p. 88)—then the same state of affairs can be said to apply 'with equal, if not greater, validity to the "traditional" societies of Africa' (p. 88). However, Conteh-Morgan suggests that, compared to their anglophone counterparts, and in spite of 'their vitality and relevance to the majority of the population', the wide range of indigenous traditions of performances 'are eclipsed in terms of sheer social and cultural power and prestige by what has become the hegemonic form in Francophone Africa, literary drama' (p. 114). Furthermore, their relative 'newness' in comparison to the indigenous traditions—the overwhelming importance of literary drama which 'only emerged in the 1930s in the French colonies and in the 1950s in the Belgian ones' (p. 114)—transcends the fact that French is a minority language in francophone African countries: 'Mediated through print culture and backed by its authority, and inspired by French literary and artistic conventions even when the latter are contested, this "Francophone" cultural production represents the contemporary official, and by implication "élite", culture. The others, expressed in African languages and through the medium of 'primary orality', are associated, in a typical case of cultural diglossia, with the "unofficial", the "popular", the "ethnic", even if they constitute a fund of technical and thematic resources for the constitution of official "national" cultures' (pp. 114–15).

In a similar vein, Luis R. Mitras's 'Theatre in Portuguese-Speaking African Countries' examines the historical nature of theatrical forms in the five countries whose official language is Portuguese: 'Angola and Mozambique, the largest two, are in Southern Africa; Guinea-Bissau is on the west coast of Africa; and the remaining two (Cape Verde and São Tomé and Príncipe) are island archipelagos in the Atlantic' (p. 380). Again, the language issue and the ways in which Portuguese 'functions as a language of "national unity" in those countries that have important regional languages', and how it 'binds the five Portuguese-speaking countries into some kind of associative unity' (p. 380), is the starting point of Mitras's contribution. That said, the linguistic situation notwithstanding, the temptation to regard them as a sort of cultural bloc should be resisted. For while the islands were uninhabited before the Portuguese settled them with slaves and white migrants, 'The three countries on the continent had ancient cultures before they were subjugated to colonial domination; these African traditions were never obliterated, and this has contributed to the way theatre is made today' (p. 380). And, while there are similarities and differences in theatrical forms between the three countries on the African mainland, the islands, on the other hand, 'have also much in common with the Creole islands in the Caribbean, and the kind of theatrical manifestations that we encounter on the islands to suggest that they operate on a different paradigm from that of the continent' (p. 380). Sharing a common bond of colonialism and the same flagrant disregard for tribal borders and cultural differences, leading to the creation of the 'post-tribal states' referred to by Omotoso above, the three Portuguese-speaking countries on the mainland share theatrical manifestations also evident in other modern African nation-states whose ethno-linguistic groups reside in more than one state.

According to Mitras two important forms of cultural expression in which theatrical elements are identifiable—the ritual dance and oral storytelling—could be said to characterize the 'embryonic theatre' of pre-colonial African society in the areas that constitute modern-day Angola, Guinea-Bissau and Mozambique. With elements derived from both African and European sources in Cape Verde, and a commensurate cultural hybridization in São Tomé and Príncipe, the political nature of the theatre experienced by the Portuguese-speaking countries, culminating in political independence in 1975, had its roots in the post-Second World War 'Anti-colonial struggle, nationalism and a new-found pride in Africa [which] were powerful themes to be deployed in literature' (p. 389). The didactic or propagandist nature of the theatre that ensued—and its aftermath—are better felt in terms of the different effects on the individual Portuguese-speaking countries: while Guinea-Bissau is the smallest of the countries on the mainland, and its theatre production the most meagre, Mitras cites a number of Angolan texts of the immediate post-revolutionary period to the late 1980s, and concludes that 'There was never a tradition of publishing plays in Mozambique' (p. 393). Again, while it could be said that the fall of the Berlin Wall, profound changes in South Africa and the collapse of the Soviet Union affected geopolitical reality in Mozambique, and ultimately the nature of the theatre in the late 1980s in Angola, in spite of the constant war—'an obvious hindrance to theatrical production and theatre' (p. 395)—'the country [Angola] seems to have a more enduring tradition of institutional theatre in the period after independence' (p. 395). In Guinea-Bissau, Mitras asserts, the situation remains as precarious as ever and, 'According to Leopold Amado, the author of a study of Guinean literature, to this day not a single European-style house has been built in Guinea-Bissau... Amateur groups continue to exist, however' (p. 397). With their similar but distinctive Creole cultures, Cape Verdean and Sãotomense societies also incarnate similar and divergent theatrical manifestations, and Mitras uses the 'romaria', a popular festival in which the boundaries between the secular and the sacred blur, to illustrate the point further: 'Traditionally, Sãotomense society was divided into two basic classes, plantation owners and slaves... Cape Verde, on the other hand, traditionally a poor country subject to periodic droughts, really only had dynastic families in the eighteenth and nineteenth centuries, but nothing on the scale of São Tomé, since Cape Verde had no agricultural riches to speak of' (p. 400). Thus, while it could be said that 'theatre occupies a central space in the cultural arena of Sãotomense society, the same is not true of Cape Verde. Here the emphasis is on music and more specifically on the unique Cape Verdean *morna*' (p. 400).

A special issue of the journal *Research in African Literatures* (*RAL* 38:i[2007]), edited by Lúcia Helena Costigan and Russell G. Hamilton, is also devoted to critical and theoretical considerations of 'Lusophone African and Afro-Brazilian Literatures'. In their introduction, Costigan and Hamilton begin with a parenthetical comment with respect to African literature in Portuguese made in David Wesley's essay, 'Choice of Language and African Literature: A Bibliographical Essay' (*RAL* 23:i [1992], pp.159–71), and the observation that 'courses on African literature began being offered in American and European universities as it became almost by definition literature in English or French (Lusophone literature being more esoteric)' (p. 5). In comparison, the editors suggest, while African literature in Portuguese 'may not have been, nor continues to be, as abstruse or recondite as the label "esoteric" implies, over the decades it certainly has been less accessible and thus not as well known as its Anglophone and Francophone counterparts' (p. 5). As the postcolonial debate becomes entangled with the language question, invariably the three languages of European origin are also subordinated to the whole notion of their colonial past or their postcolonial present—and to questions about how the three rank as world languages: 'Ironically, with regards to its "esoteric" standing vis-à-vis English and French, because in the early fifteenth century the Portuguese reached sub-Saharan Africa, their language was the first European tongue to make a social, commercial, and cultural impact on the continent.

Moreover, Portuguese-based pidgins, some of which eventually became creoles, were the first to emerge in West Africa' (pp. 5–6).

Essays on different aspects of the five lusophone African countries' literature and their historical as well as theoretical considerations, in this special issue of *RAL*, are discussed in their appropriate African regional contexts below. While the essays assembled present historical views that are applicable to all the five lusophone African countries, there are five articles that focus on Afro-Brazilian literature and culture, documenting 'the fact that the lusophone South American nations' current Afro-Brazilian literature has precursors as far back as the eighteenth century, with roots in West Africa' (p. 7). Brazil, according to the editors, 'received more slaves than any other country in the western hemisphere', and 'The sociohistorical and cultural links between Brazil and Lusophone Africa recently manifested themselves in various ways. Several Brazilian universities have faculty members who specialize in Lusophone African literature' (p. 7). The literary links between Africa and Brazil and the African diaspora are explored further in Osita Okague's 'Surviving the Crossing: Theatre in the African Diaspora' (*RAL* 38:i[2007] 430–47), which examines 'theatres from Brazil, Haiti, Martinique, Guadeloupe, Cuba and the whole of what is often referred to as the "Commonwealth Caribbean"' (p. 431). Adopting a historical rather than an analytical approach, 'placing trends, plays or playwrights within appropriate and defining historical contexts', Okagbue's article sets out, in line with the primary focus of the issue, to chronicle a history of theatre in Africa, the 'influences of African cultures and folk forms on the subsequent development of theatre in South America or the Caribbean, or in identifying dramatic trends in each country' (p. 431).

Still on drama and performance, *Theatre, Performance and New Media in Africa*, edited by Susan Arndt, Eckhard Breitinger and Marek Spitczok von Brisinski, is a collection of essays on various aspects of theatre, popular culture performances and different aspects of the new media that are used to mediate and interrogate them in Africa. In their introduction to the volume, 'Popular Culture and Media in a Globalized World: Some Introductory Thoughts' (pp. 7–10), Arndt and Brisinski observe that while 'New productions of music, theatre, literature, radio, film, newspapers, websites and other media are created daily', and while their meanings are constantly reproduced and reinvented by the populations that interpret them, it is only the 'essentialized binarisms of "high" and "low", "elite" and "the masses", "traditional" and "contemporary" [that] have been never been able to grasp and categorize the complex dynamics of popular culture' (p. 7). Edouard Glissant's theoretical notion of the 'chaos world', 'in which the different socio-historical "entanglements" of today's world no longer allow it to be predicted and planned in advance' (p. 8) presents one route towards transcending these 'essentialized binarisms'. Ostensibly, the complex, polyphonous and unpredictable nature of popular cultural forms entails that the would-be researcher should maintain an awareness that 'cultural spaces and their products cannot be separated into distinct categories that have linear roots and boundaries. . .Just as Onitsha Market Literature was inspired by the brochures from India brought to Nigeria during World War II, the global presence of Bollywood influences filmmakers in Africa and worldwide' (p. 8).

In a manner that is reminiscent of Omotoso's reference to and recapitulation of 'the same street on which both Christian and Muslim rituals and festivals took place [which] also constituted the playing spaces of the collective rituals and festivals of the Yoruba of Akure' (Banham, ed., p. 2), the editors of *Theatre, Performance and New Media in Africa* cite the example of the South African theatre duo Ellis and Bheki and their adoption of African and European theatre traditions to form the 'Township Theatre and Jacques Lecoq'. Their plays, set in Southern African villages, and drawing on global themes (such as colonialism, 9/11 and reconciliation), operate against the backdrop of their core belief that 'the essence of theatre is the actor, the audience and their relationship...When we refer to street theatre we include performing under a tree in a rural area, on a sports' field in a "no-go" area, in the swamp of Botswana or in a town square in Stavanger, Norway' (pp. 8–9). The editors suggest that Gilles Deleuze and Félix Guattari's metaphor of the 'rhizome'—'an entangled web-like organic structure, that represents multiple connections, ambivalent directions and subversive interpretations' (p. 8)—can best represent the complex dynamics of popular cultural activity and their resultant products or 'a rhizomic mode of performing the world in a way that connects local productions to global processes of cultural migration' (p. 9).

Finally, the volume of essays sets out to challenge academic narratives, especially those 'that view popular cultural forms as being instrumentally produced by dominant cultures and classes to impose their meanings on masses who consume these indifferently and are, in effect, voiceless' (p. 9). The first part of the four-part volume is entitled 'Old Wisdom and New Orality' and comprises Mineke Schipper's 'A Woman is Like the Earth: Mankind's Imagination in Proverbs Worldwide' (pp. 13–23) and Divine Neba Che's 'Performer as Tradition and Creator: The Example of the Western Grasslands of Cameroon' (pp. 25–35). Schipper contextualizes what she describes as 'probably the world's smallest literary genre'—the proverb—suggesting that proverbs are an integral aspect of oral traditions and display a global concern with issues of sex and gender: 'In Africa, the experts on traditions are referring to their ancestral legacy, the elders are supposed to be, or claim to be, the pre-eminent specialists and representatives of tradition. Quoting is an art and the skilful display of one's knowledge by quoting proverbs is a source of prestige in oral societies' (p. 14). Proverbs, according to Schipper, have striking similarities across cultures, in form as well as in content. These range from the frequent constructions they have in common to their ubiquitous cross-cultural and inter-continental occurrences: 'Thanks to its attractive form, a well-known proverb, quoted in a new situation, adequately renews people's attention to the old message as well as to its new connotations' (p. 14). Beginning with a discussion of how a literal meaning may become metaphorical and consequently invite numerous other meanings, Schipper then demonstrates the many ways in which some strikingly constant cores of meaning expressed in proverbs about women worldwide could be seen to achieve universal significance on important issues of sex and gender.

Reflecting on the intertwined nature of the local and the global in many proverbs, Schipper poses the following questions: 'Why should we be confronted with such old-fashioned, conservative ideas about gender relations in our 21st century? Does it make sense at all? My answer is an unqualified yes. We need to gain deeper insight into the processes of representation and their effects. Proverbs can be read as texts. Looking into the meanings of their messages, we can ask such questions as: Who speaks and who looks in each of those texts? Whose interests are being promoted through proverbs about women? And conversely, who does not speak, whose perspective is absent and whose interests are not represented?' (p. 21).

Echoing Schipper's concern and critical articulation of the global reaches of the world's smallest literary genre (as she defines it), *Research in African Literatures*' other special issue in the year under review (*RAL* 38:iii[2007]) is on 'The Preservation and Survival of African Oral Literature', edited by Isidore Okpewho. The volume focuses on all the concomitant effects as well as ramifications of the preservation and survival of what Okpewho describes as 'the library of tradition', appealing to 'the graphic observation by Amadou Hampaté Bâ not so long ago, that in Africa an old man dying is like a library going down in flames' (p. vii). Okpewho suggests that as a vehicle of historical memory, the oral tradition and its durability can be viewed from several perspectives: from 'an examination of the ways in which the tradition adjusts itself to more recent social and political imperatives on the one hand and to the new audiovisual technology on the other, and finally to recommendations of ways to preserve and codify the oral text as well as find a berth for them in the new hypermedia' (p. xi). Accruing from the 2004 International Society for Oral Literature in Africa (ISOLA) conference in Banjul, capital of Gambia, with the poignant theme 'The Preservation and Survival of African Oral Literature', the papers in this special issue of *RAL* are timely responses to all the seminal debates surrounding the whole notion of 'orality' and its literariness. Thus, while the final paper in the volume, Oyekan Owomoyela's 'Preservation or Mummification? The Implications of Subjecting Traditional Texts to Modern Processes' (*RAL* 38:iii[2007] 170–82), questions the validity of the union between tradition and new technologies, Leif Lorentzon's 'Is African Oral Literature *Literature*?' (*RAL* 38:iii[2007] 1–12), which opens the volume, challenges and interrogates the claim inherent in the name of the organizing association itself (the 'International Society for Oral Literature in Africa').

Following Walter Ong's groundbreaking work in *Orality and Literacy*, other more recent theoretical and polemical treatises have weighed in on the twin issues of literacy and orality, on the one hand, and what is literary about oral literature on the other. Of course, so much depends on the ways a writer or critic perceives or defines literature itself. As Lorentzon notes: 'Albert Lord, who has done so much to establish (in his epochal *The Singer of Tales*) the integrity of the oral style of narration as against writing, finally comes in his later study to accept "the paradox of 'oral literature'" on the ground that "literature can be defined as 'carefully constructed verbal expression (*The Singer Resumes the Tale*)'"' (p. xi). Lorentzon's paper sets out to address the literary quality of African oral literature and argues that it is only by rephrasing the question in his title to read 'what is it that makes one oral utterance literary, turns it into verbal art, and not another?' (p. 2) that a Malinke griot or a Luo storyteller, for example, could feature in what he further describes as the distinction 'between orature and ordinary speech' (p. 3). Previous studies, including Monro Chadwick's highly influential, monumental three-volume work, *The Growth of Literature*, according to Lorentzon, have merely applied 'a Western perspective, and terminology, even when they discuss African oral literatures in part 3 of the third volume. However, in their account of various oral genres they circuitously, and admirably, indicate how oral literature differs from mere speech in each respective culture, while also using indigenous terms for various genres when they compare them to Western ones' (p. 3). Several contemporary scholars, he suggests, following Albert Lord's theory of performance, have emphasized the performative aspects and social importance of the epic in Africa while nothing is said of its literariness: 'Okpewho does discuss form, structure and style, but consistently in the Parry–Lord tradition. This seems to exclude a more direct discussion of literary rhetoric' (p. 5). However, the absence of a question as well as an answer in Okpewho's later identification of 'literature as "creative text [and oral literature as] literature delivered by word of mouth"' (p. 6) still raises the question, 'what is an orally transmitted creative text?' (p. 6). Two scholars who take exception to the performance-centred theory are Janheinz Jahn [1966] and Karin Barber [1991]: while Jahn stands in opposition to the Whiteley and Lerner approaches, Barber 'prefers a more inclusive concept of text as a configuration of signs coherently interpretable by a community of users, which makes it possible for her to concentrate on the text, the oral text, and its potential literariness' (p. 7). Jahn's concentration on the tradition or the material/text of the Fulani storyteller and Barber's pragmatic approach to the Oríkì of the Yoruba-speaking people of Nigeria in her seminal book, *I Could Speak Until Tomorrow* [1991], along with Peter Seitel's equally rigorously theorized study of Haya verbal art in Tanzania, offer, according to Lorentzon, 'the closest that societies such as the Yorùbá or the Haya come to the concept of literature we use in Western critical discourse today, or—to use the opposite perspective—this is as close as a post-Romantic notion of literature in the West comes to Yorùbá and Haya notions of verbal art' (p. 9).

Owomoyela's paper, which closes the volume, returns to the performance theory debate from the perspective of the preservation and survival of African oral literature. The paper asks, among other epistemic and rhetorical questions, whether the present practice of 'recording a traditional oral text on tape radically transforms its nature and deprives it of the fluidity and flexibility it enjoyed in its original state'—bearing in mind the fact that the recording process 'also confers on the recorded version a sort of transcendent authenticity and authority that could be fundamentally undeserved' (p. 170). The main thrusts of Owomoyela's arguments are both aesthetic and theoretical, and they concern possible confusion in the study of oral texts and performances vis-à-vis the flexibility that translates to vitality and 'the capacity oral texts have to grow and change in response to contextual stimuli' (p. 172) during performance, against the backdrop of their potential mummification when they are recorded and preserved: 'Other distortions attend the process of making folk texts available to modern modes of preservation or dissemination. Traditionally oral texts occur naturally—as routine elements of ordinary discourse (proverbs, for example), or as routine aspects of special occasions (rituals, for example)—but the collector who wishes to record them for publication usually must set up a command performance of some sort' (p. 173). The other thirteen choice essays in this special issue of *RAL* have responded to all the practical and theoretical issues concerning the 'survival' and 'preservation' of African oral literature and again, because the majority of them have regional foci, they are discussed under the relevant regions below.

Finally, *Against All Odds: Footage and Documentary from an International Conference of African Languages and Linguistics* documents a conference held in 2000 in Asmara, Eritrea, which brought together over 250 writers, scholars, academics, cultural activists, artists and publishers from all regions of Africa, Europe and North America. Taking up the legacy of the famous African writers' conference held at Makerere University in 1962, and culminating in the formulation and ratification of the Asmara Declaration on African Languages and Literature, the conference closed with a declaration of linguistic independence for the continent. With a star line-up of literary writers and scholars intervening in the language debate from all parts of the continent and the diaspora—including Ngugi wa Thiong'o of Kenya and Nawal al Saadawi of Egypt as co-chair, Kofi Anyidoho, Abena Busia, Kassahun Checole, Akinwumi Isola and Tanure Ojaide to name just a few—the conference revisited the familiar debate on African languages and challenged the notion of 'there being no languages in Africa'. Contending that African languages, oral and written, are the continent's most valuable assets and resources, the contributors assert that their quintessential role is to advocate for African languages 'what intellectuals the world over have done for their languages; for an understanding of languages as a key link in development and democratisation processes, imperative to literary expression, cultural confidence and popular use'.

(b) West Africa

Part IV of Martin Banham, ed., *A History of Theatre in Africa*, entitled 'Anglophone West Africa', comprises 'Nigeria' by Dapo Adelugba and Olu Obafemi with additional materials by Sola Adeyemi (pp. 138–58); 'Ghana' by James Gibbs (pp. 159–70); 'Sierra Leone' by Mohamed Sheriff (pp. 171–80); and 'A Note on Recent Anglophone Cameroonian Theatre' by Asheri Kilo (pp. 181–91). Echoing Omotoso's insistence, discussed above, that any understanding of theatre must begin with a concept of local histories, Adelugba and Obafemi commence their study of the development of Nigerian theatre by asserting that 'an authentic study of Nigerian arts and of Nigerian theatre from the colonial periods is a feasible project' (p. 138). With a myriad of ancient kingdoms, several ethnic, linguistic and religious groups living within its borders, a wide range of oral traditional sources, and archaeological surveys and written documentations, there are enough grounds on which 'claims can fairly be made for an ancient ancestry of Nigeria's fine and performing arts' (p. 139). The study, however, focuses on more recent history, where evidence is more secure and where what could be described as performance spaces that are 'a *mélange* of traditional and modern heritages, architecturally and in terms of content, styles, genres and forms' (p. 139) are readily observable. In its traditional manifestation, Nigerian theatre encompasses a myriad of popular traditions, including 'the Ekpe festival as a religious festival and dance drama, the Bori spirit mediumship as ritual drama, the Alarinjo as traditional travelling theatre, the Adimu-Orisa (Eyo) funeral rites, the Gelede, the Kwagh-hir theatre, the Bornu puppet show, the Yankamanci Hausa comedy, the Ikaki Tortoise masquerade, Ezeinogbe: the Igbo masquerade play, the Okun-Okura Masquerade Ensemble, the Urhobo Udje Dance Performance and the Ozidi Saga' (p. 140). Similar to its oral traditional counterpart and the controversies surrounding its literariness, these performances have been dogged by controversy over their classification and determination as ritual or as drama. However, it is as a transmutation of ritual into entertainment, according to Adelugba and Obafemi, that Nigerian traditional theatre has realized its quintessential evolutionary trend: 'Yoruba traditional theatre (also known as *Alarinjo* or *Eegun Alare*) is one of the most reliable aesthetic formats of the Nigerian theatre—one which perceives theatre as growing out of and along with ritual' (p. 140). The same kind of metamorphosis is traceable in the Alarinjo: from 'the masque-dramaturge as a courtly and then popular theatrical form comprising song, dance, music, costume and spectacle' and its emergence in a stage-by-stage process from ritual, festival and theatre, this 'is likely to hold true for the other ethnic theatres if and when their histories are properly researched and documented' (p. 142).

What is certain is that the traditional theatre as a dominant form that has been recreated, transposed and crystallized on the contemporary Nigerian stage, among other periods, constitutes the longest properly researched and documented period, 'the cultural nationalist phase from 1860–1944' (p. 142). The period witnessed the emergence of largely mission-owned concerts and musicals, 'whose firm ideological and utilitarian purpose was to use the theatre, in this case European concerts and Christian cantatas, as an entertainment medium to "humanise" and Christianise the educated native élite' (p. 143). A cultural nationalist backlash soon followed, and the last decades of the nineteenth century and first decades of the twentieth, assert Adelugba and Obafemi, witnessed 'the emergence of the small, well-educated and cultural élite after the establishment of indigenous churches, starting with the breakaway of the native Baptist Church from its parent body in Europe in 1888' (p. 145). A syncretic theatre aesthetic ensued, and the early decades of the twentieth century saw the secularization of theatrical entertainment in southern Nigeria, which was 'sufficiently advanced for the colonial government to gazette a "Theatre and Public Performance Regulations Ordinance"' (p. 147) by 1912. The achievement of popular native drama reached its climax in the 1930s and 1940s, and the arrival of Chief Hubert Ogunde in 1944, 'with the richness and virtuosity of his stagecraft and the popularity of his early plays', inaugurated what could be described as the indigenous drama tradition, and what is now 'generally referred to as Yoruba operatic (travelling) theatre, became a veritable and established theatre tradition in Nigeria' (p. 147). Between 1944 and the mid-1980s a healthy interaction occurred, including what Omotoso has described, in the work reviewed above, as 'the playing spaces of the collective rituals and festivals of the Yoruba of Akure' (Banham, ed., p. 4). In anecdotal support, he recalls absconding from 'the boarding-house at night to go and watch a play by Hubert Ogunde and his travelling theatre at the Court Hall near the Oba's palace' (Banham, ed., p. 4) after his ordinary-level examinations in 1961. Well documented and researched by theatre historians and scholars, 'Karin Barber [for example] states that the Yoruba travelling theatre "open[s] a window onto popular consciousness that is unique in its detail and clarity", revealing "the anxieties, preoccupations and convictions that underpin ordinary people's daily experience"' (p. 147). Like the performance aesthetics of the oral literature of Owomoyela's concern discussed above, the populist aesthetics of the Yoruba travelling theatre performances—built on 'loose improvisations, the spectacles of props and costume, lively and engaging musical ensemble, and the socio-political and cultural relevance of its content' (p. 150)—could not withstand the onslaught of modern technology and 'by the 1980s Yoruba travelling theatre's fortune had fallen on hard times, as the practitioners began to take advantage of modern technologies in the arts to produce their drama as home videos' (p. 150).

Modern Nigerian theatre also encompasses its literary theatre tradition, and Adelugba and Obafemi trace the evolution of this aspect of Nigerian theatre from 1956 onwards—with discussion of the ubiquitous Onitsha market popular drama, a small segment of the Onitsha market literature that flourished from the 1940s to the start of the Nigerian civil war in 1967. It served as an important link between the indigenous travelling theatre and its literary counterpart: 'The origin of the contemporary literary tradition must be traced to the drama of Henshaw, which Yemi Ogunbiyi has also described as a more refined form of Onitsha market literature in language and style' (p. 151). Against the background of an indigenous vibrant theatre tradition, the arrowhead of theatrical activities from 1957 to 1965 was at the iconic Mbari Club, based at the University of Ibadan, 'from which the first serious and significant generation of literary dramatists including Wole Soyinka and J.P. Clark (now Clark-Bekederemo), started' (pp. 152–3). However, while the first generation of literary dramatists resorted to myth and ritual for ideological and aesthetic inspiration, their successors are notable for their materialist bent: 'At varying levels of accomplishment, the plays of these dramatists are best characterised as theatre of ideology and politics, committed to social and historical reconstruction through class struggle and a proletarian consciousness' (p. 153). The 1990s ushered in the global dynamics that have brought about the collapse of the socialist world and enthroned the largely capitalist-driven globalization phenomenon, and these have prompted a recourse to popular theatre or theatre for development: 'The popular theatre—mainly unwritten, urban, improvised vernacular travelling theatre—is gradually merging with the literary theatre, in video productions and in the works of Femi Osofisan and younger university-trained dramatists such as Felix Okolo and Ben Tomoloju' (p. 155).

James Gibbs's account of the theatrical scene from the anglophone state of Ghana begins with what he describes as 'an ever-changing link with the past through performance, spectatorship and procedure' (p. 160) provided by annual festivals. However, Gibbs asserts that while the ever-changing elements that have contributed to the 'development of a distinctive theatre tradition in Ghana include dances, rhetorical forms, symbols and symbolic acts', the trickster figure of Ananse the spider, primarily associated with the dominant Akan language group, 'has inspired several local dramatists, both Akan and non-Akan, who have transformed the tales (*anansesem*) into plays (*anansegro*), which have become part of a national tradition of narrative theatre' (p. 160). Pioneering dramatist Efua Sutherland (1927–96) epitomizes this integration of elements of local conventions into accounts of experiences of world theatre including, 'for example, Greek tragedy, Irish dramatists, Bertolt Brecht, and *Lady Precious Stream*' (p. 161). Like its Nigerian counterpart, it is probably inevitable that Ghanaian theatre should derive some of its creative energies from Greek tragedy, as it was at the coast that Africa first made contact most directly with Europe. Thus, like Ola Rotimi's seminal *The God's Are Not to Blame* (an adaptation of *Oedipus Rex* into nineteenth-century Yorubaland), Sutherland's *Edufa* [1967] 'explored the parallels between Ghanaian and classical drama' (p. 164). But it is the 'Concert Party', according to Gibbs, that 'has been synonymous with "theatre" for hundreds of thousands of Ghanaians' (p. 162) over the past seventy years, and 'As a general rule, concert parties work from ideas generated within the company and shaped by group improvisation and performance' (p. 163). Besides the 'Sekyi tradition' of playwriting that runs parallel with the 'improvisation convention' of the Concert Party, two central texts from the 1930s have also contributed immensely to the development of literary drama in Ghana: *The Third Woman* by J.B. Danquah [1939] and *The Fifth Landing Stage* [1937] by F.K. Fiawoo. While the former echoes a story found in R.S. Rattray's *Akan-Ashanti Folk-Tales*, the latter, from beginning to end, 'engages in a dialogue with Europe, specifically with the condescension of missionaries towards African society, but also with Aristotelian or neo-classicist and Shakespearean ideas of the theatre' (p. 164).

For Gibbs it was Efua Sutherland, from the late 1950s until her death in 1996, who was an influential and 'sometimes a dominating figure in the Ghanaian theatre. The experiments already referred to led eventually to *The Marriage of Anansewa* (extract published 1975) that has become a classic of African theatre' (p. 164). Besides the emergence of significant dramatists such as the 'student who then called herself "Christina Ata Aidoo"' in the 1960s, the seeds that Sutherland had sown also began to bear fruit in the 1970s and 'After the young flight lieutenant J.J. Rawlings seized power on 4 June 1979, and after his "second coming" following a coup on 31 December 1981, politics and the arts became entwined once more. Playwrights Asiedu Yirenkyi...Ama Ata Aidoo (no longer "Christina") and Ben-Abdallah all held high office, often in Information, Education or Culture' (p. 166). A period that witnessed the promotion of festivals and the construction of the national theatre ensued, and together 'they take the "story" of Ghanaian drama into the 1990s and beyond, showing the interaction of a younger generation with ideas Sutherland had espoused' (pp. 166–7). While the preponderance of drama for community development in the 1990s rode on the back the mass education and social welfare programmes of the 1930s, one of Gibbs's primary conclusions is that 'a new impetus was given to the work by contact with the international theatre for development movement and by donor agency support' (p. 168). Again, as in Nigeria where global dynamics have enthroned the largely capitalist-driven globalization phenomenon, Ghanaian theatre at the end of the millennium had 'become dependent on sponsorship of one sort or another. Productions of *Amen Corner* and *All My Sons*, supported by American dollars, adaptations of Molière, with French assistance, and the continued involvement of the British Arts Council (*Yaa Asantewa* was "shipped" from Britain to Ghana in 2001) provide further evidence of this dimension' (pp. 168–9).

Mohamed Sheriff's 'Sierra Leone' (pp. 171–81) and Asheri Kilo's 'A Note on Recent Anglophone Cameroonian Theatre' (pp. 181–91) examine similar histories of theatre in the West African states of Sierra Leone and Cameroon respectively. Sheriff contends that, as in Nigeria and Ghana, three stages in the development of theatre in Sierra Leone are discernible: there is traditional theatre from the pre-colonial era which is as old Sierra Leone's existence itself, and a second stage mediated by the colonial intrusion into Sierra Leonean societies, 'leading to the birth of a hybrid western-style African theatre as a result of both the influence of European culture and a reaction by indigenous Sierra Leoneans to the dominance of British plays' (p. 171). The post-independence era or third stage, suggests Sheriff, 'has seen an acceleration in the pace of the movement away from a purely western theatre and the further development of western-style African theatre and a revival of Sierra Leone's traditional theatrical form in the capital' (p. 171). Kilo's contribution, on the other hand, focuses on two out of the ten administrative provinces, namely the North-West and the South-West provinces, that constitute what can be referred to as anglophone Cameroon. The conditions of their history and their minority status, according to Kilo, have dictated the creative responses of anglophone dramatists: 'Compared to other Anglophone theatres in Africa and to the Francophone theatre in Cameroon itself, Anglophone theatre is under-published in terms of texts and under-performed, since the artists in western Cameroon find themselves in a disadvantaged minority position' (p. 181).

David Whittaker and Mpalive-Hangson Msiska's *Chinua Achebe's Things Fall Apart*, and Isidore Okpewho, ed., *Chinua Achebe's Things Fall Apart: A Casebook*, are two seminal works anticipating the fiftieth anniversary of the publication of Achebe's magnum opus, *Things Fall Apart* [1958]. As Okpewho notes in his introduction, since its inauguration of 'a long and continuing tradition of inquiry into the problematic relations between the West and the nations of the Third World that were once European colonies' (p. 3), Achebe's novel has attracted a whole range of critical responses and a mixed reception. While Whittaker and Msiska describe the novel as having 'sold around ten million copies worldwide and been translated into over forty-five languages'

(p. xi), Okpewho describes it as existing 'in close to sixty languages (including English), with total sales of nearly nine million copies since its publication in 1958' (p. 3). After an exhaustive, characteristically lucid introduction (pp. 3–53), chronicling all the essentials of Achebe's iconic postcolonial novel, Okpewho asserts that the choice of contributions to the casebook 'is aimed at exploring the diversity of issues that have been raised over time in the study of *Things Fall Apart*' (p. 38). Giving the first statement to Achebe himself, quoting his 1975 essay 'The African Writer and the English Language' (pp. 55–65), the casebook moves through essays that provide a variety of insights: 'ethnography, literary and critical analysis, ideology, pedagogy and theory' (p. 35). The volume ends with Charles H. Rowell's 'An Interview with Achebe' (pp. 249–72), in which Achebe 'addresses a variety of questions that students and general readers, especially in the West, have asked of this engaging novel' (p. 35).

Meanwhile, the nine seminal essays assembled by Okpewho are eloquent testimonies to the lasting legacy of *Things Fall Apart*, including the Nigerian scholar Ezenwa-Ohaeto's 'delightfully pious portrait, *Chinua Achebe: A Biography*...that will be of signal service to those investigating the development of the writer, not least in assessing Achebe's art in the context of his many commitments, both national and international' (p. 4). The volume opens with Clement Okafor's 'Igbo Cosmology and the Parameters of Individual Accomplishment in *Things Fall Apart*' ([1998] pp. 67–81); Damian U. Opata's 'Eternal Sacred Order Versus Conventional Wisdom: A Consideration of Moral Culpability in the Killing of Ikemefuna' ([1987] pp. 83–94); Harold Scheub's ' "When a man fails alone": A Man and his Chi in Chinua Achebe's *Things Fall Apart*' ([1970] pp. 95–112); and Neil Ten Kortenaar's 'How the Center Is Made to Hold in *Things Fall Apart*' ([1991] pp. 123–45). From Okafor's attempt to establish 'an appropriate epistemological framework that can profitably inform our critical discussions of *Things Fall Apart*' (p. 67) to Kortenaar's deconstruction of what is told us of the district commissioner and simultaneous reconstruction of 'a higher level where we join the author in seeing around the Europeans' (p. 124), these essays take different critical and theoretical standpoints to establish what Kortenaar describes as the overall effect of Achebe's plain style, designed to stress the everyday ordinariness of Igbo life: 'This world is comprehensible. The transition in the book from precolonization Africa to an Africa that has felt the European presence is, in terms of style, unremarkable. Indeed, because the transition is so fluid, Achebe has to draw our attention to it by means of divisions: the encroachment of the European missionaries takes place while Okonkwo is in exile during the division identified as part two' (pp. 124–5).

The other significant essays in the volume are Clayton G. Mackenzie's 'The Metamorphosis of Piety in Chinua Achebe's *Things Fall Apart*' ([1996] pp. 147–64); Rhonda Cobham's 'Problems of Gender and History in the Teaching of *Things Fall Apart*' ([1990] pp. 165–80); Biodun Jeyifo's 'Okonkwo and his Mother: *Things Fall Apart* and Issues of Gender in the Constitution of African Postcolonial Discourse' ([1993] pp. 181–200); Bu-Buakei Jabbi's 'Fire and Transition in *Things Fall Apart*' ([1975] pp. 201–19); and Ato Quayson's

'Realism, Criticism, and the Disguises of Both: A Reading of Chinua Achebe's *Things Fall Apart* with an Evaluation of the Criticism Relating to It' ([1994] pp. 221–48). Besides bringing the feminist concerns and the important issue of female authority to the fore, the last crop of essays also utilize different critical and theoretical positions to establish what Cobham has described as 'a slanging match between those who felt that texts like *Things Fall Apart* should be expurgated from the syllabus and those who wanted to tell the censorship group what they would like to do to them if he were a member of the class' (pp. 165–6). Most of the contributions to the casebook date from the 1990s and, according to Okpewho, they attest 'to the continuing appeal of *Things Fall Apart* as a classic literary statement and its significance as a paradigmatic comment on the postcolonial condition' (p. 46).

Similarly, Whittaker and Msiska's four-part guide to Achebe's *Things Fall Apart* has been designed to 'provide a scholarly exegesis of the text and introduce readers to important contextualizing historical and cultural perspectives, as well as to provide a detailed historical overview of the changing critical responses to the novel' (p. xii). Part I, entitled 'Text and Contexts', introduces the author, the novel and its literary and cultural contexts. The authors approach *Things Fall Apart* as a work that looks back at a pre-colonial culture mediated by epochal changes wrought by British colonialism and one that also looks forward to the future, 'inscribed with both the idealism and anxieties of the decade in which it was written' (p. 33). Part II, 'Critical History' (pp. 35–76), examines the history of the critical reception of the novel, and the myriad critical views and theoretical approaches used to examine it over the past five decades: 'Our argument is that despite massive differences of opinion among Achebe's critics, it is evident that the abiding question they have been raising has been: what kind of text is *Things Fall Apart*, in terms of style, mode and meaning' (p. 39). Part III is entitled 'Critical Readings' and it comprises five choice essays and excerpts from the work of a number of critics that were discussed in the first two parts: 'Extract from "The Tragic Conflict in the Novels of Chinua Achebe" ' (pp. 79–84) by Abiola Irele; 'Extract from "Sophisticated Primitivism: The Syncretism of Oral and Literate Modes in Achebe's *Things Fall Apart*" ' (pp. 85–92) by Abdul JanMohammed; 'Extract from "For Chinua Achebe: The Resilience and the Predicament of Obierika" ' (pp. 93–103) by Biodun Jeyifo; Florence Stratton's 'How Could Things Fall Apart for Whom They Were Not Together?' (pp. 104–19); and 'Extract from "Realism, Criticism, and the Disguises of Both: A Reading of Chinua Achebe's *Things Fall Apart*" ' (pp. 120–8) by Ato Quayson. Part IV, 'Further Reading and Web Resources' (pp. 129–38), contains suggestions for further reading on all the topics covered in the study guide, ranging from the number of illuminating essays that Achebe himself has published, through the turbulent history of colonialism in Africa, to the range of postcolonial literary approaches that are particularly relevant to the study of *Things Fall Apart*.

In a similar vein are two book-length studies on the equally compulsive oeuvre of Achebe's contemporary and 1986 Nobel laureate in literature, Wole Soyinka: Anjali Gera Roy, ed., *Wole Soyinka: An Anthology of Recent Criticism*, and Mpalive-Hangson Msiska's *Postcolonial Identity in*

Wole Soyinka. While Msiska's groundbreaking study examines in five lengthy chapters the whole notion of postcolonial identity in Soyinka, the former collects fifteen essays examining, from different critical and theoretical positions, the prodigious creative output of 'one of the "big men" of the African world of letters, among whom we may include fellow Nigerian giant Chinua Achebe, Senegalese poet President Leopold Senghor and Kenyan activist writer Ngugi wa Thiong'o' (Roy, ed., p. 13). The starting point for Roy's lucid introduction to the volume is the construction of the patriarchal tradition of the 'national masculine' in the postcolony, which these 'big men' of letters pioneered along with their political counterparts elsewhere in the world—Nehru, Nasser and Nkrumah. A critique of 'the essentialism of the discourse based on a politics of otherness that the big men constructed' (p. 14), against the backdrop of the different 'posts' and postcolonial theory in particular (which, suggests Roy, has challenged the claims of these patriarchal constructions to represent the people as a whole), is how Soyinka's 'brand of well-intentioned but youthful idealism has come to be increasingly inter-rogated in the wake of the "failure" of the nation' (p. 14). However, both Roy and Msiska are in agreement that Soyinka's brand of idealism—one that is described by Msiska as an 'elaboration of postcolonial identity and his attempt to ground conceptions of subjectivity in an indigenous epistemology, and Western culture and their legacies within the postcolonial formation in a hybrid world-view' (p. x)—is coterminous with the agenda of an African nationalist who has remained 'a genuine internationalist who is as keen on what happens outside Africa as he is on events in his local patch' (p. x). The volume of essays is divided into four parts. Part I, 'Biography and Autobiography', comprises Ndaeyo Uko's 'Crossing Soyinka's Path' (pp. 31–37); Chukwuma Okoye's 'Soyinka: Text, Embodied Practice and Postcolonial Resistance' (pp. 38–53); and Tunde Awosanmi's 'Wole Soyinka's Psychic Mask: Refortification and Transition into (Self)-Destination' (pp. 54–70). Together these essays explore various aspects of what Roy earlier describes as 'the titanic, almost larger than life, personality of the activist writer' (p. 14) and how his inherent activism has become the most compelling factor of Soyinka's literary and critical works. Since James Gibbs pioneered the approach of examining Soyinka from five points of view—'as a man, as a Yoruba, as an academic, as a political activist, and as a writer' (p. 15)—in his seminal *Critical Perspectives on Wole Soyinka* [1980], critical practice, according to Roy, has focused increasingly on Soyinka the man, 'the colossal figure who friends and admirers know as Kongi. This has become such a standard practice in Soyinka studies that Biodun Jeyifo, in his new book *Wole Soyinka: Politics, Poetics and Postcolonialism*, makes the strong personality of the writer the focus for examining his literary corpus' (p. 15).

Eight of the fifteen essays in the volume are collected in part II, and focus on different aspects of Soyinka's plays and dramaturgy. They include Victor Samson Dugga's 'The Yoruba Roots of *A Dance of the Forest* and *Death and the King's Horseman*' (pp. 71–84); Eckhard Breitinger's 'Wole Soyinka: *Death and the King's Horseman*' (pp. 85–99); G.A. Ioratim-Uba's 'Sound Patterns in Wole Soyinka's *The Trials of Brother Jero* and *Jero's Metamorphosis*' (pp. 100–15); Joseph McLaren's '*Kongi's Harvest* and Soyinka's Mockery of State Power' (pp. 116–29); and Ameh Dennis Akoh's 'From Ogunian Metaphysics to Proletarian Engagement: Soyinka's New Artistic Vision' (pp. 130–43). It is in Soyinka's dramatic works in particular that his cyclic view of African history is vividly evident. This is traced in the volume, beginning with what Dugga describes as the Yoruba roots of Soyinka's plays—an integral aspect of the five points approach to Soyinka studies pioneered by Gibbs— through Breitinger's study of 'the relevance of indigenous ceremonial traditions in colonial or postcolonial contexts' (p. 86) in *Death and the King's Horseman*, to Akoh's demarcation of 'the critical shift from the articulation of Ogunian metaphysics in his early plays to a mundane concern with social realities in his writings beginning with *From Zia with Love*' (p. 130). Completing the coverage of Soyinka's prodigious dramatic output are Liwhu Betiang's 'Postmodernism in Nigerian Drama: A Reading of Wole Soyinka's *The Beatification of Area Boy* as Postmodern Carnivalesque' (pp. 144–61); Hilarious N. Ambe's 'Wole Soyinka's *The Beatification of Area Boy*: Not Just a Lagosian Kaleidoscope' (pp. 162–77); and Ayan Gangopadhyay's '"Con-text" as a Problematic: Performing the "Other" in the Theater of Wole Soyinka' (pp. 178–92).

Parts III and IV are focused on Soyinka's 'Fiction' and 'Poetry' respectively, and comprise Anjali Gera Roy and Viney Kirpal's 'Men as Archetypes: Characterization in Soyinka's Novels' (pp. 193–202); Brinda Mehta's '(De)-Orientalizing the Female Self: Selected Feminine Characterizations in Wole Soyinka's *The Interpreters, Season of Anomy* and *Madmen and Specialists*' (pp. 203–26); Pushpinder Syal's 'Discourse Styles and Forms in "Idanre"' (pp. 227–42); and Ismail Bala Garba's 'Beyond Critical Orthodoxy: Wole Soyinka's *Samarkand*' (pp. 243–50). From the study of 'men as archetypes' by Roy and Kirpal to Mehta's equally illuminating articulation of their de-orientalized female counterparts in Soyinka's novels, one of the primary conclusions of the critics is that the alien reader, to paraphrase Roy and Kirpal, might miss the significance of the numerous allusions in the characterization of these men and women, and overlook the ingenuity of the writer's method: 'The deification of the male characters in the novels is accomplished by mere suggestion and through oblique references to mythical parallels. But in the portrayal of his female characters, Soyinka indulges in unabashed apotheosis' (p. 198).

In his lucid introduction, 'The Problem of Identity in Soyinka's Life and Letters' (pp. xiii–xxxvii), Msiska examines Soyinka's oeuvre against the backdrop of what is described as the writer's lifelong quest to escape from 'that moment of cultural nationalism that simply seeks to negate the Other. For him, the challenge for a radical African cultural practice begins with a fundamental reconceptualization of the relationship between Self and Other, searching for a concept of cultural authenticity that does not pander to the fiction of purity or, indeed, to the self-proclaimed supremacy of the colonial Other' (p. xxix). Recognizing the writer's search, according to Msiska, must lead the Soyinka reader or critic to an understanding of the broader epistemological and political project that his work exemplifies: 'He never simply inhabits the universal or the particular or the conjunction between the two—he occupies them strategically and parasitically, affirmatively as well as antagonistically' (p. xxxvi). Chapters 1 and 2, entitled 'Myth, History and Postcolonial Modernity' (pp. 1–44) and 'Tradition and Modernity' (pp. 45–77), examine the ways in which Soyinka deconstructs and reconstitutes the complex relationship between history and myth 'as constitutive paradigms of postcolonial modernity' (p. 1) vis-à-vis the ubiquitous roles of traditional African culture and its inevitable conflict with Western traditions. Msiska suggests that Soyinka constructs a new critical consciousness in plays such as *The Swamp Dwellers* [1964], and argues that the 'solution to the problem of Western encroachment on African tradition is neither the wholesale adoption of tradition nor modernity, but, rather, an agonistic disbelief in both and a concomitant perpetual quest for a transcendent plenitude' (p. 46).

Chapters 3 and 4 respectively examine 'The Banality of Postcolonial Power' (pp. 79–110) and 'The Abyss of Postcolonial Formation' (pp. 111–50). Soyinka's demystification of postcolonial authority and what Msiska describes as 'this promiscuous melange of identity and power that Soyinka attends to in a number of works' (p. 80) are the objects of critical focus in chapter 3. Chapter 4 examines a number of texts that attempt to 'effect . . . an enabling inhabitation of the abyss of postcolonial transition'. Msiska argues that, in *The Road* [1965], *Madmen and Specialists* [1973], and the two poetry collections *A Shuttle in the Crypt* [1972] and *Mandela's Earth and Other Poems* [1989], 'one of Soyinka's main aims is to delve deeper into the manifestation of postcolonial power as banality and to engage its metaphysical foundation' (p. 111). The final chapter, 'Resources for Redemption' (pp. 151–64), summarizes the 'clear sense of the need to imagine the possibility of change' that has been Soyinka's major preoccupation in every text he has written so far: 'There are, of course, times when his grimly satirical representation of the Nigerian and African postcolonial situation seems a little too pessimistic, but it has to be admitted that even at his most sombre, [Soyinka] still expresses a strong belief in the capacity of individuals and communities to transcend the tendency towards absorbing all difference into the dominant political imaginary of a community or nation' (p. 151).

Ezenwa-Ohaeto, *Subject, Context and the Contours of Nigerian Fiction: Studies Contrasting the Postcolonial Notion* is a collection of Ezenwa-Ohaeto's essays that appeared in different publications and academic journals from 1987 to 2001 on different aspects of Nigerian literature. The posthumous collection, edited by Eckhard Breitinger, is partly intended 'to pay homage to Ezenwa-Ohaeto as a critic, to appreciate and complement his life's work, but it is also meant not to let important insight into recent Nigerian writing disappear from the international stage of literary criticism' (p. xiv). Breitinger suggests that since his groundbreaking *Biography of Chinua Achebe* [1997] Ezenwa-Ohaeto has demonstrated how the biographical approach reveals that postcolonial writers' 'literary responses to the political turbulences are more than mere reflections to social circumstances. Individuality and the personality of the writers—both results of biographical development and growth— guarantee that their texts grow beyond the level of simple reflections of realities or perceptions of ideologically conditioned realities as Marxist social realists and critics propagate' (p. xii). Ezenwa-Ohaeto's other salient contributions to Nigerian writing and its criticism are in the areas of the vexed issue of the language debate and the relevance of gender issues in Nigerian letters. While he gives much critical attention to the work of female writers from southern Nigeria—Flora Nwapa and Buchi Emecheta— the plight of the female writer from northern Nigeria has not escaped Ezenwa-Ohaeto's critical attention. The volume is in four parts: part I, entitled 'The Contours of Criticism', comprises 'The Critic and Socio-Cultural Responses: Implications for Pragmatic Criticism' (pp. 1–9) and 'Criticism and Communication: Pidgin Literature as a Paradigm' (pp. 10–16), and these essays set the tone for Ezenwa-Ohaeto's critical standards and concerns in relation to what Breitinger has described as his lifelong attempt to 'privilege oral, spoken sources of information over western style written appreciation of literature' (p. xiii). Other essays reprinted in the collection have been reviewed in earlier volumes of *YWES*.

(c) East and Central Africa

Part V of Martin Banham, ed., *A History of Theatre in Africa*, entitled 'East Africa', comprises 'Ethiopia and Eritrea' by Jane Plastow (pp. 192–205); 'Kenya' by Ciarunji Chesaina and Evan Mwangi (pp. 206–32); 'Tanzania' by Amandina Lihamba (pp. 233–46); and 'Uganda' by Eckhard Breitinger (pp. 247–64). Plastow's survey examines the different references to Ethiopia and Abyssinia that 'litter works of literature dating back to the Bible, and are in no way reliable guides to the ancient history of the nations called Ethiopia and Eritrea' (p. 192). Plastow suggests that Ethiopia, which 'simply meant the land of black people and was therefore a reference by ancient Greeks to the African continent', should be distinguished from the first known empire in the region called the land of Punt or Sheba, 'which was converted from animism to Judaism consequent to a visit by Makeda, the Queen of Sheba, to King Solomon in the tenth century BC' (p. 192). Following the trail of legend in modern-day Ethiopia, which says that the queen had a son by Solomon, and many aspects of Ethiopian church practice which reflect a Judaic inheritance, perhaps one place to begin a chronicle of performance terms could be with the dancing priests of the Ethiopian Orthodox Church: 'Using great drums and sistrum the priests perform a religious dance or *shibsheba* in full vestments on holy days' (p. 192). After tracing early references to performance that demonstrate the power of state and church, and their wish to control the populace, Plastow suggests that specialist church performance forms 'further developed in the sixth century, when an Ethiopian priest, Saint Yared, is credited with having developed both a unique form of musical notation and *qene* poetry beloved of the Ethiopian intelligentsia' (p. 193). The formative influence of *qene* poetry over the writing style of important Ethiopian playwrights such as Kebede Mikael, Endalkachew Makonnen and Mengistu Lemma is further evidence of the dominance of these art forms: 'Over the centuries specialist church schools developed for the study of religious dance— *aquaquam*—music—*zema*—and poetry—*qene*. By the eighteenth century the *aquaquam beit* (dance house) in the imperial capital of Gondar had 276 masters, and students might study the intricacies and strict rules of their disciples for up to eight years' (p. 193). While it is relatively easy to document these elite art forms and markers of the extremely hierarchical feudal Ethiopian–Eritrean society, 'designed to impress and differentiate the ruling class from the mass of the peasantry', Plastow contends that, 'As has been the case in many cultures, it is far more difficult to find information on peasant art forms, especially before the twentieth century' (p. 194). Making up 25 per cent of the Ethiopian population, the Amhara ethnic group and the tradition of performers commonly referred to as the *azmaris* provide the only accessible information in modern Ethiopia concerning peasant art forms: 'Information on other performance art forms in the empire is meager. Only the highland peoples had a written language, and this was controlled by the church and state, so we have few records of peasant activities' (p. 194). The dawn of modern drama in Ethiopia is traceable to the return to Ethiopia in 1912 by the Amhara nobleman, Tekle Hawariat: 'By this time, it should be noted, Eritrea had become a distinct and separate entity; an Italian colony with borders delineated in 1890 . . . Tekle Hawariat's play, *Fabula: Yawreoch Commedia* (Fable: The Comedy of Animals), was a satire on the fables of La Fontaine. In its preface the playwright bemoans the absence of drama in Ethiopia' (p. 195). The new art form inaugurated by Hawariat is unique in many senses, and among its many characteristics articulated by Plastow is the link it establishes with 'common folk-story patterns, where anthropomorphic animal stories were used to teach social values' (p. 195). Plastow notes the ways in which 'the playwright had attempted, however thinly, to disguise his meaning. This conforms with Amhara linguistic conventions' (p. 195). However, in spite of being seen as an import from Europe and a literary form divorced from the music and dance traditions of the people, Ethiopian drama continues to express itself in Ethiopian languages, especially Amharic. On a continent in which the language debate has raged for more than five decades now, this development ensures the drama continues to be 'mediated through an Ethiopian sensibility from its beginning in a way that was not possible in colonized African nations' (p. 196). From 1930 when Emperor Haile Selassie came to the throne until the replacement of his imperial regime by the military Dergue in 1974, Ethiopian theatre thrived in an atmosphere of cat and mouse between the new generation of playwrights, with the emperor walking out of performances he found distasteful: 'between 1974 and 1977 a host of plays by Tsegaye, Tesfaye and Mengistu, but also by others such as Abe Gubegna, Berhanu Zerihun and Taddele Gebre-Hiwot, debated political alternatives and attracted audiences longing for information on the changing Ethiopian order' (p. 200). With the overthrow of the Dergue in 1991 by northern Tigrayan-led forces, the Amhara hegemony also came to an end and today, while 'Amharic video-making is growing rather than the theatre', according to Plastow, 'there are few works dealing with the realities of life or questioning and engaging with contemporary Ethiopian society' (p. 202).

The duo of Ciarunji Chesaina and Evan Mwangi examine the history of theatre in the equally dominant East African state of Kenya. The starting point of their study is what they describe as the indigenous roots of contemporary Kenyan drama; they consider the intricate links between Kenyan people's philosophical outlook on death and morality vis-à-vis the various myths in the people's oral tradition and the ways they have contributed significantly to the development of drama in Kenya. While these philosophical outlooks point to the origins of indigenous Kenyan drama, the drama also took diverse forms that could be categorized as follows: 'role-play and children's games; the arts of storytelling and folk-tale; impersonation; improvisation; ritual-related drama; and dance drama' (p. 208). The strong interlacing of traditional drama with the life of the particular community, suggest the authors, merely points to the need to be aware of the futility of any attempt at a discussion based on rigid categorizations: 'There are of course overlaps in the social contexts, and some of the forms intermingle to strengthen one another. It is for this reason that this overview follows a holistic approach' (p. 208). Again, while many Kenyan communities adopt different artistic means and devices in arriving at specific goals, the abiding characteristics of these traditional forms are located in their communality and close links with the various forms of ritual: 'In the traditional forms, the line between the so-called performer and the audience was very thin, but the forms introduced during the colonial era were predominantly aimed at a specific audience' (p. 216). The colonial intrusion into Kenyan communities saw the introduction of, among other characteristics, dramatic forms that were designed for the stage, and for particular audiences. Colonial forms and attributes have since intermingled with the traditional indigenous forms to produce what Chesaina and Mwangi describe further as today's post-colonial Kenyan theatre: 'By this time theatre had established itself as a tool of entertainment among the settler community and as an agent of anti-colonial struggle among indigenous Kenyans. These two strands developed side by side in post-colonial Kenya' (p. 217). Made up of over fifty ethnic communities, postcolonial Kenya has attempted to forge a national theatre, 'especially through the Kenyan Schools and Colleges Drama Festival, which brings together performances from different parts of the republic' (p. 217).

Amandina Lihamba's account of the history of theatre in neighbouring Tanzania begins with a similar examination of the 'inter-relationships between the environment, societies and peoples, their modes of production, the cultural practices and aesthetics that have supported these, inputs brought about by technological developments, population and social movements from within and outside the continent of Africa, as well as the creativity, dynamism and ingenuity of the people as they respond to developments and changes individually and collectively' (p. 233). The history of Tanzania, an integral aspect of the East African community, suggests Lihamba, 'is so intimately connected with that of the rest of East Africa that sometimes it is difficult to speak of a Tanzanian cultural history' (p. 233). Consequently, the performed poetry and dances of the various indigenous communities constituting the geopolitical entity known as Tanzania today are part and parcel of a network of several islands in the Indian Ocean, including Zanzibar and Pemba, hugging the mainland, and this geography is important 'because its features have informed performances and their content. Water and dry land, mountain and valley, the coast and the hinterland, the grassland and the forest have always provided contrasting social and aesthetic elements' (p. 233). Lihamba traces the evolution of Tanzanian theatre in three stages, beginning with the period from 200 BC to AD 1800, when 'a Bantu-speaking people [who] populated the coast of Tanzania by the year 200 BC... became part of the Swahili-speaking communities that expanded to the whole of the coastal area between the Limpopo River in the south and the Horn of Africa in the north, known as Azania' (p. 233). From 1800 to 1960, Tanzanian theatre entered what Lihamba has described as a post-Portuguese defeat era in East Africa, which ushered in other European powers to trade in the area. From 1920 to 1960, 'the theatre scene in Tanzania changed considerably after the First World War, when Germany was defeated and its colonial territories divided amongst the victors. Tanzania was given to Britain to be administered as a trust territory. A period of aggressive introduction of western theatre thus began' (p. 236). The post-independence era, 1961 to 2000, as in other parts of the continent, ushered in a period of bold innovations in Tanzania and, 'Because of the nationalistic fervor that prevailed immediately after independence, theatre performances portrayed issues that dealt with anti-colonialism, nationalism, liberation and development' (p. 239).

Eckhard Bretinger's coverage of 'Uganda' (pp. 247–64) completes this examination of the history of theatre in East Africa. According to Breitinger, two icons of Ugandan theatre, Robert Serumaga, Uganda's first internationally renowned dramatist, and Okot p'Bitek, the Acoli poet and first Ugandan director of the National theatre in Kampala, have since answered the pertinent question that has plagued Ugandan and by extension African theatre: 'whether theatre existed in Africa before the colonial powers introduced formal western theatre, performed in purpose-built theatre houses, on proscenium arch stages to paying audiences' (p. 247). While both Serumaga and p'Bitek see the national theatre as a representation of 'the "other" theatrical tradition, that of colonial cultural imposition' (p. 247), Breitinger argues that the relationship between traditional, colonial and postcolonial/modern theatre, and 'the co-existence of mutually supportive theatre in Luganda (or other Ugandan languages) and theatre in English' exist in the fact that they 'reside predominantly in different organizational structures, with their own specific histories, namely the Christian churches with their missions and their plays, the schools, the Makerere University campus, and civic organizations and public administration' (pp. 247–8).

(d) Southern Africa

Neil Lazarus's 'The South African Ideology: The Myth of Exceptionalism, the Idea of Renaissance' (*SAQ* 103:iv[Fall 2004] 607–28) and Shaun Irlam's 'Unravelling the Rainbow: The Remission of Nation in Post-Apartheid Literature' (*SAQ* 103:iv[2004] 695–718) are the predominantly literary essays in the *South Atlantic Quarterly*'s special issue on South Africa under the title, 'After the Thrill Is Gone: A Decade of Post-Apartheid South Africa'. The nature and conditions of post-apartheid South Africa is the primary concern of these articles in particular, and the special issue of the

South Atlantic Quarterly in general. Lazarus offers what he calls, at the start of his essay, 'something of an autobiographical note' (p. 607), while Irlam comments on the 'prayer and the jussive mode' that have governed and sustained the 'new' South Africa over the past ten years. After more than three centuries of white domination that began in the 1650s, the inescapable fact, according to Irlam, 'is that little has changed in the material conditions defining South African society since the end of apartheid' (p. 697). Irlam's essay explores notable trends in literature from the post-apartheid era 'in order to take the pulse of South Africa now that the first thrill of nationhood has ebbed' (p. 697). One of the starting points of his study of post-apartheid writing is Rob Nixon's analogy (in his 1996 essay 'Aftermaths') that compares South Africa after apartheid with eastern Europe after the Cold War; Nixon 'predict[ed] that writers in post-apartheid South Africa would face predicaments similar to those already encountered by writers from the old Soviet bloc' (p. 698). While the crimes of apartheid served 'as a constant goad to a *littérature engagée*, permitting the dissident writer to become a sort of folk hero at home and abroad', one of Irlam's primary conclusions is that Nixon's warning that the post-apartheid era would render the activist role of the writer irrelevant, and leave the writer marginal to the new national agendas, 'has been borne out in a kind of willed marginalization enacted in much new fiction' (p. 698). This has given birth to a new culture of introspection and 'separate development'—'a new literature of separate development is emerging, in which communities once submerged in their common resistance to apartheid now finally exercise the liberty to explore their own histories and assert their own agendas' (p. 698). As a result, he suggests, the political character of writing during the apartheid years has been replaced by more private, introspective and confessional modes: 'One observes the rise of a certain cultural chauvinism and sometimes even ethnic nationalism that was notably absent during the apartheid era, but became highly volatile in the violent clashes during the period of transition between 1990 and 1994' (p. 699).

Lazarus's equally rigorously theorized contribution considers seminal African novels of the 1960s and 1970s and how they influenced his own fledgling political awareness. He was, he writes, like many other left-wing white students at the time, struggling 'to rise to the challenge posed by the Black consciousness movement, which had sharpened the ideological lines of struggle in the country, among other lines quite rightly making it more difficult for whites to take refuge in a scrupulous *rhetoric* of nonracialism while doing absolutely nothing to oppose apartheid as a social and political *reality*' (p. 608, original italics). Lazarus notes that despite the 'pitfalls of national consciousness' represented in Ayi Kwei Armah's 1968 novel *The Beautyful Ones Are Not Yet Born*, and postcolonial African literature as a whole, 'One could scarcely fail to register . . . the disjuncture that obtained between the political valuations of time in Armah's novel and in South African radical thought' (p. 609). However, what animated the young Lazarus was the experience of decolonization that was the subject of Armah's and other postcolonial novels, and how South Africa could learn from them 'in order not to suffer the same fate as had befallen such other recently decolonized states as Algeria, Nigeria, Kenya and Uganda' (p. 610). Lazarus discusses what he calls a 'categorical differentiation', which viewed South Africa with a certain insularity and provincialism and led to the conventional wisdom that South Africa 'would be able to solve the problems of development (and maldevelopment or underdevelopment) experienced by other African states, rather than fall victim to them; to control its own fate; to write its own scripts rather than find itself written into ones not of its own devising' (pp. 610–11). The result was a complex interaction of the 'myth of exceptionalism' with the 'idea of renaissance'. This, suggests Lazarus, operated against the backdrop of 'Thabo Mbeki's latter-day annunciation as Uncle Sam's good-man-in-Africa...[and] bears intriguing implications for the cultural dimensions of the "African Renaissance," at least insofar as the matter of African identity is concerned. Scholars of African literature will of course be quite used to this subject, which has been a staple of criticism for almost half a century now, and which has characteristically announced itself in the form of the question, what does it take to be an African writer?' (p. 618).

Retrospectively reviewed is Anthony O'Brien's book-length study, *Against Normalization: Writing Radical Democracy in South Africa*, published in 2001, which examines radical impulses in South African literature and politics against the background of what he calls 'the high tide of antiapartheid struggle in the late eighties as the vivid present, both of South African culture and of its representations abroad' (p. 1). Focusing predominantly on the work of less well-known writers, most of them black, rather than the much-discussed André Brink, Breyten Breytenbach, J.M. Coetzee, Athol Fugard and Nadine Gordimer, one of O'Brien's central arguments is that 'the better-known white writers have no place in the formation of a radical democratic culture (a point argued in chapters 2 and 3 in the context of Njabulo Ndebele's cultural theory and the debates of the transition), but, against the judgement of most metropolitan critics, I do see their place as more marginal' (p. 2). What O'Brien describes as 'the neo-colonial outcome of an anticolonial struggle' (p. 3) bears remarkable resemblances to Lazarus's articulation of the complex interaction of a myth of exceptionalism with the idea of renaissance discussed above: 'By "neo-colonial" I mean to refer to the interest of foreign and local capital in preserving the structural inequalities of South African racial capitalism that oppress the everyday lives of black working people' (pp. 3–4). The whole notion of 'Radical Democracy and the Electoral Sublime', which is the object of critical focus in chapter 1, can be described as the culmination of 'Anticolonial and antiracist nationalism, feminism, the "new social movements", post-structuralist critique, and identitarian politics all [of which] contribute other questions to an unfolding meaning of the term radical democracy, as can be gauged by work such as Paul Gilroy's *The Black Atlantic*, which has deeply influenced this book' (p. 7). Chapters 2 and 3, entitled 'Njabulo Ndebele and Radical-Democratic Culture' (pp. 36–75) and 'Against Normalization: Cultural Identity from Below' (pp. 76–102) respectively, are sustained theoretical debates about what Njabulo Ndebele has described as the whole notion of 'culture from below': 'In retrospect, Ndebele's critical resumption and reworking of Black consciousness "givens" for the moment of transition beyond apartheid can be seen to have introduced a new cycle of freedom, a new political aesthetic, for South African emergent culture.

It runs parallel, as unnamed source and unfinished agenda, to the black feminism sketched out by Desiree Lewis, Lauretta Ngcobo, Nise Malange, Zoë Wicomb, and others, and is linked to other trajectories of oppositional intellectuals laid out in Kelwyn Sole's history of recent criticism ("Democratising Culture"). It is also a South African variant of a broader, international, progressive discourse of race and culture' (p. 77).

Chapters 4–7 of this rigorously theorized study are entitled 'Staging Whiteness: Beckett, Havel, Maponya' (pp. 103–32); 'Locations of Feminism: Ingrid de Kok's Familiar Ground' (pp. 133–3); 'No Turning Back: Nise Malange and the Onset of Workers' Culture' (pp. 176–214); and 'Lines of Flight: Bessie Head, Arthur Nortje, Dambudzo Marechera' (pp. 215–56). They are sustained discussions of 'Maponya and Black Consciousness theatre in chapter 4, Ingrid de Kok and white feminist poetry in chapter 5, Nise Malange and workers' culture in chapter 6, and the power of marginality in the exile writers Bessie Head, Arthur Nortje, and Dambudzo Marechera in chapter 7' (p. 7).

Two book-length publications are welcome contributions to analysis of the life and work of Bessie Head: Desiree Lewis's *Living on a Horizon: Bessie Head and the Politics of Imagining* and Huma Ibrahim, ed., *Emerging Perspectives on Bessie Head*. Lewis's focus is on what she describes as Head's mysterious biographical circumstances, which have always captivated many of her readers and 'shockingly configures the personal tragedies associated with apartheid South Africa' (p. 1). Head's major writings were published between 1968 and 1984 and Njabulo Ndebele has since described this turbulent period, when apartheid established rigid political standards for writers, as follows: 'In societies like South Africa, where social, economic and political oppression is most stark, such conditions tend to enforce, almost with the power of natural law, overt tendentiousness in the artist's choice of subject-matter and handling of subject-matter' (cited in Lewis, pp. 1–2). While Head's choice and handling of subject matter have often been seen as lacking political commitment, thereby weakening her grasp of character, one of the aims of Lewis's study 'is to reassess ways in which Head's writing represents and responds to "the political" ' (p. 2). She argues that it is precisely because Head 'avoids the progressive political models of the sixties, seventies and eighties that she develops especially acute explorations of power and resistance. Head confronts many of the political relationships and situations that other South African writers explore' (p. 2). Lewis considers Head's exploration and interpretations of universal patterns associated with power and resistance as the turbulent 1980s return to critical scrutiny (as in O'Brien's work, discussed above); this decade was, she notes, 'the high tide of antiapartheid struggle, both of South African culture and of its representations abroad' (p. 3). One of her primary conclusions is that the careful Head reader/critic should 'explore Head as the enigmatic "she", codified and appropriated in ways that often reveal more about the locations of her interpreters than about the intricacies of the writer's own texts' (p. 5).

Lewis's study is complemented by the collection of essays *Emerging Perspectives on Bessie Head*, 'which engages issues of biography/autobiography within the work of Bessie Head' (p. ix). While Ibrahim's lucid introduction to the volume describes Head as a writer who 'has been historically typecast as one who dragged her autobiography into her fictional space', these autobiographical details, she argues, have 'provided an excellent example of sociology often taught in the Western academy as a representation of Apartheid South Africa' (p. xi). The volume opens with Arlene A. Elder's 'Bessie Head: The Inappropriate Appropriation of "Autobiography"' (pp. 1–16) and Isabel Balseiro's 'Between Amnesia and Memory: Bessie Head and her Critics' (pp. 17–24). Elder explores the *izibongo* (Zulu women's oral tradition) in relation to 'the well-known complication of this kind of narrative in the works of "autobiographical fiction" by southern African, Bessie Head' (p. 1); and Balseiro considers 'what critics remember—and forget—about Bessie Head, and with the role she has come to play in the developing canon of South African literature in the post-apartheid context' (p. 17). Hershini Bhana's 'A Literature of Rejection and Reception: Bessie Head's Life, History as Fact or History as Fiction. A Report from Japan!' (pp. 33–50); Percy Mosieleng's 'The Condition of Exile and the Negation of Commitment: A Biographical Study of Bessie Head's Novels' (pp. 51–71); Craig MacKenzie's 'Bessie Head's South Africa' (pp. 73–89); and Maureen Fielding's 'The Evolution of Trauma in Bessie Head's Work' (pp. 91–108) continue this exploration from different critical and theoretical positions. Bhana discusses the effect Bessie Head's life and philosophies had on Keiko Kusunose's 'own struggles as a young middle class Japanese woman and academic' (p. 2), and MacKenzie attempts to 'draw together the various aspects of Head's experiences in South Africa and her creative responses to these' (p. 74). Mary S. Lederer and Leloba S. Molema's '"That Troublemaker": Bessie Head in Botswana' (pp. 109–20); Desiree Lewis's 'Power, Representation and the Textual Politics of Bessie Head' (pp. 121–42); Peter Mwikisa's 'Caliban's Sister: Bessie Head's *Maru* as a Rewriting of *The Tempest*' (pp. 143–65); Sisi V.M. Maquagi's 'Taboo, a Positive Transgression? A Study of Bessie Head's *The Cardinals*' (pp. 167–79); Robert Cancel's 'Gestures of Belonging and Claiming Birth Rights: Short Stories by Bessie Head and Ama Ata Aidoo' (pp. 181–98); and Huma Ibrahim's 'The Problematic Relationship of Western Canonicity and African Literature: The Not-So-Singular Case of Bessie Head' (pp. 199–215) complete these 'Emerging Perspectives' on the novelist. Finally, Ellinetie Chabwera's 'Womanhood in Bessie Head's Fiction' (*JHu* 21[2007] 13–24) is a theorized account of 'a South African woman who lived in Botswana, [and who] was a prolific writer whose interest centred on the lives of black people' (p. 13). Head's reluctance to identify herself as a feminist, according to Chabwera, could be linked to two factors: 'Firstly, it is a result of the connotations attached to the term "feminist" within most of Africa in her time, a situation that still exists to now ... Secondly, I would like to propose that in an environment of racial exclusion such as the one Bessie Head belonged to in South Africa, Head's reluctance to label herself feminist is understandable, especially considering the effect of apartheid on black people' (pp. 13–15).

Part VI of Martin Banham, ed., *A History of Theatre in Africa*, entitled 'Southern Africa', comprises two essays: 'Southern Africa' by David Kerr with Stephen Chifunyise (pp. 265–311) and 'South African Theatre' by

Yvette Hutchison (pp. 312–79). Kerr suggests that coming to terms with the conceptual boulder of indigenous performing arts constitutes the first task for scholars before any attempt at encapsulating the history of theatre in an African region: 'in most accounts of African theatre, analysts give only a passing genuflection to indigenous performance before passing on with relief to colonial and postcolonial theatre' (p. 265). Recommending painstaking research into the oral, archaeological, artistic and written evidence about pre-colonial performance, similar to that undertaken by academics attempting to recover pre-colonial religion and history, the study offers 'some tentative indicators to what the history of southern African pre-colonial theatre might look like' (p. 265). Kerr's exploration begins with an account of the Khoisan or pre-Bantu period, 'a complex period from about second century AD to modern times' (p. 265) and the study follows the current move to restore a scientific, ethnographic meaning to the term 'Bantu', which was stripped of its erstwhile ideological value under the infamous apartheid regime: 'Even in that context, however, pre-Bantu is an unsatisfactory term, given that Bantu migration into and within southern Africa was a complex process from about second century AD to modern times, and given the speculation that immigrants may have had Nilotic rather than Bantu origins' (p. 265). The rich artistic heritage of cave-paintings and engravings constitute the main evidence of San performing arts in both the 'pre-Bantu' and 'post-Bantu' periods: 'The indigenous peoples of southern Africa, a linguistically diverse but culturally similar group of hunter-gatherers, are normally given the term *San*. Some academics prefer the colonial term *bushman*, on the grounds that there are no indigenous generic names, and all others (the Khoi term *San*, the Tswana *Basarwa* or the Afrikaaner *boschjesman* from which bushman is derived) had their origins in insults' (p. 266). The numerous San rock art sites in Zimbabwe's Matopos Hills were venerated as rain shrines by both Shona and Ndebele spirit mediums for therapeutic rituals 'such as spirit possession, rainmaking, ancestral masquerades, first-fruit ceremonies, funerals, initiations and the installation of chiefs', and Kerr argues that 'The most spectacular and obviously 'theatrical' of such performances are the ancestral masquerades. Of these, the most thoroughly researched, and the one on which we expend some space, is the *Gule wa Mkulu* (Big Dance) of the *Nyau* cult found among the Chewa and Manganja people' (p. 266). In addition to the rituals of the all-male secret society known as the Nyau, female initiation ceremonies equally imbued with theatrical elements can be found 'in what is now Zambia and Malawi [where] a whole nexus of female initiation rites, variously called *chisungu* (chiBemba) or *chinamwali* (chiNyanja) provided pubescent girls with instruction in sexuality and social etiquette, often through songs, dance mimes or even short dramatic sketches' (p. 272). Finally, complementing these performances that demarcate gender roles and offer sex education are the southern African rituals that 'took on a public form and blatantly ideological functions...The eighteenth-century Lunda empire of Mwata Kazembe, for example, in the Lunda Valley, was celebrated in the *Umutomboko* ceremony...A rather different form of ideologically charged royal ritual is found in the Swazi *Incwala* ceremony' (p. 271). After a fruitful and well-researched examination of 'Indigenous Para-Dramatic Performance',

Kerr's study moves on to the more contemporary terrain of 'The Reaction of Indigenous Theatre Forms to Colonialism' (pp. 273–83) and 'Theatre in the Post-Colonial Period' (pp. 283–306) respectively. One of his primary conclusions is that 'this rather sketchy survey of colonial and post-colonial theatre may give a blurred impression of incompatible national projects and drama practices totally deracinated from pre-colonial modes of performance. However, a close examination of the actual "traditions" of theatre crystallizing in the region indicates significant continuities as well as disjuncture' (p. 306). Meanwhile, Yvette Hutchison's study focuses pre-eminently on 'South African theatre', and 'foregrounds areas of performance that have not been discussed in detail in many available South African theatre histories, and suggests how the interaction [*sic*] of these diverse forms ha[s] defined the nature of contemporary South African theatre. This choice of focus means that there is less detail on well-published mainstream South African theatre history' (p. 312).

Maurice Taonezvi Vambe's *African Oral Story-telling Tradition and the Zimbabwean Novel in English* 'traces the ways in which the African oral storytelling tradition survived in several forms within the narrative interstices of the Zimbabwean black novel in English' (p. 2). Vambe's book-length study traces the way orality as an art form was used and 'continues to be used to construct and represent African resistance to colonial culture and its legacies as variously manifested in post-independence Zimbabwean literature, history, politics and culture' (p. 2). Chapter 1, 'The Oral Artist or Sarungano in African Traditional and Modern Culture in Zimbabwe' (pp. 9–14), examines the role of the traditional artist or Sarugano vis-à-vis 'the traditional and modern contexts within which orality is used either outside or inside the novel' (p. 9). Chapter 2, 'Orality and Resistance in Post-Independence Zimbabwe' (pp. 15–23), considers the volatility of oral tradition as a cultural reality—that is, the many ways in which 'orality can be used and even manipulated to author alternative narratives of resistance' (p. 15). Chapters 4, 5 and 6 are entitled 'Romance and National Resistance' (pp. 24–46), 'Myth and the Creation of National Consciousness' (pp. 47–70), and 'Of Ancestors, Spirit Possession and Post-Colonial Resistance' (pp. 71–87) respectively, and they examine the ubiquitous roles of folktales, myth, the fantastic, the fable and the use of spirit-possession in different Zimbabwean novels of the post-independence era. Chapters 7 and 8, 'Allegory in Post-Colonial Zimbabwe' (pp. 88–99) and 'Cultural Memory and the Politics of Remembering' (pp. 100–8), are discussions of the role of allegory in Dambudzo Marechera's *Black Sunlight* [1980] and the role of remembering and the politics of memory in Yvonne Vera's *The Stone Virgins* [1992]. In chapter 9, the conclusion, Vambe evaluates 'the formal and ideological influences and functions of the African storytelling tradition within the written mode of the black novel in English' (p. 8).

A number of issues of the journal *English Studies in Africa* are belatedly reviewed here. The first (*ESA* 47:i[2004]), on 'Histories of the Book in Southern Africa', is guest-edited by Andrew van der Vlies. In 'Introduction: The Institutions of South African Literature' (*ESA* 47:i[2004] 1–15) Vlies considers the whole notion of 'Book History' suggesting that, in its broadest terms, '"book historical" studies consider the influences of historical, material, and economic variables on the making of books as physical artefacts, and the process by which the meanings of the texts they define are made and re-made' (pp. 3–4). Against the backdrop of an ever-burgeoning publishing industry and the whole notion of the materiality of the text, Vlies examines Olive Schreiner's paradigmatic *The Story of an African Farm* and the ways in which 'each publication of the novel—each instance of its repackaging and recontextualization at different historical moments for audiences with different interests and investments in the novel' (p. 3), has been more than a matter of reiterating the author's biography, reading and contexts. While literary criticism has always been concerned with the meaning of texts, 'book history', according to Vlies, 'is concerned with how these meanings are influenced by factors often beyond the control of the authors themselves, with how they are constructed, and change, and how these processes are intimately connected with publishing pressures, the ruling discourses of reviewing, censorship, abridgement, educational institutionalization, and the valorizing economics of literary prize culture (amongst other pressures)' (p. 4). The collected essays are: Peter D. McDonald's 'The Politics of Obscenity: *Lady Chatterley's Lover* and the Apartheid State' (*ESA* 47:i[2004] 31–46); Jarad Zimbler's 'Under Local Eyes: The South African Publishing Context of J.M. Coetzee's *Foe*' (*ESA* 47:i[2004]pp. 47–59); Patrick Denman Flanery's '(Re-)Marking Coetzee and Costello: *The* (Textual) *Lives of Animals*' (*ESA* 47:i[2004] 61–84): and Rita Barnard's 'Oprah's Paton, or South Africa and the Globalization of Suffering' (*ESA* 47:i[2004] 85–107). Together, these essays examine the literary provenance of what Vlies has described as 'different aspects of Southern African book culture, and the institutions which effect or police the meanings and perceived "literariness" of writing from, and writing read within South Africa' (p. 10).

Springing from a colloquium on American studies held in August 2004 at the University of Witwatersrand *ESA* 48:ii[2005] collects essays on 'American Studies in South Africa' under the title 'Exploring American Literature and Culture'. The special issue is guest-edited by David Watson and Merle A. Williams. In 'Introduction: A View of American Studies in South Africa' (*ESA* 48:ii[2005] 1–5) Watson and Williams review the whole notion of the practice of American studies in a South African context. They suggest that 'Even a cursory glance at the curricula and reading lists of English departments at South African universities indicates that, while American literature is by no means absent, it is certainly a minor player in the intellectual life of the English academy' (p. 1). While the core curriculum of most departments remains divided between canonical British and Southern African literature, the relative neglect of American studies in South Africa, according to Watson and Williams, is not 'necessarily negative, especially when that neglect arises from an increased emphasis on local products. The historical paradox remains, however, that while English departments in South Africa continue to drift in this direction, it is becoming increasingly apparent that South African culture is not itself free from the global impact and spread of American culture' (p. 2). Karen Scherzinger's '"The dilemmas that jump out at us if we look sideways": Siblings and Seriality in *The Turn of the Screw*'

(*ESA* 48:ii[2005] 7–20); Merle A. Williams's 'Henry James: Autumn in America' (*ESA* 48:ii[2005] 21–34); David Watson's 'Wallace Steven's Poems of a Different Climate' (*ESA* 48:ii[2005] 35–46); Ashleigh Harris's '"If she hollers / let her go": Toni Morrison as Public Intellectual' (*ESA* 48:ii[2005] 47–59); Deirdre Byrne's 'The Messiah versus Collective Consciousness in the *Matrix* Trilogy' (*ESA* 48:ii[2005] 61–74); and Shane Graham's 'Re-reading Leslie Marmon Silko's *Almanac of the Dead* after 9/11' (*ESA* 48:ii[2005] 75–88) examine, from a variety of critical and theoretical positions, the different aspects of what Watson and Williams have described as 'a curious impasse in South African universities' (p. 2) in which American studies appears to find itself 'an impasse perhaps most lucidly and easily explained in terms of tensions between local discourses and an increasingly transnational culture' (pp. 2–3). The final issue of *English Studies in Africa* under belated review here contains essays on a diverse range of subjects, as indicated by their titles: Gareth Cornwell's 'The Fairground Scene in *Turbott Wolfe*' (*ESA* 49:ii[2006] 1–12); Peter Shillingsburg's 'Textual Criticism, the Humanities and J.M. Coetzee' (*ESA* 49:ii[2006] 13–27); Lars Engle's 'Being Literary in the Wrong Way, Time, and Place: J.M. Coetzee's *Youth*' (*ESA* 49:ii[2006] 29–49); David Medalie's '*The Cry of Winnie Mandela*: Njabulo Ndebele's Post-Apartheid Novel' (*ESA* 49:ii[2006] 51–65); Ronit Fainman-Frenkel's 'Reconsidering Late-Apartheid Literature: The Short Stories of Agnus Sam and Jayapraga Reddy' (*ESA* 49:ii[2006] 67–82); Jamie McGregor's '"The sea, music and death": The Shadow of Wagner in Woolf's *Mrs Dalloway*' (*ESA* 49:ii[2006] 83–108); Michael Williams's '"More impious than Milton's Satan?"': Satan, the Romantics and Byron' (*ESA* 49:ii[2006] 109–22); and Lesley Finnegan's '"A completely satisfactory detective": The Detective Fiction Genre in Alexander McCall Smith's Botswana Novels' (*ESA* 49:ii[2006] 123–47).

(e) North Africa

Part II of Martin Banham, ed., *A History of Theatre in Africa*, entitled 'North Africa', comprises three essays: 'Egypt' by Ahmed Zaki (pp. 13–36), 'Morocco, Algeria and Tunisia' by Kamal Salhi (pp. 37–76) and 'Sudan' by Khalid Almubarak Mustafa (pp. 77–84). Zaki begins with what he describes as the modern construct known as 'Theatre in the form of written, staged and acted drama' (p. 13), suggesting the roots that have nurtured Egyptian theatre 'to develop its own unique style lie in the performing arts that appeared over five thousand years ago. The palimpsest of modern Egypt is, in effect, the result of its long history, different religious traditions, the influence of diverse occupying powers, an Islamic heritage and modern pan-Arab affiliations' (p. 13). In 3100 BC, under Narmer (Mena), what were known as the 'The Two Lands' of Egypt were united. The unification of the south (Upper Egypt) and the more fertile delta land in the north (Lower Egypt), which had developed separately before, 'also united the two major religions: the sun worship of the south, Amon Ra, and the nature worship of the delta, Ptah' (p. 13). According to Zaki the modern-day diversity and strength of the performing arts in Egypt, 'displaying both their origins in folk or historical or long forgotten religious traditions and incorporating new elements from local sources or abroad to make a vibrant synthesis typical of a very Egyptian approach' (p. 13), are derived from this historical merger, among other catalytic events in Egypt's long history.

Zaki demarcates four distinct periods in Egypt's historical evolution: the 'Pharaonic period' (pp. 14–18), the 'Graeco-Roman period' (pp. 18–20), the 'Christian era' (pp. 21–3) and the 'Islamic period' (pp. 23–7). He discusses the ways in which these historical periods have combined to produce 'A rich panoply of performing arts [that] was available for the inhabitants of Cairo and some principal towns, whereas the folk arts and traditions were an intrinsic part of the life of the Saidi in Upper Egypt, the *fellahin* of the delta, the Nubians, the fishermen of the coast, the Bedouins and the people of the oases. In the countryside at gatherings after the day's work was done, entertainment often took the form of the *Samer*, where those present mocked local dignitaries by mimicking them, or debating nationalistic or religious subjects using the skills of rhetoric or by epic recitation' (p. 27).

The traditional ways of life that informed this 'rich panoply of performing arts' were already in decline or at least 'beginning to undergo a complete change' (p. 27) during the period demarcated by Zaki as 'Modern: From Mohammed Aly and Napoleon' (pp. 27–34): 'Under the Ottomans, Egypt had reverted to being a province of Turkey, ruled for them by the slave caste of Mameluks. In 1798 Napoleon broke the military power of the Mameluks and took control of Egypt for the following four years' (pp. 27–8). Besides wresting power from the weakened Mameluks and creating an independent Egypt within the Ottoman empire, Mohamed Aly, who arrived from Albania in 1805, 'also sent Egyptian scholars abroad to study, principally to France and Italy... The first European-style Arabic productions were translated and adapted European classics acted in colloquial Arabic by Yacoub Sannu's National Theatre Company in 1870' (p. 28). The revolution of 1952, which removed both the monarchy and the British influence from Egypt, brought a new flourishing of the theatre and with it many highly skilled writers: 'Their work covered Egypt's historical past, its present and its role within the Arab world. They aimed not only at portraying reality, but also at reshaping it using a variety of styles ranging from realism, folk art, symbolism, naturalism and expressionism, very often with European influences from Ibsen, Chekhov, Pirandello, Brecht, Ionesco and Beckett' (p. 31). An inward-looking period that was interrupted by the October War in 1973 also saw Egypt 'busily transforming itself from a socialist semi-industrial society into a private-sector-led society that was being showered with imported consumer goods' (p. 33). One of the direct effects of the Open Door economic policy established after the October War victory of 1973 was that 'By the late 1970s and 1980s the state theatre, once the pride of the socialist/revolutionary-inspired cultural renaissance, had neither the money nor the will to compete with the private companies, television's vast output of soap operas or the cinema making films for video' (p. 34). Only the inauguration of the annual Cairo International Festival of Experimental Theatre in 1988 brought a much-needed policy change 'to promote experimental small groups of urban-centred young people's theatre, including establishing a modern dance troupe.

Nevertheless, the ephemeral nature of the many groups means that discussion among theatre people on how best to nurture the present and future theatre in Egypt continues' (p. 34).

The related but also divergent developments in the evolution of theatre in the North African countries of Morocco, Algeria and Tunisia, from the early cultural invasions to the present day, are the focus of Kamal Salhi's contribution, which 'examines the particular conception of theatre in this region, assesses the legacy of Arab and French experiences, explores influences and experimentation, and discusses the imperatives of post-colonial theatre activity' (p. 37). Before turning to the formative 'Indigenous para-dramatic performance' (pp. 40–59), Salhi examines 'The antagonist theory' (pp. 37–40), which argues that 'theatre did not exist in north Africa because of Islam. I offer evidence for a complex source of theatre in north African tradition as an ideological yet anticipative act of performance firmly grounded in Islam and secular indigenous culture' (p. 37). With the exception of a few local particularities inherited from before the arrival of Islam, almost the same situation, according to Salhi, 'can be found in Morocco, Algeria and Tunisia respectively. Numerous traditional forms of performance, game and ceremony were practiced for centuries, and some are again being practiced today, such as the Halqa (circle), which is undoubtedly the most celebrated and popular form of performance, particularly in Morocco' (p. 40). However, while popular festivals gave Moroccans and Algerians, especially, the opportunity to gain acquaintance with the art of performance, 'and the visit paid by Arab troupes helped them to learn about theatrical representations, it has to be recognized that it was the western practice of theatre that provided Moroccan and Algerian performers with their formal initiation into the art form... Beginning in 1907, Egyptian troupes began to visit Morocco, Algeria and Tunisia' (p. 56). While the dawn of 'Modern Experimentation' (pp. 59–65) witnessed considerable 'Experimental theatre in Morocco, Algeria and Tunisia [that] expresses an identification with north African culture, and thus responds to people's needs and expectations' (p. 60), the postcolonial era saw 'dramatists [who] worked within a specific problematic framed by a high degree of colonial French control over artistic expression and an overt politicisation of cultural questions' (p. 65).

Finally, Khalid Almubarak Mustafa's contribution examines the cornucopia of theatrical heritage of modern Sudan 'with its vast size (1 million square miles—almost a quarter of the area of Europe)' (p. 77). While theatre in the modern sense has a short history in Sudan, 'beginning only after the reconquest of the country and the subsequent condominium rule (1889–1955) in which Britain was the senior partner' (p. 77), performance rituals in Sudan date back to pre-Islamic rituals and 'include the trance/possession Zar that the country shares with several other African countries (e.g. Ethiopia, Egypt)... Rituals of the animist southern Sudanese ethnic groups are arguably among the finest and most effective group festivities involving whole communities. They also represent links in a chain of influences traceable to ancient Nubian and Egyptian religious ceremonies' (p. 77).

2. Australia

(a) General

Perhaps the biggest news for 2007 in Australian literary studies was that the papers of Patrick White, to date Australia's only 'home-grown' Nobel Prize winner, had not been destroyed as the author had long claimed. The story of how the material survived and a brief overview of the contents are given in Marie-Louise Ayres's essay ' "My Mss are Destroyed" ' (*AuBR* 290[2007] 8–11). In Ayres's view, the most exciting elements of the additions to the collection in the National Library of Australia are White's ten notebooks, which contain 'observations, first paragraphs, timelines, character descriptions, research notes'. She asserts that 'most of White's novels first appear in these notebooks, along with many of his plays, short stories and a surprising number of poems, most never published. It is clear that White himself valued these, and mined them—sometimes after many years—for his creative work' (p. 9). The many unpublished works include a 'novella' that runs to around 160,000 words, as well as drafts and material, especially for the later novels. Although there are very few personal letters, Ayres, an experienced critic and scholar, expresses her belief that the material is sufficiently rich to fuel productive research.

When you ask a politician to open a conference you don't normally expect anything that will survive the day. Consequently, it is a surprising delight to record that the speech by former West Australian premier and federal minister Carmen Lawrence at the 2006 ASAL conference, published as 'The Reading Sickness' (*JASAL* 6[2007] 9–18), is an interesting blend of autobiographical reading experiences, meditation on the state of Australian literature and its readership, and comment on the effect of the political climate on reading and literature. Written in the days before it became clear that the Howard government decade might one day end, the essay is a rewarding discussion of the politico-literary zeitgeist. Mark Davis's 'The Clash of Paradigms: Australian Literary Theory after Liberalism' (*JASAL* 7[2007] 7–31) presents a commanding analysis of criticism and of that zeitgeist. The essay offers a bold and lucid account of recent debates about literary 'decline', and is perhaps the most important general statement on the relationship between academic criticism and media criticism since Davis's own *Gangland* was published a decade ago. The essay opens by noting that the transformations in critical paradigms of the past forty years or so have not, in general, been taken up in the public sphere or by general readers, thus that ' "pre-revolutionary" forms of literary theory' continue, in effect, to be 'guiding forms of public knowledge' (p. 8). This frames the main contention: that 'contemporary literary theory...is losing whatever relevance it once had, not because "theory" has lost its potential force as intellectual and therefore public discourse or because its "moment" has passed, but because the contexts in which it operates have radically changed' (p. 8). These changed contexts are, principally, the crisis of liberalism engendered by the entrenching of neo-liberalism, and the concomitant restructuring of value in the public sphere and in politics over the past three decades.

A pithy survey of fiction from the late post-war period and of critical responses to it serves to illustrate the most striking element of Davis's argument: that literary theory, as well as the liberalism which is its chief target, are both grounded in the same institutions of cultural production—'the broadsheet press, public broadcasting, the literary novel and its canons'—and that their concurrent decline is a measure of theory's dependence on what it seeks to attack. Because liberalism has been entirely debilitated, 'contemporary Australian literary-critical theory has failed to produce a single figure who plays a leading public role' (p. 22). This silence of academic critics is set against the vociferous and repeated public attacks on education and, particularly, 'critical theory', by those who support 'a white, populist, majoritarian project...which seeks to undermine traditional democratic understandings of fairness, equality and wealth redistribution' (p. 24). Davis calls for an effort to make 'the new conservatism and its social texts a sustained focus of our scholarly attentions' (p. 25) and, as part of this change, he suggests the need to embrace 'low theory'. This would mean, he says, 'learning to use the logic of affect', proceeding not from the abstract but from 'accounts of people and place so as to tell stories that make our concerns real in ways that resonate with broader audiences' (p. 27). In particular, Davis urges attention to pedagogy, notably the lecture as a form, suggesting that in current conventions of teaching 'the only subject position offered students is as potential initiates into an arcane order, oriented around reverence for key theorists and critical practices that many find either alienating or simply ridiculous' (p. 27).

Some of that 'low theory' is presented in the contributions to *Translating Lives: Living with Two Languages and Cultures*, edited by Mary Besemeres and Anna Wierzbicka, which meditates on the experience of living with two languages, or attempting to acquire another language. Insidious as it might be to select individual contributions, Kim Scott's evocative and sometimes painful 'Strangers at Home' (pp. 1–11) and Eva Sallis's reflections on the emotional, social and somatic effects of learning and becoming competent in Arabic in 'Foster Mother Tongue' (pp. 150–9), which bookend the volume, are outstanding, as well as giving insight into these two writers' fiction. Scott's 'Guides and Explorers: Australia's Cultural Identity Now' (*NLitsR* 44[2005] 15–22) reflects on national identity, colonial history and his own writing practices in a way that will be helpful not only to readers of his novels, but to those interested in the questions he addresses. The transcript of a television interview with Alexis Wright following her success in the Miles Franklin Award for 2007 was published in *Hecate* (33:i[2007] 215–9). In it, Wright attends in some detail to her writing of the enormously successful novel *Carpentaria*, although her 'On Writing *Carpentaria*' in *HEAT* (13[2007] 79–95) does less in this regard than the title might seem to promise; it describes a mode or space for writing rather than detailing autobiographical facts or writing techniques. John Gatt-Rutter's 'Translating Lives: Italian-Australian Biography and Translation' (*LW* 4:i[2007] 41–58) considers the effects of translation, with the author finding that Walter Musolino's translation of Piero Genovesi's *Sebastiano Pitruzzello* emphasizes the value of 'Australianness' over 'Italianness' in subtle but pervasive ways.

Contrastingly, Leah Gerber's ' "If I've arksed youse boys once, I've arksed youse boys a thousand times! Translation Strategies in the German Translation of Phillip Gwynne's *Deadly, Unna?*' (*Papers* 17:i[2007] 51–6) contends that the German word-play of the translation renders the English text's use of distinctively colloquial language effectively, and in a manner likely to be comprehensible to German-language readers.

Ouyang Yu continues his prolific contribution to Australian literature with *Bias*, a collection of essays on literary and cultural issues, including the reception of Australian literature in China. The essays are supplemented by an interview, and a set of reviews. The most insightful of the latter are by Nicholas Birns and by Kam Louie, who discusses Ouyang Yu's multiple roles as a commentator on perceptions of China and its literature in Australia, and as a poet and scholar who is of 'the Tiananmen generation', many of whom expected better lives when they were exiled in the West. The strength of Kam's essay is that it analyses Ouyang's poetry, including its trenchant criticisms of an Australia that is seen as myopic and hostile, in the context of developments in literary themes and forms in China, and of Chinese political culture. The rest of the essays in the volume demonstrate what Birns notes is Ouyang's commitment to the vernacular and to political relevance: they largely eschew abstruse vocabulary or theoretically driven argument in favour of a set of strongly argued assertions about some aspect of literary culture or society. Most of the material has been published previously but often in small and difficult-to-obtain publications, and so the volume (notwithstanding a print run of just 200) will be a useful resource for scholars attempting to keep pace with this author.

Pradeep Trikha's *Delphic Intimations: Dialogues with Australian Writers and Critics*, a collection of interviews with sixteen writers and four critics, is a little patchy, but there is some excellent material in an innovative collection that likewise seeks to explore questions about cultural difference and cultural exchange. Implicit in some of the questions put by Trikha is an opposition between criticism and creativity. This is made explicit by the division of interviews into two sections, for creative writers and for critics, a division which looks decidedly shaky in the case of some 'creative' contributors equally distinguished as critics, among them Dennis Haskell and Jennifer Strauss. The most interesting although not the most provocative contributions are those, usually more lengthy, in which the interviewees—among them more experienced creative writers such as Carmel Bird, Kate Grenville, John Tranter and Michael Wilding—manage to combine responses that are thoughtful (in both senses of the word) with a certain level of self-deprecation and self-reflexivity. If there is a disappointment it is that the interviews can be oddly stilted, with provocative comments not really taken advantage of by the interlocutor. Nevertheless, some richly insightful remarks are likely to open up avenues for investigation for Indian students of these writers' work. These are the ostensible readers of this book, but there are some gems that deserve an (even) wider audience. Among them is the grumpy respondent on whom Trikha takes efficient revenge by printing an apparently private letter. There are also some wonderfully laconic answers to slightly too serious questions: Strauss, for example, is typically forthright in responding to an earnest enquiry about the gap between 'representation of colonized women of Asia and Aboriginal women of Australia' with the assertion that such a question 'needs a treatise, not a comment' (p. 81).

Andrew McCann offers a musingly provocative essay on the commercial, the critical and the national in his brief essay 'The International of Excreta: World Literature and its Other' (*Overland* 186[2007] 20–4). Although the author is somewhat distracted by an acerbic engagement with Ken Gelder, the more substantive point is about querying the national as a critical paradigm. McCann makes the fairly uncontentious but often ignored point that 'we have to think beyond the cognitive limits of specific national spaces and imaginaries, and work through the contradictions of borders that are permeable for capital and commodities, but impassable for all but extremely privileged populations' while acknowledging that 'an overwhelming stress on the locatability of culture has meant that affective identifications also seem to stop at the border' (p. 21). The essay condemns criticism and (particularly) fiction that seeks to promote or normalize the fantasy that 'management is opposed to coercion, and capital is opposed to violence' (p. 21). 'The trick', says McCann, speaking of a literary text whose approach he praises, is 'to remind us of globalisation's economy of affect, and then to exploit the autonomy of the literary text in order to dismantle or invert ... the initial opposition' (p. 22) between 'foreign' places—which experience violence—and western metropolitan centres, which do not. The imperative is to lose the belief that 'discrete national cultures are our only defences against a global culture industry' (p. 24), and to open up to major works of world literature. In this spirit, essays in the special issue of *Studies in Travel Writing* (11:i[2007]) on Australia raise issues of general interest to the field, being concerned with representations of Indigenous Australians; recurrent tropes and modes of travel writing; and the positioning of travel narratives in relation to other media such as film.

McCann's claims are in some respects congruent with Robert Dixon's in 'Australian Literature in International Contexts' (*Southerly* 67:i–ii[2007] 15–27), a keynote paper from an ASAL conference held to mark the retirement of professor Elizabeth Webby. Dixon's is an important call to globalize the study of Australian literature, not through promoting it in foreign places as a discrete writing practice, but rather to read, discuss and teach Australian texts in connection with other literatures, embedding them in existing 'intellectual formations and research networks' (p. 22). Lyn McCredden takes quite a different line in 'Haunted Identities and the Possible Futures of "Aust. Lit"' in a special issue of *JASAL* ([2007] 12–24), an essay which explores the implications for 'a national literature'—and its criticism—of the assertion that identity is always constituted by 'desire and lack' (p. 13). Engaging at length with the work of Gelder and, to a lesser extent, McCann, McCredden worries that Gelder's arguments imply that there is no fixed abode for argument: that the prioritizing of critique leaves no place for discussion of 'home or belonging or identity' that is not seen as 'reactionary or sentimental' (p. 16). Against such views she cites the work of scholars like John Bradley and Frances Devlin Glass, who are working in close collaboration with the Yanuyuwa community to examine Indigenous notions of the sacred. McCredden concludes by wondering what role the sacred might play in contemporary cultural and literary criticism. A different approach again is offered by Brigid Rooney, who considers David Malouf's claim to articulate formations of national identity in her essay 'Remembering Inheritance: David Malouf and the Literary Cultivation of Nation' (*JAS* 90[2007] 65–75; notes 188–9). Rooney is particularly interested in the implications of Malouf's positioning as a 'literary' writer, and in examining claims by McCann and others that 'the literary' is declining in influence in Australia. She understands Malouf's positioning as a rhetorical manoeuvre, a necessary refusal of the imperatives of a mass audience that is essential to his being recognized as a public intellectual. Methodologically different again is Susan Lever, who, in 'Surviving as a Writer: The Careers of the 1970s Generation' (*Southerly* 67:i–ii[2007] 395–407), contrasts the commercial success achieved by David Williamson and Peter Carey with the 'niche' audiences found by John Romeril and David Foster. While arguing that all four have adapted their output to cultural circumstances and new opportunities, Lever nevertheless concludes that Williamson and Carey have been more prepared to work in accessible genres (such as film and the popular novel), and to respond to the sensibilities and interests of their chosen (mainstream) audience, and have reaped benefits from doing so.

In *Making Books: Contemporary Australian Publishing* David Carter and Anne Galligan have produced a comprehensive study of the book-production industry in Australia. It is not written primarily from a literary perspective, but the media perspective of many of the articles will remind literary scholars of the context in which literary works are produced. The first section surveys the workings of Australian publishing with articles on industry aspects such as the history of publishers, bookselling, state subsidy and sponsorship of writers, and publishers' editors. Galligan's 'The Culture of the Publishing House: Structure and Strategies in the Australian Publishing Industry' (pp. 34–50; notes pp. 369–71) is a useful survey of the general pattern of movements in Australian publishing, including amalgamation and takeovers, and the sporadic emergence of important independents. Louise Poland's essay 'The Business, Craft and Profession of Book Editing' (pp. 96–115; notes pp. 375–80) is a surprisingly wide-ranging account of a part of the writing process that is still often undervalued if not overlooked. The section concludes with two rather more 'cultural' essays, Mark Davis's 'The Decline of the Literary Paradigm in Australian Publishing' (pp. 116–31; notes pp. 380–2) and Richard Flanagan's 'Colonies of the Mind; Republics of Dreams: Australian Publishing Past and Future' (pp. 132–48). Davis's pessimistic essay was discussed in *YWES* last year, when it appeared in another form. Based on his experience as a novelist, Flanagan has generally good things to say about publishers in Australia (whether local or global), although he deplores their lack of self-promotion. His most vehement argument is against large publishing advances that distract from the thoughtful reviewing and evaluation of new novels by making the books celebrity objects in a succession of overheated and vapid marketing campaigns.

The second section discusses publishing in the digital era. There are useful surveys here of print-on-demand, the importance of immediate, accurate electronic sales data for publishing, and the successes and failures of electronic forms of publishing so far, but the stand-out article is Leanne Wiseman's 'Copyright and the Regulation of the Australian Publishing Industry' (pp. 177–97; notes pp. 384–7). Wiseman points out that electronic publishers in Australia have successfully lobbied for laws that allow publishers to control the consumption of electronic texts more than general copyright laws intended, and far more than traditional publishers of printed books were able to do. The third section contains chapters on the publishing of different genres such as children's books, poetry, food and drink, financial self-help books and romance, many of which have a primary interest for literary scholars. Carter's 'Boom, Bust or Business as Usual? Literary Fiction Publishing' (pp. 231–46; notes p. 338) turns to statistics to try to put some hard evidence under the arguments of the cultural prognostications of people like Davis. Carter's source, though, is not the publisher's tool BookScan but the bibliography AustLit. Consequently, the patterns that Carter can adduce are patterns of publishing, not of sales. His data shows 'literary fiction' maintaining a steady 40 per cent of all fiction titles published. The number of new fiction books from 1990 to 2004 remained fairly stable at around 350, although there was a notable drop off in 2005 and 2006. Carter's analysis of the publishers who produce the fiction is a niche supplement to Galligan's survey earlier in the book. Although he is reluctant to generalize too widely, Carter does suggest that one reason for a diminution in the production of literary fiction since 2000 is the end of the nationalist literary project of the 1960s to the 1990s. This would put his argument in line with that of Davis: modern publishers of literary fiction are not doing anything wrong; it is just that an adventitiously golden age is now over. Although at times degenerating to a list of names and titles, Bronwyn Lea's 'Poetry Publishing' (pp. 247–54; notes p. 389) contains much valuable information precisely because poetry is often poorly marketed and hence can be elusive. Lea's conclusions are generally positive: although a subculture, poetry in Australia is remarkably resilient, and new publishers keep appearing as older ones discontinue their lists. On a per capita basis, poetry in Australia sells more impressively than in most comparable countries. John Tranter's online journal *Jacket* shows that poetry in the digital environment can accrue a significant following. Anita Heiss's 'Indigenous Book Publishing' (pp. 255–67; notes pp. 389–90) charts the commitment of some mainstream publishers to Aboriginal writing, and compares the structure and output of the three Indigenous presses, IAD, Magabala and Aboriginal Studies Press. Among them they offer a significant range of material extending from academic anthropology to oral history; from biography and autobiography to fiction; from poetry to children's books. Heiss concludes with some thoughtful remarks on issues such as the editing of Indigenous writing, and the question of audience. This book has followed surprisingly quickly on the comparable *Paper Empires: A History of the Book in Australia 1946–2005* (discussed last year) with which it shares the publisher and a number of contributors. The books are quite distinct, however, with little overlap. Whereas *Paper Empires* was a history of a fifty-year period, often using contributors who had had personal experience of the events being retailed, and depending heavily on short 'case-studies' of individual publishers, publications, awards or magazines, *Making Books* is far more a synchronic media and industry study exploring economic, political and cultural forces, and illustrating its arguments with graphs and tables rather than photographs and jacket covers. It is, however, indispensable for understanding the industry context of current Australian literature.

The politics of publishing in the contemporary era are subjected to scrutiny by Jennifer Jones in 'Editing and the Politics of Race' (*Jpub* 2[2007] 46–67), an essay highly critical of white editors who have worked with Indigenous writers. Examining three books in detail, Jones concludes that her own editions of two of these works, which restore large portions of the original manuscripts, will provide readers with more radical texts. Jones is followed by one of the main targets of her polemic, Margaret McDonell, who offers advice for editors in 'A Way of Working: Editing across Cultures' (*Jpub* 2[2007] 68–89). McDonell aims to offer a practical guide for non-Indigenous editors working with Indigenous writers, while noting the tensions between 'commercial' and 'cultural' imperatives in the preparation of manuscripts. Caroline Viera Jones's 'Historical Midwifery: The Editorial Birth of an Australian Narrative' (*Jpub* 2[2007] 26–45) uses evidence from the archive of George Robertson, the iconic Australian publisher, to put the case that Robertson's own editorial interventions in the work of some of his most important writers—among them Henry Lawson and C.E.W. Bean—encouraged a masculinist view of what was valuable in Australian culture. Viera Jones concludes that 'The body of work he commissioned, edited, published and distributed, shaped and crystallized a distinctively national voice which even today forms a significant part of a quintessentially Australian narrative' (p. 41). There is a detailed examination of the legislative and commercial contexts for the publishing of popular fiction in Toni Johnson-Woods's 'Pulp Friction: Governmental Control of Cheap Fiction, 1939–1959' (*S&P* 30:ii[2006] 103–19), which analyses the sometimes competing and sometimes congruent concerns of governments, publishers, readers and writers in restricting the flow of imported literary materials into Australia. Roger Osborne's 'Behind the Book: Vance Palmer's Short Stories and the Australian Magazine Culture in the 1920s' (*JASAL* 6[2007] 49–64) takes a volume of Palmer stories and investigates their earlier appearances in three journals, the *Bulletin*, *Triad* and the *Australian Journal*. The article contributes to our knowledge of both fiction publishing in the 1920s and the Palmer texts, but it will make more sense in the context of the larger study from which it has been excised. The materiality of books and the history of 'book loving' in the Anglo-American and Australian world are considered by Patrick Buckridge in 'Bookishness and Australian Literature' (*S&P* 30:iv[2006] 223–36). Buckridge compares the positive and pejorative connotations of the term as they are presented in fiction and criticism, largely from the first half of the twentieth century, although there is also ample reference to the nineteenth.

Queensland has been well served by scholarship in 2007, with the publication of William Hatherell's *The Third Metropolis: Imagining Brisbane through Art and Literature 1940–1970*, and Patrick Buckridge and Belinda McKay's edited collection *By the Book: A Literary History of Queensland*. *By the Book* contains four essays on the demographically dominant south-east of the state, and one essay on each of central, western and north Queensland; three essays cover the state as a whole in considering children's literature, travel writing and writing by Indigenous authors respectively. Buckridge's 'Roles for Writers: Brisbane and Literature, 1859–1975' (pp. 13–72) manages to be both magisterial and unstuffy, offering an erudite and ecumenical sweep across more than a century of published writing, with some nicely personalized detail on milieu and personalities, and a clever eye for quirky quotation. Readers will find their interest piqued in a wide variety of texts. Buckridge's approach is encapsulated in his wise comment that a historical period 'has more going on inside its arbitrary bounds—more loose ends from the past, more half-formed impulses just emerging, more marginal voices, and more difference and division among the main actors—than generalising overviews take account of' (p. 64). No other chapter is quite so rich in anecdote or so thorough, although perhaps it was editorial privilege that allowed Buckridge around double the length of most other contributors. Maggie Nolan's ' "Bitin' Back": Indigenous Writing in Queensland' (pp. 259–77; notes pp. 358–9), which takes the first part of its title from a very funny novel by Vivienne Cleven, does most to put an argument for the significance of its subject and to offer some reflections on the critical and cultural issues which arise from the consideration of this specific body of literature.

The conceptual questions arising from the use of geographical parameters to consider a body of creative writing, so troubling to McCann and Dixon, are foregrounded in Hatherell's *The Third Metropolis*, which weaves detailed analysis of representations of the city of Brisbane in the visual arts, mainly painting, and in literature, into a history of artistic movements and individuals. Hatherell considers these works in the context(s) of the city's political history, geographical features, demographic shifts and cultural movements. For example, he shows that the influx of American troops during the Second World War had a significant influence on the literary milieu; that there was a considerable Catholic intellectual circle in the city; and that there is a variety and texture to what are often assumed to be banal and uniform representations of the Brisbane landscape. Citing the careers and influence of writers and artists as diverse as Thea Astley, Jessica Anderson, Ian Fairweather and Judith Wright, the case is put that Brisbane was a rich centre of cultural debate and production during the 1940s, in particular. Hatherell's main claim is that it is the subsequent representations of the Brisbane of this period, notably in the writing of David Malouf, that have given force to pejorative modern clichés that the city is or was a 'cultural desert' or 'big country town'. The book works carefully and quietly to dispute this view, without ever becoming flag-waving.

The overwhelming concern about literary publishing evident in recent years seems to have waned somewhat, but the increasing interest in environmental issues noted in 2003 and 2004 has strengthened in 2007: more critics routinely deal with this topic, and specialist collections are starting to appear, among them Helen Tiffin's *Five Emus to the King of Siam: Environment and Empire* and CA (*sic*) Cranston and Robert Zeller's *The Littoral Zone: Australian Contexts and their Writers*, while the journal *Kunapipi* devoted its 2007 special issue (29:ii[2007]) to 'birds'. The long feature essay, Graham Barwell's fascinating forty-page discussion of 'Coleridge's Albatross and the Impulse to Seabird Conservation' (*Kunapipi* 29:ii[2007] 22–61), gives attention to the representation and engagement with the bird in the colonial cultures of the southern Pacific. While the volume as a whole has some other very fine essays, it is particularly notable for its reproduction of several sets of stunning images. Cranston and Zeller's *The Littoral Zone* has some dozen essays, most of which focus on specific regions of Australia. Somewhat anomalously, Mitchell Rolls's 'The Green Thumb of Appreciation' (pp. 93–121) examines the representation of Indigenous Australians in works that purport to express empathy with the landscape, although the essay tends to eschew reference to similar commentary (in literary studies) on this crucial topic. Other writers fall into the trap of the survey, limiting themselves to mention of a vast range of texts, but there are some very fine contributions. Tony Hughes-D'Aeth ranges widely across fiction, poetry and agricultural writing in 'The Shadow on the Field: Literature and Ecology in the Western Australian Wheatbelt' (pp. 45–69), but comes to some evocative and provocative conclusions about the ambiguous cultural/natural legacy of wheat. He draws out the 'tantalising' implications of his realization that it was the market, not the environment, which saw the 'cultural value' of wheat—dreams of bread and gold—plummet during the Depression. Hughes D'Aeth speculates that it was 'the cataclysmic intrusion of the unimaginable—that commodity prices could drop to nothing—into the imaginative fields of the 1930s psyche that helped to catalyse a fundamental reconfiguration of the relation to land and the environment' (pp. 67–8). Similarly, Ruth Blair's 'Hugging the Shore: The Green Mountains of South-East Queensland' (pp. 176–97; map p. 175) brings together lived experience (as several other writers in this volume do), precise colloquialism and vast reading to create a tone that is simultaneously ebullient and erudite. Kate Rigby provides a rich account of the 'Ecopoetics of the Limestone Plains' (pp. 153–75) which presumes the interconnectedness of geology, religion, history and literature, noting the catastrophic effects of colonization before moving on to analyse the rhetorical relationship to the environment evident in the writing of Miles Franklin, particularly her posthumously published autobiography *Childhood at Brindabella*, the poetry of David Campbell, and Marion Halligan's novel *The Point*. Two of the most reflexive essays are left until last: Cranston's own 'Islands' (pp. 219–60), and Elizabeth Leane's '"A place of ideals in conflict": Images of Antarctica in Australian Literature' (pp. 261–90). Cranston examines the trope of the islander as isolated and insular, citing examples of such assertions from literature and criticism, before examining in detail a very diverse range of texts from island cultures. Cranston's stated concern is 'ecocritical praxis' rather than a survey of nissological tropes: thus her concerns are farming, sealing, autobiography and the politics of land ownership. Leane considers the representation of Antarctica in a range of texts from the second half of the twentieth century, with the qualification that 'To identify and analyse "a literature of the Antarctic"...is to threaten the sense that this is one place on earth that the cultural has not reached, where a direct, unmediated encounter with nature can be achieved' (p. 262).

Penny van Toorn's 'Wild Speech, Time Speech, Real Speech? Written Renditions of Aboriginal Australian Speech, 1788–1850' (*Southerly* 67:i–ii[2007] 166–78) deals with questions of authenticity, giving particular attention to the representation of Indigenous speakers and speech in the journals of George Grey and Watkin Tench. The essay concludes that there is no single authentic voice and that the relationship of transcription to (likely) speech varies widely, but that 'transcription' serves as an important marker of a claim to authenticity by non-Indigenous authors. This trick of authorship appears in sources as diverse as Tench and Grey, the 'transcription' of Galmarra's 'report' of the death of Edward Kennedy, and nineteenth-century colonial poetry. The later part of the essay examines several very subtle and yet effective examples of Indigenous men smuggling their stories into narratives ostensibly produced by others; van Toorn contrasts this 'reported speech' with the 'literary ventriloquism' prevalent in journals and creative work. It is her eye for emotionally resonant examples that characterizes van Toorn's monograph *Writing Never Arrives Naked: Early Aboriginal Cultures of Writing in Australia*, a study which effectively rewrites late eighteenth- and early nineteenth-century Australian literary history. By interrogating Enlightenment views of writing as the pre-eminent technology of civilization (and on that basis incomprehensible to Indigenous peoples), and by examining in close detail Indigenous texts which, although not formally 'literary', indicate familiarity with and a capacity to deploy writing, van Toorn proposes that the notion of an Aboriginal literature which 'begins' with the publication of creative texts some time in the twentieth century is deeply flawed. Her most compelling case study, which proffers a brilliant synthesis of academic theory, personal observation and textual interpretation, is of a rock painting now called 'the Milbrodale Baiami', read in conjunction with an account of a dream of 'Jehovah' by an Awabakal scholar, Biraban, transcribed (and probably at least partially transformed) by the Reverend Lancelot Threlkeld. Detailed but admittedly inconclusive evidence is presented for the extraordinary claim that the painting, still visible, might be a visual representation of Biraban's dream (pp. 42–52, esp. 47–9). Other texts considered by van Toorn include letters and petitions to religious and government authorities, as well as some controversial 'treaties' (probably forgeries). As an exercise in book history, *Writing Never Arrives Naked* works with a sophisticated critical understanding of writing as a technology. The larger import of the study is that it demands a reconceptualizing of relationships between Indigenous peoples and Europeans in the colonial period. Not only do the arguments overturn the kinds of stereotypes of Aborigines which prevailed among those who denigrated and sought to destroy Indigenous peoples or their cultures, they lend support to the views of those who admitted—even if only in passing—their dependence on Aboriginal scholars and teachers in acquiring local knowledge. So, too, do the arguments complicate beyond recognition existing scholarly and popular beliefs about the 'beginnings' of Aboriginal literacy, the level of complexity of early cultural exchange between Indigenous and non-Indigenous peoples, and even contemporary conceptualizations of the writing of culture and of cultures of writing. In considering how individuals and communities 'have conceptualised, evaluated and used alphabetic writing from within their respective life-worlds', van Toorn offers an exemplary model of cross-cultural analysis. In denaturalizing the very notions of writing, literacy and literature, van Toorn's study remakes them from within the colonial context.

A different kind of recuperation of custodians of knowledge, albeit no less sympathetic to its subject, is offered by Sylvia Martin's biography *Ida Leeson: A Life*. Leeson, a librarian, encountered debilitating obstruction while leading collection development at Sydney's Mitchell Library, a major resource for the study of Australian and Pacific history and literature. The more specific interest for literary scholars is Martin's account of Leeson's assiduous assistance to creative writers, particularly Miles Franklin, and researchers, like E. Morris Miller, the founding bibliographer of Australian literature. Unfortunately the name index is rather selective (Morris Miller, for example, is not there), but the book does valuable work in restoring Leeson to view and giving portraits of writers like Franklin, who was clearly a good friend. One of Australia's most noted biographers, Brenda Niall, published a reflective but jaunty autobiography, *Life Class: The Education of a Biographer*, in which she reconsiders her studies of the Boyd family, noted for their work in art, literature, architecture and design, and the renowned children's writers Mary Grant Bruce and Ethel Turner, among other subjects. Niall laments the poor status of children's literature within academic institutions generally, and the study of Australian literature specifically (pp. 148–9). The book will be particularly useful for Niall's discussion of the difficulties she has experienced in writing her major works, her frank observations about the quality of her sources (archival and living), and her discussion of the constraints she sometimes experienced in 'using' them.

Some of Niall's concerns about children's literature in Australia are implicitly addressed by Clare Bradford's *Unsettling Narratives: Postcolonial Readings of Children's Literature*, a book that in a sense serves a double constituency. Bradford introduces specialists in postcolonial literatures to children's writing from Australia, Canada, Aotearoa/New Zealand and the United States, while also introducing specialists in children's writing to the premises and arguments of postcolonial criticism. One senses that Bradford's real target is teachers of children's writing, but the book might prove a little inaccessible for such a wide audience, although its survey of the field is very likely to be helpful to teachers in search of interesting texts for their students. Chapters offer detailed readings, often comparing books from two or three of the regions under study; the implicit drive is towards valuing books which Bradford sees as presenting empowering narratives for Indigenous child readers, while setting significant challenges for non-Indigenous child readers to imagine 'other worlds', other systems of value and cultural belief. A politically similar case, one which is likewise keen to argue for the greater cultural significance of children's literature, is put by Debra Dudek in 'Dogboys and Lost Things; or Anchoring a Floating Signifier: Race and Critical Multiculturalism' (*ArielE* 37:iv[2006] 1–20). The article lays out two sets of backgrounds—of multiculturalism as a policy, and of the criticism of children's literature—in order to put the case that some children's books are now entering a 'fourth phase' of what Dudek terms 'critical multiculturalism'.

In this period, attention to representation of racial difference is paramount. Sissy Helff's 'Children in Detention: Juvenile Authors Recollect Refugee Stories' (*Papers* 17:ii[2007] 67–74) considers contributions to the collection *Dark Dreams: Australian Refugee Stories by Young Writers aged 11–20 Years* within the context of a burgeoning young adult literature dealing with themes of forced migration. Helff argues that contributions to this collection, produced from entries to a national competition, challenge stereotypes of refugees and allow insight into the experience of forced flight, as well as (in some cases) some moves towards recovery from this trauma.

Undoubtedly a major achievement for the year was the publication of Nicholas Birns and Rebecca McNeer's *A Companion to Australian Literature since 1900*, a collection of thirty essays plus time-line and index. The book is more likely to be 'mined' than it is to be worked through systematically, and the editors have allowed some minor repetitions to facilitate stand-alone reading. Perhaps the more stimulating essays for later-year students and for critics are those which seek to raise rather than answer questions, and which take some room to move: Ali Gumillya Baker and Gus Worby's 'Aboriginality since Mabo: Writing, Politics and Art' (pp. 17–40) and Tanya Dalziell's 'Australian Women's Writing from 1970 to 2005' (pp. 139–53) from the first section, 'Identities', are particularly successful in this respect. Other essays in this first part of the book offer discussions of questions of Aboriginality and whiteness; multiculturalism; Asian Australian literature; hoaxes; and Jewish writers. In comparison, the contributions to part II, 'Writing across Time', feel a little more rushed, in the main surveying vast tracts of poetry and drama. The more controversial aspects of the book are perhaps parts III and V. The first of these, 'International Reputations', has essays on Patrick White, David Malouf, Les Murray, Peter Carey and Gerald Murnane, and just one woman—Christina Stead. If Judith Wright seems a disappointing omission, or perhaps Elizabeth Jolley, or Katharine Susannah Prichard (whose first name is repeatedly misspelled)—the explanation might lie in the collection's unapologetically North American focus: Wright's reputation in countries such as India, for example, or Prichard's in Europe, cut no ice here. The gender inequity is perpetuated in the next section, 'Writers and Regions', where Dorothy Hewett stands alone among Tim Winton, Xavier Herbert, Michael Wilding, Murray Bail, Rodney Hall and Frank Moorhouse, although the latter four are covered in a single essay (one which never mentions or examines the idea of region). Perhaps the problem lay in a brief that was too idiosyncratic for a reference work, not least when the work of Thea Astley is excluded, for example. Perhaps the most disappointing neglect is of Randolph Stow, a brilliant if not particularly prolific writer, one of the most discussed novelists of the 1960s, 1970s and 1980s, who might have been considered in either of these sections. The brief mentions of him in Lyn Jacobs's discussion of 'Tim Winton and West Australian Writing' (pp. 307–19; see pp. 308, 310, 319) do not make it to the index, although Geelong Grammar School does.

Perhaps what would have been useful, here, for students, is some amplification of Carolyn Bliss's very important opening to her essay 'Peter Carey' (in Birns and McNeer, eds., pp. 281–92), which meditates on questions of canonicity and the changing aesthetics of the past forty years in academic criticism. That is not to say that the editors are not intelligent about their choices—they clearly are—but readers could be forgiven for assuming that Australian literary studies is a field in which methodological issues are restricted to questions of identity (witness the contents and placement of the first section). For example, in such an explicitly canon-making volume, students might usefully have been able to read an essay that offered tools for thinking about canonicity. However, they are likely to be confused by the contents and title of the fifth and final section, 'Beyond the Canon', which seems at first to refer to genre fiction: the first two essays deal with science fiction and popular fiction respectively. But why, under this rubric, do we then have contributions on film, children's writing, environment, and gay and lesbian writing? It seems difficult to argue the case that either 'environment' or 'gay and lesbian' place us 'beyond the canon' (Judith Wright and Patrick White spring to mind). However, such problems should not be overstated, and the question of audience needs to be borne in mind: in general, the *Companion* is likely to prove very useful for undergraduate students and perhaps even general readers. The test will be the extent to which these essays prove stimulating for their audience, hence whether the collection is effective in becoming a springboard rather than an endpoint for the study of Australian literature.

A very different kind of work for students is Graham Huggan's *Australian Literature: Postcolonialism, Racism, Transnationalism*, a book which follows Bob Hodge and Vijay Mishra's *Dark Side of the Dream* in centralizing race in attempting to describe Australian literature, but which radically differs from its predecessor in calling for a return to postcolonial reading strategies. These arguments are considered further in a chapter on the history of such criticism in Australia. Huggan then discusses 'the history wars', debates about the process of colonization and about the ethics and methods of historical enquiry that have exerted a considerable force on criticism and literature over the last decade or more. Huggan's innovation here is to focus on literary history, and the co-opting of canonical figures such as Marcus Clarke, Henry Lawson and Miles Franklin, to a set of narratives of progress which presume the centrality of 'white colonial writing' (p. xiii). The third chapter, 'Interrogating Whiteness', compares canonical works by non-Indigenous authors that have Indigenous protagonists—among them Prichard's *Coonardoo* and Xavier Herbert's *Capricornia*—with Sally Morgan's *My Place* and Kim Scott's *Benang*, more recent works by Indigenous authors that focus on the search for and nature of an Indigenous identity. The final chapter engages with the problematic of the term 'multiculturalism', and the politics of its deployment.

Lyn McCredden, in ' "So you make a shadow": Australian Poetry in Review 2006–2007' (*Westerly* 52[2007] 81–98), reviews nearly twenty volumes of poetry received during the year. In contrast to McCredden's generous tone Peter Pierce finds few pleasures in his '*Westerly* Non-Fiction Review 2006–2007' (52[2007] 160–71); Anthony Hassall is Baby Bear in 'The Year's Work in Fiction' (52[2007] 187–99) for the same journal, nodding to many authors while giving warm praise to new novels by Janette Turner Hospital, Tara June Winch, Deborah Robertson and, in particular, Rodney Hall.

The 'Annual Bibliography of Commonwealth Literature 2006: Australia' (*JCL* 42:iv[2007] 5–22) was compiled by Van Ikin and Keira McKenzie, an eight-page introductory section preceding a helpfully selective list of poetry, fiction and criticism, with smaller sections covering areas such as anthologies, letters and bibliographies. The authors begin by asserting that there was a mood of 'taking stock' during 2006, a year in which 'a deep and growing disquiet at the direction of Australian literature' was expressed by 'Many critics' (p. 5). As in previous years we are indebted not only to these essays but also to the AustLit database and, in particular, to the 'Annual Bibliography of Studies in Australian Literature: 2007' compiled by Carol Hetherington and Irmtraud Petersson (*ALS* 23:i[2008] 104–20). We refer readers to this source for 'general' items as well as author-based listings, while also noting that Hetherington's 'Little Australians? Some Questions about National Identity and the National Literature' (*Antipodes* 21:i[2007] 11–15) outlines the problems of delimiting and tracking down the 'Australian' in Australian literature. Hetherington's sometimes eccentric passions animate a discussion which offers insight into the questions faced daily by the forty or so people who work on the database. Faye Christenberry compiled the annual 'Bibliography of Australian Literature and Criticism Published in North America: 2006' (*Antipodes* 21:ii[2007] 198–210), which follows a similar format to the *ALS* bibliography, albeit in reverse.

(b) Fiction

What is noticeable in 2007 is the new predominance of whiteness studies, and the extent to which this has supplanted postcolonial approaches: the constant attention in whiteness studies to the dialogue with the postcolonial can be contrasted with what seems like a certain self-satisfaction among postcolonial critics which allows them to take the validity of their methods for granted. Julie Mullaney's 'New Labours, Older Nativisms? Australian Critical Whiteness Studies, Indigeneity and David Malouf's *Harland's Half Acre*' (*JCL* 42:i[2007] 97–116) is symptomatic of this trend in offering a judicious but provocative account of the field of whiteness studies. Mullaney sees it as operating in dialogue with postcolonial studies, but in a manner which 'accentuates its... turn away from assumptions of white possession and towards new understandings of the functions of indigenous sovereignties' (pp. 100–1). She attributes this shift, in Australia at least, to the influence of the work of Aileen Moreton-Robinson. Malouf's novel seems available for a reading which focuses on the representation and rhetoric of whiteness, as per this agenda, but she also queries whether 'it is possible to argue that the agitated movements... preoccupying critical whiteness studies in its promulgation of an ever more self-questioning and constantly shifting whiteness may be *prefigured* (paradoxically) in Malouf's earlier figuring of Frank Harland and the quest for a settled white indigene' (p. 101). For Mullaney, reading *Harland's Half Acre* is a way of reflecting upon and participating in the heated debate around the reception of *Remembering Babylon*, and thus her essay engages with the larger debate around the Malouf oeuvre and its role in naturalizing or problematizing colonization. There is a productive digression into the representation of the sacred in Thomas Keneally's *The Chant of Jimmie Blacksmith* before Mullaney's conclusion, in which she quotes Ken Gelder and Jane Jacobs's *Uncanny Australia*, that Malouf's novel merely re-forms 'white needs and desire and constitutes a form of "neo-colonial racism"' in that it tends ... to "lock" Aboriginality "into a form of (spiritual) otherness necessitated by modernity and the discourse of reconciliation"' (p. 112). Frances de Groen's 'Made in England, "The Road from Singapore" and *I Think I'll Live*: Reflections on Mid-Twentieth-Century National Identity' (*Southerly* 67:i–ii[2007] 319–32) uses two captivity narratives by Australian prisoners of the Japanese to dispute Malouf's account of Australian identity in his *Quarterly Essay* 'Made in England'. De Groen reads these two stories as reinforcing Malouf's lack of interest in female identities and lives, but as radically different in offering overt expressions of anti-Britishness. The unpublished 'Road from Singapore' presents a strong endorsement of the importance of 'the bush' to the construction of Australian identity, while *I Think I'll Live* endorses an internationalist, socialist view of society. 'Read together', says de Groen, 'these texts draw attention to the omissions and elisions in Malouf's arguments about the "Englishness" of the Australian ethos' (p. 331). Students of Malouf are well served by Don Randall's *David Malouf*, published in the Contemporary World Writers series. Randall is keen to position Malouf as a postcolonial writer, but the dangers of partisanship are averted by a prudent critical sensibility. Randall achieves a nice balance of the subtly introductory (explaining plot and character) with more specialized commentary, offering original and insightful remarks on individual texts. Nor does he shrink from making negative comments on either the writer or critics, particularly in his very helpful final chapter, which offers an evaluative survey of Malouf criticism. Randall's understated deployment of theory and his judicious tone in engaging with the Malouf oeuvre—more attention is given to the later novels—stand in contrast to Jean-François Vernay's *Water from the Moon: Illusion and Reality in the Works of Australian Novelist Christopher Koch*, a study of the writing of Christopher Koch. It would be harsh to label this study 'for enthusiasts only', but Vernay does have a tendency to cheer his subject, while offering interpretations in a prose style unlikely to be tempting to the general reader. For said enthusiasts, Koch's controversial 1996 Miles Franklin Award acceptance speech was published this year under the title 'The Crusade against Beauty' (*Quadrant* 51:xii[2007] 51–2).

Maureen Clark's book *Mudrooroo, a Likely Story: Identity and Belonging in Postcolonial Australia* tackles head-on one of the most controversial and complex debates about authorship to animate Australian literary studies over the last decade. As Clark points out in her introduction, it was in part Mudrooroo's own strongly expressed criticism of Sally Morgan, specifically her claim to and representation of an Indigenous identity in her book *My Place*, which seems to have energized the controversies which have arisen about his own identity, specifically his claim to be Indigenous and to represent the views of Indigenous people in his creative writing and criticism. Notwithstanding her title, Clark refers to the author as Colin Johnson throughout the book. This is a way, she says, of respecting the formal pronouncement by the Nyoongar people of south-west Western Australia that they reject the writer's claims to kinship with them. Clark's acknowledgements indicate that she received co-operation from Mudrooroo in completing the doctoral thesis that is the basis of this study. In this context, the firmness of her consistent criticisms of his sexism is a little surprising (although they are not inapt); the larger concern, though, is with Mudrooroo's positioning as an Indigenous writer. Clark examines Johnson's cultural background and family heritage at considerable length, before going on to consider the novels in detail. Her focus in the chapters on biography is Johnson's maternal family, from whom he claimed Indigenous descent, but whom Clark and others have found to be Anglo-Irish. There are a number of strands to Clark's argument in this section of the book: that biographical information is crucial to understanding the Johnson oeuvre; that that oeuvre is a particularly significant one for Australian literary studies, and for Indigenous writers and critics in particular; and that it is necessary to consider the implications of the fact that Johnson's writings, even his once definitive critical study *Writing from the Fringe*, have more or less disappeared from school and tertiary curricula. The cornerstone of Clark's argument in the second section is that, while Johnson's work has been read as a set of engagements with the discursive strategies of colonialism, it can equally be understood as an engagement with the forces that shaped his own life. Among the more important of these are the patronage of Dame Mary Durack, which enabled the publication of his first novel *Wild Cat Falling* (in 1965), and the disproportionate success of the much later novel *Doctor Wooreddy's Prescription for Enduring the Ending of the World*. This book is about George Augustus Robinson's horribly ill-fated attempts to 'care' for a small group of Tasmanian Aborigines, all of whom eventually perished, thereby furnishing the mythology of 'the last Tasmanians'. *Wild Cat* has long been billed 'the first novel by an Aboriginal writer', while *Doctor Wooreddy* has been widely praised and taught for its apparent pioneering, among Australian Indigenous writers at least, of postmodern and/or postcolonial and/or magic realist forms. Clark wonders whether Johnson's representations of Robinson, the high-handed man of religion (and protagonist, in different guises, of several Mudrooroo novels) who made his 'fame and fortune' by claiming an authoritative speaking position in relation to Indigenous peoples, might productively be associated with the author's own claiming of a position as an arbiter of 'authentic' forms of Indigenous literary expression. Concluding that Johnson 'appears to have known all along that he is not Aboriginal', she expresses sympathy for the young man, ambitious for a writing career, who was seen by Durack as Aboriginal, an identity which in that historical period offered little in the way of cultural advantage. This sympathy is modulated, though, in the light of the controversies of thirty years later and Johnson's apparent desire in this later period to distance himself from his then newly found siblings. These were times in which, as Clark seems to see it, there was greater gain to be made from claiming Aboriginality, greater pain to be caused to others by doing so, and greater opportunity for Johnson, as an influential writer and critic, to resist interpellation. Clark hits her stride in a forceful and persuasive conclusion, which proposes ways in which the controversy might be understood, and analyses the relationship of debates about Mudrooroo's identity to the critical reception of his work, particularly the novels.

Several essays in Sheila Collingwood-Whittick's *The Pain of Unbelonging: Alienation and Identity in Australasian Literature* present discussions of recent fiction in the context of theoretical debates within and about postcolonial theory. Perhaps the most interesting and certainly the most lively of these is Marc Delrez's meditation on the politics and aesthetics of contemporary writing in 'Towards Settler Auto-Ethnography: Nicholas Jose's *Black Sheep*' (pp. 1–14). Delrez is both admiring of, and troubled by, Jose's exploration of the life of a family member who lived in the largely Indigenous-populated northern Australian town of Borroloola in the middle part of the twentieth century. In Delrez's view, Jose's attempt to find common ground with Indigenous people and concomitantly to recuperate or even 'create' a 'forefather' whose life within an Indigenous community would offer Jose a somehow more viable 'family history', or what Delrez nicely terms a search for 'redemptive affinities', might also mask or overwrite discussions of contemporary injustice and inequality. Delrez makes an even bolder argument in 'Nationalism, Reconciliation and the Cultural Genealogy of Magic in Richard Flanagan's *Death of a River Guide*' (*JCL* 42:i[2007] 117–29), where he engages with critics whom he sees as being in error in thinking that meaningful generalizations can be made about a 'national' literature. Delrez illustrates his claim with a reading of Flanagan's novel about Tasmania, the success of which he takes as proof that contemporary Australian literature demands localized readings.

The question of the relationship between history and literature which has been so central to discussions of colonial history and school curricula in Australia over recent years is given an optimistic twist by Agnes Vogler in 'Forging Heritage for the Tourist Gaze: Australian History and Contemporary Representations Reviewed' (*JAS* 91[2007] 93–106; notes pp. 189–90). The essay includes discussion of Richard Flanagan's *Gould's Book of Fish* and Alex Miller's *Journey to the Stone Country*, but is perhaps of more general interest for its exploration of the question of how to conceptualize history. Working from her argument that there is a distinction between 'history' and 'heritage', Vogler concludes that Indigenous peoples might be able to resist the forces of commodification necessary to tourism by representing history from their own points of view, in a variety of artistic and communitarian forums. Issues 5 and 6 of the API-network's online journal *Altitude* [2005], edited by Anne Brewster, collect useful case studies on the topic of *Reading Indigenous Australian Texts*. One of the best of these, Brewster's own essay on the poetry of Lisa Bellear, is revised and extended as 'Brokering Cross-Radical Feminism: Reading Indigenous Australian Poet Lisa Bellear' (*FemT* 8[2007] 209–21). Brewster uses a technically simple poem as the launching pad for a complex political and philosophical discussion of reading and whiteness.

Several useful essays on fiction appeared in a new publication, *Lemuria: A Half-Yearly Research Journal of Indo-Australian Studies* (1:i[2006]), an attractive journal that contains essays, reviews and original verse.

Paul Sharrad's 'Australian Literature and the Making of History' (*Lemuria* 1:i[2006] 55–74) criss-crosses much familiar ground but includes novelists such as Nicholas Hasluck and Rodney Hall in a generous albeit introductory survey. Former members of the Bicentennial Authority, however, will be disappointed to learn that the Australian populace thought the celebration was marking the arrival of Captain Cook, not that of the First Fleet (p. 60). Nicholas Birns, in 'Cosmopolitan Convict: Marcus Clarke's Reshuffling of the Past' (*Lemuria* 1:i[2006] 112–21), follows Andrew McCann in rejecting colonial Australia as nationalistic-in-waiting, but finds rather a displaced and fragmentary cosmopolitanism. Birns puts the case that Clarke's own strongest models are not English writers such as Dickens but French ones such as Flaubert; in fact, Clarke was 'the best nineteenth-century French novelist England never had' (p. 112). One aspect of cosmopolitanism the novel deploys is a subversive playing with history via Sylvia Vickers's reading about the Romans and the Carthaginians. The interesting if somewhat untidy argument has two other foci, the concept of 'tropicopolitan' subversion and a contrast between Atlantic history (i.e. that of slavery) and a Pacific focus on 'first contact'. Michael Cathcart's 'Lemuria and Australian Dreams of an Inland Sea' (*Lemuria* 1:i[2006] 32–47) is perhaps the most substantial contribution, re-evaluating a series of 'Lemurian novels' of the late nineteenth century which he argues were 'explicitly *imperial* stories', 'steeped in theosophical notions of race and history and...avidly read in Australia' (pp. 34, 34–5). Cathcart explains that 'Lemuria' was the name given by British scientists of the 1860s to what they posited was an ancient continent that had once joined India to Madagascar (p. 33). The stories usually feature a group of white travellers who meet with 'lost tribes' or 'lost races' that 'are living amidst the remnants of ancient customs, occult beliefs and a sophisticated technology created in the distant past' (p. 35). The engagement, here, is with critics—notably Robert Dixon, in *Writing the Colonial Adventure*—who have read the books in terms of their manifestation of colonial anxiety and paranoia. Cathcart, who disagrees with this view, suggests that there are two distinct kinds of imperial fiction: that which embodies 'necronationalism', which monumentalizes silence and death, and that which much more optimistically imagines a future of white conquest, based on mastery of the land. A number of novels are considered in some detail before the author returns to the problem of the ways in which nineteenth-century fiction represents extreme colonial violence against Aboriginal peoples. Cathcart's rather surprising but persuasive conclusion is that such tales were as concerned to promote irrigation as they were eugenics.

This discussion of the obsession with water in the context of 'national' and racial development can be juxtaposed with novelist and critic Chandani Lokuge's meditation on the deep cultural significance of water to Sri Lankan culture(s), hence to her own novels *Turtle Nest* and *If the Moon Smiled*, in her 'Waters of Desire' (*Meanjin* 66:ii[2007] 25–34). Lokuge considers the religious, geographical and cultural elements of these works, which represent encounters between Australians and Sri Lanka, in the context of her own visit to Sri Lanka just days before the horrific tsunami which devastated the country, and other parts of the region, in late December 2004. The question of audience, environment and Australian literature is also addressed in Shanthini Pillai's 'Occidental Echoes: Beth Yahp's Ambivalent Malaya' (*Hecate* 33:i[2007] 174–89). Pillai argues that the critical success of Yahp's *The Crocodile Fury* has come about not because the book challenges and diversifies ideas about Australian culture (as prize judges would have it), but because it successfully reproduces colonial tropes of landscape. The novel is set in a convent on the edge of a Malaysian jungle; in Pillai's reading, the jungle represents an unnamed and unknowable threat to 'civilization', a trope all too familiar to readers of Joseph Conrad and Somerset Maugham.

Different ways of seeing and representing the physical environment are also the subject of Paul Sharrad's 'Estranging an Icon: Eucalyptus and India' (*Interventions* 9:i[2007] 31–48). The essay investigates the proliferation of the 'quintessentially Australian' tree species in India, in dialogue with a reading of Murray Bail's novel *Eucalyptus*, a book which seems to parody the kinds of nationalism which centralize 'the bush' and its people but which also (in Sharrad's view) draws its inspiration from the spread of the tree to India and other parts of the world. After encouraging a kind of sympathy with Bail's fairytale, Sharrad turns late to ask whether the 'flow' of the story might not 'contain a sleight of hand'. He asks whether the spread of the eucalyptus was a story of magical dispersal, as Bail would seem to have it, or the very specific effect of colonial networks of administration and trade. Thus Sharrad wonders whether telling the story of the tree's proliferation in other colonial environments as a fantasy might risk recycling colonialist oppositions which depend on the notion of 'a core of *rootedness*, of nation/nature, giving depth to shallowness, authority to insecurity, rooted universality to white settler... locality' (p. 43). The conclusion is that the book's 'smooth fictional story gives it its wide success, its aesthetic appeal [but] in doing so it obscures a more real history of agents and activists' while tying 'the novel back into the national "bush" tradition it otherwise mocks' (p. 43). The consequent warning to postcolonial critics is that it is only detailed knowledge of local circumstances which will enable them to interpret texts effectively, while comparative work ensures that national and nationalist assumptions about the significance of the eucalyptus are 'defamiliarised'.

Another major essay for 2007 was Andrew McCann's 'Rosa Praed and the Vampire-Aesthete' (*VLC* 35:i[2007] 175–87), which explores the implication of its contention that Praed's 'obviously commercial novels are also intensely invested in aesthetic questions, in the dislocated character of imperial experience, in the accrual of cultural capital, and in their own relationship to the vexed question of originality vis-à-vis the market for popular fiction' (p. 175). In suggesting that Praed's deployment of the vampire figure is related to anxieties about 'cultural value and influence in an imperial economy', McCann seeks to 'diversify the provenance of the *fin-de-siècle* vampire' (p. 175). The discussion of the novels takes up arguments made by earlier Praed critics about the significance of same-sex desire to her life and work, noting Praed's representation of Oscar Wilde as a vampire figure in her novel *Affinities*. But McCann seeks to reposition Praed's novels within the imperial economy of book publishing and literary value, and thereby to reinterpret Praed's representation of aestheticism 'as a form of vampiric influence, with a figure like Wilde at its centre' (p. 176). Drawing on the work of Nicholas Daly, McCann asks whether 'far from being merely a symptom of an empire in crisis or imminent collapse...the apparent Gothicism of what Daly calls "popular middle-class fiction"...also embodies an attempt to accommodate and reflect upon aspects of cultural modernization (consumerism, professionalism, globalization, for example)' (pp. 176–7). For McCann, then, it is political economy rather than sexuality which is paramount, an argument which he pursues through a reading of Praed's *The Soul of Countess Adrian*, a book 'in which the vampire-aesthete embodies the intensely undecidable relationship between culture and commerce that is also literalized in the relationship between Praed's fiction and its potential publics' (p. 177). The conclusion of McCann's essay, which turns to the later novel *The Ghost*, has resonance for nineteenth-century Australian literary studies more generally in its assertion that this book suggests that 'Praed's solution to the problem of an aestheticism that had revealed both its profane, commercial reality and its complicity with imperial hierarchies, was a reinvestment in the notion of place as central to the expressive integrity of the literary text, to the creative process uncompromised by the commercialisation of culture' (p. 185). Julieanne Lamond's 'Rosa Praed's Readership: In Search of an Australian Audience' (*Southerly* 67:i–ii[2007] 121–34) argues that Praed had an Australian as well as a British audience and, more interestingly, that her heroines show their sensibility being formed partly by their reading. Laurie Hergenhan's 'Beautiful Lies, Ugly Truths' (*Overland* 187[2007] 42–6) is also concerned with readership, offering an informative discussion of Mark Twain's comments on Aborigines in his *More Tramps Abroad*. A briefer version of this book was published in the United States as *Following the Equator*. Noting Twain's heavy use of sources in Australian literature, including works by Praed and Marcus Clarke, Hergenhan compares the American and British editions in order to argue that the excisions 'changed understandings of Twain's attitude towards British imperialism and parallels he drew with America' (p. 43). Hergenhan wonders whether the preparation of the American edition perhaps entailed 'a kind of censorship', with Twain reluctant to hint at parallels between the brutalities of colonialism and convictism in Australia, and colonization and slavery in the United States (p. 46).

Susan K. Martin's nuanced reading of Joseph Furphy's major work in '"Us circling round and round": The Track of Narrative and the Ghosts of Lost Children in *Such Is Life*', in the special issue of *JASAL* ([2007] 77–93) is ostensibly concerned with the representation of 'Tracks, navigating and mapping' in this sprawling and eccentric novel. However, the more resonant aspects of her argument lie in Furphy's commentary on reading, place and national culture. In a carefully argued and persuasive essay, Martin makes the case that the novel 'forces the reader...self-consciously [to] enact...reading' (p. 87); the difficulty, though, is that the narrator himself is inept, and therefore cannot model successful interpretation. Likewise the sheer scope and complexity of the book mean that an individual reader will 'usually fail to notice some of the major trails' (p. 87). This is drawn together in a strong concluding section in which Martin argues that Furphy's use of the 'lost child' narrative so prevalent in Australian colonial culture 'represent[s] exactly that impossible phantasm of the unified white... Australian subject' (p. 87) and, concomitantly, that the novel must refuse narrative closure. This is a claim emphasized by its final words, which assert that the tale has been one ' "told by a vulgarian, full of slang and blanky, signifying—nothing" ' (p. 88). Elizabeth McMahon's 'The Centaur and the Cyborg: Abject Becoming on the Colonial Frontier' (*Southerly* 67:i–ii[2007] 211–25) is a bravura circling around cross-dressing in *Such Is Life* and Tasma's story 'Monsieur Caloche'. The ambitious and painfully theorized argument has some interesting moments, including comments on the awareness that Furphy shows of Zola. This introduces not only the assertion of Furphy's own naturalism in his famous rejection of Kingsleyan romance, but also ideas of degeneration and decay. ' "Oh, you're cutting my bowels out!": Sexual Unspeakability in Marcus Clarke's *His Natural Life*' (*JASAL* 6[2007] 33–48), by Damien Barlow, is a fascinating and for the most part convincing explication of the sexual undercurrents of Clarke's novel. Its particular strengths are its use of both published versions of the novel, and its setting of Clarke's novel in the discourse of the anti-transportation debate of thirty years earlier. In defiantly refusing to accept that a pipe is sometimes just a pipe, the article throws genuinely new light on well-visited themes in a well-visited novel.

In 'Riders in the Chariot: A Tale for Our Times' (*JASAL* 7[2007] 32–45), Bernadette Brennan discusses the political deployment of xenophobia and the way the term 'elites' has been mobilized to brand groups as non-Australian. The term has also been deployed in dismissing Patrick White's work. However, it can be argued that it is primarily the 'elite' quality that allows White to offer inclusiveness, and to expand the sympathetic and imaginative landscape of Australian culture. The motley four in *Riders* are united because they are ' "*different*" '; 'They are the elite because they are open to intuitive perception and an understanding of human suffering' (p. 35). Brennan finds examples of racism in recent news reports that show that the events in *Riders* are not as extreme or improbable as critics like Leonie Kramer, Michael Wilding and Simon During claim. Commensurately, she puts the case that, far from being disengaged from society, White had a consistent activist agenda for the liberalizing of Australia. Very much a writer's article, Brian Castro's 'Twice Born: Risk and Trespass in White's "Patrick" ' (*HEAT* 14[2007] 63–70) sees the Patrick White of *The Twyborn Affair* as personally and artistically secure enough to be able to project and perform aspects of opinion and personality that previously he had masked. A ruling motif of the argument is the counterfeit coin, which can have exchange value even if it is an illicit object. For an artist, that exchange value is maintained at the price of risk—a risk that the late White was ready to take. The article is full of stylish turns of phrase and thoughtful aperçus. Andrew Reimer writes a graceful tribute to Elizabeth Jolley, who passed away early in the year, noting some parallels between their respective origins, and stressing her Austrian background and her musical references in 'Songs of a Wayfarer: In Memory of Elizabeth Jolley' (*HEAT* 14[2007] 45–62). He argues that her protagonists are typically 'roamers', subject to suffering and humiliation, often eccentric or absurd; reading Jolley, one senses 'the void, something missing, puzzling and undeclared at the heart of almost everything that she wrote' (p. 61).

In 'Jewish Literature in Australia' (in Stähler, ed., *Anglophone Jewish Literature*), Elisa Morera de la Vall floats, then disposes of, the obvious definitional problems by deciding that 'this chapter will deal with halachically Jewish authors whose work expresses their Jewishness and who live in Australia' (p. 175); thereupon there is a straightforward account of eight writers and their principal works. Judah Waten still ranks highest, although Serge Lieberman's five volumes of short stories have won the Alan Marshall award three times, and Maria Lewitt won the 1986 NSW Premier's award for fiction with *No Snow in December*. Morera de la Vall argues that as well as the usual migrant themes of displacement and cultural adaptation, Jewish writers tend to revisit the Holocaust either to come to terms with loss of family, memory of the trauma, or in the case of younger writers, guilt 'for the suffering they did not share with their parents' (p. 176). David Sornig's elegantly compact and intelligent discussion of 'Specters of Berlin in A.L. [Andrew] McCann's *Subtopia* and Christos Tsiolkas's *Dead Europe*' (*Antipodes* 21:i[2007] 67–71) contends that the two novels can be read in terms of 'Derrida's exploration of the logic of the ghost, the hauntology he describes in *Specters of Marx*' (p. 67). Sornig puts the case that in both novels, 'the fall of the Berlin Wall, and Berlin itself, become a useful kind of literary landscape device in which the novels' narrators are forced to listen to some of the city's ghostly historic voices' (p. 71), voices which the reader is then forced to engage with. This remark contrasts interestingly with McCann's own comment, noted above, about the persistent concern in literature and elsewhere with the locatability of culture.

Anja Schwartz offers a reading of Tsiolkas's first novel, an indication that this writer is now receiving the kind of serious critical attention his work has long invited. The framing of the argument of 'Mapping (Un)Australian Identities: "Territorial Disputes" in Christos Tsiolkas' *Loaded*' (in Bartels and Wiemann, eds., *Global Fragments: (Dis)Orientation in the New World Order*, pp. 13–27) in terms of political debates about hostile government and popular responses to refugees on the Norwegian ship *Tampa* in 2001 perhaps stretches an argument about 'spatial logic' to its limit, but more productive interpretative ground is covered when Schwartz argues that *Loaded*'s representation of its protagonist's experience of space 'appears to echo' the opening section of Michel de Certeau's essay 'Walking the City'. Using Certeau's arguments about the contrast between the structured and legible ways in which planners understand urban environments, and the 'resourceful...tactics that people employ in everyday life to survive the city' (p. 17), the essay presents an elegant and insightful discussion of the pattern of the protagonist's movement and stasis in the city of Melbourne, considered within the specific contexts of the novel's exploration of racial politics and sexual difference. This is probably the best essay yet published on the novel, and will be of interest to any critic engaging with contemporary urban fiction and models of spatiality.

Similar topics were discussed in the work of another contemporary novelist garnering increased critical attention, Gail Jones. The title of Fiona Roughley's 'Spatialising Experience: Gail Jones's *Black Mirror* and the Contending of Postmodern Space' (*ALS* 23:ii[2007] 58–73) aptly describes the stylishly theorized argument. In the same issue, Lydia Wevers's comparative analysis, 'Fold in the Map: Figuring Modernity in Gail Jones's *Dreams of Speaking* and Elizabeth Knox's *Dreamhunter*' (pp. 187–98) does elegant work in comparing an Australian with a New Zealand novelist. The interest in postmodernism, spatiality and visual image evident in these two essays offers a useful signpost to the key concerns of Jones's work. Elsewhere, Wevers uses an autobiographical frame to compare nineteenth-century Australian and New Zealand literatures, in 'Blow the Wind Westerly: Reading Australia in New Zealand' (*Southerly* 67:i–ii[2007] 111–20), another important contribution to the special double issue of the magazine published for Elizabeth Webby. Wevers finds a much earlier sense of a coherent literature in Australia, and a far stronger sense of class in that literature; she contends that in New Zealand, race and gender have been the more important determinants of literary production.

Kalinda Ashton's ' "There's no guarantee that the future will be worth it": Government and Class in Amanda Lohrey's *The Reading Group*' (*Hecate* 33:i[2007] 154–70) is particularly interesting for its account of the reasons for the pulping of a thousand copies of the first edition of this novel. Another engaging case study, one which is specifically concerned with analysis of the vexed relationship between adult and young adult fiction, is presented in Rebecca-Anne Do Rozario's 'Don't Steal a Book by its Cover: *The Book Thief* and Who Reads It' (*S&P* 31:ii[2007] 104–16), on Marcus Zusak's best-selling novel. Do Rozario suggests that the boundaries between different kinds of audiences for literature are fragmenting, and that this fragmentation is based in part on shared experience of the book as physical object. Further discussion along these lines—of the book as an object—is contained in Paul Eggert's 'Textual Criticism and Folklore: The Ned Kelly Story and *Robbery Under Arms*' (*S&P* 31:ii[2007] 69–80), an essay which reflects on Eggert's principles and practice as a scholarly editor, and on the complex textual history of the Ned Kelly story. Julieanne Lamond likewise considers a key figure in mythologies of nation in 'The Ghost of Dad Rudd, on the Stump' (*JASAL* 6[2007] 19–32), although her argument does not consider textual/cultural questions in quite the way Eggert does. Lamond's interest is in the way different versions of the Rudd stories build different political constituencies; she argues that the 'ordinary Australian', much beloved of modern politicians, is the inheritor of the 'ghost' of Dad Rudd, as is John McIvor of Andrew McGahan's novel *The White Earth*.

(c) Poetry

A gentle and elegant discourse on the strategies, ethics and effects of borrowing images and assuming voice in creative writing is presented in Noel Rowe's ' "Will this be your poem, or mine?": The Give and Take of Story' (*ALS* 23:ii[2007] 1–14), the lead essay in a volume which celebrates Elizabeth Webby's contribution to Australian literary studies. Although the essay is not limited to poetry—it also discusses *Coonardoo*, for example, as well as modern novels such as *Dead Europe*—Rowe takes his tempo and title from poetry, notably Rosemary Dobson's 'Poems of the River Wang', in which two poets 'courteously' offer each other a story. The poignancy of the essay, intensified by the fact of its posthumous publication, is encapsulated in the anecdote with which it ends: 'As I was trying to finish this paper, I overheard a conversation in a doctor's waiting room. [The father reading the story] suddenly interrupted to ask his [ailing] daughter, "What colour is the opposite of black?" She hardly had to think before she answered, with huge confidence, "Pink". "No", he said, "The opposite of black is white, because they are so different." For all the difficulties surrounding the question of story, I hope I have succeeded in offering a small word in support of pink' (p. 12).

A tussle for the reputation of one of Australia's most popular poets occurred in *Australian Literary Studies* this year, a debate which revolves not so much around the 'facts' of biography as around the legitimacy of feminist approaches to Australian literary history. The ostensible point of difference between contributors is the significance of Henry Lawson's sojourn in England around the turn of the century which, although brief, was central to his writing career. Meg Tasker and Lucy Sussex, in ' "That wild run to London": Henry and Bertha Lawson in England' (*ALS* 23:ii[2007] 168–86), use newly available census information and records from institutions for the mentally ill to challenge biographical accounts of the illness experienced by Lawson's wife, and to reconsider beliefs about Lawson's response to her illness and even his own domestic arrangements during Bertha Lawson's long stay in hospital. They conclude that Lawson's career was influenced as much by his personal circumstances as by the literary milieu. In contrast, John Barnes argues that Lawson's London agent, J.B. Pinker, and Pinker's successful cultivation of Blackwoods (proprietor, publisher and magazine) were crucial to his literary success, in his 'Henry Lawson and the "Pinker of Literary Agents" ' (*ALS* 23:ii[2007] 89–105). Whereas Barnes attributes Lawson's literary failures to his gaucheness in dealing with his publisher and to his concern for his wife and family, Tasker and Sussex suggest that Lawson was embroiled in and debilitated by a network of gossip about his apparent infidelity, a set of problems which he later addressed in his short fiction. Philip Butterss in ' "Parnassus Slope": C.J. Dennis's First Years in Victoria' (*Southerly* 67:i–ii[2007] 254–71), aims partly to fill in the biographical details of a less successful period early in Dennis's career, and partly to defend the poet against charges of lack of originality made by influential contemporaries. Butterss also discusses Dennis's left-leaning political references in the poems, a theme which is expanded upon in ' "Your vote is wanted": C.J. Dennis at the *Call*' (*JASAL* 7[2007] 97–106). Here, Butterss examines Dennis's political contributions— poetic and other—to the satirical weekly the *Gadfly*, and to the *Call*, published by the Australian Workers' Union. And Andrew Lynch's 'C.J. Brennan's *A Chant of Doom*: Australia's Medieval War' (*ALS* 23:i[2007] 49–62) likewise offers a reconsideration, for Brennan is normally regarded as a Symbolist poet, deeply influenced by currents in nineteenth-century French and German literary thought. It comes as a surprise to learn that he also produced a volume of jingoistic verse, poems which Lynch claims make sustained use of tropes of medievalism to advance their militaristic cause.

If the reputations of some male poets were shaken during 2007, the work of critics such as Bonny Cassidy, Michael Sharkey and Anne Vickery has helped the stock of women poets to rise. Sharkey's ' "But who considers woman day by day?": Australian Women Poets and World War I' (*ALS* 23:i[2007] 63–78) finds this body of work notable for its range of themes, variety in attitude to its subject, and formal experimentation, all of which are at odds with conventional assumptions that such work was jingoistic and banal, and sought to reinforce the role of women as supportive bystanders. While noting that the majority of poems can be read this way, Sharkey puts the case that those poems which do resile from expressing such sentiments are particularly rewarding for critics. The sheer scale of Vickery's 'The Rise of "Women's Poetry" in the 1970s: An Initial Survey into New Australian Poetry, the Women's Movement, and a Matrix of Revolutions' (*AuFS* 22:liii[2007] 265–85) perhaps defeats its author's attempts to synthesize and theorize the materials which are presented in the opening pages. Vickery briefly notes major shifts in print culture, in women's liberation and in women's writing which seem to have influenced the production of poetry, but the breadth on display here seems to prefigure a larger project in which these connections will be teased out and more convincingly explained. The real strength of this essay is the scale of information about presses, poets and publication. A more closely focused recuperation of a poet who was never accepted into John Tranter's 'New Australian Poetry', the dominant poetic circle of the 1970s (a point briefly noted by Vickery), is offered in Bonny Cassidy's 'The Sounds of Sight: Jennifer Rankin's Poetics' (*JASAL* 6[2007] 33–48). Cassidy claims that the strengths and problems of Rankin's poetry cohere in her attempt to make the lyric a more direct equivalent of phenomena without stabilizing it first in a poetic consciousness, deploying some very close reading of language effects in the poems to demonstrate this. The work of complicating, recuperating and situating the writing of women poets is continued in Cassidy's ' "Mankind's old dichotomy": Gwen Harwood's Romantic Ironist' (*JAS* 90[2007] 49–63; notes pp. 186–8). Here, Cassidy is particularly concerned with Harwood's engagement with and critique of German Romanticism in her 'Professor Eisenbart' poems, a reading or set of readings that links her work to that of Brennan. This interpretation of Harwood's poetry sets Cassidy at odds with critics who have declared it to be 'anti-Romantic'. Cassidy's claim is that Harwood was seeking to explore the implications of Romantic philosophies of the self, particularly in relation to the lives and roles of women and children. Alison Hoddinott's 'Editing Gwen Harwood' (*Island* 111[2007] 29–45) offers an anecdotal account of editing Harwood's early letters and late poetry, as well as the subsequent compilation of *Gwen Harwood: Collected Poems 1943–1995*. In addition to illustrating some of the practical decisions to be made by an editor, it includes much biographical information about Harwood, who interacted with the editor during these projects.

Another broadly recuperative essay, equally in dialogue with the larger disciplinary contexts of its claims, is John O'Leary's ' "The life, the loves, of that dark race": The Ethnographic Verse of Mid-Nineteenth-Century Australia' (*ALS* 23:i[2007] 3–17). O'Leary gives detailed attention to a set of poems normally dismissed as unfortunate examples of colonialist anthropology, and puts the case that the authors of these poems—he considers about a dozen works—sought not merely to 'titillate' their audience, but to appropriate indigeneity. Whether that appropriation is an opening of cross-cultural dialogue or a crude exploitation he leaves the reader to decide; whichever is the case, though, O'Leary argues that this body of work 'deserves to be rescued from the oblivion into which it has fallen', a project well served by this essay.

Some of the themes examined in his *Victorian Literature and Culture* essay are pursued in Andrew McCann's 'Colonial Nature-Inscription: On Haunted Landscape' (in Tiffin, ed., pp. 71–83) which considers the work of Charles Harpur and Henry Kendall within the context of debates about late Romanticism, modernity, colonialism and colonial violence. The crux is McCann's claim that 'the logic of the commodity engenders representational paradigms that conveniently exploit the potentially abject nature of nature as non-identity, and thus render themselves compatible with narratives of colonization as domestication' (p. 78). In these circumstances, 'if we are to disentangle the issue of the environment or nature as an ethical concern from its imbrication with colonialism, we need to rescue a provisional sense of nature as an object of instrumental appropriation' (p. 78). For McCann, in some senses 'the nineteenth-century redeployment of nature-inscription in Australia, at what was literally the cutting edge of empire, is also the story of the erosion of the ethicality that coheres around Romanticism's elegiac idiom' (p. 78). This concomitant decline of the ethical and the Romantic because of colonization is then addressed through considerations of Charles Harpur's 'An Aboriginal Mother's Lament' and Henry Kendall's well-known piece 'The Last of his Tribe'. The poems are read as examining the possibility that colonists will be defeated by a nature 'now irrevocably associated with the threat of indigeneity' (p. 79). It is the 'commodification of Romantic intentions' that culminates in the 'formulaic production of tropes designed to capture the *frisson* of spectral alterity' (p. 80). McCann's aim is the formulation of a poetics 'that is both environmental and anti-colonial' (p. 82), grounded in the rejection of the Gothic and the (colonial) pastoral which split representations of nature into either the 'picturesque vista', which is not merely the scene but the vehicle of appropriation, or the unassimilated nature which 'remains...abject in its ugliness, although no less emphatically commodified' (p. 82). One's panic at reading that the point of view will be that of 'a poetry-lover' rather than 'an Australian literary scholar' in David Brooks' 'Charles Harpur and the Warp: Strange Happenings in "The Creek of Four Graves"' (*Southerly* 67:i–ii[2007] 151–65) quickly subsides, to be replaced by the recognition that practising poets can usually be relied on not to *glissande* across the language of the poem in a fug of tenuously related abstractions. Brooks updates the old contention that colonial poets lacked a vocabulary to deal with their 'new' landscape to a theory of the warp. The warp is revealed by the 'pressure' exerted by setting and sensibility on 'inherited forms' that have been transplanted to the colonial environment. Some clever reading of the geography in the poem follows, versions are compared, and the article concludes with a brief attempt to paint the poem as less racist than it has been traditionally read.

John Ryan and James Robert Smith's 'Manifestations of Terror: English Folklore, Winston Churchill, Les Murray and Sydney's Black Dog Institute' (*AuFolk* 21[2006] 30–47) provides a context for the theme of depression in Murray's poetry by ferreting out incidences of the motif in Anglo-Saxon folklore, in bibliography, in the biography of Winston Churchill and even in modern counselling services. The article could perhaps risk being read as implying that because the psychological state and the name are of significance to Murray's poetry, the critical world requires a catalogue of every time the phrase or a cognate has been uttered. In 'From Replication to Mutation: Barthes and the Imagery of Two Australian Poets' (*fiveb* 14:iv[2007] 38–41), Stuart Cooke uses Roland Barthes to explore the triangle of authorial persona, material quiddity and interpretative reader in relation to the poetic image. He finds Murray's ability to coalesce persona and phenomena leaves little space for suggestiveness and reader exploration; Murray expresses such a strongly normative view of the Australian landscape that readers are unable to generate from his poems their own 'individualized landscapes'. The poetry magazine *five bells* published a series of 'Australian Poems Responses', each of which is a brief critical piece on a single poem. Interesting chiefly as evidence of the tenacity of the poetry subculture, in 2007 there were readings of Dorothy Hewett's 'Sydney Postscript' by Rodney Williams (*fiveb* 14:ii[2007] 27–8), Kenneth Slessor's 'Country Towns' by Thomas Thorpe (*fiveb* 14:iii[2007] 31–2), and Ada Cambridge's 'An Answer' by Margaret Bradstock (*fiveb* 14:iv[2007] 49–50). The responses vary from the semi-autobiographical (Thorpe) to the scholarly-biographical (Bradstock).

(d) Drama

There were two major publications in the field in 2007. The positioning of Helen Gilbert and Jacqueline Lo's *Performance and Cosmopolitics: Cross-Cultural Transactions in Australasia* and Joanne Tompkins's *Unsettling Space: Contestations in Contemporary Australian Theatre*, in the Studies in International Performance series, demonstrates both the value and the limits of writing for an international audience about a minor literature. The two volumes have a similar structure—an introduction which surveys the relevant theoretical field, followed by broadly sketched case studies—and a similar problem: they are forced to reiterate commonplaces of Australian history and literary history in order to establish a basis for their own quite specialized arguments about theatre and Australian culture. Since it is common to both books this seems likely to be a publisher-driven demand for 'coverage'. But this approach risks implying that the individual work or event under discussion is not of sufficient depth or complexity to warrant the kind of detailed consideration given to a play by, say, a renowned English author, thereby threatening the claims made by both of these books to contain scholarship of significance to their discipline. Indeed, in the context of the international academic market to which these books speak, it is the use of 'Australia' as a paradigm which is seen as constituting the chief scholarly originality, whereas one senses that these three authors have quite different aims: teasing out the implications for their *discipline* of their findings about Australian theatre. As part of this interrogation of audience and its relationship to structural organization, one might ask this: if no single work or author within Australian theatre is demanding of detailed study, on what basis can the synthesizing offered here have significance for the discipline as a whole? And if proof of this problem were needed it can be found in that old signifier of colonial inferiority, poor-quality paper. Both books are marred by pictures so lacking in contrast they could be said to replace ten words rather than the regulation thousand; this is a problem when the concern is as much with stage as page, and fine-grained detail of the image is often crucial to the argument being made.

Unsettling Space argues that, while Australian space is usually represented as 'open' or 'unlimited', there are two quite different versions of this unlimitedness: 'paradisiacal' ones, and those in which Australian space is portrayed as 'vulnerable or hostile' (p. 6; it is a distinction similar to that claimed by Cathcart of nineteenth-century Lemurian novels, above). Using Freud's notion of the uncanny and the concept of methexis, 'in which space is mobile rather than fixed' (p. 12), to underpin her analysis, Tompkins distils these uncertainties in separate chapters on three key topoi: 'monuments', 'contamination' and the 'borders of identity'. Perhaps the analysis becomes a little too self-absorbed at some points—as when it is asserted that 'commodities like identity or subjectivity contribute to the study of spatiality' (p. 15), but the individual readings of plays and performances are much more convincing. The chapter on monuments considers the representation of space and spatial elements in plays about war, the theatre of the bicentenary, indigenous monuments and literal monuments. The last section of this chapter recounts a spectacular performance that used a skyscraper as a stage; Tomkins's account of the nuclear testing in Maralinga, which appears in the next chapter, is equally gripping and disturbing. The broad-ranging discussion of play texts and of performances offers the basis for a methodological argument about the necessity of considering the problematic of spatiality in criticism of Australian theatre, thence in performance more generally, and will also have application in Australian studies and Australian literary studies. The stage offers a place in which the collision between conflicting versions of spatiality can be scrutinized, by performers, critics and audiences, but what makes the poetics of spatiality used in Australian theatre particularly significant is the history of colonization, and the shape of more recent debates over the treatment of refugees (through incarceration and exile).

Gilbert and Lo's book is likewise concerned with the cultural consequences of colonization and the polemics of racial difference in contemporary theatre. In that sense, both books are recognizably heirs to the earlier Gilbert and Tompkins co-authored volume *Post-Colonial Theatre*, engaging in critical practices that could broadly be termed post-structural and postcolonial, although each represents a considerable departure from the premises and aims of the earlier work. The particular strength of *Performance and Cosmopolitics* is the comprehensiveness of its coverage of the late twentieth and early twenty-first centuries, with barely a performance or text related to its key themes not mentioned in some detail: as such, it serves not only as a learned discussion of the pertinent theoretical issues, but as an extremely useful history. That said, the prose at times betrays a somewhat unrefined historical sense, which presumes that the future will be an improvement on the past, often contradicted by individual analyses that find complication and compromise characterizing specific texts or performances. Perhaps this problem emerges because although these authors are alert to the problems of the term 'cosmopolitan', their clear preference for the 'global' over the local, and their valorization of (cultural) hybridity and transience, do not tend to allow them to consider those arguments from, say, Indigenous studies or environmental studies. Such alternative perspectives might problematize the implicit claim to the superior ethicality of cosmopolitanism that underpins the judgements offered about performances, paratexts (such as programmes and performer/ director interviews), and critical responses (media and academic) to them. Nevertheless this is an important book in documenting experimentation, change and cultural challenge in one of the country's most visible culture industries.

Relations with Europe and Britain are also foregrounded in Veronica Kelly's 'Spatialising the Ghosts of Anzac in the Plays of Sydney Tomholt: The Absent Soldier and the War Memorial' (*ALS* 23:i[2007] 18–35), in which Kelly suggests that Tomholt's little-known works can best be understood as modernist ones. Their modernist characteristics include the exploitation of new technologies of projection, and the representation of the trauma of loss generated by the catastrophic experiences of Australian troops in the First World War. The essay is attentive not only to performances of Tomholt's plays but to architecture, sculpture and popular cultural forms such as cinema, and specifically to the attempts in these media to develop a visual vocabulary which could be used to articulate not only the horrors of war but the grief which suffused so many in its aftermath. Kelly's larger claim is that the existence of Tomholt's work, because it represents an early and particularly significant attempt to deploy modernist forms and themes, calls into question conventional accounts of the 'development' of Australian theatre and the emphasis in such accounts on positioning Patrick White as the inaugurator of modernism. Ken Stewart argues that the Gilbert and Sullivan operas constitute an unacknowledged viewpoint from which to understand a whole range of Anglo-Australian relations, in 'Antipodean Topsy-Turvy: Gilbert and Sullivan in the Australian Colonies' (*Southerly* 67:i–ii[2007] 69–84). He discusses a number of successful productions of Gilbert and Sullivan operas in Australia, considering their representative claims and colonial politics, finding *Princess Ida* to be of most interest. Stewart contends that, when played in Australia, the opera was inflected to represent the 'Australian girl'. In contrast to this 'disputation' of the impact of the colonial temperament, Susan Bradley Smith argues that Miles Franklin's failure to become a successful dramatist in London was the reason for her return to Australia; it is a biographical case in which Smith raises significant questions about career, genre and nationality. In 'Miles Franklin's Dramatic Ambitions, or, Why Stella Really Came Home' (*Antipodes* 21:i[2007] 16–21) Bradley Smith notes that there are some twenty unpublished plays by Franklin which exist in manuscript, and she sets out to explain both the reasons for Franklin's lack of success and the effect of this failure on her life. The conclusion is that 'it was this cruel failure...as a professional theatre practitioner, after decades of trying, that broke her spirit and headed her squarely for home' (p. 16). The year's work in Australian drama studies, in its attention to themes of colonialism, and particularly to the resonance of colonization for contemporary culture, is symptomatic of trends across the field of Australian literary studies in 2007.

3. Canada

(a) General

Volume 3 of the *History of the Book in Canada*, edited by Carole Gerson and Jacques Michon, covering the years 1918 to 1980, completes an important collaborative project funded by the Social Sciences and Humanities Research Council of Canada. As Patricia Lockhart Fleming and Yvan Lamonde, general editors, note, the project continues to redefine the field, and includes not just the book in codex form but also oral texts, new media and other printed forms such as newspapers and music. The third volume is extensive, and is organized in seven parts: the cultural influence of books and print in Canadian society; authorship; publishing for a wide readership; publishing for distinct readerships; production; distribution; reaching readers. The editors note how the emergence of a book-publishing industry in Canada was a largely twentieth-century phenomenon, unlike the history of the book in Europe; in Canada, the publishing industry had started with other formats, such as posters and newspapers. Twentieth-century Canadian publishers are called in this volume, to use Wayne Templeton's phrase, 'architects of culture' (p. 3). Much of Canada's international influence derived from the role played by the publishing industry during the Second World War, when Quebec took over the publishing and distribution of French-language texts (p. 6). Publishing in Canada, while divided between two powerful cultural and linguistic locations—Montreal and Toronto—was multicultural, with diverse aboriginal and immigrant groups using the industry as a vehicle to promote their localized interests and concerns. Jennifer J. Connor, in 'Cohering through Books', reveals how the formation of identity took place in unexpected ways, her opening example being a community-compiled Dutch Canadian cookbook. Community is one of the wider cohering categories of the history of the book in Canada, and many of the essays in this volume are a testament to this. For example, Carole Gerson and Yvan Lamonde, in 'Books and Reading in Canadian Art', argue that artistic representations of books and reading shift from being markers of social or intellectual class to vectors of attitudes concerning the relationships between reading and gender; thus new reading communities are seen to emerge. Another important twentieth-century community is that of children and youth. Suzanne Pouliot, Judith Saltman and Gail Edwards, in 'Publishing for Children', reveal that this was a highly profitable and innovative sector of the Canadian publishing industry in Quebec. Chapter 11 of the volume explores 'Publishing and Communities' in depth, with essays on: publishing and Aboriginal communities, Allophone publishing, Jewish print culture, small press publishing, publishing by women, and publishing against the grain. Communities of readers are created through the concept of 'Best-Sellers', explored here by Klay Dyer, Denis Saint-Jacques and Claude Martin, who note that 'they provide valuable insights into the social and cultural dynamics of reading as a real-world activity' (pp. 459–60). Finally, Brendan Frederick R. Edwards, in 'Reading on the "Rez"', examines the lack of library services in Aboriginal communities during the first half of the twentieth century and beyond, despite an expressed desire and need by native peoples for improved, empowering literacy. While these review comments barely scratch the surface of this extensive volume of essays, they are indicative of the diversity and wide coverage that the third volume provides. The entire project makes a considerable contribution to history of the book scholarship.

Readers who are concerned that volume 3 of the *History of the Book in Canada* ends its coverage in 1980 will be pleased that the *Dictionary of Literary Biography*, volume 334: *Twenty-First-Century Canadian Writers*, edited by Christian Riegel, begins its coverage in 1989. While the editors of the *History* argue for a need for historical distance, as well as the transformation of Canadian publishing with the ushering in of the globalized digital era in the 1980s, Riegel notes more prosaically that *DLB* 334 covers the period from 1989 because that was when the last *DLB* on Canadian writing was published (p. xv). Riegel's introduction provides an excellent historical survey of contemporary Canadian politics and society, highlighting constitutional changes and upheavals, before moving on to literary developments, such as 'the emerging role of Canadian literature on the world stage' (p. xvi), reflected in the winning of major international prizes and a truly global book market. Creative and critical shifts are apparent: 'Issues of race, ethnicity, and gender have become increasingly important aspects of public discourse in Canadian newspapers and magazines and on television, as well as in the critical response to literary work' (pp. xvi–xvii). Riegel notes that *DLB* 334 thus contains entries on significant African Canadian and Native authors 'who have become established in the literary mainstream since the 1980s and 1990s' (p. xvii). African Canadian authors given coverage are Dionne Brand, George Elliott Clarke, Claire Harris, Dany Laferrière, Suzette Mayr, M. NourbeSe Philip (also covered in *DLB* 157) and Maxine Tynes. Native authors include Jeannette Armstrong, Tomson Highway, Thomas King and Daniel David Moses. Each chapter follows a bio-bibliographical format, giving background and critical overviews, plot summaries and descriptions, and a significant number of quotations from interviews with the authors. Highlights of the book include excellent coverage of Sandra Birdsell by Barbara Pell, who notes that 'she unsentimentally portrays the sordid lives and inarticulate longings of working-class women not frequently found in Canadian fiction' (p. 22), and a comprehensive survey of Japanese Canadian author Joy Kogawa's work, by Irene Sywenky. Theatre gets reasonable coverage, with entries on Tomson Highway, Daniel MacIvor, and Judith Thompson. Perhaps the most trans-genre entry is that on George Elliott Clarke, who is a playwright, poet, lyricist and important literary critic, developing a significant body of work on

African Canadian writing. Some mainstream authors are covered, such as Douglas Coupland, Rohinton Mistry and Carol Shields. The appendices cover literary awards in Canada, and there is a short checklist of further readings. *DLB* 334 is researched and written to a very high standard; it is an authoritative guide to contemporary Canadian writing.

Arguing that the short-story form can be considered the 'flagship genre of Canadian literature' (p. 1), Reingard M. Nischik has edited a comprehensive collection of critical essays, *The Canadian Short Story: Interpretations*. The critical apparatus includes an overview essay by Nischik, 'The Canadian Short Story: Status, Criticism, Historical Survey', further reading on the Canadian short story and a useful 'Time Chart: The Short Story in the USA, Canada, and Great Britain'. Authors selected are those most frequently anthologized, to the cost of pre-1960s short-story writing in Canada; pre-modernist short-story writing gets further written off in the overview essay, which is nevertheless strong on modernist and contemporary authors, if teleological in structure (where newer appears to be considered better). This structural weakness is reflected in the fact that there is a single essay on nineteenth-century Canadian short-story writing, Martina Seifert's 'Canadian Animal Stories: Charles G.D. Roberts, "Do See their Meat from God" (1892)'. Roberts's short-story definition is usefully cited by Seifert: 'a psychological romance constructed on a framework of natural science' (p. 43), revealing the ways in which apparently contradictory discourses come together in the animal or nature stories of the time. An essay by Heinz Antor, 'Tory Humanism, Ironic Humor, and Satire: Stephen Leacock, "The Marine Excursion of the Knights of Pythias" (1912)', follows Seifert's, before the volume jumps into Canadian modernism, with Julia Breitbach's 'The Beginnings of Canadian Modernism: Raymond Knister, "The First Day of Spring" (written 1924/25)', and the slightly later essay by Dieter Meindl, 'Modernism, Prairie Fiction, and Gender: Sinclair Ross, "The Lamp at Noon" (1938)'. All of the essays follow the same format: an introduction to the author, followed by a close reading of the selected short story; this approach is useful from a teaching perspective, and provides enough biographical and bibliographical information for the researcher. Realism is covered by: Konrad Groß, 'From Old World Aestheticist Immoralist to Prairie Moral Realist: Frederick Philip Grove, "Snow" (1926/1932)'; Paul Goetsch, 'Psychological Realism, Immigration, and City Fiction: Morley Callaghan, "Last Spring They Came Over" (1927)'; and Stefan Ferguson, 'Social Realism and Compassion for the Underdog: Hugh Garner, "One-Two-Three Little Indians" (1950)'. The complexities of generic labelling are explored well, as with the intersection of the sacred and the profane in the work of Hugh Hood, in Jutta Zimmerman's 'The Modernist Aesthetic: Hugh Hood, "Flying a Red Kite" (1962)'. Zimmerman subtly teases out the poetological site of the spiritual rather than that of the symbolic as pre-eminent in Hood's oeuvre.

The volume is strong on mainstream Canadian short-story writers, such as Margaret Atwood, Thomas King, Margaret Laurence, Alice Munro and Rudy Wiebe, yet it also reveals some less well-known aspects of 'canonical' authors, such as Sheila Watson, known almost entirely for her novel *The Double Hook* [1959]. Martin Kuester, in 'Myth and the Postmodernist Turn in

Canadian Short Fiction: Sheila Watson, "Antigone" (1959)', shows how Watson utilizes postmodern writing strategies in her short stories, in this instance to 'demythologize' *Antigone*. While the volume as a whole is sensibly structured and pedagogically useful thanks to its critical survey of heavily anthologized authors, and its close readings of selected short stories, it is a shame that key First Nations (and other minority) authors such as Eden Robinson are thereby excluded. Marta Dvořák and W.H. New, editors of *Tropes and Territories: Short Fiction, Postcolonial Readings, Canadian Writings in Context*, make up for this lack with a comprehensive collection of essays that cover Australian, Canadian and New Zealand 'short stories, tales and short fictions' (p. 3), where '*territories* prove to be landscapes of the mind, and tropes entail interstitial spaces where cultures and discourses interact' (p. 4). This expansion of the genre allows for more diverse short fictions to be analysed, most creatively in Laurie Ricou's 'The Botany of the Liar', which is the concluding essay. Ricou playfully works with the concept of 'short' in the short story as also meaning a 'surge of energy, a sudden break, a loss of power ... an embedded metaphor of surprise' (p. 346). Ricou's ecocritical approach—called a 'botanics' of reading—highlights a common theme in the collection: the resistance to forcing diverse short fictions to conform to critical expectations. Laura Moss, in 'Between Fractals and Rainbows: Critiquing Canadian Criticism', argues that much contemporary Canadian literature criticism is predicated upon the desire for social transformation which is 'consistently predicated on the political positioning of [largely] postcolonial authors' (p. 18). Put more simply, rather than looking at what Canadian authors write, there is an emphasis upon who they are. In addition to offering a new critical approach of 'fractal' criticism, where the part holistically contains the whole and the text can thus be explored in as much depth as the postcolonial, sociological contexts, Moss also offers a critique of the 'Trans.Can.Lit' movement (see below). Diana Brydon, in 'Storying Home: Power and Truth', applies William Walters's theories of 'domopolitics' to literary texts, where domopolitics is 'a reconfiguring of the relations between citizen, state, and territory' (p. 35). There are interesting comparison essays by Janice Kulyk Keefer, 'La Dame Seule Meets the Angel of History: Katherine Mansfield and Mavis Gallant', and Florence Cabaret, 'From Location to Dislocation in Salman Rushdie's *East, West* and Rohinton Mistry's *Tales from Firozsha Baag*'. Rejecting Harold Bloom's theory of the anxiety of influence in examining Mansfield's impact upon Gallant, Keefer instead argues for a pedagogic model: 'the way in which one writer influences another, not by copying, but rather by learning, one from the other, while recognising similarities of vision and perception' (p. 91). Cabaret shows how metonymy is a trope which reappropriates orientalist modes of writing, not only where the part stands in for the whole, but in terms of rethinking concepts of partition/partiality 'which appear to be part and parcel of a certain postcolonial approach to space' (p. 165). Two essays look at indigenous short prose: Warren Cariou's ' "We use dah membering": Oral Memory in Métis Short Stories', and Gerald Lynch's 'Mariposa Medicine: Thomas King's *Medicine River* and the Canadian Short Story Cycle'. The impossibility of pinning down the Métis people (i.e. homeless, they were always on the move),

means that their oral culture survived many of the assimilation attempts of the
Canadian government; orality and 're-membering' are community-based, as
Cariou reveals in an analysis of the Métis notion of 're-membering' in short
prose. Lynch reads Thomas King's *Medicine River* [1989] as a story cycle,
linking orature and the short-story-cycle genre. Canonical short-prose writers
are also covered by Robert Thacker's 'Alice Munro's Ontario'; Marta
Dvořák's 'Of Cows and Configurations in Emily Carr's *The Book of Small*';
Neil Bessner's 'Reading Linnet Muir, Netta Asher, and Carol Frazier: Three
Gallant Characters in Postcolonial Time'; Claire Omhovère's 'Roots and
Routes in a Selection of Stories by Alistair MacLeod'; and Héliane Ventura's
'Aesthetic Traces of the Ephemeral: Alice Munro's Logograms in "Vandals"'.
The collection, which is far more extensive than this review suggests, expands
the critical sense of 'short fiction', with some useful genre boundary-blurring
and -crossing; the essays as a whole develop substantial new readings of
the genre.

   A new paradigm for Canadian literary-critical and cultural studies has
developed in recent years, with the first main book of essays emerging from
shared projects called *Trans.Can.Lit: Resituating the Study of Canadian
Literature*, edited by Smaro Kamboureli and Roy Miki. The editors suggest
that, because of its institutionalization and success, the study of Canadian
literature has reached a dead end; yet something within the topic escapes the
'processes and institutions' (p. ix) in which it is embedded. What is that
something? Kamboureli and Miki suggest 'CanLit is a troubling sign' (p. ix),
where there is a constant resistance to being placed at the service of the state,
and the normalization and too easy assimilation of minority literatures into
a new canon. As the editors note, 'CanLit demands a transformation of
the codes and means of its self-representation and its representation of others.
It is to this summons for developing new terms of engagement with CanLit
and Canada as an un/imagined community that the TransCanada project
responds' (p. x). 'Trans.Can.Lit', then, is analogous to the post-structuralist
concept of *signifiance* (as theorized by Roland Barthes and Julia Kristeva),
in that it involves 'unmaking' meaning (here, 'unmaking' the nation). Diana
Brydon addresses some of the big theoretical questions raised by this book in
the first essay, 'Metamorphoses of a Discipline: Rethinking Canadian
Literature within Institutional Contexts'. Brydon theorizes Canadian literature
within institutional and global contexts, with a focus on multilayered notions
of citizenship literature; she questions the 'trans' model since this belongs to
'the nation-building narrative' (p. 13) of Canada, arguing instead for the
'planetarity' model as theorized by Gayatri Chakravorty Spivak and Wai Chee
Dimock. Defending the multicultural model as offering 'vast opportunities for
rethinking the nation and for state struggles' (p. 19) also leads to a critique of
the 'trans Canada' model in Rinaldo Walcott's 'Against Institution:
Established Law, or Purpose'. This paper is usefully read beside one later
on in the collection: Ashok Mathur's 'Transubracination: How Writers of
Colour Became CanLit'. Daniel Coleman, in 'From Canadian Trance to
TransCanada: White Civility to Wry Civility in the CanLit Project', counters
the hegemonic project of Eurocentric discourses that are foundational to
the Canadian national state, with the concept of the 'TransCanadian', which is

a 'dynamic, self-questioning concept of civility' (p. 27). Coleman's project is analysed in theoretical depth by Peter Dickinson in 'Subtitling CanLit: Keywords', where the keywords psychoanalysis, affect and performativity are examined 'as a discursive curative to the self-hypnotising talk of Canadian civility' (p. 46). Dickinson makes interesting use of Julia Kristeva's theory of the abject, as put forward in her *Powers of Horror*. Two of the contributors discuss obstacles that get in the way of understanding postcolonial texts and pedagogic issues: Lee Maracle, in 'Oratory on Oratory', and Stephen Slemon, in 'TransCanada, Literature: No Direction Home'. Globalization as one of the most important factors in the TransCanada discussion is apparent throughout the collection, with four contributors focusing on this topic: Richard Cavell, 'World Famous across Canada, or Transnational Localities'; Lily Cho, 'Diasporic Citizenship: Contradictions and Possibilities for Canadian Literature'; Lianne Moyes, 'Acts of Citizenship: Erin Mouré's *O Cidadán* and the Limits of Worldliness'; and Winfried Siemerling, 'Trans-Scan: Globalization, Literary Hemispheric Studies, Citizenship as Project'. Finally, the body as a site of repression and resistance, and the social collective as a wider body of political resistance, inform two essays: Julia Emberley's 'Institutional Genealogies in the Global Net of Fundamentalisms, Families, and Fantasies' and Len Findlay's 'TransCanada Collectives: Social Imagination, the Cunning of Production, and the Multilateral Sublime'.

Animals have featured in Canadian literature from the beginnings of the canon—and in the First Nations stories that preceded Canada's written literature. Bringing together recent scholarship in this area is Janice Fiamengo, ed., *Other Selves: Animals in the Canadian Literary Imagination*. In her introduction, '"The animals in *this* country": Animals in the Canadian Literary Imagination', Fiamengo writes a compact history of literary and critical representations of animals, with key commentary on Northrop Frye, Margaret Atwood, James Polk and more recent critics in this area such as Marian Scholtmeijer, Misao Dean and John Sandlos. The central critical question explored in the first section of the book is essentially that of anthropomorphism; as Gwendolyn Guth notes in '(B)othering the Theory: Approaching the Unapproachable in *Bear* and Other Realistic Animal Narratives': 'The vanity of anthropomorphism that was critiqued by philosopher-poet Xenophanes in 6th-century Greece and that continues to influence our present age is precisely the representation of the non-human other in human terms' (p. 30). Guth regards *Bear* as a phenomenological foregrounding of an animal's otherness, where Nature becomes analogous to the Lacanian Real, and an ethical relationship is created with the animal other. Homologies are tropes which can escape such anthropomorphism and associated anthropocentrism, as Susan Fisher argues in '"Ontological applause": Metaphor and Homology in the Poetry of Don McKay'. Cynthia Sugars, in '"Drawn from nature": Katherine Govier's Audubon and the Trauma of Extinction', constructs a theory of John James Audubon's bird paintings as 'anthropomorphic psychic dramas' which 'are neither accurate records of the wildlife nor acts of preservation, but rather are fantasy spaces for exploring the dynamics of human obsession' (p. 76). Other resistances to anthropocentric thought are sketched by Travis S. Mason in

'Lick Me, Bite Me, Hear Me, Write Me: Tracking Animals between Postcolonialism and Ecocriticism', and Jack Robinson's 'Yann Martel's *Life of Pi*: "The story with animals is the better story"'. As Mason also covers *Life of Pi*, these two essays make an interesting comparison, especially as Robinson, quoting Charlene Spretnak, argues for a 'ecological or reconstructive postmodernism' (p. 126) which in turn deconstructs the foreclosure of the animal in Freud's psychosocial drama of the origins of civilization. The philosophical and theoretical analyses of anthropocentricism provided in these essays construct a useful critical framework for the following two sections of the book: 'Animal Writers', and 'The Politics of Animal Representation'. Animal writers covered in the second section are Thomas McIlwraith, Marshall Saunders, Charles G.D. Roberts, Grey Owl (Archibald Stansfield Belaney), Timothy Findlay (in relation to his novel *The Wars* [1977]) and Dennis Lee. Ecological crises and the politics of conservation inform both Ella Soper-Jones's 'When Elephants Weep: Reading *The White Bone* as a Sentimental Animal Story' and Brian Johnson's 'Ecology, Allegory, and Indigeneity in the Wolf Stories of Roberts, Seton, and Mowat'. The politics of hunting and the ways in which patriarchal hunting narratives can be subverted are explored by Misao Dean in ' "The mania for killing": Hunting and Collecting in Seton's *The Arctic Prairies*', and Wendy Roy in 'The Politics of Hunting in Canadian Women's Narratives of Travel'. As Dean argues: 'Strategies of regulating, conserving, and studying "wildlife" have always been strategies for regulating and policing First Nations communities, and *The Arctic Prairies* [1911] demonstrates how the discourse of conservation itself has its roots in racist attitudes toward First Nations peoples' (p. 292). Roy also argues that hunting narratives written by women reveal 'differences in race, culture, class, and gender' (p. 307) and thus are a useful tool for feminist critique. What the second and third sections of the book make clear is that there are alternative modes of anthropomorphism and anthropocentrism that operate outside the romanticized, idealized and largely patriarchal discourses of exploration, hunting and the domination of Nature. When these are combined with the critical reflections in the first section, the book as a whole makes a sustained contribution to the critical discourse of animals and literature.

Translating Canada, edited by Luise von Flotow and Reingard M. Nischik, examines the translation of Canadian texts into German during the period 1967–2000, with emphasis upon literary writing but also covering broader social and political non-fiction works. The editors prepared the essay collection with four guiding questions in mind: (1) What kinds of materials are selected and 'exported' by Canada? (2) Which materials are selected by German publishers? (3) How are these materials translated? and (4) How are they received? The resulting essays are highly diverse, providing useful statistical and interpretative data. In many cases, the question of what did not get translated, and why not, is as revealing as analysis of what did get translated into German. Klaus Peter Müller, in 'Translating the Canadian Short Story into German', suggests that there are six main reasons for Canadian–German translation decisions: (1) the exotic otherness of Canada; (2) ethnicity; (3) regionalism; (4) Canada as a contemporary (post)modern nation; (5) the authors' renown and popularity; and (6) the texts' literary qualities. Reason number 4 may be the most revealing and intriguing. Müller argues that Canada is identified as sharing European values such as 'community, social security, and mutual responsibility' (p. 62), and thus its literary texts offer relevant scenarios to German readers: 'Stories about gender roles and gender relations, life in families, in cities, in peer groups, et cetera, fit into this (post)modern context' (p. 62). Of course the question of 'which' Germany the texts are being translated for also comes into this equation. This question is considered in depth by Barbara Korte in her essay '"Two Solitudes?": Anglo-Canadian Literature in Translation in the Two Germanies'. Even though fewer books were translated in the communist GDR between 1949 and 1990 than in the previously named Federal Republic of Germany, Korte notes that the literary visions of overseas, restricted worlds were highly attractive to everyday readers. Korte's essay is a fascinating glimpse into the world of communist vetting—for example, Atwood's *Surfacing* was considered a suitable novel for translation because it espoused an anti-American sentiment. Korte also provides useful comparative data concerning translation and anthologies. Genres get excellent coverage from Anglo- and French Canadian perspectives. Eva Gruber, in 'The "AlterNative" Frontier: Native Canadian Writing in German/y', examines cultural transfer in the translations of First Nations writing, noting that the first wave of translation was of works about indigenous peoples, not texts by them, thus creating a cultural frame of reference for subsequent authentic texts. Three essays on theatre—Albert-Reiner Glaap's 'Contemporary (English) Canadian Plays in German/y: Equivalence in Difference?', Andreas Jandl's 'Northern Lights in German Theatres: How Quebec Plays Come to Germany' and Brita Oeding's 'Low Motility: Transferring Montreal Playwright Stephen Orlov's *Sperm Count* to Germany'—examine the different mechanisms for the transfer of theatrical texts from Canada to Germany. In line with Müller's fourth reason for translation (above), Glaap argues that contemporary Canadian plays are relevant to German audiences because they address universal, not just Canadian, themes. Jandl notes that there is less financial and institutional support for the translation and production of Quebec plays in Germany; she traces the often highly indirect theatre translation routes from French Canada to Germany, with Daniel Danis's play *Le Chant du Dire-Dire* as a case study. Oeding provides a detailed case study of a humorous, political Jewish Canadian play, including discussion of transcultural differences and misunderstandings. This essay is usefully paired with Fabienne Quennet's 'From *Beautiful Losers* to *No Logo!* German Readings of Jewish Canadian Writing'. Canadian children's literature is a growing market, and two essays examine criteria for its translation, Martina Seifert's 'Selecting Canadiana for the Young: The German Translation of English Canadian Children's Literature' and Nikola von Merveldt's 'French, Female, and Foreign: French Canadian Children's Literature in German Translation'. Finally, the importance of women authors in German translation is addressed in three essays: Brita Oeding and Luise von Flotow's 'The "Other Women": Canadian Women Writers Blazing a Trail into Germany', Stefan Ferguson's 'Margaret Atwood in German/y: A Case Study' and Klaus-Dieter Ertler's

'Antonine Maillet in German: A Case Study'. Atwood plays a major role in
the Canadian literary scene in Germany, indicated by there being two German
translations of her novel *Surfacing*; the 'other women' who are widely read—
Margaret Laurence, Jane Urquhart, Alice Munro, Carol Shields and so on—
are often compared to Atwood in the German popular press. The difficulties in
finding financial and intellectual support for complex translations, for example
the work of Maillet, is indicative of the struggle involved in going beyond the
canonical Anglo-Canadian literatures in Germany. *Translating Canada* is
a revealing and compelling book: it has literary-critical and sociological value,
and it speaks beyond the mechanics of the Canada–Germany cultural transfer
to draw a fascinating multifaceted portrait of how Canada is perceived
through a German lens.

A monograph offering wide coverage of genre and nationality is Hugh
Hazelton's *LatinoCanadá: A Critical Study of Ten Latin American Writers of
Canada*. The introduction provides an extensive history of Latin American
writing in Canada, with prefatory historical coverage of different Latin
American immigrant groups, such as the first large-scale arrival in Canada of
political refugees fleeing the aftermath of the Spanish Civil War. Hazelton
examines key events and locations that fostered Latin American authors in
Canada, as well as giving an overview of authors and their works. While there
is inevitable and celebrated diversity in this field, Hazelton notes that 'One of
the characteristics that marks a certain amount of Latino-Canadian writing is
its relative urbanism and technical complexity' (p. 21). This is explained by the
impact of modernism: 'Literary circles in many large Latin American cities
have been far more deeply affected by twentieth-century European artistic
movements such as Futurism, Dadaism, Surrealism, and Absurdism than have
Canadian letters' (p. 21). The resulting experimentalism has been well received
in Quebec and among the English-speaking Canadian avant-garde. Authors
covered in detail, in the order of study, are: Jorge Etcheverry, Margarita
Feliciano, Gilberto Flores Patino, Alfredo Lavergne, Alfonso Quijada Urías,
Nela Rio, Alejandro Saravia, Yvonne América Truque, Pablo Urbanyi and
Leandro Urbina. Each chapter has a biographical and critical overview,
followed by primary texts, including poetry, short stories and novel extracts.
The bibliography of authors' works also gives highly useful information
concerning the various anthologies in which each author has been published.
There is a separate bibliography of Latin American Canadian authors not
covered in the main chapters. One of the most fascinating aspects of the book
is its tracing of each author's origins and lives in different Latin American
countries, followed by the personal and political decisions that led to exile,
nomadic wandering, or immediate emigration to Canada. The literature
that emerges, while often reflecting typical immigrant phases of focus and
concern, shares a complex transcultural dimension. In fact the related term
'transculturation' derives from Cuban sociologist and anthropologist
Fernando Ortiz; Hazelton notes that, for Bronislaw Malinowski, 'the
term was much more accurate than that of "acculturation," which was used
in the United States to speak of other cultures gradually accepting a
monolithic norm. In the transcultural process, both the new culture
and the old or "original" one gradually fuse, thus creating a syncretic

synthesis of both' (p. 255). Hazelton has successfully mapped the transculturation process for Latin American writers in Canada.

(b) Fiction

The question of whether Carol Shields's work proposes 'a philosophy of ordinary life' is asked by Marta Dvořák and Manina Jones in their introduction to *Carol Shields and the Extra-Ordinary*, where the extraordinary is seen 'as emerging out of the ordinary, issuing from the very matrix of everyday life, and illuminating the complexities, the indeterminacies, the contradictions, the *value* at the heart of the ordinary' (p. 4). The resulting essays edited by Dvořák and Jones were first delivered in a colloquium in Paris in 2003. The first inclusion is the text of a previously unpublished Harvard address by Shields from 1997; this is followed by sections on genre, on 'margins of otherness' and on 'extra-ordinary performances'. Archival excesses are the subject of Catherine Hobbs, 'Voice and Re-vision: The Carol Shields Archival Fonds', in particular the way in which the importance of the mundane in Shields's fiction is replicated in the focus of the archival holdings at the Library and Archives Canada, Ottawa. This excess appears to relate to Shields's own aesthetic of postmodern biographical writing, explored further by Christl Verduyn, '(Es)Saying It her Way: Carol Shields as Essayist'. Verduyn notes that Shields thought of her biography of Jane Austen [2001] as a long essay, a format in which Shields excelled. The short-story genre is covered by Christine Lorre's essay '"Dolls, dolls, dolls, dolls": Into the (Extra)ordinary World of Girls and Women'; romance fiction in Taïna Tuhkunen's 'Carol Shields's *The Republic of Love*, or How to Ravish a Genre'; and 'fictive biography' (p. 116) in Coral Ann Howells's 'Larry's A/Mazing Spaces'. There are five essays in part II: Lorna Irvine's 'A Knowable Country: Embodied Omniscience in Carol Shields's *The Republic of Love* and *Larry's Party*'; Patricia-Léa Paillot's 'Pioneering Interlaced Spaces: Shifting Perspectives and Self-Representation in *Larry's Party*'; Manina Jones's 'Scenes from a (Boston) Marriage: The Prosaics of Collaboration and Correspondence in *A Celibate Season*'; Ellen Levy's '"Artefact Out of Absence": Reflection and Convergence in the Fiction of Carol Shields'; and Héliane Ventura's 'Eros in the Eye of the Mirror: The Rewriting of Myths in Carol Shields's "Mirrors"'. Highlights from this section include Irvine's analysis of narratological enigmas, such as Shields's contraction of narrational omniscience into first-person narration, and the synchronic perspective created by simultaneously narrating characters from subjective and objective points of view. Irvine also notes that Shields's use of the rhetorical device of the oxymoron enables perspectival democracy, as multiple character perspectives are registered and accounted for. For Paillot, Shields writes using a movement that Roland Barthes calls 'the dual pattern': 'the *straight line* (development, growth, the emphasis of an idea, stance, taste or image) and the *zigzag* (opposition, counteraction, contrariety, reactive energy, denegation, the return journey, z-movement, deviant trajectory)' (p. 159). Howells notes in 'Larry's A/Mazing Spaces' that Larry's epiphanic experience in the Hampton Court maze relates to a self-splitting or doubling: 'Slipping out of the shell of his own identity, he manages for a moment to transcend the socially scripted boundaries of his identity, with all its restrictions and responsibilities' (p. 124); Paillot relates the experience of loss of subjectivity in a maze, or labyrinth, to Maurice Blanchot's notion of 'momentary exaltation' (p. 160). Three essays make up part III: Marta Dvořák's 'Disappearance and "the vision multiplied": Writing as Performance', Lorraine York's 'Large Ceremonies: The Literary Celebrity of Carol Shields' and Aritha Van Herk's 'Mischiefs, Misfits, and Miracles'. For Dvořák, the extraordinary in Shields's work can be found in her strategy of formal constraint, akin to modernist avant-garde techniques found in Raymond Queneau's OuLiPo movement (exemplified by Georges Perec's novel *La Disparition* [1969], entirely written without the use of the letter 'e'). As Dvořák argues, 'Like Perec, Shields chooses to position writing as an agonistic craft' (p. 225). York examines the binary of the ordinary/extraordinary from the perspective of Shields's media persona of a paradoxical-sounding 'ordinary' literary celebrity; York makes interesting use of William Epstein's notion of biographical 'abduction' whereby biographers represent their subject through excisions and exclusions that enable the subject to be commodified. In conclusion, the essays in this collection are most successful at charting the extraordinary in Shields's work when they engage with her writing strategies: the rhetorical devices and narratological structures, the mirroring and paradoxical discourses.

The interview format has become increasingly popular in Canadian literary studies, and Herb Wyile, in *Speaking in the Past Tense: Canadian Novelists on Writing Historical Fiction*, has compiled and edited a substantial body of work via this format, usefully supplemented by his introduction, an overview and analysis of Canadian historical narratives. Opening with a discussion of current anxieties about Canadian history and education—from the traditionalist position that political and military history are no longer adequately taught to the more liberal position that Canadian history should be viewed from a multicultural perspective—Wylie notes that the perceived overall decline in the study of history is not apparent in the field of literature, which to a large extent has become preoccupied with historical fiction. Wylie argues that 'historical fiction has grown to be one of the most popular and substantial literary genres in Canada' (p. 2). The authors interviewed are selected because of their focus on 'public history' (p. 4)—not just an engagement with traditional historical sources, but a dialogue with, and critique of, historical discourses, figures and conceptions. Noting that such dialogue is important for those traditionally excluded from grand historical narratives—'women, the working class, and racial(ized) minorities' (p. 4)—Wylie notes that they are also under-represented in his own collection of interviews, and he explores some reasons for this, such as the exclusion until relatively recently of minorities from the literary scene. While historical fiction has long been popular in Canada, especially in the nation-building period of the nineteenth century, it is the postcolonial turn that has affected the genre most profoundly in the past three decades, and which has become a distinctive feature of many recent novels. Turning to the interviews, Wylie suggests that a central focus among them is the exploration and negotiation of the relationship 'between the literary and the historical in literary representations of history' (p. 10), a self-reflexivity and foregrounding of methodology that offers genuine critical insight throughout much of the book. Guy Vanderhaeghe notes how 'there is a limited onus' (p. 35) on the historical novelist to maintain an objective relationship with the historical record, no matter how open or incomplete that record is. He argues that a foundational historical knowledge is needed before interpretations can be offered: 'To even recognize the subjectivity of history, you have to have a certain amount of information' (p. 40). Rudy Wiebe, in a wide-ranging discussion, notes that justice for Canada's First Peoples is a compelling issue in the twenty-first century; he suggests that the public exposure of historical trauma, such as the residential schools, is essential. Furthermore, this rewriting of Canadian history necessarily takes place from the perspective of 'the small person, the unimportant person' (p. 64). Another significant trauma is that of the First World War, discussed by Jane Urquhart. Joseph Boyden brings together the residential school experience and the First World War in analysis of his novels. The history of 'triply colonized' (p. 111) Newfoundland is unravelled by Wayne Johnston, and Fred Stenson also asserts the complexity of historical fiction, arguing that history is an 'incredibly dense, interconnected kind of matrix' (p. 200). Reflecting on form, George Elliott Clarke discusses his use of photography—a key element of postmodern historiographic metafiction, to use Linda Hutcheon's term—in this case the use of images from other contexts than the ones directly narrated, to indirectly reflect upon atrocities and trauma. Other conversations concerning form that are of note are those with Margaret Sweatman, on historical novels as a combination of the elegiac mode and 'ghoulish' 'necrophilia' (p. 187), and with Heather Robinson on the role of comedy and humour. The aesthetic structure of the historical novel concerns Michael Crummey. In summary, the interview format is highly productive in this book, with genuine substance and critical content, making this a worthwhile contribution to the understanding of Canadian historical fiction.

Interest in Atwood's representation of postmodern and post-human subjects receives ongoing critical attention, with an essay by Carol Merli, 'Hatching the Posthuman: Margaret Atwood's "Bluebeard's Egg"' (*JSSE* 48[2007] 83–93). Merli describes the way in which the post-structuralist play of signification in Atwood's short story is analogous to contemporary notions of the body without borders. Two sets of narrative strategies are shown to intersect: the destabilizing narrative games and puzzles and the emerging world of the cyborg. The power of play in character formation is related to a note found in the Atwood collection, University of Toronto, by Ellen McWilliams in 'The Pleasures and Dangers of Storytelling in Margaret Atwood's *The Robber Bride*' (*NConL* 37[2007] 8–10). McWilliams traces the relationship between future identity and past experiences in character formation, noting that it is the construction of multiple stories and acts of story-telling or 'narrative invention' (p. 9) that can create feminist, liberating possibilities for subjectivity. Atwood receives significant coverage in Phyllis Sternberg Perrakis, ed., *Adventures of the Spirit: The Older Woman in the Works of Doris Lessing, Margaret Atwood, and Other Contemporary Women Writers.* The figure of the 'crone' is examined by Sharon R. Wilson in 'Through the

"Wall": Crone Journeys of Enlightenment and Creativity in the Works of Doris Lessing, Margaret Atwood, Keri Hulme, and Other Women Writers', where the mythological background is reviewed before looking at specific instances in contemporary fiction, such as Atwood's 'wise trickster crone' (p. 91) in her novel *The Penelopiad*, and her use of crone wisdom in *Alias Grace* and *The Blind Assassin*. Earl G. Ingersoll, in 'Margaret Atwood's *The Blind Assassin* as Spiritual Adventure', suggests that there is a narrative tension created in the novel due to the gradually failing aged body of the narrator; the genre of the memoir (and the novel's obsession with memorials) is significant in relation to the narrator's awareness of mortality. Ageing can also lead to an overturning of propriety and regulated behaviour, a return to, or a transformation into, the 'bad girl' as argued by Debrah Raschke and Sarah Appleton in ' "And they went to bury her": Margaret Atwood's *The Blind Assassin* and *The Robber Bride*'.

Fiona Tolan explores the relationship between fiction and second-wave feminist theory (or discourse) in *Margaret Atwood: Feminism and Fiction*. The structure of the book is quite remarkable: Tolan chronologically situates each novel within a coterminous discursive field made up of feminist, theoretical and philosophical concepts and texts. This history-of-ideas approach works well, revealing that Atwood is in dialogue with, and contributes to, emerging notions of narrative, subjectivity, gender and nationality. Tolan begins with Atwood's own disavowal of feminism in her early work, and this is also the subject of the first chapter on *The Edible Woman*, which traces the influence of Simone de Beauvoir's *The Second Sex* [1949] and Betty Friedan's *The Feminine Mystique* [1963], examining also the parody of romance in Atwood's novel. The convergence of feminism, ecology and nationalism in *Surfacing*, alongside the questioning of binary oppositions, is read through theorists such as Hélène Cixous in chapter 2; there is also some interesting material on the novel's dwelling in the pre-Oedipal. The postmodern incredulity regarding metanarratives, to use Jean-François Lyotard's phrase, is the subject of the third chapter, on *Lady Oracle*; Tolan also reads this novel via Elaine Showalter's theory of gynocriticism, alongside other French feminists. The anomalous *Life Before Man* is reread in chapter 4 as being in dialogue with debates concerning sociobiology, rather than being regarded as essentialist; Tolan notes that the 'tension between postmodernism and socio-biology has continued to recur in feminist thinking' (p. 115), making the point that *Life Before Man* was in fact a novel ahead of its time. Male violence and the politics of the gaze are topics of investigation in Tolan's reading of *Bodily Harm* in chapter 5. Here the power politics of the novel is contextualized via Luce Irigaray, Laura Mulvey and John Berger, among others. Feminist utopias and dystopias help explore the liberalism/communitarian opposition in *The Handmaid's Tale* in chapter 6, which also situates the female body within political discourses; the body as read through the new French feminisms, especially *écriture féminine*, informs Tolan's analysis of *Cat's Eye* in chapter 7. The shift from a postmodern to a postcolonial discursive field takes place in chapter 8, where *The Robber Bride* is situated via the work of Homi Bhabha, Edward Said and Gayatri Chakravorty Spivak. The latter's notion of the 'subaltern' also informs the reading of *Alias Grace* in chapter 9: 'In *Alias Grace*, it is not the first world subject creating the third world object, but rather the masculine speaking subject, Simon Jordan, creating the silenced female object, Grace' (p. 227). Grace is also analysed via theorists of madness, such as Shoshana Felman, Michel Foucault and Elaine Showalter. The final two chapters examine shifts in feminist politics and theory, with the anti-feminist backlash against second-wave feminism contextualizing *The Blind Assassin*, and new theoretical models, such as Francis Fukuyama's *The End of History and the Last Man* [1992], are considered, while *Oryx and Crake* is read via theories of post-feminism and the post-human.

Three essays on Michael Ondaatje are of note: Sofie De Smyter's 'Michael Ondaatje's *Coming through Slaughter*: Disrupting Boundaries of Self and Language' (*ES* 88[2007] 682–98); Kanchanakesi Channa P. Warnapala's 'Parenthetical Desire: Michael Ondaatje's *Running in the Family*' (*SLJH* 33[2007] 97–111); and Andrew Shin's 'The English Patient's Desert Dream' (*LIT* 18[2007] 213–36). Applying Julia Kristeva's work on the semiotic and the symbolic to Ondaatje, De Smyter also manages to translate a significant body of Ondaatje criticism via Kristeva's terminology. De Smyter rejects Ajay Heble's separation of the semiotic and the symbolic in his reading of jazz and improvisation, arguing that these aspects of subjectivity are co-constitutive, concluding that while Ondaatje's characters have fragile subjectivities that finally disengage from the symbolic, the symbolic order cannot be deconstructed. Warnapala argues that Ondaatje does address Sri Lankan subjectivity, even though he has been accused by critics of evading the specifics of colonial and postcolonial history; it is in the bodily encounter with Sri Lanka that a distanced, abstracted notion of place is most thoroughly disrupted. Another bodily encounter is with the English patient in the novel and film of that name; he functions, according to Shin, as an image of the 'colonial presence' (p. 213), to use Homi Bhabha's phrase, through which the work of mourning can take place for the characters Kip and Hana. Shin examines Kip's stories as they deconstruct Rudyard Kipling's *Kim*, as well as the reworking of the Malabar Caves episode of E.M. Forster's *A Passage To India*. Kip is read as the abject, inside and outside of different cultures, as well as occupying a symbolic femininity; Kip's departure following the dropping of the atomic bomb on Hiroshima 'introduces a radical discontinuity in the novel's narrative structure, a gap that evokes the atomic bomb's erasure of history and representation' (p. 225). Finally, Shin performs a postcolonial reading of the film version of *The English Patient*, which he regards as a depoliticization of the novel. Shin's comprehensive analysis of the novel and the film is highly recommended.

A special issue of *Ahornblätter: Marburger Beiträge zur Kanada-Forschung* (19[2007]) is on 'Tales and Typescripts: Carol Shields and the Creative Process'. It includes three essays: Achim Schulze's 'Miraculous Evolution: Carol Shields's "Various Miracles" and the Creative Process' (*Ahornblätter* 19[2007] 177–94); Kristine Kuschinski and Marianne Seip's 'The Creation of a Style: Carol Shields's Short Story "A Wood" and the Creative Process' (*Ahornblätter* 19[2007] 195–206); and Christiane Struth's 'Speaking from the Margins: Abandoned Women and Magic(al) Realism in Carol Shields's *Various Miracles* and *Unless*' (*Ahornblätter* 19[2007] 207–31). Each of the essays examines archival materials to discuss different aspects of manuscript development and editing, with Schulze suggesting that such a process 'comes closer to the act of unfolding a map or looking at a picture than following a teleological narrative path' (p. 177). Ascher applies Jung's theory of synchronicity as well as the theory of quantum mechanics to the network of coincidences in *Various Miracles* before looking at the evolution of the different drafts of Shields's book, noting not just editorial changes between manuscript and published version in *Canadian Forum* [1984], but also between the latter journal and book publication. For Kuschinski and Seip, the collaborative short story 'A Wood', written by Shields and her daughter Anne, is of interest because it exists in handwritten form in the archives, making it possible for them to observe Shields's excision of 'pretty' (p. 197) language. The recovery of lost memories and narratives is central to Struth's reading of Shields's magical realism, as well as the diverse ways in which Shields's appears to suggest that language is inadequate when it attempts to represent the miraculous.

Debra Muchnik's 'Film Noir: Observations of di Michele's *Under My Skin*' (in Pivato, ed., *Mary di Michele: Essays on her Works* (poetry essays are reviewed below)), argues that Hollywood images of women are central to this Italian Canadian writer's 1994 novel, which rejects typical stereotypes of 'strong immigrant women' (p. 70) who suffer their fate in silence. Instead, di Michele creates a surreal *film noir* protagonist, a complex novel-within-a-novel structure, and a series of sexual and addictive encounters that the protagonist explores to escape from her mundane world. In her more recent novel, *Tenor of Love* [2005], the struggle to represent music through the written word grounds di Michele's poetic background in a postmodern text that, according to Ian Williams in 'Translating Voices in Mary di Michele's *Tenor of Love*', creates different artistic voices, such as the production of indirect symbolic and evocative images rather than mimetic representations of sound. Another strategy used is that of allusion to music that the reader may have heard— although such a strategy is potentially alienating since readers may not know the music in question. Williams concludes that the musical 'voice in prose, like the word, is not a mere cloak for denotation, but its very texture bristles with connotative and textural meaning' (p. 158).

Painting and photography have long been central topics in Canadian fiction, affecting not just content but also form. Travis Mason, in 'Placing Ekphrasis: Paintings and Place in *Stanley Park*' (*CanL* 194[2007] 12–32), suggests that the ekphrastic narratives of real and fictional paintings in Timothy Taylor's novel help co-ordinate the desire for a local cuisine within a global food industry. Mason explores the slippage between notions of the local and the global through the indeterminate meanings generated by ekphrasis. David Williams's essay, 'A Force of Interruption: The Photography of History in Timothy Findley's *The Wars*' (*CanL* 194[2007] 54–73), relates Walter Benjamin's notion of the photographic 'shutter-click' (p. 57) and caesura in the movement of thought, theorized in Benjamin's 'Theses on the Concept of History', with that of 'the repeated starts and stops of the opening chapters of *The Wars*' (p. 58). Such an approach leads to a reassessment of Findley's historicism.

A contribution to literary-historical understanding by Colin Hill, '*Canadian Bookman* and the Origins of Modern Realism in English-Canadian Fiction' (*CanL* 195[2007] 85–101), explores the role of little magazines from the 1920s, arguing that the *Canadian Bookman* had a more central role than critics have previously acknowledged. Hill notes that debates within the *Canadian Bookman* 'reveal that Canada's modern realists considered themselves part of the international phenomenon retrospectively termed modernism, and that, in Canada at least, literary modernism and realism are neither opposed nor conflicting aesthetics' (p. 86). Manifesto and critical writing published in the *Canadian Bookman* led to a definition of modern realism. Hill summarizes by noting that 'modern realism in Canada is to a degree a hybrid genre that incorporates techniques commonly associated with both high realism and modernism, while remaining distinct from both' (p. 96). Hill's essay reveals the importance of going back to historical sources rather than relying on secondary accounts or biased writing.

Different reading strategies for dealing with open-ended fiction are offered by John Gerlach in 'To Close or Not to Close: Alice Munro's "The Love of a Good Woman"' (*JNT* 37[2007] 146–58). Noting how Munro's stories appear to resist either/or alternatives in supplying an imagined end to her open-ended work, Gerlach suggests that the concept of 'sideshadowing' may be more useful in understanding this narrative feature. Sideshadowing is a concept drawn from Gary Saul Morson's *Narrative and Freedom: The Shadows of Time* [1994], where 'Closure is replaced by an intensified sense of presentness, of continuing uncertainty, particularly thematic uncertainty' (p. 151). Gerlach reviews the existing critical strategies used in reading the ending of 'The Love of a Good Woman' before offering his own highly effective approach based on sideshadowing.

The creation of a new genre, the traumatic pastoral, can be seen as part of the complex literary response to Nazi appropriations of the pastoral and the Holocaust. Donna Coffey, in 'Blood and Soil in Anne Michael's *Fugitive Pieces*: The Pastoral in Holocaust Literature' (*MFS* 53[2007] 27–49), describes the novel before examining the roots of the elegy and pastoral forms. Drawing upon Michael Rothberg's notion of traumatic realism, Coffey argues that traumatic pastoral keeps open the loss or the absence that is being mourned. Coffey also provides an extended section on Nazi environmentalism and the disturbing parallels that can be seen between this aspect of Nazism and contemporary environmentalist rhetoric. The essay engages in depth with issues concerning Holocaust literature, trauma and ethical responses to the Holocaust.

Ethical limits engage Smaro Kamboureli in 'The Limits of the Ethical Turn: Troping towards the Other, Yann Martel, and *Self*' (*UTQ* 76[2007] 937–61), which opens with an extended analysis of the ethical turn in theory and literary criticism, before reading Martel's novel in which the protagonist undergoes gender transformation. Kamboureli argues that 'the efficacy of an ethical turn is contingent on its relationship with conditions that instigate their own ethical questions' (p. 945). She thus questions Martel's notion that feminist theory and practice are antithetical, and also notes that Martel's paradoxical notions of the literary overcoming of his own sexism, and the subsequent failure of this project, open up debate in this area. In another essay on ethics, ' "Daringly out in the public eye": Alice Munro and the Ethics of Writing Back' (*UTQ* 76[2007] 874–89), Robert McGill suggests that the short story 'Material' is a metafictional narrative 'about the ethics of writing fiction' (p. 875), which is made complex by the 'psychological dynamism' and 'the narrator's ironic, ambivalent statements' (p. 878) evident throughout the text.

(c) Poetry and Drama

Two leading Italian Canadian poets are surveyed and critically analysed in essay collections: Joseph Pivato, ed, *Mary di Michele: Essays on her Works* and Francesco Loriggio, ed, *The Last Effort of Dreams: Essays on the Poetry of Pier Giorgio di Cicco*. Introductory and survey materials in the former include the introduction and 'Research Notes' by Joseph Pivato, as well as a short biography, bibliography and an interview. Lisa Bonato, in 'Voce Unica', traces di Michele's early poetic maturity to her 'dual language experience of Italian and English' (p. 19), which also results in her experiencing the world as an outsider, an important consideration in relation to di Michele's feminism. Multiple levels of voice and interpretation in the confessional mode is the subject of Nathalie Cooke's 'On the Integrity of Speech and Silence', where she argues that di Michele's poem 'The Primer' is a successful integration of voice and vision. Returning to questions of duality, Jon Paul Fiorentino, in 'Emergent Luminosity: The Linguistic Music of Mary di Michele', suggests that the ampersand in di Michele's work is 'both set apart from and synonymous with landscape and language' (p. 59) where 'a poetic theory of the ampersand' (p. 60) emerges in the text. Such a doubled and disjunctive poetics is also apparent in di Michele's drawing upon her childhood condition of double vision, as Barbara Godard argues in 'Refiguring Alterity in the Poetry of Mary di Michele', which also contains some interesting observations concerning the way in which a societal double standard for women informs the poems in *Immune to Gravity* [1986]. Vera F. Golini, in ' "Growing for the flight": Mary di Michele's Reception in Canada', compares and contrasts two groundbreaking Canadian anthologies, one edited by di Michele, *Anything Is Possible: A Selection of Eleven Women Poets* [1984] and the other edited by Pier Giorgio di Cicco, *Roman Candles: An Anthology of Poems by Seventeen Italo-Canadian Poets* [1978]. Golini suggests that the collection of work by women from diverse ethnic backgrounds in a single anthology was an important event in women's writing in Canada, and is a marked progression to the more nationalistic anthology *Roman Candles*. Nonetheless, in 'Di Cicco's Elusive Virgin: Hunting the Universal Feminine' (in Loriggio, ed., *The Last Effort of Dreams*), Golini notes that *Roman Candles* 'helped establish lyrical, self-reflexive Italian Canadian voices in the landscape of Canadian literature' (p. 107). In the introduction to *The Last Effort of Dreams*, Loriggio notes the irony in Northrop Frye's complaint that Canada is a nation that lacks ghosts, since the immigrant 'spectrality' (to use Jacques Derrida's phrase) of di Cicco's Italian Canadian poetry was apparent early on in his career. Another mode of haunting (from a secular perspective) is di Cicco's disappearance into the priesthood, his extended silence and then his literary reappearance in 2001 with *Living in Paradise: New and Selected Poems*. Reflective portraits are by Mary di Michele, 'Living Inside the Poem', and Albert F. Moritz, 'We Sat on the Demoted Steps of Heaven: Some Memories of Pier Giorgio Di Cicco'. Dennis Lee provides a biographical introduction and brief survey in 'Di Cicco's Paradise', which is also a witty and lively overview of a selection of di Cicco's poems. The singularity of the early narrative poems is the subject of William Boelhower's 'The Heart's Resources: Gift Paths in Pier Giorgio di Cicco's Poetry', a sophisticated reading that traces some of the theoretical tropes and discourses in his work, such as Derridean gift-giving and hospitality. Speed and intensity drive di Cicco's chronicle poetry, argues Francesco Loriggio in '*Flying Deeper into the Century*: Quick Takes'; these post-1960s poems also mark the beginning of di Cicco's 'grappling with metaphysics' (p. 66). Robert Billings, in an interview with the poet, '*Virgin Science*: The Hunt for Holistic Paradigms. An Interview with Pier Giorgio di Cicco', and William Anselmi, in 'Reading *Virgin Science*', both grapple with the cosmological vision expressed in the poetry collection that Anselmi calls 'an unusual work within the panorama of Canadian literature' (p. 97). Two essays cover core elements of di Cicco's poetics: Yaroslav Senyshyn's 'Philosophy and Music in the Art of a Poet', and Francesco Loriggio's 'Basic Stuff: Religion and Modernity in di Cicco's Later Work'. Loriggio argues in her introduction that this book offers 'a bit of all that was needed to jump-start future research on his [di Cicco's] writing' (p. xv). The resulting text achieves this and far more: the surveys are produced with finesse and close attention to the poems, while further critical analysis and contextualization are performed to a high level. Together, these editions on di Michele and di Cicco considerably enhance critical understanding of Italian Canadian poetry.

Canadian modernism comes under scrutiny by Esther Sánchez-Pardo González in 'Transitional Spaces: Constructions of the Modernist "I" In Miriam Waddington's Poetry' (*RCEI* 54[2007] 169–80). Waddington's Jewish Canadian experiences inform her poetry, although González argues that there is room for further critical research on the influence of Yiddish in her texts. Patriarchy is regarded as having been replaced by poetic enclosures, which González reveals to be modernist and feminist in construction.

Poetry, orality, translation and intellectual and ethical property rights all form a complex nexus in Nicholas Bradley's 'Remembering Offence: Robert Bringhurst and the Ethical Challenge of Cultural Appropriation' (*UTQ* 76[2007] 890–912). Examining the idealism of Bringhurst's conception of transposition of oral to written First Nations texts, Bradley moves on to look at the distance from oral performance found in Bringhurst's own translations, and the accusations of cultural appropriation and inaccuracy in his poetic versions of Haida myths. Bradley argues that to fully understand this entire intercultural encounter involves studying the specific conditions of textual 'production and reception' (p. 900). The argument is an important reminder of the controversies that surrounded the publication—and the ethical situation—of Bringhurst's version of Haida oral poetry, A *Story as Sharp as a Knife* [1999].

The role of the older woman in Atwood's poetry is the subject of Kathryn VanSpanckeren's essay 'Atwood's Space Crone: Alchemical Vision and Revision in *Morning in the Burned House*' (in Perrakis, ed., *Adventures of the Spirit*; essays on Atwood's fiction are reviewed above). VanSpanckeren traces the uncanny older woman through Atwood's use of the descent myths and other related mythological figures to argue that the post-menopausal woman in Atwood's work is 'a latent powerhouse whose wisdom and energy are sorely needed on many fronts' (p. 156). VanSpanckeren draws upon archival manuscript versions to explore not just the published poems, but the earlier drafts and unselected poems such as 'Gathering' that foreground the 'shifting manifestations' (p. 161) of ageing.

Theatre can facilitate a new understanding of violent women, argues Shelley Scott in *The Violent Woman as a New Theatrical Character Type: Cases from Canadian Drama*. This monograph focuses on 'plays by Canadian women that deal with real-life incidents of violent women' where 'the playwright is theatrically engaging with the social meaning of the woman's violent act, asking how she was interpreted in public discourse and investigating the implications of that interpretation' (p. 2). Journalistic, novelistic and theatrical discourses are compared, with Scott making the interesting observation that fictionalized representations of real murders committed by women are reacted to negatively by the very newspaper presses that obsessed over these cases in the first place. The third and fourth chapters offer close readings of the drama. Chapter 3, 'The Tragedy of Revenge', covers the Anna Project's *This Is for You, Anna*; Colleen Wagner's *The Monument*; Marie Clements's *The Unnatural and Accidental Women*; and Lorena Gale's *Angélique*. Chapter 4, 'The Making of Warriors: Women as Action Heroes', covers Sharon Pollock's *The Making of Warriors*; Sally Clark's *Jehanne of the Witches*; and Sonja Mills's *The Danish Play*. The role of teenage girls in production is studied, with consideration of Joan MacLeod's plays *The Hope Slide* [produced 1992], *Little Sister* [produced 1994] and *The Shape of a Girl* [produced 2001], which concerns the murder of Reena Virk in Victoria, BC, by a group of teenagers mostly made up of young women. Scott also talks about working with teenage actors in her production of *This Is for You, Anna* at the University of Lethbridge in 2004, where she notes that the play became 'a shared interpretive experience' (p. 69). While the individual readings of each play are rather short, this study offers a new way of thinking about Canadian theatre and representations of women that disturb and unsettle societal norms.

Previously published essays on *Space and the Geographies of Theatre*, edited by Michael McKinnie, are collected in the ninth volume in the Critical Perspectives on Canadian Theatre in English series. In the introduction, McKinnie traces spatial concern back to the first European performance in the as yet unnamed Canada, Marc Lescarbot's *The Theatre of Neptune in New France* [1606]: 'an environmental pageant, having been staged on the water and shore of the Bay of Fundy for an audience of French and Aboriginal spectators' (p. viii). McKinnie suggests that the essays in the collection can be grouped into the categories of environmental, political and cultural geography, with inevitable crossovers and intersections. The one newly commissioned 2007 essay in the collection is by Laura Levin, 'To Live with Culture: Torontopia and the Urban Creativity Script'. Opening with the spectacular *Scotiabank Nuit Blanche*, an artistic transformation of Toronto's downtown core via performances and other free artistic events, Levin explores the reinvention of urban space by the artistic and activist Torontopia movement, asking if commercial backing of such ventures might negate subcultural politics. Situationism is shown to be important for the artistic resistance to capitalism and its co-opting of urban theatre and performances; an example is the Toronto Psychogeography Society, which draws upon Guy Debord's theories in his *Society of the Spectacle* [1967] to remap urban space, although often using a masculinist discourse. A wide range of performance groups and events is described, and the essay also engages with unusual civic and artistic crossovers.

Two essays examine work by Robert LePage: Karen Fricker's 'Cultural Relativism and Grounded Politics in Robert LePage's *The Anderson Project*' (*ConTR* 17[2007] 119–41) and Steve Dixon's 'Space Metamorphosis and Extratemporality in the Theatre of Robert LePage' (*ConTR* 17[2007] 499–515). Questions of internationalism versus local theatre are explored by Fricker, who notes that globalized theatre can lead to different strategies of realizing local concerns for a wider audience. Fricker charts the production and reception of *The Anderson Project* as it travelled from Quebec City to Paris, London and Montreal between 2005 and 2006, providing a detailed and fascinating account of play development in her first main section on Quebec City. The comparisons between each performance site reveal differences in political understanding between LePage and his audiences; for example, his immigrant character, Rashid, in *The Anderson Project* is made mute so as not to appear crass in the context of immigrant unrest in Paris at the time, yet reviewers found this to be a positive character shift whereby Rashid represents liminality and the voicelessness of immigrants in France. Four plays reveal LePage's interest in 'transformative space and kinetic *mise-en-scène*' as well as 'the nature and experience of time and unity' (p. 500): *Needles and Opium* [1991], *Elsinore* [1995], *Zulu Time* [1999] and *The Far Side of the Moon* [2000]. Dixon suggests that, by comparing LePage's uses of space with those of Czech director and designer Josef Svoboda, LePage's movement into the digital era can be better understood. LePage's 'imaginative fluidity' (p. 503) is revealed in his dynamic use of staging whereby there is 'metamorphosis not only of space, but also of time, and of characters, and of genders' (p. 503). The category of the 'extratemporal' in LePage's practice is defined by Dixon as relating to a 'quasi-Jungian' mythic order that also transforms space, such as the suspension of characters in water, air and 'outer space' (p. 505). LePage's combination of high-tech postmodernism and myth, existentialism and formal experimentation, situate him, for Dixon, in the realm of the modernists and the avant-garde.

The role of sound design in Canadian theatre is the topic of *Canadian Theatre Review* 129, edited by Andreas Kahre. No longer seen as an ancillary component of theatre, Kahre suggests that sound is 'a parallel activity' (p. 6) that contributes to new modes of interdisciplinary performance. Peter Hinton, interviewed by Andreas Kahre (*CTR* 129[2007] 10–14), discusses the need for sound to gain equality in the theatre design process. The resistances to such equality are narrated in a personal and reflective essay from the perspective of sound designer Noah Drew who, in 'Tiny Heartbreaks and the Electric Creative Body' (*CTR* 129[2007] 15–18), reveals the emotional engagement involved in sound becoming more than a technical supplement. Three essays examine different aspects of technology: Stefan Smulovitz's 'Kenaxis and Diamond: Tools for Theatre Artists' (*CTR* 129[2007] 21–4); Aleksandra Dulic, Kenneth Newby and Martin Gotfrit's '*One River (running...)*: Hybrid Space—Open Composition for an Immersive Environment' (*CTR* 129[2007] 34–40); and Kenneth Newby and Aleksandra Dulic's 'Intelligent Instruments for Situated Media Performance' (*CTR* 129[2007] 41–7). Two different software environments are discussed by Smulovitz: Kenaxis, suitable for experimental theatre in alternative performance spaces, and Diamond, designed for the more conventional theatre space, yet allowing for non-linear sound layering. The ongoing Computational Poetics Research Project combined pre-recorded media with improvised performance in an interactive audiovisual installation at the Surrey Arts Centre, BC, in 2005. Drawing upon Asian performance traditions, Dulic, Newby and Gotfrit note that braided processes 'enable a form of situated media performance that integrates computation as a medium for composition, performance and improvisation' (p. 36). Braided processes are also central to the use of intelligent instruments in situated media performance, as Newby and Dulic suggest; they examine ways in which intelligent instruments can be programmed for autonomous and responsive performance, and discuss interactive music performance. An essential openness to sound designers is a key feature of the theatre group Electric Company, and this is contextualized in a short essay by David Hudgins, 'Electric Sound: Collective Creation and Sound Design' (*CTR* 129[2007] 19–20), whereas sound installations by Richard Windeyer are the topic of Bruce Barton's '*Still Ringing*: Sounds Collaborative' (*CTR* 129[2007] 25–9). A creative and reflective piece by Sue Balint, 'Into the Woods: Excavated Journal Entries from a Tent East of Peterborough' (*CTR* 129[2007] 30–3), follows her experiences with sound while helping set up R. Murray Shafer's *Patria Cycle* in a rural environment. The full range of possibilities in the sonic environment is discussed by the artistic director of New Adventures in Sound Art in Toronto, Darren Copeland, in 'Outside the Black Box: Sound Design in Non-Theatre Contexts' (*CTR* 129[2007] 48–50). He suggests that sound design outside the theatre allows the designer to comment on the world as an artist, a role often denied within the traditional theatre space. Copeland's installation *Playing on the 401* is discussed in interview with Matt Rogalsky, '*Audience* Is a Verb: A Conversation with Darren Copeland' (*CTR* 129[2007] 51–3). The script is 'Tiger of Malaya' by Hiro Kanagawa (*CTR* 129[2007] 54–83).

Spoken-word performance in Canada has become increasingly popular and diverse in recent years. In his editorial for *Canadian Theatre Review* 130 on this topic, T.L. Cowan defines spoken-word performance as 'an umbrella term which may include text-based performances where the writer/performer is performing her/his own text' (p. 7). The diversity is apparent in the essays that appear in this issue, which include performative texts by bill bissett and Adeena Karasick, 'Shards of Light' (*CTR* 130[2007] 15–20), and Klyde Durm-I Broox, 'Gestures of the Dancing Voice: Reloading the Can(n)on under the Influence of Dub' (*CTR* 130[2007] 72–82), as well as more theoretical analyses, such as Nasser Hussain's 'Consuming Language: Embodiment in the Performance Poetry of bpNichol and Steve McCaffery' (*CTR* 130[2007] 21–5). Several practitioners write reflective accounts of their art, such as Kateri Akiwenzie-Damm in '*Gitook*/Say It: An Anishnaabe Perspective on Spoken Word' (*CTR* 130[2007] 10–14), and Sheri-D Wilson in 'First Time Eyes: Unearthing Spoken Word' (*CTR* 130[2007] 26–31). A highly analytical essay by Ian Ferrier, 'Tools of Poetry in Performance in Canada' (*CTR* 130[2007] 32–7), offers some evaluative parameters for spoken-word performance, including vocal dynamics and the delivery speed, humour, improvisation, audio effects, music, dub poetry and wider theatrical tools, such as lighting, props and stage sets. Ferrier concludes that much spoken-word performance combines the techniques of the sermon, film and popular song (p. 36). Kedrick James, in 'Poetic Terrorism and the Politics of Spoken Word' (*CTR* 130[2007] 38–42), argues that spoken-word performance cannot be so easily pinned down through academic modes of analysis and assessment: 'Spoken word lacks theorization, partly because it grew up in opposition to academic poetry and critical scholarship' (p. 40). A good example of spoken word's anti-evaluative stance is the 'open mike' event, discussed by Fortner Anderson in 'All the Voices' (*CTR* 130[2007] 43–6); he suggests that at the open mike 'There is neither hierarchy nor distinction' (p. 44). Anderson goes on to compare and contrast open mike with the highly competitive slam event, the latter being the topic of Kevin Matthews's 'Site of Slam' (*CTR* 130[2007] 47–51), which he perceives as being productively enhanced by the competition: 'At least in slam, it's explicit who is setting the agenda, who is practically and ideologically judge and patron' (p. 50). Other aspects of spoken-word performance are explored in Corey Frost, 'From Wax to Bits: Spoken-Word Recordings in Canada' (*CTR* 130[2007] 52–7) and Victoria Stanton and Susanne de Lotbinière-Harwood, 'Temporal Forms Unite! A Conversation between Victoria Stanton and Susanne de Lotbinière-Harwood' (*CTR* 130[2007] 59–63), and activism is considered by Trish Salah in 'What's All the Yap? Reading Mirha-Soleil Ross's Performance of Activist Pedagogy' (*CTR* 130[2007] 64–71). The most intriguing essay in this issue is Ken Mitchell's 'Canadian Cowboy Poetry and the Oral Tradition' (*CTR* 130[2007] 83–8), which traces this folk art genre from the frontier culture of 1880 to its more recent transformation at the first Cowboy Poetry Gathering at Elko, Nevada, in 1985, thus beginning 'The postmodern era of cowboy poetry' (p. 84). Mitchell defines the genre, discusses practitioners and events, and regards the phenomenon as part of a renaissance of the spoken word. An essay on youth, Rebecca Ingalls's ' "Us" versus "Them": Performing Youth Identity through Spoken Word' (*CTR* 130[2007] 89–93), although written in an American context, still resonates within Canadian oral culture. Scripts include Skeena Reece's 'S.O.S.: Skeena of the Skeena' (*CTR* 130[2007] 94–100) and extracts from Naila Keleta Mae's 'No Knowledge College' (*CTR* 130[2007] 101–7).

Expecting essays on cutting-edge high-tech performance for an issue of *Canadian Theatre Review* (p. 131) on science, technology and theatre, editor Jenn Stephenson notes that she instead received far more cautious, introspective pieces of writing: 'rather than rushing ahead into some brave new world, we are invited to pause, to question, to weigh alternatives, to evaluate and then—to experience the wonder' (p. 5). Pondering how far science plays can truly engage with science, ethics and politics, Caroline Baillie, in 'Public Dialogue on Science: Theatre as Mediator' (*CTR* 131[2007] 6–13), suggests that the biographical focus of this type of theatre can be a barrier or a facilitator to a deeper public and educational engagement with science. The pedagogic aspects of science plays are also explored in Art Stinner's essay 'Toward a Humanistic Science Education: Using Stories, Drama and the Theatre' (*CTR* 131[2007] 14–19). Surveying the history of science plays, Christopher Innes, in 'Bridging Opposites—Drama and Science—in the Plays of John Mighton' (*CTR* 131[2007] 21–6), notes the unique situation of Canadian dramatist and mathematician John Mighton, who bridges the arts/science divide and builds 'scientific principles into the dramatic structure' (p. 22) of his plays. Scepticism about the outcome of scientific and technological futures is prevalent in little-known Canadian science fiction (SF) plays, discussed in Scott Duchesne in 'Invisible Realms: Canadian Speculative Drama' (*CTR* 131[2007] 27–32). Three essays deal with the impact of technology on theatre: Gavin McDonald's 'A Piece of String and a Little Imagination: An Interview with Chris Wheeler' (*CTR* 131[2007] 33–9); Paul Court's 'New Technology, New Technicians and an Ancient Art' (*CTR* 131[2007] 40–4); and David Feheley's 'The Canadian Opera Company's *Wozzeck* Fourteen Years Later' (*CTR* 131[2007] 45–8). Wheeler observes how theatre technicians have to keep ahead of commercially available equipment, becoming bricoleurs in the process. Court argues that theatre resists technological and industrial society while using technological advances as part of the staging; he notes that 'The challenge of introducing any new technology into an art form is to master the technology to such an extent that it becomes an artistic tool rather than an intrusive technological artefact' (p. 42). In the remount of a play, Feheley is able to compare and contrast technologies used. Technology has overtaken the search for a physical location for Canada's theatre museum, in the form of a virtual site, discussed by Kate Barris in 'To Be Virtual . . . or Not to Be: Theatre Museum Canada's Travels into the World of Technology' (*CTR* 131[2007] 49–60). Juxtaposed with this essay is Stephen Johnson's account of his visit to a museum that now exists in one man's home, 'Return of the Cabinet of Curiosities: A Tour of the Niagara Falls Museum' (*CTR* 131[2007] 53–60). Finally, Craig Walker, in 'Moral Adaptations: How Ann-Marie MacDonald's *The Arab's Mouth* became *Belle Moral*' (*CTR* 131[2007] 61–7), looks at revisions to a play which addresses issues such as Darwinism and evolution, and the opposition of the rational and the irrational. The script is Jodi Essery's 'Fathom' (*CTR* 131[2007] 68–91).

Twenty-five years after Rina Fraticelli's unpublished report 'The Status of Women in the Canadian Theatre' [1982] was written for Status of Women Canada, *Canadian Theatre Review* returns to this important topic in

'Canadian Women Playwrights: Triumphs and Tribulations' (volume 132). A new study in this area was initiated in 2003, by the Women's Caucus of the Playwrights Guild of Canada and Nightwood Theatre, which led the following year to the launch of Equity in Canadian Theatre: The Women's Initiative and the publication of *Adding It Up—The Status of Women in Canadian Theatre: A Report on the Phase One Findings of Equity in Canadian Theatre—the Women's Initiative* in 2006. Rebecca Burton, in 'Dispelling the Myth of Equality: A Report on the Status of Women in Canadian Theatre' (*CTR* 132[2007] 3–8), looks in depth at the results of these surveys and initiatives, comparing more recent data with that put forward by Fraticelli in 1982. Overall, Burton shows how notions of post-feminist equality are mythical, and that while statistics have improved, with more women working as artistic directors, directors, or playwrights, equality has not been achieved: 'The marginalization, occupational segregation and financial disparities encountered by women indicate that patriarchal ideology and conventional gender roles still hold sway' (p. 7). Yvette Nolan's essay, 'Responding: Self-Scripting for Dialogue' (*CTR* 132[2007] 9–13), celebrates the achievement of women in Canadian theatre, reporting on a conference called Canadian Women Playmakers: Triumphs and Tribulations. Presenting an opposing view to the report from 2006, Krista Dalby, in '*Adding It Up* Takes More Than Just Numbers' (*CTR* 132[2007] 14–17), argues that her experiences in the theatre industry are quite different from the picture painted in the report: 'I find our theatre community an incredibly open environment, filled with stories of men and women of different ages, sexual preferences, and diverse cultures' (p. 17). Another critique, although one that is more in tune with the 2006 report, is Bruce Barton's 'Tributes of Another Order' (*CTR* 132[2007] 18–23). Barton warns that statistical analyses are tools which can also be constrictive and which 'cannot help but further stratify and ossify and reaffirm the subject of its gaze' (p. 20). Barton, like Dalby, offers evidence of alternative modes of success: women involved in theatre and performance companies that do not fit the institutional models analysed by *Adding It Up*. Nightwood Theatre has done more than any other company in Canada to promote women in all aspects of the industry. Shelley Scott, in 'Nightwood Theatre: A Woman's Work Is Always Done' (*CTR* 132[2007] 24–9), looks at the history and range of Nightwood productions, starting with the examples of *The Danish Play* and the theatre programme called 'Busting Out!', which provides 'self esteem building and artistic expression in an open and creative, non-judgmental all-girl space' (p. 25). Scott compares and contrasts Nightwood with the feminist Redlight Theatre (1974–7), as well as examining Nightwood's involvement in festivals, and its anti-racist mandate. Naila Keleta Mae, in 'Contemporary Social Justice Theatre: Finding, Sharing, Healing' (*CTR* 132[2007] 30–3), argues for a process of symbolic reversal in the production processes of theatre, whereby theatre artists can 'occupy a socio-political position intentionally and write/create/explore the play from that perspective' (p. 32). The scripts are Collen Murphy's 'Down in Adoration Falling' (*CTR* 132[2007] 34–54) and Beverley Cooper's 'The Eyes of Heaven' (*CTR* 132[2007] 65–89).

4. The Caribbean

(a) General
The books published in the year under review continue to reconsider and enlarge the theoretical frameworks used to define the regional identity of the Caribbean. There is an increased emphasis on theories of place, space and what Peter Hulme refers to as a 'literary geography'. Critical texts focus on migrations of people and the circulation of cultural productions and influences between the US South, Central America, the Pacific islands and the Caribbean archipelago, as well as on more conventional migratory routes between the Caribbean, North America and Europe. Though there are fewer single-author studies this year there is, in the work selected, a fruitful critical dialogue with earlier texts around issues such as Caribbean modernism, a Caribbean women's aesthetic, and the relationship between literature and popular culture.

Mary Lou Emery's *Modernism, the Visual and Caribbean Literature* is a rewarding and intellectually ambitious study of the importance of seeing, vision and visual culture in twentieth-century Caribbean literature. Emery begins with a discussion of the treatment of Turner's *The Slave Ship* in three Caribbean texts: Michelle Cliff's *Free Enterprise* [1993], David Dabydeen's *Turner* [1994] and Fred D'Aguiar's novel *Feeding the Ghosts* [1997]. Threaded through her analysis of expressions of Caribbean modernism in the work of Caribbean artists Edna Manley and Ronald Moody, and writers Claude McKay and Jean Rhys, is a critique of the language of modernism's 'visually claiming and judging the black person, positioning her or him as a body to be used in one's argument' (p. 95) or, as in the case of Picasso's remark to Aubrey Williams, as an object of study. In the chapter entitled 'Exile/Caribbean Eyes 1928–1963' she begins with a sympathetic analysis of the literary production of Una Marson and C.L.R. James, including a discussion of their plays staged in London in the 1930s. She suggests that both writers use their fiction, poetry and drama to examine the 'class, gender and racial dynamics of the social acts of seeing': their texts 'see *through* colonial imitation into a freer, self-reflexive, and politically charged modernist aesthetic of the 1930s' (p. 101). She elaborates on this premise with a discussion of James's early short stories and the novel *Minty Alley* [1936] centring her argument, in relation to the novel, on representations of repeated 'act[s] of peeping' by its protagonist, Haynes. The plot is structured around what Emery defines as an act of middle-class voyeurism; she suggests that James's use of images of seeing and being seen culminates in the final scene, a moment of self-perception prompted by Haynes's return to a radically transformed number 2 Minty Alley. Peeping through the windows, Emery argues, he sees himself for the first time and, in the new inhabitants 'the replacement of a strong folk culture by the rise of the black middle class, repeating colonial conventions of respectability rather than enacting any real change' (p. 112). The chapter ends with an insightful reading of George Lamming's novels through Emery's focus on 'the significance of visuality', situating his work 'in the intersection of modernism, anti-colonial transnationalism, and literatures of exile'; this section includes close attention to 'one of the more debated aspects of Lamming's writing, the portrayal of women' (p. 153).

Emery's critical approach is sophisticated and tightly constructed, but the appeal of her work is its accessibility and its use of theoretical, contextual and socio-critical material to provide illuminating readings of familiar, if not overly scrutinized, texts. Her detailed attention to Derek Walcott's *Tiepolo's Hound* [2000] is made more interesting by its juxtaposition with her reading of the visual narrative style of Wilson Harris, the paintings of Guyanese artist Aubrey Williams and the visual tropes in Kamau Brathwaite's autobiographical essay 'Timehri' [1970]. Walcott, she suggests, 'enters the realm of the visual' in order to 'examine its epistemological claims, and critique its institutionalization in empirical science, the commodification of art and the philosophy of aesthetics' (p. 183). She looks at diverging meanings in the work of these writers, in particular the different significance given to the Amerindian presence, arguing that whereas Walcott 'discount[s] the continued Amerindian presence in the Americas as well as their past' (p. 201), Harris uses icons of Amerindian culture as a trope for 'unwritten histories of the past, through which he seeks a renewal of vision' (p. 204). Emery offers a detailed analysis of ekphrastic passages in the novels of Jean Rhys and Jamaica Kincaid, and of scenes of 'ekphrastic fear' in Michelle Cliff's *No Telephone to Heaven*, then returns to devices that emphasize 'ekphrastic hope' in Harris's fiction, focusing on his attempt to overcome the 'apparent divide between a pre-Columbian past and the written history of the Americas' (p. 222).

In the afterword to *Nationalism and the Formation of Caribbean Literature*, Leah Reade Rosenberg re-engages with Lamming's *In the Castle of My Skin* [1953] and argues that readers of fiction by writers such as Lamming and Samuel Selvon, often cited as the originators of a Caribbean literary tradition, are better placed to approach their work 'having made the acquaintance of their literary forebears' (p. 207). Her new book succeeds in its intention to acquaint readers with the nineteenth- and early twentieth-century writers and cultural activists who shaped the writing of canonical figures of Caribbean literature. Rosenberg begins her work with a close analysis of three nineteenth-century Trinidadian novels, arguing that, like Caribbean writers of the 1950s and early 1960s, these early writers were attempting the same project, 'the creation of an authentic Caribbean identity through literature' (p. 5). Whereas other recent critics such as Alison Donnell and Evelyn O'Callaghan have struggled against Brathwaite's formulation and use of 'creolization' to define both a historical Caribbean identity and the emergence of a national literature, Rosenberg uses Brathwaite's term to describe what is for her a dialectical process that shapes both the history and the cultural production on which she focuses. As the author demonstrates, three early examples—*Warner Arundell* [1838] by the Jewish émigré E.L. Joseph, *Emmanuel Appadocca* by Michel Maxwell Philip [republished in 1997] and Stephen Cobham's *Rupert Gray* [1907]—while seeking to valorize the role and status of their respective white creole, 'brown' and black protagonists, also reflect the agonistic relations of class, colour, culture and gender within which they emerge.

Rosenberg reads all the texts in this work in the context of literature published in newspapers, magazines and literary journals. She draws attention to the importance of the Institute of Jamaica, established in 1879, and the *Victoria Quarterly* (1888–92) in shaping nineteenth-century literary tastes and in articulating a form of cultural nationalism that was to define literary and cultural production well into the twentieth century. She explores the complex significance of Thomas MacDermot and H.G. de Lisser, not only as novelists and short-story writers but also as influential editors of the magazine *Planter's Punch* and, in the case of MacDermot, of the newspaper *Jamaica Times*. Many readers of this newspaper, like MacDermot, had been or were teachers and had only recently 'joined the ranks of the middle classes' (p. 53). The anxious and negative relationship that this group retained with the peasant culture they had left behind is one that characterized representations of the largely black 'folk' in the paper's public interest articles and in the short stories it published.

Aspects of subsequent chapters have appeared in recent journals; in this work however, Rosenberg's analysis of Claude McKay's fiction and poetry is enriched by its juxtaposition with the 'antilabour, antiblack' perspective of his contemporaries, MacDermot and de Lisser. Her discussion of the literature of the Beacon group begins with reference to other fiction and non-fiction by journalists such as Seepersaud Naipaul, writing for the *East India Weekly* and *Trinidad Guardian*. By reading the Beacon writers' work in the context of literature published in other newspapers and periodicals, and by including all the work published, not just the 'yard' stories, Rosenberg uncovers, in this work, a less radical class and racial politics than has previously been admitted. Though Jean Rhys did not, it seems, contribute to newspapers and journals, in her closing chapter Rosenberg examines Rhys's representations of newspaper culture in her fiction. She closes by situating Rhys in relation to her Caribbean 'peers' (p. 182), arguing that while her autobiographical and fictional writing, in its obsessive return to the figure of white creole woman as stateless, nomadic and defined by seduction, is not representative of early twentieth-century West Indian white creole womanhood, it does reflect some of the paradoxes of the literature produced by early Caribbean nationalist, anti-colonialist and modernist writers.

The aim of Joan Anim-Addo's *Touching the Body: History, Language and African-Caribbean Women's Writing* is to explore the legacy of voicelessness and silence around black women's literary expression and to 'read the body of twentieth-century texts by African-Caribbean women in a post-slavery continuum' (p. 11). This work includes writing by women based in or from Britain and Anim-Addo reads these texts within 'a convergence of theoretical tools and perspectives' also favoured by earlier critics, most notably Evelyn O'Callaghan and Édouard Glissant. The first chapter discusses the establishment of a '*pretext* of race' and various related systems and mechanisms by which the African Caribbean woman was constructed as invisible (p. 84). The challenge to invisibility and to traditions of 'speaking for' begins with a discussion of the sixteenth-century poem 'Of Ane Blak-Moir', a sustained critique of Johan Zoffany's *Portrait of Dido Elizabeth Belle and Lady Elizabeth Murray* [1779], Aphra Behn's *Oroonoko* [1688], and the poetry of the eighteenth-century African American woman writer Phyllis Wheatley. Contrary to critical assumptions that, apart from the narratives of Mary Prince and Mary Secole, black women were silent in the nineteenth century,

Anim-Addo's insightful and well-researched second chapter excavates the voices—albeit mediated—of African Caribbean women slaves in nineteenth-century anti-slavery reports. She uncovers first-person accounts wherein slave women spoke their complaints, recorded along with counter-statements in subsequent hearings. While acknowledging that the act of complaining, allowed as a hard-won reform, was in this context 'audacious', Anim-Addo is cautious about the uses of this 'gift of speech' within a system of justice that was 'only at the beginnings of assuming personhood for African-heritage peoples' (p. 113). Noting the relative silence of black women in the decades following emancipation, the author reads this period through the work of Simone Schwarz-Bart's *Telumée* [1982] and concludes with an analysis of a selection of poetry by Una Marson and Louise Bennett and with reference to Sylvia Wynter's *The Hills of Hebron* [1962].

Part II of this important work offers some fresh and revealing insights into the use of language and forms of creolization in the 'first-wave novels' (p. 190) of Caribbean women writers such as Merle Hodge, and concludes with a discussion of 'linguistic tensions' (p. 194) in the poetry and prose of Merle Collins, including *The Colour of Forgetting* [1995], Erna Brodber's *Myal* [1988] and Zee Edgell's *Beka Lamb* [1982]. Interwoven into the later sections of the book, which include an analysis of neglected contemporary black British women writers such as Beryl Gilroy, is Anim-Addo's appropriation of concepts of 'carnival masking' to demonstrate the ways that 'African-Caribbean women writers, in negotiating the written text, enter into a syncretic space, like carnival' (p. 229). The texts reflect the cultural mix out of which they emerge and demand, according to the author, an appropriate cultural reading.

Routes and Roots: Navigating Caribbean and Pacific Island Literatures, by Elizabeth M. DeLoughrey, extends and makes important departures from the work of theorists such as Antonio Benitez-Rojo, who place the island metaphor at the centre of their cultural theories of the Caribbean. The author takes a historical approach to the concept of the island in literature and history, tracing repeated emphasis on its isolation and remoteness, and pointing to the perpetuation of island myths that were circulated to conceal colonial intentions. These included, DeLoughrey argues, the provision of 'material bases for the establishment of the natural sciences' and the creation of a space to theorize racial difference and to conduct experiments in 'racial mixing, imprisonment, and enslavement' (p. 13). Her approach to reading the figure of the island in the literatures of these two cultures includes building on the work of geologist Patrick Nunn and the cultural theories of Kamau Brathwaite and Édouard Glissant, both of whom emphasize the geological depths of islands and their 'shared experience across time and space' (p. 21).

Through her deployment of Brathwaite's 'tidalectic' framework DeLoughrey focuses on ways in which the 'transoceanic imaginary fore-grounds the fluid connection between the Pacific and Caribbean islands and the role of geography...in shaping cultural production' (p. 51). Other chapters consist of close readings of a small selection of texts in ways that suggest their 'tidalectic engagement with land and sea' and their foregrounding of a 'fluid oceanic imaginary' (p. 51). Her bold and innovative reading of

John Hearne's *The Sure Salvation* [1981] begins by contextualizing the neglect of his oeuvre. She suggests, however, that in overlooking his work critics have missed this novel's attempts to destabilize discourses of Atlantic modernity and his successful subversion of 'the adventure-driven maritime novel in ways that reflect back to Melville's *Benito Cereno*' (p. 67). DeLoughrey's final chapter examines representations of the 'indigenous presence' in Michelle Cliff's *No Telephone to Heaven* [1987] and Merle Collins's *The Colour of Forgetting* [1995]. Whereas many critics have read Collins's second novel as an elaborate meditation on the failure of the Grenadian revolution, DeLoughrey, while acknowledging that the work represents the failure of 'postcolonial nationalism' (p. 233), focuses almost exclusively, and to interesting effect, on the use of metaphors of the island's flora and fauna, and the complex and ambiguous significance of Carib, the female seer. She concludes that in this novel 'In the face of globalized material progress, Amerindian presence becomes flattened sediment, receding to the alterity of the past' (p. 267).

Sarah Phillips Casteel's *Second Arrivals: Landscapes and Belonging in Contemporary Writing of the Americas* serves as a timely intervention in existing areas of 'diasporic discourse'. It attempts to counter the 'exaggerated stress on displacement, dislocation, and movement at the expense of place' in this field of study by suggesting that, paradoxically, migratory movement 'renders the need for viable forms of emplacement more, rather than less urgent' (p. 3). She argues that consequent on the emphasis on 'alienation and exile' is the repeated use of the image of the 'global city' which has come to stand for 'modern (diasporic) life itself' and the disallowing of access to rural wilderness spaces by 'minorities' and migrants (p. 5). Her book focuses on American, Canadian and Caribbean writers and artists who refuse 'to observe the carefully policed boundaries of iconic rural wilderness landscapes and the exclusionary definitions of national belonging they naturalize' (p. 6). The first chapter is a comparative study of V.S. Naipaul's *Enigma of Arrival* [1987] and Walcott's *Tiepolo's Hound* [2000]. Casteel gives less significance than Emery, in the work discussed above, to the narrative as an ekphrastic appropriation of the painting of the same name, focusing instead on Naipaul's uses of the pastoral. She suggests that, whereas Naipaul uses his encounter with the English landscape and his discovery of Wiltshire as a place he can call home as a means of ending his rootlessness, Walcott ends his encounters with the European landscape and his complex reinscriptions of a colonial pastoral by turning away from Europe. Despite the writers' critique of the 'colonial pastoral' neither, in these works, chooses displacement of the rural in favour of an urban setting; rather, 'what we find in Naipaul and Walcott is a reconfiguration of the rural that makes possible their articulation of a postcolonial sense of place' (p. 44). Other chapters include a close reading of Jamaica Kincaid's *My Garden (Book)* [1999], and discussion of the uses of 'marvelous and Gothic gardens' (p. 147) in Maryse Condé's *Crossing the Mangrove* [1995], Shani Mootoo's *Cereus Blooms at Night* [1996] and Gisèle Pineau's *The Drifting of Spirits* [1999].

In her book *All the Difference in the World: Postcoloniality and the Ends of Comparison* Natalie Melas takes an original approach to the texts she discusses. The chapter 'The Gift of Belittling All Things: Catastrophic

Miniaturization in Aimé Césaire and Simone Schwarz-Bart' traces the response of these two writers to 'transmutations of catastrophic miniaturization' defined as 'an expression of interiority, a form for possessing the world and condensing values through imagination' (p. 176). Against the 'belittling miniaturization' performed in colonial narratives, the obsessive repetition of the diminutive in the first half of Césaire's *Notebook of a Return to My Native Land* [1956] results in a reversal of these terms: 'the very force of hyperbole aggrandizes it, with the effect that the text reveals the enormity of the ontological calamity that underlies its diminutions. Smallness becomes "dazzling"' (p. 179). Melas ends a close and rewarding reading of the poem by suggesting that in using Césaire's *Notebook* as an intertext Maryse Condé and Simone Schwarz-Bart respond to its 'masculinism' by mirroring Césaire's 'insular scale', but in a way that 'conjoins it with gender' (p. 197). A version of the chapter 'Ruined Metaphor: Epic Similitude and the Pedagogy of Poetic Space in Derek Walcott's *Omeros*' was reviewed in *YWES* 86[2007].

Literature and Culture in the Black Atlantic: From Pre- to Postcolonial, by Kofi Omoniyi Sylvanus Campbell, begins with an extended critique of Paul Gilroy's seminal text, *The Black Atlantic*, the purpose of which is to 'extend the historical dimension of Paul Gilroy's original conception of the black Atlantic . . . to the black Atlantic's pre-colonial beginnings' (p. 1), thus adding a greater sense of historicity to Gilroy's original formulation. The central tenet of this work, and one that Campbell applies to his reading of the fictional texts, is that pre-colonial (1300–1600) representations paved the way for the 'future colonialist project' (p. 5). The problem with Campbell's thesis, at least as it impacts on his reading of the Caribbean texts he selects, is that 'precolonial' in this work is defined too narrowly in relation to European forms of representation. Raleigh is used in several instances as an example of a pre-colonial text, and the distinction between pre-colonial and colonial seems too fine either to 'extend' Gilroy's theories or to make possible fresh readings of these fictional texts. The strength and usefulness of this work to scholars of Caribbean literature lie in Campbell's close, sensitive readings of Wilson Harris's oeuvre, Walcott's *Dream on Monkey Mountain* [1970], Dabydeen's *Disappearance* [1993] and a text that has received little critical scrutiny, Paul Keens-Douglas's 'Ent Dat Nice' [1979].

Just Below South: Intercultural Performance in the Caribbean and the U.S. South, edited by Jessica Adams, Michael P. Bibler and Cécile Accilien, is an exciting and intellectually adventurous collection. By focusing on language and on performance as expressed in the 'intercultural region of the circum-Caribbean' (p. 11) this work aims to examine what the editors describe as the 'lingering anxious relationship between the South and the Caribbean' (p. 2). The region and its cultures, from the American South to French Guiana, are linked by histories of migration, armed struggles, 'casual contacts and prolonged relationship' (p. 2). Julian Gerstin's 'The Allure of Origins: Neo African Dances in the French Caribbean and the Southern United States' (pp. 123–45) begins with a focus on the early white and black accounts of kalenda, a dance that has been performed in parts of the Caribbean, the US mainland and South America since the end of the seventeenth century. Gerstin argues that these early descriptions of the dance served to create an image of kalenda that was more stereotype than substance and relied on a few simple traits: 'exoticism, rhythm, improvisation, and an unrestrained intensity' (p. 125). The author looks at its contemporary interpretations in Martinique, as either tourist spectacle or an attempt by 'renewalists' to return the dance to its African origins, and detects some shared, though differently expressed, characteristics: 'exoticism...a reliance on suspect texts, a predilection to glorify Africa (or what is seen as Africa) while professing global postmodernity' (p. 140). In 'Trinidad Sailor Mas' (pp. 146–66) Rawle Gibbons uses a close, historical reading of Trinidad Carnival's 'Sailor Mas' to distinguish between 'tradition mas, the category to which Sailor belongs' and commercial mas, which celebrates 'the creative relationship between communal custom and the individual imagination' (p. 150). Sailor Mas, like most traditional carnival masquerades, is a performance encoding an act of resistance that is performed beyond the sphere of the temporal but is nevertheless effective in material terms, if not as resistance, then as the management of the unequal power relations within which the Caribbean is constituted.

The essay 'Plantation America's "Alienated Cousins": Trinidad Carnival and Southern Civil War Re-enactments', by Kathleen M. Gough (pp. 167–89), makes a bold comparison between these two performances, arguing that both Southern Civil War re-enactments and the annual performance of carnival in Trinidad demonstrate that 'while slavery was eradicated in the former plantation regions of the Americas, the legacy of that history is everywhere still meaningful both at the level of institutional and of popular representation' (p. 168). She centres her discussion on the role of official institutions in the annual reproduction of carnival, arguing that their function was to subsume the traditional mas of resistance and dissent to 'pretty mas', itself used to revive old myths of the Caribbean as a 'prelapsarian, pre-civilized Garden of Eden' (p. 174). She concludes, however, that while both civil war re-enactments and the officially sponsored versions of Trinidad Carnival attempt to suppress history and the uncomfortable repetitions of historical inequalities in the present, at particular moments such as carnival 1970 there have been popular resurrections of the 'subversive power of traditional post-Emancipation forms of Carnival' (p. 181). Shirley Tolland Dix's ' "This is the horse. Will you ride?": Zora Neale Hurston, Erna Brodber, and Rituals of Spirit Possession' (pp. 191–210) looks at ways in which both writers 'explore cultural legacies of the South and the Caribbean through an African diasporic lens' (p. 191). Tolland Dix traces Brodber's self-conscious addresses to Hurston's fiction and, focusing on Brodber's third novel *Louisiana* [1994], examines the means by which one of the protagonists, Ella Townsend, becomes a channel for what Toni Morrison calls 'discredited knowledge' (p. 201): Ella attempts to connect her scientific training, with its emphasis on empirical knowledge, to her experiences of communion with the spirit world. The novel thus facilitates an interrogation of what constitutes 'valid knowledge' (p. 202). Jana Evans Braziel adds to her growing body of published criticism on Jamaica Kincaid with the essay 'Antillean Detours through the American South: Édouard Glissant's and Jamaica Kincaid's Textual Returns to William Faulkner' (pp. 239–64), a critically agile study of the echoes of Faulkner's fiction in Kincaid's *The Autobiography of My Mother*

[1996] that uses Glissant's concept of 'Antillean detours' to describe forms of historical trespass.

Narrating the Past: (Re)Constructing Memory, (Re)Negotiating History, edited by Nandita Batra and Vartan P. Messier, is a collection of conference papers published following the 2005 conference of the same name. Although the conference was hosted by the Caribbean chapter of the College English Association, only a minority of the published papers cover Caribbean literature. In contrast to scholars such as Josh Gosciak, who emphasize Claude McKay's internationalist sympathies, Tatiana Tagirova, in her paper 'The Jamaican Beginnings and World Travels of Claude McKay: A Search for Justice and Equality' (pp. 73–93), argues that McKay's autobiographical work *A Long Way from Home* [1937] and *My Green Hills of Jamaica* [published posthumously in 1979], demonstrate his preference for a 'national identification' (p. 74). Though he did not return to Jamaica, the freedom that he felt during his stay in Morocco and his perception, as he wrote in a letter to James Weldon Johnson in 1931, that the 'social side' of life in a Muslim country 'is blind to racial and colour prejudices' (p. 87), enabled him to make a fictional return home to Jamaica through the completion, while in Morocco, of the '"Jamaican book"—dealing with the customs and social life of the peasants' (p. 87). Although Dorsía Smith's short contribution 'A Violent Homeland: Recalling Haiti in Edwidge Danticat's Novels' (pp. 133–40) begins with an extensive quotation from Kim L. Worthington's work, pointing to the potential contradiction in narrative between the instability of memory and the tendency in narratives about the self towards the realization of a '"more or less readable self"' (p. 134), the essay itself does little to investigate the way in which these contradictions are either employed or evident in Danticat's fiction.

The collection of essays entitled *Caribbean Interfaces* edited by Lieven D'Hulst, Jean-Marc Moura, Liesbeth De Bleeker and Nadia Lie, is also the outcome of a conference held in the universities of Lille III and Leuven in May 2005. This work also seeks to redefine the Caribbean as a geographical space; its editors suggest that the Caribbean extends not only into the United States but also into Columbia and Venezuela. Over half of the contributions are written in French and several, such as 'Islands, Borders and Vectors: The Fractal World of the Caribbean' by Ottmar Ette (pp. 109–52), speak directly to the themes of the conference. This essay looks at ways in which the island metaphor, suggesting both isolation and the idea of 'one fragment among many, separated and at the same time in many ways still linked' (p. 111), is used by a variety of cultural and literary theorists including Derek Walcott, Édouard Glissant and George Lamming, and by Jean Bernabé, Patrick Chamoiseau and Raphaël Confiant in the influential *Éloge de la créolité* [1989]. Peter Hulme's 'Oriente: Towards a Literary Geography' (pp. 153–68) proposes an entirely new approach to literary history, one that constructs a literary geography which 'puts *place* first' (p. 154). As essays in this and other collections in the year under review have demonstrated, such an approach would include texts written about a place; the nationality and language of the writers would be secondary. Such a focus on place would then address several genres including non-fiction and any work that 'might have some topographical dimension', as well as work that uses 'literary places (*topoi*)' (pp. 155–6).

Of the 'topoi' included, however, the city, as with most critical studies of the Caribbean, is omitted. In the second half of the essay Hulme applies his theoretical framework to a study of writing from and about the area in eastern Cuba known as the Oriente, a region that includes Santiago de Cuba, the mountains of the Sierra Maestra, the Sierra del Cristal and Guantánamo. The literary geography that emerges is fascinating, unexpected and wide-ranging. Hulme ends with a reference to *Guantánamo* [2004], a play devised by Victoria Brittain and Gillian Slovo, consisting of a script compiled from transcripts of the testimonies of judges, speeches by politicians and letters from prisoners.

In the same collection, Theo D'haen's 'Cultural Memories, Literary Forms, Caribbean Revolutions' (pp. 169–84) compares Faulkner's *Absalom, Absalom!* [1936], Alejo Carpentier's *El reino de este mundo* [1949], and Albert Helman's little-known *De stille plantage* [1931], set in Dutch Surinam, arguing that each text demonstrates what Edward Said terms 'pressures from the imperium', and that these pressures imbue the novels he discusses with a distinctive form of 'Caribbean modernism' (p. 173). Vera M. Kutzinski's 'Violence and Sexual Others in Caribbean Literary History' (pp. 35–46) is concerned with probing categories that shape literary history and suggests that work such as Shani Mootoo's fiction, which 'propose[s] alternatives to identity as the central organising principle of human communities' (p. 36) is often excluded from Caribbean literary histories because its of its refusal to create stable gender categories and to create easily identifiable cultural identities. There is, however, a considerable and growing body of scholarship on Mootoo's work, and while Kutzinski provides a fruitful interpretation of *Cereus Blooms at Night*, the essay would have been strengthened by reference to this important body of critical work.

Collections and monographs from scholars based in the Caribbean, most of which attend to the literature's relationship to other forms of cultural production, are always a welcome addition to the critical material produced in the year under review. *Music, Memory, Resistance: Calypso and the Caribbean Literary Imagination* edited by Sandra Pouchet Paquet, Patricia J. Saunders and Stephen Stuempfle, is an interdisciplinary work that includes examinations of the social contexts in which calypsos emerge, calypsos as popular culture, and the uses of calypso in Caribbean literature. Gordon Rohlehr's 'Carnival Cannibalized or Cannibal Carnivalized: Contextualizing the "Cannibal Joke" in Calypso and Literature' (pp. 97–138) revisits Sparrow's controversial calypso 'Congo Man', first performed in 1964, and attempts to contextualize its representations of 'the encounter between Africa and Europe in arenas of ethnicity, culture, gender and politics' (p. 98). He suggests that, by situating his calypso in relation to the brutal events in the Congo following the departure of the Belgians in 1960, Sparrow not only revises the racial and gender relations that had dominated the media coverage of this tragedy but also performs a 'carnivalesque representation of history' that pours 'scornful laughter on everyone and everything' (p. 109). Images of cannibalism that had been the focus of the popular news coverage of the Stanleyville massacre, depicting alleged acts of cannibalism and rape, lie at the heart of this calypso. Rohlehr traces the origins of the caricatures of Africans as cannibals to representations of the 'cannibal joke' in early twentieth-century English literature and to a French Creole song that humorously depicts the ritual of Christian communion as a form of cannibalism. Rohlehr concludes that, despite its lasting popularity, Sparrow's own 'cannibal joke' is being replaced by more serious considerations of Africa in contemporary calypsos.

Clare Westall's 'Men in the Yard and on the Street: Cricket and Calypso in Caribbean Literature' (pp. 203–20) considers the function of cricket in Errol John's play *Moon on Rainbow Shawl* [1958] and V.S. Naipaul's *Miguel Street* [1955], arguing that both texts 'rely heavily upon the sounds, styles and humour of calypso to localize, unify and animate their writing' (p. 205). She notes that Naipaul uses at least fourteen calypso songs and that his characters 'operate almost entirely within the ironic idiom of calypso' (p. 206). In '(Not) Knowing the Difference: Calypso Overseas and the Sound of Belonging in Selected Narratives of Migration' (pp. 238–306) Jennifer Rahim discusses the use of calypso in Samuel Selvon's *The Lonely Londoners* [1956], Paule Marshall's *Brown Girl, Brownstones* [1959], and Lawrence Scott's *Aelred's Sin* [1988]. In Selvon's novel the music 'offers a means to more aggressively assert a collective, regional identity across ethnicities and nationalisms' (p. 285) as a way of countering British racism. Although the scene depicting calypso music in Marshall's novel is usually interpreted as symbolizing a narrow conception of Barbadian identity and Deighton's outsider status, Rahim suggests that it also serves to differentiate territorial identities among the West Indian migrant community in New York. Turning to *Aelred's Sin*, she suggests that calypso is used at the end of the novel to complicate its representations of sexual identity and desire.

Although Stewart Brown has not been based in the Caribbean for some time, the pieces in his book *Tourist, Traveller and Troublemaker: Essays on Poetry* that deal with literature from the Caribbean are all, intentionally it seems, written from the point of view of an 'insider'. This is not a scholarly collection but a series of conversational pieces that provide a lively insight into the processes of literary production in the Caribbean: it serves as a reminder that, as well as providing the basis for theoretical abstractions, geographical 'place' also refers to a material reality. Included in this collection are essays on his role as chair of the Guyana Prize when he was confronted with the fact that there were insufficient funds in the Guyana Central Bank to award the prize, a short piece on the Jamaican context of Olive Senior's poetry, and his notes for a contribution to the panel discussion 'Tidalectics of the Word', which was not included in the published conference papers reviewed below.

Gordon Rohlehr's *Transgression, Transition, Transformation: Essays in Caribbean Culture* is a collection of interlinked, interdisciplinary essays based around the components of the title. In these essays, some of which have appeared in other edited collections, Rohlehr returns to his preoccupation with cricket, calypso and their relationship to literature, popular culture and Caribbean intellectual traditions. The first essay analyses Stephen Cobham's *Rupert Gray* [1907] in relation to political events in late nineteenth-century Trinidad, including the riots of 1881, 1884, 1891 and 1903 that, according to Rohlehr, paved the way for campaigns for middle-class representation. These events, however, are notable in the novel by their absence: despite the protagonist's professed loyalty to the uplifting of Africans, the novel does not create a community of progressive Africans, merely a single, isolated protagonist, Gray himself. This essay is followed by an extended version of an earlier piece on the role of the elite Trinidadian grammar school Queens Royal College in the formation of Trinidad intellectuals, including Eric Williams, V.S. Naipaul and C.L.R. James, the figures on whom he focuses here. He includes personal reminiscences of these figures and analysis of Naipual's treatment of James through the figure of Lebrun, the protagonist of the short story 'On the Run' [1994]. Basing his findings on intersecting moments in these writers' lives rather than on a close reading of the text, he concludes, like Rhonda Cobham Sander cited below, that although the narrative repudiates James as a 'parasitical sponger, failed revolutionary and ultimately pathetic ruin' (p. 199) the narrator/author also recognizes in James a 'double and brother' (p. 213). Included in the collection is 'Dream Journeys', an extension of previously published criticism of Brathwaite's *Dream Stories* [1994].

In his book *Citing Shakespeare: The Reinterpretation of Race in Contemporary Literature and Art* Peter Erikson makes a brief reference to Caryl Phillips's use of the figure of Othello in *Extravagant Strangers: A Literature of Belonging* [1997] and *The Nature of Blood* [1997]. In the chapter entitled 'Neither Prospero nor Caliban: Derek Walcott's Revaluation of Shakespearean Fluency', he begins with a consideration of Walcott's use of the Shakespearian term 'nook shotten' to describe England in his early poem 'Ruins of a Great House', and goes on to argue that 'embedded in Walcott's attraction to "the English tongue I love" is the figure of Shakespeare, through whose work Walcott explores the nature of his divided self' (p. 44).

Patricia Moran's *Virginia Woolf, Jean Rhys and the Aesthetics of Trauma* situates an interpretation of these writers' fiction in the context of recent theories of trauma and its aftermath. She argues that Rhys and Woolf do not, on the whole, work through traumatic effects in their fictions but seem more concerned to depict 'the ways in which traumatic events impinge upon the lives of those affected by them' (pp. 4–5). Following closely Sue Thomas's work on Rhys, Moran includes a detailed reading of Rhys's autobiographical writings in the notebook she entitled 'The Black Exercise Book'. She looks at Rhys's response to Freud ' "the psychoanalytical gent" ', her account of an experience of ' "mental seduction" ' at 14, the repeated beatings by her mother and the role of all these experiences in her novels. In a later chapter she returns to what she defines as 'the pervasive masochism' in Rhys's fiction and 'its sources in traumatic events that have left her protagonists in the grip of a disabling and dehumanizing sense of shame' (p. 116).

Abigail Ward's 'Postmemories of Slavery in Fred D'Aguiar's *Bloodlines*' (in Misrahi-Barak ed., *Revisiting Slave Narratives II*, pp. 73–98) confronts two problematic issues in D'Aguiar's epic poem: the rape of the black slave, Faith, by the white male character, Christy, and the use of this act to mark the beginning of their love and, secondly, the poem's ungainly structure, in particular its inelegant use of ottava rima. The former, Ward suggests is a complex recognition of the 'inherent misogyny of slavery in nineteenth-century America' (p. 79); it also reflects a 'pervading cynicism' in D'Aguiar's text regarding the potential of relationships between black and white individuals because of the long shadow cast by slavery. The form of *Bloodlines* is, Ward offers, a way of deterring an easy reading of the poem's difficult themes. 'Rituals of "Rememory" in Paule Marshall's *The Chosen Place, The Timeless People*' (in Misrahi-Barak, ed., pp. 177–98) focuses on Marshall's use of representations of the Middle Passage in her novel, her 'interweaving of Black and Jewish diasporic figures' (p. 179) and the use of the omniscient narrator's voice to trace the 'long term effects of slavery from the vantage point of post-Holocaust consciousness' (p. 190).

Not surprisingly the book *A Breath of Fresh Eyre: Intertextual and Intermedial Reworkings of Jane Eyre*, edited by Margarete Rubik and Elke Mettinger-Shartman, contains several essays on Rhys's *Wide Sargasso Sea* [1966]. Thomas Loe's 'Landscape and Character in Jane Eyre and *Wide Sargasso Sea*' (pp. 49–61) traces both novels' encoded responses to notions of character. Antoinette's Caribbean island is represented in lush edenic imagery, whereas in the English scenes in Brontë's novel the English landscape is notable for its absence. Loe cites different types of landscape, both abstract and material, used in both novels to suggest a continuity between self and surroundings. As its unwieldy title indicates, in his essay 'The Intertextual Status of Jean Rhys's *Wide Sargasso Sea*: Dependence on a Victorian Classic and Independence as a Post-Colonial Novel' (pp. 64–77), Wolfgang G. Müller reads *Wide Sargasso Sea* as a novel that is both dependent on and independent of its pre-text *Jane Eyre*. Ulla Rahbek's 'Controlling Jean Rhys's Story "On Not Shooting Sitting Birds"' (in Rønning and Johannessen, eds., *Reading the Particular: The Postcolonial in the Postnational*, pp. 107–18), explores the ambiguities generated by a lack of narrative control in Rhys's short story.

The first essay in the collection *Economies of Representation 1790–2000: Colonialism and Commerce*, edited by Leigh Dale and Helen Gilbert, is Peter Hulme's 'Meditation on Yellow: Trade and Indigeneity in the Caribbean' (pp. 3–16). Hulme takes an interdisciplinary approach to his analysis of the relationship between commerce, trade and culture in the Caribbean; he situates his argument in relation to Olive Senior's poem 'Meditation on Yellow', from her collection *Gardening in the Tropics* [1997], and offers a detailed reading of extracts from Columbus's diaries and the 'language of investment and accounting' that frames the record of his encounter with indigenous Caribbean people at Guanahan, in what is now the Bahamas (p. 6). Moving to Dominica he looks at other moments that can be used to sketch a 'historical perspective on the five hundred intervening years' (p. 5): the retaliation of Dominican Caribs to the murder of two young Carib men by police officers raiding the Dominican Carib reserve in their search for smuggled goods, and the establishment in 1970 of a road system that brought the Caribs into the global marketplace through their involvement in banana cultivation and tourism. As members of a 'surviving indigenous population' they thus became objects of the ecotourists' gaze' (p. 13). What follows is a thought-provoking analysis of the development of a Carib Cultural Village in 2006 which, according to Hulme, presents the Caribs as 'yellow not black' and through this double difference serves to fuel the postmodern fantasy of 'authentic alterity' (p. 15).

'Sweet Beauty: West Indian Travel Narratives' (pp. 135–41), by Claudia Brandenstein, is an equally strong contribution that opens with an analysis of Matthew Lewis's account of his two visits to his slave plantation in Jamaica. On each visit he gave the slaves a holiday and 'gifts' of 'as much rum and sugar and noises and dancing as they chose' (p. 135). In the 'obverse of the gift-giving, obliging natives figured in Columbus's letter' (p. 135), his slaves stole sheep from his pen and let cattle escape to eat the cane while they sang praises to celebrate his arrival. Brandenstein then focuses on the slaves' perceived ingratitude, the focus of much of the travel writing of Lewis and other nineteenth-century writers. In their determined oblivion to the material conditions of slavery, their writing depicts the slaves as lazy, sly and fun-loving and the plantation owners as hard-working, either as labourers or as recorders of a landscape whose picturesque qualities changed, in their accounts, according to its usefulness as an economic resource. Ross Chambers's 'Text as Trading Place: Jamaica Kincaid's *My Brother*' (pp. 107–22) is a dense and not entirely rewarding reading of the text's 'agencing' of death as a figure characteristic of postcolonial 'otherness' (p. 122).

The essay 'Shifting Sands: Islescapes in Caribbean Poetry', by Jane Wilkinson (in Bottalico, Chialant and Rao, eds., *Literary Landscapes, Landscapes in Literature*, pp. 236–56) focuses on representations of island geographies in the poetry and prose of Derek Walcott and Kamau Brathwaite and, in particular, on the importance of sea and sand to their poetic vision. Both poets, she argues, use 'the circular, directionless, recursive idea of time they find in the movement of the ocean' (p. 242). For Brathwaite this movement is elaborated through his concept of 'tidalectics', reflecting the movement of the water both backwards and forwards (p. 242), whereas in Walcott's work this movement in and through water is imagined through repeated images of 'seeing' (p. 242). Wilkinson compares these representations with the use of island topography in the work of contemporary women writers, and concludes that in their work identity is located not geographically but in the 'plural, changing location of the female body' (p. 250).

William J. Maxwell's 'Banjo Meets the Dark Princess: Claude McKay, W.E.B. Du Bois, and the Transnational Novel of the Harlem Renaissance' (in Hutchinson, ed., *The Cambridge Companion to the Harlem Renaissance*, pp. 170–83) revisits the war of words between Du Bois and McKay on the publication of McKay's *Home to Harlem* [1928] and traces the much less commented on similarities in structure and in the preoccupations with transatlantic, diasporic identities in Du Bois's *Dark Princess* [1928] and McKay's novel. Like other recent critics Carl Pedersen, in 'The Caribbean Voices of Claude McKay and Eric Walrond' (in Hutchinson, ed., pp.184–97), sets out to reclaim McKay and Walrond for Caribbean literary history, seeing them as precursors of major contemporary writers such as Derek Walcott and Caryl Phillips, who 'were born in the Caribbean but have lived in the USA for much of their writing lives' (p. 184). Pedersen examines their fiction in the context of their political affiliations, arguing, for example, that it is no coincidence that Ray, a protagonist in McKay's first two novels, is from Haiti. This choice of origin is used in the novels to express the author's opposition to the American occupation of Haiti and 'to provide a counter-image to the traditional view of Haiti as the repository of chaos and savagery' (p. 191). That both writers maintain a distance from their radical contemporary Marcus Garvey, suggests, Petersen argues, a greater sympathy for a 'more class-based, anti-capitalist worldview' (p. 195).

Midori Saito's 'Gendered Negritude, Women and Representation in Novels by Claude McKay and Jean Rhys: Caribbean Authors in Modernist Europe' (in Anim-Addo and Scafe, eds., *I Am Black/White/Yellow: An Introduction to the Black Body in Europe*, pp. 37–54) juxtaposes the literary concerns of Rhys and McKay during the early twentieth-century, focusing on the differences that developed in their writing, particularly in relation to their treatment of women and their responses to Negritude. Like critics Emery and Rosenberg considered above, Saito reads these writers' work through a critique of modernism and its fascination with primitivism. 'Inventing the Self: The Black Woman Subject/Object in Britain from 1507' (in Anim-Addo and Scafe, eds., pp. 17–36) traces the absence of black women as autobiographical subjects in British writing and compares the black woman's role as object in literature and painting with moments of self-articulation in the work of Mary Prince, Beryl Gilroy, Una Marson and Thelma Perkins. '(Re)-Fashioning Identities', by Christine Checinska (pp. 55–70), is an insightful analysis of the role of dress in the negotiation of geographical, cultural and racial borders. Checinska compares the male protagonist in Olive Senior's poem 'All Clear 1928', who has returned resplendent from working in Panama, with the male migrant figures in Sam Selvon's *The Lonely Londoners* [1956] who, like Senior's 'grandee', successfully refashion their identities to reflect their new experiences and circumstances. Suzanne Scafe's 'Displacing the Centre: Home and Belonging in the Drama of Roy Williams' (pp. 71–87) locates themes of home/homelessness, belonging and identity formation in the London-based plays of dramatist Roy Williams in relation to his earlier work which, though set partly or entirely in the Caribbean, addresses similar themes of alienation and displacement.

Caribbean–Scottish Relations: Colonial and Contemporary Inscriptions in History, Language and Literature is a collection of four essays by the book's authors, Joan Anim-Addo, Velma Pollard, Giovanna Covi and Carla Sassi. It addresses versions of national and racial identity represented in a variety of Caribbean and Scottish writing and, using different critical approaches and styles, examines ways in which these representations can be used to destabilize conventional constructions of the relationship between two locations with a shared history and set of cultural relations. Covi's 'Footprints in the Sand: Attorneys, Redlegs, and the Red Haired Women in African-Caribbean Stories' looks the depiction of these figures in J.W. Orderson's recently republished *Creoleana* [*c*.1812], Mary Secole's *The Wonderful Adventures of Mrs. Secole in Many Lands* [1857], Claude McKay's *My Green Hills of Jamaica* [1979], Marlene NourbeSe Philip's *Looking for Livingstone* [1991] and selected fiction by Jamaica Kincaid. Joan Anim-Addo's 'A Brief History of Juliana "Lily" Mulzac of Union Island, Cariacou and Grenada: Creole Family Patterns and Scottish Dislocation' (pp. 46–92) constructs personal family histories along matriarchal lines. Velma Pollard's 'The Scots in Jamaica' (pp. 93–130) attempts to identify the influence of the Scots in Jamaica while remaining conscious 'of the extent of the convergence of influences from several European and African communities' (p. 93). Pollard mines a rich seam of eighteenth-century writing, including the recently republished *Marly* [1828], and includes an interesting sub-section on the retention of Scottish names in Jamaica and 'a small number of specifically Scotch loan words' that still exist in the popular language of the island (p. 118). Carla Sassi's 'Acts of (Un)Willed Amnesia: Disappearing Figurations of the Caribbean in Post-Union Scottish Literature' (pp. 131–98) begins with a reference to James Robertson's 'Suggar Heid' [2004], a poem that traces 'the long, shameful history of the involvement of Scotland in the Atlantic slave trade (p. 131), and suggests that although Scotland has been concerned with its own claims about justice and injustice, the 'shared past' of Scottish involvement in the Caribbean has been 'erased' from Scottish history (p. 133). Sassi constructs a detailed case in support of her argument, making reference to writing from the post-1833 period by the Scottish community in Jamaica in publications such as *The Daily Gleaner*, several nineteenth-century Scottish sentimental novels, the work of Creole poet Albinia Catherine Hutton, Barbadian writer Lionel Hutchinson's novel *One Touch of Nature* [1972], and a wide range of contemporary Scottish fiction.

(b) Single-Author Studies
There were very few scholarly single-author studies in the year under review. One such study is *No Land, No Mother: Essays on the Work of David Dabydeen*, edited by Lynne Macedo and Kampta Karran. In their introduction the editors describe the dominant characteristic of Dabydeen's work as 'dialogue across diversity': it reflects, they argue, a common postcolonial paradox expressed as the 'simultaneous habitation of multiple arenas' and the 'emotional need for belonging or even some form of racialised solidarity' (p. 9). The collection is divided into five subsections, each of which deals with one aspect of Dabydeen's work. Aleid Fokkema's 'Caribbean Sublime; Transporting the Slave, Transporting the Spirit' (pp. 17–31) and Tobias Döring's 'Turning the Colonial Gaze: Re-Visions of Terror in Dabydeen's *Turner*' (pp. 32–46) both address representations of the sublime in Dabydeen's poem and Turner's painting. Making reference to Edmund Burke's theories of the sublime and the beautiful and Frantz Fanon's writings on colonialism, Döring articulates the connections between the terror of the sublime in representation and the exercise of terror by imperial powers as manifested in both texts. In 'Singing Songs of Desire: Humour, Masculinity and Language in Dabydeen's *Slave Song*' (pp. 128–43) Pumla Dineo Gqola focuses on Dabydeen's provocative and self-consciously problematic representation of masculine desire in his poem *Slave Song*. She suggests that the poem is deliberately constructed to resist and mock attempts at transparency, but reads among its carnivalesque diversions a resistance to racist constructions of black masculinity and an attempt to expose 'the absurdity of the white male stereotype/fear of white female violation by black men' (p. 135). Despite the poem's use of language to 'free up male subjectivity',

however, Gqola concludes that the figure of the slave woman in the poem remains marginalised and ambiguous' (p. 140).

Christine Pagnoulle's 'A Harlot's Progress: Memories in Knots and Stays' (pp. 181–203) addresses the function and representation of memory, arguing that, in *A Harlot's Progress* [1999], the uncertainty and unreliability of memory arise both from the 'violent disruption of the slave trade' and from the text's playful engagement with 'postmodern scepticism about the possibility of any kind of reliable construction of the past' (p. 181). Ultimately, she concludes, Mungo's freedom with the 'facts' of his story is used to mirror the text's own commitment to the freedom of the writer's imagination. Gail Low's concluding essay, 'To Make Beautiful our Minds in an England Starved of Gold: Reading *The Counting House*' (pp. 205–17), also explores issues of unrepresentability in Dabydeen's work. She reads the novel *The Counting House* [1996] as a text that deliberately frustrates 'expectations of a redemptive and cathartic delivery' (p. 205).

Caribbean Culture: Soundings on Kamau Brathwaite, edited by Annie Paul, is a selection of papers from the second conference on Caribbean culture held at the University of the West Indies in 2002, the theme of which, as the title suggests, was the work of Kamau Brathwaite. Annie Paul's introduction offers a clear and comprehensive interpretation of the whole range of his work from his earliest writing to some of his latest. He is, as Paul notes, a cultural critic, historian, poet and 'founder of an intellectual tradition and methodology that articulates an influential conceptual and theoretical approach to Caribbean studies' (p. 2). The subject matter of the papers is wide-ranging and interdisciplinary. The first of seven sections, 'Ceremonies of the Word', addresses the use of orature and performance in Brathwaite's literary writings, and includes Kofi Anyidoho's 'Atumpan: Kamau Brathwaite and the Gift of Ancestral Memory' (pp. 39–53), which discusses Brathwaite's use of aspects of African oral culture and traditions. J. Edward Chamberlain's 'Keeping Your Word: Contracts, Covenants and Canticles' (pp. 76–93) links Brathwaite's poetry to traditions of Native and ethnic Canadian storytelling, and Hubert Devonish's 'When Form Becomes Substance: Discourse on Discourse in Two Calypsos' (pp. 94–112), while not addressing Brathwaite's work directly, offers a detailed analysis of the calypsos performed in the Barbadian Crop Over festival. Calypsos are defined by Devonish as performance speech events, governed by more complex rules than those of 'normal speech events'. They are characterized in part by their primary objective—which is to 'evoke admiration and pleasure' (p. 95). He then demonstrates how this objective is used to competitive effect in a selection of 'Pic-o-de-Crop' calypsos.

Lilieth Nelson's 'The Music of Kamau Brathwaite' (pp. 127–41) is, as the title suggests, a finely detailed reading of the poet's use of antiphonal structures, rhythm, melody and other musical devices in a range of poetry from *The Arrivants* [1973] to *X-Self* [1987] and a selection of poems anthologized in the journals *Caribbean Quarterly* [2000] and *Monograph* [2002]. 'Kamau Brathwaite and the Haitian Boat People: "Dream Haiti" or the Nightmare of the Caribbean Intellectual' (pp. 176–86), by Marie-José Nzengou-Tayo, is a thoughtful analysis of Brathwaite's own relationship, as a Caribbean intellectual, to Haiti. She begins with the period before 1980 when Haiti was, for the rest of the Caribbean, the locus around which black consciousness developed, and then moves to the late 1980s and the 1990s when Haiti became for the region a symbol of political failure and economic destitution. Using a dream structure that consists of 'chains of association not necessarily coherent yet developing within a symbolic framework' (p. 178), Brathwaite's poem 'Dream Haiti' describes the tragedy of the Haitian ' "boat people" ' fleeing to America. Within the poem's structure Brathwaite sets the figure of the Caribbean intellectual, linked to their suffering yet at the same time powerless and distant, 'bought and bound by the comfort of U.S. money' (p. 184).

(c) Journals

There were again several articles on Jean Rhys's work this year. One of the most interesting is Christine Britzolakis's ' "This way to the exhibition": Genealogies of Urban Spectacle in Jean Rhys's Interwar Fiction' (*TPr* 21:iii[2007] 457–82), in which she argues that Rhys critically engages surrealism's fascination with ethnography as 'a critical and diagnostic tool to be employed both within and against the institutional spaces of art' (p. 458). The spaces she defines as 'Rhysian', which are used in her work to challenge these institutional spaces, are the hotel, the exhibition and the street—sites also of the 'global modern' and of metropolitan culture 'mortgaged to a global circulation of bodies and objects' (p. 458). In a convincing and closely argued essay, 'Rum Histories: Decolonizing the Narratives of Jean Rhys's *Wide Sargasso Sea* and Sylvia Townsend Warner's *The Flint Anchor*' (*TSWL* 26:ii[2007] 309–30), Jennifer P. Nesbitt argues that 'rum' is used in Rhys's novels to signal 'points at which economic decisions are recast as cultural ones or vice-versa' (p. 312). Rum is used as a trope to reinforce Antoinette's submission to her dehumanization, and to confirm Rochester's subject position, made possible 'by his financial dependence on a rum-based economy' (p. 316). In all cases rum is used both to mask and expose the economic, material and cultural relations that shape each of the novel's characters. In 'Confronting the Abject: Women and Dead Babies in Modern English Fiction' (*JML* 29:iii[2006] 103–25) Sally Minogue and Andrew Palmer read Rhys's depiction of abortion in *Voyage in the Dark* [1934] through Mikhail Bakhtin's theories of 'grotesque realism' and Julia Kristeva's notion of the abject, and against Mary Lou Emery's interpretation of the ending of the novel as a sign of the potential for rebirth. The authors argue that Anna's miscarriage and the outpouring of blood produce an ambiguous juxtaposition of 'abject horror and carnival laughter which responds defiantly to modern rather than medieval structures of authority' (p. 109).

Victor Figueroa's thought-provoking essay 'Encomium of Helen: Derek Walcott's Ethical Twist in *Omeros*' (*TCL* 53:i[2007] 23–39) explores the changing representations of what he defines as the 'ethical twist' in Walcott's work. In the early poetry it emerges as a preoccupation with postcolonial identity and selfhood, whereas in later work ethical considerations are centred on issues of relation and power. Characters such as Plunkett are faced with the question of whether 'they can relate to other islanders in an equitable manner that relinquishes the privilege of old colonial authority or social advantage' (p. 25). Focusing on Walcott's use of Helen to represent, simultaneously, the island of St Lucia, Achilles' lover and Plunkett's maid, Figueroa explores the effectiveness of the poem's interrogation of the potential of Helen to resist attempts by both the poet/narrator and Plunkett, as island historian, to entrap her in an imperial gaze. Questions of ethics and power are articulated through the different positions that Helen occupies in relation to other characters. Figueroa concludes that *Omeros* is 'a kind of encomium of Helen: both the feminized Caribbean and the Caribbean women remain mostly mute objects of their discourses and possession' (p. 36). Through its representation of Helen's struggle against an oppressive social order and against the 'emacipatory rhetoric' of the poem itself, Walcott's poem examines its own rhetorical failure.

Pam Mordecai's 'Miss Lou—a Personal Remembrance of Louise Simone Bennett-Coverley: Poet, Folklorist, Community Worker, Lyricist, Stage and Movie Actress' (*Kunapipi* 29:i[2007] 8–18) is, as the title suggests, a praise song for Louise Bennett, and poet Pam Mordecai's personal testimony to the influence of Bennett's poetry on her own work and on the cultural production of Jamaica and the Caribbean. Though earlier writers such as McKay and Marson published poetry in Jamaican Creole, it is Bennett who 'consistently affirmed Jamaican Creole as a language for literature as well as for living' (p. 10). *Kunapipi* 29:ii[2007] is a special issue on birds. In 'Writers on the Wing: Birds and the (De/Re)construction of Cultural Memory in Patrick Chamoiseau and J.M. Coetzee's Fictional Narratives' (*Kunapipi* 29:ii[2007] 178–93) Lucile Desblanche begins her analysis of Chamoiseau's *Biblique des derniers gestes* with the statement: 'French West Indian literature hosts three types of birds: tropical birds associated with the forest, with its strong connotations of freedom: fighting birds and imaginary birds such as the soucoughan' (p. 180). Her essay continues to examine the function of these categories of birds as tropes in Chamoiseau's novel and, through his use of realistic description, to signify 'biological, linguistic and cultural move-ments' (p. 184).

Bénédicte Ledent continues her study of Caryl Phillips's writing in 'Family and Identity in Caryl Phillips's Fiction, in Particular *A Distant Shore*' (*CE&S* 29:ii[2007] 67–73). Ledent argues that, like other Caribbean writers such as Joan Riley and Jamaica Kincaid, Phillips uses the family in his fiction to crystallize the 'complexities of diasporic identity, shaped as it is by initial losses but also by undeniable gains' (p. 67). She focuses on Phillips's repeated use of surrogate kinships that, in the case of Solomon in *A Distant Shore*, only imperfectly compensate for the family and community he has left behind—an unnamed, war-torn African state. Phillips's representations of disrupted and replaced families are used to signify his desire for a more fluid and 'inclusive approach to human relationships' (p. 72).

Dorothy Booth Summers traces connections in the writers' use of the ancestral womb and folkloric kumbla in 'Pregnant Possibilities: The Boundary-Shattering Transformation of the Caribbean Woman in Brodber's

Jane and *Louisa Will Soon Come Home* and Harris's *The Whole Armour* (*JWIL*16:i[2007] 3–14). Jessica Damian's '"A novel speculation": Mary Secole's Ambitious Adventures in the New Granada Mining Company' (*JWIL* 16:i[2007] 15–36) makes a case for reading Secole's work as a text that increases our understanding of the working of nineteenth-century commerce and colonialism. 'Writing Memory: Edwidge Danticat's Limbo Inscriptions' (*JWIL* 16:i[2007]37–58), by Semia Harbawi, is a detailed examination of Danticat's critique of nationalist and patriarchal structures and the narrative's revisualization of trauma in *The Farming of Bones* [1998]. In 'Postcolonial Shamanism: Wilson Harris's Quantum Poetics and Ethics' (*JWIL* 16:i[2007] 83–97) Syed Manzu Islam revisits Harris's commitment to the use of imaginative vistas that deliberately oppose conventions of linear realism and chronological time. Roberto Strongman's 'The Colonial State Apparatus of the School: Development, Education and Mimicry in Patrick Chamoiseau's *Une enfance creole II: Chemin d'école* and V.S. Naipaul's *Miguel Street*' (*JWIL* 16:i[2007] 83–97) examines these texts' representations of the colonial school as a site from which colonial ideologies are perpetuated.

In 'Refusing "Slave Man's Revenge": Reading the Politics of the Resisting Body in Zee Edgell's *Beka Lamb* and Brenda Flanagan's *You Alone Are Dancing*' (*ChE* 14:i[2007] 23–37) Suzanne Scafe argues that these two novels intervene in a history of fictional representation which uses the figure of the 'native' woman to signify territorial, economic and sexual conquest and exploitation. Whereas the black woman, in early twentieth-century Caribbean anti-colonial fiction, silently concedes to her aggressor, whose actions ultimately end in her destruction, the female protagonists of these contemporary novels are used to provide an alternative to either victimhood or to the suggestion that, for the poor, working-class black woman, her body is her only capital.

The journal *Small Axe* continues to provide unique perspectives on Caribbean literature, culture and cultural theory. One of four review essays on Madison Smartt Bell's trilogy, Martin Munro's 'Haitian Novels and Novels of Haiti: History, Haitian Writing, and Madison Smartt Bell's Trilogy' (*Small Axe* 23[2007] 163–76), places an analysis of the American writer's fiction *about* Haiti in the context of a critical overview of Haitian fiction. He argues that the Haitian novel 'has typically sought to distance itself from history', preferring to turn inwards and to imagine 'new ways of being Haitian out of the shadows of the past' (p. 164). It tends to 'stress the unfinished, repetitive nature of their history' and to avoid repeating the 'endlessly repetitive official narrative of history' (p. 165). Perhaps because of the author's distance from the complexities of the past and its presence in the present, 'a truly epic, complex, engaged narrative of the slave uprisings, the political intrigues and the rise of Toussaint L'Ouverture' has been written by the '"white" American' Madison Smartt Bell (p. 166). 'Gendered Legacies of Romantic Nationalism in the Works of Michelle Cliff', by Jocelyn Fenton Stitt (*Small Axe* 24[2007] 57–72), contrasts Cliff's early and late novels in relation to theories of Romantic nationalism and postcolonial theory.

'In(sub)ordinate Speech: Mimicry as Bourdieuian Heterodoxy in Walcott's *Pantomime*', by Megan K. Ahern (*ArielE* 38:iv[2007] 1–24), examines relations between language and power in Walcott's play. '"Not his sort of story": Evelyn Waugh and Pauline Melville in Guyana', by Robert Ness (*ArielE* 38:iv[2007] 51–68), pays attention to the intertextual dialogue with Evelyn Waugh's *Ninety Two Days* [1934] in Pauline Melville's novel *The Ventriloquist's Tale* [1997]. In 'Landscape and Poetic Identity in Contemporary Caribbean Women's Poetry' (*ArielE* 38:iv[2007] 41–64) Denise deCaires Narain contrasts the use of landscape in the poetry of Derek Walcott and Kamau Brathwaite with visions of landscape in the poetry of Olive Senior, Lorna Goodison and Dionne Brand. Brand's poetry and prose are used to demonstrate her radical reconfiguration of the relationship between the female body, land and language.

In 'The Novels of Patricia Powell: Negotiating Gender and Sexuality across the Disjunctures of the Caribbean Diaspora' Timothy Chin argues that Powell's novels are framed within representations of permeable diasporic borders that 'break the silence surrounding issues of sexuality' (*Callaloo* 30:iv[2007] 575–93). H. Adlai Murdoch's '"All skin is not skin teeth grin": Performing Caribbean Diasporic Identity in a Postcolonial Metropolitan Frame' (*Callaloo* 30:iv[2007] 575–93) is a predominantly theoretical essay that attends to the 'multiple modernities' of the Caribbean experience in Britain with reference to Samuel Selvon's *The Lonely Londoners* [1956] and Zadie Smith's *White Teeth* [2000]. Greg A. Mullins's 'Dionne Brand's Poetics of Recognition: Reframing Sexual Rights' (*Callaloo* 30:iv[2007] 110–34) analyses Brand's representation of revolutionary politics and its defence of lesbian sexual love and desire in her novel *In Another Place Not Here* [1996].

In '"Words are all I have left of my eyes": Blinded by the Past in Turner's *Slavers Throwing Overboard the Dead and Dying* and David Dabydeen's "Turner"' (*JCL* 42:i[2007] 47–58) Abigail Ward returns to Turner's painting as an expression of what Paul Gilroy terms 'black victimage', arguing that it represents an attempt to evade the consequences of emancipation for nineteenth-century Britain. Dabydeen's poem counters Turner's use of the sublime to reinforce black victimhood by reclaiming the voices of the drowned slaves.

(d) Journals: Special Editions

Volume 5, issue ii of the electronic journal *Anthurium* is a special issue on V.S. Naipaul, who was 75 this year. In celebration of this event the University of the West Indies, St Augustine, Trinidad, organized a symposium on his writing, entitled—with deliberate irony—'V.S. Naipaul: Created in the West Indies'. 'Keeping an Eye on Naipaul: Naipaul and the Play of the Visual' (*Anthurium* 5:ii[2007] 21 paras), by Jean Antoine Dunn, looks at the influence of cinematography in the narrative style of Naipaul's early fiction and in his more recent *Half a Life* [2001]. Edward Baugh's interesting and lively contribution, '"The history that made me": The Making and Self-Making of V.S. Naipaul' (*Anthurium* 5:ii[2007] 41 paras) focuses on the vexed relationship between Naipaul and his place of birth, Trinidad and Tobago. Baugh traces the paradoxes and preoccupations that have shaped all Naipaul's writing including 'The nerves, the precariousness, the intimations of ruin, the dread of violation, taint, damage to the self' and 'The idea that people fashion identities for themselves'. These paradoxical ideas were first used to define the characters and shape the themes of his major Trinidadian novels. In 'Naipaul's Sense of History' (*Anthurium* 5:ii[2007] 13 paras) Bridget Bereton argues that, for Naipaul, 'the erasure of the past, the failure or refusal to develop researched and reasonably objective historical narratives' are the indices of intellectual impoverishment anywhere in the world.

'Consuming the Self: V.S. Naipaul, C.L.R. James and *A Way in the World*', by Rhonda Cobham-Sander (*Anthurium* 5:ii[2007] 42 paras) begins with a personal account of growing up in Trinidad in the 1950s and Cobham-Sander's recollection of the recognition with which her generation greeted Naipaul's early fiction. She traces representations of mutual recognition between Naipaul's character Lebrun, a thinly disguised C.L.R. James, and Naipaul himself in *A Way in the World* [2001]. Barbara Lalla's 'Signifying Nothing: Writing About Not Writing in *The Mystic Masseur*' (*Anthurium* 5:ii[2007] 29 paras) is a detailed exploration of ways in which 'truth-value' is dispersed in the narrative of Naipaul's first novel. 'A Mala in Obeisance; Hinduism in Select Texts by V.S. Naipaul', by Vijay Maharaj (*Anthurium* 5:ii[2007] 22 paras), argues that Naipaul's oeuvre can be described as 'folk katha'—that is, the practice of reading or reciting religious texts in relation to other texts as a way of bringing meaning to everyday life. In 'Consorting with Kali: Migration and Identity in Naipaul's "One Out of Many"', Paula Morgan engages with Naipaul's short story 'One Out of Many' and its problematic representation of the sexual consumption of its protagonist Santosh by the African American female grotesque, the goddess Kali made flesh.

Sandra Pouchet Paquet traces changing representations of indigenous peoples in Naipaul's work in 'V.S. Naipaul and the Interior Expeditions: "It is impossible to make a step without the Indians"' (*Anthurium* 5:ii[2007] 14 paras). She argues that his representations have changed from the 'imperial models' used in earlier writing to more compassionate representations and what she describes as 'overt empathy and identification with the Amerindian community' in *A Way in the World* [1994]. Jennifer Rahim investigates Naipaul's figurative evocation of the monkey figure in his early fiction in 'The Shadow of Hanuman: V.S. Naipaul and the "Unhomely" House of Fiction' (*Anthurium* 5:ii[2007] 14 paras), and in 'The Confessional Element in Naipaul's Fiction' (*Anthurium* 5:ii[2007] 55 paras) Gordon Rohlehr looks at the confessional figure and the use confessional modes of writing in the novels of the 1960s and 1970s.

'Orality in the Short Story in English' (*JSSE* 47[2006]) includes essays on Olive Senior and Edwidge Danticat. In '"My mouth is the keeper of both speech and silence ..."; or The Vocalisation of Silence in Caribbean Short Stories by Edwidge Danticat' (*JSSE* 47[2006] 155–66) Judith Misrahi Barak argues that whereas earlier generations of Caribbean fiction writers had tended to distinguish the narrative voice from the voices of characters in dialogue, the prose of contemporary writers such as Danticat is characterized by 'crossovers between orality and literacy' and a 'new Caribbean syncreticity' (p. 156).

The article examines Danticat's two collections of short stories, *Krick? Krack!* and *The Dew Breaker*, and suggests that in both these works Danticat gives voice to words and stories that 'have been bottled up for too long' (p. 156). Her stories articulate the silences of Haiti's history: the death by drowning of those who tried to flee Haiti in the 1980s, the massacre of Haitians in 1937 by the Dominican General Trujillo, and the political silences enforced by Haiti's successive dictators. Meaning emerges in these stories as a result of what Misrahi-Barak describes as 'narrative interweaving and echoing' (p. 159) produced by the stories' orality. Danticat's stories incorporate 'the orality of silence' and thus construct 'narratives of self-narration and self-empowerment' (p. 165). Marie-Annick Montout's 'The Intrinsic Written Quality of the Spoken Word in Olive Senior's Short Fiction' (*JSSE* 47[2006] 167–76) looks at the creative exploitation of a language continuum from Standard English to Jamaican Creole in a selection of stories by Olive Senior, including the unpublished 'Mad Fish'. Laurie Kruk's 'Storykeepers: Circling Family Voice in Stories by Thomas King, Olive Senior, Alistair McLeod and Guy Vanderhaeghe' (*JSSE* 47[2006] 111–26) defines Senior as a 'self-exiled writer living in Toronto but memorializing Jamaica in her fiction and poetry' (p. 113), and reads her short fiction in the context of the Canadian short-story writers of the title. Her stories are compared in detail with the short stories of Thomas King 'a mixed blood man who identifies himself as a Native writer' (p. 113). The voice of the monologue in Senior's short story 'You Tink I Mad, Miss' is described as a 'hybridized construction' (p. 115) that mixes not only two languages but also two ideological beliefs (p. 116). The writer concludes that in this short story Senior produces 'an artful "testifying" to an act of ostracism which demands new "hearing"—within the marketplace of the book' (p. 118).

'Freedom and Culture' is the title of the special edition of the journal *Moving Worlds* dedicated to work that commemorates 1807, the year in which the parliamentary Act for the Abolition of the Slave Trade was introduced. The edition includes essays by the visual artist Mary Evans, the new poem 'Empty Shell' by Olive Senior, and a selection of poems by Kwame Dawes. Gemma Robinson's 'From the Plantation Earth Subjects of Slavery and the Work of Martin Carter' (*Moving Worlds* 7:ii[2007] 46–76) traces Carter's use of slavery and the slave subject to address slavery literally or figuratively as a 'historically determined subjective experience' (p. 48). In 'Fred D'Aguiar and Denise Harris: Novels of Emancipation' (*Moving Worlds* 7:ii[2007] 77–94) Judith Misrahi-Barak uses Marianne Hirsch's concept of 'postmemory' to demonstrate how the two writers on whom she focuses 'participate in [the] "postmemorial" working through' of slavery and the transatlantic slave trade (p. 78). Her essay begins by focusing on D'Aguiar's reconfigurations of the slave narrative genre in *Feeding the Ghosts*, *Bloodlines* and *The Longest Memory*, all of which, Misrahi-Barak argues, are used not, as were nineteenth-century narratives, to document experience as history, but to create a new literary artefact that reorganizes those experiences and includes previously unimagined and unrecorded experience. Her reading of Denise Harris's novels also addresses form: she suggests that Harris's fiction opens up 'generic space' that 'cross-cuts the ghost story, the detective or crime novel, and the confessional novel' (p. 82).

ArielE 38:i[2007] is also a special issue that marks the bicentenary of 1807. In ' "Too oft allured by Ethiopic charm"? Sex, Slaves and Society in John Singleton's *A General Description of the West Indian Islands* (1767)' (*ArielE* 38:i[2007] 75–94) John Gilmore turns again to colonialist representations in his examination of this 2,470-line poem written in blank verse. Gilmore finds that Singleton's text offers insight into the complex nature of eighteenth-century Caribbean societies. ' "What time has proved": History, Rebellion and Revolution in *Hamel the Obeahman*', by Candace Ward (*ArielE* 38:i[2007] 49–74), is a consideration of this nineteenth-century narrative written from the perspective of an anti-abolitionist, the purpose of which was to 'redefine the terms of the Emancipation debate' (p. 52). By reinforcing stereotypical representations of African barbarism, the narrative suggests that African slaves were not ready for freedom. Not on the topic of slavery or the slave trade but included in this issue is an interview with Mark McWatt, 'Mark McWatt in Conversation about *Suspended Sentences: Fictions of Atonement*', with Pamela McCallum and Aritha van Herk (*ArielE* 38:i[2007] 113–19).

Small Axe 22[2007] is a special issue on Grenada that includes a new short story by Merle Collins entitled 'Tout Mounka Pléwé?' and an essay by Susan Meltzer entitled 'Decolonizing the Mind: Recent Grenadian Fiction' (*Small Axe* 22[2007] 83–94). Meltzer focuses on three examples of recent Grenadian fiction that she defines as 'resistance literature' (p. 84): Merle Collins's *The Colour of Forgetting* [1995], Lawton Pierre's self-published *Tears from Home* [1993] and *A Season of Waiting* by David Omowale [2002]. Though Omowale's novel does not specifically refer to the revolution and its aftermath, all three novels struggle to understand a past that has been shaped by Grenada's revolutionary New Jewel Movement and its violent end—whether or not these events are made explicit in the texts. All the novels are to varying degrees experimental and seek to provide and preserve alternative ways of knowing that derive from the folk culture of the island. Though Collins's is the only novel that has received some critical attention, Meltzer argues that it is *A Season of Waiting* that is 'the most far reaching and disturbing' (p. 94).

MaComère 8[2006] is a special issue on migrant writing. It contains new poems by Ramabai Espinet, 'Hook', a poem by Olive Senior, and a short story by Pam Mordecai. Diana Brydon's ' "A place on the map of the world": Locating Hope in Shani Mootoo's *He Drown She in the Sea* and Dionne Brand's *What We All Long For*' (*MaComère* 8[2006] 94–111) examines the ' "emotional geographies" of globalization' (p. 94) that are used to structure these two recent works of fiction. Brydon attends to the complex geographical identities of the novels; both might be defined as 'novels of the Trinidad diaspora', as 'simply' Canadian fiction, or as texts that deliberately resist classification. Using a more complex definition of geography, one that also includes what Katherine McKittrick defines as 'demonic grounds' to oppose the 'racial-sexual functions of the production of space' (p. 95), Brydon suggests that both novels participate in a process of remapping that reflects their desire for a 'different kind of world' (p. 97). Like Shirley Tolland-Dix, cited above, Simone Drake, in 'Gendering Diasporic Migration in Erna

Brodber's Louisiana' (*MaComère* 8[2006] 112–35), explores the novel's use of allusions to Zora Neale Hurston to make a sustained and complex critique of Western epistemology.

5. The Indian Subcontinent and Sri Lanka

(a) Books

Although 2007 marked the sixtieth anniversary of India's independence, surprisingly few studies published this year directly responded to this milestone. It is perhaps marked indirectly through the attention paid, in a number of texts, to the concept of nation, and the legacy of Nehruvian secularism in twenty-first-century India. Arguably the diversity of studies produced also reflects a key-shift change, illustrating the range of ways in which Indian fiction can now be approached and interpreted, and the variety of themes and issues at work within contemporary texts. In spite of this thematic diversity, the majority of critics still choose to focus on a few very well known authors, most prominently this year Salman Rushdie, Arundhati Roy and Vikram Seth. It is nonetheless pleasing to note that studies of less well known writers and texts are available, and these are often the source of exciting and innovative readings.

Of the few single-author studies published in 2007, a significant and substantial contribution to the field is *The Cambridge Companion to Salman Rushdie*, edited by Abdulrazak Gurnah. In tacit acknowledgement of the anniversary mentioned, this volume adopts a somewhat reflective tone, paying close attention to the role that Rushdie has played in charting developments in India since its independence, and to the dramatic events that have characterized his life as a writer. Completed not long after the publication of *Shalimar the Clown* and, of course, before the release of *The Enchantress of Florence*, the volume is similarly careful to avoid making grand pronouncements about Rushdie's body of work. As Gurnah rightly notes in his introduction, 'there are many more twists and turns to come from this writer, and it is too soon yet to be definitive about recent developments' (p. 7). The collection principally comprises discussions of key themes and issues relating to Rushdie and his work, and studies of individual texts. These are accompanied by a chronology of Rushdie's life, and a bibliography of further reading. All of its sections are as comprehensive as they can be, in a single-volume study of such a prolific and high-profile individual. The essays are similarly of reliable quality, covering topics to please a wide range of interests. A particularly valuable thematic essay is Vijay Mishra's 'Rushdie and Bollywood Cinema' (pp. 11–28), highlighting the significance of Indian popular cinema in Rushdie's work. Of the textual studies, Brendon Nicholls's 'Reading "Pakistan" in Salman Rushdie's *Shame*' (pp. 109–24) is certainly worthy of attention, and Ib Johansen's 'Tricksters and the Common Herd in Salman Rushdie's *Grimus*' (pp. 77–90) is a welcome contribution to the small body of work on this unsuccessful but illuminating early text.

Another key volume is Alex Tickell's *Arundhati Roy's The God of Small Things*, which also functions as an introductory text. Though not the first study of Roy's work, this is a welcome addition to the field, tackling a novel that has proven to be both highly influential and controversial since its publication in 1997. Tickell's guide sets out to 'preserve a sense of the different readings and...conflicting critical views' that Roy's novel has provoked (p. xiv). Meanwhile, it holds firm to the admirable aim of making academic discussions accessible to the more general reader. It achieves both through a detailed exploration of the novel's contexts, which is followed by a systematic and substantial review of critical responses to the text. Tickell is sensible to include, across both of these, reference to Roy's own non-fiction works, which offer further, illuminating, perspectives from which to view her novel. A final section introduces a selection of key articles on *The God of Small Things*, including works by Aijaz Ahmad, Brinda Bose, Emilienne Baneth-Nouailhetas and Tickell himself. Padmini Mongia's 'The Making and Marketing of Arundhati Roy' is published for the first time in the volume, and is a reasonably astute exploration of the marketing and packaging of the text. Anna Clarke's piece on language, hybridity and dialogism in *The God of Small Things* was commissioned especially for the collection, and offers a valuable discussion of language as a key and prominent concern in Roy's text.

A useful companion piece to Tickell's study is Antoinette Burton's *The Postcolonial Careers of Santha Rama Rau*. This volume explores the life of a writer who, Burton claims, was present and prominent at the beginning of the 'postwar cult of literary celebrity' that Roy has come to epitomize (p. 152). Burton commits wholeheartedly to the value and significance of Rau's work, in spite of the 'pop culture orientalism' by which, she admits, it might be characterized (p. 30). Tracing Rau's career from a childhood spent between England and India, through significant literary successes, to relative obscurity in the present day, Burton reads her as representative of a form of 'cold war cosmopolitanism' that was highly influential, particularly with audiences in the United States, on which the study primarily focuses (p. 4). Burton's chapter on Rau's *The Cooking of India* is especially illuminating. It draws on convincing connections between this text and recent writings by the critic Arjun Appadurai to uncover the 'complex circuitry' from which it emerged and the cultural politics that it is subsequently able to reveal (p. 131).

While it may from its title appear to focus solely on Salman Rushdie, Purna Chowdhury's *Between Two Worlds: Nation, Rushdie and Postcolonial Indo-English Fiction* in fact engages with the work of three writers. It takes on what Chowdhury refers to as the 'split consciousness' in Indian literature in English, as both resistant to and complicit in orientalizing projects (p. 313). In doing so it focuses on four key texts—Rushdie's *Shame* and *Midnight's Children*, Sara Suleri's *Meatless Days*, and Arundhati Roy's *The God of Small Things*—illustrating how each of these tackles the challenge of representing a nation. Chowdhury insists that Suleri handles this responsibility most effectively, and her argument is on the whole convincing, hinging on the way in which each writer manipulates language as a marker of difference, independence and occasional self-consciousness (p. 215). The study would, however, have benefited from more focused theoretical grounding, rather than the (admittedly comprehensive) history of postcolonial theory that Chowdhury deploys in her introduction.

Turning to texts that take an explicitly comparative approach, of those engaging with the legacies of Nehruvian secularism Aamir Mufti's *Enlightenment in the Colony: The Jewish Question and the Crisis of Postcolonial Culture* offers the most substantial theoretical intervention, one that is likely to have a significant impact on the field in future years. In examining the literary dimensions of India's crisis in secularism, Mufti's bold move is to read the crisis of Muslim identity in contemporary India in relation to the 'Jewish question' in post-Enlightenment Europe. Mufti begins by mapping the emergence of Jewishness as a minority culture in late nineteenth-century Europe as marking a profound crisis for modern, liberal subjectivity. The second part of *Enlightenment* charts the ways in which Muslim identity similarly unsettles Nehruvian discourses of secular citizenship, by reading a wide range of literary and political texts in English and Urdu by Jawaharlal Nehru, Abdul Kalam Azad, Sadat Hasan Manto and Faiz Ahmed Faiz. Mufti's focus is on processes of 'minoritization' – 'the *pressures* exerted on language, culture, and identity in the process of becoming minoritized' (p. 12), and a particular virtue of his theorizations is their basis in historically situated, acutely sensitive close readings. These are at their best in the analyses of the Urdu short stories and lyric poetry of Manto and Faiz; what these writers' works show is the way in which Muslim identity is placed 'at the cusp of a fatal dilemma: it can signify *either* "separate nation" or "an Indian minority"' (p. 237). Drawing upon and adapting Edward Said's notion of secular criticism, Mufti's broader aim is to elaborate a mode of critical secularism, 'whose affiliations are with the dilemmas of minority existence' (pp. 13–14) and which 'confronts Nehruvian secularism with the demand that it...*secularize* itself' (p. 30). An 'Epilogue' firmly establishes the relevance of such a critical secularism to more recent Indian fiction in English—by Rushdie, Anita Desai, Amitav Ghosh—as they negotiate the increasingly violent effort to minoritize 'the Muslim' in contemporary India.

The significance of Mufti's conceptualization of critical secularism is already evident in its prevalence in Neelam Srivastava's *Secularism in the Postcolonial Indian Novel: National and Cosmopolitan Narratives in English*. This text explores what the critic refers to as a '"secular" Indian canon in English', consisting of many of its best-known and most widely successful writers (p. 1). It argues that the 'secular genealogy' from which these canonical texts emerge stems specifically from Nehruvian rather than Gandhian or other alternative conceptions of the nation (p. 16). Srivastava acknowledges the complexity of the concept of Indian secularism in making this assertion, helpfully dedicating her opening chapter to the delineation of a range of key theoretical concepts. In addition, while being committed to the pervasiveness of Nehru's influence, Srivastava is careful to not to overlook the idiosyncrasies of the texts that she discusses. She productively mobilizes the concepts of radical and rational secularism to account for differences between some key novels, most notably Rushdie's *Midnight's Children* and Seth's *A Suitable Boy*. It is on the writings of Rushdie and Seth that Srivastava focuses predominantly, while also incorporating commentaries on Ghosh and Shashi Tharoor among others. Moving frequently between these two principal authors, Srivastava's argument can, on occasion, seem repetitive, but it equally produces some detailed critical comparisons, and astute observations. A particularly welcome chapter explores the use of Indian vernacular languages in Rushdie and Seth, and the construction of English as a 'pan-Indian' but also 'nativized' language (p. 140). Chapter 5's brief discussion of intertextuality in *Midnight's Children* is also rewarding.

Equally interested in literary negotiations of the Nehruvian legacy is Anna Guttman's *The Nation of India in Contemporary Indian Literature*. This covers a solid selection of novels including, as one might expect, works by Rushdie, Seth, Nayantara Sahgal and Roy, but also taking in Rupa Bajwa's debut novel *The Sari Shop*, and the less well known *The Last Jet-Engine Laugh* by Ruchir Joshi. What sets this study apart is the sophisticated introductory discussion of Nehru's writings that provides the lens through which Guttman views the fictional texts. Drawing out a sense of anxiety in Nehru's work, and especially in *The Discovery of India*, Guttman argues that all the novels with which she engages are 'challenged to imagine the nation as diverse' even while they pursue a representative model (p. 12). She thereby questions Nehru's designs on the nation, while acknowledging the subtleties and strengths of his ideas, not to mention their resounding impact. Guttman develops her argument through some astute close readings, which provide the key themes around which she structures the study. Moving from discussions of Indian culture in Seth and Rushdie, through the local and the global territories explored by Sahgal and Roy, to the subaltern experiences and science fiction dystopias of Bajwa and Joshi, she demonstrates the persistence of India's diversity. Guttman's case is convincing, sometimes surprising, and forward-thinking, committed to unravelling the complexities of India as a nation.

Vijay Mishra's *The Literature of the Indian Diaspora: Theorizing the Diasporic Imaginary* is noteworthy both as an exploration of Indian fiction and for the contribution that it makes to diaspora theory. This study explores the nature of diaspora in relation to two distinct waves of movement out of India: that which took place under empire and indenture, and the more recent migrations generally associated with late capitalism. Mishra argues that a clear distinction exists between the 'old' and 'new' diasporas resulting from these movements, one that it is crucial to keep in mind in order to uncover and penetrate the so-called 'diasporic imaginary'. His text is certainly ambitious, based on a detailed theoretical framework that takes in issues of mourning, travel, translation, and trauma. Moreover, it engages with an extensive selection of literary and cultural texts, many only in passing, but a considerable number in some detail. Perhaps inevitably, then, the depth of the study's analysis is sometimes sacrificed to its breadth. The critic's regular references to Bollywood film, for example, are illuminating but frustratingly brief. On the other hand, the study's wide view allows for the inclusion of a refreshingly diverse range of authors and artists—from Rushdie, through Bharati Mukherji, to Cornershop and Akram Khan—and some original insights that make it, ultimately, a rewarding read.

Also engaging diaspora communities, but from a rather different point of view, is Ruvani Ranasinha's *South Asian Writers in Twentieth-Century Britain*. It charts a history of the publication and reception of South Asian anglophone writing in Britain, working from the 1930s to the present, and focusing on changing experiences of migrancy, and attitudes towards migrant writers across this period. The text explores the work of eight authors—Nirad C. Chaudhuri, M.J. Tambimuttu, Ambalavener Sivanandan, Kamala Markandaya, Salman Rushdie, Farrukh Dhondy, Hanif Kureishi and Meera Syal—who are dealt with in pairs, according to the generations of which each formed a part. This approach produces some novel insights into the works under discussion, particularly the writings of authors such as Rushdie and Kureishi, who are more commonly set apart from rather than integrated into this history. The strength of Ranasinha's work lies in the original archival material on which it draws, obtained from a variety of publishing houses. He uses this material to illuminate the compelling and occasionally humorous discussions that surrounded the early stages of South Asian anglophone publishing, and which subsequently formed its foundations. The later sections of the study are perhaps less inventive, and the leap that Ranasinha makes from discussing literary texts to the film and television projects of Kureishi and Syal requires further justification. It is nonetheless a worthwhile and well-researched book.

Unexpectedly, Chitra Sankaran's *Myth Connections: The Use of Hindu Myths and Philosophies in R.K. Narayan and Raja Rao* explores similar territory to the above. This volume becomes, in part, an exploration of the origins of Indian English writing, in its attempt to chart the influence of Hindu mythologies and philosophies in the works of its two focal authors. While the attention paid to Rao and Narayan in this text is certainly welcome, Sankaran's argument is less successful than Ranasinha's. The concept of myth that she employs requires considerable further interrogation, as does its relationship to the Hindu religion and Indian culture more broadly. Some more up-to-date critical material would be of value in this regard. Sankaran's stated intention to trace a 'myth motif' across a selection of novels is more cogent, but she ultimately fails to follow such a clear line of thought, digressing into storytelling, and getting distracted by debates surrounding caste, race and gender.

Another somewhat disappointing collection is Nandini Sahu's *The Post-Colonial Space: Writing the Self and the Nation*. Rather than the self and nation of the title, this volume seems to be oriented around a number of topics, ranging from postmodern anxiety, to nation, to the industry of Indian English literature itself. The preface does little to explain the rationale behind this diversity, and overall the collection is characterized by a lack of analysis, coupled with some clumsy use of terms and concepts. While it may succeed in highlighting certain key issues in Indian literature, it does little to explore or resolve them.

Growing Up as a Woman Writer, a collection edited by Jasbir Jain, engages with the concept of the self more successfully, bringing together writings that explore the work and experiences of contemporary women writers in India. The collection includes poetry and prose as well as critical essays, and while

Jain is quick to point out that the volume is far from representative, it also takes in a range of different regions and languages (translated into English). Key essays are Nabaneeta Dev Sen's 'Women Writing in India at the Turn of the Century' (pp. 3–18) and Krishna Sobti's 'Discovering Hashmat' (pp. 19–26). Other contributions worthy of note include Jain's own essays, 'Feminist Writing and the Question of Readership' (pp. 504–19) and 'From Experience to Aesthetics' (pp. 361–9), and Rachel Bari's exploration of 'Dalit Feminist Experience' (pp. 471–9).

Of texts that take a comparative and transnational approach, readers will particularly welcome Ashok Bery's *Cultural Translation and Postcolonial Poetry*, a study of six poets from across the anglophone postcolonial world. Both Bery's exclusive focus on poetry and his comparative approach are productive, permitting fresh insights into the works of largely well-established writers such as Derek Walcott, Les Murray, Seamus Heaney and A.K. Ramanujan. The text is oriented around the notion of translation, as a broadly defined conceptual framework that, the author argues, allows for sound comparison across national cultural boundaries (p. 1). Bery's chapter on Ramanujan slots neatly into this theme; it recognizes the poet's work as a translator as well as the cultural translations towards which his poetry aspires. It also works well as a stand-alone piece uncovering, through selected works, a model of Indian cultures that is 'palimpsestic, reflexive and translational' and, as such, refreshingly inclusive (p. 155).

Robert P. Marzec's *An Ecological and Postcolonial Study of Literature: From Daniel Defoe to Salman Rushdie* is a timely exploration of the role and representation of land in literature from the eighteenth century to the present. It focuses on the impact that the enclosure movement, in conjunction with the rise of the British empire, had and continues to have upon humanity's relation to the land and, as a consequence, the English novel. The study takes in a broad range of authors and critics, from Daniel Defoe to Gilles Deleuze and Félix Guattari, Henry Fielding to E.M. Forster, and closes with a focus on Salman Rushdie. It sets out, through an examination of these writers' selected works, to reawaken a prediscursive 'ontological understanding' of land and inhabitancy (p. 2). Marzec's section on Rushdie focuses primarily on *Midnight's Children*, highlighting the 'parodic foregrounding of nationality' in the novel, alongside its more commonly noted experiments with language and narrative authority (p. 161). He reveals how the multitude that live out the end of this text are 'utterly colonised' by various forms of enclosure (p. 166). Working through a rather abrupt but valid connection to *The Ground Beneath Her Feet*, Marzec goes on to conclude that the enclosure movement 'continues full force in our neo-colonial era' (p. 170). In doing so, he succeeds in asserting the validity of a broadly ecocritical approach to postcolonial studies, and identifies a space worthy of considerable further discussion.

A bold and original comparative text this year is Sarah Brouillette's *Postcolonial Writers in the Global Literary Marketplace*. Brouillette takes on the industry of postcolonial literature, and the position of the postcolonial author within it, attempting to challenge the widely accepted notion that an author's complicity with market forces results in profound and permanent compromise. In setting out her stall, Brouillette revisits several key texts, and works particularly closely with Graham Huggan's *The Postcolonial Exotic*, highlighting its value as well as what she perceives as a key limitation, namely that it is rooted in its dependence on an abstract 'cosmopolitan reader'. By arguing for the partial revival of a Romantic view of the author figure, through the authorial crises commonly registered in postcolonial literature, Brouillette also confronts Roland Barthes's famous pronouncement of the death of the author. Two essays in Brouillette's book focus specifically on South Asian writers. The first, 'Salman Rushdie's "Unbelonging": Authorship and the East' (pp. 79–111), is a welcome study of Rushdie's 2001 novel *Fury*, which has received little critical attention to date. Productively reading this text alongside Rushdie's travelogue *The Jaguar Smile*, Brouillette argues that, rather than being a self-indulgent, semi-autobiographical piece, it is in fact concerned with 'the process of writing veiled memoirs' or with 'Rushdie as brand' (pp. 107–8). As such, she argues, the novel succeeds in enabling Rushdie to admit guilt and deflect criticism at the same time. In the second essay, 'Zulfikar Ghose and Cosmopolitan Authentication' (pp. 144–73), Brouillette considers the work of Zulfikar Ghose, as a writer who famously avoids engaging with any 'authenticating background' in his works (p. 144). She presents his work as a test to the 'requirement of...geographical authentication', reading it as reacting directly to the way certain modes of valuing texts have constrained Ghose's success (p. 146). The sense of balance that these two pieces evoke is retained throughout the text, making for a successful if provocative commentary on a central concern of postcolonial studies.

Nation in Imagination: Essays on Nationalism, Sub-Nationalisms and Narration, edited by C. Vijayasree, Meenakshi Mukherjee, Harish Trivedi and T. Vijay Kumar, is a cogent exploration of the concept of nation in the contemporary global moment. One of three volumes billed to document the proceedings of the thirteenth Triennial ACLALS conference, the collection boasts an impressive list of contributors, including Gayatri Chakravorty Spivak, and essays of consistently high quality. These essays collectively stress the need for contours of nation and nationalism to be 'elastic, porous and resilient' (p. xvi). Entries of particular note concerning Indian literature include Aijaz Ahmad's keynote 'Nationalism and Peculiarities of the Indian' (pp. 37–57). This explores a variety of formulations of nationalism, focusing in the latter half on the peculiarities of independent India's emergence as a democratic republic. Satish C. Aikant's 'Varieties of Nationalism: Culture and Resistance in the Indian English Novel' (pp. 57–72) picks up on Ahmad's suggestion that Indian nationalisms are closely informed by the country's pre-colonial past, to address the representation of these in the fictions of writers such as R.K. Narayan, Raja Rao and Mulk Raj Anand.

Anke Bartels and Dirk Wiemann's *Global Fragments: (Dis)Orientation in the New World Order* sets out to explore relations between globalization and new English literatures, taking as broad a definition as possible of 'literature' in order to incorporate a range of texts and approaches. Arguably the collection takes too wide a view: of the twenty-three articles it includes, the majority are too brief to achieve much in the way of a convincing argument. Moreover, in spite of its breadth, the volume is somewhat repetitive, with certain authors and texts recurring throughout. *Global Fragments* nonetheless contains some worthwhile pieces on Indian and diaspora literature. Frank Schulze-Engler's 'Black Asian and Other British: Transcultural Literature and the Discreet Charm of Ethnicity' (pp. 47–57) offers a succinct and informed reappraisal of ethnicity, particularly the concept of 'political blackness'. Justyna Deszcz-Tryhubczak's essay on Rushdie's 'At the Auction of the Ruby Slippers' (pp. 105–13) is a neat and fairly original discussion of how this short story reflects 'the uneasy frontierlessness of the globalized world' (p. 106). Dirk Wiemann's rather more substantial discussion of *Lagaan* (pp. 153–69) is a careful and illuminating exploration of the global play at work in this strikingly successful film.

Finally, Joel Kuortti and Jopi's Nyman's *Reconstructing Hybridity: Post-Colonial Studies in Transition* is a more wholeheartedly interdisciplinary collection, boasting an impressive list of contributors. It sets out to thoroughly reassess the concept of hybridity, especially as it relates to postcolonial theory and literature, in response to its 'ambiguously prominent standing in recent criticism' (p. 3). Underwriting this pursuit is a commitment to an ethical intellectual practice, one that translates into an emphasis on the practical or material potential of hybridity as a space and concept. In the first half of the collection such potential is drawn out through discussion of theories of hybridity, with articles that examine the concept in relation to issues such as human rights, whiteness, biology and transnational identity. The second half of the collection focuses on literary theorizations of the subject. Several of the articles in this latter half deal with the broad field of South Asian fiction, and all of them offer up convincing, if not always original, textual readings, which neatly intersect with the preceding theoretical pieces. Particularly enjoyable is Joel Kuortti's 'Problematic Hybrid Identity in the Diasporic Writing of Jhumpa Lahiri' (pp. 205–19), which demonstrates how 'This Blessed House' (from the *Interpreter of Maladies*) can be understood to underline 'the centrality of cultural translation in the process of possessing and repossessing the past and present' (p. 217). Perhaps more challenging but also worthy of note is Mita Banerjee's 'Postethnicity and Postcommunism in Hanif Kureishi's *Gabriel's Gift* and Salman Rushdie's *Fury*' (pp. 309–24). While this article anchors itself to the rather tiresome premise that Kureishi's and Rushdie's novels prophetically respond to the events of September 11, it traces a provocative connection between post-ethnicity (replacing hybridity) and post-communism across both texts. Reading their easily comparable east European characters as representative of a new, different, and even exotic kind of ethnicity, Banerjee raises the intriguing possibility that 'after September 11, it may no longer be safe to be postcolonial, but it is safe—even intriguing—to be postcommunist' (p. 321).

(b) Journal Articles

Among the journal articles, as with the books, there was surprisingly little explicit reflection upon the sixtieth anniversary of India's independence and partition, and a marked absence of any special issues timed to coincide with the event. Nevertheless, if books implicitly engaged with India's postcolonial progress by considering the literary legacies of Nehru's vision of nation, journal articles perhaps did so by reflecting, collectively, on the progress of Indian writing in English. Thus, while critics continue to focus the majority of their attention on Salman Rushdie, Arundhati Roy and Amitav Ghosh, there were also some timely attempts to reassess the work by pioneers of Indian writing in English such as R.K. Narayan and Raja Rao. This work is situated within an identifiable, broader trend for exploring transactions between Western, colonial English literature and Indian literature in English and the vernacular. Issues of intertextuality garnered much interest in this regard, although attention was also paid to the politics of language and translation, while the contemporary material and imaginative impacts of globalization, migration and diaspora continue to be key themes.

As ever, Rushdie's work gained substantial attention in 2007, with the politics of intertextuality emerging as a prominent strand of interest. A highlight in this area is Dirk Wiemann's 'From Forked Tongue to Forked Tongue: Rushdie and Milton in the Postcolonial Conversation' (*JCL* 42:ii[2007] 47–63). Through detailed engagement with *The History of Britain* and *Paradise Lost*, Wiemann establishes Milton as a 'distant antecedent of a rhetoric of split enunciation' so crucial to *The Satanic Verses* (p. 50). Wiemann elaborates by examining the power of description in Rushdie's text, with illuminating readings of Saladin's entrance into, and expulsion from, language. In India, Saladin's education gifts him the power to name plants in the garden, an achievement that signals both a loss of Paradise and Saladin's transformation into 'an agent of the imperial archive' (p. 56); in England, Saladin's metamorphosis repositions him 'from subject of ascription to object of description' (p. 58). Yet, Wiemann argues, this loss of the power of description acts as a 'wake-up call', and Rushdie's text, like Milton's Satan, transforms linguistic disempowerment into insurrectionary speech.

Maria Beville's 'The Gothic-Postmodernist "Waste Land" of Ellowen Deeowen: Salman Rushdie's Nightmarish Vision of a Postmodern Metropolis' (*Nebula* 4:i[2007] 1–18) offers a less focused comparative reading of *The Satanic Verses* and Eliot's *The Waste Land*, arguing that Rushdie's novel appropriates 'the Gothic mode to…represent the violence and terror of postmodernity' (p. 1). Beville rightly observes that the modern metropolis is haunted, in both texts, by 'ghostly and dehumanised characters' (p. 9), although she does not fully consider the political ramifications of such 'spectrality'.

The interest in intertextuality is continued in a 'Special Cluster' of articles on Rushdie published by *ARIEL: A Review of International English Literature*, amounting to a run of three pieces: Deepa P. Chordiya's ' "Taking on the tone of a Bombay talkie": The Function of Bombay Cinema in Salman Rushdie's *Midnight's Children*' (*ArielE* 38:iv[2007] 97–122); Daniel Roberts's 'Rushdie and the Romantics: Intertextual Politics in *Haroun and the Sea of Stories*' (*ArielE* 38:iv[2007] 123–42); and Atef Laouyene's 'Andalusian Poetics: Rushdie's *The Moor's Last Sigh* and the Limits of Hybridity' (*ArielE* 38:iv[2007] 143–65). Chordiya's piece complements Mishra's work on Rushdie and Bollywood cinema mentioned above, productively analysing the form as an 'important narrative device' (p. 97) whose generic hybridity and 'fragmentary structure...mirror and elucidate the likewise fragmentary nature of "everyday reality" in *Midnight's Children*' (p. 97). Her discussion of technique is engaging, although a consideration of the ideological moorings of Bollywood would have complicated the suggestion that its hybridity resists rarefied national narratives. The observation that Bollywood frequently 'glorifies a certain culture, namely North Indian and Hindi-speaking, and espouses an absolute system of values (usually Hindu world-view)' (p. 118), is left hanging, and is not tied to Rushdie's Muslim narrator.

In his piece, Roberts traces the interactions between *Haroun and the Sea of Stories* and two classics of Romanticism, Coleridge's 'Kubla Khan: A Vision in Dream' and De Quincey's 'The English Mail-Coach, or the Glory of Motion'. Teasing out Rushdie's engagement with these orientalist texts allows us, Roberts claims, to understand his use of fantasy to examine the fraught politics of Kashmir, and the 'profoundly *critical* interplay' he establishes between 'Romantic orientalist ideology', and the contemporary postcolonial nations of Indian and Pakistan, 'themselves guilty of imperialist attitudes to Kashmir' (pp. 137–8). In the final article in this cluster, Laouyene contributes to recent explorations of *The Moor's Last Sigh* as a self-conscious critique of discourses of secularism. Laouyene reads the 'nostalgia' for an 'ideal multicultural hybridity', epitomized by Arab Spain, as 'parodically under-cut...by Rushdie's post-exotic tropes' (p. 145). Although the idea of 'post-exotic' could have been fleshed out, Laouyene offers some fruitful readings, noting that 'the subversive value of a hybridity paradigm' is weakened when 'ungrounded in the politics of class and location' (p. 160).

Elsewhere, Rushdie's interest in public and private spaces was brought to the fore by two engaging articles: Vassilena Parashkevova's "Turn your watch upside down in Bombay and you see the time in London": Catoptric Urban Configurations in Salman Rushdie's *The Satanic Verses*' (*JCL* 42:iii[2007] 5–24), and Sara Upstone's 'Domesticity in Magic-Realist Postcolonial Fiction: Reversals of Representation in *Midnight's Children*' (*Frontiers* 28:i–ii[2007] 260–84). Identifying the 'looking-glass frontiers' (p. 5) within and between urban spaces in *The Satanic Verses*, Parashkevova develops the notion of urban 'catoptrics' to show how 'cities...unsettle the ideas of historical fixity and geographical location by continually refiguring each other' (p. 5). Although the idea of the city as a site of resistance to essentialist identity constructions is familiar, Parashkevova opens up new frameworks for reading London and Jahilia, as well as the relationship between Gibreel's dreams (refreshingly identified as *linear*) and the urban spaces in which he travels. Upstone, meanwhile, examines postcolonial rewritings of formerly colonized domestic spaces, using *Midnight's Children* as a central example. Upstone observes that colonial discourses often obscure the political implications of making home, even as they rely on the well-kept home to maintain social order. By contrast, postcolonial novels such as *Midnight's Children* repoliticize the home by insisting on a 'chaos that colonial discourse...overwrites' (p. 269). As Upstone demonstrates, Rushdie is aware of the inequalities inherent in such messiness and frequently violent disorder—especially for women—but also of the radical possibilities of a 'politicized' chaos for rethinking, and resisting, hierarchies and identities.

Repositioning Rushdie within an Anglo-American context, Robert Eaglestone's 'The Age of Reason is Over... An Age of Fury was Dawning: Contemporary Anglo-American Fiction and Terror' (*Wasafiri* 22:ii[2007] 19–22), juxtaposes *Shalimar the Clown*, Ian McEwan's *Saturday* and Jonathan Safran Foer's *Extremely Loud and Incredibly Close* in order to examine responses to the impact of the 'War on Terror'. Eaglestone's broad point—which perhaps needed further textual evidence—is that these authors fail to engage fully with the complexity of the 'other'. In these novels, 'terror is simply evil (Foer), an illness (McEwan) or stems from universally comprehensible personal motives (Rushdie)' (p. 21). A related article is Maria-Sabina Draga Alexandru's 'Salman Rushdie's America: Cities and Power in *The Ground Beneath Her Feet, Fury*, and *Shalimar the Clown*' (*RJES* 4[2007] 172–80).

Further articles on Rushdie's work include Anke Gilleir's comparative piece, 'Figurations of Travel in Minority Literature: A Reading of Hafid Bouazza, Salman Rushdie, and Feridun Zaimoglu' (*ComparativeCS* 4:xxii[2007] 255–67); Rajan Ghosh's 'Imagination, Imaging, and Revisionist Aesthetics in Rushdie's *Haroun and the Sea of Stories*: An (In)fusionist Approach' (*ILS* 8:ii[2007] 1–20); and the brief 'Writing and Chutnification in Rushdie's *Midnight's Children*' (*Expl* 65:iii[2007] 182–5), in which Todd Giles draws on Jacques Derrida's work to provide a cursory reading of acts of archivization, memory and historiography in Rushdie's novel.

In the same issue of *Wasafiri* as Eaglestone's piece, a related interview with Pankaj Mishra by Hirsh Sawhney thoughtfully grapples with the complexities of contemporary terrorism, the 'War on Terror' and the uneven impact of globalization ('An Interview with Pankaj Mishra', *Wasafiri* 22:ii[2007] 13–18). Mishra is also interviewed by Sara Fay in *Believer* 5:ii[2007] 53–63. Meanwhile, those interested in the relationship between literature and Bollywood, discussed by Chordiya and Mishra as noted above, will find a complementary discussion of a novel more firmly focused on the Bombay film industry in Suhasini Vincent's 'Celluloid Dreams in Shashi Tharoor's *Show Business*' (*CE&S* 30:i[2007] 83–92).

Joining Parashkevova's work on the city are three articles that probe the relationship between urban and national narratives, of which J. Edward Mallot's excellent comparative piece '"A land outside space, an expanse without distances": Amitav Ghosh, Kamila Shamsie, and the Maps of Memory' (*LIT* 18[2007] 261–84) deserves prominence. Both theoretically astute and textually engaged, Mallott addresses 'the narrative responsibility of maps' (p. 280), before turning to Ghosh's *The Shadow Lines* and Kamila Shamsie's *Kartography* to examine processes of 'cartographic reconstruction' that work to recuperate memory and experience as crucial ways of understanding place. Both authors, Mallott argues, highlight how official maps tend to contradict personal memory; in response, they construct a 'postnational geography' that 'transforms cartography into an intrinsically memory-based art' (p. 283). While Ghosh's protagonist moves beyond nationalist cartographies by 'trac[ing] circles of inclusion', Shamsie's work reveals maps as fuelling an essentialist politics of place. In the interactive 'internet map' that Karim and Raheen construct, however, the chasm between individual memory and official mapping—never fully bridged in *The Shadow Lines*—is closed, with a map incorporating the personal and temporal dimensions of space.

Readers will welcome Saikat Majumdar's engaging piece on the work of novelist and critic Amit Chaudhuri, 'Dallying with Dailiness: Amit Chaudhuri's Flâneur Fictions' (*SNNTS* 39:iv[2007] 448–64). Taking a cue from his introduction to *The Picador Book of Modern Indian Literature*, Majumdar convincingly argues that Chaudhuri's prose challenges the apparent hegemony of pan-Indian national allegories by foregrounding the local and everyday. Majumdar shows how Chaudhuri—and his narrators— assume a flâneur-like viewing/reading practice that recuperates the materiality of a dailiness often 'overshadowed by the spectacular history of the national allegory' (p. 460).

A complementary reading of urban identity is Karen McIntyre-Bhatty's 'Escaping the Molar: Excavating Territories in Manzu Islam's *Burrow*' (*JCL* 42:iii[2007] 25–43). McIntyre-Bhatty contributes to recent interest in Deleuzian notions of 'deterritorialization', pairing her theoretical framework with detailed textual readings that unpack *Burrow*'s concern with 'cross-cultural philosophical, historical and spiritual experiences' (p. 25). Reading Tapan Ali's 'elliptical wanderings' through the material spaces of the city and the imaginative spaces of these discourses, Bhatty argues that Islam's text formulates a 'deterritorializing' aesthetic that works with ideas of nomadic freedom (p. 30) while remaining invested in a specifically historically and politically located subject.

With the exception of Mallot's piece on *The Shadow Lines*, the majority of articles dealing with Ghosh's work focus on the generic hybridity of *In an Antique Land*, probing the strategies he uses to problematize his own authorial voice. As with Rushdie's work, intertextuality is a key critical concern. Theo D'Haen's 'Antique Lands, New Worlds? Comparative Literature, Intertextuality, Translation' (*FMLS* 43:ii[2007] 107–20) gives a nuanced account of how *In an Antique Land* 'intertextually translates' Shelley's 'Ozymandias' from a postcolonial perspective. D'Haen productively pivots his reading on the figure of the 'traveller', showing that while Shelley's narrator receives knowledge of Egypt through the filter of the traveller, Ghosh's narrator and traveller coincide, bringing into view a more complex relationship with that nation, the West, and the narratorial voice. Furthermore, as Shelley plays with the sonnet form, Ghosh plays with the novel genre, reflecting his insider/outsider relationship in a similarly ambivalent stance towards Western modernity and its literary forms.

Likewise concerned with Ghosh's hybridizing literary strategies are Eric D. Smith's '"Caught straddling a border": A Novelistic Reading of Amitav Ghosh's *In an Antique Land*' (*JNT* 37:iii[2007] 447–72), and Christi Ann Merrill's 'Laughing Out of Place: Humour Alliances and Other Postcolonial Translations in *In an Antique Land*' (*Interventions* 9:i[2007] 106–23). Smith situates *In an Antique Land* as a generically *and* ideologically conflicted *novelistic* text, whose internal dialogues between narratives and contexts counterpose the problematics of its broader project, the recovery of a subaltern subjectivity. Smith notes criticisms of Ghosh's methodologies as complicit in the very structures of historiography he seeks to challenge. But, Smith rightly suggests, reading *In an Antique Land* as a *novel* reveals, first, a distance between Ghosh as author and Ghosh as narrator, and, second, highlights how these two 'Ghoshes' are 'engaged in a heterochronic dialogue' (p. 454) in which the 'ironic distance' between the author's 'former and fictionalized self' opens up a space for self-problematization (p. 459). Merrill similarly reads Ghosh's narrator as self-consciously split between narrator and author. Drawing on Linda Hutcheon's notion of irony as 'relational, inclusive, and differential' (cited p. 118), Merrill's aim—not always successful—is to position Ghosh's use of postcolonial irony and (often uncomfortable) humour as rhetorical devices that interrogate moments of cultural translation and his own position in relation to them. An interview with the author by T. Vijay Kumar appeared in *Interventions* (' "Postcolonial" Describes You as a Negative: An Interview with Amitav Ghosh', *Interventions* 9:i[2007] 99–105).

Pursuing the complex narratorial positions of the cultural critic, Anna Guttman's 'Family Portraits and National Histories: Nayantara Sahgal's Constructions of Indira Gandhi and Jawaharlal Nehru' (*SARev* 28:ii[2007] 151–64), provides a fascinating study of Sahgal's biographies of India's former prime minister, *Indira Gandhi's Emergence and Style* and *India Gandhi: Her Road to Power*. Guttman foregrounds tensions between Sahgal's 'authority as a biographer' and her 'status as an autobiographer', a tension that threatens at once the 'intimacy and the objectivity' of her portraits (p. 153), and which reflects a broader struggle with the limits of auto/biographical and political writing.

A selection of articles focused on the transactions between 'Western', English, and colonial literatures and languages and Indian literatures in both English and indigenous languages. As Harish Trivedi amply demonstrates in 'Colonial Influence, Postcolonial Intertextuality: Western Literature and Indian Literature' (*FMLS* 43:ii[2007] 121–33), the 'Western influence on Indian literature was nothing if not dialectical and dialogic' (p. 127). Trivedi is primarily concerned with *critical discourses* surrounding issues of colonial influence and cultural hybridity, tracing a shift from an early an anxiety over influence *as* dominance, to—à la Homi Bhabha—a 'more enabling post-colonial "intertextuality" ' as a form of resistance or 'belated empowerment' (p. 131). Trivedi suggests that Indian critical practices are themselves limited by the influence of Western critical practice; his point—which will be familiar to readers of his work—is the need to shift attention from canonical English-language postcolonial writers to 'Indian-language' writers, in order to open up more complex understandings of the impact of colonial literature beyond current (Western) theoretical paradigms.

Neelam Srivastava analyses English and Bengali texts in ' "PIDGIN ENGLISH OR PIGEON INDIAN?": Babus and Babuisms in Colonial and Postcolonial Fiction' (*JPW* 43:i[2007] 55–64). Noting the Babu's centrality to concepts of colonial mimicry, Srivastava presents a fascinating genealogy of the figure through an impressive range of literature, from nineteenth-century Bengali farces and satires, to fiction by Rudyard Kipling and George Orwell, to Vikram Seth's *A Suitable Boy*. Srivastava maps the Babu as 'a quintessentially *linguistic* figure' (p. 56), whose English speech is closely connected to the appropriation and subversion of colonial language. Against Tabish Khair's contention that postcolonial Indian writing in English is marked by an elitist inauthenticity, Srivastava points out the complexities, innovative potential, and frequently self-conscious uses of English by postcolonial writers. As her readings of Rushdie and Seth demonstrate, 'recent writing has appropriated the stereotypical figure of the Babu and made its linguistic ambivalence into a profoundly creative element of the text', 'creative[ly] re-imagining' (p. 63) rather than mimicking the 'original' English of the colonial ruler.

Also concerned with language, and giving welcome attention to poetry, which remains disappointingly neglected in critical work on the subcontinent, is Tabish Khair's 'Echoes of Hieroglyphs: Language in Indian Poetry in English' (*PNR* 34:i[2007] 20–4).

Rumini Sethi resumes the interest in East–West interactions in her examination of Rao's short stories, 'Narsiga' and 'The Cow of the Barricades', in 'The Freight of Culture: The Mythicization of History in Indian Literary Tradition' (*JPW* 43:i[2007] 45–54). While recognizing their importance to Rao's work, Sethi notes that Western traditions of nineteenth-century realism present an inadequate framework through which to read the complexities of his fiction. Characterizing Rao's writing as marked by a 'double vision' of realism, caught between Western and Eastern traditions, Sethi argues that we need to view Rao in the context of Indian social realities and aesthetics, especially *puranic* story-telling traditions. A less successful attempt to relocate Indian writing in English within 'local' story-telling traditions is James Earl's 'How to Read an Indian Novel' (*LitI* 9:i[2007] 96–117).

Extending this interest in the pioneering generation of Indian writers in English, a special issue of the *Journal of Commonwealth Literature* marks the birth centenary of R.K. Narayan. As Harish Trivedi's editorial, 'R.K. Narayan at 100' (*JCL* 42:ii[2007] 1–6), suggests, the centenary offers a 'fresh stimulus for rereading and reassessing' Narayan's work, which has been eclipsed by interest in more recent postcolonial Indian writing in English (p. 3). Trivedi introduces two issues central to the symposium: the politics of writing in English, and the fraught notion of authenticity—that is, the familiar, but highly problematic, reading of Malgudi as representative of 'the real India' (p. 2). John Thieme's excellent 'The Cultural Geography of Malgudi' (*JCL* 42:ii[2007] 113–26) picks up on the latter issue in an absorbing reading of *The English Teacher*, *The Financial Expert*, *The Painter of Signs*. Rather than view Malgudi as a 'metonym for a traditional India', located outside modernity (p. 114), Thieme presents his work as 'a multi-faceted and transitional site, an interface between older and newer conceptions of "authentic" Indianness and contemporary views that stress the ubiquity and inescapability of change in the face of modernity' (p. 116).

Another highlight of the collection is Lakshmi Holmström's 'Translation Translated? *The Dark Room* in Tamil' (*JCL* 42:ii[2007] 73–87). Taking familiar discussions of the politics of language in a refreshing direction, Holmström examines Narayan's novel alongside its Tamil translation, *Iruttu Arai*.

Addressing the strategies Narayan uses to translate local (Tamil) idioms and lives into English, Holmström considers how (and how successfully) these speech styles 'travel back' into Tamil (p. 75). Through meticulous attention to subtle differences between the texts, Holmström argues that the potentially radical 'proto-feminist' themes of the English version are not accommodated by the Tamil translator, who was either 'unable to find the words to convey [them] precisely, or chose not to do so' (p. 85).

Nandini Saha's '*The World of Najaraj*: A Postmodern Malgudi?' (*JCL* 42:ii[2007] 101–12) looks at the final phase of Narayan's career, from *Talkative Men* [1986] to his last novel, *World of Najaraj* [1990]. Picking up on an increasingly self-conscious concern with authorship and authority, Saha concludes that, in Narayan's last works, 'the infiltration of postmodern self-reflexive metafictional elements that commingle with the portrayal of Malgudi life produces a new kind of Malgudi novel' (p. 111). Narayan's representations of Gandhian nationalism and the freedom movement are the focus of Satish C. Aikant's 'Colonial Ambivalence in R.K. Narayan's *Waiting for the Mahatma*' (*JCL* 42:ii[2007] 89–100). Comparing *Waiting* with Rao's *Kanthapura*, Aikant contends that the former text does not express the same ideological commitment as the latter's 'intimately Gandhian' sensibility (p. 97). Rather, Narayan's novel is detached from the social ferment of its time, appearing 'committed to his artistic vision alone' (p. 99)—a claim that appears problematic given Aikant's attention to the text's ambivalence towards Gandhian nationalism in the first place. Shashi Deshpande's 'R.K. Narayan: A Personal View' (*JCL* 42:i[2007] 65–71) presents a slightly meandering personal tribute to Narayan as a 'pioneer' of Indian writing in English (p. 71), pondering the apparent absence of interaction between Narayan's work and the vibrant Kannada cultural milieu within which he lived. The essays collected here are billed as a 'curtain-raiser' to a volume to be published by the Sahitya Akademi, which will include a wider selection from the IACLALS-Sahitya Akademi conference and a related symposium.

A number of articles published in 2007 examine the textual and extra-textual impact of globalization on South Asian literature, with two essays by Sarah Brouillette elucidating particularly valuable perspectives on the publishing market. Complementing sections of her book, reviewed above, her first article, 'Zulfikar Ghose's *The Triple Mirror of the Self* and Cosmopolitan Authentification' (*MFS* 53:i[2007] 97–119) explores Ghose's fictional presentation of the relationship between textual production and reception as a response to his own exclusion from the canons of postcolonial literature. Teasing out the tensions within Ghose's representations of the cosmopolitan writer and the 'local' subject, Brouillette deftly demonstrates the ways in which the author's fiction questions notions of local and national authenticity, and their marketability within the globalized publishing industry. In her second piece, 'South Asian Literature and Global Publishing' (*Wasafiri* 22:iii[2007] 34–8), Brouillette turns more firmly to the publishing industry. She tracks how, in the aftermath of globalization and economic liberalization, and with a growing NRI/diasporic readership, transnational firms increasingly publish the very vernacular Indian languages they once marginalized but only when the *content* fits with a marketable image of the 'local'. Brouillette cautions that not only does such 'buying up' reveal how a 'celebrated and romanticised localism is just as marketable as an ostensibly delocalised cosmopolitan English-language writing' (p. 37), but also has a potentially negative material impact on smaller (local) publishing firms and economies.

The impact of globalization is amongst the issues addressed by a handful of essays exploring Arundhati Roy's *The God of Small Things*. Perhaps the most engaging is José David Saldívar's 'Unsettling Race, Coloniality, and Caste: Anzaldua's *Borderlands/La Frontera*, Martinez's *Parrot in the Oven*, and Roy's *The God of Small Things*' (*TPr* 21:iii[2007] 339–67). Here, Saldívar reads Roy's novel within the framework of border thinking, constructing a 'cross-genealogical' treatment of 'minoritized writing' (p. 340). After readings of language use in Anzaldua's and Martinez's work, Saldívar turns to *The God of Small Things* to focus on issues of minoritization, kinship, memory, identity and experience. Roy's novel, Saldívar concludes, 'indicates the extent to which subaltern identity and experience depends upon a minor (or small) historiography' (p. 362). The ambitious attempt to build cross-cultural frameworks for reading minoritized identity is certainly welcome; however, as Saldívar notes, this approach risks acquiring a 'sweeping character' (p. 339).

In 'Performing Narrative: The Motif of Performance in Arundhati Roy's *The God of Small Things*' (*SARev* 28:ii[2007] 217–36) Parama Sarkar gives an uneven examination of Roy's critiques of globalization, and the concomitant exoticization and commodification of Indian story-telling traditions for globalized consumers, pivoting her analysis on the destructive and creative possibilities of performance in Roy's text. In the same issue, Sharmita Lahiri's 'Alternative Visions of a Feminine Space in *Clear Light of Day* and *The God of Small Things*' (*SARev* 28:ii[2007] 133–50), compares the different approaches to female emancipation taken by Roy and Anita Desai, identifying alternative visions of feminism: Desai's character Bim expounds a 'tempered feminism' that creates an independent voice without seeking to revise the dominant social codes; in Roy's novel, a 'radical rebel' explicitly challenges patriarchal norms. A related article is Pramod K. Nayar's 'The Place of the Other: Arundhati Roy's *The God of Small Things*' (*SLJH* 33:i–ii[2007] 15–28).

Feminist resistance is one subject explored in a special issue of the *Journal of Postcolonial Writing*, entitled 'Literature as Resistance: Challenging Religious, Linguistic, Casteist, Racist and Sexist Essentialism'. As the title perhaps indicates, the collection, guest-edited by Nilufer E. Bharucha and Klaus Stierstorfer, takes up the issue of 'resistance' to 'essentialism' in rather broad strokes; it collects together pieces of variable quality by creative writers, literary scholars and translators on what the editors, in 'Introduction: Literature as Resistance' (*JPW* 43:ii[2007] 121–4), refer to as a range of 'essentialist positions and fundamentalist premises'. A highlight is Catherine Pesso-Miquel's 'Addressing Oppression in Literature: Strategies of Resistance in Indian and Indian English Contemporary Literature' (*JPW* 43:ii[2007] 149–60), which offers a lively discussion of the ways in which literature attempts to resist or write against oppression suffered on the basis of differences of gender, race and religion. While Rushdie's *Shalimar the Clown* and Devi's 'Draupadi' take centre stage, Pesso-Miquel weaves in readings of work by Alka Saraogi, Monica Ali and Nadeem Aslam. At its best when discussing gender, Pesso-Miquel's central argument is that fiction 'turns the anonymous, global statistics of horror into an individualized, personal case studies' (p. 150), bearing witness to the materiality of suffering, while also complicating our understandings of oppressor and oppressed.

Nilufer E. Bharucha's 'The Earth Is Not Flat: Minority Discourses against Fundamentalisms' (*JPW* 43:ii[2007] 183–90), provides a starting point for those interested in literature of the Parsi diaspora, presenting a brief survey of writers, from the better-known fiction of Rohinton Mistry and Bapsi Sidhwa, to the poetry of Keki Daruwalla and the drama of Cyrus Mistry. While Bharucha is on safe ground arguing that these writers 'resist and challenge hegemonies . . . both external and internal' (p. 189), readers may be left wanting more detailed readings to develop this argument. Jasbir Jain's 'A Phoenix Called Resistance: Aesthetics vs Meaning' (*JPW* 43:ii[2007] 172–82) locates writing itself as an always already resistant act. Citing an ambitious range of authors—from Girish Karnad, to Hanif Kureishi, to Mahasweta Devi—Jain addresses the points of divergence and convergence between discourses of 'resistance' and 'fundamentalism'. Given the range covered, it is perhaps unsurprising that the essay—like the issue as a whole—suffers from some over-generalization, gesturing towards, without fully fleshing out, the initial suggestion that fantasy and myth are used as strategies of resistance in the writing considered.

Anisur Rahman's 'Indian Literature(s) in English Translation: The Discourses of Resistance and Representation' (*JPW* 43:ii[2007] 161–71) offers an overview of the shifting contexts for translating Indian language texts, from nineteenth-century orientalist translations to the present day. In recent decades, Rahman claims, 'conscientious' translators (Gayatri Chakravorty Spivak is a prime example) become central to projects of retrieval or theoretical engagement, and are 'concerned to voice postcolonial concerns' (p. 165). Rahman cites anthologies such as *The Oxford Anthology of Modern Indian Poetry* and *The Picador Book of Modern Indian Literature* as evidence that 'translation is fast formulating its canon and posing an alternative discourse on resistance and representation' (p. 166). It is hoped that future *YWES* volumes will reflect a growing critical interest in just such a canon.

The special issue also includes a number of more personal meditations on 'resistance'. Githa Hariharan's 'In Search of our Other Selves: Literature as Resistance' (*JPW* 43:ii[2007] 125–32) provides probably the most acute critique of essentialist discourses in the issue, focusing on the specific impact of Hindu nationalism on Indian culture. If *Hindutva* narrows the multifarious possibilities of historical figures, myths and places then, Hariharan forcefully contends, resistance is only possible through the assertion of the heterogeneity of India's cultures, languages and communities. Hariharan privileges the literary as an ideal site for such resistance, for 'The point of our using our words, ideas, images, the point of all our literary journeys, is to encounter our other selves. The resistance is in the act of our embracing these other selves' (p. 131). The Gujarati Dalit writer Dalpat Chauhan reflects on the history and literature of the Dalit community in 'I am the Witness of My History and My Literature' (*JPW* 43:ii[2007] 133–42). Chauhan notes how village dialects, as well as mythical and heroic figures, are frequently used to 'capture the form of heteroglossia' (p. 138) of Gujarati language and identities that are set against elite, Brahminic constructions of Hindu identity. Meher Pestonji's 'Troubled Times Test the Writer' (*JPW* 43:ii[2007] 143–8) gives a brief autobiographical account of her work in relation to feminist movements of the 1970s and 1980s, and the more recent rise of Hindu nationalist violence.

As in 2006, there is a continuing interest in feminist negotiations of South Asian diasporic identity, with Meena Alexander and Jhumpa Lahiri continuing to attract attention. Departing from the frequent focus on representations of *women*, however, is Bonnie Zare's 'Evolving Masculinities in Recent Stories by South Asian American Women' (*JCL* 42:iii[2007] 99–111). In an engaging piece, Zare considers the representation of complex masculinities in short stories by Mira Nair and Jhumpa Lahiri, unpacking negotiations of masculinity within the context of modernization, consumer capitalism and globalization, as well as the legacies of colonialism. In 'Meena Alexander's Transgressive/Diasporic Female Characters: Healing Wounds and Fracturing the Iconic Feminine and the Language of the Colonizer' (*SARev* 28:ii[2007] 27–46) M. Dolores Herrero takes a familiar line, examining Alexander's fictional and autobiographical work to consider how diaspora becomes a productive space from which to interrogate class and gender conflicts, as well as issues of nation and nationalism. In 'What's in a Name? Tropes of Belonging and Identity in *The Namesake*' (*SARev* 28:ii[2007] 182–200) Aparajita De draws upon the notion of polygenesis—of continual self-refashioning—to examine Gogol's (re)negotiations of his identity in relation to monolithic constructions both outside and within the diaspora. Shazia Rahman's 'Rachna Mara's Cosmopolitan (Yet Partial) Feminisms' (*ArielE* 38:ii–iii[2007] 1–18), takes us beyond these familiar writers, to consider Mara's short-story collection *Of Customs and Excise*. Unfortunately, the attempt to read Rahman's work in relation to what Ien Ang elsewhere terms a 'partial feminism' is a little unfocused. Readers will find an exceptionally brief interview with Alexander in 'A Brief Conversation with Meena Alexander' (*WLT* 81:vi[2007] 22).

Contributing to a substantial body of work examining the gendered nature of experiences of Partition, Lopamudra Basu's 'The Repetition of Silence: Partition, Rape, and Female Labor in Bapsi Sidhwa's *Cracking India*' (*SARev*28:ii[2007] 5–26) presents interesting readings of the class dynamics of sexual rivalry within Sidhwa's text, but offers little beyond the familiar in its attempt to unsettle the 'top down model of middle class feminist intervention ... posited in the novel' (p. 10).

Disappointingly, literature produced outside India and by its diaspora received scant attention in 2007. In relation to Sri Lanka, Michael Ondaatje and Shyam Selvadurai attracted most interest. Two articles continue a trend identified last year for ethical examinations of Ondaatje's fictional representations of Sri Lanka: Gillian Roberts's excellent 'Ethics and Healing: Hospital/ ity and *Anil's Ghost*' (*UTQ* 76:iii[2007] 962–76), and Hilde Staels's 'A Poetic Encounter with Otherness: The Ethics of Affect in Michael Ondaatje's *Anil's Ghost*' (*UTQ* 76:iii[2007] 977–89). Roberts's absorbing piece locates the novel's negotiation of Sri Lanka's crisis within a theoretical framework of hospitality, drawing on Derrida, Kant and Emmanuel Lévinas to illuminate Ondaatje's concern with individual and national ethics. Examining relations of hospitality and hostility in the text, between individuals, communities and nations, Roberts argues that the text 'insist[s] upon the ethical as a way to heal the nation' (p. 962). Emphasizing the merging of hospitality and medicine, Roberts identifies the hospital as a 'politically neutral space' (p. 970), in which medical care is offered as a concrete act of healing. Ethical treatment of the other becomes crucial, and Ondaatje 'presents hospitality and its embodiment in healing as necessary to the process of reconstruction, both personally and nationally' (p. 262). Taking a different theoretical approach, Staels nevertheless shares a concern for issues of Otherness and ethical healing. Staels draws on Julia Kristeva's work on alterity to illuminate how Ondaatje's 'poetic discourse disrupts the rules of "normal" communicative discourse and gives expression to the Other within the Self' (p. 978). Here, the ethical import of uncovering the 'Other within the Self' extends beyond acknowledgement of individual trauma, and points towards an 'ethical relatedness [that] implies that human beings account for the effects of unconscious drives and affects on themselves and others' (p. 988). Also interested in narratives of reconciliation in Ondaatje's novel is Shounan Hsu's 'Engaged Buddhism and Literature: The Art for Peace in Michael Ondaatje's *Anil's Ghost*' (*TkR* 37:iii[2007] 5–34). Elsewhere, Karen E. MacFarlane contributes to ongoing debates surrounding Selvadurai's negotiation of sexuality and gender in 'Taking (On) Identities: Transvestite Texts in Shyam Selvadurai's *Funny Boy*' (*OpL* 13:iii[2007] 38–46).

6. New Zealand

The year 2007 saw an unusually wide range of comments on New Zealand literature, including a thoughtful and complex re-examination of the whole field, namely Patrick Evans, *The Long Forgetting: Post-Colonial Literary Culture in New Zealand*. After some introductory material on the revolutionary impact on culture of socio-political upheavals in the 1960s, 1970s and 1980s, Evans introduces the concept of the 'sublime' (p. 47), which is to prove central to his general argument. It does not mean precisely the same as it does in late eighteenth-century and Romantic England but involves what might be called 'exalted' views of New Zealand, whether of its landscape or its society, which are as significant for what they exclude as for what they expound. The historical variants include the 'colonial sublime' initiated by the urge of settlers to find or, if necessary, create a better place than the one they left behind. The vision of Edward Gibbon Wakefield, who notoriously never saw the actual country, is an early example. The Treaty of Waitangi, whatever misunderstandings arose from it, was inspired by a wish on both sides to move towards something better than what they had known. The examples multiply. The idea that the land itself was sublime seemed to be confirmed by the 'scenic wonderlands'—at least until the North Island representatives were destroyed by a volcanic eruption. The concept of 'Maoriland' involved the idea of the indigenous made harmless, so that the settlers could acquire indigeneity for themselves. (Evans's range of reading and quotation is impressive, and yet there are curious gaps, the most obvious of which occurs at this point, where there is no reference to Jane Stafford and Mark Williams's *Maoriland* [2006]). To avoid being overwhelmed, the Maori invented their own sublime, clearly a response to the colonial version. For Evans the colonial sublime continues in some areas into our own times, and the *Te Maori* exhibition in New York in 1984 is a particularly spectacular example. In a chapter called 'Forgetting' he goes on to discuss the realities excluded by the colonial sublime. To create a pastoral paradise the axe and extensive fire were used, in effect destroying an existing natural sublime—the bush. Arcadia and Utopia, as Evans defines them, are incompatible kinds of sublime, the one pre-existing, the other created. Unlike most writers, Katherine Mansfield and Blanche Baughan, however, observed and recorded the ugliness resulting from the imposition of Utopia on Arcadia in their travel reports. H. Guthrie-Smith's *Tutira* [1926] celebrates the move from Arcadia to Utopia, only to question the entire enterprise in a brief statement in his foreword, wondering if his life's work has been an illusion. In the next chapter, 'Remembering', Evans discusses the ways in which the 'modernist' writers—such as Curnow and Sargeson—questioned the colonial sublime, only to replace it with a nationalist sublime. His story passes through 'high masculinism' (the masculine sublime), the female sublime, and the gay sublime into a postcolonial deconstruction, which, however, insists on asserting the greatness, say, of its own enterprise and strategies. All of these constructs are achieved by excluding much reality and at the risk of alienating the non-literary people who live inside that non-sublimic reality. Evans seems to detect some progress in the rise of Maori and Pacific Island literary cultures, which add new dimensions to a narrow field, but to the end of his book there is a pervasive pessimism at the way so much literature—he quotes some honourable exceptions—bypasses whole dimensions of the cultural and general human experience that could enrich it. His book is more complex than this summary can convey, and not at all an easy read, but it deserves close scrutiny, in part for the telling examples and quotations that illustrate the argument.

A volume of essays was issued to honour a prominent poet, novelist, playwright, essayist and biographer on his seventieth birthday: Bill Manhire and Peter Whiteford, eds., *Still Shines When You Think of It: A Festschrift for Vincent O'Sullivan*. The contributions that focus on the work of O'Sullivan himself tend to swarm around the question of the balance or imbalance between aesthetic qualities and moral or even political ones in the arts, or between the numinous and the terrestrial. As a student, O'Sullivan was attracted to writers of the 'art for art's sake' persuasion, and has devoted much of his academic endeavour to them. But, as Richard Mulgan lucidly explains in 'The Importance of Appearing Not To Be Earnest' (pp. 15–25), the general tendency of scholarship through the following decades was in the opposite direction, so that O'Sullivan has always run against the grain of contemporary scholarship, while at times acknowledging its seriousness. According to Mulgan, 'Within the academy, the last fifty years have seen a steady retreat of aesthetic values in the face of moral and political criticism' (p. 21), but O'Sullivan has never ceased viewing the aesthetic as primary while not denying the presence and importance of the moral and political. The result has been a tension in his writing and thinking that Mulgan and others in this volume believe has been fruitful but which might also be considered regrettable. Michael Hulse, in particular, in his contribution 'Voice and Authority in Vincent O'Sullivan's Poetry' (pp. 85–95), uses extensive quotation and close reading to demonstrate that the poet's voice denies itself authority—of the kind assumed by 'great poetry' of the past—while paradoxically achieving authority precisely by doing so. In this view, O'Sullivan's use of colloquial turns of phrase when writing of religious, philosophical or sociological matters puts him into a dialogue of equals with the reader. In response to Hulse it could, however, be argued that the colloquialisms can alienate the reader by creating fault-lines between the serious and the trivial, and that O'Sullivan's poetry is marred by its high aesthetic claims and esoteric references, on the one hand, and its sporadic slips into the demotic on the other. An unsympathetic reader might feel that the poet cannot decide between two incompatible stances. The writers in this volume, however—in keeping with the spirit of a Festschrift—are all sympathetic readers. Peter Whiteford, in 'Hic Iacet Pilatus: Vincent O'Sullivan's Pilate Tapes' (pp. 102–18), finds a wide range of meaning in the progress/regress of the man who washed his hands of Christ's blood, from the borderlands of the Roman empire to the last post of the British one, where he becomes a grocer with a bad memory in a colonial store. Murray Bramwell writes a shorter piece on O'Sullivan's 'Butcher' poems, 'Butcher at the Gates of Dawn: Choice Words for Choice Occasions' (pp. 96–101). These poems embody the contrast between vision and colloquial language, religious fervour and rough earthiness, so characteristic of O'Sullivan's manner, even more radically than others do.

Tensions of the kind hinted at here can be more readily accommodated in drama than in lyric poetry, and three further essays in the volume remind us that O'Sullivan is, as far as one can judge at this time, the most distinguished and remarkable dramatist ever to work in New Zealand. David Carnegie's 'A Lost Classic: Vincent O'Sullivan's *Lysistrata*' (pp. 168–185), describes and analyses O'Sullivan's adaptation of Aristophanes' most famous comedy. Regrettably, this theatrical tour de force has never been performed. Carnegie explains that after some delays in production, the play seemed to lose its relevance when the authoritarian rule of Prime Minister Robert Muldoon was replaced at the 1984 election by a Labour government under David Lange. Under Muldoon, the main topics of *Lysistrata*, peace and the subjection of women, were topics of hot debate. It was, by and large, the anti-nuclear issue that brought about the change of government and a woman MP in Muldoon's National Party, Marilyn Waring, created a crisis by crossing the floor of the house. Under the new government, anti-nuclear policies were legislated and a Ministry of Women's Affairs was created. This apparently deflated the issues in O'Sullivan's play. A quarter of a century later it could, however, be argued that it now deserves performance, partly for its historical interest, more significantly because the issues that Aristophanes satirized have never totally lost their *brisance* and, most significantly of all, because O'Sullivan's extraordinary language—both linguistic and theatrical—can still startle, provoke and entertain. Carnegie's essay makes that very plain. Philip Mann's reminiscence 'A Well-Flung Shuriken: Vincent in the Rehearsal

Room—A Memoir' (pp. 187–207), is a useful item of theatre history. Mann
directed the first production of O'Sullivan's *Shuriken* in 1982. It had an
enormous impact on audiences and was perhaps the most important
production in a flourishing of New Zealand theatre over a period of some
ten years. Although Mann seems to overestimate his own contribution to this
success, he is able to pass on some interesting information about the genesis of
the play and its growth during rehearsals under the theatrical conditions of the
time. O'Sullivan was present at many phases of the production's preparation
and responded sensitively to the pressures of casting and staging as they arose.
An extraordinary result of O'Sullivan's fruitful experience of Australia during
the 1980s was his play *Billy*, which places an Aboriginal mute at the centre of
the action and wittily revolves around the complexities of colonization—
'Oscar Wilde in the bush', the dramatist ironically described the play at
the time. Sebastian Black's 'Vincent O'Sullivan's *Billy* and other plays'
(pp. 208–24), shows why the play worked so well in the theatre (it was
produced just once, at Bats in Wellington) and also usefully surveys the
writer's sometimes forgotten plays for radio and theatre. My own opinion, for
what it may be worth, is that drama is the field in which this chameleon of
genres has been most successful. He is nonetheless a prolific writer of fiction,
and further essays discuss this. Owen Marshall's 'The Irresistible
Reconstruction' (pp. 283–5), is a graceful acknowledgement from one fine
practitioner of the short-story art to another; Harry Ricketts finds a wide
variety of styles and themes in the earlier stories in '"The O'Sullivan Way":
Some Reflections on Vincent O'Sullivan's Early Short Stories' (pp. 286–99),
while Paul Millar examines the author's first novel in 'Textuality and the
Grotesque in Vincent O'Sullivan's *Believers to the Bright Coast*' (pp. 300–17),
finding a similar break in sensibility to that described above in relation to the
poetry, but seeing it as a breach in society itself, where, if individuals may
follow their own inclinations to some extent without 'shattering the social
mosaic' (p. 302), the character of 'the Chow' goes further than that and does
indeed shatter the preconceptions of the other characters. Sporadically
through the volume we find items of memoir and anecdote, such as Michael
Jackson's 'Vincent' (pp. 132–6), describing encounters with the writer over
several decades. Brian Turner's view of O'Sullivan in 'A Certain "Nervous
Elegance" and All That' (pp. 161–7), is of a good 'mate', who understands that
most people can be foolish most of the time and consequently shuns
pretension. Syd Harrex writes his memories of O'Sullivan in the form of fine
verse: 'Rites of Spring: A Song & Sonnet Suite for Vincent' (pp. 223–5).
Michael Morley seems to assume the cloak of the court jester in 'Dandy with
Revolver' (pp. 252–8), telling tales of obscene language and behaviour,
sometimes with a homoerotic overtone, where O'Sullivan appears, however, in
the role of the curious observer, deliberately withholding himself from
Morley's extravagances. None of these friends seems to find the description of
O'Sullivan the man a simple task, and Don Akeson, in 'From Mount Nebo,
Vincent O'Sullivan Views the Promised Land' (pp. 364–72), appears to portray
him in a very indirect manner, not even mentioning him but rather exploring
the history of humanity in ways that might, or might not, reveal something
of both writers' views of the world.

The O'Sullivan Festschrift also includes essays on other New Zealand writers. MacDonald P. Jackson's 'Ursula Bethell's Poetry: Notes on Technique and Significance' (pp. 26–47) does what its title suggests. It takes techniques such as repetitions of various kinds, occasional recondite diction, irregular rhymes, regular and irregular metre and the shapes given to entire poems, and examines how they illuminate or transform what the poems appear to be saying. Bill Manhire, in 'Talking Points: A Note on *Man Alone*' (pp. 152–60), examines how the verb and noun 'talk' recur a surprising number of times in Mulgan's novel and speculates on what this implies about the book's intentions. In 'Three Calypsos: Baxter's Variations on a Mythic Theme' (pp. 234–48), Geoffrey Miles takes up a comment by O'Sullivan that in his poetry James K. Baxter 'thinks primarily in mythological terms' and focuses on a group of three poems on Odysseus and Calypso, written in 1957–9, to demonstrate Baxter's methods of revision.

Recently we discussed the history of Reeds New Zealand publishing house on the basis of a biography of its founder and a history of the house by Edmond Bohun. Bohun, a maverick historian, had beaten the gun, so that the official history for the centenary, Gavin McLean's *Whare Raupo: The Reed Books Story*—celebrating the hundredth anniversary of the firm (just before it changed To Raupo Publishing (NZ) Ltd)—now seems superfluous. Even though McLean's style is no less readable and witty than Bohun's, two books covering almost precisely the same ground are, frankly, an embarrassment. Specialists in publishing history may wish to use both books; even slightly more general readers will be satisfied with one—probably the unofficial version.

A fine selection of Lloyd Geering's writings is deliberately designed to show the development of his thought: *The Lloyd Geering Reader: Prophet of Modernity*, edited by Paul Morris and Mike Grimshaw. In the introduction Morris writes that the book's 'importance is that it provides another form of autobiography—the development of New Zealand's leading public intellectual and his fascinating coverage of the place and role of religion in the modern world, both nationally and internationally' (p. 21). Morris also points to Geering's insistence on clarity and conclusiveness in matters often left vague and inconclusive, and praises his 'unique, cool, hard, no-frills theological style' (p. 9). With the exception of the last adjective this is perhaps something that could be said with equal justice of the C.K. Stead who inhabits *Book Self* [2008], to be reviewed in the next edition of *YWES*, a collection of essays and writings many of which are also autobiographical. What religion is to Geering, poetry is to Stead, and perhaps there is something particularly 'New Zealand' in the crystalline style of both writers. In any case, a reading of these two books together will convey a powerful sense of the high level of intellectual endeavour possible in a community that is sometimes said to lack such qualities.

An attractive book of unusual interest is Charles Brasch's *In Egypt*, with an introduction by Margaret Scott. In 1978, three years after his death, the autobiography of this poet and fine prose stylist was published by Oxford University Press as *Indirections*, edited by James Bertram. As Scott explains, Bertram and the publisher believed that the total manuscript was simply too long to attract a general readership, and the editor undertook to cut Brasch's book down to about half its original size by leaving out material that was not directly relevant to New Zealand. Scott, a friend of Brasch, knew that there was attractive material about three archaeological trips to Egypt left out of Bertram's version of *Indirections*. It is this material that she has now published through the good offices of the Wellington publishing enthusiast, Roger Steele. The content is interesting, the prose very fine, and it seems odd indeed that no publisher can be found for the complete autobiography of one of the country's most distinguished writers.

Ever since 1907 the *New Zealand School Journal* has provided essential and entertaining reading matter for children of all ages. Its centenary was celebrated with a travelling exhibition and a book: Gregory O'Brien's *A Nest of Singing Birds: 100 Years of the New Zealand School Journal*. O'Brien has delved deeply—though selectively—in the journals themselves and in the large files from School Publications and Learning Media now in the National Archives in Wellington. He provides us with the basic historical facts over the century. He has also researched the biographies of key visual artists and writers, and argues historically about both these kinds of art as well as education itself. All this is related to a broader view of the society in which the *Journal* was embedded. Many of the visual artists and photographers—Rita Angas, Colin McCahon, Jill McDonald, Dick Frizzell, Bob Kerr, Ans Westra and others—were essential to developments in the country as a whole, and many of the writers—Fleur and Irene Adcock, James K. Baxter, Peter Bland, Alistair Te Ariki Campbell, Joy Cowley, Ruth Dallas, Marilyn Duckworth, Patricia Grace, Maurice Duggan, Denis Glover, Louis Johnson, Jack Lasenby, Margaret Mahy, Ruth Park, Frank Sargeson and others—were and are known far beyond the bounds of the *School Journal*. Just as the *Journal* reached out beyond its own limits into the broader community, the community worked back on the *Journal*. Occasionally there were fruitful scandals about the material offered to the children. O'Brien's presentation of these cases and, indeed, of the history of the *Journal*, is summary rather than detailed, and narrative rather than analytical, so that—as he explains himself—there is much more work to be done on the basis of the *Journal* archives. In the meanwhile, this attractive book will serve to stimulate thought and ideas.

The Gorse Blooms Pale was the name of Dan Davin's first book of short stories, published in 1947. Now Janet Wilson has prepared a scholarly edition of all Davin's 'Southland Stories', adding those from *Breathing Spaces* [1975] and six 'previously uncollected' stories. The edition and its notes are detailed and meticulous. The opening chronology of Davin's life covering seven dense pages (pp. 9–15) is an achievement in itself. The introduction (pp. 17–47) provides the biographical and historical context for each story and, almost incidentally, surveys the critical and academic reception of Davin's work. It is followed by a generous bibliography. The stories that follow have a dense apparatus of notes attached to them. Especially valuable are the comments on when the stories were written, published and republished. There are also notes on many terms found in them. Perhaps Wilson's enthusiasm for her subject goes a little too far here. Even relatively common turns of phrase are explained exhaustively ('a broadside' in its literal and metaphorical meanings is glossed from the *OED*). The notes, even as endnotes, can become so obtrusive that reading slows to a standstill—to some extent, of course, the reader must take responsibility for that. In fact, it seems churlish to complain about such concentrated editorial energy (there is even a map of Invercargill), and this edition might well be a model for future work from the same publisher.

Mark Williams has written an essay on the sociocultural life of the 1970s, using the death of James K. Baxter in 1972 as a starting point and focus: 'Leaving the Straight Path: Cultural Time Travel in the Seventies' (*JNZL* 4–5[2006–7] 81–9). The 'time travel' of the title refers ironically to the way people arriving in New Zealand feel that they are approaching some earlier time, commonly the 1950s. Williams uses this as a basis for some brief thoughts on the mythic ways in which New Zealanders present their country to the minds of others and often to themselves. A pristine natural world interweaves, in such myths, with an unchanging—though perhaps 'dying'— Maori culture: an ancient people in an antique world. For all the unrealities in Baxter's own vision, he was able to jolt many people into reconsidering their mythic view of the country and to face more consciously such features as its urbanism, its racial relationships and the transformations wrought on the landscape by human habitation. Williams formulates these changes in perception in terms of time and distance: 'In the seventies actual time and imaginary time struggled for dominance' (p. 88).

In 1954 New Zealand people were shocked by a matricide committed in the seemingly peaceful city of Christchurch, and its unique features, involving a conspiracy between two teenage girls deemed to be lesbians, led then and in subsequent years to much soul-searching about the nature of violence in society and its associations with sexual 'deviance'. James Bennett has surveyed the fictional and non-fictional writing on this theme in 'Fifty Years of Parker and Hulme: A Survey of Some Major Textual Representations and their Ideological Significance' (*JNZL* 4–5[2006–7] 11–38). Attitudes to the event reflect changing attitudes to sexuality and crime in the past fifty years, and these changes, rather than any underlying 'truth', are the article's concern. The texts studied are of various genres: press reports, feature articles, popular crime writing (located between fact and fiction), a play, films and scholarly articles. A major change over time has been a shift or broadening of attention from individual psychology to general sociological and political features of the reactions to this crucial event.

The 2007 issue of the online journal *Kōtare: New Zealand Notes & Queries* was not called volume 7, as might have been expected, but 'Special Issue— Essays in New Zealand Literary Biography—Series One: Women Prose Writers to World War I'. The many variations of the women's movement in the pre-war era, of which the temperance movement can be reckoned a part, have not been studied as closely as they deserve and the issue is consequently a welcome one. The writers individually covered by various authors are Lady Barker, Louisa Alice Baker ('Alien'), Edith Searle Grossmann, G.B. Lancaster (Edith Lyttelton), Jane Mander, Nelle Scanlan, Katherine Mansfield, Jean Devanny, Ngaio Marsh, Robin Hyde (Iris Wilkinson), Sylvia Ashton-Warner and Elsie Locke. It must be said at once that the last four do not fit into the stated time-frame. This is a mere quibble, however, since the essays provide a mass of biographical detail and useful summary accounts of literary texts. There is also much more to be found by following links, sometimes to other sections of the New Zealand Electronic Text Centre, of which *Kōtare* is now a part, and sometimes to external websites. There are also good bibliographies, but the fact that they are not up to date suggests that the essays were written at some time before the 2007 publication date. The essay on G.B. Lancaster, for example, makes no reference to the superb biography of that writer by Terry Sturm [2003] and the Katherine Mansfield bibliography mentions nothing later than 2001.

The journal *Ka Mate Ka Ora: A New Zealand Journal of Poetry and Poetics*, published online by the New Zealand Electronic Poetry Centre (nzepc), released its third issue in March 2007. It opens with Paul Millar's article 'James K. Baxter's Indian Poems' (*Ka Mate Ka Ora* 3[2007]). Millar has identified fourteen poems that engage immediately with Baxter's journey to India from September 1958 to April 1959, only seven of which have been published. Full texts of all fourteen are included in the issue and examined in detail in the article. Millar's concern is to relate them to the rest of Baxter's oeuvre, and he finds that they take up issues already present in the poet's adolescent work. As the son of pacifists in wartime, Baxter was already alienated and isolated, and yet he saw himself as a unit in the complex of New Zealand society. In his own words, India taught him that he was 'a man who had become, almost unawares, a member of a bigger, rougher family'. However, New Zealand was as representative of that rougher family as India or any other country. At home, too, there was poverty and exclusion, in some ways even more painful than in India. Millar comments that 'Baxter's resistance to the dehumanising aspects of the Indian status quo in the late 1950s parallels his adolescent resistance to the dehumanising aspects of New Zealand's status quo during the Second World War.' The Indian experience did not change Baxter fundamentally but added another dimension and another perspective to the concerns he had already formulated quite early in life.

The second article in the issue is Helen Sword's 'Behind the Curtain: Teaching Alistair Campbell's "Burning Rubbish"' (*Ka Mate Ka Ora* 3[2007]). In describing the reactions, skilfully prompted by her, of a group of students to Campbell's poem, she is able indirectly to explore its wide range of meaning and the way it can appeal to people with different backgrounds and preoccupations. It is an interesting approach to close reading, not as a heady analysis by the critic but as a range of responses by a group of excited readers. Nonetheless the teacher's controlling hand can be felt in the way the students are guided to examine parts of the poem and in the actual composition of the essay, which itself deserves quite close reading. Also of interest is a rather chatty survey of Hawai'ian poetry in English by Anne Kennedy, 'Hawai'i Poetry: A Tour' (*Ka Mate Ka Ora* 3[2007]). The September issue of this journal contains a valuable memoir-essay by Elizabeth Caffin, 'Poetry at Auckland University Press' (*Ka Mate Ka Ora* 4[2007]). Over a period of two decades, Caffin published much of the country's finest poetry as managing editor of the AUP. She begins by briefly surveying the background. Before her time, the press had published three of New Zealand's best-known modernist poets, Smithyman, Stead and Curnow. It went on to publish other established poets and a group of 'exuberant' poets of the 1960s and 1970s. In addition it added to the scholarship of poetry with Michelle Leggott's monumental edition of Robin Hyde, and related material. Caffin goes on to evoke in anecdotal form the wide range of personalities and poetic styles involved in her work. Of great interest to the uninitiated is her explanation of why publishing poetry is not a financial problem, as one constantly hears; rather, the AUP actually made a modest profit from the work. She is too courteous to say so, but the absence of poetry lists from most publishers' output is probably due to fear and incompetence inside the industry.

In the same issue of *Ka Mate Ka Ora*, Michelle Leggott offers a very short note on the apparently very abundant archives of Alan Brunton and Sally Rodwell. It serves as an introduction to two articles on Brunton by Murray Edmond, based extensively on the archives as well as on other sources. In 'Eating the Wind: Red Mole's Asian Itineraries' (*Ka Mate Ka Ora* 4[2007]), Murray outlines Brunton's wide-ranging journeys through Asia in the early 1970s and remarks on some of Asia's impact on the writer, notably his explicit abandonment of John Locke's idea of consciousness in favour of a 'counterfeit identity', partly drug-induced and partly created by an act of will. Murray's second article, 'From Cabaret to Apocalypse: Red Mole's *Cabaret Capital Strut* and *Ghost Rite*' (*Ka Mate Ka Ora* 4[2007]), examines the writing and stage history of two major productions by Brunton's theatre group Red Mole. *Cabaret Capital Strut* ran in Wellington's notorious transvestite nightclub for some seven months, while *Ghost Rite*, which played in Auckland's Maidment Theatre for six nights, was nothing less than a history of the world told through a parade of its ghosts. Murray examines the political satire in these pieces while not underestimating their sheer nihilist commitment to absurdity.

Stephen Hamilton supplies his customary meticulous annual bibliography of New Zealand literature, covering the year 2006 (*JCL* 42:iv[2007] 127–43). The accompanying essay notes the constant emergence of new writers and the work of small, medium and large publishers in bringing out their work, despite the extreme difficulties of the market in a small economy. He emphasizes the importance of awards and prizes in both encouraging and financing literary creativity, and surveys the recent prizewinners, as well as noting the publication of some major works of non-fiction. Another general item is Jack Ross's essay, 'Irony and After: New Bearings in New Zealand Poetry' (*Poetry NZ* 35[Sept. 2007] 95–103). Ross chronologically outlines approaches to poetry in New Zealand: 'colonial bards', 'pastoral Georgians' and 'hard-headed modernists'. Each group condemns the one it follows and, by this reckoning, the postmodernist Bill Manhire metaphorically murders alls his predecessors to promote his contemporaries. But what can follow that? Ross— 'provisionally'—claims to have found a group of young poets in whom cool deconstruction and a romantic sense of doom collide. These poets, who are 'trying to bridge the gaping abysses cutting across our culture', are named as Olivia Macassey, Will Christie, Jen Crawford, Thérèse Lloyd, Tracey Slaughter, Scott Hamilton, Richard Taylor and, by implication, Ross himself—who is from Auckland. A Wellington youngster might come up with a totally different list.

A major essay on the history of critical understanding in New Zealand is given focus by closely analysing the critical work of one writer. This is James Smithies, 'Finding the True Voice of Feeling: Kendrick Smithyman and New Criticism in New Zealand, 1961–1963' (*JCL* 42:i[2007] 59–78). By presenting Smithyman as an alternative to the stream of criticism originating with Alan Curnow, Smithies is able to range further than the title of his essay may suggest. He provides a useful survey of Smithyman's life and career and then concentrates his attention on four essays published in the journal *Mate*, which were later to become a book, *A Way of Saying* [1965]. Smithyman opposed the 'romantic'—or essentialist—view of nationalism held by Curnow and others with a nationalism or regionalism that placed New Zealand in a broader context, including the nationalisms of other countries. He was deeply, instinctively opposed to theories and systems that might solidify into dogma, and this makes him dismissive of much earlier criticism. In the second of his essays, Smithyman was also dismissive of the conflict between Romanticism and classicism embodied by Mason and Fairburn. He sees Fairburn's satire as no more than the reverse side of his Romanticism, rather than an alternative to it. Smithyman offers an alternative contrast: the 'tough-minded' Glover and Curnow as opposed to the 'tender-minded' Mason and Fairburn. He tries to apply this to New Zealand poetry as a whole and then undermines his own distinction by pointing out the changes of allegiance between the two sides, blurrings of boundaries and the like—in fact Smithies finds that Smithyman's own prose is difficult because it is 'protean', never allowing the reader to rest intellectually. Smithies explains some of Smithyman's preoccupations as oriented towards finding a place for his own poetry in a context that is not welcoming to it—the key is in responsibility to language rather than to feeling or society. This is why he was attracted to American New Criticism, which views the social function of poetry as marginal and its linguistic patterns as central. Unfortunately this devotion to language is conveyed, especially in the third essay, in language that is itself dense to the verge of incomprehensibility. The central argument here is that New Zealand poetry must be intellectual *of necessity*, because there is no tradition on which to call in order to create depth of feeling. Smithies's exposition of Smithyman's ideas is extremely useful, because in their original form they are obscurely expressed. Indeed Smithies seems more and more irritated by this as his own essay advances, and there is a note of relief when he comes to the fourth of Smithyman's essays, a study of domesticity in poetic content. Smithies points out that this poetry—exemplified by Baxter, Johnson, Dowling, Bland, Adcock and Duckworth—is quite unlike Smithyman's own, and yet he reads it with sympathy, and his own language becomes more domesticated as he advances his arguments. Much light is cast into obscurity by Smithies in this essay, which deserves to be read by any who wish to understand the nature of New Zealand criticism and, by reflection, of the poetry it debates.

In a later issue of the same journal is an essay by Doreen D'Cruz: 'Women, Time and Place in Fiona Kidman's *The Book of Secrets*' (*JCL* 42:iii[2007] 63–82). It is a feminist reading of Kidman's novel, suggesting that the female characters in a heavily patriarchal society, dominated by a kind of father-dictator, live a richer life than his design intends. They ignore the patriarchal dichotomies of culture and nature or of lyric and narrative, and focus on places intended to exclude and incarcerate women that actually provide sanctuary and a centre where alternative views of the world can be constructed.

The *British Review of New Zealand Studies*, now in its sixteenth volume, has a long and uneven period of development behind it, but the 2007 issue, a book of more than 200 pages, is valuable and substantial, consisting largely of the written versions of papers presented at a conference in Paris in 2006. Fiona Kidman's essay, 'New Zealand and France: Literature, Connections and Belonging' (*BRONZS* 16[2006/7] 13–30), offers a general overview of French writing about New Zealand and New Zealand writing about France without being either comprehensive or original. Its highest value is autobiographical, reflecting a childish awareness of the French while living in remote Northland growing into a more complex and appreciative concern based on her chance encounters with French writers and her fellowship in Menton. It is followed by a long interview with C.K. Stead conducted by Gerri Kimber, 'Black Sheep Rehabilitated: The World According to Judas and C.K. Stead' (*BRONZS* 16[2006/7] 31–52). It covers his novel *My Name Was Judas*, his poetic work, his literary criticism and his thoughts on being a writer. Consistent to all these are his loyalty to language rather than social pressures, his insistence on clarity of judgement and expression and his refusal to compromise in order to find favour with his critics.

Other essays in *BRONZS* 16, while they do not cover literary themes directly, offer much food for thought to anyone interested in the broader stream of New Zealand culture. They are concerned with the growing reception of French films in New Zealand, attitudes towards multiculturalism as exemplified by New Zealand reactions to riots in both France and Australia in October and November 2005, the concept of citizenship arising from the Treaty of Waitangi in contrast to that arising in France from the revolution, cross-influences between France and New Zealand in contemporary music and the implications of studying early modern culture in New Zealand and Australia. The volume is rounded off with a number of book reviews.

Vivian Fu writes of an American and a New Zealand doctor-poet, William Carlos Williams and Glenn Colquhoun, in 'The Poet and Doctor as One' (*Poetry NZ* 34[Mar. 2007] 97–105). She sees their poetry as a necessary complement to their medical work, adding a different and necessary mental and moral dimension to the body-based perspective of their profession. She believes that poetry enabled these doctors to cope with stresses in their daily work and, as a medical student, she finds in them a moral exemplum for her own life.

Having long occupied a pre-eminent position among New Zealand literary journals, *Landfall* seems, by comparison, to be passing through a dry and desolate phase. It still contains individual items of interest, but without a guiding editorial hand at the rudder it seems directionless. Each issue is edited by another person, chosen, it would seem, for their reputation as writers rather than for their editorial skills. Early editors, notably Charles Brasch and Robin Dudding, were devoted to the craft of editorship, quite independently of any poetry or prose they may have written. Recent editors have no such credentials. The first issue of *Landfall* for 2007 was edited by no fewer than four writers and took Russia as its theme. Despite the presence of Russian contributors, mostly living outside Russia, there is no sense that this is a comprehensive or even coherent picture of the country or its culture. The New Zealand status of *Landfall* is in no way enhanced by this formless act of homage to the exotic.

This does not exclude the presence of some interesting individual items. Of relevance here is, for example, Jacob Edmond's essay, 'No Place Like Home: Encounters between New Zealand and Russian Poetries' (*Landfall* 213[May 2007] 73–80). He draws a provocative parallel between Stalin's elimination of the old, wiping the slate clean, to create a utopia and the colonial enterprise in New Zealand that sought a substitute for the old and outworn in British culture. He traces awareness of this to Charles Brasch on a journey to Russia in 1934. Waves of New Zealand poets have attempted to 'make it new' by attacking their predecessors—an idea not unlike that described by Jack Ross above—and this is nothing less than a renewed attempt at colonialism/revolution, which can be paralleled in Russia. Edmond discusses the sense of affinity certain New Zealand poets feel for certain Russian ones—notably Anna Jackson for Mayakovsky—in these terms. The essay is thought-provoking, but the thought thus provoked needs time to mature. In the same journal, Murray Edmond (Jacob's father) writes of 'At the Crossroads: Alan Brunton's Russian Moments' (*Landfall* 213[May 2007] 89–96). Here again it is Mayakovsky who plays for the other side. Brunton's play, *At the Crossroads* [1989] is dedicated 'to the sacred memory of Vladimir Mayakovsky'. The connection between the play and the Russian poet is anything but direct and, again, Edmond sees in it the attempt to wipe away the old and substitute the new. He argues that although Brunton's encounters with Russia were sporadic and unsystematic, they can reveal some otherwise unclear depths in the dramas he wrote.

In an entertaining essay, Margarita Meklina's 'On Translating New Zealand Poetry' (*Landfall* 213[May 2007] 136–9), the insistence in the country's verse, both Maori and Pakeha, that almost everything depends on the land is questioned by a translator who finds more stimulation in computers, ipods and other modern technology than in landscapes. To translate the references to topography, flora and fauna she found the most useful resource was the internet. Finally, however, she made a journey to New Zealand and discovered that the land, indeed, dominates the world people live in there. Stephanie de Montalk discusses the background to her Pushkin-based novel, *The Fountain of Tears* [2006] in 'From "Alexander Pushkin, Lost Love and the Poetics of Distance"' (*Landfall* 213[May 2007] 162–9).

For all the doubts about the direction *Landfall* is taking, or failing to take, it may be fairly asked whether any of the articles and essays discussed here could have found an outlet in any other place. The following issue (*Landfall* 214[Nov. 2007]) was edited by Jack Ross and is totally different in content and manner. It feels much more like the original booklets, focusing on the best creative writing available, some of it very good indeed, and offering less, therefore, to this survey of secondary literature. Both issues of *Landfall*, however, include book reviews of varying interest.

Books Reviewed

Adams, Jessica, Michael P. Bibler and Cécile Accilien, eds. *Just Below South: Intercultural Performance in the Caribbean and the U.S. South.* UPVirginia. [2007] pp. 284. £15.50 ISBN 9 7808 1392 6001.

Against All Odds: Footage and Documentary from an International Conference of African Languages and Linguistics. [DVD]. Asmara.

Anim-Addo, Joan. *Touching the Body: History, Language and African-Caribbean Women's Writing.* Mango. [2007] pp. 352. £18.99 ISBN 1 9022 9423 8.

Anim-Addo, Joan, and Suzanne Scafe, eds. *I Am Black/White/Yellow: An Introduction to the Black Body in Europe.* Mango. [2007] pp. 235. £14.99 ISBN 1 9022 9431 9.

Anim-Addo, Joan, Giovanna Covi, Velma Pollard and Carla Sassi. *Caribbean–Scottish Relations: Colonial and Contemporary Inscriptions in History, Language and Literature.* Mango. [2007] pp. 208. £13.99 ISBN 9 7819 0229 4346.

Arndt, Susan, Eckhard Breitinger and Marek Spitczok von Brisinski, eds. *Theatre, Performance and New Media in Africa.* Bayreuth. [2007] pp. 217. €19.95 ISBN 9 7839 3966 1016.

Banham, Martin, ed. *A History of Theatre in Africa.* CUP. [2005] pp. 478. £91 ISBN 9 7805 2180 8132.

Bartels, Anke, and Dirk Wiemann, eds. *Global Fragments: (Dis)Orientation in the New World Order.* Rodopi. [2007] pp. xvii + 361. $106 ISBN 9 0420 2182 2.

Bartels, Anke, and Dirk Wiemann, eds. *Global Fragments: (Dis)Orientation and the New World Order.* Rodopi. [2007] pp. xvii + 361. €76 ISBN 9 7890 4202 1822.

Batra, Nandita, and Vartan P. Messier, eds. *Narrating the Past: (Re)Constructing Memory, (Re)Negotiating History.* CSP. [2007] pp. 159. £34.99 ISBN 9 7818 4718 1145.

Bery, Ashok. *Cultural Translation and Postcolonial Poetry.* Palgrave. [2007] pp. viii + 221. £48 ISBN 1 4039 3310 2.

Besemeres, Mary, and Anna Wierzbicka, eds. *Translating Lives: Living with Two Languages and Cultures.* UQP. [2007] pp. xxiv + 181. $A32.95 ISBN 9 7807 0223 6603 7.

Birns, Nicholas, and Rebecca McNeer, eds. *A Companion to Australian Literature since 1900.* CamdenH. [2007] pp. xv + 477. £50 ISBN 9 7815 7113 3496.

Bottalico, Michèle, Maria Teresa Chialant and Eleanor Rao, eds. *Literary Landscapes, Landscapes in Literature.* Carucci. [2007] pp.290. €26.20 ISBN 9 7888 4304 3170.

Bradford, Clare. *Unsettling Narratives: Postcolonial Readings of Children's Literature.* WLUP. [2007] pp. vii + 279. $C32.95 ISBN 9 7808 8920 5079.

Brasch, Charles. *In Egypt*, introd. Margaret Scott. Steele Roberts. [2007] pp. 118. NZ$24.99 ISBN 9 7818 8744 8065.

Brouillette, Sarah. *Postcolonial Writers in the Global Literary Marketplace.* Palgrave Macmillan. [2007] pp. 240. £47 ISBN 0 2305 0784 5.

Brown, Stewart. *Tourist, Traveller, Troublemaker: Essays on Poetry.* Peepal Tree. [2007] pp. 340. £16.99 ISBN 9 7818 5423 0531.

Buckridge, Patrick, and Belinda McKay, eds. *By the Book: A Literary History of Queensland.* UQP. [2007] pp. 390. $A45 ISBN 9 7807 0223 4682.

Burton, Antoinette. *The Postcolonial Careers of Santha Rama Rau.* DukeUP. [2007] pp. 216. £58 ISBN 0 8223 4071 3.

Campbell, Kofi Omoniyi Sylvanus. *Literature and Culture in the Black Atlantic: From Pre- to Postcolonial.* Palgrave. [2007] pp. viii + 200. $68.95 ISBN 9 7814 0397 2231.

Carter, David, and Anne Galligan. *Making Books: Contemporary Australian Publishing.* UQP. [2007] pp. 448. $A39.95 ISBN 9 7807 0223 4699.

Casteel, Sarah Phillips. *Second Arrivals: Landscape and Belonging in Contemporary Writing.* UPVirginia. [2007] pp. 244. £40.50 ISBN 9 7808 1392 6384.

Chowdhury, Purna. *Between Two Worlds: Nation, Rushdie and Postcolonial Indo-English Fiction.* Mellen. [2007] pp. iv + 334. £74.95 ISBN 0 7734 5347 0.

Clark, Maureen. *Mudrooroo, a Likely Story: Identity and Belonging in Postcolonial Australia.* Lang. [2007] pp. 263. €37.30 ISBN 9 7890 5201 3565.

Collingwood-Whittick, Sheila, ed. *The Pain of Unbelonging: Alienation and Identity in Australasian Literature.* Rodopi. [2007] pp. xliii + 210. €42 ISBN 9 7890 4202 1877.

Cranston, CA, and Robert Zeller, eds. *The Littoral Zone: Australian Contexts and their Writers.* Rodopi. [2007] pp. 319. €64 ISBN 9 7890 4202 2188.

Dale, Leigh, and Helen Tiffin, eds. *Economies of Representation, 1790–2000.* Ashgate. [2007] pp. xiii + 237. £55 ISBN 9 7807 5466 2570.

DeLoughrey, Elizabeth M. *Routes and Roots: Navigating Caribbean and Pacific Island Literatures.* UHawaiiP. [2007] pp. xiv + 334. £49 ISBN 9 7808 2483 1226.

D'Hulst, Lieven, Jean-Marc Moura, Liesbeth De Bleeker and Nadia Lie, eds. *Caribbean Interfaces.* Rodopi. [2007] pp. 368. €74 ISBN 9 7890 4202 1846.

Dvořák, Marta, and Manina Jones, eds. *Carol Shields and the Extra-Ordinary.* McG-QUP. [2007] pp. 275. $75 ISBN 9 7807 7353 2205.

Dvořák, Marta, and W.H. New, eds. *Tropes and Territories: Short Fiction, Postcolonial Readings, Canadian Writings in Context.* McG-QUP. [2007] pp. 368. $85 ISBN 9 7807 7353 2892.

Emery, Mary Lou. *Modernism, the Visual, and Caribbean Literature.* CUP. [2007] pp. xi + 290. £50 ISBN 9 7805 2187 2133.

Erikson, Peter. *Citing Shakespeare: The Reinterpretation of Race in Contemporary Literature and Art.* Palgrave. [2007] pp. 214. £38 ISBN 9 7814 0397 0558.

Evans, Patrick. *The Long Forgetting: Post-Colonial Literary Culture in New Zealand*. CanterburyUP. [2007] pp. 274. NZ$34.50 ISBN 9 7818 7725 7698.

Ezenwa-Ohaeto. *Subject, Context and the Contours of Nigerian Fiction*, ed. Eckhard Breitinger. Bayreuth. [2007] pp. 183. €19.95 ISBN 9 7839 3966 1016.

Fiamengo, Janice, ed. *Other Selves: Animals in the Canadian Literary Imagination*. UOttawaP. [2007] pp. 361. $45 ISBN 9 7807 7660 6453.

Flotow, Luise von, and Reingard M. Nischik, eds. *Translating Canada*. UOttawaP. [2007] pp. 340. $40 ISBN 9 7807 7660 6613.

Gerson, Carole, and Jacques Michon, eds. *History of the Book in Canada*, vol. 3: *1918–1980*. UTorP. [2007] pp. 638. $85 ISBN 0 8020 9047 8.

Gilbert, Helen, and Jacqueline Lo. *Performance and Cosmopolitics: Cross-Cultural Transactions in Australasia*. Palgrave Macmillan. [2007] pp. x + 245. €48 ISBN 9 7802 3000 3408.

Gilbert, Helen, ed. *Five Emus to the King of Siam: Environment and Empire*. Rodopi. [2007] pp. xxviii + 260. €58 ISBN 9 7890 4202 2430.

Gurnah, Abdulrazak, ed. *The Cambridge Companion to Salman Rushdie*. CUP. [2007] pp. 220. £45 ISBN 0 5218 4719 3.

Guttman, Anna. *The Nation of India in Contemporary Indian Literature*. Palgrave Macmillan. [2007] pp. vi + 230. £42.50 ISBN 1 4039 8390 9.

Hatherell, William. *The Third Metropolis: Imagining Brisbane through Art and Literature, 1940–1970*. UQP. [2007] pp. vi + 312. $A45 ISBN 9 7807 0223 5436.

Hazelton, Hugh. *LatinoCanadá: A Critical Study of Ten Latin American Writers of Canada*. McG-QUP. [2007] pp. 312. $80 ISBN 9 7807 7353 2076.

Huggan, Graham. *Australian Literature: Postcolonialism, Racism, Transnationalism*. OUP. [2007] pp. xiv + 192. £14. ISBN 9 7801 9927 4628.

Hutchinson, George, ed. *The Cambridge Companion to the Harlem Renaissance*. CUP. [2007] pp. xx + 275. £45 ISBN 9 7805 2185 6997.

Ibrahim, Huma, ed. *Emerging Perspectives on Bessie Head*. AWP. [2004] pp. 222. $19.95 ISBN 1 5922 1074 0.

Jain, Jasbir, ed. *Growing Up as a Woman Writer*. Sahitya Akademi. [2007] pp. xxii + 528. Rs220 ISBN 8 1260 2547 3.

Kamboureli, Smaro, and Roy Miki, eds. *Trans.Can.Lit: Resituating the Study of Canadian Literature*. WLUP. [2007] pp. 233. $36.95 ISBN 9 7808 8920 5130.

Kuortti, Joel, and Jopi Nyman, eds. *Reconstructing Hybridity: Post-Colonial Studies in Transition*. Rodopi. [2007] pp. x + 330. £50 ISBN 9 0420 2141 9.

Lewis, Desiree. *Living on a Horizon: Bessie Head and the Politics of Imagining*. AWP. [2007] pp. 317. pb $16.95 ISBN 1 5922 1458 4.

Loriggio, Francesco, ed. *The Last Effort of Dreams: Essays on the Poetry of Pier Giorgio di Cicco*. WLUP. [2007] pp. 207. $65. ISBN 9 7815 5458 0194.

Macedo, Lynne, and Kampta Karran, eds. *No Land, No Mother: Essays on David Dabydeen*. Peepal Tree. [2007] pp. 236. £12.99 ISBN 9 7818 4523 0203.

Manhire, Bill, and Peter Whiteford, eds. *Still Shines When You Think of It: A Festschrift for Vincent O'Sullivan*. VUP. [2007] pp. 380. NZ$40 ISBN 9 7808 6473 5713.

Martin, Sylvia. *Ida Leeson: A Life.* A&UA. [2006] pp. xiv + 242. $A29.95 ISBN 9 7817 4114 8503.

Marzec, Robert P. *An Ecological and Postcolonial Study of Literature: From Daniel Defoe to Salman Rushdie.* Palgrave Macmillan. [2007] pp. 208. $74.95 ISBN 1 4039 7640 6.

McKinnie, Michael, ed. *Space and the Geographies of Theatre.* PCP. [2007] pp. 226. $25 ISBN 9 7808 8754 8086.

McLean, Gavin. *Whare Raupo: The Reed Books Story.* Reed NZ. [2007] pp. 294. NZ$50 ISBN 9 7807 9001 1233.

Melas, Natalie. *All the Difference in the World: Postcoloniality and the Ends of Comparison.* StanfordUP. [2007] pp. xvi + 283. £21.95 ISBN 0 8047 3198 5.

Mishra, Vijay. *The Literature of the Indian Diaspora: Theorizing the Diasporic Imaginary.* Routledge. [2007] pp. xix + 286. £60 ISBN 0 4154 2417 8.

Misrahi-Barak, Judith. *Revisiting Slave Narratives II.* PULM. [2007] pp. 477. €20 ISBN 2 8426 9648 4.

Moran, Patricia. *Virginia Woolf, Jean Rhys, and the Aesthetics of Trauma.* Palgrave. [2007] pp. ix + 217. $68.95. ISBN 9 7814 0397 4822.

Morris, Paul, and Mike Grimshaw, eds. *The Lloyd Geering Reader: Prophet of Modernity.* VUP. [2007] pp. 400. NZ$40 ISBN 9 7808 6473 5478.

Msiska, Mpalive-Hangson. *Postcolonial Identity in Wole Soyinka.* Rodopi. [2007] pp. 176. £12.95 ISBN 9 7890 4202 2584.

Mufti, Aamir. *Enlightenment in the Colony: The Jewish Question and the Crisis of Postcolonial Culture.* PrincetonUP. [2007] pp. xiii + 325. £41.60 ISBN 0 6910 5731 6.

Niall, Brenda. *Life Class: The Education of a Biographer.* MelbourneUP. [2007] pp. xiv + 290. $A32.95 ISBN 9 7805 2285 3438.

Nischik, Reingard M, ed. *The Canadian Short Story: Interpretations.* CamdenH. [2007] pp. 426. $75 ISBN 9 7815 7113 1270.

O'Brien, Anthony. *Against Normalization: Writing Radical Democracy in South Africa.* DUP. [2001] pp. 333. $19.95 ISBN 0 8223 2571 3.

O'Brien, Gregory. *A Nest of Singing Birds: 100 Years of the New Zealand School Journal.* Learning Media. [2007] pp. 160. hb NZ$59.99 ISBN 9 7807 9031 9636, pb NZ$39.99 ISBN 9 7807 9032 6276.

Okpewho, Isidore, ed. *Chinua Achebe's Things Fall Apart: A Casebook.* OUP. [2003] pp. 275. pb £12.95 ISBN 0 1951 4642.

Ouyang Yu. *Bias: Offensively Chinese/Australian: A Collection of Essays on China and Australia.* Other. [2007] pp. 315. $A54.95 ISBN 0 9756 0920 3.

Paul, Annie, ed. *Caribbean Culture: Soundings on Kamau Brathwaite.* UWI. [2007]. pp. 439. £23.98 ISBN 9 7897 6640 1504.

Pivato, Joseph, ed. *Mary di Michele: Essays on her Works.* Guernica. [2007] pp. 214. $14.95 ISBN 9 7815 5071 2490.

Pouchet Paquet, Sandra, Patricia J. Saunders and Stephen Stuempfle, eds. *Music, Memory, Resistance: Calypso and the Caribbean Literary Imagination.* Randle. [2007] pp. xlii + 369. $35 ISBN 9 7897 6637 2903.

Ranasinha, Ruvani. *South Asian Writers in Twentieth-Century Britain.* OUP. [2007] pp. viii + 302. $65 ISBN 0 1992 0777 0.

Randall, Don. *David Malouf*. Contemporary World Writers. MUP. [2007] pp. xvii + 222. hb £11.99 ISBN 9 7807 1906 8324, pb ISBN 9 7807 1906 8331.

Reade Rosenberg, Leah. *Nationalism and the Formation of Caribbean Literature*. Palgrave. [2007] pp. x + 260. £42.50 ISBN 9 7814 0398 3862.

Riegel, Christian, ed. *Dictionary of Literary Biography*, vol. 334: *Twenty-First-Century Canadian Writers*. Gale. [2007] pp. 431. $254 ISBN 9 7807 8768 1524.

Rohlehr, Gordon. *Transgression, Transition, and Tranformation: Essays in Caribbean Culture*. Lexicon. [2007] pp. 507. $47.95 ISBN 978 9 7663 1049 3.

Rønning, Anne Holden, and Lene Johannessen, eds. *Readings of the Particular: The Postcolonial in the Postnational*. Rodopi. [2007] pp. vii + 274. €58 ISBN 9 7890 4202 1631.

Roy, Anjali Gera, ed. *Wole Soyinka: An Anthology of Recent Criticism*. PencraftI. [2006] pp. 271. $18 ISBN 8 1857 5377 6.

Rubik, Margarete, and Elke Mettinger-Shartmann, eds. *A Breath of Fresh Eyre: Intertextual and Intermedial Reworkings of Jane Eyre*. Rodopi. [2007] pp. 418. £60 ISBN 9 7890 4202 2126.

Sahu, Nandini. *The Post-Colonial Space: Writing the Self and the Nation*. Atlantic. [2007] pp. xxxii + 192. £25 ISBN 8 1269 0777 0.

Sankaran, Chitra. *Myth Connections: The Use of Hindu Myths and Philosophies in R.K. Narayan and Raja Rao*. Lang. [2007] pp. 326. £42.80 ISBN 3 0391 1322 4.

Scott, Shelley. *The Violent Woman as a New Theatrical Character Type*. Mellen. [2007] pp. 112. $99.95 ISBN 0 7734 5445 4.

Srivastava, Neelam. *Secularism in the Postcolonial India Novel: National and Cosmopolitan Narratives in English*. Routledge. [2007] pp. 210. £60 ISBN 0 4154 0295 8.

Stähler, Axel, ed. *Anglophone Jewish Literature*. Routledge. [2007] pp. xiv + 290. $150 ISBN 9 7804 1541 4647.

Tickell, Alex. *Arundhati Roy's The God of Small Things*. Guides to Literature. Routledge. [2007] pp. 183. £55 ISBN 0 4153 5842 2.

Tompkins, Joanne. *Unsettling Space: Contestations in Contemporary Australian Theatre*. Palgrave Macmillan. [2006] pp. xii + 204. €48 ISBN 9 7814 0398 5620.

Trikha, Pradeep. *Delphic Intimations: Dialogues with Australian Writers and Critics*. Sarup. [2007] pp. xvi + 191. $12 ISBN 8 1762 5743 5.

Vambe, Maurice Taonezvi. *African Oral Story-Telling Tradition and the Zimbabwean Novel in English*. UnisaP. [2004] pp. 130. $22.95 ISBN 1 8688 8304 3.

van Toorn, Penny. *Writing Never Arrives Naked: Early Aboriginal Cultures of Writing in Australia*. AStP. [2006] pp. ix + 270. $A32.95 ISBN 9 7808 5575 5447.

Vernay, Jean-François. *Water from the Moon: Illusion and Reality in the Works of Australian Novelist Christopher Koch*. Cambria. [2007] pp. xxii + 200. $239.95 ISBN 9 7819 3404 3356.

Vijayasree, C., Meenakshi Mukherjee, Harish Trivedi and T. Vijay Kumar, eds. *Nation in Imagination: Essays on Nationalism, Sub-Nationalisms and Narration*. Orient Longman. [2007] pp. xvi + 274. Rs850 ISBN 8 1250 3363 7.

Whittaker, David, and Msiska Mpalive-Hangson. *Chinua Achebe's Things Fall Apart*. Routledge. [2007] pp. 145. £9.99 ISBN 9 7804 1534 4562.

Wilson, Janet, ed. *The Gorse Blooms Pale: Dan Davin's Southland Stories*. UOtagoP. [2007] pp. 314. NZ$49.95 ISBN 9 7818 7737 2421.

Wyile, Herb, ed. *Speaking in the Past Tense: Canadian Novelists on Writing Historical Fiction*. WLUP. [2007] pp. 327. $26.95 ISBN 0 8892 0511 6.

XVIII

Bibliography and Textual Criticism

WILLIAM BAKER

The Papers of the Bibliographical Society of America (*PBSA* 101[2007]) running true to form, contains some fascinating and important contributions. Lynette Hunter's 'Adaptation and/or Revision in Early Quartos of *Romeo and Juliet*' (*PBSA* 101:i[2007] 5–54) contains a thorough investigation of 'the interrelationship between the [four] quarto texts' (p. 7) of *Romeo and Juliet*. In doing so, Hunter provides a most informative account of previous textual and editorial scholarship. Her focus is theatrical practice, and she concludes 'The relationship between Q1 and Q2 *Romeo and Juliet* does not require "solving," nor can it be "solved" by thinking about theatre practice, but the impact of the theatre may provide a further site for talking about the cultural materiality of the text' (p. 54).

YWES readers hardly need reminding that Jane Millgate has produced extremely important work in the field of Sir Walter Scott scholarship and early nineteenth-century publishing history. Indeed, her *Union Catalogue of Walter Scott Correspondence* may be found on the National Library of Scotland website: www.nls.uk/catalogues/resources/scott/index.html. This most generous of scholars has provided yet another important addition to our knowledge of Scott's relationships with his publishers. Her 'The Name of the Author: Additional Light on the Publication of *Ivanhoe* and the Scott–Constable Relationship' (*PBSA* 101:i[2007] 55–62) draws upon publishing agreements found in the Pierpont Morgan and the National Library of Scotland to illuminate the relationship between Scott and his publisher Archibald Constable.

Another productive and helpful scholar, Stephen Enniss, draws upon materials at the Robert W. Woodruff Library at Emory University (Enniss is the director of the wonderful special collections and archives at the university) to further inform us, in his 'Sylvia Plath, Ted Hughes, and the Myth of Textual Betrayal' (*PBSA* 101:i[2007] 63–71) of the complex relationship between Sylvia

The writer wishes to thank Professors Robin Alston, James E. May, David L. Vander Meulen and Patrick Scott for their help with this chapter.

Plath and Ted Hughes. A totally different terrain is the concern of Robert D. Armstrong in his ' "I scornfully rejected the terms": Wyoming Territory's Public Printing, 1870–74' (*PBSA* 101:i[2007] 73–89). Armstrong's work has some exceedingly lengthy footnotes containing no doubt fascinating data for those who can wade through them—see for instance note 19 on page 85!

The indefatigable Arthur Sherbo continues his explorations of 'Restoring Malone' in (*PBSA* 101:ii[2007] 125–48). On this occasion his concern is with restoring Malone's observations in his appendix to 'Volume 11 in the 1778 Johnson–Steevens *Shakespeare*, i.e., the first of the two volumes of Malone's *Supplement* thereof (1780)' (p. 127). Robert D. Armstrong continues his investigation of public printing in the western territories of what is now the United States in his ' "We have seen many a worse job done 'further east' ": Dakota's Public Printing; 1862–3' (*PBSA* 101:ii[2007] 149–66). An aspect of American nineteenth-century publishing also engages Gregory Jones and Jane Brown's 'Wilhelm Busch's Merry Thoughts: His Early Books in Britain and America' (*PBSA* 101:ii[2007] 167–204). Wilhelm Busch (1832–1908) was a German 'artist and writer from the small German kingdom of Hanover'. He had a very important influence on children's books, including *Max and Maurice*, first published in America in 1871 and his *Gingerbread* first published by Routledge in 1874. A different continent and universe is covered in Lishi Kwasitsu's 'Publishing in Victoria, Australia, 1851–1900' (*PBSA* 101:ii[2007] 205–20): 'The purpose of this study is to determine the print culture productivity, subject matter, and language distribution of the literature published locally by the pioneering settlers in the State of Victoria' (p. 205).

Kathleen Lynch's 'Religious Identity, Stationers' Company Politics, and Three Printers of *Eikon Basilike*' (*PBSA* 101:iii[2007] 285–312) draws upon printers' biographies in the *Oxford Dictionary of National Biography* in order to add to our knowledge of the printing of the *Eikon Basilike* in the middle of the seventeenth century. Arthur Sherbo's 'Edmond Malone and the Johnson–Steevens 1778 *Shakespeare*' (*PBSA* 101:iii[2007] 313–28) continues his explorations into Edmund Malone's publishing activities. Sherbo provides an extensive appendix, listing Malone's contribution to notes on individual Shakespearian plays (pp. 322–8). Norbert Schürer's 'Four Catalogues of the Lowndes Circulating Library, 1755–66' (*PBSA* 101:iii[2007] 329–58) enhances our knowledge of eighteenth-century English circulating libraries by drawing upon catalogues from the 1755–66 period.

The final number to appear in 2007 of the *PBSA* includes two contributions of direct interest to *YWES* readers and two which deal with German and French book history. Bettina Wagner's *PSA* annual address, 'Collecting, Cataloguing, and Digitizing Incunabula at the Bayerische Staatsbibliothek Munich' (*PBSA* 101:iv[2007] 451–79) is fully illustrated and of considerable interest to students of incunabula. Christopher Hunter's 'From Print to Print: The First Complete Edition of Benjamin Franklin's *Autobiography*' (*PBSA* 101:iv[2007] 481–505) draws upon marked up copies at the Library Company of Philadelphia to illuminate a fascinating printing history. Eli MacLaren's 'The Magnification of Ralph Connor: *Black Rock* and the North American Copyright Divide' (*PBSA* 101:iv[2007] 507–31) throws further light on the publishing career of the Canadian Charles William

Gordon (1860–1937)—'Ralph Connor'—and the 'copyright divide' between Canada and the United States of America in the nineteenth and twentieth centuries (p. 531). Finally, Thierry Rigogne's 'Printers into Booksellers: The Structural Transformation of the French Trades in the Age of Enlightenment' (*PBSA* 101:iv[2007] 533–61) goes some of the way to answering the important question, 'How did print spread to become a major force in eighteenth-century France?' (p. 533). In conclusion, volume 101 of *PBSA* contains the usual thorough book reviews and includes Paul Needham's review essay on 'The Bodleian Library Incunables' (*PBSA* 101:iii[2007] 359–409)—an extensive account of fifteenth-century incunabula at the Bodleian Library and elsewhere. The immediate context for Needham's learned review article is the publication of the six volumes of *A Catalogue of Books Printed in the Fifteenth Century Now in the Bodleian Library* by the Oxford University Press in 2005.

The latest volume of *Studies in Bibliography* (*SB* 57[2005–6]) has a 2008 imprint on the verso of its title page. G. Thomas Tanselle's opening essay, 'The Textual Criticism of Visual and Aural Works' (*SB* 57[2005–6] 1–37), is somewhat shorter than usual. Divided into sections focusing upon music, dance, film, video and digital art, drama and performance art, painting, drawing and calligraphy, sculpture, craft and installation art, architecture, interior design and gardening, print-making, photography and book design, Tanselle's observations 'are intended to illustrate a way of thinking, not to be comprehensive'. He stresses 'interdependence' reflecting 'the fact that all the arts are related and that thinking about the textual criticism of one art can clarify the thinking about others, including those' he has 'not touched on, such as the olfactory and gustatory arts' (p. 37). Somewhat curiously and unusually, the article lacks footnote notation or bibliographical references.

Paul Needham's 'Martin Boghardt: A Memoir' (*SB* 57[2005–6] 39–62) considers the life and work of 'Martin Boghardt [1936–98] one of the most wide-ranging and creative bibliographers of the post-World War II era' (p. 39). Although Boghardt's work was initially published in German, it has, as Needham demonstrates, relevance beyond its original language and to bibliography generally. An appendix contains an enumerative listing with some brief annotations of 'A Selection of Martin Boghardt's Major Bibliographical Writings' (pp. 60–2). Ralph Hanna's 'Verses in Sermons Again: The Case of Cambridge, Jesus College, MS Q.A. 13' (*SB* 57[2005–6] 63–83) begins with a consideration of the significance of 'Carleton Brown's contributions to the study of the early English lyric [which] remain monumental' (p. 63). However, Hanna's article 'resuscitate[s] from Brown's handling' (p. 64) the Jesus College, Cambridge MS Q.A. 13, and the conclusion of Hanna's article consists of a fresh transcription with notations of the verses found in the transcript (pp. 74–83).

Conor Fahy's 'Royal-Paper Copies of Aldine Editions, 1494–1550' (*SB* 57[2005–6] 85–113) is accompanied by five black and white illustrative figures and focuses upon Aldine editions found at the Harry Ransom Humanities Research Center at the University of Texas at Austin, at the British Library and elsewhere. An appendix lists the locations of 'Royal-Paper Copies of Aldine Octavo Editions' divided into dates: from 1514 to 1534, and 1535 to

1550 (pp. 107–11). The article concludes with a detailed alphabetically arranged listing of works cited (pp. 111–13). Andrew Zurcher's 'Printing *The Faerie Queene* in 1590' (*SB* 57[2005–6] 115–50) is a sustained account of the 1590 printing of *The Faerie Queene* and a review of previous work on the subject, especially that undertaken by F.R. Johnson and Hiroshi Yamashita. The amount of detail may be found in Zurcher's first table 'Running-titles and compositorial stints in *The Faerie Queene*, 1590' enumerated in terms of outer and inner form signatures (pp. 126–7). Zurcher provides a 'Summary of the order of printing *The Faerie Queene*, 1590' (p. 149). After all his detail, the conclusion is rather curious. Zurcher begins his final paragraph with an unanswered question. 'Is it possible that I have created here merely another insubstantial "house of cards" neatly but inconsequentially constructed from a chain of supposals?' His final sentence reads, 'A house of *cards* is also sometimes a *house* of cards' (p. 148, 150).

R. Carter Hailey's 'The Shakespearian Pavier Quartos Revisited' (*SB* 57[2005–6] 151–95) contains an account of Carter Hailey's examination of 'about 180 individual Pavier quartos—between fifteen and twenty-three copies each of the nine quartos, or five times the number of copies that Greg had seen'. Hailey's essential point is that following 'a fresh examination of the papers of the Pavier quartos' (pp. 153–4) the state of affairs is much more complex than Greg ever imagined and 'by tracing the complex patterns of the paper stocks [Carter Hailey is] able to provide new insights into the order and method of the printing of the Pavier quartos'. In a series of appendices (pp. 179–95), Carter Hailey provides 'Sequence Tables: Watermarks by Gatherings in the Plays' (pp. 179–83); 'Summary Tables: Watermarks in Individual Plays' (pp. 184–90); 'Summary Table: Watermarks in All Plays' (pp. 191–2); and a listing of 'Copies Examined' with their locations (pp. 192–5). Carter Hailey's is analytical bibliography at its most impressive: in short, the real thing.

E. Derek Taylor's 'Mary Astell's Work Toward a New Edition of *A Serious Proposal to the Ladies, Part II*' (*SB* 57[2005–6] 197–232) considers the work of Mary Astell (1666–1731) and her attempt to produce a new edition of her first published work *A Serious Proposal to the Ladies* [1694]. A detailed appendix (pp. 209–31) contains the text of her proposal. Jiaming Han's 'Henry Fielding in China' (*SB* 57[2005–6] 233–41) is a clear account of what its title suggests, accompanied by a listing of 'Chinese Translations of Fielding's Works' arranged by title and then by date (pp. 240–1). Thomas F. Bonnell's 'When Book History Neglects Bibliography: Trouble with the "Old Canon" in *The Reading Nation*' (*SB* 57[2005–6] 243–61) is a corrective to claims made and errors in William St Clair's *The Reading Nation in the Romantic Period* [2004].

In Stephen Karian's 'Authors of the Mind: Some Notes on the QSUM Attribution Theory' (*SB* 57[2005–6] 263–86), Karian considers 'the attribution theory known as cusum analysis' that is abbreviated in his article as QSUM (p. 264). Replete with statistical data, including stylometrical analysis from Jill Farringdon's *Analyzing for Authorship: A Guide to the Cusum Technique* [1996], the article reveals the limitation of Farringdon's samples and Karian proposes tests of his own. His article is accompanied by figures, statistical examples and graphs. In his conclusion, Karian writes that 'any quantitative attribution method that purports to be valid must define terms precisely and use statistical concepts in an appropriate manner. It should also offer a theoretical justification.' He hopes that the scepticism exhibited in his article will 'decrease irresponsible claims of authorship' (pp. 285–6). All in all, a very sobering account. It is somewhat of a relief, perhaps to turn to the final contribution, David Leon Hidgon and Russell (Rusty) Reed's '"Telling it unabridged": Graham Swift's Revision of *Waterland*' (*SB* 57[2005–6] 287–98). This clearly distinguishes between various editions of Graham Swift's *Waterland*, first published in 1983. It is salutary to be reminded that since 1992, with the appearance of a second version of the novel, 'discussions, interpretations and generalizations about [its] literary worth and its significance to literary movements have often been using a text to *Waterland* that differs significantly from the one used by the earlier reviewers, historians and theoreticians'. The reasons for this are that 'while reading proofs for the second British Edition, Swift was tempted into making numerous revisions, unguided by any articulated plan' (pp. 287–8). This volume of *Studies in Bibliography* contains two articles, those by Needham and Fahy, of essays that have appeared in other languages. Both are in revised form and probably would not otherwise have been noted. The volume's chronological range and serious temper, replete with a depth of bibliographical analysis of one kind or another, are not only a tribute to *Studies in Bibliography* and its editor, but reveal that serious bibliography in its various incarnations is very much alive, well and flourishing.

Book History (10[2007]), edited by Ezra Greenspan and Jonathan Rose, contains eleven articles of varying interest to *YWES* readers. Laura Cruz's 'The Secrets of Success: Microinventions and Bookselling in the Seventeenth-Century Netherlands' (*BoH* 10[2007] 1–28) may not be of immediate interest, but 'The Diffusion of Second Hand Book Auctions in the United Provinces' (p. 5), 'Bankruptcies and Book Auctions in Leiden, 1657–1698' (p. 15), and five other similar tabulations, could equally be applied to British and American bookselling activities. Of more immediate relevance is Jeffrey Glover's 'Thomas Lechford's *Plain Dealing*: Censorship and Cosmopolitan Print Culture in the English Atlantic' (*BoH* 10[2007] 29–46). Glover focuses upon the activities of Thomas Lechford and the circulation of his *Plain Dealing; or, News from New England*. This was written in Boston and in London and printed in London in two editions, the first in 1642, followed by a second edition two years later. The work 'is a report on colonial, civil and ecclesiastical institutions published by Lechford upon his reimmigration to England in 1641 after having fallen out with Bay Colony authorities' (p. 30).

Richard Yeo's 'Lost Encyclopedias: Before and After the Enlightenment' (*BoH* 10[2007] 47–68) focuses upon an idea that, as he correctly points out, in the world of the internet we are in danger of losing 'the reference function of encyclopedias' (p. 62). Keri A. Berg's 'Contesting the Page: The Author and the Illustrator in France, 1830–1848' (*BoH* 10[2007] 69–102) has relevance also to the activities across the Channel during the same period. Matt Miller's 'Composing the First *Leaves of Grass*: How Whitman Used his Early Notebooks' (*BoH* 10[2007] 103–30) is an extensive analysis of 'Whitman's attitudes towards language and artistic purpose...rooted in his discovery of

a process of composition' and his use of notebooks (p. 126). Solveig C.
Robinson's '"Sir, it is an outrage": George Bentley, Robert Black, and the
Condition of the Mid-List Author in Victorian Britain' (*BoH* 10[2007] 131–68)
resurrects the career of Robert Black (1829–1915) based upon his correspondence with his publisher George Bentley (1828–95) now in the Bentley Papers
in the British Library.

Shafquat Towheed's 'Geneva v. Saint Petersburg: Two Concepts of Literary
Property and Material Lives of Books in *Under Western Eyes*' (*BoH* 10[2007]
169–92) illuminates 'some of the contingencies of the composition, production,
and dissemination of [Joseph Conrad's] *Under Western Eyes*' (p. 186). Erin A.
Smith's '"What would Jesus do?"': The Social Gospel and the Literary
Marketplace' (*BoH* 10[2007] 193–221), on the other hand, casts an investigative eye upon 'three of the post popular social gospel novels, Mrs Humphry
Ward's *Robert Elsmere* [1888], [Charles Sheldon's] *In his Steps* and Winston
Churchill's *Inside of the Cup* [1913], all of which self-consciously represent
different modes of reading and writing in order to demonstrate the porousness
of the boundaries between literature and life for good Christian readers'
(p. 194). In places, Smith's analysis could do with less ponderous sentences,
and clarification of terminology.

The remaining three contributions may only seem to be of marginal interest
to *YWES* readers. Matthew Fishburn's 'Books Are Weapons: Wartime
Responses to the Nazi Bookfires of 1933' (*BoH* 10[2007] 223–51) deals with a
depressing subject yet has moving things to say about Anglo-American
reactions, including those of George Orwell, and Archibald MacLeish. The
other two essays focus upon China. Cynthia Brokaw, in her 'Book History in
Premodern China: The State of the Discipline I' (*BoH* 10[2007] 253–90), covers
a lot of ground. Her article is accompanied by 116 footnotes. Christopher
Reed's 'Modern Chinese Print and Publishing Culture: The State of the
Discipline II' (*BoH* 10[2007] 291–316) has only eighty-six footnotes.

The *Rare Book Review* contains the usual miscellany of materials of often
varying quality, most well illustrated, but of some interest to literary critics
and scholars and those who wish to keep up with what's going on in the rare
book and antiquarian world. Justin G. Schiller's 'The Tale of Beatrix Potter'
(*RBR* 33:vi[2006–7] 14–19) reviews a collection of works that established her
reputation, and his article concludes with a listing of 'Buying and Selling
Beatrix Potter', beginning with the privately printed *The Tale of Peter Rabbit*
[1901] of which there were only 250 copies, a flat spine, and monochrome
plates. This is priced at £65,000. On the other hand, *The Tale of Tupenny*,
published by Warne in 1973 and illustrated by Marie Angel, can be had for as
little as £5 and as much as £30 (p. 18). R.M. Healy's 'The Appliance of
Science' (*RBR* 33:vi[2006–7] 20–3) looks at the Royal Society Library. Sara
Waterson's 'Daylight Lottery' (*RBR* 33:vi[2006–7] 26–30) focuses mainly on
recent acquisitions of papers by Seamus Heaney and Salman Rushdie to be
found at the Emory Library in Atlanta. Diana Parikian's 'It Is Really
a Question of your Nose' (*RBR* 33:vi[2006–7] 35–7) is a conversation with the
distinguished bookseller and specialist in neo-Latin Renaissance literature and
other areas on the occasion of her eightieth birthday. The examination of the
surfaces of stuck down papers engages Ian Christie-Miller in 'Back to Basics'

(*RBR* 33:vi[2006–7] 43–6). Finally, the allusive Frederick Rolfe is the subject of Robert Scoble's 'The Sum of its Parts' (*RBR* 33:vi[2006–7] 48–51).

Censorship is the subject of Tabitha Barda's 'Bonfire of the Liberties' (*RBR* 34:i[2007] 16–25). Karen Cass's 'A Matter of Trust' (*RBR* 34:i[2007] 26–9) explores the riches of the Blickling Hall Library near Aylsham in Norfolk. Sara Waterson's 'A Matter of Trust' (*RBR* 34:i[2007] 31–5) continues her investigation into the buying power of US institutions when it comes to acquiring UK authors' collections (p. 31). The centenary of the birth of the poet provides the opportunity for R.M. Healey's 'Auden: Birth of a Poetic Superstar' (*RBR* 34:i[2007] 38–41). Hugo Worthy's 'The Player' (*RBR* 34:i[2007] 46–9), in addition to providing details of the British publication information of the plays of Joe Orton (1933–67), reassesses 'the extraordinary life' of the dramatist who is 'an inspiration for potential collectors' (p. 49).

The anonymously authored 'Austen Towers' (*RBR* 34:ii[2007] 12–13) provides a checklist 'of the UK's top 100 books, with *Pride and Prejudice* topping the list' (p. 13). Dr Seuss is the subject of Stanley Campbell's apparently wittily entitled 'Still Feline Fine' (*RBR* 34:ii[2007] 16–19). Anti-slavery writing by women is the topic of Elizabeth Crawford's 'Oh, let us rise and burst the Negro's chains; Yes, sisters, yes, to us the task belongs' (*RBR* 34:ii[2007] 20–4). Miniature books engage Sandra Hindman in her 'Reading the Small Print' (*RBR* 34:ii[2007] 44–8). Richard Davies's 'Like a Rowling Stone' (*RBR* 34:iii[2007] 16–19) looks at the mania surrounding and highly inflated prices fetched by the works of J.K. Rowling. Felbrigg Hall Library in Norfolk is the subject of Karen Cass's 'Keep It in the Family' (*RBR* 34:iii[2007] 28–32). Thomas Venning's 'The Autograph Man' (*RBR* 34:iii[2007] 36–40) attempts to explain that 'in the world of signed letters . . . all is not in the name' (p. 36). Annette Campbell-White, in her 'The Thrill of the Chase' (*RBR* 34:iii[2007] 46–9) explains why, after thirty years, she is now selling her collection based upon Cyril Connolly's *The Modern Movement: One Hundred Key Books from England, France and America 1880–1950*.

The death of Kurt Vonnegut at the age of 84 leads the August–September issue of (*RBR* 34:iv[2007] 10–11). The anonymous obituary is accompanied by a bibliography with pricing. Nicola Lisle's 'There and Back Again' (*RBR* 34:iv[2007] 22–6) reflects upon 'the enduring popularity of Bilbo Baggins and friends' (p. 22). R.M. Healy's 'Built to Last' (*RBR* 34:iv[2007] 28–31) considers the library of the Institution of Civil Engineers. Michou Gerits's 'Beat the Clock' (*RBR* 34:v[2007] 20–2) considers Jack Kerouac's *On the Road* fifty years after its initial publication. The article is accompanied by a useful 'Buying & Selling Jack Kerouac' (1922–69) (p. 22). The library of Denis Healey is the subject of his nephew R.M. Healey's 'A Labour of Love' (*RBR* 34:v[2007] 24–8). John Updike's prolific output concerns Stanley Campbell in his 'The Never-Ending Story' (*RBR* 34:v[2007] 32–6). This in effect is a review of Jack De Bellis and Michael Broomfield's magnificent *John Updike: A Bibliography of Primary and Secondary Materials, 1948–2007*.

Stanley Campbell's 'The Most Dangerous Man in England' (*RBR* 34:vi[2007] 20–3) is devoted to the work of Philip Pullman and contains a 'Buying & Selling Philip Pullman (b 1946)' (p. 23). James Sprague in an interview with B.T. Wolfe entitled 'People do tend to get more eccentric the longer they work at Henry Sotheran Ltd' (*RBR* 34:vi[2007] 46–52), apart from describing some of the characters who work there, does deal with the history of the distinguished London bookshop. There isn't space other than to mention contributions such as R.M. Healey's 'The Chamber of Secrets' (*RBR* 34:vi[2007] 26–31), which is a peep into the holdings at the magic circle, or Sandra Hindman's lavishly illustrated 'Times to Remember' (*RBR* 34:v[2007] 40–5), which looks at Books of Hours. Before concluding this survey of *RBR* for 2007, it should be added that in addition to its superb colour illustrations, there is an auction diary, affairs diary, auction previews and other news.

Volume 56:i[Spring 2007] of *The Book Collector* opens with an extensive essay by David McKitterick (*BC* 56:i[2007] 11–30) on 'New Needs in Libraries'. This is a judicious, historically based reflection upon the current situation in university libraries. Terry L. Meyers's ' "*Will Drew and Phil Crewe & Frank Fane*": A Swinburne Enigma'(*BC* 56:i[2007] 31–3) throws light upon a pamphlet that 'manifests the impish wit of two Swinburne enthusiasts, [Cecil Y.] Lang and John S. Mayfield' (p. 31): apparently only four copies of *Will Drew and Phil Crewe & Frank Fane* have come to light in what 'was a good joke' (p. 33). Dick Veneman's 'Joseph Strutt's *Dictionary of Engravers*' (*BC* 56:i[2007] 35–48), accompanied by four rather gruesome illustrations, examines the work of Joseph Strutt (1749–1802), and in particular his *A Biographical Dictionary; containing an Historical Account of all the Engravers, from the Earliest Period of the Art of Engraving to the Present Time*, published in two volumes in 1785 and 1786. Jeff Siemers's 'From Generation to Generation: The Story of the Stockbridge Bible' (*BC* 56:i[2007] 49–66) is a discussion of the Bible that 'belongs to the Stockbridge-Munsee band of Mohican Indians... kept in a museum on their reservation in northern Wisconsin', and is 'cherished from generation to generation' (p. 65). Robert Scoble's 'The Corvine Banquets of 1929' (*BC* 56:i[2007] 66–74) is another examination of the life of Frederick Rolfe or 'Baron Corvo'. In addition to the regular items found in each issue of *The Book Collector*, an extensive review of current bibliographical catalogues, in this case running from pages 89 to 103, 'News and Comment' (*BC* 56:i[2007] 105–28), 'Exhibitions and Catalogues' (*BC* 56:i[2007] 129–33), there are 'Obituaries'. This issue covers Rodney Dennis (1930–2006) the curator of manuscripts at Harvard's Houghton Library (*BC* 56:i[2007] 134–6), David MacNaughton (1937–2006; *BC* 56:i[2007] 136–7), 'one of the best-known figures in the Scottish second-hand book trade' (p. 136), Bent Juel-Jensen (1922–2006; *BC* 56:i[2007] 137–41), a Danish physician who had a 'long and very distinguished medical career in Oxford' (p. 138), and who was a great bibliophile and bibliographer as well as a book collector. There are the usual thorough book reviews concluding each issue of *The Book Collector*.

The Summer 2007 issue leads with a brief editorial, 'The Fifteenth-Century Book in Britain' (*BC* 56:ii[2007] 175–6), followed by A.S.G. Edwards's extensive discussion, 'Incunabula in England' (*BC* 56:ii[2007] 179–89), Martin Davies writes on '*BMC XI*' (*BC* 56:ii[2007] 191–9). Margaret Lane Ford's 'English Incunabula in the Sixteenth-Century Book Trade' (*BC* 56:ii[2007] 201–11) also draws upon the recent publication of Lotte Hellinga's *A Catalogue of Books Printed in the Fifteenth Century Now in the British*

Library—Part XI: England [2007]. A different century and different topic preoccupies Timothy d'Arch Smith's 'Aleister Crowley's *Aceldama* (1898): The "AB" Copy' (*BC* 56:ii[2007] 213–37). Arch Smith investigates vellum copies of Aleister Crowley's (1875–1947) first book, focusing upon two copies at the Warburg Institute Library at the University of London, and another in private hands. 'Obituaries' extend from Catherine Devas (no dates given), 'who founded the Panizzi Lectures' (*BC* 56:ii[2007] 281), Henri-Jean Martin (1924–2007; *BC* 56:ii[2007] 281–3) whose *L'Apparition du livre* [1958], lamely translated into English as *The Coming of the Book* [1976], was 'a miraculous book about a miraculous event' (p. 281), Elizabeth Greenhill (1907–2006; *BC* 56:ii[2007] 284–5), who 'For almost 60 years... devoted her life to making and restoring beautiful books' (p. 284), and Frank Seton (1918–2007; *BC* 56:ii[2007] 285–6), a professional performer and obsessive collector, who was, in the words of Brian Lake, 'a genuinely nice person, someone who it was always a pleasure to anticipate meeting, always a pleasure to meet—full of generous gestures, jokes and bonhomie' (p. 286).

Volume 56:iii[Autumn 2007] leads with an unsigned account of 'American Libraries' (*BC* 56:iii[2007] 311–27), stimulated by the 2007 publication of Richard Wendorf's *America's Membership Libraries* and Samuel Streit and Philip Cronenwett's *Celebrating Research*. Donald Kerr's 'Esmond de Beer: Portrait of a Bibliophile XXXIX' (*BC* 56:iii[2007] 329–51) is accompanied by seven illustrations of books de Beer collected, found today in Special Collections in the de Beer Collection at the University of Otago. There are also two photographs of de Beer, the second with his two sisters (pp. 332–3). De Beer (1895–1990), who inherited money, was born in Dunedin: his uncle Willie was a connoisseur-collector. De Beer's father moved to London in 1910, where he lived until 1990. It hardly need be said that he was a great, and obsessive, book collector and scholar, whose 'definitive six-volume edition of *The Diary of John Evelyn*' was published in 1955 (p. 334). He also collected Evelyn and John Locke amongst others. Paul A. Marquis's 'Editing and Unediting Richard Tottel's *Songes and Sonettes*' (*BC* 56:iii[2007] 353–75) is a thorough 'reassessment of the work completed by Tottel in 1557' (p. 374). There are two obituaries: Brian North Lee (1936–2007), who was addicted to the collection of book plates, and the eminent bibliographer and librarian B.J. Kirkpatrick (1919–2007) (*BC* 56:iii[2007] 431–5).

Volume 56:iv begins with the lengthy, unsigned and informative 'Balsamo, Fahy and Other Heroes of Modern Italy' (*BC* 56:iv[2007] 467–92), which is in fact a tribute to the eightieth birthday celebrations of Luigi Balsamo and Connor Fahy. Nicholas Barker explores 'The Bishop Phillpotts Library, Truro' (*BC* 56:iv[2007] 493–500) and Marvin Spevack 'The Disraeli Library at Hughenden Manor—Owners and Bookplates' (*BC* 56:iv[2007] 501–14). This is accompanied by five illustrative figures of the great man's bookplates (p. 502). Stephen Parkin is preoccupied with 'The Library of Pietro Bembo' (*BC* 56:iv[2007] 515–21), which in fact is a review of Massimo Danzi's *La biblioteca del Cardinal Pietro Bembo* [2005]. Bembo's library provides an insight into Italian libraries of the mid-sixteenth century. An annual feature of the winter issue of *The Book Collector* is the 'Christmas Catalogue' (*BC* 56:iv[2007] 523–48). If readers of *YWES* want a good chuckle, this is bound to provide it, although some of the jokes are far too recondite for the present writer! There are two obituaries. The first is devoted to Jacques Vellekoop (1926–2007; *BC* 56:iv[2007] 584–6), who 'had a distinctive place in the antiquarian book-trade, for almost forty [years], a commanding one' (p. 584). The second focuses upon the beloved and great Australian scholar of the seventeenth century, Harold Love (1937–2007; *BC* 56:iv[2007] 586–8). Harold was a most generous of eminent scholars and exceedingly humble. In short, as usual, *The Book Collector* is full of fascinating, informative information. As yet, it has not gone online. Long may this singular act of defiance continue.

The Library: The Transactions of the Bibliographical Society, eighth series [2007], maintains on a quarterly basis, its consistently high standards. John L. Flood's ' "Foreshortened in the tract of time": Towards a Bio-Bibliography of Poets Laureate in the Holy Roman Empire" (*Library* 8:i[2007] 3–24) is interesting for the idea of the laureation of poets. John L. Horden's 'The Publication of the Early Editions of Francis Quarles's *Emblemes* (1635) and *Hieroglyphikes* (1638)' (*Library* 8:i[2007] 25–32) continues his investigation of the publication of seventeenth-century emblem poetry and in particular the work of Francis Quarles (1592–1644). Pat Rogers, in his 'George Parker, Defoe, and the Whitefriars Trade: A "Lost" Edition of *A Tour thro' Great Britain*' (*Library* 8:i[2007] 35–9), examines the first reprinting (in 1734) of Defoe's *Tour thro' the Whole Island of Great Britain* [1724–6] issued in serial parts in a newspaper and then in volume form and published by George Parker (1654–1743). A different century preoccupies Randolph Ivy's 'M.E. Braddon in the 1860s: Clarifications and Corrections' (*Library* 8:i[2007] 60–9). Ivy in fact indicates inaccuracies in Robert Lee Wolfe's standard *Nineteenth-Century Fiction: A Bibliographical Catalogue* [1981–6] in its account of the novels of M.E. Braddon (1835–1915).

Maria Wakely's 'Printing and Double-Dealing in Jacobean England: Robert Barker, John Bill, and Bonham Norton' (*Library* 8:ii[2007] 119–53) is an account of competition in the London printing trade for business during the first thirty years of the seventeenth century. It is also an account of scurrilous and nefarious activities. In short, a fascinating read. Rosemary Dixon's 'The Publishing of John Tillotson's Collected Works, 1695–1757' (*Library* 8:ii[2007] 154–81) examines the publishing history of a somewhat neglected eminent prose writer, Archbishop John Tillotson (1630–94). David J. Shaw's bibliographical note, 'Serialization of *Moll Flanders* in *The London Post* and *The Kentish Post*' (*Library* 8:ii[2007] 182–92), utilizes four recently uncovered issues of the *Kentish Post*, published in 1722, that contain a serialization of Defoe's *Moll Flanders* as the basis for a discussion of the serialization of novels in 1720s newspapers. Tom Davis, in a very important article, 'The Practice of Handwriting Identification' (*Library* 8:iii[2007] 251–76), discusses in some considerable detail the methodology used for analysing handwriting in order to determine a writer's identity. Davis also explains the problems and limitations involved. Some of the limitations can be overcome through the use of web-based analyses. As he says in his conclusion, 'The comparison of handwriting for identification is not a mystery, nor an art form; it can be learned, from the observation of the practice in others.' Until recently, 'details of the forensic practice' have been restricted. Nowadays, it is easier 'to do so: to expose all of the evidence, and all of the opinions based on that evidence, so that anyone interested can observe, criticize, disagree, improve, and learn' (p. 276). As stated, the important of Davis's article should not be underestimated, especially as it deals with information that was hitherto restricted. A totally different subject and area is the concern of M.O. Grenby's 'Chapbooks, Children, and Children's Literature' (*Library* 8:iii[2007] 277–303), which scrutinizes assumptions concerning a relationship between children and chapbooks.

Michael Johnston's 'A New Document Relating to the Life of Robert Thornton' (*Library* 8:iii[2007] 304–13) is informative about the life of 'perhaps the most well-known manuscript compiler of late medieval England' (p. 304) about whom all too little is known. Gary Schneider's 'Thomas Forde, Stationers' Company Apprentice and Author: New Information about his Life and Work' (*Library* 8:iii[2007] 314–24) illuminates the life and work of Thomas Forde (b. 1624), who wrote *The Times Anatomiz'd in Severall Characters* [1647], *Lusus Fortunae* [1649] and *Virtus Rediviva* [1660–1]. Robin Alston, in an extensive review article, '*The Cambridge History of Libraries in Britain and Ireland*' (*Library* 8:iii[2007] 325–36), assesses the achievement of the publication of the three-volume *Cambridge History of Libraries in Britain and Ireland* [2006]. Alston writes that it 'is without doubt a major contribution to library history; but it might have been ultimately more useful if it had attempted less to summarize what was already known and to include more that was not generally known' (p. 336).

Stephen Tabor's 'ESTC and the Bibliographical Community' (*Library* 8:iv[2007] 367–86) is a thorough, clearly written analysis of the usage of the *English Short-Title Catalogue* freely available on the web. Peter W.M. Blayney's 'STC Publication Statistics: Some Caveats' (*Library* 8:iv[2007] 387–97) calls into question previous publication statistics for the period 1475–1640. K.A. Manley's 'The Road to Camelot: Lotteries, the Circle of Learning, and the "Circulary" Library of Samuel Fancourt' (*Library* 8:iv[2007] 398–422) shows that apparently long-lived Samuel Fancourt (*c*.1678–1768) was not in fact, as he is commonly believed to be, the founder of the first circulating library in England, and certainly not in London, but confirms that he was the first to use the phrase 'circulating library'. Jane Millgate's 'Unclaimed Territory: The Ballad of "Auld Robin Gray" and the Assertion of Authorial Ownership' (*Library* 8:iv[2007] 423–41) explores the ballad of 'Auld Robin Gray', whose author Lady Anne Lindsay, had decided not to assert her authorship of it when she composed the ballad in 1772. There are of course Sir Walter Scott connections, and it was Sir Walter who in 1823 persuaded Lady Anne to declare her authorship. This was of course disputed. For further information, readers should look at Jane Millgate's fascinating account. As usual, each issue of *The Library* contains reviews and a listing of 'Books Received' and useful enumerative surveys of items in recent periodicals.

Peter Hoare, P.S. Morrish, K.A. Manley and Alistair Black, in their 'Forty Years of *Library History*: The Editors' Testimony' (*LH* 23:i[2007] 3–15) reflect upon the changes in the journal during their editorship and the significant articles they published over the forty-year period. Evelyn Kerslake's ' "They have had to come down to the women for help!'': Numerical Feminization and the Characteristics of Women's Library Employment in England, 1871–1974' (*LH* 23:i[2007] 17–40) provides valuable insight into the late nineteenth-century library world, as well as the subsequent twentieth-century world of library work. Kerslake's analysis contains 164 footnotes and fourteen tables, including those dealing with wages. A different continent and world preoccupy J.E. Traue in his 'Reading as a "Necessity of Life" on the Tuapeka Goldfields in Nineteenth-Century New Zealand' (*LH* 23:i[2007] 41–8). Traue overturns stereotypes concerning mid-nineteenth-century gold rush townships, showing that they were also in places cultural oases and contained reading of various kinds and materials. Clara Cullen's ' "Dublin is also in great need of a library which shall be at once accessible to the public and contain a good supply of modern and foreign books": Dublin's Nineteenth-Century "Public" Libraries' (*LH* 23:i[2007] 49–61) looks at the public library facilities in Dublin in 1850.

Library History 23:ii[2007] is a special issue, edited by W. Boyd Raywood, devoted to North America. Of peripheral interest to *YWES* readers is Peter F. McNally, Glenn Brown and Nicolas Savard's discussion of the book-collecting and bibliographical activities in their 'Sir William Osler, the *Bibliotheca Osleriana* and the Creation of a History of Medicine Collection' (*LH* 23: ii[2007] 97–114). Osler (1849–1919), following a distinguished medical career in Canada and the United States, became Regius Professor at Oxford University; the authors' statistical tables show that 16.83 per cent of his collection consisted of rare literature, 6.90 per cent bibliography, 1.34 per cent incunabula and 2.09 per cent manuscripts. In fact, as tables 3–9 demonstrate, the 105 books in his incunabula collection are of particular interest. He also had an extensive collection of Francis Bacon, Isaac Newton and John Locke, and his eighteenth-century collection extended to Berkeley, Malthus and others. The nineteenth-century collection of course contained Darwin, Huxley and Spencer.

Of interest in the September issue (*LH* 23:iii[2007]) is Anna Carlsson's 'The Geography of Scientific Culture in Early Nineteenth-Century Britain: The Case of Bamburgh Castle Library' (*LH* 23:iii[2007] 179–90), revealing in 1800 an interest among the upper-class borrowers in science. Yet, by 1810, the middle classes had replaced the upper classes as borrowers of scientific books. John Crawford's 'Recovering the Lost Scottish Community Library: The Example of Fenwick' (*LH* 23:iii[2007] 201–12) examines two libraries in Fenwick in Scotland in the early nineteenth century. Felicity Stimpson's ' "I have spent my morning reading Greek": The Marginalia of Sir George Otto Trevelyan' (*LH* 23:iii[2007] 239–50) throws light upon the reading habits of George Otto Trevelyan (1838–1928) by examining his marginalia, to be found at Wallington Hall in Northumberland, which include observations on his reading of each volume of Robert Browning's *The Ring and the Book*. A great favourite was *The Notebooks of Samuel Butler Author of 'Erewhon'*. Novels that elicited marginal comment include Arnold Bennett's *The Old Wives' Tale* and various volumes by Henry James, who in fact was a friend of the Trevelyans. Felicity Stimpson observes, 'The marginalia of Sir George Otto Trevelyan give us a unique insight into the mind and reading practices of a Victorian figure' (p. 249). Volume 23:iv is a special issue devoted to the history of library automation in the UK. Each issue of *Library History* contains reviews. This December 2007 issue has Rebecca Rushforth's review of Michael Lapidge's *The Anglo-Saxon Library* [2006].

Two issues of *Publishing History* published in 2007 have come to the present writer's attention. Susan Drain's 'Family Matters: Margaret Gatty and *Aunt Judy's Magazine*' (*PubH* 61[2007] 5–45) is a thorough examination of *Aunt Judy's Magazine* under the editorship of Mrs Alfred Gatty (1809–73). The journal first appeared in May 1866 and was published by Bell and Daldy, subsequently George Bell and Sons. Drain's attention is to its first seven and a half years, when it came under Mrs Gatty's aegis, although it did survive until 1885. Drain's analysis is accompanied by 162 notes. Frederick Nesta's 'The Myth of the "Triple-Headed Monster": The Economics of the Three-Volume Novel' (*PubH* 61[2007] 47–69) contains two tables, the first outlines the 'Smith, Elder Three-Volume Novel Sales, 1858–1865' (pp. 54–5) and the second 'Novel Production, 1884–1904' (p. 59). Nesta's aim is to 'show that the three-volume novel in fact neither guaranteed profits nor benefited new novelists'. It was an artificially priced format unique to Britain and it was this price and format that would ultimately kill it' (p. 47). Kate MacDonald and Marysa Demoor focus on 'The *Dorothy* and its Supplements: A Late-Victorian Novelette (1889–1899)' (*PubH* 61[2007] 71–101). Their intention is to show that the study 'of journals such as the *Dorothy* [is] necessary for the acquisition for the full picture of print culture at the end of the nineteenth century' (p. 94).

There are four articles of interest in (*PubH* 62[2007]). In the first, Pat Rogers and Paul Baines, in 'Edmund Curll, Citizen and Liveryman: Politics and the Book Trade' (*PubH* 62[2007] 5–40), demonstrate that, especially in the city of London, 'printers, publishers and other members' of the book trade 'had significant contacts with the economic and political life of their time, often interacting regularly with the main power brokers'. The focus of the article is Edmund Curll, bookseller and 'rogue publisher' (p. 5), who was born in 1683 and died in 1747. Rogers and Baines conclude that Curll 'was a maverick, but also arguably something of a quisling, who voted with the dissidents but never hesitated to collude with the powerful' (p. 32). The meat of Ross Alloway's 'Bankrupt Books? The Aftermath of the 1825–6 Crash and the British Book Trade' (*PubH* 62[2007] 41–52) lies in its appendix, which contains a 'List of Bankrupts in the Book and Allied Trades in England and Scotland: 1826' (pp. 46–51). Samantha Matthews's 'Gems, Texts, and Confessions: Writing Readers in Late-Victorian Autographic Gift-Books' (*PubH* 62[2007] 53–80) is a thorough analysis of 'the autographic gift-book' and the reasons why the late Victorians were so fascinated with them (p. 53). Peter Robinson, on the other hand, is preoccupied with a very interesting, neglected twentieth-century poet in his 'Twists in the Plotting: Bernard Spencer's Second Book of Poems' (*PubH* 62[2007] 81–101). Robinson draws upon documents in the University of Reading's Spencer Archive. This archive 'begins in the mid-1950s and ends with letters of condolence and obituary notices in the wake of poet's, still not wholly explained, death (his body was found beside railway lines near Vienna) at the age of fifty-three on 10 September 1963' (p. 81).

The first issue of *The Huntington Library Quarterly* (*HLQ* 70:i[2007]) is devoted to *Travel Writing in the Early Modern World.* In addition to Peter C. Mancall's editorial 'Introduction: Observing More Things and More Curiously' (*HLQ* 70:i[2007] 1–10), there are nine contributions. Mary C. Fuller's 'Writing the Long-Distance Voyage: Hakluyt's Circumnavigators' (*HLQ* 70:i[2007] 37–60) throws interesting light upon Hakluyt's *Principall Navitations . . . of the English Nation*, published in 1589. Of particular interest is Anthony Parr's 'John Donne, Travel Writer' (*HLQ* 70:i[2007] 61–84). Parr starts by looking at Donne's poems concerning his 1590s naval adventures. He examines the manner in which the poems 'respond to the formal challenges of representing such experiences at a time when "travel writing" was seeking generic definition'. Parr also 'suggest[s] that Donne's interest in the new geography, the growth of tourism, and the new perspectives offered by maps and travel reports drew from him a wider set of meditations on travel experience' ('Abstract' p. 85). India is the subject of two contributions. The first, Michael H. Fisher, 'From India to England and Back: Early Indian Travel Narratives for Indian Readers' (*HLQ* 70:i[2007] 153–72), examines travel accounts authored 'by Indians about Britain intended for Indian readers' ('Abstract' p. 172). Julie F. Codell, on the other hand, in her 'Reversing the Grand Tour: Guest Discourse in Indian Travel Narratives' (*HLQ* 70:i[2007] 173–88), is preoccupied with rhetoric and the manner in which Indian travellers to Britain and other places in Europe described their travels.

Volume 70:ii of *HLQ* is devoted to 'Technologies of Illusion: The Art of Special Effects in Eighteenth-Century Britain' and is of special interest to students of the eighteenth century. In addition to two contributions on Gainsborough, eighteenth-century English cultural life is illuminated by John Brewer's well-illustrated 'Sensibility and the Urban Panorama' (*HLQ* 70:ii[2007] 229–49), and Simon During writes on 'Beckford in Hell: An Episode in the History of Secular Enchantment' (*HLQ* 70:ii[2007] 269–87). During writes insightfully on the reasons for Beckford's commitment to aestheticism, 'to the pursuit of private delight and to modes of self-undoing' ('Abstract' p. 288). William Blake's illustrator Henry Fuseli is the subject of Martin Myrone's 'Henry Fuseli and Gothic Spectacle' (*HLQ* 70:ii[2007] 289–310). *HLQ* 70:iii[2007] contains Diane Willen's 'Thomas Gataker and the Use of Print in the English Godly Community' (*HLQ* 70:iii[2007] 343–64) that throws light upon the life and publications of Thomas Gataker (1574–1654), a prolific London Puritan author. Another Puritan is the subject of David Parnham's 'Soul's Trial and Spirit's Voice: Sir Henry Vane against the "Orthodox"' (*HLQ* 70:iii[2007] 365–400). This examines the relatively neglected theological writings of Sir Henry Vane the Younger, who lived from 1613 to 1662. Perhaps the most fascinating contribution is Donald R. Dickson's account of 'Henry Vaughan's Medical Annotations' (*HLQ* 70:iii[2007] 427–52). Dickson's account is based upon an examination and transcription of Vaughan's annotations in two of his medical books found today in the Library Company of Philadelphia. Dickson also describes fourteen other books bearing Vaughan's signature and date. Each issue of *Huntington Library Quarterly* contains reviews and sometimes extensive review essays. In this issue Seth Lerer covers four recently published volumes in his 'Books and Readers in the Long Fifteenth Century' (*HLQ* 70:iii[2007] 453–60). Genevieve Guenther, in her 'New-Historical Elizabeths' considers Louis Montrose's *The Subject of Elizabeth: Authority, Gender, and Representation* [2006] (*HLQ* 70:iii[2007] 461–7). The issue concludes with Laura Stalker's very helpful 'Intramuralia: Acquisitions of Rare Materials, 2005' (*HLQ* 70:iii[2007] 491–508). This 'comprises items added to the *Huntington*'s collections of primary research materials and made available to researchers in calendar year 2005'.

Volume 70:iv has the most amusing article title of the year's bunch. Frances E. Dolan's 'Why Are Nuns Funny?' (*HLQ* 70:iv[2007] 509–34) looks at 'pornographic depictions that render the whole idea of celibacy ludicrous; a range of other denunciations of nuns as women who are not to be taken seriously, and representations of nuns actually trying to be funny' ('Abstract' p. 535). The discussion is limited to the seventeenth century. The late Nicholas Fisher writes with Matt Jenkinson on 'Rochester and the Specter of Libertinism' (*HLQ* 70:iv[2007] 537–52), an examination of Rochester's contemporary reputation. Ashley Marshall's 'Daniel Defoe as Satirist' (*HLQ* 70:iv[2007] 553–76) contains an enumerative listing of fifty-one 'Satires by Daniel Defoe' (pp. 574–6). Susan E. Whyman's 'Letter Writing and the Rise of the Novel: The Epistolary Literacy of Jane Johnson and Samuel Richardson' (*HLQ* 70:iv[2007] 577–606) considers Jane Johnson, a provincial reader from Olney, Buckinghamshire, who lived between 1706 and 1759 and was the wife of the local vicar, and her reading of Samuel Richardson. Heather McPherson's 'Caricature, Cultural Politics, and the Stage: The Case of *Pizarro*' (*HLQ* 70:iv[2007] 607–31) contains eleven illustrations, examines Sheridan's adaptation of Kotzebue's *Die Spanier in Peru* which opened at Drury Lane on 24 May 1799, and was a sensation. Susan J. Wolfson in an extensive review article, 'Charlotte Smith: "To live only to write and to write only to live"' (*HLQ* 70:iv[2007] 633–59), considers Judith Phillips Stanton's edition of *The Collected Letters of Charlotte Smith* [2006] and Stuart Curran's *The Works of Charlotte Smith* [2006]. Wolfson throws considerable light on Charlotte Smith's life and 'extraordinary accomplishments and reputation' (p. 658).

James E. May's *The Eighteenth-Century Intelligencer* (newsletter of the East-Central American Society for Eighteenth-Century Studies), NS 21, nos. i–iii (January, June and September) contains articles of considerable interest to readers of *YWES*. In his 2006 presidential address to the East-Central American Society for Eighteenth-Century studies, 'ECCO-Locating the Eighteenth Century' (*ECIntell* 21:i[2007] 1–9), Sayre N. Greenfield discusses the results of text-mining the *ECCO: Eighteenth-Century Collection Online* for evidence of when Shakespearian lines, especially from *Romeo and Juliet*, became popular. His search for the popular repetition of lines such as 'To be or not to be' or 'wherefore art thou Romeo' reveals much about the limitations and strengths of the database now revolutionizing some kinds of historical and literary studies. Greenfield also suggests that mid-century productions, especially by Garrick, increased the frequency of certain allusions. Robert D. Hume sings the praises of ECCO in a strongly phrased essay, 'The ECCO

Revolution' (*ECIntell* 21:i[2007] 9–17), encouraging research libraries to find the substantial funding needed for the database. He concludes with cautionary observations about the limitations of the publisher's (Thomson-Gale's) preparedness for revising problems in the database, as those arising from underlying problems in the ESTC and the microfilm series digitized as well as in the search software.

Penn State University's rare books curator, Sandra Stelts, offers an account of 'The Williamscote Library at Penn State: An Eighteenth-Century Survival' (*ECIntell* 21:i[2007] 17–20 + illus.), a private library of nearly 2,500 volumes once belonging to John Loveday (1711–89) and his son John (1742–1809) of Oxfordshire. Loveday senior was an antiquary and philologist, his son a Doctor of Laws, who moved the library from Caversham to Williamscote House near Banbury and continued his father's bibliophilic habits. Other volumes were added with a bequest from the poet James Merrick (1720–69). Charles Mann, former Chief of Rare Books, pursued the collection through Maggs Brothers, and Penn State has continued to add volumes as well as family portraits. Patricia Barnett provides an account of two related and important developments, the publication of Rolf Loeber and Magda Strouthamer-Loeber's *Guide to Irish Fiction, 1650–1900* (see *YWES* [2006]), and the acquisition by Notre Dame University of the extensive collection of Irish fiction developed during their long bibliographical quest (*ECIntell* 21:i[2007] 20–2). Manuel Schonhorn contributed two notes, 'St. Augustine's *Confessions* in *Clarissa* and *Tom Jones*', on shared motif of orchard thievery, and his lexical examination 'Robinson Crusoe's "Apartment"' (*ECIntell* 21:i[2007] 22–5).

The May *Intelligencer* begins with a magisterial survey by James E. Tierney, 'Resources for Locating Eighteenth-Century Periodicals: Strengths and Weakness' (*ECIntell* 21:ii[2007] 1–12), reviewing existing resources from the union catalogues and the *New Cambridge Bibliography of English Literature* (the most inclusive and convenient departure point) through printed catalogues for libraries such as the Huntington and the University of Texas at Austin. A second section examines the coverage of online resources, principally the ESTC. In 'Sterne and Young's *Conjectures on Original Composition*' (*ECIntell* 21:ii[2007] 12–17), Tim Parnell identifies a passage alluding to Young's essay and then speculates that Sterne added topicality to his *Tristram Shandy* through allusions aided by reading reviews in the major periodicals (perhaps with a particular eye to his own publisher Robert Dodsley's publications). James May contributed 'Rare Books and Manuscripts Recently Acquired and Offered' (*ECIntell* 21:ii[2007] 42–47), another of his surveys of auctions, dealer catalogues and library acquisitions. The most important acquisitions here went to Yale, but other eighteenth-century manuscripts and volumes are recorded for the Clark, McMaster, Stanford and the National Library of Scotland.

The September *ECIntell* begins with 'Samuel Johnson Revises a Debate' (*ECIntell* 21:iii[2007] 1–3), in which O.M. Brack, Jr, identifies the extent of revisions to Johnson's 'Debates in the Senate of Magna Lilliputia' within the August 1742 issue of the *Gentleman's Magazine*. Brack establishes the likelihood of Johnson's direct involvement from the nature of the changes (there are twenty-nine in all, including nineteen substantives). More significantly, Brack discovers why Johnson's revisions were limited to only twenty particular paragraphs. Brack finds that the altered section would fill 'four galley sheets', with each sheet filled with roughly 278 mm of type. In 'Gullible Lemuel Gulliver's *Banbury Relatives*' (*ECIntell* 21:iii[2007] 3–16), Hermann J. Real reports on his cemetery sleuthing in Banbury, offering illustrations of Gulliver tombstones; he then consider how Swift's choice of his protagonist's name is related to the Banbury Gullivers. All the 2007 issues include among their reviews books on authors, readers and publishing as well as reviews of critical editions, including O.M. Brack's review of Roger Lonsdale's edition of Johnson's *Lives of the Poets* (*ECIntell* 21:iii[2007] 27–33); James May's of Robert Hogan and Donald Mell's edition of *The Poems of Patrick Delany* [2006] (*ECIntell* 21:iii[2007] 39–42); and Walter Keithley's of Angus Ross's edition of *The Correspondence of Dr. John Arbuthnot* [2005] (*ECIntell* 21:i[2007] 29–32); also of note here is a review by A. Franklin Parks of *Teaching Bibliography, Textual Criticism, and Book History*, edited by Ann Hawkins [2006] (*ECIntell* 21:ii[2007] 37–9).

The *Journal of Scholarly Publishing* (*JScholP* 38–9[2007]) continues to publish material of interest. The third issue of volume 38 opens with an edited version Peter Vandenberg's keynote address to the 2005 MLA convention. Entitled 'Handoff, Dropkick, or Hail Mary Pass: Letting Go of an Academic Journal. The Council of Editors of Learned Journals' (*JScholP* 38:iii[2007] 123–33), Vandenberg draws upon his experience of editing and giving up the editorship of the award-winning journal *Composition Studies*. For Vandenberg, the successful editorial transition is the final obligation of a retiring editor, and he encourages editors to ensure that their own commitment is sustained throughout the transition by planning a practical exit strategy. Stephen K. Donovan's 'The Importance of Resubmitting Rejected Papers' (*JScholP* 38:iii[2007] 151–5) argues that a rejection provides the opportunity for reassessment, 'When the input of the editor[s] and reviewer[s], all experts in their field, should be considered and acted upon as necessary. The revitalized and improved contribution can be sent to a new journal with confidence' (p. 151). Editors and journals are the focus of Wang Feng-Nian's 'On the Innovative Spirit of Academic Journal Editors' (*JScholP* 38:iii[2007] 156–61) in which the competition amongst periodicals is assessed and discussed. Hazel K. Bell's all too brief 'Subject Indexes to Poetry: *Historical: (See Patriotis)*' (*JScholP* 38:iii[2007] 162–8) is very interesting. Bell uses *The Pageant of English Poetry*, published in 1924, as her test case in order to consider various approaches to the indexing of poetry 'and whether (serious) subject indexing of poetry is feasible' (p. 162). Bell's article tackles a much-neglected topic, that of subject indexing, and by implication the way inadequate indexing can skew a reader's or browser's response to a monograph. We at *YWES* are blessed with an excellent indexer. Of course Bell's article makes us even more aware that computer-assisted indexing is still unsatisfactory and that there is no replacement for the excellent skills of the real indexer.

Volume 38:iv [July 2007] has an interesting article by Rebecca Ann Bartlett: 'Significant University Press Titles for Undergraduates, 2006–2007' (*JScholP* 38:iv[2007] 229–48). However the articles in volume 39:i [October 2007] are probably of more relevance to those working in North America and elsewhere. Albert N. Greco, Robert F. Jones, Robert M. Wharton and Hooman Estelami, in 'The Changing College and University Library Market for University Press Books and Journals: 1997–2004' (*JScholP* 39:i[2007] 1–32), evaluate 'The economic structure of academic and non-academic libraries'. They include a discussion of the impact of the 'serials crisis' on library budgets and on university presses. Amongst other topics covered are the impact on libraries of the electronic distribution of scholarly content. In terms of analysis, this is a fascinating discussion, but few practical solutions are offered. Michael Jensen's 'Authority 3.0: Friend or Foe to Scholars?' (*JScholP* 39:i[2007] 33–43) deals with issues of authority and refereeing in internet publishing. Laurence Roth's 'MLA Regional Journals: Accountability, Innovation' (*JScholP* 39:i[2007] 44–53) provides a timely assessment of the regional journals offered by the Modern Language Association (MLA), their quality and professional place. Daniel J.J. Ross's '"An inexhaustible supply of fresh literature on the civil war"' (*JScholP* 39:i[2007] 63–71) examines the statistics of publications and book reviews in the periods 1960–4, 1980–4 and 2000–4 in terms of the production of books on the American Civil War. Each issue of *JScholP* contains short but useful reviews.

The *Bibliographical Society of Australia and New Zealand Bulletin* (*BSANZB* 30[2007]) contains much of interest of a bibliographical and textual nature. Its title is now *Script & Print*, but we shall continue to refer to it under its old abbreviations. (*BSANZB* 30:iv [2006]) is no exception. John N. Crossley's 'One Man's Library, Manila, ca. 1611—A First Look' (*BSANZB* 30:iv[2006] 201–9) provides an analysis of a personal library in the Philippines dating from around 1611. The indefatigable Wallace Kirsop considers 'Museums, Lyceums, Athenaeums and Mechanics' Institutes' (*BSANZB* 30:iv[2006] 210–22). Kirsop writes, 'The question at the heart of this paper is whether nineteenth-century British mechanics' institutes were a more or less conscious adaptation or development of late-eighteenth-century French *musées*, lycées, and *athénés*' (p. 210). Patrick Buckridge, in an analysis of the term 'bookishness' (p. 223), considers 'Bookishness and Australian Literature' (*BSANZB*30:iv[2006] 223–36). At times Buckridge's prose is rather opaque and circumlocutory. It is somewhat of a relief, then, to turn to B.J. McMullin's very specific and unpretentious, 'Silk for Posting: Sir Francis Burdett's Address to the Constituents of the City of Westminster, 6 October 1812' (*BSANZB* 30:iv[2006] 237–40). McMullin's aim is to continue his fine analysis of 'silk as a medium for printing' (p. 237) which he has been conducting in the pages of *BSANZB*. Wallace Kirsop's 'Harold Halford Russell Love 1937–2007' (*BSANZB* 30:iv[2006] 241–9) is accompanied by a photograph of Harold Love (p. 242), which for those who knew him brings back fond memories of the very kind, great scholar. Kirsop's is a detailed analysis of Harold Love's upbringing, his career and his magisterial contribution to bibliography and textual editing. Kirsop writes that Love 'enjoyed controversy and taking up contrarian positions', and adds: 'we have a massive *oeuvre* to remember him by but we must still regret that he left us too soon' (p. 249). Kirsop opens his obituary: 'The death of Harold Love on 12 August 2007, eight days after his seventieth birthday, has cut short the most remarkably sustained burst of creative work in bibliography and textual editing ever done by an Australian-born scholar' (p. 241). This issue concludes with reviews including B.J. McMullin's assessment of *Studies in Bibliography*, vol. 55 (2002 [2004]) (pp. 252–5) and a correction to his own bibliographical description found in his 'Dawson Described' in (*BSANZB* 30:iii[2006] 174–80). There are surprisingly no book reviews in (*BSANZB* 31:i[2007]).

Elaine Hoag's 'The Earliest Extant Australian Imprint, with Distinguished Provenance' (*BSANZB* 31:i[2007] 5–19) describes a playbill of 23 July 1796, which turned up in the Rare Book collection at the Library and Archives in Ottawa, Canada. 'On 11 September 2007, at Parliament House in Canberra, Canada's Prime Minister, Stephen Harper, presented the playbill to Australian Prime Minister, John Howard. The playbill has now become part of the collection of the National Library of Australia' (pp. 16–17). Clearly, it has lasted longer than politicians. Hoag's article concludes with an appendix containing a bibliographical description (p. 18). Her article contains two illustrations: the verso of the 1796 playbill (p. 9) and the recto (p. 19). Nathan Garvey's 'Selling a Penal Colony: The Booksellers and Botany Bay' (*BSANZB* 31:i[2007] 20–38) looks at the very earliest years of European colonization on the Australian continent, with particular relevance to booksellers and what became known as Botany Bay. The earliest period of Australia's early settlement is also the subject of Robert Jordan's 'The Barrington Prologue' (*BSANZB* 31:i[2007] 39–58) which he describes as 'arguably the most famous poem to have been generated by the early settlement of Australia' (p. 39). Wallace Kirsop's 'Searching for George Hughes' (*BSANZB* 31:i[2007] 58–62) explores questions raised by Elaine Hoag's Ottawa discovery of 'the oldest surviving piece of Australian printing' (p. 58).

BSANZB 31:ii[2007] appears not to have reached the present writer. However, 31:iii and 31:iv contain much of interest. Dirk H.R. Spennemann and Jon O'Neill provide an account of libraries, their development and content in the early years of the twentieth century in Micronesia in their 'A Library in Paradise: The deBrum Library on Likiep (Micronesia)' (*BSANZB* 31:iii[2007] 135–46). Joseph Rudman's 'Sarah and Henry Fielding and the Authorship of *The History of Ophelia*: A Riposte' (*BSANZB* 31:iii[2007] 147–63) is a contribution to the ongoing debate relating to the possible attribution to Sarah Fielding of 'an unfinished manuscript by her brother Henry Fielding [which she] edited and completed . . . and then published . . . in 1760 with the title *The History of Ophelia*' (p. 147). B.J. McMullin records 'An Unrecorded Title-Page Border: *The Castle of Knowledge* (1556)' (*BSANZB* 31:iii[2007] 164–71). This is accompanied by three full-page illustrations. Craig Brittain documents 'Steinbeck's Use of Ledgers in the Writing of *East of Eden* and *Journal of a Novel*' (*BSANZB* 31:iii[2007] 172–9). This number contains the usual high-quality reviews which we have come to expect from *Script & Print*.

Volume 31:iv leads with an article by Susann Liebich, ' "The books are the same as you see in London shops": Booksellers in Colonial Wellington and their Imperial Ties, ca. 1840–1890' (*BSANZB* 31:iv[2007] 197–209). This is followed by Sue Reynold's account of 'Bookbuying at the Victorian Supreme Court Library, 1853–1863: A Tale of Duplicity and Intrigue' (*BSANZB* 31:iv[2007] 210–19). John Burrows writes 'A Reply to Joseph Rudman's

"Riposte"' (*BSANZB* 31:iv[2007] 220–9), relating to the authorship of *The History of Ophelia*. Burrows's concluding paragraph is worth quoting. He comments, 'I have passed my eightieth birthday. I do not believe that Joe Rudman is much younger.' He then adds, 'We are in some danger, I fear, of behaving like two of Samuel Beckett's ancient derelicts, squabbling over a dry crust. For that reason alone, I hope to play no part in any discussion that may ensue.' To which Rudman comments, 'Amen. Ave atque vale' (p. 229).

Seemingly inexhaustibly, B.J. McMullin, whom one suspects is not yet 80, also continues to add to our knowledge. This time he writes on 'Shared Printing: James Flesher's Part in Matthew Poole's *Synopsis Criticorum*, vol. 1 (1669)' (*BSANZB* 31:iv[2007] 230–2). Patrick Spedding comments on 'To (Not) Promote Breeding: Censoring Eliza Smith's *Compleat Housewife* (1727)' (*BSANZB* 31:iv[2007] 233–42). This article is accompanied by five illustrations. The number concluded with Rory Muir's moving obituary of his mother 'Marcie Muir 1919–2007' (*BSANZB* 31:iv[2007] 243–5), the eminent historian and bibliographer of Australian book illustration. This is accompanied by a delightful illustration of 'Marcie and her dog Fanny in the mid-1980s' (p. 244). The number concludes, of course, with reviews.

This seems the appropriate place to briefly make mention of Nicholas Birns and Rebecca McNeer's *A Companion to Australian Literature since 1900*. Divided into five parts—'Identities', 'Writing Across Time', 'International Reputations', 'Writers and Regions' and 'Beyond the Canon'—this comprehensive volume contains thirty sections by different hands. It begins with a 'Chronology of Main Events in Australian History, 1901–2005' (pp. ix–xii) and 'celebrates Australian literature of the past century' (p. 1). As Birns and McNeer point out in their introduction, the book is organized deliberately 'to counteract' notions of 'narratives of emergence'. For instance, the first section, 'Cultural Foundations', convincingly disestablishes 'the settled notion of Australia as a nation of white male Crocodile Dundees' (p. 7). Obviously, with such a diverse group of topics, writers and contributors, entries will vary in quality. There are useful enumerative listings of works cited following each contribution, and a comprehensive index.

Obviously, this annual review of work in bibliography and textual criticism can only include materials which come to the compiler's attention. Its coverage does not pretend to be comprehensive, however James Hannam's article on 'The Library of Reuben Shirwoode (c.1542–1599)' (*TCBS* 13:ii[2005] 175–86) should not go unmentioned. 'Shirwoode was a Cambridge-educated schoolmaster and successful physician who lived in the second half of the sixteenth century' (p. 175). Hannam's analysis of his books provides a valuable insight into sixteenth-century reading and libraries.

The Book and Magazine Collector always has something of interest. For instance (*BMC* 278[2007]) contains William Baker's assessment of the career of the celebrated author, 'The Real Tom Stoppard' (*BMC* 278[2007] 30–41). Accompanied by illustrations, it includes an account of Stoppard's life and career, and a Stoppard primary bibliography of British and American imprints with their relative market values (pp. 41–3). The same issue contains an informative article by Dudley Chignell on 'Ernest Aris (1882–1963): The Man who Drew for Potter and Blyton' (*BMC* 278[2007] 44–62). Accompanied by fascinating colour illustrations, the article concludes with a checklist of Aris's publications for children (pp. 57–62). This is followed Mike Ashley's assessment of the life and work and publications of 'Herman Melville' (*BMC* 278[2007] 65–73). There is a 'Herman Melville Bibliography' (pp. 72–3) which indicates that if you are lucky enough to own the two-volume paper wrapper copy of Melville's *Narrative of a Four Months' Residence Among the Natives of a Valley of the Marquesas Islands*, published by John Murray in 1846, you may well value it at between £7,000 and £8,000: one suspects this is an undervaluation.

The May 2007 issue contains Mike Ashley's account of 'Blackwood's Magazine' (*BMC* 281[2007] 16–26). Richard Dalby writes on 'Wilberforce and the Abolition of the Slave Trade' (*BMC* 281[2007] 46–54) and includes a 'William Wilberforce UK Bibliography' (p. 54). David Ashford and Norman Wright's 'Colin Merrett' (*BMC* 281[2007] 62–73) is an assessment of the career of 'the best-loved of all British comic artists. . . . certainly amongst the longest of all strip artists' (p. 62), and is accompanied by an extensive 'Price Guide' (pp. 70–3). William Baker assesses the career and accomplishments of the unjustly neglected 'poet, dramatist, novelist, journalist, radio and television documentary commentator, [who] turned 80 on 28 November 2006' (p. 75), 'Bernard Kops' (*BMC* 281[2007] 74–83). The assessment concluded with 'Bernard Kops UK Bibliography' (pp. 82–3). The prices for his work, if obtainable, are still very reasonable, and perhaps the lowest for a major writer in the marketplace.

Mark Valentine's 'Francis Bourdillon—Victorian Poet' (*BMC* 283[2007] 16–21) considers the life and work of the Victorian poet who wrote the line 'The Night has a thousand eyes' (p. 17). There is a 'Francis William Bourdillon UK Bibliography' (p. 21): the prices appear to be rather low. Issue 286 [October 2007] contains Richard Dalby's 'Louis MacNeice: A Centenary Tribute' (*BMC* 286[2007] 32–41), which includes a 'Louis MacNeice UK/US Bibliography' (pp. 40–1), an examination of which indicates that prices for Louis MacNeice are far lower than those for say W.H. Auden or T.S. Eliot. Norman Wright's 'Enid Blyton: The "Five Find-Outers and Dog" Mystery Series' (*BMC* 286[2007] 62–72) considers only part of the achievement of the prolific Enid Blyton. William Baker's 'Collecting Philip Roth' (*BMC* 286[2007] 74–81) is accompanied by a 'Philip Roth US/UK Bibliography' (pp. 84–5) of the author for whom to date only the Nobel Prize remains beyond his grasp. Nicola Lisle considers the work of the prolific 'Joanna Trollope' (*BMC* 286[2007] 86–93), concluding with a 'Joanna Trollope UK Bibliography' (p. 93).

The November 2007 issue contains David Howard's very useful 'The Booker Prize: Every Winner and Runner Up' (*BMC* 287[2007] 14–29), concluding with a 'Complete Bibliography of Novels Shortlisted for the Booker Prize' (pp. 24–9), beginning in 1969. The first winner was the now forgotten P.H. Newby's *Something To Answer For*, which beat out Iris Murdoch's *The Nice and the Good*, Muriel Spark's *The Public Image*, Barry England's *Figures in a Landscape*, Nicholas Mosley's *The Impossible Object* and Gordon M. Williams's *From Scenes Like These*. Nick Hogarth gives an account of the major publications of 'The Sixties' (*BMC* 287[2007] 52–62) concluding with a '60s Bibliography' (pp. 52–62). Each article is lavishly illustrated with pictures of authors, dust-jackets, and so on. Hogarth's article contains, amongst other choice delights, the front cover of Penguin Books' *Lady Chatterley's Lover* by D.H. Lawrence, and 'Barbarella' published by Trans World (pp. 35–6). Richard Dalby explores another forgotten minor Victorian and Edwardian writer, in this instance 'William Hope Hodgson' (*BMC* 287[2007] 76–85). Hodgson (1877–1918), who 'was blown to pieces in an artillery bombardment near Ypres' (p. 83), is rather expensive. A copy of his *The Night Land* published by Eveleigh Nash in 1912 is valued at between £1,000 and £1,500 in Dalby's 'William Hope Hodgson Bibliography' (p. 85).

The Christmas 2007 issue has the interesting 'Fun, Thrills and Festive Feasts: A Potpourri of Christmas Comics' (*BMC* 289[2007] 40–54), by Norman Wright and David Ashford. This includes some fascinating illustrations of Victorian and Edwardian comics, as well as later ones. Richard Dalby writes on 'Edmund Dulac: Supreme Illustrator' (*BMC* 289[2007] 54–69). As Dalby's 'Edmund Dulac UK Bibliography' (pp. 68–9) shows, collecting Dulac is not cheap. A modern publishing phenomenon is the subject of Barbara Richardson's 'Philip Pullman's *His Dark Materials* Trilogy' (*BMC* 289[2007] 82–91). David Howard writes an eightieth-anniversary tribute for 'Simon Raven' (*BMC* 289[2007] 93–103). Howard's essay is accompanied by a 'Simon Raven UK Bibliography', which in common with the other bibliographies accompanying *Book and Magazine Collector* articles, provides a 'Guide to current values of First Editions in Fine condition without (and with) dustjackets' (p. 103). So in short, the *Book and Magazine Collector* continues to provide features of considerable interest, all of which are lavishly illustrated and scholarly. In many instances, they provide the first accounts and bibliographies of their subjects. This journal is an important one and should not be ignored by scholars and critics.

Emblematica: An Interdisciplinary Journal for Emblem Studies, volume 15, in addition to reviews, 'Research Reports, Notes, Queries, and Notices' (*Emblematica* 15[2007] 399–410), has articles of considerable interest. Jane Farnsworth's 'A Monstrous Fish Tale: Broadside Pictures and the Emblem in Sixteenth-Century England' (*Emblematica* 15[2007] 55–68), is accompanied by five illustrations of curious fish and contains interesting observations on 'the diversity of the emblem tradition', especially in sixteenth-century England (p. 67). Wim Van Dongen's rather elaborately entitled 'A Torrid Threesome: Investigating Form and Function of the Tripartite Emblem Structure in Mid-Twentieth-Century American Paperback Covers' (*Emblematica* 15[2007] 111–44) is accompanied by sixteen cover illustrations. Van Dongen has illuminating things to say about the history of paperback publication and covers. He 'shows that the tripartite structure, familiar to the seventeenth- and eighteenth-century emblem genre, also occurs in contemporary ads and on paperback covers from the mid-twentieth century' (p. 123). A special issue entitled 'Literature as Communication', under the general editorship of Roger D. Sell of the *Nordic Journal of English Studies* 6:ii[2007], contains essays by Sell on 'Wordsworthian Communication' (*NJES* 6:ii[2007] 17–45), Juha-Pekka Alarauhio on '*Sohrab and Rustum* and *Balder Dead*: Communication about Communication' (*NJES* 6:ii[2007] 47–64), Gunilla Bexar on 'John Mitchel's

The Last Conquest of Ireland (Perhaps) and Liam O'Flaherty's *Famine*: A Question of Tone' (*NJES* 6:ii[2007] 65–82), Inna Lindgrén on Kipling's '*Plain Tales from the Hills* as Emergent Literature' (*NJES* 6:ii[2007] 83–104) and Jason Finch on 'Surrey in *A Room With a View*: A Candidate for Scholarly Mediation' (*NJES* 6:ii[2007] 105–28). The issue conclude with Mirja Kuurola on 'Caryl Phillips's *Cambridge*: Discourses in the Past and the Readers in the Present' (*NJES* 6:ii[2007] 129–44) and Anthony W. Johnson's 'Ben Jonson and the Jonsonian Afterglow: Imagemes, Avatars, and Literary Reception' (*NJES* 6:ii[2007] 145–72).

1650–1850: Ideas, Aesthetics, and Inquiries in the Early Modern Era, volume 14, edited by Kevin L. Cope, in addition to extensive book reviews, has a special feature on 'Jacobite Travelers and Fellow-Travelers'. This contains Neil Guthrie on '"A Polish Lady" The Art of the Jacobite Print' (*1650–1850* 14[2007] 287–312), which is based upon a print found at Worcester College, Oxford, Library in its 'collection of prints assembled by Sir George Clarke (1661–1736), public servant, MP for the University, amateur architect, and fellow of All Souls'. Guthrie's focus is on 'a mezzotint produced by Thomas Bowles (1680–1757) in 1719 [which] depicts a young woman wearing a velvet coat trimmed with ermine and an unusual hat, with flowers behind her left ear'. Guthrie adds, 'In her right hand she holds a black mask, lined with white, a short distance from her face.' He comments, 'The mask is full-face, not a half-mask or domino, and one eye-hole is visible from the inside. The woman's hand is tilted away from the viewer, fingers spread out, which suggests she is drawing the mask away from her face rather than covering up.' Guthrie argues that 'this is the key to understanding the meaning of the print' (pp. 287–8). Guthrie's fascinating article is accompanied by four black and white illustrations.

There is a new open-access online journal, the *Journal of Illustration Studies*. Essentially the brainchild of David Skilton and produced by Cardiff University Centre for Editorial and Intertextual Research (CEIR), the articles and reports in the first issue, published in December 2007, mainly focus upon the Victorians and is treated in Chapter XIII of the present volume. As the editorial for the first issue indicates, the journal 'has been founded in an attempt to establish the systematic study of literary illustration as a discipline in its own right, having its own subject matter and its own critical and scholarly methods'. The editorial continues, 'the underlying principle is that illustration consists of text and image in privileged relation with each other, and that . . . an illustrated text is a bimedial work of art, and a full account of the meanings it produces can only arise from the reading of text and image together, in the richness of their bitextual relationship' (p. 1). One article of general interest is that of Paola Spinozzi on the 'Interarts and Illustrations: Some Historical Antecedents, Theoretical Issues, and Methodological Orientations' (*JOIS* [2007] 43 paras). Spinozzi's is an enquiry 'into the most controversial and challenging issues which have constituted 'the *paragone* of word and image throughout the centuries'. Spinozzi writes that 'Illustration can only be comprehended by showing that it has been, and still is, complicated, and that there are complex reasons for its being so. Indeed, it is a multi-layered artistic manifestation bearing witness to the intertwinement of aesthetics and ideology.' In short, this first number of the *Journal of Illustration Studies*, with its impressive, eminent editorial board, is an important addition to knowledge and research, and we wish it well.

Kevin L. Cope's *In and After the Beginning: Inaugural Moments and Literary Institutions in the Long Eighteenth Century* is the latest volume to come to attention in the AMS Studies in the Eighteenth Century series. Cope's monograph is concerned with the concept of 'eighteenth-century literature'. It begins with a chapter examining the Restoration and 'closes with a chapter on the environmental discourses of the later eighteenth century' focusing upon how 'dissimilar experimental genres (neo-Calvinist mock-heroic verse, novels about women's socialization) carry out a common project of dispersal' (p. 15). There is a good deal of jargon in this monograph, yet it does encompass in an interesting fashion major and neglected authors, and treats important subjects. There is in addition an extensive index.

Kevin L. Cope's edited *Above the Age of Reason: Miracles and Wonders in the Long Eighteenth Century* contains four texts focusing upon miracles and wonders, each with an extensive introduction. The first contains the texts of the pamphlet *A Philosophical Discourse of the Nature of Rational and Irrational Souls*, published in 1695 and attributed to Matthew Smith. As James G. Buickerood indicates in his introduction, Smith's 'purpose ... is to defend the dignity of Humane Nature against those who claim that humans and animals possess the same nature and possibly possess the same destiny' (p. 13). The text is based upon a copy at the William Andrews Clark Memorial Library 'shelf mark Pam.coll' (p. 29) and is followed by detailed notes (pp. 31–8). The second text is introduced by David Venturo and is devoted to *The School of the Eucharist ... with a Preface Concerning the Testimony of Miracles* [1687]. 'Originally written in French, by a Flemish Jesuit, Toussaint Bridoul (1595–1672)', it consists of two parts. The first is 'a preface written by' William Clagett (1646–88) an Anglican who attacked 'the Roman Catholic doctrine of miracles, especially transubstantiation', and a translation of Bridoul's 'Anthology of Beast Tales' (p. 39). The text is based upon a copy at the 'Willis Library, University of North Texas (shelf mark BX2225.B76 1687)' (p. 53) and is again accompanied by extensive notation (pp. 55–75).

The third text contains an introduction by Keith Bodner of two discourses from Thomas Sherlock's (1678–1761) *The Use and Intent of Prophecy*, published in 1725. Sherlock's work 'expresses ... anti-deistic reservations. ... the two discourses reprinted herein are reproduced' from a copy at the 'Harold B. Lee Library, Brigham Young University (shelf mark 220.15 Sh4u 1725)' (p. 93). There are also extensive footnotes following the texts (pp. 95–100). The final text of the four introduced by the editor Kevin L. Cope reproduces from the 'Special Collections Library, University of Missouri-Columbia (Rare BT364.W66 1727)' (p. 117), Thomas Woolston's *A Discourse on the Miracles of our Saviour*, published in 1727. According to Cope, 'Woolston's methods take him deep into the zone of postmodern secularism and relativism, depending as they do on an impromptu mix of anthropology and literary theory' (p. 116). Cope's notes are detailed (pp. 119–27).

The third volume of *Eighteenth-Century Thought*, edited by James G. Buickerood, contains thirteen essays edited by Earl Havens and

James G. Buickerood, stimulated by 'John Locke through the Centuries: Assessing the Lockean Legacy, 1704–2004. Beinecke Rare Book and Manuscript Library, Yale University, 28–30 October 2004'. Buickerood and Havens, in their 'Lasting Monuments to the Admiration of Posterity: Charting Locke's Legacy' (pp. 7–36), explain the background to the exhibition and Locke's significance. Jonathan I. Israel, 'John Locke and the Intellectual Legacy of the Early Enlightenment' (pp. 37–55), writes specifically on attempts to limit Locke's legacy rather than to promote it. Mark Goldie's 'The Early Lives of John Locke' (pp. 57–87) focuses upon the significance of the fact that 'no full-length biography of [Locke] appeared before 1876' (p. 57). An interesting omission from Goldie's account is any mention of the interests of Victorians such as George Henry Lewes in Locke's life and work. J.R. Milton's 'John Locke: The Modern Biographical Tradition' (pp. 89–109), on the other hand, begins not with King's *Life of John Locke* published in 1829 but with H.R. Fox Bourne's more thorough and careful 1876 biography, and includes the work of the great Peter Laslett. In his section 'What Needs To Be Done', in addition to noting that 'it is... generally agreed that there is no satisfactory biography of Locke' (p. 107), Milton notes that 'there is one field of inquiry that is still largely unexplored, the watermarks in Locke's manuscripts' (p. 109).

Justin Champion's '"A law of continuity in the progress of theology": Assessing the Legacy of John Locke's *Reasonableness of Christianity*, 1695–2004' (pp. 111–42), focuses upon the reception of one specific work of Locke, his *Reasonableness of Christianity*, published in 1695. Ian Harris's 'The Legacy of *Two Treatises of Government*' (pp. 143–67), has for its subject Locke's *Two Treatises of Government*. Harris uses the second edition of Laslett's edition published in 1967. G.A.J. Rogers's 'Locke's *Essay concerning Human Understanding*: The Philosophical Legacy' (pp. 169–87) focuses upon perhaps Locke's best-known work and argues 'that Locke's philosophical legacy was substantial and profound' (p. 169). On the other hand, Paul Schuurman's 'Locke's Modest Impact on Eighteenth-Century Natural Science: The Encyclopedic Evidence' (pp. 189–206) focuses upon the neglected area 'of Locke's contribution to eighteenth-century natural science' (p. 189). Barbara Arneil's 'Citizens, Wives, Latent Citizens and Non-Citizens in the *Two Treatises*: A Legacy of Inclusion, Exclusion and Assimilation' (pp. 207–33) 'addresses John Locke's legacy in the United States of America' (p. 207).

John Kane's 'Man the Maker *versus* Man the Taker: Locke's Theory of Property as a Theory of Just Settlement' (pp. 235–53) focuses on 'Locke's Theory of Property' (p. 235) and how he took positions which today are decidedly unfashionable. Philip Milton's 'Pierre Des Maizeaux, *A Collection of Several Pieces of Mr. John Locke*, and the Formation of the Locke Canon' (pp. 255–91), focuses upon the relation of Des Maizeaux (1673–1745) with Locke and with members of his circle. Gabriel Glickman's 'Andrew Michael Ramsay (1686–1743), the Jacobite Court and the English Catholic Enlightenment' (pp. 293–329) focuses upon Ramsay and his reputation. Glickman's aim is 'to re-evaluate the experience of English Catholics in the eighteenth century, against current historical orthodoxy' (p. 293).

Derya Gurses Tarbuck writes on 'Duncan Forbes of Culloden, Presbyterian Whig and Hutchinsonian: Towards a Reinterpretation of the History of Ideas in Eighteenth-Century Britain' (pp. 331–48). This provides her with the 'opportunities to cast light on the landscape of eighteenth-century intellectual history in Britain' (p. 331). *Eighteenth Century Thought* volume 3 contains six extensive 'Review Essays' (pp. 349–426) and two shorter 'Book Reviews' (pp. 427–35). There is also an index (pp. 437–46). This volume contains much of value on eighteenth-century and subsequent intellectual history, and, above all, prose writing.

The eighteenth volume of *The Age of Johnson: A Scholarly Annual*, edited by Jack Lynch, contains 'Korshin Memorial Essays'. These are essays dedicated to the memory of the journal's founding editor, Paul J. Korshin, who died in 2005, and who, as Jack Lynch's enumerative 'A Bibliography of Paul J. Korshin's Writings' (*AgeJ* 18[2007] 369–79) demonstrates, was a prolific writer, especially in the field of eighteenth-century studies. He authored two books, *From Concord to Dissent: Major Themes in English Poetic Theory, 1640–1700* [1973] and *Typologies in England, 1650–1820* [1982], and edited ten volumes, two journals and wrote innumerable articles and reviews. Robert Folkenflik, in the first essay, writes on 'The Politics of Johnson's *Dictionary* Revisited' (*Age of Johnson* 18[2007] 1–17), and Thomas M. Curley, at some length, on 'Samuel Johnson's Forgotten Friendship with William Shaw: Their Last Stand for Truth in the *Ossian* Controversy' (*AgeJ* 18[2007] 19–65). Johnson, one of Korshin's obsessions, is also the subject of other essays, including Arthur H. Cash's 'Samuel Johnson and John Wilkes' (*AgeJ* 18[2007] 67–130), Howard D. Weinbrot's 'Meeting the Monarch: Johnson, Boswell, and the Anatomy of a Genre' (*AgeJ* 18[2007] 131–50), and Philip Smallwood's 'Johnson's Criticism and "Critical Global Studies"' (*AgeJ* 18[2007] 151–71).

A different direction is followed in the remaining essays. James Cruise writes on 'Egypt and the Hieroglyphs in England: Secrecy in the Seventeenth and Eighteenth Centuries' (*Age of Johnson* 18[2007] 173–205), and Maximilian E. Novak on 'Novel or Fictional Memoir: The Scandalous Publication of *Robinson Crusoe*' (*AgeJ* 18[2007] 207–23). Another contribution by Jack Lynch contains the interesting title, 'Horry, the Ruffian, and the Whelp: Three Fakers of the 1760s' (*AgeJ* 18[2007] 225–42). James Gray's contribution is on 'Diderot, Garrick, and the Art of Acting' (*AgeJ* 18[2007] 243–72). Lisa Berglund writes on 'Hester Lynch Piozzi's *Anecdotes* Versus the Editors' (*AgeJ* 18[2007] 273–90). Mona Scheuermann tackles a fairly well trodden path in her 'Truths Universally Acknowledged: Social Commentary in *Mansfield Park*' (*AgeJ* 18[2007] 291–329), George Justice deals with a less well known area in his 'Schooling the Novel: John Gibson Lockhart's *Reginald Dalton*' (*AgeJ* 18[2007] 331–44), and Gloria Sybil Gross transgresses into late twentieth-century film in her 'Stanley Kubrick's Love Affair with the Eighteenth Century' (*AgeJ* 18[2007] 345–68). She does not, unfortunately, say whether Paul Korshin or Stanley Kubrick had any encounters! The remainder of the volume is taken up with ' "No writer nor scholar need be dull": Recollections of Paul J. Korshin' (*AgeJ* 18[2007] 381–442). This contains 'Personal reminiscences and tributes' from twenty-one 'friends, colleagues and former students' (p. 381). These tributes to Korshin are followed by the usual, in some instances extensive, reviews of books on the age of Johnson. Some of these constitute extensive review articles. See for instance Scott Cleary's review of Paul Baines and Pat Rogers, *Edmund Curll, Bookseller* [2007] (*AgeJ* 18[2007] 491–8).

Paul Baines and Pat Rogers's *Edmund Curll, Bookseller* is the first detailed biography of its subject since Ralph Straus's *The Unspeakable Curll* [1927], and focuses upon Curll's (1675–1747) publishing career in the years between 1706 and 1747. Baines and Rogers consider the complete extent of Curll's productions, including his often neglected distinguished antiquarian series, and draw upon archival materials to document his legal and other problems. Well illustrated, their biography 'is designed to revisit the Pope–Curll vendetta and to enter the various kinds of debate engendered by [the] resurgent interest in the history of the book with a factual, archive-based account of Curll's activities' (p. 3). The latest volume in the Stoke Newington Daniel Defoe Edition consists of an edition by Kit Kincade of *An Essay on the History and Reality of Apparitions*. Defoe's essay belongs to the end of his life and the year 1727. It illustrates its author's 'interest in the super-natural, at least as it related to the idea of divine providence' (p. xvi). Kincade's edition is replete with information on the genesis of the work, its publication history, its place in Defoe's oeuvre, its relationship to the ideas of the time, for instance Hobbes and Glanvill (pp. xvii–ci). The text is followed by extensive bibliographical data including collation based on the examination of eleven copies and a listing of textual emendations (pp. 284–319). There is an extensive essay on the work, on almost every line, by Kit Kincade and John G. Peters (pp. 320–438) followed by an index (pp. 439–63). All in all, Kincade, the general editors of the Stoke Newington Daniel Defoe Edition and the publishers, the AMS Press, New York, should be congratulated on the production of the definitive edition of this important Defoe work.

The final issue of *Studies in Scottish Literature*, volumes 35–6, edited for over four decades by the indefatigable G. Ross Roy, is a bumper one and of especial interest. Most of the essays in the volume are new, although some may have been published elsewhere in the gap between agreeing to contribute and actual publication. The front and end leaves contain a drawing of 'Professor Ross Roy, as Alasdair Gray will always see him, and drew him in 1994'. William McIlvanney's 'Burdalane' (*SSL* 35–6[2007] 1–5) is accompanied by a CD of him reading the poem. Edward J. Cowan writes on 'Chapman Billies and their Books' (*SSL* 35–6[2007] 6–25), which contains a fascinating account of the chapbook. The late K.J. Fielding and Mary Sebag-Montefiore write on 'Jane Carlyle and Sir David Davidson: Belief and Unbelief—the Story of a Friendship' (*SSL* 35–6[2007] 26–43). Mary Sebag-Montefiore is the wife of the great-grandson of Sir David Davidson (1811–1900). Margery Palmer McCulloch focuses upon '"A very curious emptiness": Walter Scott and the Twentieth-Century Scottish Renaissance Movement' (*SSL* 35–6[2007] 44–56). A recording of J. Ramsay MacDonald (1886–1937), the first Labour prime minister in 1924 and again prime minister from 1929 to 1935, of 28 November 1929 on the subject of Robert Burns is transcribed by Nicole Hopkins under the title 'J. Ramsay MacDonald on Robert Burns' (*SSL* 35–6[2007] 57–61). William Gillies writes on '"No bonnier life than the sailor's": A Gaelic Poet

Comments on the Fishing Industry in Wester Ross' (*SSL* 35–5[2007] 62–75). In fact Gillies's is a transcription of a Gaelic poem which is reproduced in Gaelic and English with a commentary.

Edwin Morgan's play *Phaedra* is the subject of J. Derrick McClure's 'Edwin Morgan's *Phaedra*: Apotheosis of Glesga?' (*SSL* 35–6[2007] 76–92). Rodger L. Tarr reflects upon his former supervisor in his lament, 'Kenneth Joshua Fielding on the Carlyle Letters: A Rumination Past and Present' (*SSL* 35–6[2007] 92–105). In his final paragraph, Tarr bids adieu to 'dear Carlyleans whoever you are' in a very bleak mood, as if all the work has been for nothing. He hopes 'against hope that the world of scholarship will return to the primacy of text' in the age of the computer screen and the demise of his old professor (p. 105). There are poems by George Bruce, '"Meeting the Woman of the North Sea"' (*SSL* 35–6[2007] 106–7) and the eminent scholar of the eighteenth century, Ian Simpson Ross, writes on 'Dr. Johnson in the *Gaeltacht*, 1773' (*SSL* 35–6[2007] 108–30). Sally Mapstone's 'Drunkenness and Ambition in Early Seventeenth-Century Scottish Literature' (*SSL* 35–6[2007] 131–55) is based upon an examination of 'the voluminous papers of William Drummond of Hawthornden' (p. 131). The Nobel Prize winner, the great poet Seamus Heaney, has translated Robert Henryson's 'The Cock and the Jasp' (*SSL* 35–6[2007] 156–63). Henryson's text is on one side of the page and Heaney's translation in modern English on the other. R.D.S. Jack writes succinctly on '"In ane uther leid": Reviewing Scottish Literature's Linguistic Boundaries' (*SSL* 35–6[2007] 164–83). Carol McGuirk's 'The Crone, the Prince, and the Exiled Heart: Burns's Highlands and Burns's Scotland' (*SSL* 35–6[2007] 184–202) focuses upon Burns's perception of the Highlands. The great Hugh MacDiarmid is the focus of Duncan Glen's 'Hugh MacDiarmid in our Time' (*SSL* 35–6[2007] 202–13). The final page consists of a reproduction of MacDiarmid's six-line poem, 'Why did they christen you Duncan Glen?'. Muriel Spark contributes a short story called '"The Girl I Left Behind Me"' (*SSL* 35–6[2007] 214–17). Maurice Lindsay writes on 'A Century of Scottish Creative Writing: Three Essays' (*SSL* 35–6[2007] 215–57). Kenneth Simpson writes on 'A Highly Textual Affair: The Sylvander–Clarinda Correspondence' (*SSL* 35–6[2007] 258–70). Peter Zenzinger's 'Cultural Paradoxes in Alexander Ross's *Fortunate Shepherdess*' (*SSL* 35–6[2007] 271–94) focuses on the neglected pastoral poet Alexander Ross (1699–1784). Robert L. Kindrick's subject is the better-known 'Robert Henryson and the Roots of Reformation' (*SSL* 35–6[2007] 295–306). Douglas S. Mack writes on 'Hogg, Byron, Scott, and John Murray of Albemarle Street' (*SSL* 35–6[2007] 307–25).

Aonghas MacNeacail contributes two 'Poems' (*SSL* 35–6[2007] 326–30) in Gaelic with an English translation. The second, 'on the red headland', is of course a play on the name of Ross Roy. Stephen W Brown writes on 'William Smellie and the Reconciliation of Maria Riddell with Robert Burns' (*SSL* 35–6[2007] 331–8). Douglas Gifford contributes 'Sham Bards of a Sham Nation? Edwin Muir and the Failures of Scottish Literature' (*SSL* 35–6[2007] 339–61). Priscilla Bawcutt writes on 'Dunbar and his Readers: From Allan Ramsay to Richard Burton' (*SSL* 35–6[2007] 362–81). A.M. Kinghorn writes on 'Old Bones Disinterred Once Again: Ramsay's Pastoral and its Legacy for the Literati' (*SSL* 35–6[2007] 382–90). Tom Leonard's poem, '*Suite* on the Page' (*SSL* 35–6[2007] 392–402) has eleven sections. It is followed by Robert D. Thornton's 'James Currie's Editing of the Correspondence of Robert Burns' (*SSL* 35–6[2007] 403–19). Trevor Royle reflects on the late 'Alan Bold: An Enduring Friendship' (*SSL* 35–6[2007] 420–5). David Hewitt predictably chooses for the subject of his contribution '"Hab nab at a venture": Scott on the Creative Process' (*SSL* 35–6[2007] 426–33). Deanna Delmar Evans writes on 'Reconsidering Dunbar's *Sir Thomas Norny* and Chaucer's *Tale of Sir Thopas*' (*SSL* 35–6[2007] 444–54). Gerard Carruthers writes on '"Tongues turn'd inside out": The Reception of "Tam o'Shanter"' (*SSL* 35–6[2007] 455–63). Edwin Morgan's contribution is 'Translation from the French' (*SSL* 35–6[2007] 464–71) and consists of a translation of three poems with their texts in French and his English translation. James Mackay writes on the interesting subject of '"That cursed tax of postage": Robert Burns and the Postal Service' (*SSL* 35–6[2007] 472–9). Alasdair Gray's contribution is a short tale on 'Three Men in Love' (*SSL* 35–6[2007] 480–6). Tom Hubbard's is '"Tell it slant": Duncan Glen and Akros' (*SSL* 35–6[2007] 487–500). In his second contribution, Ian Simpson Ross focuses upon 'La Musique Dunbarienne of Jean-Jacques Blanchot' (*SSL* 35–6[2007] 501–7). In effect, this is a consideration of the translations of Dunbar in French. Christopher Whyte focuses upon 'Sorley MacLean's "An Cuilithionn": A Critical Assessment' (*SSL* 35–6[2007] 508–25). Henry L. Fulton's subject is 'Robert Burns, John Moore, and the Limits of Writing Letters' (*SSL* 35–6[2007] 526–50), and the late Iain Crichton Smith's short tale 'Murdo Comes of Age' (*SSL* 35–6[2007] 551–3) is the concluding contribution. There are details of the contributors and an index to this volume which no doubt will become a collector's item.

Raymond Clemens and Timothy Graham's lavishly illustrated (there are 258 coloured illustrations, some of which are full-page) *Introduction to Manuscript Studies* 'aims to provide practical instructions and training in the paleography and codicology of medieval manuscripts, in particular manuscripts written in Latin'. Divided into three parts, the first, 'Making the Medieval Manuscript', 'offers an overview of the process by which manuscripts came into being'. The second part, 'Reading the Medieval Manuscript', moves the perspective to that of 'the modern student and how he or she may prepare for an encounter with manuscripts in situ and acquire the skills necessary to actively read and interpret medieval books'. The section concludes with a sampling of sixteen medieval scripts that provide illustrations of the evolution of western European handwriting from around 700 to the fifteenth century, and which consequently provides 'the opportunity' for students 'to hone their transcription skills'. The third part, 'Some Manuscript Genres', aims 'to provide an illustrated introduction to certain types of manuscripts or texts that have their own characteristic features and layout' (p. xiii). These include for instance biblical commentaries, Books of Hours, rolls and scrolls. There is an appendix by Anders Winroth, 'Tools for the Study of Medieval Latin' (pp. 259–61). After a detailed introduction, Winroth provides an annotated bibliography of useful Latin dictionaries. There is in addition an extensive and very useful glossary, beginning with an explanation of 'Acanthus' and concluding with 'Yapp Edge' (pp. 263–71).

This highly recommended book concludes with a non-descriptive bibliography (pp. 273–92) and an index (pp. 293–301). Beautifully produced with stiff, illustrated cover wrappers, Clemens and Graham's *Introduction to Manuscript Studies* is well worth its relatively inexpensive price tag. The book is full of hidden riches, for instance chapter 12, devoted to 'Liturgical Books and their Calendars' (pp. 192–202) is followed by an appendix listing 'Dominical Letters and Golden Numbers, 600–1582' (pp. 203–7): if further explanation is needed, consult the volume!

Mention should be made of an important bibliography published in 2006 by D.S. Brewer of Cambridge. In fact, its founder, the late Professor D.S. Brewer (1923–2008), a former president of the English Association, was an eminent critic of Geoffrey Chaucer who made notable contributions to medieval literature and created the small academic publishing imprint (now part of Boydell & Brewer) in 1972 which published many very valuable works of interest to *YWES* readers. In a sense, Anne F. Howey and Stephen R. Reimer's *A Bibliography of Modern Arthuriana 1500–2000* may be regarded as a tribute to Derek Brewer. The interdisciplinary annotated bibliography contains listings of the Arthurian legend in modern English-language fiction from 1500 to 2000. It encompasses literary texts, films, television, music, visual art and even games. There is an extensive general index followed by a listing of Arthurian characters and themes.

James Raven's *The Business of Books: Booksellers and the English Book Trade 1450–1850* is an extensive study replete with illustrations, figures and tables of the growth of the English book trade from the fifteenth to the nineteenth centuries. Raven writes, 'The revolution in book and print production between the mid-fifteenth and the mid-nineteenth century fundamentally changed the means of construction and circulating knowledge and intelligence' (p. 1). His concern is to trace the history of this revolution, of which he writes that 'the fundamental change to the book concerned the volume and methods of business' (p. 10). Raven writes succinctly, and his endnote annotations, found at the back of the book, are very useful. Of course, it is easy to say that there are areas which he should have concentrated on more than others. His conclusion is judicious: 'for many it is no longer sufficient to study literature without considering larger publishing strategies, professional networks, and the manner in which booksellers put the work of writers into print and created a literary market' (p. 378). Incidentally, there is a delightful front-jacket illustration of George Scharf's *Near St. Martin's [in the Fields] Church, July 1828*, consisting of a London alley surrounded by bookshops, customers and vendors. Those in the business of discarding their dust-jackets do so at their own peril.

Valerie Coghlan and Siobhán Parkinson's *Irish Children's Writers and Illustrators 1986–2006* consists of a selection of essays on thirteen Irish children's book illustrators with illustrations from their work and selected and enumerative listings of their writings. 'All the writers/illustrators are Irish by birth, background or affiliation—as indeed are the contributors. Many of the books discussed in the articles however were not published in Ireland' (p. 9). Celia Keenan writes on Eoin Colfer (pp. 20–8); Lucinda Jacob writes on Marie-Louise Fitzpatrick (pp. 30–43); Celia Keenan on Maeve Friel (pp. 46–52); Valerie on P.J. Lynch (pp. 54–69); Liz Morris on Sam McBratney (pp. 72–8); Ciara Ní Bhroin on Elizabeth O'Hara (pp. 80–8); A.J. Piesse on Mark O'Sullivan (pp. 90–6); the same writer on Siobhán Parkinson (pp. 98–108); John Short on Niamh Sharkey (pp. 110–21); Robert Dunbar on Matthew Sweeney (pp. 124–41); Dunbar again on Kate Thompson (pp. 134–43); Lucy O'Dea on Martin Waddell (pp. 146–54) and finally Carol Redford writes on Gerard Whelan (pp. 148–62). The contributions are well written and informative and do analyse their subject's work. There is a useful, title-orientated index (pp. 165–8).

The third edition of David G. Nicholls's *Introduction to Scholarship in Modern Languages and Literatures* is divided into three sections, one on 'Understanding Language', the second on 'Forming Texts' and the third on 'Reading Literature and Culture'. In his preface Nicholls comments that 'the present volume is designed to highlight relations among languages and forms of discourse' (p. vii). The first section consists of three essays: Doris Sommer on 'Language, Culture, and Society' (pp. 3–19); Paul J. Hoper on 'Linguistics' (pp. 20–47); and Heidi Byrnes on 'Language Acquisition and Language Learning' (pp. 48–69). The second section also has three essays: Susan C. Jarratt on 'Rhetoric' (pp. 73–102); David Bartholomae on 'Composition' (pp. 103–25); and Charles Bernstein on 'Poetics' (pp. 126–39). The final section has nine contributions with an epilogue. Leah S. Marcus writes on 'Textual Scholarship' (pp. 143–59); Jerome McGann on 'Interpretation' (pp. 160–70); Catherine Gallagher on 'Historical Scholarship' (pp. 171–93); J. Michael Holquist on 'Comparative Literature' (pp. 194–208); Jean Franco on 'Cultural Studies' (pp. 209–24); Anne Donadey with Françoise Lionnet on 'Feminisms, Genders, Sexualities' (pp. 225–44); Kenneth W. Warren on 'Race and Ethnicity' (pp. 245–59); Susan Stanford Friedman on 'Migrations, Diasporas, and Borders' (pp. 260–93); Lawrence Venuti on 'Translation Studies' (pp. 294–311) and finally there is Bruce Robbins's 'Epilogue: The Scholar in Society' (pp. 312–30). The volume concludes with 'Notes on Contributors' (pp. 331–3), an 'Index of Titles' (pp. 335–54), and an 'Index of Names' (pp. 355–70). Each essay is accompanied by notes (in some cases these are extensive), and by 'Works Cited and Suggestions for Further Reading'. Obviously, depending on one's interest, one contribution is going to be more engaging than the other and it would be invidious to single out any particular one for praise or criticism. In the company of such distinguished critics and scholars, the content is of the highest quality.

Thomas H. Ohlgren's *Robin Hood: The Early Poems, 1465–1560. Texts, Contexts, and Ideology* provides a thorough examination of the various Robin Hood poems based upon close examination of, wherever possible, the original manuscripts, their provenance and ownership. There is an appendix by Lister M. Matheson devoted to 'The Dialects and Language of Selected Robin Hood Poems' (pp. 189–210). Twelve illustrations accompany Ohlgren's thorough analysis. The notations to each chapter, found at the end of the book (pp. 211–49), are extensive. The enumerative 'Selected Bibliography' (pp. 250–65) is divided into 'Manuscripts', 'Early Printed Books', 'Other Primary Texts' and 'Secondary Works'. There is a detailed index to this very useful monograph.

Mary Hammond and Shafquat Towheed's *Publishing in the First World War: Essays in Book History* consists of twelve essays investigating 'the movement of information and entertainment across and between bodies and boundaries at a time when both were under extreme duress' (p. 3), that is, the period during the First World War. The volume is divided into four parts, each consisting of three essays. Part I is devoted to 'Profit and Patriotism'. Jane Potter writes succinctly on 'For Country, Conscience and Commerce: Publishers and Publishing, 1914–1918' (pp. 11–26); Stephen Colclough tackles an interesting subject for which he draws upon some archival material, ' "No such bookselling has ever before taken place in this country": Propaganda and the Wartime Distribution and Practices of W.H. Smith & Son' (pp. 27–45). Grace Brockington tackles the subject of 'Translating Peace: Pacifist Publishing and the Transmission of Foreign Texts' (pp. 46–58).

The second part is devoted to the subject of 'Reading and National Consciousness'. Santanu Das writes on 'Sepoys, Sahibs and Babus: India, the Great War and Two Colonial Journals' (pp. 61–77), the two journals being 'the colonial war journal *Indian Ink* published in Calcutta, and a special edited volume called *All About the War: The Indian Review War Book*, published in Madras' (p. 63). Rainer Pöppinghege writes on 'The Battle of the Books: Supplying Prisoners of War' (pp. 78–92), in which he draws mainly on German archives. Amanda Laugesen draws attention to 'Australian Soldiers and the World of Print during the Great War' (pp. 93–109).

In the third part, 'Writing the Trenches', Jessica Meyer writes on 'The Tuition of Manhood: "Sapper's" War Stories and the Literature of War' (pp. 113–28). John Pegum is concerned with 'British Army Trench Journals and a Geography of Identity' (pp. 129–47). He has an interesting, all too brief footnote on the differences between French and German trench journals and British ones (p. 145 n. 2). Nicholas Hiley is concerned with ' "A new and vital moral factor": Cartoon Book Publishing in Britain During the First World War' (pp. 148–77). His article, as the others, comes replete with illustrations, including some rather amusing ones: see for instance 'Coiffure in the Trenches' with its subtitle 'Keep yer'ead still, or I'll'ave yer blinkin' ear off', based on a Bairnsfather cartoon (p. 165). There are also some rather crude ones: see for instance Edmund Sullivan's '*The Kaiser's Garland*—Angel on the Chopping-Block' (p. 170).

The final part contains Kate Macdonald on 'Translating Propaganda: John Buchan's Writing During the First World War' (pp. 181–201), followed by Sara Haslam's 'Making a Text the Fordian Way: *Between St. Dennis and St. George*, Propaganda and the First World War' (pp. 202–14). Keith Grieves, in the final essay, writes on 'Depicting the War on the Western Front: Sir Arthur Conan Doyle and the Publication of *The British Campaign in France and Flanders*' (pp. 215–32). The book concludes with an enumerative, alphabetically arranged, 'Select Bibliography' (pp. 233–6) and an index (pp. 237–41). Clearly the essays differ in quality: some are far wordier than others. It is useful to see that they are accompanied not only by illustrations but informative tables such as the listings of the 'Number of Drummond novels published per year, 1921–39' and the 'Number of Drummond novels sold by price to 1939' (pp. 122–3).

Patrick H. Armstrong's two-volume *All Things Darwin: An Encyclopedia of Darwin's World* is precisely what it says it is. In his preface Armstrong admits to the impossibility of doing 'justice to' the diversity of Darwin's life and achievement. He has, however, 'attempted to highlight those parts of Darwin's life and work that, in [his] opinion, have captured the imagination: the *Beagle* voyage, his most important publications, and those who influenced and were influenced by him'. Further, he has 'included a selection of the places he visited and some of the plants and animals important to his work' (p. xv). Consequently, there are entries on sea anemones, barnacles, Chile and Peru, corals and coral reefs, igneous rocks, and sedimentary rocks. There are entries on William Buckland, Robert Chambers, Darwin's own family, Robert Fitzroy and others. The encyclopedia contains black and white illustrations, including the rather gruesome one of 'Darwin's Fungus, growing on southern beach trees, Terra del Fuego' (p. 141). Entries contain rather brief items for further reading. Some entries are clearly more detailed than others. There is an appendix introducing extracts from Darwin's work. The extracts extend over a good many pages that otherwise could have been devoted to encyclopedia entries (pp. 487–543). This helpful but uneven book concludes with a brief 'General Bibliography' (pp. 545–6) and a useful index (pp. 547–64).

Textual Cultures 2:i[Spring 2007] is a special issue edited by Martha Nell Smith. It 'features essays that focus on the interpretive consequences of any current or past editorial projects and the mutual impact of editing and traditional new historicism, history of the book, or feminist, Marxist, postcolonial, poststructural, multicultural, or queer literary theory analysis' (*TC* 2:i[2007] iii). Already problems occur with the journal. For instance, on the impressive list of 'the Board of Editorial Advisors' on the verso of the title page, the distinguished Shelley scholar Donald H. Reiman is at the 'Pforzheimber' Collection rather than at the Pforzheimer Collection, New York Public Library. A preface apologizes for errors in the actual appearance of the journal after it was returned from the compositors: in other words, there was a mess up. The author of the preface wisely observes that 'the larger question of how electronic reformatting of print purely for electronic distribution is forcing structural changes and sometimes inelegant accommodation of the limitations of electronic programs onto the layout of already established print journals is, in fact, a topic ripe for examination in this journal' (p. v). We hope that a special issue of the journal will be devoted to this specific issue. It is a crucially important one.

In the first essay of *Textual Cultures* 2:i Martha Nell Smith's 'The Human Touch Software of the Highest Order: Revisiting Editing as Interpretation' (*TC* 2:i[2007] 1–15) moves from the 'seventeenth-century architectural sense' of the 'L Word' to the need to maintain 'rigor and sharp discipline' and the embracing of 'new technologies [that are] no longer a luxury' but 'a necessity' (p. 1). John Bryant's 'Witness and Access: The Use of the Fluid Text' (*TC* 2:i[2007] 16–42) focuses upon Melville to discuss the issue of 'texts in revision—that is, "fluid texts" or any work that exists in multiple versions' (p. 16). Over two pages of Bryant's article are occupied by an enumerative alphabetical listing of 'Works Cited' (pp. 39–42). Indeed such 'Works Cited' listings are to be found at the conclusion of each essay.

Sherri Geller's 'Editing Under the Influence of the Standard Textual Hierarchy: Misrepresenting *A Mirror for Magistrates* in the Nineteenth- and Twentieth-Century Editions' (*TC* 2:i[2007] 43–77) is in effect a plea for a new edition of the text and for its incorporation 'into more classes on renaissance literature' (p. 74). Ingrid Satelmajer's 'When a Consumer Becomes an Editor: Susan Hayes Ward and the Poetry of *The Independent*' (*TC* 2:i[2007] 78–100), in relatively non-opaque language, 'examines the seminal role played by editor Susan Hayes Ward in American poetry culture in the late nineteenth and early twentieth centuries' (p. 78). America and nineteenth-century literary history are also the subject for Augusta Rohrbach's 'The Diary May Be from Dixie but the Editor Is Not: Mary Chestnut and Southern Print History' (*TC* 2:i[2007] 101–18). This is an examination of Chestnut's *Diary* 'in its five iterations in print, tracing the text from its development first as an unpublished diary to the labor of its various editors (in its serialized and published editions)' (p. 101).

The eminent Robin G. Schulze's 'How Not To Edit: The Case of Marianne Moore' (*TC* 2:i[2007] 119–35) is an examination of 'the very different edition of Moore's poems currently available'. According to Schulze, they 'underwrite very different arguments about Moore's work and career'. She is particularly critical of Grace Schulman's edition of *The Poems of Marianne Moore* (Viking Penguin [2003]). Shulze doesn't mince her words. Schulman's edition 'offers a telling example of the bad things that can happen when an editor fails to recognize the ways in which his or her presentation of the works of a given author reflect, or not, the arguments he or she wishes to make about the author, the author's work, and the issue of textuality generally' (p. 119). The final essay in this issue is Joseph Dimuro's 'The Salient Angle: Revising the Queer Case of Henry Blake Fuller's *Bertram Cope's Year*' (*TC* 2:i[2007] 136–54). Dimuro's essay is in fact an examination 'of preparing a new, annotated edition of Henry Blake Fuller's gay-themed novel, *Bertram Cope's Year* (1919)' (p. 136).

Textual Cultures 2:ii [Autumn 2007] is a special issue edited by Joe Bray and Ruth Evans on the topic of 'Definitions of Te
xtual Culture'. In their introduction, Bray and Evans attempt to explain what is meant by 'a new intellectual field "textual culture"' (p. 1). In the first essay, William Kuskin writes on '"The loadstarre of the English language": Spenser's *Shepheardes Calender* and the Construction of Modernity' (*TC* 2:ii[2007] 9–33). Kuskin contests the traditional view that 'modernity only occurred in the sixteenth century'. Kuskin 'argues for a notion of textual cultures that spans the medieval and modern, calling the very notion of historical period into question' (p. 9). Holger Shott Syme's 'The Look of Speech' (*TC* 2:ii[2007] 34–60) 'examines the visual representation of speech, and the act of speaking, in early modern Europe' (p. 34). The text is replete with illustrations, as are many others in *Textual Cultures*. In this instance, Syme draws upon fifteenth- and seventeenth-century books, and late twentieth-century comics.

John Frow's 'The Practice of Value' (*TC* 2:ii[2007] 61–76) 'seeks to think about the orders of value that govern our lives and our work as humanists engaged in the many dimensions and formations of textual culture' (p. 61).

Frow's work is conveniently divided into subsections and probably has the smallest number of 'Works Cited'—only four—of any of the articles in these issues of *Textual Culture*. Of the four cited, one is his own (*Cultural Studies and Cultural Value*), one by Hans-Georg Gadamer, an article by Paul Guyer on Immanuel Kant, and a 1987 translation of Kant's *Critique of Judgment*. It is a pity that not all the articles are so straightforward.

Kim Christian Schrøder's 'Media Discourse Analysis: Researching Cultural Meanings from Inception to Reception' (*TC* 2:ii[2007] 77–99) according to its abstract 'seeks to show the value of exploring empirically both the encoding and decoding discourse practices that mediate between media texts and socio-cultural practices, an approach that it names as a holistic "discourse ethnography" ' (p. 77). This is followed by Sally Bushell's 'Textual Process and the Denial of Origins' (*TC* 2:ii[2007] 100–17). Bushell writes that 'it is necessary to draw attention to the ways in which the discipline [i.e. English studies] in its critical (rather than text-critical) manifestation continues to privilege the published text over draft materials as the focus of criticism and analysis' (p. 100). Bushell's focus is not with Anglo-American critics but 'with influential French theories of the text' (p. 101). So we get citations from Roland Barthes, Michel Foucault and others, of course in translation. In the final essay, Clifford Siskin's 'Textual Culture in the History of the Real' (*TC* 2:ii[2007] 118–30) 'is an effort to support the launch of the University of Stirling's Textual Culture project by historicizing it. Focusing on the project's self-description [Siskin posits a] history of the real that describes how the physical became "real" in the late eighteenth and early nineteenth centuries, displacing the earlier reality of the metaphysical' (p. 118).

There are some impressive reviews in these two issues, including for instance Thomas Hallock's review of Hugh Amory's *Bibliography and the Book Trades: Studies in the Print Culture of Early New England* [2005], and Lou Burnard, Katherine O'Brien O'Keefe and John Unsworth's *Electronic Textual Editing* [2006], reviewed by David Greetham (*TC* 2:ii[2007] 131–6). The reviewer doesn't mince his words, concluding: 'Someone who did not like books designed this collection' (p. 136). One has some sympathy for Greetham's gripes. The ideas behind *Textual Cultures* are good. It's a pity the reviews are not longer: some seem to stop in full flow because of a word limitation. It is salutary to see reviews divided between 'Anglo-American Reviews' (*TC* 2:ii[2007] 131–42) and 'Continental and Mediterranean Reviews' (*TC* 2:ii[2007] 143–63). There are some distinguished contributors, but there is also quite a bit of waffle and a lack of old-fashioned clear writing. Lengthy, technologically based words are no substitute for real content and thought. Perhaps the editors of *Textual Cultures* ought to instruct their advisers to be tougher on the use of English in the journal and to remember that the electronic world is never static. What may be the flavour of the day or the month may well not be the flavour of the next month!

The Bodleian Library Record (*BLR* 20:i–ii[2007]) contains much of interest. J. Barron writes on 'The St. George's Hours' (*BLR* 20:i–ii[2007] 20–46), W. Clennell on 'The Bodleian Declaration: A History' (*BLR* 20:i–ii[2007] 47–60) and P. Croft on 'The "Mule" Portrait of Lord Burghley' (*BLR* 20:i–ii[2007] 61–75). Katherine Duncan-Jones writes interestingly on an account of

'Ms. Rawl. Poet. 185: Richard Tarlton and Edmund Spenser's "Pleasant Willy"' (*BLR* 20:i–ii[2007] 76–101). A. Vine writes on 'A New Version of Bacon's "Apologie.": Ms. Rawl. D. 672' (*BLR* 20:i–ii[2007] 102–17). There are also shorter notes, including an obituary of 'Dr. Bent Juel-Jensen (1922–2006)' (*BLR* 20:i–i[2007] 3–4), an account of 'William Croft: Autograph Manuscript' (*BLR* 20:i–ii[2007] 138) and 'Fine Bindings from the Wardington Library' (*BLR* 20:i–ii[2007] 141–3). In addition there is a description by J. Flavell of 'Two School Photographs of T.E. Lawrence' (*BLR* 20:i–ii[2007] 144–52).

An important addition to scholarship which should not go unnoticed is that published by the Royal Swedish Academy of Letters, History and Antiquities, in co-operation with the Swedish National Archives, of *The Works and Correspondence of Axel Oxenstierna*. He was the Chancellor of Sweden during its short-lived period of European supremacy. He died in 1654 and was Chancellor 'under King Gustav II Adolf (1611–32), the regency of 1632–1644 and Queen Christina (1644–54). Internationally, he is best known as the leader of Swedish foreign policy during the Thirty Years' War'. As the preface to Arne Jönsson's magisterial edition of his *Letters from Sir James Spens and Jan Rutgers* explains, 'Oxenstierna's activities in peace and war, internationally and domestically, as chancellor and magnate can be studied through his enormous correspondence'. Indeed, the edition of his works and correspondence has been going on 'since 1888 under the auspices of the Royal Swedish Academy of Letters, History and Antiquities' (p. 7).

Arne Jönsson is Professor of Latin at Lund University. His edition is the most recent to appear and encompasses Oxenstierna's correspondence with the Scottish Sir James Spens (d. 1632) and Jan Rutgers (1589–1625), the Dutch humanist jurist. Both 'played central roles in Swedish foreign politics in the 1610s and 1620s. Spens served as Swedish ambassador in Britain, as British ambassador in Sweden and as a recruiter of Scottish soldiers and officers for Gustav II Adolf's army. In the same period, Rutgers served as Swedish representative in the Dutch Republic' (p. 10). Jönsson's introduction on their lives is extremely clear, with the sources fully given. This is followed by a statement of his 'Editorial Principles' when editing the letters (pp. 10–22). Each letter (they are in Latin) is introduced by an explanation of its historical and political context as well as textual and biographical notes. 'The Letters of Sir James Spens to Axel Oxenstierna' occupies pages 23 to 224. Following the text of the Rutgers letters (pp. 225–586) there are extensive 'Biographical Notes', beginning with a note on 'Adolf Frederick I' (p. 587) and concluding with 'Zobel, Johan' (1578–1631), a diplomat in Hessian service (p. 621). This section is followed by an alphabetical listing of literature consulted (pp. 622–4) and an extensive index (pp. 625–42). The commentary of the text and all this material is in English, not Swedish, and is of considerable interest to literary and historical students of the 1610s and 1620s. The edition contains both colour and black and white illustrations, and it need hardly be said that it is splendidly produced.

Resources for American Literary Study volume 31, edited by Jackson R. Bryer and Richard Kopley, opens with Gary F. Scharnhorst's 'Prospects for the Study of Bret Harte' (*RALS* 31[2007] 1–10). Its author claims that 'The whole of Harte's canon is ripe for race, ethnicity, class, and gender studies. He was, for the record, more progressive on racial issues than, say, Twain' (p. 7). Scharnhorst's aim is to bring Bret Harte back into the canon. He concludes provocatively, 'Here's hoping... that in the twenty-third century his works are read at least as often as *Valley of the Dolls* (1966) and *The Carpetbaggers* (1961)' (p. 8). As a popular tennis commentator and former Wimbledon champion says, 'You can't be serious man!' More realistically, Todd H. Richardson writes on 'Emerson Iconography and the *Free Religious Index*' (*RALS* 31[2007] 11–29). Emron Esplin's title sums up its subject: 'From Poetic Genius to Master of Short Fiction: Edgar Allan Poe's Reception and Influence in Spanish America from the Beginnings through the Boom' (*RALS* 31[2007] 31–54). Michael Anesko and N. Christine Brookes write on 'Monsieur de l'Aubépine: The French Face of Nathaniel Hawthorne' (*RALS* 31[2007] 55–94). This article contains lengthy citations, fifty-two footnotes and an extensive listing of 'Works Cited'. Each essay in *RALS* 31 does in fact follow this procedure of notes and works cited. Sterling F. Delano and Joel Myerson write on 'Letters from Brook Farm: A Comprehensive Checklist of Surviving Correspondence' (*RALS* 31[2007] 95–123). The correspondence runs from 1840 through to 1847, lists 337 items and includes such figures as Nathaniel Hawthorne (1804–64), James Burrill Curtis (1822–95) and others. 'The present article is the first comprehensive inventory of all known surviving correspondence—published or not—from Brook Farm', and it will serve as a valuable finding aid for scholars in many fields (p. 95).

Sharon L. Dean's 'Constance Fenimore Woolson's [1840–1894] Unpublished Letters to Dr. William Wilberforce Baldwin' (*RALS* 31[2007] 125–55) publishes five letters. The first is from Cairo in Egypt dated January 18, 1890, and the last written from Venice dated December 17 [1893]. William Wilberforce Baldwin (1850–1910) was physician to Woolson and to many American ex-patriots. The five letters are selected ones: 'They have been selected to represent [Woolson's] sense of place; her friendships, especially with Henry and Alice James; her thoughts on writing and writers; and her struggle with illness and depression' (p. 133). They are followed by a 'Table of Letters from Constance Fenimore Woolson, with Supplementary Information' (pp. 141–7) and then valuable information on 'Letter Fragments and Unidentified Letters' (pp. 148–9). There is an extensive list of 'Identifications' of persons (pp. 149–51), detailed notation, and listing of works cited, including archives (pp. 152–5). Grace Farrell writes on 'Lillie Devereux Blake and Charlotte Perkins Gilman: A Collaboration' (*RALS* 31[2007] 157–68). Blake (1833–1913) was a 'novelist, essayist and suffragist' (p. 157). Robert M. Dowling's '"The Screenews of War": A Previously Unpublished Short Story by Eugene O'Neill' (*RALS* 31[2007] 169–98) is a fascinating addition to Eugene O'Neill's published works. Francis J. Bosha writes gives an extensive account of 'The John Cheever Journals at Harvard University's Houghton Library' (*RALS* 31[2007] 199–311). This constitutes another important contribution to American literary study found in this volume.

There are four review essays. Andrew Jewell assesses two electronic editions in '*Clotel, Typee*, and the Promise of Digital Scholarship' (*RALS* 31[2007]

313–17). William Pannapacker's 'The *Walt Whitman Archive*: The Body of Work Electric' (*RALS* 31[2007] 319–25) is an assessment of Ed Folsom's and Kenneth M. Price's electronic edition. Karen Ruth Kornweibel's 'Race and the Anxieties of Authorship: Two of Charles W. Chestnut's "White-Life" Novels' (*RALS* 31[2007] 327–30) assesses two editions in the ongoing 'University Press of Mississippi Press editions of Charles W. Chestnut's previously unpublished novels' (p. 327). Roger Forseth reviews two recent books on Sinclair Lewis in his 'You Can Go Home Again: Sinclair Lewis—Biography and Short Fiction' (*RALS* 31[2007] 331–45). These review articles are followed by twenty-five reviews, some of which are by distinguished hands, including Nina Bayn writing on Cecile Anne De Rocher's edition of *Elizabeth Manning Hawthorne: A Life in Letters* (*RALS* 31[2007] 343–6), Joel Myerson writing on Claudia Stokes's *Writers in Retrospect: the Rise of American Literary History, 1875–1910* (*RALS* 31[2007] 369–72), and, to mention just one other out of many, James L.W. West III writing on two books on Sherwood Anderson (*RALS* 31[2007] 375–7). The volume concludes with Heather McHale's extensive 'Author and Subject Index' (*RALS* 31[2007] 411–16). So resources for *RALS* 31 contains important contributions, especially those dealing with primary materials such as unpublished letters, checklists of surviving correspondents and unpublished short stories.

Anthologies of British literature clearly meant as competitors for the highly successful Norton Anthologies of Literature widely used in North America, continue to sprout. *The Broadview Anthology of British Literature: Concise Edition*, edited by Joseph Black et al., in its squat quarto format is clearly aimed at the North American market. The first volume, or 'Volume A', extends from the 'Medieval Period' through to the Restoration in the eighteenth century. 'Volume B' extends from the age of Romanticism to the present, the final authors included being Kazuo Ishiguro and Carol Ann Duffy. The same content can be had in six separate volumes. The preface explains that 'the rationale for publishing the *Concise Edition* . . . is, above all, pedagogical; we want to provide an alternative for those who prefer a textbook intended exclusively for use in courses that survey all of British literature over the course of two university terms' (p. xxvii). As the present writer is mentioned in the 'Acknowledgments' to these volumes, it would be invidious of him to make a value judgement about the relative merits of differing anthologies, apart from stating the facts. *The Broadview Anthology* is replete with extensive introductions, footnotes, colour illustrations and black and white illustrations, and includes notes on poetic terms in 'Imagery, Symbolism and Figures of Speech' (pp. 1587–91). There is inevitably a problem, that of copyright in producing extracts from twentieth-century writers, and to keep up to date the section 'The Late Twentieth Century and Beyond: 1945 to the Twenty-First Century' (pp. 1400 ff.) will have to be regularly updated, again, copyright allowing. There are some interesting inclusions in this section: to mention one, an all too brief extract from John Cleese and Graham Chapman's *Monty Python's Flying Circus* (pp. 1506–10). 'Volume B' concludes with a listing of 'Monarchs and Prime Ministers of Great Britain' (pp. 1158–62) and a 'Glossary of Terms', beginning with 'Accent' (p. 1563) and concluding with 'Zeugma' (p. 1585). 'Permission Acknowledgments' (pp. 1586–90) are followed by an 'Index of First Lines' (pp. 1591–5) and an 'Index of Authors and Titles' (pp. 1596–1603). Notable omissions are Harold Pinter and Tom Stoppard; one wonders why: copyright restrictions perhaps?

Archie Burnett's magnificent two-volume *The Letters of A.E. Housman* will stand the test of time. Burnett's introductory material in the first volume includes a 'Note on Editorial Principles' (pp. xv–xvii) clearly explaining the complexities involved in editing Housman. Burnett explains in his introduction that 'the decision to print every letter found has not been taken lightly . . . the main justification has been to allow as full a revelation as possible of a man whose reserve was legendary'. Burnett adds that 'even if the jigsaw is not complete, a better picture results from assembling all, rather than some, of the pieces available' (pp. xix–xx). There is a 'List of Recipients' with their details, beginning with Claude Colleer Abbott (1889–1971), who served a long reign as Professor of English Language and Literature at the University of Durham from 1932 to 1954, and concludes with W[illiam] S[iddons] Young, who authored various volumes of Latin verses (vol. 1, pp. xxiii–liv). In fact, this listing contains a panoply of mostly minor and largely forgotten late Victorian and Edwardian figures whose paths crossed with Housman's. The letters are fully annotated. Apart from textual notes, there are notes on individuals, on allusions, and on events—in fact, all that is needed to enhance one's reading of the letters. Burnett does not hesitate to acknowledge his scholarly debts, including a large one to P.G. Naiditch, seven of whose works on Housman, including an attempt to reconstruct his library, are noted in Burnett's 'Abbreviations' (vol. 1, pp. xi–xiv).

The first volume covers the letters from 1872 to 1926 and the second volume contains letters from 1927 to 1936. This second volume also includes 'Letters Undated or Approximately Dated' (pp. 534–9), an 'Index of Recipients' (pp. 541–9) and a 'General Index' (pp. 551–85). Housman is clearly an important figure, significant enough to be the subject of Tom Stoppard's drama *The Invention of Love* [1997], which examines the life and death of Housman, especially his love for his friend Moses Jackson (1858–1923). As Burnett notes in his 'List of Recipients', '"Dear Mo" was Housman's "greatest friend" who "had more influence on my life than anyone else" and who was "largely responsible for my writing poetry."' Laconically, Burnett adds, 'Only [Housman's] last letter to Jackson [19 October 1922] has come to light' (vol. 1, pp. xxxvii–xxxviii). It is worth repeating that this is a magisterial edition, magnificently produced and typeset.

Duncan Wu's welcome two-volume *The New Writings of William Hazlitt* is a collection of 205 new writings by Hazlitt collected for the first time. They give us a more rounded picture than previously known of his work as a journalist. Amongst other jewels, there are important essays on the poetry of Wordsworth, Coleridge, Byron and Shelley. There is an analysis of the various trials of William Hone, the Regency publisher and writer, and reminiscences and stories from the last years of Hazlitt's life. Wu's most informative and extensive introduction places the 205 uncollected works, 'that is to say Hazlitt did not reprint them during his lifetime' (vol. 1, p. xxv) in their social, political and biographical contexts. Wu gives a very thorough account of Hazlitt's career as a journalist (vol. 1, pp. xxix–lvii) and 'A Note on Attributions' (vol. 1, pp. lix–lxvi). 'The first part of' the first volume 'presents new writings now attributable to Hazlitt but not included in Howe's edition of the works (vol. 1, p. lxvii). There are 205 of these. In his second part, Wu presents 'Early Versions of Selected Essays' (vol. 2, pp. 431–66). This is followed by 'Questionable Attributions' (pp. 469–91). There are five useful appendices: 'Hazlitt and *The Correspondent*' (vol. 2, pp. 495–6); 'Hazlitt's Copy of *The Yellow Dwarf* and "Is There Any Hope of Reform?"' (vol. 2, pp. 597–8); 'Hazlitt's Involvement with *The White Hat*' (vol. 2, pp. 499–501); 'Hazlitt's Opera Reviews for *The Atlas, 1827–8*' (vol. 2, pp. 502–11); and 'Attribution Listings for the *Morning Chronicle, The Champion, The Examiner, The Times*, the *London Weekly Review*, and *The Atlas*' (vol. 2, pp. 512–33). The volumes conclude with a 'Subject Index' (vol. 2, pp. 535–53). The only caveat is in the extent of the annotations to the writings, although some are present. For instance, in an article published in *The Times* on 3 November 1817, page 2, Hazlitt mentions 'Sestini's celebrated Rondo' (vol. 1, p. 275). There is no entry for Sestini in the index and the reference remains unannotated.

Another monumental Clarendon Press edition to appear in what in retrospect seems to have been a vintage year for Oxford University Press, is Gary Taylor and John LaVagnino's *Thomas Middleton and Early Modern Textual Culture: A Companion to the Collected Works*. Taylor has long been an advocate for Thomas Middleton—'our other Shakespeare'—whom he regards as a major writer worthy at times, it would seem, to stand with his great contemporary William Shakespeare. Taylor writes that Middleton 'is the only other Renaissance playwright who created acknowledged masterpieces of comedy, tragedy, and history; his revolutionary English history play *A Game at Chess*, was also the greatest box-office hit of early modern London'. Taylor adds that Middleton's 'achievements extend beyond . . . traditional genres to tragicomedies, masques, pageants, pamphlets, epigrams, and biblical and political commentaries, written alone or in collaboration'. As Taylor points out, Middleton 'has influenced writes as diverse as Aphra Behn, Anthony Trollope, and T.S. Eliot'. And, one should add, Harold Pinter. 'Though repeatedly censored in his own time, Middleton has since come to be particularly admired for his representations of the intertwined pursuits of sex, money, power, and God' (p. 2).

Thomas Middleton and Early Modern Textual Culture is divided into three parts. In the first, 'The Culture', essays focus on diverse subjects such as authorship, by Macdonald P. Jackson, manuscripts, by Harold Love, legal texts, by Edward Geiskes, censorship, by Richard Burt, printing, by Adrian Weiss, visual texts, by John Astington, music, by Andrew Sabol and Gary Taylor, stationers and living authors, by Cyndia Clegg, posthumous publishing, by Maureen Bell, and early readers, by John Jowett. Some of the contributions have very suggestive titles, such as Richard Burt's 'Thomas Middleton, Uncut: Castration, Censorship, and the Regulation of Dramatic Discourse in Early Modern England' (pp. 182–94). Many of the articles are of interest to students of analytical bibliography. Adrian Weiss's account of 'Casting Compositors, Foul Cases, and Skeletons: Printing in Middleton's Age' (pp. 195–225) is replete with illustrations, gives a detailed listing of works cited (pp. 224–5), and is full of informative information, as is

John H. Ashington's 'Visual Texts: Thomas Middleton and Prints' (pp. 226–46) and Cyndia Susan Clegg's ' "I will much enrich the Company of Stationers": Thomas Middleton and the London Book Trade, 1580–1627' (pp. 247–59), to instance just some of many important and fascinating essays found in this volume.

The second part is concerned with 'The Author' and contains essays explaining the justification for works included in the edition with their background and chronology. There is a note by Macdonald P. Jackson and Gary Taylor on 'Works Excluded from This Edition' (pp. 444–6). The third part focuses on 'The Texts', and contains extensive editorial apparatus for each specific item in the *Collected Works* followed by documentation on each of them (pp. 461–1166). The volume concludes with Trish Thomas Henley's 'Index to Notes on Modernization' (pp. 1167–83), which identifies 'textual notes in Part III, which record modernizations of spelling' (p. 1167). This is followed by Molly Hand's 'A Selective Topical Index' (pp. 1175–83) recording 'proper names, references to all Middleton's works, and a selection of important topics' (p. 1175). The volume's preliminary materials include two fascinating pieces by Gary Taylor on 'How To Use This Book' (pp. 19–23) and his 'Preface: Textual Proximities' (pp. 24–8). Both most usefully combine contemporary and historical ways of looking at bibliography and succinctly explain concepts such as 'textual culture', 'texts', 'society' (pp. 24–8). All in all, this is a most exciting and important volume from which the present reviewer is learning much and will continually return to.

Andrew Murphy's *A Concise Companion to Shakespeare and the Text* aims to examine the state of thinking concerning Shakespeare's texts at the end of the twentieth century and beginnings of the new century. Divided into parts, the first part 'is an exploration of the parameters and possibilities of' the complex textual world in which we find ourselves. The second part of the book 'takes up the issue of the various strategies that have been involved in an effort to cope with the complexities of the text we have inherited from the Renaissance' (pp. 12–13). The final part of the volume deals with practical textual editorial matters. Andrew Murphy's clearly written and helpful 'Introduction: What Happens in *Hamlet*?' (pp. 1–14) is followed by the first part, entitled 'Histories of the Books'. This contains five essays: Helen Smith on 'The Publishing Trade in Shakespeare's Time' (pp. 17–34); Peter Stallybrass and Roger Chartier on 'Reading and Authorship: The Circulation of Shakespeare 1590–1619' (pp. 35–56); Thomas L. Berger on 'Shakespeare Writ Small: Early Single Editions of Shakespeare's Plays' (pp. 57–70); and Anthony James West on 'The Life of the First Folio in the Seventeenth and Eighteenth Centuries' (pp. 71–90).

The second part is devoted to 'Theories of Editing'. Andrew Murphy writes on 'The Birth of the Editor' (pp. 93–108); Paul Werstine on 'The Science of Editing' (pp. 109–27); Leah S. Marcus on 'Editing Shakespeare in a Postmodern Age' (pp. 128–44); and Michael Best on 'Shakespeare and the Electronic Text' (pp. 145–61). Part III deals with practicalities, and opens with David Bevington's very thorough account of 'Working with the Text: Editing in Practice' (pp. 165–84); Sonia Massai writes on 'Working with the Texts: Differential Readings' (pp. 185–203); and Neil Rhodes writes on 'Mapping Shakespeare's Contexts: Doing Things with Databases' (pp. 204–20). In an 'Afterword' (pp. 221–38) John Drakakis presents a comprehensive discussion exploring 'the political contexts and ramifications of many of the textual and editorial issues raised' in the rest of the book (p. 13). Murphy provides a thorough, historically arranged, enumerative bibliography (pp. 239–57) and there is a very useful index. In short, this is a very useful volume which is instructive not only for students of Shakespeare but for students of bibliography and textual criticism in general.

The Commonwealth of Books: Essays and Studies in Honour of Ian Willison is edited by Wallace Kirsop with the assistance of Meredith Sherlock. Produced by the Centre for the Book, Monash University, it is a tribute to the distinguished librarian and eminently knowledgeable and ever-helpful Ian Willison. The contributions include David McKitterick's introduction on Ian Willison (pp. 1–11). Dennis E. Rhodes adds an enumerative 'Bibliography of Ian Roy Willison['s] extensive contributions to the history of the book' (pp. 12–17). Other contributions include: J. Paul Hunter's 'Making Books, Generating Genres' (pp. 18–47); Michael F. Suarez, SJ, ' "The most blasphemous book that ever was publish'd": Ridicule, Reception, and Censorship in Eighteenth-Century England' (pp. 48–77); Richard Landon's 'Two Collectors: Thomas Grenville and Lord Amherst' (pp. 78–95); Warwick Gould's 'Biography and Textual Biography: Towards a Life of Yeats's Text' (pp. 96–119); Peter Davison's 'Impediments to Scholarship: Printing and Publishing at the Close of the Twentieth Century' (pp. 120–5); Simon Eliot's 'Whither Book History in the UK, and Beyond?' (pp. 136–48); Keith Maslen's 'The History of Print Culture in New Zealand: Report on Recent Experience' (pp. 149–63); Robin Alston's 'Bibliography and Cultural History' (pp. 164–80); Graham Shaw's 'A Pedigree Mongrel: Some Reflections on the Historical Development of the South Asian Collections of the British Library's Oriental and India Office Collections' (pp. 181–96); Terry Belanger's 'The Rare Book Program at Columbia University, 1972–1992' (pp. 197–208); Sarah Tyacke's 'Archives in a Wider World: The Culture and Politics of Archives' (pp. 209–26); Bernhard Fabian's 'Kulturwissenschaft: Einige vorläufige Notizen' (pp. 227–41); and Wallace Kirsop's 'Scholarship, Collecting and Libraries in the Old and New Worlds: A Personal Journey' (pp. 242–71). This is followed by a listing of fifteen contributors. All in all, a most worthwhile collection to celebrate its distinguished subject. Unfortunately, no doubt, the rather splendid dust-jacket will be disposed of when the book enters libraries: it shouldn't be!

Rodger L. Tarr continues his excavations into the work of the Florida writer Marjorie Kinnan Rawlings, whose novel *The Yearling* gained her the 1939 Pulitzer Prize. Tarr, an eminent Carlyle scholar, seems to have been focusing much of his attention in the last few years not on the Victorian guru but on Rawlings. His latest venture is an edition with Brent E. Kinser of *The Uncollected Writings of Marjorie Kinnan Rawlings*: 'The purpose of *The Uncollected Writings* is to reproduce the publications of Marjorie Kinnan Rawlings that have hitherto been lost to the literary scholar and general reader.' Tarr and Kinser, in their 'Editorial Note', add 'Beginning with her first publication as Marjorie Kinnan in the *Washington Post* in 1910 and ending with her last in 1953, the year of her death, these publications range from poems, to essays, to letters, to short stories, to newspaper articles, to reviews, to introductions, to blurbs.' The volume 'includes all the published material' the editors 'could find, including a few new items not listed in [Tarr's] *Marjorie Kinnan Rawlings: A Descriptive Bibliography*'. Excluded are 'excerpts and serializations of her novels', some poems, 'occasional letters she wrote to the *Washington Post*' and a few other items (p. xiii). In addition to a 'Chronology' (pp. xv–xxix), there is an extensive, well-written introduction (pp. 1–14). Writings are divided into 'Juvenilia: 1910–1914' (pp. 15–72); 'University of Wisconsin: 1914–1918' (pp. 87–152); 'The Newspaper Years: 1919–1928' (pp. 153–250); and 'Florida: 1928–1953' (pp. 251–364). In addition to a bibliography (p. 365), there is an 'Index of Titles' (pp. 367–70) and an extensive index (pp. 371–91). Annotations are found at the foot of the page, and between pages 73 and 86 may be found sixteen black and white photographs, mainly of Rawlings, from adolescence to maturity. All in all then, Tarr and Kinser have served Marjorie Kinnan Rawlings exceptionally well. Oh that other authors had the good fortune in their afterlife to find such mentors!

Martin Ray's *Joseph Conrad: Memories and Impressions. An Annotated Bibliography* 'aims to identify and annotate publications that record "memories and impressions" of Joseph Conrad by those who knew him or met him'. Alphabetically arranged and annotated, the entries begin with Lawrence F. Abbot (1859–1933), who, we are told, 'spent 32 years as the President of the Outlook Company' (p. 1), and concluding with Dr John Sheridan Zelie (1866–1942), a Princeton-born clergyman who subsequently 'served as an Army chaplain in France, 1918–1919' (p. 173). Some of the annotations are less detailed than others, and there are missed opportunities. For instance, the novelist and poet Eleanor Farjeon (1881–1965) deserves more than the very perfunctory treatment she receives (see p. 45 n. 2). Ray's annotated bibliography concludes with an extensive personal-name-orientated index (pp. 174–88). Jan Pilditch's *Catherine Carswell: A Biography* documents the life of the Scottish novelist, biographer and critic who lived between 1879 and 1946. Born Catherine Roxburgh Macfarlane in Glasgow, she travelled extensively in Europe and elsewhere and even met most of the personalities who were to become part of Stalin's cabinet in the 1930s. Carswell's *Life of Robert Burns* [1930] caused great controversy, as did her 1932 biography of D.H. Lawrence, *The Savage Pilgrimage*. This in fact was initially withdrawn amid threats of litigation. The one thing missing from Pilditch's excellent account is an extensive bibliography of Carswell's writings.

Alan Bartram's *Typeforms: A History* 'is partly based on *An Atlas of Typeforms* (which James Sutton and I wrote in 1968), abridged and mostly rewritten; to it is added a parallel story of architectural and vernacular lettering'. Bartram exemplifies nearly seventy-five different typeforms shown in their original metal forms, and places them in their historical contexts. There are photographs of contemporary inscriptions on buildings and monuments. Bartram's exploration of the correlation between the printed and the architectural extends from the Renaissance to the nineteenth century. In his 'Prologue: Then, and Now' Bartram laments what he refers to as 'a disaster' brought about by a change in technology. He points out that the compositor 'not only set the type, but made a contribution that today should be done'. The 'compositor of yesterday would correct punctuation, grammar, spelling and even query facts for they were highly trained craftsmen, having served a six-year apprenticeship in a trade that jealously guarded its skills'. Bartram notes that 'many authors today, because they own an AppleMac, believe, in their ignorance, that they can design and set their own books, which they can, of course, but badly' (p. 6). Bartram's is 'a history book' with an agenda, it is replete with fascinating information and detailed black and white illustrations (p. 8).

Books on the Move: Tracking Copies through Collections and the Book Trade, edited by Robin Myers, Michael Harris and Giles Mandelbrote, contains seven essays that were part of 'the twenty-seventh in the series of proceedings of the annual conference on book trade history, which started in 1979. This conference was held at Wesley's Chapel in City Road [London] on 1 and 2 December 2006, under the auspices of the Antiquarian Booksellers Association and with student bursaries from the Bibliographical Society' (p. x). Peter Beal writes on '"Lost": The Destruction, Dispersal and Rediscovery of Manuscripts' (pp. 1–15). He 'describes some of the mysterious ways in which printed and manuscript material can appear, disappear and reappear again' (p. viii). David Pearson, 'What Can We Learn by Tracking Multiple Copies of Books?' (pp. 17–37), has fifty-five footnotes. Pearson chooses three representative English translations of Julius Caesar 'published at approximately fifty year intervals between 1590 and 1695, to test a methodology which has been used to good effect by incunabulists but has rarely been applied to later books'. Pearson, after having traced nearly ninety copies of the three representative editions, 'compares information from as many copies as possible, looking at readers' annotations, marks of ownership, decoration and binding, to try to identify common features and changes over time in how the three editions were marketed, owned and used'. 'This approach' as the editors point out in their introduction, 'Pearson suggests, may become one of the most fruitful future directions for book history' (p. viii). Angela Nuovo's 'The Creation and Dispersal of the Library of Gian Vincento Pinelli' (pp. 39–67), replete with seventy-seven footnotes, and Astrid Balsem's 'Books from the Library of Andreas Dudith (1533–89) in the Library of Isaac Vossius (1618–89)' (pp. 69–86) concern themselves with Paduan and continental European book history, as do the three remaining essays in the volume. Jos van Heel writes on 'From Venice and Naples to Paris, The Hague, London, Oxford, Berlin. . . . The Odyssey of the Manuscript Collection of Gerard and Johan Merman' (pp. 87–111), and Cristina Dondi on 'Pathways to Survival of Books of Hours Printed in Italy in the Fifteenth Century' (pp. 113–32), in which there are seventy-six footnotes. The final essay is by Pierre Delsaerdt, focusing upon 'Bibliophily and Public–Private Partnership: The Library of Gustave van Havre (1817–92) and its Afterlife in Antwerp Libraries' (pp. 133–51). There is a useful index to the volume (pp. 153–64).

The fourth edition, edited by Hope Mayo, of Rosamond B. Loring's *Decorated Book Papers, Being an Account of their Designs and Fashions* contains eight plates, and various examples of decorated papers. Loring's work was 'first published in 1942 by the Department of Printing and Graphic Arts, Harvard College Library. The edition of 250 numbered copies was printed by the Harvard University Press, using Bembo type on ivory Glenbourn Book paper' (p. xv). Mayo's preface to the fourth edition goes on to explain at some length the three editions of the work. The second was published in 1952 and the third in 1973. 'The text remains unchanged from the first editions' (p. xvii) and essays on the author's life and work by W.M. Whitehill, D. Hunter and V. Ruzicka, with Philip Hofer's foreword, are also retained. In addition, 'illustrations...have been printed in color from new digital photography' (p. xviii). There are also essays by Hope Mayo on 'Rosamond B. Loring: Maker, Collector, and Historian of Decorated Papers' and 'Editions Bound in Paste Papers by Rosamond B. Loring: A Preliminary Checklist' (pp. xlii–xcvi). There are three appendices on 'The Art of Marbling', 'The Preparation of Paste Paper' and 'Some Early Makers of Decorated Paper Arranged Alphabetically According to the Cities in which They Worked' (pp. 105–46). Mayo's edition concludes with detailed notation and an index (pp. 147–76). This is a most valuable and deserved fourth edition of an important work on fine bookmaking during the first half of the last century.

Gabrielle H. Cody and Evert Sprinchorn's multi-volume *The Columbia Encyclopedia of Modern Drama* is bulky. It covers the period from 1860 to the present and includes Western and non-Western dramatists, claiming to have 'placed 540 individual plays, 640 playwrights and over 60 countries in their cultural and historical context'. Highly ambitious, it is sometimes confusing. 'Significant dramatists who are not given separate entries are covered in the national surveys or in articles devoted to movements or currents of thought, such as political theater, the avant-garde, philosophy and drama, and apocalyptic currents in drama.' It also claims to differ from existing reference works such as the late Myron Matlaw's *Modern World Drama: An Encyclopedia* [1972], and other standard works, by 'stressing the written drama while also providing informative articles on theater practice' (pp. ix–x). Clearly, some contributions are more extensive than others. Some are downright perfunctory, only listing select plays and very limited further reading: see for instance the entry on Arnold Wesker. In other words, Cody and Sprinchorn attempt too much and there are important omissions, such as for example Bernard Kops and Dannie Abse, to mention but two of many.

Justly praised is Owen Dudley Edwards's fascinating *British Children's Fiction in the Second World War*. In addition to a dozen illustrations, extensive footnote documentation and a thorough, fascinating bibliographical essay and epilogue, Dudley Edwards discusses in a lively manner nearly a hundred writers whom British children read during the traumatic years between 1939 and 1945. The focus is on Enid Blyton, Frank Richards, J.R.R. Tolkien, George Orwell, Richmal Crompton and some others. In addition to plot summaries and citations from their works, Edwards gives details of their lives and focuses upon the particularities of the texts and their reception. He has an interesting comparison of Second World War works for children with those produced during the First World War. All in all, this is a very important reference book and it is hardly surprising that it has already been reprinted.

Stefan Collini's *Absent Minds: Intellectuals in Britain* continues his detailed exploration of intellectuals transversing the boundaries of subject, genre and period, but focusing upon the United Kingdom in the twentieth century. There are fascinating chapters on 'New Left, New Right, Old Story' (pp. 171–200), comparisons with American, French, and other European intellectuals, and extensive discussions of, amongst others, T.S. Eliot, R.G. Collingwood, George Orwell, A.J.P. Taylor and A.J. Ayer. Collini's work is clearly written, extends beyond the subject of influence to detailed analysis of specific works and is definitive in the sense that it reflects late twentieth-century and early twenty-first-century perceptions of the work of the most perceptive cross-genre writers of the preceding generations. Another study of intellectual ideas is found in Peter Mandler's *The English National Character: The History of an Idea from Edmund Burke to Tony Blair*. Mandler attempts to follow the diverse perceptions amongst the English concerning their own national identity through two centuries. He begins more or less with Edmund Burke and concludes with Tony Blair, neither of whom, it might be argued, is necessarily 'English', Burke certainly having Anglo-Irish connections and Blair being, to put it mildly, an Anglo-Scot with an emphasis on the latter rather than the former. Mandler's account is bound of necessity to be contentious but contains material of considerable interest.

Neil Pearson's *Obelisk: A History of Jack Kahane and the Obelisk Press* is replete with coloured illustrations of jackets and black and white examples. Kahane's Obelisk Press published, amongst others, Henry Miller, Anaïs Nin, Lawrence Durrell, D.H. Lawrence and James Joyce, in addition to erotica and pulp fiction. Kahane also published under the pseudonym of the 'Marco Polo of Sex'. This is the first study of the Manchester-born Kahane (1887–1939), his authors, his activities, some of which were decidedly nefarious, and bibliography. The first section contains 'Books Published by Jack Kahane and the Obelisk Press' (pp. 79–270). Section B is devoted to 'Ephemera of the Obelisk Press' (pp. 271–80), section C focuses upon 'The Plays, Novels, Short Fiction and Non-Fiction of Jack Kahane' (pp. 281–308) and Section D is devoted to 'Translations of Jack Kahane' (pp. 309–12). This is followed by 'Author Biographies' (pp. 313–488), giving details of the authors he published. There is a listing of 'Works Consulted' (pp. 490–2) and an 'Index of Obelisk Authors' (pp. 493–527). In addition to transcribing the title pages and giving a statement of collation of pagination, Pearson in his first section gives binding and wrapper details and other bibliographical information concerning each of the Obelisk Press's publications. A thirty-two-page colour section contains illustrations of many of the original covers. Pearson's extensive 'A Very British Pornographer: The Life of Jack Kahane' (pp. 1–75), contains well-written details of its subject's interesting life and work. All in all, *Obelisk: A History of Jack Kahane and the Obelisk Press* is a fascinating account of a fascinating character and a valuable contribution to cultural history, bibliography and reference.

The second and third volumes of Jan Ross's magnificent projected seven-volume edition of *The Works of Thomas Traherne*, published by D.S. Brewer, should not go unnoticed. These two volumes make available Traherne's 'Commentaries of Heaven' from a manuscript held in the British Library.

Ross points out in her introduction (pp. xi–xl) that '*Commentaries of Heaven* is Thomas Traherne's most ambitious work, which if completed would have comprised several folio volumes.' The manuscript was 'found smoldering on a rubbish tip just outside Liverpool about 1967 [and] was rescued by Mr. Laurence Wookey' who took it to Canada with him, 'where it was identified as the work of Thomas Traherne...in 1981/1982'. Subsequently auctioned at Christie's in New York, it was bought by the British Library (vol. 2, pp. xi–xii). Volume 2, in addition to containing an extensive introduction on this discovery, its significance, dating, provenance, methods, Traherne's sources and methods of composition, methods of cross-referencing, his purpose, his ordering of its subject, the manuscript's seventeenth-century context and general editorial principles (vol. 2, pp. xxxiii–xl), contains the text. This is followed by textual emendations (vol. 2, pp. 425–512) and extensive appendices mostly devoted to Traherne's 'common place book' and cross-references (vol. 2, pp. 513–30). The text in the second volume extends from *Abhorrence* to *Alone*. The third volume, or part 2 of the text of *Commentaries of Heaven*, contains the text from *Al-Sufficient* to *Bastard*. *Commentaries*, Ross writes, 'was to be a multi-volume work, written over a period of several years'. Its author wrote it 'for specific readers: atheists, private Christians and divines' (vol. 2, p. xii).

The last volume in the twenty-one-volumes of the Cornell Wordsworth series is devoted to his dramatic poem, *The Excursion*. Worthy of its predecessors, it 'presents the first scholarly edition of' the poem to appear 'since the appearance of Ernest de Selincourt and Helen Darbishire's fifth volume of the *Poetical Works*' published by Oxford University Press in 1949. De Selincourt and Darbishire based their edition on the 1850 text. The Cornell edition of *The Excursion*, edited by Sally Bushell, James A. Butler and Michael C. Jaye, is based upon 'the poem as first published in 1814, together with cross-references enabling easy comparison of this text with the one edited by de Selincourt and Darbishire'. Extensive editors' notes are included, as are 'Wordsworth's own notes to the poem...located...as they are in 1814, after the reading texts (cross-references are given on the relevant pages of the poem itself)'. In addition to showing 'all post-publication verbal variants in manuscript and printed editions' and transcriptions of 'all *Excursion* manuscripts that were produced under the author's supervision between c.1806 and the poem's publication in 1814' (p. xi), the volume has four appendices: a 'Key to Manuscript Transcriptions' (pp. 1203–7), 'Fragments Relating to *The Excursion*' (pp. 1208–14), 'Fenwick Note to *The Excursion*' (pp. 1214–25) and finally '*The Excursion* and the Christian Miscellany' (pp. 1225–6). Assuming that books are still accessible, there is no doubt that this great edition will last more than half a century.

Simon Eliot, Andrew Nash and Ian Willison's *Literary Cultures and the Material Book*, its editors claim in their preface, 'marks a high point in the history of book history. It carries the subject around the world and back to the beginning of recorded time, yet it does not pretend to cover everything' (p. xvi). The editors also point out that the 'book has its origins in an international symposium held in London in 2004.... One of the main aims of the symposium has been to set the rapidly growing discipline of book history . . . into a much broader, international context' (p. 1). Following Simon Eliot's 'Some Material Factors in Literary Culture 2500 BCE–1900 CE' (pp. 31–52), the volume is divided into four sections. The first focuses upon 'Non-Western Traditions of the Book' and contains five essays, for instance Glen Dudbridge on 'A Thousand Years of Printed Narrative in China' (pp. 53–63) and Sheldon Pollock on 'Literary Culture and Manuscript Culture in Precolonial India' (pp. 77–94). The second section contains five essays on 'The Western Book in History' and includes David Ganz on 'Carolingian Manuscript Culture and the Making of the Literary Culture of the Middle-Ages' (pp. 147–58) and Nicholas Mann's '*Petrarca philobiblon*: The Author and his Books' (pp. 159–73). The third section, 'Language Empires', contains eight essays, including two on Spain, an essay on Spain, Portugal and Latin America, two on France and French literary culture, and one on Canadian French culture. The fourth section, on 'The Anglophone Tradition', contains essays of more immediate interest to readers of *YWES*.

John Barnard's 'Creating an English Literary Canon, 1679–1720: Jacob Tonson, Dryden and Congreve' (pp. 307–21) is an all too brief account of a fascinating topic. Barnard's aim is the reintegration of 'publishers, authors and the workings of the book trade . . . into the study of the origins of the English canon' (p. 307). Andrew Nash's 'Literary Culture and Literary Publishing in Inter-War Britain: A View from Chatto & Windus' (pp. 323–42) draws upon the Chatto archives and is illustrated, as are many of the other articles. Nash's fascinating account concludes with a brief excursion into the story of the creation of Penguin. Richard Landon's ' "The Elixir of Life": Richard Garnett, the British Museum Library and Literary London' (pp. 343–54) manages to say quite a lot about his subject and his milieu. Stephen Bury is also illuminating in his account of 'The Tradition of A.W. Pollard and the World of Literary Scholarship' (pp. 355–65). Michael Winship's ' "In the four quarters of the globe, who reads an American book?" ' (pp. 367–78) follows the reception of *Uncle Tom's Cabin* on the European continent as well as in the United States, and the subsequent treatment of Harriet Beecher Stowe. Winship raises many interesting questions which inevitably must remain unanswered, concerning 'the relationship between the study of American literary culture and book history' (p. 377). Janet B. Friskney's 'From Methodist Literary Culture to Canadian Literary Culture: The United Church Publishing House/The Ryerson Press, 1829–1970' (pp. 379–85) is an all too brief account of an interesting United Church Canadian publishing house. Sydney J. Shep's ' "The centennial racket": J.C. Beaglehole, Nationalism and the 1940 New Zealand Centennial Publications' (pp. 387–98) contains a fascinating account of 'J.C. Beaglehole [1901–1971], history professor at Victoria University College in Wellington, international scholar of Cook's voyages, labour sympathizer' and much else besides (p. 390). He was fascinated by typography and graphic design, and Friskney's account focuses upon his desire for 'a national culture', that is, a New Zealand 'national culture' (p. 390). John Barnes's ' "Heaven forbid that i should think of treating with an English publisher": The Dilemma of Literary Nationalists in Federated Australia' (pp. 399–412) focuses on the fragility in the growth of Australian publishing.

In the final essay, David McKitterick writes judiciously on 'Perspectives for an International History of the Book' (pp. 413–29). Each article in this rich volume contains extensive documentation. There is much to be learnt from it, although some of the articles are rather shorter than others. In addition, there is an extensive index (pp. 431–44). There are extensive black and white illustrations, and this important volume opens with notes on 'Contributors' (pp. xi–xv).

Simon Eliot and Jonathan Rose have edited *A Companion to the History of the Book*. This is divided into four distinct sections representing different approaches to the history of the book. The first section deals with 'Methods and Approaches' and has four contributors. The eminent T.H. Howard writes succinctly on 'Why Bibliography Matters' (pp. 9–20). David Greetham writes on 'What Is Textual Scholarship?" (pp. 21–32) and, as usual, raises very interesting issues. Solidly and statistically grounded, Alexis Weedon writes on 'The Uses of Quantification' (pp. 33–49). This section concludes with Stephen Colclough's 'Readers: Books and Biography' (pp. 50–62), which views things from the point of view of 'what people actually read in the past' (p. 50). The second section, focusing on 'The History of the Material Text' (pp. 67–176), is divided into two. The first part has two contributions, focusing on 'The World Before the Codex' (pp. 68–94); the second has seven contributions on subjects as diverse as China, 'The Hebraic Book' (pp. 153–64) and 'The Islamic Book' (pp. 165–76).

This is followed by an extensive section of eighteen contributions focusing on 'The Codex in the West 400–2000' (pp. 179–418). Unfortunately, there is not the space to individually deal with these fascinating materials. Part III, 'Beyond the Book' (pp. 421–63), contains three entries. The final one is by Charles Chadwyck-Healey on the subject of 'The New Textual Technologies' (pp. 451–63). Part IV has six contributors writing on 'Issues' (pp. 467–543). A coda is by Angus Phillips, and addresses the question: 'Does the Book Have a Future?' (pp. 547–59). Each entry is accompanied at the end by a section on 'References and Further Reading'. There is an extensive index (pp. 560–99) and at the beginning 'Notes on Contributors' (pp. x–xvi). Simon Eliot and Jonathan Rose write succinctly in their brief introduction (pp. 1–6) to the volume. They conclude that they hope the readers of the volume 'will agree that the book has had quite a past' (p. 6). Given the depth and breadth of this volume, it clearly would appear that it has a future, too!

Jack De Bellis and Michael Broomfield's *John Updike: a Bibliography of Primary and Secondary Materials, 1948–2007* celebrates Updike's seventy-fifth birthday in 2007. In a 'Foreword to My Own Bibliography', Updike, in addition to paying tribute to his bibliographers, reveals that his 'initial ambition . . . was to be a cartoonist', and that he remains 'highly susceptible to the siren call of periodical publication'. He adds, 'it pays' (p. vii). There are nine sections. By far the longest is section A, which is devoted to 'separate publications by Updike Books, broadsides, and other printed items with sole or principal text by John Updike' (pp. 1–171). These extend from Updike's first separate book publication, *The Carpentered Hen and Other Tame Creatures*, first published by Harper & Brothers in New York in 1958 (this constitutes item A1) to *Due Considerations*, published by Updike's long-time publishers Alfred A. Knopf of New York in 2007 (item A202).

While there is a wealth of detail in the description, extending from pagination to jacket description, contents and price of publication, there tends, disappointingly, to be a dearth of notes on each item, and rarely data on how many copies were printed. This may not of course be the bibliographers' fault: publishers are frequently most reluctant to supply such information. Also reviews and comments on individual books are excluded from the print version but found on the CD-ROM. Another caveat: A89 describes *Rabbit Is Rich/Rabbit Redux/Rabbit Run*, the 'one-volume photo-reproduction of the three novels' (p. 69) published in 1981, but excludes the important 'A Note on the Type' and other information found on the last two pages of the paperback.

The first (the printed) volume contains two appendices. The first is devoted to the 'Frequency of Updike's Fiction, Poetry, Article, and Review Appearances in Periodicals' (pp. 563–8). De Bellis and Broomfield note that 'there are 1642 appearances in 211 different periodicals as of December 6, 2007. Periodicals in which Updike appeared ten or more times account for 1308 items about 80% of the total' (p. 563). The second appendix lists 'Updike's Small Press Appearances' (pp. 569–70) and usefully cross-references appearances to sections in the main body of the bibliography. The work concludes with a listing of 'Works Consulted' (pp. 571–2) and a very extensive title-orientated index (pp. 573–608). Noticeably absent from the index are entries for publishers, and there are other omissions, for instance one will look in vain for Knut Hamsun.

The CD-ROM, constituting the second volume, loads easily. It contains 'Work about Updike, Appendices III–VI, and Color Images'. The CD-ROM is divided into three. The first, 'Works about Updike', has an introduction and 'Section M–N' (p. vii—the pagination then continues from the book version). Section M is devoted to 'Reviews and Comments on Individual Books' (pp. 609–787), listing 4,713 items arranged by the title of the work discussed: the sheer number explains why these are excluded from the first volume. Section N, 'General Commentary and Information' (pp. 789–832), is devoted to general commentary and information on Updike and his work, extending from 1950 to 2007, listed by year. Section O is devoted to 'Reviews or Books Edited by Updike' (pp. 833–4), listed by year, and section P, 'Thesis' (pp. 835–55), listed by year, is divided into 139 doctoral theses and then 122 Master's theses—these conclude at 2003. This section is confined to the United States and material listed in dissertation abstracts.

Updike, De Bellis and Broomfield have been splendidly served by the Oak Knoll Press, who have produced a volume worthy of its compilers and subject. The printing is clear and the spacing largely appropriate, as is the use of boldface and italics. The binding is sturdy in this 8.5 x 11 inch production. The jacket, with its cover photograph of Updike and back-cover citation from his 'Foreword to My Own Bibliography' surrounded by colour illustrations of title pages, will unfortunately be discarded when the volume reaches libraries. It is, however, an integral part of a very important definitive production that should be part of all libraries collecting *the* major late twentieth-century American authors. However, it is unfortunate that one must conclude such a brief assessment on a caveat. There is a plethora of detail in the volume and the CD-ROM, yet this is not a bibliographical history. Publication history is all too absent, and the reader is overwhelmed with a mass of detail, some of which is probably unnecessary.

John Thieme's *R.K. Narayan*, in the Contemporary World Writers series, contains a 'Select Bibliography' (pp. 233–41). It is enumerative but useful as it contains a listing of works by R.K. Narayan and selected criticism of writings about him. Charles Jencks, *Critical Modernism: Where Is Post-Modernism Going?* claims to be the first monograph devoted to the subject of 'postmodernism', although it is not clear whether Jencks is at times referring to 'postmodernism' or to critical modernism—see for instance his preface (pp. 6–13). The book is accompanied by illustrations; of course, like its subject, it could be accused of pretentiousness but does throw some light on a curious subject. Brian W. Shaffer has edited *A Companion to the British and Irish Novel, 1945–2000*, which is part of the Blackwell Companions to Literature and Culture series. First published in 2005, it now appears in paperback. Divided into two parts, 'Contexts for the British and Irish Novel, 1945–2000' and 'Reading Individual Texts and Authors', it contains forty-two individual essays. Clearly, these are of varying quality. There are some eminent contributors, and it would be invidious to single out one contribution from another. Part II begins with an essay on 'Samuel Beckett's *Watt*' (pp. 227–40) and concludes with 'Pat Barker's *Regeneration* Trilogy' (pp. 550–60). Amongst other things, the entries in Shaffer's reference work will provide a guide to what was considered important in the British and Irish novel at the start of the twenty-first century. Inevitably there are some important absentees, an obvious one being L.P. Hartley. A similar reference work is found in D.H. Figueredo's two-volume *Encyclopedia of Caribbean Literature*, first published in 2006, which includes over 700 alphabetically arranged entries covering individual authors, works, genres, cultural figures, themes and special topics. Again, the entries vary in quality. Some are exceedingly short. Each is followed by a brief further reading listing. Again, a useful reference work but not necessarily indispensable.

A.T. Tolley's analysis of *British Literary Periodicals of World War II and Aftermath: A Critical History* serves as an analytical companion to David Miller and Richard Price's largely enumerative and useful *British Poetry Magazine 1914–2000: A History and Bibliography of 'Little Magazines'*, published in 2006. Tolley's work supplements entries found in the final volume, devoted to the 1914–84 period, of the very helpful four-volume *British Literary Magazines* edited by Alvin Sullivan and published by the Greenwood Press in 1986. Tolley's critical history of British literary periodicals published during the 1939–45 war and its aftermath aims also to discuss the periodicals themselves on an individual basis and to place them in their cultural context (p. ix). Tolley's introductory first chapter (pp. 1–9), attempts to tackle the issue of why he has chosen to write the history of periodicals during this period. The reasons given range from the availability of the primary materials, the intrinsic merit of the journals and their proliferation during the 1940s, the cataclysmic events that filled those years and the consequences that attended them. Tolley notes 'the wide circulation of so many literary periodicals during the war years had been very much due to people's need to come to terms with the war and the threatening situations that came with its disruption of their lives'. Moreover, 'with the coming of peace, there was the opportunity to start up again' (pp. 8–9).

The second chapter is devoted to 'Cyril Connolly and *Horizon*' (pp. 11–25). Chapter 3 focuses on 'John Lehmann and *New Writing*' (pp. 27–47). Chapter 4 is concerned with 'Robert Herring and *Life and Letters*' (pp. 49–52). The following chapter covers more than a single periodical. 'Reginald Moore and Associates' describes Reginald Moore's activities with the seven publications connected with him: *Modern Reading, Selected Writing, Bugle Blast, The Windmill, Triad, New Saxon Pamphlets (Albion)* and *English Story* (pp. 53–71). A single editor and his influence, in this instance Denys Val Baker, is the focus of chapter 6 (pp. 73–81). This examines Baker's *Opus, Voices, Writing Today* and *The Cornish Review*. A very short seventh chapter is devoted to 'International Periodicals'—*Adam* and *The Gate* (pp. 79–81). More too could be written about the content of the eighth chapter 'Regional Periodicals' (pp. 83–100), which glides through 'Regionalism—*Wales, The Welsh Review, The Voice of Scotland, Poetry Scotland, Scots Writing, Scottish Arts and Letters, Chapbook—The Bill* and other Irish periodicals—*The West Country Magazine—The Townsman*' (p. 83). Similarly, the remaining chapters represent a missed opportunity. They survey rather than analyse. Chapter 9 glosses 'Radical Periodicals' ranging from *New, Our Time, Arena, Seven* (2nd series), and *Million* (pp. 101–14).

Chapter 10 is more focused but too brief. 'Tambimuttu and *Poetry London*' (pp. 117–24) fails to capture the spirit of Tambimuttu and his eclectic editorial methodology, or the neo-Romanticism and identification with the Apocalypse movement of *Poetry London*. Tolley's discussion of some of this is somewhat curiously left to the next chapter, 'Wrey Gardiner and the New Romanticism' (pp. 125–38). This focuses on *Seven, Poetry Quarterly, New Road, Kingdom Come, and Transformation*. Chapter 12's 'Smaller Poetry Periodicals' (pp. 141–9) includes some account of *Poetry Folios, Poets Now in the Services, Outposts, Forum, Poetry, Poetry Commonwealth, Verse, Poetry and Poverty, Prospect*. Dannie Abse's important *Verse*, a magazine that published poets of the stature of Emanuel Litvinoff, John Heath Stubbs, Denise Levertov and Kenneth Patchen, amongst others, is allotted two brief paragraphs (p. 146).

'Middle-East Periodicals' (pp. 151–9) are the subject of chapter 13, although only four of them, *Personal Landscape, Salamander, Citadel* and *Orientation*, are considered. Another missed opportunity occurs in the rather perfunctory single paragraphs devoted to each of the 'Periodicals from the Services and After' in the following chapter (pp. 161–8). Similarly, the account of 'University Periodicals' (pp. 169–75) in chapter 15 offers a mere glimpse of the content and orientation of *Kingdom Come* (first series), *Mandrake, Focus, The Critic, Politics and Letters, Imprint* and *Gambit*. Chapter 16 consists of a quick gallop through 'Younger and Newer Ventures' (pp. 177–84). Moreover, chapter 17, 'Post-War Expectations' (pp. 187–92), concentrates, again in a perfunctory manner, on three post-1945 publications: *Orion, The Mint* and *Gangrel*. There is a briefly annotated bibliography (pp. 204–12) containing a listing 'of literary periodicals of the nineteen-forties with editors and dates and place of publication' (p. 205). Regrettably, one comes away from Tolley's book with the sense that it is a survey. More information is to be gleaned from the various entries in Sullivan's volume and, often, in Wolfgang Görtshacher's *Little Magazine Profiles: The Little Magazines in Great Britain 1939–93* [1993]. Tolley's index (pp. 213–27) is useful. In spite of these limitations, all in all, he is to be commended for giving some account of selected literary periodicals during a fascinating period in British cultural history. The book is well printed. It is illustrated with the covers or title pages of selected periodicals. Priced at £10 sterling, the work is a bargain and probably should be purchased by all libraries collecting materials on twentieth-century British literary history and culture. Dean Irvine's *Editing Modernity: Women and Little-Magazine Cultures in Canada, 1916–1956* is a welcome monograph emphasizing the importance of little magazines, which in this instance are seen from a gender perspective. Irvine's aim is to stress the importance of 'women's participation in modernist literary cultures in Canada' (p. 9). Her emphasis is upon their important role in little magazines between 1916 and 1956. Irvine has some interesting, illuminating things to say, especially about writers and editors such as Dorothy Livesay, Anne Marriott, Floris McLaren, P.K. Page, Miriam Waddington, Flora Macdonald Denison, Florence Custance, Catherine Harmon, Aileen Collins and Margaret Fairley.

David Carter and Anne Galligan's *Making Books: Contemporary Australian Publishing* consists of a series of essays on the subject of the state of the Australian publishing industry in the early twenty-first century. Divided into three sections, the more than twenty-five contributors write briefly on industrial dynamics, the industry and new technologies and on the industry sectors and genre publishing. There are two appendices. The first is devoted to 'government and government-funded policy and program intervention in the value chain for print publishing' (pp. 352–7) and a listing of 'Publishers of Literary Novels, 1990–2006 (four or more titles)' (pp. 358–9). The book concludes with Anne Galligan and Kath McLean's useful glossary. Felix M. Larkin's edited *Librarians, Poets and Scholars: A Festschrift for Dónall Ó Luanaigh* is a tribute by thirty contributors to a great librarian who worked for forty-three years at the National Library of Ireland. The subjects vary from personal appreciations to perspectives on the National Library of Ireland, 'Hedge Schools, Books and Business Education in Eighteenth-Century Ireland' (pp. 85–94), 'Mrs. Jelleby's Daughter: Caroline Agnes Gray (1848–1927) and the *Freeman's Journal*' (pp. 121–9) and, to instance one out of many fascinating areas treated in the book, '"A gruesome case": James Joyce's Dublin Murder Case' (pp. 282–94). It is of course invidious to single out individual contributors. However, Owen Dudley Edwards on 'Shaw and Christianity: Towards 1916' (pp. 95–119) and 'Seamus Heaney's Five Quatrains' (p. 156) should not be ignored. No doubt the latter will prove a challenge for those involved in the updating of the Nobel Prize winner's bibliography!

William H. Martin and Sandra Mason's *The Art of Omar Khayyam: Illustrating FitzGerald's Rubaiyat* is a lavishly illustrated celebration of the 1859 publication of Edward FitzGerald's great *Rubáiyát*. The book consists of two main parts, in the first Martin and Mason look 'at the artistic and publishing history of FitzGerald's *Rubaiyat* since its first publication' and they 'follow the story of the many editions, the publishing houses and the illustrators who have been involved with the art of the *Rubaiyat* over the past century and a half'. In the second part, they take on the perspective of 'the illustrator, examining the individual quatrains and looking at what there might be in them that inspires the artist' and they 'highlight the enormous range of artistic interpretation, style and content that exists for this one poem'. Special emphasis is given to the role played by Edward Cowell, a close friend of FitzGerald 'who played a crucial role' in the poem's creation' (p. vii). There are five appendices: 'Publishers and Illustrators of FitzGerald's *Rubaiyat*' (pp. 167–8), 'Artists who Have Illustrated FitzGerald's *Rubaiyat*' (pp. 169–71), 'Published Versions of *The Rubaiyat of Omar Khayyam*' (pp. 172–4), 'Omar Khayyam and his *Rubaiyat*' (p. 174) and 'Edward FitzGerald and his *Rubaiyat*' (pp. 175–6).

Janice G. Schimmelman's *The Tintype in America, 1856–1880* is a history of the ferrotype or tintype in the history of American photography from the 1850s until around 1880. Schimmelman focuses on the improvements in image presentation, and on the inventors and businessmen who were active in the area during the period. Apparently 'the word tintype appeared in 1863. Initially it was a popular term for a tiny unmounted image measuring only $\frac{3}{4} \times 1$ inch made in multiples in a larger japanned iron plate. There is no significant material difference in the plate or in the making of a melainotype, ferrotype, or tintype. It is more a matter of historical semantics' (p. viii). In addition to her history, Schimmelman provides a glossary (pp. 253–8), including such fascinating explanations that a 'stereoscope [is] the double-lens instrument used to view stereographs. The word is derived from the Greek words *steros* and *scopeo*, which together mean "to view solid"' (p. 257). All in all, there is much to be learned from this volume.

One of the most moving books of the year is John Sutherland's *The Boy Who Loved Books: A Memoir*. Sutherland (b. 1938), as every browser of *YWES* will know, was until very recently the Lord Northcliffe Professor of Modern English Literature at University College, London. Currently he continues as Professor of English at California Institute of Technology, in addition of course to writing regularly and profusely for the *Guardian*, *Financial Times*, *New Statesman*, *Times* and other British newspapers and journals. His bibliography will really prove a challenge and he is becoming almost as prolific as the late, great Professor David Daiches (1912–2005)! *The Boy Who Loved Books* is a tear-jerking account of its author's childhood spent shuffling between Colchester and Edinburgh and between families, his father having been killed on an aircraft training flight at the start of the Second World War. Forever an outsider, out of place wherever he was, books became his lifeblood, his solace, his companions, his addiction, before being replaced later in life by alcohol. One of the strengths of Sutherland's book is his honesty. He rarely tries to cover up warts, and explains how he was able and why he was able during his youth to read so many minor obscure Victorian novels. An account of them is given so succinctly in his wonderful *Longman Companion to Victorian Fiction* (in America entitled *The Stanford Companion to Victorian Fiction*) [1989]. *The Boy Who Loved Books* reveals much not only about its subject and its times, but also about why many of us are obsessed by books and literature. Sutherland's book additionally shows how and why a period spent at Oxbridge is not necessary for a high-flying academic career; indeed the rejection by such institutions may well act not as a deterrent but as a stimulus. Sutherland's book is essential reading.

Jane Aaron's *Nineteenth-Century Women's Writing in Wales: Nation, Gender and Identity* 'aims to contribute' to the study of Welsh writing 'by introducing the reader to over 100 Welsh women who published poems, novels, essays, antiquarian and travel writings during the nineteenth century' (p. 7). Aaron especially emphasizes the influence of what she describes as the 'distinctive Non-conformist culture' (p. 192) which was pervasive throughout the nineteenth century in Wales. There is in addition in this useful study a valuable 'Selected Bibliography' (pp. 222–42). *The Oxford Companion to Black British History*, edited by David Dabydeen, John Gilmore and Cecily Jones, contains nearly 450 entries by 112 contributors on diverse topics. These range from individuals, historical periods, abolition and slavery, sports and literature to music and other activities in all walks of life. There are important gaps, especially regarding the role played by black women. The entries are arranged alphabetically, and vary in length from less than a page to almost six pages. Each concludes with a short listing of further readings. There is a 'Selected Bibliography' and a 'Chronology', in what is in fact an important reference work whose timeline extends from the second century AD to the present.

Murray Pittock has edited, in the Athlone Critical Tradition series, *The Reception of Sir Walter Scott in Europe*. The twenty-two contributors to the volume attempt to come to terms with the tremendous impact in Europe of Sir Walter Scott. Paul Barnaby contributes a 'Timeline of the European Reception of Sir Walter Scott, 1802–2005' (pp. xxiv–xxx). Murray Pittock's succinct, well-written 'Introduction: Scott and the European Nationalities Question' (pp. 1–10) is followed by essays on Scott's reception as reflected in translations in French, Spanish, Catalan, German, Hungarian, Czech, Polish, Russian, Slovene, Danish, Norwegian and Swedish, and four general essays, on the 'European Reception of Scott's Poetry: Translation as the Front Line' (pp. 268–84), 'Scott's "Heyday" in Opera' (pp. 285–92), 'Seeing with a "Painter's Eye": Sir Walter Scott's Challenge to Nineteenth-Century Art' (pp. 293–312) and, last but by no means least, 'Scotland is a Scott-Land: Scott and the Development of Tourism' (pp. 313–22) and a bibliography (pp. 323–86). *The Oxford Handbook of English Literature and Theology*, edited by Andrew W. Hass, David Jasper and Elisabeth Jay, contains articles of interest to all *YWES* readers. Divided into seven parts with fifty contributors, the subjects range from essays on 'The Bible as Literature and Sacred Text' (pp. 197–213) to essays on individual books of the Bible, to 'Theological Ways of Reading Literature' (pp. 363–516). Other entries of particular interest to students of the history of the book include, amongst many others, one on 'Vernacular Bibles and Prayer Books' (pp. 54–78). Mention must be made of the late, lamented Stephen Medcalf's brilliant 'Eliot, David Jones, and Auden' (pp. 523–42), which must be one of the last essays he penned.

In her *Print Culture and the Medieval Author: Chaucer, Lydgate, and their Books, 1473–1557*, Alexandra Gillespie examines many early printed books and late medieval manuscripts in order to compile a bibliographical history of Geoffrey Chaucer and John Lydgate in the century following the arrival of printing in England. Unfortunately, there is not space to fully assess the importance of Gillespie's monograph to the study of the history of the book and the issue of authorship. A later period is the subject of Stephen Colclough's *Consuming Texts: Readers and Reading Communities, 1695–1870*. This is an ambitious exploration of the history of reading in the British Isles during the historical period in which the printed word took over. Colclough's approach is to generally examine reading and then to discuss 'commonplace books and personal miscellanies compiled by wealthy readers in the early years of the eighteenth century'. This is followed by examination of evidence from 'further down the social scale ... private journals' and, in the final chapter, 'the emerging genre of working class autobiography before moving on to look at the "answers to Correspondents" columns that were a feature of the new penny press' (p. ix). Roger Chartier's *Inscription and Erasure: Literature and Written Culture from the Eleventh to the Eighteenth Century* is yet another work from the hand of the distinguished French historian of the book. In his introduction, 'Aesthetic Mystery and the Materialities of the Written', Chartier writes: 'The purpose of this book is to examine the manifold relationship between inscription and erasure, between the durable record and the ephemeral text, by studying', the author continues, 'the way in which writing was made literature by certain works belonging to various genres and composed in various times and places.' Chartier acknowledges his debt to the late D.F. Mackenzie, and his introduction provides an excellent introduction to recent studies of 'the sociology of texts' (p. vii). It must be confessed that Chartier's prose is at times difficult to follow. This may be the result of the fact that he writes initially in French, but not the fault of his translator, Arthur Goldhammer. In his 'Conclusion' Chartier pays tribute and cites a passage from Jorge Luis Borges to the effect that 'literature is not exhaustible, for the sufficient and simple reason that a single book is not. A book is not an isolated entity: it is a relationship, an axis of innumerable relationships' (p. 143).

Karin Littau's *Theories of Reading: Books, Bodies and Bibliomania* focuses on factors on the whole ignored by 'cultural historians of reading'. The first is 'Materiality', which is related to Littau's idea that 'when we read, we interpret semantic content and, insofar as poet or narrative structure gives form to content, we enter into a deeper level of interpretation'. She adds, 'Texts are therefore conveyors of complex and multi-layered meanings.' Secondly, Littau is concerned with 'the physicality of reading. The relation a reader has to a book is also a relation between two bodies: one made of paper and ink, the other of flesh and blood' (p. 2). These are interesting areas of enquiry, although it must be admitted that some of Littau's text makes for heavy going, especially as she's dealing with many theoretical issues. Littau also believes that of 'all the contemporary literary theories, feminist theories are unique insofar as, concerned with sexual difference, they foreground the body' (p. 154). There clearly is considerable food for thought, and for disagreement. A very specific period is examined in John Spiers's useful *Serious about Series*.

American Cheap 'Libraries', British 'Railway' Libraries, and Some Literary Series of the 1890s. Based upon the author's own collection, it carefully describes the historical, cultural and bibliographical background to the 130 titles exhibited at the University of London Senate House Library. A twenty-page introduction contains essays on the books on American cheap libraries, on British Railway libraries, and some British series of the 1890s. All in all, a most valuable addition to our knowledge in what is regrettably a reference work of which only 150 copies were produced.

Susan Weber Soros has edited a magnificently illustrated volume, *James 'Athenian' Stuart: The Rediscovery of Antiquity*. James Stuart (1753–88) began his career in London as a painter of ladies' fans and went on to become an influential skilled decorator, travelling in Rome, Naples and Athens to measure and record classical ruins. Soros's volume is the first to fully examine Stuart's diverse career and important contributions as a designer, artist and influence upon aesthetic taste. The fourteen contributors write on subjects as diverse as 'Stuart and Revett: The Myth of Greece and its Afterlife' (pp. 19–58), gardens, London houses, 'James Stuart, the Admiralty, and the Royal Hospital for Seaman at Greenwich, 1758–88' (pp. 355–84) and other fascinating areas. There is even an appendix on 'Stuart and his Craftsman' (pp. 550–78) based on an exhibition at the Bard Graduate Center for Studies in the Decorative Arts, Design and Culture from 16 November 2006 to 11 February 2007. It is difficult to overestimate the value of Soros's edition, especially given its wealth of wonderful coloured, illustrated materials. Philip W. Errington follows his magnificent descriptive bibliography of John Masefield (see *YWES* 83[2004] 1181) with an edition of *John Masefield's Great War: Collected Works*. This edition includes twenty-eight texts either written by or relating to Masefield on the subject of the Great War published in various periodicals and newspapers. Yale University Press has issued David Alan Richards's *Rudyard Kipling: The Books I Leave Behind*. This has eighty colour illustrations and is based upon Richards's Rudyard Kipling exhibition held at the Beinecke Rare Books and Manuscript Library in 2007. Richards probably owns the most extensive Kipling collection in the world, and in his introductory essay shares the difficulties and delights of its formation. There is in addition a contribution by Thomas Pinney on how Kipling and his work are a reflection of a writer's literary status.

Bridget Fowler's *The Obituary as Collective Memory* is a most welcome study of the obituary. Divided into two parts, the first focuses on the 'Theoretical, Historical and Quantitative Studies of the Obituary' (pp. 1–156) and the second on 'Memories Burnished at the Shock of Death: Discourse Analysis of Newspaper Obituaries' (pp. 157–242). The study contains an interesting account of changes in obituary writing during the last century and 'aims to demonstrate that contemporary obituaries have changed noticeably from the narrow seam mined by *The Times* in 1900. The genres of the obituary have become more diverse; the ethos developed for each newspaper's obits is in some crucial ways distinctive' (p. 22). David Seed's *A Companion to Science Fiction* consists of forty-one essays by various hands on various aspects of science fiction. It is divided into seven parts: 'Surveying the Field'; 'Topics and Debates'; 'Genres and Movements'; 'Science Fiction Film'; 'The International

Scene'; Key Writers'; and 'Readings'. Each essay is followed by a notation and supplementary reading list. Authors treated range from Mary Shelley to Aldous Huxley, Ray Bradbury, J.G. Ballard, Margaret Atwood and Iain M. Banks. In a 'Research Report' Isobel Grundy, Susan Brown and Patricia Clements give an account of '*Orlando*: The Marriage of Literary History and Humanities Computing' (*1650–1850* 14[2007] 179–253). *Orlando* is a text base 'published by subscription on the web by Cambridge University Press in June 2006' (p. 254). The report is of considerable interest and accompanied by nine illustrations. The contributors claim that they are constructing a 'new kind of reading' (p. 279). Whether *Orlando* will be ephemeral, as are so many similar ventures, remains to be seen.

Richard Wendorf's *America's Membership Libraries* consists of twenty contributions on the subject inspired by the 1731 founding of the Library Company of Philadelphia. Following a preface by Nicholas Barker, and Richard Wendorf's introduction, there are essays by Cheryl Helms on 'The Redwood Library and Athenaeum' (pp. 23–48); John C. Bernens and P.J. Gartin on 'The Charleston Library Society' (pp. 49–64); Mark Bartlett and Sara Elliott Holliday on 'The New York Society Library' (pp. 65–84); Richard Wendorf on 'The Boston Athenaeum' (pp. 85–110); Charles L. Newhall on 'The Salem Athenaeum' (pp. 111–30); Roger W. Moss on 'The Athenaeum of Philadelphia' (pp. 131–56); Tom Hardiman on 'The Portsmouth Athenaeum' (pp. 157–78); Janet Wells Greene on 'The General Society of Mechanics and Tradesmen' (pp. 179–94); Noreen Tomassi with Mary Collins on 'The Mercantile Library Center for Fiction' (pp. 195–210); Albert Pyle on 'The Mercantile Library' (pp. 211–28); Alison Davis Maxell on 'The Providence Athenaeum' (pp. 229–44); John Neal Hoover on 'The St. Louis Mercantile Library Association' (pp. 245–62); Inez Shor Cohen on 'The Mechanics' Institute Library' (pp. 263–82); Mark D. Mitchell on 'The St. Johnsbury Athenaeum' (pp. 283–98); Judy Lanier on 'The Lanier Library Association' (pp. 299–316); and Erika Torri on 'The Athenaeum Music and Arts Library' (pp. 317–36).

Tom Flynn's *The New Encyclopedia of Unbelief* has a foreword by Richard Dawkins to what is an important reference work in excess of 500 entries written by over 130 distinguished scholars. Its subject is those who live outside the boundaries of formal religion. The articles encompass aspects of atheism, agnosticism, secular humanism, secularism, religious scepticism and other areas. Each entry is accompanied by very useful bibliographies. The entries, of varying length, run from 'Abbot, Francis Ellingwood (1836–1903), American secularist and philosopher' (p. 21) to 'Zelenski, Tadeusz . . . 1874–1941), Polish iconoclastic commentator, literary critic, theater critic, and translator of masterpieces of French literature' (p. 836). Many major and minor literary figures are included within the pages of this fully indexed reference tool.

An edition of interest is Gerard Carruthers's *The Devil to Stage: Five Plays by James Bridie*, published by the Association for Scottish Literary Studies. The five plays are Bridie's *The Sunlight Sonata*, *The Anatomist*, *A Sleeping Clergyman*, *Mr. Bolfry*, and *Daphne Laureola*. There is an extensive introduction on Bridie's life and work, and comprehensive textual explanatory and critical notes on Bridie. Berthold Schoene has edited *The Edinburgh*

Companion to Contemporary Scottish Literature. This contains forty-two essays by forty scholars and critics examining the transformation in Scottish literature that has taken place since the 1997 referendum on national self-rule and the 2000 opening of the Scottish parliament. Clearly, contributions vary in length and quality, but the coverage is exceedingly comprehensive (perhaps in places too comprehensive and ought to have been more selective). Another Scots text should be mentioned, and that is Fiona Price's edition of Jane Porter's *The Scottish Chiefs*, published in 1810. Price's edition appears in Broadview Editions, replete with contemporary reviews and appendices. The text is taken from the first edition of 1810, although there were at least seven subsequent editions and 'all footnotes from the 1810 edition have been retained and selected use has been made of footnotes from later editions where they appeared useful' (p. 37).

An item which should not go ignored is Nayef Al-Joulan's sensitive study *'Essenced to Language': The Margins of Isaac Rosenberg*, which explores the social, political and ethnic background, as well as the writing, of the great poet Isaac Rosenberg (1890–1918). Unfortunately, there is not enough space to discuss further Al-Joulan's very well-written and perceptive monograph. To change tack, Steven Rothman and Nicholas Utechin have edited a delightful set of essays in memory of the distinguished Sherlock Holmes scholar and bibliographer Richard Lancelyn Green, who died in somewhat mysterious circumstances in March 2004. Not 30 years of age, Green had already co-edited a bibliography of Arthur Conan Doyle published in 1983, had served as chairman of the Sherlock Holmes Society of London and was an expert on E.W. Hornung's Raffles books. Of course, he was an obsessive collector of all things Sherlockian. The tributes to him in *To Keep the Memory Green: Reflections on the Life of Richard Lancelyn Green 1953–2004* include Owen Dudley Edwards's 'Ode to RLG' (pp. 25–35) and the same author's 'Richard and Raffles' (pp. 173–82). R. Dixon Smith writes on 'The Bibliophile and the Bookseller' (pp. 87–97), and the volume concludes with Steven Rothman's '"A great garret...stuffed with books": A Bibliographical Checklist of the Writings of Richard Lancelyn Green' (pp. 191–220). However, it is invidious to select individual items from such a volume, which constitutes a worthy tribute to its subject.

Christopher Burke's *Active Literature: Jan Tschichold and New Typography* is an extensive study by an eminent typographer, typeface designer and type historian of the modernist period of the work of Jan Tschichold (1902–74). In his foreword, 'Towards a Critical Understanding of Tschichold's Work', Robin Kinross examines perceptions of Tschichold following his death. Kinross emphasizes that attention should not be focused on 'the unquestioning recycling of the stories that surrounded him during his lifetime and the years after his death'. Instead, 'serious discussion needs to begin with the primary material: the artifacts themselves.... Tschichold also needs to be seen in his contexts, in discussion with colleagues, and engaged in the production of the "active literature" that he preferred'. Kinross concludes that 'the present book represents a notable start along this road' (p. 9). Burke's well-illustrated monograph includes a 'Select Bibliography of Tschichold's Writings' (pp. 321–2). Further volumes are added to R.C. Alston's

A Bibliography of the English Language from the Invention of Printing to the Year 1800. The first part of volume 19 covers periodical literature, 1665–1800, and in his preface Alston confesses that 'the magnitude of the task was such that compromises became necessary. At an early stage in the scanning process, it became clear that daily, semi-weekly and weekly newspapers were yielding a poor harvest of significant essays on language and the subject covered in this Bibliography.' He adds that 'Much of the non-news content in these newspapers is derivative (copied from magazine or book literature), and, for the most part, trivial.' So he 'adopted the practice of scanning a six-month period every five years' and in his *Chronological List* has provided 'a comprehensive listing of newspapers treated in this manner' (vol. 1, pp. 8–9). Also, for practical purposes, geographical coverage is more limited. In spite of these caveats, 383 titles are scanned. The second part includes facsimiles. So, in spite of the difficulties involved, we once again owe a deep debt of gratitude to R.C. Alston's prodigious efforts.

Robert Macfarlane's *Original Copy: Plagiarism and Originality in Nineteenth-Century Literature* is a brilliant, well-written examination of the concepts 'plagiarism' and 'originality' in selected nineteenth-century writers. These range from extensive discussions of George Eliot, Oscar Wilde and, to a much more limited extent, Charles Dickens. Examination of these authors is juxtaposed with a discussion of authors such as the neglected Charles Reade, Walter Pater and Lionel Johnson. In his introduction Macfarlane considers 'two theories of originality' and observes 'the key distinction between the two ideas is that of sources'; moreover, Macfarlane adds, 'according to one paradigm, the work of art is an addition to what exists, according to the other, it is an edition of it' (p. 1). Macfarlane's work is replete with documentation. His discussions of George Eliot and Charles Reade found in chapters 3 and 4 are exceedingly comprehensive. There is an extensive, enumerative alphabetically arranged bibliography (pp. 212–35) to his excellent book which provides a reading list on the subject of plagiarism, imitation and originality. Macfarlane 'reveals how, for numerous, important writers of the later Victorian years…the very elusiveness of the idea of originality—its refusal to stay still or to remain rigid as a category—was an inspiration to creativity' (p. 9).

Robert C. Hanna's *Dickens's Nonfictional, Theatrical, and Poetical Writings: An Annotated Bibliography, 1820–2000* is the second to appear in the Dickens Bibliographies published by the AMS Press under the general editorship of Duane DeVries. It is a remarkable, indeed a marvellous, volume: a real pleasure to consult. Divided into four sections, the first section consists of A, 'Full-Length Works', arranged chronologically (pp. 1–285); B, 'Works Edited or with Prefaces or Contributions by Dickens' (pp. 287–310); and C, 'Shorter Works' (pp. 311–96). The second part consists of 'Personal Writings and Speeches' (pp. 399–416). Part III is 'Plays' (arranged chronologically) (pp. 419–95) and part IV is 'Poetry' (pp. 499–512). The index (pp. 515–63) is extensive and concludes with a 'Writings Index' (pp. 565–79). Hanna's introduction (pp. xix–xxi) is short, unpretentious and to the point. His abstracts are clear, although not totally comprehensive. Interestingly, his annotations to the Dickens section on Dickens 'Juvenilia' in David C. Sutton's

Location Register of English Literary Manuscripts and Letters. Eighteenth and Nineteenth Centuries (London: The British Library [1995]) contains significant additions 'errors or misrepresentations' (see Hanna, JUV 1: 313–16). Hanna's is an important work.

Peter J. Foss's enumerative and descriptive bibliography of the lesser-known Powys brother, Llewelyn Powys (1884–1939), *A Bibliography of Llewelyn Powys*, contains a plethora of detail. It is comprehensive, covering the various genres in which Powys worked, including books and pamphlets and reviews contributed to periodicals and newspapers. There is a section on writings about Powys and even an appendix providing 'Tabulation and Variation between Early Editions of Three Books' of Powys (pp. 265–73). Foss's work concludes with a detailed index (pp. 274–92). Greg Clingham has edited *Sustaining Literature: Essays on Literature, History and Culture. 1500–1800 Commemorating the Life and Work of Simon Varey*. In addition to the individual contributions, the book concludes with an enumerative listing of 'Published Works of Simon Varey' ranging from his books, articles, notes, reviews, translation from Dutch to English and letters to periodicals (pp. 315–19). Patrick Scott's superb edition of Arthur Hugh Clough's *Amours de Voyage: An Epistolary Novella in Verse* has been published in a Fine Press Edition by the Barbarian Press in British Columbia. With an 'Afterword' by Crispin Elsted, it is published in quarter cloth with printed St Armand handmade paper over boards, with spine label, bugra endpapers, printed in Van Dijck roman with calligraphic display by Martin Jackson, Zerkall Book soft white wove with eleven wood engravings by Abigail Rorer. It is in effect a magnificent reprinting of a text from Scott's University of Queensland edition originally published in 1974, and is a fine tribute to the erudite scholar and critic Patrick Scott.

Richard B. Sher's *The Enlightenment and the Book: Scottish Authors and their Publishers in Eighteenth-Century Britain, Ireland and America* 'explores how the books of the Scottish Enlightenment were put forth into the world during the second half of the eighteenth century' (p. xv). Sher's is an extensive, erudite, well-written study that is definitive. He focuses on the explosion of activity in the later part of the eighteenth century that witnessed, amongst many others, David Hume, Adam Smith and James Boswell transform many areas of intellectual endeavour. Sher reveals the complicated and neglected relationships between authors and their publishers, throwing new light upon publishers' activities. It is difficult to do justice to Sher's learning except to say that his book is well illustrated and probably amongst the top five books published on eighteenth-century publishing history in the last decade or so. Elisabeth Daumer and Shyamal Bagchee have edited an extensive volume of eighteen essays on the subject of *The International Reception of T.S. Eliot*. The geographical compass of the essays ranges from Iceland, Italy, China, Japan and South America to Bengal, Israel and Australia. This is an important volume showing just how universal T.S. Eliot's work is. Patricia Boyle Haberstroh and Christine St Peter edited *Opening the Field: Irish Women, Texts and Contexts*, a collection of essays penned by ten critics examining a text by an Irishwoman and applying a feminist perspective. Sim Branaghan and Stephen Chibnall's *British Film Posters: An Illustrated History* is chronologically divided into the 1896–1945 and 1946–86 periods. Theirs is one of the few studies published on the subject and provides, with lavish illustration, a comprehensive assessment, including some guide to pricing of an important 'currently extremely fashionable yet very little documented' subject (p. 7). Last but by no means least, *The Byron Journal* (*ByronJ* 35:ii[2007]) is devoted to the work of the great Byron scholar and bibliographical critic Jerome McGann in appreciation of his seventieth birthday. It contains Andrew Stauffer's 'Jerome McGann's Contributions to Byron Studies 1966–2006' (*ByronJ* 35:ii[2007] 115–20), and includes an enumerative listing by years of McGann's books and articles.

Last but by no means least, mention should be made of *Collecting the Imagination: The First Fifty Years of the Ransom Center*, edited by Megan Barnard with an introduction by its director Thomas F. Staley. Splendidly illustrated in colour and black and white, in addition to Staley's erudite introduction, the tribute contains essays by Harry Huntt Ransom on 'The Collection of Knowledge in Texas' (pp. xv–xxiii); John B. Thomas III on 'Beginnings: The Rare Books Collection, 1897–1955' (pp. 1–17); Cathy Henderson on 'The Birth of An Institution: The Humanities Research Center, 1956–1971' (pp. 19–49); Richard W. Oram on 'Years of Consolidation: The Harry Ransom Humanities Research Center, 1972–1988' (pp. 51–82); and Megan Barnard on 'The Expanding Mission: The Harry Ransom Humanities Research Center, 1988–Present' (pp. 83–118). The volume closes with an enumerative bibliography (pp. 121–3) and an index (pp. 125–31). As unpopular as this may be with British readers of *YWES*, the British twentieth-century cultural inheritance is in very safe hands way down in Texas!

Books Reviewed

Aaron, Jane. *Nineteenth Century Women's Writing in Wales: Nation, Gender and Identity*. UWalesP. [2007] pp. 256. $35 ISBN 9 7807 0832 0600.

Al-Joulan, Nayef. *'Essenced to Language': The Margins of Isaac Rosenberg*. Lang. [2007] pp.287. Euro 61.60 ISBN 3 0391 0728 3.

Alston, Robin C. *A Bibliography of the English Language from the Invention of Printing to the Year 1800*, vol. 19: *Periodical Literature 1665–1800*, pt. 1. Smith Otley: printed for the author. [2007] pp. 566 (vol. 1); pp. 266 (vol. 2) facsimiles. £400 No ISBN.

Armstrong, Patrick H. *All Things Darwin: An Encyclopedia of Darwin's World*. Greenwood. [2007] pp. xxiv + 565. £74.97 ISBN 9 7803 1333 4924.

Baines, Paul, and Pat Rogers. *Edmund Curll, Bookseller*. Clarendon. [2007] pp. 400. £36.46 ISBN 9 7801 9927 8985.

Barnard, Megan. *Collecting the Imagination: The First Fifty Years of the Ransom Center*. Harry Ransom Humanities Research Center. UTexP. [2007] pp. xxviii + 132. $40 ISBN 9 7802 9271 4892.

Bartram, Alan. *Typeforms: A History*. BL/OakK. [2007] pp. 128. $55 ISBN 9 7815 8456 2221.

Birns, Nicholas, and Rebecca McNeer. *A Companion to Australian Literature since 1900*. CamdenH. [2007] pp. xvi + 477. $90 ISBN 9 7815 7113 3496.

Black, Joseph, et al., eds. *The Broadview Anthology of British Literature, Concise Edition*, volume A. Broadview Press. [2007] pp. 1,651. $54.95 ISBN 9 7815 5111 8680.

Black, Joseph, et al., eds. *The Broadview Anthology of British Literature, Concise Edition*, volume B. Broadview Press. [2007] pp. 1,603. $54.95 ISBN 9 7815 5111 8697.

Branaghan, Sim, and Stephan Chibnall. *British Film Posters: An Illustrated History*. BFI. [2006] pp. 288. $42.50 ISBN 1 8445 7221 8.

Buickerood, James C., ed. *Eighteenth-Century Thought*, vol. 3. AMS. [2007] pp. 446. $121.50 ISBN 9 7804 0463 7637.

Burke, Christopher. *Active Literature: Jan Tschichold and New Typography*. HyphenP. [2007] pp. 335. $75 ISBN 9 7809 0725 9329.

Burnett, Archie, ed. *The Letters of A.E. Housman*, 2 vols. Clarendon. [2007] pp. liv + 643 (vol. 1), pp. viii + 585 (vol. 2). £203.49 ISBN 9 7801 9818 4966.

Bushell, Sally, James A. Butler and Michael C. Jaye, eds. *The Excursion*. CornUP [2007] pp. xxix + 1,226. $79.86. ISBN 9 7808 0144 6535.

Carruthers, Gerard. *The Devil to Stage: Five Plays by James Bridie*. ASLS. [2007] pp. 330. $37.99 ISBN 9 7809 4887 7711.

Carter, David, and Anne Galligan, eds. *Making Books: Contemporary Australian Publishing*. UQP. [2007] pp. 416. $39.95 ISBN 9 7807 0223 4699.

Chartier, Roger. *Inscription and Erasure: Literature and Written Culture from the Eleventh to the Eighteenth Century*. UPennP. [2007] pp. 224. $55 ISBN 9 7808 1223 9959.

Clemens, Raymond, and Timothy Graham. *Introduction to Manuscript Studies*. CornUP. [2007] pp. 352. £22.41 ISBN 9 7808 0148 7088.

Clingham, Greg, ed. *Sustaining Literature: Essays on Literature, History, and Culture. 1500–1800, Commemorating the Life and Work of Somon Varey*. Rosemont Press. [2007] pp. 325. $59.50 ISBN 9 7808 3875 6560.

Cody, Gabrielle H., and Evert Sprinchorn. *The Columbia Encyclopedia of Modern Drama*. ColUP. [2007] pp. 1,744. $450 ISBN 9 7802 3114 0324.

Coghlan, Valerie, and Siobhán Parkinson, eds. *Irish Children's Writers and Illustrators 1986–2006: A Selection of Essays*. Church of Ireland College of Education Press and Children's Books Ireland. [2007] pp. 168. Euro 15. ISBN 0 9509 2895 X.

Colclough, Stephen. *Consuming Texts: Readers and Reading Communities, 1695–1870*. Palgrave Macmillan. [2007] pp. 256. $69.95 ISBN 9 7802 3052 5382.

Collini, Stefan. *Absent Minds: Intellectuals in Britain*. OUP. [2006] pp. 544. $35 ISBN 9 7801 9921 6659.

Cope, Kevin L., ed. *Above the Age of Reason: Miracles and Wonders in the Long Eighteenth Century*. AMS. [2007] pp. 127. $164.50 ISBN 9 7804 0459 6538.

Cope, Kevin L., ed. *In and After the Beginning: Inaugural Moments and Literary Institutions in the Long Eighteenth Century.* AMS Press. [2007] pp. 379. $93.50. ISBN 9 7804 0464 8572.

Dabydeen, David, John Gilmore and Cecily Jones, eds. *The Oxford Companion to Black British History.* OUP. [2007] pp. 562. $60 ISBN 9 7801 9280 4396.

Daumer, Elisabeth, and Shyamal Bagchee, eds. *The International Reception of T.S. Eliot.* Continuum. [2007] pp. 320. $150 ISBN 9 7808 2649 0148.

De Billis, Jack, and Michael Broomfield, eds. *John Updike: A Bibliography of Primary and Secondary Materials 1948–2007.* OakK. [2007] pp. 608. $195 ISBN 9 7815 8456 1958.

Defoe, Daniel. *The Stoke Newington Daniel Defoe Edition: An Essay on the History and Reality of Apparitions.* AMS. [2007] pp. ci + 463. £80.83 ISBN 9 7804 0464 8565.

Edwards, Owen Dudley. *British Children's Fiction in the Second World War.* EdinUP. [2007] pp. 744. $200 ISBN 9 7807 4861 6510.

Eliot, Simon, Andrew Nash and Ian Willison, eds. *Literary Cultures and the Material Book.* BL. [2007] pp. 444. $80 ISBN 9 7807 1230 6843.

Eliot, Simon, and Jonathan Rose, eds. *A Companion to the History of the Book.* Blackwell. [2007] pp. xvi + 599. £85 ISBN 9 7814 0512 7653.

Errington, Philip W., ed. *John Masefield's Great War: Collected Works.* Pen and Sword. [2007] pp. 320. £25 ISBN 9 7818 4415 6504.

Figueredo, D.H., ed. *Encyclopedia of Caribbean Literature,* 2 vols. Greenwood. [2007] pp. 1,016. $209.95 ISBN 0 3133 2742 4.

Flynn, Tom. ed. *The New Encyclopedia of Unbelief.* Prometheus Books. [2007] pp. 897. $199 ISBN 9 7815 9102 3913.

Foss, Peter J. *A Bibliography of Llewelyn Powys.* BL/OakK. [2007] pp. 256. £40 ISBN 9 7807 1234 9352.

Fowler, Bridget. *The Obituary as Collective Memory.* Routledge. [2007] pp. 312. $130 ISBN 9 7804 1536 4935.

Gillespie, Alexandra. *Print Culture and the Medieval Author: Chaucer, Lydgate, and their Books 1473–1557.* OUP. [2007] pp. 296. $95 ISBN 9 7801 9926 2953.

Haberstroh, Patricia Boyle, and Christine St Peter, eds. *Opening the Field: Irish Women, Texts and Contexts.* CorkUP. [2007] pp. 192. €39 ISBN 9 7818 5918 4103.

Hammond, Mary, and Shafquat Towheed, eds. *Publishing in the First World War: Essays in Book History.* Palgrave Macmillan. [2007] pp. 241. $69.95 ISBN 9 7802 3050 0761.

Hanna, Robert C. *Dickens's Nonfictional, Theatrical, and Poetical Writings: An Annotated Bibliography, 1820–2000.* Studies in the Nineteenth Century 35. AMS. [2007] pp. xxii + 580. $187.50 ISBN 9 7804 0464 4659.

Hass, Andrew, David Jasper and Elisabeth Jay. *The Oxford Handbook of English Literature and Theology.* OUP. [2007] pp. 889. $155 ISBN 9 7801 9927 1979.

Howey, Anne F., and Stephen R. Reimer. *A Bibliography of Modern Arthuriana 1500–2000.* Brewer. [2006] pp. xxix + 774. £113.40 ISBN 9 7818 4384 0688.

Irvine, Dean. *Editing Modernity: Women and Little-Magazine Cultures in Canada, 1916–1956*. UTorP. [2008] pp. 304. $55 ISBN 9 7808 0209 2717.

Jencks, Charles. *Critical Modernism: Where Is Post-Modernism Going?* Wiley-Academy. [2007] pp. 240. $40 ISBN 9 7804 7003 0103.

Jönsson, Arne, ed. *Letters from Sir James Spens and Jan Rutgers*. Edita Stockholm. [2007] pp. 643. ISBN 9 7891 7402 3671.

Kincade, Kit, ed. *Daniel Defoe: An Essay on the History and Reality of Apparitions*. AMS. [2007] pp. 463. $158.50 ISBN 9 7804 0464 8565.

Kirsop, Wallace, ed. *The Commonwealth of Books: Essays and Studies in Honour of Ian Willison*. OakK. [2007] pp. 271. $70 ISBN 0 7326 4002 4.

Larkin, Felix M., ed. *Librarians, Poets and Scholars: A Festschrift for Dónall Ó Luanaigh*. FCP. [2007] pp. 367. $65 ISBN 9 7818 4682 0175.

Littau, Karin. *Theories of Reading: Books, Bodies, and Bibliomania*. Polity. [2006] pp. 208. $59.95 ISBN 9 7807 4561 6582.

Loring, Rosamond B. *Decorated Book Papers: Being an Account of their Designs and Fashions*, 4th edn., ed. Hope Mayo. Blackwell. [2007] pp. 215. $50 ISBN 9 7809 7654 7266.

Macfarlane, Robert. *Original Copy: Plagiarism and Originality in Nineteenth-Century Literature*. OUP. [2007] pp. 256. $51 ISBN 9 7801 9929 6507.

Mandler, Peter. *The English National Character: The History of an Idea from Edmund Burke to Tony Blair*. YaleUP. [2007] pp. 360. $35 ISBN 0 3001 2052 4.

Martin, William H., and Sandra Mason. *The Art of Omar Khayyam: Illustrating FitzGerald's Rubaiyat*. I.B. Tauris. [2007] pp. 192. $69.95 ISBN 9 7818 4511 2820.

Murphy, Andrew ed. *A Concise Companion to Shakespeare and the Text*. Blackwell. [2007] pp. xii + 263. £56.67 ISBN 9 7814 0513 5283.

Myers, Robin, Michael Harris and Giles Mandelbrote, eds. *Books on the Move: Tracking Copies through Collections and the Book Trade*. OakK. [2007] pp. 180. $49.95 ISBN 9 7815 8456 2191.

Nicholls, David G., ed. *Introduction to Scholarship in Modern Languages and Literatures*, 3rd edn. MLA. [2007] pp. 370. $40 ISBN 9 7808 7352 5978.

Ohlgren, Thomas H. *Robin Hood: The Early Poems, 1465–1560. Texts, Contexts, and Ideology*. UDelP. [2007] pp. 278. $55 ISBN 9 7808 7413 9648.

Pearson, Neil. *Obelisk: A History of Jack Kahane and the Obelisk Press*. LiverUP. [2007] pp. 528. $39 ISBN 9 7818 4631 1017.

Pilditch, Jan. *Catherine Carswell: A Biography*. Donald. [2007] pp. 225. $26.84 ISBN 9 7808 5976 6852.

Pittock, Murray. *The Reception of Sir Walter Scott in Europe*. Continuum. [2006] pp. 396. $250 ISBN 9 7808 2647 4100.

Price, Fiona, ed. *The Scottish Chiefs: A Romance by Jane Porter*. Broadview. [2007] pp. 800. $25.94 ISBN 9 7815 5111 5986.

Raven, James. *The Business of Books: Booksellers and the English Book Trade 1450–1850*. YaleUP. [2007] pp. 448. $65 ISBN 9 7803 0012 2619.

Ray, Martin. *Joseph Conrad: Memories and Impressions. An Annotated Bibliography*. Rodopi. [2007] pp. 200. $56 ISBN 9 7890 4202 2980.

Richards, David Alan. *Rudyard Kipling: The Books I Leave Behind*. YaleUP. [2007] pp. 148. $30 ISBN 9 7803 0012 6747.

Ross, Jan. *The Works of Thomas Traherne*, vol. 2: *Part 1*. B&B. [2007]. pp. 580. $145 ISBN 9 7818 4384 1357.

Ross, Jan. *The Works of Thomas Traherne*, vol. 3: *Part 2*. B&B. [2007]. pp. 542. £73.95 ISBN 9 7818 4384 1357.

Rothman, Steven, and Nicholas Utechin, eds. *To Keep the Memory Green: Reflections on the Life of Richard Lancelyn Green 1953–2004*. The Quartering Press. [2007] pp. 222. $30. ISBN 9 7809 7955 5008.

Schimmelman, Janice. *The Tintype in America, 1856–1880*. APS. [2007] pp. 279. $29 ISBN 9 7808 7169 9725.

Schoene, Berthold, ed. *The Edinburgh Companion to Contemporary Scottish Literature*. EdinUP. [2007] pp. 424. $35 ISBN 9 7807 4862 3952.

Scott, Patrick, ed. *Amours de Voyage: An Epistolary Novella in Verse*, by Arthur Hugh Clough. Barbarian Press. [2007] pp. 88. $390 ISBN 978-0-920971-38-3.

Seed, David, ed. *A Companion to Science Fiction*. Blackwell. [2005] pp. 632. $109.95 ISBN 9 7814 0511 2185.

Shaffer, Brian W. *A Companion to the British and Irish Novel 1945–2000*. Blackwell. [2005] pp. 584. £21.90 ISBN 9 7814 0516 7451.

Sher, Richard B. *The Enlightenment and the Book: Scottish Authors and their Publishers in Eighteenth-Century Britain, Ireland, and America*. UChicP. [2007] pp. 815. $40 ISBN 9 7802 2675 2525.

Soros, Susan Weber, ed. *James 'Athenian' Stuart: The Rediscovery of Antiquity*. YaleUP. [2007] pp. 672. $100 ISBN 0 3001 1713 2.

Spiers, John. *Serious about Series: American Cheap 'Libraries' British 'Railway' Libraries and Some Literary Series of the 1890s*. Institute of English Studies. [2007] pp. 108. £20. No ISBN.

Sutherland, John. *The Boy who Loved Books: A Memoir*. Murray. [2007] pp. 272. £16.99 ISBN 9 7807 1956 4314.

Tarr, Rodger L., and Brent E. Kinser, eds. *The Uncollected Writings of Marjorie Kinnan Rawlings*. UFlorP. [2007] pp. 416. $34.95 ISBN 9 7808 1303 0272.

Taylor, Gary, and John Lavagnino. *Thomas Middleton and Early Modern Textual Culture: A Companion to the Collected Works*. OUP. [2007] pp. 1,196. £196.35 ISBN 9 7801 9922 5880.

Thieme, John. *R.K. Narayan*. ManUP. [2007] pp. 249 $74.95 ISBN 9 7807 1905 9261.

Tolley, A. Trevor. *British Literary Periodicals of World War II and Aftermath: A Critical History*. Golden Dog. [2007] pp. 227. £10 ISBN 9 7818 9490 9079.

Wendorf, Richard, ed. *America's Membership Libraries*. OakK. [2007] pp. 354. $39.95 ISBN 9 7815 8456 1996.

Wu, Duncan. *The New Writings of William Hazlitt*, 2 vols. OUP. [2007] pp. lxvi + 507 (vol. 1), pp. xiv + 553 (vol. 2). £140.25 ISBN 9 7801 9920 7060.

YWES Index of Critics

YWES - Index II Authors and Subjects

BABSON BUSINESS SCHOOL
LIBRARY